The Good Pub Guide 1999

The Good Pub Guide 1999

Edited by Alisdair Aird

Deputy Editor: Fiona Stapley

Editorial Research: Karen Fick
Research Officer: Rachel Martin
Additional Research: Robert Unsworth
Editorial Assistance: Fiona Wright

EBURY PRESS
LONDON

Please send reports on pubs to

The Good Pub Guide
FREEPOST TN1569
WADHURST
East Sussex
TN5 7BR

This edition first published in 1998 by Ebury Press,
Random House, 20 Vauxhall Bridge Road,
London SW1V 2SA

1 3 5 7 9 10 8 6 4 2

A CIP catalogue record for this book is available from the British Library.

ISBN 0 09 181476 6

Typeset from author's disks by Clive Dorman & Co.
Edited by Pat Taylor Chalmers
Printed and bound in Great Britain by Mackays of Chatham plc

Contents

Introduction

In the 17 years that we have been producing *The Good Pub Guide*, we have charted the course of a revolution in pub food. A major milestone came five years ago. It was then that, across the country, two or three dozen pubs were producing such good food that we felt the time had come to recognise their achievements by introducing our annual County Dining Pub Awards. Since then, the number of pubs offering food of this quality has multiplied many times over. There's no doubt that customers' expectations are far higher nowadays, and that to get a reputation for good food a pub has to satisfy the judgement of people whose interest in cooking and knowledge about food has been acutely sharpened by the abundance of television food programmes, with linked books and magazines.

So, in contrast with the case five years ago, the number of pubs offering imaginative and interesting cooking amounts not just to dozens but to hundreds, all over Great Britain. These are pubs which either have a licensee who cooks with flair, or have taken the trouble to find a chef who does. They track down supplies of the best local produce. What they serve changes from day to day – and from season to season.

An interesting new development is the way that some really gifted young chefs, trained in top-class restaurants, are now taking on pubs rather than restaurants. This is partly because they like a pub's more informal surroundings, and partly because a shoestring start-up can make sounder financial sense in a pub than a restaurant. Put these two reasons together and you get the surprising and very refreshing combination of a really good imaginative chef in surroundings that are the very opposite of a restaurant with all its pretensions: a classic example is Patrick Le Mesurier in the humble Royal Oak at Woodchester (Gloucs). This is the very opposite of the gastropub syndrome (where a pub gives itself all sorts of restauranty airs and graces, charging fanciful prices for fancy food). Instead, it's injecting the highest standards of cooking into a truly pubby tradition.

We have been particularly heartened this last year at the way that food scares have not weakened the appeal of classic meaty pub dishes like steak or liver – though one good result has been that many more pubs now say where their beef comes from (usually in general terms, such as 'Scottish' or 'local', and sometimes stating that it comes from a particular beef breed such as Aberdeen Angus). There is now also real recognition that people's tastes vary: all the pubs which take a good interest in food now offer a worthwhile spread of fish and vegetarian dishes. Vegetarian food has now taken its place as an entirely normal part of a pub's output, listed casually alongside other dishes – instead of being prominently labelled on menus as a sort of gastronomic ghetto.

There are of course fashions in pub food (and fashionable buzz-words – this year's has been jus). Over the last few years there's been a progression through Italian and Indian to Thai. Now, although there's less outright Thai food in pubs than there was last year, there's still a marked Thai influence, with for example widespread use of sweet chilli, lime and coconut. This has joined an interest in Middle Eastern and Mediterranean cooking to produce the current front line in pub food – characterised by robust often spicy flavours permeating the food instead of being added superficially as a separate sauce.

For unusually good food, we'd suggest the Knife & Cleaver at Houghton Conquest (Beds), the Harrow at West Ilsley (Berks), the Three Horseshoes at Madingley (Cambs), the Wheatsheaf at Beetham and Drunken Duck near Hawkshead (Cumbria), the Kings Arms at Stockland (Devon), the White Hart at Great Yeldham (Essex), the Inn For All Seasons at Little Barrington, Fox at Lower Oddington, Gumstool near Tetbury and – see above – Royal Oak at Woodchester (Gloucs), the Red Lion at Boldre (Hants), the Albion in Faversham (Kent), the Eagle & Child at Bispham Green (Lancs), the Old Barn at Glooston (Leics), the Hoste Arms in Burnham Market and Saracens Head near Erpingham (Norfolk), the Perch

& Pike at South Stoke and Kings Head at Wootton (Oxon), the Cholmondeley Riverside at Cressage (Shrops), the New Inn at Dowlish Wake (Somerset), the Froize at Chillesford (Suffolk), the Elsted Inn at Elsted, Griffin at Fletching and Horse Guards at Tillington (Sussex), the Seven Stars near Woodborough (Wilts), the Crab & Lobster at Asenby, Malt Shovel at Brearton, Blue Lion at East Witton and Three Acres at Shelley (Yorks), the Chapel and the Eagle in London, the Wheatsheaf at Swinton (Scotland), and the Nantyffin Cider Mill near Crickhowell and Walnut Tree at Llandewi Skirrid (Wales). This is distinguished company, and from it we choose as **Dining Pub of the Year** the Froize at Chillesford in Suffolk.

Among other food, the Froize does superb fish and seafood. Other pubs where fish cooking or fresh seafood is really out of the ordinary are the Fish at Bray (Berks), the Russell Arms at Butlers Cross (Bucks), the Carrington Arms at Moulsoe (Bucks), the Trinity Foot at Swavesey (Cambs), the Anchor at Beer, Drewe Arms at Broadhembury, Anchor at Cockwood and Start Bay at Torcross (Devon), Sankeys in Tunbridge Wells (Kent), the Oddfellows Arms at Mellor (Gtr Manchester), the Half Moon at Kirdford (Sussex), the George & Dragon at Rowde (Wilts), the Applecross Inn at Applecross, Loch Melfort Hotel at Arduaine, Crinan Hotel at Crinan, Cabin at St Monans, Tayvallich Inn at Tayvallich and Morefield Motel in Ullapool (Scotland) and the Walnut Tree at Llandewi Skirrid (Wales). The Carrington Arms at Moulsoe, a new main entry in Bucks, is our **Fish Pub of the Year** – it's fun choosing your food (on display, priced by weight in the Mediterranean way) and you can even have it cooked on a sophisticated indoor barbecue.

The most interesting choice of vegetarian food we've found this year has been in the King William IV at Heydon (Cambs), the Masons Arms at Cartmel Fell and Mill Inn at Mungrisdale (Cumbria), the Bottle at Marshwood (Dorset), the Victoria in Beeston (Notts) and the Snowdrop in Lewes (Sussex). The Snowdrop – an eccentric place, enjoyed by a very wide cross-section of readers for its laid-back individuality – is our **Vegetarian Pub of the Year**.

People are prepared to pay that bit extra for a really enjoyable meal. So it's a special treat to find pubs that offer good food at a low price: the Sweeney & Todd in Reading (Berks), the Eagle in Cambridge (Cambs), the Old Ale House in Truro (Cornwall), the midweek lunches at the Black Horse at Amberley (Gloucs), the Fleece at Bretforton (Herefs & Worcs), the Woolpack at Brookland (Kent), the Highbury Vaults in Bristol (Somerset), and the Dalesman in Sedbergh at lunchtime and Fat Cat in Sheffield (Yorks). In Scotland, most of our Edinburgh and Glasgow entries offer remarkably cheap food; the Babbity Bowster in Glasgow stands out among them. The Eagle in Cambridge, a pub of great character, is our **Bargain Food Pub of the Year**.

Good pubs which stand out for an excellent choice of well kept real ales are the Bhurtpore at Aston (Cheshire), the Old Ale House in Truro (Cornwall), the Watermill at Ings (Cumbria), the Alexandra and the Brunswick in Derby, the Sun at Feering (Essex), the Lytton Arms at Knebworth (Herts), the Swan in the Rushes in Loughborough (Leics), the Fat Cat in Norwich (Norfolk) and the Fat Cat in Sheffield (Yorks). The Bhurtpore at Aston (Cheshire), fresh from last year's celebrations of the 150th anniversary of the family first coming to the pub, is our **Beer Pub of the Year**.

About 40 of the pubs in this Guide now brew their own beer – often extremely good, almost always cheaper than brewery beers of similar strength. Taking quality into account, and the enthusiasm of readers' reports, we'd specially commend the Pot Kiln at Frilsham (Berks), the Brunswick in Derby, the Tally Ho at Hatherleigh and Beer Engine at Newton St Cyres (Devon), the Farmers Arms at Apperley (Gloucs), the Flower Pots at Cheriton (Hants), the Talbot at Knightwick (Herefs & Worcs), the Old Brewery at Somerby (Leics), the Three Tuns in Bishops Castle (Shrops), the Burton Bridge in Burton on Trent (Staffs), the Gribble at Oving (Sussex), the New Inn at Cropton and Sair in Linthwaite (Yorks). Though it's not been brewing for long, the Talbot in Knightwick – using hops from the owners' farm – is producing such enjoyable This, That, T'Other and Wot that it is our **Own Brew Pub of the Year**.

This year the cider industry's troubles have hit the headlines, with closures and cut-backs at producers big and small. There are still pubs that bring together a remarkable range of interesting ciders and perries: the Monkey House at Defford (Herefs & Worcs), Rose & Crown at Huish Episcopi (Somerset), Cider Centre at Brandy Wharf (Lincs) and Ram at Farncombe (Surrey). For carrying the cider flag so enthusiastically into territory that's more usually associated with G & Ts, we name the Ram at Farncombe, with its choice of 30 (and the chance of tasting them before you buy), **Cider Pub of the Year.**

When we first started *The Good Pub Guide*, virtually all the reports we had from readers about wine in pubs were decidedly unfavourable. Now, it's the opposite. Although many pubs serve wines which would not be your first choice if you were buying them by the bottle, it's rare to face outright disappointment – at least in the pubs included in this book. Many pubs now make a point of finding good value wines for their customers – and, even more important, keeping them well.

In London, the Bishops Finger and Eagle (EC1), Old Bank of England (EC4), Compton Arms (N1), Flask (NW3), Alma and Ship (SW18), Bulls Head (SW13) and White Cross (Richmond) all have a really good choice of wines by the glass. Elsewhere, pubs with a notable range are the Bell at Boxford (Berks), Five Arrows in Waddesdon (Bucks), Old Bridge at Huntingdon (Cambs), Maltsters Arms at Chapel Amble and Trengilly Wartha near Constantine (Cornwall), Nobody at Doddiscombsleigh (Devon), Green Man at Toot Hill (Essex), Fox at Lower Oddington (Gloucs), Armoury in Shrewsbury (Shrops), Crown in Southwold (Suffolk), Dun Cow at Dunchurch (Warwicks), and Starbank in Edinburgh and Auctioneers in Glasgow (Scotland). The wines at all these have drawn really warm praise from readers in recent months, but it is the exceptional choice at the Nobody in Doddiscombsleigh which has aroused most enthusiasm; the Nobody is our **Wine Pub of the Year.**

Malt whiskies come in so many subtle (and sometimes not-so-subtle) gradations of flavour that tasting unfamiliar ones can be tremendously rewarding. So pubs which take the trouble to keep more than the well known heavily promoted brands are well worth seeking out. (And, says your Scottish Editor, it is a well known scientific fact that a whisky drinker is a happy drinker.) In Scotland, quite a few of our main entries keep a fine range of up to 100 or more; the Crown at Portpatrick keeps 250, including real rarities. South of the Border, pubs which keep more than 20 or so are a good deal less common. So it's well worth knowing about the specialists: the Crown & Horns at East Ilsley (Berks), the Old Inn at St Breward (Cornwall), the Nobody at Doddiscombsleigh (Devon), the Eliot Arms at South Cerney (Gloucs), the Clarendon at Chale (Isle of Wight), the Bulls Head at Clipston (Northants), the Victoria at Beeston (Notts), the White Horse at Pulverbatch (Shrops), the Pack Horse at Widdop (Yorks) and the Dinorben Arms at Bodfari and Old House at Llangynwyd (Wales). To find over 400 single malts in a hill village pub in South Wales is such a treat that we name the Old House at Llangynwyd our **Whisky Pub of the Year.**

With all the talk of theme pubs and gastropubs, you'd be forgiven for thinking that unspoilt traditional pubs were now extinct. In fact there are plenty still to discover. A shortlist of our own favourites among the main entries (and there are many more among the Lucky Dip entries) includes the Cock at Broom (Beds), the Bell at Aldworth and Pot Kiln at Frilsham (Berks), the Chequers at Wheeler End (Bucks), the Queens Head at Newton (Cambs), the Barley Mow at Kirk Ireton (Derbys), the Square & Compass at Worth Matravers (Dorset), the Boat at Ashleworth Quay (Gloucs), the Harrow at Steep (Hants), the Fox & Hounds at Toys Hill (Kent), the Philharmonic in Liverpool (Merseyside), the Lord Nelson at Burnham Thorpe (Norfolk), the Rose & Crown at Huish Episcopi (Somerset), the Murrell Arms at Barnham (a new Sussex entry), the Haunch of Venison in Salisbury (Wilts), the Birch Hall at Beck Hole and Whitelocks in Leeds (Yorks) and the Olde Mitre (EC1, London). The Bell at Aldworth, in the same family for over 200 years, is our **Unspoilt Pub of the Year.** And anyone who finds these appealing will also relish the unique Yew Tree at Cauldon (Staffs); a simple country tavern filled with great riches of Victorian and other collectables.

The great majority of main entries now welcome children at least in some part of the pub. A few such as the Otter at Weston (Devon), the White Lion at Walkern (Herts), the Clarendon at Chale and Chequers at Rookley (Isle of Wight) and the Parkers Arms at Newton (Lancs) go to considerable lengths to suit families. We choose the Chequers at Rookley as **Family Pub of the Year** – very good facilities for children, yet leaving a good undisturbed area for adults.

This year a dozen or so pubs are on such sparkling form that we can count on readers' reports on them to cheer us up in even the darkest days of winter. They have that rare quality of making a visit to them feel quite special. They bring together a welcoming atmosphere, service that is friendly and helpful, good (often excellent) food and drink, and usually surroundings of considerable character. Most have bedrooms and are enjoyable to stay in. They are the Maltsters Arms at Chapel Amble and Trengilly Wartha near Constantine (Cornwall), the Royal Oak at Appleby and Drunken Duck near Hawkshead (Cumbria), the Cott at Dartington, Nobody at Doddiscombsleigh, Castle at Lydford and Kings Arms at Stockland (Devon), the Red Lion at Boldre and Wykeham Arms in Winchester (Hants), the Riverside at Aymestrey (Herefs & Worcs), the Three Horseshoes at Warham (Norfolk), the Lamb in Burford (Oxon), the White Hart at Ford (Wilts) and the Wheatsheaf at Swinton (Scotland). For its all-round excellence we name the Trengilly Wartha near Constantine **Pub of the Year.**

All these pubs owe their success to exceptional landlords and landladies. Other licensees of this top rank are Aubrey Sinclair-Ball of the Millstone at Barnack (Cambs), Ian and Patsy Davey of the Railway at St Agnes (Cornwall), Colin and Hilary Cheyne of the Royal Oak at Appleby and Peter Lynch of the Dukes Head at Armathwaite (Cumbria), Jamie Stuart and Pippa Hutchinson of the Duke of York at Iddesleigh and Clive and Mo Walker of the Castle at Lydford (Devon), Peter and Linda Stenson of the Allenheads Inn at Allenheads (Northumbria), Colin Mead of the Red Lion at Steeple Aston (Oxon), Stephen and Di Waring of the Wenlock Edge Inn on Wenlock Edge (Shrops), and Michael and Margaret Fox of the Buck at Thornton Watlass (Yorks). Our **Licensees of the Year** are Jamie Stuart and Pippa Hutchinson of the Duke of York at Iddesleigh in Devon.

Each year as the new inspection season rolls round we worry that, after nearly two decades of scouring the country for good new pubs, there won't be any left to find. So far (touch wood) there seems to be an inexhaustible supply. This year, we've particularly enjoyed the Hare & Hounds at Lambourn Woodlands near Lambourn (Berks), the Frog at Skirmett (Bucks), the Dysart Arms at Bunbury and Albion in Chester (Cheshire), the Old Sun in Buxton (Derbys), the George at Blackawton and Union at Dolton (Devon), the Dirty Habit at Hollingbourne (Kent), the Waggon & Horses near Doulting (Somerset), the Cornwallis Arms at Brome (Suffolk), the Murrell Arms at Barnham (Sussex), the Fiddle & Bone in Birmingham and Dun Cow at Dunchurch (Warwicks and W Midlands), the General Tarleton at Ferrensby and Jefferson Arms at Thorganby (Yorks), the Drovers at East Linton, Blackfriars in Glasgow and Glenelg Inn at Glenelg (Scotland), and the Rose & Crown at Graianrhyd (Wales). Musicians are well known for their good taste in pubs. The Fiddle & Bone, started by a violinist and trombone player in the City of Birmingham Symphony Orchestra, is such fun (with its unusual range of music including afternoon choir practices and visits by even the most exalted players) that this year our **Newcomer of the Year** is the Fiddle & Bone in Birmingham.

As we've said above, one of our finds this year has been the Cornwallis Arms at Brome. This is tied to a newish small brewery at South Elmham in Suffolk, St Peters Brewery. In its short life so far it has put together a very sympathetic small group of tied pubs, civilised yet full of character, which includes two other main entries (the De La Pole Arms at Wingfield, also in Suffolk, and Jerusalem Tavern in London). Moreover, the beers it brews for them are most enjoyable. St Peters is our **Pub Group of the Year.**

Beer prices

Last year, we saw some encouraging signs that beer prices were increasing less steeply than previously. We were beginning to hope that the measures taken to limit the power of the big brewers' monopoly (which had let them force through price increases regardless) were at last having a real effect on beer prices. This year, we were even more hopeful that we would find stability in beer prices. For a start, the brewers have been making a lot of fuss about cheap beer flooding in across the Channel (so you might have expected them to keep down their own pub prices, to compete). More importantly, the cost of malting barley – the main ingredient in beer, apart from water – has recently been falling. In real terms, barley now costs less than at any time since the 1970s. So has the price of beer been falling too?

Not a bit of it.

It's clear that the four national brewing combines (Bass, Carlsberg Tetleys, Scottish Courage and Whitbreads), and the biggest pub chains, are still exercising what amounts to a monopoly stranglehold on the market. This year they have forced up beer prices by an average of 9p a pint – a 5½% price hike. This increase is much heftier than the general increase in retail prices, which over the period of our survey (excluding mortgage interest) rose by only 3%. No wonder the biggest brewer of all, Scottish Courage, has seen its profits soar by 13% in the same year. And it is quite brazen about its intention to push prices onwards and upwards; in a recent advertisement encouraging the very farmers who now get so little for their barley to go into the pub business, it held out the carrot of 'a new business adventure where the price at which you sell your product only goes up'!

Among the Big Four national breweries, prices in Whitbreads pubs are close to the national average (and have increased by less than the other three); in pubs tied to Bass, they are now about 6p a pint more than the average; they are about 12p more in pubs tied to Carlsberg Tetleys or to Scottish Courage. Significantly, the big nationals' beer costs 10p or 11p a pint more in pubs tied to them than it does in independent pubs able to buy that same beer on their own terms.

Beer prices vary widely from area to area, largely depending on the proportion of pubs in each area that are tied to the Big Four – areas where smaller brewers have a bigger market share tend to be cheaper. How do prices in your area compare with those elsewhere? Here's the current picture, with the cheapest areas at the top of the Table, and the most expensive at the bottom:

	£/pint
Lancs (inc Manchester and Liverpool)	1.53
Derbys	1.59
Yorks	1.59
Notts	1.60
Cheshire	1.61
Cumbria	1.61
Herefs & Worcs	1.62
Staffs	1.62
Shrops	1.63
Wales	1.68
Northumbria	1.68
Gloucs	1.70
Warwicks (inc W Midlands)	1.71
Leics	1.71
Somerset	1.72
Lincs	1.74
Devon	1.75
Cornwall	1.75
Suffolk	1.77
Wilts	1.78
Essex	1.78
Beds	1.79
Cambs	1.80
Northants	1.80
Dorset	1.81
Herts	1.81
Scotland	1.83
Kent	1.84
Oxon	1.84
Sussex	1.85
Isle of Wight	1.85
Hants	1.85
Bucks	1.88
Berks	1.91
London	1.92
Surrey	1.94

Within this pattern of huge area variations, there are some real local heroes – breweries charging much less than the local average for their beer. All these stand out for big savings (the figure we give is the amount you save per pint on these brewers' beers, compared with average prices in their home county):

Savings per pint, compared with local average	(p)
Holts	42
Fullers	27
Sam Smiths	23
Clarks	23
Banks's/Hansons/Camerons	23
Bathams	22
Hook Norton	20
Wadworths	19
Donnington	16

Pubs brewing their own beer also save you on average 16p a pint, compared with prices in other pubs near them.

Sam Smiths is even more of a price hero than these figures suggest, as we've used its home county Yorkshire as the base for comparison. In fact, many of its pubs are in much more expensive areas, and here its low prices are even more striking. For carrying the Yorkshire flag of low beer prices into much higher-priced parts of Britain, Sam Smiths of Tadcaster in Yorkshire is our **Brewer of the Year.**

Food prices

Pub food price levels are at least influenced by the market leaders – the dining pub chains controlled either by the breweries or by the big pub operating companies. However, in general pubs do have rather more freedom to set the price of meals than they do in the case of beer. So perhaps it's little surprise that this year we have found pub food prices increase by more than the general level of retail price inflation but less than the increase in the price of beer. We checked prices of a standard hot dish (steak and kidney pie) and of a ploughman's in several hundred pubs spread across Britain, and found that with both they have this year increased by 4.8% – on average, for a good ploughman's you can now expect to pay £4.30, and £6.05 for a well made steak and kidney pie.

Inflexible pubs

A growing problem is that many pubs seem to have lost the ability to cope efficiently with travellers who break their journey for a quick snack. It's clear from their eloquent complaints that readers are deeply frustrated by having to wait 20 minutes for a two-minute snack, because it's had to queue behind dishes that need elaborate preparation and cooking. We'd like to see more pubs put a high priority on flexibility, so that they can respond immediately to people in a hurry.

Flexibility is also the answer to another newish problem that has been causing complaint this year. Some pubs won't accept orders for food until they are ready to serve food. That sounds sensible – until you think of all the customers who have turned up early so as to be sure of being served early. Readers are exasperated when

A note on the Good Pub Guide Annual Beer Price Survey

Each year we check the price of the cheapest cask-conditioned Bitter sold by a number of pubs right across Great Britain, and compare it with the price charged by those same pubs 12 months earlier. We make sure we get a price from every single pub in the sample. This year, there were 1,199 pubs in this year-on-year sample. This is the most accurate long-running survey of pub beer prices carried out in the UK, as it makes sure that, from one year to the next, it's the same pubs which are compared. Surveys which simply take an overall average price one year and compare it with an average for the previous year run the risk that their sample of pubs, different from one year to the next, may include a changing proportion of 'cheap' or 'expensive' pubs.

they get to a pub virtually as it opens, and then find that by the time the staff are ready to take orders umpteen other people who have arrived after them jump in ahead of them with their orders. As one reader put it: 'I don't mind waiting for food, but I do mind waiting to order it, especially while every Tom, Dick and Harry in three counties arrives in the interim and I have no guarantee that I'll be served before the people who've just arrived. After about 45 minutes we gave up and went away.' Pubs which do refuse to take orders before a certain time (and we can see no sound reason for this) should at least make sure that first comers can be first orderers.

The biggest turn-off any pub-goer faces is the attractive pub that's filled with empty tables – all with a Reserved sign. We recognise that many people like to be able to book a table. Ideally, a separate dining room is the proper place for table bookings. Pubs which instead let people reserve tables in the main bar area should be more flexible about it. First, it seems to us absurd for any pub worthy of the name to allow all its bar tables to be reserved. Secondly, surely in a bar no-one should be discouraged from sitting at an empty table, even if it is booked for later. That bossy behaviour is absolutely not what pubs are about. It may be less effort for pubs simply to scatter Reserved notices around, but instead they should make customers feel welcome to sit anywhere they want – just warning them in a friendly way that Mrs So-and-So or Mr Such-and-Such has arranged to use that table at a particular time. Publicans who feel that the flexibility and tact that this approach needs are beyond them can't be in the right job.

Another problem we have found this year is the way some pubs in popular tourist areas such as the Cotswolds have started refusing to let people book bedrooms at weekends for just one night. They insist on a two-night booking. We take such a dim view of this inflexible attitude that we are considering excluding such pubs from future editions of the *Guide*; as always, we will be guided by readers' wishes – so please let us know what you think about this.

There's no doubt that if some readers had their way any pub with piped music would be banned from the *Guide*. Certainly, piped music in pubs can arouse intense irritation. Judging by readers' reports, the bulk of customers are reasonably happy with well reproduced individually chosen music if it more or less matches the style of the pub and the general mood of the customers at the time; it can even be an important part of the appeal and character of some particular pubs. All too often (to be as repetitive as the music itself) it isn't, it isn't, it doesn't, it doesn't and it isn't: instead, it's unnecessary, unsuitable and badly reproduced. Even sheer loudness isn't the main culprit – tinny and fuzzy almost inaudible background mutterings can be even more irritating. Again, we feel the answer for pubs is more flexibility – a recognition that while piped music may not even be noticed by most people (and may contribute marginally towards keeping their staff happy), it is violently disliked by some customers. We'd urge all pubs that insist on having piped music to post a discreet notice at the bar, saying: Please tell us if you'd like us to turn off the music.

Don't let them keep your credit card

We have had disturbing reports this year of a very few pubs making readers who have ordered food leave their credit cards at the bar, as a sort of deposit. They are not entitled to do this. The credit card firms and banks which issue them warn you not to let them out of your sight; if in the meantime someone behind the counter used your card fraudulently, the card company or bank could in theory hold you liable – because of your negligence in letting a stranger hang on to the card. A publican who asks to keep your credit card is in effect saying to you: 'I don't trust you – but I'm asking you to trust me and my staff.' That's no way to do business. Suggest instead that if they feel the need for security they 'swipe' your card and give it back to you – and do 'name and shame' the pub to us.

What is a Good Pub?

The main entries in this book have been through a two-stage sifting process. First of all, some 2,000 regular correspondents keep in touch with us about the pubs they visit, and nearly double that number report occasionally. The present edition has used a total of around 40,000 reports from readers, and from users of the electronic version of the book which is available on the Internet, on Compuserve. This keeps us up-to-date about pubs included in previous editions – it's their alarm signals that warn us when a pub's standards have dropped (after a change of management, say), and it's their continuing approval that reassures us about keeping a pub as a main entry for another year. Very important, though, are the reports they send us on pubs we don't know at all. It's from these new discoveries that we make up a shortlist, to be considered for possible inclusion as new main entries. The more people that report favourably on a new pub, the more likely it is to win a place on this shortlist – especially if some of the reporters belong to our hard core of about five hundred trusted correspondents whose judgement we have learned to rely on. These are people who have each given us detailed comments on dozens of pubs, and shown that (when we ourselves know some of those pubs too) their judgement is closely in line with our own.

This brings us to the acid test. Each pub, before inclusion as a main entry, is inspected anonymously by the Editor, the Deputy Editor, or both. They have to find some special quality that would make strangers enjoy visiting it. What often marks the pub out for special attention is good value food (and that might mean anything from a well made sandwich, with good fresh ingredients at a low price, to imaginative cooking outclassing most restaurants in the area). Maybe the drinks are out of the ordinary (pubs with several hundred whiskies, with remarkable wine lists, with home-made country wines or good beer or cider made on the premises, with a wide range of well kept real ales or bottled beers from all over the world). Perhaps there's a special appeal about it as a place to stay, with good bedrooms and obliging service. Maybe it's the building itself (from centuries-old parts of monasteries to extravagant Victorian gin-palaces), or its surroundings (lovely countryside, attractive waterside, extensive well kept garden), or what's in it (charming furnishings, extraordinary collections of bric-a-brac).

Above all, though, what makes the good pub is its atmosphere – you should be able to feel at home there, and feel not just that *you're* glad you've come but that *they're* glad you've come.

It follows from this that a great many ordinary locals, perfectly good in their own right, don't earn a place in the book. What makes them attractive to their regular customers (an almost clubby chumminess) may even make strangers feel rather out-of-place.

Another important point is that there's not necessarily any link between charm and luxury – though we like our creature comforts as much as anyone. A basic unspoilt village tavern, with hard seats and a flagstone floor, may be worth travelling miles to find, while a deluxe pub-restaurant may not be worth crossing the street for. Landlords can't buy the Good Pub accolade by spending thousands on thickly padded banquettes, soft music and luxuriously shrimpy sauces for their steaks – they can only win it, by having a genuinely personal concern for both their customers and their pub.

Using the *Guide*

THE COUNTIES

England has been split alphabetically into counties, mainly to make it easier for people scanning through the book to find pubs near them. Each chapter starts by picking out the pubs that are currently doing best in the area, or specially attractive for one reason or another. Metropolitan areas have been included in the counties around them – for example, Merseyside in Lancashire. And occasionally we have grouped counties together – for example, Rutland with Leicestershire, and Durham with Northumberland to make Northumbria. When there's any risk of confusion, we have put a note about where to find a county at the place in the book where you'd probably look for it. But if in doubt, check the Contents.

Scotland and Wales have each been covered in single chapters, and London appears immediately before them at the end of England. Except in London (which is split into Central, North, South, West and East), pubs are listed alphabetically under the name of the town or village where they are. If the village is so small that you probably wouldn't find it on a road map, we've listed it under the name of the nearest sizeable village or town instead. The maps use the same town and village names, and additionally include a few big cities that don't have any listed pubs – for orientation.

We always list pubs in their true locations – so if a village is actually in Buckinghamshire that's where we list it, even if its postal address is via some town in Oxfordshire. Just once or twice, while the village itself is in one county the pub is just over the border in the next-door county. We then use the village county, not the pub one.

STARS ★

Specially good pubs are picked out with a star after their name. In a few cases, pubs have two stars: these are the aristocrats among pubs, really worth going out of your way to find. The stars do NOT signify extra luxury or specially good food – in fact some of the pubs which appeal most distinctively and strongly of all are decidedly basic in terms of food and surroundings. The detailed description of each pub shows what its special appeal is, and it's that that the stars refer to.

FOOD AND STAY AWARDS:

The knife-and-fork rosette shows those pubs where food is quite outstanding. The bed symbol shows pubs which we know to be good as places to stay in – bearing in mind the price of the rooms (obviously you can't expect the same level of luxury at £30 a head as you'd get for £60 a head). Pubs with bedrooms are marked on the maps as a square.

This wine glass symbol marks out those pubs where wines are a cut above the usual run, and/or offer a good choice of wines by the glass.

The beer tankard symbol shows pubs where the quality of the beer is quite exceptional, or pubs which keep a particularly interesting range of beers in good condition.

£

This symbol picks out pubs where we have found decent snacks at £2 or less, or worthwhile main dishes at £4.80 or less.

RECOMMENDERS

At the end of each main entry we include the names of readers who have recently recommended that pub (unless they've asked us not to). Important note: the description of the pub and the comments on it are our own and *not* the recommenders'; they are based on our own personal inspections and on later verification of facts with each pub. As some recommenders' names appear quite often, you can get an extra idea of what a pub is like by seeing which other pubs those recommenders have approved.

LUCKY DIPS

The Lucky Dip section at the end of each county chapter includes brief descriptions of pubs that have been recommended by readers, with the readers' names in brackets. As the flood of reports from readers has given so much solid information about so many pubs, we have been able to include only those which seem really worth trying. Where only one single reader has recommended a pub, we have now not included that pub in the list unless the reader's description makes the nature of the pub quite clear, and gives us good grounds for trusting that other readers would be glad to know of the pub. So with most, the descriptions reflect the balanced judgement of a number of different readers, increasingly backed up by similar reports on the same pubs from different readers in previous years (we do not name these readers). Many have been inspected by us. In these cases, LYM means the pub was in a previous edition of the *Guide*. The usual reason that it's no longer a main entry is that, although we've heard nothing really condemnatory about it, we've not had enough favourable reports to be sure that it's still ahead of the local competition. BB means that, although the pub has never been a main entry, we have inspected it, and found nothing against it. In both these cases, the description is our own; in others, it's based on the readers' reports. This year, we have deleted many previously highly rated pubs from the book simply because we have no very recent reports on them. This may well mean that we have left out some favourites – please tell us if we have!

Lucky Dip pubs marked with a ☆ are ones where the information we have (either from our own inspections or from trusted reader/reporters) suggests a firm recommendation. Roughly speaking, we'd say that these pubs are as much worth considering, at least for the virtues described for them, as many of the main entries themselves. Note that in the Dips we always commend food if we have information supporting a positive recommendation. So a bare mention that food is served shouldn't be taken to imply a recommendation of the food. The same is true of accommodation and so forth.

The Lucky Dips (particularly, of course, the starred ones) are under consideration for inspection for a future edition – so please let us have any comments you can make on them. You can use the report forms at the end of the book, the report card which should be included in it, or just write direct (no stamp needed if posted in the UK). Our address is *The Good Pub Guide*, FREEPOST TN1569, WADHURST, East Sussex TN5 7BR.

MAP REFERENCES

All pubs outside the big cities are given four-figure map references. On the main entries, it looks like this: SX5678 Map 1. Map 1 means that it's on the first map at the end of the book. SX means it's in the square labelled SX on that map. The first figure, 5, tells you to look along the grid at the top and bottom of the SX square for the figure 5. The *third* figure, 7, tells you to look down the grid at the side of the square to find the figure 7. Imaginary lines drawn down and across the square from these figures should intersect near the pub itself.

The second and fourth figures, the 6 and the 8, are for more precise pin-pointing, and are really for use with larger-scale maps such as road atlases or the Ordnance Survey 1:50,000 maps, which use exactly the same map reference system. On the relevant Ordnance Survey map, instead of finding the 5 marker on the top grid you'd find the 56 one; instead of the 7 on the side grid you'd look for the 78 marker. This makes it very easy to locate even the smallest village.

Where a pub is exceptionally difficult to find, we include a six-figure reference in the directions, such as OS Sheet 102 reference 654783. This refers to Sheet 102 of the Ordnance Survey 1:50,000 maps, which explain how to use the six-figure references to pin-point a pub to the nearest 100 metres.

MOTORWAY PUBS

If a pub is within four or five miles of a motorway junction, and reaching it doesn't involve much slow traffic, we give special directions for finding it from the motorway. And the Special Interest Lists at the end of the book include a list of these pubs, motorway by motorway.

PRICES AND OTHER FACTUAL DETAILS

The *Guide* went to press during the summer of 1998. As late as possible, each pub was sent a checking sheet to get up-to-date food, drink and bedroom prices and other factual information. By the summer of 1999 prices are bound to have increased a little – to be prudent, you should probably allow around 5% extra by then. But if you find a significantly different price *please let us know*.

Breweries to which pubs are 'tied' are named at the beginning of the italic-print rubric after each main entry. That means the pub has to get most if not all of its drinks from that brewery. If the brewery is not an independent one but just part of a combine, we name the combine in brackets. Where a brewery no longer brews its own beers but gets them under contract from a different brewer, we name that brewer too. When the pub is tied, we have spelled out whether the landlord is a tenant, has the pub on a lease, or is a manager; tenants and leaseholders generally have considerably greater freedom to do things their own way, and in particular are allowed to buy drinks including a beer from sources other than their tied brewery.

Free houses are pubs not tied to a brewery, so in theory they can shop around to get the drinks their customers want, at the best prices they can find. But in practice many free houses have loans from the big brewers, on terms that bind them to sell those breweries' beers – indeed, about half of all the beer sold in free houses is supplied by the big national brewery combines to free houses that have these loan ties. So don't be too surprised to find that so-called free houses may be stocking a range of beers restricted to those from a single brewery.

Real ale is used by us to mean beer that has been maturing naturally in its cask. We do not count as real ale beer which has been pasteurised or filtered to remove its natural yeasts. If it is kept under a blanket of carbon dioxide to preserve it, we still generally mention it – as long as the pressure is too light for you to notice any extra fizz, it's hard to tell the difference. (For brevity, we use the expression 'under light blanket pressure' to cover such pubs; we do not include among them pubs where the blanket pressure is high enough to force the beer up from the cellar, as this does make it unnaturally fizzy.) If we say a pub has, for example, 'Whitbreads-related real ales', these may include not just beers brewed by the national company and its subsidiaries but also beers produced by independent breweries which the national company buys in bulk and distributes alongside its own.

Other drinks: we've also looked out particularly for pubs doing enterprising non-alcoholic drinks (including good tea or coffee), interesting spirits (especially malt whiskies), country wines (elderflower and the like), freshly squeezed juices, and good farm ciders. So many pubs now stock one of the main brands of draught cider that we normally mention cider only if the pub keeps quite a range, or one of the less common farm-made ciders.

Meals refers to what is sold in the bar, not in any separate restaurant. It means that pub sells food in its bar substantial enough to do as a proper meal – something you'd sit down to with knife and fork. It doesn't necessarily mean you can get three separate courses.

Snacks means sandwiches, ploughman's, pies and so forth, rather than pork scratchings or packets of crisps. We always mention sandwiches in the text if we know that a pub does them – if you don't see them mentioned, assume you can't get them.

The food listed in the description of each pub is an example of the sort of thing you'd find served in the bar on a normal day, and generally includes the dishes which are currently finding most favour with readers. We try to indicate any difference we know of between lunchtime and evening, and between summer and winter (on the whole stressing summer food more). In winter, many pubs tend to have a more restricted range, particularly of salads, and tend then to do more in the way of filled baked potatoes, casseroles and hot pies. We always mention barbecues if we know a pub does them. Food quality and variety may be affected by holidays – particularly in a small pub, where the licensees do the cooking themselves (May and early June seem to be popular times for licensees to take their holidays).

Any separate *restaurant* is mentioned. But in general all comments on the type of food served, and in particular all the other details about meals and snacks at the end of each entry, relate to the pub food and not to the restaurant food.

Children's Certificates exist but in practice *Children* are allowed into at least some part of almost all the pubs included in this *Guide* (there is no legal restriction on the movement of children over 14 in any pub, though only people over 18 may get alcohol). As we went to press, we asked the main-entry pubs a series of detailed questions about their rules. *Children welcome* means the pub has told us that it simply lets them come in, with no special restrictions. In other cases we report exactly what arrangements pubs say they make for children. However, we have to note that in readers' experience some pubs make restrictions which they haven't told us about (children only if eating, for example), and very occasionally pubs which have previously allowed children change their policy altogether, virtually excluding them. If you come across this, please let us know, so that we can clarify the information for the pub concerned in the next edition. Beware that if children are confined to the restaurant, they may occasionally be expected to have a full restaurant meal. Also, please note that a welcome for children does not necessarily mean a welcome for breast-feeding in public. If we don't mention children at all assume that they are not welcome but it is still worth asking: one or two pubs told us frankly that they do welcome children but don't want to advertise the fact, for fear of being penalised. All but one or two pubs (we mention these in the text) allow children in their garden or on their terrace, if they have one. Note that in Scotland the law allows children more freely into pubs so long as they are eating (and with an adult). In the Lucky Dip entries we mention children only if readers have found either that they are allowed or that they are not allowed – the absence of any reference to children in a Dip entry means we don't know either way.

Dogs, cats and other animals are mentioned in the text if we know either that they are likely to be present or that they are specifically excluded – we depend chiefly on readers and partly on our own inspections for this information.

Parking is not mentioned if you should normally be able to park outside the pub, or in a private car park, without difficulty. But if we know that parking space is limited or metered, we say so.

Telephone numbers are given for all pubs that are not ex-directory.

Opening hours are for summer; we say if we know of differences in winter, or on particular days of the week. In the country, many pubs may open rather later and close earlier than their details show unless there are plenty of customers around (if you come across this, please let us know – with details). Pubs are allowed to stay open all day Mondays to Saturdays from 11am (earlier, if the area's licensing magistrates have permitted) till 11pm. However, outside cities most English and Welsh pubs close during the afternoon. Scottish pubs are allowed to stay open until later at night, and the Government seems increasingly likely to allow later opening in England and Wales too. We'd be very grateful to hear of any differences from the hours we quote. You are allowed 20 minutes' drinking-up time after the quoted hours – half an hour if you've been having a meal in the pub.

Bedroom prices normally include full English breakfasts (if these are available, which they usually are), VAT and any automatic service charge that we know about. If we give just one price, it is the total price for two people sharing a double or twin-bedded room for one night. Otherwise, prices before the / are for single occupancy, prices after it for double. A capital B against the price means that it includes a private bathroom, a capital S a private shower. As all this coding packs in quite a lot of information, some examples may help to explain it:

£60 on its own means that's the total bill for two people sharing a twin or double room without private bath; the pub has no rooms with private bath, and a single person might have to pay that full price
£60B means exactly the same – but all the rooms have private bath
£55(£60B) means rooms with private baths cost £5 extra
£30/£55(£60B) means the same as the last example, but also shows that there are single rooms for £30, none of which have private bathrooms

If there's a choice of rooms at different prices, we normally give the cheapest. If there are seasonal price variations, we give the summer price (the highest). This winter – 1998-9 – many inns, particularly in the country, will have special cheaper rates. And at other times, especially in holiday areas, you will often find prices cheaper if you stay for several nights. On weekends, inns that aren't in obvious weekending areas often have bargain rates for two- or three-night stays.

MEAL TIMES

Bar food is commonly served from 12-2 and 7-9, at least from Monday to Saturday (food service often stops a bit earlier on Sundays). If we don't give a time against the Meals and snacks note at the bottom of a main entry, that means that you should be able to get bar food at those times. However, we do spell out the times if we know that bar food service starts after 12.15 or after 7.15; if it stops before 2 or before 8.45; or if food is served for significantly longer than usual (say, till 2.30 or 9.45).

Though we note days when pubs have told us they don't do food, experience suggests that you should play safe on Sundays and check first with any pub before planning an expedition that depends on getting a meal there. Also, out-of-the-way pubs often cut down on cooking during the week, especially the early part of the week, if they're quiet – as they tend to be, except at holiday times. Please let us know if you find anything different from what we say!

NO SMOKING

We say in the text of each entry what if any provision a pub makes for non-smokers. Pubs setting aside at least some sort of no-smoking area are also listed county by county in the Special Interest Lists at the back of the book.

PLANNING ROUTES WITH THE GOOD PUB GUIDE

Computer users may like to know of two route-finding programmes which will show the location of *Good Pub Guide* pubs on detailed maps, work out the quickest routes for their journeys, add diversions to nearby pubs – and see our text entries for those pubs on screen. These programmes will also include material from *The Good Guide to Britain*. The programmes are NextBase® Personal Navigator™ and Microsoft® AutoRoute Express™ Great Britain 2000 Edition.

OUR NEW WEB SITE

We are working on a new Internet web site which we hope will be open at least in its first version by the time this book is published. It will use and we hope combine material from *The Good Pub Guide* and its sister publication *The Good Guide to Britain* in a way that gives people who do not yet know the books at least a taste of them. We also hope that we can use it to give readers of the books extra information (and allow them to report quickly to us), and hope to expand and improve the site significantly (for instance with pictures of the pubs) over the next year or two. You can try the site yourself at www.goodguides.com.

CHANGES DURING THE YEAR – PLEASE TELL US

Changes are inevitable, during the course of the year. Landlords change, and so do their policies. And, as we've said, not all returned our fact-checking sheets. We very much hope that you will find everything just as we say. But if you find anything different, please let us know, using the tear-out card in the middle of the book (which doesn't need an envelope), the report forms here, or just a letter. You don't need a stamp: the address is *The Good Pub Guide*, FREEPOST TN1569, WADHURST, East Sussex TN5 7BR.

Author's Acknowledgements

This book would not be possible without the enormous volume of help we get from several thousand readers, who send us reports on pubs they visit: thanks to you all. Many have now been reporting to us for a good few years, often in marvellously helpful detail, and in a number of cases have now sent us several hundred reports – even, in one or two cases, over a thousand. We rely heavily on this hugely generous help, all of it unpaid, to keep us up to date with existing entries, to warn us when standards start slipping, to build up a record of reports on the most promising Lucky Dip entries, and to uncover for us new gems that we'd otherwise never hear of.

For the exceptional help they've given us, I'm specially grateful to Ian Phillips, Richard Lewis, Gwen and Peter Andrews, CMW and JJW, George Atkinson, Roger and Jenny Huggins, Dave Irving, Ewan McCall, Tom McLean, Michael and Jenny Back, Ann and Colin Hunt, E G Parish, Peter and Audrey Dowsett, SLC, Stephen and Julie Brown, Susan and John Douglas, Phyl and Jack Street, DWAJ, Brian and Jenny Seller, the Didler, Lynn Sharpless and Bob Eardley, Ted George, Comus Elliott, M J Morgan, Tony and Wendy Hobden, Tony Scott, Gordon, Kevin Thorpe, Alan and Val Green, John Wooll, Tony and Louise Clarke, Anthony Barnes, David Carr, Bronwen and Steve Wrigley, Sue Holland and Dave Webster, Bruce Bird, Eric Larkham, Derek and Sylvia Stephenson, Joan and Michel Hooper-Immins, Martin and Karen Wake, J F M West, LM, Alan and Paula McCully, Nigel Woolliscroft, Mayur Shah, Tom Evans, Mike and Mary Carter, James Nunns, Jack and Philip Paxton, W W Burke, Pat and Tony Martin, Joy and Peter Heatherley, Marjorie and David Lamb, JDM and KM, R J Walden, John C Baker, Dave Braisted, Mrs K Clapp, R T and J C Moggridge, G Coates, J A Barker, Peter Baker, David and Tina Woods-Taylor, Andy and Jill Kassube, Michael A Butler, Tim Barrow and Sue Demont, Susan and Nigel Wilson, M Borthwick, TBB, Simon Collett-Jones, Richard Gibbs, Paul S McPherson, M Joyner, Paul and Ursula Randall, Mark Baynham and Rachael Ward, D B Jenkin, David and Carole Chapman, John Evans, Neil Townend, Rona Murdoch, John Fahy, Eric Locker, Meg and Colin Hamilton, Howard Clutterbuck, Terry Buckland, John Bowdler, Charles Bardswell, John Beeken, Nick Lawless, Gerald Barnett, I J and N K Buckmaster, Sue and Bob Ward, Iain Robertson, Vann and Terry Prime, John and Vivienne Rice, Eddie Edwards, Graham and Lynn Mason, Richard Houghton, Colin and Joyce Laffan, Neil and Anita Christopher, Thomas and Audrey Nott, Gordon Neighbour, Walter Reid and Joan Olivier.

A word of special gratitude to Steve and Carolyn Harvey, our Channel Islands Inspectors; and above all to the thousands of publicans and their staff who work so unstintingly and so warm-heartedly to give us so very many Good Pubs.

Alisdair Aird

England

Bedfordshire

Hertfordshire's loss is Bedfordshire's gain, with Ray Scarbrow moving his well tried team from the Green Man at Great Offley over the border to the Red Lion at Milton Bryan – good food in pleasant surroundings, a well deserved new main entry. The other new main entry here this year is the Globe at Linslade on the edge of Leighton Buzzard, delightfully placed by the canal. It belongs to the Old English Pub Co. chain, as does another civilised pub with good value food and drink here, the Three Cranes at Turvey. Other places for an enjoyable meal out are the Chequers at Keysoe (consistently good food) and the Fox & Hounds at Riseley (grills are its speciality – the grill room's been extended this year to meet its growing popularity). The Knife & Cleaver at Houghton Conquest, however, stands out above all other pubs in the county for the quality of its food, and for the fourth year running is our Bedfordshire Dining Pub of the Year. Other old favourites here are the delightfully traditional Cock at Broom, and the cheerful thatched Three Tuns at Biddenham – carrying on much as before, despite Alan Wilkins's virtual retirement. And a word of praise for the Bell at Odell, holding down its prices and gaining one of our cherished Bargain Awards this year. Lucky Dip pubs currently doing particularly well are the Black Horse at Ireland, Hare & Hounds at Old Warden, Rose & Crown at Ridgmont, Kings Arms in Sandy and Locomotive just outside – we have inspected nearly all of these and can vouch for their quality. Pub prices are beginning to stray a little above the national average, with beer a few pence extra a pint; we found pubs tied to Greene King cheaper than most in the area, with the Three Cranes at Turvey and Bell at Odell also good value for drinks.

BIDDENHAM TL0249 Map 5

Three Tuns

57 Main Road; village signposted from A428 just W of Bedford

Reasonably priced bar food from a fairly short straightforward menu ensures that this friendly thatched village pub continues to be especially popular at lunchtime. There are sandwiches (from £1.50), home-made soup (£1.80 – or with a choice of any sandwich £2.80), pâté (£2.20), ploughman's (£2.80), salads (from £3.50), quiche, lasagne or chilli con carne (£4.80), seafood platter, home-made steak and kidney pie or chicken casserole (£5.50), and 8oz sirloin steak (£7); usual children's menu (£1.80) and puddings (£2). The bustling lounge has low beams and country paintings, and there are darts, skittle alley, dominoes and a fruit machine in the public bar; piped music. Well kept Marston's Pedigree and Abbot on handpump. On warm summer days there are seats in the attractively sheltered spacious garden, and a big terrace has lots of picnic-sets and white doves in a dovecote; the very good children's play area has swings for all ages and a big wooden climbing frame. *(Recommended by Nigel Williamson, Ian Phillips, JKW, Gordon Theaker, Maysie Thompson)*

Greene King ~ Tenants A Wilkins and A Sullivan ~ Real ale ~ Meals and snacks (not Sun evenings) ~ (01234) 354847 ~ Children in small dining room ~ Open 11.30-2.30, 6-11; 12.30-2.30, 7-10.30 Sun

BOLNHURST TL0859 Map 5

Olde Plough 🍷

B660 Bedford—Kimbolton

As we went to press, Mrs Horridge told us that she may no longer be running this pretty 500-year-old pub by the time this Guide is published. This friendly and entertaining landlady, who has done much to create the cosy and relaxing atmosphere, is a faith-healer who throws in free healing with your pint or pie. The spacious carpeted lounge bar has little armchairs around low tables (where there are fresh flowers), a leather sofa and armchair and a log fire in the big stone fireplace. There's a big woodburning stove and a couple of refectory tables and settles in the flagstoned public bar – as well as darts, pool, hood skittles, cribbage, and dominoes. The dining room has seats around tables ingeniously made from salvaged barn oak and a wooden ceiling made with boards from a Bedford church. The restaurant upstairs is now only used on selected special occasions including Valentine's Day and Mother's Day. Good bar food from a changing menu includes home-made soup (£2.95), brie fritters with apricot coulis or large filo prawns with lemon mayonnaise (£4.15), shepherd's pie (£5.95), Lincolnshire sausages (£6.25), spinach, lentil and cheese bake (£6.95), ham and chips (£6.50), 8oz sirloin steak (£10.95), and puddings like home-made treacle tart or apple and blackberry crumble (£2.95). Well kept Courage Directors, Ruddles Best and a guest on handpump, and good selection of wines, with mulled wine in winter. In summer there may be Morris men or country dancing, with bell ringers and carol singers at Christmas. The lovely tree-shaded garden has rustic seats and tables, and a long crazy-paved terrace looks onto the pond where you can still see the remains of a moat that used to surround the pub; free plant cuttings. The cats, Blacky and Titch, the dobermann Zeus, and the other dog Lica, may occupy the best seats by the fire. *(Recommended by John Fahy, D A Norman, George Atkinson, Ian Phillips)*

Free house ~ Licensee Michael Horridge ~ Real ale ~ Meals and snacks (till 10 if busy) ~ Restaurant (not always open) ~ (01234) 376274 ~ Well behaved children welcome till 9pm ~ Open 12-2.30(3 Sat), 7-11; 12-3, 7-10.30 Sun; closed 25 and 26 Dec

BROOM TL1743 Map 5

Cock

23 High Street; from A1 opposite northernmost Biggleswade turn-off follow Old Warden 3, Aerodrome 2 signpost, and take first left signposted Broom

This friendly and delightfully unspoilt 17th-c village inn is very much the focal point of the village, attracting a strong local following as well as being popular with visitors. The four cosy rooms have simple latch doors, low ochre ceilings, stripped panelling and farmhouse-style tables and chairs on the antique tile floors; winter log fires and table skittles. There's no counter, and the very well kept Greene King IPA, Abbot, and Rayments are tapped straight from the cask. A central corridor runs down the middle of the building, with the sink for washing glasses on one side (pewter mugs hang over it) and on the other steps down to the cellar. Good bar food includes sandwiches (from £1.95), home-made soup (£2.50), ploughman's (from £3.65), proper gammon and egg or liver and bacon (£5.95), cajun chicken or mushroom stroganoff (£6.95), and puddings (from £2.95). There are picnic-sets on the terrace by the back lawn, and a fenced-off children's play area. *(Recommended by Pete Baker, Barry and Marie Males, JP, PP, DAV, Tim Heywood, Sophie Wilne, R J Bland)*

Greene King ~ Tenants Gerry and Jean Lant ~ Real ale ~ Meals and snacks (not Sun evening) ~ (01767) 314411 ~ Children welcome in family room ~ Open 12-3(4 Sat), 6-11; 12-4, 7-10.30 Sun; closed evening 25 Dec

We mention bottled beers and spirits only if there is something unusual about them – imported Belgian real ales, say, or dozens of malt whiskies; so do please let us know about them in your reports.

HOUGHTON CONQUEST TL0441 Map 5

Knife & Cleaver

Between B530 (old A418) and A6, S of Bedford

Bedfordshire Dining Pub of the Year

This is a sucessful combination of a 17-c pub with a restaurant and it's the delicious food that draws people here. In the bar, as well as regular sandwiches (from £3), they offer focaccia bread with chicken, chargrilled leeks, chorizo sausage and garlic mayonnaise (£5.95), and french bread with rib steak, red onions, rosemary and melted gruyère (£6.25). Daily specials may include chicken and pork gratin with asparagus (£5.25), sweet and sour pork with saffron rice or wild mushroom and roast tomato risotto (£6.25) and swordfish tartlet (£7.50) – and from a menu that changes regularly there might be home-made soup (£2.75), a small mixed hors d'oeuvre (£4.75; large £8.50), smoked haddock fishcake with hard-boiled egg (£6.25), spicy Merguez sausages with couscous and chickpeas (£6.50); Scottish smoked salmon with scrambled eggs (£7.95); home-made puddings such as marbled chocolate mousse, steamed lemon and sultana pudding or home-made ice creams (£3.25), and a good selection of cheeses (£3.50; you can enjoy these as a ploughman's £4). Beware, on Saturday evening if the restaurant is fully booked they may not serve bar meals. Well kept Adnams Extra and Batemans XB on handpump, Stowfod Press farm cider, 23 good wines by the glass, and a fine choice of up to 20 well aged malt whiskies; friendly, efficient service and unobtrusive piped classical music. The relaxed, comfortable bar has maps, drawings and old documents on the walls, panelling which is reputed to have come from nearby ruin Houghton House, and a blazing fire in winter; the airy conservatory no-smoking restaurant has rugs on the tiled floor, swagged curtains, cane furniture and lots of hanging plants. There are tables out in the neatly kept garden. Well equipped bedrooms in a separate building. *(Recommended by E and K Leist, Gwen and Peter Andrews, Maysie Thompson, Mike and Mary Carter, Jackie Hammond, W A Evershed, John and Enid Morris, John Cooper, Michael Sargent, Eric Locker, Derek and Maggie Washington, Maggie and Peter Shapland, Stephen, Julie and Hayley Brown, Dr B E Monk, Gordon Tong, Rita Horridge, David Shillitoe)*

Free house ~ Licensees David and Pauline Loom ~ Real ale ~ Meals and snacks (not Sun evening) ~ Restaurant (not Sun evening) ~ (01234) 740387 ~ Children in eating area of bar and in restaurant ~ Open 12-2.30(2 Sat), 7-10.30(11 Sat); 12-3 Sun (closed Sun evening); closed 27-30 Dec ~ Bedrooms: £49B/£64B

KEYSOE TL0762 Map 5

Chequers

B660 N of Bedford

It's the consistently good food which stands out at this friendly and unpretentious village local. As well as sandwiches (£2) and daily specials, the bar menu includes home-made soup (£2.50), garlic mushrooms on toast (£3.50), ploughman's (£4), chilli con carne (£5.50), home-made steak and ale pie (£6.00), chicken breast stuffed with stilton in a chive sauce (£8), steaks (from £8.75), and puddings like bread and butter pudding with cointreau raisins or kahlua flamed bananas (£2.25) which are highly recommended by readers; children's menu (£3.25). Well kept Fullers London Pride and Hook Norton Best on handpumps on the stone bar counter; some malts. The leatherette seats lend an air of the 1960s to the two neatly simple beamed rooms divided by an unusual stone-pillared fireplace; one bar is no smoking; darts; piped music. The terrace at the back looks over the garden which has a wendy house, play tree, swings and a sand-pit. *(Recommended by Jenny and Michael Back, Maysie Thompson, Margaret and Roy Randle, G Neighbour)*

Free house ~ Licensee Jeffrey Kearns ~ Real ale ~ Meals and snacks (not Tues) ~ (01234) 708678 ~ Children welcome away from main bar ~ Open 11.30-2.30, 6.30-11; 12-2.30, 7-10.30 Sun; closed Tuesdays

Soup prices usually include a roll and butter.

LINSLADE SP9225 Map 4

Globe

Globe Lane, off Stoke Rd (A4146) nr bridge; outside Linslade proper, just before you get to the town sign

Lots of traffic outside this popular early 19th-c whitewashed pub, but for once that's the attraction; it's idyllically set on its own alongside the Grand Union Canal, and the vehicles idling past are either brightly painted boats or smugly superior ducks and swans. A perfect spot to while away a sunny afternoon, it does get very busy in summer – but there are enough tables out here to cope, most of them along the towpath, with others in a very well equipped fenced-off play area with climbing forts and equipment, or in the garden under the trees alongside the car park. In summer an outdoor bar serves ice creams as well as drinks; it may be open in the afternoons when the pub itself is shut. Some readers prefer coming here in winter, when it's much quieter and the same views can be enjoyed from the warmly cosy series of beamed and flagstoned rooms. In recent years the pub has been very well regarded for its food, but when we visited in the early summer the manager was making plans to leave, and intending to take his staff with him, so we can't predict how things might change under his successors. This underlines the slight risk we always face in recommending pubs belonging to the Globe's parent group, the Old English Pub Company: staff can change fairly frequently, and sometimes no sooner has a pub established its reputation than the people responsible move on. But at the very least the summer appeal of the Globe isn't likely to alter, and nor, we're told, will the beers: Fullers London Pride, Theakstons Best and Wadworths 6X. To get to the pub you come down a little private road that seems to take you further into the countryside than you really are, and the Cross Bucks Way leads off from just along the canal. *(Recommended by Paul Cleaver, Jean and David Darby, Bill Sykes, John and Enid Morris, Andrew Scarr, Mick and Mel Smith, Marianne and Andrew Bainbridge, Graham and Karen Oddey, Ian Phillips)*

Free house ~ Real ale ~ Meals and snacks ~ Restaurant ~ (01525) 373338 ~ Open 11-3, 6-11 (though see above)

MILTON BRYAN SP9730 Map 4

Red Lion

Toddington Rd, off B528 S of Woburn

The many readers who wistfully remember this landlord's days at the Green Man at Great Offley in Hertfordshire will be pleased to learn that he's running this relaxed and comfortable pub in exactly the same way, with the help of the same efficient and friendly staff. It's already a well liked place for eating out, with the weekday lunchtime menu for the over-55s proving particularly popular at the moment: three courses are a bargain £3.95. The full menu typically includes soup (£1.75), good chunky sandwiches (£2.25), Japanese prawns (£4.50), moules marinières (£5.50), chicken casserole (£7.25), lamb hotpot (£7.50) and half a dozen or so grilled fresh fish specials like haddock or cod (£8.50), a big whole plaice (£9.50), and dover sole (£14.50). Most of the tables are set for eating, and the dining areas are all no smoking. Cool and airy on a hot day, the beamed bar area is spotlessly kept, with pristine white-painted walls, some exposed brickwork, big fading rugs on the part wood and part stone floors, a case of sporting cups, and fresh flowers on the round wooden tables; piped music. Marstons Best and Pedigree and a fortnightly changing guest on handpump. The lavatories are unusually well equipped, with shoe-shine kits and the like. In summer – when the pub is festooned with hanging baskets and plants – there's a separate bar outside, serving their own special Pimm's. Plenty of tables, chairs and picnic-sets out on the patio and on the lawn, which looks across to a delightfully thatched black and white timbered house; there's a climbing frame out here too. Woburn Abbey and Safari Park are very close by. *(Recommended by Steve and Stella Swepston)*

Marstons ~ Real ale ~ Tenant Ray Scarbrow ~ Meals and snacks ~ (01525) 210044 ~ Children welcome ~ Open 11-4, 6-11

ODELL SP9658 Map 4

Bell £

Horsefair Lane; off A6 S of Rushden, via Sharnbrook

The outside of this thatched stone village pub is as pretty as the interior where five small homely low-ceilinged rooms – some with shiny black beams – loop around a central servery and are furnished with quite a few handsome old oak settles, bentwood chairs and neat modern furniture; there's a log fire in one big stone fireplace and two coal fires elsewhere. Fairly priced bar food includes sandwiches (from £1.95), ploughman's (from £3.50), omelettes (from £3.60) ham, egg and chips (£4.00), home-made vegetable pie (£4.50), savoury pancakes (from £4.65), liver and bacon (£5.25), and daily specials from the board such as fish pie (£4.65), home-made lasagne (£5.30), spicy pork sausages in onion gravy (£5.50), and beef, bacon and wine casserole (£6.50); usual children's dishes (from £2) and home-made puddings like boozy chocolate mousse or orange cheesecake shortbread (£2). Well kept Greene King Abbot, IPA, and seasonal ales, and Rayments on handpump. There are picnic-sets on the flower-filled terrace overlooking the wooded garden that offers an attractive walk down through a wild area to a bridge over the Great Ouse. The garden is full of golden pheasants, cockatiels, canaries, and a goose called Lucy. Further along the road is a very pretty church; handy for the local country park. *(Recommended by John McDonald, Ann Bond, G Neighbour, John and Enid Morris, Ian Phillips, Maysie Thompson, Andy and Jill Kassube, Stephen G Brown, Martin and Karen Wake)*

Greene King ~ Tenant Derek Scott ~ Real ale ~ Meals and snacks (not Sun evening Sept-May) ~ (01234) 720254 ~ Children in eating area of bar only ~ Open 11-2.30, 6-11; 12-2.30, 7-10.30 Sun

RISELEY TL0362 Map 5

Fox & Hounds

High St; village signposted off A6 and B660 N of Bedford

Jan and Lynne Zielinski have been serving up highly acclaimed steaks at this cheerful little pub for almost ten years. You choose which piece of meat you want from the cabinet at one end of the bar counter, say how much you want and how you want it cooked, and you're then charged by weight – £8.96 for 8oz rump, £9.60 for 8oz of sirloin and £11.60 for fillet. Other food includes home-made soups like stilton and broccoli and leek and potato (£1.95), king prawns in filo pastry (£3.25), moules marinières (£5.95), steak and kidney pie (£6.95), local trout (£7.50), and a couple of vegetarian dishes. As we went to press, major refurbishments were taking place: the grill room will be enlarged (as will the car park), a terrace area will be built behind the pub with outside heating and wooden tables and chairs, and a comfortable lounge area will be created with leather chesterfields, low tables and wing chairs as an alternative to the more traditional pub furniture spread around among timber uprights under the heavy low beams. Well kept Charles Wells Eagle and Bombardier with regularly changing guests like Marstons Pedigree, Vaux Waggle Dance and Wadworths 6X on handpump, a decent collection of other drinks including several malts and a good range of cognacs; unobtrusive piped Glen Miller or light classics. The landlord is a real personality and helps to create the friendly and welcoming atmosphere. *(Recommended by S Markham, Michael Sargent, David Etheridge, JJW, CMW)*

Charles Wells ~ Managers Jan and Lynne Zielinski ~ Real ale ~ Meals and snacks (12-1.45, 7-10) ~ Restaurant ~ (01234) 708240 ~ Children welcome ~ Open 11.30-2.30, 6.30-11; 12-3, 7-10.30 Sun

Please keep sending us reports. We rely on readers for news of new discoveries, and particularly for news of changes – however slight – at the fully described pubs. No stamp needed: *The Good Pub Guide*, FREEPOST TN1569, Wadhurst, E Sussex TN5 7BR.

TURVEY SP9452 Map 4

Three Cranes

Just off A428 W of Bedford

Relatively little appears to have changed at this stone-built 17th-c inn since it was bought by the Old English Pub Company. Readers continue to praise bar food which now includes lunchtime sandwiches (from £1.95), soup (£2.25), beef, mushroom and ale pie (£6.25), lasagne (£6.25), trout (£7.95), and steaks (£9.50); readers enjoy the sausages (£5.50) which come from the butcher next door. The airy and spacious two-level bar has a solid-fuel stove, a quiet decor including old photographs and Victorian style prints, and an array of stuffed owls and other birds in the main dining area; there are plenty of sensible tables with upright seats. Well kept Courage Best and Directors, Fullers London Pride, Hook Norton Best, Theakstons XB, and guests on handpump. There are picnic-sets in a neatly kept garden with a climbing frame; in summer, the pub's front has been a mass of colour from carefully tended hanging baskets and window-boxes. *(Recommended by George Atkinson, Stephen Brown, L Eadon, Simon Walker, Mike Sheehan, John Saul, Maysie Thompson; more reports on the new regime, please)*

Free house ~ Managers Paul and Sheila Linehan ~ Real ale ~ Meals and snacks ~ Restaurant ~ (01234) 881305 ~ Children in eating area of bar and in restaurant till 9.30pm ~ Open 11-2.30, 6-11; 12-3, 7-10.30 Sun; closed evenings 25/26 Dec ~ Bedrooms: £39.50S/£54S

Lucky Dip

Besides the fully inspected pubs, you might like to try these Lucky Dips recommended to us and described by readers (if you do, please send us reports):

Bedford [Embankment; TL0449], *Nicholls*: Lively and fun, with good innovative food, good coffee, jazz Sun lunchtime *(Sarah Markham)*

Bromham [Bridge End; nr A428, 2 miles W of Bedford; TL0050], *Swan*: Comfortable and welcoming beamed village pub with welcoming atmosphere, quick service, lots of pictures, well kept Greene King IPA and Abbot, decent coffee, food from sandwiches to steaks, evening log fire; quiet piped music; public bar with darts and fruit machine, provision for children, pleasant garden *(Ian Phillips)*

Cardington [The Green; off A603 E of Bedford; TL0847], *Kings Arms*: Clean comfortable Brewers Fayre, usual food not too expensive; Boddingtons, Marstons Pedigree *(Ian Phillips)*

☆ **Dunstable** [A5183 S, 4 miles N of M1 junction 9; TL0221], *Horse & Jockey*: Big Chef & Brewer divided into many smaller areas, light pine furnishings, well kept ales, friendly staff, good promptly served food; children very welcome, play areas inside and out (huge garden), maybe bouncy castle *(Mick and Mel Smith, LYM)*

Houghton Conquest [B530 towards Ampthill; TL0441], *Chequers*: Proper straightforward pub with well kept Whitbreads-related and other ales, log fires, decent food from sandwiches to steaks, tables out on terrace *(Ian Phillips)*

☆ **Ireland** [off A600 Shefford—Bedford – OS Sheet 153 map ref 135414; TL1341], *Black Horse*: New management doing wide choice of good value plentiful piping hot food in pretty pub's sizeable lounge or family dining area, well kept Bass and Worthington, good coffee, helpful very friendly staff, lots of tables in lovely front garden with play area – peaceful rural setting *(Jenny and Michael Back, Maysie Thompson, Sidney and Erna Wells, BB)*

Kempston [Woburn Rd; TL0347], *Royal Oak*: Happy local atmosphere in neat little suburban pub with popular good-natured licensees, well kept Greene King IPA and sensibly priced usual food from sandwiches up *(Ian Phillips)*

Kensworth [B4540, Whipsnade end; TL0318], *Farmers Boy*: Village pub with good value food inc vegetarian, children's and Sun roast, generous and freshly made (so may be a wait), well kept Fullers, good if sometimes smoky lounge bar, good old-fashioned dining room (more restauranty evenings and Sun); dogs welcome, piped pop music, bar with fruit machine and TV; play area, maybe bouncy castle and rabbit hutches in fenced-off garden by fields with horses; children very welcome *(JJW, CMW)*

Lidlington [High St; off A421 not far from M1 junction 13; SP9939], *Green Man*: 17th-c thatched village pub, with comfortable dark-beamed lounge, real fire, good reasonably priced food in raised dining area, friendly and attentive service, Greene King IPA and Abbot; piped music; fruit machine and pool in separate bar; picnic-sets outside, boules; handy for walkers *(Tony Hobden)*

Luton [by stn; TL0921], *Bricklayers Arms*:

Convivial local atmosphere, well kept ales inc Everards, decor evokes living room/library *(Giles Francis)*; [Manchester St, opp St Georges Theatre], *Sadlers*: Smart minimalist cafe/bar with heavy bronze relief wallpaper in comfortable tartan-carpeted upstairs lounge, wide range of drinks, reasonably priced food from filled baguettes and doorstep sandwiches up, quiet piped music, discreet games machines *(Ian Phillips)*; [Tea Green, just N of Luton Airport main runway; TL1323], *White Horse*: Smallish village pub, tables tightly packed into cosy bar for good range of very popular good value food esp curries, friendly service, Flowers IPA and Wadworths 6X, big fireplace; big garden with play area *(Phil and Heidi Cook, Ian Phillips)*

Maulden [TL0538], *White Hart*: Freshly cooked good value food in friendly thatched low-beamed pub with big fireplace dividing bar, lots of tables in separate eating area, pleasant efficient service, Whitbreads-related beers *(Barry and Marie Males)*

Northill [2 Ickwell Rd; TL1546], *Crown*: Welcoming local in attractive village, well kept Charles Wells ales, games room (popular with YFC); not far from the Shuttleworth Collection *(Barry and Marie Males, D C Poulton)*

☆ **Old Warden** [High St; TL1343], *Hare & Hounds*: Welcoming beamed pub in attractive thatched village, good helpings of good if somewhat pricey food, interesting menu, lots of aircraft memorabilia, Charles Wells Eagle and Bombardier with a guest such as Morlands Old Speckled Hen, generally very friendly service, simple but comfortable decor, open fire, dining room overlooking glorious garden stretching up to pine woods, play area; piped music; handy for Shuttleworth Collection, Swiss Garden and local walks (though mucky boots and sometimes children seem frowned on) *(George Atkinson, Ian Phillips, JKW, Dr B E Monk, BB)*

Potton [4 Biggleswade Rd; TL2449], *Royal Oak*: Neatly kept traditional thatched pub with large bar, spacious dining area opening into restaurant, above-average straightforward bar food (served evenings too) inc bargain generous lunchtime roasts, very friendly service, Greene King IPA, Abbot and seasonal ales, decent wine; piped music may be loud; garden *(Graeham Broderick, Sidney and Erna Wells, Mikes Thackray)*

Pulloxhill [off A6 N of Barton le Clay; TL0633], *Cross Keys*: Modernised early 17th-c, lots of timbering and flower baskets, roomy front bars, very friendly licensee and family, good value bar food, children in big back dining room, Charles Wells ales; garden with play area, pretty part of village in nice countryside *(Mr and Mrs A Budden, MR, RR)*

☆ **Radwell** [TL0057], *Swan*: Roomy and attractive beamed and thatched pub, two rooms joined by narrow passage, woodburner, lots of prints, unobtrusive piped music, friendly service, wide choice of good food, Charles Wells Eagle, decent coffee, popular evening restaurant; pleasant garden, small quiet village *(John Saul, Maysie Thompson)*

Ravensden [B660 just N of Bedford – OS Sheet 153 map ref 065544; TL0654], *Blacksmiths Arms*: Very warm welcome, immaculate housekeeping, good food inc bargain Sun lunches, pleasant service *(Anon)*

☆ **Ridgmont** [handy for M1 junction 13; SP9736], *Rose & Crown*: Consistently good sensible pub food served quickly even when busy, choice of well kept real ales, good coffee, Rupert Bear memorabilia and old English sheepdog china in comfortable spick-and-span lounge, friendly landlady; low-ceilinged traditional public bar with open fire, games inc darts and pool; piped music, stables restaurant (not Mon or Tues evenings); long and attractive suntrap sheltered back garden; children allowed in bar eating area; easy parking, good wheelchair access *(George Atkinson, N S Holmes, Dr Paul Khan, LYM)*

☆ **Sandy** [Old London Rd; TL1649], *Kings Arms*: Attractive two-bar pub with friendly helpful staff, comfortable banquettes, lots of beams, open fire, wide choice of good reasonably priced food (veg charged separately), no-smoking eating area up steps, relaxed atmosphere, Greene King IPA, Abbot and Rayments, decent wines, friendly staff and retriever; restaurant, tiled courtyard, garden, bedrooms in well built chalets *(George Atkinson, Scott Rumery, Phil and Heidi Cook)*

☆ *nr* **Sandy** [Deepdale; B1042 towards Potton and Cambridge], *Locomotive*: Reliable pub nr RSPB HQ, packed with railway memorabilia; reasonably priced food nicely prepared and presented, friendly staff, well kept Charles Wells ales with a guest such as Greene King Abbot, no-smoking area, attractive and sizeable garden with views, barbecues and play area; piped radio; can be busy weekends; children allowed in eating area *(George Atkinson, Scott Rumery, Ian Phillips)*

Sharnbrook [High St; SP9959], *Swan With Two Nicks*: Friendly straightforward local with sensibly priced Charles Wells Eagle and Bombardier and a guest such as Morlands Old Speckled Hen, wide choice of generous food, welcoming log fire, Thurleigh Airfield WWII mementoes, games in public bar, french windows to walled terrace; dogs allowed; pretty village with interesting specialist shops *(Michael Sargent, Alison Aubrey, John Saul)*

☆ **Sharpenhoe** [Harlington Rd; TL0630], *Lynmore*: Spacious and comfortable, with friendly beamy family lounge and back dining area (good views), huge helpings of quick good value food inc children's dishes, good range of well kept ales, good garden for children, big wendy house; popular with walkers *(Sidney and Erna Wells, Eric Locker)*

☆ **Silsoe** [TL0835], *George*: Big pleasant open-plan hotel bar with public and family ends, decent bar food inc good snacks for children (and high chairs), well kept Greene King IPA and Abbot, friendly licensees, restaurant; big garden with play equipment, pets' corner; bedrooms reasonably priced *(Scott Rumery)*

☆ **Southill** [off B658 SW of Biggleswade; TL1542], *White Horse*: Well decorated comfortable lounge, dining room with spotlit well, small public bar with prints, harness and big woodburner; good value food (not Sun evening) inc wide choice of sandwiches and snacks, Whitbreads-related ales; children in eating areas; delightful big garden maybe with children's rides on diesel-engine miniature train, separate sheltered lawn with bird feeders, garden shop and good play area *(Kay Neville-Rolfe, Maysie Thompson, Scott Rumery, LYM)*

☆ **Steppingley** [Rectory Rd; TL0135], *French Horn*: Beams, flagstones, bare boards and carpet, good food inc Mon bargains, interesting real ales such as Morlands Old Rooster and Tomintoul Witches Cauldron, above-average service, woodburner, plenty of brass and pictures, restaurant; piped music *(George Atkinson, B N F and M Parkin)*

☆ **Studham** [Dunstable Rd; TL0215], *Bell*: Friendly and softly lit two-bar village pub dating from 16th c, beams, brasses, prints and plates, no smoking in half of lounge or at bar counter, plentiful good value freshly cooked food, Benskins, Flowers Original, Ind Coope Burton and Tetleys; booking advised Sat, Sun lunch very popular; handy for Whipsnade and the Tree Cathedral *(Phil and Heidi Cook, Kay Neville-Rolfe, David Gambling)*

☆ **Sutton** [village signposted off B1040 Biggleswade—Potton; TL2247], *John o' Gaunt*: Pretty pink pub nr fine 14th-c packhorse bridge – you have to go through a shallow ford; relaxing cottagey low-beamed lounge bar with log fire, well kept Greene King IPA, friendly landlord, decent food cooked by his wife (may be a wait); traditional public bar with hood skittles *(Dr Steve Feast, LYM)*

Toddington [64 High St (A5120); handy for M1 junction 12; TL0028], *Bedford Arms*: Basic but welcoming two-bar Charles Wells pub, woodburners in inglenooks, brass and beams, food inc vegetarian and children's, three real ales inc Thwaites Daniels Hammer; can get smoky, piped music; garden with play area *(CMW, JJW)*

☆ **Turvey** [Bridge St; A428 NW of Bedford – at W end of village; SP9452], *Three Fyshes*: Early 17th-c pub taken over by small dining pub chain, beams, inglenook, carpeted flagstones, well kept beer, good food, very friendly service, no-smoking restaurant, garden overlooking the Great Ouse *(Alison Aubrey, David Toulson, LYM)*

Upper Dean [TL0467], *Three Compasses*: 350-year-old beamed and thatched Charles Wells pub with good value food inc OAP special Mon (not bank hols) and children's dishes, well kept beer *(E Robinson)*

Wilden [High St; off B660 NE of Bedford; TL0955], *Victoria Arms*: Friendly and welcoming unpretentious village pub in attractive spot by green next to church, well kept Greene King, good choice of sensibly priced appetising food from club sandwiches to steaks inc bargain weekday lunches, quick service *(D C Poulton)*

☆ **Woburn** [21 Bedford St; SP9433], *Bell*: Friendly and comfortable tastefully decorated hotel with long narrow bar/dining area, well kept Greene King ales, good coffee, changing interesting food, evening restaurant; maybe piped radio; tables outside, handy for Woburn Park; bedrooms *(George Atkinson, Brian Horner, Brenda Arthur)*

The letters and figures after the name of each town are its Ordnance Survey map reference. *How to use the Guide* at the beginning of the book explains how it helps you find a pub, in road atlases or large-scale maps as well as in our own maps.

Berkshire

This county has a splendid variety of pubs, from delightfully unspoilt and welcoming country taverns (the Bell at Aldworth, in the same family for two centuries, and the Pot Kiln at Frilsham, brewing its own beer, stand out) to dining pubs that stand out for the high quality of their food. Among these, we'd particularly pick out the elegantly informal Fish in Bray (super for fish), the charming and civilised Thatched Tavern at Cheapside, the White Hart at Hamstead Marshall (Italian), the Hare & Hounds at Lambourn Woodlands between Lambourn itself and the M4 (a new main entry, traditional with a distinctively individual touch), the Harrow at West Ilsley (particularly successful combination of good food with a warm country-pub atmosphere) and the sophisticated Royal Oak at Yattendon. It's the Harrow at West Ilsley that we choose as Berkshire Dining Pub of the Year: so good to see a place with really good food keeping close to its pubby roots. Other pubs here doing particularly well these days include the pleasantly individual Horns at Crazies Hill, the Crown & Horns at East Ilsley (fantastic range of whiskies), the welcoming little Queen Victoria at Hare Hatch, the Belgian Arms at Holyport (nice spot, yet handy for the M4), the Dew Drop deep in the countryside near Hurley (new licensees winning it a place in the Guide), the Sweeney & Todd in Reading (another new Guide entry, unexpectedly pubby behind its shop-front facade, with a splendid range of pies), the fine old Bull in Sonning (back in the Guide after quite a break), and the interesting and attractive Bell at Waltham St Lawrence. The Bell at Boxford, good all round, has a quite remarkable choice of wines by the glass. Pubs in the Lucky Dip section at the end of the chapter that are currently scoring high points are the Blackbird at Bagnor, Crown in Bray, Pineapple at Brimpton, Olde Red Lion at Chieveley, Dundas Arms at Kintbury, Seven Stars at Knowl Hill, Little Angel at Remenham, Old Boot at Stanford Dingley and Crooked Billet just outside Wokingham (all inspected and confidently recommended by us). There's a fine choice for real-ale specialists in Reading. This isn't a cheap county for drinks, with a pint of beer in general costing about 15p more than the national average – but the Bell at Aldworth and Pot Kiln at Frilsham are very much cheaper, with prices that wouldn't look out of line in even the cheapest parts of Britain.

ALDWORTH SU5579 Map 2

Bell ★ £ 🍷 🍺

A329 Reading—Wallingford; left on to B4009 at Streatley

A marvellous place to start or finish a walk, this unspoilt 14th-c country pub has been run by the same family for over 200 years. It does get busy at weekends but there's always a warm welcome from the friendly licensees and a good mix of customers in the cosy bar. There's a glass-panelled hatch rather than a bar counter for service, beams in the shiny ochre ceiling, benches around the panelled walls, a woodburning stove, and an ancient one-handed clock. Incredibly good value food is confined to hot crusty rolls (apart from winter home-made soup), filled with cheddar (£1.10), ham, brie, stilton or pâté (£1.30), smoked salmon, salt beef or ox tongue (£1.80), and particularly good Devon crab in season (£1.95); salad basket and garlic dressing

(£1.60). Very well kept and very cheap Arkells BBB and Kingsdown, Morrells Bitter and Mild, and from the local West Berkshire Brewery, Old Tyler on handpump (they won't stock draught lager); particularly good house wines. Darts, shove-ha'penny, dominoes, and cribbage. The quiet, old-fashioned garden is lovely in summer, and the pub is handy for the Ridgeway. Occasional Morris dancing; Christmas mummers. *(Recommended by N Cobb, David Shillitoe, JP, PP, Ronald Harry, R Stamp, Maureen Hobbs, Liz and Ian Phillips, Sidney and Erna Wells, John Hayter, C P R Baxter, TRS)*

Free house ~ Licensee H E Macaulay ~ Real ale ~ Snacks (11-2.45, 6-10.45; not Mon) ~ (01635) 578272 ~ Well behaved children in tap room ~ Open 11-3, 6-11; 12-3, 7-10.30 Sun; closed Mon (open bank holidays), 25 Dec

BINFIELD SU8571 Map 2

Stag & Hounds

Forest Rd (B3034 towards Windsor)

There's a good buzzy atmosphere here, and at lunchtime during the week the pub quickly fills with suits and neatly dressed young women. There are lots of little rooms with interesting furnishings and pictures, log fires, extremely low black beams, soft lighting, and snugly intimate corners – the sort of place where it's easy to believe the tale that Queen Elizabeth I once watched Morris men dancing on the green outside. The walls in an airier end room on the right are hung with attractive sporting and other prints, including a fine group relating to 19th-c Royal Ascot; there's also a plusher high-ceilinged lounge on the left. One area is no smoking. Under the new managers, bar food now includes lunchtime sandwiches, vegetable wellington or steak in ale pie (£6.95), chicken supreme (£7.75), and king prawns in garlic butter or roast shoulder of lamb (£8.95). Best to book on Friday and Saturday evenings and Sunday lunch. Well kept Courage Best and Directors, Hardy Pope's and Wadworths 6X on handpump, decent wines, daily papers, and fruit machine; tables outside on front terrace and in back garden. *(Recommended by Mr and Mrs T A Bryan, G W A Pearce, A E Brace; more reports on the regime, please)*

Hardy ~ Managers Mr and Mrs B Porter ~ Real ale ~ Meals and snacks (not Sun evening) ~ (01344) 483553 ~ Children welcome away from bar areas ~ Occasional live entertainment ~ Open 11.30-3, 5.30(6 Sat)-11; 12-3, 7-10.30 Sun

BOXFORD SU4271 Map 2

Bell

Back road Newbury—Lambourn; village also signposted off B4000 between Speen and M4 junction 14

The licensees manage to keep a fine balance in this civilised and neatly kept mock-Tudor inn between somewhere notable for its very good food and accommodation, and a village pub with a country local atmosphere. It is the food that most readers come to enjoy though, and from a changing choice, there might be crab and potato balls deep-fried and served with a sesame sauce (£4.25), popular thai fishcake (£4.50), wild mushroom tortellini or smoked chicken and bacon rosti (£4.95), and half a dozen fresh Whitstable oysters (£6) or salmon on pasta with sun-dried tomatoes (£8.95), good steaks with interesting sauces such as stilton, bacon and sherry or much liked, very hot red wine and jalapeno pepper sauce (from £10.95), and lamb done with honey and pink peppercorn sauce (£13.95); they also do soup (£2.35; with a sandwich £3.95), filled french bread (£3.85), pork and leek sausage with onion gravy and mash (£4.95), home-cooked ham and eggs (£5.65), steak in ale pie (£6.95), and two roasts of the day (£6.95; 3-course roast Sunday lunch £7.95); the summer lobster dishes are great favourites (half-lobster salad £9.95, whole thermidor £21). The most serious eating takes place in the rather smart, partly no-smoking restaurant area on the left, whereas a fun place to dine in the summer is on the covered and heated terrace. The bar, round to the right, is quite long and snug, with a coal-effect fire at one end, a nice mix of racing pictures and smaller old advertisements (especially for Mercier champagne), red plush cushions for the mate's chairs, and some interesting bric-a-brac. Well kept Badger Tanglefoot, Batemans XXXB, Courage Best, and Wadworths

6X on handpump, 53 wines by the glass, a dozen champagnes, and a good choice of malt whiskies and cognacs; pool, cribbage, fruit machine, trivia, and juke box; piped music. A side courtyard had white cast-iron garden furniture; the lane is quiet enough for the main sound to be the nearby rookery. *(Recommended by Martin and Karen Wake, HNJ, PEJ)*

Free house ~ Licensees Paul and Helen Lavis ~ Real ale ~ Meals and snacks ~ Restaurant ~ (01488) 608721 ~ Children in eating area of bar ~ Open 11-3, 6(6.30 Sat)-11; 12-3.30, 7-10.30 Sun ~ Bedrooms: £56B/£65B

BRAY SU9079 Map 2

Fish 🍴 🍷

1¾ miles from M4 junction 8: A308(M), A308 towards Windsor, then first left into B3028 towards Bray; bear right into Old Mill Lane

Although food (especially the delicious, interesting fish dishes) is what this handsome tucked-away Georgian pub is so much liked for, they are happy to serve locals and occasional walkers with just a pint of beer in a relaxed and informal atmosphere. The bar servery is very much part of the scenery, its two rooms linked by a broad row of arches; above the venetian red dado, reproduction Old Master drawings and details of paintings decorate the subtly off-white walls, and on the parquet floor are most attractive caucasian rugs, well spaced tables with little sprays of fresh flowers (candles at night), and a mix of continental-style rush-seat stained-wood dining chairs and country kitchen chairs; a no-smoking conservatory (with plenty of blinds) has more tables and opens out beyond. Changing daily, the 6 or 7 choices of fresh fish might include Cornish oysters (half a dozen £7.90), deep-fried salmon with a honey, soy and ginger dressing (£10.95), roast cod with lobster sauce on saffron mash or chargrilled tuna loin with couscous and tapenade (£11.95), and grilled swordfish on lemon grass skewer with a thai dressing and coconut rice (£12.50); there's also a choice of meat dishes such as maize-fed chicken breast on a bed of spinach with bacon and gruyère sauce (£11.50) and a vegetarian dish like thai noodle and vegetable bouillon with coriander, lemon grass and mini roasted vegiskewers (£9.50); vegetables are extra, and puddings include pear tart tatin with vanilla ice cream, brandied chocolate demi-tasse with crisp biscuit, and sticky toffee pudding with hot toffee sauce (£4.95). Fullers London Pride on handpump, but the emphasis is on a fine range of mainly New World wines; very good service. *(Recommended by Penny Simpson, Susan and John Douglas, Bob and Maggie Atherton, TBB)*

Free house ~ Licensee Jean Thaxter ~ Real ale ~ Meals and snacks (not Sun evening) ~ Restaurant (not Sun evening) ~ (01628) 781111 ~ Children in bar or restaurant at lunchtime, but must be over 12 in evening ~ Open 11(11.30 Sat)-2.30, 6-11; 12-3 Sun; closed Sun evening, Mon

BURCHETTS GREEN SU8381 Map 2

Crown

Side road between A4 and A404, W of Maidenhead

To be sure of a table here, it's best to book if you want to enjoy the generous helpings of very popular, interesting food. The civilised main bar is clean, warm and comfortable with a restauranty layout and unobtrusive piped music, and there's also a very small plain bar with two or three tables for casual customers – the licensees continue to preserve an informal and very welcoming atmosphere. As well as the blackboard menu of half a dozen starters and main courses that changes twice a day, the printed menu might include sandwiches, home-made soup, warm salad of tiger prawns with a chilli and sun-dried tomato dressing (£4.65), chicken breast in a rich marsala and mushroom sauce with tomato and spring onion risotto (£8.95), poached salmon with hollandaise sauce (£9.25), calf liver with bubble and squeak, crispy bacon and onion gravy (£10.95), and twin fillets of Scottish beef in two sauces (£13.75). Presentation is careful and appetising and service is friendly and attentive. Well kept Ruddles Bitter and Charles Wells Bombardier on handpump, kept under light blanket pressure, and a good range of wines by the glass. There are tables out in a pleasant quiet garden. *(Recommended by Bob and Ena Withers, E J Locker, Mark J Hydes, J and B Cressey, Mr and Mrs B Hobden, Peter Saville)*

Morlands ~ Lease: Ian Price ~ Real ale ~ Meals and snacks (till 10pm) ~ Restaurant ~ (01628) 822844 ~ Children in restaurant ~ Open 12-2.30, 6-11

CHEAPSIDE SU9469

Thatched Tavern

Cheapside Road; off B383, which is itself off A332 and A329

There's a good bustling atmosphere in this smartly civilised dining pub – but the attentive, charming staff cope well with those coming to enjoy the huge choice of good food. There is still an area for drinkers (which fills up quickly at busy times, so best to get there early). The building is not actually thatched but does have polished flagstones, very low gnarled and nibbled beams, small windows with cheerful cottagey curtains, and an old cast-iron range in a big inglenook with built-in wall benches snugly around it. Pretty red gingham tablecloths brighten up the longish carpeted back dining area, and a vast blackboard choice covers such dishes as sandwiches (from £2.75), home-made soup (£3.50), fresh anchovy, tomato, basil and garlic oil (£8), cumberland sausages, mash and onion gravy (£9.65), home-made steak and kidney pudding (£10.50), fresh fish that's delivered daily like grilled cod or wild Tay salmon (from around £10.50), slow-roasted half shoulder of lamb (£11), local seasonal game (from £11), and lots of puddings such as fruit crumbles and bread and butter pudding (£3.95); limited bar snacks on Sunday as they do proper Sunday roasts. Well kept Greene King IPA, Abbot and Sorcerer on handpump, spotless housekeeping, and no games or piped music. Rustic seats and tables are grouped on the sheltered back lawn, around a big old apple tree; parking is not easy at busy times. Handy for walks around Virginia Water, with the Blacknest car park a mile or so down the road. *(Recommended by Derek Harvey-Piper, Susan and John Douglas, Margaret and Nigel Dennis, Martin and Karen Wake, Ian Phillips, Jerry Hughes)*

Free house ~ Licensees Robert King, Jonathan Michael Mee ~ Real ale ~ Bar meals and snacks lunchtime only ~ Restaurant (not Sun evening) ~ (01344) 620874 ~ Well behaved children welcome away from bar ~ Open 11-3.30, 6-11; 12-3.30, 7-10 Sun; closed 25 Dec

CHIEVELEY SU4774 Map 2

Blue Boar

2 miles from M4 junction 13: A34 N towards Oxford, 200 yds left for Chieveley, then left at Wheatsheaf pub and straight on until T-junction with B4494; turn right to Wantage and pub is 500 yds on right; heading S on A34, don't take first sign to Chieveley

This thatched inn has three rambling rooms furnished with high-backed settles, windsor chairs and polished tables, and decked out with a variety of heavy harness (including a massive collar); the left-hand room has a log fire and a seat built into the sunny bow window. Bar food includes soup (£2.15), sandwiches (from £2.30), ploughman's (£4.75), speciality sausages (£5.95), half chargrilled chicken (£7.70), and puddings; there's also a civilised oak-panelled restaurant. Well kept Fullers London Pride and Wadworths 6X on handpump; several malt whiskies; soft piped music. Tables are set among the tubs and flowerbeds on the rough front cobbles outside. Oliver Cromwell stayed here in 1644 on the eve of the Battle of Newbury. *(Recommended by John and Christine Simpson, Mr and Mrs I Brown, Stephen and Julie Brown, John and Elisabeth Cox, HNJ, PEJ, M Hasslacher; more reports please)*

Free house ~ Licensees Ann and Peter Ebsworth ~ Real ale ~ Meals and snacks ~ Restaurant ~ (01635) 248236 ~ Children welcome ~ Open 11-3, 6-11; 12-3, 7-10.30 Sun ~ Bedrooms: £51B/£61B

If we don't specify bar meal times for a main entry, these are normally 12-2 and 7-9; we do show times if they are markedly different.

COOKHAM DEAN SU8785 Map 2

Uncle Toms Cabin

Hills Lane, Harding Green; village signposted off A308 Maidenhead—Marlow – keep on down past Post Office and village hall towards Cookham Rise and Cookham

This pretty cream-washed cottage has a chattily informal atmosphere in its friendly series of 1930s-feeling mainly carpeted little rooms. At the front are low beams and joists, lots of shiny dark brown woodwork, and old-fashioned plush-cushioned wall seats, stools and so forth; quite a lot of breweryana, and some interesting golden discs. Bar food includes soup (£2.75), french bread or granary rolls with a wide choice of good fillings (from £2.55), filled baked potatoes (from £3.75), home-made 6oz burgers (from £4), baltis and various pasta and crêpe dishes (all from £5.25), rump steak (£9.25), and daily specials such as stuffed loin of pork with figs or cajun chicken. Well kept Benskins Best and a regularly changing guest such as Badger Tanglefoot, Fullers London Pride, Greene King Abbot, and Rebellion Mutiny on handpump; sensibly placed darts, shove-ha'penny, cribbage, and dominoes. Piped music, if on, is well chosen and well reproduced. The two cats Jess (black and white) and Wilma (black) enjoy the winter coal fire and Oggie the busy black and white dog welcomes other dogs (who get a dog biscuit on arrival). There are picnic-sets and a climbing frame in an attractive and sheltered back garden. *(Recommended by Gerald Barnett, L F Vohryzek, Martin and Karen Wake, J and B Cressey)*

Carlsberg Tetleys ~ Lease: Nick and Karen Ashman ~ Real ale ~ Meals and snacks (till 10pm) ~ (01628) 483339 ~ Well behaved children in eating area of bar until 8pm ~ Open 11-3, 5.30-11; 12-3, 7-10.30 Sun

CRAZIES HILL SU7980 Map 2

Horns

From A4, take Warren Row Road at Cockpole Green signpost just E of Knowl Hill, then past Warren Row follow Crazies Hill signposts; from Wargrave, take A321 towards Henley, then follow Crazies Hill signposts – right at Shell garage, then left

Readers enjoy the fact that this little tiled whitewashed cottage continues to have no juke box, fruit machine or piped music. Bar food has come in for warm praise this year, with filled lunchtime french bread (from £3.95, not Sunday), soup (£3.25), cambozola and pistachio nut beignets with a bramble preserve or tiger prawns in filo pastry with a chilli dip (£5.25), pasta with wild mushrooms, red pesto and cream (£6.95), steak, kidney and Guinness pie (£7.50), tuna steak niçoise (£10.95), and daily specials such as cumberland sausage with onion gravy (£6.95), fillet steak strips in a wholegrain mustard sauce (£11.95), and whole baked seabass with a green peppercorn sauce (£12.95; fish comes daily from Billingsgate); must book a table at weekends. The bars have rugby mementoes on the walls, exposed beams, open fires and stripped wooden tables and chairs; the barn room is opened up to the roof like a medieval hall. Well kept Brakspears Bitter, Old, OBJ, Special, and seasonal ales on handpump, a thoughtful wine list, and several malt whiskies. There's plenty of space in the very large garden. *(Recommended by Martin and Karen Wake, Ian and Marilyn McBeath, Gerald Barnett, D Voller, L F Vohryzek)*

Brakspears ~ Tenant A J Hearn ~ Real ale ~ Meals and snacks (not Sun evening) ~ Restaurant ~ (0118) 940 1416 ~ Children welcome lunchtime and very early evening ~ Open 11.30-2.30, 6-11; 12-3, 7-10.30 Sun; closed 25 and 26 Dec

EAST ILSLEY SU4981 Map 2

Crown & Horns

Just off A34, about 5 miles N of M4 junction 13

Although locals and stable lads are fond of this bustling old pub – it is very much in horse-training country – there is a reliably friendly welcome for visitors, too. The wide range of regularly changing real ales is reasonably priced and typically includes Adnams Broadside, Hook Norton Old Hookey, Morlands Original, Ruddles County, and Wadworths 6X on handpump. There is also an impressive collection of 160 whiskies from all over the world – Morocco, Korea, Japan, China, Spain and New Zealand. Good, interesting bar food includes sandwiches or baps (from £2.10), home-made soup (£2.95), filled baked potatoes (from £3.75), ploughman's (from £4.50), vegetable lasagne or steak and mushroom pie (£5.25), pork with apple and cider or chicken breast with stilton and mushroom sauce (£8.75), steaks (from £8.95), daily specials, and puddings (£3.25); quick, cheerful staff – even when busy. The walls of the four interesting beamed rooms are hung with racing prints and photographs, and the side bar may have locals watching the latest races on TV. There is a no-smoking area. Skittle alley, darts, pool, dominoes, cribbage, fruit machine, and piped music. The pretty paved stable yard has tables under two chestnut trees. *(Recommended by L Walker, K H Frostick, R M Sparkes, Nigel Clifton, Michael Bourdeaux, Tom McLean, Simon Penny, HNJ, PEJ, C P Baxter)*

Free house ~ Licensees Chris and Jane Bexx ~ Real ale ~ Meals and snacks (till 10pm) ~ Restaurant ~ (01635) 281545 ~ Children welcome ~ Open 11-11; 12-10.30 Sun; closed 25 Dec ~ Bedrooms: £38B/£48B

FRILSHAM SU5473 Map 2

Pot Kiln

From Yattendon take turning S, opposite church, follow first Frilsham signpost, but just after crossing motorway go straight on towards Bucklebury ignoring Frilsham signposted right; pub on right after about half a mile

Very much enjoyed by readers over the past year, this unpretentious cottagey pub appeals to a good mix of customers – all of whom are welcomed by the friendly licensees. The unchanging bar is not unsmart, with wooden floorboards and bare benches and pews, and there's a good winter log fire, too. Well kept Brick Kiln Bitter and the new Dr Hexter's Healer (from a microbrewery behind the pub) is served from a hatch in the panelled entrance lobby – which has room for just one bar stool – along with well kept Arkells BBB, and Morlands Original on handpump. Good, fairly simple food includes filled hot rolls (from £1.30), home-made soup (£2.35), a decent ploughman's (from £3.65), vegetable gratin or vegetable and cheese suet pudding (£5.65), excellent salmon and broccoli fishcake or steak and kidney pudding (£5.95), and daily specials like pasta with goat's cheese and spinach (£6.25) and fresh hot grilled salmon with hollandaise (£7.50), and sirloin steaks (£8.65); no chips, and vegetables are fresh. Rolls only on Sundays. The public bar has darts, dominoes, shove-ha'penny and cribbage. The pink, candlelit back room/dining room is no smoking. There are picnic-sets in the big suntrap garden with good views of the woods and countryside. It's a good dog-walking area and they are allowed in the public bar on a lead. *(Recommended by TBB, Tom Evans, Susan and John Douglas, Gordon, Dick Brown, R Stamp, C P R Baxter)*

Own brew ~ Licensee Philip Gent ~ Real ale ~ Meals and snacks (not Tues) ~ (01635) 201366 ~ Well behaved children in back room and public bar ~ Irish music most Sun evenings ~ Open 12-2.30, 6.30-11; 12-3, 7-10.30 Sun; closed Tues lunchtime

GREAT SHEFFORD SU3875 Map 2

Swan

2 miles from M4 junction 14; on A338 towards Wantage

There's a good local atmosphere in this neatly kept and friendly village pub. The low-ceilinged rooms of the spacious bow-windowed lounge bar are attractively and comfortably furnished and have magazines and newspapers, racing-related memorabilia and old photographs, and other bric-a-brac on the walls; the public side has darts, shove-ha'penny, dominoes, pool, a fruit machine, table skittles, and piped music. Generously served food includes filled home-baked french bread, home-made soups (£2.50), smoked fish platter (from £4.50), home-made pies (from £5.95), fresh tuna steak (£5.50), pasta dishes (from £5.95), daily specials such as various locally-made sausages, chicken in stilton sauce, fish pie, curries or lasagne (from £3.95), Scotch steaks (from £9.95), and children's menu (from £3.25). Well kept Courage Best and guests like Butts Ale (from a microbrewery in the village), and Theakstons XB on handpump; attentive service. There are tables on the terrace by big willows overhanging the River Lambourn – full waitress service here; the restaurant shares the same view. *(Recommended by John Fahy, George Atkinson, Lynn Sharpless, Bob Eardley, Clare and Chris Tooley, Paul Hilditch, Paul and Ursula Randall, N and A Chesher, Hugh Spottiswoode, Gordon)*

Courage ~ Managers Kevin Maul, Sue Jacobs ~ Real ale ~ Meals and snacks ~ Children in eating area of bar ~ Restaurant ~ (01488) 648271 ~ Open 11-3, 6-11; 12-3, 7-10.30 Sun

HAMSTEAD MARSHALL SU4165 Map 2

White Hart

Village signposted from A4 W of Newbury

If it's good, imaginative Italian food you're after, then this popular dining pub is the place to head for. The daily specials are well liked and might include a fettucine carbonara with a very tasty sauce or warm salad of marinated crispy fried lamb strips with pine nuts (£8.50), beef meatballs stuffed with mozzarella and braised in wine sauce (£9.50) or monkfish fillets in a spicy tomato and brandy sauce (£12.50); also, home-made soup (£3.75), home-made liver pâté with ciabatta toast or goat's cheese grilled with garlic and yoghurt (£4.50), various pasta dishes such as crespelle (pancakes filled with ricotta) and spinach baked with cheese and tomato (£7.50) or quadroni (mushroom and herb-stuffed ravioli with wild mushroom and cream sauce £8.50), dover sole poached in white wine with prawns and cream (£14.50), and puddings like Italian-style bread and butter pudding with chocolate, tiramisu or profiteroles prettily decorated with fresh fruit (£4.50); the food boards are attractively illustrated with Mrs Aromando's drawings, they grow many of their own herbs and some vegetables, and their beef is from a local organic farm. The restaurant is no smoking. Ringwood Best and Wadworths 6X on handpump and decent Italian wines. The L-shaped bar has red plush seats built into the bow windows, cushioned chairs around oak an other tables, a copper-topped bar counter, and a log fire open on both sides. Their newfoundland-cross dog is called Sophie, and the pony, Solo. The interesting walled garden is lovely in summer, and the quiet and comfortable beamed bedrooms are in a converted barn across the courtyard. *(Recommended by June and Tony Baldwin, Mr and Mrs Peter Smith, LM, Simon Morton, Glen and Nola Armstrong)*

Free house ~ Licensee Mr Nicola Aromando ~ Real ale ~ Meals and snacks (not Sun) ~ Restaurant (not Sun) ~ (01488) 658201 ~ Children welcome ~ Open 12-2.30, 6-11; closed Sun, 25-26 Dec, 1 Jan, 2 wks summer ~ Bedrooms: £50B/£75B

HARE HATCH SU8077 Map 2

Queen Victoria

Blakes Lane, The Holt; just N of A4 Reading—Maidenhead, 3 miles W of exit roundabout from A404(M) – keep your eyes skinned for the turning

Welcoming and friendly and liked by both cheery locals and diners, the two low-beamed rooms here have flowers on the tables, strong spindleback chairs, wall benches and window seats, and decorations such as a stuffed sparrowhawk and a delft shelf lined with beaujolais bottles; the tables on the right are no smoking. Popular bar food changes regularly and might include sandwiches, port and stilton pâté (£2.95), potato shells stuffed with spicy beef or prawns (£4.95), thai chicken, pepper and onion kebab with chilli dip (£5.95), barbecued spare ribs with herby potatoes (£6.50), and roast hock of lamb (£7.95), and puddings like home-baked fruit pies and crumbles; vegetables are fresh. Well kept Brakspears Bitter, Special and Old on handpump, a fair choice of wines by the glass, and obliging service. Dominoes, cribbage, fruit machine, video game, and three-dimensional noughts and crosses. There's a flower-filled covered terrace with tables and chairs, and a robust table or two in front by the car park. *(Recommended by Richard Houghton, J and B Cressey, Mr and Mrs C J Ward, Mark Hydes)*

Brakspears ~ Tenant Ronald Rossington ~ Real ale ~ Meals and snacks (12-2.30,

6.30-10.30; all day Sun) ~ (0118) 940 2477 ~ Children welcome ~ Open 11-3, 5.30-11; 12-10.30 Sun

HOLYPORT SU8977 Map 2

Belgian Arms

1½ miles from M4 junction 8/9; take A308(M) then at terminal roundabout follow Holyport signpost along A330 towards Bracknell; in village turn left on to big green, then left again at War Memorial shelter

In summer, sitting in the charming garden by the small lake with ducks and swans, it is hard to believe that this popular, homely pub is so close to the M4. The L-shaped, low-ceilinged bar has interesting framed postcards of Belgian military uniform and other good military prints, and some cricketing memorabilia on the walls, a china cupboard in one corner, a variety of chairs around a few small tables, and a roaring log fire. Enjoyable bar food includes sandwiches (the toasted 'special' is very well liked), a good ploughman's, pizzas with different toppings (from £4.95), home-cooked ham and eggs, good chicken pie, lasagne or chicken curry (£5.95), and duck in port or poached salmon fillet (£11.95); good Sunday lunch. You can also eat in the conservatory area. Well kept Brakspears Bitter and Special on handpump, and one or two good malts; friendly service. *(Recommended by Cyril S Brown, Lynn Sharpless, Bob Eardley, R Lake, Chris Glasson, Peter Saville, Paul and Sue Merrick, N Cobb, Peter Burton, Gerald Barnett, E J Gibson, Sue and Pete Robbins, J and B Cressey, Simon Collett-Jones)*

Brakspears ~ Tenant Alfred Morgan ~ Real ale ~ Meals and snacks (not Sun evening) ~ (01628) 34468 ~ Children in dining conservatory ~ Open 11-3, 5.30(6 Sat)-11; 12-3, 7-10.30 Sun

nr HURLEY SU8283 Map 2

Dew Drop

Just W of Hurley on A423 turn left (if coming from Maidenhead) up Honey Lane and keep going till get to T-junction, then turn right – the pub is down a right-hand turn-off at the first cluster of little houses

Although the friendly and hard-working new licensees have made a few gentle changes to this isolated brick and flint cottage, readers are glad that the genuine rustic charm still remains. The simply furnished main bar has a welcoming atmosphere, a log fire in its fine old inglenook fireplace at one end of the room, and another log fire at the other – space is rather tight in the serving area; at the back is a homely little room. Good popular bar food now includes sandwiches or rolls (from £1.95; not Sunday lunchtime), filled baked potatoes (from £2.95), ploughman's (£4.25), and daily specials such as ham and egg or macaroni cheese (£4.95), steak in ale pie (£5.95), smoked cod in parsley sauce (£6.95), assorted smoked fish (£7.95), rump steak (£8.95), and winter game dishes. Well kept Brakspears Bitter, Special and seasonal ales on handpump; darts, shove-ha'penny and dominoes. The two cats are called R2 and D2, and the dog, Sparky. The sloping garden is attractive, there are new picnic-sets and gazebo seating, and a new barbecue; good surrounding walks. *(Recommended by D A Begley, R J Mann, Gerald Barnett, R Stamp, Ian Phillips)*

Brakspears ~ Tenants Charles and Beatrice Morley ~ Real ale ~ Meals and snacks ~ Children in eating area of bar ~ (01628) 824327 ~ Open 12-3, 6-11; 12-3, 7-10.30 Sun; closed evening 25 Dec

LAMBOURN SU3278 Map 2

Hare & Hounds

5 miles from M4, junction 14: A338 N, then first left into B4000 – Baydon Rd, Lambourn Woodlands (2½ miles S of Lambourn itself)

In the heart of horse country, this stylish dining pub stands out as much for its decor as for its good quality food. Though each of the rooms leading off the narrow bar is done out in a colourful and occasionally idiosyncratic way, they still feel reassuringly traditional; this is an old-school pub at heart, but with a smart contemporary twist. Instead of bar stools are chairs that wouldn't be out of place in a cocktail lounge, and rather than, say, toby jugs you might spot strange clay models of buxom women on motorbikes. Most of the pub is painted a cosy custard yellow, with the odd pinkish stripe, and equine prints and pictures serving as a reminder of the landlord's distinguished links with the racehorse training community. Perhaps the nicest area is the rather clubby pink-hued room off to the left as you head along the central passageway; there's a lovely fireplace, and some incredible red slatted chairs. The room next to that has a mix of simple wooden and marble-effect tables, a church-style pew, and neatly patterned curtains; one wall is almost entirely covered by an elaborately gilt-edged mirror, and there's a well worn rug on the red-tiled floor. As well as sandwiches, the choice of imaginative food might include coriander, parsnip and carrot soup (£3), mussels spiced with black bean and chilli (£4.50), scallops and bacon (£5.50), warm poussin salad with spiced coconut dressing (£9), swordfish steak with citrus and caper sauce (£11), thai green curried chicken (£10.50) and rack of lamb with redcurrant gravy or calf liver and bacon (£11.50). Flowers IPA and Wadworths 6X on handpump, good wines and a choice of malt whiskies; friendly service, fresh flowers on the bar, piped music. There are a couple of benches in the garden behind. *(More reports please)*

Free house ~ Licensee David Cecil ~ Real ale ~ Meals and snacks (not Sun eve) ~ Restaurant ~ (01488) 71386 ~ Children welcome ~ Open 11-11; only 12-3.30 Sun

PEASEMORE SU4577 Map 2

Fox & Hounds

Village signposted from B4494 Newbury—Wantage

This cheerful downland pub manages to combine being a local with drawing in a dining crowd. The two bars have brocaded stripped wall settles, chairs and stools around shiny wooden tables, a log-effect gas fire (open to both rooms), and piped music. One wall has a full set of Somerville's entertaining *Slipper's ABC of Fox-Hunting* prints, and on a stripped-brick wall there's a row of flat-capped fox masks. Enjoyable bar food includes sandwiches, home-made soup, basket meals (from £2.75), a home-made pie of the day (£5.50), pork tenderloin with mozzarella and tomatoes (£7.50), vegetarian dishes, steaks, daily specials, and home-made puddings such as lemon tart and fruit crumble (from £2.50). Well kept Greene King IPA and Abbot, and Marstons Pedigree on handpump, and a good few malt whiskies. Darts, pool, dominoes, cribbage, fruit machine, discreet juke box, and football table. From the picnic-sets outside, there are views of rolling fields – and on a clear day you can look right across to the high hills which form the Berkshire/Hampshire border about 20 miles southward. *(Recommended by Julie Peters, Colin Blinkhorn, L Walker, Dick Brown, Jenny and Roger Huggins)*

Free house ~ Licensees David and Loretta Smith ~ Real ale ~ Meals and snacks (till 10pm; not Mon) ~ Restaurant ~ (01635) 248252 ~ Children welcome ~ Open 11.30-3, 6.30-11; 12-3, 7-10.30 Sun; closed Mon

READING SU7272 Map 2

Sweeney & Todd £

10 Castle Street

Walking past this delightful oddity for the first time, you'd never suspect it was somewhere to enjoy a quiet pint. From the street it looks like a simple baker's shop and take-away, selling pies, soft drinks and even fresh eggs. But hidden away past the counter and down a few steps is a far more convivial cafe-cum-pub, almost like an illicit drinking den, with their unusually flavoured pies and good choice of beers vying for attention. There's a surprising number of tiny tables squeezed into the long thin room, most of them in rather conspiratorial railway-carriage-style booths separated by curtains, and each with a leather-bound menu to match the leather-cushioned pews. Old prints line the walls, and the colonial-style fans and bare-boards floor enhance the period feel. Efficient uniformed waitresses serve pies such as chicken, honey and mustard, hare and cherry, duck and apricot, goose and gooseberry or partridge and pear (all £3.20) as well as soup (£1.50), sandwiches (from £2) and casseroles; helpings are huge, and excellent value. The small bar has well kept Adnams, Eldridge Pope Royal Oak, Wadworths 6X and a changing guest on handpump, with various wines and a range of liqueurs and cigars. You can buy the pies in the shop to take away for £1.60. *(Recommended by Richard Lewis, D J and P M Taylor, Andy Cunningham, DHV, Yvonne Hannaford)*

Free house ~ Licensee Mrs C Hayward ~ Real ale ~ Meals and snacks served all day (not Sun) ~ (0118) 958 6466 ~ Children welcome ~ Open 11-11; closed Sun

SONNING SU7575 Map 2

Bull

Village signposted on A4 E of Reading; off B478, in village

Readers tell us they have much enjoyed staying at this attractive old inn over the past year, so we feel they deserve a Stay Award. The two old-fashioned bar rooms have low ceilings and heavy beams, cosy alcoves, cushioned antique settles and low wooden chairs, and inglenook fireplaces; the back dining area is no smoking. Popular, interesting bar food is all home-made and uses fresh seasonal vegetables (no chips or deep-fried dishes). From an extensive choice of daily specials, there might be moussaka with Greek salad (£8.75), spinach and sweet pepper tart with a tomato and basil coulis (£8.95), thai crab cakes on a coconut, honey, lemon balm and cream sauce or green chicken curry with fresh mango and pineapple (£10.95), and rack of herb-crusted lamb with a redcurrant and port glaze (£12.95), with puddings such as raspberry and Drambuie meringue, treacle pudding or chocolate and pecan nut marquis (£4.25); there are also simpler pub snacks such as home-made soup (£3.95), filled french bread (from £4.50), filled baked potatoes (from £4.95), and a proper ploughman's (from £6.50); good breakfasts. Well kept Gales Best, HSB and Butser Bitter, IPA, and a guest beer on handpump; darts and fruit machine; the golden retriever is called Peri. The courtyard is particularly attractive in summer with tubs of flowers and a rose pergola resting under its wisteria-covered, black and white timbered walls. If you bear left through the ivy-clad churchyard opposite, then turn left along the bank of the river Thames, you come to a very pretty lock. *(Recommended by Bill Sykes, Mrs J Burrows, Anne and John Peacock, Mr and Mrs R Mann, Roger and Valerie Hill, I E Folkard-Evans)*

Gales ~ Lease: Dennis Mason ~ Real ale ~ Meals and snacks (all day summer Sun) ~ (0118) 969 3901 ~ Children in restaurant ~ Open 11-3, 5.30-11; 11-11 summer Sat (11-3, 5.30-11 in winter); 12-10.30 summer Sun (12-3, 7-10.30 in winter) ~ Bedrooms: £60B/£65B

STANFORD DINGLEY SU5771 Map 2

Bull

From M4 junction 12, W on A4, then right at roundabout on to A340 towards Pangbourne; first left to Bradfield, and at crossroads on far edge of Bradfield (not in centre) turn left signposted Stanford Dingley; turn left in Stanford Dingley

This is an attractive 15th-c brick pub with dark beams in the middle of the tap room and two standing timbers hung with horsebrasses dividing the room firmly into two parts. The main part has an old brick fireplace, red-cushioned seats carved out of barrels, a window settle, wheelback chairs on the red quarry tiles, and an old station clock; the other is similarly furnished but carpeted. There's also a half-panelled lounge bar with refectory-type tables, and a smaller room leading off with quite a few musical instruments. Bar food includes sandwiches, filled baked potatoes (from £2.45), soups like carrot and orange or stilton (from £2.75), garlic bacon and mushrooms on toast (£3.55), ploughman's (from £3.65), cottage pie (£6.55), tagliatelle with bacon, mushroom and wine sauce (£6.85), trout with almonds (£8.75), good beef curry, steaks (from £7.65), and daily specials including two vegetarian dishes. Well kept (and cheap for the area) Bass, Brakspears, and West Berkshire Brewery Good Old Boy on handpump; friendly, helpful staff. Ring-the-bull, occasional classical or easy listening music. In front of the building are some big rustic tables and benches, and to the side is a small garden with a few more seats. *(Recommended by Lynn Sharpless, Bob Eardley, Prof John and Mrs Patricia White, Tom Evans)*

Free house ~ Licensees Patrick and Trudi Langdon ~ Real ale ~ Meals and snacks (till 10pm; not Mon lunchtime) ~ (0118) 974 4409 ~ Children in saloon bar until 8.30pm; not Sat evening ~ Open 12-3, 7-11; 12-3, 7-10.30 Sun; closed Mon lunchtime – except bank holidays

WALTHAM ST LAWRENCE SU8276 Map 2

Bell

In village centre

Improvements have been made to the garden and terrace behind this busy timbered black and white pub – and the rabbits they keep are popular with children; the pretty hanging baskets in front have won awards for the last two years. Inside, the lounge bar has finely carved oak panelling, a log fire, and a pleasant atmosphere, and the public bar has heavy beams, an attractive seat in the deep window recess, and well kept Bass, Brakspears Bitter, Wadworths 6X and other guest beers on handpump; the small front room is no smoking. Well liked bar food includes sandwiches or filled french bread (from £2.30), ploughman's, filled baked potatoes or sausage, bacon and egg (£4.50), Tuscan bean bake or chicken tikka masala (£5), beef in ale pie (£5.50), evening extras such as sesame and ginger prawns with chilli dip (£3), venison in red wine (£6) or duck breast with orange sauce (£6.50), puddings like raspberry riffin (£2.50), and children's menu (from £2). Darts. *(Recommended by Sheila Keene, Susan and John Douglas, Mr and Mrs T A Bryan, Nicholas Holmes, Simon Collett-Jones, Linda Milbank)*

Free house ~ Licensee Mrs Denise Slater ~ Real ale ~ Meals and snacks (not Sun or Mon evenings) ~ (0118) 934 1788 ~ Children in dining room and small front room ~ Open 11-3, 6-11; 12-3, 7-10.30 Sun

WEST ILSLEY SU4782 Map 2

Harrow

Signposted at East Ilsley slip road off A34 Newbury—Abingdon

Berkshire Dining Pub of the Year

For an enjoyable meal out, eaten in a relaxed and welcoming atmosphere, this white tiled village pub is the place to head for – but it's best to get there early to be sure of a seat. The open-plan bar has dark terracotta walls hung with many mainly Victorian prints and other ornaments, big turkey rugs on the floor, and a mix of antique oak tables, unpretentious old chairs, and a couple of more stately long settles; there's also an unusual stripped twin-seated high-backed settle between the log fire and the bow window. Constantly changing, the very good home-made food might include interestingly filled french bread (from £2.95), goat's cheese on walnut salad (£4.50; main course £8.95), ploughman's with British farmhouse cheeses (from £5.50), super lamb liver and bacon (£8.50), very good scallops, fillet of salmon with vermouth sauce, chicken in a Dijon and tarragon sauce or monkfish and mussels in white wine (£8.90), shank of lamb on mashed roast potatoes (£10.95), and puddings like fresh lemon tart, fresh fruit crumbles and home-made ice creams (from £3.60); super vegetables. The dining room is no smoking. Well kept Morlands Original and Old Speckled Hen, and a guest like Flowers Original on handpump, and 8 good house wines; fruit machine. This is a lovely spot with lots of nearby walks – the Ridgeway is just a mile away – and the big garden has picnic-sets and other tables under cocktail parasols looking out over the duck pond and cricket green. *(Recommended by Steve and Sarah de Mellow, K H Frostick, D G Twyman, G W A Pearce, Julie Peters, Colin Blinkhorn, Dr R A L Leatherdale, I Maw, Dave Braisted, Mr and Mrs R A Barton, David Peakall, Simon Walker, HNJ, PEJ, R T and J C Moggridge)*

Morlands ~ Tenants Emily Hawes, Scott Hunter ~ Real ale ~ Meals and snacks ~ (01635) 281260 ~ Children welcome ~ Open 11-3(3.30 Sat), 6-11; 12-11 summer Sun; 12-3.30, 7-10.30 winter Sun

YATTENDON SU5574 Map 2

Royal Oak

The Square; B4009 NE from Newbury; turn right at Hampstead Norreys, village signposted on left

People come to this elegantly handsome inn to enjoy the very good food, and to eat in a relaxed and informal atmosphere; you should head for the panelled and prettily decorated brasserie/bar with its marvellous log fire, lovely flowers, and locally brewed West Berkshire Brewery's Good Old Boy and Banks's Bitter, well kept on handpump. Bar food includes rockfish soup with rouille and croutons (£4.50), terrine of provençal vegetables with mozzarella and pesto sauce (£5.50), warm goat's cheese salad with toasted bread (£5.75), deep-fried cod and chips (£7.50), crab salad with spicy tomato and spring onion salsa (£8.25), spicy jerk chicken with saffron risotto and bang bang sauce (£9.75), calf liver and bacon with mash and onion gravy (£11.75), chargrilled Abderdeen Angus steak (£12.50), and puddings such as treacle tart with clotted cream, hot chocolate fondant with amarula ice cream or caramelised apple, almond and plum crumble with cinnamon ice cream (from £4.50); vegetables are extra, the restaurant is no smoking, and there's a good wine list. Best to book. In summer, you can eat at tables in the pleasant walled garden – and there are more in front on the village square. The attractive village is one of the few still owned privately.
(Recommended by Stephen Brown, Mr and Mrs C R Little, C P R Baxter; more reports please)

Free house ~ Managers Corinne Macrae, Steven Hall ~ Real ale ~ Meals and snacks (till 10pm Fri and Sat) ~ Restaurant (not Sun evenings) ~ (01635) 201325 ~ Well behaved children allowed ~ Open 11-3, 6-11; 12-3, 7-10.30 Sun; closed evening 26 Dec ~ Bedrooms: £90B/£100B

Lucky Dip

Besides the fully inspected pubs, you might like to try these Lucky Dips recommended to us and described by readers (if you do, please send us reports):

Aldworth [Haw Lane; B4009 towards Hampstead Norreys; SU5579], *Four Points*: Recently refurbished, with friendly young landlord, good range of freshly made food inc some unusual specials, dining area off small bar; well kept beers, neat garden over road *(Stan Edwards, HNJ, PEJ, LYM)*

Aston [Ferry Lane; signed off A4130 Henley—Maidenhead; SU7884], *Flower Pot*: Nice, friendly but sophisticated pubby hotel with great garden – views over meadows to cottages and far side of Thames; well kept Brakspears inc Mild, reasonably priced food, friendly young staff, bare-boards public bar with lots of stuffed fish in glass cases, darts, unobtrusive piped music; popular Sun lunchtimes, handy for riverside strolls *(Comus Elliott, Simon Collett-Jones, J and B Cressey)*

☆ **Bagnor** [quickest approach is from Speen on edge of Newbury; SU4569], *Blackbird*: Chatty traditional pub in very peaceful setting nr Watermill Theatre – they do a pre-show menu; bar simple and unfussy with plates around walls, leaded lamps, dried flowers in fireplace, plain wooden furnishings, old farm tools and firearms hanging from ceiling; more formal eating area opens off; changing beers such as Brakspears, Shepherd Neame Spitfire, Ushers Best and brews from West Berkshire Brewery, well prepared straightforward food; tables in side garden and on green in front; regular backgammon nights *(HNJ, PEJ, BB)*

☆ **Bracknell** [Church Rd; SU8769], *Old Manor*: Big open-plan Wetherspoons pub, one of their few that welcome children, with usual good value food, sensibly priced real ales, big no-smoking area, good solid decor inc original oak beams, twice-yearly beer festival with up to 30 different beers, relatively quiet tables outside; very useful for the M4/M25 short cut via M3 *(D J and P M Taylor)*

☆ **Bray** [High St; handy for M4 junction 9; SU9079], *Crown*: Upmarket 14th-c pub with good atmosphere, low beams, timbers and panelling, leather seats, popular food in bar and restaurant, Courage Best and Wadworths 6X, decent wines, friendly helpful service, log fires; well behaved children allowed, plenty of seating outside inc flagstoned vine arbour *(TBB, Chris Glasson, Martin and Karen Wake, LYM)*

Bray [High St], *Hinds Head*: Handsome Tudor pub, panelling and beams, with good food (esp upstairs restaurant), Courage beers *(TBB, A Hepburn, S Jenner, J and B Cressey, LYM)*

☆ **Brimpton** [Brimpton Common; B3051, W of Heath End; SU5564], *Pineapple*: Friendly thatched and low-beamed country pub doing well under new landlord, cosy bar with stripped brick and timbering, tiled floor, heavy elm furnishings, open fire, new no-smoking dining extension, good service, seven well kept Whitbreads-related ales, usual food noon-9, side games area, maybe piped pop music; lots of tables on sheltered lawn, play area; open all day; children in eating area, folk music first Sun of month *(Tony and Wendy Hobden, R M Sparkes, LYM)*

Chaddleworth [off A338 Wantage—Hungerford; SU4177], *Ibex*: Quiet village pub with enjoyable low-priced food (not Sun evening), well kept Morlands Original and Old Speckled Hen, cheerful landlord; traditional games in public bar, maybe piped pop music; tables out on sheltered lawn and floodlit terrace *(Elizabeth and Klaus Leist, Julie Peters, Colin Blinkhorn, LYM)*

Charvil [Lands End Lane; SU7776], *Lands End*: Warm welcome, friendly staff and cats, open fire, Brakspears and Boddingtons, good generous food; nice garden, summer barbecues *(Lynne Fowler, Richard Hanson)*

☆ **Chieveley** [East Lane – handy for M4 junction 13 via A34 N-bound; SU4774], *Olde Red Lion*: Bustling local with lots going on from Weds steak night and Thurs fish and chip night to occasional evening hypnotist; well kept Arkells beers, good value straightforward food, comfortable low-beamed L-shaped bar with well worn furnishings, lots of brasses around walls, couple of old sewing machines, roaring log fire; piped music, fruit machine, pool, TV; parking immediately outside can be a squeeze – easier in overflow opp *(HNJ, PEJ, A and M Marriott, Chris Sutton, John and Christine Simpson, BB)*

☆ **Cookham** [The Pound – former White Hart; SU8884], *Spencers*: Imaginative reasonably priced food, cosy relaxed atmosphere, good solid furniture, friendly service, big garden with boules, good Thames walks; can be crowded esp Sun lunchtime *(Roger Stamp, Dr Gerald Barnett)*

Cookham [High St], *Bel & the Dragon*: This fine old building has been well refurbished, with more emphasis on the food side (and an interesting menu), and a new gallery in the larger dining room, which now has a big grill on one side; sadly though, the new landlord has been blankly unwilling to give any information for our readers, bringing to an abrupt end 16 unbroken years of recommendation by us *(LYM)*

☆ **Cookham Dean** [Church Lane, off Hills Lane; SU8785], *Jolly Farmer*: Traditional small rooms, open fires, well kept Courage Best and two guest beers, attractive dining room, unhurried feel, traditional games, no music or machines, good quiet garden with play area; well behaved children welcome away from bar *(Gerald Barnett, Phoebe Thomas, Ellie Weld, LYM)*

Cookham Dean [Dean Lane], *Chequers*: Small pubby-feeling dining bar with beams, flagstones, old fireplace, country furniture and decorations, imaginative reasonably priced food, well kept real ale, very helpful service, tiny garden, and seats out among hanging baskets *(Susan and John Douglas, J and B Cressey)*; *Inn on the Green*: Inviting atmosphere, good solid furniture with attractive tables, unspoilt rambling layout, stripped beams, two-sided log fires, good genuine food, well kept ales inc Fullers London Pride, attractive restaurant; maybe piped music *(Martin and Karen Wake, Ron Leigh)*

☆ **Curridge** [3 miles from M4 junction 13: A34 towards Newbury, then first left to Curridge, Hermitage, and left into Curridge at Village Only sign – OS Sheet 174 map ref 492723; SU4871], *Bunk*: Nicely prepared good interesting food (not cheap, not Sun evening) in stylish dining pub with smart stripped-wood tiled-floor bar on left, elegant stable-theme bistro on right with wooded-meadow views and conservatory; four well kept ales inc Fullers London Pride, good choice of wines, cheerful efficient service, tables in neat garden *(Phyl and Jack Street, BB)*

Datchet [The Green; not far from M4 junction 5; SU9876], *Royal Stag*: Good friendly local with above-average food, log fire, welcoming retriever, well kept Tetleys-related and guest beers; bar partly panelled in claret case lids, occasional juke box *(Bruce Braithwaite)*

☆ **East Ilsley** [SU4981], *Swan*: Spacious, neat and well decorated in a slightly hotelish way, with interesting things to look at; wide range of bar food inc vegetarian (busy with families Sun – best to book), well kept Morlands Original and Charles Wells Bombardier, friendly efficient service, daily papers; no-smoking restaurant, tables in courtyard and walled garden with play area; good bedrooms, some in house down road *(Graham and Lynn Mason, LYM)*

☆ **Eton** [82 High St; SU9678], *Eton Wine Bar*: Very good food, nice house wines, good friendly service, plain wood tables, some pews, tiled floor, bar stools; can be very busy if there's an event at the school *(Heather Martin)*

☆ **Great Shefford** [Shefford Woodland; less than ½ mile N of M4 junction 14, by junction B4000/A338; SU3875], *Pheasant*: Good relaxing motorway break, friendly service in four neat rooms, good generous food inc Sun lunches (choice perhaps over-wide), well kept Brakspears and Wadworths IPA and 6X, decent wines and coffee, log fires; public bar with games inc ring the bull; children welcome, attractive views from garden *(Paul Hilditch, J H Jones, Roger and Pauline Pearce, LYM)*

Halfway [A4 Hungerford—Newbury; SU4168], *Halfway*: Wide choice of imaginative food, great attention to detail and colour, cajun and Chinese dishes, fresh veg, good children's dishes (and children's helpings of most main ones); good range of wines and beers, friendly helpful staff, partitions dividing dining room into cosy areas *(David Parsons)*

Hampstead Norreys [SU5276], *White Hart*: Friendly low-beamed Morlands pub with wide range of reasonably priced good food, good sandwiches and take-aways, real ales, decent coffee, children welcome; darts, pool and fruit machine in public bar, soft piped music; back terrace and garden *(Joan Olivier, Sidney and Erna Wells)*

☆ **Holyport** [The Green; 1½ miles from M4 junction 8/9, via A308(M)/A330; SU8977], *George*: New landlord doing good food esp fish and seafood in low-ceilinged open-plan bar with nice old fireplace, friendly bustle, Courage ales; picnic-sets outside, lovely village green *(D J and P M Taylor, David Dimock, Paul and Sue Merrick)*

Hungerford [Charnham St; 3 miles from M4 junction 14; town signposted at junction; SU3368], *Bear*: Varied, reasonably priced and plentiful bar food, pleasant period atmosphere, fantastic huge clock, open fires, well kept real ales such as Wadworths 6X, efficient service; restaurant, bedrooms comfortable and attractive *(Meg and Colin Hamilton, LYM)*

☆ **Hungerford Newtown** [A338 ½ mile S of M4 junction 14; SU3571], *Tally Ho*: Quiet, roomy and well appointed, with good well presented home-made food from sandwiches to steaks (popular with older people at lunchtime), small no-smoking area, well kept ales such as Boddingtons and Wadworths 6X, decent house wines, friendly efficient service, subdued piped music; children if eating. *(J S Green, Mr and Mrs Peter Smith)*

Hurley [A404; SU8283], *Black Boy*: Old-fashioned cottagey pub concentrating on wide-ranging food, but a few tables for drinkers, with well kept Brakspears PA and SB, open fire, attractive garden by paddock, picnic-sets looking over countryside rolling down to Thames *(SCCJ)*

Hurley *Olde Bell*: Handsome and unusual old-fashioned timbered inn with some remarkable ancient features inc Norman doorway and window; small but comfortable bar with decent food, very friendly staff; good restaurant, fine gardens, very civilised gents'; keg beer, tolerable piped music; bedrooms *(Mike and Heather Watson, TBB, LYM)*

☆ **Inkpen** [Lower Inkpen], *Swan*: Rambling beamed pub, good food from recently enlarged kitchen in neat bar and new restaurant extension, welcoming service, good interesting choice of well kept ales, local farm cider; also has organic food shop *(HNJ, PEJ, LYM)*

☆ **Kintbury** [SU3866], *Dundas Arms*: Clean, tidy and welcoming, with comfortably upmarket feel, good fresh home-made food (not Mon evening or Sun) from sandwiches up, well kept real ales from smaller breweries, good coffee and wines by the glass, no piped music, remarkable range of clarets and burgundies in evening restaurant; tables out on deck above Kennet & Avon Canal, children welcome, pleasant walks; comfortable bedrooms with own secluded waterside terrace *(HNJ, PEJ, GLD, R M Sparkes, Nigel Wilkinson, LM, TBB, LYM)*

☆ **Knowl Hill** [A4; SU8279], *Seven Stars*: Simple old-fashioned relaxing place with good honest bar food from sandwiches to steaks at sensible prices, well kept Brakspears (full range), good choice of wines, a lot of panelling, roaring log fire, sleepy dog and cat; friendly helpful service, fruit machine, flowers, big garden with summer barbecue; may have relaxed live music Sun *(Chris Glasson, TBB, J and B Cressey, BB)*

Knowl Hill [Bath Rd], *Old Devil*: Roomy yet cosy, with wide choice of well cooked food, Badger IPA, Best and Tanglefoot; good view from pleasant verandah above attractive lawn with tables and colourful awnings, swings and slide for children; piped music, fruit machine, quiz Mon; joke board outside *(Roger Stamp)*

☆ **Littlewick Green** [3¾ miles from M4 junction 9; A404(M) then left on to A4, from which village signposted on left; SU8379], *Cricketers*: Charming spot opp cricket green, friendly service, well kept Brakspears and Fullers London Pride, decent food, neat housekeeping, lots of cricketing pictures. Very much as 1998 book; beautiful quiet spot overlooking village cricket green, with Fullers London Pride and Summer ale and Brakspears beers – but watch for short measures from silly sparklers; average food; trays of drinks on the edge of cricket green; all the ashtrays are filled with sand *(LM, TBB, Gerald Barnett, LYM)*

Littlewick Green [A4], *Ring o' Bells*: Spacious main road pub with wide range of home-cooked blackboard food, very friendly staff, well kept Boddingtons and guest beer *(Nigel and Sue Foster)*

Maidenhead [Lee Lane; Pinkneys Green, just off A308 N; SU8582], *Stag & Hounds*: Friendly refurbished pub with carpeted dining lounge, small side bar, Gales and good guest ales; skittle alley *(Chris Glasson)*

☆ **Marsh Benham** [off A4 W of Newbury; SU4267], *Water Rat*: Attractive thatched country dining pub (not really a place just for a drink) which has had good food inc unusual vegetarian dishes, welcoming service and well kept ales such as Brakspears and Wadworths 6X; seats on terrace or in charming garden with play area; reports on current management please *(June and Tony Baldwin, Ian Hepburn, Sue Everett, R M Sparkes, Fiona Maclean, LYM)*

Midgham [Bath road (N side); SU5567], *Coach & Horses*: Main-road pub with good food under new landlord; garden behind *(R M Sparkes, BB)*

☆ **Newbury** [towpath, nr main st; SU4666], *Lock Stock & Barrel*: Briskly efficient modern Fullers pub standing out for canalside setting, with tables on suntrap terrace looking over a series of locks towards handsome church; spacious popular wood-floored bar with antique-effect lights and fittings, and quite a sunny feel – lots of windows; reliable food all day, well kept Fullers beers, plenty of newspapers, lots of tables and chairs, good mix of customers; no-smoking back bar; pop music may be loudish; canal walks *(Peter and*

Audrey Dowsett, Phyl and Jack Street, C R L Savill, BB)

☆ **Old Windsor** [17 Crimp Hill; off B3021 – itself off A308/A328; SU9874], *Union*: Appealing old pub with interesting collection of nostalgic show-business photographs, well kept ales such as Fullers London Pride, good bar food from sandwiches up, consistently good friendly service, woodburner in big fireplace, fruit machine; good value attractive copper-decorated restaurant, white plastic tables under cocktail parasols on sunny front terrace (heated in cooler weather), country views; comfortable bedrooms *(Mr and Mrs T A Bryan, Mayur Shah, PCZ, Ian Phillips, BB)*

☆ **Old Windsor** [Crimp Hill], *Oxford Blue*: Welcoming extended family pub packed with aeroplane memorabilia inc lots of suspended model aeroplanes, big new family room, chintzy dining room in conservatory extension, food all day, Fullers London Pride and Wadworths 6X, decent wines by the glass, friendly service, piped music; play fort and giant toadstool in garden, with picnic-sets, also sets on sheltered front terrace overlooking field *(Andy and Jill Kassube, Piotr Chodzko-Zajko, John and Elisabeth Cox, Lin and Roger Lawrence, BB)*

Old Windsor [next to river], *Bells of Ouzeley*: Busy Harvester dining pub with pleasant staff, good choice of reasonably priced food, Bass *(R B Crail)*

☆ **Reading** [Kennet Side – easiest to walk from Orts Rd, off Kings Rd; SU7273], *Fishermans Cottage*: Quiet backwater by canal lock and towpath, with lovely big back garden, friendly atmosphere, modern furnishings of character, pleasant stone snug behind woodburning range, light and airy conservatory, waterside tables; good value lunches (very busy then but service quick), evening food inc Mexican, well kept Fullers ales, small choice of wines, small darts room, SkyTV; dogs allowed (not in back garden) *(C P Scott-Malden, D J and P M Taylor, Tony and Wendy Hobden)*

Reading [10 Forbury Rd], *Corn Stores*: Imaginative split-level conversion, lots of stone and wood, chandler's equipment, Fullers full range excellently kept (inc their bottled beers), friendly staff and locals, wheelchair access; open all day weekdays, cl Sun, no food Fri/Sat evening *(Richard Lewis)*; [Tudor Rd], *Flyer & Firkin*: Several well kept ales inc unusual specials (eg Vanilla Ice Cream), two farm ciders, bare boards, railway and brewing decor, lots of seating, friendly staff, pub games, usual food; open all day *(Richard Lewis)*; [2 Broad St], *Hobgoblin*: Popular and friendly, with four interesting guest beers and a couple of farm ciders as well as their well kept Wychwood ales, bare boards, raised side area, alcovey panelled back rooms, hundreds of pumpclips on ceiling; open all day *(Richard Lewis, Dr and Mrs A K Clarke)*; [120 Castle Hill], *Horse & Jockey*: Comfortable and friendly open-plan bar, half a dozen well kept real ales from changing small breweries (two you tap yourself down in the cellar), farm cider, good staff, wide choice of good value food; TV; open all day *(Richard Lewis)*; [163 Friar St], *Monks Retreat*: Good L-shaped Wetherspoons pub, nicely furnished, with upper bar wrapping around towards the back, nine well kept ales, Weston's farm cider, friendly efficient staff, plenty of seating inc no-smoking areas; open all day *(Richard Lewis)*; [Friar St], *Newt & Cucumber*: Roomy and comfortable open-plan chain pub, open all day, with half a dozen well kept mainly national beers, good choice of food, friendly staff *(Richard Lewis)*; [163 Southampton St], *Red Lion*: Superb choice of excellently kept Hop Back ales, also their bottled beers and a farm cider, and occasional Reading Lion beers from pub's own microbrewery; basic local feel, pool, darts *(Richard Lewis)*; [Rly Stn, Platform 4], *Three Guineas*: Large friendly railway-theme pub in what seems to have been former booking office building, central bare-boards bar with pleasant furnishings, plenty of seating, wide choice of food inc lots of specials, well kept ales such as Bass and Bass GWR, Brakspears Best, Elgoods Golden Newt, Gales HSB and Youngs Special, friendly staff; piped music, games machines, tables on terrace; open from 7.30am *(Richard Lewis)*

☆ **Remenham** [A4130, just over bridge E of Henley; SU7683], *Little Angel*: Low-beamed dining pub with panelling and darkly bistroish decor, good food – mainly restauranty, but snacks from sandwiches up too, friendly landlord, efficient service, good atmosphere; splendid range of wines by the glass, well kept Brakspears, floodlit terrace *(James Nunns, Gordon, Christopher Glasson, LYM)*

Shurlock Row [SU8374], *White Hart*: Two traditional relaxing rooms separated by inglenook fireplace, friendly service, Brakspears, Fullers London Pride and Wadworths 6X, decent food, panelling, flying memorabilia inc squadron badges, old pictures and brasses; soft piped music, fruit machine; tables in garden *(Simon Collett-Jones, J and B Cressey)*

☆ **Stanford Dingley** [SU5771], *Old Boot*: Stylish 18th-c beamed pub, two roaring log fires, one in an inglenook, assorted old country tables and chairs smelling nicely of furniture polish, stagecoach scenes on attractive linen curtains and prints; unpretentiously upmarket dining room, public bar, good choice of imaginative not cheap food inc several fish dishes, vegetarian and children's – very generous sandwiches too; well kept ales such as Archers and Brakspears, good measures of good wine, chatty landlord, big suntrap back garden, lovely village *(Susan and John Douglas, Dr M Ian Crichton, Roger Byrne, Dr Wendy Holden, G C Hackemer, LYM)*

Stanford Dingley, *Travellers Friend*: Small and cosy popular local *(Roger Stamp)*

☆ **Swallowfield** [S of Reading on Farley Hill lane; SU7364], *George & Dragon*: Cosy old country pub attractively and comfortably modernised, good value generous food inc imaginative dishes, well kept Wadworths 6X and other ales (staff bring drinks to table), good choice of wines, good friendly service; can get very busy, best to book *(John and Julia Hall)*

☆ **Theale** [Church St; SU6371], *Volunteer*: Open-plan, with flagstones in public bar, comfortable carpeted lounge with historical military prints, nice wooden furniture, well kept Fullers, reasonably priced generous bar food (not Sun evening), friendly considerate staff, quiet piped music, free Sun nibbles; children at reasonable times, small garden *(C P Scott-Malden, Chris and Andy Crow, Bruce Bird)*

Upper Basildon [village signposted from Pangbourne and A417 Pangbourne—Streetley; SU5976], *Beehive*: Bee-theme black-beamed front bar with flagstones, bare boards and big log fire, middle section with settees and easy chairs, back restaurant; generous freshly made food from filled baguettes up, old timbers, tasteful decor, good friendly service; small garden *(Mr and Mrs David Holt, LYM)*

Wargrave [High St; off A321 Henley—Twyford; SU7878], *Bull*: Quietly friendly and cottagey low-beamed pub popular for good if not cheap food beyond the usual range; well kept Brakspears, good log fires, tables on pretty covered terrace; bedrooms *(M Borthwick, LYM)*

Warren Row [SU8180], *Crooked Inn*: Small but welcoming bar in corner of what's really a rather smart and far from cheap restaurant, dark varnished floor, crisp white tablecloths and cream napkins, Mediterranean and Pacific Rim food inc lunchtime snacks, unusual wine list *(Martin and Karen Wake)*

☆ **Wickham** [3 miles from M4 junction 14, via A338, B4000; SU3971], *Five Bells*: Neatly kept local in racehorse-training country, big log fire, tasty food, tables tucked into low eaves, well kept ales inc Ringwood, friendly landlord, garden with good play area; children in eating area, good value bedrooms *(Gordon, Jeff Davies, LYM)*

Windsor [Market St; SU9676], *Three Tuns*: Particularly well kept Courage, food inc good sandwiches (same baker as the Queen), quick service; piped music, can be busy with tourists *(Marjorie and Malcolm Sykes)*; [Vansittart Rd], *Vansittart Arms*: Victorian, period decor in three rooms inc coal-fired range, good home-made food, well kept Fullers, interesting range of wines by the glass; paved terrace, small play area *(Kaye Carver, Malcolm Kinross)*

Winkfield [Church Rd (A330); SU9072], *White Hart*: Neatly modernised Tudor pub with ex-bakery bar and ex-courthouse restaurant, good food esp Sun lunch, real ales such as Brakspears and Fullers London Pride, good wine choice; sizeable attractive garden *(A Hepburn, S Jenner, LYM)*

☆ **Winterbourne** [not far from M4 junction 13; SU4572], *Winterbourne Arms*: Pretty black and white pub with pleasantly old-fashioned decor, good rather restauranty food, friendly helpful service, good choice of real ales; tables in attractive front garden and on green over quiet village lane, play area, nearby walks *(Julie Peters, Colin Blinkhorn, D E Kent, Jerry Hughes, LYM)*

☆ **Wokingham** [Gardeners Green, Honey Hill – OS Sheet 175 map ref 826668; SU8266], *Crooked Billet*: Homely country pub with pews, tiles, brick serving counter, crooked black joists, big helpings of good value genuinely home-cooked lunchtime food, well kept Brakspears, friendly service, small no-smoking restaurant area where children allowed, cosy local atmosphere; nice outside in summer, very busy weekends *(J W Joseph, Andy Cunningham, Yvonne Hannaford, LYM)*

Wokingham [Nine Mile Ride], *Wh'd A Tho't It*: Big pub very popular for food (not Mon evening), decent helpings and wide choice, polite service *(K and E Leist)*

☆ **Woodside** [off A332 Windsor—Ascot, S of B3034; SU9270], *Duke of Edinburgh*: Perfectly cooked good value fish and other generous food (not Sun evening, but good Sun lunch) in unpretentious refurbished pub with well kept Arkells 2B, 3B and Kingsdown, cheerful service; children welcome, some tables outside *(Mr and Mrs T A Bryan, A Hepburn, S Jenner, LYM)*;

☆ **Woodside**, *Rose & Crown*: Thriving dining pub with good (not cheap) interesting meals, plenty of space for eating with most tables set for diners, wider choice in evenings; neatly painted low beams in long narrow bar, Charles Wells Bombardier, Marstons Best and Ruddles on handpump, big jugs of Pimm's, good service; tables and swing in side garden, attractive setting; bedrooms (not Sun) *(TAB, N S Holmes, BB)*

Woolhampton [Station Rd (off A4 opp Angel); SU5767], *Rowbarge*: Big canalside family dining place with beamed bar, panelled side room, small snug, bric-a-brac, candlelit tables, good choice of well kept ales; no-smoking back conservatory, tables in big garden with fish pond; piped pop music may obtrude, lots of children, service can lack personal touch *(C P R Baxter, R M Sparkes, DHV, D E Twitchett, Roger Byrne, LYM)*

Post Office address codings confusingly give the impression that some pubs are in Berkshire, when they're really in Oxfordshire or Hampshire (which is where we list them).

Buckinghamshire

This year's front runners here, all doing particularly well in recent months, are the Mole & Chicken at Easington (a charmingly relaxed and informal dining pub), the very distinctive old Royal Standard of England at Forty Green, the beautifully placed Stag & Huntsman at Hambleden, the Rising Sun at Little Hampden (outstanding imaginative food, nice setting), the friendly and homely Shoulder of Mutton at Little Horwood, the Angel at Long Crendon (gaining our Food Award for the first time this year), the Carrington Arms at Moulsoe (distinctive food, really helpful service – a new main entry), the White Hart at Preston Bissett (another newcomer, traditional character), the bustling well run Polecat at Prestwood, the Frog at Skirmett (yet another new entry – one of our most enjoyable finds this year, and a nice place to stay in), and the very welcoming and traditional Chequers at Wheeler End. Other pubs for good food include the Russell Arms at Butlers Cross and Red Lion at Great Kingshill (under the same management – fresh fish is their thing), the attractively placed Walnut Tree at Fawley, the Hampden Arms at Great Hampden, the Green Dragon at Haddenham (quite elaborate cooking), the civilised Five Arrows in Waddesdon (excellent wines, too), and the Chequers at Wooburn Common. The place that gains our award as Buckinghamshire Dining Pub of the Year is the Mole & Chicken at Easington – a pub where the atmosphere contributes as much to your enjoyment as the food itself. The Lucky Dip section at the end of the chapter has some good prospects in it, too, especially the Bull & Butcher at Akeley, Old Swan at Astwood, Bottle & Glass near Aylesbury, Blue Flag at Cadmore End, Bell at Chearsley, Kings Head at Little Marlow, Two Brewers in Marlow, Red Lion at Marsworth, Black Boy at Oving, Crown at Penn, Hit or Miss at Penn Street, Old Crown at Skirmett, Cock and Bull in Stony Stratford (competition between these two famously neighbouring inns seems to be doing them both a lot of good at the moment), Old Swan at The Lee, Chequers at Weston Turville and Cock at Wing; we have inspected and so can vouch for most but not all of these. Against a background of generally very high drinks prices in this county, the Cross Keys in Great Missenden (tied to Fullers) stood out as cheap; and prices were relatively low in the White Hart at Preston Bissett.

---

nr AMERSHAM SU9495 Map 4

Queens Head

Whielden Gate; pub in sight just off A404, 1½ miles towards High Wycombe at Winchmore Hill turn-off; OS Sheet 165 map reference 941957

Unchanging and unpretentious, this old brick and tile pub has a low-beamed, friendly bar with traditional furnishings, horsebrasses, and lots of brass spigots; flagstones surround the big inglenook fireplace (which still has the old-fashioned wooden built-in wall seat curving around right in beside the woodburning stove – with plenty of space under the seat for logs), and there's also a stuffed albino pheasant, old guns, and a good cigarette card collection. The family room is no smoking. Bar food includes sandwiches, home-made soup (£2.25), sweet pickled trout (£3.50), omelettes (£4), and pies such as steak in ale, spicy lamb or venison (£5.50). Well kept Adnams Bitter,

Brakspears Hop Demon, Courage Best, and Rebellion IPA on handpump, and several malt whiskies; darts, shove-ha'penny, dominoes, cribbage, fruit machine, and piped music. The garden is quite a busy place with bantams running around, an aviary with barn owls, children's play equipment, a golden labrador called Tanner, and a jack russell called Ellie. *(Recommended by Gerald Barnett, Ian Phillips; more reports please)*

Free house ~ Licensees Les and Mary Anne Robbins ~ Real ale ~ Meals and snacks (till 10pm; not Sun evening) ~ (01494) 725240 ~ Children in family room ~ Open 11-3, 5.30(6 Sat)-11; 12-3, 7-10.30 Sun

BEACONSFIELD SU9490 Map 2

Greyhound

A mile from M40 junction 2, via A40; Windsor End, Old Town

This cosy, pleasant and neatly kept two-bar former coaching inn is well liked locally, and the entertaining landlord and his staff will give you a warm welcome. Food is quite a draw too: filled french or granary bread (from £3.45), home-made burgers (from £5.75), home-made pork, apple, bacon and cider, steak and kidney or garlic mushroom with a creamed spinach sauce and parmesan topping (from £5.75), popular bubble and squeak with cold rare roast beef, honey roast ham or cheese (from £6.45), daily changing pasta dishes, daily specials, and puddings (£2.95); there's a partly no-smoking back bistro-like restaurant. Well kept Courage Best, Fullers London Pride, Wadworths 6X, and two guest beers on handpump; no piped music or games machines and no children. *(Recommended by Gerald Barnett, Geoff and Sylvia Donald, Kevin Thomas, Janet and Colin Roe)*

Free house ~ Licensees Jamie and Wendy Godrich ~ Real ale ~ Meals and snacks (till 10pm; not Sun evening) ~ Restaurant ~ (01494) 673823 ~ Open 11-3, 5.30-11; 12-3, 7-10.30 Sun

BLEDLOW SP7702 Map 4

Lions of Bledlow

From B4009 from Chinnor towards Princes Risborough, the first right turn about 1 mile outside Chinnor goes straight to the pub; from the second, wider right turn, turn right through village

From the bay windows of the attractive low-beamed rooms in this 16th-c pub there are fine views over a small quiet green to the plain stretched out below. The inglenook bar has attractive oak stalls built into one partly panelled wall, more seats in a good bay window, and an antique settle resting on the deeply polished ancient tiles; log fires and a woodburning stove. Bar food includes home-made soup (£2), filled french bread (from £3.25), ploughman's (£4), spinach and stilton lasagne (£4.95), steak and Guinness pie (£5.50), chicken tikka masala (£6.25), Scotch rump steak (£8.95), daily specials like lamb liver and bacon (£4.75), spinach-stuffed plaice fillet (£5.95), and duck breast in raspberry jus with basmati rice (£6.50), and children's menu (£3.50); the restaurant is no smoking. Well kept Brakspears Bitter, Courage Best, Marstons Pedigree, Rebellion Mutiny, John Smiths, and Wadworths 6X on handpump. One of the two cottagey side rooms has a video game and fruit machine. There are seats on the sheltered crazy-paved terrace and more on the series of neatly kept small sloping lawns – a good place to relax after a walk in the nearby Chilterns. *(Recommended by Tim Brierly, Greg Kilminster, Gerald Barnett, JP, PP, B R Sparkes, K Leist)*

Free house ~ Licensee Mark McKeown ~ Real ale ~ Meals and snacks ~ Restaurant ~ (01844) 343345 ~ Well behaved children in eating area of bar and in restaurant ~ Open 11.30-3, 6-11; 12-3.30, 7-10.30 Sun (may open longer hours in summer)

BOLTER END SU7992 Map 4

Peacock

Just over 4 miles from M40 junction 5; A40 to Stokenchurch, then B482

For 20 years Mr and Mrs Hodges have been running this bustling little pub. The brightly modernised bar has a rambling series of alcoves, a good log fire, and a cheerful atmosphere; the Old Darts bar is no smoking. Good home-made bar food includes lunchtime sandwiches and ploughman's (not Sunday lunchtime or bank holidays), three changing daily specials such as spicy Spanish meatballs (£5.50), thai green chicken curry (£6.95), and griddled English lamb steak with mediterranean vegetables (£8.20), as well as local butcher sausages (£5.50), home-made lasagne (£5.70), cheesy mushroom pancakes (£5.90), steak and kidney pie (£6.80), stincotto (a big lean gammon hock with lamon beans, £7.50 or £10.30), fillet of fresh salmon with herby mayonnaise (£8.20), Aberdeen Angus steaks (from £9), and puddings like home-made syllabub or lemon and almond tart with lemon sauce (£3). Well kept Brakspears Bitter, Tetleys Bitter, and Youngs Special on handpump, decent wines, and freshly squeezed orange juice. In summer there are seats around a low stone table and picnic-sets in the neatly kept garden. The 'no children' rule is strictly enforced here and there is no piped music. *(Recommended by Gerald Barnett, Mr and Mrs T A Bond, Mark Hydes)*

Carlsberg Tetley ~ Lease: Peter and Janet Hodges ~ Real ale ~ Meals and snacks (not Sun evening) ~ (01494) 881417 ~ Open 11.45-2.30, 6-11; 12-3 Sun (closed Sun evening)

BRILL SP6513 Map 4

Pheasant 🍷

Windmill St; village signposted from B4011 Bicester—Long Crendon

You can enjoy a meal here overlooking the windmill opposite the pub (one of the oldest post windmills still in working order) from both the verandah and the garden – and there are fine views, on a clear day, of nine counties. The quietly modernised and neatly kept beamed bar has a friendly, unpretentious atmosphere, refectory tables and windsor chairs, a woodburning stove, and a step up to a dining area which is decorated with attractively framed prints. The views from both rooms are marvellous. Bar food includes vegetarian dishes (from £3.40), home-cooked ham with eggs (£5.45), marinated strips of chicken breast with garlic bread (£5.60), fresh salmon fillet on a bed of sautéed potatoes (£6.95), five different types of chicken breast (£7.95), and rump steak with six different types of sauce (£9.50). Well kept Marstons Pedigree and Tetleys on handpump, and at least six good wines by the glass; piped music. No dogs (they have two golden retrievers themselves). Roald Dahl used to drink here, and some of the tales the locals told him were worked into his short stories. *(Recommended by L Walker, Michael Sargent, K H Frostick, Piotr Chodzko-Zajko, Andy and Jill Kassube, Steve de Mellow, E J Gibson, Mr and Mrs T Bryan)*

Free house ~ Licensee Mike Carr ~ Real ale ~ Meals and snacks ~ Restaurant ~ (01844) 237104 ~ Children welcome ~ Open 11-3, 6-11; 11-11 summer Sat; 12-11 Sun; closed 25 Dec ~ Bedrooms: £43S/£64S

BUTLERS CROSS SP8406 Map 4

Russell Arms

Chalkshire Rd; off A4010 S of Aylesbury, at Nash Lee roundabout; or off A413 in Wendover, passing station

The licensee who made another of our main entries, the Red Lion at Great Kingshill so successful, has also taken on this small brick and flint roadside pub. As with the Red Lion, the main emphasis is on the really fresh, very good fish dishes. Changing every day, there is a fine choice of oysters (80p each), scallops or king prawns (£6 for four), and bass, swordfish, turbot, monkfish, dover sole and so forth (£8-£14), and the landlord will cook it however you want it. The small bar is entirely straightforward, with standard pub furnishings and a few pictures, and there is a small but light and airy dining room opening off it. ABC Best and Flowers Original on handpump, and good house wines. Out in front are picnic-sets, with more in a garden screened from the road by tall hedges. The pub is well placed for Chilterns walks. *(Recommended by George Atkinson; more reports on the new regime, please)*

Pubmaster ~ Tenant Jose Rivero-Cabrera ~ Real ale ~ Meals and snacks (see below) ~

Restaurant (not Sun evening or Mon) ~ (01296) 622618 ~ Children welcome ~ Open 11-3, 6-11; 12-3, 7-10.30 Sun; closed Mon lunchtime

CADMORE END SU7892 Map 4

Old Ship

B482 Stokenchurch—Marlow

The attraction here is that this has remained a good straightforward country pub with the full range of Brakspears ales tapped from the cask, a warm welcome, and simple, well liked food. The furnishings in the tiny low-beamed two-room bar are pretty basic – leatherette wall benches and stools in the carpeted room on the right, and on the left scrubbed country tables, bench seating (one still has a hole for a game called five-farthings), bare boards and darts, shove-ha'penny, cribbage, dominoes, and chess. Bar food includes filled rolls (from £1.40), vegetable soup (£1.95), ploughman's (£3.25), filled baked potatoes (£3.50), chilli beef (£4.25), and chicken casserole (£6.95); they offer more substantial meals at the weekend; a fair choice of malt whiskies and traditional cider. There are seats on the terrace (with more in the sheltered garden), a large pergola with picnic-sets, and an enclosed play area for children (who may not be allowed inside). Parking is on the other side of the road. *(Recommended by Peter Plumridge, JP, PP, Dave Irving, Ewan McCall, Roger Huggins, Tom McLean, Pete Baker, Mark Hydes, Mayur Shah, Gordon)*

Brakspears ~ Tenants Ken and Diane Smith ~ Real ale ~ Meals and snacks ~ (01494) 883496 ~ Open 12-2.30(3 Sat), 5.30(6 Sat)-11; 12-3, 7-10.30 Sun

CHEDDINGTON SP9217 Map 4

Old Swan

58 High St

In summer, the garden with its very good enclosed play area, furnished wendy house and child-size wooden bench and tables, is liked by families; the hanging baskets and tubs are pretty, too. Inside this attractive thatched pub, the neatly kept and quietly civilised bar rooms on the right have quite a few horsebrasses and little hunting prints on the walls, old-fashioned plush dining chairs, a built-in wall bench, a few tables with nice country-style chairs on the bare boards, and a big inglenook with brass in glass cabinets on either side of it. On the other side of the main door is a room with housekeeper's chairs on the rugs and quarry tiles and country plates on the walls, and a step up to a carpeted part with stripy wallpaper and pine furniture. Decent bar food includes sandwiches (from £2; 4oz rump steak £4.50), filled baked potatoes (from £2.75), vegetable lasagne or liver and bacon (£4.95), gammon and egg (£5.25), home-made steak and mushroom pie (£6.25), daily specials, children's dishes (£2.50), and puddings; the restaurant is partly no smoking. Well kept ABC Best, Adnams Bitter, Ridgeway Bitter (from Tring), and Youngs Special on handpump, quite a few malt whiskies, and quite a few wines; pleasant staff. Fruit machine, dominoes, and piped music. *(Recommended by Ian Phillips, Mel Smith, Shirley Cannings, C A Hall, Ted George, Monica Shelley, Laura Darlington)*

Carlsberg Tetleys ~ Lease: Maurice and Joyce Cook ~ Real ale ~ Meals and snacks (12-2.30, 7-9 weekdays, 12-4, 7-9.30 weekends) ~ Restaurant ~ (01296) 668226 ~ Children welcome ~ Regular live music ~ Open 11-11; 12-10.30 Sun

DINTON SP7611 Map 4

Seven Stars

Stars Lane; follow Dinton signpost into New Road off A418 Aylesbury—Thame, near Gibraltar turn-off

Tucked away in a quiet village, this pretty white pub is a friendly place and is well worth the effort it takes to find it. The characterful public bar (known as the Snug here) is notable for the two highly varnished ancient built-in settles facing each other across a table in front of the vast stone inglenook fireplace. The spotlessly kept lounge bar, with its beams, joists and growing numbers of old tools on the walls, is comfortably and simply modernised – and although these rooms are not large, there is a spacious and comfortable restaurant area. Popular, good value bar food includes sandwiches (from £1.80; toasties 25p extra), soup (£2.25), filled baked potatoes (from £3), ploughman's (£4), gammon and egg (£5.75), daily specials such as peppered pork (£5.50), minted lamb chop (£5.75), and seafood medley (£6), and puddings (from £2.25). Well kept ABC, and Vale Notley and Edgars on handpump; dominoes and piped music. There are tables under cocktail parasols on the terrace, with more on the lawn of the pleasant sheltered garden. The pub is handy for the Quainton Steam Centre. *(Recommended by Quentin Williamson, Marjorie and David Lamb, Michael Sargent, S J Sloan, Douglas Miller, Ian Phillips, Duncan Satterly, Mark Hydes)*

Free house ~ Licensees Rainer and Sue Eccard ~ Real ale ~ Meals and snacks (not Sun or Tues evenings) ~ Restaurant ~ Children in eating area of bar and in restaurant ~ (01296) 748241 ~ Open 12-3, 6-11; 12-3, 7-10.30 Sun

EASINGTON SP6810 Map 4

Mole & Chicken

From B4011 in Long Crendon follow Chearsley, Waddesdon signpost into Carters Lane opposite the Chandos Arms, then turn left into Chilton Road

Buckinghamshire Dining Pub of the Year

This year, the licensees have added quite a few more seats and tables to their garden where they aim to hold summer barbecues and pig and lamb roasts. But it's the very good food that remains the big draw to this bustling country dining pub, and it's almost essential to book a table. Although the inside is open-plan, it is very well done, so that all the different parts seem quite snug and self-contained without being cut off from what's going on, and the atmosphere is chatty and relaxed. The beamed bar curves around the serving counter in a sort of S-shape – unusual, as is the decor of designed-and-painted floor, pink walls with lots of big antique prints, and even at lunchtime lit candles on the medley of tables to go with the nice mix of old chairs; good winter log fires. Served by friendly staff, the generous helpings of food might include baked artichoke hearts with hollandaise (£4.50), duck breast and pistachio pâté (£5.95), seafood crêpes or fresh asparagus and stilton quiche (£7.95), chicken tikka (£8.95), and king prawn thai curry or lamb and vegetable casserole with fresh mint dumplings (£9.95). Decent French house wines (and a good choice by the bottle), lots of malt whiskies, and well kept Morlands Old Speckled Hen, Ruddles Best, and Wadworths 6X on handpump. No dogs. *(Recommended by Bob and Maggie Atherton, Marion Turner, Joan Yen, Michael Sargent, James Chatfield, G R Braithwaite, B R Sparkes, Liz Bell, Graham and Karen Oddey, Peter Saville, Abigail Dombey, Kate Nash)*

Free house ~ Licensees Tracey Gardner, Allan Heather ~ Real ale ~ Meals and snacks (till 10pm) ~ (01844) 208387 ~ Children welcome ~ Open 12-3, 6-11; 12-10.30 Sun; closed 25 Dec

FAWLEY SU7586 Map 2

Walnut Tree

Village signposted off A4155 (then right at T-junction) and off B480, N of Henley

This is the sort of place that people come back to year after year to enjoy the good, well presented food. You can choose to eat in the bar with its stripy red wallpaper and red carpet, the no-smoking conservatory or the restaurant. From the bar menu, there are dishes like baked stuffed aubergine (£5.50), home-made burgers (£6.50), home-baked hot ham with parsley sauce (£6.50), and a home-made pie of the day (£6.95) or you can choose from the restaurant menu: a terrine of the day (£4.25), baked Cornish crab (£4.95), chicken with stilton and walnuts (£9.95), whole roast guinea fowl (£10.75), daily specials like home-made ravioli (£8.25) or grilled lemon sole (£12.95), and puddings such as home-made cheesecake or spiced apple torte (from £2.95). Well kept Brakspears Bitter, Special and seasonal ales on handpump, and a good range of wines. The big lawn around the front car park has some well spaced tables made from elm trees, with some seats in a covered terrace extension – and a hitching rail for riders. *(Recommended by Bob and Maggie Atherton, Susan and John Douglas, Gerald Barnett, Mike and Mary Carter, Gwen and Peter Andrews, Alan Morton, Mary and Des Kemp, Mayur Shah, Mark Hydes, Gordon)*

Brakspears ~ Tenants Ben and Diane Godbolt ~ Real ale ~ Meals and snacks ~ Restaurant ~ (01491) 638360 ~ Children in eating area of bar, in restaurant, and conservatory but must be over 5 in evening ~ Open 12-3.30, 6-11; 12-3.30, 7-10.30 Sun; closed winter Sun evenings ~ Bedrooms: £35S/£50S

FORD SP7709 Map 4

Dinton Hermit

Village signposted between A418 and B4009, SW of Aylesbury

You can be sure of a friendly welcome from the licensees of this characterful stone cottage. The attractively traditional partly tiled public bar on the left has scrubbed tables, a woodburning stove in its huge inglenook, and prints of a lady out hunting. The lounge on the right, with a log fire, has red plush banquettes along the cream walls and red leatherette chairs around polished tables, and red leatherette seats built into the stripped stone walls of a small room leading off. Mrs Tompkins cooks the good bar food, and at lunchtime, when they don't take reservations, this might include (with prices unchanged since last year) sandwiches (from £1.50), soup (£2.25), ploughman's (from £3.50), smoked haddock in mushroom and cheese sauce (£5.25), a vegetarian hotpot or home-made lasagne (£5.25), chicken curry or stilton and asparagus pancake (£5.95), and puddings such as home-made fruit pie or bread pudding (£2.75); in the evening (when you must book), dishes are slightly more expensive and include more grills and fish. Well kept ABC Best, Adnams, and Wadworths 6X on handpump; darts, shove-ha'penny, cribbage and dominoes. The sheltered and well planted garden opposite (they don't serve food out there in the evenings) has swings, a slide and a seesaw. *(Recommended by Michael Sargent, Graham Tayar, Catherine Raeburn, Peter and Jan Humphreys, S J Sloan, Quentin Williamson, Mark Hydes, Comus Elliott, Douglas Miller)*

Free house ~ Licensees John and Jane Tompkins ~ Real ale ~ Meals and snacks (not Sun, Mon or Tues) ~ (01296) 748379 ~ Well behaved children welcome ~ Open 11-2.30, 6-11; 12-2, 7-10.30 Sun; closed Mon lunchtimes

FORTY GREEN SU9292 Map 2

Royal Standard of England

3½ miles from M40 junction 2, via A40 to Beaconsfield, then follow sign to Forty Green, off B474 ¾ mile N of New Beaconsfield

This is a lovely old pub that has enormous appeal both to locals and visitors. The rambling rooms have huge black ship's timbers, finely carved old oak panelling, roaring winter fires with handsomely decorated iron firebacks, and a massive settle apparently built to fit the curved transom of an Elizabethan ship; also, ancient pewter and pottery tankards, rifles, powder-flasks and bugles, lots of brass and copper, needlework samplers, and stained glass. Two areas are no smoking. Enjoyable bar food includes home-made mediterranean fish soup (£3.25), Italian antipasto salad (£3.95), ploughman's (£5.25), vegetable curry or beef in ale pie (£7.25), poached salmon fillet with watercress sauce or sesame stir-fried chicken (£8.25), rib-eye steak (£8.95), and puddings like cinnamon and marmalade bread and butter pudding (£3.25). Well kept Adnams Best, Brakspears Bitter, Marstons Pedigree and Owd Rodger, Morlands Old Speckled Hen, and Vale Notley on handpump, and country wines. There are seats outside in a neatly hedged front rose garden, or in the shade of a tree. *(Recommended by Michael Taylor-Waring, Susan and John Douglas, Mark J Hydes, Greg Milminster, JP, PP, George Atkinson, Gerald Barnett, Lawrence Pearse, Mayur Shah, DFL, J and B Cressey)*

Free house ~ Licensees Cyril and Carol Cain, Georgina Oxenbury ~ Real ale ~ Meals and snacks ~ (01494) 673382 ~ Children in three areas for them ~ Open 11-3, 5.30-11; 12-3, 7-10.30 Sun; closed evening 25 Dec

FRIETH SU7990 Map 2

Prince Albert

Village signposted off B482 in Lane End; turn right towards Fingest just before village

No noisy machines or piped music disturb the quietly chatty atmosphere in this pretty little tiled cottage. On the left there are hop bines on the mantlebeam and on the low black beams and joists, brocaded cushions on high-backed settles (one with its back panelled in neat squares), a big black stove in a brick inglenook with a bison's head looking out beside it, copper pots on top, and earthenware flagons in front, and a leaded-light built-in wall cabinet of miniature bottles. The slightly larger area on the right has more of a medley of chairs and a big log fire; magazines, books and local guides to read. Well kept Brakspears Bitter, Special, Mild, Old and OBJ on handpump, good wines, and decent whiskies on optic include Smiths Glenlivet and Jamesons. Bar food includes good home-made soup (£3.25), a fine choice of filled french bread (£3.95) such as cheese and onion, giant sausage, black pudding and bacon or pastrami and cucumber, ham and egg (£4.45), and daily specials such as steak and kidney pudding, fresh fish and chips, home-made curries and stews or boiled bacon with parsley sauce (£5.95). Shove-ha'penny and cribbage. The lovely dog is called Leo. A nicely planted informal side garden has views of woods and fields, and there are plenty of nearby walks. Please note, children are not allowed inside.

(Recommended by Maureen Hobbs, Susan and John Douglas, Pete Baker, Anthony Longden, Mark Hydes, DJW, Mayur Shah, TBB)

Brakspears ~ Tenant Frank Reynolds ~ Real ale ~ Lunchtime meals and snacks ~ (01494) 881683 ~ Light folk/blues some Sun evenings ~ Open 11-3, 5.30-11; 12-3, 7-10.30 Sun

GREAT HAMPDEN SP8401 Map 4

Hampden Arms

Village signposted off A4010 S of Princes Risborough; OS Sheet 165 map reference 845015

Set in a lovely quiet spot opposite the village cricket pitch, this civilised dining pub offers two menus. At lunchtime, dishes are priced at £4.95 and might include filled baked potatoes, cottage pie, chicken and ham bake, seafood pancake or lemon sole with baby prawns in a robust cheese and lobster sauce. In the evening, meals are more substantial: burger topped with pâté and covered with pastry (£6.95), chicken in cider and apples and topped with stilton (£9.95), and beef stroganoff, salmon and prawn bake or steak stuffed with bacon and pâté in a rich brandy and mushroom sauce (£13.95). There are puddings such as sticky toffee pudding and treacle pudding (£3.50). A small corner bar has well kept Greene King Abbot, Tetleys, and Wadworths 6X on handpump, and Addlestones cider; service is quietly obliging. The cream-walled front room has broad dark tables, with a few aeroplane pictures and country prints; the back room has a slightly more rustic feel, with its pink-cushioned wall benches and big woodburning stove. There are tables out in the tree-sheltered garden; on the edge of Hampden Common, the pub has good walks nearby.

(Recommended by Greg Kilminster, Gill and Keith Croxton, Gerald Barnett, B R Sparkes, George Atkinson, Francis and Deirdre Gevers, Gordon Tong)

Free house ~ Licensees Terry and Barbara Matthews ~ Real ale ~ Meals and snacks ~ (01494) 488255 ~ Children welcome ~ Open 12-2.30, 6.30-11; 12-3, 6.30-10.30 Sun

GREAT KINGSHILL SU8798 Map 4

Red Lion

A4128 N of High Wycombe

At first sight, this seems like an unassuming local as the furnishings are unpretentious, the walls are hung with decorative plates and old photographs of the pub, and there's not much room for standing around – but to all intents and purposes, it is a fish restaurant with all the tables laid for eating. The Spanish staff serve very fresh fish from Billingsgate, which might include oysters, fresh calamares, skate, king prawns, swordfish, dover soles, lobsters, and much more (around £8-£16); the chips are freshly cut and good, and there's a bargain Sunday lunch; service charge is added automatically. Tetleys on handpump, good house wines, and freshly squeezed orange juice. *(Recommended by Mark Girling, TBB, Bob and Maggie Atherton, Paul Coleman, John and Hazel Waller; more reports please)*

Pubmaster ~ Tenant Jose Rivero-Cabrera ~ Real ale ~ Meals and snacks ~ Restaurant ~ (01494) 711262 ~ Children welcome ~ Open 12-3, 6-11; closed Sun evening, Mon

GREAT MISSENDEN SP8900 Map 4

Cross Keys

High St

This is a friendly and old-fashioned little town pub with wooden standing timbers dividing the bar. One half has old sewing machines on the window sill, collectors' postcards, various brewery mirrors, lots of photographs, and horse bits and spigots and pewter mugs on the beams by the bar counter, and the other half has a bay window with a built-in seat overlooking the street, a couple of housekeeper's chairs in front of the big open fire, and a high-backed settle. The food is all Italian and at lunchtime in the bar, there is soup (£2.95), cold grilled vegetables (£3.40), meatballs cooked in tomato sauce (£4.20), various pasta dishes with sauces (from £4.20), and a selection of salami and cheeses (£4.50); more elaborate food in the restaurant. Well kept Fullers Chiswick, London Pride, and ESB on handpump, very cheap for the area. Cribbage, dominoes, fruit machine, and piped music. The terrace at the back of the building has picnic-sets with umbrellas – and you can eat out here, too. *(Recommended by Ian Phillips, Dave Braisted; more reports please)*

Fullers ~ Tenant Martin Ridler ~ Real ale ~ Lunchtime meals and snacks ~ Restaurant ~ Well behaved children in restaurant ~ (01494) 865373 ~ Open 11-3, 5-11; 12-3, 7-10.30 Sun; closed 25 Dec

George

94 High St

In the 15th c, this friendly inn was built as a hospice for the nearby abbey. It has a cosy two-roomed bar with attractively moulded heavy beams, timbered walls decorated with prints, little alcoves (including one with an attractively carved box settle – just room for two – under a fine carved early 17th-c oak panel), and Staffordshire and other figurines over the big log fire. A snug inner room has a sofa, little settles and a smaller coal fire; shove-ha'penny, cribbage, dominoes, shut-the-box, and Jenga. The new chef has introduced quite a few daily specials, such as smoked haddock and spinach bake (£5.75), curried lamb rissoles (£5.95), gammon and egg (£6.25), bass with parsley and lemon butter (£8.25), and duck breast in a plum and redcurrant sauce (£9.25); also, home-made soup (£2.25), sandwiches (from £2.15; not Sunday), filled baked potatoes (from £2.95), chicken balti (£5.75), steak and kidney pie (£6.80), and steak (£10.50). A huge Sunday roast, and if you are staying, breakfasts are served until 10am. The restaurant is no smoking. Well kept Adnams Bitter, Chiltern Beechwood Bitter, Fullers London Pride, and Wadworths 6X on handpump kept under light blanket pressure, mulled wine in winter, sangria in summer, and several malt whiskies; prompt and cheerful service. Plenty of seats on the terrace and garden area. *(Recommended by Ian Phillips, Gill and Keith Croxton, Simon Penny)*

Greenalls ~ Lease: Guy and Sally Smith ~ Real ale ~ Snacks (served all day) and meals; not Sun or evenings 25-26 Dec ~ Restaurant ~ (01494) 862084 ~ Children welcome ~ Open 11-11; 12-3.30, 7-10.30 Sun; closed evenings 25-26 Dec and between 3 and 7pm 31 Dec ~ Bedrooms: £65.75B/£72.75B

Children – if the details at the end of an entry don't mention them, you should assume that the pub does not allow them inside.

HADDENHAM SP7408 Map 4

Green Dragon

Village signposted off A418 and A4129, E/NE of Thame; then follow Church End signs

The main area in this civilised dining pub – two high-ceilinged communicating rooms – has been decorated in warm Tuscan blues and yellows, they have added to their attractive still lifes and country pictures, lighting has been improved, and tablecloths are now a blue and terracotta checked design; log fire on cool days. There is a respectable corner for people wanting just a drink, with a few blond cast-iron-framed tables, some bar stools and well kept Marstons Pedigree and Vale Notley on handpump; piped music. But the main emphasis is certainly on food, with lunchtime dishes such as home-made soup (£3), home-made pâté of local wood pigeon and chicken with a spicy fresh fish chutney (£4.85), grilled skewers of marinated swordfish with tabouleh (£5.25, main course £7.50), various omelettes (from £6.50), a vegetarian dish of the day (£7.65), and grilled Scottish salmon wrapped in dover sole on fresh noodles with balsamic vinegar sauce (£12.45), with evening specials like roulade of oriental chicken breast and shitake mushrooms with a teriyaki dressing (£4.85), bouillabaisse with rouille and croutons (£3.25), calf liver with a ragout of jerusalem artichokes and leeks on a caper and chive sauce (£12.85), and grilled magred of duck with home-made wild mushroom tortellini on a port and morrel sauce (£13.15); puddings include bread and butter pudding, mandarin and kumquat iced soufflé with a warm passion fruit coulis or baked individual rice pudding flavoured with cinnamon and served with pistachio ice cream (from £3.45). The wine list is well chosen and sensibly priced, with a good choice by the glass. There are white tables and picnic-sets under cocktail parasols on a big sheltered gravel terrace behind, with more on the grass, and a good variety of plants; this part of the village is very pretty, with a duck pond unusually close to the church. *(Recommended by Bob and Maggie Atherton, Brian Atkin; more reports please)*

Whitbreads ~ Lease: Julian Ehlers ~ Real ale ~ Meals and snacks ~ (01844) 291403 ~ Children welcome lunchtimes only (unless by prior arrangement and must be over 6) ~ Open 11.30-2.30, 6.30-11; 12-2.30 Sun (closed Sun evening)

HAMBLEDEN SU7886 Map 2

Stag & Huntsman

Turn off A4155 (Henley—Marlow Rd) at Mill End, signposted to Hambleden; in a mile turn right into village centre

Readers very much enjoy this charming brick and flint pub. It's in an especially pretty village, set opposite the church, and is just a field's walk from the river (appreciated by those with boats). The half-panelled, L-shaped lounge bar has low ceilings, a large fireplace, upholstered seating and wooden chairs on the carpet, and a friendly bustling atmosphere. The attractively simple public bar has darts, shove-ha'penny, dominoes, cribbage, and quiz night every second Monday, and there's a cosy snug at the front, too. Good home-made bar food includes soup (£2.95), ploughman's (£5.25), liver and bacon (£6.15), mediterranean pasta (£6.50), fresh salmon fishcakes or marinated chargrilled chicken (£6.95), pork medallions (£7.95), steaks (from £11.25), and puddings like fresh fruit crumble (£2.75); the dining room is pretty. Well kept Brakspears Bitter and Special, Old Luxters Barn Ale, and Wadworths 6X on handpump, farm ciders, and good wines served by cheerful staff. The spacious and neatly kept country garden is where they hold their popular big barbecues – cajun salmon, pork and apple burgers, pork and leek sausages, and various kebabs. The bedrooms are a little old-fashioned. *(Recommended by Gordon, Dave Carter, Elizabeth and Klaus Leist, Glen and Nola Armstrong, Christine and Geoff Butler, Gerald Barnett, Mike and Mary Carter, Graham and Karen Oddey, P J and J E F Caunt, D Voller, TBB, Chris and Ann Garnett)*

Free house ~ Licensees Hon Henry Smith and Andrew Fry ~ Real ale ~ Meals and snacks ~ Restaurant ~ (01491) 571227 ~ Children in eating area of bar ~ Open 11-3(3.30 Sat), 6-11; 12-3.30, 7-10.30 Sun; closed bank hol Mon evenings ~ Bedrooms: £38.50S/£48.50S

IBSTONE SU7593 Map 4

Fox

1¾ miles from M40 junction 5: unclassified lane leading S from motorway exit roundabout; pub is on Ibstone Common

Smart but friendly, this 17th-c country inn gives a warm welcome to all. The comfortable low-beamed lounge bar has high-backed settles and country seats, old village photographs on the walls, and log fires. In the public bar – which has darts, dominoes, and fruit machine – the pine settles and tables match the woodblock floor; piped music. Decent bar food includes enjoyable sandwiches, ploughman's, and changing hot meals like crispy duck salad with raspberry dressing (£4.30 starter, £6.50 main course), beef and Guinness pie (£7.15), smoked haddock with mustard sauce (£7.60), lamb steak on ratatouille with a rosemary and red wine sauce (£9.35), and puddings such as plum crumble; efficient service. The small dining area is no smoking; there's also a smart restaurant. Well kept Brakspears Bitter and weekly changing guest beers on handpump. From the neat rose garden, you can overlook the common, with rolling fields and the Chilterns oak and beech woods beyond; the village cricket ground is close by. *(Recommended by Gerald Barnett, Susan and John Douglas, Simon Collett-Jones, Peter Plumridge, M J Dowdy)*

Free house ~ Licensee Ann Banks ~ Real ale ~ Meals and snacks (till 10pm) ~ Restaurant ~ (01491) 638722 ~ Children in eating area of bar and in restaurant ~ Open 11-3, 6-11; 12-3, 7-10.30 Sun; closed evenings 25/26 Dec, 1 Jan ~ Bedrooms: £45B/£58B

LITTLE HAMPDEN SP8503 Map 4

Rising Sun

Village signposted from back road (ie W of A413) Great Missenden—Stoke Mandeville; pub at end of village lane; OS Sheet 165 map reference 856040

The food in this smart dining pub remains consistently excellent and imaginative. From a constantly changing menu, there might be gently braised ginger and honey duck leg with a hoisin sauce (£4.75), scallops and bacon with anchovy fillets (£4.95), excellent woodman's (a bowl of soup with a warm roll and cheddar, brie, stilton and pâté, mixed salad and pickles, £6.50), casserole of smoked rabbit or charcoal grilled tuna steak with a provençal tomato sauce (£8.45), roast home-smoked pork joint with a red wine and plum sauce or rump steak with a Guinness and pickled walnut sauce (£8.95), hickory smoked Deben duck with a cinnamon and pear sauce (£9.95), and puddings such as raspberry and amaretti flummery or Jamaican toffee banana pancake (£3.25). Well kept Adnams, Brakspears Bitter, Marstons Pedigree, and Morlands Old Speckled Hen on handpump, with home-made mulled wine and spiced cider in winter, and a short but decent wine list; efficient service. One part of the interlinked bar rooms is no smoking, and there's also a separate no-smoking dining room (which enjoys the same food as the bar). No noisy games machines or piped music. The secluded setting, with tracks leading through the woods in different directions, is delightful – walkers are welcome as long as they leave their muddy boots outside. There are some tables on the terrace by the sloping front grass. *(Recommended by Peter Saville, Peter and Christine Lea, Maysie Thompson, B R Sparkes, Stephen and Tracy Groves, David and Ruth Shillitoe, Miss G Hume)*

Free house ~ Licensee Rory Dawson ~ Real ale ~ Meals and snacks (not Sun evening, not Mon) ~ (01494) 488393 ~ Children welcome ~ Open 11.30-2.30, 6.30-11; 12-3 Sun; closed Sun evenings and Mon – except for lunchtime bank holidays ~ Bedrooms: £25(£35B)/£40(£58B)

LITTLE HORWOOD SP7930 Map 4

Shoulder of Mutton

Church St; back road 1 mile S of A421 Buckingham—Bletchley

You can be sure of a really friendly welcome in this partly thatched and half-timbered old pub. The rambling T-shaped bar is attractively but simply furnished with sturdy seats around chunky rustic tables on the quarry-tiles, has a huge fireplace at one end with a woodburning stove, and a showcase of china swans; the friendly, well trained black labrador-cross (who loves children) is called Billy, and the black cat, Trouble. Well kept ABC Best and Marstons Pedigree on handpump; shove-ha'penny, cribbage, dominoes, and fruit machine in the games area. Much enjoyed, good value bar food includes home-made soup (£1.90), sandwiches (from £1.90), filled baked potatoes (from £2.50), ploughman's (from £3.90), home-made dishes like chilli con carne, diced leg of lamb cooked in ale or steak and kidney pie (from £4.20), all-day breakfast (£4.30), home-made nut cutlet (£4.90), steaks, and children's meals (from £1.60). French windows look out on the pleasant back garden where there are plenty of tables. From the north, the car park entrance is tricky. *(Recommended by Ted George, CMW, JJW, S Markham, Susan and John Douglas, Klaus and Elizabeth Leist, Michael Bourdeaux, Graham and Karen Oddey, Gill and Keith Croxton)*

Pubmaster (Allied) ~ Tenant June Fessey ~ Real ale ~ Meals and snacks (not Sun evening, not Mon) ~ Restaurant ~ (01296) 712514 ~ Children in restaurant until 8.30pm ~ Open 11-2.30(3 Sat), 6-11; 12-3, 7-10.30 Sun; closed Mon lunchtime

LITTLE MISSENDEN SU9298 Map 4

Crown

Crown Lane, SE end of village, which is signposted off A413 W of Amersham

The same family have been running this bustling small brick cottage for over 90 years now – the present licensees are the third generation. The bars are thoroughly traditional and sparkling clean, there's a good mix of customers, and the atmosphere is very chatty and relaxed. There are old red flooring tiles on the left, oak parquet on the right, built-in wall seats, studded red leatherette chairs, a few small tables, and a complete absence of music and machines. The Adnams Broadside, Hook Norton Best, and a guest such as Marstons Pedigree or Morrells Varsity on handpump are kept particularly well; they also have farm ciders and decent malt whiskies. Bar food is simple but all home made, majoring on a wide choice of generous very reasonably priced sandwiches (from £2.20), as well as ploughman's (£3.75), pasties and Buck's bite (a special home-made pizza-like dish, £4.10); darts, shove-ha'penny, cribbage, dominoes. There are picnic-sets and other tables in an attractive sheltered garden behind. The village is pretty, with an interesting church. No children. *(Recommended by Ian Phillips, Peter and Christine Lea, John and Hazel Waller)*

Free house ~ Licensees Trevor and Carolyn How ~ Real ale ~ Lunchtime snacks (not Sun) ~ (01494) 862571 ~ Open 11-2.30, 6-11; 12-2.30, 7-10.30 Sun

LONG CRENDON SP6808 Map 4

Angel

Bicester Rd (B4011)

There's quite a choice of very good popular food in this partly 17th-c civilised dining pub. At lunchtime, there might be crispy duck and bacon salad with hoisin vinaigrette (£4.50), salad of smoked chicken and sun-dried tomatoes, topped with toasted pine kernels (£4.95), chargrilled lamb liver and crispy bacon in a shallot and sage sauce (£6.95), or leek and smoked cheddar risotto flavoured with saffron and topped with toasted pine kernels (£8.95); evening extras such as terrine of local pheasant, pigeon and partridge with orange compote (£4.75) or chicken breast on garlic mash with a tarragon and mustard grain sauce (£10.75), daily specials like home-made carrot and orange soup (£3.50), Spanish sardines with chilli butter (£4.25), poached fillet of smoked haddock on leek and mustard mash and glazed with a cheese sabayon (£10.75) or king prawn and vegetable stir-fry with garlic and ginger (£11.75), and puddings such as sticky toffee pudding with toffee ice cream, double espresso brûlée or chocolate fallen angel with white and dark chocolate sauces (£4.50). Well kept Hook Norton Old Hookey, Jennings Bitter, Ridleys Rumpus, and Shepherd Neame Spitfire on handpump, quite a few malt whiskies and an extensive wine list. There are capacious sofas in a comfortable and pleasantly decorated lounge, sturdy tables and chairs in another area, and a no-smoking conservatory dining room at the back looking out on the garden; also, a terrace for summer eating out; piped music. *(Recommended by Joan Yen, Francis and Deirdre Gevers, Tim Heywood, Sophie Wilne, Mark Hydes)*

Free house ~ Licensees Trevor Bosch, Angela Good ~ Real ale ~ Meals and snacks (not Sun evening) ~ Restaurant ~ (01844) 208268 ~ Children welcome ~ Open 12-3, 6-11; 12-3 Sun (closed Sun evening) ~ Bedrooms: £45B/£55B

MOULSOE SP9041 Map 4

Carrington Arms 🍷

1¼ miles from M1, junction 14: A509 N, first right signed Moulsoe; Cranfield Rd

Choosing your food at this well refurbished old brick house is far more interesting than simply studying a menu: the delicious meats and fresh fish that are the highlight of any visit are irresistibly displayed in a refrigerated glass case, and the friendly staff are particularly good at guiding you through what's on offer. As well as excellent rump, fillet and sirloin steaks, a typical choice might include local lamb and venison, duck breasts marinated in gin with chillies, and fish and seafood such as salmon, seabass, scallops, lobster, tiger prawns, marlin or a colourful strawberry grouper. They're happy to let you try little bits of everything, and as the meat and fish are sold by weight (in pounds and ounces), you can have as much or as little as you like. Meals are cooked on an adjacent grill, rather like a sophisticated indoor barbecue. There's also a bar menu with ploughman's (from £4.15), brie and apple omelette (£5.50), various thai meals like green chicken (£6.50) or a spicy vegetable crumble (£7.25), and puddings like Egyptian bread and butter pudding done with coconut milk and grape juice (£3). Furnishings are comfortable and traditional, with a mix of wooden chairs and cushioned banquettes around the tables and flame-effect fire, and up some steps a cosier seating area with hops hanging from the ceiling and a big mirror along the back wall; soft piped music, and discreetly placed TV. A separate oyster bar has caviar as well as oysters (£1 each or £9.50 a dozen), the shells of which are stacked up in a growing pile outside the front door. Well kept Adnams Southwold, Charles Wells Bombardier and Theakstons Old Peculier on handpump, good range of bottled wines, a choice of champagnes by the glass, good coffee in nice mugs. Behind the pub a long garden has a couple of tables, and there are bedrooms in a separate building alongside. The licensees recently opened the Fitzwilliam Arms at Castor in Cambridgeshire, with the same enjoyably distinctive culinary approach. *(Recommended by Howard and Margaret Buchanan, Mike and Mary Carter, John and Enid Morris, Stephen, Julie and Hayley Brown, Cliff Blakemore, David and Mary Webb, A Sutton, Mark Hydes)*

Free house ~ Licensee Edwin Cheeseman ~ Real ale ~ Meals and snacks (till 10) ~ (01908) 218050 ~ Children welcome ~ Open 11-2.30, 6-11 ~ Bedrooms: /£44B

NORTHEND SU7392 Map 4

White Hart

On back road up escarpment from Watlington, past Christmas Common; or valley road off A4155 Henley—Marlow at Mill End, past Hambleden, Skirmett and Turville, then sharp left in Northend itself

In summer, the garden of this little 16th-c pub is rather charming and full of flowers and fruit trees. In winter, the quiet bar has good log fires (one in a vast fireplace), as well as very low handsomely carved oak beams, some panelling, and comfortable window seats. A small choice of food (with prices almost unchanged since last year) includes sandwiches, home-made soup with fresh baked bread or home-made pâté (£2.95), cumberland sausage with mash and onion gravy (£4.95), various home-made pies, fresh salmon, king prawns (£7.50), and two Sunday roasts (and a home-made nut roast; £5.50); fresh vegetables. Well kept Brakspears Bitter, Special and OBJ on handpump or tapped from the cask; shove-ha'penny, cribbage and dominoes; no piped music. *(Recommended by Gordon; more reports please)*

Brakspears ~ Tenants Derek and Susie Passey ~ Real ale ~ Meals and snacks (not Sun or Mon evenings) ~ Restaurant ~ (01491) 638353 ~ Children in eating area of bar ~ Open 11.30-3, 5.30-11; 12-3, 7-10.30 Sun

PRESTON BISSETT SP6529 Map 4

White Hart

Pound Lane; village can be reached off A421 Buckingham bypass via Gawcott, or from A4421 via Chetwode or Barton Hartshorn

So many dogs have been known to accompany their owners to this friendly 18th-c thatched and timbered white-painted house that they sell dog biscuits at the tiny central bar counter. Throughout our last visit their own golden retriever lay slumbering contentedly beside the log fire, its faithful teddy bear close at hand. The three cosy little rooms have a genuinely traditional feel, with old lamps hanging from the low beams, captain's chairs, red banquettes and stools nestling around the tables, and local prints and memorabilia from the local Tetleys-related Aylesbury Brewing Company around the walls. ABC Best, Greene King IPA and Marstons Pedigree on handpump, around a dozen malt whiskies, country wines, and home-made lemonade and elderflower spritzer. The largest room, with a well polished wooden floor and high-backed wooden settle, is the nicest place to enjoy the tasty bar food, listed on a big blackboard menu covering most of one wall. Dishes might include soup (£2.50), goat's cheese crostini on a bed of mixed leaves (£4.50), mussels in cider and cream (£4.95), sausage and mash with red onion marmalade (£6.50), wild rabbit and bacon pie or linguine with red pesto and sun-dried tomatoes (£6.95), and red mullet fillets with caper and lemon dressing (£8.95); lunchtime snacks like filled baguettes (from £2.95) and Aga-baked potatoes (from £3.95); they recommend booking at busy times. Service is chatty and helpful: the landlord drew us a map to our next destination. There are tables behind in a yard and on a small grassy area. They occasionally have barbecues or wine tastings. *(Recommended by George Atkinson, D and J McMillan, Mr and Mrs Grimes, Marjorie and David Lamb)*

Pubmaster ~ Tenants Duncan Rowney and Lisa Chapman ~ Real ale ~ Meals and snacks (not Mon evening, not Tues) ~ (01280) 847969 ~ Children in dining room ~ Open 12-2.30, 6.30-11; closed lunchtime Tues

PRESTWOOD SP8700 Map 4

Polecat

170 Wycombe Rd (A4128 N of High Wycombe)

A good mix of customers fills this attractive, extended pub – at lunchtime there are chatty crowds of middle-aged lunchers, with a broader mix of ages in the evening. Several smallish rooms open off the low-ceilinged bar, with a good medley of tables and chairs, all sorts of stuffed birds as well as the stuffed white polecats in one big cabinet, small country pictures, rugs on bare boards or red tiles, a couple of antique housekeeper's chairs by a good open fire in another; the Galley room is no smoking. A good choice of well presented bar food includes soup (£2.70), sandwiches (from £2.70), filled baked potatoes (from £4), baked mushrooms with blue cheese and port (£4.20), ploughman's (£4.50), courgette and mushroom rissoles (£6.20), home-made steak and kidney pie (£7.60), grilled fillet of red snapper marinated in fresh ginger and coriander (£8.20), braised lamb shank with smoked bacon, tomato and rosemary (£8.80), daily specials such as peppered chicken with lemon, coriander, butter sauce (£7.90), fried crab cakes in lemon crumb with chilli jam (£8.40), and magret of duck with prunes and cider (£10.20), and puddings like raspberry shortcake or apple, honey and walnut crumble (£3.50). Well kept Marstons Pedigree, Morlands Old Speckled Hen, Theakstons Best and XB, and Wadworths 6X on handpump at the flint bar counter, a list on a board of wines by the glass, and at least 20 malt whiskies; quick friendly service. As well as picnic-sets on neat grass out in front beneath a big fairy-lit apple tree, and more on a big well kept lawn behind, the licensees have planted pretty hanging baskets and window boxes, and 300 herbaceous plants. *(Recommended by Peter Saville, Maysie Thompson, B R Sparkes, Mark Hydes)*

Free house ~ Licensee John Gamble ~ Real ale ~ Meals and snacks (not Sun evening) ~ (01494) 862253 ~ Children in eating area of bar ~ Open 11.30-2.30, 6-11; 12-3 Sun (closed Sun evening)

SKIRMETT SU7790 Map 2

Frog

From A4155 NE of Henley take Hambleden turn and keep on; or from B482 Stokenchurch—Marlow take Turville turn and keep on

Our most recent visit to this brightly modernised country inn was a little after the last advertised time for food, but the briskly efficient bar staff were happy to rustle up a baguette or two. Better still, they didn't mind serving puddings, which proved to be easily among the best we'd had for quite some time. Though it's understandably the food that draws most people here, it's an appealing place to come just for a drink, with something of the atmosphere of a smart rural local; leaflets and posters near the door advertise local raffles and the like. Obviously well cared for, the beamed bar area has a striking hooded fireplace with a bench around the edge (and a pile of logs sitting beside it), big rugs on the wooden floors, a mix of comfortable furnishings, and sporting and local prints around the salmon painted walls. The function room leading off, with a fine-looking dresser, is sometimes used as a dining overflow. Already proving popular with readers, the generously served meals include soup (£2.50), lunchtime baguettes, chicken liver pâté (£4.25), warm tartlet of roast peppers, basil and mozzarella (£4.95), pork loin with onions and mushrooms in a green peppercorn sauce or baked marrow and ratatouille topped with goat's cheese (£8.95), chicken breast stuffed with soft cheese, pine nuts and coriander warpped in parma ham with vegetable risotto (£10.25), and puddings (£3.25); they do a three-course set meal for £16.50. Service stays slick even at busy times. The restaurant is no smoking; piped music. Adnams Best, Brakspears, Fullers London Pride and a weekly changing guest on handpump, a good range of bottled wines, and various coffees; the strength of the beers and wines is clearly chalked up above the bar. Through a gate at the side is a lovely garden, with a large tree in the middle, and unusual pentagon-shaped tables well placed for attractive valley views. The bedrooms are engaging, and it's a nice base for the area; Henley is close by, and just down the road the windmill at Ibstone is delightful. *(Recommended by Peter Plumridge, Mr and Mrs B Thomas, Dave Carter, Anthony Longden)*

Free house ~ Licensees Jim Crowe, Noelle Green ~ Real ale ~ Meals and snacks (not Sun evening Oct-May) ~ Restaurant ~ (01491) 638996 ~ Children in eating area of bar and restaurant ~ Open 11.30-3(4 Sun), 6.30-11 ~ Bedrooms: £43.50B/£53.50B

TURVILLE SU7690 Map 2

Bull & Butcher

Valley road off A4155 Henley—Marlow at Mill End, past Hambleden and Skirmett

Set among cottages in a lovely Chilterns valley, this pretty black and white timbered pub has a comfortable and atmospheric low-ceilinged bar – partly divided into two areas – beams from ships seized from the Spanish Armada, cushioned wall settles, and an old-fashioned high-backed settle by one log fire; there's also an inglenook fireplace. A good choice of enjoyable bar food includes home-smoked pastrami on rye bread (£4.95), game in ale pie (£7.95), cod in beer batter (£8.95), chicken divon (£10.95), venison medallions with forestière sauce or scallops in a thai or lime and thyme sauce (£14.95), and whole grilled turbot with a white wine sauce (£18.50). Well kept Brakspears Bitter, Mild, Special, Old, and a guest beer on handpump, and around four dozen wines, most by the glass; efficient service. Shove-ha'penny, dominoes, cribbage, and occasional piped music. This is a fine place to finish a walk, and the attractive garden has tables on the lawn by fruit trees and a neatly umbrella-shaped hawthorn; good summer barbecues. Once a month (Tuesday evenings) the MG car club meet here. It does get crowded at weekends. *(Recommended by Gordon, Simon Collett-Jones, JP, PP, Dave Carter, Gerald Barnett, Graham and Karen Oddey, TBB, Peter Saville, T G Brierly)*

Brakspears ~ Tenant Nicholas Abbott ~ Real ale ~ Meals and snacks ~ (01491) 638283 ~ Children in eating area of bar ~ Open 11-3, 6-11; 12-3, 7-10.30 Sun

WADDESDON SP7417 Map 4

Five Arrows

A41 NW of Aylesbury

Part of the Rothschild Estate, this rather grand small hotel is an ideal base for visiting Waddesdon Manor, the grounds, and aviary. The informally pubby bar is an open-plan series of light and airy high-ceilinged rooms with a relaxed but civilised atmosphere, and a handsome bar counter carved with the five arrows of the Rothschild crest which symbolise the dispersal of the five founding sons of the international banking business. There are also family portrait engravings and lots of old estate-worker photographs on the leafy green wallpaper, heavy dark green velvet curtains on wooden rails, mainly sturdy cushioned settles and good solid tables on parquet flooring (though one room has comfortably worn-in armchairs and settees), and newspapers and copies of *Country Life* in an antique magazine rack. It's the daily specials that come in for most praise: delicious aubergine, feta and tomato pancake, hot smoked goat's cheese on a garlic croûte (£4.25), fried pork escalope with apple, cream and calvados (£11.50), and chargrilled emu steak with rosemary and sesame oil with creamed pearl barley (£13.95); good home-made puddings, and no sandwiches or snacks on Sunday. The country-house style restaurant is no smoking; must book at busy times. The formidable wine list naturally runs to Rothschild first-growth clarets as well as less well known Rothschild estate wines. Well kept Adnams Bitter, Chiltern Beechwood, and Fullers London Pride on handpump; other drinks including many malt whiskies are exemplary; efficient service, unobtrusive piped music. The sheltered back garden has attractively grouped wood and metal furnishings. *(Recommended by Martin and Barbara Rantzen, Maysie Thompson, W W Burke, Graham and Karen Oddey, Susan and John Douglas, Michael Long, Comus Elliott, Michael and Lorna Bourdeaux)*

Free house ~ Licensees Julian Alexander-Worster, Fabia Bromovsky ~ Real ale ~ Meals and snacks ~ Restaurant ~ (01296) 651727 ~ Children welcome ~ Open 11.30-3, 6-11; 12-3, 7-10.30 Sun ~ Bedrooms: £60B/£75B

WEST WYCOMBE SU8394 Map 4

George & Dragon

High St; A40 W of High Wycombe

By the time this Guide is published, the licensees of this handsome Tudor inn hope to have refurbished several of the bedrooms and be well on the way to extending the no-smoking family bar. The comfortable and colourfully decorated rambling main bar has massive beams, sloping walls, and a big log fire; the magnificent oak staircase is said to be haunted by a wronged girl. Bar food includes lunchtime sandwiches, home-made soup (£1.95), potted stilton (£4.25), home-made nut cutlet with a red pesto salsa (£5.45), chicken and asparagus pie (£6.25), seafood and potato gratin (£7.45), super pies, beef wellington (£8.25), and home-made puddings like fresh fruit crumble or walnut and toffee tart (from £2.35). Well kept Courage Best and Directors and guests like Bass, Gales HSB, Marlow Rebellion, Ushers Founders or Youngs Special on handpump, and quite a few malt whiskies; dominoes and cribbage. The arched and cobbled coach entry leads to a spacious, peaceful garden with picnic-sets, and a fenced in play area with a climbing frame; you can park through here, too. The inn does get crowded at weekends, so it's best to get there early then. Nearby you can visit West Wycombe Park with its fine furnishings and classical landscaped grounds (it is closed on winter Saturdays). *(Recommended by Chris Glasson, Allan Engelhardt, Gerald Barnett, Kevin Thomas, Susan and John Douglas, TBB, Alan Morton)*

Courage ~ Lease: Philip Todd ~ Real ale ~ Meals and snacks (not 25 Dec) ~ (01494) 464414 ~ Children in family bar ~ Open 11-2.30(3 Sat), 5.30-11; 12-3, 7-10.30 Sun ~ Bedrooms: £56B/£66B

Children welcome means the pubs says it lets children inside without any special restriction; readers have found that some may impose an evening time limit – please tell us if you find this.

WHEELER END SU8093 Map 4

Chequers

Village signposted off B482 in Lane End NW of Marlow, then first left also signposted Wheeler End; or can be reached by very narrow Bullocks Farm Lane (sign may be defaced) from A40 layby just W of W Wycombe

The Robinsons continue to run this small white-painted tiled house as a good traditional village pub – this is becoming quite a rarity now, with so many places aiming at the dining market. They are intent on preserving a really welcoming atmosphere to locals and visitors alike, and offering a fine range of real ales and other drinks, and good straightforward pub food. Under its low ochre ceiling the bar has what might be called an inherently friendly layout: it's so small, and shaped in such a way, that you can't help but feel part of the general conversation. It angles back past a good inglenook log fire (that the black cat favours), and a little roomlet with a fruit machine, to a bigger back room with a couple of dart boards. Furniture is mainly scrubbed country-kitchen with a few board-backed wall benches, and the ochre walls have a liberal sprinkling of local notices alongside small hunting prints, cartoons and so forth; darts, shove-ha'penny, cribbage, dominoes, and fruit machine. There are good malt whiskies and excellent coffee as well as well kept Adnams, Bass, Brakspears PA, Fullers London Pride and Greene King IPA and Abbot on handpump, with a guest such as Brains Dark Mild tapped from the cask. Food includes excellent hot and cold filled rolls (the 'small' bacon and black pudding roll at £2.50 will set you up nicely for a stroll on the nearby common), good soups such as jerusalem artichoke or leek and potato with thyme (£2.95), a pasta dish, meaty or vegetarian chilli or late breakfast (all £4.95), ploughman's (from £4.95), and liver and bacon or bangers and mash (choice of cumberland or Abbot Ale sausage – £5). There are a few tables outside; no car park to speak of, but plenty of parking nearby. *(Recommended by Susan and John Douglas, Simon Collett-Jones, Anthony Longden, TBB)*

Free house ~ Licensees David and Patsy Robinson ~ Real ale ~ Snacks and lunchtime meals (not Sun or Mon) ~ (01494) 883070 ~ Children in eating area of bar until 9pm ~ Live blues Tues evening ~ Open 11-3, 5.30-11; 11-11 Sat; 12-10.30 Sun; closed Mon lunchtime

WOOBURN COMMON SU9187 Map 2

Chequers

2 miles from M40 junction 2; A355 towards Slough, first right, then right again; Kiln Lane, Widmoor – OS Sheet 175, map reference 910870

This smart country local does undoubtedly get a lot of its custom from the flourishing hotel and restaurant side (though it is none the worse for that) but keeps an unchanging traditional atmosphere in its bar. This is low-beamed and partly stripped brick, and has standing timbers and alcoves to break it up, lived-in sofas on its bare boards, a bright log-effect gas fire, and various pictures, plates and tankards. There's an attractive brasserie on the left (they also have another more formal restaurant), and very good food such as sandwiches and ploughman's, home-made burger (£6.50), strips of chicken with a thai sauce (£7.95), home-made steak and kidney pie, and excellent monkfish and king scallops with ginger or tuna with caper sauce (£10.95). Well kept Fullers London Pride, Marstons Bitter and Pedigree, and Morlands Old Speckled Hen on handpump, a sizeable wine list, Scrumpy Jack cider, and a fair range of malt whiskies and brandies; spacious garden away from the road, with cast-iron tables. The attractive stripped-pine bedrooms are in a 20th-c mock-Tudor wing; breakfasts are good. *(Recommended by David and Helen Wilkins, Susan and John Douglas, Bob and Maggie Atherton, Simon Collett-Jones, Terry Buckland, Kevin Thomas)*

Free house ~ Licensee Peter Roehrig ~ Real ale ~ Meals and snacks ~ Restaurant ~ (01628) 529575 ~ Children welcome ~ Open 11-11; 12-10.30 Sun ~ Bedrooms: £87.50B/£92.50B

Lucky Dip

Besides the fully inspected pubs, you might like to try these Lucky Dips recommended to us and described by readers (if you do, please send us reports):

☆ **Adstock** [Main St (off A413); SP7330], *Old Thatched Inn*: Friendly and comfortable beamed and flagstoned pub/restaurant, cosy corners and open fires, generous food from good value baguettes up, well kept mainly Scottish Courage and guest ales (at a price), decent wines, friendly attentive staff; piped music; seats out in sheltered back garden, children in restaurant and eating area *(Gill and Keith Croxton, Graham and Karen Oddey, K Frostick, LYM)*

☆ *nr* **Adstock** [Verney Junction, Addington – OS Sheet 165 map ref 737274], *Verney Arms*: Cheery and cottagey, more bistro than pub, with imaginative decor, colourful walls and chairs, plates on bright red dado, fresh flowers; very good food, also small bar area around tiny brick counter; well kept Greene King Rayments, soft piped jazz, smartly relaxed atmosphere, open fire, good friendly service *(Stuart Archer, BB)*

☆ **Akeley** [The Square, just off A413; SP7037], *Bull & Butcher*: Genuine village pub, cheerful cricket-loving landlord, landlady cooks good value food, also lunchtime buffet (not Sun) inc wide range of help-yourself salads, several puddings, and evening steak bar (not Sun or Mon); three good fires in long open-plan beamed bar with red plush banquettes, well kept Fullers London Pride, Marstons Pedigree, Morlands Original and a guest beer, decent house wines, winter spiced wine, two friendly dogs, traditional games; children allowed in eating area, tables in attractive garden, occasional live entertainment; handy for Stowe Gardens *(Ian Phillips, B J Smith, Graham and Karen Oddey, LYM)*

☆ **Amersham** [High St, Old Town (A413); SU9597], *Eagle*: Good helpings of tasty bar food inc rather more imaginative specials, well kept ales such as Marstons Pedigree, reliably quick very friendly service even on busy lunchtimes, clean pleasant rambling low-beamed bars, log fire; maybe soft piped music, fruit machine; more lively young person's pub evenings; back garden overlooking football pitch *(David Clifton, M J Dowdy, TBB)*

☆ **Amersham** [High St], *Kings Arms*: Picture-postcard timbered building in charming street, lots of heavy beams and snug alcoves, big inglenook, high-backed antique settles and other quaint old furnishings among more standard stuff; low-priced bar food inc vegetarian, restaurant, pleasant service, well kept Tetleys-related and other ales, children in eating area; open all day, rather a young person's pub evening; nice garden *(Nina Randall, LYM)*

Amersham [Whealden St (A404)], *Saracens Head*: 17th c, with decent food, well kept Everards and Ruddles; bedrooms *(Gordon Neighbour, LYM)*

☆ **Aston Clinton** [119 Green End St; SP8712], *Oak*: Cosy and attractively refurbished Fullers pub, good choice of home-made food, decent wine list, real fire, no music or machines, good efficient service *(Andrew Scarr, Helen Hazzard)*

Aston Clinton, *Bell*: More restaurant than pub, comfortable and smart with nice atmosphere, short choice of good interesting food (very good choice of cheeses), well chosen wines; a comfortable place to stay *(Mr and Mrs Starling, M J Dowdy)*

☆ **Astwood** [off A422; SP9547], *Old Swan*: Friendly bar, spacious and airy dining area, good generous food from bacon sandwiches to Sun roasts, well kept Scottish Courage and guest ales such as Shepherd Neame, efficient service, cosy old-fashioned atmosphere; small covered terrace, large garden *(George Atkinson, Sidney and Erna Wells, LYM)*

☆ *nr* **Aylesbury** [Gibraltar; A418 some miles towards Thame, beyond Stone – OS Sheet 165 map ref 758108], *Bottle & Glass*: Welcoming low-beamed thatched pub, tiled floor, rambling layout, wide choice of good imaginative food from sandwiches to seafood, lively atmosphere, helpful service, well kept Morrells Oxford and Varsity, good choice of wines, neat garden *(Michael Sargent, Marion Turner, Tim Heywood, Sophie Wilne, LYM)*

Beachampton [Main St; SP7737], *Bell*: Large pub with modern extension, terrace and play area in big garden, wide choice of reasonably priced generous food inc good sandwiches, ales such as Caledonian Golden Promise, Marstons Pedigree, Ridleys, Tetleys and Youngs Special, helpful service, small games room, piped classical music; nice little village with stream along street *(George Atkinson, Michael and Jenny Back)*

Bourne End [Coldmoorholme Rd; lane towards Thames off A4155; SU8888], *Spade Oak*: Useful Brewers Fayre, three well kept Whitbreads ales and Brakspears, pictures and books, piped music, a few benches outside; no dogs *(CMW, JJW, G Barnett)*

Buckingham [Mkt Sq; SP6933], *Whale*: Good Fullers pub with changing beers, friendly staff, good atmosphere, often live music Sat *(Mrs Jess Cowley)*

☆ **Cadmore End** [B482 towards Stokenchurch; SU7892], *Blue Flag*: Smartened-up beamed village pub, comfortable and civilised, with separate modern hotel wing; very attentive polite service, well kept Fullers London Pride, Marlow Rebellion, Morlands Original and Wadworths 6X, wide choice of good value interesting generous food inc fresh fish, lots of proper big dining tables; decent wines, expert unobtrusive service, fascinating vintage MG pictures in side room; attractive little restaurant; bedrooms *(Simon Collett-Jones, Peter Saville, G Barnett, Cyril S Brown, BB)*

Chackmore [SP6835], *Queens Head*: Comfortable village pub with welcoming antipodean landlord, good value varied lunchtime food from toasties and baguettes up, well kept real ales, small separate dining room *(Bernard and Marilyn Smith)*

☆ **Chalfont St Giles** [London Rd; SU9893], *Ivy House*: Attractive pub with wide range of food from sandwiches to elaborate dishes, big restaurant extension, tables in pretty little courtyard, several ales such as Brakspears, Fullers London Pride and Tallyshooter, good range of wines, pretty little courtyard; piped music *(P J Keen, Ian Phillips, Cyril Brown, Peter Saville)*

☆ **Chearsley** [The Green; N of Thame; SP7110], *Bell*: Warmly welcoming cottagey thatched pub on village green, small beamed bar with lots of tankards and decorative plates, inviting settle by woodburner; excellent service, wide choice of good value home-made food (not Mon lunchtime) from sandwiches up, inc vegetarian, well kept Fullers London Pride and a seasonal ale, good coffee, summer weekend barbecues in sizeable garden; children and dogs welcome *(Heather Couper, B R Sparkes, Gill and Keith Croxton, Marjorie and David Lamb)*

☆ **Chenies** [Chesham Rd – off A404 nr M25 junction 18; TQ0198], *Red Lion*: Pleasant and unpretentious L-shaped bar, small back snug and dining room, popular food from filled baps to pies, steaks and so forth, well kept Benskins Best, Rebellion Lion Pride (brewed for the pub) and Wadworths 6X; no children, machines or piped music *(Peter Saville, Ian Phillips, Andrew Life, LYM)*

Colnbrook [1¼ miles from M4 junction 5 via A4/B3378, then 'village only' rd; TQ0277], *Ostrich*: Striking Elizabethan pub, modernised but still signs of its long and entertaining history; good open fire, real ale and prompt friendly service, though emphasis primarily on food side – good range of bar food, separate restaurant *(Simon Collett-Jones, LYM)*

☆ **Denham** [3/4 mile from M40 junction 1; follow Denham Village signs; TQ0486], *Swan*: Pretty pub in lovely village, bright and tidy, with prints on timbered walls, picture windows overlooking splendid floodlit back garden with play area; comfortable seats, open fires, decent food and wines, well kept Courage Best, John Smiths and Wadworths 6X, good choice of food from lots of sandwiches up *(Ian Phillips, Stan Edwards, Mayur Shah, LYM)*

☆ **Downley** [Downley Common – OS Sheet 165 map ref 849959; SU8495], *Le De Spencers Arms*: Unpretentious 18th-c Fullers pub hidden away on common, fairy-lit loggia overlooking lawn with picnic-sets, prompt cheerful service, good bar food; woodland walks to nearby Hughenden Manor *(Mark Percy, Lesley Mayoh, Ian Phillips, LYM)*

☆ **Fingest** [signed off B482 Marlow—Stokenchurch; SU7791], *Chequers*: Civilised and old-fashioned Tudor pub with new licensees (family link to main entry White Hart at Northend); several rooms, sunny lounge by good-sized charming country garden, small no-smoking room, interesting furniture, Brakspears PA, SB and Old, dominoes and cribbage, attractive restaurant; children in eating area; interesting church opp, good walks *(Gordon, JP, PP, G Barnett, LYM)*

☆ **Flackwell Heath** [3½ miles from M40 junction 4; A404 towards High Wycombe, 1st right to Flackwell Heath, right into Sheepridge Lane; SU8988], *Crooked Billet*: Cosy and comfortable old-fashioned 16th-c pub in lovely country setting, low beams, good choice of lunchtime food (not Sun), eating area spread pleasantly through alcoves, friendly prompt service, well kept Brakspears and Whitbreads-related ales, good open fire; juke box; delightful little front garden with quiet views *(G and M Stewart, Ian Phillips, Simon Collett-Jones, J and B Cressey, G Barnett, BB)*

☆ **Frieth** [signed off B482 in Lane End], *Yew Tree*: Concentration on the food side, but locals still dropping in for a drink – enjoyable atmosphere, exemplary service (now a family connection to the Highwayman at Exlade Street, Oxon), well kept ales such as Brakspears PA, Fullers London Pride and Gibbs Mew Bishops Tipple; unobtrusive piped music; walkers with dogs welcome *(Sheila Keene, Simon Collett-Jones, LYM)*

☆ **Great Linford** [4½ miles from M1, junction 14; from Newport Pagnell take Wolverton Rd towards Stony Stratford; SP8542], *Black Horse*: Large pub rambling through different levels, good range of good value food, well kept Tetleys-related and guest beers, Addlestone's cider, friendly staff, open fire, upstairs restaurant, interesting nooks and crannies devoted to Grand Union Canal alongside – drinks can be taken out on the towpath (good walks along here), and sizeable lawn with well spaced picnic-sets and biggish play area; children allowed away from bar *(Bill Sykes, LYM)*

Haversham [2 High St; SP8343], *Greyhound*: Quiet and pleasant 17th-c village pub in attractive countryside, some stripped stone and beams in newly refurbished bar and lounge, well kept Greene King IPA and Abbot and a guest beer, good generous reasonably priced food inc doorstep sandwiches, friendly staff; small garden with picnic-sets and swing; live music Tues *(Tony and Gabbie Church, George Atkinson)*

☆ **Hedgerley** [SE of M40 junction 2; SU9686], *White Horse*: Friendly old country local with enjoyable food inc sandwiches, bangers and mash, home-made fishcakes, particularly well kept Charles Wells Eagle, Greene King IPA and six unusual changing ales tapped from the cask, friendly service; relaxed atmosphere in charming small public bar, jugs, ball cocks and other bric-a-brac, log fire, larger lounge with cold food display cabinet, occasional barbecues in big pleasant back garden, lovely window boxes, occasional beer festivals; no dogs, can be very busy; attractive village,

good walks nearby *(Iain Robertson, CMW, JJW, Dave Carter, Ron Gentry)*
Hedgerley [Village Lane], *One Pin*: Small, warm, friendly pub with very mixed group of locals from Rolls-Royce to bicycle; catering side now run separately, doing thai meals *(Colin Draper, M J Dowdy)*
High Wycombe [Amersham Rd, Terriers; SU8792], *Beech Tree*: Cosy little red brick local, vastly expanded conservatory eating area at the back, Courage Best and Wadworths 6X, friendly staff, reasonably priced food; quiet piped music; good value for families, big children's play area, lots of picnic-sets on grassy area, pleasant semi-rural setting *(Tony Dickinson, Gerald Barnett, Ian Phillips)*
☆ **Iver** [TQ0381], *Gurkha*: Gurkha paintings and trophies in pleasant bar, spacious yet cosy and individual; good choice of reasonably priced home cooking, well kept beer, good atmosphere and service, big restaurant *(N S Holmes)*
☆ **Lacey Green** [Parslows Hillock; from A4010 High Wycombe—Princes Risborough follow Loosley signpost, then Gt Hampden, Gt Missenden signpost; OS Sheet 165 map ref 826019; SP8201], *Pink & Lily*: Charming old-fashioned tap room (apostrophised sillily by Rupert Brooke – poem framed here) in much-extended Chilterns pub with airy and plush main bar, well kept ales such as Boddingtons, Brakspears PA, Courage Best and Glenny Hobgoblin, good wines, friendly efficient service, open fire, cheapish food (not Sun evening) from sandwiches up, dominoes, cribbage, ring the bull; piped music, children over 5 if eating; conservatory, big garden *(B R Sparkes, Mick Hitchman, M J Dowdy, Joan and Andrew Life, Ted George, LYM)*
Lacey Green [Pink Rd; SP8100], *Whip*: Cheery pubby local just below windmill, mix of simple traditional furnishings, reliable food from good lunchtime sandwiches to Sun lunches, well kept beer, friendly service; fruit machine, TV; tables in sheltered garden *(Margaret Dyke, Maureen Hobbs, Gerald Barnett, BB)*
Lavendon [High St; A428 Bedford—Northampton; SP9153], *Green Man*: Spacious and aiming upmarket, with woodburner, hops around bar, Adnams, Courage Directors and Ruddles County, good range of food inc interesting soups, particularly friendly attentive staff, restful atmosphere; piped classical music *(George Atkinson)*
Ley Hill [signed off A416 in Chesham; SP9802], *Swan*: Snugs and alcoves, heavy black beams and timbers, bar food cooked to order inc thoughtful children's dishes, maybe veg from their garden, no-smoking evening restaurant, well kept Tetleys-related and guest ales; piped music; picnic-sets outside with play area, lovely setting by green; children in eating area, open all day at least in summer *(Dr and Mrs B T Marsh)*
Little Horwood [SP7930], *Old Crown*: Old thatched and beamed village pub, small bar, dining area with small room off, Marstons Pedigree and Tetleys, good food inc snacks and children's (not Sun evening, Mon lunch), daily papers; picnic-sets in side garden, juke box, fruit machine, TV, quiz nights *(CMW, JJW)*
☆ **Little Marlow** [Church Rd; off A4155 about two miles E of Marlow, pub signed off main rd], *Kings Head*: Welcoming flower-covered old free house, homely and cosy open-plan interior, popular generous reasonably priced bar food from good toasties up, well kept ales Boddingtons, Brakspears, Fullers London Pride and Wadworths 6X, prompt pleasant service; good farm shop opp, charming walk down to church *(Don Mather, Simon Collett-Jones, Derek Harvey-Piper, Kevin and Nina Thomas)*
Little Marlow [cul de sac reached by turning off A4155 nr Kings Head], *Queens Head*: Quiet and pleasant, in peaceful attractive spot, decent food *(TBB)*
Little Missenden [SU9298], *Red Lion*: 15th-c small and genuine local, well kept Tetleys-related and other real ales, decent wines, limited but generous cheap food from sandwiches up; piped music may obtrude; sunny garden with pets' corner *(Cyril Brown, M J Dowdy)*
☆ **Littleworth Common** [Common Lane; 3 miles from M40 junction 2, off A355 towards village then left after Jolly Woodman; SU9487], *Blackwood Arms*: Lively and friendly family atmosphere, well kept real ales, good value simple food, roaring log fire, tables outside; good walks all around *(Alan Vere, Gordon Prince, LYM)*
Littleworth Common [Littleworth rd, off A355], *Jolly Woodman*: Busy Whitbreads pub by Burnham Beeches, beamed and cottagey, wide range of food, usual Whitbreads-related beers, quick pleasant service, bar billiards, useful tourist leaflets *(Gordon Prince, LYM)*
Longwick [Thame Rd; SP7805], *Red Lion*: Pleasant and welcoming, with attractive end restaurant; bedrooms *(Iain Robertson)*
Ludgershall [The Green; off A41 Aylesbury—Bicester; SP6617], *Bull & Butcher*: Quiet and cool little beamed country pub with usual food freshly prepared (so may be a delay if busy), reasonable prices, well kept Fullers London Pride and Tetleys, good service; plain seating, maybe loudish radio; children allowed in back dining room, tables in nice front garden, attractive setting *(D and J McMillan, Marjorie and David Lamb)*
☆ **Maids Moreton** [just off A413 Towcester—Buckingham; SP7035], *Wheatsheaf*: Thatched and beamed, with lots of pictures, posters and bric-a-brac in old part, friendly atmosphere and service, interesting food from sandwiches to superb steaks, well kept Hook Norton Best; newspapers in gents', quaint conservatory with woodburner, pleasant enclosed garden; piped music, opens noon *(George Atkinson, Gill and Keith Croxton, Graham and Karen Oddey)*
☆ **Marlow** [St Peter St; first right off Station Rd

from double roundabout; SU8586], *Two Brewers*: Low-beamed bar with shiny black woodwork, nautical pictures, gleaming brassware, new landlord putting emphasis on well kept Brakspears, Flowers IPA, Fullers London Pride, Wadworths 6X and a guest like Cotleigh Rebellion, good wines, well cooked food (unusual crypt-like dining area), considerate service, tables in sheltered back courtyard, front seats with glimpse of the Thames (pub right on Thames Path); children in eating area *(David Shillitoe, Gordon, T R and B C Jenkins, LYM)*

☆ **Marlow** [Henley Rd (A4155 W)], *Hare & Hounds*: Pretty ivy-clad dining pub, cosy corners, inglenook log fire, comfortable armchairs, decent food, well kept Brakspears, Rebellion Smuggler and a guest beer, good house wines, darts, cribbage, dominoes; piped music; no-smoking restaurant, children welcome; new back garden *(Chris Glasson, Susan and John Douglas, J and B Cressey, G Barnett)*

Marlow [High St], *Hogshead*: Nice and spacious but not posh, with good choice of real ale, wholesome food; SkyTV, very popular with young people *(Roger Stamp, J S Green)*

☆ **Marsworth** [Vicarage Rd; signed off B489 Dunstable—Aylesbury; SP9214], *Red Lion*: Low-beamed partly thatched village pub with cheerful service, well kept ales such as Bass, Fullers London Pride, Hancocks HB and Morlands Old Speckled Hen, decent wines, good value food inc good vegetarian dishes, quiet lounge with two open fires, steps up to snug parlour and lively games area; sheltered garden, provision for children; not far from impressive flight of canal locks *(Bill Sykes, Andrew Scarr, LYM)*

☆ **Medmenham** [A4155 Henley—Marlow; SU8084], *Dog & Badger*: Comfortably modernised low-beamed bar with open fire, brasses and soft lighting, usual food (not Sun evening) inc Fri fish and chips and proper old-fashioned puddings, well kept Brakspears PA and SB, Flowers Original and local Rebellion IPA, restaurant; children in eating area; piped music *(Val Stevenson, Rob Holmes, DHV, G Barnett, Gordon, LYM)*

Milton Keynes [not far from M1 junctions 13 and 14; SP9137], *Leathern Bottel*: Friendly welcoming landlord; very popular lunchtime for good straightforward food *(David and Mary Webb)*; [Shenley Lodge; SP8335], *Old Beams*: Tastefully converted 17th-c farmhouse, McMullens ales with a guest such as Courage Directors, bright, friendly and efficient staff, good snacks and meals; very popular with local office staff *(E J and M W Corrin)*; [Broughton Rd, Milton Keynes village; SP8839], *Swan*: Spacious dark-beamed thatched pub with big back dining extension, no-smoking area; Boddingtons, Courage Best and Wadworths 6X, wide choice of food inc vegetarian, friendly attentive service, attractive furnishings, log-effect gas fire in inglenook; popular with businesspeople lunchtime, very busy Sun; picnic-sets in back garden, footpaths to nearby lakes *(Graham and Karen Oddey, Ian Phillips)*

☆ **Newport Pagnell** [Tickford St (B526), 2 miles from M1 junction 14; SP8743], *Bull*: Busy, unspoilt town pub, not unlike a Dutch 'brown bar', in welcoming 17th-c coaching inn, eight properly kept changing real ales inc rarities for the area, generous well priced straightforward food (not Sun evening) inc a fine vegetarian balti, daily papers, friendly staff, softly lit low-ceilinged lounge decorated with front pages on famous events, bar with darts, juke box and pool; tables in pleasant courtyard; next to Aston Martin works, cars on show weekdays; bedrooms *(John C Baker, Simon Walker, CMW, JJW, Richard Houghton, Ian Phillips)*

Northall [Leighton Rd; A4146 Hemel Hempstead—Leighton Buzzard; SP9520], *Northall*: 16th-c beamed coaching inn, good reasonably priced food in dining bar, cosy public bar, well kept beers, big garden and courtyard; handy for Whipsnade and local walks *(Ken and Thelma Mitchell)*

Oakley [Oxford Rd; SP6312], *Royal Oak*: Lively village pub with good food, reasonable prices, John Smiths and Marstons Pedigree *(David Lamb)*

Olney [9 Mkt Pl; SP8851], *Bull*: Spacious pub, clean and tidy, HQ of the town's famous Shrove Tuesday pancake race, largely refurbished giving one more restauranty room, but still has two small front bar rooms; Charles Wells ales with a guest such as Youngs Winter Warmer, popular food, good coffee, log-effect gas fires, very friendly chatty landlord *(George Atkinson, Stephen G Brown)*; [12 High St (A509)], *Swan*: Cosy mix of beamed pub and bistro, with very good choice of food from sandwiches up inc vegetarian, five well kept ales, decent choice of wine, candles on pine tables, log fire *(CMW, JJW, David and Mary Webb, Penny and Ron Westwood)*; [34 High St], *Two Brewers*: Very wide choice of generous popular food inc good home-made pies and Sun lunches, big dining area with plenty of different-sized tables, well kept beer, good coffee, friendly prompt service, attractive courtyard decorated to show its brewery past, tables in garden too *(Stephen Brown, George Atkinson)*

☆ **Oving** [Church Lane; off A413 Winslow rd out of Whitchurch; SP7821], *Black Boy*: Friendly and interesting old pub nr church, magnificent collection of jugs, log fire, well kept Whitbreads-related beer, good generous food esp fish, cheerful service, superb views from extended back dining area over terrace and big sloping garden; TV in small bar; children welcome *(George Atkinson, JCW, Mr and Mrs B Edwards)*

☆ **Penn** [Witheridge Lane; SU9193], *Crown*: Friendly Chef & Brewer transformed by new licensee, good interesting generous food in three low-ceilinged refurbished bars, one with medieval flooring tiles, well kept Scottish Courage ales, good service; children in eating areas, piped music; perched on high ridge with distant views, lots of tables in attractive gardens with good play area, weekend barbecues; open all day *(Dr Gerald Barnett, Mark J Hydes, LYM)*

Penn, *Horse & Jockey*: Friendly and reliable, with good range of promptly served daily changing bar food, most home-made, well kept beers *(Michael Tucker, G Barnett)*

☆ **Penn Street** [SU9295], *Hit or Miss*: Amazing range of good generous food from ploughman's to seafood inc lobster, well presented by good chef, in well laid out low-beamed three-room pub with own cricket ground, good cricket and chair-making memorabilia, friendly bustling atmosphere and welcoming service, well kept ales such as Brakspears, Fullers and Hook Norton, good wines, log fire, no piped music or machines, occasional live music; separate restaurant, pleasant setting *(Peter Saville, N Bushby, W Atkins, G Barnett, Michael Tucker, Joan and John Fuller, Cyril Brown, LYM)*

Pitstone Green [Pitstone Wharf; SP9215], *Duke of Wellington*: Two rooms divided by log fire, Brakspears, Fullers London Pride and Marstons Pedigree, reasonably priced food; on Grand Union Canal *(Ian Phillips)*

☆ **Princes Risborough** [Whiteleaf; Upper Icknield Way, Whiteleaf (off A4010) – OS Sheet 165 map ref 817040; SP8104], *Red Lion*: Friendly old-fashioned bar with good log fire, nautical antiques, winged settles, sporting and coaching prints, home-made bar food from sandwiches to steaks, well kept Brakspears PA, Hook Norton Best, Morlands Old Speckled Hen, and a guest beer, traditional games, tables in garden; children in restaurant, good Chilterns walks; bedrooms *(Simon Penny, M J Dowdy, Helen Hazzard, Graham and Karen Oddey, R T and J C Moggridge, LYM)*

☆ **Skirmett** [High St; Fingest rd off B482 at Bolter End, then follow Skirmett sign; SU7790], *Old Crown*: Cosy and attractive dining pub, interesting decor in small pleasantly simple rooms, huge log fire, charming garden, good rich well presented but expensive food, well kept Brakspears, good house wines (not a place for just a drink); service generally very good – just the occasional question-mark *(Mayur Shah, Mick Hitchman, JP, PP, Mr and Mrs C Moncreiffe, Yavuz and Shirley Mutlu, Graham and Karen Oddey, Gerald Barnett, Christine and Geoff Butler, Gregor Macdonald, Helen Pickering, James Owen, J and B Cressey, Peter Saville, LYM)*

Slapton [Horton Rd; SP9320], *Carpenters Arms*: Small pub doubling as fascinating book shop, inside divided into four, inc a dining room; very friendly staff, ales inc Morlands Old Speckled Hen, attractively served good food (not cheap – and may stop serving Sun) *(D Billingham, Andrew Scarr)*

Stoke Goldington [B526 NW of Newport Pagnell; SP8348], *White Hart*: Friendly thatched and beamed pub with two smartly modernised bars and restaurant, new licensees doing good value well presented usual food, Charles Wells beers with a guest such as Adnams Broadside, Badger Tanglefoot or Morlands Old Speckled Hen; picnic-sets on sheltered back lawn with play area, footpath network starts just across rd *(John Saul, George Atkinson, Ian Phillips, LYM)*

☆ **Stony Stratford** [72 High St; SP7840], *Cock*: Quiet and comfortable old-fashioned hotel with leather settles and library chairs on bare boards, good bar food, very friendly service, six well kept ales such as Boddingtons, Brains, Fullers London Pride, Greene King Abbot, Jennings and Theakstons; tables out in attractive back courtyard, barbecues; bedrooms *(Ian and Nita Cooper, Ian Phillips, LYM)*

☆ **Stony Stratford** [High St], *Bull*: Famous old hotel, recently smartened up but keeping panelling and beams, comfortable lounge bar, nice little area used for (good) coffee with open fire, small dining room, separate more rustic flagstoned bar with country hardware; decent food, well kept Gales, friendly service; bedrooms *(George Atkinson, Graham and Karen Oddey, LYM)*

☆ **The Lee** [Swan Bottom (back rd 3/4 mile N), OS Sheet 165 map ref 902055; SP9055], *Old Swan*: Four simply but attractively furnished interconnecting rooms, low beams and flagstones, cooking-range log fire in inglenook, relaxed civilised atmosphere, particularly well kept Brakspears and guests such as Adnams, Batemans and Morlands, decent wines, long-serving landlord cooks very good interesting food (sandwiches too), friendly efficient service; spacious prettily planted back lawns with play area, good walks *(Mr and Mrs A Hoyle, Peter and Christine Lea, Peter Saville, George Atkinson, John and Carol Rees, LYM)*

☆ **Thornborough** [just off A421 4 miles E of Buckingham, outside village – pub name on OS165; SP7433], *Lone Tree*: Very interesting range of quickly changing and often recherché real ales, wide choice of food from sandwiches up inc fish and vegetarian, good choice of wines and good coffee in spotless long stripped-brick bar with old-fashioned tables and chairs, inglenook log fire, pub-related books and magazines, friendly service, no-smoking dining area; not large, so can fill quickly; quiet piped music; garden with play area (road noise) *(George Atkinson, Keith Croxton)*

☆ **Twyford** [E of village; Calvert—Gawcott rd, just N of Twyford—Steeple Claydon one – OS Sheet 165 map ref 676268; SP6726], *Seven Stars*: Rambling low-beamed country pub popular for varied imaginative food in lounge bar and separate dining area (not Sun evening; fish and meat from London markets daily), friendly service, well kept Hook Norton Best and Old Hookey with two weekly changing guests, open fires, pictures and old farm tools; pool in games room, tables on pleasant lawn with animals for children, entertainment Sun evening; handy for Claydon House *(Marjorie and David Lamb)*

☆ **Waddesdon** [High St; SP7417], *Lion*: Village local with entertaining French landlord doing good generous French country food inc fish and vegetarian, splendid helpings, premier-league chips, quick very friendly service, good choice of beers, lovely local atmosphere, nice wooden furniture in long bar/eating area, guest beers *(Paul and Sarah Gayler, Gill and Keith Croxton)*

☆ **Weston Turville** [Church Lane; SP8510], *Chequers*: Concentration on good interesting food (not Mon) from sandwiches up in relaxing low-beamed flagstoned two-level bar and attractive restaurant, good house wines and good range of malt whiskies, well kept Tetleys-related and other ales, open fire, stylish solid wooden furniture; tucked away in attractive part of village, some tables outside *(Tim Heywood, Sophie Wilne, Ann and Les Kibble, Michael Sargent)*

☆ **Weston Underwood** [off A509 at Olney; SP8650], *Cowpers Oak*: Charming old creeper-clad pub, beams and stripped stone, open fire, real ales such as Hook Norton Best and Tomintoul Scottish Bard, good value food inc good soup, back restaurant, friendly service, tropical fish tank, games area with darts and hood skittles; unobtrusive piped music; big attractive garden (no dogs) with play area, handy for Flamingo Gardens *(George Atkinson, G R Braithwaite, Maysie Thompson)*

☆ **Wing** [High St; SP8822], *Cock*: Doing well under welcoming current management, with unusual range of consistently well kept changing ales, good food in comfortable bar and separate dining areas, friendly efficient service even when busy, real fires *(Richard Houghton, John Poulter, Ted George)*

Winslow [Market Sq; SP7627], *Bell*: Unpretentious former coaching inn with comfortable modernised lounge, efficient landlord, friendly obliging staff, good value food, Greene King Abbot and IPA, no music; bedrooms good value too, dogs allowed *(Ian Phillips, LYM)*

☆ **Wooburn Common** [Wooburn Common Rd, about 3½ miles from M40; SU9387], *Royal Standard*: Wide choice of enjoyable good value bar food, good friendly service, well chosen wines, well kept Brakspears and Wadworths, open fire, mix of old and new decor with popular restaurant area, unobtrusive piped music; tables outside *(Roger Huggins, Cyril Brown, Peter Saville, Mr and Mrs T A Bryan, LYM)*

Wooburn Green [14 The Green; SU9188], *Red Cow*: Friendly old inn with French bistro, good food, helpful staff, well kept ales, garden with wonderful views *(H Low)*

☆ **Worminghall** [Clifden La, not far from M40 junction 8; SP6308], *Clifden Arms*: Very picturesque 16th-c beamed and timbered thatched pub in pretty gardens, old-fashioned seats and rustic memorabilia in lounge bar with roaring log fire, another in public bar, well kept Adnams Broadside, Boddingtons, Fullers ESB and London Pride, Hook Norton and interesting guest beers, traditional games, food (not Sun evening) from sandwiches to steaks; good play area, Aunt Sally, some live music; attractive village *(Roger and Valerie Hill, LM, Ted George, P A Legon)*

The letters and figures after the name of each town are its Ordnance Survey map reference. *How to use the Guide* at the beginning of the book explains how it helps you find a pub, in road atlases or large-scale maps as well as in our own maps.

Cambridgeshire

Several first-class dining pubs set a high tone for this county, and food is well worth while in many other pubs which have more of an all-round appeal. For a really satisfying meal out, our top shortlist would consist of the White Hart at Bythorn (its friendly landlord always well in evidence), the smart Chequers at Fowlmere, the Old Bridge in Huntingdon (with a very enterprising approach to guest beers for a place that's so strong on wines), the Pheasant at Keyston, the Three Horseshoes at Madingley (excellent wines at both these two), and the Anchor at Sutton Gault (flourishing under a new management team fresh from Conran's Mezzo in London). All these have been scoring very high points with readers in the last few months – particularly the Three Horseshoes at Madingley, which is our choice as Cambridgeshire Dining Pub of the Year. Other pubs currently doing particularly well include the Millstone at Barnack (a splendid all-rounder), the Eagle in Cambridge (a real favourite), the John Barleycorn at Duxford (new licensees bringing it back into the Guide after a break), the engagingly traditional Fountain in Ely (another new entry), the Woodmans Cottage at Gorefield (legendary for its puddings – and its warm-hearted landlady), the King William IV at Heydon (excellent for vegetarians, with lots to fascinate the rest of us), the Plough & Fleece at Horningsea (a magnet for lunchers), the Queens Head at Kirtling (another new entry – a companion pub to the very successful Beehive at Horringer just over the Suffolk border), and the Trinity Foot on the A14 at Swavesey (an excellent break from that trunk road). Another old favourite, the ancient Old Ferry Boat at Holywell, changed hands not long before we went to press – too soon for a judgement, but such a fine old place that we've kept it among the main entries with our fingers crossed. Pubs in the Lucky Dip section that are particularly worth knowing these days (almost all inspected by us) include the Royal Oak at Barrington, Duke of Wellington at Bourn, Kings Head at Dullingham, Oliver Twist at Guyhirn, Pear Tree at Hildersham, George at Spaldwick, White Horse at Swavesey and Tickell Arms at Whittlesford; the White Pheasant at Fordham is a very promising newcomer, and there's an excellent variety to choose from in Cambridge. Drinks prices are holding relatively steady in the area but are still a bit higher than the national average; we found the Anchor at Sutton Gault surprisingly cheap, and beer prices were also low at the Live & Let Live in Cambridge, on Charters the boat-pub in Peterborough, and at the Black Bull at Godmanchester. A big surprise for us this year was the discovery that no less than one in three of our Cambridgeshire entries now do freshly squeezed juices – a welcome boon for people who want to go easy on the alcohol.

Post Office address codings confusingly give the impression that some pubs are in Cambridgeshire, when they're really in Leicestershire or the Midlands group of counties (which is where we list them).

BARNACK TF0704 Map 5

Millstone

Millstone Lane; off B1443 SE Stamford; turn off School Lane near the Fox

If he's not busy in the kitchen cooking his famous pies – perhaps chicken and leek, fish, fresh salmon and broccoli or steak and kidney (all £6.75) – it's quite likely that Aubrey, the very welcoming landlord at this friendly village local, will greet you himself. Try and arrive early as the good reliable food is very popular and seats fill up quickly, even midweek. Good value filled french bread with hot sausage and mushrooms (£2.95) is another favourite, there's also filled baked potatoes (from £3.95), fresh battered fish (£5.25), spare ribs, balti or cajun chicken (£6.95), and puddings like lemon and lime cheesecake or chocolate mousse with rum (from £2.75); smaller helpings for OAPs, and a straightforward children's menu. No less important here is the very well kept Everards Old Original and Tiger, two guest beers on handpump, and country wines, all served in the traditional, timbered bar which is split into comfortably intimate areas, with cushioned wall benches on the patterned carpet and high beams weighed down with lots of heavy harness. A little snug is decorated with the memorabilia of a former regular, including his medals from both World Wars. The snug and dining room are no smoking; very soft piped music, darts and dominoes. *(Recommended by L Walker, Mike and Maggie Betton, Jenny and Michael Back, M Morgan, P Stallard, Simon Collett-Jones, F J Robinson, Eric Locker)*

Everards ~ Tenant Aubrey Sinclair Ball ~ Real ale ~ Meals and snacks (not Sun evening) ~ Restaurant (not Sun evening) ~ (01780) 740296 ~ Children in snug and dining room ~ Open 11-2.30, 5.30(6 Sat)-11; 12-4, 7-10.30 Sun

BYTHORN TL0575 Map 5

White Hart

Village signposted just off A14 Kettering—Cambridge

The good value imaginative specials board changes weekly at this warmly run country pub. Bill Bennett the friendly landlord was busy in the kitchen preparing meals for lunch when we rang early in the morning but readers tell us he's often in evidence, cheerily roaming the pub, glass in hand. A very helpful barman told us that bar food might include home-made chicken soup (£2.50), cumberland sausage, chicken and prawn balti, tomato and garlic pasta, oriental chicken salad, rib steak with peppercorn sauce, smoked duck salad, toasted brie and bacon, swordfish with tomato and garlic, tuna steak, crab thermidor and eel terrine (all £7.50), with puddings like chocolate rum parfait, blackcurrant sorbet, apple tarts and pear gateaux (£4.50); four-course Sunday lunch (£16.50). There's an unpretentious mix of furnishings in the homely main bar and in the several linked smallish rooms, such as a big leather chesterfield, lots of silver teapots and so forth on a carved dresser and in a built-in cabinet, and wing armchairs and attractive tables. One area with rugs on stripped boards has soft pale leather studded chairs and stools, and a cosy log fire in a huge brick fireplace; cookery books and plenty of magazines for reading. Well kept Greene King IPA and Abbot on handpump, and a good, no-nonsense, well chosen wine list. The restaurant is no smoking. *(Recommended by Stephen Brown, R Wiles, Joan and Michel Hooper-Immins, Ian Phillips, J F M West, John C Baker, Maysie Thompson; more reports please)*

Free house ~ Licensees Bill and Pam Bennett ~ Real ale ~ Meals and snacks (till 9.30; no bar meals Saturday evening, set menu only Sunday lunchtime) ~ Restaurant ~ (01832) 710226 ~ Children welcome ~ Open 11-3, 7-11; 12-3 Sun; closed Sun evening, closed Monday and 26 Dec

CAMBRIDGE TL4658 Map 5

Anchor £

Silver St

You can lazily watch punts drifting along the River Cam from the delightfully placed suntrap terrace of this cheery pub, and perhaps hire one here yourself later on. It's set on four levels with two bars, and the area around the entrance is sectioned off to create a cosy atmosphere with lots of bric-a-brac and church pews, and a brick fireplace at each end. The upstairs bar (no smoking during food service times) is pubby, with pews and wooden chairs and good river views. The cafe-bar downstairs has enamel signs on the walls and a mix of interesting tables, settles, farmhouse chairs, and hefty stools on the bare boards. Steps take you down to a simpler flagstoned room, and french windows lead out to the terrace. Simple good value bar food includes home-made soup (£1.95), filled baked potatoes (from £2.95), ploughman's (£4.20), salads (£4.50), scampi (£5.25), four home-made daily specials such as aubergine and pasta bake, barbecue chicken casserole, sweet and sour pork, or lamb and apple pie (all £4.50), and puddings like hot chocolate fudge cake (£2.25); Sunday roasts (£5). Lots of well kept real ales might include Boddingtons Bitter, Flowers Original, Fullers London Pride, Marstons Pedigree, Morlands Old Speckled Hen, Wadworths 6X, Whitbread Castle Eden and Youngs Special tapped from the cask, and there's a good range of foreign bottled beers; friendly young service, and various trivia, video games and fruit machines, juke box and piped music. *(Recommended by David Carr; more reports please)*

Whitbreads ~ Managers Alastair and Sandra Langton ~ Real ale ~ Meals and snacks (12-8, till 4 Fri and Sat, 12-2.30 Sun) ~ (01223) 353554 ~ Children in eating area of bar during food service hours ~ Open 11-11; 11-10.30 Sun

Eagle 🍷 £

Bene't Street

Readers really love this comfortably bustling old stone-fronted town centre coaching inn which often provides a civilised haven from the summer tourist crowds outside. Its five rambling and relaxing rooms (one no smoking) retain many charming original architectural features intact. There are lovely worn wooden floors and plenty of original pine panelling, two fireplaces dating back to around 1600, two medieval mullioned windows, and the remains of two possibly medieval wall paintings. The high dark red ceiling has been left unpainted since the war to preserve the signatures of British and American airmen worked in with Zippo lighters, candle smoke and lipstick. The furniture is nicely old and creaky. Screened from the street by sturdy wooden gates is an attractive cobbled and galleried courtyard with heavy wooden seats and tables and pretty hanging baskets. Straightforward but good value well liked food is served from a display counter in a small room at the back. At lunchtime, there might be pasty, chips and beans (£3.95), ploughman's, quiche or ham and eggs (£4.25) and chilli, lasagne or roast chicken (£4.50), with evening burgers (from £3.95), barbecue chicken wings, fish and chips or breaded plaice (£4.95); daily specials, too. A neat little booklet lists up to 20 wines, sparkling wines and champagnes by the glass. Well kept Greene King IPA, Abbot, and Rayments and seasonal ales on handpump. This was the local of Nobel Prize winning scientists Crick and Watson, who discovered the structure of DNA; friendly service from well dressed staff. *(Recommended by John Wooll, A Hepburn, S Jenner, Anthony Barnes, Andy and Jill Kassube, Robert Gomme, A J Bowen, John A Barker, Michael and Lynne Gittins, Keith and Janet Morris, Jeff Davies, Norma and Valerie Housley, G W Stephenson, J F M West, Scott Rumery)*

Greene King ~ Managers Peter and Carol Hill ~ Real ale ~ Meals and snacks (12-2.30, 5.30-8.45; not Fri, Sat, Sun evenings) ~ (01223) 505020 ~ Children in eating area of bar only ~ Open 11-11; 12-10.30 Sun

Free Press

Prospect Row

Just being a completely no-smoking pub is enough to make this the perfect place for a good many of our readers, but happily it's also a wonderfully unspoilt unpretentious inn that's been run by the same friendly licensee for over 20 years. The collection of oars and rowing photographs in its friendly chatty bare-board rooms reflects its status as a registered boat club. Good wholesome home-made bar food served in generous well priced helpings from a fairly short menu includes two vegetarian soups (£2.25), chilli con carne or vegetarian pâté (£4.25), at least two meat and two vegetarian specials like pork and cider casserole, beef in beer, mushroom stroganoff or leek croustade (£4.25-£4.50), and puddings like fig, prune and yoghurt bar, apple and mincemeat tart or lemon torte (£1.95). Well kept Greene King IPA, Abbot and Mild on handpump, with a good selection of malt whiskies and freshly squeezed orange juice; cribbage and dominoes behind the bar. The sheltered paved garden at the back is quite a suntrap; friendly cat. *(Recommended by Andy and Jill Kassube, Ian Phillips, John A Barker, A J Bowen, M A Buchanan, John Fahy, Mark J Hydes, David Carr, J F M West, Jeff Davies, Keith and Janet Morris, Hazel and Michael Duncombe, Pat and Tony Martin, T L Rees)*

Greene King ~ Tenant Christopher Lloyd ~ Real ale ~ Meals and snacks (12-2(2.30 Sat and Sun), 6(7 Sun)-9) ~ (01223) 368337 ~ Well behaved children welcome ~ Open 12-2.30(3 Sat and Sun), 6-11; 12-3, 7-10.30 Sun; cl 25, 26 Dec evening

Live & Let Live £

40 Mawson Road; off Mill Road SE of centre

There's a particularly friendly welcome at this unpretentious little backstreet local. The heavily timbered brickwork rooms have sturdy varnished pine tables with pale wood chairs on bare boards, lots of interesting old country bric-a-brac and posters about local forthcoming events; cribbage, bagatelle and piped music. The eating area is no smoking, and basic but generous bar food includes big sandwiches (from £1.50, not Sunday), hot filled baguettes (from £2.50), filled yorkshire pudding (£3.60), vegetable curry or ploughman's (from £3.75), lasagne or vegetable lasagne (£3.95), as well as daily specials; Sunday breakfast (£3.50). Well kept Adnams Southwold, Batemans Mild, Brunos Bitter (brewed for the pub by Banks & Taylor) Everards Beacon Tiger, Nethergate Umbel and a guest on handpump, and local cider and English wines; friendly service. On Sunday evenings they serve free garlic bread and potato wedges and dips with the live music. There is now a small terrace; well behaved dogs are welcome. *(Recommended by Ian Phillips, Tessa Stone, P and D Carpenter, David Carr)*

Free house ~ Licensee Peter Gray ~ Real ale ~ Meals and snacks ~ (01223) 460261 ~ Children in eating area till 8.30 by prior arrangement ~ Folk duo most Sun evenings ~ Open 11(12 Sat)-2.30, 5.30(6 Sat)-11; 12-2.30, 7-10.30 Sun

DUXFORD TL4745 Map 5

John Barleycorn

Moorfield Rd; village signposted off A1301; pub at far end of village

The new licensees at this enchanting thatched cottage might be South African but they seem to know all the elements that combine to make a well run English pub. Readers speak highly of courteous welcoming service, a very friendly atmosphere and big helpings of good home-cooked food. With a log fire in winter, and candlelit at night, the attractive bar is nicely furnished with high-backed booth-type oak settles and chunky country tables. The menu includes ploughman's (from £4.60), open sandwiches – the hot black pudding with gooseberries is recommended by one reader – (from £4.90), grilled sardines (£6.40), irish stew with parsley dumplings (£8.20), pork in mushroom sauce (£8.50), chilled poached salmon with dill dressing (£9.60), 8oz sirloin (£11), and puddings like chocolate orange pudding, pear and almond flan or figs with vodka (from £3.80); a slightly different evening menu has starters such as salmon roulade (£5.20) and a couple more main courses like lamb curry (£9.60). If you eat and leave your table before 8pm there's a special price of £11 for two courses. It can get busy so it's worth arriving early (one reader found that service had stopped early as the kitchen was overloaded with orders). Well kept Greene King IPA, Abbot and Rayments Special under light blanket pressure; South African wines. The little front terrace has hanging baskets, tubs and flowerbeds around picnic-sets, and there are more tables surrounded by roses and flowering shrubs in the back garden. A pretty little barn with ancient timbers and some back-to-back seats has an attractive brick barbecue and mini bar. The staffordshire terrier is called Jess. *(Recommended by Christopher Reeves, Anthony Barnes, Jackie Orme, Robert Price, A P Smith, Ron Gentry, Comus Elliott, TRS, Susan and Nigel Wilson, D W Twitchett, Brian and Jill Bond)*

Greene King ~ Tenants Pat and Heather Green ~ Real ale ~ Meals and snacks (till

9.45; 9.30 Sun) ~ (01223) 832699 ~ Children by prior arrangement with licensees ~ Open 12-2.30, 6.30-11(7-10.30 Sun)

ELSWORTH TL3163 Map 5

George & Dragon

Off A604 NW of Cambridge, via Boxworth

You can make the most of this civilised dining pub by visiting on a Monday lunchtime when they offer a very good value three-course set menu (£7) – you will need to book. Otherwise, the carefully prepared fresh food served by friendly uniformed waitresses includes good home-made soups (£2.50), smoked salmon and prawn pâté (£4.50), chicken breast in mushroom and white wine sauce, mushroom and spinach lasagne or scampi (£7.50), gammon (£8), salmon fillet topped with prawn and anchovy butter (£8.50), mixed grill (£11), 16oz scotch rump (£14.50) and home-made puddings (£3). Set back from the quiet village street, this brick-built pub has been transformed inside, the characterful panelled main bar opening on the left to a slightly elevated no-smoking dining area with comfortable tables and a good woodburning stove. From here are steps down to a another quiet no-smoking section behind, with more tables here overlooking the back garden. On the right is a more formal restaurant; soft piped music. Well kept Greene King IPA and Ruddles County on handpump, decent wines. There are attractive terraces and so forth in the back garden. *(Recommended by Margaret and Roy Randle, Jenny and Michael Back, Ian Phillips, John Fahy, Maysie Thompson, E A George)*

Free house ~ Licensees Barry and Marion Ashworth ~ Real ale ~ Meals and snacks (not Sun evening) ~ Restaurant ~ (01954) 267236 ~ Children in eating area of bar and restaurant ~ Open 11-2.30, 6-11; 12-2.30 Sun (closed Sun evening, closed 25 Dec)

ELY TL5380 Map 5

Fountain

Corner of Barton Square and Silver Street

Beautifully refurbished and redecorated by its current owner, this spotless town pub is very traditional in its approach: a good range of particularly well kept beers, no food, and a welcoming atmosphere that attracts a real mix of age groups. Though very close to the cathedral it escapes the tourists, and indeed on the lunchtimes when it's open you might have the place almost to yourself; it's delightfully peaceful then. Things get busier in the evenings, especially on Fridays and Saturdays, but even then this is the kind of place to come to for a chat rather than to shout over music or fruit machines. Old local photographs, regional maps and mementoes of the neighbouring King's School punctuate the elegant dark pink walls, and neatly tied-back curtains hang from golden rails above the big windows. Above one fireplace is a stuffed pike in a case, and there are a few antlers dotted about – not to mention a duck at one end of the bar. Adnams Southwold, Fullers London Pride, Woodfordes Wherry and a changing guest such as Everards Tiger on handpump; very efficient service. A couple of tables are squeezed on to a tiny back terrace. Note the limited opening times. *(Recommended by John Baker, Dr Andy Wilkinson, D H Taillat, Sue Holland, Dave Webster)*

Free house ~ Licensees John and Judith Borland ~ Real ale ~ (01353) 663122 ~ Children welcome ~ Open 5-11 (from 6 on Sat, and 7 on Sun), plus 12-2 wknds and bank holidays

ETTON TF1406 Map 5

Golden Pheasant

Village just off B1443, just E of Helpston level crossing; and will no doubt be signposted from near N end of new A15 Peterborough bypass

There's enthusiastic local support for this cheerfully bustling 19th-c stone-built manor house. It's well known for its seven or eight well kept real ales on handpump, usually Adnams, Bass, Batemans XXXB, Shepherd Neame Bishops Finger and Spitfire,

Timothy Taylor Landlord and Woodfordes Wherry. Quite a few malt whiskies, too. The comfortable homely bar has an open fire, high-backed maroon plush settles built against the walls and around the corners, and prints on the walls. In the airy, glass-walled, no-smoking side room are some Lloyd Loom chairs around glass-topped cane tables. Pool, dominoes, fruit machine, and piped music. Tasty bar food includes home-made soup (£3), garlic mushrooms (£3.75), filled yorkshire pudding (£5.95), stir-fry vegetables (£7.25), stilton chicken or minted lamb bake (£7.95), fillet medallions (£11.50) and puddings (£2.75). The stone-walled garden looks out across flat countryside, and has boules, an adventure playground, an aviary with about 70 golden pheasants, quail, cockatiels, rosella parakeets and budgerigars, and a big paddock. The golden labrador is called Bonnie. *(Recommended by Anthony Barnes, M J Morgan, John C Baker, John Fahy; more reports please)*

Free house ~ Licensee Mrs H M Wilson ~ Real ale ~ Meals and snacks (12-3, 6.30-10) ~ Restaurant ~ (01733) 252387 ~ Children in eating area of bar and conservatory ~ Open 11.30-11; 12-10.30 Sun ~ Bedrooms: £20/£40

FEN DRAYTON TL3368 Map 5

Three Tuns

High Street; village signposted off A14 NW of Cambridge

It's thought that this notably ancient thatched building may once have housed the trade or Guildhall of Fen Drayton. The delightfully atmospheric bar (well kept Greene King IPA and Abbot and a monthly guest on handpump as well as a range of malt whiskies) has two inglenook fireplaces, particularly interesting heavy-set moulded Tudor beams and timbers, comfortable cushioned settles and a nice variety of chairs. It's decorated with old local photographs, old song-sheets of local folk songs, big portraits, sparkling brass plates, fresh flowers, and old crockery in a corner dresser. Very welcoming licensees and staff serve generous helpings of good value bar food including soup (£1.80), chicken liver and bacon pâté (£2.75), ploughman's (£3.75), chicken curry, pie of the day, meat or vegetarian lasagne (£4.75), scampi (£6) and 8oz rump steak (£8). Sensibly placed darts, shove-ha'penny, cribbage, dominoes and fruit machine. A well tended lawn at the back has tables under cocktail parasols, apple and flowering cherry trees, and some children's play equipment. It can get very crowded, so it's best to arrive early if you want to eat. *(Recommended by Ian Phillips, J I Davies, Elizabeth and Klaus Leist, Gordon Theaker, B N F and M Parkin, Dr and Mrs B Baker, Barry and Anne, Rona Murdoch, Maysie Thompson, F J Robinson)*

Greene King ~ Tenant Michael Nugent ~ Meals and snacks (not 25-31 Dec, 1 Jan) ~ (01954) 230242 ~ Children welcome until 8pm ~ Open 11-2.30, 6.30-11; 12-2.30, 7-10.30 Sun; closed evening 25 Dec

FOWLMERE TL4245 Map 5

Chequers 🍴 🍷

B1368

It's the high standard of imaginative cooking and very pleasant service that are the main draws at this civilised 16th-c country pub. The menu (more than one reader described it as good value) embraces starters like split pea soup with moroccan spiced butter and croutons (£2.90), mushrooms creamed with white wine and tarragon with croutons (£3.90), smoked chicken, avocado and pink grapefruit salad (£4.90), and main courses like confit of barbary duck on oriental ginger, anise and chilli sauce with strips of cucumber and spring onion (£5.80), roast salmon fillet on noodles with creamed basil and white wine sauce (£9.60), slices of monkfish fried in sesame egg coating on cream thai sauce with stir fried pak choi and basmati rice (£9.90), boiled ham hock coated with creamed pommery mustard and chive sauce with spinach and new potatoes (£10.70), lightly peppered fillet steak on white wine, brandy, tarragon, dijon mustard and cream sauce (£14.90). Puddings include chocolate truffle cake on dark chocolate sauce with vanilla ice cream in a chocolate cup (£4), hot polenta and almond cake on lime sauce with a tuile basket filled with lemon sorbet or hot date sponge on a sticky toffee sauce (£3.80), Irish farmhouse cheeses (£3.80). There's an excellent choice of very well priced fine wines by the glass (including vintage and late-bottled ports), a very good list of malt whiskies, well kept Adnams and a guest which might be Adnams Broadside, Courage Directors or Morlands Old Speckled Hen on handpump, freshly squeezed orange juice, and a good choice of brandies. Two warm and cosy comfortably furnished communicating rooms downstairs have an open log fire – look out for the priest's hole above the bar. Upstairs there are beams, wall timbering and some interesting moulded plasterwork above the fireplace. The airy no-smoking conservatory overlooks white tables under cocktail parasols among flowers and shrub roses in a pleasant well tended floodlit garden. *(Recommended by G Neighbour, M and C Starling, Tony Beaulah, Tina and David Woods-Taylor, R Wiles, Pat and Tony Hinkins, Dr Paul Khan, Hilary Edwards, F C Johnston, TRS, Nick and Meriel Cox, Derek Patey)*

Free house ~ Licensee Norman Rushton ~ Real ale ~ Meals and snacks (till 10pm) ~ Restaurant ~ (01763) 208369 ~ Well behaved children welcome ~ Open 11.30-2.30, 6-11; 12-2.30, 7-10.30 Sun; closed 25 Dec

GODMANCHESTER TL2470 Map 5

Black Bull

Post St; follow village signposts off A14 (was A604) just E of Huntingdon

There's a really friendly welcoming atmosphere at this well run and lively old pub by the church. The heavily beamed main bar has seats built into the inglenook of the enormous fireplace which has a roaring winter log fire; settles form booths by leaded-light windows and there is quite a bit of glinting brassware. A side room up a step is hung with lots of black agricultural and other rustic ironwork. Courteous staff serve good reasonably priced bar food such as home-made soup (£1.75), ploughman's (£3.90), ham and egg (£4.95), turkey curry, home-made steak and ale pie or a vegetarian dish (£6.50), spicy chicken (£7.45), mixed grill (£9.25), and daily specials like peppered pork or poached salmon, and puddings like apple crumble with toffee and pecan (£2.25). Well kept Black Bull (brewed for the pub locally), Boddingtons, Flowers Original and Wadworths 6X kept under light blanket pressure; freshly squeezed apple and cranberry juice; unobtrusive piped pop music, dominoes and fruit machine; no-smoking dining room. There's a big courtyard and pretty garden behind the car park. *(Recommended by Ian Phillips, A J Bowen, Anthony Barnes, Mark O'Hanlon, Ian and Jane Irving, CMW, JJW, D Byng, J R Morris, Dr and Mrs B Baker)*

Whitbreads ~ Lease: Colin Dryer ~ Real ale ~ Meals and snacks (till 10pm; all day Sun) ~ Restaurant ~ (01480) 453310 ~ Children welcome ~ Open 11-2.30(3 Sat), 6-11; 12-10.30 Sun; closed 25 Dec ~ Bedrooms: £19/£35

GOREFIELD TF4111 Map 8

Woodmans Cottage

Main St; off B1169 W of Wisbech

Lucille, the buoyantly cheerful landlady at this friendly village local, employs a full time pudding girl to make the amazing number of puddings on offer here – you can expect up to 50 at the weekend. Other bar food includes toasties (from £1.25), omelettes or ploughman's (£4), steak and kidney pie, gammon and pineapple and about eight vegetarian dishes like mushroom stroganoff (all £6.25), cajun chicken (£6.75), mixed grill (£7.25), daily specials like chicken and mushroom pie, lamb and walnut casserole, tuna bake or turkey, ham and stilton casserole (all £6.25), and children's dishes (from £1.25); roast Sunday lunch (£6; children £4). The spacious modernised bar, with leatherette stools and brocaded banquettes around the tables on its carpet, rambles back around the bar counter. A comfortable side eating area has a big collection of china plates, as well as 1920s prints on its stripped brick walls. There's space for non-smoking diners called the Cellar, with a display of Lucille's paintings. Beyond is an attractive pitched-ceiling restaurant – best to book some time ahead. At the other end of the pub, a games area has darts, pool, cribbage, dominoes and a juke box; Monday bridge nights, and piped music. Well kept Bass, Greene King IPA and Worthington on handpump and quite a lot of Australian wines. There are tables out in a sheltered back terrace, with a few more on a front verandah.

(Recommended by Jenny and Michael Back, Bernard and Marjorie Parkin, Stephen Brown; more reports please)

Free house ~ Licensees Lucille and Barry Carter ~ Real ale ~ Meals and snacks (till 10pm) ~ Restaurant (cl Sun evening) ~ (01945) 870669 ~ Supervised children welcome away from the bar counter ~ Open 11-2.30, 7-11; 12-3, 7-10.30 Sun; closed evenings 25 and 26 Dec

GREAT CHISHILL TL4239 Map 5

Pheasant

Follow Heydon signpost from B1039 in village

The traditionally attractive beamed split-level flagstoned bar at this little country pub (it's part of the Old English Pub Company) has some elaborately carved though modern seats and settles, a few plates on timbered walls, bar stools with decent backs and, at one end, dining chairs around tables. A good choice of bar food, all listed on blackboards, might include interestingly filled sandwiches or baguettes (from £2.95, rump steak or hot chicken and bacon £4.50), home-made soup or chicken liver pâté (£3.25), spinach and aubergine lasagne (£5.95), steak in ale pie (£6.25), battered cod or thai spiced chicken on noodles with oriental sauce (£6.50), game pie (£6.75), vegetable strudel (£7.50), pheasant supreme with caramelised apple with shallot and red wine sauce (£8), baked monkfish on potato rosti with tarragon and white wine sauce (£8.95) or rump steak (£10.95). Well kept Adnams, Courage Best and Directors and Theakstons on handpump, and a decent wine list; darts, cribbage, dominoes, and piped music. The attractive rising lawn behind the pub has seats among flowering cherries and a weeping willow, and there's a small children's play area. There is quiet farmland beyond the back rose hedge. *(Recommended by Gwen and Peter Andrews, Enid and Henry Stephens, M R D Foot, Stephen Brown, John Fahy)*

Free House ~ Managers Mandy and Malcolm Drewery ~ Real ale ~ Meals and snacks ~ Restaurant ~ (01763) 838535 ~ Open 12-2.30(3 Sat), 6-11; 12-3, 7-10.30 Sun

HEYDON TL4340 Map 5

King William IV

Village signposted from A505 W of M11 junction 10; bear right in village

All the cooking is good at this atmospheric pub but there's a notably imaginative choice of about a dozen vegetarian dishes such as pine kernel stir fry with noodles and crackers or wild mushroom and apricot fettucine with sun-dried tomatoes and split almonds in a creamy sauce, asparagus, broccoli and rocquefort lattice puff pastry or vegetable masala with wild rice and poppadums (from £7.45). Other good value bar food in generous helpings includes lunchtime sandwiches (from £2.45), filled french bread (from £3.55), soup (£3.25), devilled mushrooms with a hot mustard, garlic and horseradish sauce (£4.75), bangers and mash (£5.95), steak and kidney pie (£6.95), prawn stir fry (£7.65), salmon and scallops with saffron and ginger on a puff pastry pillow (£7.95), beef and mushrooms in stout with herb dumplings or pork loin with brandy and wholegrain mustard cream sauce (£8.45), 8oz sirloin (£10.95), and roast duck breast with blackberries soaked in sloe gin (£13.95); spotted dick, pancakes with vanilla ice cream and syrup or fresh berries and fruit in a chocolate shell (from £3.95 to £4.45); part of the restaurant is no smoking. The beamed rambling nooked and crannied rooms, warmed in winter by a log fire, are crowded with a lovely collection of country life implements like ploughshares, yokes, iron tools, cowbells, beer steins, as well as samovars, cut-glass, brass or black wrought-iron lamps, copper-bound casks and milk ewers, harness, horsebrasses, smith's bellows, and decorative plates and china ornaments. Well kept Adnams, Boddingtons, Greene King IPA and Abbot and Marstons Pedigree on handpump; friendly, efficient staff. There are seats in the pretty garden. *(Recommended by Sarah Markham, Zoe Morrell, Andrew Anderson, M A Buchanan, S Markham, Sidney and Erna Wells, Keith and Janet Morris, B N F and M Parkin, Stephen Horsley)*

Free house ~ Licensees Elizabeth and Edward Nicholls ~ Real ale ~ Meals and snacks (till 10pm) ~ Restaurant ~ (01763) 838773 ~ Children in eating area of bar and restaurant ~ Open 12-3, 6.30(6 Sat)-11; 12-3, 7-10.30 Sun

HINXTON TL4945 Map 5

Red Lion

2 miles from M11 junction 9, 3½ miles from junction 10; just off A1301 S of Great Shelford

We're always pleased when we come across a pub that serves real chips, as they do at this pretty pink-washed twin-gabled old building. The good solid bar menu includes reasonably priced home-made soup (£2.75), prawn cocktail (£3.75), leek and mushroom pasta bake or baked stuffed aubergine (£5.95), lamb moussaka (£6.50), sausages and mashed potatoes or chicken and lime masala (£6.95), lamb, smoked bacon and apricot pie (£7.95), skate wing (£9.25), 8oz sirloin (£9.75), seabass provençale (£10.95), dover sole (£14.95) and puddings like jam roly poly, crème caramel or belgian apple pie (£2.50). Part of the restaurant is no smoking. The mainly open-plan bustling bar is filled with clocks, mirrors and pictures, grandfather and grandmother clocks, and a chatty Amazon parrot called George. Well kept Adnams, Adnams Extra, Greene King IPA and Woodfordes Wherry on handpump, and Adnams wines, as well as trivia and unobtrusive piped classical music. The neatly kept garden has picnic-sets; handy for Duxford Aeroplane Museum. *(Recommended by Anthony Barnes, Mr and Mrs R Head, Bill and Sheila McCardy, Keith and Janet Morris, Luke Worthington)*

Free house ~ Licensees James and Lynda Crawford ~ Real ale ~ Meals and snacks (till 10pm; 9.30pm Sun and Mon) ~ Restaurant ~ (01799) 530601 ~ Children over ten in restaurant if eating ~ Open 11-2.30, 6-11; 12-2.30, 7-10.30 Sun; closed 25/26 Dec evening

HOLYWELL TL3370 Map 5

Old Ferry Boat

Village and pub both signposted (keep your eyes skinned, it's easy to go wrong!) from Needingworth, which is just off the A1123

This lovely rambling old thatched building is charmingly set in a remote part of the fens, with lazy tables and cocktail parasols on a manicured rose lawn (more on a front terrace) by the Great Ouse – where there's mooring for boats. The site was once that of a monastic ferry house and it's said to be one of the country's oldest pubs. Marstons had just bought the pub as we went to press and couldn't give us firm details about opening times or food so it is worth checking with the pub before you set out (as it's such an attractive place we felt we couldn't leave it out of the Guide completely). There are six characterful open-plan bar areas with very low beams and timbered and panelled walls. Window seats overlook the river, and one of the four open fires has a fish and an eel among rushes moulded on its chimney beam, and a stone in the bar marks the ancient grave of the resident ghost Juliette, said to return every year on 17 March. An interesting collection of photographs depict scenes from the very bad fire they had here a couple of years ago; most of the pub is now no smoking. Six real ales include Marstons Best and Pedigree, and guests like Greene King Abbot, Exmoor Gold, Morlands Old Speckled Hen and Timothy Taylor Landlord; friendly, attentive, efficient service even when it gets very busy in summer and at weekends. Fruit machine and piped music. Bar food might include soup (£2.50), filled french sticks (from £3.25), ploughman's (from £3.75), chicken liver pâté (£4.25), scampi (£6.95), beef in beer (£7.50) and 8oz sirloin steak (£10.95). *(Recommended by M A Buchanan, Paul and Pam Penrose, E Robinson, Ian Crichton, Ian Phillips, John Fahy, E Robinson, Mr Gibson Warner, Julian Holland, David Carr, Charles and Pauline Stride, Nick and Meriel Cox, Jenny and Michael Back; more reports on the new regime please)*

Marstons ~ Manager ~ Real ale ~ Meals and snacks ~ (01480) 463227 ~ Well behaved children in children's area ~ Open 11.30-3, 6-11; 12-10.30 Sun (12-3, 7-11 winter Sun) ~ Bedrooms

By law pubs must show a price list of their drinks. Let us know if you are inconvenienced by any breach of this law.

HORNINGSEA TL4962 Map 5

Plough & Fleece ★

Just NE of Cambridge: first slip-road off A45 heading E after A10, then left at T; or take B1047 Fen Ditton road off A1303

Just ten minutes' drive from the centre of Cambridge, this rambling country pub is a very popular place for business lunches. The homely low black-beamed public bar has comfortably worn high-backed settles and plain seats on the red tiled floor, a stuffed parrot and a fox by the log fire, and plain wooden tables including an unusually long pine one with an equally elongated pew to match. Enjoyable bar food includes lunchtime sandwiches (from £1.70; toasties £2), home-made soup (£2.20), home-made pâté or stilton and broccoli flan (£3.50), home-cooked ham and egg (£4.50), delicious ham hotpot (£5.50), steak, kidney and mushroom pie (£6.50), rabbit with bacon (£7.50), barbary duck breast with hot, spicy sauce (£9.50), sirloin steak (£11), and puddings like cherry cobbler or treacle tart (£2.50); prices are higher in the evening; friendly service. There's a good no-smoking dining room with lots of wood and old bricks and tiles, linked by a terrace to the garden, and a conservatory at the back. Well kept Greene King IPA and Abbot on handpump; dominoes and cribbage. The mix of wild and cultivated flowers in the garden is a nice touch; picnic-sets beyond the car park. *(Recommended by J F M West and Dr M West, Sarah Markham, Keith and Janet Morris, Mark Hydes, Dr I Crichton, Nigel Clifton, P and D Carpenter, Chris and Ann Garnett, Stephen Brown, Malcolm Taylor)*

Greene King ~ Tenant Kenneth Grimes ~ Real ale ~ Meals and snacks (till 1.30 Sun, not Sun or Mon evenings) ~ Restaurant ~ (01223) 860795 ~ Children over 5 in restaurant only ~ Open 11.30-2.30, 7-11; 12-2, 7-10.30 Sun; closed Mon evening, evenings 25 and 26 Dec

HUNTINGDON TL2371 Map 5

Old Bridge

1 High St; just off B1043 entering town from the easternmost A604 sliproad

This very well run civilised hotel has a particularly creative menu, an outstanding wine list (including an excellent choice by the glass) and this year we've discovered that alongside Adnams Best and City of Cambridge Hobsons Choice they also rotate about 250 guest beers a year; freshly squeezed orange juice and good coffee, too. Tucked away in a good spot by the River Great Ouse, it has its own landing stage, and tables on the well kept garden's waterside terraces. The charming bar – panelling and plush with a good log fire – has a chatty friendly atmosphere, the spaciously comfortable restaurant is no smoking. Changing monthly, the menu might include curried parsnip soup (£3.75), spinach and ricotta gnocchi (£4.25), rabbit terrine with greek vegetables (£4.50), carpaccio (£6.25), feta, spinach, red onion and filo pie with marinated tomato salad (£7.50), salmon fillet with cucumber, shi-itake mushrooms and oriental sauce (£9.95), roast monkfish with mashed potato, spinach, shallots and red wine sauce (£12.95), roast quail with red wine sauce and french bean and hazelnut salad (£11.50) and veal kidneys with celeriac purée and red wine sauce (£13.50); there's also a nice choice of extra vegetables like fennel with braised tomato (£1.25-£1.95), and puddings like caramelised pear pizza with mascarpone, sticky toffee and date pudding or chocolate and hazelnut tart with crème fraîche (from (£3.75); they do small helpings for children, an unlimited-choice lunchtime cold table (£10.50) and Sunday roast lunch (£11.95); very good waitress service. *(Recommended by Stephen Brown, Ian Phillips, R Wiles, John Fahy, J F M West)*

Free house ~ Licensee Nick Steiger ~ Real ale ~ Meals and snacks (till 10.30) ~ Restaurant ~ (01480) 452681 ~ Children welcome ~ Live music first Fri of month Feb-Nov ~ Open 11-11; 12-10.30 Sun ~ Bedrooms: £79.50B/£89.50B-£139.50B

Planning a day in the country? We list pubs in really attractive scenery at the back of the book.

KEYSTON TL0475 Map 5

Pheasant

Village loop road; from A604 SE of Thrapston, right on to B663

Very well run on similar lines to the Old Bridge above (they're part of the same small group), this thoroughly enjoyable and civilised restauranty pub is the place to come for a particularly good meal, with fine wines and efficient courteous service. The same menu is on offer throughout the building, with linen napkins and bigger tables in the no-smoking Red Room. Imaginative changing dishes might include leek and potato soup with crème fraîche and chives (£3.75), double baked goat's cheese soufflé with apple and walnut salad (£3.95), fried scallops with stir fried vegetables, old balsamic vinegar and coriander (£5.95), fresh tagliatelle with olives, sun-dried tomato, pesto and parmesan (£7.95), wild boar casserole (£8.95), halibut with swiss chard, seed mustard, parsley and tomato (£11.75), seared bass with linguini pasta, courgette, rosemary, chilli and olive oil (£13.75), pigeon breasts with wild mushroom risotto (£12.95), fillet steak with roast tomatoes, artichokes, basil and chips (£14.25); smaller helpings for children; extra vegetables (£1.50-£1.75). A very tempting pudding list might include steamed ginger pudding with egg custard, hot vanilla soufflé with raspberry compote and vanilla ice cream or iced nougat glace with Grand Marnier and orange sauce (£3.50-£5.95); Sunday roast sirloin of beef (£11.25). The exceptionally good wine list has an interesting choice of reasonably priced bottles – though to make the most of their list you need quite a deep pocket – with around 14 by the glass, plus sweet wines and ports; freshly squeezed juices like carrot, orange and ginger; also well kept Adnams Bitter and a changing guest like Adnams Broadside, Fenland Doctors Orders or Fullers London Pride. A friendly low-beamed room has old photographs, leather slung stools and a heavily carved wooden armchair; another room, with high rafters, used to be the village smithy – hence the heavy-horse harness and old horse-drawn harrow there. Wooden tables are set in front of the pub. *(Recommended by John Fahy, G Neighbour, M Morgan, Michael Sargent, Rita Horridge, Sarah Markham, R Gorick, Gordon Theaker, J F M and Dr M West, Jane Kingsbury, R Wiles, Stephen Brown, R K Sledge, M J Morgan, Paul and Maggie Baker, Deborah Weston)*

Free house ~ Licensees Martin Lee and John Hoskins ~ Meals and snacks (till 10pm) ~ Restaurant ~ (01832) 710241 ~ Children welcome ~ Open 12-3, 6(7 Sun)-11; closed evening 25 Dec

KIRTLING TL6857 Map 5

Queens Head

Village signposted off B1063 Newmarket—Stradishall, though pub reached more quickly from Newmarket on the Saxon Street road; OS Sheet 154 map reference 690570

Recently re-opened after a long closure, this peacefully set charming 16th-c building has been discreetly refurbished in period style. Particularly splendid blackboard-listed daily changing bar food follows the pattern of its long-established sister pub the Beehive in Horringer (just over the border in Suffolk) and might include cream of spinach soup (£3.25), toasted steak or thai prawn sandwiches (£5.95), deep fried brie with plum and gooseberry sauce or beef tomato and fresh mozzarella salad (£4.25), king prawns in spicy lemon grass thai sauce (£6.95) and main courses like fresh vegetables with pasta in a creamy herb sauce (£7.50), strips of chicken breast in a creamy mushroom and peppercorn sauce or haddock fillet with asparagus and red pepper butter (£8.95), mignons of beef fillet in creamy stilton sauce (£12.50) and fresh lobster (£18.95, half £11.95), puddings (all £3.50) might include baked date and rum cheesecake or coconut and treacle tart; well kept Greene King IPA and a guest like Mansfield Old Baily under light blanket pressure, and a decent wine list with over half a dozen by the glass. *(Recommended by D E Twitchett, G and R Barber, Geoffrey and Ro Baber; more reports please)*

Free house ~ Licensee Gavin Howard ~ Real ale ~ (01638) 731737 ~ Meals and snacks (till 10, not Sun evenings) ~ Children welcome ~ Open 12-3, 7-11; closed Sun evening

MADINGLEY TL3960 Map 5

Three Horseshoes

Off A1303 W of Cambridge

Cambridgeshire Dining Pub of the Year

Well run and comfortably furnished, this smartly civilised thatched white pub has a well established reputation for its stylishly imaginative food and exceptional wine list – with about 17 wines by the glass, sweet wines and ports. The charmingly traditional bar is pleasantly relaxed with an open fire and efficient attentive service. In summer it's nice to sit out on the lawn, surrounded by flowering shrubs, roses and trees. Particularly well prepared food from a regularly changing menu might include sweetcorn and saffron soup (£3.75), Indian spiced shrimp with crab and corn salad and green chilli poppadum or warm salad of grilled beef, thai basil, mint, coriander, chilli and lime with Asian noodles (£5.50), blackened pork belly with beetroot, chard and courgette stir fry, black bean salsa and tamari and mustard vinaigrette (£9), grilled chicken with potato and garlic cake, grilled okra, sweetcorn salsa, yoghurt dressing and mint oil (£9.75), fried john dory with braised cabbage, potatoes, black mushrooms and rosemary (£11.75), grilled rump steak marinated in red wine, balsamic vinegar, thyme and garlic with horseradish mashed potato, roast red onions, fried onions and red wine butter (£12.50); and puddings like cappuccino brûlée and truffles, mango and passion fruit trifle or malted milk chocolate chip ice cream (£3-£4.75). Four well kept real ales on handpump might be Adnams Southwold, Batemans XXXB, Elgoods Cambridge, Everards Tiger, Fullers London Pride or Morlands Old Speckled Hen, Shepherd Neame Spitfire or Wadworths 6X on handpump. *(Recommended by John Saul, Charles Bardswell, Michael Sargent, Maysie Thompson, J F M West, Mrs D Ball, Colin Barnes, R H Davies, R Wiles, Sebastian Leach, Derek and Sylvia Stephenson, Nick and Meriel Cox, Gwen and Peter Andrews, Paul McPherson)*

Free house ~ Licensee Richard Stokes ~ Real ale ~ Meals and snacks ~ Children welcome ~ Restaurant ~ (01954) 210221 ~ Open 11.30-2.30, 6-11; 12-2.30, 7-10.30 Sun

NEWTON TL4349 Map 5

Queens Head ★

2½ miles from M11 junction 11; A10 towards Royston, then left on to B1368

'Basic, with no frills but bags of atmosphere' is how one reader described this unchanged little gem of a pub; another said it's 'a real find, an enthusiast's pub'. The well worn friendly main bar – run by the same licensee for more than a quarter of a century – has a low ceiling and crooked beams, bare wooden benches and seats built into the walls and bow windows, a curved high-backed settle on the yellow tiled floor, a loudly ticking clock, paintings on the cream walls, and a lovely big log fire. The little carpeted saloon is similar but cosier. Don't expect anything elaborate to eat – food is limited to a range of very good value sandwiches (from £1.80 to £2) including very good roast beef ones and excellent beef dripping on toast (£1.80), mugs of lovely home-made soup (£2) and filled baked potatoes (£2); in the evening and on Sunday lunchtime they serve plates of excellent cold meat, smoked salmon, cheeses and pâté (from £2.80). Adnams Bitter, Broadside and Extra are tapped straight from the barrel, with Old Ale in winter and Tally Ho at Christmas; country wines, Crone's and Cassells ciders and fresh orange juice. Darts in a no-smoking side room, with shove-ha'penny, table skittles, dominoes, cribbage, and nine men's morris. There are seats in front of the pub, with its vine trellis and unusually tall chimney, or you can sit on the village green. Belinda the goose who used to patrol the car park now sits stuffed in a glass case, but lives on in the pub sign, painted by the licensee's father and son; no-smoking games room. *(Recommended by M A Buchanan, M A and C R Starling, Peter and Christine Lea, Tony Beaulah, Bob and Maggie Atherton, Anthony Barnes, Ian and Liz Phillips, Nick and Meriel Cox, Owen and Rosemary Warnock, Charles Bardswell, Gregor Macdonald)*

Free house ~ Licensees David and Juliet Short ~ Real ale ~ Snacks ~ (01223) 870436 ~ Well behaved children in games room ~ Open 11.30-2.30, 6-11; 12-2.30, 7-10.30 Sun; closed 25 Dec

PETERBOROUGH TL1999 Map 5

Charters

Town Bridge, S side

This friendly bustling place is a remarkable conversion of a sturdy 1907 commercial Dutch barge. The well timbered sizeable bar is housed below decks in the cargo holds, and above deck a glazed no-smoking restaurant replaces the tarpaulins that used to cover the hold. Twelve handpumps serve six quickly changing microbrewery guests alongside well kept Bass, Everards Tiger, Fullers London Pride and beers from the owner's own microbrewery: JHB, Bishops Farewell and one of their seasonal ales; two farm ciders in summer; bar food includes filled french bread (from £1.75), filled yorkshire puddings (£2.95), steak sandwich (£3.95), chilli, spinach, tomato and mushroom lasagne, steak and ale pie or chicken, gammon and leek topped with puff pastry (£4.75), scampi (£4.95), 10oz rump steak (£7.50); piped music. Landlubbers can opt for tables in one of the biggest pub gardens in the city. *(Recommended by JP, PP, Andy and Jill Kassube, Dagmar Junghanns, Colin Keane)*

Own brew ~ Licensee Paul Hook ~ Real ale ~ Lunchtime bar meals and snacks ~ Evening restaurant ~ (01733) 315700 ~ Children in restaurant ~ Open 12-11(10.30 Sun); closed 25-26 Dec, 1 Jan

STILTON TL1689 Map 5

Bell

High Street; village signposted from A1 S of Peterborough

It's said that Dick Turpin hid from the law for nine weeks at this rather elegant 16th-c old stone coaching inn. It has a fine coach-arch that opens on to tables in a lovely sheltered courtyard which has a well that's believed to date back to Roman times. The two neatly kept friendly bars have sturdy upright wooden seats on flagstone floors, plush-cushioned button-back banquettes built around the walls, bow windows, big prints of sailing and winter coaching scenes on the partly stripped walls, and a large warm log fire in a handsome stone fireplace. Good seasonal bar food might include stilton and celery soup (£2.25), stilton pizza made with ciabatta (£3.50), chicken supreme with stilton, cider and cream sauce (£7.50), seared salmon fillet on a bed of artichokes and roasted new potatoes (£7.75), roasted cod fillet with parsley crust (£7.95), mediterranean lamb stew (£8.50) and 10oz rib-eye steak (£9.50); extra vegetables (£1.50), with puddings such as summer fruit pudding with red fruit nectar or sticky toffee pudding with sticky toffee sauce (£2.95) or stilton cheese with plum bread (£3.95); the eating area of the bar and part of the restaurant are no smoking. Well kept Greene King Abbot and Marstons Pedigree and one or two guests like Iceni Fine Soft Day or Oakham Jeffrey Hudson on handpump, and a good selection of wines by the glass; good friendly service; dominoes, backgammon, cribbage and Scrabble; attractive chintzy bedrooms. *(Recommended by M Morgan, Joy and Peter Heatherley, Paul and Diane Edwards, Alan and Heather Jacques, Ian Phillips, Paul and Sandra Embleton, Andy Cunningham, Yvonne Hannaford, Lady M H Moir, John Tyzack, Nick and Meriel Cox, Barry and Anne, P Rome, Mr Miller, Dr B and Mrs P B Baker, Simon Collett-Jones, F J Robinson)*

Free house ~ Licensee Liam McGivern ~ Real ale ~ Meals and snacks ~ Restaurant ~ (01733) 241066 ~ Children in eating area of bar at lunchtime ~ Open 12-2.30, 6-11; 11-3, 6-11 Sat; 12-3, 7-10.30 Sun; closed evenings 25 and 26 Dec ~ Bedrooms: £45B/£59B

SUTTON GAULT TL4279 Map 5

Anchor ★

Village signed off B1381 in Sutton

This very well run riverside pub is best known for its particularly good food, and perhaps feels more like a restaurant than a pub. The imaginative menu changes daily but might include broccoli soup (£3.75), grilled dates wrapped in bacon on a mild mustard cream sauce (£4.75), herring fillets marinated in lemon and lime with tomato and fennel salad (£5.50), baked polenta with aubergine, tomato, basil and mozzarella (£9.50), seafood crêpe with white wine and parsley sauce (£9.95), chicken, leek and bacon crumble, or steak, kidney and Guinness pie (£10.95), guinea fowl braised in red wine and mushrooms (£12.95), venison steak with celeriac mash and red wine sauce (£14.50), puddings like mixed berry pavlova, sticky toffee and walnut pudding or steamed banana and coconut pudding with banana and caramel sauce (£4.25), Jersey ice creams (£3.75) and a particularly good changing cheeseboard (£4.25). A good time to visit is Monday to Friday (not bank holidays) lunchtimes when there's a very good value two-course menu (£7.50). Very sensibly, children can have most of their dishes in half-helpings. There's a thoughtful wine list (including a wine of the week and 10 by the glass), winter mulled wine, a local cider and freshly squeezed orange. Well kept City of Cambridge Hobsons Choice, Elgoods Cambridge, Nethergate IPA, and Wolf Bitter tapped from the cask. There's a cosy intimate atmosphere in the four heavily timbered stylishly simple rooms, with three log fires, lighting by gas and candles, antique settles and well spaced scrubbed pine tables on the gently undulating old floors, and good lithographs and big prints on the walls; three-quarters of the pub is now no smoking. In summer you can sit outside at the tables or on the bank of the Old Bedford River watching the swans and house martins; the river bank walks are lovely. No dogs. *(Recommended by Chris Miller, K F Mould, A J Bowen, Gwen and Peter Andrews, Michael Sargent, Mr and Mrs A Brooks, R Wiles, Steve and Sarah Pleasance, Mrs C Archer, M J Brooks, Keith and Janet Morris, James Nunns, Luke Worthington, Gordon Theaker, Julian Holland, P and D Carpenter, P A Devitt, M Brooks, M C and S Jeanes)*

Free house ~ Licensee Robin Moore ~ Real ale ~ Meals and snacks (till 9.30 on Sat) ~ (01353) 778537 ~ Children in eating area of bar till 8.30pm ~ Open 12-3, 7(6.30 Sat)-11 ~ Bedrooms: £47.50B/£59.50B

SWAVESEY TL3668 Map 5

Trinity Foot

A14; to reach it from the westbound carriageway, take Swavesey, Fen Drayton turnoff

They serve an incredible range of fresh fish – delivered daily from the East Coast ports – at this bustling pub, and at their shop next door (open Tuesday-Saturday 11-2.30, 6-7.30). Depending on the day's catch, there might be spiced herring fillets or soft herring roe on toast (£3.95), 6 oysters (£5), grilled butterfish, haddock or cod (all £7.50), grilled skate wings (£8.25), john dory (£8.50), dover sole, monkfish with pernod and cream or grilled tuna steak (£9.75), and fresh lobster (£13-£18); also, sandwiches (from £1.75), soup (£2.50), ploughman's (£4.25), omelettes (£6), mixed grill (£9.95), and generously served daily specials like mushroom and pepper quiche (£6.50), chicken curry (£7) and steak and kidney pie (£7.50); puddings (£3). Well kept Boddingtons and Flowers on handpump, decent wines, and freshly squeezed fruit juice. Service is cheerfully efficient, and there are well spaced tables, fresh flowers, and a light and airy flower-filled conservatory; no-smoking dining room. There are shrubs and trees in the big enclosed garden. *(Recommended by C J Darwent, R and M Bishop, Anthony Barnes, Michael Hyde, Gordon Theaker, P and D Carpenter, Jane Kingsbury, Ian Crichton)*

Whitbreads ~ Lease: H J Mole ~ Real ale ~ Meals and snacks (till 10 Fri and Sat) ~ (01954) 230315 ~ Children welcome ~ Open 11-2.30, 6-11; 12-3 Sun (cl Sun evenings)

WANSFORD TL0799 Map 5

Haycock ★ 🛏 🍷

Village clearly signposted from A1 W of Peterborough

The fine flagstoned main entry hall at this famous old coaching inn has antique hunting prints, seats and a longcase clock. This leads into the panelled main bar with its dark terracotta walls, sturdy dado rail above a mulberry dado, and old settles. Through two handsome stone arches is another attractive area, while the comfortable front sitting room has some squared oak panelling by the bar counter, a nice wall clock, and a big log fire. The airy stripped brick Orchard room by the garden has dark blue and light blue basketweave chairs around glass-topped basket tables, pretty flowery curtains and nice modern prints; doors open on to a big sheltered terrace with lots of tables and cream Italian umbrellas; piped music. As well as a very good range of around 11 well chosen house wines by the glass, there's an exceptional wine list, properly mature vintage ports by the glass and well kept Adnams Southwold, Bass, Ruddles Best, and a guest like Morlands Old Speckled Hen on handpump. They only serve ciabatta or bread sandwiches in the bar (£3.95), but you can have a full meal in the Orchard room: soup (£3.60), chicken liver pâté (£4.95), smoked haddock risotto (£5.75), steak and kidney pie or baked pork chop with crispy sage and onion coating (£8.95), baked fillet of sole rolled with leeks with white wine sauce (£10.50), 10oz sirloin (£11.95). The spacious walled formal garden has boules and fishing as well as cricket (they have their own field). The restaurant is no smoking. *(Recommended by R Wiles, Bob and Maggie Atherton, Paul and Sandra Embleton, Gordon Neighbour, Tony Dickinson, Julian Holland, O K Smyth)*

Free house ~ Licensees Simon Morpuss and Louise Dunning ~ Real ale ~ Meals and snacks (12-10.30) ~ Restaurant ~ (01780) 782223 ~ Children welcome ~ Jazz first Fri in the month ~ Open 10-11; 12-10.30 Sun ~ Bedrooms: £85B/£120B

WOODDITTON TL6659 Map 5

Three Blackbirds

Village signposted off B1063 at Cheveley

The two simple but snug little stone-floored bars in this very pretty thatched village pub have high winged settles or dining chairs around fairly closely spaced neat tables, cigarette cards, Derby-Day photographs, little country prints, and winter fires – the room on the left has the pubbier atmosphere; piped music. Good bar food includes sandwiches (from £2 – not Sunday), home-made soups like braised lamb shank and barley with rosemary cream (£3.25), charred red pepper with somerset goat's cheese and basil oil dressed leaves (£4.25), warm fresh crab, aubergine and mushroom tart with lime and ginger dressing (£4.50), roast cod fillet with garlic and parsley crust and saffron butter (£8.95), caramelised pork fillet with chinese greens and sweet and sour sauce (£9.95), honey glazed norfolk duckling (£11.95), local beef fillet topped with mushroom compote and straw potatoes (£13.95), and home-made puddings such as treacle tart, summer fruit crème brûlée or bakewell tart (£2.70); the restaurant is no smoking. Two changing real ales like Adnams Regatta, Greene King IPA, Flowers Original or Whitbreads Castle Eden well kept on handpump, and wines from the Adnams list. The attractive front lawn, sheltered by an ivy-covered flint wall, has flowers, roses, and a flowering cherry. *(Recommended by Ian Phillips, Mark Hydes, John and Elizabeth Cox; more reports please)*

Whitbread/Carlsberg Tetleys ~ Tenant Mark Roberts ~ Real ale ~ Meals and snacks ~ Restaurant ~ (01638) 730811 ~ Well behaved children in eating area of bar ~ Open 11.30-3, 6.30-11; 12-10.30 Sun; they may open bedrooms this year

Lucky Dip

Besides the fully inspected pubs, you might like to try these Lucky Dips recommended to us and described by readers (if you do, please send us reports):

☆ **Alconbury** [Vinegar Hill, Alconbury Weston – handy for A1, nr A14/M11 turnoffs; TL1875], *White Hart*: Friendly and comfortable respite from trunk roads, good value generous food inc home-made chips, eating areas left and right, John Smiths, Wadworths, Websters and local Dons Dilemma, back bar with darts, very helpful licensees; charming village, ducks on stream *(Jenny and Michael Back, Norma and Keith Bloomfield, Irene and Geoffrey Lindley)*

☆ **Barrington** [West Green – from M11 junction 11 take A10 to Newton, turn right; TL3949], *Royal Oak*: Rambling thatched Tudor pub, heavy low beams and timbers, lots of character, pleasant no-smoking dining conservatory, tables out overlooking charming green; well kept Adnams, Courage Best and Directors and Greene King IPA, prompt service, food inc wide vegetarian range; maybe piped music, children in one area *(James Nunns, TRS, Jeff Davies, Malcolm Taylor, P and D Carpenter, LYM)*

☆ **Bourn** [signed off B1046 and A1198 W of Cambridge; at N end of village; TL3256], *Duke of Wellington*: Consistently good range of generous imaginative food inc good home-made puddings in quiet and civilised relaxing bar divided by arches and so forth – where the locals come to dine out; well spaced tables, pleasant attentive staff, well kept Greene King; cl Mon *(Maysie Thompson, Mr and Mrs A Martin, John Fahy, BB)*

Boxworth [TL3463], *Golden Ball*: Attractive building and setting, pleasant helpful staff, good food, well kept Greene King and Nethergate, separate restaurant/family room; piped music may obtrude; no children in main bar, seats and a few children's playthings in big well kept garden *(K and J Morris)*

Buckden [High St, just off A1; TL1967], *Lion*: Lovely partly 15th-c coaching inn, oak beams and carvings in small comfortable bar, John Smiths and Ruddles on electric pump, pleasant staff, good well presented food, attentive staff, no music or machines; bedrooms *(Gordon Theaker, George Atkinson)*

☆ **Cambridge** [Ferry Path; car park on Chesterton Rd], *Old Spring*: Good individual atmosphere, cosy old-fashioned furnishings and decor, bare boards, gas lighting, lots of old pictures, decent straightforward bar food inc Sun roasts, well kept Greene King IPA and Abbot, two log fires, long back conservatory, summer barbecues; children till 8, has been open all day Sat *(David Carr, Keith and Janet Morris, Stephen Brown, LYM)*

☆ **Cambridge** [14 Chesterton Rd], *Boathouse*: Eight or so well kept beers, good choice of ciders, decent coffee and generous food in easy-going pub with verandah overlooking river (wonderful playground on opp bank), L-shaped main room with varnished wood tables, framed prints and rowing memorabilia; juke box; children welcome, pretty garden with hungry ducks, open all day; no dogs *(John A Barker, David Carr, LYM)*

☆ **Cambridge** [Mill Lane], *Mill*: Recently decorated sturdy but attractive alehouse interior, overlooks mill pond where punts can be hired; eight changing ales inc Adnams and Nethergate Old Growler, farm ciders, country wines, simple lunchtime bar food from sandwiches up, fruit machine, piped pop; children in eating area, open all day; very popular waterside garden *(Robert Lester, David Carr, Andy and Jill Kassube)*

☆ **Cambridge** [85 Gwydir St], *Cambridge Blue*: Comfortable, small, simply furnished, interesting university sports photographs and local paintings, well kept Nethergate and frequently changed guest beers, bargain popular fresh food (not Sun evening – fee charged if you pay by cheque) inc vegetarian; one room no smoking, welcoming knowledgeable staff, sheltered terrace with children's climbing frame and entertaining model train *(Sandy McIlwain, Andy and Jill Kassube, LYM)*

☆ **Cambridge** [129 King St], *St Radegund*: Smallest pub in town, unusual decor with interesting former-student memorabilia, friendly landlord, well kept ales such as Fullers London Pride, Hook Norton Best and Nethergate, good malt whisky collection *(Keith and Janet Morris)*

Cambridge [19 Bridge St], *Baron of Beef*: Peaceful and friendly traditional front bar, old wooden furnishings, scrubbed floor, panelling, lots of old photographs, well kept Greene King ales from uncommonly long counter, buffet food *(John A Barker)*; [King St], *Bun Shop*: Atmospheric studenty pub, popular food, Boddingtons and Marstons Pedigree *(Anon)*; [Castle St], *Castle*: Large, airy and well appointed local, with full Adnams range kept well and guests such as Wadworths Farmers Glory, good value usual lunchtime food inc burgers and vegetarian, no-smoking area with easy chairs upstairs, friendly staff; maybe piped pop music; picnic-sets in good garden *(Keith and Janet Morris, P and D Carpenter, Ian Hydes, Robert Gomme)*; [68 King St], *Champion of the Thames*: Basic small and cosy pub with friendly welcome, good atmosphere, wonderfully decorated windows, padded walls and seats, painted Anaglypta ceiling, lots of woodwork, no music, well kept Greene King IPA and Abbot *(Keith and Janet Morris)*; [Clarendon St], *Clarendon Arms*: Popular unpretentious partly flagstoned local with well kept Greene King and Rayments, friendly staff, wide choice of cheap but adventurous bar lunches inc giant crusty sandwiches; open all day; bedrooms simple but clean and comfortable *(G Coates, Jeff Davies)*; [Kings St], *Finnegans*: Pleasant Irish-theme bar with Courage ales; same building includes wine bar and restaurant *(Anon)*; [16 Chesterton Rd], *Fresher & Firkin*: Bare boards and beer drinkers (brews its own), but quieter at lunchtime with good value food and friendly helpful service; back windows overlook river *(Richard Houghton, Terry Buckland)*; [17 Bridge St, opp St Johns Coll], *Mitre*: Friendly attentive service, half a dozen real ales, well priced wines and food from fine sandwiches and hot beef baps up, no-smoking area, log-effect fire, back-to-basics alehouse decor *(Keith and Janet Morris)*; [43 Panton St], *Panton Arms*: Newly refurbished, with good inexpensive lunchtime food esp very fresh help-yourself salads, pleasant landlord, quick service *(John A Barker)*

Clayhithe [TL5064], *Bridge*: Picturesque spot by River Cam with pretty waterside garden, cosy beamed and timbered bar with good log fire, well kept Adnams Bitter and Broadside and Elgoods, quick friendly service, wide changing choice of food esp curries, restaurant; comfortable bedrooms in motel extension *(R C Vincent, LYM)*

☆ **Downham** [Main St (B1411); sometimes known as Little Downham – the one near Ely; TL5283], *Plough*: Welcoming little village local, lots of pictures of regulars but very friendly to visitors, short range of good value home-made food, Greene King beers under light top pressure, good choice of malt whiskies, busy atmosphere, friendly golden retriever, framed banknotes; tables in front and in garden behind *(Basil Minson, Roy Bromell, BB)*

☆ **Dry Drayton** [Park St, opp church; signed off A428 W of Cambridge; TL3862], *Black Horse*: Recently redecorated village local with very generous food inc wide vegetarian choice, well kept Greene King and other ales inc weekly changing guests, friendly prompt service, welcoming fire in central fireplace, games area, tables on pretty back terrace and neat lawn; camping/caravanning in meadow behind, maybe geese at end of car park *(E Robinson, Keith and Janet Morris, LYM)*

☆ **Dullingham** [50 Station Rd; TL6357], *Kings Head*: Cosy dining pub in pretty village, wide range of food inc sandwiches, plenty of vegetarian and lots of puddings at very reasonable prices; coal fires, well kept ABC Bitter and Flowers IPA, good choice of fairly priced wines, friendly helpful staff, no-smoking room; fairy-lit seats out above the broad village green, adventure playground, no dogs; children in restaurant, and separate family room *(Liz and Ian Phillips, Mark Hydes, LYM)*

Elsworth [1 Brockley Rd; TL3163], *Poacher*: Old thatched local in beautiful surroundings, comfortable lounge, small back bar, lots of carving inc nicely done birds on bar front, loads of brassware and pleasant pictures, very friendly staff, wide choice of good food, Adnams *(Gordon Theaker)*

☆ **Eltisley** [signed off A428; TL2659], *Leeds Arms*: Knocked-through beamed bar overlooking peaceful village green, huge log fire, plenty of dining tables, nicely presented substantial food, Greene King IPA and Hook Norton Best under light blanket pressure, no-smoking restaurant; children in eating area, pleasant garden with play area; simple comfortable bedrooms in separate block *(E Robinson, AB, LYM)*

☆ **Ely** [Annesdale, off A10 on outskirts; TL5380], *Cutter*: Lovely riverside setting, with plenty of tables outside and a genuine welcome for children; friendly series of unpretentious bars, generous attractively priced food, real ales, good house wines, willing service; best to book Fri/Sat in boating season *(Frank Davidson, Mark and Heather Williamson, LYM)*

Ely [2 Brook St (Lynn rd)], *Lamb*: Impressively panelled hotel lounge bar, well kept Tetleys Imperial, friendly staff, good restaurant; shame about the piped music; bedrooms *(Sue Holland, Dave Webster)*; [62 Silver St], *Prince Albert*: Friendly town pub worth knowing in summer for attractive garden with two aviaries; full range of Greene King ales kept well, tasty snacks, no juke box *(Charles and Pauline Stride, Ian Phillips)*

☆ **Fen Ditton** [High St; TL4860], *Ancient Shepherds*: Good value generous bar food inc imaginative dishes, good atmosphere, comfortable and immaculate old-world lounge with settees and no music or fruit machines; friendly helpful staff, cosy restaurant (not Sun) *(J F M West)*

☆ **Fordham** [TL6270], *White Pheasant*: Good choice of good food in well converted dining pub (same management as Red Lion at Icklingham – Suffolk main entry – and Crown & Punchbowl at Horningsea), friendly helpful service, well kept beers, good wines, log fire, nice mix of mismatched furniture inc good big tables; opens noon *(Nicholas Law, J F M West, Bob and Maggie Atherton, Wayne Brindle)*

☆ **Fowlmere** [High St; TL4245], *Swan House*: Friendly and comfortable local with enormous log fire, good interesting reasonably priced bar food, good choice of well kept ales, attentive landlord, piano *(JF, TRS)*

Friday Bridge [TF4604], *Chequers*: Village pub doing well under very welcoming newish landlord, reasonably priced bar food from enormous filled cobs up, Fri steak night, Elgoods real ale, red plush seats, lots of beer mats on beams; restaurant – must book Sun lunch; neat garden *(Michael and Jenny Back)*

Fulbourn [1 Balsham Rd; TL5156], *White Hart*: Stripped brick and farm tools, good choice of enjoyable food inc vegetarian and crisp grease-free chips, comfortable seats, flame-effect fire, cheerful service, real ales, reasonable wine range; piped music *(P and D Carpenter)*

Godmanchester [London Rd; TL2470], *Exhibition*: Flagstones, plain furniture, flowers on tables, mural of village shops, amazingly wide and interesting choice of well priced food *(Comus Elliott)*

Grantchester [junction Coton rd with Cambridge—Trumpington rd; TL4355], *Rupert Brooke*: Friendly and cosy renovated beamed pub with Whitbreads-related ales, good varied food inc vegetarian, very reasonable prices, nice atmosphere; discreet piped music *(Mr and Mrs R Head, Julian Holland)*

Great Abington [off A1307 Cambridge—Haverhill, and A11; TL5348], *Three Tuns*: Low-ceilinged village local with open fires, interesting old photographs, real ales such as Fullers and Greene King IPA, cheerful, helpful and most welcoming service, good basic food from sandwiches up prepared to order, reasonable prices; lovely peaceful setting *(P J Keen)*

Great Gransden [off B1046 Cambridge—St Neots; TL2755], *Crown & Cushion*: Thatch, old beams, log fire, Charles Wells Bombardier and Shepherd Neame Spitfire, genial landlord, food inc really fresh sandwiches; small garden, pretty thatched village *(Ian Phillips)*

☆ **Guyhirn** [off B1187 nr A47/A141 junction S of Wisbech; TF3903], *Oliver Twist*: Comfortable open-plan lounge with well kept sturdy furnishings, good range of good value home-made generous food from huge crusty warm rolls to steaks, well kept Everards Beacon and Tiger with a weekly guest beer, cheerful service, big open fire; restaurant, very popular as lunchtime business meeting place; opp River Nene embankment *(Mrs J Shillington, E Robinson, Anthony Barnes, Jenny and Michael Back, BB)*

Hemingford Abbots [High St; TL2870], *Axe*

& Compass: Friendly new young licensees in comfortable old-world 15th-c two-bar thatched pub with flagstones, inglenook seats, brasses, farm tools and local photographs, Scottish Courage ales, usual food; piped radio *(Gwen and Peter Andrews)*

☆ **Hildersham** [off A604 N of Linton; TL5448], *Pear Tree*: Busy straightforward village local with odd crazy-paved floor, huge woodburner, generous genuine home cooking inc home-baked bread, some unusual dishes, good vegetarian ones and children's helpings; cheerful service, well kept Greene King IPA and Abbot, decent wines, daily papers, board games, tables in back garden with aviary; children welcome *(Jenny and Michael Back, Peter and Mavis Brigginshaw, Keith and Janet Morris, BB)*

☆ **Horningsea** [TL4962], *Crown & Punchbowl*: Dining pub with good food inc wonderful puddings, well kept ales inc Adnams, decent wine, lots of young enthusiastic staff; piped music; bedrooms *(J F M West, Maysie Thompson)*

☆ **Kennett** [Bury Rd; TL7066], *Bell*: Busy 16th-c heavy-beamed and timbered Marstons pub with their ales and Banks's Mild kept well (served through sparkler), neat plush furnishings, good reasonably priced bar food, friendly efficient staff; very busy weekends; bedrooms *(John Baker, LYM)*

Kimbolton [2 Stow Rd, Newtown; TL0968], *White Horse*: Olde-worlde two-bar pub with log fire as well as central heating, friendly family atmosphere, good food from bar snacks to full restaurant meals inc three Sun roasts; conservation village *(Patrick and Melvynne Johnson)*

Little Shelford [TL4451], *Navigator*: Attractive village pub, well kept Greene King, nice open fire, obliging landlord, thai food, reasonable prices *(Comus Elliott)*

Littleport [Sandhill Rd; TL5686], *Black Horse*: Quiet panelled lounge with copper-topped tables, decorative plates and pictures, separate bar, Boddingtons and Wolf, bar food, restaurant; riverside garden *(Jenny and Michael Back)*

March [Wimblington Rd; TL4195], *Stars*: Former Seven Stars completely refurbished under new Greene King tenants, attractively priced well cooked food; open all day (Sun afternoon closure) *(E Robinson)*

Milton [33 High St; off A10 N of Cambridge; TL4762], *Waggon & Horses*: Friendly village local with L-shaped lounge, good value food, up to six faultlessly kept real ales, three farm ciders, efficient service; piped music, TV, fruit machine; attractive garden with slide and swing, apple trees, barbecues, picnic-sets and boules *(John Baker)*

☆ **Needingworth** [Overcote Lane; pub signed from A1123; TL3472], *Pike & Eel*: Marvellous peaceful riverside location, with spacious lawns and marina; two separate eating areas, one a carvery, in extensively glass-walled block overlooking water, boats and swans; easy chairs, settees and big open fire in room off separate rather hotelish plush bar, well kept Adnams, Bass, and Greene King Abbot, good coffee, friendly and helpful staff, provision for children; clean simple bedrooms, good breakfasts *(D E Twitchett, Julian Holland, LYM)*

☆ **Peakirk** [12 St Pegas Rd; TF1606], *Ruddy Duck*: Low beams, plush seats, copper-topped tables, central fire, vast choice of generous food inc filling baguettes, fresh fish and vegetarian (and late lunches), Bass, Ruddles Best, John Smiths and guest beers such as Wadworths 6X and Woodfordes Nelsons Revenge, plenty of malt whiskies, friendly helpful service, restaurant, terrace; children in end dining room by prior arrangement, piped music may obtrude; handy for Wildfowl Trust, open all day *(Jenny and Michael Back, Brian and Jill Bond, Keith and Janet Morris)*

☆ **Peterborough** [465 Oundle Rd (A605 SW), Orton Longueville; TL1797], *Botolph Arms*: Attractive ivy-covered flagstone-floored pub doing well under friendly and efficient new Yorkshire couple, huge helpings of good value food inc proper pies, cheap Sam Smiths, family atmosphere, thick walls, open fires; good disabled facilities, tables outside, safe play area *(Elizabeth and Jeremy, R and M Bishop)*

Peterborough [80 Westgate], *Brewery Tap*: New alehouse-style pub, tap for Oakham with three of their beers and two or three guests, bare boards, brewery memorabilia, maybe brewery trips; same owners as Charters, open all day *(Not yet seen by us, included on strength of owners' track record)*; [17 North St], *Bogarts*: At least six well kept ales such as Adnams and Bass, good simple food, fine mix of customers in basic but genuine pub handy for the Westgate shopping centre; friendly staff, open all day *(JP, PP)*; [Westgate], *Bull*: Rambling hotel with numerous bar rooms, nooks and crannies with plush armchairs, low tables and liveried staff; ales inc Adnams, decent house wine, limited food bar menu inc good sandwiches; bedrooms *(John Wooll)*

Purls Bridge [TL4787], *Ship*: Courteous and friendly newish landlord doing good value varied delicious food in old pub at end of long fenland road, overlooking Old Bedford River and RSPB reserve *(John and Sally Clarke)*

Ramsey St Marys [B1040; TL2588], *Lion*: Attractive creeper-clad three-room pub, five real ales, food lunchtime and evening (all day weekends), small fish tank, pool and darts, fruit machine, restaurant; piped music; well kept garden with picnic-sets and play area *(JJW, CMW)*

Six Mile Bottom [A1304 SW of Newmarket; TL5756], *Green Man*: Particularly good reasonably priced food, well presented in generous helpings, with good variety and frequent changes; polite staff, well kept beers *(K A Swatman)*

☆ **Spaldwick** [High St, just off A14; TL1372], *George*: Refurbished 16th-c village inn with very friendly and helpful landlord, very popular for good value well presented food esp fish and summer buffet, well kept Charles Wells ales, decent wines, good coffee, lots of pictures, brasses and dried flowers, three interconnecting restaurant rooms, darts and pool in public bar; very busy – booking needed Fri/Sat *(Margaret and Roy Randle, Mrs E Buckman, David and Mary Webb, D and M T Ayres-Regan)*

Stibbington [off A1 northbound; TL0898], *Sibson*: Neatly kept beamed and carpeted bars, well kept Courage Directors, Ruddles and a guest such as Fullers London Pride, friendly staff, tempting if not cheap food, attractive garden; bedrooms *(James Nunns)*

Stow Cum Quy [Main St; on B1102 follow sign to Anglesey Abbey; TL5260], *White Swan*: Unpretentious village pub, comfortable and cosy; good value generous food cooked to order so may be a wait, vegetarian dishes, no-smoking dining room, Adnams and Courage Directors *(Keith and Janet Morris)*

Stretham [Elford Closes; off A10 S of Stretham roundabout; TL5072], *Lazy Otter*: Big family pub in fine spot on the Great Ouse, with waterside conservatory and neat terrace tables; generous food inc good value children's meals, warm fire in bar, Greene King, Marstons Pedigree and a guest ale, matey service; piped music, can get busy weekends; open all day *(Hilary Edwards, LYM)*

Swaffham Bulbeck [High St; TL5562], *Black Horse*: Wide choice of reasonably priced home-made food, vast helpings, friendly staff, good choice of beers, very relaxing atmosphere (though there may be piped music), restaurant; bedrooms on ground floor of converted stable block *(P and D Carpenter, Christopher Hart)*

☆ **Swaffham Prior** [B1102 NE of Cambridge; TL5764], *Red Lion*: Welcoming and attractive local in pleasant village, well kept Greene King ales, wide range of generous fresh food from sandwiches and baked potatoes to steaks, comfortably divided dining area, quick cheerful service; unusually plush gents' *(Maysie Thompson)*

☆ **Swavesey** [High St/Market Pl; signed off A14 NW of Cambridge; TL3668], *White Horse*: Good fresh home-cooked food from sandwiches to steaks inc vegetarian dishes and notable steak and kidney pie and curries (not Sun evening or Mon lunch) in welcoming village local with attractive traditional furnishings in public bar, more straightforward spacious lounge and no-smoking eating room; three Whitbreads-related ales, enterprising wines, good range of malt whiskies, winter Gluhwein, log fire, friendly service, children allowed; maybe discreet piped music *(Ian Phillips, J I Davies, P and D Carpenter, BB)*

Thriplow [2 Lower St (off A505 nr M11 junction 12 and Duxford air museum); TL4346], *Green Man*: Well kept ales such as Woodfordes Wherry, attractive food inc interesting dishes (worth booking w/e), interesting pictures, renovated garden *(Keith and Janet Morris)*

Trumpington [High St (A1309); TL4454], *Coach & Horses*: Reopened after spacious tasteful refurbishment, with sandwiches, baked potatoes and baguettes though more emphasis on well cooked and presented meals with tasty sauces; dining area, open fire, plenty of young eager to please staff, no piped music *(P and D Carpenter)*

Upware [off A1123 W of Soham; (full name Five Miles From Anywhere, No Hurry); TL5370], *Five Miles From Anywhere*: Aptly named spacious modern free house, brightly refurbished under new management, in fine riverside site with elaborate play area, extensive moorings and public slipway (day boats for hire), seats on heated waterside terrace and in newly landscaped garden; three real ales, open fire, restaurant, pool room, video games, children welcome; live music Fri/Sat and bank hols; disabled facilities *(LYM)*

Waresley [Eltisley Rd; TL2454], *Duncombe Arms*: Comfortable and welcoming old pub, long main bar, fire one end, good range of reasonably priced bar food, consistently well kept Greene King ales, restaurant *(D H Heath)*

☆ **Whittlesford** [off B1379 S of Cambridge; handy for M10 junction 10, via A505; TL4748], *Tickell Arms*: Great character and atmosphere, ornate heavy furnishings, dim lighting, lovely log fires, attractive flower-filled Victorian-style conservatory and formal garden, wide range of imaginative bar food, friendly service, well reproduced classical music, decent wines, well kept Adnams; cl Mon (exc bank hols), no credit cards *(Kevin Thorpe, Wilma and Ian Smith, J Fahy, LYM)*

☆ **Wicken** [High St; TL5670], *Maids Head*: Neatly kept dining pub in lovely village-green setting, good food in bar and no-smoking restaurant, well kept Bass, Charrington, Hancocks HB and a guest beer, fair-priced wines, quiet piped music; tables outside, handy for Wicken Fen nature reserve (NT) *(Lesley Sones, H F Drake, R C Morgan)*

Wilburton [TL4875], *Kings Head*: Well prepared food inc shellfish specials last three days of month, well kept Adnams Bitter and Broadside, Greene King IPA, welcoming licensees, efficient service; public bar with bar billiards *(Nicholas Law, Sue Holland, Dave Webster)*

☆ **Wisbech** [North Brink; TF4609], *Red Lion*: Hospitable and civilised long front bar in lovely Georgian terrace on River Nene, nr centre and NT Peckover House; very popular lunchtime for good range of good value home-cooked food inc several vegetarian and fish, Fri bargain salad bar, well kept local Elgoods beer, decent wines *(M Morgan)*

☆ **Wisbech** [53 North Brink], *Rose*: Gimmick-free pub in same splendid riverside spot, interesting changing range of well kept beers from small breweries, good cheerful service, and steady trickle of regulars; cheap fresh filled french bread *(Peter Plumridge, Geoff Tomlinson)*

Cheshire

Four attractive new entries here this year are the Dysart Arms at Bunbury (an attractively laid out dining pub with good food and drink), the Albion in Chester (a strikingly individual place, decent food, excellent beer), the Fox & Barrel at Cotebrook (a newly done extensive dining pub, with a civilised and attractive bar area too), and the Crown in Nantwich, a fine old building with a successful mix of pubby bar and good restaurant side. On the food side, other pubs doing very well here are the stylish Grosvenor Arms at Aldford, the restauranty Cholmondeley Arms at Bickley Moss, the Calveley Arms at Handley (it's the specials which win real praise here), the delightfully placed Bells of Peover at Lower Peover (its refurbished kitchens have given the food quite a boost), the rambling out-of-the-way Cheshire Hunt at Pott Shrigley, and the very well run Plough at Whitegate. Of these, the Bells of Peover gains our award as Cheshire Dining Pub of the Year (as well as a new Food Award). It's incidentally worth noting that Cheshire pubs are normally very generous with their size of helpings. Particular changes or events to mention include new landladies at the Old Harkers Arms in Chester and the Hanging Gate at Langley (already lots of praise from readers for both), and more recently new licensees at the Swan at Marbury; a new dining room at the Dog at Peover Heath; and the Bhurtpore at Aston celebrating the 150th anniversary of the family first coming to the pub – wonderful range of drinks here, enjoyable food too. In the Lucky Dip section at the end of the chapter, pubs standing out prominently in recent months (and all inspected and approved by us) are the Maypole at Acton Bridge, Stanley Arms at Bottom of the Oven, Boot among several others in Chester, Alvanley Arms at Cotebrook, Thatch at Faddiley (a really worthwhile dining pub), Copper Mine at Fullers Moor, George & Dragon at Great Budworth, Dun Cow at Ollerton, Olde Park Gate at Over Peover, Bulls Head at Smallwood, Swettenham Arms at Swettenham, Swan at Tarporley, Ferry just outside Warrington and Swan at Wybunbury. Although we've not yet visited it ourselves, we'd add the Boot at Willington Corner to this list on the strength of recent reports from readers. Drinks prices in Cheshire are substantially lower than the national average; we found pubs tied to the regional brewer Robinsons particularly cheap for beer, as were the Bhurtpore at Aston and Grosvenor Arms at Aldford – proof yet again that high quality needn't mean high prices.

ALDFORD SJ4159 Map 7

Grosvenor Arms ★ 🍴 🍷 🛏

B5130 S of Chester

Pubs Limited, the small chain to which this pub belongs, aims to foster character – they have certainly succeeded at the Grosvenor which for a large pub has an unusually friendly and individual atmosphere. Don't be put off by the imposing exterior, inside traditional decor is cleverly combined with a spacious open-plan layout; the best room is probably the huge panelled library with floor-to-ceiling book shelves along one wall. Buzzing with conversation, this also has long wooden floor boards, lots of well spaced substantial tables, and quite a cosmopolitan feel. Several quieter rooms are well furnished with good individual pieces including a very comfortable parliamentary type leather settle. Throughout there are plenty of interesting pictures, and the lighting's exemplary. The airy terracotta-floored conservatory has lots of huge low-hanging flowering baskets and chunky pale wood garden furniture; it opens on to a large elegant suntrap terrace and neat lawn with picnic-sets, young trees and a tractor. Bar food is very good, but it's not at all the kind of place where eating dominates to the exclusion of all else – indeed the range of drinks at the good solid bar counter is excellent. Batemans XB, Boddingtons, Buckleys, Flowers IPA and Jennings well kept on handpump, 35 malt whiskies, and each of the remarkable collection of wines – largely New World – is served by the glass. The menu changes every day, but might include home-made soup or sandwiches (£2.95), vegetable and potato cakes with tomato salsa (£3.95), ploughman's (£4.95), salmon and haddock fishcakes with a tomato and onion salad and lemon mayonnaise (£5.95), mushroom and courgette stroganoff with basmati rice (£7.25), home-made steak, ale and mushroom pie (£7.95), chicken with a white wine, mushroom, tomato, tarragon and thyme sauce (£8.95), roast half shoulder of lamb with a mint and apricot sauce (£10.95), steaks (from £11.45), and puddings such as home-made banoffi pie and peanut butter cheesecake (£3.75); good service, even when busy (which it usually is). Two log fires, bar billiards, cribbage, dominoes and trivia machine. *(Recommended by W C M Jones, SLC, D Bryan, Tim Harper, Sue Holland, Dave Webster, Pat and Tony Hinkins, Ray and Olive Hebson, Lorna and Howard Lambert, E G Parish, Roger and Christine Mash, Mike and Wena Stevenson, Joan Yew, Richard Lewis, Rosemary Johnston, S Williamson, Brian and Anna Marsden)*

Free house ~ Licensees Gary Kidd and Jeremy Brunning ~ Real ale ~ Meals and snacks (all day) ~ (01244) 620228 ~ Children in eating area of bar till 6pm ~ Open 11.30-11; 12-10.30 Sun; closed 25 Dec

ASTON SJ6147 Map 7

Bhurtpore

Off A530 SW of Nantwich; in village follow Wrenbury signpost

1999 will be the 150th anniversary of the landlord's family originally coming to the Bhurtpore. His great grandfather sold the pub in 1901; Simon George bought it back as a bare shell ninety years later and has created what one reader describes as 'A real ale enthusiast's dream.' They have 10 handpumps serving a rotating choice (over 700 last year) of well kept beers like Adnams Oyster Stout, Hanby Drawwell Bitter, Itchen Valley Godfathers, Keltek Magik, Marston Moor Brewers Droop and Woody Woowards Gobstopper; around 5,500 pints were supped at last year's beer festival (unfortunately not to be repeated in 1999.) They have dozens of good bottled beers, too, including Belgian Friart, Liefmans Cherry Ale and Rodenbach fruit beers (and fruit-flavoured gins), keep a changing farm cider or perry, and try to encourage people to try malt whiskies they've not had before (there's a choice of around 90). The wine list is interesting and attractively priced. The pub's unusual name comes from a town in India where local landowner Lord Combermere won a battle, and there's a slightly Indian theme to the decor and the menu. The carpeted lounge bar has a growing collection of Indian artefacts (one statue behind the bar proudly sports a pair of Ray-Bans), as well as good local period photographs, and some attractive furniture. As well as very good home-made curries and baltis on the specials board (from £5.75), enjoyable bar food includes home-made soup (£1.75), sandwiches (from £1.75; toasties £2.25), Shropshire sausages and egg (£3.25), ploughman's (from £2.95), steak, kidney and ale pie or mushroom stroganoff (£5.50), haddock fillets with lemon and parsley butter (£5.95), 10oz gammon with egg (£5.95), chicken with tarragon sauce (£6.25), steaks (from £7.95), and puddings like chocolate fudge cake or sticky toffee pudding (from £2.75); children's menu. It can get packed at weekends, but earlyish on a weekday evening or at lunchtime the atmosphere is cosy and civilised. Tables in the comfortable public bar are reserved for people not eating, snug area and dining room are non-smoking; darts, dominoes, cribbage, pool, fruit machine, and piped folk, jazz or blues; enthusiastic and friendly landlord and staff; tables in garden. *(Recommended by Derek and Sylvia Stephenson, Richard Lewis, Sue Holland, Dave Webster, E G Parish, Sue and*

Bob Ward, Chris Gabbitas, Hugh McPhail, SLC, Nigel Wolliscroft, Comus Elliott, M Joyner, Andy Chetwood, Howard Harrison, Andy Lace)

Free house ~ Licensee Simon George ~ Real ale ~ Meals and snacks (no snacks Fri and Sat evenings)~ Restaurant ~ (01270) 780917 ~ Well behaved children welcome till 8.30 ~ Folk night third Tues of month ~ Open 12-2.30, 6.30-11; 12-3, 7-10.30 Sun

BARTHOMLEY SJ7752 Map 7

White Lion ★ £

A mile from M6 junction 16; take Alsager rd and is signposted at roundabout

This delightfully unpretentious black and white timbered pub has a timeless, peaceful character; from seats and picnic-sets on the cobbles outside you can relax as life in the attractive village drifts by. Inside the simply furnished main bar has a welcoming open fire, heavy oak beams dating back to Stuart times, attractively moulded black panelling, Cheshire watercolours and prints on the walls, latticed windows, and wobbly old tables. Up some steps, a second room has another open fire, more oak panelling, a high-backed winged settle, a paraffin lamp hinged to the wall, and shove-ha'penny, cribbage and dominoes; a third room is very well liked by local societies. The straightforward lunchtime bar food fits in splendidly with the overall style of the place: cheese and onion oatcakes with beans and tomato (£1.80), pie, peas and gravy (£2.50), a particularly good home-made hotpot or hot lamb sandwich with redcurrant jelly and mint sauce (£3), hot beef sandwich (£3.30) and ploughman's (£3.95). Very well kept Burtonwood Bitter, Buccaneer, James Forshaws, and Top Hat on handpump; no noisy games machines or music. The cats are friendly. They provide hostel-type accommodation in a converted grain store for walkers and cyclists (£4.50 per night including bacon sandwiches and coffee for breakfast). There's a barbecue area in the improved back terrace. The early 15th-c red sandstone church of St Bertiline across the road is worth a visit. *(Recommended by Andy and Jill Kassube, D Bryan, John Saul, J and P Maloney, Nigel Woolliscroft, Dr D J Walker, Sue Holland, Dave Webster, Chris and Ann Garnett, Jenny and Brian Seller, Stan and Hazel Allen, Howard Harrison, Dr and Mrs A K Clarke, John Honnor, Richard Lewis, Liz and Graham Bell)*

Burtonwood ~ Tenant Terence Cartwright ~ Real ale ~ Lunchtime meals and snacks (not Thurs) ~ (01270) 882242 ~ Children welcome except in main bar – must be gone by 9pm ~ Spontaneous folk music first Sun lunchtime of month ~ Open 11.30-11; 12-10.30 Sun; closed Thurs lunchtime

BICKLEY MOSS SJ5549 Map 7

Cholmondeley Arms ★ 🍴 🛏 🍷

Cholmondeley; A49 5½ miles N of Whitchurch; the owners would like us to list them under Cholmondeley Village, but as this is rarely located on maps we have mentioned the nearest village which appears more often

It's the imaginative and popular food that draws people to this converted Victorian schoolhouse with steeply pictched roof, gothic windows and the huge radiators that keep it really warm in winter. The atmosphere is much more relaxed than you'd expect from the style of cooking and there's plenty to look at in the cross-shaped and high-ceilinged bar, such as old school desks above the bar on a gantry, masses of Victorian pictures (especially portraits and military subjects), and a great stag's head over one of the side arches; seats from cane and bentwood to pews and carved oak settles, patterned paper on the shutters to match the curtains. Despite the obvious concentration on food there is well kept Boddingtons, Greene King Abbot, and Marstons Best and Pedigree on handpump. From a daily changing menu there might be carrot or celery soup, hot baked prawns in sour cream and garlic (£4.25), cold spinach roulade with mushroom, cream and garlic filling or goat's cheese soufflé with devilled tomato sauce (£4.50), farfalle with porcini and oyster mushrooms and parmesan cheese (£7.75), fillet of whitby cod with butter and herbs (£7.75), rabbit braised with wine, mustard and lemon thyme (£7.95), kashmiri lamb curry (£8.95), rare lightly peppered rib-eye steak (£10.95), and puddings like rhubarb and ginger crumble or strawberry pavlova. Unless you can spare the time to wait booking ahead is a good idea, especially on a Saturday. An old blackboard lists ten or so interesting and often uncommon wines by the glass; big (4 cup) pot of cafetière coffee, teas, and hot chocolate; friendly service but can be slow when busy. The bedrooms are across the old playground in the head master's house. There are seats out on a sizeable lawn, and Cholmondeley Castle and gardens are close by. *(Recommended by W C M Jones, Derek and Margaret Underwood, Nigel Woolliscroft, Mike and Mary Carter, Roger and Christine Mash, C H Mauroy, R Wiles, Richard and Margaret Peers, Lorna and Howard Lambert, Mike and Karen England, GLD, Gwen and Peter Andrews, David and Judy Walmsley, Wendy Arnold, Prof B L Underwood, Liz and Graham Bell, Andrew Shore, Dr Jim Mackay, Arthur and Margaret Dickinson, SLC, B J P Edwards, Wayne Brindle)*

Free house ~ Licensees Guy and Carolyn Ross-Lowe ~ Real ale ~ Meals and snacks (till 10 Sat; not 25 Dec) ~ (01829) 720300 ~ Well behaved children welcome ~ Ocassional jazz nights ~ Open 11-3, 7(6.30 Sat)-11; 11-3, 7-11 Sun ~ Bedrooms: £45S/£60S

BROXTON SJ4754 Map 7

Egerton Arms

A41/A534 S of Chester

The balcony terrace here has lovely views over the surrounding sandstone countryside, as far as the River Dee. Inside, the roomy and attractive dark-panelled bar has well polished old furniture, brasses, antique plates and prints; the neatly kept and recently extended no-smoking dining area opens off here. A good choice of bar food includes soup (£1.70), sandwiches, half a roast chicken (£4.85), steak and ale pie (£4.95), gammon and egg (£5.25), lasagne (£5.65), steaks (from £6.95), and puddings (£2.45); children's menu and Sunday lunch. Well kept Burtonwood Bitter, James Forshaw's and Top Hat on handpump, decent wines by the glass; service is consistently friendly and efficient. Popular with families, there is a play area with a wendy house as well as picnic-sets in the garden; piped music, fruit machine. We still have not yet had reports on the bedrooms here. *(Recommended by Paul and Maggie Baker, SLC)*

Burtonwood ~ Manager Jim Monaghan ~ Real ale ~ Meals and snacks (all day weekends) ~ Restaurant ~ (01829) 782241 ~ Children welcome ~ Open 11-11; 12-10.30 Sun; closed evening 25 Dec ~ Bedrooms: £40.25S/45.50S

BUNBURY SJ5758 Map 7

Dysart Arms 🍷

Bowes Gate Road; village signposted off A51 NW of Nantwich; and from A49 S of Tarporley – coming this way, coming in on northernmost village access road, bear left in village centre

Reopened in 1997 as an addition to the small group of Pubs Ltd pubs that includes the Grosvenor Arms at Aldford, this is primarily an informal but smart dining pub, with good interesting food such as cream of leek and potato soup (£2.95), chicken liver pâté flavoured with Cointreau and orange (£4.75), ploughman's (£5.45), gammon steak (£6.95), spaghetti tossed in a garlic and smoked applewood cheese sauce (£7.95), chicken breast filled with brie and walnut pesto with a lemon and chive cream sauce (£8.95), shoulder of lamb with thyme and coarse grain mustard (£10.45) and puddings such as rhubarb and orange crumble or vanilla crème brûlée (£3.95). On our midweek evening inspection visit virtually everyone was eating, but one or two people sat drinking and chatting at the pleasantly lit central bar, near a big inglenook fireplace with a small coal fire. Well kept Boddingtons, Fullers London Pride, Plassey and a weekly changing guest on handpump, with good interesting wines by the glass and farmhouse cider; friendly well trained young uniformed staff. Cosy small areas ramble around this central part of the extended former farmhouse, with several other fires, red and black tiles, some stripped boards and some carpet, a comfortable variety of well spaced solid wooden tables and chairs, a couple of big bookcases, some interesting bric-a-brac (by no means an excess), properly lit pictures, deep venetian red ceilings; the atmosphere is convivial, as all these separate parts are in view of each other yet give a feeling of intimacy; one area is no smoking. An end extension is more restauranty: a big raftered room with its end wall lined with more books. There are tables out on the terrace and in the attractive and immaculate slightly elevated garden; a nice spot by the splendid church at the end of a picturesque village, with distant views of the Peckforton Hills. *(Recommended by Derek and Sylvia Stephenson, E G Parish, Rod and Moyra Davidson, Graham and Lynn Mason, Joan Yen)*

Free house ~ Licensee Catryn Devaney ~ Real ale ~ Meals and snacks (12-9.30) ~ Restaurant ~ (01829) 260183 ~ Children welcome till 6pm ~ Open 11.30-11; 12-10.30 Sun

CHESTER SJ4166 Map 7

Albion

Park Street

A delightful find, run quietly and very individually. It is decorated throughout in a muted post-Edwardian style, with floral wallpaper, appropriate lamps, leatherette and hop-back chairs, period piano, cast-iron-framed tables: two communicating rooms in the candlelit dining section on the right, three in the bar on the left. The decoration is all carefully related to different aspects of World War I: one room with big engravings of men leaving for war, another with similarly striking prints of wounded veterans, others with the more expected aspects – really most interesting. The bar atmosphere is friendly and chatty (no piped music), with maybe a serious game of cards in one corner. Well kept Cains, Greenalls Bitter, Youngs Bitter and a weekly guest such as Titanic White Star on handpump, friendly service (though they don't like people rushing in just before closing time – and won't serve crisps or nuts, let alone children). The food quality is above average, with proper robust home cooking including lamb and vegetable casserole, Staffordshire oatcakes filled with stilton and broccoli, chicken madras curry and basmati rice with mango chutney or lamb liver and bacon with cider gravy (most at £4.95), and puddings such as rice pudding with cinnamon and rhubarb coulis or home-made ice cream (£2.95). No children. The landlord informs us that two bedrooms are planned for 1999 – we await reports. The pub is in a quiet part of town, just below the Roman wall. *(Recommended by Richard Lewis, Sue Holland, Dave Webster, David and Kathy Holcroft, Derek and Sylvia Stephenson, Bill Sykes, Tony and Wendy Hobden, Brian Wainwright)*

Greenalls ~ Lease: Michael Edward Mercer ~ Real ale ~ Meals (12-2, 5-8; not Mon evening) ~ (01244) 340345 ~ Open 11.30-3, 5(6 Sat)-11; 12-2.30, 7-10.30 Sun

Old Harkers Arms

1 Russell St, down steps off City Rd where it crosses canal – under Mike Melody antiques

Little appears to have changed since Barbie Hill took over as landlady at this attractive conversion of an early Victorian canal warehouse. The lofty ceiling and tall windows give a feeling of space and light, yet the seats and tables are carefully arranged to allow a sense of privacy too; it's pleasant watching the canal and cruise boats drifting by outside. There's a good variety of things to look at inside too; attractive lamps, sepia nudes, accordion, and a well stocked library for Sunday morning reading at one end of the bar. The bar counter, apparently constructed from salvaged doors, dispenses well kept Boddingtons, Cheriton Diggers Gold, Fullers London Pride, Timothy Taylor Landlord and a guest on handpump; there are 31 malt whiskies, 13 flavoured Polish vodkas, and decent well described wines. The good choice of well presented food might include sandwiches (from £2.95), soup (£2.95), chicken liver pâté (£4.50), ploughman's (£4.95), pasta with broccoli and stilton sauce (£5.95), fish pie or gammon and egg (£6.95), steak, mushroom and Guinness pie or pan-fried chicken breast (£7.95), steak (£11.45) and puddings like steamed coconut sponge pudding or sticky apricot pudding with butterscotch sauce (£3.45). Helpings are generous; friendly service; and high marks for housekeeping – often what lets city pubs down. *(Recommended by Dr P A Sutton, D Bryan, Brad W Morley, SLC, Jason Wilding, Liz and Graham Bell, Paul Barnett; more reports on the new regime, please)*

Free house ~ Barbie Hill ~ Real ale ~ Meals and snacks (all day) ~ (01244) 344525 ~ Children at weekends only in eating area of bar ~ Open 11.30-11; 12-10.30 Sun; closed 26 Dec and 1 Jan

COTEBROOK SJ5865 Map 7

Fox & Barrel

A49 NE of Tarporley

Reopened in 1997 after a thorough-going refurbishment, this has an interesting decor and good mix of tables and chairs, with cosy distinct areas – we liked the part with an oriental rug in front of the very big log fireplace, others might go for the comfortable banquette corner, or perhaps the part with shelves of rather nice ornaments and china jugs (or that good run of Jersey cattle annual registers). Silenced fruit machine, unobtrusive piped music. Beyond the bar, where friendly neatly uniformed staff serve decent wines, and (through a sparkler) Boddingtons, Marstons Pedigree, Tetleys and a guest such as Ash Vine Black Bess on handpump, a huge candlelit dining area spreads away, with well spaced varying-sized tables, comfortable dining chairs, attractive rugs on bare boards, rustic pictures above the panelled dado, and one more extensively panelled section; part of the dining area is no smoking. Good food might include sandwiches (from £2.35), home-made soup (£2.25), ploughman's (£5.25), beef and ale pie (£5.95), lentil and spinach croquettes with a sweet chilli sauce (£6.25), chicken balti with rice, nan bread, chutney and pickle, pan-fried breast of chicken with red wine, shallot and bacon sauce (£8.95), steaks (from £11.95) and home-made puddings (£3.75). *(Recommended by W C M Jones, Mr and Mrs H Pearson)*

Greenalls ~ Lease: Martin Cocking ~ Real ale ~ Meals and snacks (not 25 Dec) ~ Restaurant ~ (01829) 760529 ~ Children welcome in restaurant ~ Open 12-3, 5.30-11; 12-11 Sat; 12-10.30 Sun; closed evening 25 Dec

DELAMERE SJ5669 Map 7

Fishpool

A54/B5152

A pleasant, relaxed atmosphere pervades this attractive and well liked pub. The four comfortable small room areas are bright with polished brasses and china, and have neatly polished tables, upholstered stools and wall settles. Well kept Greenalls Bitter, Mild and Original on handpump. Good bar food includes sandwiches, and hot dishes such as cod and chips or lamb chops with a port sauce (£5.95), and braised steak with mushroom and onions (£6.50). No games or music; picnic-sets outside on the lawn. As the pub is so well placed near the pike-haunted lake and Delamere Forest it can be particularly busy at weekends – best to go early. *(Recommended by Sue Holland, Dave Webster, Olive and Ray Hebson, W C M Jones, SLC, John McDonald, Ann Bond)*

Greenalls (Allied) ~ Tenant Richard Lamb ~ Real ale ~ Meals and snacks ~ (01606) 883277 ~ Children welcome ~ Open 11.30-3, 6-11; 12-3, 7-10.30 Sun

HANDLEY SJ4758 Map 7

Calveley Arms

Village loop road, just off A41 Chester—Whitchurch

Readers note the welcoming and friendly service at this attractive black and white country pub. The food is good and the menus themselves are novel: they come in the covers of old children's annuals. Interesting and original daily specials might include pan-fried pheasant with hedgerow sauce (£7.25), scallops with mangetout and ginger teriyaki (£9.00) and steak with port and wild mushroom sauce (£11.25); the standard menu includes sandwiches, home-made soup (£1.95), pâté and toast (£2.95), home-made steak and kidney pie or breaded plaice (£4.95), gammon steak and egg (£5.95), chicken with mustard sauce (£6.50), steaks (from £7.50), and home-made puddings such as meringues with mango purée (£2.50). It might be wise to book on Friday or Saturday night. They have well kept Boddingtons Bitter and Mild, Wadworths 6X, Whitbread Castle Eden, and occasional guests including Fullers London Pride, Greene King Abbot and Morland Old Speckled Hen on handpump. The well furnished roomy beamed lounge has leaded windows, an open fire at one end and some cosy alcove seating; shove-ha'penny, dominoes, cribbage and bar skittles. Out in the secluded garden you can play boules in the summer and there are tables and a barbecue.

(Recommended by Graham and Lynn Mason, SLC, Joan Yen, Mrs P J Carroll, Sue Holland, Dave Webster, David and Judy Walmsley, Sarah Evans)

Enterprise Inns ~ Managers Grant Wilson and Chrissy Manley ~ Real ale ~ Meals and snacks ~ Children in eating area of bar ~ (01829) 770619 ~ Open 12-3, 6-11; 12-3, 7-10.30 Sun; closed evening 25 Dec

HIGHER BURWARDSLEY SJ5256 Map 7

Pheasant

Burwardsley signposted from Tattenhall (which itself is signposted off A41 S of Chester) and from Harthill (reached by turning off A534 Nantwich—Holt at the Copper Mine); follow pub's signpost on up hill from Post Office; OS Sheet 117 map reference 523566

The views across the Cheshire plain from this half-timbered and sandstone pub are quite absorbing, although you will have to share the window that affords the best view with Sailor – the pub parrot. The walls of the beamed and timbered bar are covered with pictures and rosettes of the licensees' own highland cattle (they guarantee their beef BSE free) from shows they've won prizes in, and there are plenty of reminders of the landlord's previous career as a ship's pilot, such as his Merchant Navy apprenticeship papers, some ship photographs, a brass ship's barometer and of course the parrot. Other decorations include a stuffed pheasant, a set of whimsical little cock-fighting pictures done in real feathers, and big colour engravings of Victorian officials of the North Cheshire Hunt. There are some plates above the high stone mantlepiece of the see-through fireplace (said to house the biggest log fire in the county), and around the fire is a tall leather-cushioned fender. Other seats include red leatherette or plush wall seats and one or two antique oak settles; there's a pleasant non-smoking conservatory. Bar food includes sandwiches (from £2.25), soup (£2.70), chicken liver pâté and toast (£3.40), their own highland steaks and fresh fish (from £8) and home-made puddings (£2.80); they charge 50p for cheques or cards. Well kept Bass, Batemans XB, Brains Bitter and a guest beer on handpump, and a choice of over 40 malts; friendly staff; cribbage. Picnic-sets on a big side lawn and barbecue on some summer weekends. The bedrooms are in an attractively converted sandstone-built barn, and all have views. The pub is well placed for walks along the Peckforton Hills, and the nearby Candle Workshops are quite a draw in summer. *(Recommended by SLC, Gillian Jenkins, Sue Holland, Dave Webster, E G Parish, D A Norman, Graham and Lynn Mason, Andrew Hodges, J C Brittain-Long, C Sinclair, JCW, David and Judy Walmsley)*

Free house ~ Lease: David Greenhaugh ~ Real ale ~ Meals and snacks ~ Restaurant ~ (01829) 770434 ~ Children in conservatory till 9pm ~ Horses welcomed, and pony and trap rides can be arranged ~ Open 11-3, 6-11; 11-11 Sat; 12-10.30 Sun ~ Bedrooms: £45B/£70B

nr LANGLEY SJ9471 Map 7

Hanging Gate

Meg Lane, Higher Sutton; follow Langley signpost from A54 beside Fourways Motel, and that road passes the pub; from Macclesfield, heading S from centre on A523 turn left into Byrons Lane at Langley, Wincle signpost; in Sutton (half-mile after going under canal bridge, ie before Langley) fork right at Church House Inn, following Wildboarclough signpost, then two miles later turning sharp right at steep hairpin bend; OS Sheet 118 map ref 952696

The new owner is proving to be a friendly host at this cosy old drovers' pub perched high in the Peak District. The three low-beamed rooms are spotlessly kept, simply and traditionally furnished, have big coal fires, and some attractive old prints of Cheshire towns around the walls. Down some stone steps is an airier garden room. Bar food includes sandwiches (from £2.50), soup, meat and potato pie (£4.95) ploughman's (£4.75), gammon and egg (£5.75) and steaks (from £7.95); daily specials include chicken and apricot curry (£4.95) and beef in Guinness casserole or grilled local trout (£5.95). Well kept Cains Formidable Ale and Marstons Bitter and Pedigree on handpump; quite a few malt whiskies. The blue room is no smoking. Seats outside on a crazy-paved terrace have lovely views looking out beyond a patchwork of valley pastures to distant moors (and the tall Sutton Common transmitter above them).

(Recommended by Jackie Lawler, Stephen, Julie and Hayley Brown, Dr D J Walker, Nigel Woolliscroft, Jack Morley, Mike Ridgeway, Sarah Miles, Mark J Hydes, Philip and Ann Falkner; more reports please on the new regime)

Free house ~ Licensee Carole Marshall ~ Real ale ~ Meals and snacks ~ (01260) 252238 ~ Children in family room ~ Open 12-3, 7-11; 12-11 Fri and Sat; 12-10.30 Sun

LANGLEY SJ9471 Map 7

Leathers Smithy

From Macclesfield, heading S from centre on A523 turn left into Byrons Lane at Langley, Wincle signpost; in Langley follow main road forking left at church into Clarke Lane – keep on towards the moors; OS Sheet 118 map reference 952715

Another pub in a lovely setting, with fine views across the Ridgegate Reservoir. The room with perhaps the most character is the lively, partly flagstoned right-hand bar with its bow window seats or wheelback chairs, and roughcast cream walls hung with motoring memorabilia. On the left, there are more wheelback chairs around cast-iron-framed tables on a turkey carpet and a locomotive name-plate curving over one of the two open fires. Bar food (with prices again unchanged since last year) includes sandwiches (from £2), black pudding and mushy peas (£3.95), ploughman's, vegetarian dishes such as spinach and walnut pancake (£4.95), lasagne (£5.20), home-made steak pie (£5.50), halibut or gammon and egg (£6.75), steaks (from £8.95), and puddings. Banks's Bitter and Mild, Camerons Strongarm, Marstons Pedigree, and Morrells Graduate and Varsity on handpump; Scrumpy Jack cider, Gluhwein in winter from a copper salamander, and a decent collection of spirits, including around 80 malt whiskies and 10 Irish; faint piped music. Close to Macclesfield Forest and Teggs Nose country park, the pub is a popular stop for walkers. *(Recommended by Stephen, Julie and Hayley Brown, Jackie Lawler, P and M Rudlin, David and Judy Walmsley, Michael Butler, Philip and Ann Falkner, Mike Howes)*

Free house ~ Licensee Paul Hadfield ~ Real ale ~ Meals and snacks (limited Mon lunchtime, not Mon evening; till 8.30 other evenings, though Fri and Sat till 9.30) ~ (01260) 252313 ~ Occasional pianola music ~ Open 12-3, 7(5.30 Fri)-11; all day Sat and summer Sun

LOWER PEOVER SJ7474 Map 7

Bells of Peover ★

The Cobbles; from B5081 take short cobbled lane signposted to church

Cheshire Dining Pub of the Year

Tucked away in a tranquil village and next to a lovely 14th-c black and white timbered church, the setting of this wisteria-covered pub is delightful; a spacious lawn beyond the old coachyard at the side spreads down through trees and rose pergolas to a little stream, and there are seats on the sheltered crazy-paved terrace in front. Inside is very neatly kept and full of character; the little tiled bar has side hatches for its serving counter, toby jugs, and comic Victorian prints, and the original lounge has antique settles, high-backed windsor armchairs and a spacious window seat, antique china in the dresser, pictures above the panelling, and two small coal fires. There's a second similar lounge. The kitchens were fully refurbished last year and good bar food includes interesting daily specials, home-made soup (£2.25), sandwiches (from £2.90), vegetarian dishes (from £5.75), home-made pie of the day (£6.25), gammon and egg (£6.55), chicken in a tomato and basil sauce (£7.25), steaks (from £10.95), and puddings (£2.95); enjoyable Sunday lunch. Polite and efficient service even when busy; most people wear a jacket and tie in the restaurant. Well kept Boddingtons and Greenalls Bitter and Original on handpump; dominoes. *(Recommended by Mayur Shah, W C M Jones, RJH, Mrs Caroline Cole, Colin Barnes, Roger and Christine Mash, JP, PP, Graham and Lynn Mason, M A Godfrey, P R and S A White, G McGrath, Liz and Graham Bell, James Nunns, Mrs E E Sanders, David and Judy Walmsley, Basil Minson)*

Greenalls (Allied) ~ Managers Ken and Wendy Brown ~ Real ale ~ Meals and snacks ~ Restaurant ~ (01565) 722269 ~ Children in restaurant ~ Open 11-3, 5.30-11; all day Sat and Sun

MACCLESFIELD SJ9271 Map 7

Sutton Hall Hotel ★

Leaving Macclesfield southwards on A523, turn left into Byrons Lane signposted Langley, Wincle, then just before canal viaduct fork right into Bullocks Lane; OS Sheet 118 map reference 925715

The interior here reflects the fact that this pub is a civilised 16th-c baronial hall; there's a suit of armour by a big stone fireplace in the bar which is divided into separate areas by tall black timber and also has some antique squared oak panelling, lightly patterned art nouveau stained-glass windows, broad flagstones around the bar counter (carpet elsewhere), and a raised open fire. It is furnished mainly with straightforward ladderback chairs around sturdy thick-topped cast-iron-framed tables, though there are a few unusual touches such as an enormous bronze bell for calling time, a brass cigar-lighting gas taper on the bar counter itself and a longcase clock. Readers find the atmosphere friendly and unpretentious. Home-made bar food includes soup (from £1.45), pâté (£3.25), lasagne (£4.95), steak and kidney pie or spinach pancakes filled with ratatouille with a sour cream dressing (£5.25), daily specials such as grilled smoked quail wrapped in bacon with warm redcurrant jelly (£4.25), beef in ale (£6.25), and lamb liver and bacon (£6), and puddings like apple and blackberry crumble or sticky toffee pudding (£2). Well kept Bass, Marstons Best, Stones Best and a guest beer on handpump, 40 malt whiskies, decent wines, and a proper Pimm's. It's set in lovely grounds with tables on a tree-sheltered lawn; they can arrange clay shooting, golf or local fishing for residents. *(Recommended by JP, PP, E G Parish, Nigel Woolliscroft, Kate and Robert Hodkinson, James Nunns, David and Ruth Hollands)*

Free house ~ Licensee Robert Bradshaw ~ Real ale ~ Meals and snacks ~ Restaurant ~ (01260) 253211 ~ Children in restaurant ~ Open 11-11; 12-4, 7-11 Sun ~ Four-poster bedrooms: £75B/£90B

MARBURY SJ5645 Map 7

Swan

NNE of Whitchurch; OS Sheet 117 map reference 562457

The Sumners retired in March 1998 after well over 25 years at this creeper-covered white pub and it is to be hoped that the new licensees will be able to retain the buoyantly cheerful atmosphere that they did so much to create. The neatly kept, partly panelled lounge has upholstered easy chairs and other country furniture, a copper-canopied fireplace with a good winter fire (masses of greenery in summer), and discreet lighting. The bar food menu now changes every other day but might include soup (£1.95), sandwiches (from £2), stilton and gammon pâté (£2), ploughman's (£4.50), wild mushroom pancake or home-made steak and kidney pie (£6.95), chicken in mushroom and vermouth sauce (£7.95), steaks (from £8.95), scallops with ginger and spring onion (£8.95), and puddings such as jam roly-poly and spotted dick (£2.50). Greenalls Original and Tetleys Bitter on handpump, 40 malt whiskies. Darts, pool, cribbage and dominoes; no machines or piped music. Rebuilt in 1884, the pub is in a quiet and attractive village, a half-mile's country walk from the Llangollen Canal, Bridges 23 and 24. The nearby church is worth a visit. *(Recommended by Sue Holland, Dave Webster, Nigel Woolliscroft, E G Parish, Joan Yen, David and Judy Walmsley, Lorna and Howard Lambert, John Cockell; more reports on the new regime please)*

Greenalls (Allied) ~ Lease: Sandy, Pam and Colin Yule ~ Real ale ~ Meals and snacks (all day Sat and Sun but not Mon lunchtime) ~ Restaurant (non-smoking) ~ (01948) 663715 ~ Children welcome ~ Open 12-3, 7-11; all day Sat and Sun; closed Mon lunchtime

NANTWICH SJ6552 Map 7

Crown

High Street; in pedestrian-only centre, close to church; free public parking behind the inn

It's hard to resist wandering inside this black and white Elizabethan timbered inn which is strikingly quaint, with its overhanging upper galleries and uncertain perpendiculars and horizontals. There are beams, timbered walls and sloping creaky floors in the cosy rambling bar which is simply furnished with various antique tables and chairs. Good bar food includes a lunchtime carvery, home-made soup (£1.95), sandwiches (from £2.25), filled baked potatoes (from £2.75), ploughman's (£3.50), cumberland sausage (£3.50), plaice (£3.95), steaks (£8.50) and puddings (£2.25); children's menu (£2.25); the restaurant specialises in Italian food. Boddingtons Bitter and Whitbread Flowers Original on handpump; friendly service; very busy weekend evenings; piped music; part of the small Pubs Ltd chain. *(Recommended by Richard Lewis, E G Parish, Pamela and Merlyn Horswell)*

Free house ~ Licensee Phillip Martin ~ Real ale ~ Meals and snacks ~ Restaurant ~ (01270) 625283 ~ Children welcome ~ Open 11-11; 12-10.30 Sun; closed 25 Dec ~ Bedrooms: £64.95B/£84.90B

OVERTON SJ5277 Map 7

Ring o' Bells £

Just over 2 miles from M56, junction 12; 2 Bellemonte Road – from A56 in Frodsham take B5152 and turn right (uphill) at Parish Church signpost

In summer this friendly early 17th-c pub is a mass of colour from the hanging baskets which adorn its exterior. It's very much the sort of place where drinkers stand around the bar chatting and is popular with locals and visitors alike. Redecorated this year but retaining its old-fashioned charm, it has a couple of little rambling rooms with windows looking past the stone church to the Mersey far below; one at the back has some antique settles, brass-and-leather fender seats by the log fire, and old hunting prints on its butter-coloured walls; a beamed room with antique dark oak panelling and stained glass leads through to a darts room (there's also dominoes, cribbage and shove-ha'penny). Good value waitress-served bar food is served at lunchtime only, and includes sandwiches and toasties (from £1.50), omelettes (£2.50) filled jacket potatoes (£2.75), chicken curry (£3.45), home-made beef, mushroom and Guinness pie, lemon sole, rainbow trout or cumberland sausage with mash and onion gravy (£3.95). Greenalls Bitter and around four guest ales per week on handpump or tapped from the cask, and about 80 different malt whiskies served from the old-fashioned hatch-like central servery; piped music. The cats are Tilly and Flora, and a very friendly recently acquired stray called Ambrose. At the back is a secluded garden with tables and chairs, a pond, and lots of trees. *(Recommended by Gillian Jenkins, David and Judy Walmsley, D A Goult)*

Greenalls (Allied) ~ Tenant Shirley Wroughton-Craig ~ Real ale ~ Lunchtime meals and snacks ~ Children welcome away from bar area ~ (01928) 732068 ~ Open 11.30-3(4 Sat), 5.30(6 Sat)-11; 12-4, 7-10.30 Sun

PEOVER HEATH SJ7973 Map 7

Dog

Off A50 N of Holmes Chapel at the Whipping Stocks, keep on past Parkgate into Wellbank Lane; OS Sheet 118 map reference 794735; note that this village is called Peover Heath on the OS map and shown under that name on many road maps, but the pub is often listed under Over Peover instead

Recently refurbished and extended, with a new non-smoking dining room and two more bedrooms planned, this civilised inn continues to develop without detriment to the comfortable and genial atmosphere. In the main bar logs burn in one old-fashioned black grate, a coal fire opposite is flanked by two wood-backed built-in fireside seats, and there are comfortable easy chairs and wall seats (one built into a snug alcove around an oak table). Well liked bar food includes sandwiches (from £2.70), home-made soup (£2.50), mushrooms in beer batter with garlic dip (£3.95), hot sandwiches (from £4), roast beef and yorkshire pudding, chicken in mushroom and brandy sauce, leek, stilton and mushroom pancake or local rabbit (all £8.95), sirloin steaks (from £12.95) and puddings such as home-made fruit crumble or sticky toffee pudding (£2.95). Well kept Boddingtons, Flowers IPA, Tetleys and Weetwood Old Dog on handpump, Addlestones cider, over 50 malt whiskies, decent and expanding wine list and freshly squeezed orange juice; friendly and efficient service; darts, pool, dominoes, cirbbage, juke box, and piped music; quiz nights on Thursdays and Sundays. Advisable to book at weekends. There are picnic-sets out on the quiet lane, underneath the pub's pretty hanging baskets, and an attractive beer garden, nicely lit in the evenings. The licensees also run the Swettenham Arms, Swettenham. *(Recommended by Colin Barnes, Bronwen and Steve Wrigley, Roger and Christine Mash, G McGrath, Dr Phil Putwain, Dr Jim Mackay)*

Free house ~ Licensee Frances Cunningham ~ Real ale ~ Meals and snacks ~ (01625) 861421 ~ Children welcome in eating area of bar ~ Pianist Tues ~ Open 11.30-3(4 Sat), 5.30-11; 12-3.30, 7-10.30 Sun ~ Bedrooms: £50B/£70B

PLUMLEY SJ7175 Map 7

Smoker

2½ miles from M6 junction 19: A556 towards Northwich and Chester

Taking its name from a favourite racehorse of the Prince Regent, this partly thatched pub provides a useful escape from the M6. The same menu covers both the bar and brasserie (though they will reserve tables and give full waitress service in the brasserie); this has created a relaxed atmosphere, with the brasserie becoming even more part of the pub. The three well decorated connecting rooms have dark panelling, open fires in impressive period fireplaces, some military prints, a collection of copper kettles, an Edwardian print on the wall capturing a hunt meeting outside (which shows how little the appearance of the pub has changed over the centuries) and a painting of the first Lord de Tabley mounted on 'Smoker'; also, comfortable deep sofas, cushioned settles, windsor chairs, and some rush-seat dining chairs. A glass case contains an interesting remnant from the Houses of Parliament salvaged after it was hit by a bomb in World War II. Enjoyable bar food includes home-made soup (£2.10), sandwiches (from £2.30), black pudding with a mustard and white wine sauce (£3.85), mushrooms stuffed with pâté (£3.95), vegetable curry (£6.35), home-made seafood bake (£6.75), gammon and egg or steak and kidney pie (£6.95), monkfish in a brandy, mustard and cream sauce (£7.95), steaks (from £8.95), and daily specials such as aubergine stuffed with chicken, tomato, onion, mushrooms and garlic or diced lamb balti (£6.55). Well kept Robinsons Best, Hatters Mild, Frederics, and Old Stockport on handpump, 30 malt whiskies and a good choice of wines; friendly and helpful service; no-smoking areas in bar and brasserie; may be piped music. Outside there's a sizeable side lawn with roses and flower beds, and a children's play area in the extended garden. *(Recommended by Roger Byrne, W C M Jones, L Cherry, Graham and Lynn Mason, M A Godfrey, Bronwen and Steve Wrigley, SLC, J Roy Smylie, John Stanfield, Dr Jim Mackay, Peter Walker, Liz and Graham Bell, Keith and Judith Ashcroft, Derek and Sylvia Stephenson)*

Robinsons ~ Tenants John and Diana Bailey ~ Meals and snacks ~ Restaurant ~ (01565) 722338 ~ Children in eating area of bar and in restaurant ~ Open 11-3, 5.30-11; 12-10.30 Sun

POTT SHRIGLEY SJ9479 Map 7

Cheshire Hunt

At end of B5091 in Bollington, where main road bends left at Turners Arms, fork straight ahead off it into Ingersley Road to follow Rainow signpost, then up hill take left turn signposted Pott Shrigley; OS Sheet 118 map reference 945782

This isolated stone pub retains its homely rustic atmosphere from the days when it was a farmhouse, but it's the popular food that is the main draw today. As well as daily specials, there might be sandwiches, home-made soup (£2.20), mushrooms poached in beer with a cream and white wine sauce (£4.25), Portuguese sardines (£5.50), home-cooked ham on toast with two eggs (£4.95), omelettes (from £5.50), gammon and egg (£5.95), home-made spinach and cottage cheese pancake or lemon chicken (£7.50), pan-fried lamb liver and bacon (£6.95), half a roasted duckling (£9.90), steaks (from £8.95), and puddings like home-made bilberry pie or lemon brûlée (from £2.80); Sunday lunch carvery (best to book); table d'hôte menu Tues-Fri 6-8pm (3 courses £8.95); children's dishes (from £2.50). There are several small rooms (one no smoking) that ramble up and down steps with spindleback and wheelback chairs, beams and black joists, hunting pictures and roaring log fires. Well kept Bass, Boddingtons, and Marstons Pedigree on handpump; friendly and efficient service even when busy. No games machines or piped music. Outside, there are seats on three terraces, gardens, and views over pastures. *(Recommended by R H Rowley, Leo and Barbara Lionet, Graham and Lynn Mason, Bronwen and Steve Wrigley, Nick Lawless, Dave and Deborah Irving, Philip and Ann Falkner, Wendy and Ian Phillips, Mrs E E Sanders, Stephen, Julie and Hayley Brown, Stephen Brown)*

Free house ~ Licensee Alan James Harvey ~ Real ale ~ Meals and snacks (till 10pm; not Mon lunchtime) ~ Restaurant ~ (01625) 573185 ~ Children welcome ~ Open 11.30-3, 5.30-11; 12-3, 7-10.30 Sun; closed Mon lunchtime (except bank holidays)

TARPORLEY SJ5563 Map 7

Rising Sun

High St; village signposted off A51 Nantwich—Chester

Pretty in summer with its mass of hanging baskets and flowering tubs, this bustling village pub is enjoyed by locals and visitors alike. Inside, well chosen tables are surrounded by character seats including creaky 19th-c mahogany and oak settles, and there's also an attractively blacked iron kitchen range (and three open fires), sporting and other old-fashioned prints on the walls, and a big oriental rug in the back room. Generously served lunchtime bar food includes sandwiches (from £2), filled baked potatoes (from £2.30), home-made cottage pie (£5.25), home-made steak and kidney pie (£5.40), gammon and egg (£5.95), pork and apple in cider or beef in ale (£6.30); more elaborate dishes in the evening from the restaurant menu. Well kept Robinsons Best and Mild on handpump; fruit machine, maybe piped music (usually drowned by conversation). *(Recommended by W C M Jones, Dave Braisted, Sue Holland, Dave Webster, Paul Barnett, Brian Wainwright, Alan and Paula McCully, Philip and Ann Falkner, David and Judy Walmsley)*

Robinsons ~ Tenant Alec Robertson ~ Real ale ~ Meals and snacks ~ Restaurant ~ (01829) 732423 ~ Open 11.30-3, 5.30-11; 11.30-11 Sat; 12-10.30 Sun

WESTON SJ7352 Map 7

White Lion 🛏

3½ miles from M6 junction 16; A500 towards Crewe, then village signposted on right

From the road all you can see is the pretty black and white timbered old inn, the comfortable hotel part is discreetly hidden away at the back. Originally a Tudor farmhouse, the inn has a busy low-beamed main room divided up into smaller areas by very gnarled black oak standing timbers. There's a varied mix of seats from cushioned modern settles to ancient oak ones, plenty of smaller chairs, and a friendly, relaxing atmosphere. In a smaller room on the left are three fine settles, well carved in 18th-c style. The well balanced bar menu includes home-made soup (£1.65), sandwiches (£1.95), filled french bread (from £2.50), smoked salmon pâté (£3.15), vegetarian quiche (£3.95), ploughman's or a daily roast (£4.75), poached local Dee salmon (£6.75), steak (£8.50), and home-made puddings (£2.25). Get there early at lunchtime as it can fill up quickly then; advisable to book at weekends. Well kept Bass and Boddingtons on handpump, and a sizeable wine list; dominoes, cribbage, trivia, and piped music. Two side rooms are no smoking. Picnic-sets shelter on neat grass behind, by the pub's own bowling green. *(Recommended by Colin Draper, E G Parish, Neville Kenyon, Kate and Robert Hodkinson, D A Goult, S Williamson)*

Free house ~ Licensee Alison Davies ~ Real ale ~ Meals and snacks (12-2, 5.30-9.30 weekdays; 12-1.45, 7-9.30 weekends; no food Sat lunchtime or 25 Dec) ~ Restaurant ~ (01270) 500303 ~ Children welcome ~ Open 11-3, 5.30(6.30 Sat)-11; 12-3, 7-11 Sun ~ Bedrooms: £49B/£59B

Please let us know what you think of a pub's bedrooms. No stamp needed: *The Good Pub Guide*, FREEPOST TN1569, Wadhurst, E Sussex TN5 7BR.

WETTENHALL SJ6261 Map 7

Boot & Slipper

From B5074 on S edge of Winsford, turn into Darnhall School Lane, then right at Wettenhall signpost: keep on for 2 or 3 miles

There's a pleasant and relaxed atmosphere in the knocked-through beamed main bar here, as well as three shiny old dark settles and more straightforward chairs, and a fishing rod above the deep low fireplace with its big log fire. The modern bar counter also serves the left-hand communicating beamed room with its shiny pale brown tiled floor, cast-iron-framed long table, panelled settle and bar stools; darts, dominoes, and piped music. An unusual trio of back-lit arched pseudo-fireplaces forms one stripped-brick wall and there are two further areas on the right, as well as a back restaurant with big country pictures. Good value bar food includes home-made soup (£1.60), sandwiches (from £2.65; steak batch £2.95), steak and Guinness pie (£5.25), seafood pancake (£4.95), gammon steak or lamb chops (£6.45); generous portions; friendly service. Well kept Marstons Pedigree and Bass on handpump, good selection of malt whiskies and a decent wine list. Outside there are picnic-sets on the cobbled front terrace by the big car park; children's play area. *(Recommended by John Cockell, John McIver, E G Parish, J Roy Smylie, Ann Griffiths, S Williamson)*

Free house ~ Licensee Joan Jones ~ Real ale ~ Meals and snacks ~ Restaurant ~ (01270) 528238 ~ Children welcome till 8.30pm ~ Open 12-3, 5.30-11; 12-11 Sat; 12-10.30 Sun ~ Bedrooms: £36S/£48S

WHITEGATE SJ6268 Map 7

Plough

Foxwist Green; along Beauty Bank, opp Methodist chapel – OS Sheet 118 map reference 624684; from A556 at W end roundabout of Northwich bypass take Whitegate road, bear right in village and then take Foxwist Green turn left; or from A54 W of Winsford turn off at Salterswell roundabout, then first left

Readers report that there is always a warm welcome at this bright and cheerful pub. The old building has several rooms with comfortably straightforward furnishings – including an intimate little dining room with just half a dozen tables. A wide range of good value home-made food using fresh produce includes soup (£1.95), sandwiches (from £2.75), filled jacket potatoes (from £4.75), ploughman's (£4.95), steak pie or mushroom and sweetcorn stroganoff (£5.50), honey roasted chicken (£5.75) and daily specials like chicken wrapped in bacon with an asparagus sauce (£6.75), salmon and asparagus en croûte (£7.50), lemon sole (£8.25) or rib eye steak (£7.95); two sittings for Sunday lunch. Well kept Robinsons Best and Hatters Mild; good considerate service; quiz night on Mondays; darts and piped music. The Whitegate Way – a former railway track – is one of several popular walks nearby. No children. *(Recommended by Miss I Nielson, Sarah Jolley, Ray and Liz Monk, N Revell, John Broughton)*

Robinsons ~ Tenant David Hughes ~ Real ale ~ Meals and snacks (all day Sun) ~ (01606) 889455 ~ Open 11.30-3.30, 5.30-11; 11-11 Sat; 11.30-10.30 Sun

WINCLE SJ9666 Map

Ship

Village signposted off A54 Congleton—Buxton

Said to be one of the oldest in Cheshire, this quaint 16th-c pub is tucked away in scenic countryside with good walks all around. There's friendly service in the old-fashioned and simple little rooms which have thick stone walls, a coal fire, and two constantly rotating guest ales such as Eccleshall HiDuck and Goose Eye Bitter; decent wines. Good bar food includes home-made soup, filled french bread (£3.95), fresh fish on Wednesdays such as local trout (£5.75), well liked gammon and eggs (£5.95), game casserole (£6.95) and home-made puddings. No smoking in dining room; no piped music or games machines. *(Recommended by Stephen Brown, Colin Barnes, Nigel Woolliscroft, Stephen, Julie and Hayley Brown, Roger and Christine Mash, James Nunns, John and Christine Lowe, Philip and Ann Falkner, J F West)*

Free house ~ Licensees Andrew Harmer and Penelope Hinchliffe ~ Real ale ~ Meals and snacks (not winter Mon) ~ Restaurant ~ (01260) 227217 ~ Children in family room ~ Open 12-3ish (maybe longer if busy), 7-11 (10.30 Sun); closed Monday Nov-Mar

WRENBURY SJ5948 Map 7

Dusty Miller

Village signposted from A530 Nantwich—Whitchurch

Perfectly positioned in a peaceful spot by the Llangollen branch of the Shropshire Union Canal and next to a striking counter-weighted drawbridge, this handsomely converted 19th-c mill is attractive and welcoming. The main area is comfortably modern, with a series of tall glazed arches facing the water, long low hunting prints on the white walls, and varied seating including tapestried banquettes, an ornate church pew and wheelback chairs flanking rustic tables. Further in, there's a quarry-tiled standing-only part by the bar counter, which has well kept Robinsons Best, Frederics, Hartleys XB, Old Stockport Old Tom on handpump. The good bar food includes home-made soup (£2.50), deep-fried feta cheese with cranberry sauce (£4.95), pizzas (from £4.75), oatcakes filled with spinach, mushrooms and garlic or beef and ale pie (£6.95), plaice stuffed with prawns, mushroom and lemon and baked cheese sauce (£7.50), ham and eggs (£7.95), steaks (from £9.25), puddings and children's menu; the upstairs dining area is no smoking. Dominoes and piped music. In summer it's pleasant to sit outside at the picnic-sets on a gravel terrace among rose bushes by the water; they're reached either by the towpath or by a high wooden catwalk above the River Weaver. *(Recommended by Paul and Maggie Baker, Sue and Bob Ward, Nigel Woolliscroft, E G Parish, Comus Elliott, David and Judy Walmsley)*

Robinsons ~ Tenant Mark Sumner ~ Real ale ~ Meals and snacks ~ Upstairs restaurant ~ (01270) 780537 ~ Children in eating area of bar ~ Open 11-3, 6-11; 12-3, 7-10.30 Sun

Lucky Dip

Besides the fully inspected pubs, you might like to try these Lucky Dips recommended to us and described by readers (if you do, please send us reports):

☆ **Acton Bridge** [Hilltop Rd; B5153 off A49 in Weaverham, then right towards Acton Cliff; SJ5975], *Maypole*: Civilised beamed dining pub very popular for wide choice of good varied generous food, roomy and pleasant dining area with lots of brass, copper and china, some antique settles as well as more modern furnishings, two coal fires, friendly staff, well kept Greenalls Bitter and Mild, gentle piped music; attractive outside with hanging baskets and tubs, seats in well kept garden with orchard behind *(Graham and Lynn Mason, John Mallen, LYM)*

Alpraham [Chester Rd (A51); SJ5959], *Tollemache Arms*: Good value family pub under enthusiastic new young licensees, farmhouse food all day, real ales inc Burtonwood Buccaneer; warm and comfortable, saloon being extended in style of ancient forge *(E G Parish, Graham and Lynn Mason)*; *Travellers Rest*: Particularly well kept Tetleys Bitter and Mild and McEwans 70/- in unchanging four-room country local in same family for three generations, leatherette, wicker and Formica, some flock wallpaper, fine old brewery mirrors, darts, back bowling green; no food, cl weekday lunchtimes *(E G Parish, Richard Lewis)*

Alsager [Station Rd; SJ7956], *Lodge*: Refurbished lounge with log fire, pool and games in busy bar with piped music, well kept ales such as Sam Allsopps, Greene King Abbot, Marstons Pedigree, Titanic Best, Premium and Bitter; happy hour Mon-Sat 5-6pm, reasonably priced bar food *(Richard Lewis)*; [Crewe Rd; SJ8048], *Plough*: Spacious Big Steak pub, low beams and country decor, good facilities for children (inside and out) and disabled, good service, well kept Marstons Pedigree and Tetleys; open all day *(Sue Holland, Dave Webster, Richard Lewis)*; [Crewe Rd], *Poachers Pocket*: Country-theme family pub in former mill, beams and lots of bric-a-brac, open fires, lounge bar, supervised indoor play area, upstairs bar and dining area, friendly staff, good menu, well kept Banks's and Camerons Strongarm; open all day; bedrooms *(Richard Lewis)*; [Sandbach Rd N], *Wilbraham Arms*: Large comfortable open-plan pub with well kept Hartleys XB and Robinsons Bitter and Hatters Mild from long bar, good choice of food, conservatory dining area, play area with pets corner; popular jazz Thurs *(Richard*

Lewis, Sue Holland, Dave Webster)
Alvanley [Manley Rd – OS Sheet 117 map ref 496740; SJ4974], *White Lion*: Remarkably wide changing choice of generous food from sandwiches up inc vegetarian and children's dishes in comfortable, civilised yet homely dining pub, friendly service, plush seats in low-ceilinged lounge, busy restaurant extension (booking recommended), games in smaller public bar, Greenalls Mild, Bitter and Original, tables and play area outside with some small farm animals *(Graham and Lynn Mason, LYM)*
Ashley [3 miles S of Altrincham – OS Sheet 109 map ref 776843; SJ7784], *Greyhound*: Roomy Greenalls pub with well organised family dining area, generous food (all day w/e), well kept Greenalls and Tetleys, decent wines, unlimited well served coffee; games room *(Geoffrey and Brenda Wilson, Mr and Mrs C Roberts)*
Ashton [B5393, off A54 nr Tarvin; SJ5169], *Golden Lion*: Pleasant village pub with well furnished three-tier lounge, well kept Greenalls and a guest beer, good food from sandwiches hot and cold through huge salad bowls to steaks and Sun lunch, very friendly staff; children in eating areas, popular with walkers *(Graham and Lynn Mason)*
Barbridge [just off A51 N of Nantwich; SJ6156], *Barbridge Inn*: Friendly and well run open-plan Greenalls Millers Kitchen family dining pub in pretty setting by lively marina at junction of Shropshire Union and Middlewich canals, with play area in busy riverside garden, conservatory, no-smoking area, usual hygienic food, well kept Boddingtons, Cains and weekend guest beers, games room, quiet piped music; good disabled facilities, open all day, quiz Tues, jazz Thurs, barbecue *(Graham and Lynn Mason, E G Parish, W C M Jones, Richard Lewis, LYM)*
Beeston [SJ5459], *Boars Head*: Imposing black and white hotel, superb if a little pricy bar food, fine restaurant, excellent service; bedrooms *(P J Taylor)*
Bell O Th Hill [just off A41 N of Whitchurch; SJ5245], *Blue Bell*: Cosy and attractive two-roomed heavily beamed country local with decent food, Sun papers, well kept real ales such as Hanby Drawwell, generous coffee, friendly dogs; piped music; nice garden, attractive surroundings *(Sue Holland, Dave Webster, LYM)*
Bickerton [Bulkeley; A534 E of junction with A41; SJ5052], *Bickerton Poacher*: Rambling old poacher-theme family pub with good reasonably priced food, well kept Greenalls Bitter and Original, good choice of food, open fires, friendly staff, copper-mining memorabilia, attractive barbecue extension around sheltered courtyard, play area and horseshoe quoits pitch; children welcome *(E G Parish, Richard Lewis, LYM)*
Bollington [Church St; SJ9377], *Church House*: Small friendly village pub with wide choice of good value quickly served lunchtime food, well kept Marstons and Tetleys, furnishings inc pews and working sewing-machine treadle tables, roaring fire, separate dining room; can book tables for busy lunchtimes *(Bill Sykes, Pat and Tony Young, Joanne Morris)*
☆ **Bottom of the Oven** [off A537 Buxton—Macclesfield, 1st left past Cat & Fiddle – OS Sheet 118 map ref 980723; SJ9872], *Stanley Arms*: Isolated moorland pub with cosy rooms, lots of shiny black woodwork, plush seats, dimpled copper tables, open winter fires, dining room (children allowed here), small choice of generous well cooked traditional food, well kept Marstons beers and a guest, piped music, picnic-sets on grass behind; may close Mon in winter if weather bad *(Leo and Barbara Lionet, Geoffrey and Irene Lindley, Nigel Woolliscroft, LYM)*
Bradfield Green [A530 NW of Crewe; SJ6859], *Coach & Horses*: Attractive cottagey pub with well kept Greenalls, good choice of very pleasantly served reasonably priced food, horse pictures, friendly staff; discreet piped music *(E G Parish)*
Brereton Green [set back off A50 2 m S of Holmes Chapel; SJ7864], *Bears Head*: Handsome and quite individual old heavily timbered inn, a long-standing main entry under its very long-serving Italian owners; but now taken over as a managed house by Bass – we await the results with some trepidation, as this has been such a favourite; bedrooms in modern block *(LYM)*
☆ **Brownlow** [off A34 S of Congleton; SJ8260], *Brownlow Inn*: Popular extended Whitbreads dining pub, exposed timbers and several alcoves, good range of food from good ploughman's up (busy lunchtime), Boddingtons and Flowers, choice of wines by the glass, reasonable prices, good service; handy for Little Moreton Hall *(Sue Holland, Dave Webster, Janet Pickles)*
Broxton [Nantwich Rd; A543, nr junction with A41; SJ4754], *Durham Heifer*: Welcoming and comfortable beamed dining pub with good food from usual pub dishes to particularly good fish, reasonable prices; small bar (can get quite crowded), good range of drinks, separate restaurant, unobtrusive piped music; pleasant views *(Graham and Lynn Mason)*
Burleydam [A525 Whitchurch—Audlem; SJ6143], *Combermere Arms*: 16th-c beamed pub with Bass, Worthington and guest beers from unusual circular bar, bar food from sandwiches up, jovial landlord, pub games and big indoor adventure play area, restaurant; piped music; open all day *(Nigel Woolliscroft, LYM)*
☆ **Chester** [Eastgate Row N], *Boot*: Lovely old Rows building, heavy beams, lots of woodwork, oak flooring and flagstones, even some exposed Tudor wattle and daub, black-leaded kitchen range in lounge beyond good value food servery, no-smoking oak-panelled upper area, good atmosphere and service, cheap well kept Sam Smiths; piped music may be rather loud, children allowed *(E G Parish,*

Martin Hickes, SLC, Rona Murdoch, Sue Holland, Dave Webster, LYM)

☆ **Chester** [Upper Northgate St], *Pied Bull*: Good atmosphere in roomy attractively furnished open-plan carpeted bar, attractive mix of individual furnishings, divided inner area with china cabinet and lots of pictures, nice snug by entrance, imposing intriguingly decorated fireplace; Greenalls Bitter and Original, attentive welcoming staff, wide choice of generous reasonably priced food inc afternoon teas (food Sun evening, too), no-smoking area; fruit machines, maybe piped music; handsome Jacobean stairs up to bedrooms *(Sidney and Erna Wells, SLC, BB)*

☆ **Chester** [Watergate St], *Watergates*: Wide range of quickly served good food from ploughman's up in lovely rambling medieval crypt, good wine list, espresso coffee machine, real ales such as Boddingtons and Cains, efficient service, candlelight, sturdy old tables; late evenings fills with young people and loud music *(Rona Murdoch, SLC, Andrew Hodges, BB)*

☆ **Chester** [Lower Bridge St], *Falcon*: Striking building with good bustling atmosphere, handsome beams and brickwork, well kept Sam Smiths, decent basic bar meals (not Sun), fruit machine, piped music; children allowed lunchtime (not Sat) in airy upstairs room; jazz Sat lunchtime, open all day Sat, interesting tours of the vaults; can get packed *(Sue Holland, Dave Webster, SLC, LYM)*

☆ **Chester** [Watergate St], *Old Custom House*: Traditional bare-boards bar well furnished with settles, high chairs and leatherette wall seats, lounge with cosy corners, prints, etchings, panelling and coal-effect gas fire, well kept Banks's, Marstons Bitter, Pedigree and Head Brewer's Choice, well reproduced piped music, fruit machine; open all day *(BB)*

Chester [94 Lower Bridge St], *Bear & Billet*: Handsome timbered building with interesting features and a lot of potential inc some attractive furnishings in open-plan bar; up to six real ales such as Boddingtons, Bushys Old Shunter, Theakstons Black Bull and Best; open fire, pool, piped pop music, TV; Indian restaurant upstairs; open all day *(SLC, BB)*; [Grosvenor Pk Terr, The Groves], *Boathouse*: Modern pub by River Dee next to rowing clubs, super views, large airy family room, good range of food promptly served to numbered tables, ales such as Morlands Old Speckled Hen, Ruddles County and Theakstons XB (more in back bar, which specialises in them), fruit machines; good disabled facilities; picnic-sets on small terrace *(SLC)*; [Lower Bridge St], *Clavertons*: Popular beamed cellar bar, cosy, comfortable and intimate, with friendly staff, enjoyable food noon-8, well kept Lees Best and Moonraker, local prints; piped music *(SLC)*; [Frodsham St], *Firkin & Fortress*: By canal, usual Firkin bare boards etc, sensibly priced usual food, SkyTV, upstairs bar for parties; open all day *(SLC)*; [Lower Bridge St], *Kings Head*: Ancient softly lit beamed Greenalls pub, bar food, restaurant, nice atmosphere; bedrooms *(SLC)*; [Milton St], *Mill*: Pleasantly relaxed real ale bar in ex-mill hotel, fine changing choice such as Coach House, Weetwood and Woods, friendly efficient staff, enjoyable bar food till late evening, good value Sun lunch, restaurant overlooking canal; piped music – some live; good with children, waterside tables, boat trips; bedrooms *(Derek and Sylvia Stephenson, Richard Lewis, SLC)*; [Bridge St], *Olde Vaults*: Panelling and leaded lights, well kept Greenalls, upstairs lounge *(Sue Holland, Dave Webster)*; [Tower Wharf, Raymond St – behind Northgate St, nr rly], *Telfords Warehouse*: Converted canal building, bare brick and boards, high pitched ceiling, big wall of windows overlooking water, massive iron winding gear in bar, some old enamelled advertisements, good photographs for sale; Courage Directors, Theakstons Best and XB and a guest such as Weetwood Old Dog, steps to heavy-beamed restaurant area with more artwork; live music Fri/Sat *(Bill Sykes, M Phillips, BB)*

Church Lawton [Liverpool Rd W; SJ8155], *Lawton Arms*: Recently refurbished homely two-room pub with welcoming licensees, lots of brass and pictures, Robinsons Best and (particularly popular here) Hatters Mild well kept, dining room with wide choice of popular food, traditional games; open all day Fri *(Richard Lewis)*

☆ **Comberbach** [off A553 and A559 NW of Northwich, pub towards Great Budworth; SJ6477], *Spinner & Bergamot*: Cosy plush beamed dining pub with log fire, hunting prints and toby jugs, softly lit back dining room with country-kitchen furniture and big inglenook, red-tiled public bar, usual food, well kept Greenalls Bitter, Original and Mild; piped music; picnic-sets on sloping lawn, lots of flowers, bowling green *(Keith and Judith Ashcroft, Ray Hebson, LYM)*

☆ **Cotebrook** [junction A49/B5152 N of Tarporley; SJ5765], *Alvanley Arms*: Handsome old creeper-covered Georgian inn with two rooms (one no smoking) off chintzy hall, big open fire, neat high beams, interesting sporting and other prints, plenty of tables, well kept Robinsons Mild and Best, decent house wines, several malt whiskies, good value waitress-served food from sandwiches to excellent fish (may be a wait unless you arrive early), attractive fairy-lit garden by pond with geese; children in restaurant; good value bedrooms *(Paul Barnett, John McDonald, Ann Bond, W C M Jones, SLC, S Williamson, David and Judy Walmsley, Mr and Mrs R Allan, Sue Holland, Dave Webster, LYM)*

☆ **Crewe** [Nantwich Rd (A534) opp rly stn; SJ7056], *Crewe Arms*: Victorian businessmen's hotel with comfortable and spacious lounge, marble-topped tables, alabaster figurines, period pictures, curtained alcoves, ornate ceiling; good pubby public bar with pool, well kept Ind Coope Burton or Tetleys, good value bar meals, popular

restaurant, friendly staff, open all day; bedrooms *(E G Parish, Richard Lewis)*
Crewe [1 Pedley St], *Albion*: Enjoyable corner local in area awaiting redevelopment, well kept Tetleys Bitter and Dark Mild and two ever-changing interesting guest beers, friendly staff, railway-theme lounge, lively bar with games and pool room; piped music, open 7(4 Mon, 2 Fri, 12 Sat)-11, 12-3, 7-10.30 Sun *(E G Parish, Richard Lewis, Sue Holland, Dave Webster)*; [Nantwich Rd], *Bank*: Bank to Banks's – conversion by them of spacious former Barclays, with their Bitter and Mild, friendly staff; piped music *(Richard Lewis)*; [58 Nantwich Rd], *British Lion*: Snug local known as the Pig, with comfortable partly panelled bar, back snug, well kept Tetleys-related ales and a guest such as Fullers London Pride, friendly staff; can get smoky when busy *(Sue Holland, Dave Webster, E G Parish, Richard Lewis)*; [71 Nantwich Rd], *Brunswick*: Two-floor Whitbreads Beer Engine pub with lots of bare wood, pool room, SkyTV sports, interesting guest beers, friendly staff; live music Thurs, quiz nights; busy w/e and evenings *(Richard Lewis)*; [332 Crewe Rd (B5071), Shavington], *Cheshire Cheese*: Comfortably refurbished Greenalls Millers Kitchen family dining pub, good friendly service, above-average bar food, OAP bargains, well kept Boddingtons, Greenalls Original, Tetleys and a guest beer, good disabled access, high chairs, baby-changing; tables outside, play area *(Richard Lewis, E G Parish)*; [25 Earle St], *Crown*: Sociable down-to-earth pub with busy main front bar, two lounges (service bell pushes), back games room with pool and juke box, drinking corridor; welcoming landlady and locals, well kept Robinsons, high ceilings, old-fashioned furnishings and wallpaper; handy for Railway Heritage Centre *(E G Parish, Sue Holland, Dave Webster, PB)*; [Nantwich Rd/Ruskin Rd], *Earl of Crewe*: Big mock-Tudor pub interestingly divided into small panelled areas, some curtained off with settles; lots of railway prints and beer memorabilia, good choice of ever-changing real ales kept well, good service, reasonably priced lunchtime food popular with older people; evenings more a young people's meeting place, busy esp weekends with loud music then *(E G Parish, Sue Holland, Dave Webster)*; [56 Earle St], *Kings Arms*: Several friendly rooms, nice tiling and panelling, well kept Whitbreads-related ales, pool, darts, dominoes and cribbage; very busy lunchtime, no food *(Sue Holland, Dave Webster)*; [Earle St], *Orient Express*: Reopened by Hydes, with their Best, Light and Mild (or a guest beer) kept very well, simple but roomy bar, back lounge, food inc Sun lunch, friendly atmosphere; live bands *(Richard Lewis)*; [Middlewich Rd (A530), Wolstanwood], *Rising Sun*: Well refurbished, with panelling, prints and comfortable seating in lots of separate areas, raised eating area, children's facilities; good service and bar food, well kept Greenalls, Tetleys and an interesting guest beer; tables and play area outside, open all day, good disabled access (inc lift), bedrooms *(E G Parish)*; [Weston Gate, Duchy Rd (A5020 SE)], *Rookery Wood*: Imposing new Tom Cobleigh family pub, plush and roomy open-plan lounge with Grecian marble effect, big bar, lots of wood, prints and artefacts, their usual menu inc children's, vegetarian and early-evening bargains, well kept ales such as Bass, Boddingtons, Morlands Old Speckled Hen and Worthington, log fire; lots of tables outside, supervised play area, friendly staff; open all day (but cl Sat if Crewe FC playing at home), good disabled facilites *(Richard Lewis, E G Parish)*; [Thomas St], *Sleepers*: Small compact bar with good choice of beers, good reasonably priced food at well spaced tables in dining room, good very friendly service, flowered terrace; bedrooms *(E G Parish)*; [240 Sydney Rd], *Sydney Arms*: Wide choice of bar food inc bargain daily roast, well kept ales, fast friendly service, garden with play area *(E G Parish)*; [Earle St], *Three Lamps*: Comfortably refurbished, lots of woodwork and attractive prints, relaxed atmosphere, friendly staff; back food area, well kept Banks's ales inc Mild; piped music, games machines, live music some nights; open all day, overlooking Town Lawn and handy for Lyceum Theatre *(E G Parish, Sue Holland, Dave Webster)*
Daresbury [Old Chester Rd; SJ5983], *Ring o' Bells*: Cosy and welcoming, with roaring log fire, good choice of reasonably priced good food inc vegetarian, well kept Greenalls Bitter, Original and Mild and a weekly guest beer, friendly efficient service, big garden and play area; short walk from canal; village church has window showing all the characters in *Alice in Wonderland*; bedrooms *(Dave and Deborah Irving, Sue Kelly)*
☆ **Dean Row** [102 Adlington Rd; SJ8781], *Unicorn*: Well enlarged, with roomy bar on left and lower no-smoking dining area on right, rustic stripped brickwork and stripped pine furniture, tempting generous food, friendly staff, Whitbreads-related ales, lots of tables in pleasant garden; children allowed, no dogs *(Dave and Deborah Irving)*
Disley [up side road by Rams Head Hotel; SJ9784], *White Horse*: Clean and civilised friendly local with well kept Robinsons, efficient service and enjoyable home-cooked food using fresh local produce – incredible value OAP lunches Mon and Thurs, very busy then *(Pat and Tony Young, R Davies)*; [A6], *White Lion*: Very well kept cheap Holts and Wilsons in relaxing refurbished pub with comfortable carpeted lounge areas off polished-floor bar area, glazed dark wood screens forming booths, back pool room, friendly staff, bar food; bedrooms *(Richard Lewis)*
Eaton [Beech Lane; the one nr Tarporley, at SJ5763], *Red Lion*: Nicely decorated comfortable country pub, pleasant restaurant, wide choice of good generous food inc

vegetarian, lots of sandwiches and OAP bargains, efficient service, no-smoking areas, separate bar with pool and darts, floodlit bowling green, barbecues and play area; well kept Greenalls and Stones, unobjectionable piped music; children welcome, open all day *(N Revell)*

☆ **Faddiley** [A534 Wrexham—Nantwich; SJ5753], *Thatch*: Attractive cottagey thatched, beamed and timbered dining pub, warm and comfortable, with particularly good food, pricy but worth it, from imaginative sandwiches (home-baked bread) to perfectly cooked main dishes and fresh puddings; popular with older people, with good friendly service, cosy open fire, well kept ales such as Courage Directors, John Smiths and Weetwood Old Dog; piped music may be intrusive, children welcome *(Bob Smith, E G Parish, Clive Gilbert, Sue Holland, Dave Webster, LYM)*

Frodsham [Chester Rd; SJ5278], *Netherton Arms*: Converted town-edge farmhouse popular for good imaginative food, with interesting real ales and good choice of wines; friendly attentive young staff *(Pat and Tony Hinkins)*

☆ **Frodsham** [Church St; SJ5278], *Rowlands*: Friendly single-roomed pub with several well kept quickly changing real ales (well over 1,000 in last five years), as well as bottled wheat beers and good choice of wines by the glass; sensibly short choice of good simple bar food, upstairs bistro, children welcome, open all day *(Richard Lewis, Andy and Jill Kassube, Derek and Sylvia Stephenson)*

☆ **Fullers Moor** [A534 – OS Sheet 117 map ref 500542; SJ5054], *Copper Mine*: Busy and comfortable dining pub, light and airy, with pine furnishings, interesting copper-mining memorabilia, pretty nooks and crannies, wide choice of well presented tasty food from big lunchtime sandwiches to good Sun lunches, well kept Bass and Burtonwood Best, friendly staff, children welcome; spacious garden with barbecues and lovely views; handy for Sandstone Trail *(Paul Robinshaw, Graham and Lynn Mason, Arthur and Margaret Dickinson, LYM)*

☆ **Gawsworth** [nr Macclesfield; SJ8969], *Harrington Arms*: Farm pub's two small rooms with bare wooden floorboards, fine carved bar counter, well kept Robinsons Best and Hatters Mild served in big old enamelled jugs, friendly service, benches on small front cobbled terrace *(Richard Lewis, JP, PP, LYM)*

Goostrey [Station Rd, towards A535; SJ7870], *Red Lion*: Friendly modernised open-plan bar and back family restaurant with enjoyable food, well kept Boddingtons, Tetleys and a guest beer, friendly efficient service, nice garden with play area; piped music, fruit machines, quiz night, videos, can seem a bit smoky; children welcome *(Derek Stafford, LYM)*

☆ **Great Budworth** [signed off A559 NE of Northwich; SJ6778], *George & Dragon*: Attractive 17th-c building in delightful village, rambling panelled lounge, beams hung with copper jugs, red plush button-back banquettes and older settles, no-smoking area, games in public bar, upstairs restaurant, sensibly priced bar food (generally good), well kept Tetleys and two weekly changing guest beers, farm cider, decent coffee, helpful service; children welcome, open all day Sat/Sun *(D S and A R Hare, Bill and Sheila McLardy, Andy and Jill Kassube, S P Watkin, P A Taylor, I Maw, Graham and Lynn Mason, S J Barber, Dr Oscar Puls, David and Judy Walmsley, LYM)*

Gurnett [just S of Macclesfield; SJ9271], *Olde Kings Head*: Split-level pub by Macclesfield Canal aqueduct (moorings), old-fashioned unlit kitchen range, very generous reasonably priced food, Banks's, Boddingtons and Camerons, great service *(Bill Sykes, S G Brown)*

Haslington [58 Crewe Rd; SJ7355], *Fox*: Roomy and hospitable village pub, very friendly, good food from well filled fresh sandwiches to original well presented hot dishes; real ale, good house wines, good helpful service; lavatories for the disabled *(E G Parish)*

☆ **Hassall Green** [SJ7858], *Romping Donkey*: Picturesque black-and-white pub by locks on Trent & Mersey Canal, with timbers, bevelled beams and ledged doors in delightful bar neatly furnished to match appearance; very civilised bar meals, Ansells real ale, welcoming atmosphere *(E G Parish, LYM)*

Haughton Moss [Long Lane; off A49 S of Tarporley; SJ5856], *Nags Head*: Friendly black and white pub with low beams, pristine furnishings, tempting food inc reasonably priced lunches, welcoming staff, real ales, big garden with unobtrusive play area, bowling green for hire; children welcome, no dogs *(E G Parish, Sue Holland, Dave Webster)*

Heatley [Mill Lane; SJ7088], *Railway*: Friendly former railway pub with four distinct rooms, good cheap bar food, particularly well kept Boddingtons and usually Timothy Taylor Landlord, topped up before being served; good soup and hot lunches, good fresh filled barm cakes other times *(M Smith)*

Hooton [A41 (Hooton crossroads); SJ3678], *Chimneys*: Recently refurbished Gothic-style hotel with handsomely made bar counter, conservatory, consistently well kept Bass-related beers, friendly staff, good food, good prices; comfortable bedrooms *(S J Biggins)*

☆ **Little Bollington** [the one nr Altrincham, 2 miles from M56 junction 7: A56 towards Lymm, then first right at Stamford Arms into Park Lane – use A556 to get back on to M56 westbound; SJ7286], *Swan With Two Nicks*: Busy refurbished beamed village pub full of brass, copper and bric-a-brac, cheerful atmosphere, snug alcoves, some antique settles, log fire, emphasis on popular generous food served quickly, well kept Whitbreads-related ales, tables outside; attractive hamlet by Dunham Hall deer park *(R Davies, Andy and Jill Kassube, LYM)*

☆ **Little Leigh** [A49, just S of A533; not far from

M56 junction 10; SJ6276], *Holly Bush*: Cosy thatched pub, good value food in no-smoking restaurant with busy young waitresses, pleasant friendly landlady, well kept Burtonwood and guest beers, traditional old-fashioned public bar; bedrooms *(Chris Walling, Graham and Lynn Mason, LYM)*
Little Stanney [Cheshire Oaks factory outlet village; SJ4174], *Cheshire Old Hall Farm*: Recently refurbished Banks's Milestone chain pub with good pub food, very pleasant helpful young staff, Banks's and Marstons ales, decent house wines; very busy lunchtime *(J F M West)*
Lymm [Eagle Brow; nr M6 junction 20; SJ6787], *Spread Eagle*: Character beamed village local with traditional decor, big comfortable lounge, cosy snug with real fire, cheery atmosphere, good freshly made reasonably priced lunches, particularly well kept Lees, juke box in public bar *(M Smith, Colin and Sue Graham)*
Macclesfield [Brook St; SJ9273], *Boar Hound*: Very well kept Robinsons Best and Hatters Mild in big comfortable local with two lounge areas, bar and separate pool room, friendly welcome and busy landlord *(Richard Lewis)*; [27 Churchwallgate], *Castle*: Firmly run deceptively big pub with small public bar, two lounges and end glass-roofed area up steps, well kept Courage Directors and Theakstons Bitter and Mild, simple lunchtime food *(Richard Lewis, JP, PP, BB)*; [Mill St], *Filigree & Firkin*: Three well kept Firkin ales and a farm cider, usual Firkin decor, big screen TV, games machines, daily papers, friendly staff; open all day *(Richard Lewis)*; [Waters Green], *Millstone*: Large Marstons pub with their beers inc seasonal kept very well, interesting glass partitions, separate comfortable lounge areas off bar, back pool room, friendly staff and locals; open all day *(Richard Lewis)*; [Waters Green], *Queens*: Recently taken over by Holts and superbly restored, two big rooms with high ceilings, comfortable plush seating, friendly staff and locals, and well kept Bitter and Mild at wonderfully low prices; open all day *(Richard Lewis)*; [Byrons Lane], *Railway View*: Good range of unusual changing ales in pair of 1700 cottages knocked into roomy pub with lots of intimate attractively furnished areas, farm cider, good choice of food, friendly staff and locals; back terrace overlooking railway, remarkably shaped gents'; cl lunchtime Mon-Thurs *(Richard Lewis, P A Legon)*; [Coronation St], *Travellers Rest*: Two big lounges, popular good value weekday lunches, well kept Robinsons Best and Hatters Mild, friendly staff and locals; bedrooms *(Richard Lewis)*; [96 Waters Green], *Waters Green*: Boddingtons and three interesting quickly changing guest beers kept very well, basic layout with back and side lounges, lunchtime bar food (not Sun), friendly staff and locals; may get smoky; open all day *(Richard Lewis)*
Marston [Ollershaw Lane; SJ6775], *Salt Barge*: Bright and friendly extended pub by Trent & Mersey Canal, reasonably priced food running up to ostrich, well kept Burtonwood Top Hat and Buccaneer *(Dr P A Sutton, Joan and Michel Hooper-Immins)*
☆ **Mobberley** [opp church; SJ7879], *Church*: Recently comfortably refurbished, with more emphasis on its wide choice of good value food, but keeping friendly atmosphere and style; well kept Greenalls, big log fire, cheerful service; tables outside, play area, own bowling green; children welcome *(Leo and Barbara Lionet)*
Mobberley [Knolls Green (B5085 towards Alderley)], *Bird in Hand*: Cosy low-ceilinged rooms with comfortably cushioned heavy wooden seats, warm coal fires, small pictures on Victorian wallpaper, little panelled snug, no-smoking top dining area, promptly served food from sandwiches up, summer afternoon teas, helpful staff, well kept Sam Smiths, lots of malt whiskies, pub games; occasional piped music; children allowed, open all day *(Philip and Ann Falkner, Dr Jim Mackay, Dr and Mrs J H Hills, LYM)*; [Pepper St – Ashley rd out towards Altrincham], *Chapel House*: Small, clean and comfortable, nicely carpeted, darkish woodwork, upholstered stools and wall settles, short choice of good value simple lunchtime food (not Sun/Mon) inc superb chips, good friendly service, well kept Boddingtons, two open fires, small games room; courtyard seats *(Mr and Mrs C Roberts)*; [Faulkners Lane], *Frozen Mop*: Brewers Fayre dining pub with good food, well kept Boddingtons, Marstons Pedigree and Whitbreads Fuggles Imperial, cheerful friendly service, family area *(Mr and Mrs C Roberts)*
☆ **Nantwich** [51 Beam St; SJ6552], *Red Cow*: Well renovated former Tudor farmhouse, good relaxed atmosphere, smallish lounge and bar, no-smoking dining area, good range of good value home-made food esp vegetarian, also children's and weekday OAP bargain lunch, well kept Robinsons Best, Mild, Old Tom, Frederics and Hartleys XB, real fire; back pool table *(E G Parish, SLC, Sue Holland, Dave Webster, Chris Gabbitas, Hugh McPhail)*
☆ **Nantwich** [Hospital St – by side passage to central church], *Lamb*: Warmly civilised hotel bar with leather chesterfields and other comfortable seats, well kept Burtonwood Forshaws, decent malt whiskies, good value nicely served generous home-cooked food inc outstanding fish and chips in bar and traditional upstairs dining room, welcoming attentive staff, unobtrusive piped music; bedrooms *(E G Parish, Sue Holland, Dave Webster, Olive and Ray Hebson, BB)*
Nantwich [The Gullet, behind church], *Bowling Green*: Well set in pedestrian area, beams and panelling, good choice of reasonably priced food, well kept Scottish Courage ales, friendly staff; side pool room, piped music, games machine, can get smoky w/e; back garden with lots of tables *(Richard*

Lewis); [A530 towards Middlewich], *Farmhouse*: Large family dining pub with wide food choice, prompt friendly service *(Janet Pickles)*; [4 Oatmarket], *Frog & Ferret*: Fine choice of well kept ales, some tapped from the cask, lunchtime food, friendly young staff, front terrace; piped music, games; open all day (Sun afternoon closure) *(Richard Lewis, SLC)*; [97 Welsh Row], *Oddfellows Arms*: Low ceilings, real fires, friendly service, Burtonwood ales, reasonably priced food inc vegetarian, garden; lovely street, antique shops *(Sue Holland, Dave Webster)*; [221 Crewe Rd (A534)], *Peacock*: Roomy and comfortable Greenalls Millers Kitchen family dining pub, good helpings of decent food, friendly staff, well kept ales with a guest such as Caledonian 80/-, big lawn with lots of picnic-sets and good play area; facilities for disabled, open all day; bedrooms behind *(Richard Lewis)*; [Welsh Row], *Wilbraham Arms*: Family-run, with real ales and food in recently refurbished bars; bedrooms *(E G Parish)*

Neston [19 Quayside; down track SW of Little Neston – OS Sheet 117 map ref 290760; SJ2976], *Harp*: Charming tiny old pub in marvellous spot by ruined quay on the Burton Marshes looking out over the River Dee to Wales; cosy beamed and tiled-floor bar with real fire, simple comfortable lounge, well kept ales such as Chesters Mild, Flowers IPA, Whitbreads Trophy and Timothy Taylor Landlord, friendly landlord, good straightforward bar food lunchtime and early evening inc Sun roast; plenty of seats outside with play area, open all day from noon *(Richard Lewis)*

No Mans Heath [A41 N of Whitchurch; SJ5148], *Wheatsheaf*: Civilised and chatty, with low beams, lots of pictures, brasses, wrought iron, comfortable seats, cosy fires, friendly staff, well kept Bass, Ruddles County, Theakstons Best and Worthington Best, proper food; piped music; play area in garden *(Sue and Bob Ward)*

☆ **Ollerton** [A537; SJ7877], *Dun Cow*: Attractive country pub recently reopened after refurbishment, small snug rooms, two fine log fires (and they've kept the famous suit of armour), good choice of food (booking advised for restaurant), really pleasant welcoming service, well kept Greenalls and a guest such as Shepherd Neame Spitfire, decent wines; no longer open all day *(E G Parish, Leo and Barbara Lionet, Douglas Miller, LYM)*

☆ **Over Peover** [off A50 S of Knutsford; SJ7674], *Olde Park Gate*: Quiet comfort in immaculate small black-beamed rooms with some attractive furnishings inc fine Macclesfield oak chairs and lots of pictures, lounge with dining area (good sensibly priced food), well kept cheap Sam Smiths, warmly welcoming service, darts in locals' back room; family room, tables outside *(Leo and Barbara Lionet, B Adams, BB)*

Over Peover [Stocks Lane, by A50], *Whipping Stocks*: Several rooms, good oak panelling and fittings, solid furnishings, well kept cheap Sam Smiths, popular straightforward food from good sandwiches up; can be dominated weekday lunchtime by people from nearby Barclays Bank regional HQ, but relaxing evenings; children in eating area, picnic-sets in garden with safe play area, easy parkland walks *(J F M West, Dave Braisted, BB)*

☆ **Parkgate** [1 The Parade, Parkgate Rd (B5135); village signed off A540; SJ2878], *Boathouse*: Black and white timbered dining pub with several interesting connecting rooms and big dining conservatory (booking needed weekends), spectacular views to Wales over silted grassy estuary behind, usual generous food inc children's, efficient young staff, well kept Greenalls, Tetleys and guest beers; nearby marshes good for birdwatchers *(Liz Bell, R Moorehead)*

Parkgate [The Parade], *Old Quay*: Roomy modern single-storey Brewers Fayre family dining pub facing Dee and Welsh hills, comfortable banquettes, sensible tables, old prints, big picture windows, food all day, helpful staff, Whitbreads Castle Eden; indoor play area *(Richard Lewis, R Moorehead)*; [Boathouse Lane (B5135)], *Parkgate Hotel*: Cosily furnished country house hotel well placed on Dee estuary, stylish pubby bar, warm welcome, good value tasty food, sensible drinks prices, good wines and service; comfortable bedrooms *(R Moorehead)*; [The Parade], *Red Lion*: Comfortable and welcoming Victorian-feel pub on attractive waterfront with same great view, good value sandwiches and home-cooked main dishes, well kept Tetleys-related ales, 19th-c paintings and beer-mug collection, open fire, good service, darts and pool; chatty parrot called Nelson *(Richard Lewis, R Moorehead)*

☆ **Plumley** [Plumley Moor Lane; off A556 by the Smoker; SJ7175], *Golden Pheasant*: Very friendly management (6th generation), wide choice of food inc interesting dishes, well kept Lees Bitter and Mild, spacious series of comfortably modernised rooms, roomy restaurant and conservatory overlooking back children's garden, pub gardens and bowling green; children welcome, good well equipped bedrooms *(E G Parish, LYM)*

Poynton [Shrigley Rd N, Higher Poynton, off A523; SJ9283], *Boars Head*: Doing well under current licensee, welcoming walkers (good area), with Boddingtons and a guest such as Wadworths 6X; popular midweek lunchtime with pensioners from nearby golf club *(Brian and Anna Marsden)*

Prestbury [SJ9077], *Legh Arms*: Striking long heavy-beamed 16th-c building with lots of woodwork, gallery, smart atmosphere, tables laid with cloths and cutlery in main dining bar, wide choice of food inc decent sandwiches and vegetarian, cosy comfortable separate lounge bar, well kept Robinsons Best and Frederics, friendly service; open all day, children welcome *(E G Parish)*

☆ **Rainow** [NE of village on A5002 Whaley Bridge—Macclesfield; SJ9576], *Highwayman*:

Timeless unchanging moorside pub with small rooms, low 17th-c beams, good winter fires (electric other times), plenty of atmosphere, lovely views; Thwaites real ales, bar food inc good sandwiches, rather late opening *(JP, PP, Philip and Ann Falkner, LYM)*

Sandbach [High St; SJ7661], *Old Black Bear*: 16th-c black and white thatched pub, low beams, panelling, well kept Marstons Pedigree and Tetleys, Addlestone's cider, convivial bar, sectioned-off dining areas with ample reasonably priced food, friendly staff; games machines and juke box, busy on Thurs market day *(E G Parish, Richard Lewis)*

Scholar Green [off A34 N of Kidsgrove, towards Mow Cop; SJ8356], *Rising Sun*: Good country-pub atmosphere, generous good value home-made food, friendly service, well kept Marstons Bitter and Pedigree, family room, small no-smoking dining room; separate games room, unobtrusive piped music *(Bill Sykes, Richard and Anne Lewis, Kate and Robert Hodkinson)*

Scholar Green [Congleton Rd (A34)], *Bleeding Wolf*: Popular thatched pub, cosy and comfortable separate areas inc carvery and conservatory, lots of wood and brass, good menu, well kept Robinsons Best, Hatters Mild and Hartleys XB *(Richard Lewis)*

Shocklach [off A534 from Wrexham at crossrds with Farndon; SJ4449], *Bull*: Good food inc interesting dishes and wide range of puddings, changing daily, conservatory; can be very busy *(Rita and Keith Pollard)*

Smallwood [Newcastle Rd (A50)], *Bulls Head*: Attractive interestingly decorated dining pub, neat and tidy, with lots of space inc two conservatories, and particularly good garden with play area; well kept Marstons Pedigree, decent wines, good choice of well presented generous food inc interesting salads and excellent puddings, welcoming service; piped music, children welcome; plants for sale, quite handy for Biddulph Grange (NT) *(R C Vincent, LYM)*

Sproston Green [nr M6 junction 18 – A54 towards Middlewich; SJ7367], *Fox & Hounds*: Pleasant modernised pub with good choice of food and Greenalls beers *(Dick Brown)*

Sutton [Higher Sutton, off A54 Congleton—Buxton, 2¾ miles E of A523 – OS Sheet 118 map ref 942694; SJ9469], *Ryles Arms*: Large popular dining pub in fine countryside, wide choice of food from sandwiches to game in season, no-smoking dining area and family room, some attractively individual furnishings, french windows to terrace, well kept Coach House Best, Marstons Pedigree, and Ruddles Best and County, good choice of whiskies, welcoming long-serving Irish landlord, no music or games *(Jackie Lawler, LYM)*

Swettenham [off A54 Congleton—Holmes Chapel or A535 Chelford—Holmes Chapel; SJ8067], *Swettenham Arms*: Attractive and prettily placed old country pub with wide choice of popular food efficiently served in charming series of individually furnished rooms inc no-smoking dining area (must book Sun), well kept Greenalls Original and Tetleys, picnic-sets on quiet side lawn; children welcome, live music Weds; loses its place among the main entries this year only through a relative lack of readers' reports *(JFMW, Dr Jim Mackay, JP, PP)*

☆ **Tarporley** [50 High St (off A49); SJ5563], *Swan*: Tastefully modernised Georgian inn with cosy little spaces, well kept Ruddles and three guests such as Adnams, Charles Wells Bombardier and Jennings, bottled Belgian beers, lots of malt whiskies, civilised informal brasserie with rather smart food inc superb goat cheeses (also lunchtime sandwiches and snacks), separate restaurant, polite service; tables outside, provision for children; comfortable well equipped bedrooms *(Derek and Sylvia Stephenson, E Parish, M Joyner, Sue Holland, Dave Webster, LYM)*

☆ *nr* **Tiverton** [Wharton's Lock, Bates Mill Lane – OS Sheet 117 map ref 532603; SJ5660], *Shady Oak*: Canalside country pub with plenty of seats and good play area in waterside garden and terrace, fine view of Beeston Castle, airy lounge, small carpeted conservatory, pleasant young licensee, well kept Scottish Courage ales, decent generous Chef & Brewer food all day, summer barbecues, moorings *(Graham and Lynn Mason, LYM)*

Walgherton [London Rd; A51 between Bridgemere Gdn Centre and Stapeley Water Gdns; SJ6949], *Boars Head*: Large family pub with local farming-theme decor, pleasant layout of small dining areas, prints and boars' heads, nice conservatory, generous quick food all day from sandwiches up, Boddingtons and Greenalls, friendly young uniformed staff, games; big garden with children's play area; bedrooms *(E G Parish, Sue and Bob Ward)*

☆ **Walker Barn** [A537 Macclesfield—Buxton; SJ9573], *Setter Dog*: Warm, clean and civilised stonebuilt pub with windswept moors view, well kept real ales such as Bass, Marstons and Timothy Taylor Landlord in small pubby bar, small separate restaurant with appetising food inc good value roasts, good friendly service, roaring fire; handy for Teggs Nose Country Park, open all day *(Dave and Deborah Irving)*

☆ **Warmingham** [School Lane; SJ7161], *Bears Paw*: Good food inc lots of specials and enormous filled baguettes, plush seating around marble-top tables in raised areas, well kept Bass, Boddingtons, Flowers IPA and Marstons Pedigree, relaxed atmosphere, friendly and helpful staff, charming restaurant, pool room, children very welcome; good spot by river and ancient church in small hamlet, seats in front garden *(E G Parish)*

☆ *nr* **Warrington** [Fiddlers Ferry; leave A562 in Penketh – park in Station rd off Tannery Lane – OS Sheet 108 map ref 560863], *Ferry*: Picturesquely isolated between St Helens Canal and Mersey, four well kept real ales inc very quickly changing guest beers, over 100 whiskies, good home-cooked food in nice upstairs dining room (not Sun evening), friendly service, cosy low-beamed bar, log fires, provision for children; tables outside with play area, pets corner, pony paddock *(Mike and Mary Carter, LYM)*

☆ **Waverton** [A41 S of Chester; SJ4663], *Black Dog*: Clean and inviting old Greenalls dining pub done out in modern pine and light oak style, good choice of popular food, real ales inc guests, cordial licensees, big tasteful lounge, small garden; occasional jazz evenings, piped music *(SLC, Graham and Lynn Mason)*

Weaverham [SJ6274], *Wheatsheaf*: Well kept beer, good food and wine, good atmosphere *(G Washington)*

Wheelock [SJ7559], *Commercial*: Old-fashioned unspoilt four-room local, one no smoking, high ceilings, Boddingtons, Thwaites and a guest beer, real fire, firmly efficient service; pool, occasional informal live music *(Sue Holland, Dave Webster)*

Whiteley Green [Hole House Lane – OS Sheet 118 map ref 924789; SJ9278], *Windmill*: Roomy modernised lounge and partly no-smoking dining area, Tetleys and a guest such as Morlands Old Speckled Hen, newspapers, friendly service, bar food from lunchtime sandwiches up inc good vegetarian dishes and popular themed food nights; provision for children; spacious attractive garden with summer bar and barbecues, nice countryside with canal and other walks *(R F Grieve, Rev John Hibberd, BB)*

Wildboarclough [OS Sheet 118 map ref 982685; SJ9868], *Crag*: Old stonebuilt pub hidden in charming little sheltered valley below the moors, pleasant genuine welcome, well kept beer, enjoyable food in bar and restaurant; plastic shoe covers in the entrance porch for ramblers, pretty terrace *(Dave and Deborah Irving, LYM)*

Willaston [Newcastle Rd, Blakelow – OS Sheet 118 map ref 680517; SJ6851], *Horseshoe*: Panelled lounge with fire, dining room and no-smoking restaurant extension, public bar, decent food, Robinsons; garden with swings *(Sue Holland, Dave Webster)*

☆ **Willington Corner** [Boothsdale, off A54 at Kelsall; SJ5367], *Boot*: Good interesting food (all day w/e) from sandwiches, vegetarian and children's dishes to pheasant casserole, fresh veg, charming restaurant with log fire, friendly helpful service, very acceptable prices, Greenalls and guest ales; lovely views, picnic-sets on terrace, handy for the picturesque walking area known locally as Little Switzerland *(Mrs K Forber, Graham and Lynn Mason, Mrs P J Carroll)*

☆ **Wilmslow** [Rex Buildings; SJ8481], *Samuel Finney*: Well done pastiche of comfortable Victorian pub, sharing converted old cinema with addictive bookshop; darkish wood, various alcoves and levels, very friendly good service, separate areas of counter for beer, wine, orthodox food inc sandwiches, and their speciality cheese and pickles – generous good value *(Mr and Mrs C Roberts, J F M West, Dave and Deborah Irving)*

Wilmslow [A34], *King William*: Robinsons pub with cosy alcoves opening off bar, well kept real ales, lunchtime food, friendly atmosphere; children welcome *(Dave and Deborah Irving)*

Winnington [off A533 NW of Northwich; SJ6474], *Winnington Hall*: Formerly ICI Club, and in centre of ICI complex – founders' home, part 16th c, with a 1780 wing with appropriate decor, and a Victorian section; bar open to the public 12-3, 5-11 (cl Sun evening), restaurant Fri/Sat evening, Sun lunchtime; good fresh well chosen modestly priced food, remarkable low-priced wine list *(Stephen Williamson)*

☆ **Wistaston** [Nantwich Rd; SJ6853], *Old Manor*: Former mansion, now a comfortable olde-worlde dining pub with reliable food inc children's, pleasing service, pubby atmosphere, Bass, Stones and Worthington; supervised playroom *(E G Parish)*

☆ **Wybunbury** [Main Rd (B5071); SJ6950], *Swan*: Well run bow-windowed pub with nooks and crannies in rambling lounge, snug dining areas, pleasant public bar, well kept Marstons, Boddingtons, Thwaites and two interesting guest beers, enjoyable reasonably priced home cooking, warmly welcoming staff, tasteful furnishings inc plenty of bric-a-brac – shop at the back; seats in garden by beautiful churchyard; bedrooms *(E G Parish, Sue Holland, Dave Webster, Graham and Lynn Mason, SLC, LYM)*

Post Office address codings confusingly give the impression that some pubs are in Cheshire, when they're really in Derbyshire (and therefore included in this book under that chapter) or in Greater Manchester (see the Lancashire chapter).

Cornwall

We've never been able to understand why it is that some years – and this changes year by year – some parts of the country seem quite dull from a pub point of view, while others really shine. For Cornwall's pubs, this is certainly a vintage year: lots of character and interest, friendly licensees, some fine positions, and food markedly better than it used to be. No wonder readers have been reaching for the superlatives in their reports to us. This success is reflected in the number of new entries (or pubs back among them after an absence): the friendly Old Ferry in its most attractive position at Bodinnick; the Olde Plough House at Duloe (neat, comfortable and relaxed, with an emphasis on food); the unpretentious Lamorna Wink at Lamorna, just a stroll up from the cove; the ancient Bush at Morwenstow, one of the county's most interesting pubs, its kind landlady doing good simple home-made food; the friendly and attractive Old Mill House in Polperro, a really nice find in that honeypot of a seaside village; and the well set Port Gaverne Hotel near Port Isaac. Other pubs on peak form here this year are the Maltsters Arms at Chapel Amble (gaining a Star Award for all-round enjoyment), the Trengilly Wartha near Constantine (unanimous praise all round – it gains a coveted Food Award this year, and is our choice as Cornwall Dining Pub of the Year), the Earl of St Vincent at Egloshayle (good food and atmosphere, nice collections), the Royal Oak in Lostwithiel (pleasant country feel in a town pub, good all round), the Crown at St Ewe (particularly popular for food), the Victory at St Mawes (an exemplary seaside local), the Springer Spaniel at Treburley (very well run, good all round – the only other Cornish pub with a Food Award) and the Old Ale House in Truro (huge choice of real ales, nice bustling atmosphere, enjoyable food). Other places we'd pick out for an enjoyable meal include the Halzephron south of Helston, the Halfway House at Kingsand, the friendly Crown at Lanlivery (some refurbishment, but just as much character as before), the White Hart at St Keverne (lots of improvements under very hard-working newly wed licensees), and the engaging Eliot Arms at Tregadillett (a barometer collection starting, to join all the other things there). There are quite a few changes of licensee here this year, with consequent changes in style. Among them, that ace landlady Mo Law, who won lots of friends for the China House in Plymouth when she was there, has now crossed the water to the beautifully set Edgcumbe Arms at Cremyll. There's an excellent choice of pubs in the Lucky Dip section at the end of the chapter, too. Padstow in particular has several good ones, as do Fowey and Polperro. The Napoleon at Boscastle and Rising Sun at St Mawes both stand out, and others doing well at the moment (almost all inspected and approved by us, too) are the Borough Arms just outside Bodmin, Falcon in Bude, Chain Locker in Falmouth, Ferryboat at Helford Passage, Fox & Hounds at Lanner, Ship at Lerryn, Top House at Lizard, Olde Salutation in Looe, Bullers Arms at Marhamchurch, Red Lion at Mawnan Smith, Fort in Newquay, Notter Bridge at Notter, Punch Bowl & Ladle at Penelewey, Royal Oak at Perranwell, Weary Friar at Pillaton, Lugger at Portloe, Logan Rock at Treen, Wig & Pen in Truro, New Inn at Veryan and Tinners Arms at Zennor, with several worthwhile places on the Isles of Scilly. Drinks prices here are close to the national average, with pubs supplied by the local St Austell brewery usually rather cheaper; good beers from another much smaller and newer local brewer, Sharps, are now widely available here, and this year we enjoyed our first taste of yet another new local brew, Cornish Rebellion. Our cheapest pubs for beer were the Lugger at Polruan, Cobweb at Boscastle, Ship at Mousehole and Old Mill House in Polperro. The Blue Anchor in Helston, which brews its own, has now refurbished its ancient back brewhouse (as well as the bars), and is distributing its interesting ales to other pubs.

BODINNICK SX1352 Map 1

Old Ferry Inn

On a steep slope close to the River Fowey, this friendly old inn has three simply furnished little rooms with wheelback chairs, built-in plush pink wall seats, an old high-backed settle, quite a few bits of nautical memorabilia, a couple of half model ships mounted on the wall, and several old photographs. The games room at the back is actually hewn into the rock and has darts, dominoes, and piped music. Bar food includes good home-made daily specials such as stilton and leek pasta bake, various curries, and pies such as fish, steak in ale or venison (all from £5.95), as well as more straightforward things such as home-made soup (£2.95), sandwiches (from £2.05; toasties 25p extra), ploughman's (from £4.95), quite a few dishes with chips (from £2.95; home-cooked ham and egg £3.95), chicken tikka masala (£5.95), rump steak (£6.95), and children's meals (from £1.95); the restaurant is no smoking. Well kept Sharps Own on handpump kept under light blanket pressure. Make sure your brakes work well if you park on the steep lane outside. Some of the bedrooms look out over the river. *(Recommended by A J Thomas, J and F Gowers, Mr and Mrs D Humphries)*

Free house ~ Licensees Royce and Patricia Smith ~ Real ale ~ Meals and snacks ~ Restaurant ~ (01726) 870237 ~ Children welcome ~ Open 11-11; 12-10.30 Sun; 11-3, 6-11 in winter ~ Bedrooms: £30(£55B)/£40(£60B)

BOSCASTLE SX0990 Map 1

Cobweb

B3263, just E of harbour

In a pretty village close to the tiny steeply cut harbour, this bustling old pub is friendly to locals and visitors alike and has plenty of atmosphere in its lively public bar where hundreds of old bottles hang from the heavy beams; there are also two or three curved high-backed winged settles against the dark stone walls, a few leatherette dining chairs, and a cosy log fire. Well kept Bass, Greene King Abbot, St Austell Tinners, HSD, and guest beers on handpump, and several malt whiskies. Bar food (with prices unchanged since last year) includes sandwiches (from £1.50), ploughman's (from £3.25), vegetarian dishes or a daily roast (£4.50), steaks (from £7), and mixed grill (£9.75); the restaurant is no smoking. Darts, pool, dominoes, cribbage, video game, fruit machine, and juke box; the big communicating family room has an enormous armchair carved out of a tree trunk as well as its more conventional windsor armchairs, and another winter fire. Opening off this is a good-sized children's room and more machines. *(Recommended by Keith Stevens, John and Vivienne Rice, David Carr, Barry and Anne, Mr and Mrs P Stubbs, Jo and Gary Charlton, Val Stevenson, Rob Holmes, Ann and Colin Hunt, Wayne Wheeler, Barry Perfect)*

Free house ~ Licensees Ivor and Adrian Bright ~ Real ale ~ Meals and snacks (11.30-2.30, 6-10) ~ Restaurant ~ (01840) 250278 ~ Children in own room ~ Live entertainment Sat evening ~ Open 11-11

CHAPEL AMBLE SW9975 Map 1

Maltsters Arms ★ 🍷

Village signposted from A39 NE of Wadebridge; and from B3314

Readers have consistently enjoyed their visits to this well run, friendly pub, particularly over this past year, so we have decided to award the pub a star this year. The attractively knocked-together rooms have a relaxed, pleasant atmosphere, black oak joists in the white ceiling, partly panelled stripped stone walls, heavy wooden tables on the partly carpeted big flagstones, and a large stone fireplace; the bar extension is hung with ship pictures and a growing collection of seafaring memorabilia. There's also a no-smoking side room with windsor chairs and a no-smoking upstairs family room. Popular bar food includes lunchtime sandwiches, home-made soup (£2.25), sardines fried in garlic butter (£3.95 or £7.95), lunchtime ploughman's (from £4.25), Cornish crab cocktail (£4.95), cottage pie (£4.50), vegetable curry (£4.95), squat lobster tails in breadcrumbs (£7.25), pasta with roasted vegetables and black olives (£7.95), sirloin steak (£8.95), chicken livers with mustard, sherry and cream (£9.25), skate wing with capers and parsley (£10.25); they also do afternoon cream teas (£2.50) and a Sunday lunchtime carvery (£5.25); good, attentive service. The main restaurant is no smoking. Well kept Sharps Cornish, Maltsters Special (brewed specially for the pub by Sharps), and Everards Beacon Bitter, Ruddles County, and Wadworths 6X on handpump kept under light blanket pressure; 21 wines by the glass and 21 malt whiskies. Cribbage, dominoes, backgammon, and piped music. Benches outside in a sheltered sunny corner, and pretty hanging baskets and tubs. *(Recommended by Peter and Daphne Ross, Mr and Mrs S Groves, John Barker, M J Dowdy, R and S Bentley, D Martin, David Carr, Graham Tayar, Catherine Raeburn, John Westlake, D R Eberlin, M G Hart, M Borthwick, D B Jenkin, Ted George, C P Scott-Malden, John and Jackie Chalcraft, I H Baker, P H Boot, M A Borthwick, Mr and Mrs M N Greenwood, Mr and Mrs B Hobden, Pamela and Merlyn Horswell, Mr and Mrs A C Curry, Andy and Jill Kassube, Iain Robertson, Rita Horridge, Ian Wilson, Mr and Mrs G McNeill, Jenny and Brian Seller, Val Stevenson, Rob Holmes, Brian Skelcher)*

Free house ~ Licensees David and Marie Gray and David Coles ~ Real ale ~ Meals and snacks ~ Restaurant ~ (01208) 812473 ~ Children in family room and in restaurant (must be over 8) ~ Open 10.30-11; 12-10.30 Sun; 10.30-2.30, 6-11 in winter; closed evening 25 Dec

CONSTANTINE SW7229 Map 1

Trengilly Wartha ★ 🍴 🍷 🍺 🛏

Constantine signposted from Penryn—Gweek rd (former B3291); in village turn right just before Minimarket (towards Gweek); in nearly a mile pub signposted left; at Nancenoy, OS sheet 204, map reference 731282

Cornwall Dining Pub of the Year

Unanimous praise again from a wide mix of our readers for this extremely well run inn, tucked away down narrow lanes. Families have felt genuinely welcomed, the range of beers from local breweries changes constantly, the food is imaginative and very good, the atmosphere most enjoyable – and it's a particularly nice place to stay. The low-beamed main bar has a woodburning stove and modern high-backed settles boxing in polished heavy wooden tables, and the lounge has cushioned wall benches, a log fire and some harness. Up a step from the bar is an eating area with winged settles and tables, and there's also a bright no-smoking conservatory family room. Super bar food (we've added a Food Award to their list this year) includes weekly changing specials like smoked mackerel and cheese pot (£3.50), good mixed fried fish (£4), pork and cider sausages (£4.20), king prawns in a saffron beer batter (£4.50), mediterranean cassoulet with mixed pulses and harissa mash (£6), baked cod fillet on a bed of caramelised onions (£7.30) or pork and apricot with a cider, grain mustard and apricot cream sauce (£7.80), as well as home-made soup (£2.30), meaty or vegetarian pasty (£3.30), their own sausage or pâté such as chicken liver and port or devon blue cheese and walnut (£3.80), ploughman's (from £4.50), shank of lamb braised in a sherry and anise flavoured gravy (£6.80), stir-frys (from £7.60), crab cakes (£9.30), and home-made puddings such as steamed chocolate and orange pudding, treacle tart or a plate of 6 in miniature (from £2.60); they do a children's menu (from £2.40) but will give small helpings of adult food where possible and have marked the weekly specials with a smiley face to indicate dishes that are more appropriate to smaller appetites. On winter Wednesday evenings they do a bargain home-made steak and kidney pudding and a pint of beer offer (£5.40); good breakfasts with home-made jam and marmalade. They keep an unusually wide choice of drinks for the area, such as well kept Ind Coope Burton, Keltek Golden Lance and King (a new local brewery), St Austell HSD, and Sharps Cornish on handpump with regularly changing ales from smaller brewers tapped from the cask such as Cotleigh Tawny, Exmoor Gold, Gibbs Mew Bishops Tipple, Hook Norton, Otter Bright, Smiles, and so forth. Also, over 50 malt whiskies (including several extinct ones), lots of interesting wines (over 20 by the glass), and 10 armagnacs. Darts, pool, cribbage, shove-ha'penny, dominoes, fruit machine, and video and trivia machines. The pretty landscaped garden has some new tables with large parasols, an international sized piste for boules, and a lake; lots of walks. Two new deluxe bedrooms have been added this year. *(Recommended by John, Lindy and Katy Voos, RB, N Cobb, R and S Bentley, Dave and Deborah Irving, Michael Sargent, Dr and Mrs A J Newton, W K Wood, Steve Willey, John Woodward, Paul and Pam Penrose, P and N Rudlin, Mr and Mrs A Scrutton, Walter and Susan Rinaldi-Butcher, Tim Barrow, Sue Demont, Brian Skelcher, Anthony Barnes, Iain Robertson, Philip Orbell, Nigel Flook, Betsy Brown, John and Joan Calvert, Nick Wikeley, S E Dark, Bryan Taylor, John and Christine Lowe, David and Jane Russell; also in the Good Hotel Guide)*

Free house ~ Licensees Nigel Logan, Michael Maguire ~ Real ale ~ Meals and snacks (not 25 Dec) ~ Restaurant ~ (01326) 340332 ~ Children welcome ~ Open 11-3, 6.30-11; 12-3, 7-10.30 Sun ~ Bedrooms: £39(£44B)/£52(£66B)

CREMYLL SX4553 Map 1

Edgcumbe Arms

End of B3247, off A374 at Crafthole (coming from A38) or Antony (from Torpoint car ferry)

We were delighted to discover that Mo Law who used to run the China House in Plymouth just across the water, has now turned up here. This bustling pub is in a super setting by the foot ferry from Plymouth, with good Tamar views from its bow-window seats and from waterside tables outside. Inside, there are lots of old-fashioned small rooms with panelling, beam-and-plank ceilings, slate flagstones and bare boards, and furnishings to match – big stripped high-backed settles, pews, fireside sofa, housekeeper's chairs, pretty cushions and the like, with candles on tables and plenty of decorative china, copper, brass and old pictures. At lunchtime, bar food includes ploughman's (£3.95), filled french bread or baked potatoes (from £3.95), vegetarian dishes of the day (from £4.50), real ham and egg or chicken lasagne (£4.95), home-made steak and kidney pie (£5.95), with evening dishes like scallops in cream and wine (£3.95), salmon steak in lemon, ginger and cream or lamb cutlets with fresh rosemary and cranberry (£7.95), pork fillet with apricots (£8.50), and home-made puddings such as treacle tart or bread and butter pudding (£2.75). Well kept St Austell HSD, Tinners and Trelawny's Pride on handpump. There are splendid walks in nearby waterfront parkland. *(Recommended by A Browne, Shirley Mackenzie, Tim Jacobson, June and Perry Dann, S Parr, P Birch, Mike Woodhead, James Cartwright)*

St Austell ~ Manageress Mo Law ~ Real ale ~ Meals and snacks (all day Sun until 5pm) ~ (01752) 822294 ~ Children welcome ~ Live jazz, rhythm and blues planned ~ Open 11-11; 12-10.30 Sun; 11-3, 6-11 in winter weekdays ~ Bedrooms: £32.50S/£45S

CROWS NEST SX2669 Map1

Crows Nest

Signposted off B3264 N of Liskeard; or pleasant drive from A30 by Siblyback/St Cleer rd from Bolventor, turning left at Common Moor, Siblyback signpost, then forking right to Darite; OS Sheet 201 map reference 263692

New licensees have taken over this old-fashioned 17th-c pub set on the southern slopes of Bodmin Moor. There are lots of stirrups, bits and spurs hanging from the bowed dark oak beams, an interesting table converted from a huge blacksmith's bellows (which still work), and an unusually long black wall settle by the big log fire as well as other more orthodox seats. On the right, and divided by a balustered partition, is a similar area with old local photographs. Good value bar food includes pasties (£1.40), sandwiches (from £1.75), ploughman's (from £3.25), and daily specials such as a vegetarian dish or pies like beef in Guinness or chicken and mushroom (£4.75). Well kept St Austell Tinners and HSD on handpump kept under light blanket pressure; euchre on Monday evenings, and piped music. On the terrace by the quiet lane there are picnic-sets. No children. *(Recommended by Ian Phillips, Miss G Glen, Ted George, Dr and Mrs B D Smith; more reports on the new regime, please)*

St Austell ~ Tenants R and S Hughes ~ Real ale ~ Meals and snacks (not Sun evenings) ~ (01579) 345930 ~ Open 11-3, 6-11; 12-3, 7-10.30 Sun

DULOE SX2358 Map 1

Olde Plough House

B3254 N of Looe

One reader was mildly alarmed, after ordering but before tackling his food, to find in the floor the gravestone of someone by the same name as him – not a perfect pre-lunch omen, but the food itself (the main draw) is an immediate reassurance. The good choice at lunchtime includes home-made soup (£1.95), filled rolls (from £1.95), ploughman's (from £3.95), fried mushrooms with smoked bacon topped with cheese (£4.45), pasta with stilton, cream and chives or a roast of the day (£4.65), battered cod (£4.85), and lasagne (£5.65), with evening dishes like scallops poached in cream and white wine with mushrooms (£4.10), chicken liver parfait (£4.25), tropical vegetable curry (£5.95), chicken strips fried in a honey and lime sauce (£7.65), breast of duck with plum sauce (£9.65), daily specials based on fresh fish such as yellow seabass with sweet peppers on a tomato coulis (£9.25) or medley of seafood with a thermidor sauce (£9.45), their speciality sizzler dishes (meat cooked on hot stones from £6.95), and home-made puddings like banana and lime tart or sticky toffee pudding (£3). Very neatly kept, the pub has a lovely dark polished Delabole slate floor in both communicating rooms, some turkey rugs, a mix of pews, modern high-backed settles and smaller chairs, foreign banknotes on the beams, three woodburning stoves, and a restrained decor – some prints of waterfowl and country scenes, a few copper jugs and a fat china pig perched on window sills. The public side (just as comfortable) has darts and pool; cribbage and piped music. Bass, Fullers London Pride and Sharps Doom Bar on handpump, sensibly priced wines, good attentive service. There is a small more modern carpeted dining room, and a few picnic-sets out by the road. The two friendly jack russells are called Jack and Spot, and the cat, Willow. *(Recommended by R Turnham, Ian Phillips, W W Burke, Keith Archer, Mr and Mrs R F E Smith)*

Free house ~ Licensees Gary and Alison Toms ~ Real ale ~ Meals and snacks ~ (01503) 262050 ~ Children in eating area of bar only ~ Open 12-2.30, 6.30-11(7-10.30 Sun)

EDMONTON SW9672 Map 1

Quarryman

Village signposted off A39 just W of Wadebridge bypass

Built around a carefully reconstructed slate-built courtyard of former quarrymen's quarters, this relaxed pub has three beamed rooms (one is no smoking) with simple pleasant furnishings, fresh flowers on tables, a woodburner, and a couple of bow windows (one with a charming stained-glass quarryman panel) looking out to a distant wind farm; there's some interesting sporting memorabilia – particularly the Roy Ullyett menu cartoons for British Sportsman's Club Savoy lunches for visiting cricket and rugby international teams. Good bar food includes sandwiches (from £2.50; a bumper bacon butty £3), filled baked potatoes or ploughman's (from £3.50), a pasta dish or home-made pie of the day (£4.90), chargrilled sardines (£5.50), outstanding Aberdeen Angus sizzle steaks (from £9.50), fresh locally caught fish, daily specials, and very tempting puddings (£2.50). Well kept Bass, Sharps Doom Bar, and guest beers on handpump, decent house wines and some interesting good value bottles, and good malt whiskies; pool, darts, fruit machine. The dog's called Floyd. There's a cosy no-smoking bistro on the other side of the courtyard. This interesting pub forms part of an attractively understated small health and holiday complex; it's a pleasant spot, and just a good brisk walk from the sandy Camel estuary. *(Recommended by P and M Rudlin, David Carr, Andy and Jill Kassube, Mr and Mrs R Searston)*

Free house ~ Licensees Terry and Wendy De Villiers Kuun ~ Real ale ~ Meals and snacks ~ Restaurant ~ (01208) 816444 ~ Children in eating area of bar ~ Open 12-11; 12-10.30 Sun

EGLOSHAYLE SX0172 Map 1

Earl of St Vincent

Just outside Wadebridge, off A389 Bodmin road

In a quiet spot behind the church, this friendly pub is comfortable and civilised with a combination of rich furnishings and a fascinating collection of antique clocks (all in working order), golfing memorabilia and art deco ornaments; piped music. Well kept St Austell Tinners, HSD or Trelawneys Pride, and good food such as sandwiches (super crab), soup (£2.10), pâté (£2.50), mushroom and broccoli au gratin (£4.75), scallops in white wine (£5.20), good liver and bacon, chicken in leek and stilton sauce (£9.35), steaks (from £9.60), salmon poached in cream (£9.90), roast duckling (£10.45), beef stroganoff (£12), and three-course Sunday lunch (£7); friendly service. The snug is no smoking. In summer, there are picnic-sets in the lovely garden here and marvellous flowering baskets and tubs. No children. *(Recommended by G S and E M Dorey, David Carr, H J Gray, Chris Parsons, Pat and Tony Martin, Mr and Mrs B Hobden, Mike and Heather Watson, John A Barker, John Westlake, Jenny and Brian Seller, Andy and Jill Kassube, Val Stevenson, Rob Holmes, Rita Horridge)*

St Austell ~ Tenants Edward and Anne Connolly ~ Real ale ~ Meals and snacks (not Sun) ~ (01208) 814807 ~ Open 11-3, 6.30-11; 12-3, 7-10.30 Sun

FALMOUTH SW8032 Map 1

Quayside

Arwenack St

Next to the handsome Georgian harbour-master's office, this pub is known for its fine range of real ales: Bass, Courage Directors, Flowers Original, Sharps Special Ale, Doom Bar, and Own, and Tetleys on handpump, with up to another 14 tapped from the cask; they hold beer fesitvals during the Spring and Autumn half-terms. Scrumpy Jack cider and country wines. There are lots of beer mats on the panelled walls, book matches on the black ceiling, malt sacks tacked into the counter, a big white ensign, a mix of ordinary pub chairs on the bare boards, and a log-effect gas fire in the stripped stone fireplace; piped music. Upstairs is the lounge bar (which you enter from the attractively bustling shopping street) with comfortable armchairs and sofas at one end, more straightforward tables and chairs at the other, and picture windows overlooking the harbour. Bar food includes home-made doorstep sandwiches (from £2.65), filled baked potatoes (from £3.25), ploughman's (from £3.65), sausage and mash (£3.85), vegetable stir-fry (£3.95 regular, £4.95 large), and sizzling beef with ginger and spring onion in oyster sauce, five spice chicken or cantonese prawns (£4.65 regular, £5.95 large). There are picnic-sets on the tarmac by the Custom House Quay. *(Recommended by Nigel Woolliscroft, Ted George, Eamonn and Natasha Skyrme, Andy and Jill Kassube, J and B Cressey, Dr S P Willavoys, John Wooll, P and M Rudlin)*

Greenalls ~ Manager Ray Gascoigne ~ Real ale ~ Meals and snacks ~ (01326) 312113 ~ Children welcome until 9pm ~ Live music Fri and Sat evenings ~ Open 11-11; 12-10.30 Sun

If we know a pub does summer barbecues, we say so.

HELFORD SW7526 Map 1

Shipwrights Arms

Off B3293 SE of Helston, via Mawgan

The terraces outside this thatched pub are quite a draw in summer as they are set above a lovely wooded creek, and in summer they hold barbecues in the evening with cajun pork chops (£7.25), marinated lamb fillet or swordfish (£7.95), steaks (from £8.40), and prawns in garlic or monkfish (£9.40). Inside there's quite a nautical theme with navigation lamps, models of ships, sea pictures, drawings of lifeboat coxswains and shark fishing photographs – as well as a collection of foreign banknotes behind the bar counter. A dining area has oak settles and tables; winter open fire. Well kept Flowers IPA and Whitbreads Castle Eden on handpump, and bar food such as starters (from £2.40), good ploughman's, summer salads including lobster and crab (from £6.75), winter stews such as steak and mushroom in ale, and home-made puddings (£3.75). It does get crowded at peak times. *(Recommended by Mike and Wena Stevenson, C Robinson, Ted George, D P and J A Sweeney, John Woodward, Carol Fellowes, J and B Cressey, S P Watkin, P A Taylor, P and S White, John and June Freeman, Nigel Flook, Betsy Brown, Brian Skelcher)*

Greenalls ~ Lease: Charles Herbert ~ Real ale ~ Meals and snacks (not winter Sun evenings) ~ (01326) 231235 ~ Children in eating area of bar ~ Parking only right outside the village in summer ~ Open 11-2.30, 6-11; 12-2.30, 7-10.30 Sun; closed winter Sun evenings

HELSTON SW6527 Map 1

Blue Anchor £

50 Coinagehall Street

Now that the brewery in this characterful old thatched town pub has been refurbished (it is probably the oldest brewing house in the country), the very good Middle, Best, 'Spingo' Special, and Easter and Christmas Special ales are also being distributed to other pubs; they also sell farm cider. A series of small, low-ceilinged rooms opens off the central corridor, with simple old-fashioned furniture on the flagstones, interesting old prints, some bared stone walls, and in one room a fine inglenook fireplace. A family room (to be refurbished this year) has darts; dominoes and fruit machine. Bar food includes rolls and sandwiches (from £1.20), home-made soup (£1.50), ploughman's (from £3.25), ham and eggs (£3.15), liver and bacon hotpot (£3.25), steak and kidney pie or curry (£4.25), and daily specials. Past an old stone bench in the sheltered little terrace area is a skittle alley which you can hire. At lunchtimes you can usually go and look round the brewery and the cellar. *(Recommended by Jeanne Cross, Paul Silvestri, Brian Skelcher, James Nunns, Jim Reid, Sue Holland, Dave Webster, Colin Draper, David Carr)*

Own brew ~ Licensee Kim Corbett ~ Real ale ~ Lunchtime meals and snacks (12-4) ~ (01326) 562821 ~ Children in family room ~ Jazz 1st Mon of month; folk 2nd Thurs of month and usually Fri or Sat ~ Parking sometimes difficult ~ Open 11-11; 12-10.30 Sun

Halzephron

Gunwalloe, village about 4 miles S but not marked on many road maps; look for brown sign on A3083 alongside perimeter fence of RNAS Culdrose

Once a well known smugglers' haunt, this popular inn has lots of surrounding unspoilt walks with fine views of Mount's Bay, Gunwalloe fishing cove just 300 yards away, and a sandy beach one mile away at Gunwalloe Church Cove. The bustling and pleasant bar is spotlessly clean with comfortable seating, copper on the walls and mantlepiece, and maybe the two cats (Humphrey the gentle black one and a lively marmalade one called Mr Chivers) sitting by the warm fire in the big hearth; there's also a quite a small no-smoking family room. Good bar food includes good sandwiches (lunchtimes, from £2.40; crab £5.50), home-made soup (£3), grilled goat's cheese on garlic bread (£4), ploughman's (from £4), enjoyable daily specials such as seafood pancakes (£4.10), crab au gratin (£4.80), vegetarian quiche (£5.80), steak and kidney pudding (£8.80), rack of lamb (£9.10), chargrilled sirloin steak (£10.10), and fresh lemon sole (£10.30); the restaurant amd the snug are no smoking. Well kept Dartmoor Best and Sharps Own and Doom Bar on handpump, a good wine list, 40 malt whiskies, and around 35 liqueurs; darts, dominoes and cribbage. Small but comfortable and well equipped bedrooms – and huge breakfasts. *(Recommended by John Voos, Freda Macnamara, C Robinson, D B Jenkin, Cliff Blakemore, James Nunns, Brian Skelcher, J and B Cressey, John and Sally Clarke, Bryan Taylor, Paul and Pam Penrose, RB, Peter and Gwyneth Eastwood, Gwen and Peter Andrews)*

Free house ~ Licensees Harry and Angela Davy Thomas ~ Real ale ~ Meals and snacks (not 25 Dec) ~ Restaurant ~ (01326) 240406 ~ Children in family room and in restaurant if over 8 ~ Open 11-3(2.30 in winter), 6(6.30 in winter)-11; 12-3, 7-10.30 Sun; closed 25 Dec (and no accomm 24 Dec) ~ Bedrooms: £35B/£59B

KINGSAND SX4350 Map 1

Halfway House

Fore St, towards Cawsand

The simply furnished but quite smart bar in this attractive old inn is neatly kept and cosy and rambles around a huge central fireplace. It's low-ceilinged, softly lit, and mildly Victorian in style, popular with locals but with a warm welcome for the many summer visitors. Bar food is good and enjoyable and includes daily specials such as scallops wrapped in parma ham with warm basil dressing (£4.50), fishcakes with fresh tomato sauce (£6.45), grilled duck breast with mango and ginger sauce (£8.95), and roast garlic monkfish (£9.50); from the menu, there might be filled french bread (from £1.95), soup (£2.20), filled baked potatoes (from £3.20), garlic mushrooms with a bacon and cheese topping (£3.85), ploughman's (from £4.80), home-cooked ham and egg (£5.40), a curry of the day or spicy vegetable salsa (£6.50), steaks (from £8.95), and puddings like dark and white chocolate profiteroles, summer pudding or tarte citron (£3.25); vegetables are fresh and carefully cooked. There are often attractive fresh flowers on the tables. Well kept Bass, Boddingtons, Flowers Original and Sharps Cornish on handpump kept under light blanket pressure, and decent wines. Service is quick and friendly, and the bar staff add a lot to the enjoyable atmosphere; the landlord himself is a man of strong opinions, not shy of stating them – though always courteous. The piped music is generally unobtrusive; cribbage, dominoes, backgammon, chess, and fruit machine. The village is well placed for marvellous cliff walks on Rame Head, or for visiting Mount Edgcumbe. *(Recommended by Charles Gray, R Turnham, Ted George, Jacquie and Jim Jones, Roy and Judy Tudor Hughes)*

Free house ~ Licensees Sarah and David Riggs ~ Real ale ~ Meals and snacks ~ Restaurant ~ (01752) 822279 ~ Children welcome ~ Choir Weds evenings, quiz winter Thurs evenings ~ Open 11-4, 7-11; 12-4, 7-10.30 Sun; winter weekday opening 12 ~ Bedrooms: £24S/£48S

LAMORNA SW4424 Map 1

Lamorna Wink

After a bracing walk along the coastal path and a short walk up from the attractive little cove this neatly kept local is a fine place for a lunchtime break. It's simply furnished, and has one of the best collections of warship mementoes, sea photographs and nautical brassware in the county. Bar food includes locally made pasty (£1.50), sandwiches (from £1.40; fresh local crab £4), a choice of home-made quiche (£3.50), ploughman's (£4), and fresh local crab salad (in season, £9.50). Pool, dominoes, fruit machine, and piped music. There are front benches outside where you can just hear the sound of the sea and the burble of the stream behind. *(Recommended by Michael and Lorna Bourdeaux, Simon Williams, Jack and Gemima Valiant, Brian Smart, Kevin Thorpe)*

Free house ~ Licensee Bob Drennan ~ Meals and snacks (not winter evenings) ~ Children in pool room ~ Open 11-11; 12-10.30 Sun; 11-4, 5-11 in winter

LANLIVERY SX0759 Map 1

Crown

Signed off A390 Lostwithiel—St Austell

In a quiet village, this is one of Cornwall's oldest inns. It's run by genuinely helpful and friendly licensees who have redecorated the whole place throughout this year, but have kept the character of the rambling series of rooms unchanged – no noisy games machines, music or pool tables. The small, dimly lit public bar has heavy beams, a slate floor, and built-in wall settles and attractive alcove seats in the dark former chimney; darts. A much lighter room leads off here with beams in the white boarded ceiling, some comfortable plush sofas in one corner, cushioned black settles, a small cabinet with wood turnings for sale, owl and badger pictures, and a little fireplace with an old-fashioned fire; there's another similar small room. Good bar food includes sandwiches (from £1.60), pasty (£2.10), home-made soup (£2.50), ploughman's (from £2.85), home-made curries (from £5.15), and daily specials such as fresh haddock in batter (£5.25), lamb's kidneys in three-mustard sauce (£5.95) or monkfish thermidor (£10.50); the restaurant is partly no smoking. Well kept Bass, Sharps Own and Coaster on handpump; dominoes, cribbage, euchre, and shove-ha'penny. The slate-floored porch room has lots of succulents and a few cacti, and wood-and-stone seats. In the sheltered garden are some granite faced seats as well as white cast-iron furniture and picnic-sets, and the fruit and herb gardens have been added to. (*Recommended by D B Jenkin, P P Salmon, Klaus and Elizabeth Leist, R J Walden, Howard Clutterbuck, J K Lefeaux, Ian Phillips, Anthony Barnes, Peter and Audrey Dowsett, John Woodward, Joan and Michael Johnstone, P and M Rudlin, Lawrence Bacon, Jean Scott, P and S White*)

Free house ~ Licensees Ros and Dave Williams ~ Real ale ~ Meals and snacks ~ Restaurant ~ (01208) 872707 ~ Children in restaurant ~ Trad jazz once a month, handbell ringing Sun evening in summer ~ Open 11-3, 6-11; 12-3, 7-10.30 Sun ~ Bedrooms: £25S/£40S

LOSTWITHIEL SX1059 Map 1

Royal Oak

Duke St; pub just visible from A390 in centre

Although this is a town centre pub, it has the relaxed feel of an inn in the country. The staff are really friendly and welcoming and keep a fine range of real ales on handpump: Bass, Fullers London Pride, Hoskins & Oldfield EXS Bitter, Marstons Pedigree, and Sharps Own and Doom Bar – as well as lots of bottled beers from around the world. Good, popular bar food includes sandwiches, soup (£1.95), good stuffed mushrooms (£3.25), broccoli pie (£5.95), scallops in garlic and butter (£8.25), steaks (from £8.35), daily specials such as a curry (£5.95), steak and kidney in ale pie (£6.25), fresh salmon in a cucumber and cream sauce (£8.50), and garlic king prawns (£9.25), and puddings like cherry pie or treacle tart (£1.85). The neat lounge is spacious and comfortable, with captain's chairs and high-backed wall benches on its patterned carpet, and a couple of wooden armchairs by the gas-effect log fire; there's also a delft shelf, with a small dresser in one inner alcove. The flagstoned and beamed back public bar has darts, dominoes, cribbage, fruit machine and juke box, and is popular with younger customers. On a raised terrace by the car park are some picnic-sets. (*Recommended by B M and P Kendall, Ted George, A J Thomas, P and S White, P H Boot, Charles Gysin*)

Free house ~ Licensees Malcolm and Eileen Hine ~ Real ale ~ Meals and snacks ~ Restaurant ~ (01208) 872552 ~ Children welcome ~ Open 11-11; 12-10.30 Sun ~ Bedrooms: £33.50B/£55B

Stars after the name of a pub show exceptional quality. One star means most people (after reading the report to see just why the star has been won) would think a special trip worth while. Two stars mean that the pub is really outstanding – many that for their particular qualities cannot be bettered.

LUDGVAN SW5033 Map 1

White Hart

Churchtown; off A30 Penzance—Hayle at Crowlas – OS Sheet 203 map reference 505330

This is a marvellously unspoilt old place and the small, cosy beamed rooms are full of interest: masses of mugs and jugs glinting in cottagey corners, bric-a-brac, pictures and photographs (including some good ones of Exmoor), soft oil-lamp-style lighting, stripped boards with attractive rugs on them, and a fascinating mix of interesting old seats and tables; the two big woodburning stoves run radiators too. Simple bar food includes sandwiches (from £1.50), village-made pasties (£1.80), ploughman's (from £3.25), omelettes (£4.25), ham and egg (£4.40), home-made vegetable or meaty lasagne (£4.75), steaks (from £8), and daily specials. Well kept Bass, Flowers IPA, and Marstons Pedigree tapped from the cask, and quite a few whiskies; cribbage, dominoes. *(Recommended by R J Walden, Jack and Gemima Valiant, John and Christine Lowe, James Nunns, P Williams, P and M Rudlin, Mr and Mrs G McNeill)*

Greenalls ~ Tenant Denis Churchill ~ Real ale ~ Meals and snacks (not Mon evening Oct-Whitsun) ~ (01736) 740574 ~ Children in restaurant ~ Open 11-2.30, 6-11; 12-3, 7-10.30 Sun

MITHIAN SW7450 Map 1

Miners Arms

Just off B3285 E of St Agnes

Under the new licensee, plans are afoot to open up another room and redecorate and alter the dining room in this 16th-c pub. The small back bar has an irregular beam and plank ceiling, a wood block floor, and bulging squint walls (one with a fine old wall painting of Elizabeth I); another small room has a decorative low ceiling, lots of books and quite a few interesting ornaments, and there are warm winter fires. Bar food includes sandwiches, home-made soup (from £2.95), home-made pâté (£3.25), ploughman's (from £3.95), courgette and mushroom pasta (£4.95), lamb curry (£5.50), steak, kidney and oyster pie (£5.95), and steaks (£7.95). The dining room is no smoking. Bass, Flowers IPA, and Wadworths 6X on handpump kept under light blanket pressure, and decent wines. Darts, shove-ha'penny, dominoes, fruit machine, trivia, and piped music. There are seats on the back terrace, with more on the sheltered front cobbled forecourt. *(Recommended by Patrick Hancock, Roger and Christine Mash, James Nunns, Brian Skelcher, David and Jane Russell, Mr and Mrs J D Marsh; more reports on the new regime, please)*

Greenalls ~ Lease: Richard Baylin ~ Real ale ~ Meals and snacks ~ (01872) 552375 ~ Children welcome away from bar ~ Open 12-3, 6-11; 12-11 Sat; 12-10.30 Sun; closed between 3 and 6pm winter weekends

MORWENSTOW SS2015 Map 1

Bush

Village signposted off A39 N of Kilkhampton

Part of this ancient place dates back just over 1,000 years and it was once a monastic rest house on a pilgrim route between Wales and Spain. There are ancient built-in settles, flagstones, and a big stone fireplace, and a cosy side area with antique seats, a lovely old elm trestle table, and a wooden propeller from a 1930 De Havilland Gipsy Moth. An upper bar, opened at busy times, is decorated with antique knife-grinding wheels, miners' lamps, casks, funnels, and so forth. Well kept St Austell HSD and Winter Brew (December and January only) both on handpump; quite a few malt whiskies and Inches cider. Simple, genuinely home-made lunchtime bar food includes good soup (£2), sandwiches (from £2), locally-made pasties, ploughman's (from £3), winter stews (£3.50), crab salad (£5.50), and occasional puddings like spotted dick or apple pie; no chips. Darts, and Charlie the friendly cat. Seats outside shelter in the slightly sunken yard. Within a few hundred yards is the famous village church, with a wrecked ship's figurehead as a gravestone for its crew, and Vicarage Cliff, one of the grandest parts of the Cornish coast (with 400-ft precipices) is a ten-minute walk away. No children. *(Recommended by Mike and Mary Carter, Sam Samuells, Lynda Payton, Prof A N Black, Brian and Jenny Seller, Basil Minson)*

Free house ~ Licensee B A J Moore ~ Real ale ~ Lunchtime snacks (not Sun) ~ (01288) 331242 ~ Open 12-3, 7-11; closed Mon Oct-Apr, except bank holidays

MOUSEHOLE SW4726 Map 1

Ship

Follow Newlyn coast rd out of Penzance; also signposted off B3315

Right by the harbour in a lovely village, this fisherman's local has a cheerful bustling atmosphere and is welcoming to both regulars and holiday-makers. The opened-up main bar has black beams and panelling, built-in wooden wall benches and stools around the low tables, photographs of local events, sailors' fancy ropework, granite flagstones, and a cosy open fire. Bar food includes sandwiches (crab £4.75), fisherman's lunch (£4.50), local mussels (£4.70), and seafood platter (£10.95). On 23 December they bake Starry Gazy pie to celebrate Tom Bawcock's Eve, a tradition that recalls Tom's brave expedition out to sea in a fierce storm 200 years ago. He caught seven types of fish, which were then cooked in a pie with their heads and tails sticking out. Well kept St Austell BB, Tinners, HSD and Trelawny's Pride on handpump, and several malt whiskies; friendly staff. The elaborate harbour lights at Christmas are worth a visit; best to park at the top of the village and walk down. *(Recommended by R J Walden, Bronwen and Steve Wrigley, H Thomson, Dr and Mrs Cottrell, Tim Barrow, Sue Demont, David Warrellow, Gwen and Peter Andrews)*

St Austell ~ Tenants Michael and Tracey Maddern ~ Meals and snacks ~ Restaurant ~ (01736) 731234 ~ Children welcome away from bar ~ Summer parking can be difficult ~ Open 10.30am-11pm; 12-10.30 Sun ~ Bedrooms: /£50B

nr MYLOR BRIDGE SW8036 Map 1

Pandora ★★🍷

Restronguet Passage: from A39 in Penryn, take turning signposted Mylor Church, Mylor Bridge, Flushing and go straight through Mylor Bridge following Restronguet Passage signs; or from A39 further N, at or near Perranarworthal, take turning signposted Mylor, Restronguet, then follow Restronguet Weir signs, but turn left down hill at Restronguet Passage sign

The sheltered waterfront position of this charming medieval thatched pub is lovely and you can sit at picnic-sets in front or (more fun) on the long floating jetty. Quite a few people arrive by boat and there are showers for visiting yachtsmen. The several rambling, interconnecting rooms are marvellously atmospheric and have low wooden ceilings (mind your head on some of the beams), beautifully polished big flagstones, cosy alcoves with leatherette benches built into the walls, a kitchen range, and a log fire in a high hearth (to protect it against tidal floods); half the bar area is no smoking – as is the restaurant. Bar food includes home-made soup (from £1.95), sandwiches (from £2.95, delicious local crab £6.25), vegetable stew and parsley dumplings (£4.50), fish pie (£5.75), daily specials, puddings like home-made treacle tart (£2.50); Sunday roast (from £5.25), and children's dishes (from £1.75). Bass, St Austell Tinners, HSD, and Trelawny's Pride on handpump from a temperature controlled cellar, 20 good wines by the glass, and local cider; dominoes, winter pool, and cribbage. It does get very crowded in summer, and parking is difficult at peak times. *(Recommended by Pat and Tony Martin, Tim Jacobson, Mr and Mrs B Hobden, Mrs Maria Furness, Michael Sargent, Ted George, J Henry, Patrick Hancock, H and D Payne, Catherine Lloyd, Gethin Lewis, George Atkinson, Nigel Flook, Betsy Brown, Louise Lyons, Peter Elliot, J H Bell, Sybille Weber, RB, Dr B and Mrs B B Baker, P P and J Salmon, Brian Skelcher)*

St Austell ~ Tenant Helen Hough ~ Real ale ~ Meals and snacks (till 10pm in summer) ~ Evening restaurant ~ (01326) 372678 ~ Children in eating area of bar ~ Open 11-11; 12-10.30 Sun; 12-2.30, 7-11 winter weekdays; closed evening 25 Dec

PELYNT SX2055 Map 1

Jubilee 🛏

B3359 NW of Looe

The relaxed, beamed lounge bar in this neatly kept 16th-c inn has mementoes of Queen Victoria, such as a tapestry portrait, old prints, and Staffordshire figurines of the Queen and her consort, an early 18th-c Derbyshire oak armchair, cushioned wall and window seats, windsor armchairs around oak tables, and a good winter log fire in the stone fireplace; the Victorian bar has some carved settles and more mementoes. The flagstoned entry is separated from the bar by an attractively old-fangled glass-paned partition. Bar food includes sandwiches (from £1.60), home-made soup (£2.40), ploughman's (from £2.80), chicken tikka (£4.80), fresh cod (£5.60), gammon and egg (£7.50), sirloin steak (£10.50), and puddings (from £2.20). Well kept Bass and St Austell Trelawny's Pride on handpump. The quite separate public bar has sensibly placed darts, pool, fruit machine, and piped music. A crazy-paved central courtyard has picnic-sets with red and white striped umbrellas and pretty tubs of flowers, and there's a well equipped children's play area. *(Recommended by Mayur Shah, T Rowntree, Bernard Stradling, June and Perry Dann, Terry and Eileen Stott, Edward Froggatt, Janet and Colin Roe, Eamonn and Natasha Skyrme, Paul and Pam Penrose, Peter and Audrey Dowsett, the Sandy Family)*

Free House ~ Licensee Tim Williams ~ Real ale ~ Meals and snacks ~ Restaurant ~ (01503) 220312 ~ Children welcome ~ Open 11-3, 6-11; 11-11 Sat; 12-10.30 Sun ~ Bedrooms: £36B/£59B

PENZANCE SW4730 Map 1

Turks Head

At top of main street, by big domed building (Lloyds Bank), turn left down Chapel Street

Popular with locals and visitors alike, this friendly little pub has a bustling bar with old flat irons, jugs and so forth hanging from the beams, pottery above the wood-effect panelling, wall seats and tables, and a couple of elbow rests around central pillars. The menu has quite an emphasis on seafood, with crab soup (£2), fish pie (£5.75), crab salad (mixed meat £7.25, white meat £8.50), and cold seafood platter (£9.50), as well as sandwiches (from £1), filled baked potatoes (from £2.50), ham and egg (£3.60), ratatouille topped with cheese (£3.50), meaty or vegetarian lasagne (£4.75), steak and kidney pie (£4.95), good steaks (from £6.95), and daily specials like cod in beer batter (£4.95), half a pheasant (£7.50) or duck breast with plum sauce (£8.95). They keep four real ales on handpump from a choice of Boddingtons, Flowers Original, Sharps Doom Bar or Cornish, Ringwood Bitter, and Wadworths 6X on handpump; country wines, and helpful service. The suntrap back garden has big urns of flowers. There has been a Turks Head here for over 700 years – though most of the original building was destroyed by a Spanish raiding party in the 16th c. *(Recommended by Simon Williams, G P Reeves, S P Watkin, P A Taylor, D J Priestley, P and M Rudlin)*

Greenalls ~ Tenant William Morris ~ Real ale ~ Meals and snacks (11-2.30, 6-10) ~ Restaurant ~ (01736) 363093 ~ Children in cellar dining room ~ Open 11-3, 5.30-11; 12-3, 5.30-10.30 Sun; closed 25 Dec

PHILLEIGH SW8639 Map 1

Roseland ★

Between A3078 and B3289, just E of King Harry Ferry

A new licensee has taken over this charming little pub. The low beamed bar has a good chatty atmosphere, a nice oak settle and antique seats around the sturdy tables on the flagstones, an old wall clock, and a good winter fire; several friendly cats. Popular home-made bar food includes sandwiches, ploughman's, filled baked potatoes, and daily specials such as steak and mushroom in ale pudding (£5.95), and shoulder of lamb with rosemary and thyme gravy or guinea fowl with a cranberry and chestnut sauce (£6.95). Well kept Bass, Greenalls Bitter, Marstons Pedigree, Morlands Old Speckled Hen, and Sharps Cornish and Doom Bar on handpump, local cider, and quite a few malt whiskies; cribbage and dominoes. The pretty paved front courtyard is a lovely place to sit in the lunchtime sunshine beneath the cherry blossom, and the back garden has been converted into a small outdoor children's play area. Handy for the King Harry ferry and Trelissick Gardens. *(Recommended by R Inman, W K Wood, Ian and Deborah Carrington, Mrs L E Phillips, Romey Heaton, D P and J A Sweeney, D Martin, Mr and Mrs Peter Smith, Keith and Margaret Kettwell, Michael Sargent, Mr Parkes, Christopher Wright, Christine and Geoff Butler, William and Julie Ryan, Mike and Wena Stevenson, B M and P Kendall, Brian Skelcher; more reports on the new regime, please)*

Greenalls ~ Licensee Colin Phillips ~ Real ale ~ Meals and snacks ~ Restaurant ~ (01872) 580254 ~ Children welcome ~ Open 11-3, 5.30-11; 12-3, 6-10.30 Sun

POLKERRIS SX0952 Map 1

Rashleigh

Signposted off A3082 Fowey—St Austell

The position here is smashing. From seats on the stone terrace you can enjoy the views towards the far side of St Austell and Mevagissey bays, and the isolated beach with its restored jetty is just a few steps away. Inside, the front part of the bar has comfortably cushioned seats, with local photographs on the brown panelling of a more simply furnished back area; winter log fire and piped classical music. Enjoyable bar food includes soup (£2.50), sandwiches (from £1.85; open ones from £4.75), ploughman's (from £4), beef curry (£5.25), pasta and mushroom bake (£5.50), fish pie (£6.75), a lunchtime cold buffet (£6.50), daily specials such as scallops and tiger prawns in garlic butter or lemon sole, and puddings (£2.50). Badger Tanglefoot, Bass, Dartmoor Best, Otter Ale, St Austell HSD, Sharps Doom Bar and two weekly guest beers on handpump or tapped from the cask, decent wine list and several whiskies. Though parking space next to the pub is limited, there's a large village car park, and there are safe moorings for small yachts in the cove. This whole section of the Cornish Coast Path is renowned for its striking scenery. *(Recommended by Pete and Rosie Flower, A J Thomas, R Turnham, Mr and Mrs A Scrutton, B J Harding, Pamela and Merlyn Horswell, Christopher Turner, C and E M Watson, Luke Worthington, Brian Skelcher)*

Free house ~ Licensees Bernard and Carole Smith ~ Real ale ~ Meals and snacks (till 10pm in summer) ~ Restaurant ~ (01726) 813991 ~ Well behaved children in eating area of bar ~ Pianist Sat evening ~ Open 11-4.30, 5.30-11; 12-4.30, 5.30-10.30 Sun; 11-3, 6.30-11 in winter

POLPERRO SX2051 Map 1

Old Mill House

Mill Hill; bear right approaching harbour

A nice civilised feel here, with polished boards, solid stripped pine furniture, dado and stall dividers, a couple of housekeeper's chairs and some hefty rustic implements by the big log fireplace, fishing-boat pictures, netting and some nautical hardware overhead. There are flagstones by the serving counter, which has well kept Bass, Ind Coope Burton, St Austell Trelawnys Pride Exmoor Gold on handpump, and farm cider. Service is very friendly, and bar food includes sandwiches, home-made soup (£2.50), home-made hummus with warm pitta bread (£3.30), grilled sardines with fresh herbs and piri-piri sauce (£3.50), crab claws (£5.75), vegetarian chilli (£6.50), pasta with fresh and smoked seafood in a creamy white wine sauce or cajun chicken (£7.25), steaks (from £7.65), and daily specials with fresh fish straight from the boats in Looe; in winter they only do food in the evenings (not Sunday) but they do offer Sunday lunch. Round the corner is an area with darts and pool, shove-ha'penny, cribbage, dominoes, shut the box, and chess; piped music. A cosy little bistro opens off on the left, and down a long bright-painted corridor is a little children's room with seaside murals and a box of toys. There's a picnic-set by the very narrow lane in front of the pretty white cottage (hung with flowering baskets in summer), and more under parasols in a streamside garden with a terrace behind. We have not yet heard from readers using the bedrooms here, but the inn does have its own parking further up the village – a real boon. Dogs are welcomed with a dog biscuit. *(Recommended by Ted George, Michael Sandy)*

Free house ~ Licensees Jane Fletcher and Patricia Carroll ~ Real ale ~ Meals and snacks ~ Restaurant ~ (01503) 272362 ~ Children in own room, snug, and restaurant ~ Live entertainment most Fri or Sat evenings ~ Open 11-11; 12-10.30 Sun; winter opening 12 ~ Bedrooms: £22.50B/£45B

POLRUAN SX1251 Map 1

Lugger

Reached from A390 in Lostwithiel; nearby parking expensive and limited, or steep walk down from village-edge car park; passenger/bicycle ferry from Fowey

It's rather fun to leave your car in Fowey and take the foot passenger ferry to get to this friendly local. From the quay there's a flight of steep stone steps, and once there, you can enjoy fine views of the little harbour. Inside, the two knocked-together bars have beams, high-backed wall settles, wheelback chairs, and a slightly nautical theme with big model boats and local boat photographs. Good bar food includes sandwiches (from £1.40), ploughman's (from £3.40), fresh battered cod (£4.50), stilton and leek pie (£4.75), beef and Guinness pie (£5.45), and steaks (from £6.45); the restaurant is no smoking. St Austell BB, Tinners, Trelawnys Pride, HSD and XXXX Mild on handpump; darts, fruit machine, and piped music. Good surrounding walks. Self-catering cottage available. *(Recommended by Dr and Mrs B D Smith, A J Thomas, Peter and Audrey Dowsett, Janet and Colin Roe, P and M Rudlin, D and J Tapper, R A Cullingham)*

St Austell ~ Managers Colin and Shelagh Dolphin ~ Real ale ~ Meals and snacks (not Sun evening) ~ Restaurant ~ Children welcome ~ (01726) 870007 ~ Occasional live duo ~ Open 11-11; 12-10.30 Sun

PORT ISAAC SW9980 Map 1

Golden Lion

Fore Street

Set high over the harbour in a lovely steep village, this unspoilt bustling pub has seats in the windows of the cosy rooms that enjoy the view – or you can sit out on the terrace. The bar has a fine antique settle among other comfortable seats, decorative ceiling plasterwork, and perhaps the pub dog Hollie. Bar food includes sandwiches (lunchtime only; good crab £4.25), ploughman's (£4.75), proper fish and chips (£5.95), good fish pie (£6.25), and steak in ale pie (£6.75); during the summer, evening meals are served in the bistro. Well kept St Austell Tinners, HSD and Trelawny's Pride on handpump and several malt whiskies. Darts, shove-ha'penny, dominoes, a fruit machine in the public bar, and piped music. You can park at the top of the village unless you are luckly enough to park on the beach at low tide. The very steep narrow lanes of this working fishing village are most attractive. *(Recommended by Ted George, Barry and Anne, A J Thomas, Mr and Mrs P Stubbs, Pat and Tony Martin, J Henry, David Carr, Graham Tayar, Catherine Raeburn, Jenny and Brian Seller, Andy and Jill Kassube, Nigel Flook, Betsy Brown, D and J Tapper, Alan and Paula McCully, Jo and Gary Charlton, K Flack)*

St Austell ~ Tenants Mike and Nikki Edkins ~ Real ale ~ Meals and snacks (not 31 Dec) ~ Evening restaurant ~ (01208) 880336 ~ Children in eating area of bar ~ No parking nearby ~ Open 11.30-11; 12-10.30 Sun; closed evening 25 Dec

nr PORT ISAAC SX0080 Map 1

Port Gaverne Hotel

Port Gaverne signposted from Port Isaac, and from B3314 E of Pendoggett

Just back from the sea and close to splendid clifftop walks, this early 17th-c inn has big log fires and low beams in the neat bars, flagstones as well as carpeting, some exposed stone, and an enormous marine chronometer. In spring the lounge is filled with pictures from the local art society's annual exhibition, and at other times there are interesting antique local photographs. Bar food includes sandwiches (from £1.60; crab £3.85), home-made soup (£2.60), ham and egg (£2.85), ploughman's (from £3.05), cottage pie (£3.35), vegetarian lasagne (£3.60), and deep-fried local plaice

(£5.65), and is served in the bar or 'Captain's Cabin' – a little room where everything except its antique admiral's hat is shrunk to scale (old oak chest, model sailing ship, even the prints on the white stone walls); the restaurant is no smoking. Well kept Bass, Flowers IPA and Sharps Doom Bar on handpump, a good bin-end wine list with 60 wines, a very good choice of whiskies and other spirits. The Green Door Bar across the lane, which has a big diorama of Port Isaac, is open on summer afternoons. *(Recommended by Brian and Jenny Seller, Graham Tayar, Catherine Raeburn, K Stevens, M J Dowdy, John Westlake, Sue and Bob Ward, John and Jackie Chalcraft, Freda Macnamara, Dr H V Hughes, D Marsh, Nigel Flook, Betsy Brown, Edward Froggatt)*

Free house ~ Licensee Mrs M Ross ~ Real ale ~ Meals and snacks (till 10pm) ~ Restaurant ~ (01208) 880244 ~ Children in restaurant (must be over 7 in evening) ~ Open 11-11; 12-10.30 Sun; closed early Jan to mid-Feb ~ Bedrooms: £51.50B/£103B; restored 18th-c s/c cottages

PORTHALLOW SW7923 Map 1

Five Pilchards

SE of Helston; B3293 to St Keverne, then village signposted

Just 20 yards from the beach, this sturdy stone-built pub has a new licensee this year who has enlarged the kitchens and bar – but in sympathy with the old interior. The walls and ceilings of the bars are hung with an abundance of salvaged nautical gear, lamps made from puffer fish, and interesting photographs and clippings about local shipwrecks. Lunchtime food now includes home-made soup (£2.50), vegetable pasta bake (£4.50), ploughman's (from £4.50; crab £5.95), and fish pie (£5.95), with evening dishes such as seafood chowder (£3.50), grilled lemon sole or sirloin steak (£8.95), and scallops in wine and saffron (£9.50). Well kept Greene King Abbot and weekly guest beers like Elgoods, Morlands Old Speckled Hen or Sharps Doom Bar on handpump. Tides and winds allowing, you can park on the foreshore. *(Recommended by Nigel Woolliscroft, Tim Barrow, Sue Demont, P and J Shapley, John and Sally Clarke, S P Watkin, P A Taylor; more reports on the new regime, please)*

Free house ~ Licensee Brandon Flynn ~ Real ale ~ Meals and snacks ~ (01326) 280256 ~ Children in eating area of bar ~ Open 12-3, 7-11(10.30 Sun); closed winter Sun evening and winter Mon

PORTHLEVEN SW6225 Map 1

Ship ★

To get to this old fisherman's pub you have to climb a flight of rough stone steps – it's actually built into the steep cliffs. There are marvellous views over the pretty working harbour and out to sea from inside the pub and from the terraced garden; at night, the harbour is interestingly floodlit. The knocked-through bar has log fires in big stone fireplaces and some genuine character, and there's a warmly chatty atmosphere and happy mix of locals and visitors; the family room is a conversion of an old smithy and has logs burning in the huge open fireplace. Popular bar food includes sandwiches (from £2.50; fine toasties from £2.95; excellent crusty loaf from £3.95), filled oven-baked potatoes (from £2.50), ploughman's (from £4.95), pot meals like vegetable curry, steak and kidney pudding or fish pie (from £6.25), interesting daily specials like fish and tomato bake or chicken tikka, sirloin steak (£9.95), puddings like home-made apple torte, evening extras, and children's meals; the candlelit dining room also enjoys the good view. Well kept Courage Best, Greene King Abbot, Morlands Old Speckled Hen, and Sharps Doom Bar on handpump, and several malt whiskies; dominoes, cribbage, fruit machine and piped music. *(Recommended by Jack and Gemima Valiant, Dave and Deborah Irving, Tim Jacobson, Pete and Rosie Flower, P P Salmon, Paul and Pam Penrose, Michael and Lorna Bourdeaux, Cliff Blakemore, Bronwen and Steve Wrigley, D B Jenkin, James Nunns, John and Sally Clarke, Brian Skelcher, P and J Shapley, Ewan and Moira McCall, RB, CB, John and Christine Lowe)*

Free house ~ Licensee Colin Oakden ~ Real ale ~ Meals and snacks ~ (01326) 572841 ~ Children in family room ~ Parking can be difficult in summer ~ Open 11.30-11; 12-10.30 Sun; 11.30-3.30, 6.30-11 in winter; 12-3, 7-10.30 winter Sun

RUAN LANIHORNE SW8942 Map 1

Kings Head

Village signposted off A3078 St Mawes road

In summer, this attractive and neatly kept pub is a fine place to be with seats in the suntrap, sunken garden and views down over the pretty convolutions of the River Fal's tidal estuary. Inside, the beamed bar has a welcoming local atmosphere, and is decorated with hanging china and framed cigarette cards, and there's an attractive family room with lots of mirrors next door. With prices unchanged since last year, bar food includes soups such as courgette and tomato (£2.25), ploughman's or potted shrimps (£3.95), good open sandwiches (from £3.95), moussaka, fish gratin with pasta and leeks in a mustardy cheese sauce or chicken pasta bake in provençale sauce (all £4.95), lots of salads (from £4.95), trout meunière (£6.95), grilled salmon fillet marinated in sun-dried tomatoes and yoghurt (£7.95), very good fillet steak (£10.95), super puddings like fruit and nut torte, various cheesecakes and popular tiramisu (£2.50), daily specials, good Sunday roasts (£4.95), and excellent steaks; the dining room is no smoking. Well kept Hardy Country and Sharps Special Ale on handpump or tapped from the cask, with Worthington Best kept under light blanket pressure, quick service, and unobtrusive radio. The pub is opposite the fine old church in this pleasant out-of-the-way village. *(Recommended by John and Jackie Chalcraft, Michael Sargent, Roger and Christine Hyde, Christopher Wright, Mayur Shah, Keith and Margaret Kettwell, Peter and Gwyneth Eastwood, DJW, Ian and Deborah Carrington, John and Joan Calvert, Julia Constable, Dr B and Mrs B Baker, C and E M Watson, Brian Skelcher)*

Free house ~ Licensees Peter and Shirley Trenoweth-Farley ~ Real ale ~ Meals and snacks ~ (01872) 501263 ~ Children in eating area of bar ~ Open 12-2.30, 7-11(10.30 Sun); closed winter Mon, closed Mon lunchtime in summer (except bank holidays)

ST AGNES SW7250 Map 1

Railway

10 Vicarage Rd; from centre follow B3277 signs for Porthtowan and Truro

You can be sure of a really friendly welcome from the helpful licensees in this busy little local – and the various nooks and crannies are full of interest. There is a remarkarkable collection of shoes in the older part – minute or giant, made of strange skins, fur, leather, wood, mother-of-pearl, or embroidered with gold and silver, from Turkey, Persia, China or Japan, and worn by ordinary people or famous men; also, some splendid brasswork that includes one of the finest original horsebrass collections in the country – and a notable collection of naval memorabilia from model sailing ships and rope fancywork to the texts of Admiralty messages at important historical moments, such as the announcement of the ceasefire at the end of the First World War. Enjoyable bar food includes lunchtime sandwiches (from £2.25), as well as home-made soup (£2.25), filled baked potatoes (from £3.50), ploughman's (from £4.35), cannelloni (£5.95), fisherman's platter with five different sorts of fish (£6.95), steaks (from £8.95), daily specials such as steak and kidney pie (£3.95) or fresh plaice (£6.95), a winter Sunday roast (two courses £4.95), and OAP specials (two courses with coffee £3.95). Well kept Bass, Boddingtons and Flowers IPA on handpump kept under light blanket pressure; darts, fruit machine, juke box, and piped music. This year, they have built a new terrace area. *(Recommended by Mayur Shah, Romey Heaton, John Woodward, Mrs M Furness, Chris and Margaret Southon)*

Greenalls ~ Tenants Patsy and Ian Davey ~ Real ale ~ Meals and snacks ~ (01872) 552310 ~ Children in family room and eating areas ~ Open 11-3, 6-11; 12-3, 7-10.30 Sun ~ Bedrooms: £14/£30

Anyone claiming to arrange or prevent inclusion of a pub in the *Guide* is a fraud. Pubs are included only if recommended by genuine readers and if our own anonymous inspection confirms that they are suitable.

ST AGNES (Isles of Scilly) SV8807 Map 1

Turks Head

The Quay

Britain's most south-westerly pub, this little slate-roofed white cottage is a smashing place to unwind. From the few tables on a patch of lawn across the sleepy lane from the pub are wonderful views over the bay, and there are steps down to the slipway so you can walk down with your drinks and food and sit right on the shore. Inside, the simply furnished but cosy and very friendly pine-panelled bar has quite a collection of flags, helmets and headwear and banknotes, as well as maritime photographs and model ships; the dining extension is no smoking, the cats are called Taggart and Lacey, and the collie, Tina. At lunchtime, the decent bar food includes legendary huge locally made pasties (though they do sell out; £3.25), open sandwiches (from £1.95; local crab £4.25), ploughman's (from £4.25), salads (from £5.25; local crab £6.75), cold roast beef with chips (£4.95), vegetable pasta bake (£5.25), and puddings like sticky toffee pudding (£2.65), with evening gammon in port wine sauce (£6.25), fresh fish of the day, and sirloin steak (£8.95); children's meals (from £2.50). Ice cream and cakes are sold through the afternoon, and in good weather they do good evening barbecues (£3-7 Tuesday, Thursday and Sunday, July/August only), arranging special boats from St Marys – as most tripper boats leave by 5-ish. Remarkably, they also have real ale which arrives in St Agnes via a beer supplier in St Austell and two boat trips: Dartmoor Best, Flowers Original and IPA, Ind Coope Burton, and Tetleys well kept on handpump, besides decent house wines, a good range of malt whiskies, and hot chocolate with brandy. Darts, cribbage, dominoes and piped music. In spring and autumn hours may be shorter, and winter opening is sporadic, given that only some 70 people live on the island; they do then try to open if people ask, and otherwise tend to open on Saturday night, Sunday lunchtime (bookings only, roast lunch), over Christmas and the New Year, and for a Wednesday quiz night. *(Recommended by Pete and Rosie Flower, R J Walden, Michael Sargent, John and June Freeman, D J Priestley, David Mead, Steve and Carolyn Harvey)*

Free house ~ Licensees John and Pauline Dart ~ Real ale ~ Meals and snacks ~ (01720) 422434 ~ Well behaved children welcome ~ Open 10.15am-11pm; 10.15am-10.30pm Sun (see text for winter) ~ Bedroom: /£50B

ST BREWARD SX0977 Map 1

Old Inn

Old Town; village signposted off B3266 S of Camelford, also signed off A30 Bolventor—Bodmin

To find this friendly little country pub, just head for the church which is a landmark for miles around. There's a lot of character in the two-roomed bar with fine broad slate flagstones, banknotes and horsebrasses hanging from the low oak joists that support the ochre upstairs floorboards, and plates on the stripped stonework. The outer room has fewer tables (old ones, of character), an open log fire in big granite fireplace, a piano and sensibly placed darts. The inner room has cushioned wall benches and chairs around its tables, a good log fire, and a glass panel showing a separate no-smoking games room with darts, pool, juke box, trivia, and fruit machine, where children are allowed; cribbage. Big helpings of popular home-made bar food include lunchtime baps and sandwiches (from £2.25) and ploughman's (£4), filled baked potatoes (from £3), ham and eggs (£4.50), local plaice (£5), home-made chicken curry or vegetable chilli (£5.50), home-made pie of the day (£5.75), a huge mixed grill (£8.50 or £9.50), and children's menu (from £2.75); in winter there are roast Sunday lunches (£4.95), and they hold monthly themed food evenings in the no-smoking restaurant. Well kept Bass, Ruddles County, and Sharps Doom Bar and Special Ale on handpump; the landlord is from the West Highlands and his range of over 100 malt whiskies reflects this – in winter, there are monthly malt whisky tastings. A thoughtful wine list, and fast, efficient service. Picnic-sets outside are protected by low stone walls. There's plenty of open moorland behind, and cattle and sheep wander freely into the village. In front of the building is a very worn carved stone; no one knows exactly what it is but it may be part of a Saxon cross. *(Recommended by Dr D J Walker, Ted George, Howard Clutterbuck, Jeff Davies, Andy and Jill Kassube, Jo and Gary Charlton)*

Free house ~ Licensees Iain and Ann Cameron ~ Real ale ~ Meals and snacks (not 25 Dec) ~ Restaurant ~ (01208) 850711 ~ Children in eating area of bar and in own room ~ Open 12-3(2.30 in winter), 6-11; 12-3, 7-10.30 Sun

ST EWE SW9746 Map 1

Crown

Village signposted from B3287; easy to find from Mevagissey

One reader has been visiting this popular unspoilt cottage in its quiet village setting for 40 years (which is almost as long as Mr Jeffery has been running it) and finds it as welcoming as ever. The traditional bar has 16th-c flagstones, a very high-backed curved old settle with flowery cushions, long shiny wooden tables, an ancient weight-driven working spit, and a relaxed atmosphere; the fireside shelves hold plates, and a brass teapot and jug. The eating area has cushioned old church pews and velvet curtains. Bar food (they tell us that prices have not increased this year) includes good, fresh pasties, sandwiches (from £1.95, local crab in season £4.25, open sandwiches from £4.25), soup (£2), ploughman's or filled baked potatoes (from £3.95), gammon and egg or fresh seasonal crab salad (£7.50), tasty steaks (from £8.50), grilled lemon sole (£9.95; evenings only), daily specials, and puddings like home-made fruit or very good mincemeat and brandy pies (from £2.10). Well kept St Austell Tinners and HSD on handpump, several malt whiskies, and local wine; fruit machine and piped music. Several picnic-sets on a raised back lawn. Handy for the Lost Gardens of Heligan. Please note, they no longer do bedrooms. *(Recommended by David Carr, R Inman, Christopher Wright, Roger Huggins, Ewan McCall, Nick Lawless, John A Barker, Peter and Daphne Ross, Pete and Rosie Flower, Maria Furness, A Cowell, Brian Skelcher, Rita Horridge, DJW, David and Jane Russell, Mr and Mrs A C Curry, John and June Freeman, Wayne Wheeler)*

St Austell ~ Tenant Norman Jeffery ~ Real ale ~ Meals and snacks ~ Restaurant ~ (01726) 843322 ~ Children in eating area of bar and in restaurant ~ Open 11-3, 6-11; 12-3, 7-10.30 Sun

ST JUST IN PENWITH SW3631 Map 1

Star 🛏

Fore Street

Almost of a different era, this friendly old village inn remains quite unchanged with its informal, very relaxed atmosphere and bearded, characterful regulars. The dimly lit L-shaped bar has appropriately old-fashioned furnishings, tankards hanging over the serving counter, some stripped masonry, and a good many mining samples and mementoes; there's also a small separate snug. Good value bar food includes sandwiches, pasties (£2), home-made soup with garlic bread or cheese melties (£3.50), home-made fishcakes with herby potatoes or chicken and mushroom pie (£4.20), and crab averock (£5.50); no chips. Well kept St Austell Tinners and HSD tapped from the cask, with XXXX Mild and Trelawnys Pride on handpump; farm cider in summer, mulled wine in winter, and old-fashioned drinks like mead, lovage and brandy or shrub with rum; shove-ha'penny, cribbage, dominoes, bar billiards, table skittles, fruit machine, shut the box, euchre, and juke box. Attractive back yard with roses, a gunnera, and tables. The bedrooms are simple but comfortably furnished in period style, with notable breakfasts; the pub's not far from the coast path. *(Recommended by Ian and Jacqui Ross, Dave and Deborah Irving, John McDonald, Ann Bond, Anthony Barnes, Bronwen and Steve Wrigley, Wayne Wheeler, Val Stevenson, Rob Holmes)*

St Austell ~ Tenants Rosie and Peter Angwin ~ Real ale ~ Meals and snacks ~ (01736) 788767 ~ Children in snug ~ Live music Mon, all comers Thurs and Sat, occasional singing Fri ~ Open 11-11; 12-10.30 Sun; 11-3, 6-11 Mon-Thurs in winter ~ Bedrooms: £18/£30(£40B)

ST KEVERNE SW7921 Map 1

White Hart

The Square; at the end of B3293 SE of Helston – the village is well signposted

The old coaching house at the back of this friendly inn has been turned into a Sports Bar with darts, juke box, an additional pool table and satellite TV; this will overlook a partly covered raised terrace extension to the garden filled with herbs and creepers. The black beams of the bar are hung with horsebrasses, there's a mix of wall seats, mate's chairs and some heavy rustic small wooden seats around sturdy tables on the bare boards, a relaxed, chatty atmosphere, and an open fire. As well as summer daily special fish dishes and winter game, good enjoyable bar food includes lunchtime filled baked potatoes (from £3), and sandwiches or french bread (from £3.25), plus soup (£2.50), garlic mushrooms (£3.95), home-made lasagne (£5; spinach and goat's cheese £5.50), sizzling platters of marinated meat with floured tortillas, sour cream and avocado salsa (from £6.50), salads (from £6), seafood platter (£6.50/£8.50), and puddings like mango and white chocolate cheesecake or treacle tart (from £3); children's menu (from £3). A monthly newsletter keeps people up to date with events. Well kept Flowers Original and a guest ale with Morlands Old Speckled Hen and Wadworths 6X as summer additions. Outside are some picnic-sets on a narrow front terrace, with more on a side lawn. Dogs welcome – their own black labrador bitch is called Incie. *(Recommended by Tim Barrow, Sue Demont, Paul and Pam Penrose, Mr and Mrs Harris, Sylvia Sutherland, A Evans, P Boultwood, R Moon, Mr and Mrs D T Deas, Vicki Berry, Alex Roberts, David and Rachael Padfield)*

Greenalls ~ Tenants Nick and Pippa Botting ~ Real ale ~ Meals and snacks ~ Restaurant ~ (01326) 280325 ~ Children welcome ~ Open 11-11; 12-10.30 Sun; 12-2.30, 6-11 in winter ~ Bedrooms: /£50B

ST KEW SX0276 Map 1

St Kew Inn

Village signposted from A39 NE of Wadebridge

A new licensee has taken over this rather grand-looking old stone building set in a peaceful hamlet. The neatly kept and friendly bar has winged high-backed settles and varnished rustic tables on the lovely dark Delabole flagstones, black wrought-iron rings for lamps or hams hanging from the high ceiling, a handsome window seat, and an open kitchen range under a high mantlepiece decorated with earthenware flagons. At lunchtime, bar food includes sandwiches, soup (£1.95), filled baked potatoes (£3.75), ploughman's (£3.95), leeks and bacon in a cheese sauce (£4.50), a pie of the day (£5.50), vegetarian dishes, and sirloin steak (£9.50), with evening extras like cold cured mackerel (£3.50), king prawns in garlic (£3.95), curry of the day (£5.95), fish of the day, duck with a plum and port sauce (£9.50), daily specials such as chicken parmigiana (£5.95), fried fresh haddock (£6.95), and fillet of sole stuffed with smoked salmon mousse and prawn sauce (£9.50), and children's menu (from £3.25). Well kept St Austell Tinners and HSD tapped from wooden casks behind the counter (lots of tankards hang from the beams above it). The big garden has seats on the grass and picnic-sets on the front cobbles. Parking is in what must have been a really imposing stable yard. The church next door is lovely. Please note, they no longer do bedrooms. *(Recommended by John A Barker, David Carr, Mike and Heather Watson, Richard Cole, L Granville, Graham Tayar, Catherine Raeburn, Jacquie and Jim Jones, D Marsh, Andy and Jill Kassube, Jo and Gary Charlton, Pamela and Merlyn Horswell, Brian and Bett Cox, Jenny and Brian Seller, Iain Robertson, James and Ruth Morrell; more reports on the new regime, please)*

St Austell ~ Tenant Desmond Weston ~ Real ale ~ Meals and snacks ~ Restaurant ~ (01208) 841259 ~ Well behaved children in restaurant ~ Open 11-2.30, 6-11; 12-2.30, 7-10.30 Sun

Most pubs in the *Guide* sell draught cider. We mention it specifically only if they have unusual farm-produced 'scrumpy' or even specialise in it.

ST MAWES SW8433 Map 1

Victory

One reader told us that this was the type of place he always hoped for in a Cornish coastal village – an unpretentious and friendly little fisherman's local. It's tucked away up a steep lane just up from the harbour and Falmouth ferry, and is well liked by regulars as well as visitors. The simple bar is full of sailing and other sea photographs, and there's a carpeted back part with comfortable seats, an antique settle and old prints of Cornish scenes. Good bar food includes home-made soup (£2.75), sandwiches (from £2.80; crab £5.50), filled baked potatoes (from £3.30), local pasty (£3.35), lasagne or steak and kidney pie (£5.50), cashew nut paella (£5.55), steak (£8.75), children's dishes (from £2.70), and daily specials; the restaurant is no smoking. Well kept Bass, Flowers Original, and Greenalls Original on handpump. Benches outside on the cobbles give glimpses of the sea. *(Recommended by D P and J A Sweeney, John Woodward, Nigel Wikeley, A Ball, DJW, G W Stevenson)*

Greenalls ~ Lease: Phillip and Marie Bridget Savage ~ Real ale ~ Meals and snacks ~ Restaurant ~ (01326) 270324 ~ Children welcome ~ Occasional live entertainment ~ Parking in public car park ~ Open 11-11; 12-10.30 Sun ~ Bedrooms: /£40(£50B)

ST MAWGAN SW8765 Map 1

Falcon

NE of Newquay, off B3276 or A3059

In a quiet tree-lined village, this pretty wisteria-covered pub has a big friendly bar with a log fire, small modern settles and large antique coaching prints on the walls, and plenty of space for eating the enjoyable bar food, which might include lunchtime sandwiches such as smoked salmon and cottage cheese with chives (£3.25), fresh cod or plaice (£4.95), venison sausages in red wine and juniper berries (£5.75), prawns in garlic butter (£8.75), and steaks (from £8.95). The restaurant is no smoking. Well kept St Austell Tinners, HSD and Trelawny's Pride on handpump; efficient service even when busy. As well as being quite a summer suntrap, the peaceful, pretty garden has plenty of seats, a wishing well, play equipment for children, and good views of the village; also, stone tables in a cobbled courtyard. A handsome church is nearby. *(Recommended by Patrick Hancock, Mr and Mrs R Head, Klaus and Elizabeth Leist, David Carr, Neil and Anita Christopher, Mrs M Furness, Edward Frogatt, Andy and Jill Kassube, Pamela and Merlyn Horswell)*

St Austell ~ Tenant Andy Banks ~ Real ale ~ Meals and snacks (not 25 Dec) ~ Restaurant ~ Children in restaurant ~ (01637) 860225 ~ Open 11-3, 6-11; 12-3, 7-10.30 Sun ~ Bedrooms: £17/£45(£55S)

TREBARWITH SX0585 Map 1

Port William

Trebarwith Strand

The setting here is lovely and the views over the beach, Gull Rock, and out to sea can be enjoyed from the picnic-sets across the road or from the covered terrace; the sunsets are marvellous. Inside, there's quite a nautical theme with fishing nets and maritime memorabilia decorating the walls, a separate gallery area with work by local artists, and the no-smoking 'marine room' which has three different fish tanks showing a live reef with corals, one with seahorses, and another with marine fish (proving popular with both adults and children). Bar food includes daily specials such as home-made celery and stilton soup (£2.95), good mussels in cider and cream (£4.75), mushroom stroganoff (£6.45), steak and kidney pie (£6.95), halibut with mustard, cream and cheese sauce (£9.75), duck breast in green peppercorn sauce (£10.95), and whole grilled dover sole (£14.50); from the menu, there might be pasties (£2.95), filled rolls (from £3.25), cold platters (from £5.95; crab £7.95), and evening roast duckling (£10.95), and steaks (from £11.95); children's meals (from £1.65). Bass, Boddingtons, Flowers, and St Austell Tinners on handpump, kept under light blanket pressure. Darts, pool, cribbage, dominoes, fruit machine, video game and piped music.

(Recommended by Rita Horridge, Dennis Stevens, John Westlake, R J Walden, Mr and Mrs Archibald, Tim Barrow, Sue Demont, Andy and Jill Kassube, Barry Perfect, Jeff Davies, Anna Ralph, K Flack)

Free house ~ Licensee Peter Hale ~ Real ale ~ Meals and snacks ~ Restaurant ~ (01840) 770230 ~ Children welcome away from main bar ~ Folk music Fri evening ~ Open 11-11; 12-10.30 Sun ~ Bedrooms: £43.50(£67B)

TREBURLEY SX3477 Map 1

Springer Spaniel

A388 Callington—Launceston

It isn't just the very good food that readers like so much in this well run pub, but the friendly welcome, thoughtful little wine list, decent beer, and relaxed atmosphere. The bar has a lovely, very high-backed settle by the woodburning stove in the big fireplace, high-backed farmhouse chairs and other seats, and pictures of olde-worlde stage-coach arrivals at inns; this leads into at room with chintzy-cushioned armchairs and sofa in one corner, and a big solid teak table; bagatelle. Up some steps from the main bar is the beamed, attractively furnished, no-smoking restaurant. The enjoyable bar food includes sandwiches or rolls (from £2; roast duck £3.50), macaroni with bacon (£4.75), vegetable laksa (£5.25), cassoulet of pork and beans or steak and kidney pie (£5.95), chicken and prawn gumbo (£6.95), venison and game pie (£8.50), and puddings such as chocolate mousse with a light and dark chocolate sauce, frozen peach yoghurt with raspberries, honey and a raspberry coulis or bread and butter pudding (from £2.95). Well kept Dartmoor Best and St Austell HSD on handpump, several malt whiskies, and a good choice of spirits; very good service. *(Recommended by J C Perry, Jacquie and Jim Jones, John and Vivienne Rice, Miss G Glen, R J Walden, Mrs H Murphy, R A Cullingham, Bett and Brian Cox, Mrs R Pearson, Patrick Freeman, Sarah Jones, Gay Richardson)*

Free house ~ Licensee John Pitchford ~ Real ale ~ Meals and snacks ~ Restaurant ~ (01579) 370424 ~ Children welcome ~ Open 11-3, 5.30-11; 12-3, 7-10.30 Sun

TREGADILLETT SX2984 Map 1

Eliot Arms ★★

Village signposted off A30 at junction with A395, W end of Launceston bypass

The welcoming licensees have laid old Delabole slate floors in some of the charming little softly lit rooms here. They have also started a collection of barometers (10 so far) to add to the 72 antique clocks (including 7 grandfathers), 400 snuffs, hundreds of horsebrasses, old prints, old postcards or cigarette cards grouped in frames on the walls, and shelves of books and china. There's a fine old mix of furniture, from high-backed built-in curved settles, through plush Victorian dining chairs, armed seats, chaise longues and mahogany housekeeper's chairs, to more modern seats, open fires, flowers on most tables, and a lovely ginger cat called Peewee; inoffensive piped music. Generous helpings of good home-made food (they now use mostly local produce and smoke their own chicken and ham) includes open sandwiches or locally made chargrilled burgers (from £3.95), ploughman's (from £4.25), vegetable moussaka (£5.75), steak, kidney and mushroom pie (£5.95), half home-smoked chicken (£7.95), steaks (from £8.75), and daily specials like liver and bacon (£5.95), local game pie or local crab salad (£6.95), and oriental platter (£9.50), and bass in cream with prawns (£10.95); enjoyable Sunday lunch. Well kept Dartmoor Best, St Austell Trelawny's Pride and HSD, and a summer guest beer on handpump, a fair choice of wines, several malt whiskies, farm cider, and friendly service; darts, shove-ha'penny, and fruit machine. A garden beyond the car park has picnic-sets, a good climbing frame, swing and playhouse. A new 4-poster room has been added this year. *(Recommended by Graham Tayar, Catherine Raeburn, M G Hart, David Carr, J Henry, Nigel Wikeley, Roger and Christine Mash, Paul and Judith Booth, D B Jenkin, Roy Smylie, Edward Froggatt, P and J Shapley, P and J Salmon, Brian Skelcher, Christopher Turner, James Nunns, Dr and Mrs A Whiteway, S Watkin, P Taylor, Mrs M Furness, Philip Orbell, Jeff Davies, James and Ruth Morrell, Brian and Bett Cox)*

Free House ~ Licensees John Cook and Lesley Elliott ~ Real ale ~ Meals and snacks (not 25 Dec) ~ (01566) 772051 ~ Children in eating area of bar ~ Open 11-2.30(3 Sat), 6-11; 12-2.30, 7-10.30 Sun ~ Bedrooms: £25(£30B)/£40(£50B)

TRESCO (Isles of Scilly) SV8915 Map 1

New Inn

New Grimsby

A good mix of locals and visitors creates a fine bustling atmosphere in this old inn, once a row of fishermen's cottages. The light and airy bars are attractively refurbished with lots of washed-up wood from a ship's cargo, solid pine bar chairs, farmhouse chairs and tables, a collection of old telescopes, and a model yacht. Good bar food includes sandwiches, and lots of changing daily specials such as filling French-style fish soup (£5), monkfish in grain mustard sauce (£7.95), and seafood salad or casserole (£8.90). The well regarded and cheerfully decorated no-smoking restaurant also has a separate children's menu. On handpump, there may be a choice of Flowers Original, Fullers London Pride, St Austell HSD, Marstons Pedigree, and Whitbreads Castle Eden on handpump, interesting wines, 30 malt whiskies, and 10 vodkas. Darts, pool, juke box, cribbage, dominoes and piped music. There are picnic-sets in the garden. *(Recommended by Michael Sargent, Kevin Flack, R J Walden, John and Vivienne Rice, Dr Alan Green, Nigel Abbott, Cliff Blakemore, Steve and Carolyn Harvey)*

Free house ~ Licensee Graham Shone ~ Real ale ~ Meals and snacks ~ Restaurant ~ (01720) 422844 ~ Children in eating area of bar until 9.30 ~ Live entertainment every 3 weeks ~ Open 11-11; 12-3, 6-10.30 Sun; 12-2.30, 7-11 in winter ~ Bedrooms: /£146B – this includes dinner

TRURO SW8244 Map 1

Old Ale House ★ £

7 Quay St/Princes St

Back-to-basics, old-fashioned pubs don't always appeal to a wide mix of customers, but this bustling, friendly place manages to do just that. Perhaps it has something to do with the fact that they keep up to 24 constantly changing real ales on handpump or tapped from the cask such as Boddingtons, Bass, Cotleigh Old Buzzard and Tawny, Courage Best and Directors, Exmoor Gold, Ale and Beast, Fullers London Pride, Glentworth Dizzy Blonde, Kings Head Golden Goose, Marstons Owd Rodger, Morlands Old Speckled Hen, RCH East St Cream, Sharps Own, Skinners Betty Stogs and Cornish Knocker Ale, John Smiths Bitter, Shepherd Neame Spitfire, Smiles Heritage, Theakstons Old Peculier, and Westwood Oasthouse Gold; also country wines. The dimly lit bar has an engaging diversity of furnishings, some interesting 1920s bric-a-brac, beer mats pinned everywhere, matchbox collections, newpapers and magazines to read, and a barrel full of monkey nuts whose crunchy discarded shells mix affably with the fresh sawdust on the floor; piped music. Highly enjoyable bar food, freshly prepared in a spotless kitchen in full view of the bar includes doorstep sandwiches (from £2.65; delicious hot baked garlic bread with melted cheese from £1.95), filled oven-baked potatoes (from £2.95), ploughman's (from £3.65), very good hot meals served in a skillet pan like oriental chicken, sizzling beef or vegetable stir-fry (small helpings from £3.50, big helpings from £3.95), lasagne or steak in ale pie (£4.55), daily specials, and puddings (£2.25). *Recommended by John A Barker, Ted George, W W Burke, Mayur Shah, Klaus and Elizabeth Leist, Pat and Tony Martin, Stephen Horsley, Mr and Mrs B Hobden, B M and P Kendall, Andy and Jill Kassube, Catherine Lloyd, Philip Orbell, Peter Baggott, Keith and Janet Morris, P and M Rudlin, Mr and Mrs A Curry, Jacquie and Jim Jones)*

Greenalls ~ Managers Howard Grave, Julie Marshall ~ Real ale ~ Meals and snacks (not Sun evening) ~ (01872) 271122 ~ Children in eating area of bar until 8.30 ~ Live bands Mon, Weds, Thurs evenings, duo Sat evening ~ Open 11-11; 12-10.30 Sun

Lucky Dip

Besides the fully inspected pubs, you might like to try these Lucky Dips recommended to us and described by readers (if you do, please send us reports):

Angarrack [SW5838], *Angarrack*: Welcoming village local tucked below railway viaduct in little secluded valley, three well kept St Austell beers, good value food inc local fish, no machines or music; good gig racing team *(Dave and Deborah Irving, D Cheesbrough)*

☆ **Bodmin** [Dunmere (A389 NW); SX0467], *Borough Arms*: Neat and friendly, with stripped stone, open fire, lots of railway photographs and posters, well kept Bass, Boddingtons and Whitbreads, decent wines, friendly atmosphere, speedy service and plenty of room even when busy, big helpings of good value straightforward food (no sandwiches), unobtrusive piped music, fruit machine; children in side room, picnic-sets out among shady apple trees *(David Carr, John and Jackie Chalcraft, BB)*

Bodmin [Crockwell St], *Hole in the Wall*: Former debtors' prison, masses of bric-a-brac inc old rifles, pistols and swords, old stonework, well kept Bass, Boddingtons, Worthington and Wadworths 6X, good value generous bar food inc fish (not Sun or winter evenings) meals, upstairs dining bar; yard behind with small stream running past *(Dr D J Walker)*

☆ **Boscastle** [upper village, stiff climb from harbour; SX0990], *Napoleon*: Appealing 16th-c pub, comfortable and welcoming little low-beamed rooms, interesting Napoleon prints, good generous bar food inc fresh veg and vegetarian, no-smoking restaurant, well kept Bass and St Austell tapped from the cask, decent wines, good coffee, friendly staff and locals, polished slate floor, big open fire, pool room, children allowed; piped music, maybe folk music; sheltered terrace, second larger family garden; may close early if quiet *(Jeanne Cross, Paul Silvestri, Jeff Davies, Ann and Colin Hunt, John and Vivienne Rice, Richard Houghton, A Addington, LYM)*

Breage [3 miles W of Helston; SW6128], *Queens Arms*: Popular local with long narrow bar, open fire, beams festooned with plates, no-smoking dining room, generous popular hot food, sandwiches (sometimes hefty), vegetarian and children's dishes, Whitbreads-related ales, welcoming landlord; tables and children's games room outside, another play area and garden over the lane; quiz night Weds; bedrooms, interesting church opp *(D B Jenkin)*

Bude [Vicarage Rd; SS2005], *Brendon Arms*: Friendly canalside pub with two big bars, back family room, Bass and Sharps Own, good standard food and interesting specials, tables on front grass; bedrooms *(P and M Rudlin)*

☆ **Bude** [Falcon Terrace; SS2005], *Falcon*: Bustling bar overlooking canal in impressive 19th-c hotel, lots of quick good value food inc crunchy veg, daily roast, local fish and good puddings, well kept Bass and St Austell Tinners and HSD, attentive friendly staff, big family room with two pool tables; bedrooms comfortable and well equipped, good breakfast *(Gerry Hollington, Dr and Mrs N Holmes, Rita Horridge, David Carr)*

☆ **Cadgwith** [SW7214], *Cadgwith Cove*: Friendly local open all day at least in summer, roomy and clean, local seascapes, snacks in lounge inc sandwiches, ploughman's and lots of well priced plain food with chips, well kept beer, lively sing-song Fri; big front terrace overlooking fish sheds and bay, outstanding village; separate restaurant *(Paul and Pam Penrose, Ewan and Moira McCall)*

☆ **Camborne** [B3303 out towards Helston; SW6440], *Old Shire*: Homely family pub with popular carvery, usual pub meals in dining area (small fee for extra plate to share generous helpings), young efficient staff, modern back extension with lots of easy chairs and sofas, Bass and Dartmoor Best, decent wines, pictures for sale and great coal fire; children welcome, pleasant garden with summer barbecues, five bedrooms *(Gwen and Peter Andrews, K H Frostick, Eamonn and Natasha Skyrme, Dave and Deborah Irving, P and M Rudlin, Stephen Horsley)*

Camelford [Main St (A39); SX1083], *Masons Arms*: Unpretentious heavy-beamed stonebuilt pub with well kept St Austell ales, good food inc children's dishes, local photographs, advertising mirrors, houseplants; pool and juke box in one bar; children allowed *(G Washington)*

Canons Town [Rose-an-Grouse; A30 Hayle—Penzance; SW5335], *Lamb & Flag*: Some concentration on good food, good choice inc vegetarian; well kept beer, warm welcome *(James and Wendy Timms)*

Cargreen [the Quay; off A388 Callington—Saltash; SX4362], *Crooked Spaniard*: Big smart river-view dining area, small panelled bar, huge fireplace in another smallish room, well kept ales, good generous food; lovely spot, with waterside tables on terrace by Tamar – always some river activity, esp at high tide *(Ted George, M Joyner)*

Charlestown [by Pier House Hotel; SX0351], *Harbour*: Small well managed bar with good varied food and first-class location alongside and looking over the classic little harbour; interesting film-set conservation village with shipwreck museum *(W W Burke)*; *Rashleigh Arms*: Large pub focused on good generous quick straightforward food inc fresh fish and popular puddings, seats out by the little harbour; well kept ales inc Sharps, friendly service, big restaurant, good canalside family room; piped music may be loud; good value bedrooms *(N Lawless, D B Jenkin)*

Coverack [SW7818], *Paris*: Friendly old-fashioned pub above harbour, spectacular bay views, well kept ale, food esp local fish and seafood, also children's, good Sun lunch and teas, interesting wooden moulds from Falmouth churchyard; restaurant, garden; bedrooms *(Colin Gooch, Eamonn and Natasha Skyrme, Tim Barrow, Sue Demont)*

☆ **Crackington Haven** [SX1396], *Coombe Barton*: Huge clean open-plan pub in tiny village, spectacular sea view from roomy lounge/dining area, friendly helpful service, good value food inc local fish, well kept local and other ales, good coffee, back family room, tables on big terrace, games room with pool tables; bedrooms *(Jenny and Brian Seller)*

Crantock [Langurroc Rd; SW7960], *Old Albion*: Pleasantly placed thatched village pub with old-fashioned tastefully decorated bar, friendly relaxed atmosphere, good range of generous home-made food, up to five real ales *(Patrick Hancock, LYM)*

Cripples Ease [SW5036], *Engine*: Former counting house of old tin mine, popular with locals and visitors; well kept Marstons Pedigree, decent food, pool; superb moorland location, views of the sea on all sides from nearby hill; bedrooms good value *(Susan and Nigel Wilson)*

Devoran [SW7939], *Old Quay*: Friendly old local idyllically placed in creekside village, unpretentious decor, welcoming obliging licensees, wide choice of generous cheap food, well kept ale; good value bedrooms *(Maria Furness)*

☆ **Falmouth** [Custom House Quay; SW8032], *Chain Locker*: Well placed overlooking inner harbour, with welcoming atmosphere and strongly nautical decor, well kept Bass, Flowers Original, and Worthington Best, food majoring on fresh local fish, good value sandwiches etc too, good separate darts alley; fruit machine, piped music; well behaved children welcome, open all day; self-catering accommodation; well up to main entry standard, but no recent reports *(LYM)*

Falmouth [Dracaena Ave/Grenville Rd (A39)], *Four Winds*: Spotless and roomy, bright plants in warm airy conservatory, good generous food inc particularly good value puddings (may be big tourist parties for late lunches, so get there on time), bargain two-sitting Sun carvery with help-yourself veg – worth booking, friendly staff, french doors to terrace, pleasant shady garden *(D B Jenkin, Mr and Mrs B Hobden)*

☆ **Fowey** [Fore St; SX1252], *Ship*: Friendly and pubby local, good choice of good value generous food from sandwiches through local fish and chips to steak, comfortably worn-in cloth-banquette main bar with coal fire, pool/darts room, family dining room with big stained-glass window; well kept St Austell Tinners and HSD, juke box or piped music (may obtrude), dogs allowed; bedrooms old-fashioned, some oak-panelled *(R W A Suddaby, A J Thomas, Dr S P Willavoys, G Washington, Catherine Lloyd, BB)*

☆ **Fowey** [Town Quay; from centre follow Car Ferry signs], *Galleon*: Superb spot overlooking harbour and estuary, well refurbished with solid pine, generous fresh good value food inc generous fresh local fish, well kept and priced Bass, Flowers IPA and Sharps, fast friendly service, tables out on extended waterside terrace *(P and M Rudlin, JDM, KM, BB)*

Fowey [Town Quay], *King of Prussia*: Upstairs bay windows looking over harbour to Polruan, well kept St Austell ales, good welcoming service, piped pop music (may obtrude), side family food bar with wide choice of fish and seafood, seats outside; bedrooms *(Ted George, M Jeanes, LYM)*; *Lugger*: Unpretentious locals' bar, comfortable small dining area popular with older people for good inexpensive food, cheap St Austell beers, friendly service, big waterfront mural, tables outside; bedrooms *(Ted George, Janet and Colin Roe, BB)*

Goldsithney [B3280; SW5430], *Crown*: Tidy pub with bargain lunches and Sun roasts, L-shaped bar and small restaurant/function room, St Austell ales, decent house wines, friendly service; pretty suntrap glass-roofed front loggia, masses of flowers outside *(Jack and Gemima Valiant, J and B Cressey)*

☆ **Grampound** [Fore St; A390 St Austell—Truro; SW9348], *Dolphin*: Small village inn with very friendly helpful staff, good value generous straightforward food inc OAP lunches Weds and home-made pasties, well kept St Austell ales, decent house wines, comfortable chintzy settees and easy chairs, interesting prints; children allowed, pool, fruit machine; handy for Trewithen Gardens; bedrooms *(Andy and Jill Kassube, Howard Clutterbuck, D B Jenkin, Gwen and Peter Andrews)*

Gulval [SW4831], *Coldstreamer*: Busy but very clean and civilised local, comfortable dining atmosphere, very enjoyable food (dover sole, pork and venison sausages and puddings all recommended), well kept Bass and Greenalls, a welcome from cheerful polite staff, unusual high ceilings, cosy restaurant; quiet pleasant village but very handy for Scillies heliport – turn right opp entrance *(John and Kathleen Potter, D Allen)*

☆ **Gurnards Head** [B3306 Zennor—St Just; SW4338], *Gurnards Head*: Unspoilt flagstoned pubby bar, real fires each end, real ales such as Bass, Flowers Original and Fullers London Pride, friendly service, substantial home-made food (not Mon evening); plain family room, piped music may sometimes obtrude, some live music; bedrooms, glorious walks in wonderful NT scenery, inland and along the cliffy coast *(Bronwen and Steve Wrigley, Lawrence Bacon, Jean Scott, Simon Williams, Jeanne Cross, Paul Silvestri)*

Gweek [SW7027], *Gweek Inn*: Happy family pub, large low-ceilinged bar with open fire, good reasonably priced home-made food, good service, moderate prices, lots of motoring trophies (enthusiast licensees); separate restaurant Tues-Sat (summer); children welcome, short walk from seal sanctuary *(John and Wendy Allin, Tim Barrow, Sue Demont)*

☆ **Helford Passage** [signed from B3291; SW7627], *Ferryboat*: Extensive bar in great summer spot by sandy beach with swimming, small boat hire, fishing trips and summer ferry to Helford, full St Austell range kept well, wide choice of generous food inc fresh fish, comfortable no-smoking restaurant, prompt cheerful service; piped music, games area with juke box and SkyTV; suntrap waterside terrace, barbecues, usually open all day summer (with cream teas and frequent live entertainment), welcome new car park; about a mile's walk from gate at bottom of Glendurgan Garden (NT); children allowed; can seem a bit brash and loud in summer *(G L Carlisle, C and E M Watson, Peter and Daphne Ross, S P Watkin, P A Taylor, Guy Consterdine, R J Bland, Nigel Woolliscroft, Ewan and Moira McCall, Sybille Weber, Carol Fellowes, John and Joan Calvert, LYM)*

Hessenford [A387 Looe—Torpoint; SX3057], *Copley Arms*: Spacious and attractive streamside garden and terrace, pleasant alcoves in eating area (some emphasis on food), well kept St Austell ales; piped music, dogs allowed in one small area, big plain family room, play area; bedrooms *(D B Jenkin)*

Kingsand [village green; SX4350], *Rising Sun*: Welcoming unpretentious local, generous food from sandwiches and pasties to local seafood, well kept ales such as Bass, Brains and Cornish Rebellion, open fire; can get packed, on one of Cornwall's best walks *(Dr and Mrs B D Smith, Roy and Judy Tudor Hughes, M Joyner)*

Langdon [B3254 N of Launceston; SX3089], *Countryman*: Well kept beer, bar food inc good snacks, friendly staff; very busy Sun lunchtime *(D B Jenkin)*

☆ **Lanner** [Comford (A393/B3298); SW7240], *Fox & Hounds*: Relaxed rambling bar with very friendly helpful staff, black beams, stripped stone, dark panelling, high-backed settles and cottagey chairs, warm fires, good choice of generous food from sandwiches up inc plenty of vegetarian, well kept Bass and St Austell Tinners, HSD and Winter Warmer tapped from the cask, partly no-smoking restaurant, children in dining area; pub games, piped music (may be loud); great floral displays in front, neat back garden with pond and play area; open all day weekends *(Mr and Mrs G R Parker, P and S White, C and E M Watson, Mr and Mrs J D Marsh, LYM)*

Launceston [15 Broad St; SX3384], *White Hart*: Civilised and popular old-fashioned dining room with home-made food from good sandwiches up inc good value help-yourself fresh salad bar, low prices; bar with Courage Best and Directors, button-back banquettes, flame-effect fire, darts, fruit machine and TV (shame about the piped pop music); bedrooms *(M Joyner, Brian Websdale, Guy Consterdine, BB)*

Lelant [Fore St; SW5437], *Badger*: Attractively furnished panelled pub, decent bar food inc daily fresh fish, St Austell Tinners and other beers, friendly efficient service; bedrooms good value, prettily decorated; wonderful breakfast *(Heather and Julio Louro)*; *Watermill*: Mainly upstairs restaurant, with well kept Tetleys in downstairs bar, black beams, dried flowers, local watercolours for sale, working waterwheel behind with gearing inside *(Dave and Deborah Irving)*

☆ **Lerryn** [signed from A390 in Lostwithiel; SX1457], *Ship*: Partly no smoking, with wide choice of reasonably priced popular bar food from sandwiches and good pasties up, well kept ales such as Bass, Courage Best, Morlands Old Speckled Hen and Sharps Doom Bar, local farm cider, fruit wines and malt whiskies, huge woodburner, games room with pool, children welcome; service – normally speedy – can slow; picnic-sets outside, play area; famous stepping-stones and three well signed waterside walks nearby; nice bedrooms in adjoining building, wonderful breakfast *(Iain Robertson, R Turnham, Edward Froggatt, A J Thomas, D B Jenkin, Dr and Mrs B D Smith, Peter and Daphne Ross, Peter and Audrey Dowsett, Stephen Horsley, Catherine Lloyd, P and M Rudlin, Patrick Freeman, LYM)*

☆ **Linkinhorne** [off B3257 NW of Callington; SX3173], *Church House*: Neatly modernised bar, part rustic furniture and flagstones, part plush and carpet, with customer snapshots, some decorative china etc, woodburner, darts; well kept Sharps Doom Bar and Skinners Cornish Knocker, low mark-ups on wine, popular home-made food inc vegetarian and some bargains for children, also plush restaurant; piped pop music may be loudish; nice spot opp church, has been cl Mon *(JDM, KM, R A Cullingham, J C Perry, BB)*

☆ **Lizard** [SW7012], *Top House*: Spotless well run pub particularly popular with older people; in same family for 40 years, lots of interesting local sea pictures, fine shipwreck relics and serpentine craftwork in neat bar with generous good value bar food inc good local fish and seafood specials, interesting vegetarian dishes, well kept Bass, Marstons Pedigree, Flowers IPA and Sharps, decent wines, sincere friendly staff, roaring log fire, big no-smoking area, no piped music (occasional live); fruit machine, darts, pool; tables on terrace, interesting nearby serpentine shop *(Paul and Pam Penrose, Tim Barrow, Sue Demont, Jeanne Cross, Paul Silvestri, Colin and Pat Bristow, John and Joan Calvert, Paul and Maggie Baker, Gwen and Peter Andrews, BB)*

☆ **Longrock** [old coast rd Penzance—Marazion; SW5031], *Mexico*: Imaginative range of generous good value food from substantial sandwiches up, plenty of local fish and shellfish, no-smoking dining extension, cheerful local atmosphere, well kept Bass and Marstons Pedigree, comfortable surroundings; former office of Mexico Mine Company, with massive stone walls *(Jack and Gemima Valiant, P and M Rudlin, Brian Skelcher)*

☆ **Looe** [Fore St, E Looe; SX2553], *Olde Salutation*: Big squareish beamed and tiled room with red leatherette seats and neat tables, nice old-fashioned fireplace, lots of local fishing photographs, side snug with olde-worlde harbour mural and fruit machine, step down to simple family room; consistently good simple food (not Sat evening) esp crab sandwiches or salads and Sun roasts, also vegetarian dishes, fast friendly service, well kept Ushers Best; piped music may be obtrusive, forget about parking; popular locally as The Sal – open all day, handy for coast path *(M E Williamson, D P and J A Sweeney, M Joyner, Dr and Mrs B D Smith, BB)*

Ludgvan [Lower Quarters; SW5033], *Old Inn*: Clean, comfortable and well run, with very welcoming landlord, good reasonably priced food; bedrooms *(Mr and Mrs B W Twiddy)*

☆ **Malpas** [off A39 S of Truro; SW8442], *Heron*: Genuine and friendly, in stunning setting above wooded creek; thriving atmosphere, good variety of generous quick fresh food inc good crab sandwiches – good value; St Austell Tinners and HSD, log fire, lots of local photographs; pool, machines, piped music; suntrap slate-paved terrace; children welcome, can be very busy *(Mr and Mrs J O Hicks, R Turnham, MF, LYM)*

☆ **Manaccan** [down hill signed to Gillan and St Keverne; SW7625], *New Inn*: Attractive old thatched local, friendly landlady, well kept ales such as Flowers IPA and Wadworths 6X tapped from the cask, wide choice of food inc local seafood and sandwiches (service even of these can slow when busy), traditional games – but modern tables and chairs; children and dogs welcome, winter darts and euchre nights, big garden with swing, pretty waterside village *(Brian Skelcher, Adrian Hastings, John and Sally Clarke, John and June Freeman, LYM)*

☆ **Marhamchurch** [off A39 just S of Bude; SS2203], *Bullers Arms*: Friendly atmosphere, oak beams and settles in pleasant rambling L-shaped bar, food inc unusual dishes as well as ploughman's and so forth (not cheap, but good), good choice of well kept beers inc Bass, Morlands Old Speckled Hen and Sharps, decent wine by the glass, good CD juke box, darts in flagstoned back part, restaurant; children welcome; tables and play area in sizeable garden, a mile's walk to the sea; bedrooms *(C P Scott-Malden, R J Walden, LYM)*

Mawgan [St Martin; SW7323], *Old Courthouse*: Spacious and comfortable open-plan split-level pub, well kept Whitbreads-related ales, food from enormous ploughman's, fried food and so forth to cheap Sun lunches; pool, piped music may be obtrusive; pleasant garden; bistro Thurs-Sat evenings and Sun lunchtime; children welcome *(Gwen and Peter Andrews, Nigel Woolliscroft, Mrs Maria Furness)*

☆ **Mawnan Smith** [W of Falmouth, off Penryn—Gweek rd – old B3291; SW7728], *Red Lion*: Big helpings of well cooked and presented food, lots of choice inc seafood (should book summer evening) in pleasantly furnished old thatched dining pub with open-view kitchen, pictures, plates and bric-a-brac in cosy softly lit interconnected beamed rooms inc no-smoking room behind restaurant, lots of wines by the glass, well kept Bass, Greenalls, Worthington and a guest beer, helpful staff; piped music, children allowed, handy for Glendurgan and Trebah Gardens *(Mrs Maria Furness, Pam Honour, Mr and Mrs J Pitts, R J Bland, Brian Skelcher, Nick Wikeley, Sybille Weber, Gwen and Peter Andrews, Chris and Margaret Southon, Mr and Mrs Treagust, Mr and Mrs Soar, LYM)*

☆ **Mevagissey** [off Fore St by Post Office; SX0145], *Fountain*: Welcoming unpretentious slate-floored local with good simple food inc fresh fish, well kept St Austell ales, obliging service, plenty of atmosphere, lots of old local prints and photographs, cosy side room off back alley; piano sing-songs some evenings, good fish in popular upstairs restaurant; SkyTV sports, pretty frontage *(Nick Lawless, Iain Robertson, David Carr, Christopher Wright, Pete and Rosie Flower)*

Mevagissey, *Kings Arms*: Small and welcoming, cheap cheerful food *(Pete and Rosie Flower)*; [Fore St, nr harbour], *Ship*: 16th-c pub with good generous quickly served food, full range of well kept St Austell beers, genial landlord, neat efficient staff; big comfortable room with small interesting areas, low ceilings, flagstones, nice nautical decor, open fire; fruit machines, juke box or piped music (may be loud), regular live music; bedrooms *(Christopher Wright, Pete and Rosie Flower, Edward Froggatt, M Rutherford, David Carr, Keith and Janet Morris)*

Mount Hawke [Old School Rd; SW7147], *Old School*: Three real ales and good cheap food (landlord catches fish) in unusual building – ex primary school; family skittles Sun, Tues, Thurs *(Martin Pacey)*

☆ **Mullion** [SW6719], *Old Inn*: Thatched and beamed village inn with emphasis on usual Greenalls bar food (all day Jul/Aug) from sandwiches to evening steaks, extensive eating areas, interesting nooks and crannies, lots of brasses, nautical items and old wreck pictures, big inglenook fireplace, no-smoking room, well kept Bass and guests such as Wadworths 6X and Whitbreads Castle Eden; children welcome, open all day Sat/Sun and Aug; can be very busy (esp on live music nights), service can slow, darts, fruit machine; picnic-sets in pretty garden; good bedrooms *(Jenny and Roger Huggins, Jo and Gary Charlton, Gwen and Peter Andrews, Edward Froggatt, Pam Honour, LYM)*

Newlyn [SW4628], *Tolcarne*: Clean and well kept traditional pub, good choice of food, well kept Morlands Old Speckled Hen and

Sharps Doom Bar; good parking – useful here *(Cliff Blakemore)*

☆ **Newquay** [Fore St; SW8061], *Fort*: Former master mariner's house in good setting high above beach and small harbour, brass and comfortable seating in roomy front bar, two further bars inc one for back conservatory, concentration on good food all day from sandwiches, hot baguettes and baked potatoes to chargrills, inc vegetarian and children's dishes, very reasonable prices, Bass, St Austell HSD and Wadworths 6X; big garden, good bedrooms *(Tony Scott, Mayur Shah, David and Carole Chapman)*

Newquay [Mellanvrane Lane], *Tavern*: Very comfortable, partly 14th-c, with great atmosphere, friendly staff and locals, Bass, Stones and guest beers, family room, nice garden; open all day *(David and Carole Chapman)*

☆ **Notter** [Notter Bridge; just off A38 Saltash—Liskeard; SX3861], *Notter Bridge*: Lots of old photographs and paintings in knocked-through bar/lounge, conservatory making the most of lovely riverside spot, wide choice of food esp particularly good home-made curries, good value children's meals and puddings inc delicious local farm ice creams, warmly welcoming bustling atmosphere, well kept beer, tables out on waterside terrace; children very welcome, friendly fat tortoiseshell cat; must book Fri/Sat, very handy for nearby holiday parks *(Bronwen and Steve Wrigley, Ted George)*

☆ **Padstow** [Lanadwell St; SW9175], *London*: Wonderfully unspoilt fishermen's local with a real welcome for strangers, lots of pictures and nautical memorabilia, good buzzing atmosphere (get there early for a table), full St Austell range kept well, decent choice of malt whiskies, good food in small back dining area (moules hotly tipped), great real fire; games machines but no piped music; open all day; bedrooms good value – but check that there isn't going to be a late party on the night of your stay *(Ian Pendlebury, Ted George, Val Stevenson, Rob Holmes, David Carr, Neil Franklin, John and Christine Simpson, Catherine Lloyd, Paul and Sharon Sneller, Pat and Tony Martin, LYM)*

☆ **Padstow** [Lanadwell St], *Golden Lion*: Friendly and cosy backstreet local with pleasant black-beamed front bar, high-raftered back lounge with plush banquettes against ancient white stone walls; reasonably priced simple lunches inc very promptly served good sandwiches, evening steaks and fresh seafood, well kept Cornish Original, coal fire, good staff, pool in family area; piped music or juke box, fruit machines; bedrooms *(R R and J D Winn, Ted George, David Carr, Brian Skelcher, BB)*

Padstow [South Quay], *Old Custom House*: Spacious open-plan seaside bar with conservatory and big family area, decent unpretentious food inc fresh fish and vegetarian, evening restaurant, St Austell Tinners and HSD, quick service, pool; good spot by harbour, attractive sea-view bedrooms *(Andy and Jill Kassube, M L Hodge, Paul and Sharon Sneller, Ted George, David Carr, BB)*

☆ **Penelewey** [Feock Downs, B3289; SW8240], *Punch Bowl & Ladle*: Much extended thatched pub in picturesque setting, bar with cosy rooms, big settees and rustic artefacts, strong emphasis on plush and spreading dining side, with US-style hostess allocating seating and taking orders for the wide choice of good fresh generous food, inc good help-yourself salads, fish and vegetarian; Bass and Flowers original, helpful and friendly quick service, unobtrusive piped music, children welcome in restaurant; handy for Trelissick Gardens; open all day summer, live music winter Fri *(Romey Heaton, Mrs Maria Furness, Brian Skelcher, A Ball, LYM)*

Pentewan [just off B3273 St Austell—Mevagissey; SX0147], *Ship*: Friendly two-bar local opp harbour, comfortable and clean, with St Austell HSD, good bar food and reasonably priced Sun lunch, open fire, pool room, nostalgic piped music; nr good sandy beach and caravan park *(Pete and Rosie Flower)*

Penzance [Chapel St; SW4730], *Admiral Benbow*: Elaborately nautical decor, friendly staff, decent food inc good curries, Scottish Courage ales, children allowed, downstairs restaurant, pleasant view from top back room; open all day summer *(Ted George, LYM)*

Perranuthnoe [signed off A394 Penzance—Helston; SW5329], *Victoria*: Good atmosphere in comfortable L-shaped bar with coastal and wreck photographs, some stripped stonework, well kept Ushers Best and Founders, good value bar food, neat coal fire, booth seating in family area, games area; handy for Mounts Bay; bedrooms *(Cliff Blakemore, Jeremy and Kate Honeybun)*

☆ **Perranwell** [off A393 Redruth—Falmouth and A39 Falmouth—Truro; SW7839], *Royal Oak*: Welcoming village pub with large attractive old black-beamed bar, cosy seats, buoyant atmosphere, good value food inc sandwiches, well kept Whitbreads-related ales and good wines by the glass, good log fire, provision for children, garden with picnic-sets *(John Wooll, James and Ruth Morrell, Gwen and Peter Andrews, Ted George, LYM)*

Phillack [Church Town Rd; SW5638], *Bucket of Blood*: Welcoming busy village pub done out in stripped pine, generous attractive food, well kept St Austell beers, jolly gruesome ghost stories, tables outside *(Dave and Deborah Irving, LYM)*

☆ **Pillaton** [off Callington—Landrake back rd; SX3664], *Weary Friar*: Pretty tucked-away 12th-c pub with four neatly kept knocked-together rooms (one no smoking), comfortable seats around sturdy tables, easy chairs one end, well kept Bass, Courage Directors, Morlands Old Speckled Hen and Wadworths 6X, farm cider, country wines, bar food inc lunchtime sandwiches (service stops on the dot), children's helpings and good puddings; big back restaurant (not Mon), children in eating area, helpful service; piped music; tables outside, Tues bell-ringing in church next door; comfortable bedrooms *(Bronwen and Steve Wrigley, Ted George, W R Cunliffe, Iain Robertson, R A Cullingham, Mayur Shah, LYM)*

☆ **Polperro** [The Quay; SX2051], *Blue Peter*: Cosy and unpretentious little low-beamed wood-floored local up narrow steps from harbour, nautical memorabilia, well kept St Austell and guest beers such as Sharps Doom Bar, farm cider, log fire, traditional games, some seats outside, family area upstairs with video game; open all day, can get crowded, and piped music – often jazz or nostalgic pop – can be loudish; no food (but maybe a Bonio for dogs) *(Emma Kingdon, Ted George, Kerry Law, Annemarie Firstbrook, Bronwen and Steve Wrigley, Tony Scott, Michael Sandy, LYM)*

☆ **Polperro** [Quay], *Three Pilchards*: Low-beamed fishermen's local high over harbour, lots of black woodwork, dim lighting, simple furnishings, generous good value food inc lots of seafood, open fire in big stone fireplace, neat helpful and chatty staff, Ushers Best and Founders, tables on upper terrace up steep steps; piped music can be fairly loud, open all day *(M Joyner, Ted George, Michael Sandy, Dennis Stevens, BB)*

☆ **Polperro** [top of village nr main car park], *Crumplehorn Mill*: Friendly service and good value generous food inc local fish in converted mill, dark cosy corners inc upper gallery, beams, stripped stone, flagstones, log fire, comfortable seats, well kept Bass and St Austell HSD and XXXX, farm cider; pool area, piped music (can be fairly loud); families welcome, good value bedrooms *(Bronwen and Steve Wrigley, Terry and Eileen Stott, Ted George, BB)*

Polperro, *Manor*: Friendly little wood and stone inn tucked away in back street, well kept beers, nice back eating room, tasty reasonably priced bar food *(Ted George)*; [Llansallos St; bear R approaching harbour], *Noughts & Crosses*: Steps down to cosy and cheerful beamed terraced pub with flagstoned woody servery, small food bar, more steps to bigger tiled-floor stripped stone streamside bar, upstairs family room; Ushers seasonal ale, decent food inc local crab sandwiches, good specials and cheap children's food, friendly young staff; children welcome, open all day w/e *(Bronwen and Steve Wrigley, Michael Sandy, Dr and Mrs A Whiteway, A J Thomas, Ted George, I J and N K Buckmaster, BB)*; [Fore St], *Ship*: Very welcoming service in big comfortable bar, well kept Ushers, generous good value fresh food, steps down to well furnished family room, small back terrace *(Ted George, Mr and Mrs B Hobden)*

Port Isaac [The Terrace; SX0080], *Shipwright*: Great clifftop views from small hotel's restaurant, snooker table brings young people to lively public bar, friendly staff, good home-cooked food esp seafood, real ale, warm solid fuel stove; bedrooms *(Graham Tayar, Catherine Raeburn)*; *Slipway*: Built into cliff on several floors, pleasant decor, more restauranty than pub, but good Sharps beer, good food inc wonderful fish and seafood, particularly helpful staff; tables out by harbour; bedrooms *(Mike and Heather Watson)*

Porthleven [SW6225], *Harbour*: Large pub/hotel close to beach with tables out on big harbourside terrace – fantastic setting; good choice of food in dining lounge and restaurant, separate bar, quick friendly service, well kept St Austell ales inc XXXX Mild, comprehensive wine list; comfortable bedrooms *(Tim Barrow, Sue Demont, Andy and Jill Kassube, Ewan and Moira McCall)*

☆ **Portloe** [SW9339], *Lugger*: Delightful setting in unspoilt almost souvenir-free village above cove; not really pubby, and its restaurant licence means you can't go just for a drink, but has well presented bar lunches inc children's, simple easy chairs, two fires, good evening restaurant, decent wines, quick efficient service even when busy; tables on terrace, bedrooms (not all with sea view) *(R W Suddaby, R Inman, LYM)*

Portloe, *Ship*: Pleasantly unfussy welcoming atmosphere, well kept St Austell Tinners and HSD, small sensible choice of home-made food, sheltered streamside garden – useful alternative to Lugger for people on coast path; bedrooms *(June and Perry Dann, DJW, Christopher Wright)*

☆ **Portmellon Cove** [SX0144], *Rising Sun*: Fine spot overlooking sandy cove nr Mevagissey, flagstoned bar with unusual open fire, Birmingham City FC and nautical memorabilia, big upper family/games room and dining room, generous food inc children's, vegetarian and good value Sun roast, well kept Boddingtons, Marstons Pedigree and Wadworths 6X, good coffee and hot chocolate, seats outside; comfortable beamed bedrooms, most with sea view; cl Oct-Easter *(Nick Lawless, DJW, P P Salmon, Pete and Rosie Flower, BB)*

Portreath [SW6545], *Basset Arms*: Comfortable and welcoming terraced village local with good food in bar and restaurant, well kept beers, unobtrusive piped music; short stroll from beach *(Dave and Deborah Irving)*

Portscatho [SW8735], *Plume of Feathers*: Friendly and comfortable, with good value food, side locals' bar, well kept St Austell, helpful smiling staff, evening restaurant; well reproduced loudish pop music, dogs allowed; pretty fishing village, very popular with summer visitors *(R Inman, LYM)*

☆ **Poughill** [SS2207], *Preston Gate*: Welcoming modernised local with log fires, well kept Tetleys-related ales and Marstons Pedigree, well cooked nicely presented good value bar food (evenings get there early or book), chatty landlord, darts, some seats outside; children welcome, dogs looked after well *(Brian and Jenny Seller, James Flory, Richard Cole, LYM)*

☆ **Praze an Beeble** [B3303 Camborne—Helston; SW6336], *St Aubyn Arms*: Quiet and pleasant, with well kept Bass and Wadworths, limited but good choice of enjoyable bar food inc children's, Sun roasts, curry and steak nights – can be eaten in upstairs restaurant; family room, garden *(Colin Gooch, K H Frostick)*

Quintrel Downs [East Rd; SW8560], *Two Clomes*: Attractive largely unspoilt former cottage with apt furnishings, friendly staff and regulars, well kept Sharps Doom Bar, reasonably priced food from good choice of soups and filling sandwiches up, very welcoming fire, pleasant landlord; family room *(M G Hart)*

☆ *nr* **Redruth** [Tolgus Mount; SW6842], *Tricky Dickies*: Well converted isolated former tin-mine smithy, dark inside, with forge bellows, painting of how it might have looked; buoyant atmosphere, well kept beers, good choice of wines by the glass, good value food, good service, a welcome for children, friendly cat called Josie; partly covered terrace with barbecues, aviary, adjoining squash and fitness centre; jazz Tues, other entertainment Thurs; bedrooms being built, motel-style *(Dave and Deborah Irving, P and M Rudlin)*

Scorrier [B3298, off A30 just outside Redruth; SW7244], *Fox & Hounds*: Long partly panelled well divided bar, big log fires, comfortable furnishings, stripped stonework and creaky joists, with large no-smoking section, picnic-sets out in front; has been a popular main entry, with a good range of good food and well kept Boddingtons and Flowers IPA and Original, but sadly the very popular tenants who ran it so enjoyably have now left *(LYM)*

Sennen Cove [SW3526], *Old Success*: Old but radically modernised – the setting's the best part, by clean beach with glorious view along Whitesand Bay; big bustling nautical-theme bar, perhaps best out of season, lots of old photographs, well kept Bass, St Austell and Sharps Doom Bar, piped music, bar food, carvery restaurant; gents' past car park; children welcome, attractive bedrooms, good breakfasts *(Dave and Deborah Irving)*

St Cleer [SX2468], *Market*: Large village pub opp church, clean and comfortable, with stone fireplace in lounge, friendly efficient service, good value food, pleasant garden *(P and M Rudlin)*

St Columb Major [Market Sq/Bank St; SW9163], *Ring o' Bells*: Friendly town pub with good range of real ales inc Sharps Own and Coaster, food inc vegetarian and children's; several rooms going back from narrow road frontage – front bar with juke box, lounge bar and snug bar, tables out behind; Tues quiz night *(G Coates, BB)*

☆ **St Dominick** [Saltash; a mile E of A388, S of Callington – OS Sheet 201 map ref 406674; SX3967], *Who'd Have Thought It*: Spick and span, with flock wallpaper, tasselled plush seats, Gothick tables, gleaming pottery and copper; well kept Bass and Whitbreads-related ales, decent wines, friendly staff, generous food inc fresh fish, impeccable lavatories, superb Tamar views from roomy attractively furnished family conservatory; quiet countryside nr Cotehele *(Jacquie and Jim Jones, Ted George)*

☆ **St Issey** [SW9271], *Ring o' Bells*: Neatly modernised village inn with consistently good home-made food inc children's helpings, well kept Courage, open fire; darts, pool, some tables in flowery courtyard; can get packed in summer; bedrooms *(Mr and Mrs B Hobden, David Carr, LYM)*

☆ **St Ives** [The Wharf; SW5441], *Sloop*: Refurbished and can get packed in season but still has snug pews, slate floor and beams in cosy old right-hand front bar, interesting pictures (some for sale), well cooked down-to-earth food inc lots of fish, Ruddles and Theakstons Old Peculier, decent wines, some drinks bargains, benches out facing harbour; open all day, handy for Tate Gallery; bedrooms *(John Wooll, Ted George, Michael Sargent, Tim Barrow, Sue Demont, Alan and Heather Jacques, Liz and John Soden, Brian Skelcher, Dr and Mrs Cottrell)*

St Ives [Fore St], *Castle*: Comfortable and friendly two-room local, well priced bar food, Whitbreads-related ales, pine panelling, old local photographs, maritime memorabilia, unobtrusive piped music; best out of season *(B J Harding)*

☆ **St Just in Penwith** [Mkt Sq; SW3631], *Wellington*: Busy and friendly, with well kept St Austell beers, generous food inc local fish, vegetarian, good big ploughman's and toasties, fine steaks, polite cheerful service, good local atmosphere, decent wines; bedrooms, good breakfast *(Dr B and Mrs P B Baker, Jack and Gemima Valiant, Mr and Mrs D T Deas, Simon Williams, Stephen Horsley)*

St Just in Penwith, *Kings Arms*: Friendly local, comfortable and clean, with good bar meals, St Austell ales *(G J Gibbs)*

☆ **St Keverne** [The Square; SW7921], *Three Tuns*: Relaxing local by church, pleasantly refurbished, with generous well presented food, well kept Whitbreads-related ales, quick friendly service, picnic-sets out by square; bedrooms *(Ted George, Tim Barrow, Sue Demont, Gwen and Peter Andrews, LYM)*

☆ **St Mabyn** [SX0473], *St Mabyn Inn*: Good interesting food inc lots of fish in sympathetically refurbished pub/restaurant, all cooked freshly so may be a wait; warm welcome *(J and F Gowers)*

☆ **St Mawes** [SW8433], *Rising Sun*: The helpful and sociable landlord who made this charmingly placed waterside hotel so popular in the 1980s has just returned, and first reports indicate that it's firmly back on track for a main entry, with a fine choice of interesting food in its recently refurbished big comfortable open-plan bar and restaurant, smiling efficient staff, well kept St Austell ales and wines, good coffee; attractive conservatory, slate-topped tables on sunny terrace just across lane from harbour wall; open all day summer, pretty bedrooms *(John Crafts, Tim Barrow, Sue Demont, D B Jenkin, LYM)*

☆ **St Teath** [B3267; signed off A39 SW of Camelford; SX0680], *White Hart*: Proper cheerful village pub with marine and naval mementoes in slate-floored bar, popular bar food from good bacon and cheese rolls to steaks and Sun roasts, no-smoking restaurant, well kept Bass, Ruddles County and Ushers Best, coal fire, front games bar with darts, two pool tables, dominoes, and fruit machine; children welcome, recently refurbished bedrooms; open all day *(Rita Horridge, J and F Gowers, Mrs Jill Silversides, Barry Brown, Graham Tayar, Catherine Raeburn, LYM)*

Sticker [just off A390; SW9750], *Hewas*: Lovely floral displays, genuinely warm welcome, reasonably priced food, St Austell beers *(Andy and Jill Kassube)*

☆ **Stratton** [A3072; SS2406], *Kings Arms*: Thriving old well kept three-room 17th-c local with well kept Exmoor, Sharps Own and Cornish Coaster and three or more guest beers, well served good value food, attentive helpful staff; children welcome *(P and M Rudlin, R Houghton, Mr and Mrs P Stubbs, James Flory)*

Threemilestone [W of by-pass outside village; SW7844], *Oak Tree*: Spacious yet cosy and cheerful, Whitbreads-related ales, decent wines, good quickly served food, caring friendly staff *(Stephen Horsley)*

Tintagel [Fore St; SX0588], *Cornishman*: Good food from sandwiches up, well kept St Austell ales, flower-filled back terrace *(John Westlake)*

☆ **Trebarwith** [signed off B3263 and B3314 SE of Tintagel – OS Sheet 200 map ref 058865; SX0585], *Mill House*: Marvellously placed in steep streamside woods above sea, darkish bar with fine Delabole flagstones and interesting local pictures, games room with pool table and children's play area, food inc children's dishes, real ales, decent coffee, friendly owners (and Millie the spaniel), evening restaurant (not Mon-Weds in winter); dogs welcome, tables out on terrace and by stream; five comfortable bedrooms *(SED, Dennis Stevens, Alan and Paula McCully, LYM)*

☆ **Treen** [just off B3315 Penzance—Lands End; SW3824], *Logan Rock*: Relaxed local nr fine coast walks, low beams, high-backed modern oak settles, wall seats, hot coal fire, popular food (all day in summer) from sandwiches up inc children's and cream teas, well kept St Austell Tinners, HSD and Trelawnys Pride, lots of games in family room, pub dog; may be juke box or piped music, dogs allowed on leads; tables in small sheltered garden *(Kevin Thorpe, Val Stevenson, Rob Holmes, Ewan and Moira McCall, Brian Smart, P and S White, Gwen and Peter Andrews, Peter and Gwyneth Eastwood, Susan and Nigel Wilson, Brian Skelcher, LYM)*

Tregony [B3287; SW9245], *Kings Arms*: Welcoming and relaxed old coaching inn, two chatty bars, dining area, decent food at reasonable prices, well kept Boddingtons and Wadworths 6X *(DJW, Christopher Wright, Mr and Mrs Peter Smith)*

☆ **Trelights** [signed off B3314 Wadebridge—Delabole; SW9979], *Long Cross*: Coastal hotel with fine restored Victorian garden, recently refurbished bar continuing the gardening theme, family room, further dining bar, good play area; friendly landlord and staff, well kept St Austell ales, good food esp wide choice of curries, afternoon teas; bedrooms comfortable and well furnished, many with good views *(Tim Jacobson, BB)*

Trematon [Stoketon Cross; SX3959], *Crooked Inn*: Good generous straightforward home cooking, good range of Whitbreads-related ales and cider, big sloping garden with lots of play equipment, various animals inc friendly pot-bellied pig; children very welcome; pretty bedrooms, reasonably priced *(Bronwen and Steve Wrigley, Ted George)*

Tresparrett [SX1491], *Horseshoe*: Welcoming traditional village local, well kept beers, imaginative choice of good value food, friendly and helpful licensees *(Rita Horridge, Richard Houghton)*

☆ **Truro** [Frances St/Castle St], *Wig & Pen*: Lots of well spaced comfortable tables around big horseshoe bar, good choice of good value well prepared and presented food inc vegetarian, several wines by the glass inc good New World ones, good range of beers, daily papers, good-humoured welcoming licensees and staff; unobtrusive piped music; tables out on busy street *(Richard and Janet Fleming, John Wooll, John A Barker, Ted George)*

Truro [Kenwyn Rd/Hendra Lane], *City*: Small friendly local with genuine character, cosy atmosphere, attractive bric-a-brac, particularly well kept Courage *(Simon Walker, John A Barker)*; [Kenwyn St], *William IV*: Busy recently refurbished panelled split-level bar with well kept St Austell beers, decent wine, good value food inc hot dishes in elegantly tiled airy two-level conservatory dining room opening into small flowery garden; evening piped music may be loud *(Steve Willey)*

Upton Cross [B3254 N of Liskeard; SX2872], *Caradon*: Pleasant country local with built-in banquettes and dark chairs, carpet over 17th-c flagstones, woodburner, pewter hanging from joists, Castella card collection, decorative plates, fish tank; cheery landlord, good value generous home-made food, Flowers Original, Sharps Own and St Austell HSD, airy and comfortable public bar with games and juke box; children welcome, some picnic-sets outside *(Trevor Ashenden, Andy and Jill Kassube, BB)*

☆ **Veryan** [SW9139], *New Inn*: Interesting choice of good value nourishing food with fresh veg in neat, welcoming and homely one-bar pub, popular with locals and visitors; leisurely atmosphere, genial landlord, well kept St Austell Tinners and HSD tapped from the cask, good value house wine, good coffee, dachshund called Boris, quiet garden behind; bedrooms, lovely village *(A J Thomas, Chris and Margaret Southon, Mr and Mrs Peter Smith, Nick Wikeley, Christopher Wright, DJW)*

☆ **Zennor** [SW4538], *Tinners Arms*: Gently extended bare old country local in lovely windswept setting by church nr coast path, limited but good value food (all day in summer), normally welcoming, with well kept ales such as Sharps and Wadworths 6X from casks behind bar, Lane's farm cider, decent coffee, rather spartan feel with flagstones, lots of granite and stripped pine; real fires each end, back pool room (where children may be allowed), cats everywhere, friendly dogs, no music, tables in small suntrap courtyard; limited parking *(Jacquie and Jim Jones, Stephen Horsley, Tim Barrow, Sue Demont, Simon Williams, Brian Skelcher, David Warrellow, Lawrence Bacon, Jean Scott, Russell Grimshaw, Kerry Purcell, Gwen and Peter Andrews, Jeanne Cross, Paul Silvestri, LYM)*

Isles of Scilly

Bryher [SV8715], *Hell Bay*: Warm welcoming low-ceilinged granite-walled bar with sea views from deep window recesses, pleasant atmosphere, friendly staff, good quickly served cheap bar food inc fine crab sandwiches, attractive gardens with sheltered play area and pitch-and-putt, stroll from beaches; keg beers; well equipped bedrooms *(Kevin Flack, BB)*

St Martins – Lower Town [SV9215], *Seven Stones*: Worth knowing that there is a pub here, but it doubles as the village hall and looks it; keg beers, basic food and friendly atmosphere; superb view, tables outside *(Dr Alan Green)*

☆ **St Marys – Hugh Town** [The Strand; SV9010], *Atlantic*: Big low-beamed L-shaped bar packed with locals and tourists – and with interesting nautical bric-a-brac, wreck salvage and photographs; wonderful harbour views, good cheery atmosphere (esp on live music nights), wide choice of simple generous bar food inc sandwiches and lots of local fish, well kept St Austell Tinners and Trelawnys; piped music (may be obtrusive); family room, no-smoking restaurant; good views, esp from small back terrace over harbour; bedrooms in adjacent hotel *(Dr Alan Green, David Mead, Kevin Flack, John and Kathleen Potter, Michael Sargent, BB)*

☆ **St Marys – Hugh Town** [Silver St (A3110)], *Bishop & Wolf*: Very wide choice of good value well presented generous food esp fish (should book, attractive upstairs restaurant), helpful staff, well kept St Austell Tinners and HSD, lively local atmosphere, interesting sea/boating decor with gallery above rd, nets, maritime bric-a-brac, lifeboat photographs; piped music may obtrude, popular summer live music *(Peter and Gwyneth Eastwood, AG, Steve and Carolyn Harvey, John and Kathleen Potter)*

St Marys – Hugh Town [The Quay], *Mermaid*: Venerable feel, with rough timber, stone floor, lots of seafaring relics and dim lighting; picture-window harbour view, well kept Boddingtons, bar food, big stove; cellar bar with boat counter, pool table and music for young people (live at weekends); restaurant *(John and Kathleen Potter, Steve and Carolyn Harvey)*

St Marys – Old Town [SV9111], *Lock Stock & Barrel*: Friendly cross between locals' bar and social club, Badger and Fullers London Pride, sandwiches and big pizzas; open all day *(Dr Alan Green)*

The letters and figures after the name of each town are its Ordnance Survey map reference. *How to use the Guide* at the beginning of the book explains how it helps you find a pub, in road atlases or large-scale maps as well as in our own maps.

Cumbria

This area's pubs cover an excellent mix, from simple pubs beautifully placed for walkers, with heartening decent food to match, to some really ambitious foody places, with cooking right at the front of modern trends. On top of that, there are good local breweries, well supported by Cumbrian pubs. This spread is reflected in this year's clutch of new entries (some of them old friends, welcomed back after a break): the welcoming Barbon Inn at Barbon just below the fells, something for all tastes; the Bridge at Buttermere, very popular with walkers; the enterprisingly run Oddfellows at Caldbeck, showing that sheer quality can fill even an out-of-the-way place with customers; the Pheasant at Casterton (good food, a pleasant place to stay in); the lively and unpretentious Dog & Gun in Keswick; the charmingly placed Mill Inn at Mungrisdale (very helpful young licensees – unusually for the area, their good food includes plenty of vegetarian and even vegan dishes), and the cheerful and nicely restored Agricultural in Penrith. Other pubs currently doing particularly well here are the Royal Oak in Appleby (excellent all round), the Dukes Head at Armathwaite (good food, really helpful service), the Wheatsheaf at Beetham (new licensees doing such good imaginative food that they gain a Food Award this year – and they've refurbished the whole place), the Hare & Hounds at Bowland Bridge (friendly, well run, nice to stay at), the quaint old Hole in t' Wall in Bowness (lots to look at), the Britannia at Elterwater (adored by walkers – it does get very busy), the Travellers Rest at Grasmere (good food, nice spot), the Drunken Duck up above Hawkshead (very good all round, winning a Food Award and a Stay Award this year – and it brews its own beers), the Watermill at Ings (lots of real ales), the Old Dungeon Ghyll in Langdale (another magnet for walkers), the Tower Bank Arms at Near Sawrey (still much as it looked in Jemima Puddleduck), the bustling Dalesman in Sedbergh (cheap lunches), the friendly Kings Arms at Stainton, the Queens Head at Tirril (good food, enterprising owners) and the engaging but very busy Queens Head at Troutbeck. Some other places to mention for good meals are the Punch Bowl at Crosthwaite, the Snooty Fox in Kirkby Lonsdale, the Bay Horse outside Ulverston and the Gate at Yanwath. For Dining Pub of the Year we had a very difficult final choice between the Wheatsheaf at Beetham, with its new owners making such a promising impact, and the Drunken Duck up near Hawkshead – already very well known to readers, and hugely enjoyed. In the end, as the changes it's made on the kitchen side are working out so well, we have chosen the Drunken Duck as Cumbria Dining Pub of the Year this time around – but watch this space! Current highlights in the Lucky Dip at the end of the chapter are the Queens Head at Askham, Fish at Buttermere, Trout in Cockermouth, Sun at Coniston, Royal at Dockray, King George IV at Eskdale Green, Sawrey at Far Sawrey, Old Crown at Hesket Newmarket and Wasdale Head Inn at Wasdale Head; we have already inspected all of these and can confirm their reported merits. Drinks prices here are well below the national average, particularly in pubs tied to smaller local or regional breweries such as Jennings, Thwaites or Sam Smiths; the Blacksmiths Arms near Broughton in Furness and George & Dragon at Garrigill were also very cheap.

AMBLESIDE NY3804 Map 9

Golden Rule

Smithy Brow; follow Kirkstone Pass signpost from A591 on N side of town

Walkers and their dogs are welcome in this honest Lakeland local. It's a friendly place with lots of local country pictures and a few fox masks decorating the butter-coloured walls, horsebrasses on the black beams, built-in leatherette wall seats, and cast-iron-framed tables; dominoes and cribbage. The room on the left has darts and a fruit machine, and the one down a few steps on the right is a quieter sitting room (no smoking until 9pm). Well kept Hartleys XB and Robinsons Best, Old Stockport, and Hatters Mild on handpump; pork pies (50p), filled rolls (£1.50), and winter soup (£1.75). There's a back yard with tables, a small pretty summer garden, and wonderfully colourful window boxes. The golden rule referred to in its name is a brass measuring yard mounted over the bar counter. *(Recommended by Roger Stamp, R J Bland, Mick Hitchman, Mr and Mrs Richard Osborne, Tim Heywood, Sophie Wilne, David Carr, H K Dyson, Andy and Jill Kassube, Pete and Sue Wells, Jeanne Cross, Paul Silvestri)*

Hartleys (Robinsons) ~ Tenant John Lockley ~ Real ale ~ Limited snacks ~ (015394) 32257 ~ Children welcome until 9pm ~ Nearby parking virtually out of the question in summer ~ Open 11-11; 12-10.30 Sun

APPLEBY NY6921 Map 10

Royal Oak ★

Bongate; B6542 on S edge of town

'One of our favourite all-rounders' is how one well travelled reader describes this very popular old-fashioned coaching inn – and it's this that appeals so much to people. There is some emphasis on the good imaginative food but not at the expense of the proper pubby atmosphere (especially in the oak-panelled public bar with its good open fire), and the fine range of beers in top condition is not overshadowed by the thoughtful wine list (which has around 8 by the glass). The welcome from the diligent licensees and their friendly staff remains as genuine as ever. The beamed lounge has old pictures on the timbered walls, some armchairs and a carved settle, and a panelling-and-glass snug enclosing the bar counter; dominoes. Good enjoyable food from a changing menu includes sandwiches (from £1.60), home-made soups like wild mushroom or roast tomato (£1.95), stilton, celery and walnut tart with sweet onion jam (£3.95), smoked salmon, cream cheese and chive pâté (£4.95), black pudding with glazed apples or smoked haddock and bacon fishcakes with parsley sauce (£6.95), garlic roast breast of chicken with a tomato and white wine sauce (£8.95), fresh sardines griddled with fresh rosemary and garlic butter (£9.95), lobster cooked three different ways (from £16.95), home-made puddings, and properly kept cheeses. One of the dining rooms is no smoking. There are usually eight real ales on handpump: Bongate Special Pale Ale (their own beer made locally) and Theakstons Best, with regular visitors such as Black Sheep Bitter, Caledonian Deuchars IPA, John Smiths, Tetleys, Yates Bitter, and Youngers Scotch; several malt whiskies, Stowford Press cider, and a carefully chosen wine list with quite a few half bottles. In summer the outside is very colourful, with seats on the front terrace among masses of flowers in tubs, troughs and hanging baskets. You can get here on the scenic Leeds/Settle/Carlisle railway (best to check times and any possible delays to avoid missing lunch). *(Recommended by Vann and Terry Prime, Karen Eliot, Ann and Colin Hunt, John and Jackie Chalcraft, Roger and Christine Mash, Helen Pickering, James Owen, Liz Bell, Susan and John Douglas, Richard Fallon, Keith Wright, Richard Houghton, Tom McLean, Roger Huggins, Mr and Mrs D Wilson, Derek and Sylvia Stephenson, Malcolm Taylor, David and Margaret Bloomfield, D Knott)*

Free house ~ Licensees Colin and Hilary Cheyne ~ Real ale ~ Meals and snacks (12-2, 6-9) ~ Restaurant ~ (017683) 51463 ~ Well behaved children in eating area of bar ~ Open 11-11; 12-10.30 Sun ~ Bedrooms: £33B/£70B

See also entry under nearby BRAMPTON

ARMATHWAITE NY5146 Map 10

Dukes Head

Off A6 a few miles S of Carlisle

Mr Lynch is a particularly welcoming and helpful landlord and readers enjoy their visits here very much. The civilised lounge bar has oak settles and little armchairs among more upright seats, oak and mahogany tables, antique hunting and other prints, and some brass and copper powder-flasks above its coal fire. Consistently good bar food includes sandwiches and ploughman's, black pudding in a mild mustard sauce (£3.50), smoked salmon and prawns (£4), home-boiled ham (£6.90), grilled salmon (£7.70), grilled venison (£9.90), super roast duckling (£10.50), and puddings like sticky toffee or bread and butter puddings (£2.95). Out of season, they do themed food evenings and offer three-course set meals; the breakfasts are huge. Well kept Boddingtons and a guest such as Tetleys on handpump; piped music and dominoes; separate public bar with darts, pool, juke box, and fruit machine. There are tables out on the lawn behind. *(Recommended by Chris and Ann Garnett, Malcolm Taylor, Simon and Amanda Southwell, Mrs Frances Gray, Jackie Moffat, P Cox, N Sarbutts, Joy and Peter Heatherley)*

Pubmaster ~ Licensee Peter Lynch ~ Real ale ~ Meals and snacks ~ Restaurant ~ (016974) 72226 ~ Children welcome ~ Open 11-3, 6-11; 12-3, 6-10.30 Sun ~ Bedrooms: £26.50B/£48.50B

ASKHAM NY5123 Map 9

Punch Bowl

Village signposted on right from A6 4 miles S of Penrith

Some changes to this attractive pub this year include a new open log fireplace between the lounge and games room (which is also new), the extension of the dining room, and the addition of private bathrooms to the bedrooms; the juke box has been removed. The rambling bar has an antique settle by another log fire, interesting furnishings such as Chippendale dining chairs and rushwork ladder-back seats around sturdy wooden tables, and well cushioned window seats in the white-painted thick stone walls; there are coins stuck into the cracks of the dark wooden beams (periodically taken out and sent to charity), and local photographs and prints of Askham. The old-fashioned woodburning stove, with its gleaming stainless chimney in the big main fireplace, is largely decorative. Bar food includes home-made soup (£2.75), lunchtime sandwiches (£2.70), chicken terrine (£3.85), cumberland sausage (£5.90), beef in stout pie (£6.20), Mexican beanpot (£6.65), seafood Italian (£7.20), steaks (from £9.20), daily specials such as whole plaice, Chinese stir-frys, and fresh Scottish lobster, and children's dishes (£3). Boddingtons, Marstons Pedigree, Morlands Old Speckled Hen, Wadworths 6X, and Whitbreads Castle Eden on handpump; dominoes and piped pop music, and in the separate public bar darts, pool, and fruit machine. There are tables out on a flower-filled terrace. *(Recommended by Sheila and John French, Eric Locker, Richard Lewis, RJH, A Preston, H Dyson, Angus Lyon)*

Whitbreads ~ Lease: David and Frances Riley ~ Real ale ~ Snacks (lunchtime) and meals ~ (01931) 712443 ~ Children welcome until 9pm ~ Open 11.30-3, 6.30-11; 11.30-11 Sat; 12-10.30 Sun; 12-3, 7-11(10.30 Sun) in winter ~ Bedrooms: £28.50B/£53B

BARBON SD6383 Map 10

Barbon Inn

Village signposted off A683 Kirkby Lonsdale—Sedbergh; OS Sheet 97, map reference 628826

There's always a friendly welcome in this 17th-c coaching inn and a good mix of locals and visitors. Plenty of tracks and paths leading up to the fells (the hospitable licensee may provide a friendly dog for your walk), and the inn is at the start of a beautiful drive to Dent. Several small rooms lead off the simple bar with its blackened range, each individually and comfortably furnished: carved 18th-c oak settles, deep chintzy sofas and armchairs, a Victorian fireplace. Decent bar food includes sandwiches (from £2.25), home-made soup (£2.50), cumberland sausage (£5.95), lasagne (£6.25), daily specials such as battered cod (£5.50), lamb pie (£6.25), steak in ale pie (£6.50), steaks (from £10), and puddings like fruit crumble or sticky toffee pudding (from £2.50). Well kept Theakstons Best and Old Peculier on handpump, and a respectable wine list; dominoes, trivia and piped music. The lovely sheltered garden here is very prettily planted and neatly kept. *(Recommended by Alan J Morton, Paul Robinshaw, B Edgeley, E G Parish, Sue Holland, Dave Webster, Denis and Margaret Kilner)*

Free house ~ Licensee Lindsey MacDiarmid ~ Real ale ~ Meals and snacks ~ Restaurant ~ (015242) 76233 ~ Children welcome ~ Open 12-3, 6.30-11; 12-3, 7-10.30 Sun ~ Bedrooms: £30(£35B)/£55(£60B)

BASSENTHWAITE NY2332 Map 9

Sun

Village signposted off A591 a few miles NW of Keswick

Originally a farmhouse, this pleasant inn has a rambling bar with low 17th-c black oak beams, two good stone fireplaces with big logs burning in winter, built-in wall seats and plush stools around heavy wooden tables, lots of brasses, and areas that stretch usefully back on both sides of the servery. The enjoyable bar food draws on both the licensees' backgrounds – the landlady is from the Lakes, while her husband is Italian: minestrone soup (£2), spicy prawns in breadcrumbs (£3), lunchtime ploughman's (£4), lancashire hotpot (£5), home-made steak pie or home-made lasagne (£5.50), pork steaks in mushroom sauce (£6.50), sirloin steak (£8.50), and puddings such as syrup sponge or sticky toffee pudding (£2.50). Well kept Jennings Bitter on handpump. A huddle of white houses looks up to Skiddaw and other high fells, and you can enjoy the view from the tables in the pub's front yard by the rose bushes and honeysuckle; no dogs. *(Recommended by D and N Towle, Ewan and Moira McCall, William Cunliffe, David and Judy Walmsley, H K Dyson; more reports please)*

Jennings ~ Tenants Giuseppe and Josephine Scopelliti ~ Real ale ~ Meals and snacks (12-1.30, 6.30-8.30ish; not Sun evening) ~ (017687) 76439 ~ Children in side rooms whenever possible ~ Open 12-2.30, 6-11; 12-2.30, 7-10.30 Sun; may close earlier winter lunchtimes if very quiet; closed Mon and Weds lunchtimes Nov-Mar

BASSENTHWAITE LAKE NY1930 Map 9

Pheasant ★

Follow Wythop Mill signpost at N end of dual carriageway stretch of A66 by Bassenthwaite Lake

The little bars in this civilised and rather smart hotel are pleasantly old-fashioned and pubby, and have persian rugs on the parquet floor, rush-seat chairs, library seats, and cushioned settles, hunting prints and photographs on the fine ochre walls, and well kept Bass, Jennings Cumberland, and Theakstons Best on handpump; quite a few malt whiskies, too. Another new licensee has taken over this year and lunchtime bar food now includes home-made soup (£2.50), ploughman's or cumberland sausage platter with home-made chutney (£4.95), potted Silloth shrimps (£5.25), cheesecake of smoked cheddar, apple and celery with home-made spicy tomato chutney (£5.45), smoked local trout with roasted sweet red pepper and balsamic vinaigrette (£5.60), and home-made puddings (£2.95); the elegant restaurant is no smoking. If the bars are full, you might want to move to the large and airy beamed lounge at the back, which has easy chairs on its polished parquet floor and a big log fire on cool days; there are also some chintzy sitting rooms with antique furniture (one is no smoking). The hotel is surrounded by very attractive woodlands, with beeches, larches and Douglas firs, and you can walk into them from the garden. This is a fine walking area. *(Recommended by David and Kathy Holcroft, H Thomson, Maysie Thompson, Christine and Geoff Butler, Nigel Woolliscroft, Paul S McPherson, Liz Bell, Neville Kenyon, William Cunliffe, Alan Risdon, SLC, Mr and Mrs D Wilson; more reports on the new regime, please)*

Free house ~ Licensee Christopher Curry ~ Real ale ~ Lunchtime bar meals and snacks ~ Restaurant ~ (017687) 76234 ~ Children in restaurant only ~ Open 11-3, 5.30-10.30(11 Sat); 12-3, 7-10.30 Sun; closed 24/25 Dec ~ Bedrooms: £66B/£104B

BEETHAM SD5079 Map 7

Wheatsheaf

Village (and inn) signposted just off A6 S of Milnthorpe

Friendly new licensees have taken over this fine 17th-c coaching inn with its striking timbered cornerpiece, and readers have been quick to give warm praise. The bedrooms have been refurbished (as has the pub itself), and the food is now aimed at modern British ideas using the best local produce. The relaxed, partly no-smoking lounge bar has lots of exposed beams and joists, and new tables and chairs and soft furnishings, and the upstairs no-smoking restaurant (candlelit at night) is elegantly redecorated. Changing regularly, the imaginative food includes a warm salad of goat's cheese with chard, aubergine and basil oil (£3.50), smoked mackerel and crab fishcakes with tomato chutney (£3.95), lamb liver and crispy bacon with onion gravy (£5.95), grilled lemon sole with crab and rocket dressing (£7.25), roast loin of pork with honey and sage roasted shallots in local ale gravy (£7.50), braised lamb shank with damsons and rosemary (£7.95), and puddings such as wensleydale and apple crumble with creamy custard or baked egg and nutmeg tart (from £3). Well kept Greene King Abbot, Jennings Cumberland, and Tetleys on handpump, New World wines, and quite a few malt whiskies; darts. *(Recommended by M A Buchanan, Neil Townend, A D Ryder, G Washington, Dr A McArthur Bennie, Geoff and Angela Jaques; more reports on the new regime, please)*

Free house ~ Licensees Donald and Diane Munro ~ Real ale ~ Meals and snacks ~ Restaurant ~ (015395) 62123 ~ Children in eating area of bar till 8.30pm ~ Open 11-3, 6-11; 12-3, 7-10.30 Sun ~ Bedrooms: £55S/£70S

BOOT NY1801 Map 9

Burnmoor

Village signposted just off the Wrynose/Hardknott Pass road, OS Sheet 89 map reference 175010

Surrounded by peaceful fells, this is a simple inn with Lakeland hospitality, and a popular place to stay; lots of attractive tracks to walk along, and the pub is close to Dalegarth Station (the top terminus of the Ravenglass and Eskdale light steam railway), and to a restored watermill, said to be the oldest in the country. The beamed and carpeted white-painted bar has an open fire, red leatherette seats and settles, and small copper-topped tables. Mrs Foster is Austrian and there are always some speciality dishes on the menu. With prices unchanged since last year, there might be sandwiches, delicious soup (£1.50), lunchtime ploughman's (£3.60), several flans such as cheese and onion or Austrian smoked ham and cheese (from £3.80), home-cooked cold meats (£4.20), cumberland game pie (£5.80), wienerschnitzel (£6.40), sirloin steak (£8.20), and daily specials such as cauliflower and broccoli crumble (£4) and gammon steak (£5.80); children's helpings. They grow a lot of the vegetables themselves, and keep hens and pigs; the restaurant is no smoking. Well kept Jennings Bitter, Cumberland and Snecklifter on handpump, Austrian wines, and Gluhwein in winter; good, quick service. Pool, dominoes, cribbage, and juke box. There are seats outside on the sheltered front lawn. *(Recommended by H K Dyson, Mick Hitchman, WAH, Mike and Mary Carter, Jenny and Brian Seller, J H Bell, Brian Wainwright, Simon Watkins, David and Judy Walmsley)*

Free house ~ Licensees Tony and Heidi Foster ~ Real ale ~ Meals and snacks (12-2, 6-9) ~ Restaurant ~ (019467) 23224 ~ Children welcome till 9pm ~ Open 11-2.30, 4.30-11(10.30 Sun) ~ Bedrooms: £26/£52(£58B)

BOUTH SD3386 Map 9

White Hart

Village signposted off A590 near Haverthwaite

This small village inn (run by a particularly helpful, friendly landlord) is well placed in good walking country, and there are tables out in the attractively planted and well kept garden, with occasional summer barbecues. Inside, sloping ceilings and floors show the building's age, and there are lots of old local photographs and bric-a-brac – farm tools, stuffed animals, a collection of long-stemmed clay pipes – and two log fires, one in a fine old kitchen range. The games room has darts, pool, pinball, dominoes, fruit machine, video game, and juke box; piped music. A fair choice of home-made food includes sandwiches, pizzas (from £2.95), cod (£5.50), 1lb gammon (£5.95), barnsley chops (£6.95), good authentic curries, daily specials, and puddings like blackberry and apple crumble or sticky toffee pudding. Well kept Boddingtons, Highgate Mild, Jennings Bitter, and Tetleys on handpump, and 50 malt whiskies. *(Recommended by JDM, KM, Margaret and Roy Randle, Paul and Georgina Swinden, Andy and Jill Kassube, Dr J Morley, Stan and Hazel Allen)*

Free house ~ Licensee Dave Trotter ~ Real ale ~ Meals and snacks (not Mon lunchtime) ~ Restaurant ~ (01229) 861229 ~ Children welcome until 8.30pm ~ Open 12-2(3 Sat), 6-11; 12-3, 7-10.30 Sun; closed Mon lunchtime (exc bank holidays) ~ Bedrooms: £20(£30B)/£30(£40B)

BOWLAND BRIDGE SD4289 Map 9

Hare & Hounds

Village signposted from A5074; OS Sheet 97 map reference 417895

Readers enjoy staying at this attractive white-painted inn, quietly set in the Winster Valley. It's run by ex-international soccer player Peter Thompson and his wife Debbie who offer a genuinely warm welcome to their customers. The comfortably modernised bar, divided into smaller areas by stone walls, has Liverpool and England team photographs and caps, oak beams, ladder-back chairs around dark wood tables on the spread of turkey carpet, reproduction hunting prints, a stuffed pheasant, and open fires. Bar food includes soup (£1.80), sandwiches (from £2.25), pizzas (from £4.25), ploughman's (£5.25), mushroom and vegetable stroganoff (£5.95), giant yorkshire pudding filled with cumberland sausage and onion gravy (£6.25), venison in red wine with cranberries (£6.75), poached swordfish steak with prawn sauce (£7.25), steaks (from £10.80), daily specials, 4-course Sunday roast lunch, and children's menu (£3.25); very good, prompt service. Well kept Tetleys and a weekly guest beer on handpump, and several malt whiskies from a long bar counter with a cushioned red leatherette elbow rest for people using the sensible backrest-type bar stools. Dominoes and piped music. The climbing roses, window boxes and hanging baskets are pretty in summer, and there are picnic-sets in the spacious garden at one side, with more by the road. The pub is set by the bridge itself. *(Recommended by David Carr, John and Jackie Chalcraft, Mick Hitchman, Steve Goodchild, David and Kathy Holcroft, Bill and Elsa Wood, John Honnor, Mr and Dr J Harrop, Malcolm Taylor, P A Legon, A Lock, Mark Fennell, R D Knight, Chris Walling)*

Free house ~ Licensees Peter and Debbie Thompson ~ Real ale ~ Meals and snacks ~ Restaurant (residents only) ~ (015395) 68333 ~ Children welcome ~ Open 11-11; 11-10.30 Sun ~ Bedrooms: £35B/£50B

BOWNESS ON WINDERMERE SD4097 Map 9

Hole in t' Wall

Lowside

Well worth the effort to find it, this tucked away stone tavern is very much liked by readers. It's full of interest and character, and the beamed bar has lots to look at – giant smith's bellows, old farm implements and ploughshares, and jugs hanging from the ceiling, and a room upstairs has handsome plasterwork in its coffered ceiling; another long, narrow room has hops and chamber pots, stuffed animals, and old pictures. On cool days a splendid log fire burns under a vast slate mantlebeam. The tiny flagstoned front courtyard (where there are sheltered seats) has an ancient outside flight of stone steps to the upper floor. Mrs Mitton decides what to cook each day once she gets into her kitchen. There might be sandwiches (from £2), vegetarian chilli or broccoli and cauliflower bake (£5.50), steak and kidney pudding or a hotpot (£5.75), whisky chicken (£6.25), fish pie (£5.75), sirloin steak (£7.50), popular whole roast pheasant with red wine sauce (£7.50), and puddings like home-made apple pie

(£2.50). Hartleys XB and Robinsons Fredericks and Best on handpump in excellent condition, home-made lemonade and very good mulled winter wine; darts, pool, fruit machine and juke box upstairs. If you'd rather catch it on a quiet day, it's better to visit out of season. *(Recommended by Karen Eliot, G Coates, Roger Stamp, Mrs S Miller, David Carr, Kerry Law, Simon Smith, SLC, Roy Bromell, H K Dyson, Richard Lewis, Dr and Mrs A K Clarke, Alan Risdon, A Lock)*

Hartleys (Robinsons) ~ Tenants: Andrew and Audrey Mitton ~ Real ale ~ Meals and snacks (not Sun evening) ~ (015394) 43488 ~ Children in family room off tap room until 9pm ~ Live music Sun lunchtime and evening ~ Parking nearby can be difficult ~ Open 11-11; 12-10.30 Sun

BRAITHWAITE NY2324 Map 9

Coledale Inn

Village signposted off A66 W of Keswick; pub then signed left off B5292

Much of the emphasis here is on the hotel side, but those dropping in for a drink while out walking are made very welcome. The inn is perfectly placed at the foot of Whinlatter Pass, so walkers can start their hike straight from the door. The left-hand bar has fine views of Skiddaw and the much closer bracken-covered hills from the window seats, a winter coal fire, and little 19th-c Lakeland engravings; the green-toned bar on the right, with a bigger bay window, is more of a dining bar. Bar food includes home-made soup (£1.75), lunchtime sandwiches (from £2), filled baked potatoes (from £3.40), platters (from £4.20), home-made vegetable chilli (£5.75), cumberland sausage (£5.90), gammon and egg (£6.50), sirloin steak (£8.95), daily specials, and puddings (from £2.35). Well kept Jennings Bitter, Theakstons XB, Yates Bitter, and Youngers on handpump; darts, dominoes, and piped music. The dining room is no smoking. The garden has tables and chairs on the slate terrace beyond the sheltered lawn, and a popular play area for children. *(Recommended by H K Dyson, Lesley Bass, David J Cooke, Sheila Keene, D and N Towle, Colin Draper, SLC, David Yandle, Maurice Thompson, IHR)*

Free house ~ Licensees Geoffrey and Michael Mawdsley ~ Real ale ~ Meals and snacks ~ (017687) 78272 ~ Children welcome ~ Open 11-11; 12-10.30 Sun; closed Mon-Thurs winter weekdays until 6.30 ~ Bedrooms: £22.50S/£55S

BRAMPTON NY6723 Map 10

New Inn

Note: this is the small Brampton near Appleby, not the bigger one up by Carlisle. Off A66 N of Appleby – follow Long Marton 1 signpost then turn right at church; village also signposted off B6542 at N end of Appleby

The two cosy little rooms in this attractively traditional inn have nice stripped and polished old pine benches with upholstered cushions and old pine tables, a good range of local pictures (mainly sheep and wildlife), a stuffed fox curled on top of the corner TV, and a red squirrel poking out of a little hole in the dividing wall. The particularly interesting flagstoned dining room has horsebrasses on its low black beams, well spaced tables, and a splendid original black cooking range at one end, separated from the door by an immensely sturdy old oak built-in settle. Good bar food includes lunchtime sandwiches (from £1.30; steak £3.25), home-made soup (£1.95), potted Morecambe Bay shrimps (£3.45), pizzas (from £3.50), ploughman's (£3.75), home-made nut roast or steak and kidney pie (£5.20), chicken and cheese crunch (£5.95), seafood gratinée (£6.95), half roast duck in orange sauce (£7.95), sirloin steak (£8.30), and puddings (£2.50); 3-course Sunday lunch (£6.95; children £3.25). Well kept Boddingtons, Theakstons Best, and Youngers Scotch on handpump, and a good choice of whiskies with some eminent malts; friendly service, darts, dominoes and piped music. There are seats on the lawn and a barbecue area. In June, the Appleby Horse Fair tends to use the pub as its base, so things tend to get crowded then. Incidentally, another Brampton near Chesterfield has a pub of the same name. *(Recommended by Mr and Mrs A Bull, Maureen and Bryan Cully, Judith Hirst, Mr and Mrs R Ray, Richard Fallon; more reports please)*

Free house ~ Licensees Roger and Anne Cranswick ~ Real ale ~ Meals and snacks ~ Restaurant ~ (017683) 51231 ~ Children in eating area of bar until 9pm ~ Open 12-3, 6-11; 12-11 Sat and Sun (though closed 10.30 Sun); closed 25 Dec ~ Bedrooms: £20/£40

BROUGHTON IN FURNESS SD2290 Map 9

Blacksmiths Arms

Broughton Mills; off A593 N

The hanging baskets and tubs of flowers in front of this small friendly pub are very pretty in summer, and the position is peaceful – tucked away in a charming hamlet in pretty countryside that's never too overrun with summer visitors. There are four simply but attractively refurbished little rooms with open fires in three of them, ancient slate floors, and well kept Coniston Bluebird, Derwent Bitter, and Theakstons Best on handpump. Enjoyable lunchtime food (not served in the bar itself) includes open sandwiches (from £2.25), ploughman's (from £3.25), steak and ale pie or lasagne (£4.95) and trout (£5.25). Evening dishes are more elaborate: devilled mushrooms (£2.95), black pudding in cranberry sauce (£2.45), New Zealand mussels with garlic and mozzarella cheese (£2.95), Italian baked fish (£5.75), poacher's pie (£6.25), good steak diane, steak au poivre or steak with stilton and cream sauce (£8.75), puddings like apple or rhubarb crumble (£2.25), and children's menu; there are two smallish dining rooms (the back one is no smoking). Darts and dominoes. *(Recommended by Dr and Mrs B Baker, H K Dyson, Derek Harvey-Piper, RJH)*

Free house ~ Licensee Philip Blackburn ~ Real ale ~ Meals and snacks ~ Restaurant ~ (01229) 716824 ~ Children welcome ~ Open 12-11(12 Sat); 12-10.30 Sun; cl 25 Dec

BUTTERMERE NY1817 Map 9

Bridge Hotel

Some of the best steep countryside in the county surrounds this friendly inn, so it's naturally popular with walkers – and the flagstoned area in the bar is good for walking boots. The beamed bar has built-in wooden settles and farmhouse chairs around traditional tables, a panelled bar counter and a few horsebrasses, and there's a dining bar with brocaded armchairs around copper-topped tables, and brass ornaments hanging from the beams. Lunchtime snacks include a big soup (£3.15), filled baked potatoes (£3.95), ploughman's (£4.10), and battered chicken pieces with a honey and mustard dressing (£4.15); they also serve creamed garlic mushrooms (£2.75), butterbean casserole (£5.75), liver, bacon and onion casserole (£5.95), cumberland hotpot or steak and mushroom in ale pie (£6.75), salmon steak with chive butter (£7.25), and sirloin steak (from £9.25); the restaurant is no smoking. Well kept Black Sheep, Marstons Pedigree, Tetleys Bitter, and Theakstons Old Peculier on handpump, quite a few malt whiskies, and a decent wine list. Outside, a flagstoned terrace has white tables by a rose-covered sheltering stone wall. The views from the bedrooms are marvellous; self-catering, too. *(Recommended by Walter and Susan Rinaldi-Butcher, Gail Coskery, K F Mould, W W Burke, Colin Draper, SLC)*

Free house ~ Licensee Peter McGuire ~ Real ale ~ Meals and snacks ~ Restaurant ~ (017687) 70252 ~ Children welcome ~ Open 10.30am-11pm; 11-10.30 Sun ~ Bedrooms: £45B/£90B; also, s/c apartments

CALDBECK NY3239 Map 9

Oddfellows

B5299 SE of Wigton

In the village where John Peel is buried, this comfortably extended pub is surprisingly large and busy – considering that it's not exactly on the beaten track. It owes its success – and its good thriving atmosphere – entirely to the hard work put in by the friendly young landlord and his pleasant staff, and in the last few years has improved no end, with immaculate lavatories and now a newly and attractively refurbished dining room. A wide choice of good cheap generous food, nicely presented, includes rolls filled to overflowing with good side salads, nourishing soups, lunchtime sandwiches or baked potatoes (from £2.70), particularly good cumberland sausage (£4.50), ploughman's, steak pie or a vegetarian dish (£5.50), roast beef with yorkshire pudding (£5.95), evening steaks (from £9.50), and puddings like sherry trifle or sticky toffee pudding (from £2.95); the restaurant is no smoking. Well kept Jennings Bitter, Cumberland and maybe Cocker Hoop on handpump, good wines. Darts, pool, dominoes, fruit machine, juke box and piped music. We have not yet heard from readers who have tried the new bedrooms (they've extended into the next-door building), but would expect this to be a nice place to stay in. *(Recommended by David and Margaret Bloomfield, Peter and Pat Frogley, David Heath, W Blatchford, Peter and Jan Humphreys, Dr Rod Holcombe)*

Jennings ~ Manager Mr D Graham ~ Real ale ~ Meals and snacks ~ Restaurant ~ (016974) 78227 ~ Children welcome ~ Open 11-11; 12-10.30 Sun; 12-3, 6.30-11 in winter ~ Bedrooms: £22.50S/£45S – they also do self-catering

CARTMEL SD3879 Map 7

Cavendish Arms

Off main sq

Cartmel's oldest pub has now been run by Mr Murray for over 20 years. It's a friendly place with an open fire, farmhouse and other chairs and stools around traditional tables in the relaxed bar, and Bass, Lakeland Gold (brewed by Mr Murray's son), Shepherd Neame Spitfire and guests on handpump, and a fair choice of malt whiskies. For those here on a walking break, the landlord will give advice and maps about the area. As well as sandwiches (from £3.25) and light lunches such as soup (£2.75), ploughman's (£6.45), and hot smoked salmon with prawns (£6.95), there might be spinach and ricotta cheese cannelloni (£5.55), stuffed cod wrapped in vine leaves with a tomato sauce (£6.75), steak in ale pie (£6.95), chicken kebab in an orange, honey and ginger glaze (£7.15), steaks (from £10.95), and daily specials such as good liver and onions; they still do Sunday roasts on the spit in the no-smoking restaurant; helpful staff. There are tables in front of the pub, with more at the back by the stream, and their flower displays tend to win awards. *(Recommended by Emma Collins, Vann and Terry Prime, SLC, Duncan Small, Jack and Gemima Valiant, E A George, David and Judy Walmsley, Stan and Hazel Allen, Phill and Elaine Wylie, Peter Richards, Mark Fenell, S Watkin, P Taylor, Jane Taylor, David Dutton)*

Free house ~ Tom Murray ~ Real ale ~ Meals and snacks (11-2.15, 6-9.30; all day Sun) ~ Restaurant ~ (015395) 36240 ~ Children in eating area of bar and in restaurant ~ Open 11.30-11; 12-10.30 Sun ~ Bedrooms: £32B/£54(£64B)

CARTMEL FELL SD4288 Map 9

Masons Arms

Strawberry Bank, a few miles S of Windermere between A592 and A5074; perhaps the simplest way of finding the pub is to go uphill W from Bowland Bridge (which is signposted off A5074) towards Newby Bridge and keep right then left at the staggered crossroads – it's then on your right, below Gummer's How; OS Sheet 97, map reference 413895

From the terrace in front of this popular pub, there are rustic benches and tables with an unrivalled view overlooking the Winster Valley to the woods below Whitbarrow Scar. The main bar has low black beams in the bowed ceiling, country chairs and plain wooden tables on polished flagstones, and a grandly Gothick seat with snarling dogs as its arms. A small lounge has oak tables and settles to match its fine Jacobean panelling, and a plain little room beyond the serving counter has pictures and a fire in an open range; the family room has an old-parlourish atmosphere, and there's also an upstairs room which helps at peak times. A fine range of real ales includes their own Hoadstock Bitter and bottled Damson Ale, as well as Anchor Steam (from San Francisco), Barnsley Bitter, Brains SA, Mitchells Original Bitter, and Morrells Oxford Bitter on handpump, quite a few Belgian fruit beers, and Normandy cider; carefully chosen mainly New World wines, too. Wholesome food includes sandwiches (from £3.55), light meals such as cajun sausage and black pudding or lentil and hazelnut pâté (£4.95), and ploughman's (£5.95), plus home-made soup (£2.90), Morecambe Bay potted shrimps (£4.95), vegetable burritos or lamb rogan josh (£6.95), steak pie (£7.95), and daily specials such as fennel and westmoreland smoked cheese bake or roasted pepper and black olive lasagne (£6.95), cod and crab gratin (£7.50), and normandy pork chop (£7.95). They sell leaflets outlining local walks of varying lengths and difficulty. The bar does get extremely crowded at weekends. *(Recommended by Prof P A Reynolds, Nigel Woolliscroft, Mick Hitchman, Paul S McPherson, Barbara Wensworth, Ewan and Moira McCall, Mrs S Kingsbury, Steve Goodchild, Ann and Colin Hunt, Phil and Heidi Cook, Liz Bell, Bronwen and Steve Wrigley, Tina and David Woods-Taylor, LM, Hugh Roberts, Arthur and Margaret Dickinson, David and Judy Walmsley, Andy and Jill Kassube, Richard May, Jack and Gemima Valiant)*

Own brew ~ Licensee Helen Stevenson ~ Real ale ~ Meals and snacks (12-2, 6-8.45) ~ (015395) 68486 ~ Children welcome till 9 ~ Open 11.30-11; 12-10.30 Sun; 11-3, 6-11 in winter; closed 25 Dec and evening 26 Dec ~ Four s/c flats and two s/c cottages available

CASTERTON SD6279 Map 10

Pheasant

A683 about a mile N of junction with A65, by Kirkby Lonsdale; OS sheet 97, map reference 633796

With plenty to do nearby, this civilised inn is a popular place to stay. The neatly kept and attractively modernised beamed rooms of the main bar have padded wheelback chairs, plush wall settles, newspapers and magazines to read, an open log fire in a nicely arched bare stone fireplace with polished brass hood, and souvenir mugs on the mantlepiece; there's a further room (which is no smoking during meal times) across the passage with a piano. Good bar food includes home-made soup (£2.25), sandwiches (from £2.25), freshly made greek salad (£4.25), steak and kidney pie (£5.75), spinach, feta cheese and mushroom strudel or gammon and egg (£6.25), steaks (from £11), and daily specials such as goat's cheese and sun-dried tomatoes grilled on a fresh bread crouton (£4.25), lamb liver and bacon (£6.95), home-made lasagne (£7.25), fresh sardines (£7.95), shoulder of lamb with a sweet mint marinade (£9.50), and fresh hake steak Dieppe style (£12.95); hearty breakfasts; the restaurant is no smoking. Well kept Theakstons Best and a weekly changing guest beer on handpump, over 30 malt whiskies, and a good wine list. Darts, dominoes, a popular weekly winter quiz night in aid of the Guide Dogs, and piped music. There are some tables with cocktail parasols outside by the road, with more in the pleasant garden. The nearby church (built for the girls' school of Brontë fame here) has some attractive pre-Raphaelite stained glass and paintings. *(Recommended by Michael Butler, Karen Eliot, Alan J Morton, David and Kathy Holcroft, K H Richards, Neil Townend, R Bouran)*

Free house ~ Licensees Melvin and May Mackie ~ Real ale ~ Meals and snacks ~ Restaurant ~ (015242) 71230 ~ Children welcome ~ Open 11-3, 6-11(10.30 Sun) ~ Bedrooms: £37.50B/£68B

CHAPEL STILE NY3205 Map 9

Wainwrights

B5343

In a charming fellside spot, this white-rendered pub has plenty of good surrounding walks and picnic-sets on the terrace with fine views. Inside, there's a relaxed and friendly atmosphere and plenty of room in the characterful slate-floored bar with its old kitchen range and cushioned settles. Under the new licensee, bar food includes home-made soup (£1.95), sandwiches (from £2.05), filled baked potatoes (£3.75), ploughman's or quiche (£5.20), cannelloni filled with spinach and ricotta cheese (£6.50), lamb shoulder with honey and mint (£7.50), children's dishes (£2.95), and daily specials; good, prompt service. The dining area is no smoking. Well kept Jennings Bitter, Cumberland Ale, and Sneck Lifter, and a guest beer on handpump; darts, dominoes, fruit machine, video game, and piped music. *(Recommended by Roy Butler, David Cooke, SLC, Colin Draper, Suzanne and Steve Griffiths)*

Free house ~ Licensee David Banks ~ Real ale ~ Meals and snacks ~ Restaurant ~ (015394) 38088 ~ Children welcome until 9.30 ~ Open 11.30-11; 12-10.30 Sun; 11.30-3, 6-11 winter weekdays

COCKERMOUTH NY1231 Map 9

Bitter End

15 Kirkgate

As in all the best town pubs, this interestingly refurbished place has a different atmosphere in each of its three main rooms from quietly chatty to sporty, with the decor reflecting this – unusual pictures of a Cockermouth that even Wordsworth might have recognised to more up-to-date sporting memorabilia. There's a tiny Victorian style shop window view of the little brewery behind the back room where the landlord brews Cockersnoot and Skinners Old Strong – you can see the equipment without even getting up from your seat. He also keeps Jennings Bitter, Theakstons Best, Old Peculier, and XB and two guest beers on handpump, in good condition; quite a few bottled beers from around the world. At lunchtime, simple snacks include home-made soup (£1.50), filled rolls (from £1.65; spicy chicken £2.50), and filled baked potatoes (from £1.95), with a larger evening choice such as home-made chicken tikka (£4.65), lasagne, steak pie or three cheese pasta with broccoli (£4.75), puddings like home-made sticky toffee pudding (£1.95), children's meals (from £1.95), and roast Sunday lunch (£3.95). Service is very welcoming; piped music; the public car park round the back is free after 6. *(Recommended by H K Dyson, Richard Houghton; more reports please)*

Own brew ~ Licensee Susan Askey ~ Real ale ~ Meals and snacks (12-2, 6-8.30) ~ (01900) 826626 ~ Children in eating area of bar at meal times ~ Quiz night Tues, live folk/jazz on Sun at end of month ~ Open 12-2.30, 6-11.30; 11.30-3, 6-11 Sat; 12-3, 7-10.30 Sun

CONISTON SD3098 Map 9

Black Bull

Yewdale Rd (A593)

Donald Campbell stayed here while attempting his water speed records and there's quite a lot of memorabilia devoted to him. They also brew a beer on the premises named for his Bluebird – as well as Coniston Old Man, Opium, and Blacksmiths (and keep Jennings and Yates as guests). The beamed and carpeted front part of the building has cast-iron-framed tables, comfortable red banquettes and stools, an open fire, and a relaxed, comfortable feel, while the cheerful back area has slate flagstones – so walkers (and dogs) are welcome here; the restaurant and part of the bar are no smoking. Filling bar food, good if not cheap, includes home-made soup (£1.95), sandwiches (from £2.95; toasties £3.25), filled baked potatoes (from £3.50), ploughman's (£5.95), cumberland sausage (£5.95), spicy chilli con carne (£6.80), vegetable moussaka (£7.45), local smoked trout (£7.95), sirloin steak (£10.95), daily specials, puddings like home-made apple pie (£2.50), and children's menu (£3.50). Service is prompt and friendly even under pressure; dominoes, cribbage, and unobtrusive piped music. There are tables out in the former coachyard, and the inn is well placed at the foot of the Old Man of Coniston. Parking may not be easy at peak times. *(Recommended by G Coates, JCW, SLC, Pamela and Merlyn Horswell, V W Prime, Wm Van Laaten, Richard Houghton; more reports please)*

Own brew ~ Licensee Ronald Bradley ~ Real ale ~ Meals and snacks (all day) ~ Restaurant ~ (015394) 41335 ~ Children welcome till 9pm ~ Open 11-11; 12-10.30 Sun ~ Bedrooms: £37.50B/£65B

> Looking for a pub with a really special garden, or in lovely countryside, or with an outstanding view, or right by the water? They are listed separately, at the back of the book.

CROSTHWAITE SD4491 Map 9

Punch Bowl

Village signposted off A5074 SE of Windermere

Although Mr Doherty has moved to the Spread Eagle at Sawley (Lancashire) he continues to run this idyllically placed 16th-c inn through managers. Most people do come here to eat (booking is strongly advised) but those wanting just a drink are welcomed too. There are several separate areas carefully reworked to give a lot of space, and a high-raftered central area by the serving counter with an upper minstrels' gallery on either side; several no-smoking areas. Steps lead down into a couple of small dimly lit rooms on the right, and there's a doorway through into two more airy rooms on the left. It's all spick and span, with lots of tables and chairs, beams, pictures, and an open fire. Very good food includes cream of tomato and basil soup with croutons (£2.25), rabbit terrine with home-made pickles and chutney (£4.25), deep-fried goat's cheese salad (£4.50), chargrilled breast of chicken with crisp air-dried cumbrian ham (£8.50), chargrilled tuna with a soy, ginger and sesame dressing (£8.75), braised shank of lamb (£9.25), steak (£10.25), and puddings like banana tart tatin or chocolate nemesis (from £3). Well kept Jennings Cumberland and Sneck Lifter, Theakstons Best, and Charles Wells Bombardier on handpump. The upper gallery is no smoking. There are some tables on a terrace stepped into the hillside. *(Recommended by Tina and David Woods-Taylor, G Coates, Gwen and Peter Andrews, Sheelia Curtis, K F Mould, David Carr, JDM, KM, Mick Hitchman, Prof P A Reynolds, Ann and Colin Hunt, Karen Eliot, IHR, Peter Walker, RJH, Malcolm Taylor, Jack Morley, Tim and Sue Halstead, Dr Stewart Rae, Joan Yew, John and Barbara Burns, Mr and Mrs A C Chapman, Tony Hall, Melanie Jackson; more reports please)*

Free house ~ Licensees Duncan Collinge, Dawn Brackstone ~ Real ale ~ Meals and snacks (12-2, 6-9) ~ (015395) 68237 ~ Children welcome ~ Open 11-11; 12-10.30 Sun; closed 25 Dec, evenings 26 Dec, 1 Jan ~ Bedrooms: £35B/£50B

DENT SD7187 Map 10

Sun

Village signposted from Sedbergh; and from Barbon, off A683

Just a few miles up in the dale is the Dent Brewery that supplies this pretty pub with its own real ales: Bitter, T'Owd Tup, and Kamikazee Strong Ale on handpump. There's a pleasant, traditional atmosphere in the bar, fine old oak timbers and beams studded with coins, simple furniture, quite a few local snapshots, and a coal fire; one of the areas is no smoking. Through the arch to the left are banquettes upholstered to match the carpet (as are the curtains). Straightforward bar food includes home-made soup (£1.80), sandwiches (£1.85), ploughman's (£4.05), home-made steak and kidney pie or lasagne (£4.75), gammon and egg (£6.05), rump steak (£6.45), puddings (£1.95), and children's helpings (£2.75); prompt service. Darts, pool, bar billiards, dominoes, fruit machine, video game, and juke box (in the pool room). There are rustic seats and tables outside and the surrounding fells are popular with walkers. *(Recommended by Paul and Sandra Embleton, JP, PP, Susan and Nigel Wilson, Derek and Sylvia Stephenson, Alan J Morton, Denis and Margaret Kilner, R H Rowley, Andy and Jill Kassube, David and Judy Walmsley)*

Own brew ~ Licensee Martin Stafford ~ Real ale ~ Meals and snacks ~ (015396) 25208 ~ Children in eating area of bar until 9pm ~ Open 11-11; 11-2, 7-11 in winter; 12-10.30 Sun; closed 25 Dec ~ Bedrooms: £20/£37

ELTERWATER NY3305 Map 9

Britannia Inn ★

Off B5343

Walkers love this pub. It's set at the heart of the Lake District with numerous tracks over the surrounding fells, and chairs and slate-topped tables on the front terrace looking across the village green; dogs are welcome everywhere except the dining room. At the back is a small and traditionally furnished bar, while the front bar has winter coal fires and settles, oak benches, windsor chairs, a big old rocking chair, and a couple of window seats looking across to Elterwater itself through the trees on the far side; there's also a comfortable no-smoking lounge. Well kept Coniston Bluebird, Dent Aviator, Jennings Bitter, and two guest beers on handpump, quite a few malt whiskies, a well chosen, good value wine list, country wines, and farm cider. Popular bar food includes filled rolls and ploughman's, home-made soup (£2), home-made cumberland pâté with cumberland sauce (£2.50), home-made chicken balti or hungarian bean goulash (£6), home-made steak and mushroom pie (£6.50), poached fresh salmon with lemon and dill butter (£6.75), puddings such as sticky toffee pudding with toffee sauce or home-made raspberry and white chocolate ice cream (£2.75), daily specials such as roast chicken breast stuffed with ham and stilton or roast loin of pork with dijon mustard and rosemary (£6.50), and children's meals with activity sheet and crayons (£3.25; they also offer small helpings of the daily specials); super breakfasts and home-baked fruit scones for afternoon cream teas. The restaurant is no smoking; dominoes, cribbage, several board games, and Sunday evening quiz night. In summer, people flock to watch Morris and Step and Garland dancers. They've opened a car park for residents only. *(Recommended by Nick Lawless, Tina and David Woods-Taylor, Mrs Frances Gray, SLC, Prof P A Reynolds, Michael A Butler, Ewan and Moira McCall, Jenny and Brian Seller, V W Prime, Wm Van Laaten, Andy and Jill Kassube, Mr and Mrs Richard Osborne, David Carr, H K Dyson, Alan Risdon, Colin and Sue Graham, David Hoult)*

Free house ~ Judith Fry and Julie Carmichael ~ Real ale ~ Meals and snacks (snacks are sold all afternoon) ~ Restaurant ~ (015394) 37210 ~ Children welcome until 9 ~ Summer parking may be difficult ~ Open 11-11; 12-10.30 Sun; closed 25 Dec and evening 26 Dec ~ Bedrooms: £24/£48(£62B)

ESKDALE GREEN NY1300 Map 9

Bower House

½ mile W of village towards Santon Bridge

There's a good winter log fire in the lounge bar of this old stone-built inn, as well as cushioned settles and windsor chairs that blend in well with the original beamed and alcoved nucleus around the serving counter, and a quietly relaxed atmosphere – no noisy machines or piped music; also, a separate lounge with easy chairs and sofas. Decent bar food includes sandwiches, cumberland sausage (£6), vegetarian dishes (from £6), and daily specials such as pheasant in whisky sauce (£7.25). Well kept Hartleys XB, Theakstons Best, and three changing real ales on handpump, and a reasonably priced wine list; friendly staff. The restaurant is no smoking. The nicely tended sheltered garden is a pleasant place to relax and on summer Sundays you can watch the cricket on the field alongside the pub. Some of the comfortable bedrooms are in the annexe across the garden. *(Recommended by Tina and David Woods-Taylor, Mrs S Kingsbury, H K Dyson, Martin, Patricia and Hilary Forrest, Rob Holt, B J P Edwards)*

Free house ~ Licensees Derek and Beryl Connor ~ Real ale ~ Meals and snacks (12-2, 6.30-9.30) ~ Restaurant ~ (019467) 23244 ~ Children welcome ~ Open 11-11; 12-3, 7-11 Sun ~ Bedrooms: £51B/£70B

GARRIGILL NY7441 Map 9

George & Dragon

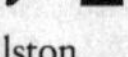

Village signposted off B6277 S of Alston

Set opposite a small tree-shaded village green, this simple stonebuilt inn is liked by walkers as the Pennine Way passes the door. Inside on the right, the bar has solid traditional furnishings on the very broad polished flagstones, a lovely stone fireplace with a really good log fire, and a friendly, relaxed atmosphere; there's a separate tartan-carpeted games room with sensibly placed darts, pool and dominoes; piped music. Good value straightforward bar food includes soup (£1.70), sandwiches (from £1.45), filled yorkshire pudding (from £1.95), filled baked potatoes (from £2.20), cumberland sausage and egg (£4.60), home-made steak pie (£5.10), broccoli and cream cheese bake (£5.10), sirloin steak (£7.95), daily specials, and children's dishes (from £1.95). The dining room is no smoking. Well kept Boddingtons, Marstons

Pedigree, Whitbreads Castle Eden, and guest beers on handpump. *(Recommended by Dr G Sanders, M J Morgan, R T and J C Moggridge, K F Mould, Comus Elliott, John Fazakerley)*

Free house ~ Licensees Brian and Jean Holmes ~ Real ale ~ Meals and snacks ~ Restaurant ~ (01434) 381293 ~ Children welcome ~ Open 11.30-4, 6-11; 12-4, 6.30-10.30 Sun; 12-3, 7-11 in winter ~ Bedrooms: £15/£30(£37B)

GRASMERE NY3406 Map 9

Travellers Rest

Just N of Grasmere on A591 Ambleside—Keswick rd; OS sheet 90, map ref 335089

In a lovely spot and surrounded by wonderful scenery and good walks, this attractive little 16th-c pub has picnic-sets in the side garden from which you can admire the marvellous views while enjoying a pint of well kept Jennings Bitter, Cumberland, Mild and Snecklifter, and Marstons Pedigree on handpump. Inside, the comfortable, beamed lounge bar has a warming log fire, banquettes and cushioned wooden chairs around varnished wooden tables, local watercolours and suggested walks and coast-to-coast information on the walls, and a relaxed atmosphere; piped classical music. The games room is popular with families: pool, dominoes, and fruit machine. There's quite an emphasis on the enjoyable bar food which includes home-made soup (£1.95), sandwiches (from £2.45; open ones from £5.25), crunchy garlic mushrooms (£2.95), five bean chilli (£5.25), fish and chips with mushy peas (£5.75), ploughman's or steak and kidney pie (£5.95), lamb rogan josh (£6.25), crispy fried duck in a basket (£6.95), chargrilled steaks (from £10.45), puddings (£2.75), daily specials such as braised beef in ale, hock of bacon with fresh parsley sauce or fresh fish like tuna, halibut or red snapper, and a good children's menu (from 75p); the restaurant is no smoking. They keep at least a dozen malt whiskies; friendly, efficient service. *(Recommended by Nick Lawless, Ann and Colin Hunt, Tim and Ann Newell, SLC, K F Mould, Michael A Butler, David and Tina Woods-Taylor, Derek and Sylvia Stephenson, Susan and Nigel Wilson, David Carr, Dr A C Williams, Dr F M Ellard, V W Prime, Wm Van Laaten, Andy and Jill Kassube, Norman and Angela Harries, Mark Fennell, Judith Erlandsen)*

Free house ~ Licensees Lynne, Derek and Graham Sweeney ~ Real ale ~ Meals and snacks (12-9.30 in summer) ~ (015394) 35604 ~ Children welcome ~ Open 12-11; 12-10.30 Sun; 12-3, 6-9.30 in winter ~ Bedrooms: /£53.90(£59.90B)

nr HAWKSHEAD NY3501 Map 9

Drunken Duck ★

Barngates; the hamlet is signposted from B5286 Hawkshead—Ambleside, opposite the Outgate Inn; or it may be quicker to take the first right from B5286, after the wooded caravan site; OS Sheet 90 map reference 350013

Cumbria Dining Pub of the Year

We get more reports on this attractive 17th-c Lakeland pub than almost any other in the Guide. It's a super place to stay with little thoughtful extras in the bedrooms, the food is particularly good (we've given them Food and Stay awards this year, which is quite an achievement), their own real ale from Barngates Brewery is proving a winner, and the staff are especially helpful. One change this year is that they felt the kitchen was being stretched too much and that customers were not getting the standard of service they were accustomed to here, so bookings are now taken in the restaurant (which takes up the three main rooms of the pub) and the menu has altered quite a bit – no fried dishes any more. Food is simpler at lunchtime and includes lovely home-made soup such as curried cauliflower or cream of tomato and pepper (£2.75), sandwiches (£2.95; grilled open ones £4.25), liver or hummus pâté (£3.95), quiche (£4.95), nice ploughman's (£5.50), and good country lamb or cheese, onion and potato pies (£5.95); in the evening, the choice is more elaborate and there might be grilled black pudding on sautéed leeks with a chervil butter sauce (£3.50), crispy duck and watercress salad with a sesame, balsamic and ginger dressing (£5.50), stir-fried vegetables in a black bean sauce (£6.95), liver and gammon with thyme mashed potato and onion and marsala gravy (£7.50), steamed steak pudding with honey roast vegetables (£8.95), medallions of salmon on gingered courgette ribbons, champagne sauce and chive dorphine (£9.95), Aberdeen Angus steak with watercress mousse and glazed shallots (£13.95), and puddings such as pear and brazil nut crumble, black cherry frangipane strudel or sticky toffee pudding (from £2.95). As well as Cracker brewed in their cellar, they now have Chesters Strong & Ugly Ale, too, and also keep Jennings Bitter, Theakstons Old Peculier, and Yates Bitter on handpump; over 50 malt whiskies. The bar and snug are traditional pubby beamed rooms with good winter fires, cushioned old settles and a mix of chairs on the fitted turkey carpet, pictures, cartoons, cards, fox masks, and cases of fishing flies and lures, and maybe the multi-coloured cat. All of the pub is no smoking except the bar. Darts, dominoes, and cribbage. Seats on the front verandah look across to Lake Windermere in the distance; to the side there are quite a few rustic wooden chairs and tables, sheltered by a stone wall with alpine plants along its top, and the pub has fishing in a private tarn behind. *(Recommended by Simon and Amanda Southwell, SLC, Ann and Colin Hunt, Vann and Terry Prime, Mr and Mrs D W Mitchell, Tina and David Woods-Taylor, George Picton, Brian Green, Neil Townend, Prof P A Reynolds, Larry and Karen House, JP, PP, R W Tapsfield, Roger and Christine Mash, Bronwen and Steve Wrigley, Phil and Heidi Cook, Nick Lawless, David J Cooke, Derek and Sylvia Stephenson, Liz Bell, Andy and Jill Kassube, Alastair Campbell, JDM, KM, Jerry and Alison Oakes, John Honnor, JCW, Walter and Susan Rinaldi-Butcher, Jack Morley, P H Roberts, Richard Houghton, Alan Risdon)*

Free house ~ Licensee Stephanie Barton ~ Real ale ~ Meals and snacks ~ Restaurant ~ (015394) 36347 ~ Children in eating area of bar ~ Occasional jazz or folk ~ Open 11.30-3, 6-11; 12-3, 6-10.30 Sun; closed evening 25 Dec ~ Bedrooms: £55B/£75B

HEVERSHAM SD4983 Map 9

Blue Bell

A6 (now a relatively very quiet road here)

Civilised and comfortable, this partly timbered old country inn has a lounge bar with warm winter fires, pewter platters hanging from the beams, an antique carved settle, cushioned windsor armchairs and upholstered stools on the flowery carpet, and small antique sporting prints and a display cabinet with two stuffed fighting cocks on the partly panelled walls. One big bay-windowed area has been divided off as a children's room, and the long, tiled-floor public bar has darts, pool, cribbage, dominoes, fruit machine, piped music, and TV. Good bar food based on fresh local produce includes home-made soup (£2.25), sandwiches (from £2.75), lovely Morecambe Bay potted shrimps (£4.50), local venison casserole (£6.50), roast breast of duck, sizzling sirloin steak platter (£9.95), and puddings like sticky toffee pudding (£2.45). The restaurant is no smoking. Well kept Sam Smiths OB on handpump kept under light blanket pressure, several malt whiskies, a decent wine list, and their own cider; helpful staff. Crossing over the A6 into the village itself, you come to a picturesque church with a rambling little graveyard; if you walk through this and on to the hills beyond, there's a fine view across to the estuary of the River Kent. The estuary itself is a short walk from the pub down the country road that runs by its side. *(Recommended by SLC, Mr and Mrs C Roberts, D Bryan, Roger and Christine Mash, Alan Risdon)*

Sam Smiths ~ Managers Richard and Susan Cowie ~ Real ale ~ Meals and snacks (all day) ~ Restaurant ~ (015395) 62018 ~ Children welcome ~ Open 11-11 ~ Bedrooms: £42B/£64B

INGS SD4599 Map 9

Watermill

Just off A591 E of Windermere

Just a couple of miles from Windermere, this ivy-covered Lakeland stone inn has a good mix of visitors and locals keen to enjoy the marvellous range of 14 real ales perfectly kept on handpump: Black Sheep Special, Coniston Bluebird, Jennings Cumberland, Lees Moonraker, and Theakstons Best, Old Peculier and XB, with changing guests like Caledonian Murrays Summer Ale, Dent Ramsbottom, Fullers London Pride, Hesket Newmarket Doris's 90th Birthday Ale, Hop Back Summer Lightning, Marstons Pedigree, and Moorhouses Black Cat and Pendle Witches Brew;

Old Rosie cider, bottled beers, and up to 50 malt whiskies; thirsty dogs are kindly catered for, too, with a biscuit and bowl of water. There's a friendly welcome from the chatty landlord and his staff and a bustling atmosphere – no noisy machines or juke box. The bars have a happy mix of chairs, padded benches and solid oak tables, bar counters made from old church wood, open fires, and amusing cartoons by a local artist on the wall; some tables in the extension are no smoking. The spacious lounge bar, in much the same traditional style as the other rooms, has rocking chairs and a big open fire. Decent bar food includes lunchtime snacks such as sandwiches (from £2.25), filled baked potatoes (from £3.25), and ploughman's (from £4.25; with soup £5.75), plus soup (£2), deep-fried mushrooms with garlic dip (£2.95), ham and chips (£5.75), roast chicken (£5.95), 1lb cumberland sausage (£6.95), steaks (from £9.75), and daily specials like beef in ale pie or lamb and apricot balti (£6), chicken and cheese in a wild mushroom sauce (£7), and poached halibut and salmon with a smoked salmon sauce (£7.90); children's menu (£3.25). Darts, table skittles, dominoes, Jenga, and card games. There are seats in the front garden. Lots of climbing, fell-walking, fishing, boating of all kinds, swimming and pony-trekking within easy reach. *(Recommended by Lesley Jones, David and Helen Wilkins, Dick Brown, ALC, Sheila Keene, K F Mould, Ann and Colin Hunt, R J Bland, David and Kathy Holcroft, SLC, David Carr, G Coates, Roger Stamp, Bronwen and Steve Wrigley, Richard and Robyn Wain, M Thompson, JDM, KM, Mark Fennell, Ian and Villy White, Dr J Morley, Andy and Jill Kassube, Colin Draper, Alan Risdon, John Scarisbrick, Richard Houghton)*

Free house ~ Licensees Alan and Brian Coulthwaite ~ Real ale ~ Meals and snacks (not 25 Dec) ~ (01539) 821309 ~ Children in lounge until 9pm ~ Story telling first Tues of month ~ Open 12-2.30, 6-11; 12-3, 6-10.30 Sun; closed 25 Dec ~ Bedrooms: /£45S

KESWICK NY2624 Map 9

Dog & Gun

Lake Road; off top end of Market Square

Well liked by walkers, hikers and climbers, this lively and unpretentious town local has low beams, a partly slate floor (the rest are carpeted or bare boards), some high settles, a fine collection of striking mountain photographs by the local firm G P Abrahams, coins in beams and timbers by the fireplace, and log fires. Well kept Theakstons Best and Old Peculier on handpump, and good food such as home-made soup (£2.25), filled french bread (from £2.25), baked trout in garlic butter with prawns, venison in red wine or the house speciality, goulash (all £5.95), and puddings such as sticky toffee pudding (£1.90); no grills or chips. 25 malt whiskies, piped music and fruit machine. *(Recommended by David and Kathy Holcroft, David Carr, SLC, Tim and Ann Newell, Kevin Thorpe, Alan Risdon)*

Scottish Courage ~ Licensee John Wiener ~ Real ale ~ Meals and snacks (12-9.30) ~ (01768) 773463 ~ Children welcome until 9pm ~ Open 11-11; 12-10.30 Sun; closed 25 Dec

KIRKBY LONSDALE SD6278 Map 7

Snooty Fox

Main Street (B6254)

The food in this rambling pub is very good indeed, but there's also a bustling pubby atmosphere and plenty of interest in the various rooms: mugs hang from beams, and the walls are full of eye-catching coloured engravings, stuffed wildfowl and falcons, mounted badger and fox masks, guns and a powder-flask, stage gladiator costumes, and horse-collars and stirrups. The bar counters are made from English oak, as is some panelling, and there are also country kitchen chairs, pews, one or two high-backed settles and marble-topped sewing-trestle tables on the flagstones, and two coal fires. From a changing menu, there might be sandwiches, home-made soup with their own walnut and apricot bread (£2), a terrine with redcurrant and orange sauce (£4.75), cumberland sausage with caramelised onion gravy (£5.95), steak and kidney pudding (£6.25), broccoli, stilton and apple lasagne with home-made pasta (£6.95), rib-eye steak with dauphinoise potatoes and caesar salad (£9.95), roast barbary duck with a passion fruit, honey and orange glaze (£11.95), and whole bass with a coriander and citrus butter (£15.25). The dining annexe is no smoking. Well kept Hartleys XB, Theakstons Best, and Timothy Taylor Landlord on handpump, several malt whiskies, and country wines; fruit machine and good juke box in back bar only. There are tables out on a small terrace beside the biggish back cobbled stableyard, with more in a pretty garden; small play area for children. *(Recommended by Neil Townend, Paul S McPherson, K H Frostick, JDM, KM, Mrs J Kemp, John Fazakerley, Roger and Lynda Goldstone, Jackie Laister, Angela and Humphry Crum Ewing, Paul Robinshaw)*

Free house ~ Licensee Jack Shone ~ Real ale ~ Meals and snacks (12-2.30, 6.30-10) ~ Restaurant ~ (015242) 71308 ~ Children in eating area of bar and in restaurant ~ Open 11-11; 12-10.30 Sun; closed evening 25 Dec ~ Bedrooms: £32.50B/£50B

Sun

Market St (B6254)

Turner stayed here in 1818 while painting *Ruskin's View* and this friendly and bustling little pub is still a popular place to stay; some of the bedrooms are in a stone barn with lovely views across the Barbon Fells. The rambling low-beamed rooms (one of which is no smoking) have a good local atmosphere, window seats, cosy pews, and good winter fires, and are filled with a collection of some 500 banknotes, maps, old engravings, and other interesting antiques on the walls (some of which are stripped to bare stone or have panelled dados). Very well kept Black Sheep Bitter, Boddingtons, Dent Bitter, and Wadworths 6X on handpump, and 60 malt whiskies, a good choice of coffees, and Havana cigars; dominoes, trivia and piped music. Generous helpings of tasty bar food include home-made soup (£1.75), sandwiches (from £2.25), black pudding with a wholegrain mustard sauce (£2.95), devilled lamb kidneys on a crispy potato rosti (£3.95), bubble and squeak (£4.50), crêpes (£4.95), pizzas (from £4.95; you can choose your topping), home-made chicken, leek and wensleydale cheese pie (£5.95), Aberdeen Angus steak (£7.95), and children's meals (£2.95). Good personal service and super breakfasts. There's an unusual pillared porch; the steep cobbled alley is also attractive. *(Recommended by R J Walden, Prof P A Reynolds, A Hepburn, S Jenner, Andy and Jill Kassube, Alan Risdon, Noel and Roni Flatley, John and Beryl Knight, Graham Prodger)*

Free house ~ Licensee Andrew Wilkinson ~ Real ale ~ Meals and snacks (11-2, 6-10) ~ Restaurant ~ (015242) 71965 ~ Children welcome ~ Open 11-11; 12-10.30 Sun ~ Bedrooms: £24.50(£29.50B)/£45.50(£49.50B)

LANERCOST NY5664 Map 9

Abbey Bridge Inn

Follow brown Lanercost Priory signs from A69 or in Brampton

The actual pub part of this attractive inn – set by a strikingly arched medieval bridge – is in a side building (formerly a 17th-c smithy) with high pitched rafters and knobby whited stone walls, an understated rustic decor that includes charming Ashley Boon prints as well as a large woodburning stove, and a relaxed but rather stylish atmosphere. Bar food includes sandwiches, home-made soup (£2.99), potted brown shrimps (£4.25), deep-fried camembert with a sweet and sour sauce (£4.35), home-made vegetable pie (£7.50), thai vegetable schnitzel or beef in ale pie (£9.99), roast beef with yorkshire pudding (£10.99), coq au vin or Scottish salmon fillet with a prawn and cream sauce (£11.99), rack of lamb (£12.99), and puddings like chocolate rumpots, home-made apple pie or sticky toffee pudding (from £2.30); it's normally served restaurant-style in a no-smoking gallery up spiral stairs. Well kept Adnams, Fullers Chiswick, and Shepherd Neame Spitfire from a choice of nine weekly changing ales, other good drinks such as the excellent Fentimans ginger beer, and quite a few malt whiskies; welcoming service. Very faint piped pop music, chess, cribbage, and dominoes. There are a few seats outside, and the pub is set in lovely quiet off-the-beaten-track countryside just up the lane from the great 12th-c priory. *(Recommended by Ian and Jane Irving, H Dickinson, Ann Williams, Tony Hughes, Canon David Baxter, Justin*

Hulford, Ian Phillips, David and Margaret Bloomfield, Bob and Marg Griffiths, Vann and Terry Prime, June and Tony Baldwin)

Free house ~ Licensee Philip Sayers ~ Real ale ~ Meals and snacks ~ Evening restaurant ~ (016977) 2224 ~ Children welcome ~ Open 12-2.30, 7-11(10.30 Sun); closed 25 Dec ~ Bedrooms: £25(£35B)/£50(£60B)

LANGDALE NY2906 Map 9

Old Dungeon Ghyll

B5343

For those who love walking, this simply furnished unchanging pub is just the place to be. There's a good bustling atmosphere and plenty of stories of days on the hills from cheerful customers. The position is marvellous – at the heart of the Great Langdale Valley and surrounded by fells including the Langdale Pikes flanking the Dungeon Ghyll Force waterfall – and there are grand views of the Pike of Blisco rising behind Kettle Crag from the window seats cut into the thick stone walls of the bar. Straightforward food (with prices unchanged since last year) includes lunchtime sandwiches (£2), filled baked potatoes (£3.25), home-made pizzas (£4.20), cumberland sausage (£5.25), chilli con carne (£5.75), puddings (£2.25), and children's meals (£3.25); if you are not a resident and want to eat in the no-smoking restaurant you must book ahead. Well kept Jennings Cumberland and Mild, Theakstons XB and Old Peculier, Yates Bitter, and guest ales on handpump, and farm cider; darts, cribbage and dominoes. It can get really lively on a Saturday night (there's a popular National Trust campsite opposite). *(Recommended by R J Bland, SLC, N Cobb, Nigel Woolliscroft, Roy Butler, Ewan and Moira McCall, Liz Bell, Bronwen and Steve Wrigley, H K Dyson, Tim Heywood, Sophie Wilne, G Oglanby)*

Free house ~ Licensee Neil Walmsley ~ Real ale ~ Meals and snacks (12-2, 6-9) ~ Evening restaurant ~ (015394) 37272 ~ Children welcome until 9 ~ Open 11-11; 12-10.30; closed 24-26 Dec ~ Bedrooms: £29.50(£33B)/£59(£66B)

LITTLE LANGDALE NY3204 Map 9

Three Shires

From A593 3 miles W of Ambleside take small road signposted The Langdales, Wrynose Pass; then bear left at first fork

The three shires are Cumberland, Westmorland and Lancashire, which used to meet at the top of the nearby Wrynose Pass, and the views over the valley from seats on the terrace to the partly wooded hills below Tilberthwaite Fells are lovely; there are more seats on a well kept lawn behind the car park, backed by a small oak wood. Inside, the comfortably extended back bar has antique carved oak settles, country kitchen chairs and stools on its big dark slate flagstones, stripped timbers and a beam-and-joist stripped ceiling, Lakeland photographs lining the walls, and a warm winter fire in the modern stone fireplace with a couple of recesses for ornaments; an arch leads through to a small, additional area. Decent bar food includes soup (£2.20), duck liver pâté with citrus fruit salad (£3.95), good cumberland sausage (£5.95), pie of the day (£6.50), lamb liver with bubble and squeak or a parcel of four cheeses and spinach with a sage, walnut and raspberry dressing (£7.25), chicken breast with a fennel and basil pancake and a fresh tomato sauce (£8.50), sirloin steak (£10.95), daily specials, home-made puddings like sticky toffee pudding or lemon and lime tart (£2.95), and children's dishes (£3; they can also have small helpings of most meals). The restaurant and snug are no smoking. Well kept Black Sheep Special, Coniston Old Man, Jennings Bitter, and Theakstons XB on handpump; darts and dominoes. *(Recommended by K F Mould, Nigel Woolliscroft, Tina and David Woods-Taylor, W W Burke, David Carr, JDM, KM, Philip and Ann Falkner, Julie Peters, Malcolm Taylor, Colin Blinkhorn)*

Free house ~ Licensee Ian Stephenson ~ Real ale ~ Meals and snacks (no evening food Dec/Jan) ~ Evening restaurant ~ (015394) 37215 ~ Children welcome until 9pm ~ Open 11-11; 12-10.30 Sun; 12-3, 8-10.30 in winter ~ Bedrooms: £33B/£66B

LOWESWATER NY1222 Map 9

Kirkstile

From B5289 follow signs to Loweswater Lake; OS Sheet 89, map reference 140210

From picnic-sets on the lawn and from the very attractive covered verandah in front of this friendly little country pub, there are views of the spectacular surrounding peaks and soaring fells; it's a haven for walkers and there's plenty of room for wet boots and gear – and a roaring log fire to dry in front of. The bar is low-beamed and carpeted, with comfortably cushioned small settles and pews, and partly stripped stone walls; from the bow windows in one of the rooms off the bar are more lovely views. Decent bar food includes sandwiches or rolls, filled baked potatoes, ploughman's, deep-fried brie (£3.95), mixed game casserole or braised lamb with rosemary (£6.75), children's menu, and afternoon tea with home-made scones and cakes; big breakfasts. Well kept Derwent Mutineer, and Jennings Bitter and Cocker Hoop on handpump, and several malt whiskies; darts, cribbage, dominoes, and a slate shove-ha'penny board; a side games room called the Little Barn has pool, fruit machine, video game and juke box. *(Recommended by Nick Lawless, Roger and Christine Mash, DC, H K Dyson, John Honnor, William Cunliffe, Peter Walker, Nick and Meriel Cox, Andy and Jill Kassube, John and Christine Lowe, Simon Watkins, David Hoult)*

Free house ~ Licensees Ken and Shirley Gorley ~ Real ale ~ Meals and snacks (12-9) ~ Restaurant ~ (01900) 85219 ~ Children welcome ~ Open 11-11; 12-10.30 Sun ~ Bedrooms: £37(£47B)/£47(£57B)

MELMERBY NY6237 Map 10

Shepherds ★ 🍷

About half way along A686 Penrith—Alston

Run by hard-working, friendly people, this bustling place has a bar divided up into several areas; the heavy-beamed no-smoking room to the left of the door is carpeted and comfortable with bottles on the mantlebeam over the warm open fire, sunny window seats, and sensible tables and chairs, and to the right is a stone-floored drinking part with a few plush bar stools and chairs. At the end is a spacious room with a high-raftered ceiling and pine tables and farmhouse chairs, a woodburning stove, and big wrought-iron candelabra, and steps up to a games area with pool and darts; shove-ha'penny, dominoes, fruit machine and juke box. Enjoyable food includes weekly specials such as curried winter vegetable soup (£2.20), duck liver pâté (£3.60), beef in Guinness with dumplings (£6.80), vegetable couscous or finnan haddock and broccoli pancakes (£6.40), pork with a mushroom and ginger sauce (£7.80), and half a roast duckling with orange and kumquat sauce (£8.80), as well as ploughman's with a choice of three cheeses from their fine range (£5.20), favourites such as cumberland sausage hotpot (£5.80), and barbecued spare ribs (£7.50), and steaks (from £11.50); half helpings for children, and traditional Sunday roast. Much of the main eating area is no smoking. Well kept Black Sheep Rigwelter, Eccleshall Slaters Bitter, Hartleys XB, Holts Bitter, and Jennings Cumberland on handpump, as well as over 50 malt whiskies, a good wine list, country wines, and quite a few bottled continental beers. Hartside Nursery Garden, a noted alpine and primula plant specialist, is just over the Hartside Pass, and there are fine views across the green to the Pennines. *(Recommended by K F Mould, Monica Shelley, Paul S McPherson, Andy and Jill Kassube, Richard Holloway, Malcolm Taylor, Jerry and Alison Oakes, Mr Miller, David Carr, Nick and Meriel Cox, F J Robinson, Peter Richards, Bob and Marg Griffiths, June and Tony Baldwin)*

Free house ~ Licensees Martin and Christine Baucutt ~ Real ale ~ Meals and snacks (11-2.30, 6-9.45) ~ (01768) 881217 ~ Children welcome away from bar until 9 ~ Open 10.30-3, 6-11; 12-3, 7-10.30 Sun; closed 25 Dec ~ Several holiday cottages

> We accept no free drinks or payment for inclusion. We take no advertising, and are not sponsored by the brewing industry – or by anyone else. So all reports are independent.

MUNGRISDALE NY3630 Map 10

Mill Inn

Village signposted off A66 Penrith—Keswick, a bit over a mile W of A5091 Ullswater turn-off

In a lovely village, this very hospitable inn based on a 16th-c building nestles among trees in a high, secluded valley below soaring fells that climb eventually to Blencathra. It's not surprisingly popular with walkers, and in the past had guests like Charles Dickens, Wilkie Collins, and John Peel (who is buried a few miles away). The main bar is simply furnished and has a warm fire in the stone fireplace, and the games room has lots of paragliding pictures (the licensees are very keen on the sport), and darts, pool, board games, and carpet bowls; piped music; the separate restaurant is no smoking. Bar food is good and all home-made (they make their own bread, use local produce, and offer vegetarian and vegan dishes): soup (£2.50), sandwiches (from £2.95), black pudding and bacon with mustard sauce (£3.95), good ploughman's (their speciality; you can choose three cheeses from a choice of 14 to have with home-made chutneys or pâté and hummus £3.95), a medley of field and forest mushrooms in a cream sauce (£4.95), a burger made from vegetables, pulses, fruit and nuts or spinach and feta cheese pie (£6.95), chicken breast wrapped in smoked bacon with a stilton sauce (£7.95), pies such as duckling, apple and calvados or chicken, pheasant and apricot (£8.45), seared tuna steak in lime on a tomato salsa base (£9.95), and puddings like chocolate parfait, fresh fruit pavlovas or sticky toffee pudding (from £2.45); children's menu (from £3.45). Well kept Jennings Bitter and Cumberland on handpump, and a good wine list with 10 by the glass; really friendly, helpful service. There are seats on a gravel forecourt, and down on a neat and very sheltered lawn that slopes towards the little river. Note that there is a separate Mill Hotel in this same hamlet. *(Recommended by Tim Brierly, Monica Shelley, Laura Darlington, Lesley Bass)*

Free house ~ Licensees Melissa Townson, John McKeever ~ Real ale ~ Meals and snacks (12-9) ~ Restaurant ~ (017687) 79632 ~ Children welcome ~ Open 11-11; 12-10.30 Sun; closed 25 Dec ~ Bedrooms: £26/£47(£57B)

NEAR SAWREY SD3796 Map 9

Tower Bank Arms

B5285 towards the Windermere ferry

Featured in *Jemima Puddleduck*, this bustling pub backs on to Beatrix Potter's Hill Top Farm (owned by the National Trust), and so can get busy at peak times. The low-beamed main bar has a fine log fire in the big cooking range, high-backed settles on the rough slate floor, local hunting photographs and signed photographs of celebrities on the walls, a grandfather clock, and good traditional atmosphere. Good bar food includes lunchtime snacks such as home-made soup (£2), filled rolls (from £2.50), ploughman's (from £4.25), and home-made cheese flan (£5), plus a home-made pie of the day or cumberland sausage (£5.25), duckling à l'orange (£7.50), and daily specials such as cottage pie (£5.25), fillet of plaice (£5.60), and local venison in red wine (£7.50). Well kept Theakstons Best, XB, and Old Peculier and weekly changing guest beers on handpump, as well as 24 malt whiskies, and Belgian fruit beers and other foreign beers; darts, shove-ha'penny, cribbage, dominoes, backgammon, and shut-the-box. Seats outside have pleasant views of the wooded Claife Heights. This is a good area for golf, sailing, birdwatching, fishing (they have a licence for two rods a day on selected waters in the area), and walking, but if you want to stay at the pub, you'll have to book well in advance. *(Recommended by Tina and David Woods-Taylor, SLC, P Thompson, Dr Rod Holcombe, Nick Lawless, DHV, JDM, KM, Jacquie Kirk, Dr J Morley, Colin Draper)*

Free house ~ Licensee Philip Broadley ~ Real ale ~ Meals and lunchtime snacks (not 25 Dec) ~ Restaurant ~ (015394) 36334 ~ Children welcome in eating area of bar at lunchtime, in restaurant in evening ~ Open 11-3, 5.30(6 in winter)-11; 12-3, 5.30-11 Sun; closed evening 25 Dec ~ Bedrooms: £35B/£48B

PENRITH NY5130 Map 10

Agricultural Hotel

Castlegate; ¾ mile from M6 junction 40 – A592 into town, just off entrance roundabout

Jennings bought this Victorian market-town hotel from Marstons a few years ago, and have sensibly refurbished it so as to preserve much of the original charm of the comfortable L-shaped beamed lounge – even keeping the curved sash windows over the bar. There's partly glazed panelling, plenty of seating, a lovely log fire, and a good down-to-earth local atmosphere with a thorough mix of customers. It can get extremely busy, staying cheerful and lively. Jennings Bitter, Dark Mild, Cumberland and Sneck Lifter on handpump are particularly well kept; prompt service, thoughtful and helpful, with a good chatty landlord; darts, piped music and fruit machine (in hall not in bar). A wide choice of reasonably priced food includes a home-made soup (£1.50), lunchtime sandwiches (from £1.80), cumberland sausage with onion gravy or home-made shepherd's pie (£4.25), ploughman's (£4.75), steak and kidney pie (£4.95), chicken, mushroom and tomato lasagne (£5.25), steaks (from £6.95), and puddings like sticky toffee pudding (£2.20); separate restaurant. There are good views from the picnic-sets out at the side. We have not yet heard from readers who have stayed here overnight. *(Recommended by John C Baker, Richard Lewis, Colin and Sue Graham, Jenny and Brian Seller, Bronwen and Steve Wrigley)*

Jennings ~ Tenants James and Margaret Hodge ~ Real ale ~ Meals and snacks ~ (01768) 862622 ~ Children welcome ~ Open 11-11; 12-10.30 Sun ~ Bedrooms: £25/£40

SCALES NY3427 Map 9

White Horse

A66 1½ miles NE of Threlkeld: keep your eyes skinned – it looks like a farmhouse up on a slope

Pretty in summer with its flowering window baskets and tubs, this traditional Lakeland pub is in a lovely dramatic setting under Blencathra. The little snug and old kitchen have all sorts of kitchen implements such as a marmalade slicer, butter churns, kettles, and a black range, and the comfortable beamed bar has warm winter fires, hunting pictures and local hunting cartoons on the walls; a small area is no smoking. There's quite an emphasis on eating with many of the tables set for dining, and bar food at lunchtime includes home-made soup (£1.95), chicken liver pâté (£3.95), cheese omelette (£4.75), ploughman's (£4.95), sultana, apple and butter bean casserole (£5.50), Waberthwaite sausage with pickled red cabbage (£5.90), and daily specials; evening dishes such as grilled black pudding with whisky and red wine sauce (£2.95), air-dried cumberland ham (£3.85), chicken in a sauce of shallots, cream and calvados (£7.95), roast duckling (£8.95), sirloin steak (£10.50), and puddings like sticky toffee pudding or home-made gingerbread topped with rum butter and whipped cream (from £2.50). Well kept Jennings Bitter with guests from Hesket Newmarket Brewery – Blencathra Bitter and Skiddaw Special Bitter on handpump; no noisy games machines or piped music. From the cluster of pub and farm buildings, tracks lead up into the splendidly daunting and rocky fells with names like Foule Crag and Sharp Edge; muddy boots should be left outside. *(Recommended by Roger and Christine Mash, F J Robinson, David and Judy Walmsley, Elizabeth Barraclough, Dorothy Hind, Ann and Frank Bowman; more reports please)*

Free house ~ Licensee Bruce Jackson ~ Real ale ~ Meals and snacks ~ (017687) 79241 ~ Well behaved children welcome, must be over 5 in evening ~ Open 12-2.30, 6.45-11(10.30 Sun); closed Mon Nov-Easter, 2 wks Jan

SEATHWAITE SD2396 Map 9

Newfield

Duddon Valley, nr Ulpha (ie not Seathwaite in Borrowdale)

Good walks lead from the doorstep of this little 16th-c cottage, so it's not surprising that climbers and walkers crowd in at weekends. There's a genuinely local and informal atmosphere in the slate-floored bar as well as a comfortable side room and a games room with darts and dominoes. Good value bar food includes filled granary french bread or proper home-made soup (£1.95), big cumberland sausages (£5.35), home-made steak pie or a vegetarian dish (from £4.95), huge gammon steaks with local farm eggs (£7.25), and good steaks; the restaurant is no smoking. Well kept Theakstons Best, XB and Old Peculier and a guest such as Fullers ESB, Greene King Abbot, Marstons Pedigree or Morlands Old Speckled Hen on handpump, several Polish vodkas and 24 malt whiskies; good service. Tables out in the nice garden have good hill views. The pub owns and lets the next-door cottages and has self-catering flats. *(Recommended by David Cooke, Derek Harvey-Piper; more reports please)*

Free house ~ Licensee Chris Burgess ~ Real ale ~ Meals and snacks ~ Restaurant ~ (01229) 716208 ~ Well behaved children welcome ~ Open 11-11; 11-10.35 Sun; 12-3, 6-11 winter weekdays

SEDBERGH SD6692 Map 10

Dalesman £

Main St

Even on a Sunday evening, you're likely to find this bustling, nicely modernised pub full of customers as the licensees and their staff offer a cheerful welcome as well as good beer and enjoyable food. There's quite a mix of decorations and styles in the rooms – lots of stripped stone and beams, cushioned farmhouse chairs and stools around dimpled copper tables, and a raised stone hearth with a log-effect gas fire; also, horsebrasses and spigots, Vernon Stokes gundog pictures, various stuffed animals, tropical fish, and a blunderbuss. Through stone arches on the right a no-smoking buttery area serves good value lunchtime food (it's for these meals that our Bargain Award is given) such as home-made soup (£1.50), a big choice of filled rolls (from £1.30; grilled bacon and egg £2.30, steak and onions £4), lots of filled baked potatoes (from £3), breakfast (£3.50), and lasagne (£4); a more substantial menu offers chicken liver and pistachio nut pâté (£3.95), home-made cumberland sausage with two eggs (£5.95), cannelloni ricotta or steak and kidney pie (£6.50), local grilled trout or lamb and rosemary casserole (£7.50), steaks (from £9.90), daily specials such as chicken satay (£3.50), lamb rogan josh (£8) or ostrich fillet (£12), and good value Sunday roast beef (£5.50); children's menu (from £2.90). The restaurant is no smoking. Well kept Tetleys Bitter and Theakstons Best on handpump; dominoes and piped music. There are some picnic-sets out in front; small car park. *(Recommended by Dick Brown, Katherine Williams, Ann and Colin Hunt, Paul S McPherson, K F Mould, Paul Cowburn, R F and M K Bishop, Sheila Dunsire, David Warrellow)*

Free house ~ Licensees Michael Garnett, Graham Smith ~ Real ale ~ Meals and snacks (12-2.30, 6-9.30) ~ Restaurant ~ (015396) 21183 ~ Children welcome ~ Open 11-11 ~ Bedrooms: £30S/£60B

STAINTON NY4928 Map 10

Kings Arms

1¾ miles from M6 junction 40: village signposted from A66 towards Keswick, though quickest to fork left at A592 roundabout then turn first right

The friendly landlord in this pleasantly modernised pub goes out of his way to make you feel welcome, and readers have enjoyed their visits over this past year here very much. The neatly kept open-plan bar has leatherette wall banquettes, stools and armchairs around wood-effect tables, brasses on the black beams, and prints and paintings of the Lake District on the swirly cream walls; one room is no smoking during mealtimes. Enjoyable traditional bar food includes home-made soup (£1.50), lunchtime sandwiches (from £1.80; good toasties from £1.95; open sandwiches from £3.10) or filled baked potatoes (from £3.30), cumberland sausage with egg (£4.20), home-made steak and kidney pie (£4.95), breast of chicken with sage and onion stuffing or vegetable lasagne (£6), sirloin steak (£9.45), puddings (from £1.70), children's dishes (£2.50), daily specials (from £4.20), and roast Sunday lunch. Well kept Wadworths 6X and Whitbreads Castle Eden on handpump; sensibly placed darts, dominoes, fruit machine, and piped music. There are tables outside on the side terrace and a small lawn. *(Recommended by Ann and Colin Hunt, Basil J Minson, John and Cath Howard, W Blachford, Nick Lawless, Carol and Philip Seddon, Neil Townend, IHR, Jenny and Roger Huggins, B J P Edwards, Colin Draper, Alan Risdon)*

Whitbreads/Carlsberg-Tetleys ~ Tenants James and Anne Downie ~ Real ale ~ Meals and snacks (not winter Mon lunchtime) ~ (01768) 862778 ~ Children welcome till 9pm ~ Open 11.30-3, 6.30(7 in winter)-11; 12-3, 7-10.30 Sun; closed winter Mon lunchtime

THRELKELD NY3325 Map 9

Salutation

Old main rd, bypassed by A66 W of Penrith

There's nothing fancy about this little village local, but walkers are fond of it and the tiled floor is used to muddy boots. The low-beamed connecting rooms have simple furnishings, a good atmosphere and a roaring log fire, plus Courage Directors, Marstons Pedigree, Ruddles County, and Theakstons Best and XB on handpump. Bar food includes sandwiches (from £2), soup (£2.25), basket meals (from £3.95), large ploughman's (from £4.95), meaty or vegetarian lasagne, steak and mushroom pie, local trout or hungarian goulash (all £5.85), steaks (from £10.85), daily specials, and puddings like sticky toffee pudding (£2.85). The spacious upstairs children's room has a pool table and juke box (oldies); also, cribbage, dominoes, fruit machine, trivia, video game and piped music. The owners let a couple of holiday cottages in the village. *(Recommended by Nigel Woolliscroft, David and Margaret Bloomfield, Bob and Marg Griffiths, T M Dobby, Maurice Thompson)*

Scottish Courage ~ Tenants Ken and Rose Burchill ~ Real ale ~ Meals and snacks (not 25 Dec) ~ (017687) 79614 ~ Well behaved children welcome ~ Open 11-3, 5.30-11; 11-11 Sat; 12-10.30 Sun; 12-3, 6-11(10.30 Sun) winter weekends

TIRRIL NY5126 Map 10

Queens Head

3½ miles from M6 junction 40; take A66 towards Brough, A6 towards Shap, then B5320 towards Ullswater

Now that the hard-working licensees have finished exposing the original flagstones and floorboards in the bars and part of the restaurant here, they aim to upgrade the bedrooms. The oldest parts of the bar have low bare beams, black panelling, high-backed settles, and a roomy inglenook fireplace (once a cupboard for smoking hams); piped music. At lunchtime, bar snacks include filled french bread (from £2.50), filled baked potatoes (from £2.95), pasta dishes (£3 half helping, £6 main course), OAP lunches (£3.95), ploughman's (from £4.50), and cumberland sausage or home-made pie of the day (£5.95), gammon and egg (£7.25). Also, home-made soup (£2.25), garlic mushrooms (£2.95), lamb liver and bacon (£6.25), thai chicken curry (£6.95), smoked haddock in cheese and chives (£7.50), wild boar chops or shoulder of lamb (£8.50), steaks (from £8.95), barbary duck breast (£9.50), and puddings like chocolate and orange torte or sticky ginger pudding (from £2.50); most of the restaurant is no smoking. Well kept Theakstons Best and XB and guests like Black Sheep Bitter, Coniston Bluebird, Hesket Newmarket Doris's 90th Birthday Ale, and Jennings Cumberland on handpump, over 40 malt whiskies, a carefully chosen wine list, and some country wines; darts, pool, and dominoes in the back bar. They hold an annual beer and sausage festival in mid-August with around 16 real ales and 14 varieties of sausage. The Wordsworth family owned the building for over 20 years until 1836. The pub is very close to a number of interesting places, such as Dalemain House at Dacre. *(Recommended by A Hepburn, S Jenner, ALC, Yvonne and Mike Meadley, Ian and Jane Irving, Mick Hitchman, David and Ruth Shillitoe, Ian Jones, D G Twyman, Roger Byrne, June and Tony Baldwin, Malcolm Taylor, Peter and Ann Mumford, D Knott, Ewan and Moira McCall, Neville Kenyon, Kevin Thorpe, Alan Risdon, Bob and Marg Griffiths, Keith Kelly)*

Free house ~ Licensees Chris and Jo Tomlinson ~ Real ale ~ Meals and snacks ~ Restaurant ~ (01768) 863219 ~ Children welcome ~ Open 12-3, 6-11; 12-11 Sat; 12-10.30 Sun ~ Bedrooms: £35B/£45B

TROUTBECK NY4103 Map 9

Mortal Man

Upper Rd, nr High Green – OS Sheet 90, map ref 411035

New licensees have taken over this neatly kept inn, surrounded by marvellous scenery. The partly panelled bar has a big roaring fire, a nice medley of seats including a cushioned settle and some farmhouse chairs around copper-topped tables, horsebrasses on the dark beams, and piped music; there's also a small, cosy no-smoking room leading off, set for eating. Bar food includes sandwiches and snacks (from £2.25), steak or fish sizzlers or thai curry (£5.25), vegetarian dishes, 6oz fillet steak (£6.95), and puddings. The restaurant, with its big picture windows, is no smoking. Well kept Marstons Pedigree and Theakstons Best on handpump, and several malt whiskies; darts and dominoes. Walkers' boots must be left outside. *(Recommended by JDM, KM, IHR, David Carr, Tim and Ann Newell, W W Burke, Pat Bruce, Alan Risdon, RJH)*

Free house ~ Licensee Mrs Audrey Brogden ~ Real ale ~ Meals and snacks (12-9.30) ~ Restaurant ~ (015394) 33193 ~ Children welcome ~ Open 11-11; 12-10.30 Sun ~ Bedrooms: £60B/£80B

Queens Head ★ 🍴 🛏

A592 N of Windermere

This very popular gabled 17th-c coaching inn has a big rambling bar with some half-dozen attractively decorated rooms, including an unusual lower gallery, a comfortable dining area, and lots of alcoves and heavy beams; two rooms are no smoking. A massive Elizabethan four-poster bed is the basis of the serving counter, and there's also some other fine antique carving, cushioned antique settles among more orthodox furniture, and two roaring log fires in imposing fireplaces. Very good bar food includes lunchtime filled french bread (from £2.95) and a light lunch special such as fried pork with cabbage, bacon and new potatoes with a port wine jus (£5.50), plus a terrine of salmon, langoustine, crab and fresh asparagus on red pepper chutney and dill yoghurt (£5.50), supreme of chicken marinated in coriander with lemon grass and soya sauce (£8.25), a platter of roasted vegetables with a thyme dressing, a tomato and goat's cheese mille feuille, and parmesan crumb coating (£8.95), fillet of salmon topped with a pesto crumb baked on to a tagliatelle of vegetables with a black olive butter sauce (£9.95), and puddings like blackberry and cassis parfait with a fresh fruit coulis (£3.50). Well kept Boddingtons, Black Sheep, Coniston Old Man, Jennings Bitter, Mitchells Lancaster Bomber, and Tetleys on handpump. Darts, dominoes, and piped music. Plenty of seats outside have a fine view over the Trout valley to Applethwaite moors. The bedrooms over the bar can be a bit noisy. *(Recommended by W W Burke, Phil and Dilys Unsworth, Phil and Heidi Cook, David and Tina Woods-Taylor, David and Helen Wilkins, R F Gale, Mrs S Miller, Nick Lawless, Anne and Colin Hunt, Helen Pickering, James Owen, Mrs S Kingsbury, R J Heslop, Vann and Terry Prime, Walter and Susan Rinaldi-Butcher, Mrs Frances Gray, Maysie Thompson, JDM, KM, John and Christine Lowe, S P Watkin, P A Taylor, H K Dyson, Mr and Mrs R Osborne, Brian and Anna Marsden, Ewan and Moira McCall, David Carr, Mark Fennell, David and Judy Walmsley, Mr and Mrs A G Leece, Mr and Mrs D Wilson)*

Free house ~ Licensees Mark Stewardson and Joanne Sherratt ~ Real ale ~ Meals and snacks (12-2, 6.30-9) ~ Restaurant ~ (015394) 32174 ~ Children welcome ~ Open 11-11; 12-10.30 Sun; closed 25 Dec ~ Bedrooms: £40B/£60B

ULVERSTON SD2978 Map 7

Bay Horse Hotel 🍴 🍷

Canal Foot signposted off A590 and then you wend your way past the huge Glaxo factory

The no-smoking conservatory restaurant in this civilised hotel has fine views over Morecambe Bay (as do the bedrooms) and there are some seats out on the terrace. But it remains the imaginative cooking that draws people here. In the bar, food is served at lunchtime only and might include sandwiches (from £1.75), home-made soup (£2.50), home-made herb and cheese pâté or savoury terrine with cranberry and ginger purée (£5.50), button mushrooms in a tomato, cream and brandy sauce on a peanut butter crouton (£7.95), flakes of smoked haddock in a rich cheddar cheese and mustard sauce, strips of pork, pineapple and red chilli peppers glazed with honey, sherry and white wine vinegar or cooked ham, pear and stilton baked in a cheese and chive pastry (all £8.25), and home-made puddings (£3.50); it's essential to book for the restaurant. Well kept Courage Directors, Morlands Old Speckled Hen, and Theakstons Best on handpump, a decent choice of spirits, and a carefully chosen and interesting wine list. The bar has a relaxed atmosphere and a huge stone horse's head, as well as attractive wooden armchairs, some pale green plush built-in wall banquettes, glossy hardwood traditional tables, blue plates on a delft shelf, and black beams and props with lots of horsebrasses. Magazines are dotted about, there's a handsomely marbled green granite fireplace, and decently reproduced piped music; darts, bar billiards, shove-ha'penny, cribbage. *(Recommended by Paul Bailey, A D Ryder, David Carr, Karen Eliot, R Gorick, Dr B Williams, Derek Harvey-Piper, JDM, KM)*

Free house ~ Licensee Robert Lyons ~ Real ale ~ Lunchtime bar meals and snacks (not Mon) ~ Separate lunchtime and evening restaurant (not Mon lunchtimes) ~ (01229) 583972 ~ Children in eating area of bar only ~ Open 11-11; 12-10.30 Sun ~ Bedrooms: £85B/£170B inc dinner

YANWATH NY5128 Map 9

Gate

2¼ miles from M6 junction 40; A66 towards Brough, then right on A6, right on B5320, then follow village signpost

A welcome break from the M6, this unpretentious village local is well liked for its surprisingly imaginative food: sandwiches, home-made soup (£2.25), good 'black devils' (sliced black pudding in a thin mildly peppery cream sauce – an excellent starter or very light snack at £2.95), herby mushrooms en croûte (£3.50), kidney bean and black bean casserole, fish pie or chicken, ham and egg in a parsley sauce with puff pastry top (all £5.80), stir-fried vegetables in a crispy pancake with a tomato sauce and mozzarella cheese (£7.75), butter baked salmon with red pepper sauce (£8.75), steaks (from £9.75), excellent gin and lime duck (£10.50), and puddings such as squidgy chocolate roulade, lemon cheesecake or sticky gingerbread pudding (£2.75). The simple turkey-carpeted bar, full of chatting regulars, has a log fire in an attractive stone inglenook and one or two nice pieces of furniture and middle-eastern brassware among more orthodox seats; or you can go through to eat in a two-level no-smoking restaurant. Well kept Theakstons Best and a local beer brewed for them called Creaking Gate Bitter on handpump, and obliging service; darts, dominoes, a quiz night on the last Sunday of the month, and unobtrusive piped music; the friendly border collie is called Domino and is good with children. There are a few picnic-sets outside. *(Recommended by John and Cath Howard, Neil Towend, R C Morgan, K F Mould, Mike and Maggie Betton, Mr and Mrs D Wilson)*

Free house ~ Licensees Ian and Sue Rhind ~ Real ale ~ Meals and snacks ~ Restaurant ~ (01768) 862386 ~ Children welcome ~ Open 12-3(2.30 winter), 7(6 Sat and Sun)-11(10.30 Sun)

Lucky Dip

Besides the fully inspected pubs, you might like to try these Lucky Dips recommended to us and described by readers (if you do, please send us reports):

Ainstable [off B6413 Brampton—Castle Carrock; NY5346], *New Crown*: Redecorated under current owners, spotless and attractive, with generous well presented usual food in light and airy dining room, simple flagstoned bar; two bedrooms *(J and H Coyle)*
Ambleside [next to Bridge House; NY3804], *Glasshouse*: New cafe/bar, fantastic conversion with marvellous indoor waterwheel, great coffee, food, wine and bottled beer, seats outside *(ALC)*
nr **Ambleside** [A592 N of Troutbeck; NY4007], *Kirkstone Pass*: Worth knowing for its position and fine surrounding scenery – Lakeland's highest inn, best out of season, with lots of old photographs and bric-a-brac, good coffee, well kept Tetleys, open fire, lively amusements, simple food, maybe piped radio *(Ann and Colin Hunt, LYM)*
☆ **Askham** [lower green; NY5123], *Queens Head*: Warmly welcoming two-room lounge, open fire, lots of beams, copper and brass, generous good home-made food from sandwiches to steaks and fresh fish inc plenty of fresh veg and good pudding choice, well kept Wards Sheffield Best, wide choice of wines, friendly young local licensees; children welcome, pleasant garden; bedrooms comfortable with creaking floorboards, splendid breakfast *(Mrs B Couzens, Bob Ellis, A N Ellis, David Cooke, Chris Brown, LYM)*
☆ **Bampton** [NY5118], *St Patricks Well*: Pretty little village local, friendly landlord, well kept Jennings Bitter and Mild, bar food (not Sun lunchtime) inc good shepherd's pie and steaks, big open fire, pool room, darts, juke box; a couple of seats outside; bedrooms good value, huge breakfast *(H K Dyson, BB)*
Bardsea [SD3074], *Bradylls Arms*: Plushly refurbished village inn, some stripped stone, wide choice of good food from sandwiches to fresh seafood, very popular well furnished back conservatory restaurant with lovely Morecambe Bay views; Boddingtons and Theakstons, friendly landlady; garden with play area *(David Carr)*
Baycliff [A5087 Barrow—Ulverston; SD2972], *Farmers Arms*: Real local, with lunchtime sandwiches, Hartleys XB, colourful window boxes *(Margaret and Roy Randle)*; *Fishermans Arms*: Well presented tasty food popular with older people midweek lunchtime, efficient service; garden with play area, comfortable bedrooms *(Margaret and Arthur Dickinson)*
Boot [NY1700], *Brook House*: Wide choice of good generous home-cooked food served cheerfully in small family-run hotel, small plush bar, comfortable hunting-theme lounge, open fires, well kept Black Sheep and Theakstons, friendly knowledgeable landlord, good views; handy for Ravenglass rly and great walks, good value bedrooms *(Eddie Edwards, H K Dyson)*
Borrowdale [NY2515], *Borrowdale Inn*: Good roomy bar, good value varied food from sandwiches up, pleasant staff *(Daphne Watson)*
Bowness on Windermere [Rayrigg Rd; SD4097], *Olde John Peel*: Attractively refurbished lounge, panelled bar and upstairs family room, country artefacts, good value family bar food inc vegetarian, Theakstons ales, friendly staff; darts, games machines, juke box, quiz and karaoke nights; handy for World of Beatrix Potter *(Richard Lewis, SLC)*; [Brantfell Rd], *Royal Oak*: Whitbreads and guest beers, dining area, slightly raised games area, front garden; children welcome *(SLC)*; [Lake Rd], *Village*: Busy opened-up town pub, low beams and red plush banquettes, partitions with some stained glass, bar food all day inc good vegetarian choice, well kept ales such as Jennings Cumberland, Marstons Pedigree, Whitbreads Castle Eden and weekend guests, good service even under pressure, air conditioning; restaurant, tables out in front *(G Coates, John Baker)*
Brampton [Market Pl; just off A69 E of Carlisle; NY5361], *Nags Head*: Roomy and friendly, with old-world decor, food lunchtime and evening, well kept Boddingtons and Whitbreads Castle Eden, smaller family room down a few steps, dogs; open afternoons; bedrooms basic but good value *(Judith Hirst)*; [High Cross St], *White Lion*: Warm and friendly old-world Victorian hotel, well kept ales inc Yates Premium, good generous home-cooked food, two comfortable well decorated rooms with coal fires, pleasant service; bedrooms *(RT and JC Moggridge, David and Margaret Bloomfield)*
Branthwaite [off A595 at Winscales; NY0625], *Riverside*: Dining pub with stone fireplace and Venetian pictures in nice bar area, Jennings and Tetleys, good range of pastas and grills (Italian chef), efficient service, river-view restaurant *(William Cunliffe)*
☆ **Broughton in Furness** [The Square; SD2187], *Manor Arms*: 18th-c inn with six well kept changing ales mixing interesting microbrews with the nationals; good rolls and sandwiches, comfortable relaxed atmosphere, friendly owners and locals; well appointed good value bedrooms, big breakfast *(Derek Harvey-Piper, Margaret and Roy Randle, Dr and Mrs B Baker)*
☆ **Broughton in Furness** [Church St], *Old Kings Head*: Big helpings of good moderately priced food from sandwiches and children's dishes up in smart but relaxed old-world pub with stone fireplace, chintz and knick-knacks, friendly obliging service, Boddingtons, Hartleys XB and Whitbreads Castle Eden, separate games area with pool, small cosy no-

smoking restaurant, tables outside; comfortable spacious bedrooms *(P and D Finlay)*

Broughton in Furness [Princes St], *Black Cock*: Olde-worlde pub dating from 15th c, good value food, friendly service, cosy fireside, well kept Courage-related ales; open all day Tues; bedrooms *(Margaret and Roy Randle, H K Dyson)*

Burneside [SD5096], *Jolly Anglers*: Good food with generous veg, well kept Theakstons; bedrooms good value *(David Edwards)*

☆ **Buttermere** [NY1817], *Fish*: Spacious, fresh and airily refurbished former coaching inn on NT property between Buttermere and Crummock Water, wide range of good value generous food from fresh sandwiches to delicious fish, well kept Jennings and Theakstons and guests such as Charles Wells Bombardier, friendly leisurely service, fine views, tables out on terrace; can get crowded; bedrooms *(Michael A Butler, W W Burke, SLC, Don and Shirley Parrish, BB)*

Calder Bridge [NY0506], *Golden Fleece*: Village pub with bar food, well kept Theakstons, very obliging staff, seats out in front; open all day Sat *(Gwyneth and Salvo Spadaro-Dutturi)*

☆ **Cartmel** [The Square; SD3879], *Kings Arms*: Picturesque pub nicely placed at the head of the attractive town square – rambling heavy-beamed bar, mix of furnishings from traditional settles to banquettes, usual generous bar food and no-smoking restaurant all day, good friendly service, well kept Wards Darleys Thorne, children welcome (get lollipops), seats outside; teashop, craft and gift shop upstairs *(Jane and Richard Doe, Alan Risdon, LYM)*

Castle Carrock [B6413 S of Brampton; NY5455], *Weary Sportsman*: Reasonably priced well presented food inc some interesting dishes and good choice of puddings, lovely old open fire, sporting memorabilia, beers such as Theakstons Chairmans, no piped music; bedrooms *(Jack and Heather Coyle)*

☆ **Cockermouth** [Crown St; NY1231], *Trout*: Solid old fishing hotel with pink plush sofas, captain's chairs and open fire in comfortable and friendly bar, good bar food from good sandwiches up inc a vegetarian dish, well kept Jennings Cumberland, Marstons Pedigree and Theakstons Best, over 50 malt whiskies, decent wines, freshly squeezed juices, attentive staff; coffee lounge and restaurant (best to book Sun lunch) both no smoking; piped music; nice gardens down to river; children welcome, good bedrooms *(Chris Rounthwaite, RB, LYM)*

☆ **Coniston** [signed from centre; SD3098], *Sun*: Attractively placed below mountains (doubling as rescue post), with interesting Donald Campbell and other Lakeland photographs in basic walkers' and locals' back bar, friendly staff, good log fire, enjoyable home-made bar food with good fresh veg, Coniston Old Man (from back microbrewery), Jennings Cumberland and Old Smoothy and Tetleys; children in carpeted no-smoking eating area and restaurant, darts, dominoes, piped music; open all day; comfortable bedrooms *(Tina and David Woods-Taylor, S P Watkin, P A Taylor, Ewan and Moira McCall, H K Dyson, Alan Risdon, William Cunliffe, David Carr, Jeanne Cross, Paul Silvestri, LYM)*

☆ **Crook** [B5284 Kendal—Bowness; SD4795], *Sun*: Wide choice of surprisingly inventive fresh food in open-plan village local with good atmosphere, well kept Jennings and Theakstons, good value wines, briskly efficient staff, welcoming fire; orders may stop before 2 *(Bruce Braithwaite, David Dolman, Cyril E Higgs, ALC, LYM)*

Dacre [between A66 and A592 SW of Penrith; NY4626], *Horse & Farrier*: Well renovated 18th-c inn with jovial landlord, friendly helpful staff, varied well prepared good food, particularly well kept Bass; integral post office *(D Cooke, Patrick Herratt)*

Dalton in Furness [Holmes Green, Broughton Rd; SD2376], *Black Dog*: Low beams, good choice of real ales, farm cider, two real fires, good home-cooked food all day (air-dried hams hanging over bar), friendly atmosphere; bedrooms *(Anon)*

☆ **Dent** [Main St; SD7187], *George & Dragon*: Clean and comfortable pub/hotel, Dent Bitter, Ramsbottom and T'Owd Tup, also Scottish Courage ales, good generously served bar food, bargain Sun lunch, reasonably priced evening restaurant, no piped music; pleasant staff and friendly locals, pool, darts; bedrooms comfortable *(Paul S McPherson)*

☆ **Dockray** [A5091, off A66 W of Penrith; NY3921], *Royal*: Surprisingly plush and open-plan for the area, but comfortable, with bar food from lunchtime rolls and baked potatoes to good interesting specials and home-made puddings; children's helpings, Black Sheep, Boddingtons Bitter, Jennings Cumberland, Marstons Pedigree, Timothy Taylor Landlord and Whitbreads Castle Eden, good wines by the glass, prompt service, two dining areas (one no smoking), walkers' part with stripped settles on flagstones; darts, cribbage and dominoes; piped music; picnic-sets in garden; open all day, comfortable bedrooms *(JCB, Mark Fennell, D S and J M Jackson, T Loft, Susan and Nigel Wilson, Timothy Galligan, LYM)*

☆ **Dufton** [NY6925], *Stag*: Small, basic pub in lovely unspoilt village on Pennine Way; friendly licensee, good choice of food inc breakfasts and good lunchtime sandwiches, well kept ales such as Boddingtons, Black Sheep Best and Riggwelter, Dent Best and Jennings (less choice in winter), good coffee, sensible prices, splendid early Victorian kitchen range; children, walkers and dogs welcome; open all day summer (cl winter Mon lunchtime), garden with shetland ponies; bedrooms *(Richard Lewis)*

Eskdale [Bleabeck, E of Boot; NY1900],

Woolpack: Last pub before the notorious Hardknott Pass, a whitewashed beacon for travellers and walkers with usual reasonably priced home-cooked food, well kept Jennings, nice garden with mountain views; children welcome; bedrooms *(H K Dyson)*

☆ **Eskdale Green** [E of village; NY1400], *King George IV*: Cheerful bustling beamed and flagstoned bar, comfortable lounge, back games room, wide choice of quickly served good generous food from sandwiches to steaks, well kept Bass, Jennings Cumberland and Theakstons Best, XB and Old Peculier, good collection of malt whiskies, restaurant; friendly staff, log fire, fine views from garden – idyllic spot, lots of good walks; children abundantly welcome, open all day summer; good value bedrooms *(Neil Townend, H K Dyson, Jenny and Brian Seller, Bronwen and Steve Wrigley, LYM)*

☆ **Far Sawrey** [B5285 across from Bowness ferry; SD3893], *Sawrey*: Comfortable, warm and welcoming stable bar with tables in wooden stalls, harness on rough white walls, big helpings of good simple lunchtime bar food inc well presented inexpensive sandwiches, well kept Black Sheep Bitter and Special and Jennings, pleasant staff, attractive prices; separate hotel bar, evening restaurant; seats on nice lawn, beautiful setting, walkers, children and dogs welcome; bedrooms comfortable and well equipped *(JDM, KM, N J Lawless, SLC, LYM)*

Grasmere [NY3406], *Tweedies*: Big functional bar and separate family dining room, food inc good baguettes and vegetarian choice, well kept Jennings Bitter and Cumberland and Theakstons, friendly staff, pleasant hotel garden; bedrooms *(David Cooke, Alan Risdon, Tim and Ann Newell)*

Great Strickland [NY5623], *Strickland Arms*: Pleasantly refurbished comfortable and civilised old village inn, fine original food such as thai red prawn curry, well kept Jennings and Tetleys-related ales served via sparkler, competitive prices; may be cl Weds *(John Baker)*

☆ **Great Urswick** [Church Rd; SD2674], *General Burgoyne*: Small flagstoned early 18th-c village pub overlooking small tarn; bar and lounges with log fires, country atmosphere, Hartleys XB and Robinsons, friendly efficient service, good food; exemplary lavatories *(W D Christian, David Carr)*

☆ **Hawkshead** [SD3598], *Queens Head*: Some concentration on food in bustling red plush low-beamed and panelled bar and no-smoking snug and restaurant, from lunchtime sandwiches and usual pub things (but no nuts or crisps) to quite elaborate evening dishes; open fire, well kept Hartleys XB and Robinsons Bitter, Frederics and Mild, dominoes, cribbage, service generally good; piped music, children in eating areas and snug, open all day; good bedrooms *(R W Tapsfield, D Stokes, Alan Risdon, SLC, Peter and Pat Frogley, LYM)*

☆ **Hawkshead**, *Kings Arms*: Relaxed yet lively and chatty local with low-ceilinged bar, open fire, bar food from sandwiches up, well kept Coniston, Greenalls Original, Tetleys, Theakstons XB and guest beers, summer cider, darts, dominoes, cribbage; no-smoking restaurant; fruit machine, piped pop music, tables on terrace overlooking little square of lovely Elizabethan village; well behaved children welcome, open all day, bedrooms (bar can be noisy till late), car park some way off *(SLC, Mark Fennell, Colin Draper, LYM)*

Hawkshead, *Red Lion*: Friendly modernised local with some old-fashioned touches, good log fire, well kept Courage-related ales with guests such as Jennings, good range of usual food, piped music; open all day, bedrooms *(SLC, BB)*; *Sun*: Friendly staff, big dining area, well kept Courage-related and maybe a guest ale; piped music, TV; bedrooms *(SLC)*

Hayton [A69 E of Carlisle; NY5158], *Lane End*: Quite foody, with pleasant flagstoned bar, log fire, good bustling atmosphere, welcoming service, well kept Boddingtons and Tetleys, conservatory restaurant; open all day *(David Heath)*

☆ **Hesket Newmarket** [signed from B5299 in Caldbeck; NY3438], *Old Crown*: Relaxed and homely unfussy local in attractive village, decent reasonably priced food inc good curries, friendly landlord, six unusual beers brewed in back barn; outside lavatories, cl weekday lunchtimes exc school hols; bedrooms *(Richard Houghton, Peter and Pat Frogley, Alan Risdon, H Eastwood, LYM)*

High Newton [just off A590 Lindale—Newby Bridge, towards Cartmel Fell; SD4082], *Duck & Crown*: Well kept Jennings, helpful friendly staff, good value food with plenty of veg served separately, nice open fire; children welcome; bedrooms *(Paul and Georgina Swinden)*

Hoff [B6260 Orton—Appleby; NY6718], *New Inn*: Simple low-beamed roadside local with well kept Black Sheep, generous straightforward food, friendly atmosphere, no music or machines *(Ann and Colin Hunt)*

☆ **Howtown** [NY4519], *Howtown Hotel*: Unrivalled position on Ullswater's quieter shore, pre-war feel in both back walkers' bar (good lunchtime sandwiches) and cosy very red hotel bar – waitresses have starched aprons (but come from Australia and S Africa as well as Cumbria); restaurant (book for good Sun lunch), morning coffee and afternoon tea; welcoming very long-serving owners, keg Theakstons but decent wines by the glass, pleasant garden; charming old-fashioned bedrooms, early morning tea ladies *(Monica Shelley, Christine and Geoff Butler, Alan Risdon)*

Kendal [98 Highgate; SD5293], *New Inn*: . Vaux Bitter, bar food, pool and TV; open all day *(SLC)*; [Highgate], *Olde Fleece*: Much refurbished, with pleasant atmosphere and service, well kept Scottish Courage ales, good helpings of usual food till 9.30, upstairs dining area; open all day *(SLC)*

Keswick [47 Main St; NY2624], *Bank*: Popular local welcoming visitors, clean and comfortable, full Jennings range kept well, professional service; bedrooms *(P and M Rudlin, SLC)*; [St Johns St], *George*: Attractive traditional black-panelled side room with interesting Wordsworth connection (and good log fire), open-plan main bar with old-fashioned settles and modern banquettes under Elizabethan beams; under new ownership, with well kept Jennings, bar food inc children's, restaurant; bedrooms comfortable *(P and M Rudlin, David Carr, LYM)*; [Main St], *Oddfellows Arms*: Pleasant staff, wide range of well kept Jennings ales, plenty of food, town-centre atmosphere – piped music may be obtrusive, but does draw young people *(Peter and Pat Frogley, G Washington)*

☆ *nr* **Keswick** [Crosthwaite Rd; by A66, a mile out], *Pheasant*: Small friendly beamed pub with lots of local cartoons, good value generous food lunchtime and early evening, fast service, well kept Jennings beers, no-smoking dining room; children if eating; bedrooms *(P and M Rudlin, H K Dyson, SLC)*

☆ *nr* **Keswick** [Newlands Valley – OS Sheet 90 map ref 242217], *Swinside*: Clean and friendly modernised pub in peaceful valley with stunning views of crags and fells, well kept Bass and Jennings, decent wines, good fires, welcoming service, good value generous freshly made bar food, restaurant; dogs allowed, tables outside with best view, open all day Sat and summer; bedrooms *(H K Dyson, David Yandle, Sylvia and Tony Birbeck, Mrs M Grimwood, LYM)*

Langdale [by car park for Stickle Ghyll; NY2906], *Stickle Barn*: Lovely views from walkers' and climbers' bar, good choice of food inc packed lunches, well kept Scottish Courage beers; fruit machines, maybe loud piped music; big pleasant terrace, open all day; bunkhouse accommodation, live music in loft *(Alan Risdon, SLC)*

☆ **Lazonby** [NY5539], *Joiners Arms*: Small spotless pub with pleasant local atmosphere, roaring fire, brasses and china, well presented food inc sandwiches and good curries, well kept Bass and Stones (landlord was a head brewer there), consistently friendly service, pool table in lower bar; clean comfortable bedrooms, good breakfasts *(R T and J C Moggridge, Jack and Heather Coyle)*

☆ **Levens** [off A590; SD4886], *Hare & Hounds*: Village pub handy for Sizergh Castle, with partly panelled low-beamed lounge bar (part is no smoking), front tap room with coal fire and darts, cribbage and dominoes, pool room down steps with juke box and fruit machine, well kept Vaux Waggle Dance and Wards Darleys Thorne, friendly service, usual bar food inc lunchtime sandwiches and a vegetarian dish, restaurant; children in eating area, good views from terrace *(Ann and Colin Hunt, Andy and Jill Kassube, IHR, Jenny and Brian Seller, LYM)*

☆ **Levens** [Sedgwick Rd, by Sizergh Castle gates – OS Sheet 97 map ref 500872], *Strickland Arms*: Wide choice of generous imaginative well cooked food, friendly prompt service even when very busy, well kept Scottish Courage ales with a guest such as Masons Amazon, log fire; piped music, pool table; no-smoking upstairs restaurant, children allowed, good garden *(ALC)*

Lindale [B5277 N of Grange over Sands; SD4180], *Lindale Inn*: Newish chef doing good generous reasonably priced food (sandwiches too), nice big oak-beamed dining area (children welcome here), well kept Whitbreads-related ales and a guest such as Red Pike, dozens of malt whiskies, friendly atmosphere, good service; fruit machine, pool and TV in bar area up a few steps; open all day Fri and Sat in summer, reasonably priced good bedrooms *(J Perrott, SLC)*

Lorton [Low Lorton (B5289 Buttermere—Cockermouth); NY1525], *Wheat Sheaf*: Bar and dining lounge, good food inc huge filled yorkshire puddings and big helpings of other traditional dishes, very well kept Jennings, service highly efficient but still friendly; caravan park behind *(Vann and Terry Prime, H K Dyson, DC, BB)*

Low Hesket [A6 Carlisle—Penrith; NY4646], *Rose & Crown*: Clean and welcoming Jennings pub, simple food inc good value toasties, efficient service *(David Cooke)*

☆ **Lowick Bridge** [just off A5084; SD2986], *Red Lion*: Family food pub, warm, comfortable and clean, very busy in summer, with two spacious and attractive areas, well kept Hartleys XB and Robinsons, good choice of generous tasty bar food inc vegetarian and Sun roasts, half helpings if you want, pleasant helpful service, open fire; tables outside, charming spot, open all day Sun and summer Sat, quiz night Thurs; bedrooms *(David Heath, T M Dobby, Alan Risdon, SLC, Julie Peters, Colin Blinkhorn, Mr and Mrs M F Norton)*

☆ **Lowick Green** [A5092 SE of village; SD2985], *Farmers Arms*: Charming cosy public bar with heavy beams, huge slate flagstones, big open fire, cosy corners and pub games (also piped music, TV; this part may be cl winter), some interesting furniture and pictures in plusher hotel lounge bar across yard, tasty well presented food in bar and restaurant inc two-person bargains, well kept Theakstons XB, friendly attentive staff; children welcome, open all day Sat/Sun; piped music; comfortable bedrooms *(B J P Edwards, SLC, K H Frostick, LYM)*

Nether Wasdale [OS Sheet 89 map ref 125041; NY1204], *Screes*: Big friendly bar, very good value food, particularly well kept Black Sheep and Yates, interesting piped music; five bedrooms, great views *(Jenny and Brian Seller)*

Newby Bridge [just off A590; SD3786], *Swan*: Fine setting next to river with waterside picnic-sets by old stone bridge, hotelish atmosphere even when very busy, decent food inc Sun roasts, Boddingtons ale; bedrooms *(Maysie Thompson)*

Outgate [B5286 Ambleside—Hawkshead; SD3699], *Outgate Inn*: Attractively placed country pub with three comfortably modernised rooms, well kept Hartleys XB and Robinsons Bitter and Frederics, friendly staff, usual food inc sandwiches; open all day, bedrooms *(SLC, JM, LYM)*

Patterdale [NY3916], *White Lion*: Well kept Whitbreads-related ales, usual bar food, friendly service; busy with walkers in summer; bedrooms *(R T and J C Moggridge)*

☆ **Penrith** [Devonshire St; NY5130], *George*: Well run family hotel with decorous beamed and oak-panelled lounge hall, fine plasterwork, oak settles and easy chairs around good open fire, big bow windows; short choice of reasonably priced lunchtime bar food, well kept Marstons Pedigree, friendly and lively plain back bar with good juke box, restaurant; comfortable good value bedrooms *(B Lake, Kevin Thorpe, E Howbrook, LYM)*

Penrith [Cornmarket], *Gloucester Arms*: Cosy low-beamed local, lots of wood and panelling, comfortable seats, big open fire, friendly landlord, cheap filling food, well kept Flowers IPA and Whitbreads Castle Eden; open all day *(R T and J C Moggridge)*; [Queen St], *Lowther Arms*: Friendly and comfortable local popular for wide range of very cheap lunchtime food inc a vegetarian dish, Scottish Courage beers with guest ales such as Marstons Pedigree, Morlands Old Speckled Hen, Timothy Taylor Landlord, Wadworths 6X, real fire *(Ann and Colin Hunt)*; [16 Victoria Rd], *Salutation*: Felt more like a club than a pub, with friendly staff, well kept beers, lots of basic seating, events posters, pool, juke box, tables outside; children very welcome, live music Fri; bedrooms *(Richard Lewis)*

☆ **Penruddock** [NY4327], *Herdwick*: Carefully restored 18th-c inn with consistently good well priced food esp Sun roast and good fresh veg, good atmosphere, quiet leisurely service, Theakstons real ale, interesting menu in attractive restaurant with upper gallery – worth booking evenings; five bedrooms *(Malcolm Taylor, Canon David Banter, Mr and Mrs D Wilson, J and H Coyle)*

Pooley Bridge [former Swiss Chalet; NY4724], *Pooley Bridge*: Now open all day, with real ales inc Marstons Pedigree and Tetleys and a guest beer, good choice of freshly cooked food *(M J Morgan)*; *Sun*: Small lounge bar with plush settee by fire fills quickly, steps past servery to bigger bar with games and piped music (can obtrude), simple bar food inc sandwiches, well kept Jennings ales, restaurant; tables in garden *(Nick Lawless)*

Ravenglass [SD0996], *Ratty Arms*: Ex-railway bar in main line station (a bit of a trek from the narrow-gauge steam railway) with well kept Lakeland Gold and other ales, interesting food, good value restaurant, service friendly and efficient even when busy; pool table in busy public bar; cl Sun *(John Baker, P A Legon, LYM)*

☆ **Ravenstonedale** [signed off A685 Kirkby Stephen—M6; NY7204], *Black Swan*: Genteel bar with open fire and some stripped stone, Black Sheep, Jennings Cumberland and Cockerhoop and Timothy Taylor Landlord, lots of country wines, good set food inc some interesting dishes; dogs welcome, tables in pretty tree-sheltered streamside garden over road; bedrooms inc some for disabled, peaceful setting *(Michael Tucker, PY, Arthur and Margaret Dickinson, Ann and Colin Hunt, John Saul, Mrs Frances Gray, Guy Vowles, BB)*

Ravenstonedale, *Kings Head*: Cheerful, with beams, button-back banquettes and dining chairs, good range of generous food, well kept Jennings, log fires; public side with games room, popular with young people – music there may be loud; bedrooms *(Ann and Colin Hunt, T M Dobby, LYM)*

nr **Ravenstonedale** [Crossbank; A683 Sedbergh—Kirkby Stephen; SD6996], *Fat Lamb*: Remote inn with pews in brightly modernised bar, log fire in traditional black kitchen range, good local photographs; usual bar food, well kept Mitchells, maybe piped classical music, restaurant, seats out by sheep pastures; facilities for disabled, children really welcome; comfortable bedrooms with own bathrooms, good walks from inn *(T M Dobby, BB)*

☆ **Rosthwaite** [NY2615], *Scafell*: Extended slate-floored pubby back public bar with tables out overlooking beck, well kept Theakstons Best and XB and a guest such as Busheys Export, log fire, wide choice of good value food from hotel's kitchens, children's helpings of most dishes; welcoming and well run, coping even when packed with walkers; afternoon teas, piped music; hotel has cosy sun-lounge bar and dining room; bedrooms not big but good *(Peter and Pat Frogley)*

Santon Bridge [NY1102], *Bridge*: Relaxed traditional pub with good range of Jennings ales, good reasonably priced straightforward home-made food inc children's, friendly service; can get very busy in summer; bedrooms *(Nick Lawless)*

☆ **Satterthwaite** [SD3492], *Eagles Head*: Small and unpretentious but very welcoming, with imaginative vegetarian menu alongside more conventional good value generous home-made lunchtime food esp soup, sandwiches and home-made pies (also Fri/Sat summer evenings), big log fire, helpful landlord, well kept Thwaites, pool, darts; papers and guidebooks for sale; handy for Grizedale Forest; a welcome for small children; bedrooms comfortable and clean, shared bathroom; maybe some closures winter esp Mon, but usually open all day at least Thurs-Sat in summer *(JCW, Margaret and Roy Randle)*

Shap [A6, S end; NY5615], *Greyhound*: Friendly and unpretentious, with wide range of generous good value traditional food inc good Sun roast, really quick service, Tetleys real ale, farm cider; popular with coast-to-coast walkers; bedrooms *(A and A Dale)*

Southwaite [Broad Field; away from village, towards Gaitsgill; NY4046], *Crown*: Very welcoming, with good food from sandwiches and home-made soup up, open fire, Theakstons; handy for Carlisle races *(David J Cooke)*

☆ **Staveley** [SD4798], *Eagle & Child*: Simple good value home-cooked bar food with fresh veg, well kept Theakstons and guest beers, lots of malt whiskies, friendly service, bright but comfortable little modern front lounge and more spacious carpeted bar; well kept, with small neat riverside garden; good value bedrooms, good breakfast *(Dr B and Mrs P B Baker, BB)*

☆ **Stonethwaite** [Borrowdale; NY2613], *Langstrath*: Welcoming, neat and clean, more restaurant than pub but good fresh interesting food in bar as well as dining room, plenty of walkers and locals, well kept Black Sheep and Theakstons, lots of malt whiskies, open fires, good service; delightful peaceful village, pleasant bedrooms *(Hazel Nicholson, Mr and Mrs Woods, Brian Seller, Nigel Woolliscroft, S O'Connor)*

Tebay [very handy for M6 junction 38; NY6204], *Cross Keys*: Friendly and comfortable roadside pub with pleasant staff, good cheap food in separate eating area, coal fire, darts, pool, cribbage; bedrooms *(Ann and Colin Hunt)*

Threlkeld [NY3325], *Horse & Farrier*: Unspoiled 17th-c inn popular with locals, big bar with wooden settles, games room, small panelled snug, unpretentious and genuinely friendly licensees, well kept Jennings; bedrooms with own bathrooms, good breakfast *(Judith Hirst)*

Ulverston [King St; SD2978], *Rose & Crown*: Friendly and busy open-plan local with good home-made food all day inc interesting vegetarian dishes, well kept Hartleys XB, Robinsons Best Mild and Bitter, quick service even when busy on Sat market day, pleasant garden and pavement tables *(Tim and Ann Newell, David Carr)*

☆ **Wasdale Head** [NY1808], *Wasdale Head Inn*: Mountain hotel in marvellous fellside setting, spacious panelled main bar with cushioned settles on slate floor and great mountain photographs, no-smoking snug and children's/pool room; good value food inc interesting dishes in bar and restaurant, well kept Jennings, Theakstons Best and Old Peculier and Yates, decent choice of wines and malt whiskies, lively helpful staff; open all day, cl much of winter; comfortable bedrooms, well equipped self-catering accommodation *(Nigel Woolliscroft, P and M Rudlin, David Honeyman, LYM)*

Watermillock [A592, Ullswater; NY4422], *Brackenrigg*: 19th-c inn opened up but keeping rustic style, with particularly well kept Black Sheep Special and Jennings Cumberland, attractive food, friendly if scarcely quiet mix of holiday-makers and locals *(John Baker)*

Wetheral [off A69 at Warwick Bridge; NY4654], *Crown*: On village green, mixing English country house style with traditional pub, and even Scandinavian touches, with lots of exposed light wood; good imaginative food, Thwaites Bitter and Scallywag; good bedrooms *(Walter Reid)*

☆ **Winster** [A5074 S of Windermere; SD4293], *Brown Horse*: Open-plan dining place, light and comfortable if not full of atmosphere, with well spaced tables and good log fire; popular especially among older people for attractively priced food, prompt friendly service, well kept Jennings Cumberland and Theakstons, decent wines; children welcome (own menu, toys), booking essential in season *(Phil and Heidi Cook, Diane and Maurice Flint, Philip and Ann Falkner, John Logan, Rachel Thomas, SLC, LYM)*

Real ale may be served from handpumps, electric pumps (not just the on-off switches used for keg beer) or – common in Scotland – tall taps called founts (pronounced 'fonts') where a separate pump pushes the beer up under air pressure. The landlord can adjust the force of the flow – a tight spigot gives the good creamy head that Yorkshire lads like.

Derbyshire

New entries here include the Trout at Barlow and Red Lion at Hognaston, both of them very sympathetically reworked as attractive dining pubs; the Old Sun in Buxton, a civilised and very successful entry by Marstons into the wide-choice alehouse stakes (good house wines and enjoyable food, too); the Castle Hotel in Castleton, a very comfortable retreat from the village's open-air pursuits; and the Quiet Woman at Earl Sterndale, an archetypal simple country tavern of the sort that's nowadays all too rare, though Derbyshire is very fortunate in having two more splendid examples of that endangered species, in the Barley Mow at Kirk Ireton (excellent choice of real ales) and the Three Stags Heads near Wardlow. Other pubs in the county that are currently doing particularly well are the Devonshire Arms at Beeley (enjoyable food all day), the friendly Waltzing Weasel at Birch Vale (very good if not cheap food, and a nice place to stay), the atmospheric Olde Gate at Brassington (nice food), the welcoming Old Crown just outside Shardlow (good value home cooking) and the White Horse at Woolley Moor (a well judged balance between good food and well kept beer – its new conservatory restaurant has charming views). The restauranty Druid at Birchover scores high points for its very wide choice of good food, and the Hardinge Arms at Kings Newton, always popular for its carvery, now has a good choice of fresh fish too. From the very wide choice here it's the Waltzing Weasel at Birch Vale, clearly on top form these days, that we choose as Derbyshire Dining Pub of the Year. An important value for money point about Derbyshire pubs is that the food they serve usually comes in pretty hefty helpings – indeed, some of our smaller-appetite readers have often been overwhelmed. In many parts of England, town pubs can't hold a candle to the surrounding country pubs: not so in Derbyshire. Derby itself has three excellent main entries (besides several very rewarding places in the Lucky Dip at the end of the chapter), and elsewhere Smiths Tavern in Ashbourne and the Derby Tup at Whittington Moor on the edge of Chesterfield are exemplary town pubs. In the Lucky Dip at the end of the chapter, we'd give particular prominence to the Olde Nags Head in Castleton, Barrel near Foolow, Lantern Pike near Hayfield, Colvile Arms at Lullington, Royal Oak at Millthorpe, Monsal Head at Monsal Head, Bulls Head at Monyash and George at Tideswell (all inspected and vouched for by us), and the Plough in Hathersage (still awaiting that pleasure). Derby as we've said has a fine choice, especially for beer connoisseurs, with the Flower Pot and Standing Order at the top of the Dip list. Drinks prices here are well below the national average. In Derby, the Brunswick beers brewed on the premises are particularly good value, and other pubs with really cheap beer are the Alexandra there, and the Barley Mow at Kirk Ireton, Navigation at Buxworth and Three Stags Heads near Wardlow.

The knife-and-fork rosette distinguishes pubs where the food is of exceptional quality.

ASHBOURNE SK1846 Map 7

Smiths Tavern

St Johns St; bottom of market place

This nicely old-fashioned town tavern has five daily newspapers for customers to enjoy in a relaxed, chatty atmosphere. The attractive bar has horsebrasses and tankards hanging from heavy black beams, a delft shelf of antique blue and white china, old cigarette and drinks advertisements, and a plush wall seat facing the bar counter. Steps take you up to a middle room with more plush seating around solid tables, a log-effect gas fire and a piano, and beyond that a light and airy end dining room. Well kept Marstons Best and Pedigree and a guest on handpump, around 36 malt whiskies, and a range of vodkas. Popular and generously served bar food includes soup (£1.95), freshly cut sandwiches (from £1.70), ploughman's (£3.95) and daily specials like moussaka (£4.50), vegetable balti (£4.75) and home-made pies like fresh fish pie or steak and kidney (£4.95); homely puddings like deep dish apple pie or gateaux (£2.25); Sunday roast with good fresh vegetables (£5.50). Very friendly service, and dominoes. *(Recommended by David Carr, Stephen, Julie and Hayley Brown, Graham and Karen Oddey; more reports please)*

Marstons ~ Tenant John Bishop ~ Real ale ~ Meals and snacks ~ Restaurant ~ (01335) 342264 ~ Children in restaurant ~ Open 11-11; 12-10.30 Sun

BARLOW SK3474 Map 7

Trout

Valley Road; off B6051 NW of Chesterfield

Recently refitted as a dining pub, this turns out inside to be a good deal more inviting than you might have guessed from the road. The major part is given over to the food operation, and is carpeted, with neat good-sized tables and comfortable brocaded banquettes, old-world prints and beamery; this part is candlelit at night, and a second smaller dining room opens off. It's best to book at weekends. The other side of the bar has a good properly pubby atmosphere, with big stripped and scrubbed tables on bare boards, more banquettes and cushioned stools, and a big brick fireplace. The food, which you can eat round here among the drinkers too, is good and genuinely home-made. The lunchtime menu includes soup (£2.50), substantial sandwiches (from £3.25), pâté (£3.50), prawn and crab salad (£3.95), filled baguettes (£4.50), ravioli with tomato and herb sauce (£5.50), fresh fish fillet of the day with herb crust or main course salads (£5.95), braised lamb knuckle, pork fillet with tarragon, mushroom and sherry cream sauce or chicken supreme with crab and lobster sauce (£6.95) and 10oz rump steak (£7.50), delicious puddings include caramel apple crumble and crêpes with orange and brandy sauce (£2.75). The evening menu has several additional dishes including grilled avocado with prawn and blue cheese dressing (£3.25) and lamb and ginger marinated salmon (£7.50); no-smoking restaurant. Service is very welcoming, quick and competent; well kept Boddingtons, Flowers IPA, Marstons Pedigree and Trout brewed for the pub by Coach House under light blanket pressure and good house wines; unobtrusive well reproduced piped music. There are tables out on the terrace. *(Recommended by Joy and Peter Heatherley, Steve Goodchild, Steve and Irene Law, Frank Gorman)*

Free house ~ Licensee John Redfearn ~ Real ale ~ Meals and snacks ~ Restaurant ~ (0114) 289 0893 ~ Children if eating ~ Folk music Thurs evening ~ Open 12-3, 6-11; 12-3, 7-10.30 Sun; closed 25 Dec, 26 Dec lunchtime

BEELEY SK2667 Map 7

Devonshire Arms

B6012, off A6 Matlock—Bakewell

Beautifully set in a pretty Peak District village, this very handsome old stone building – it's handy for Chatsworth – was very successfully converted back in 1741 from three early 18th-c cottages to a prosperous coaching inn. Big warming log fires burn in the characterful black-beamed rooms which also have comfortably cushioned stone seats along their stripped walls and antique settles and simpler wooden chairs on the flagstoned floors; the restaurant and one area in the bar are no smoking. Very enjoyable bar food which is served all day includes home-made soup (£2.20), good sandwiches (from £2.40), smoked mackerel fillet with gooseberry sauce (£3.25), a selection of smoked and pickled seafoods (£5.50), a good value ploughman's (£5.75), steak and ale pie, cumberland sausage, trout with lemon and herb stuffing or haggis and neeps (£5.95), chicken breast with stilton sauce or potato, leek and cheese bake (£6.95), sirloin steak (£10.50), and puddings displayed in a cold counter (from £2.50). Friday night is fish night with butterfly king prawns or crab (£6.95), scampi (£8.95) and seafood platter (£16.95). On Sundays they do a special Victorian breakfast with a glass of bucks fizz and the Sunday newspapers (£9.50). You will need to book for the Sunday breakfast, and probably at the weekends. Well kept Black Sheep Special and Best, Boddingtons, Theakstons XB and Old Peculier, and guest beers on handpump and about three dozen malt whiskies; shove-ha'penny. *(Recommended by Rita and Keith Pollard, Janet Pickles, K and B Forman, JP, PP, David Carr, Paul and Maggie Baker, Martin and Catherine Snelling, John and Annette Derbyshire, Jeanne Cross, Paul Silvestri, John and Mary Holderness)*

Free house ~ Licensee John Grosvenor ~ Real ale ~ Meals and snacks (12-9.30) ~ Restaurant ~ (01629) 733259 ~ Children welcome ~ Open 11-11; 12-10.30 Sun

BIRCH VALE SK0286 Map 7

Waltzing Weasel

A6015 E of New Mills

Derbyshire Dining Pub of the Year

Going from strength to strength, this warmly welcoming civilised inn gains a food award this year. The beautifully kept, very comfortable bar has cosy chatty areas, some handsome oak settles and tables among more usual furniture (Mr and Mrs Atkinson used to deal in antiques), plenty of houseplants on corner tables, lots of nicely framed mainly sporting Victorian prints, a good longcase clock, and a cheerful fire; there are daily papers on sticks, maybe classical piped music and a friendly old dog, Sam, pottering about. Though not cheap, bar food is really well liked by readers, with a lunchtime spread taking in soup (£2.50), duck pâté (£4.50), vegetable tart (£6.75), home-baked ham or lamb and walnut pie (£7.75), seafood tart or meat pie (£8.95). In the evening there might be hot buttered shrimps on toast, hare pâté or mussels in wine (£4.50), mixed bean chilli (£6.75), roast garlic lamb (£9.75), fish of the day (about £11.50) and lobster or barnsley chop (£12.50); puddings (£3.50) and fine cheeses; well kept Marstons Best and Pedigree on handpump, and a good choice of decent wines and malt whiskies. The charming back restaurant has picture-window views of Kinder Scout and the Peak District – these are shared by a pretty garden and terrace. Spacious comfortable bedrooms are well furnished and lovely breakfasts include home-made marmalade. *(Recommended by Tony and Joan Walker, Bronwen and Steve Wrigley, Mike and Karen England, G Wheeler, DAV, Margaret and Roy Randle, Sue Holland, Dave Webster, Julie Peters, Tim Brierly, Vann and Terry Prime, J F M West, David Hoult, Peter Marshall, Joan and Tony Walker, G V Price, Brian and Anna Marsden, Colin Blinkhorn, Stephen Brown, Martin and Karen Wake)*

Free house ~ Licensee Mike Atkinson ~ Real ale ~ Meals and snacks ~ Restaurant ~ (01663) 743402 ~ Children welcome (must be over 5 in evening restaurant) ~ Open 12-3, 5.30-11(10.30 Sun) ~ Bedrooms: £38.78B/£65.95B

BIRCHOVER SK2462 Map 7

Druid

Village signposted from B5056

There's an astonishing choice of imaginative dishes written up on the blackboards that line the long fairly narrow bar at this creeper-covered dining pub. These might include thai fish cakes with chilli, garlic and honey dip (£4.60), steak and kidney pudding (£7.90), aubergine stuffed with peppers, rice, mushroom, hazelnuts and cheese with peanut and garlic sauce (£7.30), hungarian lamb stew or chinese five spice steamed duck shredded and served with sliced ginger, pineapple, onion and garlic on steamed noodles with spinach (£8.80), fish stew (£8.90) or baked halibut with orange and garlic, black olives and water chestnuts (£10.70); half-price helpings for children. The spacious and airy two-storey dining extension, candlelit at night, is really the heart of the place, with pink plush seats on olive-green carpet, and pepper-grinders and sea salt on all the tables. It's unlikely you'll be able to sit down if you're not eating as the emphasis is very much on dining, and it's advisable to book for evening and weekend meals. The small plain bar (dominoes) has plush-upholstered wooden wall benches around straightforward tables, and a big coal fire; the Garden Room, tap room and part of the bar are no smoking. Well kept Mansfield Bitter, Marstons Pedigree, Morlands Old Speckled Hen and a guest on handpump, and a good collection of malt whiskies; well reproduced classical music. There are picnic-sets in front and good walks in the area. *(Recommended by Joy and Peter Heatherley, JP, PP, Mr Cameron, Ann Tross, Nigel Woolliscroft, Mr and Mrs C Pink, Sue and Geoff Price, Simon Walker, Wilma and Ian Smith, S P Watkin, P A Taylor, J Gibbs, John and Christine Lowe, Victoria Herriott, John and June Freeman, J F Knutton, Paul Robinshaw, Rona Murdoch, JDM, KM)*

Free house ~ Licensee Brian Bunce ~ Real ale ~ Meals and snacks ~ Restaurant ~ (01629) 650302 ~ Children in dining area till 8 ~ Open 12-3(2.30 in winter), 7-11(10.30 in winter)

BRASSINGTON SK2354 Map 7

Olde Gate

Village signposted off B5056 and B5035 NE of Ashbourne

The peaceful public bar at this well liked traditional old country pub has gleaming copper pots on the lovely old kitchen range, pewter mugs hanging from a beam, embossed Doulton stoneware flagons on a side shelf, an ancient wall clock, and rush-seated old chairs and antique settles (one ancient, partly reframed, black oak solid one). Stone-mullioned windows look across lots of garden tables to small silvery-walled pastures. On the left of a small hatch-served lobby, another cosy beamed room has stripped panelled settles, tables with scrubbed tops, and a roaring fire under a huge mantlebeam. Promptly served good bar food includes very tasty grilled baguettes (£4.50), big open sandwiches (from £4.75), fresh crab (£4.95), spinach and mushroom lasagne or cheese bake (£7.95), steak and mushroom pudding (£8.15), chicken balti (£9.25), king prawn balti (£10.75) and a popular summer barbecue, with lamb steaks, cajun chicken, swordfish and tuna (£8.95-£12.75); good puddings (£2.95). The dining room is no smoking. Well kept Marstons Pedigree and a guest on handpump, and a good selection of malt whiskies; cribbage and dominoes. The small front yard has a couple of benches. It's five minutes' drive from Carsington reservoir which is ideal for water sports and so forth. *(Recommended by Jason Caulkin, JP, PP, Peter Marshall, the Didler, Patrick Hancock, JDM, KM, P Honour, Derek and Sylvia Stephenson, Dr R F Fletcher, John and Christine Lowe, John and June Freeman, Andy and Jill Kassube, J K Knutton, Gillian Russell, Paul Robinshaw, Jerry and Alison Oakes)*

Marstons ~ Tenant Paul Burlinson ~ Real ale ~ Meals and snacks (not Mon, not Sun evenings in winter) ~ (01629) 540448 ~ Children over 10 in bar ~ Open 12-2.30(3 Sat), 6-11(10.30 Sun); closed Mon lunchtimes

nr BUXTON (Derbys) SK0673 Map 7

Bull i'th' Thorn

Ashbourne Road (A515) six miles S of Buxton, nr Hurdlow; OS Sheet 119 map reference 128665

It's worth coming here to see the fascinating medieval hall that's survived since 1472. A massive central beam runs parallel with a forest of smaller ones, there are panelled window seats in the embrasures of the thick stone walls, handsome panelling, and old flagstones stepping gently down to a big open fire. It's furnished with fine long settles, an ornately carved hunting chair, a longcase clock, a powder-horn, and armour that includes 17th-c German helmets, swords, and blunderbusses and so forth. Look out too for the lively old carvings at the main entrance: one shows a bull caught in a thornbush, and others an eagle with a freshly caught hare, and some spaniels chasing a rabbit. Despite all this, the atmosphere is that of any straightforward roadside pub. Served all day, bar food might include haddock or cod (£5), swordfish (£6), barnsley chop (£6.50), sirloin steak, ostrich, crocodile or wild boar (£8.50); Sunday lunch (£5). An adjoining room has darts, pool, shove-ha'penny, dominoes and juke box; piped music. Robinsons Best on handpump. The simple family room opens on to a terrace and big lawn, with swings, and there are more tables in a sheltered angle in front. The pub is handy for the High Peak Trail. *(Recommended by JP, PP, Tony and Wendy Hobden, Paul McPherson, Maurice and Pauline Kean, Eddy and Emma Gibson, David Hoult, D O Savidge)*

Robinsons ~ Tenant Mrs Annette Maltby-Baker ~ Real ale ~ Meals and snacks (9.30-9pm) ~ Restaurant ~ (01298) 83348 ~ Children in children's room ~ Occasional live bands ~ Open 9.30-11(10.30 Sun) ~ Two bedrooms: £18/£36

BUXTON SK0673 Map 7

Old Sun

33 High St

This old coaching inn has been carefully reworked by Marstons as the first of an interesting new venture: well furnished traditional pubs to run virtually as free houses under a Union Taps flag. On the basis of this example, it's well worth while. Several small cosy softly lit rooms lead off the central bar, with open fires, low beams, bare boards or comfortable leather armchairs and chesterfields, fresh flowers, stripped wood screens, old local photographs, and some carefully chosen bric-a-brac (such as the 19th-c Guinness bottles found during refurbishment of the cellar). It is perhaps no surprise that the Marstons Bitter, Pedigree and Regimental, and four or five guest beers such as Exmoor Gold, Whim Hartington, Magic Mushroom Mild and Timothy Taylor Landlord on handpump are kept well; but the use of lined oversized glasses is an unexpected plus point, as is the great range of bottled beers and of malt whiskies, with Bulmer's Old Hazy farm cider, and a good choice of wines, with about a dozen by the glass (in huge glasses). Food too is above average, adventurous and up-to-date, including home-made soup (£1.60), sandwiches (from £3), fried mushrooms on crostini (£3), prawn and buxton blue cheese tart (£3.50), shortcrust steak, kidney and mushroom pie (£6.50), grilled local lamb cutlets with mint and redcurrant (£6.95), monkfish, prawn and pepper kebab with herb butter on a bed of noodles (£10.95), daily specials like wild boar, ostrich steak or swordfish (from £9.50) and excellent puddings like grilled banana and chocolate (£1.70), fruit crumble (£2) and Derbyshire cheese board (£2.75). Staff are friendly (and may offer drinks tasters). They have a beer festival in the week leading up to Easter; cribbage. *(Recommended by Paul Mason, Mike Ridgway, Sarah Miles, Steve Godrich, Tim Barrow, Sue Demont, Richard Lewis)*

Marstons ~ Manager Graham Taylor ~ Real ale ~ Meals and snacks (12-2.30, 5-8.30 (maybe all day in summer); 12-8.30 Sat/Sun) ~ (01298) 23452 ~ Children in back bar till 8pm ~ Open 11-11; 12-10.30 Sun

BUXWORTH SK0282 Map 7

Navigation

Silkhill, off B6062, which itself leads off the A6 just NW of Whaley Bridge roundabout – OS Sheet 110 map ref 022821

Tucked down by a former canal basin, the car park at this homely early 18th-c free house was originally the site of the old Peak Forest Tramway which would have connected the canal with the limestone quarries in nearby Dove Holes. An ambitious restoration project is nearing completion. The cosy linked low-ceilinged rooms do have some canalia, but bring the bargees' days back to life more vividly in their bright clutter of brassware, china and lacy curtains, all neat and shiny as a new pin. It's a smashing place to wander around at quiet times (some of the prints are particularly interesting), and when it's busy there are plenty of snug corners to tuck yourself into, with good coal and log fires and flagstone floors. Good value generous food includes soup (£1.90), sandwiches (from £2), ploughman's (£4.50), dishes called 'golden oldies' such as ham hock with parsley sauce, bubble and squeak, chicken, leek and stilton pie or cumberland sausage (all £5-£6), a huge grilled meat platter (£14), and puddings such as apple pie or bread and butter pudding (£2.25), with vegetarian and children's dishes. Well kept Marstons Pedigree, Timothy Taylor Landlord, Websters Yorkshire and one or two guest beers on handpump, farm ciders in summer and winter Gluhwein; cheery staff. A games room has pinball, pool, darts, dominoes, and TV; quiet piped music. There are tables out on a sunken flagstoned terrace, with a side play area and pets corner. *(Recommended by B Adams, Bill Sykes, M A Buchanan, Pete Yearsley, G Coates, J F M West, Jack Morley)*

Free house ~ Licensees Alan and Lynda Hall ~ Real ale ~ Meals and snacks (12-9.30) ~ Restaurant ~ (01663) 732072 ~ Children welcome away from bar ~ Occasional live entertainment ~ Open 11-11; 12-10.30 Sun ~ Bedrooms: £25(£28B)/£35(£38B)

CASTLETON SK1583 Map 7

Castle Hotel

High Street at junction with Castle Street

A good day to visit this historic hotel is Saturday 29th May when the colourful Garland Ceremony procession, commemorating the escape of King Charles II from the Roundheads, stops and dances outside. The neatly kept atmospheric bar has stripped stone walls with built-in cabinets, an open fire, finely carved early 17th-c beams and, in one room, ancient flagstones. Good bar food includes chicken soup (£1.95), lunchtime sandwiches (from £3.50), smoked seafood platter (£4.65), sausage and mash (£4.75), beef and Bass pie, cod and chips or lemon chicken (£5.25), stilton, chestnut and stout bake (£5.65), minted lamb cutlets (£7.25), with one or two additional evening dishes like mixed grill (£7.95) and peppered rump steak (£8.25); well kept Bass, Stones and Worthington on handpump; shove-ha'penny, cribbage, dominoes, fruit machine and piped music; seats outside. *(Recommended by Richard and Ann Higgs, David Carr, Katherine Williams, Mike and Wendy Proctor, Dr F M Halle, Peter Blake, Mrs S Miller)*

Bass ~ Lease: Paul Brady ~ Real ale ~ Meals and snacks (11-10) ~ Restaurant ~ (01433) 620578 ~ Children welcome ~ Occasional jazz in the garden in summer ~ Open 11-11; 12-10.30 Sun ~ Bedrooms: £39.50B/£59B

DERBY SK3435 Map 7

Alexandra £

Siddals Rd, just up from station

The enthusiastic landlord at this friendly two-roomed Victorian town pub will happily advise you about his half a dozen or so often unusual and quickly changing guest beers which are particularly well kept alongside Batemans XB, Castle Rock Hemlock and Marstons Pedigree. Also, country wines, around two dozen malt whiskies, a good range of Belgian bottled beers, and changing continental beers on draught. The fairly basic but lively bar has lots of railway prints and memorabilia – it's just two minutes away from Derby station – good heavy traditional furnishings on dark-stained floorboards and shelves of bottles, and a fine choice of real ales. Simple remarkably priced bar food includes filled hot or cold rolls (from £1.20), pie and peas (£1.80) and ploughman's, roast or grilled liver and bacon (£3.50); friendly service and locals; dominoes and piped music. *(Recommended by ALC, Richard Lewis, JP, PP, Nigel Williamson, SLC, the Didler, JDM, KM, Andy and Jill Kassube, Chris Raisin, Mrs A Haswell)*

Free house ~ Licensee Mark Robins ~ Real ale ~ Lunchtime meals and snacks (not Sun) ~ (01332) 293993 ~ Open 11-11; 12-3, 7-10.30 Sun ~ Bedrooms: £25B/£35B

Though we don't usually mention it in the text, most pubs will now make coffee – always worth asking. And many – particularly in the North – will do tea.

Brunswick £

1 Railway Terrace; close to Derby Midland railway station

This traditional old railwaymen's pub is home to an incredible 17 constantly used handpumps. Seven of the beers – including Recession Ale, First Brew, Second Brew, the highly-praised Railway Porter, Triple Hop, Festival Ale, and Old Accidental – are from their own Brunswick Brewery (the workings of which are visible from a viewing area), with prices well below the average for the area. The other pumps serve guest beers which are sourced from independent brewers countrywide. They have beer festivals in February and the first week in October; draught farm cider. The very welcoming high-ceilinged serving bar has heavy, well padded leather seats, whisky-water jugs above the dado, and a dark blue ceiling and upper wall, with squared dark panelling below. The no-smoking room is decorated with little old-fashioned prints and swan's neck lamps, and has a high-backed wall settle and a coal fire; behind a curved glazed partition wall is a quietly chatty family parlour narrowing to the apex of the triangular building. Darts, cribbage, dominoes, fruit machine; good friendly service. Lunchtime bar food includes filled salad rolls with turkey, beef, ham, cheese or tuna and sweetcorn (£1.10), hot beef, hot turkey, cheese and bacon or hot traditional sausage beef cobs (£1.60), home-made celery and stilton soup (£1.95), ploughman's (£2.95), home-made chicken, leek, mushroom and celery pie (£3); they do only snacks in the evening and rolls on Sunday. There are seats in the terrace area behind.

(Recommended by Kerry Law, Simon Smith, Richard Lewis, Derek and Sylvia Stephenson, SLC, JP, PP, the Didler, JDM, KM, Sue Holland, Dave Webster, Mrs A Haswell, Chris Raisin, Andy and Jill Kassube)

Own brew ~ Licensee Trevor Harris ~ Real ale ~ Lunchtime meals and snacks (11.30-2.30; evening meals by arrangement) ~ Restaurant ~ (01332) 290677 ~ Children in family room and no-smoking room ~ Jazz Thurs evenings ~ Open 11-11; 12-10.30 Sun

Olde Dolphin £

6 Queen St; nearest car park King St/St Michaels Lane

Perhaps the best time to visit this quaint little place is mid-afternoon when you can quietly enjoy the snugly old-fashioned atmosphere. Its four cosy rooms – two with their own separate street doors – are traditionally decorated with varnished wall benches in the tiled-floor public bar and a brocaded seat in the little carpeted snug; there are big bowed black beams, shiny panelling, cast-iron-framed tables, a coal fire, lantern lights and opaque leaded windows; the atmosphere is friendly and quietly chatty, and they have the daily papers and board games (no piped music). Well kept Bass and a couple of guests; very cheap food includes sandwiches (from £1.35; toasties £1.75), filled baked potatoes (from £2), omelettes (from £2.80), all-day breakfast (£2.95), gammon and egg and a generous mixed grill (£3.99), with dishes of the day such as liver and onion or braised steak. There is a no-smoking restaurant upstairs.

(Recommended by JDM, KM, JP, PP; more reports please)

Bass ~ Manager Paul Needham ~ Real ale ~ Meals and snacks (11-9.45 Mon-Thurs, till 6.30 Fri/Sat; 12-5.30 Sun) ~ Restaurant ~ (01332) 267711 ~ Children in eating area of bar ~ Live music Sun, Mon and Tues evenings ~ Open 10.30am-11pm; Sun 12-10.30

EARL STERNDALE SK0967 Map 7

Quiet Woman

Village signposted off B4053 S of Buxton

A treasure for those who like their pubs really basic and old-fashioned, properly rooted in their locality, this is one of those very rare places where you can buy free-range bantam and goose eggs, local cheese, or even silage as easily as a pint of beer, and where the landlord may rush through in boots and overalls on his way to an emergency fencing job. There are hard seats, plain tables (we liked the sunken one for dominoes or cards), low beams, quarry tiles, lots of china ornaments and a good coal fire. Food is limited to good sandwiches (£1.50) and home-made pork pies (70p; using their own pork), with maybe a winter hotpot. Particularly well kept Batemans Mild, Marstons Best, Pedigree and Owd Rodger and Timothy Taylor Landlord on handpump, cribbage, darts and pool in the family room. There are picnic-sets out in front, with various small animals to keep children amused. A classic. *(Recommended by Jenny and Roger Huggins, Paul Robinshaw, DC, the Didler, JP, PP, John Beeken)*

Free house ~ Licensee Kenneth Mellor ~ Real ale ~ Snacks ~ (01298) 83211 ~ Children in family room ~ Open 11-3, 6.30-11; 12-3, 7-10.30 Sun; cl 25 Dec evening

EYAM SK2276 Map 7

Miners Arms

Signposted off A263 Chesterfield—Chapel en le Frith

Eyam is famous for its suffering during the plague years when the villagers, after a tailor had received a parcel from London and developed the plague, isolated themselves to save the lives of others in the area. These days it makes a very good base for exploring the Peak District, and this well run little local is a handy lunchtime stop. Well served by attentive staff the reliable home-cooked food might include sandwiches (from £2.25), ploughman's or cumberland sausages (£3.95), braised lamb cutlets (£5.95), salmon with white wine sauce (£6.25), crispy roast duck (£6.50) and puddings like sherry trifle or bakewell pudding (£2.25). There's a pleasant restful atmosphere in the three little plush beamed rooms, each of which has its own stone fireplace. In the evening (when they don't do bar food) it gets busy with locals dropping in for the well kept Stones and Tetleys on handpump. Decent walks nearby, especially below Froggatt Edge. *(Recommended by Joy and Peter Heatherley, IHR, JP, PP, Norma and Keith Bloomfield, Barry and Anne, David Carr, Peter Marshall, C Smith, Pat and Tony Martin, Pat and Tony Young, B, M and P Kendall)*

Free house ~ Licensees Nicholas and Ruth Cook ~ Real ales ~ Lunchtime meals and snacks (not Sun) ~ Evening restaurant (they do Sunday lunch too) ~ (01433) 630853 ~ Children welcome ~ Open 12-3, 7-11; closed Sun evening, Mon lunchtime and first 2 weeks Jan ~ Bedrooms: £25B/£50B

FENNY BENTLEY SK1750 Map 7

Coach & Horses

A515 N of Ashbourne

The little back room at this pleasantly friendly 17th-c rendered stone house has ribbed green built-in wall banquettes and old prints and engravings on its dark green leafy Victorian wallpaper. There are more old prints in the friendly front bar, which has flowery-cushioned wall settles and library chairs around the dark tables on its turkey carpet, waggonwheels hanging from the black beams, horsebrasses and pewter mugs, and a huge mirror. Popular reliable bar meals include soup (£2.25), lunchtime sandwiches (from £2.75), filled baked potatoes (from £3.95), lunchtime ploughman's (from £4.95), yorkshire pudding filled with cumberland sausages (£5.95), mushroom and pepper stroganoff or roast of the day (£6.25), grilled salmon steak, pork fillet with smoked bacon and creamy sherry and herb sauce with mushrooms or chicken breast in leek and stilton sauce (£7.50); puddings like lemon meringue pie or treacle tart (£2.25), as well as several daily specials. The dining room and one area of the bar are no smoking. Very well kept Black Bull, Dovedale (brewed a couple of fields away), Mansfield Riding and Morlands Old Speckled Hen on handpump, and lots of malt whiskies; dominoes and piped music. There are picnic-sets on the back grass by an elder tree, with rustic benches and white tables and chairs under cocktail parasols on the terrace in front. *(Recommended by C J Fletcher, Derek and Margaret Underwood, George Atkinson, Jill Bickerton, JP, PP, Colin Fisher, Justin Hulford, Derek and Sylvia Stephenson, John Scarisbrick, Eric Locker, Dorothee and Dennis Glover)*

Free house ~ Licensees John and Matthew Dawson ~ Real ale ~ Meals and snacks ~ (01335) 350246 ~ Children in restaurant ~ Open 11-3, 5-11; 11-11 Sat; 12-10.30 Sun

FROGGATT EDGE SK2477 Map 7

Chequers

B6054, off A623 N of Bakewell; Ordnance Survey Sheet 119, map reference 247761

Readers particularly enjoy staying in the nicely furnished comfortable bedrooms at this beautifully placed country inn, with Froggatt Edge just up through the woods behind. The fairly smart bar has library chairs or small high-backed winged settles on the well waxed floorboards, an attractive, richly varnished beam-and-board ceiling, antique prints on the white walls (partly stripped back to big dark stone blocks), and a big solid-fuel stove; one corner has a nicely carved oak cupboard. Bar food includes soup (£1.75), tortilla or smoked mackerel pâté (£2.95), sandwiches (from £3.25) with very enjoyable filling hearty sandwiches (from £4.25, steak £5.50), spinach, mozzarella, tomato and feta cheese cake or stuffed aubergine (£5.75), liver and bacon (£5.85), cottage pie with mustard thatch (£5.95), smoked haddock and broccoli pie (£6.25), 8oz sirloin (£8.95) and daily specials like green thai curry (£6.95), pork fillet stuffed with ginger and apricot (£8.95), braised lamb shank (£9.95) and fried king scallops with mushroom and tarragon sauce (£10.50); part of the dining area is no smoking. Well kept Wards Best and Thorne on handpump, over 20 malt whiskies and a changing wine board; piped music. There are seats in the peaceful back garden. *(Recommended by David and Mary Webb, Mike and Mary Carter, Sue Holland, Dave Webster, Martin and Karen Wake, Leonard Robinson, Barry and Anne, R H Rowley, IHR, John and Chris Simpson, Margaret and Nigel Dennis, Richard Fallon, John Fahy, Paul Barnett, John Davis, Mike and Karen England, JDM, KM)*

Wards ~ Lease: Tony Dipple and Mr R Graham ~ Real ale ~ Meals and snacks ~ (01433) 630231 ~ Children in eating area of bar ~ Open 11-3, 5.30-11; 11-11 Sat; 12-10.30 Sun; closed 25/26 Dec evening ~ Bedrooms: £46B/£58B

HARDWICK HALL SK4663 Map 7

Hardwick Inn

2¾ miles from M1 junction 29: at roundabout A6175 towards Clay Cross; after ½ mile turn left signed Stainsby and Hardwick Hall (ignore any further sign for Hardwick Hall); at Stainsby follow rd to left; after 2½ miles staggered rd junction, turn left

This well proportioned National Trust owned 17th-c golden stone lodge is a particularly handy stop as it's just four miles from the M1, they serve their very generous helpings of popular bar food all day and service remains prompt and friendly even when it's busy: soup (£1.45), sandwiches (from £2.35), ploughman's (from £3.90), lincolnshire sausage with egg (£4.25), home-made steak and kidney pie (£5), a daily vegetarian dish (£5.50), grilled trout (£5.50), and daily specials such as game and ale pie or rabbit casserole (£5.75); children's menu (from £2.50), and afternoon teas (from £2.75). The carvery restaurant is no smoking. Its separate rooms have a relaxed old-fashioned atmosphere and stone-mullioned latticed windows; the most comfortable is the carpeted lounge with its upholstered wall settles, tub chairs and stools around varnished wooden tables; one room has an attractive 18th-c carved settle. Well kept Courage Directors, Morlands Old Speckled Hen, Theakstons XB and Old Peculier and Youngers Scotch on handpump, and over 100 malt whiskies. Tables in the garden outside offer a very nice view. The pub can get crowded, especially at weekends. *(Recommended by R M Macnaughton, Martin, Jane and Laura Bailey, Piotr Chodzko-Zajko, Jack Morley, IHR, Don and Shirley Parrish, Richard Cole, Minda Alexander, Ann and Bob Westbrook, C Booth, Andy and Jill Kassube, DC, R H Rowley)*

Free house ~ Lease: Peter and Pauline Batty ~ Real ale ~ Meals and snacks (11.30-9.30; 12-9 Sun) ~ Carvery restaurant ~ (01246) 850245 ~ Children in restaurant and three family rooms ~ Open 11.30-11; 12-10.30 Sun

If you have to cancel a reservation for a bedroom or restaurant, please telephone or write to warn them. A small place – and its customers – will suffer if you don't.

HOGNASTON SK2350 Map 7

Red Lion

Village signposted off B5035 Ashbourne—Wirksworth

Close to Carsington Reservoir, this carefully renovated open-plan oak-beamed dining pub has a good relaxed atmosphere, friendly and welcoming. There is an attractive mix of old tables (candlelit at night) on its ancient flagstones, with old-fashioned settles among other seats, and no less than three open fires. A modicum of bric-a-brac includes a growing collection of teddy bears; dominoes, piped music. Good well presented imaginative food includes filled baguettes (from £3.50), home-made smoked salmon pâté (£3.65), warm tart filled with ricotta cheese and caramelised red onions (£4.20), grilled rib of beef with redcurrant, red wine and juniper berry sauce or sun-dried tomato and parsley pancakes filled with spinach and cream cheese, topped with wild mushroom sauce (£6.95), fried prawns in garlic butter (£8.95), glazed duck breast on coriander, lime and lemon sauce or smoked haddock on a bed of spinach with tomato and basil sauce (£10.95) and steak or rack of lamb with garlic and rosemary crust (£11.95); booking is recommended for weekends. Despite the emphasis on food (with almost a bistro feel around the dining tables), this is still very much a pub where locals drop in for a drink, with well kept Marstons Pedigree, Morlands Old Speckled Hen and a guest on handpump; country wines. Staff are helpful and attentive. *(Recommended by Geoffrey and Karen Berrill, Clare Jones, Jonathon Smith, John and Christine Lowe, M R Bennett)*

Free house ~ Licensee P J Price ~ Real ale ~ Meals and snacks (not Mon lunchtime or Sun evening) ~ (01335) 370396 ~ Children in eating area of the bar till 8.30 ~ Open 12-3, 6-11(10.30 Sun); cl Mon lunchtime ~ Bedrooms: £40B/£65B

HOPE SK1783 Map 7

Cheshire Cheese

Edale Road

During the autumn and winter months they arrange guided walks from this very friendly 16th-c village pub set in fine walking country in the heart of the Peak District. Three very snug oak-beamed rooms, up and down steps and divided by thick stone walls, are particularly cosy in cool weather as each has its own coal fire. Very tasty home-cooked bar food with lots of fresh vegetables includes good soup like cauliflower and stilton (£2.25), lunchtime sandwiches (from £3), moules marinières in cream and white wine (£5.25), chicken supreme in cream and white wine sauce (£7.50), smoked salmon scrambled egg and garlic spinach (£7.95), duck breast in orange and red wine sauce (£9.75) and 8oz sirloin (£10.95) with daily specials like yorkshire pudding filled with vegetables (£4.95, filled with beef casserole £7.95), game dishes – often courtesy of the chef's own marksmanship – such as rabbit pie (£6.95), and lamb knuckle in mint and red wine (£7.45); puddings like chocolate fudge cake or syrup sponge (£3); Sunday lunch (£6.95). The lower dining room is no smoking. Service is particularly efficient and cheerful, even when it gets busy; well kept Wards Best and a couple of guests like Theakstons and Thwaites on handpump, a good choice of house wines. Parking can be a problem at busy times. Beautifully furnished bedrooms. *(Recommended by Antonia Weeks, JP, PP, David Carr, Richard Medhurst, Audrey Preston, Simon Watkins, Alan Thwaite, Jeanne Cross, Paul Silvestri, Sam Samuells, Lynda Payton)*

Free house ~ Licensees Mandy and Peter Eustace ~ Real ale ~ Meals and snacks ~ (01433) 620381 ~ Children welcome ~ Open 12-3, 6.30-11; 12-11 Sat; 12-4, 6.30-10.30 Sun; closed winter Sun evening and winter Mon lunchtime ~ Two bedrooms: /£50B

KINGS NEWTON SK3826 Map 7

Hardinge Arms

5 miles from M1 junction 23A; follow signs to E Midlands airport; A453, in 3 miles (Isley) turn right signed Melbourne, Wilson; right turn in 2 miles to Kings Newton; pub is on left at end of village

A new fresh-fish board lists four or five dishes a day at this well run attractive old inn. There might be red snapper on stir fry with chilli sauce (£7.95) or lemon sole with tarragon cream and butter sauce (£10.50). There's also a popular carvery (pork £5.95, beef £6.25, lamb £6.75), as well as home-made soup (£1.90), open sandwiches (from £3.35; not Sunday), cod and chips (£4.25), chicken curry (£5.95), 8oz sirloin steak (from £7.95). About two dozen puddings are displayed in a cold counter (£2.75). The friendly rambling front bar has open fires, beams, a fine panelled and carved bar counter, and blue plush cushioned seats and stools – some in a pleasantly big bow window. At the back is a stately and spacious lounge. Well kept Boddingtons, Flowers IPA and Wadworths 6X under light blanket pressure, and several malt whiskies; piped music. *(Recommended by B Adams, Theo, Anne and Jane Gaskin; more reports please)*

Free house ~ Licensee Mel Stevens ~ Real ale ~ Meals and snacks (till 10 Sat) ~ (01332) 863808 ~ Children in eating area of bar ~ Open 11.30-2.30, 6-11; 12-2.30, 7-10.30 Sun ~ Bedrooms: £35B/£45B

KIRK IRETON SK2650 Map 7

Barley Mow

Signposted off B5023 S of Wirksworth

One reader staying here found it hard to find their way round the rambling interior of this timeless tall gabled Jacobean building with its dimly lit passageways and little stairwells. Probably little changed since it became an inn 200 years ago, the timelessly relaxing pubby small main bar has antique settles on the tiled floor or built into the panelling, a coal fire, slate-topped table, shuttered mullioned windows – and a modest wooden counter behind which are the casks of Hook Norton Best and Marstons Pedigree and three or four guests from brewers like Black Sheep, Charles Wells, Cottage and Eccleshall, all costing quite a bit less than you'd usually pay for a pint in this area; farm ciders. Another room has built in cushioned pews on oak parquet flooring and a small woodburner, and a third has more pews, tiled floor, beams and joists, and big landscape prints. One room is no smoking. Popular filled lunchtime rolls; good value imaginative evening meals for residents only. Civilised old-fashioned service, a couple of friendly pugs and a somnolent newfoundland. There's a good-sized garden, as well as a couple of benches out in front. The charming village is in good walking country. *(Recommended by Mrs M A Stevenson, Steve Riches, the Didler, Pete Baker, G Wheeler, JP, PP, J Roy Smylie, Jo and Gary Charlton, J F Knutton, Neil Ferguson-Lee)*

Free house ~ Licensee Mary Short ~ Real ale ~ Lunchtime sandwiches ~ (01335) 370306 ~ Children at lunchtime, not in bar ~ Open 12-2, 7-11(10.30 Sun) ~ Bedrooms: £25B/£42B

LADYBOWER RESERVOIR SK1986 Map 7

Yorkshire Bridge

A6013 N of Bamford

There's a very cheery atmosphere, and friendly efficient service at this bustling roadside hotel which is prettily situated with pleasant views across a valley to steep larch woods from its no-smoking Garden Room. Good bar food is popular (you do need to get there early in summer) and includes particularly generous helpings of soup (£1.95), lunchtime sandwiches (from £2.60), filled baked potatoes (£2.75), ploughman's (£4.95), steak and kidney pie (£5.90), steamed chicken breast with stilton and onion sauce (£5.95), filled yorkshire pudding (£6.25) and puddings like lemon meringue pie or double chocolate cake (£2.65). Well kept Bass, Stones and Theakstons Best and Old Peculier on handpump, and good coffee with real cream. Floral wallpaper gives its rooms a cottagey feel, one area has sturdy cushioned wall settles, Staffordshire dogs and toby jugs on a big stone fireplace with a warm coal-effect gas fire, china on delft shelves, a panelled dado and so forth. A second extensive area, with another fire, is lighter and more airy with pale wooden furniture, good big black and white photographs and lots of plates on the walls. A small no-smoking conservatory has wicker chairs; darts, cribbage, dominoes, fruit machine, and piped music; disabled loos, and newly decorated bedrooms; lots of nice walks nearby.

(Recommended by G Washington, Pat and Tony Young, Norma and Keith Bloomfield, David Carr, Ewan and Moira McCall, Mr and Mrs G Turner, Gwen and Peter Andrews, Bill and Brenda Lemon)

Free house ~ Licensee Trevelyan Illingworth ~ Real ale ~ Meals and snacks (all day Sun) ~ (01433) 651361 ~ Children welcome ~ Open 11-11; 12-10.30 Sun ~ Bedrooms: £38B/£56B

LITTLE HUCKLOW SK1678 Map 7

Old Bulls Head

Pub signposted from B6049

The two neatly kept main rooms of this friendly little country pub have old oak beams, thickly cushioned built-in settles, antique brass and iron household tools, local photographs, and a coal fire in a neatly restored stone hearth. One room is served from a hatch, the other over a polished bar counter; there's also an unusual little 'cave' room at the back. Tasty bar food includes home-made soup (£2.25), lasagne or scampi or stilton and vegetable bake (£6.25), chicken with apricots and walnuts (£7.95), barnsley chop (£8.95), sirloin steak (£10.95), mixed grill (£12.95) and puddings like spotted dick or fruit crumble (£2.25). Well kept John Smiths Magnet, Tetleys and Wards from carved handpumps, and several malt whiskies; darts, dominoes. There are tables in the neatly tended garden, which is full of an unusual collection of well restored and attractively painted old farm machinery; we haven't yet heard from readers about the new bedrooms. *(Recommended by Stephen, Julie and Hayley Brown, Robin Smith, R H Rowley, JP, PP, David Hoult, Michael Butler)*

Free house ~ Licensee Julie Denton ~ Real ale ~ Meals and snacks ~ (01298) 871097 ~ Children welcome ~ Open 12-3, 6(6.30 Sat)-11(10.30 Sun) ~ Bedrooms: £40B/£49.90B

nr MELBOURNE SK3825 Map 7

John Thompson

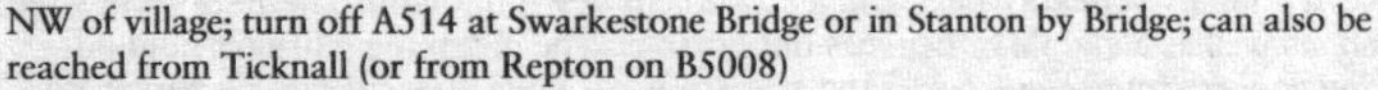

NW of village; turn off A514 at Swarkestone Bridge or in Stanton by Bridge; can also be reached from Ticknall (or from Repton on B5008)

The splendid own-brewed real ales – JTS, Summer Gold and winter Porter – at this enthusiastically run enjoyable pub are very good indeed, as is the popular food. The big, pleasantly modernised lounge has ceiling joists, some old oak settles, button-back leather seats, sturdy oak tables, antique prints and paintings, and a log-effect gas fire; a couple of smaller cosier rooms open off, with pool, a fruit machine, video game, and a juke box in the children's room, and a no-smoking area in the lounge; piped music. Straightforward but good and well priced bar food consists of sandwiches or rolls (from £1.20, nothing else on Sundays; the beef is excellent), home-made soup (£1.50), salads with cold ham or beef (£4), excellent roast beef with yorkshire puddings (£5, not Mondays) and well liked puddings (£1.50). The pub is in a lovely setting above the River Trent, with lots of tables on the well kept lawns by flowerbeds, and on a partly covered outside terrace with its own serving bar. *(Recommended by JDM, KM, JP, PP, J and P Halfyard, Ian Phillips, Andy and Jill Kassube, Michael Marlow, Peter and Audrey Dowsett, Pamela and Merlyn Horswell, Jean and Richard James, Colin Fisher, Jean Bernard Brisset)*

Own brew ~ Licensee John Thompson ~ Real ale ~ Lunchtime meals and snacks (sandwiches only Sun; cold buffet only, Mon) ~ (01332) 862469 ~ Children in separate room ~ Open 10.30-2.30, 7-11; 12-2.30, 7-10.30 Sun

OVER HADDON SK2066 Map 7

Lathkil

Village and inn signposted from B5055 just SW of Bakewell

The little hillside hamlet of Over Haddon is possibly the best situated Derbyshire village, and this comfortable hotel reaps the benefit of its breathtaking views. Steeply down below is Lathkil Dale, one of the quieter dales, with an exceptionally harmonious spread of pastures and copses and plenty to interest the nature lover; paths from the village lead straight into this tempting landscape. Walkers will find a place for their muddy boots in the pub's lobby, and further in some good civilised comforts. The airy room on the right has a warming fire in the attractively carved fireplace, old-fashioned settles with upholstered cushions or plain wooden chairs, black beams, a delft shelf of blue and white plates on one white wall, original prints and photographs, and big windows. On the left is the spacious and sunny family dining area – partly no smoking – which doubles as a restaurant in the evenings; it's not quite as pubby as the bar, but there isn't a problem with shorts or walking gear. At lunchtime the bar food is served here from a buffet and includes home-made soup (£2), salads (from £4.95), fish pie or a vegetarian dish (£5.25), lasagne (£5.35), lamb liver and bacon casserole (£5.55), steak and kidney pie (£5.60) and puddings like treacle tart and strawberry and apple pie (£2.50). Well kept Cottage Golden Arrow, Marstons Pedigree, Wards Best, Whim Hartington and Vaux Waggle Dance on handpump; select malt whiskies and new world wine; piped classical music or jazz, darts, bar billiards, shove-ha'penny, dominoes, cribbage. It does get very busy so it's best to get here early in good weather. *(Recommended by Michael Sargent, JP, PP, Tim and Beryl Dawson, TBB, M Joyner, Mrs M A Stevenson, Roger and Christine Mash, Nigel Woolliscroft, Richard W Marjoram, Dr F M Halle, Mrs A Haswell, Paul Robinshaw, Roy Y Bromell, Michael Graubart, JDM, KM, Charley and Ann Hardwick, Andy and Jill Kassube)*

Free house ~ Licensee Robert Grigor-Taylor ~ Real ale ~ Meals and snacks ~ Restaurant (evenings) ~ (01629) 812501 ~ Children in family room at lunchtime; in restaurant if eating evenings ~ Open 11.30-3, 6.30(7 in winter)-11; 11-11 Sat; 12-10.30 Sun ~ Bedrooms: £35S/£70B

SHARDLOW SK4330 Map 7

Old Crown

Cavendish Bridge

The bar at this thriving 17th-c village pub is packed with bric-a-brac, including hundreds of jugs and mugs hanging from the beamed ceiling, brewery and railway memorabilia, and lots of pictures. Well kept real ales include Bass, Exmoor Gold, Marstons Pedigree, and Taps Best Tipple which was brewed for the pub by Batemans to celebrate the birth of the landlord's son; a nice choice of malt whiskies. Daily specials are really popular, with a good choice of dishes like very tasty pasties with mushy peas and gravy (£5), beef and kidney pie (£5.25), lamb casserole (£5.95), lamb chops with a port and orange sauce or calf liver with sherry, smoked bacon and soured cream sauce (£6.75) and beef topside stuffed with minced veal, onion and breadcrumbs and roasted in red wine (£6.95); shove-ha'penny, cribbage, dominoes and piped music. The pub is next to the River Trent and was once the deportation point for convicts bound for the colonies. *(Recommended by Sue Holland, Dave Webster, JDM, KM, Dr and Mrs B Baker, JP, PP, R Inman, Henry Paulinski, M A Buchanan, B A Lord, the Didler, Alistair Forsyth, Susan and John Douglas, Stephen Brown, Jo and Gary Charlton, Andy and Jill Kassube, Roger Bellingham)*

Free house ~ Licensees Peter and Gillian Morton-Harrison ~ Real ale ~ Lunchtime meals and snacks (till 3) ~ (01332) 792392 ~ Children in eating area of bar only ~ Open 11-3, 5-11; 12-5, 7-10.30 Sun; cl evenings 25/26 Dec ~ Bedrooms: /£40B

WARDLOW SK1875 Map 7

Three Stags Heads

Wardlow Mires; A623 by junction with B6465

Genuinely rather than fashionably traditional, this unspoilt little stone cottage is certainly not the sort of place that pleases everyone – although it's one that we're fond of. Be warned that you might find several dogs taking a hopeful interest in your meal, let alone hogging the fire, that the antiques here look elderly rather than venerable and the loos are a bit scruffy. It's firmly run by a very down to earth landlord (who may not be impressed if you park in the road outside instead of in the car park across the road). The well kept beer here is pretty no nonsense too with Abbeydale Black Lurcher (brewed for the pub) at ABV 8%, Matins and Springhead, and a guest like Abbeydale Last Rites at ABV 10.5% on handpump, as well as lots of bottled continental and English bottled beers. The tiny unassuming flagstoned parlour bar, warmed right through the winter by a cast-iron kitchen range, has old leathercloth seats, a couple of antique settles with flowery cushions, two high-backed windsor armchairs and simple oak tables; one curiosity is the petrified cat in a glass case. Tables in the small no-smoking dining parlour – where there's an open fire – are bookable. They try to vary the seasonal menu to suit the weather so dishes served on their hardy home-made plates (the barn is a pottery workshop) might include a leek and stilton hotpot or vegetable curry (£5.50), lamb and spinach curry (£6.50), steak and kidney pie (£7), seasonal game (£8.50), and fillet steak (£12.50). Cribbage and dominoes, nine men's morris and backgammon. Walkers, their boots and dogs are welcome. The front terrace outside looks across the main road to the distant hills. *(Recommended by JP, PP, the Didler, Sue Holland, Dave Webster, Patrick Hancock, Nigel Woolliscroft, David Carr, Victoria Herriott, Richard Fallon, John Plumridge)*

Free house ~ Licensees Geoff and Pat Fuller ~ Real ale ~ Meals and snacks (7.30pm-9.30pm; 12.30-3.30, 7.30-9.30 Sat/Sun) ~ (01298) 872268 ~ Children welcome away from bar room until 8.30 ~ Folk/Irish music most Sat evenings ~ Open 7pm-11pm weekdays; 12-11 Sat; 12-10.30 Sun; closed Mon except bank holidays

WHITTINGTON MOOR SK3873 Map 7

Derby Tup £

387 Sheffield Rd; B6057 just S of A61 roundabout

This very straightforward corner house is an unspoilt reminder of the way town pubs used to be. The plain but sizeable rectangular bar, with frosted street windows and old dark brown linoleum, has simple furniture arranged around the walls (there's a tremendously long red plastic banquette) leaving lots of standing room. There are two more small no-smoking rooms. There are daily papers, possibly piped rock and blues, trivia machine, darts, dominoes and cribbage. An incredible eleven real ales are kept on handpump, with regulars like Batemans XXXB, Everards Tiger, Greene King Abbot, Marstons Pedigree, Theakstons Old Peculier and Whim Hartington and five quickly changing guest beers such as Ash Vine Casablanca, Gibbs Mew Bishops Tipple, Woodfordes Wherry, and Youngs Special. They also have lots of continental and bottle-conditioned beers, changing ciders, and decent malt whiskies. Besides good sandwiches, the daily changing bar food might include mushroom soup (£2), bean chilli (£3.25), spaghetti bolognese or cauliflower cheese (£3.75), chilli, chicken casserole, Somerset pork or thai minted lamb (£4.25). Despite the remote-sounding name, Whittington Moor is on the northern edge of Chesterfield. *(Recommended by ALC, JP, PP, JJW,CMW; more reports please)*

Free house ~ Licensee Peter Hayes ~ Real ale ~ Meals and snacks (12-2, 5-7.30; not Sun or Mon evenings) ~ (01246) 454316 ~ Children in two side rooms ~ Folk/blues every Thurs evening ~ Open 11.30-3, 5-11 Mon/Tues; 11.30-11 Wed-Sat; 12-4, 7-10.30 Sun

WOOLLEY MOOR SK3661 Map 7

White Horse

Badger Lane, off B6014 Matlock—Clay Cross

There are views to nearby Ogston reservoir from the new no-smoking conservatory at this attractive, bustling old pub. It's very well run by friendly enthusiastic licensees who keep a good balance between its dining areas and the original tap room where the cheerful locals gather to organise their various teams – darts, dominoes, and two each for football and boules (they have their own pitch and piste); cribbage. Readers love the home-made bar food which is prepared with fresh local produce and includes soup (£1.95), sandwiches (from £2.75), steak and kidney pie or ploughman's (£4.25), as well as several sensibly imaginative daily changing specials like courgettes stuffed with cream cheese and basil and a pecan crust (£5.75), chicken fillet stuffed with sun-dried tomatos and ricotta cheese wrapped in smoked bacon, rosemary and chilli lamb casserole or roast pork loin with damson and juniper sauce (all £6.75), fresh salmon and asparagus fricassee (£6.95), and puddings (£2.25); children's meals (£2) come with a puzzle sheet and crayons; puddings (£2.30). Well kept Bass and four weekly changing guests on handpump, and a decent wine list; piped classical music in the lounge; the restaurant is no smoking. Picnic-sets in the garden have lovely views across the Amber Valley, and there's a very good children's play area with wooden play train, climbing frame and swings. A booklet describes eight walks from the pub, and the landlord is a keen walker. *(Recommended by JP, PP, KDM, KM, Paul and Sandra Embleton, Geoffrey and Irene Lindley, Joy and Peter Heatherley, Derek and Sylvia Stephenson, Keith and Margaret Kettwell, Don and Shirley Parrish, M A Buchanan, Mike and Mary Carter, Peter Marshall, M Buchanan, John and Christine Lowe, David Carr, J Warren, Luke Worthington, Mike and Sue Walton, Neil Porter, Peter and Audrey Dowsett, Norma and Keith Bloomfield, Pat and Roger Fereday, Sue and Geoff Price, Andrew Pashley, G P Kernan)*

Free house ~ Licensees Bill and Jill Taylor ~ Real ale ~ Meals and snacks (11.30-2(2.30 Sat/Sun), 6.30-9(5.30-8.30 Sun)) ~ (01246) 590319 ~ Children in lounge and conservatory ~ Open 11.30-2.30(3 Sat), 6-11; 12-3, 5-10.30 Sun

Lucky Dip

Besides the fully inspected pubs, you might like to try these Lucky Dips recommended to us and described by readers (if you do, please send us reports):

Apperknowle [45 High St; SK3878], *Yellow Lion*: Welcoming 19th-c stonebuilt village local, comfortable banquettes in L-shaped lounge with TV, old organ, brass lamps, fruit machine; no-smoking dining room, wide choice of good value food from sandwiches and toasties up inc vegetarian, five real ales, good choice of wines by glass, caring licensees, garden with play area; Weds quiz night; children welcome; bedrooms – very cheap *(CMW, JJW)*

☆ **Ashbourne** [Ashbourne Green (A515 towards Matlock); SK1846], *Bowling Green*: Well kept Bass, Worthington and two other changing ales, wide choice of good value home-cooked food inc vegetarian, friendly atmosphere, straightforward comfort; good bedrooms *(David Carr)*; [Market Pl], *George & Dragon*: Good simple food (all day Sat/Sun) inc bargain Sun lunch, very friendly atmosphere; open all day *(David Carr)*; [central], *Green Man*: Well kept Mansfield beers, friendly welcoming landlord, good reasonably priced pub food; good value bedrooms *(Bill and Pam Baker, David Carr)*; [Market Sq], *White Lion*: Well kept Vaux Samson and Waggle Dance, good choice of food inc interesting fish, good steaks and vegetarian; friendly and welcoming; bedrooms *(Bill and Pam Baker, David Carr)*

☆ **Ashford in the Water** [SK1969], *Bulls Head*: Cosy and homely comfortable lounge with a good pubby atmosphere, well kept Robinsons ales, home-made food from good soup and sandwiches up, reasonable prices, friendly service, no piped music; tables out in front *(Sue and Geoff Price, John Waller, David and Mary Webb, IHR, Rita and Keith Pollard, Jeremy Burnside)*

Ashford in the Water [Church St], *Mill House*: New name and new style for the former Ashford Hotel (the licensees who ran it then as a successful main entry can now be found at the Coach & Horses, Fenny Bentley); extended seating inside and out (no dogs in garden, part of which has gone into enlarging car park), family meals, colouring sets for children *(LYM)*

Bakewell [Bridge St; SK2168], *Castle*: Good value food, newspapers to read, smart wine-bar feel but good choice of ales, friendly staff *(David Carr)*; [Market Pl], *Peacock*: Clean, bright and cheerful, Wards ales, wide choice of good popular meals, good prices and service *(Mrs C Dale)*

Baslow [Chesterfield Rd (off A619); SK2672], *Robin Hood*: Nice pub in good walking country, nr Baslow Edge; fairly modern, well decorated and comfortable; uncarpeted bar for climbers (where boots and dogs welcome), good reasonably priced food, Mansfield ales, brisk friendly service; bedrooms *(Julia Cooper)*

Bonsall [off A6012 Cromford—Hartington – right at the Pig of Lead, then left in village; SK2858], *Barley Mow*: Friendly nicely furnished pub of character, with particularly well kept Vaux, Whim and a guest beer, good if not cheap food made freshly – service can be slow when busy, with no queue-jumping for simple dishes such as sandwiches; has been cl weekday lunchtimes (may open Fri by arrangement) *(Derek and Sylvia Stephenson, Paul Robinshaw, JP, PP)*; *Kings Head*: Cosy and friendly 17th-c pub under newish management, with good village-pub atmosphere, scrubbed tables in two rooms, log fires, interesting choice of good value food, Bass, Marstons and Tetleys, good house wines; handy for Limestone Way and other walks *(Judith and Richard Thorpe, Mr and Mrs J K Miln)*

Bradwell [Brough Lane Head; A625/B6049, N of village; SK1882], *Travellers Rest*: Recently bought by local farmer for preservation as true country local; lots of character, well kept Bass, Boddingtons and Stones *(J F M West)*; [Church St (B6049)], *Valley Lodge*: Half a dozen well kept changing ales such as Barnsley Best, Hobsons Best, Mansfield Old Baily, Stones Best, Vaux Samson and Wards Best in surprisingly red brick pub with foyer bar, comfortable lounge, big public bar with darts and pool, weekend food, friendly staff, seats outside; cl weekday lunchtimes, bedrooms *(Richard Lewis)*

☆ **Brassington** [SK2354], *Miners Arms*: Very welcoming and pubby, with good food from hot pork rolls up, well kept Marstons Pedigree and guest beers, good service, tables out among flower tubs; open all day, children welcome, live music some nights; bedrooms *(Miss S Watkin, P Taylor, David Carr, Paul Robinshaw, JDM, KM)*

Breaston [SK4634], *Navigation*: Character landlady, attractive decor, good value usual food, well kept ales inc Marstons Pedigree; fine old buildings, genuine atmosphere *(Bill and Sheila McLardy)*

Bullbridge [off A610 W of Ripley; SK3652], *Lord Nelson*: Clean and pleasant mid 19th-c pub with beamed lounge, friendly landlord, Mansfield real ales, good value home-made lunchtime food – second bar has comfortable tables for diners; piped music; picnic-sets in small garden *(JDM, KM, JJW, CMW)*

Buxton [Water St; SK0673], *Clubhouse*: Very spacious, giving some feel of the town's 19th-c opulence (despite the varnish over the glorious woodwork), with comfortable armchairs, several levels, ample solid food inc fine steak and kidney pie; well kept Ind Coope Burton and Tetleys, cheerful long-serving staff; opp Opera House *(Robert Gomme, G Curtis)*; [Spring Gdns], *Miltons Head*: Small bar, larger back lounge and front restaurant, decent food, friendly chatty service *(Mr and Mrs C Roberts)*; [Bridge St], *Railway*: Large welcoming railway-theme food pub under viaduct, very good choice of good value food, huge helpings, well kept Hardys & Hansons, prompt service *(David Carr)*

nr **Buxton** [Hurdlow Town; A515 Ashbourne Rd, about half a mile from the Bull i'th' Thorn; SK1166], *Duke of York*: Clean and comfortable, with Robinsons real ale, wide choice of good value generous food inc children's dishes (all day in summer), coal fire, pleasant staff; lovely views, well spaced tables outside *(Geoffrey Lindley)*

Calver [off A623 N of Baslow; SK2474], *Bridge*: Quick good value food from newly refurbished kitchen, but resisting pressure to become just another dining pub – unspoilt but clean, comfortable and roomy, with particularly well kept Hardys & Hansons Best and Classic, pleasant landlord, old brass and local prints; tables in nice big garden by River Derwent *(Vann and Terry Prime, M Joyner, IHR, DC)*; *Derwentwater Arms*: Nicely refurbished, welcoming and attentive staff, good freshly cooked food esp fish and fresh veg *(E Hopkins)*

☆ **Castleton** [Cross St; SK1583], *Olde Nags Head*: Small but solid hotel dating from 17th c, civilised turkey-carpeted main bar with interesting antique furnishings, coal fire, faint piped music, friendly staff, well kept ales, good coffee, impressive bar food from sandwiches up inc vegetarian dishes, cosy Victorian restaurant; open all day, comfortable bedrooms *(Justin Hulford, Simon Watkins, Jeremy Burnside, LYM)*

Castleton [How Lane], *Peak*: Recently refurbished airy lounge, leather wall seats in smaller bar, dining room with high ceiling and picture-window view of Peak hills, wide choice of reasonably priced food inc vegetarian, huge helpings, particularly well kept Tetleys and Marstons Pedigree, friendly service; bedrooms – a friendly place to stay *(Justin Hulford, DC, Dr F M Halle)*; *George*: Good atmosphere and good value simple food in roomy bars with friendly helpful staff, well kept Bass; tables on wide forecourt; popular with young people – nr YHA; dogs welcome *(DC, Jeremy Burnside)*

Chelmorton [between A6 and A515 SW of Buxton; SK1170], *Church*: Comfortable split bar, ample space for diners, good range of reasonably priced generous food inc fresh veg, friendly landlord and golden labrador, well kept Marstons Bitter, Pedigree, seasonal ale and a guest such as Adnams, tables out on terrace, well tended flower boxes; piped music, outside lavatories; superb walking country *(Alan and Heather Jacques)*

☆ **Chesterfield** [43 Chatsworth Rd; SK3871], *Royal Oak*: Friendly pub, always a good atmosphere, fine choice of well kept beers, enthusiastic young landlord *(David Carr, JP, PP)*

Chesterfield [23 Stephenson Pl], *Rutland*: Very old L-shaped pub next to crooked spire church, now a Hogshead, with rugs and assorted wooden furniture on bare boards, a dozen real ales and a farm cider, good value food, darts, pinball machine, old photographs; children welcome, open all day *(CMW, JJW)*

☆ **Chunal** [A624 a mile S of Glossop; SK0391], *Grouse*: Pleasant open-plan but cosy moorland pub, good food esp home-made pies, also lunchtime and early evening OAP bargains, good chips and interesting specials, huge helpings; well kept Thwaites, friendly service, spectacular views of Glossop, real fires, old photographs of surrounding countryside, traditional furnishings and candlelit tables; unobtrusive piped music, quiz night Thurs; children allowed in upstairs restaurant *(J F M and M West, David Hoult)*

Clifton [off A515 S of Ashbourne; SK1644], *Cock*: Comfortable family pub with good value home-cooked food, massive helpings, very friendly staff keen to please; children really welcome *(Gail and Simon Rowlands)*

Coxbench [Alfreton Rd; off B6179 N of Derby; SK3743], *Fox & Hounds*: Pleasantly pubby, with wide choice of good interesting if not cheap freshly made food inc vegetarian,

Mansfield and a guest beer such as Shepherd Neame Spitfire; piped music may obtrude *(JDM, KM, J F Knutton)*

☆ **Cromford** [Scarthin – one-way st behind mkt pl; SK2956], *Boat*: 18th-c traditional local in quaint village, long narrow low-beamed bar with stripped stone, bric-a-brac and books, very welcoming staff, friendly relaxed atmosphere, well priced inventive food from black pudding to wild boar inc good Sun lunch, log fire, real ales such as Bass, Leatherbritches Bespoke, Morlands Old Speckled Hen, Townes Muffin and one brewed for the pub; TV may be on for sports; children welcome, garden *(G Coates, DC)*

☆ **Cutthorpe** [NW of Chesterfield; B6050 well W of village; SK3273], *Gate*: Picture-window views over eastern Peak District from chatty area around bar, neat and comfortable no-smoking dining lounge down steps, decent fair-priced food (not Sun-Tues evenings) inc bargain lunches popular with older people, well kept ales such as Bass, Boddingtons, Flowers Original and Mansfield Riding, friendly efficient staff, lots of biggish pictures; children welcome if eating, no dogs *(JJW, CMW, Dr F M Halle, BB)*

☆ **Dale** [Main St, Dale Abbey; off A6096 NE of Derby; SK4339], *Carpenters Arms*: Attractive village pub with panelling, low beams, riding prints, well kept Ansells BB, Ind Coope Burton, Marstons Pedigree and Ruddles County, good value food in bar, lounge (no dogs here) and restaurant, real fire, family room, darts, fruit machine; garden with play area (camping ground behind), good walking country – popular with walkers, can get very busy; pleasant village with Abbey ruins and unusual church attached to house *(John Beeken, JJW, CMW, JP, PP)*

☆ **Derby** [25 King St], *Flower Pot*: Very popular extended real-ale pub with outstanding range of up to two dozen kept well, some behind glass and feeding gravity taps, helpful landlord, friendly staff and locals, good value generous food from sandwiches and cheap burgers up into afternoon, daily papers, comfortable back bar with lots of books and old Derby photographs, three other simply furnished rooms, traditional games, no piped music or machines; good live bands Sat, pleasant garden; open all day *(Chris Raisin, Richard Lewis, Joan and Michel Hooper-Immins, SLC)*

☆ **Derby** [Irongate], *Standing Order*: Vast Wetherspoons conversion of imposing bank, central bar, booths down each side, elaborately painted plasterwork, pseudo-classical torsos, high portraits of mainly local notables; usual popular food all day, good range of well kept ales, reasonable prices, daily papers, neat efficient young staff, no-smoking area; rather daunting acoustics; disabled facilities *(JDM, KM, Chris Raisin, SLC, Richard Lewis, BB)*

☆ **Derby** [Ley St, Darley Abbey; SK3438], *Abbey*: Interesting for including massive stonework remnants of 11th-c abbey; brick floor, studded oak doors, big stone inglenook, stone spiral stair to upper bar with handsome oak rafters; well kept cheap Sam Smiths, decent lunchtime bar food, children allowed; opp Derwent-side park, riverside walk to centre *(Jeremy Burnside, LYM)*

Derby [114 Friargate], *Friargate*: Comfortable and relaxing, part carpeted, light green decor, heavily panelled central bar, lunchtime food, good choice of well kept ales (some tapped from the cask), disabled facilities; open all day; same ownership as Flower Pot *(Richard Lewis)*; [Meadows Rd], *Smithfield*: Friendly bow-fronted riverside pub with big bar, two smaller rooms, up to nine well kept ales mainly from interesting small breweries, helpful staff, filled rolls and lunchtime meals, pub games inc table skittles; open all day, children welcome, Derwentside garden; same family as Flower Pot *(Richard Lewis, Chris Raisin, G Coates)*; [Irongate], *Vaults*: Long vaulted cellar bar, flagstones and bare brick, with well kept ales such as Bass, Boddingtons, Fullers London Pride, Jennings Sneck Lifter and Marstons Pedigree (some tapped from the cask); pool, piped music, SkyTV, open all day; food upstairs in P J Peppers *(Richard Lewis)*

Dronfield [Pentland Rd/Gorsey Brigg, Dronfield Woodhouse; off B6056; SK3378], *Jolly Farmer*: Extensive bar tastefully done as Greenalls Country Ale House, old pine, bare bricks, polished boards and carpet, alcoves and cosy corners, bric-a-brac and fresh flowers, very friendly staff and atmosphere, daily papers, comfortable seats, open fire, six real ales, decent food all day; piped pop music, games area with pool and TV, quiz and ale-tasting nights; children at lunchtime if eating *(CMW, JJW)*; [91 Chesterfield Rd (B6057)], *Old Sidings*: Railway-theme pub by main line, upstairs lounge with lots of local railway memorabilia, no-smoking part up a couple of steps, games inc revolving pool table past narrow bar, well kept Bass and Stones Bitter and Mild, wide choice of reasonably priced food inc children's, vegetarian and bargains for early suppers or students; open all day *(JJW, CMW, Mr and Mrs Smith)*

Duffield [Duffield Bank; across River Derwent, off Holbrook rd; SK3543], *Bridge*: Newly refurbished Mansfield family pub in lovely setting by River Derwent, superb play areas indoors and out, riverside terrace, above-average usual food, well kept ales, shelves of knick-knacks *(JDM, KM, Rona Murdoch)*

Eckington [126 High St (B6052); SK4379], *Bird in Hand*: Friendly, pleasant and chatty late Victorian pub, fresh flowers in comfortable lounge, good value bargain lunches (may have to book Sun), attentive quick service, well kept ales such as Adnams or Ridleys, cheap tea and coffee; lovely hanging baskets, swing in small back garden; piped music, big games room with pool and SkyTV; children welcome *(JJW, CMW)*

Edale [SK1285], *Old Nags Head*: Useful walkers' pub at start of Pennine Way, basic food, open fire, S&N and other ales; can be very busy, piped music sometimes loud; children in airy back family room, tables on front terrace and in garden – short path down to pretty streamside cottages *(Simon Watkins, David Hoult, Tim Barrow, Sue Demont, LYM)*

☆ **Elton** [SK2261], *Duke of York*: Unspoilt old-fashioned local, like stepping back in time, lovely little quarry-tiled back tap room with coal fire in massive fireplace, glazed bar and hatch to corridor, two front rooms – one like private parlour with dining table (no food, just crisps); Mansfield and occasional guest beer; open 8.30-11, and Sun lunchtime *(the Didler, Richard Lewis, JP, PP)*

☆ **Fenny Bentley** [A515 N of Ashbourne; SK1750], *Bentley Brook*: Big open-plan bare-boards bar/dining room, log fire, communicating airy carpeted restaurant; one or two changing own-brewed Leatherbritches ales and several guest beers, marquee for beer festival spring bank hol, usual food (maybe free meals for children eating with adults early evening), well reproduced piped music, games machines; picnic-sets on terrace with proper barbecue area, skittles, kitchen shop; open all day, handy for Dovedale; bedrooms *(Richard Lewis, JP, PP, John Scarisbrick, BB)*

Flagg [off A515 S of Buxton, at Duke of York; SK1368], *Plough*: Reopened and refurbished, in beautiful Peak District village, lovely countryside; log fire, usual food inc beautifully presented sandwiches, play area; bedrooms planned *(A M Pring)*

Foolow [signed off A623 just E of B6465 junction; SK1976], *Bulls Head*: Attractive moorland village pub, friendly atmosphere, good welcoming service, Wards and Vaux beers and one or two guests, food in bar and pleasant no-smoking restaurant area; bedrooms, fine views *(JM, DC, LYM)*

☆ *nr* **Foolow** [Bretton, signed from Foolow; SK2077], *Barrel*: Splendid site on ridge edge, seats on breezy front terrace, five-county views and good walks; cosy beamed bar with snug areas and log fire, sensibly short choice of good generous cheap food from sandwiches up, well kept real ales, restaurant *(DC, IHR, JDM, KM, Dr F M Halle, Nigel Woolliscroft, Eddy and Emma Gibson, LYM)*

Ford [off B6054 S of Sheffield; SK4080], *Bridge*: Good service, four real ales, popular food (not Sun/Mon evenings) inc good sandwiches, log fire; no dogs, machines or piped music; TV in front lobby, picnic-sets in garden, children welcome; pretty millpond village, walks *(JJW, CMW, Dr F M Halle)*

Glapwell [The Hill; A617 a mile E of M1 junction 29; SK4866], *Young Vanish*: Small no-smoking dining area, decent standard food, five real ales; fruit machine, piped pop music; play area in garden *(Patrick Hancock)*

☆ **Great Hucklow** [SK1878], *Queen Anne*: Comfortable beamed bar with home-cooked food inc fresh veg, well kept beer, good atmosphere, friendly staff, open fire, walkers' bar, small terrace and pleasant garden with lovely views; children welcome, handy for walks; two newly done bedrooms *(JP, PP, DC, Jeanne Cross, Paul Silvestri)*

Great Longstone [SK2071], *White Lion*: Friendly, with quite wide choice of food inc oriental and interesting puddings, OAP discounts, well kept beer; charming stone village, beautiful countryside *(Philip and Ann Falkner)*

☆ **Grindleford** [B6521 N of village; SK2478], *Maynard Arms*: Spacious high-ceilinged hotel bar with dark panelling, local and autographed cricketing photographs, wide choice of food from sandwiches to steaks, well kept Boddingtons and Whitbreads Castle Eden, friendly staff; no-smoking restaurant overlooking neat gardens; piped music; children in eating areas, open all day Sun, comfortable bedrooms, nice setting *(IHR, Margaret and Nigel Dennis, Alan and Heather Jacques, Derek and Sylvia Stephenson, Dr F M Halle, LYM)*

Grindleford [B6001], *Sir William*: Comfortable and friendly, with wide choice of good value food, well kept ales, good coffee, pool table in spacious room; splendid view esp from terrace, walking nearby *(Don and Shirley Parish, DC, IHR, Dr F M Halle)*

Hartington [SK1360], *Charles Cotton*: Scottish Courage ales, good value food, roaring coal fires; bedrooms *(JP, PP, Monica Shelley, Laura Darlington)*; [The Square], *Devonshire Arms*: Good choice of tasty food worth the price, well kept beer, good welcoming service even under pressure; bedrooms comfortable *(DC, Robert Gomme)*

Hartshorne [Ticknall Rd; SK3322], *Old Mill Wheel*: Interesting conversion of old screw mill, big working water wheel, bar and dining area on ground floor, small bar and more extensive dining area upstairs, Marstons Pedigree and weekly guest beers, good-sized helpings of good interesting food inc reasonably priced genuine Thai set meals, very friendly atmosphere *(Caroline Lengyel)*

☆ **Hathersage** [Leadmill Bridge; A622 (ex B6001) towards Bakewell; SK2380], *Plough*: Beautifully placed ex-farm with Derwentside garden, good helpings of good fresh varied food in bar and two dining areas (ex-butcher landlord), good atmosphere, charming prompt service even when very busy; well kept Tetleys and Wadworths 6X, good value wines *(Don and Shirley Parrish, Mr and Mrs R Head, Rose, Richard and Sally Melvin, Dr F M Halle, IHR, Mrs C M Smalley)*

☆ **Hathersage** [A625], *George*: Substantial comfortably modernised old inn, good value well presented food, calm atmosphere, well kept Boddingtons, decent wine, attentive service, neat flagstoned back terrace by rose garden; a nice place to stay (the back bedrooms are the quiet ones) *(T L Rees, LYM)*

☆ **Hathersage** [Church Lane], *Scotsmans Pack*: Big clean welcoming open-plan local, good choice of generous nicely presented interesting food (best to book Sun lunch), reasonable prices, well kept Burtonwood Bitter and Forshaws, decent wines, good service; some seats on pleasant side terrace by trout stream; good bedrooms, huge breakfast *(Mrs E Haynes, Jeanne Cross, Paul Silvestri, Mr and Mrs R Head, DC)*

Hayfield [Little Hayfield – A624 N; SK0388], *Lantern Pike*: Cosily unpretentious and welcoming, with plush seats, lots of brass, china and toby jugs, well kept Boddingtons, Flowers IPA, and Timothy Taylor Landlord, good choice of malt whiskies, decent bar food from sandwiches up inc children's and OAP weekday lunches; no-smoking back dining room, darts, dominoes, maybe piped nostalgic music; back terrace looking up to Lantern Pike, great spot for walkers; children welcome, open all day w/e, good value bedrooms *(Ewan and Moira McCall, Mr and Mrs N Thorp, Eddie Edwards, D Irving, Jenny and Roger Huggins, T McLean, Philip and Ann Falkner, Amanda and Simon Southwell, Stephen Brown, Stephen Holman, LYM)*

Heage [94 Ripley Rd (B6374); SK3750], *Heage Tavern*: Comfortable, with good value food, Bass and Marstons Pedigree (good measure), public area with pool, TV and juke box; no dogs, some seats outside *(JJW, CMW)*

Holmesfield [Lydgate; B6054 towards Hathersage; SK3277], *Robin Hood*: Neatly extended moorland pub with wide choice of promptly served popular food (all day w/e) from sandwiches to steaks, half helpings for OAPs and children, well kept Charles Wells Bombardier, smart pleasant staff, good open fires, beams, partly carpeted flagstones, plush banquettes, high-raftered restaurant with big pictures; children in eating areas, piped music, stone tables out on cobbled front courtyard *(Dr F M Halle, G P Kernan, LYM)*

Hope [1 Castleton Rd; SK1783], *Woodroffe Arms*: Several friendly rooms inc conservatory, wide choice of good value food inc children's dishes and Sun lunch, Whitbreads-related ales and Addlestone's cider, real fire, polite service; Sun quiz night, garden with swings; bedrooms *(Dave Braisted, DC, Dr F M Halle)*

Ilkeston [Bridge St, Cotmanhay; off A609/A6007; SK4543], *Bridge*: Two-room local by Erewash Canal, popular with fishermen and boaters for early breakfast and sandwich lunches; extremely well priced Hardys & Hansons Best Mild and Best, big carp in lounge tank; nice back garden with play area, well behaved children allowed, open all day *(the Didler)*

Little Longstone [off A6 NW of Bakewell via Monsal Dale; SK1971], *Packhorse*: Snug 16th-c cottage with old-fashioned country furnishings in two cosy beamed rooms, well kept Marstons Best or Pedigree, decent food, pub games, terrace in steep little garden *(Joy and Peter Heatherley, Nigel Woolliscroft, R H Rowley, Jeremy Burnside, LYM)*

☆ **Lullington** [Coton Rd; SK2513], *Colvile Arms*: 18th-c village pub with basic panelled bar, plush beamed lounge, pleasant atmosphere, friendly staff, piped music, four well kept ales inc Bass, Marstons Pedigree and a Mild, good value snacks (no cooking), picnic-sets on small sheltered back lawn overlooking bowling green; cl weekday lunchtimes *(CMW, JJW, C J Fletcher, LYM)*

☆ **Makeney** [Holly Bush Lane; A6 N, cross river Derwent, before Milford turn right, then left; SK3544], *Holly Bush*: Unspoilt two-bar village pub, cosy and friendly, with five well kept ales brought from cellar in jugs, besides Ruddles County and one named for the pub – also annual beer festival; three roaring open fires (one by curved settle in snug's old-fashioned range), flagstones, beams, tiled floors, good value basic meals inc lunchtime snacks, Thurs steak night, dining area; games machines in lobby; children allowed in back conservatory, dogs welcome, aviary on small terrace *(Richard Houghton, JP, PP, Chris Raisin)*

Marshlane [B6056 S of Sheffield; SK4079], *Fox & Hounds*: Cosy dark-beamed pub with pictures, plates and brass, open fire, separate tap room with darts, four well kept Burtonwood ales, good coffee, good value food inc children's and Sun lunch, friendly staff and dogs; piped music may obtrude a bit; big garden with picnic-sets, good play area, good views *(CMW, JJW, Dr F M Halle, DC)*

Matlock [Smedley St E/Rutland St; SK2959], *Gate*: 19th-c corner local, banquettes in long lounge, good choice of reasonably priced food from filled rolls up, four real ales, real fire, bar with pool and games, juke box, small garden; Tues quiz night *(CMW, JJW)*; [48 Jackson Rd, Matlock Bank], *Thorn Tree*: Homely two-room 19th-c stonebuilt local, superb views over valley and town from front picnic-sets; well kept Bass, Mansfield Old Baily and Whim Hartington, chatty licensees, sensibly priced lunchtime food from sandwiches up, darts, dominoes; TV, piped nostalgic music, outside gents'; cl Mon/Tues lunchtime *(CMW, JJW, DC, the Didler, JP, PP, Derek and Sylvia Stephenson)*

Melbourne [222 Station Rd; towards Kings Newton/Islay Walton; SK3825], *Railway*: Good old-fashioned chatty local, tiled and wooden floors, cast-iron gas fireplaces, good value simple fresh food, attractive dining room, well kept Marstons Pedigree, Timothy Taylor Landlord, Wards and guest beers mainly from very small breweries, own brewery being built behind; well behaved children allowed; bedrooms good value *(the Didler)*; [Derby Rd (B587 N, between Stanton by Bridge and Kings Newton)], *Sir Francis Burdett*: Very popular for wide range of real ales inc guest beers, good stock of whiskies; big choice of food inc help-yourself veg from hot counter; basic bar, big family room off, American billiards room, tables outside *(Brian and Genie Smart)*

☆ **Millthorpe** [Cordwell Lane; SK3276], *Royal Oak*: Stripped stone, quarry tiles, oak beams, relaxed welcome for all inc walkers, cosy snug, real fires, mix of simple chairs and plush banquettes, good value lunchtime home cooking inc proper Bakewell pudding, well kept Wards, good helpful service, no piped music; no children inside, tables out on pleasant terrace; good walks nearby, cl Mon lunchtime exc bank hols *(Joy and Peter Heatherley, DC, LYM)*

☆ **Milltown** [off B6036 SE of Ashover; SK3561], *Miners Arms*: Comfortable dining pub with good home-made food inc several unusual vegetarian dishes, main dishes served with separate dishes of potatoes and vegetables in interesting variety, tempting puddings, attractive prices, well kept Mansfield ales and a guest such as Batemans XXXB, good value wines, good friendly service, quiet piped classical music; lovely countryside, good walks right from the door; cl Mon, Tues, usually have to book a day or so ahead *(JDM, KM, Mr and Mrs Smith)*

Milton [just E of Repton; SK3126], *Coach House*: Converted Georgian dower house almost too well furnished for a pub, with ample helpings of good food inc bargain suppers, three well kept ales, fresh flowers in bar and dining areas, nice garden *(Brian and Genie Smart)*

☆ **Monsal Head** [B6465; SK1871], *Monsal Head*: Extended Victorian hotel with valley views from front terrace or upstairs lounge, side stable bar with ski-lodge feel (steps up to crafts gallery), well kept Marstons Pedigree, John Smiths, Theakstons Best, Old Peculier and XB, Whim Hartington and a beer brewed for the pub, bar food (usually good) all day from sandwiches up, log fire, relaxed friendly service, separate spacious high-ceilinged front bar, no-smoking restaurant; children welcome till 7, back garden with play area, winter folk nights Fri, good bedrooms with views *(Jo and Gary Charlton, A Bradbury, Joy and Peter Heatherley, Mrs A Haswell, Paul and Maggie Baker, Phil and Heidi Cook, Kevin and Amanda Earl, Hilarie Dobbie, Paul and Sandra Embleton, Mr M Joyner, Dave and Deborah Irving, LYM)*

☆ **Monyash** [SK1566], *Bulls Head*: Homely and friendly high-ceilinged two-room bar with oak wall seats and panelled settle, horse pictures, shelf of china, roaring log fire, mullioned windows, impressive generous low-priced home-cooked food inc sandwiches, vegetarian and good salads, Black Sheep and Tetleys Mild and Bitter, efficient staff; nicely set tables in plush two-room dining room, pool in small back bar, maybe quiet piped music; long pews outside facing small green, friendly ginger cat, children and muddy dogs welcome; simple bedrooms, nice village *(Julia Hiscock, M G Hart, Paul Robinshaw, Mrs M A Stevenson, BB)*

Mugginton [back rd N of Weston Underwood – OS Sheet 119 map ref 287439; SK2843], *Cock*: Clean, comfortable and relaxing, with tables and settles in L-shaped bar, big dining area, friendly efficient staff, well kept weekly changing ales such as Timothy Taylor Landlord and Wadworths 6X, sensibly priced wines, good value food from lunchtime sandwiches and snacks to more adventurous specials inc vegetarian, interesting fresh veg; tables outside, nice surroundings, walks *(JDM, KM)*

New Mills [Brookbottom – OS Sheet 109 map ref 985864; SJ9886], *Fox*: Friendly and unspoilt characterful old country pub cared for well by long-serving landlord, open fire, well kept Robinsons, good range of basic food inc sandwiches, darts, pool; children welcome, handy for walkers; splendid tucked-away hamlet down single-track lane *(David Hoult)*; [Mellor Rd, N of town; SJ9987], *Pack Horse*: Popular and friendly unpretentious pub with plentiful good value food, lovely views across broad valley, well kept Tetleys; open all day; bedrooms *(Michael Graubart, Stephen, Julie and Hayley Brown)*

Old Brampton [SK3372], *George & Dragon*: Comfortable stonebuilt village local, wide choice of well presented good value lunchtime food popular with older people, well kept Marstons Bitter and Pedigree, good coffee, jovial Irish landlord, quick service, two real fires, L-shaped dining room, panelling, plates, brasses and paintings; maybe piped Classic FM, monthly live music; count the minutes on the church clock's S face opp; disabled access *(CMW, JJW)*

Old Tupton [Derby Rd; A61 S of Chesterfield; SK3965], *Royal Oak*: Friendly three-room pub with up to six real ales in lined glasses, discount on four-pint jugs, reasonable choice of good value freshly made lunchtime (and early evening Fri/Sat), pleasant service, picnic-sets in garden with swings; TVs, darts, fruit machine, maybe piped music; quiz night Mon, skittles Tues *(CMW, JJW)*

☆ **Pilsley** [off A619 Bakewell—Baslow; SK2471], *Devonshire Arms*: Welcoming tastefully refurbished local with good value generous home-made fresh food, carvery some evenings (may need to book), well kept Mansfield Riding and Old Baily and a guest such as Batemans, public bar area for walkers and children; lovely village handy for Chatsworth Farm and Craft Shops *(IHR, Norma and Keith Bloomfield, M Joyner)*

☆ **Rowarth** [off A626 in Marple Bridge at Mellor sign, sharp left at Rowarth sign, then follow Little Mill sign; OS Sheet 110 map ref 011889 – but need Sheet 109 too; SK0189], *Little Mill*: Beautiful tucked-away setting, unusual features inc working waterwheel, vintage Pullman-carriage bedrooms; cheap cheerful plentiful bar food all day (may be a wait), big open-plan bar with lots of little settees, armchairs and small tables, Banks's, Hansons, Robinsons Best Mild and Bitter and a guest beer, hospitable landlord, busy upstairs restaurant; can be smoky, pub games, juke box; children welcome, pretty garden dell across stream great for them, with good play area; bedrooms *(Bronwen and Steve Wrigley, Martin and Karen Wake, Eddie Edwards, LYM)*

☆ **Rowsley** [A6; SK2566], *Grouse & Claret*: Spacious and comfortable if unpubby Mansfield Landlords Table family dining pub in well refurbished old stone building, good reasonably priced food (all day weekends) from carvery counter with appetising salad bar, friendly helpful efficient service, no-smoking area, decent wines, open fires; tap room popular with walkers, tables outside; good value bedrooms, small camp site behind nr river *(Brian Marsden, DC, G Washington, David and Mary Webb, R Moorehead, Mr Cameron)*

☆ **Shardlow** [3½ miles from M1 junction 24 The Wharf, off A6 towards Derby; SK4330], *Malt Shovel*: Old pub in 18th-c former maltings attractively set by canal, good cheap changing lunchtime food, well kept Marstons and guest ales, welcoming quick service; odd-angled walls, good open fire; no small children, seats out by water *(JDM, KM, Roger Bellingham, P R White, LYM)*

Shardlow, *Clock Warehouse*: Very child-oriented dining pub in handsome 18th-c brick-built warehouse with picture windows overlooking attractive canal basin, well kept Mansfield real ales, play areas indoors and out, tables outside too; bedrooms *(LYM)*

☆ **Shottlegate** [Ashbourne Rd (A517 W of Belper); SK3247], *Hanging Gate*: Charming much improved Bass Tavern dining pub, above-average food all day inc limited but interesting vegetarian choice, also pleasant bar with attractive settles, Bass and a guest ale, and decent choice of sensibly priced wines esp New World; polite helpful staff, garden *(JDM, KM, Jo and Gary Charlton, Louise Medcalf)*

☆ **Smalley** [A608 Heanor—Derby; SK4044], *Bell*: Refreshing warmly welcoming village pub, good atmosphere in two rooms, one split for diners – good changing food from new chef; well kept ales such as Marstons Pedigree, Ruddles County and Whim Hartington and Mushroom Mild, good choice of wines, particularly neat polite staff, post office annexe, tables out in front and on big relaxing lawn with play area, beautiful array of hanging baskets; attractive bedrooms behind *(Jack and Philip Paxton, David and Kay Ross, the Didler)*

Sparklow [SK1266], *Royal Oak*: Friendly, with well kept Burton Bridge, Mansfield and other guest beers, very varied good food inc vegetarian; children genuinely welcome, on Tissington Trail *(Terry King)*

Spitewinter [Matlock Rd; A632 SW of Chesterfield; SK3366], *Three Horse Shoes*: Very well run, with Mansfield beers, good food inc good range of puddings, no-smoking restaurant; panoramic views of Chesterfield *(Frank Gorman)*

Stanton in Peak [off A6 Matlock—Bakewell; SK2464], *Flying Childers*: Cosy and unspoilt right-hand room with coal fire, Wards Sheffield Best and a guest beer, good value filled rolls, very welcoming landlord; in delightful steep stone village, overlooking verdant valley *(the Didler)*

nr **Sudbury** [Aston Bridge; A515, about 2 miles S; SK1631], *Boars Head*: Rambling pub/hotel handy for Sudbury Hall, good value lunchtime carvery and well presented bar food, well kept Bass and Ruddles County, cheerful efficient service despite the bustle; restaurant; bedrooms (motel-type) *(Norma and Keith Bloomfield)*

Taddington [SK1472], *Queens Arms*: Attractively furnished and decorated, varied generous enjoyable food from sandwiches up inc good children's dishes, well kept Marstons Pedigree, John Smiths and Theakstons, very friendly staff; quiet village in good walking country *(Rita and Keith Pollard, R Davies)*

Ticknall [B5006 towards Ashby de la Zouch; SK3423], *Chequers*: Small, friendly and full of atmosphere, with vast 16th-c inglenook fireplace, bright brass, old prints, well kept Marstons Pedigree and seasonal beers, Ruddles Best and County; nice garden, good walking area *(the Didler, JP, PP, LYM)*; [7 High St (Ashby rd)], *Staff of Life*: Neat and friendly local with well kept beer, good generous food at most attractive prices, very wide choice, meat cooked wonderfully; open fire, restaurant *(C A Hall, Joan and Michel Hooper-Immins)*

☆ **Tideswell** [SK1575], *George*: Spacious and comfortably refurbished, with simple traditional decor and furnishings, separate room areas with nice balance between eating and drinking, wide choice of good value simple but generous home cooking (super ploughman's), well kept Hardys & Hansons, open fires, welcoming staff; tables in front overlooking pretty village, sheltered back garden; children welcome; 60s music Fri, good value bedrooms, pleasant walks *(Mrs M A Stevenson, Norma and Keith Bloomfield, Tony and Wendy Hobden, BB)*

Tintwistle [Old Rd; off A628, N side; SK0297], *Bulls Head*: Good value generous food, well kept ales and reasonable prices in low-beamed character 16th-c pub, suitable decor, big log fire, very friendly staff, no juke box or machines; handy for Woodhead Pass, but may be cl some weekday lunchtimes *(David Hoult, Aileen and Mervyn Winstanley)*

☆ **Wardlow** [B6465; SK1874], *Bulls Head*: Plushly comfortable smart country dining pub with short menu of decent food, good specials and steaks, Wards ale, helpful landlord and welcoming staff, provision for children; no dogs or walking boots *(Geoffrey Lindley, DC, LYM)*

Weston on Trent [Weston Hall, 5 miles SE of Derby; SK4028], *Coopers Arms*: Tall and imposing early 17th-c manor house converted in early 1990s, massive stonework and ancient beams, comfortable carpeted bars in former rhubarb-forcing cellar, good food counter with changing menu from hot filled rolls and good home-made soup up, Bass, Worthington and a guest beer such as Fullers London Pride, huge log fire; conservatory, tables outside, fishing in lake; bedrooms *(JDM, KM)*; *Old Plough*: Village pub with Edwardian decor, well kept Ansells and guest beers, good choice of food and of wines, no-smoking eating area, helpful staff, children's/games room, good back lawns with play area and barbecues *(M Joyner)*

Winster [B5056 above village; SK2460], *Miners Standard*: Welcoming local doing well under newish landlord and his friendly family, well kept Mansfield Mild and Bitter, Marstons Pedigree and Wadworths 6X, reasonably priced bar food, big open fires, interesting lead-mining photographs and minerals, ancient well; restaurant, attractive view from garden; children allowed away from bat *(Alan and Heather Jacques, IHR)*

☆ **Youlgreave** [Church St; SK2164], *George*: Handsome yet unpretentious stonebuilt local opp church, quick friendly service, good range of reasonably priced home-made food, comfortable banquettes, well kept Scottish Courage ales; flagstoned locals' and walkers' side room, games room, juke box; attractive village, roadside tables outside; handy for Lathkill Dale and Haddon Hall *(DC, Jeanne Cross, Paul Silvestri)*

Youlgreave, *Bulls Head*: Traditional big village pub with atmosphere, hearty food from tasty toasties up, well kept Marstons ales inc changing Head Brewers Choice, darts and pool; popular with walkers and locals *(Mark and Heather Williamson, DC)*; [High St], *Farmyard*: Comfortable low-ceilinged local with well kept Mansfield Bitter and Riding and a guest such as Charles Wells Bombardier, fire in impressive stone fireplace, old farm tools, cheap food, big upstairs restaurant; children, walkers and dogs welcome, TV, tables in garden *(Kerry Law, Paul Robinshaw, DC)*

If a service charge is mentioned prominently on a menu or accommodation terms, you must pay it if service was satisfactory. If service is really bad you are legally entitled to refuse to pay some or all of the service charge as compensation for not getting the service you might reasonably have expected.

Devon

For yet another year this favoured county has come up trumps with an excellent crop of new entries: the Anchor in the nice seaside village of Beer, notable for excellent fish and seafood; the relaxed and unspoilt George at Blackawton, with splendid beers and good food; the George at Chardstock – friendly licensees, and a nice place to stay (bouncing happily back into the main entries after an absence); the welcoming Wild Goose tucked away in Combeinteignhead (good jazz nights); the civilised, relaxed and very individual Union at Dolton (particularly enjoyable food); the Boathouse opposite lovely Instow beach – an exemplary seaside pub; the Bickley Mill nestling into its lush valley just outside Kingskerswell, a good relaxed dining pub; the Dolphin at Kingston, another former main entry making good again under really friendly licensees; the Church House at Marldon, another justly popular dining pub; and the quietly comfortable Rising Sun at Umberleigh, an excellently run fishing inn with good food. This year, Devon's top six pubs for food are the Cott at Dartington (a very popular all-rounder), the very well run Castle at Lydford (on a really hot streak at the moment – with the first vegetarian table d'hôte we've seen in a pub), the New Inn at Coleford (hard-working licensees make the most of the West Country's fine local produce), the Old Rydon at Kingsteignton (really good food in surroundings of considerable character), the Kings Arms at Stockland (a magnificent choice of food) and the Maltsters Arms at Tuckenhay (new licensees turning up trumps on the food side, and restoring a truly pubby atmosphere). Of these, the Kings Arms at Stockland is currently proving so enjoyable for meals out that it is our choice as Devon Dining Pub of the Year. Other pubs here that are currently doing particularly well are the Sloop at Bantham (enjoyable food, a nice spot), the unspoilt Fountain Head at Branscombe (brews its own beers), the Masons Arms there (successful refurbishment, good food), the Coach & Horses at Buckland Brewer (a popular all-rounder now in the safe hands of the previous landlord's son), the unpretentious Butterleigh Inn at Butterleigh (enjoyable food), the Five Bells at Clyst Hydon (good food, very hard-working licensees), the Anchor at Cockwood (splendid for seafood), the Nobody Inn at Doddiscombsleigh (a first-class all-rounder), the Drewe Arms at Drewsteignton (surprising us by developing good imaginative food without losing its preciously unspoilt character), the civilised and restful Rock at Haytor Vale (good food), the very unmanorial Manor at Lower Ashton (cheerful combination of good beer with enjoyable food), the nicely isolated chatty Warren House near Postbridge on Dartmoor, the lovely old Church House at Rattery (good simple food), the well set and distinctive Journeys End at Ringmore (good food), the tiny little creekside Millbrook at South Pool (good food), the distinguished old Oxenham Arms at South Zeal, the friendly (and child-friendly) Otter at Weston, and the unspoilt Rugglestone just far enough outside touristy Widecombe to be tracked down only by those in the know. Among the Lucky Dip entries at the end of the chapter, current front runners, all inspected and approved by us, are the Watermans Arms at Ashprington, Fishermans Cot at Bickleigh, Poltimore Arms at Brayford,

Bridford Inn at Bridford, Coppa Dolla at Broadhempston, Linny at Coffinswell, Hunters Lodge at Cornworthy, Union at Denbury, Ferry Boat at Dittisham, Anglers Rest near Drewsteignton, Pyne Arms at East Down, Stags Head at Filleigh, Rock at Georgeham, Church House at Holne, Rising Sun in Lynmouth, White Hart at Moretonhampstead, Old Ship in Sidmouth, Bridge just outside Topsham, Old Church House at Torbryan, Kingsbridge in Totnes, Westleigh Inn at Westleigh and Kings Arms at Winkleigh. Devon drinks prices are around the national average; we found the Imperial, a showpiece Wetherspoons pub in Exeter, much the cheapest for beer, and the Fountain Head at Branscombe (brewing its own), Anchor at Beer and Union at Dolton (getting beer from small local breweries) were also much cheaper than average.

ABBOTSKERSWELL SX8569 Map 1

Court Farm

Wilton Way; look for the church tower

This is an attractive 17th-c farmhouse with quite a bit of character in its various rooms. The long bar has a mix of seats on the polished crazy flagstones, a nice big round table by an angled black oak screen, a turkey rug in one alcove formed by a low granite wall with timbers above, a long rough-boarded bar counter, and a woodburning stove in a stripped red granite fireplace; a further small room is broadly similar with stripped kitchen tables and more spindleback chairs; piped music. On the right of the entrance is the two-roomed public bar with a woodburning stove and fruit machine, and a simple end room with darts, cribbage and dominoes. Bar food includes good daily specials plus home-made soup (£1.95), sandwiches (from £2.50; toasties from £2.20), home-made pâté (£3.35), ploughman's (from £4.35), ham and egg or good vegetable and cashew nut stir-fry (£5.25), home-made steak and kidney pie or whole grilled fresh local plaice (£6.75), steaks (from £7.95), roast rack of lamb with rich madeira sauce (£9.95), and puddings (£2.75); half helpings for children. Well kept Bass, Boddingtons, Flowers Original and IPA, and Wadworths 6X on handpump, and helpful staff. The garden is pretty, and they have their own cricket team. *(Recommended by Mr and Mrs A Scrutton, Jeanne Cross, Paul Silvestri, Chris Reeve, M Joyner, David and Brenda Begg, Andrew Hodges)*

Heavitree (who no longer brew) ~ Tenant Robin Huggins ~ Real ale ~ Meals and snacks (11.30-2.30, 6.30-10; not 25 Dec) ~ (01626) 361866 ~ Children welcome ~ Open 11-11; 12-10.30 Sun

ASHPRINGTON SX8156 Map 1

Durant Arms

Village signposted off A381 S of Totnes; OS Sheet 202 map reference 819571

A new terrace with wooden garden furniture has been added here and there are also seats on the sheltered back garden. It's a friendly and neatly kept inn with a beamed open-plan bar, several open fires, lamps and horsebrasses, fresh flowers, and a mix of seats and tables on the red patterned carpet; there's a lower no-smoking carpeted lounge too, with another open fire. There's quite an emphasis on the good bar food which includes sandwiches, soup (£2.40), seafood pancake (£4.25), ham and eggs, lamb pepperpot, avocado and corn bake or steak and kidney pie (all £5.95), beef stroganoff (£8.75), scallops with bacon and cream sauce (£8.95), poached salmon with lemon and dill (£9.75), sliced barbary duck with gooseberry sauce or sirloin steak (£10.95), and pudddings like rhubarb and apple crumble or bread and butter pudding (£2.95); best to book if you want to be sure of a table. Well kept Flowers Original and IPA, and Wadworths 6X on handpump, and local cider; no games machines or piped music. They have a self-catering cottage in the grounds. The church is opposite and this is a pretty village. *(Recommended by Dr A J and Mrs P G Newton, P Haines, Andrew Hodges, J S Evans, Iain Robertson, B J Harding, David Carr)*

Free house ~ Licensees Graham and Eileen Ellis ~ Real ale ~ Meals and snacks ~ (01803) 732240 ~ Children welcome ~ Open 11.30-2.30, 6(6.30 winter)-11; 12-2.30, 7-10.30 Sun ~ Bedrooms: £25S/£50S

AVONWICK SX7157 Map 1

Avon Inn

B3210, off A38 E of Plymouth, at South Brent

Emphasis is very much on the enjoyable food in this busy dining pub, so to be sure of a table, it's best to book. Listed on boards in the small back bar, there might be filled french bread (from £1.95), home-made soup (£2.25), home-made pâté (£3.25), salad of smoked duck breast with an orange vinaigrette (£4.50), stir-fry of quorn with chinese vegetables and noodles (£8), rabbit and venison pie (£8.50), whole grilled lemon sole (£10.25), loin of pork stuffed with spinach and gorgonzola in calvados and cider sauce (£11), steak (£12.50), and daily specials such as crostini (£2.50), seafood risotto (£5.95), veal valdostano (£10.25), and monkfish with pesto and cream (£11.50); there may be Italian dishes on the menu as the licensee is from Italy; authentic espresso coffee. Some decent Italian wines alongside the well kept Badger Best and Bass on handpump; fruit machine and piped music. Decor and furnishings are comfortable and pleasant in a fairly modern style. There are tables out in a pleasant garden by the River Avon. *(Recommended by John Evans, DJW, Stan Edwards; more reports please)*

Free house ~ Licensees Mario and Marilyn Velotti ~ Real ale ~ Meals and snacks (not winter Sun evenings) ~ Restaurant (not winter Sun evenings) ~ (01364) 73475 ~ Children in restaurant ~ Open 11.30-2.30, 6-11; 12-3, 7-10.30 Sun

AXMOUTH SY2591 Map 1

Harbour

B3172 Seaton—Axminster

Popular locally, this thatched stone pub is in a pretty setting, and has some tables in the neat back flower garden. The Harbour Bar has a friendly atmosphere, black oak beams and joists, fat pots hanging from pot-irons in the huge inglenook fireplace, brass-bound cask seats, a high-backed oak settle, and an antique wall clock. A central lounge has more cask seats and settles, and over on the left another room is divided from the no-smoking dining room by a two-way log fireplace. At the back, a big flagstoned lobby with sturdy seats leads on to a very spacious and simply furnished family bar. Well kept Flowers IPA and Original, Otter Ale, and Wadworths 6X on handpump; darts, pool, and winter skittle alley. Good bar food (they tell us prices are unchanged from last year) includes sandwiches (from £1.45), ploughman's (from £3.50), vegetarian dishes (from £4.75), fresh fish (from £5.25), puddings (from £2), and children's menu (£2.25); cheerful service even when busy, and friendly cat. They have a lavatory for disabled people, and general access is good. The handsome church has some fine stone gargoyles. *(Recommended by Paul White, Mr and Mrs McKay, Galen Strawson, Peter and Audrey Dowsett, P and S White)*

Free house ~ Licensees Dave and Pat Squire ~ Real ale ~ Meals and snacks (not winter Sun evenings) ~ (01297) 20371 ~ Children in eating area of bar and in family room ~ Open 11-2.30, 6-11; 12-2.30, 7-10.30 Sun

BANTHAM SX6643 Map 1

Sloop 🛏 🍷

Off A379/B3197 NW of Kingsbridge

Being so close to a lovely sandy beach (just 300 yards over the dunes) and on the South West Coastal Path, this popular 16th-c inn does get very busy at peak times. The black-beamed bar has country chairs around wooden tables, stripped stone walls and flagstones, a woodburning stove, and easy chairs in a quieter side area with a nautical theme. Good bar food includes sandwiches, tasty home-made soup

(£2.30), hot potted shrimps (£3.95), liver and onions (£4.85), scallop mornay (£4.95), mediterranean hotpot (£5.45), good salads (from £6.15), venison casserole (£6.75), Devon lamb steak with cumberland sauce (£8.35), steaks (from £9.65), lots of fish like skate wing (£8.55), monkfish with a light chilli sauce (£9.95), and turbot with a tomato and basil sauce (£10.45), and puddings like home-made lemon crunch, summer pudding or treacle tart (£2.80); hearty breakfasts. Well kept Bass, Blackawton Bitter, Ushers Best and a guest beer on handpump, Churchward's cider from Paignton, 20 malt whiskies, 10 wines by the glass from a carefully chosen wine list (including some local ones), and a good choice of liqueurs and West Country drinks like rum and shrub or brandy and lovage. Darts, dominoes, cribbage, table skittles, and piped music. There are some seats at the back. The bedrooms in the pub itself have the most character. *(Recommended by Nick Lawless, Richard and Robyn Wain, JDM, KM, Andrew Low, Peter and Audrey Dowsett, Dr A J and Mrs P G Newton, A M Stephenson, J L Hall, Andrew Woodgate, Jeanne Cross, Paul Silvestri, Andrew Hodges, Jo and Gary Charlton, Michael Marlow, David Carr)*

Free house ~ Licensee Neil Girling ~ Real ale ~ Meals and snacks (till 10pm) ~ Restaurant ~ (01548) 560489/560215 ~ Children in eating area of bar ~ Open 11-2.30, 6-11; 12-2.30, 7-10.30 Sun; closed evenings 25/26 Dec ~ Bedrooms: £31B/£62B; s/c cottages also

BEER ST2389 Map 1

Anchor 🍷

Fore St

In a charming village with a stream running along one side of the main street, this spreading inn has a good mix of locals (especially those with dinghies) and visitors. It's just up from the beach where you can hire motor boats. The two rooms of the public bar have the most character (one half is more simply furnished than the other): lots of nice old local photographs mostly of sailing and fishing boats on the pale green walls, cushioned wooden wall benches, a couple of nice bow window seats, and a relaxed local feel; well produced piped music, and Otter Bitter and Ale and a guest such as Robinsons Best on handpump; local cider. The lounge bar (leading off the sizeable no-smoking restaurant) has some ropework and ship pictures and mate's and wheelback chairs around a few tables; steps lead up to another area. It's the very good changing fresh fish that customers enjoy most here – moules marinières (£4.95), good oysters (half-a-dozen £5.95), fillet of tuna wrapped in filo pastry with sun-dried tomatoes and fresh tarragon (£10.95), lobster salad (from £11.25), fillet of bass with a saffron sauce garnished with king prawns (£11.50), and grilled fillet of red mullet on red and green pepper sauces (£12); also, bar snacks like sandwiches (from £1.75; the crab are generous, £3.30), chicken and coconut soup or crab bisque (£2.10), ploughman's (£3.95), and home-made burger (£4.50), and more elaborate dishes such as warm spicy Italian sausage with mixed bean braise and marinated red peppers (£4.95), grilled lamb cutlets with a bacon and port sauce (£10.95), medallions of pork with prawns and apricots in a brandy sauce (£11.50), and puddings with clotted cream (£3.10). Darts, cribbage, dominoes, and fruit machine. *(Recommended by Basil Minson, Gerald Barnett, J H James, Peter and Audrey Dowsett, Andy and Jill Kassube, Don and Thelma Beeson)*

Free house ~ Licensee David Boalch ~ Real ale ~ Meals and snacks (12-2, 7-9.30) ~ Restaurant ~ (01297) 20386 ~ Children in eating area of bar until 8.30 ~ Open 11-11; 12-10.30 Sun; 11-2.30, 5.30-11 in winter; closed evening 25 Dec ~ Bedrooms: £40B/£53B

BERRYNARBOR SS5646 Map 1

Olde Globe ★ £

Village signposted from A399 E of Ilfracombe

Children are made welcome in this rambling 13th-c pub – there's a play frame and ball pool inside, and an activity house in the garden. The series of dimly lit homely rooms have low ceilings, curved deep-ochre walls, and floors of flagstones or of ancient lime-ash (with silver coins embedded in them). There are old high-backed oak settles (some carved) and plush cushioned cask seats around antique tables, and lots of cutlasses, swords, shields and fine powder flasks, a profusion of genuinely old pictures, priests (fish-coshes), thatcher's knives, sheep shears, gin traps, pitchforks, antlers, and copper warming pans. Well kept Courage Directors, Ushers Best and a guest beer on handpump, and several country wines; sensibly placed darts, pool, skittle alley, dominoes, cribbage, fruit machine, and piped music. Bar food includes sandwiches (from £1.35), pasty (£1.50), home-made soup (£1.65), ploughman's (£2.80), vegetable lasagne (£4.40), steak and kidney pie (£4.45), gammon and pineapple (£5.70), steaks (from £6.95), daily specials, puddings (from £1.90), children's dishes (£2), and popular main course Sunday lunch (£4.10, children £2); quick, friendly service. The restaurant is no smoking. The crazy-paved front terrace has some old-fashioned garden seats. *(Recommended by R V G Brown, Gerald Barnett, Karen and Garry Fairclough, Ian Phillips, Tony Dickinson, Rita Horridge, R J Walden, Tony Gayfer, Philip and Jude Simmons, Dr A J and Mrs P G Newton)*

Courage ~ Lease: Phil and Lynne Bridle ~ Real ale ~ Meals and snacks ~ Gaslit restaurant ~ (01271) 882465 ~ Children in family/function room with toys ~ Open 11.30-2.30, 6-11; 12-2.30, 7-11 Sun; winter evening opening 7pm

BLACKAWTON SX8050 Map 1

George

Main Street, village signposted off A3122 W of Dartmouth, and off A381 S of Halwell

In a quiet village, this unspoilt pub keeps a changing choice of interesting beers from all over the country such as Princetown Dartmoor IPA and Stout on handpump and a couple of guests like Bank Top Spinning Jenny, Mauldons May Bee or Sutton XSB, as well as Bitberger Pils and Hoegaaden Weissbier on tap and dozens of Belgian bottled beers; they hold a beer festival around the late May bank holiday with live bands. The main bar has some timbering, a mix of cushioned wooden chairs, cushioned wall benches, and wheelbacks on the bare boards, mounted butterflies and a collection of beer mats and pump clips, and hop bines above the bar; another bar has train pictures and a big Loch Lomond station sign on the cream Anaglypta walls, and red Rexine-seated chairs on the dark blue and red patterned carpet. On one wall is a quaint old bow-windowed panel with little drawings of customers scratched on the black paint. There's also a cosy end lounge with an open fire and big bow window with a pleasant view. Good bar food includes lunchtime sandwiches, garlic bread with cheese topping (£1.75), soup (£1.95), chick pea curry (£3.95), two sizes of pizza (from £3.95), haddock fillet in beer batter (£4.25), a choice of organic sausages such as lamb, bacon and garlic or pork and apple (from £4.25), home-baked ham with egg (£4.50), ploughman's or chilli con carne in a tortilla with salsa and sour cream (£4.95), sizzling skillets (from £5.25), steak and kidney pie (£5.30), and puddings (from £2.30). Darts and euchre, and a young alsatian called Oscar. The garden, set below the pub, has several picnic-sets and nice views (but they may be going to extend the pub across it). *(Recommended by Andrew Hodges, Mrs G Tuckey, Mrs M Gaze, Mark Tabbron, Jim Cornish, Elven Money)*

Free house ~ Licensees Mr and Mrs S J O'Dell ~ Real ale ~ Meals and snacks ~ (01803) 712342 ~ Children in eating area of bar ~ Occasional live music Fri evenings ~ Open 12-2.30, 7-11; 12-10.30 Sun; closed Mon lunchtimes

Normandy Arms

OS Sheet 202 map reference 807509

The name of the pub comes from when this whole village was commandeered as a training ground to prepare for the Normandy landings. The quaint main bar has an interesting display of World War II battle gear, a good log fire, and well kept Blackawton Bitter, 44 Special, Devon Gold, and Shepherd's Delight, Ind Coope Burton, and occasional guest beers on handpump. Good bar food includes home-made soup (£1.95), sandwiches (from £1.95), vegetable pancake (£3.25), ploughman's (£3.95), home-made chicken liver pâté (£4.50), steak and kidney pie

(£4.95), whole lemon sole or pork in cider and cream (£8.95), steaks (from £8.95), and home-made puddings like tipsy cake or apple pie (from £2.75); children's menu (from £2.75). The restaurant is no smoking. Sensibly placed darts, pool, shove-ha'penny, cribbage, dominoes, and piped music. Some tables out in the garden. *(Recommended by Mr and Mrs A Scrutton, JP, PP, D B Jenkin, A M Stephenson, J D Cloud, C Sinclair, Sheila and John French, Elven Money, John and June Freeman; more reports please)*

Free house ~ Licensees Jonathan and Mark Gibson ~ Real ale ~ Meals and snacks (not Sun evenings Nov-Mar) ~ Restaurant ~ (01803) 712316 ~ Children in restaurant and games room ~ Open 12-2.30, 6.30-11 (10.30 winter Mon-Thurs); 12-11 Sat; 12-3, 7-10.30 Sun; closed 25 Dec ~ Bedrooms: £30/£48B

BRANSCOMBE SY1988 Map1

Fountain Head

Upper village, above the robust old church; village signposted off A3052 Sidmouth—Seaton

Readers are fond of this unspoilt 14th-c local, looking down a lane lined by thatched cottages. The own-brewed beers are popular too – Branoc, Jolly Geff (named after Mrs Luxton's father, the ex-licensee), summer Summa'that, and winter Hells Belles, plus summer guest beers, and their midsummer weekend beer festival which comprises three days of spitroasts, barbecues, live music, Morris men, and over 30 real ales. The room on the left – formerly a smithy – has forge tools and horseshoes on the high oak beams, a log fire in the original raised firebed with its tall central chimney, and cushioned pews and mate's chairs. On the right, an irregularly shaped, more orthodox snug room has another log fire, white-painted plank ceiling with an unusual carved ceiling-rose, brown-varnished panelled walls, and rugs on its flagstone-and-lime-ash floor; the children's room is no smoking, the airedale is called Max, and the black and white cat, Casey Jones (who has two new hips this year). Bar food includes cockles or mussels (£1.75), sandwiches (from £2; good fresh crab when available £2.95), ploughman's (£3.95), steak and kidney pie or home-cooked ham and eggs (£5.25), evening grills (from £6.50), daily specials like fried sardines (£3.95), fresh battered cod (£5.25, on Fridays), pork steak in mustard sauce (£6.50), and children's dishes (from £1.50). Darts, shove-ha'penny, cribbage, dominoes. There are seats out on the front loggia and terrace, and a little stream rustling under the flagstoned path. *(Recommended by S Tait, S Lonie, Comus Elliott, Peter and Audrey Dowsett, JP, PP, Andy and Jill Kassube)*

Free house ~ Licensee Mrs Catherine Luxton ~ Real ale ~ Meals and snacks ~ (01297) 680359 ~ Children in own small room; must be over 10 in Forge in evening ~ Solo/duo guitar summer Thurs evenings with barbecue ~ Open 11-3, 6-11; 12-3(2.30 in winter), 6(7 in winter)-10.30 Sun; 11.30-2.30, 7-11 in winter ~ S/c available

Masons Arms

Main St; signed off A3052 Sidmouth—Seaton

Quite a few changes to this popular inn this year – the main one being that the enthusiastic licensee is now taking more of a back seat and has employed able new managers. The no-smoking Old Worthies bar now has a slate floor, a new fireplace with a two-sided woodburning stove, and woodwork that has been stripped back to the original pine. The newly redecorated no-smoking restaurant (warmed by one side of the woodburning stove) has been stripped back to dressed stone in parts, and is used as bar space on busy lunchtimes. The rambling low-beamed main bar has a massive central hearth in front of the roaring log fire (spit roasts on Tuesday and Sunday lunch and Friday evenings), windsor chairs and settles, and a good bustling atmosphere. They have reduced their choice of popular bar food to improve quality and reduce waiting time: lunchtime sandwiches, soups like carrot, honey and ginger or cauliflower and almond (from £2.50), chicken and pistachio terrine with a crispy bacon and chicory salad (£3.95), marinated roast prawns or langoustines with crisp vegetables and a soy and lime sauce (£4.25), steak and kidney pudding (£6.95), cod cakes with wilted leaves and a red pepper and coriander sauce (£7.95), braised pork with root vegetables, calvados and prunes (£8.25), monkfish with potato rosti, spinach and a red wine sauce (£8.50), fillet of beef with gratin dauphinois and a basil and garlic dressing (£12.95), and puddings like raspberry crème brûlée, passion fruit and hazelnut or chocolate steamed pudding or blackcurrant and apple crumble; polite, attentive staff. Well kept Bass, Otter Bitter and Masons, and two guest beers like Greene King Abbott, Morlands Old Speckled Hen or Teignworthy Beachcomber on handpump or tapped from the cask; they hold a summer beer festival and keep 30 malt whiskies, 14 wines by the glass, farm cider, freshly squeezed orange juice. Darts, shove-ha'penny, cribbage, dominoes, and skittle alley. Outside, the quiet flower-filled front terrace has tables with little thatched roofs, extending into a side garden. The bedrooms have been redecorated and refurbished. *(Recommended by Peter and Audrey Dowsett, Comus Elliott, M Clifford, Revd A Nunnerley, Nick Lawless, TP, Paul White, Gerald Barnett, John and Vivienne Rice, L H and S Ede, A Hepburn, S Jenner, L W King, Alan and Barbara Mence, George Atkinson, MCG, P Williams, Gordon, R Boyd)*

Free house ~ Licensees Murray Inglis and Andy Painter ~ Real ale ~ Meals and snacks ~ Restaurant ~ (01297) 680300 ~ Children welcome ~ Occasional live bands ~ Open 11-11; 12-10.30 Sun; 11-3, 6-11 in winter ~ Bedrooms (some in cottage across road): £22(£37B)/£44(£60B)

BROADCLYST SX9897 Map 1

Red Lion

B3121, by church

This is an enjoyable old pub with long-standing licensees and a quiet relaxed atmosphere – no noisy machines or piped music. The long red-carpeted bar has heavy beams, cushioned window seats, some nice chairs around a mix of oak and other tables, and a collection of carpenter's planes; a flagstoned area has cushioned pews and low tables by the fireplace, and at the end of the L-shaped room are big hunting prints and lots of team photographs. Good bar food includes home-made soup (£2), sandwiches (from £2.10), home-made chicken liver pâté (£3.50), lamb kidneys in sherry (£3.95), ploughman's (from £4.85), vegetable lasagne (£4.95), steak and kidney pie or pork and apple in cider casserole (£5.50), rump steak (£8.25), daily specials, puddings (£3), children's meals (from £2.40), and roast Sunday lunch (£5.50). Well kept Bass, Eldridge Pope Royal Oak, Worthington Best, and a guest like Greene King Abbot on handpump; beamed skittle alley. There are picnic-sets on the front cobbles and more seats in a small enclosed garden across the quiet lane. *(Recommended by Jeanne and George Barnwell, S Gregory, Dr D J Walker, Stan Edwards, S Gregory, Wayne Wheeler, Lynn Sharpless, Bob Eardley, Alan Kitchener, E V M Whiteway, James Flory, Anthony Barnes; also in the Good Hotel Guide)*

Free house ~ Licensees Stephen and Susan Smith ~ Real ale ~ Meals and snacks (till 10pm) ~ Restaurant ~ (01392) 461271 ~ Children welcome if quiet ~ Open 11-3, 5.30(6 Sat)-11; 12-3, 7-10.30 Sun

BROADHEMBURY ST1004 Map 1

Drewe Arms ★ 🍴 🍷

Signposted off A373 Cullompton—Honiton

Thatched and very pretty, this 15th-c inn is in a charming village of similar cream-coloured cottages. The chatty bar has neatly carved beams in its high ceiling, and handsome stone-mullioned windows (one with a small carved roundabout horse). On the left, a high-backed stripped settle separates off a little room with three tables, a mix of chairs, flowers on sturdy country tables, plank-panelled walls painted brown below and yellow above with attractive engravings and prints, and a big black-painted fireplace with bric-a-brac on a high mantlepiece; some wood carvings, walking sticks, and framed watercolours for sale. The flagstoned entry has a narrow corridor of a room by the servery with a couple of tables, and the cellar bar has simple pews on the stone floor. It's the fresh fish that draws in most customers, though locals are quite happy to drop in for just a chat and drink. From the bar menu, there might be fillet of plaice (£9), sea bream with chilli and orange butter or whole griddled lemon sole (£9.50), fillet of brill (£10.50), half a crab salad (£11), and half a lobster salad (£12.50), as well as pea, ham and mint soup (£4), open sandwiches (from £5.25), hot chicken and bacon salad (£8), and puddings like pear tarte tatin or chocolate marquis; there's also a three-course menu (£21) which can be eaten anywhere in the pub – or in the flower-filled garden. Well kept Otter Bitter, Ale, Bright and Head tapped from the cask, and a very good wine list laid out extremely helpfully – including 10 by the glass. There are picnic-sets in the lovely garden which has a lawn stretching back under the shadow of chestnut trees towards a church with its singularly melodious hour-bell. (*Recommended by Patrick Hancock, Jacquie and Jim Jones, Comus Elliott, Alan and Paula McCully, John Askew, Basil Minson, JP, PP, Karen Jeal, Howard and Margaret Buchanan, Peter and Margaret Frost, John and Sally Clarke, Galen Strawson, T L Rees, S Rolt, Philip Vernon, Kim Maidment, James Flory, Helen Morton, Liz Bell, R J Walden, Mavis and Robert Harford)*

Free house ~ Licensees Kerstin and Nigel Burge ~ Real ale ~ Meals and snacks (till 10pm; not Sun evening) ~ Restaurant (not Sun evening) ~ (01404) 841267 ~ Children in restaurant ~ Open 11-3, 6-11; 12-3, 7-10.30 Sun; closed 25 and 31 Dec, 1 Jan

BUCKLAND BREWER SS4220 Map 1

Coach & Horses ★ 🛏

Village signposted off A388 S of Bideford; OS Sheet 190 map reference 423206

Now that Mr Wolfe has retired, his son and partner are fully in charge of this friendly thatched pub, but any changes they have made have been minimal. There's an easy going mix of chatty locals and visitors in the attractively furnished bar with its heavy oak beams, comfortable seats (including a handsome antique settle), and woodburning stove in the inglenook; a good log fire also burns in the big stone inglenook of the cosy lounge. A small back room serves as a children's room; Harding is the friendly cat. Good bar food now includes home-made soup, sandwiches and ploughman's, with daily specials like liver and bacon casserole or local fish pie (£5.50), four home-made curries (£6.50), fresh fish such as sole, skate, trout or bass (from £7.95), and home-made puddings (£2.50). Well kept Flowers Original, Fullers London Pride, and Wadworths 6X on handpump; friendly and efficient service. Darts, pool, cribbage, fruit machine, video game, skittle alley, and piped music. There are tables on a terrace in front, and in the side garden. (*Recommended by Rita Horridge, Steven M Gent, Richard and Robyn Wain, Bett and Brian Cox, Anthony Barnes, R J Walden, Betsy and Peter Little, Mike and Mary Carter, Miss D Buckley, Patrick Renouf, Mr and Mrs G McNeill, Desmond and Pat Morris, Mr and Mrs J Marsh, Mr and Mrs D Ross, Wayne Wheeler, Mrs M Furness, Ann and Colin Hunt, Ben and Sheila Walker, Roger and Jenny Huggins, D B Jenkin)*

Free house ~ Licensees Oliver Wolfe, Nicola Barrass, Ken Wolfe ~ Real ales ~ Meals and snacks ~ Restaurant ~ (01237) 451395 ~ Well behaved children welcome until 9pm ~ Open 12-3, 6-11; 12-3, 7-10.30 Sun; closed evening 25 Dec ~ Bedrooms: £25B/£50B

BUTTERLEIGH SS9708 Map 1

Butterleigh Inn

Village signposted off A396 in Bickleigh; or in Cullompton take turning by Manor House Hotel – it's the old Tiverton road, with the village eventually signposted off on the left

Interesting decorations fill the little rooms in this unpretentious and friendly village pub: pictures of birds and dogs, topographical prints and watercolours, a fine embroidery of the Devonshire Regiment's coat-of-arms, and plates hanging by one big fireplace. One room has a mix of Edwardian and Victorian dining chairs around country kitchen tables, another has an attractive elm trestle table and sensibly placed darts, and there are prettily upholstered settles around the three tables that just fit into the cosy back snug. Tasty bar food includes filled lunchtime rolls, deep-fried vegetables with pesto mayonnaise (£2.95), good thai fishcakes or lentil and mushroom bake (£4.95), chicken and bacon kebab, yorkshire pudding filled with braised steak or steaks (from £7.95), and puddings with clotted cream such as chocolate and ginger timbale, pancakes with hot toffee sauce or meringue glace with fresh fruit coulis (£2.50). Well kept Cotleigh Tawny, Barn Owl and occasional Old Buzzard on handpump; darts, shove-ha'penny, cribbage, dominoes, and piped music; jars of snuff on the bar. Outside are tables on a sheltered terrace and neat small lawn, with a log cabin for children. *(Recommended by Andy and Jill Kassube, B J Harding, R J Walden, Charles Gray, Mr and Mrs P Stubbs, Catherine Lloyd, Gordon, James Flory, Val and Rob Farrant, R T and J C Moggridge)*

Free house ~ Licensees Mike and Penny Wolter ~ Real ale ~ Meals and snacks ~ (01884) 855407 ~ Children welcome lunchtimes only ~ Open 12-2.30, 6(5 Fri)-11; 12-3, 7-10.30 Sun ~ Bedrooms: £20/£34

CHAGFORD SX7087 Map 1

Ring o' Bells

Off A348 Moretonhampstead—Whiddon Down

A brisk breakfast, early morning coffee and snack trade has built up in the friendly old pub which has created a pleasant, relaxed atmosphere for visitors and locals who can borrow the daily papers for a quiet read. The oak-panelled bar has black and white photographs of the village and local characters past and present on the walls, comfortable seats, a big fireplace full of copper and brass, and a log-effect gas fire; there's a small no-smoking candlelit dining room with another fireplace. Good value bar food includes sandwiches with a generous side salad and coleslaw (from £2.50), home-made soup (from £2.50; soup and pudding £4.50), vegetarian dishes, fresh fish (around £6.95), puddings with clotted cream (£2.50), and Sunday roasts (£5.50). Well kept Butcombe Bitter and Wilmots Premium Ale, and St Austell Tinners on handpump, Addlestones cider, and quite a few malt whiskies. Darts, shove-ha'penny, dominoes, and quiet piped music. The sunny walled garden behind the pub has seats on the lawn; dogs are welcome – the pub cats Coriander and Casper will keep them in control. Good moorland walks nearby. *(Recommended by John and Christine Simpson, R J Walden, John Wilson, Mike Doupe, Mike Gorton, Basil Minson, John and Vivienne Rice)*

Free house ~ Licensee Mrs Judith Pool ~ Real ale ~ Meals and snacks (all day – see hours below) ~ Restaurant ~ (01647) 432466 ~ Well behaved children in eating area of bar ~ Open 11-3, 4.30-11; 12-3, 4.30-10.30 Sun; may close earlier on winter weekday evenings ~ Bedrooms: £20/£40(£45B)

CHARDSTOCK ST3004 Map 1

George 🛏

Village signposted off A358 S of Chard

This thatched 13th-c inn is an enjoyable place to stay with friendly, helpful licensees and very good generous breakfasts. The two-roomed original bar has massive beams, ancient oak partition walls, character furnishings, stone-mullioned windows, well converted old gas lamps, and two good log fires; there's also an interestingly laid out two-level back bar. Good bar food includes home-made soup (£2.25), sandwiches (from £3.25), ploughman's (£4.25), vegetarian dishes (from £5.65), liver and bacon, ham and egg and steak and kidney pie, and daily specials such as pheasant with juniper (£9.95), steak with prawns (£11.95), lots of fresh fish dishes like local grilled Membury trout (£8.65), grilled fillets of bream (£9.95), poached lemon sole (£11.95), and scallops and prawns in garlic (£12.95), and puddings (from £2.75). Well kept Boddingtons, Butcombe Bitter, Fullers London Pride, and Charles Wells Bombardier on handpump; skittle alley and piped music. There are some tables out in a back loggia by a flint-cobbled courtyard sheltered by the rather attractive modern extensions to the ancient inn, with more in a safely fenced grass area with a climber and swings. The bedrooms are in a well converted back stable block. Excellent walks nearby. *(Recommended by Steve and Maggie Willey, Mr and Mrs R Hatfield, Nigel Clifton, Mr and Mrs S Barrington)*

Free house ~ Licensee Lin Watkins ~ Real ale ~ Meals and snacks (11-2.30, 6-10) ~ Restaurant ~ (01460) 220241 ~ Children welcome ~ Open 11.30-3, 6-11; 12-3, 7-10.30 Sun ~ Bedrooms: £39B/£49.50B

CHERITON BISHOP SX7793 Map 1

Old Thatch

Village signposted from A30

Very handy for drivers from the busy A30, this popular old pub has redecorated bar and dining areas this year. A large open stone fireplace (lit in the cooler months) separates the rambling, beamed bar from the lounge, local ales such as Beer Engine Rail Ale, Branscombe Vale Branoc and a guest beer are kept on handpump, and they hold a beer festival on May Day bank holiday weekend. Bar food includes sandwiches, fresh fish platter (£4.95), home-made steak and kidney pudding (£5.50), fried skate wings with basil and garlic (£8.95), breast of duck with a raspberry and redcurrant jus (£9.95), and chargrilled monkfish on a red pepper and basil coulis (£11.95). Dominoes, cribbage, and piped music. *(Recommended by K Stevens, Andy and Jill Kassube, Kevin Flack, Paul White, Klaus and Elizabeth Leist, Mr and Mrs S Groves, P and M Rudlin, R Inman, Ewan and Moira McCall, John and Sally Clarke, Lyn and Geoff Hamilton, Ian Phillips, Dr A J and Mrs P G Newton)*

Free house ~ Licensee Stephen Horn ~ Real ale ~ Meals and snacks ~ (01647) 24204 ~ Children in eating area of bar ~ Open 11.30-3, 6-11; 12-3, 7-10.30 Sun ~ Bedrooms: £34.50B/£46B

CHITTLEHAMHOLT SS6521 Map 1

Exeter Inn

Village signposted from A377 Barnstaple—Crediton and from B3226 SW of South Molton

Exmoor National Park is almost on the doorstep of this pleasant thatched 16th-c inn, so there are plenty of outdoor activities nearby. The bars are full of matchboxes, bottles and foreign banknotes, and there's an open woodburning stove in the huge stone fireplace, and cushioned mate's chairs, settles and a couple of big cushioned cask armchairs. A side area has seats set out as booths around the tables under the sloping ceiling. Good bar food includes nice leek and mushroom soup (£1.95), sandwiches (from £1.85; filled french bread from £2.40), filled baked potatoes (from £2.45), home-made chicken liver pâté (£2.75), ploughman's and salads (from £3.95), vegetarian cheese and nut croquettes or hog (haggis-like) pudding (£4.95), local trout (£6.95), good local steaks (£9.95), daily specials, children's meals (from £2.95), and home-made puddings with clotted cream (£2.35); Sunday roast (£5.50; children £4.25). The restaurant is no smoking. Well kept Dartmoor Best, Greene King Abbot, Marstons Pedigree, and Tetleys Bitter on handpump or tapped from the cask, and farm ciders; darts, shove-ha'penny, dominoes, cribbage, fruit machine, trivia, and piped music. The dog is called Alice and the cat, Clyde. The terrace has benches and flower baskets. The pub's cricket team play on Sundays. *(Recommended by J M Lefeaux, D J Tomlinson, C P Scott-Malden, R J Walden, Dr A J and Mrs P G Newton)*

Free house ~ Licensees Norman and Margaret Glenister ~ Real ale ~ Meals and snacks ~ Restaurant ~ (01769) 540281 ~ Children welcome ~ Open 11.30-2.30, 6-11; 12-3, 7-10.30 Sun ~ Bedrooms: £28S/£46S; s/c cottages available

CLYST HYDON ST0301 Map 1

Five Bells

Off B3181 S of Cullompton, via Westcott and Langford

The cottagey garden in front of this very attractive white-painted thatched pub (with its reed pheasants on top) is a fine sight with its thousands of spring and summer flowers, big window boxes and pretty hanging baskets; up some steps is a sizeable flat lawn with picnic-sets, a slide, and pleasant country views. Inside, the long bar is spotlessly kept and divided at one end into different seating areas by brick and timber pillars; china jugs hang from big horsebrass-studded beams, there are many plates lining the shelves, lots of sparkling copper and brass, and a nice mix of dining chairs around small tables (fresh flowers and evening candles in bottles), with some comfortable pink plush banquettes on a little raised area; the pretty no-smoking restaurant is up some steps to the left. Past the inglenook fireplace is another big (but narrower) room they call the Long Barn with a pine dresser at one end and similar furnishings. Popular home-made daily specials might include mussels in cider and cream (£4.95), fresh scallops with bacon and coriander (£6), venison and apricot pie, savoury vegetable crumble or chicken curry with chutneys and poppadums (£6.95), cod fillet topped with tomato, onion and mint, venison and apricot pie or steak and kidney pudding (£7.25), and puddings such as treacle tart, peach and honey sponge or raspberry and sloe gin mousse (£3.25); also, sandwiches (from £2), home-made soup (£2.45), ploughman's (from £4), smoked prawns with garlic mayonnaise (£4.25), cold rare roast beef with chips (£6.95), sirloin steak (from £8.95), and children's menu (from £2.50); there may be a wait for food if they are busy. Well kept Cotleigh Tawny, Dartmoor Best, and Wadworths 6X on handpump, a thoughtful wine list, and several malt whiskies. *(Recommended by R J Walden, Tony Beaulah, Stan Edwards, Catherine Pocock, G Washington, Ewan and Moira McCall, Basil Minson, S Tait, S Lonie, Dr M Owton, James Flory, Alan McQuillian, John Franklin, Evelyn and Derek Walter, Alan Kitchener, Mike and Maggie Betton, Mrs J E Hilditch, Jacquie and Jim Jones)*

Free house ~ Licensees Robin Bean and Charles Hume Smith ~ Real ale ~ Meals and snacks (till 10pm) ~ Restaurant ~ (01884) 277288 ~ Well behaved children in eating areas, but must be over 6 in evening restaurant ~ Open 11.30-2.30, 6.30(7 winter weekdays)-11; 12-2.30, 7-10.30 Sun

COCKWOOD SX9780 Map 1

Anchor

Off, but visible from, A379 Exeter—Torbay

This is a delightful pub with something for everyone – and all are made welcome by the friendly, attentive landlord. The small, low-ceilinged, rambling rooms have black panelling, good-sized tables in various alcoves, and a cheerful winter coal fire in the snug, and the cosy restaurant is no smoking. It's the wide choice of good fresh fish that draws most comments: 30 different ways of serving mussels (£5.95 normal size helping, £9.95 for a large one), 12 ways of serving scallops (from £5.25 for a starter, from £12.95 for a main course), and 10 ways of serving oysters (from £5.95 for starter, from £12.95 for main course); other fresh fish dishes might include fried shark steak (£5.50), locally caught cod (£5.95), whole grilled plaice (£6.50), local crab platter (£6.95), and maybe red snapper, bream, grouper and parrot fish. Non-fishy dishes feature as well, such as sandwiches (from £2.65), home-made chicken liver paté (£3.85), ratatouille (£3.95), home-made steak and kidney pudding (£4.95), 8oz rump steak (£8.95), and children's dishes (£2.10). Well kept Bass, Hardy Royal Oak, Flowers Original, Marstons Pedigree, and two guests on handpump (under light blanket pressure) or tapped from the cask, with rather a good wine list (10 by the glass – they do monthly wine tasting evenings September-June), a good choice of brandies, 50 malt whiskies, and West Country cider; darts, dominoes, cribbage, fruit machine, and piped music. From the tables on the sheltered verandah here you can look across the road to the bobbing yachts and crabbing boats in the landlocked harbour. Nearby parking is difficult when the pub is busy – which it usually is. *(Recommended by Peter Burton, Keith Louden, Jeanne Cross, Paul Silvestri, John Beeken, Susan and Nigel Wilson, John and Christine Simpson, John and Vivienne Rice, Jean and Douglas Troup, Basil Minson, R J Walden, Peter and Rosie Flower, Peter and Jenny Quine)*

Heavitree (who no longer brew) ~ Tenants T Morgan, Miss A L Sanders ~ Real ale ~ Meals and snacks (12-3, 6.30-10) ~ Restaurant ~ (01626) 890203 ~ Children in eating area of bar ~ Open 11-11; 12-10.30 Sun

COLEFORD SS7701 Map 1

New Inn

Just off A377 Crediton—Barnstaple

For 10 years, the friendly licensees have been running this 600-year-old inn, one of the oldest 'new' inns in the country. They remain as enthusiastic as ever and continue to promote good fresh produce using local suppliers for their fish, meat, free range eggs, cheese and so forth. From the seasonally changing menus, there might be cream of local crab soup (£3.50), grilled goat's cheese with walnuts and walnut oil salad (£4.25), Brixham fish pie, wild mushroom, crouton and cashew nut salad with garlic potato cake or venison sausages with cumberland sauce (all £6.95), chicken stroganoff (£8.95), seafood platter (£9.95), braised guinea fowl in a tomato and herb sauce (£10.25), and puddings like chocolate cups filled with chocolate rum mousse with orange sauce, treacle tart with clotted cream or ginger steamed pudding (£2.95); the restaurant is no smoking. Well kept Badger Best, Otter Ale, Wadworths 6X, and a guest beer on handpump, an extensive wine list (some from a local vineyard), quite a range of malt whiskies, and ports and cognacs. Four interestingly furnished areas spiral around the central servery with ancient and modern settles, spindleback chairs, plush-cushioned stone wall seats, some character tables – a pheasant worked into the grain of one – and carved dressers and chests, as well as paraffin lamps, antique prints and old guns on the white walls, and landscape plates on one of the beams and pewter tankards on another; the resident parrot is chatty and entertaining. The servery itself has settles forming stalls around tables on the russet carpet, and there's a winter log fire; fruit machine (out of the way up by the door), darts, and piped music. Big car park. There are some benches and seats outside by the stream. *(Recommended by R J Walden, J M Lefeaux, Guy Vowles, David and Ruth Shillitoe, Dr A J and Mrs P G Newton, D B Jenkin, M Fynes-Clinton, T Pascall, David and Mandy Allen, Neil and Anita Christopher)*

Free house ~ Licensees Paul and Irene Butt ~ Real ale ~ Meals and snacks ~ Restaurant ~ (01363) 84242 ~ Children in eating area of bar and in restaurant ~ Open 12-3, 6-11; 12-3, 7-10.30 Sun; closed 25-26 Dec ~ Bedrooms: £46B/£60B

COMBEINTEIGNHEAD SX9071 Map 1

Wild Goose

Just off unclassified coast road Newton Abbot—Shaldon, up hill in village

On our Monday evening inspection, the regular jazz session was in full swing and this old pub had a marvellously buoyant atmosphere. The hard-working licensees have been here 13 years and have built up a good solid regular trade – this is home to the local cricket club, dogs are welcome, and there is no juke box or piped music. The spacious back beamed lounge has a mix of wheelbacks, red plush dining chairs, a decent mix of tables, and french windows to the garden; the front bar has some red Rexine seats in the window embrasures of the thick walls, flagstones in a small area by the door, some beams and standing timbers, and a step down on the right at the end, with dining chairs around the tables and a big old fireplace with a woodburning stove. The main part has standard lamps in corners, a small carved oak dresser with a big white goose, and a fruit machine; darts, pool, cribbage, backgammon, and shove-ha'penny; a cosy section on the left has an old settee and comfortably well used chairs. They have 30 well kept, monthly rotating beers on six handpumps: Exe Valley Devon Glory, Hop Back Summer Lightning, Otter Ale, Princetown Dartmoor Best, and Teignworthy Reel Ale; a good collection of 30 malt whiskies. Good bar food includes well liked daily specials as well as home-made soup (£2.25), sandwiches (from £2.25), king prawns in filo pastry with sesame and ginger dip (£4.25), ploughman's (from £4.25), ham and egg or home-made vegetarian lasagne (£5.25), home-made steak and kidney pie or jumbo cod fillet (£5.50), steaks (from £8.95), home-made puddings, and Sunday roast lunch (£5.25). *(Recommended by John Wilson, John Barker, Stan Edwards)*

Free house ~ Licensees Rowland and Thelma Honeywill ~ Real ale ~ Meals and snacks (till 10pm) ~ Restaurant ~ (01626) 872241 ~ Well behaved children over 6 in restaurant ~ Trad jazz Mon evenings and annual festival in Sept ~ Open 11.30-2.30, 6.30-11; 12-2.30, 7-10.30 Sun

If you report on a pub that's not a main entry, please tell us any lunchtimes or evenings when it doesn't serve bar food.

DALWOOD ST2400 Map 1

Tuckers Arms

Village signposted off A35 Axminster—Honiton

Down narrow high-hedged lanes is this cream-washed thatched medieval longhouse in a pretty village. The fine flagstoned bar has lots of beams, a log fire in the inglenook fireplace, a woodburning stove, and a random mixture of dining chairs, window seats, and wall settles – including a high-backed winged black one. A side lounge has shiny black woodwork and a couple of cushioned oak armchairs and other comfortable but unpretentious seats, and the back bar has an enormous collection of miniature bottles. You can choose to have a one-course (£9.95), two-course (£13.50 or £16.50) or three-course menu (£16.50 or £19.50), with starters such as celery and leek soup with stilton, terrine of duck with bacon served on a green and orange salad, warm salad of wild mushrooms and garlic prawns or kidneys in red wine, and main courses like red sea bream with oysters in cream muscadet and dill, chicken with wild mushrooms, calvados and cream, rack of lamb with roasted shallots, steaks or sautéed king scallops with tarragon, cider, mustard and cream. Well kept Flowers Original, and Otter Ale and Bitter on handpump kept under light blanket pressure; skittle alley and piped music. The flowering tubs, window boxes and hanging baskets are lovely in summer. *(Recommended by Basil Minson, Mr and Mrs J Bishop, M Clifford, Yavuz and Shirley Mutlu, John and Vivienne Rice, Mike Gordon, Richard and Robyn Wain, L H and S Ede, John and Elspeth Howell, James Nunns, Anthony Barnes, Martin Pritchard, R Walden)*

Free house ~ Licensees David and Kate Beck ~ Real ale ~ Meals and snacks (till 10pm; not evenings 25-26 Dec) ~ Restaurant ~ (01404) 881342 ~ Children in eating area of bar, in restaurant, and in skittle alley ~ Open 12-3, 6.30-11; 12-3, 7-10.30 Sun ~ Bedrooms: £27S/£45S

DARTINGTON SX7762 Map 1

Cott ★ (food) (stay) (wine)

In hamlet with the same name, signposted off A385 W of Totnes opposite A384 turn-off

'A terrific pub' is how one reader describes this lovely thatched 14th-c place – and a huge number of customers agree with this; indeed, it remains one of the most popular pubs in our book – as somewhere to stay, to enjoy a good meal, and to feel genuinely welcomed by the caring licensees and their staff. The communicating rooms of the traditional, heavy-beamed bar have big open fires, flagstones, and polished brass and horse-harnesses on the whitewashed walls; one area is no smoking. Food changes daily and may include soups such as tomato, carrot and chive or cream of mushroom and spinach (£3.50), chargrilled baby squid with chilli jam and aioli dip (£5.95), duck and orange terrine with a kumquat confit (£4.25), vegetable moussaka with a feta cheese salad (£7.25), steak and kidney pie (£7.95), game casserole (£8.25), half shoulder of lamb in a redcurrant, madeira and rosemary sauce (£10.95), sirloin steak (£11.95), Cornish scallops with bacon and shallots in a cream and pernod sauce (£12.95), and bass with ginger, lemon, chives, and roast almonds (£13.50); it is essential to book; ample breakfasts. The restaurant is no smoking. Well kept Bass, Butcombe Bitter and Otter Bitter on handpump, Inch's cider, 11 interesting wines by the glass from a very good wine list, and a good selection of malt whiskies. There's a pub cricket team – they'd welcome enquiries from visiting teams. Harvey the cat still likes to creep into bedroom windows in the middle of the night (despite advancing age), and Minnie and Digger the jack russells have been joined by Molly the black labrador and remain keen to greet visitors. There are picnic-sets in the garden with more eating on the terrace amidst the attractive tubs of flowers. Good walks through the grounds of nearby Dartington Hall, and it's pleasant touring country – particularly for the popular Dartington craft centre, the Totnes—Buckfastleigh steam railway, and one of the prettiest towns in the West Country, Totnes. *(Recommended by Gethin Lewis, Nick Lawless, Andrew Hodges, W W Burke, Bett and Brian Cox, John Askew, Revd A Nunnerley, J F M West, Richard and Robyn Wain, Mike and Karen England, Jacquie and Jim Jones, Mrs Mary Woods, Mick*

Hitchman, Mr and Mrs D Price, Miss L Hodson, John and Christine Simpson, Nigel Flook, Betsy Brown, Mr and Mrs W Welsh, D H and M C Watkinson, Chris Nelson, Ian Phillips, P Rome, S C Nelson, Michelle Matel, Ted George, Mr and Mrs D Wilson, David and Nina Pugsley, Alan McQuillian, DAV, Catherine Lloyd, Liz Bell, J D Cloud, DWJ)

Free house ~ Licensees David and Susan Grey and Mark Annear ~ Real ale ~ Meals and snacks (12-2.15, 6.30-9.30; not 25 Dec) ~ Restaurant ~ (01803) 863777 ~ Children in restaurant ~ Live entertainment Sun evenings ~ Open 11-2.30, 5.30-11; 12-3, 7-10.30 Sun; closed 25 Dec ~ Bedrooms: £52.50B/£65B

DARTMOUTH SX8751 Map 1

Cherub

Higher St

Although only a pub for some 30 years, this is Dartmouth's oldest building and is Grade II* listed, with each of the two heavily timbered upper floors jutting further out than the one below (and hung with pretty summer flowering baskets). Inside, the bustling bar has tapestried seats under creaky heavy beams, leaded-light windows, and a big stone fireplace; upstairs is the low-ceilinged no-smoking dining room. Well kept Morlands Old Speckled Hen, Summerskills Old Cherub Bitter, Wadworths 6X and a guest beer on handpump, quite a few malt whiskies, and Addlestones cider. Bar food includes sandwiches (from £2), soup (£2.50), filled baked potatoes (from £3.50), ploughman's (£4), ratatouille, chilli con carne or smoked haddock in white wine and cheese sauce (£5), tiger prawns in filo pastry, and steak sandwich or seafood risotto (£6.50). In summer (when it does get packed), the flower baskets are very pretty. *(Recommended by John and Christine Simpson, Nick Lawless, John Barker, John Askew, Colin Thompson, I Buckmaster, Ted George, J D Cloud, Alan McQuillian, Mr and Mrs I Buckmaster, Luke Worthington, David Carr, Peter and Rosie Flower, K and J Brooks, Mary Woods, Catherine Lloyd, Ian and Jane Irving, TBB, M Joyner, Simon Penny, Simon Walker, Alan and Paula McCully, Jo and Gary Charlton)*

Free house ~ Licensee Alan Jones, Manager Jilly Sanbrooke ~ Real ale ~ Meals and snacks (till 10pm) ~ Evening restaurant ~ (01803) 832571 ~ Children over 10 in restaurant lunchtime only ~ Open 11-11; 12-10.30 Sun; 11-3, 6-11 in winter

Royal Castle

11 The Quay

There's always a good bustling atmosphere in this rambling 17th-c hotel, overlooking the inner harbour. The left-hand local bar has a balanced mix of locals and visitors, navigation lanterns, glass net-floats and old local ship photographs, and a mix of furnishings from stripped pine kitchen chairs to some interesting old settles and mahogany tables; one wall is stripped to the original stonework and there's a big log fire. On the right in the more sedate, partly no-smoking carpeted bar, they may do winter spit-roast joints on some lunchtimes; there's also a Tudor fireplace with copper jugs and kettles (beside which are the remains of a spiral staircase), and plush furnishings, including some Jacobean-style chairs. One alcove has swords and heraldic shields on the wall. Well kept Boddingtons, Blackawton Bitter, Courage Directors, and Flowers Original on handpump, a wide choice of malt whiskies, and local farm cider; welcoming staff. Dominoes, fruit machine, and piped music. Enjoyable, good value bar food includes toasted sandwiches (from £2.95), home-made soup, pasties, deep-fried brie with gooseberry sauce, ploughman's, gammon and egg (£5.50), steak and kidney pie (£5.95), very good seafood pie and nice prawn and crab salad, daily specials and steaks. *(Recommended by Peter and Audrey Dowsett, Mrs Mary Woods, Lawrence Pearse, E G Parish, M Joyner, B A Gunary, Mike Gorton, Alan and Paula McCully, Simon Penny, David Carr)*

Free house ~ Licensees Nigel and Anne Way ~ Real ale ~ Meals and snacks (11.30-10) ~ Restaurant ~ (01803) 833033 ~ Children in first-floor library lunchtimes only ~ Live music Sun, Mon, Tues and Thurs ~ Open 11-11; 12-10.30 Sun ~ Bedrooms: £55.50B/£91B

DODDISCOMBSLEIGH SX8586 Map 1

Nobody Inn ★ ★

Village signposted off B3193, opposite northernmost Christow turn-off

Still one of the most popular pubs in our book, this atmospheric inn is probably best loved for its marvellous cheeses and exceptional choice of drinks. They keep perhaps the best pub wine cellar in the country – 800 well cellared wines by the bottle and 20 by the glass kept oxidation-free; there's also properly mulled wine and twice-monthly tutored tastings (they also sell wine retail, and the good tasting-notes in their detailed list are worth the £3 it costs – anyway refunded if you buy more than £30-worth); also, a choice of 250 whiskies, local farm ciders, fresh orange juice, and well kept Bass, Nobody's (brewed by Branscombe), Cotleigh Tawny and a guest beer on handpump or tapped straight from the cask. Well liked bar food includes good home-made soup (£2.20), sausage and mash with onion gravy or hot filled panini bread (an Italian bread which when cooked becomes crisp and crunchy on the outside and soft in the middle, £3.50), an incredible choice of around 50 West Country cheeses (half a dozen £4.20; you can buy them to take away as well), and daily specials such as local ostrich and juniper pâté, chicken with orange and ginger, tasty butterbean casserole, venison and stout pudding, salmon fishcake, mediterranean tuna, and mutton in a turmeric, cinnamon and prune sauce (from £5), and puddings such as apple and lovage strudel, treacle tart, and delicious rhubarb and ginger crumble (£3). The restaurant is no smoking. The two rooms of the lounge bar have a relaxed, friendly atmosphere, handsomely carved antique settles, windsor and wheelback chairs, benches, carriage lanterns hanging from the beams, and guns and hunting prints in a snug area by one of the big inglenook fireplaces. There are picnic-sets on the terrace, with views of the surrounding wooded hill pastures. The medieval stained glass in the local church is some of the best in the West Country. No children are allowed inside the pub. *(Recommended by Jacqueline Orme, Dr R Price, Colin Thompson, John Askew, Gordon, Dr and Mrs G H Lewis, Mike and Mary Carter, JP, PP, Guy Vowles, Peter Burton, Jasper Sabey, Basil Minson, Dr Rod Holcombe, G Washington, John Evans, John and Christine Simpson, Richard and Robyn Wain, Andrew Low, Steve Whalley, N P Bayliss, Dallas Seawright, Nigel Flook, Betsy Brown, Catherine Lloyd, David and Nin Pugsley, Mrs F A Ricketts, Alan and Barbara Mence, Comus Elliott, Susan and Nigel Wilson, Lynn Sharpless, Bob Eardley, D H and M C Watkinson, M Fynes-Clinton, Mr and Mrs J B Bishop, Helen Morton, M and J Madley, Catherine Lloyd, Christopher Turner, John Mackeonis, Mr and Mrs D Deas, J Mustoe, Jo and Gary Charlton, E V Whiteway, R J Walden)*

Free house ~ Licensee Nicholas Borst-Smith ~ Real ale ~ Meals and snacks (till 10pm) ~ Evening restaurant (not Sun) ~ (01647) 252394 ~ Open 12-2.30, 6-11; 12-3, 7-10.30 Sun; closed evenings 25-26 Dec ~ Bedrooms (some in distinguished 18th-c house 150yds away): £23(£33B)/£33(£64B)

DOLTON SS5712 Map 1

Union

B3217

The good, interesting and genuinely home-made food in this comfortable and relaxed 17th-c pub benefits from the landlord's interest in shooting, fishing and fungi-foraging, and it's he who does the cooking, while friendly Mrs Fisher is front of house. From the menu, there might be garlic stuffed mushrooms (£4), moules marinières (£4.25), tomato pasta filled with cheese topped with a fresh tomato and herb sauce and fresh grated parmesan (£5.25), breast of chicken with a fresh lime, honey and ginger sauce (£6.95), escalope of pork with marsala wine and cream (£7.50), rib-eye steak (£8.95), king scallops in a cream and vermouth reduction (£9.50), and puddings such as rum pot, special bread and butter pudding or treacle sponge (from £2.50); they also do bar snacks such as home-made soup, lamb-burger in a soft bap (£2), freshly baked french bread (from £2.50), ploughman's (from £3.95), and home-cooked ham with egg (£4.10), with daily specials like tempura prawns with sweet chilli dip (£4), good Italian antipasti, spinach and sweet pepper tart (£6.75), home-made game pie flavoured with port and juniper (£6.95), and mixed seafood stir-fry or grilled halibut steak with lemon butter sauce (£8.50). The restaurant is no smoking. Well kept Barum BSE (from a small new Barnstaple brewery), Sharps Doom Bar, and St Austell HSD, and decent wines. The little lounge bar has a comfortably cushioned window seat, a pink plush chesterfield, a nicely carved priest's table and some dark pine country chairs with brocaded cushions, and dagging shears, tack, country prints, and brass shell cases. On the right and served by the same stone bar counter, is another bar with a chatty, enjoyable atmosphere and liked by locals both eating or dropping in for just a drink: heavy black beams hung with brasses, an elegant panelled oak settle and antique housekeeper's chairs, a small settle snugged into the wall, and various dining chairs on the squared patterned carpet; the big stone fireplace has some brass around it, and on the walls are old guns, two land-felling saws, antlers, some engravings, and a whip. Outside on a small patch of grass in front of the building are some rustic tables and chairs. (*Recommended by David Wallington, DJW*)

Free house ~ Licensees Ian and Irene Fisher ~ Real ale ~ Meals and snacks ~ Restaurant ~ (01805) 804633 ~ Children in eating area of bar and in restaurant ~ Open 12-2.30, 6(7 Sun)-11 ~ Bedrooms: /£45B

DREWSTEIGNTON SX7390 Map 1
Drewe Arms

Signposted off A30 NW of Moretonhampstead

Readers enjoy coming to this old thatched pub with its unpretentious character and friendly licensees. The small rooms have serving hatches, an assortment of simple tables and chairs clustered around huge fireplaces, and well kept Flowers IPA, Marstons Pedigree, Wadworths 6X, and Whitbreads Castle Eden and Grays cider kept on racks in the tap room at the back. Good bar food includes sandwiches, ploughman's, venison sausage with braised red cabbage or baked ham with mustard mash (£5.95), fresh crab and mushroom bake (£6.50), monkfish in parma ham with saffron dressing or grilled bass with salsa verdi and straw chips (£10), and baked fillet steak with fresh horseradish crust (£12.95). Castle Drogo nearby (open for visits) looks medieval, though it was actually built earlier this century. *(Recommended by Robert Gomme, JP, PP, Alan and Paula McCully, Guy Vowles, John Barker, Philip Vernon, Kim Maidment, Neil and Anita Christopher, John and Sally Clarke, Catherine Lloyd, Kerry Law, Annemarie Firstbrook, John Franklin)*

Whitbreads ~ Lease: Janice and Colin Sparks ~ Real ale ~ Meals and snacks ~ Restaurant ~ (01647) 281224 ~ Children in restaurant ~ Jazz Fri evening in barn behind pub ~ Open 11-3, 6-11; 12-3, 7-10.30 Sun ~ Bedrooms: /£50B

DUNSFORD SX8189 Map 1
Royal Oak

Village signposted from B3212

There's a friendly village atmosphere in the light and airy bar of this Victorian pub, and windows look out over the thatched white cottages of this small hill village, and beyond to the fringes of Dartmoor. The central bar, flanked by two dining areas (one is no smoking), dispenses the well kept Flowers IPA and Original, Fullers London Pride, and Greene King Abbot on handpump. Good, well presented home-made bar food includes soup, sandwiches, vegetarian dishes, home-cooked ham and egg (£4.50), and beef and stilton pie (£5.95). Darts, pool, cribbage, dominoes, video game, and piped music; dogs welcome. *(Recommended by Ian Wilson, MRSM, Mike Gorton, Val and Rob Farrant, C and E M Watson; more reports please)*

Free house ~ Licensees Mark and Judy Harrison ~ Real ale ~ Meals and snacks ~ (01657) 252256 ~ Children in eating area of bar ~ Live entertainment monthly Fri evening ~ Open 12-2.30, 6.30-11; 12-2.30, 7-10.30 Sun ~ Bedrooms: £22.50(£27.50)/£40(£45B)

EXETER SX9292 Map 1

Double Locks ★

Canal Banks, Alphington; from A30 take main Exeter turn-off (A377/396) then next right into Marsh Barton Industrial Estate and follow Refuse Incinerator signs; when road bends round in front of the factory-like incinerator, take narrow dead end track over humpy bridge, cross narrow canal swing bridge and follow track along canal; much quicker than it sounds, and a very worthwhile diversion from the final M5 junction

For the younger customers, this remote old lockhouse is a lively place to be with its Thursday evening jazz and 10 real ales. Tapped from the cask or on handpump, the beers might include Adnams Broadside, Branscombe Branoc, Everards Old Original, Fullers London Pride, Greene King Abbot, Smiles Best, Golden Ale, and Heritage, and Youngs Special; Grays farm cider. Bar food includes sandwiches and soup, hot ciabatta topped with roasted vegetables and mozzarella (£3.75), feta and spinach pie (£4.40), and turkey and mushroom pie (£4.65). There's quite a nautical theme in the bar – with ship's lamps and model ships – and friendly service; there have been a few comments from readers about housekeeping this year. Darts, shove-ha'penny, cribbage, dominoes, trivia, and piped music. There are picnic-sets outside and cycle paths along the ship canal. *(Recommended by Paul White, Andy and Jill Kassube, JP, PP, Hilary Dobbie, Vivienne and John Rice, Simon Walker, R J Walden, Catherine Lloyd, Mike Gorton, Barry and Anne)*

Smiles ~ Managers T Stearman and I Williams ~ Real ale ~ Meals and snacks (all day) ~ (01392) 56947 ~ Children welcome ~ Jazz Thurs evening ~ Open 11-11; 12-10.30 Sun

Imperial

New North Road; just off A377 nr St Davids Station

To get to this sumptuous place, you must pass the gated lodge and along a sweeping drive. It was built in 1801 as a private mansion and stands in a 6-acre hillside park with plenty of picnic-sets in the grounds and elegant metal garden furniture in an attractive cobbled courtyard. Inside, there are all sorts of areas such as a couple of little clubby side bars and a great island bar looking into a light and airy former orangery – the huge glassy fan of its end wall is lightly mirrored – and a glorious ex-ballroom filled with elaborate plasterwork and gilding brought here in the 1920s from Haldon House (a Robert Adam stately home that was falling on hard times). The furnishings give Wetherspoons' usual solid well spaced comfort, and there are plenty of interesting pictures and other things to look at. Well kept and very cheap Bass, Courage Directors, Exmoor Stag, Morlands Old Speckled Hen, Theakstons Best, Timothy Taylor Best, and three or four guests. Good bar food includes soup (£1.95), filled french bread (from £2.25; with soup as well £2.75), filled baked potatoes (from £2.70), burger with stilton and bacon sauce (£3.15), mozzarella and tomato pasta (£4.45), pork, ham, apple and cider pie or chicken and pasta in a creamy pepper, sun-dried tomato and cheese sauce (£4.95), and puddings such as exotic fruit salad or lemon and ginger cheesecake (£1.99); between 2pm and 10pm, two people can eat for £5.95. The two fruit machines are silenced and there's no piped music. No under-18s. *(Recommended by Ian Phillips, Jim and Maggie Cowell, Mike and Mary Carter, Mike Gorton, Andrew Hodges, E V M Whiteway)*

Free house ~ Manager Jonathon Randall ~ Real ale ~ Meals and snacks (11-10; 12-9.30 Sun) ~ (01392) 434050 ~ Open 11-11; 11-10.30 Sun

White Hart ★

66 South St; 4 rather slow miles from M5 junction 30; follow City Centre signs via A379, B3182; straight towards centre if you're coming from A377 Topsham Road

For centuries, people have been meeting in the rambling atmospheric bar of this nicely old-fashioned 14th-c inn. There are windsor armchairs and built-in winged settles with latticed glass tops to their high backs, oak tables on the bare oak floorboards (carpet in the quieter lower area), heavy bowed beams in the dark ochre terracotta ceiling hung with big copper jugs, and a log fire in one great fireplace with long-barrelled rifles above it. In one of the bay windows is a set of fine old brass beer engines, the walls are decorated with pictorial plates, old copper and brass platters, and a wall cabinet holds some silver and copper. From the latticed windows, with their stained-glass coats-of-arms, one can look out on the cobbled courtyard – lovely when the wisteria is flowering in May. The Tap Bar, across the yard, with flagstones, candles in bottles and a more wine-barish feel, serves soup (£2.50), rolls filled with cheese (£2.75), hot pastrami, dill pickles and salad (£2.95), local ostrich steak (£4.95) or fillet steak with five spices (£5.95), pasta with courgettes, olives and prawns with a fresh tomato sauce or garlic and herb tagliatelle with sun-dried tomatoes (£5.25), and puddings like treacle tart with clotted cream or chocolate brandy fudge cake with pecan nut sauce (£2.95). There is yet another bar, called Bottlescreu Bill's, even more dimly candlelit, with bare stone walls and sawdust on the floor. It serves much the same food, as well as a respectable range of Davy's wines, and in summer does lunchtime barbecue grills in a second, sheltered courtyard. On Sundays both these bars are closed. Bass, Davy's Old Wallop (served in pewter tankards in Bottlescreu Bill's) and John Smiths on handpump. Bedrooms are in a separate modern block. *(Recommended by D J and P M Taylor, Mark Girling, Mr and Mrs J Pitts, Ian Phillips, R J Walden, E V Whiteway, Barry and Anne, Comus Elliott, Brian and Bett Cox, R T and J C Moggridge, Mrs H Murphy, Anthony Barnes)*

Free house ~ Licensee Graham Stone ~ Real ale ~ Meals and snacks (till 10pm) ~ Restaurant ~ (01392) 279897 ~ Children in eating area of bar and in lounges ~ Open 11-3, 5-11; 11-11 Sat; 12-3, 7-10.30 Sun; closed 24-26 Dec ~ Bedrooms: £57.50B/£84B – not 24-26 Dec

EXMINSTER SX9487 Map 1

Turf ★

Follow signs to Swan's Nest, signposted from A739 S of village, then continue to end of track, by gates; park, and walk right along canal towpath – nearly a mile

Set by the last lock of the Exeter Canal before the estuary of the River Exe, this isolated, friendly pub cannot be reached by car. You can either walk (which takes about 20 minutes along the ship canal) or take a 40-minute ride from Countess Wear in their own boat, the *Water Mongoose* (bar on board; £4 adult, £2.50 child return, charter for up to 56 people £140). They also operate a 12-seater and an 8-seater boat which bring people down the Exe estuary from Topsham quay (15 minute trip, adults £3, child £2). For those arriving in their own boat there is a large pontoon as well as several moorings. From the bay windows of the pleasantly airy bar there are views out to the mudflats – which are full of gulls and waders at low tide – and mahogany decking and caulking tables on the polished bare floorboards, church pews, wooden chairs and alcove seats, and big bright shorebird prints by John Tennent and pictures and old photographs of the pub and its characters over the years on the walls; woodburning stove and antique gas fire. Bar food includes sandwiches (from £2.25; toasties from £2.80), home-made soup (£2.75), garlic bread with melted cheese (£2.95), homity pie (£4.25), lasagne (£6.50), daily specials such as garlic bread topped with goat's cheese, pesto and tomatoes (£4.25), aubergine and lentil moussaka (£5.50) or popular chicken enchiladas (£6.50), and puddings like sticky toffee pudding or apple crumble (from £2.50); on the new deck area you can also have chargrilled steaks and fish (£7.50). The dining room is no smoking. Well kept Dartmoor Best and Morlands Old Speckled Hen on handpump, and Green Valley farm cider; darts, shove-ha'penny, cribbage, dominoes, and piped music. The garden has a children's play area. *(Recommended by Mike Gorton, Mrs F A Ricketts, Catherine Lloyd, EML, Jeanne Cross, Paul Silvestri; have readers stopped coming here? We'd really like reports on this nice pub)*

Free house ~ Licensees Clive and Ginny Redfern ~ Real ale ~ Meals and snacks (not Sun evening) ~ (01392) 833128 ~ Children welcome ~ Open 11-11; 12-10.30 Sun; closed Nov-March (maybe open weekends) ~ Bedrooms: £22.50/£45

HARBERTON SX7758 Map 1

Church House

Village signposted from A381 just S of Totnes

Parts of this ancient pub may be Norman, when it was probably used as a chantry-house for monks connected with the church. There is some magnificent medieval oak panelling, and the latticed glass on the back wall of the open-plan bar is almost 700 years old and one of the earliest examples of non-ecclesiastical glass in the country. Furnishings include attractive 17th- and 18th-c pews and settles, candles, and a large inglenook fireplace with a woodburning stove; one half of the room is set out for eating. The family room is no smoking. Most people choose to eat the daily specials which might include deep-fried brie wrapped in bacon with a spicy redcurrant jelly (£3.95), fresh battered cod (£5.95), mushroom stroganoff (£6.75), steak picado or seafood piri-piri (£7.95), mussel and clam casserole (£15.90) or lamb kleftico (£17.90 for two people), and sticky toffee pudding with clotted cream (£2.95); the standard menu includes home-made soup (£2.35), sandwiches (from £2.50), ploughman's (from £3.95), three locally made sausages with chips (£4.75), a fry-up (£5.95), prawn curry (£7.50), grilled whole plaice (£7.95), and steaks (from £7.95). Well kept Bass, Courage Best, and Charles Wells Bombardier and a guest beer such as Greene King Abbot, Hardy Royal Oak or St Austell HSD on handpump, Churchward's cider, and several malt whiskies; dominoes. *(Recommended by Bob Medland, Margaret and Roy Randle, Paul S McPherson, Jo and Gary Charlton, Richard May, Mr and Mrs D Wilson, Patrick Freeman, Dr and Mrs A Whiteway, DWJ, Dr A J and Mrs P G Newton)*

Free house ~ Licensees David and Jennifer Wright ~ Real ale ~ Meals and snacks (12-1.45, 7-9.30) ~ (01803) 863707 ~ Children in family room ~ Occasional Morris men in summer ~ Open 12(11.30 Sat)-3, 6-11; 12-3, 7-10.30 Sun; closed evenings 25-26 Dec and 1 Jan ~ Bedrooms: £20/£36

HATHERLEIGH SS5404 Map 1

George ♀

A386 N of Okehampton

The little front bar in the original part of this pleasant old pub has huge oak beams, stone walls two or three feet thick, an enormous fireplace, and easy chairs, sofas and antique cushioned settles. The spacious L-shaped main bar was built from the wreck of the inn's old brewhouse and coachmen's loft, and has more beams, a woodburning stove, and antique settles around sewing-machine treadle tables; dominoes, piped music. The right-hand bar, liked by younger customers, has pool, juke box, fruit machine and darts. Well kept Bass, Dartmoor Best and HSD and a guest beer such as Adnams Broadside or Greene King Abbot on handpump, plus Inches cider. Bar food includes soup, sandwiches (from £1.90), filled baked potatoes (from £2.95), garlic chicken livers on toast (£3.40), ploughman's (£3.50), vegetarian stir-fry (£4.95), gammon and egg (£5.25), bacon-wrapped scallops (£6.75), and steaks (from £8.75); daily specials and children's menu. In summer, the courtyard is very pretty with hanging baskets and window boxes on the black and white timbering, and rustic wooden seats and tables on its cobblestones; there's also a walled cobbled garden. *(Recommended by Rita Horridge, JP, PP, David Carr, John Askew, Lynn Sharpless, Bob Eardley, Richard and Rosemary Hoare, Rob Cope, Mrs B Sugarman, Mr and Mrs J D Marsh, Catherine Lloyd, Mrs H Murphy, Dr A J and Mrs P G Newton)*

Free house ~ Licensees David and Christine Jeffries ~ Real ale ~ Meals and snacks (11.30-2.30, 6.30-9.30) ~ Restaurant ~ (01837) 810454 ~ Children in eating area of bar ~ Open 11-3, 6-11; 12-3, 7-11 Sun ~ Bedrooms: £28(£48B)/£49.50(£69.50B)

Places with gardens or terraces usually let children sit there – we note in the text the very very few exceptions that don't.

Tally Ho

Market St (A386)

The own-brewed beers in this friendly pub can be enjoyed here or taken away in bottles or cartons: Potboiler, Jollop (winter only), Tarka Tipple, Thurgia, Nutters, and Master Jack's Mild (spring only); 20 malt whiskies, and Italian grappas. The opened-together rooms of the bar have heavy beams, sturdy old oak and elm tables on the partly carpeted wooden floor, decorative plates between the wall timbers, shelves of old bottles and pottery, and two woodburning stoves. Bar food includes lunchtime sandwiches on a fresh bagel or warm french bread (from £2.75), omelettes (from £3.25), and ploughman's (from £3.50), as well as home-made soup, home-made game pâté (£3.90), trout (£8.75), steaks (from £9.50), and daily specials like pasta with thai-style vegetables (£5.25), steak and kidney in ale pie (£6.95), and chicken breast with herby mozzarella and grilled vegetables and topped with tomato sauce or salmon on crisp courgette ribbons with a watercress sauce (£7.95); pizzas on Wednesdays (from £3.95) and a Swiss fondue on Thursdays (£20 per couple; not summer). The restaurant is no smoking. Darts, shove-ha'penny, dominoes, cribbage, trivia, and piped music. There are tables in the sheltered garden. *(Recommended by Mr and Mrs Croall, John and Vivienne Rice, JP, PP, David Carr, R J Walden, Phil and Anne Smithson, Lynn Sharpless, Bob Eardley, Rob Cope, Catherine Lloyd, Andy and Jill Kassube, Mr and Mrs J D Marsh, John Perry)*

Own brew ~ Licensee Miss M J Leonard ~ Real ale ~ Meals and snacks ~ Restaurant ~ (01837) 810306 ~ Well behaved children welcome ~ Open 11-3(2 in winter), 6-11; 12-2.30, 7-10.30 Sun ~ Bedrooms: £30B/£50B

HAYTOR VALE SX7677 Map 1

Rock ★

Haytor signposted off B3387 just W of Bovey Tracey, on good moorland road to Widecombe

The two communicating, partly panelled bar rooms in this rather civilised inn have a quiet, restful atmosphere (no noisy games machines or piped music), fresh flowers, easy chairs, oak windsor armchairs and high-backed settles, candlelit, polished antique tables, old-fashioned prints and decorative plates on the walls, and good winter log fires (the main fireplace has a fine Stuart fireback); all rooms apart from the bar are no smoking. A wide choice of very good bar food includes home-made soup (£2.75), sandwiches (from £3.20), duck and port pâté (£5.45), ploughman's and platters (from £5.75), local rabbit in a grain mustard sauce (£6.30), steak and kidney pie (£6.50), warm scallops with a roasted red pepper and saffron dressing (£6.85), spinach and mushroom pie (£7.20), whole grilled plaice with pink peppercorn butter (£8.75), chicken filled with devon stilton wrapped in bacon with a leek sauce (£9.85), steaks (from £13), and puddings like lemon crème brûlée and treacle and walnut tart (from £3.55). Well kept Dartmoor Best and Hardy Royal Oak on handpump, and several malt whiskies; courteous, friendly service. In summer, the pretty, well kept large garden opposite the inn is a popular place to sit and there are some tables and chairs on a small terrace next to the pub itself. The village is just inside the National Park, and golf, horse riding and fishing (and walking, of course) are nearby. *(Recommended by I Maw, Mike Doupe, R J Walden, Andy and Jill Kassube, Alan and Paula McCully, B J Harding, Dr A J and Mrs P G Newton, P D Kudelka, Comus Elliott, Mr and Mrs C R Little, Ted George, Liz Bell)*

Free house ~ Licensee Christopher Graves ~ Real ale ~ Snacks (not Sun or bank hol) ~ Restaurant ~ (01364) 661305 ~ Children in restaurant ~ Open 11-11; 12-10.30 Sun ~ Bedrooms: £47(£55B)/£71B

All *Guide* inspections are anonymous. Anyone claiming to be a *Good Pub Guide* inspector is a fraud, and should be reported to us with name and description.

HOLBETON SX6150 Map 1

Mildmay Colours

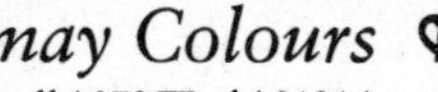

Signposted off A379 W of A3121 junction

Between 6 and 7pm they have a 'happy hour' at this neatly kept pleasant pub with their own-brewed ales (Mildmay SP and Colours) for £1 pint; they also keep local farm cider. The bar has plenty of bar stools as well as cushioned wall seats and wheelback chairs on the turkey carpet, various horse and racing pictures on the partly stripped stone and partly white walls, and a tile-sided woodburning stove; an arch leads to a smaller, similarly decorated family area. One area is no smoking. The separate plain back bar has pool, sensible darts, dominoes, and fruit machine. Bar food includes sandwiches (from £2.60), home-made soup (£2.75), home-made chicken liver pâté (£2.95), filled baked potatoes (from £2.75), ham and chips (£3.95), ploughman's (from £4.95), mushroom stroganoff (£5.40), Mexican chicken enchilada (£6.25), pork chops with apple sauce (£6.60), steaks (from £9.95), daily specials, puddings (£2.90), and children's meals (£2.70); they hold regular themed food evenings on Wednesdays. The well kept back garden has picnic-sets, a swing, and an aviary, and there's a small front terrace. *(Recommended by JDM, KM, Paul White, David Lewis, Sarah Lart, Mr and Mrs C Roberts, Elven Money, Mrs M Rolfe, Andy and Jill Kassube, Hugh Roberts, Nick Lawless, Mr and Mrs C R Little)*

Own brew ~ Licensee Louise Price ~ Real ale ~ Meals and snacks (served throughout opening hours) ~ Upstairs restaurant ~ (01752) 830248 ~ Children welcome ~ Open 11-3, 6-11; 12-3, 7-10.30 Sun ~ Bedrooms in two cottages opposite: £35B/£50B

HORNDON SX5280 Map 1

Elephants Nest ★

If coming from Okehampton on A386 turn left at Mary Tavy Inn, then left after about ½ mile; pub signposted beside Mary Tavy Inn, then Horndon signposted; on the Ordnance Survey Outdoor Leisure Map it's named as the New Inn

Happily, little changes in this 400-year-old pub. There's a good log fire, large rugs and flagstones, a beams-and-board ceiling, and cushioned stone seats built into the windows, with captain's chairs around the tables; the name of the pub is written up on the beams in 60 languages. Another room – created from the old beer cellar and with views over the garden and beyond to the moors – acts as a dining or function room or an overspill from the bar on busy nights. Good home-made bar food at lunchtime includes soup (£1.50), filled granary rolls (from £1.60), home-made chicken liver pâté or salmon and cucumber mousse (£3.20), chicken fillet burger (£3.50), ploughman's (from £3.50; the elephant's lunch (£3.80) is good), steak and kidney pie (£5.40), and local game pie (£6.90), with evening dishes like deep-fried brie with gooseberry conserve or crab and potato fritters with mango chutney (£3.20), beef curry (£5.25), steak and kidney pie (£5.40), and sweet and sour chicken with apricot (£5.45); daily specials such as bean bourguignonne (£4.50), kidney and bacon casserole or lamb vindaloo (£5), and fresh grilled plaice (£8.50), and puddings like treacle and walnut tart, sticky butterscotch slice or chocolate and brandy crunch cake (£2.20 with clotted cream). Well kept Boddingtons Bitter, Palmers IPA, St Austell HSD, and two changing guest beers on handpump; Inch's cider. Sensibly placed darts, cribbage, dominoes, and piped music. Wooden benches and tables on the spacious, flower-bordered lawn look over the walls to the pastures of Dartmoor's lower slopes. You can walk from here straight on to the moor or Black Down, though a better start (army exercises permitting) might be to drive past Wapsworthy to the end of the lane, at OS Sheet 191 map reference 546805. They have four dogs, one cat, ducks, chickens, rabbits, and horses; customers' dogs are allowed in on a lead. *(Recommended by Dr and Mrs N Holmes, Paul and Heather Bettesworth, Jeanne Cross, Paul Silvestri, JP, PP, John and Vivienne Rice, Andy and Jill Kassube, R A Cullingham, Alan and Heather Jacques, Tom McLean, R Huggins, E McCall, Kerry Law, Annemarie Firstbrook, Emma Kingdon, R J Walden)*

Free house ~ Licensee Nick Hamer ~ Real ale ~ Meals and snacks (11.30-2, 6.30-10) ~ (01822) 810273 ~ Children welcome away from bar ~ Open 11.30-2.30, 6.30-11; 12-2.30, 7-10.30 Sun

HORSEBRIDGE SX3975 Map 1

Royal

Village signposted off A384 Tavistock—Launceston

This prettily-set pub was known as the Packhorse Inn until the Civil War when Charles I visited the pub and left his seal in the granite doorstep. And the simple slate-floored rooms haven't changed much since Turner slept on a settle in front of the fire so that he could slip out early to paint the nearby bridge. There's a peaceful atmosphere with no music or fruit machines, interesting bric-a-brac, and pictures of the local flood; the side room is no smoking. From their microbrewery, they produce their own brewed ales: Horsebridge Right Royal, Tamar and the more powerful Heller – plus Bass, Sharps Doom Bar, and Wadworths 6X on handpump. Darts, bar billiards, and dominoes. Tasty bar food includes filled baked potatoes or ploughman's, ham and egg (£3.75), home-made lasagne (£4.25), pasta royal (£4.75), chilli cheese tortillas (£5), and sirloin steak (£8.95). The big garden is gradually being done up and there is a new terrace at the back. No children in the evening. *(Recommended by D B Jenkin, Jacquie and Jim Jones, Paul and Heather Bettesworth, Bruce Bird, JP, PP, John and Vivienne Rice, Patrick Freeman, T Pascall, J R Hawkes, R J Walden)*

Own brew ~ Licensee Paul Eaton ~ Real ale ~ Meals and snacks ~ (01822) 870214 ~ Children in eating area of bar lunchtime only ~ Live duo monthly Sat ~ Open 12-3, 7-11(10.30 Sun)

IDDESLEIGH SS5708 Map 1

Duke of York

B3217 Exbourne—Dolton

The friendly licensees in this old thatched pub go out of their way to make both locals and visitors feel welcome. The atmosphere is relaxed and friendly, and the bar has rocking chairs by the roaring log fire, cushioned wall benches built into the wall's black-painted wooden dado, stripped tables, and other homely country furnishings, and well kept Adnams Broadside, Cotleigh Tawny, Sharps Doom Bar, Smiles Golden, and Wye Valley Dorothy Goodbodys tapped from the cask; farm cider, Irish whiskies, local wine, and freshly squeezed orange and pink grapefruit juices. Good bar food includes sandwiches, home-made soup (£3), home-made port and stilton pâté (£4), turkey and mushroom pie (£5.50), good steak and kidney pudding (£6), and puddings like sticky toffee pudding (£2.80); three-course menu in the dining room (£17.50), and good breakfasts. Darts, shove-ha'penny, cribbage, and dominoes. Through a small coach arch is a little back garden with some picnic-sets. Good fishing nearby. *(Recommended by R J Walden, Rachel Martin, Bett and Brian Cox, JP, PP, Mr and Mrs Croall, Richard and Ann Higgs, Mr and Mrs J D Marsh, David Wallington, Ron and Sheila Corbett, Brian Skelcher, Dr A J and Mrs P G Newton)*

Free house ~ Licensees Jamie Stuart, Pippa Hutchinson ~ Real ale ~ Meals and snacks (11-10; 12-10 Sun) ~ Restaurant ~ (01837) 810253 ~ Children welcome ~ Open 11-11; 12-10.30 Sun ~ Bedrooms: £25(£25B)/£50(£50B)

INSTOW SS4730 Map 1

Boathouse

Marine Parade

In summer particularly, this simple modern and friendly little pub's position is a huge bonus – it's across a small road from a huge sandy tidal beach. There's just one bar with high ceilings and an airy feel, black mate's chairs around black tables, red plush cushioned small settles against the wall and built into the high vertical-panelled dado, and big old-fashioned nautical paintings on wood hung on the stripped stone wall facing the long wooden bar counter (lined by green plush bar stools). Well kept Bass, Flowers IPA, and Shepherd Neame Spitfire on handpump, and good bar food such as sandwiches or home-made soup (£1.80), filled french bread (from £2.90), mussels (£3.90), chicken breast wrapped in smoked bacon with a brandy and cream sauce, fresh fish (from the beach opposite) such as skate, sole or monkfish (£7.90) and lobster (£14.90), puddings (£2.40), and roast Sunday lunch (£4.70); they don't take bookings; good service, piped music. *Recommended by Roger and Pauline Pearce, Neil Townend, Mr and Mrs J Marsh)*

Free house ~ Licensees Robert and Elizabeth Thompson ~ Real ale ~ Meals and snacks ~ (01271) 861292 ~ Children welcome ~ Open 11.30-3, 6-11; 12-3, 7-10.30 Sun

KINGSKERSWELL SX8767 Map 1

Barn Owl

Aller Mills; just off A380 Newton Abbot—Torquay – inn-sign on main road opposite RAC post

The large bar in this 16th-c converted farmhouse has some grand furnishings such as a couple of carved oak settles and old-fashioned dining chairs around the handsome polished tables on its flowery carpet, an elaborate ornamental plaster ceiling, antique dark oak panelling, and a decorative wooden chimney piece; lots of pictures and artefacts, and old lamps and fresh flowers on the tables. The other rooms have low black oak beams, with polished flagstones and a kitchen range in one, and an inglenook fireplace in the other. Good popular bar food includes home-made soup (£2.50), sandwiches with side salad (from £3.25), filled baked potatoes (from £3.50), deep-fried camembert with a gooseberry and apple purée (£4.25), ploughman's (from £4.50), quite a few cold platters (from £6.25; fresh local crab £7.75), fresh fillet of lemon sole (£7.50), gammon and pineapple (£8.25), steaks (from £8.25), and daily specials like poached hake on a bed of leeks with beurre blanc sauce or fillet of pork stuffed with prunes in a rich armagnac and cream sauce. Well kept Dartmoor Best, Ind Coope Burton, and Marstons Pedigree on handpump, 15 malt whiskies, and 18 wines by the glass. There are picnic-sets in a small sheltered garden. No children. *(Recommended by D I Baddeley, Mr and Mrs A Scrutton, Brian and Bett Cox, John Wilson, Andrew Hodges, P Rome, Jean and Douglas Troup, Ian and Jane Irving)*

Free house ~ Licensees Derek and Margaret Warner ~ Real ale ~ Meals and snacks (till 10pm) ~ Restaurant ~ (01803) 872130 ~ Open 11.30-2.30, 6(6.30 in winter)-11; 12-2.30, 6-10.30 Sun; closed evening 25 Dec, closed 26-27 Dec ~ Bedrooms: £49.50B/£65B

Bickley Mill

Towards N Whilborough

Once a flour mill, this attractive pub has lovely summer hanging baskets, a courtyard with tables under a eucalyptus tree and small cabbage palms, and a series of sheltered hillside terraces creating a sub-tropical effect with dracaenas among the shrubs on this steep slope. Inside, there's a spreading series of beamed rooms with lots of copper and brass implements on the walls, on shelves and by the fireplace, built-in brocaded wall benches and solid wooden chairs, candles on the tables, toby jugs on a shelf with plants on the window sills, and a log fire in the stone fireplace; a similarly furnished no-smoking room leads off this main bar, and up some steps is another area with plates and pictures on the walls; piped music. Good bar food includes home-made soup (£2.25), sandwiches (from £2.75), home-made chicken liver pâté or green-lipped mussels in a provençal sauce (£3.50), ploughman's (£4.75), home-cooked ham and eggs (£5.50), chicken curry (£6), mushroom stroganoff (£6.25), grilled local trout (£7.50), steaks (from £9), around a dozen daily specials, puddings (£2.95), and children's meals (from £2.75). Well kept Bass, Charles Wells Bombardier, and a guest like Elgoods Cambridge on handpump or tapped from the cask, and a good choice of wines; darts, fruit machine and piped music. *(Recommended by Gordon, Mr and Mrs D Wilson, John Wilson, Dr A J and Mrs P G Newton)*

Free house ~ Licensees Mr H Hayes, Mrs G Perkins ~ Real ale ~ Meals and snacks (12-1.45, 6-9.35) ~ Restaurant ~ (01803) 873201 ~ Children in family room and restaurant ~ Open 11-2.30, 6-11; 12-3, 7-10.30 Sun ~ Bedrooms: £22S/£44S

KINGSTEIGNTON SX8773 Map 1

Old Rydon ★ 🍴

Rydon Rd; from A381/A380 junction follow signs to Kingsteignton (B3193), taking first right turn (Longford Lane), go straight on to the bottom of the hill, then next right turn into Rydon Rd following Council Office signpost; pub is just past the school, OS Sheet 192 map reference 872739

It isn't easy to find this busy old farmhouse – and when you do, its location in the middle of a residential area is rather a surprise – but readers much enjoy their visits here. The small, cosy bar has a big winter log fire in a raised fireplace, cask seats and upholstered seats built against the white-painted stone walls, and lots of beer mugs hanging from the heavy beam-and-plank ceiling. There are a few more seats in an upper former cider loft facing the antlers and antelope horns on one high white wall; piped music. Very good bar food includes filled baked potatoes or toasted muffins with various toppings (from £2.95), ploughman's (from £4.25), a vegetarian dish (£5.95), mixed leaf salad with fried potatoes and croutons and topped with charcoal grilled tandoori chicken (£5.65), Brixham plaice fillets (£5.95), 6oz sirloin steak (£6.95) or grilled king prawns (£8.85), and daily specials such as warm asparagus, leek and goat's cheese tart with red pepper sauce (£3.95), smoked haddock and chive fishcakes with a curried apple chutney (£5.95), lamb liver and black pudding on bubble and squeak with red wine, rosemary and onion sauce (£6.30), pasta with venison and pink peppercorn meatballs in a tomato sauce (£6.50), and pork steaks with ginger, honey and soy sauce with egg noodles, stir-fried vegetables and a five-spice and tomato salsa (£7.60); children's menu (£2.95). The restaurant is no smoking (though you may smoke in the restaurant lounge). Well kept Bass, Wadworths 6X, and a changing guest ale on handpump, and helpful, friendly service. The nice biggish sheltered garden has seats under parasols, with more on the terrace, and a much liked conservatory with its prolific shrubbery: two different sorts of bougainvillea, a vine with bunches of purple grapes, and lots of pretty geraniums and busy lizzies. *(Recommended by John and Christine Simpson, D I Baddeley, Keith Loudon, Stan Edwards, Liz Bell, Andrew Hodges, B Ferris Harms, Chris Reeve)*

Free house ~ Licensees Hermann and Miranda Hruby ~ Real ale ~ Meals and snacks ~ Restaurant ~ (01626) 354626 ~ Children upstairs and in conservatory, but no under 8s after 8pm ~ Open 11-2.30, 6-11; 12-3, 7-10.30 Sun

KINGSTON SX6347 Map 1

Dolphin 🛏

Off B3392 S of Modbury (can also be reached from A379 W of Modbury)

Half a dozen tracks lead from this peaceful shuttered 16th-c inn down to the sea, and the friendly licensees are very helpful about giving advice on other local walks, too. The several knocked-through beamed rooms have a relaxed, welcoming atmosphere (no noisy games machines or piped music), amusing drawings and photographs on the walls, and rustic tables and cushioned seats and settles around their bared stone walls; one small area is no smoking. Good honest bar food includes sandwiches (from £1.95; crab £3.95), soup such as curried lentil (£2.25), ploughman's (from £3.75), deep-fried camembert and gooseberry sauce or sausages with apricot and dill sauce (£3.95), spinach and walnut bake or chicken in a cider and apple sauce (£5.50), fish pie (£5.95), lamb casserole with apricot (£6.50), gammon and egg (£7.50), steaks (from £8.50), and home-made treacle tart or chocolate banana bread pudding (£2.50); children's meals (from £1.50). Well kept Courage Best and Ushers Founders and seasonal beers on handpump. Outside, there are tables and swings. *(Recommended by B J Harding, Jacquie and Jim Jones, Richard and Robyn Wain, Paul White, C C Jonas, Brian Coad, Michael Marlow)*

Ushers ~ Tenants Neil and Annie Williams ~ Real ale ~ Meals and snacks (till 10pm) ~ (01548) 810314 ~ Children in eating area of bar ~ Open 11-3(2.30 in winter), 6-11; 12-3, 6.30-10.30 Sun ~ Bedrooms: £37.50B/£49.50B

KNOWSTONE SS8223 Map 1

Masons Arms ★ 🍷

Village signposted off A361 Bampton—South Molton

For many people, this quiet 13th-c inn is a special place with a great deal of character and atmosphere – and although the casually personal way it's run doesn't of course appeal to everyone, most really like the difference from more standardised places. The unspoilt small main bar has heavy medieval black beams hung with ancient bottles of all shapes and sizes, farm tools on the walls, substantial rustic furniture on the stone floor, and a fine open fireplace with a big log fire and side bread oven. A small lower sitting room has pinkish plush chairs around a low table in front of the fire, and bar billiards. Bar food can be very good: widely praised home-made soup and home-made pâté like cheese and walnut or smoked mackerel, ploughman's with proper local cheese and butter, good pies, and daily specials such as smoked chicken and avocado salad (£4.50), grilled mackerel with gooseberry sauce (£4.95), venison ragoût (£5.25), cider cassoulet (£5.50), grilled Exmoor lamb chops (£7.95), and puddings like apple cake (£2.50); Sunday lunch and occasional themed food nights with appropriate music. The restaurant is no smoking. They often sell home-made marmalades, fruit breads or hot gooseberry chutney over the counter. Well kept Badger Best and Cotleigh Tawny tapped from the cask, farm cider, a small but well chosen wine list, and a fair choice of malt whiskies; several snuffs on the counter; darts, shove-ha'penny, dominoes, cribbage, and board games. *(Recommended by Karen and Garry Fairclough, Jeremy Brittain-Long, Julian Holland, Sarah Laver, Tim Barrow, Sue Demont, the Didler, N Cobb, John A Barker, J F M West, JP, PP, S G Bennett, Mr and Mrs Pyper, H Thomson, S Tait, S Lonie, Philip and Jude Simmons, Neil and Anita Christopher, Mr and Mrs G R Turner, Jo and Gary Charlton, Mr and Mrs G McNeill, M and M Carter, R J Walden, Dr and Mrs I H Maine, A and G Evans, Sheila and John French, Dr A J and Mrs P G Newton)*

Free house ~ Licensees David and Elizabeth Todd ~ Real ale ~ Meals and snacks ~ Restaurant ~ (01398) 341231/341582 ~ Children in eating area of bar and in restaurant ~ Open 11-3, 6(7 in winter)-11; 12-3, 7-10.30 Sun; closed evenings 25-26 Dec ~ Bedrooms: £21/£55B; dogs £1.50

LITTLEHEMPSTON SX8162 Map 1

Tally Ho!

Signposted off A381 NE of Totnes

Although new licensees have taken over this bustling little pub, Mr Hitchman (the manager) is the son of the previous licensee, so things shouldn't change too much. The neatly kept and cosy rooms have low beams and panelling, fresh flowers and candles on the tables, and bare stone walls covered with lots of porcelain, brass, copperware, mounted butterflies, stuffed wildlife, old swords, and shields and hunting horns and so forth; there's also an interesting mix of chairs and settles (many antique and with comfortable cushions), and two coal fires; no noisy machines or piped music. Good bar food includes home-made soup (£3.25), sandwiches (from £2.95), mussels in cream and white wine (£3.95), ploughman's (£4.75), rabbit casserole (£6.95), steak and kidney pie or whole local plaice (£7.75), pork with a cider, almond, apple and cream sauce (£8.50), Brixham fish pie (£9.75), steaks (from £9.75), fresh roast duckling (£11.95), home-made puddings with clotted cream (from £2.75), and lots of lunchtime daily specials (£5.95). Well kept Dartmoor Best, Palmers Tally Ho!, and Teignworthy Reel Ale on handpump from a temperature controlled cellar, and several malt whiskies. The friendly dog is called Morph, the nice ginger cat, Priscilla, and the farm cat, Elvis. The terrace is a mass of flowers in summer. Please note, they now do bedrooms. *(Recommended by Andrew Hodges, Ian and Jane Irving, Jean and Douglas Troup, Bill and Brenda Lemon; more reports please)*

Free house ~ Licensees Phillip Saint, Andrew Greenwood, Dale Hitchman ~ Real ale ~ Meals and snacks (till 10pm) ~ (01803) 862316 ~ Children in special area of bar ~ Open 12-2.30, 6(6.30 in winter)-11; 12-3, 7-10.30 Sun; closed 25 Dec ~ Bedrooms: £35S/£45S

LOWER ASHTON SX8484 Map 1

Manor

Ashton signposted off B3193 N of Chudleigh

This is a good, enjoyable pub run by friendly licensees who take real care over their food and drink. The left-hand room has beer mats and brewery advertisements on the walls and is more for locals enjoying the well kept Wadworths 6X tapped from the cask and RCH Pitchfork, Teignworthy Reel Ale, Theakstons XB and a changing guest ale on handpump, or perhaps the local Grays farm cider. On the right, two rather more discreet rooms have a wider appeal, bolstered by tasty home-made food including soup (£1.85), sandwiches (from £1.85), filled baked potatoes (from £2.95), burgers with various toppings (from £3.40), ploughman's (from £4), vegetable bake (£4.70), home-cooked ham and egg (£5.50), steak, mushroom and ale pie (£5.75) and steaks (from £8.95), with a good choice of changing specials such as mushroom, stilton and almond tart (£5.25), lasagne (£5.50), pork with mushrooms and cream or chicken curry (£5.95), smoked fish bake (£6.75), grilled lemon sole (£7.35), lamb steak with a redcurrant sauce (£7.95), and local ostrich steak (£9.95); service is quick. Shove-ha'penny, spoof. The garden has lots of picnic-sets under cocktail parasols (and a fine tall scots pine). No children. *(Recommended by Mike Gorton, G Wall, Edward Nicol, G Washington, N Wills)*

Free house ~ Licensees Geoff and Clare Mann ~ Real ale ~ Meals and snacks (12-1.30, 7-9.30; not Mon) ~ (01647) 252304 ~ Open 12-2.30, 6(7 Sat)-11(10.30 Sun); closed Mon exc bank holidays

LUSTLEIGH SX7881 Map 1

Cleave

Village signposted off A382 Bovey Tracey—Moretonhampstead

In a pretty village, this friendly old thatched pub has a low-ceilinged lounge bar with attractive antique high-backed settles, pale leatherette bucket chairs, red-cushioned wall seats, and wheelback chairs around the tables on its patterned carpet, and a roaring log fire. A second bar has similar furnishings, a large dresser, harmonium, an HMV gramophone, and prints, and the no-smoking family room has crayons, books and toys for children. Enjoyable bar food includes home-made soup (£2.95), sandwiches (£3.25), ploughman's (from £3.95), home-made chicken liver pâté (£4.45), very good local sausages (£5.95), home-made steak, kidney and Guinness pie (£6.95), good roast pork with apple sauce or home-made nut roast with spicy tomato sauce (£7.50), daily specials like pasta dishes (from £4.95), whole fresh local trout or fillet of salmon with a lemon and tarragon sauce (£9.25), and half a honey-roast duckling with black cherry sauce (£11.95), puddings (£2.50), and children's dishes (from £3.25). Well kept Bass, Flowers Original and Wadworths 6X on handpump kept under light blanket pressure. The hanging baskets are lovely in summer, and the neat sheltered garden is full of cottagey flowers, and has a wendy house. *(Recommended by R J Walden, Edward Leetham, Richard and Ann Higgs, B J Harding, Dr A J and Mrs P G Newton, Richard and Rosemary Hoare, Barry and Anne, John and Vivienne Rice, Comus Elliott)*

Heavitree (who no longer brew) ~ Tenant Alison Perring ~ Real ale ~ Meals and snacks ~ (01647) 277223 ~ Children in family room ~ Parking may be difficult ~ Open 11-11; 12-10.30 Sun; 11-3, 6.30-11 in winter

LUTTON SX5959 Map 1

Mountain

Off Cornwood—Sparkwell road, at W end of village

Both the licensees and their dogs and cats will make you feel welcome in this friendly local. The bar has a high-backed settle by the log fire and some walls stripped back to the bare stone, with windsor chairs around old-fashioned polished tables in a larger connecting room. Well kept Summerskills Best Bitter, Suttons XSB, and two weekly guest beers on handpump, several malt whiskies, and farm cider; darts, cribbage, and dominoes. Simple, good value straightforward bar food includes soup and cheese (£3.20), ploughman's (£3.80), beef and ham rolls (£4), and ham and egg (£4.50). From seats on the terrace (and from one room inside) there is a fine view over the lower slopes of Dartmoor. *(Recommended by the Sandy Family, John Poulter, D Cheesebrough, Elven Money)*

Free house ~ Licensees Charles and Margaret Bullock ~ Real ale ~ Meals and snacks ~ (01752) 837247 ~ Children in eating area of bar ~ Open 11-3, 6(7 winter Mon-Weds)-11; 12-3, 7-10.30 Sun

LYDFORD SX5184 Map 1

Castle ★

Signposted off A386 Okehampton—Tavistock

The hard-working, friendly licensees are continually improving this charming pink-washed Tudor inn, and this year, three new bedrooms have been added, one with its own terrace garden. The twin-roomed bar has a relaxed atmosphere, and country kitchen chairs, high-backed winged settles and old captain's chairs around mahogany tripod tables on big slate flagstones. One of the rooms (where the bar food is served) has low lamp-lit beams, a sizeable open fire, masses of brightly decorated plates, some Hogarth prints, an attractive grandfather clock, and, near the serving-counter, seven Lydford pennies hammered out in the old Saxon mint in the reign of Ethelred the Unready, in the 11th c; the second room has an interesting collection of antique stallion posters; unusual stained-glass doors. The lounge area for diners and residents has stylishly old-fashioned sofas and attractive antique tables on the slate flagstoned floor, a Stewart oak dresser, a high backed settle, lots of pictures and plates on the walls, local oak beams supporting the bowed ceiling, and an open fire in the granite fireplace. Using fresh local produce and their own herbs (including lemon grass, chillis, borage and chervil) and some garden vegetables, the constantly changing menu might have soup (£2.50; crab £2.90), ploughman's (from £4.10), steak and kidney pie or gammon with an apricot and mango sauce (£6.15), wild mushroom and pine nut tagliatelle with a mascarpone sauce (£6.20), fresh salmon and trout fishcakes with a wine and prawn sauce (£6.40), thai chicken curry with fresh basil, cucumber and yoghurt dip (£6.55), casserole of pheasant in a cream and brandy sauce (£7.20), lemon sole with a coriander and lime sauce (£10.25), and home-made puddings (from £2.95); roast Sunday lunch (£6.10, children £4.20), and good breakfasts. The partly no-smoking restaurant has a fixed-price menu, plus a new vegetarian-only one (2 courses £12.45). Well kept Blackawton Bitter and Fullers London Pride with regular guests such as Bass, Jennings Cumberland, Palmers IPA and Smiles on handpump or tapped from the cask, and around 17 wines by the glass from a carefully chosen wine list; sensibly placed darts, cribbage, shove-ha'penny, and dominoes. The garden has a terrace with a pets corner for residents' children with ducks, chickens and goats. The pub is next to the village's daunting, ruined 12th-c castle and close to a beautiful river gorge (owned by the National Trust; closed Nov-Easter); the village itself was one of the four strong-points developed by Alfred the Great as a defence against the Danes. *(Recommended by Dr Rod Holcombe, JP, PP, John Askew, Jacquie and Jim Jones, Ted George, John and Christine Simpson, Walter and Susan Rinaldi-Butcher, Gordon, Tony and Joan Walker, R J Walden, Mr and Mrs P M Board, John and Vivienne Rice, Nigel Flook, Betsy Brown, Catherine Lloyd, Neil Franklin, Mrs M Rolfe, Andy and Jill Kassube, Liz Bell, Lynn Sharpless, Bob Eardley, Mike Gorton, Anthony Barnes, David and Mandy Allen, Elven Money, Nigel Wikeley)*

Free house ~ Licensees Clive and Mo Walker ~ Real ale ~ Meals and snacks ~ Evening restaurant ~ (01822) 820242 ~ Children in snug and, if over 7, in restaurant ~ Open 11.30-3, 6-11.30; 12-3, 7-10.30 Sun; closed evening 25 Dec ~ Bedrooms: £34.50B/£62B

> You are now allowed 20 minutes after 'time, please' to finish your drink – half-an-hour if you bought it in conjunction with a meal.

MARLDON SX8663 Map 1

Church House

Just W of Paignton

After the hurly-burly of Torquay and Paignton, this well run and attractive shuttered inn has a good relaxed atmosphere and is set in a quiet spot near the church. The spreading bar wraps itself around the big semi-circular bar counter and divides into different areas. The main bar has interesting windows with swagged curtains, some beams, dark pine chairs around solid tables on the turkey carpet, and green plush-seated bar chairs; leading off here is a cosy little candlelit room with just four tables on the bare-board floor, a dark wood dado, and stone fireplace, and next to this is the attractive, dimly lit, no-smoking restaurant with hops on the beams and dried flowers in the big stone fireplace. At the other end of the building is a characterful room split into two parts with a stone floor in one bit and a wooden floor in another (with a big woodburning stove). Good popular bar food includes soup (£2.15, cod and corn chowder £2.50), pasta with tomato sauce and olives and topped with mozzarella (£2.25), club-style sandwiches or filled french bread (from £2.95; crab £3.25), omelettes or filled baked potatoes (from £3.25), ploughman's (£4.50), lasagne (£4.95), sirloin steak (£8.65), and daily specials such as home-made game pâté (£2.95), stir-fried prawn or chicken with cajun spcies (£5.25), grilled cod fillet with a smoked salmon and prawn sauce (£5.90), and steak and kidney pudding or marinated lamb with artichokes and ciabatta topped with fresh tomato salsa (£6.25). They hold speciality evenings, too: stir-fries on Monday, Mexican dishes on Tuesday, curries on Wednesday, and pasta on Thursday. Well kept Bass, Boddingtons, Fullers London Pride on handpump; there are three grassy terraces with picnic-sets behind. (*Recommended by Mr and Mrs Marsden Howell, Dr A J and Mrs P G Newton, Mrs B Faulkner, Margaret and Ian Taylor, Mr and Mrs C Roberts, Mr and Mrs K Rose, Mr and Mrs A Hedges)*

Whitbreads ~ Lease: Sue and David Armstrong ~ Real ale ~ Meals and snacks ~ Restaurant ~ (01803) 558279 ~ Children in restaurant ~ Open 11.30-2.30, 5-11; 12-3, 7-10.30 Sun ~ Bedrooms: £15B/£30B in s/c flat

MEAVY SX5467 Map 1

Royal Oak

Off B3212 E of Yelverton

Attractively set on the village green, this friendly traditional old pub has a carpeted L-shaped bar with pews from the next door church, red plush banquettes and old agricultural prints and church pictures on the walls; a smaller bar – where the locals like to gather – has a big fireplace and side bread oven, and red-topped barrel seats. Bar food includes sandwiches (£1.90), smoked salmon pâté (£3.25), ploughman's (£3.95), cumberland sausage (£5.25), ham and egg (£5.50), meaty or vegetarian lasagne (£5.95), chicken curry (£6.50), daily specials such as bacon and spinach quiche (£5.50), crab salad (£6) or rump steak (£7.95), Sunday roast, and puddings like spotted dick and custard (£2.25). Well kept Bass, Courage Best, and Meavy Valley Bitter on handpump kept under light blanket pressure, and three draught ciders. Dominoes, euchre, and piped music. There are picnic-sets and benches outside or on the green. No children. *(Recommended by B J Harding, Dr Rod Holcombe, Neil Spink, Jacquie and Jim Jones, Joan and Michel Hooper-Immins, Barry and Anne, Emma Kingdon, A and G Evans, R J Walden)*

Free house ~ Licensees Roger and Susan Barber ~ Real ale ~ Meals and snacks (11.30-2.30, 6.30-9.30) ~ (01822) 852944 ~ Open 11.30-3, 6.30-11; 12-3, 7-10.30 Sun

Ideas for a country day out? We list pubs in really attractive scenery at the back of the book – and there are separate lists for waterside pubs, ones with really good gardens, and ones with lovely views.

NEWTON ST CYRES SX8798 Map 1

Beer Engine

Sweetham; from Newton St Cyres on A377 follow St Cyres Station, Thorverton signpost

You can now take the good own-brewed real ales home with you, as well as enjoying them at this friendly old station hotel. Kept on handpump, there is Rail Ale, Piston Bitter, Return Ticket (Mild), and the very strong Sleeper. The spacious main bar has partitioning alcoves, and windsor chairs and some cinnamon-coloured button-back banquettes around dark varnished tables on the brown carpet; the eating area is no smoking. Decent bar food includes chicken in barbecue sauce (£5.50), speciality sausages (£4.25), steak in their own ale pie (£5.50), home-made steak and kidney pudding (£5.95), and rump steak; roast Sunday lunch (£5.25 one course, £6.95 two courses). Darts, shove-ha'penny, dominoes and cribbage; fruit machine and video game in the downstairs lobby. The hanging baskets and window boxes are very pretty in summer, and there's lots of sheltered seating in the large sunny garden where they hold popular summer barbecues. *(Recommended by John and Bryony Coles, Andy and Jill Kassube, Stan Edwards, Alan and Paul McCully, R J Walden, Catherine Lloyd, A and G Evans, Ian Jones, Dr A J and Mrs P G Newton)*

Own brew ~ Licensee Peter Hawksley ~ Real ale ~ Meals and snacks (till 10pm) ~ (01392) 851282 ~ Children in eating area of bar ~ Open 11-11; 12-10.30 Sun

PETER TAVY SX5177 Map 1

Peter Tavy

Off A386 nr Mary Tavy, N of Tavistock

New licensees again for this attractive 15th-c stone inn, but happily, there are no plans for any major changes. The low beamed friendly bar has a lot of atmosphere, high-backed settles on the black flagstones by the big stone fireplace (a good log fire on cold days), smaller settles in stone-mullioned windows, and a snug no-smoking side dining area. Good bar food at lunchtime includes soup such as tomato and basil (£1.95), filled french bread (from £3.20), baked avocado and crabmeat (£3.75), steak and kidney pudding (£5.95), cashew nut paella (£6.25), and venison casserole (£6.95); in the evening there might be port and stilton pâté (£3.20), prawns with a garlic dip (£3.95), mushroom and asparagus stroganoff (£5.95), roast rack of lamb with minted gooseberry sauce or pork tenderloin with peppercorn sauce (£8.95), seared salmon with citrus sauce (£9.95), and puddings such as home-made blackberry and apple crumble, treacle tart or rhubarb lattice pie (£2.75). Five well kept real ales on handpump, kept under light blanket pressure, such as Bass, Cotleigh Tawny, Otter Ale, Princetown Jail Ale, and a guest such as Princetown Dartmoor IPA; 30 malt whiskies; darts and piped music. From the picnic-sets in the pretty garden there are peaceful views of the moor rising above nearby pastures. *(Recommended by Dr and Mrs N Holmes, JP, PP, R J Walden, John Askew, Paul and Heather Bettesworth, Ewan and Moira McCall, Lynn Sharpless, Bob Eardley, Iain Robertson, Barry and Anne, H Paulinski, James Bailey, Richard and Rosemary Hoare, John Evans, Elven Money, S E Dark, Dr A J and Mrs P G Newton; more reports on the new regime, please)*

Free house ~ Licensees Graeme and Karen Sim ~ Real ale ~ Meals and snacks ~ Restaurant ~ (01822) 810348 ~ Children in restaurant ~ Open 11.30(12 in winter)-2.30(3 Fri and Sat), 6.30(7 in winter)-11; 12-3, 7-10.30 Sun

PLYMOUTH SX4755 Map 1

China House ★

Marrowbone Slip, Sutton Harbour, via Sutton Road off Exeter Street (A374)

The position here – overlooking Sutton Harbour and over to the Barbican – is marvellous, and there are picnic-sets and benches on the heated verandah, so you can enjoy the view all year round. It's the oldest warehouse in Plymouth and got its name from the fact that Cookworthy started his porcelain factory here in 1768. Inside, the bar is lofty and very spacious but cleverly partitioned into smaller booth-like areas, with great beams and flagstone floors, bare slate and stone walls, and lots of nets, kegs and fishing gear; there's even a clinker-built boat. On the left is the main bar with plain wooden seats around dark tables in front of a good log fire – all very comfortable and relaxed. Bar food includes sandwiches, home-made soup (£3.25), butterfly king prawns with a sesame and ginger coating (£4.75), chilli con carne or steak and kidney pie (£5.75), cumberland sausage with onion gravy or nutty broccoli and pesto pasta bake (£6.50), roast cod in orange butter sauce (£8.50), duck supreme with a honey sauce and dried apricots (£10.95), and puddings (£3.25); cold food is served all day. Well kept Dartmoor Best, Marstons Pedigree, and Tetleys on handpump; fruit machine, trivia and piped music. *(Recommended by Ian Phillips, John Wilson, Ted George, Andrew and Hazel Summerfield, Andrew Hodges, R A Cullingham, P and M Rudlin, Steve and Maggie Willey, David Carr, Anthony Barnes)*

Carlsberg-Tetleys ~ Manageress Nicole Quinn ~ Real ale ~ Meals and snacks (all day) ~ Restaurant ~ (01752) 260930 ~ Children in eating area of bar ~ Jazz Sun lunchtime, live bands and DJ Fri/Sat evenings ~ Open 11-11 Mon-Thurs (till 12.30 Fri/Sat); 12-10.30 Sun

nr POSTBRIDGE SX6780 Map 1

Warren House

B3212 1¾ miles NE of Postbridge

In glorious solitude on a pleasant moorland road, this friendly place is a welcome oasis for walkers and birdwatchers and a popular meeting place for the scattered communities. The cosy bar has a fireplace at either end (one is said to have been kept almost continuously alight since 1845), and is simply furnished with easy chairs and settles under a beamed ochre ceiling, wild animal pictures on the partly panelled stone walls, and dim lighting (fuelled by the pub's own generator). Good no-nonsense home cooking includes locally made meaty or vegetable pasties (£1.60), home-made soup (£1.90), sandwiches (from £2.50), filled baked potatoes (from £2.75), good ploughman's with local cheeses (£4.50), mushroom and nut fettucine (£5.25), and home-made pies like rabbit (£6) or steak in ale pie (£6.50), with evening dishes such as spicy prawns, lemon sole with a home-made prawn and mushroom sauce (£7.50), and Scottish salmon (£8.50), and puddings such as toffee apple sponge pudding or lemon and lime parfait with a Crunchie base (£2.80). Well kept Badger Tanglefoot, Butcombe Bitter, Gibbs Mew Bishops Tipple, and St Austell HSD on handpump, farm cider, and local country wines. Darts, pool, cribbage, dominoes, and video game. *(Recommended by R J Walden, John Beeken, Barry and Anne, Mayur Shah, Mr and Mrs D E Powell, John and Vivienne Rice, M G Hart, A N Ellis, Hanns P Golez, Andrew Hodges)*

Free house ~ Licensee Peter Parsons ~ Real ale ~ Meals and snacks (noon-9.30 in summer) ~ (01822) 880208 ~ Children in family room ~ Open 11-11; 11-2.30, 5.30-11 winter weekdays; 12-10.30 Sun

RACKENFORD SS8518 Map 1

Stag

Off A361 NW of Tiverton

The entrance to this little thatched inn (dating in part from 1237 and perhaps Devon's oldest) is along a marvellous old cobbled entrance corridor between massive stone and cob walls, and the bar lives up to this first impression. The shiny dark ochre ceiling is very low, and a couple of very high-backed old settles face each other in front of the massive fireplace with its ancient bressumer beam (and good log fire). The bar counter is a grand piece of oak, and there are some other interesting old pieces of furniture as well as more modern seats; a narrow sloping side area has darts, and leading off is a cottagey dining room. Good bar food includes sandwiches (from £1.75), filled baked potatoes (from £2.95), ham and egg (£3.75), omelettes (£4.20), rump steak (£7.95), daily specials such as home-made lasagne or spinach and ricotta canelloni (£3.95), home-made pies like steak and kidney or lamb and apricot (£4.95), and salmon fillets with a mushroom and cream sauce (£6.50), puddings (£2.50), and children's menu (from £1.95). Well kept Adnams Broadside, Cotleigh Tawny and a guest such as Shepherd Neame Spitfire on handpump, good house wines, very friendly service – a nice relaxed atmosphere; darts, pool, alley skittles, cribbage, dominoes, and piped music. The dog is called Spanner, and the cat, Mr Pudge. *(Recommended by Tony Gayfer, Peter Churchill; more reports please)*

Free house ~ Licensees Norman and Jennie Foot ~ Real ale ~ Meals and snacks ~ (01884) 881369 ~ Evening restaurant ~ Local musicians weekends, monthly trad jazz ~ Children welcome ~ Open 12-2.30, 6-11; 12-11 Sat; 12-10.30 Sun ~ Bedrooms: £17.50(£18.50B)/£35(£37B)

RATTERY SX7461 Map 1

Church House

Village signposted from A385 W of Totnes, and A38 S of Buckfastleigh

This is a lovely old pub with a restful atmosphere and plenty of history. It is one of the oldest pub buildings in Britain and the spiral stone steps behind a little stone doorway on your left as you go in probably date from about 1030. There are massive oak beams and standing timbers in the homely open-plan bar, large fireplaces (one with a little cosy nook partitioned off around it), windsor armchairs, comfortable seats and window seats, and prints on the plain white walls; the dining room is separated from this room by heavy curtains; Shandy the golden labrador is very amiable. Good bar food includes filled rolls and ploughman's with local cheeses, and daily specials such as turkey and pineapple curry (£6.15), local grilled trout stuffed with prawns (£6.95), and chicken and coconut balti (£7.25); children's meals. Well kept Dartmoor Best, Marstons Pedigree, and a weekly guest beer on handpump, around 40 malt whiskies, and a decent wine list. Outside, there are peaceful views of the partly wooded surrounding hills from picnic-sets on a hedged courtyard by the churchyard. *(Recommended by JKW, I J and N K Buckmaster, Steve and Maggie Willey, JP, PP, Jacquie and Jim Jones, B J Harding, Mike and Karen England, Andrew Hodges, Andy and Jill Kassube, Mr and Mrs D Wilson, Jo and Gary Charlton, Mike Gorton, M Joyner, David and Nina Pugsley, Dr A J and Mrs P G Newton)*

Free house ~ Licensees Brian and Jill Evans ~ Real ale ~ Meals and snacks ~ (01364) 642220 ~ Children in eating area of bar and in dining room ~ Open 11-2.30, 6-11; 12-2.30, 7-10.30 Sun

RINGMORE SX6545 Map 1

Journeys End

Off B3392 at Pickwick Inn, St Anns Chapel, nr Bigbury

This friendly partly medieval thatched inn originally housed the masons working on the nearby church. The tidy carpeted main bar has an unusual partly pitched ceiling, some panelling, soft lighting from a nice mix of lamps, and a blazing log fire; the small outer snug has flagstones, and the carpeted conservatory has unusual wall lamps and a large fish tank. Good bar food includes lunchtime sandwiches (from £2), ploughman's (£4), leek and stilton bake or ham and egg (£4.50), local trout or lamb chops (£6.50), steaks (from £8.50), enjoyable daily specials, and puddings like treacle tart or home-made apple pie (£2.50); smashing breakfasts and nice candlelit no-smoking restaurant; pleasant efficient staff. Well kept Adnams Broadside, Badger Tanglefoot, Exmoor Ale, Otter Ale, and Wye Valley HPA on handpump or tapped from the cask, and they hold two beer festivals – usually April and September; Stancombe farm cider, and dominoes and fruit machine. The big, attractively planted garden has plenty of seats. The circular walks to the beach and cliffs (National Trust) are a must, and it's worth a wander around the pretty village, too. *(Recommended by Peter and Audrey Dowsett, Lorna and Howard Lambert, Richard and Robyn Wain, Mick Hitchman, David Lewis, Sarah Lart, Mike and Wena Stevenson, Dr Rod Holcombe, S P Goddard, B J Harding, Mark Fennell, Mr and Mrs C R Little, T G Brierly, David Wallington)*

Free house ~ Licensee James Parkin ~ Real ale ~ Meals and snacks (not evening 25 Dec) ~ Restaurant ~ (01548) 810205 ~ Children in conservatory ~ Open 11.30-3, 6-11; 12-10.30 Sun; closed evening 25 Dec ~ Bedrooms: £25B/£45B

SHEEPWASH SS4806 Map 1

Half Moon 🛏 🍷 £

Off A3072 Holsworthy—Hatherleigh at Highampton

Since 1958, this civilised inn has been owned by the same friendly family. It's a most enjoyable place to visit and has lots of fishing pictures on the white walls of the neatly kept carpeted main bar, solid old furniture under the beams, and a big log fire fronted by slate flagstones. Lunchtime bar snacks are traditionally simple and good and include sandwiches (£1.50, toasties £2.25), super home-made vegetable soup (£1.75), home-made pasties (£3), ploughman's (£3.50), home-cooked ham salad (£3.75), and home-made puddings (from £2). Well kept Courage Best, Jollyboat Mainbrace Bitter (brewed locally), Marstons Pedigree, and an occasional guest on handpump (well kept in a temperature-controlled cellar), a fine choice of malt whiskies, and an extensive wine list; darts, fruit machine, and separate pool room. This is the place to stay if you love fishing as they have 10 miles of private fishing on the River Torridge (salmon, sea trout and brown trout) as well as a rod room, good drying facilities and a small shop stocking the basic things needed to catch fish. *(Recommended by R J Walden, Dr A J and Mrs P G Newton, Sheila and John French, George Barnwell, Mr and Mrs J D Marsh)*

Free house ~ Licensees Benjamin Robert Inniss and Charles Inniss ~ Real ale ~ Snacks (lunchtime) ~ Evening restaurant ~ (01409) 231376 ~ Children welcome lunchtime only ~ Open 11-2.30(3 Sat), 6-11 ~ Bedrooms: £36B/£57.50B

SIDFORD SY1390 Map 1

Blue Ball ★ 🛏 🍽

A3052 just N of Sidmouth

From midday, this bustling and very popular thatched inn fills up quickly – but the helpful staff cope well with the rush. It's been owned by the same friendly family since 1912, and there's a good atmosphere in the low, partly panelled and neatly kept lounge bar, as well as a lovely winter log fire in the stone fireplace (two other open fires also), heavy beams, upholstered wall benches and windsor chairs, and lots of bric-a-brac; the snug is no smoking. Quickly served bar food includes soup (£1.95), sandwiches with several choices of bread (from £1.90; crab £2.95), lots of ploughman's and salads (from £3.50), omelettes (£4.50), mushroom and nut fettucine (£5.25), steak and mushroom pie (£5.95), chicken balti (£6.50), steaks (from £8.75), daily specials, children's dishes, and puddings (£2.50); the two-course OAP lunches on Wednesdays are well attended, and they hold themed food evenings with appropriate music. Bass, Boddingtons, Flowers IPA, Otter Ale, and Wadworths 6X on handpump, kept well in a temperature-controlled cellar; helpful staff. A plainer public bar has darts, dominoes, cribbage and a fruit machine; piped music. Tables on a terrace look out over a colourful front flower garden, and there are more seats on a bigger back lawn – as well as in a covered area next to the barbecue; safe swing, see saw and play house for children. *(Recommended by Joyce Cottrell, Paul White, W W Burke, L H and S Ede, Basil Minson, Peter and Audrey Dowsett, Arnold Day, Klaus and Elizabeth Leist, G G Lawrance, Stan Edwards, R Boyd)*

Greenalls ~ Tenant Roger Newton ~ Real ale ~ Meals and snacks (10.30-2, 6-9.30) ~ Restaurant ~ (01395) 514062 Well behaved children in restaurant and own room ~ Live music monthly ~ Open 10.30-2.30(3 Sat), 5.30-11; 12-3, 6(7 in winter)-10.30 Sun ~ Bedrooms: £24/£40

SOURTON SX5390 Map 1

Highwayman ★

A386 SW of Okehampton; a short detour from the A30

Nothing can prepare you for the sensation of your first visit here. For 40 years, the friendly owners have put great enthusiasm into this pub's remarkable design. The porch (a pastiche of a nobleman's carriage) leads into a warren of dimly lit stonework and flagstone-floored burrows and alcoves, richly fitted out with red plush seats discreetly cut into the higgledy-piggledy walls, elaborately carved pews, a leather porter's chair, Jacobean-style wicker chairs, and seats in quaintly bulging small-paned bow windows; the ceiling in one part, where there's an array of stuffed animals, gives the impression of being underneath a tree, roots and all. The separate Rita Jones' Locker is a make-believe sailing galleon, full of intricate woodwork and splendid timber baulks, with white antique lace-clothed tables in the embrasures that might have held cannons. They only sell keg beer, but specialise in farm cider, and food is confined to a range of meaty and vegetarian pasties (£1.50); service is warmly welcoming and full of character; old-fashioned penny fruit machine, and 40s piped music; no smoking at the bar counters. Outside, there's a play area in similar style for children with little black and white roundabouts like a Victorian fairground, a fairy-tale pumpkin house and an old-lady-who-lived-in-the-shoe house. You can take children in to look around the pub but they can't stay inside. The period bedrooms are attractive. *(Recommended by Gordon, JP, PP, James and Ruth Morrell)*

Free house ~ Licensees Buster and Rita Jones and Sally Thomson ~ Snacks (11-1.45, 6-10) ~ (01837) 861243 ~ Open 11-2, 6-10.30; 12-2, 7-10.30 Sun; closed 25/26 Dec ~ Bedrooms: /£36

SOUTH POOL SX7740 Map 1

Millbrook

Off A379 E of Kingsbridge

Even when it's raining, you can sit outside this tiny, spotlessly kept pub, as both the front courtyard and the terrace by the stream (where you can sit and watch the Aylesbury ducks) are covered by canopies. It's one of the smallest pubs in the book and does get pretty packed – parking can be difficult. The charming little back bar has handsome windsor chairs, a chintz easy chair, drawings and paintings (and a chart) on its cream walls, clay pipes and lots of calling cards on the beams, and fresh flowers; there's also a top bar. Good home-made bar food includes sandwiches, cumberland sausages (£4.95), smoked salmon pasta (£5.95), halibut au poivre (£7.25), seafood paella (£7.95), and Scottish sirloin steak (£9.50). Well kept Bass, Ruddles Best, Wadworths 6X and a guest ale on handpump, and local farm ciders; good, friendly service even when busy. Darts and euchre in the public bar in winter. *(Recommended by Mrs Mary Woods, Dr Rod Holcombe, Nick Lawless, D I Baddeley, Peter and Audrey Dowsett, Ann and Frank Bowman, TBB, DJW, Mr and Mrs W Welsh, Peter and Rosie Flower)*

Free house ~ Licensees Victoria Green and Liz Stirland ~ Real ale ~ Meals and snacks ~ (01548) 531581 ~ Children in top bar ~ Open 11(11.30 in winter)-2.30(3 Sat), 5.30(6.30 in winter)-11; 12-3, 7-10.30 Sun – these times depend on high tide

SOUTH ZEAL SX6593 Map 1

Oxenham Arms ★ 🛏 🍷

Village signposted from A30 at A382 roundabout and B3260 Okehampton turn-off

Readers very much enjoy their visits to this fine old inn – for its friendly welcome and for the unhurried atmosphere and sense of history. It was first licensed in 1477 and has grown up around the remains of a Norman monastery, built here to combat the pagan power of the neolithic standing stone that still forms part of the wall in the family TV room behind the bar (there are actually twenty more feet of stone below the floor). It later became the Dower House of the Burgoynes, whose heiress carried it to the Oxenham family. And Charles Dickens, snowed up one winter, wrote a lot of *Pickwick Papers* here. The beamed and partly panelled front bar has elegant mullioned windows and Stuart fireplaces, and windsor armchairs around low oak tables and built-in wall seats. The small no-smoking family room has beams, wheelback chairs around polished tables, decorative plates, and another open fire. Popular bar food includes soup (£2.25), sandwiches (from £2.25), good ploughman's (£3.95), fish and chips (£5.25), home-made steak, kidney, Guinness and mushroom pie (£6.25), fish and chips (£5.25), daily specials such as vegetable quiche (£4.75), lamb moussaka (£5.45), and smoked fish platter (£6.25), evening steaks (£9.25), and puddings (from £2.45). Well kept Princetown IPA, Jail Ale (brewed locally), and Dartmoor Gold on handpump or tapped from the cask, and an extensive list of wines including good house claret; darts, shove-ha'penny, dominoes, and cribbage. Note the imposing curved stone steps leading up to the garden where there's a sloping spread of lawn. *(Recommended by JP, PP, Mike and Heather Watson, John Mcdonald, Ann Bond, John Askew, Anne and Michael Corbett, Catherine Lloyd, Bernard Stradling, John and Christine Simpson, Jacquie and Jim Jones, R R and J D Winn, A Hepburn, S Jenner, R J Walden, Dallas Seawright, Nigel Flook, Betsy Brown, John and Sally Clarke, Mrs H Murphy, Klaus and Elizabeth Leist, George and Jeanne Barnwell, Jeff Davies, Alan and Paula McCully, Mrs M Rolfe, Jane and Adrian Tierney-Jones, Mr and Mrs G McNeill, IHR, Brian and Bett Cox)*

Free house ~ Licensee James Henry ~ Real ale ~ Meals and snacks ~ Restaurant ~ (01837) 840244 ~ Children in family room ~ Open 11-2.30, 6-11; 12-2.30, 7-10.30 Sun ~ Bedrooms: £45B/£60B

STAVERTON SX7964 Map 1

Sea Trout

Village signposted from A384 NW of Totnes

A good mix of locals and visitors enjoys this friendly old village inn, just a few hundred yards from the River Dart. The neatly kept rambling beamed lounge bar has seatrout and salmon flies and stuffed fish on the walls, cushioned settles and stools, and a stag's head above the fireplace, and the main bar has low banquettes, soft lighting and an open fire. There's also a public bar with pool, darts, table skittles, shove-ha'penny, and juke box; the conservatory is no smoking. Good bar food includes home-made soup (£2.35), sandwiches (from £2.75), home-made pâté (£3.50), ploughman's (from £3.95), pork and apple sausages or vegetable hotpot (£4.70), home-cooked ham and egg (£4.95), smoked haddock and prawn crumble (£5.75), whole Brixham plaice (£7.25), lamb cutlets (£7.95), steaks (from £8.95), daily specials, puddings, children's meals (from £2.85), and good Sunday lunch. Well kept Bass, Dartmoor Best, Wadworths 6X, and guest beers like Blackawton Best, Exmoor Best or Fullers London Pride on handpump; efficient, helpful staff. There are seats under parasols on the attractive paved back garden. A station for the Torbay Steam Railway is not far away. *(Recommended by D B Jenkin, Dr Rod Holcombe, I Buckmaster, Julie Peters, Colin Blinkhorn, J H Bell, Andrew Hodges, Dr A J and Mrs P G Newton)*

Free house ~ Licensees Andrew and Pym Mogford ~ Real ale ~ Meals and snacks ~ Restaurant ~ (01803) 762274 ~ Children in eating area of bar ~ Occasional Spanish guitar Fri evenings ~ Open 11-3, 6-11; 12-3, 6.30(7 in winter)-11 Sun; closed evenings 25-26 Dec ~ Bedrooms: £42.50B/£64B

STOCKLAND ST2404 Map 1

Kings Arms

Village signposted from A30 Honiton—Chard

Devon Dining Pub of the Year

This year, praise for the marvellous choice of excellent food in this busy 16th-c pub is even warmer than ever. The blackboard specials are explained by one of the licensees to expectant diners in mouth-watering detail and served by friendly, professional staff: vegetable mousse or mediterranean-style fish soup (£3.50), gaelic king scallops or assiette gourmet (£4.50), vegetable surprise or excellent pigeon breasts with game sauce (£7.50), fillet of cod portugaise or lovely fresh plaice (£8.50), king prawn brochette (£9.50), Cotley rack of lamb (£9.50), venison medallions (£10.50), marvellous duck or ostrich fillet (£12.50), and puddings like gooseberry crunch gateau, crêpes suzette or blueberry and raspberry cheesecake (£3.50); from the lunchtime snack menu, there might be sandwiches (from £1.75), soup (£2), ploughman's (£4), omelettes (from £4.50), steak and kidney pie, sausages with onion gravy or gammon and egg (£5.50), a vegetarian pasta dish (£7.50), and children's menu (or they can have half-size helpings of adult meals £3.50). Booking

is essential; good breakfasts. The dark beamed, elegant dining lounge has solid refectory tables and settles, attractive landscapes, a medieval oak screen (which divides the room into two), and a great stone fireplace across almost the whole width of one end; the cosy restaurant with its huge inglenook fireplace and bread oven has the same menu as the bar. Well kept Exmoor Ale, Otter Ale, John Smiths, and a changing guest such as Marstons Pedigree on handpump, over 40 malt whiskies (including island and west coast ones; large spirit measures), a good wine list with house wines and special offers by the bottle or glass chalked up on a board, and farm ciders. At the back, a flagstoned bar has captain's-style tub chairs and cushioned stools around heavy wooden tables, and leads on to a carpeted darts room with two boards, another room with dark beige plush armchairs and settees (and a fruit machine), and a neat ten-pin skittle alley; table skittles, cribbage, dominoes, fruit machine, and quiet mainly classical piped music. There are tables under cocktail parasols on the terrace in front of the white-faced thatched pub and a lawn enclosed by trees and shrubs. The bedrooms have been refurbished.
(Recommended by Karen Jeal, Richard and Margaret Peers, J H Jones, Richard and Robyn Wain, Michael and Anne Corbett, John and Christine Simpson, G and P Dixon, Yavus and Shirley Mutlu, Roger Price, Mike Gorton, R J Walden)

Free house ~ Licensees Heinz Kiefer and Paul Diviani ~ Real ale ~ Snacks (lunchtime) and meals ~ Restaurant ~ (01404) 881361 ~ Well behaved/supervised children welcome ~ Live music Sun evenings and bank hol Mon evenings ~ Open 12-3, 6.30-11; 12-3, 7-11 Sun ~ Bedrooms: £25B/£40B

STOKE FLEMING SX8648 Map 1

Green Dragon 🍷

Church Rd

This is a very relaxed and friendly pub set opposite a church with an interesting tall tower. The main part of the flagstoned and beamed bar has two small settles, bay window seats, boat pictures, and maybe Electra or Maia the burmese cats or Rhea the relaxed german shepherd; down on the right is a wooden-floored snug with throws and cushions on battered sofas and armchairs, a few books (20p to RNLI), adult board games, a grandfather clock, and cuttings about the landlord (who is a long-distance yachtsman), and maps of his races on the walls. Down some steps is the Mess Deck decorated with old charts and lots of ensigns and flags, and there's a playbox of children's games; darts, shove-ha'penny, cribbage, and dominoes; piped music. Good home-made bar food includes soup (£1.90), sandwiches (from £2.40), ploughman's with three cheeses (£3.50), Malaysian stuffed mushrooms, fish wellington, salmon en croûte, Wiltshire plait, and pepper pithivers (all £5.50), and puddings and children's menu; winter roast lunch every third Sunday – must book. Well kept Bass, Hardy Royal Oak, Flowers IPA and Wadworths 6X on handpump (all except Bass kept under light blanket pressure), big glasses of six good house wines from Australia, California, France and Germany, and a decent range of spirits; you can take the beer away with you. There's a back garden with swings, a climbing frame and picnic-sets and a front terrace with some white plastic garden tables and chairs. *(Recommended by Peter Cook, B J Harding, Elven Money, D G Clarke, A M Stephenson, Patricia Dodd; more reports please)*

Heavitree (who no longer brew) ~ Tenants Peter and Alix Crowther ~ Real ale ~ Meals and snacks ~ 01803 770238 ~ Children in eating area of bar, in restaurant, and snug ~ Open 11-3, 5.30-11; 12-3, 6(7 in winter)-10.30(11.30 in winter) Sun

STOKE GABRIEL SX8457 Map 1

Church House ★

Village signposted from A385 just W of junction with A3022, in Collaton St Mary; can also be reached from nearer Totnes; nearby parking not easy

Out of season, this is very much an unspoilt and enjoyable local – in season, of course, there's more of a mix of customers, but the friendly staff remain welcoming and helpful. The lounge bar has an exceptionally fine medieval beam-and-plank ceiling, a black oak partition wall, window seats cut into the thick butter-colour walls, decorative plates and vases of flowers on a dresser, and a huge fireplace still used in winter to cook the stew. The mummified cat in a case, probably about 200 years old, was found during restoration of the roof space in the verger's cottage three doors up the lane – one of a handful found in the West Country and believed to have been a talisman against evil spirits. Home-made bar food (they tell us prices have not changed) includes soup (£1.95), a huge choice of sandwiches and toasties (from £1.75; good cheese and prawn toasties, lovely local river salmon and local crab), ploughman's (from £3.25), daily specials like tuna and broccoli bake or home-made steak, kidney and ale pie (£5.50), fresh Dart salmon (£7.25), and puddings (from £2.25); well kept Bass, Worthington Best, and a weekly guest ale on handpump, and quite a few malt whiskies. Cribbage in the little public locals' bar. There are picnic-sets on the little terrace in front of the building. No children. *(Recommended by Ian and Deborah Carrington, W W Burke, Mike and Mary Carter, David Carr, M Joyner, Ian and Jane Irving, Mike Gorton, John and June Freeman)*

Free house ~ Lease: Glyn Patch ~ Real ale ~ Meals and snacks (till 10pm) ~ (01803) 782384 ~ Open 11-3, 6-11; 11-11 Sat; 11-3.30, 7-10.30 Sun

STOKENHAM SX8042 Map 1

Tradesmans Arms

Just off A379 Dartmouth—Kingsbridge

In a charming village, this pretty thatched cottage is run by a character landlord. The little beamed bar has plenty of nice antique tables and neat dining chairs – with more up a step or two at the back, window seats looking across a field to the village church, and a big fireplace. Good bar food includes lunchtime sandwiches and toasties (from £2.65), ploughman's (from £3.65), and sardines (£3.85), as well as home-made french onion soup (£2.50), home-made chicken liver or avocado and herb pâté (from £3.65), sausages (£4.75), pasta with a courgette and tomato sauce (£5.50), sirloin steak (£11.75), and daily specials such as fresh fish delivered daily from Brixham or Plymouth (crab or mixed seafood salads (£6.75), scallops grilled with garlic butter (£8.50), halibut steak with pink pepper, cream and wine sauce (£9.50), plus bacon hock with mustard and onion sauce (£7.50), pork steaks with cider and rosemary sauce (£8.50), and rack of lamb with redcurrant and wine sauce (£9.50). Well kept Adnams Southwold and perhaps Bass, Brakspears Bitter, Greene King Abbot, Hook Norton Best or Youngs IPA on handpump, 50 good malt whiskies, and Heron Valley cider. Dogs are welcome – their Italian sheepdog is called The Blanket, and there are four cats: Flotsam, Jetsam, Gregory and Harry. There are some seats outside in the garden. *(Recommended by B J Harding, Lynn Sharpless, Bob Eardley, TBB, DJW, Mr and Mrs Welsh, Elven Money)*

Free house ~ Licensee Peter Henderson ~ Real ale ~ Meals and snacks ~ Restaurant ~ (01548) 580313 ~ Well behaved children in restaurant only ~ Open 12-3, 6-11(10.30 Sun); closed Mon and closed evenings (except Fri/Sat) Nov-March

TOPSHAM SX9688 Map 1

Passage House

2 miles from M5 junction 30: Topsham signposted from exit roundabout; in Topsham, turn right into Follett Road just before centre, then turn left into Ferry Road

Pleasant and attractive waterside pub with seats on the quiet shoreside terrace (and more on the front courtyard). Inside, the traditional bar has wall pews and bar stools and is decorated with electrified oil lamps hanging from big black oak beams in the ochre ceiling, and the lower dining area still has its slate floor; best to book if you want to be sure of a table. Bar food includes filled rolls (from £1.95), ploughman's (from £4.75), ham and eggs (£4.25), crab or prawn platters (£4.95), steaks (from £7.95), and fresh fish dishes (£6.50-£12.95); the restaurant is no smoking. Well kept Bass, Boddingtons, Flowers IPA, and Wadworths 6X on handpump. As the car park is small, you can park on the quay and walk the 150 yards to the pub. No children. *(Recommended by JP, PP, G Washington, Mayur Shah, Dr*

A J and Mrs P G Newton, John and Vivienne Rice, John and Sally Clarke, Klaus and Elizabeth Leist, Mrs F A W Ricketts, Basil Minson)

Heavitree (who no longer brew) ~ Tenant David Evans ~ Real ale ~ Meals and snacks (not winter Sun evening) ~ Restaurant ~ (01392) 873653 ~ Parking can be a problem ~ Open 11-11

TORCROSS SX8241 Map 1

Start Bay

A379 S of Dartmouth

For 20 years Mr Stubbs has been running this immensely popular dining pub. It's the particularly good fresh fish and the fine position right on the beach that continue to pull in the crowds and in summer there may be queues before the doors open. Picnic-sets on the terrace look out over the three-mile pebble beach, and there are plenty of nearby walks. A local trawler catches the fish, a local crabber drops the crabs at the back door, and the landlord enjoys catching plaice, scallops, and bass: cod and haddock (medium £3.95; large £5.20; jumbo £6.50 – truly enormous), whole lemon sole (from £4.75), skate (£5.50), whole dover sole (in four sizes from £6.75), local scallops (£7.90), brill (from £8.50), and whole bass (small £9.25; medium £9.95; large £11.50). Other food includes sandwiches (from £1.95), ploughman's (from £3.20), vegetable lasagne (£4.75), gammon and pineapple (£5.95), steaks (from £7.95), puddings (£2.75), and children's meals (£3.25); they do warn of delays at peak times (and you will probably have to wait for a table); the sachets of tomato sauce or tartar sauce are not to everyone's taste. Well kept Bass and Flowers Original on handpump, Luscombe cider and fresh apple juice, and local wine. The unassuming main bar (which has a small no-smoking area) is very much set out for eating with wheelback chairs around plenty of dark tables or (round a corner) back-to-back settles forming booths; there are some photographs of storms buffeting the pub and country pictures on its cream walls, and a winter coal fire; a small chatty drinking area by the counter has a brass ship's clock and barometer. The children's room is no smoking. The good winter games room has pool, darts, shove-ha'penny, and juke box; there's more booth seating in a family room with sailing boat pictures. Fruit machine in the lobby. The freshwater wildlife lagoon of Slapton Ley is just behind the pub. *(Recommended by JDM, KM, June and Perry Dann, Andrew Hodges, Richard and Robyn Wain, I Buckmaster, Pat and Robert Watt, TBB, B J Harding, Peter and Rosie Flower, Liz Bell, A M Stephenson, P and J Shapley, Mary Woods)*

Heavitree (who no longer brew; Whitbreads tie) ~ Tenant Paul Stubbs ~ Real ale ~ Meals and snacks (all day in summer; 11.30-2, 6-9 in winter) ~ (01548) 580553 ~ Children in restaurant and own room ~ Open 11.30-11; 12-10.30 Sun; 11.30-2.30, 6-11 in winter; closed evening 25 Dec

TORRINGTON SS4919 Map 1

Black Horse

High St

Both General Fairfax and Lord Hopton are thought to have stayed at this pretty twin-gabled inn during the civil war, and the present licensee is planning to theme the lounge bar along civil war lines. The bar on the left has a couple of fat black beams hung with stirrups, a comfortable seat running right along its full-width window, chunky elm tables, and an oak bar counter; on the right, the no-smoking lounge has a striking ancient black oak partition wall, a couple of attractive oak seats, muted plush easy chairs, and a settee. The oak-panelled restaurant has an aquarium. Generously served, the good value bar food might include sandwiches (from £1.65; filled french bread from £2.50; triple decker toasties with chips £3.10), filled baked potatoes (from £2.85), ploughman's (from £3.45), vegetable lasagne (£4.25), steak and kidney pie (£4.40), prawns marinated in garlic and ginger, breadcrumbed and deep-fried (£4.45), gammon and egg (£4.50), rib-eye steak (£6.25), puddings (£1.95), and children's meals (from £1.95). Well kept Courage Best and Directors and John Smiths, with a changing guest beer on handpump;

darts, shove-ha'penny, cribbage, dominoes, fruit machine, and well reproduced piped music; friendly cat and dogs. Handy for the RHS Rosemoor garden and Dartington Crystal. *(Recommended by Karen and Garry Fairclough, G Washington, R J Walden, Roger and Jenny Huggins, M R Austen, J P Lee, Dr A J and Mrs P G Newton)*

Ushers ~ Lease: David and Val Sawyer ~ Real ale ~ Meals and snacks (not Sun evening Easter-end Sept) ~ Restaurant (not winter Sun evening) ~ (01805) 622121 ~ Children in eating lounge and in restaurant ~ 60s/70s singer 1st Sat of month ~ Open 11-3, 6-11; 11-11 Sat; 12-4, 7-10.30 Sun ~ Bedrooms: £18B/£32B

TUCKENHAY SX8156 Map 1

Maltsters Arms

Take Ashprington road out of Totnes (signed left off A381 on outskirts), keeping on past Watermans Arms

It was quite a surprise to discover that the enthusiastic new licensees here have come from managing one of our successful main entries in London. This, however, is their own pub in a lovely spot by a peaceful wooded creek with tables by the water and moorings for boats. Their aim is to ensure that the pub remains just that – a place where you can just pop in for a pint and a glass of wine without feeling obliged to eat (though the food promises to be so good, that you will probably be quickly tempted). The menu changes daily, using the best local produce – seafood from Brixham, locally caught game and locally reared ostrich and wild boar, and organic ice cream. At lunchtime, there might be filled french bread (from £3.25), butternut squash and ginger soup (£3.50), field mushrooms stuffed with tuna, anchovy and black olive couscous (£4.25), ploughman's (from £4.50), baby onion and celery quiche (£6.25), greek-style shepherd's pie (£6.95), wild boar sausages with mash and onion gravy (£7.25), rabbit casseroled in ale with wholegrain mustard (£7.95), ostrich fillet with a kumquat and peach brandy glaze (£9.95), and puddings like cassis and pink champagne sorbets drenched in pink champagne, rhubarb tart or white chocolate and white rum mousse (from £3.50); in the evening dishes include chicken liver and cranberry pâté with a winter berry chutney (£4.75), pigeon breasts with a redcurrant and madeira glaze (£4.95), gnocchi in a tomato, olive and caper sauce (£6.75), calf liver in a rich madeira sauce (£9.95), venison haunch steak with a stilton glaze (£11.50), and fresh tuna steak with a tomato and avocado salsa (£10.75). Well kept Blackawton Special and Princetown Dartmoor IPA and changing guests on handpump, a thoughtful wine list with a dozen by the glass (they are aiming for many more) including retsina, an Indian methode-champenoise, and a local sparkling wine, and farm cider. The long, narrow bar links two other rooms – a little snug one with an open fire (where the big black dog likes to sit) and plenty of bric-a-brac, and another with red-painted vertical seats and kitchen chairs on the wooden floor, and a second open fire. Darts, shove-ha'penny, cribbage, dominoes, chess, and backgammon.The quayside area is to be smartened up and they hold weekend barbecues here in summer. The bedrooms in the next door Old Winery are pretty special; plenty of bird life. *(Recommended by Andrew Hodges, Mrs Mary Woods, John Wilson, John E Thomason, Margaret and Roy Randle, Mike and Karen England; more reports on the new regime, please)*

Free house ~ Licensees Denise and Quentin Thwaites ~ Real ale ~ Meals and snacks ~ Restaurant ~ (01803) 732350 ~ Children in two rooms and part of restaurant ~ Regular jazz piano Sun evening ~ Open 11-3, 6-11; 11-11 Sat; 12-10.30 Sun; 12-3, 7-10.30 winter Sun; closed from 3pm 25 Dec ~ Bedrooms: /£55B

UGBOROUGH SX6755 Map 1

Anchor

Off A3121 – village signposted from A38 W of South Brent

Happily, this nice old pub has an unchanging and pleasantly relaxed oak-beamed public bar with a log fire in its stone fireplace, and wall settles and seats around wooden tables on the polished woodblock floor; there are windsor armchairs in the comfortable restaurant (the top area is no smoking). The wide choice of good food continues to attract customers, and you can eat from either the bar or restaurant menus and sit anywhere in the pub (apart from Saturday night when there are no bar snacks in the restaurant). Unusual things such as ostrich, alligator, emu, bison, and wild boar rub shoulders with home-made soup (£2.95), devilled mushrooms (£4.50), crab and kiwi cocktail (£5.50), vegetarian kiev (£7.50), steaks (from £12.50), pork in chilli and tomato sauce (£12.65), duck simmered in kirsch with a black cherry sauce (£12.85), and rack of lamb (£16.50); courteous service. Well kept Bass tapped from the cask and Wadworths 6X and three local guest beers on handpump, and quite a few malt whiskies. Darts, dominoes, and fruit machine. There's a small outside seating area. *(Recommended by Mike Gorton, P H Boot, Walker and Debra Lapthorne, J Burrage, Mr and Mrs J Brown, Stephen and Susan Breen)*

Free house ~ Licensees Sheelagh and Ken Jeffreys-Simmons ~ Real ale ~ Meals and snacks ~ Restaurant ~ (01752) 892283 ~ Children welcome ~ Live music most Mons and Sats ~ Open 11-11; 11.30-10.30 Sun ~ Bedrooms: £30B/£40B

UMBERLEIGH SS6023 Map 1

Rising Sun

A377 S of Barnstaple

This comfortable, friendly inn is just across the road from the River Taw (they have five salmon and sea trout beats) and there are plenty of photographs in the bar of happy anglers holding enormous fish. A low stone wall with cushions on top divides the bar into two parts; at one end are some brocaded stools and spindleback chairs around traditional tables on the flowery carpet, a small stone fireplace with a log-effect fire and hops above the hunting horn on the bressumer beam, and a cushioned window seat. The stone bar counter has a row of graded pewter tankards and lots of hops on the gantry, and serves well kept Tetleys plus guests like Courage Directors, Dartmoor Best, Theakstons and Wadworths 6X on handpump; thoughtful little wine list. The other end of the room has high bar stools on the flagstones, a pine built-in wall bench and long cushioned wall seat by a big mural of the river valley, and a woodburning stove with logs stacked on either side. Good bar food includes home-made carrot and coriander soup (£1.95), sandwiches or baked potatoes (from £2), venison sausages (£2.45), tagliatelle in a garlic, cream, mushroom and white wine sauce (£3.15), vegetable chilli (£4.15), ploughman's (from £4.25), lamb crumble (£4.75), pheasant casserole or steak, Guinness and mushroom pie (£4.95), cold poached salmon with minted New Jersey potatoes (£5.25), and home-made puddings (£2.20); you can also eat dishes from the restaurant menu in the bar. There are some green seats under parasols outside, and Umberleigh railway station is just a couple of hundred yards away, over the bridge. *(Recommended by Colin Thompson, Clive Skilton, Mr and Mrs J McCurdy)*

Free house ~ Licensee Roy David ~ Real ale ~ Meals and snacks ~ Restaurant ~ (01769) 560447 ~ Children in restaurant and river room ~ Open 11-3, 6-11; 12-3, 7-10.30 Sun ~ Bedrooms: £40B/£77B

WESTON ST1400 Map 1

Otter ★ 𝕐

Village signposted off A30 at W end of Honiton bypass

Even when really busy, this rambling pub keeps its happy and very relaxed atmosphere and the hard-working staff remain friendly and helpful. The low-beamed main bar has an interesting mix of polished wooden antique tables with fresh flowers and candles in bottles, wooden chairs and handsome chapel pews, chamberpots and jugs hanging from beams, and comfortable chairs by the log fire (that stays alight right through from autumn to spring); each day a page of the Bible on the lectern that ends one pew is turned, and attractive bric-a-brac includes some formidable arms and armour, horse collar and bits, quite a few pictures, and an old mangle; a veritable library leads off, with quite a few readable books and magazines, as well as board games, darts, dominoes, bar billiards, pool, fruit machine, video game, trivia, and piped music; skittle alley. Tasty bar food includes sandwiches (from

£2.50), filled baked potatoes (from £3.75), ploughman's (£4.85), lunchtime specials like home-made prawn and asparagus flan or sausage and mash (£5.95), home-made steak and kidney pie (£6.85), and prawn or salmon salad (£6.95), and evening specials such as red mullet fillet in fresh crab and orange sauce (£7.95), chicken breast stuffed with asparagus, wrapped in bacon and served with different sauces (£9.95), and half honey-roast duck (£12.95); 3-course Sunday lunch, and maybe spit roasts on Thursday evenings from 8pm. Well kept Bass, Boddingtons, and Hardy Country on handpump, good inexpensive wines, and farm cider. They are very kind to children, with high chairs (children sitting in them get a free meal), a children's menu (with a picture to colour and free lollipop), a box of toys, rocking-horse, a bike, and a climbing frame and slide. The sizeable lawn (where there are often quacking ducks) runs down to the little River Otter, and has picnic-sets, pretty climbing plants, hanging baskets and flowering tubs. *(Recommended by Mrs Mary Woods, Jacquie and Jim Jones, Peter and Audrey Dowsett, Brian and Jenny Seller, Joyce Cottrell, R and S Bentley, the Sandy family, Jerry and Alison Oakes, Iain Robertson, Richard Dolphin, R J Walden, Alan and Paula McCully, Mavis and Robert Harford, Mark and Mary Fairman, G R Sunderland, Nigel Wikeley, Mrs M Furness)*

Free house ~ Lease: Brian and Susan Wilkinson ~ Real ale ~ Meals and snacks (till 10pm) ~ (01404) 42594 ~ Children welcome ~ Open 11-3, 6-11; 12-3, 7-10.30 Sun

WIDECOMBE SX7076 Map 1

Rugglestone

Village at end of B3387; pub just S – turn left at church and NT church house, OS Sheet 191 map reference 720765

A little no-smoking dining room has been opened up in this unspoilt local, just up the lane from the bustling tourist village. The small bar has just four small tables, a few window and wall seats, a one-person pew built into the corner by the nice old stone fireplace, and a rudimentary bar counter dispensing well kept Butcombe Bitter and Dartmoor Best tapped from the cask; local farm cider. The room on the right is a bit bigger and lighter-feeling, and shy strangers may feel more at home here: another stone fireplace, beam-and-plank ceiling, stripped deal tables, a built-in wall bench; darts, shove-ha'penny, cribbage, dominoes, and euchre. Good simple bar food includes home-made soup (£2.15), hot locally salted beef or roast pork in a large cottage roll (£2.75), ploughman's (£3.75), cauliflower cheese (£3.90), daily specials such as cheesy leek and potato bake (£3.95), steak and kidney pie (£4.65), and beef stew with dumplings or scrumpy wild rabbit casserole (£4.85), and puddings like treacle tart or apple pudding with clotted cream (£2.75); friendly service. The two cats are called Marbles (who is now 18) and Elbi, there's a flat-coated retriever, Mogul, and two terriers, Tinker and Belle. Outside across the little medieval leat bringing moor water down to the village is a field with lots of picnic-sets (and some geese and chickens); old-fashioned outside lavatories. No children inside (though they have constructed a large shelter with tables and chairs in the garden). *(Recommended by I Maw, Jeanne Cross, Paul Silvestri, P and M Rudlin, JP, PP, Andy and Jill Kassube, Comus Elliott, Paul and Heather Bettesworth)*

Free house ~ Licensees Lorrie and Moira Ensor ~ Real ale ~ Meals and snacks (not Sun evening, not Mon in winter) ~ (01364) 621327 ~ Open 11-2.30(3 Sat), 6(7 winter; 5 Sat)-11; 12-3, 6.30-10.30 Sun

WONSON SX6790 Map 1

Northmore Arms 🍷 🛏

Off A382 half mile from A30 at Whiddon Down; turn right down lane signposted Throwleigh/Gidleigh. Continue down lane over humpback bridge; turn left to Wonson; OS Sheet 191 map reference 674903

Tucked away down narrow high-hedges lanes, this remote country cottage appeals very much to those who like simple unspoilt locals. It's a friendly place with two small connected beamed rooms – modest and informal but civilised – with wall settles, a few elderly chairs, five tables in one room and just two in the other. There are two open fires (only one may be lit), and some attractive photographs on the stripped stone walls; darts and cribbage. Besides well kept ales such as Adnams Broadside, Cotleigh Tawny and Exe Valley Dobs, they have good house wines, and food (with unchanging prices) such as sandwiches, pâté (£2.45), home-made duck and orange pie (£3.95), steak and kidney pudding (£4.50), Sunday lunch (£4.95), and sticky toffee pudding (£1.95). Tables and chairs sit precariously in the steep little garden – all very peaceful and rustic; excellent walking from the pub (or to it, perhaps from Chagford or Gidleigh Park). No children. *(Recommended by R J Walden, Catherine Lloyd, Bett and Brian Cox, Dallas Seawright, David and Jane Russell, Helen Morton, Mike Gorton)*

Free house ~ Licensee Mo Miles ~ Real ale ~ Meals and snacks (12-9; 12-2, 7-9 Sun) ~ (01647) 231428 ~ Open 11-11; 12-10.30 Sun ~ Two bedrooms: /£25

WOODBURY SALTERTON SY0189 Map 1

Digger's Rest

3½ miles from M5 junction 30: A3052 towards Sidmouth, village signposted on right about ½ mile after Clyst St Mary; also signposted from B3179 SE of Exeter

For quarter of a century, the same friendly licensees have been running this pleasant thatched village pub. The heavy beamed bar has a log fire at one end with an ornate solid fuel stove at the other, comfortable old-fashioned country chairs and settles around polished antique tables set with fresh flowers, a dark oak Jacobean screen, a grandfather clock, and plates decorating the walls of one alcove. The big skittles alley can be used for families, and there's a games room with pool, fruit machine, and video game. Well kept Bass and Dartmoor Best on ancient handpumps, and local farm ciders; sensibly placed darts and dominoes in the small brick-walled public bar. Decent bar food includes home-made soup (£1.85), sandwiches with home-cooked meats (from £2.95; good local hand-picked crab), home-made pâté (£3.45), filled baked potatoes (from £3.65), ploughman's (from £3.85), cold roast beef with chips (£4.85), liver and bacon with onion gravy or home-made lasagne (£4.95), steaks, daily specials, and Sunday roasts (£5.45); it does get busy, so best to get here early at lunchtime. The terrace garden has views of the countryside. *(Recommended by Alan and Paula McCully, John Askew, G Washington, Mr and Mrs J Bishop, Elven Money, Basil Minson, Mr and Mrs C R Little, Dr A J and Mrs P G Newton)*

Free house ~ Licensee Sally Pratt ~ Real ale ~ Meals and snacks (12-1.45, 7-9.45) ~ (01395) 232375 ~ Children in eating area of bar ~ Open 11-2.30, 6.30-11; 12-2.30, 7-10.30 Sun; closed evenings 25-26 Dec

WOODLAND SX7968 Map 1

Rising Sun

Village signposted off A38 just NE of Ashburton – then keep eyes peeled for Rising Sun signposts

This is an unexpected place in such an isolated spot – a considerable expanse of softly lit red plush button-back banquettes and matching studded chairs, partly divided by wooden balusters, masonry pillars and the odd high-backed settle. A forest of beams is hung with thousands of old doorkeys, and a nice part by the log fire has shelves of plates and books, and old pictures above the fireplace. Bar food is very good and includes sandwiches (from £2), home-made pasties (£2.50), home-made soup (£2.95), stilton and pear bruschetta with mixed leaves (£3.95), smoked duck breast with red onion compote (£4.50), ploughman's with home-made chutney (from £5; good local cheeses), pasta with tomato and basil sauce (£5.25), spiced aubergine and red pepper stew with couscous, home-made pies or home-cooked gammon with home-made chips and free range egg (£5.95), pork cutlet with a prune and ginger glaze (£7.95), fried grey mullet with a tomato and balsamic vinegar dressing (£8.25), rack of lamb glazed with dijon mustard and rosemary or local venison steak with berry fruit and sloe gin compote and red wine (£10.95), and puddings like sticky toffee pudding with butterscotch sauce, rhubarb fool or Devon apple sponge (£2.95); children have home-breaded chicken breast, home-made fishcakes or local sausages (£2.50; they can also have small helpings of some adult dishes); super afternoon teas with home-made scones. You can have pies, cakes and pastries baked to order to take home, too, and there are regular themed food evenings. A couple of real ales are well kept on handpump – Bass, Dartmoor Best, Exmoor Gold or Jennings Cocker Hoop – and service is very cheerful; two family areas include one up a couple of steps with various toys (and a collection of cookery books). The dining area is no smoking. There are some picnic-sets in the spacious garden, which has a play area including a redundant tractor. *(Recommended by Dr A J and Mrs P G Newton; more reports please)*

Free house ~ Licensee Heather Humphreys ~ Real ale ~ Meals and snacks (12-2.15, 6-9.15) ~ (01364) 652544 ~ Children in family areas ~ Open 11(12 Sun)-4.30, 6-11(10.30 Sun); 11.30-2.30, 6(7 Sun)-11(10.30 Sun) in winter; closed winter Mon lunchtime

Lucky Dip

Besides the fully inspected pubs, you might like to try these Lucky Dips recommended to us and described by readers (if you do, please send us reports):

Abbotskerswell [SX8569], *Butchers Arms*: Well used, with dark alcovey stone walls, well kept Bass, Boddingtons, Flowers and Hardy Royal Oak, friendly staff, good food; garden with very good play area *(Mr and Mrs C Roberts, Chris Reeve)*

Alswear [A373 South Molton—Tiverton; SS7222], *Butchers Arms*: Well kept friendly local, bright lounge, generous good value food esp steaks, guest ales such as Butcombe, helpful staff; good for children; bedrooms *(the Hilton family)*

Appledore [Irsha St; SS4630], *Beaver*: Great estuary views from raised area in light airy pub, good value food (esp fish), friendly staff, well kept changing ales such as Bass, Butcombe, Flowers, pool in smaller games room, views from outdoor tables; children welcome *(Dr A J and Mrs P G Newton, Neil Townend, Philip and Jude Simmons)*

☆ **Ashburton** [West St], *Exeter*: Friendly atmosphere in pleasing old-fashioned pub with welcoming Scottish licensees, well kept Badger, good value food inc small helpings for older people *(Tom Rowntree, Dr B and Mrs P B Baker)*

Ashburton [11 West St], *London*: This main entry hotel, which brewed its own ales, closed after fire damage last year *(LYM)*

☆ **Ashprington** [Bow Bridge, towards Tuckenhay; SX8156], *Watermans Arms*: Nicely placed pub now part of a West Country chain, wide choice of food from well filled baguettes up inc children's, partly no-smoking restaurant, well kept Bass, Dartmoor Best, Palmers IPA, and Tetleys, farm cider, good quick service, heavy beams, tiles, stripped stone, log fires, some high-backed settles; pretty garden by river with ducks; children in side area, dogs allowed, comfortable bedrooms with good breakfast *(D Barlow, A J Goddard, Andrew Hodges, DC, John Wilson, P and J Shapley, Ian Shorthouse, Pat and Robert Watt, Liz Bell, LYM)*

Avonwick [B3210 ½ mile from A38; SX7157], *Mill*: Good value food inc fresh veg, children's helpings and generous Thurs and Sun lunchtime carvery in roomy and pretty converted mill, friendly service, Bass; reasonable disabled access, high chairs; play area in big lakeside garden *(JE)*

☆ **Aylesbeare** [Sidmouth Rd; A3052 Exeter—Sidmouth, junction with B3180; SY0392], *Halfway*: Spotless dining pub with high views over Dartmoor, interesting sporting prints and memorabilia, good food esp fish and vegetarian, well kept ales inc changing guest beers, good very friendly service *(Alan and Paula McCully, Dr and Mrs D J Walker)*

Beer [ST2389], *Barrel of Beer*: Drinkers' pub but also serves food; open all day, parking nearby *(Peter and Audrey Dowsett)*; *Dolphin*: Friendly open-plan local with good collection of bric-a-brac, particularly well kept beer, good food and wine – nothing expensive; quite large, but locally popular and can get busy; maybe antiques fair behind; restaurant, bedrooms, quite near sea *(Peter and Audrey Dowsett, Jeanne Cross, Paul Silvestri)*

Beesands [SX8140], *Cricket*: Friendly local by sea wall, with tables outside; good value standard food inc fish, well kept Whitbreads-related and other ales such as Wadworths 6X, log fire, unobtrusive piped music; family room; bedrooms *(Pat and Robert Watt)*

Berry Head [SX9456], *Berry Head*: Currently doing well, with enjoyable food inc good carvery, panoramic Torbay views *(D I Baddeley)*

☆ **Bickleigh** [A396/A3072 N of Exeter; SS9406], *Fishermans Cot*: Lots of tables on acres of turkey carpet in greatly extended thatched fishing inn, attractively broken up with pillars, plants and some panelled parts, charming view over shallow rocky race below 1640 Exe bridge, more tables out on terrace and waterside lawn; good well served food inc popular reasonably priced carvery, well kept Bass and Wadworths 6X, friendly efficient service; piped pop music; comfortable bedrooms looking over own terrace to river *(John and Vivienne Rice, E Robinson, Alan Kitchener, Neil Townend, Mr and Mrs R Head, BB)*

☆ **Bickleigh**, *Trout*: Thatched pub with comfortable easy chairs in huge bar and dining lounge, sizeable buffet counter with good choice of food from sandwiches up and tempting puddings cabinet, well kept ales such as Cotleigh Tawny, Bass, Boddingtons, Exmoor Gold, nice coffee, efficient friendly service; tables on pretty lawn, car park across rd; five well equipped bedrooms, good breakfast *(G Washington, E Robinson, Basil Minson, Alan and Barbara Mence, LYM)*

Bideford [The Quay; SS4526], *Kings Arms*: Well kept Whitbreads-related and other ales, decent food from good filled rolls up, cheerful atmosphere, Victorian harlequin floor tiles in alcovey front bar, back raised family area; pavement tables *(Karen and Garry Fairclough)*

Bigbury [SX6647], *Royal Oak*: Welcoming village pub with particularly well kept Bass tapped from the cask, enjoyable food inc fresh fish *(Brian Coad)*

☆ **Bishops Tawton** [signed off A377 outside Barnstaple; SS5630], *Chichester Arms*: 15th-c cob and thatch pub with low bowed beams, large stone fireplace, old local photographs, plush banquettes, open fire, well priced food from home-made soup and sandwiches up, well kept Dartmoor Best, Ind Coope Burton and Tetleys, games in family room, partly no-smoking restaurant; picnic-sets on front terrace and in back garden; open all day *(Sheila and John French, R J Walden, Sue and Bob Ward, Rita Horridge, Dr A J and Mrs P G Newton, Alan and Heather Jacques)*

☆ **Bolberry** [Bolberry Down – OS Sheet 202 map ref 691392; SX6939], *Port Light*: Former radar station alone on dramatic NT clifftop – one reader who spent several weeks of his RAF service here wishes the food had been as good then; bright, clean, spacious and busy, with superb picture-window views and varied tasty well presented food, not too expensive; well kept Dartmoor, friendly efficient service, restaurant, conservatory, tables in garden, good play area; well behaved children allowed; five bedrooms, nr fine beaches, right on the coast path *(JDM, KM, A M Stephenson, Ian and Jane Irving, B J Harding)*

Bovey Tracey [SX8278], *Cromwell Arms*: Popular local with reasonably priced food piled high, friendly quick service, good range of well kept well priced beers, several areas with high-backed settles, no piped music *(E G Parish)*

Brampford Speke [off A377 N of Exeter; SX9299], *Agricultural*: Dining pub doing well under new management, very enjoyable, with good interesting nicely presented bar food, frequent special events such as wine tastings, very friendly staff, gallery restaurant (children allowed); picnic-sets on sheltered terrace *(Sue and Adrian Upton)*

☆ *nr* **Brayford** [Yarde Down; 3 miles from Brayford, on Simonsbath rd over Exmoor; SS7235], *Poltimore Arms*: Chatty and pubby old two-bar local with friendly cheerful staff, good value bar food, well kept Cotleigh Tawny and Wadworths 6X tapped from the cask, basic traditional furnishings, inglenook; maybe piped music, simple games room; children allowed in restaurant, picnic-sets in side garden; no dogs inside *(Dr A J and Mrs P G Newton, Mrs V A Knight, D Rooke, R J Walden, LYM)*

Brendon [Rockford; Lynton—Simonsbath rd, off B2332 – OS Sheet 180 map ref 755477; SS7547], *Rockford*: Newish licensees in homely and friendly little inn well set for walkers (and fishermen) by East Lyn river, summer afternoon refreshments as well as generous usual bar food inc vegetarian and fish; well kept Cotleigh Barn Owl, Courage Best and a guest beer, darts, pool, shove-ha'penny, cribbage, dominoes; piped music; restaurant, children in eating areas, folk night every 3rd Sat, bedrooms; open all day summer *(Steven M Gent, Piotr Chodzko-Zajko, R V G Brown, LYM)*; *Staghunters*: Idyllic setting with garden by East Lyn river, popular substantial food from filled baguettes up inc fresh veg, well kept Wadworths 6X and Addlestone's cider; friendly to walkers; can get very busy; restaurant, bedrooms *(Richard and Ann Higgs, Barry and Anne, Terry Morgan)*

☆ **Bridestowe** [old A38; SX5189], *White Hart*: Unpretentious friendly local, partly flagstoned beamed main bar with grandfather clock and games end, some nice old furnishings in lounge, panelled restaurant; good value bar food, well kept Palmers, decent wines, friendly staff, informal streamside back garden, peaceful Dartmoor village; bedrooms *(Bett and Brian Cox, LYM)*

☆ **Bridford** [off B3193 Dunsford—Chudleigh; SX8186], *Bridford Inn*: Attractive family-run pub, friendly and cheerful, with consistently good sensibly priced food inc imaginative dishes and popular Sun lunch (worth booking), well kept beers, local cider; dark beams, some well polished antiques, turkey carpet, log fire in big stone fireplace; cl Tues, does not open till 12 and 7 (6.30 Sat); tables on fairylit terrace above charming quiet village with pretty valley views, well behaved dogs allowed *(Nigel Wikeley, Jean and David Hall, LYM)*

Brixham [Bolton St; SX9255], *Vigilance*: New Wetherspoons conversion of former shop, sizeable well furnished open-plan bar with no-smoking area, good reasonably priced food and drink, no music; nearby parking difficult *(Andrew Hodges)*

☆ **Broadhempston** [off A381, signed from centre; SX8066], *Coppa Dolla*: Good ambitious food in comfortable and welcoming beamed bar divided by sturdy timber props, very reasonable prices, well kept ales such as Bass, Dartmoor Best and Morlands Old Speckled Hen, decent wines, cheery service, log fires, pleasant upstairs restaurant; Sun quiz night; well spaced picnic-sets in attractive garden with pleasant views; two apartments *(Andrew Woodgate, Colin McKerrow, E R Cowtan, Dr and Mrs Rod Holcombe, BB)*

☆ **Buckfastleigh** [Totnes Rd, handy for A38; SX7366], *Dartbridge*: Big family pub, prettily placed opp Dart Valley Rly – very popular in summer; good food, well kept Butcombe, above-average house wines, friendly young staff; reasonable disabled access, tables in neatly kept roadside garden, ten letting chalets *(John*

Evans, John and Vivienne Rice, Mr and Mrs Buckmaster)

☆ **Buckland Monachorum** [SX4868], *Drakes Manor*: Well kept Courage and Ushers, consistently good reasonably priced food, good friendly service, good house wine; beams and oak panelling, separate public bar *(F T and S M Simonds)*

☆ **Budleigh Salterton** [Chapel St; SY0682], *Salterton Arms*: Wide range of reasonably priced good food, well kept Bass, John Smiths and Theakstons Old Peculier, good choice of malts and Irish whiskeys, lots of jazz musician and other prints, nautical mementoes, small open fires, neat uniformed staff, upper dining gallery; children and dogs welcome, can get very busy summer; jazz winter Sun evenings, open all day w/e *(Peter and Audrey Dowsett, Neil Spink, Basil Minson, Paul White, Mark and Heather Williamson, LYM)*

☆ **Burgh Island** [SX6443], *Pilchard*: The star's for the setting, high above sea on tidal island with great cliff walks; not at all smart, but atmospheric, with blazing fire; Courage and Ushers, basic food (all day summer, lunchtime only winter), piped music, children in downstairs bistro, dogs welcome, some tables down by beach *(Neil Spink, JP, PP, LYM)*

☆ **Chagford** [Mill St; SX7087], *Bullers Arms*: Small but cheery panelled local with food servery doing very wide range inc vegetarian, well kept Dartmoor Best and Ind Coope Burton, decent coffee, very friendly licensees, militaria, copper and brass, darts; can get smoky at night; summer barbecues *(Neil and Anita Christopher, Guy Vowles, LYM)*

Chagford, *Three Crowns*: Ancient thatched building of great potential, but rather unsympathetic furnishings; popular generous food, welcoming service, well kept Bass and Flowers Original, big fire, stripped-stone public bar with pool and darts; dogs welcome, tables on front cobbles and in back garden; good old-fashioned bedrooms *(Guy Vowles, Ted George, Jeanne Cross, Paul Silvestri, BB)*

☆ **Christow** [signed off B3193 N of A38; SX8385], *Artichoke*: Pretty thatched local with open-plan rooms stepped down hill, low beams, some black panelling, flagstones, straightforward food inc decent specials, vegetarian, fish and game, big log fire (2nd one in no-smoking end dining room), mainly Whitbreads-related ales; rather prominent games machine; tables on back terrace, pretty hillside village nr Canonteign Waterfalls and Country Park *(Dr and Mrs A K Clarke, BB)*

Chudleigh [Fore St; SX8679], *Bishop Lacey*: Partly medieval, with Boddingtons, Flowers IPA, Fullers London Pride and Princetown Jail, some tapped from casks in back bar; good value food, no-smoking dining room, open all day *(the Didler)*

Chudleigh Knighton [SX8477], *Claycutters Arms*: Thatched village pub promisingly taken over recently by licensees of the Anchor at Cockwood (main entry), with very wide choice of food from sandwiches up, inc game, venison and speciality steamed puddings, pleasant restaurant; seats on side terrace and in orchard *(LYM; reports please)*

☆ **Churchstow** [A379 NW of Kingsbridge; SX7145], *Church House*: Long character bar with heavy black beams, stripped stone, cushioned settles, back conservatory with floodlit well feature, seats outside; Bass, Fullers London Pride, Morlands Old Speckled Hen and changing guest ales, food from filled baps to mixed grill, pleasant waitresses *(JKW, Peter and Audrey Dowsett, LYM – more reports on new regime please)*

Churston Ferrers [SX9056], *Churston Court*: Attractive Elizabethan former manor house in lovely setting next to village church, nr Elbury Cove, good food inc good fresh fish; three big bull mastiffs add to the setting; bedrooms *(Dave and Sue Norgate)*

Clearbrook [off A386 Tavistock—Plymouth, edge of Dartmoor; SX5265], *Skylark*: Friendly old Dartmoor-edge local under new licensees, big and often busy with walkers, generous good value food, Bass and Courage Best and Directors, simple furnishings, log fire, children's room; good Dartmoor and Plymouth Sound views, big back garden *(Jacquie and Jim Jones)*

Clovelly [SS3225], *Red Lion*: Worth knowing for lovely position on curving quay, with character back bar, food from sandwiches up, real ale; restaurant, simple attractive bedrooms *(Ann and Colin Hunt, MJ)*

☆ **Clyst St Mary** [nr M5 junction 30; SX9790], *Half Moon*: Attractive old pub next to multi-arched bridge over Clyst, well kept ales such as Bass and Wadworths 6X tapped from the cask, good home-made food inc some local dishes and local produce; wheelchair access, bedrooms *(Mrs Sally Britnell, Ken and Janet Bracey, G Washington, Pat and Robert Watt)*

Cockington [Cockington Lane; SX8963], *Drum*: Busy and cheerful olde-worlde pastiche thatched and beamed tavern in quaintly touristy Torquay-edge village by 500-acre park, with Dartmoor Bitter and Legend, roomy bar (can be smoky) and two family eating areas, quick service, Weds summer barbecues, winter skittle evenings and live music; piped music; tables on terrace and in attractive back garden *(Dr A J and Mrs P G Newton, Ian and Jane Irving, E G Parish, Nick Lawless)*

☆ **Cockwood** [SX9780], *Ship*: Comfortable and welcoming 17th-c inn overlooking estuary and harbour, seafaring memorabilia, food from open crab sandwiches up inc good evening fish dishes (freshly made so takes time), Ushers BB and Founders, reasonable prices, good steep-sided garden *(Colin Thompson, DAV, John Beeken, Stan Edwards)*

☆ **Coffinswell** [off A380 N of Torquay; SX8968], *Linny*: Very pretty partly 14th-c thatched country pub, relaxed and cheerful big beamed bar, settles and other old seats, smaller areas off; some concentration on wide choice of good value bar food inc fine crab salad; well kept Bass, Morlands Old Speckled Hen and Tetleys, cosy log fires, lots of twinkling brass, neat friendly service, no-smoking area, children's room, upstairs restaurant extension, some

tables outside; picturesque village *(Gordon, John Wilson, Stan Edwards, John Barker, Andrew Hodges, BB)*
Colaton Raleigh [A376 Newton Poppleford—Budleigh Salterton; SY0787], *Otter*: Well cooked food in long bar and restaurant, hard-working friendly licensees, children's room, lovely big garden. Friendly service, well cooked food, children's room, restaurant, long bar, good garden, new licensees *(Mark and Heather Williamson, John Askew, Stan Edwards)*
Colyford [Swan Hill Rd; A3052 Exeter—Lyme Regis, by tramway stn; SY2492], *White Hart*: Good food inc wonderful Italian menu in bistro with opera memorabilia, constantly changing real ales, wide choice of wine, very friendly, children's games room, skittle alley; garden, boules; trad jazz Sun night *(Brian Websdale)*
Colyton [Dolphin St – village signed off A35 and A3052 E of Sidmouth; SY2493], *Kingfisher*: Friendly staff, hearty popular food from good sandwiches and baked potatoes up, stripped stone, plush seats and elm settles, beams and big open fire, well kept Badger Best and Tanglefoot, Charles Wells Bombardier and changing guests, low-priced soft drinks; pub games, upstairs family room, skittle alley, tables out on terrace, garden with water feature *(George Atkinson, Peter and Rosie Flower, R Boyd, R T and J C Moggridge, Derek and Iris Martin)*
Combe Martin [Seaside; SS5847], *Fo'csle*: Fantastic beach setting, very welcoming staff, generous helpings of good varied food; John Smiths; bedrooms reasonably priced, recently pleasantly decorated, superb breakfast *(Sue and John Woodward)*
Combeinteignhead [SX9271], *Coombe Cellars*: Big bustling family Brewers Fayre open all day, with lots for children inc indoor play area, their own menu, baby-changing, fun days and parties with entertainment, outside play galleon and fenced-in playground; lovely estuary setting, tables on pontoons, jetties and big terraces, water-sports; roomy and comfortable bar with plenty of sporting and nautical bric-a-brac, usual food all day, well kept Whitbreads-related ales, lots of wines by the glass, friendly efficient staff, various events; good disabled facilities *(Dr Rod Holcombe, Chris Reeve, Andrew Hodges, Basil Minson, JWGW, LYM)*
Cornwood [off A38 E of Plymouth; SX6059], *Cornwood*: Badger Tanglefoot, Bass and Courage in big L-shaped lounge with no-smoking eating area, generous food inc bargain Sun lunch, lots of ornamental plates, old photographs, separate bar with pool; dogs welcome, quiet Dartmoor-edge village *(Neil Spink)*
Cornworthy [off A381 Totnes—Kingsbridge; can also be reached direct from Totnes via Ashprington—Dittisham rd; SX8255], *Hunters Lodge*: Pleasant and comfortable genuine country local, snug and chatty, with wide choice of food from sandwiches to often extremely good genuine home cooking (very popular, worth booking); well kept Blackawton Special and Forty-four, John Smiths and Ushers Best, local Pig Squeal cider, helpful service, good log fire, darts, dominoes, shove-ha'penny, children's games; piped music; picnic-sets on terrace and big lawn, good walks *(Liz Bell, D I Baddelely, B J Harding, Dr S P Willavoys, Jo and Gary Charlton, LYM)*
☆ **Countisbury** [A39, E of Lynton – OS Sheet 180 map ref 747497; SS7449], *Exmoor Sandpiper*: Beautifully set rambling and friendly heavy-beamed pub with antique furniture, several log fires, good choice of usual food from sandwiches to steaks, well kept Bass, Exmoor Best and Hardy Royal Oak, restaurant with weekend smorgasbord and carvery; children in eating area, garden tables, open all day; comfortable bedrooms, good nearby cliff walks *(Richard Gibbs, Pat and Robert Watt, LYM)*
☆ **Croyde** [B3231 NW of Braunton; SS4439], *Thatch*: Lively rambling thatched pub nr great surfing beaches, with laid-back feel and customers to match (can get packed in summer); wide choice of reasonably priced generous food, well kept Bass, St Austell HSD and Tetleys, cheerful young staff, tables outside; restaurant, children in eating area, open all day; piped music may be a bit loud, can be packed in summer; bedrooms simple but clean and comfortable *(Sue and John Woodward, Paul and Ursula Randall, I J and N K Buckmaster, LYM)*
☆ **Dartmouth** [Smith St; SX8751], *Seven Stars*: Crowded beamed and panelled local, well priced popular food, well kept ales such as Norman Conquest and Wadworths 6X, coal fire, end family area with sensible tables and settles; service can slow, maybe piped pop music, fruit machine; upstairs restaurant *(Mr and Mrs C Roberts, DC, BB)*
Dartmouth [Bayards Cove], *Dartmouth Arms*: Warm friendly local (popular with naval students evening) with well kept beer, good value basic bar food inc lots of pizzas, log fire, panelling and boating memorabilia; tables out in prime spot overlooking Dart estuary *(I J and N K Buckmaster, Andrew Hodges)*; [Sandquay], *Floating Bridge*: Clean and friendly, with well kept Scottish Courage ales, good choice of food, cheery landlord, nice atmosphere; good views of Dart and higher ferry *(I J and N K Buckmaster)*
☆ **Denbury** [The Green; SX8168], *Union*: Spotless and comfortable low-beamed local on edge of old village green, good food from sandwiches to steaks inc interesting dishes, vegetarian, fresh fish and lots of puddings, two eating areas, well kept Flowers, Brains Dark Mild and Wadworths 6X, good coffee, charming service; tables in garden by green, quietly pretty sheltered village *(Mr and Mrs C Roberts, Clare and Roy Head, Jean and Douglas Troup, BB)*
☆ **Dittisham** [best to park in village – steep but attractive walk down; SX8654], *Ferry Boat*: Big windows make the most of beautiful waterside spot, nr little foot-ferry you call by bell; good range of low-priced bar food, well kept Ushers, friendly staff *(I and N Buckmaster, Patricia Dodd, Jo and Gary Charlton, Liz Bell, LYM)*
Dolton [The Square; SS5712], *Royal Oak*:

Attractive bar and restaurant, very extensive bar menu inc fresh fish, good range of beers inc some local, good hospitable service; bedrooms *(Simon and Jane Williams, R J Walden)*

☆ **Down Thomas** [follow HMS *Cambridge* signs from Plymouth; SX5149], *Langdon Court*: Interesting old country-house hotel with friendly landlord, good meals in lounge bar and family room, reasonable prices, good fire, country views, well kept Bass and Wadworths 6X from ornate servery, subdued piped music, picnic-sets outside; dogs allowed; comfortable bedrooms *(Mr and Mrs G Little, P Broughton)*

☆ *nr* **Drewsteignton** [Fingle Bridge, off A38 at Crockernwell via Preston or Drewsteignton; OS Sheet 191 map ref 743899; SX7489], *Anglers Rest*: Idyllic wooded Teign valley spot by 16th-c pack-horse bridge, lovely walks; much extended former tea pavilion, with tourist souvenirs and airy cafe feel, but has well kept Cotleigh and Dartmoor Gold and reliable food inc children's meals (not Sun); friendly helpful service, log fire, waterside picnic-sets; cl winter evenings *(Alan and Paula McCully, John Franklin, Tony Dickinson, L H and S Ede, David and Ruth Shillitoe, BB)*

☆ **East Budleigh** [SY0684], *Sir Walter Raleigh*: Small neat village inn with faultless service, good range of nicely presented hot and cold food inc help-yourself salad bar and good Sun lunch, friendly staff and locals, cosy charming dining room, Flowers IPA and Marstons Pedigree; nice village and church; bedrooms *(Basil Minson, F J Willy, LYM)*

☆ **East Down** [off A39 Barnstaple—Lynton nr Arlington – OS Sheet 180 map ref 600415; SS5941], *Pyne Arms*: Low-beamed bar with very wide choice of generous food from sandwiches up, lots of nooks and crannies, attractive furnishings inc high-backed curved settle, small no-smoking galleried loft (where children allowed), well kept Bass and Worthington, decent house wines, flagstoned games area with unobtrusive juke box; handy for Arlington Court, good walks *(Richard and Ann Higgs, Dr A J and Mrs P G Newton, Donald Mather, LYM)*

Ermington [SX6353], *First & Last*: Beautifully set local, lots of well tended hanging baskets, friendly service, limited choice of good cheap food with ample veg, Bass *(John Evans, B J Harding)*

Exbourne [SX6002], *Red Lion*: Good value food inc authentic Thai and other oriental dishes (new Singaporean licensee), warm friendly service, well kept Badger, Fullers London Pride and guest ales *(R J Walden)*

☆ **Exeter** [The Close, attached to Royal Clarence Hotel], *Well House*: Big windows looking across to cathedral in open-plan bar divided by inner walls and partitions; lots of Victorian prints, well kept changing ales such as Blackawton Special and Forty-four, Hart Off Your Trolley and Crouch Vale Millennium Gold, popular bar lunches inc good salads, daily papers, good service; Roman well beneath (can be viewed when pub not busy); piped music *(Ian Phillips, D J and P M Taylor, BB)*

Exeter [Iron Bridge, North Gate; SX9192], *City Gate*: Former Crown & Sceptre spaciously refurbished, with ornate ceiling, good food bar, very attentive staff, tables on terrace *(A Addington)*; [Iron Bridge], *Fizzgig & Firkin*: Huge brick-floored warehouse bar, popular with locals, brewing its own Floozie and Fizzgig; interesting music nights – modern, rock, blues *(Dallas Seawright)*; [St Davids Hill], *Great Western*: Warm and friendly, with a comfortable relaxed feel, attractively priced honest food from sandwiches up, daily papers, Scottish Courage ales; peanuts in the shell, no music *(Ian Phillips, E V M Whiteway)*; [Little Castle St], *Hole in the Wall*: Pleasantly refurbished Eldridge Pope pub *(R J Walden)*; [14 Exe St, off Bonhay Rd], *Papermakers*: Bistro pub with charming continental atmosphere, wide choice of good if not cheap unusual food running up to bass and venison, friendly efficient service, Tetleys and a guest beer, good choice of wines; maybe piped music *(Ian Phillips)*; [The Quay], *Port Royal*: Extensive bar and eating area with river views, economical bar food *(D J and P M Taylor)*; [The Quay], *Prospect*: Overlooking waterfront, with beams, panelling and settles, old safari pictures and local prints, comfortable upper river-view dining area (food from good doorstep sandwiches up), well kept Bass, Boddingtons and Wadworths 6X; lower bar with games machines, piped music *(Mr and Mrs C Roberts, Alan and Heather Jacques, D J and P M Taylor, Vivienne and John Rice)*; [Martins Lane – just off cathedral close], *Ship*: Pretty 14th-c pub with substantial comfortable furniture in heavy-beamed busy but atmospheric bar, well kept Bass and Boddingtons, farm cider, good service, decent generous food, quieter upstairs restaurant *(Galen Strawson, G Washington, Dr A J and Mrs P G Newton, LYM)*

Exton [SX9886], *Puffing Billy*: Consistently good food, careful friendly management *(N Rimmer)*

☆ **Filleigh** [off A361 N Devon link rd; SS6627], *Stags Head*: Pretty 16th-c thatched pub with old rustic tables out in fairy-lit honeysuckle arbour by big tree-sheltered pond with lots of ducks and fish; friendly local bar with crack darts team, banknotes on beams, Corgi toy collection, very high-backed settle, good food, generous if not cheap, pleasantly cottagey dining room up a couple of steps; well kept Barum Original, Bass and Tetleys, reasonably priced wines, welcoming landlord, maybe piped nostalgic pop; bedrooms comfortable and good value, good breakfast *(Peter Churchill, Karen and Garry Fairclough, Don and Thelma Beeson, BB)*

Folly Gate [A386 Hatherleigh—Okehampton; SX5797], *Crossways*: Wide range of good value interesting food inc fresh lobster and crab, well kept St Austell ales, friendly landlord *(R J Walden, Brian and Bett Cox)*

☆ **Fremington** [B3233 Barnstaple—Instow; SS5132], *New Inn*: Good choice of generous home-cooked food at very popular prices inc three daily roasts in bar and restaurant, well kept Courage, John Smiths and Ushers, pleasant service; bedrooms *(Dr A J and Mrs P G Newton, Mr and Mrs D Beeson, Mrs A Adams)*

Frogmore [A379 E of Kingsbridge; SX7742], *Globe*: Wide range of good food esp local fish in spacious comfortable dining room, well kept beer, lots of circumnavigator pictures, friendly staff, relaxed atmosphere, children welcome; bedrooms *(Gilly and Frank Newman, Lorna and Howard Lambert)*

☆ **George Nympton** [SS7023], *Castle*: Homely yet comfortably stylish two-bar village inn with good range of generous above-average home cooking inc vegetarian, welcoming service, well kept Flowers IPA and a guest beer; bedrooms comfortable too, fishing rights *(C A Parker)*

☆ **Georgeham** [Rock Hill, above village – OS Sheet 180 map ref 466399; SS4639], *Rock*: Good value food from huge baguettes up in well restored oak-beamed pub, well kept Marstons Pedigree, Morlands Old Speckled Hen, Tetleys, Theakstons and Ushers Best, local farm cider, decent wines, good service, convivial atmosphere, old red quarry tiles, open fire, pleasant mix of rustic furniture, lots of bric-a-brac; children in pleasant back room, piped music, darts, fruit machine, pool room; tables under cocktail parasols on front terrace, pretty hanging baskets *(Richard and Ruth Dean, E A Moore, Paul Richards, Richard and Ann Higgs, Philip and Jude Simmons, N and A Chesher, Dr A J and Mrs P G Newton, Alan and Heather Jacques, BB)*

☆ **Hartland Quay** [end of toll rd; SS2224], *Hartland Quay*: Mildly redecorated though not smart, with outstanding cliff scenery, rugged coast walks, real maritime feel with fishing memorabilia and shipwreck pictures; good value generous basic food (dogs treat you as honoured guests if you're eating), maybe well kept Sharps Doom Bar (often keg beer only), Inch's cider, efficient service, small no-smoking bar, lots of tables outside – very popular with holidaymakers; good value bedrooms, seawater swimming pool *(Richard and Robyn Wain, Jenny and Brian Seller, C P Scott-Malden)*

☆ **Holne** [signed off B3357 W of Ashburton; SX7069], *Church House*: Ancient country inn well placed for attractive walks, open log fires, interesting building, log fires in both rooms, home-made food from lunchtime sandwiches to good fish and enjoyably homely puddings, no-smoking restaurant, Dartmoor Bitter and Legend, Palmers IPA and 2000, and Wadworths 6X, Gray's farm cider, country wines, decent house wines, traditional games in public bar; well behaved children in eating area; good bedrooms *(John and Christine Simpson, Dr S P Willavoys, Miss L Hodson, Mike Gorton, Catherine Lloyd, Mrs M Rolfe, Abigail Dombey, Kate Naish, R J Walden, Mark and Heather Williamson, LYM)*

☆ **Honiton** [43 High St; ST1500], *Red Cow*: Welcoming local, very busy on Tues and Sat market days, scrubbed tables, pleasant alcoves, log fires, good choice of Scottish Courage and local ales, decent wines and malt whiskies, wide choice of good value home-made food inc some enterprising dishes, friendly Welsh licensees (may have Radio Wales), loads of chamber-pots and big mugs on beams, pavement tables; bedrooms *(K R Harris, JP, PP, Stan Edwards, BB)*

nr **Honiton** [Fenny Bridges, 4 miles W; SY1198], *Greyhound*: Big thatched dining pub, now taken over by Old English Pub Co; heavy beams, lots of red plush, deliberately old-fashioned style, food from good open sandwiches and baked potatoes to meals in attractive restaurant, quick friendly service, well kept Scottish Courage ales, provision for children; bedrooms *(Vivienne and John Rice, LYM)*

Hope Cove [SX6640], *Hope & Anchor*: Simple seaside inn, warm and comfortable, with good open fire, good value food, Wadworths 6X, no piped music; bedrooms *(Peter and Audrey Dowsett, LYM)*

☆ **Horns Cross** [A39 Clovelly—Bideford; SS3823], *Hoops*: Attractive much modernised thatched dining pub with wide choice of Whitbreads-related ales and of good food, pleasant friendly service, big inglenook log fire each end, eating area in central courtyard as well as cosy restaurant and bar, decent wines and coffee, Easter beer festival, aircraft-minded landlord, provision for children and disabled; Easter beer festival; open all day, comfortable bedrooms *(JP, PP, Andy and Jill Kassube, R J Walden, Dr and Mrs Cottrell, H J Gray, LYM)*

Horns Cross [A39], *Coach & Horses*: Small family-run country pub, attractive old building with good old-fashioned atmosphere, warm woodburner, friendly chatty licensees, reasonably priced food (short on vegetarian); low-priced bedrooms in well converted outbuildings *(BL, PDL)*

☆ **Ilfracombe** [SS5147], *George & Dragon*: Oldest pub here, handy for harbour, with plenty of olde-worlde character, soft lighting, lots of ornaments, china etc; very friendly, with good food inc Sun lunch and lots for vegetarians, well kept Courage and Ushers; piped music *(Kevin Blake, M Joyner)*

Ilfracombe [155 High St], *London & Paris*: Small cosy bar with green decor, wooden tables, relaxed atmosphere, food from snacks to steaks and fish; children welcome till 8 *(Mrs A Pompilis)*

Ilsington [SX7876], *Carpenters Arms*: Friendly and pleasantly unspoilt local in quiet backwater, good food very reaonably priced, courteous service, well kept Whitbreads; no music *(Dr Rod Holcombe)*

☆ **Kilmington** [A35; SY2797], *Old Inn*: Thatched pub with character front bar (dogs allowed here), back lounge with leather armchairs by inglenook fire, good value bar food and good Sun lunch, well kept Bass and Worthington BB, traditional games, small no-smoking restaurant; maybe piped radio; children welcome, two gardens *(John and Elspeth Howell, Colin Thompson, Brian and Bett Cox, LYM)*

Kings Nympton [SS6819], *Grove*: Friendly

thatched and beamed family local, well kept Ushers and farm cider, good value food (fish and chips Tues); lots of games, skittle alley, picturesque village *(Mr and Mrs J Marsh, LYM)*

☆ **Kingsbridge** [quayside, edge of town; SX7344], *Crabshell*: Lovely waterside position, charming when tide in, with big windows and tables out on the hard, wide choice of bar food inc lunchtime shrimp or crab sandwiches; hot food (ambitious, concentrating on very wide choice of local fish and shellfish) may be confined to upstairs restaurant, with good views; quick friendly staff, Bass and Charrington IPA, good farm cider, warm fire; can get a bit smoky *(D G Clarke, Mrs B Sugarman, Liz Bell, Peter and Audrey Dowsett, Simon Barriskell, Tina Rossiter, BB)*

Kingsbridge [Mill St], *Hermitage*: Friendly, usual food inc good home-made soup, log fire, well kept Bass, Flowers IPA, Wadworths 6X and Whitbreads Castle Eden, good coffee *(John Barker)*; [Fore St], *Kings Arms*: Timbered bar with modern settles in big partly 16th-c hotel, friendly service, well kept beer, unobtrusive piped music; good food inc local seafood in small restaurant; bedrooms, many with four-posters – heated indoor swimming pool for residents *(Nick Lawless)*; [Fore St], *Ship & Plough*: Companionable olde-worlde local, Fullers London Pride and Whitbreads Castle Eden *(John Barker)*

Kingskerswell [by road bridge over main road; SX8767], *Lord Nelson*: Small two-bar local with friendly landlord, Courage Best and Rocketeer *(John Barker)*

Kingswear [SX8851], *Royal Dart*: Fine setting by ferry and Dart Valley Railway terminal, good restaurant food upstairs *(I J and N K Buckmaster)*; [Higher St], *Ship*: Tall and attractive old inn with unpretentious local atmosphere, good quickly served food, well kept Bass, friendly efficient service; one table with Dart views, a couple outside *(B A Gunary, I J and N K Buckmaster)*

Knowle [the one nr Budleigh Salterton; SY0583], *Britannia*: Recently cosily refurbished, with friendly licensees, well kept Bass, low drinks prices, great main bar with open fire *(R Price)*

Knowle [the N Devon one, just off A361 2 miles N of Braunton; SS4938], *Ebrington Arms*: Lots of bric-a-brac and relaxed olde-worlde atmosphere in comfortable main bar, bar food and attractive candlelit evening restaurant; new licensees also doing theme nights, and plan to open longer in summer *(Frank and Kathy Mathison, LYM)*

Lamerton [A384 Launceston—Tavistock; SX4476], *Blacksmiths Arms*: Welcoming local with good value generous fresh food, friendly efficient service, well kept ales; children very welcome *(Paul and Heather Bettesworth)*

Landkey [Church St; just off A361; SS5931], *Ring o' Bells*: Old small pub that's centre of village life, good home cooking, Bass and Wadworths 6X *(K R Harris)*

Lapford [SS7308], *Olde Malt Scoop*: Cosy, old-fashioned and friendly, with huge log fire, good choice of good food *(Mr and Mrs K F Brame)*

☆ **Littleham** [SS4323], *Crealock Arms*: Friendly family local in lovely tucked-away village nr Sandy Bay holiday site, with good range of good affordable food, well kept beers and ciders, comfortable plush bar, pleasantly modernised dining room, children's room, picnic-sets under cocktail parasols in sheltered garden with play area and pets corner *(Dr J D Grice, M J Winterton)*

Littlehempston [A381; SX8162], *Pig & Whistle*: Large pub with long bar, big dining area, separate pool room, talkative welcoming landlord, lots of reasonably priced home-made food, well kept local beer *(Jackie Orme, Robert Price)*

☆ **Longdown** [B3212 W of Exeter; SX8690], *Lamb*: Open-plan bar with wide choice of imaginative reasonably priced home-made food in dining area, settees in front alcove, ales such as Dartmoor, Exmoor Gold, Ind Coope Burton *(Mr and Mrs L Rees)*

Lympstone [The Strand; SX9984], *Globe*: Clean and pleasant two-room local, popular food inc good seafood specialities, friendly licensees, Flowers IPA, small pleasant restaurant; pretty waterside village *(Stan Edwards)*; *Redwing*: Friendly two-bar local with Bass, Dartmoor Best and Greene King, local farm ciders, reasonably priced food inc fresh fish, interesting specials, good puddings; discreet piped music; no-smoking dining area and pretty garden, live music Tues, Fri *(Jeanne Cross, Paul Silvestri)*

☆ **Lynmouth** [Mars Hill; SS7249], *Rising Sun*: Wonderful position overlooking harbour, good bedrooms in cottagey thatched terrace stepped up hill; concentration on the hotel side and the attractive no-smoking restaurant, so people just dropping in to the modernised beamed and panelled bar can feel a bit left out, but they have well kept Courage Directors, Exmoor Gold, Ruddles County and Theakstons XB, decent lunchtime bar food and a nice dog called Sophie; charming gardens up behind, children may be allowed in eating areas *(Nigel Flook, Betsy Brown, Paul Barnett, I J and N K Buckmaster, James House, Sheila O'Donnell, Jerry Hughes, Tony Gayfer, Neil and Anita Christopher, R J Walden, Dr A J and Mrs P G Newton, M G Hart, LYM)*

Lynmouth [middle of harbour], *Rock House*: Small relaxing bar popular with locals, friendly staff, good value simple food; restaurant, pleasant bedrooms with good breakfast, very attractive spot *(Sue and John Woodward)*; [19 Lynmouth St], *Village Inn*: Good reasonably priced home cooking lunchtime and evening, pleasant bar, quick welcoming service, good wine list, great location; piped music; bedrooms recently redecorated to very high standard, good value *(Vivienne Coombs, Sue and John Woodward)*

Lynton [Castle Hill; SS7149], *Royal Castle*: Immaculate quiet but interesting Edwardian decor with dining area and comfortable food-free lounge off central bar, particularly well kept ales such as Adnams Broadside, Badger

Tanglefoot, Butcombe and Cotleigh Tawny, polite service, great views from back terrace and garden – at night you can see the lights on the Welsh coast; bedrooms *(Mark Matthewman, DJW, Dr A J and Mrs P G Newton)*

Malborough [SX7039], *Old Inn*: Big refurbished open-plan dining pub with very wide choice of food majoring on fish; charming quick service, Courage, Flowers IPA and Marstons Pedigree, good house wine, pleasant children's room; lovely village *(Nick Lawless, DC)*; *Royal Oak*: Cosy and friendly local, log fire, Ushers ales *(Nick Lawless)*

Marldon [SX8663], *Old Smokey House*: Restored old pub, food inc good Sun carvery, good range of beers inc Bass *(Pam and Derek Higham)*

☆ **Marsh** [signed off A303 Ilminster—Honiton; ST2510], *Flintlock*: Comfortable 17th-c inn doing well under current welcoming management, wide choice of good varied reasonably priced food inc vegetarian, well kept beer and cider, armoury and horsebrasses *(Mr and Mrs Peter Smith, Howard Clutterbuck, Mr and Mrs W B Walker)*

Mary Tavy [Lane Head; A386 Tavistock—Okehampton; SX5079], *Mary Tavy Inn*: Friendly landlord (ex fire service) and locals, well kept Bass, St Austell HSD and Mild with a guest such as Princetown Jail, woodburner; good value bedrooms, big breakfast *(Tom McLean, R Huggins, E McCall, Bruce Bird, JP, PP)*; *Royal Standard*: New owners settled in well, with well kept Otter and guest beers, good home-made bar food inc good curry *(Dr and Mrs N Holmes)*

Meeth [A386 Hatherleigh—Torrington; SS5408], *Bull & Dragon*: 16th-c beamed and thatched village pub, well kept Fullers London Pride, decent wines, good value freshly cooked food, friendly effective staff, unobtrusive piped music; children and dogs welcome, exemplary lavatories *(R J Walden, Elaine Hawkins)*

Miltoncombe [off A386 ¾ mile S of Yelverton; SX4865], *Who'd Have Thought It*: Attractive 16th-c black-panelled bar with woodburner, barrel seats and high-backed winged settles, separate lounge, no-smoking room, picnic-sets in reworked streamside garden; new licensees doing decent usual food, well kept Blackawton Headstrong, Cornish Rebellion, Exmoor, Princetown Jail and Wadworths 6X; children are now allowed in (but so is piped music), and they have a new garden with water feature, and tables out in front; folk club Sun *(Jacquie and Jim Jones, Ted George, Mr and Mrs J Brown, LYM)*

Monkton [A30 NE of Honiton; ST1803], *Monkton Court*: Imposing stone house with neatly kept, warm and comfortable spacious main bar with beams, panelling and stone or slate walls, snug side areas, well kept Courage, log fire, good choice of food in bar and restaurant (children allowed till 7), spacious relaxing garden; bedrooms *(Mark and Heather Williamson, LYM)*

Moretonhampstead [A382 N of Bovey Tracey; SX7585], *White Hart*: Oak settles and old clocks in cosy but lively carpeted back bar, more ordinary big lounge bar, attractive no-smoking restaurant, warmly welcoming atmosphere and staff, well kept Butcombe, Dartmoor Gold and Princetown Jail, farm cider, wide choice of generous food from sandwiches up, cream teas; children welcome, open all day; well equipped bedrooms, well placed for Dartmoor, good walks *(Sam Samuells, Lynda Payton, R C Morgan, Mike Gorton, C and E M Watson, Dr and Mrs A K Clarke, LYM)*

☆ **Mortehoe** [off A361 Ilfracombe—Braunton; SS4545], *Ship Aground*: Welcoming open-plan village pub with big family room, well kept Cotleigh ales, Hancock's cider in summer, decent wine, bar food inc good pizzas, two log fires, friendly if not always speedy service; massive rustic furnishings, interesting nautical brassware, friendly cross-eyed cat, pool, skittles and other games, tables on sheltered sunny terrace with good views; piped music; by interesting church, wonderful walking on nearby coast footpath *(Ian and Nita Cooper, M Joyner, Dr A J and Mrs P G Newton, Mrs Mary Woods, LYM)*

☆ *nr* **Newton Abbot** [A381 2 miles S, by turn to Abbotskerswell], *Two Mile Oak*: Atractively quiet and old-fashioned, with good log fire, black panelling, low beams, stripped stone, lots of brasses, comfortable candlelit alcoves, cushioned settles and chairs; wide choice of enjoyable generous food, cosy little dining room, well kept Bass, Flowers IPA, Hardy Royal Oak and guest beers, friendly service, seats on back terrace, attractive garden *(Mr and Mrs C Roberts, Jess and George Cowley, LYM)*

☆ **Newton Ferrers** [Riverside Rd E; SX5448], *Dolphin*: Friendly pub in lovely village overlooking yachting harbour, good value food *(David Lewis, Sarah Lart)*

Newton Poppleford [High St; SY0889], *Cannon*: Doing well under experienced new landlord, redecorated and refurbished; pleasant service, reasonably priced food inc speciality steaks *(L H and S Ede)*

Newton Tracey [5 miles S of Barnstaple on B3232 to Torrington; SS5226], *Hunters*: Friendly old pub with four real ales, log fire, skittle alley/games room, food inc vegetarian, children's and evening restaurant; juke box, fruit machines; tables outside, play area; provision for children *(Angela and Derek Wood, BC)*

☆ **No Mans Land** [B3131 Tiverton—South Molton; SS8313], *Mount Pleasant*: Cosy traditional country pub with wide range of good inexpensive home-made food from huge sandwiches up, well kept ales such as Bass and Butcombe, decent wines, good friendly staff, open fires, ex-forge restaurant; children's room, tables outside *(Paul and Heather Bettesworth)*

☆ **North Bovey** [SX7483], *Ring of Bells*: Bulgy-walled 13th-c thatched inn, well kept Dartmoor Pride, Ind Coope Burton, Marstons Pedigree and Wadworths 6X, Gray's farm cider, games etc, good log fire, decent bar food from ploughman's and filled baguettes up, friendly if not always speedy service, restaurant; children welcome; seats outside by lovely tree-covered village green below Dartmoor; big bedrooms with four-posters *(John and Vivienne Rice, Dr and Mrs A K Clarke, Tony Dickinson, LYM)*

☆ **Noss Mayo** [off A379 via B3186, E of Plymouth; SX5447], *Old Ship*: Charming setting with tables on waterside terrace by own quay in picturesque village, two thick-walled friendly bars, bar food from sandwiches to steaks inc local fish, well kept Bass, Dartmoor and a changing guest beer, swift helpful service; darts, fruit machine, piped music; children welcome, no-smoking restaurant upstairs with Sun carvery; watch the tide if you park on the slipway *(Mick Hitchman, Lyn and Geoff Hallchurch, EM, LYM)*

☆ **Noss Mayo** [off Junket Corner], *Swan*: Small pub with lovely waterside views, good range of bar food inc fresh fish, well kept Courage Best and Directors, old beams, open fire; can get crowded, with difficult parking; dogs on leads and children welcome, tables outside *(David Lewis, Sarah Lart)*

Otterton [Fore St; SY0885], *Kings Arms*: Comfortably refurbished open-plan pub in charming village, good value straightforward home-made food from sandwiches and baked potatoes up, plenty of room, good skittle alley doubling as family room, beautiful evening view from picnic-sets in good-sized back garden *(David Hoult)*

Paignton [3 Colin Rd; SX8960], *Embassy*: Welcoming licensees, pleasant staff, well kept beer, good food inc daily fresh local fish and good value Sun lunch, family holiday entertainment; handy for beach *(Stefan Spencer, Louise McLaughlin)*

Paignton [Torquay Rd; SX8960], *Isaac Merritt*: Well furnished Wetherspoons conversion of former shopping arcade, varied seating inc no-smoking area in spacious open-plan bar, good reasonably priced food and drink, no music *(Andrew Hodges)*

Plymouth [Barbican], *Dolphin*: Good lively unpretentious atmosphere, good range of beers inc particularly well kept Bass tapped from the cask; Beryl Cook paintings *(John Poulter, DC, John Barker)*; [21 Breton Side], *Kings Head*: Enjoyable pub with Summerskills ales (inc one at low price); opens 10 *(Andrew and Hazel Summerfield)*; [The Quay, Barbican], *Ship*: Friendly waterside pub with harbour views from upstairs restaurant, good carvery with two-for-one, OAP and early evening offers, Scottish Courage beers *(W R Cunliffe)*

Plymtree [ST0502], *Blacksmiths Arms*: Friendly atmosphere, good value interesting home-made food, good choice of well kept beers *(C G Dingley, Mr and Mrs P Williams)*

Portgate [Launceston Rd (old A30); SX4185], *Harris Arms*: Bright, friendly and comfortable, well kept ales such as Bass, Dartmoor Best and Morlands Old Speckled Hen, prompt informal service, good food inc superb South Devon steaks and wonderful mixed grill *(J C Perry, T Pascall)*

☆ **Poundsgate** [between Ashburton and B3357; SX7072], *Tavistock*: 13th-c Dartmoor-edge village local with narrow-stepped granite spiral staircase, original flagstones, ancient fireplaces and beams, Courage Best and Ushers Best and Founders, local farm cider, bar food, pub games, family room, tables outside *(Paul and Heather Bettesworth, Mike Gorton, Barry and Anne, Lyn and Geoff Hallchurch, LYM)*

Pyworthy [SW of Holsworthy; SS3102], *Molesworth Arms*: Popular country pub with attractively priced food inc good curries in bar or restaurant, well kept Bass and a guest beer, friendly staff *(Mr and Mrs J D Marsh, Mr and Mrs P Stubbs)*

☆ **Rockbeare** [SY0295], *Jack in the Green*: Recently refurbished, with log fire in snug bar, good varied food, local fish and game, delicious puddings, competitive prices, well kept Bass and three local ales, good value wines, pleasant staff, back restaurant; tables out in courtyard, skittle alley *(G P Reeves, Mr and Mrs J B Bishop)*

☆ **Salcombe** [off Fore St nr Portlemouth Ferry; SX7338], *Ferry*: The star is for the fine estuary position, with tiers of stripped-stone bars rising from sheltered flagstoned waterside terrace, inc top one opening off street, and middle dining bar; well kept Palmers and farm cider; piped music can be too loud, can get busy, may be cl part of winter *(David Carr, G Washington, Hilarie Dobbie, Nick Lawless, B J Harding, LYM)*

Salcombe [Union St, end of Fore St], *Fortescue*: Sizeable very popular five-room pub nr harbour, nautical theme throughout, lots of old local black and white shipping pictures, well kept Scottish Courage ales, reliable food, quick pleasant service, relaxing atmosphere, good woodburner, big games room, no piped music; restaurant, terrace *(Peter and Audrey Dowsett, Nick Lawless, Jo Rees, DC, G W Stevenson, B J Harding)*; [Fore St], *Victoria*: Well placed, friendly and attractive, with bare-boards bar, comfortable lounge, pleasant upstairs dining room, copious good food cooked to order, jovial landlord, Bass, Courage and Worthington, no piped music; segregated children's room, bedrooms *(Peter and Audrey Dowsett, B J Harding, DC, John Barker)*

Sampford Peverell [16 Lower Town; a mile from M5 junction 27, village signed from Tiverton turn-off; ST0214], *Globe*: Spacious and comfortably modernised bar, handy for good range of home-made food from sandwiches to steaks inc fish, vegetarian, children's and popular Sun lunch, well kept Otter and Wadworths 6X, piped music, games in public bar, pool room, skittle alley, tables in front; open all day; children allowed in eating area and family room *(K R Harris, W H and E Thomas, Nick Wikeley, LYM)*

☆ **Sandy Park** [SX7189], *Sandy Park*: Thatched country local with old-fashioned small bar, stripped old tables, built-in high-backed wall seats, big black iron fireplace, decent food, well kept ales such as Cotleigh Tawny, Eldridge Pope Hardy and Wadworths 6X, decent wines and farm cider; children in eating area, cosy restaurant; simple clean bedrooms *(Dr and Mrs G K Blackwell, DBJ, LYM)*

☆ **Shaldon** [The Strand; SX9372], *Ferryboat*: Quaint little pub, basic but comfortable, long bar overlooking mouth of River Teign, welcoming landlord, Courage Best and Directors and Youngs, big helpings of home-made food; terrace across narrow street overlooks the water, with Teignmouth ferry and lots of boats off sandy beach *(John Beeken, R Moorehead, Stan Edwards)*

Shaldon [Fore St], *Clifford Arms*: Small and attractive 18th-c pub in pleasant seaside village, good value home-made food inc fresh local fish, well kept Bass and Dartmoor Best, farm ciders, friendly atmosphere, pub games, family room; colourful little front courtyard, pleasant back terrace *(Stan Edwards, Mr and Mrs W Welsh)*; *London*: Friendly village pub, good food and beer *(P Lewis)*

☆ **Shiphay**, Devon [off A380/A3022, NW edge of Torquay; SX8865], *Devon Dumpling*: Open-plan farmhouse pub with atmospheric cosy corners, tasteful wall adornments, popular locally for good value straightforward food inc vegetarian served very quickly and cheerfully, well kept Courage Directors, Ruddles County, John Smiths and maybe Branscombe Vale; plenty of space inc upper barn loft; aquarium, occasional live music, no dogs inside *(Mr and Mrs C Roberts, Reg Nelson)*

☆ **Sidbury** [Putts Corner; A375 Sidbury—Honiton; SY1595], *Hare & Hounds*: Roomy and relaxed lounge bar, wood-and-tiles tap room, two fine old chesterfields and more usual furnishings, stuffed birds, huge log fire; four or five well kept changing ales, very friendly staff, wide choice of quick inexpensive well cooked food in bars and restaurant with Sun carvery, pool in side room, another with giant sports TV; big garden, good views of valley below *(Peter and Audrey Dowsett, V Jenner)*

☆ **Sidmouth** [Old Fore St; SY1287], *Old Ship*: Partly 14th c, with low beams, mellow black woodwork and panelling, ship pictures, wide choice of food (good but not cheap) inc vegetarian and home-made specials, well kept ales such as Boddingtons, Marstons Pedigree, Wadworths 6X, friendly atmosphere, good service even when busy; close-set tables but roomier raftered upstairs bar with family room, dogs allowed; just moments from the sea (note that around here parking is limited to 30 mins) *(Jim and Maggie Cowell, Peter and Rosie Flower, E V M Whiteway, Alan and Paula McCully, BB)*

Sidmouth [Old Fore St], *Anchor*: Friendly high-ceilinged local with good generous cheap food inc unusual daily specials in no-smoking dining area, second bar downstairs, Bass-related beers; tables in good outdoor area, open all day – full of folk music in festival week *(Peter and Audrey Dowsett, Comus Elliott)*

nr **Sidmouth** [Bowd Cross; junction B3176/A3052; SY1089], *Bowd*: Big thatched family dining pub recently well done up, with lovely garden, quick friendly service even when busy, well kept Bass and Flowers Original, indoor and separate outdoor play areas; open all day *(Mrs G Greenslade, P and M Rudlin, Basil Minson, L W King, BB)*

☆ **Slapton** [SX8244], *Tower*: Ancient low-ceilinged flagstoned pub with open fires, family room, generous food, half a dozen well kept ales such as Badger Tanglefoot, Exmoor and Gibbs Mew Bishops Tipple, interesting wines, good service, cosy family atmosphere, peaceful pretty garden overhung by romantic ivy-covered ruined jackdaw tower; bedrooms *(Mr and Mrs C R Little, EM, I Buckmaster, Roger Wain-Heapy, D R Eberlin, M and J Madley, Pat and Robert Watt, LYM)*

Slapton, *Queens Arms*: Comfortable and snug old inn with good value food, well kept Bass, Exmoor and Palmers, informative landlady, lovely suntrap garden with plenty of tables *(Roger Wain-Heapy, Pat and Robert Watt, B J Harding)*

☆ **South Molton** [SS7125], *George*: Choice of well kept real ales and very well cooked bar food, buzzing atmosphere reminiscent of the old Trust House town-centre coaching inns in their hey-day – very relaxing; cinema club in upstairs Assembly Room Sun, summer jazz nights; bedrooms *(DJW)*

☆ **South Tawton** [off A30 at Whiddon Down or Okehampton, then signed from Sticklepath; SX6594], *Seven Stars*: Friendly and unpretentious local in attractive village, good range of well prepared good value food, well kept Bass, Boddingtons and a guest beer, decent wines; pool and other bar games, restaurant (cl Sun and Mon evenings winter); children welcome; bedrooms *(R J Walden, LYM)*

Starcross [SX9781], *Atmospheric Railway*: Named for Brunel's experimental 1830s vacuum-powered steam railway here, new landlord has kept the mass of associated memorabilia, prints and signs; Bass, Boddingtons, Flowers Original and Wadworths 6X, good choice of home-made food (served in dining car), log fire, family room, skittle alley; garden with tables and play area *(John Beeken, BB)*; [The Strand], *Courtenay Arms*: 17th-c family pub, bar one end of big lounge, Bass and Greene King, well presented basic bar food and enterprising specials, enormous choice of Devon ice creams, welcoming log fires in double fireplace *(John Beeken)*

☆ **Sticklepath** [off A30 at Whiddon Down or Okehampton; SX6494], *Devonshire*: Well used 16th-c thatched village inn with easy-going low-beamed slate-floored bar, big log fire, friendly old furnishings, good filling low-priced snacks, bookable Sun lunches and evening meals, welcoming owners and locals, well kept St Austell Tinners and HSD tapped from the cask, farm cider, magazines to read; open all day Fri/Sat; bedrooms *(Andy and Jill Kassube, John Cockell, LYM)*

☆ **Stokeinteignhead** [SX9170], *Church House*: Civilised and friendly 13th-c thatched pub with dining lounge and restaurant area, well presented food, well kept Bass, Flowers IPA and Wadworths 6X, farm cider, good coffee;

delightful spiral staircase in small character public bar; nice back garden with little stream, lovely unspoilt village *(John Wilson, Andrew Hodges, Gordon, Stan Edwards, LYM)*

☆ **Stokeinteignhead** *Chasers Arms*: Good value often interesting food inc imaginative veg and unusual puddings in busy 16th-c thatched pub/restaurant (you can't go just for a drink, but they do bar snacks too and the style emulates a country pub); fine range of house wines, quick friendly service *(Mr and Mrs W Welsh, D I Baddeley)*

☆ **Stokenham** [just off A379 at E end of village; SX8042], *Church House*: Comfortable firmly run open-plan pub, good if not cheap food inc fresh local seafood, well kept Bass, Eldridge Pope Hardy and Flowers Original, farm cider, good wines, no-smoking dining room, unobtrusive piped music; front children's room with writing/drawing materials, attractive recently extended garden with enjoyably individual play area, fishpond and chipmunks *(the Sandy family, Dr A J and Mrs P G Newton, Colin Draper, Mary Woods, LYM)*

Swimbridge [nr Barnstaple; SS6130], *Jack Russell*: Good changing good bar food inc children's and fantastic choice of vegetarian food (non-greasy veggie fry-up breakfast served from 10), big helpings, well kept Scottish Courage ales, plainly furnished but informal and comfortable bar, lounge and pool room, very friendly staff, relaxed atmosphere; terrace, opp church in pleasant village *(Jamie Thomson)*

Thelbridge Cross [B3042 W of Tiverton; SS7912], *Thelbridge Cross*: Welcoming lounge bar with log fire and plush settees, good generous food inc some unusual dishes in extensive dining area and separate restaurant, pleasant service, particularly well kept Bass and Butcombe; bedrooms *(John Evans, G S B G Dudley, Alan Kitchener, Dr A J and Mrs P G Newton, BB)*

Thorverton [SS9202], *Thorverton Arms*: Nicely appointed pub with very well prepared restaurant meals, gracious welcome even for big parties with noisy small children, well kept Bass and Whitbreads-related ales; pleasant village, enjoyable strolls by River Exe *(Dr Harding E Smith, John and Bryony Coles, J and B Coles)*

Thurlestone [SX6743], *Village Inn*: Much refurbished but convivial pub emphasising food (cool cabinet, open kitchen behind servery, blackboards, etc) – wide choice inc vegetarian and lots of fish, reasonable prices; well kept Marstons Pedigree, Palmers and Wadworths 6X, comfortable new country-style furnishings, dividers forming alcoves, pleasant helpful staff; children and dogs catered for, darts, quiz nights, live music, handy for coast path *(DJW, Colin McKerrow, Richard and Ann Higgs)*

Tipton St John [off B3176 Sidmouth—Ottery St Mary; SY0991], *Golden Lion*: Has been a long-standing popular main entry, with good generous food in bar and restaurant, attractive mix of furnishings, open fire, and well kept Bass, Boddingtons, Hardy and Wadworths, farm cider, and decent wines, opening all day Sat, with two comfortable bedrooms; but just as we went to press the tenants told us they were leaving, after 28 years here – obviously no chance yet of judging how the new regime will turn out *(LYM – reports please)*

☆ **Topsham** [from centre head towards Exmouth via Elmgrove Rd; SX9688], *Bridge*: Unchanging, unspoilt and very relaxing 16th-c pub, in same family for a century and visited by the Queen in 1998 (the only pub she has visited by design); fine old traditional furnishings in friendly little no-smoking lounge partitioned off from inner corridor by high-backed settle, log fire, bigger lower room open at busy times, cosy regulars' inner sanctum with at least six or seven beers tapped from the cask, decent wine; lunchtime pasties, great sandwiches and huge ploughman's, no music or machines, children welcome *(Jo and Gary Charlton, Dallas Seawright, Catherine Lloyd, JP, PP, the Didler, G Washington, Alan and Paula McCully, LYM)*

☆ **Topsham** [Fore St (2 miles from M5 junction 30)], *Globe*: Substantial traditional inn dating from 16th c, good solid furnishings and log fire in friendly heavy-beamed bow-windowed bar, low-priced straightforward home-cooked food, well kept Bass, Ushers Best and Worthington BB, decent reasonably priced wine, snug little dining lounge, separate restaurant, back extension; children in eating area, open all day; good value attractive bedrooms *(G Washington, the Didler, Alan and Paula McCully, LYM)*

☆ **Topsham** [The Quay], *Lighter*: Spacious and comfortably refurbished family pub, panelling and tall windows looking out over tidal flats, more intimate side room, well kept Badger Best, Tanglefoot and a beer brewed for the pub, good friendly staff, good quickly served bar food inc local fish, open fire; games machines; tables out on old quay, good value bedrooms *(John Beeken, R J Walden, James Nunns, Alan and Paula McCully, BB)*

Topsham [High St], *Lord Nelson*: Lots of sea prints, sails over big dining area, smaller side seats up steps, good choice of reasonably priced bar food, very attentive service, Bass; piped pop music may obtrude *(John Beeken, Dr A J and Mrs P G Newton)*; [Monmouth Hill], *Steam Packet*: Cheap bar food, several well kept ales, dark flagstones, scrubbed boards, panelling, stripped masonry, a lighter dining room; on boat-builders' quay *(the Didler, LYM)*

☆ **Torbryan** [most easily reached from A381 Newton Abbot—Totnes via Ipplepen; SX8266], *Old Church House*: Atmospheric early 15th-c inn by part-Saxon church, quaint bar on right with benches built into Tudor panelling, high-backed settle and big log fire, also series of comfortable and discreetly lit lounges, one with a splendid inglenook fireplace; helpful service, bar food from sandwiches to guinea fowl, well kept Bass, Flowers IPA and Original, Marstons Pedigree, Wadworths 6X, and Worthington Best, good choice of malt whiskies, decent wines; piped music; children welcome, well equipped bedrooms, roomy and immaculate *(John Robertson, Mr and Mrs A Scrutton, Andrew Woodgate, John and Vivienne Rice, Dr*

A J and Mrs P G Newton, LYM)
Torquay [Park Lane, opp clock tower; SX9264], *Hole in the Wall*: Ancient unpretentious low-beamed two-bar local nr harbour, well kept Courage, Blackawton cider, friendly service, flagstones, lots of naval memorabilia, old local photographs, chamber-pots; open all day *(Reg Nelson, John Barker)*
Torquay [Beach Rd, Babbacombe; SX9265], *Cary Arms*: Good sea and cliff views, cheerful service, decent straightforward food inc lots of sandwiches, well kept beers, pleasant piped music, tables on terrace; bedrooms *(Ian and Jane Irving, Andrew Hodges)*; [Ilsham Rd (off B3199)], *Kent*: Nicely decorated largeish pub with wide choice of good food, pleasant atmosphere, good landlord, real ales such as Bass, Courage Rocketeer, Mendip Gold, John Smith and Theakstons Old Peculier *(John Barker)*; [Strand], *London*: Vast Wetherspoons conversion of former NatWest bank overlooking harbour and marina, no-smoking upper mezzanine bar, big local ship paintings and a couple of reproduction ship's figureheads, good value food, no piped music *(Andrew Hodges)*; [Union St], *Pig in Black*: May be contrived, but well done, with lots of wood fittings, good atmosphere, real ales *(Reg Nelson)*
Totnes [9 Leechwell St; SX8060], *Kingsbridge*: Low-beamed rambling bar with timbering and some stripped stone, plush seats, small no-smoking area, home-made food from nicely presented sandwiches to steaks and local fish, well kept Badger Best and Tanglefoot, Bass, Courage Best, Dartmoor Best, and Theakstons Old Peculier, local farm cider, decent house wines, prompt pleasant service; children in eating area, some live music *(Mr and Mrs G Little, Dr S P Willavoys, Paul White, Jo and Gary Charlton, DC, LYM)*
Totnes [Fore St, The Plains], *Royal Seven Stars*: Civilised old hotel with late 1960s decor in big character lounge, impressive central hall below sunny skylight and stairs off, Bass and Courage Best, cheerful helpful service, cheap food, tables out in front – ideal on a Tues market day when the tradespeople wear Elizabethan dress; bedrooms, river on other side of busy main road *(Nick Lawless, DC)*
Trusham [signed off B3193 NW of Chudleigh – 1½ very narrow miles; SX8582], *Cridford*: Interesting 14th-c longhouse, with Britain's oldest domestic window in its bar, lots of stripped stone, flagstones and stout timbers, appropriate furnishings; bedrooms; changed hands 1998, and the few reports we've had since don't yet give a clear enough indication of how we should rate it for food, drink and service *(LYM)*
Turnchapel [SX4952], *New Inn*: Bass, Ind Coope Burton, Doom Bar, Hook Norton Best and Shepherd Neame Spitfire, piped music *(Anon)*
Two Bridges [B3357/B3212; SX6175], *Two Bridges*: Friendly and gently refurbished rambling 18th-c hotel in protected central Dartmoor hollow, nice log fire in cosy bar, another in spacious beamed lounge, good choice of food in bars and restaurant, afternoon tea, well kept Princetown IPA and Jail; comfortable bedrooms, good walks – a romantic winter hideaway, but very busy with tourists and their children in summer *(Bruce Bird, Janet and Colin Roe, Dr and Mrs A K Clarke, Gordon Neighbour)*
Tytherleigh [A358 Chard—Axminster; ST3103], *Tytherleigh Arms*: Spacious and comfortable, with good range of usual food inc local fish, Eldridge Pope ales, small restaurant *(Howard Clutterbuck, J H Jones)*
Walkhampton [SX5369], *Walkhampton*: 16th-c Dartmoor-edge village pub, stripped stone and beams, well kept Princetown IPA and Jail and a guest beer, good choice of food inc many freshly cooked specials, friendly staff; piped music quieter in no-smoking area; bedrooms *(Bruce Bird)*
Welcombe [Darracott; village signed off A39 S of Hartland; SS2217], *Old Smithy*: Thatched pub in lovely setting by lane leading eventually to attractive rocky cove, completely refurbished inside, with rows of tables in relaxed if rather noisy open-plan family bar, functional modern decor, good value food, quick friendly service, well kept Boddingtons and Marstons, renovated restaurant; plenty of seats in pretty terraced garden, handy for nearby campsite *(Mr and Mrs P Stubbs, Dr A J and Mrs P G Newton, Mike and Mary Carter, LYM)*
Wembworthy [Lama Cross; SS6609], *Lymington Arms*: Big helpings of reasonably priced home-made food inc vegetarian in clean and bright pub with well kept beers such as Brakspears, Inch's cider, fair range of wines; garden, pleasant country setting; children welcome *(Richard Harris)*
☆ **Westleigh** [½ mile off A39 Bideford—Instow; SS4628], *Westleigh Inn*: Huge neatly kept hillside garden with good play area gives gorgeous views down over the Torridge estuary; old local pictures in very welcoming single room split by serving bar, well kept Ruddles County and Ushers, farm cider, wide changing choice of good straightforward home-cooked food, family atmosphere, pub dog *(Piotr Chodzko-Zajko, M Joyner, LYM)*
Whiddon Down [Exeter Rd, off A30; SX6992], *Post*: Friendly local with good relaxed atmosphere, enthusiastic and welcoming newish landlady, good value food inc good vegetarian dishes, well kept Whitbreads-related ales, separate bar with darts, pool and skittles, small garden *(Revd L Melliss, B J Cox)*
☆ **Widecombe** [SX7176], *Olde Inne*: Friendly and comfortable, with stripped 14th-c stonework, big log fires in both bars, some concentration on wide choice of good generous food cooked to order with fresh veg, prominent restaurant area, well kept Ushers and other beers, local farm cider, decent wines, good friendly service, family room; in pretty moorland village, very popular with tourists though perhaps at its best out of season; room to dance on music nights, good big garden; great walks – the one to or from Grimspound gives spectacular views

(Jeanne Cross, Paul Silvestri, JP, PP, Comus Elliott, John Askew, LYM)

☆ **Winkleigh** [off B3220 Crediton—Torrington; SS6308], *Kings Arms*: Attractive and comfortable, with beams, flagstones, scrubbed pine tables, woodburner and big log fire, good range of well cooked enjoyable food, reasonable prices, well kept Princetown Jail and other ales, local Inch's farm cider, good efficient service, well reproduced piped music, no-smoking restaurant (popular for Sun lunch); small sheltered side courtyard with pool *(Dr A J and Mrs P G Newton, Michael and Joan Melling, Mrs B Sugarman, R J Walden, John Askew, LYM)*

☆ **Woolfardisworthy** [called Woolsery locally; SS3321], *Farmers Arms*: Spotless 14th-c thatched local with very low ceiling, big stone fireplace, model ships, local pictures and horsebrasses, very welcoming staff and locals, well kept Bass, guest beers and Thatcher's cider, decent food inc generous Thurs bargain OAP lunch; public bar with pool room, restaurant *(Richard and Robyn Wain)*

☆ **Wrafton** [A361 just SE of Braunton; SS4935], *Williams Arms*: Modernised thatched family dining pub, two big bars divided into several cosy areas, children very welcome, interesting wall hangings, wide choice of good value bar food, unlimited self-service from good carvery in attractive separate restaurant, quick friendly service, Bass; pool, darts, piped music, discreet TV; picnic-sets outside with play area and aviary *(Roger and Pauline Pearce, DJW, M Joyner, K R Harris)*

Yarcombe [A30; ST2408], *Yarcombe*: Attractive and welcoming 14th-c thatched pub, good choice of food from tasty ploughman's up, cheerful licensee, separate dining room, nice little spotless front bar, well kept local guest beers; quiet piped music *(D B Jenkin)*

Yelverton [by roundabout on A386 halfway between Plymouth and Tavistock; SX5267], *Rock*: Spacious extended pub with wide choice of food, friendly efficient service, good range of ales and ciders, games room and good facilities for children, popular terrace, safe play area; open all day, bedrooms *(Paul Redgrave)*

Bedroom prices normally include full English breakfast, VAT and any inclusive service charge that we know of. Prices before the '/' are for single rooms, after for two people in double or twin (B includes a private bath, S a private shower). If there is no '/', the prices are only for twin or double rooms (as far as we know there are no singles).

Dorset

Pubs doing particularly well here these days are the individualistic little Fox at Corscombe (particularly good food including lots of fish), the Cock & Bottle at East Morden (good food in its attractive and civilised dining side), the distinctively run Museum at Farnham (imaginative well presented food), the welcoming Loders Arms at Loders (well presented food here too), the Pilot Boat in Lyme Regis (a very popular dining pub just over the road from the sea), the Bottle at Marshwood (a new entry, unchanging in style, but up to the minute in content – even vegan food, organic drinks), the warmly welcoming Marquis of Lorne at Nettlecombe (an excellent all-rounder, gaining a Food Award this year), the archetypically English Thimble at Piddlehinton (very reasonably priced meals), the Brace of Pheasants at Plush (another nice old country dining pub), the welcoming old Crown prettily set at Puncknowle (another new entry, a nice simple place to stay), and the very well run Langton Arms at Tarrant Monkton (wholesome food, interesting real ales). From among these front-runners we choose as Dorset Dining Pub of the Year the Cock & Bottle at East Morden: it's been giving many readers really enjoyable meals out in recent months. The Halfway at Norden Heath has lost its Greek landlord (and distinctive Greek dishes), but gained well tried new licensees who are doing a more catholic range of home-made food. There's new management too at the Royal Oak at Cerne Abbas, the Acorn at Evershot (lots of changes under way – promises well), the Scott Arms at Kingston (doing well, big helpings of popular food), and the Smugglers at Osmington Mills (now tied to Badger). The attractively old-fashioned Digby Tap in Sherborne has been winning warm approval for its good value policy of attractively priced decent food and good changing beers. In general drinks prices in Dorset are higher than the national average. Of the local breweries, we generally found Palmers cheaper than Badger, with the Greyhound in Corfe Castle and Bottle at Marshwood standing out as cheap for drinks. Among the Lucky Dip entries at the end of the chapter, pubs which have been earning particular praise from readers in the last few months are the Winyards Gap at Chedington, Weld Arms at East Lulworth, Inn in the Park in Poole, Three Horseshoes at Powerstock, New Inn at Stoke Abbott, Bankes Arms at Studland, Springhead at Sutton Poyntz, Crown at Uploders and Castle at West Lulworth; we have already inspected and given the thumbs up to all but two of these.

ABBOTSBURY SY5785 Map 2

Ilchester Arms 🛏

B3157

There have been considerable changes at this rambling stone inn since the last edition of the *Guide*. It's been enthusiastically decked out as servants' quarters, with a cook's sitting room, a potting shed, a scullery and parlour, each area with themed decorations and bric a brac, as well as a new Aga and a couple of new fireplaces. A nice mix of old pine furniture stands on wood and parquet floors. The collection of

prints depicting the famous swans from the nearby abbey has been joined by prints of local scenes and characters. Changing bar food is now all home-made and might include soup (£1.55), kedgeree with prawns (£2.25), breaded brie with redcurrant sauce (£2.95), pâté or half a pint of prawns (£3.25), ploughman's (£4.50), lamb cutlets with home-made mint sauce or chicken and broccoli pie (£5.95), baked stuffed trout wrapped in bacon (£6.45) or pork chop with apple and mint chutney (£6.95); home-made puddings include apple pie and summer pudding (£2.25). Well kept Bass, Flowers Orginal and Thomas Greenalls Original; darts, winter pool, cribbage, dominoes, shut the box and chess, fruit machine, and piped music. Service can be slow in the sizeable and attractive no-smoking conservatory restaurant.
(Recommended by JKW, Galen Strawson, Karen Eliot, Richard Gibbs, DAV, John and Vivienne Rice, John Knighton, Jo and Gary Charlton, P and J Caunt, David Mead, Paul Seligman)

Greenalls ~ Manager Hugh McGill ~ Real ale ~ Meals and snacks ~ Restaurant ~ (01305) 871243 ~ Children in eating area of bar ~ Open 11-11; 11-3, 6-11 winter Mon-Thurs ~ Bedrooms: £47.90B/£52.85B

ASKERSWELL SY5292 Map 2

Spyway ★ 🍷 £

Village signposted N of A35 Bridport—Dorchester; inn signposted locally; OS Sheet 194 map reference 529933

The cosy little rooms at this well liked delightfully unspoilt country inn have old-fashioned high-backed settles, cushioned wall and window seats, a vast collection of china teacups, harness and a milkmaid's yoke, and a longcase clock; there's also a no-smoking dining area decorated with blue and white china, old oak beams and timber uprights. Promptly served very reasonably priced good bar food includes a range of generous and tasty ploughman's such as hot sausages and tomato pickle or home-cooked ham (from £3.50), breaded haddock (£3.90), 8oz rib eye steak (£8.95) and daily specials such as quiche or chilli (£3.95) and chicken, game or steak pie (all £4.50). There's a fine choice of drinks including Adnams Best and Southwold, Branscombe Vale Branoc and Morlands Old Speckled Hen on handpump, 24 reasonably priced decent wines by the glass, 20 country wines, around 40 whiskies and some unusual non-alcoholic drinks. Shove-ha'penny, table skittles, dominoes and cribbage. There are plenty of pleasant nearby walks along the paths and bridleways. Eggardon Hill, which the pub's steep lane leads up, is one of the highest in the region and there are marvellous views of the downs and to the coast from the back terrace and gardens (where you can eat on warm days). No children.
(Recommended by John and Vivienne Rice, Dr and Mrs G H Lewis, B and E Clements, S and R Preston, Pete and Rosie Flower, Nigel Hyde, Karen Eliot, P R and S A White, Geoffrey Lawrence, Galen Strawson, C Robinson, Nigel Flook, Betsy Brown, Peter and Audrey Dowsett, George Atkinson, James and Lynne House, Simon and Jane Williams, JM, SM, Dr and Mrs J H Hills, D B Jenkin, C A Hall)

Free house ~ Licensees Don and Jackie Roderick ~ Real ale ~ Meals and snacks ~ (01308) 485250 ~ Open 11-2.30(3 Sat), 6-11; 12-3, 7-10.30 Sun; cl Mon except bank holidays

BRIDPORT SY4692 Map 1

George

South St

The licensee has been at this good old-fashioned town local for 22 years now – sadly his longstanding barman of 20 years has left to go and live in Wales. Divided by a coloured tiled hallway, the two sizeable bars – one is served by a hatch from the main lounge – are full of friendly old-fashioned charm and atmosphere. There are nicely spaced old dining tables and country seats and wheelback chairs, big rugs on tiled floors, a mahogany bar counter, fresh flowers, and a winter log fire, along with an interesting pre-fruit-machine ball game. Thursday night chess club – all welcome. Well kept Palmers Bridport, IPA and 200 on handpump, fresh orange, grapefruit and apple, several malts, decent wines, and hot toddies and proper Pimm's. Bar food includes home-made fishcakes with tomato sauce (£2.95), home-made chicken liver or smoked mackerel pâté (£3.30), home-made lamb and turnip, game or ham, chicken and mushroom pie or local fresh fish (£4.50), and puddings or English cheeses; vegetables are extra (£1.50); you can usually see the licensee at work preparing your meal. You can only have an evening meal out of season if you make a reservation; piped classical radio or jazz *(Recommended by Karen Eliot, Galen Strawson, Mick and Hilary Stiffin, Simon and Jane Williams, Jo and Gary Charlton, Michael Graubart)*

Palmers ~ Tenant John Mander ~ Real ale ~ Meals and snacks (not Sun) ~ (01308) 423187 ~ Children in eating area ~ Open 10am-11pm (8am for coffee every day); 12-10.30 Sun; closed 25 Dec ~ Bedrooms: £25/£50

BURTON BRADSTOCK SY4889 Map 1

Three Horseshoes

Mill St

Like the George at Bridport above, the licensees at this friendly thatched inn have been here for over 20 years. It's a useful place to know with a homely atmosphere in its pleasant roomy bar, an open fire, comfortable seating, and Palmers 200, Bridport, IPA and Tally Ho (kept under light blanket pressure in winter). Nicely presented promptly served bar food from a menu full of groan-inducing jokes includes battered cod (£4.80), chicken and ham or steak and ale pie (£5.20), vegetable curry (£6.45), gammon (£6.80), seafood platter (£10.95), puddings like raspberry pavlova gateau (£2.75), and usual children's meals (£3) and daily specials like pork and cider pie, Chinese spicy noodles or chilli. The dining room is no smoking; table football and pool in family room, and carom in the bar; sporadic piped music. There are tables on the lawn, and Chesil beach and cliff walks are only 400 yards away. *(Recommended by Eddie Edwards, Pat and Tony Martin, Ian Phillips, R Shelton, C A Hall, David Mead, John and Vivienne Rice)*

Palmers ~ Tenant Bill Attrill ~ Real ale ~ Meals and snacks ~ Restaurant ~ (01308) 897259 ~ Children in eating area of bar ~ Open 11-2.30, 6-11; 12-3, 7-10.30 Sun ~ Bedrooms: £27B/£40B

CERNE ABBAS ST6601 Map 2

Red Lion 🍷

Long St

There's an unhurried atmosphere at this genteel and neatly kept cottagey inn. Parts of the comfortable building are a lot older than the unassuming mid-Victorian frontage suggests – the fine fireplace in the quietly relaxing bar for instance is 16th c. There's also some rare Groves Brewery windows, a handsome wooden counter, wheelback chairs on the green patterned carpet, a good deal of china, plants on tables and two more little areas leading off the bar. The friendly white terrier Gemma may sit waiting for titbits. Most of the popular meals are available in a reduced size for those with smaller appetites. The menu includes soup (£1.95), sandwiches (from £2.50), filled baked potatoes (from £3.75), good ploughman's (from £4.40), omelettes (from £4.40), pancakes (from £4.95), several vegetarian pasta dishes (£5.45), local trout (£7.60), grilled loin of pork (£8.25) and steaks (from £9.80), with puddings such as apricot strudel (from £1.75), with daily specials such as sautéed lamb kidneys or cod or haddock in ale batter (£6.40), pork medallions in mushroom sauce or pheasant breast in cumberland sauce (£6.80), delicious fresh Portland crab salad (£7.50) and duck breast in orange and port sauce (£8.75). Some of the vegetables come from local gardens and allotments. Well kept Adnams, Bass and Wadworths IPA and 6X, a decent wine list, with several available by the glass, and a fair choice of malt whiskies. Darts, skittle alley, shove-ha'penny, cribbage, and piped music. There's a secluded flower-filled garden. *(Recommended by David Heath, Joan and Michel Hooper-Immins, Ann and Colin Hunt, Basil J S Minson, P G Bardswell, N J Lawless, Mrs T A Bizat, Jack and Gemima Valiant, Andy and Jill Kassube, Joan and Michel Hooper-Immins)*

Free house ~ Licensees Brian and Jane Cheeseman ~ Real ale ~ Meals and snacks (roast only on Sun) ~ (01300) 341441 ~ Children in eating area of bar ~ Open 11-2.30, 6.30-11; 12-3, 7-10.30 Sun; cl 25 Dec evening

Royal Oak 🍷

Long Street

There are seats at the front of this cosy looking creeper-covered Tudor inn where you can quietly sit and watch the world go by. Inside, an incredible range of small ornaments covers the stone walls and ceilings – local photographs, antique china, brasses and farm tools. The three friendly flagstoned communicating rooms have sturdy oak beams, lots of shiny black panelling, an inglenook with an oven, warm winter log fires. The very friendly barmaid Jenny serves well kept Bass, Flowers Original, Mansfield Bitter, Morlands Old Speckled Hen, Otter Bitter, and Palmers IPA on handpump from the uncommonly long bar counter, as well as 16 wines by the glass, and a decent range of malt whiskies. Bar food under the new licensees includes sandwiches (from £1.95), soup (£2.20), whitebait (£3.50), ploughman's (from £4.25), breaded plaice (£4.95), 8oz sirloin (£10.75), as well as daily specials like moussaka (£5.65), steak and stilton pie (£5.95), lamb curry (£6.25) or chicken chasseur (£6.75); puddings like hot chocolate fudge cake or cheesecake (from £2.60). There are also seats and tables in the enclosed back garden. *(Recommended by Paul and Sue Merrick, Gordon, Joy and Peter Heatherley, Simon Williams, Galen Strawson, Ann and Colin Hunt, P A Legon, N J Lawless, Simon and Jane Williams, DAV, Tim and Ann Meaden, Jack and Gemima Valiant, Joan and Michel Hooper-Immins, Dr and Mrs J H Hills)*

Free house ~ Licensees Stuart and Noreen Race ~ Real ale ~ Meals and snacks ~ Children in eating area of bar ~ (01300) 341797 ~ Open 11-3, 6-11; 12-3, 7-10.30 Sun

nr CHIDEOCK SY4292 Map 1

Anchor

Seatown; signposted off A35 from Chideock

Splendidly situated, just a few steps from a nearly idyllic cove beach and nesting dramatically beneath the 617-foot Golden Cap pinnacle, this well run old inn almost straddles the Dorset Coast path. Seats and tables on the spacious front terrace are ideally placed for the stunning sea and cliff views, but you'll have to get there pretty early in summer to bag a spot as it can get almost ridiculously busy. Out of season when the crowds have gone the cosy little bars seem especially snug with warming winter fires, some sea pictures and lots of interesting local photographs, a few fossils and shells, simple but comfortable seats around neat tables, and low white-planked ceilings; the family room and a further corner of the bar are no smoking, and there are friendly animals (especially the cats). Good bar food includes sandwiches (from £1.95), filled baked potatoes (from £3.25), ploughman's (£3.95), breaded plaice (£4.95), baked avocado filled with crabmeat topped with melted cheese (£6.25), and evening seafood platter (£9.25). Well kept Palmers 200, Bridport, IPA and Tally Ho on handpump, under light blanket pressure in winter only; freshly squeezed orange juice, and a decent little wine list. Darts, shove-ha'penny, table skittles, cribbage, dominoes, fruit machine (summer only), a carom board, and piped, mainly classical, music. There are fridges and toasters in the bedrooms to make your own breakfast and eat it looking out over the sea. The licensees now also run the Ferry at Salcombe. *(Recommended by Peter and Pat Frogley, G and T Edwards, Ian Phillips, Marjorie and David Lamb, Martyn and Helen Webb, R C Morgan, R J Walden, George Atkinson, Eric Locker, Jeff Davies, C A Hall, Peter and Audrey Dowsett, John and Sally Clarke, David Eberlin, Trevor Swindells, Jo and Gary Charlton, JM, SM, Michael Graubart, Lynn Sharpless, Bob Eardley)*

Palmers ~ Tenants David and Sadie Miles ~ Real ale ~ Meals and snacks (12-9.30 during summer; not winter Sun evenings or 25 Dec) ~ (01297) 489215 ~ Well behaved children welcome ~ Folk, blues or jazz Sat evenings and Wed evenings during school holidays ~ Open 11-11; 11-2.30, 7-11 in winter; 12-10.30 Sun; closed evening 25 Dec ~ Bedrooms: £17.50/£35 nr CHRISTCHURCH SZ1696 Map 2

Fishermans Haunt

Winkton: B3347 Ringwood road nearly 3 miles N of Christchurch

They've recently smartened up the bar at this friendly little hotel by knocking two interconnecting rooms into one, fitting a new dark patterned carpet, re-upholstering the furniture and freshening up their choice of ornaments. At one end big windows look out on the neat front garden, and at the other there's a fruit machine. Good value straightforward bar food includes sandwiches (from £2.25; toasties from £2.75), filled baked potatoes (from £3.50), salads (from £5.25), steak and kidney pie or mushroom and nut fettucine (£5.50), and children's dishes (£2.95). Well kept Bass, Gales HSB, IPA and Ringwood Fortyniner on handpump, and lots of country wines; cheerful staff; disabled loos. The quiet back garden of this creeper-covered hotel has tables among the shrubs, roses and other flowers, and is close to weirs on the river Avon. *(Recommended by Dr C C S Wilson, D P and J A Sweeney, Andy and Jill Kassube, R Moorehead, Colin Fisher, G P Reeves, Paul Davies, David and Jo Williams, Mrs M A Newman)*

George Gale & Co Ltd ~ Manager Kevin A Crowley ~ Real ale ~ Meals and snacks (till 10) ~ Restaurant ~ Children welcome ~ (01202) 477283 ~ Open 10.30-2.30, 5-11; 10.30-11 Sat; 12-10.30 Sun ~ Bedrooms: £45B/£64B

CHURCH KNOWLE (Isle of Purbeck) SY9481 Map 2

New Inn 🍷

Fresh fish is delivered daily to this very attractive partly thatched 16th-c pub. Prices vary according to the market but there might be very tasty crab soup (£3.50), six grilled sardines (£5), mediterranean bouillabaisse, half pint prawns or moules marinières (£5.50), local trout (£6.95), fresh dressed crab (£7.50), very popular haddock in beer batter (£8.50) and dover sole (£12.50). A fairly traditional menu includes sandwiches (from £2.80), much liked home-made blue vinney soup (£2.65), ploughman's (from £4.25), home-made steak and kidney pie (£5.95), broccoli and cream cheese bake (£6.50), game pie (£7), chicken tikka masala (£7.75) and 8oz fillet steak (£12.50), puddings like spotted dick or blackberry and apple pie and children's meals (£3). The two main bar areas are nicely furnished with farmhouse chairs and tables and lots of bric-a-brac on the walls, and there's a log fire at each end; the dining lounge has a good relaxed atmosphere. Well kept Flowers Original and Wadworths 6X and a changing guest beer on handpump; a dozen or so very reasonably priced wines are all available in two sizes of glass, and around 20 malt whiskies and bourbons; skittle alley, darts, and piped music. When the local post office closed recently this became the first pub in the county to serve as local village post office and shop, and you can generally buy locally made cheese to take away. There are plenty of tables in the good-sized garden, which has fine views of the Purbeck hills. No dogs; camping in two fields at the back but you need to book beforehand; good disabled facilities. *(Recommended by Mike and Heather Watson, Joy and Peter Heatherley, DAV, Nigel Flook, Betsy Brown, Carol and John Fage, Ian and Nita Cooper, Eric Locker, Derek Patey, E A George, Andrew Rogers, Amanda Milsom)*

Greenalls ~ Tenant Maurice Estop ~ Meals and snacks ~ Restaurant ~ (01929) 480357 ~ Children in eating area of bar ~ Open 11-3, 6(7 in winter)-11; 12-3, 6-11 Sun; closed Mon Jan-March

COLEHILL SU0302 Map 2

Barley Mow

From roundabout junction of A31 Ferndown bypass and B3073 Wimborne rd, follow Colehill signpost up Middlehill Rd, pass Post Office, and at church turn right into Colehill Lane; Ordnance Survey Sheet 195 map reference 032024

This lovely old thatched dining pub is particularly attractive in summer, when there are colourful tubs of flowers in front, and more flowers in hanging baskets set off vividly against the whitewash. At the back is a pleasant and enclosed big lawn sheltered by oak trees; boules; good nearby walks. The cosy beamed main bar has a good fire in the huge brick fireplace and attractively moulded oak panelling, and is decorated with some Hogarth prints; the cat is called Misty. Bar food includes soup (£2.50), open sandwiches (from £2.95), mushrooms in creamy stilton sauce topped with crispy croutons (£3.50), ploughman's (£4.50), steak and kidney pie or turkey and gammon pie with sliced leek and cream sauce (£6.25), chicken breast wrapped in smoked bacon and stuffed with stilton with port sauce (£7.75), tiger prawns (£8.75), pork topped with creamy stilton and mushroom sauce (£9.95); puddings like blackberry and apple pie (£2.95). The family dining area is no smoking. Well kept Badger Best and Tanglefoot on handpump; fruit machine and piped music. *(Recommended by G Washington, M J Dowdy, Maurice Southon, A E Brace; more reports please)*

Badger ~ Managers Bruce and Sue Cichocki ~ Real ale ~ Meals and snacks ~ (01202) 882140 ~ Children in family room ~ Singer/guitarist every other Wednesday ~ Open 11-3, 5.30-11; 12-3, 7-10.30 Sun

CORFE CASTLE (Isle of Purbeck) SY9681 Map 2

Fox

West Street, off A351; from town centre, follow dead-end Car Park sign behind church

The evocative ruins of Corfe Castle rise up behind the very pleasant suntrap garden – reached by a pretty flower-hung side entrance, and divided into secluded areas by flower beds and a twisted apple tree – at this characterful old pub. The fabric of the pub exhibits much of the same stone as the castle, particularly in an ancient alcove with a number of fossils, and a pre-1300 stone fireplace. An ancient well in the lounge bar has been glassed over and lit from within. The tiny atmospheric front bar has closely set tables and chairs, a painting of the castle in its prime among other pictures above the panelling, old-fashioned iron lamps, and hatch service. Well kept Eldridge Pope Thomas Hardy and Royal Oak, Gibbs Mew Bishops Tipple, Greene King Abbot, Ind Coope Burton and Wadworths 6X are tapped straight from the cask. Bar food includes sandwiches (from £1.95), home-made soup (£1.95), home-made steak and kidney pie or fresh cod (£4.95), and daily specials like lamb rogan josh (£4.95) or turkey caribbean (£6.45), and puddings (from £2.20). The countryside surrounding this National Trust village is worth exploring, and there's a local museum opposite. No children. *(Recommended by Alastair Tainsh, Jeremy Burnside, R Moorehead, Mr and Mrs N A Spink, Gordon, D P and J A Sweeney, David and Carole Chapman, Ian and Jacqui Ross, Geoffrey Lawrance, Stephen Brown, James and Lynne House, David Carr, Howard England, Eric Locker, B and K Hypher, D Eberlin)*

Free house ~ Licensees Miss A L Brown and G B White ~ Real ale ~ Meals and snacks ~ (01929) 480449 ~ Open 11-3, 6.30-11; 12-3, 7-10.30 Sun

Greyhound

A351

Standing right next to the castle, this bustling old pub was originally two early 16th-c cottages, and a stable at the back has some 12th-c timbers and stone. The garden borders the castle moat and has fine views of both the castle battlements and the surrounding Purbeck hills, and the courtyard (which opens on to the castle bridge) has lots of pretty climbing and flowering shrubs. The three small low-ceilinged areas of the main bar have mellowed oak panelling and lots of paintings, brasses, and old photographs of the town on the walls. Popular bar food includes filled rolls (from £1.50), filled baked potatoes (from £2.75; local crab £3.75), ploughman's (from £3.25), home-made pizzas (from £3.85), home-made chilli (£4.50), home-made steak in ale pie (£5.95), daily specials such as home-made faggots in rich onion gravy (£4.75), Scotch salmon steaks in a hollandaise sauce (£5.95), Scotch rump steak (£7.95), and local bass (£12.50), puddings (£2.50), and children's meals (£2.50); Sunday roast beef or pork (two courses £5.75). Well kept Boddingtons, Flowers Original, local Poole Best on handpump. Sensibly placed darts, winter pool, cribbage, dominoes, Purbeck shove-ha'penny on a 5ft mahogany board, TV, and piped music; the family room is no smoking. *(Recommended by J and B Cressey, D P and J A Sweeney, John and Vivienne Rice, R Moorehead, Mr and Mrs N A Spink, David and Carole Chapman, Chris Reeve, Gordon, Stephen Brown, Kath Wetherill, David Carr)*

Whitbreads ~ Lease: Mike and Louisa Barnard ~ Real ale ~ Meals and snacks ~ (01929) 480205 ~ Children in eating area of bar and in family room ~ Folk music Sun lunchtime ~ Open 11-11; 12-10.30 Sun

CORSCOMBE ST5105 Map 2

Fox

On outskirts, towards Halstock

The daily specials are what people enjoy most at this cosy thatched rural pub. They might include fresh vegetable soup (£3.25), provençal fish soup, moules marinières, fried squid with chilli and garlic or warm salad of pheasant breast and bacon (£4.95), fish pie (£7.75), salmon fishcakes with fresh tomato sauce or local rabbit braised in cider, mustard and cream (£7.95), roast cod with anchovies, garlic and olive oil (£8.95), chicken breast in green thai curry (£9.25), moroccan-style lamb tagine with couscous (£9.50), brill fillet with lemon and chive butter or medallions of venison with red wine and damson sauce (£11.50) or seafood grill with oysters, crab, stuffed clams and mussels (£15); puddings such as treacle tart, sticky toffeee pudding and meringues with clotted cream (all £2.95). The flagstoned room on the right has lots of beautifully polished copper pots, pans and teapots, harness hanging from the beams, small Leech hunting prints and Snaffles prints, Spy cartoons of fox hunting gentlemen, a long scrubbed pine table (a highly polished smaller one is tucked behind the door), and an open fire. In the left-hand room there are built-in wall benches, candles in champagne bottles on the cloth-covered or barrel tables, an assortment of chairs, lots of horse prints, antlers on the beams, two glass cabinets with a couple of stuffed owls in each, and an L-shaped wall settle by the inglenook fireplace; darts, dominoes, cribbage. Readers particulary enjoy the flower-filled conservatory which has a huge oak table. Well kept Exmoor Ale, Fullers London Pride and Shepherd Neame Spitfire on handpump, a thoughtful wine list, local cider and home-made elderflower cordial, damson vodka, and sloe gin. The labrador Bramble loves a bit of attention but unfortunately doesn't mix well with other dogs, so no dogs allowed. There are seats across the quiet village lane, on a lawn by the little stream. This is a nice area for walks. *(Recommended by Basil Minson, Karen Eliot, Mr and Mrs N Heleine, Colin Thompson, Tim and Ann Meaden, E A George, James and Lynne House, Desmond and Pat Morris, N Latham, Jo and Gary Charlton, Nigel Wilkinson)*

Free house ~ Licensee Martyn Lee ~ Real ale ~ Meals and snacks ~ (01935) 891330 ~ Well behaved children in eating area of bar ~ Open 12-2.30, 7-11; 12-4.30, 7-11 Sat; 12-4, 7-10.30 Sun ~ Bedrooms: £50B/£60.70B

CRANBORNE SU0513 Map 2

Fleur-de-Lys

B3078 N of Wimborne Minster

The walls of this 17th-c inn are lined with historical documents and mementoes of some of the people who have stayed here over the centuries, from Thomas Hardy while writing *Tess of the d'Urbervilles* to Rupert Brooke, whose poem about the pub takes pride of place above the fireplace. The oak-panelled lounge bar is attractively modernised, and there's also a more simply furnished beamed public bar with well kept Badger Best and Tanglefoot on handpump, farm cider, and some good malt whiskies. Well liked bar food includes soup (£2.25), sandwiches (from £2.35), pâté (£3.30), ploughman's (£4.25), nutty mushroom layer or smoked haddock bake (£5.25), liver and bacon casserole (£5.75), steak pie or steak and kidney pudding (£5.95), chicken breast with red and green pepper sauce (£6.95), chicken breast filled with stilton cheese and wrapped in bacon or noisettes of lamb in rosemary and redcurrant sauce (£8.95) and puddings like crème brûlée and treacle tart (£2.95); best to arrive early for Sunday lunch. Darts, dominoes, cribbage, fruit machine, and piped music. A pair of ancient stone pillars in the car park are said to have come from the ruins of a nearby monastery, and there are swings and a slide on the lawn behind the car park. Bedrooms are comfortable but one reader was disturbed by traffic noise. *(Recommended by Tom and Joan Childs, Gerald Barnett, R J Walden, Ann and Colin Hunt, D G Twyman, Peter Meister, Colin Fisher, Tim and Ann Meaden, Mike and Heather Watson)*

Badger ~ Tenant Charles Hancock ~ Real ale ~ Meals and snacks ~ (01725) 517282 ~ Children over 5 in restaurant ~ Open 11-3, 6.30(7 winter)-11; 12-3, 7-10.30 Sun ~ Bedrooms: £30(£35B)/£45(£50B)

DORCHESTER SY6890 Map 2

Kings Arms

High East St

The spaciously comfortable bar at this pleasantly old-fashioned Georgian coaching inn has some interesting old maps and pictures, a capacious fireplace, and plenty of tables full of eaters enjoying the well presented fairly straightforward bar food: soup (£1.90), sandwiches (from £2.40), filled baked potatoes (£3.70), cauliflower cheese (£4.95), fried lamb liver and bacon (£4.95), lasagne (£5.25), gammon steak (£5.75), steak, mushroom and ale pie (£5.95) and grilled salmon (£6.95). Well kept Bass, Courage Directors, Flowers Original and Tetleys on handpump, a range of malt whiskies and fruit wines from the long mahogany bar counter; consistently friendly service from neatly dressed staff. Fruit machine, piped music. *(Recommended by Greg Kilminster, Gordon, Simon Penny, Jack and Gemima Valiant, J F M and M West, David Carr, D B Jenkin, Janet and Colin Roe, JM, SM, Miss R Kingsmill)*

Greenalls ~ Manager Stephen Walmsley ~ Real ale ~ Meals and snacks ~ Restaurants ~ (01305) 265353 ~ Children welcome in eating area of bar, restaurant and conservatory ~ Live band Thurs evening ~ Open 11-3, 5.30-11; 11-11 Sat; 12-3, 7-10.30 Sun ~ Bedrooms: £49.90B/£54.85B

EAST CHALDON SY7983 Map 2

Sailors Return

Village signposted from A352 Wareham—Dorchester; from village green, follow Dorchester, Weymouth signpost; note that the village is also known as Chaldon Herring; Ordnance Survey sheet 194, map reference 790834

The cheerfully welcoming bar at this popular thatched pub still keeps much of its original character, and the newer part has open beams showing the roof above, uncompromisingly plain and unfussy furnishings, and old notices for decoration; the dining area has solid old tables in nooks and crannies. It's tucked away in a tranquil spot near Lulworth Cove, and from nearby West Chaldon a bridleway leads across to join the Dorset Coast Path by the National Trust cliffs above Ringstead Bay. Benches, picnic-sets and log seats on the grass in front look down over cow pastures to the village. Even when busy, service remains as good as ever but it is best to get here early if you plan to eat, especially on Sunday, when the good value roast is popular. Bar food includes sandwiches (from £1.60), filled baked potatoes (from £3.50), and popular daily specials such as mushroom risotto or vegetable curry (£4.95), fisherman's pie (£5.95), whole gammon hock (£7.25), whole local crab (£8.95), whole local plaice (£7.95), and half a shoulder of lamb or pig roast (£8.95) or leg of lamb (£12.50). Half the restaurant is no smoking. Well kept Flowers IPA and Fullers London Pride and three or four guests like Cottage Normans Conquest, Quay Bombshell and Palmers IPA on handpump, country wines, and farm cider. Darts, shove-ha'penny, dominoes, and piped music. *(Recommended by James Nunns, John and Vivienne Rice, E A George, P G Bardswell, Marjorie and David Lamb, James and Lynne House, Tim and Ann Meaden, David Carr, Sue Cutler, Alan and Barbara Mence, Pat and Robert Watt, JM, SM)*

Free house ~ Licensees Bob and Pat Hodson ~ Real ale ~ Meals and snacks ~ Restaurant ~ (01305) 853847 ~ Children in restaurant ~ Open 11-11; 12-10.30 Sun in summer; 11-2.30, 6.30-11; 11-2.30, 6.30-11 Sun October-May

EAST KNIGHTON SY8185 Map 2

Countryman

Just off A352 Dorchester—Wareham; OS Sheet 194 map reference 811857

Readers particularly enjoy the comfortable bedrooms and the very friendly welcome at this well run bustling pub. There's a relaxing atmosphere in the neatly comfortable, long main bar, with a mixture of tables, wheelback chairs and relaxing sofas, and a fire at either end. It opens into several other smaller areas, including a no-smoking family room, a games bar with pool and darts, and a carvery (£10.25 for a roast and pudding). Generous helpings of bar food include sandwiches or filled rolls (from £2), home-made soup (£2.20), omelettes (from £3.45), ploughman's (from £4.75), vegetable curry (£5.75), tomato and lentil lasagne (£5.95), sardines in garlic butter (£6.50), gammon and pineapple (£8.75), steaks (from £10), daily specials like chicken curry or steak and kidney pie (£5.95), home-made puddings (£2.50) and children's meals (from £2.70); nice breakfasts. Well kept Courage Best and Directors, Morlands Old Speckled Hen, Ringwood Best and Old Thumper and Theakstons XB on handpump; farm cider, good choice of wines, and courteous well trained staff; piped music. There are tables and children's play equipment out in the garden as well as some toys inside; dogs welcome. *(Recommended by James and Lynne House, P and J Caunt, Bruce Bird, Tim and Ann Meaden, Mr and Mrs N A Spink, GDS, E H and R F Warner, Stephen, Julie and Hayley Brown, Marjorie and David Lamb, David Carr, John and Beryl Knight, Ann and Colin Hunt, Brian and Anna Marsden, Nigel Clifton, Andrea Carr)*

Free house ~ Licensees Jeremy and Nina Evans ~ Real ale ~ Meals and snacks ~ Restaurant ~ (01305) 852666 ~ Children welcome ~ Open 11-2.30, 6-11; 12-3, 6.30-10.30 Sun; closed 25 Dec ~ Bedrooms: £40B/£50B

EAST MORDEN SY9195 Map 2

Cock & Bottle

B3075 between A35 and A31 W of Poole

Dorset Dining Pub of the Year

Reports on this very attractive old red brick inn have been particularly good over the last year. Its handsome interior is divided into several communicating areas, with a warmly rustic feel – heavy rough beams, some stripped ceiling boards, some squared panelling, a nice mix of old furnishings in various sizes and degrees of antiquity, small Victorian prints and some engaging bric-a-brac. There's a good log fire, intimate corners each with just a couple of tables, plenty of no-smoking space, and a separate proper lino-floored public bar (with piped music, dominoes, a fruit machine and a sensibly placed darts alcove); this in turn leads on to yet another dining room, again with plenty of character. There's plenty of praise for the sensibly imaginative very well prepared bar food which readers describe as good value: sandwiches (from £2), home-made pâté (£4.25), faggots with onion gravy (£5.40), ploughman's (£5.25), home-made beefburger topped with smoked bacon and stilton (£5.75), leek and mushroom crumble (£6.50), Scotch sirloin steak (£10.25), and daily specials such as spinach and mushroom pancake with fresh tomato sauce (£6.50), home-made curries or pork and apricot casserole (£6.75), steak and kidney pudding (£8.50), large whole plaice with parsley butter (£8.75), red bream with cajun spices and stir-fried vegetables with a light soy dressing (£9.95), roast partridge (£10.25), grilled tuna steak with sun-dried tomatoes (£11.95) and puddings like champagne and strawberry ice cream, apple and crème fraîche slice with Grand Marnier sauce and lemon tart with citrus sauce (£3.25), and children's dishes (from £2.95). Well kept Badger IPA, Best and Tanglefoot on handpump, a good choice of decent house wines including several by the glass, cordial service (though when it's busy food can take a time to come), disabled facilities. There are a few picnic-sets outside, a garden area, and an adjoining field with a nice pastoral outlook. *(Recommended by Geoffrey and Joanne Camp, Howard and Margaret Buchanan, Alastair Tainsh, WHBM, James and Lynne House, Jack Triplett)*

Badger ~ Tenant Peter Meadley ~ Real ale ~ Meals and snacks ~ Restaurant ~ (01929) 459238 ~ Children in restaurant ~ Open 11-3, 6-11; 12-3, 7-10.30 Sun

EVERSHOT ST5704 Map 2

Acorn

Village signposted from A37 8 miles S of Yeovil

Martyn Lee, the new landlord at this village pub, is known to us already for his high standard of work at the Fox at Corscombe which appears earlier in this chapter. He's planning gentle alterations to return the building to a more attractive original state – removing the carpet in the back bar has already revealed a nice stone floor. The comfortable L-shaped bar has tapestry covered wooden benches, two fine old fireplaces, and copies of the inn's deeds going back to the 17th c on the partly hessian covered bare stone walls; another lounge has a woodburning stove. Lunchtime bar food includes carrot and orange soup (£3.25), chargrilled vegetable tart (£4.50), filled baguettes (£3.50), home-made beefburger (£5.50), venison and apricot pie (£6.50) and chicken casserole (£7.50), with more substantial evening dishes like rabbit in white wine and mustard sauce (£9.50), lamb rump with shallots and spring greens (£10.95) and lemon sole with thyme butter (£11.50); no-smoking dining room. Well kept Exmoor, Fullers London Pride and Wadworths 6X on handpump as well as farm cider, home-made elderflower cordial, damson vodka and sloe gin; pool, darts, shove-ha'penny, skittle alley, dominoes, cribbage and juke box. Outside, there's a terrace with dark oak furniture. It's a nice village to stay in and there are lots of good surrounding walks. *(Reports on the new regime please)*

Free house ~ Licensee Martyn Lee ~ Real ale ~ Meals and snacks ~ Restaurant ~ (01935) 83228 ~ Children in games room ~ Open 12-2.30(3 Sat), 6.30-11; 12-3, 7-10.30 Sun ~ Bedrooms: £55B/£80B

FARNHAM ST9515 Map 2

Museum

Village signposted off A354 Blandford Forum—Salisbury

Many readers have been impressed with the good service, well prepared food and welcoming atmosphere at this unassuming looking pub. A particularly well prepared and presented wide range of daily specials might include home-made minestrone or chilled tomato and basil soups (from £2.95), butterfly prawns with sweet and sour sauce (£4.95), scrambled eggs with smoked salmon (£5.25), roast vegetables with polenta (£6.25), home-made fish pie (£6.95) and gammon steak with parsley sauce (£7.25) at lunchtime, with evening dishes like grilled aubergine with parmesan and rocket or cassoulet of snails (£5.25), pork provençale (£10.95), osso bucco (£11.25), salmon fishcakes with crab sauce (£11.95), and breast of duck with olives and fresh mango (£12.25). The attractive Coopers Bar has green cloth-cushioned seats set into walls and windows, local pictures by Robin Davidson, an inglenook fireplace with bread oven, and piped classical music. Very well kept Wadworths 6X and changing guests such as Butcombe, Fullers London Pride, and Hook Norton on handpump, around 20 malt whiskies, and a large wine list (the licensee may like to recommend one for you); darts, pool, juke box. There's a most attractive small brick-walled dining conservatory, leading out to a sheltered terrace with white tables under cocktail parasols, and beyond an arched wall is a garden with swings and a colourful tractor. The bedrooms are in converted former stables. *(Recommended by Pamela Turner, Stephen, Julie and Hayley Brown, Ian Phillips, Ann and Alex Tolputt, Simon Williams, Gwen and Peter Andrews, B and K Hypher, Phil and Heidi Cook, Chris Elford, Dave Braisted)*

Free house ~ Licensee John Barnes ~ Real ale ~ Meals and snacks ~ Restaurant ~ (01725) 516261 ~ Children welcome away from bar ~ Live music 3rd Thurs of month ~ Open 11-3, 6-11; 12-3, 7-10.30 Sun; cl 25 Dec ~ Bedrooms: £45B/£65B

GODMANSTONE SY6697 Map 2

Smiths Arms

A352 N of Dorchester

There are only six tables inside this tiny 15th-c thatched building which measures just 12 by 4 metres. The quaint little bar has some antique waxed and polished small pews hugging the walls (there's also one elegant little high-backed settle), long wooden stools and chunky tables, National Hunt racing pictures and some brass plates on the walls, and an open fire. Very well kept Ringwood Best tapped from casks behind the bar; friendly, helpful staff (the landlord is quite a character); dominoes, trivia, cribbage and piped music. Simple but tasty home-made food might be sandwiches (from £1.70; the roast beef is lovely), giant sausage (£3.10), ploughman's (from £3.50), quiche or chilli (£4.55), a range of salads (from £4.35), home-cooked ham (£5.45), and daily specials such as curried prawn lasagne or topside of beef and steak and kidney pie (£5.45) and puddings (£2). There are seats and tables set outside on a crazy-paved terrace and on the grassy mound by the narrow River Cerne. A pleasant walk leads over Cowdon Hill to the River Piddle. No children. *(Recommended by Carole Smart, Andrew Jeeves, Joy and Peter Heatherley, JP, PP, Dr and Mrs A K Clarke, James and Lynne House)*

Free house ~ Licensees John and Linda Foster ~ Real ale ~ Meals and snacks (till 9.45) ~ (01300) 341236 ~ Open 11-3, 6-11; 12-3, 7-10.30 Sun; closed Jan

KINGSTON (Isle of Purbeck) SY9579 Map 2

Scott Arms

B3069

There are wonderful views of Corfe Castle and the Purbeck hills from the well kept garden of this popular creeper-clad stone house. Inside, its rambling warren-like rooms have old panelling, stripped stone walls, warming fires, some fine antique prints and a friendly, chatty feel; an attractive room overlooks the garden, and there's a decent extension which is well liked by families. Popular lunchtime bar food in generous helpings includes tasty home-made soup (£3.25), sandwich platters (from £3.25), ploughman's (£4.75), lasagne (£6.95), as well as specials such as lamb and apricot casserole or pork and stilton stroganoff (£7.95), and lots of fresh fish like lemon or dover sole, john dory or bass (all about £8.95). The evening menu is slightly different with mushrooms in cream and garlic (£3.95), steak and ale pie (£7.95) and 8oz sirloin (£9.95); children's meals (£2.95); no-smoking dining area; they do afternoon cream teas in summer. Well kept Greenalls Original and Ringwood Best on handpump, and lots of wines; darts, fruit machine, and piped music. *(Recommended by Simon Williams, JP, PP, K Stevens, John and Vivienne Rice, Mr and Mrs A R Hawkins, David and Carole Chapman, J Boucher, Simon and Jane Williams, Andy and Jill Kassube, Jeff Davies, Stephen, Julie and Hayley Brown, JM, SM, S J and C C Davidson, Stephen Brown, DAV, JDM, KM, B and K Hypher)*

Greenalls ~ Manager Neil Robert Cann ~ Real ale ~ Meals and snacks ~ (01929) 480270 ~ Children in restaurant ~ Open 11-11; 12-10.30 Sun; 11-3, 6-11 in winter, 12-3, 7-10.30 winter Sun ~ Bedrooms: /£60B

LANGTON HERRING SY6182 Map 2

Elm Tree

Village signposted off B3157

This lovely old beamed pub is popular for its interesting well prepared daily specials such as creamed fennel and celery soup (£2.65), roasted red pepper and goat's cheese bruschetta (£4.95), pasta with fresh asparagus, leeks and pecorino cheese (£5.25), loin of pork with creamed shallot and rosemary sauce (£8.50), roasted red snapper fillet in a moroccan marinade (£9.25), sirloin steak with a creamed oyster mushroom sauce (£9.75), and puddings such as treacle tart and clotted cream or hot banana fudge biscuit (from £2.95). More standard dishes from the bar menu include sandwiches (from £2), soup (£2.50), filled baked potatoes (from £2.50), ploughman's or ciabatta with goat's cheese and tomatoes (£3.75), hot garlic bread filled with hot roast beef (£3.45), lasagne (£6.50), steak and ale pie (£6.95), creamy cider, pork and apple casserole (£7.50) and baked crab mornay (£7.95), puddings including a very chocolatey chocolate pudding (from £2.95) and the usual children's menu (from £2.25); good Sunday roasts. There may be a bit of a wait for food when they get busy. The Portland spy ring is said to have met in the main beamed and carpeted rooms, which have walls festooned with copper, brass and bellows, cushioned window seats, red leatherette stools, windsor chairs, and lots of tables; one has some old-fashioned settles and an inglenook. The traditionally furnished extension gives more room for diners. Greenalls Original and a guest such as John Smiths or Marstons Pedigree under light blanket pressure; country wines. Outside in the pretty flower-filled sunken garden are colourful hanging baskets, flower tubs, and tables; a track leads down to the Dorset Coast Path, which here skirts the eight-mile lagoon enclosed by Chesil Beach. *(Recommended by Karen Eliot, Basil Minson, Joy and Peter Heatherley, David Mead, Pete and Rosie Flower, Galen Strawson, John and Vivienne Rice, Anthony Barnes, Richard and Rosemary Hoare, Mrs A Wiseman, James and Lynne House, B and K Hypher)*

Greenalls ~ Tenants Roberto D'Agostino, L M Horlock ~ Real ale ~ Meals and snacks ~ (01305) 871257 ~ Children in eating area of bar ~ Open 11-3, 6-11; 12-3, 6.30-10.30 Sun

LODERS SY4994 Map 1

Loders Arms

Off A3066 just N of Bridport; can also be reached off A35 E of Bridport, via Uploders

This pretty stonebuilt village of largely thatched cottages is tucked into a sheltered fold of steep Dorset hills. The smallish long bar at this relaxing pub, which is still well used by local people, is welcoming and comfortable, with a log fire, maybe piped classical music, and amiable dogs. Well kept Palmers Bridport, 200 and IPA, a good choice of wines, good service. The good interesting food here is a large part of the reason that this is such a popular place. The menu changes daily and might include huge filled french bread (from £3, smoked salmon and cream cheese £3.95), devilled kidneys (£3.95), tiger prawns in garlic or fresh anchovies with tomato and basil salad (£4.25), sausage, mash and onion gravy (£4.95), lemon and ginger chicken (£5.95), mushroom and aubergine risotto or rabbit in cider (£6.95), pork tenderloin with a cream and horseradish sauce (£8.95), venison steak with gin and juniper berry sauce (£10.95), and puddings like chocolate and brandy mousse, fruit crumbles or apricot pudding (£3); no-smoking dining room. There's a skittle alley; cribbage. *(Recommended by Nigel Wikeley, Anthony Barnes, Galen Strawson, Gethin Lewis, R Shelton, Simon and Jane Williams, Hugh Robertson, Brian Lister, Brian and Bett Cox, Dr B and Mrs P B Baker, Jo and Gary Charlton, R C Morgan)*

Palmers ~ Tenants Roger and Helen Flint ~ Real ale ~ Meals and snacks ~ Restaurant ~ (01308) 422431 ~ Children welcome until 9pm ~ Open 11.30(11 Sat)-3, 6-11; 12-10.30 Sun ~ Bedrooms: £25B/£40S(£45B)

LYME REGIS SY3492 Map 1

Pilot Boat ♀

Bridge Street

Perfect after a day on the beach or at sea, the bar at this simple airy seaside pub is decorated with local pictures, navy and helicopter photographs, lobster-pot lamps, sharks' heads, an interesting collection of local fossils, a model of one of the last sailing ships to use the harbour, and a notable collection of sailors' hat ribands. At the back, there's a long and narrow lounge bar overlooking the little River Lym; skittle alley and piped music. Popular bar food includes reasonably priced ploughman's (£3.75), lentil nut loaf (£5.25), steak, kidney and ale pie (£5.95) and local fish such as fried bass with white wine sauce (£10.75). The dining area is no smoking. Well kept Palmers Bridport, IPA and 200 on handpump, and a decent wine. The licensees run another Lyme Regis pub, the Cobb Arms, which has bedrooms. There are seats on a terrace outside. *(Recommended by Mr and Mrs J E Lockwood, M Brooks, Andy and Jill Kassube, Mike Doupe, Paul and Judith Booth, Pat and Tony Martin, Greg Kilminster, Ann and Colin Hunt, Joan and Michel Hooper-Immins, Peter and Pat Frogley, Simon Williams, M G Hart, JM, SM, Tim and Ann Meaden, David Gittins, Simon and Jane Williams, Stephen, Julie and Hayley Brown)*

Palmers ~ Tenants Bill and Caroline Wiscombe ~ Real ale ~ Meals and snacks (12-10)

~ (01297) 443242 ~ Children welcome ~ Occasional live entertainment ~ Open 11-11; 12-10.30 Sun

MARNHULL ST7718 Map 2

Blackmore Vale

Burton Street; quiet side street

One of the main draws at this warmly welcoming old pub is the enjoyable food, which might include sandwiches or soup (£2.25), prawn and egg mayonnaise or breaded brie with fruits of the forest sauce (£3.95), Indian vegetable curry (£5.75), steak and kidney pie or chilli (£5.85), game pie (£6.95), lamb and mango curry (£7.45), whole grilled plaice (£7.75), seafood parcel (£7.85), steaks (from £8.95), and daily specials such as various stir fries – chicken in cajun spices, prawn in Chinese green curry sauce, cashew nuts in a sweet and sour sauce, and beef in black bean sauce (all £5.95), and lots of home-made puddings; Friday is fish night, and they offer six good roasts on Sundays (£3.95-£4.25). They will bring your food to the garden, where one of the tables is thatched. The comfortably modernised lounge bar is decorated with fourteen guns and rifles, keys, a few horsebrasses and old brass spigots on the beams, and there's a log fire; one bar is no smoking. Well kept Badger Best and Tanglefoot on handpump, farm cider and a good wine list. Cribbage, dominoes, shove-ha'penny, and a skittle alley. No children. *(Recommended by Charles and Pauline Stride, Mrs Laura Gustine, R H Rowley, W Burke, Lynn Sharpless, Bob Eardley, R J Walden, Gregor Macdonald, G G Lawrance, Mrs M L Carter)*

Badger ~ Tenants Roger and Marion Hiron ~ Real ale ~ Meals and snacks (till 10pm) ~ (01258) 820701 ~ Open 11.30-2.30, 6.30-11; 12-2.30, 7-10.30 Sun

MARSHWOOD SY3799 Map 1

Bottle

B3165 Lyme Regis—Crewkerne

Enthusiastic new licensees have chosen not to spruce up the simple interior of this thriving village local, which they reckon is pretty much the same as it was 30 years ago (so perhaps a little worn in places), and an enjoyable mix of customers from businessmen to bikers, and hikers to farmers seems to appreciate the genuinely friendly character here. Simple furnishings including cushioned benches and one high-backed settle stand on a bare composition floor, and there's an inglenook fireplace with a big log fire in winter. They've introduced a particularly interesting range of unusual vegetarian and vegan dishes, many international-style dishes, organic lagers and wines, and they can cater for people with food allergies. There might be organic pork and chive sausages and mash, steak and mushroom pie, butterbean and carrot pâté with tomato and basil coulis or buckwheat pancakes with ratatouille (£6.95), spinach and feta pie, Carribean sweet potato curry with coconut milk or fresh cod and herb fishcakes with tomato and herb sauce (£7.95), organic lamb chops with cranberry and orange sauce (£8.50) or sirloin steak (£14.95); well kept Morlands Old Speckled Hen, Otter and Wadworths 6X on handpump; darts, pool, and a fruit machine in a smaller side room, also shove-ha'penny, dominoes and cribbage, a skittle alley and piped music. They have a craft shop with local wickerwork, pottery and paintings. A good big back garden has a well equipped play area, and beyond it a camp site. The pub is surrounded by pretty walking country and close to Lambert's Castle (a National Trust hill fort). *(Recommended by Basil Minson, Mr and Mrs J Bishop, A Fisher, Marjorie and David Lamb)*

Free house ~ Licensees: Sim Pym and Chloe Fox-Lambert ~ Real ale ~ Meals and snacks ~ (01297) 678254 ~ Children welcome ~ Bands and comedy once a month ~ Open 12-3, 6.30(7 in winter)-11(10.30 Sun); closed Tues in winter

> Post Office address codings confusingly give the impression that some pubs are in Dorset, when they're really in Somerset (which is where we list them).

MILTON ABBAS ST8001 Map 2

Hambro Arms

Village signposted from A354 SW of Blandford, in Winterborne Whitechurch and Milborne St Andrew

This pretty pub nestles in the heart of a late 18th-c landscaped village, its gently winding lane lined by lawns and cream-coloured thatched cottages. Its beamed front lounge bar has a bow window seat looking down over the attractive village houses, captain's chairs and round tables on the carpet, and in winter an excellent log fire. Well kept Bass and Boddingtons on handpump, and several malt whiskies; darts in the cosy back public bar. Big helpings of good bar food include soup (£2.50), pâté (£2.95), sandwiches (£3.25), grilled rump sandwich (£4.95), ploughman's (£5.25), beef, Guinness and mushroom pie (£8.50), sirloin steak (£10.95) and puddings like lemon tart with lemon sorbet or apple strudel with vanilla custard (all £3.95), as well as daily specials like fresh battered or grilled cod (£6.55), grilled whole plaice, fillet of sea bream, poached salmon or pheasant in mushroom and red wine sauce (£7.65), halibut with white wine and mushroom sauce or venison steaks in a rich madeira sauce (£8.75); roast Sunday lunch (£12.65). The outside terrace has some tables and chairs. *(Recommended by Geoffrey Lawrance, Lynda Katz, James and Lynne House, Paul Seligman, G G Lawrence, Andy and Jill Kassube, Mr and Mrs M Budd, M J Dowdy, Stephen Brown, WHBM)*

Greenalls ~ Tenants Ken and Brenda Baines ~ Real ale ~ Meals and snacks ~ Restaurant ~ (01258) 880233 ~ Children in restaurant ~ Open 11-3, 6(7 in winter)-11; 12-3, 7-10.30 Sun ~ Bedrooms: £35B/£55B

NETTLECOMBE SY5195 Map 2

Marquis of Lorne

Turn E off A3066 Bridport—Beaminster Road 1½ miles N of Bridport. Pass Mangerton Mill and 1m after West Milton go straight across give-way junction. Pub is on left 300 yards up the hill.

Although it's quite a tortuous drive to get to this delightful country pub, it is a very pleasant journey through lovely peaceful countryside, and you are guaranteed a warm welcome on arrival. The comfortable bustling main bar has a log fire, mahogany panelling and old prints and photographs around its neatly matching chairs and tables; two dining areas lead off, the smaller of which has another log fire and is no smoking. A good range of very well cooked changing bar food might include broccoli and stilton soup (£2.25), avocado with curried chicken (£3.95), cold leek, stilton and walnut pie (£5.25), spinach and walnut lasagne (£5.95), fish pie or beef cooked in Guinness (£6.25), pork steak marinated in orange and basil (£6.95), roast duck breast with orange and ginger sauce (£9.95), and puddings such as almond and apricot strudel or sticky toffee pudding (£3); good vegetables, and they may have locally-made chutneys and marmalade for sale. Well kept Palmers Bridport and IPA on handpump with 200 tapped straight from the cask, and good wine list with usually around eight by the glass. A wooden-floored snug has cribbage and table skittles; the piped music is mainly classical. Outside, the summer hanging baskets are pretty, and the big garden has a rustic style play area among the picnic-sets under its apple trees. The earth-fort of Eggardon Hill is close by. *(Recommended by Galen Strawson, Simon Williams, David Heath, Mrs M E Bell, P J Hanson, Pete and Rosie Flower, Dr and Mrs G H Lewis, Mrs M Rolfe, Desmond and Pat Morris, Michael Graubart, J R Williams, Jo and Gary Charlton, Peter and Audrey Dowsett, C A Hall, Brian Lister, Dr and Mrs J H Hills, Mick and Hillary Stiffin, Lynn Sharpless, Bob Eardley, George Atkinson, Simon and Jane Williams, Philip Cooper)*

Palmers ~ Tenants Ian and Anne Barrett ~ Real ale ~ Meals and snacks ~ (01308) 485236 ~ Children in eating area of bar (must be over 10 if staying) ~ Open 11-2.30, 6(6.30 winter)-11; 12-3, 7-10.30 Sun ~ Bedrooms: £38S/£58S

NORDEN HEATH SY9483 Map 2

Halfway

Furzebrook – A351 Wareham—Corfe Castle

New licensees at this pretty mainly thatched 16th-c house have introduced a new menu which uses fresh produce and might include lamb shank cooked in onion, garlic, thyme, potato and red wine (£9), duck breast with red onion, cranberry and orange relish (£9.75), steak (£11.95), and fresh fish, served with interesting vegetables like creamed parsnip with sage and onion and dijon swede. The homely carpeted back bar, decorated with hops and hop sacks, has a narrow little room leading snugly off, and a hatch to serve a flagstoned front room with shiny tables and wheelback chairs, plates over its big fireplace (log fire in winter, flowers in summer), and a boarded ceiling. On the right as you go in, another pair of no-smoking front rooms have a pleasant mix of tables and small dining chairs on their carpet, local pictures, bird prints and colourful plates on stripped stone walls, another log fire. Well kept Badger Dorset Best and Tanglefoot and two guests like Adnams Southwold or Wadworths 6X on handpump or tapped from casks behind the bar; country wines. Darts, shove-ha'penny, cribbage, fruit machine and piped music. There are some tables and play equipment out in a sheltered back courtyard, and more tables out in front. *(More reports on the new regime please)*

Badger ~ Managers Rod, Claire and Amanda Brough ~ Real ale ~ Meals and snacks ~ (01929) 480402 ~ Children in eating area of bar ~ Open 11-11; 12-10.30 Sun

OSMINGTON MILLS SY7341 Map 2

Smugglers 🍷

Village signposted off A353 NE of Weymouth

Although this partly thatched inn has been taken over by Badger and has new managers, the plan is to make no changes and keep it running along the same successful lines as before. Its spacious interior has shiny black panelling and woodwork dividing the relaxing bar into cosy, friendly areas. Soft red lantern-lights give an atmospheric hue to the stormy sea pictures and big wooden blocks and tackle on the walls, and there are logs burning in an open stove. Some seats are tucked into alcoves and window embrasures, with one forming part of an upended boat. As well as a snack menu with home-made soup (£2), filled soft french sticks (from £3.25), ploughman's (£4.50), and home-made steak, kidney and mushroom pie (£6), popular daily specials include tandoori chicken legs (£4), lovely spare ribs (£4.50), potted fresh lobster with a thermidor sauce (£6.50), and lots of fish like roast monkfish with bacon on a sweet pepper and vermouth cream sauce, local crab, grilled bass on fresh tomato pasta with a cider vinegar dressing, grilled grey mullet with a fresh mango and chilli salsa, whole lemon sole, and brill fillet with a tomato and basil cream sauce (between £10 and £12). Service stays efficient and friendly even when they're busy. Over half the restaurant area is no smoking. Well kept Courage Best and Directors and Bagder Tanglefoot as well as guests like Ringwood Old Thumper and Theakstons on handpump, and about six wines by the glass. Darts, pool and fruit machine are kept sensibly out of the way; piped music. There are picnic-sets out on crazy paving by a little stream, with a thatched summer bar where they have summer barbecues, and a good play area over on a steep lawn. It gets very busy in high season (there's a holiday settlement just up the lane). *(Recommended by Pat and Tony Martin, Mr and Mrs D E Powell, J and B Cressey, Tony Scott, C Robinson, Andy and Jill Kassube, David and Carole Chapman, J F M West, P Eberlin, Tony Scott, M Rutherford, Simon Penny, Kath Wetherill, Simon and Jane Williams)*

Badger ~ Managers David and Jacqui Southward ~ Real ale ~ Meals and snacks ~ Restaurant ~ (01305) 833125 ~ Children in eating area of bar and in restaurant ~ Occasional Sunday lunchtime jazz or steel bands in summer ~ Open 11-11; 12-10.30 Sun; 11-2.30, 6.30-11 in winter; 12-2.30, 6.30-10.30 winter Sun ~ Bedrooms: £30B/£65B

PIDDLEHINTON SY7197 Map 1

Thimble

B3143

This pretty thatched pub is many readers' idea of the perfect English pub. It's delightfully tucked away down winding lanes, and approached by a little footbridge over the River Piddle, and the flower-filled garden (attractively floodlit at night) is a charmingly restful place to enjoy lunch. Inside, the neatly kept and friendly low-beamed bar is simpler than the exterior suggests, although nicely spacious so that in spite of drawing quite a lot of people in the summer, it never feels too crowded – service doesn't falter when it's busy either. There's a handsome open stone fireplace, and a deep well. Good value tasty bar food includes sandwiches (from £2, hot chicken breast £5.35), soup (£2.35), ploughman's (from £3.80), spinach and ricotta canelloni or breaded trout (£5.50), steak and kidney pie or pudding (£5.90), sirloin steak (£9.70), as well as daily specials like venison sausages (£3.30), game pie or pigeon, beef and mushroom pudding (£6.10), grilled salmon on hollandaise (£6.45), and puddings like blueberry muffin and clotted cream or warm apple strudel and cream (£3.25); two Sunday roasts (£5.95). Well kept Badger Best and Tanglefoot, Hardy Country and Ringwood Old Thumper on handpump, along with quite a few malt whiskies; friendly service; darts, shove-ha'penny, dominoes, cribbage, and piped music. *(Recommended by David Lamb, Mr and Mrs A R Hawkins, G Neighbour, Bronwen and Steve Wrigley, Simon Williams, R J Walden, M G Hart, Basil Minson, Pat and Robert Watt, Tim and Ann Meaden, Richard and Rosemary Hoare, Mrs M Rolfe, Ian and Nita Cooper, Galen Strawson)*

Free house ~ Licensees N R White and V J Lanfear ~ Real ale ~ Meals and snacks ~ (01300) 348270 ~ Children in eating area of bar ~ Open 12-2, 7-11(10.30 Sun); closed 25 Dec, 26 Dec evening

PLUSH ST7102 Map 2

Brace of Pheasants (🍴)

Village signposted from B3143 N of Dorchester at Piddletrenthide

The unusual pub sign at this charming long low 16th-c thatched inn is a glass case containing two stuffed pheasants. The airy beamed bar – popular with locals and visitors – has good solid tables, windsor chairs, fresh flowers, a heavy-beamed inglenook at one end with cosy seating inside, and a good log fire at the other (although a couple of readers have found it a bit chilly in winter). Well kept Bass, Fullers London Pride and Smiles Golden straight from the cask; the friendly black labrador is called Bodger, and the gold retriever Molly. A wide choice of very well prepared imaginative bar food might include soup (£2.25), crab savoury (£3.50), ploughman's (from £3.95), warm salad of queen scallops and lardons of bacon tossed in garlic butter (£5.95), game pie (£10.25), pork tenderloin with grain mustard and basil sauce or steamed supreme of salmon with a lobster, tarragon and prawn sauce (£10.75), duck breast with fresh orange and Grand Marnier sauce (£11.75), and daily specials like lamb and rosemary pie (£6.95) and pork fillet with blue cheese and sherry (£10.75). The restaurant and family room are no smoking. There's a decent-sized garden and terrace with an aviary, a rabbit cage and a lawn sloping up towards a rockery. Originally a row of cottages that included the village forge, the pub lies alongside Plush Brook, and an attractive bridleway behind goes to the left of the woods and over to Church Hill. *(Recommended by Pat and Robert Watt, Miss E A Blease, Joy and Peter Heatherley, G and T Edwards, Anthony Barnes, Karen Eliot, Mr and Mrs Broadhurst, R M Wickenden, Mike and Heather Watson, James and Lynne House, Jack Triplett, Sharon Hancock, Louie Eze, Tim and Ann Meaden)*

Free house ~ Licensees Jane and Geoffrey Knights ~ Real ale ~ Meals and snacks (till 9.45) ~ Restaurant ~ (01300) 348357 ~ Children in family room ~ Open 12-2.30, 7-11; 12-3, 7-10.30 Sun

PUNCKNOWLE SY5388 Map 2

Crown 🛏

Church Street; village signposted off B3157 Bridport—Abbotsbury; or reached off A35 via Chilcombe

Prettily set opposite a partly Norman village church and its rookery, this long 16th-c thatched and flint inn has a neat and welcoming rambling public bar with a pleasantly informal mix of furnishings, darts, table skittles and a comfortable family room opening off. The stripped stone lounge bar has red plush banquettes and stools; both rooms have heavy beams, and log fires in big stone fireplaces, and there are paintings by local artists for sale. There's a nice view from the partly paved back garden, which has tables under three venerable fairy-lit apple trees. Attractive food includes sandwiches (from £1.60), soup (£2), ploughman's (from £3.95), spinach and feta goujons (£2.55), curried prawns (£4.50), steak and kidney pie, cod and smoked haddock casserole in cream sauce or beef and parsnip casserole (£5.50), mushroom, chestnut and stilton casserole (£5.60), chicken and cashew nut casserole or lamb, orange, rosemary and wine casserole (£5.70), salmon steak topped with avocado and tarragon butter (£7.20) and rump steak (£8.95), and lots of tasty puddings like syrup sponge pudding, toffee crunch ice cream or almond meringue with fruit filling (£2.40); filling breakfasts. Well kept Palmers Best, Bridport, 200 and Tally Ho on handpump, Taunton Vale farm cider and country wines, good friendly service, no piped music. The village, incidentally, is pronounced Punnell.

(Recommended by Geoffrey Lawrance, Mick and Hillary Stiffin, George Atkinson, Richard Burton, Jo and Gary Charlton)

Palmers ~ Tenant Michael Lawless ~ Real ale ~ Meals and snacks ~ Children in family room ~ (01308) 897711 ~ Open 11-3, 6.30(7 in winter)-11; 12-3, 7-10.30 Sun; closed evening 25 Dec ~ Bedrooms: £20B/£40B

SHAVE CROSS SY4198 Map 1

Shave Cross Inn ★

On back lane Bridport—Marshwood, signposted locally; OS Sheet 193, map ref 415980

The original timbered bar at this charming partly 14th-c flint and thatch inn is a lovely flagstoned room, surprisingly roomy and full of character, with one big table in the middle, a smaller one by the window seat, a row of chintz-cushioned windsor chairs, and an enormous inglenook fireplace with plates hanging from the chimney breast. The larger carpeted side lounge has a dresser at one end set with plates, and modern rustic light-coloured seats making booths around the tables, and is partly no smoking. Bass, Badger Best and Eldridge Pope Royal Oak well kept on handpump, and local cider in summer. The pretty flower-filled sheltered garden has a thatched wishing-well, a goldfish pool, and a children's play area. Served by friendly staff, bar food includes ploughman's (£3.25), spinach and mushroom lasagne (£4.45), two sweet and sour pork and spicy lamb kebabs (£6.65), salmon steak (£7.75), sirloin steak (£8.45), and daily specials such as mushroom and nut fettucine (£4.45), lasagne (£4.45), rack of ribs (£6.35) and seafood pancakes (£6.95), and puddings like hot Dorset apple cake (£2.05). Darts, skittle alley, dominoes and cribbage.

(Recommended by Mick and Elizabeth Leyden, Galen Strawson, Joy and Peter Heatherley, Anthony Barnes, Colin Thompson, Marjorie and David Lamb, JP, PP, Yavuz and Shirley Mutlu, George Atkinson, JM, SM, E A George, Stephen, Julie and Hayley Brown, Brian Lister, Michael Graubart, Dr and Mrs J H Hills)

Free house ~ Licensees Bill and Ruth Slade ~ Real ale ~ Meals and snacks (not Mon, except bank holidays) ~ (01308) 868358 ~ Children in lounge bar ~ Open 12-3(2.30 in winter), 7-11(10.30 Sun); closed Mon except bank holidays

Pubs with particularly interesting histories, or in unusually interesting buildings, are listed at the back of the book.

SHERBORNE ST6316 Map 2

Digby Tap £

Cooks Lane; park in Digby Road and walk round corner

With four or five well kept real ales on handpump at a time, they work through about two dozen different ales a week – possibly Exmoor Ale, Hook Norton Best, Oakhill Mendip Gold, Ringwood Best and Teignworthy Reel Ale – at this simple uncluttered old-fashioned town ale house. An easy mix of customers enjoys the pleasant relaxed atmosphere in the flagstone-floored main bar which has plenty of bygone character and traditional seating. Huge helpings of very reasonably priced bar food include soup (£1.50), good sandwiches (from £1.50), cheesy stuffed mushrooms (£2.25), ploughman's (from £3), sausages, beans, carbonara pasta or home-made pasty (£3.25), chilli with cheese topping (£3.50), omelettes or gammon and egg (£3.75), and daily specials like prawn and pesto pasta (£5.25). There are several small games rooms with pool, darts, dominoes, fruit machine, and a video game; piped music; there are some seats outside. The pub is handy for the glorious golden stone abbey. *(Recommended by Gordon, Lynn Sharpless, Bob Eardley, Tony and Wendy Hobden, Stephen Brown, Pat and Tony Martin, Andy and Jill Kassube, Jo and Gary Charlton, W W Burke, Ian Mauger, Gregor Macdonald, Brian Chambers)*

Free house ~ Manager Peter Lefeure ~ Real ale ~ Lunchtime meals and snacks (not Sun or bank holiday Mons) ~ (01935) 813148 ~ Children in eating area of bar ~ Open 11-2.30, 5.30(6 Sat)-11; 12-2, 7-10.30 Sun

TARRANT MONKTON ST9408 Map 2

Langton Arms

Village signposted from A354, then head for church

An interesting range of five rotating well kept real ales at this 17th-c thatched country inn might include well kept Goldfinch Midnight Blunder, Hampshire Richard Lionheart, Morlands Old Speckled Hen, Ringwood Best and Tisbury Best; decent wines by the glass. Generous helpings of popular bar food might include filled french bread (from £3), lasagne or venison sausages (£5.65), steak pie (£5.95), chicken curry (£6.25), fillet of salmon (£6.45) and minted lamb cutlets (£6.95). The well run comfortable beamed main bar has settles that form a couple of secluded booths around tables at the carpeted end, window seats, and another table or two at the serving end where the floor's tiled. There's a big inglenook fireplace in the public bar, and an old stable is the no-smoking restaurant area; darts, dominoes, cribbage, pool, fruit machine, juke box and piped music. The skittle alley doubles as a no-smoking family room during the day, and there are children's play areas in here and in the garden. Tracks lead up to Crichel Down above the village, and Badbury Rings, a hill fort by the B3082 just south of here, is very striking. *(Recommended by Dr C C S Wilson, Ian Phillips, Mr and Mrs A R Hawkins, Stephen, Julie and Hayley Brown, JDM, KM, Tim and Ann Meaden, Joy and Harold Dermott, Phil and Heidi Cook, K H Frostick, Martin and Karen Wake)*

Free house ~ Licensee James Cossins ~ Real ale ~ Meals and snacks (till 10pm) ~ Restaurant ~ (01258) 830225 ~ Children in family room ~ Open 11.30-11; 12-10.30 Sun ~ Bedrooms: £40B/£60B

UPWEY SY6684 Map 2

Old Ship

Ridgeway; turn left off A354 at bottom of Ridgeway Hill into old Roman Rd

Very well prepared bar food at this warmly friendly dining pub includes soup and sandwiches, creamy garlic mushrooms (£3.95), grilled liver and bacon (£6.95), chicken breast with a wine and onion sauce, venison steak with red wine and cranberry sauce (£10.95), and a big range of salads. Several attractive interconnected beamed rooms have a peacefully welcoming atmosphere, as well as a mix of sturdy chairs, some built-in wooden wall settles, fresh flowers on the solid panelled wood bar counter and tables, china plates, copper pans and old clocks on the walls, a couple of comfortable armchairs, and an open fire with horsebrasses along the mantlebeam; well kept Bass, Boddingtons, Greenalls Original and a guest like Wychwood Dogs Bollocks on handpump, and a good wine list that always includes a dozen or so by the glass; attentive service. There are colourful hanging baskets outside, and picnic-sets and umbrellas in the garden. *(Recommended by Simon Williams, Joan and Michel Hooper-Immins, J and B Cressey, Galen Strawson, Anthony Barnes, P G Bardswell, J F M and Dr M West, George Atkinson, Michael Tucker, Simon and Jane Williams, Desmond and Pat Morris)*

Greenalls ~ Tenant Paul Edmunds ~ Real ale ~ Meals and snacks (not 25-26 Dec) ~ (01305) 812522 ~ Children in eating area of bar ~ Open 11-2.30, 6-11; 12-3, 7-10.30 Sun

WEST BEXINGTON SY5387 Map 2

Manor Hotel

Village signposted off B3157 SE of Bridport, opposite the Bull in Swyre

It's just a short stroll to the beach from this well run and very relaxing old stone hotel. You can see the sea from the bedrooms, and from the garden, where there are picnic-sets on a small lawn with flower beds lining the low sheltering walls; a much bigger side lawn has a children's play area. The bustling downstairs cellar bar (on the same level as the south-sloping garden) has small country pictures and good leather-mounted horsebrasses on the walls, red leatherette stools and low-backed chairs (with one fat seat carved from a beer cask) under the black beams and joists, as well as heavy harness over the log fire. A smart no-smoking Victorian-style conservatory has airy furnishings and lots of plants. Very good but not cheap bar food includes moules marinières (£6.35), thai curry or mushroom stroganoff (£8), steak and kidney pudding (£8.35), pork wellington (£9.85), roast cod in garlic and cranberries (£9.95), and puddings like chocolate roulade or raspberry meringue; good breakfasts. Well kept Hardy Country and Royal Oak, Smiles and Wadworths 6X on handpump, quite a few malt whiskies and several wines by the glass. Helpful courteous service. *(Recommended by Galen Strawson, Chris Reeve, John and Vivienne Rice, Basil Minson, Mrs M L Carter, Joy and Harold Dermott, R M Wickenden, Brian and Jill Bond, Brian Lister, Nigel Wilkinson)*

Free house ~ Licensee Richard Childs ~ Real ale ~ Meals and snacks (till 10pm) ~ Restaurant ~(01308) 897616 ~ Children in eating area of bar ~ Open 11-11; 12-10.30 Sun; closed evening 25 Dec ~ Bedrooms: £51B/£82B

WORTH MATRAVERS (Isle of Purbeck) SY9777 Map 2

Square & Compass

At fork of both roads signposted to village from B3069

Little has changed at this basic but fascinating small pub which has been run by the Newman family for 90 years. The low ceilinged old-fashioned main bar has simple wall benches around the elbow-polished old tables on the flagstones, interesting local pictures, and well kept Badger Tanglefoot, Quay Old Rott, Ringwood Fortyniner, and Whitbreads Castle Eden tapped from a row of casks behind a couple of hatches in the flagstoned corridor which leads to a more conventional summer bar; farm cider. Bar food is limited to Cornish, cheese and onion or pork and chilli pasties (£1), served when they're open; cribbage, shove-ha'penny and dominoes. On a clear day the view from the peaceful hilltop setting is hard to beat, looking down over the village rooftops to the sea between the East Man and the West Man (the hills that guard the coastal approach), and on summer evenings the sun setting out beyond Portland Bill. There are benches in front of the pub with views over the countryside to the sea, and free-roaming hens, chickens and other birds may cluck happily around your feet. There are good walks from the pub. Perhaps best to park in the public car park 100 yards along the Corfe Castle road. *(Recommended by Anthony Barnes, Andy and Jill Kassube, David and Carole Chapman, Jeremy Burnside, JP, PP, Simon Williams, Nigel Flook, Betsy Brown)*

Free house ~ Licensee Charlie Newman ~ Real ale ~ Snacks ~ (01929) 439229 ~ Children welcome ~ Occasional live music ~ Open 11-3, 6-11; 11-11 Sat; 12-3, 7-10.30 Sun

Lucky Dip

Besides the fully inspected pubs, you might like to try these Lucky Dips recommended to us and described by readers (if you do, please send us reports):

☆ *nr* **Almer** [B3075, just off A31 towards Wareham; SY9097], *Worlds End*: Outstanding play area outside comfortable and roomily rebuilt open-plan thatched family dining pub, good decor with panelled alcoves, very wide choice of generous food, well kept Badger Best and Tanglefoot, good service (can slow when it's crowded); open all day, picnic-sets out in front and behind *(Howard and Barbara Clutterbuck, WHBM, Dennis Stevens, G G Lawrance, Bruce Bird, Mrs J Lockhart, BB)*

Beaminster [The Square; ST4701], *Greyhound*: Doing well under current management, with friendly locals, wide choice of decent reasonably priced food esp fish (proper chips, too), congenial service, well kept Palmers, pleasant decor, attractive layout; unobtrusive piped music *(Mark Matthewman, Glen and Nola Armstrong)*

Bere Regis [High St; SY8494], *Drax Arms*: Comfortable village pub improved by present helpful licensees (eg rediscovered big open fire in left-hand bar area), well kept Badger ales and farm cider, limited choice of good reasonably priced food esp home-made pies and casseroles; good walking nearby *(John and Joan Nash, G Washington)*

☆ **Bishops Caundle** [A3030 SE of Sherborne; ST6913], *White Hart*: Nicely moulded dark beams, ancient panelling, attractive furnishings, sizeable no-smoking family area with french windows to big prettily floodlit garden with fine play area and all sorts of games; kind and friendly helpful service, Badger Best and Tanglefoot, food from sandwiches to steaks inc cut-price smaller helpings and children's menu; darts, skittle alley, fruit machine, piped pop music; reasonably priced bedrooms *(Marjorie and David Lamb, James and Lynne House, Anthony Barnes, Brian Chambers, D B Jenkin, LYM)*

Blandford Forum [ST8806], *Dolphin*: Nine well kept real ales in single friendly bar *(Dr and Mrs A K Clarke)*; *Kings Arms*: Redecorated flagstoned pub on various levels, well kept real ales *(Dr and Mrs A K Clarke)*

☆ **Bournemouth** [4 Exeter Rd; SZ0991], *Moon in the Square*: Spacious and well fitted Wetherspoons pub, no-smoking upstairs bar, well kept beers inc Ringwood Fortyniner and three guests, awesome helpings of good value bar food inc good baguettes and off-time bargains, friendly service, no piped music; can get crowded – popular with young people but in no sense exclusively their preserve; tables on terrace *(B and M Kendall, P A Legon, Jill Bickerton, Chris and Margaret Southon, R Moorehead)*

Bournemouth [The Square], *Criterion*: Busy and welcoming, with well kept real ales *(Dr and Mrs A K Clarke)*; [Wimborne Rd], *Dean Park*: Well kept Wadworths, quiet part of town; bedrooms *(P A Legon)*; [Durley Chine], *Durley*: A chain dining pub, but a model of its type; great spot right on the beach, for very enjoyable pub lunches – good service, good choice of wines by the glass *(Nigel Flook, Betsy Brown, Jill Bickerton, Audrey and Peter Reeves)*; [by International Conference Centre], *Edwards*: Ultra-modern bistro bar with well kept beer, convivial surroundings *(Dr and Mrs A K Clarke)*; [West Hill Rd], *Goat & Tricycle*: Amalgamation of former Pembroke Arms and Pembroke Shades, done out with cluttered memorabilia; well kept beer *(Dr and Mrs A K Clarke)*; [Old Christchurch Rd], *Jug of Ale*: Well kept Whitbreads-related and other changing ales, reasonable prices, straightforward food inc good value Sun lunch; open all day, busy weekend evenings *(Dr and Mrs A K Clarke, P A Legon)*

Bradford Abbas [ST5814], *Rose & Crown*: Popular country local with well kept Hardy beers, interesting generous food; bedrooms *(Pat and Robert Watt)*

☆ **Broadwindsor** [ST4303], *White Lion*: Very welcoming 17th-c pub/restaurant, carefully and comfortably renovated, with well spaced tables, a modicum of china, fresh and dried flowers, big woodburner; good choice of home-made food inc generous starters, fresh fish, a fine bread and butter pudding, lovely choice of ice creams, well kept Palmers, darts, plenty of locals; no machines, well behaved dogs welcome, unobtrusive piped music *(Ray Williams, Mrs T A Bizat)*

Burton Bradstock [B3157; SY4889], *Anchor*: Unassuming but roomy and comfortable, well kept Ushers Best and Founders, good choice of good value bar food esp local fish, good wine list, particularly friendly attentive service *(George Atkinson, David Newman, Sherry Rollinson)*; [Southover], *Dove*: Thatched local with two simple little bars, some stripped stone, inglenook fireplace, well kept Branscombe Vale ales, Thatcher's farm cider, darts, piped nostalgic pop music (may be loud), a few 1960ish theatrical photographs from Steve Berkoff to Frank Sinatra, rather smarter dining rooms; picnic-sets on steeply terraced back grass, rabbits and fancy fowl *(George Atkinson, Richard Houghton, Eddie Edwards)*

Charminster [former New Inn; SY6793], *Inn For All Seasons*: Newish owners doing good value food inc fresh veg in bright airy dining room, well kept Hardy Country Popes and Royal Oak and Otter, attentive service *(Joan and Michel Hooper-Immins)*

☆ **Chedington** [A356 Dorchester—Crewkerne; ST4805], *Winyards Gap*: Spectacular view from tables in front of tastefully modernised pub, very welcoming new owners doing wide choice of good home-made food esp pies and fish, well kept ales such as Exmoor Stag, Flowers Original and Wadworths 6X, country wines, no-smoking area, skittle alley, also darts, pool etc; children in dining area; pleasant walks nearby *(Megan Howell, E A George, G Washington, LYM)*

Chesil [follow Chiswell signposts off A354 at N edge of Portland; SY6873], *Cove House*: Modest bare-boards pub listed for its superb position just above the miles-long Chesil pebble beach, with three tables out by sea wall; friendly staff, Whitbreads-related ales, usual food inc good crab sandwiches; piped music may be obtrusive *(Simon Williams, David Carr, Tim and Ann Meaden, LYM)*

Chickerell [East St; SY6480], *Turks Head*: Busy stonebuilt village pub with pleasant beamed bar and spacious eating area, wide choice of good generous freshly cooked food inc children's and wonderful puddings, lots of old local photographs, pictures and decorative plates, cheerful service, restaurant; children welcome, comfortable bedrooms, good breakfast *(David Mead)*

☆ **Chideock** [A35 Bridport—Lyme Regis; SY4292], *George*: Welcoming thatched 17th-c pub with neat rows of tables in simple front bar, plusher lounge, hundreds of banknotes on beams, various bric-a-brac, big log fire, good choice of food inc vegetarian and good puddings, reasonable prices, well kept Palmers, efficient staff, big restaurant, no piped music; tables in back garden, bedrooms *(Mark Matthewman, R Boyd, Galen Strawson, LYM)*

☆ **Child Okeford** [Gold Hill – village signed off A350 Blandford Forum—Shaftesbury and A357 Blandford—Sherborne; ST8313], *Saxon*: Cosy and friendly old village meeting place, quietly clubby bar with log fire and more spacious side room (where children allowed), well kept Bass, Butcombe and a guest beer, country wines, traditional games, reasonably priced food (not Tues evening, not winter Sun evening) inc sandwiches and children's dishes; piped music, dry dogs on leads welcome; quite a menagerie in attractive back garden, also friendly golden retrievers and cats; good walks on neolithic Hambledon Hill *(Martin Sandercombe, A Homes, Joy and Harold Dermott, LYM)*

Christchurch [High St; SZ1593], *Ship*: Dark and low-beamed Hogshead, with good choice of well kept ales and fine range of Belgian draught beers; good honest bar food, reasonably priced *(Ian Baillie, Andy and Jill Kassube, W W Burke)*

☆ **Corfe Castle** [SY9681], *Bankes Arms*: Big and busy but welcoming, with flagstones and comfortable traditional decor, subtle lighting, well kept Wadworths 6X, generous good value food, friendly service, restaurant; tables on terrace and in long garden with play area, running down to tourist railway; children and dogs welcome; bedrooms, on attractive village square *(Mr and Mrs N A Spink, J and B Cressey)*

Cranborne [The Square; SU0513], *Sheaf of Arrows*: Welcoming two-bar village local with simple good value bar food from toasties and good ham ploughman's to fish, cheerful service, Cranborne Quiver and Old Shafter from their own back brewhouse (brewery visits encouraged) and other ales such as Ringwood Best; friendly dogs and cats, children welcome, bedrooms *(Ann and Colin Hunt, Mrs V Brown)*

☆ **Dorchester** [40 Allington Ave; A352 towards Wareham, just off bypass; SY6890], *Trumpet Major*: Bright and airy big-windowed modern lounge bar, empasis on food inc good help-yourself salad bar, vegetarian and children's dishes, speciality apple cake, well kept Hardy Country ales, good choice of wines by the glass; handy for Max Gate (Thomas Hardy's house, now open to the public); conservatories, garden, children welcome, very busy lunchtime *(Joan and Michel Hooper-Immins, J F M West, Dr B and Mrs P B Baker)*

Dorchester [Weymouth Ave; by Dorchester Sth Stn], *Station Masters House*: Spacious open-plan railway-theme pub with friendly service, well kept Hardy Country ales, full range straight from the handsome adjacent brewery; plush Victorian-style decor, courteous young staff, generous sensibly priced food from filled warm baguettes and baked potatoes up; games area with darts, fruit machines and pool tables, piped music; open all day Weds-Sat, busy Weds (market opp) *(DC, Pat and Tony Martin, Dr B and Mrs P B Baker)*

☆ **East Lulworth** [B3070; SY8581], *Weld Arms*: Friendly, vivacious yet relaxed, with nice mix of individual furnishings, attractive little snug, good interesting food from well filled rolls up inc good puddings, tables out in big garden; good value bedrooms *(Phil Putwain, Paul S McPherson, Veronica Brown, LYM)*

☆ **Ferndown** [Wimborne Rd E; SU0700], *Pure Drop*: Large Hardy Country pub, warm and friendly, with their beers kept well, consistently good food, sizeable restaurant, good wines *(F Mundy, John and Vivienne Rice)*

Ferndown [Wimborne Rd, Uddens Cross (off A31)], *Old Thatch*: Rather smart pub/restaurant, nice secluded seating out at the back surrounded by woods, good choice of sensibly priced enjoyable food and of wines inc interesting bin ends, no-smoking area *(Michael Brookes)*

☆ **Fiddleford** [A357 Sturminster Newton—Blandford Forum; ST8013], *Fiddleford Inn*: Comfortable and spacious refurbished pub, ancient flagstones and some other nice touches, well kept Scottish Courage ales, friendly service, unobtrusive piped music, quickly served food from good sandwiches up in lounge bar, restaurant area and back family area; big garden with play area *(Pat and Robert Watt, G Neighbour, Brian Chambers, LYM)*

☆ **Furzehill** [B3078 N of Wimborne; SU0101], *Stocks*: Busy extended thatched dining pub, attractive and welcoming, with masses of brass and copper, old prints and even a lobster pot and fishing net, wide range of good food inc good value OAP lunch Thurs, friendly and attentive young staff; spacious back restaurant *(M Reading, Gordon)*

Holt [SU0304], *Old Inn*: Well appointed and very friendly dining pub with good generous food inc fresh fish, two restaurants, winter fires, Badger beers *(J Morris, Gerald Barnett)*

☆ **Horton** [SU0207], *Drusillas*: Picturesque renovated 17th-c beamed pub, food inc good fish and OAP bargains, nice new thatched dining extension, Boddingtons, Flowers IPA and Wadworths 6X, log fire, separate games bar with two pool tables; piped pop music; children welcome, adventure playground, open all day *(Ian Phillips, John and Vivienne Rice, Dave Braisted)*

Hurn [village signed off A338, then follow Avon, Sopley, Mutchams sign; SZ1497], *Avon Causeway*: Big rather touristy pub, but civilised and comfortable, with well kept Wadworths beers and guests such as Gales HSB, Highgate Old, Ringwood Old Thumper and Woodfordes Norfolk Nog, good range of bar food, good choice of wines and spirits, interesting railway decorations, good disabled access; Pullman-coach restaurant by former 1870s station platform; piped music, jazz Tues, open all day; roomy bedrooms *(G Coates, LYM)*

Langton Matravers [B3069 nr junction with A351; SY9978], *Ship*: Robust basic local with lively Purbeck Longboard shove-ha'penny, pool, darts, Courage-related ales; children welcome, handy for Putland Farm; bedrooms *(Jeremy Burnside, LYM)*

Lower Burton [Old Sherborne Rd, N of Dorchester; SY6894], *Sun*: Comfortable 17th-c beamed pub well decorated with lots of pictures, wide choice of well kept ales, decent wines, good home-made food inc vegetarian, quick service, big well kept enclosed garden with limited play area, front terrace with summer live bands and good barbecues *(Chris Reeve)*

☆ **Lyme Regis** [25 Marine Parade, The Cobb; SY3492], *Royal Standard*: Right on broadest part of beach, with suntrap courtyard (own servery and wendy house); bar serving area dominated by pool table and piped pop, but has some fine built-in stripped high settles, and there's a quieter no-smoking area with stripped brick and pine; well kept Palmers Bitter, Best and 200, good value food inc sensibly priced sandwiches, local crab and fish, good cream teas, darts; three bedrooms *(B R Shiner, Pat and Tony Martin, Dr and Mrs J H Hills, BB)*

Lyme Regis, *Harbour*: Simple pub with back food bar, tasty good value food inc good generous fish soup, no piped music, friendly service, Theakstons beers, seats on verandah and a couple of tables on adjacent beach *(Greg Kilminster)*

☆ **Marnhull** [B3092 N of Sturminster Newton; ST7718], *Crown*: Part-thatched 17th-c inn with oak beams, huge flagstones, old settles and elm tables, window seats cut into thick stone walls, and logs burning in a big stone hearth; small more modern lounge, friendly service, reasonably priced bar food inc good thick sandwiches, Badger Best and Tanglefoot, skittle alley and pub games, maybe piped music; restaurant, tables in peaceful enclosed garden, children welcome; good value bedrooms, good breakfast *(E A George, Dave Braisted, LYM)*

Martinstown [SY6488], *Brewers Arms*: Friendly village pub, quite large, with reasonable choice of food prepared to order inc vegetarian and even vegan, Flowers tapped from the cask, tables outside with barbecue area *(Dr G J Richards, Marjorie and David Lamb)*

Morecombelake [A35 Bridport—Lyme Regis; SY4093], *Ship*: Friendly roadside local with built-in wall seats, plush-cushioned chairs, lots of photographs and woodburner, open fire in waxed-tablecloth two-level eating area, well kept Palmers IPA, Tally Ho and 200, home-made food inc fresh local fish, vegetarian, children's, small helpings available; piped music may be loud; picnic-sets outside; bedrooms *(Mrs Best, Ian Phillips, BB)*

Moreton [B3390 nr stn; SY7889], *Frampton Arms*: Quiet and relaxed, with good choice of good value food from sandwiches up, Boddingtons and Flowers IPA, log fire, friendly landlord, steam railway pictures in lounge bar, Warmwell Aerodrome theme in public bar, bright and airy conservatory restaurant; comfortable bedrooms *(Joan and Michel Hooper-Immins, J S M Sheldon)*

Mudeford [SZ1892], *Ship in Distress*: Very popular under current ownership, emphasis almost exclusively on the wide choice of very fresh carefully cooked fish and seafood; good wine list; best to book *(Nigel Flook, Betsy Brown)*

☆ **North Wootton** [A3030 SE of Sherborne; ST6514], *Three Elms*: Lively and welcoming, with wide range of good food esp vegetarian, well served sandwiches, plenty of vegetarian choice, reasonable prices, half a dozen well kept ales inc Fullers London Pride, Shepherd Neame Spitfire and one brewed for the pub, jovial barman, enormous number of Matchbox and other model cars; interesting gents'; three comfortable bedrooms, shared bathrooms, good breakfast, big garden *(Michael and Hazel Lyons, Stephen Brown)*

☆ **Piddletrenthide** [B3143 N of Dorchester; SY7099], *Poachers*: Welcoming landlord and staff, well kept John Smiths, Websters, Worthington and summer guest ales, generous tasty food, good atmosphere in recently extended bar, good value restaurant; well furnished chalet-style bedrooms around outside pool *(Brian and Jill Bond, Mark Seymour, Jackie Roberts)*

☆ **Poole** [Pinewood Rd, Branksome Park; off A338 on edge of Poole, towards Branksome Chine – via The Avenue; SZ0590], *Inn in the Park*: Popular oasis of cheer – pleasantly redecorated small hotel bar, well kept Adnams Broadside, Bass and Wadworths 6X, good value generous bar food (not Sun evening) from good sandwiches up, polite young staff, attractive dining room (children allowed), log fire, tables on small sunny terrace; comfortable bedrooms, quiet pine-filled residential area above sea *(Jill Bickerton, B and K Hypher, M J Dowdy, John and Vivienne Rice, LYM)*

☆ **Poole** [The Quay], *Portsmouth Hoy*: Enjoyable nautical theme, lots of interesting brassware and ships' insignia, bustling atmosphere, well kept Hardy Country and guest beers, cheerful service, wide choice of usual food inc good value fish and chips special, nice back dining area, separate no-smoking area; shame about the piped music and games machine; on lively quay, handy for aquarium *(Howard and Margaret Buchanan, Nigel Flook, Betsy Brown, Paul and Sue Merrick)*

Poole [Market St; SZ0190], *Crown*: Warm and friendly, with very good value plentiful food esp fresh fish, two-for-one bargains some days, well kept Bass and Hardy Country; unpretentious very helpful service *(Anthony Bathurst, Tom Espley)*; [The Quay], *Custom House*: Interesting cafe/bar conversion of original customs house, pastel walls, pews and cast-iron cafe furniture on bare boards, several rooms, Victorian fireplaces, trompe l'oeil painting in lavatories; full range of beers, french-style menu in bar, young friendly enthusiastic staff, tables out on small terrace overlooking quay; upstairs restaurant *(Sam Samuells, Lynda Payton)*; [Market St], *Guildhall*: Good freshly made food esp local fish in bright family eating pub, very pleasant service *(Dr R A L Leatherdale)*; [Longfleet Rd/Fernside Rd (A35)], *Shah of Persia*: Spacious comfortably refurbished roadhouse, well kept Hardy Country Bitter, Popes and Royal Oak with a guest such as Websters, wide choice of generous food inc vegetarian and outstanding mixed grill, big no-smoking area, relaxed friendly service and pleasant atmosphere; may be delays on busy evenings *(Joan and Michel Hooper-Immins, Audrey and Peter Reeves, Betty Davey)*

Portesham [Front St (B3157); SY6086], *Kings Arms*: Large extended pub in pretty village, good reasonably priced food inc some unusual dishes, well kept Bass and Wadworths 6X, welcoming service, sizeable attractive garden with play area, pond and trout stream *(Mike and Hilary Stiffin)*

☆ **Portland Bill** [SY6870], *Pulpit*: Rather bare but comfortable and particularly welcoming food pub in great spot nr Pulpit Rock, short stroll to lighthouse and cliffs; generous food inc vegetarian, good pies and pizzas, local shellfish and interesting puddings, four well kept Gibbs Mew ales, good service; piped music *(Simon Williams, David Carr, Tony Scott, David and Carole Chapman, P G Bardswell)*

☆ **Powerstock** [off A3066 Beaminster—Bridport via W Milton; SY5196], *Three Horseshoes*: Country pub in delightful setting, should do well again under friendly new licensees, landlord cooking good individual food inc fresh fish, no-smoking restaurant, small panelled L-shaped bar, warm fires, well kept Palmers Bridport and IPA, good choice of wines by the glass, freshly squeezed fruit juice; lovely views from garden above with play area; bedrooms *(Keith and Peggy Frew, LYM)*

☆ **Shaftesbury** [St James St; ST8622], *Two Brewers*: At bottom of steep famously photogenic Gold Hill, with good atmosphere in well divided open-plan turkey-carpeted bar, lots of decorative plates, very wide choice of reasonably priced popular bar food (children's helpings of any dish) freshly prepared inc vegetarian, good puddings and good Sun roasts, chatty landlord and good service, well kept Courage Best and Directors, Wadworths 6X and guests such as Batemans XB and Brains SA, quiet piped music in restaurant; picnic-sets in attractive good-sized garden with pretty views *(Alan and Paula McCully, Bruce Bird, Tim and Ann Meaden, Marjorie and David Lamb, BB)*

☆ **Shaftesbury** [Bleke St], *Ship*: Traditional 17th-c local, cosy and simple, with black panelling, oak woodwork, well kept Badger Best and Tanglefoot, farm cider, bar food, separate eating area, helpful friendly service, pool and other games in public bar (crowded with young people weekend evenings), tables on terrace *(Brian Chambers, Carole Smart, Andrew Jeeves, Howard England)*

Shaftesbury [Salisbury Rd (A30)], *Half Moon*: Comfortably busy Badger pub with well presented fairly priced generous food, quick service; garden with adventure playground *(David and Marjorie Lamb)*

Sherborne [88 Cheap St; ST6316], *Cross Keys*: Comfortably refurbished local, with separate areas, sensible choice of food, quick cheerful service, well kept Hardy Country and Royal Oak; interesting display of postal history, postbox in corridor; talking fruit machine; open all day Sun *(Ann and Colin Hunt, Joan and Michel Hooper-Immins)*

☆ **Sixpenny Handley** [High St; ST9917], *Roebuck*: Plain but enviable village local with good fish, meat and game cooked by the landlord's French wife, with home-grown veg; Ringwood Porter, Hop Back Special and Tisbury Bitter, no piped music, seats outside *(Geoffrey Lawrance, Joan and Michel Hooper-Immins)*

☆ **Stoke Abbott** [off B3162 and B3163 2 m W of Beaminster; ST4500], *New Inn*: Present friendly tenants doing well in 17th-c thatched pub with beams, brasses, stripped stone alcoves on either side of one big log fireplace, another with handsome panelling; well kept Palmers Bridport, IPA and 200, sensibly limited choice of good food inc vegetarian and generous fish, no-smoking dining room, well kept attractive garden with play area, nice setting in unspoilt quiet village; children welcome, bedrooms; cl Mon in July/Aug *(Mark Matthewman, Galen Strawson, Basil Minson, T A Bizat, Anthony Barnes, Dr and Mrs J Hills, Miss R Kingsmill, LYM)*

☆ **Studland** [SZ0382], *Bankes Arms*: Very popular spot above fine beach, outstanding country, sea and cliff views from huge pleasant garden; comfortable, friendly and easy-going big bar with raised drinking area, substantial decent simple food all day inc local fish, good choice of well kept beers inc Flowers, local Poole Bosun and Wadworths 6X, attractive log fires, darts and pool in side games area; children welcome, just off Coast Path; can get very busily trippery at weekends and in summer, parking can be complicated or expensive if you're not a NT member; big comfortable bedrooms, has been cl winter *(David and Carole Chapman, Ian and Nita Cooper, DC, PV, KM, Nigel Flook, Betsy Brown, D P and J A Sweeney, Michael Dunn, P G Bardswell, Jeremy Burnside, Simon Williams, G Coates)*

Sturminster Marshall [A350; SY9499], *Black*

Horse: Comfortable long bar, interesting pictures and local artefacts in dining area, well kept Badger ales, good evening food esp fish and particularly good value puddings *(Paul and Sue Merrick)*

☆ **Sutton Poyntz** [off A353 SE of Weymouth; SY7083], *Springhead*: Good quick friendly service, beams, dark decor, comfortable mix of furnishings, log fires, daily papers, well kept ales such as Bass, Flowers IPA and Wadworths 6X, good value wines, good range of malt whiskies, decent choice of freshly made food (not cheap) in bar and separate restaurant area; bar billiards, well chosen piped music – often jazz; lovely spot opp willow stream in quiet village, entertaining ducks, good play area in big garden, walks to White Horse Hill and Dorset Coastal Path *(Liz and John Soden, Simon Williams, Tony Scott)*

☆ **Swanage** [Shore Rd; SZ0278], *Mowlem*: First-floor theatre cafe and restaurant, not a pub, but good straightforward food inc bar lunches, well kept Badger Best and Tanglefoot, good service, great bay views *(Joan and Michel Hooper-Immins, David and Carole Chapman)*

Swanage [159 High St], *Black Swan*: Quaint old pub with open fire each end, well kept changing beers such as Fullers London Pride, Theakstons Old Peculier, Wadworths 6X (widest choice at weekends), decent house wines, good value generous food inc unusual ice creams, friendly landlady; maybe piped radio, occasional live music, can get crowded and smoky; dinosaur footprints in back yard, garden nr millpond, well priced bedrooms *(Veronica Brown, Peter and Audrey Dowsett, Jeremy Burnside)*; *Red Lion*: Snug two-bar pub, beams densely hung with mugs and keys, lots of blow lamps, decent inexpensive food, well kept Ringwood and Whitbreads, friendly staff; children's annexe, partly covered back terrace *(Jeremy Burnside)*; [417 High St], *Royal Oak*: Pleasant local with friendly newish landlord, good food, two well kept real ales, pool; children welcome, tables outside *(Jeremy Burnside)*

Tolpuddle [SY7994], *Martyrs*: Well kept Badger beers, friendly staff, home-made food in bar and busy restaurant, nice garden with ducks, hens and rabbits *(Francis Johnston, R Shelton, R Moorehead)*

☆ **Uploders** [signed off A35 E of Bridport; SY5093], *Crown*: Friendly and homely brightly furnished low-beamed village pub, mainly no smoking, festooned with polished bric-a-brac; wide choice of very good value genuine food (not Sun evening) inc vegetarian dishes and fine home-made puddings, well kept Palmers BB and 200, good service, log fires, pictures by local artists, tables in pleasant two-tier garden; bedrooms *(Galen Strawson, Mrs M E Bell, Brian Lister, Ian and Deborah Carrington, Richard and Rosemary Hoare, Ian and Anne Barrett, P Furse, BB)*

☆ **Wareham** [41 North St(A351, N end of town); SY9287], *Kings Arms*: Friendly and lively traditional thatched town local, back serving counter and two bars off flagstoned central corridor, well kept Whitbreads-related ales, reasonably priced bar food (not Fri—Sun evenings), back garden *(Tim and Ann Meaden, R Moorehead, LYM)*

☆ **Wareham** [South St], *Quay*: Comfortable, light and airy stripped-stone bars, bar food from soup and sandwiches up, open fire, well kept Whitbreads-related and other ales, friendly staff, children allowed away from main bar; picnic-sets out on quay, parking nearby can be difficult *(DC, Jeremy Burnside)*

Wareham [14 South St], *Black Bear*: Bow-windowed 18th-c hotel with pleasant bar on right of through corridor, well kept Eldridge Pope Royal Oak and Hardy Country, good choice of well priced bar food, decent coffee, picnic-sets in back yard; bedrooms *(David Carr, J and B Cressey)*; [East St], *Duke of Wellington*: Small 18th-c pub, friendly and unpretentious, with enjoyable food inc interesting dishes; popular with family groups *(Bill and Sylvia Trotter)*

☆ **Waytown** [between B3162 and A3066 N of Bridport; SY4697], *Hare & Hounds*: Attractively refurbished 17th-c pub, good value well presented food inc OAP bargains, well kept Palmers, helpful friendly service, simple garden with good play area *(R Shelton, Ian and Anne Barrett, Desmond and Pat Morris, Galen Strawson, Tim and Ann Meaden)*

West Bay [SY4590], *Bridport Arms*: Thatched pub on beach of Bridport's low-key holiday village, generous good value food esp fish, friendly staff, well kept Palmers BB, big fireplace in basic flagstoned back bar, no music *(Mr and Mrs J E Lockwood, DC)*; [18 George St], *George*: Red plush banquettes, mate's chairs, masses of shipping pictures, some model ships and nautical hardware; roomy L-shaped public bar with games and juke box, separate restaurant; food inc lots of local fish, well kept Palmers BB, Best and 200, cheery service; tables outside, bedrooms *(Joan and Michel Hooper-Immins, BB)*

☆ **West Knighton** [off A352 E of Dorchester; SY7387], *New Inn*: Biggish neatly refurbished pub, very busy in summer, with interesting range of reasonably priced food, small restaurant, quick friendly staff, real ales, country wines, skittle alley, good provision for children; big colourful garden, pleasant setting in quiet village with wonderful views *(Geoffrey Lawrance, Tim and Ann Meaden)*

☆ **West Lulworth** [B3070; SY8280], *Castle*: Pretty thatched inn in lovely spot nr Lulworth Cove, good walks; flagstoned bar bustling with summer visitors, maze of booth seating, usual food inc children's, well kept Devenish Wessex, Flowers Original and Marstons Pedigree, decent house wines, farm cider, piped music (may be loud), video and board games; cosy more modern-feeling lounge bar, helpful landlord, pleasant dining room, splendid ladies', popular garden with giant chess boards, boules, barbecues *(P G Bardswell, Kath Wetherill, Gordon, Andrew Rogers, Amanda Milsom, Galen Strawson, Mrs V Brown, Louie Eze, LYM)*

West Moors [Pinehurst Rd; SU0802], *Fryer*

Arms: Good home-made food inc good specials such as trout, salmon on watercress mousseline, pheasant, rack of lamb – children eat free if adults eating *(Rev J Hibberd)*

☆ **West Stafford** [signed off A352 Dorchester—Wareham; SY7289], *Wise Man*: Comfortable 16th-c local nr Hardy's cottage, very busy in summer; thatch, beams and toby jugs, with wide choice of good value generous standard food (not Sun evening) inc fish from Poole, happy staff, well kept Greenalls, decent wines and country wines; piped light classics, public bar with darts; children not encouraged *(Geoffrey Lawrance, Howard Clutterbuck)*

West Stour [ST7822], *Ship*: Good generous food, good value, well kept local beer, attractive furnishings, big log fire, tremendous local atmosphere, attentive service, intimate split-level restaurant; garden behind, comfortable bedrooms *(Pat and Robert Watt)*

☆ **Weymouth** [Barrack Rd; SY6778], *Nothe Tavern*: Roomy and comfortable well run local with good atmosphere, wide range of food inc local fresh fish specialities and children's dishes, friendly service, well kept Hardy Country, Popes and Royal Oak, decent wines; distant harbour glimpses from garden *(Joan and Michel Hooper-Immins, David and Carole Chapman, Tony Scott, Peter and Audrey Dowsett, J F M West, DC, Tony Scott, BB)*

Weymouth [Hope Sq], *Dorset Brewers*: Well kept Badger Best, Bass, Courage Directors, Ringwood Old Thumper and Smiles, quickly served simple meals, fishing stuff all over the ceiling, bare boards; tables outside, opp smart touristy Brewers Quay complex in former brewery *(Joan and Michel Hooper-Immins)*; [15 Trinity Rd], *Kings Arms*: Popular and friendly two-bar quayside pub, one local and lively, one more comfortable; well kept beer, considerable character *(P G Bardswell, David Carr)*; [Trinity Rd], *Old Rooms*: Bustling low-beamed pub, well priced straightforward food (some all day at least in summer), friendly staff, John Smiths and Worthington, old nautical lamps and maps, unpretentious restaurant; front terrace with harbour views over part-pedestrianised street; piped music may be loud, no nearby parking *(Tony Scott, David and Carole Chapman, Joan and Michel Hooper-Immins, DC, Eric Locker)*

Whitchurch Canonicorum [SY3995], *Five Bells*: Useful Palmers local, decent food, pool, very friendly licensees, tables out under cocktail parasols; plenty of camping ground *(Marjorie and David Lamb)*

Wimborne St Giles [SU0212], *Bull*: Imaginative food inc fish fresh daily from Cornwall in comfortable red-carpeted bar, well kept Badger ales, farm cider *(G Washington)*

Winterborne Zelston [A31 Wimborne—Dorchester; SY8997], *Botany Bay*: Attractive restaurant-oriented pub with good range of bar snacks, well kept Ringwood, lots of books, friendly service, decent coffee; tables on back terrace *(John and Vivienne Rice)*

The letters and figures after the name of each town are its Ordnance Survey map reference. *How to use the Guide* at the beginning of the book explains how it helps you find a pub, in road atlases or large-scale maps as well as in our own maps.

Durham *see* Northumbria

Essex

New entries here this year include the White Harte in Burnham on Crouch, a charming and cheerful nautical inn looking out over the Crouch estuary – cheap, too; the Jolly Sailor at Heybridge Basin, an altogether smaller-scale seaside pub; the friendly and extremely well run Wheatsheaf near High Ongar; and the pretty Punchbowl tucked away at Paglesham – good modest comfort. Among longer-serving main entries, there's particularly good food to be had at the Bull at Blackmore End, the Swan at Chappel (heating for its pretty courtyard now), the Cricketers at Clavering, the Compasses near Coggeshall (moving upmarket), the Black Bull at Fyfield, the Green Man at Gosfield, the White Hart at Great Yeldham, the Bell at Horndon-on-the-Hill, the Eight Bells in Saffron Walden, the Green Man at Toot Hill and the Green Dragon at Youngs End. For sound value on a simpler scale, we'd add the very popular Sun at Feering, the Rainbow & Dove at Hastingwood (so handy for the motorway), the cheerful Green Man at Little Braxted, the charming little Flitch of Bacon at Little Dunmow and the Prince of Wales at Stow Maries, so very strong on its beer side. From among all these, for the third year running we choose as Essex Dining Pub of the Year the outstanding White Hart at Great Yeldham – a remarkable record of unbroken success. All this makes Essex sound a very foody county: it is, in the sense that enjoyable food has now become an important part of the appeal of most of its best pubs. But don't lose sight of the fact that most of the pubs we've mentioned so far appeal in other ways, too – just as food is also a plus in the all-round appeal of pubs we haven't mentioned, such as the very well liked Bell at Castle Hedingham or Square & Compasses at Fuller Street (building new kitchens as we go to press). Pubs in the Lucky Dip section at the end of the chapter that we've noted as being on good form these days (the great majority inspected and approved by us) are the Queens Head at Boreham, Theydon Oak at Coopersale Common, Three Horseshoes at Duton Hill, Seabrights Barn at Great Baddow, White Hart at Great Saling, Cock at Hatfield Broad Oak, Rose at Peldon, White Horse at Pleshey, Volunteer near Waltham Abbey and Bell at Woodham Walter. There's a good choice in Coggeshall – and connoisseurs of the ideal in pubby station buffets won't want to miss the one at Manningtree. Drinks prices in the county are just a shade higher than the national average, particularly in pubs getting their beers from the big national brewers; the cheapest places we found were the White Harte in Burnham on Crouch and Sun at Feering.

Post Office address codings confusingly give the impression that some pubs are in Suffolk, when they're really in Essex (which is where we list them).

ARKESDEN TL4834 Map 5

Axe & Compasses ★ 🍷

Village signposted from B1038 – but B1039 from Wendens Ambo, then forking left, is prettier; OS Sheet 154 map reference 482344

There's a fine old-fashioned and relaxed atmosphere in this rambling thatched country pub. The carpeted lounge bar dating back to the 17th c is the oldest part with beautifully polished upholstered oak and elm seats, easy chairs and wooden tables, as well as a warm fire, lots of beautifully polished brasses on the walls, and a friendly cat called Spikey. The smaller uncarpeted characterful public bar, with cosy built-in settles, has darts and cribbage. Bar food might include home-made soup (£2.75), grilled sardines (£3.25), baked avocado with prawns and cheese (£4.75), lamb liver and bacon or home-made steak and kidney pie (£6.95), chicken, leek and bacon crumble or stir fry vegetables in a pastry case with mustard sauce (£7.75), lemon sole or steak (£9.95) and monkfish cooked on roasted pepper sauce (£10.95); impressive pudding trolley (£2.75); helpful and friendly service. Well kept Greene King IPA and Abbott on handpump and a very good wine list. There are seats outside on a side terrace with pretty hanging baskets; parking at the back.

(Recommended by A and M Marriott, A E Brace, Tony Beaulah, Richard Siebert, A Bradbury, DFL, Gwen and Peter Andrews, Ian and Liz Phillips, Peter Plumridge)

Greene King ~ Tenants: Themis and Diane Christou ~ Real ale ~ Meals and snacks (till 9pm) ~ Restaurant ~ (01799) 550272 ~ Children welcome in restaurant until 8.30 ~ Open 11-2.30, 6-11; 12-3, 7-10.30 Sun

BLACKMORE END TL7430 Map 5

Bull 🍴 🍷

Signposted via Beazley End from Bocking Church Street, itself signed off A131 just N of Braintree bypass; pub is on Wethersfield side of village

It's the consistently well prepared food that brings readers back again and again to this comfortable dining pub. There's a refreshingly good range of sandwiches (from £2.95, french sticks £3.50), and ploughman's (£4.50) but the real draw is the very well prepared specials menu neatly written up on blackboards every two weeks, possibly including beautifully presented fresh mushroom and thyme soup with wild mushrooms (£2.95), tiger prawns and wild mushrooms in garlic and parsley butter on a crouton (£5.95), pan-fried lamb liver topped with avocado and garlic butter or chicken collops with glazed shallots and thyme and white wine cream sauce (£8.50), breast of guinea fowl on parsnip and apple purée with cider cream sauce (£10.95), mignons of fillet steak with stilton and port sauce (£10.95), venison cutlet with pink peppercorns and red wine cherry sauce (£13.95) (readers have also reported finding ostrich and kangaroo on the menu), all served in generous helpings with fresh vegetables in separate dishes. There are lots of tempting home-made puddings such as bread pudding with rum, whipped cream and toasted nuts, meringue filled with kiwi and pineapple with kirsch cream, hot apple and apricot strudel or pear and ginger sponge (from £3.50). The flowery-carpeted dining bar has red plush built-in button-back banquettes, low black beams and lots of menu blackboards; maybe piped music but this is often inaudible when the pub is full. Beyond a massive brick chimney-piece is a pretty cosy cottagey restaurant area (no cigars or pipes). Well kept Adnams, Greene King IPA, Mauldons Whiteadder and changing guest ales on handpump; ten wines by the glass from a wine list of about 70 which includes some enterprising bin-ends, vintage ports and dessert wines; picnic-sets outside.

(Recommended by B N F and M Parkin, Gwen and Peter Andrews, Richard and Robyn Wain, Tony Beaulah, Paul and Sandra Embleton, Richard Siebert, M W Bond)

Free house ~ Licensees Christopher and Mary Bruce ~ Real ale ~ Meals and snacks (till 9.30 Tues-Sat; no sandwiches or snacks Sat evening) ~ Restaurant ~ (01371) 851037 ~ Children welcome in restaurant ~ Open 12-3, 6.30-11(7-10.30 Sun); cl Mon (except bank holidays)

BURNHAM ON CROUCH TQ9596 Map 5

White Harte £

The Quay

With a friendly and genuinely nautical atmosphere, a wonderful outlook over the yachting estuary of the River Crouch and its own private jetty, this hearty old inn is popular with boating people. The decor in the partially carpeted bars reflects this: there are replicas of Royal Navy ships, a ship's wheel, a barometer, and a compass in the hearth of the welcoming log fire; comfortably cushioned seats around oak tables. Other traditionally furnished, high-ceilinged rooms have sea pictures decorating the panelled or stripped brick walls. Straightforward but attractively priced bar food includes steak and kidney pie, lasagne or toad in the hole (£4.50), pan-fried locally caught skate or cod (£6.80) and hot puddings (£1.80). Well kept Adnams, Crouch Vale Best and Tolly Cobbold Bitter on handpump. *(Recommended by Nigel Wikeley, Gwen and Peter Andrews, A F Keary)*

Free house ~ Licensee G John Lewis ~ Meals and snacks ~ Restaurant ~ (01621) 782106 ~ Children welcome away from main bar ~ Open 11-11, 11-10.30 Sun ~ Bedrooms: £19.80(£36.30B)/£39.00(£59.40B)

CASTLE HEDINGHAM TL7835 Map 5

Bell

B1058 E of Sible Hedingham, towards Sudbury

Sandra Ferguson has been providing a warm welcome at this historic old coaching inn for over 30 years and her cheerful character contributes much to the pub's friendly and congenial atmosphere. The beamed and timbered saloon bar remains unchanged over the years, with Jacobean-style seats and windsor chairs around sturdy oak tables, and beyond the standing timbers left from a knocked-through wall, some steps lead up to an unusual little gallery. Behind the traditionally furnished public bar a games room has dominoes and cribbage. One bar is no smoking, and each of the rooms has a good welcoming log fire; piped music. Well liked bar food from a fixed menu includes tomato soup (£2.20), lamb or beefburger (£3), ploughman's or home-made chicken liver pâté and toast (£3.50), liver and bacon casserole (£5.50), chicken or vegetarian kebabs, steak and Guinness pie, or thai chicken curry (£6), rainbow trout or salmon steak (£6.50), sirloin steak (£8), and puddings like treacle tart or banoffi pie (from £2.20). Greene King IPA and Abbot, and a guest beer tapped from the cask. In summer it is pleasant to sit outside in the big walled garden behind the pub – an acre or so, with grass, trees and shrubs; there are more seats on a small terrace; quiz on Sunday evenings. The nearby 12th-c castle keep is worth a visit. *(Recommended by Richard and Valerie Wright, G Neighbour, Ronald G Dodsworth, Paul Edwards, Gwen and Peter Andrews, Ian Phillips)*

Grays (Greene King, Ridleys) ~ Tenant Mrs Sandra Ferguson ~ Real ale ~ Meals and snacks (no food Mon evenings and winter Sun evenings) ~ (01787) 460350 ~ Children welcome except in public bar ~ Trad Jazz last Sun of month, acoustic guitar group Fri evening ~ Open 11.30-3(3.30 Sat), 6-11; 12-3.30, 7-10.30 Sun, closed 25 Dec

CHAPPEL TL8927 Map 5

Swan

Wakes Colne; pub visible just off A604 Colchester—Halstead

Fabulously set, with the River Colne running through the garden and on down to a splendid Victorian viaduct below, parts of this friendly timbered old pub date back to 1390. The spacious and low-beamed rambling bar has standing oak timbers dividing off side areas, banquettes around lots of dark tables, one or two swan pictures and plates on the white and partly panelled walls, and a few attractive tiles above the very big fireplace which is filled with lots of plants in summer. Fresh fish is the speciality here and as well as specials there might be rock eel (£5.45, large £7.45), plaice (£5.95, large £7.95), haddock (£6.25, large £8.50) and trout grilled with almonds (£6.45). Other good value and popular bar food includes filled french rolls or sandwiches (from £1.60, well liked rare roast beef £2.95), ploughman's (from £3.50), home-made chicken and mushroom pie or gammon with pineapple (£4.95), home-made chicken kiev (£6.45, large £8.95), sirloin steak (£9.95), and good puddings (from £2.50); children's menu; no-smoking area in restaurant. Well kept Greene King IPA and Abbot and Mauldons on handpump, a good selection of wines by the glass and just under two dozen malt whiskies served by cheery helpful staff; cribbage, maybe piped music. The sheltered suntrap cobbled courtyard has a rather continental feel with parasols, big tubs overflowing with flowers, and french street signs; gas heaters have recently been installed to extend its use beyond the summer season. The nearby Railway Centre (a must for train buffs) is just a few minutes' walk away. *(Recommended by Gwen and Peter Andrews, Ian Phillips, B N F and M Parkin, Anthony Barnes, R A Buckler, DFL)*

Free house ~ Licensees Terence Martin and Mark A Hubbard ~ Real ale ~ Meals and snacks (till 10.30) ~ Restaurant ~ (01787) 222353 ~ Children welcome away from main bar ~ Open 11-3, 6-11; 12-3, 7-10.30 Sun

CLAVERING TL4731 Map 5

Cricketers

B1038 Newport—Buntingford, Newport end of village

The wide choice of interesting and elaborate home-made bar food attracts a well heeled set to this comfortably modernised 16th-c dining pub. There are sandwiches (from £2.25) and starters include soup (£3), sautéed lamb kidneys with spicy turbigo sauce and saffron rice (£4.25), avocado with poached chicken breast, mango, coriander and a light curry mayonnaise (£4.95) and brochette of beef fillet marinated in coriander seeds and olive oil, grilled and served with a satay sauce (£6); main courses might include steak and kidney pie or a filo pastry parcel of spinach, mushrooms and mozzarella served with a watercress sauce (£8.75), grilled salmon with prawns and tarragon and tomato butter sauce (£9.75), pan fried calf liver (£10.75) and rack of lamb with a fresh thyme and garlic jus (£12); home-made ice creams and sorbets (£2.50) and mouth-watering puddings (£3). The spotlessly kept and roomy L-shaped beamed bar has standing timbers resting on new brickwork, and pale green plush button-backed banquettes, stools and windsor chairs around shiny wooden tables on a pale green carpet, gleaming copper pans and horsebrasses, dried flowers in the big fireplace (open fire in colder weather), and fresh flowers on the tables; one area is no smoking; piped music. Adnams, Boddingtons, Flowers Original and IPA and Wadworths 6X on handpump. The attractive front terrace has picnic-sets and umbrellas amongst colourful flowering shrubs. Pretty and traditionally furnished bedrooms. *(Recommended by Charles and Pauline Stride, Mrs D Ball, Ian Phillips, Mr and Mrs N Chesher, Maysie Thompson, Quentin Williamson)*

Free house ~ Licensees Trevor and Sally Oliver ~ Real ale ~ Meals and snacks ~ Restaurant ~ (01799) 550442 ~ Children in eating area of bar and in restaurant ~ Open 10.30-3, 6-11; cl 25-26 December ~ Bedrooms: £60B/£80B

nr COGGESHALL TL8522 Map 5

Compasses

Pattiswick; signposted from A120 about 2 miles W of Coggeshall; OS Sheet 168 map reference 820247

It's the friendly atmosphere and the consistently good value food that readers enjoy at this remote country pub. The neatly kept and spaciously attractive comfortable beamed bars have tiled floors and lots of brass ornaments, Greene King IPA, Abbot and Rayments on handpump under light blanket pressure, and darts and piped music. Home-made bar food in generous helpings includes sandwiches and filled baguettes (from £3.85), filled baked potatoes (from £4.50), ploughman's (£5.75), turkey curry (£6.95), battered cod (£7.25), ham and eggs (£7.50), toad in the hole (£7.95), fisherman's pie or steak and kidney pie (£8.95) and tasty puddings. More elaborate dishes are served in the new barn restaurant. Outside there are seats on the lawns, and an adventure playground. *(Recommended by Ronald G Dodsworth, Richard Siebert, Richard and Robyn Wain, Tony Beaulah, Joan and Andrew Life, G Neighbour, Peter Meister, A Hepburn, S Jenner, Evelyn and Derek Walter, Roger and Pauline Pearce, Michael Hyde)*

Free house ~ Licensees Chris and Gilbert Heap ~ Real ale ~ Meals and snacks ~ Restaurant ~ (01376) 561322 ~ Children welcome in eating area of bar and restaurant ~ Pianist Friday and Sunday nights ~ Open 11-3, 6.30(6 Sat)-11; 12-3, 7-10.30 Sun

DEDHAM TM0533 Map 5

Marlborough Head

Recently taken over by the Olde English Pub Company; it is to be hoped that the new manager will be able to retain the relaxed and friendly atmosphere of this lovely old timbered pub in the heart of Constable's old town. Little has so far changed and the lovely old central lounge still has lots of beams and pictures, a wealth of finely carved woodwork, and a couple of roaring log fires. The beamed and timbered bar is set out for eating with lots of tables in wooden alcoves around its plum-coloured carpet. Bar food includes sandwiches (from £2.95), soup (£2.50), deep-fried brie (£3.95), marinated herring fillets (£3.85), rabbit with prunes or chicken and mushroom pasta bake (£6.95), lasagne (£7.55), roast duck (quarter £7.95, half £11.95), chicken with mustard sauce (£9.45), shank of lamb (£9.75) and specials such as chicken with lobster sauce (£9.25). Adnams and Greene King IPA on handpump. Family room no smoking; may be piped music. Seats on the terrace or in the garden at the back; nice comfortable bedrooms. *(Recommended by Anthony Barnes, Ian Phillips, J and P Maloney, Joan and Andrew Life, Gwen and Peter Andrews, B N F and M Parkin, John Kirk, Mark Baynham)*

Free house ~ Manager Angela Coulwill ~ Real ale ~ Meals and snacks (till 10 Fri and Sat) ~ (01206) 323250/323124 ~ Children welcome in family room ~ Open 11-11 (11-3, 6-11 winter weekdays); 12-10.30 Sun ~ Bedrooms: £45S/£55S

FEERING TL8720 Map 5

Sun

3 Feering Hill; before Feering proper, B1024 just NE of Kelvedon

Originally part of a 16th-c mansion; readers enjoy the good food, beer and atmosphere at this friendly gabled old inn. Standing timbers break up the several areas of the low beamed bar which has plenty of neatly matching tables and chairs, and green-cushioned stools and banquettes around the walls. Carvings on the beams in the lounge are said to be linked with Catherine of Aragon, and there's a handsome canopy with a sun motif over the woodburning stove; newspapers to read, shove-ha'penny, table skittles, cribbage, dominoes and piped music. Five very well kept real ales change virtually daily, with up to 20 different brews passing through the handpumps each week, possibly Charles Wells Bombardier, Fullers London Pride, Jennings Cumberland, Wadworths 6X or Wolf Coyote. They also have a changing farm cider, and over 40 malt whiskies. Their Easter and August bank holiday beer festivals have a regional theme, when they'll stock ales from a particular county or area. The very big choice of bar meals is written up on blackboards over the fireplace and might include sandwiches (from £1.55), ploughman's (from £4.25), home-made soup or melon with a cherry and port coulis (£2.20), Maltese ricotta and pea pie (£5.50), steak and kidney pie, chicken in an asparagus and wine sauce or pork chop in an orange, apricot and cider sauce (£5.95), and puddings such as spotted dick (£2.40) and white chocolate and coconut parfait (£3.20); children's menu; friendly and efficient service. There are quite a few seats and tables on a partly covered paved patio behind; there may be barbecues out here on sunny weekends. There are more tables in an attractive garden beyond the car park. *(Recommended by George Atkinson, Eddie Edwards, John Fahy, Ian Phillips, Pete Yearsley, Graham Simpson, Ronald G Dodsworth, Pat and Tony Martin, M A and C R Starling, Peter Baggott)*

Free house ~ Licensees Charles and Kim Scicluna ~ Real ale ~ Meals and snacks (till 3pm Sunday lunch, not 25-26 Dec and 1 Jan or evenings 24 and 31 Dec) ~ Well behaved children welcome away from the main bar ~ Open 11-3, 6-11; 12-3, 6-10.30 Sun; closed evenings 25/26 Dec and 1 Jan

FULLER STREET TL7416 Map 5

Square & Compasses

From A12 Chelmsford—Witham take Hatfield Peverel exit, and from B1137 there follow Terling signpost, keeping straight on past Terling towards Great Leighs; from A131 Chelmsford—Braintree turn off in Great Leighs towards Fairstead and Terling

The licensees have now bought this friendly and civilised little country pub from Ridleys and at the time of going to press work was beginning on new kitchens and a new bar servery. It's to be hoped that this won't disrupt the pleasant and quietly welcoming atmosphere in the open-plan L-shaped beamed bar, which is comfortable and well lit, has a woodburner as well as a big log fire, and an understated rural decor – stuffed birds including an albino pheasant above the mantlepiece, traps, old country photographs, brasses; shove-ha'penny, table skittles, cribbage, dominoes and maybe piped music. Good if not cheap food all cooked to order (so there may be a wait, although the new kitchens should reduce this) from a very extensive menu includes filled rolls and sandwiches (from £1.50), well liked tomato soup (£3.50), ploughman's (from £5.75), potted brown shrimps and toast (starter £5, main £6.75), smoked cod's roe with hot buttered toast, chicken leg stuffed with gammon, pork, sage and onion and topped with bacon or home-made mushroom and onion quiche (£5.75), ham and eggs (£6), home-made steak and kidney pie (£7), grilled halibut with salsa (£10.50), steaks (from £10.50) and calf liver and bacon (£10.75); main courses come with lots of fresh vegetables, and as the landlord shoots (the pub is much used by shooting parties) there is usually game in season, such as whole roast partridge (£11) and roast grouse (£14.50). Tables can be booked. Well kept Ridleys IPA and Mauldons Best tapped from the cask, decent French regional wines, good coffee, attentive service. There are tables outside with gentle country views. *(Recommended by Gwen and Peter Andrews, Paul and Ursula Randall, Eddie Edwards)*

Free house ~ Licensees Howard and Ginny Austin ~ Real ale ~ Meals and snacks ~ (01245) 361477 ~ Well behaved children welcome ~ Open 11.30-3, 6.30(7 in winter)-11; 11.30-3.30, 6-11 Sat; 12-3, 7-10.30 Sun

FYFIELD TL5606 Map 5

Black Bull £

B184, N end of village

It's the daily specials which offer the best value at this comfortably welcoming 15th-c vine-covered pub which is popular for its wide range of very tasty bar food. They might include chicken curry or mushroom stroganoff, both with coriander rice (£4), home-made steak and mushroom pie or home-made chicken and leek pie (£4.15), liver, bacon and onions (£4.50) and gammon steak (£4.85). In addition, the standard menu offers home-made soup (£2), soft roes (£3), well liked green-lip mussels with black bean sauce (£3.75), spinach and mushroom lasagne (£3.65), chicken roasted with cider, mustard, ginger and spice (£7), excellent steak and kidney pudding (£7.25), lemon sole with prawns and mushrooms (£7.95), steaks (from £8.50) and breast of duck cooked pink with an orange, green ginger and red pepper sauce (£8.95); generous portions, efficient and friendly service; recommended to book at busy times. The series of communicating rooms has low ceilings, big black beams, standing timbers, and cushioned wheelback chairs and modern settles on the muted maroon carpet; warm winter fire; no-smoking area in restaurant. Well kept Courage Directors, Theakstons Best and Wadworths 6X under light blanket pressure; darts, shove-ha'penny, cribbage, dominoes, fruit machine and piped music. Outside there is white garden furniture and lots of barrels filled with flowers; by the car park is an aviary with budgerigars and cockatiels. There are also picnic-sets on a nearby stretch of grass, as well as to the side of the building. *(Recommended by Dave Braisted, Gwen and Peter Andrews, Tina and David Woods-Taylor, R Wain, Joy and Peter Heatherley, Stephen Brown)*

Free house ~ Licensees Alan Smith and Nicola Eldridge ~ Real ale ~ Meals and snacks ~ Restaurant ~ (01277) 899225 ~ Open 11-2.30(3 Sat), 6.30-11; 12-3, 7-10.30 Sun

GOSFIELD TL7829 Map 5

Green Man

3 m N of Braintree

As well as particularly good food, you can expect a warm welcome from the cheerfully efficient staff and Banjo the dog in this smart, well run dining pub. One of the main attractions is the splendid lunchtime cold table which has a marvellous help-yourself choice of home-cooked ham, tongue, beef and turkey, dressed salmon or crab in season, game pie, salads and home-made pickles (£6.95). Well cooked English style menu includes soups like stilton and celery (£3.10), home-made duck and brandy pâté (£3.25), fresh battered cod (£6.50), lamb liver and bacon (£6.75), home-made steak and kidney pudding (£6.95), sirloin of beef (£7), lamb chops in port and cranberry sauce (£8.50), venison in beer (£8.95) and half roast duck with orange sauce (£10.25). A fabulous range of puddings might include raspberry pavlova or steamed marmalade pudding (£3), vegetables are fresh and the chips home-made; advisable to book at busy times. The two little bars have a relaxed conversational atmosphere, Greene King IPA and Abbot on handpump, and decent nicely priced wines, many by the glass; darts, pool, dominoes, cribbage, fruit machine and juke box. *(Recommended by Gwen and Peter Andrews, R Wiles, Dr Oscar Puls, Ronald G Dodsworth, Evelyn and Derek Walter, Mike and Heather Watson, R C Morgan)*

Greene King ~ Lease: John Arnold ~ Real ale ~ Meals and snacks (not Sun evening) ~ Restaurant ~ (01787) 472746 ~ Children in eating area of bar ~ Open 11-3, 6.30-11; 12-3, 7-10.30 Sun

GREAT YELDHAM TL7638 Map 5

White Hart

Poole Street; A1017 Halstead—Haverhill

Essex Dining Pub of the Year

This black and white timbered pub walks the tightrope between pub and restaurant and according to readers, despite the emphasis on the exceptionally good and inventive food, still manages to satisfy devotees of both. You can make your meal as smart or informal as you choose as the same menu is available in the bar or restaurant. There is a very good value set menu (two course £7.50, three course £10.50) which might include french onion soup, salmon and courgette tempura with a teriyaki sauce, chargrilled pork cutlet with couscous, baked aubergine with stir-fried vegetables and pesto and blackcurrant ice cream with shortbread biscuits. From the main menu starters might be flavoursome thai-style mussel soup with lemon grass, spring onion and noodles (£3.95), terrine of game with grape and apple chutney and toasted herb brioche (£4.25), spinach and parmesan tart with tomato and chilli confit and a tossed rocket salad (£4.75), with main courses such as ploughman's (£4.95), chicken curry with lemon rice and spicy yoghurt (£8), mediterranean vegetable and mozzarella tart with warm new potato salad and a balsamic dressing (£7.95), breast of pigeon with parsnip mash, roasted baby onions and a redcurrant jus (£8.50), grilled marinated brill with deep-fried artichoke hearts and ratatouille or breast of chicken with chestnut stuffing, braised leeks, cranberry and apple tartlet and roast potatoes (£9.50), and grilled seabass with tagliatelle, pine nuts, marinated wild mushrooms and wilted rocket or chargrilled sirloin steak with roasted plum tomatoes, button mushrooms and chips (£13.95). Irresistible puddings might include well liked home-made ice cream served in an almond tuile (£3.50), plum pudding with prunes in brandy and vanilla ice cream or warm rice pudding with plum jam (£3.95), or a selection of unpasteurised cheeses (£5.50); smaller helpings for children; no-smoking restaurant. As well as an impressive list of about 100 well described wines there are 17 wines by the glass including a good selection of pudding wines. The well kept real ales on handpump change frequently but might include Adnams and Wells Bombardier Premium. The main areas have stone and wood floors with some dark oak panelling especially around the fireplace and watch your head – the door into the bar is very low. The pretty well kept garden has seats among a variety of trees and shrubs on the lawns. *(Mrs M Dixon, Gwen and Peter*

Andrews, G Neighbour, John Askew, Richard Siebert, Paul and Sandra Embleton, B and M Parkin, R Wiles, Michael Sargent, Quentin Williamson, John Fahy, Paul and Ursula Randall, Hazel R Morgan, Mr Sommerville)

Free house ~ Licensees Roger Jones and John Hoskins ~ Real ale ~ Meals and snacks (12-2, 6.30-10; 12-2, 6.30-9.30 Sun) ~ Restaurant ~ (01787) 237250 ~ Well behaved children welcome ~ Open 11-3, 6-11; 12-2, 7-10.30 Sun; cl 25-26 Dec and 1 Jan evenings

HASTINGWOOD TL4807 Map 5

Rainbow & Dove

¼ mile from M11, junction 7; Hastingwood signposted after Ongar signs at exit roundabout

There is always a friendly welcome at this 17th-c rose-covered cottage which offers a relaxing break from the busy motorway nearby. There are cosy fires in the three homely little low-beamed rooms which open off the main bar area; the one on the left is particularly snug and beamy, with the lower part of its wall stripped back to bare brick and decorated with brass pistols and plates. Popular bar food (they tell us details are exactly the same as last year) includes sandwiches (from £1.75), ploughman's (from £3.60), steak and kidney pie (£4.75) and lots of fresh fish like cod mornay, well liked brill in lemon sauce, hake and skate on a specials board. Well kept Ansells and Flowers Original; may be piped music. Picnic-sets under cocktail parasols, on a stretch of grass hedged off from the car park. *(Recommended by Stephen Brown, Tony Beaulah, LMM, Mr and Mrs N Chesher, Joy and Peter Heatherley)*

Carlsberg Tetleys ~ Tenant J A Keep ~ Meals and snacks ~ (01279) 415419 ~ Children welcome ~ Open 11.30-3, 6-11; 12-4, 7-10.30 Sun

HEYBRIDGE BASIN TL8707 Map 5

Jolly Sailor

Basin Rd (B1026 E of Maldon)

There's a very welcoming atmosphere at this cheerful down-to-earth little place. With simple furnishings, nautical charts and lots of boating and marine pictures, it's tucked in by the high sea wall of the popular boating estuary, with seats out on a nice little terrace beside the wall. The chef himself usually brings out the good value food, including sandwiches (from £2.10), filled baked potatoes (from £2.20), ploughman's (£4.50), mushroom and fresh cream tart (£4.95), steak and stout pie (£5.50), and huge helpings of delicious fresh Lowestoft fish with superb chips (from £4.95); well kept Greene King IPA, Marstons Pegidree and one or two guests on handpump; home-made lemonade in summer and mulled wine in the winter; friendly chatty staff, darts, dominoes, cribbage, games machines and piped music. There are shoreside walks from here, and this could make a good finish for longer walks by the Rivers Blackwater and Chelmer. Parking is limited, especially on summer weekends. *(Recommended by George Atkinson, John Wilmott, Paul and Ursula Randall, Pete Yearsley)*

Carlsberg Tetley ~ Licensee Andrea Wiley ~ Real ale ~ Meals and snacks (12-2, 7-9; from 6pm in summer) ~ Restaurant ~ 01621 854210 ~ Children welcome away from the bar ~ Pianist some Fri and Sat evenings ~ Open 11.30-3, 6-11; 11-11 (11-3, 6-11 winter) Sat; 12-10.30 (12-4, 7-10.30 winter) Sun; closed evenings 25/26 Dec

HIGH ONGAR TL5603 Map 5

Wheatsheaf

King St, Nine Ashes; signposted Blackmore, Ingatestone off A414 just E of Ongar

The nicest seats indoors here are in the four unusual booths or stalls built into the big front bay window, each with an intimate little lamp and fresh flowers on its broad round-ended polished table. We say indoors, because on a fine day the spacious back garden is practically irresistible, with a variety of well spaced tables and plenty of room for children to run around in, as well as a 'giant' play house and other play equipment. Unusually, the landlord and landlady take the kitchen and front-of-house turn and turn about, which seems to help keep the welcome really fresh; other staff are always cheerful too – and efficient. A wide choice of good home-made food includes sandwiches (from £1.70), soup (£2.25), filled jacket potatoes (from £3.10), ploughman's (from £3.50), garlic mushrooms (£3.65), crab and vegetable parcels (£3.95), vegetable lasagne (£6.50), lamb chops (£7.75), mixed grill (£10.95), steaks (from £11.95); specials might include lamb steak in garlic and rosemary (£8.95), duck breast with blueberry and brandy sauce (£10.95), and fresh fish such as whole plaice stuffed with prawns and cheese (£8.95) or halibut steak with a stilton crust (£9.95); good vegetables and excellent chips (usually a choice of other types of potato too); small helpings on request. Well kept Flowers IPA and Original, Marstons Pedigree and a guest which may be from Youngs, Fullers or Everards on handpump; a log fire each end of the beamed bar; darts and cribbage; no children inside. *(Recommended by Peter Baggott, Gwen and Peter Andrews, Rex Miller, Sandra Iles, Joy and Peter Heatherley)*

Free house ~ Licensees Tony and Sue Streeter ~ Real ale ~ Meals and snacks (not Sunday evenings and Monday lunchtimes) ~ (01277) 822220 ~ Open 11-3, 5.30-11; 11-4, 6-11 Sat; 12-10.30 Sun; closed Mon lunchtime

HORNDON ON THE HILL TQ6683 Map 3

Bell

M25 junction 30 into A13, then left into B1007 after 7 miles, village signposted from here

This lovely old flower bedecked medieval inn has been meticulously run by the same enthusiastic family for over 60 years. Imaginative carefully home-prepared bar food which tends towards English country style might include spinach and oyster soup (£2.80), warm tuna salad niçoise (£4.50), poached seafood with saffron and garlic mayonnaise (£10.40), breast of chicken with leeks and morels or pigeon breast with dried apricots and haggis (£10.50), grilled salmon with welsh rarebit, tomatoes and chives (£10.80), lamb cutlets in pastry with tarragon (£11.95) and beautifully presented puddings such as poached pear with vanilla ice cream in a marzipan basket and chocolate marquise with caramelised pineapple. There's a wine list of over 100 well chosen wines from all over the world with about 13 by the glass listed on a blackboard with suggestions on what to drink with your food; you can also buy them off-sales; Bass and Fullers London Pride, Greene King IPA, and guests such as Crouch Vale Millennium Gold and Youngs Special on handpump. The heavily beamed bar has some antique high-backed settles and plush burgundy stools and benches, rugs on the flagstones or highly polished oak floorboards, and a curious collection of hot cross buns hanging from a beam. On the last weekend in June the High Road outside is closed (by Royal Charter) for period-costume festivities and a crafts fair; the pub holds a feast then. Very attractive beamed bedrooms; no smoking in restaurant. *(Recommended by H Dickinson, Gwen and Peter Andrews, Joy and Peter Heatherley, G Neighbour, John and Enid Morris, Thomas Nott, Richard Siebert, K Flack, DFL)*

Free house ~ Licensee John Vereker ~ Real ale ~ Meals and snacks (12-1.45, 6.30-9.45; not 25/26 Dec) ~ Restaurant ~ (01375) 642463 ~ Children welcome in eating area of bar and restaurant ~ Open 11-2.30(3 Sat), 6-11; 12-3, 7-10.30 Sun ~ Bedrooms: /£83B

LANGHAM TM0233 Map 5

Shepherd & Dog

Moor Rd/High St; village signposted off A12 N of Colchester

Make sure that you are really hungry before seeking out this cheerful friendly inn, as the reasonably priced food portions are very generous. The not over elaborate but reliably interesting menu, which changes daily and is chalked on boards around the bar, might include home-made leek and potato soup (£1.95), home-made chicken liver pâté or deep-fried brie (£3.50), ploughman's (from £3.95), home-made curries, well liked salads or spinach and feta cheese filo parcels (£5.95), roasted rainbow trout with almonds and tarragon (£6.95), grilled halibut with anchovy and caper butter (£7.50), breast of chicken with cashew nut sauce (£7.95), breast of duck roasted with honey and sesame seeds (£10.95) and puddings such as home-made bread and butter pudding or apricot crumble (£2.50). Well kept Greene King IPA and Abbot, Mauldons Best, Moles Best and Nethergate Bitter and Old Growler on handpump, and a short but decent wine list. An engaging hotch potch of styles, the spick and span L-shaped bar has an interesting collection of continental bottled beers, and there's often a sale of books for charity. Tables outside. *(Recommended by Gwen and Peter Andrews, Paul and Sandra Embleton, A C Morrison, Pete Yearsley, Richard and Robyn Wain, Margaret and Maurice Peterson, Quentin Williamson, Thomas Nott)*

Free house ~ Licensees Paul Barnes and Jane Graham ~ Real ale ~ Meals and snacks (12-2.15, 6-9.30) ~ Restaurant ~ (01206) 272711 ~ Children welcome ~Live music every fourth Sunday ~ Open 11-3, 5.30(6 Sat)-11; 12-3, 7-10.30 Sun; cl 26 Dec

LITTLE BRAXTED TL8314 Map 5

Green Man

Kelvedon Road; village signposted off B1389 by NE end of A12 Witham bypass – keep on patiently

Readers report that it is well worth the journey up the quiet lane to this tucked away and isolated brick house. The cosy welcoming little lounge houses an interesting collection of bric-a-brac, including some 200 horsebrasses, some harness, mugs hanging from a beam, a lovely copper urn, and an open fire. In the tiled public bar friendly staff dispense well kept Ridleys IPA and Rumpus from handpumps in the form of 40mm brass cannon shells, also several malt whiskies; darts and video machine. Good, well presented and reasonably priced food includes sandwiches (from £1.80), filled french bread (£2.50), filled baked potatoes (from £2.55), and daily specials like liver and apple casserole (£4.25), tuna and sweetcorn pasta pot, mushroom stroganoff or chicken breast in mushroom sauce, lasagne or fidget pie (£5.50), steak and ale pie (£5.95) and puddings like chocolate mousse or blackberry and apple coconut crumble (£1.95). There are picnic-sets and a pretty pond in the delightfully sheltered garden behind. No children. *(Recommended by Mike and Maggie Betton, Mrs M Dallisson, Tina and David Woods-Taylor, Mike and Mary Carter, Evelyn and Derek Walter, A E Brace, Gwen and Peter Andrews)*

Ridleys ~ Tenant Tony Wiley ~ Real ale ~ Meals and snacks ~ (01621) 891659 ~ Open 11.30-3, 6-11; 12-3, 7-10.30 Sun; closed evening 25 Dec

LITTLE DUNMOW TL6521 Map 5

Flitch of Bacon

Village signposted off A120 E of Dunmow, then turn right on village loop road

There's a warm welcome for all at this delightfully unspoilt rural tavern where country characters rub shoulders with visiting businessmen. The small timbered bar has a genuinely friendly atmosphere and is simply but attractively furnished, mainly with flowery-cushioned pews, and has prettily arranged flowers on the tables, and ochre walls. Quietly relaxing at lunchtime during the week, it can be vibrantly cheerful in the evenings – especially on one of the Saturdays they're singing through a musical around the piano at the back. The sensibly small range of unpretentious and tasty bar food is all freshly cooked by the landlady and might include generous sandwiches (£2.20) – including excellent home-carved ham (£2.20), soup (£2.50), ploughman's (£3.50), anchovies on toast (£3.50), local ham and eggs with a crusty roll (£4), Friday fish and chips (£4.50), smoked salmon and scrambled eggs (£5.50), and three or four changing hot dishes such as sausage hotpot (£4.95) game dishes, pork and apple or steak and kidney pie (£6.50), and a couple of puddings; good buffet lunch only on Sunday. Greene King IPA and two guests such as Fullers London Pride or Nethergate Umbel Magna on handpump. Cribbage, dominoes, no games machines or piped music; bedrooms basic but clean and comfortable. The pub looks across the quiet lane to a broad expanse of green, and has a few picnic-sets on the edge; the nearby church of St Mary is well worth a visit (the pub has a key).

(Recommended by Mrs Cynthia Archer, Dr Oscar Puls, Mike and Karen England, Tony Beaulah, Stephen Brown, Gwen and Peter Andrews, Neville Kenyon, Charles and Daniele Smith, Michael Gittins, John Fahy)

Free house ~ Licensees Bernard and Barbara Walker ~ Real ale ~ Meals and snacks (not Sun evening) ~ Restaurant ~ (01371) 820323 ~ Children welcome in restaurant ~ Open 12-3(3.30 Sat), 6-11; 12-5(3 winter) Sun ~ Bedrooms: £35S/£49.60S

MILL GREEN TL6400 Map 5

Viper

Mill Green Rd; from Fryerning (which is signposted off north-east bound A12 Ingatestone bypass) follow Writtle signposts; OS Sheet 167 map reference 640019

Almost hidden by overflowing hanging baskets and window boxes in summer, this cosy little pub has a simple and quaint charm. Two timeless little lounge rooms have spindleback seats, armed country kitchen chairs, and tapestried wall seats around neat little old tables, and a warming log fire. The fairly basic parquet-floored tap room (where booted walkers are directed) is more simply furnished with shiny wooden traditional wall seats, and beyond there's another room with country kitchen chairs and sensibly placed darts; shove-ha'penny, dominoes, cribbage and a fruit machine. Very well kept changing real ales such as Burtonwood Bitter, Hook Norton Old Hookey, Mansfield Bitter, Ridleys IPA, Wells Eagle IPA and Wolf Best on handpump are served from an oak-panelled counter. Simple lunchtime bar snacks include soup (£2.50), good sandwiches (from £1.75), chilli (£3.25), and ploughman's (from £3.80). Pleasant service even when busy; no children. Tables on the lawn overlook the marvellously cared for cottage garden. *(Recommended by Mike and Karen England, Pete Baker, Richard and Robyn Wain, James Nunns, John Fahy, R H Rowley, Quentin Williamson)*

Free house ~ Licensee Fred Beard ~ Real ale ~ Lunchtime snacks ~ (01277) 352010 ~ Open 11.30-2.30(3 Sat), 6-11; 12-3, 7-10.30 Sun

NORTH FAMBRIDGE TQ8597 Map 5

Ferry Boat

The Quay; village signposted from B1012 E off S Woodham Ferrers; keep on past railway

The River Crouch is nearer than you think to this genuinely unpretentious 500-year-old weatherboarded pub – it sometimes creeps up the lane towards the car park. The bar is simply furnished with traditional wall benches, settles and chairs on its stone floor, nautical memorabilia, old-fashioned lamps, and a few historic boxing-gloves. There's a log fire at one end, and a woodburning stove at the other, although the fact that most of the buildings rest only on a bed of reeds allowing the old wood and plaster to move around according to the climate means that it can still be a bit draughty. Straightforward bar food includes sandwiches (from £1.80), soup (£1.80), ploughman's (from £3.50), deep-fried cod or plaice (£3.75), roast chicken (£4.95), lemon sole (£7.50), venison in port and red wine or fried chicken stuffed with prawns and lobster (£7.50). Well kept Flowers IPA on handpump and guests like Morlands Old Speckled Hen or Wadworths 6X; friendly chatty landlord; shove ha'penny, table skittles, cribbage, dominoes, fruit machine and piped music. There's a pond with ducks and carp, and seats in the garden. *(Recommended by Paul and Sandra Embleton, Mike and Karen England, Peter Baggott, George Atkinson, Richard Siebert)*

Free house ~ Licensee Roy Maltwood ~ Real ale ~ Meals and snacks ~ Restaurant ~ (01621) 740208 ~ Children welcome in family room and restaurant ~ Open 11-3, 6-11 (7-11 winter); 12-10.30 Sun; 12-3, 7-10.30 winter Sun

Most pubs in this book sell wine by the glass. We mention wines only if they are a cut above the – generally low – average. Please let us know of any good pubs for wine.

PAGLESHAM TQ9293 Map 3

Punchbowl

Church End; from the Paglesham road out of Rochford, Church End is signposted on the left

Beautifully kept, this pretty white weatherboarded pub has a very peaceful outlook over the fields – a reward for the long drive down country lanes. It's a very genuine place, with cosy beamed bar and dining area with pews, barrel chairs and other seats, lots of bric-a-brac, and a very friendly feel – thanks to the particularly hospitable landlord. Good standard food includes superb filled crusty rolls (from £1.75, prawn £2.75), filled baked potatoes, soup (£1.95), cheese and ham toasties (£2.25), ploughman's (from £3.25), steak and ale pie (£5.50) and good fresh fish including plaice (£5.25), skate (£6.95), lemon sole (£9.50) and dover sole (£10.25). Well kept Adnams, Morlands Old Speckled Hen, a changing Ridleys ale and a guest on handpump; piped music; music quiz some Friday evenings in winter. There are some tables in the small garden, with a couple out by the quiet road. *(Recommended by George Atkinson, Tim Heywood, Sophie Wilne)*

Free house ~ Licensees Bernie and Pat Cardy ~ Real ale ~ Meals and snacks ~ (01702) 258376 ~ Children welcome in dining area ~ Open 11.30-3, 7-11(10.30 Sun); closed evening 25 Dec

RICKLING GREEN TL5029 Map 5

Cricketers Arms 𝕐

Just off B1383 N of Stansted Mountfichet

Overlooking the cricket green where Essex CC play once a year, this friendly family run inn is much older than it looks from the outside – the fairly plain Victorian façade veils a mass of Elizabethan timbering. Not surprisingly there's lots of cricket memorabilia inside, with masses of cricket cigarette cards on the walls of the softly lit and comfortable saloon bar, the two bays of which are divided by standing timbers; in winter chestnuts are roasted on the log fire. As well as sandwiches, good bar food from the blackboard menu might include soft roes (starter £2.25, main £5.50), potato skins (£3.25), smoked trout with horseradish (£5.50), roast leg of duck or deep-fried cod (£5.95), bacon and onion pudding (£6.95), lemon sole (£7.75), tuna steak (£8.75), lamb en croûte or crab thermidor (£8.95); puddings include well liked fruit crumble (£2.30) and steamed syrup sponge pudding (£2.70). Well kept Flowers IPA, Fullers ESB and Wadworths 6X tapped from the cask, 10 wines by the glass and in summer about two dozen bottle conditioned beers from all over Britain; pool, darts, cribbage, dominoes, fruit machine and juke box. A sheltered front courtyard has picnic-sets; the bedrooms are in a modern block behind and are handy for Stansted Airport, with a courtesy car for guests. *(Recommended by Gwen and Peter Andrews, Quentin Williamson, Charles and Pauline Stride, G Neighbour, Lynne Gittins)*

Free house ~ Licensees Tim and Jo Proctor ~ Real ale ~ Meals and snacks (till 10) ~ Restaurant ~ (01799) 543210 ~ Children welcome in restaurant ~ Open 12-2.30, 7-11; all day Sat and Sun ~ Bedrooms: £50B/£60B

SAFFRON WALDEN TL5438 Map 5

Eight Bells

Bridge Street; B184 towards Cambridge

Despite its size this handsomely timbered black and white Tudor inn is cosy and welcoming. As well as daily specials, good bar food includes home-made soup (£2.10), ploughman's (from £4.45), Cromer crab (£5.25), home-made lasagne or cheese, leek and potato pie with mushroom sauce (£5.95), well liked home-made steak and kidney pie (£6.35), grilled whole fresh plaice with parsley butter or gammon and egg (£6.75), calf liver with smoked ham, mushroom and cream sauce (£8.85), and steaks (from £10.30). Well kept Adnams, Ind Coope Burton, Marstons Pedigree, Tetleys and a changing guest on handpump, and half a dozen decent wines by the glass (with a choice of glass size). The neatly kept friendly open-plan bar is divided by old timbers, with modern oak settles forming small booths around the tables; games machines may be noisy. The bar leads into the old kitchen which is now a carpeted family room with an open fire. The partly no-smoking restaurant is in a splendidly timbered hall with high rafters, tapestries and flags. There are seats in the garden. Nearby Audley End makes a good family outing, and the pub is close to some good walks. *(Recommended by A and M Marriott, Paul and Sandra Embleton, Peter Smith, Mayur Shah, G Washington, Ronald G Dodsworth, Maysie Thompson, Andy Cunningham, Yvonne Hannaford)*

Carlsberg Tetley ~ Manager David Gregory ~ Real ale ~ Meals and snacks (all day) ~ Restaurant ~ (01799) 522790 ~ Children welcome in restaurant and family room ~ Open 11-11; 12-10.30 Sun

STOCK TQ6998 Map 5

Hoop

B1007; from A12 Chelmsford bypass take Galleywood, Billericay turn-off

Remaining happily unsophisticated and with a refreshingly mixed clientele, the little bar of this well liked village local has a really friendly atmosphere. As well as a fine range of about six changing real ales that might be from Adnams, Crouch Vale, Fullers, Hop Back or Nethergate, on handpump or tapped from the cask (during May they hold a beer festival when there might be around 150), there are farm ciders and winter mulled wine. There's a coal-effect gas fire in the big brick fireplace, brocaded wall seats around dimpled copper tables on the left and a cluster of brocaded stools on the right; sensibly placed darts (the heavy black beams are studded with hundreds of wayward flights), dominoes and cribbage. Reasonably priced bar food includes sandwiches (from £1.20), soup (£1.50), ploughman's (from £3.50), steak and kidney pie (£3.50), vegetable pie or well liked lancashire hotpot (£4), chicken curry (£4.50), and specials which might include braised steak and dumpling, steak and oyster pie, skate or lemon sole (fresh fish is delivered daily); vegetables are charged in addition to these prices. Picnic-sets in the big sheltered back garden, prettily bordered with flowers. No children; over 21s only in bar. *(Recommended by Tina and David Woods-Taylor, Dr Oscar Puls, Gwen and Peter Andrews, Paul Barstow, Karyn Taylor, John and Enid Morris, John Wilmott, Beryl and Bill Farmer, D E Twitchett)*

Free house ~ Licensees Albert and David Kitchin ~ Real ale ~ Meals and snacks (all day) ~ (01277) 841137 ~ Open 11-11; 12-10.30 Sun

STOW MARIES TQ8399 Map 5

Prince of Wales

B1012 between S Woodham Ferrers and Cold Norton

It's the landlord's knowledge and enthusiasm for beer that makes this Essex marshland pub worth searching out. He runs a beer wholesaling business (supplying rare ales for local beer festivals), and changes his five or six real ales weekly. As well as a Fullers seasonal ale, you might find Dent Aviator, Fullers London Pride or Mitchells Original; they also have a growing range of Belgian draught beers, and a particularly unusual range of continental bottled beers, Belgian fruit beers, farm cider, and a good choice of malt whiskies and vintage ports. There's a friendly chatty atmosphere in the several cosy low-ceilinged rooms which although seemingly unchanged since the turn of the century were carefully restored in genuinely traditional style only a few years ago; few have space for more than one or two tables or wall benches on the tiled or bare-boards floors, though the room in the middle squeezes in quite a jumble of chairs and stools. One room used to be the village bakery, and in winter the oven there is still used to make bread and pizzas. A new Italian chef means that the reasonably priced home-made bar food has a continental theme, the Belgian ploughman's includes three different Belgian cheeses (the landlord brings some of them back from Belgium himself) and Belgian style pickles (£4.80); blackboard specials might include spaghetti and spinach omelette or baked aubergine, tomatoes and parmesan (£4.80), and puddings such as home-made tiramisu (£2.25) There are seats and tables in a garden behind and in summer the gap between the white picket fence and the pub's weatherboarded frontage is filled with beautiful dark red roses, with some scented pink ones at the side. *(Recommended by George Atkinson, Ian Nicolson, Peter Baggott)*

Free house ~ Licensee Rob Walster ~ Real ale ~ Meals and snacks ~ (01621) 828971 ~ Children in family room ~ Occasional live music ~ Open 11-11; 12-10.30 Sun; cl evening 25 Dec

TOOT HILL TL5103 Map 5

Green Man 🍷

Village signposted from A113 in Stanford Rivers, S of Ongar; and from A414 W of Ongar

It's the tremendous choice and variety of wines that makes this pub stand out among country dining pubs – the list offers around 100 well chosen varieties, 20 half bottles and many by the glass; they also have free monthly tastings and talks by visiting merchants. The main emphasis is on the newly refurbished and now much more plush long dining lounge; in the evenings they take bookings for tables in here, but only for 7.30; after that, when you turn up they put you on a queue for tables that come free. The ambitious bar food is freshly cooked to order (they warn of delays when busy) and might include ploughman's, wild rabbit casserole with herb dumplings (£7.90) or maize fed chicken stuffed with mushrooms (£7.50). The landlord plans to refurbish the simply furnished area by the bar at some point this year, retaining little except the open fire and well kept Crouch Vale IPA and a weekly changing guest such as Fullers London Pride on handpump; darts, shove-ha'penny, dominoes and cribbage; no-smoking area. In summer, the outside is a lovely mass of colourful hanging baskets, window boxes and flower tubs, prettily set off by the curlicued white iron tables and chairs and wooden benches; more tables behind. A couple of miles through the attractive countryside at Greensted is St Andrews, the oldest wooden church in the world. *(Recommended by Gwen and Peter Andrews, M A Starling, A Hepburn, S Jenner, Martin and Jane Bailey, GL, A Bradbury, Mr and Mrs N Chesher, Joy and Peter Heatherley, Mrs S Lamprecht, DFL, J H Gracey)*

Free house ~ Licensee Peter Roads ~ Real ale ~ Meals and snacks ~ Restaurant ~ (01992) 522255 ~ Open 11-3, 6-11; 12-3, 7-10.30 Sun

WENDENS AMBO TL5136 Map 5

Bell

B1039 just W of village

There is a veritable menagerie at this jolly little beamed village pub with Thug the friendly black cat, Kate the dog and in the garden Gertie the goat, who has been joined by two new pigmy goats called Reggie and Ronnie. Goats apart, the extensive back garden itself is quite special with a big tree-sheltered lawn, lots of flower borders and unusual plant-holders; the wooden wendy house, a proper tree swing, and a sort of mini nature-trail wandering off through the shrubs should keep children happily engaged. Inside, spotlessly kept small cottagey low-ceilinged rooms are filled with interesting knick-knacks; as well as a friendly open fire there are brasses on ancient timbers, wheelback chairs around neat tables, comfortably cushioned seats worked into snug alcoves, and quite a few pictures on the cream walls. Well presented bar food includes filled rolls (from £1.90), particularly good ploughman's (£3.75), vegetarian dishes (£5.50), chillies and curries (£5.95), beef and Guinness pie or venison casserole (£6.75), mixed grill (£7) and puddings such as spotted dick or treacle tart (£2.25); the dining room is no smoking. Four well kept real ales which might be from Adnams, Ansells, Everards, Mauldons, Ridleys, Shepherd Neame or Wadworths are well kept on handpump or tapped straight from the cask by the cheery landlord or motherly barmaid; darts, dominoes, cards, Monopoly and cribbage; piped music. *(Recommended by Gwen and Peter Andrews, John Wooll, Richard and Robyn Wain, Ian Phillips, Maysie Thompson, Wayne Brindle, B N F and M Parkin)*

Free house ~ Licensees Geoff and Bernie Bates ~ Real ale ~ Meals and snacks (not

Mon evening) ~ Restaurant ~ Children welcome in restaurant ~ (01799) 540382 ~ Open 11.30-2.30(3 Sat), 6-11; 12-3, 7-10.30 Sun

WOODHAM WALTER TL8006 Map 5

Cats

Back road to Curling Tye and Maldon, from N end of village

As the landlord would rather we didn't include his pub in the *Guide* we can't be too specific with factual information about this pleasantly relaxed timbered black and white country cottage; we can only tell you as much as we've been able to glean from readers' reports in the last year or so (in our defence we must say that letting licensees decide for us which pubs *not* to include would damage our independence almost as much as allowing other landlords to pay for their inclusion). Stone cats prowl across the roof and the feline theme is continued in the cosy interior with shelves of china cats in the rambling low-ceilinged bar; the low black beams and timbering are set off well by neat white paintwork, and there are interesting nooks and crannies as well as two log fires. Well kept Greene King Abbot and IPA and a guest on handpump; good simple bar food; friendly service. No children or piped music. There are seats outside in the pretty garden with views across the surrounding farmland. *(Recommended by Lynn Sharpless, Bob Eardley, Pete Yearsley, Mike and Karen England, R Morgan, Peter Baggott, Sam Clark; more reports please)*

Free house ~ Real ale ~ Lunchtime snacks (Thurs-Sat but see note above) ~ Open 11-2.30ish, 6ish-11; possibly closed Tues and Wed lunchtimes and all day Mon; may close if not busy in winter

YOUNGS END TL7319 Map 5

Green Dragon

A131 Braintree—Chelmsford, just N of Essex Showground

It's the very good bar food that draws people to this well run dining pub. Besides sandwiches and ploughman's the extensive bar menu might include home-made soup (£2.25), chicken liver pâté (£3.95), ham and eggs (£5.50), leek, mushroom and potato cakes (£6.50), excellent steak and kidney pie (£6.50), chicken dumplings (£7.25), kleftiko (£8.55), sirloin steak (£12.75) and fresh fish specials such as cod fishcakes with parsley sauce (£5.50), six rock oysters (£6), skate (£8.50), baked rainbow trout stuffed with prawns and mushrooms (£7.95), monkfish kebabs with ratatouille (£9.50) and bass baked with oranges and coriander (£9.95); fresh vegetables; good puddings like spotted dick or treacle sponge and a pudding trolley (£2.95); fixed price set menu available. The restaurant area has an understated barn theme – stripped brick walls and a manger at one end; a new non-smoking eating area has been created in the 'hayloft'. The bar part has normal pub furnishings in its two rooms, with a little extra low-ceilinged snug just beside the serving counter. At lunchtime (not Sunday) you can have bar food in part of the restaurant, where the tables are a better size than in the bar. Well kept Greene King IPA, Abbot and their seasonal beers and a guest on handpump; unobtrusive piped music (jazz on our inspection visit). The neat back garden has lots of picnic-sets under cocktail parasols, a big green play dragon, climbing frame and budgerigar aviary. *(Recommended by John Fahy, Angela Copeland, Paul and Ursula Randall; more reports please)*

Greene King ~ Lease: Bob and Mandy Greybrook ~ Real ale ~ Meals and snacks (till 10 Fri and Sat) ~ Restaurant ~ (01245) 361030 ~ Children welcome in eating area till 8 ~ Open 11.30-3(3.30 Sat), 6(5.30 Sat)-11; 12-3.30, 6.30-10.30 Sun

> The letters and figures after the name of each town are its Ordnance Survey map reference. *How to use the Guide* at the beginning of the book explains how it helps you find a pub, in road atlases or large-scale maps as well as in our own maps.

Lucky Dip

Besides the fully inspected pubs, you might like to try these Lucky Dips recommended to us and described by readers (if you do, please send us reports):

Abridge [London Rd (A113); TQ4696], *Maltsters Arms*: Snug and friendly low-beamed partly 16th-c pub with well kept Greene King IPA and Abbot, open fires; public side with darts and bar billiards; popular with young people evenings *(Robert Lester, Mr and Mrs N Chesher)*

☆ **Althorne** [Green Lane; TQ9199], *Huntsman & Hounds*: Thatched low-beamed rustic pub, occasional barbecues in lovely big garden, well kept Greene King ales, farm cider, good food and coffee, good friendly service; piped music *(John Wilmott, BB)*

☆ **Ardleigh** [A137 towards Colchester; TM0529], *Wooden Fender*: Good choice of promptly served home-made food inc Sun lunch and well kept Greene King IPA, Abbot and Rayments in friendly beamed bar, open-plan but traditional; friendly service, log fires, restaurant allowing children, a pool in back garden; immaculate lavatories *(Quentin Williamson, LYM)*

Ashdon [back rd Saffron Walden—Haverhill; TL5842], *Rose & Crown*: 17th-c, softly lit small beamed rooms, one with original gothic lettering and geometric patterns; enjoyable food (fresh fish Fri) in bar and restaurant, real fire, Greene King Abbot with a guest such as Ind Coope Burton; pool room *(Gwen and Peter Andrews)*

Bannister Green [TL6920], *Three Horseshoes*: Comfortable country local, well kept Ridleys, good value food inc good veg and Sun lunch (booking advised in small restaurant), tables out on broad village green and in garden; children welcome *(Tony Beaulah, LYM)*

Barnston [A130 SE of Dunmow; TL6419], *Bushel & Sack*: Cheerful 19th-c bar and comfortable restaurant beyond sitting room, well kept interesting guest beers, no piped music *(Gwen and Peter Andrews)*

Bicknacre [Main Rd; TL7802], *White Swan*: Good value straightforward food all day in homely central eating area, huge collection of mugs, jugs and tankards, well kept Boddingtons, Flowers IPA and guest ales, pleasant wall lamps, tables out on side terrace *(Paul Barstow, Karyn Taylor)*

Billericay [Chapel St, off High St; TQ6794], *Coach & Horses*: Well run comfortable local, good service from long bar even when busy, Greene King IPA and Abbot and at least one guest beer, simple good value lunchtime food, lots of artefacts, darts; maybe quiet piped music *(John Wilmott)*; [Southend Rd, South Green], *Duke of York*: Pleasant beamed local with real fire, longcase clock, local photographs, upholstered settles and wheelback chairs, good value food in bar and modern restaurant, long-serving licensees, Greene King and occasional guest beers, maybe unobtrusive piped 60s pop music *(David Twitchett)*

Birdbrook [TL7041], *Plough*: Pretty thatched pub with hard-working newish young licensees doing good value food, good choice of well kept ales, nice open fire in public bar, dining area *(Richard and Valerie Wright)*

☆ **Boreham** [Church Rd; TL7509], *Queens Head*: Homely traditional pub with very welcoming licensees, well kept Greene King IPA and Abbot, decent wines, good simple cheap food (not Sun evening) inc Weds roast and Sun lunch; snug beams-and-brickwork saloon (fills quickly), more tables down one side of long public bar with darts at end; maybe piped music; small garden *(Gwen and Peter Andrews)*

Braintree [A120, by Wyevale garden centre; TL7622], *Fowlers Farm*: Built attractively to resemble an old farmhouse that once stood here, floorboards and old farm equipment, well kept Hancocks HB, good value generous food from sandwiches up served quickly, plenty of seating inc no-smoking area, pleasant young staff; piped music not too obtrusive; rabbit run in attractive garden *(Keith and Janet Morris)*

☆ **Broxted** [TL5726], *Prince of Wales*: Softly lit L-shaped dining pub, low beams, brick pillars, some settees, food from hearty sandwiches up, good choice of wines by the glass, Friary Meux and an interesting changing guest beer, smiling service; piped music; conservatory, good garden with play area *(Gwen and Peter Andrews, Paul and Sandra Embleton, John Fahy)*

Bulmer Tye [TL8438], *Fox*: More restaurant than pub, Italian-run, with good welcoming service, well kept Greene King IPA and decent wine from small bar on left, popular lunchtime carvery and Italian dishes *(David Regan, Gwen and Peter Andrews)*

Chelmsford [29 Rainsford Rd; TL7006], *County*: Smallish hotel bar, pubby but always civilised (prices keep the yobs out), well kept Adnams, Greene King IPA and Wadworths 6X, good straightforward bar food inc sandwiches, friendly barman, no music; bedrooms *(Gwen and Peter Andrews, Paul and Ursula Randall)*; [Baddow Rd], *Nags Head*: Well kept Greene King IPA, basic well priced food, friendly service *(R T and J C Moggridge)*

☆ **Chignall Smealy** [TL6711], *Pig & Whistle*: Solid furniture and soft lighting, beams, brasses and stripped brick, enjoyable enterprising food inc Sun lunch, music-free partly no-smoking restaurant, changing well kept ales such as Adnams, Courage Best and Directors, Greene King IPA, Morlands Old Speckled Hen, Ruddles County and Theakstons Best, good choice of house wines; children welcome away from bar, smiling service, fine views *(Gwen and Peter Andrews, Tony Beaulah)*

Chignall St James [TL6609], *Three Elms*: Small open-plan country pub, off the beaten track; food cooked to order inc good local ham and egg, real ale *(Paul and Ursula Randall)*

☆ **Chigwell** [High Rd (A113); TQ4693], *Kings Head*: Beautiful 17th-c building with interesting Dickens memorabilia, some antique furnishings; Chef & Brewer bar food, quick friendly service, well kept ales, upstairs restaurant; piped music, can get very crowded weekend evenings; attractive garden *(JF)*

Chigwell Row [57 Lambourne Rd (A112); TQ4693], *Two Brewers*: Recently refurbished, comfortable and friendly, with Flowers Original, extended restaurant, day's paper up in gents' *(Robert Lester)*

Clacton on Sea [211 London Rd; TM1715], *Robin Hood*: Carefully refurbished in traditional style but with emphasis on wide choice of decent food inc interesting vegetarian, first-class friendly service, fine range of beers, good choice of sensibly priced wines, tables in nice garden; children welcome *(John Wilmott, Judy Wayman, Bob Arnett)*

☆ **Coggeshall** [West St], *Fleece*: Handsome and friendly Tudor local, well kept Greene King IPA and Abbot, decent wines, reliable straightforward bar food (not Tues or Sun evenings) from sandwiches up, cheery service, children welcome, open all day; spacious sheltered garden with play area, next to Paycocke's *(Gwen and Peter Andrews, C L Kauffman, LYM)*

☆ **Coggeshall** [TL8522], *White Hart*: Lots of low Tudor beams, antique settles among other more usual seats, prints and fishing trophies on cream walls, wide choice of food, Adnams, decent wines and coffee; bedrooms comfortable *(JF, Paul and Sandra Embleton, D E Twitchett, BB)*

Coggeshall [Church St], *Woolpack*: Handsome timber-framed 15th-c inn opp church, charming softly lit period lounge with big log fire, interesting bar food, well kept Adnams; comfortable bedrooms *(C L Kauffman, LYM)*

☆ **Colchester** [East St; TM0025], *Rose & Crown*: Plush tastefully modernised Tudor inn, timbered and jettied, parts of a former gaol preserved in its rambling beamed bar, pew seats, decent food, nice afternoon teas, well kept Adnams Broadside, Tetleys and a beer brewed for them; can get smoky; comfortably functional bedrooms, many in modern extension, with good breakfast *(George Atkinson, Tony and Ann Allen, LYM)*

Colchester [4 St Johns St], *Playhouse*: Flamboyant Wetherspoons conversion of former theatre – good fun, on top of all the usual virtues *(John Fahy)*; [Fingringhoe Rd, S edge – Donyland, nr Rowhedge; TM0222], *Walnut Tree*: Modest friendly local opp woods, carefully kept changing real ales, good value home cooking inc vegetarian; dogs welcome, chickens, birds and a goat outside; limited opening hrs *(Lindi Burroughs)*

☆ **Coopersale Common** [off B172 E of Theydon Bois; TL4702], *Theydon Oak*: Welcoming beamed pub with lots of brass and copper, old handpump collection, well kept Bass, Hancocks HB, Greene King and Wadworths 6X, friendly service, ample cheap food in large eating area with interesting old maps; no piped music (not even the boss's), popular with all ages; tables in garden with play area *(Eddie Edwards, Tony Gayfer, A Hepburn, S Jenner)*

Cressing [TL7920], *Three Ashes*: Very pleasant new licensees, comfortable new furnishings, good reasonably priced food, well kept Greene King ales, decent house wines, no piped music *(Gwen and Peter Andrews)*

Danbury [Runsell Green; N of A414, just beyond green; TL7905], *Anchor*: Lots of beams, timbering, brickwork and brasses, two log fires, separate games bar, attractive dining conservatory, friendly new licensees, generous food inc daily fresh Lowestoft fish, well kept Ridleys, decent house wines *(Gwen and Peter Andrews, LYM)*

☆ **Dedham** [High St; TM0533], *Sun*: Roomy and comfortably refurbished Tudor pub, cosy panelled rooms with log fires in huge brick fireplaces, handsomely carved beams, good range of well kept ales, decent wines, generous food inc bargains Tues/Weds evening, Thurs fish night, Fri steak specials, cheerful staff, good piped music; tables on back lawn, car park behind reached through medieval arch, wonderful wrought-iron inn sign; panelled bedrooms with four-posters, good walk to or from Flatford Mill *(Quentin Williamson, LYM)*

☆ **Duton Hill** [off B184 Dunmow—Thaxted, 3 miles N of Dunmow; TL6026], *Three Horseshoes*: Welcoming licensees in quiet country pub gently updated to keep traditional atmosphere, decent low-priced food inc good value big Lincs sausages with choice of mustards in wholemeal baps, well kept Elgoods Cambridge, Ridleys IPA and two guest beers, aged armchairs by fireplace in homely left-hand parlour, interesting theatrical memorabilia and enamel advertising signs; pool in small public bar, fine views from garden where local drama groups perform in summer *(M Creasy, Gwen and Peter Andrews, JF, BB)*

☆ **Fiddlers Hamlet** [Stewards Green Rd, a mile SE of Epping; TL4700], *Merry Fiddlers*: Long low-ceilinged 17th-c country pub, lots of copper and brass, chamber-pots, beer mugs and plates, Adnams, Greene King IPA and Morlands Old Speckled Hen, usual pub food, attentive friendly staff, unobtrusive piped music, occasional live sessions; big garden with play area (can hear Mway) *(George Atkinson, A Hepburn, S Jenner, Mr and Mrs N Chesher)*

Finchingfield [TL6832], *Fox*: Splendidly pargeted late 18th-c building (older in parts), straightforward dining pub inside, clean and spacious, with jugs and brass, Greene King IPA and Abbot, pleasant service, good value food (not winter Sun evening); steps down to lavatories; open all day, tables in garden, very photogenic village *(Gwen and Peter Andrews, A Hepburn, S Jenner)*

Fordstreet [A604 W of Colchester; TL9126], *Shoulder of Mutton*: Pretty Elizabethan pub by River Colne, cosy beamed bar with log fire and country prints, welcoming service, well kept Greene King ales, food from good ploughman's to enjoyable suppers; piped music *(Clare and Roy Head, Quentin Williamson)*

☆ **Fyfield** [Church St (off B184); TL5606], *Queens Head*: Traditional welcoming local, low beams, bare boards, high-backed upholstered settles forming cosy areas, good value food counter, well kept ales such as Adnams Broadside, Elgoods, Timothy Taylor Landlord and

Thwaites Chairman, good house wine, no music *(Joy and Peter Heatherley, Gwen and Peter Andrews)*

Galleywood [Galleywood Common; TL7003], *Horse & Groom*: Greene King IPA and Abbot with a guest such as Tetleys, welcoming landlord, reasonably priced simple hearty lunchtime food *(Gwen and Peter Andrews)*

Goldhanger [B1026 E of Heybridge; TL9009], *Chequers*: Friendly old village pub with good variety of food inc extremely fresh Friday fish, well kept ales such as Greene King and Ind Coope Burton; good walks and birdwatching nearby *(Colin and Joyce Laffan, Pete Yearsley, G Neighbour)*

☆ **Great Baddow** [Galleywood Rd; or off B1007 at Galleywood Eagle; TL7204], *Seabrights Barn*: Fine Greenall Millers Kitchen family dining pub in rustic raftered barn conversion, lots for children though also a spacious child-free bar, good food (all day Sun), good friendly service, well kept ales inc a weekly guest, good choice of wines by the glass, summer barbecues; piped music may be obtrusive *(Mr and Mrs N Chesher, Peter and Gwen Andrews, LYM)*

Great Baddow [High St], *White Horse*: Friendly beamed bar and restaurant (up steps; more steps down to lavatories), well kept Hancocks HB; unobtrusive piped music, fruit machines *(Gwen and Peter Andrews)*

Great Burstead [South Green; A129 Billericay—Wickford; TQ6892], *Duke of York*: Very comfortable, with interesting local photographs, good value food from sandwiches (fine range) and baked potatoes up, wide vegetarian choice, well kept real ales, restaurant; intriguing pub booklet *(D E Twitchett)*

☆ **Great Easton** [Mill End Green; pub signed 2 miles N of Dunmow, off B184 towards Lindsell; TL6126], *Green Man*: Dates from 15th c, smart but cosy and interesting beamed bar, conservatory, decent food inc good interesting specials, welcoming service, well kept ales such as Greene King IPA and Fullers London Pride, quiet piped music; children welcome, attractive garden in pleasant rural setting *(Gwen and Peter Andrews, Quentin Williamson, John Fahy)*

nr **Great Henny** [Henny Street; Sudbury—Lamarsh rd E; TL8738], *Swan*: Cosy well furnished darkly timbered pub with well kept Greene King IPA and Abbot and Marstons Pedigree, decent wines, good coffee, partly no-smoking conservatory restaurant; children allowed, maybe unobtrusive piped music; tables on lawn by quiet river opp *(Gwen and Peter Andrews, LYM)*

☆ **Great Saling** [signed from A120; TL7025], *White Hart*: Friendly and distinctive Tudor pub with dining area in dimly lit upper gallery, ancient timbering and flooring tiles, lots of plates, brass and copperware, good speciality giant filled baps inc hot roast beef and melted cheese and other snacks served till late, well kept Adnams and Ridleys, decent wines, good service, restaurant Tues-Sat evenings, well behaved children welcome; seats outside *(Tony Beaulah, JF, Paul and Sandra Embleton, LYM)*

☆ **Great Waltham** [old A130; TL6913], *Beehive*: Neatly kept pub very popular with older people for lunch (freshly cooked, so there may be a wait), well kept Ridleys, welcoming service, good log fire; tables outside, opp attractive church – pleasant village, peaceful countryside *(PGP, Paul and Ursula Randall, Gwen and Peter Andrews)*

Great Warley Street [TQ5890], *Thatchers Arms*: Pretty Chef and Brewer in attractive village, reliable food, well kept Scottish Courage ales, helpful service *(JF)*

Harwich [Kings Head Rd; TM2632], *Alma*: Pewter, hurricane lamps and old local photographs, well kept Greene King Abbot, good basic food *(R T and J C Moggridge)*

☆ **Hatfield Broad Oak** [High St; TL5416], *Cock*: Character 15th-c beamed village pub with well kept Adnams Best, Nethergate IPA and changing guest beers, Easter beer festival, decent wines, friendly and attentive young staff, light sunny L-shaped bar with open fire, music hall song sheets and old advertisements, enjoyable food (not Sun evening) from sandwiches to interesting hot dishes, restaurant; bar billiards, juke box and darts; children in eating area *(Jackie Orme, A Nicholls, Joy and Peter Heatherley, Gwen and Peter Andrews, LYM)*

Hatfield Heath [B1054 E of Saffron Walden; TL6337], *Bluebell*: Comfortable bar with two small rooms off and restaurant, wide choice of hugely generous if not cheap food, real ales such as Morlands Old Speckled Hen; outside seating *(John Fahy, DC)*

Hatfield Heath [A1005 towards Bishops Stortford; TL5215], *Thatchers*: Friendly refurbished beamed and thatched pub with woodburner, copper kettles and brasses, well kept Greene King ales and decent house wines from long bar, wide food choice; piped music; tables out under cocktail parasols *(Gwen and Peter Andrews)*

Heybridge Basin [Lockhill; TL8707], *Old Ship*: The smarter of the two pubs here, with lots of nautical bric-a-brac, well kept ales inc Adnams Broadside and Nethergate IPA, reasonably priced food, blond wooden furniture, unobtrusive piped music; well behaved dogs welcome, no children; seats outside, some overlooking water by canal lock – lovely views of the saltings and across to Northey Island; can be very busy, esp in summer when parking nearby impossible (but public park five mins' walk) *(George Atkinson, David Dimock)*

☆ **High Easter** [off A1060 or B184 nr Leaden Roding; TL6214], *Cock & Bell*: Tudor pub with grand old beams and timbers, attractive decor, dining area up steps from lounge, log fire in second bar, cheery staff, generous home-cooked straightforward food, beers such as Batemans, Crouch Vale, Fullers London Pride, Morlands Old Speckled Hen; children welcome; piped radio may obtrude; comfortable bedrooms *(R Jupp, Eddie Edwards, LYM)*

Kirby Le Soken [B1034 Thorpe—Walton; TM2222], *Red Lion*: Attractive and pleasantly furnished 14th-c pub, relaxing at lunchtime, with friendly helpful service, good range of food inc imaginative dishes and good vegetarian choice, well kept Scottish Courage and guest ales; piped music can obtrude, predominantly young people in the evenings; good garden *(John Wilmott, Rev J Hibberd, Thomas Nott)*

Knowl Green [TL7841], *Cherry Tree*: Small thatched local on edge of pretty village, step down to rustic split-level bar, 15th-c beams, guns, brass trays, cricket photographs and vases, well kept Adnams, Greene King and guest ales, great value food, genial licensees, steps to back bar with darts and pool; garden with rustic seats and good play area *(Richard and Valerie Wright, Gwen and Peter Andrews)*

☆ **Lamarsh** [take Station Rd off B1508 Sudbury—Colchester – Lamarsh then signed; TL8835], *Lion*: Abundant timbering, pews in stalls with red velvet curtain dividers, local pictures, big log fire, no-smoking area, limited choice of hearty food (not Sun evening) from huge filled rolls to tender steaks, fresh fish Thurs/Fri, Nethergate Suffolk and guest beers such as Fullers London Pride and Greene King IPA, decent house wines, friendly staff, restaurant; children in eating area, unobtrusive piped music, pool, darts, machines; sheltered sloping garden, quiet country views *(Gwen and Peter Andrews, Ian Phillips, LYM)*

☆ **Leigh on Sea** [51 High St; TQ8385], *Crooked Billet*: Homely old pub with waterfront views from big bay windows, local fishing pictures and bric-a-brac, and still some character despite flowery-cushioned refurbishment, new panelling and rather overt piped music; well kept Tetleys-related ales and a good choice of others, peaking at spring and autumn beer festivals, home-made lunchtime food (not Sun) inc vegetarian, friendly service; open all day, new side garden and terrace, nice spot; live music nights *(Tim Heywood, Sophie Wilne, John and Enid Morris, LYM)*

Leigh on Sea [Old Leigh], *Ship*: Local with cheap drinks, a welcome for visitors, caring staff, playroom; quiz and folk nights *(Caroline Wright)*

Little Hallingbury [Hall Green, A1060 Hatfield Heath—Bishops Stortford; TL5017], *Sutton Arms*: Good interesting generous food in pleasant extended beamed and thatched pub with quick friendly service, well kept beers; fruit machine; close to M11, can get very busy *(A Hepburn, S Jenner, Gwen and Peter Andrews)*

☆ **Little Walden** [B1052; TL5441], *Crown*: Neat low-beamed L-shaped bar with big log fire, well kept Greene King IPA, Theakstons Old Peculier and Wadworths 6X tapped from the cask, decent wine, wide choice of enjoyable food from sandwiches up inc generous veg, smiling helpful service, good relaxed atmosphere; small, can get crowded *(Gwen and Peter Andrews, G Washington)*

☆ **Little Waltham** [TL7012], *Dog & Gun*: Long L-shaped timbered bar and suntrap conservatory, good food well worth the price inc good fresh veg, well kept Greene King IPA and Rayments, decent wine, good service, comfortable banquettes, unobtrusive piped music; garden with elegant willow *(Gwen and Peter Andrews)*

Littlebury [High St (B1383 NW of Saffron Walden); TL5139], *Queens Head*: New management in unassuming pub, appealing tiled area with sofa by bar, simple furnishings, partly no-smoking restaurant, good plain food (not Sun evening), well kept ales such as Bass and Marstons Bitter and Pedigree, decent wines, pleasant staff, traditional games; maybe piped music; tables out in a nicely planted walled garden with play area, open all day (Sun late afternoon closure) *(Mayur Shah, Richard Siebert, Gwen and Peter Andrews, R Wiles, H Dickinson, Mr and Mrs G Turner, LYM)*

Littley Green [2 miles SE of Felsted; TL6917], *Compasses*: Unpretentious country pub with tables in back garden and benches out in front, big huffers and ploughman's a speciality *(Tony Beaulah)*

Loughton [99 Smarts Lane; TQ4296], *Carpenters Arms*: Friendly and comfortable, with Flowers Original, carpentry tools in public bar *(Robert Lester)*

☆ **Manningtree** [Manningtree Stn, out towards Lawford; TM1031], *Station Buffet*: Clean and warm, with nostalgic early 1950s long marble-topped bar, three little tables and a handful of unassuming seats, interesting well kept ales such as Adnams, Mauldons Squire and maybe a distant guest such as Brandysnapper (all the way from Worcs), delicious sandwiches, traditional hot dishes, friendly helpful service *(Pat and Tony Martin)*

Matching Green [TL5311], *Chequers*: Quiet and friendly country local in nice spot overlooking pretty cricket green, good generous cheap food, well kept Adnams, Greene King and Fullers London Pride, good choice of wines, welcoming landlord, two bars, one with TV and lots of aircraft pictures; garden *(Gwen and Peter Andrews, A Hepburn, S Jenner)*

☆ **Mill Green** [TL6401], *Cricketers Arms*: Popular country pub/restaurant in picturesque setting, comfortable and spruce, no-smoking area, well kept Greene King IPA and Abbot tapped from the cask, cheerful staff, lots of cricketing memorabilia, some farm tools, friendly jack russell called Bonney; best to book evenings; plenty of seats out in front *(Gwen and Peter Andrews, Neil Spink, Keith and Janet Morris, Paul and Ursula Randall)*

☆ **Moreton** [signed off B184 at Fyfield or opp Chipping Ongar school; TL5307], *White Hart*: Wide choice of enjoyable briskly served food inc enormous ploughman's, good fish and veg and very popular Sun lunch (dining room should be booked then) in rambling multi-level local with small rather functional bars, sloping floor and ceilings, old local photographs, well kept ales such as Adnams, Courage Best and Directors and Everards Tiger, decent house wines, lovely log fire (with dogs), staff very friendly and helpful even when busy; pleasant circular walk from pub; bedrooms *(Joy and Peter Heatherley, Martin and Karen Wake, H O Dickinson, A Hepburn, S Jenner, M A Starling, Mr and Mrs N Chesher)*

Mundon [Roundbush Rd; B1018 S of Maldon; TL8601], *Roundbush*: Little pub with old wooden benches, no music, Greene King beers tapped from the cask, good value food Thurs-

Sat inc giant mussels and Indian dishes, helpful landlord; mainly locals *(John Wilmott)*

☆ **Navestock** [Navestock Heath – follow Sabines Green signpost off main rd; TQ5397], *Plough*: Friendly no-frills country pub with usually around eight rotating well kept ales such as Adnams, Burtonwood, Boddingtons, Brakspears, Flowers IPA and Fullers London Pride, big divided beamed room, open fire, good value usual food (not Sun evening, not Mon), small no-smoking restaurant, traditional games; unobtrusive piped music; children welcome, good garden, open all day *(John Fahy, Ted George, Dr Oscar Puls, JF, LYM)*

☆ **Newney Green** [off A414 or A1060 W of Chelmsford; TL6507], *Duck*: Comfortable dining pub with keen and friendly new owners, neat young staff, engaging rambling bar full of beams, timbering and panelling, well kept ales such as Batemans XB, Morlands Old Speckled Hen, Ridleys SX and Shepherd Neame, decent food inc vegetarian; attractive garden *(Gwen and Peter Andrews, LYM)*

Newport [Cambridge Rd (B1383); TL5234], *Coach & Horses*: Great food, five real ales inc lots of guests *(M Creasy)*

North Shoebury [Parsons Corner; TQ9485], *Angel*: Attractive conversion of timbered and partly thatched former post office, good bar food, Fullers London Pride, Greene King IPA and Abbot and a guest such as Ushers Winter Storm, restaurant popular for business lunches; jazz nights *(Richard and Robyn Wain)*

☆ **Peldon** [junction unclassified Maldon road with B1025 Peldon—Mersea; TL9916], *Rose*: Cosy low-beamed bar with creaky close-set tables, some antique mahogany, chintz curtains and leaded lights, brass and copper, well kept Flowers IPA and Wadworths 6X, decent wines, separate food counter (wide range from good sandwiches up), friendly service; children welcome away from bar, restaurant Fri/Sat evening, big no-smoking conservatory, spacious relaxing garden with geese, ducks and two ponds; bedrooms, good breakfast *(B N F and M Parkin, Hazel R Morgan, R T and J C Moggridge, E A George, LYM)*

☆ **Pleshey** [signed off A130 Dunmow—Chelmsford; TL6614], *White Horse*: Cheerful recently refurbished 15th-c pub with nooks and crannies, big dining room (should book w/e), enjoyable bar food from good big hot filled baps up, well kept Ridleys, local cider, decent wines, no music; children welcome, tables out on terrace and in garden with small safe play area; pretty village with ruined castle *(Maysie Thompson, Gwen and Peter Andrews, Tony Beaulah, Paul and Ursula Randall, Peter Baggott, DFL, LYM)*

☆ **Purleigh** [TL8401], *Bell*: Cosy rambling beamed and timbered pub up by church, fine views over the marshes and Blackwater estuary; beams, nooks and crannies, big inglenook log fire, well kept Adnams, Benskins Best, Greene King IPA and Marstons Pedigree, decent house wines, good reasonably priced home-made lunchtime food, magazines to read, welcoming staff, Benares brass and other bric-a-brac, friendly dog; picnic-sets on side grass *(Gwen and Peter Andrews, LYM)*

☆ **Radwinter** [B1053 E of Saffron Walden – OS Sheet 154 map ref 612376; TL6137], *Plough*: Neatly kept red plush open-plan black-timbered beamed bar with central log fire and separate woodburner; good popular food inc vegetarian, well kept Greene King IPA and Rayments, guests such as Shepherd Neame Spitfire, kind landlord, friendly staff, no music; children and dogs on lead welcome, very attractive terrace and garden, open countryside; bedrooms *(Gwen and Peter Andrews, C S Stolings, BB)*

Saffron Walden [Gold St; TL5438], *Old English Gentleman*: New licensees in welcoming, busy and atmospheric 16th-c town pub, good reasonably priced food from sandwiches up *(John Fahy, Geoff Meek)*

☆ **Shalford** [TL7229], *George*: Exposed beams and brickwork, decorative plates and brassware, good solid tables and chairs, log fire in enormous fireplace, good home cooking (worth the wait) inc sandwiches and vegetarian, well kept Adnams Broadside, Greene King IPA and guests, cheerful service, lots of children at weekends, unobtrusive piped music; tables on terrace *(Gwen and Peter Andrews)*

☆ **South Hanningfield** [South Hanningfield Rd; TQ7497], *Old Windmill*: Attractive 18th-c beamed and timbered building opp reservoir, areas off spacious L-shaped bar, very friendly staff, good freshly cooked food, exceptional choice of wines by the glass, well kept Theakstons Best and XB, lots of hop bines; piped music turned down on request *(Gwen and Peter Andrews)*

South Weald [Weald Rd (off A1023 – handy for M25 junction 28); TQ5793], *Tower Arms:* Above-average food all day in thoughtfully refurbished Chef & Brewer, several small high-ceilinged rooms, conservatory restaurant (not Sun-Tues evenings), well kept Scottish Courage ales with a guest such as Greene King IPA, friendly staff, family area; extensive secluded garden with boules; opp church in picturesque village *(Thomas Neate, JF)*

Southminster [2 High St; TQ9599], *Kings Head*: Clean, comfortable and friendly old pub, well cooked pub food inc vegetarian, several real ales, very helpful service *(John Wilmott, P Hunkin)*; [Althorne Rd], *Queens Head*: Good choice of drinks and of bargain food cooked by landlady, esp good pastry; very friendly landlord, big play area *(Stan and Vera Thorogood)*

St Osyth [The Bury (signed to Point Clear); TM1215], *White Hart*: Small family-run pub in row of pretty weatherboarded houses, very friendly and welcoming, with good value food, well kept ales such as Adnams, Theakstons, John Smiths and Woodfordes; small garden and barbecue *(Ian Phillips)*

Stanford Rivers [149 London Rd (A113); TL5300], *White Bear*: Small friendly bare-boards pub with well kept Greene King Abbot, good coffee, good simple food esp home-made puddings, very welcoming service, restaurant, big side garden; Weds is bikers' night – they're said to behave like angels *(Gwen and Peter Andrews, Robert Lester)*; [London Rd (A113), Little End], *Woodman*: Delightful cosy country pub with real ales such as Hop Back Summer Lightning and Nethergate Old Growler, big garden *(Robert Lester)*

Stapleford Abbotts [Oak Hill Rd (B175); TQ5096], *Royal Oak*: Attractive bar with pleasant old-fashioned atmosphere, well furnished verandah restaurant, good generous food inc Italian specialities and fine roast of the day with fresh veg, varied well kept beers, long-serving licensees, very friendly service *(Dr Oscar Puls)*

☆ **Stapleford Tawney** [about 2 miles N on Tawney Common – OS Sheet 167 map ref 500013; TL5001], *Mole Trap*: Delightful tiny low-beamed country pub, friendly landlord, well kept McMullens, rustic artefacts and framed account of how the pub got its name, two long settles for the tables in its small bar, limited basic food, pleasant seats outside; popular with walkers and cyclists *(Robert Lester, A Hepburn, S Jenner, J H Gracey, Mr and Mrs N Chesher)*

☆ **Stock** [Common Rd; just off B1007 Chelmsford—Billericay; TQ6998], *Bakers Arms*: Busy open-plan low-beamed pub with smart banquettes, above-average home-made food inc vegetarian, reasonable prices, attractive airy dining room with french windows to charming well kept small garden, good pleasant service, no piped music *(Phyl and Jack Street, S E Paulley)*

Thaxted [Bullring; TL6130], *Swan*: Thriving and attractively renovated Tudor pub opp lovely church, well kept Adnams and Greene King, warm atmosphere in extended bar areas, plenty of well spaced tables, no music, restaurant; bedrooms *(JF, Gwen and Peter Andrews)*

☆ **Theydon Bois** [Coppice Row (B172); TQ4599], *Queen Victoria*: Cosy beamed and carpeted lounge with roaring fire, local pictures, mug collection, McMullens ales, very friendly accommodating staff, well presented quick straightforward good value food, bright end dining area with interesting knick-knacks, smaller no-smoking front bar, pleasant bustle; tables on terrace *(George Atkinson, Quentin Williamson, Joy and Peter Heatherley, Roger and Pauline Pearce)*

Tillingham [South St; B1021; TL9903], *Cap & Feathers*: Low-beamed and timbered 15th-c pub, attractive old-fashioned furniture, well kept Crouch Vale Best, IPA, Best Dark and an interesting guest beer, traditional games, home-cooked bar food, no-smoking family room, picnic-sets on side terrace; three bedrooms *(John Wilmott, LYM)*

☆ **Tolleshunt Major** [TL9011], *Bell*: Country pub with beams and studwork, comfortable banquettes and bay windows in L-shaped saloon with woodburner, good smiling service even when very busy, well kept Greene King with guests such as Brains SA and Shepherd Neame Spitfire, good coffee, food inc good value Sun lunch, no music, public bar with fruit machine; children welcome, verandah and garden with big rustic pond, barbecue and play area, disabled facilities *(Colin and Joyce Laffan, Gwen and Peter Andrews)*

☆ *nr* **Waltham Abbey** [very handy for M25 junction 26; A121 towards Waltham Abbey, then follow Epping, Loughton sign from exit roundabout; TL3800], *Volunteer*: Good genuine chow mein and big pancake rolls (unless Chinese landlady away Mar/Apr) and generous more usual food in well run roomy open-plan McMullens pub, swift service even when very busy, attractive conservatory, guest beer; piped music; some tables on side terrace, pretty hanging baskets, nice spot by Epping Forest *(Joy and Peter Heatherley, Sue and Mike Todd, D and J Tapper, BB)*

Witham [Albert Rd/B1018, nr stn; TL8214], *Albert*: Straightforward open-plan town pub worth knowing for good value lunchtime bar food; well kept beer, pleasant staff; big-screen TV *(Tina and David Woods-Taylor)*; [113 Hatfield Rd (B1389); TL8214], *Jack & Jenny*: Quiet, spacious and comfortable haven just off busy A12, wide choice of good food from filled rolls and first-class ploughman's up, well kept beers, efficient friendly staff, dining conservatory, garden with shady seats *(M Clifford)*

☆ **Wivenhoe** [Black Buoy Hill, off A133; TM0321], *Black Buoy*: Charming 16th-c building, open-plan bar, cool, dark, roomy and convivial, well separated dining area with wide choice of good food inc sandwiches, local fish and interesting vegetarian dishes, well kept Greene King and weekly guest ale, open fires; piped music; tucked away from water in conservation area, but has river views *(John Fahy, Paul and Ursula Randall, Ian Phillips)*

☆ **Wivenhoe** [Quayside; TM0321], *Rose & Crown*: Friendly unspoilt Georgian pub in delightful quayside position on River Colne, genuine nautical decor with low beams, scrubbed floors and log fire, well kept Adnams Broadside, Friary Meux Best and Shepherd Neame Spitfire, local and nautical books, no piped music, waterside seats (when the tide's in) *(Quentin Williamson, John Fahy, Rev J Hibberd)*

Woodham Mortimer [A414 Danbury—Maldon; TL8104], *Royal Oak*: Well kept Benskins Best, Flowers IPA and Tetleys, adventurous menu of impressively cooked and presented food with some emphasis on fish, good service, friendly atmosphere; film industry decor, restaurant *(Rev Tom Jordan, Gwen and Peter Andrews)*

☆ **Woodham Walter** [signed off A414 E from Chelmsford; TL8006], *Bell*: Striking 16th-c pub with beams and timbers, decorative plates and lots of brass, comfortable alcoves on various levels, log fire, wide choice of well presented enjoyable bar food (not Mon) from sandwiches to steaks, pretty second dining room in partly panelled upper gallery, friendly service, Adnams, Friary Meux Best and a guest beer; children in eating areas *(David Hanstead, R Morgan, R Turnham, Beryl and Bill Farmer, Mrs M Dallisson, LYM)*

Gloucestershire

Newcomers to the main entries in this favoured county are the Five Mile House at Duntisbourne Abbots (remarkably successful extension of a gloriously old-fashioned tavern, greatly broadening its appeal without losing character), the Hollow Bottom at Guiting Power (individualistic country pub now owned by a syndicate of horse-racing notables), the friendly and prettily placed Carpenters Arms at Miserden (doing very well under new ownership), the Egypt Mill at Nailsworth (stylish conversion of a sizeable watermill), the Churchill at Paxford (very good interesting food in a rather restauranty dining pub), the Old Black Bear in Tewkesbury (the county's most ancient pub, very picturesque) and the Royal Oak at Woodchester (new licensees doing excellent food in pleasantly unpretentious surroundings – quite a find). Other pubs doing particularly well here this year include the delightfully unspoilt Boat at Ashleworth Quay, the friendly and relaxed Bear at Bisley, the engaging little Red Hart at Blaisdon (friendly young licensees, good interesting food and beers), the foody Kings Head at Bledington, the bustling Eight Bells in Chipping Campden (new licensee settling in well), the welcoming little Plough at Cold Aston, the smart and civilised New Inn at Coln St Aldwyns, the enjoyably traditional old Plough at Ford (great asparagus feasts in May), the neatly run and foody Harvest Home at Greet, the interesting Royal Oak at Gretton (gains a Beer Award this year, good food and nice surroundings too), the stylish Inn For All Seasons at Little Barrington, the busy Fox at Lower Oddington (excellent wines to go with the imaginative food), the Anchor at Oldbury on Severn (a fine traditional all-rounder, in the same hands for the last 27 years), the unpretentious Boat by the Wye at Redbrook (you cross the Welsh border when you walk over the bridge) and the cheerful prettily set Butchers Arms at Sheepscombe. The pubs on this honours roll-call underline Gloucestershire's dual strengths: a fine choice of pubs for very civilised and enjoyable meals out, as well as some splendid simple country inns and taverns. Among the foodier places, our final choice as Gloucestershire Dining Pub of the Year is the Fox at Lower Oddington; the New Inn at Coln St Aldwyns is a close rival, but the Fox carries the day with its friendlier prices. On price, we should mention the exceptional value bargain weekday lunches from the Black Horse at Amberley. A couple of changes to mention are the good new landlord at the Red Hart at Awre (bedrooms now), and new people tidying up and extending the very popular Bakers Arms at Broad Campden. Pubs scoring high points with readers these days among the Lucky Dip entries at the end of the chapter are the Red Lion at Ampney St Peter, Horse & Groom at Bourton on the Hill, Lygon Arms in Chipping Campden, Tunnel House at Coates, Highwayman near Elkstone, Glasshouse at Glasshouse, Thames Head at Kemble, Golden Ball at Lower Swell, Catherine Wheel in Marshfield, Snowshill Arms at Snowshill, Swan at Southrop, Queens Head in Stow on the Wold, Bell in Tewkesbury, Farriers Arms at Todenham (the only one of these that we have not yet been able to inspect and approve ourselves) and Ram at Woodchester. Drinks prices here are a little below the national average, particularly in pubs tied to small brewers such as Smiles, Wadworths and the local Donnington. Pubs supplied by the national combines tended to be the most expensive.

ALMONDSBURY ST6084 Map 2

Bowl

1¼ miles from M5, junction 16 (and therefore quite handy for M4, junction 20); from A38 towards Thornbury, turn first left signposted Lower Almondsbury, then first right down Sundays Hill, then at bottom right again into Church Road

Very handy for the M5, this bustling pub keeps a good range of real ales and is well liked for its wide choice of bar food: sandwiches (£2.50; toasties from £2.75; filled french bread £3.75), home-made soup (£2.95), burgers (from £3.75), popular rack of ribs (£5.75 or £8.95), fish and chips or mushroom-filled pasta with pesto, white wine and cream sauce (£5.95), cajun chicken fajitas (£6.95), pork chop in a honey, mustard and walnut crust or steak and stilton pie (£7.95), vegetarian or meaty lasagne (from £7.25), luxury fish bake (£8.95), and puddings (£3.35); service can slow down under pressure but remains pleasant. They charge extra if you eat bar meals in the restaurant. The long neatly kept beamed bar has blue plush-patterned modern settles, pink cushioned stools and mate's chairs around elm tables, quite a few horsebrasses, stripped bare stone walls, and a big winter log fire at one end, with a woodburning stove at the other; one area of the bar and another in the restaurant are no smoking. Well kept Courage Best and Directors, Morlands Old Speckled Hen, Otter Bright, Smiles Best, and Theakstons XB on handpump, several malt whiskies, and a decent wine list; fruit machine, piped music. The brown spaniel is called Charlie, another dog Corrie, and there's a black and white cat. The flowering tubs, hanging baskets and window boxes are pretty, a back terrace overlooks a field, and there are some picnic-sets across the quiet road. *(Recommended by D Parkhurst, Gwen and Peter Andrews, Dave Braisted, John and Christine Simpson, Lawrence Pearse, Michael and Lorna Bourdeaux, N P Cox, Peter Neate, Paul Barnett, Mr and Mrs R Maggs, Alan and Paula McCully, J and B Cressey, Daren Haines, Ian and Jane Irving, Amanda and Simon Southwell, Mr and Mrs M J Bastin)*

Courage ~ Lease: John Alley ~ Real ale ~ Meals and snacks (till 10pm) ~ Restaurant ~ (01454) 612757 ~ Children welcome ~ Open 11-3, 5(6 Sat)-11; 11-3, 7-10.30 Sun; closed evening 25 Dec ~ Bedrooms: £32.50B/£52.50B

AMBERLEY SO8401 Map 4

Black Horse £

Village signposted off A46 Stroud—Nailsworth; as you pass village name take first very sharp left turn (before Amberley Inn) then bear steeply right – pub on your left

It's not surprising that this pub gets so busy on Monday-Thursday as they offer many of the dishes on their menu for £3.95. Bar food includes soup (£1.95), tapas (£2.95), ploughman's (£3.25), sausages and chips (£3.95), steak in ale pie, ham and egg, vegetable pie or lasagne (all £4.95), cajun chicken (£5.95), swordfish steak (£6.95), vegetable or chicken fajitas (from £6.95), and steaks (from £7.95); fish and chips on Friday £3.50, brunch on Saturday £4.95, and Sunday lunch £4.95. The dining bar has wheelback chairs, green-cushioned window seats, a few prints on the plain cream walls, and a fire in a small stone fireplace, and there's a conservatory, and a family bar on the left which is no smoking. A good range of well kept real ales on handpump such as Archers Village, Best and Golden, Dartmoor Best, Ind Coope Burton, Moles Bitter, Uley Bitter, and Wadworths 6X. Darts, pool, and skittle alley. A back terrace has teak seats, picnic-sets, and a barbecue and spit roast area, and on the other side of the building, a lawn with pretty flowers and honeysuckle has more seats. There are remarkable views of the surrounding hills. *(Recommended by D Irving, R Huggins, T McLean, E McCall, Peter and Audrey Dowsett, Michael Gittins, Dave and Deborah Irving, Andy and Jill Kassube, Deborah and David Rees)*

Free house ~ Licensee Patrick O'Flynn ~ Real ale ~ Meals and snacks ~ (01453) 872556 ~ Children welcome ~ Occasional live duo ~ Open 12-3, 6-11; 12-11 Sat; 12-10.30 Sun – closed winter weekend afternoons

AMPNEY CRUCIS SP0602 Map 4

Crown of Crucis

A417 E of Cirencester

By the time this book is published, the spacious bar here will have been redecorated and refurnished to give a more modern feel; they also plan to install a disabled lavatory and baby changing facilities. The no-smoking restaurant has also been revamped with a fresh blue and yellow theme to go with the stripped oak tables and wooden floor. It's a friendly place with a hospitable licensee and pleasant staff, and good popular food: home-made soup (£2.60), sandwiches (from £3), grilled chicken, bacon and avocado salad (small £4.30, large £6.10), ploughman's (£4.50), mushroom stroganoff (£6), chicken balti (£6.25), salmon in a chive and cream sauce (£5.90), sirloin steak (£9.75), a lunchtime home-made special (£4.25) with other daily specials such as crostini of goat's cheese (£4.30), or confit of salmon with caramelised onions (£5.90), home-made puddings (£2.70), and children's menu (£2.60). Well kept Archers Village, Marstons Pedigree, and Wadworths 6X on handpump. This is a nice place to stay with some rooms overlooking the village cricket pitch and stream with ducks and maybe swans; the back grass has lots of tables with the same view. *(Recommended by Mike and Heather Watson, David and Helen Wilkins, Simon Collett-Jones, R C Watkins, W Osborn-King, Mrs S Evans, Dorsan Baker, Tony Dickinson, TRS, TBB, NWN)*

Free house ~ Licensee Ken Mills ~ Real ale ~ Meals and snacks (12-2.30, 6-10) ~ Restaurant ~ (01285) 851806 ~ Children welcome until 8.30 ~ Open 11-11; 12-10.30 Sun; closed 25 Dec ~ Bedrooms: £56B/£82B

APPERLEY SO8628 Map 4

Farmers Arms

Lower Apperley; nr Apperley on B4213, which is off A38 N of Gloucester

If you ask, you can usually look round the little thatched, modern brick brewhouse in the grounds of this extended friendly local. They brew Mayhems Oddas Light and Sundowner Heavy, and also keep Wadworths 6X on handpump. The bar has guns lining the beams, old prints, horseshoes and stuffed pheasants dotted about, coal-effect gas fires, and plenty of room – though you'll generally find most people in the comfortable and spacious dining lounge; piped music. Fresh fish is delivered daily, which leads to several interesting blackboard specials, and there's also open sandwiches (from £2.60), ploughman's (from £3.75), lasagne, lamb in rosemary and red wine, pork in cider and sage or beef in ale pie (all £5.95), mushroom stroganoff (£6.95), steaks (from £7.75), and puddings (£2.95); friendly service. The neat garden has picnic-sets by a thatched well, with a wendy house and play area. *(Recommended by Alan and Paula McCully, Simon Hulme, Iain Robertson, Tom Evans, Sue and Bob Ward, Mike and Mary Carter, Daren Haines, Andy and Jill Kassube)*

Own brew/Wadworths ~ Manager Geoffrey Adams ~ Real ale ~ Meals and snacks (till 10pm) ~ Restaurant ~ (01452) 780307 ~ Children welcome ~ Open 10.30-3, 6-11; 12-3.30, 7-10.30 Sun

ASHLEWORTH QUAY SO8125 Map 4

Boat ★

Ashleworth signposted off A417 N of Gloucester; Quay signed from village

The charming landladies work hard at preserving the unique character of this gentle, unspoilt old cottage. It has been in the same family since it was originally granted a licence by Charles II – this must be a record for continuous pub ownership. Spotlessly kept, the little front parlour has a great built-in settle by a long scrubbed deal table that faces an old-fashioned open kitchen range with a side bread oven and a couple of elderly fireside chairs; there are rush mats on the scrubbed flagstones, houseplants in the window, fresh garden flowers, and old magazines to read; shove-ha'penny, dominoes and cribbage (the front room has darts and a game called Dobbers). A pair of flower-cushioned antique settles face each other in the back room where Arkells BBB, Oakhill Yeoman, and Smiles Best and guests like Bath SPA, Brandycask Whistling Joe, Cottage Southern Bitter, Hambleton Bitter, RCH East Street Cream and Pitchfork, and Wye Valley Bitter are tapped from the cask, along with a full range of Westons farm ciders. They usually do good lunchtime rolls (from £1.50) or ploughman's with home-made chutney (£4.60) during the week. This is a lovely spot on the bank of the River Severn and there's a front suntrap crazy-paved courtyard, bright with plant tubs in summer, with a couple of picnic-sets under cocktail parasols; more seats and tables under cover at the sides. The medieval tithe barn nearby is striking; some readers prefer to park here and walk to the pub. *(Recommended by Iain Robertson, JP, PP, Mrs A Oakley, P and S White, Pete Baker, Dave Irving, Roger Huggins, Tom McLean, Ewan McCall, D H and M C Watkinson, Stephen Pine, Alfred Lawrence, Andy and Jill Kassube, Peter and Anne Cornall, Mike and Mary Carter, Daren Haines)*

Free house ~ Licensees Irene Jelf and Jacquie Nicholls ~ Real ale ~ Lunchtime snacks ~ (01452) 700272 ~ Children welcome till 8pm ~ Open 11-2.30(3 Sat), 6-11; 12-3, 7-10.30 Sun; winter evening opening 7pm; closed Weds lunchtime Oct-Mar

AUST ST5789 Map 2

Boars Head

½ mile from M4, junction 21; village signposted from A403

Two extra rooms have been opened up here – a small dining room and a sitting room. The neatly kept and comfortable main bar has well polished country kitchen tables and others made from old casks, old-fashioned high-backed winged settles in stripped pine, decorative plates hanging from one stout black beam, some walls stripped back to the dark stone, big rugs on dark lino, and a large log fire. Another room has a second log fire, while a third has more dining tables with lace tablecloths, fresh flowers and candles. Popular bar food includes sandwiches, good soup (£2.95), melted brie and redcurrant jelly (£4), spinach and mushroom lasagne or sausage and mash (£5.95), deep-fried spicy prawns (£6.25), smoked haddock and eggs (£6.95), gammon and egg (£7.50), steaks (£9.25), daily specials such as lancashire hotpot (£6.95), half roast pheasant (£7.95), and salmon steak (£9.25), and puddings like fruit crumble or chewy chocolate cheesequake (£3.25). Part of the eating area is no smoking; piped music. Well kept Bass, Courage Best and Directors, and Hardy Royal Oak on handpump; quite a few malt whiskies. There's a medieval stone well in the pretty sheltered garden, which has an aviary and rabbits. Also a touring caravan site. *(Recommended by James and Ruth Morrell, Philip and Jude Simmons, S H Godsell, Charles and Pauline Stride, Simon and Amanda Southwell, Jack and Gemima Valiant, Mrs B Sugarman, Meg and Colin Hamilton, Stan Edwards; more reports please)*

Hardy ~ Manageress Mary May ~ Real ale ~ Meals and snacks (not Sun evening) ~ (01454) 632278 ~ Children allowed anywhere away from bar ~ Open 11-3, 6.30-11; 12-3, 7-10.30 Sun

AWRE SO7108 Map 4

Red Hart

Village signposted off A48 S of Newnham

Welcoming, helpful new licensees have taken over this attractive and surprisingly tall country pub, and have introduced a new menu and raised the number of real ales they keep to five. The neat L-shaped main part of the bar has a deep glass-covered illuminated well, an antique pine bookcase filled with their cookery books, an antique pine display cabinet with Worcester china, an upholstered wall settle, and wheelback chairs; there are plates on a delft shelf at the end, as well as a gun and a stuffed pheasant over the stone fireplace, and big prints on the walls. Good bar food now includes sandwiches or filled baked potatoes (from £3.95), ploughman's (£5.25), tortillas with chilli con carne, home-baked ham and egg or broccoli and cream cheese bake (£5.95), seafood pancake (£6.95), and daily specials such as tomato and tarragon soup (£2.40), home-made smoked trout pâté (£3.75), mushroom stroganoff (£5.25), french bread filled with spicy smoked sausage or steak (from £5.25), moussaka (£5.75), stir-fried chicken with peppers and cashews or steak and kidney pie (£5.95), beef carbonnade or cold poached salmon (£6.95), steaks (from £9.25); the restaurant is no smoking. Well kept Bass, plus four changing guests like Cottage Champflower Ale, Everards Tiger, Freeminers Speculation, and Hampshire Pride of Romsey on handpump, a growing collection of malt whiskies, and varied wine list; darts, cribbage, dominoes, fruit machine and piped music. In front of the building are some picnic-sets. *(Recommended by Neil Townend, Alan and Paula McCully, S H Godsell, Daren Haines; more reports on the new regime, please)*

Free house ~ Licensees Nicola and Jerry Bedwell ~ Real ale ~ Meals and snacks ~ Restaurant ~ (01594) 510220 ~ Children welcome ~ Open 11-11; 12-10.30 Sun; 12-3, 5.30-11 in winter ~ Bedrooms: /£55B

BARNSLEY SP0705 Map 4

Village Pub

A433 Cirencester—Burford

Enjoyable food and a friendly welcome are what readers like about this relaxing pub. Served by helpful staff, the menu might include sandwiches (from £2.25), filled bagels or toasted muffins (from £3.25), grilled fresh sardines (£3.50), smoked trout and cream cheese pâté (£3.75), ploughman's (from £3.75), cold gammon and egg (£5.45), home-made steak and kidney pie (£6), chicken curry (£6.45), and daily specials such as quorn tikka masala (£5.75), beef in Guinness or lamb and apricot casserole (£7.25), with evening steaks (from £9.25); the dining area is no smoking. Well kept Hook Norton Bitter and Wadworths 6X on handpump, and country wines. The walls of the comfortable low-ceilinged communicating rooms are decorated with country pictures, gin-traps, scythes and other farm tools, and there are several winter log fires, as well as plush chairs, stools and window settles around the polished tables (which have candles in the evening). Darts, cribbage, dominoes, and piped music. The sheltered back courtyard has plenty of tables, and its own outside servery. The pub is handy for Rosemary Verey's garden in the village. *(Recommended by Gordon, Sidney and Erna Wells, Maysie Thompson, Dave Irving, Roger Huggins, Tom McLean, Ewan McCall, Paul S McPherson, Simon Collett-Jones, D H and M C Watkinson, N C Hinton, Richard and Stephanie Scholey, Derek Wilkinson, Dorsan Baker)*

Free house ~ Licensee Mrs Susan Wardrop ~ Real ale ~ Meals and snacks ~ Restaurant ~ (01285) 740421 ~ Children welcome ~ Open 11-3, 6-11; 12-3, 6-10.30 Sun; closed 25 Dec ~ Bedrooms: £25(£30B)/£35(£45B)

BISLEY SO9006 Map 4

Bear

Village signposted off A419 just E of Stroud

In a steep and attractive stone-built village, this elegant rather gothic little building has a good relaxed atmosphere and friendly staff and locals. The meandering L-shaped bar has a long shiny black built-in settle and a smaller but even sturdier oak settle by the front entrance, and an enormously wide low stone fireplace (not very high – the ochre ceiling's too low for that); a separate no-smoking stripped-stone area is used for families. Good home-made bar food includes soup (£2.25), lots of filled french bread (from £3; black pudding, tomato and fried egg £4), burgers like sweet and sour pork, smoked haddock and caper or lamb liver, apple and sage or sautéed potatoes with various toppings (from £4.25), home-made pies and casseroles – rabbit and vegetable stew with herb dumplings, vegetable pasty or Moroccan spiced lamb hotpot (from £5), and puddings (£2.25); small helpings for children, and good breakfasts. Well kept Bass, Flowers Original, Tetleys, Whitbread Castle Eden, and a weekly guest beer on handpump; helpful, attentive service. Darts, table skittles, cribbage, and dominoes. A small front colonnade supports the upper floor of the pub, and the sheltered little flagstoned courtyard made by this has a traditional bench; as well as the garden across the quiet road, there's quite a collection of stone mounting-blocks. *(Recommended by Richard Gibbs, Mike and Mary Carter, Greg Kilminster, Mike and Heather Watson, P and S White, Nick and Meriel Cox, Tim and Linda Collins, Mr and Mrs D Hack, George Atkinson, F and A Parmenter, Daren Haines, CLS, RMB)*

Pubmaster ~ Tenant Nick Evans ~ Real ale ~ Meals and snacks (till 10pm; not Sun evening or 25-26 Dec) ~ (01452) 770265 ~ Children in family room ~ Open 11-3, 6-11; 12-3, 7-10.30 Sun; open all day Sat and Sun if busy in summer; closed evenings 25-26 Dec ~ Bedrooms: £18/£36

BLAISDON SO7017 Map 4

Red Hart

Village signposted off A4136 just SW of junction with A40 W of Gloucester; OS Sheet 162 map reference 703169

Very much enjoyed by readers, this bustling pub is a warmly friendly place with attentive, chatty licensees, a fine choice of real ales, and good, interesting food. The flagstoned main bar has pink-cushioned wall and window seats, traditional pub tables, a big sailing-ship painting above the good log fire, and a thoroughly relaxing atmosphere – helped along by well reproduced piped bluesy music, and maybe Spotty the perky young jack russell. There are always five real ales on handpump that change regularly from a list such as Cottage, Exe Valley, Goff's, RCH, Timothy Taylor, Uley, Woods and Wychwood, and so forth; a decent wine list. On the right, an attractive two-room no-smoking dining area with some interesting prints has good home-cooked specials such as ham, egg and bubble and squeak (£4.75), smoked chicken and avocado salad or good salmon and coriander fishcakes with hollandaise sauce (£3.75 starter, £5.95 main course), hickory smoked rib of pork, chicken, ham and sweetcorn pie, good curries, roast monkfish with parma ham on a bed of spinach (£8.50), rack of lamb with port and cranberries (£9.50), and steaks; sandwiches and children's menu. A comfortable little separate games room has a well lit pool table, cribbage, dominoes, and table skittles; piped music. There are some picnic-sets out beside flower beds by the quiet road, and more in a pretty garden up behind (where they have developed a barbecue area). Dogs welcome on a lead. *(Recommended by F J and A Parmenter, Stephen and Tracey Groves, Mike and Mary Carter, Ted George, Neil and Anita Christopher, S Godsell)*

Free house ~ Licensee Guy Wilkins ~ Real ale ~ Meals and snacks ~ Restaurant ~ (01452) 830477 ~ Children welcome ~ Open 12-3(7 Sun), 6-11(10.30 Sun)

BLEDINGTON SP2422 Map 4

Kings Head ★

B4450

Although there is quite an emphasis on dining in this bustling pub in its pretty setting by the village green, the friendly licensees are keen that customers do just drop in for a pint of beer and a chat, and there are usually tables that have not been reserved. The spotlessly kept, smart main bar is full of ancient beams and other atmospheric furnishings, such as high-backed wooden settles, gateleg or pedestal tables, and there's a warming log fire in the stone inglenook (which has a big black kettle hanging in it); the lounge looks on to the garden, and to the left of the bar is a carpeted sitting room with comfortable new sofas, magazines to read, views of the village green from a small window, and some attractive antiques and old gilt-edged paintings on the walls. At lunchtime, bar food includes home-made soup (£2.25), sandwiches served with straw potatoes and salad (from £3.25; cumbrian ham on a warm brioche with egg and sloeberry jelly £4.25), tatin of basil, mozzarella and tomato (£3.95), vegetable frittata (£4.25), braised chicken and cider, marinated pork honeyed ribs or sautéed liver with calvados cream (£5.95), mussel and monkfish pot (£6.95), and children's menu (from £1.50); in the evening, there might be pork crackling and apple cider dip (£1.95), spaghetti carbonara tossed with smoked herring (£3.25), black pudding grilled and layered on to a potato rosti with fresh king scallop and pepper sauce (£4.95), steak and mushroom pie (£6.95), pork fillet fried with oranges, vanilla and saffron risotto (£8.95), steaks (from £9.95), half a honey-roast duck with a peppered sherry sauce and pear and parsnip purée (£12.95), specials like haddock and courgette cakes presented on to iced bloody mary (£4.95), various pasta dishes (£6.95), pigeon and quail breasts with redcurrant juices (£8.95), red mullet baked with garlic, pink grapefruit and whisky (£9.95), good value three-course meals (£9.95). An antique bar counter dispenses well kept Adnams Broadside, Hook Norton Best, Shepherd Neame Spitfire, Timothy Taylor Landlord, Uley Old Spot, and Wychwood Hobgoblin, an excellent extensive wine list, with 10 by the glass, and 50 or so malt whiskies; efficient, friendly service. Part of the restaurant area is no smoking; piped music. The public bar has bar billiards, shove-ha'penny, table skittles, dominoes, and piped music. The back garden has tables that look over to a little stream with lots of ducks. *(Recommended by Stephen and Julie Brown, Martin and Catherine Snelling, Sandra and Keith Abbley, D W Evans, RJH, J H Jones, Bett and Brian Cox, Keith and Margaret Kettell, Maysie Thompson, Phil and Caroline Welch, Eddie Edwards, Pam Adsley, Susan and John Douglas, John and Betty Howe, Mrs C Fielder, Dave Irving, Roger Huggins, Tom McLean, Ewan McCall, Liz Bell, Tony Hall, Melanie Jackson, John Bowdler, Kevin Plant, Robert Whittle, Derek Hayman, John and Hazel Waller, Michael Kirby, Andrew Hudson)*

Free house ~ Licensees Michael and Annette Royce ~ Real ale ~ Meals and snacks (12-2, 6.30-10) ~ Restaurant ~ (01608) 658365 ~ Children in restaurant ~ Open 11-3, 6-11; 12-2.30, 7-10.30 Sun; closed 24/25 Dec ~ Bedrooms: £45B/£65B

BLOCKLEY SP1634 Map 4

Crown ★

High Street

There's a relaxed and civilised atmosphere in this golden stone Elizabethan inn and the three rooms of the split-level bar tend to fill up quickly with customers keen to enjoy the very good food – though locals do drop in for just a drink and a chat. There are comfortable padded green leather chairs and plush stools around pubby tables, padded window seats, various prints on the walls, and an open fire; a sitting room has newspapers to read, comfortable sofas and chairs, and another open fire, and the brasserie is now upstairs; piped music. Bar food includes home-made soup (£2.95), good pâté, sandwiches (from £3.50 for 1½ rounds), popular cod in beer batter with home-made chips (£7.95), macaroni with morilles au gratin or chicken and bacon with roast peppers and chutney on a baguette (£7.95), sardines stuffed with asparagus and bacon, braised knuckle of lamb with garlic and ginger, home-made steak and kidney pudding or chicken korma with a pineapple fritter (£8.95), local seasonal game (£12.95), and home-made puddings (£3.95); good Sunday lunch (£9.95). Well kept Goff's Jouster, Hook Norton Best, and Wadworths 6X on handpump, a large choice of wines, several malt whiskies, and freshly squeezed fruit juice; friendly staff. The terraced coachyard is surrounded by beautiful trees and shrubs, and there's a hatch to hand drinks down to people sitting out in front, by the lane. The inn is handy for Batsford Park Arboretum. *(Recommended by Rob Whittle, N Christopher, SLC, David Edwards, Joy and Peter Heatherley, Lawrence Pearse, LM, Dorothy and Leslie Pilson, Liz Bell, Mick and Jeanne Shillington, Mike and Maggie Betton, John and Hazel Waller, E V Walder, D P Brown, Martin and Karen Wake, Ted George, M and C Starling, D and M Watkinson, Bob and Maggie Atherton, J Rankin, R Davies)*

Free house ~ Licensees John and Betty Champion ~ Real ale ~ Meals (not in bar Sat evening) and snacks ~ Restaurant ~ (01386) 700245 ~ Well behaved children welcome ~ Open 11-11; 12-10.30 Sun ~ Bedrooms: £64B/£89B

If you enjoy your visit to a pub, please tell the publican. They work extraordinarily long hours, and when people show their appreciation it makes it all seem worth while.

BRIMPSFIELD SO9312 Map 4

Golden Heart

Nettleton Bottom; A417 Birdlip—Cirencester

As well as a good choice of real ales on handpump or tapped from the cask, this extended partly 16th-c pub also has a wide range of wines by the glass and quite a few whiskies: Bass, Hook Norton, Marstons Pedigree, Timothy Taylor Landlord and various guests. They hold beer festivals during the May and August bank holidays. The main low-ceilinged bar is divided into three cosily distinct areas, with a roaring log fire in the huge stone inglenook fireplace in one, traditional built-in settles and other old-fashioned furnishings throughout, and quite a few brass items, typewriters, exposed stone, and wood panelling. A comfortable parlour on the right has another decorative fireplace, and leads into a further room that opens on to the terrace; two rooms are no smoking. Served by friendly staff, bar food might include good sandwiches, generous ploughman's, steak and Guinness pie, stuffed breast of chicken or kangaroo and black cherry (all £7.95), wild boar casserole, ostrich steak (£10.95), and crocodile and mango (£12.95). There are pleasant views down over a valley from the rustic cask-supported tables on its suntrap gravel terrace; good nearby walks. *(Recommended by JP, PP, Chris and Ann Garnett, N Christopher, P and S White, Dave Irving, Ewan McCall, Roger Huggins, Tom McLean, David Ling, D G King, Jo Rees, Neil and Anita Christopher, Tony Dickinson, Lynda Payton, Sam Samuells)*

Free house ~ Licensee Catherine Stevens ~ Real ale ~ Meals and snacks (till 10pm) ~ (01242) 870261 ~ Children welcome ~ Open 11-3, 6-11; 12-3, 7-10.30 Sun ~ Bedrooms: £35B/£55B

BROAD CAMPDEN SP1637 Map 4

Bakers Arms ★

Village signposted from B4081 in Chipping Campden

New licensees have taken over this traditional village pub and are building an extension – though they aim to preserve the unpretentious character and have no noisy games machines, juke box or piped music. The tiny beamed bar has a pleasant mix of tables and seats around the walls (which are stripped back to bare stone), and an inglenook fireplace at one end. The oak bar counter is attractive, and there's a big framed rugwork picture of the pub. Bar food at lunchtime includes sandwiches (from £2.95), ploughman's (from £3.25), cottage pie, chicken curry or smoked haddock bake (£4.50), and a pie of the day (£5.95), with evening dishes such as a couple of vegetarian choices (£4.50), local bangers and mash with a port and onion gravy (£4.95), chicken supreme (£5.95), pork steak in cider (£6.25), and fish pie (£6.75); Sunday roast lunch (£4.95). Well kept Adnams Bitter and Marstons Pedigree with changing guests like Fullers London Price, Morlands Old Speckled Hen, Shepherd Neame Bishops Finger or Spitfire, and Charles Wells Bombardier on handpump or tapped from the cask. Darts, cribbage, dominoes. There are white tables under cocktail parasols by flower tubs on a side terrace and in the back garden, some seats under an arbour, and a play area. The tranquil village is handy for the Barnfield cider mill. *(Recommended by Jenny and Michael Back, Mrs G Connell, Ann and Bob Westbrook; more reports on the new regime, please)*

Free house ~ Licensees Ray and Sally Mayo ~ Real ale ~ Meals and snacks ~ (01386) 840515 ~ Children in eating area of bar ~ Folk night 3rd Tues of month ~ Open 11.30-2.30, 6(6.30 in winter)-11; 12-3, 7-10.30 Sun; closed 25 Dec, evening 26 Dec

CHEDWORTH SP0511 Map 4

Seven Tuns

Queen Street, Upper Chedworth; village signposted off A429 NE of Cirencester; then take second signposted right turn and bear left towards church

This is rather a useful stop after a visit to the nearby famous Roman villa. The cosy little lounge on the right has comfortable seats and decent tables, sizeable antique prints, tankards hanging from the beam over the serving bar, a partly boarded ceiling, a good winter log fire in the big stone fireplace, and a relaxed, quiet atmosphere; no muddy boots in here. The basic public bar on the left is more lively, and opens into a games room with darts, pool, cribbage, dominoes, pinball, fruit machine, video game, and juke box; there's also a skittle alley (which can be hired). Bar food changes daily and includes home-made gloucester old spot pork and apple pie (£5.95), fresh and smoked salmon fishcakes with parsley sauce or fresh dressed Cornish crab with a ginger and orange scented mayonnaise (£6.95), chicken with a crisp parma ham crust and chunky salsa or grilled marinated lamb steaks (£7.95), dover sole (£9.95), and steaks (24 hours notice); the bread with the soup or ploughman's is home-made. Well kept George's Traditional and Premium (from a small Bristol brewery) and Theakstons XB on handpump; friendly, helpful staff. Across the road is a little walled raised terrace with a waterwheel and a stream, and there are plenty of tables both here and under cocktail parasols on a side terrace. *(Recommended by Simon Collett-Jones, Tom McLean, Roger Huggins, Ewan McCall, Dave Irving, Nick and Meriel Cox, Neil and Anita Christopher, Paul and Judith Booth, JKW, J H Kane, Alan and Barbara Mence, Liz Bell, John and Lynn Busenbark, Tony Dickinson)*

Free house ~ Licensee B Eacott ~ Real ale ~ Meals and snacks (not Sun evening or Mon lunchtime) ~ (01285) 720242 ~ Well behaved children in eating area of the bar ~ Open 12-2.30, 6.30-11; 11.30-11 Sat; 12-10.30 Sun; closed winter Mon

CHIPPING CAMPDEN SP1539 Map 4

Eight Bells

Church Street (which is one way – entrance off B4035)

Under a new licensee, this handsome inn, dating from the 13th or 14th c, has a good bustling atmosphere. There are cushioned pews and solid dark wood furniture on the broad flagstones, stripped stone walls (with caricatures of regulars and photographs of pub events), heavy oak beams with massive timber supports, and log fires in up to three restored stone fireplaces – one enormous one has a painting of the pub in summer; the bar extension has a fine rug on the wall and a glass inlet in the floor showing part of the passage from the church by which Roman Catholic priests could escape from the Roundheads. Several areas are no smoking. Good bar food now includes cauliflower soup with stilton cream and sage oil (£2.95), breast of pigeon with foie gras and toasted pine kernels (£4.75), pasta in red pepper sauce with two pestos (£6.25), scallops with a salad of artichokes, capers and crisp bacon (£6.50), escalope of salmon with smoked salmon, white wine and cream chive sauce (£8), good calf liver with creamed leeks, port and green pepper sauce (£10.50), nice red mullet, and puddings like poached pear and blackcurrant coulis with strawberry ice cream, iced pineapple and coconut terrine with melon and banana or sticky toffee pudding (£3.50). Well kept Adnams, Marstons Pedigree and Morlands Old Speckled Hen on handpump on a striking oak bar counter, and a decent wine list. A fine old courtyard surrounded by roses and climbers has picnic-sets. *(Recommended by Gwen and Peter Andrews, P and W White, Wendy Arnold, H Dickinson, Paul S McPherson, Martin Jones, David Shillitoe, Roger and Fiona Todd, IHR, R Davies, Nick Lawless, Andrew and Ruth Triggs)*

Free house ~ Licensees Kirstie Sykes ~ Real ale ~ Meals and snacks ~ Restaurant ~ (01386) 840371 ~ Children in eating area of bar ~ Open 11-11; 12-10.30 Sun; 11-3, 5.30-11 in winter; closed 25 Dec ~ Bedrooms: £42B/£45B

Noel Arms

Charles II is reputed to have stayed here after the Battle of Worcester in 1651 – the inn was already 300 years old by then. It's a smart place with old oak settles, attractive old tables, seats and newer settles among the windsor chairs, casks hanging from the beams, armour, and farm tools, horseshoes and gin-traps on the bare stone walls; there's a winter coal fire, and a conservatory behind. The small lounge areas are comfortable and traditionally furnished with coach horns, lantern lighting, and some stripped stonework, and the reception area has its quota of pikes, halberds, swords, muskets, and breastplates. Well kept Bass, Hook Norton Best, and a guest beer on handpump kept under light blanket pressure, and quite a few malt whiskies; piped music. Decent bar food includes sandwiches or filled french bread (from £3), filled baked potatoes (from £3.25), ploughman's (£4.75), smoked mackerel salad (£3.95), ham and egg (£4.75), lasagne (£4.95), steak and kidney pie (£5.95), chicken with a rich red wine sauce (£7.25), steaks, daily specials, and puddings; the restaurant is no smoking. The sunny enclosed courtyard has lots of pretty hanging baskets. No children. *(Recommended by Mr and Mrs L Pilson, Pam Adsley, Andrew and Ruth Triggs, Neil and Anthony Huxter, George Atkinson, SLC, M Joyner)*

Free house ~ Licensee Paul Rees ~ Real ale ~ Lunchtime bar meals and snacks ~ Restaurant ~ (01386) 840317 ~ Open 11-3, 6-11; 11-11 Sat; 12-10.30 Sun; 11-3, 6-11 in winter ~ Bedrooms: £70B/£99B

CLEARWELL SO5708 Map 4

Wyndham Arms

B4231, signposted from A466 S of Monmouth towards Lydney

Well placed for exploring the area, this 600-year-old family run inn has three acres of lovely gardens, and seats on the neat terraces. The smart and friendly beamed bar has red plush seats and velvet curtains, a collection of flat-irons in its spacious inglenook fireplace, and two big unusual patchwork pictures on its bared stone walls. Well kept Bass on handpump, 30 malt whiskies, a very good range of generously served wines by the glass (12) or half bottle – and gherkins, onions and olives on the counter; good service from smartly turned-out staff. Good bar food includes home-made soup (£2.50), sandwiches (from £3; open ones from £4.25), ploughman's (£4.25), home-made pâtés like cheese and fresh herb or chicken liver (£3.45), poached haddock (£3.95), filled giant yorkshire pudding (£4.95), a pasta dish of the day (£5.95), a generous breakfast (£7.50), spinach and cheese roulade or deep-fried fillet of fresh lemon sole (£9.25), lamb liver and bacon (£9.75), steaks (from £11.50), sweet and sour duck breast (£12.50), and puddings like profiteroles or sherry trifle (£3); the restaurant is no smoking, and there's also a Grill Room. The huge black newfoundland is called Brian. This is a comfortable place to stay, with excellent breakfasts, and you can stay free on Sundays if you eat in the restaurant. *(Recommended by Gwen and Peter Andrews, Alan and Barbara Mence, Dave Irving, Roger Huggins, Tom McLean, E McCall, E H and R F Warner, Wayne Brindle, G and T Edwards, LM; more reports please)*

Free house ~ Licensees John and Robert Stanford ~ Real ale ~ Meals and snacks ~ Restaurant ~ (01594) 833666 ~ Children welcome ~ Open 11-11; 12-10.30 Sun ~ Bedrooms: £54.50B/£70B

COLD ASTON SP1219 Map 4

Plough

Village signposted from A436 and A429 SW of Stow on the Wold; beware that on some maps the village is called Aston Blank, and the A436 called the B4068

Cool on a hot summer's day and warm and cosy in winter, this welcoming and tiny 17th-c pub is divided into snug areas by standing timbers. There are low black beams, a built-in white-painted traditional settle facing the stone fireplace, simple old-fashioned seats on the flagstone and lime-ash floor, and a happy mix of customers. Good bar food at lunchtime includes filled rolls (from £2.75), ploughman's (£4.25), filled baked potatoes (from £4.50), tasty spinach and ricotta cannelloni (£5.25), steak in ale pie (£5.50), and scampi and king prawn platter (£6.96), with evening dishes such as fresh salmon on a bed of leeks with a dill sauce or calf liver and bacon with garlic mash and onion gravy (£8.95), duck breast with an orange sauce (£9.50), pork with calvados sauce or enjoyable half a shoulder of lamb (£9.95), and medallions of fillet steak with a dijon mustard sauce (£11.95); you must book for the no-smoking restaurant. Well kept Hook Norton Best, John Smiths, and Theakstons Best on handpump kept under light blanket pressure; darts and piped music. The small side terraces have picnic-sets under parasols, and there may be Morris dancers out here in summer. *(Recommended by Simon Collett-Jones, Chris*

Mawson, Dave Irving, Ewan McCall, Roger Huggins, Tom McLean, Stephen and Julie Brown, Gwen and Peter Andrews, Liz Bell, Ted George, DFL, Mr and Mrs M F Norton, Dorothy and Leslie Pilson, Martin and Karen Wake, I R Bell, Tim Brierly)

Free house ~ Licensees Ernest and Christine Goodwin ~ Real ale ~ Meals and snacks ~ Restaurant ~ (01451) 821459 ~ Children welcome ~ Open 11-2.30, 6.30-11; 12-3, 7-10.30 Sun

COLN ST ALDWYNS SP1405 Map 4

New Inn

On good back road between Bibury and Fairford

Of course most of the emphasis in this civilised ivy-covered inn is on the very good food – which can be eaten either in the relaxed bar or the smarter restaurant – but those wanting just a drink are made very welcome, too. The two neatly kept main rooms are most attractively furnished and decorated, and divided by a central log fire in a neat stone fireplace with wooden mantlebeam and willow-pattern plates on the chimney breast; there are also low beams, some stripped stonework around the bar servery with hops above it, oriental rugs on the red tiles, and a mix of seating from library chairs to stripped pews. Down a slight slope, a further room has a log fire in an old kitchen range at one end, and a stuffed buzzard on the wall. From the bar menu, dishes might include soup (£2.95), sun-dried tomato risotto with shaved parmesan (£3.95), rich chicken liver parfait with toasted brioche and onion marmalade (£5.50; you may be charged extra for more bread), fish and chips (£7.95), smoked haddock with poached egg, spinach and a grain mustard sauce (£8.25), lamb liver with bacon and onion gravy (£9.25), steak and kidney pudding (£10.95), sirloin steak with red wine, shallot and mushroom sauce (£12.50), and puddings like treacle tart with vanilla egg custard, steamed white chocolate and Grand Marnier pudding with orange marmalade syrup or a crumble of the day (£3.95); vegetarian choices and children's meals. The restaurant is no smoking. Well kept Hook Norton Best, Morlands Original, and Wadworths 6X on handpump, half a dozen good wines by the glass, and several malt whiskies; dominoes. The split-level terraced garden has plenty of seats. The peaceful Cotswold village is pretty, and the surrounding countryside is good for walking – the riverside walk to Bibury is not to be missed. *(Recommended by Tom McLean, Roger Huggins, Dave Irving, Ewan McCall, Bronwen and Steve Wrigley, N J Worthington, S L Tracy, W Burke, Liz Bell, Mr and Mrs Boradhurst, Simon Collett-Jones, G V Price, George and Jean Dundas, B J Cox, John Bowdler, Liz Bell, Karen Pagínton, Pat and John Millward, John and Barbara Burns; also in the Good Hotel Guide)*

Free house ~ Licensee Brian Evans ~ Real ale ~ Meals and snacks ~ Restaurant ~ (01285) 750651 ~ Children in eating area of bar and over 10 in restaurant ~ Open 11-11; 12-10.30 Sun ~ Bedrooms: £68B/£93B

CRANHAM SO8912 Map 4

Black Horse

Village signposted off A46 and B4070 N of Stroud; up side turning

For 12 years, the same friendly licensees have run this old-fashioned 17th-c pub. A cosy little lounge has just three or four tables, and the main bar is quarry-tiled, with cushioned high-backed wall settles and window seats, and a good log fire. Most people come to enjoy the good food: sandwiches and ploughman's (£2-£4), smoked salmon and asparagus quiche (£5.50), pasta provençale (£6.25), sausage and bacon toad-in-the-hole or chicken breast in wine, cream and mustard sauce (£6.95), mediterranean-style cod or duckling legs with whisky and orange glaze (£7.25), kleftico (£9.25), and pheasant and game in season; Sunday roast lunches. You can eat the same menu in the upstairs dining rooms (best to book at weekends). Very well kept Boddingtons, Flowers Original, Hook Norton Best, Marstons Pedigree, and Wickwar BOB on handpump, and country wines. Shove-ha'penny, cribbage, and piped music; Truffle the brittany spaniel is quite a character. Tables in the sizeable garden behind have a good view out over the steep village and wooded valley, and they keep chickens and rabbits. *(Recommended by Richard and Jean Phillips, NC, AC, IHR, Stephen Pine, Alfred Lawrence, Tony Dickinson, Mike and Mary Carter, Daren Haines)*

Free house ~ Licensees David and Julie Job ~ Real ale ~ Meals and snacks (not Sun evening) ~ (01452) 812217 ~ Children welcome ~ Occasional Irish music or Morris men ~ Open 11.30-2.30, 6.30-11; 12-3, 7-10.30 Sun; may close Mon mornings Jan/Feb

DUNTISBOURNE ABBOTS SO9709 Map 4

Five Mile House

Just off A417 5 miles N of Cirencester (new bypass)

When this old place closed after the death in 1995 of Ivy Ruck its long-serving landlady, everyone feared that its engaging traditional character was lost for ever – especially with the talk that followed, of its new owners plunging into a £500,000 refurbishment. Reopened in 1997, it's proved the doubters wrong. The front has a companionable bare-boards drinking bar on the right, with wall seats around the big table in its bow window and just one other table; on the left is a flagstoned hallway tap room snug formed from two ancient high-backed settles by a (new) woodburning stove in a tall carefully exposed old fireplace. The thoroughly old-fashioned feel of this part is preserved by the landlord's tactful insistence that if you want to eat even a sandwich you should move to one of the other areas, such as the lounge behind the left-hand snug. There's a new small cellar bar (piped music on request down here – it's a perfect size for a group celebration), a back restaurant down steps, and a refurbished family room on the far side. The lounge and cellar bar are no smoking. Well kept Marstons Best and Timothy Taylor Landlord on handpump (the cellar is temperature-controlled), interesting wines (strong on New World ones). Generous fairly priced bar food (cooked by the landlord) at lunchtime includes home-made soup (£2.50), open sandwiches (from £2.50), ploughman's (£4.25), stilton, spinach and mushroom lasagne, 6oz rump steak baguette or home-cooked smoked ham with two eggs (£5.95), and whole local trout with prawn and lemon butter (£6.95); in the evening, there might be hot chicken liver and bacon salad (£4.25), chicken breast stuffed with stilton and wrapped in bacon on a brandy and mushroom cream sauce (£7.95), shoulder of lamb stuffed with redcurrant and mint with a redcurrant and port gravy or fillet of red snapper with a white wine and chive cream sauce (£8.50), 12oz Aberdeen Angus rump steak with sauces (£9.95), and puddings such as home-made American chocolate cheesecake, good lime pie or fruit crumbles (£2.50); children's helpings where possible, and Sunday roast lunch (£5.95). Service is thoughtful and friendly. Quoits. *(Recommended by Jenny and Roger Huggins, Tom McLean, Dave Irving, Ewan McCall, Giles Francis, Guy Vowles, Nick and Alison Dowson, JP, PP, Christopher Mobbs, Gordon)*

Free house ~ Licensee Jo Carrier ~ Real ale ~ Meals and snacks (not winter Sun evenings) ~ Restaurant ~ (01285) 821432 ~ Children welcome away from bar ~ Open 12-3, 6-11; 12-3, 7-10.30 Sun

EBRINGTON SP1840 Map 4

Ebrington Arms

Signposted from B4035 E of Chipping Campden; and from A429 N of Moreton in Marsh

This unpretentious place is very much an old-fashioned local – which makes quite a change from the many smart dining pubs around here. The little bar has some fine old low beams, stone walls, flagstoned floors and inglenook fireplaces (the one in the dining room still has the original iron work), plus sturdy traditional furnishings, some seats built into the airy bow window, and a slightly raised woodfloored area. A lower room, also beamed and flagstoned, has stripped country-kitchen furnishings. Enjoyable simple bar food (chalked up on the beams) might include sausage and onion bap, soup or egg and chips (£2.50), omelettes (from £3.75), ploughman's or home-made ratatouille (£4.25), home-made lasagne (£4.95), good fresh cod or home-made steak, mushroom and Guinness pie (£5.95), and steaks; decent breakfasts. Well kept Donnington SBA, Hook Norton Best and a guest beer on handpump (kept under light blanket pressure); they have a pianola (absolutely no piped music or games machines). Trophies bear witness to the success of the pub's dominoes team, and you can also play cribbage, darts and shove-ha'penny. An arched stone wall shelters a terrace with picnic-sets under cocktail parasols. No dogs – at least at mealtimes, when the licensees' friendly welsh springer is also kept out. Handy for Hidcote and Kiftsgate. *(Recommended by G Washington, David Edwards, Dr D E Granger, P and S White, Martin Jones, David Heath, Mr and Mrs C Roberts, Geoffrey and Penny Hughes, Peter and Anne Hollindale, E V Walder, Ted George)*

Free house ~ Licensee Gareth Richards ~ Real ale ~ Meals and snacks (not Sun evening) ~ (01386) 593223 ~ Children in dining room ~ Open 12-2, 7-11; 12-3, 7-10.30 Sun; closed 25 Dec ~ Bedrooms: /£35B

EWEN SU0097 Map 4

Wild Duck ★ 🍷

Village signposted from A429 S of Cirencester

Rather like an old manor house, this popular and civilised 16th-c inn has a high-beamed main bar with a nice mix of comfortable armchairs and other seats, candles on the tables, paintings on the coral walls, crimson drapes, magazines to read, and an open winter fire; another bar has a handsome Elizabethan fireplace and antique furnishings, and looks over the garden. Bar food includes soup (£2.95), chicken liver pâté or ploughman's (£4.95), fish and chips or gnocchi in a rich stilton sauce (£6.95), smoked haddock risotto (£7.95), chicken with pasta and pesto sauce (£8.95), knuckle of ham (£9.95), and steaks (£12.95); there may be a wait when service is pushed. As well as Duckpond Bitter, brewed especially for the pub, well kept beers might include Courage Directors, Smiles Best, and Theakstons Best and Old Peculier on handpump, kept under light blanket pressure. Good wines, several malt whiskies, and shove-ha'penny. There are attractive white painted cast-iron tables and seats in the neatly kept and sheltered garden. *(Recommended by Dave Irving, Roger Huggins, Tom McLean, Ewan McCall, Stephen Brown, RJH, Ian Phillips, B Berfect, G Francis, Paul S McPherson, Greg Kilminster, Keith and Margaret Kettell, Andrew and Eileen Abbess, Tim and Linda Collins)*

Free house ~ Licensee Brian Mussell ~ Real ale ~ Meals and snacks (till 10pm) ~ Restaurant ~ (01285) 770310 ~ Children in eating area of bar and in restaurant ~ Open 11-11; 12-10.30 Sun ~ Bedrooms: £49.50B/£69.50B

FORD SP0829 Map 4

Plough

B4077

Doing very well at the moment, this pretty stone pub has a good bustling atmosphere and a happy mix of customers. The beamed and stripped-stone bar has racing prints and photos on the walls, old settles and benches around the big tables on its uneven flagstones, oak tables in a snug alcove, and three welcoming log fires (one is log-effect gas). The gallops for local stables are opposite, so there's quite a racing feel – particularly on the days when the horse owned by a partnership of locals is running at Cheltenham. Dominoes, cribbage, shove-ha'penny, fruit machine, and piped music. Enjoyable home-made bar food includes good sandwiches, home-made soup (£2.95), home-made pâté (£4.25), mixed cheese platter (£4.95), home-cooked ham and eggs (£6.50), lamb and apricot pie or steak, mushroom and Guinness casserole (£7.25), knuckle of lamb (£9.25), and steaks, (from £9.50). They still have their traditional asparagus feasts every April-June, when the first asparagus spears to be sold at auction in the Vale of Evesham usually end up here. Well kept Donnington BB and SBA on handpump, Addlestone's cider, a few malt whiskies, and decent wines. There are benches in front, with rustic tables and chairs on grass by white lilacs and fairy lights, and a play area at the back. Look out for the llama farm between here and Kineton. *(Recommended by Richard Gibbs, Bernard and Becky Robinson, H Dickinson, JP, PP, Martin Jones, Stan and Hazel Allen, Stephen and Julie Brown,*

Mrs C Fielder, Peter and Audrey Dowsett, Tim and Linda Collins, Edward and Richard Norris, J Dwane, BHP, Jackie Orme, RKP, Wayne Wheeler, Daren Haines, Pat and Roger Fereday, Guy Vowles, Dr and Mrs J Hills, Liz Bell, R Watkins)

Donnington ~ Tenant W Skinner ~ Real ale ~ Meals and snacks ~ (01386) 584215 ~ Children welcome ~ Open 11-11; 12-10.30 Sun; closed 25 Dec ~ Bedrooms: £35B/£55B

GREAT BARRINGTON SP2013 Map 4

Fox

Village signposted from A40 Burford—Northleach; pub between Little and Great Barrington

The terrace outside this simple pub is heated, so even on a chilly evening you can enjoy the pretty setting by the River Windrush; there's a landscaped pond in the orchard. Inside, the low-ceilinged little bar has rustic wooden chairs, tables and window seats, stripped stone walls, and two roaring log fires; sensibly placed darts, pool, dominoes, cribbage, fruit machine, and piped music. Donnington BB and SBA on handpump, and Addlestone's cider. The pub dog is called Bruiser (though he's only little). Bar food includes sandwiches (not Sundays), warm chicken, bacon and brie salad (£4.95), home-made fresh salmon fishcakes or red thai chicken curry (£6.95), and home-made beef in ale pie (£7.25). There's a skittles alley out beyond the sheltered yard, and they have private fishing. *(Recommended by David Lamb, Jenny and Michael Back, Tim and Linda Collins, George Atkinson, Geoffrey and Penny Hughes, Ted George, Liz Bell, John and Shirley Dyson, Stephen Pine, Alfred Lawrence, Daren Haines, Margaret Dyke)*

Donnington ~ Tenants Paul and Kate Porter ~ Real ale ~ Meals and snacks (not winter Mon evenings) ~ (01451) 844385 ~ Children welcome ~ Open 11-11; 12-10.30 Sun ~ Bedrooms: £25/£42.50

GREAT RISSINGTON SP1917 Map 4

Lamb 🛏 🍷

There are lots of things to look at in the cosy two-roomed bar of this rather civilised partly 17th-c inn: part of a propeller from the Wellington bomber that crashed in the garden in October 1943, an interesting collection of old cigarette and tobacco tins, photographs of the guide dogs the staff and customers have raised money to buy (over 20), a history of the village, and various plates and pictures. Wheelback and tub chairs with cushioned seats are grouped around polished tables on the light brown carpet, a table and settle are hidden in a nook under the stairs, and there's a log-effect gas fire in the stone fireplace. Good bar food includes sandwiches (on request), home-made soup (£2.50), home-made chicken liver pâté (£4.25), home-made pork and leek sausages with mash and onion gravy (£5.50), lamb liver and bacon (£5.75), steak and Guinness pie (£5.95), salmon steak with a dill sauce (£8.75), and daily specials such as a roast half shoulder of lamb with a rosemary and redcurrant gravy (£10.50); you can also eat from the more extensive menu of the partly no smoking restaurant. Well kept Smiles and Wadworths 6X on handpump, a good wine list, and several malt whiskies; helpful service, piped classical music. You can sit out in the sheltered hillside garden or really take advantage of the scenery and walk (via gravel pits now used as a habitat for water birds) to Bourton on the Water. Readers enjoy staying here but bedrooms do vary tremendously in quality and price – check when booking. *(Recommended by Mike and Heather Watson, Walter Reid, John and Jackie Chalcraft, Bronwen and Steve Wrigley, Ted George, Martin and Karen Wake, Ian and Jane Irving, M S Catling, Andrew and Ruth Triggs, Arnold Day, John and Shirley Dyson, Stephen and Yvonne Agar)*

Free house ~ Licensees Richard and Kate Cleverly ~ Real ale ~ Meals and snacks ~ Restaurant ~ (01451) 820388 ~ Children welcome ~ Open 11.30-2.30, 6.30-11; 12-3, 7-10.30 Sun; closed 25-26 Dec ~ Bedrooms:/£50-£85B

GREET SP0230 Map 4

Harvest Home

B4078 just N of Winchcombe

Although this looks a little ordinary from the outside, once inside it's rewarding to find a warm welcome from the friendly licensees and good food and drink in the spotlessly kept rooms. The bar has a dozen or so well spaced tables, with seats built into the bay windows and other sturdy blue-cushioned seats; there are pretty flower prints and country scenes on the walls, and several dried-flower arrangements. The lounge bar is linked to the dining room by a servery with a bric-a-brac shelf, a big cartwheel centre light, and lots of hop bines to the exposed beams. Enjoyable bar food includes home-made soup (£1.75), filled french bread (from £2.50), garlic mushrooms (£3.25), ploughman's (from £4.25), omelettes (£4.50), three local spicy sausages (£4.75), ham and eggs (£5.75), chicken tikka (£5.95), tasty duck and bacon pie or fresh local trout (£6.25), steaks (from £6.75), pork schnitzel (£7.25), daily specials such as salmon wellington with mushrooms and chives (£6.95), vegetarian dishes, puddings like wonderful apple strudel with vanilla sauce or nice white chocolate pudding (£2.50), and children's menu (from £2.25). Well kept Boddingtons, Fullers London Pride, Hook Norton Best, and Wadworths 6X on handpump, decent wines, and several malt whiskies; darts down at one end and a good open fire at the other; shove-ha'penny, cribbage, dominoes, and unobtrusive piped classical music; helpful and pleasant young staff. There's a big beamed pitched-roof side restaurant (same food; no smoking). The sizeable garden has a play area and boules, a terrace with access to the restaurant, and a narrow-gauge GWR railway that passes it. The miniature schnauzers are called Oscar and Boris. The pub is not far from medieval Sudeley Castle. *(Recommended by Stephen and Julie Brown, J H Kane, Sue and Steve Griffiths, G R Williams, Nigel and Rita Cooke, Martin Jones, Steve Corrigan, Derek and Sylvia Stephenson, Norman and Angela Harries, John Bowdler, Mr and Mrs J Brown)*

Whitbreads ~ Lease: Heinz and Lisa Stolzenberg ~ Real ale ~ Meals and snacks ~ Restaurant ~ (01242) 602430 ~ Children in eating area of bar ~ Open 11-3, 6-11; 12-3, 6-10.30 Sun

GRETTON SP0131 Map 4

Royal Oak

Village signposted off what is now officially B4077 (still often mapped and even signed as A438), E of Tewkesbury; keep on through village

This is an enjoyable pub – both inside and out. From seats on the flower-filled terrace you can enjoy the wonderful views over the village and across the valley to Dumbleton Hills and the Malverns. There are more seats under a giant pear tree, a neatly kept big lawn running down past a small hen-run to a play area (with an old tractor and see-saw), and even a bookable tennis court. The series of bare-boarded or flagstoned rooms here – the pub was once a pair of old stone-built cottages – have a friendly bustle and soft lighting (including candles in bottles on the mix of stripped oak and pine tables); also, dark ochre walls, beams (some hung with tankards, hop bines and chamber-pots), old prints, and a medley of pews and various chairs; the friendly setter is called George and there are two cats. The well liked no-smoking dining conservatory has stripped country furnishings, and a broad view over the countryside. Good bar food includes soup (£2.95), mussels grilled with stilton (£3.25), ploughman's (£4.50), chicken rogan josh, leek and mushroom pasta bake or baked ham and cauliflower cheese (all £5.95), salmon steak with yoghurt and chives or rack of lamb with red wine and cranberry sauce (£8.95), rump steak (£10.75), and puddings (£2.95). Well kept Archers, Goff's Jouster, John Smiths, Morlands Old Speckled Hen, Theakstons Old Peculier, and Wickwar BOB on handpump, and a decent wine list; shove-ha'penny, fruit machine, and piped music. *(Recommended by Dr A Drummond, George Atkinson, Gordon, Martin Jones, Stephen and Julie Brown, P and S White, Lawrence Pearse, Derek and Sylvia Stephenson, E V Walder, G and M Stewart, Daren Haines, Ted George)*

Free house ~ Licensees Bob and Kathy Willison ~ Real ale ~ Meals and snacks ~ Restaurant ~ (01242) 602477 ~ Well behaved children welcome ~ Folk Weds evening ~ Open 11-2.30, 6-11; 12-3, 7-10.30 Sun; closed 25-26 Dec

GUITING POWER SP0924 Map 4

Hollow Bottom

Village signposted off B4068 SW of Stow on the Wold (still called A436 on many maps)

If you are interested in race horses and racing, then this snug old cottage is the place to head for. It's owned by a small syndicate that includes Peter Scudamore and two trainers, and the comfortable beamed bar has lots of racing memorabilia including racing silks, tunics and photographs, and a winter log fire in an unusual pillar-supported stone fireplace; the public bar has flagstones and stripped stone masonry. Bar food includes sandwiches, home-made soup (£2.50), whitebait (£4.25), buffalo shrimps (£4.50), home-made steak and kidney pie (£5.75), steaks (from £9.50), and Sunday roast (£6.50); afternoon teas. Well kept Bass, Hook Norton, and Goff's Jouster on handpump. From the pleasant garden behind are views towards the peaceful sloping fields. Decent walks nearby. *(Recommended by Gavin Smith, M L Berryman, Lawrence Pearse, NWN, W Osborn-King; more reports please)*

Free house ~ Licensees Jason Dohse, Marilyn Scudamore ~ Real ale ~ Meals and snacks ~ Restaurant ~ (01451) 850392 ~ Well behaved children in restaurant ~ Irish band occasionally ~ Open 11-11; 12-10.30 Sun; closed evening 25 Dec ~ Bedrooms: £25B/£45B

HYDE SO8801 Map 4

Ragged Cot

Burnt Ash; Hyde signposted with Minchinhampton from A419 E of Stroud; or (better road) follow Minchinhampton, Aston Down signposted from A419 at Aston Down airfield; OS Sheet 162 map reference 886012

At each end of the rambling bar in this relaxed old place is a log fire – one has a traditional dark wood settle by it. There are black beams and quite a bit of stripped stone, red cushioned wheelback chairs and bar stools, cushioned window seats, and a stuffed owl; there's a new no-smoking eating area. Good value bar food includes sandwiches and rolls (from £1.25; hot granary rolls from £3.75), home-made soup (£2), chicken liver pâté (£3.25), sausage, egg and chips (£3.35), filled baked potatoes (£3.95), a pasta dish, battered cod or a pie of the day (all £4.95), rump steak (£6.45), daily specials such as moules marinières (£3.75 starter, £5.95 main course), liver and bacon (£5.25), salmon in a lemon salsa (£6.50), and duck breast in plum and ginger (£6.75); vegetarian dishes, puddings, and 3-course Sunday lunch (£7.95). Well kept Bass, Theakstons Best, Uley Old Spot, Wadworths 6X, and guest beers on handpump, a thoughtful wine list, 55 malt whiskies, and Westons cider; shove-ha'penny, cribbage, dominoes, backgammon, Scrabble, and fruit machine. There are picnic-sets (and an interesting pavilion) in the garden, and bedrooms in an adjacent converted barn. *(Recommended by Dave Irving, Roger Huggins, Tom McLean, Ewan McCall, W M and J M Cottrell, Peter and Audrey Dowsett, Simon Penny, Andy and Jill Kassube, John and Shirley Dyson)*

Free house ~ Licensee Nicholas Winch ~ Real ale ~ Meals and snacks (not 25-26 Dec) ~ Restaurant ~ (01453) 884643 ~ Children in eating area of bar and in restaurant ~ Open 11-2.30, 6-11; 12-3, 7-10.30 Sun ~ Bedrooms: £38B/£55B

KILKENNY SP0018 Map 4

Kilkeney Inn

On A436, 1 mile W of Andoversford, nr Cheltenham – OS Sheet 163 map reference 007187

People do drop into this pleasant place for just a drink, but this is very much a comfortable dining pub with specials that change twice a day. At lunchtime, there are light dishes such as filled french bread (from £2.95), ploughman's (£4.15), local pork sausage with mash and onion gravy (£4.85), and fish pie (£5.95); also, soup (£2.25), cheese fritters with cumberland sauce or confit of duck legs glazed with orange and honey (£3.95), steak and kidney pie (£6.50), aubergine and wild mushroom cannelloni with a tomato coulis (£6.95), pork fillet, peach and pistachio roulade with a pear and brandy sauce (£8.75), roast fillet of lamb on a parsnip and potato cake with a fresh herb and redcurrant sauce (£10.95), chargrilled medallions of beef fillet on a pâté crouton with madeira sauce (£11), and puddings like lemon and lime frangipane tart, toffee pudding with caramel sauce or chocolate délice (£3). Booking is recommended, especially at weekends. The extended and modernised bar, quite bright and airily spacious, has neatly alternated stripped Cotswold stone and white plasterwork, as well as gleaming dark wheelback chairs around the tables, and an open fire. Up at the other end of the same long bar is more of a drinking area, with well kept Ruddles Best and Tetleys on handpump, an excellent range of decent wines and lots of malt whiskies. It opens into a comfortable no-smoking dining conservatory. Attractive Cotswold views, and good parking. *(Recommended by Mr and Mrs B J Edwards, Greg Kilminster, Dr and Mrs A Newton, W M and J M Cottrell, Mr and Mrs J Brown, Gordon Tong, D H and M C Watkinson, NWN, Stephen Pine, Alfred Lawrence, Gwen and Peter Andrews)*

Free house ~ Licensees John and Judy Fennell ~ Real ale ~ Meals and lunchtime snacks ~ (01242) 820341 ~ Well behaved children in eating areas ~ Open 11.30-2.30, 6.30-11; 12-2.30, 7-10.30 Sun; closed Sun evenings Jan-March; 25-26 Dec, 2nd Mon/Tues in Jan

KINETON SP0926 Map 4

Halfway House

Village signposted from B4068 and B4077 W of Stow on the Wold

Surrounded by good walks, this pretty little stone house has a sheltered back lawn with some seats, and more on the narrow flagstoned front terrace (separated from the slow, quiet village lane by tubs of bright flowers on top of a low stone wall). Inside, the unpretentious bar has a warm winter log fire, attractive plates and colourful posters on the walls, and some ancient farm tools and pictures at one end, with beams at the other; one area of the dining room is no smoking. Well kept Donnington BB and SBA (fresh from the nearby brewery) on handpump, and bar food such as sandwiches, home-made soup (£2.60), black pudding with mango chutney (£2.95), chicken and pineapple kebabs, home-made curry or local trout (£6.95), steak and kidney pie (£7.25), steaks (from £9.25), and children's meals (£3). Darts, cribbage, dominoes, fruit machine, juke box, and piped music. The pub is handy for Sudeley Castle and Cotswold Farm Park. *(Recommended by J Dwane, Gwen and Peter Andrews, Rob Whittle; more reports please)*

Donnington ~ Tenant Paul Hamer ~ Real ale ~ Meals and snacks ~ (01451) 850344 ~ Children in eating area of bar until 9pm ~ Open 11.30-2.30, 6.30-11; 12-2.30, 7-10.30 Sun ~ Bedrooms: £25/£40

LITTLE BARRINGTON SP2012 Map 4

Inn For All Seasons

A40 3 miles W of Burford

We've given this friendly and civilised old inn a Food Award this year as readers have been warmly enthusiastic about the imaginative dishes and high standard of cooking. But this isn't just a dining pub – it's a really enjoyable pub to come to (and a nice place to stay) with attentive staff and a good relaxed atmosphere. The attractively decorated mellow lounge bar has low beams, stripped stone, and flagstones, old prints, leather-upholstered wing armchairs and other comfortable seats, country magazines to read, and a big log fire (with a big piece of World War II shrapnel above it); maybe quiet piped classical music. The licensee has a fish business in Brixham, so their half dozen fresh fish dishes are particularly good: turbot, red mullet, poached skate, squid and scallop salad, Dart salmon, lobster, sea bass and so forth (£8-£11). Other good bar food might include sandwiches (£2.95), home-made soup (£3.25), crispy confit of duck with a fruit, balsamic and plum vinaigrette (£4.75), gravadlax of Dart salmon flavoured with brandy and served with dill mustard mayonnaise (£4.95), open hereford steak sandwich with home-made chips (£6.95), braised Italian vegetables on a granary crouton glazed with melted ricotta and goat's cheese (£7), mild tomato and duck curry with raita, mango chutney and poppadums (£7.25), confit of pork on a garlic mash with a green peppercorn sauce (£9.50), roast rack of Cotswold lamb with caramelised shallots and garlic on a rich red wine sauce (£10.95), and puddings like hot ginger and treacle tart, iced banana parfait with mocha sauce or chocolate mousse cake; good breakfasts. Well kept Glenny Wychwood Special, and Wadworths 6X on handpump, a good wine list, and over 60 malt whiskies. Cribbage, dominoes and piped music. The pleasant garden has tables, and there are walks straight from the inn – if you're staying, you may be asked to take the owners' two well trained dogs along with you. It's very busy during Cheltenham Gold Cup Week – when the adjoining field is pressed into service as a helicopter pad. *(Recommended by Liz Bell, Simon Collett-Jones, Nigel Williamson, J H Kane, Susan and John Douglas, Peter and Audrey Dowsett, Rob Whittle, Gordon)*

Free house ~ Licensees Matthew and Heather Sharp ~ Real ale ~ Meals and snacks (11-2.30, 6-9.30) ~ Restaurant ~ (01451) 844324 ~ Children welcome ~ Open 11-2.30, 6-11; 12-2.30, 7-10.30 Sun; closed 25-26 Dec ~ Bedrooms: £42.50B/£79B

LITTLE WASHBOURNE SO9933 Map 4

Hobnails

B4077 (though often mapped still as the A438) Tewkesbury—Stow on the Wold; 7½ miles E of M5 junction 9

You can be sure of a friendly welcome in this partly 15th-c cheerful pub, and the landlord's family have been here since 1743. The snug little front bar has low sway-backed beams hung with pewter tankards, lots of old prints and horsebrasses, and old wall benches by a couple of tables on its quarry-tiled floor; there's a more modern, carpeted back bar with comfortable button-back leatherette banquettes and newspaper cuttings about the pub and the family; open fire. Bar food includes their speciality baps (from £1.60; liver £3.10; steak in wine £5.25; you can build your bap with extras like fried banana, melted stilton, fried egg, and so forth), home-made soup (£2.75), ploughman's (£4.25), cashew nut and mushroom loaf (£6.60), lasagne or goulash (£6.75), daily specials, home-made puddings (£3.45), children's menu (from £1.25), and their special cider cake with cheese (£2.55); fresh vegetables £2.55. Both dining rooms are no smoking. Well kept Boddingtons, Flowers Original, Hook Norton, and Wadworths 6X on handpump; darts, shove-ha'penny, quiet piped music. A separate skittle alley (with tables) can be hired weekday evenings. Between the two buildings, and beside a small lawn and flower bed, there's a terrace with tables, and children's playground. *(Recommended by Sue and Steve Griffiths, Sheelia Curtis, Stephen and Julie Brown, Andrew and Ruth Triggs, Mr Miller, Hugh and Sarah McShane, Mrs Jeane Dundas, Ted George, John Barnwell, JCW, Lawrence Bacon, Jean Scott)*

Whitbreads ~ Lease: Stephen Farbrother ~ Real ale ~ Meals and snacks (till 10pm) ~ Restaurant ~ (01242) 620237 ~ Children welcome ~ Open 11-2.30, 6-11; 12-2.30, 6-10.30 Sun; closed 25-26 Dec

LITTLETON UPON SEVERN ST5990 Map 2

White Hart

3½ miles from M4 junction 21; B4461 towards Thornbury, then village signposted

There's a lot of character in this carefully restored and very popular old farmhouse, and although extensions have been made to the original 17th-c building, the old-fashioned feel has not been much harmed. The three atmospheric main rooms have some fine furnishings that include long cushioned wooden settles, high-backed settles, oak and elm tables, a loveseat in the big low inglenook fireplace, flagstones in the front, huge tiles at the back, and smaller tiles on the left, some old pots and pans, and a lovely old White Hart Inn Simonds Ale sign. By the black wooden staircase are some nice little alcove seats, there's a black-panelled big fireplace in the front room, and hops on beams. An excellent no-smoking family room, similarly furnished, has some sentimental engravings, plates on a delft shelf, and a couple of high chairs, and a back snug has pokerwork seats and table football; darts, cribbage, fruit machine, chess, backgammon and Jenga. There's another new manager this year, and food now includes sandwiches, leek and stilton pie (£5.25), minted lamb casserole (£6.25), and thai chicken curry or pork in cider (£6.75). Well kept Smiles Best, Golden and Heritage, Greene King Abbot, and changing guest beers on handpump. Picnic-sets sit on the neat front lawn, intersected by interesting cottagey flowerbeds, and by the good big back car park are some attractive shrubs and teak furniture on a small brick terrace. Several walks from the pub itself. *(Recommended by M G Hart, A Hughes, D L Parkhurst, Alan Johnson, Steve Willey, Ian and Villy White, Dr and Mrs A Whiteway, Andrew Shore, Tom McLean, Ewan McCall, Roger Huggins, Dave Irving, Simon and Amanda Southwell, S H Godsell)*

Smiles ~ Manager Jonathan Swift ~ Real ale ~ Meals and snacks ~ (01454) 412275 ~ Children in family area ~ Open 11-2.30(3 Sat), 6-11; 12-3, 6-10.30 Sun ~ Bedrooms: £34.50B/£44.50B

LOWER ODDINGTON SP2325 Map 4

Fox (🍴) 🍷

Nr Stow on the Wold

Gloucestershire Dining Pub of the Year

To be sure of a table in this well run, stylish dining pub, you need to get here early – even on a winter weekday. The simply and spotlessly furnished rooms have fresh flowers and flagstones, a woodburning stove, a display cabinet with pewter mugs and stone bottles, and a relaxed but smart feel; there's a lovely dining room, and piped classical music. Efficiently served by friendly staff, the good, interesting food might include mint, pea and lettuce soup (£2.95), filled french bread (from £2.95), onion tart with mango chutney (£3.50), aubergine, pepper and warm goat's cheese salad (£3.95), spinach and ricotta cannelloni (£6.50), kidneys with meaux mustard (£6.95), chicken breast wrapped in bacon with garlic cream sauce (£7.95), rack of local lamb with shrewsbury sauce (£8.95), rib-eye steak (£9.95), daily specials like lovely warm chicken, bacon and avocado salad, super spare ribs, fine trout baked in newspaper or salmon fishcakes with parsley sauce (£7.95), puddings such as petit pot au chocolat, french lemon tart or apple and cinnamon pie (£2.95), and Sunday roast sirloin of beef with yorkshire pudding (£8.95). The wine list is excellent and they keep good Hook Norton Best, Marstons Pedigree and a guest beer on handpump. A good eight-mile walk starts from here (though a stroll around the pretty village might be less taxing after a fine meal). *(Recommended by Hugh Spottiswoode, Liz Bell, Lawrence Pearse, J H Kane, Andrew Shore, G Neighbour, Dr Wendy Holden, Tom and Joan Childs, RJH, James Garvey, George Atkinson, Jackie Lawler, Hazel McCarthy, R Crockett, Michael Bourdeaux, Martin Jones, Paul Barnett, K Jeavons, A Turner, Mike and Maggie Betton, Peter Dubois, Wilma and Ian Smith, Mike Gorton, D Irving, R Huggins, T McLean, E McCall, John Bowdler, Rob Whittle)*

Free house ~ Licensees Vicky Elliot and Luli Birch ~ Real ale ~ Meals and snacks (till 10pm) ~ (01451) 870555 ~ Children in eating area of bar ~ Open 12-3, 6.30-11; 12-3, 7-10.30 Sun; closed 25 Dec and evenings 26 Dec and 1 Jan

MEYSEY HAMPTON SU1199 Map 4

Masons Arms

High Street; just off A417 Cirencester—Lechlade

Pleasantly placed by the village green, this friendly 17th-c stonebuilt inn has a longish open-plan bar with a good parquet floor, solid part-upholstered built-in wall seats with some matching chairs, good sound tables, a big inglenook log fire at one end, carefully stripped beams, daily newspapers, and a few steps up to the no-smoking restaurant. There's a properly pubby atmosphere and John Smiths, Wadworths 6X, Wychwood Shires, and guests like Badger Tanglefoot, Berkeley Early Riser, Exmoor Stag, Goff's Jouster, and Shepherd Neame Spitfire on handpump, decent wines including several ports; dominoes, cribbage, maybe piped music. Bar food includes home-made soup (£2.45), good filled sandwiches (from £1.95; filled french bread from £3.95), filled baked potatoes (from £2.45), stilton and bacon garlic mushrooms (£3.60), ploughman's (from £4.25), ham and two eggs or vegetable stir fry (£4.95), steak and kidney pie (£5.65), haddock and chips (£5.95), chicken curry (£6.25), duck in a honey and plum sauce (£8.65), steaks (from £9.25), daily specials such as spicy chicken goujons (£3.65), cod au gratin (£5.85), and cotswold chicken (£7.25), and children's menu (£3.25); 2-course weekday lunch £6.50; good breakfasts. *(Recommended by D Irving, E McCall, R Huggins, T McLean, A Wright, MRSM, Kevin Thorpe, TRS, George Atkinson, D H and M C Watkinson)*

Free house ~ Licensees Andrew and Jane O'Dell ~ Real ale ~ Meals and snacks (not Sun evening) ~ (01285) 850164 ~ Children welcome lunchtimes and until 9pm in restaurant ~ Open 11.30-3, 6-11; 12-4, 7-10.30 Sun ~ Bedrooms: £32S/£48S

MINCHINHAMPTON SO8600 Map 4

Old Lodge

Minchinhampton Common; from centre of common take Box turn-off then fork right at pub's signpost

Doing well at the moment, this former hunting lodge stands in the middle of a common, and there are tables on a neat lawn by an attractive herbaceous border that look over grey stone walls to the grazing cows and horses. Inside, the small and snug central bar has a relaxed, friendly atmosphere and substantial pine tables and chairs, and opens into a pleasant bare-brick-walled room and an airy stripped-stone dining area, both of which are no smoking; no noisy games or piped music; skittle alley. Good, interesting bar food includes lunchtime sandwiches, fried chicken livers and black pudding on a potato pancake with an onion marmalade or a tartlet filled with lettuce, chicory and parma ham with a warm roquefort dressing (£4.65), strips of lamb liver with peppers and spring onions in a ginger and black bean sauce on a bed of noodles (£4.75; main course £7.25), millefeuille filled with sautéed mushrooms and spinach and a puy lentil curry sauce (£8.45), chicken breast stuffed with brie and redcurrants in filo pastry with red wine sauce (£8.50), salmon topped with crab and coriander under a lemon crust with a lobster and smoked prawn sauce (£8.75), and puddings like summer pudding or vanilla crème brûlée with a berry compote (£3.75). Well kept Marstons Pedigree and Thwaites Bitter with a guest like Tetleys on handpump, and a good range of wines; friendly, helpful service. They share car parking with the adjoining golf club, so lots of cars outside doesn't necessarily mean the pub is full. *(Recommended by Neil and Anita Christopher, D and C Cosgrove, P Hedges, D G King, D Etheridge, M G Hart, Wendy, Liz and Ian Phillips)*

Free house ~ Licensees David Barnett-Roberts and Eugene Halford ~ Real ale ~ Meals and snacks (till 10pm; not Mon) ~ (01453) 832047 ~ Children welcome (no food for them after 8pm) ~ Open 11-3, 6.30-11; 12-3, 7-10.30 Sun; closed Mon (except bank holidays)

MISERDEN SO9308 Map 4

Carpenters Arms

Village signposted off B4070 NE of Stroud; also a pleasant drive off A417 via the Duntisbournes, or off A419 via Sapperton and Edgeworth; OS Sheet 163 map reference 936089

Beautifully placed in an idyllic Cotswold estate village above the Golden Valley, this cheerful local has recently been taken over by the landlord of the Butchers Arms at Sheepscombe. Its two open-plan bar areas have nice old wooden tables, seats with the original little brass name plates on the backs, bare boards, stripped stone walls with some interesting bric-a-brac, and two big log fires, and there's a small no-smoking dining room with dark traditional furniture; the sizeable collage (done with Laurie Lee) has lots of illustrations and book covers signed by him. Well kept ales on handpump such as Brakspears and Wadworths 6X, darts, cribbage and dominoes. Good honest home-made food includes sandwiches (from £2), home-made soup

(£2.50), filled baked potatoes (from £3.95), ploughman's (from £4.50), five vegetarian dishes such as spinach, lentil and nut wellington (£5.75), a pie of the day (£5.95), changing fresh fish dishes (from £5.95), home-made salmon and potato cakes, Guinness and beef sausages with malt whisky or gammon and egg (£6.50), pot-roast casserole of kangaroo (£7.95), steaks (from £8.50), and home-made puddings like a daily crumble or sticky toffee pudding (£2.75); the friendly staff do their best for hungry and muddy walkers. There are tables out in the garden and occasional summer Morris men. The nearby gardens of Misarden Park, open midweek summer, are well worth visiting. *(Recommended by Giles Francis, Alec Hamilton, Peter and Audrey Dowsett, D Irving, E McCall, R Huggins, T McLean, Guy Vowles, Margaret Dyke, D G King, Mrs G Connell)*

Free house ~ Licensee Johnny Johnston ~ Real ale ~ Meals and snacks ~ (01285) 821283 ~ Children welcome ~ Open 11-2.30, 6-11; 12-3, 7-10.30 Sun; closed evening 25 Dec

NAILSWORTH ST8599 Map 4

Egypt Mill

Just off A46 S of Stroud; left and left again at roundabout

Very different, this: a three-floor stonebuilt mill which still has working waterwheels and the millstream flowing through. It's been attractively converted, with the brick-and-stone-floored split-level bar giving good views of the wheels, and big pictures and lots of stripped beams in the comfortable carpeted lounge, along with some hefty yet elegant ironwork from the old mill machinery. It's now emerged from a spell during which it had karaoke nights and so forth, with a pleasant almost bistro-ish feel these days. Although it can get quite crowded on fine weekends, it's actually spacious enough to feel at its best when it's busy – with good service to cope. There's a civilised upstairs restaurant, and a no-smoking area. Tetleys, Wadworths 6X, and a guest beer on handpump, and a wide choice of nicely presented good generous food such as lunchtime sandwiches and filled french bread (from £2.20), ploughman's (£4.70), and omelettes, as well as soup (£2.30), chicken liver, pork and bacon terrine (£3.80), moules marinières (£3.95), spicy vegetable filo parcels (£6.20), macaroni cheese (£6.80), chicken pie (£6.90), home-made steak and mushroom pudding (£7.45), crispy pork belly with braised red cabbage (£7.90), lamb balti (£7.80), duck cassoulet (£8.20), steaks (from £9.90), daily fresh Cornish fish, children's menu (from £2), and Sunday roast lunch. No dogs; the floodlit terrace garden by the millpond is most attractive, and there's a little bridge over from the car park. *(Recommended by Andy and Jill Kassube, D G King, Keith and Margaret Kettell)*

Free house ~ Licensee Stephen Webb ~ Real ale ~ Meals and snacks ~ Restaurant ~ (01453) 833449 ~ Children welcome ~ Open 11-3, 6.30-11; 11-11(10.30 summer Sun) summer Sat ~ Bedrooms: £45.50B/£75B

Weighbridge

B4014 towards Tetbury

Over many years, this well liked pub has remained unchanged. The friendly bar has three cosily old-fashioned rooms with stripped stone walls, antique settles and country chairs, and window seats; one even has a bell to ring for prompt service. The black beam-and-plank ceiling of the left-hand room is thickly festooned with black ironware – sheepshears, gin-traps, lamps, cauldrons and bellows – while up some steps a raftered loft has candles in bottles on an engaging mix of rustic tables, as well as unexpected decorations such as a wooden butcher's block; no noisy games machines or piped music. Good bar food includes filled french bread (from £1.80), ploughman's (from £3.60), meaty or vegetarian lasagne (£4.30), a two-in-one pie with cauliflower cheese in one half and steak and mushroom or chicken, ham and leek in the other (small £5.20, big £6.20; lovely pastry), and puddings like treacle tart or cherry crumble (£2.40); helpful service. Well kept Marstons Pedigree, Smiles Best, Theakstons Best, and Wadworths 6X on handpump, and up to 10 wines by the glass. Behind is a sheltered garden with swings and picnic-sets under cocktail parasols. Back in the days when the landlord used to run the bridge from which the pub takes its name, it would cost you 3d for each score of pigs you wanted to take along the turnpike. *(Recommended by Dave Irving, Tom McLean, Roger Huggins, Ewan McCall, Peter and Audrey Dowsett, Tony Dickinson, T L Rees)*

Free house ~ Licensee Richard Kulesza ~ Real ale ~ Meals and snacks ~ (01453) 832520 ~ Children in eating area of bar ~ Open 11-2.30, 7(6.30 Sat)-11; 12-3, 7-10.30 Sun; closed 25 Dec

NAUNTON SP1123 Map 4

Black Horse

Village signposted from B4068 (shown as A436 on older maps) W of Stow on the Wold

Lovely after a walk on the blowy hills (leave muddy boots outside), this friendly old inn has a comfortable bar with black beams, stripped stonework, simple country-kitchen chairs, built-in oak pews, polished elm cast-iron-framed tables, and a warming open fire. Decent bar food includes filled french bread, home-made soup (£2.60), home-made pâté (£3.75), filled baked potatoes (from £4.25), ploughman's with lots of salad (from £4.50), broccoli cheese bake (£5.95), steak and kidney pudding (£6.50), lamb casserole (£8.95), steaks (from £11.25), and puddings (£2.95); the restaurant is no smoking. Well kept and well priced Donnington BB and SBA on handpump, and sensibly placed darts, cribbage, shove-ha'penny, dominoes, and piped music. Some tables outside. *(Recommended by Stephen and Julie Brown, K Neville-Rolfe, Mr and Mrs Head, Lawrence Pearse, Andy and Jill Kassube, Eddie Walder, Marjorie and David Lamb, James and Wendy Timms, Joan Morgan, D J and P M Taylor, Guy Consterdine, Graham and Karen Oddey, R Davies, Dr and Mrs J Hills, Margaret Dyke, Rob Whittle, Glen and Nola Armstrong)*

Donnington ~ Tenant Martin Macklin ~ Real ale ~ Meals and snacks ~ Restaurant ~ (01451) 850565 ~ Children in eating area of bar ~ Open 11.30-3, 6-11; 12-3, 7-10.30 Sun ~ One bedroom: /£45B

NORTH CERNEY SP0208 Map 2

Bathurst Arms

A435 Cirencester—Cheltenham

They've cleverly found a good balance between diners and drinkers in this handsome old inn – with those wanting a pint and a chat being made just as welcome as customers coming for a meal. The beamed and panelled bar has a friendly, relaxed atmosphere, a fireplace at each end (one quite huge and housing an open woodburner), a good mix of old tables and nicely faded chairs, old-fashioned window seats, and some pewter plates. There are country tables in a little carpeted room off the bar, as well as winged high-backed settles forming booths around other tables. A good choice of bar food might include sandwiches (from £2), home-made pâté (£3.60), warm cerney goat's cheese salad (£4.50), various pasta dishes (£5.50), home-made pies (£6.25), home-made salmon fishcakes (£6.95), steaks with good sauces (from £8.50), duck with a sweet and sour sauce (£10.50), and monkfish in bacon and cream or ostrich with red wine sauce (£10.95). Well kept Arkells BBB, Hook Norton Best, Wadworths 6X and three guest beers on handpump, and good wines by the glass. The Stables Bar has darts, pool, cribbage, dominoes, and juke box; piped music. The attractive flower-filled front lawn runs down to the little River Churn, and there are picnic-sets sheltered by small trees and shrubs; plenty of surrounding walks. *(Recommended by J Taylor, P and S White, Dr and Mrs B D Smith, John Fahy, Gwen and Peter Andrews, Dr and Mrs A K Clarke, MRSM, Joan Olivier, Oliver Hill, Lynn Sharpless, Bob Eardley)*

Free house ~ Licensee Mike Costley-White ~ Real ale ~ Meals and snacks ~ Restaurant ~ (01285) 831281 ~ Children in eating area of bar ~ Occasional weekend live entertainment ~ Open 11-3, 6-11; 12-2, 7-10.30 Sun; closed 25 Dec ~ Bedrooms: £35B/£45B

NORTH NIBLEY ST7596 Map 4

New Inn

Waterley Bottom, which is quite well signposted from surrounding lanes; inn signposted from the Bottom itself; one route is from A4135 S of Dursley, via lane with red sign saying Steep Hill, 1 in 5 (just SE of Stinchcombe Golf Course turn-off), turning right when you get to the bottom; another is to follow Waterley Bottom signpost from previous main entry, keeping eyes skinned for small low signpost to inn; OS Sheet 162 map reference 758963; though this is the way we know best, one reader suggests the road is wider if you approach directly from North Nibley

Perhaps this friendly pub is best at lunchtime or on an early summer evening when you can enjoy the country setting. At the far end of the garden is a small orchard with swings, slides and a timber tree-house, and they may serve afternoon teas on the neatly kept terrace. Inside, the carpeted lounge bar has cushioned windsor chairs and varnished high-backed settles against the partly stripped stone walls, and sensibly placed darts, dominoes, shove-ha'penny, cribbage, table skittles, and trivia in the simple public bar. Particularly well kept Berkeley Dicky Pearce, Cotleigh Tawny and WB (a beer brewed specially for the pub), Greene King Abbot, Smiles Best, and Theakstons Old Peculier are either dispensed from Barmaid's Delight (the name of one of the antique beer engines) or tapped from the cask; the character landlady is quite a real-ale expert; lots of malt whiskies, and Inch's cider. Bar food (they tell us prices have not changed since last year) includes filled brown baps or toasties, curry or steak and onion pie (£4.15), lasagne (£4.40), and puddings like peach and banana crumble (£1.95); piped music. No children. *(Recommended by Tom McLean, Roger Huggins, Dave Irving, Ewan McCall, JP, PP, Gill Cathles, Patrick Hancock, Peter and Jenny Quine, Malcolm Taylor, T L Rees)*

Free house ~ Licensee Ruby Sainty ~ Real ale ~ Meals and snacks ~ (01453) 543659 ~ Open 12-2.30(3 Sat), 7-11; 12-3, 7-10.30 Sun ~ Two bedrooms: £25B/£35B

OAKRIDGE LYNCH SO9102 Map 4

Butchers Arms

Village signposted off Eastcombe—Bisley road, E of Stroud, which is the easiest approach; with a good map you could brave the steep lanes via Frampton Mansell, which is signposted off A419 Stroud—Cirencester

In summer, the flowering tubs and hanging basket in front of this neatly kept pub are very pretty, and picnic-sets on a stretch of lawn look down over the valley. Inside, the spacious rambling bar has a few beams in its low ceiling, some walls stripped back to the bare stone, old photographs, comfortable, traditional furnishings like wheelback chairs around the neat tables on its patterned carpet, and three open fires. Bar food includes rolls, ploughman's, tasty hot french sticks filled with things like melted brie and salami (£4.25), garlic prawns (£4.95), haddock in celery sauce (£6.50), nice curries, rib-eye steak (£8.95), and daily specials (£4.95-£6.95); popular Sunday lunch (£7.95; 3 courses £11.95). Best to book at the weekend; the restaurant is no smoking. Well kept Archers Best, Goff's Jouster, Hook Norton Old Hookey, Marstons Pedigree, and Tetleys Bitter on handpump; a little room off the main bar has darts, fruit machine, and trivia, and there's a skittle alley. There are good walks in the valley along the old Thames & Severn canal. Usefully, the pub's car park is up on the level top road, so you don't have to plunge into the tortuous network of village lanes. *(Recommended by Nick and Meriel Cox, Mr and Mrs Spencer, Pat and John Millward, P R and S A White, Neil and Anita Christopher)*

Free house ~ Licensee Peter Coupe ~ Real ale ~ Meals and snacks (not Sun evening) ~ Restaurant (Weds-Sat evenings, Sun lunch) ~ (01285) 760371 ~ Children in small anteroom and in restaurant ~ Open 11-3, 6-11; 12-3.30, 7-10.30 Sun; closed 25 Dec

The details at the end of each main entry start by saying whether the pub is a free house, or if it's tied to a brewery (which we name).

ODDINGTON SP2225 Map 4

Horse & Groom

Upper Oddington; signposted from A436 E of Stow on the Wold

The garden here is a good place for families in summer. There's a little water-garden beyond a rose hedge, picnic-sets on the neat lawn below the car park, apple trees, Aunt Sally, and a fine play area including an enormous log climber and pet rabbits and other animals. Inside, the bar has pale polished flagstones, a handsome antique oak box settle among other more modern seats, some horsebrasses on the dark 16th-c oak beams in the ochre ceiling, stripped stone walls with some harness and a few brass platters, an inglenook fireplace, and a fish tank. Good bar food includes sandwiches, filled french bread and filled baked potatoes (from £3.25), ploughman's (£4.50), and soups like roasted tomato and aubergine (£2.95), chicken, wild mushroom and spinach terrine with apple chutney or salmon fishcakes with a tomato and tarragon sauce (£3.95), confit of pork with an apple and cider sauce (£4.25), home-made lasagne (£7.95), strips of chicken in a creamy wild mushroom sauce (£8.95), rack of lamb with crisp potato cake and rosemary jus (£10.95), and puddings like bread and butter pudding, baked lemon tart and fruit crème brûlée (£3.25); children's menu (£3.25); the no-smoking candlelit dining room is pretty. Well kept Hook Norton Best and guests like Fullers London Pride, Ledbury Goldings Best, Wadworths 6X, Charles Wells Bombardier, and Wychwood Hobgoblin on handpump, and a good wine list with 8 by the glass. *(Recommended by D G Clarke, Dorothee and Dennis Glover, Chris Mawson, P Ridley, Dr and Mrs J Hills, R Vincent, Ted George, Dr A Y Drummond, J H Kane, Liz Bell)*

Free house ~ Licensees David and Jill South ~ Real ale ~ Meals and snacks ~ Restaurant ~ (01451) 830584 ~ Children in eating area of bar and in restaurant until 9pm ~ Open 11.30-2.30, 6-11; 12-2.30, 7-10.30 Sun ~ Bedrooms: £40S/£55S

OLD SODBURY ST7581 Map 2

Dog

Not far from M4 junction 18: A46 N, then A432 left towards Chipping Sodbury

This is a handy pub for the M4, and seems to be constantly busy with people coming to eat. There are fresh fish dishes like plaice, red mullet, halibut, shark or tuna, whole fresh sole, Devon scallops or clam fries, several different ways of serving mussels (from £3.25), and squid (£4.95), as well as sandwiches (from £1.75), ploughman's (£4.25), cottage pie or cheese and onion flan (£4.95), home-made steak and kidney pie (£5.25), Mexican tamales with chilli sauce (£5.95), sweet and sour pork or Hawaiian chicken creole (£6.50), steaks (from £6.95), puddings (from £1.95), children's menu (from £1.50), and daily specials. The two-level bar and smaller no-smoking room both have areas of original bare stone walls, beams and timbering, low ceilings, wall benches and cushioned chairs, open fires, and a bustling atmosphere. Well kept Bass, Boddingtons, Flowers Original, Wadworths 6X, and Wickwar BOB on handpump, and several malt whiskies; good service. Darts, dominoes, fruit machine, video game, juke box, and skittle alley. Trophy, the border collie, likes playing football with customers. There's a large garden with lots of seating, a summer barbecue area and pets corner, climbing frames, swings, slides, football net, and see-saws, and a bouncy castle most bank holidays. Lots of good walks nearby. *(Recommended by Mayur Shah, Pat Crabb, Paul and Diane Burrows, Phyl and Jack Street, Carole Smart, Andrew Jeeves, Roy Smylie, Tom Evans, Meg and Colin Hamilton, B J Harding, S Godsell, Neville Kenyon, Hugh Roberts, Keith Waters, Miss Helen Osborne, M G Hart, Charles and Pauline Stride, Mr and Mrs R Maggs, Lyn and Geoff Hallchurch)*

Whitbreads ~ Lease: John and Joan Harris ~ Real ale ~ Meals and snacks (served all day Mon-Sat) ~ (01454) 312006 ~ Children welcome ~ Open 11-11; 12-3.30, 7-10.30 Sun ~ Bedrooms: £22.50/£38

Please let us know of any pubs where the wine is particularly good.

OLDBURY ON SEVERN ST6292 Map 2

Anchor

Village signposted from B4061

After 27 years, the licensees are happy to tell us that this still remains a traditional village pub with a good welcome, and no music, no games machines, and no chips. There's a good mix of customers – locals who enjoy their nightly summer games of boules (they have over 100 members now), walkers who have trod the many paths over the meadows to the sea dyke overlooking the tidal flats (Sunday lunch is now served until 4pm to accommodate them), and those out to have a good relaxing meal. The lounge has modern beams and stone, a mix of tables including an attractive oval oak gateleg one, cushioned window seats, winged seats against the wall, pictures in gilt frames, and a big winter log fire. Diners can eat in the lounge or bar area or in the no-smoking dining room at the back of the building (good for larger groups) and the menu is the same in all rooms: no sandwiches but wholemeal bread with cheeses, beef, home-baked ham, pâté or smoked mackerel (from £2.75), salads (from £3.75), sliced aubergine rolled and stuffed with cheese, black olives, pine nuts and oregano with a tomato sauce (£4.75), bean bourguignon or large yorkshire pudding filled with beef and onion gravy (£5), salmon in a creamy wine sauce or pepperpot beef (£5.95), fresh cod with tomato and chilli sauce (£6.25), chargrilled chicken (£6.75), sirloin steak (£8.25), daily specials like pork au poivre (£5.95), fresh marinated salmon (£6.95) or popular chargrilled ostrich with a port and plum sauce (£11.95), and puddings like raspberry brûlée, tarte à l'orange or caramel apple granny (from £2.30); as they don't do chips, they do offer dauphinois or don quixote (sliced and cooked with cheese and onion), new potatoes or baked ones. Well kept Bass, Black Sheep, Butcombe Bitter, Theakstons Best and Old Peculier, and Worthington Best on handpump or tapped from the cask, all well priced for the area. Also over 75 malts, a decent choice of good quality wines, and Inch's cider; darts, shove-ha'penny, dominoes and cribbage; they have wheelchair access and a disabled lavatory. There are seats in the pretty garden. St Arilda's church nearby is interesting, on its odd little knoll with wild flowers among the gravestones (the primroses and daffodils in spring are lovely). *(Recommended by Simon and Amanda Southwell, Tom Evans, S H Godsell, Christopher and Mary Thomas, Meg and Colin Hamilton, R C Morgan, Gwen and Peter Andrews, Andrew Shore, Ian Wagg, James and Ruth Morrell, Tom McLean, Roger Huggins, Ewan McCall, Dave Irving, M G Hart)*

Free house ~ Licensees Michael Dowdeswell, Alex de la Torre ~ Real ale ~ Meals and snacks ~ Restaurant ~ (01454) 413331 ~ Children in restaurant only ~ Open 11.30-2.30, 6.30-11; 11.30-11 Sat, 12-10.30 Sun; closed 25 Dec, evening 26 Dec

PAXFORD SP1837 Map 4

Churchill

B4479, SE of Chipping Campden

A decade ago this quaint out-of-the-way Cotswold stone pub was a basic little Hook Norton local. That brewery sold it to Whitbreads, who in turn sold it as a free house. Recently it's been taken over and reworked as a charming dining pub by two skilled restaurateurs, who have married cooking of real talent to a decor that entirely suits the surroundings. There's understandable concentration on the newish restaurant extension, but the atmosphere has stayed pleasantly pubby, particularly in the small side drinks bar evidently formed from two tiny knocked-together rooms. There are flagstones, assorted old tables and chairs, and a snug warmed by a good log fire in its big fireplace. In the best pub tradition they don't take bookings; your name goes on a chalked waiting list if all the tables are full. And full they are often likely to be, as word gets around about the quality of the cooking here. The generously served food might include good starters such as scallops, smoked fish and charcuterie, as well as home-made soup (£2.95), hot cheese fritter with sweet chilli sauce (£4), pigeon breast salad with leeks, orange and peppers (£5), plaice with rocket butter and soy sauce (£9), roast breast of guinea fowl with wild mushroom sauce (£9.50), fried calf liver with lentil and pistachio nut jus (£9.90), lamb with ginger and rosemary (£12), and puddings like mango mousse with white peach sauce and vanilla ice cream or sticky toffee pudding (from £2.95). Well kept Arkells BBB, Hook Norton Best, and a guest like Boddingtons on handpump, a reasonable medium-priced wine list with 8 by the glass, good nicely served coffee; dominoes, cribbage. There are some tables outside; Aunt Sally. *(Recommended by J H Kane, Martin Jones, H Dickinson, Alex)*

Free house ~ Licensee Leo Brooke-Little ~ Real ale ~ Meals and snacks ~ (01386) 594000 ~ Well behaved children allowed away from bar ~ Open 11-3, 6-11; 12-2.30, 7-10.30 Sun; closed evening 25 Dec ~ Bedrooms: £40B/£60B

REDBROOK SO5410 Map 4

Boat

Pub's car park is now signed in village on A466 Chepstow—Monmouth; from here 100-yard footbridge crosses Wye (pub actually in Penallt in Wales – but much easier to find this way); OS Sheet 162 map reference 534097

This little pub does get very full at peak times, but you can sit on the sturdy home-built seats by the interestingly shaped tables in the garden here and listen to the waters of the River Wye spilling down the waterfall cliffs into the duck pond below – it's a popular spot with walkers. Inside, the unpretentious bar still has lots of landscapes and pictures of the pub during floods, simple seating, and a woodburning stove on the tiled floor. They have a fine choice of around 8 well kept beers, tapped straight from casks behind the bar counter that might include Adnams Broadside, Butcombe Bitter, Freeminer Bitter and Speculation, Fullers London Pride, Hook Norton Best, Theakstons Old Peculier, and Wadworths 6X; a range of country wines, too. Decent bar food includes home-made soup (£2), filled baked potatoes (from £2), ploughman's (£4), vegetable curry (£4.50), leek and roast parsnip stilton bake (£4.70), boozy beef pie (£4.80), Moroccan honeyed lamb (£4.85), pork, chestnut and Guinness casserole (£4.95), and puddings (£2.15); children's dishes (from £1.25). Darts, shove-ha'penny, table skittles, cribbage, and dominoes. *(Recommended by Sidney and Erna Wells, JP, PP, Barry and Anne, Edward Leetham, Dr and Mrs P Baker, J and F Gowers, David Lewis, Sarah Lart, JKW, Mark Percy, Lesley Mayoh, P Fowler, G and T Edwards, Daren Haines, Wayne Brindle, Ted George, Nick and Meriel Cox, Liz Bell)*

Free house ~ Licensees Steffan and Dawn Rowlands ~ Real ale ~ Meals and snacks (all day on bank holidays and summer hol Sun) ~ (01600) 712615 ~ Well behaved children welcome ~ Folk Tues evening, blues Thurs ~ Open 11.30-3, 6-11; 11-11 Sat; 12-10.30 Sun; 12-4, 6.30-10.30 winter Sun

SAPPERTON SO9403 Map 4

Daneway

Village signposted from A419 Stroud—Cirencester; from village centre follow Edgeworth, Bisley signpost; OS Sheet 163 map reference 939034

Lots of seats in front of this friendly old pub look down over the canal and the valley of the little River Frome, and the lovely sloping lawn is bright with flower beds. There are good walks along the canal banks in either direction, and it's particularly worth the short stroll to the entrance of the Sapperton Tunnel, which was used at the end of the 18th c by the 'leggers', men who lay on top of the canal boats and pushed them through the two-and-a-half mile tunnel with their feet. The welcoming bar has a remarkably grand and dominating fireplace, elaborately carved oak from floor to ceiling, racing and hunting prints on the walls, and Polly the talking parrot. Bar food includes winter soup (£1.95), baps filled with things like Aberdeen Angus steak or good bacon and mushrooms (from £2.75), ploughman's (from £4.25), home-made chilli or lasagne (£5.75), beef and Guinness pie (£6.25), gammon and egg (£7.95) and steaks (from £9.50); afternoon teas in summer. Well kept Wadworths IPA, 6X, and seasonal beers on handpump, and Westons Old Rosie cider; darts, dominoes, cribbage, shove-ha'penny, and ring-the-bull in the public bar, which has a big inglenook fireplace; table skittles and quoits. They hold a vintage motorcycle club meeting twice a year. Camping by arrangement. *(Recommended by Gordon, Dr and Mrs A K Clarke, Dave Irving, Roger Huggins, Tom McLean, Ewan McCall, Dr A Drummond, Barry and Anne, Kay Neville-Rolfe, Peter and Audrey Dowsett)*

Wadworths ~ Tenants Richard and Liz Goodfellow ~ Real ale ~ Meals and snacks ~ (01285) 760297 ~ Children in small no-smoking family room off lounge ~ Open 11-2.30(5.30 Sat), 6.30-11; 12-5.30, 7-10.30 Sun; 11-3, 6.30(7 Sun)-11 winter weekends

SHEEPSCOMBE SO8910 Map 4

Butchers Arms 🍷

Village signposted from B4070 NE of Stroud, and A46 N of Painswick (narrow lanes)

They have a sensible policy here not to reserve tables in the bar (though many customers do wish to eat there) as this ensures that casual diners and their locals and regulars have a welcoming area in which to enjoy their drinks. It's a friendly place with a good bustling atmosphere in the bar (no noisy games machines or piped music), seats in big bay windows, flowery-cushioned chairs and rustic benches, log fires, and lots of interesting oddments like assorted blow lamps, irons, and plates. Good lunchtime bar food includes soup (£2.25), filled rolls (from £2.75; hot crispy bacon £3.50), filled baked potatoes (from £3.50), ploughman's (from £4.50), smoked salmon pâté (£3.95), big Gloucester sausages (£4.75), vegetable curry or home-cooked honey-roast ham with chips (£5.75), home-made steak and kidney pie (£5.95), and mixed grill (£8.50), with evening dishes like tiger prawns in filo pastry with a spicy sauce (£4.50), big New Zealand green-lip mussels in white wine and garlic (£5), mushroom and lentil cannelloni (£5.75), halibut steak (£7.50), double breast of chicken in Jamaican spices (£7.95), and steaks (from £9.75), and daily specials such as oriental vegetable stir fry (£5.75), loin of pork with an apricot stuffing and apricot sauce (£6.25), venison medallions with a rich red wine gravy (£6.75), and grilled red snapper with a lemon and dill dressing (£7.85). The restaurant and a small area in the bar are no smoking. Well kept Archers Best Bitter, Hook Norton Best, Uley Old Spot, and guest beers on handpump, decent wines, traditional ciders, and country wines; darts, cribbage, dominoes. The views are marvellous and there are teak seats below the building, tables on the steep grass behind, and a cricket ground behind on such a steep slope that the boundary fielders at one end can scarcely see the bowler. *(Recommended by P and S White, Martin Jones, Dave Irving, Roger Huggins, Tom McLean, Ewan McCall, IHR, Pat and John Millward, Mrs G Connell, Liz Bell, Neil and Anita Christopher, Pat and Roger Fereday, George Atkinson, Dr and Mrs J H Hills, James Nunns, Kay Neville-Rolfe, Stephen Pine, Alfred Lawrence, Daren Haines, Steve Goodchild)*

Free house ~ Licensees Johnny and Hilary Johnston ~ Real ale ~ Meals and snacks (till 10pm) ~ Restaurant ~ (01452) 812113 ~ Children welcome until 9pm ~ Open 11-11; 12-10.30 Sun; 11-2.30, 6.30-11 in winter

SIDDINGTON SU0399 Map 4

Greyhound

Ashton Rd; village signposted from A419 roundabout at Tesco

This pleasant, smartened-up pub has two connected rooms with a friendly bustling atmosphere. The biggish lounge bar has two big log fires, high dining chairs, chapel seats and so forth on the old herringbone brick floor, and good tables – mainly stripped pine, but one fine circular mahogany one. The beams and ochre walls are covered with lots of copper and brass, as well as a few hunting prints, some black-lacquered farm tools, and china and other bric-a-brac; the public bar has darts, cribbage, dominoes, trivia, and piped music, and there's a skittle alley at the back. Well liked bar food includes home-made soup (£2.50), sandwiches or filled baked potatoes (from £2.95), home-made chicken liver pâté (£3.15), good ploughman's (from £4.25), chilli con carne or macaroni cheese (£4.95), home-made pie of the day, chicken and mango curry (£5.95), pork steak with cider, cream and apple sauce (£6.25), steaks (from £8.95), and grilled salmon steak with lemon butter (£9.25); popular Sunday carvery. Well kept Wadworths IPA and 6X, and Badger Tanglefoot on handpump. There are seats among lilacs, apple trees, flower borders and short stone walls behind the car park. *(Recommended by Dave Irving, Roger Huggins, Ewan McCall, Tom McLean, G W Pearce, Martin and Karen Wake, P and S White, W W Burke, Simon Collett-Jones, F J and A Parmenter, Peter and Audrey Dowsett)*

Wadworths ~ Managers Mike and Louise Grattan ~ Real ale ~ Meals and snacks ~ (01285) 653573 ~ Children in eating area of bar ~ Open 11.30-3, 6.30-11; 12-3, 7-10.30 Sun

SOUTH CERNEY SU0497 Map 4

Eliot Arms

Village signposted off A419 SE of Cirencester; Clarks Hay

There's an unusal layout (and a good welcoming atmosphere) in this handsome wisteria-draped stone inn. On the right is the small solid pale wooden counter, and on the left is the main bar with sturdy plush-cushioned captain's chairs, built-in corner seats, plush round stools, and lots of shiny copper pots and jugs and some enamel water pots hanging from high beams – tastefully arranged. Lots of separate snug places to sit are linked by short passages lined with decorative plates, and the back room is packed with carpentry tools, stirrups, and horse bits hanging from the ceiling, hundreds of dug-up ancient bottles on the mantlepiece over the log fire (with little snug pews tucked in beside it), a housekeeper's chair, and some interesting racing-car pictures from Fangio and Moss to Mansell. Bar food includes sandwiches (from £2.75; french bread from £4.25), home-made chicken liver pâté (£3.95), filled baked potatoes (from £3.95), ploughman's (from £5.50), home-made lasagne, chicken in a white wine sauce or pies such as steak and mushroom or chicken, ham and leek pies (all £6.95), salmon with prawn sauce (£7.95), and steaks (from £8.95). As well as the cosily attractive little dining room down a step or two, there's a smart separate no-smoking restaurant, and a coffee shop. Well kept Boddingtons, Flowers Original, Marstons Pedigree, and Wadworths 6X on handpump, 120 malt whiskies, a variety of foreign bottled beers, and helpful service; shove-ha'penny, cribbage, dominoes, a tucked-away fruit machine, and piped music; skittle alley. There are picnic-sets and a swing in the neat back garden. *(Recommended by Malcolm Thomas, Roger Huggins, Tom McLean, Dave Irving, Ewan McCall, Mr and Mrs B Craig, P and S White, Neil and Anita Christopher, David Peakall, S P Bobeldijk, Mrs B Sugarman)*

Free house ~ Licensees Duncan and Linda Hickling ~ Real ale ~ Meals and snacks (till 10pm) ~ Restaurants ~ (01285) 860215 ~ Children welcome till 9pm ~ Open 10.30-11; 12-10.30 Sun ~ Bedrooms: £39.95B/£52.50B

ST BRIAVELS SO5605 Map 4

George

Not far from Tintern Abbey, this attractive little pub has tables on a flagstoned terrace at the back overlooking the grassy former moat of the silvery stone 12th-c castle built as a fortification against the Welsh; there are more seats among roses and shrubs, and an outside chessboard. Inside, the three rambling rooms have old-fashioned built-in wall seats, some booth seating, green-cushioned small settles, toby jugs and antique bottles on black beams over the servery, and a large stone open fireplace; a Celtic coffin lid dating from 1070, discovered when a fireplace was removed, is now mounted next to the bar counter. A dining area is no smoking. Enjoyable home-made bar food includes soup (£2.50), pâté or spicy chicken wings (£3.95), ploughman's (£4.50), filled baked potatoes (£4.95), moussaka (£5.95), steak and kidney pie, chilli or crunchy nut loaf (£6.95), fresh grilled tuna steak (£7.95), steaks (from £7.95), duck breast in madeira sauce (£8.95), daily specials, puddings such as bread and butter pudding or banoffi pie (£3.25), and Sunday roast lunch (£7.95). The dining room is no smoking. Well kept Marstons Pedigree, Shepherd Neame Spitfire, Wadworths 6X, and a guest such as Batemans on handpump, and lots of malt whiskies. Lots of walks start nearby. *(Recommended by R T and J C Moggridge, Donald Godden, Rona Murdoch, LM, Paul Barnett, Wayne Brindle, Peter and Gwyneth Eastwood, JKW, Brian and Liz Whitford)*

Free house ~ Licensee Bruce Bennett ~ Real ale ~ Meals and snacks ~ Restaurant ~ (01594) 530228 ~ Children welcome ~ Open 11-3, 6.30-11; 12-3, 7-10.30 Sun ~ Bedrooms: /£40B

STANTON SO0634 Map 4

Mount

Village signposted off B4632 (the old A46) SW of Broadway; Old Snowshill Road – take the no through road up hill and bear left

The best view down across the lovely golden stone village and (on a good day) on to the Welsh mountains, is from seats on the pretty terrace in front of this pub; boules on the lawn. Inside, the original simple bar has black beams, cask seats on big flagstones, heavy-horse harness and racing photographs, and a big fireplace. A spacious extension, with some big picture windows, has comfortable oak wall seats and cigarette cards of Derby and Grand National winners, and another extension (no smoking) is used in winter as a restaurant and in summer as a more informal eating bar. Donnington BB and SBA on handpump kept under light blanket pressure and farm cider; darts, shove-ha'penny, dominoes, cribbage, bar billiards, and piped music. Decent bar food includes sandwiches (£2.75; toasties £3.95), ploughman's (£4.25), broccoli and cheese bake, thai green chicken curry or seafood lasagne (all £5.25), daily specials, evening steaks and fish dishes, and puddings (£2.75). *(Recommended by Paul S McPherson, Miss V Kavanagh, D G Haines, Martin Jones, David Walker, Rob Whittle, Graham and Karen Oddey, Kay Neville-Rolfe, Peter and Audrey Dowsett, Ted George, Andrew and Ruth Triggs, Liz Bell, Sally Shaw)*

Donnington ~ Tenant Colin Johns ~ Real ale ~ Meals and snacks (not Sun evening) ~ (01386) 584316 ~ Well behaved children welcome until 9pm ~ Open 11-3, 6-11; 11-11 Sat; 12-10.30 Sun; closed 25 Dec

TETBURY ST8394 Map 4

Gumstool

Part of Calcot Manor Hotel; A4135 W of town, just E of junction with A46

By no means a straightforward pub, this civilised dining bar is not somewhere to come to for a quick drink, though there are concessions to this – a couple of marble-topped pub tables beyond one screen, leather armchair by the big log fire, daily papers, well kept Bass, Wadworths 6X, and Wickwar BOB and Coopers on handpump, and dominoes, shove-ha'penny, and cribbage. The layout is well divided to give a feeling of intimacy without losing the overall sense of contented bustle, the lighting is attractive, and materials are old-fashioned (lots of stripped pine, flagstones, gingham curtains, hop bines) though the style is neatly modern. The changing menu has plenty of sensibly priced starters that for a little extra would do as a snack lunch – soups (£2.75; generous £4.25), local English cheeses with celery, grapes and crusty bread (£4.70; generous £7.20), salad of black pudding, crispy bacon and poached egg (£5.20; generous £7.70), slow roasted duck salad with pickled ginger and carrot and sweet and sour dressing (£6.70; generous £9.20); also, beer sausages with mash and onion gravy (£6.90), ham, cabbage and onion hash with poached egg and mustard sauce (£7.55), breast of chicken with garlic and herb mushrooms and crispy bacon (£8.55), lamb and cumin tagine with lemon and couscous (£9.20), and puddings like warm chocolate and cherry cake, bread and butter pudding or home-made ices and sorbets (from £3.75); extra vegetables £1.50. Best to book. A very wide choice of interesting wines by the glass spans a wide price range; piped music. The neat side lawn has a couple of picnic-sets; Westonbirt Arboretum is not far. *(Recommended by Pat and John Millward, Charles and Pauline Stride, Simon and Amanda Southwell, Dr and Mrs A Newton, Peter Neate, D G King)*

Free house ~ Licensees Paul Sadler, Richard Ball ~ Real ale ~ Meals and snacks ~ Restaurant ~ (01666) 890391 ~ Children welcome ~ Occasional live jazz ~ Open 11.30-2.30, 6-11; 11.30-11 summer Sat and Sun ~ Bedrooms: £95B/£110-£155B

TEWKESBURY SO8932 Map 4

Old Black Bear

High Street (N end, just before the bridge)

One look at this picturesque timbered pub and you're happily convinced of the truth of its reputation: it's said to be the county's oldest. Inside lives up to the promise, with rambling ancient rooms off black-timbered tiled corridors, some with low heavy beams, others light and sunny, inviting yet not too crowded. Furnishings are much as you'd expect from a town pub, with a log fire in one room, fruit machine and TV in the public bar; piped music. Flowers IPA and Original and Greenalls Original, and guest beers such as Marstons Pedigree, Smiles and Wadworths 6X tapped on handpump or from casks behind the bar in the main front room; country wines; very friendly if not always brisk service. Enjoyable food includes sandwiches (from £1.75), ploughman's (from £3.95), gammon and egg (£6.20), giant battered cod (£6.30), steak and kidney pie (£6.35), vegetarian lasagne (£5.50), steaks (from £7.95), puddings (from £1.80), and 3-course roast Sunday lunch (£6.50). Picnic-sets in the pleasant back garden overlook the River Avon; play area. *(Recommended by Martyn and Helen Webb, Andrew and Ruth Triggs, Andy and Jill Kassube, Ian Phillips, Gordon, Peter and Audrey Dowsett, Daren Haines, Mr and Mrs P Stubbs)*

Greenalls ~ Managers Jean-Claude and Helen Bourgeois ~ Real ale ~ Meals and snacks (not Sun evening) ~ Restaurant ~ (01684) 292202 ~ Well behaved children welcome ~ Open 11-11; 12-10.30 Sun

WITHINGTON SP0315 Map 4

Mill Inn

Village signposted from A436, and from A40; from village centre follow sign towards Roman villa (but don't be tempted astray by villa signs before you reach the village!)

The setting for this mossy-roofed old stone inn is charming – it stands virtually alone in a little valley surrounded by beech and chestnut trees and a rookery. The pretty garden with the River Coln running through it is bridged, and there are seats and tables on the small island and on the main lawn. Inside, the beamed and flagstoned bar and other wooden floored rooms have little nooks and corners with antique high-backed settles and large stone fireplaces; two rooms are no smoking. Good bar food (with prices unchanged since last year) includes cheese, a roll and pickle or ham, a roll and mustard (£2.95), ploughman's (£3.95), very good local goat's cheese wrapped in filo pastry with a tomato coulis (£3.95), pasta with mixed seafood in a creamy dill and cucumber sauce or nut roast with tomato provençale (£5.95), chicken in honey and mustard with chinese noodles (£6.50), gigot of lamb with cranberry and sage (£6.75), duck breast with apple and blackberry gloop (£8.95), and puddings like gooseberry crunch or apricot crumble (£2.65). Well kept Sam Smiths OB on handpump, a decent wine list, and quite a few malt whiskies; piped jazz and classical music. *(Recommended by J Dwane, Dr Ian Crichton, Dr Paul Kitchener, Tom McLean, Roger Huggins, E McCall, Rob Whittle, J H Kane, Daren Haines)*

Sam Smiths ~ Managers Peter Nielson and Robin Collyns ~ Real ale ~ Meals and snacks ~ (01242) 890204 ~ Children in eating area of bar until 9pm ~ Open 12-2.30, 6-11; 12-11(10.30 summer Sun) summer Sat ~ Bedrooms: £25B/£49.50B

WOODCHESTER SO8302 Map 4

Royal Oak

Church Road, North Woodchester; signposted off A46 on S edge of Stroud

This plain stonebuilt pub doesn't look in the least bit special from outside, and inside seems pretty straightforward, too, with a small simple local-feeling bar, a few highly varnished tables in the rather bright and equally small eating area on the left, and a few more towards the back; the Acrow props supporting the massive fireplace lintel, split down the middle, look a little ominous. The restaurant is no smoking; shove-ha'penny, cribbage, dominoes, and cards. The first clue that you're on to something good comes with the warm welcome, and the discovery that as well as well kept ales on handpump such as Archers Best, Berkeley Old Friend, Hook Norton Best, Uley Old Spot, and Wychwood Special, they have good house wines and good proper coffee. But it's with the food, served deftly and cheerfully, that they really score, using fresh ingredients cooked with real flair by one of the partners (who, it emerges, trained at Le Gavroche, Gavvers, and the Roux brothers' classy hotel in New York). At lunchtime, there might be sandwiches (from £2.60; the club chicken breast, bacon and poached egg is good; they bake their own bread each day), cream of asparagus soup (£3.25), goat's cheese salad (£4), ploughman's (£4.25), corned beef hash with poached eggs (£4.75), poached salmon salad, home-made beer sausages with mash or beef stroganoff (£5.50), fresh whole lobster salad (£11.25), changing seasonal daily specials, and evening dishes like timbale of ratatouille, wild mushrooms and tomato concassé (£6), braised leg and fried breast of duck with jus (£10.25), sirloin steak (£11.25), and puddings like baked lemon tart or crème brûlée (£3.50); you can eat the evening à la carte menu in the bar; they do good value weekday set lunches. Try this place soon; opened in 1997, it's already quite busy at weekends, and we predict will soon be humming midweek too. They hold occasional themed food and music evenings. The jack russell is called Dylan, and the young black labrador puppy, Jasmine. *(Recommended by Peter Shaw, Kate Naylor, HP, Tom Rees)*

Free house ~ Licensees Patrick Le Mesurier and Tony Croome ~ Real ale ~ Meals and snacks (not Sun evening) ~ (01453) 872735 ~ Well behaved children welcome ~ Open 11-3, 5.30-11; 11-11 Sat; 12-10.30 Sun; closed evening 25 Dec

Lucky Dip

Besides the fully inspected pubs, you might like to try these Lucky Dips recommended to us and described by readers (if you do, please send us reports):

☆ **Aldsworth** [A433 Burford—Cirencester; SP1510], *Sherborne Arms*: Much-extended relaxing modernised dining pub, many tables booked, with cheerful obliging service, beams, bric-a-brac and spacious and attractive no-smoking conservatory dining area, wide choice of good fresh food from baked potatoes and ploughman's up esp fish and very popular Sun lunch, well kept ales such as Archers, Bass, Boddingtons and Brakspears SB, log fire; darts, fruit machine; lovely garden, lavatory for disabled *(Simon Collett-Jones, David and Marjorie Lamb, Neil and Anita Christopher)*

☆ **Ampney St Peter** [A417, ½ mile E of village; SP0801], *Red Lion*: Unspoilt traditional 17th-c country local, clean and polished, with old-fashioned benches facing open fire, well kept Flowers IPA and Hook Norton Best served over corner bench, welcoming long-serving landlord and chatty regulars, hatch to corridor; separate room with wall benches around single table, darts, cards and dominoes; cl weekday lunchtimes *(Gordon, Tom McLean, Mrs S Evans, Dave Irving, Kevin Thorpe, Ewan McCall, JP, PP, Roger Huggins, Pete Baker, TRS, BB)*

Andoversford [Old Gloucester Rd; signed just off A40; SP0219], *Royal Oak*: Cosy beamed village local, lots of stripped stone, nice galleried dining room, big open fire, Boddingtons and Wadworths 6X, pool, darts, good choice of basic bar food from toasties and baked potatoes up *(Neil and Anita Christopher, BB)*

Arlingham [SO7111], *Old Passage*: Spacious, relaxing and well furnished, good value food, good range of Marstons ales, small restaurant; games machines, service can be slow, live music Fri; french windows to big garden with play area, extending down to River Severn *(Dr A Drummond, Tom Rees)*

☆ **Ashleworth** [signed off A417 at Hartpury; SO8125], *Queens Arms*: Comfortable and friendly, with remarkably wide choice of food inc some unusual dishes, particularly good veg and very popular Sun lunch (booking advised) in bar or attractive restaurant, helpful cheerful landlord, quick service, well kept Donnington; skittle alley *(P A Barnett, S H Godsell)*

Avening [High St; ST8897], *Bell*: Country pub done up with fitted carpets and pretty wallpaper, welcoming real fire, good helpings of simple well priced food inc vegetarian, well kept Marstons, Wickwar BOB and guest beers *(Andy and Jill Kassube, D Irving, R Huggins, T McLean, E McCall)*

Bibury [Arlington – B4425 NE of Cirencester; SP1106], *Catherine Wheel*: Friendly old low-beamed stripped-stone pub, open-plan main bar with quieter smaller room and dining area at back, well kept Archers Village, Courage Best and Directors and Hardy Country, decent wines, good log fire, food from sandwiches up, traditional games; fruit machine, piped music; picnic-sets in attractive quiet and spacious garden with play area, famously beautiful village, handy for country and riverside walks; open all day (Sun afternoon closure), children welcome, bedrooms *(Gordon, LYM)*

Birdlip [A417/A436 roundabout; SO9316], *Air Balloon*: Useful much extended Whitbreads Wayside Inn dining pub, sound value for family groups, with good service, pubbier front bar with open fire, Bass and Wadworths 6X; tables on terrace and in garden *(Neil and Anita Christopher, A E Brace, E A George)*; [SO9214], *Royal George*: Spacious beamed dining pub, on two levels, divided into areas with good waitress service; Bass and Greenalls, wide range of reasonably priced bar and restaurant food from sandwiches up; fine garden, pleasant setting, bedrooms *(D G King, Neil and Anita Christopher, A C Morrison)*

☆ **Blockley** [Station Rd; SP1634], *Great Western Arms*: Peaceful, comfortable and spacious modern-style lounge, wide choice of reasonably priced home-cooked food, well kept Flowers, Hook Norton and Marstons Pedigree, welcoming service, no piped music, busy public bar with games room; attractive village, lovely valley view *(G W A Pearce)*

☆ **Bourton on the Hill** [A44 W of Moreton in Marsh; SP1732], *Horse & Groom*: Old Cotswold stone inn redecorated by new owners, pine furniture on flagstones and hessian in main bar, settees and easy chairs around log fire in lounge, attractive dining room, well kept Bass, Hook Norton Best and Morlands Old Speckled Hen, home-made food inc delicious lunchtime snacks; bedrooms *(David and Ruth Hollands, NWN, LYM)*

Bourton on the Water [Bridge End Walk; SP1620], *Old Manse*: Lovely setting with front garden and beamed bar overlooking River Windrush, good log fire, pictures and tapestries (shame about the piped music and end games machines), well kept Morlands Old Speckled Hen, Ruddles County and Wadworths 6X, good coffee, generous well cooked food inc doorstep sandwiches, courteous service, friendly helpful staff, pretty restaurant; good bedrooms *(Mike and Heather Watson, Peter and Audrey Dowsett, Tony Scott, George Atkinson)*; [Riverside], *Parrot & Alligator*: Big airy stone pub being renamed Kingsbridge Inn, in nice spot overlooking river, friendly, clean and tidy L-shaped bar, very wide choice of food to suit this popular tourist spot, real ales such as Bass, Boddingtons, Morlands Old Speckled Hen, obliging staff; piped music, children welcome in dining area, big no-smoking part, no dogs, plenty of space outside *(Ted George, Richard Lewis, Clare Jones, Jonathon Smith, Neil and Anita Christopher)*

Brimscombe [A419 SE of Stroud; SO8602], *Ship*: Named for former shipping canal here (its trans-shipment port, England's biggest in 1700s, now an industrial estate); well laid out to combine roominess with feeling of snugness, good value food, well kept Bass and Boddingtons *(D Irving, R Huggins, T McLean, E McCall, Dr and Mrs A K Clarke)*

☆ **Broadwell** [off A429 2 miles N of Stow on the Wold; SP2027], *Fox*: Attractive local opp broad green, with good generous food, well kept Donnington BB, SB and SBA, Addlestone's cider, friendly service, stripped stone and flagstones, darts, dominoes and chess, pool room extension, piped music; good big back garden with Aunt Sally, field behind for Caravan Club members; bedrooms, nice village *(Rob Whittle, Peter and Anne Hollindale, D Irving, E McCall, R Huggins, T McLean, A Y Drummond)*

☆ **Brockhampton** [signed off A436 Andoversford—Naunton – OS Sheet 163 map ref 035223; SP0322], *Craven Arms*: Popular for lunch, particularly among retired people, with good value well presented food in homely interlinked rooms inc restaurant, Bass, Hook Norton Best and Wadworths 6X, low beams, sturdy stripped stone, pine furniture with some wall settles, tub chairs and a log fire, darts, shove-ha'penny; children welcome, swings in sizeable garden, attractive gentrified hillside village with lovely views *(David and Nina Pugsley, DMT, Roger and Jenny Huggins, P and S White, LYM)*

☆ **Brockweir** [just off A466 Chepstow—Monmouth; SO5401], *Brockweir*: Wye Valley walkers' pub with beams and stripped stonework, quarry tiles, sturdy settles, snugger carpeted alcoves with brocaded seats, food inc sandwiches and vegetarian, well kept Fullers London Pride, Greene King Abbot, Hook Norton Best and Thwaites, farm ciders, games and piped music in public bar; covered courtyard, sheltered terrace, garden; open all day Sat, children in eating area; bedrooms *(Daren Haines, Paul Barnett, David Lewis, Sarah Lart, Wayne Brindle, Barry and Anne, LYM)*

Brockworth [Shurdington Rd; A46, off A417 E of Gloucester; SO8816], *Cross Hands*: Brewers Fayre with usual value food in roomy dining area, more pubby separate bar *(Daren Haines)*

Cambridge [3 miles from M5 junction 13 – A38 towards Bristol; SO7403], *George*: Busy and welcoming, with two spacious dining extensions, good value bar food, well kept Hook Norton Best and Marstons Pedigree; restaurant, garden with barbecues, aviaries and play area; open all day Sun *(Alan and Paula McCully, M Hasslacher)*

Camp [B4070 Birdlip—Stroud, junction with Calf Way; SO9109], *Fostons Ash*: Open-plan refurbished Cotswold pub with comfortable well spaced tables, open woodburners each end, good value ample home-made food, well kept Scottish Courage beers with a guest such as Morlands Old Speckled Hen, prompt friendly service; piped music can be obtrusive; children and walkers welcome, garden with play area *(A Y Drummond, Kay Neville-Rolfe)*

Cerney Wick [SU0796], *Crown*: Roomy modernised lounge bar, neat and clean, opening into comfortable semi-conservatory extension, public bar with pool, darts, fruit machine and log fire, popular straightforward food inc good Sun roasts, well kept Whitbreads-related ales, helpful service; children welcome, good-sized garden with swings, small motel-style bedroom extension *(G W A Pearce, D Irving, R Huggins, T McLean, E McCall)*

☆ **Charlton Kings** [Cirencester Rd (A435); SO9620], *Little Owl*: Concentration on carefully cooked imaginative food in much extended and smartened up pub, using fresh ingredients inc carefully bred free-range pork from their own nearby farm; Boddingtons,

Hook Norton and Wadworths 6X, friendly staff – bar still has traditional feel *(John and Joan Wyatt)*

Charlton Kings [A435], *Clock Tower*: Useful Milestone Tavern, with their standard menu done well, well kept Banks's ales, decent wines (given a taste before buying), good service *(Stephen and Julie Brown, E A George)*; [London Rd (A40)], *London*: Reliable lunch stop with good food range from filled baps and baked potatoes up, plush lounge-restaurant, big public bar, real ales such as Archers, Fullers, Morlands Old Speckled Hen and Wadworths 6X; pleasant walled garden *(John and Joan Wyatt)*

Cheltenham [Bath Rd; SO9422], *Bath*: Basic unspoilt 1920s two-bar layout and simple furnishings, locals' smoke room, well kept Bass and Uley *(D Irving, E McCall, R Huggins, T McLean, PB, JP, PP)*; [1-3 Montpellier Villas], *Beehive*: Enjoyable bare-boards atmosphere, welcoming service, coal fire, wide range of beers and spirits, good house wines, wide choice of good food inc imaginative baguette fillings and Sun lunch *(Mr and Mrs P Goldman)*; [Fairview St], *Kemble Brewery*: Well kept Archers, sensible prices; not a lot of space *(E McCall, R Huggins, D Irving, T McLean)*; [Montpellier Walk], *Rotunda*: Lively old-fashioned high-ceilinged pub with particularly well kept Tetleys-related ales and Wadworths 6X, good service, friendly atmosphere *(E McCall, R Huggins, D Irving, T McLean)*; [Suffolk Rd], *Suffolk Arms*: Dark-decor pub with comfortable wall seats, well kept beers such as Brakspears, Goff's Jouster and Wickwar Brand Oak; food lunchtime and evening, sports TV, skittles alley *(G Coates)*; [Montpellier Walk], *Whole Hog*: Well kept beer, some comfortable armchairs, rather trendy pop-art decor – like some other pubs here can be very crowded or very empty *(N P Cox, Mark and Elaine Weightman)*

☆ **Chipping Campden** [High St; SP1539], *Lygon Arms*: Welcoming locally popular stripped-stone bar with lots of horse pictures, open fires, well kept Donnington SBA, Hook Norton Best, Wadworths 6X and interesting guest beers, helpful service, interesting range of plentiful food till late evening from well filled rolls and good ploughman's up, back dining area, raftered evening restaurant beyond shady courtyard with tables; children welcome, open all day exc winter weekdays; good bedrooms *(Nick Lawless, E V Walder, Janet and Peter Race, Chris Mawson, LYM)*

☆ **Chipping Campden** [Lower High St], *Volunteer*: Early 18th-c pub with cosy little lounge, busy public bar, friendly family staff, good range of food from ploughman's up, well kept beers such as Marstons Pedigree and Theakstons, log fire, military memorabilia, books, lots of bric-a-brac, games room (children allowed here); tiny attractive courtyard with beautiful garden running down to river *(N Christopher, Lawrence Pearse, Richard Lewis, Nick Lawless, R Davies)*

☆ **Cirencester** [Black Jack St; SP0201], *Golden Cross*: Backstreet 1920s local with longish comfortable bar, sensible tables, simple cheap generous food, three well kept Arkells ales, good friendly service, good beer mug collection; piped music; skittle alley, tables in back garden *(Mr and Mrs C Roberts, D Irving, E McCall, R Huggins, T McLean)*

☆ **Cirencester** [Lewis Lane], *Twelve Bells*: Lively backstreet pub with friendly simple but comfortable back rooms, coal fires, pictures for sale, clay pipe collection, particularly well kept Archers Best, Uley and two or three very quickly changing guests, good bar food esp fish; small garden with fountain *(D Irving, E McCall, R Huggins, T McLean, Dr and Mrs A K Clarke)*

Cirencester [Castle St], *Black Horse*: Refurbished pub with decent lunchtime food, Scottish Courage ales; lively evenings, popular with young people then; bedrooms *(D Irving, E McCall, R Huggins, T McLean)*; [Dollar St/Gloucester St], *Corinium Court*: Not so youthful – character building, warmly welcoming, cosy and comfortable, with big log fire, well kept ales such as Hook Norton Old Hookey and Wadworths 6X, decent wine, food in bar and attractive restaurant, friendly landlord; no piped music; entrance through charming courtyard with tables; bedrooms *(Peter and Audrey Dowsett, D Irving, R Huggins, T McLean, E McCall)*

☆ **Coates** [follow Tarleton signs from village (right then left), pub up rough track on right after rly bridge, OS Sheet 163 map ref 965005; SO9600], *Tunnel House*: Idyllically placed idiosyncratic beamed country pub by interesting abandoned canal tunnel, very relaxed management style, mix of well worn armchairs, sofa, rustic benches, enamel advertising signs, stuffed mustelids, race tickets, real ales such as Archers Best, Morlands Old Speckled Hen, Smiles and Wadworths 6X, basic food inc good home-made soup, Sunday barbecues, log fire, pub games, big juke box much appreciated by Royal Agricultural College students; children welcome (good safe play area), camping facilities *(Rick and Torti Friedberger, John Fahy, D Irving, E McCall, R Huggins, T McLean, Pat Crabb, LYM)*

Coberley [A436 Brockworth—Andoversford, just SW of junction with A435 Cheltenham—Cirencester – OS Sheet 163 map ref 968168; SO9616], *Seven Springs*: Spacious and airy Hungry Horse dining pub, lofty ceiling hung with fishing nets and hurricane lamps, big windows, snugger side areas and sizeable sloping pond-side garden; generous food (all day Sun), Bass and Greene King Abbot, cheery piped music; children allowed daytime *(Neil and Anita Christopher, LYM)*

☆ **Codrington** [handy for M4 junction 18, via B4465; ST7579], *Codrington Arms*: Refurbished village pub with several comfortable rooms, wide choice of inexpensive food, quick friendly service, impressive housekeeping, good range of beers inc Hardy Country and Wadworths 6X, good house wines, big log fire, big garden with good views and play area; piped music *(Peter and Audrey Dowsett)*

☆ **Coleford** [Joyford; best approached from Christchurch 5-ways junction B4432/B4428, by church – B4432 towards Broadwell, then follow signs; or from Berry Hill PO crossroads; OS Sheet 162 map ref 580134 – keep eyes skinned for pub sign hidden in hedge; SO5813], *Dog & Muffler*: Very prettily set, with open-plan lounge, beamed and flagstoned back extension with games area (and juke box), pleasant back sun lounge dining room and verandah, well kept Sam Smiths and a guest beer, cheerful service, food from sandwiches up; well spaced picnic-sets on sheltered lawn, play area, nice walks; children welcome, good bedrooms *(Charles and Pauline Stride, LYM)*

Coleford [Christchurch; SO5712], *New Inn*: Smallish open-plan stripped-stone pub, discreetly lit, with big log fire, ales such as Boddingtons, Flowers IPA, Marstons Pedigree and Otter, interesting quickly served food, friendly staff and parrot *(Pat and Tony Martin, R J Walden)*

☆ **Cowley** [Cockleford; off A435 S of Cheltenham at Elkstone signpost; SO9714], *Green Dragon*: Attractive old-fashioned country pub in nice spot, formerly very popular, with beams, flagstones, bare boards, huge fireplace and plenty of character; the reopening mentioned in our last edition was postponed, and as we went to press the pub was still under refurbishment, but a huge new car park suggested that reopening was at last imminent *(News please)*

☆ **Didmarton** [A433 Tetbury rd; ST8187], *Kings Arms*: Quietly decorated front rooms with individual character, Bass, John Smiths and local beers, open fire, imaginative choice of good value food, polite and friendly young staff, candlelit restaurant with white linen and relaxed atmosphere, big barn-like back extension; children and dogs welcome, tables out behind *(D G Clarke, Meg and Colin Hamilton, D Irving, E McCall, R Huggins, T McLean, Dr and Mrs A K Clarke, Jacquie and Jim Jones)*

☆ **Dursley** [May Lane/Hill Rd, by bus stn; ST7598], *Old Spot*: Relaxed real-ale pub with well kept Bass, Worthington, Uley Old Spot and Old Ric and two guest beers, lots of malt whiskies, friendly landlord, doorstep sandwiches and home-made pasties, pig paraphernalia, quarry tiles and bare boards – several rooms inc one no smoking; bar billiards, cribbage, dominoes and boules, no music or machines *(R Huggins, D Irving, E McCall, T McLean, Giles Francis, John and Audrey Butterfield)*

☆ **Eastleach Turville** [off A361 S of Burford; SP1905], *Victoria*: Unusually good reasonably priced home cooking in unpretentious local with pleasant back dining extension off small lounge, pool in big public bar, welcoming staff, well kept Arkells, nice views; quiet midweek lunchtime, busy evenings; pleasant front garden overlooking picturesque buildings opp, delightful village esp at daffodil time *(Mr and Mrs J Brown, Peter and Audrey Dowsett, G W A Pearce, Gordon, Dick Brown, Patrick Hancock, E McCall, R Huggins, T McLean)*

☆ **Edge** [A4173 N of Stroud; SO8509], *Edgemoor*: The star is for the position, with panoramic valley view from simple tidy modernised picture-window dining area; wide choice of decent food (lunchtime service stops 2), well kept Smiles, Uley Old Spot and Wickwar BOB, no-smoking area, children welcome, pretty terrace, good walks nearby; cl Sun evening *(M and I Bayley, Alan and Paula McCully, Kay Neville-Rolfe, Martin and Karen Wake, LYM)*

☆ *nr* **Elkstone** [Beechpike; A417 6 miles N of Cirencester; SO9610], *Highwayman*: Well kept Arkells ales, good house wines, big back eating area (wide choice inc vegetarian), good friendly staff, and considerable character in rambling 16th-c warren of low beams, stripped stone, alcoves, antique settles among more modern furnishings, big log fires, rustic decorations; quiet piped music; disabled access, good family room, outside play area *(G Coates, Jack and Philip Paxton, LYM)*

Fairford [Market Pl; SP1501], *Bull*: Friendly beamed hotel, enormous choice of reasonably priced good food, no-smoking dining areas, helpful efficient service, well kept Arkells 3B and Kingsdown; piped music; bedrooms, charming village, church has remarkable stained glass; bedrooms small but fresh, all different, with a bright decor *(Robert Gomme)*

☆ **Frampton Mansell** [off A491 Cirencester—Stroud – OS Sheet 163 map ref 923027; SO9202], *Crown*: Quiet but welcoming stripped stone lounge bar with dark beam-and-plank ceiling, flagstones, well kept ales such as Archers Village, Oakhill Farmers, Wadworths 6X, public bar with darts, good food in bar and attractive restaurant; lovely views over village and steep wooded valley; children in eating area, teak seats outside; bedrooms *(Dr and Mrs A K Clarke, D Irving, E McCall, R Huggins, T McLean, BB)*

Frampton on Severn [The Green; SO7407], *Bell*: Clean and welcoming Whitbreads dining pub by compact cricket pitch, good range of fairly priced lunchtime food, decent service, real ales inc interesting guests, separate locals' bar with pool *(Pete and Rosie Flower)*; *Three Horseshoes*: Cracking old cider house, wonderful banter between landlady and locals, three pub dogs and visiting ones – very welcoming *(Pete Flower)*

☆ **Glasshouse** [by Newent Woods; first right turn off A40 going W from junction with A4136; SO7121], *Glasshouse*: Newish owners carefully preserving small country tavern with changing well kept ales tapped from the cask, flagstone floors, log fire in vast fireplace, good basic food esp thick sandwiches, interesting decorations, darts and quoits, lovely hanging baskets, seats on fenced lawn with big weeping willow loved by children; fine nearby woodland walks *(Mike and Mary Carter, LYM)*

Gloucester [68 Southgate St], *Black Swan*: Fine building, comfortable back room, fireplace and chandelier giving character, cheap food, well kept Donnington *(Anon)*; [Westgate St/Berkeley St], *Fountain*: Thriving Italian-run 17th-c pub handy for cathedral, very popular lunchtime for simple enjoyable food at reasonable prices; very attentive staff, Flowers Original *(D G King)*; [Westgate St], *New Inn*: Chef & Brewer in four separate areas of lovely medieval building with courtyard, rather over-restored but keeping some atmosphere – worth a visit if you're near; good value food, warm welcome and several well kept ales; piped pop music; bedrooms *(Steve Willey, George Atkinson)*

☆ **Guiting Power** [off B4068 SW of Stow on the Wold; SP0924], *Farmers Arms*: Popular traditional local in lovely village, stripped stone, mix of carpet and flagstones, good log fire, well kept Donnington BB and SBA, decent home-made bar food; skittle alley, games area with darts, pool, cribbage, dominoes, fruit machine; piped music; seats (and quoits) in garden, good walks; children welcome, bedrooms *(Neil and Anita Christopher, S G N Bennett, Guy Consterdine, Stephen and Julie Brown, Tim Brierly, Jo Rees, MRSM, LYM)*

☆ **Horsley** [B4058 just S of Stroud; ST8397], *Bell & Castle*: Friendly village pub with wide choice of ample reasonably priced food inc innovative touches and good vegetarian dishes, good service, pub games *(D G King)*

Iron Acton [High St; ST6884], *Rose & Crown*: Good functional village pub, cosy lounge, basic public bar, wide choice of real ale inc some local gems; bedrooms *(Dr and Mrs A K Clarke)*; [High St], *White Hart*: Traditional village pub popular for food, with good range of real ales inc national ones and Smiles *(Dr and Mrs A K Clarke)*

☆ **Kemble** [outside village; A433 Cirencester—Tetbury – OS Sheet 163 map ref 981986; ST9897], *Thames Head*: Very well served good food inc wide puddings choice, well kept Arkells Bitter, 2B and 3B, pleasant owners and staff, stripped stone, timberwork, cottagey back area with pews and log-effect gas fire in big fireplace, country-look dining-room with another big gas fire, real fire in front area; seats outside, children welcome *(C and A Moncreiffe, B Perfect, LYM)*

☆ **Kingscote** [A4135 Dursley—Tetbury; ST8196], *Hunters Hall*: Civilised Tudor dining pub with attractive layout – series of comfortable and relaxing individually furnished rooms on two floors, part no smoking, also cosy old flagstoned public bar with pool and other games; food inc sandwiches (not Sunday lunch), buffet and various good hot dishes, friendly young staff (service can slow when busy), well kept Bass, Courage Directors, Theakstons Best and Uley Hogs Head, garden with ingenious play area; children welcome, live music Sun evening, open all day; bedrooms *(Stephen Brown, Pete and Rosie Flower, Andy and Jill Kassube, Janet and Peter Race, R Davies)*

Lechlade [SU2199], *Crown*: Nicely updated bare-boards pub with good food in back restaurant area, well kept ales such as Hook Norton and Morlands Old Speckled Hen *(Dr and Mrs A K Clarke)*; [The Square (A361)], *New Inn*: Big and busy, with good range of well kept ales and of very generous well cooked food, not expensive, very friendly staff, huge log fire, back restaurant; pity about the piped music; play area in big garden extending to Thames; bedrooms *(Peter and Audrey Dowsett)*; *Red Lion*: Down-to-earth local with wide range of good value food inc good Sun lunches, friendly service, well kept Arkells, restaurant with log fire; gents' due for updating *(Michael and Hazel Duncombe, Mick and Mary Clark)*

☆ *nr* **Lechlade** [St John's Bridge; A417 a mile E], *Trout*: Low-beamed three-room pub dating from 15th c, with some flagstones, stuffed fish and fishing prints, big Thamesside garden with boules, Aunt Sally and a simple summer family bar; Courage Directors and maybe related beers, popular well presented food from ploughman's through pizzas to steaks, friendly staff, no-smoking dining room; children in eating areas, jazz Tues and Sun, fishing rights; very busy in summer – open all day Sat then *(R Huggins, D Irving, E McCall, T McLean, David Carr, LYM)*

Longborough [signed off A424; SP1729], *Coach & Horses*: Basic honest Donnington pub *(Tom McLean)*

☆ **Longhope** [Ross Rd (A40); SO6919], *Farmers Boy*: Heavy beams, warm fire, relaxing atmosphere and candles in attractive two-room country restaurant with curry specialities, good specials, OAP bargains Thurs; well kept ales such as Boddingtons, Marlow Rebellion, Smiles Best, Theakstons and Thwaites; piped music, separate public bar with big screen TV and electric organ; pleasant garden and terrace *(Mike and Mary Carter, F J and A Parmenter, BB)*

☆ **Lower Swell** [B4068 W of Stow on the Wold; SP1725], *Golden Ball*: Sprucely unspoilt local with friendly new landlady, log fire, well kept Donnington BB and SBA from the pretty brewery just 20 mins' walk away, good range of ciders and perry, games area with fruit machine and juke box behind big chimneystack, generous food inc home-made dishes, small evening restaurant (not Sun evening), small garden with occasional barbecues, Aunt Sally and quoits; maybe piped classical music, no dogs or children, decent simple bedrooms; pretty village, good walks *(John Fahy, John and Joan Wyatt, R Huggins, D Irving, E McCall, T McLean, Colin Fisher, LYM)*

☆ **Lower Wick** [off A38 Bristol—Gloucester just N of Newport; ST7196], *Pickwick*: Wide choice of attractively priced food in carpeted bar with woodburner and lots of wheelback chairs around shiny dark tables, brocaded small settles and more of the wheelbacks in dining room, some stripped stone, well kept Smiles Best and Golden with a guest such as Bass, traditional games inc antique table skittles; piped music may be loud; picnic-sets and play fort by back paddock – Mway noise out here; children welcome, cl 2.30 sharp weekdays *(Peter and Audrey Dowsett, Charles and*

Pauline Stride, BB)

☆ **Marshfield** [signed off A420 Bristol—Chippenham; ST7773], *Catherine Wheel*: Interesting and attractive old pub with plates and prints on stripped stone walls, medley of settles, chairs and stripped tables, open fire in impressive fireplace, cottagey back family bar, charming no-smoking Georgian dining room, flower-decked back yard; cheerful service, wide choice of good food inc imaginative dishes and Thurs fresh fish, (not Sun), well kept Ruddles County and Wadworths IPA and 6X, farm cider, decent wines; golden labrador called Elmer, darts, dominoes; provision for children, unspoilt village *(Mr and Mrs R Maggs, Susan and John Douglas, Rowan and Melanie Hardy, LYM)*

☆ **Mickleton** [B4632 (ex A46); SP1543], *Kings Arms*: Comfortable, clean, relaxed and civilised, popular food inc notable ploughman's and Sun roasts, nice puddings, vegetarian dishes; considerate service, Whitbreads-related ales, farm cider, small log fire; some tables outside, handy for Kiftsgate and Hidcote *(M G Swift, Pat and Robert Watt, BB)*

Minsterworth [A48 S of Gloucester; SO7716], *Apple Tree*: Friendly and comfortable roadside Whitbreads dining pub based on extended oak-beamed 17th-c farmhouse, decent standard food, open fires, prompt service, unobtrusive piped music, well kept ales; big garden with enclosed play area; open all day – lane beside leads down to the Severn, a good way of avoiding east bank crowds on a Bore weekend *(Mr and Mrs B Craig)*

☆ **Mitcheldean** [SO6718], *Lamb*: Two unspoilt bars with pleasant atmosphere, decent fresh food, quick friendly service, well kept beer; refurbished restaurant, good bedrooms – well placed for Forest of Dean *(Alan Meecham)*

☆ **Moreton in Marsh** [High St; SP2032], *White Hart Royal*: Relaxing old-world inn, partly 15th c, with interesting Civil War history, oak beams, stripped stone, big inglenook fire in flagstoned smaller bar, roomy carpeted main bar, particularly well kept Bass and Worthington BB, good value food, simple but pleasant restaurant, efficient friendly staff; a real welcome for children, can get crowded esp on Tues market day; good value bedrooms *(Andrew and Ruth Triggs, Gordon)*

Moreton in Marsh [High St; SP2032], *Bell*: Pleasant pub with real ales such as Boddingtons, Flowers IPA, Marstons Pedigree and Wadworths 6X, good value food inc afternoon tea, efficient uniformed staff; bar covered with banknotes and beermats, solid fuel stove, no-smoking family area, tables (some under cover) in attractive courtyard; bedrooms *(Neil and Anita Christopher, SLC, LM)*; [Market Pl], *Black Bear*: Full range of local Donnington ales, big stripped-stone carpeted bar with TV and darts one end, bare-boards dining room (not Sun evening) *(Joan and Michel Hooper-Immins, N Christopher)*

Nailsworth [ST8599], *Cross*: Newly opened, big and open-plan, with stripped stone walls, wide mix of customers, comfortable feel, pool *(D Irving, E McCall, R Huggins, T McLean)*

☆ **Naunton** [Stow Rd (B4068); just W of village – OS Sheet 163 map ref 099232; SP1123], *Foxhill*: Comfortable little old stone pub, good generous home-cooked food at sensible prices, quiet pleasant atmosphere *(Graham Tayar, Catherine Raeburn)*

Newent [Church St; SO7225], *George*: Nice location opp Shambles museum, well kept Bass and related beers, open fire, decent inexpensive food, children welcome; bedrooms *(G Washington)*

☆ **Newland** [B4231 Lydney—Monmouth; SO5509], *Ostrich*: Partly 13th c, nr fine church; plenty of atmosphere, attractive mix of furnishings, fine range of real ales such as Hook Norton Best, Monmouth Rebellion, RCH Pitchfork, Shepherd Neame Spitfire, Timothy Taylor Landlord and one brewed for them by Freeminer, good choice of other drinks inc fresh fruit juices, big fireplace, good bustling atmosphere; if anything too wide a choice of food (inc vegetarian), can be a delay; small garden, dogs allowed on lead; no children, two bedrooms *(Maureen Hobbs, Alan and Barbara Mence, R Michael Richards, R V G Brown, James Nunns, Phil and Heidi Cook, Paul Barnett, LYM)*

Newnham [Station Rd; SO6912], *Railway*: Friendly down-to-earth local, good home-made food *(Mrs Susan Dunning)*

☆ **North Nibley** [B4060; ST7496], *Black Horse*: Good straightforward village local with wide range of generous good value home-made food, well kept Whitbreads-related ales and an interesting guest beer, good log fire, maybe piped music; popular restaurant Tues-Sat evenings, Sun lunchtime, tables in pretty garden; good value cottagey bedrooms, good breakfast *(R Huggins, D Irving, E McCall, T McLean, DAV, BB)*

Northleach [Market Pl; SP1114], *Red Lion*: Good value generous food from good sandwiches to Sun roasts with thoroughly cooked veg in straightforward bar with open fire, well kept Scottish Courage ales, decent house wine, good coffee, very friendly service, restaurant; unobtrusive piped music *(Mr and Mrs J Brown)*; [Cheltenham Rd], *Wheatsheaf*: More hotel than pub, with sober atmosphere, quiet piped classical music, polite friendly staff; good if not cheap lunchtime bar food, real ales inc Marstons Pedigree; restaurant, lovely terraced garden; well equipped modern bedrooms *(Sidney and Erna Wells, IHR)*

☆ **Nympsfield** [signed off B4066 Stroud—Dursley; SO8000], *Rose & Crown*: Stonebuilt village inn, open all day, with well kept ales such as Bass, Boddingtons, Severn Boar, Smiles Best, Theakstons Old Peculier, Uley Old Spot, Wadworths 6X and Wickwar BOB, decent wines, pink plush banquettes and lots of brass in pubby beamed bar with log fire and fruit machine, dark pews around tables in back saloon opening into dining room, picnic-sets in side yard and on sheltered lawn with good play area; bedrooms, handy for Cotswold walks *(DAV, Peter Neate, Ken Hull, Vanessa Mudge,*

T L Rees, Dr and Mrs A K Clarke, M Joyner, Gill Cathles, Dorothy and Leslie Pilson, Tom Evans, BB)

☆ **Painswick** [St Mary's St; SO8609], *Royal Oak*: Thriving old-fashioned town local with interesting layout and furnishings inc some attractive old or antique seats, huge helpings of good reasonably priced food (bar nibbles only, Sun) from sandwiches up, well kept Whitbreads-related ales, friendly family service, small sun lounge by suntrap pretty courtyard; children in eating area; can get crowded, nearby parking may be difficult *(Anthony Hoyle, LYM)*

Painswick [New St; SO8609], *Falcon*: Big main room, largely panelled, with wooden floor, tables and comfortably padded seats on left, high bookshelves by fire, well kept Flowers and other changing ales from bar on right, wide range of home-made food inc good baguettes and pies, daily papers, carpeted dining area beyond stained glass and panelling divider, separate locals' bar; bedrooms *(D Irving, E McCall, R Huggins, T McLean, D G King)*

Parkend [just off B4234; SO6208], *Fountain*: Homely and welcoming, with assorted chairs and settles, real fire, old local tools and photographs, good freshly made usual food inc good range of curries, efficient landlord, well kept local Freeminer and guest beers; children welcome *(Pete Baker)*

Pennsylvania [4 miles from M4 junction 18 – A46 towards Bath; ST7373], *Swan*: Small friendly unspoilt local, well kept ales such as Archers and Bunces, good food inc bargain two-course lunch, interesting fireplace depicting battle *(Giles Francis, Meg and Colin Hamilton, Luke Worthington)*

☆ **Prestbury** [Mill St; SO9624], *Plough*: Welcoming well preserved thatched village local, good generous food in cosy and comfortable oak-panelled front lounge, basic but roomy flagstoned back tap room with grandfather clock and big log fire, good value homely food, well kept Whitbreads-related ales tapped from casks, pleasant back garden *(Lew Badger, E McCall, R Huggins, D Irving, T McLean)*

Rodborough [Rodborough Common; SO8404], *Bear*: Flagstoned bar with pleasant window seats, welcoming log fire, decent bar food, well kept local beer, children welcome; comfortable hotel – good base for touring Cotswolds *(Dave and Deborah Irving)*

☆ **Sapperton** [signed off A419 Stroud—Cirencester; SO9403], *Bell*: Neat village pub with extending stripped stone lounge, good log fire, sturdy pine tables, well kept Flowers Original, Tetleys and Wadworths 6X, simple food from sandwiches to steaks, friendly service, traditional public bar with games, skittle alley, tables outside; children welcome *(R Huggins, D Irving, E McCall, T McLean, LYM)*

Shipton Moyne [off B4040 Malmesbury—Bristol; ST8989], *Cat & Custard Pot*: Enormous food choice from bread and cheese to game and steaks, good drinks range, reasonable prices; picturesque village *(L G Howlett, BB)*

Shipton Oliffe [just off A40/A436 S of Andoversford; SP0218], *Frogmill*: Roomy yet cosy 17th-c stone coaching inn with flagstoned bar, no-smoking area, friendly service, food inc ploughman's, filled hot baguettes and hot dishes, two-course weekday bargains, Scottish Courage ales; tables on streamside terrace with waterwheel, big play area; bedrooms *(Neil and Anita Christopher)*

Slad [B4070 Stroud—Birdlip; SO8707], *Woolpack*: Small hillside village local with imaginative freshly cooked food such as duck and bacon pie, Weston's Old Rosie cider, well kept Bass and Uley Old Spot, lovely valley views *(Pat and Jim Halfyard, D Irving, E McCall, R Huggins, T McLean)*

Slimbridge [Shepherds Patch – OS Sheet 162 map ref 728042; SO7303], *Tudor Arms*: Well kept Hook Norton Best, Tetleys, Uley Bitter and Pigs Ear and Wadworths 6X, fair range of generous food from sandwiches and ploughman's up inc children's dishes, typical modernised lounge, bar with billiards and TV, skittle alley, family room, evening restaurant; handy for Wildfowl Trust and canal boat trips, snacks all day w/e; bedrooms in small annexe *(Alan Drummond, Steve Thomas)*

☆ **Snowshill** [SP0934], *Snowshill Arms*: Handy for Snowshill Manor (which closes lunchtime), with good popular sensibly priced food, well kept Donningtons BB and SBA, efficient friendly service, spruce and airy carpeted bar with neat array of tables, local photographs, stripped stone, log fire; charming village views from bow windows and from big back garden with little stream and play area, friendly local feel midweek winter, can be very crowded other times – get there early; skittle alley, good play area; children welcome if eating, nearby parking may be difficult; beautiful village *(Neil and Anita Christopher, Ian and Liz Phillips, David Walker, SLC, M G Swift, Maysie Thompson, George Atkinson, Dorothee and Dennis Glover, DFL, Roger and Jenny Huggins, Peter and Audrey Dowsett, LYM)*

Somerford Keynes [OS Sheet 163 map ref 018954; SU0195], *Bakers Arms*: Homely partly stripped-stone local in lovely Cotswold village, wide choice of enjoyable food inc good specials, vegetarian and Sun lunch, well kept Bass and other frequently changing ales, knowledgeable friendly barman; busy lunchtime (booking recommended), big garden *(D Irving, E McCall, R Huggins, T McLean)*

☆ **Southrop** [signed off A417 and A361, nr Lechlade; SP2003], *Swan*: Cottagey seats and log fire in low-ceilinged dining lounge with generally good and often interesting food, small no-smoking restaurant (not Sun evening), friendly efficient staff; stripped stone skittle alley, public bar, Morlands Original and guests such as Marstons Pedigree, good wines; children welcome; pretty village esp at daffodil time *(W Burke, D H and M C Watkinson, Guy Vowles, Peter and Audrey Dowsett, George Atkinson, Mary Walters, Kay Neville-Rolfe, LYM)*

Staunton [A4136 NW of Coleford; SO5412], *White Horse*: Well kept real ales inc Flowers IPA, good quickly served food in bar and small restaurant inc unusual dishes and Sun lunch, friendly service, big well kept garden with penned wildfowl and adventure play area, good walks *(S P Watkin, P A Taylor, Dick Brown)*

☆ **Stow on the Wold** [The Square; SP1925], *Queens Head*: Chatty old local with heavily beamed and flagstoned traditional back bar, high-backed settles, big log fire, horse prints, piped classical or opera, usual games, nice dogs; lots of tables in civilised stripped stone front lounge, good value straightforward fresh food (not Mon evening or Sun), well kept Donnington BB and SBA, mulled wine, quick helpful service; children welcome, tables outside, occasional jazz Sun lunchtime *(Wendy Arnold, Liz Bell, Rob Whittle, Neville Kenyon, Pam Adsley, Peter Baggott, Tim and Linda Collins, Wayne Wheeler, D Irving, E McCall, R Huggins, T McLean, Joan and Michel Hooper-Immins, Albert and Margaret Horton, LYM)*

☆ *nr* **Stow on the Wold** [Ganborough (A424 N); SP1729], *Coach & Horses*: Straightforward pub alone on old coach road, nicely decorated with hops on beams, flagstones, central log fire, steps up to carpeted dining area with high-backed settles; well kept Donnington BB and SBA, very wide choice of good food (all day summer Fri/Sat), friendly service; children welcome, open all day Sun and summer Sat *(George Atkinson, E V Walder, Peter and Anne Hollindale, Colin McKerrow, John Fahy, Walter Reid, Peter and Audrey Dowsett, LYM)*

Stroud [1 Bath Rd; SO8504], *Clothiers Arms*: Extended but still genuine 18th-c pub with well kept Tetleys-related ales in busy bar with old Stroud brewery decorations, pleasant airy dining room, garden *(D G King, Dave and Deborah Irving)*; [Nelson St, just E of centre], *Golden Fleece*: Small old terrace pub, fairly dark inside, with daily papers, cheerfully musical decor, unobtrusive piped jazz, well kept beer, unspoilt feel, separate smaller upstairs room *(Dave and Deborah Irving)*; [top end of High St], *Retreat*: Pink walls, polished wooden floors and tables, small choice of well kept ales, imaginative lunchtime food, children welcome; can get crowded evenings, tiny courtyard now covered in as attractive extension *(Dave and Deborah Irving)*; [Stratford Rd], *Stratford*: Modern refurbished pub with well kept ale, food inc good baguettes all day, decor commemorating popular former local GP *(D G King)*

☆ **Tetbury** [Gumstool Hill, Mkt Pl; ST8893], *Crown*: 17th-c town pub popular with older people for good value bar lunches with upmarket touches, well kept Hook Norton Best and Whitbreads-related ales, long oak-beamed front bar with big log fire and attractive medley of tables, very efficient service, unobtrusive piped music; pleasant back no-smoking family dining conservatory with lots of plants, picnic-sets on back terrace; comfortable bedrooms, sharing bathroom *(Paul and Judith Booth, Brian Kirby, Ann and Colin Hunt, D Irving, E McCall, R Huggins, T McLean, D G King)*

Tetbury [Market Pl], *Snooty Fox*: Wide and unusual food choice in welcoming high-ceilinged hotel lounge with medieval-style chairs and elegant fireplace, friendly staff, restaurant; bedrooms good value *(Alan and Paula McCully, Ann and Colin Hunt)*

☆ **Tewkesbury** [52 Church St; SO8932], *Bell*: Plush but interesting hotel bar under new ownership, black oak beams and timbers, neat 17th-c oak panelling, medieval leaf-and-fruit frescoes, armchairs, settees and tapestries; good choice of inexpensive food inc vegetarian, attractive restaurant, well kept Badger Best and Courage Directors, good coffee, quick service, big log fire; garden above Severnside walk, nr abbey; good bedrooms *(Peter and Audrey Dowsett, Andrew and Ruth Triggs, Joan and Michel Hooper-Immins, Lawrence Bacon, Jean Scott, BB)*

☆ **Thornbury** [Chapel St; ST6390], *Wheatsheaf*: Newish licensees doing good fresh home-made food in straightforward 1930s local (the evening specials may run out early); obliging service, wide range of real ales, children's helpings, minimal music *(Meg Hamilton, Catherine Waite, K R Harris)*

Tirley [SO8328], *Hawbridge*: Lovely riverside setting, friendly staff, good food on very big plates, well kept Wadworths at sensible prices *(Iain Robertson)*

Tockington [ST6186], *Swan*: Spacious pub with beams, standing timbers, bric-a-brac on stripped stone walls, good range of reasonably priced food (dragon pie tipped if you like hot food), friendly staff, Bass and Boddingtons on handpump, guests such as Smiles and Theakstons Best tapped from the cask, country wines; piped music; tables in tree-shaded garden, quiet village *(Meg and Colin Hamilton, Simon and Amanda Southwell)*

Toddington [A46 Broadway—Winchcombe, junction with A438 and B4077; SP0432], *Pheasant*: Quickly served good food and lots of veg, local real ale; but don't offend the staff by sitting in the wrong place *(John and Joan Wyatt, Martin Jones)*

☆ **Todenham** [between A34 and A429 N of Moreton in Marsh; SP2436], *Farriers Arms*: Extensively refurbished Cotswold dining pub by church in quiet village, good generous home-made food inc fresh veg and interesting evening dishes, pleasant old-world bar, Scottish Courage ales with a guest such as Hook Norton, good friendly service; bedrooms *(J Kane, Tim and Linda Collins, John Bowdler)*

Tolldown [under a mile from M4 junction 18 – A46 towards Bath; ST7577], *Crown*: Tidy but largely unspoilt, with usual food inc good steaks and fresh veg in heavy-beamed stripped stone bar, no-smoking area, well kept Wadworths, woodburner or coal fire, quick friendly service; dominoes, darts and fruit machine, piped music, good garden with play area; no dogs (friendly cat), children in eating area and restaurant; comfortable bedrooms *(Mark and Heather Williamson, Ian and Nita Cooper, Andrew Shore, Alan Kilpatrick, LYM)*

Tormarton [v near M4 junction 18; ST7678], *Compass*: Busy extended off-motorway hotel/conference centre with choice of rooms inc cosy local-feeling bar open all day for wide choice of food, pleasant conservatory, well kept Archers, Bass and Smiles, friendly staff, rather pricy restaurant; open all day, children in eating areas, comfortable bedrooms *(Peter and Audrey Dowsett, LYM)*; *Portcullis*: Unassuming pub with several real ales such as Otter and Wychwood, food inc vegetarian (nothing expensive), friendly landlord, beams and stonework, log fire (sometimes two), panelled dining room; tables in garden, quiet village *(Peter and Audrey Dowsett, Luke Worthington)*

Upper Framilode [Saul Rd; not far from M5 junction 13; SO7510], *Ship*: Recently renovated, in relaxing setting by disused canalside offshoot from Severn with ducks and swans, good choice of Tetleys-related ales, wide range of food from sandwiches to fish and steaks inc wide vegetarian choice and lots for children, restaurant extension *(D G King)*

Wick [High St (A420); ST7072], *Rose & Crown*: Busy and roomy recently refurbished Chef & Brewer with character, good service, very wide food range, good beer range *(Mark and Heather Williamson)*

☆ **Winchcombe** [High St (B4632); SP0228], *Old Corner Cupboard*: Recently refurbished, beams, stripped stone and good inglenook log fire, some concentration now on good reasonably priced food (not Sun or Mon evenings) from good sandwiches to generous main dishes inc steaks and good vegetarian range, small helpings for children, well kept ales such as Flowers IPA and Original, Fullers London Pride, Goff's Jouster, Wadworths 6X; bedrooms in self-contained wing; open all day weekends, at top of charming village *(James Cooper, IHR, Meg and Colin Hamilton)*

☆ **Winchcombe** [Abbey Terr], *Plaisterers Arms*: Split-level 18th-c pub with stripped stonework, beams, and open fire, dim-lit lower back part, dining area; now Ushers, with their beers and a guest such as Goff's Jouster, new tenant (a former chef) doing short but interesting choice of good food; good play area in attractive garden, long and narrow; bedrooms comfortable and reasonably priced, handy for Sudeley Castle *(Derek and Sylvia Stephenson, Lew Badger, Dr P Lavender)*

Winchcombe [Gretton Rd], *Bell*: Good local beer at low prices, good lunchtime snacks inc freshly cut sandwiches, very friendly atmosphere and locals *(Mrs Elizabeth Turner)*; [High St], *White Harte*: Comfortable stone-built beamed inn with usual food, real ales such as Boddingtons, Marstons Pedigree and Stanway Oatmeal Stout, pleasant staff; bedrooms spacious with good facilities *(George Atkinson)*

Winterbourne Down [Down Rd; ST6679], *Cross Hands*: Good family pub with interesting collection of sewing machines, good range of local real ales *(Dr and Mrs A K Clarke)*

☆ **Woodchester** [South Woodchester, signed off A46 Stroud—Nailsworth; SO8302], *Ram*: Fine choice of ales such as Archers Best, Boddingtons, John Smiths and Uley Old Spot with several interesting guest beers, in relaxed L-shaped beamed bar with nice mix of traditional furnishings, some stripped stonework and three open fires, darts, bar food from sandwiches to steaks, restaurant; children welcome, open all day Sat/Sun, spectacular views from terrace tables *(DC, Stephen Pine, Alfred Lawrence, Miss K Law, Simon Smith, Conor Smith, Alec Hamilton, Geoffrey and Penny Hughes, D Irving, R Huggins, T McLean, E McCall, Stephen Brown, J and P Halfyard, Roger and Valerie Hill)*

Woodchester [Bath Rd, Rooksmoor; A46 a mile S of Stroud; SO8403], *Old Fleece*: Wide choice of good freshly made bar food inc interesting light meals, particularly well kept Bass, Boddingtons and Greene King, good wines, local non-alcoholic drinks, good friendly service, big log fire, daily papers, popular golden labrador; well laid candlelit tables in bistro dining areas *(D G King)*

Post Office address codings confusingly give the impression that some pubs are in Gloucestershire, when they're really in the Midlands (which is where we list them).

Hampshire

This county's pubs embrace a good spectrum from that most appealing type of local (the type that immediately makes strangers feel at home) to some very popular dining pubs. Among the pubs doing best here these days are the bustling and lively Hobler at Battramsley (good food), the Red Lion at Boldre (some sensible new refurbishments, really nice interesting food), the friendly White Hart in Cadnam (enjoyable food), the very pretty Red Lion at Chalton (Hampshire's oldest), the delightful and unpretentious Flower Pots at Cheriton (good beer brewed there), the Peat Spade at Longstock (a new main entry – friendly newish licensees doing imaginative food), the Royal Oak at North Gorley (another new entry – a fine all-rounder, charmingly placed), the Bush at Ovington (another lovely spot; rather upmarket food now), the Ship up on the downs at Owslebury (good views, popular with walkers; good family garden), the welcoming thatched Tichborne Arms at Tichborne, the Brushmakers Arms at Upham (excellent new licensees – moving from the Five Bells at Buriton), the very well run White Lion at Wherwell (the lounge and public bar are being knocked together as these words are written, so we await readers' views on whether this is an improvement – or not), and the engaging Cartwheel tucked away at Whitsbury (another new main entry). There have been changes of management at other pubs, too: perhaps most notably at that great favourite, the Wykeham Arms in Winchester (so far, so good, enjoyable on all fronts), but also at the Jolly Sailor at Bursledon (plans for extension, new garden), the friendly Queen at Dummer, the Royal Oak at Langstone (the waterside position's the thing, here), the Leather Bottle at Mattingley (as relaxed as ever, very popular), the Dever Arms at Micheldever (friendly people doing good food), and the Coach & Horses at Rotherwick (he's from South Africa, and people like the handful of South African dishes they've introduced). Most of the county's best pub food is to be found among the pubs we've mentioned so far; others to pick out for enjoyable meals are the friendly rambling White Horse at Droxford, the Hen & Chicken at Froyle (imaginative, not cheap), the very relaxed and local-feeling Hawkley Inn at Hawkley, and the Fleur de Lys at Pilley (the sort of place that's best at quiet times). From among the wide range of possibilities it's the Red Lion at Boldre that we congratulate as Hampshire Dining Pub of the Year, carrying off our award for the second year running. There are some fine pubs too among the Lucky Dip entries at the end of the chapter: the Ship at Bishops Sutton, Tally Ho at Broughton, Five Bells at Buriton, Fox & Hounds at Bursledon, Sir John Barleycorn in Cadnam, Chairmakers Arms at Denmead, Hampshire Bowman at Dundridge, New Forest at Emery Down, Foresters Arms at Frogham, Olde Whyte Harte in Hamble, High Corner at Linwood, Trusty Servant at Minstead, Rose & Thistle at Rockbourne, Bear & Ragged Staff at Timsbury, and two that (unlike those so far mentioned) we've not yet had the pleasure of inspecting, the Oak at Bank and Queens Head at Dogmersfield. There's a good choice in and around Portsmouth, and in Winchester. Hampshire drinks prices are well above the national average, with pubs tied to more or less local brewers such as Badger, Eldridge Pope (Hardy), Gales and Wadworths no cheaper than the rest; the cheapest places we found were the Flower Pots at Cheriton (brewing its own beer), the Brushmakers Arms at Upham (a free house with a much lower price on its Gales than we found in pubs tied to that brewery) and the Peat Spade at Longstock (getting its excellent value Hampshire King Alfred from nearby Romsey).

ALRESFORD SU5832 Map 2

Globe 🍷

The Soke, Broad Street (extreme lower end – B3046 towards Old Alresford); town signposted off A31 bypass

Terrace doors here give access to the terrace and garden – and give a good view over the Alresford Ponds, a sizeable stretch of water created in the 12th c and now a lovely haven for wildlife; some of the birds hope for scraps in the attractive garden, and in summer offer endless amusement for small children. Inside, the pub is comfortably refurbished, with big log fires at each end, a bustling atmosphere, and a clean and uncluttered decor – old local photographs, information about the ponds. Bar food includes soup (£2.45), sandwiches (from £2.75), ploughman's (£3.75), chicken liver parfait or stilton and walnut pâté (£3.95), bangers and mash (£4.75), lamb meatballs on couscous (£4.95), home-made meatloaf, feta cheese and spring onion flan or steak and kidney pie (£5.75), chicken ballotine with a bacon and basil stuffing (£6.95), and crab and lobster cakes (£7.95). Part of the restaurant is no smoking. Well kept Courage Best with a guest such as Marstons Pedigree, John Smiths or Wadworths 6X on handpump, a wide choice of decent wines by the glass, winter mulled wine, and country wines; board games. Nearby parking is rather limited; there's plenty about 100 metres away, at the bottom of truly named Broad St. *(Recommended by Ann and Colin Hunt, Dr Alan Green, Mike Hayes, Lynn Sharpless, Bob Eardley, F Johnston, Patricia and Anthony Daley, Jo and Gary Charlton, Howard Allen)*

Scottish Courage ~ Lease: Lyn O'Callaghan and Terry McTurk ~ Real ale ~ Meals and snacks ~ Restaurant (Tues-Sat evenings) ~ (01962) 732294 ~ Children welcome ~ Open 11-3, 6-11; 12-3, 6.30-10.30 Sun

BATTRAMSLEY SZ3099 Map 2

Hobler

A337 a couple of miles S of Brockenhurst; OS Sheet 196 map reference 307990

To be sure of an evening table in this bustling, popular pub, it would be wise to book – and it's worth arriving early at lunchtime as well. The black-beamed bar – divided by the massive stub of an ancient wall – has a very relaxed feel, and is furnished with pews, little dining chairs and a comfortable bow-window seat. Guns, china, New-Forest saws, the odd big engraving, and a growing collection of customer photographs decorate the walls, some of which are stripped back to timbered brick; the cosy area on the left is black-panelled and full of books. Enjoyable food (they tell us prices have not changed since last year) might include ploughman's (£3.95), stuffed jalapeno chillies (£5.50), home-made pies (£5.95), peppers in pasta or half shoulder of lamb (£7.95), lamb kidneys in a thick bacon and wholegrain mustard sauce (£8.95), bass in a lemony butter sauce or their popular 'Hot Rocks', a hot stone on a plate upon which you cook your own sirloin steak or chicken breast (£9.95), and scallops (£10.95). Meat is especially well looked after – the landlord is also the local butcher. Well kept Flowers IPA, Wadworths 6X and guest beers like Bass, Gibbs Mew Deacon, Morlands Old Speckled Hen, and Ringwood Fortyniner on handpump, a good range of malt whiskies (over 75) and country wines; cribbage, dominoes, chess, scrabble, and piped music. In summer, a spacious forest-edge lawn has a summer bar, a huge timber climbing fort in the very good play area, and picnic-sets, as well as a paddock with ponies, pigs, donkeys, a peacock and hens. Note children aren't allowed inside. *(Recommended by David Gregory, J and P Halfyard, R Inman, Dr and Mrs A K Clarke, Ann and Colin Hunt, Mr and*

Mrs A J Woolstone, Lynn Sharpless, Bob Eardley, D Marsh)

Whitbreads ~ Lease: Pip Steven ~ Real ale ~ Meals and snacks (till 10pm) ~ (01590) 623291 ~ Jazz Tues evening, blues every 2nd Thurs evening ~ Open 10.30-2.30(3 Sat), 6-11; 12-3, 7-10.30 Sun

BEAUWORTH SU5624 Map 2

Milbury's

Turn off A272 Winchester/Petersfield at Beauworth ¾ Bishops Waltham 6 signpost, then continue straight on past village

Handy for the South Downs Way, this popular pub is a good place to end up after a walk, and the garden has fine views. Inside, the bar has a 600-year-old well with a massive 250-year-old treadmill – if you drop an ice cube into the spotlit shaft it takes eight full seconds to reach the bottom, which apparently means it is 300 feet deep. Sturdy beams and panelling, stripped masonry, interesting old furnishings, and massive open fireplaces (with good winter log fires) offer other reminders of the building's age. Well kept Cheriton Diggers Gold, Four Rivers Moondance, Hampshire Arthur Pendragon, and a beer named for the pub on handpump, Addlestone's cider, and country wines. Enjoyable bar food includes home-made soup (£2.65), filled french bread or baked potatoes (£4.20), home-made lasagne (£5.25), home-made steak and kidney pie (£6.25), poached salmon in a white wine and prawn sauce (£8.25), ragoût of wild mushrooms in a puff pastry case or monkfish provençale (£8.95), puddings like treacle tart or apple pie (from £2.45), and children's meals (from £2.50); Sunday roasts. There's usually a ginger and a tabby cat, and a big dog; fruit machine, skittle alley. The name of this pub was at first only a nickname, coming from the Millbarrow, a Bronze Age cemetery surrounding it, briefly famous back in 1833 when a Norman hoard of 6,000 silver coins was found here. *(Recommended by Tony and Wendy Hobden, Ann and Colin Hunt, Steve Power, Lynn Sharpless, Bob Eardley, Martin and Karen Wake, Eddie Edwards, Sheila and Robert Robinson, Mr and Mrs Jonathan Russell, Mrs F A W Ricketts, Michael Inskip, N E Bushby, W E Atkins, Jo and Gary Charlton, Joy and Harold Dermott)*

Free house ~ Licensees Jan and Lenny Larden ~ Real ale ~ Meals and snacks (till 10pm) ~ Restaurant ~ (01962) 771248 ~ Children in eating area of bar ~ Open 10.30-3.30, 6-11; 12-4, 7-10.30 Sun ~ Bedrooms: £27.50/£38.50

BENTWORTH SU6740 Map 2

Sun

Sun Hill; from the A339 coming from Alton the first turning takes you there direct; or in village follow Shalden 2¼, Alton 4¼ signpost

The two tiny traditional communicating rooms in this unspoilt and friendly old country cottage have open fires in big fireplaces, high-backed antique settles, pews and schoolroom chairs, olde-worlde prints and blacksmith's tools on the walls, and bare boards and scrubbed deal tables on the left. An arch leads to a brick-floored room with another open fire and hanging baskets. Home-made bar food includes sandwiches (from £1.90), home-made soup (£2.25), ploughman's (£3.50), smoked salmon pasta (£5.50), pies such as chicken, ham and leek or steak and kidney or lamb casserole (£6.50), lamb with port and redcurrants (£6.95), and puddings £2.50). Well kept Badger Best, Brakspears Bitter, Bunces Pigswill, Cheriton Pots Ale, Ringwood Best, and Timothy Taylor Landlord on handpump, and several malt whiskies. There are a few seats in the garden. *(Recommended by Jasper Sabey, Miss V Brown, Howard Allen, Lynn Sharpless, Bob Eardley, Phyl and Jack Street, Martin and Karen Wake, Christopher Wade, Gordon Prince, Ann and Colin Hunt, Thomas Nott, Jo and Gary Charlton)*

Free house ~ Licensee Mary Holmes ~ Real ale ~ Meals and snacks ~ (01420) 562338 ~ Children welcome ~ Open 12-3, 6-11; 12-10.30 Sun

BOLDRE SZ3298 Map 2

Red Lion ★ 🍴 🍷

Village signposted from A337 N of Lymington

Hampshire Dining Pub of the Year

The careful refurbishments have now been completed here and readers are happy to report that they haven't changed the character of this friendly pub. The entrance and a new terrace lead off the car park, the bar has been extended and the small entrance lobby is now a cosy little bar with a fine old cooking range given by a customer. The four black-beamed rooms are filled with heavy urns, platters, needlework, rural landscapes, and so forth, taking in farm tools, heavy-horse harness, needlework, gin-traps and even ferocious-looking man-traps along the way; the central room has a profusion of chamber-pots, and an end room has pews, wheelback chairs and tapestried stools, and a dainty collection of old bottles and glasses in the window by the counter. The dining areas are no smoking. Good, very popular bar food includes home-made soup (£2.80), sandwiches (£2.90), crostini of cured ham, poached egg and cream of stilton or rabbit terrine with pear chutney (£4.50), smoked haddock fishcakes (£4.80), ploughman's (£5.50), good salads such as salmon and prawns with fresh coriander with a lime and chilli dressing or niçoise (from £5.90), mixed seafoods on squid ink pasta or vegetable casserole (£6.50), lamb liver (£7.20), breast of chicken with devilled sauce and chorizo sausage (£8.50), navarin of lamb (£9.20), confit of duckling with marinated red cabbage (£9.50), and puddings like chocolate truffle torte, whisky bread and butter pudding, and cherry and almond mousse (£3.20); get there early to be sure of a seat. Well kept Bass and Hardy Royal Oak on handpump, a range of malt whiskies, and up to 20 wines by the glass; prompt and friendly service. In summer, the flowering tubs and hanging baskets are lovely and there's a cart festooned with colour near the car park. This is a fine area for walking, with 1,000 acres of Raydon Wood Nature Reserve. No children. *(Recommended by John and Christine Simpson, Roger J Trott, R Inman, Phyl and Jack Street, W Osborn-King, Patrick Renouf, Dr and Mrs A K Clarke, R H Rowley, Dave Braisted, Mr and Mrs A R Hawkins, Ann and Colin Hunt, J and P Halfyard, Tim and Linda Collins, Jo and Gary Charlton, M J Dowdy, Betsy Brown, Nigel Flook, D Marsh, Mrs F A Ricketts, Pat and Roger Fereday, P and S White)*

Hardy ~ Lease: John and Penny Bicknell ~ Real ale ~ Meals and snacks (11.30-2.30, 6.30-10) ~ (01590) 673177 ~ Open 11-11; 12-10.30 Sun; closed 25 and evening 26 Dec

BRAMDEAN SU6128 Map 2

Fox

A272 Winchester—Petersfield

The open-plan and carefully modernised bar here has black beams, tall stools with proper backrests around the L-shaped counter, and comfortably cushioned wall pews and wheelback chairs; the fox motif shows in a big painting over the fireplace, and on much of the decorative china. At least one area is no smoking. There's quite a firm emphasis on eating, with lunchtime sandwiches (from £2.50), soup (£2.95), brandied mushrooms with bacon on a crouton (£4.75), mushrooms with dolcellate cheese or ploughman's (£4.95), fresh deep-fried cod in batter (£7.95), and fresh salmon with tarragon sauce or rump steak (£8.95), with evening dishes like chicken breast with parma ham in boursin sauce (£10.95), roast rack of lamb (£12.95), and fresh frilled bass with a red pepper salsa (£13.95). Well kept Marstons Pedigree on handpump; piped music. At the back of the building is a walled-in terraced area, and a spacious lawn spreading among the fruit trees, with a good play area – trampoline as well as swings and a seesaw. No children inside. *(Recommended by Ron Shelton, Betty Laker, Iain Robertson, Phyl and Jack Street, Janet and Colin Roe; more reports please)*

Marstons ~ Tenants Jane and Ian Inder ~ Real ale ~ Meals and snacks ~ (01962) 771363 ~ Open 11-3, 6-11; 12-3, 7-10.30 Sun; closed 25 Dec

BURSLEDON SU4809 Map 2

Jolly Sailor

2 miles from M27 junction 8; then A27 towards Sarisbury, then just before going under railway bridge turn right towards Bursledon Station; it's best to park round here and walk, as the lane up from the station is now closed to cars

An extension to the front of this pub is planned, the kitchens are to be enlarged, and the banks are to be landscaped. You can sit out at the tables under the big yew tree or on the wooden jetty, watching all the goings on in the rather pretty harbour or enjoy the same view from the window seat inside. The airy front bar has ship pictures, nets and shells, as well as windsor chairs and settles on the floorboards. The atmospheric beamed and flagstoned back bar, with pews and settles by its huge fireplace, is a fair bit older. Under the new managers, bar food includes sandwiches, mushroom and butterbean lasagne (£6.95), wild boar and apple sausage salad (£7.75), thai green chicken curry (£7.95), and bouillabaisse (£10.95). The dining area is no smoking. Well kept Badger Best, IPA, and Tanglefoot and Oving Bitter on handpump, and country wines; fruit machine and piped music. The path down to the pub (and of course back up again) from the lane is steep. *(Recommended by Jess and George Cowley, Bruce Bird, Ian Phillips, Ann and Colin Hunt, John and Christine Simpson, D Marsh, Martin and Karen Wake, James Flory, Stephen, Julie and Hayley Brown, Eric and June Heley)*

Badger ~ Managers Adrian Jenkins, Jackie Cosens ~ Real ale ~ Meals and snacks (12-9.30) ~ (01703) 405557 ~ Children in dining area ~ Open 11-11; 12-10.30 Sun; closed 25 Dec

CADNAM SU2913 Map 2

White Hart

½ mile from M27 junction 1; A336 towards village, pub off village roundabout

The enjoyable food is the main draw here – and it does get particularly busy on weekend lunchtimes. Attractively presented, there might be soup (£3.25), cheese, bread and pickle (£4.75), open sandwiches or chicken satay (£5.25), sausages with onion gravy or freshly battered cod (£7.25), a daily pasta dish or aubergine fritters with grilled vegetables and pesto (£8.25), gammon and egg (£9.25), duck breast with orange and cranberry sauce or medallions of venison with bacon and mushroom sauce (£11.25), specials such as seared scallops with bacon and mushrooms (£10.25), Sunday lunch half roast shoulder of lamb with minted gravy (£8.75), and home-made puddings. The spacious multi-level dining lounge has good solid furnishings, soft lighting, country prints and appropriate New Forest pictures and mementoes; well kept Courage Best, Flowers Original, Morlands Old Speckled Hen, and Wadworths 6X on handpump, and decent wines; efficient, friendly service. There are picnic-sets under cocktail parasols outside. *(Recommended by David Gregory, Paul White, David Shillitoe, Lynn Sharpless, Bob Eardley, Dennis Stevens, Eric and Charlotte Osgood, Ian and Jacqui Ross, Brian Mills, Martin and Karen Wake, Phyl and Jack Street, Steve Power, Derek and Margaret Underwood, Dr C S Wilson, D B Jenkin, Philip Vernon, Kim Maidment, Ian Phillips, D Marsh, Mark and Heather Williamson)*

Whitbreads ~ Lease: Nick and Sue Emberley ~ Real ale ~ Meals and snacks ~ (01703) 812277 ~ Children welcome ~ Open 11-3, 6-11; 12-3, 6-10.30 Sun

CHALTON SU7315 Map 2

Red Lion 🍷

Village signposted E of A3 Petersfield—Horndean

Particularly pretty – especially in summer with its colourful hanging baskets – this timbered thatched pub is Hampshire's oldest and was first licensed in 1503. The most characterful part is the heavy-beamed and panelled front bar with high-backed traditional settles and elm tables and an ancient inglenook fireplace with a frieze of burnished threepenny bits set into its mantlebeam. Popular bar food includes sandwiches and snacks, and daily specials such as fried lamb liver and bacon

(£6.95), rack of lamb glazed in honey and ginger (£7.05), guinea fowl in calvados (£7.95), and mahi-mahi (a fish) marinated in lime and coconut (£8.50). Families are usually directed to a modern no-smoking dining extension. Well kept Gales BBB, Best, HSB, Winter Brew, and a guest beer on handpump, a good choice of wines by the glass or bottle, country wines, and over 40 malt whiskies; efficient service; piped music. The garden is pretty in summer and the pub is popular with walkers and riders as it is fairly close to the extensive Queen Elizabeth Country Park and about half a mile down the lane from a growing Iron Age farm and settlement; it's only about 20 minutes to the car ferry, too. *(Recommended by N E Bushby, W E Atkins, Mike and Mary Carter, Mr and Mrs Buckler, Ian Phillips, Tony and Wendy Hobden, J and P Halfyard, Dennis Stevens, Brad Morley, Richard Dolphin, P and S White)*

Gales ~ Managers Mick and Mary McGee ~ Real ale ~ Meals and snacks (not Sun evening) ~ (01705) 592246 ~ Children in family dining room ~ Open 11-3, 6-11; 12-3, 7-10.30 Sun; closed evenings 25-26 Dec

CHERITON SU5828 Map 2

Flower Pots ★

Pub just off B3046 (main village road) towards Beauworth and Winchester; OS Sheet 185 map reference 581282

'Delightful' is how several readers describe this bustling village local – and even though it does get busy, there's still a marvellous friendly atmosphere created by the charming licensees. There are two little rooms and the one on the left feels almost like someone's front room, with pictures of hounds and ploughmen on its striped wallpaper, bunches of flowers, and a horse and foal and other ornaments on the mantlepiece over a small log fire; it can get smoky in here. Behind the servery there's disused copper filtering equipment, and lots of hanging gin-traps, drag-hooks, scaleyards and other ironwork. Good value straightforward bar food includes sandwiches (from £1.80, toasties or big baps from £2), ploughman's (from £3.30), and chilli con carne, lamb and apricot casserole or beef and ale stew (from £4.10). Their own-brewed beers from the Cheriton Brewhouse are very good indeed: Diggers Gold, Pots Ale and Cheriton Best Bitter. Darts in the neat extended plain public bar (where there's a covered well), also cribbage, shove-ha'penny and dominoes. On the pretty front and back lawns are some old-fashioned seats – very useful in fine weather as it can quickly fill up inside; they sometimes have Morris dancers out here in summer. Near the site of one of the final battles of the Civil War, the pub once belonged to the retired head gardener of nearby Avington Park, which explains the unusual name. *(Recommended by Ann and Colin Hunt, Lynn Sharpless, Bob Eardley, Mr and Mrs Peter Smith, Eddie Edwards, A R and B E Sayer, Michael Hasslacher, Howard Allen, John Knighton, John and Christine Simpson, Ron Shelton, Mrs G Connell, Susan and John Douglas, Ron Gentry, Thomas Nott, Martin and Karen Wake, Stephen Harvey, Mrs F A W Ricketts, J S M Sheldon)*

Own Brew ~ Licensees Patricia and Joanna Bartlett ~ Real ale ~ Meals and snacks (not Sun evening) ~ (01962) 771318 ~ Children in small sitting room off lounge bar ~ Open 12-2.30, 6-11; 12-3, 7-10.30 Sun ~ Bedrooms: £27B/£45B

DROXFORD SU6018 Map 2

White Horse

4 miles along A32 from Wickham

Doing very well at the moment, this rambling 16th-c inn has a relaxed and friendly atmosphere. The atmospheric lounge bar is made up of several small cosy rooms – low beams, bow windows, alcoves, and log fires, while the public bar is larger and more straightforward: pool, table football, table skittles, shove-ha'penny, cribbage, dominoes, video game, and CD juke box. Good, reasonably priced bar food includes sandwiches (from £1.80; hot crusty french sticks from £2.75), home-made soup (£2), ploughman's (from £3.50), Portuguese sardines (£5.15), spicy cumberland sausage or vegetable curry (£5.25), a home-made pie of the day (from £6), a brace of locally smoked quail (£6.25), gammon and egg (£6.75), steaks (from £9.50), daily specials like home-made fish pie with salmon, trout, prawns, smoked haddock and white fish (£6.50), home-made steak, mushroom and Guinness pie (£7.95), and lots of game such as snipe, partridge, hare, pheasant, rabbit and venison (£5.75-£11.50), home-made puddings, and children's menu (£2.10). Both restaurant areas are no smoking. Well kept Morlands IPA and Old Speckled Hen plus Flowers Original, Greene King Abbot, and Ruddles Best on handpump. One of the cubicles in the gents' overlooks an illuminated well. There are tables in a secluded flower-filled courtyard comfortably sheltered by the building's back wings. *(Recommended by Ann and Colin Hunt, A R and B E Sayer, Brad W Morley, Lynn Sharpless, Bob Eardley, Mrs F A Ricketts, David Heath, Gwen and Peter Andrews, T W Fleckney, Dave Braisted, Steven Tait, Susie Lonie)*

Morlands ~ Tenant Paul Young ~ Real ale ~ Meals and snacks (till 9.45; all day at weekends/bank holidays) ~ Restaurant ~ (01489) 877490 ~ Children in family room and eating area of bar ~ Open 11-11; 12-10.30 Sun ~ Bedrooms: £25(£40B)/£35(£50B)

DUMMER SU5846 Map 2

Queen

Half a mile from M3, junction 7; take Dummer slip road

New licensees have taken over this tiled white cottage but no major changes have taken place. The bar is open-plan, but has a pleasantly alcovey feel, with a liberal use of timbered brick and plaster partition walls, as well as beams and joists and an open fire. There are built-in padded seats, cushioned spindleback chairs and stools around the tables on the dark blue patterned carpet, and pictures of queens, old photographs, small steeplechase prints and advertisements. Decent bar food includes home-made soup (£2.50), sandwiches (from £3.25 with chips and salad), filled baked potatoes (from £4.25), several types of burgers (from £6.50), cod in their own beer batter (£6.95 medium, £8.95 large), bangers and mash or lasagne (£6.95), steak and kidney pudding (£10.95), steaks (from £10.95), daily specials, puddings (£4), and roast Sunday lunch (from £6.95); friendly service. Well kept Courage Best and Directors, Fullers London Pride, and sometimes Marstons Pedigree on handpump; fruit machine in one corner, and piped music. Picnic-sets under cocktail parasols on the terrace and in a neat little sheltered back garden. *(Recommended by Ian Phillips, Martin and Karen Wake, Tony Gayfer, M C Girling, Howard Allen, G C Wilkinson, Mrs H Murphy, Nigel and Sue Foster, J and B Cressey, Susan and John Douglas)*

Courage ~ Managers John and Beverly Simm ~ Real ale ~ Meals and snacks (till 10 on Thurs, Fri, Sat) ~ Restaurant ~ (01256) 397367 ~ Children in restaurant until 9pm ~ Open 11-3, 5.30-11; 12-3, 7-10.30 Sun

EAST TYTHERLEY SU2929 Map 2

Star

Off B3084 N of Romsey, via Lockerleigh – turn off by railway crossing nr Mottisfont Abbey

There's always a friendly bustle here – and plenty going on. The bar is pleasantly informal with an unassuming mix of comfortably homely furnishing, log fires in attractive fireplaces, a no-smoking lower lounge bar, and a cosy and pretty restaurant; despite the very relaxed feel of the place, staff are smart and efficient – an excellent balance. Enjoyable home-made food includes soup (£1.95), sandwiches (from £3.25), ploughman's (£4.25), steak and kidney pie, lasagne or chilli con carne (£5.95), daily specials such as game pie or mushrooms in stilton (£5.95), roast pheasant in red wine (£8.95), vegetarian dishes, and puddings such as apple and blackberry crumble, treacle sponge or spotted dick and custard (£2.95). The restaurant is no smoking. Well kept Courage Directors, Gales HSB and Ringwood Best on handpump, and country wines. The garden has a play area, and there are picnic-sets on the forecourt; full size chess and draughts; skittle alley. *(Recommended by Howard Allen, John and Joan Calvert, Adrian and Mandy Bateman, D Marsh)*

Free house ~ Licensee Carol Mitchell ~ Real ale ~ Meals and snacks ~ Restaurant ~ (01794) 340225 ~ Well behaved children welcome ~ Open 11-2.30(3 Sat), 6-11; 12-3, 7-10.30 Sun ~ Bedrooms: £35S/£50S

FROYLE SU7542 Map 2

Hen & Chicken

A31 Alton—Farnham

The three interconnecting rooms in this old coaching inn have beams hung with hops, candles on the tables, chestnuts roasting on the fire in the inglenook fireplace, daily papers, soft piped music and a discreetly positioned fruit machine. Served by staff in neat waistcoats, the imaginative good food includes home-made soup (£3.75), sandwiches (from £3.50; filled french bread from £4.25), mushrooms in a brandy and cream sauce or chargrilled peppers on pesto (£4.95), ploughman's (£5.50), omelettes (from £5.50), chilled duck breast with a red onion compote and pine nut dressing (£5.75), sun-dried tomato couscous and fresh basil with parmesan (£8.50), chicken breast on chargrilled vegetables with a sweet chilli dressing (£9.25), confit of duck on a potato rosti with a mushroom and silver onion sauce (£10.25), steaks (from £10.95), puddings like white chocolate and strawberry parfait, coconut crème brûlée or bread and butter pudding (£3.95), and children's menu (£2.95); part of the restaurant is no smoking. Well kept Badger Best, Courage Best, Fullers London Pride, Hogs Back Hop Garden Gold, Hook Norton Old Hookey, Timothy Taylor Landlord, and Tisbury Nadderjack Ale on handpump kept under light blanket pressure, and several malt whiskies; cheerful, friendly service. The big garden has children's play equipment. *(Recommended by Ann and Colin Hunt, Guy Consterdine, Nick Wikeley, Thomas Nott, Jo and Gary Charlton, Simon Collett-Jones, V Harris, Chris and Ann Garnett, E G Parish, Victor Harris)*

Free house ~ Licensee Bill Thompson ~ Real ale ~ Meals and snacks (11-2.30, 6-10) ~ Restaurant ~ (01420) 22115 ~ Children welcome ~ Jazz Weds evening ~ Open 11-11; 12-10.30 Sun

HAWKLEY SU7429 Map 2

Hawkley Inn

Pococks Lane; village signposted off B3006, first turning left after leaving its junction with A325 in Greatham; OS Sheet 186 map reference 746292

Very much a local – with a friendly welcome for visitors, too – this unpretentious pub is tucked away in attractive countryside. The opened-up bar and back dining room have a good mix of customers, simple decor – big pine tables, a moose head, dried flowers, and prints on the mellowing walls – and a relaxed atmosphere. Parts of the bar can get a bit smoky when it's busy, but there is a no-smoking area to the left of the bar. Good, promptly served bar food includes various types of ploughman's (from £4.85), baked potato with garlic mushrooms and stilton, scallops in a tarragon sauce, Tunisian fish tart, ham and leek pancakes or tarte provençale (all £7.85), beef stew (£9.25), spicy minced lamb (£10.45), and puddings like fresh fruit crumble or nougat glace (£3.25). Helpings are generous, and service is friendly. Well kept local ales such as Ballard's Best, Cheriton Flower Pots, Hogs Back Hop Garden Gold, Hop Back Summer Lightning, Itchen Valley Godfathers, and RCH Hewish IPA on handpump; they make their own scrumpy. There are tables and a climbing frame in the pleasant garden behind, and the pub is on the Hangers Way Path. *(Recommended by Martin and Karen Wake, Lynn Sharpless, Bob Eardley, Derek Harvey-Piper, Ann and Colin Hunt, Philip and Trisha Ferris, Mr Sedgewick, Mr and Mrs Kirkwood)*

Free house ~ E N Collins and A Stringer ~ Real ale ~ Meals and snacks (not Sun evening) ~ Restaurant ~ (01730) 827205 ~ Children in eating area of bar till 8pm ~ Occasional blues/folk ~ Open 12-2.30(3 Sat), 6-11; 12-3, 7-10.30 Sun

IBSLEY SU1509 Map 2

Old Beams

A338 Ringwood—Salisbury

Far bigger than it looks from outside, this black and white thatched pub is very much somewhere to come for a meal. The big main room is divided by wooden panelling and a canopied log-effect gas fire, and there are lots of varnished wooden tables and country-kitchen chairs under the appropriately aged oak beams; the small formal partly no smoking restaurant has its own bar, and the buffet area and conservatory are no-smoking. From a wide menu chalked on boards, there might be lunchtime sandwiches (from £2.80), vegetarian pasta bake (£4.50), a popular cold buffet (from £4.50), curried beef or turkey (£5.20), home-made steak and kidney pie or a roast of the day (£7.20), steaks (from £9.50), and puddings (from £2.40); they shout your order when it's ready. Well kept Gibbs Mew Bishops Tipple, Hop Back Summer Lightning, Ringwood Best and Old Thumper, and Wadworths 6X on handpump, country wines, and a decent wine list. Fruit machine. *(Recommended by Jill Bickerton, Mr and Mrs A R Hawkins, W W Burke, W Osborn-King, Peter Meister, Paul and Sue Merrick, G C Wilkinson, N Cobb, Dr D Twyman, Phyl and Jack Street, Lord Sandhurst, Richard and Rosemary Hoare, Colin Draper, P J and J E F Caunt, Simon Penny, Klaus and Elizabeth Leist)*

Free house ~ Licensee Clive Newell ~ Real ale ~ Meals and snacks (till 10pm in summer) ~ Restaurant ~ (01425) 473387 ~ Children in eating area of bar ~ Open 10.30-2.30, 6-11; 12-3, 6.30-10.30 Sun

LANGSTONE SU7105 Map 2

Royal Oak

High Street (marked as cul-de-sac – actually stops short of the pub itself); village is last turn left off A3023 (confusingly called A324 on some signs) before Hayling Island bridge

Charmingly placed on the edge of a landlocked natural harbour, this popular pub has fine views from seats on the terrace; be careful you don't get marooned by the tide. Inside, the spacious and atmospheric flagstoned bar has windows from which you can see the ancient wadeway to Hayling Island, and simple furnishings like windsor chairs around old wooden tables on the wooden parquet and ancient flagstones, and two winter open fires. There's a new manager again this year, and food now includes sandwiches, filled baked potatoes, ploughman's, duck and port pâté (£3.95), smoked halibut in a caper mayonnaise (£4.25), chicken satay (£5.50), various fresh fish dishes (from £6), broccoli and tomato bake (£6.25), lamb curry (£6.95), and rump steak (£8.65); the dining area is no smoking. Well kept Boddingtons, Flowers Original, Gales HSB, Morlands Old Speckled Hen, and Wadworths 6X on handpump, decent wine, Bulmer's cider, and country wines; monthly fun quiz, no noisy piped music or games machines. Morris dancers in summer; good coastal paths nearby. *(Recommended by Lynn Sharpless, Bob Eardley, Val and Alan Green, Ian Phillips, Dennis Stevens, J and P Halfyard, Phyl and Jack Street, A E Brace, A G Drake, D Marsh, Martin and Karen Wake, Ann and Colin Hunt)*

Whitbreads ~ Manager Chris Ford ~ Real ale ~ Meals and snacks (bar snacks all day) ~ (01705) 483125 ~ Children in eating areas ~ Folk 1st Weds evening of month ~ Parking at all close may be very difficult ~ Open 11-11; 12-10.30 Sun

LOCKS HEATH SU5006 Map 2

Jolly Farmer

2½ miles from M27 junction 9; A27 towards Bursledon, left into Locks Rd, at end T-junction right into Warsash Rd then left at hire shop into Fleet End Rd; OS Sheet 196 map reference 509062

In an area of largely modern development, this white-painted inn with its pretty hanging baskets is a welcome sight. Much of the emphasis is on eating, though there is a little drinking area (popular at lunchtime). The small bar on the right and extensive series of softly lit rooms on the left have nice old scrubbed tables, cushioned oak pews and smaller chairs; their ochre walls and beams are hung with a veritable forest of country bric-a-brac, racing prints, Victorian engravings and so on, making for a very cosy feeling that's amplified by the coal-effect gas fires. A wide choice of bar food includes filled baps (from £3.25), soup (£2.95), ploughman's (from £4.15), home-baked ham and eggs or steak and kidney pie (£5.95) and specials such as fresh fish dishes (from £5.95), ham, mushroom and cream tagliatelle or omelettes (£6.95), steaks (from £10.25), and puddings (£2.95). One restaurant is no smoking. Well kept Flowers Original, Gales HSB, and Morlands Old Speckled Hen on handpump, and country wines; silenced fruit machine, piped music. Neat friendly staff. There are tables under cocktail parasols on two sheltered terraces, one with a play area. *(Recommended by John and Christine Simpson, Ann and Colin Hunt, Mr and Mrs B Craig, Michael Inskip, Stephen, Julie and Hayley Brown)*

Whitbreads ~ Lease: Martin O'Grady ~ Real ale ~ Meals and snacks (till 10pm) ~ Two restaurants ~ (01489) 572500 ~ Children welcome ~ Open 11-11; 12-10.30 Sun ~ Bedrooms: £40S/£52S

LONGPARISH SU4344 Map 2

Plough

B3048 – off A303 just E of Andover

The terrace to the side of this pretty creeper-covered village inn is full of hanging baskets and flower tubs, and the garden has been smartened up and extended – plenty of seats as well as guinea pigs and rabbits for children. Inside, the dining lounge spreads through a series of low wide arches which gives a feeling of snugness: wheelbacks and built-in wall seats on the patterned carpet, fringed lamps, and a few farm tools, copper implements, and prints; there is a small pubby part with hops around the cream-painted walls, but the feel of the place is quite restauranty. A large choice of quickly served bar food might include good home-made watercress soup (£2.75), sandwiches (from £3.50), ploughman's (£3.95), gammon and pineapple (£5.75), cod, chips and mushy peas (£6.25), vegetarian dishes like cream and mushroom pasta or vegetable bake (£6.95), steaks (from £7.25), daily specials like liver and bacon (£5.50) or cod provençale (£6.25), puddings such as home-made pineapple cheesecake or strawberry pavlova (£2.75), and children's menu (£3.25); the restaurant is partly no smoking; friendly service. Well kept Boddingtons, Flowers Original, Wadworths 6X and a guest such as Hampshire King Alfreds on handpump, and country wines; piped music. The two persian blue cats are called Chalis and Chardonnay, and the yellow labrador, Honey. *(Recommended by Graham and Lynn Mason, Martin and Karen Wake, Mike Gorton, JCW, Mr and Mrs D Price, Lynn Sharpless, Bob Eardley)*

Whitbreads ~ Lease: Pauline and Christopher Dale ~ Real ale ~ Meals and snacks ~ Restaurant ~ (01264) 720358 ~ Children in eating area of bar ~ Occasional live entertainment ~ Open 11-3.30, 6-11; 12-4, 7-10.30 Sun ~ Bedrooms: £20/£40

LONGSTOCK SU3537 Map 2

Peat Spade

Village signposted off A30 on W edge of Stockbridge, and off A3057 Stockbridge—Andover

Very well run under its newish licensees, this lively and popular dining pub has a roomy and attractive squarish main bar, airy and high-ceilinged, with pretty windows, well chosen furnishings and a nice show of toby jugs and beer mats around its fireplace. A rather elegant smaller dining room leads off; one area is no smoking. Good food includes imaginative dishes such as filled ciabatta bread or home-made soup (£3.50), English cheese with bread and home-made pickles (£4.75), lunchtime dishes like home-made pork and bacon faggots (£5.50), various pasta dishes (from £5.50), and tabbouleh and smoked salmon salad on a bed of rocket (£5.95), as well as baked goat's cheese with a fricassee of sweet peppers and oyster mushrooms with a balsamic dressing (£7.95), Dorset scallops with a shrimp and mussel sauce, breast of Gressingham duck with garlic, chilli and ginger dressing or sirloin steak (all £10.50), and puddings like walnut and raisin fudge tart or coffee parfait with home-made shortbread biscuits (£3.50); children's helpings, and two Sunday roasts (£7.50). Well kept Hampshire King Alfred's, Ringwood Fortyniner, and a winter guest on handpump, and a decent wine list; shove-ha'penny, dominoes, cribbage and maybe Classic FM. There are tables (and free range chickens) out in the garden, not large but pleasant, and the River Test is only about 100 yards away; they have a friendly diabetic dog Mollie (who is not allowed to be fed) and three cats. The quiet village is on the 44-mile Test Way long-distance path, and the pub is also handy for bracing downland walks up around the Danebury hillfort. *(Recommended by Phyl and Jack Street, Mrs J Taylar)*

Free house ~ Licensees Bernie Startup and Sarah Hinman ~ Real ale ~ Meals and snacks (not Sun evening or Mon) ~ Restaurant ~ (01264) 810612 ~ Children welcome ~ Open 11-3, 6-11; 12-3 Sun; closed Sun evening and all day Mon ~ Bedrooms: £54.25B/£58.75B

MATTINGLEY SU7357 Map 2

Leather Bottle

3 miles from M3, junction 5; in Hook, turn right-and-left on to B3349 Reading Road (former A32)

New licensees have taken over this brick and tiled pub, and happily, little seems to have changed. It's a simple, peaceful place with a friendly and relaxed beamed main bar – brocaded built-in wall seats, some sabres on the cream walls, and a ticking metal clock over one of the inglenook fireplaces (both have good winter log fires). At the back is the characterful cottagey second bar with lots of black beams, an antique clock, country pictures on the walls (some stripped to brick), lantern lighting, and sturdy inlaid tables with seats; newspapers to read. Good popular bar food includes sandwiches (from £2.20; hot ciabatta rolls £4.25), home-made soup (£2.50), deep-fried camembert with cumberland sauce (£3.80), ploughman's (£4.50), home-cooked ham and egg (£6.25), meaty or vegetarian lasagne (£7.25), chicken korma (£7.50), fish pie (£7.95), chicken in a mild mustard cream and white wine sauce (£8.50), lime and peppercorn steak (£8.95), steaks (from £12.50), and puddings such as toffee apple and pecan crumble (from £3). Well kept Courage Best (tapped from the cask) and Directors, and guest beers such as Hardy Royal Oak and Country on handpump; fruit machine and piped music. The flowering baskets and tubs are pretty in summer, and there are seats in the tree-sheltered garden. *(Recommended by G D Sharpe, Ian Phillips, KC, TBB, Comus Elliott, Jess and George Cowley, Susan and John Douglas, G and M Stewart, Chris and Ann Garnett, D Voller, Andy Cunningham, Yvonne Hannaford; more reports on the new regime, please)*

Courage ~ Lease: David Meredith, Jane Evans ~ Real ale ~ Meals and snacks (till 10pm) ~ (01189) 326371 ~ Children in dining room ~ Open 11-2.30, 6-11; 12-3, 7-10.30 Sun

MICHELDEVER SU5138 Map 2

Dever Arms

Village signposted off A33 N of Winchester

Friendly new licensees again for this attractive country pub. The simply decorated and beamed bar has heavy tables and good solid seats – a nice cushioned panelled oak settle and a couple of long dark pews as well as wheelback chairs – and a woodburning stove at each end; a no-smoking area with lighter-coloured furniture opens off. Good bar food includes sandwiches (from £2.50), home-made soup (£3.45), filled baked potatoes (from £3.50), omelettes (£4.50), ploughman's or vegetable lasagne (£4.95), lamb with redcurrants (£5.95), steak in ale pie (£6.95), roast partridge or poached salmon (£7.95), steaks (from £8.95), puddings like sticky toffee pudding or summer pudding (£3.50), and children's menu (£3.50). Well kept Batemans Mild, Marstons Best, and Pedigree, and a guest beer every two weeks on handpump; darts, pool and piped music – the landlord plays the saxophone, and was hoping to get a licence for live music as we went to press; they have an alsatian called Brew, and four cats. There are seats on a small sheltered back terrace, and some more widely spaced picnic-sets and a play area on the edge of a big cricket green behind; also, rabbits and chickens and a pony. This is a good starting point for exploring the Dever Valley (there are lots of good walks nearby). *(Recommended by Mike Gorton, P R and S A White, Mrs Y M Lippett, W W Burke, R W Allan, Shirley Mackenzie, Jess and George Cowley, C Sinclair, Ann and Colin Hunt, Stephen and Jean Curtis, J L Hall, G Freemantle; more reports on the new regime please)*

Marstons ~ Tenants Ray and Belinda Douglas ~ Real ale ~ Meals and snacks ~

Restaurant ~ (01962) 774339 ~ Children welcome ~ Open 12-3, 6(7 Sun)-11(10.30 Sun)

NORTH GORLEY SU1611 Map 2

Royal Oak

Ringwood Rd; village signposted off A338 S of Fordingbridge

This welcoming 17th-c thatched pub looks over the road and green to a big pond on the edge of the New Forest. On the left is a quiet, comfortable and neatly refurbished no-smoking lounge, though our own preference is for the busier main bar on the right: carpeted too, with pews, mate's chairs, a corner woodburning stove, old engravings and other pictures, with steps down to an attractive L-shaped eating area. This has a mix of dark pine tables and pleasant old-fashioned chairs, with big rugs on bare boards, and a further part with pine booth seating. There are french windows to a neatly kept sheltered back garden, with a play area. Generous enjoyable food includes snacks (from £1.50 to £3.50), vegetarian dishes, curries or chilli (£5.50), steak and stilton pie (£6.25), fresh fish (£6.50), gammon (£6.95), steaks (£8.95), mixed grill (£9.25), and children's dishes. Well kept Fullers London Pride, Gales HSB, Ringwood Best, and Wadworths 6X on handpump, decent wines, quite a few malt whiskies, friendly and efficient young staff; sensibly placed darts, CD juke box, fruit machine; cribbage, dominoes, and skittle alley. *(Recommended by P Gillbe, D Marsh, N B Thompson, John and Vivienne Rice)*

Whitbreads ~ Lease: Ron Newsham ~ Real ale ~ Meals and snacks ~ Children in two areas ~ Restaurant ~ (01425) 652244 ~ Open 11-2.30(3 Sat), 6-11; 12-10.30 Sun

OVINGTON SU5531 Map 2

Bush

Village signposted from A31 on Winchester side of Alresford

Readers are fond of this charming little cottage set in a lovely spot with seats in the garden behind running down to the River Itchen, and more on a tree-sheltered pergola dining terrace with a good-sized fountain pool. The low-ceilinged bar has cushioned high-backed settles, elm tables with pews and kitchen chairs, masses of old pictures in heavy gilt frames on the walls, and a roaring fire on one side with an antique solid fuel stove opposite. Bar food includes sandwiches, home-made soup, ploughman's, good prawn and salmon salad, ratatouille with melted goat's cheese (£6.95), tiger prawns in filo pastry or local trout fillets (£7.95), Greek fish stew (£9.95), steaks, and home-made puddings. Well kept Wadworths IPA, 6X and Farmers Glory and a guest such as Badgers Tanglefoot on handpump; trivia. The pub is handy for the A31, and there are nice walks nearby. *(Recommended by R J Walden, John and Christine Simpson, Peter and Audrey Dowsett, Ann and Colin Hunt, J and B Cressey, Nigel Wikeley, D P and J A Sweeney, Howard Allen, Martin and Karen Wake, Jo and Gary Charlton, Stephen, Julie and Hayley Brown, P R and S A White, Mrs F A W Ricketts)*

Wadworths ~ Managers Les and Bunty Morgan ~ Real ale ~ Meals and snacks (not Sun evening) ~ (01962) 732764 ~ Nearby parking may be difficult ~ Children in eating area of bar ~ Open 11-2.30, 6-11; 12-3, 7-10.30 Sun

OWSLEBURY SU5123 Map 2

Ship

Whites Hill; village signposted off B2177 between Fishers Pond and Lower Upham; can also be reached from M3 junction 10 via Morestead, or from A272 2½ miles SE of A31 junction

As there are lots of good surrounding walks, this well organised pub is naturally popular with walkers, especially at weekends. Both garden areas have fine views – one side looks right across the Solent to the Isle of Wight, the other gives a view down to Winchester; there's an aviary, sheep, a summer marquee, a children's play area, and a weekend bouncy castle. Inside, the knocked-through bar has a friendly bustling atmosphere, varnished black oak 17th-c ship's timbers as beams and wall props, and built-in cushioned wall seats and wheelback chairs around wooden tables, and a big central fireplace. Good food includes sandwiches (from £2.50), soup (£2.50), seafood mornay (£3.95), lunchtime ploughman's (from £4.75), ham and egg (£4.95), steak and kidney pie (£5.95), meatloaf with blue cheese (£6.95), vegetarian stuffed peppers (£7.95), cajun chicken tortillas or stuffed lamb with fresh mint and port wine gravy (£8.95), thai duck (£9.95), and children's menu (£2.25). Well kept Batemans Mild, Marstons Best and Pedigree, and a guest beer on handpump; cribbage, dominoes, and piped music. *(Recommended by Jenny and Brian Seller, Lynn Sharpless, Bob Eardley, Peter and Audrey Dowsett, Ann and Colin Hunt, John and Christine Simpson, Phyl and Jack Street, P R White, Iain Robertson)*

Marstons ~ Lease: Clive Mansell ~ Real ale ~ Meals and snacks ~ Children welcome ~ Open 11-3, 6-11; 11-11 summer Sat; 12-10.30 Sun; closed 25 Dec

nr PETERSFIELD SU7423 Map 2

White Horse ★

Priors Dean – but don't follow Priors Dean signposts: simplest route is from Petersfield, leaving centre on A272 towards Winchester, take right turn at roundabout after level crossing, towards Steep, and keep on for four miles or so, up on to the downs, passing another pub on your right (and not turning off into Steep there); at last, at crossroads signposted East Tisted/Privett, turn right towards East Tisted, then almost at once turn right on to second gravel track (the first just goes into a field); there's no inn sign; alternatively, from A32 5 miles S of Alton, take road by bus lay-by signposted Steep, then, after 1¾ miles, turn off as above – though obviously left this time – at East Tisted/Privett crossroads; OS Sheet 197 coming from Petersfield (Sheet 186 is better the other way), map reference 715290

The two charming and idiosyncratic parlour rooms in this fine old farmhouse have various old pictures, farm tools, drop-leaf tables, oak settles, rugs, stuffed antelope heads, a longcase clock, and a fireside rocking-chair, and so forth. A fine range of beers on handpump includes the very strong No Name Bitter and Strong, as well as Ballards Best, Bass, Gales Best and HSB, Ringwood Fortyniner, and two or three changing guests. Shove-ha'penny, dominoes, cribbage. Bar food includes soup (£2.95), sandwiches (from £3.50), ploughman's or mushroom stroganoff (£5.95), liver and bacon or steak and kidney pie (£6), cajun chicken (£6.50), sirloin steak (£8.95), and puddings such as orange and ginger sponge or apple pie (£2.95). Rustic seats (which include chunks of tree-trunk) and a terrace outside; as this is one of the highest spots in the county it can be quite breezy. If trying to find it for the first time, keep your eyes skinned – not for nothing is this known as the Pub With No Name. Dogs are welcome. *(Recommended by Lynn Sharpless, Bob Eardley, Dennis Stevens, Dan Wilson, Ann and Colin Hunt, MCG, David Cullen, Emma Stent, John and Elizabeth Cox, Jo and Gary Charlton, Mrs F A W Ricketts, Tom Evans, John Beeken)*

Gales ~ Managers Stephen and Lynn Tickner ~ Real ale ~ Meals and snacks (not Sun evening) ~ (01420) 588387 ~ Children in dining room ~ Open 11-2.30(3 Sat), 6-11; 12-3, 7-10.30 Sun

PILLEY SZ3298 Map 2

Fleur de Lys

Village signposted off A337 Brockenhurst—Lymington

Most people do come here to eat and it does get fairly hectic at peak times. It is the oldest pub in the New Forest and was established as an inn in 1096. The characterful lounge bar has heavy low beams, lots of bric-a-brac and a huge inglenook log fire, and in the entrance-way is a list of landlords that goes back to 1498; a large part of the pub is no smoking. From a comprehensive menu, good bar food includes lunchtime sandwiches, game pâté or giant mushrooms (£4.50), ploughman's (£6.25), venison and herb sausages (£6.75), spinach and stilton pancake (£6.99), poached salmon salad (£7.55), chicken wrapped in ham topped with mozzarella on spinach with a lemon and wine sauce (£8.99), half shoulder of lamb or cod wrapped in bacon (£9.99), spicy duck breast with a honey hoisin sauce with stir-fried vegetables (£10.25), daily specials, and fillet steak (£12.75). The heated marquee restaurant is used both in summer and winter. Five well kept ales on handpump or tapped from the cask such as Boddingtons, Flowers Original, Marstons Pedigree, Morlands Old Speckled Hen, and Wadworths 6X, good wines, and farm ciders; courteous service. There are seats in the garden, and fine forest and heathland walks nearby. *(Recommended by David Gregory, W Osborn-King, Martin and Karen Wake, J and P Halfyard, Sam Samuells, Lynda Payton, Gwen and Peter Andrews, Keith and Margaret Kettell, Nigel Flook, Betsy Brown, Terry and Eileen Stott, Colin Fisher, Jack Triplett, J and B Cressey, John and Chris Simpson, John Corless, Phyl and Jack Street, Lyn Sharpless, Bob Eardley, Mrs F A W Ricketts, John and Vivienne Rice)*

Free house ~ Licensee Craig Smallwood ~ Real ale ~ Meals and snacks ~ Restaurant ~ (01590) 672158 ~ Children welcome ~ Open 12-3, 6-11(10.30 in winter); 12-3, 7-10.30 Sun

PORTSMOUTH SZ6501 Map 2

Still & West

Bath Square; follow A3 and Isle of Wight Ferry signs to Old Portsmouth water's edge

It's the marvellous position that readers enjoy here: from the terrace or upstairs restaurant, there are wonderful views as far as the Isle of Wight, and the boats and ships fighting the strong tides in the very narrow mouth of Portsmouth harbour seem almost within touching distance. The bar is decorated in nautical style, with ship models, old cable, and photographs of famous ships entering the harbour; well kept Gales HSB, GB, IPA, Varsity, Anniversary Ale, and Festival Mild tapped from the cask, and a guest beer on handpump, along with some aged whiskies and country wines; piped music, fruit machine. Bar food includes sandwiches, traditional fish and chips wrapped in newspaper, ploughman's, and home-made pies; there's a wider range of meals upstairs, with quite a few fresh fish dishes; part of the dining area is no-smoking. The pub is quite near to HMS *Victory*, and can get busy on fine days. Nearby parking can be difficult. *(Recommended by Derek Stafford, Mrs Mary Woods, Simon and Amanda Southwell, Ann and Colin Hunt, Tony and Wendy Hobden, David Heath, J Warren)*

Gales ~ Managers Mick and Lynn Finnerty ~ Real ale ~ Meals and snacks ~ (01705) 821567 ~ Children welcome ~ Open 11-11; 12-10.30 Sun

ROTHERWICK SU7156 Map 2

Coach & Horses

4 miles from M3, junction 5; follow Newnham signpost from exit roundabout, then Rotherwick signpost, then turn right at Mattingley, Heckfield signpost; village also signposted from B3349 N of Hook

After several changes of management here, the present licensees seem to be settling in well. The two small beamed front rooms (one is tiled, the other flagstoned, and one is no smoking) have a relaxed, friendly atmosphere, a roaring fire in the stripped brick fireplace, newspapers to read, oak chairs and other interesting furniture, and attractive pictures. Good bar food includes home-made soup (£2.50), creamy garlic mushrooms (£3.25), filled french bread (£4.95 with chips and salad), mediterranean galette (layers of vegetables topped with cheese, served with Greek salad £5.50), a home-made pie (£5.75), gammon and two eggs (£5.95), swordfish steak (£6.95), sirloin steak (£9.25), and as the landlord is from South Africa, a few specialities such as boerwors (spicy sausage £5.95) and perhaps ostrich or crocodile; puddings such as home-made banana and toffee pie or chocolate and nut brandy cake (£3.25). Well kept real ales on handpump at the servery in the parquet-floored inner area include Badger Best, IPA, and Tanglefoot, Gribble Black Adder II and Reg's Tipple, and Oving Dick Turpin; cribbage, dominoes, and piped music. The back garden has seats and pretty summer tubs and hanging baskets. *(Recommended by Francis Johnston, J and B Cressey, Ian Phillips, G K Smale, Martin and Karen Wake, TBB, Mrs P J Pearce, Andy Cunningham, Yvonne Hannaford, Mr and Mrs A J Woolstone)*

Badger ~ Managers Lisa and Riaan De Wett ~ Real ale ~ Meals and snacks (12-3, 6-10) ~ (01256) 762542 ~ Children welcome ~ Open 11-11; 12-10.30 Sun

SOPLEY SZ1597 Map 2

Woolpack

B3347 N of Christchurch; can be reached off A338 N of Bournemouth, via B3073 Hurn exit and minor road from Hurn roundaboat

In summer, the garden here is a pleasant place to enjoy a drink and you can watch the ducks dabbling about on the little chalk stream under the weeping willows, by the little bridge. Inside, the rambling open-plan bar has low beams, red leatherette wall seats and simple wooden chairs around heavy rustic tables, a woodburning stove, and a small black kitchen range; there's also a no-smoking conservatory. Bar food includes soup (£2.95), open rolls (from £3.50), ploughman's (£4.50), vegetable lasagne (£6.25), steak and kidney pudding, thai curry or cod in beer (£6.95), gammon steak (£8.95), steaks (from £10.95), puddings (£2.95), and Sunday roast beef (£5.95). Well kept Flowers Original, Ringwood Best and Wadworths 6X on handpump; piped music. *(Recommended by Mr and Mrs W G Turner, David Gregory, Annette and Stephen Marsden, Howard Allen, Andy and Jill Kassube, John Knighton, John and Vivienne Rice)*

Whitbreads ~ Lease: C L and C E Hankins ~ Real ale ~ Meals and snacks ~ (01425) 672252 ~ Children in eating area of bar ~ Open 11-11; 12-10.30 Sun

SOUTHSEA SZ6498 Map 2

Wine Vaults

Albert Rd, opp Kings Theatre

It's worth coming to this simple, welcoming pub on any night between Monday and Thursday as they have a double happy hour at 5.30 to 7.30pm when their five real ales are £1 a pint (in fact, on Monday it's £1 all night), and if you are coming to eat on those days and arrive before 7.30, you get a free drink. As well as their own brewed Spikes Best, Golden and Bitter & Twisted on handpump, guest beers might include Bass, Hop Back Summer Lightning, Ringwood Best and Fortyniner, Ruddles Best and County, and Theakstons Old Peculier; they may hold beer festivals in May and November. The busy straightforward bar has wood-panelled walls, a wooden floor, Wild West saloon-type swing doors, and an easy-going, chatty feel; pool. Bar food is good value and served in decent sized helpings, with plenty of vegetarian choices (all priced at £4.95), and lots of filled french bread, baked potatoes and ploughman's. Friendly hard-working staff. The one-eyed black labrador is called Ziggy; other dogs are welcome. This year there's a new small garden with paving and a wooden gazebo. *(Recommended by Alan Green, Brad W Morley, Ann and Colin Hunt, Mr and Mrs D Lawson, Jess Cowley, Ian Phillips, Tom Evans, J Warren)*

Own brew ~ Licensees Jeremy Stevens and Mike Huges ~ Real ale ~ Meals and snacks (all day) ~ (01705) 864712 ~ Children welcome ~ Open 11-11(10.30 Sun)

SPARSHOLT SU4331 Map 2

Plough ♀

Village signposted off A272 a little W of Winchester

At lunchtime in particular, there's a good bustling atmosphere in this attractive, neatly kept and efficiently run pub. The main bar area has an interesting mix of wooden tables and chairs, with farm tools, scythes and pitchforks attached to the ceiling; one area is no smoking. Good, popular bar food includes sandwiches, broccoli, stilton and mushroom pie (£6.25), seafood, avocado and tomato casserole with oatmeal crust (£6.95), tuna steak with roasted tomatoes or supreme of chicken with port, wine and bacon jus (£10.50), and monkfish with red wine and leeks (£12.95); it might be best to book a table. Well kept Wadworths IPA, 6X, Badger Tanglefoot, and Hartleys Bitter on handpump, and a good wine list. A new children's play area has been created and there are plenty of seats outside on the lawn. *(Recommended by R J Walden, W W Burke, Howard Allen, Terry and Linda Moseley, Patrick Renouf, John and Joan Calvert, Mrs J A Taylar)*

Wadworths ~ Tenants R C and K J Crawford ~ Real ale ~ Meals and snacks ~ (01962) 776353 ~ Children in eating area of bar ~ Murder mystery evening every 3 months; must book ~ Open 11-3, 6-11; 12-3, 6-10.30 Sun; closed 25 Dec

STEEP SU7425 Map 2

Harrow

Take Midhurst exit from Petersfield bypass, at exit roundabout first left towards Midhurst, then first turning on left opposite garage, and left again at Sheet church; follow over dual carriageway bridge to pub

For nearly 70 years, this charming old-fashioned pub has been in the same friendly family. Happily, nothing changes here, and the little public bar has hops and dried flowers hanging from the beams, built-in wall benches on the tiled floor, stripped pine wallboards, a good log fire in the big inglenook, and maybe wild flowers on the scrubbed deal tables (and on the tables outside); cribbage, dominoes. Generous helpings of good simple home cooked bar food include home-made scotch eggs (£1.70), sandwiches (from £2.30), excellent soups such as ham, split pea and vegetable (£3), huge ploughman's (from £4, some come with home-cooked meats), home-made quiches or ham lasagne (£5.75), and puddings such as delicious treacle tart or seasonal fruit pies (£2.60). Well kept Ballards, Cheriton Diggers Gold and Best, Ringwood Best, and Tisbury Best tapped from casks behind the counter, country wines, and Bulmers cider; polite and friendly staff, even when under pressure. The big garden is left free-flowering so that goldfinches can collect thistle seeds from the grass. The Petersfield bypass doesn't intrude on this idyll, though you will need to follow the directions above to find it. No children inside. *(Recommended by Lynn Sharpless, Bob Eardley, Dr Alan Green, Brad W Morley, Wendy Arnold, David Cullen, Emma Stent, James Nunns, Derek Harvey-Piper, M J Hydes, Mrs D M Gray, Ann and Colin Hunt)*

Free house ~ Licensee Ellen McCutcheon ~ Real ale ~ Meals and snacks (limited Sun evening) ~ (01730) 262685 ~ Open 12-2.30, 6-11; 11-3, 6-11 Sat; 12-3, 7-10.30 Sun; closed evening 25 Dec

TICHBORNE SU5630 Map 2

Tichborne Arms

Village signed off B3047 since the building of the Alresford by-pass

Run by attentive and helpful licensees, this neat and attractive thatched pub is much enjoyed by readers at the moment. The comfortable, square-panelled room on the right has a log fire in an attractive stone fireplace, pictures and documents on the walls recalling the bizarre Tichborne Case (a mystery man from Australia claimed fraudulently to be the heir to this estate), wheelback chairs and settles (one very long), and latticed windows with flowery curtains. On the left, a larger and livelier room, partly panelled and also carpeted, has sensibly placed darts, shove-ha'penny, cribbage, dominoes and a fruit machine. Good bar food might include sandwiches (from £1.65; toasties from £2.20), home-made soup (£2.50), liver and bacon nibbles with a home-made dip (£2.75), lots of baked potatoes (from £3.60), ploughman's (£4), daily specials such as stilton and mushroom quiche (£4.95), braised beef with chestnuts or casserole of guinea fowl (£5.95) or home-made fish pie (£6.25), and puddings like home-made profiteroles, raspberry jam sponge or fudge and walnut flan (£2.50). Well kept Flowers IPA, Wadworths 6X, and Whitbread Fuggles IPA tapped from the cask, and country wines; excellent friendly service. There are picnic-sets outside in the big well kept garden, and plenty of surrounding walks. Dogs are welcome, but not children. *(Recommended by Mrs G Connell, Lynn Sharpless, Bob Eardley, Sheila and Robert Robinson, Ann and Colin Hunt, A R and B E Sayer, Prof A N Black, D P and J A Sweeney, J S M Sheldon, Philip and Trisha Ferris, Lady M H Moir, Michael Inskip, TBB, Glen and Nola Armstrong)*

Free house ~ Licensees Chris and Peter Byron ~ Real ale ~ Meals and snacks (12-1.45, 6.30-9.45) ~ (01962) 733760 ~ Open 11.30-2.30, 6-11; 12-3, 7-10.30 Sun

TITCHFIELD SU5305 Map 2

Fishermans Rest

Mill Lane, Segensworth; off A27 W of Fareham at Titchfield Abbey sign

On a sunny day, you can sit at tables behind this comfortably extended dining pub and enjoy a drink by the River Meon. Inside, separate warm cosy rooms including a mellow eating area and a no-smoking family room, lead off the long bar; there are two log fires, light wood furnishings, daily papers, and a good deal of fishing memorabilia including stuffed fish. A wide choice of food includes cob rolls with chips, filled baked potatoes, fish and chips, lasagne, and daily specials such as pasta napolitana (£5.50), chicken Mcginty (£5.75), Aberdeen beef (£6.25), and salmon Paris (£7.50). Well kept Boddingtons Bitter and Mild, Flowers Original, Gales HSB, Morlands Old Speckled Hen, and Wadworths 6X on handpump, and several decent wines by the glass; dominoes. Titchfield Abbey is opposite. *(Recommended by R Inman, Val and Alan Green, Charles and Pauline Stride, John and Christine Simpson, Ann and Colin Hunt, Stephen, Julie and Hayley Brown, A E Green, Michael Inskip)*

Whitbreads ~ Manager Harry Griffiths ~ Real ale ~ Meals and snacks (12-9.30) ~ (01329) 842848 ~ Children in no-smoking area ~ Open 11-11; 12-10.30 Sun

UPHAM SU5320 Map 2

Brushmakers Arms

Shoe Lane; village signposted from Winchester—Bishops Waltham downs road, and from B2177 (former A333)

Hard-working and warmly welcoming new licensees have taken over this neatly attractive old pub, and readers have been quick to send us favourable reports. There's a good mix of regulars and visitors in the comfortable L-shaped bar that is divided into two by a central brick chimney with a woodburning stove in the raised two-way fireplace; also, comfortably cushioned wall settles and chairs, a variety of tables including some in country-style stripped wood, a few beams in the low ceiling, and quite a collection of ethnic-looking brushes; a snug has been opened up. Well kept Ballards Best, Bass, Gales Best, and Ringwood Best on handpump, country wines, and Thatchers cider. Reasonably priced bar food at lunchtime now includes sandwiches (£2.95; toasties £3.50), and filled baked potatoes and ploughman's (£3.50), as well as ham and egg (£4.95), and chicken curry, vegetable chilli and tacos (£5.50), plus evening dishes like garlic prawns or baked brie in filo pastry (£3.50), salmon with chive and mustard, pork tenderloin with syrup and apples, sirloin steak with stilton and madeira or rack of lamb (from £8.95); daily specials, and home-made puddings (£2.50). Sensibly placed darts, dominoes, shove-ha'penny, fruit machine and piped music. The big garden is well stocked with mature shrubs and trees, and there are picnic-sets on a sheltered back terrace among lots of tubs of flowers, with more on the tidy tree-sheltered lawn. Good walks nearby – though not much parking. *(Recommended by Ann and Colin Hunt, Phyl and Jack Street, A R and B E Sayer, Lynn Sharpless, Bob Eardley, Dennis Stevens, D G King, Mrs G Connell, John and Joan Nash, Luke Worthington, Mrs F A W Ricketts, P and S White, Lorraine Cornelius-Brown, Don and Carole Kane)*

Free house ~ Tenant Tony Mottram ~ Real ale ~ Meals and snacks ~ (01489) 860231 ~ Children in eating area of bar ~ Live Irish folk monthly Thurs evening ~ Open 11-2.30(3 Sat), 5.30-11; 12-3.30, 5.30-10.30 Sun

WELL SU7646 Map 2

Chequers

5 miles W of Farnham; off A287 via Crondall, or A31 via Froyle and Lower Froyle (easier if longer than via Bentley); from A32 S of Odiham, go via Long Sutton; OS Sheet 186 map reference 761467

There's been yet another change of management here – but apart from tidying up the garden, the new people don't plan any major alterations. The low beamed cosy rooms have lots of alcoves, wooden pews, old stools, and GWR carriage lamps, and the panelled walls are hung with 18th-c country-life prints and old sepia photographs of locals enjoying a drink. Bar food changes daily and now includes home-made soup (£2.75), asparagus tortellini with pesto cream (£4.25), moules marinières (£5.25), Italian-style meatballs (£6.25), fresh tuna with tarragon sauce or wild boar sausage with mash (£6.50), turkey escalope with mushroom sauce (£7.95), fillet of red snapper with garlic butter (£8.50), sirloin steak with green peppercorn sauce (£9), and puddings such as raspberry crème brûlée, plum tart or bread and butter pudding (from £3). Well kept Badger Best, Tanglefoot and IPA on handpump. In the back garden are some chunky picnic-sets, and at the front, there's a vine-covered arbour. The pub can get busy at weekends. *(Recommended by Lynn Sharpless, Bob Eardley, Roger and Valerie Hill, R M Sparkes, Mayur Shah, Martin and Karen Wake, June and Malcolm Farmer, TBB; more reports on the new regime, please)*

Badger ~ Manager P Simmonds ~ Meals and snacks (till 10pm) ~ (01256) 862605 ~ Children in eating area of bar only ~ Open 11-3, 6-11; 11-11 Sat; 12-10.30 Sun

nr WHERWELL SU3839 Map 2

Mayfly 🍷

Testcombe (i.e. not in Wherwell itself); A3057 SE of Andover, between B3420 turn-off and Leckford where road crosses River Test; OS Sheet 185 map reference 382390

On a warm day, the charming position by the River Test does draw the crowds to this popular pub. There are plenty of tables from which to watch the swans, ducks and maybe plump trout, and the efficient staff seem able to handle huge numbers of people without any fuss. The spacious, beamed and carpeted bar has fishing pictures and bric-a-brac on the cream walls above its dark wood dado, windsor chairs around lots of tables, two woodburning stoves, and bow windows overlooking the water; there's also a no-smoking conservatory. Bar food from a buffet-style servery includes a wide range of cheeses (around three dozen) or home-made quiche (£4.20), a good choice of cold meats such as rare topside of beef, pork or smoked chicken (from £4.20), smoked trout (£4.50), vegetable curry or macaroni cheese (£5.50), winter pies and casseroles (from £5.95), chicken tandoori (£6), winter steaks (from £9.95), and puddings (from £3); salads are an extra 70p a spoonful which can bump up prices a bit. You'll usually find queues at busy periods. Well kept Boddingtons, Flowers Original, Morlands Old Speckled Hen, and Wadworths 6X on handpump, a wide choice of wines, and country wines; fruit machine and piped music. *(Recommended by David Shillitoe, Brian and Jenny Seller, Anthony Barnes, A R and B E Sayer, Andy and Sarah Gillett, Dennis Stevens, R J Walden, C Robinson, Joy and Peter Heatherley, Ian Phillips, G C Brown, R Lake, Mrs P J Pearce, Dr D G Twyman, Michael Inskip, Derek Harvey-Piper, Luke Worthington)*

Whitbreads ~ Managers Barry and Julie Lane ~ Real ale ~ Meals and snacks (11.30-9) ~ (01264) 860283 ~ Children welcome ~ Open 11-11; 12-10.30 Sun

White Lion

B3420, in village itself

The planned changes here have now taken place. Apart from redecorating and refurbishing the bars and dining areas, the public bar and lounge have been opened up to create a new dining room, a new fire has been opened up in the Village Bar, and the bedrooms have been upgraded; the lower dining room is no smoking. The multi-level beamed bar still has plates on delft shelves, sparkling brass, and fresh flowers, and well kept Adnams Best, Flowers Original, Greenalls Bitter, and Worthington bitter on handpump. Good homely bar food includes lunchtime sandwiches (not Sunday), filled baked potatoes or ploughman's, and daily specials like cheese, onion and potato pie (£5.40), lamb kidneys and sausages in wine (£5.60), smoked ham and mushroom tagliatelle (£5.80), locally smoked trout (£5.95), pheasant casserole (in season) or breast of chicken with lemon and tarragon (£6.20), salmon and broccoli bake (£7.40), and half shoulder of minted lamb or pork hock roasted with juniper berries and glazed with honey (£7.90); Sunday roasts (worth booking for these). The licensees are caring people, and the two friendly black labradors are called Sam and Guinness. There are plenty of seats in the courtyard and on the terrace. The village is well worth strolling through, and there's a nice walk over the River Test and meadows to Chilbolton. *(Recommended by Colin Laffan, Phyl and Jack Street, Ann and Colin Hunt, R T and J C Moggridge, Joy and Peter Heatherley, John and Joan Nash)*

Greenalls ~ Lease: Adrian and Patsy Stent ~ Real ale ~ Meals and snacks (not Sun evening) ~ (01264) 860317 ~ Children in eating area of bar ~ Irish folk Mon evening, folk 1st and 3rd Thurs of month ~ Open 10-2.30(3 Sat), 6(7 Mon-Tues)-11; 12-3, 7-10.30 Sun ~ Bedrooms: £25/£40

WHITSBURY SU1219 Map 2

Cartwheel

Follow Rockbourne sign off A354 SW of Salisbury, turning left just before Rockbourne itself; or head W off A338 at S end of Breamore, or in Upper Burgate – we got mildly lost trying to find it direct from Fordingbridge!

This tucked-away pub has a cheerful village-local atmosphere; it's opened up inside, with pitched high rafters in one part, lower beams elsewhere, antlers, military prints, country pictures, what looks like a steam-engine's jockey wheel as a divider, and simple but comfortable cloth-cushioned wall seats and other chairs. There's a snug little room by the door, with a couple of tables either side of the fire; a small side room has darts, pool, fruit machine, and cribbage, and dogs seem very welcome. Generous food includes good sandwiches, king prawns in filo pastry (£4.25), warm chicken liver salad (£4.95), sausages, mash and onion gravy (£5.50), steak and kidney pudding (£5.75), and seared tuna steak with garlic butter (£6). Adnams Broadside, Fullers London Pride, Ringwood True Glory, Smiles Golden and April Fool and Tisbury Archibald Beckett on handpump, in top condition, with beer festivals around the second week in August and in late October; efficient service. The garden, sheltered by a shrubby steep slope, has weekly summer barbecues and a particularly good play area that children really enjoy. It's good walking country. *(Recommended by Dr M Smith, Ann and Colin Hunt, Jerry and Alison Oakes, Simon Bobeldijk, Rev John Hibberd, John Moate)*

Free house ~ Licensee Patrick Lewis ~ Real ale ~ Meals and snacks (not Tues evening mid Oct-mid May) ~ Restaurant ~ (01725) 518362 ~ Children in eating area of bar and in restaurant ~ Open 11-2.30(3 Sat), 6-11; 12-3, 7-10.30 Sun

WINCHESTER SU4829 Map 2

Wykeham Arms ★

75 Kingsgate Street (Kingsgate Arch and College Street are now closed to traffic; there is access via Canon Street)

Graeme Jameson who built this pub up into something special over the 14 years he was in charge, is no longer a tenant and the pub has been sold to Gales, but Mr Jameson is still there in the background, in a consultative capacity, and it's clear that all is well under the new manager (who actually trained under Mr Jameson anyway). A series of stylish bustling rooms radiating from the central bar has 19th-c oak desks retired from nearby Winchester College, a redundant pew from the same source, kitchen chairs and candlelit deal tables and big windows with swagged paisley curtains; all sorts of interesting collections are dotted around. A snug room at the back, known as the Watchmakers, is decorated with a set of Ronald Searle 'Winespeak' prints, a second one is panelled, and all of them have a log fire; several areas are no smoking. Particularly good food includes lunchtime sandwiches (from £2.60; toasties £2.95), good soups like lentil, tomato and thyme (£2.65), salmon and herb terrine (£4.50), curried mango chicken (£5.25), British cheese platter (£5.50), cottage pie or pasta with spinach and bacon sauce (£5.75), smoked haddock kedgeree (£5.75), lamb and redcurrant casserole (£5.95), Aberdeen Angus steaks (from £10.95), evening dishes such as gougere of tomato, mozarella and olives (£9.95), fried calf liver with bacon, black pudding and spring onion mash with a red wine sauce (£11.25) or roasted duck breast marinated in orange and ginger with roast sweet potatoes and carrots and citrus dressing (£11.75), and puddings like walnut fudge tart, almond and raspberry trifle or praline mousse (from £4.25); courteous service. There's an excellent seasonally-changing list of around 100 wines including 20 by the glass, quite a few half-bottles, helpful tasting notes, and a fine choice of brandies, armagnacs and liqueurs. Also, well kept Gales Bitter, Best, HSB, and Bass on handpump. There are tables on a covered back terrace, with more on a small but sheltered lawn. The lovely bedrooms in the pub are thoughtfully equipped, and the Saint George, a 16th-c annexe directly across the street (and overlooking Winchester College Chapel) has more bedrooms, a sitting room with open fire, a post office/general stores, and a Burgundian wine store; you can enjoy the good breakfasts either in your room there or at the pub. No children. *(Recommended by J F Reay, Wendy Arnold, Ann and Colin Hunt, Dr and Mrs A K Clarke, David Shillitoe, Keith Louden, John Moate, Nick Rose, Charles Gysin, Lynn Sharpless, Bob Eardley, Mr and Mrs A R Hawkins, Mr and Mrs Jon Corelis, David Dimock, Helen Grundy, Martin Seymour, Pamela Turner, Philip Vernon, Kim Maidment, Comus Elliott, Tim Barrow, Sue Demont, David Cullen, Emma Stent, Canon and Mrs M Bourdeaux, Mrs F Ricketts, Gregor Macdonald, J L Kelly, P and S White, A E Green, N Matthews, Francis Johnston, Karen Eliot, John Beeken, Jim and Maggie Cowell, Colin and Alma Gent, Jo and Gary Charlton, M J Dowdy)*

Gales ~ Manager Tim Manktelow-Gray ~ Real ale ~ Meals and snacks ~ Restaurant ~ (01962) 853834 ~ If the small car park is full local parking may be difficult – don't be tempted to block up Kingsgate Street itself ~ Open 11-11; 12-10.30 Sun; closed 25 Dec ~ Bedrooms: £69.50B/£79.50B

Lucky Dip

Besides the fully inspected pubs, you might like to try these Lucky Dips recommended to us and described by readers (if you do, please send us reports):

Abbotts Ann [Little Ann, A343 Andover—Salisbury; SU3343], *Poplar Farm*: Spacious Brewers Fayre, good service of almost clinical efficiency, attractive building, amusements inside and out for children, good well served reasonably priced food, piped music *(Phyl and Jack Street)*

Aldershot [Weybourne Rd; SU8650], *Duke of York*: Good food inc children's in bar and small conservatory restaurant, friendly service, particularly well kept beers inc Courage, Youngs and guests *(Jill and Andy Kassube)*; [Ash Rd], *Red Lion*: Worth knowing for the quality of the real ale; lunches *(Andy and Jill Kassube)*

☆ **Alresford** [Broad St; SU5832], *Horse & Groom*: Friendly open-plan spreading bar with beams, timbers and some stripped brickwork, nice bow window seats, half a dozen Whitbreads-related ales under light blanket pressure, good value food from sandwiches to steaks, coal-effect gas fire, unobtrusive piped music; children welcome, open all day at least in summer *(Dr M Ian Crichton, A R and B E Sayer, Mrs H Murphy, Ann and Colin Hunt, Thomas Nott)*

Alresford [West St], *Bell*: Relaxing Georgian coaching inn with extended bar, smallish dining room, quickly served good value food inc children's helpings, well kept Greene King Abbot, decent tea and coffee, friendly service, daily papers, log fire, attractive back courtyard; comfortable bedrooms *(Ann and Colin Hunt, Ron Shelton)*; [Jacklyns Lane], *Cricketers*: Large pub, cottagey eating area with good value straightforward food, well kept Flowers Original, garden with play area *(Ann and Colin Hunt)*; [11 West St], *Swan*: Very neatly kept long narrow panelled hotel bar with games machine, good restaurant; bedrooms clean and comfortable, in adjoining block *(David Gittins)*

Ampfield [off A31 Winchester—Romsey; SU3923], *White Horse*: Vastly extended open-plan Whitbreads dining pub with very wide choice of reasonably priced food, period-effect furniture, log fire, well kept ales (but served through sparkler), decent wine, efficient courteous service, Victorian prints and advertising posters in dining room; pub backs on to golf course and village cricket green; handy for Hillier arboretum, good walks in Ampfield Woods *(Phyl and Jack Street, Stephen Harvey, B M Baker, Douglas and Ann Hare)*

Arford [SU8336], *Crown*: Tastefully refurbished local with good affordable food and lovely atmosphere inc children's and vegetarian in big clean candlelit eating area, hospitable welcome, well kept Tetleys-related and guest beer, log fire, riverside garden *(E M Steinitz)*

Avon [B3347 N of Sopley; SZ1498], *New Queen*: Modern chain family dining pub with different areas and levels, low pitched ceiling, good range of popular reasonably priced food, well kept Badger ales, helpful staff; tables out on spacious covered terrace and lawn, bedrooms; *(Paul and Sue Merrick)*

Axford [SU6043], *Crown*: Small comfortable two-bar local, a favourite with walkers; very friendly service, open fires, Badger Best and other real ales, good range of pub food, separate dining area; juke box *(John Vigar, David Lamb)*

☆ **Bank** [signed off A35 S of Lyndhurst; SU2807], *Oak*: Cleanly refurbished New Forest local, friendly staff, good choice of generous well prepared food inc real doorstep sandwiches and exceptional puddings, interesting changing chilled real ales tapped from the cask; piped music, very busy evenings and weekends; goats in tidied-up garden, lovely spot for walks and a haven for thirsty cyclists; village attractive and untouristy though within earshot of A35 (ponies stroll through) *(Paul and Sue Merrick, M Joyner, W W Burke, Dr and Mrs A K Clarke, David Gregory, D Marsh, Jess Cowley, John and Joan Calvert)*

Barton Stacey [High St; SU4341], *Swan*: Friendly village local with beamed front bar, smaller eating area off, real ales inc Wadworths 6X, back restaurant, tables on front lawn – pleasant spot *(Ann and Colin Hunt)*

Basingstoke [81 Bounty Rd; SU6352], *Bounty*: Country feel (with adjoining cricket ground) marks it out; good well priced food, well kept Ushers; limited parking *(Andy and Jill Kassube)*; [off Mkt Sq], *Feathers*: Fairly lively with TV, juke box and fruit machine, but swift friendly service, well kept Theakstons XB, good value food esp club sandwiches; nice building, older than the beamery suggests *(R T and J C Moggridge)*

☆ **Beaulieu** [almost opp Palace House; SU3802], *Montagu Arms*: Civilised comfortable hotel in attractive surroundings; separate more basic Wine Press bar, open all day, has simple lunchtime bar food, well kept Greene King and Ringwood Fortyniner, good wines, lots of malt whiskies, picnic-sets out on front courtyard, piped pop music (maybe loud); children welcome; comfortable bedrooms, good spot for walks *(D H and M C Watkinson, J and P Halfyard)*

☆ **Bentley** [A31 Alton—Farnham dual carriageway, a mile E; SU8044], *Bull*: Civilised low-beamed respite from the noisy trunk road, welcoming service, traditional furnishings, lots of interesting pictures, soft lighting, log-effect gas fire, good choice of well presented food from sandwiches to fresh fish and seafood, well kept Courage Best, Fullers London Pride and Gales HSB, darts, fruit machine, piped music; children in eating area and restaurant; open all day, tables on side terrace, play area, jazz Sun lunchtime *(C and E M Watson, Pat Martin, TBB, J S M Sheldon, HNJ, PEJ, LYM)*

☆ **Bighton** [off B3046 in Alresford just N of pond, or off A31 in Bishops Sutton; SU6134], *Three Horseshoes*: Good cheap simple lunchtime food (not Mon, maybe just sandwiches in summer) in modest but well run old-fashioned village local with unusual thatched fireplace in small lounge, well kept Gales HSB, BBB, winter 5X and Prize Old Ale, lots of country wines, friendly family service, police memorabilia, darts; children welcome, geese in garden, good walks nearby *(Jo and Gary Charlton, Ron Shelton, John H L Davis, J Sheldon, Ann and Colin Hunt, Lynn Sharpless, Bob Eardley)*

☆ **Bishops Sutton** [former A31 Alresford—Alton; SU6031], *Ship*: Pleasantly relaxed two-bar local, good reasonably priced bar food inc tempting puddings, Boddingtons, Ruddles and Worthington in highly polished glasses, attentive staff, cosy back restaurant; tables in garden with a couple of thatched parasols; handy for Watercress Line, pleasant walks *(Phyl and Jack Street, J Sheldon, LYM)*

Bishops Waltham [Basingwell St; SU5517], *Barleycorn*: Georgian or earlier, pleasant mix of dark oak and cream, well kept Marstons, log fire, friendly people, games in public bar, separate dining room – good value simple home-made food inc two-for-one lunch bargains Mon and Weds, children's dishes and good vegetarian choice; garden *(Val and Alan Green)*; *White Swan*: Welcoming village local, courteous staff, simple good value bar food from sandwiches up, Scottish Courage beers *(Dennis Stevens)*

Botley [Station Hill, nr stn; SU5213], *Railway*: Railway-themed Marstons Tavern Table dining pub, usual vast range of food, efficient quick uniformed service even when busy; quiet piped music *(Val and Alan Green)*

Braishfield [Newport Lane; SU3725], *Newport*: Fine example of old-fashioned unsmart two-bar village local, particularly well kept Gales HSB, Best and Butser, simple good value food inc huge sandwich and good value ploughman's, country wines, decent coffee, down-to-earth licensees, weekend singsongs; good summer garden with geese, ducks and chickens *(Lynn Sharpless, Bob Eardley)*; *Dog & Crook*: Cottagey, with good choice of freshly cooked food inc vegetarian, fish specialities, well kept Wadworths 6X, good house wine; garden with play area *(Mr and Mrs G Tobin)*

Brambridge [Church Lane, just off B3335 Twyford—Winchester; SU4721], *Dog & Crook*: Modernised open-plan L-shaped bar with welcoming landlady, quick service, real ales, country wines, enjoyable food from fresh sandwiches to mixed grill and steaks, vegetarian choice, Thurs fish night; restaurant; handy for Itchen Way walks *(E U Broadbent)*

☆ **Bransgore** [Ringwood Rd, off A35 N of Christchurch; SZ1897], *Three Tuns*: Pretty little thatched whitewashed pub, much restored inside with beamery etc; friendly, chatty and busy, with comfortable dining area popular with older people at lunchtime for wide range of food inc vegetarian and good Sun menu, good service, well kept Ringwood Best and Fortyniner, tasteful bar, fresh flowers, small restaurant; pleasant back garden with play area and open country views, flower-decked front courtyard; bedrooms *(Sue and Mike Todd, Ann and Alex Tolputt, D Marsh, Peter Walters, John and Vivienne Rice)*

Brockenhurst [Lyndhurst Rd; SU3002], *Snakecatcher*: Thriving well run pub with interesting split-level bar and restaurant areas inc cosy bit with log fire and easy chairs, decent food from sandwiches to steaks cooked to order (so may be a wait), good Sat fish specials and children's food, well kept Hardy ales, good choice of wines by the glass, good service, candles at night; good walks nearby *(Phyl and Jack Street, Jess and George Cowley)*

Brook [SU2714], *Bell*: Really a hotel (with thriving golf club), but does good bar lunches, with prompt friendly service, well kept Wadworths 6X and lovely log fire; big garden, delightful village; comfortable bedrooms *(John and Joan Calvert, TBB)*

☆ **Broughton** [opp church; signed off A30 Stockbridge—Salisbury; SU3032], *Tally Ho*: Sympathetically renovated local, big plain modern flagstoned bar with darts (they don't mind walking boots), comfortable hunting-print lounge, sensibly priced home cooking inc good sandwiches and curries, homely fire in each room, entertaining landlord, well kept beers such as Cheriton Pots and Ringwood True Glory, decent wines in two glass sizes; tables in pretty garden behind, good walks *(Martin and Karen Wake, Howard Allen, J L Hall, Phyl and Jack Street, Tony Hobden, Lynn Sharpless, Bob Eardley, BB)*

Bucks Horn Oak [A325 Farnham—Petersfield; SU8041], *Halfway House*: Good if not cheap food, well kept beers, big cosy bar with separate restaurant area *(G C Hackemer, Iain Robertson)*

Burgate [Lower Burgate; about a mile N of Fordingbridge – OS Sheet 184 map ref 152155; SU1515], *Tudor Rose*: Quaint and cottagey outside, recently refurbished in – roomy and beamy, with traditional food; on Avon Valley Path *(Phyl and Jack Street)*

☆ **Burghclere** [Harts Lane, off A34 – OS Sheet 174 map ref 462608; SU4660], *Carpenters Arms*: Pleasantly furnished small pub with good country views from attractively laid-out dining conservatory, big helpings of bar food from well presented sandwiches up, well kept Arkells, unobtrusive piped music; garden; handy for Sandham Memorial Chapel (NT) *(F C Johnston)*

☆ **Buriton** [High St, signed off A3 S of Petersfield; SU7320], *Five Bells*: Small rooms, low beams, big log fire, some stripped masonry, old-fashioned furnishings; now a Badger managed house, with their beers and a local guest, enjoyable food (same chef as before) in bar and restaurant, daily papers, traditional games; tables in garden with sheltered terraces; self-catering; pretty village, children welcome away from bar, live music Weds *(Phyl and Jack Street, Lynn Sharpless, Bob Eardley, Brad W Morley, Ann and Colin Hunt, LYM)*

☆ **Burley** [Bisterne Close, ¾ mile E; SU2003], *White Buck*: Reliably good Gales pub, with their beers and others such as Ringwood and Wadworths 6X, elegant and spacious high-ceilinged plush bar extending into family room, smaller restaurant (should book), good reasonably priced food, courteous efficient staff; dogs allowed, hitching posts, pleasant front terrace and spacious lawn; well equipped bedrooms, superb Forest walks towards Burley itself and over Mill Lawn *(Phyl and Jack Street, D Marsh)*

☆ **Bursledon** [Hungerford Bottom; SU4809], *Fox & Hounds*: Carefully refurbished rambling oak-beamed 16th-c Chef & Brewer, flagstones and carpet, log fires, piped classical music, friendly polite staff, newspapers, Scottish Courage ales with a guest such as Wychwood Mistletoad, good value if not cheap food from sandwiches to steak inc fish; linked by family conservatory area to ancient back barn with cheerful rustic atmosphere, immense refectory table, lantern-lit side stalls, lots of interesting and authentic farm equipment, wide choice from food bar; children allowed *(Val and Alan Green, Gill and Mike Grout, LYM)*

Bursledon [Southampton Rd], *Ship*: Comfortable Gales pub, marine memorabilia, lower restaurant, good Sun bar nibbles, good service *(Ann and Colin Hunt)*; [Bridge Rd], *Yachtsman*: Extended 1930s Whitbreads Wayside Inn, cream, red and oak, boaty decor, welcoming new management, wide-ranging food inc some attractive touches, separate dining room, Whitbreads-related ales, no piped music, good well signed disabled facilities, children welcome *(Alan Green, Mr and Mrs D Price)*

☆ **Cadnam** [by M27, junction 1; SU2913], *Sir John Barleycorn*: Attractive low-slung long thatched Whitbread Wayside Inn dating from 12th c, dim lighting, low beams and timbers, rustic decor, Whitbreads-related ales with a guest such as Lees Scorcher, reasonably priced wines, big helpings of good value standard food, good landlord, helpful efficient service, two log fires, no-smoking restaurant end; can be very busy; suntrap benches in front, eye-catching flowers *(C Gilbert, Dr and Mrs A Whiteway, W W Burke, John Beeken, Dr and Mrs A K Clarke, M Joyner, Eric and Charlotte Osgood, BB)*

Chawton [SU7037], *Greyfriar*: Fine well run basic village local with low Tudor beams, standing timbers studded with foreign coins, reasonably priced varied food from very well filled home-baked bread sandwiches up, quick efficient service, well kept beer, good coffee, small garden behind with barbecue; opp Jane Austen's house, good walks *(A Cowell, Phyl and Jack Street)*

Chilworth [A27 Romsey Rd; SU4118], *Clump*: Useful extended Whitbreads dining pub, well run and open all day, good big garden; the attractive quaint old village is tucked away *(Phyl and Jack Street, John and Chris Simpson, Stephen Harvey, D Marsh)*

Colden Common [B3354 – OS Sheet 185 map ref 488210; SU4821], *Fishers Pond*: Big refurbished Brewers Fayre open all day, smiling waitresses, attentive landlord, decent food inc children's menu; pretty setting by pond with ducks, handy for Marwell Zoo *(Phyl and Jack Street, Dennis Stevens)*

Cove [90 Fleet Rd; SO8555], *Plough & Horses*: Big Steak pub with good competitively priced food, well kept Tetleys-related and guest ales, decent wines *(Andy and Jill Kassube)*

☆ **Crawley** [signed from A272 and B3420 NW of Winchester; SU4234], *Fox & Hounds*: This attractive place no longer does bar food; though the bar survives much as before (they've taken down the curtains) its new owners prefer not even to think of it as a pub, with its entire focus now on the (de-carpeted) bistro restaurant – where we can recommend the good if pricy French cooking; bedrooms big and comfortable, good breakfast, French staff polite and cheerful *(Pam Izzard, Phyl and Jack Street, Howard Allen, Tim Barrow, Sue Demont, LYM)*

Crawley [A272 Stockbridge—Winchester, about 5 miles N of Winchester], *Rack & Manger*: Comfortably extended Marstons pub with dining lounge, big no-smoking area, traditional public bar, good choice of beers, wide food range popular with local office workers, Sun bar nibbles, friendly landlord, courteous staff, quiet piped music; good-sized garden *(D M Brumfit, Ann and Colin Hunt)*

Crondall [SU7948], *Hampshire Arms*: Unpretentious welcoming local, good choice of food from sandwiches up, well kept Morlands and Ruddles, pleasant service, open fires, traditional games, boules *(R T and J C Moggridge, Iain Robertson)*; [The Borough], *Plume of Feathers*: Fine 15th-c village pub, cosy and attractive, with beams and dark wood, prints on cream walls, open fire in big brick fireplace, welcoming landlord, Morlands and other ales such as Everards Tiger and Ruddles Best, generous food from hot filled baguettes and double-decker sandwiches up, smarter restaurant end; no piped music or juke box, dogs and children welcome; two red telephone boxes in garden, picturesque village *(Geoffrey Lawrance, Nigel and Sue Foster)*

☆ **Curbridge** [Botley Rd (A3051); SU5211], *Horse & Jockey*: Beautiful setting by River Hamble tidal tributary at start of NT woodland trail, well refurbished with separate dining area; two spotless bars, well presented good value home-made food inc vegetarian and imaginative specials, well kept Gales ales, country wines, cheerful licensees, prompt friendly service; lovely garden with small terrace, trees and fenced play area *(Ann and Colin Hunt, Phyl and Jack Street)*

Curdridge [Curdridge Lane (B3035), just off A334 Wickham—Botley; SU5314], *Cricketers*: Open-plan country pub popular for food inc good specials, nice dining area, banquettes in refurbished lounge area, little-changed public part, welcoming licensee, good service even when busy, Marstons ales; quiet piped music, tables on front lawn, pleasant footpaths *(John and Christine Simpson, Jo and Gary Charlton, Ann and Colin Hunt, Phyl and Jack Street)*

Damerham [SU1016], *Compasses*: 16th c, carefully refurbished by present owners, wide choice of food from sandwiches up inc vegetarian and children's, local ingredients, interesting cheeses, five changing ales inc their own (they hope to restore the pub's antique tower brewhouse), good range of malt whiskies, good wines; separate public bar, big garden; children in dining room; bedrooms carefully furnished and well equipped *(Anon)*

☆ **Denmead** [Forest Rd, Worlds End; SU6211], *Chairmakers Arms*: Simple roomy country pub surrounded by paddocks and farmland, comfortable bar but most space given over to bays of tables for good value generous food, no-smoking area, well kept Gales BBB, HSB and XXXL, decent wine, quick polite service, log fires; no music, plenty of tables in garden with attractive pergola, nice walks *(HNJ, PEJ, Dennis Stevens, Ann and Colin Hunt, LYM)*

☆ **Dogmersfield** [Pilcot Lane; SU7853], *Queens Head*: Friendly 17th-c coaching inn in attractive country setting, concentration on tasty well priced food from filled baguettes through lots of salads to interesting restauranty main dishes; good choice of wines, real ales, faultless service; gets very busy, booking advised evenings *(Mr and Mrs M J Bastin, Andy Cunningham, Yvonne Hannaford, G W Stevenson, Francis Johnston)*

Dummer [old A30; SU5846], *Sun*: Friendly atmosphere, good reasonably priced food inc good sandwiches, well kept Courage Best and Fullers London Pride, log fire in lounge *(John and Vivienne Rice)*

☆ **Dunbridge** [Barley Hill; SU3126], *Mill Arms*: Friendly and cosily refurbished, good well presented food inc fine Sunday beef, four real ales, open fire, conservatory, tables in pleasant garden *(Bernadette Williams, Mr and Mrs B Craig)*

☆ **Dundridge** [Dundridge Lane; off B3035 towards Droxford, Swanmore, then right towards Bishops Waltham – OS Sheet 185 map ref 579185; SU5718], *Hampshire Bowman*: Friendly and cosy downland pub, not too smart, with remarkable mix of customers (children, dogs and walkers welcome, usually some classic cars or vintage motorcycles); well kept Archers Golden, King & Barnes Festive and Ringwood Best and Fortyniner tapped from the cask, decent house wines, country wines, good straightforward home cooking inc vegetarian, sensible prices, efficient staff; tables on spacious and attractive lawn *(Ann and Colin Hunt, Jo and Gary Charlton, LYM)*

☆ **Durley** [Heathen St (Curdridge rd); SU5116], *Farmers Home*: Village inn with good food inc pies, fresh fish, vegetarian, children's, traditional and more exotic puddings; well kept Bass, Boddingtons, Flowers Original and Ringwood Best, decent wine, log fire in small bar, big dining area, relaxed atmosphere, good quick thoughtful service; piped music may intrude rather; children welcome, big garden with good play area and pets corner; pleasant walks *(D M Brumfit, Ann and Colin Hunt, Peter and Audrey Dowsett, Phyl and Jack Street, Mr and Mrs A G Leece)*

☆ **Durley** [Durley Street; just off B2177 Bishops Waltham—Winchester], *Robin Hood*: Friendly and homely two-bar Marstons dining pub, log fire, impressive food running up to kangaroo and crocodile, cheerful waitresses, reasonably priced wines; darts and quiz evenings; back terrace and pleasant garden with play area *(Val and Alan Green, Ann and Colin Hunt, Mike and Sally Serridge, A R and B E Sayer, Jo and Gary Charlton)*

☆ **East Boldre** [SU3700], *Turf Cutters Arms*: Roomy and relaxed dim-lit New Forest pub with good original atmosphere, lots of beams and pictures, elderly furnishings, two log fires, Flowers Original, Wadworths 6X and a guest such as Gales HSB, several dozen malt whiskies, character landlord, friendly service and very enjoyable food – worth waiting for a table; no children, live jazz first Sun lunchtime of month; tables in garden; three big old-fashioned bedrooms, reasonable price, huge breakfast *(Lynn Sharpless, Bob Eardley, D Marsh, Sandra Childress)*

☆ **East Meon** [Church St; signed off A272 W of Petersfield, and off A32 in West Meon; SU6822], *George*: Rambling country pub, heavy beams and inglenooks, four log fires, cosy areas around central bar counter, deal tables and horse tack; well kept Badger Tanglefoot, Ballards, Bass, Flowers and Gales HSB, decent wines, country wines, substantial straightforward food in bar and restaurant, summer cream teas, obliging service; children welcome, good outdoor seating arrangements, quiz night Sun; small but comfortable bedrooms, good breakfast; pretty village with fine church, good walks *(Susan and John Douglas, Jo and Gary Charlton, Phyl and Jack Street, Ann and Colin Hunt, LYM)*

East Meon [High St; SU6822], *Izaak Walton*: Straightforward two-bar local in delightful village, helpful service, smart lounge mainly for eaters (good value fresh food inc vegetarian and children's), well kept Ruddles County, darts and pool in public bar; nice table out by front stream, massive back garden (maybe unusual rabbits); children welcome, open all day Sun, quiz night most Weds *(Susan and John Douglas, Ann and Colin Hunt)*

East Stratton [SU5439], *Plough*: Simply furnished pub in attractive village, reasonably priced home-made food with fresh veg from garden, Gales BBB and HSB, cosy little lounge with adjoining restaurant, basic public bar, friendly service; tables on lawn over road *(A Jones, Ann and Colin Hunt)*

Easton [SU5132], *Chestnut Horse*: Comfortable rambling beamed dining pub in lovely sleepy village, wide choice of good value food, Bass, Courage Best, a beer brewed for the pub and a guest beer, quick friendly service, down-to-earth landlord, good log fire, smart prints and decorations; small terrace with very colourful flowers, good Itchen valley walks *(S A Edwards, Lynn Sharpless, Bob Eardley)*; [off B3047], *Cricketers*: Friendly open-plan village local, small bright restaurant off, current licensees combining wide choice of good interesting food with well kept ales such as Cottage Southern, local Moondance, Otter, Ringwood Best and Shepherd Neame Spitfire, and good range of decent wines; darts and shove-ha'penny one end *(Lynn Sharpless, Bob Eardley, Ann and Colin Hunt, June and Peter Gregory)*

☆ **Ellisfield** [Fox Green Lane, Upper Common; SU6345], *Fox*: Two-bar village local with wide choice of well priced standard food, good changing of beers such as Fullers London Pride, Hampshire King Alfred, Marstons Pedigree and Ringwood Porter, decent wines and country wines, very pleasant landlord, relaxed atmosphere, open fire, daily papers; attractively screened-off raised restaurant area, pleasant garden, good walks *(Phyl and Jack Street, Lynn Sharpless, Bob Eardley, Guy Consterdine, C P Baxter)*

☆ **Emery Down** [signed off A35 just W of Lyndhurst; SU2808], *New Forest*: Good position in one of the nicest parts of the Forest, with good walks nearby; attractive softly lit separate areas on varying levels with log fires, Whitbreads-related ales, wide choice of house wines, good popular food, service efficient even when busy; children allowed, small but pleasant three-level garden *(Dr and Mrs A K Clarke, W W Burke, G W Stevenson, Tim and Linda Collins, M Joyner, John Fahy, Alan and Barbara Mence, P G Bardswell, LYM)*

☆ **Emsworth** [19 Havant Rd; SU7406], *Kings Arms*: Comfortable friendly local popular for generous well priced interesting food inc vegetarian cooked by landlady, fresh veg, good choice of wines, friendly service, Gales and a guest ale such as Timothy Taylor Landlord, small restaurant area; pleasant garden behind *(Ann and Colin Hunt, K and F Giles, Brian Lock, J F Freay)*

Emsworth [High St], *Crown*: Good range of ales, good food and friendly service in bar and restaurant, competitive prices; bedrooms *(Mr and Mrs B Craig)*

Eversley [SU7762], *White Hart*: Lovely genuine local, old posters and pictures, reasonably priced food from snacks up, three different areas suiting darts crowd, smart set and doggie set, back dining area, good long-serving tenant; open all day *(Dick Brown)*

☆ **Exton** [signed from A32; SU6120], *Shoe*: Smart facade and decor, brightly refurbished with red carpets and curtains, attractive panelled room off bar, log fire in cosy restaurant (may find all tables booked for Sun lunch – very popular with older people), friendly efficient service, well kept Bass; piped music; tables on lawn down to River Meon – pretty village, good walks *(Lynn Sharpless, Bob Eardley, N Smith, Phyl and Jack Street, R Michael Richards)*

☆ **Faccombe** [SU3858], *Jack Russell*: Smart yet comfortably homely bar with lots of pictures, attractive dining conservatory with good interesting food (not cheap), helpful service, tables in lovely garden, nice setting opp village pond by flint church; piped music may be obtrusive; disabled facilities; bedrooms spotless and cheerful, good breakfast, good walks with rewarding views *(HNJ, PEJ, Ann and Colin Hunt, Philip and Trisha Ferris, G Gallagher, Douglas Rough, Jayshree Joshi)*

Fareham [1 Wallington Shore Rd, Wallington – nr M27 junction 11], *Cob & Pen*: Recently refurbished, with pleasant pine furnishings, flagstones and carpets, Hook Norton Best and Ringwood ales tapped from the cask, wide choice of good value food in new dining room; large garden *(Ann and Colin Hunt, Val and*

Alan Green); [Porchester Rd (A27)], *Delme Arms*: Pleasant good value two-bar Victorian local with decent food, well kept Bass, Fullers London Pride, Worthington and a guest beer such as Badger, friendly service; opp splendidly restored Cams Hall *(Val and Alan Green, Ann and Colin Hunt)*; [Trinity St], *Fareham*: Former Cheese & Ale, rethemed as Greenalls Ale & Hearty pub with Bass, Boddingtons, Greenalls Original and Marstons Pedigree on handpump, several changing guest beers tapped from the cask such as Archie Beckett and Ringwood Fortyniner; food inc vegetarian and children's; piped music may be intrusive *(Val and Alan Green)*

☆ **Farnborough** [Rectory Rd, nr Farnborough North stn; SU8753], *Prince of Wales*: Lively and friendly local with up to ten real ales in top condition, inc Badger Tanglewood, Hogs Back TEA, Ringwood Fortyniner and guests such as Cheriton Pots and Kelham Pale Rider; good choice of whiskies, good service and lunchtime food; three small connecting rooms, can get very crowded *(Andy and Jill Kassube)*

Fordingbridge [14 Bridge St; SU1414], *George*: Superb position, conservatory bar facing River Avon, waterside terrace, pleasant interior; good range of local beers *(Eddie Edwards)*

Four Marks [A31 Alton—Alresford; SU6634], *Windmill*: Large main-road family dining pub, good value food, lots of choice, quick pleasant service, carvery Sat evening and Sun lunch, OAP bargains Thurs; good range of real ales, adventure playground, skittle alley *(A M Pring, Kerry)*

☆ **Freefolk** [N of B3400 – sharp lane uphill at W end of village; SU4848], *Watership Down*: Genuine unaffected village pub, partly brick-floored, nicely placed above grassy bank, very welcoming landlord, good choice of ale such as Archers Best, Brakspears PA and Mild and even Bunny Hop, popular food inc a couple of tasty specials, functional furnishings; games area with plenty of old-fashioned slot machines and table football; piped music, Sun quiz night; attractive garden with play area and rabbit pen, pleasant walks *(JCW, Jess and George Cowley, Rick and Torti Friedberger)*

☆ **Fritham** [village signed from exit roundabout, M27 junction 1; SU2314], *Royal Oak*: Spartan thatched New Forest pub in same family for 80 years, no concessions to modernity; well kept Ringwood Best and Fortyniner tapped from the cask (sometimes run out), maybe Wadworths 6X, odd assortment of furniture inc high-backed settles, pots and kettles hanging in wide old chimney, log fires – but there is a video game; tables in basic garden with climbing frame, all sorts of passing animals; no food beyond crisps, nuts, seafood in jars and occasional barbecues, bring your own sandwiches; children in back room, lovely walks *(Pete Baker, Andy and Jill Kassube, Phyl and Jack Street, Howard Allen, LYM)*

☆ **Frogham** [Abbotswell Rd; SU1712], *Foresters Arms*: Very friendly landlady and staff in extensively refurbished New Forest pub, flagstones and small woodburner, well kept Wadworths and guest ales, decent wines, good food esp lamb shoulder, extended dining room; children welcome, pleasant garden and front verandah; small camp site adjacent, good walks *(Phyl and Jack Street, John and Joan Calvert, G Gibbs, LYM)*

Gosport [Stokes Bay Rd, Alverstoke; SZ6099], *Alverbank House*: Civilised but pubby bar with changing ales such as Mordue Working Ticket and Ringwood Best in immaculate hotel set in woods at end of Walpole Park, over rd from promenade; good choice of food with plenty of veg, friendly staff, big garden with play area, Solent and Isle of Wight views; piped music; bedrooms very well appointed *(Val and Alan Green, Peter and Audrey Dowsett, Michael and Jeanne Shillington)*; [Fort Rd, Alverstoke], *Dolphin*: Comfortable nautical theme, well kept beers inc Gales HSB, good wine, popular food, no piped music, big well laid out garden with huge play area; nr sea, views to Isle of Wight *(Peter and Audrey Dowsett)*; [Alverstoke], *Old Lodge*: Locally popular for attractive bar menu, Scottish Courage ales, and no piped music – despite jazz portraits in intimate bar; restaurant, tables outside, summer marquee; bedrooms, nr sea *(Peter and Audrey Dowsett)*; [Queens Rd], *Queens*: Popular real-ale pub with five well kept beers, basic food inc huge filled rolls, good service, nice atmosphere, cosy fire, sensibly placed darts, family area with TV; parking may be difficult *(Ann and Colin Hunt, Val and Alan Green)*; [Brockhurst Rd (A32)], *Queens Head*: Attractive town pub with fairly big L-shaped bar, one end done like small lounge, Boddingtons and two weekly guests such as Greene King Abbot or Wadworths 6X; sensibly placed darts, pool *(Ann and Colin Hunt)*

☆ **Griggs Green** [Longmoor Rd (off A3 S of Hindhead); SU8231], *Deers Hut*: Pleasantly laid out L-shaped bar, welcoming licensees, nice atmosphere, Morlands ales; picnic-sets in pretty front garden, attractive woodland setting; touring caravan site behind *(P R White, Dennis Stevens)*

☆ **Hamble** [3 miles from M27 junction 8; SU4806], *Olde Whyte Harte*: Friendly down-to-earth yachtsmen's pub, low beams, flagstones, blazing inglenook log fire, welcoming landlady, reasonably priced good home-made food, Gales Best, BBB and HSB, lots of country wines, decent coffee; children in eating area, some seats outside; handy for nature reserve *(Ann and Colin Hunt, Dr Alan Green, LYM)*

Hamble [High St], *King & Queen*: Lively atmosphere, welcoming staff, well kept beers, good value generous food *(Michael and Jeanne Shillington)*

☆ **Hambledon** [West St; SU6414], *Vine*: Particularly well cooked generous food (not Sun evening) in friendly beamed pub, open-plan but traditional, with panelling, old prints, china, ornaments, farm tools, high-backed settles, log fire – even a well in one of its four areas; good range of beers such as Charles Well Bombardier, Fullers London Pride, Gales HSB and BBB, Hampshire Hare, country wines, long-serving landlord, welcoming helpful staff; shove-ha'penny, darts; pretty downland village *(Martin and Nicki Lampon, P R White, Jo and Gary Charlton, R M Corlett, Ann and Colin Hunt)*

Hambledon [West St], *New Inn*: Simple two-bar village pub with Ringwood ales at low prices, pool room with darts, friendly landlord and locals – conversation comes first *(Ann and Colin Hunt)*

☆ *nr* **Hambledon** [Broadhalfpenny Down; about 2 miles E towards Clanfield; SU6716], *Bat & Ball*: Extended dining pub opp historic cricket pitch doing well under newish landlord, comfortable modern furnishings in three rooms and panelled restaurant, some old cricketing photographs, log fire; several Gales ales, good interesting food inc fresh fish, lovely downs views *(R M Corlett, David Heath, W A Evershed, LYM)*

Havant [South St; SU7106], *Old House At Home*: Enlarged and much modernised low-beamed Tudor pub, two fireplaces in lounge, well kept Gales BBB and HSB, welcoming licensees; piped music (live Sat), back garden *(Ann and Colin Hunt, Tony and Wendy Hobden, LYM)*; [North St, nr stn], *Perseverance*: Comfortable Whitbreads pub with Victorian theme, long banquettes, Fullers London Pride and Wadworths 6X, good range of food from chip butties up, cheerful regulars *(Val and Alan Green)*; [6 Homewell], *Robin Hood*: Cosy old pub with low ceilings in rambling open-plan bar, good mix of customers, Gales ales tapped from the cask, reasonably priced bar meals, open fire; sensibly placed darts *(Ann and Colin Hunt)*

Hazeley [B3011 N of H Wintney; SU7459], *Shoulder of Mutton*: Warmly friendly dining pub, home-made food from ploughman's to good steaks, good vegetarian choice, efficient service, good fire in cosy lounge, no-smoking area, real ales such as Courage, Marstons Pedigree, Morlands Old Speckled Hen and Wadworths 6X, quiet piped music; attractive building, terrace and garden *(D and J Tapper, Francis Johnston)*

Highclere [Andover Rd (A343); SU4360], *Red House*: Recently refurbished with some concentration on good if not cheap food inc children's, spotless and relaxing lounge with pine furniture, friendly staff and dogs Czar and Murphy, Ushers Best and a seasonal ale, bar with pool; couple of tables out in front *(Jane Wright, Mandy Dancocks, E A George)*

☆ **Hill Head** [67 Hill Head Rd; SU5402], *Osborne View*: Picture windows and rebuilding on three stepped-back levels make the most of exceptional Solent views in modern clifftop pub by Titchfield Haven bird reserve, with generous bar food inc children's and Sun roasts (best to book then), well kept Badger Best, Tanglefoot and ales from the Gribble at Oving, efficient service, no music; spacious and roomy, completely refurnished last year with red plush and ship theme; evening restaurant; open all day, garden and beach access, good walks *(Phyl and Jack Street, A R and B E Sayer, Michael Inskip, Ann and Colin Hunt, Eric and June Heley, Val and Alan Green)*

☆ **Horsebridge** [off A3057 Romsey—Andover, just SW of Kings Somborne; SU3430], *John o' Gaunt*: Friendly village local very popular with walkers for good attractively priced food, simple L-shaped bar, well kept Palmers IPA, Ringwood Fortyniner and a guest beer, prompt friendly service, new licensees; picnic-sets outside, by mill on River Test; dogs welcome, no piped music *(Thomas Nott, John Fahy, Sheila and Robert Robinson, Lynn Sharpless, Bob Eardley)*

Houghton [S of Stockbridge; SU3432], *Boot*: Quiet pub with garden running down to lovely stretch of River Test, newish licensees, well kept Ringwood Best, usual bar food, restaurant; muted Classic FM *(John Fahy)*

Hursley [A3090 Winchester—Romsey; SU4225], *Kings Head*: Large open-plan food pub, rather elegant decor, good fresh interesting food inc vegetarian, well kept ales such as Bass and Fullers London Pride, cellar bar with skittle alley; bedrooms *(Lynn Sharpless, Bob Eardley, Thomas Nott, M J Dowdy)*

☆ **Itchen Abbas** [4 miles from M3 junction 9; A34 towards Newbury, fork right on A33, first right on B3047; SU5333], *Trout*: Smallish country pub with discreet low-key lounge bar (partly no smoking), chatty public bar with darts and bar billiards, well kept Marstons Bitter and Pedigree, decent wines, good value food esp fish (decorative trout plates), friendly service, restaurant; pretty side garden with good play area; roomy comfortable bedrooms, good breakfast, pleasant village with good river and downland walks nearby *(Phyl and Jack Street, BB)*

☆ **Keyhaven** [SZ3091], *Gun*: Well run 17th-c nautical-theme beamed pub overlooking boatyard, popular at lunchtime particularly with older people for wide choice of generous bar food, well kept Whitbreads-related ales and allies; children welcome, garden with swings and fishpond *(W W Burke, D Marsh)*

☆ **Langstone** [A3023; SU7105], *Ship*: Plenty of seats out on quiet quay by waterside pub with lovely view from roomy pleasantly decorated bar and upstairs restaurant, fast friendly service, full Gales range kept well, good choice of wines by the glass, country wines, log fire, generous food; children's room, long opening hours *(John Saul, Alan Skull, J F Freay, D Marsh, Francis Bugg, Dennis Stevens, Phyl and Jack Street)*

☆ **Lasham** [SU6742], *Royal Oak*: Thriving two-bar village pub, friendly and comfortable, with well kept Hampshire King Alfred, Ringwood Best and interesting guest beers, good range of home-made food inc vegetarian, log fire, quiet piped music, friendly cat, much talk of aircraft and gliding (airfield nearby); pleasant garden by church, attractive village, good walks *(Phyl and Jack Street, Ann and Colin Hunt)*

Lee on the Solent [Manor Way; SU5600], *Bun Penny*: Low beams and flagstones, separate areas inc conservatory and restaurant, good choice of food inc vegetarian, Whitbreads-related ales, daily papers, efficient staff; garden *(Val and Alan Green)*

☆ **Linwood** [signed from A338 via Moyles Court, and from A31; keep on – OS Sheet 195 map ref 196107; SU1910], *High Corner*: Big rambling pub very popular for its splendid New Forest position, with extensive neatly kept lawn and sizeable play area; some character in original upper bar, lots of back extension for the summer crowds, large helpings of well prepared and served food from sandwiches to steaks inc Sun carvery (nicely partitioned restaurant open all day Sun), well kept Whitbreads-related and other ales such as Hampshire King Arthur, decent wine, no-smoking verandah lounge; children and dogs welcome in some parts, open all day Sat; bedrooms *(C A Hall, M J Dowdy, John Fahy, John and Vivienne Rice, David Gregory, Dennis Stevens, LYM)*

☆ **Linwood** [up on heath – OS Sheet 195 map ref 186094], *Red Shoot*: Nice New Forest setting, lots of space, some attractive old furniture and rugs on bare boards (perhaps less seating than you might expect), generous good value food inc good sandwiches and special sausage dishes, six well kept ales inc Wadworths and now a beer brewed at the pub, friendly staff, children and dogs (and muddy boots) welcome; very touristy in summer (by big campsite and caravan park), can get smoky *(G J Gibbs, Jo and Gary Charlton, John and Vivienne Rice, Mr and Mrs N A Spink, M Joyner)*

Liss [Farnham Rd, West Liss (A325); SU7728], *Blue Bell*: Good French food (two French chefs) in bar and well appointed restaurant, good wine list *(C L Kauffmann)*

Little London [Silchester Rd (off A340 N of Basingstoke); SU6359], *Plough*: Cosy unspoilt local with tiled floor, low beams, friendly landlord, well kept Wethereds, Ringwood and a guest such as Greene King Abbot, log fire, darts, bar billiards; attractive garden, handy for Pamber Forest and Calleva Roman remains *(G Coates)*

☆ **Lower Froyle** [signed off A31; SU7643], *Anchor*: Well run, warm and attractive brightly lit traditional pub with wide range of good reasonably priced food inc sandwiches and fish, cheerful informal service, well kept Hardy Royal Oak, decent malt whiskies; well in one of the two connecting bars, restaurant; piped music; seats outside *(R B Crail, G and M Stewart)*

☆ **Lower Wield** [SU6340], *Yew Tree*: Recently renovated dining pub opp village cricket pitch in peaceful walking country, good original well presented food in partly stripped-brick dining room or small cottagey bar; cheerful and friendly, with well kept Marstons Pedigree, fresh flowers; cl Sun evening, Mon *(Phyl and Jack Street, P and J Ferris, Miss U Brown)*

☆ **Lymington** [Ridgeway Lane, Lower Woodside, marked as dead end just S of A337 roundabout in Pennington W of Lymington, by White Hart; SZ3294], *Chequers*: Simple but stylish young yachtsmen's local with polished boards and quarry-tiles, attractive pictures, plain chairs and wall pews; reasonably priced food (fish enjoyed, also garlic bread with cheese and prawns), Marstons Pedigree and Wadworths 6X, good wines, fine rums; friendly landlord, well if not quietly reproduced piped pop music, traditional games, tables in neat garden with terrace; well behaved children allowed *(Mrs V Brown, D Marsh, Lydia Cahill, G W Stevenson, Mrs F A W Ricketts, James Flory, LYM)*

Lymington [Station St], *Bosuns Chair*: Light and airy high-ceilinged rooms, food inc fish cooked plainly or with options, well kept Wadworths ales; bedrooms *(Thomas Nott, Tony and Wendy Hobden)*

Lyndhurst [22 High St; SU2908], *Fox & Hounds*: Big cheery much modernised dining pub with lots of exposed brickwork, standing timbers as divisions, family room beyond former coach entry, games room with pool, darts etc, welcoming staff, Whitbreads-related and local guest ales, usual food from good ploughman's and brunch to steaks *(Simon Penny, Jess and George Cowley)*

☆ **Mapledurwell** [Tunworth Rd, off A30 Hook—Basingstoke; SU6851], *Gamekeepers*: Badger pub doing well under new landlord, with their IPA and Tanglefoot and a guest such as Hardy Country, good value wines, roomy and interesting old bar, attractive dining area with good food, friendly efficient staff; views from nice open garden, in lovely thatched village with duckpond *(Phyl and Jack Street, Roger Byrne)*

Meonstoke [SU6119], *Bucks Head*: Dark red banquettes and good log fire in popular dining lounge, well kept Bass and Morlands Old Speckled Hen, country wines, good value substantial bar food, friendly service, comfortable public bar, log fire; pleasant walled garden, lovely village setting with ducks on pretty little River Meon, good walks *(Phyl and Jack Street, A R and B E Sayer, Ann and Colin Hunt)*

☆ **Minstead** [just off A31 nr M21 junction 1; SU2811], *Trusty Servant*: In pretty New Forest village with wandering ponies; small bare-boards public bar, unsophisticated back lounge (also small), wide choice of good food from enormous sandwiches to fresh fish (nice seafood chowder) and imaginative main dishes, well kept changing ales such as Flowers Original, Fullers London Pride and Ringwood Best, Thatcher's farm cider, country wines; sizeable attractive restaurant, airy by day, candlelit by night; piped music, and rather a take-us-as-you-find-us feel; bedrooms simple, good breakfast *(Mike and Heather Watson, Ann and Colin Hunt, D Marsh, David Gregory, Gwen and Peter Andrews, R T and J C Moggridge, Jasper Sabey, BB)*

New Cheriton [A272 nr B3154 junction; SU5828], *Hinton Arms*: Roomy pub doing well under newish owner, some concentration on wide choice of good food running up to bass, fresh veg, real ales such as local Itchen Valley; very handy for Hinton Ampner House (NT) *(John and Joan Calvert, Ron Shelton)*

Newnham [Newnham Green; handy for M3

junction 5; SU7054], *Old House At Home*: Pleasantly old-fashioned peaceful bay-windowed house in secluded hamlet, good fire, very friendly welcome, food inc generous servings of very wide range of speciality sausages, delicious puddings, well kept Courage and Ushers; pleasant walks nearby *(Tony Beaulah, James and Geraldine Russell)*
Newtown [Church Rd; off A32 N of Wickham; SU6112], *Travellers Rest*: Uncomplicated country pub gently enlarged but still cosy, with log fires, traditional furnishings, chatty local atmosphere, friendly service, real ales; pretty back garden *(J and P Halfyard, LYM)*
☆ **North Warnborough** [nr M3 junction 5; SU7351], *Swan*: Friendly and comfortable village local with good choice of well priced straightforward food cooked to order, well kept Scottish Courage beers *(A E Brace, Ian Phillips)*
Overton [Red Lion Lane; SU5149], *Red Lion*: Village pub with wide choice of food inc good vegetarian dishes in sizeable eating area, well kept changing ales in lively little locals' bar, open fires, garden with good play area; children welcome *(Mrs Jess Cowley)*
Park Gate [Bridge Rd; A27, a mile from M27 junction 9; SU5108], *Talisman*: Busy Badger dining pub, beams, oak panels, boards and carpets, flame-effect fire, big helpings, their ales inc one from the Gribble at Oving, no-smoking area, children's seating, quiet piped music; garden *(Val and Alan Green)*
Pennington [Milford Rd; SZ3194], *White Hart*: Whitbreads Wayside Inn, modernised in character, with separate rooms around central core, real ales such as Flowers Original, Fullers London Pride, Gales HSB and Wadworths 6X, good range of food, friendly service; terrace and garden *(W W Burke)*
☆ **Petersfield** [College St; SU7423], *Good Intent*: 16th-c core with low oak beams and oak tables, four Gales ales and a guest such as Fullers London Pride, food inc sandwiches, baguettes, lots of unusual sausages, a good imaginative vegetarian dish, friendly welcoming service; children in cosy former restaurant area *(Val and Alan Green, Derek and Margaret Underwood, C A Stanbridge)*
☆ *nr* **Petersfield** [old coach rd NW past Steep – OS Sheet 186 map ref 726273], *Trooper*: Doing well under current management, with generous good food esp fish, well kept Bass, Ringwood and guest beers such as Wadworths, Czech lager on tap, interesting good value wines, friendly service, candlelight and fresh flowers, scrubbed pine tables and bare boards; new restaurant in former back stables; tables out on terrace, country views *(Wendy Arnold, Terry Morgan)*
Plaitford [A36 S'ton—Salisbury; SU2819], *Shoe*: Attractively lit, with Ringwood Best, bar food, big games room off, garden behind *(Ann and Colin Hunt)*
☆ **Portsmouth** [High St, Old Town], *Dolphin*: Spacious and genteel old timber-framed inn with ten or more Whitbreads-related and other ales, wide range of food, good log fire, cosy snug; video games; open all day Sat, children welcome in eating area, small terrace *(Reg Nelson, Andy and Jill Kassube, Chris and Ann Garnett, Ann and Colin Hunt)*
Portsmouth [Camber Dock; SU6501], *Bridge*: On the wharf, quiet and relaxing, with lots of wood fittings, maritime theme, good water views, bar food, upstairs fish bistro, Boddingtons and Marstons Pedigree *(Reg Nelson, Ann and Colin Hunt)*; [Portsdown Hill Rd, Widley; SU6606], *Churchillian*: Smallish open-plan dining pub, oak, cream and red carpet, big windows overlooking Portsmouth and Solent, usual food, Gibbs Mew ales; quietish piped music; handy for Fort Widley equestrian centre and nature trail *(Alan Green)*; [Penhale Rd], *Connaught Arms*: Attractive Tudor corner pub with straightforward food inc pasties, well kept ales such as Bass, Cheriton Pots and Fullers London Pride, friendly long-serving licensees and locals, sensibly placed darts; terrace *(Ann and Colin Hunt)*; [King Henry I St], *Fleet & Firkin*: Usual Firkin style with naval additions, roomy interior with first floor, friendly staff, large choice of real ales, simple bar food *(Ann and Colin Hunt, Paul and Sue Merrick)*; [Portsdown Hill Rd, Widley], *George*: Friendly unspoilt Georgian local with well kept ales such as Fullers London Pride, Goachers 1066, Marstons Pedigree, Morlands Old Speckled Hen and Whitbreads, lunchtime food inc good soups and club sandwiches – can be crowded then; handy for Portsdown Hill nature reserve, wonderful views of Hayling Island, Portsmouth and Isle of Wight from terrace *(Alan Green)*; [Surrey St], *Hogshead & Bucket*: Roomy pub nr main shops, 10 real ales, usual food, polite service, no-smoking area, comfortable lounge, nice mirrors, old prints and mixed furniture *(Ann and Colin Hunt, Jess and George Cowley)*; [Highland Rd, Eastney; SU6899], *Mayflower Beer Engine*: The cat's like the pub – good pedigree but friendly; two bars, tasteful decor, subdued lighting, good prints, lots of original wood fittings, careful modern refurbishments, engaging atmosphere, well kept Tetleys and other ales, simple bar food; darts, juke box, garden *(Reg Nelson, Ann and Colin Hunt)*; [Port Solent marina], *Mermaid*: Smart pub on exclusive marina with Boddingtons beer and limited bar snacks; plenty of seating inside and out, lots to look at *(Dennis Stevens)*; [Pembroke St], *Pembroke Arms*: Old-fashioned feel, with well kept ales such as Greene King Abbot; fruit machine *(Derek Stafford)*; [High St, Old Portsmouth], *Sally Port*: Spick-and-span, sympathetically modernised and still interesting, with good atmosphere, soft lighting, reasonably priced bar food esp fish, well kept Marstons, upstairs restaurant; comfortable bedrooms *(Zoe Morrell, Andrew Anderson, Robert and Gladys Flux, Ann and Colin Hunt, Reg Nelson)*; [Victory Rd, The Hard, Portsea], *Ship Anson*: Relaxing Whitbreads pub with related ales, food; handy for HMS *Victory* etc *(Ann and Colin Hunt)*; [Bath Sq, Old Town], *Spice Island*: Vast modernised waterside Whitbreads pub with seafaring theme, dark panelling, big

windows and outside seats overlooking passing ships, well kept ales, food all day inc vegetarian, family room (one of the few in Portsmouth), bright upstairs restaurant; can be very crowded *(Richie Berryman, Jess and George Cowley, Reg Nelson)*; [Surrey St], *Surrey Arms*: Backstreet local popular lunchtime for good food, well kept beer; bedrooms *(Reg Nelson)*; [off Grand Parade, Old Portsmouth], *Wellington*: Friendly and busy little traditional pub nr seafront, good bar food esp reasonably priced fresh fish dishes, friendly landlord, relaxing atmosphere, well kept beer *(Ann and Colin Hunt)*; [opp Guildhall], *Wetherspoons*: Roomy new pub with smart decor, simple food, good choice of ales, sensible prices *(Ann and Colin Hunt, Jess and George Cowley)*

☆ **Ringwood** [The Bridges, West St, just W of town; SU1505], *Fish*: Several quiet and cosy areas (some away from bar perhaps a bit dark), intriguing fishy decorations, well kept Boddingtons, Brakspears, Flowers and Fullers, coffee and tea, wide choice of good value generous food maybe inc bargains, log fire, friendly if not always speedy service, no-smoking eating area allowing children, no dogs; tables on riverside lawn with play area and budgerigar aviary, open all day *(P A Legon, Anette and Stephen Marsden, DC, LYM)*

Ringwood [12 Meeting House Lane], *Inn on the Furlong*: Several rooms, flagstones, stripped brick and oak timbering, simple decor, full range of Ringwood beers kept well, friendly service, limited bar food, conservatory; live music some nights, Easter beer festival *(Bruce Bird, Paul and Sue Merrick)*

☆ **Rockbourne** [signed off B3078 Fordingbridge—Cranborne; SU1118], *Rose & Thistle*: Attractive thatched 17th-c pub with good if pricy home-made food inc vegetarian in civilised bar with booth seating, old engravings and good log fire, well kept Courage Best, Marstons Pedigree, Ushers seasonal brews, Wadworths 6X and Youngers Scotch, good range of wines, normally pleasant service, traditional games, no-smoking area, restaurant; maybe piped classical music; children welcome, tables by thatched dovecot in neat front garden, charming setting in lovely village, good walks *(Mike and Heather Watson, M J Dowdy, P J and J E F Caunt, Jamie and Ruth Lyons, Hilarie Taylor, Colin Thompson, Ann and Colin Hunt, G Neighbour, LYM)*

☆ **Rockford** [OS Sheet 195 map ref 160081; SU1608], *Alice Lisle*: Friendly modernised open-plan pub attractively placed on green by New Forest (can get very busy), emphasis on big conservatory-style family eating area with generous helpings of good food inc sandwiches, some interesting dishes and sensible children's menu; well kept Gales and guest beers, country wines, helpful staff, baby-changing facilities; garden with extensive play area, peacock and other birds, ponies wander nearby; handy for Moyles Court *(Rev John Hibberd, WWB, BB)*

☆ **Romsey** [23 Mainstone; SU3521], *Old Horse & Jockey*: Individually decorated small rooms around central servery, emphasis on good reasonably priced food similar to that of White Hart at Cadnam (family link); Courage Directors, John Smiths and Theakstons Old Peculier, decent house wines, friendly attentive service; piped music *(Lynn Sharpless, Bob Eardley, J L Kelly)*

Romsey [Greatbridge; A3057 towards Stockbridge; SU3422], *Dukes Head*: Attractive dining pub festooned with flowering baskets in summer; smart efficient waitresses, well kept Whitbreads-related ales and guests such as local Pride of Romsey, decent house wines, good value well prepared food, inglenook eating places, no piped music, charming back garden wth old tractor and rabbits *(Ian Phillips, Paul Ransom, Brian Mills)*; [Botley Rd; A27 towards N Baddesley – handy for M27 junction 3; SU3720], *Luzborough House*: Extensive Whitbreads family dining pub with interesting smaller rooms leading off high-raftered rather sparsely furnished flagstoned main bar, generous food all day, well kept ales, big log fire, cheerful staff; piped music; children welcome away from bar, tables and play area in spacious walled garden *(Dennis Stevens, LYM)*

☆ **Rotherwick** [The Street; SU7156], *Falcon*: Smart and lively welcoming country pub, recently given open-plan refurbishment, with good food inc enjoyable specials, interesting spicy dishes and Sun roasts, themed food nights, particularly well kept ales such as Archers Golden, Brakspears and Morrells Varsity, bright prompt service, log fire, darts, bar billiards; children welcome, big garden with swings *(Andy and Jill Kassube, Tracy Conway, Simon Collett-Jones)*

Selborne [SU7433], *Queens*: Unpretentious village pub with interesting local memorabilia, well kept Ushers, good value standard food from hot filled rolls up inc children's, open fires; children welcome, occasional jazz; bedrooms, very handy for Gilbert White's home, carriage rides from here *(Thomas Nott, Dave Braisted, Jo and Gary Charlton, J S M Sheldon, LYM)*; *Selborne Arms*: Well kept real ales, good range of enjoyable food, friendly staff cope very well even when very busy, twinkly landlord, log fire in fine inglenook; tables in garden with good play area, right by walks up Hanger *(Ian Phillips)*

Shedfield [A334 Wickham—Botley; SU5512], *Wheatsheaf*: Busy little family-run two-bar local, well kept ales such as Archers, Cheriton Pots, Hampshire and Hop Back, satisfying lunchtime food, reasonable prices; garden, handy for Wickham Vineyard *(Ann and Colin Hunt, Val and Alan Green)*

☆ **Soberton** [School Hill; signed off A32 S of Droxford; SU6116], *White Lion*: Unaffected 16th-c country pub in nice spot by green, rambling no-smoking bistro area with enjoyable straightforward food, irregularly shaped public bar with built-in wooden wall seats and traditional games, well kept Gales HSB, Morlands Old Speckled Hen, Wadworths 6X and a beer brewed for them by Hampshire Brewery, decent house wine, eager collie called

Spike; small sheltered pretty garden and sun-trap fairy-lit terrace; children in eating areas, open all day *(Jo and Gary Charlton, Martin and Karen Wake, Lynn Sharpless, Bob Eardley, Brad W Morley, Ann and Colin Hunt, LYM)*

Southampton [The Common; SU4212], *Cowherds*: Long low chain pub pleasantly set on common, well restyled to give numerous alcoves and rooms with individual decor, tables in nice little bay windows, lots of Victorian photographs, carpets on polished boards, log fires; good food, Bass ales, efficient staff, restaurant, tables outside, tie-ups for dogs, with water for them *(Ian Phillips)*; [Highcrown St, Highfield; SU4214], *Crown*: Warmly relaxed atmosphere, good range of good generous food, very reasonable prices, helpful staff, ice buckets for wine; open fires, dogs allowed in main bar (giving country feel in the city) *(Jennifer Robertson)*; [Welbeck Ave, Portswood; SU4313], *Drummond Arms*: Friendly local with pleasant licensees and staff, bar food, lots of events *(Paul Fleckney)*; [Moorgreen Rd, West End (off B3035); SU4714], *Southampton Arms*: Friendly jolly local with good food *(L A Knott)*; [Above Bar], *Square Balloon*: Shoppers and business people lunchtime, young people later evening, in vast comfortable pub converted from cinema, plenty of tables on raised galleries, good decor, soft lighting, wide range of drinks, decent food, smart, efficient and welcoming staff, attractive range of coffees; enormous balloon over the circular bar, no trainers allowed *(Phyl and Jack Street)*; [20 High St], *Standing Order*: A formula, with standardised Wetherspoons menu and make-believe decor, but it works, with reasonably priced food inc popular bargain Sun lunch, well kept beers inc interesting guests, helpful efficient young staff, strange and interesting collection of books in one corner, no-smoking area *(Sue and Mike Todd, John and Christine Simpson)*; [101 Waterloo Rd], *Waterloo Arms*: Small 1930s pub tied to Hop Back with their full beer range kept well, some lunchtime food, open fires, plenty of light-coloured wood, ochre walls with brewing awards, traditional games, back garden with boules, plans for conservatory; very busy weekends (local CAMRA branch meets Sun lunchtime), Tues quiz night *(G Coates)*; [Woolston, just S of Itchen toll bridge; SU4310], *Yacht*: Unassuming modern pub done up with nets, blocks and tackle etc, worth knowing for friendly welcome, simple fairly cheap food, and proximity to Jubilee Yard – building first modern timber-framed sailing ship, with viewing gallery *(C P Scott-Malden)*

☆ **Southsea** [15 Eldon St/Norfolk St; SZ6498], *Eldon Arms*: Roomy, comfortable and relaxing rambling bar with old pictures and advertisements, attractive mirrors, lots of enjoyable bric-a-brac; half a dozen Hardy and other changing well kept ales, decent wines, friendly new manager, good changing range of promptly served food, sensibly placed darts; pool and fruit machine, restaurant, tables in back garden *(Ann and Colin Hunt, Reg Nelson)*

Southsea [Albert Rd], *5th Hampshire Volunteers*: Very approachable backstreet local, military memorabilia *(Reg Nelson)*; [Auckland Rd], *Auckland Arms*: Superb original frontage, very interesting old local photographs *(Reg Nelson)*; [King St], *Diamond*: Backstreet local with glorious original frontage, nice atmosphere *(Reg Nelson)*; [Victoria St], *Fuzz & Firkin*: One of the best Firkins: police theme, usual bare boards and solid furnishings, friendly staff, good beer brewed at the pub, lively atmosphere; loud music and lots of young people Sat night, cheaper drinks Thurs night *(Ann and Colin Hunt, Reg Nelson, Jess and George Cowley)*; [68 Osborne Rd], *Osborne*: Handy workaday pub with good value food from cheap sandwiches to low-priced hot dishes in L-shaped bare-bricks bar, well kept ales such as Boddingtons and Courage Directors; children away from main bar, no dogs *(David Dimock, Ann and Colin Hunt)*

Southwick [High St; SU6208], *Red Lion*: Newly done up by Gales, emphasis on dining room, well priced food, low beams, very friendly prompt service, mainly no smoking *(Dr Alan Green, Ann and Colin Hunt)*

St Mary Bourne [B3048; SU4250], *George*: Plushly refurbished dining pub, well kept ales inc guest such as Morlands Old Speckled Hen, good food inc seafood specials, thai curry, good mixed grill, welcoming landlord, very pleasant service, restaurant; tables outside, attractive village *(R T and J C Moggridge, M Hasslacher, Ann and Colin Hunt)*

☆ **Stockbridge** [High St; SU3535], *Grosvenor*: Good atmosphere and quick cheerfully courteous service in pleasant and comfortable old country-town hotel's two smallish bars and dining room, decent food, Courage Directors and Whitbreads Best, log fire; big attractive garden behind; bedrooms good value *(R J Walden, BB)*

Stockbridge [High St], *Three Cups*: Coaching inn dating from 1500, now a pub, friendly, comfortable and unpretentious, with Fullers and Worthington, well prepared quickly served food from sandwiches to generous hot dishes *(Gareth Morris)*; [High St], *Vine*: Busy pub/restaurant, old beams and woodwork, stripped bricks and purple wallpaper, delft shelf of china and pewter, bright floral curtains, popular food from huge sandwiches up, half helpings for children, restaurant (smoking allowed), well kept Boddingtons, Brakspears and Flowers Original, good wine list, unobtrusive piped music; open all day, tables in nice big garden, weekend barbecues *(Anna and Martyn Carey, John and Vivienne Rice, LYM)*; [High St (A272/A3057 roundabout)], *White Hart*: Cheerful and welcoming divided bar, oak pews and other seats, antique prints, shaving-mug collection, good reasonably priced home-made bar food, Sun lunches, well kept Ringwood Fortyniner, country wines, nice licensees; children allowed in comfortable beamed restaurant with blazing log fire; bedrooms *(Phyl and Jack Street, Pat and Kay McCaffrey, LYM)*

Stubbington [Crofton Lane; SU5402], *Crofton*: Two bars, friendly staff, Ushers ales, usual bar food, wider choice in dining room with red plush, pink wallpaper, wrought iron; piped music inc popular classical *(Val and Alan Green)*

☆ **Swanmore** [Hill Pound Rd; SU5815], *Rising Sun*: Welcoming and comfortable beamed pub, good log fires, good choice of popular food (booking advised weekends), well kept Whitbreads-related ales, decent wines, good courteous service, recently extended restaurant area; pleasant garden with play area, good walks *(Phyl and Jack Street, Ann and Colin Hunt, Jo and Gary Charlton, P Harbut)*

Swanmore [Hill Grove], *Hunters*: Popular plush dining pub with big family room, wide choice of decent straightforward food inc vegetarian and children's, Courage Directors, good house wine, country wines, lots of carpentry and farm tools, beams and banknotes; plenty of picnic-sets, good big play area; very busy weekends *(A R and B E Sayer)*

Swanwick [Swanwick Lane (A3051); handy for M27 junction 9; SU5109], *Elm Tree*: Neat and comfortably refurbished, with two bars and dining room off, Courage, Gales HSB, Ruddles and Wadworths 6X, wide range of home-made food inc vegetarian and fish, quiet piped music; children welcome, tables in garden; handy for Hampshire Wildlife Reserve *(Alan Green)*

☆ **Sway** [Durns Town – just off B3055 SW of Brockenhurst; SZ2898], *Hare & Hounds*: Well spaced tables in airy and comfortable New Forest pub with friendly new licensees, redecorated dining room, good range of food, well kept Flowers Original, Fullers London Pride and Ringwood Best, picnic-sets and play frame in sizeable neatly kept garden; open all day Sat *(JC, Dr and Mrs A K Clarke, LYM)*

Thruxton [SU2945], *White Horse*: Very friendly 16th-c thatched local rather dwarfed by A303 overpass, soft lighting, very low beams, horse-racing decor, log fire, well kept Fullers London Pride and Greene King IPA, decent food inc good sandwiches, separate dining area, relaxed informality, very obliging landlord *(Mark Matthewman)*

☆ **Timsbury** [Michelmersh; A3057 towards Stockbridge; SU3424], *Bear & Ragged Staff*: Very busy beamed Whitbreads country dining pub, much modernised, airy and comfortable, with wide choice of food all day inc good value ploughman's and good vegetarian dishes, quick service even when busy, several well kept ales, lots of wines by the glass, country wines, tables out in garden, good play area; children in eating area; handy for Mottisfont *(Ian and Deborah Carrington, Gordon, R Lake, Thomas Nott, LYM)*

Titchfield [High St (off A27 nr Fareham; SU5305], *Queens Head*: Sympathetically restored ancient pub, cosy and friendly 1930s-feel bar with window seats and central brick fireplace, changing well kept ales such as Fullers London Pride and Morlands Old Speckled Hen, sparkling glasses, good choice of nicely prepared food esp fish cooked by landlord, pleasant restaurant; bedrooms, pleasant conservation village nr nature reserve and walks to coast *(Phyl and Jack Street, Ann and Colin Hunt, Eric and June Heley)*; [East St], *Wheatsheaf*: Pleasantly pubby, with long bow-windowed sitting room, small dining room and snug, back terrace, reasonably priced ales such as Brakspears, Fullers London Pride, Hook Norton Old Hookey and Woodfordes Wherry, simple food, log fires, daily papers, piped radio *(Val and Alan Green, Ann and Colin Hunt)*

Totford [B3046 Basingstoke—Alresford; SU5738], *Woolpack*: Friendly, warm and cosy pub/restaurant with well kept Gales HSB, Palmers IPA and local Cheriton Pots, stripped-brick bar, large dining room, decent food inc vegetarian and good Sun roast, open fire; tables outside, lovely setting in good walking country; bedrooms *(Ann and Colin Hunt)*

Twyford [SU4724], *Bugle*: Friendly open-plan pub done up in rich post-Victorian style, wide choice of generous reasonably priced good food inc good value Sun lunch, well kept Hardy ales, decent wines by the glass *(Michael and Gillian Ford, Alan Green)*; [High St], *Phoenix*: Friendly open-plan local redecorated in red and dark wood, with white walls and big end inglenook; changing choice of good generous straightforward food inc shortcrust pies, enthusiastic cheerful landlord, well kept Marstons, decent wines, back room with skittle alley, garden; children allowed up one end *(Lynn Sharpless, Bob Eardley, Stephen Harvey, Ann and Colin Hunt)*

☆ **Upton Grey** [SU6948], *Hoddington Arms*: Consistently good value interesting food inc good puddings in unpretentious two-bar local; well kept Morlands and other ales, Australian wines by glass, friendly atmosphere and service, family room, bar billiards; piped music; garden, attractive village *(G and M Stewart, Francis Johnston)*

☆ **Vernham Dean** [off A343 via Upton, or off A338 S of Hungerford via Oxenwood; SU3456], *George*: Relaxed and neatly kept rambling open-plan beamed and timbered bar, carefully refurbished, with some easy chairs, inglenook log fire, good value bar food (not Sun evening) from toasties to steaks inc good home-made puddings, well kept Marstons Best and Pedigree; darts, shove-ha'penny, dominoes and cribbage; well behaved children allowed in no-smoking eating area, tables in pretty garden behind *(Glen and Nola Armstong, Gordon, E V Walder, LYM)*

Wallington [nr M27 junction 11; SU5806], *White Horse*: Neat and cosy well furnished two-bar local with pictures of old Fareham, well kept Bass tapped from the cask and changing guest ales such as Hook Norton, Exmoor Hart, Rugby Summer Lightning; darts *(Terry and Eileen Stott, Ann and Colin Hunt)*

Waltham Chase [Winchester Rd (B2177) – OS Sheet 196 map ref 562162; SU5616], *Chase*: Large house converted to bar and dining room, very welcoming hard-working newish licensees, very wide choice of food, real ales such as Fullers London Pride, Marstons Bitter and

Ringwood Fortyniner, machines and billiards *(Alan Green)*

Warsash [Shore Rd; SU4806], *Rising Sun*: Waterside pub, lively and attractive, open all day for well presented food inc seafood specialities, efficient service, Marstons and Whitbreads-related ales, decent wines, long bar part tiled-floor and part boards, fine Hamble estuary views esp from restaurant up the spiral stairs; Solent Way walk passes pub, handy for Hook nature reserve *(Phyl and Jack Street, Michael Inskip, Ann and Colin Hunt, D Marsh)*

Whitchurch [London Rd; SU4648], *Red House*: Ancient flagstones under 14th-c beams by inglenook fireplace, good value food inc fresh veg, home-baked rolls and restaurant dishes, well kept ales inc Courage, welcoming staff; marvellous terrace with play area *(Francis Johnston)*

Wickham [Kingsmead; A32 towards Droxford; SU5711], *Roebuck*: Well appointed Gales pub (even a white grand piano) doing well under experienced new tenants, good food in bar and restaurant, library of books *(A R and B E Sayer)*

☆ **Winchester** [The Square, between High St and cathedral; SU4829], *Eclipse*: Picturesque but unpretentious small partly 14th-c pub with massive beams and timbers, well worn fittings, oak settles, well kept Boddingtons, Hampshire Pendragon and Ringwood Old Thumper, well done generous lunchtime bar food inc good value toasties, staff welcoming and helpful even when very busy (can get smoky); children in back room, seats outside, very handy for cathedral *(Ann and Colin Hunt, Sue and Mike Todd, Mr and Mrs Jon Corelis, LYM)*

☆ **Winchester** [Royal Oak Passage, off upper end of pedestrian part of High St], *Royal Oak*: Cheerful well kept Hogshead real-ale tavern with ten or so kept well, little rooms (some raised) off main bar, beams and bare boards, scrubbed tables, no-smoking areas, well priced straightforward quick food, cheerful service; the cellar bar (not always open) has massive 12th-c beams and a Saxon wall which gives it some claim to be the country's oldest drinking spot *(Jim and Maggie Cowell, Ann and Colin Hunt, DJW, Dr and Mrs A K Clarke, LYM)*

Winchester [Stockbridge Rd/Andover Rd], *Albion*: Small imaginatively renovated traditional city pub, inexpensive simple lunchtime bar food, Bass, Worthington Best and Hook Norton, friendly landlord; open all day, can get smoky *(Lynn Sharpless, Bob Eardley)*; [Wharf Hill], *Black Boy*: Beamed L-shaped bar with all sorts of interesting bric-a-brac and memorabilia, pleasantly quirky atmosphere, unusual games in separate part, good food running up to tuna steaks, well kept beer and decent wines (good mulled wine in winter), welcoming licensees, dogs welcome, attractive secluded terrace *(Tom Espley, Ann and Colin Hunt, Anthony Bathurst, LYM)*; [57 Hyde St (A333)], *Hyde*: Unspoilt 15th-c local with hardly a true right-angle, friendly welcome, sensible prices, particularly well kept Marstons Pedigree; can get a bit smoky *(Ann and Colin Hunt)*; [11 Saxon Rd, Hyde; SU4830], *King Alfred*: Victorianised Marstons pub, unfussy decor, wood and opaque glass dividers, interesting choice of good food from lunchtime baguettes and baked potatoes up, helpful friendly new tenants, attentive staff, very wide choice of wines by the glass; TV and piped music, and can get a bit smoky, but big enough to get away *(Lynn Sharpless, Bob Eardley)*; [Kingsgate Rd], *Queen*: Modestly comfortable and roomy refurbished pub in attractive setting opp College cricket ground, dark dado, cricketing prints on cream walls, well kept Marstons, decent wines, enjoyable food inc popular Sun lunch, disabled facilities; open all day Fri-Sun *(Lynn Sharpless, Bob Eardley, Paul McPherson, Dr and Mrs A K Clarke)*

☆ **Woodgreen** [SU1717], *Horse & Groom*: Several beamed rooms around servery, nature photographs, log fire in nice Victorian fireplace, comfortable eating area, games in simple locals' bar on left; good choice of home-cooked food inc lovely old-fashioned puddings and good value Sun roast, real ales such as Hampshire Arthur Pendragon, Ringwood Best and Tisbury Archibald Beckett, brisk service; picnic-sets on front terrace and in spreading back garden with good aviaries *(Lyn and Geoff Hallchurch, Jim and Liz Meier, Phyl and Jack Street, BB)*

Real ale to us means beer which has matured naturally in its cask – not pressurised or filtered. We name all real ales stocked. We usually name ales preserved under a light blanket of carbon dioxide too, though purists – pointing out that this stops the natural yeasts developing – would disagree (most people, including us, can't tell the difference!).

Hereford & Worcester

Quite a lot of changes here this year include new licensees at the grand old Fleece at Bretforton (food more of a bargain than in the past), thorough redecoration at the Walter de Cantelupe at Kempsey (imaginative food), good beers brewed on the premises using hops grown on their own farm at the attractive Talbot at Knightwick, a new landlord at another popular dining pub, the Hunters at Longdon, new people too at the Slip at Much Marcle (they've taken on a gardener, to keep the gardens here in the very top rank of pub gardens), a takeover at the Kings Arms at Ombersley, by an outfit called the Quintessential English Pub Co (misgivings evaporate – very favourable reports on the new regime's food), a natural disaster at the Ancient Camp at Ruckhall (landslides following the Easter 1998 storms, a lot of work needed), planning permission granted for bedrooms at the charming Three Crowns at Ullingswick, and a new licensee at the tucked-away Butchers Arms at Woolhope. The ancient Pandy out at Dorstone has been doing very well recently, and rejoins the main entries after a few years' break. The newish owners of the Roebuck at Brimfield have settled in very well, putting this dining pub among the area's tops for eating out – a select group which, besides pubs already mentioned, includes the Riverside at Aymestrey (gaining one of our Food Awards this year), the Feathers in Ledbury, the Crown & Anchor at Lugwardine, the Crown & Sandys Arms at Ombersley, and the Olde Salutation in the delightful village of Weobley. The atmosphere here is perhaps rather more formal than in many other pubs, but this isn't necessarily a bad thing for a special meal out, and can even add to the sense of occasion: the Olde Salutation at Weobley is our Hereford & Worcestershire Dining Pub of the Year. In general, pub food in this area is good value, with prices that compare well with those elsewhere. A special mention for the very attractive food prices at the Farmers Arms at Birtsmorton, the King & Castle in Kidderminster (great for steam buffs), and the Fleece at Bretforton. Drinks prices in the area are also well below the national average (especially if you go for the area's local speciality, farm cider). The beers brewed by the Talbot at Knightwick stand out as exceptionally cheap, but prices were also particularly good at the Crown at Woolhope, the Slip at Much Marcle, the Cottage of Content at Carey and the Farmers Arms at Birtsmorton – all getting beers from more or less distant small independent brewers. In the Lucky Dip section at the end of the chapter, pubs that stand out (most of them already inspected by us) are the Little Pack Horse in Bewdley, Crown & Trumpet in Broadway, Live & Let Live at Cutnall Green, New Inn at Pembridge, Brandy Cask in Pershore, Hope & Anchor in Ross on Wye and Peacock near Tenbury Wells.

Post Office address codings confusingly give the impression that some pubs are in Hereford and Worcestershire, when they're really in the Midlands, Shropshire, Gloucestershire or even Wales (which is where we list them).

AYMESTREY SO4265 Map 6

Riverside Inn

A4110; N off A44 at Mortimers Cross, W of Leominster

There is no shortage of warm log fires at this black and white timbered riverside inn. There is a lovely laid-back atmosphere in the rambling beamed bar, with several cosy areas and decor drawn from a pleasant mix of periods and styles: from fine antique oak tables and chairs to stripped pine country kitchen tables, from flowers on the tables to hops strung from a ceiling waggon-wheel, from horse tack through a Librairie Romantique poster for Victor Hugo's poems to a cheerful modern print of a plump red toadstool. The ambitious bar food is a good eclectic mix, too: changing daily, it might include an excellent creamy fish soup as well as say roast tomato soup (£2.95), liver and bacon casserole, lasagne or fried squid with garlic and parsley (£4.95), fish bake or monkfish provençale (£5.95), pheasant breast with caramelised apples and chestnuts (£9.95), spiced duck breast with honey and soy (£10.95) and venison with damson compote (£11.95). Well kept own-brew beers Woodhampton Dipper, Jack Snipe and Kingfisher Ale; local farm cider, decent house wines, and friendly obliging service. There's a big restaurant area; shove-ha'penny and table skittles but no machines. Outside are waterside picnic-sets, and rustic tables and benches up above in a steep tree-sheltered garden; up beyond, also beautifully sheltered, is a former bowling green. Recent reports on the bedrooms are very favourable and residents are offered fly-fishing (they have fishing rights on a mile of the River Lugg) and a free taxi service to the start of the Mortimer Trail. Busy at weekends, when booking would be wise. *(Recommended by Mr and Mrs Head, Ian Jones, A Caffyn, Sarah and Peter Gooderham, Sue and Bob Ward, Brian Pohill, D Etheridge, Kevin Thorpe, Mary and Andrew Leach, Chris Walling)*

Own Brew ~ Licensees Val and Steve Bowen ~ Real ale ~ Meals and snacks ~ Restaurant ~ (01568) 708440 ~ Children over five welcome in eating area of bar ~ Open 12-3, 6.30-11; 12-3, 7-10.30 Sun ~ Bedrooms: £30B/£45.60B)

BIRTSMORTON SO7935 Map 4

Farmers Arms £

Birts Street, off B4208 W of Birtsmorton

Readers report that the warmth of the welcome at this neatly kept black and white timbered local wards off any chill of winter. On the right a big room rambles away under low dark beams, with some standing timbers, and flowery-panelled cushioned settles as well as spindleback chairs; on the left an even lower-beamed room seems even snugger, and in both the white walls have black timbering. Good value home-made bar food includes sandwiches (from £1.35), ploughman's (from £2.45), soup (£1.60) cauliflower cheese (£3.15), chicken and vegetable curry (£4), fish and chips (£4.10), chicken and chips (£4.35), steak and kidney pie (£5), gammon steak (£6.30) and mixed grill (£7.80); puddings (from £1.75). Well kept Hook Norton Best and Old Hookey and a guest which may be from Brandy Cask, Cottage or Ledbury on handpump; darts in a good tiled area, shove-ha'penny, cribbage, and dominoes. There are seats out on the grass. *(Recommended by Simon Watkins, Tim and Linda Collins, JKW, Stephen Pine, Alfred Lawrence, Alan and Paula McCully, Derek Hayman)*

Free house ~ Licensees Jill and Julie Moore ~ Real ale ~ Meals and snacks (11-2, 6-10) ~ (01684) 833308 ~ Children welcome ~ Open 11-2.30, 6-11; 12-3, 7-10.30 Sun; cl evening 25 Dec

BREDON SO9236 Map 4

Fox & Hounds

4½ miles from M5 junction 9; A438 to Northway, left at B4079, then in Bredon follow To church and river signpost on right

This prettily set and neatly thatched pub has gradually become more and more restauranty over the years and readers suggest that a visit is likely to include a full sit-down meal. The very wide choice of popular food includes home-made soup

(£2.95), ploughman's (from £4.25), avocado, excellent stilton and port pâté (£4.25), brie and sautéed bacon pieces, breadcrumbed and deep fried with a redcurrant sauce (£4.50), mushroom stroganoff (£6.50), chilli (£6.95), thai-style chicken (£9.75), lamb shoulder roasted on rosemary with mint and honey glaze (£11.25), beef and bacon stroganoff (£11.95) and half duckling (£12.75), as well as a seasonal daily specials board; Sunday roast. The comfortable and well modernised carpeted bar has a friendly atmosphere, dressed stone pillars and stripped timbers, a central wood-burning stove, upholstered settles, wheelback, tub, and kitchen chairs around attractive mahogany and cast-iron-framed tables, dried grasses and flowers, a toy fox dressed in hunting scarlet, and elegant wall lamps. A smaller side bar has assorted wooden kitchen chairs, wheelbacks, and settles, and an open fire at each end. Well kept Banks's Bitter, Marstons Pedigree and Morlands Old Speckled Hen on handpump, several malt whiskies and wines by the glass; dominoes, shove-ha'penny, cribbage, fruit machine and piped music. No smoking in the restaurant and part of the bar. The pub is pretty in summer with its colourful hanging baskets, and some of the picnic-sets are under Perspex. *(Recommended by David and Nina Pugsley, F J Robinson, Ian Phillips, W W Burke, C Moncreiffe, J F Knutton, M A Borthwick, Paul and Maggie Baker)*

Whitbreads ~ Lease: Michael Hardwick ~ Real ale ~ Meals and snacks ~ Restaurant ~ (01684) 772377 ~ Children welcome ~ Open 11.30-3, 6.30-11; 12-10.30 Sun (12-3.30, 6.30-10.30 winter Sun)

BRETFORTON SP0943 Map 4

Fleece ★ ★ £

B4035 E of Evesham: turn S off this road into village; pub is in centre square by church; there's a sizeable car park at one side of the church

There's a new landlord here and they have put in a cigarette machine which we think rather a desecration of this splendid old pub, especially in light of the fact that when she bequeathed it to the National Trust in 1977 Lola Taplin wished traditional ways to be perpetuated and even stipulated that no crisps, peanuts and so forth should be sold. The fine country rooms remain filled with original antique furnishings (readers suggest that these alone are well worth a visit): a great oak dresser holds a priceless 48-piece set of Stuart pewter, there's a fine grandfather clock, ancient kitchen chairs, curved high-backed settles, a rocking chair, and a rack of heavy pointed iron shafts, probably for spit roasting, in one of the huge inglenook fireplaces. There are massive beams and exposed timbers, worn and crazed flagstones (scored with marks to keep out demons), and plenty of oddities such as a great cheese-press and set of cheese moulds, and a rare dough-proving table; a leaflet details the more bizarre items, and there are three warming winter fires. The room with the pewter is no smoking. Well kept Cannon Royall Buckshot, M & B Brew XI, Highgate Fox's Nob, Hook Norton Bitter, Uley Old Spot and Pigs Ear, on handpump, over a dozen country wines and farm cider. Simple generously served bar food (which may be a bit slow on busy days owing to limited kitchen facilities) is ordered through a hatch and includes sandwiches (from £1.70), ploughman's (from £3.60), chilli (£3.70), lasagne or ratatouille lasagne (£4.50), steak and kidney pie or chicken and leek pie (£4.75), locally cured gammon (£5.50), and steak (£6.50); puddings such as cheesecake or apple pie and cream (from £2). Darts, cribbage, dominoes, shove-ha'penny. In summer, when it gets very busy, they make the most of the extensive orchard, with seats on the goat-cropped grass that spreads around the beautifully restored thatched and timbered barn, among the fruit trees, and at the front by the stone pump-trough. There's also an adventure playground, an aviary, and an enclosure with geese and goats. There may be Morris dancing and they hold the village fête and annual asparagus auctions at the end of May; annual beer festival in July. *(Recommended by Peter and Audrey Dowsett, Mike and Hazel Lyons, JP, PP, Gwen and Peter Andrews, Andy and Jill Kassube, Mrs G Connell, Greg Kilminster, Alan Eames, Peter Baggott, Nick and Meriel Cox, Sheila and John French, Chris Reeve, Denys Gueroult, Chris and Andy Crow, Liz Bell, Tom Evans, Michael and Hazel Lyons; more reports on the new regime please)*

Free house ~ Licensee: Graham Brown ~ Real ale ~ Meals and snacks ~ (01386) 831173 ~ Children welcome ~ Open 11-3, 6-11; 11-11 Sat; 12-3, 6-10.30 Sun

BRIMFIELD SO5368 Map 4

Roebuck

Village signposted just off A49 Shrewsbury—Leominster

Whilst the gentle relaxed atmosphere has been retained at this smart country dining pub the food has veered towards the upmarket in terms of both complexity of the dishes and price. The stylish bar menu now includes starters such as soup (£2.95), duo of duck pâtés, gin-cured salmon with crème fraîche, or creamy garlic mushrooms with boursin in a puff pastry case (£5.25); main courses might include steamed pigeon suet pudding (£6.95), steamed steak and mushroom suet pudding (£7.25), pork fillet stuffed with apricots served with an orange sauce or pan-fried duck breast with a fresh raspberry, honey and lime sauce (£10.95), moroccan spiced lamb wrapped in spinach and filo (£11.25) and fillet steak with a red wine and shallot jus (£11.25). The interesting reasonably priced wine list is sourced from several merchants, also well kept Morland Old Speckled Hen, Tetleys and a guest like Greene King Abbot on handpump; local farmhouse cider. The quiet and old-fashioned locals snug has an impressive inglenook fireplace, and two other quietly civilised bars have decorative plates mounted over dark ply panelling and a small open fire. Kind intelligent landlord and caring, pleasant staff; dominoes, cribbage and shove-ha'penny; piped music; no-smoking dining room. Seats outside on the enclosed terrace. *(Recommended by Helen Pickering, James Owen, Liz Bell, J H Jones, Rob Whittle, Mike and Wena Stevenson, Arthur and Margaret Dickinson, Jacquie and Jim Jones, R Davies)*

Free house ~ Licensees David and Sue Willson-Lloyd ~ Real ale ~ Meals and snacks ~ Restaurant ~ (01584) 711230 ~ Children welcome ~ Open 11.30-3, 6-11; 12-3, 7-10.30 Sun ~ Bedrooms: £45B/£60B

CAREY SO5631 Map 4

Cottage of Content

Village signposted from good road through Hoarwithy

This very pretty and out-of-the-way medieval country cottage is charmingly set, with picnic-sets on the flower-filled front terrace and a couple more on a back terrace looking up a steep expanse of lawn, and just the little lane running past by a stream. Inside there are characterful rooms with a nice mix of country furnishings – stripped pine, country kitchen chairs, long pews by one big table and a mix of other old-fashioned tables. One room has flagstones, another bare boards, and there are plenty of beams and prints; darts and dominoes. Readers have found all tables laid for dining at weekends, when it is advisable to book. Daily specials might include vegetarian dishes (£5.50), pie of the day (£5.95), fresh fish and game in season (£8.50-£12.50), or saltmarsh lamb in season (£12.50). Well kept Hook Norton Best on handpump, around 80 wines by the bottle and 40 malt whiskies. The two samoyed dogs are called Shadow and Storm. *(Recommended by Mrs G Connell, David Edwards, Andy and Jill Kassube, G Washington, J Goodrich, Wayne Brindle, Chris Philip, David Peakall, Denys Gueroult, Dr M Smith)*

Free house ~ Licensee Mike Wainford ~ Real ale ~ Meals and snacks (till 10pm Fri and Sat) ~ Restaurant ~ (01432) 840242 ~ Well behaved children welcome ~ Open 12-2.30, 7-11(10.30 Sun); cl Mon and Tues lunchtime in winter and 25 Dec ~ Bedrooms: £35B/£48B

> If you see cars parked in the lane outside a country pub have left their lights on at night, leave yours on too: it's a sign that the police check up there.

DEFFORD SO9143 Map 4

Monkey House

Woodmancote; A4104 towards Upton – immediately after passing Oak public house on right, there's a small group of cottages, of which this is the last

The only sign that this pretty black and white thatched cottage is a pub is a notice by the door saying 'Licensed to sell cider and tobacco'. More accurately it is one of the few remaining absolutely traditional cider-houses – very cheap Bulmer's Medium or Special Dry cider is tapped from barrels and poured by jug into pottery mugs and served from a hatch beside the door. Beer is sold in cans – a concession to modern tastes. They don't do food (except crisps and nuts), but allow you to bring your own. In good weather, you can stand outside in the garden with Anna the bull terrier and Tapper the jack russell, and hens and cockerels that wander in from an adjacent collection of caravans and sheds; there's also a pony called Mandy. Alternatively you can retreat to a small and spartan side outbuilding with a couple of plain tables, a settle and an open fire; darts and dominoes. The name came from a drunken customer some years ago who fell into bramble bushes and insisted he was attacked by monkeys. *(Recommended by Pete Baker; more reports please)*

Free house ~ Licensee Graham Collins ~ (01386) 750234 ~ Children welcome in one room ~ Open 11-2.30, 6-10.30; 12-2, 7-10.30 Sun, closed Mon evening, all day Tues

DORSTONE SO3141 Map 6

Pandy

Pub signed off B4348 E of Hay on Wye

Said to be the oldest in the county, this half-timbered pub was built in 1185 by Richard de Brico to house workers constructing a chapel of atonement for his part in the murder of Thomas à Becket. The neatly kept main room (on the right as you go in) is friendly and welcoming with heavy beams in the ochre ceiling, stout timbers, upright chairs on its broad worn flagstones and in its various alcoves, and a vast open fireplace with logs; no-smoking area; a side extension has been kept more or less in character. The cats are called Amadeus, Mellow and Elsie. Well liked and reasonably priced bar food includes sandwiches (with chips £2.95), soup (£2.25), hummus and hot pitta bread (£3.25), smoked salmon mousse (£3.75), ploughman's (£4.95), crêpes filled with broccoli and pecan nuts or indian-style garlic chicken (£6.25), steak and kidney or wild rabbit pie (£6.75), lamb and apricot casserole (£6.95), and local steaks (from £9.25). Well kept Bass and Wye Valley HPA on handpump, lots of malt whiskies and all the Irish ones; darts, quoits, maybe piped music. Surrounded by pretty countryside, there are picnic-sets and a play area in the neat side garden. *(Recommended by G Robinson, David Gregory, Victoria Herriott, N H E Lewis, C Park, Ian Jones)*

Free house ~ Licensees Chris and Margaret Burtonwood ~ Real ale ~ Meals and snacks ~ (01981) 550273 ~ Children welcome ~ Open 12-3, 7-11(10.30 Sun)

KEMPSEY SO8548 Map 4

Walter de Cantelupe 🍷

Main Road; 3¾ miles from M5 junction 7: A44 towards Worcester, left on to A4440, then left on to A38 to roundabout

There is a friendly and welcoming atmosphere at this roadside pub where a great deal of care and effort goes into the imaginative bar food menu. On offer there might be sandwiches (from £1.95), soup with locally baked bread (£2.35), hot soft roes with a shallot, white wine and cream sauce (£3.50), smooth chicken liver pâté spiked with brandy and served with redcurrant jelly and hot toast (£3.25), lamb, mint and date pie (£5.80), roasted peppers, wild mushroom and fennel stroganoff (£5.90), lamb liver and bacon with onion gravy (£6.20), steak and mushroom pie (£6.25), chicken breast stuffed with stilton, wrapped in bacon and served with a white wine sauce (£6.95), steaks (from £7.20), baked smoked haddock with red onions, lemon and cream (£7.35), and puddings (£2.50); good value Sunday lunch

(£7.20 for 2 courses, £8.50 for 3); no-smoking dining area. Over the last year the interior has been boldly redecorated in deep red and gold; the dining area is pleasantly furnished with a mix of plush or yellow leather dining chairs, an old settle, a sonorous clock and candles and flowers on the tables. The bar side is friendly and relaxed, with an informal mix of furniture, a couple of steps up to a carpeted area, an old wind-up HMV gramophone and a good big fireplace. Well kept Marstons Bitter, Timothy Taylor Landlord, Woods Shropshire Lad and frequently changing guest beers on handpump, good choice of wines by the glass (they import direct from Italy and have regularly changing bin ends as well as English wines from a local vineyard); hard-working young landlord – and no music or games machines; cribbage. There are tables in a pretty walled garden at the back, and the friendly labrador Monti may be around. *(Recommended by G Coates, M Joyner, Michael Coates, Mike and Mary Carter)*

Free house ~ Licensee Martin Lloyd-Morris ~ Real ale ~ Meals and snacks (till 10pm Fri and Sat; not Mon or winter Sun evenings) ~ Restaurant ~ (01905) 820572 ~ Children welcome till 8.15 in eating area ~ Open 11.30-2.30, 6-11; 12-3, 7-10.30 Sun; cl Mon except bank holidays

KIDDERMINSTER SO8376 Map 4

King & Castle £

Railway Station, Comberton Hill

Not only a cheery and welcoming pub, this is also a fascinating re-creation of a classic station refreshment room, set on the terminus of Britain's most lively private steam railway and perfectly conjuring up the feel of a better-class Edwardian establishment that has unbent a little to greet the more informal ways of the 1920s. The cheery good-humoured landlady and her friendly staff cope well with the bustle of bank holidays and railway gala days (when it can be very difficult to find a seat). Furnishings are solid and in character (even to the occasional obvious need for a touch of re-upholstery), and there is the railway memorabilia that you would expect. The atmosphere is lively and sometimes noisily good-humoured (and again in character can sometimes be rather smoky). With steam trains right outside, some railway-buff readers are quite content to start and end their journeys right here; others have used a Rover ticket to shuttle happily between here and the Railwaymans Arms in Bridgnorth (see Shropshire chapter). Either way you can take your pint outside on to the platform and watch the trains steam by. They serve well kept Bathams and Marstons Pedigree and two guests such as Enville, Wye Valley or Wyre Piddle on handpump, Addlestone's farm cider and a wide choice of straightforward good value bar food such as filled rolls (£1.50), filled baked potatoes (from £2.25), ploughman's (£4.35), lasagne (£4.25), beef and beer pie (£4.75) and chicken kiev (£4.95). *(Recommended by John C Baker, Phil Putwain, John Price, Andy and Jill Kassube)*

Free House ~ Licensee Rosemarie Hyde ~ Real ale ~ Meals and snacks (not Mon-Weds evenings, till 8 Thurs and Fri) ~ (01562) 747505 ~ Children welcome till 9pm ~ Open 11-3, 5-11; 11-11 Sat; 12-10.30 Sun

KNIGHTWICK SO7355 Map 4

Talbot

Knightsford Bridge; B4197 just off A44 Worcester—Bromyard

The well kept This, That, Wot and T'other ales on handpump at this 14th-c coaching inn are brewed locally from hops grown on the licensees' own small farm; also well kept Hobsons Bitter. Many of the ingredients for the almost completely home-made food are also grown on the farm or in the pub's organic garden. Besides sandwiches and ploughman's (£4.25), meals are priced according to the number of courses you have (at lunchtime 1 course £8.95, 2 courses £10.95, 3 courses £12.95, more in the evenings), although we were assured that there was room for flexibility within this. Starters might include celery soup, hot smoked eel or pork orange and cognac pâté; main courses venison pudding, rabbit pie, black-eyed bean stew or pig kidneys; steamed jam pudding or sticky date and toffee pudding; although the food's not cheap readers suggest that the quality and generous helpings give good value; over 25 wines by the glass. The heavily beamed lounge bar has entertaining and rather distinguished coaching and sporting prints and paintings on its butter-coloured walls, a variety of interesting seats from small carved or leatherette armchairs to the winged settles by the tall bow windows, and a vast stove which squats in the big central stone hearth; there's another log fire. The well furnished back public bar has pool on a raised side area, darts, fruit machine, video game and juke box; dominoes and cribbage. There are some old-fashioned seats outside, in front, with more on a good-sized lawn over the lane by the river (they serve out here too); boules. Some of the bedrooms are above the bar. *(Recommended by Eddie Walder, Stephen and Tracey Groves, Rob Whittle, Dr Stephen Feast, Ian Jones, Mavis and Robert Harford, John Bowdler)*

Free house ~ Licensee A C Clift ~ Real ale ~ Meals and snacks ~ Restaurant ~ (01886) 821235 ~ Children welcome ~ Open 11-11(11.30 Sat); 12-10.30 Sun; cl evening 25 Dec ~ Bedrooms: £30(£37B)/£50(£67.50B)

LEDBURY SO7138 Map 4

Feathers

High Street, Ledbury, A417

Although this elegant and striking timbered inn increasingly styles itself more as a hotel than a pub, there is a congenial mix of drinkers and diners in the atmospheric and rather civilised Fuggles bar, with locals gathered at one end of the room or at stools by the bar counter, uninhibited by those enjoying the imaginative food and fine wines. There are some very snug and cosy tables with nicely upholstered seats with bays around them off to one side, as well as beams and timbers, hop bines, some country antiques, 19th-c caricatures and fowl prints on the stripped brick chimney breast (lovely winter fire), and fresh flowers on the tables. Very attractively presented good food includes home-made soup (£3.25), stir-fry button mushrooms with cumin, cashews and soy (£4.25), warm grilled pear on a watercress and walnut salad with blue cheese gratin (£4.25), garlic and herb tagliatelle with chilli prawns and sun-dried tomatoes (£4.25) and main courses such as hamburgers (£7.25), salmon and cumin fishcakes (£7.95), wild mushrooms and ricotta filo parcel (£9.50), chicken supreme filled wtih fresh basil leaves and garlic cheese (£11.75), walnut coated lamb cutlets (£12.25), spiced tenderloin of pork with cranberry and orange suace (£12.95) and home-made puddings such as very sticky toffee pudding with butterscotch sauce or dark chocolate and orange truffle pot with Grand Marnier sauce (all £4.25); friendly, attentive service. They do excellent if not cheap afternoon teas in the more formal quiet lounge by the reception area with comfortable high-sided armchairs and sofas in front of a big log fire, and newspapers to read. Well kept Bass, Everards Tiger Best, Fullers London Pride, Shepherd Neame Spitfire and Worthington Best on handpump, a fine wine list, various malt whiskies, and farm cider. Abundant pots and hanging baskets adorn the lawn at the back, they have their own squash courts and more bedrooms have been added this year. *(Recommended by Tim and Linda Collins, Liz Bell, NWN, Paul and Sandra Embleton, Stephen and Tracey Groves, Andy and Jill Kassube, P Lloyd, Tony Beaulah, June and Mike Coleman, K J Jeavons, A Turner, G S and E M Dorey, Alan and Paula McCully, John and Christine Lowe, Helen Morton, Denys Gueroult, Chris Philip, Mavis and Robert Harford, John Bowdler, Pamela and Merlyn Horswell, W A and S Rinaldi-Butcher, Joan and Tony Walker)*

Free house ~ Licensee David Elliston ~ Real ale ~ Meals and snacks (till 10pm Fri/Sat) ~ Restaurant ~ (01531) 635266 ~ Children welcome in eating area of bar ~ Jazz/blues/folk jazz Weds evening ~ Open 11-11; 12-10.30 Sun ~ Bedrooms: £69.50B/£89.50B

If we know a pub does sandwiches we always say so – if they're not mentioned, you'll have to assume you can't get one.

LONGDON SO8336 Map 4

Hunters 🍷

B4211 S

Beautifully set in five and a half acres of grounds (complete with its own helicopter landing pad), although rather grand from the outside, this civilised pub has a relaxed, friendly atmosphere in its bar rooms. On the right as you go in there are two comfortable armchairs in a bay window, one-person pews and wheelbacks around a mix of tables, a warm open fire, and so forth; on the left is a similarly furnished room with polished flagstones and a big woodburning stove – a small dining room leads off here, and there's a smart heavily beamed restaurant as well. Under the new licensees bar food includes sandwiches (from £2.50), home-made soup (£2.20), button mushrooms in stilton sauce (£3.95), ploughman's (£4.50), steak and kidney pie (£7.25), fresh vegetarian filled pasta in tomato and herb sauce (£6.95), chicken curry (£6.95), salmon with prawns in lobster sauce (£9.25), individual roasted loin of pork or half shoulder of lamb with port, orange and wine sauce (£9.95) and Aylesbury duck with orange and Grand Marnier (£12.95); home-made puddings (£3.75). Well kept and regularly rotating real ales might include Bass, Fullers London Pride, Greene King Abbot Ale, Ledbury Challenger SB, Marstons Pedigree and Thwaites on handpump; 40 malt whiskies, farm cider and good wine by the glass; piped music. The attractive back garden has some picnic-sets on the crazy-paved terrace, with more on the big lawn. *(Recommended by Sue and Steve Griffiths, Andy and Jill Kassube, Mr and Mrs Broadhurst, Joy and Peter Heatherley, J H Kane, John and Moira Cole, S Holder; more reports on the new regime please)*

Free house ~ Licensee Gareth Rees ~ Real ale ~ Meals and snacks ~ Restaurant ~ (01684) 833388 ~ Children welcome in eating area of bar ~ Open 11-3, 6-11; 12-3, 7-10.30 Sun

LUGWARDINE SO5541 Map 4

Crown & Anchor 🍷

Cotts Lane; just off A438 E of Hereford

A friendly and comfortable atmosphere pervades at this attractive old black and white timbered inn. There are several smallish characterful rooms (one suitable for families), with an interesting mix of furnishings and a big log fire. There's well kept Bass, Hobsons Best, Worthington Best and maybe a guest on handpump and decent wines, including a clutch of usefully priced bin ends. Good bar food includes home-made soup (£2.50), deep-fried brie with cranberry sauce (£3.25), ploughman's (£4), battered cod (£4.75), several vegetarian dishes such as mixed bean goulash (£5.50), grilled trout, steak and kidney pie or gammon and egg (£6.50), chicken with apple and brandy sauce (£6.90), chargrilled Herefordshire sirloin steak (£10.00) and quite a few daily specials including game in season; puddings (£2.75), children's menu; small no smoking area. *(Recommended by Prof P A Reynolds, Gary Benjamin, David Edwards, David Gittins)*

Free house ~ Licensees Nick and Julie Squire ~ Real ale ~ Meals and snacks (till 10pm, not 25 Dec) ~ (01432) 851303 ~ Children welcome ~ Jazz first Weds of month ~ Open 11.30-11; 12-10.30 Sun

MUCH MARCLE SO6633 Map 4

Slip Tavern 🍷

Off A449 SW of Ledbury; take Woolhope turning at village stores, then right at pub sign

There is a new landlord at this quiet country pub but we have been assured that they fully intend to continue the tradition of fine horticulture established by their predecessor: the gardens that stretch out behind the building are really quite splendid and full of interesting plants; the hanging baskets and big urns in front are very pretty too. The cosy chatty bar is popular with older people at lunchtime with a more villagey local atmosphere in the evening. There are ladderback and wheelback upholstered chairs around the black tables and little country prints on neat cream walls; well kept Hook Norton Best and Wadworths 6X on handpump; very friendly service. Bar food includes faggots (£5.35), vegetable lasagne (£5.75), lemon sole or cod in parsley (£5.95), steak pie (£6.25), or beef in ale (£7.10). There's more space for eating in the attractively planted conservatory, though it's best to book. There's a well separated play area. *(Recommended by Mr and Mrs I Brown, Derek Stafford, R Michael Richards, June and Malcolm Farmer, P G Topp, Denys Gueroult, Daren Haines, Stephen Pine, Alfred Lawrence; more reports on the new regime please)*

Free house ~ Licensee D Templeman ~ Real ale ~ Meals and snacks ~ Restaurant ~ (01531) 660246 ~ Children welcome in eating area of bar and restaurant ~ Open 11.30-2.30, 6.30-11; 12-2.30, 7-11 Sun

OMBERSLEY SO8463 Map 4

Crown & Sandys Arms 🍷

Coming into the village from the A4133, turn left at the roundabout in middle of village, and pub is on the left

It's the range of consistently well cooked and unusual meals that draws the crowds that gather at this pretty Dutch-gabled white inn on busy evenings. The blackboard menu might include sandwiches (from £1.95), soup (£2.25), smoked salmon terrine (£3.10), ploughman's (from £3.75), prawn cocktail (£3.95), home-cooked ham (£5.50), steak and kidney pie or curry (£5.75), vegetarian quiche (£5.95), cajun chicken (£6.50) and steaks (from £8.95), as well as daily specials which include lots of fresh fish such as sole, hake, tuna, monkfish, and cod, vegetarian dishes, seasonal game, and pot-roast lamb; all served with a choice of chips, new potaotes or a different potato dish which changes each day. The lounge bar has a friendly and welcoming atmosphere, black beams and some flagstones, comfortable windsor armchairs, antique settles, a couple of easy chairs, old prints and maps on its timbered walls, log fires, and daily newspapers; half is no smoking. Two to four well kept real ales rotate constantly and might be from Beowolf, Fullers, Hobsons, Hook Norton, or Woods; around six wines by the glass, litre or half-litre, and country wines. There are picnic-sets in the garden behind the building; no dogs; bedrooms no-smoking. *(Recommended by Ron Fletcher, DAV, Richard and Margaret Peers, Joan and Michel Hooper-Immins, Ian and Jacqui Ross, Dennis Stevens, Mike Gorton, Richard and Robyn Wain, Dr I Crichton, Nigel Clifton, G Robinson, C I Harvey, Colin Draper, A G Drake, G S and E M Dorey, Paul and Maggie Baker, F J Robinson, Alan Morton, Chris Philip, J Boucher, Stephen Pine, Alfred Lawrence, Chris and Shirley Machin, John and Joan Nash)*

Free house ~ Licensee R E Ransome ~ Real ale ~ Meals and snacks (12-2, 6-9.45) ~ Restaurant ~ (01905) 620252 ~ Well behaved children welcome until 7pm ~ Open 11-3, 5.30-11; 12-3, 7-10.30; closed 25 Dec and evenings 26 Dec and 1 Jan ~ Bedrooms: £35S/£55S

Kings Arms 🍴

Reports suggest that, recently taken over by the Quintessential Pub Company, this big black-beamed and timbered Tudor pub is going from strength to strength under new management. The excellent and varied bar food menu includes home-made soup or potato skins with sour cream (£2.50), grilled goat's cheese and bacon salad (£4.25), tortellini with mushrooms, cream, chervil and crusty bread (£5.95), honey-glazed spring chicken (£7.50), pork chop with caramelised shallot and bramley apple (£7.75), turkey steak with mozzarella, avocado, tomato and fresh basil (£7.95), chargrilled sirloin steak with horseradish butter (£8.95) and puddings (£3.50); also blackboard specials which always include fresh fish; all snacks pleasantly served with linen napkins. The comfortably informal rambling rooms have a friendly, bustling feel, and the various cosy nooks and crannies are full of stuffed animals and birds, a collection of rustic bric-a-brac and four open fires; one room has Charles II's coat of arms moulded into its decorated plaster ceiling – he's reputed to have been here in 1651. Well kept Banks's Bitter, Bass, Fullers London Pride, Marstons Pedigree and Wadworths 6X on handpump; no piped music. A tree-sheltered courtyard has tables under cocktail parasols, and colourful hanging baskets and tubs in summer, and there's also a terrace. *(Recommended by G and E Dorey, G Neighbour, Joy and Peter Heatherley, Alan and Paula McCully, Mike and Mary Carter, J Barnwell, D A Norman, P Neate, Mrs C Fielder, Chris Philip, John Bowdler, John and Joan Nash, Denys Gueroult, G S and E M Dorey, Theo, Anne and Jane Gaskin; more reports on the new regime please)*

Free house ~ Manager D Pendry ~ Real ale ~ Meals and snacks (12-2, 6-10) ~ (01905) 620142 ~ Children welcome away from the main bar ~ Open 11-2.30, 5.30-11; 12-2.30, 5.30-10.30 Sun; cl 25 Dec

PENSAX SO7269 Map 4

Bell

B4202 Abberley—Clows Top, S of village

Readers find this roadside mock-Tudor pub welcoming and unpretentious. The friendly landlord is happy to chat about his enthusiasm for real ale – the four handpumps quickly rotate around 500 well kept beers a year including many from small and local breweries; also farmhouse cider. This is by no means exclusively a pub for real-ale fans: the mostly home-made food is served with an impressive range of vegetables and besides sandwiches might include vegetable curry (£4.95), chicken, ham and leek pie, steak and kidney pudding or pork with orange and ginger casserole (£5.75), gammon steak with egg and pineapple or halibut in a light garlic and tomato sauce (£6.50), beef stroganoff (£6.95) and steaks (from £6.95). The L-shaped main bar has a restrained traditional decor, with long cushioned pews on its bare boards, good solid pub tables, and a woodburning stove. Beyond a small carpeted area on the left with a couple more tables is a more airy dining room added in the late 1980s, with french windows opening on to a wooden deck that on hot days can give a slightly Californian feel; it has a log fire for our more usual weather; cribbage, dominoes and piped music; no-smoking restaurant. In the back garden, picnic-sets look out over rolling fields and copses to the Wyre Forest. *(Recommended by Joy and Peter Heatherley, John Bowdler, Mike and Mary Carter, Kerry Law, Hilary Soms, Denise Harbord, Peter and Rosie Flower, Patrick Herratt, Robert Whittle)*

Free house ~ Licensee Graham Titcombe ~ Real ale ~ Meals and snacks ~ Restaurant ~ (01299) 896677 ~ Children welcome in snug and restaurant ~ Open 12-2.30, 5-11; 12-10.30 Sun

RUCKHALL SO4539 Map 4

Ancient Camp

Ruckhall signposted off A465 W of Hereford at Belmont Abbey; from Ruckhall pub signed down private drive; can reach it too from Bridge Sollers, W of Hereford on A438 – cross Wye, then after a mile or so take first left, then left again to Eaton Bishop, and left to Ruckhall

Landslides caused by severe storms at Easter 1998 caused this smart country dining pub to close, but as we went to press repair work was in progress and the friendly licensees assured us that they would soon be fully operational again. There's quite some emphasis on the stylish (not cheap) food which might include spinach and watercress soup (£2.95), home-cured gravadlax with citric dressing (£4.50), chicken liver parfait (£6), crispy duck on celeriac purée with port and orange sauce (£6.50), warm smoked chicken salad (£6.50), fish pie with tomato coulis or fresh dressed selsey crab (£7.50), tenderloin pork with sweet pepper sauce (£12.75), seabass (£13.50) and lamb fillet on rosti with mint béarnaise (£14.50). The very civilised central beamed and flagstoned bar is simply but thoughtfully furnished with comfortably solid green-upholstered settles and library chairs around nice old elm tables. On the left, a green-carpeted room has matching sofas around the walls and kitchen chairs around tripod tables. On the right, there are simple dining chairs around stripped kitchen tables on a brown carpet, and stripped stonework; nice log fire. Well kept Hook Norton Best, Woods Parish and guests on handpump, and fine wines and vintage port; piped classical music; no-smoking restaurant. The long front terrace has tables and chairs among the roses that look down on a picturesque rustic landscape with the River Wye curling gently through the foreground. If you stay the night ask for the room at the front which shares this view; the licensee owns a stretch of the river so you could combine your stay with some fishing. *(Recommended by Richard and Julia Tredgett, Richard and Margaret Peers, Mike and Mary Carter, Chris Philip, Bob Arnett, Judy Wayman, Victoria Herriott, James Andrew, Denys Gueroult)*

Free house ~ Licensees Pauline and Ewart McKie ~ Real ale ~ Meals and snacks (not Mon) ~ Restaurant (not Mon) ~ (01981) 250449 ~ Children welcome lunchtime in eating area of bar ~ Open 12-3, 7-11(10.30 Sun); cl Monday ~ Bedrooms: £45B/£60B

ST OWENS CROSS SO5425 Map 4

New Inn

Harewood End

There are fine views over rolling countryside to the distant Black Mountains from this old timbered black and white coaching inn which is bedecked with colourful hanging baskets in summer. Both the characterful lounge bar and the no-smoking restaurant have huge inglenook fireplaces, intriguing nooks and crannies, settles, old pews, beams, and timbers. Hearty pies such as steak and kidney (£6.45) are the highlight of the bar menu which also includes soup (£2.45), deep-fried brie with cranberry sauce (£3.50), home-made lasagne (£4.95), mushroom and asparagus pancake or gammon steak (£6.95), breast of chicken in a white wine and cream sauce with smoked bacon, garlic, mushrooms and tomatoes (£7.95), whole lemon sole (£8.95), honey roast rack of lamb (£9.95), and steaks (from £10.45); specials board and children's meals; efficient and friendly service. Bass, Fullers London Pride, Smiles Best and Golden Brew, Tetleys Bitter, Wadworths 6X and guest beers on handpump, and a fair choice of malt whiskies; darts, shove-ha'penny, cribbage, dominoes, and piped music. The three dobermans are called Baileys, Tia Maria and Ginnie. *(Recommended by Jill Bickerton, Hugh and Shirley Mortimer, K H Frostick, Mark Percy, Lesley Mayoh, Wayne Brindle, Patrick Freeman, JKW, David Gregory, S P Watkin, P A Taylor, Dr and Mrs R Booth)*

Free house ~ Licensee Nigel Donovan ~ Real ale ~ Meals and snacks ~ Restaurant ~ (01989) 730274 ~ Children welcome ~ Open 12-2.30, 6-11; 12-3, 7-10.30; closed 25 Dec ~ Bedrooms: £40B/£70B

SELLACK SO5627 Map 4

Lough Pool Inn ★ 🍷

Back road Hoarwithy—Ross on Wye; OS Sheet 162 map reference 558268

Readers report a warm welcome at this attractive black and white timbered country cottage with plenty of picnic-sets on its neat front lawn and pretty hanging baskets. The well liked and interesting food menu includes soup (£2.25), stilton and port pâté (£3.35), ploughman's (£3.95), Caribbean fruit curry, gammon with pineapple or home-made steak and kidney pie (£5.95), medallions of pork with a white wine and garlic sauce (£8.75), popular greek-style goat casserole (£9.25), local steaks (from £9.25), daily specials such as wild boar casserole or seafood bake, and puddings like date and walnut pudding or lemon syllabub (from £2.95); the restaurant is no smoking. The beamed central room has kitchen chairs and cushioned window seats around plain wooden tables on the mainly flagstoned floor, sporting prints and bunches of dried flowers, and a log fire at each end. Other rooms lead off, with attractive individual furnishings and nice touches like the dresser of patterned plates. Well kept Bass, John Smiths and Wye Valley Hereford on handpump, as well as a good range of malt whiskies, local farm ciders and a well chosen reasonably priced wine list; piped classical music. *(Recommended by Bernard Stradling, Richard and Jean Phillips, Neil and Anita Christopher, Dr J A Harvey, Daren Haines, Ted George, Dr M Smith, June and Malcolm Farmer, Dorothy and Leslie Pilson, Pamela and Merlyn Horswell, S P Watkin, P A Taylor, JKW, Mark Percy, Lesley Mayoh, Wayne Brindle, D H and M C Watkinson)*

Free house ~ Licensees Malcolm and Janet Hall ~ Real ale ~ Meals and snacks ~ Restaurant ~ (01989) 730236 ~ Children welcome in restaurant and snug ~ Open 11.30-2.30, 6.30-11; 12-2.30, 7-10.30 Sun; cl 25 Dec, evening 26 Dec

STOCKTON CROSS SO5161 Map 4

Stockton Cross Inn

Kimbolton; A4112, off A49 just N of Leominster

There is an excellent range of enjoyable food at this beautifully kept black and white timbered pub. The blackboard menu includes rabbit caught by Percy the local rabbit catcher which the landlady prepares in so many enterprising ways (rabbit casserole £8.95) that a local radio station runs slots with her recipes; also vegetable rosti with red cabbage and apples (£7.50), gammon steak (£8.25), steaks (from £8.50), chicken breast with brandy, orange and tarragon sauce (£8.95), wild duck with port and damsons (£10.95), mixed grill or wild venison with port and red wine (£11.50) and tenderloin of pork filled with spinach, wrapped in bacon and served with a cream and white wine sauce (£11.95). The long heavily beamed bar's old-fashioned feel is perhaps at its best on a cold winter's day, when it's really snug at the top end: a handsome antique settle facing an old black kitchen range, and old leather chairs and brocaded stools by the huge log fire in the broad stone fireplace. There's a woodburning stove at the far end too, with heavy cast-iron-framed tables and sturdy dining chairs; there are more tables and chairs up a step in a small no-smoking side area. Old-time prints, a couple of épées on one beam and lots of copper and brass complete the picture.Well kept Flowers Original, Whitbreads Castle Eden and a guest on handpump; good welcoming service; no-smoking eating area; tables out in the garden, with maybe a fine summer show of sweet peas. It can get busy at weekends. *(Recommended by W C Jones; more reports please)*

Free house ~ Licensee Mr R Wood ~ Real ale ~ Meals and snacks ~ (01568) 612509 ~ Well behaved children welcome in eating area of bar (must be over 6 on weekdays) ~ Open 12-3, 7-11; cl Mon evening

ULLINGSWICK SO5949 Map 4

Three Crowns 🍷

Village off A465 S of Bromyard (and just S of Stoke Lacy) and signposted off A417; pub at Bleak Acre, towards Little Cowarne

Readers report this to be a successful combination of a pub and restaurant, with the landlord dressed in full chef's clothing producing excellent food and dispensing beer to the local farmers. As well as a few lunchtime sandwiches and snacks the extensive seasonally changing menu might include cauliflower and lovage soup (£3.50), monkfish and scallops on a rosemary stick with courgettes, anchovy and rosemary sauce (£4.75), ratatouille pancake gateau (£7), grilled chicken breast with polenta, mozzarella and dragoncello (£10), well liked rack of lamb with braised chick peas and garlic sauce (£11), grilled ribeye steak with salsa verde and chorizo potatoes (£12), or bouillaibaisse (£13); they grow their own vegetables and other produce is purchased locally. The charmingly cosy traditional interior has hops strung along the low beams of its smallish bar, a couple of traditional settles besides more usual seats, open fires and one or two gently sophisticated touches like candles on tables and napkins; half is no smoking. Service is very welcoming; well kept Hobsons Best, Tetleys and a guest on handpump; farmhouse cider and good house wines; cribbage. There are tables out on the lawn, not large but attractively planted, with good summer views. An extension with four bedrooms is planned – we await reports. *(Recommended by Chris Philip, John Hackett; more reports please)*

Free house ~ Licensees Derrick and Sue Horwood and Brent Castle ~ Real ale ~ Meals and snacks (no sandwiches or snacks evenings and Sun lunchtime ~ (01432) 820279 ~ Open 12-2.30, 7-11; 12-3, 7-10.30 Sun; closed Tues

Children welcome means the pubs says it lets children inside without any special restriction; readers have found that some may impose an evening time limit – please tell us if you find this.

UPTON BISHOP SO6527 Map 4

Moody Cow

2 miles from M50 junction 3 westbound (or junction 4 eastbound), via B4221; continue on B4221 to rejoin at next junction

Set in the quiet village of Upton Bishop this friendly pub has several snug separate areas angling in an L around the bar counter, a pleasant medley of stripped country furniture, stripped floorboards and stonework, a few cow ornaments and naive cow paintings, and a big log fire. On the far right is a biggish no-smoking restaurant, rustic and candlelit, with hop-draped rafters and a fireside area with armchairs and sofas. The far left has a second smaller dining area, just five or six tables with rush seats, green-stained woodwork, shelves of country china; piped music. The large and changing choice of well cooked food might include starters like soup (£3.65), stilton and garlic stuffed mushrooms wrapped in filo pastry with a basil and tomato sauce (£4.65), and main courses like lasagne (£4.95), chilli (£6.45), battered cod and chips in newspaper (£6.95), steak, kidney, sprouts, carrots, potatoes and gravy pie (£7.75), wild oyster mushroom risotto (£7.75), lamb liver and bacon (£9.75), steaks (from £7.95) and breast of duck with a sweet blackberry sauce (£13.95); puddings (£2.95) include bread and butter pudding and home-made ice creams; pleasant service. Boddingtons, Flowers IPA, Smiles Best, and Wadworths 6X on handpump. ***(Recommended by Mike and Mary Carter, Neil and Anita Christopher, Steve Marchant, David Ling, D H and M C Watkinson)***

Free house ~ Licensee James Lloyd ~ Real ale ~ Meals and snacks (not Sun lunchtime or Mon) ~ Restaurant ~ (01989) 780470 ~ Well behaved children welcome ~ Jazz Thurs evening ~ Open 12-2.30, 6.30-11; 12-3, 7-10.30 Sun; cl Mon lunchtime

WALTERSTONE SO3425 Map 6

Carpenters Arms

Village signposted off A465 E of Abergavenny, beside Old Pandy Inn; follow village signs, and keep eyes skinned for sign to pub, off to right, by lane-side barn; OS Sheet 161, map reference 340250

With a friendly landlady who always has time for a chat, this delightful little stone cottage is the best sort of unspoilt homely country tavern. There are ancient settles against stripped stone walls, some pieces of carpet on broad polished flagstones, a roaring log fire in a gleaming black range (complete with pot-iron, hot water tap, bread oven and salt cupboard), pewter mugs hanging from beams, well kept Wadworths 6X and one of their seasonal ales tapped from the cask, farm cider, the slow tick of a clock, a big vase of flowers on the dresser in the snug dining room with its mahogany tables and oak corner cupboards, and the promising aroma of stock simmering in the kitchen. Food might include rolls and sandwiches (from £1.60), soup (£2.50), prawn cocktail (£2.80), ploughman's (£3.50), sausage and chips (£3.50), vegetarian chilli (£4.50), beef curry (£5), scampi (£5), lamb chop with redcurrant sauce (£8.50) and pepper fillet steak (£10); puddings (£2.50). There's a separate pool room with fruit machine and juke box; the outside lavatories are cold but in character. ***(Recommended by John Cockell; more reports please)***

Free house ~ Licensee Vera Watkins ~ Real ale ~ Meals and snacks (12-3, 7-10) ~ (01873) 890353 ~ Children welcome ~ Open 11-11; 12-10.30 Sun

WEOBLEY SO4052 Map 6

Olde Salutation

Village signposted from A4112 SW of Leominster; and from A44 NW of Hereford (there's also a good back road direct from Hereford – straight out past S side of racecourse)

Hereford and Worcestershire Dining Pub of the Year

This beautifully kept 500-year-old hotel is popular for its lovely setting, atmospheric well equipped bedrooms and good bar food. The changing menu might include soup (£2.75), filled french bread (from £3.50), deep-fried brie wedges with a redcurrant and port wine sauce (£4.65), ploughman's (from £4.95), lamb liver and bacon

(£6.25), steak and stout pie, gammon steak with egg and pineapple or leek and mushroom strudel (£6.50), thai chicken curry £6.75), pheasant with red wine, mushrooms and herbs or salmon (£7.95) and steak (£10.75); lovely home-made puddings include apple tart with a walnut crumble and calvados ice cream (£3.85), bread and butter pudding with apricot purée (£3.95); well cooked and generous breakfasts; efficient service. The two areas of the quiet, comfortable lounge – separated by a few steps and standing timbers – have a relaxed, pubby feel, brocaded modern winged settles and smaller seats, a couple of big cut-away cask seats, wildlife decorations, a hop bine over the bar counter, and logs burning in a big stone fireplace; more standing timbers separate it from the neat no-smoking restaurant area, and there's a separate smaller parquet-floored public bar with sensibly placed darts, juke box, and a fruit machine; dominoes and cribbage. Well kept Hook Norton Best, Fullers London Pride and a guest on handpump, an interesting extensive wine list and quite a good collection of whiskies. On a sheltered back terrace are tables and chairs with parasols. The village is pretty and quaint – even the bus shelter is black and white timbered. *(Recommended by Dr Stephen Feast, Mike and Wena Stevenson, Mr and Mrs McKay, Steve Whalley, Courtney and Elaine West, Dorothee and Dennis Glover, Peter Shaw, Karen Naylor, P M Potter, Denys Gueroult, JKW, MRSM, Mrs Jill Jones, Chris Philip, Victoria Herriott, Nigel Clifton, Mrs J E Hilditch, Andrew Shore, Mr and Mrs D Jackson, Glenn and Gillian Miller, Ian Jones, P P and J Salmon, Wayne Brindle, David Gregory; also in the Good Hotel Guide)*

Free house ~ Licensees Chris and Frances Anthony ~ Real ale ~ Meals and snacks ~ Restaurant ~ (01544) 318443 ~ Children welcome in eating area of bar ~ Open 11-11; 12-10.30 Sun; closed 25 Dec ~ Bedrooms: £40B/£65B

WINFORTON SO2947 Map 6

Sun

Mrs Hibbard does the cooking at this neatly kept little dining pub where the wide ranging menu changes daily but might include cream of watercress and spinach soup (£2.95), camembert filo parcels with elderflower and cranberry sauce (£3.85), warm salad of local woodpigeon, bacon and mushrooms (£4.99), wild mushrooms and spinach strudel (£6.50), maize fed guinea fowl with wild mushroom sauce (£9.75) and half shoulder of welsh lamb with cider, leek and lentil gravy (£11.99); puddings (£3.85) include goosberry and elderflower fool and tipsy bread and butter pudding with hot fruit compote. The two friendly beamed areas on either side of the central servery have an individual assortment of comfortable country-kitchen chairs, high-backed settles and good solid wooden tables, heavy-horse harness, brasses and old farm tools on the mainly stripped stone walls, and two log-burning stoves; no-smoking area. Well kept Brains Bitter, Morlands Old Speckled Hen and Charles Wells Bombardier on handpump, several malt whiskies, and local cider; sensibly placed darts, cribbage, dominoes, maybe piped music. As well as sheltered tables and a good play area the garden has an 18 hole pitch-and-putt/crazy golf course. *(Recommended by Sarah and Peter Gooderham, Mrs L Minchella, P Mapstone; more reports please)*

Free house ~ Licensees Brian and Wendy Hibbard ~ Real ale ~ Meals and snacks (not Tues) ~ (01544) 327677 ~ Children welcome in eating area of bar ~ Open 11-3, 6-11; closed Tues and 2 weeks in Jan ~ Bedrooms: £30B/£48B

WOOLHOPE SO6136 Map 4

Butchers Arms

Signposted from B4224 in Fownhope; carry straight on past Woolhope village

The friendly new licensees assure us that they will continue to run this relaxed and atmospheric place very much along the same lines as their predecessors; reports suggest that apart from a lick of paint little has changed in the spaciously welcoming bars. One has very low beams decorated with hops, old-fashioned well worn built-in seats with brocaded cushions, captain's chairs and stools around small tables and a brick fireplace filled with dried flowers. The other, broadly similar though with less beams, has a large built-in settle and another log fire; there are often fresh flowers. Good bar food includes home-made soup (£2.95), chicken liver pâté cooked with brandy (£3.95), ploughman's (from £4.25), mushroom, butterbean and basil stew or breaded plaice (£4.95), lasagne (£5.75), venison sausages and mash or chicken curry (£6.25), home-made steak and kidney or well liked rabbit and cider pie (£6.50), gammon steak (£7.25) and rump steak (£8.95); puddings include treacle tart (£2.95) and chocolate brandy cake (£3.25); good breakfasts; the restaurant is no smoking. Well kept Hook Norton Best and Old Hookey, Woodhampton Kingfisher and Wye Valley Bitter on handpump, local ciders, quite a few malt whiskies, and decent wines. Sliding french windows lead from the bar to a little terrace with teak furniture, a few parasols and cheerful flowering tubs; there's also a tiny willow-lined brook. The countryside around is really lovely – to enjoy some of the best of it, turn left as you come out of the pub and take the tiny left-hand road at the end of the car park; this turns into a track and then into a path; the view from the top of the hill is quite something. *(Recommended by Martin Wyss, David Gittins, Paul and Sue Merrick, J Goodrich, Don Bryan, Tony Beaulah, Andy and Jill Kassube, Lynn Sharpless, Bob Eardley, D A Norman, Sarah and Peter Gooderham, Mike and Mary Carter, Daren Haines, John Bowdler, Chris Philip, Wayne Brindle, Ian and Nita Cooper, Luke Worthington, Denys Gueroult, Dr M Smith, JKW, Gwen and Peter Andrews; more reports on the new regime please)*

Free house ~ Licensees Sian and Mark Vallely ~ Real ale ~ Meals and snacks ~ Restaurant ~ (01432) 860281 ~ Children welcome ~ Open 11.30-3, 6-11; 12-3, 7-10.30 Sun; cl evening 25 Dec ~ Bedrooms: £32/£42

Crown 🍷

In village centre

There are picnic-sets under cocktail parasols on the neat front lawn of this carefully managed old pub, and in summer they play quoits. The neatly kept lounge bar has plush button-back built-in wall banquettes and dark wood tables and chairs. There's also an open fire, a timbered divider strung with hop bines, good wildlife photographs and little country pictures on the cream walls, and lots of attention to details like flowers on tables; darts. The good value and very extensive bar menu includes home-made soup (£2.25), home-made potted stilton with mushrooms (£3.75), deep-fried camembert with raspberry sauce (£4.50), ploughman's (from £4.50), stilton, apple walnut pasta bake (£5.95), steak and kidney pie, chilli or sweet and sour chicken (£6.20), home-made fish pie or gammon steak (£6.50), home-made salmon and broccoli au gratin (£7.20), steaks (from £8.95) and mixed grill (£10.20); home-made puddings (£2.95) include apple, cinnamon and walnut cake with custard and summer pudding; the dining area is no smoking. Well kept Hook Norton Best, Smiles Best, Tetleys Bitter and a guest beer on handpump, decent wine list, and farm cider. *(Recommended by D A Norman, Andy and Jill Kassube, David Ling, Chris Philip, Wayne Brindle, Denys Gueroult, Daren Haines)*

Free house ~ Licensees Neil and Sally Gordon ~ Real ale ~ Meals and snacks (till 10pm, not 25 Dec) ~ Restaurant ~ (01432) 860468 ~ Well behaved children welcome in eating areas till 8pm, though customers are asked to check beforehand because of limited space ~ Open 12-2.30, 6.30(6 Sat)-11; 12-3, 6.30-10.30 Sun; winter evening opening 7; cl evening 25 Dec

WYRE PIDDLE SO9647 Map 4

Anchor

B4084 NW of Evesham

The spacious lawn behind this 17th-c pub runs down to the River Avon, offering ringside seats for the kind of blissfully unspectacular activities that on a lazy day seem so compelling: summer barges tying up on the moorings alongside, or ducks scuttling about on the water. Beyond there are views spreading out over the Vale of Evesham as far as the Cotswolds, the Malverns and Bredon Hill. The friendly and well kept little lounge has a good log fire in its attractively restored inglenook fireplace, comfortably upholstered chairs and settles, and two beams in the shiny ceiling; the big airy back bar affords the same marvellous views as the lawn. Good bar food (as all food is cooked to order service can be a little slow when they are very busy in the summer months) includes soup (£2.75), filled baps and french bread (from £3), home-made chicken, mushroom and brandy pâté (£3.95), ploughman's (from £4.25), moules marinières (£5.25), lasagne (£5.75), steak and kidney pie or Caribbean fruity vegetable curry (£6.25), gammon steak (£7.75) and steaks (from £11); blackboard specials include a selection of Indian dishes and seasonal asparagus dishes; home-made puddings (£2.50). Well kept Boddingtons, Banks's Best, Flowers Best and Original and Marstons Pedigree under light blanket pressure, a few whiskies, and country wines; fruit machine. *(Recommended by G Braithwaite, Iona L Thomson, Pat and Tony Martin, Ian and Nita Cooper, J and P Daggett, S H Godsell, Brian and Anna Marsden, Mark Fennell, Mavis and Robert Harford, Nick Lawless, Sheila Keene)*

Whitbreads ~ Lease: Michael Senior ~ Real ale ~ Meals and snacks ~ River-view restaurant (not Sun evening) ~ (01386) 552799 ~ Children welcome ~ Open 11-2.30, 6-11; 12-3, 6-11 Sat; 12-3, 7-10.30 Sun

Lucky Dip

Besides the fully inspected pubs, you might like to try these Lucky Dips recommended to us and described by readers (if you do, please send us reports):

Aston Crews [SO6723], *Penny Farthing*: Partly 15th c, roomy and relaxing, lots of beams with horsebrasses, harness and farm tools, well in bar with skeleton at bottom; good choice of food inc interesting puddings, well kept Marstons, decent wines, good service, easy chairs, log fires, two restaurant areas, one with pretty valley and Forest of Dean views (shared by tables in charming garden), subdued piped music; bedrooms *(Andrew and Celia Rose, BB)*

Baughton [A4104; SO8742], *Gay Dog*: Wide range of delicious food cooked by landlord inc mouth-watering puddings, reasonable prices, friendly atmosphere, good wines, well kept beer; two comfortable sensibly priced bedrooms *(Anon)*

Belbroughton [SO9277], *Holly Bush*: Comfortable beamed pub with food inc Sun roast, Tetleys and Woods Shropshire Lad; no music *(James Nunn)*

☆ **Bewdley** [31 High St; SO7875], *Little Pack Horse*: Ancient low-beamed heavily timbered building, cosily pubby and bustling, with candles and woodburner, masses of inriguing bric-a-brac and old photographs and advertisements, pleasant mix of old furnishings, good value food; now owned by Ushers, but still has Ind Coope Burton, and its trademark Little Puck and Lumphammer – and the same manager; children in eating area, open all day w/e; only reason this nice and very individual pub misses the main entries this year is a lack of recent reports *(Roger and Pauline Pearce, Dorothee and Dennis Glover, Peter and Audrey Dowsett, Daren Haines, Peter and Rosie Flower, LYM)*

Bewdley [64 Load St; SO7477], *George*: Handy for Severn Valley Rly, with breakfasts and light snacks from 10 am as well as bar lunches; bedrooms *(DMT)*

Bournheath [Doctors Hill; SO9474], *Nailers Arms*: Useful refurbished Big Steak pub, with wide choice of reasonably priced specials, well kept beers, very courteous staff, safely enclosed play area, extra terrace seating for those without children *(Ian Shorthouse)*

☆ **Bransford** [Powick rd; off A4103 SW of Worcester; SO7852], *Bear & Ragged Staff*: Largely a dining pub (but still keeping darts and other traditional games), with country views from relaxed interconnecting rooms inc no-smoking restaurant; has had good food, Boddingtons and Wadworths 6X and a good range of other drinks, and a welcome for children, but no reports since it changed hands towards the end of last year *(LYM)*

☆ **Broadway** [Church St; SP0937], *Crown & Trumpet*: Cosy unspoilt beamed and timbered local with dark high-backed settles, big log fire, well kept Boddingtons, Flowers IPA and Original, Morlands Old Speckled Hen, local Stanway and Wadworths 6X, seasonal made drinks, good value home-made food, cheerful efficient staff, good range of pub games but also intrusive fruit machine and piped music; Thurs quiz night, Sat duo; children welcome, open all day Sat, seats on front terrace; bedrooms *(David and Nina Pugsley, Meg and Colin Hamilton, Norma and David Hardy, Nick Lawless, SLC, LYM)*

☆ **Broadway** [Collin Lane; follow Willersey sign off A44 NW – marked Gt Collin Farm on OS Sheet 150 map ref 076391], *Collin House*: Wide choice of good interesting freshly done bar food inc traditional puddings in lovely bar of small country hotel, very relaxed and civilised – good log fires, no machines or piped music (but no sandwiches or ploughman's either), very accommodating; nice restaurant not overpriced (wise to book), good wines, local beers, proper coffee, pleasant staff; tables outside; comfortable bedrooms *(IHR)*

Broadway [High St (A44)], *Lygon Arms*: Stately Cotswold hotel well worth visiting for the strikingly handsome ancient building itself, with interesting old rooms rambling away from the attractive if pricy oak-panelled bar; sandwiches available all day, also imaginative if pricy food in adjoining Goblets wine bar; young cheerful staff, tables in prettily planted courtyard, well kept gardens; children allowed away from bar; bedrooms smart and comfortable; open all day in summer *(Wendy Arnold, LYM)*

Bromsgrove [78 Birmingham Rd; SO9570], *Hop Pole*: Homely and welcoming local nr football ground, well kept real ale, wide range of reasonably priced sandwiches and other snacks *(Richard Houghton)*

Canon Pyon [SO4549], *Nags Head*: Good interesting food in traditional flagstoned bar with two huge log fires, and in beautifully decorated restaurant with tables set around well; well kept Brains, Flowers IPA and Wadworths 6X, superb wine list, sensible prices; wise to book, esp weekends *(G Priday)*

Catshill [Stourbridge Rd; SO9573], *Crown*: Busy Greenalls Ale & Hearty pub, lively friendly atmosphere, good choice of handpump beers inc Banks's, lots of bottled ones, wide choice of good value generous food on huge plates, children's dishes, large family area; big garden with play area *(Ian Shorthouse, Phillip Whitlock)*

Charlton [Strand; the one nr Evesham; SP0145], *Gardeners Arms*: Straightforward local on green of pretty thatched village, good value generous fresh food, welcoming atmosphere and service, lots of tables in lounge, spartan public bar with darts, Whitbreads-related ales, decent choice of wines; quiet piped music *(June and Mike Coleman)*

Checkley [SO5938], *Yewtree*: Good food in restaurant, very varied, imaginative and inexpensive; friendly service *(Avril Tolond)*

Clifton upon Teme [Main St; SO7261], *Old Lion*: Civilised and comfortable, with friendly staff and licensee, good choice of drinks, wide choice of food, central log fire in big bar; attractive beamed bedrooms, pretty village *(R G Lewis)*

Cookley [Wolverhampton Rd; SO8479], *Cafe Rene*: French theme taken to Little Pub Co's usual extreme, even full-size model French people, thousands of bottles in ceiling; good food and drink, friendly atmosphere, helpful staff, maybe piped Frank Sinatra *(B Adams)*

☆ **Crowle** [SO9256], *Old Chequers*: Smart and busy yet relaxing, with more modern restaurant extension opening off old pubby core of some character, interesting choice of good generous food (no sandwiches etc, but good value light lunches), well kept Bass and other ales, good house wines, very friendly prompt service; nice spot in small village *(G S and E M Dorey, Mrs Ursula Hofheinz, Mike and Mary Carter)*

☆ **Cutnall Green** [A442 Kidderminster—Droitwich; SO8768], *Live & Let Live*: Small, busy and unpretentious converted cottages, first-rate service, Bass and Tetleys, wide range of good reasonably priced home-made food from lots of sandwiches and interesting light meals to Sun roasts in new no-smoking timbered dining room or popular open-sided summer marquee; small but pretty garden *(W H and E Thomas, Brian and Genie Smart, Mrs G Connell)*

Dodford [Whinfield Rd; SO9372], *Dodford Inn*: Unpretentious Greenalls country pub in extensive grounds, lovely setting overlooking wooded valley, lots of footpaths; relaxed peaceful atmosphere, reasonably priced home cooking inc vegetarian and plenty of snacks, well kept ales inc guests; children welcome, tables on shady terrace, big play area; camp and caravan site *(Anon)*

Droitwich [Celvestune Way; SO8861], *Pillar of Salt*: Good individual modern estate pub with warmly welcoming Australian landlord, theme food nights, live bands, quiz nights *(Ian Colley)*; [Kidderminster Rd], *Railway*: Small friendly traditional local with railway memorabilia in two-room lounge bar, canal basin and park views from big balcony, well kept Banks's Mild, Marstons Pedigree and guest ales, limited but imaginative choice of freshly made lunches, friendly landlords and customers, pub games; open all day Fri/Sat *(Dr B and Mrs P B Baker, Ian Colley)*

Dunhampstead [just SE of Droitwich; pub towards Sale Green – OS Sheet 150 map ref 919600; SO9160], *Firs*: Pretty, with flower-filled terrace, small grassy garden, lots of hanging baskets, comfortable conservatory; good food from doorstep sandwiches up, well kept Banks's and Marstons, prompt welcoming service, friendly dogs, flowers on tables; nice spot not far from canal *(Stephen Pine, Alfred Lawrence, LYM)*

Eckington [Church St (B4080); SO9241], *Bell*: Attractive and inviting village pub, central servery for pleasant bar and big dining area, cool dining conservatory, wide choice of good value well cooked food, quick helpful staff, real ales, pool table in bar, unobtrusive piped music; charge for credit cards *(Malcolm Thomas, P Lloyd, Margaret and David Watson)*

Evesham [Oat St; off High St at Barclays, follow Library signs; SP0344], *Green Dragon*: 16th-c coaching inn, formerly part of monastery, brewing own Asum and Gold (glass panel shows brewery); small dining lounge, big comfortable public bar, back pool room and skittle alley, old well in corridor, friendly staff, attractive prints, cheap food, quiet at lunchtime; evening piped music, maybe TV, karaoke, live music, bouncers; good value bedrooms, good breakfast *(Chris Reeve, Pete Baker, G Coates, Dr and Mrs B Baker)*

☆ **Flyford Flavell** [Radford Rd; ½ mile off A422 Worcester—Alcester; SO9754], *Boot*: Unpretentious beamed country pub with 18th-c front but core dating from 13th c, plenty of character, wide range of consistently good generous food (cooked to order so may be a short wait) inc vegetarian and popular Sun lunch, beamed dining rooms (one no smoking) with open fires and glass-topped well; well kept Bass, Boddingtons, Marstons Pedigree and a couple of less common guest beers, good wine choice, darts in plain traditional public bar, conservatory; children welcome to eat, garden with play area, lovely surroundings; bedrooms *(Ian Shorthouse, June and Mike Coleman, Andrew Cameron)*

Forhill [Lea End Lane/Icknield St, handy for

M42 junctions 2 and 3; SP0575], *Peacock*: Small recently refurbished low-beamed pub on the edges of Birmingham yet tucked away in picturesque countryside, with good walks; good affordable French cooking, smoking and no-smoking dining rooms, good beer choice inc changing guests, friendly service; children welcome, jazz last Tues of month *(Michael and Hazel Lyons)*

☆ **Fownhope** [B4224; SO5834], *Green Man*: Striking 15th-c black and white inn, often very busy (so the friendly service can slow), with big log fire, wall settles, window seats and armchairs in one beamed bar, standing timbers dividing another, popular well priced food from sandwiches to steak inc children's and Sun carvery (no-smoking main restaurant), well kept Courage Directors, Hook Norton Best, Marstons Pedigree, John Smiths and Sam Smiths OB, Weston's farm ciders, attractive prices; children welcome, quiet garden with play area; comfortable bedrooms, good breakfast *(John Bowdler, Stephen Pine, Alfred Lawrence, Mr and Mrs P Stainsby, DAV, Wayne Brindle, N C Hinton, LYM)*

☆ **Gorcott Hill** [off A435 3 miles S of M42 junction 3; SP0868], *Hollybush*: Quietly placed country pub (easy to find after you've arrived – map on back of bill) with wide range of generous good value home-made food inc seafood and filled yorkshire puddings, well kept Scottish Courage ales, good service; busy with office people weekday lunchtime *(Dave Braisted)*

Hadley [Hadley Heath, off A4133 Droitwich—Ombersley; SO8664], *Bowling Green*: Large but cosy beamed bar in attractively refurbished 16th-c inn, wide range of reasonably priced food inc enterprising filled baguettes, interesting hot dishes and good value Sun carvery; well kept Banks's Bitter and Mild, Marstons Pedigree and Hook Norton, good value wines, big log fire, attractive restaurant, comfortable bedrooms; children welcome, tables outside, has UK's oldest bowling green *(Chris Philip, Martin and Karen Wake, Denys Gueroult)*

Hampton Bishop [SO5638], *Bunch of Carrots*: Busy spaciously refurbished beamed country pub with good value imaginative daily specials inc fish, popular Sun lunch, well kept ales inc Boddingtons, local farm cider, friendly efficient service; play area *(D H Gittins, David and Nina Pugsley, Richard and Cathy Barker)*

Hanbury [Woodgate; SO9663], *Gate Hangs Well*: Much extended dining pub alone in farmland, open-plan but well divided, with good value attractively presented generous food inc carvery and enormous home-made pies, well kept Bass and Worthington, friendly service; very popular, best to book *(David and Helen Wilkins)*

☆ **Hanley Castle** [Church End, off B4211 N of Upton upon Severn; SO8341], *Three Kings*: Genuinely unspoilt friendly country local, well worn in, with huge inglenook and hatch service in very traditional little tiled-floor tap room, well kept Butcombe, Thwaites and usually three guest beers, farm cider, dozens of malt whiskies, two other larger rooms, low-priced homely food (not Sun evening – singer then; be prepared for a maybe longish wait other times), seats of a sort outside; family room, bedroom *(Pat and Tony Martin, Dr I Crichton, Alan and Paula McCully, M Joyner, R J Walden, D Eberlin, LYM)*

Hanley Swan [B4209 Malvern—Upton; SO8142], *Swan*: Neatly run and friendly traditional pub by village green and duck pond, varied reasonably priced food running up to steaks, well kept Theakstons, decent wine, prompt service, nice locals' bar, small attractive restaurant evenings and Sun lunch; tables on lawn, play area *(S Holder, D A Hughes, Bill and Brenda Lemon, Mr and Mrs M J E Pearson)*

☆ **Harewood End** [A49 Hereford—Ross; SO5327], *Harewood End*: Attractive panelled dining lounge with old candlelit tables, big log fire, old prints and antiques, good range of consistently enjoyable home-made food inc children's and massive mixed grill, well kept beers, decent wines; very busy weekends; good value bedrooms *(S Watkin, P Taylor, Mrs C M Smalley, John and Joan Hilliard)*

Harvington [A450; SO8774], *Dog*: Wide choice of good value food inc Sun carvery, Banks's and Marstons Pedigree; interesting sample of pub architecture over the ages *(W and E Thomas)*

Hereford [Kings Acre Rd; SO5139], *Bay Horse*: Attractive biggish pub with quick friendly service and cleverly presented good food (from enjoyable sandwiches and soup up), good colour coordination of food and decor, pleasant piped music throughout *(Margaret and Andrew Leach)*; [1 Broad St], *Green Dragon*: Pleasant bar and decent buffet-style lunches in long-established hotel *(EGP)*

Himbleton [SO9458], *Galton Arms*: Friendly old-fashioned country pub, log fires, oak beams, well kept Bass and Banks's, bar food, restaurant; play area outside *(Ian Shorthouse)*

Hopwood [A441 N of Alvechurch; SP0275], *Hopwood House*: Converted to Milestone chain dining pub, but keeping some individuality, with imposing stairs to main entrance (back door for disabled car users); reasonably priced food, Banks's ales *(Dave Braisted)*

☆ **Howle Hill** [coming from Ross fork left off B4228 on sharp right bend, first right, then left at crossroads after a mile – OS Sheet 162 map ref 603204; SO6020], *Crown*: Immaculate little hidden-away pub with good range of well priced tasty food inc exceptional value puddings (not Sun evening, Mon; no sandwiches), well kept Whitbreads-related ales, friendly landlord and labradors (no visiting dogs), very cheery staff, padded pews; bar skittles, tables in garden; winter opening may be limited *(Malcolm Taylor, J Goodrich)*

Inkberrow [High St; SP0157], *Bulls Head*: Welcoming Georgian pub with beams, flagstones, ancient settles and log fire, Banks's, Bass, Boddingtons and guest beers, food inc vegetarian and good roasts *(Sarah and Peter Gooderham, Patricia Tovey)*

☆ **Kemerton** [Bredon—Beckford; SO9437], *Crown*: Welcoming 18th-c local in upmarket village, bustling L-shaped lounge bar, panelled benches, well kept Whitbreads-related ales, enjoyable food from good sandwiches and light meals to special food events with emphasis on fish; pretty garden *(Michael Herman, Mrs A Oakley)*

Kington [Victoria Rd; SO3057], *Olde Tavern*: Wonderful time-warp old place, ornate exterior (without inn sign), small plain often enjoyably crowded parlour and public bar, dark brown woodwork, old settles and other antique furniture, china, pewter and curios; well kept Ansells, no music, machines or food; children welcome, though not a family pub *(PB, JP, PP)*

Kinnersley [off A38 S of Worcester; SO8643], *Royal Oak*: Short changing choice of very imaginative food inc generous starters; Bass and Heroes Bitter, compact bar with local characters *(Dave Braisted)*

Ledbury [Homend; SO7137], *Horse Shoe*: Pretty timbered pub bright with hanging baskets etc, very warm and cosy, with six real ales, good bar food, log fire *(Tracy Dawson, Gary Benjamin)*

☆ **Leintwardine** [Rosemary Lane, just off A4113; SO4174], *Sun*: Delightful treasure for lovers of unspoilt pubs, three benches by coal fire in decades-old red-tiled front parlour off hallway, venerable landlady brings you your pint (maybe Tetleys, Ansells or Woods, from casks in her kitchen), also small settee and a couple of chairs in her sitting room; no food *(Kevin Thorpe, JP, PP, Pete Baker)*

Leintwardine [High St], *Lion*: Beautiful spot by packhorse bridge over River Teme, nice safely fenced riverside garden with play area, well kept Whitbreads-related ales, good value bar food esp fish, popular restaurant, welcoming efficient staff; very busy in main holiday season; bedrooms attractive and not too pricy *(Rob Whittle)*

☆ **Leominster** [West St; SO4959], *Talbot*: Comfortable and hospitable old coaching inn in charming town, heavy beams and standing timbers, antique carved settles, log fires with 18th-c oak-panelled chimneybreasts, sporting prints; decent straightforward home-made bar food inc good sandwiches, well kept Scottish Courage ales, good coffee, efficient cheerful service; piped music; bedrooms *(E G Parish, BB)*

Leominster [74 South St], *Black Horse*: Big bustling bar with comfortably rustic furniture, snug lounge/restaurant (no food Sun); tap for Marches Brewery, with their Jenny Piped Summer Ale, BHB, Best and Forever Autumn, guest beers, traditional games *(G Coates, Gwyneth and Salvo Spadaro-Dutturi)*; [nr stn], *White Lion*: Cottagey pub with comfortable beamed bar/lounge area, friendly staff and locals, well kept Bass, side eating room *(Richard Lewis)*

Lulsley [signed a mile off A44; SO7455], *Fox & Hounds*: Tucked away, smallish parquet-floored bar stepping down into neat dining lounge, bar food inc good steak baguette, well kept Bass and a local beer, open fire; garden with play area *(J H Peters, BB)*

Lyonshall [SO3355], *Royal George*: Unpretentious village inn, clean and friendly, with good food inc Sun lunch nicely served, decent reasonably priced house wine, three rooms off central servery, pleasant partly no-smoking dining room; comfortable bedrooms, outstanding floral decorations outside *(W Buxton)*

Malvern [Abbey Rd; SO7845], *Abbey*: Good soup and sandwiches in comfortable hotel bar with fine views, friendly staff; bedrooms *(P Lloyd)*

☆ **Mamble** [just off A456 Bewdley—Tenbury Wells; SO6971], *Sun & Slipper*: Friendly, attractively refurbished and well run 16th-c inn in small village, good set lunches and bar food; village has interesting church and superior craft centre; bedrooms *(R Morgan, BB)*

☆ **Mathon** [A419; SO7345], *Cliffe Arms*: Very low heavy beams in three unpretentious little rooms, flowery-cushioned pews and comfortable kitchen chairs, good relaxed local atmosphere, wide choice of home-made food, enormous helpings, efficient service, well kept Courage-related and a guest ale, back dining room with minstrels' gallery; streamside garden, lovely setting; children welcome *(Joy and Peter Heatherley)*

☆ **Michaelchurch Escley** [off back rd SE of Hay on Wye, along Escley Brook valley; SO3134], *Bridge*: Remote homely black-beamed riverside inn delightfully tucked away in attractive valley; has been an enjoyable main entry, with several well kept ales and farm ciders, fairly priced wines and good simple food from sandwiches to steaks, with a welcome for children and open all day Sat; but being sold as we go to press *(LYM – reports please)*

Mordiford [just off B4224 SE of Hereford; SO5737], *Moon*: Lounge with roaring fire, good value food from filled baked potatoes to unusual dishes of the day, front restaurant, friendly relaxed service, Bass, Boddingtons, Flowers IPA and Wye Valley Bitter, local farm ciders, reasonably priced wines; back bar popular with young locals *(M G Hart, R A Buckler)*

Much Dewchurch [SO4831], *Black Swan*: Roomy partly 14th-c pub, attractive and friendly, with limited but enjoyable well cooked food, several well kept ales such as Bass, Hook Norton Best, Woods Special and one brewed for the pub, decent wines; can get smoky *(John Goodrich)*

New End [SP0559], *Nevill Arms*: Brewers Fayre chain pub, a cut above the norm *(Dave Braisted)*

Orleton [just off B4362 W of Woofferton; SO4967], *Boot*: Character haunted 16th-c pub doing well under helpful new licensees, lovely inglenook in small bar, big beamed dining lounge with exposed wattle and daub, old photographs of villagers and cider-making, very friendly largely local atmosphere, good sensibly priced food, real ales inc Hobsons, good wines; pleasant garden, attractive village *(Rob Whittle)*

☆ **Pembridge** [Mkt Sq (A44); SO3958], *New Inn*: Ancient inn overlooking small black and white town's church, comfortable and atmospheric three-room bar, antique settles, worn flagstones, substantial log fire, one room with sofas, pine furniture and books, good food from sandwiches up inc some interesting dishes, attentive friendly staff, well kept Ruddles Best and County, Theakstons and a guest beer, farm cider, traditional games; quiet little family dining room (not Sun evening); outside lavatories, simple bedrooms *(Glenn and Gillian Miller, A J Bowen, N H E Lewis, Brian Skelcher, LYM)*

Pembridge, *Red Lion*: Good bar food, very friendly *(Sarah and Peter Gooderham)*

☆ **Pershore** [Bridge St; SO9445], *Brandy Cask*: Own-brewed generously hopped Brandysnapper and John Baker, guest beers, Aug beer festival, good freshly made food from sandwiches up inc pies and curries in bar and quaintly decorated no-smoking brasserie, quick friendly service; well behaved children allowed; long attractive garden down to river, with terrace and koi pond *(Kerry Law, Pat and Tony Martin, Graham Reeve, Dr and Mrs B Baker)*

Peterstow [A49 Ross—Hereford, N; SO5625], *Red Lion*: Good food in pleasant dining area, attentive licensee *(K H Frostick)*

☆ **Priors Frome** [off A438 E of Hereford; SO5739], *Yew Tree*: Traditional country pub with Tetleys-related ales, occasional guests such as Shepherd Neame or Smiles, good imaginative generous food in bar and rather more ambitious cellar restaurant, friendly service; fine Frome Valley views *(Paul and Sue Merrick, Felicity Toube)*

Radford [Alcester Rd; S of A422 Worcester—Stratford; SP0055], *Wheelbarrow Castle*: Popular extended beamed pub with wide choice of good generous home cooking inc bargain cod and chips Mon, Weds and Fri, good value Sun carvery, friendly service, well kept Banks's, Hook Norton and Theakstons *(D Conway)*

Rashwood [A38, ½ mile SW of M5 junction 5; SO9165], *Robin Hood*: Busy Bass dining pub with good English plain food, very pleasant staff, well kept Bass and Hancocks HB, log fire *(Mr and Mrs T A Bryan, Ian Shorthouse)*

☆ **Ross on Wye** [Riverside; coming in from A40 W side, 1st left after bridge; SO6024], *Hope & Anchor*: Big-windowed family extension looking out on well kept flower-lined lawns leading down to river, plenty of tables out here (and summer ice-cream bar and barbecues), thorough-going boating theme in cheery main bar, cosy upstairs parlour bar and Victorian-style dining room, generous good value food inc good choice for children, well kept Banks's ales, farm cider, good house wine, hard-working new licensees; open all day, can be crowded weekends *(E G Parish, IHR, Tom L Rees, Michael and Gillian Ford, Steve Thomas, Mike and Mary Carter, LYM)*

Ross on Wye [8 High St], *Kings Head*: Comfortably old-fashioned locally popular beamed and panelled hotel lounge bar, generous good value food inc home-made soup, good sandwiches and toasties, some hot dishes, swift friendly service, evening restaurant; open all day; bedrooms *(P Lloyd, Derek Bartlett)*; [Walford Rd (B4234), Tudorville], *Vine Tree*: Very good value home cooking by landlord's wife *(D Conway)*

Shatterford [Bridgnorth Rd (A442); SO7981], *Bellmans Cross*: Big pub/restaurant recently refurbished by new owners (he is a French chef), interesting bar meals with strong French influence, good restaurant dishes, Bass and guest beer *(Neil and Jane Kendrick)*; [A442], *Red Lion*: Comfortable olde-worlde pub with gleaming copper and brass, lively coal fire, partly no-smoking dining extension, Banks's Mild and Bitter and local ales such as Herefordshire Classic and Woods Shropshire Lad, wide choice of good generous well presented food inc vegetarian and properly cooked veg, good atmosphere, very friendly staff; fine views *(Ian Phillips, Phil Putwain)*

Stoke Heath [44 Hanbury Rd (A38 2½ miles from M5 junction 5); SO9468], *Hanbury Turn*: Good short range of bar food inc tapas and other good light meals, mainly Tetleys-related ales *(Dave Braisted)*

☆ **Stoke Prior** [Hanbury Rd (B4091); the one nr Bromsgrove, SO9468], *Country Girl*: Friendly country pub with comfortable lounge, rustic brickwork, light oak beams, farm tools, soft lighting, new licensees keeping up tradition of enterprising choice of specials inc quite a few vegetarian, friendly efficient service, well kept Whitbreads-related and other ales such as Wadworths 6X, unobtrusive piped music; enclosed garden, walks on Dodderhill Common *(Dave Braisted, Ian Shorthouse)*

Stoke Works [SO9365], *Boat & Railway*: Popular and unpretentious canalside Banks's pub with good lunchtime snacks, pretty hanging baskets *(Dave Braisted, BB)*

Stonehall Common [S of Norton, via Hatfield; SO8749], *Fruiterers Arms*: Very homely, with chesterfields and open fires, interesting guest beers such as Exmoor Hart and Smiles Best, food in panelled bar and extension restaurant inc good carvery lunchtime and early evening *(Kerry Law, Simon Smith, W E and E Thomas)*

Stourport on Severn [Mitton Walk; SO8171], *Holly Bush*: Cosy little pub with well kept Everards Tiger and Enville and Hobsons ales, big helpings of reasonably priced bar food inc bargain Sun lunch, small dining area; pool room off main bar *(Dr and Mrs B Baker)*

Symonds Yat [Symonds Yat E, by ferry – ie over on the Gloucs bank; SO5615], *Saracens Head*: Riverside beauty spot next to ferry, busy down-to-earth flagstoned bar popular with canoeists, mountain bikers and hikers, cheerful staff, reasonably priced nourishing food inc vegetarian, for people with big appetites, Theakstons ales, settles and window seats; cosy carpeted restaurant, games bar with pool, piped jazz and blues, SkyTV, lots of waterside tables outside, live music Thurs; summer boat trips, parking cheaper beyond Royal Hotel *(Rona Murdoch, Arthur and Margaret Dickinson)*

Tenbury Wells [Worcester Rd, Newnham; A456 about 1½ miles E – so inn actually in Shrops; SO6168], *Peacock*: Beautiful 14th-c roadside inn with several separate rooms, heavy black beams, big log fire in front lounge, comfortable kitchen chairs and ex-pew settles; good attractively presented food with lots of fresh veg, good friendly service, well kept ales, decent wines, back family room, charming bistro; picnic-sets on terrace, lovely setting by River Teme; good bedrooms *(Helen Winter, C H Wood, Mr and Mrs Woolnough, LYM)*

☆ **Tenbury Wells** [Oldwood, A4112 S], *Fountain*: Quaint low timbered pub with lots of black beams in open-plan lounge bar, red and gold flock wallpaper, big brass platters, delft shelf of bright china, masses of artificial flowers, coal-effect gas fire, big dining room beyond, side bar with pool; quickly served home-cooked food inc sandwiches, children's and fine specials, well kept Ruddles and a guest beer, decent wines by the glass, friendly service, maybe unobtrusive piped music; picnic-sets on side lawn with lots of play equipment *(Andrew Rogers, Amanda Milsom, Chris Wrigley, BB)*

☆ **Tenbury Wells** [Teme St], *Ship*: Small L-shaped bar with lots of dark wood inc fine Elizabethan beams, little hunting prints and other pictures, well kept Ansells and guests such as Exmoor Gold and Hobsons Best, decent wines, good coffee, good imaginative bar food and Sun lunch in bright no-smoking dining room with fresh flowers, reasonable prices, friendly landlord and staff, good relaxed atmosphere; piped music; picnic-sets in coach yard and on neat sheltered back lawn; comfortable bedrooms *(G Coates, Luke Worthington, BB)*

Tillington [SO4645], *Bell*: Good range of food from good baguettes to generous home-made hot dishes, Bass, Fullers London Pride and Wadworths 6X, comfortable banquettes in lounge extension, warm welcome; big garden with play area *(Mr and Mrs J Brassington, Courtney and Elaine West)*

☆ **Trumpet** [A438; SO6639], *Verzons*: Cheerful and welcoming small hotel, good choice of decent food in long comfortable bar-cum-bistro on left, well kept Hook Norton, friendly relaxed staff, restaurant on right; lovely garden with Malvern views, tasteful bedrooms *(Mr and Mrs Pilson)*

Uphampton [off A449 N of Ombersley; SO8364], *Fruiterers Arms*: Small country local (looks like a private house with a porch) brewing its own Cannon Royall Arrowhead, Buckshot and good strong Mild, also has John Smiths and farm cider; Jacobean panelled bar serving lounge with beamery, log fire, lots of photographs and local memorabilia, comfortable armchairs; good basic lunchtime food, no music, plain pool room, garden *(G Coates, Dr and Mrs B Baker)*

☆ **Upton upon Severn** [High St; S08540], *Olde Anchor*: Picturesque and rambling but neat and tidy 16th-c pub with helpful service, old-fashioned furnishings, black timbers propping its low beams, lots of copper, brass and pewter, good fire in unusual central fireplace; well kept Scottish Courage ales, enjoyable low-priced food; has been open all day summer, can get crowded evenings then *(Mrs F A W Ricketts, P and M Rudlin, LYM)*

Upton upon Severn [Riverside], *Kings Head*: Lovely riverside setting, plenty of Severn-side seating, friendly young efficient staff; popular lunchtime for generous food, with extended well furnished lounge bar, Whitbreads-related ales, separate eating area; dogs allowed *(Alan and Paula McCully, Mrs F A W Ricketts)*; [Old St, far end main st], *Little Upton Muggery*: Thousands of mugs on the ceiling, simple furnishings, open fires, pool in third room, unusual beer, good value generous food, good friendly service; piped radio may be loud, basic lavatories *(Joy and Peter Heatherley, P and M Rudlin)*; [Riverside], *Swan*: Straightforward low-beamed bar in charming riverside setting, well kept Banks's and Marstons Pedigree, two open fires, boating memorabilia, fruit machine, games machines in anteroom; small smarter bar with sizeable dining room off, good value interesting food; garden with summer barbecues *(Mrs F A W Ricketts, Alan and Paula McCully, Michael and Gillian Ford, BB)*

☆ **Weatheroak Hill** [Icknield St – coming S on A435 from Wythall roundabout, filter right off dual carriageway a mile S, then in village turn left towards Alvechurch; not far from M42, junction 3; SP0674], *Coach & Horses*: Roomy country pub popular for its wide choice of interesting well kept ales, most from small breweries; plush-seated low-ceilinged two-level lounge bar, tiled-floor public bar, bar food inc very generous fish and chips, modern restaurant, plenty of seats out on lawns and upper terrace; piped music; children allowed in eating area *(W H and E Thomas, LYM)*

☆ **Welland** [towards Upton; SO7940], *Anchor*: Long low building covered in roses and other colourful climbers, pretty front garden, spotless rustic bar with well kept ales such as Batemans XXXB, good choice of food inc enormous baguettes, very friendly landlord; pleasant restaurant *(Alan and Paula McCully, Michael Tucker)*

Wellington [off A49 N of Hereford; SO4948], *Wellington Inn*: Recently refurbished, with well kept real ales, good food in bar with log fire and candlelit restaurant, quiet classical piped music, good service *(Mr and Mrs M Wade)*

Worcester [31 Friar St; SO8555], *Cardinals Hat*: Several small ancient-feeling rooms, good food inc good baguettes, service quick and friendly even when busy, Banks's beers *(Barry and Anne)*; [30 The Tything], *Lamb & Flag*: Irish pub nr racecourse, famous for its radical customers; well kept Marstons, as well as Irish Guinness served carefully *(Dr and Mrs B Baker)*

Wychbold [A38 towards Bromsgrove; SO9267], *Thatch*: Not a pub (part of Webbs Garden Centre, open 10-5, with wines licence) but useful for good value soup and ploughman's, or a hot dish, and first-class tea, in pleasant surroundings; doing well under new chef, with new larger restaurant opened summer 1998 *(D Green)*

☆ **Wythall** [Icknield St; SP0775], *Peacock*: Good food from baps to chargrilled steaks (just roasts, Sun) and well kept Banks's with a guest such as Hobsons or Solicitors Ruin in reliable country pub with old tiled floors; no-smoking area, open all day *(Dave Braisted, Jack Barnwell)*

Hertfordshire

Pubs doing notably well here these days are the friendly and charmingly placed Greyhound at Aldbury (a new main entry), the well run Jolly Waggoner at Ardeley (good food), the White Horse at Burnham Green (attractively priced food, very popular at lunchtime), the Bull at Cottered (same good management as the Jolly Waggoner, food good too), the George & Dragon at Watton at Stone (attractive dining pub) and the Sword in Hand at Westmill (very careful cooking at this sympathetically rebuilt pub, qualifies for a Food Award this year). The Bricklayers Arms at Flaunden is also enjoyable for meals out; and the Rose & Crown in St Albans deserves a special mention for its American landlord's super big transatlantic-style sandwiches. The White Lion at Walkern stands out for families, with plenty of summer entertainments for children. In the Lucky Dip at the end of the chapter, the Bridgewater Arms at Little Gaddesden, Nags Head at Little Hadham and Coach & Horses at Newgate Street (all inspected and approved by us) are showing particularly well these days. Drinks prices are higher than the national average; much the cheapest place we found was the prettily set Boat at Berkhamsted, tied to Fullers.

ALDBURY SP9612 Map 4

Greyhound

Stocks Road; village signposted from A4251 Tring—Berkhamsted, or reached directly from roundabout at E end of A41 Tring bypass

In a prime spot below the Chilterns backdrop of the Ashridge Estate (National Trust), this attractive country pub has tables outside facing the village green, complete with stocks, duckpond – and plenty of vociferous ducks. It has a handsome Georgian frontage (especially so in autumn, when the Virginia creeper is a brilliant counterpoint to the bronzing leaves of the beechwoods on the slopes behind). Inside, there are signs of an older building, for instance around the copper-hooded inglenook. There's a thriving atmosphere in the two main rooms that ramble off each side of the drinks and food serving areas, with plenty of tables. The blackboards show a wide and changing range of good food such as sandwiches (from £2.20), soup (£3.45), ploughman's (from £3.95), griddle cooked beef burger and chips (£4.65), jacket potatoes (from £4.95), mushroom stroganoff, ham and double egg or lasagne (£6.95), chicken tikka (£7.35), salmon with a tarragon sauce (£7.50) and rump steak (£8.95). Well kept changing real ales from Greene King and Marston and a beer brewed for the pub by Tring Brewery on handpump (weekday early evening happy hour), good welcoming service – smiling and efficient even under pressure. They don't mind well behaved dogs, and keep plastic bags by the entrance for muddy boots; no-smoking area. The garden is pleasant, and good walks abound nearby, for instance around the monument to the 3rd Duke of Bridgewater, the canal mogul, up on the escarpment; for the more sedentarily inclined, the toll road through the Ashridge Estate is very attractive. We haven't heard recently from readers who have stayed here, but would expect the bedrooms to be good value. *(Recommended by Gwen and Peter Andrews, R C Morgan, JJW, CMW, Klaus and Elizabeth Leist, Francis Bugg, LYM)*

Free house ~ Licensee Martin Roberts ~ Real ale ~ Meals and snacks ~ Restaurant ~ (01442) 851228 ~ Children welcome ~ Open 6am(8am Sun)-11pm ~ Bedrooms: £50B/£55B

ARDELEY TL3027 Map 5

Jolly Waggoner

This charming little pink-washed inn is well liked for its very good bar food – nothing too fancy or complicated but carefully prepared usuing fresh produce from local suppliers. In addition to sandwiches (from £2.20) and soup (£4), there might be fried goat's cheese and tomato salad (£5), home-made burgers (from £5.50), vegetable and pasta bake (£5.95), omelette filled with smoked haddock and topped with cheese (£6.50), calf liver with sage and butter or roquefort cheese and horseradish (£11.50) and fillet steak (£13.50), and delicious puddings; booking is essential for their Sunday lunch, and there's a £1 surcharge for credit cards. The comfortable bar has lots of open woodwork and a relaxed and civilised atmosphere, while the restaurant (extended into the cottage next door) is decorated with modern prints. Well kept Greene King IPA tapped from the cask and Abbot on handpump, a good range of wines and freshly squeezed orange juice in summer; darts and maybe piped music. Peacefully set in a pretty tucked-away village and handy for Cromer Windmill; the landlord also runs a main entry pub at Cottered. *(Recommended by Charles Bardswell, Andrew Scarr; more reports please)*

Greene King ~ Tenant Darren Perkins ~ Real ale ~ Meals and snacks (not Mon) ~ Restaurant ~ (01438) 861350 ~ Children over seven welcome ~ Open 12-2.30(3 Sat), 6.30-11; 12-3, 7-10.30 Sun; cl Monday

ASHWELL TL2639 Map 5

Bushel & Strike

Off A507 just E of A1(M) junction 10, N of Baldock, via Newnham; also signposted off A1 southbound; and off A505 Baldock—Royston; in village turn off High St into Gardinders Lane, pub is opposite the Church (car park can be reached down Swan Lane)

The front part of this cheerful village pub is devoted to eating with a large salad bar and pudding display cabinet as well as neatly laid tables with fresh flowers, attractive hunting and coaching prints, and local colour photographs. There is an enchanting trompe l'oeil Edwardian conservatory restaurant – it's actually an old school hall – with abundant painted foliage, horses and rolling hills; leather chesterfields on polished floorboards in front of an open fire lend a civilised air to the bar. The wide choice of food includes home-made soup (£2.50), grilled goat's cheese with gooseberry conserve (£4.25), pork chop grilled with soy sauce, cloves and honey (£5.25), steak, kidney, mushroom and ale pie (£6.95), chicken breast stuffed with pâté, wrapped in bacon with a port wine, redcurrant and stilton cream sauce (£7.75) and loin of pork with braised pears and prunes marinated in armagnac (£8.95); the restaurant is no smoking as is a small area of the bar. Well kept Charles Wells Bombardier and Eagle and a guest such as Adnams Broadside on handpump, as well as freshly squeezed fruit juice, hot toddies, mulled wine and half a dozen wines by the glass. There are tables out on a small terrace and more spacious fenced lawn; maybe barbecues or hog roasts in summer. *(Recommended by Stephen, Julie and Hayley Brown, Wayne Brindle; more reports please)*

Charles Wells ~ Tenant Michael Mills-Roberts ~ Real ale ~ Meals and snacks (not Sun evening) ~ Restaurant ~ (01462) 742394 ~ Children welcome in eating area of bar and restaurant ~ Open 11-3, 6-11; 11-11 Sat; 12-10.30 Sun ~ Bedrooms: /£30

Three Tuns

High St

The lounge at this flower-decked 18th-c inn is opulently Victorian, with lots of pictures, stuffed pheasants and antiques; there are comfortable chairs, and some big family tables; the atmosphere is akin to that of a pleasantly old-fashioned but unstuffy hotel. Well presented food includes sandwiches (from £2.25), ploughman's (from £3.95), soup (£2.50), home-made pâté (£2.95), blue cheese and broccoli quiche (£5.95), well liked steak and kidney pie (£6.50), gammon and egg or baked chicken breast with hickory and herbs (£7.95), grilled lamb chops with tomato and mushrooms (£8.95), and steaks (from £9.95). Greene King IPA, Abbot and Rayments under light blanket pressure, a good choice of wines. It can get very busy, especially on summer weekends. The simpler more modern public bar has pool, darts and a fruit machine; piped music, boules. We haven't had reports from readers on the bedrooms here, but they were fully refurbished in 1998 and we would imagine that it would be a pleasant place to stay. *(Recommended by G Neighbour, T Loft, Sheila Samuels)*

Greene King ~ Tenants C M and D E Stanley ~ Real ale ~ Meals and snacks (all day at weekends) ~ Restaurant ~ (01462) 742107 ~ Children in eating area of bar ~ Open 11-11; 12-10.30 Sun ~ Bedrooms: £35(£55B)/£45(£55B)

AYOT ST LAWRENCE TL1916 Map 5

Brocket Arms

B651 N of St Albans for about 6 miles; village signposted on right after Wheathampstead and Mid Herts golf course; or B653 NE of Luton, then right on to B651

Don't be surprised to hear mysterious voices and footsteps in the two very traditional low-ceilinged rooms of this peacefully set ancient pub – it's said to be haunted by the ghost of a Catholic priest who was tried and hanged here during the Reformation. More tangible features include sturdy oak beams, a big inglenook fireplace (with a woodburning stove in the back room), old-fashioined furnishings and magazines to read; darts, dominoes, cribbage, piped classical music. Adnams Broadside, Brakspear Special, Greene King Abbot and IPA, and Wadworths 6X under light blanket pressure and two guests tapped from the cask; around 8 wines by the glass. Straightforward lunchtime bar food includes soup (£2.50), sandwiches (£2.50), filled jacket potatoes (£3.00), ploughman's (from £4), pasties (£4.75), steak and kidney pie or spaghetti bolognese (£6), and 8oz sirloin steak (£9.50). The evening menu is a bit different with 4oz steak in french bread or scampi (£5), salads (£5), steaks (£9.95), chicken with a tia maria sauce, salmon with lobster and brandy sauce or home-made vegetable nut roast (£11.50), and roast duck, pheasant or venison (£12.50); no-smoking area in restaurant. It can get very crowded at weekends. The extensive south-facing suntrap walled garden has a summer bar and a children's play area; this is attractive countryside, near Shaw's Corner. *(Recommended by Ian Phillips, Mick and Hilary Stirrin, Barry and Marie Males, BG, CH)*

Free house ~ Lease: Toby Wingfield Digby ~ Real ale ~ Meals and snacks (reduced menu Sun and Mon evenings ~ Restaurant ~ (01438) 820250 ~ Children in eating area of bar and restaurant ~ Open 11-11; 12-11 Sun ~ Bedrooms: £45B/£60(£65B)

BERKHAMSTED SP9807 Map 5

Boat

Gravel Path

Again under new management; readers report that this beautifully set little canalside pub is full of character despite being only 10 years old. Recent refurbishment has increased the dining area and besides sandwiches (from £2.65), soup (£2.95) and ploughman's (£4.95), the changing food menu might include spinach, mozzarella and tomato tarte (£5.95), steak and ale pie (£6.50), fresh cod in beer batter (£6.95), and chicken filled with brie and wrapped in bacon (£7.75). Friendly staff serve well kept and reasonably priced Fullers Chiswick, ESB, London Pride and Fullers seasonal ale on handpump; good wine list. Fruit machine and piped music; no-smoking area at lunchtime. Over 21s only on Friday and Saturday nights when they don't serve food because it's so busy. A terrace overlooks the canal. *(Recommended by Quentin Williamson, Ian Phillips, David and Ruth Shillitoe, Simon Penny; more reports please)*

Fullers ~ Manager Jane Brovey ~ Real ale ~ Meals and snacks (12-3, 6-9; not Fri and Sat evenings) ~ (01442) 877152 ~ Children welcome till 9pm ~ Open 11-11; 12-10.30 Sun; 11-3, 5-11 Mon-Thurs in winter

It is illegal for bar staff to smoke while handling your drink.

BURNHAM GREEN TL2516 Map 5

White Horse £

Off B1000 N of Welwyn, just E of railway bridge by Welwyn Station

This thriving and civilised dining pub fills up quickly at lunchtime and readers suggest you should arrive in good time to secure a table. The nicest part is the original black-beamed bit by the bar, with solid traditional furnishings, hunting prints, corner china cupboards and log-effect gas fires in two small communicating areas. There are many more tables in a two-floor extension with pitched rafters in its upper gallery, no smoking downstairs. Good value lunchtimes bar food includes sandwiches (from £1.75), soup (£2.25), local sausages (£3.25), ploughman's or deep-fried brie with toast and cranberry sauce (£3.50), scampi, omelettes, vegetable lasagne or broccoli and cream cheese bake (£4.60), home-made steak and kidney pudding (£5.25), chargrilled breast of chicken (£8.95), rack of lamb in mustard and herbs (£10.95) and beef wellington (£11.95). There's a more elaborate restaurant menu. A back brick terrace by a fountain, with a gentle country view, has neat green garden furniture, large umbrellas and outdoor heaters, so you can eat outside even on cooler evenings; there are rustic benches on grass by a pond beyond. Children under 16 are not allowed in this garden unless they stay seated as the pond is deep, but there is lots of room to play on the broad green in front. Well kept Adnams, Greene King IPA and Abbot, Theakstons Old Peculier and Tetleys on handpump, quick friendly service even when busy; maybe piped music. *(Recommended by Barry and Marie Males, G Neighbour, Greg Kilminster, A C Morrison, Paul and Sandra Embleton, Phil and Heidi Cook, George Atkinson, K Leist)*

Free house ~ Licensee Richard Blackett ~ Real ale ~ Meals and snacks (12.30-2, 6.30-8) ~ Restaurant ~ (01438) 798416 ~ Children welcome in restaurant ~ Open 11.30-3, 6-11; 12-4, 7-10.30 Sun

COTTERED TL3129 Map 5

Bull

A507 W of Buntingford

There's a relaxed and welcoming atmosphere at this old tree-surrounded inn, which is prettily placed opposite a row of thatched cottages. It shares the same landlord as the Jolly Waggoner at Ardeley and readers report that the bar food is of a similarly high standard: sandwiches (from £2.40), soup (£4), ploughman's (£5.50), steak and kidney pie (£7), stir-fry vegetables or vegetarian pasta dishes (£7.50), roast rack of lamb or garlic chicken (£10) and beef fillet (£13). There's a £1 surcharge for credit cards. There are antiques on a stripped wood floor in the roomy and comfortable low-beamed front lounge as well as lots of horsebrasses, and a good fire. A second bar has darts, shove-ha'penny, cribbage, dominoes; unobtrusive piped music. Well kept Greene King IPA and Abbot on handpump, decent wines; quick pleasant service. There are benches and tables in the sizable garden; also a play area and maybe boules. *(Recommended by B and M Kendall, Prof John and Patricia White, E J Cutting, D Barlow, A J Goddard, Charles Bardswell, Phil and Heidi Cook, Gwen and Peter Andrews, Ian Phillips)*

Greene King ~ Lease: Darren Perkins ~ Real ale ~ Meals and snacks ~ Restaurant ~ (01763) 281243 ~ Children over 7 welcome ~ Open 12-3, 6.30-11; 12-3, 7-10.30 Sun

FLAUNDEN TL0100 Map 5

Bricklayers Arms

Village signposted from A41; Hogpits Bottom – from village centre follow Boxmoor, Bovingdon road and turn right at Belsize, Watford signpost

Roaring log fires and snug cottagey rooms ensure that this is a cosy and welcoming place to enjoy well prepared food and a very well kept pint from a range of half a dozen or so real ales. The warmly decorated low-beamed bar has dark brown painted traditional wooden wall seats and stubs of knocked-through oak-timbered walls that maintain a feeling of intimacy in the three areas that used to be separate rooms. The life-size bronze dogs and model gorilla at the bar certainly catch the eye. Good value bar snacks include soup (£1.95), sandwiches (from £2.95), ploughman's (from £3.95), chilli or chicken and mushroom pie, (£5.95) and steak and kidney pudding, gammon steak or fajitas (£6.95). The more elaborate restaurant menu which can be eaten throughout the pub includes garlic prawns and mushrooms or home-made crab cakes (£5.25), warm duck salad (£5.45) and main courses such as mushroom and three pepper stroganoff (£8.50), lemon sole (£10.50), steamed chicken stuffed with asparagus or lamb liver and bacon (£10.75), half a roasted pheasant (£11.95) and steaks (from £12.75). Half a dozen well kept beers on handpump might include Brakspear Bitter, Fullers London Pride, Marstons Pedigree, Ringwood Old Thumper, Vale Edgar's Golden Ale, or Youngs Special and there's a good range of wines; friendly and efficient service; cribbage, dominoes. It gets very busy at the weekends, so arrive early for a table. In summer tables in the old-fashioned garden are surrounded by foxgloves against sheltering hawthorn and ivy hedges. Just up the Belsize road there's a path on the left, through woods, to more Forestry Commission woods around Hollow Hedge. *(Recommended by R C Morgan, Comus Elliott, David and Ruth Shillitoe, Peter and Mavis Brigginshaw, Bob and Maggie Atherton, Nigel and Amanda Thorp, Roger Bellingham, Cyril Brown, Wayne Brindle, Joan and Andrew Life)*

Free house ~ Licensees R C Mitchell and D J Winteridge ~ Real ale ~ Meals and snacks ~ Restaurant ~ (01442) 833322 ~ Children welcome in restaurant ~ Jazz in the garden some summer Sunday lunchtimes ~ Open 11-2.30(3 Sat), 6-11; 12-10.30 Sun; 12-4, 7-10.30 winter Sun

KNEBWORTH TL2320 Map 5

Lytton Arms

Park Lane, Old Knebworth, 3 miles from A1(M) junction 7; A602 towards Stevenage, 2nd roundabout right on B197 towards Knebworth, then right into Old Knebworth Lane; at village T-junction, right towards Codicote

Over the past decade more than 2300 real ales have been rotated through the handpumps at this friendly Victorian brick pub. At any one time, besides 10 guests you should find well kept Bass, Fullers London Pride, Theakstons Best and Woodfordes Wherry; also Staropramen beer from Prague on draught, about 50 Belgian bottled beers, country wines, about 50 malt whiskies, Weston's Old Rosie farm cider, and hot chocolate and herb teas as well as coffee; in the winter, hot gluhwein served by the log fire, with chestnuts roasting, and regular beer festivals. Several solidly furnished simple big-windowed rooms, some panelled and each with a slightly different decor (railway memorabilia here, old Knebworth estate photographs there), ramble around the big central servery, ending in a newish no-smoking conservatory with orderly pale tables on its shiny brown tiles. In addition to daily specials bar food includes soup (£2.40), sandwiches (from £1.80), stilton mushrooms (£3.60), ploughman's or chilli (£4.80), cauliflower and broccoli with stilton cheese sauce (£4.95), breaded plaice (£5.90), steak and kidney pie (£6.20), home-made lasagne (£6.30), mixed grill (£8.50); there may be a delay at busy times. There are picnic-sets on a terrace in front, and the back garden has a play area. Dominoes, shove-ha'penny, table skittles and maybe piped music; two new cats called Aitkin and Noggin. *(Recommended by Peter Saville, George Atkinson, John Fahy)*

Free house ~ Licensee Stephen Nye ~ Real ale ~ Meals and snacks (not 25 Dec) ~ Restaurant ~ (01438) 812312 ~ Well behaved children welcome in eating area of bar ~ Open 11-3, 5-11 Mon-Wed; 11-11 Thurs-Sat; 12-10.30 Sun; closed evening 25 Dec

ST ALBANS TL1507 Map 5

Rose & Crown

St Michaels Street; from town centre follow George Street down past the Abbey towards the Roman town

American-style gourmet sandwiches are the speciality at this relaxed and civilised Victorian town pub. Made under the supervision of the friendly American landlord they range from straightforward cheese (£1.60), through Royalty sandwiches served with potato salad, crisps and pickled cucumber on a granary or white loaf or bap filled with for example beef, salami, swiss cheese, onion and English mustard (£3.95) or peanut butter, honey, watercress and salted peanuts (£2.95), to toasted double-deckers like roast beef, horseradish, mustard, tomato, American cheese and salad or salami, swiss cheese, tomato, chicken, whole grain mustard, lettuce and mayonnaise (£3.95). A few other dishes include soup (£1.95), chilli (£3.75) or lasagne (£4.65). The very traditional beamed public bars have unevenly timbered walls, old-fashioned wall benches, chintzy curtains and cushions and black cauldrons in a deep fireplace which houses a big fire in winter; no-smoking area at lunchtime. Well kept Adnams, Tetleys, Wadworths 6X and a guest on handpump; a dozen or so malt whiskies; efficient service. Darts (placed sensibly to one side), dominoes, cribbage. Lots of tables and benches along the side and at the back of the pub with shrubs and roses, flower beds and hanging baskets. *(Recommended by Maggie and Peter Shapland, M A and R C Starling, Michael Hyde; more reports please)*

Greenalls ~ Tenant Neil Dekker ~ Real ale ~ Lunchtime meals and snacks (not Sun) ~ (01727) 851903 ~ Children welcome in eating area of bar ~ Live music Mon and Thurs nights ~ Open 11.30-3, 5.30(6 Sat)-11; 12-3, 7-10.30 Sun

WALKERN TL2826 Map 5

White Lion

B1037

With a very different atmosphere to our usual entries this popular 17th-c brick pub is geared towards families. Children will be happily occupied by the exciting wooden play area through conifers in the pleasant garden (which is fully enclosed so they can't wander off), a bouncy castle, football nets (the football-playing dog is called Mr Bobby), and the satellite cartoon channel on the terrace in summer. They have recently added a smaller bouncy castle, sand pit and crawl through tent in an effort to amuse even the youngest members of the family. Greene King IPA and Abbot under light blanket pressure is served in the comfortable open-plan bar; jugs of Pimms in summer. Bar food includes soup (£2.95), hot bacon and avocado salad (£3.95), garlic sardines (£3.45), moules marinières (£4.25), liver and bacon or steak and kidney pie (£5.95), fresh fish and chips (£6.95), chicken with mango and coconut (£7.95) and 8oz sirloin steak (£9.95); there is also a small separate no-smoking restaurant. *(Recommended by Charles Bardswell; more reports please)*

Greene King ~ Lease: Gerry Diaz and Helen Ward ~ Meals and snacks (5-9.50; 12-9.30 Sat; 12-3.30 Sun) ~ Restaurant ~ (01438) 861251 ~ Children welcome ~ Open 11-3, 5-11; 11-11 Sat; 12-5 Sun; cl Mon except bank holidays; closed for 10 days in Oct and Jan

WATTON AT STONE TL3019 Map 5

George & Dragon ★ (🍴)

Village signposted off A602 about 5 miles S of Stevenage, on B1001; High St

It's mainly the excellent bar food that draws so many people to this popular country dining pub (they do get busy so book or arrive early). With a wide range of changing daily specials, besides sandwiches (from £1.60), soup (£2.45) and ploughman's (£3.85), the imaginative bar food might include half avocado filled with cream cheese, radish and horseradish (£3.85), home-made burger (£4.35), deep-fried brie served with cranberry and ginger sauce (£4.75), tomato and basil quiche, turkey, mushroom and tarragon pie or mediterranean-style pork balls with tomato and sweet pepper sauce (£5.75), fillet of lemon sole with white wine and asparagus sauce (£7.25), chicken breast with sautéed leeks in a creamy white wine and herb sauce served in a puff pastry shell (£8.45), fresh swordfish steak with garlic and chilli butter (£8.75), and Aberdeen Angus sirloin steak (£11.45); home-made puddings (£2.75). Service is friendly and attentive and the atmosphere is pleasantly sophisticated with kitchen armchairs around attractive old tables, dark blue cloth-upholstered seats in the bay windows, an interesting mix of antique and modern prints on the partly timbered ochre walls, and a big inglenook fireplace. A quieter room off the main bar has spindleback chairs and wall settles cushioned to match the green floral curtains, a hunting print and old photographs of the village above its panelled dado. Proper napkins, antiques and daily newspapers add to the smart feel. As well as a very good wine list they have Greene King Abbot, IPA and seasonal ales under light blanket pressure and several malt whiskies; the small dining room is no smoking; fruit machine, Sunday quiz nights and boules in the pretty extended shrub-screened garden. The pub is handy for Benington Lordship Gardens. *(Recommended by Peter Saville, Charles Bardswell, R Wiles, Bob and Maggie Atherton, Dr and Mrs G H Lewis, Miss J Reay, Gordon Tong, Maysie Thompson)*

Greene King ~ Lease: Kevin Dinnin ~ Real ale ~ Meals and snacks (till 10; not Sun evening) ~ Restaurant ~ (01920) 830285 ~ Children welcome in eating area of bar and restaurant until 9pm ~ Open 11-2.30, 6-11; 11-11 Sat; 12-3, 7-10.30 Sun; closed evenings 25/26 Dec

WESTMILL TL3626 Map 5

Sword in Hand

Village signposted W of A10, about 1 mile S of Buntingford

Delightfully set in a very attractive village, this 14th-c colour-washed listed building is full of character with exposed beams, log fires and traditional style furniture. The dining room (with no-smoking area) has unspoilt views over the church, garden and fields beyond. Well cooked and beautifully presented bar food includes sandwiches (£3), crispy camembert on a bed of salad with port and cranberry sauce or grilled goat's cheese salad (starter £3.95, snack £5.95), well liked ham, egg and chips (£4.95), sausage and mash (£5.95), home-made burger with roquefort cheese or bacon, avocado and mayonnaise (£6.95), avocado and corn bake with spicy taco and cheese sauce (£7.50), steaks (from £7.95) and kiln-smoked salmon (£9.95); Sunday roast (2 courses £11.95), 3 courses £15.50); as everything is home-made to order there may be delays at busy periods, but readers suggest that the quality of the food when it arrives far outweighs any wait. Well kept Greene King IPA and Abbot and Marstons Pedigree on handpump, and a changing range of wines; piped music. There are seats on a terrace surrounded by climbing roses and clematis, and more in the partly crazy-paved side garden running down to the fields, where a play area has a log cabin, slide, and an old tractor to climb on; nice walks nearby. *(Prof John and Patricia White, Mr and Mrs J Richardson; more reports please)*

Free house ~ Licensees David and Heather Hopperton ~ Real ale ~ Meals and snacks ~ Restaurant ~ (01763) 271356 ~ Children welcome (no young children in the restaurant after 8pm) ~ Open 12-3, 5.30-11; 12-4 Sun; closed Sun evening and Mon except bank holidays

Lucky Dip

Besides the fully inspected pubs, you might like to try these Lucky Dips recommended to us and described by readers (if you do, please send us reports):

☆ **Aldbury** [Trooper Rd; SP9612], *Valiant Trooper*: Lively beamed and tiled bar with woodburner in inglenook, some exposed brick in carpeted middle bar, far room (no smoking at lunchtime), well kept Bass, Fullers London Pride, John Smiths, Youngs Special and a guest beer, popular food (not Sun or Mon evenings; good Sun lunch in restaurant), good prices, good friendly service, traditional games, tables in pretty safely fenced garden – good walks nearby; children and dogs welcome (the pub's is called Alexander) *(R C Morgan, Sue Grossey, Ted George, LYM)*

Ashwell [69 High St; TL2639], *Rose & Crown*: Homely and comfortable open-plan local, 16th-c beams, lovely log fire, decent usual food, candlelit restaurant, well kept Greene King IPA, Abbot and Rayments, pleasant staff, darts and machines at plainer public end of L-shaped bar; tables in big pretty country garden *(T Loft, Barry and Marie Males, Nicholas Holmes)*

☆ **Barley** [High St (B1368); TL3938], *Fox & Hounds*: Sold to a chain after 20 years under previous landlady (main entry nearly as long); no longer brews its own beer, and tidied up under new people (the bar billiards have gone, as has some of the individuality), but still has nooks and crannies, log fire, very wide choice of food inc good vegetarian dishes, helpful friendly service, well kept ales such as Morlands Old Speckled Hen *(Shaun Flook, Heather*

Campbell, Susan and Nigel Wilson, R Turnham, Charles Bardswell, Mike and Jennifer Marsh, Bernard and Marjorie Parkin, LYM)

Batford [Lower Luton Rd; B653, S of B652 junction; TL1415], *Gibraltar Castle*: Large Fullers pub doing well under welcoming new landlord, old-fashioned style, low beams, cosy window alcoves, open fire, good atmosphere, interesting militaria, hearty reasonably priced home-made food inc popular Sun roast, well kept beers, good wines and Irish coffee; some tables on front roadside terrace *(N S Doolan, R A Buckler)*

Bishops Stortford [North St; TL4820], *Tap & Spile*: Good changing choice of well kept beers, lots of country wines, very helpful friendly staff, good lunchtime food, lovely old building with rooms of different sizes and levels, decor tastefully in keeping; no music *(Bruce Bird, Elaine Pugh, Steve Mitchell)*

Bourne End [Winkwell; just off A41 Berkhamsted—Hemel, by Texaco at E end; TL0206], *Three Horseshoes*: 16th-c pub worth knowing for its charming canal setting by unusual swing bridge, tables out by water, bay-windowed extension overlooking canal; cosy and homely low-beamed three-room core with inglenooks, one with an Aga, good range of well kept Tetleys-related and guest ales, friendly staff – service can slow when busy; children welcome, open all day (no food Sun evening) *(Bill Sykes, Wayne Brindle, LYM)*

Braughing [The Street, just off B1368; TL3925], *Axe & Compass*: Cricket-oriented pub in pretty village, two roomy and pleasant bars (one an unusual corner-shape) and restaurant, good food inc generous specials, good range of well kept beers, pleasant staff *(N E and M A Jolley)*

☆ **Brickendon** [1 Brickendon Lane, S of Hertford; TL3208], *Farmers Boy*: Roomy refurbished village pub in attractive spot nr village green, friendly service, good range of Whitbreads-related and other ales and of wines, wide choice of good value food from sandwiches up, dining area; seats in back garden and over road *(B N F and M Parkin, Chris Mawson)*

Bricket Wood [off Smug Oak Lane – off A5183 at bridge over M25; TL1502], *Moor Mill*: Spectacular 18th-c restored watermill, central working wheel, largely pine decor, good value lunchtime food servery downstairs, upstairs carpeted lounge bar with real fire, pictures and artefacts, top restaurant with good choice of food lunchtime and evening inc children's dishes, up to nine real ales, picnic-sets in big waterside garden with play area; open all day, piped music *(CMW, JJW)*

Bushey [25 Park Rd; turning off A411; TQ1395], *Swan*: Homely atmosphere in rare surviving example of unspoilt single-room backstreet terraced pub, reminiscent of 1920s *(Pete Baker, BB)*

Charlton [TL1727], *Windmill*: Pleasant streamside setting in small village, food cooked by landlord (mainly lunchtime, evening by arrangement) inc winter game, well kept Charles Wells and guest beers; garden with ducks *(Barry and Marie Males)*

Chorleywood [Dog Kennel Lane, the Common – signed The Swillet off A404 nr lights; TQ0295], *Black Horse*: Nice seating under low dark beams in attractively divided room with thick carpet, two massive log fires, good choice of well prepared food (not Mon) from sandwiches up, real ales such as Adnams and Greenalls Original, friendly welcoming staff, no music; family area, dogs welcome (popular walking territory), biscuits on bar *(Ian Phillips, E R Cowtan)*; [Long Lane, Heronsgate (off M25 at junction 17)], *Land of Liberty Peace & Plenty*: Friendly simply decorated local with particularly well kept Courage-related and interesting guest ales from far afield, half a dozen Belgian beers on tap; limited range of freshly made bar food *(Mr and Mrs S Groves)*; [Long Lane, Heronsgate Rd], *Stag*: Clean and friendly open-plan dining pub, welcoming too for a drink, with well kept Courage Directors, Fullers London Pride and McMullens, good sensibly priced food; quiet piped music, machines tucked around corner; tables on back lawn, children's play area; good walking area, busy weekends *(Ian Phillips, E R Cowtan)*

Colney Heath [Sleapshyde; just off back rd N, between A414 and A1057; TL2007], *Plough*: Popular pleasantly refurbished 18th-c beamed pub, warm and cosy at front with good log fire, Greene King and Fullers ales, enjoyable food *(G Neighbour, Carole Smart, Andrew Jeeves)*

☆ **Datchworth** [Watton Rd; TL2718], *Tilbury*: Two-bar pub with pleasant atmosphere, friendly polite service, good range of up to ten changing well kept beers, good value home-made food inc vegetarian and a pie of the day, bookable restaurant, big garden *(R Turnham, Norma and David Hardy, Robert Turnham)*

☆ *nr* **Datchworth** [Bramfield Rd, Bulls Grn; TL2717], *Horns*: Pretty 15th-c country pub well refurbished and extended into roomy dining area with alcoves, lots of woodwork, writings painted on the beams, inglenook log fire, rugs on brick floor, china and pictures; good choice of food in bar and restaurant, charming service, Whitbreads-related ales *(Charles Bardswell, Enid and Henry Stephens, LYM)*

Epping Green [back rd Cuffley—Little Berkhamsted; TL2906], *Beehive*: Cosy and popular local with huge helpings of good food esp fish, friendly service, Greene King ales *(Gordon Neighbour, Bernard and Marjorie Parkin)*

Flamstead [High St (just off A5); TL0714], *Three Blackbirds*: Cosy low-beamed partly Tudor pub, old dark wood and brickwork, pictures, brass and copper, two real fires; well kept Scottish Courage ales from central bar, friendly service, good value usual food from sandwiches up, no-smoking area; pool, darts and fruit machine in games area, piped music; good walks nearby, children welcome *(Ian Phillips, David Shillitoe, George Atkinson)*

Furneux Pelham [TL4327], *Brewery Tap*: Welcoming licensees and enjoyable food esp fish in friendly refurbished bar with well kept

Greene King IPA and Abbot; pool table, children welcome, back garden room and terrace overlooking neat attractive garden *(Gwen and Peter Andrews)*

Graveley [27 High St; TL2327], *Waggon & Horses*: Former coaching inn with reasonably priced straightforward food inc good Sun roast, comfortable beamed and timbered lounge, big open fire, locals' snug by door, Whitbreads-related ales; plenty of seats in secluded attractive garden and big terrace overlooking duckpond, summer lunchtime barbecues *(Prof John and Mrs Patricia White)*

☆ **Great Amwell** [TL3712], *George IV*: Clean and pleasant pub in pretty spot by church and river, generous helpings of good value varied reasonably priced food inc fish, vegetarian and good puddings, friendly attentive staff, Adnams and other ales *(R E and P Pearce, Mr and Mrs Williams, Mr and Mrs N Chesher)*

Great Gaddesden [off A4146 NW of Hemel; TL0211], *Cock & Bottle*: Main bar and dining area attractively and sensitively decorated – dado rails, warm colours, clever lighting; enterprising food inc theme nights, strong commitment to real ale inc regular beer festivals *(Anon)*

Great Offley [TL1427], *Green Man*: Reopened after refurbishment as roomy Chef & Brewer family dining pub with very wide choice of food, good choice of real ales, conservatory, pleasant back terrace and garden, front play area; the landlord and team who made it a popular main entry in its former guise can now be found at the Red Lion, Milton Bryan (Beds) *(B, M, and P Kendall, LYM)*

☆ **Halls Green** [NW of Stevenage; TL2728], *Rising Sun*: Well restored 18th-c beamed country pub with reliable food in bar or pleasant conservatory restaurant inc special evenings (booking recommended weekends), convivial atmosphere, well kept McMullens and a guest ale, big open fire in small lounge, good big garden with terrace, summer barbecues and play area *(Charles Bardswell)*

☆ **Harpenden** [Luton Rd, Kinsbourne Green; 2¼ miles from M1 junction 10; A1081 towards town, on edge; TL1015], *Fox*: Beamed and panelled lounge with pews and plusher seats, lots of bric-a-brac and masses of prints, smaller tiled public bar; food still good value under new management, wider choice of wine if fewer ales – Benskins, Greene King Abbot, Ind Coope Burton, Marstons Pedigree and Tetleys; log fires, no music, part of lounge now no smoking; children welcome, garden with lots of tables and play area *(Phil and Heidi Cook, BB)*

Harpenden [15 Leyton Green], *Oak Tree*: Refurbished pub with ever-changing real ales, good value lunchtime snacks; can get busy with older people (keen prices for them) *(N S Doolan)*; [Southdown Rd], *Plough & Harrow*: Large open-plan pub with wide choice of food inc huge Sun lunches, real ales such as Courage Directors and Ruddles, respectable wines, friendly licensees; Sun quiz night, big play area *(Steve and Sue Griffiths)*

☆ **Hatfield** [Park St, Old Hatfield; TL2308], *Eight Bells*: Quaint and attractive old beamed pub with well kept Tetleys-related and guest ales, decent bar food, couple of tables in back yard, piped music; open all day w/e, occasional live music; best at quiet times, crowded Fri/Sat nights *(Anon)*

☆ *nr* **Hemel Hempstead** [Bridens Camp; leaving on A4146, right at Flamstead/Markyate signpost opp Red Lion – OS Sheet 166 map ref 044111; TL0411], *Crown & Sceptre*: Country pub keeping some character, with three rooms, roaring fire, well kept Greene King and Rayments BBA with Fullers London Pride and ESB, friendly staff, reasonably priced food from doorstep sandwiches to steaks, tables outside *(Ian Phillips, LYM)*

nr **Hemel Hempstead** [Gaddesden Row; N, towards Markyate; TL0512], *Old Chequers*: Pleasant country pub with good value good home cooking, nice atmosphere *(SF)*

Hertford Heath [B1197, signed off A414 S edge of Hertford; TL3510], *Silver Fox*: Bustling well kept local under new management, friendly service, wide choice of food inc vegetarian and lots of fish, Marstons beers; relaxing sheltered back terrace with fountain *(Nigel and Amanda Thorp, Paul and Sandra Embleton, Chris Mawson, BB)*

☆ **Hexton** [signed off B656; TL1230], *Raven*: Friendly plush rambling pub with four bar areas inc long tidy public bar (open fire, pool one end), big no-smoking room, plenty of dining tables; wide range of good well presented food inc lots of starters, vegetarian and two children's menus, four well kept ales inc Boddingtons and Morlands Old Speckled Hen; children welcome, big garden with terrace, barbecue, well segregated play area *(Phil and Heidi Cook, Barry and Marie Males, Brian Lock, Sidney and Erna Wells)*

High Wych [TL4614], *Rising Sun*: Particularly well kept Courage Best and Directors tapped from the cask, woodburner in one room, log fire in the other, very friendly landlord and locals *(Jack and Philip Paxton)*

☆ **Hinxworth** [High St, just off A1(M); TL2340], *Three Horseshoes*: Friendly and well run thatched, beamed and timbered 18th-c dining pub with good value food (not Sun evening, Mon) inc children's, big brick inglenook, small dining extension, well kept Greene King IPA and Abbot, decent wines, no music; children welcome, big garden with play area *(Anthony Barnes)*

Hunton Bridge [Bridge Rd; just off A41 N of Watford; TL0800], *Kings Head*: Several levels inc galleried dining area, good range of food, helpful flexible service, Benskins and Marstons; big canalside garden excellent for children, handy for canal walks *(Tony Hobden)*

☆ **Little Gaddesden** [Nettleden Rd, off B4506; SP9913], *Bridgewater Arms*: Very civilised dining pub with padded seats, friendly, attentive and helpful staff, wide choice of good food ordered from separate counter in bar and separate restaurant, good wines, well kept ales such as Fullers London Pride, Marstons Pedigree and John Smiths, good coffee; darts at uncarpeted public end; good walks straight from the pub *(Gwen and Peter Andrews, BB)*

☆ **Little Hadham** [The Ford, just S of A120 W of Bishops Stortford; TL4322], *Nags Head*: Cosy and relaxed 16th-c dining pub with very wide choice of good fresh changing food inc lots of fish and al dente veg, very generous helpings and sensible prices, well kept Greene King IPA, Abbot, Rayments and a seasonal beer tapped from the cask, decent wines, freshly squeezed orange juice, efficient friendly staff; comfortable heavily black-beamed interconnecting rooms, old local photographs, guns, copper pans, no music; restaurant down a couple of steps; must book Sun lunch, children welcome, handy for Hopleys nursery *(Joy and Peter Heatherley, Michael Fullagar, Michael Gittins, Paul and Sandra Embleton, Gwen and Peter Andrews, BB)*

Little Wymondley [TL2127], *Bucks Head*: Friendly and pleasantly decorated timbered pub with several well kept real ales, decent food, good staff; attractive garden *(Barry and Marie Males, LYM)*

London Colney [High St; TL1704], *Fox*: Good choice of good generous food and of wines (specialist choice), nice atmosphere, good decor, service and prices; plenty of room *(Lucy Robinson)*

☆ **Much Hadham** [Widford Rd (B1004 S); TL4319], *Jolly Waggoners*: Mock-Tudor dining pub, very family-oriented; beautiful lawn with complex play equipment, also friendly donkeys, horses, sheep, goats, ducks and geese; good range of home-cooked food inc vegetarian and children's dishes, popular Sun lunch, attentive service, McMullens AK and IPA, good range of malt whiskies, nice window seats; attractive countryside nr Hopleys nursery, some live jazz *(Carrie Morley, George Atkinson, Paul and Sandra Embleton, John Wooll, Ted George)*

☆ **Newgate Street** [1 mile N of Cuffley; TL3005], *Coach & Horses*: Attractively refurbished heavy-beamed country pub by church, doing well under current management; cosy rambling small flagstoned bars, reasonably priced food, well kept real ales, two open fires; picnic-sets in sheltered garden, good walks nearby *(D H Heath, LYM)*

Northchurch [High St (A4251 Berkhamsted—Tring); SP9708], *George & Dragon*: Traditional family-run low-beamed 18th-c coaching inn, log fire, warm welcome, good range of reasonably priced home-cooked lunchtime food (not Sun), well kept Bass and Tetleys-related ales, good choice of bottled beers; tables in big garden with aviary, beautiful floral display in yard; opp church where Peter the Wild Boy is buried *(Peter and Mavis Brigginshaw, David and Eileen Lush)*

☆ **Nuthampstead** [TL4034], *Woodman*: Out-of-the-way but welcoming thatched and weatherboarded village local, good range of well kept ales, generous home-cooked food in extended restaurant, good service, inglenook log fire, interesting USAF memorabilia (nearby WWII airfield); pleasant garden, lovely setting *(S Horsley)*

Park Street [A5183 S of St Albans; TL1403], *Overdraft*: Brass, bric-a-brac, prints and old photographs in homely beamed and panelled front room, stripped brick, two bottle gardens and chamber-pot garden, good value lunchtime food inc reasonably priced Sun lunch, three well kept changing ales, fresh flowers; TV in back room; garden and play area; children welcome, open all day *(JJW, CMW, Stephen and Tracey Groves)*

☆ **Perry Green** [B1004 Widford—Much Hadham; TL4317], *Hoops*: Cosy and friendly, in small village opp the Henry Moore Foundation (can be visited by appt; good food from freshly baked baguettes up, real ales, children allowed in no-smoking dining area, tables in garden *(B and M Parkin, Paul and Sandra Embleton, Elaine Pugh, Steve Mitchell)*

Potten End [TL0109], *Red Lion*: Exceptional value food esp giant doorstep sandwiches; well kept Hancocks HB *(Pat and Robert Watt)*

☆ **Potters Crouch** [off A4147; TL1105], *Holly Bush*: Clean and spacious old farmhouse-style country pub, unusual furnishings inc highly varnished good-sized tables, lots of pictures, brasses and antlers, crockery on welsh dresser, old-fashioned lighting; particularly well kept Fullers Chiswick, London Pride and ESB, simple mainly snacky food (not Sun), decent wines; busy weekends; no dogs, good big garden with picnic-sets *(CMW, JJW, CE, Mick and Hilary Stiffin)*

☆ **Radlett** [14 Cobden Hill (A5183); opp Tabard RUFC; TL1600], *Cat & Fiddle*: Fine old building converted from cottages, three small attractive rooms, fire in each, low red banquettes, cat theme throughout inc lots of china ones; five well kept ales, fairly wide choice of good value lunchtime food (one room no smoking then), picnic-sets in small tree-sheltered garden; fruit machine, darts *(CMW, JJW)*

Reed [High St, just off A10 S of Royston; TL3636], *Cabinet*: Ancient tiled and weatherboarded country pub with log fire in little rustic parlourish public bar, pleasant lounge, tables in charming big garden with pond and flowers; no reports since new owners took over late 1997 *(LYM; news please)*

Rushden [village signed off A507 W of Cottered; TL3031], *Moon & Stars*: Unspoilt cottagey beamed country pub, a main entry under previous tenant, with no-smoking lounge bar, inglenook log fire, well kept Greene King ales, popular food, pleasant garden; no reports yet on new regime *(LYM; news please)*

☆ **Sarratt** [The Green; TQ0499], *Boot*: Friendly and attractive early 18th-c tiled pub in pleasant spot facing green, cosy rambling rooms, unusual inglenook fireplace, well kept Tetleys-related ales, good if not cheap bar food; handy for Chess Valley walks *(J S M Sheldon, Ian Phillips, LYM)*

Sarratt [Church Lane], *Cock*: Prettily refurbished 17th-c country pub with good mix of old and new, plenty of tables, inglenook log fire, pleasant garden, restaurant in nicely restored thatched barn, pub games; now a Badger managed pub, with IPA, Best and

Tanglefoot and guests such as Brakspears and Shepherd Neame Spitfire, wide choice of food; piped music, children in eating areas, open all day w/e *(Cyril S Brown, LM, Ian Phillips, Pat and Robert Watt, LYM)*; [The Green], *Cricketers*: Big busy dining pub with good choice of food inc impressive range of fish and seafood, well kept Courage Directors, Marstons Pedigree, Ruddles County and Tring Sun, plenty of friendly uniformed staff, pleasant decor; tables out by pond, open all day *(H H Liesner, J W G Nunns)*

Sawbridgeworth [81 London Rd; TL4814], *Gate*: Roomy pub with lots of quickly changing ales, all in peak condition; bank hol beer festivals, cheap fresh lunchtime food, sports teams from darts to soccer *(Jack and Philip Paxton)*

Sawbridgeworth [Station Rd/Knight St; TL4814], *King George IV*: Old-fashioned, with photographs and bric-a-brac, pleasant licensees, well kept real ales, bar food, good value wines, good range of well priced food in newer restaurant (Sun and evenings); open all day w/e *(Gwen and Peter Andrews)*

☆ **St Albans** [off George St, through abbey gateway – you can drive down; TL1507], *Fighting Cocks*: Odd-shaped former abbey gatehouse, much modernised inside but still showing the sunken area which was a Stuart cockpit, some low and heavy beams, inglenook fires, and pleasant nooks, corners and window alcoves; eight well kept Tetleys-related and changing guest ales, farm cider, bar food (not Sun and Mon evenings) from filled baps up, daily papers; piped music and machines may obtrude, can get packed with summer visitors; children welcome, attractive public park beyond garden, open all day *(Ian Phillips, Allan Engelhardt, David and Ruth Shillitoe, LYM)*

☆ **St Albans** [Sopwell Lane, off Holywell Hill], *Goat*: Surviving fragment of substantial 18th-c inn, old pews, lots of bric-a-brac, books and prints in rambling areas around central servery, open fire, cheery atmosphere, Adnams, Courage Directors, Greene King IPA, Marstons Pedigree and Worthington Best, good range of malt whiskies, cheapish home-made bar food (not Fri-Sun evenings) inc Sun lunch, games machines, piped music, tables in neat back garden; children in eating area, jazz Sun lunchtime, open all day *(Ian Phillips, LYM)*

St Albans [26 St Peters St], *Blacksmiths Arms*: Real ales such as Boddingtons and Wadworths 6X, various guest beers; can be rather crowded Fri/Sat night *(Anon)*; [Fishpool St], *Blue Anchor*: Small warmly welcoming locals' bar on left, newspapers to read, well kept McMullens ales inc Mild, attractive prices, sensibly placed darts, friendly service, real fire; comfortable lounge opening on to sizeable garden, good value bar food (not Sun evening) from sandwiches up, coffee, wines; handy for Roman remains *(Richard Houghton)*; [Hatfield Rd], *Crown*: All-day food till 9 in beamed pub with Courage Best, Greene King IPA, Marstons Pedigree and Wadworths 6X; quiz night Mon and Thurs, juke box *(Anon)*; [61 Albert St; left turn down Holywell Hill past White Hart – car park left at end], *Garibaldi*: New managers in this useful and friendly Fullers pub, with Chiswick, London Pride and ESB and a guest such as Adnams, usual food (not Mon); children welcome, piped nostalgic pop music, open all day *(Klaus and Elizabeth Leist, Ian Phillips, LYM)*; [Sopwell Lane], *Hare & Hounds*: Plenty of seats outside, bar food lunchtime and evening, beers inc Boddingtons and Fullers London Pride *(Anon)*; [98 Hatfield Rd], *Mermaid*: Recently refurbished, neat and tidy, doesn't feel contrived; several pleasant seating areas inc quiet window seat, well kept Everards, relaxed atmosphere *(Anon)*

nr **St Albans** [Tyttenhanger Green; from A414 just under 2 miles E of A6/A1081 roundabout, take B6426 signed St Albans, then first left; TL1805], *Barley Mow*: Spacious sunny-windowed welcoming bar, big log fire, well kept ales such as Adnams, Bass, Courage Directors, Fullers ESB and London Pride and Tring Ridgeway, usual food, friendly service; children welcome, tables in garden with pond overlooking paddocks *(Mick and Hilary Stiffin, LYM)*; [Tyttenhanger Green], *Plough*: Spacious and friendly village pub, polite prompt service, lovely longcase clock, good log fire, well kept Fullers ESB and London Pride, Greene King Abbot, Marstons Pedigree and rotating guest beers, basic lunchtime food, good collection of old beer bottles and other bric-a-brac, pleasant young staff; big garden with play area *(Dr and Mrs G H Lewis)*

Tewin [Upper Green Rd, signed off B1000 NE of Welwyn; N end of village – OS Sheet 166 map ref 273153; TL2715], *Plume of Feathers*: Has been one of Hertfordshire's best pubs, with very individual furnishings and layout, as well as unusual food in bar and restaurant; but summer 1998 bought by Marstons, and being extensively refurbished as we went to press – so fingers crossed! *(LYM; news please)*

☆ **Therfield** [off A505 Baldock—Royston; TL3336], *Fox & Duck*: Pleasantly refurbished beamed village pub with rugs on old tiled floor, solid old-fashioned tables and chairs, good value bar food and more pricy dishes (dining room extension), Adnams, Courage Directors, Greene King IPA and Ruddles, decent wines, unobtrusive piped music; good children's garden with climbing frames, swings and tree house *(Sidney and Erna Wells, Gwen and Peter Andrews)*

Titmore Green [TL2126], *Hermit of Redcoats*: Large open-plan village pub, four cosy rooms recently refurbished under new management, old prints, candles on tables, open fire, interesting choice of good value food, Greene King IPA and Abbot, Marstons Pedigree and a seasonal beer, good wine choice, friendly obliging service; no-smoking area, small upstairs dining room, big terrace and garden *(Phil and Heidi Cook)*

Tring [Bulbourne; B488 towards Dunstable, next to BWB works; SP9313], *Grand Junction Arms*: Very friendly open-plan canalside pub with real ales such as Jennings Cocker Hoop and Thwaites Daniels Hammer, reasonably priced food in raised side eating area, canal photographs and memorabilia; play area in big garden overlooking canal, barbecues and Sat evening live music out here *(Ian Phillips);* [King St; SP9211], *Kings Arms*: Unspoilt genuine backstreet local with no juke box or video screens, simple wholesome food, five well kept ales inc local Tring brews, green decor, friendly welcome *(Stephen and Tracey Groves)*

☆ **Wadesmill** [Poles Lane, Thundridge; A10, N of Ware; TL3517], *Sow & Pigs*: Cheery central bar with pig decor, spacious pleasantly rustic beamed dining room off, well kept Adnams, Shipstones, Wadworths 6X and one or two guest beers, very generous food from sandwiches up; no dogs, children in eating areas, tables outside; open all day *(Nigel Wikeley, Paul and Sandra Embleton, Bernard and Marjorie Parkin, LYM)*

Walkern [B1036; TL2826], *Yew Tree*: Wide choice of well cooked good food in ancient pub recently comfortably refurbished, McMullens ales, good unpretentious atmosphere *(Charles Bardswell)*

Ware [TL3614], *Old Bulls Head*: Refurbished as Festival Ale House without losing character, comfortable and cosy, with nice raised area and the odd easy chair, good choice of well kept real ales *(Anon)*

☆ **Watton at Stone** [113 High St (A602); TL3019], *Bull*: Picturesque and comfortably rebuilt 15th-c beamed coaching inn doing well under its young licensees, massive inglenook, good varied food (separate dining room), friendly attentive staff, Tetleys-related ales, good house wines, attractive prices, public bar with darts and unobtrusive juke box; very busy weekends; pleasant flowered terrace overlooking big well kept back garden *(Sidney and Erna Wells, Mrs E E Sanders, R Turnham, Charles Bardswell)*

Welwyn Garden City [19 Howardsgate; TL2312], *Cask & Glass*: Well converted bank, two well decorated floors; lively, with well kept Boddingtons and other ales, lunchtime food *(Dr and Mrs A K Clarke)*; [Church Rd], *Cottage*: Spacious, lively and interesting conversion of old school/cottage hospital, the library style working very well; well kept Greene King, food most of the day *(Dr and Mrs A K Clarke)*

nr **Wheathampstead** [Gustard Wood; off B651 1½ miles N – OS Sheet 166 map ref 172164; TL1716], *Tin Pot*: Good friendly small 17th-c country pub by rough common, wide range of good home-made food, well kept ales such as Wadworths 6X and Youngs, comfortable beamed lounge, tiled-floor public; dogs welcome; bedrooms excellent, good breakfast *(N S Doolan, Neil Fletcher)*

Post Office address codings confusingly give the impression that some pubs are in Hertfordshire, when they're really in Bedfordshire or Cambridgeshire (which is where we list them).

Isle of Wight

The Clarendon at Chale, its bar part known as the Wight Mouse, stands out as a great family pub, with a real welcome for children (and a new indoor play area), as well as family suites. It's a good all-round pub, too, with a thriving evening atmosphere, and a splendid collection of malt whiskies; the new bedrooms in the converted adjoining farm are a welcome addition. Another pub with very good facilities for children is a new entry, the Chequers at Rookley; people like the way that the children's side here is kept quite separate – and the very good food. Other places with good food are the White Lion at Arreton, the Crab & Lobster in Bembridge (another new entry, an attractive place just above the shore), the somewhat idiosyncratic Italian-run Bonchurch Inn at Bonchurch, the well run Seaview Hotel in Seaview (with its nice contrast between the genteel front dining bar and the much pubbier back part), and the Spyglass perched above the sea in Ventnor. But best of all for an enjoyable meal out is the Red Lion at Freshwater – our Isle of Wight Dining Pub of the Year. With a high proportion of the island's pubs still tied to the big national brewers, drinks prices here are higher than average, but recently have not been increasing as much as elsewhere. Badger and Gales, from the near mainland, have quite a presence on the island now, but for a real local flavour the main beer to look for is Goddards from Ryde, with the reborn Burts also having quite a showing, and the quite separate Ventnor Brewery also worth trying. The cheapest beer we found was at the Seaview Hotel (one of the growing number of island pubs to use a blanket of carbon dioxide to keep their beers fresh – a practice frowned on by real-ale purists, though only the bravest would claim to be able to detect any taste difference). This year we have pruned the Isle of Wight's Lucky Dip entries (at the end of the chapter) rather severely, so as to concentrate attention on pubs such as the White Horse at Whitwell that we have good up-to-date evidence of being really worthwhile – so please let us know if we have missed out any places that are really deserving.

ARRETON SZ5486 Map 2

White Lion

A3056 Newport—Sandown

It's the good, straightforward and reasonably priced food that draws people to this cosy white village pub. Besides soup (£1.95), sandwiches and filled french bread (from £2.15), jacket potatoes (from £3.65) and ploughman's (from £3.10), the menu includes home-made pâté (£3.75), vegetable pie (£4.75), cod (£5.25), home-made steak and kidney pie (£5.95), gammon steak and egg or pineapple (£6.95) and steaks (from £6.95); daily specials might include lunchtime fish and chips (£3.50), chicken and chips (£3.75) or boozy bangers and mash (£4.50); children's menu. The pleasant beamed lounge bar has shining brass and horse-harnesses on the partly panelled walls, and cushioned wheelback chairs on the red carpet; piped music, fruit machine, shove ha'penny, table skittles, darts, dominoes and bar billiards in winter. The restaurant is no smoking. Well kept Badger Dorset Best, Fullers London Pride, Goddards Fuggle-Dee-Dum and Wadworths 6X tapped from casks behind the bar with an interesting cask-levelling device or on handpump (maybe under light blanket pressure). The pleasant garden has a children's play area and aviary, and you can also sit out in front by the tubs of flowers – you may need to as it does get very busy. *(Recommended by Alan Skull, Jack Barnwell, Martin and Julie Robinson, Andy and Jill Kassube, Mary Aldersey-Williams, June and Malcolm Farmer, Derek and Sylvia Stephenson)*

Whitbreads ~ Lease: Mark and Rucky Griffith ~ Real ale ~ Meals and snacks (all day during summer and Easter holidays) ~ (01983) 528479 ~ Children welcome in family room ~ Open 11-11; 12-10.30 Sun; 11-3, 7-11 winter; 12-3, 7-10.30 winter Sun

BEMBRIDGE SZ6587 Map 2

Crab & Lobster

Foreland Fields Road, off Howgate Road (which is off B3395); OS Sheet 196 map reference 655873

Tucked away on a bluff above the shore, this looks past the Foreland coastguard station to the Channel, with great sea and shipping views from window seats and particularly from the many tables in its garden down towards the beach – an easy walk down. It's attractively decorated in a civilised almost parlourish style, with lots of old local photographs and yachting memorabilia. There's more room inside than you'd expect from the frontage (prettily decked out with flower baskets), with a separate restaurant. Here and in the bar there is some emphasis on good local seafood, such as crab sandwiches, huge Bembridge prawns, crab salad (£7.50) and lobster salad (£9.75); other bar food, served generously, includes sandwiches (from £2), soup (£2.25), lobster soup (£3.75) and daily specials such as vegetable lasagne (£5.75) and steak and kidney pie (£6.95), with a better than average choice of puddings (£2.50). Three real ales on handpump might include Flowers Original, Goddards Fuggle-Dee-Dum and Whitbreads Castle Eden, decent house wines, country wines from the barrel, good coffee, friendly helpful staff; piped music (even in the lavatories). It does get very popular, and is on coach trip itineraries, so best to get there early or late at lunchtime (the lunchtime coaches tend to leave at 2). *(Recommended by D P and J A Sweeney, N Zurick, SLR, Michael A Butler, Phil and Heidi Cook, I R Goodwin)*

Whitbreads ~ Lease: Keith Terrell ~ Real ale ~ Meals and snacks ~ Restaurant ~ (01983) 872244 ~ Children in eating area of bar ~ Open 11-3, 6-11; 12-3, 7-10 Sun; all day weekends in summer

BONCHURCH SZ5778 Map 2

Bonchurch Inn

Bonchurch Shute; from A3055 E of Ventnor turn down to Old Bonchurch opposite Leconfield Hotel

Formerly the stables for the nearby manor house this old stone inn is made up of a separate bar, restaurant, rooms and kitchens all spread around a central courtyard. There's a warm welcome from the friendly Italian landlord and locals in the furniture-packed Victorian bar, which conjures up an image of salvaged shipwrecks with its floor of narrow-planked ship's decking, and seats of the sort that old-fashioned steamers used to have. There's a separate entrance to the very simple no-smoking family room which is a bit separate from the welcoming atmosphere of the public bar, making this not the best place on the Island for families. Courage Best and Directors tapped from the cask, Italian wines by the glass, a few bottled french wines, and coffee; darts, bar billiards, shove-ha'penny, table tennis, dominoes and cribbage. Good bar food includes sandwiches (from £2.50), minestrone soup (£2), ploughman's (from £3.50), chicken and chips (£4.95), well liked Italian specials such as spaghetti bolognese, lasagne or canelloni with spinach (£5), seafood risotto (£5.50), grilled halibut steak (£7), duckling with orange sauce (£7.25) and steaks (from £7.25); puddings such as zabaglione (£3.50); children's menu (£2). They only open the restaurant across the courtyard for reservations in the evenings; bedrooms are simple but comfortable. *(Recommended by Richard Dolphin, Alan Skull, O and J Smith, G and J Wheeler, Lynn Sharpless, Bob Eardley, HNJ, PEJ, Gifford and Annabelle Cox, James and Susie McQuhae)*

Free house ~ Licensees Ulisse and Aline Besozzi ~ Real ale ~ Meals and snacks (11.30-2.15, 6.30-10) ~ Restaurant ~ (01983) 852611 ~ Children welcome in family room ~ Open 11-3, 6.30-11; 12-3, 7-10.30 Sun; cl 25 Dec ~ Bedrooms: £20B/£40B

CHALE SZ4877 Map 2

Clarendon / Wight Mouse

In village, on B3399; also access road directly off A3055

With a toddler play area, swings, slides, a bouncy castle, a junior adventure challenge, tricyles, shetland pony rides from Sid and Arthur, a pets corner and maybe even punch and judy shows in the spacious back garden, this rambling family pub may even be a better value afternoon out with the kids than Blackgang Chine across the road; and don't worry if it's raining – there is a new indoor play area where under 12s can let off steam whatever the weather (admission £1). Considering how well geared up to children it is, the original core of the pub is surprisingly traditional, with musical instruments, guns, pistols and so forth hanging over an open log fire. One end opens through sliding doors into a pool room with dark old pews, large antique tables, video game, juke box, darts, dominoes, fruit machine and pinball. At the other end there's a woody extension with more musical instruments, lots of china mice around a corner fireplace, decorative plates and other bric-a-brac, and even oars from old lifeboats hanging from its high pitched ceiling; piped music; no-smoking area. A very good range of drinks includes well kept Boddingtons, Gales HSB, Marstons Pedigree, Morlands Old Speckled Hen, Wadworths 6X, Whitbreads Fuggles Imperial and an occasional guest on handpump, an outstanding choice of around 365 whiskies, over 50 wines, and some uncommon brandies, madeiras and country wines. Bar food includes sandwiches (from £2.50), soup (£2.10), jacket potatoes (from £2.90), ploughman's (from £3.50), burgers (from £4.10), vegetable mornay (£4.80), chicken curry (£5.50), moules marinières (£6.20), mixed grill (£8.70) and daily specials; and of course a children's menu. The landlord is very friendly and service is always efficient and smiling; no-smoking dining area. There's live music every evening; more restful souls can soak up the lovely views out towards the Needles and Tennyson Downs. The bedrooms are beautifully decorated and now include three luxury two-bedroom family suites; they have also converted the adjoining farm, creating ten new en-suite bedrooms. *(Recommended by John Kirk, C J Fletcher, Dennis Stevens, Michael and Jeanne Shillington, Phil and Heidi Cook, David and Carole Chapman, Mike Starke, Andy and Jill Kassube)*

Free house ~ Licensees John and Jean Bradshaw ~ Real ale ~ Meals and snacks (all day) ~ Restaurant ~ (01983) 730431 ~ Children welcome ~ Live music every night ~ Open 11-12; 12-10.30 Sun ~ Bedrooms: £37B/£74B

nr COWES (EAST) SZ5092 Map 2

Folly

Folly Lane – which is signposted off A3021 just S of Whippingham

It's the delightful setting and nautical atmosphere that draw people to this shipshape old pub on the bank of the estuary; big windows, and seats on a waterside terrace offer bird's-eye views of the boats. Its maritime connections go back a long way; the original building was based around a beached sea-going barge and the roof still includes part of the deck. These days it's a very handy and well known yachting stop, with moorings, a water taxi, long-term parking, and showers; they even keep an eye on weather forecasts and warnings. The nautically themed opened-out bar has a wind speed indicator, barometer and a chronometer around the old timbered walls, as well as venerable wooden chairs and refectory-type tables, shelves of old books and plates, railway bric-a-brac and farm tools, old pictures, and brass lights. It gets very busy at weekends during the summer. Straightforward bar food; Boddingtons, Flowers IPA and Original, Marstons Pedigree and Morlands Old Speckled Hen under light blanket pressure; no-smoking area, pool, darts, fruit machine. There's a bouncy castle in the landscaped garden in summer, and it's not far to Osborne House. If you're coming by land, watch out for the sleeping policemen along the lane. *(Recommended by D P and J A Sweeney, Joy and Peter Heatherley, Andy Cunningham, Yvonne Hannaford, A E Bruce, Andy and Jill Kassube)*

Whitbreads ~ Managers Andrew and Cheryl Greenwood ~ Real ale ~ Meals and snacks (9-11 for breakfast, then 12-10) ~ (01983) 297171 ~ Children welcome in eating area of bar ~ Live entertainment evenings Sat and summer Thurs and Sun ~ Open 11-11(9 for breakfast); 12-10.30 Sun

FRESHWATER SZ3487 Map 2

Red Lion

Church Place; from A3055 at E end of village by Freshwater Garage mini-roundabout follow Yarmouth signpost, then take first real right turn signed to Parish Church

Isle of Wight Dining Pub of the Year

There is an interesting and extensive range of food at this carefully run civilised pub – listed on a big blackboard behind the bar this might include soup (£2.50), herring roes on toast (£4.25), crab and stilton stuffed mushrooms (£4.95), steak and kidney pie, gammon steak with parsley sauce or mushroom stroganoff (£6.95), chicken breast with bacon and mushroom sauce (£7.50), pan-fried trout with almonds (£8.95), sirloin steak (£9.50), swordfish in herb butter (£9.95) or baby leg of lamb for two (£15.50); puddings include apple and ginger crumble, chocolate sponge pudding and home-made ice creams. The comfortably furnished open plan bar has open fires, low grey sofas and sturdy country-kitchen style furnishings on mainly flagstoned floors with bare boards at one end, and lots of local pictures and photographs and china platters on the walls. Flowers Original, Fullers London Pride, Goddards Best and Wadworths 6X under light blanket pressure; small but carefully selected wine list; fruit machine, darts, shove-ha'penny, dominoes, piped classical music. As it can get very busy it is advisable to book. Tables on a grassy area at the back and a couple of picnic-sets in a quiet tucked away square at the front, near the church; no children. There are good walks nearby, especially around the River Yar. *(Recommended by Alan Skull, Michael Hasslacher, Philip Vernon, Kim Maidment, Pamela Turner, A C Brace, E Baxter, John Beeken, Joy and Peter Heatherley, Jeanne Cross, Paul Silvestri, Derek and Sylvia Stephenson, Mrs V Brown, D C T and E A Frewer, D P and J A Sweeney)*

Whitbreads ~ Lease: Michael Mence ~ Real ale ~ Meals and snacks ~ (01983) 754925 ~ Open 11.30-3, 5.30-11; 11-4, 6-11 Sat; 12-3, 7-10.30 Sun

ROOKLEY SZ5084 Map 2

Chequers

Niton Road; signposted S of village

The main attraction of this former customs and excise house is the consistently good food. The exceptionally good facilities for families – including a mother and baby room, a large no-smoking family room with Lego table, colouring competitions, a separate building behind with table tennis and a ball pool and a large play area, toboggan run and bouncy castle in the garden – are a bonus. It's all carefully designed so as to avoid the mayhem that large numbers of children can entail, and restricted to one area of the pub; more mature readers are pleased to find that they can enjoy a quiet meal or drink in child-free surroundings. The comfortable carpeted lounge bar is decorated with cottagey ornaments, and has a group of easy chairs and settees down at one end by the good winter log fire; inland views of rolling downland. The lively flagstoned public bar beyond retains its local character and is popular with young farmers; sensibly placed darts, dominoes, fruit machine, trivia and maybe piped music. Well kept Courage Best and Directors, John Smiths, Morland Old Speckled Hen and Wadworths 6X on handpump; friendly and efficient service even when busy. The very extensive bar menu includes sandwiches (from £1.90), jacket potatoes (from £3.40), ploughman's (from £4.10), home-made steak and ale pie, chicken curry, spinach and ricotta tortellini with cream and mushroom sauce or broccoli and cheese bake (£4.95), open steak sandwich topped with fried onions and mushrooms (£5.25), deep-fried seafood platter (£5.65), grilled lamb steak with garlic butter (£5.85), fresh cod (£5.95), rainbow trout (£6.65), chicken supreme with a green peppercorn sauce (£6.75), mixed grill or gammon steak with pears and stilton (£8.95) and a very good children's menu that includes steaks and jacket potatoes besides the more usual sausages, fish fingers and chips; Sunday roasts and a weekday lunchtime carvery. *(Recommended by Michael and Jeanne Shillington, HNJ, PEJ, M Lockett, J Barnwell)*

Free house ~ Licensees RG and S L Holmes ~ Real Ale ~ Meals and snacks (12-10) ~ (01983) 840314 ~ Children welcome in family room ~ Open 11-11; 12-10.30 Sun

SEAVIEW SZ6291 Map 2

Seaview Hotel

High Street; off B3330 Ryde—Bembridge

The continental-style terraces on either side of the path to the door of this bustling little place do indeed look out over the sea, as do some of the bedrooms. The nautical back bar is a lot pubbier than you might expect from the hotel-like exterior, with traditional wooden furnishings on the bare boards, and lots of seafaring paraphernlia around its softly lit ochre walls, and a log fire; it can be busy with young locals and merry yachtsmen. The civilised airier bay-windowed bar at the front has a splendid array of naval and merchant ship photographs, as well as Spy nautical cartoons for *Vanity Fair*, original receipts fom Cunard's shipyard payments for the *Queen Mary* and the *Queen Elizabeth*, and a line of close-set tables down each side on the turkey carpet. The very popular freshly made bar food includes soup (£2.95), very well liked crab with cream and spices grilled with cheese (£4.50), melted goat's cheese with walnut, apple and red onion mash (£4.95), spiced saffron moules marinières (£5.50), broccoli and cheese puff with tomato and tarragon vinaigrette (£6.95), knuckle of lamb with shredded beetroot, port and potatoes or steak and kidney pie (£7.95) and steak (£10.95); puddings include home-made hot chocolate sponge (£3.50) and steamed treacle pudding (£2.95); friendly landlord and young staff. Flowers IPA and Goddards under light blanket pressure, good wine list and a choice of malt whiskies; darts, cribbage, dominoes, shove-ha'penny and piped music. Tables on the terraces at the front and in a sheltered inner courtyard. *(Recommended by J Barnwell, Alan Skull, Mrs Romey Heaton, D P and J A Sweeney, Michael and Jeanne Shillington, J F M and M West, Yvonne and Peter Griffiths, Joy and Peter Heatherley, A E Brace, Andy and Jill Kassube)*

Free house ~ Licensees Nicholas and Nicola Hayward ~ Real ale ~ Meals and snacks ~ Restaurant ~ (01983) 612711 ~ Children welcome ~ Open 10.30-2.30, 6-11; 12-3, 7-10.30 Sun ~ Bedrooms: £55B/£85B

SHANKLIN SZ5881 Map 2

Fishermans Cottage

Bottom of Shanklin Chine

Although only a few minutes' walk from busy Shanklin's Esplanade, this simple thatched cottage enjoys one of the nicest and most unusual settings of any pub we know, peacefully tucked into the cliffs and quite literally on Appley beach; it's a lovely walk to here along the zigzagged path down the steep and sinuous chine, the beautiful gorge that was the area's original tourist attraction. Tables on the terrace soak up the sun by day and later moonlight romantically shimmers on the lapping waves. Inside, the clean low-beamed and flagstoned rooms have photographs, paintings and engravings on the stripped stone walls. Very simple bar food includes sandwiches (from £2.20), ploughman's (from £3.50), filled jacket potatoes (from £3.20), and a few hot dishes such as vegetable lasagne (£4.40), cod (£4.80) and steak and kidney pie (£5.35). Courage Directors under light blanket pressure, coffee all day, and a range of local country wines. Maybe piped music; wheelchair access. Do remember before starting out that the pub is closed out of season. *(Recommended by David and Carole Chapman, D P and J A Sweeney, more reports please)*

Free house ~ Licensees Mrs A P P Springman and Mrs E Barsdell ~ Real ale ~ Meals and snacks (11.30-3.30, 7-9) ~ (01983) 863882 ~ Children welcome ~ Live entertainment Mon, Wed, Fri and Sat evenings ~ Open 11-3, 7-11; 12-3, 7-10.30 Sun; cl Nov-Feb

SHORWELL SZ4582 Map 2

Crown

B3323 SW of Newport; OS Sheet 196 map reference 456829

In an attractive rural setting on the prettier south eastern side of the island, this friendly old place draws summer crowds to its peaceful tree-sheltered garden, where picnic-sets and white garden chairs and tables look over a little stream that broadens out into a wider trout-filled pool with prettily planted banks; a decent children's play area blends in comfortably. There is a traditional atmosphere in the four friendly rooms that wander round a central bar. The characterful, warm and cosy beamed two-room lounge has blue and white china in an attractive carved dresser, old country prints on the stripped stone walls, other individual furnishings, a cabinet of model vintage cars, and a winter log fire with a fancy tilework surround. Black pews form bays around tables in a stripped-stone room off to the left, with another log fire; the stone window ledges are full of houseplants; several areas are no smoking. Bar food includes steak and kidney pie (£5.95), beef in red wine casserole (£6.95), sea bream with crab sauce (£7.95) and duck breast with orange sauce (£9.50). Well kept Badger Tanglefoot, Boddingtons, Flowers Original and Wadworths 6X on handpump; efficient service; darts, fruit machine, trivia, piped music. *(Recommended by I R Goodwin, Michael and Jeanne Shillington, Alan Skull, Jack Barnwell, Phil and Heidi Cook, Penny and Peter Keevil, D P and J A Sweeney, Andy and Jill Kassube, Martin and Julie Robinson, L G Milligan, John Hayter)*

Whitbreads ~ Lease: Mike and Sally Grace ~ Real ale ~ Meals and snacks ~ (01983) 740293 ~ Children welcome ~ Open 10.30am-11pm; 11.30-10.30 Sun; 10.30-3, 6-11 in winter

VENTNOR SZ5677 Map 2

Spyglass

Esplanade, SW end; road down very steep and twisty, and parking can be difficult

This splendidly placed pub is perched on the top of the sea wall with wonderfully relaxing views out to sea, and readers tell us that the spacious sunny terrace is a delightful place to have lunch. Inside the snug separate areas of the mostly quarry-tiled bar are filled with a genuinely interesting jumble of memorabilia that includes wrecked rudders, ships' wheels, old local advertisements, rope makers' tools, stuffed seagulls, an Admiral Benbow barometer and an old brass telescope. Furnishings include pews around traditional pub tables; no-smoking area. Good bar food includes sandwiches (from £2.10) – the fresh local crab (£3.50) are especially praised by readers – ploughman's (from £3.75), burgers (from £4.25), deep-fried potato shells filled with vegetable chilli (£4.95), home-made cottage pie (£5.25), lasagne (£5.30), lemon and pepper butterfly chicken (£5.95), steaks (from £8.95) and daily specials like pork and apple casserole (£5.95) and seafood tart or beef braised in red wine (£6.25). Well kept Badger Dorset Best and Tanglefoot and Ventnor Golden on handpump; on special occasions such as a lifeboat support week there may be half a dozen or more guests tapped from the cask. Fruit machine; they have no objection to dogs or muddy boots. *(Recommended by Alan Skull, Mrs Mary Woods, John Kirk, D P and J A Sweeney, David and Carole Chapman, J F M West, Andy and Jilly Kassube, Derek and Sylvia Stephenson, David Heath)*

Free house ~ Licensees Neil and Stephanie Gibbs ~ Real ale ~ Meals and snacks; afternoon tea in summer ~ (01983) 855338 ~ Children in eating area of bar ~ Live traditional Irish, blues or jazz every night ~ Open 10.30-11(10.30 Sun); 10.30-3, 7-11 winter weekdays ~ Bedrooms: /£40B

If we know a pub has a no-smoking area, we say so.

YARMOUTH SZ3589 Map 2

Wheatsheaf

Bridge Rd

Don't be put off by the slightly unprepossessing street frontage – inside this pub is comfortably relaxed and spacious, with four eating areas including a light and airy no-smoking conservatory. Reliably good and generously served bar meals include soup (£2), prawn cocktail (£3.75), vegetarian kiev or home-cooked ham (£5.95), chicken tikka masala (£6.95), pasta with a sauce (£6.95), giant garlic and cheese crunch mussels (£6.95); efficient service. Beers include Brakspears, Goddards Fuggle-Dee-Dum, Morlands Old Speckled Hen and Wadworths 6X on handpump or under light blanket pressure; pool (winter only) and juke box (in public bar); garden; the nearest pub to the ferry. *(Recommended by D P and J A Sweeney, Mrs S Quekett, David Heath, Joy and Peter Heatherley, Thomas Nott, Andy Cunningham, Yvonne Hannaford, Andy and Jill Kassube, Dr and Mrs A K Clarke, Sheila and Robert Robinson)*

Whitbreads ~ Lease: Anthony David and Suzanne Keen ~ Real ale ~ Meals and snacks (11-10; 12-10 Sun) ~ (01983) 760456 ~ Children welcome in harbour lounge and conservatory ~ Open 11-11; 12-10.30 Sun; 11-3, 6-11 weekdays in winter; 12-3, 6-10.30 Sun in winter; cl 25 Dec, 26 Dec evening

Lucky Dip

Besides the fully inspected pubs, you might like to try these Lucky Dips recommended to us and described by readers (if you do, please send us reports):

☆ **Bembridge** [Station Rd; SZ6487], *Row Barge*: Friendly outspoken landlord, good home-made pizzas and wide range of well kept Whitbreads-related and other ales in open-plan pub with unpretentious nautical decor, farm cider; children welcome, bedrooms, nr harbour *(Alan Skull, Keith Stevens)*

☆ **Carisbrooke** [High St; SZ4888], *Eight Bells*: Plainly refurbished dining pub, big and busy, well worth knowing for its good generous straightforward food with sparkling fresh veg, good vegetarian and puddings; reasonable prices, well kept Whitbreads-related and other beers such as the well priced local Goddards, quiet piped music, children welcome; set at foot of castle, with charming garden behind running down to lovely lake with lots of waterfowl, also play area *(P G Bardswell, HNJ, PEJ, L G Milligan, Bruce Bird)*

Carisbrooke [Park Cross, Calbourne Rd; B3401 1½ miles W; SZ4687], *Blacksmiths Arms*: Quiet hillside pub with welcoming Bavarian landlord doing varied and imaginative food (Bavarian-sized helpings, too) inc continental dishes, also German wines and beers on draught as well as changing ales such as Archers, Batemans, Fullers London Pride and Ventnor Gold, helpful polite service; neatly kept prewar bars facing road, homely upper bar, panoramic Solent views from dining extension and terraced back garden, play area *(John Beeken, HNJ, PEJ, Derek and Sylvia Stephenson)*

Godshill [SZ5282], *Cask & Taverners*: Comfortable dining pub with good service and good food inc OAP bargains in bar and restaurant, Burts ales, log fire, garden with play area; quiz nights, jazz Thurs *(D P and J A Sweeney)*

Havenstreet [off A3054 Newport—Ryde; SZ5690], *White Hart*: Cosy bar with lots of locomotive prints in ancient building, tidy and comfortable, well kept Badger and Flowers, varied generous food inc good fresh veg and splendid salads, friendly staff; interesting beer-bottle collection *(D P and J A Sweeney, Martin Wright)*

Lake [Lake Hill; SZ5983], *Old Manor House*: Pleasant pub useful for usual food, nice dining room *(A M Pring)*

☆ **Limerstone** [B3399 towards Brighstone; SZ4382], *Countryman*: Large bright high-ceilinged open-plan bars and restaurant area, airy and welcoming, with mock dark beams, horse/farming equipment and pictures, good value straughtforward food inc vegetarian, prompt polite service, well kept Badger Best and Tanglefoot, Hampshire and guest ales; front garden with view over fields to sea *(Derek and Sylvia Stephenson, HNJ, PEJ)*

Newport [8 Carisbrooke Rd; SZ4988], *Cask & Crispin*: Small, friendly Burts local with good food and well kept ales *(D P and J A Sweeney)*

☆ **Niton** [off A3055 just S of village, towards St Catherines Point; SZ5075], *Buddle*: Extended former smugglers' haunt, heavy black beams, big flagstones, broad stone fireplace, no-smoking areas, good range of Whitbreads-related and guest ales, some tapped from the cask, local farm cider, bar food inc good seafood and griddled dishes (service can slow at busy times), family dining room/games annexe, friendly dogs; well cared for sloping garden and terraces, good walks; open all day, some live jazz *(Andy and Jill Kassube, June and Malcolm Farmer, A E Brace, LYM)*

Sandown [St Johns Rd; aka Old Comical; SZ5984], *Sandown Brewery*: Tap for Burts brewery (can be visited), cask and other tables, panelled wall bench and mate's chairs in traditional bar, comfortable lounge area, food inc big range of sausages, garden with play area and boules *(D P and J A Sweeney)*

Seaview [Esplanade; B3340, just off B3330 Ryde—Brading; SZ6291], *Old Fort*: Spacious, light and airy, with commanding sea views, interesting choice of food, Ruddles *(Alan Skull)*

Shalfleet [A3054 Newport—Yarmouth; SZ4189], *New Inn*: Traditional beamed and panelled bar, carpeted dining lounge and restaurant, no-smoking family area, Bass, log fire; piped music may be loud; open all day summer *(Penny and Peter Keevil, D P and J A Sweeney, LYM)*

☆ **Shanklin** [Chine Hill; SZ5881], *Chine*: Great clifftop setting, tastefully refurbished, with flagstones, beams, good food (not Sun evening, Tues or Sat), well kept Bass and local Goddards; bright family conservatory and small terrace overlooking beach and chine (which is illuminated at dusk) *(David and Carole Chapman, D P and J A Sweeney)*

Shanklin [The Esplanade], *Longshoreman*: Large comfortable low-beamed seafront pub with old island photographs, friendly staff, good food, garden overlooking Sandown Bay; entertainment some nights *(David and Carole Chapman, D P and J A Sweeney)*; [Old Village], *Village Pub*: Big helpings of good value food inc memorable puddings, obliging service, upstairs dining room open if downstairs bar full, small pleasant back garden with wendy house; children allowed in family area if eating, open all day *(A M Pring)*

☆ **Whitwell** [High St; SZ5277], *White Horse*: Welcoming ancient pub with wide range of good value home-made food inc vegetarian, huge helpings, full range of Gales ales kept well, well furnished big interconnected beamed bars with separate comfortable family areas; cheerful quick service, country decor, horsebrasses, log fire *(Alan Skull, David Heath)*

Bedroom prices normally include full English breakfast, VAT and any inclusive service charge that we know of. Prices before the '/' are for single rooms, after for two people in double or twin (B includes a private bath, S a private shower). If there is no '/', the prices are only for twin or double rooms (as far as we know there are no singles). If there is no B or S, as far as we know no rooms have private facilities.

Kent

Quite a flush of new entries here this year: the attractive Kings Head just across from the Deal seafront, the Red Lion in Hernhill (new licensees since this was last in the Guide, doing imaginative food), the interesting and ancient Dirty Habit at Hollingbourne, altogether more appealing than its unattractive name (we much prefer either of its previous names, the Pilgrims Rest or Kings Head – but then we've never much liked trendy name-changes), the Duke William at Ickham (good food, excellent choice of wines by the glass), the relaxed and chatty Woodcock just outside Iden Green, the friendly old Bull at Linton (good all round, lovely views from its garden), and the Beacon out on the edge of Tunbridge Wells (nice mix of town and country). Other pubs doing particularly well here these days are the Wheatsheaf at Bough Beech (good all round, some very nice touches), the Dove tucked away at Dargate (earning a Food Award this year, for its careful use of fresh local ingredients), the Albion in Faversham (concentration on very good imaginative food, but still a friendly place to sit at the bar for a drink), the nicely placed Crown at Groombridge (attractive inside, with very good food for that area), the George at Newnham (food improved under newish licensees), the Bottle House out on the edge of Penshurst (good all round – and an excellent choice of fresh fish), the Ringlestone at Ringlestone (great character, good all round – and nice bedrooms in the farmhouse opposite), and the very friendly Rose & Crown prettily set at Selling. Besides several of these where we've picked out the food as a strong point, the Dering Arms at Pluckley, Sankeys in Tunbridge Wells and Pearsons in Whitstable also stand out for enjoyable meals out. From the county's very good choice of foody places, we name as Kent Dining Pub of the Year the Albion in Faversham. In the Lucky Dip section at the end of the chapter, pubs currently showing particularly well are the Ship at Conyer Quay, Plough at Ivy Hatch (very restauranty), Chequers at Smarden and Tiger at Stowting; we have inspected and approved all of these. In Canterbury, the Canterbury Tales looks to be the current pick. Drinks prices in the county have stayed more stable than elsewhere, particularly in free houses (a good effect of cross-Channel competition?), but are still higher than the national average. We found the Cock at Luddesdown and Red Lion at Hernhill cheaper than most; pubs tied to the local brewer, Shepherd Neame of Faversham, also tended to be relatively cheap for drinks. A lot of Kent pubs stock farm ciders, often local – well worth keeping an eye open for.

BARFRESTON TR2650 Map 3

Yew Tree

A huge yew tree obscures the unassuming exterior of this very friendly tucked away country local. Although the licensee, Pamela, is new here, we're expecting the comfortable easy going atmosphere to continue unchanged as she is the sister of Angie, the old licensee (they've swopped pubs). The chatty main bar has a log fire, upholstered pine chairs and wall seats around a mix of old pine tables on the bare boards, candles in bottles, cream walls with old local photographs, lots of hops draped over a large beam, and a delft shelf with an ancient wooden yoke and a few horsebrasses; fresh flowers on the bar counter. There's a second, simply furnished little bar, and a cosy dining room with just four tables, a piano, and an open fire in the stone fireplace – you can book this for a private party. Bar food includes doorstep sandwiches (£2.75), good soups such as curried parnsip or celery (£2.75), tasty pies such as pork and cider, game, steak and kidney, chicken and mushroom, mushroom and seafood (£5.95), and evening steaks (£7.95); puddings (£2.50); popular Sunday roast (£6). They keep seven real ales, well kept on handpump such as Black Sheep, Fullers ESB, Greene King IPA and Dark Mild, Timothy Taylor Landlord, farm ciders, several malt whiskies, and several different fresh coffees; cribbage, piped music and a table-top skittles game called daddlums. *(Recommended by Anthony Barnes, Digby Linnett, Douglas and Ann Hare, B J Harding, Stephen G Brown, David and Margaret Bloomfield, Patricia Dodd)*

Free house ~ Licensee Pamela White ~ Real ale ~ Snacks (all day) and meals ~ (01304) 831619 ~ Children welcome ~ Live music Thurs evening and Sun from 5 ~ Open 11-11; 12-10.30 Sun ~ Bedrooms: £15/£30

nr BIDDENDEN TQ8538 Map 3

Three Chimneys

A262, a mile W of village

There's a wonderfully unspoilt atmosphere at this characterful old country pub. The rambling and low oak beamed series of small, very traditional rooms have simple wooden furniture and old settles on flagstones and coir matting, some harness and sporting prints on the exposed brick walls, and good winter log fires. The simple public bar has darts, shove-ha'penny, dominoes and cribbage, and the good range of well kept real ales tapped from the cask might include Adnams Best, Brakspears, Harveys Best (and Old in winter), Marstons Pedigree and Morlands Old Speckled Hen along with Biddenden local cider, a carefully chosen wine list with a range of half bottles (as well as local wine), and about twenty malt whiskies. Bar food is limited to four starters, four main courses, and four puddings each day: soup such as seafood chowder (£3.75), curried crab mousse (£3.75), duck and orange pâté (£3.95), prawn and mushroom quiche (£5.50), mushroom stroganoff (£5.95), chicken in cheese, wine and tarragon sauce (£6.85), duck and pheasant casserole (£7.25), and pear and nut tart (from £2.95). You can book tables in the Garden room. At the back the lusciously growing garden has nut trees at the end, and densely planted curving borders with flowering shrubs and shrub roses. Sissinghurst gardens are just down the road. *(Recommended by Mrs J Burrows, G Neighbour, Kevin Thorpe, Joan and Andrew Life, Janet and Colin Roe, Peter Meister, JP, PP, Chris Brace, Douglas and Ann Hare, Mr and Mrs P Eastwood, Nigel Wikeley, Ian and Nita Cooper, A Homes, C Sinclair, Paula Williams, J Tross, John Le Sage, K Flack)*

Free house ~ Licensees C F W Sayers and G A Sheepwash ~ Real ale ~ Meals and snacks (till 10pm) ~ (01580) 291472 ~ Children in Garden room ~ Open 11-2.30, 6-11; 12-2.30, 7-10.30 Sun; closed 25-26 Dec

BOUGH BEECH TQ4846 Map 3

Wheatsheaf

B2027, S of reservoir

This delightful old hunting lodge is stylishly well run with plenty of attention to detail, enthusiastic service, and very nice food. There are thoughtful touches like piles of smart magazines to read, nice nibbles, chestnuts to roast in winter, summer Pimms and mulled wine in winter. The neat central bar and the long bar (with an attractive old settle carved with wheatsheaves, shove-ha'penny, dominoes, and board games) have unusually high ceilings with lofty oak timbers, a screen of standing timbers and a revealed king post. Divided from the central bar by two more rows of standing timbers – one formerly an outside wall to the building – is the snug, and another bar. Other similarly aged features include a piece of 1607 graffiti, '*Foxy Galumpy*', thought to have been a whimsical local squire. There are quite a few horns and heads, as well as a sword from Fiji, crocodiles, stuffed birds, swordfish spears, and the only manatee in the south of England on the walls and above the massive stone fireplaces. Really well liked bar food – served all day – includes houmous with black olives and pitta bread (£2.95), faggots (£4.50), moules (£7.95), home-baked honey roast ham (£7.50) and monkfish tails (£10.50). Well kept Flowers Original, Fullers London Pride, Morlands Old Speckled Hen, Shepherd Neame Master Brew and Wadworths 6X on handpump, decent wines including local wine, and several malt whiskies; piped music. There's a rustic cottage in the garden, lovely garden furnitre and swings for children to play on, and flower beds and fruit trees fill the sheltered side and back gardens. *(Recommended by LM, Derek Harvey-Piper, Paul and Sharon Sneller, Mr and Mrs D Mullett, Howard England, Simon Small, Timothy Galligan, Tim Barrow, Sue Demont, Susan and John Douglas, B J Harding, D E Twitchett, Paul Hilditch)*

Whitbread ~ Lease: Elizabeth Currie ~ Real ale ~ Meals and snacks (noon-10pm) ~ (01732) 700254 ~ Folk music Weds evening ~ Open 11-11; 12-10.30 Sun

BOUGHTON ALUPH TR0247 Map 3

Flying Horse

Boughton Lees; just off A251 N of Ashford

This lovely old pub was built on the ancient Canterbury Pilgrims' Way, probably to capture the hungry pilgrim trade. A few clues to the building's age still remain, mainly in the shiny old black panelling and the arched windows (though they are a later Gothic addition), and its two ancient glass-covered and illuminated spring-water wells. The open-plan bar has fresh flowers, hop bines around the serving area, horsebrasses, stone animals on either side of the blazing log fire, lots of standing room (as well as comfortable upholstered modern wall benches), and a friendly atmosphere; two more open fireplaces. From the no-smoking back room, big doors open out on to the spacious rose filled garden, where there are seats and tables; summer barbecues. Bar food under the new licensees includes escargot, potted shrips or whitebait (£3.75), avocado baked with spinach, prawns and cheese (£6.95), poached salmon and tarragon sauce or duck breast with mushroom and pepper sauce (£7.50) and home-made puddings (£2.60). Well kept Courage Best and Directors, Fullers London Pride, Morlands Old Speckled Hen, Theakstons XB and Youngs Special on handpump, and good wines. Shove-ha'penny, cribbage, dominoes, fruit machine, and piped music. The Shuttle is only 8 miles away. *(Recommended by Alan and Judith Gifford, Ian Phillips, Janet and Colin Roe, Stephen Brown, Elizabeth and Klaus Leist, Mrs G Sharman, Stephen Brown, Gregor Macdonald, D and J Tapper, Mr and Mrs Jonathan Russell)*

Courage ~ Lease: Timothy Chandler and Francis Hartnett ~ Real ale ~ Meals and snacks (11.45-2.15, 6-10; all day Sat and Sun) ~ Restaurant ~ (01233) 620914 ~ Children in eating area of bar and restaurant till 9pm ~ Open 12-3, 6-11; 12-11 Sat; 12-10.30 Sun ~ Bedrooms: £25/£40

BOYDEN GATE TR2265 Map 3

Gate Inn ★

Off A299 Herne Bay—Ramsgate – follow Chislet, Upstreet signpost opposite Roman Gallery; Chislet also signposted off A28 Canterbury—Margate at Upstreet – after turning right into Chislet main street keep right on to Boyden; the pub gives its address as Marshside, though Boyden Gate seems more usual on maps

One of the most fun photographs (alongside some ancient sepia ones) at this splendidly welcoming old-style local is a picture of Mr Smith, the landlord, running a race in a dress – so we know he's got a sense of humour. There's also a good winter log fire (which serves both quarry-tiled rooms), flowery-cushioned pews around tables of considerable character, hop bines hanging from the beam and attractively etched windows. Tasty bar food includes sandwiches (from £1.60; fried egg, sausage and bacon £2.60), generous ploughman's (£3.95), vegetable flan (£4.60), spicy hotpots with toppings like grilled sausage chunks (£4.60), gammon and pineapple (£4.80), steak (£4.80), and puddings; they use organically grown local produce where possible, and you can generally buy local honey and free-range eggs. The eating area is no smoking at lunchtime. Well kept Shepherd Neame Bitter, Spitfire, 1698 Celebration Ale and seasonal ales tapped from the cask, with country wines and local apple juice. Shove-ha'penny, dominoes, trivia and cribbage. On a fine evening, it's marvellously relaxing to sit at the picnic-sets on the sheltered side lawn listening to the contented quacking of what seems like a million happy ducks and geese (they sell duck food inside – 10p a bag). *(Recommended by David Carr, David Shillitoe, Kevin Thorpe, Comus Elliott, Ian and Nita Cooper, Mr and Mrs A Budden, Ian Phillips, Gregor Macdonald, David Gregory)*

Shepherd Neame ~ Tenant Christopher Smith ~ Real ale ~ Meals and snacks ~ (01227) 860498 ~ Children in eating area of bar and in family room ~ Open 11-2.30(3 Sat), 6-11; 12-3, 7-10.30 Sun

BROOKLAND TQ9926 Map 3

Woolpack £

On A259 from Rye, as you approach Brookland, take the first right turn just after the expanse of Walland Marsh

It's quite easy to imagine smugglers sheltering from the winter marsh mists in the simply decorated bar at this ancient marshland inn. The tremendous age of this crooked white cottage is immediately apparent in the ancient entrance lobby with its uneven brick floor and black painted pine panelled walls. On the right, the simple but homely softly lit main bar has a good warming log fire and basic cushioned plank seats in the massive inglenook fireplace itself, a painted wood effect bar counter hung with lots of water jugs, and some ship's timbers in the low-beamed ceiling that may date from the 12th c. On the quarry tiled floor is a long elm table with shove-ha'penny carved into one end, other old and new wall benches, chairs at mixed tables, and characterful photos of the locals (and perhaps their award winning sheep) on the walls. To the left of the lobby there's a sparsely-furnished little room, and an open-plan games room with central chimney stack, modern bar counter, and young locals playing darts or pool; dominoes, fruit machine, piped music. Well kept Shepherd Neame Bitter and Spitfire on handpump. Generous helpings of good value, straightforward bar food include sandwiches (from £1.50), soup (£2.50), ploughman's (£3.75), pint of prawns or steak pie (£4.25), chilli, lasagne or cod and chips (£4.50), pork chops (£5.95), sirloin steak (£8.25) and daily specials. Tables outside look down the garden to a stream where the pub has fishing rights. *(Recommended by Kevin Thorpe, D and J Tapper, Anthony Barnes, Quentin Williamson, Paul Davis, Comus Elliott, Carl and Jackie Cranmer, Neil Hardwick, Thomas Nott)*

Shepherd Neame ~ Tenants John and Pat Palmer ~ Real ale ~ Meals and snacks ~ (01797) 344321 ~ Children in games room ~ Open 11-2.30, 6-11; 12-3, 7-10.30 Sun

CHIDDINGSTONE TQ4944 Map 3

Castle 🍷

Village signposted from B2027 Tonbridge—Edenbridge

The long standing licensee and staff at this rambling old place lend a sense of comfortable continuity and care. You can order drinks and food in the very prettily laid out suntrap back garden which bears witness to the cheerful input of Chris King, who has doubled as head waiter and gardener for about eighteen years now. Inside, the handsome, carefully modernised beamed bar has well made settles forming booths around the tables, cushioned sturdy wall benches, an attractive mullioned window seat in one small alcove, and latticed windows. Well kept Harveys Best, Larkins Traditional (brewed in the village), and Youngs Bitter on handpump, a good range of malt whiskies, and a very good wine list (the quality is reflected in the prices, though the house wines should suit all pockets). Darts, shove-ha'penny, dominoes and cribbage. Bar food (served all day) includes home-made soup (£3.15), prawn cocktail (£4.50), filled baguettes (from £4.95), half a pint of shell-on prawns (£5.65), open sandwiches (from £3.85), ploughman's (from £5.95), very hot chilli con carne or beef and vegetable curry (£4.35), local sausages (£5.75) and children's dishes (from £2.95). There are tables at the front opposite the church, and it's worth a walk around the village to look at the marvellously picturesque cluster of unspoilt Tudor houses; the countryside around here is lovely. *(Recommended by R and S Bentley, Peter Meister, Nigel Wikeley, B and M Parkin, Brian and Anna Marsden, J S Evans, Pat and Tony Martin, Mrs M Furness, A Homes, Paul Hilditch, Mr and Mrs C G Fraser)*

Free house ~ Licensee Nigel Lucas ~ Real ale ~ Meals and snacks (served all day) ~ Restaurant ~ (01892) 870247 ~ Children welcome (not in public bar) ~ Open 11-11; 12-10.30 Sun

DARGATE TR0761 Map 3

Dove

Village signposted from A299

Changing daily, and using fresh seasonal local ingredients, the popular imaginative menu at this friendly pub might include french bread with prawns and spring onion (£3.75), minute steak in ciabatta bread or smoked haddock fishcakes or salad niçoise (£4.50), grilled fillet of salmon with provençale vegetables (£9), steak with shallot and bacon sauce (£12), lamb cutlets with ratatouille (£12.50), whole grilled bass with marinated artichokes and olives (£15) or whole fresh lobster with samphire (£17-£21), and puddings such as iced grand marnier soufflé, baked chocolate pudding or orange and lemon crème brûlée (from £3.50). Well kept Shepherd Neame Bitter, and Spitfire in summer on handpump. The rambling rooms have photographs of the pub and its licensees throughout the century on the walls, a good winter log fire, and plenty of seats on the bare boards; piped music. The sheltered garden has roses, lilacs, paeonies and many other flowers, picnic-sets under pear trees, a dovecot with white doves, a rockery and pool, and a swing. A bridlepath leads up from the pub (along the charmingly named Plumpudding Lane) into Blean Wood. *(Recommended by Mark Percy, Lesley, Mayoh, David Gittins, David Gregory, Stephen Brown, Kevin Thorpe, Ian Phillips, Dave Braisted)*

Shepherd Neame ~ Tenants Nigel and Bridget Morris ~ Real ale ~ Meals and snacks (not Mon or Sun evening) ~ (01227) 751360 ~ Well behaved children welcome ~ Open 11.30-3, 6-11; 12-3, 7-10.30

DEAL TR3752 Map 3

Kings Head £

9 Beach Street, just off A258 seafront roundabout

This handsome three-storey Georgian inn is particularly attractive in summer, decorated with stunning hanging baskets and window boxes, with picnic-sets out on a broad front paved terrace area just across the road from the promenade and sea. The four comfortable bar rooms around the central servery have a good bustling atmosphere, with a couple of flame-effect gas fires. The walls, partly stripped masonry, are interestingly decorated with marine architectural drawings, other maritime and local pictures and charts, and other material underlining connections with the Royal and Merchant navies. A wide choice of enjoyable good value food includes soup (£1.65), sandwiches (from £1.95), pâté (£2.35), cottage pie (£4), breaded plaice (£4.20) and steak and kidney pie (£4.35), as well as a good value two course lunch (£4.95). Well kept Courage Best, Shepherd Neame Master Brew and Bishops Finger and Wadworths 6X on handpump, helpful friendly staff. One room has darts and a fruit machine, and there may be quiet piped music. Beware that traffic wardens here are vigilant; there's pay-and-display parking nearby. This is probably a good place to stay (you have to use pay-and-display parking even if you're staying) but we haven't yet heard from enough readers to judge for sure. An exemplary seaside pub. *(Recommended by David Shillitoe, Mrs P Pearce, David Gregory, George Jonas, Sue Holland, Dave Webster, Thomas Nott, Kevin Thorpe, E G Parish)*

Free house ~ Licensee Graham Stiles ~ Real ale ~ Meals and snacks (possibly all day in summer) ~ (01304) 368194 ~ Open 11-11; 12-10.30 Sun; cl evening 25 Dec ~ Bedrooms: £35B/£46B

FAVERSHAM TR0161 Map 3

Albion

Follow road through town and in centre turn left into Keyland Road; just before Shepherd Neame Brewery walkway over road turn right over bridge, bear right, first right into public car park

Kent Dining Pub of the Year

Although there's quite a lot of emphasis on the popular bar food at this cheerful creekside pub there's still a good pubby atmosphere around the bar area. Alterations to the building mean that there's even more space for drinkers to perch comfortably on bar stools, in the light and airy open-plan bar, and take in the working waterside views through the big new french windows. A more spacious feeling is the only really noticeable change; the simple but solid mixed old pine furniture on wood and sisal flooring, pale pea green walls with nautical paraphernalia and old pine mirrors all remain intact; piped music. Very popular imaginative bar food prepared by the French chef/licensee Patrick, might include excellent fish soup, aioli and croutons or roquefort and nut terrine (£3.25), warm salad of chicken liver and wild mushrooms with raspberry vinegar dressing or ploughman's (£4.25), smoked haddock and asparagus pancake with creamy sauce (£4.75), pork and prune shortcrust pie (£6.50), beef, mushroom and tomato loaf with wild mushroom sauce or beef, mushroom and ale pie (£6.95), chick pea and okra with rice (£7.25), grilled marlin steak with salsa fresca – avocado, chilli, spring onion, cucumber and olive oil (£9.75), fried calf liver with lime and sage butter (£11.50), crispy half roast duck with fruit and brandy sauce (£11.75), and puddings like dark chocolate pudding with white chocolate and amaretto sauce, little marmalade puddings with citrus sauce or hazelnut and meringue roulade with mango crème fraîche and cointreau sauce (from £3.15); well kept Shepherd Neame Bishops Finger, Bitter, Spitfire and seasonal ales kept under light blanket pressure; a decent French wine list, too. There are picnic-sets out on the river walkway and you can stroll along the bank for about an hour; new disabled loos. *(Recommended by David Gittins, JP, PP, Stephen Brown, Mark Percy, Lesley Mayoh, Douglas and Ann Hare, David Gregory, A Cowell, Peter Smith, Geoffrey Stephenson, Mr and Mrs D Ross)*

Shepherd Neame ~ Tenants Patrick and Josephine Coevoet ~ Real ale ~ Meals and snacks ~ (01795) 591411 ~ Children in eating area of bar ~ Open 11-3, 6.30(6 Sat)-11; 12-3, 7-10.30 Sun

FORDCOMBE TQ5240 Map 3

Chafford Arms

B2188, off A264 W of Langton Green

Unchanging over the years, this tile-hung old pub is an absolute mass of flowers in summer, with cascading creepers and carefully tended shrubs and perennials – very inviting. Most of the flowers are in front; behind is a sheltered lawn, with plenty of shade from attractive shrubbery and arbours, and a fine big tree. It's been so carefully extended inside as to seem all of a piece, with plenty of room between the neat tables and comfortable seats, and the uncluttered decor includes some show-jumping pictures and memorabilia. Popular food includes sandwiches (from £2.15; fresh crab £3.50), sausage and chips (£3.45), ploughman's with good cheese (£4.45), rib-eye steak (£8.95), and a good range of fresh fish and seafood (picked up from Hastings by the landlord) such as moules marinières (£5.95), skate (£9.45), crab (£9.95), dover sole (from £11.95), and seafood platter (£23.95 for two people); Sunday roast (£6.95). Tables can be booked. Unusually for a foody pub, it has a thriving local side, the pubby bar often getting busier towards the close of the evening while the dining side winds down. Well kept Fullers London Pride, King & Barnes Sussex and Larkins, on handpump, local farm cider, and decent house wines; friendly and very attentive long-serving licensees and staff; two amiable old labradors, their natural interest in the food kept politely in check. Darts, shove-ha'penny, cribbage, dominoes and fruit machine. Just up the (steepish) lane is an archetypal village cricket green. *(Recommended by Peter Meister, Geoffrey Lawrance, B J*

Harding, Eddie Edwards, Mr and Mrs C Moncreiffe, Mr and Mrs R D Knight, G G Lawrence, K H Frostick)

Whitbreads ~ Lease: Barrie Leppard ~ Real ale ~ Meals and snacks ~ Restaurant ~ (01892) 740267 ~ Children welcome ~ Open 11-3, 6-11; 12-4, 7-10.30 Sun

GROOMBRIDGE TQ5337 Map 3

Crown

B2110

For many readers this quaint Elizabethan inn is their idea of the perfect Kentish pub. It's very prettily set at the end of a row of sweet cottages overlooking a steep village green. There are several beamed snug rooms, lots of old teapots, pewter tankards, and antique bottles, and large logs burning in the big brick inglenook; locals tend to crowd around the long copper-topped serving bar. The walls, mostly rough yellowing plaster with some squared panelling and some timbering, are decorated with small topographical, game and sporting prints, and a circular large-scale map with the pub at its centre; a little no-smoking dining area leads off the main bar. The end room, normally for eaters, has fairly close-spaced tables with a variety of good solid chairs, and a log-effect gas fire in a big fireplace. At lunchtime, very good value – particularly for this part of the world – tasty bar food includes home-made soup (£1.80), ploughman's (from £3), filled baked potatoes (from £3.80), vegetable lasagne (£4.50), good local sausages (£4.80), steak and mushroom pie (£5.50), prawn curry (£6), poached salmon (£7), and puddings (£2.25); a different evening menu includes avocado and scallop salad with sweet pepper coulis (£4), moules marinières (£5.50), leg of lamb with red wine, honey and rosemary sauce (£7), butter fish steak (£7.50), sirloin steak (£8). Well kept Courage Directors, Harveys IPA and Swale Kentish Pride on handpump, and local farm cider; scrabble. There are picnic-sets on the sunny front brick terrace or on the green. Across the road is a public footpath beside the small chapel which leads, across a field, to moated Groombridge Place and fields beyond. *(Recommended by Richard Gibbs, G Francis, Peter Meister, Pat and Tony Martin, Colin Laffan, LM, K Flack, J S M Sheldon, Tony and Wendy Hobden, Quentin Williamson, B J Harding, Ian and Nita Cooper)*

Free house ~ Licensees Bill and Vivienne Rhodes ~ Real ale ~ Meals and snacks (not Sun evening) ~ Evening restaurant (not Sun) ~ (01892) 864742 ~ Children in eating area of bar and in restaurant ~ Open 11-3, 6-11; 11-11 summer Sat; 12-10.30 summer Sun ~ Bedrooms: £25/£40

HERNHILL TR0660 Map 3

Red Lion

Off A299 at Highstreet roundabout via Dargate; or off A2 via Boughton Street and Staplestreet; follow Hernhill church signs

New licensees are doing very well at this pretty Tudor inn which is charmingly set next to the church and attractive village green. The long narrow characterfully beamed and flagstoned interior with new pine tables throughout is often crowded with people gathering for the well liked bar food (order from one side of the bar): soup (£1.95), pâté of the day (£3.25), moules marinières (£4.75), fisherman's pie or fried vegetable patties with spicy tomato chutney (£5.95), mushroom and tarragon stroganoff (£6.25), meat pudding of the day or strips of chicken and beef in cream and peppercorn sauce (£7.75), loin of pork in bacon, french mustard and cream sauce (£8.95), bass baked in foil with sliced mushrooms and tomatoes or duck breast with raspberry sauce on caramelised onions (£10.75); puddings (£2.95). There is a restaurant upstairs. Well kept real ales include Courage Directors, Fullers London Pride, Shepherd Neame Master Brew and Wadworths 6X, and country wines; log fires in winter; very good play area in garden; boules; piped pop music which can be quite loud; darts. There may be two Bassetts around, Webster and Murphy. *(Recommended by Jeff Seaman, David and Doreen Gregory, Stephen and Julie Brown, Kevin Thorpe, A Homes)*

Free house ~ Licensees Iain Styles Murray and Gary Greenaway ~ Real ale ~ Meals and snacks (11-3, 6-10.30) ~ Restaurant (not Sun eve) ~ (01227) 751207 ~ Children welcome away from bar ~ Open 11-3, 6-11; 12-3, 7-10.30 Sun

HODSOLL STREET TQ6263 Map 3

Green Man

Hodsoll Street and pub signposted off A227 S of Meopham; turn right in village

A small framed board by the front door of this well run friendly village pub, and another inside, give a brief but interesting account of the myth of the Green Man. There's a peacefully relaxing atmosphere in the big airy carpeted rooms which work their way round a hop-draped central bar, with a turkey rug in front of a log fire at one end. Neat tables are spaced tidily around the walls, with interesting old local photographs and antique plates on the creamy walls above. Popular dependable bar food from the menu listed on three boards in front of the bar might include filled rolls (from £2.75), ploughman's (£4.75), lamb and rosemary or steak and kidney pie (£5.50) and fish platter (£9.50). One of the main draws here is the incredible choice of puddings temptingly laid out in a big glass display cabinet (£2.75). Four well kept real ales such as Fullers London Pride, Greene King Abbot, Shepherd Neame Masterbrew and Wadworths 6X on handpump; friendly staff; fruit machines and piped pop music; walkers are welcome but are asked to remove their boots. Behind the back car park are picnic-sets under parasols on a well tended lawn, as well as a play area and aviary. *(Recommended by Jenny and Brian Seller, Ian Phillips, A E Bruce, Gwen and Pip Piper, T Neate)*

Whitbreads ~ Lease: Mr and Mrs Colin McLeod ~ Real ale ~ Meals and snacks (not Sun evening, not Mon evening Oct-May) ~ (01732) 823575 ~ Well behaved children welcome away from the bar till 9pm ~ Open 11(11.30 Sat)-3, 6.30-11; 12-3, 7-10.30 Sun

HOLLINGBOURNE TQ8455 Map 3

Dirty Habit

Eyhorne St; B2163 off A20

Originally a monastic house (and called the Pilgrims Rest), this early 15th-c inn has an attractive Georgian façade and is on the North Downs Way. Inside, there's quite a bit of character in the various rooms. The main bar has a profusion of hops over the counter, four deeply comfortable old armchairs with tables on which to rest your drinks, some high bar chairs, and heavy beams, and a long, very low beam leading to a panelled, dimly lit room with candles on sizeable tables, a very high-backed plush red cusioned settle with rather grand arms set opposite a big brown sofa, and a mix of dining chairs. Another little area has long settles, some chunky dining chairs, a brick fireplace, and newspapers on racks; a door from here leads up steps to a brick-tiered terrace with stone slab tables, green plastic chairs, statues, chimney pots filled with flowers, and a pergola. At the other end of the bar is a lighter room with more panelling, a relaxed, chatty atmosphere, a mix of chairs and tables, and a woodburning stove. Well kept Fullers London Pride, Greene King IPA, Shepherd Neame Spitfire, and Wadworths Farmers Glory on handpump kept under light blanket pressure, and country wines; piped music. A wide choice of good bar food includes filled french bread (from £3.50), chicken satay (£4.50), ploughman's (from £4.50), warm salad of pigeon breast (£4.95), lasagne or stir-fried vegetables (£7.95), beef in ale pie or pasta carbonara (£8.95), bacon-wrapped chilli prawns with squid and garlic (£10.95), thai turkey kebabs (£11.95), rump steak (£13.95), and daily specials. *(Recommended by Mark Percy, Lesley Mayoh, Thomas and Audrey Nott, B J Harding)*

Free house ~ Licensee John Brown ~ Real ale ~ Meals and snacks ~ (01622) 880880 ~ Children welcome away from bar ~ Band Mon evenings ~ Open 11.30-3, 6.30-11; 12-3, 7-10.30 Sun; closed evening 25 Dec

ICKHAM TR2257 Map 3

Duke William 🍷

Village signposted off A257 E of Canterbury

The big draw at this friendly and comfortable family-run pub is the very wide choice of good food, such as sandwiches (from £1.90), filled french sticks (from £3.95), soup (£3), ploughman's (£4.50), about a dozen pizzas (£4.95-£10.50), fajitas (£4.95-£6.25), about a dozen different pasta dishes including stir-fried squid (£5.45-7.95), steak and kidney pie or baked chicken breast with lemon, herbs and onion (£5.95), and puddings from a trolley (£3.50). The pub's bigger than it looks from outside. The open-plan carpeted bar extends on either side of the serving counter (which faces you as you enter), with a comfortably lived-in feel in this front part, helped by the big inglenook, all the brasses, copper and other bric-a-brac, a longcase clock and even gas lighting. There's more formal seating behind, with a rather smart air-conditioned restaurant area, and a no-smoking well shaded Victorian-style conservatory. Well kept beers such as Adnams, Fullers London Pride, Shepherd Neame Masterbrew and Youngs Special on handpump, as well as a dozen wines by the glass; darts, pool, fruit machine and juke box. The attractive garden, overlooking fields, is very neatly kept; this is a picturesque village. *(Recommended by Alan Thwaite, Kevin Thorpe, Derek Hayman)*

Free house ~ Licensees Mr and Mrs A R McNeill ~ Real ale ~ Meals and snacks (till 10) ~ Restaurant ~ (01227) 721308 ~ Children welcome ~ Open 11-3, 6-11; 12-5, 7-10 (possibly all day in summer) Sun; cl Mon morning except bank holidays

IDEN GREEN TQ8031 Map 3

Woodcock

Iden Green is signed off A268 E of Hawkhurst and B2086 at W edge of Benenden; in village at crossroads by bus shelter follow Standen Street signpost, then fork left at pub signpost – beware that there is an entirely different Iden Green just 10 miles away near Goudhurst.

There always seems to be a friendly cluster of locals chatting happily to the bar staff or jovial landlord at the corner bar counter of this unaffected little country pub, and the piped local radio or pop music seems to suit the informal atmosphere here better than in other pubs. Its cosy little exposed brick bar has very low ceilings bearing down heavily on a couple of big timbers on its stone floor, as well as a comfy sofa and armchairs by a warming woodburner, and a couple of good sized old pine tables tucked snugly into little nooks. Real ales include well kept Greene King Abbot and IPA and three guests like Fullers London Pride, Harveys and Rother Valley Level Best on handpump. Fairly straightforward bar food served in generous helpings with lots of vegetables, and often served by quirky local waitresses, includes pâté (£2.95), prawn cocktail (£3.50), lemon sole goujons or fried lamb liver and bacon (£7), steak, kidney, mushroom and ale pie or grilled plaice with white wine and prawn sauce (£7.50), sirloin steak (£8.50), and puddings like profiteroles and cream or chocolate gateaux (£2.95-£3.50); darts. *(Recommended by Digby Linnett, Janet and Colin Roe, B and M Parkin)*

Greene King ~ Lease: Frank Simmonds ~ Real ale ~ Meals and snacks ~ Restaurant ~ (01580) 240009 ~ Well behaved children away from bar ~ Open 11-11; 12-10.30 Sun; cl 25 Dec lunchtime

IGHTHAM COMMON TQ5755 Map 3

Harrow

Signposted off A25 just W of Ightham; pub sign may be hard to spot

Smartened up a little since the last edition, this characterful creeper-covered country pub has a good traditional local public bar (a big screen TV shows sports events only), a pleasant mix of customers, and an easy going atmosphere. Assorted country furniture stands on nice old brick flooring in two unpretentious rooms, one cheerfully painted a sunny yellow above the dark green dado, both warmed by log fires in winter. Careful but natural attention to detail means there are daily papers, and fresh flowers and candles on the tables. Tasty bar food includes spicy vegetable soup (£3.95), ploughman's (£4.75), grilled goat's cheese salad (£4.95), moules marinières (£5.50), steak and kidney pie (£5.95), warm leek tart (£6.50), salmon and dill fishcakes or wild boar sausages (£6.95), crevettes in garlic, lime and ginger butter or steak and kidney pie (£7.95), grilled swordfish with tomato and basil sauce (£8.95); puddings (£3.95). There's a good wine list, with plenty of good wines by the glass reasonably priced, and well kept Greene King Abbot, IPA and Marstons Pedigree, and an occasional guest on handpump. A lush grapevine grows around the delightful little antiquated conservatory which leads off an attractive dining room; piped rock music, pleasant young bar staff; tables and chairs on a pretty little pergola-enclosed back lawn. *(Recommended by Pat and Tony Martin, John and Elspeth Howell, Ian Phillips, Derek Thomas, Catherine Kanter, Eddy and Emma Gibson)*

Free house ~ Licensee John Elton and Claire Butler ~ Real ale ~ Meals and snacks (not Sun evening) ~ Restaurant ~ (01732) 885912 ~ Children welcome in one room ~ Open 12-3, 5.30-11; 12-11 Sat; 12-10.30 Sun; cl 1 Jan, drinks only 26 Dec lunchtime ~ Bedrooms: £28B/£48B

LANGTON GREEN TQ5538 Map 3

Hare 🍷

A264 W of Tunbridge Wells

The knocked-through ground floor of this spacious Victorian house is light and airy, with good-sized rooms, high ceilings and lots of big windows. There are dark-painted dados below light walls and dark ceilings, with oak furniture and turkey carpets on stained wooden floors, old romantic pastels and plenty of bric-a-brac (including a huge collection of chamber-pots). Old books, pictures and two big mahogany mirror-backed display cabinets crowd the walls of a big chatty room at the back which has lots of large tables (one big enough for at least 12) on a light brown carpet. From here french windows open on to a heated terrace with picnic-sets looking out on to a tree-ringed green (you don't see the main road). It's very popular for its interesting bar menu which might include sandwiches (from £3.50), open smoked bacon and gruyère sandwich (£4.95) and ploughman's (£6.95), there might be home-made soup (£3.25), button mushrooms sautéed in garlic and herb butter topped with smoked cheddar sauce (£4.75), fried strips of coconut chicken with mango dressing (£4.95), salmon and smoked haddock fishcakes with tomato and spring onion salad (£6.25), penne with chorizo sausage, black olives, peppers and tomato sauce (£6.95), steak burger with tomato, mozzarella and garlic mayonnaise (£7.95), shortcrust steak and kidney pie (£9.95), salmon escalope with coriander and lime crust with warm sun-dried tomato dressing (£10.25), roast shoulder of lamb with herb crust and red wine, rosemary and grain mustard sauce (£10.95), and puddings like bread and butter pudding, summer pudding and sticky toffee pudding with butterscotch sauce (£3.95). Well kept Greene King IPA, Abbot, Rayments and a guest on handpump or staight from the barrel, 14 wines by the glass, and over 40 malt whiskies; piped pop music in the front bar area, shove-ha'penny, cribbage, dominoes, and trivia. *(Recommended by Janet and Colin Roe, Tina and David Woods-Taylor, David Cullen, Emma Stent, J Sheldon, Margaret and Nigel Dennis, David and Lynne Cure, Hilarie Dobbie, Mr and Mrs G Turner)*

Greene King ~ Tenant Brian Keeley-Whiting ~ Real ale ~ Meals and snacks (all day) ~ Restaurant ~ (01892) 862419 ~ Children in restaurant ~ Open 11.30-11; 12-10.30 Sun; cl 25 Dec/1 Jan evening

LINTON TQ7550 Map 3

Bull

A229, Linton Hill

On our summer evening inspection, there were Morris men on the terrace in front of this country pub, and marvellous views down over the farmland to the reservoir with its big fountains; plenty of picnic-sets, and an attractive sheltered side garden with more seats and the spire of the church peeking over the trees. Inside, the relaxed bar is divided into two rooms with brocaded stools, dining chairs and carved wooden settles on the stripped wooden floor, a few standing timbers with horsebrasses, guide dog photographs, and some guns and plates above the fine old fireplace; up a step, the second room has plenty of standing room, some big bar stools, one long table with a dark bench, and hops above the bar counter. Well kept Shepherd Neame Master Brew, Spitfire, and seasonal beers on handpump kept under light blanket pressure; fruit machine. Decent bar food includes sandwiches (from £1.95), soup (£2.25), brie-stuffed mushrooms or mussels in garlic and white wine (£3.95), chicken breast stuffed with cheese and wrapped in bacon with a port and red wine sauce (£8.50), half shoulder of lamb (£10.95), sirloin steak (£12.95), nice fish such as trout or salmon (£6.95), and puddings (£2.75); friendly staff. The sizeable attractive no-smoking restaurant is divided up by standing timbers and has its own bar; piped music. (*Recommended by Comus Elliott, D Twitchett)*

Shepherd Neame ~ Manager Bob Earl ~ Real ale ~ Meals and snacks (not Sun evening) ~ Restaurant ~ (01622) 743612 ~ Children welcome ~ Open 11-3, 6-11; 12-3, 6-10.30 Sun

LUDDESDOWN TQ6667 Map 3

Cock £

Henley Street, OS Sheet 177 map reference 664672; Luddesdown signposted with Cuxton off A227 in Meopham, and off A228 in Cuxton (first real turn-off S of M2 junction 2); Henley Street is off the N end of Luddesdown village

The landlord at this tucked-away country inn keeps a good balance between his well kept real ales, and very good value bar food – he's determined that this should remain a pub that serves food. Light pours through a huge bay window into the calmly comfortable, neat and tidy little red-carpeted lounge with copper- or wood-topped tables. A couple of locals perch at the bar chatting to the landlord or chef and sample the well kept ales such as Adnams Southwold, Goachers, Greene King IPA and Abbot, O'Hanlons Blakeleys Best No 1, Welton Old Cocky and Youngs Special. They also keep two farm ciders. There's a very traditional pubby atmosphere in the attractive quarry-tiled back bar which now has a conservatory leading off, as well as pews, an antique bar billiards table, shove-ha'penny, cribbage, darts, TV, sports photographs and a glass case of model cars. Big helpings of well liked bar food include a pint of prawns (£2.50), sandwiches (from £2.60), sausage and mash (£3.50), vegetable moussaka (£3.90), chilli or steak and kidney pudding (£4.50), pizzas (from £5.20) and daily specials like chicken curry or battered haddock (£5.90). There are some tables outside, and boules. *(Recommended by Robert Gomme, Ian Phillips, Comus Elliott, Andy Stedman)*

Free house ~ Licensee Andrew Turner ~ Real ale ~ Meals and snacks (not Sun or Mon evenings) ~ (01474) 814208 ~ Open 12-11(10.30 Sun)

NEWNHAM TQ9557 Map 3

George

44 The Street; village signposted from A2 just W of Ospringe, outside Faversham

In the last edition we asked for more reports on the new licensees, and over the year readers have told us that this 16th-c country pub is now even better than before. There's particular praise for the freshly prepared bar food which includes soup (£2.50), chicken liver, orange and Grand Marnier pâté (£3.25), avocado pear and seafood medley (£3.95), beef suet pudding (£5.95), quiche of the day (£6.75), baked New Zealand mussels in provençal sauce topped with parmesan cheese (£7.50), chicken balti (£8.95), salmon fillet poached in white wine and lemon juice, 8oz sirloin (£9.75); three course Sunday roast (£12.50). The spreading series of atmospheric rooms have dressers with lots of teapots, prettily upholstered mahogany settles, dining chairs and leather carving chairs around candlelit tables, table lamps and gas-type ceiling chandeliers, and rugs on the waxed floorboards; hop bines hang from the beams and there are open fires and fresh flowers. The dining room has been completely redesigned. Well kept Shepherd Neame Master Brew, Spitfire and seasonal beers on handpump, and piped music. There are picnic-sets in a spacious sheltered garden with a fine spreading cobnut tree, below the slopes of the sheep pastures. Dogs allowed (drinking bowl in lobby). Good walks nearby. *(Recommended by Tina and David Woods-Taylor, June and Tony Baldwin, John E Thomason, Geoffrey Stephenson, Michael Tucker, David Gregory)*

Shepherd Neame ~ Tenants Tony and Jackie Richards ~ Real ale ~ Meals and snacks ~ Restaurant ~ (01795) 890237 ~ Children welcome ~ Jazz and Mon evening, live 60s music last Tues of month ~ Open 11-3, 6.30-11; 12-3.30, 7-10.30 Sun

OARE TR0163 Map 3

Shipwrights Arms £

Ham Road, Hollow Shore; from A2 just W of Faversham, follow Oare—Luddenham signpost; fork right at Oare—Harty Ferry signpost, drive straight through Oare (don't turn off to Harty Ferry), then left into Ham Street on the outskirts of Faversham, following pub signpost

Electricity is produced by a generator, and water is pumped from an artesian well at this marvellously unaltered white weatherboarded and tiled 17th-c inn. Its setting is quite striking, with small front and back gardens leading up a bank to the path above the creek where lots of boats are moored, and the Saxon Shore Way running right past. Many people still arrive by boat, or you can walk there from the village through a tangle of boatyards and scrapheaps. The surrounding salt marshes are designated as areas of Special Scientifc Interest and populated by rare birds. Three unspoilt little bars are characterfully dark and cosy, and separated by standing timbers and wood part-partitions or narrow door arches. There's a medley of seats from tapestry cushioned stools and chairs through some big windsor armchairs to black wood-panelled built-in settles forming little booths, hops and pewter tankards hanging over the bar counter, boating jumble and pictures, flags or boating pennants on the ceilings, several brick fireplaces, and a woodburning stove. Simple home-made but good value bar food such as sandwiches (from £2), soup (£1.95), filled baked potatoes (from £2.10), pizzas (from £3), macaroni cheese (£3.50), ploughman's (£3.95), chilli (£4.25), steak and kidney or chicken and leek pudding (£5.95), and puddings like spotted dick (£2.50); part of the eating area is no smoking. Well kept beers such as Coachers Mild, Shepherd Neame Bitter and Spitfire, and a guest like Adnams or Youngs tapped from the cask (they may have a beer festival at the end of May), and strong local farm cider; darts, table skittles, table football, cards, board games and fruit machine. *(Recommended by JP, PP, Gordon Tong, Howard Allen, Paul Hilditch, Thomas Nott)*

Free house ~ Landlords Rod and Simon Carroll ~ Real ale ~ Meals and snacks (12-3, 7-9.30) ~ (01795) 590088 ~ Children welcome ~ Live bands Sat evening ~ Open 11-11; 12-10.30 Sun

PENSHURST TQ5243 Map 3

Bottle House

Coldharbour Lane, Smarts Hill; leaving Penshurst SW on B2188 turn right at Smarts Hill signpost, then bear right towards Chiddingstone and Cowden; keep straight on

We've given this welcoming 15th-c pub a food award this year for their really impressive choice of over a dozen well prepared fish dishes that might include grilled sardines or thai fishcakes with chilli jam (£7.95), cajun swordfish with prawn salsa and sour cream (£9.50), skate wing with lemon butter and capers (£9.95) and bass with ginger lemon grass and spring onion sauce (£10.95); starters like soup (£3.25). Other dishes, just as good and served in really generous helpings, might include pâté en croûte with cumberland sauce and toast or devilled whitebait (£3.95), smoked salmon with horseradish fromage frais (£5.95), crispy duck (£6.50) and main courses like chilli or wild mushroom stroganoff (£7.95), roast stuffed chicken (£8.95), calf liver with horseradish mash (£11.95) and 10oz rump (£12.95). The neatly kept low beamed front bar has a well worn brick floor that extends to behind the polished copper-topped bar counter. Big windows look on to a terrace with climbing plants and hanging baskets around picnic-sets under cocktail parasols, and beyond to views of quiet fields and oak trees – there are lovely walks round here. Down a step, the unpretentious main red-carpeted bar has massive hop-covered supporting beams, two large stone pillars with a small brick fireplace (with a stuffed turtle to one side), and old paintings and photographs on mainly plastered walls. To the far right, an isolated extension forms a small pine-panelled snug hung with part of an extensive collection of china pot lids; the rest are in the low ceilinged dining room; well kept Harveys Best, Larkins and Fullers on handpump; cider from Chiddingstone, and local wine; unobtrusive piped music. Dogs welcome (they may offer them biscuits). *(Recommended by Derek Harvey-Piper, Tony Crafter, Peter Meister, Tim and Pam Moorey, Gwen and Peter Andrews, B J Harding, DFL, R and S Bentley, B and M Parkin, D H and M C Watkinson, Nigel Wikeley, A Homes)*

Free house ~ Licensees Gordon and Val Meer ~ Real ale ~ Meals and snacks (till 10pm) ~ Restaurant ~ (01892) 870306 ~ Children welcome ~ Open 11-3, 6-11; 12-3, 7-10.30 Sun

Spotted Dog

Smarts Hill; going S from village centre on B2188, fork right up hill at telephone box: in just under ½ mile the pub is on your left

This quaint old tiled house is in a spectacular spot with twenty-mile views of untouched countryside from picnic-sets on its tiered garden slopes (get there early as they do fill up early on fine days, as do tables in the bar at weekends). The neatly kept, heavily beamed and timbered bar has some antique settles as well as wheelback chairs on its rugs and tiles, a fine brick inglenook fireplace, and attractive moulded panelling in one alcove. It's quite small, so there may be an overflow into the restaurant at busy times. Enjoyable and imaginative food listed on several blackboards (with prices unchanged since last year) might include lovely celery and stilton soup (£2.95), avocado and wild mushroom bake or spinach, cream cheese and green peppercorn roulade (£6.25), pork and mushroom stroganoff (£7.25), chicken breast in lemon garlic (£8.25), good fresh fish dishes like tasty lemon sole (£8.45), red snapper (£8.95), or bass grilled with lime, ginger and coriander butter (£9.25), half a shoulder of lamb braised in red wine, garlic and rosemary (£10.25), and puddings such as cherry strudel or treacle tart (£3.25); staff stay smiling amidst the cheery bustle. Well kept Adnams, Eldridge Pope Royal Oak and King & Barnes Sussex on handpump, along with Old Spotty – a Best Bitter brewed specially for them; decent wine list. Lots of room for children to play outside. *(Recommended by Peter Meister, Tina and David Woods-Taylor, R J Walden, Janet and Colin Roe, Howard England, Liz Bell, Paul Hilditch, Dr Richard Crane, B and M Parkin, James House, D P Brown, Mrs M Furness)*

Carlsberg-Tetley ~ Lease: Andy and Nikki Tucker ~ Real ale ~ Meals and snacks (not Mon evening) ~ Restaurant ~ (01892) 870253 ~ Children in restaurant ~ Open 12(11.30 Sat)-2.30, 6-11; 12-3.30, 7-10.30 Sun; closed 25-26 Dec

PLUCKLEY TQ9243 Map 3

Dering Arms

Pluckley Station, which is signposted from B2077 in village

The handsome exterior of this old hunting lodge is reminiscent of a fairytale castle with its massive grey stone blocked walls, dutch-gables outlined against the sky and heavy studded oak doors. The stylishly plain high ceilinged bar has a variety of good solid wooden furniture on stone floors, and a roaring log fire in the great fireplace. It's popular with locals and there's a good pubby atmosphere; dominoes and cribbage. A smaller panelled bar with wood floors has similar furnishings. There is quite some emphasis on very well cooked fresh fish such as mussels in cider and cream sauce (£3.95), crab newberg (£4.45), grilled plaice (£6.95), monkfish in creamy bacon and orange sauce, fillet of red bream meunière or fresh tuna baked with saffron onions (£9.65), and scallops with garlic butter or grilled lemon sole (£10.95); also, sandwiches (£1.70), home-made soup (£2.95), ploughman's (£3.50), ham and chips (£3.75), pasta with stilton and basil sauce (£6.95), a home-made pie (£7.45), rabbit in mustard and ale (£9.65), roast partridge (£10.65), and puddings like chocolate parfait or sherry trifle (£2.50). Well kept Goachers's Maidstone Porter and Dering ale (a beer brewed specially for them) on handpump, a very good extensive wine list, home-made lemonade, local cider and quite a few malt whiskies. There's a vintage car rally once a month, and maybe summer garden parties with barbecues and music; bedrooms are quite simple. *(Recommended by Kevin Thorpe, JP, PP, Mr and Mrs R Lawson, Peter Meister, Hilary Dobbie, Ian Phillips, Mr and Mrs Jonathan Russell, D H Gittins, J Tross, C and M Starling, Lin Stephens, Thomas Nott, Jennie Munro, Jim Wingate)*

Free house ~ Licensee James Buss ~ Real ale ~ Meals and snacks (not Sun evening) ~ Restaurant ~ (01233) 840371 ~ Children welcome ~ Open 11-3.30, 6-11; 12-3.30, 7-10.30 Sun; closed 26-27 Dec ~ Bedrooms: £30/£40

RINGLESTONE TQ8755 Map 3

Ringlestone ★

M20 Junction 8 to Lenham/Leeds Castle; join B2163 heading N towards Sittingbourne via Hollingbourne; at water tower above Hollingbourne turn right towards Doddington (signposted), and straight ahead at next crossroads; OS Sheet 178 map reference 879558

With its happy, relaxed atmosphere, fine choice of good food, well kept real ales and hardworking friendly staff, this characterful old place is probably readers' favourite pub in Kent. It's surrounded by eight acres of land, including two acres of beautifully landscaped lawns, with shrubs, trees and rockeries, a water garden with four pretty ponds and cascading waterfalls, a delightful fountain, and troughs of pretty flowers along the pub walls; plenty of seats. The central room has farmhouse chairs, cushioned wall settles, and tables with candle lanterns (and bowls of shell-on peanuts) on its worn brick floor, and old-fashioned brass and glass lamps on the exposed brick and flint walls; there's a woodburning stove and small bread oven in an inglenook fireplace. An arch from here through a wall – rather like the outside of a house, windows and all – opens into a long, quieter room with cushioned wall benches, tiny farmhouse chairs, three old carved settles (one rather fine and dated 1620), similar tables, and etchings of country folk on its walls (bare brick too). Regulars tend to sit at the wood-panelled bar counter, or liven up a little wood-floored side room; dominoes, cribbage, and piped music. Bar food (served buffet style at lunchtime – there may be a queue) includes chicken, vegetable and bean soup with sherry and croutons (£3.85), herrings in dill or mussels provençale (£5.45), macaroni with tuna and clams or shepherd's pie (£6.95), lamb, coconut and banana curry (£7.95), lots of pies including vegetable and nut (£9.25), fish in elderflower wine (£9.65), and game pie with redcurrant wine (£10.25); vegetables are extra (£3.25). Puddings such as home-made cheesecake, treacle, orange and nut tart or fruit crumble (£3.95). Three or four changing well kept real ales (they list them on a blackboard) might include Adnams, Fullers London Pride, Marstons Pedigree or Ringlestone Bitter on handpump or tapped from the cask; two dozen country wines (including sparkling ones), local cider and fresh fruit cordials. Well behaved dogs welcome. *(Recommended by G Neighbour, Timothy Galligan, June and Tony Baldwin, Gwen and Peter Andrews, Douglas and Ann Hare, Maria Furness, Richard Gibbs, Val and Alan Green, Peter Meister, Tina and David Woods-Taylor, David and Kay Ross, Thomas Nott, J Tross, Evelyn and Derek Walter, Ian Phillips, Comus Elliott, Mr Miller, Kay Neville-Rolfe, Lin Stephens)*

Free house ~ Licensees Michael Millington-Buck and Michelle Stanley ~ Real ale ~ Meals and snacks (till 10 in summer) ~ Restaurant ~ (01622) 859900 ~ Children welcome ~ Open 12-3, 6-11; 12-11 Sat; 12-10.30 Sun; closed 25 Dec ~ Bedrooms: £85B/£95B

SANDGATE TR2035 Map 3

Clarendon

Head W out of Sandgate on main road to Hythe; about 100m after you emerge on to the seafront park on the road across from a telephone box on the right; just back from the telephone box is an uphill track.

With new licensees this year, this very simple little local is set half way up a steep lane from the sea. Visitors will probably feel most comfortable in the big windowed lounge on the left – you can just see the sea through one window. Decor is unaffected, with copper topped or new pine tables on a light patterned carpet, a few impressions of the pub, and a coal-effect gas fire. There's a very simple chatty atmosphere and a winter open fire in the straightforward right hand bar (popular with locals), and the well kept real ales include Shepherd Neame Best, Bishops Finger, Spitfire and seasonal ales on handpump from a rather nice Victorian mahogany bar and mirrored gantry, as well as 16 wines by the glass, and 16 malts; shove-ha'penny, cribbage, dominoes, chess, draughts and piped music. Bar food includes home-cured ham sandwiches (£2; crab £3), ploughman's (£3.50), chicken in beer or wine (£5.25), steak, kidney and mushroom pie (£5.75). The hanging baskets and boxes are lovely. *(Recommended by Ian Phillips, Thomas Nott; more reports please)*

Shepherd Neame ~ Tenants Keith and Shirley Barber ~ Real ale ~ Meals and Snacks (12-2, 7-8.30) ~ (01303) 248684 ~ Children in eating area of bar ~ Open 11.45-3, 6(7 Sat)-11; 12-3, 7-10.30 Sun; they will open all day in summer if busy

SELLING TR0455 Map 3

Rose & Crown

Selling signposted from exit roundabout of M2 junction 7: keep right on through village and follow Perry Wood signposts; or from A252 just W of junction with A28 at Chilham follow Shottenden signpost, then right turn signposted Selling, then right signposted Perry Wood

The hard-working and genuinely welcoming licensees here ensure that a visit to this flower bedecked 16th-c farmhouse is a delightful experience. There's all sorts of attention to detail, with pretty fresh flowers by each of the sturdy corner timbers in the relaxing central servery, hop bines strung from the beans, and an interesting variety of corn-dolly work – there's more of this in a wall cabinet in one cosy side alcove, and much more again down steps in the comfortably cottagey restaurant (which has been redecorated with stencils hand-made by Mrs Prebble of woodland animals). Apart from a couple of old-fashioned housekeeper's chairs by the huge log fire (which is replaced in summer by an enjoyably colourful mass of silk flowers interlaced with more corn dollies and so forth), the seats are very snugly cushioned. Good generously served bar food includes filled rolls (from £3.50), ploughman's (£4), steak and kidney pie (£5.75), chicken tikka masala or China Town platter (£7.50), fisherman's platter (£9), daily specials such as prawn creole, beef in red wine, and Jamaican chicken (£7.50), and a tremendous display of puddings on show in a cold cabinet down steps in a small family room: toffee apple tart, pecan and maple pie with local honey ice cream and Italian white chocolate (£2.90). Well kept changing ales such as Adnams Southwold, Goacher's Maidstone, Harveys Best, and guests such as Bass or Fullers London Pride on handpump, local cider, a good range of malts and decent wines in good measures; informal, helpful service; cribbage, shove-ha'penny, dominoes and piped music; the local TVR club meets here on the first Sunday lunch of the month. The sizeable garden behind is lovely and full of flowers, has a very good children's wooden play frame, lots of picnic-sets, bat and trap, and a small aviary. *(Recommended by David Gittins, Kevin Thorpe, Dr Robert Perks, Douglas and Ann Hare, Maria Edwards, Geoffrey Stephenson, Heidi Conroy, Stephen Brown, D J Roseveare, Comus Elliott)*

Free house ~ Licensees Richard and Jocelyn Prebble ~ Real ale ~ Meals and snacks (not Sun or Mon evenings) ~ Restaurant ~ (01227) 752214 ~ Children in family area and in restaurant ~ Open 11-3, 6.30-11; 12-3, 7-10.30 Sun; closed evening 25 Dec

nr SMARDEN TQ8842 Map 3

Bell ★

From Smarden follow lane between church and The Chequers, then turn left at T-junction; or from A274 take unsignposted turn E a mile N of B2077 to Smarden

It's worth visiting this ancient rose-covered 16th-c pub with its massive chimneys to get the feel of a pub as it might have been years ago. The dimly lit snug little back rooms have low beams, ancient walls of bare brick or rough ochre plaster, brick or flagstone floors, pews and the like around simple tables, and warm fires in inglenook fireplaces; one room is no smoking. The larger white painted and green matchboarded bar has a beamed ceiling and quarry tiled floor, a woodburning stove in the big fireplace, and a games area with darts, pool, cribbage, dominoes, fruit machine and juke box at one end. Bar food includes lasagne (£5), steak and kidney pudding (£5.95), wild boar sausages (£6.25), battered cod or chicken with cheese (£6.95) and cajun salmon (£7.50). Well kept Boddingtons, Flowers Original, Fullers London Pride, Harveys Best, Marstons Pedigree, Morlands Old Speckled Hen and Shepherd Neame Bitter on handpump, local cider, country wines, and winter mulled wine. There's a pleasant garden with mature fruit trees and shrubs; bedrooms are quite simple. *(Recommended by Anthony Barnes, G Neighbour, Bruce Bird, R and M Bishop, JP, PP, Janet and Colin Roe, Paula Williams, Serena Hebeler, Thomas Nott, Graham and Lynn Mason, Mrs M Furness, Colin Laffan, C Sinclair)*

Free house ~ Licensees Mr and Mrs C J Smith ~ Real ale ~ Meals and snacks (till 10pm) ~ Restaurant ~ (01233) 770283 ~ Children in restaurant ~ Open 11.30-3, 6-11; 12-3, 7-10.30 Sun ~ Bedrooms: £30/£42

TOYS HILL TQ4751 Map 3

Fox & Hounds £

Off A25 in Brasted, via Brasted Chart and The Chart

The fairly firm but kind Mrs Pelling – who doesn't allow mobile phones, and has little notices by the open fires warning against 'unofficial stoking' – refers to the 'great battle of 1986' when she fought the brewery's campaign to upgrade this slightly eccentric down-to-earth country local. When your eyes have adjusted to the dim lighting you'll see letters and press cuttings on the walls that describe this campaign, and photographs depicting the thirty years of the Pellings' tenancy here. Quite rightly, Mrs Pelling made a piece of local history, and little has changed in the two homely rooms here since the 60s (including the service which isn't necessarily geared for a mid-summer tourist rush). You can sit comfortably on one of the well worn old sofas or armchairs which are scattered with cushions and throws, and read the latest *Country Life*, *Hello* or *Private Eye*. Lunchtime bar food is at an absolute minimum with pre-wrapped filled rolls (from £1.50) and one or two simple dishes like ploughman's, cauliflower cheese or sausage and tomato pie (£3.95), and well stocked chocolate shelves. Well kept Greene King IPA and Abbot on handpump; occasional sing-songs around the piano; darts, shove-ha'penny, cribbage and dominoes. The garden is particulary lovely with picnic-sets on a good area of flat lawn surrounded by mature shrubs. As you approach this peaceful retreat from the pretty village (one of the highest in the county) you will catch glimpses through the trees of one of the most magnificent views in Kent. There are good walks nearby, and it's handy for Chartwell and for Emmetts garden. *(Recommended by Jenny and Brian Seller, D E Twitchett, TBB, Ian Phillips)*

Greene King ~ Tenant Mrs Hazel Pelling ~ Real ale ~ Lunchtime snacks (filled rolls only Sun and bank holidays) ~ (01732) 750328 ~ Children in side room at lunchtime ~ Open 11.30(12 in winter)-2.30(3 Sat), 6-11; 12-3, 7-10.30 Sun; closed 25 Dec

People don't usually tip bar staff (different in a really smart hotel, say). If you want to thank them – for dealing with a really large party say, or special friendliness – offer them a drink.

TUNBRIDGE WELLS TQ5639 Map 3

Beacon 🍷

Tea Garden Lane; leaving Tunbridge Wells westwards on A264, this is the left turn off on Rusthall Common after Nevill Park.

As this airy Victorian building is tucked away in a quiet lane away from the town centre there are some nice country touches like volley ball, boules and rounders, and sweeping hillside views from the terrace and dining area which juxtapose nicely with a gently urbanised atmosphere in the bar. There's usually a couple of business gents conversing at the sweeping bar counter with its ranks of shiny bottles and up to nine wines by the glass, ladies chatting on the comfy sofas by the fire, with possibly a table of jovial old chaps lunching in the dining area. The dining area, bar and small conservatory run freely into each other with stripped paneling, lovely wood floors, ornately built wall units and glowing lamps giving a solidly comfortable feel. Not cheap but popular bar food includes soup (£2.95), filled baguettes or baked potatoes (from £3.50), chicken and duck liver pâté with marsala and sultanas (£3.95), spinach and dolcelatte tart with gruyère sauce (£4.50), rump steak (£6), fried calf liver and onion (£10.95), pork fillet with grapes, almonds and cream (£12.75), bass with saffron, samphire and martini (£12.95), dover sole with prawns, coriander, lime and white wine (£13.95), as well as daily specials like grilled goat's cheese with raspberry vinaigrette (£4.95), avocado and gravadlax (£5.95), tortellini with asparagus and garlic (£8.95), 6oz sirloin with black pepper sauce (£10.50) and medallions of monkfish with pernod (£11.95). Well kept Fullers London Pride, Harveys and Larkins kept under light blanket pressure; lots of board games and piped music. *(Recommended by Hilarie Dobie, Janet and Colin Roe; more reports please)*

Free house ~ Licensee John Cullen ~ Real ale ~ Meals and snacks ~ (01892) 524252 ~ Children welcome away from bar ~ Open 11-11; 12-10.30 Sun

Sankeys 🍴 🍷

39 Mount Ephraim (A26 just N of junction with A267)

There's a friendly bustling atmosphere in the downstairs wine bar of this popular seafood restaurant. It's furnished with lots of sturdy old pine tables on the York stone floor, and decorated with old mirrors, prints, enamel advertising signs, antique beer engines and other bric-a-brac (most of which has been salvaged from local pub closures); french windows lead to a small suntrap terrace with white tables and chairs under cocktail parasols. Good, enjoyable food includes cheeses with biscuits (£3.50), a plate of charcuterie (£4.50), moules and frites (£5), pork and leek sausages (£4.50), Kentish lamb cutlets with mustard sauce (£10), and daily specials; you can also eat from the restaurant menu, too: warm salad of king scallops with wild mushrooms and tagliatelle or Loch Fyne langoustines tossed in garlic butter (£6.50), skate wing with black butter (£10), lovely Cornish cock crab (£14.50), roast monkfish with sweet pepper sauce, tuna steak griddled mediterranean style or halibut grilled with herbs (£15), and fruits de mers (£17.50). Shepherd Neame Masterbrew and guests from an antique beer engine, though most people seem to be taking advantage of the superb wine list; they also have quite a choice of unusual teas. You need to get there very early for a table in the bar; the restaurant is no smoking. *(Recommended by Tina and David Woods-Taylor; more reports please)*

Free house ~ Licensee Guy Sankey ~ Real ale ~ Meals and snacks (12-3, 7-10) ~ Restaurant ~ (01892) 511422 ~ Children welcome ~ Open 11-11; 11-3, 6-11 Sat; cl Sun and bank holidays

ULCOMBE TQ8550 Map 3

Pepper Box

Fairbourne Heath (signposted from A20 in Harrietsham; or follow Ulcombe signpost from A20, then turn left at crossroads with sign to pub)

Jones, the pub's tabby tom, is likely to be hogging one of the two armchairs or sofa by the splendid inglenook with its warm log fire at this cosy old country inn (there are two more cats and a collie called Rosie). The friendly homely bar also has standing timbers and low beams hung with hops, copper kettles and pans on window sills, and some very low-seated windsor chairs and wing armchairs. A side area is more functionally furnished for eating, and there's a very snug little no-smoking dining room. A short but good list of enjoyable daily specials includes crab pâté (£4.50), mixed thai starter for two (£9.80), beef and ale pudding (£6.50), lamb liver and bacon with sage and onion gravy (£7.50), chicken breast with rosemary and chargrilled pepper and tomato sauce (£8.50), bass steak steamed with ginger and lime (£9); they also do lunchtime sandwiches, good puddings, and a Sunday roast. Very well kept Shepherd Neame Masterbrew, Bishops Finger and Spitfire tapped from the cask, and country wines; efficient, courteous service. The pub is very nicely placed on high ground above the weald with views from a new terrace over a great plateau of rolling arable farmland, and if you're in the garden, with its small pond, swing and tables among trees, shrubs and flower beds, you may catch a glimpse of the deer that sometimes come up. The name of the pub refers to the pepperbox pistol – an early type of revolver with numerous barrels. No children inside. *(Recommended by Mr and Mrs Archibald, Comus Elliott, Mr and Mrs Peter Smith, Mrs M Furness, Carl and Jackie Cranmer, Quentin Williamson, Mrs P J Pearce, Janet and Colin Roe)*

Shepherd Neame ~ Tenants Geoff and Sarah Pemble ~ Real ale ~ Meals and snacks (12-1.45, 7-9.45; not Sun or Mon evenings) ~ Restaurant ~ (01622) 842558 ~ Open 11-3, 6.30-11; 12-4, 7-10.30 Sun

WHITSTABLE TR1166 Map 3

Pearsons

Sea Wall; follow main road into centre as far as you can, turning L into Horsebridge Rd; pub opposite Royal Free Fishers & Dredgers; parking limited

This weatherboard seaside pub keeps its place in the *Guide* for the very good fresh fish served in the little upstairs restaurant with its nicely relaxed atmosphere and fine sea views. There might be cockles (£1.75), mussels or battered rock (£4.95), grilled king prawns (£5.95), six local oysters in season (£6), fresh battered cod, skate or plaice (from £6.95; not Sun lunchtime), vegetarian meals like spinach and mushroom lasagne (£8.50), seafood platter (£10.95), Pearsons paradise – a huge meal for two involving lobster, crab, prawns, oysters, mussels and more (£36), and changing fresh fish (excellent plaice) or shellfish specials; children's menu (from £3.25). They serve a few seaside lunchtime snacks in the bar downstairs such as rollmops (£2.25), smoked mackerel (£2.50) and platter of prawns (£2.95), as well as the usual reasonably priced bar food. Well kept Boddingtons, Flowers Original, Youngs and Whitbread Best and a changing guest like East Kent Brewery Best on handpump; decent house wines; piped pop music, fruit machine. There are some picnic-sets outside between the pub and the sea. *(Recommended by Ian Phillips; more reports please)*

Whitbreads ~ Lease: Linda Wingrove ~ Real ale ~ Meals and snacks (11.30-2.30, restaurant meals only in the evening) ~ Restaurant ~ (01227) 272005 ~ Children welcome away from bar ~ Open 11-3, 6-11; 11-11 Sat; 12-10.30 Sun; closed 25-26 Dec

Children welcome means the pub says it lets children inside without any special restriction. If it allows them in, but to restricted areas such as an eating area or family room, we specify this. Places with separate restaurants usually let children use them, hotels usually let them into public areas such as lounges. Some pubs impose an evening time limit – let us know if you find this.

Lucky Dip

Besides the fully inspected pubs, you might like to try these Lucky Dips recommended to us and described by readers (if you do, please send us reports):

Appledore [15 The Street; TQ9529], *Black Lion*: Friendly pub locally popular for huge range of good value food served all day esp local fish, partitioned eating area, real ales inc Morlands Old Speckled Hen and John Smiths *(Janet and Colin Roe, R E Swainson, Rev John Hibberd, Roy Agombar)*

☆ **Ashford** [Silverhill Rd, Willesborough; TR0241], *Hooden Horse on the Hill*: Dim lighting inc candles, walls covered with old hop sacks and advertisements, cheerful often high-spirited atmosphere, well kept ales, farm ciders, country wines, good original food esp squid special and chicken jalfrezi, competent enthusiastic service *(John C Baker)*

☆ **Aylesford** [19 High St, not far from M2 junction 3 and M20 junction 6; TQ7359], *Little Gem*: 12th-c pub, Kent's smallest, cosy and quaint unassuming survivor, with tiny front door, lots of atmosphere, interesting upper gallery; good range of interesting ales and farm ciders, bar lunches and evening snacks, flame-effect fire; children welcome, SkyTV *(Thomas Nott, LYM)*

Aylesford [High St], *Chequers*: Straightforward comfort in welcoming riverside pub with generous well priced food, well kept Whitbreads-related ales, charming views from riverside terrace; open all day, parking some way off *(Rev J Hibberd)*

Barham [Elham Valley Rd; former B2065; TR2050], *Palm Tree*: Attractive country free house with good range of beers, reasonably priced food, tasteful decor, olde-worlde atmosphere; big garden *(M Chaloner)*

Basted [TQ6055], *Plough*: Old beams, friendly locals, good range of beers inc interesting guests, food inc good value bacon sandwich; unusual inn sign *(Jenny and Brian Seller)*

Boughton Street [nr M2 junction 7; TR0559], *White Horse*: Carefully restored dark-beamed bars and timbered dining room, well prepared food all day inc early breakfast and good value carvery Thurs, Fri, Sat, well kept Shepherd Neame beers, decent wines, good tea and coffee, friendly service; tables in garden, children allowed; good value bedrooms (back ones quieter), good breakfast *(Stephen Brown, LYM)*

Brabourne [Canterbury Rd; East Brabourne; TR1041], *Five Bells*: Big open-plan bar with comfortable banquettes, excellent service, wide choice of good value fresh food inc good sandwiches, well kept ales, continental beers, log fire; tables in garden with play area *(Alan Thwaite)*

☆ **Brasted** [A25, 3 miles from M25 junction 5; TQ4654], *White Hart*: Spacious dining lounge and extension sun lounge with large no-smoking area, substantial food inc very generous ice-cream concoctions and good sponge puddings, pleasant staff, Bass and Hancocks HB served through chiller, Battle of Britain bar with signatures and mementoes of Biggin Hill fighter pilots; children welcome, big neatly kept garden with well spaced tables and play area; bedrooms, pretty village with several antique shops *(E G Parish, Tina and David Woods-Taylor, B J Harding, D E Twitchett, Margaret and Nigel Dennis, LYM)*

Brenchley [Horsmonden Rd; TQ6841], *Halfway House*: Pleasant welcoming staff and surroundings, wide choice of good freshly made food inc fish and some vegetarian at sensible prices; locally very popular *(R D and S R Knight)*

Broadstairs [by quay; TR3967], *Tartar Frigate*: Huge helpings of seafood in busy upstairs restaurant with good harbour view, Victorian tile-and-plush style, well kept beer, fishing memorabilia *(Howard Allen, Sue Holland, Dave Webster)*

☆ **Canterbury** [12 The Friars, just off main St Peters St pedestrian area], *Canterbury Tales*: Clean and airy, more winebar feel than traditional pub, but a good range of well kept ales such as Harveys Best and Shepherd Neame 30/-, enjoyable food inc good sandwiches, vegetarian and Mexican tapas, books, games and chess table, theatrical memorabilia, more noise from conversation than the piped jazz, staff cheerily friendly and efficient; peaceful at lunchtime, busier with young people evening, some live jazz *(Mr and Mrs D Ross, Howard England, Mark Matthewman, Janet and Colin Roe, Kevin and Sarah Foster, Martin, Pat and Hilary Forrest, Tony and Wendy Hobden, David Carr)*

Canterbury [St Stephens Green, N of centre; TR1459], *Olde Beverlie*: Built 1570 with adjoining almshouses, beam and wattle open-plan rooms with flagstones, old prints, brasses, jugs etc, varied food, Shepherd Neame ales, small restaurant, nice walled garden with bat and trap; piped music *(Kevin Thorpe)*; [18 The Friars], *Pilgrims*: Partly 18th-c hotel, busy bar with Ind Coope Burton and Wadworths 6X, good food with veg served separately; bedrooms *(R F and M K Bishop)*; [3 Church Lane], *Simple Simons*: Step down into basic pub in 14th-c building, beams, broad floorboards and flagstones, huge log fire, nine well kept ales such as Bass, Courage, Mansfield, Morlands and Theakstons, impressive pump clip collection, simple lunchtime food, more studenty evening; good piped music, live blues Tues, jazz Thurs, courtyard, open all day *(Kevin Thorpe)*; [24 Watling St], *Three Tuns*: Interesting building in nice location, Scottish Courage ales, food popular with tourists lunchtime; bedrooms *(G P Kernan, Stuart Brown)*

☆ **Chiddingstone Causeway** [B2027; TQ5146], *Little Brown Jug*: Heavily refurbished in olde-brick-and-beam style, spacious, clean and comfortable even when busy, well kept Fullers London Pride, Harveys, and Hook Norton Old Hookey, decent wines, prompt friendly service, no-smoking area, generous popular food (no sandwiches), restaurant; children welcome if eating, attractive garden with play area; bedrooms *(John C Baker, Robert Gomme)*

Chipstead [Chevening Rd; TQ4956], *Bricklayers Arms*: Attractive old pub overlooking lake and green, heavily beamed bar with open fire, larger back restaurant, good choice of appetising food (not Sun evening), full range of Harveys beers tapped from casks behind long counter, good atmosphere *(Mike Gorton)*

☆ **Conyer Quay** [from A2 Sittingbourne—Faversham take Deerton St turn, then at T-junction left towards Teynham, then follow Conyer signs; TQ9664], *Ship*: Rambling collection of cosily nautical little rooms in cheery unspoilt creekside pub, good straightforward home-made food inc vegetarian, friendly landlord, well kept Adnams, Boddingtons, Courage Directors and Wadworths 6X, tea, coffee and hot chocolate, decent wines, restaurant; open all day, tables outside facing waterfront – road outside can flood at spring tides *(Kevin Thorpe, K Flack, Howard Allen, LYM)*

☆ **Cowden** [Cowden Pound; junction B2026 with Markbeech rd; TQ4642], *Queens Arms*: Unspoilt two-room country pub like something from the 1930s, with splendid landlady, well kept Whitbreads, darts; strangers quickly feel like regulars *(JP, PP, PB)*

Detling [TQ7958], *Cock Horse*: Pretty tiled and weatherboarded village local, well kept Whitbreads-related and other ales, good value food, restaurant, good landlord; tables in yard behind *(Neville Kenyon, Comus Elliott, Ian Phillips)*

Dover [Cannon St; TR3141], *Eight Bells*: Medium-sized new Wetherspoons, with the chain's characteristic good choice of well priced beers, food and wines, interesting decor *(Thomas and Audrey Nott, W M and J M Cottrell)*

☆ **Dunks Green** [Silver Hill; TQ6152], *Kentish Rifleman*: Welcoming atmosphere in cosy early 16th-c local, wide choice of good freshly cooked food, friendly service, well kept real ales such as Fullers and Marstons Pedigree, decent wine, plenty of character, no machines; dogs welcome; plenty of seats in unusually well designed garden behind *(A Cowell, Anthony Quinsee, Anthony Bradbury)*

East Farleigh [by stn; TQ7353], *Victory*: Large open-plan pub with end dining area, good usual food, beers inc local Goachers, tables in garden and on terrace overlooking road *(Tony and Wendy Hobden)*; [Dean St], *White Lion*: Chef/landlord doing superbly presented good reasonably priced food using local produce in cosy old pub, good choice of wines by the glass, pleasant landlady, nice atmosphere, log fire; has been cl Mon *(Pat Turvill, Peter Bethune, Mrs B Gibbons)*

East Malling [N of stn, back rd between A20 at Larkfield and A26; TQ7057], *King & Queen*: 14th-c building, much altered, popular for wide choice of food inc lots of fish, modern furnishings, some handsome panelling, Boddingtons, Brakspears, Fullers London Pride, Wadworths 6X, decor involving Henry VIII *(Thomas and Audrey Nott, James Nunns)*; [Rocks Rd], *Prince of Wales*: Good bar and restaurant food inc plenty of veg, good vegetarian choice, lots of fish and carvery Sun lunch, also popular theme nights *(Mick and Glenda Lambert)*

Eynsford [TQ5365], *Malt Shovel*: Neatly kept spacious old-fashioned dining pub handy for castles and Roman villa, generous bar food inc lots of good value seafood (lobster tank), Pilgrims ales, friendly service, nice atmosphere; car park across busy road *(Margaret and Nigel Dennis, BJH)*

Farningham [High St; TQ5466], *Chequers*: Old open-plan village local with full range of Fullers ales and guests such as Timothy Taylor Landlord, home-made bar food (can take a time) from simple well presented sandwiches and ploughman's up, friendly welcome, reasonable prices; quiet lunchtime *(Tony Gayfer)*

Faversham [Abbey St; TR0161], *Anchor*: Smallish friendly two-room local nr quay, well kept Shepherd Neame Bitter and winter Porter, good quiet relaxed atmosphere, bare boards and individual furniture, hall with bench seats, a couple of picnic-sets outside, attractive old street *(David Gittins, Mrs M Hall)*; [31 The Mall], *Elephant*: Picturesque flower-decked terrace town pub with very good choice of well kept changing ales, thoughtful staff, simple but attractive furnishings on stripped boards, home-made food inc vegetarian and summer barbecues *(Richard Houghton, Judy Tolman, GS)*; [99 Abbey St], *Phoenix*: Olde-worlde pub with good food inc imaginative daily specials, real ale, very pleasant ambiance *(Geoffrey Stephenson, Mark Percy, Lesley Mayoh)*

☆ **Finglesham** [The Street; just off A258 Sandwich—Deal; TR3353], *Crown*: 16th-c country pub attractively refurbished keeping character, wide choice of good value food in bar and popular olde-worlde restaurant with inglenook fireplace and flagstones; good friendly service, lovely garden *(Douglas and Ann Hare)*

☆ **Four Elms** [B2027/B269 E of Edenbridge; TQ4648], *Four Elms*: Busy dining pub, welcoming and comfortable, wide choice of consistently good value generous food inc fresh fish and fine rabbit pie in attractive recently redecorated dining room, well kept Scottish Courage ales such as Theakstons, decent wine, friendly service, several rambling rooms, two big open fires, huge boar's head, no music, pleasant restaurant; family room, tables outside; juke box, fruit machine; handy for Chartwell *(Colin Laffan, Margaret and Nigel Dennis, R Waters)*

☆ **Goudhurst** [TQ7238], *Star & Eagle*: Attractively timbered medieval inn with settles and Jacobean-style seats in relaxing heavily beamed open-plan bar, well kept Whitbreads-related ales, decent wine, separate servery for bar food, restaurant; lovely views esp from tables out behind; children welcome, bedrooms comfortable *(Thomas Nott, Janet and Colin Roe, Ken Frostick, LYM)*

☆ *nr* **Goudhurst** [A262 W; TQ7037], *Green Cross*: Not very pubby, but popular particularly with older people for good value genuine home cooking inc good Sat night carvery (summer cold cuts, winter roasts), well kept Harveys and other ales, well chosen wines; bar with open fires, big beamed back restaurant with different evening menu; bedrooms light and airy, good value; handy for Finchcocks *(Dr I Crichton, M and C Starling)*

Greenhithe [High St, Old Town; TQ5874], *Pier*: Riverside position the main thing, fine views of the Dartford Bridge; Courage ales, cheap food, big log fire, children in room off bar, terrace *(Ian Phillips)*

☆ **Hadlow** [Hamptons, 4 miles SE of Plaxtol – OS Sheet 188 map ref 627524; TQ6252], *Artichoke*: Dating from 13th c, with ancient low beams, high-backed wooden settles, some unusual wrought-iron glass-topped tables, huge welcoming inglenook log fire, gleaming brass, country pictures and bric-a-brac, bar food inc good home-made pies, no-smoking restaurant, well kept Adnams, Fullers London Pride, Greene King Abbot and Youngs Special, good range of spirits; children in eating area, seats outside inc pews in shower-proof arbour, quiet rural setting; a very nice pub, but the way they keep booked tables empty isn't exactly friendly; cl winter Sun evenings *(Tina and David Woods-Taylor, Tim Barrow, Sue Demont, A Homes, Martin, Pat and Hilary Forrest, Peter Meister, LYM)*

Hadlow [Maidstone Rd], *Harrow*: Well run Shepherd Neame pub with their Bitter, Spitfire and 1698 well kept and reasonably priced, wide variety of freshly made food inc memorable fish stew, friendly efficient service, darts around corner, dining area *(Brian and Anna Marsden)*

Harvel [David St; TQ6563], *Amazon & Tiger*: Simple but charming old two-bar local in pretty village, interesting beers such as Frolicking Farmer, decent food, friendly service, restaurant, nightly entertainment esp jazz; beautiful countryside *(Jenny and Brian Seller, Eddie Edwards, BB)*

☆ **Hawkhurst** [Pipsden – A268 towards Rye; TQ7730], *Oak & Ivy*: Immaculate refurbished and extended pub, well kept Whitbreads-related ales, friendly efficient staff, generous good value home cooking inc popular Sun roasts, heavy low beams and timbers, dark brown terracotta walls and ceilings, roaring log fires (one in massive inglenook), dark tables on quarry tiles; farm tools, piped music, fruit machine; tables outside, good play area *(G G Lawrance, B R Sparkes)*

Hawkhurst [The Moor (A229 SW); TQ7529], *Eight Bells*: Good range of unusual beers, generous well cooked and served food, bright, clean and pleasant surroundings, efficient pleasant staff *(Mr and Mrs Kemp-Elmes)*; [Moor Hill (A229)], *Kent Cricketers*: Old small roadside pub with good very cheap bar food inc filled baked potatoes *(Jason Caulkin)*; [Rye Rd (A268)], *Queens Head*: Very good value quickly produced food, helpful friendly staff, huge log fire, Harveys and another real ale; bedrooms comfortable *(Jason Caulkin, B R Sparkes)*

☆ **Heaverham** [Watery Lane; TQ5758], *Chequers*: Wide choice of good food with adventurous touches, well kept Shepherd Neame, friendly service in quietly attractive two-bar country pub with hops on beams; lots of birds in big garden *(LM)*

Herne Bay [East St/Central Parade; TR1768], *Old Ship*: Useful Whitbreads pub with window tables for sea view over fairly quiet road, eight well kept beers, good inexpensive food, fairly bright open space, curved rustic brickwork *(Howard Allen)*

☆ **Hever** [outside gates of Hever Castle; TQ4744], *Henry VIII*: Comfortable and friendly pub dating from 14th c, some fine oak panelling and heavy beams, inglenook fireplace, Henry VIII decor, tables out on terrace and pondside lawn; now a Shepherd Neame managed pub under efficient new licensees, usual bar food (all day Mar-Nov) inc good ploughman's and half-helpings for children, restaurant *(B, M and P Kendall, Mrs S Miller, Martin, Pat and Hilary Forrest, LYM)*

☆ **Ide Hill** [off B2042 SW of Sevenoaks; TQ4851], *Cock*: Pretty village-green local with well kept Greene King, fine log fire, bar billiards, straightforward bar food (not Sun evening, only sandwiches Sun lunchtime), piped music, some seats out in front; handy for Chartwell and nearby walks – so gets busy, with nearby parking sometimes out of the question; no children *(David Dimock, W Ruxton, Robert Gomme, Timothy Galligan, LYM)*

☆ *nr* **Iden Green** [A262 E of Goudhurst; TQ7437], *Peacock*: Traditional low-beamed lounge, flagstones and massive fireplace, well kept Shepherd Neame ales, good snacks and meals, friendly staff, plain public bar with music and games, good big garden; packed with young people Sat night *(Comus Elliott, BB)*

☆ **Ivy Hatch** [off A227 N of Tunbridge; TQ5854], *Plough*: More restaurant than pub, by no means cheap, but it's good (and often fully booked), with fastidious French cooking, good wines (and well kept Greene King IPA), attractive candlelit surroundings – upmarket in a friendly informal style; very efficient well turned out staff, delightful conservatory and garden *(Comus Elliott, Jason Caulkin, Eddy and Emma Gibson, M J Dowdy, Maysie Thompson, LYM)*

Kemsing [Cotmans Ash Lane; TQ5558], *Rising Sun*: Attractive old country pub like something out of one of H E Bates's lighter works, several guest beers, interesting range of generous bar food, informal garden with toys and aviary *(John C Baker, Paul and Sharon Sneller)*

Kingsdown [Cliffe Rd; TR3748], *Rising Sun*: Attractive 17th-c clapboard pub by shingle beach, mainly modern inside but keeping some old brickwork and beams; Whitbreads-related ales, log fire, decent straightforward food, darts in back bar, quiet piped music; small cottage garden, good walks *(Kevin Thorpe)*; [off A258 Dover—Deal], *Zetland Arms*: Great spot on storm beach (access by rough shingle track), sea view from big open-plan room, friendly service, usual food, four real ales inc Morlands Old Speckled Hen and Shepherd Neame, some interesting photographs *(Sue Holland, Dave Webster)*

Knockholt [Star Hill; TQ4658], *Harrow*: Enjoyable atmosphere, food from good hot baguettes to hot home-made dishes, pleasant beamed dining room, well kept beer; lovely walks *(Janet and Colin Roe)*

Laddingford [TQ6948], *Chequers*: Friendly village local with real ales such as Adnams, Boddingtons and Whitbreads, varied enjoyable food catering strongly for children; big garden *(A W Lewis)*

☆ **Lamberhurst** [B2169, off A21 nr entrance to Scotney Castle; TQ6735], *Brown Trout*: Useful dining pub specialising in fish, lots of tables in biggish extension off small beamed bar, well kept Fullers London Pride and Marstons Pedigree, fair choice of wines, picnic-sets in large safe garden with play area; children in eating areas, open all day Sun and summer *(Mrs J Burrows, Brenda and Stuart Naylor, G Simpson, LYM)*

☆ *nr* **Lamberhurst** [Hook Green (B2169 towards T Wells); TQ6535], *Elephants Head*: Ancient rambling timber-framed country pub with wide choice of food inc vegetarian, well kept Harveys inc seasonal brews, friendly landlord, heavy beams, brick or oak flooring, log fire and woodburner, plush-cushioned pews etc; darts and fruit machine in small side area, quiet piped music, picnic-sets in big back garden with terrace and play area (peaceful view), and by front green; nr Bayham Abbey and Owl House, very popular with families weekends *(Dr S P Willavoys, Peter Meister, TBB, LYM)*

☆ **Littlebourne** [4 High St; TR2057], *King William IV*: Straightforward character and decor, but welcoming relaxed atmosphere and unusual range of good interesting freshly prepared food running up to ostrich and kangaroo; generous helpings, reasonable prices, good friendly service, well kept ales, interesting wines inc New World ones; small but good restaurant, good value bedrooms, good breakfast; handy for Howletts Zoo *(Desmond and Gillian Bellew, David Gregory, Mr and Mrs R E M Lawson)*

Lower Hardres [TR1552], *Three Horseshoes*: This attractive and individualistic old-fashioned country pub has been closed following the death of its landlord *(LYM)*

Lydd [Lydd Airport; TR0621], *Biggles Bar*: Close to runway, very popular with plane-spotters; Morlands Old Speckled Hen, aircraft paintings, tables outside *(Ian Phillips)*

Maidstone [Penenden Heath Rd; ¼ mile from M20, junction 7, towards Maidstone; TQ7757], *Chiltern Hundreds*: Refurbished as upmarket Chef & Brewer dining pub, well done with restrained decor easy on the eye, food all day, Scottish Courage ales; conservatory, terrace *(Thomas and Audrey Nott, BB)*

Marden Thorn [Pagehurst Lane; TQ7842], *Wild Duck*: Neat and friendly country pub concentrating on wide choice of good well presented food in attractive bar and big smart dining room, well kept ales inc Fullers London Pride and Harveys, good range of wines, plenty of atmosphere despite piped pop music *(Comus Elliott, BB)*

Marshside [TR2265], *Hog & Donkey*: Idiosyncratic small pub, quiet, plain and simple, with Whitbreads-related ales, no food, cottagey front room with unsmart mix of tables, chairs, sofas and bright cushions strewn around, coal fire, maybe 60s radiogram music; car park may be full of cars even if pub empty – landlord collects them; handy for Stour Valley and Saxon Shore walks *(Kevin Thorpe)*

Minster [42 Station Rd; the one nr Ramsgate; TR3164], *Mortons Fork*: Attractive country-style small bar and linked dining area in well kept small hotel, settles and sewing-machine tables, log fire, helpful friendly staff, good choice of varied good value unusual bar food inc exotic puddings, decent wine, good housekeeping; restaurant, tables outside; three luxurious bedrooms *(Douglas and Ann Hare)*

Oad Street [nr M2 junction 5; TQ8662], *Plough & Harrow*: Unpretentious local opp craft centre, with collection of brewery advertisements, jugs hanging from dark beams, careful lighting, well kept Shepherd Neame and changing guest beers, limited inexpensive menu (not winter weekday evenings); children welcome, picnic-sets in secluded back garden *(Thomas and Audrey Nott)*

☆ **Otford** [66 High St], *Horns*: Friendly and cosy, 15th-c beams and timbers, big inglenook log fire, blue plush seats and wheelback chairs, neatly cottagey decorations, second room on left, attentive welcoming service, tables set for short choice of good well presented standard food from well filled sandwiches up, well kept Fullers London Pride and Harveys, cheerful service *(Janet and Colin Roe, David Friett, BB)*

Paddlesworth [TR1939], *Cat & Custard Pot*: Reasonably priced well kept beer, good value food *(Dave Braisted)*

☆ **Painters Forstal** [signed off A2 at Ospringe; TQ9958], *Alma*: Attractive weatherboarded village local, busy but neat and tidy, with good varied food, well kept Shepherd Neame inc winter Porter, friendly efficient service, largeish dining lounge, small bare-boards public bar, maybe piped classical music, picnic-sets on lawn *(June and Tony Baldwin)*

☆ **Penshurst** [centre; TQ5243], *Leicester Arms*: Busy pub in charming village by Penshurst Place, cosy old bars and original dining room up steps, with country views, plainer back extension eating area, good choice of generous reasonably priced food, well kept Fullers London Pride, Larkins and Wadworths 6X, willing young staff; children welcome, tables in back garden, economical bedrooms *(Colin Laffan, Robert Gomme, A M Pring)*

☆ *nr* **Penshurst** [Hoath Corner – OS Sheet 188

map ref 497431], *Rock*: Charmingly old-fashioned untouristy atmosphere in tiny beamed rooms, wonky brick floors, woodburner in inglenook, good value sandwiches and generous home cooking, well kept local Larkins and Shepherd Neame, friendly staff, ring the bull; children and dogs welcome (pub dog very shy); front terrace, back garden, beautiful countryside nearby *(LM, Jenny and Brian Seller)*

☆ **Pett Bottom** [off B2068 S of Canterbury, via Lower Hardres; TR1552], *Duck*: Remote tile-hung cottage with two small bars, big 17th-c fireplace, plain furnishings – can get packed out for wide choice of bar food inc interesting pies and pasta; Greene King ales, decent wines by the glass, local cider; restaurant, children allowed in smaller room; tables in sizeable garden *(Kevin Thorpe, LYM)*

Plaxtol [Sheet Hill; TQ6054], *Golding Hop*: Secluded country pub, good in summer with suntrap streamside lawn; small and simple inside, with Adnams and Youngs tapped from the cask, farm ciders (sometimes even their own), limited bar food (not Mon evening), woodburner, billiard table, game machine, good friendly service *(LM, LYM)*

Pluckley [TQ9245], *Black Horse*: Open-plan bar with roomy back dining area in attractive old house, hops on beams, vast inglenook, usual furnishings and food, cheery atmosphere, Whitbreads-related and guest ales; piped music may seem rather loud, fruit machine; children allowed if eating; picnic-sets in spacious informal garden by tall sycamores, good walks *(CM, JP, PP, BB)*

Pluckley [Munday Bois; TQ9144], *Rose & Crown*: Welcoming little pub with nicely furnished dining room, good varied food esp fresh fish, soups, puddings and Sun lunch, interesting wines and country wines, well kept ales, farm cider, plenty of malt whiskies, reasonable prices, helpful service; friendly dog *(Pat Turvill, Dominic Dunlop)*

Rochester [10 St Margarets St; TQ7467], *Coopers Arms*: Cosy and quaint ancient local, good bustling atmosphere with fine mix of customers, friendly staff, comfortable seating, generous low-priced bar lunches, well kept Scottish Courage ales; handy for castle and cathedral *(A E Brace)*

Ruckinge [B2067 E of Ham Street; TR0233], *Blue Anchor*: Well kept and friendly, with Whitbreads-related ales, wide choice of reasonably priced well presented food, tastefully furnished dining conservatory; former smuggling associations, garden with pretty pond *(Janet and Colin Roe)*

Sandgate [High St; TR2035], *Ship*: Old-fashioned, not smart but cosy and welcoming, ten or so quickly changing real ales tapped from the cask, good reasonably priced food, good service, seafaring theme, great atmosphere, friendly landlord; seats outside *(LMM, Kay Macara, John Havery)*

Sandwich [12 Moat Sole; TR3358], *Red Cow*: Two carefully refurbished open-plan bars and eating area, old beams and pictures, changing ales such as Boddingtons, Fullers London Pride, Greene King Abbot, King & Barnes, Morlands Old Speckled Hen and Whitbreads, good value food, good atmosphere, friendly staff, lovely log fire; soft piped music; guide dogs only, garden bar, hanging baskets *(Kevin Thorpe, D and J Tapper)*

☆ **Sarre** [A28 Canterbury—Margate; TR2565], *Crown*: Carefully restored pub making much of its long history as the Cherry Brandy House, two attractive beamed bars, pictures of celebrity guests, good choice of reasonably priced home-cooked food, well kept Shepherd Neame beers, log fires, quiet restaurant; garden, open all day; comfortable spacious bedrooms *(Kevin Thorpe, Stephen and Julie Brown, R and M Bishop)*

☆ **Selling** [village signed from exit roundabout, M2 junction 7, also off A251 S of Faversham; TR0456], *White Lion*: 17th-c pub with wide choice of popular food (all day Sat/Sun), well kept Shepherd Neame Bitter and Spitfire, decent wines, comfortable bar with two big log fires (one with a spit), pews on stripped boards, unusual semi-circular bar counter, back restaurant; children welcome; rustic picnic-sets in attractive garden, colourful hanging baskets *(Quentin Williamson, Paul and Sharon Sneller, KT, LYM)*

☆ **Sevenoaks** [Godden Green, just E; TQ5555], *Bucks Head*: Picturesque old village-green local in pretty spot by duckpond, surrounded by cherry blossom in spring; good value food from sandwiches up, welcoming service and atmosphere, cosy furnishings, full Shepherd Neame range; children welcome away from bar; in attractive walking country nr Knole *(Mr and Mrs A Budden, Brian and Anna Marsden, Paul and Sharon Sneller, Robert Gomme)*

Sevenoaks [London Rd, nr stn, 2½ miles from M25 junction 5], *Halfway House*: Quiet and friendly partly 16th-c local with beams and brasses, well kept Greene King IPA, Abbot and Rayments, wide range of reasonably priced home-made food inc fresh fish Weds, good service; parking may be difficult *(Tim and Pam Moorey)*

Shadoxhurst [Woodchurch Rd; TQ9737], *Kings Head*: Lots of hops, copper and brass, stripped pine tables, tiled-floor dining area, good food, Shepherd Neame ales, pleasant staff, games area with bar billiards; garden *(Neil and Anita Christopher)*

Shoreham [High St; TQ5161], *Olde George*: Simply furnished old beamed pub nr church in pretty village, very friendly chatty landlord, superbly kept Greene King IPA, roaring open fire, decent sandwiches, ploughman's, home-made soup; children and dogs welcome, good walking country, nr Darent Trail

☆ **Smarden** [TQ8842], *Chequers*: Carefully prepared tasty food from fine filled baguettes to quite exotic main dishes inc vegetarian and lots of fish in cosy and relaxed traditional beamed local, one small eating area with a good deal of rustic character off main turkey-carpeted bar, another at the back more orthodox; second parquet-floored bar largely laid for diners; Bass, Morlands Old Speckled Hen, Ruddles County,

Worthington and Youngs Special, decent wines and spirits, good friendly service, log fire, local-interest books, no music or machines; pleasant tables outside; bedrooms simple (and some within earshot of bar) but good value, with huge breakfast, lovely village *(Pam and Tim Moorey, Mrs J Evans, Janet and Colin Roe, Mark Baynham, Rachael Ward, BB)*

☆ **Snargate** [B2080 Appledore—Brenzett; TQ9928], *Red Lion*: Delightfully old-fashioned and unspoilt 19th-c Romney Marsh pub, bare boards and old kitchen furniture, marble bar top, well kept Adnams and Batemans tapped from the cask or via antique handpumps, classic landlady, traditional games, sawdust on the floor, no music or food *(Kevin Thorpe, JP, PP)*

Sole Street [this is the Sole Street nr Wye; TR0949], *Compasses*: Big neatly kept garden with rustic tables, play area and various pets, easy-going low-ceilinged rambling bars with bare boards or flagstones, antique or reclaimed furnishings, massive brick bread oven, enamel advertisements, well kept Fullers ESB, London Pride, Shepherd Neame and Stour Valley Kentish Pride, local farm cider, fruit wines, hearty unpretentious food, loudly cheery landlord, children welcome in extended garden room; bar billiards, piped music; good walks *(Mark Percy, Lesley Mayoh, LYM)*

☆ **Speldhurst** [signed from A264 W of Tunbridge Wells; TQ5541], *George & Dragon:* Fine timbered building, partly 13th-c, panelling, massive beams and flagstones, huge log fire, high-backed settles, sofa, banquettes, handsome upstairs restaurant; well kept Harveys PA and Best and a guest such as M&B Brew XI, lots of malt whiskies, good wines, bar food (not Sun evening) inc good boar or venison sausages and fish pie; pub games, piped music, service (usually good) can slow at busy times; provision for children, tables in garden; blues Sun evening, open all day (not Mon-Thurs in winter) *(E and K Leist, Pat and Tony Martin, Paul and Pam Penrose, Peter Meister, LM, Quentin Williamson, Thomas Nott, LYM)*

St Margarets at Cliffe [High Street; TR3644], *Cliffe Tavern Hotel*: Attractive clapboard-and-brick inn opp church with well worn in bar and open-plan lounge, good log fire, well kept Greene King and Shepherd Neame ales, interesting filled baguettes and other food, secluded back walled garden, separate dining room; open all day Sat, well behaved children allowed; bedrooms, inc some in cottages across yard, good walks nearby *(C Elliott, Hilarie Dobbie, LYM)*; *Hope*: Friendly local, simple food, good range of Shepherd Neame ales; pastel panelling in one room *(Sue Holland, Dave Webster, Colin McKerrow)*; *Smugglers*: Friendly staff in tiny bar, good cooking esp Mexican, Indian and pizzas in attractive dining room and conservatory *(John Prescott)*

St Margarets Bay [TR3844], *Coastguard*: Tremendous views to France from cheery modernised seaside pub, open all day in summer; children welcome, lots of tables on balcony below NT cliff *(Howard Allen, BB)*

St Nicholas at Wade [just off A299; TR2666], *Bell*: 16th c, with four olde-worlde beamed rooms, friendly staff, open fires, good well priced seafood and other food, well kept Shepherd Neame *(R and M Bishop, Paul and Sharon Sneller)*

Stanford [B2068, ½ mile from M20 junction 11; TR1238], *Drum*: Welcoming, with Courage, Marstons Pedigree, good sandwiches; pool, piped music, children's garden; very handy for Channel Tunnel *(Peter Frost)*

Staple Street [off A2 via Boughton Street, or A299, nr M2 junction 7; TR0560], *Three Horseshoes*: Friendly brick and clapboard local with open fire, gas mantles, Shepherd Neame tapped from casks out at the back, bare boards, simple food; open all day Fri *(Kevin Thorpe)*

☆ **Staplehurst** [Chart Hill Rd; TQ7847], *Lord Raglan*: Sypathetically refurbished traditional country pub, friendly staff and locals, well kept Goachers and guests such as Shepherd Neame Spitfire and Youngs Special, imaginative well presented food inc wide choice for Sun lunch, coal fires; reasonable wheelchair access, good-sized garden *(John C Baker, Sylvia Law, Janet and Colin Roe)*

☆ **Stodmarsh** [High St; TR2160], *Red Lion*: Well rebuilt, with hops on beams, flagstones and bare boards, log fires, pine furniture, pictures and rustic bric-a-brac, good food inc chargrills, helpful landlord, friendly staff; well kept Greene King IPA and occasional guest beers such as Stour Valley Kentish Pride tapped from the cask, farm cider, winter mulled wine, pub games; open all day, can get busy w/e, some live music, garden with bat and trap; bedrooms, handy for bird sanctuary *(Kevin Thorpe, I Pritchard, Alex Smith)*

☆ **Stone in Oxney** [off B2082 S of Tenterden; TQ9427], *Crown*: Cosy family pub with newish owners doing innovative good sensibly priced food, not a big choice but well cooked and presented, also modest range of sandwiches; pleasant friendly service, Shepherd Neame and Otter ales, good coffee, Penshurst English wine as house white *(Janet and Colin Roe, Roy Agombar)*

Stone in Oxney, *Stone Ferry*: Classic untouched traditional pub, former smugglers' haunt by what used to be the landing for the Oxney ferry – simple old-fashioned cottage with no fuss or frills, pleasantly worn feel; big garden *(Roy Agombar)*

☆ **Stowting** [off B2068 N of M20 junction 11; TR1242], *Tiger*: Character country pub, partly 17th c, with attractive unpretentious furniture, candles on tables, faded rugs on bare boards, friendly hard-working licensees, three or more well kept real ales, Biddenden farm cider, well prepared and presented food, good log fire, tables outside with occasional barbecues; well behaved children allowed, good jazz Mon (cl Mon lunchtime) *(Martin Hickes, Mrs Anne-Marie Logan, LYM)*

Sundridge [Main Rd (A25); TQ4854], *White Horse*: Pleasant and clean, with prints and carpeted dining area, welcoming service, bar food, evening meals (not Mon-Weds), Sun

lunch; tables under cocktail parasols in small garden *(A M Pring)*
Swanley [TQ5168], *Lamb*: Particularly well kept ales such as Shepherd Neame Bishops Finger and winter Porter, food inc good pies, pleasant service, friendly atmosphere *(R T and J C Moggridge)*
Tenterden [High St; TQ8833], *Eight Bells*: Old building recently reopened, traditional long bar, central courtyard now glazed in as no-smoking eating area, good reasonably priced food inc interesting dishes, very friendly efficient service; easy wheelchair access *(Sylvia Law, Brenda and Stuart Naylor)*; [West Cross (top of High St)], *William Caxton*: Cosy oak-beamed 15th-c pub, inglenook log fire, wide choice of food inc vegetarian in bar or pleasant restaurant, Shepherd Neame beers; tables in garden, open all day; children welcome; bedrooms *(Kevin Thorpe)*
Teynham [Lewson St; TQ9562], *Plough*: Picturesque beamed pub in quiet village, comfortably and tastefully furnished, full range of Shepherd Neame ales, good wines, wide choice of food from ploughman's to lobster bisque, log fires, good friendly staff; attractive gardens and setting *(Jeff Seaman)*
Trottiscliffe [The Street; TQ6460], *Plough*: Traditional two-bar village local with good choice of beers inc many guests, good value food, friendly licensees, quiet flower-covered terrace *(John E Vigar)*
Tunbridge Wells [Spa Hotel, Mt Ephraim; TQ5839], *Equestrian Bar*: Relaxing hotel bar by common, unusual equestrian floor-tile painting and steeplechasing pictures, good polite helpful service, bar food such as sandwiches and excellent bangers and mash, well kept Bass; hotel lounge takes overflow; bedrooms *(Janet and Colin Roe, BB)*; [Chapel Pl/Castle Sq], *Grapevine*: Cellar bar/restaurant handy for Pantiles, under new ownership and refurbished to give more room; good enterprising food inc light dishes and vegetarian (may be a wait, booking essential Sat night), Harveys ales, good range of wines by the glass *(Hilarie Dobbie, Pat and Tony Martin)*; [The Common], *Mount Edgcumbe*: Pleasant setting with common views, lots of bricks, hops and wood, good choice of food from ploughman's and good baguettes up, obliging service; bedrooms *(Janet and Colin Roe, LYM)*; [Mount Ephraim], *Royal Wells*: Well lit hotel bar with comfortable settees and chairs, cosy corners, views over T Wells, well kept Courage Directors, Harveys Best and Wadworths 6X, good value enterprising lunchtime brasserie menu, friendly efficient staff; bedrooms *(John Beeken)*
Under River [SE of Sevenoaks, off B245; TQ5551], *White Rock*: Friendly old-fashioned two-bar pub with well kept ales such as Adnams Broadside, good choice of well presented good value bar food (delicious steak sandwich), popular restaurant, chatty landlord, interesting bar games as well as pool and bar billiards; good big garden, not far from Ightham Mote *(Mr and Mrs A Budden, Martin, Pat and Hilary Forrest, A E Brace)*
☆ **West Farleigh** [B2010 SW of Maidstone; TQ7152], *Tickled Trout*: Good value food in pleasant bar and attractive dining room, decor gently toned down, well kept Whitbreads-related ales, good service; colourful flowers and hanging baskets outside, Medway views (esp from big garden with play area), path down to river with good walks *(Thomas Nott, Simon Small, LYM)*
West Peckham [TQ6452], *Swan*: Good value straightforward food, well kept Harveys and Morlands Old Speckled Hen, friendly staff, some character in cosy right-hand bar (welcoming to booted walkers); tables out by road through peaceful village-green hamlet – popular on summer weekends *(Paul Hilditch, Brian and Anna Marsden)*
Westbere [just off A18 Canterbury—Margate; TR1862], *Yew Tree*: Very heavily beamed early 14th-c pub, real ales, straightforward food, cosy atmosphere, friendly staff; back garden *(Kevin Thorpe)*
Westerham [A25 just W; TQ4454], *General Wolfe*: Excellently kept Greene King, good inexpensive food, delightfully unspoilt; nice licensees *(D E Twitchett)*
Wormshill [The Street; TQ8757], *Blacksmiths Arms*: Comfortably old-fashioned and relaxed renovation of isolated low-beamed country cottage, tiled floors, open fire, friendly staff, well kept Shepherd Neame and changing ales such as Goachers Dark and Greene King IPA, good varied food (not Tues evening) inc vegetarian and doorstep sandwiches in end dining area; Fri nostalgic 60s music (same man, same records for 25 yrs), pretty garden with country views *(Thomas Nott, Jeff Seaman)*
☆ **Worth** [The Street; signed off A258 S of Sandwich; TR3356], *St Crispin*: Stripped brickwork, bare boards, low beams, central log fire, real paraffin lamps, simple but interesting good food in bar and restaurant, well kept changing ales such as Brakspears SB, Gales HSB, Marstons Pedigree, Shepherd Neame and Charles Wells Bombardier, local farm cider, cheerful service, piped satellite music; charming big garden with barbecue, lovely village position not far from beach; bedrooms *(Kevin Thorpe, Howard Allen, Alan Thwaite, Patricia Dodd, Richard Farmer)*
Yalding [Yalding Hill; TQ7050], *Walnut Tree*: Pleasant brightly lit beamed bar on several levels with inglenook and interesting pictures, friendly efficient staff, food inc good fresh fish and bargain OAP weekday lunch, wide restaurant choice, Fremlins, Harveys and Wadworths 6X; piped music not over-intrusive, live music Sun evening; bedrooms, handy for Organic Garden *(Joy and Peter Heatherley)*

Lancashire

This is a wonderful area for real value in pubs, with food usually good value and often a real bargain, and drinks prices well below the national average – drinkers here generally save over 20p a pint, and pubs tied to Holts have exceptionally cheap beer. Pubs doing particularly well here these days include the White House on Blackstone Edge (remarkably cheap food considering it's in such a remote spot), the Stork at Conder Green (great spot, and as one reader puts it almost a Jamaica Inn feel – a new main entry), the Bushells Arms at Goosnargh (good food at this decorous dining pub), the Wheatsheaf at Raby (lots of character, good simple food – the pub seems to be growing a little more each year), and the Inn at Whitewell (a splendid all-rounder). The fine choice of fish at the Oddfellows Arms in Mellor is becoming a decided draw. There's particularly good imaginative food to be had too at the Eagle & Child at Bispham Green, a charming pub with beers brewed in their other pub over in Liverpool; the Eagle & Child is our Lancashire Dining Pub of the Year. For exceptional cheeses, head for Manchester – where the Mark Addy has an outstanding choice in very generous servings, and the Royal Oak and Dukes 92 are also good. Pubs showing well in the Lucky Dip section at the end of the chapter include the Old Packet House in Altrincham, Rams Head at Denshaw, Irby Mill at Irby, Ship at Lathom and Royal Oak at Riley Green (we have inspected and approved all of these). There's a splendid choice in Manchester, with a good sprinkling of Holts pubs (especially in Eccles); the choice in Liverpool isn't so wide, but those who know Cains beers will need little persuasion to try the Cains Brewery Tap there. We've also had very promising reports on the food at the Spread Eagle at Sawley, and the Saddle at Lea Town sounds nice; we'd be very grateful for more reports on these. Incidentally, please note that we include in this chapter those places around Stockport which have for the last couple of decades been absorbed into the Greater Manchester area – and those parts of the Wirral which were at the same time 'pinched' from Cheshire by Merseyside.

BELMONT (Lancs) SD6716 Map 7

Black Dog £ 🛏

A675

The original cheery and traditional small rooms at this friendly 18th-c farmhouse are packed with antiques and bric-a-brac, from railwaymen's lamps, bedpans and chamber-pots to landscape paintings, as well as service bells for the sturdy built-in curved seats, rush-seated mahogany chairs, and coal fires. The atmosphere is perhaps best on a winter evening, especially if you're tucked away in one of the various snug alcoves, one of which used to house the village court. On New Year's Day at lunchtime a small orchestra plays Viennese music. Very popular, generously served bar food includes home-made soup (£1.30), sandwiches (from £2), local black pudding or pâté (£2.80), breaded cod (£4.20), quiche (£4.40), ploughman's (from £4), vegetarian or chicken rogan josh (£4.80), 8oz sirloin (£6.20), salmon fillet in lobster sauce (£6.50), well liked salads with various fruits like grape, banana and strawberry, and daily specials like deep-fried camembert or whitebait (£2.50), spinach and ricotta cheese lasagne (£4.50), swordfish steak in lemon and herb butter (£6), venison in red wine (£6.50) or goose breast in plum sauce (£7); well kept Holts Bitter and Holts Mild. We like the way they've kept it pubby by not taking bookings, but it does tend to fill up quickly so get there early for a table. An airy extension lounge with a picture window has more modern furnishings; morning coffee, darts, pool, shove-ha'penny, dominoes, cribbage, and fruit machine; softly piped classical music. From two long benches on the sheltered sunny side of the pub there are delightful views of the moors above the nearby trees and houses; there's a track from the village up Winter Hill and (from the lane to Rivington) on to Anglezarke Moor, and paths from the dam of the nearby Belmont Reservoir. *(Recommended by Brian Wainwright, Peter Haines, Humphry and Angela Crum Ewing, Gordon Tong, T M Tomkinson, Jack Morley)*

Holts ~ Tenant James Pilkington ~ Real ale ~ Meals and snacks (till 8pm Sun; not Mon or Tues evenings except for residents) ~ (01204) 811218 ~ Children welcome ~ Open 12-4, 7-11; 12-4, 6.30-10.30 Sun ~ Bedrooms: £29.50B/£38B

BISPHAM GREEN (Lancs) SD4914 Map 7

Eagle & Child

Maltkiln Lane (Parbold—Croston rd) off B5246

Lancashire Dining Pub of the Year

We particularly enjoyed the stylishly simple interior of this striking red brick pub which has been very attractively refurbished in an understated old-fashioned style. The civilised bar is largely open-plan, but well divided by stubs of walls. There are fine old stone fireplaces, oriental rugs and some coir matting on flagstones, old hunting prints and engravings, and a mix of individual furnishings including small oak chairs around tables in corners, several handsomely carved antique oak settles – the finest apparently made partly from a 16th-c wedding bed-head, and an oak coffer. The snug area is no smoking. The owner's family farm much of the land around Parbold, so there may be well hung meat from their various herds. Imaginative bar food might include soups like smoked chicken and almond (£1.80), coronation chicken salad and mango (£6), warm crispy duck salad with mortadella, lardons and croutons and walnut dressing (£7), beef bourguignon or sautéed chicken fillet and mustard mascarpone (£8.50), fried pigeon breast with roquefort and pear dressing, roasted wild salmon with tomato and basil or seafood in a mild cream curry sauce (£9), grilled lamb neck fillet with couscous salad, grilled brill with lemon (£11), fresh king scallops with garlic and cream or fillet steak with button onions, white wine and cream (£12), and puddings like sticky toffee pudding (£2.50) or raspberry shortbread (£3). A particularly good range of well kept beers on handpump consists of Coach House Gunpowder Dark Mild, Theakstons Best, Thwaites, Timothy Taylor Landlord, with three or four changing guest ales one of which might be from their newly aquired own-brew pub, the Liverpool Brewing Co in the centre of Liverpool. Also farm cider, decent wines, and a good collection of malt whiskies. Friendly and interested service; maybe piped pop radio. There is a neat bowling green behind (with croquet in summer), and the pub garden has a lovely wild garden with crested newts and nesting moorhens. The two new oxford sandy and black pigs will have piglets this year, and Harry the dog is not the most sober individual. *(Recommended by M A Buchanan, Phil and Dilys Unsworth, David and Kathy Holcroft, Steve Whalley, Comus Elliott, Keith and Judith Ashcroft, Brian Kneale, Janet Pickles)*

Free house ~ Manager Monica Evans~ Real ale ~ Meals and snacks (12-2, 6-8.30) ~ (01257) 462297 ~ Children in eating area of bar ~ Jazz in the garden on summer Sun evenings ~ Open 12-3, 5.30-11; 12-11 Sat; 12-10.30 Sun; 12-3, 5.30-11 Sat in winter

BLACKSTONE EDGE (Gtr Manchester) SD9716 Map 7

White House £

A58 Ripponden—Littleborough, just W of B6138

There are impressive views over the moors from the lounge at this very popular 17th-c pub, which is spectacularly set 1,300 feet above sea level on the Pennine Way. The busy, welcoming and cheery main bar has a turkey carpet in front of a blazing coal fire and a large-scale map of the area (windswept walkers hardly know whether to head for the map or the fire first). The snug Pennine Room opens off here, with brightly coloured antimacassars on its small soft settees, and there's a new extension. A spacious room on the left has a big horseshoe window looking over the moors, as well as comfortable seating. Good helpings of good value homely bar food served with good vegetables include vegetable soup (£1.50), sandwiches (from £2.50), recommended cumberland sausage with egg (£3.90), steak and kidney pie, roast chicken breast or vegetarian quiche (£4.30), chilli, beef curry or lasagne (£5), daily specials like haddock and prawn mornay (£5) and lamb steak with herbs and garlic (£6.50), and home-made apple pie (£1.40); children's meals (£1.65). Prompt friendly service. Two well kept beers on handpump such as Black Sheep, Marstons Pedigree, Moorhouses Pendle Witches Brew, farm cider, and malt whiskies; fruit machine. Muddy boots can be left in the long, enclosed porch. *(Recommended by M A Buchanan, R T and J C Moggridge, Bronwen and Steve Wrigley, Graham and Lynn Mason, Derek and Sylvia Stephenson, Ian and Nita Cooper, David and Judy Walmsley, Alison Wills)*

Free house ~ Licensee Neville Marney ~ Real ale ~ Meals and snacks (11.30-2; 7-10) ~ (01706) 378456 ~ Children welcome till 9pm ~ Open 12-3, 6.30-11; 12-3, 6-10.30 Sun

BRINDLE (Lancs) SD6024 Map 7

Cavendish Arms

3 miles from M6 junction 29; A6 towards Whittle le Woods then left on B5256

With luck the brewery will continue to hold fire on their plans to upgrade and enlarge this snug old building with its several unchanging characterful little rooms which ramble round a central servery. There's a lovely cosy atmosphere, and the licensees are really friendly and welcoming. Some of the woodwork partitions contain fascinating stained-glass scenes with lively depictions of medieval warriors and minstrels. Many of them commemorate the bloody battle of Brundenburg, a nasty skirmish between the Vikings and Anglo-Saxons on the Ribble estuary. There are lots of pictorial plates and Devonshire heraldic devices in plaster on the walls, as well as comfortable seats and discreet flowery curtains. Two well kept Burtonwood beers on handpump, and a good choice of malt whiskies; darts. Simple bar food includes soup (£2), open sandwiches (from £3.95) home-made beef pie or breaded haddock (£4.95), peppered prawns (£5.50), spinach and mushroom lasagne (£5.65), chicken balti (£6.50), and daily specials like broccoli and pasta bake (£4.50) or fish pie (£5.50). There are white metal and plastic tables and chairs on a terrace by a rockery with a small water cascade, with another table on a small lawn behind. It's nicely set in a tranquil little village, and there's a handsome stone church across the road. *(Recommended by Miss J E Winsor, Roger and Jenny Huggins, Janet Pickles, G Armstrong, F C Johnston, M Buchanan, Brian Kneale, Dave Braisted)*

Burtonwood ~ Manager Peter Bowling ~ Real ale ~ Meals and snacks (12-2, 5.30-9 Thurs-Sat; not Mon, not Sun evening) ~ Restaurant ~ (01254) 852912 ~ Children in eating area of bar till 9.30 ~ Open 11-2.30, 5.30-11; 12-3, 7-10.30 Sun

CHIPPING (Lancs) SD6243 Map 7

Dog & Partridge 🍷

Hesketh Lane; crossroads Chipping—Longridge with Inglewhite—Clitheroe, OS Sheet 103 map reference 619413

Good food is the main draw at this comfortably relaxed and spotlessly kept dining pub. At lunchtime this includes soup (£2), sandwiches (from £2.95), prawn cocktail (£3.50), leek and mushroom crumble or curried nut roast with tomato chutney (£5.50), steak and kidney pie (£6.50) and grilled pork chop with apple sauce and stuffing (£7). The evening menu has a couple more dishes like poached salmon with prawn sauce (£7.50), roast beef (£8) and sirloin steak (£9.75); the home-made chips are particularly well liked and they do various fish and game specials. Parts of the building date back to 1515, though it's been much modernised since, with the eating space now spreading over into a nearby stable. The main lounge is comfortably furnished with small armchairs around fairly close-set low wood-effect tables on a blue patterned carpet, brown-painted beams, a good winter log fire, and multi-coloured lanterns; service is friendly and helpful. Tetley Bitter and Mild and a weekly changing guest on handpump, over 40 wines, and a good range of malt whiskies; piped music. Jacket and tie are preferred in the restaurant; dining areas are no smoking. *(Recommended by Roger and Christine Mash, Gillian Jenkins, J F M West, Sue and Geoff Price, Margaret and Peter Brierley, Arthur and Margaret Dickinson, J Boucher, Brian and Sue Wharton)*

Free house ~ Licensee Peter Barr ~ Real ale ~ Meals and snacks (12-1.45, 7-9; 12-9 Sun) ~ Restaurant ~ (01995) 61201 ~ Children welcome ~ Open 12-3, 7-11; 12-10.30 Sun

CONDER GREEN (Lancs) SD4556 Map 7

Stork

3 miles from M6 junction 33: A6 towards Lancaster, first left, then fork left; just off A588

This rambling white-painted ancient inn is in a fine spot, with tables outside looking out over the marshes and watery wastes where the River Conder joins the Lune estuary, and an added feel of isolation from the cries of the waterfowl out there when the winds (and tides) are right. It's convivial and unspoilt inside, with several cosy panelled rooms (one has a list of licensees going back to 1660), and a good fire. Although it's a place where people come to eat out, the atmosphere is pleasantly informal and relaxed, with service that stays cheerful (and efficient) even on a busy Saturday night. Food served in the bar and separate dining room includes good value sandwiches (£1.75), excellent potted shrimps (£2.50) and a mixed starter of locally smoked fish such as trout, mackerel, salmon and mussels (£2.50), with good generous home cooking including cumberland sausage with fried egg (£4.25), ploughman's (£4.75), steak and mushroom pie (£4.95), seabass (£6.50) and sirloin steak (£8.50). Their vegetarian dishes such as wild mushroom bake (£3.95) or roasted vegetable lasagne (£4.25) are well liked. Hot dishes are served with a choice of potatoes and of salad or vegetables; puddings (£1.95). Well kept Boddingtons, a beer named after the pub and interesting guest beers such as Crown Buckley Reverend James and Eccleshall Slaters on handpump; good coffee; darts, pool, fruit machine, trivia and a juke box; dogs welcome. The inn is just a mile from Glasson Dock, and a handy quiet retreat from Lancaster. *(Recommended by Jacqueline Morley, Dr and Mrs D Awbery, Ann Franklin, P J Rowland, David Cooke, R T and J C Moggridge)*

Free house ~ Licensees Mr and Mrs Tony Cragg ~ Real ale ~ Meals and snacks (12-2.30, 6.30-9; 12-9 Sun) ~ Restaurant ~ (01524) 751234 ~ Children away from main bar ~ Open 11-11; 12-10.30 Sun; cl 25 Dec ~ Bedrooms: £22.50B/£36B

CROSTON (Lancs) SD4818 Map 7

Black Horse £

Westhead Road; A581 Chorley—Southport

A new lounge extension with a log-burning stove at this very friendly village free house has been decorated in a quietly comfortable Victorian style in keeping with the rest of the building. The neatly kept bar has patterned carpets, attractive wallpaper, solid upholstered wall settles and cast-iron-framed pub tables, a fireplace tiled in the Victorian manner and reproduction prints of that period (also a couple of nice 1950s street-scene prints by M Grimshaw), as well as darts, pool, cribbage, dominoes, fruit machine, juke box, satellite TV and piped music. Very reasonably priced reliable home cooking is popular with local pensioners and includes sandwiches (from £1.80), ploughman's (£2.95), chilli (£3.60), steak in ale or mushroom stroganoff (£3.95), 6oz sirloin (£4.95), puddings (£1.85) and daily specials; no-smoking dining area. A surprising seven well kept real ales might include Black Sheep, Courage Directors, Jennings Bitter, Hancocks HB, Moorhouses Pendle Witches Brew, Ridleys IPA, Ruddles Best or Theakstons Bitter. There are picnic-sets outside, and a good solid safely railed-off play area; the pub has its own crown bowls green and boules pitch (boules available from the bar). *(Recommended by Ellis Heaton, B Kneale, Carl Reid, Richard Lewis, John Fazakerley; more reports please)*

Free house ~ Licensee Graeme Conroy ~ Real ale ~ Meals and snacks (12-2.30, 5.30-9; 12-7 Sun) ~ Restaurant ~ (01772) 600338 ~ Children welcome till 9pm ~ Open 11-11; 12-10.30 Sun

nr DARWEN (Lancs) SD6922 Map 7

Old Rosins

Pickup Bank, Hoddlesden; from B6232 Haslingden—Belthorn, turn off towards Edgeworth opposite the Grey Mare – pub then signposted off to the right; OS Sheet 103 map reference 722227

Served all day, the good value bar food at this remotely set but popular friendly pub includes sandwiches (from £1.95), cod and chips (£4.45), ploughman's (£3.25), turkey broth and dumplings (£3.50), good value beef in Old Peculier (£4.95), chicken tikka (£5.25) and puddings (from £1.90). There's a good pubby atmosphere in the open-plan bar which is comfortably furnished with red plush built-in button-back banquettes, and stools and small wooden chairs around dark cast-iron-framed tables. Lots of mugs, whisky-water jugs and so forth hang from the high joists, while the walls are decorated with small prints, plates and old farm tools; there's also a good log fire. Parts of the bar and restaurant are no smoking. Well kept Boddingtons, Flowers Original, Marstons Pedigree and Theakstons Old Peculier on handpump, plenty of malt whiskies, and coffee; fruit machine and maybe piped music. There are picnic-sets on a spacious crazy-paved terrace, and lovely views over the moors and down into the wooded valley on clear days. *(Recommended by M Buchanan, Andy Hazeldine, Charlotte Wrigley, K and B Forman, Steven and Denise Waugh, Vicky and David Sarti, Carl Travis)*

Free house ~ Licensee Bryan Hankinson ~ Meals and snacks (all day) ~ Restaurant ~ (01254) 771264 ~ Children welcome ~ Open 11-11; 12-10.30 Sun ~ Bedrooms: £42.50B/£52.50B

DOWNHAM (Lancs) SD7844 Map 7

Assheton Arms

From A59 NE of Clitheroe turn off into Chatburn (signposted); in Chatburn follow Downham signpost; OS Sheet 103 map reference 785443

Window seats and picnic-sets outside this charmingly set village dining pub, which takes its name from the family who bought this delightful stonebuilt village in 1558 and preserved it in traditional style ever since, look across to the church. Inside, the rambling, beamed and red-carpeted bar has olive plush-cushioned winged settles around attractive grainy oak tables, some cushioned window seats, and two grenadier busts on the mantlepiece over a massive stone fireplace that helps to divide the separate areas; part of the bar is no smoking. As well as seasonal fish specialities such as oysters, monkfish, crab and lobster, popular if not cheap bar food includes ham and vegetable broth (£2.25), sandwiches (from £3.25; not Saturday evening or Sunday lunchtime), brie and lancashire cheese deep fried in batter with gooseberry sauce or ploughman's (£3.95), mushrooms and cream with pasta (£5.50), steak and kidney pie (£5.95), venison, bacon and cranberry casserole (£7.95), halibut steak with cream cheese sauce (£8.95), scampi (£10.25) and strips of beef fillet stir-fried with ginger and spring onion (£11.50). Well kept Boddingtons and Whitbreads Castle Eden under light blanket pressure; decent wines by the glass or bottle; piped music. *(Recommended by Mrs Ursula Hofheinz, Ken and Joan Bemrose, Bronwen and Steve Wrigley, Peter Miatee)*

Whitbreads ~ Tenants David and Wendy Busby ~ Real ale ~ Meals and snacks (till 10pm) ~ (01200) 441227 ~ Children welcome ~ Open 12-3, 7-11(10.30 Sun)

FENCE (Lancs) SD8237 Map 7

Forest

Cuckstool Lane; off A6088 opp B6248 to Brierfield

You will need to book at the weekend to try the inventive cooking at this smartly attractive dining pub. Ceilings are painted a striking red, there's heavy panelling, lots of paintings, vases, plates and books, and a cosy comfortable feel, thanks to its big open fire and subdued lighting. The open-plan bar has two rooms opening off it, and a side restaurant. Good varied food uses fresh local produce where possible – salmon from the river instead of a fish farm, perhaps pork from a free-range Gloucester Old Spot instead of some modern genetic wonder. And the cooking is inventive: soup of the day (£2.40), hot chicken sandwich (£3.95), crispy black pudding with sautéed cider apples (£4.75), scallops with garlic and gruyère (£5.50), herb baked polenta with fresh tomato sauce, salsa and julienne of vegetables (£7.50), tagliatelle with fresh mussels, chorizo and tomato sauce with fresh herbs (£7.95), Indonesian chicken satay (£8.95), Scottish rump steak (£9.95), rack of lamb with potato purée, confit of root vegetables and rich mint lamb jus or bass steak with provençal vegetables (£11.50), puddings and ice creams are home made and come in combinations like caramelised rice pudding with red berry compote and caramel ice cream (£4.25); there is no children's menu but they will do small helpings of suitable dishes; no-smoking area in conservatory dining room; quiet piped music. Ruddles and Theakstons Best on handpump as well as a couple of guests like Marstons Pedigree or Morlands Old Speckled Hen, a good choice of wines, friendly helpful service. *(Recommended by M A Buchanan, Brian Kneale; more reports please)*

Free house ~ Licensee Clive Seedall ~ Real ale ~ Meals and snacks (12-2.30, 5.30-9.30; 12-9 Sun) ~ Restaurant ~ (01282) 613641 ~ Children welcome ~ Open 12-11(10.30 Sun); cl 25 Dec evening

GARSTANG (Lancs) SD4845 Map 7

Th'Owd Tithebarn ★

Signposted off Church Street; turn left off one-way system at Farmers Arms

This converted, creeper-covered canalside tithe barn is a fascinating and unique old building. In some ways it's a bit like a simple old-fashioned farmhouse kitchen parlour with an old kitchen range, prints of agricultural equipment on the walls, stuffed animals and birds, and pews and glossy tables spaced out on the flagstones under the very high rafters – we're told that only the York Museum has a bigger collection of antique farming equipment. Waitresses in period costume with mob-caps complete the vintage flavour. There are lots of benches on the big flagstoned terrace that overlooks ducks and boats wending their way along the Lancaster Canal, beside this beautifully set creeper-covered barn. It does get busy here, as it's something of a tourist attraction. Simple but well prepared bar food includes soup (£1.95), garlic mushrooms (£2.95), filled cottage loaves (from £3.25, lunchtime only), spicy bean tortilla bake (£4.95), steak and kidney pudding (£5.75) and lamb cobbler (£5.95), and specials like breaded lobster or ham topped with cheese and pineapple (£5.95) or 10oz rump with spicy herb and tomato sauce (£6.45). They do afternoon teas in summer. Well kept Mitchells Original and Lancaster Bomber on handpump; lots of country wines, dominoes, piped music. *(Recommended by Mrs S Kingsbury, Ian Phillips; more reports please)*

Mitchells ~ Manager Gordon Hutchinson ~ Real ale ~ Meals and snacks (12-9.30(10 Sat); 12-2.30, 6-9.30(10 Sat) in winter; 12-9.30 Sun) ~ (01995) 604486 ~ Children in dining area ~ Open 11-11; 11-3, 6-11 Mon-Sat in winter; 12-10.30 Sun

GOOSNARGH (Lancs) SD5537 Map 7

Bushells Arms

4 miles from M6 junction 32; A6 towards Garstang, turn right at Broughton traffic lights (the first ones you come to), then left at Goosnargh Village signpost (it's pretty insignificant – the turn's more or less opposite Whittingham Post Office)

The landlord at this rather special and very good value dining pub sets a civilised tranquil scene for diners to chat in peace over good food, well kept beer and sound wines. The menu tends towards Mediterranean and Middle Eastern food with daily specials determined by the availability of good fresh ingredients, and fresh fish from Fleetwood. As well as an unusual soup like Dutch pea with ham and garlic sausage (£1.30), recent daily specials have included local black pudding (£2), cinnamon flavoured minced lamb layered with pasta and topped with savoury custard (£5), vegetable cobbler or pork, apple, prune and walnut meatballs braised in cider sauce (£5.50), Moroccan chicken, fresh salmon marinated in red wine, blackberries and mint and chicken fillet in mild spicy curry sauce with sliced peppers, sultanas and thyme (£6). The bar menu includes spring rolls, samosas or falafel (£2), steak and kidney pie (£5.50), and salmon and broccoli parcel, stifatho (a Greek beef stew), or chicken fillet filled with smoked bacon, asparagus, grated cheese in hollandaise sauce and wrapped in puff pastry (£6). Crisp and fresh vegetables include tasty potatoes done with garlic, cream, peppers and parmesan, and there's a good range of puddings like pecan pie and pecan ice cream or orange bread and butter pudding (£2). The spacious, modernised bar has lots of snug bays, each holding not more than two or three tables and often faced with big chunks of sandstone (plastic plants and spotlit bare boughs heighten the rockery effect); also soft red plush button-back banquettes, with flagstones by the bar. Two areas are no smoking. The well chosen and constantly developing wine list is excellent, with some New World ones and several half bottles, as well as changing wines of the month and helpful notes. Also well kept Timothy Taylor Best on handpump, and several malt whiskies. Tables in a little back garden, and hanging baskets at the front. The signal for opening the doors at lunchtime is the tolling of the church clock, and haunted Chingle Hall is not far away. *(Recommended by N Stansfield, J Perry, Brian and Anna Marsden, Mr and Mrs J E Murphy, Steve Whalley, Neil Townend, Wendy Fairbank, Margaret and Roy Randle, M Buchanan, Arthur and Margaret Dickinson, Peter Miatee, Michael Tucker, Dave Braisted, John and Moira Cook)*

Whitbreads ~ Lease: David Best ~ Real ale ~ Meals and snacks (not Goosnargh Field Day) ~ (01772) 865235 ~ Well behaved children in eating area of bar ~ Open 12-3, 6-11(7-10.30 Sun); cl 25 Dec and occasional Mondays

Horns 🍷

Pub signed from village, about 2 miles towards Chipping below Beacon Fell

This pleasantly positioned old coaching inn is well run with great care and attention by friendly welcoming licensees and staff. Its neatly kept snug rooms are dotted around with a number of colourful flower displays, and all have log fires in winter. Beyond the lobby, the pleasant front bar opens into attractively decorated middle rooms with antique and other period furnishings. At lunchtime it's mostly popular with people enjoying the tasty bar food such as beef and vegetable soup (£2.25), beautifully presented sandwiches (from £2.75), ploughman's (£4.25), steak and kidney pie (£5.95), plaice or roast pheasant (£6.25) and sirloin steak with mushrooms (£9.50), all nicely served with freshly cooked, piping hot chips; home-made puddings like sherry trifle or an excellent sticky toffee pudding (£3.25). A very good range of up to ten or so wines by the glass, an extensive wine list and a fine choice of malt whiskies; cheerful and helpful young staff, piped music. *(Recommended by RJH, Dr Michael Allen, W W Burke, John Fazakerley, Mike and Mary Carter, J A Boucher, K C and B Forman, Brian and Sue Wharton)*

Free house ~ Licensee Mark Woods ~ Meals and snacks (not Sun/Mon lunch or Sat evening) ~ Restaurant ~ (01772) 865230 ~ Children in eating area of bar and restaurant ~ Open 11.30-3, 6-11; 12-3, 6-10.30 Sun; cl Mon lunchtime ~ Bedrooms: £45B/£70B

LIVERPOOL SJ4395 Map 7

Philharmonic ★ £ ☕

36 Hope Street; corner of Hardman Street

There's tremendous historical interest at this magnificent old Victorian gin palace – properly known as the Philharmonic Dining Rooms – with its wonderfully opulent rooms still exquisitely decorated in their original style, and happily bustling with theatre-goers, students, locals and tourists. The heart of the building is a mosaic-faced serving counter, from where heavily carved and polished mahogany partitions radiate under the intricate plasterwork high ceiling. The echoing main hall is decorated with stained glass including contemporary portraits of Boer War heroes such as Baden-Powell and Lord Roberts, rich panelling, a huge mosaic floor, and copper panels of musicians in an alcove above the fireplace. More stained glass in one of the little lounges declares *Music is the universal language of mankind* and backs this up with illustrations of musical instruments; there are two plushly comfortable sitting rooms. Lavatory devotees may be interested to know that the famous gents' are original 1890s Rouge Royale by Twyfords: all red marble and glinting mosaics; some readers have long felt these alone earn the pub its star. Well kept Marstons Pedigree, Morlands Old Speckled Hen and Tetleys Bitter on handpump, some malt whiskies and cask cider; fruit machine, video game and piped music. Good value home-made bar food includes soup (£1.25), filled baguettes (from £2.15, hot £2.35), and various well priced dishes like lasagne, steak and kidney pie or haddock (all £3.95), gammon, cajun chicken or cod and prawn pie (£4.95), mixed grill (£8.45) and puddings (£1.85); they do a very well priced three-course Sunday lunch; no-smoking area in restaurant. Friendly service. *(Recommended by Ray Hebson, JP, PP, G Dunstan, Alan and Paula McCully, Gillian Jenkins, Brian Kneale, Richard Fallon, Chris Raisin)*

Carlsberg Tetleys ~ Manager John Sullivan ~ Real ale ~ Meals and snacks (12-2.30, 5-8) ~ Restaurant ~ (0151) 709 1163 ~ Children in eating area of bar ~ Open 11.30-11; 12-3, 7-10.30 Sun; cl Sun lunchtime

LYTHAM (Lancs) SD3627 Map 7

Taps £

A584 S of Blackpool; Henry Street – in centre, one street in from West Beach

There are usually eight well kept beers at this cheery ale house. There might be Bunces Pigswill, Hopback Summer Lightning, Timothy Taylor Landlord, Woods Shropshire Lad and Wychwood Dogs Bollocks. The enthusiastic landlord is forever hunting out new beers, and every time he changes a barrel it's to something different – so far he's had over 1,000. Boddingtons is more or less a regular fixture, and they usually have some country wines. The Victorian-style bare-boarded bar has a really friendly and unassuming atmosphere, as well as plenty of stained-glass decoration in the windows, with depictions of fish and gulls reflecting the pub's proximity to the beach; also captain's chairs in bays around the sides, open fires, and a coal-effect gas fire between two built-in bookcases at one end. As well as a TV for special sporting events there's a bit of a rugby theme, with old photographs and portraits of rugby stars on the walls; piped music, shove-ha'penny, dominoes, fruit machine and juke box. Anyone who's taken sampling the beers a little too seriously will appreciate the seat belts on the bar stools, and the headrest in the gents'. The home-made bar food is simple but good value, with the most popular dishes including a good pea and ham soup (95p), hot roast beef sandwich (£2.35), beer sausages and mash or chilli (£2.95) and chicken curry or ploughman's (£3.25); the ham and beef is home cooked. There are no meals on Sunday, but instead they have free platters of food laid out, with tasty morsels like black pudding, chicken wings or minted lamb. There are a few seats outside. *(Recommended by ALC, Kate and Robert Hodkinson; more reports please)*

Whitbreads ~ Manager Ian Rigg ~ Real ale ~ Lunchtime meals and snacks (free snacks only on Sun) ~ (01253) 736226 ~ Open 11-11; 12-10.30 Sun

MANCHESTER SJ8498 Map 7

Dukes 92 £

Castle Street, below the bottom end of Deansgate

Stylishly converted from old canal-horse stables, in a superbly atmospheric setting by locks and under railway arches in the rejuvenated heart of old industrial Manchester, this spacious old building has black wrought-iron work contrasting boldly with whitewashed bare plaster walls, a handsome marble-topped bar, and an elegant spiral staircase to an upper room and balcony. Up here are some modern director's chairs, but down in the main room the fine mix of furnishings is mainly rather Edwardian in mood, with one particularly massive table, elegantly comfortable chaises-longues and deep armchairs. It's under the same ownership as the well established Mark Addy (see entry below), and has a similar excellent choice of over three dozen cheeses and several pâtés – some quite unusual – served in huge helpings with granary bread (£3.50); soup

(£2.50), toasted sandwiches (from £2.95), sandwiches like pastrami with coarse grain mustard and gherkin on rye bread (£3.95), pasta (£4.75), mixed mezze (£7.95) and oriental platter (£9.95). Well kept Boddingtons and a guests like Timothy Taylor Landlord on handpump, along with the Belgian wheat beer Hoegarden, and quite a few Belgian fruit beers; decent wines and a large selection of malts, friendly staff; piped classical music. There are tables out by the canal basin which opens into the bottom lock of the Rochdale Canal. On bank holiday weekends events in the forecourt may include jazz and children's theatre, and there's a permanent theatre in the function room. *(Recommended by Ian Phillips, David Carr, John McDonald, Ann Bond, ALC, Dr M Bridge, Stephen and Julie Brown, John Fazakerley, Meg Hamilton)*

Free house ~ Licensee Louise Ratcliffe ~ Real ale ~ Snacks (all day) ~ (0161) 839 8646 ~ Children welcome ~ Open 11.30-11; 12-10.30 Sun

Lass o' Gowrie £

36 Charles Street; off Oxford Street at BBC

Seats around a sort of glass cage give a view of the brewing process in the cellar microbrewery where they produce the lightly flavoured LOG35 and the meatier LOG42 at this tiled Victorian pub. There's also well kept Marstons Pedigree, Wadworths 6X, Whitbreads Castle Eden and several guest beers on handpump, and Old Hazy cider; it might take some while to get served at busy periods. The simple but characterful long bar has gas lighting and bare floorboards and lots of exposed brick work. Hop sacks drape from the ceiling, and the bar has big windows in its richly tiled arched brown facade. Good value bar food includes sandwiches (from £1.75), bacon bap (£2), burger, steak and kidney pie or a choice of five types of sausage with mash (£2.85) and lasagne (£3.75); efficient cheery service. The volume of the piped pop music really depends on the youth of the customers at the time; fruit machine; the snug is no smoking at lunchtime. At really busy periods (usually only Friday and Saturday nights during term times), the bar may be so full of good-natured university students you'll have to drink your own-brew pint on the pavement outside in true city-centre pub style; no children. *(Recommended by Sue Holland, Dave Webster, David Carr, John McDonald, Ann Bond, Wayne Brindle, Richard Lewis)*

Own brew (Whitbreads) ~ Manager David McGrath ~ Real ale ~ Meals and snacks (11.30-7) ~ (0161) 273 6932/2896 ~ Open 11-11; 12-10.30 Sun; cl 25 Dec

Marble Arch £

73 Rochdale Rd (A664), Ancoats; corner of Gould St, just E of Victoria Station

They are now producing half a dozen very reasonably priced own- brew beers at this beautifully preserved Victorian pub: Dades, Dobber, Ginger Marble, IPA, Marble and Totally Marbelled are well kept alongside a good choice of bottled beers (including Belgian Trappist beers), Biddenden cider, and a selection of country wines. There's a magnificently restored lightly barrel-vaulted high ceiling and extensive marble and tiling, amongst which the frieze advertising various spirits and the chimney breast above the carved wooden mantlepiece particularly stand out. A mosaic floor slopes down to the bar, and some of the walls are partly stripped back to the glazed brick. There are armchairs by a fire in the back bar. Remarkably low-priced bar food, served in the lounge extension at the back, includes beer sausages (from £1.75), lasgane, sausage and ale pie and half a dozen curries (£2.50). Darts, alley skittles, table skittles, chess, cards, pinball, fruit machine, juke box and lively background music. The Laurel and Hardy Preservation Society meets here on the third Wednesday of the month and show old films. *(Recommended by The Didler, Richard Lewis, Ian Phillips, David Carr, JP, PP, Peter Plumridge)*

Free house ~ Manager Mark Dade ~ Real ale ~ Meals and snacks 11.30-4 ~ (0161) 832 5914 ~ Live music some evenings ~ Open 11.30(12 Sat)-11; cl Sun, 25/26 Dec, 1 Jan

Mark Addy 🍷 £

Stanley Street, Salford, Manchester 3 (if it's not on your street map head for New Bailey St); look out not for a pub but for what looks like a smoked-glass modernist subway entrance

Served in huge helpings with granary bread, you can choose from an incredible choice of almost 50 different cheeses and pâtés from all over Britain and Europe (all carefully described on the menu) at this atmospheric cheese pub. It's £3.50 for a helping and they automatically give you a doggy bag. There's also toasted sandwiches (£2.50). Well converted from waiting rooms for boat passengers, the pub has quite a civilised and trendy atmosphere, especially in the flower-filled waterside courtyard from where you can watch the home-bred ducks. Inside, the series of barrel-vaulted red sandstone bays is furnished with russet or dove plush seats and upholstered stalls, wide glassed-in brick arches, cast-iron pillars, and a flagstone floor; piped music. Well kept Boddingtons and two changing guests like Marstons Pedigree or Timothy Taylor Landlord kept under light blanket pressure; quite a few wines too, with a sign by the entrance recommending which go best with particular cheeses. They get very busy, so it is worth getting there early, and they prefer smart dress. The pub is run by the same people as another Manchester main entry, Dukes 92 (see above). *(Recommended by Ian Phillips, David Carr, Meg and Colin Hamilton, Martin McGowan, Dr M Bridge)*

Free house ~ Licensee Thomas Joyce ~ Real ale ~ Snacks (all day) ~ (0161) 832 4080 ~ Children welcome ~ Open 11.30-11; 12-10.30 Sun

Royal Oak £

729 Wilmslow Road, Didsbury

This bustling end-of-terrace pub is famous for its incredibly vast array of cheese served with a substantial chunk of bread and extras such as olives and pickled onions (£3.50 for a choice of two cheeses). They are rarely served in less than a pound helping, and take-away bags are provided. Well kept Batemans Mild, Marstons Bitter and a fortnightly changing guest beer on handpump, and some sherries and ports from the wood; efficient, friendly service. Antique theatre bills and so forth cover the walls of the busy bar which is very popular with drinkers. There are some seats outside and lots of hanging baskets cheer up its simple exterior. *(Reports on the new regime please)*

Marstons ~ Manager Norma Hall ~ Real ale ~ Lunchtime snacks (not weekends or bank holidays) ~ (0161) 434 4788 ~ Children over 14 allowed 12-2 ~ Open 11-11; 12-10.30 Sun

MELLOR (Gtr Manchester) SJ9888 Map 7

Oddfellows Arms

73 Moor End Road; follow Mellor signpost off A626 Marple—Glossop and keep further on up hill – this is the Mellor near Stockport

Fresh fish is something of a speciality at this lovely old country pub, with up to nine different dishes like natural cured haddock poached in white wine (£7.95), monkfish fried with mixed sweet peppers, spring onions and oyster sauce (£10.55), and Cantonese steamed bass with ginger and soy (£11.95). Other very carefully prepared bar food includes three or four soups (£1.75), sandwiches (from £1.95), hot rump steak sandwich (£3.45), ploughman's (from £4.75), beef masala (£5.45), roast of the day (£5.75), chicken fried with celery and stilton cream (£7.50), pork fillet and mushrooms fried with green peppercorns, brandy and cream (£8.95), strips of beef fillet with mushrooms, cashew nuts and black bean cakes with rice cake (£9.25); puddings like Caribbean crumble bread (£2.95); three course Sunday lunch (£7.95); no-smoking restaurant. With no piped music or games, there's a pleasantly civilised buzz of conversation in the two fine old flagstoned bars, with low ceilings, open fires, and well kept Adnams, Marstons Pedigree and a weekly changing guest on handpump. There's a small restaurant upstairs, and a few tables out by the road. *(Recommended by David Hoult, Richard and Ruth Dean, Stephen and Julie Brown, Tony Young)*

Free house ~ Licensee Robert Cloughley ~ Real ale ~ Meals and snacks ~ Restaurant ~

(0161) 449 7826 ~ Children welcome till 8.30 ~ Open 12-3, 5.30-11; 12-3, 7-10.30 Sun; cl Mon except bank holidays, cl Tues after bank holidays

NEWTON (Lancs) SD6950 Map 7

Parkers Arms

B6478 7 miles N of Clitheroe

The very friendly licensees at this delightfully set timbered pub have added a well stocked animal garden (with pygmy goats, rabbits, guinea pigs, hens, pheasants, parrots and lots more birds) for children to enjoy while their parents take in the view from well spaced picnic-sets on the big lawn looking down towards the river, and beyond to the hills. There's also a play area, and two amiable black labradors (who have been known to bring customers a stick to throw). Inside there are plenty of stuffed animals and paintings, as well as red plush button-back banquettes, a mix of new chairs and tables, and an open fire. Beyond an arch is a similar area with sensibly placed darts, pool, dominoes, bar billiards, fruit machine, and discreet piped music. Well kept Boddingtons and Flowers IPA and guests like Marstons Pedigree or Theakstons on handpump, a good range of malt whiskies, and regularly changing wine list. Generous helpings of bar food might include soup (£2.50), very generous sandwiches (from £2.75), big ploughman's (£5.50), and a wide choice of daily blackboard specials like home-made shortcrust beef and ale pie (£5.75), home-cooked ham salad or Turkish aubergine (£5.95), fillet of plaice with prawns and cheese sauce or Morrocan chicken tagine (£6.95), fresh poached salmon salad (£7.50) and wild boar steak (£9.25); big well prepared breakfasts; no-smoking restaurant. *(Recommended by David J Cooke, Arthur and Margaret Dickinson, Gary and Sarah Goldson, John and Joan Wyatt, Julie and Steve Anderton, Sue and Geoff Price)*

Whitbreads ~ Lease: Barbara Clayton ~ Real ale ~ Meals and snacks (all day in summer, and all day Sat/Sun in winter) ~ Restaurant ~ (01200) 446236 ~ Children welcome in eating area of bar and restaurant ~ Open 11-11; 12-10.30 Sun; 11-2.30, 5-11 weekdays in winter ~ Bedrooms: £35B/£50B

RABY (Merseyside) SJ3180 Map 7

Wheatsheaf

The Green, Rabymere Road; off A540 S of Heswall

The tremendously characterful low-ceilinged rooms at this charming half-timbered, thatched and whitewashed country cottage (known locally as the Thatch and not easy for strangers to find) are simply furnished with an old wall clock and homely black kitchen shelves in the cosy central bar, and a nice snug formed by antique settles built in around its fine old fireplace. A second, more spacious room has upholstered wall seats around the tables, small hunting prints on the cream walls, and a smaller coal fire. Straightforward but tasty bar food includes soup (£1.80), lots of toasted sandwiches (from £2.20), ploughman's (£4.35), breaded plaice (£5.10), steak and ale pie (£5.50), 8oz sirloin (£8.50). The spacious restaurant (with more elaborate evening menu) is in a converted cowshed that leads into a larger no-smoking conservatory. Well kept beers on handpump include Cains Original, Tetleys, Theakstons Best, Old Peculier and XB, Thwaites Best and Daniel Hammer and Youngers Scotch, and there's also a good choice of malt whiskies. The landlord (who used to farm the land next door) has added a patio area with picnic-sets behind. *(Recommended by E G Parish, Sue and Bob Ward, Tom and Joan Childs, Ian Phillips, Ray Hebson, Graham and Lynn Mason, Dr Jim Mackay, Liz and Graham Bell)*

Free house ~ Licensee Thomas Charlesworth ~ Real ale ~ Lunchtime meals and snacks ~ Evening restaurant ~ (0151) 336 3416 ~ Children in eating area of bar ~ Open 11.30-11; 12-10.30 Sun

Real ale to us means beer which has matured naturally in its cask – not pressurised or filtered.

RIBCHESTER (Lancs) SD6435 Map 7

White Bull

Church Street; turn off B6245 at sharp corner by Black Bull

There's plenty of Roman history in the vicinity of this stately stone dining pub (built in 1707). The Tuscan pillars that guard its entrance porch have been in the area for nearly 2,000 years, there are the remains of a Roman bath house behind it, and a small Roman museum nearby. The spacious and attractively refurbished main bar has comfortable old settles, and is decorated with Victorian advertisements and various prints, as well as a stuffed fox in two halves that looks as if it's jumping through the wall; most areas are set out for eating during the day, and you can also eat out in the garden behind. Half the dining area is no smoking. Service is friendly and attentive, even during busy periods, and children are made particularly welcome. Good value bar meals include soup (£1.60), open sandwiches (from £2.60), prawn cocktail (£3.20), steak and kidney pie (£4.95), meat or vegetable lasagne (£5), ploughman's (£5.20), various steaks with a choice of toppings (from £7), braised shoulder of lamb (£8.50), and changing specials such as swordfish with garlic and prawns; children's menu. Well kept Boddingtons, Flowers IPA, Marstons Pedigree and Wadworths 6X under light blanket pressure, a good range of malt whiskies, and a blackboard list of several wines by the glass or bottle; they also do coffees, tea, and hot chocolate. It can get busy, so it's worth arriving early for a table. TV, darts, pool, juke box, dominoes and fruit machine in the games room; piped music. *(Recommended by Brian and Anna Marsden, Bronwen and Steve Wrigley, M Buchanan, Peter Walker, Sue and Geoff Price; more reports please)*

Whitbreads ~ Lease: Neil Sandiford ~ Real ale ~ Meals and snacks (not Mon evening) ~ (01254) 878303 ~ Children in eating area of bar till 9pm ~ Open 11.30-3, 6.30-11; 12-10.30 Sun

STALYBRIDGE (Gtr Manchester) SJ9698 Map 7

Stalybridge Station Buffet £

Much loved by readers, this classic Victorian platform bar is not smart but comfortably nostalgic with a marble-topped bar counter, roaring fire below an etched-glass mirror, newspapers and magazines to read, old photographs of the station in its heyday and other railway memorabilia – even a little conservatory. It's expanded along the platform into what was the ladies' waiting room and part of the station-master's quarters, original ornate ceilings and a dining/function room with Victorian-style wallpaper; dominoes, cribbage, draughts. On a sunny day you can sit out on the platform. As well as good coffee and tea made freshly by the pot, there are good cheap old-fashioned snacks such as sandwiches (from £1.30), ploughman's (£1.75), and three or four daily specials like much loved black peas, pasta bake, liver and onions or fish pie (£1.75-£2.50). A very good range of well kept beers includes Boddingtons, Flowers IPA, Wadworths 6X and up to six interesting changing guest beers like Mallard Drake and Salopian Gingersnap on handpump, as well as farm cider, Belgian and other foreign bottled beers; beer festivals in early May and late November. Readers who knew it before will welcome one innovation – neat inside lavatories. *(Recommended by the Didler, Ian Phillips, JP, PP, Pat and Tony Martin, Mr J and Dr S Harrop, Stephen Brown, Richard Fallon, David Hoult, Richard Lewis)*

Free house ~ Licensees Sylvia Wood and John Hesketh ~ Real ale ~ Snacks (12-9) ~ (0161) 303 0007 ~ Children welcome ~ Folk singers Sat evening ~ Open 11-11; 12-10.30 Sun; cl 25 Dec

WHARLES (Lancs) SD4435 Map 7

Eagle & Child

Church Road; from B5269 W of Broughton turn left into Higham Side Road at HMS Inskip sign; OS Sheet 102 map reference 448356

Dotted throughout the neatly kept rooms of this delightfully timeless thatched ale house is the landlord's marvellous collection of lovely antique furnishings. The most interesting are in the L-shaped bar, where a beamed area round the corner past the counter has a whole cluster of them. One of the highlights is a magnificent, elaborately carved Jacobean settle which originally came from Aston Hall in Birmingham, carrying the motto *exaltavit humiles*. There's also a carved oak chimneypiece, and a couple of fine longcase clocks, one from Chester, and another with a nicely painted face and an almost silent movement from Manchester. The plain cream walls are hung with modern advertising mirrors and some older mirrors, and there are a few exotic knives, carpentry tools and so forth on the plastered structural beams; even when it's not particularly cold, there should be a good fire burning in the intricate cast-iron stove. Well kept Boddingtons and three regularly changing guests such as Cains Traditional, Wadworths 6X or Wards on handpump; darts in a sensible side area, pool, dominoes, friendly cat. One or two picnic-sets outside. *(Recommended by Ian and Nita Cooper; more reports please)*

Free house ~ Licensee Brian Tatham ~ Real ale ~ No food ~ (01772) 690312 ~ Children over 14 ~ Open 7-11; 12-4, 7-10.30 Sun

WHITEWELL (Lancs) SD6546 Map 7

Inn at Whitewell ★ ★

Most easily reached by B6246 from Whalley; road through Dunsop Bridge from B6478 is also good

Perhaps most dramatically approached from Abbeystead, this civilised country house hotel is beautifully set deep in the Forest of Bowland and surrounded by well wooded rolling hills set off against higher moors. It houses a wine merchant (hence the unusually wide range of around 180 wines available – the claret is recommended) and an art gallery, and owns several miles of trout, salmon and sea trout fishing on the Hodder; with notice they'll arrange shooting. Although it gets very busy, it's very spacious inside and out, so usually stays peaceful and relaxing. The old-fashioned pubby bar has antique settles, oak gateleg tables, sonorous clocks, old cricketing and sporting prints, log fires (the lounge has a very attractive stone fireplace), and heavy curtains on sturdy wooden rails; one area has a selection of newspapers, dominoes, local maps and guide books. There's a piano for anyone who wants to play. Down a corridor with strange objects like a stuffed fox disappearing into the wall is the pleasant suntrap garden, with wonderful views down to the valley. Very highly praised bar food includes soup (£2.90), open sandwiches (from £3.80), warm salad with steaky bacon, grilled goat's cheese and avocado (£4.90), haddock with welsh rarebit (£5.90), herb risotto (£6.50), sausage and mash (£7.20), daube of beef (£9.50), fish pie (£7.90), roast guinea fowl breast (£11.50), home-made puddings like chocolate roulade (£3.50) and hand-made farmhouse cheeses (from £3.50); the evening menu is just slightly different; they serve coffee and cream teas all day; very civil service. Well kept Boddingtons and Marstons Pedigree on hand. Some of the spacious and beautifully refurbished bedrooms even have their own CD players. *(Recommended by David J Cooke, Roger and Christine Marsh, Guy Vowles, M Meadley, Nigel Woolliscroft, Dorothee and Dennis Glover, Jean and Peter Walker, W W Burke, Karen Eliot, J S M Sheldon, Kathleen Newton, Peter Walker, John and Barbara Burns, D M Sayers, Mr Miller, Sarah Bradbury, J A Boucher, Richard Fallon, Keith and Judith Ashcroft)*

Free house ~ Licensee Richard Bowman ~ Real ale ~ Meals and snacks ~ Restaurant ~ (01200) 448222 ~ Children welcome ~ Open 11-3, 6-11; 12-3, 7-11 Sun ~ Bedrooms: from £52B/£74B

YEALAND CONYERS (Lancs) SD5074 Map 7

New Inn

3 miles from M6 junction 35; village signposted off A6 N

Even on Sunday when this simple ivy-coloured stone pub is busy with fell walkers here for the good value Sunday lunch, the atmosphere is tranquil and soothing. Although the emphasis is very clearly on the very well prepared bar food, there's still a cosy village atmosphere: filled baguettes (from £4.50), starters such as soup (£2.95), fried chicken livers with garlic, mushroom and marsala on a date crouton (£4.95), green-lipped mussels cooked with cream, parmesan and garlic or babotie (£4.95), main courses like cumberland sausage on white onion and sage purée (£7.50), broccoli, leek, potato, cheese and garlic bake or ham baked with honey and orange (£7.95), Caribbean pork with pineapple and coconut (£8.95), chicken breast filled with cheese and herb pâté and topped with white onion sauce or sole St Germain with fresh herb cream sauce (£9.50), and puddings like bread and butter pudding, orange and lemon mousse or crème brûlée (from £3.50). On the left is a simply furnished little beamed bar with a log fire in the big stone fireplace, and on the right are two communicating cottagey dining rooms (one no smoking) with black furniture to match the shiny beams, an attractive kitchen range and another winter fire. Robinsons Best, Hartleys XB, Hatters Mild and Old Tom under light blanket pressure, a good choice of around 30 malt whiskies, home-made lemonade in summer and mulled wine in winter. Dominoes, cribbage, piped music. A sheltered lawn at the side has picnic-sets among roses and flowering shrubs. *(Recommended by IHR, Paul Bailey, Bronwen and Steve Wrigley, Roger and Christine Mash, David Atkinson, David and Kathy Holcroft, Gwen and Peter Andrews, John Voos, Neil Townend, Paul and Maggie Baker, A C Chapman, M Buchanan, Peter Walker, Sue and Bob Ward, C McKerrow, Chris Walling, Malcolm Taylor, E Locker, P A Legon, David and Judy Walmsley)*

Hartleys (Robinsons) ~ Tenant Annette Dutton ~ Real ale ~ Meals and snacks (all day in summer) ~ Restaurant ~ (01524) 732938 ~ Children welcome ~ Open 11-11; 12-10.30 Sun; winter weekdays 11-3, 5.30-11

Lucky Dip

Besides the fully inspected pubs, you might like to try these Lucky Dips recommended to us and described by readers (if you do, please send us reports):

Accrington [Burnley Rd; SD7528], *Whitakers Arms*: Tastefully decorated and spacious newly opened pub with good generous food cooked by landlord's young son, very speedy service, friendly welcome, well kept Theakstons; tables outside *(Geoff Chadwick)*

Adlington [5A Market St (A6); SD5912], *White Bear*: Basic town local with well kept Black Sheep and Scottish Courage ales, wide choice of generous cheap food inc good value Sun lunch, quick cheery service, pool table in back bar; can be smoky; safely enclosed back terrace with lots of play equipment, four bedrooms *(Ellis Heaton, BB)*

☆ **Altrincham** Gtr Man [Navigation Rd, Broadheath; junction with Manchester Rd (A56); SJ7689], *Old Packet House*: Pleasantly restored local with attractive Victorianised decor, shiny black woodwork, good solid furnishings, turkey carpet, well kept Boddingtons and Websters, open fires, good bar food inc lots of sandwiches, well presented salads and interesting specials, nice plush back dining room, prompt friendly service; fruit machines, juke box; under same ownership as Dog at Peover Heath (see Cheshire main entries); small sheltered back terrace, well equipped bedrooms, good breakfast *(Ian Phillips, Bruce Braithwaite, BB)*

Altrincham [153 Manchester Rd, Broadheath], *Railway*: Early Victorian, with lounge, bar, games room (darts and dominoes), snug and dining room, church pews, Boddingtons Bitter and Dark Mild, Holts Bitter and Mild, food inc snacks, good choice of simple main dishes and (7-11) huge breakfast, low prices, very friendly managers, tables on back terrace; open all day, new bedrooms *(Alan Gough)*

☆ **Balderstone** [Whalley Rd, Samlesbury; A59 Preston—Skipton, over 3 miles from M6 junction 31; SD6332], *Myerscough*: Reliable refuge, with solid furnishings in relaxed softly lit beamed bar, well kept Robinsons Best and Mild, maybe Hartleys XB, traditional games, good bar food from sandwiches up, no-smoking front room (children allowed there, mealtimes); picnic-sets, bantams and rabbits outside, Weds quiz night, bedrooms *(Alyson and Andrew Jackson, LYM)*

☆ **Barnston** Mer [Barnston Rd (A551); SJ2883], *Fox & Hounds*: Partly flagstoned long lounge bar with blacked range, copper kettles, china on delft shelf, intriguing hat collection, plush wall banquettes, good value quickly served straightforward food from ploughman's up inc very popular Sun lunch, well kept Scottish Courage and guest ales, lots of malt whiskies, comfortable restaurant area; pretty summer courtyard and garden with outside bar; by farm and lovely wooded dell *(Liz and Graham Bell, Douglas and Jean Troup)*

Barrowford [Barnoldswick Rd (A682); about 2 miles from M65 junction 13; SD8640], *Cross Gaits*: 18th c, with well kept Burtonwood, good range of reasonably priced food, friendly service *(Brian Wainwright)*

☆ **Bashall Eaves** [NW of Clitheroe, off B6478 or B6243; SD6943], *Red Pump*: Tucked-away partly 18th-c country pub, recently refurbished and expanded, with very relaxed unpretentious atmosphere, friendly service, shortish choice of good interesting bar food from new kitchen inc good value Sun lunch, Whitbreads-related ales, two roaring log fires, no piped music, roomy smartly decorated restaurant; two bedrooms, good breakfast, own fishing on River Hodder

(KC, M and A Dickinson, J A Boucher)

☆ **Bilsborrow** [off A6 N of Preston; at S end of village take Myerscough Coll of Agriculture turn; SD5139], *Owd Nells*: Purpose-built pub in busy expanding thatched canalside tourist complex inc hotel, craft and teashops and so forth, best for families; easy-going rustic feel, high pitched rafters at either end, lower beams (and flagstones) by the bar counter in the middle, a big welcome for children (maybe bread for feeding the ducks), wide choice of generous bar food inc two-for-one bargains, prompt professional service, half a dozen Whitbreads-related and other ales, country wines, malt whiskies, tea and coffee, popcorn machine, plenty of games, adjacent restaurant; good play area outside (even cricket and bowls); open all day, live music Thurs/Fri, comfortable bedrooms *(Emma Critchley, W W Burke, SLC, Ian Phillips, LYM)*

Bilsborrow, *Roebuck*: Wide choice of reasonably priced good food, pleasant service and surroundings *(Mr and Mrs T Taylor)*

☆ **Blacko** [A682 towards Gisburn; SD8541], *Moorcock*: Beautifully placed moorland pub with spaciously comfortable bar, big picture windows for breathtaking views, tables set close for the huge range of popular and often enterprising food inc lamb from their own flock, excellent beef and some German dishes, decent wine but nitrokeg beers, hillside garden with various animals; open all day for food Sun, children welcome, bedrooms *(Roger and Christine Mash, Gwen and Peter Andrews, Paul S McPherson, Brian Wainwright, Dr G Sanders, Sarah Bradbury, Karen Eliot, LYM)*

Blackpool [Red Bank Rd; SD3035], *Bispham*: Civilised, with well kept Sam Smiths *(John and Audrey Butterfield)*; [204 Talbot Rd, opp Blackpool North stn], *Ramsden Arms*: Attractive decor with masses of bric-a-brac and pictures, friendly helpful staff, no-smoking area, well kept cheap house beer, also Boddingtons, Jennings, Tetleys and guest ales, over 40 whiskies, CD juke box, games; good value bedrooms *(Patrick Hancock)*

Blacksnape [Blacksnape Rd; Roman rd above Darwen – OS Sheet 103 map ref 712215; SD7121], *Red Lion*: Cosy bar, well kept Burtonwood and occasional guest beers, wide range of good food esp giant filled yorkshire puddings, good puddings, dining area; high moorland setting *(Mrs M Mcgurk, M A Buchanan, Dr K M Buchanan)*

Bolton Gtr Man [Deansgate; SD7108], *Hen & Chickens*: Open-plan corner pub with huge helpings of hearty food, efficient friendly service, well kept Burtonwood *(Alan and Heather Jacques)*; [107 Folds Rd (A676 NE)], *Lord Clyde*: Traditionally laid out local, sympathetically refurbished and very welcoming to visitors, with well kept Hydes on electric pump; good value home-cooked lunches Fri *(Pete Baker)*

☆ *nr* **Broughton** [Station Lane, Eaves; A6 N through Broughton, 1st left about a mile after traffic lights – OS Sheet 102 map ref 495374; SD4937], *Plough at Eaves*: Two homely low-beamed carpeted bars, friendly and good value, well kept Thwaites ales, lots of malt whiskies, small choice of usual food inc children's helpings, darts, pool and other games, piped music, well equipped play area outside; cl Mon/Tues *(Prof P A Reynolds, LYM)*

Burnley [2 Manchester Rd; SD8332], *Old Red Lion*: Spacious recently refurbished Thwaites pub, consistently good value low-priced food 10-2.30 (not Sun), pleasant staff, very relaxed atmosphere *(Arthur and Margaret Dickinson)*

☆ **Burton in Kendal** [Station Lane (just off A6070 between M6 junctions 35 and 36); SD5376], *Dutton Arms*: Pub/restaurant now under same management as New Inn at Yealand Conyers – see main entries; Boddingtons and Dent ales in pleasant bar (no food there), very good roomy two-level restaurant, partly no smoking, good friendly service, garden with play area; open all day Sun and summer weekdays *(P A Legon)*

☆ *nr* **Bury** [Nangreaves; off A56/A666 N under a mile E of M66 junction 1, down cobbled track; SD8115], *Lord Raglan*: Notable for its lonely moorside location, with great views; enjoyable varied food from cheap bar snacks to good meals with fresh veg, well kept mainly Scottish Courage ales, interesting foreign bottled beers, lots of bric-a-brac in traditional front bar, big open fire in cosy back room, plainer blond-panelled dining room (where children allowed) *(Bronwen and Steve Wrigley, RJH, BB)*

Claughton [A683 Kirkby Lonsdale—Lancaster; SD5666], *Fenwick Arms*: Olde-worlde black and white pub with Tetleys and related beers, good range of usual food inc good home-made soup, friendly landlord and staff, restaurant *(Ann and Bob Westbrook)*

Colne [Skipton Old Rd, Black Lane Ends – NE, towards Lothersdale; SD9243], *Hare & Hounds*: Timothy Taylor ales, good choice of usual food (not Tues evening) inc take-aways – served late Fri, friendly staff, some live jazz *(A Keys)*

Crank Mer [Red Cat Lane; SJ5099], *Red Cat*: New landlady doing good if not cheap food, freshly cooked and generous, in front lounge and nicely decorated dining room – must book *(Mrs E V Pennington, Don and Pat Wilson)*

Crosby Mer [College Ave, Gt Crosby; SJ3199], *Crows Nest*: Dim-lit spotless and interesting Victorian-style lounge, well kept Higsons, Boddingtons and a worthwhile guest beer *(Alan and Paula McCully)*; [Bath St, Waterloo; SJ3298], *Royal*: Pleasantly refurbished in library-look style, with comfortable sofas away from the bar and TV, well kept Boddingtons, relaxing atmosphere *(Alan and Paula McCully)*; [East St, Waterloo], *Volunteer Canteen*: Cosy and friendly sidestreet Higsons pub, lounge all Victorian sparkle and old photographs, waiter service the norm; known as the Volly *(Alan and Paula McCully)*

Delph Gtr Man [Huddersfield Rd (A62); SE0009], *Old Bell*: Good if not cheap restaurant food with emphasis on seafood, comfortable bar, good choice of beers such as Boddingtons and Timothy Taylor Landlord, friendly efficient service *(Ian and Karen*

Hargreaves, Bronwen and Steve Wrigley)

☆ **Denshaw** Gtr Man [Ripponden Rd; 2 miles from M62 junction 2; A672 towards Oldham, pub N of village; SD9710], *Rams Head*: Cosy and comfortable moorland farm/pub with several small rooms mainly for diners (good meals, altogether more sophisticated than you'd expect from location), with well kept Theakstons, Timothy Taylor and maybe a guest beer, good range of wines by bottle and glass, bric-a-brac on beams and panelling, log fires, traditional settles; children welcome, unobtrusive piped music; on special days eg Mothering Sunday dining room may be fully booked with no bar snacks served, but otherwise popular with walkers – lovely scenery, good walking; has been cl weekday lunchtimes *(Nancy Cleave, Edward Leetham, Bronwen and Steve Wrigley, K and B Forman, LYM)*

☆ **Diggle** Gtr Man [Diglea Hamlet, Sam Rd; village signed off A670 just N of Dobcross; SE0008], *Diggle Hotel*: Bustling atmosphere in modernised three-room hillside pub popular lunchtime and early evening for good value food (can be a wait) from sandwiches up inc generous Sun roasts and children's dishes; well kept Timothy Taylor Golden Best and Landlord, decent wines, good choice of malt whiskies, good coffee, friendly service, soft piped music, rustic fairy-lit tables among the trees, quiet spot just below the moors; children welcome, opens noon; bedrooms *(Bronwen and Steve Wrigley, BB)*

Dunham Woodhouses Gtr Man [B5160 E of Altrincham; SJ7288], *Vine*: Welcoming country-style pub handy for Dunham Massey, carefully refurbished to keep olde-worlde atmosphere, with coal fires in both smallish character back rooms (one no smoking), one front room mainly for dining – popular home cooking from soup and sandwiches up (can get busy Sun); well kept low-priced Sam Smiths, coal fires in character back rooms, one no smoking; seats outside *(Pete Baker)*

Eccles Gtr Man [Liverpool Rd; SJ7698], *Crown & Volunteer*: Popular local with cheap Holts Bitter and Mild in unfussy panelled bar and good compact lounge *(the Didler)*; [Liverpool Rd], *Golden Cross*: Open-plan lounge, popular plain bar, well kept low-priced Holts Bitter and Mild; live music nights *(the Didler)*; [439 Liverpool Rd, Peel Green – A57 ½ mile from M63 junction 2], *Grapes*: Classic Edwardian local with superb glass and tiling, lots of mahogany, brilliant staircase, cheap Holts Bitter and Mild, fairly quiet roomy lounge and smoke room, pool room, vault with Manchester darts (can get quite loud and smoky), drinking corridor; open all day *(the Didler, Pete Baker, JP, PP)*; [33 Regent St (A57 – handy for M602 junction 2)], *Lamb*: Untouched Edwardian three-room Holts local with splendid etched windows, fine woodwork, tiling and furnishings, admirable trophies in display case; cheap well kept Bitter and Mild, full-size snooker table; popular with older people *(the Didler, JP, PP)*; [Liverpool Rd], *Stanley Arms*: Busy corner local with cheap Holts Bitter and Mild, small bar, snug, drinking corridor *(the Didler)*; [133 Liverpool Rd, Patricroft], *White Lion*: Classic Edwardian local with drinking corridor, games in lively vaults bar, separate smoke room (with weekend sing-songs) and quiet lounge, great value Holts Bitter and Mild *(PB, the Didler, JP, PP)*

Eccleston [Towngate; B5250, off A581 Chorley—Southport; SD5117], *Farmers Arms*: Big friendly low-beamed pub/restaurant, wide choice of consistently good generous food all day, not cheap but good value; modernised but keeping character – black cottagey furniture, red plush wall seats, rough plaster covered with plates, pastoral prints, clocks and brasses; well kept largely Whitbreads-related ales, helpful service, darts; parking can be a problem when busy; bedrooms *(Maurice and Pauline Kean, Derek Stafford, Mrs E V Pennington and friends)*

☆ **Entwistle** [Overshores Rd, by stn; village signed off Blackburn Rd N of Edgworth – OS Sheet 109 map ref 726177; SD7217], *Strawbury Duck*: Cosy dim-lit traditional beamed and flagstoned country pub by isolated station – trains from Blackburn and Bolton; well kept changing ales such as Boddingtons, Moorhouses Pendle Witches Brew, Timothy Taylor Best and Landlord and a house beer, friendly service, bar food (all day Sat and Sun) inc children's; games room, no-smoking lounge, restaurant, good unobtrusive piped music (live Thurs), some seats outside; children till 8.30, open all day w/e and July/Aug, cl Mon exc bank hols, jazz Thurs (same band for 18 yrs); comfortable good value bedrooms, big sizzling breakfasts, good Pennine walks *(Bronwen and Steve Wrigley, Vicky and David Sarti, LYM)*

Euxton [Wigan Rd; SD5519], *Bay Horse*: Bass, Stones and Worthington, bar food (all day Sun), pool *(SLC)*; [Dawbers Lane (A581 well towards Croston)], *Rose & Crown*: Small and welcoming, several rooms, good value basic food, big garden with lots of swings and interesting climber *(Bronwen and Steve Wrigley)*

Foulridge [SD8842], *New Inn*: 16th-c Thwaites pub with comfortable lounge, views from no-smoking room, separate snug, good basic food inc solid soups, proper home-made pies and interesting salads *(Charles and Pauline Stride)*

Garstang [A6, nr Knott End signs; SD4845], *Flag*: Spacious, plush and relaxing, well done in old-fashioned style, with good value tasty food from good filled baguettes to appetising puddings, friendly accommodating staff; open all day, pleasant conservatory *(Bronwen and Steve Wrigley)*; [northbound section of one-way system], *Wheatsheaf*: Small and cosy neatly kept low-beamed pub with gleaming copper and brass, good range of well priced freshly cooked good food inc notable specials (esp fish), good service, decent malt whiskies *(P A Legon, BB)*

Great Mitton Gtr Man [Mitton Hall, Mitton Rd; B6246 NW of Whalley; SD7238], *Owd Neds*: Good value generous usual food all day inc vegetarian in roomy partly raised dining area and conservatory, well kept Boddingtons and Jennings, helpful staff, flagstoned bar (can be rather smoky), tables on terrace, plenty of space for children in informal grounds with stream and woodland; part of mansion which includes restaurant, frequent entertainment, bedrooms *(Derek and Sylvia Stephenson)*

Grindleton [off A69 via Chatburn; SD7545], *Duke of York*: Smart, cheery and bright old upmarket village local in attractive Ribble Valley countryside, personable landlady, various areas inc one with open fire, Tetleys and Whitbreads Castle Eden, good if not cheap food from good sandwiches to carefully cooked main dishes, friendly attentive staff, separate dining room; tables in front, garden behind *(Margaret and Arthur Dickinson, RJH)*

Haigh Gtr Man [Red Rock Lane; SD6009], *Crawford Arms*: Nice spot by Leeds & Liverpool Canal, own moorings, friendly welcome, basic food, quiz night Thurs *(Charles and Pauline Stride)*

Hambleton [A588 Blackpool—Lancaster; SD3741], *Shovels*: Good atmosphere in pleasant old beamed bar with well kept Boddingtons, good food well priced and served *(R T and J C Moggridge)*

Hazel Grove Gtr Man [Jackson Lane; SU9287], *Three Bears*: Clean pub with pleasant atmosphere, good service, particularly well kept Robinsons, good helpings of decent lunchtime food *(Stephen and Julie Brown, P A Legon)*

Hest Bank [2 Hest Bank Lane; SD4766], *Hest Bank*: Doing well under present landlord, good range of good food (served through longer hours), guest beers as well as Boddingtons; pleasant canalside setting *(P A Legon)*

Heswall Mer [Lower Heswall; SJ2782], *Sheldrakes*: Unusual hacienda-style pub-restaurant with masses of geraniums on low whitewashed walls of tiled terrace, superb views over River Dee to Wales, steps down to beach; very popular in summer for good value barbecues inc fish from trout to bass, tiger prawns and lobster with good help-yourself salad bar; good value lunchtime sandwiches, four-course winter buffets; children very welcome *(Liz Bell)*; [45 Gayton Rd, Lower Heswall], *Victoria*: Two big Victorian-style bars overlooking River Dee and Welsh hills, curtained recesses, sensible comfortable furniture, good choice of food, Bass ales, friendly caring service, nice garden behind; bedrooms *(E G Parish)*

High Lane Gtr Man [Buxton Rd; A6 Stockport—Disley; SJ9585], *Red Lion*: Pub with emphasis on extended restaurant, big helpings of substantial food inc refrigerated display of speciality fresh fish; well kept Robinsons, sandwiches too, good friendly service; six bedrooms *(J F M West)*

☆ **Holden** [the one up by Bolton by Bowland – OS Sheet 103 map ref 777494; SD7749], *Copy Nook*: Spick-and-span roomy and well renovated roadside pub with friendly landlord, efficient obliging staff, wide choice of good food, well kept Tetleys *(GLD, HMD)*

Hornby [SD5869], *Castle*: Comfortable, with good range of well priced food inc well prepared veg, Mitchells real ales *(B, M and P Kendall)*

Hoscar [off A5209 Parbold—Burscough; SD4611], *Railway*: Small very friendly country pub with well kept beers inc good guests, lots of whiskies, good choice of good value food, open fire; occasional barbecues, Thurs quiz night *(Malcolm and Judith Mentha)*

Hoylake Mer [Stanley Rd, Kings Gap; SJ2289], *Green Lodge*: Pleasantly refurbished old hotel associated with nearby Royal Liverpool golf links, usual bar food inc enjoyable home-made specials, Burtonwood ales; handy for the beautiful Hoylake beach and Red Rocks Nature Reserve; bedrooms *(Liz Bell, Mark O'Hanlon)*

Hurst Green [Whalley Rd (B6243 E); SD6838], *Shireburn Arms*: Quiet comfortable 17th-c hotel in idyllic setting with panoramic Ribble valley views, good reasonably priced food, Thwaites and other ales; separate tea room, occasional pianist, lovely neatly kept back garden and terrace, safe low-key play area; bedrooms *(Arthur and Margaret Dickinson)*

Inglewhite [Silk Mill Lane; 3 miles from A6 – turn off nr Owd Nells, Bilsborrow; SD5440], *Green Man*: Sparklingly clean and well polished, with good generous food served piping hot at attractive prices (children's menu and small helpings available), wide choice of good sandwiches, well kept Greenalls, friendly attentive service, red plush seating, log fire, pool, darts, games machines; unspoilt countryside nr Beacon Fell country park; bedrooms with own bathrooms, camp site behind *(J F M West, Ken and Joan Bemrose)*

☆ **Irby** Mer [Irby Mill Hill, off Greasby rd; SJ2684], *Irby Mill*: Well kept Bass, Boddingtons, Cains Bitter and Dark Mild, Jennings and two interesting weekly guest beers, good house wines and generous good value fresh-cooked lunchtime food (not Sun) inc huge cheap cod and chips in four low-beamed largely flagstoned rooms, comfortable pub furniture, coal-effect gas fire, relaxed local atmosphere, interesting old photographs and history of the former mill, a few tables outside *(Robert Campbell, R Moorehead, Sue and Bob Ward, Graham and Lynn Mason, BB)*

☆ **Lathom** [Wheat Lane, off A5209; Parbold Rd after Ring o' Bells heading into Burscough; SD4511], *Ship*: Big busy well run pub tucked below canal embankment, several separate rooms with decor varying from interestingly cluttered canal memorabilia through naval pictures and crests to hunting prints, lots of copper and brass, cheap popular lunchtime food (not Sun) served promptly, friendly staff, ten well kept changing ales, often interesting; games room with pool; open all day Fri-Sun *(Julie and Steve Anderton, David and Kathy Holcroft, Nancy Cleave, Edward Leetham, Richard Lewis, BB)*

☆ **Lea Town** [Sidgreaves Lane (N towards Woodplumpton); SD4832], *Saddle*: Recently refurbished country pub with wide choice of home-made bar food cooked to order from sandwiches up, inc vegetarian and children's, five real ales, sensibly priced wines, restaurant; tables outside, play area; bedrooms *(Anon)*

Leigh Gtr Man [Twist Lane; SJ6699], *Waterside*: Converted 19th-c canalside warehouses handy for indoor and outdoor markets, popular lunchtime for wide choice of food, Boddingtons and Robinsons Hatters Mild; plenty of tables by Leigh branch of Liverpool—Leeds Canal, lots of ducks and swans *(Colin and Sue Graham)*

Little Eccleston [Cartford Lane; off A586 Garstang—Blackpool, by toll bridge; SD4139], *Cartford*: In scenic countryside by toll bridge on River Wyre (hosts fishing nights), brewing its own interesting Hart beers; well kept Theakstons too, oak beams, plenty of atmosphere, pleasant service, two of its three floors set with tables for good choice of reasonably priced generous food inc vegetarian and children's; quiet juke box, pool, tables outside (not by water), play area; very busy esp weekends; well equipped bedrooms *(Harry Gleave, R T and J C Moggridge)*

Littleborough Gtr Man [A58 Rochdale—Halifax; SD9316], *Stubley Hall*: Surprisingly attractive spot, Tudor hall set back from main rd – Yates's pub with well kept beer, friendly service, food *(Alice Venner, Timothy Horsley)*

☆ **Liverpool** [Grafton St], *Cains Brewery Tap*: Splendidly restored Victorian architecture with nicely understated decor, wooden floors, plush raised side snug, lots of old prints, wonderful bar, flame-effect gas fire, newspapers; cosy relaxing atmosphere, friendly staff, good well priced food, and above all well kept attractively priced Cains ales with guest beers from other small breweries; popular brewery tour ending here with buffet and singing; sports TV *(Richard Lewis, JP, PP)*

☆ **Liverpool** [Albert Dock Complex], *Pump House*: Relaxing multi-level conversion of dock building, good Mersey views, lots of polished dark wood, bare bricks, mezzanine and upper gallery with exposed roof trusses; marble counter with bulbous beer engines and brass rail supported by elephants' heads, tall chimney; wide choice of generous cheeses, some hot food, friendly efficient service; waterside tables, boat trips in season; keg beers, busy weekend evenings *(John Fazakerley, David Carr, Brian Kneale, Gillian Jenkins)*

Liverpool [13 Rice St], *Cracke*: Attractively basic, bare boards, walls covered with posters for local events and pictures of local buildings, unusual Beatles diorama in largest room, juke box and TV, very cheap lunchtime food, well kept Marstons Pedigree; popular mainly with young people; sizeable garden *(JP, PP)*; [17 Cases St], *Globe*: Welcoming traditional local, good service, well kept Bass, Cains Bitter and Dark Mild, good port, tiny sloping-floor back lounge, friendly licensees, lots of prints of old Liverpool; lunchtime filled baps *(Roy Moorehead)*; [25 Matthew St], *Grapes*: Lively and friendly, with well kept Boddingtons and Cains, good value lunchtime bar food, open-plan but cottagey decor (flagstones, old range, wall settles, gas-effect lamps); open all day, can get crowded Fri/Sat, cl Sun *(JP, PP)*; [4 Hackins Hey, off Dale St], *Hole In Ye Wall*: Well restored 18th-c pub, several different areas in pleasant high-beamed panelled bar, beer unusually fed by gravity via oak pillars from upstairs cellar *(Roy Moorehead)*; [Water St], *Oriel Chamber*: Good Italian food, well kept beer, good wine and service *(Roy Moorehead)*; [93 Rice Lane, Walton], *Prince Arthur*: Victorian alehouse, well kept Walkers *(R Moorehead)*; [Lunt Rd, Sefton], *Punch Bowl*: Nice village pub, reputedly haunted, done out as Whitbreads Roast Inn *(Roy Moorehead)*; [Derby Sq], *Queens*: Well kept beer, good food, daily papers; two bars, no music *(Roy Moorehead)*; [Roscoe St], *Roscoe Head*: Three tiny rooms, friendly, quiet and civilised, with outstandingly well kept Tetleys and maybe Jennings, huge and growing tie collection *(R Moorehead)*; [Charlotte Row], *Tess Riley*: Food inc good value Sun roast, good service, free juke box *(Roy Moorehead)*; [1 Charlotte Row], *Wetherspoons*: Roomy Wetherspoons (in former department store) with good service, good value food, well kept beer, decent wine *(Roy Moorehead)*

☆ **Longridge** [Thornley; 1½ miles N on back rd to Chipping – OS Sheet 103 map ref 607393; SD6039], *Derby Arms*: Comfortable and sincerely welcoming old stonebuilt country pub, bustling relaxed atmosphere in several dining rooms off small entrance bar, good choice of fresh food in good-sized helpings – duck and fish recommended; willing service, well kept Greenalls, decent wine, occasional jazz; very popular w/e; barn restaurant *(Sue and Brian Wharton, R L Gorick)*

Lower Bartle [off B5411 just NW of Preston; SD4832], *Sitting Goose*: Taken over by the Gallaghers, whose hard work and friendly enthusiasm made their previous pub the Rock at Tockholes a popular main entry; this country pub gives them more room (inc a conservatory), and should turn out very well *(Anon)*

Lydgate Gtr Man [51 Stockport Rd; SD9603], *White Hart*: Tastefully refurbished inn overlooking Saddleworth Moor, with Boddingtons and Lees, log fires, good food from chicken and pesto sandwiches or home-made sausages up – wide choice in bar and restaurant; bedrooms nice, pretty village *(Robin Knapp)*

☆ **Manchester** [50 Great Bridgewater St; corner of Lower Mosley St], *Britons Protection*: Chatty, genuine and well run by long-serving licensees, with fine tilework, solid woodwork and elaborate plastering in rather plush front bar, attractive softly lit inner lounge with coal-effect gas fire and unusual ceiling, battle murals in passage leading to it; exceptional choice of whiskies, well kept Jennings, Robinsons and Tetleys, good wines, good home-cooked bar lunches, reasonable prices, no juke box or machines, tables outside behind; old-time music hall first Tues of month, otherwise quiet and relaxed evenings, handy for Bridgewater Hall and GMEX centre *(Richard Lewis, Peter*

Plumridge, Ian Phillips, Tim Barrow, Sue Demont, BB)

☆ **Manchester** [127 Gt Bridgewater St (Oxford St side)], *Peveril of the Peak*: Three traditional rooms around central servery, busy lunchtime but welcoming and homely evenings, with cheap basic lunchtime food (not Sun), very welcoming family service, log fire, well kept Scottish Courage ales; lots of mahogany, mirrors and stained glass, sturdy furnishings, interesting pictures, pub games inc pool, table football, juke box; splendidly lurid green external tilework, seats outside; children welcome, cl weekend lunchtimes *(Richard Lewis, JP, PP, Ian Phillips, Peter Plumridge)*

☆ **Manchester** [40 Chorlton St], *Mash & Air*: Futuristic bar, not cheap but good value, with lime-green walls, purple seating and bright lights, upstairs bistro and top-floor restaurant; microbrewery running up centre of all three bars, producing usually filtered beers, but interesting and enjoyable others (eg Blackcurrant Porter or Peach), kept under light carbon dioxide blanket; good food esp pizzas, friendly staff, rather a young wine bar feel; open all day *(J F M West, Richard Lewis, ALC)*

☆ **Manchester** [52 Cross St], *Mr Thomas Chop House*: Welcoming Victorian city pub with small bare-boards oak-panelled bar, back eating area with crisp tilework, interesting period features inc wrought-iron gates, good innovative approach to classic English dishes (even sausage and mash), well kept Boddingtons and Flowers, decent wines, no-smoking area; open all day, packed at lunchtime *(Mike Ridgway, Sarah Miles, Richard Lewis, Andrew Jarvis)*

☆ **Manchester** [6 Angel St; off Rochdale Rd], *Beer House*: Lively basic real-ale pub with splendid well kept range, mainly unusual, farm ciders and perry, several Belgian beers on tap, good range of bottled foreign beers, country wines, cheap spirits doubles (wide choice); bare boards, lots of seating, friendly helpful staff, old local prints, good CD juke box (may be loud), bar billiards, darts, robust cheap bar food inc vegetarian and various bargains; tables outside, ceilidh band Tues, open all day (Sun afternoon closure) *(the Didler, Ian Phillips, Richard Lewis, JP, PP, Stephen Brown)*

☆ **Manchester** [Oxford Rd/Whitworth St, basement of handsome Palace Hotel], *Copper Face Jacks*: Stylish basement bar full of copper inc huge carefully lit dome over island serving counter; calls itself Irish, but the Celtic references are pleasantly understated (soda bread, Irish smoked salmon), there's no trace of scruffiness, the friendly service may be Australian, and tasty tagliatelle comes with garlic bread and designer salad – food all day; live music (late licence) *(GLD)*

Manchester [John Dalton St], *Ape & Apple*: Smart newish Holts pub with their fantastic value beer kept well, comfortable seats in bare-boards bar with nice lighting and interesting pictures, armchairs in upstairs lounge; good mix on busy weekend evenings (unusually for city centre, over-25s won't feel out of place), quieter lunchtime or midweek *(Brian Wainwright, Paul Mason)*; [Deansgate, Castlefield end], *Atlas*: Good modern food and lots of good beers in modern bar under railway arches, nice sitting out behind *(ALC)*; [opp Dukes 92, other side of Rochdale Canal, Castlefields area], *Barca*: Great modern canalside bar with good modern food *(ALC)*; [66 Oldham St], *Castle*: Unspoilt traditional front bar, small snug, back games room, full Robinsons range inc Hartleys and the unusual Old Stockport from fine bank of handpumps, nice tilework outside; children's room till 7, blues Thurs, open all day (Sun afternoon closure) *(the Didler, Alex Koval)*; [86 Portland St], *Circus*: Two tiny rooms, back one panelled with leatherette banquettes, very well kept Tetleys from minute corridor bar, friendly landlord, no music or machines; often looks closed but normally open all day weekdays (you have to knock) *(Richard Lewis, Peter Plumridge, Ian Phillips)*; [48 Kennedy St], *City Arms*: Well kept Ind Coope Burton, Tetleys and interesting changing guest beers, Belgian bottled beers, occasional beer festivals, popular bar lunches, quiet evenings; bare boards, wheelchair access but steps down to back lounge, open all day (cl Sat afternoon, Sun) *(Richard Lewis, Peter Plumridge)*; [95 Cheetham Hill Rd (A665)], *Derby Brewery Arms*: Huge showpiece Holts pub with well kept cheap beer from the nearby brewery, cheap lunchtime food from hatch *(Peter Plumridge)*; [852 Wilmslow Rd, Didsbury], *Didsbury*: Elegant Chef & Brewer, roomy yet surprisingly intimate, with lots of alcoves, softly lit rooms, candles, at least two coal fires; Scottish Courage ales with a guest such as Shepherd Neame Early Bird, good choice of changing hot dishes, also sandwiches, baked potatoes, topped ciabatta etc *(Ian Phillips)*; [57 Mosley St], *Forgery & Firkin*: Typical recent Firkin conversion from bank, well kept Dogbolter and other ales, bare boards and woodwork, barrels, bottles, brewery prints etc, friendly staff, good choice of food, long bar, games and machines, TV; open all day *(Richard Lewis)*; [80 Portland St], *Grey Horse*: Cosy traditional Hydes local, welcoming and busy, with timbering, pictures and plates, well kept Bitter and Mild, some unusual malt whiskies, popular lunchtime food; no juke box or machines, open all day *(Richard Lewis)*; [Cross St], *Grinch*: Good food esp mussels, great buzz about the place, good wine *(ALC)*; [64 High St], *Hogshead*: Roomy bare-boards alehouse conversion with cask seats, good interesting range of real ales, Belgian and US bottled beers, country wines, barrel tables, food all day; pool, juke box, games machines, friendly staff; open all day, cl Sun evening *(Richard Lewis)*; [47 Ducie St], *Jolly Angler*: Unpretentious backstreet local, small and friendly, with well kept Hydes Bitter and Strong, coal fire, darts, pool and TV; informal folk singing Mon *(Richard Lewis, Peter Plumridge, JP, PP, PB, BB)*; [Canal St], *Metz*: Enjoyable bar over a little bridge, east European cooking, good drinks *(ALC)*; [68

Deansgate], *Moon Under Water*: Britain's biggest pub, well done Wetherspoons cinema conversion, beautifully fitted and decorated, with superb ceiling, lovely plasterwork, very long bar, balcony seating, no-smoking area; good range of real ales, bustling atmosphere, friendly efficient staff, good choice of popular food all day *(Sue Holland, Dave Webster, Richard Lewis)*; [520 Manchester Rd (A6), Wardley, W of Swinton], *Morning Star*: Busy Holts local, well kept ales, good value basic food weekday lunchtime, lively games-oriented bar, usually some Sat entertainment in lounge *(PB)*; [33 Back Piccadilly], *Mother Macs*: Comfortably solid backstreet local, very welcoming to strangers, with tall etched glass windows, old local photographs, cheap weekday bar food inc huge baps and generous cheap hot dishes, Boddingtons, Chesters Best and Flowers IPA; piped music, TV; open all day (12-3 Sun) *(Peter Plumridge)*; [90 Portland St], *Old Monkey*: Traditional Holts pub, built 1993 but you'd never guess from the etched glass and mosaic tiling; interesting memorabilia, well kept cheap Bitter and Mild, low-priced food, upstairs lounge, warm hospitality, wide mix of customers *(Ian Phillips, JP, PP, P A Legon)*; [36 New Mount St], *Pot of Beer*: Small friendly refurbished two-bar pub with bare boards, stripped bricks and timber, interesting changing guest beers some tapped from the cask in unusual stillage system (casks fronts projecting from temperature-controlled chamber), Thatcher's farm cider, continental beers – one on draught; open all day, cl Sun *(Richard Lewis, JP, PP)*; [Wilmslow Rd, Withington], *Red Lion*: Long low cottage-style pub much bigger than it looks, opening into huge two-level complex of plush seating; well kept Marstons ales inc interesting seasonal ones, popular good value food (not Sun evening), big conservatory overlooking immaculate bowling green; machines at the back *(Ian Phillips)*; [Grosvenor St], *Sand Bar*: Pair of Georgian houses with relaxed well decorated series of varied areas, well kept changing ales such as Bass, Boddingtons, Coach House Gunmaker Mild, Lees Moonraker, Marstons Pedigree, Phoenix Bantam and Robinsons Frederics, good choice of foreign bottled beers *(Richard Lewis)*; [Shambles Sq, Arndale Centre], *Sinclairs*: This timeless 18th-c pub has been carefully dismantled, for re-erection a short distance away, as part of the Arndale reconstruction project – as has its neighbour the Old Wellington *(LYM)*; [49 Piccadilly], *Wetherspoons*: Good range of beers and wines, usual efficient service and pleasant decor, good lunchtime menu with special offers *(P A Legon)*; [Portland St], *White Horse*: Unspoilt city pub with jovial atmosphere, Hyde beers at sensible prices; small bar *(Peter Plumridge)*; [43 Liverpool Rd, Castlefield], *White Lion*: Busy but friendly Victorian pub, tables for eating up one side of three-sided bar, some home-made food inc good curries, real ales such as Batemans, Boddingtons and Ushers, decent house wine, good tea, friendly service, pleasant outdoor seating among excavated foundations of Roman city overlooking fort gate; handy for Museum of Science and Industry and Royal Exchange Theatre *(Ian Phillips, John Wooll)*; [Bury Old Rd, Prestwich; A665 by Heaton Pk main gate, just S of A6044], *Woodthorpe*: Huge Victorian pile, former home of Holts brewing family, impressively converted 1993 without altering character, open-plan but keeping distinct areas (and original ornate fireplaces – shame they don't have real fires); good value simple home-made lunches, well kept cheap Holts Bitter and Mild, guest beers, friendly young staff, restaurant; disabled access and facilities *(Pete Baker, Alan Gough)*

☆ **Marple**, Gtr Man [off A626 via Church Lane, following The Ridge signs – OS Sheet 109 map ref 963862; SJ9686], *Romper*: Remarkable to have such a beautifully placed country pub so near urban development; above Peak Forest Canal in Goyt Valley, dining pub in four softly lit knocked-through oak-beamed rooms, reliable generous food (all day Sun) inc plenty of vegetarian, well kept Boddingtons, Marstons Pedigree, Theakstons Old Peculier and Timothy Taylor Landlord, decent wines and malt whiskies, efficient friendly staff; tables outside, opens noon *(Simon Hulme, M Buchanan, Roger and Christine Mash, DAV, Kathy and Steven Barker, Pat and Tony Martin, LYM)*

☆ **Mawdesley** [Bluestone Lane; follow Eccleston sign from village which is signed off B5246 Parbold—Rufford; SD5016], *Robin Hood*: Busy, neat and comfortable open-plan dining pub with button-back wall banquettes, reproduction Victorian prints, decorative plates, stained-glass seat dividers, some stripped stone; good value generous straightforward home cooking with fresh veg and cheap children's helpings, small pretty upstairs restaurant (often booked well ahead), good friendly service, well kept Whitbreads-related and good guest ales, decent wines, children's room; piped nostalgic pop music, fruit machine; picnic-sets on neat side terrace, good fenced play area *(Kevin Potts, R Moorehead, David and Kathy Holcroft, BB)*

Mawdesley [Hall Lane; SD4915], *Black Bull*: Lovely village pub, partly 13th c, good food and beer *(Roy Moorehead)*

Mellor Gtr Man [Longhurst Lane; this is the Mellor near Marple, S of Manchester; SJ9888], *Devonshire Arms*: Old favourite under new management, cheerful front bar with old leather-seated settles among other seats, lots of old local photographs, a couple of small period back rooms (one no smoking), Victorian fireplaces all round, well kept Robinsons Best and Mild, usual lunchtime food, cribbage, shove-ha'penny and dominoes; picnic-sets out in front and in back garden, well behaved children in eating area *(David Hoult, LYM)*

Mellor [Mellor Lane; this is the Mellor up near Blackburn; SD6530], *Traders Arms*: Tasteful, charming and spotless, with no-smoking area, enjoyable low-priced food (all day Sun) cooked to order inc vegetarian and fresh fish, well kept Thwaites; seats outside, play area *(Arthur and Margaret Dickinson)*

Ormskirk [Burscough St; SD4108], *Buck i'th Vine*: Close to parish church, takes you back in time: lots of rooms, nooks and crannies, low serving window at bar – you have to stoop to order; decent food, well kept Bitter and Mild; live music and quiz some nights, tables in yard surrounded by old stables and old pub brewery building; oldest part dates from 1650 *(David Carr)*; [County Rd], *Hayfield*: Relaxing pub attractively rebuilt using some old materials, good choice of nine or so real ales such as Courage Directors, Fullers London Pride, Timothy Taylor Landlord, good range of food, very nice atmosphere, character American manager and charming helpful staff; always a lot going on, occasional live music *(Ian Phillips, Julie and Steve Anderton)*

Preston [99 Fylde Rd; SD5329], *Hogshead*: Former millowner's house well restored by Whitbreads as one of the best in their bare-boards wood-and-bricks alehouse chain, a dozen or more changing well kept ales mainly from small breweries, big window into cellar where casks tilt automatically, also bottle-conditioned beers, farm cider and country wines; no music or games, lots of old photographs, friendly staff, food served 11-7 (not Sun), chef happy to make things not on menu; open all day, lots of picnic-sets outside *(Comus Elliot, Richard Lewis)*; [35 Friargate (by Ringway)], *Old Black Bull*: Big open-plan extended Tudor-fronted alehouse with main lounge, leather-seat snug and side public bar, half a dozen well kept interesting changing ales from small breweries and farm cider, barrels racked behind servery, big back open fireplace, relaxing atmosphere, friendly staff and locals, wide choice of reasonably priced food, games room, darts; open all day *(Richard Lewis)*

Rainford Mer [Church Rd (B5203); SD4700], *Golden Lion*: Nice village pub with good food, well kept beer *(Roy Moorehead)*

Ramsbottom Gtr Man [Bye Rd, Twine Valley; signed off A56 N of Bury at Shuttleworth; SD7916], *Fishermans Retreat*: Surrounded by well stocked trout lakes, good interesting well presented reasonably priced food with proper chips, generous helpings, good choice of changing beers (and of whiskies), busy restaurant, games room with two pool tables and games machines; open all day from 8am *(Martyn Smith, V Bateson, M A Buchanan)*; [Lumb Carr Rd (B6214), Holcombe], *Shoulder of Mutton*: Quaint country pub with nicely presented well cooked food, well kept guest beers; worth booking weekends *(Alan Eaves)*

☆ **Riley Green** [A6061/A675 Preston—Bolton; SD6225], *Royal Oak*: Cosy low-beamed three-room pub nr canal, reliably good food inc superb puddings, Thwaites Bitter and Mild, friendly efficient service; ancient stripped stone, open fires, seats from high-backed settles to red plush armchairs, lots of nooks and crannies, turkey carpet, soft lighting, impressive woodwork, fresh flowers, interesting model steam engines; short walk from Leeds & Liverpool Canal, can be packed Fri night and w/e *(M A Buchanan, Dr and Mrs D E Awbery, Charles and Pauline Stride, Roger and Pauline Pearce, BB)*

Rimington [OS Sheet 103 map ref 806457; SD8045], *Black Bull*: Spotless popular dining pub, tasteful dining area (bar tables may be booked too), flower arrangements and other nice touches, comfortable furniture, real fire, lots of wildlife paintings, railway memorabilia, impressive model trains; good food from sandwiches with real chips through salmon, pheasant etc to three-course Sun lunch, well kept Theakstons, faultless service, well chosen piped music; cl Mon exc bank hols, no food Sun evening *(Margaret and Arthut Dickinson)*

Sale Gtr Man [Britannia Rd; SJ8092], *Kings Ransom*: Large well furnished newish pub on Bridgewater Canal, individual seating areas inc no smoking, roaring fires, antique oil paintings, candlelight, well kept Boddingtons, Courage Directors and Ruddles County, lots of malt whiskies, food lunchtime and evening; open all day *(Alex Koval, Pat and Robert Watt)*

☆ **Sawley** [signed off A59 NW of Clitheroe; SD7746], *Spread Eagle*: 16th-c pub that's jumping into the big time as a dining pub, with excellent cooking by Stephen Doherty (in his hands the Punch Bowl at Crosthwaite was our Cumbria Dining Pub of the Year last year), giving sensibly priced interesting food (his marinated seafood is particularly good) inc very good value weekday set lunches; well kept real ales, good house wines, pleasant service *(K F Mould, Warwick and Jillian Green)*

Scarisbrick [Southport Rd; SD3813], *Morris Dancers*: Good value food and real ale in Beefeater pub/restaurant with nice atmosphere *(Roy Moorehead)*

☆ **Slaidburn** [B6478 N of Clitheroe; SD7152], *Hark to Bounty*: Relaxed country atmosphere, decor a quietly luxurious mix of old and new, open fire, brasses, wide choice of good value bar food (lots of tables), full Theakstons range kept well, decent wines; bedrooms – a nice place to stay in a charming Forest of Bowland village, pleasant garden behind, good walks *(P J Taylor, Margaret and Arthur Dickinson, LYM)*

Southport Mer [Bold St/Lord St; SD3316], *Bold*: Popular and spacious lounge bar leading to front terrace, well kept Tetleys from long counter, decent wines, good value varied food all day inc very good fish, good service; comfortable bedrooms *(Roy Moorehead, David Carr)*; [93 Lord St], *Wetherspoons*: Well placed, with good choice of food all day *(David Carr)*

Stockport Gtr Man [23 Millgate St, behind Asda; SJ8991], *Arden Arms*: Traditional and welcoming, with several room areas inc old-fashioned snug through servery, good value limited lunchtime bar food, well kept Robinsons, several grandfather clocks, Dinky toy collection *(Brian Wainwright, PB)*; [1 Avenue St], *Railway*: Porters Bitter, Dark Mild, Rossendale, Porter, Sunshine, Young Tom and Timmys Ginger Beer kept well in comfortable L-shaped bar with old Stockport prints, bottles and memorabilia, friendly staff, decent straightforward food, no music or machines;

tables out behind *(Richard Lewis)*

☆ **Tockholes** [just N of village, which is signed off A666 and A675 S of Blackburn; SD6623], *Rock*: Cosy interestingly decorated two-room beamed moorland inn with great views (as far as coast) from restaurant, friendly newish landlady, well kept Thwaites Bitter and Mild, decent generous food from sandwiches up; unobtrusive piped music, children welcome, tables on a small terrace; has been cl Mon lunchtime *(GLD, B Adams, LYM)*

Tockholes [signed off A6062 S of Blackburn], *Royal Arms*: Friendly and old-fashioned little rooms, one no smoking, with big open fires, rustic decorations, well kept Thwaites Bitter and Mild, sandwiches and varied home cooking, piped popular classics, views from sheltered terrace, play area in garden, nature trail opp; children welcome, open all day Fri-Sun and summer *(Richard Lewis, LYM)*

West Kirby Mer [SJ2187], *Ring o' Bells*: Very old village pub with good fair-priced food, Whitbreads-related ales, decent wines; tables in garden *(Roy Moorehead)*

Wheelton [Blackburn Rd (A674); SD6021], *Red Cat*: Mainly an Italian eating house, but with cosy and friendly bar; good value nicely served food *(Charles and Pauline Stride)*

Whittle le Woods [Preston Rd (A6, not far from M61 junction 7); SD5721], *Sea View*: This friendly inland pub really does have a sea view (from upstairs); spacious but cosy and comfortable, with well kept Courage Directors, Morlands Old Speckled Hen, Theakstons and Manx Bitter, good traditional reasonably priced food inc real chips, dining rooms (one no smoking), beams, horsebrasses and coach horns, big stone fireplace in extension; piped music *(Dr and Mrs B Baker)*

Wigan Gtr Man [Wallgate, opp Wigan NW Stn; SD5805], *Swan & Railway*: Traditional unspoiled town pub that reverberates with passing trains, high ceilings, mosaic tiling depicting swan and railway train, usual food, Banks's ales, dominoes, TV *(Tony Hobden)*

Woodford Gtr Man [550 Chester Rd; A5149 SW of BAe entrance; SJ8882], *Davenport Arms*: Down-to-earth convivial country pub in same family for 60 years, simple but comfortable, with small rooms, coal fires, well kept Robinsons Best and Best Mild, good house wines, good reasonably priced lunchtime home cooking inc fine toasties and chips, good games room, no-smoking room; children allowed in back no-smoking snug, live music Tues/Sat; tables on front terrace and in attractive back garden with play area *(J F M West)*

Wycollar [Laneshawbridge—Haworth rd, overlooking village – OS Sheet 103 map ref 946391; SD9339], *Herders*: Welcoming licensees and locals, enjoyable food *(Paul McPherson)*

Post Office address codings confusingly give the impression that some pubs are in Lancashire when they're really in Yorkshire (which is where we list them).

Leicestershire (with Rutland)

Pubs doing specially well here are the White Horse at Empingham (it's the food and accommodation which shine here), the nicely placed Fox at Exton (again, warm feelings about the food), the Monckton Arms at Glaston (good all round, some useful bedroom refurbishment), the Old Barn at Glooston (another fine all-rounder), the Old White Hart at Lyddington (the newish owners have settled in very well, gaining a Food Award this year – increasingly a dining pub but keeping plenty of character), the Nevill Arms at Medbourn (very popular as a place to stay), the Peacock at Redmile (a fine distinctive dining pub), the Bakers Arms at Thorpe Langton (another very good dining pub, now open on weekday lunchtimes too), the Finches Arms overlooking Rutland Water at Upper Hambleton (new owners doing such good food that this new rather chic main entry comes straight in with a Food Award), and the attractively remodelled ancient Kings Arms at Wing (another new entry – good all round). People who want good pub food really are spoilt for choice in this part of the world; from among this splendid choice it's the Old Barn at Glooston that we name Leicestershire Dining Pub of the Year. (It's closed on weekday lunchtimes – indeed, this area seems to be lagging behind many others in the trend to weekday pub lunching which has now caught on so much elsewhere, particularly among older people.) In Leicester itself, it's noticeable that many of the most promising entries in the Lucky Dip section at the end of the chapter seem to be bars rather than pubs, and the Welford Place which rates so highly is very unpubby. This can also be said of two of the three most prominent Dips elsewhere: the Barnsdale Lodge at Barnsdale, and Ram Jam at Stretton. However the third, the Noel Arms at Whitwell, does have a very properly pubby core. Beer prices in the area are close to the national average – just a few pence a pint below. Much the cheapest pub we found was the Old Brewery at Somerby, brewing its own fine Parish ales. The Swan in the Rushes in Loughborough (a great real-ale pub, with good food too) was also cheap, as were the Rose & Crown at Hose and Peacock at Redmile. A particularly sad blow to the area's beer lovers this last year has been the closing of the Ruddles brewery in Langham, Rutland (by its new owners Morlands, the Oxfordshire brewers).

BRAUNSTON SK8306 Map 4

Old Plough 🍷

Village signposted off A606 in Oakham

Despite an emphasis on well presented and imaginative food this flower-decked stone pub is not exclusively a dining pub. The atmosphere is still pubby and friendly, they hold lots of social and sporting events for locals and the well kept real ales are generally all brewed locally: besides John Smiths these include Ruddles Best and County, and brews from the Grainstore Brewery. Also a well noted wine list, fruit punches in summer, Scrumpy Jack cider, and a choice of teas and coffees. The menu changes every season, but might include tasty dishes such as home-made soup (£2.25), really big filled rolls (from £3.15), baked potatoes (from £3.25), baked field mushrooms with spinach and goat's cheese (£3.95), home-made lasagne or sweet potato and broccoli cake with sweet pepper sauce (£6.95), duo of tagliatelle with smoked salmon and avocado sherry sauce or steak and kidney pie (£7.95), roast fillet of pork sliced over apple mash with black pudding and sage crust and mustard sauce (£9.25), seared salmon steak with carrot and courgette noodles and a lemon and chive sauce (£8.95), lamb cutlets with a three bean and rosemary casserole and parsnip chips (£10.25), marinated duck breast with forest fruit sauce (£11.95) and blackboard specials. The traditional bars have upholstered seats around cast-iron-framed tables under the heavy and irregular back beams, and plenty of brass ornaments on the mantlepiece. At the back is a stylish modern no-smoking conservatory dining room. The carpeted public bar has darts in winter; maybe piped music. In the garden picnic-sets shelter among fruit trees, and there's a boules pitch. *(Recommended by L Walker, Derek and Sylvia Stephenson, D Goodger, Jenny and Michael Back, David and Anne Culley, Eric Locker, Mrs J Burrows, Brian Atkin, J R Morris)*

Free house ~ Licensees Andrew and Amanda Reid ~ Real ale ~ Meals and snacks (till 10) ~ Restaurant ~ (01572) 722714 ~ Children welcome ~ Open 11-3, 6-11(12 Sat); 12-3.30, 7-10.30 Sun

EAST LANGTON SP7292 Map 4

Bell

The Langtons signposted from A6 N of Market Harborough; East Langton signposted from B6047

Described by one reader as a model country pub, this pretty creeper covered inn serves good imaginative home-cooked food at plain wooden tables in its long stripped-stone bar; good log fire and warm and inviting atmosphere. The menu changes seasonally but might include sandwiches (from £1.95), home-made soup (£2.55), pheasant pâté or ploughman's (£4.25), broccoli and stilton quiche (£5.50), pork with dijon mustard sauce or a brie, cheddar and celeriac savoury cheesecake with redcurrant jelly glaze (£7.95), Whitby wholetail scampi (£8.25), chicken breast stuffed with smoked leicester cheese and wrapped in bacon with a wild mushroom sauce (£7.75), seafood brochettes (£9.95) and steaks (from £10.95); also blackboard specials; Sunday carvery and weekday senior citizens' lunches. Well kept Greene King IPA and Abbot, Jennings Cumberland and Ridleys Rumpus on handpump and regularly changing guests tapped from the cask; friendly and efficient service; no-smoking green-hued dining room. The bedrooms are very well appointed. There are tables out in the garden; the village is attractive and set in peaceful countryside. *(Recommended by Stephen and Julie Brown, Barbara and James Woods, O K Smyth, Bernard and Becky Robinson, Mrs E Lorey, John Peet, Owen and Rosemary Warnock)*

Free house ~ Licensee Alistair Chapman ~ Meals and snacks (till 10pm) ~ Restaurant ~ (01858) 545278 ~ Well behaved children welcome till 8.30pm ~ Open 10-2.30, 7(6 Sat)-11; 12-3, 7-10.30 Sun; cl 25 Dec ~ Bedrooms: £37.50S/£49.50S

EMPINGHAM SK9408 Map 4

White Horse

Main Street; A606 Stamford—Oakham

Close to the edge of Rutland Water, Europe's largest man-made lake, this attractive and bustling old inn is a particularly nice place to stay. Some of the bedrooms are in a delightfully converted stable block, the breakfasts are very good and they offer deep freezing facilities for lucky anglers. The open-plan carpeted lounge bar has a big log fire below an unusual free-standing chimney-funnel, lots of fresh flowers, and a very relaxed and comfortable atmosphere. Very popular well cooked bar food includes filled french bread, soup (£2.35), stilton mushrooms (£3.95), spicy tomato and vegetable curry (£5.95), seafood crêpes (£6.75), steak and kidney pie or chicken breast wrapped in oak-smoked bacon with a local cheese and chive cream sauce (£6.95), lamb cutlets with a sweet red onion, wild mushroon and redcurrant port wine sauce (£7.25), steaks (from £8.95) and home-made puddings which look almost too good to eat; vegetables are served separately in a little dish; they also do morning coffee and afternoon tea. The restaurant and the Orange Room are no-smoking. Well kept Courage Directors, Grainstore Triple B, John Smiths and Ruddles County on handpump; fruit machine and piped music; friendly service. Outside are some rustic tables among urns of flowers. *(Recommended by Joy and Peter Heatherley, George Atkinson, David and Anne Culley, Keith and Margaret Kettwell, Mrs M Dixon, Michael Butler, Gwen and Peter Andrews, Mr Bewley, R and M Bishop, R Inman, Brian Horner, Brenda Arthur, D W Atkinson, Michael and Lynne Gittins, Jenny and Michael Back)*

Scottish Courage ~ Tenant Roger Bourne ~ Real ale ~ Meals and snacks (till 9.45) ~ Restaurant ~ (01780) 460221 ~ Children in eating area of bar ~ Open 11-11(10.30 Sun) ~ Bedrooms: £50B/£63B

EXTON SK9211 Map 7

Fox & Hounds

Signposed off A606 Stamford—Oakham

Prettily set right on the village green, this rather grand old coaching inn is a striking reminder of the days when this now quiet and characterful village was part of the main coach route to Oakham. The comfortable high-ceilinged lounge bar has some dark red plush easy chairs as well as wheelback seats around lots of dark tables, maps and hunting and military prints on the walls, brass and copper ornaments, and a winter log fire in a large stone fireplace; piped music. Well presented and reasonably priced bar food includes, lasagne or liver, bacon and onions (£6.75), plaice and prawns (£7.75), sautéed chicken with sherry, cream and mushroom sauce or steak and kidney pie (£7.50) and honey roasted local trout (£8.95); maybe Sunday roast. The lively and quite separate public bar has darts, pool, cribbage, dominoes, juke box, fruit machine, and video game. One well kept changing real ale such as Batemans XB, Fullers London Pride or Morland Original on handpump might increase to three on busy weekends. There are seats among large rose beds on the well kept back lawn, overlooking paddocks. Rutland Water is only a couple of miles away and it's very handy for walkers on the Viking Way. *(Recommended by L Walker, Steven M Gent, F R Robinson, M J Morgan, Paul and Sandra Embleton, David and Anne Culley, Michael Butler, Eric Locker, Gordon Theaker, Bill and Sheila McLardy, Jo and Gary Charlton)*

Free house ~ Licensees David and Jennifer Hillier ~ Real ale ~ Meals and snacks ~ Restaurant (not Sun evening) ~ (01572) 812403 ~ Children welcome ~ Open 11-3, 6-11; 12-3, 6.30-10.30 ~ Bedrooms: £22/£36

GLASTON SK8900 Map 4

Monckton Arms

A47 Leicester—Peterborough, E of Uppingham

As we went to press they were just beginning work on refurbishing the bedrooms at this stone roadside inn that readers particularly like as a place to stay. Part of the Old English Pub Company chain, it was originally a 16th-c farmhouse, most of which now forms the bar and snug area, and there's a sizeable modern extension. The nicest seats are by a big woodburner in an inglenook fireplace. Well liked bar food includes sandwiches (from £2.75), filled baguettes (from £2.95), baked potatoes (from £3.50), ploughman's (£5.25), chicken curry (£6.75), beef or vegetable lasagne or gammon, pineapple and egg (£6.95), salmon and sole bake (£7.25), local Rutland trout (£8.95), steaks (from £8.95) and mixed grill (£9.95); friendly and efficient service. Courage Directors, John Smiths, Marstons Pedigree and Ruddles Best and County under light blanket pressure; dominoes, cribbage, piped music; no-smoking restaurant. There are picnic-sets on a sheltered terrace; the licensee is an *X-Files* fan – the popular black Labrador is called Scully. Rutland Water is ten minutes' drive away, it's also handy for Burghley House and Rockingham Castle. *(Recommended by D Sinclair, J Dawson, John Wooll, Duncan Cloud, Ash, Samantha and Josie Wright, J F Knutton, A Bradbury)*

Free house ~ Licensee Spencer Dainton ~ Real ale ~ Meals and snacks (12-10) ~ Restaurant ~ (01572) 822326 ~ Children welcome ~ Open 11(12 Sun)-11; 12-4, 7-11 winter Sun; cl 25 Dec evening ~ Bedrooms: £40B/£50B

GLOOSTON SP7595 Map 4

Old Barn ★

From B6047 in Tur Langton follow Hallaton signpost, then fork left following Glooston signpost

Leicestershire Dining Pub of the Year

Readers tell us that this carefully restored 16th-c pub continues to deserve all of its awards. Although not cheap, every dish on the very inventive monthly changing menus is tempting – there might be soup (£3.25), gorgonzola tartlet with salad leaves drizzled with a saffron, honey and pistachio dressing (£4.95), thai fishcakes with a sweet and sour cucumber sauce (£5.50), roasted red pepper filled with cannellini beans, courgettes, onions and fresh herbs, served with a mixed salad and a yoghurt and coriander salsa (£8.95), medallions of pork marinated in elderflowers and honey with an apple, elderflower and chive stuffing (£11.50), lemon sole poached and garnished with white crab meat served with a fresh crab and chive sauce (£12.75), chargrilled fillet steak in a rich red wine sauce with an oat and stilton rissole (£14.95); home-made puddings and ice creams (£3.50); their 3 course Sunday lunch is good value (£13.50). It's worth taking careful note of their opening times given below as they close on weekday lunchtimes, and they only serve snacks on Saturday lunchtimes. The warm and welcoming lower beamed main bar has stripped kitchen tables and country chairs, pewter plates, Players cricketer cigarette cards, and an open fire; dominoes. Four well kept real ales on handpump rotated from a wide choice of beers like Adnams Broadside, Buttcombe Bitter, Fullers London Pride, Wadworths 6X; good wine list (with half a dozen by the glass), champagne by the glass. The dining area is no smoking. There are a few old-fashioned teak seats and picnic-sets in front. Breakfasts are good and the bedrooms are comfortable with French-style shower-and-wash cabinets that please most readers, but might perhaps suit best those with at least a modest degree of mobility. Well behaved dogs welcome. *(Recommended by M Borthwick, Eric Locker, Duncan Cloud, Stephen, Julie and Hayley Brown, Peter Smith, Patrick Hancock, David Child, Ed Miller, Alan J Morton, Barbara and James Woods, D Goodger, Ted George, Anthony Longdon, Joyce McKimm, Anthony Barnes, Mary Wood, Simon Walker, Brian Atkin, Mrs S F Front)*

Free house ~ Licensees Charles Edmondson-Jones and Stewart Sturge ~ Real ale ~ Meals and snacks (not weekday lunchtimes or Sun evening, till 1.30 Sat) ~ Restaurant ~ (01858) 545215 ~ Children in eating area of the bar (if there is a bedroom available they offer baby listening service) ~ Open 7pm-11pm only during the week; 12-2.30, 7-11 Sat; 12-3 Sun, cl Sun evening and weekday lunchtimes ~ Bedrooms: £37.50S/£49.50S

HALLATON SP7896 Map 4

Bewicke Arms ★

On good fast back road across open rolling countryside between Uppingham and Kibworth; village signposted from B6047 in Tur Langton and from B664 SW of Uppingham

This ancient thatched inn is prettily set on the edge of the village green; the front windows have a lovely view out into the village and from the back you can look out towards the hills. The unpretentious beamed main bar has two small oddly shaped rooms with farming implements and deer heads on the walls, pokerwork seats, old-fashioned settles (including some with high backs and wings), wall benches, and stripped oak tables, and four copper kettles gleaming over one of the log fires. Well kept Marstons Pedigree, Ruddles Best and County and a guest beer under light blanket pressure; darts; piped music. Popular bar food includes sandwiches (from £1.50), home-made soup (£2.70), ploughman's (£4.20), breaded plaice (£5.60), scampi (£6.20), 10oz rump steak (£9.20), as well as weekly changing specials such as deep-fried brie and cranberry dip (£4.45), warm goat's cheese salad (£4.60), aubergine and chick pea moussaka (£6.20), creamy seafood pancake or lasagne (£6.80), grilled salmon fillet with lemon and dill butter, pheasant and venison sausage casserole or beef and ale casserole (£7.20) and chicken breast with herb and garlic cheese (£7.80); you can book a table most days, otherwise get there early; jovial landlord and very friendly staff. No dogs. They now have a gift shop and tea room behind and are planning a children's pets farm. On Easter Monday after the famous pagan 'Hare Pie Scrambling' has taken place the 'bottle-kicking race' procession sets out from the green for Hare Hill, and in the summer there may be Morris dancing here. *(Recommended by JP, PP, Duncan Cloud, John Wooll, George Atkinson, Eric Locker, Ted George, CMJ, JJW, Stephen, Julie and Hayley Brown, Brian Atkin)*

Free house ~ Licensee Neil Spiers ~ Real ale ~ Meals and snacks (till 9.45) ~ Restaurant ~ (01858) 555217 ~ Children welcome ~ Open 12-3(3.30 Sat), 7-11; 12-4, 7-11 Sun

HOSE SK7329 Map 7

Rose & Crown

Bolton Lane

The eight regularly changing and well kept real ales are the main attraction at this atmospheric old place. You won't find Carl's Tipple anywhere else – it's brewed exclusively by Butterknowle for its namesake, the landlord here. There might also be ales from Bantham, Butterknowle, Burton Bridge, Jennings and Greene King; around a dozen malt whiskies. There's a relaxed lighthearted atmosphere in the more-or-less open-plan bar which has pool, dominoes, cribbage, a fruit machine and juke box; no-smoking areas in restaurant and lounge bar. Good straightforward bar food includes filled rolls (from £1.60), garlic mushrooms (£1.80), home-made soup (£2.25), ploughman's (from £3.75), well liked home-made chicken and ham or steak and ale pies (£5.50), mushroom stroganoff (£5.50), lots of steaks (from £6.55), home-cooked ham (£7.75); blackboard specials might include brie with sweet and sour coulis (£2.50), medallions of pork with port and mustard sauce or chicken with stilton and bacon cream sauce (£7.95) and duck with plum sauce (£8.50). There are tables on a fairy-lit sheltered terrace behind the building and a fenced family area at the rear of the car park. *(Recommended by June and Malcolm Farmer, Norma and Keith Bloomfield, The Didler, Dr and Mrs J H Hills, R M Taylor, D C Roberts, Rona Murdoch, Chris Raisin, Graham Doyle)*

Free house ~ Licensee Carl Routh ~ Meals and snacks (not evening 26 Dec) ~ Restaurant ~ (01949) 860424 ~ Children in eating area of bar and restaurant till 9 ~ Open 11.30-2.30, 7-11; 12-3, 7-10.30 Sun; closed 25 Dec

KEGWORTH SK4826 Map 7

Cap & Stocking ★ £

Under a mile from M1 junction 24: follow A6 towards Loughborough; in village, turn left at chemists' down one-way Dragwall opposite High Street, then left and left again, into Borough Street

Readers feel instantly comfortable and very welcome at this old-fashioned small town local, a handy stop-off from the M1. Each of the two determinedly simple but cosy front rooms has its own coal fire, and a friendly and easy-going feel; on the right there's lots of etched glass, big cases of stuffed birds and locally caught fish, fabric-covered wall benches and heavy cast-iron-framed tables, and a cast-iron range; cribbage, dominoes, trivia and piped music. Well kept beers include Draught Bass tapped from the cask and Hancocks HB and M & B Mild on handpump. Good value bar food includes filled rolls (from £1); hot sausage and onion (£1.10), soup (£1.65), burgers (from £2.20), ploughman's (from £4), pizzas (from £4), chilli or vegetable curry (£4.20), hungarian goulash (£5.25), beef stroganoff (£5.60) and daily specials such as thai chicken curry or beef in Guinness (£5.75). The back room has french windows to the pleasant garden where there may be floodlit boules. *(Recommended by Peter Hancock, JP, PP, Duncan Cloud, Roger and Abigail Huggins, The Didler, G P Kernan, Vicky and David Sarti, Pete Baker, K and J Brooks, Val Stevenson, Rob Holmes, Jack and Jemima Valiant, Peter and Anne Hollindale, K Fell, Jo and Gary Charlton, P V Burdett, Adam and Joan Bunting)*

Bass ~ Lease: Graham and Mary Walsh ~ Real ale ~ Meals and snacks (11.30-2.15, 6.30-8.45) ~ (01509) 674814 ~ Children in eating area of bar ~ Open 11.30-2.30, 6.30-11; 12-3, 7-10.30 Sun

LOUGHBOROUGH SK5319 Map 7

Swan in the Rushes £

The Rushes (A6)

This is predominantly a drinker's pub, and it's the fine collection of beers that draws people to its rather spartan but welcoming town premises. There are interesting German, Belgian and other bottled beers, and on handpump changing ales might include well kept Archers Golden, Bramcote Hemlock, Marstons Pedigree and Tetley; also two ciders, a good range of malt whiskies, and country wines. The several neatly kept and simply furnished room areas all have their own style – the most comfortable seats are in the left-hand bay-windowed bar (which has an open fire) and in the snug no-smoking back dining room. It can get very crowded, but service is good. Very reasonably priced home-made bar food includes filled rolls, baked potatoes (from £2), a choice of ploughman's (from £3.50), chilli (£3.95), and specials such as spinach and ricotta brioches (£4.50), tandoori chicken curry, pork, apple and cider casserole or braised liver and onions (£4.95). Shove-ha'penny, cribbage, dominoes, juke box. The simple bedrooms are clean and cosy although they may suffer from motorway noise; generous breakfasts. There are tables in an outside drinking area. *(Recommended by The Didler, Tim Barrow, Sue Demont, Ian Phillips, Joan and Michel Hooper-Immins, Bruce Bird, JP, PP, Barry and Anne, John Voos, Stephen Brown, JJW, CMW, Jack and Gemima Valiant)*

Free house ~ Licensee Andrew Hambleton ~ Real ale ~ Meals and snacks (12-2, 6-8.30; not Sat/Sun evenings) ~ (01509) 217014 ~ Children in dining room ~ Local bands Fri evening, blues Sat evening, folk Sun evening ~ Open 11-11; 12-10.30 Sun; closed evening 25 Dec ~ Bedrooms: £20(£25B)/£30(£40B)

LYDDINGTON SP8797 Map 4

Old White Hart

Village signposted off A6003 N of Corby

Although increasingly a dining pub, this traditional 17th-c village inn has not lost its considerable character. The cosy softly lit bar has just three close-set tables in front of the warm log fire, with heavy bowed beams and lots of attractive dried flower arrangements. The bar opens into an attractive restaurant with corn dollies and a big oak dresser, and on the other side is a tiled-floor room with some stripped stone, cushioned wall seats, mate's chairs and a woodburning stove; darts, a thriving dominoes school, bar billiards, shove-ha'penny, cribbage, fruit machine and piped music. Lunchtime food includes home-made soup (£2.95), filled french bread (£4.95), tagliatelle with pesto and parmesan (£7.25), home-made steak and kidney suet pudding (£7.95), grilled salmon with lemon and parsley butter (£9.25), chicken breast wrapped in ham with a sage and lemon split butter sauce (£9.50), sautéed fillet of lamb with oyster mushrooms and Drambuie cream (£10.95) and sirloin steak (£12.95); the evening menu has slightly more elaborate dishes including boned oxtail with madeira sauce served on crispy vegetables (£9.25), saddle of lamb stuffed with apricot and hazelnut with a red wine sauce (£10.95) and duck with pears and port sauce (£11.25); one of the restaurants is no smoking. Well kept Greene King IPA and Abbot and a guest such as Marstons Pedigree, Timothy Taylor Landlord or Black Sheep Best on handpump. There are picnic-sets in the safe and pretty walled garden which has twelve floodlit boules pitches – on Thursday you can listen to the church bell ringers. Good nearby walks; handy for the Bede House. *(Recommended by Rona Murdoch, Sue and Mike Loseby, RB, David and Anne Culley, O K Smyth, M J Morgan, Anthony Barnes, Stephen Brown, George Atkinson)*

Free house ~ Licensee Stuart East ~ Real ale ~ Meals and snacks (not Sun evening) ~ Restaurant ~ (01572) 821703 ~ Children welcome ~ Open 12-3, 6-11; 12-4, 7-10.30 Sun

Cribbage is a card game using a block of wood with holes for matchsticks or special pins to score with; regulars in cribbage pubs are usually happy to teach strangers how to play.

MEDBOURNE SP7993 Map 4

Nevill Arms

B664 Market Harborough—Uppingham

You reach this handsome old mullion-windowed pub, especially popular with readers as a place to stay, via a footbridge over the duck-filled River Welland. Last year they converted two neighbouring cottages to provide additional rooms, and good breakfasts are served in the sunny conservatory. The appealing main bar has a cheerful atmosphere, as well as two winter log fires, chairs and small wall settles around its tables, a lofty, dark-joisted ceiling and maybe a couple of dogs or a cat; piped music. A spacious back room by the former coachyard has pews around more tables (much needed at busy times), and some toys to amuse the children. In summer most people prefer eating at the tables outside on the grass by the dovecote. Well kept Adnams, Ruddles Best and County and two changing guests under light blanket pressure; about two dozen country wines. Good value bar food includes home-made soups like curried parsnip or cauliflower and stilton (£2.30); blackboard specials (£5.25) might include smoked haddock and spinach bake, chicken in lime and mango, pork in white wine and mushrooms, lamb in honey and ginger or beery beef. Darts, shove-ha'penny, cribbage, table skittles, hood skittles, dominoes and other board games on request. The church over the bridge is worth a visit. *(Recommended by Jeff Davies, Alan J Morton, Joan and Michel Hooper-Immins, Sue and Mike Loseby, M Morgan, Eric Locker, Dorsan Baker, Barbara and James Woods, Rona Murdoch, CMW, JJW, D Goodger, Jo and Gary Charlton, Mr and Mrs J T V Harris, R Murdoch, Dr Jim Mackay)*

Free house ~ Licensees E F Hall and partners ~ Real ale ~ Meals and snacks (till 9.45) ~ (01858) 565288 ~ Children welcome ~ Open 12-2.30, 6-11; 12-3, 7-10.30 Sun; closed evening 25 Dec ~ Bedrooms: £40B/£50B

OLD DALBY SK6723 Map 7

Crown ★

By school in village centre turn into Longcliff Hill then left into Debdale Hill

As we went to press this smart creeper-covered former farmhouse was up for sale – the licensees want to concentrate all of their energy on their other pub, the Martins Arms at Colston Bassett (see Notts chapter). Readers praise the food under the present regime – it isn't cheap but then they do grow their own herbs and make their own bread, vinegars and ice creams. As well as soup (£2.95), sandwiches (from £2.95) and ploughman's (£7.95), the menu might include starters like pan-fried black pudding with apple mustard cream sauce or chicken terrine studded with red peppers and asparagus (£5.95), and main courses like spicy grilled aubergine with a tomato fondue sauce and pesto dressing (£7.95), smoked salmon tagliatelle with white wine, herbs, cream and cheese (£8.95), roast of cod on minted mushy peas, with red onion and dill vinaigrette (£11.95), roast pheasant in bourguignon sauce (£12.95), fillet of pork on a confit of cabbage, with honey and clove jus (£13.95), roast loin of venison with chocolate and raspberry sauce or rib of beef with red wine and bay leaf sauce (£14.95); puddings like banana, pear and toffee crumble or chocolate crêpe with hot chocolate sauce (£4.50). The atmosphere is fairly formal with staff in black and white uniforms and bow ties. Three or four intimate little rooms have black beams, one or two antique oak settles, William Morris style armchairs and easy chairs, hunting and other rustic prints, fresh flowers, and open fires; the snug and one dining area are no smoking; cribbage and dominoes. A good range of beers tapped from the cask might include Adnams, Batemans XB and XXB, Black Sheep, Greene King Abbot, Marstons Pedigree, Morlands Old Speckled Hen, Smiles and Timothy Taylor Landlord and Vaux Waggle Dance; they also have an interesting wine list, quite a few malt whiskies, and several brandies and Italian liqueurs. There are rustic tables and chairs on a terrace, with a big, sheltered lawn sloping down among roses and fruit trees; you can play boules out here. No credit cards. *(Recommended by G Neighbour, Mike and Mary Carter, Ted George, GL, Paul and Sharon Sneller, Julie Sage, George Green, Stephen and Julie Brown, Alan J Morton, JP, PP, J H Kane, John Poulter, Tim Barrow, Sue Demont, D J and P M Taylor, M Buchanan)*

Free house ~ Licensees Lynne Strafford Bryan and Salvatore Inguanta ~ Real ale ~ Meals and snacks (till 10; not Sun evening) ~ Restaurant ~ (01664) 823134 ~ Children welcome away from bar ~ Open 12-3, 6-11; 12-3, 7-10.30 Sun

PEATLING MAGNA SP5992 Map 4

Cock

Village signposted off A50 S of Leicester

Visitors feel warmly welcome at this chatty little village local where there's a cheery start to the evening with discounted beers and spirits and free cut-your-own sandwiches, from loaves of good crusty bread and hunks of excellent stilton or red leicester on the bar (weekdays 5.30-7). During the evening the friendly and energetic landlord likes the kitchen to send out little snacks like free baked potatoes. The narrow main bar has horsey pictures and plates above the coal-effect gas fire and on some beams, cushioned wall benches and plush stools; there's a neat country dining area in the right-hand room; well kept Courage Directors and John Smiths on handpump, and decent house wines. Good straightforward bar food includes home-made soup (£1.95), sandwiches such as local ham and cheese with a salad garnish and chips (£3) and home-made specials such as curry, chilli, lasagne or haddock and chips (£4.95). The very popular Sunday lunch has three bookable sittings; maybe piped pop music. *(Recommended by Ed Miller, Stephen and Julie Brown, Rona Murdoch, David W Atkinson; more reports please)*

Free house ~ Licensee Max Brown ~ Real ale ~ Meals and snacks (not Sun or Mon evenings) ~ Restaurant ~ (0116) 247 8308 ~ Well behaved children welcome ~ Open 5.30-11 (closed weekday lunchtimes); 10-2.30, 6-11 Sat; 12-4, 7-10.30 Sun

REDMILE SK7935 Map 7

Peacock

Off A52 W of Grantham; at crossroads follow sign for Belvoir Castle, Harlby, and Melton

Although it's increasingly a dining pub, reader reports suggest that this place continues to go from strength to strength. The very imaginative freshly prepared bar food might include soup (£2.75), open ciabatta sandwiches such as cajun spiced chicken legs with plum chutney (£5.95), warm deep-fried goat's cheese in herb crust with pineapple and sun-dried tomato salsa (£4.75), poached salmon wrapped in smoked salmon with dill and potato salad (£5.95), smoked chicken risotto or spaghetti tossed with sun-dried tomatoes and herbs (£6.75) and blackboard specials such as penne tossed with crab and cockles in a cheese sauce (£5.50), seared fillet of cod on a cucumber and salsa bed with tomato and basil oil (£7.25), and pan roasted breast of guineafowl with a cassoulet of sausage, pinto beans and baby pear or chargrilled tuna loin with pistachio and apricot salad drizzled with balsamic glaze (£7.50); delicious puddings include fresh summer fruit Italian gateaux with lemon sorbet and mascarpone cheese tartlet with fresh double cream (£3.95). Service is friendly and helpful, but can slow down at busy times; booking advisable. The range of well kept beers on handpump includes Tetleys, Timothy Taylor Landlord, and local guests, and they have an interesting wine list including fairly priced bottles and some by the glass; occasional special events such as cookery demonstrations or wine tastings. The four spotless beamed pubby rooms have an easy-going feel, with open fires, pews, stripped country tables and chairs, the odd sofa and easy chair, some stripped golden stone, old prints, chintzy curtains for the small windows, and a variety of wall and table lamps; no-smoking area; dominoes, piped music, and tables outside. Spacious, nicely decorated bedrooms; good breakfasts. The pub is in an extremely pleasant tranquil setting near Belvoir Castle. *(Recommended by Alan Caudell, Mr and Mrs P Johnson, RB, David and Helen Wilkins, J F Knutton, June and Malcolm Farmer, Dr and Mrs J Hills, R Clare, J A Hodgson)*

Free house ~ Licensees Celia and Colin Craword ~ Real ale ~ Meals and snacks (12-3, 7-10; afternoon teas) ~ Restaurant ~ (01949) 842554 ~ Children welcome ~ Open 11-11; 12-10.30 Sun ~ Bedrooms: £75B/£90B

SIBSON SK3500 Map 4

Cock

A444 N of Nuneaton

There was a cock pit here until 1870 and this quaint thatched pub dates back to the 13th c; though it's changed a fair bit over the years, proof of its age can still be seen in the unusually low doorways, ancient wall timbers, heavy black beams, and genuine latticed windows. An atmospheric room on the right has comfortable seats around cast-iron tables, and more seats built in to what was once an immense fireplace where Dick Turpin is rumoured to have hidden. The room on the left has country kitchen chairs around wooden tables, and there's a no-smoking dining area. Well kept Bass and M & B Brew XI on handpump; fruit machine and piped music. Good value bar food includes home-made soup (£1.90), sandwiches (from £2.20), home-made pâté (£2.30), steak and kidney pie, lasagne, chilli or beef curry (£6), honey roast ham and egg or chicken kiev (£6.50), steaks (from £8.50), and daily specials such as fresh cromer crab salad or roast minted shank of lamb (£6.95), duck legs with apricot and walnut stuffing (£8.75) and lobster thermidor (£16); on Sunday the only food is roasts in the restaurant. A little garden and courtyard area has tables and maybe summer barbecues; summer hanging baskets and a flower filled dray cart in front. The restaurant (in a former stable block) is popular, and they have a caravan field (certified with the Caravan Club). *(Recommended by Simon Hulme, Eric Locker, Paul and Sandra Embleton, Ted George, R W Allan, Tim Phillips, Ian Blackwell, JP, PP, Tony and Joan Walker)*

Bass ~ Lease: Graham and Stephanie Lindsay ~ Real ale ~ Meals and snacks (till 9.45; not in bar Sun lunchtime) ~ Restaurant (not Sun evening) ~ (01827) 880357 ~ Children in eating area of bar and restaurant ~ Open 11.30-2.30, 6.30-11; 11.30-3, 6-11 Sat; 12-3, 7-10.30 Sun

SOMERBY SK7710 Map 4

Old Brewery

Off A606 Oakham—Melton Mowbray, via Cold Overton, or Leesthorpe and Pickwell; can also be reached direct from Oakham via Knossington

The attraction here is the interesting range of good value award-winning beers brewed by the landlord; Baz's Bonce Blower at 12% is listed in the *Guinness Book of Records* for its awesome strength. There's also Parish Mild, a Special, Poachers Ale, Somerby Premium and Farm Gold all on handpump. Groups can book tours of the little brewery in the former stables. The comfortable L-shaped main bar has red plush stools and banquettes and plush-cushioned captain's chairs, a sofa in one corner, and a good log fire in the big stone fireplace; another bar has bays of button-back red seating. There's a cheerful relaxed atmosphere, with a much broader mix of customers than you might expect. Straightforward bar food includes soup (£1.95), pâté (£2.75), garlic mushrooms (£2.95), delicious local sausages (£4.95), ploughman's, lasagne, steak pie or vegetarian nuggets (£4.95), three minted lamb chops or breaded plaice (£5.95), fresh Rutland Water trout (£6.95) and 8oz sirloin (£7.95); no-smoking area in restaurant. Juke box, fruit machine, and piped music. A fenced-off area by the car park has white plastic tables and a climbing frame. *(Recommended by Norma and Keith Bloomfield, Anthony Barnes, Stephen Brown, Ed Miller, Rona Murdoch, Sue Brodrick, Joan and Michel Hooper-Immins)*

Own brew ~ Licensee Baz Parish ~ Real ale ~ Meals and snacks ~ Restaurant ~ (01664) 454866 ~ Children welcome ~ Live entertainment most Thursdays ~ Open 11-3, 6-11; 12-10.30 Sun ~ Bedrooms: £20/£30

THORPE LANGTON SP7492 Map 4

Bakers Arms

Village signposted off B6047 N of Market Harborough

Although some readers suggest that this is now more like a restaurant than a pub the atmosphere here is still pubby and furnishing is simple, with straightforward seating and stripped pine tables – you'll probably find just about all the tables given over to eating – in lots of nooks and crannies. Well presented and made with fresh ingredients the good bar food might include grilled goat's cheese with dressed leaves (£4.50), seared scallops with parma ham and vinaigrette dressing (£4.95), monkfish dusted with five spice and served with a red wine sauce (£9.95), breast of duck carved pink with oyster mushrooms and couscous (£11.95), lamb studded with garlic and rosemary (£12.95) and home-made chocolate and orange truffle or sticky toffee pudding (£3.35); booking advisable. Well kept Tetleys on handpump, and an extensive wine list with five by the glass; good friendly service, and no games or piped music. The snug is no smoking. There are picnic-sets in the garden – the only place where they allow children (must be over 12 in evenings). *(Recommended by Duncan Cloud, Stephen Brown, G Neighbour, Patrick Tailyour, Brian Atkin, Henry Paulinski, George Atkinson)*

Carlsberg Tetley ~ Lease: Kate Hubbard ~ Real ale ~ Meals and snacks (not Sun evening or Mon) ~ Restaurant ~ (01858) 545201 ~ Pianist Fri evenings ~ Open Tues-Sat 12-2.30, 6.30-11; 12-3 Sun; cl Sun evening and Mon

UPPER HAMBLETON SK9007 Map 4

Finches Arms

Village signposted from A606 on E edge of Oakham

The emphasis is very much on the good, interesting and upmarket food at this delightfully positioned stone pub with fine views over Rutland Water. The same menu is served in the bar and the more modern no-smoking restaurant; both have stylish cane furniture on wooden floors, and the various oils and watercolours on the walls are for sale. There is a mediterranean slant to the menu, which besides sandwiches (£5.25), includes soup (£2.95), calf liver salad with lime and coriander or chargrilled sardines with apricot and greek yoghurt (£6), smoked haddock tart (£6.25), spring vegetable noodles with soy sauce (£7.95), chicken breast with orange and red cabbage on a whipped mash (£10), grilled seabass with blackened butter (£11) and rack of lamb with pesto crust, rosemary and garlic butter (£12.95); home-made puddings include sticky toffee pudding with cream and butterscotch sauce and chocolate truffle parfait set on coffee anglaise (£3.95). Charles Wells Bombardier, Greene King Abbot, Marstons Pedigree and Theakstons Best under light blanket pressure; piped music. We haven't yet heard from readers who have stayed here, but would expect the bedrooms to be very pleasant. The twin village of Lower Hambleton is now somewhere below the expanse of Rutland Water. *(Recommended by M J Morgan, Jacqueline Orme, Rona Murdoch)*

Free house ~ Licensee David Ventor ~ Real ale ~ Meals and Snacks (12-3, 6.30-10)~ Restaurant ~ (01572) 756575 ~ Children welcome ~ Maybe live entertainment Fri and Sun evenings ~ Open 10.30-4, 6-11.30; 11am-11.30pm Sat and Sun (11-4, 6-11.30 winter Sat and Sun) ~ Bedrooms: £65B/£75B

WING SK8903 Map 4

Kings Arms

Top Street, signed off A6003 S of Oakham

There's a friendly and relaxed atmosphere at this simple early 17th-c inn. The bar has a traditional feel with wooden beams and a flagstone floor, as well as two large log fires, captain's chairs around pine and darker wood tables, old local photographs and a collection of tankards and old-fashioned whisky measuring pots; in the snug there are fishing rods and tackle. Good food includes sandwiches (from £1.95), prawns and mushrooms pan fried in garlic butter (£3.95), a trio of local herb sausages with red onion gravy and rosti potatoes (£4.95), ploughman's or fish stew (£5.95), roasted aubergine filled with vegetable risotto and topped with mozzarella (£6.50), chicken supreme stuffed with rutland cheese in a mushroom and cream sauce (£9.25) and steaks (from £9.75); home-made puddings (£2.40-£4.50) include bread and butter pudding, crème brûlée with a chocolate base and praline and sugar topping and raspberry cranachan. Well kept Batemans XXXB and Valiant and Ruddles County and two guests on handpump; darts and background music. The bedrooms and the restaurant are no smoking. Seats in the sheltered garden; a medieval turf maze some 17 yards across is just up the road. *(Recommended by Roger Brady, Kathy Burke, Rona Murdoch, Joe Besso, R P and P F Edwards)*

Free house ~ Licensees Karen and Neil Hornsby ~ Real ale ~ Meals and snacks ~ Restaurant ~ (01572) 737634 ~ Children welcome ~ Open 11-11; may be closed Sunday evenings in winter ~ Bedrooms: £35B/£60B

Lucky Dip

Besides the fully inspected pubs, you might like to try these Lucky Dips recommended to us and described by readers (if you do, please send us reports):

Arnesby [SP6192], *Old Cock*: Recently refurbished to high standard, good food, well kept Tetleys, front dining room, back locals' bar, no-smoking room *(Stephen, Julie and Hayley Brown)*

Ashby Folville [SK7011], *Carington Arms*: Simple, welcoming and comfortable Tudor-style country pub, generous plain cooking with good chips, well kept Adnams, Everards Tiger and Beacon; children welcome, nice garden, maybe calves or horses in back paddock, live music weekends and some weekdays; annual veteran car rally *(O K Smyth)*

Barkby [35 Brookside; off A607 6 miles NE of Leicester, towards Beeby; SK6309], *Brookside*: Warmly welcoming unpretentious pub in pretty village with a brook running past the front door, homely, welcoming and cosy, reasonably priced food, real ales inc interesting guest beer; lounge, bar and extended dining area, lots of toby jugs, brass and copper *(Rona Murdoch, Duncan Cloud)*

☆ **Barnsdale** [just off A606 Oakham—Stamford; SK9008], *Barnsdale Lodge*: Extensive conservatory dining bar with good choice of generous if not cheap attractively presented food, charming decor, comfortable sitting-roomish coffee lounge, real ales such as Morlands Old Speckled Hen, Ruddles County and Tetleys, cream teas, friendly attentive staff; bedrooms comfortable and attractive, with good breakfast, adjacent antiques centre *(George Atkinson, M J Morgan, Janet Pickles, BB)*

Barrow upon Soar [87 Mill Lane, off South St (B5328); SK5717], *Navigation*: Extended split-level pub based on former barge-horse stabling, attractive and comfortable, with lovely canal view from small back terrace with moorings; good value home-made food (may be limited winter) inc interestingly filled baguettes (only these Sun lunchtime), unusual bar top made from old pennies, central open fire, friendly service, family room; well kept ales such as Ash Vine, Courage Directors and Shipstones Mild, skittle alley; maybe piped music, SkyTV *(Keith and Janet Morris, Norma and Keith Bloomfield)*

Barrowden [Main St; just off A47 Uppingham—Peterborough; SK9400], *Exeter Arms*: Beautiful rambling pub built with local stone in super setting with front terrace overlooking big village green and distant duck pond; long lounge/dining area, limited but good lunchtime food from doorstep sandwiches up inc vegetarian choice, changing real ales such as Hoskins & Oldfields Ginger Tom, prompt cheery service, lively public bar, restaurant; folk club, good R&B nights *(George Atkinson, RB)*

Belmesthorpe [Shepherds Walk; TF0410], *Bluebell*: Quaint and friendly olde-worlde village pub with good fire, well kept Marstons Pedigree and Ruddles County, good traditional home cooking, generous and sensibly priced, inc game, poultry and fresh fish *(J Overton, A L Blowers)*

Billesdon [Church St; SK7202], *Queens Head*: Beamed and partly thatched pub with wide range of good well priced food, Everards and guest ales, comfortable lounge bar with warm log fire, unspoilt public bar, small conservatory eating area and upstairs restaurant, friendly efficient staff; children welcome, pretty stone village *(John Wooll, Ted George)*

Botcheston [off B5380 E of Desford; SK4805], *Greyhound*: Traditional village pub with warmly welcoming new management doing good freshly cooked food inc bargain lunches, children's food and Sun carvery *(Mr and Mrs R R Thompson)*

Bottesford [SK8038], *Red Lion*: Well kept Hardys & Hansons and Frolicking Farmers, simple food choice inc good home-made specials, very pleasant helpful friendly staff *(Francis Johnston, M J Brooks)*

☆ **Braunston** [6 Cedar St; off A606 in Oakham; SK8306], *Blue Ball*: Relaxed and informal feel in recently rethatched pub with individually furnished separate rooms, food from sandwiches to interesting hot dishes inc children's helpings, service good even when busy, well kept Bass, Courage Directors, John Smiths, Ruddles County and a guest beer; no-smoking areas inc restaurant; dominoes, shove-ha'penny, piped music; children welcome, open all day Sun *(J F Knutton, David and Anne Culley, Anthony Barnes, LYM)*

☆ **Breedon on the Hill** [A453 Ashby—Castle Donington; SK4022], *Holly Bush*: Comfortably plush, with low black beams, lots of brass, sporting plates etc, well kept Marstons Pedigree and Tetleys, bar food (stops early lunchtime; not Sun), restaurant (may be fully booked Sat, cl Sun), no-smoking area, friendly efficient staff; piped music; some tables outside, nice bedrooms; interesting village with Anglo-Saxon carvings in hilltop church above huge limestone face; bedrooms *(Theo, Anne and Jane Gaskin, JP, PP, BB)*

☆ **Castle Donington** [Hill Top; A453, S end;

SK4427], *Nags Head*: Good atmosphere in beamed dining pub with range of rooms from small and cosy up inc busy separate no-smoking restaurant, beautifully cooked and presented food inc imaginative dishes, well kept beer, decent wine, friendly service (can slow rather when busy) *(Sue Holland, Dave Webster, M Kershaw, G Washington)*

Castle Donington [Bondgate/Mkt St; SK4427], *Turks Head*: Corner local handy for car museum and circuit, lots of good value snacks and light meals, comfortable lounge, second bar downstairs, games machines, darts, juke box; karaoke, disco and pop quiz nights *(CMW, JJW)*

Catthorpe [just off A5 S of M1/M6/A14 interchange; SP5578], *Cherry Tree*: Welcoming and attractive country local, cosy, clean and warm, with good value generous mainly traditional food from heavily garnished sandwiches up (even take-away curries), well kept Bass-related ales with guests such as Black Sheep and Hook Norton Best, attentive service, dark panelling, lots of plates and pictures, coal-effect fire; hood skittles, no juke box, machines or pool table, but maybe piped radio; cl Mon/Tues lunchtimes *(P Tailyour, Rona Murdoch, DAV, John C Baker)*

Church Langton [B6047 about 3 miles N of Mkt Harborough; just off A6; SP7293], *Langton Arms*: Extended village pub with good mix of customers, good service even when busy, well kept Marstons Pedigree and fortnightly guest beers, wide choice of good food; piped music; garden with play area *(Rona Murdoch, Duncan Cloud)*

☆ **Cottesmore** [Main St; SK9013], *Sun*: 17th-c village pub with good sensibly priced food served well by friendly staff in attractive bar with decent sporting prints, plush button-back banquettes, blazing fire in stone inglenook; quieter side rooms, piped music and fruit machine, tables in garden; children welcome *(Michael Betton, BB)*

Croxton Kerrial [1 School Lane; A607 SW of Grantham; SK8329], *Peacock*: 17th-c pub doing very well under current licensees, particularly good generous home cooking in bar and small restaurant inc fine choice of puddings, interesting changing guest beers, long bar with real fire partitioned off at one end, some bric-a-brac, quiet piped music, pool; well behaved children welcome, skittle alley, picnic-sets in garden *(Wojclech Kierstan)*

Foxton [94 Main St; SP7090], *Black Horse*: Biggish pub by bridge in village, short walk from locks; bar, lounge, no-smoking dining conservatory, reasonably priced food from good sandwiches up inc bargain lunches, Marstons Pedigree, big garden *(George Atkinson)*

Frisby on the Wreake [Main St; SK6917], *Bell*: Friendly roomy pine-beamed local with brass, oil paintings and real fire, family room in back extension, consistently well cooked and presented food inc superb soups, good choice of well kept ales, fair range of wines, decent coffee; smaller back family room; piped music, smart dress required; tables outside *(Richard Gregory)*

Great Easton [6 Cross Bank; signed from Caldecott off A6003 Uppingham—Corby; SP8493], *Sun*: Welcoming unpretentious local, low beams, polished tables, well kept Bass, Marstons Pedigree and Tetleys, friendly dog, attractively priced lunchtime food (not Sun); darts, pool, fruit machine, juke box (not too loud); open all day Sat, cl Tues lunchtime *(Mike Loseby)*

☆ **Greetham** [B668 Stretton—Cottesmore; SK9214], *Wheatsheaf*: Extremely wide choice of good value generous food served till 11 inc lots of chargrills, Fri bargain steak suppers and fish take-aways, nicely redecorated welcoming L-shaped communicating rooms, well kept Tetleys and Whitbreads-related ales, attentive staff, roaring woodburner, odd pivoted clock, soft piped music; pool and other games in end room, restaurant, picnic-sets on side grass; bedrooms in annexe *(Jenny and Michael Back, Bill and Sheila McLardy, BB)*

Harby [SK7531], *Nags Head*: Rambling old open-plan pub, lots of beams, Mansfield ales, good value food cooked by landlady (not Sun or Mon, not Tues evening), separate dining area; interesting Vale of Belvoir village *(Norma and Keith Bloomfield)*

Heath End [follow coach signs from main rd, next to Staunton Harold Hall entry; SK3621], *Saracens Head*: Basic unspoiled two-room farm pub by Staunton Harold Reservoir visitor centre, handy for Calke Abbey; well kept Bass served by jug from the cask, great value filled rolls and toasties, cosy coal fires, picnic-sets on nice grass area *(Chris Raisin, Graham Doyle, John Beeken, JP, PP)*

Hemington [21 Main St; SK4528], *Jolly Sailor*: Very welcoming village local with well kept Bass, Mansfield, Marstons Pedigree and two guest ales, farm cider, good range of malt whiskies and other spirits, good big fresh rolls; good open fire each end, big country pictures, brasses, blow-torches and bric-a-brac, table skittles; beautiful hanging baskets and tables outside *(JP, PP)*

Hose [Bolton Lane; SK7329], *Black Horse*: Friendly local with well kept real ale, quarry tiles, darts, open fire *(JP, PP, RMT)*

Houghton on the Hill [36 Main St; SK6703], *Old Black Horse*: Good atmosphere, good range of Everards and guest ales, good value interesting food (no hot food Mon lunchtime) inc vegetarian, friendly helpful staff, separate restaurant; big garden *(Mrs E Lambert, Eric Locker, Prof and Mrs H Prins)*

☆ **Kegworth** [towards West Leake; actually just over the Notts border – OS Sheet 129 map ref 501268; SK5026], *Station*: Busy well refurbished pub with bare brick and woodwork, coal fires, two rooms off small bar area, well kept Bass, Courage Directors, Worthington and guest beers, upstairs restaurant with good home cooking; big back lawn, play area; simple good bedrooms, sharing bathroom *(the Didler, Trevor Millum, JP, PP)*

Kegworth [24 High St], *Red Lion*: Four small

character rooms in busy village local with very cheap beers such as Bass, Batemans XB, Marstons Pedigree, Theakstons Best and guest beers inc a Mild, wholesome food, big garden with play area; open all day *(the Didler)*

Ketton [High St; A6121 SW of Stamford; SK9704], *Northwick Arms*: Pleasant and well run, in lovely limestone village; well kept real ales inc Mansfield, wide range of good value food inc sandwiches, fine walks nearby *(D Stokes)*

Kibworth Beauchamp [Leicester Rd; SP6893], *Coach & Horses*: Very good choice of popular generous food in tastefully decorated pub with well kept ales inc Bass, snug main bar (less atmosphere in back room), log fires, very friendly staff *(H Paulinski, Eric Locker)*; [5 High St], *Old Swan*: Friendly pub/restaurant with wide range of good value food inc popular Mon/Tues curry nights and fish and chip suppers Weds, well kept Marstons Pedigree, efficient service *(Rona Murdoch)*

☆ **Knipton** [signed off A607 Grantham—Melton Mowbray; SK8231], *Red House*: Attentive and friendly new licensees doing ambitious food in handsome Georgian hunting lodge looking over pretty village close to Belvoir Castle, hunting prints in roomy bar divided by central hearth, restaurant with attractive conservatory, well kept Marstons, John Smiths and a guest beer, traditional games in public end; pretty gardens, children welcome, open all day, comfortable bedrooms with lovely views *(Joan Morgan, Tony Gayfer, LYM)*

☆ **Leicester** [9 Welford Pl, corner Newarke St/Welford Rd], *Welford Place*: High standards in spacious former Constitutional Club, up impressive flight of stone steps; quiet, comfortable and clubby semicircular Victorian bar, more lively some evenings; well kept Adnams and Marstons Pedigree, good choice of Italian wines and other drinks, fresh orange juice, obliging management, friendly service even under pressure, imaginative changing food 8am-11pm in bar and attractive dining room (children allowed here), daily papers, no piped music, jazz Weds; same management as Wig & Mitre, Lincoln *(O K Smyth, Duncan Cloud, J Middis, P Stallard)*

Leicester [17 Market St], *Bar Beristo*: Bright and airy with plush seats (no standing allowed at bar), upper mezzanines, Morlands Independent and Old Speckled Hen with guests such as Flowers Original and Ruddles Best, good range of food all day inc bargains some afternoons, efficient service *(Joan and Michel Hooper-Immins)*; [90 High St], *Cafe Bruxelles*: Former bank with tall Victorian bar gantry, ornate domed ceiling with painted scenes between gold filigree plasterwork, back area done out as Belgian cafe with more plasterwork, check oilcloth tablecloths, old labels and coloured tiles on walls, good service, short choice of well presented food inc Belgian snacks (Sun limited to roast, filled baguettes and ciabattas), lots of bottled beers and several continentals on draught, coffees, good budget wines, small downstairs bar; jazz Mon night, may have bouncer *(John Wooll, Rona Murdoch, Joan and Michel Hooper-Immins, Ted George)*; [Granby St], *Edwards*: Very light and airy, polished wood floors, good modern prints, real ales such as Bass, good house wines, cappuccino etc from long bar, good value generous food, pleasant efficient service *(John Wooll)*; [Silver St/Carts Lane], *Globe*: Old-fashioned three-room local with lots of woodwork, gas lighting, coal-effect gas fire, good value simple generous lunchtime food from sandwiches up, more peaceful upstairs dining room with friendly service; well kept Everards and guest beers; juke box in sometimes noisy back room, can be smoky, children allowed in some parts *(Nigel and Sue Foster, John Wooll, Ted George, R Cooper, BB)*; [139 London Rd], *Marquess of Wellington*: Carefully restored, with splendid gold and black Edwardian exterior, horsey prints, quiet comfort, Everards ales with a guest such as Hampshire Pendragon, reasonably priced food, colourful back courtyard with murals and attractive plants *(Joan and Michel Hooper-Immins)*; [185 Charles St], *Rainbow & Dove*: Convivial open-plan bare-boards bar nr station with enterprising new manager, well kept Banks's Bitter, Hansons Mild, Camerons Strongarm, Marstons Pedigree and three or four changing guest ales, farm cider, limited weekday lunchtime food; students evening, professionals too lunchtime, regular beer festivals, open all day *(Joan and Michel Hooper-Immins)*; [1 Wellington St], *Vaults*: Very basic concrete-floored former cellar wine bar now linked to Leatherbritches Brewery of Fenny Bentley, with their and other changing microbrews, some tapped from the cask; buoyant atmosphere, friendly staff, low ceiling with iron pillars, settle seating, stripped brick walls with old signs rather reminiscent of a railway station; cl Mon-Thurs lunchtime, has been open all day Fri-Sun, may be entrance fee for weekend live bands *(Rona Murdoch, the Didler, G Coates)*; [29 Market St], *Wilkies*: Bare yet cheerful, with imaginative lunchtime food inc German and Spanish, well kept Adnams, Boddingtons and other ales, up to three German or Belgian beers, farm cider, lots of continental bottled beers; open all day, cl Sun *(the Didler)*

Little Bowden [edge of Mkt Harboro, nr Sainsburys; SP7487], *Cherry Tree*: Attractive low-beamed thatched and timbered pub with two sitting rooms, lots of pictures, well kept Everards Beacon, Tiger and Old Original with a guest beer, good value food (not Sun evening) from filled baked potatoes up, games room, limited no-smoking dining room; can be a bit smoky elsewhere when busy, piped pop music may obtrude a bit; children welcome, garden with picnic-sets and play area, open all day Sat/Sun, nr 12th-c church *(Bryan and Betty Southwell, Stephen, Julie and Hayley Brown, George Atkinson)*

Loughborough [The Rushes (A6); SK5319], *Black Lion*: Wide range of Hoskins and other beers, stripped pine and pews, bare boards and sawdust in front bar area, cosier back lounge; very helpful bar service, good value simple food, peaceful at lunchtime but noisy evenings; handy for canal basin *(R Cooper)*; [Canal Bank, Meadow Lane], *Boat*: Picturesque refurbished canalside pub with good atmosphere, very obliging service, good food at reasonable prices inc bargain Sun lunch, good range of beers, boating memorabilia; very popular with local office staff weekday lunchtimes *(R Cooper)*; [36 Nottingham Rd], *Tap & Mallet*: Fairly plain pub distinguished by five or six changing microbrews, farm cider, occasional beer festivals; back garden, open all day Sat/Sun *(the Didler)*; [Churchgate], *Three Nuns*: Good range of beers and country wines, good value food the main lunchtime draw, popular with students at night *(R Cooper)*; [Sparrow Hill], *Windmill*: Oldest pub here, carefully restored, with good reasonably priced food inc tapas and other Spanish dishes, good atmosphere, friendly staff, Marstons Bitter and Pedigree, Spanish wine *(R Cooper)*

☆ **Market Bosworth** [1 Park St; from centre follow Leicester and Hinckley signs; SK4003], *Olde Red Lion*: Clean and plushly tidy black-beamed beamed split-level pub, with reasonable low-priced food inc vegetarian, obliging staff, Victorian tap room with real ales such as Banks's Bitter and Mild, Camerons, Marstons Pedigree, Ridleys Rumpus and Theakstons XB and Old Peculier, choice of ciders; piped light classics, occasional live music, children welcome, tables and play area in sheltered courtyard; bedrooms, attractive village *(Keith Day, George Atkinson, Joan and Michael Hooper-Immins, LYM)*

☆ **Market Overton** [Teigh Rd, nr church; SK8816], *Black Bull*: Attractive thatched pub with thriving lounge bar, good helpings of well cooked reasonably priced food here and in small back restaurant, very prompt welcoming service, well kept Ruddles Best, Theakstons and a guest such as Hook Norton, artificial pool and waterfall by entrance, nice atmosphere combining village pub and eating house; get there early Sun and in summer; pretty village, some tables out in front; bedrooms *(Bill and Sheila McLardy, Anthony Barnes)*

☆ **Markfield** [A50 just under a mile from M1 junction 22; SK4810], *Field Head*: Huge beamed lounge/dining area around hotel's island bar, pictures and tasteful bric-a-brac, friendly nooks and corners; good value generous food in bar and restaurant, well kept Hoskins and other ales, decent house wine; bedrooms, big breakfast *(Ash Samanta, Josie Wright, O K Smyth)*

Melton Mowbray [Burton St; by St Mary's Church; SK7518], *Anne of Cleves*: Medieval stonebuilt pub recently re-Tudorised, with exposed beams, nice fireplace, scrubbed tables – even Tudor piped music; plenty of atmosphere, enjoyable food, daily papers *(Chris Raisin, Graham Doyle, Meg and Colin Hamilton, Duncan Cloud)*

Mowsley [off A50 S of Leicester; SP6489], *Staff of Life*: Refurbished village pub, clean and attractive, with comfortable lounge bar, big back dining conservatory, good range of enjoyable freshly cooked food inc fresh fish and chargrills, well kept Bass, Boddingtons and Marstons Bitter and Pedigree; lovely back garden with terrace *(Stephen, Julie and Hayley Brown, Dorsan Baker)*

Muston [Church Lane; just off A52 W of Grantham; SK8237], *Muston Gap*: Former traditional village local stripped out (some mourn the loss of all those ancient features), now smartly and expensively extended into thriving Brewers Fayre, reliable reasonably priced food, play area outside (and a small one inside); wheelchair access *(R C Vincent)*

Nether Broughton [A606 Nottingham—Mowbray; SK6925], *Red Lion*: Comfortable food pub, wide choice inc good value Sun lunch, generous helpings, well kept ales, separate dining area; rabbits in garden *(Peter and Jenny Quine, Roger and Ruth Airey)*

☆ **Newton Burgoland** [Main St, off B586 W of Ibstock; SK3708], *Belper Arms*: Ancient rambling pub said to date from 13th c, friendly and interesting, with good reasonably priced food esp fish, also vegetarian, in roomy lounge and low-beamed areas off, masses of bric-a-brac, well kept Adnams, Marstons Pedigree and a guest beer, farm cider, good choice of malt whiskies, beer festivals (with live music), chatty landlord and staff, restaurant; children and locals' dogs welcome, resident ghost, big garden with play area *(Rona Murdoch, John Hancock)*

Oadby [Stoughton Farm Pk, Stoughton Rd – follow Farmworld signs off A6; SK6200], *Cow & Plough*: Pub in working farm open to the public 5-9 (and to farm patrons 12-2), up to seven real ales such as Belvoir Star, Fullers London Pride and Steamin' Billy, good choice of bottled beers, wines by the glass, Weston's cider; three rooms filled with brewing memorabilia, enamel signs, old church pews – no food; can watch milking and so forth *(Andy and Jill Kassube, Duncan Cloud, JP, PP)*

Oadby [Florence Wragg Way; SK6200], *Grange Farm*: Roomy and sympathetically converted attractive early 19th-c farmhouse, open fires, old local photographs, newspapers, wide range of imaginative generous food, no-smoking area, well kept Bass-related ales, decent wines, good choice of whiskies, good mix of customers *(Christopher Evans)*

Oakham [Station Yard; SK8508], *Grainstore*: Bare brick and boards, ex-Ruddles brewer producing his own Cooking, Triple B, Tom Cribb Winter Ale and Ten Fifty here; filled rolls, good service *(Joan and Michel Hooper-Immins, JP, PP)*; [S of Rutland Water, off A606 E, nr Empingham], *Normanton Park*: Refreshingly informal waterside hotel's Sailing Bar with interestingly varied choice of good if pricy food inc 'healthy' menu, well kept Morlands Old Speckled Hen, Ruddles Best and County and Tetleys; bedrooms, fine views *(M J Morgan, Gwen and Peter Andrews)*

Osgathorpe [SK4320], *Royal Oak*: Good all round, with fine big collection of horsebrasses; bedrooms excellent *(Mrs Gillian Connell)*

Packington [High St; SK3614], *Bull & Lion*: Quietly placed family-run pub with particularly well kept Marstons inc fortnightly specials, unpretentious and relaxed *(Mark Baynham, Rachael Ward)*

Peggs Green [just N of Swannington; nr junction A512/B587; SK4117], *New Inn*: Masses of bric-a-brac and farming memorabilia in two main rooms and snug, particularly well kept ales, friendly licensees with interesting Irish background; food limited to rolls *(B Adams)*

Preston [Uppingham Rd; SK8602], *Kingfisher*: Attractive flower-decked pub under friendly new landlord, lots of exposed stone, beams, plates, jugs, etc, all immaculate; very friendly efficient service, Marstons Pedigree, Tetleys and Worthingtons, comfortable chairs and sofas, reasonably priced usual food; games room, maybe piped music; tables in garden with slide *(Patrick Tailyour, Rona Murdoch)*

Ratcliffe Culey [signed off A444 Nuneaton—Burton; SP3299], *Gate*: Cosy low-ceilinged two-bar village pub with well kept Burtonwood, wide choice of reasonably priced good food, friendly staff, open fires; separate dining room; children welcome, swings in garden *(Mr and Mrs P K Cornock)*

Redmile [off A52 Grantham—Nottingham; SK8036], *Olde Windmill*: Welcoming and comfortable lounge and dining room, well kept Boddingtons and Ruddles, good house wines, good value bar food, pleasant restaurant and staff; tables outside *(Norma and Keith Bloomfield, K H Frostick)*

Ryhall [The Square; TF0310], *Green Dragon*: Village pub with consistently good generous food and service, attractive pillared lounge, close-set tables and open fire in plush dining area, separate public bar and plain games room; well kept Ansells Mild, Bass, Boddingtons, Greene King IPA and Tetleys, helpful service *(Jenny and Michael Back, K H Frostick)*

☆ **Saddington** [S of Leicester between A50 and A6 – OS Sheet 141 map ref 658918; SP6591], *Queens Head*: Welcoming, popular and very well run, with good food inc fresh mussels and good Sun lunch in recently built no-smoking dining room, separate smaller one for smokers, OAP bargain lunches, well kept Adnams, Everards Beacon and Tiger and a guest such as McMullens, quick service, daily papers; long sloping garden with lovely reservoir view *(John Saul, Patrick Tailyour, R Murdoch, Jean Cloud)*

Shawell [not far from M6 junction 1; village signed off A5/A427 roundabout – turn right in village; SP5480], *White Swan*: 17th-c beams, open fire, good bar food inc home-made pies, good hot beef baguettes and some unusual specialities, four real ales, friendly helpful service; some emphasis on good no-smoking panelled restaurant; cl lunchtime exc Sun *(Dr Alan Sutton, DAV)*

☆ **Sileby** [Swan St; SK6015], *White Swan*: Wide choice of interesting good value generous home-cooked food (not Sun eve or Mon lunchtime) in friendly and unspoilt sidestreet pub with comfortable and welcoming dining lounge; well kept Ansells and Marstons Pedigree, good house wines, entertaining boxer dogs, small tasteful restaurant (booking needed); children's playroom in converted back bowling alley with closed-circuit TV *(Stan and Hazel Allen)*

Somerby [Main St; SK7710], *Stilton Cheese*: Consistently good value food (three chefs in the family) inc game in season and good soups, in comfortable and friendly 16th-c stonebuilt pub with Marstons Pedigree, Ruddles County, Tetleys and a guest beer; upstairs restaurant, on edge of pretty village *(Joan and Michel Hooper-Immins, Denise and Quentin Thwaites)*

☆ **South Luffenham** [10 The Street; signed off A6121 nr Halfway House, then first right; SK9402], *Boot & Shoe*: Spotless village inn with comfortable rambling stripped-stone bar, good log fire, good value fish and pasta from Italian chef/patron, Tetleys, no-smoking eating area, evening restaurant; seats in neat small garden, pool in public bar; children welcome; four simple bedrooms, sharing two bathrooms – good breakfasts *(Howard and Margaret Buchanan, LYM)*

☆ **Stretton** [just by A1; SK9416], *Ram Jam*: Not a pub, but a good A1 stand-in – a civilised and relaxing modern version of a Great North Road coaching stop: mix of sofas and neat contemporary seating in airy modern upmarket cafe-restaurant, open fire, good unusual food from light snacks up, efficient service, good wines, freshly squeezed orange juice, fresh-ground coffee and so forth, daily papers; children welcome, comfortable bedrooms, open all day, food 7am-10pm *(Paul and Ursula Randall, John C Baker, Sue Blackburn, John Fahy, Lesley Sones, Francis Johnson, Eddy and Emma Gibson, Luke Worthington, Frank Davidson, Mr and Mrs D Powell, LYM)*

Stretton *Jackson Stops*: Thatched pub in quiet village, well kept Ruddles and Theakstons, decent wines, good range of generous freshly cooked standard food inc good puddings, log fire, old farm tools, pleasant landlord, bar on left kept for drinkers; local for three-nation fighter squadron at RAF Cottesmore with lots of relevant memorabilia; may cl at 2 *(M J Brooks, RB, LYM)*

Tur Langton [off B6047; follow Kibworth signpost from village centre; SP7194], *Crown*: Attractive pub with decent food inc lunchtime, well kept Bass and other ales, very welcoming landlord, traditional lounge bar, plush public bar with juke box, machines and TV (popular with younger customers), separate restaurant with own bar, tables under cocktail parasols on terrace; no food Sun or Mon evenings *(P Devitt, LYM)*

Ullesthorpe [Main St; SP5087], *Chequers*: Big country inn popular with lunchtime businessmen, beamed and flagstoned bar and most of lounge areas with emphasis on very wide choice of reasonably priced food from large servery (pay as you order), real ales such as Batemans XXXB, Gales HSB and Theakstons Old Peculier, faint semi-classical music, no-smoking areas; normally prompt service; children welcome, family room and play area; comfortable bedrooms *(Nigel Wilson, PT)*; [Main St], *Swan*: Nicely refurbished with upmarket touches, wide choice of food from sandwiches or hot baguettes up inc vegetarian, pasta and Scotch beef, attentive staff *(Anon)*

Uppingham [High St East/Market Sq; SP8699], *Falcon*: Fine old-fashioned town-centre hotel with comfortable and light lounge, big windows over market sq, civilised light lunches, good coffee and afternoon tea, serious dailies and fashionable magazines; well kept real ales in oak-panelled bar; bedrooms *(John Bowdler)*; [Market Sq], *Vaults*: Attractive pub overlooking square, tables outside; well kept Marstons Pedigree, popular food; bedrooms *(Margaret and Roy Randle)*; [High Street W], *White Hart*: Wide choice of good value simple tasty food using local produce, inglenook fire in panelled front lounge, quite a warren of passages and rooms, three well kept real ales, reasonably priced wines, good service, back restaurant; bedrooms *(E J Locker)*

Walton on the Wolds [Loughborough Rd; SK5919], *Anchor*: Long rambling open-plan pub popular lunchtime with businessmen for straightforward food; friendly and unpretentious local evening atmosphere, well kept ales such as Exmoor Gold, Timothy Taylor Landlord and a seasonal beer from Marstons; can get smoky Sat night; tables outside, nice village *(Rona Murdoch)*

☆ **Welham** [off B664 Mkt Harboro—Uppingham; SP7692], *Old Red Lion*: Popular dining pub (part of small local chain) with several beamed rooms and attractive if rather dark barrel-vaulted back area, limited choice of low-priced good food inc good steaks, Courage Best and Directors, decent wines, efficient hard-working staff, no-smoking areas, lovely fire; piped music may be loudish *(Stephen and Julie Brown)*

☆ **Whitwell** [A606 Stamford—Oakham; SK9208], *Noel Arms*: Wide choice of good food (till 10) esp fish and delicious puddings, in spaciously extended plush dining lounge, smart customers; cheerful local atmosphere in original unpretentious little front rooms, well kept Marstons Pedigree and Timothy Taylor Landlord, charming quick service, suntrap tables outside, occasional barbecues; piped music, can get busy; handy for Rutland Water, children welcome; bedrooms *(David Eberlin, Mr and Mrs M Reeve, LYM)*

Wigston [Leicester Rd; SK5900], *Bell*: Open-plan, with old local photographs, interesting good value food, real ales inc guests (a Festival Ale House), good choice of malt whiskies *(Veronica Brown)*; [114 Leicester Rd], *Star & Garter*: Interesting good value food in quiet and cosy little two-bar pub, Everards and guest ales, several good malt whiskies, back garden and tables out in front *(Veronica Brown)*; [84 Leicester Rd], *William Wygston*: Roomy new Wetherspoons in converted supermarket (you'd never know), bright and airy, with their usual well presented food and six well kept real ales (more during beer festivals); accessible if not exactly riveting books *(Veronica Brown, Joan and Michel Hooper-Immins)*

Wing [3 Top St, signed off A6003 S of Oakham; SK8903], *Cuckoo*: Welcoming thatched open-plan pub, good value generous food (not Tues) esp curries, well kept Bass, Marstons Pedigree and interesting guest beers, nice log fires, midsummer beer festival, cuckoo clock, darts and pool at one end, dining area with small fishtank the other; children and dogs welcome, weekend live music, plenty of tables in tidy garden *(Jack and Gemma Valiant, JJW, CMW)*

☆ **Woodhouse Eaves** [Church Hill; main street, off B591 W of Quorndon; SK5214], *Pear Tree*: Attractive upper flagstoned food area with pitched roof and pews forming booths, open kitchen doing enjoyable food (not Sun night) from sandwiches up; more conventional turkey-carpeted lower pub part with conservatory, log fire, Ansells, Bass, Ind Coope Burton and Marstons Pedigree, good choice of malt whiskies, decent wines; children welcome, open all day bank hol weekends, picnic-sets and summer bar outside, good nearby walks *(Jenny and Michael Back, LYM)*

☆ **Woodhouse Eaves** [Brand Hill, beyond main st – OS Sheet 129 map ref 533148], *Wheatsheaf*: Plush and busy open-plan beamed country pub, smart customers, pleasant service, good if not cheap home-cooked food inc sandwiches and vegetarian, Bass, Ruddles County, Timothy Taylor Landlord and several well kept weekly changing guest ales, decent wines, log fires, upstairs restaurant; floodlit tables outside, dogs welcome but no motor-cyclists or children *(P J Caunt, Alan Johnson, Joan and Michel Hooper-Immins, Duncan Cloud, LYM)*

Post Office address codings confusingly give the impression that some pubs are in Leicestershire, when they're really in Cambridgeshire (which is where we list them).

Lincolnshire

Several pubs here have exceptional individual claims to fame: the cheerful Cider Centre at Brandy Wharf with its unique range of ciders and perries; and the Beehive in Grantham, a nice little pub with very cheap food, and the unique living beehive inn-sign which it's had for centuries (we remember a few years ago the landlord leaving us drinking in the bar as he went off to retrieve a swarm – not from his hive, as it turned out – from a neighbour's tree). Other pubs doing particularly well in the county are the Wishing Well at Dyke (good food and beer – they'll soon have topped the thousand mark, in the number of different guest beers they've had), the Chequers at Gedney Dyke (very good food, especially fish), the Victoria in Lincoln (a new main entry, a fine old-fashioned alehouse really flourishing under the landlord who took it over a couple of years ago), the more decorous Wig & Mitre there (an unusual place, with enjoyable food all day), the civilised Red Lion at Newton (first-class buffet, top-quality meats and fish – good salads too), the good value Abbey Lodge at Woodhall Spa, and that grand old inn the George in Stamford. This last place has good food, good beer, good wine, and rooms and courtyard of great character: the George of Stamford is our choice as Lincolnshire Dining Pub of the Year. The Lucky Dip at the end of the chapter shows a good choice of places in Lincoln; outside, the places currently generating the widest support from readers are the Leagate outside Coningsby, Vine in Skegness and White Hart at Tetford – all inspected and approved by us. Drinks prices in Lincolnshire have gone up more than elsewhere this year, and are now closely in line with the national average. The own-brews at the Brewers Arms in Snaith were much cheaper than average – as were the beers at the Victoria in Lincoln. The proudly independent local family brewer Batemans is a great source of delight for beer-loving visitors to Lincolnshire, with beers as distinctive as many of its charming little red brick tied pubs.

ALLINGTON SK8540 Map 7

Welby Arms

The Green; off A1 N of Grantham, or A52 W of Grantham

There's a warm and relaxing atmosphere, good straightforward food and a fine range of ales at this pleasantly set village local; it's an excellent respite from the A1. A stone archway divides the two rooms of the bar; there are comfortable burgundy button-back wall banquettes and stools, some Lloyd Loom chairs, black beams and joists, red velvet curtains, a coal fire in one stone fireplace and logs burning in an attractive arched brick fireplace. One area has lots of signed celebrity photographs (Phil Collins, Gary Lineker etc); the dining lounge off to one side is no smoking; piped music. Tasty home-cooked food might include home-made soup (£2.45), garlic mushrooms (£3.25), chicken and broccoli bake or home-made lasagne (£5.65), steak and ale pie (£5.95), gammon and egg or pineapple (£6.25), steaks (from £8.45) and mixed grill (£8.95); the fresh Grimsby haddock in beer batter is especially well liked by readers; advisable to book especially at weekends. Bass, John Smiths, Timothy Taylor Landlord and up to six guests such as Oakham Old Tosspot or Phoenix Wobbly Bob served through a sparkler but kept well, decent wines and a good range of country wines; tables on the sheltered terrace at the back and picnic-sets on the lawn in front. *(Recommended by John Fahy, Tony Gayfer, P W Taylor, P Stallard, H Bramwell, D S and A R Hare, John Baker, DC, Steven M Gent, Joy and Peter Heatherley, Derek and Sylvia Stephenson, Avis Spencer, Stephen Brown, Chris Mawson, Keith and Norma Bloomfield, Colin and Sue Graham, Keith Wright)*

Free house ~ Licensee Bob Dyer ~ Real ale ~ Meals and snacks (not Sun evening) ~ Restaurant ~ (01400) 281361 ~ Children welcome in restaurant ~ Open 12-2.30(3 Sat), 6-11; 12-3, 7-10.30 Sun

ASWARBY TF0639 Map 8

Tally Ho

A15 S of Sleaford (but N of village turn-off)

The new licensees at this handsome 17th-c stone-built inn are planning few changes and hope to retain its gently civilised atmosphere. The country style bar has dark oak beams and cast-iron-framed tables, a big log fire, some stripped masonry and country prints; maybe piped music. Well kept Bass, Batemans XB and a guest on handpump, good house wines; daily papers. Besides soup (£2.25), lincolnshire sausage (£3.50), ploughman's or filled french bread (£3.95), blackboard specials might include four-cheese tartlet or smoked mackerel pâté (£3.50), warm duck leg salad (£3.75), mediterranean vegetable lasagne (£5.75), chicken pieces in pepper and orange sauce (£6.50), salmon fillet with pesto or lamb kebabs and rice (£6.75) and steak (£8.95); they take great care and attention with the home-made puddings which might include German cheesecake or plum pie (£2.50). It's wise to book for the attractive pine-furnished restaurant. There are tables out behind among fruit trees, and usually sheep in the meadow beyond. The bedrooms are in a neatly converted back block, formerly the dairy and a barn. Over the road, the pretty estate church, glimpsed through the stately oaks of the park, is worth a visit. *(Recommended by JCW, M Morgan, Dr G Sanders, June and Malcolm Farmer, Bill and Brenda Lemon, Humphry and Angela Crum Ewing, Sue and Bob Ward, Julia and Peter Baker, Stephen Brown, F and A Parmenter; more reports on the new regime please)*

Free house ~ Licensees Peter and Christine Robertson ~ Real ale ~ Meals and snacks ~ Restaurant ~ (01529) 455205 ~ Children in eating area of bar and in restaurant ~ Open 12-3, 6-11; 12-3, 7-10.30 Sun ~ Bedrooms: £33B/£48B

BRANDY WHARF TF0197 Map 8

Cider Centre

B1205 SE of Scunthorpe (off A15 about 16 miles N of Lincoln)

Set in four acres of orchard and meadow, this unusual pub is a shrine to cider. The main bar is a simple room with wheelback chairs and brown plush wall banquettes, cheery customer photographs, a good little coal fire, and – most importantly – Addlestone's, Scrumpy Jack and Weston's Old Rosie on handpump, and some five dozen other farm ciders and perries – up to 8 tapped from casks, the rest from stacks of intriguing bottles and small plastic or earthenware kegs on shelves behind the bar; they also keep country wines and mead. The friendly landlord's very happy to talk cider, and will on request show you his extraordinary collection of hundreds of different cider flagons, jugs and bottles. A dim-lit lounge bar has all sorts of cider memorabilia and good-humoured sidelights on cider-making and drinking (not to mention the foot of 'Cyril the Plumber' poking down through the ceiling); there is also a small museum. Good value generous plain food includes sandwiches (£1.80), ploughman's (from £3), pork and cider sausage (£4.20), home-made steak and vegetable pie (£5.20), and chicken curry (£5.20), with wonderful real chips; piped British folk music. A simple glazed verandah overlooks the river, and there's lots of space outside with an orchard, a caravan site, moorings and slipway; quite a few appropriate special events. No children. *(Recommended by JP, PP, CMW, JJW, M J Morgan, Pat and Tony Martin, Andy and Jill Kassube)*

Free house ~ Licensee Ian Horsley ~ Meals and snacks (not Tues lunchtime or Mon in winter) ~ (01652) 678364 ~ Open 12-3(maybe 2.30 in winter), 7-11(10.30 Sun); cl Mon lunchtimes mid Oct-Easter; cl Fri before Christmas-early Jan

COLEBY SK9760 Map 8

Bell

Far Lane; village signposted off A607 S of Lincoln, turn right and right into Far Lane at church

Generously served and well presented food is always complemented by a very warm welcome and friendly service at this 18th-c dining pub. The bar menu includes spicy chicken wings, pâté or crispy mushrooms (£2.95), beef, mushroom and Murphy's pie (£6.50), asparagus strudel (£7.25), mushroom stroganoff (£5.25), gammon steak with egg or pineapple (£7.50), chicken kiev (£8.25), boeuf stroganoff (£8.95), pork fillet with a creamy dijon sauce (£9.25), steaks (from £11.95) and mixed grill (£15.95). salmon fillet (£8.25), chicken topped with smoked salmon and prawns en croûte with cream and mushroom sauce (£8.95), steaks (from £9.95), and specials like pork, apple and cider casserole (£5.95) and chicken breast with asparagus sauce (£8.25). Wednesday night is fish night with fresh fish delivered from Grimsby, and on Saturday and Sunday morning from 9.30 to 11.45 they serve a big breakfast with Sunday newspapers; no-smoking restaurant. The three communicating carpeted rooms have roaring winter log fires and low black joists, and the lounge is decorated with horsebrasses, a variety of small prints, and lots of number plates from around the world. Well kept Bass, Flowers Original, and Tetleys on handpump, and several malt whiskies. Several picnic-sets outside, and walks along the Viking Way. *(Recommended by F J Willy, M Morgan, Tony and Wendy Hobden, John Cooper, M J Morgan, Ken and Jenny Simmonds, Brian Skelcher, Stephen G Brown, Simon Collett-Jones, David and Ruth Hollands, Andy and Jill Kassube, Canon and Mrs M Bourdeaux, Brian Horner)*

Pubmaster ~ Tenants Robert and Sara Pickles ~ Real ale ~ Meals and snacks (served all day) ~ Restaurant ~ (01522) 810240 ~ Children welcome in eating area of bar ~ Live bands Fri evenings ~ Open 11-11; 12-10.30 Sun ~ Bedrooms: /£38.45B

DYKE TF1022 Map 8

Wishing Well

21 Main Street; village signposted off A15 N of Bourne

They keep a running tally over the bar of the number of different real ales served at this welcoming black and white village inn – as we went to press they had almost reached the thousand mark. The landlord is quite a beer buff and the well kept changing real ales are sometimes quite unusual; there might be Batemans Jawbreaker, Everards Tiger, Greene King Abbot, Morlands Aunt Sally, Tetleys Bitter, Woodfordes Wherry and possibly one brewed for the pub by Enderby called Going Down Well, all on handpump. Well liked and good value food includes home-made soup (£2.10), sandwiches (from £2.30), jacket potatoes (from £3.10), ploughman's (from £4.75), lincolnshire sausages with chips, egg and peas (£4.75), home-made pies, home-made meat or vegetarian lasagne, seafood platter, gammon and egg, or chicken tikka (£5.95), steak (£6.95), children's meals (£2.50) and a wide range of daily specials; popular Sunday lunch (£8.50; children £5.50; must book). There is a wishing well at the dining end of the long, rambling bustling front bar – as well as lots of heavy beams, dark stone, brasswork, candlelight and a cavern of an open fireplace. The carpeted lounge area has green plush button-back low settles and wheelback chairs around individual wooden tables. The quite separate public bar, smaller and plainer, has sensibly placed darts, pool, fruit machine, video game and piped music. There's a small conservatory and tables in the garden; play area. *(Recommended by M Morgan, Jenny and Michael Back, Eric Locker, Paul and Ursula Randall, Mark J Hydes, Jill Bickerton, M J Morgan)*

Free house ~ Licensee Barrie Creaser ~ Real ale ~ Meals and snacks ~ Restaurant ~ (01778) 422970 ~ Children welcome ~ Open 11-2.30, 6.30-11(10.30 Sun) ~ Bedrooms: £25S/£49S

Pubs brewing their own beers are listed at the back of the book.

GEDNEY DYKE TF4125 Map 8

Chequers

Village signposted off A17 Holbeach—Kings Lynn

Although this stylish but friendly and informal Fenland pub is popular with readers for its good imaginative food, the bar retains a comfortable mix of locals, drinkers and diners. Everything's kept spotless, with an open fire in the bar, a small rather old-fashioned no-smoking restaurant area at one end, and an elegant dining conservatory at the other, overlooking a garden with picnic-sets. A speciality is the really fresh fish and seafood specials such as cromer crab salad, seared monkfish with herb crumb and coriander relish and seabass fillet with beurre blanc sauce; there may also be gloucester old spot pork or gressingham duck. There's a wide choice of other well cooked and attractively presented food, including home-made soup (£2.50), open sandwiches (from £3.95), ploughman's, pâté or warm goat's cheese salad (£4.50), chestnut and vegetable roast (£6.50), cajun spiced chicken supreme (£6.95), seared supreme of guineafowl with caramelised shallots and balsamic dressing (£8.95) and pan-fried aberdeen angus sirloin on a crispy crouton with smoked salmon and creamy horseradish sauce (£9.50); good home-made puddings; roast Sunday lunch; service is friendly and professional. Well kept Adnams Bitter, Bass, Elgood Pageant, and Morlands Old Speckled Hen on handpump, about ten decent wines by the glass, elderflower pressé and apple juice. *(Recommended by R Macnaughton, Alan Morton, JDM, KM, W K Wood, R Wiles, Geoffrey Lawrance, Stephen G Brown, Derek and Sylvia Stephenson, Peter Burton, Geoff Tomlinson, Chris and Shirley Machin, Mr and Mrs N Thorp, John Wooll)*

Free house ~ Licensee Judith Marshall ~ Real ale ~ Meals and snacks ~ Restaurant ~ (01406) 362666 ~ Children welcome ~ Open 12-2, 6(7 winter weekdays)-11; 12-3, 7-10.30 Sun; cl 25/26 Dec

GRANTHAM SK9135 Map 7

Beehive £

Castlegate; from main street turn down Finkin Street opposite St Peter's Place

This simple no-frills pub's real claim to fame is its remarkable sign – a hive full of living bees, mounted in a lime tree. It's been here since at least 1830, and probably the eighteenth century, making this one of the oldest populations of bees in the world and if the landlord is not behind the bar he is probably up a ladder checking them out. The comfortably straightforward bar which is popular with students has a bustling, friendly atmosphere, and Batemans XB, and two guests like Shepherd Neame Spitfire and South Yorkshire Barnsley Bitter on handpump. Very good value bar food includes home-made soup (£1.50), sandwiches or good value basic ploughman's (from £1.80), filled baked potatoes (from £2.30), burgers (from £2.35), omelettes, crispy fried vegetables or home-made chilli (£2.95), lincolnshire sausages (£3.25), gammon and egg (£3.30), breaded haddock (£3.40) and puddings like hot chocolate fudge cake and spotted dick (£1.60); cheerful service. Fruit machine, pinball, trivia, video game and piped music. *(Recommended by Shirley Mackenzie, JP, PP, Stephen Brown, Andy and Jill Kassube)*

Free house ~ Licensee Stuart J Parkes ~ Real ale ~ Lunchtime meals and snacks (not Sun) ~ (01476) 404554 ~ Well behaved children welcome till 8pm ~ Open 11-11; 7-10.30 Sun; closed 25 Dec

HECKINGTON TF1444 Map 8

Nags Head

High Street; village signposted from A17 Sleaford—Boston

The landlady prepares consistently good homely bar food at this low white-painted 17th-c village inn. The changing selection might include sandwiches or carrot and orange soup (£2.50), garlic mushrooms on a crouton or pâté (£3.25), pears and stilton grilled on toast (£3.50), hot beef or pork and stuffing sandwich (£4.25), ploughman's (£4.50), smoked salmon, salmon and prawn quiche (£5.25), potato, cheese and leek pie (£5.50), lincolnshire sausage pie (£5.75) and warm salmon with cream, lemon and chives or grilled tuna steak with tomato and basil (£6.50) as well as puddings like rhubarb crumble (all £2.50). The snug two-roomed bar has a comfortable lived-in feel; the left-hand part of has a coal fire below a shiny black wooden chimney-piece in what must once have been a great inglenook, curving into the corner and taking up the whole of one end of the small room – it now houses three tables, one of them of beaten brass. On the right there are red plush button-back built-in wall banquettes, small spindleback chairs, and an attractive bronze statuette-lamp on the mantlepiece of its coal fire; also, a lively watercolour of a horse-race finish (the horses racing straight towards you), and a modern sporting print of a problematic gun dog. Well kept Wards Sheffield Best and Double Maxim, and a guest beer on handpump; darts, pool, shove-ha'penny, shut the box, fruit machine, and juke box. The garden behind has picnic-sets, and it's not far to an unusual eight-sailed windmill. *(Recommended by Stephen Brown, Don and Shirley Parish, John Watt, Tony and Wendy Hobden, G G Lawrence, Andy and Jill Kassube, R E and P Pearce, K and J Brooks)*

Wards ~ Lease: Bruce Pickworth ~ Real ale ~ Meals and snacks ~ (01529) 460218 ~ Well behaved children welcome at lunchtime ~ Open 11-3, 5-11; 12-3, 7-10.30 Sun ~ Bedrooms: £22/£32

LINCOLN SK9771 Map 8

Victoria

6 Union Road

Tucked away in a back street behind the castle, this is a proper alehouse – a classic quaint early Victorian local, with no airs and graces, and few concessions to comfort. The atmosphere is really buoyant – homely, warm and chatty. The plainly furnished little front lounge has a coal fire and some good Queen Victoria pictures. It's always bustling, and can get very crowded at lunchtime and in the later part of the evening – especially when the city's Christmas Fair is on, when you can scarcely squeeze in; darts. Besides well kept Batemans XB, Brains SA, Castlelock Hemlock, Everards Old Original, and Timothy Taylor Landlord on handpump, they have around half a dozen interesting changing guest beers such as Caledonian Murrays Summer Ale, Castlelock Elsi Mow, Hook Norton Haymaker, Jennings Dark Mild or Ruddles Best, also foreign draught and bottled beers, and country wines; there are beer festivals the third week in June and the last week in November. Lunchtime food includes well filled cobs (from £1.20, the bacon ones, £2.25, are a meal in themselves), ploughman's (£3.25), all-day breakfast and basic home-made hot dishes such as beef stew, steak and kidney pie, chilli or curry (£3.50); Sunday roast; friendly staff; no children. *(Recommended by Gwyneth and Salvo Spadaro-Dutturi, B R Shiner, Andrew Young, Mark J Hydes, Jon Hale, JP, PP, the Didler)*

Free house ~ Manager: Neil Renshaw ~ Real ale ~ Lunchtime meals and snacks ~ Restaurant (Sunday lunchtime only) ~ (01522) 536048 ~ Impromptu folk/rock jam sessions first Sun lunchtime in month ~ Open 11-11; 12-10.30 Sun; closed 25 Dec

Wig & Mitre ★

29 Steep Hill; just below cathedral

As we went to press the licensees told us that they were in the process of buying this welcoming old pub from Sam Smiths. They serve an incredible range of very well prepared food from several different menus – including a full breakfast menu (English breakfast £7.50) – from 8 o'clock in the morning to closing, and even when busy the service is always cordial and efficient. The various menus differ in style and none are particularly cheap. Dishes might include sandwiches (from £4.95), lightly curried parsnip soup (£3.50), warm salad of chicken liver with shallots and balsamic vinegar (£6), baked cheese soufflé with stilton and mushrooms (£6.25), home-made lasagne (£6.50), coq au vin (£6.95), roasted vegetable risotto with saffron and herbs (£9), roast fillet of halibut with garlic crumb on a red pepper and tomato sauce (£14.50), saddle of venison with cabbage and bacon with a cracked peppercorn sauce (£15.50) and pan-fried fillet steak with oyster mushrooms and roquefort butter (£16.50); puddings include tiramisu or raspberry and mascarpone crème brûlée (£3.75). There's an excellent and extensive, if somewhat pricy, selection of over 95 wines, many of them available by the glass. Sam Smiths OB on handpump, lots of liqueurs and spirits, and freshly squeezed orange juice. Many of the building's original 14th-c features have been carefully preserved: there's a section of the original lime-ash and reed floor, exposed oak rafters, and part of the medieval wattle-and-daub by the stairs. Downstairs, the cheerful, simpler bar has pews and other more straightforward furniture on its tiles, and a couple of window tables on either side of the entrance; the civilised upstairs dining room has settees, elegant small settles, Victorian armchairs, shelves of old books, and an open fire, and is decorated with antique prints and more modern caricatures of lawyers and clerics, with plenty of newspapers and periodicals lying about. *(Recommended by Shirley Mackenzie, Meg and Colin Hamilton, R Wiles, Neil Glover, Christopher Beadle, Francis Johnson, Maysie Thompson, JP, PP, Peter and Pat Frogley, Robert Gomme, Peter Burton, M Kershaw, David and Ruth Hollands, Canon and Mrs M Bourdeaux, J Oglanby, Walter and Susan Rinaldi-Butcher, Ian Phillips, Tony Dickinson, Chris Raisin, Graham Doyle)*

Free house ~ Licensees Michael Hope and Paul Vidic ~ Real ale ~ Meals and snacks (8-11; 8-10.30 Sun) ~ Restaurant ~ (01522) 535190 ~ Children welcome in restaurant ~ Open 8-11(10.30 Sun)

NEWTON TF0436 Map 8

Red Lion ★ (🍴)

Village signposted from A52 E of Grantham; pub itself also discreetly signed off A52

The licensee at this impeccably kept civilised old place used to be a butcher, and it does show – the meat and fish could hardly taste better. Besides blackboard specials such as vegetarian pasta and ratatouille (£5.95), steak pie, hotpot, liver and onions or chicken curry (£6.95), fisherman's hotpot (£7.50), lamb cutlets, gammon and egg, or pork chops (£8), they offer an impressive cold buffet with a splendid choice of meats, fish and salads – you help yourself to as much as you like, a small helping is £8.95, normal £9.95, and large £12.95, with children's helpings £4.50. On Saturday evening and Sunday lunchtime there are also four roasts; no-smoking area in dining room. The welcoming communicating rooms have fresh flowers, old-fashioned oak and elm seats and cream-rendered or bare stone walls covered with farm tools, malters' wooden shovels, a stuffed fox, stag's head and green woodpecker, pictures made from pressed flowers, and hunting and coaching prints. Well kept Bass and Batemans XXXB on handpump; friendly service, piped music, a fruit machine, and a nice dog. During the day and at weekends two squash courts run by the pub can be used by non-members. The neat, well sheltered back garden has some seats on the grass and on a terrace, and a good play area. The countryside nearby is ideal for walking, and acccording to local tradition this village is the highest point between Grantham and the Urals. *(Recommended by M Morgan, G Neighbour, M J Morgan, R Wiles, Andy and Jill Kassube, Brian and Jill Bond, RB, James Nunn)*

Free house ~ Licensee Graham Watkin ~ Real ale ~ Meals and snacks ~ (01529) 497256 ~ Children welcome ~ Open 12-3, 6-11(7-10.30 Sun); closed 25 Dec

STAMFORD TF0207 Map 8

George ★ (🍴) 🛏 🍷

71 High St, St Martins

Lincolnshire Dining Pub of the Year

Steeped in history, this smartly bustling old coaching inn has retained its character despite now having every modern comfort. It was built in 1597 for Lord Burghley, though there are surviving parts of a much older Norman pilgrim's hospice – and a crypt under the cocktail bar that may be 1000 years old. There's a medley of seats in its civilised, but relaxed rooms ranging from sturdy bar settles through leather, cane and antique wicker to soft settees and easy chairs, while the central lounge has sturdy timbers, broad flagstones, heavy beams, and massive stonework; some claim that you can see a ghostly girl's face in the wooden panelling in the London room. The nicest place for lunch (if it's not a warm sunny day) is the indoor Garden Lounge, with well spaced white cast-iron furniture on herringbone glazed bricks around a central tropical grove. Not cheap but very good bar food includes soup of the day with Italian bread (£3.95), chicken liver pâté with orange and redcurrant sauce (£5.55), pasta and gnocchi dishes or warm salad of chicken strips, smoked bacon, avocado, spinach and cherry tomatoes (£8.95), fresh haddock from Billingsgate (£9.95), deep-fried rabbit, chicken and mediterranean vegetables with a trio of sauces (£11.95) and seared salmon on a bed of couscous with a yoghurt and basil sauce or chargrilled sirloin steak (£12.45), or a splendidly tempting help-yourself buffet (£12.95); in the York bar there are lighter snacks such as ciabatta sandwiches (from £3.50), cheddar and stilton platter with ciabatta bread (£5.55), and open ham and cheese toasted sandwiches (£4.75). Well kept Adnams Broadside, Ruddles Best and a guest on handpump, but the best drinks are the Italian wines, many of which are good value and sold by the glass; also freshly squeezed orange juice, filter, espresso or cappuccino coffee; friendly and very professional staff. There's waiter drinks service in the cobbled courtyard at the back which is lovely in summer, with comfortable chairs and tables among attractive plant tubs and colourful hanging baskets; there's also a neatly maintained walled garden, with a sunken lawn where croquet is often played. *(Recommended by R Wiles, Brian Wainwright, Maysie Thompson, Christine and Geoff Butler, D Stokes, Paul and Pam Penrose, John Fahy, G Neighbour, J F M West, Neville Kenyon, David and Ruth Hollands, Deborah Weston, Rona Murdoch, Stephen Holman, Sue Holland, Dave Webster, Joan and Tony Walker, Julian Holland, Angela Copeland; also in the Good Hotel Guide)*

Free house ~ Licensees Ivo Vannocci and Chris Pitman ~ Real ale ~ Meals and snacks (all day) ~ Two restaurants ~ (01780) 750750 ~ Children welcome ~ Open 11-11; 12-10.30 Sun ~ Bedrooms: £78B/£100B

WOODHALL SPA TF1963 Map 8

Abbey Lodge

Tattersall Rd, Kirkstead (B1192 Woodhall Spa—Coningsby)

Readers report this solid roadside inn a reliable and popular place for a good meal. The discreetly decorated bar has some Victorian or older furnishings, and pictures showing its World War II connections with RAF Coningsby – Squadron 627, based at the former airfield opposite, still holds reunion dinners here. Good reasonably priced bar food includes sandwiches (from £1.25), omelettes (from £4), macaroni cheese (£4.25), ploughman's (£4.50), lamb lasagne (£4.95), haddock (£5.25), boneless pink trout (£6.25) chicken with garlic butter or sweet and sour sauce (£6.50), steaks (from £8.95), blackboard specials and a wide selection of puddings; the restaurant has good Sunday roasts. Well kept Bass and Worthington on handpump; affable licensee; friendly and efficient service; no children. *(Recommended by Mark J Hydes, Richard Cole, W W Burke, Bill and Sheila McLardy, G W Stephenson, G G Lawrence)*

Free house ~ Licensee Mrs A J Inglis ~ Real ale ~ Meals and snacks (till 10pm Fri, Sat) ~ Restaurant ~ (01526) 352538 ~ Open 11-2.30, 6.30-11; 12-2.30 Sun

Lucky Dip

Besides the fully inspected pubs, you might like to try these Lucky Dips recommended to us and described by readers (if you do, please send us reports):

Alford [26 West St (A1004); TF4576], *Half Moon*: Good choice of well kept ales and decent cheap food inc adaptable menu for children in decorous lounge, dining area and spacious L-shaped bar; children welcome, back games area, nice fairy-lit back garden with barbecues *(P and R Baker, BB)*

Ancaster [High St (B6403); SK9843], *Ermine Way*: Well kept beers and good value food inc generous Sun lunch in bar and lounge/restaurant; bedrooms *(Mrs J Nuttall)*

☆ **Barholm** [off A16 Stamford—Mkt Deeping; TF0810], *Five Horseshoes*: Old-fashioned relaxed village local, clean, cosy and friendly, with well kept Adnams, Batemans and interesting guest beers, mini beer festivals, decent wines, comfortable seats, rustic bric-a-brac, maybe weekend food; tables out under shady arbour, weekend barbecues, paddocks behind *(M J Morgan, Alan and Heather Jacques, BB)*

☆ **Barnoldby le Beck** [SW of Grimsby; TA2303], *Ship*: Warm well furnished nautical-theme country pub with good sensibly priced home cooking inc game, vegetarian, esp fresh Grimsby fish, friendly attentive service, good range of wines, comfortable dining room, pleasant village setting; bedrooms *(Maggie Middleton, John Cooper, Marie and Edwin Legard)*

Belchford [E of A153 Horncastle—Louth; TF2975], *Blue Bell*: Three well kept interesting guest beers, simple food inc delicious home-made pies, good local trout and good value Sun lunch, nicely refurbished bar, pleasant atmosphere *(M J Morgan)*

☆ **Boston** [Wormgate; TF3244], *Goodbarns Yard*: Wide choice of good value home-made food from filled french bread and baked potatoes to steaks inc interesting snacks in popular and comfortable place, well kept Theakstons and guest ales, old beams in original core (former riverside cottages looking up to Boston Stump), modern but matching back extension, plenty of alcoves, terrace overlooking river *(Tony Albert, O K Smyth)*

Bracebridge Heath [St Johns Park; A15 S of Lincoln; SK9867], *Homestead*: Tom Cobleigh pub rather reminiscent of a Wetherspoons, with no-smoking area, wide choice of ales, decent food inc children's and vegetarian, friendly staff *(Tony and Wendy Hobden)*

Candlesby [A153 Skegness—Horncastle; TF4567], *Royal Oak*: Consistently good home-made food, lots of imagination, local game, fish and veg, particularly well kept Batemans XB, coffee ad lib, no rush; handy for Gunby Hall *(Steven Gent)*

Carlton le Moorland [Church St; SK9058], *White Hart*: Friendly and comfortable beamed village pub with good choice of good reasonably priced freshly prepared food inc Sun lunch; children welcome, Thurs quiz night; fruit machine, TV, piped pop music; garden with play area *(CMW, JJW)*

☆ **Castle Bytham** [High St; SK9818], *Castle*: Warm welcome, consistently good generous well presented food (not Mon evening), imaginative if not cheap, efficient service, Ansells Mild, Boddingtons Best and Gold, Tetleys, Theakstons Best and guests such as Shepherd Neame Bishops Finger and York Stonewall, roaring log fire, no-smoking dining room with huge pig collection; soft piped music, no children at the bar; CCTV for parked cars *(Jenny and Michael Back, E J Locker)*

Caythorpe [SK9348], *Red Lion*: Friendly and homely 16th-c pub in pleasant surroundings, wide choice of fair-priced food from sandwiches to good fresh Grimsby fish and Whitby scampi, well kept ales inc Boddingtons, Greene King Abbot, Timothy Taylor Landlord and Youngs Special, no piped music, attentive service *(Peter Burton)*

Cleethorpes [High Cliff Rd; south promenade; TA3008], *Willys*: Modern bistro-style pub with cafe tables, tiled floor and painted brick walls; brews its own good beers, also well kept guest beers and well priced basic lunchtime food; friendly staff, quiet juke box, Humber estuary views; annual beer festival *(R M Taylor, JP, PP)*

Coleby [Hill Rise; SK9760], *Tempest Arms*: Roomy, friendly and comfortable local, with well kept Batemans XB, nicely presented interesting food Thurs-Sat, good service, friendly spaniel, lots of hanging baskets, wonderful view from pretty garden; on Viking Way *(M J Morgan, M Kershaw, Mike and G Turner)*

☆ **Coningsby** [Boston Rd (B1192), ¾ mile NW of village; TF2458], *Leagate*: Dark old heavy-beamed fenland local with three linked areas, ageing medley of furnishings inc great high-backed settles around the biggest of the three log fires; friendly licensees, prompt good value home-made food, well kept ales such as Batemans and Exmoor Gold; piped jazz or pop music (not at lunchtime), fruit machine; rustic garden with play area; children if eating *(M J Morgan, Mr and Mrs B James, Bill and Sheila McLardy, LYM)*

Corby Glen [A151 Colsterworth—Bourne; SK9924], *Woodhouse Arms*: Pleasant stone building tastefully modernised, well kept Ruddles and Theakstons, good food in bar and restaurant inc Sardinian specialities; three bedrooms in converted outbuildings *(M J Morgan)*

Cowbit [Barrier Bank; A1073 S of Spalding; TF2618], *Olde Dun Cow*: Welcoming 17th-c local reopened under new owners, good range of economical meals, well kept Theakstons Best and other ales, pleasant black and white split-level bar with old oak beams, antique notices, restaurant one end, family games area at the other; tables in garden with play area, bedrooms *(E Robinson)*

Denton [SK8632], *Welby Arms*: Cosy and comfortable well run Mansfield pub in attractive village nestling in Vale of Belvoir; good food at reasonable prices, attentive service, separate dining room; reasonable wheelchair access *(Geoffrey Lindley)*

☆ **Donington on Bain** [between A153 and A157, SW of Louth; TF2382], *Black Horse*: Relaxed atmosphere and pleasant layout, with low-beamed snug back bar and softly lit inner room (with murals of carousing Vikings) off main village bar, log fires, bar food from filled baked potatoes to steaks inc children's dishes (£1.95), Ruddles Best and John Smiths; no-smoking restaurant, games room off public bar, juke box or piped music; children in eating areas, picnic-sets in back garden; bedrooms, good for walkers – on Viking Way *(Humphry and Angela Crum Ewing, Geoffrey Lawrance, Bill and Sheila McLardy, LYM)*

☆ **Edenham** [A151; TF0621], *Five Bells*: Welcoming family service, wide choice of reliable generous food in neat busy modernised dining lounge, well kept Bass and Tetleys, two log fires, dominoes, piped music, lots of foreign banknotes, soft lighting; back restaurant/function room, tables in garden with good play area; children and walkers welcome *(NS, Francis Johnson, LYM)*

Epworth [The Square; SE7804], *Red Lion*: Lively, welcoming, comfortable and spacious, with several separate beamed areas inc no-smoking eating area, roaring fire, well kept Tetleys and a couple of other ales, good value food inc lots of vegetarian dishes, special coffees, friendly efficient waitress service; children welcome, piped music and machines; bedrooms, handy for Old Rectory, John Wesley's birthplace *(CMW, JJW)*

☆ **Ewerby** [TF1247], *Finch Hatton Arms*: Substantial plushly furnished well decorated mock-Tudor pub with good home-made food esp fresh fish, well kept Stones Best and Wards Sheffield Best, coal fire, decent bar food, smart restaurant, comfortable back locals' bar; bedrooms *(F J and A Parmenter, BB)*

Folkingham [Market Pl; TF0733], *Greyhound*: 17th-c coaching inn with Georgian facade, pleasant atmosphere in bar, atrium area and restaurant, enjoyable interesting food with good veg, sensibly priced wines; bedrooms *(Mr and Mrs A Lumley-Wood)*

Frognall [155 Spalding Rd; A16 E of Mkt Deeping; TF1610], *Goat*: Geared to cheap and cheerful straightforward food (all day Sun) inc fish and vegetarian, with Adnams, Bass and several interesting guest beers, low beams, stripped stonework, two dining lounges, restaurant, no piped music; big garden with play equipment (no children inside) *(R F and M K Bishop)*

Gainsborough [Ships Ct, Caskgate Lane; SK8189], *Eight Jolly Brewers*: Eight superbly kept locally produced ales in fine unpretentious pub, easy to strike up conversation; limited food such as sausage sandwich *(Mr and Mrs A Turk)*; [Morton Terr], *Elm Cottage*: An oasis in this part of the world – nice local atmosphere, comfortable cottagey interior, friendly staff, well kept Bass, good straightforward food at remarkably low prices *(Geoffrey Lawrance)*

Gedney Drove End [B1359; TF4629], *New Inn*: Friendly two-room pub with pig theme, Elgoods Cambridge, basic food, real fire in one room with darts, TV and fruit machine in the other; piped music; fresh produce stall from own small farm, camping *(CMW, JJW)*

☆ **Grantham** [High St; SK9135], *Angel & Royal*: Remarkable worn medieval carved stone facade, ancient oriel window seat in upstairs plush bar on left, massive inglenook in friendly high-beamed main bar opp, well kept Bass and occasional guest beers, bar food; bedrooms in comfortable modern hotel block extending behind *(JP, PP, LYM)*

Grantham [Vine St], *Blue Pig*: Another of the few buildings here to survive the great fire of 1660, beams, character, well kept beer, welcoming service, simple lunchtime bar food, three rooms – one with machines *(RB, JP, PP)*

Grimsby [88 Freeman St; TA2609], *Corporation*: Well kept Bass and Worthington in traditional town pub with nice back lounge – original panelling, leather seats, old Grimsby shipping photographs; second lounge, lively public bar with games and TV *(PB)*; [Victoria St], *Hope & Anchor*: Basic relaxing traditional bar and lounge off central servery, friendly staff and locals, reasonably priced lunchtime food inc hot filled rolls, well kept real ales with ambitious two-week beer festival *(R M Taylor)*; [Garth Lane], *Tap & Spile*: Spartan stone floors and heavy wooden chairs and tables, basic but welcoming; good choice of ales with tasting samples, unusual dishes on the light menu *(R M Taylor)*

☆ **Grimsthorpe** [A151; TF0422], *Black Horse*: Doing well after complete refurbishment and reopening by new owners, good enterprising food inc fish and game in bar and restaurant, three Batemans ales; good bedrooms, excellent breakfast *(Mike and Heather Watson, M J Morgan)*

Hagworthingham [TF3469], *George & Dragon*: Batemans ales, good well presented food changing daily from sandwiches up, good service *(M J Morgan)*

Hainton [A157 Wragby—Louth; TF1884], *Heneage Arms*: Good food inc top value Sun lunch, well kept Highwood Tom Wood ales, warm friendly atmosphere, good service, open fires; handy for Cadwell Park *(Derek and Sylvia Stephenson, M J Morgan)*

Haltham [A163 Horncastle—Coningsby; TF2463], *Marmion Arms*: Pleasant village pub with good atmosphere, decent well cooked reasonably priced food, well kept ales inc Mansfield Old Baily; informal music Fri, not noisy *(Bill and Sheila McLardy)*

☆ **Halton Holegate** [B1195 E of Spilsby; TF4165], *Bell*: Pretty village local, simple but comfortable and consistently friendly, with wide choice of decent home-made food inc outstanding fish and chips, vegetarian dishes and Sun lunches, well kept Bass, Batemans and Mansfield Old Baily, aircraft pictures, pub games, maybe piped music; children in eating area and restaurant *(JP, PP, LYM)*

Hatton [A158 Wragby—Horncastle; TF1776], *Midge*: Good value well presented fresh-cooked food (not Mon) in bar and candlelit restaurant, Bass, Stones and a guest ale served through sparkler *(R A Nuttall, B Adams)*

Haxey [31 Church St (B1396); SK7699], *Loco*: Flagstoned shop conversion full of railway memorabilia inc large chunk of a steam loco, lots more inc clocks and armour; reasonably priced bar food, Sun lunches, occasional gourmet evenings, restaurant (Thurs-Sat, Sun lunch), warm friendly atmosphere; children welcome, cl Mon-Weds lunchtime in winter *(CMW, JJW, Ian and Nita Cooper)*

Hemingby [off A158/B1225 N of Horncastle; TF2374], *Coach & Horses*: Old-fashioned village local, long, low and attractive, with central fireplace dividing bar – games on left, eating area with sewing-machine tables on right; comfortable pews, oak beams, very helpful service, reasonably priced food from sandwiches to steaks inc vegetarian and children's, well kept ales such as Batemans XB and Blackawton Shepherds Delight, friendly licensees and cat; Sun quiz night *(Jenny and Michael Back, Geoffrey Lawrance)*

Holbeach [Spalding Rd; TF3524], *Red Lion*: Doing well under helpful new licensees, with enjoyable low-priced food served piping hot, Bass, John Smiths, Tetleys and a guest such as Batemans' current monthly beer, very friendly welcoming staff, massive beams in no-smoking dining room *(Jenny and Michael Back)*

Horncastle [Bull Ring; TF2669], *Bull*: Country-town hotel, former posting inn, with good value bar food inc generous vegetarian, helpful friendly staff, well kept real ales; SkyTV; bedrooms *(Meg and Colin Hamilton)*
Kirkby la Thorpe [TF0945], *Queens Head*: Good choice of good home-made food inc fresh fish, interesting changing specials, delicious puddings and home-baked bread; particularly well kept Batemans and Marstons, small cosy no-smoking restaurant, friendly staff *(Geoff Clarke, Mr and Mrs D Lightfoot)*
Kirkby on Bain [TF2462], *Ebrington Arms*: Low beams and partitions, eating areas each side, copper-topped tables, wall banquettes, aircraft and racing car pictures, nicely set out restaurant; prompt welcoming service, five or more changing ales from small breweries far and wide, good choice of sensibly priced food inc generous cheap Sun lunch *(Jenny and Michael Back, Derek and Sylvia Stephenson)*
☆ **Lincoln** [Steep Hill], *Browns Pie Shop*: Wide choice of good food inc popular chunky pies; restaurant licence only, but does have a beer such as Charles Wells as well as decent wines, comfortable seats, friendly efficient staff, pleasant traditional atmosphere *(Francis Johnson, M Morgan)*
☆ **Lincoln** [Bunkers Hill], *Lincolnshire Poacher*: Roomy and comfortable, with old chairs and books, Lincolnshire memorabilia inc interesting prints, big dining part with no-smoking areas, good range of food inc local dishes, Mansfield Riding and Old Baily ale, attentive considerate service; play areas inside and (with video surveillance) outside; open all day Sun *(M Morgan)*
Lincoln [7 Langworthgate], *Bull & Chain*: Popular unpretentious local with comfortable banquettes, decorative plates, cheap food (all day Sun) inc vegetarian, friendly staff, Bass and John Smiths ales, good darts team, dominoes, juke box, machines; children welcome, big garden overlooking tennis court, not far from cathedral *(JJW, CMW, Geoffrey Lindley)*; [Exchange Arcade], *Cornhill Vaults*: Rare underground pub with cheap well kept Sam Smiths, bar lunches inc unusual sandwiches, pool table in separate area, friendly staff; juke box after 3, live music evenings *(Chris Raisin, Graham Doyle, the Didler, JP, PP)*; [21 High St], *Golden Eagle*: Cheerfully busy basic two-bar town pub with wide choice of well kept changing ales, good choice of country wines, good value lunchtime food inc vegetarian *(John Baker, JP, PP)*; [11 Greetwellgate], *Morning Star*: Unspoilt well scrubbed pub handy for cathedral, friendly atmosphere, good value lunches, well kept reasonably priced Bass, Ruddles Best and guest beers, coal fire, aircraft paintings, nice outside area; piano nights, open all day (Sun closure 5-7) *(the Didler)*; [off Whisby Rd], *Pride of Lincoln*: Open-plan country-style Tom Cobleigh pub built around restored windmill, comfortable seating, carpets, lots of wood and artefacts, real ales such as Bass, Boddingtons, Shepherd Neame Spitfire, John Smiths, Theakstons Mild and Worthington Best, good choice of food inc carvery, efficient friendly service; play area, summer bouncy castle, open all day; bedrooms *(Richard Lewis)*; [Brayford Wharf], *Royal William IV*: Wide choice of decent food and well kept Scottish Courage real ales, tables overlooking canal *(M J Morgan)*; [26 Melville St, opp bus stn], *Sippers*: Quiet little pub with good food (not w/e evenings), Courage Directors, Marstons Pedigree, John Smiths, Wilsons Mild and guest beers, very friendly licensees; cl Sun lunchtime *(the Didler)*; [Hungate], *Tap & Spile*: Good changing choice of well kept ales and Crone's farm cider from central bar, framed beer mats, prints and breweriana, bare boards and stone floors, friendly atmosphere; open all day *(Richard Lewis)*
Long Sutton [Main St; off bypass A17 Kings Lynn—Holbeach; TF4222], *Crown & Woolpack*: Good generous cheap home cooking (well filled baguettes only, Mon-Weds) in attractively decorated lively local with panelled back dining room, good Sun lunch (must book), Bass and Worthington BB, roaring fire; dominoes, piped music (may be rather loud, bar may be smoky) *(Jenny and Michael Back)*
Louth [Mercer Row; TF3387], *Kings Head*: Large unfussy bar, well kept beer, good range of good value bar food inc roasts and traditional puddings *(Mike and Maggie Betton)*; [Cornmarket], *Masons Arms*: Edwardian pub with well restored woodwork and fancy glass, friendly landlord, well kept ales wuch as Bass, Batemans XB, XXB and Dark Mild, Bass, Fullers London Pride and Marstons Pedigree, good home-made food inc vegetarian, good upstairs dining room (remarkably decorated former masonic lodge meeting room); bedrooms *(David and Michelle James, Stephen, Julie and Hayley Brown)*
Mareham le Fen [A115; TF2861], *Royal Oak*: Pretty partly thatched 14th-c building with well kept Batemans XB and guest ales and limited good value food in pleasant friendly bar – TV too; small attractive unpubby dining area *(M J Morgan, Dorothy and Leslie Pilson)*
☆ **Market Deeping** [Market Pl; TF1310], *Bull*: Bustling local, warmly friendly, with cosy low-ceilinged alcoves, little corridors, interesting heavy-beamed medieval Dugout Bar; well kept Everards Tiger and Old Original and guest beers, amiable landlord, popular food (not Sun or Mon evening), attractive eating area, restaurant (booking now advised); no piped music lunchtime, seats in pretty coachyard; children in eating areas; open all day Fri, Sat *(Mr and Mrs N M Cook, M Morgan, Sue and Bob Ward, LYM)*
☆ **Navenby** [High St; SK9858], *Kings Head*: Small village pub with decent food inc good varied puddings in pleasant no-smoking area off bar, interesting knick-knacks, books, quick friendly service, well kept Bass, unobtrusive piped music *(Geoffrey Lawrance, Paul McPherson)*
☆ **Nettleham** [A46 N of Lincoln; TF0075], *Brown Cow*: Comfortable civilised lounge bar, kept

spotless, with wide range of good value generous food inc two-course bargain lunch, pleasant helpful staff; Sun lunch very popular; pleasant village *(B P White, G G Lawrance, M Morgan)*

Nettleham [14 High St, off A46], *White Hart*: Simple friendly pub with welcoming licensee, wide range of good value food inc unusual dishes; in centre of pleasant village *(Geoffrey Lawrance)*

North Kelsey [Middle St; off B1434 S of Brigg; TA0401], *Butchers Arms*: Busy reopened village local, tastefully refurbished and opened up but not too modern, with five well kept Highwood beers (brewed by owner on his farm), good lavish sensibly priced food (no hot dishes evening) and enthusiastic cheerful service; no juke box *(John C Baker, E M Jones)*; [High St], *Royal Oak*: Comfortable old village pub with good value straightforward food, well kept ales inc Batemans, bar, snug with TV, games room with darts and pool; real fire, fruit machine, quiz night Tues *(Geoffrey Lawrance)*

North Scarle [off A1133 Newark—Gainsborough; SK8567], *White Hart*: Good choice of generous food in bar and restaurant, well kept beer, live music Sun *(Geoffrey Lawrance)*

☆ **Norton Disney** [off A46 Newark—Lincoln; SK8859], *St Vincent Arms*: Attractive and welcoming village pub with well kept Batemans Mild and XXXB, Marstons Pedigree, three guest beers, open fire, good cheap generous plain food from sandwiches up inc beautifully cooked veg, pleasant landlord; tables and big adventure playground out behind *(JP, PP, D J and P M Taylor, Geoffrey Lawrance)*

☆ **Old Somerby** [B1176 E of Grantham; SK9633], *Fox & Hounds*: Enjoyable bar food from sandwiches to steaks inc good fish in spacious rambling pub with big no-smoking area, hunting-theme decor, well kept Marstons Pedigree, Ruddles Best and County and a guest beer, friendly staff, restaurant; piped music, darts, machines; children welcome, tables in big garden with DIY barbecue, tennis court for hire, jazz alternate Thurs; cl Mon exc bank hols *(Andy and Jill Kassube, Paul Mallett, Sue Rowland, RB, LYM)*

Pinchbeck [Glenside S; West Pinchbeck; TF2425], *Packing Shed*: Cosy and friendly, with beautiful fire and brasses, wide choice of good food *(M Morgan)*

Raithby [TF3767], *Red Lion*: Lovely setting, attentive staff, decent food *(M Kershaw)*

Ropsley [SK9934], *Green Man*: Genuine two-bar village local, good range of beers, friendly welcome, snacks, darts, dominoes *(RB)*

☆ **Rothwell** [Caistor Rd (off B1225 S of Caistor); TF1599], *Nickerson Arms*: Cheerful open-plan bar divided by arches and good coal fire, attractive wildlife prints, heavy beams, spacious dining area, well presented food (either sandwiches and basic snacks or much more expensive things like steaks and fresh fish), Batemans XB and XXXB, Courage Directors, Fullers London Pride, Marstons Pedigree and a guest beer, plenty of malt whiskies, pleasant small dining room, friendly service; piped music, darts and dominoes; children welcome, tables outside *(Andy and Jill Kassube, Mike and Sue Walton, M J Morgan, Michael Butler, LYM)*

☆ **Skegness** [Vine Rd, Seacroft (off Drummond Rd); TF5660], *Vine*: Handsome extended country house dating mainly from late 18th c, comfortable well run bar overlooking drive and own bowling green, imposing antique seats and grandfather clock in turkey-carpeted hall, juke box in inner oak-panelled room; three well kept Batemans ales, good value food in bar and restaurant, friendly staff, tables on big back sheltered lawn with swings; pleasant bedrooms, peaceful suburban setting not far from beach and birdwatching *(Christine and Geoff Butler, Geoffrey Lawrance, JP, PP, LYM)*

Skellingthorpe [High St; SK9272], *Stone Arms*: Small simple village local, warm and welcoming, with willing service and carefully cooked generous fresh food at low prices (small helpings available) inc popular Sun lunch in plush restaurant; opp church and meadow *(Kate and Arthur Moreton, Geoffrey Lawrance)*

Sleaford [1 Mareham Lane; TF0645], *Carre Arms*: Hotel with pub part, good generous enterprising food in brasserie and good value restaurant, decent wines, good service; bar can be smoky; bedrooms *(June and Malcolm Farmer)*

South Witham [High St; off A1 S of Colsterworth; SK9219], *Blue Cow*: Fine unspoilt pub brewing its own beers behind, two bars, one seeming largely for diners, first-class service, a welcome for newcomers *(Richard Houghton)*

Stamford [5 Cheyne Lane; between High St and St Marys St; TF0207], *Hole in the Wall*: Cosy and busy old L-shaped room with old tables, chairs and settles, central servery, well kept ales such as Adnams, Bass, Caledonian 70/-, Courage Directors and Fullers London Pride, decent reasonably priced wine, friendly helpful staff, lunchtime food (may be a wait) *(Julian Holland, Paul and Ursula Randall, Joan and Michel Hooper-Immins)*; *Periwig*: Recently opened quality pub with gallery above narrow single bar, good range of beers, limited choice of well filled good value baguettes; baked potatoes, ploughman's, salads, chequered tablecloths in bistro-style eating area, unobtruside piped music *(Michael Gittins)*; [St Peters St], *St Peters*: Well kept Marstons Best and Pedigree and several guest beers, good food inc pasta, oriental and vegetarian, cosy bar and bistro, quiet music, friendly staff *(Tony and Wendy Hobden)*

Stickford [A16; TF3560], *Red Lion*: Good reasonably priced home-made food inc lots of Greek and other mediterranean dishes, in separate dining room or garden; bedrooms *(Mrs C Hall)*

☆ **Stow** [4 Stow Pk Rd (B1241 NW of Lincoln); SK8882], *Cross Keys*: Prettily set village pub, tastefully modernised and extended, with attractive dining areas, interesting reasonably priced food inc unusual vegetarian choices and puddings, good range of beers and wines, big woodburner; nr Saxon minster church *(Mr and Mrs A Turk, Mr and Mrs G A Hargreaves)*

Surfleet [A16 N of Spalding; TF2528], *Mermaid*: Welcoming food stop, with wide choice from sandwiches to good value Sun lunch, generous veg, two dining areas, well kept ales such as Adnams, Robinsons and John Smiths, friendly helpful staff; by river with footpaths, interesting church nearby with leaning tower; garden with play area; bedrooms *(Bill and Sheila McLardy)*

Surfleet Seas End [154 Reservoir Rd; off A16 N of Spalding; TF2728], *Ship*: Unspoilt 17th-c riverside pub, flagstone bar, open fires, well kept Marstons Bitter and Pedigree and guests such as Fullers London Pride, good home-cooked meals (delicious seafood platter needs 24 hrs' notice), no-smoking dining room; bedrooms *(M J Morgan)*

Swinderby [A46 Newark—Lincoln; SK8663], *Half Way House*: 17th-c coaching inn with good generous home-made food in comfortably refurbished roomy lounge, helpful friendly staff, well kept real ale; piped music; disabled facilities, play area *(M J Morgan)*

Swineshead Bridge [A17, nr A1121 junction; TF2142], *Barge*: Useful lunch stop, relaxing uncrowded front room, good value food, friendly staff, lots of interesting knick-knacks and old beer bottles, pool table in public bar, quiet garden with swing; children given puzzle and picture to colour *(Bronwen and Steve Wrigley)*

Tealby [11 Kingsway; off B1203; TF1590], *Kings Head*: 14th-c thatched and beamed pub in quiet and attractive Wolds village, handy for Viking Way walk; food freshly prepared to order inc sandwiches, vegetarian and meaty home-made pies, real ale, farm cider, restaurant *(John Ringrose, A R Moore, JP, PP)*; [Cow Lane], *Olde Barn*: Pleasant pub handy for Viking Way, cheerfully served good straightforward food inc fresh fish in bar and restaurant, well kept Everards Old Original and Tiger, guest beers, big attractive back garden with lawn *(Derek and Sylvia Stephenson, M J Morgan)*

☆ **Tetford** [off A158 E of Horncastle; TF3374], *White Hart*: Early 16th-c pub with good atmosphere, fine mix of people, well kept Mansfield Riding and a guest beer, wide choice of food from good value sandwiches to popular Sun lunches; old-fashioned settles, slabby elm tables and red tiled floor in pleasant quiet inglenook bar, no-smoking snug, basic games room; seats and swings on sheltered back lawn, simple bedrooms *(Sue and Bob Ward, Geoffrey Lawrance, JP, PP, M J Morgan, LYM)*

Thorpe St Peter [TF4860], *Queen Victoria*: Good bar food from sandwiches and burgers to fish etc, good restaurant; children very welcome *(P and R Baker)*

☆ **Threekingham** [just off A52 12 miles E of Grantham; TF0836], *Three Kings*: Big entrance hall, two small bars and dining room; warm and comfortable, good service, wide choice of good attractively priced food, well kept Bass, M&B Brew XI and Stones; tables outside *(R Vincent, F J and A Parmenter, M J Morgan, Mr and Mrs D Lightfoot)*

Torksey [A156; SK8478], *Hume Arms*: Much extended comfortable dining pub/hotel with well kept Marstons and Whitbreads Castle Eden, good choice of food *(M J Morgan)*

Uffington [Bertie Lane; TF0607], *Bertie Arms*: Beautifully kept thatched pub with good food, excellent landlord *(Gibson-Warner, M J Morgan)*

Wellingore [High St; off A607 Lincoln—Grantham; SK9856], *Marquis of Granby*: Attractive and neatly kept old pub, friendly and welcoming, with good value food from good filled rolls to interesting specials, well kept Theakstons Best and XB and changing guest ales, comfortable button-back banquettes, log fire; music may obtrude in bar, but much quieter dining area; bedrooms, tiny pretty village *(F J and A Parmenter)*

West Ashby [TF2672], *George & Dragon*: Friendly, with good beer, plentiful reasonably priced usual food in attractive dining area *(Dorothy and Leslie Pilson)*

West Deeping [King St; TF1109], *Red Lion*: Long low bar with plenty of tables, roaring coal fires each end, old stonework and beams, well kept ales such as Adnams Broadside, Bass, Fullers London Pride and Tetleys, wide choice of generous food from appetising bacon baps to piping hot dishes inc vegetarian, puddings from cold cabinet, prompt welcoming service, friendly alsatian called Prince; big pool room, open all day, tables in back garden *(Jenny and Michael Back)*

Witham on the Hill [Main St; TF0516], *Six Bells*: Currently doing well, with varied interesting food, Bass and Tetleys, good service and ample accommodation *(K H Frostick)*

Woodhall Spa [Stixwould Rd; TF1963], *Village Limits*: Don't be put off by Motel tag – good home cooking, pleasant ambiance with pink plush banquettes and aeroplane prints, a real ale, humorous Scots landlord; bedrooms *(Meg and Colin Hamilton)*

Bedroom prices normally include full English breakfast, VAT and any inclusive service charge that we know of. Prices before the '/' are for single rooms, after for two people in double or twin (B includes a private bath, S a private shower). If there is no '/', the prices are only for twin or double rooms (as far as we know there are no singles).

Norfolk

In the last few years this has become one of the nicest parts of Britain for pub lovers, with a good many pubs of real individuality, good food and drink, and some lovely surroundings. We add three new entries this year: the unspoilt and relaxed Hare & Hounds at Hempstead, good all round under its present licensees (it gains a Beer Award); the pleasantly smartened-up Red Lion at Upper Sheringham (another good all-rounder responding well to its present management); and the friendly Wheatsheaf at West Beckham. Among longer-established main entries, the current stars are the bustling and friendly old Kings Head at Bawburgh (good interesting food), the White Horse in Blakeney (an enjoyable small hotel), the very civilised Hoste Arms in Burnham Market (super food – gains a Food Award this year), the highly individual Saracens Head near Erpingham (excellent food here too), the attractive little Earle Arms tucked away in a delightful spot at Heydon (enjoyable food, and the sort of place that quickly becomes a special favourite), the very well run Tudor Rose in Kings Lynn (decent food, good prices), the Angel at Larling (a roadside pub lifted right out of the ordinary by the people who run it – gains a Place to Stay Award this year), the bustling old Crown in Mundford (good food), the ancient Adam & Eve in Norwich (good all round) and for real ale the chatty Fat Cat there, the Ferry by the water at Reedham, the thriving and pleasantly individual Red Lion at Stiffkey, the attractive Hare Arms at Stow Bardolph (reliably good food), Darbys at Swanton Morley (a good farm building conversion), the unspoilt traditional Three Horseshoes at Warham, friendly and well run, with good food (it's a pub several readers use as a yardstick for judging other places – and we can see why), and the Fur & Feather at Woodbastwick (tap for Woodfordes' super beers – and for that reason it's quite a surprise to find such a dining-pub feel). Among all these, the Hoste Arms at Burnham Market stands out as a place for a special meal out: it's our Norfolk Dining Pub of the Year. A special mention for the Lord Nelson just down the road from there at Burnham Thorpe, with all its Nelson memorabilia. This county also has a fine choice of places in the Lucky Dip section at the end of the chapter: the most prominent these days are the Chequers at Binham, Jolly Sailors at Brancaster Staithe, Ratcatchers at Cawston, Feathers at Dersingham, Walpole Arms at Itteringham (the only one of this group that we have not yet been able to inspect and approve ourselves, but it does sound very promising), and Crown at Stanhoe. Many readers will be pleased to hear that the attractive old Chequers at Thompson has reopened. Drinks prices in Norfolk are a bit higher than the national average; we found the Fat Cat in Norwich particularly cheap for beer.

People don't usually tip bar staff (different in a really smart hotel, say). If you want to thank someone – for dealing with a really large party, say, or special friendliness – offer them a drink. Common expressions are: 'And what's yours?' or 'And won't you have something for yourself?'

BAWBURGH TG1508 Map 5

Kings Head

Pub signposted down Harts Lane off B1108, which leads off A47 just W of Norwich

Even when this old pub is really busy, the friendly licensee and his staff will find the time to make you feel welcome. The four linked rooms have low beams, some standing timbers, a log fire in a large knocked-through canopied fireplace, a woodburner and dried flowers in the attractive inglenook in the end room, and comfortable green or rust plush banquettes. Ample helpings of attractively presented food include home-made soup (£1.85), sandwiches or filled french bread (from £3), danish-style fishcakes with mustard and dill sauce (£3.95), a good salad niçoise or pasta carbonara (£4.50), lamb kebabs with minted yoghurt (£5.95), ploughman's or vegetable balti (£6), steak and kidney or fish pies or honey and lime chicken (£6.95), fresh scampi tails in coconut batter (£8.50), weekly changing specials such as fried chicken livers with cream and brandy (£3.95), carpaccio of duck breast with basil and chilli oil (£4.25), good glazed ham hock with leek and potato gratin (£9) or roast seabass with lime, ginger, chilli and garlic (£12.25), puddings like treacle tart or summer pudding (from £3), and children's menu (£3.95); no-smoking restaurant. Three well kept real ales on handpump such as Adnams Bitter, Boddingtons, Courage Directors, Oldershaw Caskade, Theakstons Old Peculier, and Woodfordes Wherry and Great Eastern Ale on handpump; good quick service; cribbage, dominoes and piped music. There are rustic tables and benches on the gravel outside. *(Recommended by MDN, Tony Albert, Bob Arnett, Judy Wayman, Stephen Horsley, John McDonald, Ann Bond, Martin and Karen Wake, Bill and Sheila McLardy, Anthony Barnes, Ian Phillips, David Gregory, Bob Arnett, Judy Wayman)*

Free house ~ Licensees Anton and Pamela Wimmer ~ Real ale ~ Meals and snacks (till 10pm) ~ Restaurant ~ (01603) 744977 ~ Children in eating area of bar and in restaurant ~ Solo singer every other Mon evening, jazz on certain Sun afternoons ~ Open 11.30-11; 12-10.30 Sun

BLAKENEY TG0243 Map 8

Kings Arms

West Gate St

The three simply furnished, knocked-together rooms in this popular pub have some interesting photographs of the licensees' theatrical careers, other pictures including work by local artists, and what's said to be the smallest cartoon gallery in England in a former telephone kiosk; two small rooms are no smoking; the airy extension is liked by families and diners. Bar food includes sandwiches (from £1.50), soup (£2.25), filled baked potatoes (from £3.50), ploughman's (from £3.95), vegetarian curry (£4.95), local cod or haddock (£5.50), and evening salads (from £5.75); enjoyable breakfasts. Very well kept Marstons Pedigree and Websters Yorkshire on handpump with Woodfordes Wherry tapped from the cask; darts, shove-ha'penny, dominoes, and fruit machine. The large garden has lots of tables and chairs and a separate, equipped children's area; there are baby-changing facilities, too. The son and daughter-in-law have recently taken over the day-to-day management, and initially things were not perhaps running as smoothy as readers have come to expect here; we hope they'll soon pick up the knack for points of detail that Mr and Mrs Davies have shown so strongly in the past. *(Recommended by A C Curry, Bernard and Marjorie Parkin, Mrs D Rathbone, Nigel Woolliscroft, Peter Plumridge, Klaus and Elizabeth Leist, Jeremy Burnside, M Morgan, Chris Rounthwaite, John Fahy, Dr Jim Mackay, R Suddaby, J F Knutton, Sue Holland, Dave Webster)*

Free house ~ Licensees Howard and Marjorie Davies ~ Meals and snacks (all day in summer) ~ (01263) 740341 ~ Children welcome ~ Open 11-11; 12-10.30 Sun ~ Bedrooms: /£50S, and self-catering flats upstairs £50

If you stay overnight in an inn or hotel, they are allowed to serve you an alcoholic drink at any hour of the day or night.

White Horse

4 High Street

This small hotel is an enjoyable place and run by friendly people and their helpful staff. The long main bar has a good mix of visitors and locals, a good chatty atmosphere, and is predominantly green (despite the venetian red ceiling), with a restrained but attractive decor – including two big reproductions of Audubon waterfowl up at the far end; well kept Adnams, Bass, and Boddingtons on handpump, and a wide choice of reasonably priced wines (wine tastings in spring and winter); cribbage. There's wheelchair access, though a short flight of steps to the back part of the bar. Good bar food includes sandwiches (from £2.25), home-made soup (£2.50; the cockle chowder is very good, £3.25), home-made pâté (£3.25), fish pie (£5), sirloin steak (£10.75), daily specials such as crab thermidor or tagliatelle with seafood sauce (£6.25) and grilled fillet of salmon with crab sauce (£6.50), children's meals (£3.25), and home-made puddings (£2.50); no-smoking area. The attractive conservatory restaurant is much liked by readers (as is the food there). Tables out in a suntrap courtyard. The bedrooms are well equipped, if small. *(Recommended by George Atkinson, K H Frostick, MDN, Peter and Anne Hollindale, Keith and Janet Morris, Lesley Kant, Mark O'Hanlon, M J Morgan, O K Smyth, Charles Bardswell, George and Shirley Campey, Norman and Valerie Housley, Dr B and Mrs P B Baker, Frank Davidson, Sue Holland, Dave Webster)*

Free house ~ Licensee Daniel Rees ~ Real ale ~ Meals and snacks ~ Restaurant (Tues-Sat evenings only) ~ (01263) 740574 ~ Children in gallery room and eating area of bar ~ Open 11-3, 6(5.30 Sat)-11; 12-3, 5.30(7 in winter)-10.30 Sun ~ Bedrooms: £35B/£70B

BLICKLING TG1728 Map 8

Buckinghamshire Arms

Off B1354 N of Aylsham

Owned by the National Trust, this bustling and handsome Jacobean inn stands at the entrance to Blickling Hall. The small front snug is simply furnished with fabric-cushioned banquettes, while the bigger lounge has neatly built-in pews, stripped deal tables, and Spy pictures. Lunchtime bar food includes home-made soup (£2.95), open sandwiches or filled french bread (from £2.95), filo king prawns with garlic mayonnaise or ploughman's (£4.50), home-made steak and kidney pie (£6.25), and smoked chicken and avocado salad with a blue cheese dressing (£6.75), with evening dishes such as home-made smoked mackerel pâté (£3.95), vegetable tagliatelle with mediterranean vegetables and mozzarella (£6.75), thai-style chicken curry (£6.75), fresh local trout (£7.95), beef sizzler (£8.75), sirloin steak (£10.95), and puddings (£2.95). Adnams Best, Reepham Granary Bitter, Tolly & Cobbold Bitter, and a beer brewed for the pub by Woodfordes on handpump, and a good range of wines; shove-ha'penny. There are lots of tables on the big lawn, and they serve food from an out-building here in summer. Blickling Hall is open 1-4.30pm Wednesday-Sunday; the garden is the same days as the house, 10.30-5.30. No children in the pub. *(Recommended by Steve and Sarah Pleasance, A Bowen, R M Macnaughton, J R Hughes-Lewis, John Fahy, Bob Arnett, Judy Wayman, Colin Barnes, John Wooll)*

Free house ~ Licensee Pip Wilkinson ~ Real ale ~ Meals and snacks ~ Evening restaurant ~ (01263) 732133 ~ Open 11-3, 6-11; 12-3, 7-11 Sun ~ Bedrooms: £45S/£60S

BURNHAM MARKET TF8342 Map 8

Hoste Arms

The Green (B1155)

Norfolk Dining Pub of the Year

A long way from your average village local, this handsome 17th-c hotel is much enjoyed by the many who like their pubs civilised but informally smart. The boldly decorated bars have massive log fires, and a good mix of people, especially at the weekend. The panelled bar on the right has a series of watercolours showing scenes from local walks, there's a bow-windowed bar on the left, a nice sitting room, a little art gallery in the staircase area, and well kept Greene King Abbot and IPA, Sherwood Forest Lionheart Ale, and Woodfordes Wherry on handpump, a good wine list including champagne by the glass, a decent choice of malt whiskies, and freshly squeezed orange juice. Good, well presented lunchtime food (we feel they deserve a Food Award this year) is served in the no-smoking conservatory and includes home-made soup (£3.25), sandwiches (from £3.50), half a dozen local oysters (£5.75), a selection of charcuterie, black olives and roasted peppers and sun-dried tomatoes (£5.25), pot-roasted ham hock with dauphinoise potato and café au lait sauce (£7.95), whole roast baby chicken with sautéed globe artichokes (£8.95), seatrout fillet with ratatouille and pesto dressing (£9.25), rump steak (£11.95), daily specials such as sushi with wasabi, pickled ginger and soy (£5.75), fried lamb liver, kidney and chorizo with olive mash and red onion (£7.95), baked cod with buttered spinach and celeriac gateaux (£8.95), and puddings like walnut and hazelnut chocolate tart, banoffi pie or baked apple and sultana roll with crème anglaise (£3.95); efficient, friendly service. The Gallery restaurant is no smoking. At the back is a pleasant walled garden with tables on a terrace. *(Recommended by Anthony Barnes, M J Morgan, R J Bland, Bernard and Marjorie Parkin, Mrs Jill Silversides, Barry Brown, JP, PP, Nigel Woolliscroft, Steve and Sarah Pleasance, MDN, Eric Locker, David Heath, J F Knutton, John Fahy, P and M Pumfrey, David and Anne Culley, Robert and Anne Lees, Dennis and Barbara Cook, Minda and Stanley Alexander, Sebastian Leach, Sue Holland, Dave Webster, Chris Rounthwaite, Mark Hydes, Ken and Jenny Simmonds, M A and C R Starling, Howard and Margaret Buchanan; also in the Good Hotel Guide)*

Free house ~ Licensees Paul Whittome, Mrs Jeanne Whittome, Miss Rebecca Mackenzie ~ Real ale ~ Meals and snacks ~ Restaurant ~ (01328) 738777 ~ Children welcome ~ Occasional live entertainment Fri evenings ~ Open 11-11; 12-10.30 Sun ~ Bedrooms: £60B/£86B

BURNHAM THORPE TF8541 Map 8

Lord Nelson

Village signposted from B1155 and B1355, near Burnham Market

There's no bar counter here, so you have to order your pint of well kept Greene King IPA, Abbot and Mild and Woodfordes Nelsons Revenge which is then tapped from the cask in a back stillroom; they also have an unusual rum concoction called Nelson's Blood. Nelson was born in this village, so it's no surprise to find lots of pictures and memorabilia of him lining the walls. The characterful little bar has well waxed antique settles on the worn red flooring tiles and smoke ovens in the original fireplace, and an eating room has flagstones, an open fire, and more pictures of the celebrated sailor; there's only one room for smokers. Bar food at lunchtime includes sandwiches (from £2.10), garlic mushrooms (£2.95), breakfast (£3.95), and ploughman's (£4.95), as well as breaded plaice (£4.95), gammon and egg (£7.50), daily specials and vegetarian choices, children's meals (from £2.50), and puddings; friendly staff, and shove-ha'penny, dominoes, draughts, cards, and children's toys. They have baby changing facilities and a disabled lavatory. There's a play area with basketball and a climbing frame outside. *(Recommended by John Beeken, Mick Hitchman, JP, PP, John Woolf, R J Bland, Bill Pemberton, F G Drain, Dennis and Barbara Cook, Ian Phillips, D J Hayman, Mrs S F Front, Quentin Williamson, Michael Switzer)*

Greene King ~ Lease: Lucy Stafford ~ Real ale ~ Meals and snacks ~ (01328) 738241 ~ Children in all areas except the smoking room ~ Live music first Fri of month ~ Open 11-3, 6-11; 12-3, 7-10.30 Sun

COLKIRK TF9126 Map 8

Crown

Village signposted off B1146 S of Fakenham; and off A1065

In a peacefully prosperous village, this bustling pub is popular with friendly locals – but there's a warm welcome for visitors, too. The public bar and small lounge both have open fires, solid straightforward country furniture, rugs and flooring tiles, and sympathetic lighting; the no-smoking dining room leading off is pleasantly informal. Well kept Greene King IPA, Abbot, Mild, Rayments, and winter Dark Ale on handpump, several malt whiskies, and 50 wines (all are available by the glass). Well presented bar food includes home-made soup (£2.30), lunchtime filled french bread (from £2.95) and ploughman's (£4.05), and daily specials such as chicken liver pâté (£3.55), ratatouille and pasta cheese bake (£5.95), fresh grilled skate wine (£6.25), steak and kidney pie (£6.50), and grilled duck breast with ginger sauce (£8.65); the dining room is no smoking. Darts, shove-ha'penny, cribbage, dominoes, and fruit machine. There's a garden and sun-trap terrace with picnic-sets. *(Recommended by Steve and Sarah Pleasance, Maurice and Jean George, Frank Davidson, Chris and Ann Garnett, Jeremy Gough, Dr B and Mrs P B Baker)*

Greene King ~ Tenant Patrick Whitmore ~ Real ale ~ Meals and snacks (12-1.45, 7-9.30; not 25-26 Dec) ~ (01328) 862172 ~ Children welcome ~ Open 11-2.30, 6-11; 12-2.30, 7-10.30 Sun

DOCKING TF7637 Map 8

Hare Arms

Station Rd (B1153 towards Brancaster)

The two smallish main bar rooms here are attractively and individually decorated in unusual relaxing deep colours, with lots of entertaining bric-a-brac and Victorian pictures; there's also a cosy and pretty end dining room. Enjoyable food cooked by the licensee's son changes day by day and might include good soups (£2.75), lunchtime sandwiches (from £1.95), ploughman's (from £4.95), home-made steak and kidney pie or vegetable stir-fry (£6.50), daily fresh fish such as cod in beer batter (£4.95) or strawberry grouper, parrot fish or shark steaks (£9-£16), steaks (from £11.95), and puddings such as sticky toffee pudding or fruit pies (£2.75). Well kept Adnams Broadside, Greene King Abbot, and Ushers Twelve Bore on handpump, decent wines, good log fire, welcoming service, and piped music; the jack russell is called Jessie. There's a small site for touring caravans behind. *(Recommended by John Wooll; more reports please)*

Free house ~ Licensee Christine Milner ~ Real ale ~ Meals and snacks ~ Restaurant ~ (01485) 518402 ~ Children welcome away from bar ~ Occasional live entertainment ~ Open 11-3, 6-11; 12-3, 7-10.30 Sun

ERPINGHAM TG1631 Map 8

Saracens Head

Address is Wolterton – not shown on many maps; Erpingham signed off A140 N of Aylsham, keep on through Calthorpe, then where road bends right take the straight-ahead turn-off signposted Wolterton

Imaginative, reliably good food served in a relaxed and informal atmosphere continues to draw warm praise from readers for this civilised and rather remote pub – and proves again, that originality doesn't need to cost the earth. Changing regularly, there might be creamy seafood bisque (£2.95), baked egg with smoked salmon and cream (£3.70), crispy fried aubergine with garlic mayonnaise (£4.25), grilled goat's cheese on a croûte topped with marinated mediterranean vegetables (£7.50), braised twin pigeons with red fruit, fried chicken breast with banana and marsala or baked local crab with mushrooms (£8.50), fried escalope of veal with pernod and cream (£8.95), wok-sizzled strips of sirloin with basil and tomato (£9.50), local venison medallions with wild mushroom and bacon sauce (£10.50), and puddings such as chocolate pot with a rich orange jus, treacle tart or spicy apple pie (£2.95); very good value two-course weekday lunch (£5); booking is almost essential. The two-room bar is simple and stylish, with high ceilings and tall windows giving a feeling of space, though it's not large, and around the terracotta walls are a mix of seats from built-in leather wall settles to wicker fireside chairs, solid-colour carpets and curtains, log fires and flowers on the mantlepieces. It looks out on a charming old-fashioned gravel stableyard with picnic-sets. There's a pretty little four-table parlour on the right – cheerful nursery colours, and another big log fire. Well kept Adnams, a beer named for the pub (brewed by Woodfordes), and occasional guest beers on handpump; decent malt whiskies. The wine list is really quite interesting, with some shipped direct from a French chateau. *(Recommended by Miss M Hamilton, Ian Phillips, K F Mould, Peter and Pat Frogley, Charles Bardswell, Marion Turner, Anthony Barnes, Mick Hitchman, D Twitchett, G Neighbour, Rita Horridge, Dr Jim Mackay, Bob Arnett, Judy Wayman)*

Free house ~ Licensee Robert Dawson-Smith ~ Real ale ~ Meals and snacks ~ Restaurant ~ (01263) 768909 ~ Well behaved children welcome ~ Open 11.30-2.30, 6-11; 12-2.30, 7-10.30 Sun; closed 25 Dec ~ Bedrooms: £40B/£60B

FAKENHAM TF9229 Map 8

Wensum Lodge

Bridge St (B1146 S of centre)

The original mill here was still in operation in the 1970s – which is quite a surprise. Careful new development has been built around it, but the former grain store now makes up the very roomy and relaxing civilised bar: lots of pictures, mate's chairs grouped around polished tables; Manchester Gold, and Theakstons XB on handpump, kept under light blanket pressure; fruit machine and piped music. Two beamed dining areas (one is no smoking) lead off, with more dark tables and chairs, prints and houseplants. A wide choice of interesting bar food includes sandwiches (from £1.90; filled french bread from £3.25), home-made soup (£2.75), filled baked potatoes (from £2.75), filled pancakes (£5.75), home-made steak, mushroom and Guinness pie or spicy mixed bean and pepper parcel (£7.25), grilled swordfish steak in lime, coriander and ginger with home-made spicy salsa (£8.75), caramelised fillet of pork in a roast cherry tomato sauce (£9.75), sizzlers (£10.75), roast duck breast with a home-made redcurrant compote and cranberry jus (£10.95), and steaks (from £10.95), and king prawn parcel on a bed of straw vegetables and fresh herbs (£11.50); children's menu (£2.95) and puddings like steamed chocolate sponge with home-made marmalade ice cream or warm apricot and almond tart or home-made chocolate ice cream (from £2.95); attentive service. There's a lounge area with a conservatory leading to a new bedrooms development. There are tables outside, with grass running down to the river, weeping willows along its banks. *(Recommended by Charles Bardswell, Mrs Dorothy Smith, George Atkinson)*

Free house ~ Licensees Dawn Woods, P and G Hobday ~ Real ale ~ Meals and snacks (11-3, 6.30-10) ~ Restaurant ~ (01328) 862100 ~ Children welcome ~ Open 11-11; 12-10.30 Sun ~ Bedrooms: £45B/£60B

GREAT BIRCHAM TF7632 Map 8

Kings Head

B1155, S end of village (which is called and signposted Bircham locally)

A friendly Italian licensee runs this rather grand looking place, handy for the very striking windmill. The unassuming lounge bar (two room areas) has a pleasantly quiet and relaxed atmosphere and a mix of high and low tables suiting both diners and drinkers, with a good hot fire in a third more homely bit round behind. Reliably good bar food includes lunchtime sandwiches (from £2.70), ploughman's (£4.80), steak and kidney pudding (£7.50), smoked haddock mornay or home-made fishcakes with crab sauce (£7.90), and quite a few Italian specialities such as fresh spaghetti or tortellini (£5.90); tempting puddings. The dining area is no smoking. Besides well kept Adnams and Bass there's a good choice of malt whiskies, and decent wines; maybe unobtrusive piped music, dominoes. The somnolent alsatian is called Brandy. The big side lawn, with a well kept herbaceous border, has picnic-sets and play things. The attractive village has a decent art gallery, and Houghton Hall is not far off. *(Recommended by John Wooll, Charles Bardswell; more reports please)*

Free house ~ Licensees Isidoro and Iris Verrando ~ Real ale ~ Meals and snacks ~ Restaurant ~ (01485) 578265 ~ Children in eating area of bar and in restaurant ~ Open 11-3, 6.30-11; 12-3.30, 7-10.30 Sun ~ Bedrooms: £38B/£59B

HEMPSTEAD TG1137 Map 8

Hare & Hounds

Towards Baconsthorpe – and actually closer to that village, though just inside the Hempstead parish boundary; village signposted from A148 in Holt; OS Sheet 133 map reference 115372

This unspoilt and relaxed pantiled flint cottage is doing well at the moment. There are two simple bars (the charming no-smoking snug is down a step) with a mix of old-fashioned furnishings and lots of pine, beams, newspapers to read, and a big woodburning stove in the broad low-beamed fireplace. Well kept Batemans XB, Shepherd Neame Spitfire, Woodfordes Wherry, and a guest beer on handpump; darts, cribbage, dominoes, dice, and piped music. Enjoyable bar food includes home-made soup (£2.50), filled french bread (from £2.95), ham and egg (£3.95), ploughman's (from £4.25), steak and kidney pie (£5.50), broccoli and cream cheese bake (£5.75), chicken stuffed with mature stilton (£7.95), steaks (from £8.50), and fish specials such as poached salmon with a lemon, herb and cream sauce or a trio of fish – plaice, dab and sole – in a stilton cream sauce (£7.95), or poached bass (£9.25), and puddings such as apple crumble, bread and butter pudding and profiteroles (£2.95). There are some picnic-sets on the side grass facing a pond and rockery, and a children's play area. This isn't the easiest pub to find, but it's well worth tracking down.
(Recommended by Ian Phillips, Frank Davidson)

Free house ~ Licensee Ashley Brewster ~ Real ale ~ Meals and snacks (not winter Mon evening) ~ (01263) 713285 ~ Children welcome ~ Occasional live entertainment ~ Open 11-3, 6-11; 12-3, 7-10.30 Sun ~ S/c barn sleeping 4, £50

HEYDON TG1127 Map 8

Earle Arms

Village signposted from B1149 about midway between Norwich and Holt

The village here is quite special and has hardly changed since the 1630s, and this imposing yellow-painted brick pub faces the green lined with charming cottages and houses. Inside, two carpeted rooms, one with hatch service, open off a small lobby with a handsomely carved longcase clock, and are individually furnished and decorated, with pretty rosehip wallpaper over a stripped dado, china on shelves, deep tiled-floor cupboards with interesting bric-a-brac, attractive prints and good log fires; dominoes, shove-ha'penny, and cribbage. There's a tiny homely dining room, and a simple but well heated no-smoking conservatory beyond; booking is advised for weekends. Food is good and at lunchtime (when all dishes are £4.95) there might be ploughman's, baked Cromer crab, home-cooked gammon and egg, pigeon, duck and orange pie, aubergine and sweet pepper parmesan or basque chicken on couscous; in the evening dishes may include chestnut and potato kugel (£8.25), seafood in a white wine sauce on choux pastry (£8.95), salmon steak with a thai topping or Italian garlic duck breast (£9.95), fillet of steak au poivre (£10.95), and turbot fillet with butter and lemon (£12.95); home-made puddings include fresh fruit crumbles, chocolate pecan pie or maple bread and butter pudding (£2.95). Well kept Morlands Old Speckled Hen and Woodfordes Wherry, Great Eastern, and Norfolk Nog on handpump, a decent wine list, and several malt whiskies; a friendly and enthusiastic licensee, and good service. The well behaved dogs sometimes in evidence are called Barnaby and Bendoodle. There are picnic-sets in a small and prettily cottagey back garden, and on the wall above the colourful front flower borders is what looks like a figurehead – the licensees think it is Ceres the Mother Earth symbol. This is Norfolk's only fully licensed pub theatre, and there's also a gallery for local artists. *(Recommended by David and Anne Culley, John Wooll, Sue and Mike Loseby, Peter and Pat Frogley, Mick Hitchman, David Gregory, Brian Horner, Brenda Arthur, D E Twitchett, Frank Davidson)*

Free house ~ Licensees Keith and Sara Holman-Howes ~ Real ale ~ Meals and snacks (not Sun evening, not Mon except bank holidays) ~ (01263) 587376 ~ Children in eating area of bar only ~ Gaelic band first Thurs of month, 8.30 ~ Open 12-3, 7-11; closed Mon (except bank holidays)

HORSEY TG4522 Map 8

Nelson Head

Signposted off B1159 (in series of S-bends) N of Gt Yarmouth

After a wet walk or a spot of chilly birdwatching, this genuine country pub is a warm, welcoming haven. The two unpretentious rooms, divided by a slung-back red velvet curtain, have simple but comfortable seats (including four tractor-seat bar stools), lots of shiny bric-a-brac and small local pictures for sale, geraniums on the window sill and a relaxed cottagey feel. Besides usual dishes such as ploughman's (£4.25), ham and egg (£4.50), breaded cod or vegetarian tagliatelle (£4.75), steaks (from £8.75), and children's dishes (£2.95), the Austrian managers do several good specialities such as znaimer goulash (£7.50), wiener schnitzel (£7.75), sacher torte and apple strudel (£2.95). Woodfordes Wherry and (of course) Nelsons Revenge on handpump, decent coffee, good fire; piped music. There's a homely family dining room, the garden has picnic-sets and an outside marquee, and dogs on leads are allowed. The beach is just down the road. *(Recommended by Anthony Barnes, Bronwen and Steve Wrigley, Minda and Stanley Alexander, John McDonald, Ann Bond, Maureen Hobbs, Eric Locker, David and Anne Culley)*

Free house ~ Licensee Reg Parsons ~ Real ale ~ Meals and snacks ~ (01493) 393378 ~ Children in eating area of bar only ~ Open 11-2.30, 6(7 in winter)-11; 12-3, 7-11 Sun

HUNWORTH TG0635 Map 8

Blue Bell

Village signposted off B roads S of Holt

Called the Hunny Bell for several years, this cosy village local has a pleasantly welcoming L-shaped bar with windsor chairs around dark wooden tables, comfortable settees (some of which are grouped around the log fire) and Norfolk watercolours and pictures for sale hanging above the panelling dado; the dining room is no smoking. Well kept Adnams Best and Greene King Abbot on handpump, quite a few malt whiskies, and decent wines. Bar food includes sandwiches (from £2.50), home-made soup or home-made pâté (£2.75), ploughman's (£3), local sausages (£4), home-cooked ham and eggs (£4.75), steak and kidney or chicken and ham pies (£4.95), sirloin steak (£8.50), and daily specials such as chicken curry, ham hock or crab salad (£4.95). Darts, dominoes, and cribbage. In summer, the garden is very pleasant and there's bar service to the tables on the lawn; children's play area. *(Recommended by Ian Phillips, Minda and Stanley Alexander, Mrs M Sloper, Mrs J Hale; more reports please)*

Free house ~ Licensees Sally and Thomas King ~ Real ale ~ Meals and snacks ~ Restaurant ~ (01263) 712300 ~ Children welcome ~ Open 11-3, 5-11; 11-11 Sat; 12-4, 6-11 Sun

KINGS LYNN TF6220 Map 8

Tudor Rose £

St Nicholas St (just off Tuesday Market Place – main square)

The quite separate back bar in this bustling half-timbered pub is to be refurbished with panelling, old-style furniture, and medieval-style tapestries. The old-fashioned snug little front bar has high beams, reproduction squared panelling, a big wrought-iron wheel-rim chandelier, newspapers to read, and a really warm welcome from the friendly staff; fruit machine and piped music. Good food includes cheap home-made food such as sandwiches (from £1.35), home-made soup (£2.25), cheese topped mushrooms (£2.99), local pork sausages (£3.50), crispy vegetables in a sweet and sour sauce or ploughman's (£3.75), home-made chilli con carne (£3.95), ham and egg (£3.99), with more elaborate dishes from the restaurant menu (available in the bar) like lamb balti (£7.25), steak and kidney pie (£7.50), pork steaks with tarragon and madeira sauce (£8.25), and fish kebabs (£8.50). Well kept Bass, Batemans XB, Woodfordes Wherry, and a guest beer on handpump, a fine choice of whiskies, and decent wines. The upstairs raftered restaurant and a small area of the lounge are no smoking. There are seats in the courtyard garden. Bedrooms are simple and modern but comfortable, and some have a pretty view of St Nicholas's Chapel. *(Recommended by R C Vincent, Margaret and Allen Marsden, John Wooll, Anthony Barnes, David and Ruth Hollands, Charles Gysin, Mr and Mrs R Maggs)*

Free house ~ Licensees John and Andrea Bull ~ Real ale ~ Meals and snacks (not Sun lunchtime) ~ Restaurant ~ (01553) 762824 ~ Children in eating area of bar only ~ Open 11-11; 12-2, 7-10.30 Sun (closed winter Sun lunchtimes) ~ Bedrooms: £30(£38.50B)/£50B

LARLING TL9889 Map 5

Angel

A11 S of Attleborough

Run by very pleasant and friendly licensees (the same family have been here since 1913), this neatly kept pub is a welcoming oasis on a rather barren trunk road. The comfortable 1930-style lounge on the right has cushioned wheelback chairs, a nice long cushioned panelled corner settle, some good solid tables for meals and some lower ones, squared panelling, a collection of whisky-water jugs on the delft shelf over the big brick fireplace which houses a big woodburner, a couple of copper kettles, and some hunting prints; there are two dining rooms (one of which is no smoking). Reliable bar food includes sandwiches and toasties (from £2.25; the bacon and banana toastie is popular), mushroom pot (£3.95), ploughman's (£4.95), home-made burgers (from £4.95), chicken balti, tuna pasta bake or ham and egg (£5.95), grilled lamb chops (£6.95), local grilled trout (£7.95), steaks (from £9.95), daily specials such as fresh cod in beer batter or good steak and kidney pie (£6.25), home-made puddings (£2.95), children's dishes (£3.25), and Sunday roasts (from £6.50). Well kept Adnams Best and beers from local brewers like Iceni Mild and Scotts Blues and Bloater on handpump, and over 100 malt whiskies; friendly helpful service. The quarry-tiled black-beamed public bar has a good local atmosphere, with darts, dominoes, cribbage, juke box and fruit machine; piped music. A neat grass area behind the car park has picnic-sets around a big fairy-lit apple tree, and a safely fenced play area. Peter Beale's old-fashioned rose nursery is nearby. *(Recommended by Bill and Sheila McLardy, Sue Holland, Dave Webster, B and M Parkin, A N Ellis, K H Frostick, Richard Houghton, James and Pam Benton, Beryl and Bill Farmer, M and D Beard, Ian Phillips, Frank Davidson, John Baker)*

Free house ~ Licensee Brian Stammers ~ Real ale ~ Meals and snacks (till 10pm Fri/Sat) ~ (01953) 717963 ~ Children welcome ~ Live music monthly Sun afternoon ~ Open 10am-11pm; 12-10.30 Sun ~ Bedrooms: £30B/£50B

MUNDFORD TL8093 Map 5

Crown

Crown Street; village signposted off A1065 Thetford—Swaffham

Handy for Thetford Forest, this attractive 17th-c posting inn is well liked by a good mix of locals and visitors. The beamed lounge bar has a huge open fireplace in a flint wall, captain's chairs around highly polished tables, interesting local advertisements and other memorabilia, and a friendly bustling atmosphere. If the pub is full, a spiral iron staircase with *Vanity Fair* cartoons beside it leads up to the club room, an elegant restaurant and the garden. There are more heavy beams in the separate red-tiled locals' bar on the left, which has cast-iron-framed tables, another smaller brick fireplace with a copper hood, sensibly placed darts, cribbage, dominoes, fruit machine, a juke box and a screened-off pool table. Well kept Courage Directors, Iceni Boadicea Chariot Ale, Marstons Pedigree, and Woodfordes Wherry on handpump, and over 50 malt whiskies. Kind staff serve bar snacks such as sandwiches or wholemeal hoagies (from £1.50), home-made soup (£1.85), ploughman's (£5.25), burgers (from £3.25), local herb sausage (£4.25), daily specials like fried cherry tomatoes and mushrooms on a bed of courgette ribbons (£3.85), hot and spicy cajun style prawns with chilli salsa (£3.95), chicken curry, beef in ale or lamb rogan josh (£5.95), and paupiettes of plaice filled with prawns and smoked halibut (£8.50), steaks (from £8.95), and puddings such as chocolate and cointreau bavarois, treacle and nut tart of apple bakewell tart (from £2.75); Sunday roast beef (£5.95), and children's helpings of most meals.

(Recommended by Lesley Kant, B and M Parkin, MDN, Muriel and Peter Gleave, John Fahy, Nigel Clifton, P A Devitt, Roger and Fiona Todd)

Free house ~ Lease: Barry Walker~ Real ale ~ Meals and snacks (12-3, 7-10) ~ Restaurant ~ (01842) 878233 ~ Children welcome ~ Open 11-11; 12-10.30 Sun ~ Bedrooms: £32.50B/£49.50B

NORWICH TG2308 Map 5

Adam & Eve 🍷

Bishopgate; follow Palace Street from Tombland N of the Cathedral

Being so close to the city centre, it's unusual to find a pub with a nice cottagey feel and a genuinely friendly chatty atmosphere. This is Norwich's oldest pub and is thought to date back to at least 1249 – though the striking Dutch gables were added in the 14th-15th c. The little old-fashioned characterful bars quickly fill at lunchtime with a good mixed crowd of people, and there are antique high-backed settles (one handsomely carved), cushioned benches built into partly panelled walls, and tiled or parquet floors; the snug room is no smoking. Enjoyable, good value food includes sandwiches, granary baps or filled french bread (from £2.05), cheese and ale soup with a pastry top (£2.95), filled baked potatoes (from £3), ploughman's (from £3.55), shepherd's pie or vegetable bake (£4.05), chilli (£4.15), fish pie or ham and egg (£4.30), pork in cider and rosemary (£4.35), game pie (£4.40), daily specials like sausage and mash (£2.90) or salmon and leek fishcakes (£3.90), and puddings like home-made spicy bread and butter pudding (from £2); good Sunday roasts. Well kept Adnams Bitter, Greene King IPA, Marstons Pedigree, Theakstons Old Peculier, and guest beers on handpump, a wide range of malt whiskies, about a dozen decent wines by the glass or bottle, and Addlestone's cider. There are tableclothed picnic-sets in front of the pub and very pretty summer tubs and hanging baskets. *(Recommended by Sue Holland, Dave Webster, Tina and David Woods-Taylor, Muriel and Peter Gleave, Ian Phillips, Anthony Barnes, R J Bland, Mick Hitchman, John McDonald, Ann Bond, John Wooll, Robert and Anne Lees, A Albert, JDM, KM, Mr and Mrs N Chesher, Tim Barrow, Sue Demont, Jim Cowell)*

Courage ~ Lease: Colin Burgess ~ Real ale ~ Meals and snacks (12-7; till 2.30 Sun) ~ (01603) 667423 ~ Children in snug ~ Open 11-11; 12-10.30 Sun

Fat Cat

49 West End Street (A1074 W of centre, but inside ring road)

Coming to this traditional alehouse is like a visit to a private little beer festival with everyone talking to each other and trying a half of this and a half of that. They keep a fantastic range of around 25 changing well kept ales such as Adnams Bitter, Fullers London Pride and ESB, Greene King Abbot, Hop Back Summer Lightning, Kelham Island Pale Rider, Woodfordes Nelsons Revenge and Wherry, and so forth. About half are on handpump, while the rest are tapped from the cask in a still room behind the bar – big windows reveal all. They also keep two draught Belgian beers (a wheat and a fruit), draught lagers from Germany and the Czech Republic, bottled Belgian beers, eight country wines, and local cider. The no-nonsense furnishings include plain scrubbed pine tables and simple solid seats, lots of brewery memorabilia, bric-a-brac and stained glass, and there's a good lively bustling atmosphere – no music or machines. Not unexpectedly, customers are predominantly male; bar food consists of a dozen or so rolls at lunchtime (60p; not Sunday). There are tables outside. No children. *(Recommended by Mark J Hydes, David Twitchett, Ian Phillips, Sue Holland, Dave Webster, Jim Cowell, D Rumney, Tim Barrow, Sue Demont)*

Free house ~ Licensee Colin Keatley ~ Real ale ~ Snacks ~ (01603) 624364 ~ Open 12-11(10.30 Sun)

Most pubs in this book sell wine by the glass. We mention wines only if they are a cut above the – generally low – average. Please let us know of any good pubs for wine.

REEDHAM TG4101 Map 5

Ferry

B1140 Beccles—Acle; the ferry here holds only two cars but goes back and forth continuously till 10pm, taking only a minute or so to cross

Many people come to this splendidly placed Broads pub by boat – either by the working chain ferry (£2.25 per car plus 20p per passenger) or on a holiday hire boat (if you eat in the pub, they give you free mooring and showers); there are plenty of well spaced tables on the terrace overlooking the water. Inside, the long front bar has big picture windows, comfortable banquettes and some robust rustic tables carved from slabs of tree-trunk; the secluded back bar has antique rifles, copper and brass, and a fine log fire. Good food includes home-made soup (£2.60), chicken satay with spicy peanut sauce (£3.25), vegetable kiev (£5.50), home-made curry (£5.90), home-made steak and mushroom pie or lasagne (£5.95), home-cured gammon with pineapple (£6.75), steaks (£10.75), daily specials, and home-made puddings; children's menu (from £2.50), and good fresh vegetables. The restaurant and family room are no smoking. Well kept Adnams Bitter, Greene King Abbot, and Woodfordes Wherry on handpump, quite a few malt whiskies, country wines, and good cheerful staff; piped music. They're well geared up for families, with arrangements for baby food, and changing facilities. The woodturner's shop next door is worth a look. *(Recommended by M A Buchanan, Simon Penny, June and Malcolm Farmer, Bronwen and Steve Wrigley, Tina and David Woods-Taylor, Tim Barrow, Sue Demont, Ian Phillips, Mike and Mary Carter, Paul and Sandra Embleton, June and Perry Dann, Anthony Barnes)*

Free house ~ Licensee David Archer ~ Real ale ~ Meals and snacks ~ Restaurant ~ (01493) 700429 ~ Children welcome ~ Open 11-3, 6.30(6 Sat)-11; 12-10.30 Sun; 11-2.30, 7-11 in winter

RINGSTEAD TF7040 Map 8

Gin Trap

Village signposted off A149 near Hunstanton; OS Sheet 132 map reference 707403

A good steady trade of both visitors and locals gives this attractive white painted pub a bustling, friendly atmosphere. Copper kettles, carpenter's tools, cartwheels, and bottles hang from the beams in the lower part of the well kept friendly bar, there are toasting forks above the woodburning stove, a couple of gin-traps ingeniously converted to electric candle-effect wall lights, and captain's chairs and cast-iron-framed tables on the green-and-white patterned motif carpet; part of this bar is no smoking, and a small no-smoking dining room has quite a few chamber pots suspended from the ceiling, and high-backed pine settles; you can book a table in here. Well kept Adnams Bitter, Woodfordes Nog and Great Eastern Ale, and Gin Trap Bitter brewed by Woodfordes for the pub on handpump. Decent bar food includes lunchtime sandwiches (£2), filled baked potatoes (from £3), and ploughman's (from £3.25), as well as local sausages (£4.50), nut cutlet (£4.95), ham and chips (£5.50), home-made lasagne or steak and kidney pie (£5.75), steaks (from £8.50), daily specials, puddings, and children's meals (from £2). A handsome spreading chestnut tree shelters the car park, and the back garden has seats on the grass or small paved area and pretty flowering tubs. The pub is close to the Peddar's Way; hikers and walkers are welcome, but not their muddy boots. There's an art gallery next door, and boules in the back car park. *(Recommended by M Morgan, Paul Craddock, Chris Mawson, John Wooll, Bob Arnett, Judy Wayman, John Beeken, Mrs J Burrows, R Vincent, A F Gifford, Anthony Barnes)*

Free house ~ Brian and Margaret Harmes ~ Real ale ~ Meals and snacks (not winter Sun evenings) ~ (01485) 525264 ~ Children welcome away from bar until 9pm ~ Occasional piano player or Morris dancers ~ Open 11.30-2.30, 6.30(7 in winter)-11; 12-2.30, 7-10.30 Sun

SCULTHORPE TF8930 Map 8

Sculthorpe Mill

Pub signed off A148 W of Fakenham, opposite village

On a summer day, the garden in front of this converted watermill is a lovely place to sit with the River Wensum emerging from the bridge and ducks wandering around. Inside, the three small genteel rooms of the bar have soberly attractive furnishings, with good well polished tables, sensible chairs for diners (food is the main thing here), black beams and joists, and generous open fires in winter. The reception desk on the left of the bar and the neatly uniformed staff add a touch of dignity. Under the new licensees, bar food includes sandwiches or filled french bread (from £3.25), ploughman's (from £4.95), cajun chicken, steak and mushroom in ale pudding or fish pie (£6.95), rump steak (£7.95), tuna steak (£8.25), puddings (£2.75). Well kept Courage Directors, Greene King IPA, Morlands Old Speckled Hen and Woodfordes Wherry on handpump; decent wines; piped music. *(Recommended by M J Morgan, P M Sheard, Mark, Amanda, Luke and Jake Sheard, George Atkinson, R C Vincent, Ian Phillips; more reports on the new regime, please)*

Free house ~ Managers Roger Aston, Antoinette Riseborough ~ Real ale ~ Meals and snacks ~ Restaurant ~ (01328) 856161 ~ Children welcome ~ Open 11-11; 12-10.30 Sun; 11(12 Sun)-3, 6(7 Sun)-11(10.30 Sun) in winter ~ Bedrooms: £50B/£60B

SNETTISHAM TF6834 Map 8

Rose & Crown 🍷

Village signposted from A149 Kings Lynn—Hunstanton Rd, just N of Sandringham

Smartened up considerably over the last year or two, this pretty and warmly friendly white cottage continues to please readers. The Back Bar has cushioned seats on the dark wooden floor, the landlord's sporting trophies, old rackets and real tennis rackets, golf clubs and fishing rods, and a big log fire. The no-smoking Small Bar has a fine collection of prints of local interest, including Queen Victoria leaning from her window at Sandringham to acknowledge the gentlemen of the Snettisham hunt, and a newspaper rack; this room is popular with eaters. Some lovely old pews and other interesting furniture sit on the wooden floor of the Old Dining Room, and there are shelves with old bottles and books, and old prints and watercolours. The old-fashioned beamed front bar has lots of carpentry and farm tools, cushioned black settles on the red tiled floor, and a great pile of logs by the fire in the vast fireplace (which has a gleaming black japanned side oven). Weekly changing bar food includes home-made soup (£2.50), home-made pork and chicken liver pâté with pistachio nuts (£3.50), fillet of smoked haddock with a poached egg and glazed cheese sauce (£3.75; main course £5.75), pasta with prawns, clams and tarragon (£4.50; main course £6.75), lamb kidneys with mash and crispy bacon and red wine gravy (£6.95), chargrilled marinated loin of pork with beanshoots and black bean sauce (£7.75), roast duck breast with roasted mixed peppers and yellow pepper sauce (£8.25), and chargrilled fillet steak with casseroled onions and a pink peppercorn sauce (£11.75). Five real ales on handpump kept under light blanket pressure include Adnams Bitter, Bass, Greene King Abbot and IPA and Woodfordes Wherry. Lots of wines by the glass and freshly squeezed orange juice. The colourful garden is particularly attractive, with picnic-sets among the flowering shrubs, and two spectacular willow trees; summer barbecues. There's a good adjoining adventure playground, and maybe guinea pigs and budgerigars. We would be grateful to hear from readers who have stayed here. *(Recommended by John Wooll, Mr and Mrs G Turner, Mike and Wena Stevenson, M Morgan, Rita and Keith Pollard, G Neighbour, Steve and Sarah Pleasance, R C Vincent, Mr and Mrs C Fraser)*

Free house ~ Licensee Anthony Goodrich ~ Real ale ~ Meals and snacks ~ Restaurant ~ (01485) 541382 ~ Children in large family room ~ Blues every second Thurs ~ Open 11-11; 12-10.30 Sun ~ Bedrooms: £40B/£55B; s/c cottage, too

STIFFKEY TF9743 Map 8

Red Lion

A149 Wells—Blakeney

Even when the birdwatchers and walkers crowd in, the service in this friendly old pub remains cheerful and efficient. There's a very traditional atmosphere in the three fairly spartan interestingly shadowy bars; the oldest parts have a few beams, aged flooring tiles or bare floorboards, open fires, a mix of pews, small settles, built-in wooden wall seats and a couple of stripped high-backed settles, a nice old long deal table among quite a few others, and oil-type or lantern wall lamps. Bar food includes sandwiches (not Sunday lunchtime), steak and kidney pie (£6.25), rump steak (£7.25), and local whitebait (£4.50), mussels (£4.95) and crab (£6.25), with fresh local fish (£5.95-£7.95), and roast Sunday lunch (£6.50). Well kept Adnams Bitter, Elgoods Black Dog Mild, Greene King Abbot, Woodfordes Great Eastern Ale on handpump with Woodfordes Wherry tapped from the cask, Adnams wines, and Stowford Press cider; darts, dominoes, cribbage, and board games. The back restaurant leads into a no-smoking conservatory, and there are wooden seats and tables out on a back gravel terrace, with more on grass further up beyond. There's a pretty steam with ducks and swans across the road, and some pleasant walks from this unspoilt village.
(Recommended by Charles Bardswell, M Morgan, Fiona Wynn, Pete Stroud, Anthony Barnes, Tony Albert, Charles Gysin, MDN, Frank Davidson, O K Smyth, Peter Frogley, Keith and Janet Morris, JP, PP, R Suddaby, John Bowdler, Dennis and Barbara Cook, Mark Hydes, David Gregory, P and M Pumfrey)

Free house ~ Licensee Matthew Rees ~ Real ale ~ Meals and snacks (12-1.45, 7-8.45) ~ (01328) 830552 ~ Children in eating area of bar ~ Blues every other Fri evening ~ Open 11-3, 6.30-11; 12-3, 7-10.30; winter evening opening 7

STOW BARDOLPH TF6205 Map 5

Hare Arms 🍷

Just off A10 N of Downham Market

'Reliably enjoyable' is how several readers describe this pretty creeper-covered pub. There's a good bustling atmosphere, and the welcoming bar is decorated with old advertising signs and fresh flowers, has plenty of tables around its central servery, and a good log fire; maybe two friendly ginger cats and a sort of tabby. This bar opens into a spacious heated and well planted no-smoking conservatory, and that in turn opens into a pretty garden with picnic-sets under cocktail parasols and wandering peacocks, turkeys and chickens. Good bar food includes sandwiches (from £1.75), filled baked potatoes (from £3.60), ploughman's (from £5.25), home-made mushroom stroganoff (£6.25), gammon and pineapple (£7.95), steaks (from £12.50), daily specials such as leek and potato soup (£2.75), fresh deep-fried cod (£4.95), smoked haddock mornay or nut cutlet in tomato sauce (£6.25), pork steak in peppercorn sauce (£6.75), and lamb in redcurrant and port sauce (£8.45); efficient staff, even when pushed. Well kept Greene King IPA, Abbot, Rayments and their seasonal ales on handpump plus guests such as Caledonian 80/- and Smiles Heritage, a good range of wines, and quite a few malt whiskies; maybe cockles and whelks on the bar counter; fruit machine. *(Recommended by Charles Bardswell, Dr Andy Wilkinson, John Wooll, P M Millikin, Basil Minson, Jenny and Michael Back, Anthony Barnes, June and Malcolm Farmer, M Morgan, R Wiles, Lesley Kant, Quentin Williamson, Brian and Jill Bond, M A and C R Starling)*

Greene King ~ Tenants Trish and David McManus ~ Real ale ~ Meals and snacks (till 10pm) ~ Restaurant ~ (01366) 382229 ~ Children in conservatory and on Sundays in Old Coach House ~ Open 10.30-2.30, 6-11; 12-2.30, 7-10.30 Sun; cl 25-26 Dec

Looking for a pub with a really special garden, or in lovely countryside, or with an outstanding view, or right by the water? They are listed separately, at the back of the book.

SWANTON MORLEY TG0117 Map 8

Darbys

B1147 NE of Dereham

Carefully converted from two derelict farm cottages, this creeper-covered brick pub has a good lively village atmosphere and a fine mix of customers. The bar has lots of gin-traps and farming memorabilia, photographs on the left-hand end wall of the pub conversion, a good log fire (with the original bread oven alongside), tractor seats with folded sacks lining the long, attractive serving counter, and fresh flowers on the pine tables; maybe papers to read. Well kept Adnams Bitter and Broadside, Badger Tanglefoot, Greene King IPA, and Theakstons Old Peculier on handpump. Enjoyable bar food includes soup (£1.95; thai tom yum £2.95), tempura with sweet chilli sauce (£2.50), filled french bread or baked potatoes (from £3.25), ploughman's (£4.75), blue cheese pasta bake (£5.50), sweet and sour pork (£5.75), popular cod in beer batter (£5.95), salmon and prawn tagliatelle (£6.25), steaks (from £8.95), thai seafood (£9.50), daily specials, and puddings; children's menu (£2.75). The restaurant is no smoking; neat, friendly staff. Two dogs – a labrador and a border collie; darts, dominoes, cribbage, piped music, children's room with toy box (and a glassed-over well), and a really good play area out in the garden; they hold cook-your-own barbecues in summer. The bedrooms are in carefully converted farm buildings a few minutes away, and there's plenty to do if you're staying – the family also own the adjoining 720-acre estate, and can arrange clay pigeon shooting, golf, fishing, nature trails, and craft instruction. *(Recommended by Jenny and Michael Back, Anthony Barnes, John Wooll, Muriel and Peter Gleave, Lesley Kant, Ron and Sheila Corbett, David Gregory, Mike and Sue Davis, John Fahy, Eric Locker)*

Free house ~ Licensee John Carrick ~ Real ale ~ Meals and snacks (till 9.45) ~ Restaurant ~ (01362) 637647 (bedroom reservations 01362 637457) ~ Children welcome ~ Open 11-2.30, 6-11; 11-11 summer Sat; 12-3, 7-10.30 Sun; closed evening 25 Dec ~ Bedrooms: £22(£25B)/£35(£43B)

THORNHAM TF7343 Map 8

Lifeboat

Turn off A149 by Kings Head, then take first left turn

Perhaps at its best in winter when it's not so busy, this rambling old white-painted stone pub has a lot of genuine character. The main bar, dimly lit with antique paraffin lamps, has low settles, window seats, pews, and carved oak tables on the rugs on the tiled floor, great oak beams hung with traps and yokes, and masses of guns, swords, black metal mattocks, reed-slashers and other antique farm tools; there are a couple of little rooms leading off here, five open fires and no noisy games machines or piped music, though they still play the ancient game of 'pennies', outlawed in the late 1700s, and dominoes. Bar food includes soup (£2.75), game pâté with port and redcurrant sauce (£3.75), huge open sandwiches (£4.25), ploughman's (£4.75), mussels (£4.95; main course £6.95), butterbean and vegetable stew (£5.95), home-made burger or fish pie (£6.95), game casserole (£7.95), steaks (from £11.95), and children's menu (from £2.95). Well kept Adnams, Bass, Greene King IPA and Abbot, and Woodfordes Wherry on handpump. Up some steps from the smart conservatory is a sunny terrace with picnic-sets, and further back is a children's playground with fort and slide. The pub faces half a mile of coastal sea flats – plenty of surrounding walks. *(Recommended by Paul Craddock, Colin McKerrow, Martin Chambers, M Morgan, N Cobb, John Wooll, G Neighbour, Steve and Sarah Pleasance, MDN, A C Curry, O K Smyth, P and M Pumfrey, M Rutherford, Michael Switzer, John Bowdler, Pat and Clive Sherriff, Eric Locker, Mrs J Burrows, Sam Samuells, Lynda Payton, A Austin, Sue Holland, Dave Webster, Quentin Williamson, Ken and Jenny Simmonds)*

Free house ~ Licensees Charles and Angie Coker ~ Real ale ~ Meals and snacks ~ Restaurant ~ (01485) 512236 ~ Children welcome ~ Live entertainment most Fridays ~ Open 12-11; 12-10.30 Sun ~ Bedrooms: £56B/£72B

TITCHWELL TF7543 Map 8

Manor Hotel

A149 E of Hunstanton

A very nice place to stay, this comfortable hotel is very well run and popular with birdwatchers as it overlooks Titchwell RSPB reserve; lots of good walks and footpaths all round, and championship golf courses only moments away. From the end bar there are wonderful views over the salt marshes to the sea from the seats by the picture windows. The tranquil lounge has magazines, an open fire, and a good naturalists' record of the wildlife in the reserve. The pretty no-smoking restaurant leads into a conservatory which opens on to the sheltered neatly kept walled gardens. Good bar food includes Brancaster oysters (£1 each), home-made soup such as french onion with cheese crouton or sandwiches (£3.50), seared king scallops with basil and pine nut pesto (£5.95), vegetarian pasta parcels with tomato and herb sauce (£8), fillet of cod in beer batter (£8.95), rump steak burger with bacon, scallops and relish (£9.95), roast beef and yorkshire pudding (£10.95), and loin of fresh tuna (£13.50); children's menu. Greene King IPA and Abbot on handpump. *(Recommended by Paul Craddock, M Morgan, Charles Bardswell, Brian and Jill Bond, Deborah and Miles Protter, John Bowdler)*

Free house ~ Licensees Ian and Margaret Snaith ~ Real ale ~ Meals and snacks ~ Restaurant ~ (01485) 210221 ~ Children welcome ~ Open 12-2.30, 6.30-11(10.30 Sun); closed 18-31 Jan ~ Bedrooms: £55B/£90B

TIVETSHALL ST MARY TM1686 Map 5

Old Ram 🍷

Ipswich Rd; A140 15 miles S of Norwich

Carefully refurbished and well run, this is very much somewhere to come for a reliable meal rather than a quick drink. Served by friendly staff, the wide choice of food includes filled rolls (from £2.25), filled baked potatoes (from £2.75), ploughman's (£4.95), steak and kidney pie, chicken curry or lasagne (£7.50), skate wing with black butter or gammon and pineapple (£8.95), steaks (from £10.95), daily specials like baked crab (£3.95), tagliatelle carbonnade (£7.95), chicken stir fry (£9.95), tiger prawns with thai vegetables (£10.95), and roast duck breast on a mango and lime leaf sauce (£11.95); puddings like sticky toffee pudding (from £2.75), and children's menu (from £2.95). They also offer an Over Sixty Club Menu with main courses at £5.95. Well kept Adnams, Boddingtons, Woodfordes Wherry, and Worthingtons on handpump, 13 wines including champagne by the glass, and freshly squeezed orange juice; unobtrusive fruit machine and piped music. The spacious main room, ringed by cosier side areas, has standing-timber dividers, stripped beams and brick floors, a longcase clock, antique craftsmen's tools on the ceiling, and a huge log fire in the brick hearth; other rooms ramble off. An attractive, no-smoking dining room has an open woodburning stove, and leads to a second comfortable no-smoking dining room and gallery. Seats on the sheltered flower-filled terrace (which has heaters for eating outside on cooler days). No dogs. *(Recommended by Tina and David Woods-Taylor, Andy and Sarah Gillett, Beryl and Brian Farmer, Mrs D P Dick, John Wooll, Brian Horner, Brenda Arthur, Ian and Nita Cooper)*

Free house ~ Licensee John Trafford ~ Real ale ~ Meals and snacks (from 7.30 for breakfast – non-residents welcome – till 10pm) ~ (01379) 676794 ~ Children welcome but under 7s must leave by 8pm ~ Occasional live entertainment ~ Open 11-11; 12-11 Sun; closed 25-26 Dec ~ Bedrooms: £49B/£68B

UPPER SHERINGHAM TG1441 Map 8

Red Lion

B1157; village signposted off A148 Cromer—Holt, and the A149 just W of Sheringham

The very good food is the main draw to this delightfully simple but relaxing little flint cottage. This might include home-made soup, home-made pâté (£3.50), stilton-stuffed mushrooms (£3.75), mushroom stroganoff or vegetable curry (£5.50), steak and kidney or chicken and leek pies (from £5.95), winter pigeon, rabbit and pheasant (from £6.75), lots of fresh fish like haddock with cheese sauce (£6.75), whole plaice with herb butter (£6.95), and halibut with a thai sauce or skate with caper butter (£7.25), steaks (from £8.50), and puddings such as home-made bakewell tart or home-made bread and butter pudding with whisky (£2.50). Well kept Greene King IPA, and Woodfordes Wherry and Great Eastern Ale on handpump, with over 60 malt whiskies and decent wines. The two quiet small bars have stripped high-backed settles and country-kitchen chairs on the red tiles or bare boards, plain off-white walls and ceiling, a big woodburning stove, and newspapers to read; one area is no smoking. Dominoes and cribbage, and maybe some cats. *(Recommended by George Atkinson, Malcolm Taylor, Alan and Judith Gifford, Marion Turner, Colin Barnes, Peter and Pat Frogley, D Twitchett, J F Knutton)*

Free house ~ Licensee I M Bryson ~ Real ale ~ Meals and snacks ~ (01263) 825408 ~ Children welcome ~ Open 11.30-3, 6-11; 12-3, 7-10.30 Sun ~ Bedrooms: £23/£36

WARHAM TF9441 Map 8

Three Horseshoes

Warham All Saints; village signposted from A149 Wells next the Sea—Blakeney, and from B1105 S of Wells

Unanimous praise again for this unspoilt, old-fashioned country local. It's very well run and neatly kept by the friendly licensees, and even when really busy, service remains cheerful and efficient. The three rooms have stripped deal or mahogany tables (one marked for shove-ha'penny) on the stone floor, red leatherette settles built around the partly panelled walls of the public bar, and open fires in Victorian fireplaces; an antique American Mills one-arm bandit is still in working order (it takes 5p pieces; there's a 1960s one that takes 1p pieces), there's a big longcase clock with a clear piping strike, and a twister on the ceiling (you give it a twist and according to where it ends up you pay for the next round). One area is no smoking. Reasonably priced and generously served, the enjoyable bar food includes lunchtime snacks like sandwiches and filled rolls (from £2.50), filled baked potatoes (from £3), and ploughman's (from £4.20), as well as local mussels, cockles and prawns in a cheddar sauce (£3.50), baked mushrooms (£4.20), fish cheese bake (£6.80), beef in beer or game pie (£7.20), nice daily specials such as mushroom and tomato pie (£4.80), liver and onions (£5.20), and cream garlic lamb pie (£6.80), and puddings like rhubarb crumble; good vegetables. The dining room is no smoking. Notably well kept Greene King IPA and Abbot, Woodfordes Wherry, and a weekly guest on handpump or tapped from the cask, good home-made lemonade, and local cider. Darts, cribbage, shove-ha'penny, dominoes, and one of the outbuildings houses a wind-up gramophone museum – opened on request. There are rustic tables out on the side grass. *(Recommended by John Beeken, David and Helen Wilkins, John C Baker, Charles Bardswell, David and Anne Culley, Paul Craddock, John Honnor, John Wooll, M Morgan, Mr and Mrs Dennis Cook, Jeff Davies, Derek and Sylvia Stephenson, Anthony Longden, Robert and Anne Lees, Mrs M Sloper, Mrs J Hale, Dennis and Barbara Cook, Stephen Harvey, P and M Pumfrey, Dr B and Mrs P B Baker, Chris and David Stephenson)*

Free house ~ Licensee Iain Salmon ~ Real ale ~ Meals and snacks (not 25-26 Dec) ~ (01328) 710547 ~ Children in eating area of bar ~ Open 11.30-2.30, 6-11; 12-3, 6-10.30 Sun ~ Bedrooms: £22/£44(£48B)

WELLS NEXT THE SEA TF9143 Map 8

Crown

The Buttlands

This big black and white Georgian-faced inn has a pubby front bar with bowed beams showing that it's a fair bit older than the frontage suggests, and the two quieter back rooms have some interesting pictures on the wall over the roaring log fire, including several big Nelson prints and maps showing the town in the 18th and 19th centuries. Waitress-served bar food includes sandwiches (from £1.60), soup (£2.25), ploughman's (£4.75), vegetable curry (£4.75), ham and egg (£5.25), steak and kidney pie or grilled trout (£5.75) lamb chops (£6.75), rump steak (£10.50), and daily specials like moules marinières (£5.25), crab mornay (£6.25), and tuna steak with lemon butter (£8.25); children's dishes. Adnams, Bass, and a guest beer on handpump, and several malt whiskies; piped music. A neat conservatory has small modern settles around the tables. The central square of quiet Georgian houses is most attractive, and archers used to practise on the tranquil village green opposite. *(Recommended by M J Morgan, Charles Bardswell, Ian Phillips, R Suddaby, Sue Holland, Dave Webster)*

Free house ~ Licensee Wilfred Foyers ~ Real ale ~ Meals and snacks ~ Restaurant ~ (01328) 710209 ~ Children in eating area of bar ~ Open 11-2.30, 6-11; 12-2.30, 7-10.30 Sun ~ Bedrooms: £35(£55B)/£59(£69B)

WEST BECKHAM TG1339 Map 8

Wheatsheaf

Church Road; village signposted off A148 Holt—Cromer

This attractive village inn with its flint walls and cottagey doors has been sensibly renovated inside – not too excessively, keeping separate beamed areas and a pleasantly homely feel. There's a roaring feature log fire in one part, a smaller coal one in another, comfortable chairs and banquettes, and an enormous black cat. Service is deft, and the landlord and his staff are so welcoming that the mix of local people and holiday-makers works really well. Well kept Bass, Woodfordes Wherry, Nelsons Revenge, Norfolk Nog and Headcracker, and a weekly changing guest beer, a good choice of wines in generous measures, and country wines. Reasonably priced food includes good sandwiches and filled french bread (from £1.75), winter home-made soup (£2.25), ploughman's (from £4.25), calamari (£3.75), deep-fried brie with cumberland sauce (£3.95), giant yorkshire pudding with sausage and beans or good ham and egg (£5.25), steaks (from £8.95), and lunchtime specials such as steak and kidney or chicken and mushroom pies (£5.25), fried gammon strips with wine and cream sauce (£6.50), chicken with a mustard and mushroom cream sauce (£6.95); in the evening the specials are more elaborate with duck and port pâté with cumberland sauce or black pudding with apple and bacon (£3.75), home-made herb pancakes stuffed with vegetables (£5.50), lamb cutlets with a mustard crust and a port and mushroom sauce (£7.25), quail stuffed with tomato, onion, and garlic and served with a whisky cream sauce (£7.50), and puddings like home-made bakewell tart, apple crumble or chocolate sponge with chocolate sauce (£2.95); on Fridays they do fresh fish in beer batter (£5.25); popular Sunday lunch. The two dining rooms are no smoking. Darts, pool, bar billiards, shove-ha'penny, cribbage, dominoes, fruit machine, video game, and piped music. There are tables out in the partly terraced front garden, which may have a bouncy castle and wandering chickens (there's a shorter menu if you want to eat outside); behind is a small craft centre. *(Recommended by John Wooll, Frank Davidson, Malcolm Taylor, George Atkinson, Derek Field, R C Morgan)*

Free house ~ Licensee Paul Fletcher ~ Real ale ~ Meals and snacks (not Sun evening or winter Mon lunchtime) ~ (01263) 822110 ~ Well behaved children welcome ~ Occasional live entertainment ~ Open 11.30(12 in winter)-3, 6.30(7 in winter)-11; 12-3, 7-10.30 Sun; closed winter Mon lunchtime

WINTERTON ON SEA TG4919 Map 8

Fishermans Return

From B1159 turn into village at church on bend, then turn right into The Lane

The front terrace in front of this traditional brick and flint pub has been extended this year and has attractive wrought-iron and wooden benches; there's a pond and pets corner with ornamental chickens and bantams. Run by friendly people and with a relaxing atmosphere, the white-painted panelled lounge bar has neat brass-studded red leatherette seats and a winter log fire, while the panelled public bar has low ceilings and a glossily varnished nautical air. Good home-made bar food includes daily specials such as spinach-stuffed cannelloni on a mushroom and pesto base or bean casserole with smoked ham and sausage (£4.75), chicken in coriander and lime sauce with pasta (£6.75), fresh salmon fishcakes with tomato sauce (£7.25), and puddings such as apricot upside-down pudding or tiramisu cheesecake (£2.50); also, toasties (from

£1.75), filled baked potatoes (from £3.25), burgers (from £5), omelettes (from £5.50), steaks (from £9.50); children's dishes (£2.75). Well kept Scotts Blues and Bloater and Strong Mild, and Woodfordes Wherry and Great Eastern on handpump, decent wines, around 30 malt whiskies, and James White cider; darts, dominoes, cribbage, pool, fruit machine, video game, and juke box. Seats in front by a quiet lane have nice views, as do the sheltered garden and terrace, which opens out from the back bar. The characterful bedrooms, up the steep curving stairs, have low doors and uneven floors; no-smoking garden room. The pub is not far from the sandy beach, with good birdwatching. *(Recommended by Sue and Mike Loseby, Klaus and Elizabeth Leist, David and Anne Culley, Chris Brace, Revd and Mrs A Smith, Robert and Anne Lees, JDM, KM, Derek and Sylvia Stephenson)*

Free house ~ Licensees John and Kate Findlay ~ Real ale ~ Meals and snacks ~ (01493) 393305 ~ Children in small dining room in winter, in family room in summer ~ Open 11-2.30, 6.30-11; 11-11 Sat; 12-10.30 Sun ~ Bedrooms: £30/£50

WOODBASTWICK TG3315 Map 8

Fur & Feather

Off B1140 E of Norwich

As this converted thatched cottage is set next door to Woodfordes Brewery, the marvellous range of beers is the primary draw. Tapped from the cask they include Broadsman Bitter, Great Eastern Ale, Wherry, Mardlers Mild, Baldric, Norfolk Nog (a strong dark ale, good for keeping out the winter cold), very strong Head Cracker, and Nelsons Revenge; you can take some home with you. There's quite an emphasis on food and the rooms are set out in the style of a dining pub: sandwiches (from £2.50), home-made chicken liver pâté (£3.50), filled baked potatoes (from £3.50), ploughman's or home-made chilli (£5.50), burgers (£5.75), home-cooked ham and chips or leek and butterbean nut crumble (£5.95), tuna and pasta bake, chicken breast wrapped in bacon with a stilton sauce or steak and kidney pudding (£6.75), sirloin steak (£9.95), puddings (from £2.50), and children's meals (£3.15); friendly, helpful staff. The restaurant and part of the bar are no smoking; piped music and cribbage. There are tables out in the garden. This estate village is lovely. *(Recommended by K and E Leist, D Bryan, Lesley Kant, James Nunns, Mike Gorton, Andrew Barker, Claire Jenkins, Sue Holland, Dave Webster, JP, PP, Martin and Karen Wade, Brian Horner, Chris and Shirley Machin, Jenny and Michael Back)*

Woodfordes ~ Tenants John and Jean Marjoram ~ Real ale ~ Meals and snacks ~ Restaurant (Tues-Sat evenings) ~ (01603) 720003 ~ Children in eating area of bar and in restaurant ~ Open 11(12 in winter)-3, 6-11; 12-3, 7-10.30 Sun

Lucky Dip

Besides the fully inspected pubs, you might like to try these Lucky Dips recommended to us and described by readers (if you do, please send us reports):

Attleborough [London Rd (off A11); TM0495], *White Lodge*: Good value enjoyable food in low and pretty partly thatched beamed cottage, two roaring log fires, several rooms, Adnams and Hoskins beers *(Brian Horner, Brenda Arthur, Ian Phillips)*

Beachamwell [off A1122 Swaffham—Downham Mkt; TF7505], *Great Danes Head*: Cosy and friendly, with helpful licensees, real ales inc Greene King Abbot, good house red, good varied food; children and dogs welcome, small separate public bar with pool, restaurant; by green of tiny village *(Philip and Caroline Pennant-Jones)*

Beeston [TF9015], *Ploughshare*: Pleasantly renovated big sunny bar with old tables, benches, woodburner in big fireplace, magazines to read, small no-smoking area, separate restaurant, pool room; fairly wide choice of food inc good choice of puddings; Greene King IPA, Abbot, Rayments and guest beers, decent house wines *(John Wooll, Ted George)*

☆ **Binham** [B1388 SW of Blakeney; TF9839], *Chequers*: Long beamed bar with coal fires each end, one in inglenook, sturdy plush seats, ales such as Adnams, Bass, Greene King IPA and Abbot, enterprising promptly served home-made food from good rolls and sandwiches up using local produce (Sun lunch very popular), reasonable prices, small no-smoking dining area, efficient cheerful staff, picnic-sets on grass behind; open all day, interesting village with huge priory church; bedrooms *(Robert and*

Anne Lees, R Vincent, John Beeken, George Atkinson, BB)

Blakeney [TG0243], *Manor*: Small attractive hotel in own grounds with civilised, comfortable and peaceful pub part, popular with older people for good generous waitress-served bar food from well filled crab sandwiches up, not expensive; decent house wines; sunny tables outside, bedrooms; opp wildfowl reserve and sea inlet *(Frank Davidson, Charles Bardswell)*; *Red Lion*: Cosy narrow carpeted pub, Morlands Old Speckled Hen, Websters Pennine and Woodfordes Wherry *(James Nunn)*

☆ **Brancaster Staithe** [A149 Hunstanton—Wells; TF7743], *Jolly Sailors*: Good freshly cooked specials and good range of home-made puddings in simple but stylish and rather upmarket old-fashioned pub, popular with yachtsmen and the local gentry; well kept Bass and Greene King, good wines, provision for children, log fire, attractive restaurant, sheltered tables in nice garden with terrace, enclosed play area and tennis court, open all Sun in summer *(Howard and Margaret Buchanan, M Morgan, Charles Bardswell, JJW, CMW, R Suddaby, LYM)*

Brancaster Staithe, *White Horse*: Light and airy refurbishment under newish owners, with lots of wood, spotlights, jazzy piped music, blue and yellow dining room with highly colour-coordinated tables and crockery, enjoyable gently trendy meals inc plenty of fresh fish and local seafood, crunchy veg, bar food too; good reasonably priced wine list, cheery helpful staff *(Louise Medcalf, J D Hodgson, Paul Munton)*

Brisley [B1145; TF9521], *Bell*: 16th-c pub in good spot on edge of green, olde-worlde long beamed bar with some stripped brick, Whitbreads-related ales, good service, wide choice of popular food inc fresh veg and children's dishes, small evening fish restaurant; tables out on green; children and dogs welcome; bedrooms *(CMW, JJW)*

☆ **Briston** [B1354, Aylsham end of village; TG0532], *John H Stracey*: Welcoming, clean and well run country dining pub, wide choice of good reasonably priced quickly served food inc fresh fish Tues and other good value speciality nights, well kept Greene King Abbot, decent house wines, comfortable seats, log fire, long-serving landlord, friendly obliging staff, dog and cat; popular pleasant restaurant, a few tables in small well kept garden; good value bedrooms with good breakfast – nice for people who like being part of family *(John and Julia Hall, John Wooll)*

Burnham Overy Staithe [A149; TF8442], *Hero*: Pleasant service, generous usual food, Flowers Original and Tetleys, friendly atmosphere, interesting bygones *(M J Morgan)*

Burston [Crown Green; TM1383], *Crown*: Genuine country pub with relaxed and friendly staff and locals, lots of old woodwork, good food all freshly made inc some creative dishes, well kept Adnams, Greene King Abbot and Burston Strike brewed for the pub by Old Chimneys, all tapped from the cask; faultless service *(John C Baker)*

Caister on Sea [Victoria St; TG5211], *Ship*: Busy old-fashioned fishing-theme local with magnificent hanging baskets, well kept Whitbreads and guest beers, decent house wine, good value satisfying food inc cheap fresh local fish *(John Kirk, Mr and Mrs T Drake)*

☆ **Castle Acre** [Stocks Green; village signed off A1065 N of Swaffham; TF8115], *Ostrich*: Interesting ungentrified pub prettily placed overlooking a tree-lined green, odd mix of utilitarian furnishings and fittings with some ancient beams, masonry and huge fireplace, well kept Greene King ales; at best the food's very enjoyable and good value (with plenty of vegetarian dishes), and service individual and welcoming; dominoes, cribbage, fruit machine, piped music, family room, picnic-sets in sheltered garden; jazz 2nd and 3rd Weds of month, folk last Weds, attractive village with castle and monastery remains *(Charles Bardswell, Nigel Clifton, R J Bland, Ann and Mike Bolton, LYM)*

Castle Rising [TF6624], *Black Horse*: Comfortable and spotless Beefeater family dining pub by church and almshouses in pleasant unspoilt village, good furnishings inc sofas, usual reliable food, mainly Whitbreads-related ales, friendly unhurried service, long hours; children welcome, own menu and play packs; no dogs, pleasant tables out under cocktail parasols, play area *(John Wooll, R C Vincent, M Morgan)*

☆ **Cawston** [Eastgate, S of village – on B1149 from Norwich turn left towards Haveringland at crossroads ½ mile before the B1145 Cawston turn; TG1323], *Ratcatchers*: Bustling pub-restaurant very popular for good freshly prepared food from sandwiches with own-baked bread to steaks, with good fish and vegetarian choice, good value if not cheap; well kept Adnams Extra, Bass, Hancocks HB and a guest, good range of wines and country wines, several malt whiskies; L-shaped beamed bar with open fire, quieter no-smoking candlelit dining room (not Sun evening); darts, cribbage, dominoes, piped music; children welcome; bedrooms *(David Atkinson, Frank Davidson, Anthony Barnes, Bill and Brenda Lemon, Marion H Turner, J F Knutton, Ann and Mike Bolton, LYM)*

☆ **Cley next the Sea** [Holt Rd, off A149 W of Sheringham; TG0443], *George & Dragon*: Edwardian pub, comfortable if a bit faded, popular with salt-marsh birdwatchers, cosy locals' bar, lounge and dining area, St George artefacts, wide choice of generally good bar food inc good vegetarian choice, well kept Greene King IPA, Abbot and a seasonal ale; sizeable garden over road, with boules pitch; bedrooms *(Stephen Pine, Alfred Lawrence, Peter Frogley, David and Anne Culley, Rita and Keith Pollard, Eric Locker, LYM)*

☆ **Cley next the Sea** [Holt Rd, Newgate Green, nr church], *Three Swallows*: Homely unostentatious take-us-as-you-find-us village local tucked off main rd facing green, banquettes around long high leathered tables, roaring fire, steps up to second simpler bar, good generous quickly served simple home-made food from sandwiches (good crab) to fresh fish, well kept Flowers Original, Greene King IPA and Tetleys from extraordinary carved bar, good wines; dogs welcome, wandering tabbies; barbecues in big attractive garden with croquet, aviary, dogs, cats and lovely view of church; bedrooms simple but clean and comfortable, handy for the salt marshes *(Nick May, Paul Hilditch, M Morgan, George Atkinson, Charles Bardswell, G Staple)*

☆ **Coltishall** [Church St (B1354); TG2719], *Red Lion*: Friendly modernised family pub, away from water but pleasant setting; decent straightforward generous food inc good puddings, real ales such as Adnams, Boddingtons, Flowers Original, Fullers Chiswick, Greene King Abbot, Morlands Old Speckled Hen and Weasel brewed for them by Woodfordes, several attractive split-level rooms (main bar effectively in cellar), restaurant; tables out under cocktail parasols by fountain, good play area; bedrooms *(Ian Phillips, M A Buchanan)*

☆ **Denver Sluice** [signed via B1507 off A1122 Downham Mkt bypass; TF6101], *Jenyns Arms*: Extensive and well laid out roadhouse-style pub in fine spot by the massive hydraulic sluices which control the Great Ouse, tables out by the waterside with strutting peacocks, ales such as Adnams, Boddingtons, Flowers Original, Fullers London Pride, Greene King IPA and Websters Yorkshire, generous usual food from sandwiches to steaks inc vegetarian; big light and airy games area, piped music; handy for Welney wildfowl reserve *(John and Elizabeth Cox, Charles Bardswell, BB)*

Dereham [42 Norwich St; TF9913], *Kings Head*: Decent value bar food, which you can eat in the dining room if the bar's full *(Frank Davidson)*

☆ **Dersingham** [Manor Rd; B1440 towards Sandringham; TF6830], *Feathers*: Solid Jacobean sandstone inn with relaxed modernised dark-panelled bars opening on to attractive garden with elaborate play area; well kept Adnams, Bass and a quickly changing guest beer, log fires, generous bar food from sandwiches up, restaurant (not Sun evening); good range of pub games in third bar, children welcome, can get very busy in season; some live music in barn; comfortable well furnished bedrooms *(John McDonald, Ann Bond, John Fahy, Muriel and Peter Gleave, John Wooll, Sheila and Robert Robinson, Edward Froggatt, LYM)*

Dersingham [nr church], *Gamekeepers Lodge*: Pleasantly refurbished old building, friendly staff, well cooked and presented generous food inc good value carvery, nice dining room (children welcome here); tables outside *(Albert and Margaret Horton)*

Diss [TM1179], *Saracens Head*: Good food, well kept Woodfordes Wherry; can be fully booked w/e *(Rita and Keith Pollard)*

Docking [High St; TF7637], *Pilgrims Reach*: Warm and comfortable small bar (can be busy), well kept Adnams Bitter and Broadside and Boddingtons, good generous food inc interesting soups, friendly landlady and staff, quiet restaurant, children's room; tables on attractive sheltered back terrace *(Mrs J Burrows, O K Smyth, A F and J Gifford, M Morgan)*

Downham Market [Bridge St; TF6103], *Crown*: 17th-c coaching inn with log fire in small homely oak-panelled bar, well kept changing ales such as Buckleys and Theakstons Mild, speedy service, good food inc attractively presented veg (can be eaten in restaurant); comfortable bedrooms, big breakfast *(R C Vincent)*

East Barsham [B1105 3 miles N of Fakenham; TF9133], *White Horse*: Pleasantly refurbished and extended, long main bar with big log fire, attractive dining area, well kept ales such as Woodfordes, reasonably priced food in bar and restaurant; piped music, darts; children welcome; bedrooms *(M Morgan)*

Foulsham [TG0224], *Queens Head*: Long bar, partly partitioned dining area on right, lots of china, crockery and brassware, wide choice of enjoyable freshly cooked food, comfortable wall seats, cast-iron-framed tables, friendly staff and cat, real ales such as Adnams and Elgoods Golden Newt; children welcome – family room/back games room, big back garden *(Jenny and Michael Back)*

Fritton [Beccles Rd (A143); TG4600], *Fritton Decoy*: Good choice of food inc children's, high chairs, courteous helpful licensees, Tetleys; tables in garden, opp country park *(Quentin Williamson)*

☆ **Garboldisham** [The Street; TM0081], *Fox*: Popular food inc fresh tasty unusual sandwiches and full Adnams range kept well in sympathetically updated old pub with original beams, old pews, massive woodburner in deep brick hearth, super landlord, friendly helpful staff; daily papers; small back garden *(Ian and Liz Phillips)*

☆ **Gayton** [B1145/B1153; TF7219], *Crown*: New landlord and chef doing wide-ranging bar food inc Spanish specialities and superb hot winter lunchtime buffet in attractive flower-decked pub, simple yet stylish inside, with some unusual old features; well kept Greene King IPA, Abbot and Mild, friendly relaxed atmosphere, comfortable seats, games room; tables in sheltered garden *(Bob King, LYM)*

☆ **Great Cressingham** [Water End; just off A1064 Swaffham—Brandon – OS Sheet 144 map ref 849016; TF8401], *Windmill*: Roomy family pub with three beamed bars, cosy nooks and crannies, huge log fireplace, lots of farm tools, conservatory, games room; good value generous food, quick service, well kept Adnams, Batemans, Bass, Sam Smiths and guest beers, decent wines; well kept big garden, dogs allowed *(Anthony Barnes, Frank Davidson, Charles and Pauline Stride)*

☆ **Great Ellingham** [Church St; pub signed off B1077, which is off A11 SW of Norwich; TM0196], *Crown*: Neatly kept open-plan bar well divided into quiet alcoves, comfortable plush and other seats, soft lighting, relaxed atmosphere, enjoyable food inc good fresh fish and seafood, home-made bread and pickles, bargain lunches, three small attractive dining rooms (one for families), well kept Adnams, John Smiths, Woodfordes Wherry and local Wolf, very friendly and professional young landlord, tables in garden; no dogs *(Bill and Sheila McLardy, Gwen and Peter Andrews, BB)*

Great Ryburgh [TF9527], *Boar*: Friendly and comfortable, well kept Adnams, food inc good main dishes and puddings in bar and restaurant (should book Sat night) *(R Vincent)*

nr **Great Yarmouth** [St Olaves; A143 towards Beccles, where it crosses R Waveney; TM4599], *Bell*: Busy extensively modernised riverside pub (still has attractive Tudor brickwork and heavy timbering), with good varied bar food, well kept Whitbreads-related ales from long bar counter, decent wines, games and juke box on public side, restaurant where children allowed; garden with good play area and barbecues *(M A Buchanan, LYM)*; [Berney Arms Stn; TG4604], *Berney Arms*: Accessible only by boat, 8-min train ride from Gt Yarmouth or long walk across fields; great spot, exceptionally friendly landlord, well kept Greene King IPA, straightforward food, good atmosphere, interesting decor, flagstones, woodburner, ex-cask settles; tables out by towpath, cl winter *(Simon Penny)*

Haddiscoe [A143; TM4497], *Crown*: Spacious and comfortable bars and dining room, interesting bric-a-brac, good home-made food inc Fri fish and chip suppers and Sun lunch, well kept Courage Directors and Greene King IPA, good service *(Sue Rowland, Paul Mallett)*

Hainford [Stratton Rd; TG2218], *Chequers*: Comfortable and friendly rebuilt thatched cottage in charming setting, well prepared food from filled baguettes up, real ales such as Courage Directors, Fullers ESB and John Smiths, big airy bar area and rooms off, pleasant staff, well laid-out gardens with play area; piped music; children welcome *(Ian Phillips)*

Happisburgh [by village church; TG3830], *Hill House*: Friendly heavy-beamed village pub with plush seats, woodburner in big inglenook, open fire other end, bar billiards in games area, well kept changing ales such as Marstons Pedigree and Shepherd Neame Spitfire, wide choice of popular generous food inc good value sandwiches and original dishes, dining area (children allowed here); tables outside front and back; bedrooms, pleasant setting *(K Flack, Anthony Barnes, BB)*

☆ **Hethersett** [Old Norwich Rd; TG1505], *Kings Head*: Cheerful and homely traditional pub with well kept Courage Directors, Marstons Pedigree, Morlands Old Speckled Hen and Woodfordes Wherry, good reasonably priced food (very popular weekdays with older people), comfortable carpeted lounge, obliging staff, old chairs and tables, big log-burning stove in inglenook, traditional games in cosy public bar, attractive and spacious back lawn, good play area *(Ian Phillips, Charles Bardswell, LYM)*

☆ **Hilborough** [A1065 S of Swaffham; TF8100], *Swan*: Welcoming early 18th-c pub with good simple home cooking done to order (so may be a wait), well kept Batemans, Greene King IPA and Abbot and guest beers, pleasant helpful staff, plenty of old-fashioned pub and board games, no music, small back restaurant; picnic-sets on pleasant sheltered lawn *(Norman S Smith, Anthony Barnes, James Nunn, BB)*

Hillington [TF7225], *Ffolkes Arms*: Useful roomy roadside stop for Sandringham visitors, wide range of beers, popular Sun carvery, good choice of bar food, garden behind; reasonably priced bedrooms in former barn *(M Morgan)*

☆ **Holkham** [A149 nr Holkham Hall; TF8943], *Victoria*: Relaxed and simply furnished brick-and-flint inn with communicating bar rooms, interesting pictures, well kept Adnams, Greene King IPA and Tetleys, decent house wine, family food from sandwiches up, good service; dominoes, cribbage, piped music; children allowed in restaurant, tables outside; bedrooms, handy for coastal nature reserves, open all day Sat *(C J Machin, John Wooll, Charles Bardswell, Michael Switzer, LYM)*

Holme next the Sea [Kirkgate St; TF7043], *White Horse*: Good value straightforward generous food inc tasty fish and chips, welcoming licensees and locals, useful two-glass wine bottles, big garden; cl Mon lunchtime *(John Wooll)*

Honingham [just off A47; TG1011], *Buck*: Beamed pub with very good range of enjoyable food inc huge sandwiches, vegetarian dishes, lunchtime bargains; welcoming licensees *(Don and Shirley Parrish)*

Horning [Lower St; TG3417], *Swan*: Busy popular Brewers Fayre by paddle-boat cruiser stop, open all day, worth knowing for its splendid views, with riverside picnic-sets; well kept Whitbreads-related ales, pleasant efficient service, bedrooms *(P A Legon, Beryl and Bill Farmer, Paul and Sharon Sneller)*

☆ **Itteringham** [off B1354 NW of Aylsham; TG1430], *Walpole Arms*: Delightfully old-fashioned village pub on River Bure, interesting varied food, generous, reasonably priced and beautifully presented, staff quick, friendly and helpful even though very busy, well kept ales such as Adnams Regatta and Broadside and Boddingtons, good lively atmosphere; children welcome *(Mr and Mrs M A Steane, Malcolm Taylor, A Larter)*

Kings Lynn [Tuesday Mkt Pl; TF6220], *Maydens Heade*: Centrally placed Scottish Courage pub, cosmetically refurbished, popular with all ages at lunchtime and a younger set in the evening; tasty bar food, separate good value carvery restaurant *(R C Vincent, Tony Hobden)*; [Gayton Rd, Gaywood; TF6320], *Wildfowler*: Useful Big Steak pub, smart but comfortable and relaxed even when busy, popular food inc children's menu (fun packs for them), well kept Tetleys-related beers, good choice of wines in big glasses, very friendly swift staff, separate non-food adult area *(R C Vincent, John Wooll)*

☆ **Letheringsett** [A148 just W of Holt; TG0538],

☆ *Kings Head*: Set well back from the road like a private house, with plenty of tables on spacious lawn, informally furnished bar (not smart) with sepia prints of Norfolk life, friendly staff, well kept Adnams, Greene King IPA and Abbot and Woodfordes Wherry, usual food from sandwiches to steaks inc children's, log fire, small lounge, games room with darts, pool, shove ha'penny, dominoes, cribbage, fruit machines; piped music, occasional live; children and dogs welcome, open all day *(John Beeken, Bernard and Marjorie Parkin, LYM)*

Litcham [B1145; TF8817], *Bull*: Big two-bar village pub with no music, decor mixing old and new, good value usual food, decent wine by the glass, friendly landlord *(John Wooll)*

Little Cressingham [TF8700], *White Horse*: Small pub with Flowers Original and Wadworths 6X, very nice freshly prepared snacks, obliging service *(Ian Phillips)*

Loddon [just off A146 Norwich—Lowestoft; TM3698], *Swan*: Cosy and pleasant 17th-c coaching inn in attractive village not far from the water, long bar with lounge at one end and upstairs bar with pool table and video games, good choice of generous home-made food, good range of real ales, friendly service, seats in yard outside *(A J Thomas)*

Newton [A1065 4 miles N of Swaffham; TF8315], *George & Dragon*: Distinctive roadside pub with good value food inc imaginative dishes, obliging staff, good choice of beers, back restaurant *(Keith Day, R Vincent)*

☆ **North Elmham** [B1110/B1145 N of E Dereham; TF9820], *Kings Head*: Welcoming old-fashioned inn, neat and tidy, with wide choice of good value home-cooked food in log-fire lounge or lovely small dining room; friendly efficient service even when busy, Scottish Courage ales and Greene King IPA, good coffee, unusual hat collection and coaching prints, no-smoking room, restaurant, games room with pool and darts; children welcome, quiet piped music; garden with play area; bedrooms, pleasant walks *(JJW, CMW , E G Drain, John Beeken)*

Northrepps [TG2439], *Parsons Pleasure*: Converted tithe barn with well kept Greene King IPA and Abbot in lively and friendly bar, welcoming landlord, restaurant; bedrooms *(D E Twitchett)*

☆ **Norwich** [Wensum St, S side of Fye Bridge], *Ribs of Beef*: Warm and welcoming high-ceilinged old pub, well kept ales such as Adnams, Boddingtons Mild, Fullers London Pride and Woodfordes Wherry, farm cider; deep leather settees and small tables upstairs, attractive smaller downstairs room with river view and some local river paintings, generous cheap reliable food from filling pitta breads up (served till 5 Sat/Sun), quick friendly service; can be studenty evenings, but without deafening music *(John Wooll, Tony and Wendy Hobden, Sue Holland, Dave Webster, Ian Phillips)*

Norwich [Old Post Office Yard], *Bedfords*: Wine bar not pub, with keg or nitrokeg beers, but worth knowing for good reasonably priced food in beamed upstairs room; good choice of good wines *(John Wooll)*; [5 Orford Hill], *Bell*: Weatherspoons – no music, good value, pleasant furnishings and atmosphere, with well kept ales inc Adnams Extra and Woodfordes Wherry *(Simon Penny)*; [Hall Rd, off inner ring rd nr A11], *Billy Bluelight*: Friendly real-ale local tied to Woodfordes, with their full beer range and interesting guests kept well, cheapish food, real fire *(Richard Houghton, Sue Holland, Dave Webster)*; [82 Thorpe Rd], *Coach & Horses*: Tap for the Chalk Hill brewery, with their own Bitter, CHB, Dreadnought, Flint Knappers and Old Tackle, also guests such as Boddingtons and Timothy Taylor, reasonably priced food inc breakfast with limitless coffee *(Ian Phillips)*; [Prince of Wales Rd], *Compleat Angler*: T & J Bernard pub opp River Wensum boat station, friendly service, lunchtime food inc good home-made soup and sandwiches, good beer range *(JDM, KM, Jim Cowell)*; [Mount Pleasant], *Eaton Cottage*: Very tidy and well run, with comfortable lounge and nice atmosphere *(R Houghton)*; [King St], *Ferryboat*: Well cared-for riverside Greene King pub with their beers kept well, limited generous tasty food, helpful service, a good deal of character – traditional beamed old-fashioned front part, steps down through spacious raftered and flagstoned back dining area to riverside garden with play area and barbecue *(Robert Gomme, LYM)*; [Pembroke Rd], *Garden House*: Good freshly prepared food, friendly staff *(M Kempe)*; [Warwick St], *Mad Moose*: Good food inc interesting Asian menu, well kept beer *(M Kempe)*; [Spixworth Rd, Old Catton], *Maids Head*: Hotel with lots of character in 17th-c smoking room and bar, small range of real ales, comfortable old-fashioned surroundings; good bedrooms, well equipped yet with plenty of individuality *(Ian Phillips)*; [41 Earlham Rd], *Pickwick*: Converted 1830s town house, raised lounge on right, darts and pool on left, real ales such as Boddingtons, Greene King Abbot and Tetleys, wide choice of good value food from sandwiches up *(Ian Phillips)*; [Prince of Wales Rd], *Prince of Wales*: Comfortable, with bright friendly service, wide range of beers and other drinks, trendy decor, food till later than some other pubs here; popular with young people *(Ian Phillips)*; [St Andrews Hill, next to Cinema City], *Take Five*: Not a pub (in the evenings you can only get in through Cinema City for which it serves as the cafeteria), but very pleasant relaxed atmosphere, and has real ales inc one brewed for them, also farm cider; good choice of wines, good value very health-and-trend-conscious food, relaxed atmosphere, changing local art, piped classical music, tables in nice old courtyard *(Tim Barrow, Sue Demont, J Middis)*; [Castle St], *Walnut Tree Shades*: Quirky and colourful, with pop memorabilia, outstanding juke box inc 60s rock, well kept beers inc Marstons Pedigree, good fast food; relaxed and enjoyable *(Tim Barrow, Sue Demont)*; [St Martin, nr Palace

Plain], *Wig & Pen*: Real ales such as Buffeys, John Smiths, Smiles Holly Hops, Woodfordes Wherry in big partly modernised old beamed bar opp cathedral close, lawyer and judge prints, roaring stove with horsebrasses on overmantle, filling cheap bar food, good value wine, quick service; loudish piped music *(Ian Phillips, John Wooll)*

☆ **Old Hunstanton** [part of L'Estrange Arms Hotel, Golf Course Rd; TF6842], *Ancient Mariner*: Relaxed friendly atmosphere in attractively furnished old bar, comfortable and interesting, with lots of dark wood, bare bricks and flagstones, several little areas inc upstairs gallery, good value usual food, up to half a dozen well kept ales inc Adnams and Broadside and Bass, unusually good wines by the glass, open fires, papers and magazines; bedrooms *(John Wooll)*

Potter Heigham [A1062 Wroxham Rd; TG4119], *Falgate*: Charmingly refurbished, good food inc vegetarian, very friendly service, well kept Flowers IPA and Original and Greene King Abbot, restaurant; piped music, fruit machine; aviaries at back; bedrooms, not far from river *(Paul and Sharon Sneller, John and Joyce Smethurst, Don and Shirley Parrish)*

Pulham Market [TM1986], *Crown*: Wide choice of home-made food inc good ploughman's, enticing walk-through hot and cold buffets and popular restaurant Sun lunch (must book), well kept beer, service attentive and friendly even when very busy *(Mike and Mary Carter, Bill Shorten)*

Pulham St Mary [TM2085], *Kings Head*: Doing well under current hard-working landlord, wide choice of food inc take-aways and popular generous Sun lunch, friendly staff, thriving happy feel *(Maggie and Derek Washington)*

Reedham [17 The Havaker; TG4101], *Railway*: Friendly and comfortable, with good range of real ales, dozens of whiskies, log fire, good bar and restaurant food, games room with darts, pool etc *(Anthony Barnes, A J Thomas)*

☆ **Reepham** [Market Sq; TG0922], *Old Brewery House*: Sizeable rambling Georgian hotel with big sundial over two-columned porch, imaginative well prepared fresh food inc good fish in roomy eating areas, well kept ales inc Adnams and local Reepham brews in small cosy inner bar, regular beer festivals, good friendly service, restaurant with theme nights; appealing bedrooms with use of sports club *(Mrs Mandy Littler, Mr and Mrs T Lyons, J Barber, R C Vincent)*

Reepham [Market Pl], *Kings Arms*: Pleasant decor with stripped brickwork, open fire and farm tools, well kept ales such as Adnams, Fullers and Woodfordes Wherry, three open fires, reasonably priced good food inc occasional theme nights, friendly atmosphere, games area one end, steps to restaurant; jazz some nights, tables outside front and back, quiet village, bedrooms *(CMW, JJW)*

Rollesby [A149; TQ4416], *Horse & Groom*: Straightforward renovated pub worth knowing for good value generous home-made food esp seafood; clean and comfortable, with well kept Flowers Original, good friendly service; restaurant, decent wines; well equipped bedrooms in motel wing *(Beryl and Bill Farmer)*

Roydon [the one nr Kings Lynn; TF7022], *Three Horseshoes*: Homely two-bar local with good value food inc Sun lunch (reduced price for children), pleasant restaurant, Flowers Original, Greene King IPA and Abbot, good service *(R C Vincent)*

Roydon [the one on Thetford Rd (A1066); TM0980], *White Hart*: Attractive old pub, partly 15th c, brasses on beams, good food inc phenomenal choice of puddings, big bar and restaurant *(June and Perry Dann)*

Salthouse [A149 Blakeney—Sheringham; TG0743], *Dun Cow*: Extensively refurbished country local looking over salt marshes, good bar food, well kept Greene King and other ales from new bar counter, open fires, newly stripped beams and cob walls; children welcome, big attractive walled garden with figs, apples and play area, good walks and birdwatching nearby (also seafood/samphire shack) *(Anon)*

☆ **Sedgeford** [B1454, off A149 Kings Lynn—Hunstanton; TF7136], *King William IV*: Relaxed and friendly local with energetic landlord, simple cheap well presented food inc Sun roast with good veg, warm woodburner, fast service, well kept Bass and Worthington, decent wine, restaurant; children allowed in lounge if eating, weekly music and quiz nights *(John Wooll, Ted George)*

Sheringham [High St; TG1543], *Lobster*: Almost on seafront, old Singer treadle tables in nice lounge, welcoming service, good cheap food (discounts for early lunchers) inc crab, lobster and fish specials, warm fire; dogs on leads allowed *(David and Jane Culley)*; [promenade], *Two Lifeboats*: Lovely sea view from comfortable lounge and terrace tables, big helpings of good value usual food inc fresh fish (no-smoking dining area), well kept Greene King ales, helpful friendly service; bedrooms; reasonably priced *(Sue Holland, Dave Webster, R C Vincent)*

South Creake [B1355 Burnham Mkt—Fakenham; TF8535], *Ostrich*: Friendly and efficient newish owners doing imaginative fresh bar food inc local fish, pine tables in long narrow bar and lounge, well kept beers such as Adnams Broadside and Bitter, Bass, Boddingtons, Woodfords Wherry *(Mr and Mrs B James, Dr B and Mrs P B Baker)*

South Lopham [The Street; A1066 Diss—Thetford; TM0481], *White Horse*: Beamed pub with good choice of enjoyable home-made food inc Sun lunch, good staff (holiday visitors treated like regulars), Adnams, Greene King IPA and Marstons Pedigree, big garden; handy for Bressingham Gardens *(M Clifford)*

South Walsham [18 The Street (B1140); TG3713], *Ship*: New licensees in small friendly village pub, good chef-served food inc ideal shepherd's pie, good choice of fresh fish and (till 4.30) Sun roasts, stripped bricks and

beams, well kept Adnams and Woodfordes Wherry; pool in separate bar; tables on front elevated terrace and more in back garden; children's room, play area *(Dave Holcroft)*

South Wootton [Grimston Rd (A148/A149); part of Knights Hill Hotel; TF6422], *Farmers Arms*: Olde-worlde conversion of barn and stables, wide choice of tasty reasonably priced food all day in bar and restaurant inc vegetarian, Scottish Courage ales with a guest such as Marstons Pedigree, good wines, abundant coffee, friendly service; children welcome, open all day; comfortable motel bedrooms, health club *(John Wooll, M Morgan, R C Vincent)*; [Nursery Lane], *Swan*: Good value home cooking in small old-fashioned two-bar pub overlooking village green, duckpond and bowling green; conservatory dining area, well kept Scottish Courage ales and Greene King IPA, small enclosed garden with play area *(Ted George)*

Sporle [TF8411], *Squirrels Drey*: Open fire in comfortable lounge, enormous antique round table in bar, above-average food inc good puddings, restaurant *(Nigel Clifton, Bernard and Marjorie Parkin)*

☆ **Stanhoe** [B1155 towards Burnham Mkt; TF8036], *Crown*: Good friendly atmosphere in small bright country local, popular good value home cooking inc game, well kept Elgoods Cambridge, decent wine and coffee, convivial licensees, central log fire, one beam studded with hundreds of coins; well behaved children allowed; tables on side lawn, lots of fancy fowl (and chicks) outside; caravan site, s/c cottage available *(Charles Bardswell, John Wooll, Ted George, BB)*

☆ **Surlingham** [village signed off A146 just SE of A47 Norwich ring rd, then Coldham Hall signed; TG3206], *Coldham Hall*: Well kept ales such as Batemans XB, Shepherd Neame Spitfire and Woodfordes Wherry, wide choice of enjoyable food, comfortable high-backed settles, friendly service, woodburner, pool in games area, Broads-view dining area, sensible dress code, well reproduced piped music (also juke box); picnic-sets by big well kept waterside lawn with shrubs, weeping willows and moorings; children in family room *(A J Thomas, BB)*

Tasburgh [A140; TM1996], *Countryman*: Welcoming main-road pub with reasonably priced food inc good sandwiches, willing service, well kept Adnams and Courage Best, decent wine *(Anthony Barnes, Frank Davidson)*

☆ **Thompson** [Griston Rd, off A1075 S of Watton; TL9296], *Chequers*: Long, low and picturesque 15th-c thatched house reopened by new owners, delightful series of olde-worlde quaint rooms, interesting food at reasonable prices; good choice of beer and wines *(Mr and Mrs Peter Chance, LYM)*

☆ **Thornham** [Church St/A149; TF7343], *Kings Head*: Pretty old pub with lots of hanging baskets, low-beamed bars with banquettes in well lit bays, decent food inc vegetarian and fresh fish, Greene King IPA and Abbot, Marstons Pedigree and Tetleys, friendly efficient service, open fire, no-smoking area; dogs allowed; well spaced tables on back lawn with barbecues, three homely and comfortable bedrooms *(Michael Switzer, MDN, Mrs J Burrows)*

Titchwell [Main St; TF7543], *Briarfields*: Good bar food inc vegetarian, well kept Adnams and moderately priced house wines in hotel's comfortable back bar; obliging staff, terrace overlooking salt marshes, telescope and bird-sightings book; bedrooms comfortable and well appointed – a nice place to stay *(O K Smyth, Chris Rounthwaite)*

Walcott [Stalham Rd, nr church; B1159 S of village; TG3532], *Lighthouse*: Friendly and busy, with wide range of good generous food freshly cooked to order inc interesting vegetarian dishes, Adnams and other well kept changing ales, prompt helpful service; children in no-smoking dining room and family room with toys, inexpensive slot machine and pool; tables outside, good walks nearby *(Eamonn and Natasha Skyrme, Jim Cowell)*

☆ **Walsingham** [Common Place/Shire Hall Plain; TF9236], *Bull*: Good friendly atmosphere and comfortable straightforward interior, walls covered with clerical visiting cards; welcoming landlord, well kept Flowers and Tolly Original and Flowers, decent food; attractive flowery terrace on busy village square *(George Atkinson)*

☆ **West Rudham** [A148 Fakenham—Kings Lynn; TF8127], *Dukes Head*: 17th c, with three attractively homely rooms, short choice of generous fresh home-made food from sandwiches up inc interesting fish dishes, well kept Adnams, Woodfordes Wherry and a guest such as Shepherd Neame Spitfire, decent wines, friendly service, newspapers and plenty of books *(Derek and Sylvia Stephenson, John Wooll, R C Vincent)*

☆ **West Walton** [School Rd; N of Wisbech; TF4713], *King of Hearts*: Comfortably refurbished dining pub with wide choice of good genuine food in smartly furnished bar and restaurant, good hot buffet (as much as you want), quick friendly service copes well even with big parties, full range of Elgoods and a guest; holds key for lovely next-door church *(John Child)*

Weston Longville [signed off A1067 Norwich—Bawdswell in Morton; TG1115], *Parson Woodforde*: Clean and spacious beamed pub popular for food, with lots of alcoves, willing service, well kept Adnams Extra, Woodfordes Wherry and a Bass beer brewed for the pub, evening carvery *(Michael Hyde)*

☆ **Wighton** [The Street; TF9340], *Carpenters Arms*: 17th-c flint village pub regaining old name (spent some years as Sandpiper) under friendly and energetic new landlord, central stove and small bar area in long room, woodworking tools etc, photographs of old village life, Adnams ales with a guest such as Fullers London Pride, good choice of enterprising reasonably priced bar food from filled baguettes up, pool, tables in large charming garden *(John Beeken, George Atkinson)*

☆ **Wiveton** [B1156 Blakeney—Holt; TG0342], *Bell*: Big open-plan local with lots of Jaguar and other motoring mementoes (even an engine in the fireplace), dozens of model planes, usual food with interesting specials, well kept beers such as Morlands Old Speckled Hen, Wolf BB, Woodfordes Wherry and ones brewed for them in Suffolk and given Jaguar-related names, daily papers, piped music (may be loud); more automania in carpeted no-smoking conservatory, picnic-sets on lawn and small garden behind with personal hibachi-substitutes apparently made from car bits; dogs welcome; bedrooms *(Jenny and Michael Back, Frank Davidson, BB)*

☆ **Wreningham** [off B1113 SW of Norwich; TM1598], *Bird in Hand*: Roomy but cosy tastefully refurbished dining pub with very wide choice of good varied reasonably priced food from sandwiches up inc unusual vegetarian dishes and well presented Sun lunch; well kept Whitbreads-related and Woodfordes ales, good friendly service, local bygones and Lotus car photographs, choice between formal Victorian-style panelled restaurant and more tea-roomish farmhouse one; picnic-sets in delightful garden *(Paul Mallett, Sue Rowland, Christine Seager)*

Wroxham [Bridge Precinct; TG3018], *Hotel Wroxham*: Modern building with large bar and dining area, picture windows and terrace overlooking River Bure, waterfowl hoping for food, good value generous carvery with help-yourself veg and cut-priced children's helpings, well kept ales such as Adnams, Woodfordes Wherry and Nog, maybe a bargain guest *(JDM, KM)*

Wymondham [TG1101], *Station*: Interesting converted station, real trains stop at beautiful flower-decked platform; decent food, very reasonable prices, well kept beer, wheelchair access *(Margaret Watkinson)*

Post Office address codings confusingly give the impression that some pubs are in Norfolk when they're really in Suffolk (which is where we list them).

Northamptonshire

This county has some fine pubs, often with considerable character, in lovely spots. Those which have been shining most strongly in recent months include the attractively set Windmill at Badby (its cooking wins it a Food Award this year), the George & Dragon at Chacombe (good food here too, and very handy for the M40), the friendly Bulls Head at Clipston (good all round), the redecorated Eastcote Arms at Eastcote (they've extended the food range and are now doing some adventurous specials on Friday and Saturday nights), the atmospheric Kings Arms at Farthingstone (imaginative cooking at sensible prices gains it a Food Award, and it wins a Beer Award too this year), the Snooty Fox at Lowick (new management bringing this engaging place back into the Guide after several years' break), the charming Star at Sulgrave (good food here too), the delightfully placed Kings Head at Wadenhoe, and the White Swan at Woodnewton, a well run dining pub that joins the main entries for the first time this year. The Falcon at Fotheringhay has been taken over by Huntsbridge, the very small family-run group of pubs which won our award last year for Britain's best pub chain, and the new regime was looking promising in its early weeks, before we went to press. Our choice as Northamptonshire Dining Pub of the Year is the Kings Arms at Farthingstone; nothing too fancy, but a really enjoyable place for a meal out. The Lucky Dip section at the end of the chapter has a lot of strong entries; we'd particularly mention the New Inn at Abthorpe, Navigation at Cosgrove, White Horse at Old and Vane Arms at Sudborough. Drinks prices in the area are a little higher than the national average, with pubs getting their beers from the smaller breweries tending to be relatively cheap; the cheapest we found were the Eastcote Arms at Eastcote and Falcon at Fotheringhay.

ASHBY ST LEDGERS SP5768 Map 4

Olde Coach House

4 miles from M1, junction 18; A5 S to Kilsby, then A361 S towards Daventry; village is signposted left. Alternatively 8 miles from M1 junction 16, then A45 W to Weedon, A5 N to sign for village.

Originally a farmhouse and converted into a pub when Sir Edwin Lutyens restyled the village and the estate farm workers lost their watering-hole, this handsome creeper-covered stone inn has a wonderfully traditional feel. The several comfortable, rambling little rooms have high-backed winged settles on polished black and red tiles, old kitchen tables, harnesses on a few standing timbers, hunting pictures (often of the Pytchley, which sometimes meets outside), Thelwell prints, and a big winter log fire. A front room has darts, pool, TV (very popular for sport) and piped music. A fine drinks selection includes well kept Everards Old Original, Flowers Original, Greene King IPA and a couple of guests on handpump, with lots more during their spring beer festivals; also over a dozen wines by the glass and an unusual choice of non-alcoholic drinks; straightforward bar food. There are seats among fruit trees and under a fairy-lit arbour (maybe summer barbecues), and an activity centre for children; disabled entrance and baby-changing facilities. They have a very full diary of events throughout the year, with everything from Indian food festivals to firework displays and bank holiday pig roasts. The nearby manor house was owned by one of the gunpowder plotters. *(Recommended by Susan and John Douglas, Joan and Michel Hooper-Immins, B J Harding, Susan and Nigel Wilson, Allan and Philippa Wright, Mike and Wena Stevenson, E J Locker, A Sutton, John McIver, Bernard and Becky Robinson, N Cobb, JP, PP, Andy and Jill Kassube, Jo and Gary Charlton, David Carr, Andy Cunningham, Yvonne Hannaford, Barbara Wensworth)*

Free house ~ Licensees Brian and Philippa McCabe ~ Real ale ~ Meals and snacks ~ Restaurant ~ (01788) 890349 ~ Children welcome ~ Open 12-2.30, 6-11; 12-11 Sat; 12-10.30 Sun; closed 25 Dec ~ Bedrooms: £51B/£65B

BADBY SP5559 Map 4

Windmill

Village signposted off A361 Daventry—Banbury

On sunny days it's pleasant to sit outside in front of this attractive old thatched village inn, where traditional and unsophisticated pubby charm is carefully blended with efficient management and modern hotel facilities for staying guests – an unobtrusive modern extension is well hidden at the back. The two friendly beamed and flagstoned bars are popular with locals and businessmen and have cricketing and rugby pictures and appropriately simple country furnishings in good solid wood; there's an enormous inglenook fireplace in one area and a cosy and comfortable lounge. Good promptly served wholesome bar food in generous helpings includes home-made soup (£1.95), sandwiches (from £1.95, open topside of beef £5.25), stilton mushrooms or pork liver, bacon and brandy pâté (£3.50), ploughman's (£4.25), lasagne (£5.50), pasta with stir-fried vegetables (£6.25), curry of the day (£6.50), chicken and ham pie or venison burgers (£6.95), steaks (from £6.95), chicken breast with a white wine and stilton sauce (£7.75) and roast barbary duck with orange and port sauce (£10.25); daily specials, puddings (from £2.95), and children's meals (£2.50). There's a pleasant restaurant and marquee in summer. Well kept Bass, Boddingtons, Flowers Original, Highgate Dark Mild and Wadworths 6X on handpump; video game, piped music. *(Recommended by K H Frostick, George Atkinson, Howard and Margaret Buchanan, E Locker, D Wall, Roy Bromell, Mr and Mrs Andrew Barsby and friends, Brenda and Rob Fincham, John Bowdler, Mrs K V and Miss J Weeks)*

Free house ~ Licensees John Freestone and Carol Sutton ~ Real ale ~ Meals and snacks ~ Restaurant ~ (01327) 702363 ~ Children in eating area of bar ~ live jazz one Friday in the month ~ Open 11.30-3, 5.30-11; all day Sat and Sun in summer ~ Bedrooms: £45B/£59B

CHACOMBE SP4943 Map 4

George & Dragon

2½ miles from M40 junction 11: A361 towards Daventry, then village signposted on right; Silver Street

There's a really welcoming atmosphere at this genuinely relaxing village pub – just what we always hope to find near a motorway, but hardly ever do. In the bar there are comfortable seats, beams, flagstones, and logs burning in a massive fireplace, and Marstons Pedigree, Morlands Old Speckled Hen, and Theakstons XB and Best on handpump; fruit wines. Carefully cooked bar food includes mushroom and asparagus pancake (£7.25), baked breast of chicken in red wine and mushrooms (£8.95), crispy duck pancake with honey and ginger (£9.75) and a selection of fresh fish such as baked red snapper with pepper relish and chilli sauce or roasted seabass (£9.95); friendly and attentive service that can cope with people who need to get back on the road fairly quickly yet doesn't hurry those who have more time to spare. Afternoon teas and snacks; no-smoking area in restaurant; darts, dominoes and piped music; friendly black and white cats. *(Recommended by K H Frostick, Ted George, Ian Phillips, Mr and Mrs C Moncreiffe, R J Frearson, David Regan, John and Shirley Dyson, James Nunn)*

Free house ~ Licensee Ray Bennett ~ Real ale ~ Meals and snacks (12-9.30) ~ Restaurant ~ (01295) 711500 ~ Children welcome ~ Open 12-11(10.30 Sun) ~ Bedrooms: £38B/£55B

CHAPEL BRAMPTON SP7266 Map 4

Brampton Halt

Pitsford Road; off A50 N of Northampton

The friendly new licensee was beginning to settle in at this attractive Victorian station master's house as we went to press. Inside, one low-ceilinged area with a woodburning stove has wash drawings of steam trains; by the bar counter, a high-raftered dining area has dagging shears and other agricultural bygones; there's Victorian-style floral wallpaper throughout, with matching swagged curtains, and furnishings are sturdily comfortable. There are a few tables in a small sun lounge. Under the new regime bar food includes soup (£2.50), garlic mushrooms (£2.95), prawn cocktail (£3.50), mushroom stroganoff (£6.95), chicken supreme or sirloin steak (£8.50) and salmon steak in tarragon (£8.75); home-made puddings (£2.50-£3.50). Well kept Adnams, Everards Tiger and Fullers London Pride on handpump; decent wines; friendly service; trivia, piped music and maybe TV showing sporting events. A stop here by the little Northampton & Lamport Railway makes part of a terrific day out for the family. There are train rides at the weekends with additional bank holiday and Santa specials, and there's a 14-mile walk and cycle-way along an adjacent converted old track through pretty countryside. During the week you may see enthusiasts working on the rolling stock. *(Recommended by Ted George, Penny and Martin Fletcher, George Atkinson, Ian Phillips, Stephen, Julie and Hayley Brown, David and Mary Webb; more reports on the new regime please)*

Free house ~ Licensee Richard David Hobbins ~ Real ale ~ Meals and snacks (till 9.45; not Mon evening or Sun lunch) ~ Restaurant ~ (01604) 842676 ~ Children welcome in eating area of bar ~ Open 11-3, 5-11; 12-3, 7-10.30 Sun; maybe less in winter

CLIPSTON SP7181 Map 4

Bulls Head

B4036 S of Market Harborough

There is a warm and convivial atmosphere at this lovely village inn and if they are not too busy you can expect a personal greeting as you walk in. The bar is cosily divided into three snug areas leading down from the servery, with comfortable seats, sturdy small settles and stools upholstered in red plush, a grandmother clock, some harness and tools, and a log fire; the black beams glisten with countless coins, carrying on an odd tradition started by US airmen based nearby in World War II – they used to wedge the money waiting for their next drink in cracks and crannies of the ancient woodwork. Well kept Batemans, Timothy Taylor Landlord, Wadworths 6X, Whitbread Best and Wychwood Dogs Bollocks on handpump, and an incredible choice of about 530 malt whiskies. A new dining area has been created in the room at the back with oak settles, high-back chairs and a grandfather clock keeping time; the walls are hung with china meat plates. Good food includes sandwiches and other light snacks, and daily specials such as drunken bull pie or home-baked ham and eggs (£5.95), cumberland sausage (£6.50), haddock (£6.95), surf and turf, hawaiian gammon with pineapple and cheese or chicken filled with stilton wrapped in bacon with mustard and wine sauce (£7.95). Fruit machine and piped music; there may be a couple of friendly dogs. Slightly saucy pin-ups decorate the gents', and indeed the ladies'. Outside, a terrace has a few white tables under cocktail parasols. *(Recommended by Sue and Mike Loseby, Mr and Mrs A Bull, Greg Kilminster, Ted George, Chris Gabbitas, Hugh McPhail, B Adams, Eric Locker, Joy and Peter Heatherley, Stephen Brown, L Eadon)*

Free house ~ Licensees Colin and Jenny Smith ~ Real ale ~ Meals and snacks (not Mon) ~ (01858) 525268 ~ Children in eating area ~ Occasional live entertainment ~ Open 11.30-2.30, 6.30-11; 12-3, 7-10.30 Sun; cl Mon lunchtime ~ Bedrooms: £29.50B/£39.50B

We say if we know a pub has piped music.

CRICK SP5872 Map 4

Red Lion

A mile from M1 junction 18; A428

There's a relaxed friendly atmosphere at this unpretentious old thatched pub – offering pleasant respite from the M1. It's quietest and snuggest in the inner part of the low-ceilinged bar. Four well kept changing beers might include Morlands Old Speckled Hen, Marstons Pedigree, Theakstons Best and Websters Yorkshire on handpump. No noisy games machines or piped music. Lunchtime snacks include sandwiches, ploughman's, and chicken and mushroom pie, moussaka, lasagne or a roast (£3.90); in the evening they offer a wider range of dishes including gammon or rainbow trout (£6), lamb cutlets (£6.25), steaks (from £8.50) and roast duckling with apple sauce (£9). There are a few picnic-sets under cocktail parasols on grass by the car park and in summer you can eat on the terrace in the old coach yard which is sheltered by a Perspex roof; lots of pretty hanging baskets. *(Recommended by Ian Phillips, Ted George, Val and Alan Green, Bob and Maggie Atherton, James Nunns)*

Free house ~ Lease: Tom Marks ~ Real ale ~ Meals and snacks (not Sun evenings) ~ (01788) 822342 ~ Children welcome in snug at lunchtime ~ Open 11-2.30, 6.30-11; 12-3, 7-10.30 Sun

EAST HADDON SP6668 Map 4

Red Lion

High St; village signposted off A428 (turn right in village) and off A50 N of Northampton

With so many interesting old *objets* dotted around, walking into this rather smart substantially-built golden stone hotel is rather like going to an antique shop. The well appointed neat lounge bar has oak panelled settles, library chairs, soft modern dining chairs, and a mix of oak, mahogany and cast-iron-framed tables; also, white-painted panelling, recessed china cabinets, old prints and pewter, and little kegs, brass pots, swords and so forth hung sparingly on a couple of beams. The small public bar has sturdy old-fashioned red leather seats. Very well kept Charles Wells Eagle and Bombardier and Morlands Old Speckled Hen on handpump, and decent wines; attentive, friendly service; piped music. Most people visit for the good bar food from a well balanced daily changing menu: soups (£3), sandwiches (from £3.50), ploughman's or pâté (£6.95), vegetable risotto (£7.95), goat's cheese toasties on a bed of leaves, seafood lasagne or steak and kidney pie (£8.95), smoked salmon slices on a crisp crouton topped with scrambled eggs or sautéed lamb liver (£9.95), grilled sirloin steak with whisky and peppercorn sauce (£12.95) and puddings like lemon bread and butter pudding or sherry trifle (£3.50); it's worth booking for their three-course set Sunday lunch and there's a more elaborate menu in the pretty restaurant; good breakfasts. The walled side garden is a pleasant place to enjoy coffee after a meal, with lilac, fruit trees, roses and neat little flower beds; it leads back to the bigger lawn, which has well spaced picnic-sets. There are more tables under cocktail parasols on a small side terrace, and a big copper beech shades the gravel car park. *(Recommended by Anthony Barnes, Ian Phillips, Maysie Thompson, Geoffrey and Penny Hughes, J and P Maloney, L Eadon, Kim and Sara Tidy)*

Charles Wells ~ Tenant Ian H Kennedy ~ Real ale ~ Meals and snacks (not Sun evening) ~ Restaurant ~ (01604) 770223 ~ Children in eating area of bar and restaurant, must be over 14 in evenings ~ Open 11-2.30, 6-11; 12-2.30, 7-10.30 Sun; closed Sun evening in winter ~ Bedrooms: £60B/£75B

EASTCOTE SP6753 Map 4

Eastcote Arms

Gayton Rd; village signposted from A5 3 miles N of Towcester

The inside of this welcoming village pub has been fully redecorated over the last year but there's still a good cheerful villagey atmosphere and there are lots of rugby prints above the maroon dado in the bar, as well as traditional furnishings with two imitation log fires, cottagey curtains, fresh flowers; dominoes, cribbage, and

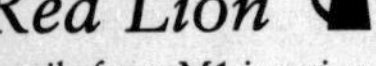

unobtrusive piped music. Lunchtimes snacks include sandwiches (from £1.80), filled french bread (from £2), filled baked potatoes (from £2.75), ploughman's (from £3.50), fish and chips (£2.95), double egg and chips (£3.25) and steak and ale pie (£5.45). On Friday and Saturday evenings there are now much more adventurous specials such as marinated smoked trout fillet with a potato and gherkin salad (£3.25), grilled goat's cheese en croûte (£3.85), poached salmon with potato and chive mash and lemon butter sauce (£8.25), pan-fried chicken supreme with sautéed mushrooms and dijon mustard glaze (£8.75), calf liver with braised red cabbage and crème fraîche and balsamic vinegar (£11.95) or angus beef with a celeriac and chestnut purée and a wild mushroom ketchup (£12.95); Sunday lunchtime roasts; no-smoking dining room. Well kept Adnams Bitter, Fullers London Pride, Thwaites and a guest on handpump. There are picnic-sets and other tables in an attractive back garden, with roses, geraniums and so forth around the neat lawn. *(Recommended by George Atkinson, Bruce Bird, CMW, JJW, K H Frostick, Richard and Maria Gillespie, John Baker, Tom Evans)*

Free house ~ Licensees John and Wendy Hadley ~ Real ale ~ Meals and snacks (not Mon lunch or evenings Sun-Thurs) ~ Restaurant ~ (01327) 830731 ~ Children in eating area of bar and restaurant ~ Open 12-2.30, 6-11; 12-3, 7-10.30 Sun; closed Mon lunchtime except bank holidays

FARTHINGSTONE SP6155 Map 4

Kings Arms

Off A5 SE of Daventry; village signposted from Litchborough on former B4525 (now declassified)

Northamptonshire Dining Pub of the Year

Readers enjoy the wide choice of good imaginative and freshly cooked food at this handsome 18th-c well weathered stone pub. It might include home-made soup (£2.10), leek and feta cheese tartlet with pine nuts (£3.25), hot game pâté (£3.75), yorkshire pudding filled with steak and kidney (£4.50), lentil bake with salad and cheese bread (£5.65), Moroccan chicken with garlic bread and couscous or smoked haddock and crab bake (£5.95), fillet of plaice with stilton sauce (£6.15), venison casserole with apricots and cranberries (£6.25), breast of barbary duck with redcurrant and raspberry sauce (£7.25); good home-made puddings include hot gingerbread with maple syrup, Tunisian lemon pudding or bread pudding (£2.65). There's a huge log fire in the small atmospheric flagstoned bar, with comfortably homely sofas and armchairs near the entrance; whisky-water jugs hang from oak beams, and there are lots of pictures and decorative plates on the walls. In the more spacious dining area there is a smoking area and there may be local crafts for sale (booking advisable at busy times); a games room at the far end of the bar has dominoes, cribbage, table skittles and board games. Four or five well kept real ales might include Adnams, Hook Norton Best, Jennings Cumberland and Timothy Taylor Landlord; decent wines and fruit wines, friendly licensees and good informal service; no credit cards. There are tables in a neatly kept sheltered garden; interesting decor in outside gents'. It's a pretty village, with good walks nearby (including the Knightley Way). *(Recommended by Francis Johnson, R M Corlett, George Atkinson, Pete Baker, Mike and Jennifer Marsh, David Mead, K H Frostick, D I Williams)*

Free house ~ Licensees Paul and Denise Egerton ~ Real ale ~ Meals and snacks (till 1.45; not Sun evening, all day Mon, Tues lunchtime) ~ Restaurant ~ (01327) 361604 ~ Children welcome in eating area of bar, restaurant and games rooms ~ Open 12-2.30(3 Sat), 6.30-11; closed Mon, Tues lunchtime; 12-3, 7-10.30 Sun

FOTHERINGHAY TL0593 Map 5

Falcon ★

Village signposted off A605 on Peterborough side of Oundle

Now part of the small but highly successful Huntsbridge group which includes several of our main entries in Cambridgeshire and Essex, this stylish but relaxed old country pub attracts a mix of locals and visitors with its well prepared, varied and interesting food. Besides lunchtime sandwiches (from £2.50), ploughman's (£4) and lunchtime roasts (from £6.50), the seasonally changing menu might include green pea soup with crème fraîche (£2.50), chicken liver pâté with onion chutney and toast (£3.50), steak, mushroom and Guinness pie or lamb liver and bacon (£6), pasta with spring vegetables, herbs, chilli oil and parmesan (£7), chargrilled chicken with mustard and beer sauce (£8), steaks (from £9.50) and roast monkfish with rosemary and garlic (£12.50); tempting puddings include sticky toffee pudding with rum and raisin ice cream and caramel sauce (£3.50) and fresh cherries in kirsch with lemon syllabub (£4); can get very busy, advisable to book. The comfortable lounge has cushioned slatback armchairs and bucket chairs, winter log fires in stone fireplaces at each end, fresh flower arrangements, and a hum of quiet conversation; the pleasant conservatory is popular for Sunday lunch and in summer the terrace is a particularly nice place for an al fresco meal. There is a much smaller tap bar for locals with darts, shove-ha'penny and dominoes; the dining room and conservatory are no smoking. Well kept Adnams Bitter and Broadside, Greene King IPA, and a guest on handpump. The vast church behind is worth a visit, Richard III was born in the village, and the site of Fotheringhay Castle is nearby (where Mary Queen of Scots was executed in 1587). *(Recommended by Michael and Jenny Back, Tina and David Woods-Taylor, Andy and Jill Kassube, Ted George, A Sutton, John Bowdler, Eric Locker, R Wiles, R Inman, David and Mary Webb, Maysie Thompson, Tony Dickinson, P and D Carpenter, Quentin Williamson, Sue Holland, David Webster, Peter Burton, Edward Froggatt, Brian and Jill Bond; more reports on the new regime please)*

Free house ~ Licensees Ray Smikle and John Hoskins ~ Real ale ~ Meals and snacks (till 10) ~ Restaurant ~ (01832) 226254 ~ Children welcome ~ Open 12-2.30, 6(7 Sun)-11

GREAT BRINGTON SP6664 Map 4

Fox & Hounds ★

Signposted off A428 NW of Northampton, near Althorp Hall; can also be reached via Little Brington, off A45 (heading W from M1 junction 16 it's the first right turn, signed The Bringtons)

Hopefully the expected deluge of visitors to Great Brington and Althorp following the death of the Princess of Wales will not spoil the character of this carefully restored golden stone thatched village inn. The bar has a delightfully relaxed informal feel, with lots of old beams and saggy joists, an attractive mix of country tables and chairs on its broad flagstones and bare boards, plenty of snug alcoves, some stripped pine shutters and panelling, two fine log fires, and an eclectic medley of bric-a-brac and country pictures; well reproduced piped music. Good changing range of around a dozen well kept real ales such as Brakspears, Greene King IPA, Hook Norton Old Hooky, Hop Back Summer Lightning, Jennings, Marstons Fever Pitch, Theakstons Best and XB, Ushers Summer Madness and Wadworths 6X; country wines. Bar food includes good hot open sandwiches at lunchtime (from £4.50), chicken terrine or smoked salmon (£3.95), pan-fried pork or chicken (£8), duck legs (£8.95) or steak (£10.50). A cellarish games room down steps has pool; quiz Monday evenings. A coach entry goes through to an attractive paved courtyard with sheltered tables, and there are more, with a play area, in the side garden. *(Recommended by John C Baker, Brian and Anna Marsden, Ted George, J W G Nunns, Penny and Martin Fletcher, L Granville, Francis Johnson, Maysie Thompson, P J Robbins, Stephen Brown, Andrew Shore, Bob and Maggie Atherton, Simon Walker, D Etheridge, Joy and Peter Heatherley, Stephen and Brenda Head, Neville Kenyon)*

Free house ~ Licensee Chris Murray ~ Real ale ~ Meals and snacks (not Mon, Tues and Sun evenings) ~ (01604) 770651 ~ Live jazz, blues and country Tues ~ Open 11.30-11 (12-3, 5.30-11 Mon-Thurs in winter); 12-10.30 Sun

HARRINGWORTH SP9298 Map 4

White Swan

Seaton Road; village SE of Uppingham, signposted from A6003, A47 and A43

As we went to press we heard that there were new licensees at this stone-built Tudor inn that still shows signs of its coaching days in the blocked-in traces of its central carriage-entry arch. Inside, the central bar area has good solid tables, an open fire, and old village photographs (in which many of the present buildings are clearly recognisable). There are comfortable settles in the roomy and welcoming lounge/eating area, which is decorated with a collection of carpenter's planes and other tools; in a quieter no-smoking dining room there is a collection of old jugs, dried flower arrangements and locally painted watercolours. Bar food might include home-made soup (£2.50), deep-fried butterfly prawns with lemon garnish (£3.95), home-made lasagne (£5.75), home-made steak and kidney pie or asparagus au gratin (£5.95), tuna, prawn and pasta baked in a mornay sauce or slivers of lamb liver flash fried with wine and herbs (£6.25), chicken stuffed with onions and mushrooms and grilled with stilton (£6.95), steaks (from £7.95). Well kept Greene King IPA and Abbot, Marstons Pedigree and maybe a guest beer on handpump. Darts, dominoes, cribbage and piped music; tables outside on a little terrace. The attractive village is dominated by the famous 82-arch railyway viaduct. *(Recommended by Anthony Barnes, Joan and Michel Hooper-Immins, PGP, Stephen Brown, more reports on the new regime please)*

Free house ~ Licensees John and Carol Harding ~ Real ale ~ Meals and snacks (till 10) ~ Restaurant ~ (01572) 747543 ~ Children welcome in restaurant ~ Open 11.30-2.30, 6.30-11; 12-3, 7-10.30 Sun; cl evening 25, 26 Dec and 1 Jan ~ Bedrooms: £38.50B/£52B

LOWICK SP9780 Map 4

Snooty Fox

Village signposted off A6116 Corby—Raunds

The softly floodlit picnic-sets on the grass in front of this imposing 17th-c inn are very inviting on a warm evening. On cooler days there will be a roaring log fire in the huge stone fireplace in the atmospheric two-roomed lounge, as well as handsomely moulded dark oak beams and stripped stone walls decorated with a series of prints by Terry Thomas of Guinness advert fame entitled 'A Day in the Life of the Snooty Fox'. Neat and attractive dining chairs are set around the well spaced tables – with plenty of space too along the formidable monumentally carved bar counter. Good food from the blackboard menu might include filled french bread (from £1.95), soup (£1.95), ploughman's (£4.95), cheese ratatouille or steak pie with fresh chillis (£5.95), fresh plaice or cod (£6.95), spicy cajun swordfish or lemon sole (£7.95) and steaks (from £7.95); puddings (£2.95). Well kept Adnams Best, Bateman Hill Billy and Everards Beacon and Tiger on handpump; fruit machine and piped music. *(Recommended by C Ferguson, Francis Johnston, Joan Morgan, Miss J Torte)*

Free house ~ Licensee Geoff Monks ~ Real ale ~ Meals and snacks (till 10pm Mon-Sat) ~ Restaurant ~ (01832) 733434 ~ Well behaved children welcome ~ Karaoke Weds evening, singer Thurs evening ~ Open 12-3, 7-11; 12-3, 7-10.30 Sun

OUNDLE TL0487 Map 5

Mill

Barnwell Rd out of town; or follow Barnwell Country Park signs off A605 bypass

There's a mill on this site recorded in the Doomsday Book and the waterwheel at the present buiding, which dates from the early 17th c, did not stop turning until 1930. Nowadays it's popular with diners enjoying the wide choice of well served and carefully prepared (but not cheap) meals in the upstairs Trattoria that has stalls around tables with more banquettes in bays, stripped masonry and beams, and a millstone feature; its small windows look down over the lower millpond and the River Nene; large no-smoking area. The extensive menu might include soup (£2.95), New England clam chowder (£3.25), baby camembert baked with garlic served with rosemary pizza bread (£5.80), chargrilled burgers (from £5.55), pizzas (from £5.75), spinach and ricotta cannelloni or venison and redcurrant sausages (£7.95), steak and kidney pie (£8.55), steaks (from £9.95) and duck à l'orange (£10.55); also a large range of Mexican dishes including chilli (£7.55), chimichanga (£8.55), and fajitas (from £9.95); fish dishes include mussels (£7.95) and swordfish (£8.95); large selection of liqueur coffees. A ground-floor bar (only open at weekends and in summer) has red leatherette button-back built-in wall banquettes against its stripped-stone walls; on the way in a big glass floor panel shows the stream race below the building. Courage Directors on handpump, bar billiards, piped music; the beamed no-smoking top-floor restaurant houses the corn hoist. There are picnic-sets under cocktail parasols among willow trees by the mill pond, with more on the side grass, and some white cast-iron tables on a flagstoned terrace. *(Recommended by Paul and Sandra Embleton, Dorothee and Dennis Glover, Howard and Margaret Buchanan)*

Free house ~ Licensees Noel and Linda Tulley ~ Real ale ~ Meals and snacks ~ Restaurant ~ (01832) 272621 ~ Children in eating area of bar ~ Open 11-3, 6.30-11

Ship £

West St

The bustling yet friendly and genuinely welcoming atmosphere at this cheerful and unpretentious local attracts a pleasantly mixed clientele at lunchtimes. The heavily beamed lounge bar is made up of three rooms that lead off the central corridor on the left: up by the street there's a mix of leather and other seats including a very flowery piano stool (and its piano), with sturdy tables and a log fire in a stone inglenook, and down one end a panelled snug has button-back leather seats built in around it; the snug is no smoking. Well kept Bass, Fullers London Pride, Hopback Summer Lightning and Tetleys on handpump, a good range of malt whiskies, cappuccino and espressos. Very good value bar food might include soup (£2), smoked salmon or chicken liver pâté (£3.25), ham, egg and chips (£3.75), seafood pie (£4.95) and lunchtime specials (£3.50-£4.50); puddings £2. Smiling, efficient service. Dominoes, maybe free Sunday nuts and crisps on the bar. The tiled-floor public side has darts, pinball, fruit machine, juke box and piped music. Wooden tables and chairs outside on a series of small sheltered terraces, lit at night. Several of the clean and comfortable bedrooms are in a new extension. The pub can get busy with a lively young crowd in the evenings. *(Recommended by Michael Sargent, Peter Plumridge, David and Mary Webb, Quentin Williamson, Sue Holland, David Webster, A L and J D Turnbull)*

Free house ~ Licensees Andrew and Robert Langridge ~ Real ale ~ Meals and snacks (till 10) ~ (01832) 273918 ~ Children welcome ~ Jazz Sunday evening ~ Open 11-11; 12-10.30 Sun; may close in the afternoon in winter; cl 25 Dec evening ~ Bedrooms: £25(£30B)/£40(£50B)

SULGRAVE SP5545 Map 4

Star

E of Banbury, signposted off B4525; Manor Road

There are plenty of things to look at in the bar of this creeper-covered stonebuilt inn: newspaper front pages record events such as Kennedy's assassination, the death of Churchill and the first Kentucky Derby, and a rather quirky collection of stuffed animals including the rear end of a fox, a hare's head fitted with little antlers to make it look like a miniature stag and a kangaroo with an Ozzie hanging-corks hat. The part by the big inglenook fireplace (with a paper skeleton on its side bench) has polished flagstones, the other part a red carpet, and furnishings are mainly small pews, cushioned window seats and wall benches, kitchen chairs and cast-iron-framed tables. Generous helpings of seasonal dishes from the changing blackboard menu might include very good double-decker sandwiches (£2.75), soup (£3.50), Orkney rollmops, filo wrapped tiger prawns, smoked halibut, houmous with pitta bread or guacamole (£3.50-£4.50), main courses like ploughman's (£5.25), black eye bean and tomato goulash, watercress and goat's cheese tart, cod and chips or spinach and ricotta wholemeal tart (£6.95) or grilled smoked chicken breast (£8.95) and home-made puddings like bread and butter pudding, treacle tart or tipsy trifle (£3.25). Well kept Hook Norton Best, Generation and Old Hookey and a monthly changing guest beer on handpump; no-smoking back restaurant; piped music; no children. The staff are welcoming and friendly, as are one or two very regular locals. There are some tables outside. Good views from some of the clean and comfortable bedrooms. The pub is on the road to George Washington's ancestral home. *(Recommended by Patrick Hancock, R*

Macnaughton, Penny and Martin Fletcher, Anthony Barnes, Mike and Mary Carter, R M Corlett, Anne P Heaton, Mr and Mrs J E Lockwood, Ian Phillips, Mr and Mrs C Moncrieffe, Stephen Brown, Mr and Mrs R Jones)

Hook Norton ~ Tenant Andrew Willerton ~ Real ale ~ Meals and snacks ~ Restaurant ~ (01295) 760389 ~ Open 11-2.30, 6-11; 12-3, 7-11 Sun; 12-5 Sun in winter; closed 25 Dec ~ Bedrooms: £30S/£50S

WADENHOE TL0083 Map 5

Kings Head

Church Street; village signposted (in small print) off A605 S of Oundle

This stone-built pub is attractively set in a village of thatched stone cottages, with picnic-sets among willows and aspens on a rough swathe of grass sloping down to boat moorings on the River Nene. The welcoming and atmospheric partly stripped-stone main bar has pleasant old worn quarry-tiles, solid pale pine furniture with a couple of cushioned wall seats, and a leather-upholstered chair by the woodburning stove in the fine inglenook. The bare-boards public bar has similar furnishings and another fire, with steps down to a games room with darts, dominoes and hood skittles, and there's yet more of the pale pine furniture in an attractive little beamed dining room. In the summer lunchtime bar food is limited to soup (£2.50), sandwiches (£2.75 – £1 extra with soup), filled french bread (from £3.25), welsh rarebit (£3.50) and ploughman's (£5), but in the evening and at lunchtime in winter there's a sensible choice of imaginative well cooked dishes that might include onion tart or chicken liver pâté with onion marmalade (£3.75), chorizo and black pudding salad (£4.50), pasta (£7), steak and kidney casserole with herb dumplings (£7.75), wild mushroom and aubergine risotto (£8) and baked salmon on a fresh herb cream sauce (£9.75); they do good winter Sunday roasts; pleasant service. Well kept Adnams Southwold and Broadside, and Marstons Pedigree on handpump, freshly squeezed orange juice, home-made lemonade and an extensive wine list; magazines to read, no piped music; no-smoking restaurant. Well equipped bedrooms look out over the garden. *(Recommended by Francis Johnson, E J Locker, Peter Plumridge, John Bowdler, G Noel, Stephen, Julie and Hayley Brown, John Coulter)*

Free house ~ Licensees Catherine and Alasdair Belton ~ Real ale ~ Meals and snacks (not Sun or Mon evening) ~ Restaurant ~ (01832) 720024 ~ Children welcome ~ Open 12-3, 6-11(10.30 Sun); closed Mon lunchtime; closed Sun evening in winter ~ Bedrooms: £35S/£50S

WOODNEWTON TL0394 Map 5

White Swan

Main Street; back roads N of Oundle, easily reached from A1/A47 (via Nassington) and A605 (via Fotheringhay)

It doesn't look big from the road, but this friendly country dining pub is surprisingly long and roomy inside. Despite the concentration on food, there's still space for drinkers at one end, with well kept Fullers London Pride, Oakham JHB and a guest on handpump, and a flame-effect gas fire. The main focus is on the attractively set-out dining area at the other end, which has double tablecloths and fresh flowers on all the tables, and attentive service from cheerful waitresses, obviously very well trained by the friendly licensees; there's careful attention to detail throughout. The blackboard changes daily, but the good carefully cooked food might include filled french bread (from £3.95), a good steak and kidney pudding (£7.95), lemon sole with prawns, cream, brandy and lobster sauce (£9.95), pan-fried duck or spring lamb (£10.95) and steaks (from £11.95); main courses are served with lots of freshly cooked vegetables. It's best to book in the evening or at weekends. There may be local radio. There are tables on the back lawn, which has a boules pitch. *(Recommended by John Bowdler, Rev J E Cooper, George Atkinson)*

Free house ~ Licensees George and Ann Dubbin ~ Real ale ~ Meals and snacks (till 10; possibly not Sun evening) ~ Restaurant ~ (01780) 470381 ~ Children welcome in restaurant ~ Open 12-3, 6.45-11; Sun 12-3, 7-10.30

Lucky Dip

Besides the fully inspected pubs, you might like to try these Lucky Dips recommended to us and described by readers (if you do, please send us reports):

☆ **Abthorpe** [Silver St; signed from A43 at 1st roundabout S of A5; SP6446], *New Inn*: Tucked-away partly thatched country local, rambling take-us-as-you-find-us dim-lit bars, beams, stripped stone, inglenook log fire, masses of pictures and old family photographs, attractively priced home cooking (not Sun/Mon) inc good cheap crab sandwiches, well kept Hook Norton Best, Old Hookey and Double Stout, good choice of malt whiskies, hospitable landlord, lots of old family photographs etc; big garden with goldfish pool, rabbits and aviary, quiet village *(George Atkinson, Mr and Mrs A Bull, BB)*

Apethorpe [Kings Cliffe Rd; TL0295], *Kings Head*: Roomy stonebuilt pub in attractive conservation village, comfortable lounge with real fire, ales such as Fullers London Pride, Marstons Bitter and Pedigree and Wadworths 6X, obliging landlord and staff, arch to big dining area with big helpings of good food inc good fish choice, other interesting dishes, plenty of veg, also (not Mon) separate bar food menu; cosy bar with pool; children welcome, picnic-sets in small enclosed garden *(David and Mary Webb, L Eadon)*

Arthingworth [just above A14 by A508 junction; SP7581], *Bulls Head*: Refurbished pub, with good value freshly cooked food in bar and restaurant inc vegetarian and popular Sun lunch, jovial landlord, well kept ales such as Brains SA; open all day summer *(John Liddell, Stephen Brown, Bryan and Betty Southwell)*

Ashley [SP7990], *George*: Unpretentious, friendly and unspoilt village pub, huge beam in lounge with comfortable settles and tables set for dining, more basic bar with welcoming locals, darts, dominoes and team photographs, well kept Mansfield beers, decent cheap standard food *(Rona Murdoch)*

Ashton [the one NE of Oundle, signed from A427/A605 island; TL0588], *Chequered Skipper*: From outside still a handsome thatched pub in elegant estate village, but rebuilt internally (after fire) as light and airy continental-feel cafe/bar with ultra-modern fittings; real ales such as Bass, Oakham JBH and Shepherd Neame Spitfire, reasonably priced food (not Mon), young lively staff *(GA)*

☆ **Aynho** [B4100/B4031 SE of Banbury; SP5133], *Cartwright Arms*: Friendly former posting inn, good home-made food in neatly modernised lounge and bar, well kept ales, helpful staff, reasonably priced restaurant, a few tables in pretty corner of former coachyard; bedrooms comfortable and attractive *(Kathy Henshaw, R J Frearson, BB)*

Barby [SP5470], *Arnold Arms*: Doing well under current licensees, with pleasant atmosphere, good range of beers, traditional food inc good old-fashioned puddings, garden with barbecues *(David Mead)*

☆ **Blakesley** [High St (Woodend rd, off old coach rd Towcester—Southam); SP6250], *Bartholomew Arms*: Cosy and attractive beamed pub with lots of dark panelling in bar and lounge, stuffed birds and bric-a-brac, good food, friendly service, well kept Ansells, Marstons Pedigree and Tetleys, soft lighting; piped music, children welcome in dining area; fine tranquil sheltered garden set some way back with summer house; next to interesting little art gallery *(George Atkinson)*

Braunston [Dark Lane, Little Braunston, just N of canal tunnel; SP5466], *Admiral Nelson*: Popular 18th-c ex-farmhouse in peaceful setting by Grand Union Canal Lock 3 and hump bridge, with pleasant waterside garden and towpath walks; well kept Courage Directors, good friendly service, good quick reasonably priced food inc children's and sandwiches, restaurant; bedroom overlooking lock *(David and Karen Berry, George Atkinson, Gordon)*

Brigstock [1 Hall Hill; off A6116; SP9485], *Green Dragon*: Very pleasant, clean and warm, with friendly staff, reasonably priced food *(Anon)*

Broughton [SP8375], *Red Lion*: Very clean dining pub, lounge/restaurant laid out for eating, varied menu inc lunchtime and early evening meal bargains for two; pleasant staff, areas for smokers and non-smokers, separate bar and games area, pleasant garden with play area *(David and Mary Webb)*

☆ **Buckby Wharf** [A5 N of Weedon; SP6065], *New Inn*: Simple welcoming pub under friendly new licensees, fresh paint, new carpets and furniture in several rooms radiating from central servery, inc small dining room with nice fire; short choice of sensibly priced food from steak sandwiches and hot filled rolls up, Marstons Pedigree; tables out on pleasant terrace by Grand Union Canal *(George Atkinson, LYM)*

Burton Latimer [Bake House Lane, off Church St; SP9075], *Olde Victoria*: Spacious mix of genuine and contrived old-world inc ornate gas lamps and lots of china, with nice atmosphere, well kept ales such as Marstons Pedigree, Morlands Old Speckled Hen, Shepherd Neame Spitfire and John Smiths, enjoyable food from baked potatoes up (sandwiches come at a price with salad and chips), friendly staff; quiet piped music, machines, back restaurant with cover charge; garden and terrace with picnic-sets under cocktail parasols *(George Atkinson, Stephen, Julie and Hayley Brown)*

Chapel Brampton [SP7266], *Spencer Arms*: Very big recently refurbished Chef & Brewer family dining pub, wide choice of good food inc well cooked veg, courteous staff, real ales inc Theakstons Old Peculier *(Patrick Tailyour)*

Cogenhoe [Whiston Rd; SP8360], *Royal Oak*: Village local with five real ales and good choice of reasonably priced food (not Sun evening), public bar with darts, pool, hood skittles, juke box and TV; picnic-sets in garden *(JJW, CMW)*

☆ **Cosgrove** [Thrupp Wharf, towards Castlethorpe – off A508 just NW of Milton Keynes; SP7942], *Navigation*: Lovely canalside setting, bustling rambling open-plan bar up steps with chesterfield and armchairs around open fire, lots of canal prints and memorabilia, character landlord, competent service, real ales inc Wadworths 6X and local Frog Island Shoemaker, usual food done well inc good toasties; summer jazz, children welcome, lots of tables out by water (a long way round from front entrance), moorings; can be very busy weekends and school hols *(John C Baker, George Atkinson, BB)*

Cranford St John [High St; 3 miles E of Kettering just off A14; SP9277], *Red Lion*: Good range of good value generous food inc bargain OAP lunches in welcoming and attractive two-bar stone pub, well kept Ind Coope and Tetleys, decent house wine, good-humoured service; pleasant garden, quiet village *(Anthony Barnes, Pete Yearsley)*

Culworth [off B4525 NE of Banbury; SP5446], *Red Lion*: Done-up 17th-c pub with lots of highly polished brassware in cosy and comfortable well heated lounge, Marstons Pedigree *(Tom Evans)*

Daventry [Brook St; SP5762], *Dun Cow*: Interesting former coaching inn, log fire and lots of old local photographs in down-to-earth cosy character bar (no piped music), roomier more peaceful rare Elizabethan gallery bar, cheap lunchtime food (not Sun) inc home-made steak and kidney pie, back family eating room, attentive service, well kept Bass, Davenports and a guest such as Elgoods *(Patrick Tailyour, Pete Baker)*

☆ **Duddington** [A43 just S of A47; SK9800], *Royal Oak*: Attractive stone inn, more hotel than pub, spotless and comfortable, with plush banquettes, fresh flowers, gleaming brass inc wartime shell cases, lots of pictures, open fire; wide choice of good popular food, Ruddles County, very friendly and efficient Portuguese family (Portuguese wines strong on the list); nice garden and terrace; good bedrooms *(Dorothy and Leslie Pilson)*

Evenley [The Green; SP5834], *Red Lion*: Small friendly local with strong cricket connections, opp attractive village green; some flagstones, Banks's and Marstons Pedigree, decent choice of wines, good usual food inc good sandwiches and Sun lunch; piped music *(K H Frostick, George Atkinson)*

☆ **Grafton Regis** [A508 S of Northampton; SP7546], *White Hart*: Quite smart, with friendly landlord, obliging service, good home-made food in lounge bar inc several good soups, Greene King IPA and Abbot, most space given over to bookings-only restaurant with open fire – very popular for flamboyant chef's good imaginative cooking; big garden (food not served there), in lovely thatched village *(George Atkinson, P A Evans)*

Great Houghton [Cherry Tree Lane; up No Through Road just before the White Hart; SP7958], *Old Cherry Tree*: Cosy old pub in quiet village spot, stone, low beams and dark panelling, limited range of good value lunchtime bar food, well kept Charles Wells Eagle and Bombardier, good friendly service, no music; good garden *(George Atkinson)*

Great Oxendon [Harborough Rd (A508); SP7383], *George*: Civilised L-shaped bar/lounge, pleasant no-smoking conservatory overlooking big garden and terrace, friendly staff, Adnams and Bass, great choice of good reasonably priced food inc good assorted cheese ploughman's, restaurant; bedrooms *(George Atkinson, Shirley Fletcher)*

Hardingstone [61 High St; SP7657], *Crown*: Two-bar pub with good value lunchtime food, well kept Theakstons, games room, fruit machine; children welcome, picnic-sets in sizeable garden with play area, dovecot and pets corner *(CMW, JJW)*

Harpole [High St; nr M1 junction 16; SP6860], *Bull*: Comfortable old-fashioned village pub with good value generous food in cosy front lounge and eating area, well kept Scottish Courage ales with three guests, good service, log fire in big inglenook, locals' basic back bar and games room, small terrace; no dogs *(T A Bryan)*

☆ **Harrington** [High St, off A508 S of Mkt Harboro; SP7779], *Tollemache Arms*: Good home-cooked fresh food in civilised beamed Tudor pub, friendly and obliging service, well kept Charles Wells Eagle and Bombardier, open fires, small back garden; children welcome, clean and attractive bedrooms, quiet stonebuilt village *(K H Frostick, Pete Yearsley)*

☆ **Hellidon** [off A425 W of Daventry; SP5158], *Red Lion*: Clean, cosy and comfortable, good value food inc good Weds OAP lunch in bars and restaurant, well kept Bass and Worthington, two farm ciders, welcoming landlord and above-average service, roaring log fire, friendly labradors, games room; bedrooms, beautiful setting by village green, tables outside, pleasant walks nearby *(John Brightley, Mr and Mrs A Bull)*

Higham Ferrers [4 College St; SP9668], *Green Dragon*: Outstanding range of well kept interesting real ales, low-priced food inc good steaks bought by weight, friendly service, really big garden with dovecote in walls *(Stephen Brown)*

☆ **Holcot** [Main St; nr Pitsford Water, N of Northampton; SP7969], *White Swan*: Attractive partly thatched two-bar village inn with hospitable series of rooms, good reasonably priced food (not Sun-Weds evenings) from baked pots up inc good value Sun lunch, Fullers London Pride, Greene King IPA and Tetleys from thatched servery, maybe Hook Norton and Morlands Old Speckled Hen, efficient smiling service even when very busy, games room with darts, skittles and pool; open all day Sun and summer, children welcome; bedrooms *(George Atkinson, Eric Locker, Michael and Jenny Back, Rona Murdoch)*

Islip [just off A14, by bridge into Thrapston; SP9879], *Woolpack*: Friendly and comfortable old inn, armchairs and prints in spacious beamed and stripped-stone lounge, Adnams, Bass, Greene King IPA and Abbot and Marstons Pedigree, usual food, woodburner, chatty landlord, Sun restaurant lunch; bedrooms *(George Atkinson)*

Kettering [1 Sheep St, Market Pl; SP8778], *Cherry Tree*: Welcoming local with good reasonably priced home-cooked food all day (not after 6 Tues, afternoon break Sun) inc vegetarian choice and two-person bargains, friendly staff, gas fire, well kept Charles Wells Eagle; piped music may be rather loud, unobtrusive fruit machines *(Keith and Janet Morris)*

Kilsby [Main Rd; A5/A361, handy for M1 junction 18; SP5671], *Red Lion*: Attractive pub in beautiful thatched village, good choice of good food, several real ales, real fire, pictures, plants and fresh flowers, public bar with pool and darts area, lots of picnic-sets on terrace and lawn with play area; piped music may be rather loud, quiz night, children welcome *(CMW, JJW)*

Kings Cliffe [TL0097], *Cross Keys*: Well kept Bass, Worthington and another ale such as Frolicking Farmers, simple but nicely served food, good atmosphere *(Francis Johnston)*

Kings Sutton [SP4936], *Butchers Arms*: Well kept village pub with decent reasonably priced food, well kept Hook Norton Best, Old Hookey and Generation in fine condition, also their Christmas 12 Days; in neat sandstone village easily spotted by spire *(Giles Francis, Dick and Jan Chenery)*

Kislingbury [6 Mill Rd; off A45 W of Northampton; SP6959], *Sun*: Out-of-the-way thatched stone village pub, four small cosy linked rooms, Ind Coope Burton, Morlands Old Speckled Hen and Tetleys, decent food from refurbished kitchen (not Sun; service can slow when busy), real and gas fires, charity book swap; darts, SkyTV, fruit machine, piped radio, no dogs; back terrace and garden with waterfall and fish pond, barbecues; river walks nearby *(CMW, JJW)*

Little Addington [High St; SP9573], *Bell*: Roomy and elegant stonebuilt dining pub with wide choice of interesting and fair-priced food in bar and restaurant – delicious sauces, a touch of nouvelle cuisine, not a chip in sight; good service, linen napkins even with the bar meals, which you can eat in the restaurant; well kept beers inc Marstons *(Howard and Margaret Buchanan)*

☆ **Little Brington** [4½ miles from M1 junction 16, first right off A45 to Daventry; also signed from A428; SP6663], *Saracens Head*: Well kept real ales inc local Frog Island Best, Fullers London Pride and Hook Norton Best, welcoming staff, some emphasis on good generous quickly served food; extended no-smoking restaurant area, roomy lounge with alcoves, lots of pictures, books and odds and ends, even a red telephone box, lovely log fire, games bar; piped pop music; tables in neat back garden, handy for Althorp House and Holdenby House *(George Atkinson, K H Frostick, Simon Walker, Bruce Bird, BB)*

☆ **Little Harrowden** [Orlingbury Rd/Kings Lane – off A509 or A43 S of Kettering; SP8771], *Lamb*: Spotlessly refurbished 17th-c pub, cosy three-level lounge with log fire, brasses on beams, intimate no-smoking dining area, hard-working jovial landlord, wife cooks good nicely presented food (not Sun evening) inc good Sun lunch, game and vegetarian dishes, veg extra, well kept Charles Wells Eagle and Bombardier and guests such as Badger Best, decent coffee, quiet piped music; small public bar, games room with darts and hood skittles, theme and quiz nights; children welcome, small terrace and garden, delightful village *(George Atkinson, L Eadon, CMW, JJW, David Etheridge)*

Loddington [SP8178], *Chequered Flag*: Good range of well kept ales inc Marstons Pedigree, well cooked food inc good fresh pies *(Stephen G Brown)*

☆ **Marston Trussell** [Main St – off A427, 2 miles W of Mkt Harboro; SP6985], *Sun*: More hotel than pub, with comfortable good value bedrooms, but well worth knowing for wide choice of beautifully presented home-made food in bar, lounge/dining area and restaurant, well kept Bass, decent house wines, unusual malt whiskies, helpful uniformed staff; good bedrooms, pleasant village *(George Atkinson, Bruce Cooper)*

Mears Ashby [Wilby Rd; SP8466], *Griffins Head*: Quiet pleasantly refurbished country pub with two rooms off central bar, good friendly service, good food from sandwiches to good value Sun roasts, generous OAP lunches Mon-Fri, attractive views and hunting prints, full range of Everards ales inc Mild, also Marstons Pedigree and a guest such as Frog Island, huge fireplace; games room with darts, skittles and piped music; seats out in small garden, on edge of attractive thatched village *(George Atkinson, CMW, JJW, Peter and Pat Frogley)*

☆ **Milton Malsor** [Towcester Rd (old A43); SP7355], *Greyhound*: Big busy pub, well refurbished in olde-worlde mode, 15th-c beams, old paintings and china, pewter-filled dresser etc; very popular locally for imaginative choice of good generous food all day from wide range of filled rolls and hot cobs to steak and duck, vegetarian dishes, quick cheery service, John Smiths, Theakstons Best and XB, good choice of wines, candlelit tables, good log fire, piped classical music; open all day, spreading front lawn with duck pond *(George Atkinson, Mrs S Parsons, K Campbell, Barry Perfect, Dave Braisted, Gill and Keith Croxton)*

Nassington [2 Fotheringhay Rd – 2½ miles S of A1/A47 interchange W of Peterboro; TL0696], *Black Horse*: Civilised 17th-c beamed and panelled dining pub in nice village, wide choice of food from sandwiches up, with children's helpings; splendid big stone fireplace, panelling, easy chairs and small settees in two rooms linked by bar servery, well kept Scottish Courage ales, friendly landlord, good varied wine list; attractive garden, open all day summer weekends *(Maysie Thompson, Quentin Williamson, Brian Wainwright, LYM)*

Newnham [The Green; SP5859], *Romer Arms*:

Light and airy pub on green, very welcoming ebullient new landlord, lots of stripped pine, open fire, back conservatory, good generous home cooking inc popular Sun lunch (no snacks then), real ales such as Batemans Jollys Jaunts, Greene King IPA, Jennings and Mansfield Old Baily; piped music, opens noon or so *(George Atkinson)*

Northampton [Fish St; SP7560], *Beamhouse*: Newish central open-plan pub with carpet on polished boards, comfortable chairs and banquettes, good value food (not Sun) from very well filled toasties to good value hot dishes and tasty puddings in big dining area, pleasant helpful service, Mansfield ales, newspapers, piped pop, games machines; disabled access *(JJW, CMW, Mr and Mrs J Brown)*; [Old Bedford Rd, 3¾ miles from M1 junction 15], *Britannia*: Rambling pub with massive beams, mix of flagstones, bare boards and carpet, attractive 18th-c kitchen, Scottish Courage ales, lunchtime food with no-smoking area, conservatory; machines, piped music; picnic-sets by River Nene *(CMW, JJW, LYM)*; [11 Fish St], *Fish*: Nice bustling atmosphere, good value weekday lunches, more limited evening food, eight real ales inc unusual ones (not cheap), farm cider, bare boards, newspapers; games machines, piped pop music; disabled access; bedrooms *(CMW, JJW)*; [121 Bridge St], *Malt Shovel*: Recently refurbished 1914 pub opp Carlsberg Brewery, long pine and brick bar with Banks's, Boddingtons Mild, Frog Island Natterjack, Whitbreads Castle Eden and guest ales from small breweries, imported bottles, lots of whiskies, farm cider, occasional beer festivals, enthusiastic landlord, daily papers, good home-made usual food lunchtime, expanding collection of breweriana; piped music, darts; picnic-sets on small back terrace *(George Atkinson, Bruce Bird, CMW, JJW)*; [Mkt Sq], *Moon on the Square*: Civilised Wetherspoons, with pews and masses of books, good range of real ales from long bar, interesting good value food all day, good coffee, no-smoking back conservatory; no music, a quiet haven *(George Atkinson)*; [4 St Giles Sq], *Rat & Parrot*: Scottish Courage chain pub in converted bank, food all day, Courage Directors and Theakstons, upstairs seating, back terrace with tubs and statuary; fruit machines, piped pop music (may be loud), young people's evening pub; disabled facilities *(CMW, JJW)*

☆ **Old** [Walgrave Rd; N of Northampton between A43 and A508; SP7873], *White Horse*: Wide choice of enjoyable sensibly priced food inc some interesting dishes, cosy and comfortable lounge with welcoming log fire, lots of pictures and plates, friendly service, well kept Banks's and Morrells, decent wines, good coffee, restaurant, unusual theme nights; piped radio may obtrude; lovely garden overlooking 13th-c church *(K H Frostick, Rona Murdoch, Roy Bromell)*

Orlingbury [signed off A43 Northampton—Kettering, A509 Wellingborough—Kettering; SP8572], *Queens Arms*: Large airy Tetleys pub doing well under current friendly young landlord, four or five well kept guest ales from small breweries, good food lunchtime and evening, stylish furnishings, good atmosphere; nice garden with play area *(Leo Eadon)*

Oundle [52 Benefield Rd; A427 towards Corby; TL0388], *Black Horse*: Small roadside local popular for good value straightforward food (skip breakfast if you want to try their mixed grill), well kept Bass, Batemans XXXB and John Smiths, lots of up-to-date paperbacks to borrow, growing collection of talking toys and dolls, simple plush seating, new restaurant area, friendly prompt service, quiet piped music; picnic-sets in garden behind, Sat karaoke *(Jenny and Michael Back, BB)*

Polebrook [just SE of Oundle – OS Sheet 142 map ref 067871; TL0687], *Kings Arms*: Welcoming young licensees, good friendly atmosphere in big partly divided open-plan lounge, good choice of food inc really good value sandwiches, real ales such as Adnams, Bass and Greene King, good value food, separate dining room, spotless lavatories; piped music can be rather loud *(Peter Plumridge)*

Ravensthorpe [Church Lane; SP6670], *Chequers*: Wide range of bar food inc good well priced Sun lunch (worth booking this), well kept cheap Sam Smiths OB and other northern ales, lots of bric-a-brac in spotless L-shaped bar with jugs and mugs on beams, friendly locals, good service, restaurant (Weds-Sat); TV, fruit machine, piped music, monthly quiz night; quiet garden with play area *(Ted George, CMW, JJW)*

Rothwell [Sun Hill (A6); SP8181], *Rowell Charter*: Ancient pub with two open fires, good choice of home-cooked food, friendly service, unusual range of consistently well kept beers, sensible prices *(Patrick Tailyour, Stephen and Julie Brown)*

Rushton [SP8482], *Thornhill Arms*: Pleasantly refurbished pub opp attractive village's cricket green, open fire, decent low-priced food, well kept ales inc Ruddles, restaurant *(Stephen, Julie and Hayley Brown)*

☆ **Sibbertoft** [Welland Rise, off A4303 or A508 SW of Mkt Harboro; SP6782], *Red Lion*: Cosy and civilised, increasingly a dining pub, with all lounge tables set for good generous food inc vegetarian; big tables and comfortably cushioned wall seats, well kept Batemans, decent wines, good friendly service, piano, magazines; lovely beamed restaurant; may be cl Weds lunchtime *(Rona Murdoch, Dorsan Baker)*

Stoke Albany [1 Harborough Rd; SP8088], *White Horse*: Recently refurbished, clean and tidy, popular for good value well cooked food inc wide vegetarian choice; well kept Bass and Worthington *(Stephen Brown)*

☆ **Stoke Bruerne** [3½ miles from M1 junction 15 – A508 towards Stony Stratford then signed on right; SP7450], *Boat*: Ideal canal location by beautifully restored lock opp British Waterways Museum and shop; little character flagstoned bar by canal, more ordinary back lounge without the views (children allowed in this bit), tables by towpath; well kept ales such as Marstons Best and Pedigree, Sam Smiths OB, Theakstons XB, Wadworths 6X and guests, skittle alley; bar snacks, no-smoking restaurant (not Mon lunchtime) and all-day tearooms, pub open all day summer Sats, canal boat trips *(Charles and Pauline Stride, LYM)*

☆ **Sudborough** [High St (off A6116); SP9682], *Vane Arms*: Cheerily take-us-as-you-find us thatched pub notable for its fine choice of well kept ales mostly from interesting small breweries and often strong, friendly helpful service from enthusiastic landlord and daughter; also Belgian fruit beers, farm cider, country wines; stripped stonework, inglenook fires, games in public bar (can be noisy), food (not Sun evening, Mon lunch) from sandwiches to steaks inc lots of Mexican dishes; piped music, and Nelson the dog gets around; lounge, dining area and upstairs restaurant (not Sun evening) all no smoking; children in eating area, bedrooms; cl Mon lunchtime *(L Eadon, Stephen and Julie Brown, Joan and Michel Hooper-Immins, JP, PP, Rona Murdoch, John McDonald, Ann Bond, Julian Holland, Christopher Beadle, Roger and Pauline Pearce, LYM)*

Sutton Bassett [B664; SP7790], *Queens Head*: Peaceful village pub with good if not cheap food inc children's using herbs from own garden, changing well kept ales such as Adnams, Butcombe Wilmots, Morlands Original, Oakham Grainstore VP1000 (brewed to celebrate welcoming Irish landlord's 1000th different real ale here), Ruddles Best and County, Thwaites Chairmans, upstairs restaurant; some seats out beyond car park *(Stephen and Julie Brown, Joan and Michel Hooper-Immins)*

Syresham [off A43 Brackley—Towcester; SP6241], *Kings Head*: Family dining pub with beams, brasses, pictures, motor-racing memorabilia – also toys, high chairs, baby-changing; food from good sandwiches up, friendly service, real fire, well kept Banks's and Marstons ales; piped music, separate bar with games and juke box; tables in garden, children welcome *(George Atkinson, J Warren)*

☆ **Thornby** [Welford Rd – A50 Northampton—Leicester, handy for A14; SP6775], *Red Lion*: Friendly old bar with decorative china, pews and some leather armchairs, amiable dogs, log fire, good home-made bar food from sandwiches to steaks inc Sun roasts and children's helpings, well kept Greene King IPA, Marstons Pedigree, Robinsons Best and Thwaites, good range of traditional games; piped music; open all day weekends, children welcome *(George Atkinson, M J Morgan, David Heath, LYM)*

☆ **Thorpe Mandeville** [former B4525; SP5344], *Three Conies*: Cosy and attractive, with brasses, low beams, some stripped stone, gin-trap over inglenook fireplace, horse-racing photographs and conversation, furnishings to suit the old building; good reasonably priced food, well kept Hook Norton and Old Hookey, good choice of wines and spirits, friendly efficient service, games room, appealing restaurant; children welcome, lots of seats in big garden *(David Carr, Ted George, LYM)*

Thorpe Waterville [A605 Thrapston—Oundle; TL0281], *Fox*: Pleasantly extended old pub with wide range of food, Charles Wells ales, log-effect fire, quiet piped music, no-smoking dining area, friendly prompt service; children allowed, no dogs, small garden with play area *(Dave Braisted)*

Titchmarsh [signed from A14 and A605, just E of Thrapston; TL0279], *Wheatsheaf*: Welcoming village local popular for evening food inc good home-made dishes as well as usual fish and steaks, Hook Norton and Marstons Pedigree, lots of exposed stonework, golfing memorabilia, pool room, restaurant, cat and dogs, piped music; children allowed in eating areas; cl Mon evening, weekday lunchtimes *(Francis Johnston, LYM)*

Twywell [off A14 W of Thrapston; SP9478], *Old Friar*: Neat and tidy, with good range of beers, big front eating area, smaller one off lounge bar, helpful staff, good reasonably priced food *(Ted George, Simon Watkins, LYM)*

Wakerley [Main St (off A43); SP9599], *Exeter Arms*: Good range of ales, enjoyable food (not Mon), two connecting rooms with woodburner, local photographs; piped music, fruit machine, occasional live music; garden with swings, good views and walks over Welland Valley *(David and Mary Webb)*

Watford [Watford Gap; B4036 towards Daventry; SP5968], *Stags Head*: Attractive boat-shaped bar with open fire, enjoyable food inc good steak and kidney pie, white cast-iron tables on terrace overlooking garden by Grand Union Canal, cellar public bar, restaurant; long-serving Portuguese licensees *(Patrick Tailyour)*

Weedon [junction A5/A45; SP6458], *Globe*: Atractive and friendly family-run country hotel with reliable fresh food inc vegetarian and take-aways, small helpings for children or OAPs, quick friendly service, well kept Marstons Bitter and Pedigree, Websters Yorkshire and usually a northern guest beer, log fire, restaurant; picnic-sets outside, live music Mon; bedrooms *(P A Evans, George Atkinson)*; [Daventry Rd (A45)], *Heart of England*: Big pub much extended from 18th-c core, partly no-smoking panelled eating area, busy attractively refurbished lounge bar with small areas off, three Mansfield real ales, good value food inc children's, restaurant with conservatory, lively family room; piped pop music; big garden leading down to Grand Union Canal, good value pine-furnished bedrooms *(CMW, JJW)*; [Stowe Hill (A5 S)], *Narrow Boat*: Plain decor with canal prints, high-raftered ex-kitchen family dining room, good straightforward bar food, well kept Charles Wells ales; fruit machine, skittles and quiet piped music, very busy in summer; spacious terrace, big garden by canal, barbecues; bedrooms in back motel extension, narrowboat hire next door *(Norma and Keith Bloomfield, LYM)*; [Bridge St/West St, Weedon Bec], *Plume of Feathers*: New licensees doing good choice of good food in friendly old village local, several real ales, picnic-sets and play area in garden, canal and walks nearby; quiet piped music *(CMW, JJW)*

☆ **Welford** [High St (A50); SP6480], *Shoulder of Mutton*: Friendly and spotless low-ceilinged pub nr canal marina, partly divided by standing timbers and arches, plenty of tables and wheelback chairs, copper and brass, decent food inc imaginative and children's dishes, well kept Bass, Batemans XB and Ruddles Best, good house wines and coffee, eager service; piped music; skittle room, exemplary lavatories, good back garden with play area; cl Thurs *(Frank Davidson, E J Cutting, BB)*

Wellingborough [Cannon St; SP8968], *Cannon*: Friendly, with up to six real ales from their own back microbrewery, several well kept guest beers, lunchtime snacks, real fire, 1980s decor, rare beer bottle collection in pillared and partitioned lounge; piped music can be loud, fruit machine, games room with bar billiards; open all day *(Richard Lewis, G Coates)*; [Sheep St], *Horseshoe*: Limited choice of consistently good reasonably priced food and real ales such as Bass and Marstons Pedigree in comfortably traditional no-frills pub *(Mr and Mrs D Ely)*

☆ **Weston** [Helmdon Rd; the one N of Brackley; SP5846], *Crown*: Spacious and very welcoming no-frills 17th-c stonebuilt ex-farmhouse, log fires, beams and flagstones, lots of agricultural bric-a-brac, pictures and sporting trophies, well kept Judges Barristers and Grey Wig and one or two other ales such as Ushers 12-bore, good coffee, unusual long room (former skittle alley) with cubicle seating, enjoyable simple food (not Sun evening or Mon lunch); pool room, darts alcove; bedrooms, handy for NT Canons Ashby and Sulgrave *(George Atkinson, Tom Evans, JJW, CMW)*

Yardley Gobion [30 High St (off A508); SP7644], *Coffee Pot*: Charming roomy low-beamed village local with well kept Scottish Courage ales, real fires, friendly local licensees, good freshly cooked standard food, children in eating area, tables outside; pool, live music most weekends, challenging quiz nights *(Mr and Mrs D S Price, Bill Sykes)*

Yardley Hastings [just off A428 Bedford—Northampton; SP8656], *Rose & Crown*: Relaxed and spacious 18th-c pub in pretty village, great character, flagstones, beams and stripped stonework, lots of pictures and brasses, nooks and crannies for a quiet drink, cheerful staff, good value freshly made food from excellent sausage baps up, vegetarian and children's dishes, Thurs OAP lunches, Tues evening bargain carvery; Charles Wells ales, comfortable family area, seats in courtyard *(T G Saul, Terry and Tina Jeffery, George Atkinson, Penny and Ron Westwood)*

Stars after the name of a pub show exceptional quality. One star means most people (after reading the report to see just why the star has been won) would think a special trip worth while. Two stars mean that the pub is really outstanding – many that for their particular qualities cannot be bettered.

Northumberia

Scattered over this huge area are some rewarding finds. There's the Allenheads Inn at Allenheads with its amazing decor, a treasure-trove of bric-a-brac – and an enjoyable place to stay; the Blue Bell at Belford, a lovely traditional small hotel, making a come-back to the Guide after careful refurbishment; the Lord Crewe Arms at Blanchland, certainly the most striking building among Northern inns; the Percy Arms at Chatton, much enjoyed by readers, as is the Fox & Hounds at Cotherstone – which has good food, and is a nice place to stay in; the Jolly Fisherman at Craster (try that crab soup); the Dipton Mill at Diptonmill, a classic atmospheric local that we wish was closer than 332 miles from our office; the Tankerville Arms at Eglingham, a comfortable dining pub currently doing well; the friendly and attractive thatched Black Bull at Etal; the Queens Head at Great Whittington, gaining a Food Award this year, with well kept beers too; the cosy Milecastle near Haltwhistle, with good home cooking; the very efficiently run Masons Arms at Rennington, with its charming landlord; the friendly Feathers at Hedley on the Hill (good food, great atmosphere, cheap beer); the attractively placed Rose & Crown at Romaldkirk, a tremendous favourite with readers – good all round; the Waterford Arms at Seaton Sluice (currently doing so well that it's back in these pages after an absence, with good fresh fish); and the Three Wheat Heads at Thropton, a charmingly placed inn doing particularly well under new licensees – another new main entry. Among all these, and other pubs here with good food, the Rose & Crown at Romaldkirk stands out as Northumbria Dining Pub of the Year. We'd urge your attention on the Lucky Dip entries at the end of the chapter, too – a good many interesting ones, particularly several in Beamish, the Black Bull at Corbridge, Hadrian at Wall and Bay Horse at West Woodburn. There's a decent choice in Durham, and in Newcastle the Cooperage stands out among a mass of other tempting prospects. The Keelman in Newburn is notable as sharing a building with the Big Lamp Brewery, and this year we've been pleased to find the good local Mordue beers getting about more widely. Drinks prices in the area have been increasing more than elsewhere recently, but are still rather below the national average. Please note that redrawn county boundaries mean that some pubs S of the Tees which previously appeared in this chapter will now be found in the Yorkshire one.

ALLENDALE (Northumberland) NY8355 Map 10

Kings Head 🛏

Market Place (B6295)

Dating from the beginning of the 18th c the Kings Head is the oldest pub in the area, but despite its years it stands up well to the keen competition from the other half a dozen pubs and inns in this rambling town square. The spacious bar/lounge has a big log fire, straightforward pub furnishings, and Greene King Abbot, Tetleys, Theakstons Best, and four or five guest ales on handpump, all kept well in a temperature-controlled cellar. Good value bar food includes sandwiches (from £1.80), hot filled french bread (£3.25), beef in ale or jester chicken (£4.95), mushroom and nut fettucine (£5.25), fried wild salmon or chicken fillets with leeks and stilton in a port sauce (£5.95), king prawns in a mediterranean sauce (£7.95), duck with a citrus sauce (£8.50), steaks (from £10.80) and puddings (£1.95); children's menu (£1.95). Darts and piped pop music; quoits on clay pitches in the back garden. There are good walks in the area, and the road through the valley is a fine scenic drive. *(Recommended by M P and K T Guy, M A Buchanan, Paul S McPherson, JJW, CMW, Steve and Marianne Webb-Phillips, Eric Larkham)*

Free house ~ Licensee Margaret Taylor ~ Real ale ~ Meals and snacks ~ Children welcome ~ (01434) 683681 ~ Folk music 2nd and 4th Fridays in the month ~ Open 11-11; 12-10.30 Sun ~ Bedrooms: £23B/£45B

ALLENHEADS (Northumberland) NY8545 Map 10

Allenheads Inn £

Just off B6295

The decor at this pub is so extraordinary that the four-foot wooden chicken that stands on one of the tables in the dining room somehow doesn't look out of place. The ever growing collection of antiques, bric-a-brac and junk covers every available space – the bar, walls and ceiling. In the loosely themed rooms you can find stuffed animals, mangles, old radios, typewriters, long silenced musical intruments, a ship's wheel and engine-room telegraph, brass and cooper bygones, a plastic lobster, brooms, birdcages and even shoes – the list is endless and it's all clean and enthusiastically well cared for. The games room (with darts, pool, cribbage and antique juke box) has perhaps the most effervescent collection, and the car club discs and number plates on the panelling are a symptom of the fact that members of a classic car club try to persuade their vehicles to wend their way up here every other Tuesday; the naval room is no smoking. They do huge helpings of good value straightforward food such as soup (£1.50), sandwiches (from £1.50), cod, vegetarian curry or vegetarian or meat chilli (£4.50), lasagne, scampi or sweet and sour chicken (£5), steak pie (£5.25) and puddings (from £1.50); also maybe special offer of two steaks and a bottle wine (£12); roast Sunday lunch (£4.25); one room is no smoking. Well kept Ind Coope Burton, Tetleys, locally brewed Old Barn Brewery Sheep Dog and a changing guest from Tetleys on handpump; decent coffee, real fire, piped music, friendly alsatian, very warm-hearted service from the cheerful and eccentric licensees. Readers report the bedrooms to be warm and comfortable. There are tables outside, flanked by more hardware – the sorts of machinery that wouldn't fit inside, including a Vintage Rolls-Royce parked in front; it's on the Sustrans C2C cycle route. *(Recommended by Jonathan Rowe, Louise Ezzard, Dennis Stevens, Mr and Mrs W Donworth, Byron and June Etherington, Pat and John Denby, Margaret Whitaker, Mr and Mrs J Beard)*

Free house ~ Licensees Peter and Linda Stenson ~ Real ale ~ Meals and snacks ~ Restaurant (bookings only) ~ (01434) 685200 ~ Children in the games room ~ Open 11-3(4 Sat), 7-11; 12-4, 7-10.30 Sun; cl Mon and Tues lunchtimes in winter ~ Bedrooms: £25B/£43B

ALNMOUTH (Northumberland) NU2511 Map 10

Saddle

Northumberland Street (B1338)

This unpretentious stonebuilt hotel is bigger than you'd expect from the outside, rambling through several areas including a spacious dining area. All are clean, friendly and attractively decorated, with a seascape over the tiled fireplace in the bar, brocaded stools, built-in wall benches and neat shiny dark tables. A wide choice of food includes soup (£1.80), pâté (£3.25), northumberland sausage (£3.75), chicken curry (£5.25), steak and kidney pie (£5.50), ploughman's (£5.95), barnsley lamb chops (£7.95), gammon with peach, pineapple or egg (£8.25) and steak (£9.95); good puddings (from £2.40) or an outstanding cheese board (£3.75). Ruddles Best and Theakstons Best, decent wines, friendly helpful staff; darts, pool, dominoes, cards and table tennis;

unobtrusive piped music; no-smoking restaurant. This seaside village has attractive beaches, good coastal walks, and plenty for summer visitors. *(Recommended by Nigel Thompson, Diana Crawford, Jack and Heather Coyle, June and Tony Baldwin, Guy Consterdine)*

Free house ~ Licensee Michael McMonagle ~ Real ale ~ Meals and snacks ~ Restaurant ~ (01665) 830476 ~ Children in family room, snug and lounge ~ Open 11-3, 6-11; 12-3, 6-10.30 Sun; closed Mon lunchtime in winter ~ Bedrooms: £37B/£64B

BAMBURGH (Northumberland) NU1835 Map 10

Lord Crewe Arms

This spotlessly kept inn is prettily set in a charming coastal village dominated by the impressive Norman castle. The back cocktail bar, with comfortably upholstered banquettes, windsor armchairs and the like around cast-iron traditional pub tables, has a bar counter studded with hundreds of pre-decimal polished copper coins, and its beams are festooned with swordfish swords, armadillo skins, miners' lamps, lobster pots, fishing nets and lots more; there's a winter log fire. A more modern side bar has hunting murals; dominoes and piped music. Bass and Stones kept under light blanket pressure; friendly helpful staff. Lunchtime bar food includes home-made soup (£2.15), sandwiches (from £2.15), basket meals (£3.95), ploughman's (£4.50), local haddock fillet deep-fried (£5.25), smoked local kippers or chicken kiev (£5.95), steak in ale pie or gammon and pineapple (£6.25), with evening dishes such as vegetarian pasta (£5.75), crunchy lamb casserole (£6.25), poached salmon (£7.75) and sirloin steak (£10.95); the restaurant is no smoking. The castle is still lived in and has a large collection of arms and armour, and it's only a few minutes' walk to the splendid sandy beach. *(Recommended by Ray and Chris Watson, Martin and Helen Hickes, Kevin Thorpe, Geoffrey and Brenda Wilson)*

Free house ~ Licensee Malcolm Eden ~ Real ale ~ Meals and snacks ~ Evening restaurant ~ (01668) 214243 ~ Children in eating area of bar ~ Open 11.30-10.30(11 Sat); hotel is closed end Oct-week before Easter ~ Bedrooms: £37(£49B)/£52(£74B)

BELFORD (Northumberland) NU1134 Map 10

Blue Bell

Market Place

Readers report a feeling of time standing still at this lovely traditional hotel; a welcome refuge from the A1. In the comfortable lounge bar there are upholstered seats standing on the turkey carpet, coaching prints on the walls and a log fire; the bar counter itself was taken from the Theatre Royal in Newcastle. Good bar food includes sandwiches (from £1.75), soup (£1.80), green salad (£2.20), mushrooms with bacon and brandy (£3.25), home-made steak and kidney pie, stir-fried quorn or paella (£5.25), chicken or lamb balti (£5.75), and 12oz sirloin steak (£11.95); home-made puddings such as kiwi pavlova or summer pudding (£2.75). Well kept Belhaven St Andrews, Northumberland Secret Kingdom, Theakstons XB and Wadworths 6X on handpump; darts, pool, table skittles, cribbage, dominoes and fruit machine; large garden. *(Recommended by M J Morgan, Comus Elliott, Martin and Helen Hickes, R T and J C Moggridge)*

Free house ~ Licensee Paul Shirley ~ Meals and snacks ~ Restaurant ~ (01668) 213543 ~ Children welcome ~ Live music at wekends ~ Open 11-2.30, 6.30-11; 12-2, 7-10.30 Sun ~ Bedrooms: £40B/£80B

BLANCHLAND (Northumberland) NY9750 Map 10

Lord Crewe Arms

Full of character and delightfully set in a very picturesque village this pub is steeped in history: originally built in 1235 as part of the guest-house of a Premonstratensian monastery – part of the cloister still stands in the neatly terraced gardens – it was later a manor house and one of the bedrooms is said to be haunted. The unusual barrel-vaulted crypt bar has plush bar stools, built-in wall benches, ancient flagstones, and stone and brick walls that are eight feet thick in some places; Vaux Samson on handpump; darts. Upstairs, the quietly welcoming Derwent Room has low beams, old settles, and sepia photographs on its walls, and the Hilyard Room has a massive 13th-c fireplace once used as a hiding place by the Jacobite Tom Forster (part of the family who had owned the building before it was sold to the formidable Lord Crewe, Bishop of Durham). Lunchtime bar food includes soup (£1.85), filled rolls (mostly £2.90), ploughman's (from £4.40), cumberland sausage (£5.25), salmon fishcakes (£5.40), breaded chicken escalope with crushed tomatoes and melted emmental (£5.85) and wild boar and pheasant pie (£6.50); in the evening, there might be baked salmon steak (£8), brie and broccoli bake (£8.25), or sirloin steak (£10) and puddings (£3). There's a pleasant enclosed garden. *(Recommended by Bill Wood, M J Morgan, M Morgan, Martin Hickes, Steve and Marianne Webb-Phillips, Paul and Ursula Randall, Richard Fallon)*

Free house ~ Licensees A S Todd, Peter Gingell, Ian Press ~ Real ale ~ Meals and snacks ~ Restaurant ~ (01434) 675251 ~ Children welcome ~ Open 11-3, 6-11.30; 12-3, 7-10.30 Sun; closed winter Tues and Weds lunchtimes ~ Bedrooms: £80B/£110B

CARTERWAY HEADS (Northumberland) NZ0552 Map 10

Manor House

A68 just N of B6278, near Derwent Reservoir

They have redecorated the bar and lounge at this long and simple stone house, stripping back the beamed ceiling in the locals' bar to expose the original wooden boards; also pine tables, chairs and stools, old oak pews, and a mahogany bar. The comfortable lounge bar has picture windows with fine southerly views over moorland pastures, and a woodburning stove. Well kept Courage Directors and Theakstons Best with guest beers from often local breweries such as Border, Butterknowle, Durham and Northumberland on handpump, draught scrumpy, around 20 malt whiskies, and decent wines; darts, dominoes and piped music. Popular food from a wide and changing menu might include chicken breast stuffed with smoked salmon (£9.95), red snapper with black olive and anchovy pesto or sirloin steak (£10.50), guinea fowl with wild mushrooms and garlic (£11) and home-made puddings such as sticky toffee pudding or apple crumble (£2.85); part of the restaurant is no smoking. Rustic tables out on a small side terrace and lawn. Clean and comfortable bedrooms and good breakfasts. The friendly and enthusiastic licensees have plans to extend the lounge to create an additional dining area. *(Recommended by M J Morgan, John Oddey, M Morgan, John Prescott, E J Locker, Jack Morley, R Stanley, R Macnaughton, Paul S McPherson, Brenda and Stuart Naylor, Chris Rounthwaite, Colin Ferguson, Walter and Susan Rinaldi-Butcher, Jack and Heather Coyle, M Borthwick, Joy and Peter Heatherley, Richard Dolphin, Eric Larkham, Mrs M Hughes, T M Dobby, Roger Bellingham, Dave Braisted, Graham and Karen Oddey, M Hughes)*

Free house ~ Licensees Chris and Moira Brown ~ Real ale ~ Meals and snacks ~ Restaurant ~ (01207) 255268 ~ Children in lounge and restaurant till 8.30 ~ Open 11-3, 6-11; 12-3, 7-10.30 Sun ~ Bedrooms: £25/£45

CHATTON (Northumberland) NU0628 Map 10

Percy Arms

B6348 E of Wooller

The attractively lit and neatly kept bar at this popular stone local has green stripy upholstered wooden wall seats, cushioned farmhouse chairs and stools, horse bits and brasses on beams, maps and country pictures on the walls. Through a stone arch is a similar room with a woodburning stove. The panelled dining room with its pretty plates on a delft shelf is most attractive. Tasty bar food at lunchtime includes good filled french bread (£2.65), home-made soup (£1.95), sweet pickled herring salad (£3.55), ploughman's (£4.55), filled baked potatoes (from £4.55), a vegetarian dish of the day, haddock or steak and kidney pie (£5.75), with evening dishes like smoked haddock on a bed of spinach with cheese and nutmeg sauce (£6.95), lamb chops glazed with redcurrant, orange and mint sauce (£9.25), Aberdeen Angus steaks (from £10.45) and half a roast duckling with cranberry and orange sauce (£11.45); puddings (from £1.95); good breakfasts. Well kept Theakstons XB or Morland Old Speckled Hen on handpump, a wine of the month plus blackboard specials, and a fine choice of about two dozen malt whiskies; unobtrusive piped music; public bar with darts, pool, dominoes, fruit machine, video game and juke box. There are picnic-sets on the small front lawn above the village road; bedrooms and a holiday cottage. No dogs in public areas. Residents have the use of a sauna, sunbed, keep-fit equipment and 12 miles of private fishing, where there may be salmon, sea trout or stocked rainbow trout. *(Recommended by JKW, Iain Patton, Chris Rounthwaite, CE, K McManus, T J Smith, June and Tony Baldwin, J H and S A Harrop, Steve and Marianne Webb-Phillips, Dr and Mrs J H Hills, Michael Wadsworth)*

Free house ~ Licensees Pam and Kenny Topham ~ Real ale ~ Meals and snacks (12-1.30, 6.30-9.30) ~ Restaurant ~ (01668) 215244 ~ Children welcome ~ Open 11-3, 6-11; 12-3, 7-10.30 Sun ~ Bedrooms: £25B/£50B

COTHERSTONE (Durham) NZ0119 Map 10

Fox & Hounds

B6277 – incidentally a good quiet route to Scotland, through interesting scenery

Readers enjoy staying at this simple white-painted old country pub which is prettily placed overlooking the village green. The beamed bar has various alcoves and recesses, with comfortable furnishings such as thickly cushioned wall seats, local photographs and country pictures on the walls, and a warming winter open fire. Well liked home-made bar food – served in the L-shaped lounge – includes omelette (£4.95), yorkshire pudding filled with cumberland sausage, fillet steak sandwich or gammon and egg (£5.95), haddock or chicken curry (£6.95) and pasta in a tomato and basil sauce (£7.95); coffee (95p) is served with home-made fudge; you can also eat from the more adventurous (and pricy) restaurant menu in the bar; one of the restaurants is no smoking. Well kept Black Sheep Best and Special and a guest under light blanket pressure, a fair choice of malt whiskies, and a useful wine list; helpful, friendly staff. Good nearby walks. *(Recommended by M J Morgan, DAV, Kim Maidment, Philip Vernon, Mr and Mrs D Wilson, Mr Crichton, Ian and Karen Hargreaves, Phil Putwain, Anthony Barnes, Richard Dolphin)*

Free house ~ Licensees Michael and May Carlisle ~ Real ale ~ Meals and snacks (11.30-3, 6-10) ~ Restaurant ~ (01833) 650241 ~ Children welcome ~ Open 11-3, 6-11; closed 25 Dec ~ Bedrooms: £37.50B/£55B

CRASTER (Northumberland) NU2620 Map 10

Jolly Fisherman £

Off B1339 NE of Alnwick

Readers are unanimous in their praise of the splendid crabmeat soup with whiskey and cream (£2.25) served up at this unpretentious local. The well filled crab sandwiches are also highly praised and other simple but popular bar snacks include sandwiches (from £1.60) and home-made craster kipper pâté (£2.25). From the big picture windows or the little garden there are lovely views over the harbour and out to sea and there is a nice mix of locals and visitors in the atmospheric bar: the snug by the entrance is popular with workers from the harbour or the kippering shed opposite. Well kept Marstons Pedigree, Vaux How's Your Father and Wards Thorne Best Bitter on handpump, and a range of malt whiskies; friendly service. Darts, pool, dominoes, cribbage, fruit machine and juke box. The pub can get crowded on sunny days, but unlike places in similar settings never begins to feel like a tourist attraction. There's a lovely clifftop walk to Dunstanburgh Castle. *(Recommended by Chris Rounthwaite, Peter Meister, Rev J Hibberd, GLD, C A Hall, JP, PP, Comus Elliott, A W and K J Randle, R T and J C Moggridge, Denis and Margaret Kilner, Richard Dolphin, Jack and Philip Paxton, Roger Wain-Heapy, Pauline and Bleddyn Davies, Jenny and Brian Seller, John and June Gale)*

Vaux ~ Lease: William P Silk ~ Real ale ~ Snacks (all day in summer) ~ (01665) 576461 ~ Children in eating area of bar till 9 ~ Open 11-11; 11-3, 6-11 in winter; 12-10.30 Sun; 12-3, 7-10.30 winter Sun

DIPTONMILL (Northumberland) NY9361 Map 10

Dipton Mill ◖

Off B6306 S of Hexham at Slaley, Blanchland and Dye House, Whitley Chapel signposts and HGV route sign

There's bags of atmosphere in the snug little bar of this small country local, with its dark ply panelling, red furnishings and open fires. The friendly landlord really knows his ales and is a partner in the Hexhamshire Brewery, hence the good choice of their well kept beers: Hexhamshire Shire Bitter, Devil's Water and Whapweasel; they also keep Theakstons Best and a guest, 25 malt whiskies and farm cider. Good wholesome bar food includes filled rolls, soup such as carrot and celery (£1.60), ploughman's (£3.50), cheese and broccoli flan or tomato, bean and vegetable casserole (£4.50), steak and kidney pie or turkey, bacon and mushroom crumble (£5.50), lamb steak in a wine and mustard sauce or chicken breast in sherry sauce (£5.50) and puddings like bread and butter pudding or syrup sponge (£1.60); home-made cakes and coffee (£1.65); pleasantly brisk service. Darts, bar billiards, shove-ha'penny and dominoes. You can sit at seats on the sunken crazy-paved terrace by the restored mill stream, or by the garden's pretty plantings and aviaries. It's in a very peaceful wooded valley and there are easy-walking footpaths nearby. *(Recommended by M J Morgan, Mr and Mrs A Bull, Dr B and Mrs P B Baker, M Morgan, GSB, Eric Larkham, Joy and Peter Heatherley, Mr Miller)*

Free house ~ Licensee Geoffrey Brooker ~ Real ale ~ Meals and snacks (12-2.30, 6.30-8.30; 12-2.30, 7.30-8.30 Sun) ~ (01434) 606877 ~ Children in small games room ~ Open 12-2.30, 6-11; 12-4.30, 7-10.30 Sun; closed 25 Dec

EGLINGHAM (Northumberland) NU1019 Map 10

Tankerville Arms

B6346 NW of Alnwick

Doing very well under its newish management, this busy village pub now has very well cooked and presented food. The blackboard changes daily and might include soup (from £1.95), sandwiches (from £2.75), ploughman's (£4.95), cream and mushroom rosti (£5.25), fresh battered cod (£5.80), home-made pie of the day (£5.95), chicken with stilton and cream (£7.45), steaks (from £8.95) and puddings such as home-made jelly with passion fruit ice cream and buttercake with poached pears in kirsch (£3.25); the cheviot lamb, quail, pigeon, liver and bacon, fresh fish and huge helpings of luscious puddings all have their devotees, and side salads are impressively generous. The long stone building stepped down the village street has coal fires at each end of the dining bar, black joists, some walls stripped to bare stone and hung with brassware, and plush banquettes and captain's chairs around cast-iron-framed tables on the turkey carpet; there's a snug no-smoking area. Friendly service, three well kept real ales such as Bateman XB, Theakstons Best and Timothy Taylor Landlord under light blanket pressure, a decent range of wines and malt whiskies; maybe piped music. There are tables in the garden. *(Recommended by K McManus, GSB, Tim and Sue Halstead)*

Free house ~ Licensee Dawn Thorpe ~ Real ale ~ Meals and snacks ~ Restaurant ~ (01665) 578444 ~ Well behaved children welcome ~ Open 11-3, 6-11; 12-3, 6-10.30 Sun; closed evening 25 Dec

ETAL (Northumberland) NT9339 Map 10

Black Bull

Off B6354, SW from Berwick

At the only thatched pub in Northumberland they are not allowed real fires in the stone fireplaces – the roof caught fire in 1979 and the whole building was reduced to a shell. The spacious open-plan lounge bar nowadays has a friendly relaxed atmosphere, windsor chairs around the tables on its carpet, and glossily varnished beams. Enjoyable food includes home-made soup (£1.80), filled rolls and baked potatoes, northumbrian sausage or steak and kidney pie (£5.95), chicken tikka masala or giant yorkshire pudding with various fillings (£6.95), gammon and pineapple (£8.50), a huge seafood platter with crab, smoked salmon, herring, mussels, calamari and so forth (£10.50), 12oz steaks (from £14.95), and puddings such as white chocolate and whiskey torte or rhubarb and redcurrant crumble. Well kept Lorrimers Scotch, Vaux Samson and Wards Thorne on handpump. Darts, dominoes, pool, juke box and piped music in the pool room. There are a few picnic-sets in front. A three-mile light railway runs between Heatherslaw (where there's a working watermill from which you can buy flour ground on the premises) and the bare ruins of Etal Castle on the banks of the River Till at the far end of this particularly picturesque village. *(Recommended by Kevin Thorpe, GLD, Andy and Jill Kassube, Roger Wain-Heapy, K M Thorpe, A W and K J Randle, Eric Larkham, Jenny and Brian Seller, Chris Rounthwaite, R T and J C Moggridge)*

Vaux ~ Tenant: Fiona Anderson ~ Real ale ~ Meals and snacks (12-3, 7-9) ~ (01890) 820200 ~ Children welcome ~ Open 11-11; 12-10.30 Sun; winter 12-3, 7-11(10.30 Sun); closed lunchtimes Mon-Fri in winter; closed 25 Dec

GREAT WHITTINGTON (Northumberland) NZ0171 Map 10

Queens Head

Village signposted off A68 and B6018 just N of Corbridge

Readers so enjoy the well cooked and imaginative food at this simple stone inn that this year we have given it a Food Award. The wide choice in the bar might include sandwiches, ploughman's, lamb liver and smoked bacon with shallots (£7.95), breast of chicken stuffed with spinach mousse or fillet of salmon with a lobster and prawn sauce (£8.95) and breast of duck with a compote of berries (£10.95); the restaurant is no smoking. Despite the emphasis on food the two beamed rooms retain a pubby atmosphere, both are comfortably furnished and neatly decorated with some handsome carved oak settles among other more modern furnishings, a mural over the fireplace near the bar counter, old prints and a collection of keys, and log fires. Well kept Queens Head (now brewed for them by Hambleton Brewery), Hambleton Bitter and Black Sheep Best on handpump, 30 malt whiskies, and decent wines; friendly attentive service, maybe unobtrusive piped music. There are six picnic-sets on the small front lawn, and the surrounding partly wooded countryside is pretty. *(Recommended by John Prescott, A Denniss, Paul and Ursula Randall, Chris Rounthwaite, Eric Larkham, Ian Phillips, John Honnor, John Oddey, Dr Peter Smart, R Shepherd)*

Free house ~ Ian Scott ~ Real ale ~ Meals and snacks (not Mon lunchtime) ~ Restaurant ~ (01434) 672267 ~ Children in restaurant ~ Open 12-3, 6-11; 12-3, 7-10.30 Sun; closed Mon lunchtime

nr HALTWHISTLE (Northumberland) NY7164 Map 10

Milecastle

Military Rd; B6318 NE – OS Sheet 86 map reference 715660

A warm coal fire makes this small 17th-c pub a welcome refuge on a cold winter's night. Standing alone on the remote moorland road running alongside Hadrian's Wall, it gets surprisingly busy, especially in season (or when the local farmers crowd in); there's a lunchtime overflow into the small comfortable restaurant. Popular bar food might include lunchtime sandwiches (from £2.40) and ploughman's (£4.75), home-made soup (£1.90), chicken wings (£3.25), vegetable curry (£5.25), tasty venison sausage (£6.25), pies such as wild boar and duckling, steak and kidney or turkey, ham and chestnut (from £5.95), gammon and egg (£7.20), sirloin steak (£9.50); home-made puddings (from £2.50). The local meat is well hung and the fresh local vegetables good. The snug little rooms of the beamed bar are decorated mainly with brasses, horsey and local landscape prints and attractive dried flowers; well kept Butterknowle Banner, Hexhamshire Bitter, Northumberland Castles Bitter and Tetleys on handpump, a fair collection of malt whiskies, and a good wine list. Friendly service; walkers welcome (but no rucksacks allowed). No games or music. There are some white plastic seats and tables outside in a sheltered walled garden with a dovecote. *(Recommended by Justin Hulford, Dr and Mrs B Baker, Martin, Jane and Laura Bailey, Penny and Martin Fletcher, Ian Phillips, L Dixon, Chris Rounthwaite, D J and P M Taylor, Joy and Peter Heatherley)*

Free house ~ Licensees Ralph and Margaret Payne ~ Real ale ~ Meals and snacks ~ Restaurant ~ (01434) 320682 ~ Children over 5 welcome if eating ~ Open 12-3, 6.30-11

HALTWHISTLE (Northumberland) NY6860 Map 10

Wallace Arms

Rowfoot, Featherstone Park – OS Sheet 86 map reference 683607

Visitors and locals alike can expect a genuinely warm welcome from the friendly licensee and Molly the old english sheepdog at this cosy rambling former farmhouse. There are five interlinked rooms with simple furnishings and unpretentious decorations. The small beamed main bar has dark oak woodwork, some stripped stone, comfortable seats, and a good log fire; the side games room has another fire (also darts, pool, shove-ha'penny, table skittles and juke box), and there's a third in the middle of the big no-smoking dining room (a former barn), which has its own interesting menu. At lunchtime good value bar food includes soup (£1.95), sandwiches (from £2.50), filled baked potatoes (£2.95), vegetarian quiche (£4.50), cumberland sausage (£4.75), Whitby haddies (crumbed haddock pieces, £5.50), poacher's pie (£6.50), home-made puddings (£2.75), and children's menu (£2.25); in the evening there might be beef in ale pie (£5.95), gammon and egg (£6.95), chicken in lemon sauce (£7.75) and sirloin steak (£9.50). Good Sunday roasts and vegetarian choices. Well kept ales from Four Rivers on handpump, and several malt whiskies; quizzes every second Wednesday. Access for disabled people is fairly easy. Picnic-sets outside on both sides of the quiet lane have lovely fell views; one good walk from the pub is along the former Alston railway line; there's a play area at the back and quoits. *(Recommended by Mrs M Wood, John Oddey, Ian Phillips, A W and K J Randle, Eric Larkham)*

Free house ~ Licensees John and Mary Stenhouse ~ Real ale ~ Meals and snacks (not Mon or Tues lunchtime or Sun evening) ~ Restaurant ~ (01434) 321872 ~ Children in snug and games room ~ Open 4-11 Mon/Tues; 12-2.30, 4-11 Wed/Thurs; 12-11 Fri/Sat; 12-4, 7-10.30 Sun

HEDLEY ON THE HILL (Northumberland) NZ0859 Map 10

Feathers

Village signposted from New Ridley, which is signposted from B6309 N of Consett; OS Sheet 88 map reference 078592

It's the splendid combination of a friendly, relaxed and genuinely pubby atmosphere and well cooked food that draws people to this attractive little stone local. Loyal and enthusiastic locals mix happily with visitors in the three well kept turkey-carpeted traditional bars, with beams, woodburning stoves, stripped stonework, solid brown leatherette settles and old black and white photographs of local places and country folk working the land. Well kept Boddingtons and three guest beers such as Big Lamp Prince Bishop, Butterknowle Banner, Hexhamshire Devils Water or Mordue Workie Ticket on handpump; they hold a mini beer festival around Easter with thirteen real ales on at any one time, which ends with a barrel race on Easter Monday; around 30 malt whiskies. The range of good imaginative food changes weekly and might include tomato and mint soup (£1.95), cumberland sausage with grainy mustard sauce (£3.95), parsnip, leek and tomato crumble or ragoût of fennel, aubergine, red pepper and onion (£4.50), smoked cod and cheese filled pancake or home-cooked ham with mango chutney (£5.95) and beef casseroled with herbs, mushrooms, port and brandy (£6.50); puddings include home-made ice creams and spiced fig, honey and almond tart or cinnamon apple pancakes (£2.35). Shove-ha'penny, table skittles, cribbage, and dominoes. From picnic-sets in front you can watch the world drift by. *(Recommended by GSB, Joy and Peter Heatherley, L M Anderson, John Fazakerley, Joan Bunting; more reports please)*

Free house ~ Licensee Marina Atkinson ~ Real ale ~ Meals and snacks (not weekday lunchtime or Mon) ~ (01661) 843607 ~ Children in lounge and family room until 9pm ~ Open 6-11; 12-3, 6-11 Sat; 12-3, 7-10.30 Sun; closed weekday lunchtimes except bank holidays and 25 Dec

NEW YORK (Tyne & Wear) NZ3370 Map 10

Shiremoor House Farm ★

Middle Engine Lane/Norham Road; from A1 going N from Tyne Tunnel, right into A1058 then next left signposted New York, then left at end of speed limit (pub signed); or at W end of New York A191 bypass turn S into Norham Road, then first right (pub signed)

Marvellously transformed from derelict farm buildings almost a decade ago, the pub keeps many pleasing references to its origins in the smartly relaxed bar. There's a charming mix of interesting and extremely comfortable furniture, a big kelim on the broad flagstones, warmly colourful farmhouse paintwork on the bar counter and several tables, conical rafters of the former gin-gan, a few farm tools, and good rustic pictures such as mid-West prints, big crisp black and white photographs of country people and modern Greek bull sketches. Gentle lighting in several well divided spacious areas cleverly picks up the surface modelling of the pale stone and beam ends. Besides Stones and Theakstons Old Peculier well kept real ales might include Hull Northern Pride and Mordue Workie Ticket; decent wines by the glass. Bar food includes sandwiches, steak, ale and mushroom pie (£4.45), beef stroganoff (£5.45), cajun spiced chicken breast in ciabatta bread with southern fries (£5.45) and sizzling strips of chicken in black bean sauce (£7.95). The no-smoking granary extension is good for families, including high chairs, with bottles or baby food warmed on request. Popular with businessmen at lunchtime when there is a good bustling atmosphere; no games or piped music. There are picnic-sets on neat grass at the edge of the flagstoned farm courtyard, by tubs and a manger filled with flowers. *(Recommended by Ian Phillips, Roger Bellingham, Andy and Jill Kassube, Gregg Davies, Eric Larkham, Peter Lewis, Joy and Peter Heatherley)*

Free house ~ Licensee C W Kerridge ~ Real ale ~ Meals and snacks (12-9) ~ Restaurant ~ (0191) 257 6302 ~ Children in eating areas of bar and in restaurant ~ Open 11-11; 12-10.30 Sun

NEWCASTLE UPON TYNE (Tyne & Wear) NZ2266 Map 10

Crown Posada £

31 The Side; off Dean Street, between and below the two high central bridges (A6125 and A6127)

This is Newcastle's second oldest pub and undoubtedly the city's finest specimen in terms of pub architecture. At night the pre-Raphaelite stained-glass windows catch the eye from across the steep street, and by day the golden crown adds grandeur to an already imposing carved stone facade. Inside there's an elaborate coffered ceiling, stained glass in the counter screens, a line of gilt mirrors each with a tulip lamp on a curly brass mount which match the great ceiling candelabra, and Victorian flowered wallpaper above the brown dado; below this are fat heating pipes – a popular footrest when the east wind brings the rain off the North Sea. It's a very long and narrow room, making quite a bottleneck by the serving counter, and beyond that, a long soft green built-in leather wall seat is flanked by narrow tables. Well kept Bass, Boddingtons, Butterknowle Conciliation, Jennings, Theakstons Best and a guest on handpump; lunchtime sandwiches (£1). Friendly barmen, chatty customers; fruit machine and an old record player that provides background music when the place is quiet. Best to visit during the week when regulars sit reading the papers put out in the front snug; at the weekend it's usually packed. No children. A few minutes' stroll to the castle. *(Recommended by Eric Larkham, Denis and Margaret Kilner; more reports please)*

Free house ~ Licensee Malcolm McPherson ~ Real ale ~ Lunchtime snacks ~ (0191) 232 1269 ~ Open 11-11; 12-3, 7-10.30 Sun

People named as recommenders after the main entries have told us that the pub should be included. But they have not written the report – we have, after anonymous on-the-spot inspection.

NEWTON ON THE MOOR (Northumberland) NU1605 Map 10

Cook & Barker Arms

Village signposted from A1 Alnwick—Felton

The restaurant part of this long stone pub used to be a blacksmith's shop – nowadays the extra space is really needed as this place is popular for its very good imaginative food. The bar menu includes warm brie salad or tunisian bean salad (£3.95), pink grapefruit in white wine (£4.25), moules marinières (£4.75), pie of the day or lamb liver and bacon (£4.95), escalope of pork (£8.95), casserole of seafood thermidor (£9.95) and sirloin steak (£11.25). The unfussy, long beamed bar has stripped, partly panelled walls, brocade-seated settles around oak-topped tables, framed banknotes and paintings by local artists on the walls, brasses, a highly polished oak servery, and a coal fire at one end with a coal-effect gas fire at the other; another room has tables, chairs, an old settle, and darts (popular with locals), and the games room has scrubbed pine furniture and french windows leading on to the terrace; the lounge is no smoking. Well kept rotating ales on handpump include Courage Directors, Fullers London Pride, Ruddles County, and Theakstons Best, quite a few malt whiskies, and a comprehensive wine list. *(Recommended by G Neighbour, Penny and Martin Fletcher, R F and M K Bishop, GLD, M Borthwick, Chris and Ann Garnett, D Knott, Bruce Jamieson, R A Underwood, A Twyford, A J Morton)*

Free house ~ Licensee Phil Farmer ~ Real ale ~ Meals and snacks (12-2, 6-8) ~ Restaurant ~ (01665) 575234 ~ Children in eating area of bar ~ Open 11-3, 6-11; 12-3, 6-10.30 Sun ~ Bedrooms: £37.50B/£70B

RENNINGTON (Northumberland) NU2119 Map 10

Masons Arms

Stamford Cott; B1340 NE of Alnwick

Readers report that this friendly old coaching inn is run with military-stle precision. It's the good value, generously served bar food that draws most people here – there might be lunchtime sandwiches, home-made soup (£1.95), home-made duck liver or craster kipper pâté (£3.95), fried haddock (£4.95), pasta and blue cheese grill (£5.95), gammon steak or lamb cutlets (£6.55), game casserole (£6.75), barbary duck breast with an apricot and orange sauce (£9.95) and steaks (from £11.95). The comfortably modernised beamed lounge bar has wheelback and mate's chairs around solid wooden tables on the patterned carpet, plush bar stools, lots of brass, pictures and photographs on the walls, and a relaxed atmosphere; the dining rooms (one is no smoking) have pine panelling and wrought-iron wall lights. Courage Directors, Ruddles Best and Theakstons Best on handpump, efficiently served by friendly, helpful staff. Shove-ha'penny, dominoes and piped music. The comfortable, spotlessly clean bedrooms are in an adjacent stable block. There are sturdy rustic tables on the little front terrace, surrounded by lavender. *(Recommended by Martin and Helen Hickes, Jack and Heather Coyle, Peter Guy, Gerald Barnett, Chris Rounthwaite, Peter Meister, Sarah and Peter Gooderham, June and Tony Baldwin, T Loft, A W and K J Randle, J H and S A Harrop, John Cockell)*

Free house ~ Licensee Frank Sloan ~ Real ale ~ Meals and snacks ~ Restaurant ~ (01665) 577275 ~ Children in restaurant (must be over 5 in evening) ~ Open 12-2, 6.30-11; 12-2.30, 7-10.30 Sun ~ Bedrooms: /£50B

ROMALDKIRK (Durham) NY9922 Map 10

Rose & Crown

Just off B6277

Northumbria Dining Pub of the Year

The friendly licensees continue to make improvements at this stone three-storey pub which combines best aspects of a good hotel and fine restaurant with those of a pleasant country pub. This year we have awarded them a Wine Award for their increased selection of wines by the glass. The beamed traditional bar has been fully redecorated but there are still old-fashioned seats facing the log fire, a Jacobean oak settle, lots of gin-traps, some old farm tools and black and white pictures of

Romaldkirk on the walls, as well as a grandfather clock, and lots of brass and copper. The smart Crown Room, where bar food is served, has more brass and copper, original etchings of game shooting scenes and farm implements. The hall is hung with wine maps and other interesting prints and a photograph of the Hale Bopp comet over Romaldkirk church that was taken by a guest; no smoking oak-panelled restaurant. As we went to press they were beginning to refurbish the bedrooms. Besides lunchtime filled brown baps (from £2.95) and ploughman's (£5.25), the particularly good bar food from a changing menu might include home-made soup (£2.95), chicken liver pâté (£3.85), chargrilled pork sausages with black pudding and onions (£4.35), creamed scrambled eggs with ribbons of smoked Scotch salmon and hot buttered toast (£4.85), chicken livers sautéed with smoked bacon (£5.95) and steak, kidney, mushroom and ale pie (£7.75); weekly changing blackboard specials include salmon pâté with cucumber and yoghurt salsa (£4.25), courgette, tomato and basil fritatta (£4.50), pan-fried breasts of wood pigeon with juniper berries and onion confit (£8.50), baked monkfish tails with grain mustard and gruyère cheese (£8.95) and chargrilled escalope of veal with roasted vegetables, capers and flat-leaf parsley (£9.95); puddings include lemon and elderflower mousse and crème caramel with poached pears; children's dishes (from £1.75) and good three-course Sunday lunch (£12.95). Well kept Marstons Pedigree and Theakstons Best on handpump; good, friendly service. Tables outside look out over the village green, still with its original stocks and water pump. The village is close to the superb Bowes Museum and the High Force waterfall, and has an interesting old church. *(Recommended by Ian Phillips, David Philcox, K F Mould, H H Liesner, Chris Brace, M J Morgan, Dr T Hothersall, Joy and Peter Heatherley, Richard Fallon, Mr and Mrs D Powell, David and Ruth Hollands, Paul and Ursula Randall, Sue and Geoff Price, June and Tony Baldwin; also in the Good Hotel Guide)*

Free house ~ Licensees Christopher and Alison Davy ~ Real ale ~ Meals and snacks (12-1.30, 7-9) ~ Restaurant (not Sun evening) ~ (01833) 650213 ~ Children welcome ~ Open 11-3, 5.30-11; 12-3, 7-10.30 Sun; closed 25/26 Dec ~ Bedrooms: £60B/£82B

SEAHOUSES (Northumberland) NU2232 Map 10

Olde Ship ★

B1340 coast road

Still very much a fisherman's local, the atmospheric and welcoming bar here is a treasure-trove of seafaring memorabilia: shiny brass fittings, sea pictures and model ships (including a fine one of the North Sunderland lifeboat and a model of Seahouses' lifeboat *The Grace Darling*), as well as ship's instruments and equipment, and a knotted anchor made by local fishermen; all the items are genuine. Even the floor of the saloon bar, with its open fire, is scrubbed ship's decking. The one clear window (the others have stained-glass sea pictures) looks out across the harbour to the Farne Islands, and as dusk falls you can watch the Longstones lighthouse shine across the fading evening sky; there's another low-beamed snug bar. The cabin bar and dining room are no smoking. Good value bar food includes soup (£1.50), roast beef and yorkshire pudding, steak and kidney pie, haddock bake, creamy lemon pork, liver and onion casserole or chicken and asparagus casserole (all £5); three course dinner (£13). A good choice of real ales takes in Bass, Fountain McEwans 80/-, Marstons Pedigree, Morlands Old Speckled Hen, Ruddles Best, John Smiths, Theakstons Best, and guest beers in summer; an improved selection of wines and 20 malt whiskies; dominoes and piped music. Pews surround barrel tables in the back courtyard, and a battlemented side terrace with a sun lounge looks out on the harbour; putting and quoits. An anemometer is connected to the top of the chimney. You can book boat trips to the Farne Islands Bird Sanctuary at the harbour, and there are bracing coastal walks, particularly to Bamburgh, Grace Darling's birthplace. The pub is not really suitable for children. *(Recommended by Chris Brace, Andy and Jill Kassube, JP, PP, Comus Elliot, M A Buchanan, Judith Hirst, John Honnor, Richard Fallon, Guy Consterdine, Eric Larkham, John Cockell, A Twyford, Archie and Thelma Jack, Jack and Philip Paxton)*

Free house ~ Licensees Alan and Jean Glen ~ Real ale ~ Meals and snacks (12-2, 7-8.30) ~ Restaurant ~ (01665) 720200 ~ Open 11-3, 6-11; 12-3, 7.30-10.30 Sun ~ Bedrooms: £37.50B/£75B

SEATON SLUICE (Northumberland) NZ3477 Map 10

Waterford Arms

Just off A193 N of Whitley Bay

It's the very good food – especially the fresh fish – that draws readers to this very restauranty pub. Double doors now open from the restaurant into the comfortable and homely bar, where it is likely that all the tables will be laid for dining. The same menu covers both areas and might include soup (£1.50), garlic mushrooms (£3.95), Mexican nachos (£3.05), mushroom stroganoff or vegetarian chilli (£4.95), very well liked fish and chips (£5.50-£14.50 depending on size), Mexican chicken burito (£6.75), seafood platter (£8.95), steak diane (£13.50) and seafood feast (£14.95); puddings include jam roly poly (£2.30) and speciality ice creams (£2.95); no-smoking area, friendly and efficient service. Vaux Samson, Wards Best and Waggledance and a guest under light blanket pressure. *(Recommended by Dr L H Groves, Graham and Karen Oddey, Eric Larkham, Ian Phillips, Richard Dolphin, David Honeyman, John Oddey)*

Vaux ~ Tenant Michael Naylor ~ Real ale ~ Meals and snacks (whenever open) ~ Restaurant ~ Children ~ (0191) 237 0450 ~ Open 12-2, 5-10; 12-10 Sat; 12-9 Sun ~ Bedrooms: £25B/£50B

STANNERSBURN (Northumberland) NY7286 Map 10

Pheasant

Kielder Water road signposted off B6320 in Bellingham

Originally built as a farm in the early 17th c, this unpretentious inn was the post house for the back road over the hills. The traditional and comfortable lounge is partly stripped stone and partly panelled, and the separate public bar, similar but simpler, opens into a games room with darts, pool, and dominoes. There's a good mix of visitors and locals in the evening, when the small no-smoking dining room can get crowded. Bar food includes sandwiches, haddock, home-made steak pie or lasagne (£6.95), smoked salmon salad (£7.50), game pie (£7.95) and cider baked gammon with cumberland sauce (£8.50). Well kept Ind Coope Burton, Tetleys, Theakstons and Timothy Taylor Landlord on handpump, 34 malt whiskies. Unobtrusive yet attentive service. It's in a peaceful valley with picnic-sets in the streamside garden, a pony paddock behind, and quiet forests all around. *(Recommended by John Poulter, John and Kathleen Potter, D Knott, Tim and Sue Halstead, Paul and Ursula Randall, Graham and Karen Oddey, Humphry and Angela Crum Ewing; more reports please)*

Free house ~ Licensee W R C Kershaw ~ Real ale ~ Meals and snacks ~ Restaurant ~ (01434) 240382 ~ Children welcome in eating areas until 9 ~ Open 11-3, 6-11; 12-3, 7-10.30 Sun; 12-2, 6.30-11 winter weekdays; closed Mon and Tues in Jan/Feb ~ Bedrooms: £40B/£58B

THROPTON (Northumberland) NU0302 Map 10

Three Wheat Heads

B6341

Doing well under its new licensees, this stonebuilt 17th-c village inn is attractively placed in the heart of Coquetdale, with lovely views towards the Simonside Hills from its attractive garden, which has a play area and dovecot. Inside, the refurbished carpeted bar on the right and the pleasant and roomy dining area have good fires (there's a fine tall stone fireplace), wheelback chairs around neat rows of dark tables, more heavily cushioned brocaded seats, comfortable bar stools with backrests, and an elaborate longcase clock; darts. Good home-made food, served in huge helpings with copious vegetables, includes sandwiches (from £1.65), cod (£4.95, jumbo £6.50), a selection of vegetarian dishes (£5.95), steak and kidney pudding or chicken breast (£6.50) and steaks (from £9.50); puddings (£2.25). Three changing Vaux ales on handpump, 10 malt whiskies, welcoming obliging service, decent juke box. *(Recommended by T Dobby, J Wheeler, Mr and Mrs T A Bryan, GLD)*

Vaux ~ Tenant: Gordon Young ~ Real ale ~ Meals and snacks (all day in summer) ~

Restaurant ~ (01669) 620262 ~ Open 11-11(11-3, 6-11 in winter); 12-10.30 Sun ~ Bedrooms: £35B/£47.50B

WARENFORD (Northumberland) NU1429 Map 10

Warenford Lodge

Just off A1 Alnwick—Belford, on village loop road

Although there's no pub sign outside this comfortable stone house it is well worth seeking out for the attractively presented and interesting home-made food. The menu includes home-made soup or eggy rice cakes (£2.25), prawn fritters with oriental sauce (£3.75), leek roly poly (£4.90), beef, smoked ham and tomato cannelloni (£6.05), thai-style prawn and potato curry (£8.20), northumbrian fish soup (£8.70) or sirloin steak (£12.30); puddings such as spiced apple fritters with apple strudel ice cream or baked lemon pudding (£2.70), and they have an impressive range of local cheese. A decent selection of wines and malt whiskies, and a good choice of teas. The bar looks modern but is actually quite old, with cushioned wooden seats around pine tables, some stripped stone walls, and a warm fire in the big stone fireplace; steps lead up to an extension which now has comfortable dining tables and chairs, and a big woodburning stove. *(Recommended by Martin and Helen Hickes, John Cockell, Jenny and Brian Seller; more reports please)*

Free house ~ Licensee Raymond Matthewman ~ Meals and snacks (not lunchtimes, except weekends when lunchtime service stops 1.30, or all day Mon) ~ Evening restaurant ~ (01668) 213453 ~ Children in restaurant only ~ Open 7-11 (closed weekday lunchtimes and all day Mon except bank holidays), plus 12-2 Sat and Sun

Lucky Dip

Besides the fully inspected pubs, you might like to try these Lucky Dips recommended to us and described by readers (if you do, please send us reports):

Anick N'land [signed NE of A69/A695 Hexham junction; NY9665], *Rat*: Quaint little pub, friendly and nicely refurbished, with well kept ales inc one brewed for the pub, lovely north Tyne views, good service, good value food; children welcome, pretty garden with well planted boots *(Bill and Sheila McLardy)*

Bamburgh N'land [NU1835], *Mizen Head*: A hotel, but welcoming and comfortable pubby lounge bar, quiet at lunchtime; good choice of good value food, Theakstons, quiet piped music; bedrooms *(Alan Kilpatrick)*; [Front St], *Victoria*: Done up with style and panache, caring young staff, good food and atmosphere, good prices; comfortable bedrooms *(Neil Hunter)*

Barnard Castle Dur [The Bank; NZ0617], *Old Well*: Friendly landlady, good atmosphere, big helpings of good food cooked by daughter from sandwiches, baked potatoes and extremely good chips to gourmet evenings, well kept Courage and Tetleys ales, decent wines, restaurants inc no-smoking room (well behaved children allowed here); terrace over town walls, comfortable bedrooms *(M Smith)*

☆ **Beamish** Dur [off A693 towards museum; NZ2254], *Shepherd & Shepherdess*: Very useful for its position nr outstanding open-air heritage museum; good range of quick fairly priced straightforward food, standard layout with tables around walls, but comfortable, with good service, well kept Vaux Samson and Wards Sheffield Best, decent wines, coal fires; can get crowded, piped music; children welcome, tables and play area with Fibreglass monsters out among trees; has been open all day *(D W and J W Wilson, Pete Yearsley, LYM)*

☆ **Beamish** [far side of Beamish Open Air Museum – paid entry], *Sun*: Turn-of-the-century pub moved from Bishop Auckland as part of the museum; very basic real period feel at quieter times, with well kept McEwans 80/-, Theakstons Best and Youngers No 3, filled rolls *(Pete Yearsley, Penny and Martin Fletcher, Paul S McPherson, LYM)*

Beamish [Front St, No Place; off A693 signed No Place and Cooperative Villas, S of museum], *Beamish Mary*: Friendly down-to-earth 1960s pub, quiet lunchtime, with Durham NUM banner in games room, very assorted furnishings and bric-a-brac in bar with Aga; huge choice of good value very generous basic bar food and Sun lunch, up to seven well kept Scottish Courage or guest ales, annual beer festival; piped music, two dogs, children allowed until evening; live music in converted stables concert room (Weds, Fri, Sat); bedrooms *(John Oddey, Matthew Mardling)*

☆ **Belsay** N'land [A696 NW of Ponteland; NZ1079], *Highlander*: Good range of food in extensively refurbished side bar and open-plan dining area, nice plain wood tables, reasonable prices, good welcoming service, well kept Scottish Courage ales, good log fires *(John Oddey, Christopher Turner, Graham and Karen Oddey)*

Berwick upon Tweed N'land [Promenade; The Spittal; NT9953], *Galleon*: Small genuine local nr caravan site with good neighbourhood atmosphere, wide range of good value food, pleasant service and good coffee; darts etc, live music Sat evening *(Paul McPherson)*

Billy Row Dur [Old White Lea; off A689; NZ1638], *Dun Cow*: Place of pilgrimage for lovers of unspoilt pubs, in same family for 100 years, cosy old-fashioned front room with warming range, comfortable wall settles, photographs of long-gone and more recent local football teams; bar in back room serving a well kept ale such as local Darwin Hodges Original, very friendly character landlord and locals; folk music last Fri of month, cl lunchtime exc Sun *(Bruce Bird, JP, PP)*

Birtley T&W [Ravensworth Terr; NZ2756], *Moulders Arms*: Pleasantly refurbished local by church in old part of village, popular for substantial reasonably priced straightforward lunches – book Sun; garden *(M Borthwick)*

Castleside Dur [NZ0849], *Smelters Arms*: Welcoming village pub with well kept Vaux, simple food well cooked and presented, prompt service, long lounge with tap room off, adjoining chip shop; may be music Sat *(Pete Yearsley)*

☆ **Catton** N'land [B6295 N of Allendale; NY8358], *Crown*: Cosy bustling traditional local with bargain home-cooked lunches and other good value food till 10 inc children's and lots of sandwiches, newish dining area, roaring log fire, four ales such as Butterknowle and Theakstons, good teas and coffee, jovial landlord, pool, darts, piped music; small garden; well behaved children and dogs welcome *(John Oddey, CMW, JJW, Jack and Heather Coyle)*

Chester le Street Dur [Front St; NZ2752], *Red Lion*: Large pleasantly furnished traditional pub, simple substantial low-priced food from hot counter, cheerful staff; busy on market days (Tues, Fri, Sat), smoke can drift into eating area *(M Borthwick)*

☆ **Corbridge** N'land [Middle St; NY9964], *Black Bull*: Roomy old-fashioned low-ceilinged pub with good choice of generous well priced pub food, well kept Whitbreads-related and guest ales, reasonably priced wines, big no-smoking restaurant area; stone-floored bar with traditional settles, mix of comfortable chairs, roaring fire, efficient staff, friendly civilised atmosphere even on crowded Fri/Sat night; open all day *(A Denniss, L Dixon, Liz and John Soden)*

Corbridge [Newcastle Rd], *Angel*: Small hotel with welcoming and attentive neat staff and good value bar food in plushly comfortable lounge; locals' back bar, restaurant, Scottish Courage ales; bedrooms *(Eric Locker, LYM)*; [Station Rd], *Dyvels*: Unassuming but pleasant and friendly, with particularly well kept changing beers such as Black Sheep and Smiles, tables outside; good value well equipped bedrooms *(Dr and Mrs B Baker)*; [Watling St/St Helens St, just N of centre], *Wheatsheaf*: Open-plan pub with comfortable banquettes, wide choice of food in pleasantly decorated dining lounge and big conservatory, well kept Darleys Thorne and Vaux Waggledance, good choice of wines and malt whiskies, friendly licensees; pub games, piped music (can obtrude), children welcome, some picnic-sets outside; bedrooms *(Mrs G M Steiner, LYM)*

nr **Corbridge** [East Wallhouses, Military Rd (B6318 5 miles NE); NZ0568], *Robin Hood*: Popular for generous food (choice widest in restaurant); three real ales, blazing real fires, friendly staff, interesting carved settles in saloon; piped music *(John Prescott, John Oddey)*

Cornsay Dur [Old Cornsay; NZ1443], *Black Horse*: Recently refurbished, with welcoming enthusiast landlord, cheerful staff, well kept Hancocks and Wards, good range of malt whiskies, well presented straightforward food; hilltop hamlet with great views; cl lunchtime exc Sun *(Pete Yearsley)*

Darlington Dur [Coniscliffe Rd; NZ2915], *No 22*: Good service, eight well kept real ales inc three brewed on the premises, very friendly atmosphere; good food, but though the pub's been extended there's talk of cutting this to give more space for the hugely popular ale side *(Mike and Sue Walton)*

Dinnington N'land [NZ2173], *White Swan*: Friendly helpful staff, very wide choice of reasonably priced good food in busy dining area, great atmosphere *(Laurie McCall)*

Durham [Hawthorn Terr; NZ2642], *Colpitts*: Basic and friendly, with particularly cheap Sam Smiths, sandwiches, open fires, pool in one room, TV and machines *(Eric Larkham, the Didler)*; [Court Lane, next to courts], *Court*: Bass and a guest beer, good cheap generous food inc fine chips all day (not Sun), helpful outside price list, big L-shaped room with seats outside *(Eric Larkham)*; [Darlington Rd, S of Nevilles Cross on A167], *Duke of Wellington*: Busy but spacious Victorian-style local useful for wide range of hearty good value bar food inc vegetarian and Sun lunch, generous veg, well kept Bass, Worthington and a guest such as Adnams, attentive service, pleasant separate restaurant; children welcome *(M Borthwick, P A Legon)*; [37 Old Elvet], *Dun Cow*: Unsmart but enjoyable traditional town pub in pretty black-and-white timbered cottage, tiny front bar with wall benches, larger back bar with machines etc, particularly well kept Whitbreads Castle Eden and a guest ale, warm welcome, cheap soup and sandwiches etc; children welcome, open all day *(Eric Larkham, LYM)*; [86 New Elvet], *Half Moon*: Split-level pub handy for castle and cathedral, well kept Bass and a weekly guest beer, good service from bare-boards top bar, some basic snacks even on Sun, separate comfortable unpretentious lower room; machines, TV, can get very busy *(Eric Larkham)*; [Saddler St], *Hogshead*: Closest to castle and cathedral, newly refurbished (former Brewer & Firkin), jolly atmosphere, real ales such as Boddingtons, Flowers Original, Fullers London Pride, Marstons Pedigree, Timothy Taylor Landlord and Whitbreads Abroad

Cooper and Castle Eden, good range of reasonably priced food; may have loud modern music *(David and Kay Ross, Alyson and Andrew Jackson)*; [12 Crossgate], *Old Elm Tree*: Big pub with three linked rooms on steep hill opp castle; unpretentious but warm welcoming atmosphere, prompt cheerful service, open fires, Vaux and occasional guest beers, farm cider, seats outside; TV, machines, juke box; regulars can clock in and out *(Eric Larkham)*; [86 Hallgarth St – A177 nr Dunelm House], *Victoria*: Three small and attractive unspoilt rooms packed with Victoriana, Darwin Hodges Original, Marstons Pedigree, McEwans 80/- and Theakstons Best, no juke box or TV, coal fires in bar and back room; bedrooms *(Eric Larkham, the Didler)*

Eachwick N'land [S of village; extension of B6324 NW of Newcastle; NZ1271], *Plough*: Large, well furnished and clean, with lots of pictures inc landlady's racehorse, good choice of above-average well presented generous food inc roast of the day, good value house wine, friendly staff; garden with wishing well and peacocks *(J and H Coyle, Cynthia Waller)*

☆ **Ebchester** Dur [B6309 N of Consett, outside village; NZ1055], *Derwent Walk*: Welcoming staff, full Jennings range kept well and a guest such as Theakstons Black Bull, good wine range, wide choice of generous home-made food inc interesting and vegetarian dishes *(Catherine and Martin Snelling)*

☆ **Ellingham** N'land [signed off A1 N of Alnwick – OS Sheet 75 map ref 167257; NU1726], *Pack Horse*: Dining pub in quiet village, newish owners and friendly helpful staff, wide choice of good food all cooked to order (so may be a wait) in bar or roomy eating area, friendly helpful staff, well kept Scottish Courage ales; good value well equipped bedrooms *(Dr Gerald Barnett, Nigel Thompson)*

Embleton N'land [NU2323], *Dunstanburgh Castle*: Enjoyable dining room meals – curry, game, fresh fish and so forth – in comfortable hotel attractively placed nr magnificent coastline, good waitress service, nice cocktail bar with several malt whiskies; keg beers; bedrooms clean and well furnished *(C A Hall)*

Esh Dur [Front St; NZ1944], *Cross Keys*: Friendly local with good home-made food from sandwiches to steaks inc vegetarian and lovely chips, well kept Vaux beers, decent wines, simple clean dining area; country views *(William Cunliffe)*

Falstone N'land [NY7287], *Blackcock*: Cosy and old-fashioned friendly local, well run, with open fires, good value food esp baked potatoes and vast yorkshire puddings, well kept ales inc Boddingtons, Whitbreads Castle Eden and their own cheap Blackcock; children allowed in pool room, quiet juke box; bedrooms, handy for Kielder Water *(John and Kathleen Potter, Rita and Keith Pollard, Denis and Margaret Kilner)*

Frosterley Dur [A689; NZ0337], *Black Bull*: Small pub with L-shaped stripped stone bar, open fire, hunting memorabilia, games room, SkyTV, small dining room; well kept John Smiths, and simple good value generous bar food (not Tues evening); bedrooms *(M J Morgan)*

Gateshead T&W [Low Eighton – A167, just off A1; NZ2657], *Angel View*: Former Barn Inn, renamed for exceptional view of controversial nearby Angel of the North; old buildings sympathetically refurbished, several small attractively furnished areas, good value food from sandwiches to interesting specials and Sun lunch (superb chips), helpful friendly staff; restaurant; bedrooms *(M Borthwick)*; [Whitemore Pool, Wardley, just off A1; NZ3161], *Green*: Large modern-style lounge, separate bar, restaurant area, Bass, Theakstons Best and XB and an interesting guest beer such as Mordue, huge helpings of freshly prepared food; light piped music, bright lighting *(Andrew Jefferies)*; [Eighton Banks, quite handy for A1(M); NZ2758], *Ship*: Popular and comfortable open-plan pub with good choice of food inc unusually good side salads, Sun lunch, well kept Vaux Samson, friendly staff, south-facing garden with play area, great moor views inc interesting animals opp *(M Borthwick, Andrew Jefferies)*; [Kells Lane, Low Fell, just off A167; NZ2559], *Victoria*: Large nicely furnished two-bar local with good value food (not Sun evening) inc sandwiches, children's and vegetarian, OAP and Tues supper bargains, eating areas, friendly obliging staff *(M Borthwick)*; [Galloping Green Rd, Eighton Banks], *Waggon*: Recently refurbished and extended, good value food from sandwiches and baked potatoes to full meals inc Sun lunch, comfortable airy eating areas inc conservatory, friendly staff; handy for Bowes Railway, nr Angel of the North *(M Borthwick)*

☆ **Greta Bridge** Dur [hotel signed off A66 W of Scotch Corner; NZ0813], *Morritt Arms*: Interesting and prettily placed old hotel, not cheap but enjoyable, with unusual Pickwickian mural in sturdily traditional civilised bar, well kept ales such as Butterknowle Conciliation, Stones, Tetleys, Theakstons Best and Timothy Taylor Landlord, friendly staff; attractive garden with play area, restaurant; comfortable bedrooms *(James Nunns, Philip Cooper, LYM)*

Hart Dur [just off A179 W of Hartlepool; NZ4735], *White Hart*: Interesting, with old ship's figurehead outside, nautical theme in; popular for wide choice of reasonably priced food, one changing real ale *(Norma and Keith Bloomfield)*

Hartlepool Dur [Marina Way; NZ5133], *Jacksons Wharf*: Very well kept Camerons in new pub given 18th-c look, maritime interior, decent straightforward food; next to Historic Quay Museum *(Penny and Martin Fletcher)*

Heddon on the Wall N'land [NZ1367], *Swan*: Varied and interesting good food in attractively refurbished pub with lots of separate areas, welcoming efficient staff, good choice of Scottish Courage ales *(John Oddey)*

☆ **High Force** Dur [B6277 about 4 miles NW of Middleton; NY8728], *High Force*: Beautifully placed high-moors hotel, named for England's highest waterfall nearby and doubling as mountain rescue post; brews its own good value Teesdale Bitter and Forest, also Theakstons and good choice of bar food (and of malt whiskies), good service, friendly atmosphere, quiz night Fri; children allowed, comfortable bedrooms *(Kevin Thorpe, Maurice Thompson, LYM)*

☆ **Holy Island** N'land [Marygate; NU1343], *Ship*: Cosy bar with eating area off, beamery, wooden furniture, bare boards, panelling, maritime/fishing memorabilia and pictures; good value food inc vegetarian and local seafood, quick chatty service, well kept real ales in summer such as Border Blessed, Holy Island and Sacred Kingdom, good choice of whiskies; children welcome, nice setting; three comfortable Victorian-decor bedrooms, may close for a while Jan/Feb *(Denis and Margaret Kilner, Paul McPherson, Brian and Jenny Seller, Comus Elliott, I Polsik, N Haslewood)*

Horsley N'land [B6528; just off A69 Newcastle—Hexham; NZ0966], *Lion & Lamb*: Transformed by recent refurbishment – stripped stone, flagstones, timbering, untreated tables and chairs; good well presented food inc bargain specials, Whitbreads and guest ales *(John Oddey)*

Lanchester Dur [NZ1647], *Queens Head*: Good generous often interesting food (sandwiches on request), well kept Vaux beers, decent wines and friendly and attentive Swedish landlady in village pub with smallish locals' bar and plushly comfortable dining room *(C A Hall)*

Longbenton T&W [Front St; NZ2768], *Benton Ale House*: Comfortably refurbished, with six or seven real ales inc guests (lined glasses), home-made lunchtime food (not Sat), friendly staff, TV alcove, back room with pool, juke box and machines; good disabled facilites, open all day *(Eric Larkham)*

☆ **Longframlington** N'land [A697 N of Morpeth; NU1301], *Granby*: Comfortably modernised family-run two-room bar very popular for very wide choice of generous food inc good vegetarian dishes, Worthingtons real ale, good collection of malt whiskies, decent wines, pleasant staff, restaurant; bedrooms in main building good (but it's a busy road), with big breakfast *(Mike and Di Saxly, Mr and Mrs A Bull, LYM)*

☆ **Longhorsley** N'land [Linden Hall Hotel, off A697 N of Morpeth; NZ1597], *Linden Pub*: Gradually extending friendly ex-granary pub behind country house conference hotel in extensive grounds; briskly served limited but generous bar food, a couple of well kept Whitbreads-related ales, gallery restaurant and conservatory, interesting old enamel advertising signs, uniformed staff; children welcome, bedrooms in main hotel *(GSB, GLD, LYM)*

Lowick N'land [2 Main St (B6353); off A1 S of Berwick upon Tweed; NU0139], *Black Bull*: Busy country pub with comfortable main bar, small back bar, back dining room locally popular for decent food inc vegetarian, well kept Scottish Courage ales, welcoming service; three attractive bedrooms, on edge of small pretty village *(Mr and Mrs A Bull, R T and J C Moggridge)*

☆ **Matfen** N'land [off B6318 NE of Corbridge; NZ0372], *Black Bull*: Striking stone building by the green of an interesting out-of-the-way estate village; local eating-out atmosphere in extended turkey-carpeted bar with plush banquettes, comfortable restaurant (no smoking at lunchtime), efficient service, nicely presented good food from sandwiches up inc good fresh veg, 1940s *Picture Post* photographs, well kept Morlands Old Speckled Hen, Theakstons Black Bull and guest beers, log fires; children in eating area, separate games bar, juke box – may be loud; picnic-sets outside; bedrooms, open all day Sun and summer *(Chris Rounthwaite, T Dobby, K F Mould, Ian Phillips, J S Reed and J Reed, Simon Barriskell, Tina Rossiter, LYM)*

Netherton N'land [NW of Rothbury – OS Sheet 81 map ref 989077; NT9807], *Star*: Remote local, spartan but clean, well kept Whitbreads Castle Eden tapped from the cask, friendly staff and regulars; no food *(JP, PP)*

Newbrough N'land [NY8768], *Red Lion*: Pleasant pub now doing decent standard food at reasonable prices from lunchtime toasties to evening steaks *(John Oddey)*

☆ **Newburn** T&W [Grange Rd, by Tyne Riverside Country Park; NZ1665], *Keelman*: Shares attractive granite-built 19th-c former pumping station with Big Lamp Brewery; high ceiling, wooden gallery, no-smoking area, lofty windows, their full range of beers at attractive prices, limited but good waitress-served bar food (not Sun evening) inc vegetarian and children's; brewery open to visitors; fruit machine, piped pop music; open all day, tables outside; bedrooms in new block *(Eric Larkham, John Oddey, L Dixon)*

☆ **Newcastle upon Tyne** [32 The Close, Quayside], *Cooperage*: One of the city's oldest buildings, all bare stone and wooden beams; a Bass managed pub with a good range of other ales such as Ind Coope Burton, Marstons Owd Rodger, Stones, Timothy Taylor Landlord and Tetleys, with Addlestone's cider and a good choice of good well presented food at sensible prices; pool, juke box, machines; restaurant, night club *(Eric Larkham, Mr and Mrs J Pitts, M Phillips, Denis and Margaret Kilner, LYM)*

☆ **Newcastle upon Tyne** [33 Shields Rd, Byker – former Tap & Spile; NZ2664], *Ouseburn Tavern*: The well run original Tap & Spile, renamed when the namesake chain of pubs was sold off; nine interesting well kept real ales, three farm ciders, decent lunchtime bar food inc sandwiches, quiet and solidly comfortable back lounge, front bar with pool, machines and TV; jazz Mon, quiz Tues, occasional live music; open all day *(Eric Larkham, LYM)*

Newcastle upon Tyne [High Bridge East, between Pilgrim St and Grey St], *Bacchus*: Two beautifully fitted rooms with lovely old mirrors, panelling and elbow-height tables (but a refurbishment looming), well kept Bass, Stones, Tetleys, Theakstons XB and two guest beers, cheap hot lunches (not Sun); piped music, machines; cosy and comfortable when not too busy, open all day (cl Sun lunchtime) *(Eric*

Larkham); [125 Westgate Rd], *Bodega*: Beautifully refurbished partly divided Edwardian drinking hall, bare boards, colourful walls and ceiling, two magnificent original stained-glass domes; good value lunchtime food inc interesting vegetarian, six well kept mainly local beers tapped from the cask, friendly staff; open all day, juke box or piped music may be loudish, machines, TV, Tues quiz night, busy evenings (and if Newcastle Utd at home or on TV); next to Tyne Theatre *(Eric Larkham, GSB)*; [Broad Chare, by river], *Bonded Warehouse*: Former Baltic Tavern, spacious and comfortably converted warehouse, lots of stripped brick and flagstones or bare boards (as well as plusher carpeted parts) in warren of separate areas, good value bar food, well kept Whitbreads and guest beers, farm cider; open all day (cl Sun) *(Eric Larkham, LYM)*; [Castle Garth, next to high level bridge], *Bridge*: Big high-ceilinged room divided into several areas leaving plenty of space by the bar with replica slatted snob screens, six well kept ales, decent lunchtime food, welcoming staff, magnificent fireplace; sports TV, piped music, fruit machines, some live music upstairs; tables on flagstoned back terrace with great views of river, bridges and section of old town wall; open all day *(Eric Larkham, John Oddey, LYM)*; [Chillingham Rd, Heaton; NZ2765], *Chillingham*: Two big rooms, fine panelling and furnishings, six well kept ales inc guests, occasional mini beer festivals, good cheap food lunchtime and early evening; piped music, pool tables in room off, juke box, TV, machines; children in lounge (cl afternoon – rest open all day) *(Eric Larkham)*; [High Bridge West, between Grey St and Bigg Mkt], *Duke of Wellington*: Often crowded L-shaped Victorian-style pub lined with photographs, well kept Tetleys-related beers and a good choice of guests, occasional beer festivals, hot and cold lunchtime sandwiches and baked potatoes; juke box, machines, TV; open all day (cl Sun afternoon) *(Eric Larkham, Graham and Karen Oddey, Denis and Margaret Kilner)*; [127 Albion Rd], *Fighting Cocks*: Basic pub tied to Hadrian with their beers kept well, good bridge views, keen staff, free juke box, fruit machine; couple of steps down to bar, open all day (cl Sun afternoon) *(Eric Larkham)*; [City Rd nr Milk Mkt, opp Keelmans Hosp], *Fog & Firkin*: Striking Victorian-style decor in big open-plan two-level pub overlooking quayside, bare boards, nautical decorations, real ales brewed for the pub (by Fly & Firkin brewpub), friendly service even when busy, basic good value food inc vegetarian; disabled facilities *(Eric Larkham, Penny and Martin Fletcher)*; [St Lawrence Rd, Byker – off A186 Walker Rd into what looks like industrial estate; NZ2765], *Free Trade*: Great atmosphere in basic split-level pub with awesome river and bridge views, local Mordue and Scottish Courage beers, lunchtime sandwiches, real fire, interesting free juke box; tables outside, open all day *(Eric Larkham)*; [103 Percy St], *Hotspur*: Light and airy open-plan Victorian pub, big front windows and decorated mirrors, Scottish Courage and up to three guest beers, farm cider, lots of bottled Belgian beers, good value wine; machines, big-screen sports TV, piped music; open all day, sandwiches and hot snacks all day till 9; can get packed, esp pre-match *(Eric Larkham, John Wooll, Ted George)*; [Stepney Bank; NZ2664], *Ship*: Traditional local beside Byker city farm, Whitbreads-related beers, sandwiches, pin table, pool, juke box, fruit machine, TV; seats outside, open all day; popular with craft and music workers from nearby arts centre *(Eric Larkham)*; [52 Clayton St W], *Tut 'n' Shive*: Deliberately basic (mismatched carpets, doors fixed to ceiling etc), with well kept Whitbreads and up to five guest ales, lunchtime sandwiches, juke box, machines, TV; open all day, live music upstairs most nights – a major draw *(Eric Larkham)*; [1 Maling St], *Tyne*: Single-room pub below Glasshouse Bridge at confluence of Ouseburn and Tyne, local Mordue and Whitbreads-related ales, hot or cold sandwiches, decor of band posters, free juke box, fruit machine, sports TV; tables out under arch of Glasshouse Bridge, barbecue Sun lunch, early Fri evening; open all day, can get very full *(Eric Larkham)*

☆ **Newton by the Sea** N'land [The Square, Low Newton; NU2426], *Ship*: Good genuine local quaintly tucked into top corner of courtyard of old cottages facing beach and sea, friendly effective service even when busy (as it can be on a hot day), good reasonably priced crab sandwiches and ploughman's, coffee, tea, real ale in summer, pool table, ices served outside in summer; children welcome, tables out on green *(Denis and Margaret Kilner, Iain Patton, John Cockell, Chris Wrigley)*

☆ **North Shields** T&W [1 Camden St; NZ3468], *Magnesia Bank*: Big brightly lit bar in well run Victorian pub overlooking Tyne, well kept Mordue, Vaux and guest beers, vast choice of cheerful home-made food (not Sun evening), friendly staff, open fire, quiet piped pop music, TV, fruit machines; children welcome, tables outside, open all day, live music Thurs and Sun *(Eric Larkham, Andy and Jill Kassube)*

North Shields [New Quay], *Chain Locker*: Close to pedestrian ferry, simple nautical-theme Victorian pub with half a dozen well kept ales inc unusual local ones, farm cider, open fire; food (not Sun evening) from lunchtime sandwiches up; piped music (may be loud), fruit machine; children welcome, open all day Thurs-Sun, Fri folk night *(Jim and Maggie Cowell, Eric Larkham, LYM)*; [25 Charlotte St], *Colonel Linskill*: Up to six beers kept well by keen manager, TV, fruit machine; open all day *(Eric Larkham)*

Piercebridge Dur [B6275 just S of village, over bridge – so actually in N Yorks; NZ2116], *George*: Three comfortably worn-in bars with five open fires between them, Scottish Courage ales, decent wines, wide choice of generous bar food from sandwiches up inc vegetarian, the famous clock that stopped short never to go again, river-view restaurant, fine waterside garden; so rambling as not to suit disabled people; children in eating areas, piped music; open all day, good value bedrooms *(John Poulter, D Kay, Dr P D Smart, Beryl and Bill Farmer, Lynne Gittins, LYM)*

Ponteland N'land [Street Houses (A696 SE); NZ1871], *Badger*: Rustic-theme conversion of 18th-c house by garden centre, well decorated and furnished rooms and alcoves, flagstones, carpet or bare wood, timbered ceilings, stripped stone, brick and timbering, real fires, three Bass-related ales, welcoming efficient uniformed staff, quiet piped music; most people eating *(GSB)*; [Higham Dykes – A696 towards Belsay; NZ1375], *Waggon*: New licensees doing good choice of nice reasonably priced food, mainly Scottish Courage real ales, log fires, beams and some stripped stone, comfortable settles *(John Oddey)*

Riding Mill N'land [NZ0262], *Wellington*: Large chain dining pub carefully refurbished in line with its 17th-c date, beams, two big log fires and mix of tables and chairs, some upholstered, some not; four Scottish Courage real ales, wide choice of interesting food cooked to order, friendly welcome and service, disabled access; piped classical music, children welcome, play area and picnic-sets outside *(John Oddey)*

☆ **Romaldkirk** Dur [just off B6277 NW of Barnard Castle; NY9922], *Kirk*: Cosy and very friendly little two-room pub, well worn but clean, with wide choice of interesting good value food (not Tues), well kept ales such as Black Sheep and Butterknowle, good coffee, 18th-c stonework, good log fire, darts, piped popular classics; picnic-sets out by green of attractive moorland village; doubles as PO *(M J Morgan)*

Rothbury N'land [Main St; NU0602], *Newcastle House*: Comfortably refurbished lounge and separate dining area, well kept Tetleys and Timothy Taylor Landlord, friendly service, good popular food; comfortable bedrooms, imposing spot at end of green – handy for Cragside (NT) *(Dave Braisted, R J Bland, Bob and Marg Griffiths)*

Shincliffe Dur [A177 a mile S of Durham; NZ2941], *Seven Stars*: Comfortable and welcoming village inn, remarkable fireplace in one bar, well kept Wards and Vaux Samson, good service, inexpensive good value food, restaurant, some tables outside; attractive village, bedrooms *(Margaret and Allen Marsden)*

Shotton Dur [off A19 – 1st left after taking 1st Peterlee exit heading N; NZ4140], *Black Bull*: Cosy and comfortable Brewers Fayre, nicely decorated with lots of wood; four well kept Whitbreads ales, friendly efficient staff, good menu inc children's; play area outside *(Richard Lewis)*

Stanhope Dur [89 Front St (A689); NY9939], *Queens Head*: Friendly two-room local, well kept Theakstons Bitter and XB, good value bar meals, Sun lunch; bedrooms *(M J Morgan)*

Stannington N'land [just off A1 N of Newcastle; NZ2279], *Ridley Arms*: Good straightforward food at reasonable prices in spacious open-plan main bar, pleasant and cosy in rustic style, efficient helpful staff, quiet lounge, restaurant; well kept Whitbreads Castle Eden *(BB)*

Sunniside T&W [Sun St; NZ2159], *Potters Wheel*: Fine light and airy pub with good lunchtime food, three real ales; fruit machines; open all day Tues-Sat, handy for Tanfield steam railway *(Eric Larkham)*

☆ **Tynemouth** T&W [Tynemouth Rd (A193); ½ mile W of Tynemouth Metro stn; NZ3468], *Tynemouth Lodge*: Genuine-feeling friendly little Victorian-style pub very popular for particularly well kept ales and farm ciders, quiet on weekday afternoons, can be packed evenings; cheap lunchtime filled rolls, coal fire, no juke box or machines, no dogs or children; open all day, tables outside *(Eric Larkham, LYM)*

☆ **Wall** N'land [A6079 N of Hexham; NY9269], *Hadrian*: Solidly cushioned two-room beamed lounge with wide choice of good generous well presented food inc fresh fish and local cheeses, well kept Vaux Samson and Wards Thorne, good house wine, interesting reconstructions of Romano-British life, woodburner, smart efficient staff, unobtrusive piped music, games in public bar, no-smoking Victorian dining room; children welcome, neat garden; roomy comfortable bedrooms – back ones quieter, with good views *(Phil and Heidi Cook, Lise Kerslake, BB)*

Warden N'land [½ mile N of A69; NY9267], *Boatside*: Extended dining pub with good range of good food, attentive service, real ale *(John Oddey, CR)*

☆ **Warkworth** N'land [23 Castle St; NU2506], *Hermitage*: Rambling pub with interesting decor, old range for heating, well kept Jennings and John Smiths, generous food from sandwiches to good fresh local fish reasonably priced, good service, friendly dry-humoured landlord and staff, small plush upstairs restaurant *(Brian and Jenny Seller, Jack and Heather Coyle, Eric Larkham, BB)*

Warkworth [Bridge St], *Black Bull*: Well kept Lambtons, Northumbria Castle, Theakstons Best and a guest such as Adnams, huge choice of good food esp Italian and seafood, small helpings for children, no music *(Rev J Hibberd)*; [3 Dial Pl], *Masons Arms*: Welcoming and comfortable thriving local, quick service, good generous food inc good fish choice, well kept Courage Directors, Newcastle Exhibition and Youngers, good coffee, local pictures; attractive back flagstoned courtyard *(Kevin Thorpe, GLD, Comus Elliott)*; [Castle St], *Warkworth House*: Friendly atmosphere in cosy bar with comfortable sofas, helpful staff, good choice of spirits, well kept Bass and Stones, decent bar meals; dogs welcome; bedrooms comfortable *(Philip and Caroline Pennant-Jones)*

☆ **West Woodburn** N'land [A68; NY8987], *Bay Horse*: Welcoming service in open-plan bar with red plush banquettes and other seats, open fire, well kept Theakstons XB, good coffee, limited choice of good well served bar food inc vegetarian, children's and Sun roasts; airy dining room, games room, children welcome, riverside garden, play area; cl Mon/Tues lunchtime in winter; comfortable well equipped bedrooms, good breakfast *(Revd Richard and Revd Kathleen Allen, T M Dobby, Kay Neville-Rolfe, LYM)*

☆ **Whalton** N'land [B6524 SW of Morpeth; NZ1382], *Beresford Arms*: Tudoresque decor in dining pub particularly popular with older people for genuine home cooking at reasonable prices; friendly helpful staff, well kept Vaux Lorimers Scotch and Wards, pretty village *(Chris Rounthwaite, M Borthwick)*

Whickham T&W [Derwenthaugh Rd, Swalwell; NZ1962], *Skiff*: Modern pub useful for cyclists and walkers on Keelmans Way along S bank of River Tyne, usual food inc sandwiches, garden *(M Borthwick)*

Whitley Bay T&W [71 The Links; NZ3672], *Briardene*: Spotless brightly decorated and very well furnished two-room seaside pub with friendly efficient staff, several well kept real ales and frequent mini beer festivals, wide range of good food; seats outside with play area, open all day *(Eric Larkham)*; [2 South Parade], *Fitzgeralds*: Big main room with raised dining area, smaller more intimate snug, five or six well kept changing beers, decent food choice; can get very busy in the evenings with live music Weds, DJ Thurs-Sat; open all day (cl Sun afternoon), children well catered for *(Eric Larkham, Jim and Maggie Cowell)*

☆ **Whittonstall** N'land [B6309 N of Consett; NZ0857], *Anchor*: Attractively refurbished stonebuilt beamed village pub, comfortable banquettes in L-shaped lounge and dining area with high-raftered pitched roof, well kept Scottish Courage ales, huge choice of good generous food from sandwiches through interesting hot dishes to popular Sun lunch, service efficient and friendly even coping with big coach party, piped music; pool, darts and fruit machine in public bar; nice countryside *(Mrs C Sawyer, GSB, CMW, JJW, Pete Yearsley, Bob and Marg Griffiths)*

Wolsingham Dur [Tow Law Rd; NZ0737], *Bay Horse*: Quiet and comfortable, with humorous Irish landlord, well kept Tetleys and Ruddles County, generous home-made food inc vegetarian; lots of good walks – not far from the Tees waterfalls *(Bruce Bird)*

Wooler N'land [A697 northwards; NT9928], *Tankerville Arms*: Pleasant hotel bar in tastefully modernised old building, good choice of homely food inc local produce (small helpings on request), Border Farne Islands, Marstons Pedigree and Theakstons Best, very helpful service, restaurant (with maybe local folk music Sun lunchtime); bedrooms *(Jenny and Brian Seller, Joan Bunting)*

Children welcome means the pub says it lets children inside without any special restriction. If it allows them in, but to restricted areas such as an eating area or family room, we specify this. Some pubs may impose an evening time limit.

Nottinghamshire

The pubs currently doing best here include the Victoria in Beeston (gaining a Food Award this year, though it's a true pub-lovers' pub rather than a dining pub), the Caunton Beck at Caunton (this newcomer undeniably is a dining pub, and a good one, but has very good drinks too), the Robin Hood at Elkesley (a good refuge from the A1, but the landlord's thinking of leaving), the Square & Compass at Normanton on Trent (very much a local), and the French Horn at Upton (another reliable dining pub). There's also good food at the Martins Arms at Colston Bassett (at a price), and more straightforwardly at the Nelson & Railway in Kimberley, the Dovecote at Laxton, and the Lincolnshire Poacher in Nottingham – which has a splendid choice of really well kept beers. The Three Horseshoes up at Walkeringham also rates highly – we wish more readers were able to get to this nice but out-of-the-way pub. From among all these, it's the Caunton Beck at Caunton which is our Nottinghamshire Dining Pub of the Year – rare for a new entry to achieve this status so quickly. Pubs currently standing out in the Lucky Dip section at the end of the chapter are Tom Browns at Gunthorpe, Beehive at Maplebeck, Market in Retford, Bramley Apple in Southwell, Cross Keys at Upton and Star at West Leake (all inspected and approved by us). We've also heard good things about the Chequers at Ranby, and there's a fine choice, particularly for real-ale drinkers, in Nottingham, with a growing number of pubs linked to Tynemill who operate the Lincolnshire Poacher. Food is often a bargain in the county, and drinks prices are well below the national average, with Fellows Morton & Clayton in Nottingham standing out as particularly cheap for beer – it brews its own. Pubs supplied by the local Hardys & Hansons brewery are also generally good value for beer.

BEESTON SK5338 Map 7

Victoria

Dovecote Lane, backing on to railway station

Readers report such an excellent choice of beer and food at this once-derelict railway hotel that this year we have awarded them a Food Award too. 12 well kept changing real ales on handpump might include Batemans XB, Bramcote Hemlock, Everards Tiger, Marstons Pedigree, a guest Mild, a guest Porter or Stout, and up to six other guest beers; also, two traditional ciders, 105 malt whiskies, 20 Irish whiskies, and half a dozen wines by the glass. The menu changes daily but good interesting food served in the no-smoking dining area might include sandwiches (from £1.30), wild mushroom and pesto tortellini with potato and tomato salsa (£5.95), pepper pork casserole with cider, onions, red peppers, sage, mushrooms and orange (£6.95), chargrilled Welsh lamb with garlic and rosemary (£7.25), seared monkfish wrapped in pancetta (£8.95), trio of game birds in madeira and redcurrant jus (£9.50) and puddings like apple and blackberry pie or jam roly-poly (£2.50). The three downstairs rooms in their original long narrow layout have simple solid traditional furnishings, very unfussy decor, stained-glass windows, stripped woodwork and floorboards (woodblock in some rooms), newspapers to read, and a good chatty atmosphere; dominoes, cards, piped music. The lounge and bar back on to the station, and picnic-sets in a pleasant area outside look over on to the station platform – the trains pass within feet. *(Recommended by Martin Wyss, Mike and Wena Stevenson, JP, PP, Mark and Heather Williamson, R M Taylor, Roger and Jenny Huggins, Dr David Webster, Sue Holland, Simon Walker, Derek Martin, Andy and Jill Kassube, Paul Barnett)*

Free house ~ Licensee Neil Kelso ~ Real ale ~ Meals and snacks (12-9; not 25 Dec) ~ Restaurant ~ (0115) 925 4049 ~ Children in eating area until 8 ~ Jazz every 2nd Sunday ~ Open 11-11; 12-10.30 Sun; closed evening 25 Dec

CAUNTON SK7460 Map 7

Caunton Beck

Main Street; village signposed off A616 Newark—Ollerton

Nottinghamshire Dining Pub of the Year

This started looking promising a few years ago, when what amounts to a virtually new (but not new-looking) pub was reconstructed around the bones of the old Hole Arms here. Then in early 1997 it was taken over by the people who run the Wig & Mitre in Lincoln, and the large number of readers who have enjoyed that so much won't be surprised to hear that this new venture has also hit the button. It's a pleasant relaxed environment, with scrubbed pine tables and country-kitchen chairs, low beams and rag-finished paintwork; more atmosphere will develop as it all wears in more. They do good food all day from 8am to 11pm, changing what's available to suit the time of day. Lunchtime and evening food includes sandwiches (£3.25), soup (£3.50), steak and kidney pie (£6.95), pan-fried venison sausages with bubble and squeak (£8.50), vegetarian dishes such as fresh asparagus bake in filo pastry with oyster mushrooms and mozzarella with saffron and tomato dressing (£9), grilled fillet of plaice with mustard seed mash and herb butter sauce (£11.25), pan-fried strip of duck breast with coriander and pine-nut couscous (£11.50), pan-fried whole lemon sole with prawns and lemon nut brown butter (£13.95) and enterprising salads such as black pudding and smoked chicken; puddings include white chocolate and toffee cheesecake, rice pudding with fresh strawberries, and strawberry crème brûlée (£3.50); with a good value set meal for two. Well kept Adnams and Timothy Taylor Landlord on handpump, good house wines and usually a fine choice of half bottles, freshly squeezed orange juice; welcoming service, daily papers and magazines, no music or games. There are tables out on delightful terraces with lots of flowers and plants. *(Recommended by David and Ruth Hollands, Jack Morley, June and Malcolm Farmer, Kevin Blake)*

Free house ~ Licensees Adam Morgan and Paul Vidic ~ Real ale ~ Meals and snacks (all day) ~ Restaurant ~ (01636) 636793 ~ Children welcome in restaurant and family area ~ Open 9-11; 9-10.30 Sun

COLSTON BASSETT SK7033 Map 7

Martins Arms

Signposted off A46 E of Nottingham

There is an air of gentility at this pleasant dining pub where smart uniformed staff serve very good food. It isn't cheap, but is carefully prepared to order from fresh, daily-delivered produce: home-made soup (£2.95), sandwiches (from £2.95; on fresh ciabatta bread from £4.95), roast plum and feta cheese tartlets (£4.95), rich game terrine with toasted brioche and mango chutney (£5.95), ploughman's or potato cake filled with local stilton or cheddar with mango chutney (£6.95), fresh egg linguini with smoked bacon and cream and parmesan sauce (£7.95), pan-fried turkey escalopes with fried crushed new potatoes, smoked bacon, chives and a thyme jus (£10.95), cassoulette of roasted fillets of cod with tomato fondue (£11.95), roast rump of lamb on ratatouille with coriander pesto or spiced breast of duck with shallot and bramble compote and lime leaf jus (£13.95), sirloin steak diane (£14.95); home-made puddings include banoffee pie with warm butterscotch sauce and vanilla ice cream or glazed orange tart with citrus sorbet (£4.50). A good choice of real ales on handpump might include Bass, Batemans XB and XXXB (and a beer brewed by Batemans for them, Martins Arms Beer), Black Sheep Bitter, Fullers London Pride, Marstons Best and Pedigree, Morlands Old Speckled Hen, Timothy Taylor Landlord and Smiles Best; a good range of malt whiskies and cognacs, and an interesting wine list. There are two open fires in one of the comfortable, attractively decorated bars, and a proper snug; cribbage and dominoes. The well laid out restaurant is decorous and smart, with well spaced tables. Sizeable garden where croquet may be played; no children. *(Recommended by Mike Brearley, Joan and Michel Hooper-Immins, JP, PP, J H Kane, Chris Raisin, David Atkinson, Peter and Jenny Quine, M Buchanan, Brian and Jill Bond, June and Malcolm Farmer, Roy Bromell)*

Free house ~ Licensees Lynne Strafford Bryan and Salvatore Inguanta ~ Real ale ~ Meals and snacks (till 10pm; not Sun evenings) ~ Restaurant (not Sun evening) ~ (01949) 81361 ~ Open 12-3, 6-11; 12-11 Sat; 12-3, 7-10.30 Sun ~ Bedrooms: £35B/£60B

ELKESLEY SK6975 Map 7

Robin Hood

High Street; village well signposted just off A1 Newark—Blyth

As we went to press we heard that the licensee may soon be leaving this friendly village local which provides an excellent refuge from the A1. Under the present regime well cooked, reasonably priced bar food includes hot filled rolls (from £1.70) such as sausage (good local pork and sage ones), home-made soup (£2.40), home-made chicken liver pâté or winter moules marinières (£3.60), a daily vegetarian dish (from £4.50), sautéed liver with onion, garlic and parsley (£5), chicken breast or gammon and eggs (£5.50), steaks (from £6.50), daily specials, and home-made puddings such as chocolate truffle cake or tiramisu (£2.50); a good choice of fresh fish might run from basic cod in batter (£4.95) to baby halibut or stir-fried monkfish (from £6.70). The roomy and comfortably furnished carpeted family dining lounge has pictures, some copper pans and so forth – even a small collection of handcuffs. There's also a plain but neatly kept public bar, with pool, dominoes, cribbage and trivia machines; well kept Boddingtons on handpump and a guest such as Wadworths 6X under light blanket pressure; friendly and efficient service, unobtrusive piped music. The garden is moderately well screened from the A1 and has picnic-sets and a play area. *(Recommended by Richard Cole, Kevin Thorpe, Derek and Sylvia Stephenson, Andy and Jill Kassube, Eddy and Emma Gibson, Jason Warren)*

Whitbreads ~ Lease: Alan Draper ~ Real ale ~ Meals and snacks (not Sun evening) ~ Restaurant ~ (01777) 838259 ~ Children welcome ~ Open 11-3, 6-11; 11-11 Sat; 12-3, 7-10.30 Sun; closed evening 25 Dec

KIMBERLEY SK5044 Map 7

Nelson & Railway £

3 miles from M1 junction 26; at exit roundabout take A610 to Ripley, then signposted Kimberley; pub in Sation Rd, on right from centre

This splendid two-roomed Victorian pub used to stand between two competing railway stations and its unusual name comes from a shortening of its original title, the Lord Nelson, Railway Hotel. The beamed bar and lounge have an attractive mix of Edwardian-looking furniture, interesting brewery prints and railway signs on the walls, and a relaxed atmosphere – though it can get busy; no-smoking area. With the brewery directly opposite, the Hardys & Hansons Bitter, Classic and seasonal ales on handpump and Mild on electric pump are particularly well kept; several malt whiskies. Good value straightforward bar food includes soup (£1.30), sandwiches (from £1.30; hot rolls from £1.60), baked potatoes (£2.25), cottage pie (£2.75), cod in batter, mushroom stroganoff, lasagne or steak and kidney pie (£4.45), chicken tikka masala (£4.85), gammon and egg (£4.95), sirloin steak (£5.95), puddings (£1.85) and children's meals (£1.65); Sunday lunch (£3.95 adults, £2.95 children). Darts, pool, alley skittles, dominoes, cribbage, fruit machine and juke box. There are tables and swings out in a good-sized cottagey garden. *(Recommended by R T and J C Moggridge, Derek and Sylvia Stephenson, John and Elspeth Howell, D Parkhurst, JP, PP, John Honnor, Jenny and Roger Huggins, Dr and Mrs Baker, Alan Morton, Andy and Jill Kassube, K Fell)*

Hardys & Hansons ~ Tenant Harry Burton ~ Real ale ~ Meals and snacks (12-6 Sun)

~ (0115) 938 2177 ~ Children in eating area of bar ~ Open 10.30-3, 5-11 Mon-Weds; 11-11 Thurs-Sat; 12-10.30 Sun ~ Bedrooms: £19/£33

LAXTON SK7267 Map 7

Dovecote

Signposted off A6075 E of Ollerton

Laxton is one of the few places in the country still farmed using the open field system and this redbrick house stands next to the three huge medieval fields. A former stable block behind the pub has a visitor centre explaining it all and as part of this ancient farming system the grass is auctioned for haymaking in the third week of June, and anyone who lives in the parish is entitled to a bid – as well as to a drink. The central room has brocaded button-back built-in corner seats, stools and chairs, and a coal-effect gas fire, and opens through a small bay, which was the original entry, into another similar room. Around the other side a simpler room with some entertaining Lawson Wood 1930s tourist cartoons leads through to a pool room with darts, fruit machine, pool, dominoes and piped music; no-smoking area. Straightforward but popular good value food includes sandwiches, home-made soup, home-made steak and mushroom or chicken and mushroom pie (£5), fresh fish (from £5.20), strips of steak in mushroom and pepper sauce (£5.40) and mixed grill (£6.75); friendly and efficient service. Two weekly changing guest ales might include Charles Wells Bombardier or Mansfield. There are white tables and chairs on a small front terrace by a sloping garden with a disused white dovecote, and a children's play area; also, a site for six caravans with lavatories and showers. *(Recommended by Bill Fisher, John Fahy, Angela Copeland, CMW, JJW; more reports please)*

Free house ~ Licensees Stephen and Betty Shepherd ~ Real ale ~ Meals and snacks ~ (01777) 871586 ~ Children welcome ~ Open 12-3, 6.30-11; 12-3, 7-10.30 Sun

NORMANTON ON TRENT SK7969 Map 7

Square & Compass £

Signposted off B1164 S of Tuxford

Popular with locals, this low-beamed village pub is old-fashioned and friendly. The bar has an attractive grandfather clock, and is divided by an enormous woodburning stove in a central brick fireplace. There are several more or less separate snug areas, alcoves and bays, mainly with green plush furnishings, farming photographs, a flowery red carpet, red curtains and roughcast shiny cream walls; piped music. Good value bar food includes chip butties (85p), sandwiches or rolls (from £1.20), baked potatoes (from £1.20), soup (£1.30), burgers (from £1.50), home-made pâté (£2.85), battered cod (£4.10), home-made steak and kidney pie (£4.25, large £6.30), gammon and egg with pineapple (£4.50), mushroom and nut fettucine, lasagne or chicken kiev (£4.75), 8oz sirloin steak (£7.75), with a couple of blackboard specials like gingered beef or chicken in whiskey sauce (£4.50) and rabbit pie (£5.50), puddings (from £1.60), and children's meals (from £1.60); Sunday roast. The landlord is keen on shooting, so game features on the menu quite often. Well kept Adnams Bitter and guests such as Springhead Bitter, Theakstons Best or Ushers Best on handpump. The public side has pool, table skittles, dominoes. Outside, there are seats and a well equipped children's play area, and you can camp here. *(Recommended by Ian and Nita Cooper, Derek and Sylvia Stephenson, Alan and Brenda Williams, Angela Copeland, Mary and David Webb, Ian Phillips)*

Free house ~ Licensee Janet Lancaster ~ Real ale ~ Meals and snacks ~ Restaurant ~ (01636) 821439 ~ Children welcome ~ Open 12-3, 6-11; 12-11 Sat; 12-4, 7-10.30 Sun ~ Bedroom: £23S/£26S

Pubs close to motorway junctions are listed at the back of the book.

NOTTINGHAM SK5640 Map 7

Fellows Morton & Clayton

54 Canal Street (part of inner ring road)

This carefully converted old canal building brews its own beer (which is very reasonably priced for the area); from a big window in the quarry tiled glassed-in area at the back you can see the little brewery: Samuel Fellows and Matthew Claytons. They also have well kept Boddingtons, Burtonwood Top Hat, Timothy Taylor Landlord, Wadworths 6X and Whitbreads Castle Eden on handpump. Popular good value lunchtime bar food includes filled rolls (from £1.20), home-made soup (£1.75), burgers (from £2.25), pasta bows in rich cheese and tomato sauce with broccoli or chicken curry (£4.25), home-made lasagne (£4.50), home-made steak and kidney pie (£4.95), battered haddock (£5.25), and rump steak (£5.95); prompt, friendly service. The softly lit bar has dark red plush seats built into alcoves, wooden tables, some seats up two or three steps in a side gallery, and bric-a-brac on the shelf just below the glossy dark green high ceiling; a sympathetic extension provides extra seating. Maybe well reproduced nostalgic pop music, trivia, fruit machine and daily newspapers on a rack. Outside there's a terrace with seats and tables. Buzzing with businessmen and lawyers at lunchtime, it's popular with a younger crowd in the evening. The canal museum is nearby, and Nottingham station is just a short walk away. *(Recommended by Patrick Hancock, Norma and Keith Bloomfield, D Parkhurst, Derek and Sylvia Stephenson, Ian Phillips, JP, PP, SLC, M Rutherford, Andy and Jill Kassube, Roger Huggins)*

Own brew (Whitbreads) ~ Lease: Les Howard and Ihor Najdan ~ Real ale ~ Lunchtime meals and snacks (12-6) ~ Restaurant ~ (0115) 950 6795 ~ Children welcome in restaurant ~ Open 11-11; 12-10.30 Sun; closed 25 Dec

Lincolnshire Poacher

Mansfield Rd; up hill from Victoria Centre

A splendid arrangement with Batemans allows this bustling and homely town pub to serve Bass, Marstons Pedigree and up to six guest ales alongside perfectly kept Batemans XB, XXXB, Dark Mild and Victory Ale on handpump; also good ciders, and around 70 malt whiskies and 10 Irish ones. The traditional big wood-floored front bar has wall settles and plain wooden tables, and is decorated with breweriana; it opens on to a plain but lively room on the left, from where a corridor takes you down to the chatty panelled back snug – newspapers to read; cribbage, dominoes, cards, piped Irish music; no-smoking area at lunchtime. Good reasonably priced daily specials might include hummus and pitta bread with olives and salad or hazelnut pâté (£3.95), harvest pie or sausage and mash (£4.50), lasagne, Italian meat balls or vegetarian kofta kebabs (£4.95) and lamb chops (£5.50); no chips, and efficient, pleasant service. It can get busy in the evenings when it's popular with a younger crowd. A conservatory overlooks tables on a large terrace behind. *(Recommended by JP, PP, R M Taylor, David Atkinson, Roger and Jenny Huggins, Andy and Jill Kassube, Irene and Geoffrey Lindley, Dr and Mrs J H Hills, Mr and Mrs J T V Harris, Derek and Sylvia Stephenson, Simon Walker, M Rutherford)*

Batemans/Tynemill ~ Lease: Paul Montgomery ~ Real ale ~ Meals and snacks (12-3 Mon-Sat; 12-4 Sun; 5-8 Tues-Thurs; no food Fri, Sat, Sun and Mon evenings) ~ (0115) 9411584 ~ Children welcome in conservatory till 8pm ~ Open 11-11; 12-10.30 Sun

Olde Trip to Jerusalem ★

Brewhouse Yard; from inner ring road follow The North, A6005 Long Eaton signpost until you are in Castle Boulevard then almost at once turn right into Castle Road; pub is up on the left

The unique upstairs cavern bar here – thought to have served as cellarage for an early medieval brewhouse which stood here – is cut into the sandstone rock below the castle, its panelled walls soaring narrowly into the dark chasm above. The friendly downstairs bar is also mainly carved from the rock, with leatherette-cushioned settles built into the dark panelling, tables on tiles or flagstones, and more low-ceilinged rock alcoves; also a parlour/snug and two more caves open to the public. Well kept real ales include Hardys & Hansons Kimberley Best, Best Mild, Classic and their cellarman's cask (brewed every two months or so), and Marstons Pedigree on handpump. Home-made bar food includes sandwiches and filled french bread or burgers (from £2.29), filled baked potatoes (from £2.79), giant yorkshire pudding filled with roast beef, pork, lamb or sausages, steak and kidney pudding, courgette and mushroom lasagne or liver and onions (£4.99), fisherman's medley (£5.99), and puddings (from £1.99). Cribbage, fruit machine; seats outside. No children. *(Recommended by Derek and Sylvia Stephenson, Tim Barrow, Sue Demont, JP, PP, Brad W Morley, Ian Phillips, R M Taylor, Sidney and Erna Wells, Rona Murdoch, Timothy Smith, Sue Holland, Dave Webster, Chris Raisin, Mr and Mrs J T Harris, M Rutherford, SLC, Paul Barnett)*

Hardys & Hansons ~ Manager Patrick Dare ~ Real ale ~ Lunchtime meals and snacks (11-6; 12-6 Sun) ~ (0115) 9473171 ~ Open 11-11; 12-10.30 Sun

UPTON SK7354 Map 7

French Horn

A612

This friendly dining pub is so popular that you may need to book even on a weekday lunchtime, when most of the tables will be laid for eating. Well cooked and presented food might include sandwiches (from £2.95), soup (£2.95), mushrooms stuffed with stilton in a port and redcurrant sauce (£3.25), steak pie (£5.25), and good specials like grilled sardines with a lemon and herb stuffing (£5.95), brie and broccoli crèpes with a spicy tomato sauce (£6.25), beef bourguignon (£7.25), medley of salmon, sea trout and shark in a white wine and cream sauce, poached salmon in a cream and dill sauce or grilled loin of lamb filled with mustard sauce and a redcurrant jus (£7.95), and puddings like home-made chocolate truffle torte or lemon meringue pie (£2.95). Usefully they also do a range of sandwiches and hot snacks all afternoon; helpful and efficient staff even when busy. The neat and comfortable open-plan bar has a nicely relaxed feel, with cushioned captain's chairs, wall banquettes around glossy tables, and watercolours by local artists on the walls (some may be for sale). Well kept Vaux Waggle Dance, Thorne Best, and a guest like Shepherd Neame Spitfire on handpump, and several wines by the glass; piped music. Picnic-sets on the big sloping back paddock look out over farmland. *(Recommended by G Neighbour, J H Kane, Joy and Peter Heatherley, Ian Phillips, Irene and Geoffrey Lindley, Alan Wilcock, Christine Davidson, Andy and Jill Kassube, J F Knutton, Lawrence Bacon, Luke Worthington, David and Ruth Hollands, David and Lynne Cure, Paul Barnett, Angela Copeland)*

Wards ~ Tenant Joyce Carter ~ Real ale ~ Meals and snacks (12-2, 6-9.30; light snacks 2-6) ~ Restaurant ~ (01636) 812394 ~ Children welcome ~ Open 11-11; 12-10.30 Sun

WALKERINGHAM SK7792 Map 7

Three Horseshoes

High Street; just off A161, off A631 W of Gainsborough

The licensees are justifiably proud of the award winning flowers and hanging baskets that adorn this pleasant village pub in summer. Using 9,000 plants, the display is really quite amazing, and it combines attractively with the slight austerity of the simple old-fashioned decor inside – not to mention the menu and blackboard of dishes of the day to greet you in the hall. Well kept Bass, Stones, Worthington Best and a guest beer are served from handpumps in the warmly welcoming bar. Of the two brothers who run it, John keeps the bar, while Ray is responsible for the often inventive cooking: a wide choice that might include lunchtime sandwiches, home-made soup (£1.40), spinach and courgette lasagne, liver, bacon and sausage casserole (£5.50), gammon and pineapple or home-made steak and kidney pie (£5.95), escalope of chicken with cheese and tomato or roast stuffed breast of lamb (£6.60), medallions of pork in a white wine, herb, mustard and cream sauce (£7.50), steaks (from £8.75) and possibly game, monkfish, brill or dover sole specials; vegetables are fresh and lightly cooked. Darts, dominoes, fruit machine, video game, and piped music. There are seats on a lawned area. *(Recommended by M Godfrey, D E Twitchett, J and M Hall)*

Free house ~ Licensees Ray and John Turner ~ Real ale ~ Meals and snacks (not Sun evening or Mon) ~ Restaurant ~ (01427) 890959 ~ Children welcome ~ Open 11.30-3, 7-11; 12-4, 7-10.30 Sun

Lucky Dip

Besides the fully inspected pubs, you might like to try these Lucky Dips recommended to us and described by readers (if you do, please send us reports):

Bagthorpe [Church Lane; off B600, nr M1 junction 27; SK4751], *Red Lion*: Comfortable and spacious open-plan split-level refurbishment of 17th-c village pub, Home and Theakstons ales with a guest beer, some tables set aside for reasonably priced food inc OAP lunches, open fire, pictures, penny arcade machine, no piped music; picnic-sets and big play area in big garden with terrace, attractive setting; open all day Thurs-Sat *(Alan Bowker, CMW, JJW)*; [Lower Bagthorpe], *Shepherds Rest*: Former traditional mining pub, extensively refurbished but keeping character, cheerfully enterprising landlord, very pleasant staff, well kept Theakstons and guest beers, wide choice of good home-made food inc OAP lunches, early evening bargains, monthly theme nights; occasional live music; pretty surroundings *(Alan Bowker)*

Bleasby [Gypsy Lane; SK7149], *Waggon & Horses*: Comfortable banquettes in carpeted lounge, open fire in character bar, Banks's and Marstons Pedigree, reasonably priced fresh lunchtime food from snacks up, Fri fish and chips night, chatty landlord, tables outside, back lobby with play area and comfortable chairs to watch over it; piped music; small camping area behind *(CMW, JJW, Jeremy Burnside)*

Blyth [SK6287], *White Swan*: Well kept Whitbreads-related ales, helpful welcoming service, good food from sandwiches up inc good fresh fish, in cosy neatly kept pub with big open fires; piped music; good A1 break, by duck pond *(Mr and Mrs D Graham)*

Carlton on Trent [Ossington Rd; signed just off A1 N of Newark; SK7964], *Great Northern*: Large busy local next to railway line, comfortable and welcoming, with lots of railway memorabilia, toys in large family room; Mansfield Riding, local Springhead and guest ales, decent food inc good fish and chips, small dining area, good service; play area in garden *(JP, PP)*

Caythorpe [Main St; SK6845], *Black Horse*: Small intimate unspoilt country pub run by same family for many years, good food inc Mon curry night, microbrewery producing its own Dover Beck ales, modest prices, distinctive landlady; opp pottery *(D A Begley, Jeremy Burnside)*

Clayworth [High St; SK7388], *Blacksmiths Arms*: Smart tasteful dining pub with open fire, friendly professional service, good choice of good generous food, Ruddles, Stones and a guest such as Shepherd Neame Spitfire; bedrooms *(Andrew Lingham, Amanda Parry)*

Costock [off A60 Nottingham—Loughborough; SK5726], *Generous Briton*: Very good value food from filled baps up inc OAP bargain lunches Mon-Weds in two-bar beamed pub, couple of no-smoking tables up two steps, three Mansfield real ales, good choice of soft drinks, friendly chatty landlady, children allowed if eating, very quiet piped music *(JJW, CMW)*

Cuckney [High Croft; SK5671], *Greendale Oak*: Good range of reasonably priced well cooked and served food (not weekend evenings) from sandwiches up, helpful licensees, swift service even when very busy midweek lunchtime, roomy but cosy and friendly L-shaped bar, good coffee, popular evening restaurant; bedrooms *(Brenda and David Tew)*

Drakeholes [signed off A631 Bawtry—Gainsborough; SK7090], *Griff Inn*: Civilised plush lounge bar, partly no smoking, bar food from sandwiches up, airy brasserie-style summer restaurant, separate no-smoking restaurant, Courage and John Smiths; children in eating area, piped music; neat landscaped gardens with pretty view above Chesterfield Canal, comfortable bedrooms *(Julie Peters, LYM)*

East Bridgford [Kneeton Rd, off A6075; can also be reached from A46; SK6943], *Reindeer*: Popular village local refurbished under new management, with new kitchen and back public bar, improved beamed front dining bar, John Smiths and Marstons Pedigree and a guest beer, decent food, log-effect gas fires; children welcome *(Derek and Sylvia Stephenson, Norma and Keith Bloomfield, BB)*

Eastwood [Nottingham Rd, Giltbrook, not far from M1 junction 26; SK4845], *Hayloft*: Character split-level Hogshead ale house, converted loft full of farm tools, alcoves, low lighting, comfortable armchairs, good atmosphere, good if not cheap choice of beers tapped from the cask *(Kevin Blake)*

☆ **Gunthorpe** [Trentside, off A6097 E of Nottingham; SK6844], *Tom Browns*: Modern family-run brick bar over road from River Trent (pleasant walks), wok cooking in glass booth, decent bar food too (good Sun lunch – must book), six Scottish Courage and interesting guest beers, good choice of wines, easy-going atmosphere, log fire; well reproduced pop music (may be loud evening), fruit machine, no dogs; enjoyable restaurant, seats outside *(JJW, CMW, Clive Bonner, BB)*

Hickling [SK6929], *Plough*: Interesting pub by

Grantham Canal basin (locally navigable), extended around old cottage; very cosy snug, Theakstons and a local guest ale, inexpensive food, friendly service; handy for towpath walks; children welcome *(Norma and Keith Bloomfield)*

Hoveringham [Main St; SK6946], *Reindeer*: Open fires in bar and lounge, lots of beams, some antiques; friendly and unpretentious, with popular bar food, well kept Marstons Pedigree *(Chris Raisin, Graham Doyle, JP, PP)*

Kirkby in Ashfield [Park Lane (B6018 S); SK5056], *Countryman*: Great traditional atmosphere in upgraded former miners' local, attractive bas relief murals of shooting scenes, mining memorabilia, well kept Theakstons and guest beers, beer festivals, generous bar food (not Sun evening), low prices; popular with walkers, music nights *(Peter and Audrey Dowsett, the Didler, JP, PP)*

Linby [Main St; SK5351], *Horse & Groom*: Theakstons XB, bar food (restricted Tues to good choice of hot and cold filled rolls); in attractive village nr Newstead Abbey *(David Atkinson, JP, PP)*

☆ **Maplebeck** [signed from A616/A617; SK7160], *Beehive*: Unspoiled beamed country tavern doing very well under current owners, tiny front bar, rather bigger side room, traditional furnishings, open fire, free antique juke box, well kept Mansfield Riding and Old Baily, cheese or ham rolls, tables on small terrace with flower tubs and grassy bank running down to little stream, play area with swings; may be cl Mon lunchtime, delightfully peaceful spot weekday lunchtimes, very busy w/e and bank hols *(Chris Raisin, Graham Doyle, A M Pring, JP, PP, LYM)*

Mapperley [Plains Rd (B684); SK6043], *Travellers Rest*: Lots of nooks and crannies in friendly bar with interesting feature curtains, good choice of changing ales, good wine choice, wide range of good value food all day (not after 2 Sun/Mon) from filled baguettes to interesting main dishes, candlelit tables, popular lunchtime no-smoking area, friendly welcoming staff, back family building with adjacent play area, garden; open all day *(M Rutherford)*

Moorgreen [SK4847], *Horse & Groom*: Good choice of food inc OAP bargains, well kept Hardys & Hansons *(Geoffrey Lindley)*

Morton [back rd SE of Southwell; SK7251], *Full Moon*: Comfortable L-shaped lounge in 16th-c local with wide choice of good value standard food inc lots of puddings, well kept Theakstons and guest beers, friendly staff; children welcome, pool and TV in separate games room, no piped music or dogs; big garden with terrace, picnic-sets, play area; delightfully out-of-the-way hamlet not far from River Trent *(Irene and Geoffrey Lindley, JJW, CMW)*

Newark [off A46 SW; SK8054], *Lord Ted*: A Tom Cobleigh pub, with enjoyable food from their usual menu inc children's and vegetarian, good decor, very pleasant efficient service, wide choice of well kept beers such as Boddingtons and Courage Directors; open all day *(Bill and Sheila McLardy)*; [25 North Gate], *Malt Shovel*: Welcoming and comfortably refurbished old-fashioned local with good doorstep sandwiches and lunchtime hot dishes inc fresh veg, well kept ales inc good beer brewed for them by Rudgate, choice of teas, cheerfully laid-back atmosphere and service *(John C Baker)*; [Lincoln Rd], *Roman Way*: Recently opened big Brewers Fayre with wide choice of good food, well kept Whitbreads-related ales, popular indoor play area and soft play area, friendly efficient staff, garden; disabled facilities, open all day; bedrooms *(Richard Lewis)*

☆ **Nottingham** [1 Ilkeston Rd (A52 towards Derby)], *Sir John Borlase Warren*: Several connecting traditional rooms, lots of old prints, interesting Victorian decorations and fittings, exceptional value lunchtime food, no-smoking eating area, very friendly staff, well kept Greenalls Original, Shipstones, Tetleys, also guests tapped from the cask; tables in back garden with barbecues; children welcome (not Fri/Sat evenings) *(Chris Raisin, Graham Doyle, Roger and Jenny Huggins, LYM)*

☆ **Nottingham** [Sheriffs Way, Queensbridge Rd], *Vat & Fiddle*: Former Tom Hoskins reopened 1997 as Tynemill pub (similar to Lincolnshire Poacher) beside the new Castle Rock brewery, with good food, good range of malt whiskies and wide choice of particularly well kept beers such as Archers Golden, Castle Rock Hemlock, Hook Norton Best, Marstons Pedigree, Whim Hartington IPA; small semi-circular character bar with tiled floor, scrubbed tables, old local pictures, daily papers, upstairs function room used for lunches *(the Didler, Steve Godrich, R M Taylor)*

Nottingham [Wollaton Rd, Wollaton; SK5139], *Admiral Rodney*: Large panelled pub with well kept real ales, limited but popular weekday lunchtime food Mon-Fri inc tempting bacon baps *(D J Atkinson)*; [18 Angel Row; off Market Sq], *Bell*: Quaint low-beamed 15th-c pub with Boddingtons, Jennings Mild, Marstons Pedigree, Theakstons XB, Ruddles County and a guest like Black Sheep Special kept well in extraordinarily deep sandstone cellar, three bustling timbered and panelled bars (very crowded and maybe smoky), ancient stairs to attractive calmer raftered room with nice window seats used as lunchtime family restaurant for good value simple well presented lunchtime food; good value wines; trad jazz Sun lunchtime (rolls only then), Mon and Tues evenings; open all day weekdays *(JP, PP, R M Taylor, SLC, M Rutherford, LYM)*; [36 Hockley], *Bunkers Hill*: Former bank, effective and unusual green decor, beams, comfortable traditional feel, up to ten real ales from small breweries far and wide, good value home-made food inc speciality curries; quiz nights, no machines or juke box *(Alan Bowker, the Didler, R M Taylor)*; [Angel Row], *City Gate*: Well kept Bass, Shipstones, Tetleys and a weekly guest such as Nethergate Old Growler, speciality wonderful doorstep sandwiches with over a hundred fillings *(D L Parkhurst)*; [3

Porchester Rd, Thornywood; SK5941], *Coopers Arms*: Superb solid old Victorian local with three unspoilt rooms, Home Mild and Bitter, Theakstons XB; small family room in skittle alley; cl Weds lunchtime *(the Didler)*; [Mansfield Rd], *Forest*: Rather spartan conversion (by Tynemill – same small group as Lincolnshire Poacher), splendid ales such as Castle Rock, Greene King Abbot, Marstons Pedigree, Woodfordes Wherry and (associated with Tynemill) Hemlock Stone, varied food inc wide range of light snacks with international flavour; back rooms now form nightclub *(Alan Bowker)*; [Lincoln St, Old Basford; SK5442], *Fox & Crown*: Pleasantly refurbished open-plan local with back microbrewery producing its own Fiddlers Bitter, Mild, Finest and Porter; freshly prepared reasonably priced meals in dining area, helpful staff *(Richard Houghton, JP, PP, Alan Bowker)*; [273 Castle Bvd, Lenton; SK5438], *Grove*: Flagstones and bare boards, panelled dado, some stripped red stone, old casks on shelves, Scottish Courage beers with guests such as Batemans and Marstons Owd Rodger, interesting bottled beers and brewery memorabilia, simple well priced food from sandwiches and baked potatoes up *(Jenny and Roger Huggins)*; [63 North Sherwood St; SK5640], *Hole in the Wall*: Mansfield Bitter and Old Baily and three guest beers, long room with scrubbed tables and bare wood, good value usual food (not after 7) inc Sun lunch, SkyTV sports; popular with students, open all day (cl Sun afternoon) *(the Didler)*; [Radford Rd, New Basford; SK5541], *Horse & Groom*: Doing well after tasteful refurbishment by new owners, six good value beers such as Bass, Belvoir Star and Marstons Pedigree, fresh food from sandwiches to restaurant meals, old Shipstones Brewery memorabilia; open all day *(the Didler)*; [Wellington Circus], *Limelight*: Extended convivial bar and restaurant attached to Playhouse theatre, well kept Adnams, Batemans XB, Courage Directors, Marstons Pedigree, Theakstons XB and guests inc a Mild, reasonably priced food from rolls to full meals (not Sun lunchtime), pleasant efficient staff, theatre pictures, occasional modern jazz, attractive continental-style outside seating area; open all day, live blues and jazz, same group as Lincolnshire Poacher *(Kevin Blake, R M Taylor, JP, PP, SLC, M Rutherford, the Didler)*; [Lower Mosley St, New Basford], *Lion*: Refurbished in contemporary open-plan spartan style, bare bricks and boards, up to 18 real ales from one of city's deepest cellars (visible through glass panel – can be visited at quiet times), tasty food inc doorstep sandwiches, live jazz and blues; open all day *(the Didler, Alan Bowker, JP, PP, R M Taylor)*; [St Nicholas St, Castlegate], *Royal Children*: Open-plan, busy but relaxed, three basic but comfortable areas with bare boards, lots of panelling, old pictures, converted gas lamps, brass water fountains on bar, eight well kept ales such as Home, Theakstons and Timothy Taylor Landlord, good bar meals *(Jenny and Roger Huggins, M Rutherford)*; [Maid Marion Way], *Salutation*: Ancient back part with beams, flagstones and cosy corners, plusher modern front, good range of reasonably priced nicely presented food, up to a dozen or more changing ales, sensible prices and good atmosphere – can get a bit noisy *(Roger and Jenny Huggins, Derek and Sylvia Stephenson, M Rutherford, R M Taylor, SLC, Patrick Hancock, BB)*; [Stamford Rd (A606), W Bridgford; SK5936], *Willow Tree*: Large busy suburban local with good well cooked food in friendly lounge and restaurant, well kept ales inc full Batemans range *(Norma and Keith Bloomfield)*

Nuthall [Nottingham Rd (B600, away from city), off A610 nr M1 junction 26; SK5144], *Three Ponds*: Friendly and tastefully refurbished Hardys & Hansons roadhouse with wide range of good value food inc OAP bargains, well kept Best, Best Mild and Classic, good coffee, good staff; piped music may obtrude; big back garden with play area *(JP, PP)*

Orston [Church St; SK7741], *Durham Ox*: Welcoming local opp church, well kept Home and Theakstons ales, good value beef, ham and other rolls; split-level open-plan bar with interesting RAF/USAF memorabilia, collection of whisky bottles; tables outside (and hitching rail for ferrets as well as for horses) *(Norma and Keith Bloomfield, R M Taylor)*

☆ **Ranby** [just off A1 by A620 Worksop—E Retford; SK6580], *Chequers*: Nice building in superb canalside spot, delightful waterside terrace, some mooring, weekend boat trips; well kept beer, cheerful service, attractive and comfortable inside, dining room with farm tools and bric-a-brac; children very welcome, open all day, good value substantial food noon-10 from sandwiches to main dishes with Italian emphasis *(A M Pring, P and R Baker, Mike and Grete Turner)*

☆ **Retford** [off West Carr Rd, Ordsall; follow Leisure Centre signs from A620 then just after industrial estate sign keep eyes skinned for pub sign on left; SK6980], *Market*: Good choice of well kept ales, comfortable plush banquettes, splendid range of good value generous home cooking inc great fresh haddock, friendly helpful service; very busy Fri/Sat night, jazz 3rd Sun in month *(Pat and Tony Martin, D Parkhurst, Geoffrey and Irene Lindley, John C Baker, Sue and Mike Loseby, JP, PP, LYM)*

☆ **Southwell** [Church St (A612); SK6953], *Bramley Apple*: Friendly prompt service, generous good value food inc good w/e carvery (two sittings Sun), fresh fish and vegetarian, very crisp veg, well kept Mansfield and guest ales, good atmosphere, attractively worked Bramley apple theme, eating area screened off by stained glass, TV zone; bedrooms *(Norma and Keith Bloomfield, Chris Raisin, Graham Doyle, Rona Murdoch, BB)*

Southwell [King St], *Earl Rodney*: Two largish low-beamed rooms with central bar, decent food inc vegetarian, real ales inc Batemans, Boddingtons and Greene King, good house wine, quick friendly service *(John Wooll)*

Strelley [Main St; off A6002 nr M1 junction 26; SK5141], *Broad Oak*: Good value dining pub, Hardys & Hansons Bitter, Classic and Mild, lots of partitioned areas, comfortable banquettes, OAP specials, no piped music, picnic-sets outside, play area in back garden; no dogs *(Geoffrey Lindley)*

Thurgarton [Southwell Rd; A612; SK6949], *Red Lion*: Enjoyable generous food, well kept ales, lovely fire, roomy bars and restaurant; pleasant garden, children welcome *(Paul McPherson)*

☆ **Upton** [Main St (A612); SK7354], *Cross Keys*: Rambling heavy-beamed bar with good welcoming service, lots of alcoves, central log fire, masses to look at from sporting cartoons and local watercolours to decorative plates and metalwork, interesting medley of furnishings; well kept Batemans XXXB, Boddingtons, Brakspears, Marstons Pedigree and local Springhead, decent wines; friendly dog, unobtrusive piped music, Sun folk night; children in back extension with carved pews or upstairs restaurant *(Keith Wells, David Carr, June and Malcolm Farmer, JP, PP, LYM)*

☆ **Watnall Chaworth** [3 miles from M1 junction 26: A610 towards Nottingham, left on to B600, then keep right; SK5046], *Queens Head*: Tastefully extended old pub with wide range of good value food, well kept Home Bitter and Mild, Theakstons XB and Old Peculier and a guest beer, efficient friendly service; intimate snug, dining area, beams and stripped pine, coal fires; fruit machine, piped music; picnic-sets in spacious and attractive back garden with big play area; open all day Fri/Sat *(the Didler, JP, PP)*

☆ **Wellow** [Eakring Rd, just off A616 E of Ollerton; SK6766], *Olde Red Lion*: New landlord in low-beamed and panelled 16th-c pub by green with towering maypole which gives its name to the local brewery that brews Lions Pride for the pub, alongside well kept changing beers such as Mansfield, Ruddles Best and Wadworths 6X; reasonably priced food from sandwiches up inc vegetarian and Sun roasts, no-smoking restaurant and dining area; children welcome, picnic-sets outside *(D Parkhurst, J W G Nunns, LYM)*

☆ **West Leake** [off A6006; SK5226], *Star*: Traditional beamed and quarry-tiled country bar with a good deal of character, hunting trophies, wall settles, comfortable partly panelled lounge with good log fire, short choice of good value simple weekday lunchtime food, well kept Bass and Marstons Pedigree; children in eating area *(Chris Raisin, Roger and Ruth Airey, JP, PP, LYM)*

West Stockwith [Canal Lane opp marina, off A161; SK7995], *Waterfront*: Extended two-bar pub with big dining area, five well kept ales, good value food inc Sun carvery, garden with barbecue and tyre swings – excellent waterside spot on basin between River Trent and Chesterfield Canal; TV, fruit machine, piped music; open all day w/e, crowded summer evenings with jolly boating types; caravan park behind *(JJW, CMW)*

Wilford [Main Rd, off B679 S of Nottingham; SK5637], *Ferry*: Good lunchtime pub, with good bar meals, low beams and bare boards, bays of comfortable banquettes, chesterfield, pictures, two snugs, four well kept sensibly priced ales, restaurant with lofted roof and imposing fireplace; piped pop music; tidy back terrace, garden with play area, view over River Trent to Nottingham Castle *(Peter and Jenny Quine, JJW, CMW)*

Real ale may be served from handpumps, electric pumps (not just the on-off switches used for keg beer) or – common in Scotland – tall taps called founts (pronounced 'fonts') where a separate pump pushes the beer up under air pressure. The landlord can adjust the force of the flow – a tight spigot gives the good creamy head that Yorkshire lads like.

Oxfordshire

Oxfordshire has some excellent pubs, with a good mix from simple country taverns to very restauranty places, verging on the hotelish. It's by no means a cheap area, with food often expensive, and drinks prices well above the national average – and tending to rise more quickly than elsewhere. Much the cheapest place we found was the Romany at Bampton, with the Five Bells at Broadwell also cheap for drinks, and the local Hook Norton Brewery reliable for good value attractively priced beer. Of the other local breweries, Brakspears, famous for its charmingly rustic pubs, tends to price its beers high. A threat to choice came in summer 1998 when the Morrells brewery in Oxford announced that it was up for sale – the worry is that it seems more valuable as a city property site than as a brewery. By contrast, however, Morlands of Abingdon (average prices) seems to be expanding happily on the back of its famously named Old Speckled Hen beer. There have been quite a few changes among the pubs this year, with new licensees at the Boars Head at Ardington (opening up another room at this popular dining pub), the pretty Clanfield Tavern, the cricket-filled Bat & Ball at Cuddesdon (gains a Place to Stay Award), the Half Moon at Cuxham (little change), the White Horse at Duns Tew, the Pear Tree in Hook Norton (tap for the brewery), the Olde Leathern Bottel at Lewknor (friendly people, doing well), the Lamb at Shipton under Wychwood, the Star at Stanton St John (good reports on them), and the roomy Talk House there. Pubs doing particularly well in recent months are the friendly Five Bells at Broadwell (hard-working licensees, enjoyable food), the Lamb at Buckland (nice atmosphere, interesting food – a new main entry), the lovely old Lamb in Burford (very well run, good all round), the Wheatsheaf at East Hendred (a good New Zealand chef bringing it back into the Guide after a few years' break), the stylish Blowing Stone at Kingston Lisle (another new main entry with good food), the neat thatched Nut Tree at Murcott, the Turf Tavern tucked away in the heart of Oxford, the friendly Perch & Pike at South Stoke (good interesting food, nice wines), the welcoming Trout on the Thames at Tadpole Bridge, and the warm-hearted Crown at Toot Baldon (really enjoyable accomplished homely cooking). A good many other pubs are giving plenty of enjoyment, too, but it's from among these favourites that we choose as Oxfordshire Dining Pub of the Year the Lamb at Burford. The Lucky Dip section at the end of the chapter also seems particularly strong at the moment, with very firm support for the Maytime at Asthall, Bull in Burford, Hand & Shears at Church Hanborough, Deddington Arms at Deddington, Trout at Godstow, Maybush at Newbridge, Perch in Oxford, Crown at Pishill and Six Bells at Warborough – all inspected and approved by us. We've also had good reports on the new regime at the Fishes at North Hinksey, but have not yet been able to try it ourselves.

Please let us know what you think of a pub's bedrooms. No stamp needed: *The Good Pub Guide*, FREEPOST TN1569, Wadhurst, E Sussex TN5 7BR.

ARDINGTON SU4388 Map 2

Boars Head

Village signposted off A417 Didcot—Wantage, 2 miles E of Wantage

A friendly new licensee has taken over this civilised dining pub and has opened up another room and introduced a new menu. The good popular food now includes chicken, lemon grass and sweetcorn soup (£3.50), tomato pudding with tomato vinaigrette (£3.75), smoked duck with a hazelnut and juniper dressing (£4.50), creamy smoked haddock risotto or double baked soufflé with broccoli and stilton (£9), guinea fowl with baked apples and a cider cream sauce (£10), fried scallops with lentils and chardonnay (£14), and puddings like rich dark chocolate and mascarpone cheesecake or hot bilberry crèpe with blackcurrant sorbet (£3.50); they also offer a lighter menu with ciabatta bread with changing fillings (£2.80), insalata di mare (£3.75; main course £5), hot smoked chicken and caesar salad (£4.25; main course £6.50), and steak escalope with tomato and feta cheese salad (£5; main course £8); the restaurant is no smoking. Well kept Mansfield Original, Ruddles County, and Wadworths 6X on handpump kept under light blanket pressure, and a good wine list. The three simply furnished but smart interconnecting rooms have low beams and timbers, fresh flowers, and a pleasant light-coloured wood block floor. One room is primarily for eating, with pine settles and well spaced big pine tables, the others have smaller country tables and chairs – still with room for drinkers. Darts, cribbage, dominoes, and piped music. In a peaceful and attractive village, the pub is part of the Ardington estate; good walks nearby. *(Recommended by R C Watkins, Dr D Twyman, Gordon, R V G Brown)*

Free house ~ Licensee Mark Stott ~ Real ale ~ Meals and snacks (not Sun evening, not Mon) ~ Restaurant ~ (01235) 833254 ~ Well behaved children welcome ~ Open 11.30-2.30, 6-11; 12-3, 7-10.30 Sun; closed Mon

BAMPTON SP3013 Map 4

Romany £

Bridge St; off A4095 SW of Witney

In this area particularly, it would be hard to find better value meals (or cheaper beer) than those served in this 17th-c pub. The comfortable bars have plush cushioned windsor chairs and stools around wooden tables, foreign currency notes from all over the world, plates and prints on the partly stripped stone walls, and a winter open fire. Bar food includes sandwiches, soup (£1.75), pâté or whitebait (£1.95), ham and egg (£3.95), steak in ale pie (£4.35), and thai chicken curry or lamb rogan josh (£4.50); roast Sunday lunch. The restaurant is no smoking. Well kept Archers Village, Courage Directors, Donnington SBA, Hook Norton Best, and Marstons Pedigree handpumped from the Saxon cellars below the bar; cribbage, fruit machine, and piped music. The big garden has picnic-sets, Aunt Sally, and a children's play area with tree house, see-saw, and mushroom slide and house. *(Recommended by Stephen Brown, Marjorie and David Lamb, John Higgins, Anthony Barnes, Patrick Hancock, Tom McLean, Mrs Kay Neville-Rolfe, Derek and Sylvia Stephenson)*

Free house ~ Licensees Robert and Tessa Smith ~ Real ale ~ Meals and snacks (11.30-2.30, 6-9.30) ~ Restaurant ~ (01993) 850237 ~ Well behaved children welcome ~ Open 11-11; 12-10.30 Sun ~ Bedrooms: £22.50(£26B)/£39B

BANBURY SP4540 Map 4

Reindeer £

47 Parsons Street, off Market Place

Pretty in summer with its flowering baskets around the big sash windows, this nice old pub has a long front room with heavy 16th-c beams, very broad polished oak floorboards scattered with rugs, a magnificent carved overmantle for one of the two roaring log fires, and traditional solid furnishings. Ask to be shown the Globe Room – a beautifully proportioned room, where Cromwell held court before the Battle of Edgehill, with original gloriously carved 17th-c panelling. Well kept Hook Norton Best, Old, Mild, and Generation and a guest ale on handpump, country wines, 30 Irish whiskeys, good coffee, and even snuffs and clay pipes for the more adventurous. Lunchtime bar food (they tell us prices have not changed) includes doorstep or hot sandwiches (from £1.80), home-made chicken liver pâté (£2.80), bubble and squeak with ham, egg and baked beans (£3), filled baked potatoes (from £3), ploughman's (from £3.20), shepherd's pie (£3.30), steak in ale pie (£4.50), and daily specials; they do a Thursday OAP special. A smaller back room up steps is no smoking at lunchtime. Efficient cheerful service; unobtrusive piped music. The grey fluffy cat is called Cromwell and the tabby, Oliver. Small back courtyard with picnic-sets under parasols, and Aunt Sally; no under-21s (but see below). *(Recommended by Ted George, Charles Gysin, George Atkinson, Kevin and Penny McDonald; more reports please)*

Hook Norton ~ Tenants John and Hazel Milligan ~ Real ale ~ Lunchtime meals and snacks ~ (01295) 264031 ~ Children in Globe Room lunchtime only if eating ~ Open 11-11; closed Sun and 25 Dec

BARNARD GATE SP4010 Map 4

Boot

Village signposted off A40 E of Witney

Quite a few more boots have been added to the existing celebrities' collection in this attractive neatly kept pub. The decor is pleasant and civilised, with flowers on the good solid country tables and chairs, bare boards, and stout standing timbers and stub walls with latticed glass breaking up the main area; there's a huge log fire. Good, if not cheap, food might include sandwiches (from £2.95), soup (£3.25), grilled king prawns with dip and garlic bread (£3.95; main course £8.95), pasta with minute steak with pepper sauce (£8.95), stir-fry of mixed mushrooms (£9.95), steak and kidney pudding (£10.75), grilled fillet of salmon with caesar salad or thai chilli chicken curry (£10.95), Aberdeen Angus steak (£12.75), daily specials such as whole grilled lemon sole with lemon parsley butter (£12.50) and brochette of monkfish and king prawns (£12.95), puddings like sticky toffee pudding (£3.50), and children's menu (from £4.75); part of the restaurant is no smoking. Well kept Hook Norton Best and a guest beer on handpump, and decent wines. There are tables out in front of the stone-tiled stone pub, which despite being so handy for the A40 is out of earshot. *(Recommended by Michael Sargent, Maureen Hobbs, Peter and Audrey Dowsett, Stephen and Julie Brown, Simon Collett-Jones, H W Clayton, TRS, John and Hazel Waller, D G Hayman)*

Free house ~ Manager Jonathan Flint ~ Real ale ~ Meals and snacks ~ Restaurant ~ (01865) 881231 ~ Children welcome ~ Piano Mon, Weds, Fri evenings, Sun lunchtime ~ Open 11-3, 6-11; 12-3, 7-10.30 Sun; closed 26 Dec)

BINFIELD HEATH SU7478 Map 2

Bottle & Glass ★

Village signposted off A4155 at Shiplake; in village centre fork right immediately after Post Office (signposted Harpsden) and keep on for half mile

A pub for 287 years, this very pretty thatched and black and white timbered pub is 15th-c in parts and was probably three little farm cottages. The neatly kept low beamed bar has attractive flagstones, scrubbed, ancient tables, a bench built into black squared panelling, spindleback chairs, a fine fireplace, and a window with diamond-scratched family records of earlier landlords. The smaller, relaxed side room is similarly decorated. Written up on blackboards, the range of promptly served bar food might include lunchtime sandwiches and a good ploughman's, potted shrimps (£4.95), large mussels (£5.25), pasta with prawns in a cheese sauce (£5.95), smoked salmon salad (£6.75), steak in red wine with apricots (£7.75), roast English lamb or loin of pork with apple sauce and stuffing (£8.25), venison in red wine (£9.95), and home-made puddings; friendly staff. Well kept Brakspears Bitter, and seasonal Old or Special on handpump, and quite a few malt whiskies. The lovely big garden has old-fashioned wooden seats and tables under little thatched roofs (and an open-sided shed like a rustic pavilion). No children or dogs. *(Recommended by Chris Glasson, Mike and Heather Watson, Roger and Valerie Hill)*

Brakspears ~ Tenants Mike and Anne Robinson ~ Real ale ~ Meals and snacks (12-

1.45, 7-9.30; not Sun evening) ~ (01491) 575755 ~ Open 11-4, 6-11; 12-4, 7-10.30 Sun

BIX SU7285 Map 2

Fox

On A4130 Henley—Wallingford

To enjoy a quiet drink in a relaxed pubby atmosphere, it's best to come to this creeper-clad pub during the week – it does get busier at weekends. The cosy L-shaped lounge bar has panelling, beams, armchairs and settles making the most of the big log fires, and gleaming brasses. There's another log fire and some settles in the connecting wood-floored farmers' bar, with darts, dominoes and a fruit machine. Bar food includes sandwiches, filled baked potatoes (from £3.25), ploughman's (from £3.75), ham and eggs or ratatouille (£4.95), cheese and broccoli pasta bake (£5.50), bacon chop with parsley sauce (£5.75), and Sunday roast (£5.95). Well kept Brakspears Bitter and seasonal Old or Special on handpump, picnic-sets in the good-sized garden behind. The friendly dog is called Henry, and there's a much-used hitching rail for horses outside. No children. *(Recommended by Gerald Barnett, Jack Barnwell, Joan Olivier, Chris Glasson, Gordon Prince, Bill Ingham, TBB)*

Brakspears ~ Tenants Richard and Sue Willson ~ Real ale ~ Meals and snacks (not Mon) ~ (01491) 574134 ~ Open 11-3, 7-11; 12-3, 7-10.30 Sun; closed Mon and 25 Dec

BLEWBURY SU5385 Map 2

Red Lion

Take the lane with the tree in the middle; off the A417

No noisy games machines or music disturb the relaxed atmosphere in this pleasant village pub. The engaging beamed bar has upholstered wall benches and armed seats on its scrubbed quarry tiles, cupboards and miniature cabinets filled with ornaments, and foreign banknotes on the beams; in winter you can maybe roast chestnuts over the big open fire. Good bar food includes filled french bread (not Friday or Saturday evening or Sunday lunch), moules (£3.50), smoked salmon and smoked halibut salad (£4), chicken provençale or lemon sole (£7), sirloin steak with pepper sauce (£9.50), and pheasant (£10); the restaurant is no smoking. Well kept Brakspears Bitter, Old Ale and Special on handpump; attentive service, and dominoes. The extended garden has a terrace with quite a few seats and tables. *(Recommended by Richard Gibbs, TBB, Mary Walters; more reports please)*

Brakspears ~ Tenant Roger Smith ~ Real ale ~ Meals and snacks ~ Restaurant (weekends) ~ (01235) 850403 ~ Children in restaurant ~ Open 11-2.30(3 Sat), 6-11; 12-3, 7-10.30 Sun ~ Bedrooms: £25/£35

BLOXHAM SP4235 Map 4

Elephant & Castle £

Humber Street; off A361, fairly hndy for M40 junction 11

This is an imposing Cotswold village and this friendly pub has a relaxed and elegantly simple public bar with a striking 17th-c stone fireplace and a strip wood floor; the comfortable lounge is divided into two by a very thick wall, and has a good winter log fire in its massive fireplace, too; sensibly placed darts, dominoes, cribbage, fruit machine, and trivia, and shove-ha'penny on a hardy board they have been using for over a century. Good value straightforward lunchtime bar food includes sandwiches or filled french bread (from £1.30), sausage, eggs and beans (£3), and steak and kidney pie or vegetable or meaty lasagne (£3.50). Well kept and cheap Hook Norton Best, Old Hookey, Generation, summer Haymaker, Twelve Days, and Double Stout, Bulmers cider (guest ciders in summer), and around 30 malt whiskies. The flower-filled extended yard has Aunt Sally in summer and maybe weekend barbecues. *(Recommended by Jenny and Roger Huggins, Ted George, David Carr, Gordon)*

Hook Norton ~ Tenants Chas and Simon Finch ~ Real ale ~ Lunchtime meals and snacks (not Sun) ~ (01295) 720383 ~ Children welcome ~ Open 10-3, 6(5 Sat)-11; 12-10.30 Sun

BROADWELL SP2503 Map 4

Five Bells

Village signposted off A361 N of Lechlade, and off B4020 S of Carterton

In summer, the hanging baskets and flower tubs in front of this Cotswold stone inn are very pretty. Inside, the friendly hard-working licensees will make you most welcome, and the neatly kept series of well furnished rooms have a pleasant mix of flagstones and carpeting, low beams, antique pistols, and plates and rural pictures on the walls; big warming log fires. The sizeable dining room to the right of the lounge, and the small conservatory (both no smoking), overlook the spacious, attractive garden – where they play Aunt Sally, and grow some of the vegetables used in the kitchen. Enjoyable bar food includes sandwiches (from £1.50), soup (£2.25), stilton mushrooms (£3.50), ploughman's (£3.75), cajun prawns (£3.95), ham, egg and chips (£4.25), lamb kidneys in sherry sauce (£5.75), almond nut roast or chicken chasseur (£5.95), steak and kidney pudding (£6.25), honey-glazed lamb steak or swordfish (£6.50), sirloin steak (£8.95), puddings (£2.50), and Sunday lunch (£5.25); good vegetables in separate tureens. Well kept Hook Norton Best, Wadworths 6X, and a guest such as Hampshire Brewery King Alfred on handpump, and decent house wine. The public bar has darts. Wheelchair access. *(Recommended by Joan Olivier, Ted George, Marjorie and David Lamb, P and S White, Kay Neville-Rolfe, HNJ, PEJ, G W A Pearce)*

Free house ~ Licensees Trevor and Ann Cooper ~ Real ale ~ Meals and snacks (12-1.45, 7-9.15; not Mon) ~ Restaurant (not Mon) ~ (01367) 860076 ~ Children in restaurant; must be over 7 Sat evening ~ Open 11.30-2.30, 6.30-11; 12-3, 7-10.30 Sun; closed Mon except bank hol lunchtimes ~ Chalet bedrooms; /£45B

BUCKLAND SU3497 Map 4

Lamb

Village signposted off A420 NE of Faringdon

Sunday lunch at this smartly refurbished and extended 18th-c stone-built inn is clearly a regular treat for some people; on our summer visit, several customers left with a cheery 'See you next week'. Opening off a hallway, and divided in two by dark painted timbers, the neatly civilised little bar has plush blue furnishings, potted plants around the windows, and a few carefully chosen sheep and lamb pictures and models around the cream-painted walls – not to mention the carpet. On a piano are newspapers to read, and examples of their own chutneys and jams. The good food (restaurant quality as well as prices) might include sandwiches (weekdays only; from £2), soup (£3.25), hasenpeffer (a rich winter hare casserole, £12.25), fillet of roast lamb with cumin in a spicy tomato and coriander sauce (£15.95), and warm lobster, scallop and ginger salad with soy sauce (£16.95); the three-course Sunday lunch – with coffee and petit fours – is £19.25. Three well kept real ales such as Adnams Broadside, Bass and Wadworths 6X, a dozen or so wines by the glass, and carefully mixed Pimms or Bucks Fizz; very friendly service. There are a couple of white plastic tables on a terrace, and a good few wooden picnic-sets in the very pleasant tree-shaded garden. The village is pretty, with good walks nearby. *(Recommended by GL, J Tross, A C Morrison, Hugh Spottiswoode, Angus Lyon, Dr Irvine Loudon and others)*

Free house ~ Licensees Paul and Peta Barngard ~ Real ale ~ Meals and snacks ~ Restaurant ~ (01367) 870484 ~ Children welcome ~ Open 11-3, 5.30-11; 12-3, 7-11 Sun ~ Bedrooms: /from £35B

The symbol shows pubs which keep their beer unusually well or have a particularly good range.

BURCOT SU5695 Map 4

Chequers

A415 Dorchester—Abingdon

The friendly Weeks have been at this attractive black and white thatched pub for 20 years now. The smartly comfortable and surprisingly spacious lounge has beams, an open fire, a very relaxed and friendly atmosphere, and well kept Brakspears, Flowers IPA, and Wadworths 6X on handpump, with some good whiskies, unusual liqueurs, and a large collection of miniatures in display cabinets. Good enjoyable food is all home-made (they also bake all their own bread) and includes home-made soup (£2.75), big filled rolls (from £2.75), pepper, parsnip and blue cheese pasta or pork, lime and celery bake (£5.95), steak and kidney pudding (£6.25), lamb, bacon and apricot pie (£6.75), escalope of chicken in white wine and cream with a mushroom or stilton sauce (£8.25), sirloin steak (£8.95), and puddings like Mary's disaster cake or blueberry pudding with custard (£2.50); they will be starting a hearty monthly Sunday brunch. There are seats on the terrace (lit at night), lots of pretty pots, hanging baskets, and bedding plants, tables and chairs among roses and fruit trees on the neatly kept roadside lawn, and a vegetable patch at the lower end of the garden to grow their own salad and herb produce. They have their own decent little no-smoking art gallery. *(Recommended by Ian Phillips, Brad W Morley, Nicholas Holmes, Iain Robertson, B and K Hypher, Jenny and Brian Seller)*

Free house ~ Lease: Mary and Michael Weeks ~ Real ale ~ Meals and snacks (not Sun evening) ~ (01865) 407771 ~ Children in eating area of bar and in gallery ~ Grand piano Sat evenings ~ Open 11-2.30, 6-11; 12-3, 7-10.30 Sun

BURFORD SP2512 Map 4

Lamb ★ ★

Sheep Street; A40 W of Oxford

Oxfordshire Dining Pub of the Year

It isn't just the timeless and tranquil feel of this civilised 15th-c Cotswold stone inn that appeals to so many people, but the fact that the staff remain friendly and helpful even when under pressure, the beer is well kept, the bar food good, and it is an enjoyable place to stay. The spacious beamed main lounge has distinguished old seats including a chintzy high winged settle, ancient cushioned wooden armchairs, and seats built into its stone-mullioned windows, bunches of flowers on polished oak and elm tables, oriental rugs on the wide flagstones and polished oak floorboards, and a winter log fire under its fine mantlepiece. Also, a writing desk and grandfather clock, and attractive pictures, shelves of plates and other antique decorations. The public bar has high-backed settles and old chairs on flagstones in front of its fire. There may be nibbles on the bar counter, as well as good bar lunches such as sandwiches or filled french bread (from £2.50; roast lamb with mint mayonnaise £2.95), home-made soups like cream of asparagus (£3.25), ploughman's (£4.95), turban of sole and smoked scallops with dill mayonnaise (£5.25), sautéed chicken livers with crispy bacon or fresh herb pancake filled with seafood and leeks in a dijon mustard cream (£6.75), braised wild boar and apple sausages in marsala (£7.50), steak and mushroom pie or grilled gammon steak with apricot compote (£7.95), and puddings like lemon and nutmeg brûlée, chocolate and mint mousse or cherry and almond sponge pudding (£3.25); on Sundays there are proper roasts but no bar meals; the restful formal restaurant is no smoking. Well kept Adnams, Hook Norton Best and Wadworths 6X are dispensed from an antique handpump beer engine in a glassed-in cubicle; good wines. A pretty terrace leads down to small neatly-kept lawns surrounded by flowers, flowering shrubs and small trees, and the garden itself can be really sunny, enclosed as it is by the warm stone of the surrounding buildings. *(Recommended by Adam and Elizabeth Duff, Lynn Sharpless, Bob Eardley, James and Wendy Timms, Stephen Brown, C M F Redlich, E A and D C Frewer, P and S White, Walter Reid, Nigel Woolliscroft, Stephen and Julie Brown, Peter Neate, J H Jones, Gillian Jenkins, P M Millikin, Jackie Hammond, TBB, Simon Collett-Jones, Gordon, Peter Saville, Rona Murdoch, John and Chris Simpson, Paula Williams, Alan and Paula McCully, Pam Adsley, Rob Whittle, Liz Bell, Paul*

McPherson, John and Hazel Waller, James Nunns)

Free house ~ Licensee Richard de Wolf ~ Real ale ~ Lunchtime bar meals and snacks (not Sun) ~ Evening restaurant ~ (01993) 823155 ~ Children welcome ~ Open 11-2.30, 6-11; 12-3, 7-10.30 Sun; closed 25-26 Dec ~ Bedrooms: £57.50B/£100B

Mermaid

High St

Some parts of this bustling dining pub date back to the 14th c and it has a handsome Tudor-style frontage – the other High Street buildings are mainly 18th c. Inside, the attractive long and narrow bar has beams, polished flagstones, brocaded seats in bays around the single row of tables down one side, and pretty dried flowers. The inner end, with a figurehead over the fireplace and toby jugs hanging from the beams, is panelled, the rest has stripped stonework; there's an airy dining room and a no-smoking upstairs restaurant. Bar food is usefully served all day and might include soup (£3.25), filled french bread (from £3.75), filled baked potatoes (£4.95), omelettes (from £4.95), fish of the day (from £4.95), filled yorkshire puddings (£5.50), chicken curry (£5.95), a roast of the day (from £5.95), fish pie (£6.50), daily specials, children's menu (£3.95), puddings (from £3), and afternoon cream teas. Well kept Bass, Morlands Old Speckled Hen, and Ruddles on handpump; pool, fruit machine, and piped music. There are picnic-sets under cocktail parasols. *(Recommended by David and Nina Pugsley, Gordon, Stephen Brown, Liz Bell, Mr and Mrs N Spink)*

Morlands ~ Lease: John Titcombe ~ Real ale ~ Meals and snacks (noon-9.45pm) ~ Restaurant ~ (01993) 822193 ~ Children in restaurant ~ Parking may be difficult ~ Open 11-11; 12-10.30 Sun

CHALGROVE SU6396 Map 4

Red Lion

High St (B480 Watlington—Stadhampton)

The local church (which has some notable medieval wall paintings) has owned this charming pub since it first appeared in written records in 1637, and probably a good deal longer: some of the timbers date back to the 11th c. The decor is smartly modern and attractive with all the walls painted a crisp white which contrasts sharply with the simple dark furnishings, the windows have neatly chequered green curtains and fresh flowers, and there's an old woodburner and a log fire. Across from the fireplace is a painting of the landlady's aunt, and there are a few carefully collected prints and period cartoons; piped music, cribbage, and darts in the tiled public bar. There's quite an emphasis on the imaginative and very well presented bar food: sandwiches, soup (£2.75), garlic mushrooms with a herb topping (£3.40), dressed Cromer crab baked with garlic butter, cream and cheese (£5.50), roasted scallops tossed in chervil and garlic butter on dressed rocket (£5.95), tagliatelle with bacon, cream and stilton or steak, mushroom and ale pie (£6.95), lamb liver and bacon with caramelised onion gravy (£8.90), roasted half shoulder of lamb marinated in mint and hoisin sauce with a plum compote and rosemary jus (£9.90), game casserole with herb dumplings (£10.95), roasted cod fillet with a saffron bouillabaisse (£11.80), and home-made puddings (£3.25); potatoes usually come in a separate side dish. The helpful landlord will generally open a bottle of wine and buy back the remainder if you don't finish it. Well kept Brakspears, and Fullers London Pride and ESB on handpump; attentive individual service. The back dining room (sometimes used for functions) is no smoking. There's a good big replanted garden behind with a new pergola, quite a few seats, and play equipment, and picnic-sets in front, attractively floodlit at night. *(Recommended by Kevin Thorpe, Dick and Jan Chenery, Marjorie and David Lamb, Joan Olivier)*

Free house ~ Licensees Jonathan and Maggi Hewitt ~ Real ale ~ meals and snacks (not Sun evening) ~ Restaurant (not Sun evening) ~ (01865) 890625 ~ Well behaved children welcome ~ Open 12-3, 5.30(6 Fri, Sat, Sun)-11(10.30 Sun)

CHECKENDON SU6684 Map 2

Black Horse

Village signposted off A4074 Reading—Wallingford; coming from that direction, go straight through village towards Stoke Row, then turn left (the second turn left after the village church); OS Sheet 175 map reference 666841

Tucked away into woodland, this delightfully unpretentious country local is well liked by walkers. It has been in the same family for many decades and has a marvellously relaxed atmosphere, plus well kept Brakspears and a few local guests like Rebellion IPA and West Berkshire Good Old Boy tapped from casks in a back still room. The room with the bar counter has some tent pegs ranged above the fireplace, a reminder that they used to be made here; a homely side room has some splendidly unfashionable 1950s-look armchairs, and beyond that there's a third room. They'll usually do fresh filled rolls (from £1.25), and keep pickled eggs. There are seats out on a verandah and in the garden. *(Recommended by Pete Baker, JP, PP, Dr D E Granger, David Warrellow)*

Free house ~ Licensees Margaret and Martin Morgan ~ Real ale ~ Snacks ~ (01491) 680418 ~ Children welcome ~ Open 12-2(3.30 Sat), 7-11; 12-3.30, 7-10.30 Sun; cl evening 25 Dec

nr CHINNOR SU7698 Map 4

Sir Charles Napier 🍴 🍷

Spriggs Alley; from B4009 follow Bledlow Ridge sign from Chinnor; then, up beech wood hill, fork right (signposted Radnage and Sprigg Alley) then on right; OS Sheet 165 ref 763983

Don't be fooled by the inauspicious plain outside of this Cotswold pub. It's a decidedly civilised place that is not *quite* a restaurant as it does have the relaxed approach of a pub, and at quiet moments during the week you'll generally feel quite welcome coming for just a drink, particularly in the cosy and simply furnished little front bar. At other times you may find the whole place is virtually dedicated to the stylish back partly no-smoking restaurant, and there's little point coming at weekends unless you want to eat. This is definitely somewhere to come for a treat, and a typical day's bar menu might include goat's cheese mousse with olives (£6), seared tuna with lentil salsa (£6.50), crab cakes with lime, coriander and avocado salsa (£7), fried calf liver with balsamic vinegar and crème fraîche (£12.50), whole steamed Cornish crab with basil oil (£13.50), crispy Gressingham duck with soy, ginger and papaya salsa (£15.50), chargrilled rib-eye of beef with basil sauce (£16.50), puddings (£5.50), and English cheeses (£6.50); service is not included. Two-course set lunch (£15.50), and Sunday lunch is distinctly fashionable – in summer it's served in the crazy-paved back courtyard with rustic tables by an arbour of vines, honeysuckle and wisteria (lit at night by candles in terracotta lamps). An excellent range of drinks takes in well kept Wadworths 6X, IPA and Summersault tapped from the cask, champagne on draught, an enormous list of exceptionally well chosen wines by the bottle (and a good few half-bottles), freshly squeezed juice, Russian vodkas and quite a few malt whiskies. Piped music is well reproduced by the huge loudspeakers, and there's a good winter log fire. The croquet lawn and paddocks by the beech woods drop steeply away to the Chilterns, and there's a boules court out here too. *(Recommended by B R Sparkes, Dave Carter, Karen Eliot, Graham and Karen Oddey, KC; more reports please)*

Free house ~ Licensee Julie Griffiths ~ Real ale ~ Lunchtime bar meals (not Sat or Sun) ~ Restaurant ~ (01494) 483011 ~ Children welcome by prior arrangement only ~ Open 12-2, 6.30-11; 12-2 Sun; closed Sun evening and all day Mon

People named as recommenders after the main entries have told us that the pub should be included. But they have not written the report – we have, after anonymous on-the-spot inspection.

CHURCH ENSTONE SP3724 Map 4

Crown

From A44 take B4030 turn-off at Enstone

This cottagey Cotswold stone inn has a comfortable beamed bar with open fires, gleaming brasses, windsor chairs, local prints on the bare stone walls, and Hampshire Brewery King Alfred's, Hook Norton Best, and Wadworths 6X on handpump from the horseshoe-shaped bar; a good wine list with around nine by the glass. Popular bar food is served throughout the two bars and conservatory, and includes filled ciabatta bread or french sticks, home-made soup (£2.95), filled baked potatoes or bowl of chipolatas with mustard dip (£3.50), ploughman's (£3.75), campanelle with wild mushrooms (£4.95), steak and kidney pie or kashmiri lamb (£6.50), and puddings (£2.95). Cribbage, dominoes, and piped music. There are some white metal tables and chairs on a front terrace and more seats in the attractive back garden. Lots of nearby walks and the medieval church is worth a visit. *(Recommended by John Bowdler, Mike and Jennifer Marsh, Adam and Elizabeth Duff, Lynn Sharpless, Bob Eardley, Prof P A Reynolds, Tim Barrow, Sue Demont, Joan and John Fuller, Mike and Wena Stevenson, G Neighbour, Ted George, Marjorie and David Lamb, P and J Shapley, Sir Nigel Foulkes, Tony Dickinson, Eddie Edwards, Pam Adsley)*

Free house ~ Licensees Stephen Marnham and Keith Maby ~ Real ale ~ Meals and snacks (not 25 Dec) ~ Restaurant ~ (01608) 677262 ~ Children in conservatory and upper bar area ~ Open 12-3, 7-11(10.30 Sun) ~ Bedrooms: £30(£32B)/£42(£45B)

CLANFIELD SP2802 Map 4

Clanfield Tavern

A4095 5 miles S of Witney

As we went to press, new licensees had just taken over this pretty village inn. The busy main bar has several flagstoned, heavy-beamed and stone-walled small rooms leading off it, with a good mix of seats, brass platters, hunting prints, and a handsome open stone fireplace crowned with a 17th-c plasterwork panel. Well kept Courage Best, Hook Norton Best and John Smiths on handpump; there's a no-smoking conservatory that links the pub to a barn with a courtyard and fountain just outside it. Bar food includes sandwiches (from £3), chicken liver pâté (£3.25), deep-fried brie parcels with cranberry sauce (£3.75), ploughman's (£4.95), burgers with various toppings (£6.75), avocado and mushroom pancakes with a light mornay sauce (£6.95), king prawn tails with garlic, rosemary and wine (£8.50), daily specials such as confit of duck (£9.95) and monkfish in white wine (£14.25), and puddings such as lemon tart or banoffee pie (£3.25); the ices and sorbets are home-made. It's attractive in summer, with tiny windows peeping from the heavy stone-slabbed roof and tables on a flower-bordered small lawn that look across to the village green and pond. *(Recommended by Peter and Audrey Dowsett, Mike and Mary Carter, TRS, Liz Bell, Kay Neville-Rolfe, John and Hazel Waller, Maureen Hobbs, Gordon, Pat and Derek Westcott)*

Free house ~ Licensee Andron Ingle ~ Real ale ~ Meals and snacks (11.30-2, 6-10) ~ Cottagey restaurant ~ (01367) 810223 ~ Children welcome ~ Open 11.30-2.30(3 Sat), 6-11; 12-3, 7-10.30 Sun

CLIFTON SP4831 Map 4

Duke of Cumberlands Head

B4031 Deddington—Aynho

Five new ensuite bedrooms have been added to this friendly pub this year, a new kitchen will be ready by the time this Guide is published, a front porch is to be built, a disabled lavatory installed, and the bar and no-smoking restaurant have been redecorated. It's a stylish but relaxed place with a spacious, simply furnished lounge with a lovely log fireplace and well kept Adnams Southwold, Hampshire King Alfred's, Hook Norton Best, and Warden Brewery CHB on handpump, a good wine list, and 30 malt whiskies. Enjoyable bar food includes lunchtime sandwiches (not Sun), soup (£3.25), home-made smoked mackerel or duck liver pâté (from £3.75), deep-fried haddock or cod, steak and stout pie, pork in dijon sauce or wild mushroom stroganoff (small helping £4, big helping £7.50), chicken korma (small helping £4.50, big helping £8), salmon steak with a white wine and prawn sauce (£8.50), and puddings such as sticky toffee pudding, apple and raspberry crumble or honey and ginger cheesecake (£3.50); decent breakfasts. There are tables out in the garden, and the canal is a short walk away. *(Recommended by Prof P A Reynolds, E A and D C Frewer, Penny and Martin Fletcher, Richard Gibbs, Dave Braisted, Sir Nigel Foulkes, Joan Olivier, Simon Collett-Jones, John Bowdler)*

Free house ~ Licensee Nick Huntington ~ Real ale ~ Meals and snacks (not Sun evening, not winter Mon) ~ Restaurant (not Mon) ~ (01869) 338534 ~ Children welcome until 9pm ~ Open 12-2.30(3 Sat), 6-10.30(11 Sat); 12-3, 7-10.30 Sun; closed Mon ~ Bedrooms: £27.50/£42.50(£60B)

CLIFTON HAMPDEN SU5495 Map 4

Plough

On A415 at junction with Long Wittenham turn-off

The lack of piped music and games machines and the fact that this pub is totally no smoking, appeals to quite a few readers. It's run by a helpful and charming licensee, and the opened-up bar area has beams and panelling, black and red floor tiles, antique furniture, attractive pictures, and a friendly, relaxed atmosphere. It is very much a place people come to for a meal, with light dishes such as home-made soup (£3.95), seafood salad with lime, lemon and coriander (£5.25), spinach, tomato and tarragon roulade or grilled goat's cheese (£6.95), tagliatelle with bolognese sauce or chicken curry (£7.25), stir-fried beef with spring onion, ginger and bean sprouts (£8.75), grilled minute steak (£8.95), and home-made puddings like treacle tart or crème brûlée (£3.70); 2-course Sunday lunch (£10.95); the restaurant has an engaging portrait of the licensee and a much more comprensive menu. Well kept Courage Best and Directors, and John Smiths on handpump, plenty of good wines, and a dozen malt whiskies. Some tables and seats outside. Several of the bedrooms in the converted building across the courtyard have 4-poster beds. *(Recommended by TBB, Mrs J Burrows, JP, PP, Ian Phillips, Roger Huggins, Dave Irving, Ewan McCall, Tom McLean, Dr and Mrs A Newton, Kim Darnes, Dr and Mrs Mervyn Jaswon, Mrs I Folkard-Evans, Hazel and Michael Duncombe, Mike and Mary Carter)*

Courage ~ Lease: Yuksel Bektas ~ Real ale ~ Meals and snacks (served all day) ~ Restaurant ~ (01865) 407811 ~ Children welcome ~ Open 11-11 ~ Bedrooms: £55B/£75B

CUDDESDON SP5903 Map 4

Bat & Ball

S of Wheatley; if coming from M40 junction 7 via Gt Milton, turn towards Little Milton past church, then look out for signpost

Anyone interested in cricket would be interested in the decor here – every inch of wall-space is covered with cricketing programmes, photographs, porcelain models in well-lit cases, score books, cigarette cards, pads, gloves and hats, and signed bats, bails and balls. The immaculately kept L-shaped bar has beams and low ceilings, comfortable furnishings, a partly flagstoned floor, and a relaxed, friendly atmosphere. Under the new licensee, bar food includes home-made soup (£2.75), filled french sticks (from £3.95), gammon, egg and pineapple (£6.75), bangers and mash (£6.95), vegetarian dishes and pies, darne of salmon (£9.25), and fillet steak forestière (£12.50). The restaurant is no smoking. Well kept Marstons Pedigree and Original and a guest beer on handpump, and a decent wine list; cribbage, dominoes, and piped music. A very pleasant terrace at the back has seats, Aunt Sally, and good views over the Oxfordshire plain. *(Recommended by Dr T E Hothersall, James Chatfield, TBB, Miss A Aronica, Don Bryan, Mrs J Burrows; more reports on the new regime, please)*

Marstons ~ Tenant Tony Viney ~ Real ale ~ Meals and snacks ~ Restaurant ~ (01865) 874379 ~ Well behaved children in eating area of bar ~ Open 11-11; 12-10.30 Sun ~ Bedrooms: £39.95S/£49.95S

CUMNOR SP4603 Map 4

Bear & Ragged Staff

19 Appleton Road; village signposted from A420: follow one-way system into village, bear left into High St then left again into Appleton Road – signposted Eaton, Appleton

There's a decidedly civilised but relaxed atmosphere in this smart old place, and the comfortably rambling, softly lit bar has roaring log fires, easy chairs, sofas and more orthodox cushioned seats, and wall banquettes; one part has polished black flagstones, another a turkey carpet; the dining area of the bar is no smoking. Very good food includes home-made soup (£3.45), potted ham with parsley and piccalilli (£5.45), lunchtime sandwiches (from £5.45), seared Cornish scallops and tuna fish carpaccio (£7.95), fricassée of lamb livers, kidneys and sweetbreads with lamb cutlets and mustard sauce (£13.75), several fish dishes like hot bean salad with bass and a dark chilli glaze or breast of duck with fig tatin and five spices (£15), and puddings like summer pudding with seasonal sorbets (£5.50). Well kept Morrells Oxford Bitter, Graduate, and Varsity, and a changing guest beer on handpump, plus up to 10 wines by the glass from a good wine list. Service is pleasant and obliging. The building is named for the three-foot model of a Warwick heraldic bear which guards the large open fire. *(Recommended by TBB, D C amd E A Frewer, Dr D Twyman, TRS, Dr and Mrs A Whiteway, Mr and Mrs R Maggs, Roger Crisp, Tim Barrow, Sue Demont; more reports please)*

Morrells ~ Tenants Bruce and Kay Buchan ~ Real ale ~ Meals and snacks (till 10pm) ~ Restaurant ~ (01865) 862329 ~ Children in eating area of bar and in restaurant ~ Open 11.30-3, 5.30-11; 12-3, 7-10.30 Sun; closed several days between Christmas and New Year

CUXHAM SU4588 Map 2

Half Moon

4 miles from M40, junction 6; S on B4009, then right on to B480 at Watlington

Friendly new licensees have taken over this thatched and rather cottagey village pub, and reports from readers suggest that, happily, little has changed. The comfortable low-beamed bars have country-style furnishings, books and prints, an inglenook fireplace with winter log fires, and Brakspears Bitter and Special on handpump. Bar food now includes home-made soup (£2.75), home-made pâté (£3.50), breaded brie with cranberry sauce (£4.25), home-cooked ham and eggs (£5.95), lasagne (£6.95), chicken tikka masala with mint and cucumber relish (£7.25), rack of barbecued ribs (£9.95), sirloin steak (£10.95), vegetarian and fish dishes, and lunchtime filled baked potatoes and french bread. Darts, shove-ha'penny, table skittles, cribbage, and dominoes. There are seats sheltered by an oak tree on the back lawn, as well as a climbing frame and maybe summer barbecues. Across the road, a stream runs through this quiet village. *(Recommended by John and Kathleen Potter, Kevin Thorpe, Martin and Karen Wake, TBB, Maggie Washington, Helen Hazzard, James Waller, Marjorie and David Lamb)*

Brakspears ~ Tenants Robert West and Jane Webb ~ Real ale ~ Meals and snacks ~ (01491) 614110 ~ Children in family room ~ Open 12-2.30(3 winter Sat), 6-11; 12-11 summer Sat; 12-10.30 summer Sun; 12-8 winter Sun

DORCHESTER SU5794 Map 4

George

High St; village signposted just off A4074 Maidenhead—Oxford

First used as a brewhouse for the Norman abbey which still stands opposite, this lovely timber and tile house later flourished as a posting and then a coaching inn. There's lots of old-fashioned charm in the civilised beamed bar with its fresh flowers on the tables, roaring winter log fire, comfortable seats and fine old furniture (including cushioned settles and leather chairs), and copies of *Country Life*. Good bar food includes sandwiches, confit of guinea fowl on a warm green bean salad and truffle scented dressing (£5), risotto of roast peppers and red onion with pepper coulis and parmesan (£5.50), grilled chicken breast filled with a leek and basil mousse on herbed polenta cakes with sautéed shii-take mushrooms and soy jus (£11), peppered skate wing with roast cherry tomatoes and basil and balsamic dressing (£12), roast saddle of lamb with an apple and spinach stuffing, rosemary potatoes, and rosemary and redcurrant jus (£14.50); roast Sunday lunch (no bar food then). Well kept Brakspears Bitter and a guest beer on handpump, good wine by the glass from a quite exceptional wine list, and a range of malt whiskies. Pleasant and welcoming service. *(Recommended by Gordon, Peter Burton, Mike and Heather Watson, Sheila and John French)*

Free house ~ Licensees B Griffin and M Dinder ~ Real ale ~ Meals and snacks ~ Restaurant ~ (01865) 340404 ~ Children in restaurant only ~ Open 11.30-11(10.30 Sun) ~ Bedrooms: £62.50B/£80B

DUNS TEW SP4528 Map 4

White Horse

Off A4260 N of Kidlington

A good mix of locals and visitors enjoys this 16th-c beamed inn. The main part of the bar has simple wooden tables and chairs around rugs on the flagstoned floor, a pile of newspapers to read, and a big inglenook fireplace up by a side room used as an overflow for eating. Towards the terrace the low ceiling gives way to a carefully added raftered area. Under the new licensee, bar food includes sandwiches (from £2.75; filled french bread from £3.25), filled baked potatoes (from £2.95), ploughman's, steak in ale pie (£6.30), asparagus tortelli (£7.95), seafood mornay (£8.95), steaks (from £9.95), and puddings (£2.95); roast Sunday lunch. The smart little oak-panelled side restaurant is candlelit at night, and no smoking. Courage Best, Hook Norton Best, and Theakstons Best on handpump, and several malt whiskies; service is friendly and efficient. Darts and piped music. There are tables squeezed on to the little terrace behind the pub and they play Aunt Sally on Thursday evenings. The bedrooms are in a sympathetically converted stable block behind; they organise special golfing breaks. The country lanes around here are very pleasant. This is part of the Old English Pub Co chain. *(Recommended by Charles and Pauline Stride, Brian Smart, Martin Jones, Adam and Elizabeth Duff; more reports on the new regime, please)*

Free house ~ Licensee Richard Bailey ~ Real ale ~ Meals and snacks ~ Restaurant ~ (01869) 340272 ~ Children in eating area of bar and in restaurant ~ Folk/jazz/country music Weds evenings ~ Open 12-11; 12-3.30, 7-10.30 Sun ~ Bedrooms: £45B/£55B

EAST HENDRED SU4588 Map 2

Wheatsheaf Ῡ

Chapel Square; village signposted from A417

Set just below the downs, this attractive black and white timbered 16th-c village pub has a good mix of visitors and locals. The bar has been redecorated but still has high-backed settles and stools around tables on quarry tiles by an inglenook fireplace, some wall panelling, and a tiny parquet-floored triangular platform by the bar; low, stripped deal settles form booths around tables in a carpeted area up some broad steps. Food at the moment is very good: sandwiches or baps (from £1.70), home-made soup (£1.95), ham and egg (£4.50), fettucine with vegetables in a spinach sauce or chicken, ham and leek pie (£4.95), ploughman's (from £4.95), cumberland sausage with leek mash (£5.25), Asian pork with spring onions and ginger on egg noodles (£6.50), breast of chicken with mushroom sauce (£6.95), fillet steak with bacon and mushrooms in a red wine sauce (£9.95), and puddings such as fruit crumble, summer pudding or treacle and nut tart (£2.25). Well kept Morlands Original and Old Speckled Hen, and Ruddles County on handpump, and a decent wine list. Dominoes, cribbage and Aunt Sally teams, and piped music. The black labrador is called Bob and the springer spaniel, Harry. The garden behind is colourful with roses and other flowers beneath conifers and silver birch. The nearby church is interesting – its Tudor clock has elaborate chimes but no hands. *(Recommended by Ron and Barbara Watkins, Justin Hulford, John E Vigar, Steve Goodchild)*

Morlands ~ Tenant Neil Haywood ~ Real ale ~ Meals and snacks ~ Restaurant ~ (01235) 833229 ~ Children welcome ~ Open 11-11; 12-10.30 Sun

EXLADE STREET SU6582 Map 2

Highwayman

Signposted just off A4074 Reading—Wallingford

Some parts of this rambling inn are 14th c, though it's mostly 17th c, and the two beamed rooms of the bar have quite an unusual layout, with an interesting variety of seats around old tables and even recessed into a central sunken inglenook; an airy no-smoking conservatory dining room has more seats (mainly for eating) and overlooks the garden. Bar food includes sandwiches, home-made soup (£3.75), garlic mushrooms with bacon (£5.25), grilled sardines in garlic butter (£5.75), fresh penne with tomato concassé (£6.95), steak, Guinness and mushroom pie (£8.95), smoked haddock rarebit (£9.95), salmon fishcakes (£11.95), half roast duck and prune sauce or rack of lamb and parsnip mash (£13.95), steaks (from £13.95), puddings like toffee apple tart or sticky toffee pudding with fruit, and 3-course Sunday lunch (£13.95). Well kept Adnams Broadside, Brakspears, Fullers London Pride, Gibbs Mew Bishops Tipple, and a guest beer on handpump, several malt whiskies, decent wines, freshly squeezed orange juice, winter mulled wine, and summer Pimms; piped music. The friendly mongrel is called Gurty and the black and white spaniel, Saigon. The surrounding wooded countryside is lovely, and the attractive garden has tables and fine views. *(Recommended by Dick Brown, Roger and Valerie Hill, G Neighbour, JP, PP, Nicholas Holmes, Margaret Dyke, Maureen Hobbs, Gordon)*

Free house ~ Licensees Carole and Roger Shippey ~ Real ale ~ Meals and snacks (12-2.30, 6-10.30) ~ Restaurant ~ (01491) 682020 ~ Children in restaurant ~ Open 11-3, 6-11; 11-11 Sat; 12-10.30 Sun ~ Bedrooms: £50S/£60S

FINSTOCK SP3616 Map 4

Plough

The Bottom; just off B4022 N of Witney

Surrounded by attractive hilly scenery (plenty of good walks), this neatly kept thatched pub is a friendly and enjoyable place. The long, low-beamed rambling bar is comfortable and relaxed and nicely split up by partitions and alcoves, with an armchair by the open logburning stove in the massive stone inglenook, tiles up at the end by the servery (elsewhere is carpeted), and walls decorated with rosettes the licensees have won at Crufts and other doggy-related paraphernalia. Their llasl apso is called Jumbo, and other dogs are welcome in the garden (on a lead) and in the public bar. Good bar food includes sandwiches, and specials such as lamb cutlets with red onion sauce (£7.95), vegetable crèpes with double cream and mature cheddar (£8.45), good steak and kidney pudding, and chicken breast stuffed with cream cheese and stilton wrapped in puff pastry (£8.65). A comfortable low-beamed stripped-stone dining room is on the right. Adnams Bitter, Fullers London Pride, Greene King Abbot, Hook Norton Best, Marstons Pedigree, and Morlands Old Speckled Hen on handpump or tapped from the cask, and farm ciders (when they can get it). A separate games area has darts, bar billiards, and dominoes. There are tables (and Aunt Sally) in the good, sizeable garden and several rare specimen roses (heavily scented). *(Recommended by N Cobb, D Bryan, Mrs S Evans, Sandra Childress, H W Clayton, Nigel Clifton, Wayne Brindle, Liz Bell, Gill and Keith Croxton, John and Shirley Dyson, Mike and Mary Carter, W W Burke, H T Flaherty, Paul Barnett)*

Free house ~ Licensee Keith and Nigel Ewers ~ Real ale ~ Meals and snacks ~ Restaurant ~ (01993) 868333 ~ Children welcome ~ Open 12-2.30, 6-11; 12-11 Sat; 12-3.30; closed Sun evenings ~ One bedroom: £30B/£50B

Please keep sending us reports. We rely on readers for news of new discoveries, and particularly for news of changes – however slight – at the fully described pubs. No stamp needed: *The Good Pub Guide*, FREEPOST TN1569, Wadhurst, E Sussex TN5 7BR.

FYFIELD SU4298 Map 4

White Hart

In village, off A420 8 miles SW of Oxford

It's quite a surprise to find that this humble-looking building has an impressive medieval interior with soaring eaves, huge stone-flanked window embrasures, and an attractive carpeted upper gallery making up the main room – a grand hall rather than a traditional bar, though the atmosphere is informal and relaxed. A low-ceilinged side bar has an inglenook fireplace with a huge black urn hanging over the grate, and a framed history of the pub on the wall. The priests' room and barrel-vaulted cellar are dining areas – most of which are no smoking. Well kept Boddingtons, Fullers London Pride, Hook Norton Best, Theakstons Old Peculier, Wadworths 6X, and guest beers on handpump or tapped from the cask, Westons cider, and country wines. Good bar food includes lunchtime sandwiches, home-made soup (£2.75), home-made chicken liver pâté (£3.50), fried sardines (£3.95; main course £6.50), spicy cashew nut and vegetable stir fry (£6.25), steak, mushroom and Guinness pie (£6.50), chicken piri-piri (£6.95), steaks (from £9.50), half a roast duck with black cherry and orange sauce (£9.95), daily specials, and home-made puddings (£3.25); friendly, attentive service. Darts, shove-ha'penny, dominoes, cribbage, and piped music. A heavy wooden door leads out to the rambling, sheltered and flowery back lawn, which has a children's playground. *(Recommended by Sandra Childress, TBB, Tony and Joan Walker, Andy and Sarah Gillett, TBB, Ted George, D and D Savidge, W H Bruton, Roger Byrne, Wayne Brindle)*

Free house ~ Licensees John and Sherry Howard ~ Real ale ~ Meals and snacks (till 10pm) ~ Restaurant ~ (01865) 390585 ~ Children in eating area of bar ~ Open 11-3, 6-11; 12-3, 7-10.30 Sun; closed 25-26 Dec

HOOK NORTON SP3533 Map 4

Pear Tree

Village signposted off A361 SW of Banbury

As this is the brewery tap for Hook Norton (the brewery is barely 100 yards down the lane), they keep the full range of their ales on handpump: Hook Norton Best, Old Hookey, Generation, and Mild along with the seasonal Haymaker and Stout. The knocked together bar area has country-kitchen furniture on the nicely timbered floor, some long tables, a well-stocked magazine rack, and open fires; maybe locals drifting in with their dogs. Under the new licensee, bar food includes home-made soups, sandwiches, home-cooked ham and eggs or beef in ale casserole (£4.95), and thai red chicken curry (£5.50). The attractive, sizeable garden has plenty of seats, and Aunt Sally. *(Recommended by Robert Gomme, JP, PP, Tom Evans, Helen Pickering, James Owen, Penny and Martin Fletcher, John Bowdler, Ray Blake, Chris Raisin, Graham Doyle; more reports please)*

Hook Norton ~ Licensee J Sivyer ~ Real ale ~ Meals and snacks (not Sun or Tues evenings) ~ (01608) 737482 ~ Children welcome until 9pm ~ Open 11.30-2.30(4 Sat), 6-11; 12-4, 7-10.30 Sun ~ Bedrooms: £28S/£45S

nr HOOK NORTON SP3533 Map 4

Gate Hangs High 🍷

Banbury Rd; a mile N of village towards Sibford, at Banbury—Rollright crossroads

Really worth the effort to find it, this tucked away pub is quite a sight in summer with spectacular flowering tubs and wall baskets around the picnic-sets in front; at the back, the broad lawn with holly and apple trees has swings for children to play on and fine views. Inside, there's a warm welcome from the friendly licensee, and quite an emphasis on the popular, weekly changing food: sandwiches, home-made fresh asparagus soup (£2.50), stilton and walnut pâté (£3.95), beef in red wine (£6.75), fresh smoked haddock in lemon butter (£6.95), home-cooked ham and asparagus with cheese sauce (£7.95), chicken breast wrapped in bacon with sausage stuffing (£8.75), barbary duck breast with cranberry and orange sauce (£9.25), venison medallions with port and stilton sauce (£9.95), and home-made puddings (£2.95). The bar has joists in the long, low ceiling, a brick bar counter, stools and assorted chairs on the carpet, and a gleaming copper hood over the hearth in the inglenook fireplace. Well kept Hook Norton Best, Old Hookey, Haymaker, and Twelve Days on handpump, a good wine list, and a range of malt whiskies; dominoes. Five miles south-west of the pub are the Bronze Age Rollright Stones – said to be a king and his army who were turned to stone by a witch. *(Recommended by M and C Starling, Sue and Steve Griffiths, Marjorie and David Lamb, Hugh Spottiswoode, E A George, Chris Raisin, Graham Doyle, Sir Nigel Foulkes, John Bowdler)*

Hook Norton ~ Tenant Stuart Rust ~ Real ale ~ Meals and snacks (not Sun evening) ~ Restaurant (not Sun evening) ~ (01608) 737387 ~ Children in eating area of bar and in restaurant ~ Open 11.30-3, 6.30-11; 12-3, 7-10.30 Sun; closed 25 Dec

KELMSCOT SU2499 Map 4

Plough

NW of Faringdon, off A417 or A4095

As this pretty pub is minutes from the Thames and the Thames Path is so popular, walkers are fond of dropping in here for a drink or a meal; the pub is also on the Oxfordshire cycleway and has both fresh and coarse fishing available locally. There are moorings for boats, too, and the attractive garden has seats amongst the unusual flowers. Inside, the small traditional front bar has ancient flagstones and stripped stone walls, and a relaxed chatty atmosphere, and there's also a larger cheerfully carpeted lounge bar with interesting prints on the walls, and a second lounge (which has been the restaurant); dogs are allowed in the public bar (where there is satellite TV for sport). The licensee is happy to offer advice on local walks. A wide choice of home-cooked food includes sandwiches (from £2.50; toasties from £3, filled french bread from £3.50), soup (£2.50), filled baked potatoes (from £3.75), ploughman's (from £4.50), ham and egg (£4.95), filled pancakes (from £5.95), beef and Guinness pie (£6.95), daily specials like chicken in calvados and cream sauce, lamb kidneys in madeira sauce, and plenty of fish like bass, sea bream, swordfish, and shrimp creole, steaks, and home-made puddings like chocolate sponge with chocolate sauce, fruit fool and toasted bananas with butterscotch sauce (from £3). On Sunday they only serve snacks and a roast. Well kept Morlands Original and Ruddles Best on handpump; darts, shove-ha'penny, cribbage, dominoes, fruit machine, trivia, and piped music. *(Recommended by Edward Leetham, Peter and Audrey Dowsett, Ted George, Jenny and Roger Huggins, J and P Maloney, Peter Neate)*

Free house ~ Licensees Trevor and Anne Pardoe ~ Real ale ~ Meals and snacks (not Sun evenings Jan-Easter) ~ (01367) 253543 ~ Children in eating area of bar until 9pm ~ Live music Sat evening ~ Open 12-11; 12-3, 7-10.30 Sun; closed Sun evenings Jan/Feb ~ Bedrooms: £30B/£50B – no accomm 24-30 Dec

KINGSTON LISLE SU3287 Map 4

Blowing Stone 🍷

Village signposted off B4507 W of Wantage

The licensees at this comfortable brick-built dining pub have a background in well regarded restaurants, so it's no surprise to find the meals here imaginative and carefully prepared – readers rate them very highly indeed. It takes its name from a stone pierced with holes on the edge of the village, said to have been used by King Alfred as a horn to summon his troops (your Editor as a teenager used to be able to make a tremendous blast on it). Popular with locals as well as visiting diners, the brightly modernised bar has quite a light, fresh feel thanks to the orange-painted walls, as well as simple wooden tables and red-cushioned chairs on the neatly polished red-tiled floor; next to the fireplace is a table with newspapers, graced on our last visit by a striking display of flowers. A little room leading off is filled by its pool table, while over towards the restaurant and conservatory are a comfortable lounge, and a small area with a piano – unusually for a pub, it's in tune. Bar meals might include mushroom and coriander soup (£3), baked cheese soufflé with tomato and artichoke salad (£5.50), pork and apple sausages (£6.50), filo parcels of spinach, feta cheese and garlic with warm tomato and basil vinaigrette (£6.95), grilled chicken breast with mushroom and bacon tagliatelle (£9.50), and monkfish with a parsley crust and braised lentils (£11.50); good Sunday lunches (main course £8, three courses £14.50). Food service can stop promptly. Bass, Morlands Original and a seasonal guest on handpump, several malt whiskies, and a very good choice of wines – they import their own (some are available off-sale). A few tables behind look over a pond with koi and goldfish, and maybe the peacock who regularly visits from his home in the pleasant village. Handy for Uffington Castle hill fort and the other ancient sites up on the downs above the village. We haven't yet heard from readers about this aspect, but would expect this to be a good place to stay. *(Recommended by Robert Tapsfield, F J Willy, Dr Irvine Loudon, Michael Sargent, Mr and Mrs J Chaffe, Lynn Sharpless, Bob Eardley, HNJ, PEJ)*

Free house ~ Licensees Charles and Carol Trevor-Roper ~ Real ale ~ Meals and snacks (12.30-2.15, 7.30-9.30; no food Mon – exc bank holidays – or Sun eves) ~ Restaurant ~ (01367) 820288 ~ Children welcome ~ Open 11.30-3, 6.30-11; 12-3, 7-11 Sun; closed Mon lunch (exc bank holidays) ~ Bedrooms: /£60B

LEWKNOR SU7198 Map 4

Olde Leathern Bottel

Under a mile from M40 junction 6; just off B4009 towards Watlington

In a charming village, this neatly kept pub has a good bustling atmosphere and a warm welcome from the new licensee. The two rooms of the bar have heavy beams in the low ceilings, rustic furnishings, open fires, and an understated decor of old beer taps and the like; the no-smoking family room is separated only by standing timbers, so you don't feel cut off from the rest of the pub. Popular and generously served bar food includes lunchtime sandwiches and snacks as well as penne with mozzarella and tomato or beef in ale pie (£5.95), good fresh haddock and mussels in cream sauce, large salads, spare ribs in barbecue sauce (£6.95), steaks (from £8.95), and puddings like treacle tart or cheesecake; quick, obliging service. Well kept Brakspears Bitter, SB and winter Old on handpump; dominoes and piped music. There are tables on the sizeable lawn alongside the car park. *(Recommended by Kevin Thorpe, Gordon, B R Sparkes, Mr and Mrs C Moncreiffe, Karen Eliot, Paula Williams, Elizabeth and Klaus Leist, M Mason, D Thompson, Hazel and Michael Duncombe, Phyl and Jack Street, Neville Kenyon, Mr C Crichton, TBB)*

Brakpears ~ Tenant L S Gordon ~ Real ale ~ Meals and snacks (till 10pm Fri/Sat) ~ (01844) 351482 ~ Children in eating areas and in family room ~ Open 11-2.30(3 Sat), 6-11; 12-3, 7-10.30 Sun

MAIDENSGROVE SU7288 Map 2

Five Horseshoes

W of village, which is signposted from B480 and B481; OS Sheet 175, map reference 711890

In summer, this popular pub is an especially nice place to be – there are lovely views from the sheltered back garden (which also has a rockery and some interesting water features), and they have an outside bar where summer barbecues are held serving tuna, shark, half shoulder of lamb, cumberland sausages and so forth with a choice of at least 12 different salads. The rambling bar is furnished with mostly modern wheelback chairs around stripped wooden tables (though there are some attractive older seats and a big baluster-leg table), and has a good log fire in winter; the low ceiling in the main area is covered in bank notes from all over the world, mainly donated by customers. There's also a separate bar for walkers where boots are welcome – plenty of surrounding walks – and a partly no-smoking dining conservatory (booking is pretty much essential in here at weekends). Quite an emphasis is placed on the good bar food with dishes like home-made soup (£3.25), chicken liver parfait with home-made fruit chutney (£5.25), grilled goat's cheese on chargrilled sweet peppers with toasted pine nuts and lemon dressing (£6.50), carpaccio of tuna (£6.95), steak and kidney pie (£7.95), salmon and crab cakes with piquant tomato sauce (£8.95), braised knuckle of parma ham finished with herbs and honey (£9.95), chargrilled calf liver with sage butter (£11.50), roast tail of monkfish with caramelised shallots (£13.50), and steaks (from £14); they also do a winter set three-course menu (£12.50). Well kept Brakspears Bitter, Special and seasonal ales on handpump, and a dozen wines by the glass. *(Recommended by Michael Bourdeaux, Mark Percy, Lesley Mayoh, Michael Sargent, R C Morgan, Gerald Barnett, Gordon, David Burgner, Graham and Karen Oddey, John Dickson)*

Brakspears ~ Tenant Graham Cromack ~ Real ale ~ Meals and snacks ~ Conservatory restaurant ~ (01491) 641282 ~ Children in eating area of bar and in restaurant ~ Open 11.30-2.30, 6.30-11; 12-3, 7-10.30 Sun; closed 25 Dec

MURCOTT SP5815 Map 4

Nut Tree ♀

Off B4027 NE of Oxford, via Islip and Charlton on Otmoor

Neatly thatched and pretty in summer with its hanging baskets and tubs, this is a fine pub with a good friendly atmosphere and welcoming landlord. The civilised beamed lounge has a long polished bar with brasses, antiques and pictures all round, fresh flowers on its tables (set for food), and a winter log fire; there's also a small back partly no-smoking conservatory-style restaurant. Good bar food includes soup (£2.75), sandwiches (from £3.50), garlic mushrooms (£3.95), ploughman's or ham and egg (£4.95), vegetarian moussaka or fresh cod (£6.50), cajun chicken (£8.50), calf liver and bacon (£9.50), rack of lamb (£9.95), steaks (from £10.50), duck breast with madeira sauce (£10.50), daily specials, and puddings (£3.50) or good cheeses (£4). Well kept Hook Norton Best and Morrells Oxford, and guests like Wychwood Hobgoblin on handpump, a fair number of malt whiskies, and a decent range of wines with several by the glass. Darts, shove-ha'penny, cribbage, dominoes, and frequent Sunday quiz nights. There are usually ducks on a front pond, and plenty of animals such as donkeys, peacocks and rabbits; also Aunt Sally, and an unusual collection of ten gargoyles, each loosely modelled on one of the local characters, and carved into a magnificently grotesque form from a different wood. Nine of them hang in the walnut tree and one from a pillar overlooking the well. The pub is handy for walks through the boggy Otmoor wilderness. Roundhead soldiers came here extensively when Cromwell had his headquarters at nearby Boarstall. *(Recommended by Keith and Margaret Kettwell, Steve and Sarah de Mellow, Ted George, NWN, Michael Sargent, John McDonald, Ann Bond, Derek and Sylvia Stephenson, D S and A R Hare, Gordon, Marjorie and David Lamb, D and J McMillan)*

Free house ~ Licensee Gordon Evans ~ Real ale ~ Meals and snacks (not Sun) ~ Restaurant ~ (01865) 331253 ~ Children in conservatory (not Sun evenings) ~ Open 11-3, 6.30-11; 12-3, 7-10.30 Sun

OXFORD SP5016 Map 4

Kings Arms £

40 Holywell St

There's always a good mix of students and visitors in this bustling 16th-c pub – but staff remain friendly and efficient even when really pushed. There's a big rather bare main room, with a no-smoking coffee room just inside the Parks Road entrance, and several cosy and comfortably worn-in side and back rooms, each with a different character and customers. An extra back room has a sofa and more tables and there's a tiny room behind that. They still keep a dictionary for the crossword buffs in the Dons Bar, with its elderly furnishings and tiled floor; fruit machine and video game. There's a mix of old prints and photographs of customers, and sympathetic lighting. Well kept Youngs Bitter, Special and seasonal ales and Wadworths 6X on handpump, a good choice of wines with 18 by the glass, 20 malt whiskies, and decent bar food such as sandwiches (from £1.75), home-made soup (£1.95), filled baked potatoes (from £2.95), six types of greasy spoon dishes (£3.50), a large slice of crusty loaf with various toppings (£3.95), spinach and mushroom lasagne (£4.50), and steak and mushroom pie (£5.25); on Sundays they open at 10.30 for breakfast and coffee; daily papers, tables out on the pavement. *(Recommended by Robert Gomme, Walter Reid, TBB,*

Stephen and Julie Brown, Anthony Barnes, SLC, Christopher Gallop, Gordon, James Nunns, John and Hazel Waller, J and P Maloney)

Youngs ~ Manager David Kyffin ~ Real ale ~ Meals and snacks (11.30-3, 5.30-9) ~ (01865) 242369 ~ Children welcome ~ Open 10.30-11; 12-10.30 Sun; closed 25-26 Dec

Turf Tavern

Bath Place; via St Helen's Passage, between Holywell Street and New College Lane

To get to this small pub, you have to stroll down little passageways and alleys and it feels a million miles from the bustle of the city. There's a cheerful atmosphere and a cosy feel in the two little rooms with their dark beams and low ceilings, which are much as Hardy described them when Jude the Obscure discovered that Arabella the barmaid was the wife who'd left him years before; there's also a bar in one of the courtyards. A changing range of real ales might include Archers Golden, Boddingtons, Morlands Old Speckled Hen, Whitbreads The Abroad Cooper, and nine guest beers on handpump; also, Belgian beers, a few country wines and a couple of farm ciders; video game. Straightforward bar food includes doorstep sandwiches (from £2.75), filled baked potatoes (from £2.90), basket meals (from £2.95), a vegetarian dish (£4.95), and steak in ale pie (£5.25); the top food area is no smoking. This is a pretty place – especially in summer, when there are tables in the three attractive walled-in flagstoned or gravelled courtyards around the old-fashioned building; in winter you can huddle around the braziers in the courtyard. *(Recommended by Tony Scott, TBB, Nigel Woolliscroft, Liz, Wendy and Ian Phillips, Stephen and Julie Brown, Lawrence Pearse, R J Bland, Giles Francis, Brad W Morley, A C Morrison, Mark Percy, Lesley Mayoh, Rona Murdoch, Gordon, Tony Scott, Tony Dickinson, Dr and Mrs A Whiteway, Hazel and Michael Duncombe, D Voller, Simon Penny, Ian and Villy White, John Hill, Simon Ludlow)*

Whitbreads ~ Manager Trevor Walter ~ Real ale ~ Meals and snacks (noon-8pm; 12-3, 6-8 in winter) ~ (01865) 243235 ~ Children allowed away from bar areas ~ No nearby parking ~ Open 11-11; 12-10.30 Sun

RAMSDEN SP3515 Map 4

Royal Oak

Village signposted off B4022 Witney—Charlbury

Whilst there's quite an emphasis on the good, popular food in this busy village inn, they have a fine choice of well kept real ales on handpump, too: Archers Golden, Arkells Kingsdown, Fullers London Pride, Goff's White Knight, and Hook Norton Best and Old Hookey. Enjoyable house wines. Served by helpful staff, the bar food might include home-made soup (£2.75), chicken, liver and cointreau pâté (£3.25), lunchtime sandwiches (from £3.95; not Sunday), a pie of the week, chicken tikka masala or lasagne (£5.75), home-made burgers (from £5.75), stilton, leek and mushroom puff (£7.75), game casserole (£7.95), steaks (from £9.25), daily specials like sausage, mash and onion gravy (£5.45), fresh crab and smoked salmon fishcakes (£9.25), and half shoulder of lamb with sage and cider sauce (£10.95), and puddings; on Thursday evenings they offer a steak, pudding and glass of wine special (£10.95); roast Sunday lunch (no snacks then). The traditional beamed bar is simply furnished and decorated but comfortable, and has fresh flowers, and a cheery winter log fire. The evening dining room is no smoking. The cosy bedrooms are in separate cottages. *(Recommended by Peter and Audrey Dowsett, George Atkinson, Paul and Ursula Randall, Mike and Mary Carter, Ronald Harry, M G Hart, M S Catling, Roger Crisp)*

Free house ~ Licensee Jon Oldham ~ Real ale ~ Meals and snacks (till 10pm) ~ Restaurant ~ (01993) 868213 ~ Children in eating area of bar and in restaurant ~ Open 11.30-2.30, 6.30-11; 12-3, 7-10.30 Sun ~ Bedrooms: £30B/£45B

If we don't specify bar meal times for a main entry, these are normally 12-2 and 7-9; we do show times if they are markedly different.

ROKE SU6293 Map 2

Home Sweet Home

Village signposted off B4009 Benson—Watlington

Rather smart and pleasantly old-fashioned, this picturesque pub has a welcoming, relaxed feel in the two smallish rooms of the bar. There are heavy stripped beams, leather armed chairs on the bare boards, a great high-backed settle with a hefty slab of a rustic table in front of it, a few horsey or game pictures such as a nice Thorburn print of snipe on the stone walls, and a big log fire. On the right, a carpeted room with low settees and armchairs and an attractive corner glass cupboard leads through to the restaurant. Good bar food includes sandwiches, fresh cod in beer batter (£6.25), warm crab and saffron tart or crispy prawn and cream cheese mushrooms (£6.95), fresh salmon fishcakes or steak and kidney pudding (£7.25), calf liver with crispy bacon (£8.25), and chicken with gorgonzola (£8.95). Well kept Brakspears Bitter and Hardy Royal Oak on handpump, and a good choice of malt whiskies. The low-walled front garden is ideal for eating on a sunny day; there are lots of flowers around the tables out by the well. *(Recommended by Marjorie and David Lamb, Kevin Thorpe, B R Sparkes, Dr Ian Crichton, Adam and Elizabeth Duff, John and Hazel Waller)*

Free house ~ Licensees Jill Madle, Peter and Irene Mountford ~ Real ale ~ Meals and snacks ~ Restaurant ~ (01491) 838249 ~ Well behaved children welcome ~ Open 11-3, 6-11; 12-3, 7-10.30 Sun; closed 25 and 26 Dec

SHENINGTON SP3742 Map 4

Bell

Village signposted from A422 W of Banbury

If you enter this 17th-c pub through the door marked 'restaurant' you come into the heavy-beamed and carpeted lounge with its cushioned wall and window seats, vases of flowers on the tables, and horsebrasses and an old document on the cream walls; the wall in the flagstoned area on the left is stripped to stone and decorated with heavy-horse harness, and the right side opens into a little pine-panelled room (popular with locals) with decorated plates; darts, cribbage, dominoes, coal fire. Decent bar food includes sandwiches, terrine of four cheeses (£3.25), mushrooms in cream, garlic and brandy (£5.75), pork with apple, cider and herbs (£7.25), lamb and mint casserole (£7.50), salmon with watercress sauce (£7.95), and duck in a port and black cherry sauce (£8.95). Well kept Boddingtons and Hook Norton Best on handpump. There's a west highland terrier, Lucy and a labrador, Daisy. The tables at the front look across to the green. *(Recommended by John Bowdler, M and C Starling, J H Kane, Maysie Thompson, R Watkins, Sir Nigel Foulkes, Mr and Mrs C Moncreiffe, Sharon Hancock, Suzanne and John Jones, Mr and Mrs Vancourt Carlyle-Lyon, John Read, Tony Ingham)*

Free house ~ Licensee Jennifer Dixon ~ Real ale ~ Meals and snacks ~ (01295) 670274 ~ Children in eating area of bar ~ Open 12-3, 6.30-11; 12-4, 7-10.30 Sun ~ Bedrooms: £20/£40B

SHIPTON UNDER WYCHWOOD SP2717 Map 4

Lamb 🍷 🛏

Just off A361 to Burford

This civilised old place has a relaxed beamed bar with a fine oak-panelled settle, a nice mix of solid old farmhouse-style and captain's chairs on the wood-block floor, polished tables, cushioned bar stools, an oak bar counter, pictures on old partly bared stone walls, newspapers on rods to read, and an open fire. Under the new licensees bar food now includes home-made soup (£2.95), home-made terrines (from £3.95), grilled goat's cheese with olives and cherry tomatoes (£4.50), a lunchtime buffet (from £7.50; not Sunday), baked cod with tomatoes and cream (£7.95), fillet of pork with stilton and brandy sauce (£8.95), supreme of chicken with leeks and bacon (£9.95), venison steak in port (£11.50), fillet steak with horseradish butter (£14.95), and puddings like banoffee pie or home-made apple pie (£3.75). The restaurant is no smoking; best to reserve a table at weekends. Well kept Hook Norton Best and Marstons Pedigree on handpump, several malt whiskies, and a good wine list (champagne by the glass). The garden has been extended this year, and the bedrooms have been redecorated. This is part of the Old English Pub Co chain. *(Recommended by Catherine Pocock, Walter Reid, Maysie Thompson, A Sutton, Stephen and Tracey Groves, J H Kane, Sandra Childress, S H Godsell, Jackie Hammond, T L Rees, Liz Bell, Scott Antel, M A and C R Starling, Pam Adsley, Mrs Jean Dundas, Michael Kirby, H T Flaherty, John Bowdler, BHP, M S Catling; more reports on the new regime, please)*

Free house ~ Managers Michael and Marnie Frith ~ Real ale ~ Meals and snacks ~ Restaurant ~ (01993) 830465 ~ Children welcome ~ Open 11-3, 6-11; 12-2.30, 7-10.30 Sun ~ Bedrooms: £65B/£75B

Shaven Crown

Little has changed in the medieval courtyard garden behind this grand old place since it was used as an exercise yard by monks – originally, this was a hospice for the monastery of Bruern in the 14th c. There are old-fashioned seats set out on the stone cobbles and crazy paving, with a view of the lily pool and roses; the pub has its own bowling green. Inside, there's a magnificent double-collar-braced hall roof, lofty beams and a sweeping double stairway down the stone wall, and the beamed bar has a relief of the 1146 Battle of Evesham, as well as seats forming little stalls around the tables and upholstered benches built into the walls. Bar food includes sandwiches, soup (£2.65), smoked salmon mousse with oatcakes (£3.50), ploughman's (£4.75), aubergine lasagne (£5), venison sausages in red wine or Scottish salmon fishcakes with a rich tomato sauce (£6.25), lamb cutlets (£6.90), and sirloin steak or roasted leg of English lamb (£8.95); children's helpings, and Sunday lunch. The restaurant is no smoking. Well kept Adnams, Benskins, and Hook Norton Best on handpump; shove-ha'penny, dominoes and cribbage. *(Recommended by Sue and Steve Griffiths, Sidney and Erna Wells, Gordon, Marjorie and David Lamb, Pam Adsley, John Bowdler, Dr S P Willavoys, George Atkinson, Colin and Sarah Pugh, A J Carter)*

Free house ~ Licensees Robert and Jane Burpitt ~ Real ale ~ Meals and snacks (not Dec 25) ~ Restaurant ~ (01993) 830330 ~ Children welcome ~ Open 12-2.30, 5-11; 12-11 Sat; 12-10.30 Sun; closed 25-26 Dec ~ Bedrooms: £40(£53B)/£82B

SOUTH STOKE SU5983 Map 2

Perch & Pike

Off B4009 2 miles N of Goring

There's quite an emphasis on the good interesting food in this friendly little brick and flint building. From the lunchtime menu there might be sandwiches (from £3.50), ploughman's, chargrilled ham with sliced avocado on french bread (£5.95), sliced smoked salmon on cream cheese and date (£6.25), and fresh dressed crab salad (£10.95); also, from their seasonal changing menu, home-made soup (£3.50), tart of goat's cheese and spinach (£5.25), fresh anchovies, chargrilled bacon and chopped egg on poached leeks (£5.75), mediterranean tart with chargrilled vegetables and mozzarella (£9.50), beef and mushroom casserole with port and Guinness (£9.75), roast baby chicken with a tarragon, garlic and lemon stuffing (£10.50), chargrilled Aberdeen Angus steaks (from £12.95), roast honey glazed duck breast with a kumquat and chilli marmalade (£14.50), and puddings like sticky toffee pudding, raspberry and chocolate roulade and banana and toffee crème brûlée (from £3.95). Diners have linen table napkins in old napkin rings and bone-handled cutlery gleaned from antique markets. Well kept Brakspears Bitter and Special on handpump, and a good wine list with quite a few by the glass served from the old oak bar counter. The relaxing bar has comfortable seats, open fires, and a nice assortment of tables; half the pub is no smoking. The window boxes are pretty, there are seats out on the large flower-bordered lawn, and more on a new Cotswold stone terrace. The Thames is just a field away. *(Recommended by T R and B C Jenkins, TBB, JP, PP, Herbert and Susan Verity, Sarah Bemrose)*

Brakspears ~ Tenants Michael and Jill Robinson ~ Real ale ~ Meals and snacks (not Sun evening) ~ (01491) 872415 ~ Children in eating area of bar only ~ Open 12-2.30, 6-11; 12-3 Sun; closed Sun evening, 25-26 Dec

STANTON ST JOHN SP5709 Map 4

Star

Pub signposted off B4027; village is signposted off A40 heading E of Oxford (heading W, you have to go to the Oxford ring-road roundabout and take unclassified road signposted to Stanton St John, Forest Hill etc); bear right at church in village centre

New licensees have taken over this popular country pub, and early reports from readers have been most favourable. There's a well refurbished extension on a level with the car park which has rugs on flagstones, pairs of bookshelves on each side of an attractive inglenook fireplace, old-fashioned dining chairs, an interesting mix of dark oak and elm tables, shelves of good pewter, terracotta-coloured walls with a portrait in oils, and a stuffed ermine; down a flight of stairs are little low-beamed rooms – one has ancient brick flooring tiles and the other quite close-set tables. Good bar food includes sandwiches (£1.95), home-made soup (£2.40), ploughman's (£3.95), home-made quiche (£5.50), gammon and pineapple (£7.50), fresh salmon steak (£7.45), daily specials such as broccoli and mushroom quiche (£5.50), spinach and mushroom strudel with basil sauce or beef in Guinness or cheesy tuna bake (£5.95), salmon and asparagus pie (£6.25), lamb shank in redcurrant and rosemary (£7.95), and lots of puddings (£2.95). Well kept Wadworths IPA, Farmers Glory, 6X and Summersault, and a guest such as Badger Tanglefoot on handpump, and country wines. The family room is no smoking. The walled garden has new seats among the rockeries, and upgraded children's play equipment. *(Recommended by Robert Gomme, R T and J C Moggridge, Paul and Sarah Gayler, TBB, David Lamb, Joan Olivier, Maureen Hobbs)*

Wadworths ~ Managers Michael and Maria Urwin ~ Real ale ~ Meals and snacks (11-2.30, 6.30-10) ~ (01865) 351277 ~ Children in eating area of bar and in family room ~ 11-2.30, 6.30-11; 12-2.30, 7-10.30 Sun

Talk House 🍷 🛏

Wheatley Road (B4027 just outside village)

It takes a lot of people to fill this capacious series of linked areas – and most do come here to eat. There are lots of oak beams, flagstoned and tiled floors, stripped 17th-c stonework, simple but solid rustic furnishings, and attractive pictures and other individual and often light-hearted decorations. Under the new licensees, bar food includes sandwiches, home-made soup (£2.95), grilled goat's cheese toasts (£4.95), skewers of chicken satay and prawns (£5.95), pesto pasta (£6.95), ham and eggs (£7.95), chicken curry or steak and kidney pie (£8.95), Scotch salmon steak (£9.95), Scotch sirloin steak (£11.95), a half shoulder of lamb with rosemary and honey (£10.95), half a Gressingham duck with orange suace (£11.95), and fresh fish dishes. Well kept Brakspears Special, Marstons Pedigree, and Morlands Original and Old Speckled Hen on handpump, good house wines, and several malt whiskies. The sheltered courtyard has tables around an impressive fountain. *(Recommended by Mark and Heather Williamson, Mike and Mary Carter, Ian Jones, David Oakes, Peter and Audrey Dowsett)*

Free house ~ Licensees Shane Ellis, Alan Heather ~ Real ale ~ Meals and snacks ~ Restaurant ~ (01865) 351648 ~ Children welcome ~ Jazz band Sun lunchtime ~ Open 11-3, 5.30-11; 12-11 Sun ~ Bedrooms: £40B/£49.50B

STEEPLE ASTON SP4725 Map 4

Red Lion 🍷

Off A4260 12 miles N of Oxford

Mr Mead continues to warmly welcome all his customers to this civilised little village pub – he's been here for 26 years now. The comfortable partly panelled bar has beams, an antique settle and other good furnishings, and under the window a collection of interesting language and philosophy books that crossword fans find compelling. Enjoyable lunchtime bar food might include tasty stockpot soup (£2.30), sandwiches (£2.50, the rare beef is good), smoked pork in a large roll with tomato and shallot (£3.40), excellent ploughman's with nicely ripe stilton (£3.90), home-made pâté (£4.20), goulash with ham and smoked sausage (£5.20), fresh salmon salad or whole fresh baby crab (£5.50), and puddings (from £2.10); the evening no-smoking restaurant is more elaborate with a good three-course meal (£21). Well kept (and reasonably priced) Badger Tanglefoot, Hook Norton Best and Wadworths 6X on handpump, a choice of sixty or so malt whiskies, and a fine wine list of over 100 different bottles. The suntrap front terrace with its lovely flowers is a marvellous place to relax in summer. *(Recommended by Ian Phillips, E A and D C Frewer, Tim Barrow, Sue Demont, Michael Sargent, D and J Tapper, Hugh Spottiswoode, Gordon, Peter Baggott, Mr and Mrs C Moncreiffe, Maysie Thompson, Martin and Karen Wake, James Nunns)*

Free house ~ Licensee Colin Mead ~ Real ale ~ Lunchtime bar meals and snacks (not Sun) ~ Evening restaurant (not Sun) ~ (01869) 340225 ~ Children in restaurant ~ Open 11-3, 6-11; 12-3, 7-10.30 Sun

TADPOLE BRIDGE SP3300 Map 4

Trout

Back road Bampton—Buckland, 4 miles NE of Faringdon

Bustling and friendly, this Thames-side pub is liked by a good mix of people. The small L-shaped original bar with plenty of seats on the flagstones is dedicated only to enjoying the Archers Village and Golden, Batemans XXXB, Fullers London Pride, Greene King Abbot, and Hook Norton Old Hookey on handpump, several malt whiskies, and darts, dominoes, cribbage, and backgammon; there's a small but comprehensive wine list. Tasty bar food includes lunchtime snacks such as filled french bread (£3.50), ploughman's (£4.35), a pie of the day (£5.50), and fish pie (£6.50), as well as home-made soup (£2.65), crab and pepper cakes with a spicy tomato salsa (£4.25), cumberland sausage, herb and mustard mash and onion gravy (£6.50), grilled sea trout with a herb crust (£8.25), honey-roasted barbary duck breast with a tart lime sauce (£9.55), peppered pork fillet in a stilton and chive cream (£9.75), Aberdeen Angus rump steak (£10.25), and puddings; piped music. The garden (with Aunt Sally) is pretty in summer with small fruit trees, attractive hanging baskets, and flower troughs, and you can fish on a two-mile stretch of the river (the pub sells day tickets); moorings for boaters, too. *(Recommended by TBB, Anthony Barnes, Calum and Jane Maclean, Joan Olivier, Gordon, Daren Haines, David Carr, Peter Holman, Val Stevenson, Rob Holmes)*

Free house ~ Licensee Christopher Green ~ Real ale ~ Meals and snacks ~ (01367) 870382 ~ Children in eating area of bar ~ Open 11.30-3, 6-11; 12-3.30, 7-10.30 Sun; closed Sun evening Nov-Easter

TOOT BALDON SP5600 Map 4

Crown

Village signed from A4074 at Nuneham Courtenay, and B480

This is a thoroughly enjoyable place to come and savour really good, honest, accomplished cooking in a warm and welcoming atmosphere. As well as sandwiches and ploughman's, there might be good home-made soup, pork chop with stilton sauce (£7.50), venison in wine sauce, chicken supreme with fresh herbs or halibut in cream and mustard sauce (all £8.50), nice mixed grill and chicken breast stuffed with garlic and mushrooms, puddings like super apple and blackberry pie, and Sunday roast lunch; they use home-grown herbs and other produce whenever possible. Best to book, especially at weekends. The simple beamed bar has a log fire, solid furnishings on the tiled floor, and a pleasant atmosphere. Well kept Mansfield Bitter and Ruddles County on handpump; darts, shove-ha'penny, and dominoes. Aunt Sally, summer barbecues, and tables on the terrace. *(Recommended by Ian Jones, Glen and Nola Armstrong, TBB, Keith and Margaret Kettell, Peter Brueton, Robert Turnham, Mr and Mrs W Welsh, Kendall Davis, D C and E A Frewer, Canon M A Bourdeaux, G T Hughes, Ian and Villy White)*

Free house ~ Licensees Liz and Neil Kennedy ~ Real ale ~ Meals and snacks (not Sun or Mon evenings) ~ Restaurant ~ (01865) 343240 ~ Well behaved children welcome ~ Open 11-3, 6.30-11; 12-3, 7-10.30 Sun

WATLINGTON SU6894 Map 4

Chequers

3 miles from M40, junction 6; take B4009 towards Watlington, and on outskirts of village turn right into residential rd Love Lane which leads to pub

The relaxed rambling bar in this tucked away pub has a low panelled oak settle and character chairs such as a big spiral-legged carving chair around a few good antique oak tables, a low oak beamed ceiling darkened to a deep ochre by the candles which they still use, and red and black shiny tiles in one corner with rugs and red carpeting elsewhere; steps on the right lead down to an area with more tables. A conservatory with very low hanging vines looks out over the garden. Popular bar food includes toasties (£2.50), ploughman's (£4), deep-fried camembert (£4.20), filled baked potatoes (£4.80), aubergine and lentil moussaka (£5.50), cauliflower cheese or fish pie (£5.70), steak and kidney pie or chicken curry (£6.70), calf liver and bacon or half a duck with orange sauce (£9.60), and steaks (from £9.60); good Sunday lunch. Well kept Brakspears Bitter, Special, and OBJ and seasonal ales on handpump, a decent little wine list, and friendly staff. The cheese shop in Watlington itself is recommended. The garden is notably pretty – quite refreshing after the bustle of the main street – with picnic-sets under apple and pear trees, and sweet peas, roses, geraniums, begonias, and rabbits. No children inside. *(Recommended by Gordon, P J Keen, Sidney and Erna Wells, Michael Sargent, Hazel and Michael Duncombe, Bill Ingham, Simon Collett-Jones, TBB)*

Brakspears ~ Tenants John and Anna Valentine ~ Real ale ~ Meals and snacks (not Sun evening) ~ (01491) 612874 ~ Open 11.30-2.30, 6-11; 12-3, 7-10.30 Sun; closed 26 Dec

WESTCOTT BARTON SP4325 Map 4

Fox

Enstone Road; B4030 off A44 NW of Woodstock

This lovely stone-built village pub likes to call itself 'a pasta and ale house' – the landlord and his brother are Italian, and the good enjoyable bar food is a mix of Italian and English dishes: filled ciabatta bread or rolls (from £2.25), filled baked potatoes (£3.25), ploughman's (£3.75), omelettes (£3.95), pasta with sausage, mushroom, bacon and mozzarella (£4.95), seafood pasta with mussels, calamari, clams and king prawns or home-made steak in ale pie (£5.25), and puddings such as treacle sponge or tiramisu (from £2.25); Sunday roast and children's meals. Hops hang from the low beams in the deceptively small and very relaxed bar, above snug little window seats, high-backed settles and pews around tables on flagstones, and the odd trap or horsebrass on the stone walls; open fires, juke box. A narrow corridor leads to a tucked-away back room with a faded tapestry and an old coach wheel, and an elegant restaurant. Well kept Hook Norton and two changing guests like Hampshire 1066 or Theakstons XB on handpump; espresso and cappuccino. There are a few tables out in front, and more in the very pleasant garden behind, overlooking a verdant sheep-filled field. There's a wooden play fort out here for children, and quite a few trees. Watch your head as you go inside – the porch is very low. *(Recommended by George Atkinson, Tim Barrow, Sue Demont, D C T and E Frewer; more reports please)*

Free house ~ Licensee Vito Logozzi ~ Real ale ~ Meals and snacks ~ Restaurant ~ (01869) 340338 ~ Children welcome ~ Occasional live music ~ Open 12-3, 5-11; 12-3, 7-10.30 Sun

WOODSTOCK SP4416 Map 4

Feathers

Market St

Many readers head for the old-fashioned and quietly relaxed garden bar at the back of this civilised Cotswold stone hotel. It has oils and watercolours on its walls, stuffed fish and birds (a marvellous live parrot, too), and a central open fire, and opens on to a splendid sunny courtyard with a small water feature, and attractive tables and chairs among geraniums and trees. Good, imaginative food from a short but thoughtful menu might include home-made soup (£3.95), warm goat's cheese salad with basil and garlic (£5.50), risotto with pesto and parmesan (£5.95), sausage and mash with onions and deep-fried cabbage (£7.95), salad niçoise (£8.25), baked salmon with roasted peppers and olive salsa (£8.50), and puddings such as hazelnut tart or vanilla cassanade (£4.15); the restaurant is no smoking. Well kept (rather pricy) Wadworths 6X on handpump, a good choice of malt whiskies, home-made lemonade, and freshly squeezed orange juice; excellent service; piped music. Get there early for a table. Five new bedrooms have been added. *(Recommended by Steve Power, M Borthwick, C Gilbert, Paul Barnett, M J Dowdy; also in the Good Hotel Guide)*

Free house ~ Licensees Martin Godward, Andrew Leeman, Howard Malin ~ Real ale ~ Meals and snacks (not Sat or Sun evenings) ~ Restaurant ~ (01993) 812291 ~ Children welcome ~ Open 11-3, 6-11; 12-3, 7-10.30 Sun; closed to non-residents evening 25 Dec ~ Bedrooms: £88B/£105B

WOOTTON SP4419 Map 4

Kings Head

Chapel Hill; off B4027 N of Woodstock

Most people do come to this pretty 17th-c Cotswold stone house to enjoy the very good food – which can be eaten either in the bar, no-smoking restaurant or garden. Best to book to be sure of a table. The civilised and relaxing beamed no-smoking lounge bar has a nice mix of old oak settles and chairs around wooden tables, comfortable armchairs and chintzy sofas, an open log fire, and old prints and ceramics on the pale pink walls. Well presented and changing frequently, the food might include sandwiches (not Saturday evening or Sunday lunchtime), home-made soup (£3.25), warm goat's cheese on a garlic crouton topped with bacon and served with a balsamic dressing (£4.25), crispy duck with a plum sauce (£5.25), vegetarian pancakes in a cream stilton sauce (£6.95), roast magret of duck on a rosti potato with caramelised pears and juniper berries and rich red wine jus (£11.50), peppered fillet steak on anna potato with a creamy pepper sauce (£14.95), steamed turbot fillets on a bed of green vegetables with lime and ginger (£15.95), and home-made puddings like lemon tart with gin and lavender ice cream, sticky toffee pudding, and three-tiered chocolate terrine with a mulled wine compote (from £3.50). Well kept Ruddles Best and County and Wadworths 6X on handpump, and decent wines, including glasses served in 'normal' or 'friendly' sizes. The bedrooms (two of which have their own private sitting rooms) have been redecorated this year. *(Recommended by J H Kane, Sir Nigel Foulkes, Tim Brierly, G V Holmes, Audrey and Peter Dowsett, Heather Couper, M Hasslacher, J Oakes, C Barrett, Mr and Mrs Peter Smith, B Haywood, Alan Tye, Pam Adlsey)*

Free house ~ Licensees Tony and Amanda Fay ~ Real ale ~ Meals and snacks (till 10pm) ~ Restaurant ~ (01993) 811340 ~ Well behaved children welcome ~ Open 11-3, 6-11; 12-3, 7-10.30 Sun ~ Bedrooms: £54B/£65B

WYTHAM SP4708 Map 4

White Hart

Village signposted from A34 ring road W of Oxford

Swathed in creepers, this 17th-c stone pub is charmingly placed in an unspoilt village with houses owned and preserved by Oxford University. The partly panelled, flagstoned bar has high-backed black settles built almost the whole way round the cream walls, a shelf of blue and white plates, and a winter log fire with a fine relief of a heart on the iron fireback; there's a small no-smoking area. Well kept Adnams Best, Greene King Abbot, Morlands Old Speckled Hen and a guest beer on handpump, and a fair choice of malt whiskies. Bar food from the food servery includes cheese or pâté with bread (from £2.95), filled baked potatoes or help-yourself salads (around £3.95), steaks (from £8.80), fresh fish like plaice, trout or salmon, swordfish and tuna (from £9), daily pasta and vegetarian specials, and puddings (£3.20); it does get busy on weekday lunchtimes. They may hold barbecues in the lovely walled rose garden. The pub's name is said to have come from a badge granted to the troops of Richard II after the Battle of Radcot Bridge in 1390. *(Recommended by Caroline Wright, Alan Green,*

Gordon, TBB, R T and J C Moggridge, Wayne Brindle, Tim Brierly, Pat and Roger Fereday, Joan Olivier, Hazel and Michael Duncombe, Joan and Tony Walker, J I Davies)

Carlsberg-Tetleys ~ Managers Donald and Louise Tran ~ Real ale ~ Meals and snacks ~ (01865) 244372 ~ Children in eating area of bar ~ Open 11.30-11; 12-10.30 Sun; 11.30-2.30, 6-11 in winter

Lucky Dip

Besides the fully inspected pubs, you might like to try these Lucky Dips recommended to us and described by readers (if you do, please send us reports):

☆ **Abingdon** [St Helens Wharf; SU4997], *Old Anchor*: Faultless Morlands in little front bar looking across Thames, flagstoned back bar with shoulder-height serving hatch, roomy lounge, panelled dining room overlooking neat almshouse gardens; warm fire, some comfortable leather armchairs, decent food inc children's, friendly service; charming spot *(Mrs I Folkard-Evans, Tony and Wendy Hobden, P Legon)*

☆ **Adderbury** [A4260 S of Banbury, fairly handy for M40 junction 11; SP4635], *Red Lion*: Smartly civilised, with friendly new landlord, big inglenook, high stripped beams, stripped stone, prints and comfortable chairs, cosy dining area on left, no-smoking back dining room, well kept Hook Norton Best, Marstons Pedigree and Theakstons Best, several wines by the glass, daily papers; comfortable bedrooms, children in eating area, tables out on well kept terrace; open all day summer *(Dr T E Hothersall, Mrs H Davis, Mr and Mrs S Sloan, Kevin Thorpe, E A and D C Frewer, LYM)*

Adderbury [just off A4260; turn opp Red Lion], *Bell*: Unpretentious largely unspoilt beamed village local with chiming grandfather clock, sofa by huge log fire, generous good fresh food, well kept Hook Norton inc seasonal ales; second bar with character old settles, candlelit back restaurant *(Pete Baker, Giles Francis)*

Alvescot [B4020 Carterton—Clanfield; SP2604], *Plough*: Partly 17th-c beamed village pub with friendly new licensees, plentiful good value modest food inc vegetarian and Sun lunch (must book), well kept Boddingtons and Wadworths 6X, decent wines, good coffee, end dining area, old maps and plates, log fire (but cool and pleasant on hot days), quiet piped music; separate public bar *(Marjorie and David Lamb, Peter and Audrey Dowsett, John Higgins, Kay Neville-Rolfe)*

Appleton [50 Eaton Rd; SP4401], *Thatched*: Attractive two-room Brakspears pub (actually tiled now), one room furnished for the enjoyable food from sandwiches up, soft piped music, very friendly licensees – she's Canadian; small garden *(Joan Olivier)*

Ardley [B430 (old A43); just SW of M40 junction 10; SP5427], *Fox & Hounds*: Old stone pub with small cosy lounge bar, snug beyond, and long opened-up dining area, low beams, lots of horsebrasses, pictures and old glassware, flowers on tables, open fires, Banks's and Marstons Pedigree or Morlands, good Australian wines by the glass, food inc Sun roasts and old-fashioned puddings; keen and very friendly new young licensees; piped music, Sun evening singalong *(Val and Alan Green, D and E Frewer, Marjorie and David Lamb)*

Ashbury [B4507/B4000; SU2685], *Rose & Crown*: Comfortable open-plan beamed pub nr Ridgeway with highly polished woodwork, settees, pews and oak tables and chairs, traditional pictures, unpretentious sensibly priced food, well kept Arkells, friendly helpful staff, neat lavatories; bedrooms *(Peter Neate, Robert Tapsfield)*

☆ **Asthall** [off A40 at W end of Witney bypass, then 1st left; SP2811], *Maytime*: Genteel and comfortable dining pub with very wide choice of good value well served meals inc plenty for vegetarians, some bar snacks, slightly raised plush dining lounge neatly set with tables (best ones down by fire may be booked for overnight guests), airy conservatory restaurant (children allowed behind screen), Morrells and Wadworths 6X, decent wines, prompt service, interesting pictures, small locals' bar; piped music; in tiny hamlet, nice views of Asthall Manor and watermeadows from garden, big car park; quiet comfortable bedrooms around charming back courtyard, attractive walks *(Paul McPherson, Pam Adsley, Jean and George Dundas, Gillian Jenkins, P and J Shapley, BB)*

Bampton [Mkt Sq; SP3103], *Talbot*: Quaint pub, welcoming and comfortable, with good-sized open fire, well kept Tetleys and Wadworths 6X, decent choice of food, attractive prices; quiet piped music; clean old-fashioned bedrooms, lovely village *(Peter and Audrey Dowsett)*

Banbury [9 North Bar; A41 just S of Banbury Cross; SP4540], *Cromwell Lodge*: Welcoming and relaxed bars, well kept Theakstons, good value food inc fish specialities and weekend summer barbecues in courtyard and garden; bedrooms *(D N Ling)*; [Parsons Lane], *Wine Vaults*: Basic bare boards and seating, exceptional range of well kept beers, good range of bottled ones; cheap basic wholesome food *(Ted George)*

☆ **Barford St Michael** [Lower St; off B4031 S of Banbury; SP4332], *George*: Pretty 17th-c thatched local, rambling modernised beamed bar with well kept Adnams Broadside, Fullers London Pride and Morlands Original and Old Speckled Hen, country wines, pizzas and other food (not Mon) inc vegetarian, log fires, tie collection, some interesting decorations; pub games, piped music; pleasant garden with giant chess set, boules, adventure playground; children welcome, blues Mon, open all day Sat in summer *(Gordon, Brian and Anna Marsden, CMW, JJW, Simon Collett-Jones, Daren Haines, LYM)*

☆ **Beckley** [High St; signed off B4027; SP5611], *Abingdon Arms*: Comfortably modernised simple lounge with interesting old photographs, smaller public bar with a couple of antique carved settles, food inc interesting dishes (not Sun evening), well kept Hook Norton Best and Wadworths 6X, good range of wines, bar billiards, dominoes, cribbage, shove-ha'penny; floodlit terrace, extensive pretty garden dropping away into orchard; good walks, no children, generally taciturn service *(B J P Edwards, W Ruxton, D C T and E A Frewer, Adam and Elizabeth Duff, George Atkinson, Martin and Karen Wake, LYM)*

Begbroke [A44 Oxford—Woodstock; SP4613], *Royal Sun*: Friendly and busy much refurbished open-plan stripped-stone pub with emphasis on prompt good value food; well kept Tetleys-related and guest ales, piped music and machines, tables on terrace and in small garden *(Dr and Mrs A K Clarke, P and S White)*

Bicester [Sheep St; SP5822], *Penny Black*: Spacious and attractive new Wetherspoons conversion of former 1920s main post office, four competitively priced ales, good cheap coffee, good choice of wines (not so cheap), books and newspapers; usual food *(E A and D C T Frewer)*

Bletchingdon [Station Rd; B4027 N of Oxford; SP5017], *Blacks Head*: Friendly local overlooking village green, good value food, well kept Flowers IPA, Tetleys and guest beers, some sympathetic refurbishment to give dining area and conservatory (no pool room now), big woodburner, darts, cards and dominoes in public bar; garden with Aunt Sally, informal singalong Thurs *(Pete Baker)*

☆ **Blewbury** [London Rd; SU5385], *Blewbury Inn*: Friendly and comfortable character downland village pub with mellowed old furniture and attractive log fire in cosy beamed bar, good food in small dining room, friendly landlord; bedrooms *(Calum and Jane Maclean)*

Bloxham [High St (A361); SP4235], *Red Lion*: Beamed dining pub with lots of flowers, dozens of whisky-water jugs, Adnams and Wadworths 6X, good coffee, open fire, friendly atmosphere *(George Atkinson)*

Boars Hill [between A34 and B4017; SP4802], *Fox*: Clean and attractive timbered pub in pretty countryside, largely refurbished with rambling rooms on different levels, huge log fireplaces, poems on the wall, food inc vegetarian and children's, Tetleys-related and other changing ales, decent wine, family area, polite service; maybe piped music; restaurant, pleasant raised verandah, big well designed sloping garden with play area *(Paul Robinshaw, Dick Brown, D C T and E A Frewer)*

☆ **Brightwell Baldwin** [signed off B480 Chalgrove—Watlington and B4009 Benson—Watlington; SU6595], *Lord Nelson*: Civilised and friendly turkey-carpet pub with dining chairs around country-kitchen tables, most laid for the good value food (may be a delay when busy), Courage Best, Ruddles Best and Charles Wells Bombardier, decent house wines, no-smoking restaurant, simple decor with some maritime pictures; piped music, well behaved children allowed; front verandah, back terrace and attractive garden *(DHV, G S B G Dudley, M A and C R Starling, LYM)*

Britwell Salome [B4009 Watlington—Benson; SU6793], *Red Lion*: Friendly, with huge range of good freshly made food esp pies (may be a slight delay at busy times), Brakspears PA and Marstons Pedigree, separate back restaurant area *(Marjorie and David Lamb, J and B Cressey)*

Broughton [B4035 SW of Banbury; SP4238], *Saye & Sele Arms*: Greenalls pub with odd mix of new and old, inc row of sewing machines and child's penny-farthing; interesting food, ales inc Tetleys *(Dave Braisted)*

Bucknell [handy for M40 junction 10; SP5525], *Trigger Pond*: Neat stone-built pub opp the pond, young American landlord with English wife, home cooking inc old-fashioned puddings, well kept changing ales such as Adnams, Badger Best and Tanglefoot and Hook Norton Best; piped music; pleasant terrace and garden *(E A and D C Frewer)*

☆ **Burford** [Lower High St (A361); SP2512], *Bull*: Comfortable sofas in interestingly restored dimly lit lower beamed and panelled lounge bar, Scottish Courage and a guest ale, woodburner, good choice of wines by the glass, wide choice of bar food inc lunchtime buffet, back restaurant; piped music; children welcome, open all day, seats out in old coach entry; comfortable bedrooms *(Gordon, David Regan, Mr and Mrs N Spink, LYM)*

Burford [14 Witney St], *Angel*: Long narrow dining pub, heavy beams, panelling and flagstones, tastefully simple spotless furnishings, interesting food inc good value Sun lunch, no-smoking candlelit back dining room, big log fire, Bass, Marstons Pedigree and Morlands Old Speckled Hen, reasonably priced wines, prompt service, friendly cats; piped music, no children, open all day; clean comfortable bedrooms *(Jo Rees, SCCJ, Nigel Woolliscroft, Mark Percy, Lesley Mayoh, Paul Bailey, John Bowdler, Charles Faragher, Sarah Corlett, Dr S P Willavoys, Liz Bell, LYM)*; [Sheep St], *Bay Tree*: Attractive old village inn with very pubby hotel bar, smart yet informal and comfortable, roaring fire, leaded lights, windsor chairs and window seats; imaginative reasonably priced bar food, enchanting walled terraced garden; bedrooms *(Susan and John Douglas, Paul McPherson)*

Caulcott [Lower Heyford Rd (B4030); SP5024], *Horse & Groom*: Friendly new licensees doing rather different food inc sandwiches, ploughman's, filled baked potatoes and speciality sausages in part-thatched creeper-covered 16th-c pub, cosy and homely L-shaped beamed bar, blazing coal fire in stone fireplace, Brakspears, Morlands Old Speckled Hen and

Charles Wells Bombardier; front sun lounge, pretty garden with picnic-sets under cocktail parasols *(E A and D C T Frewer, Ian Phillips)*

☆ **Chadlington** [Mill End; off A361 S of Chipping Norton, and B4437 W of Charlbury; SP3222], *Tite*: Comfortable and welcoming rambling food-oriented local with well kept ales such as Archers Village and Wychwood Brambling, log fire in huge fireplace, settles, wooden chairs, prints, rack of guidebooks; good if not cheap food inc lovely puddings, vine-covered restaurant evenings and Sun lunchtime, superb garden full of shrubs, some quite unusual, with stream running under pub – lovely views, pretty Cotswold village, good walks nearby; children welcome, cl Mon exc bank hols, car park right beyond garden *(George Atkinson, Pam Adsley, P and M Rudlin)*

☆ **Charlbury** [Sheep St; SP3519], *Bull*: Very good bistro-style atmosphere and surroundings, restaurant on left and freshly furnished dining bar on right, good range of well presented good food in generous helpings – not really a place for just a drink; cl Mon *(John and Judy Fennell, BB)*

Charney Bassett [SU3794], *Chequers*: Popular 18th-c two-room village-green local with very wide choice of freshly made food, well kept ales such as Morlands, Ruddles Best and Wadworths 6X; some singalongs, pool, piped music; children welcome, cl Mon *(PB)*

Checkendon [SU6682], *Four Horseshoes*: Attractive partly thatched local, good pub food, friendly landlord, music-free stripped-floor dining lounge (where children allowed), local public bar with pool table and piped music; well kept Brakspears, good simple wine list; big garden with picnic-sets, super hanging baskets *(G V Price, JP, PP)*

☆ **Chipping Norton** [Goddards Lane; SP3127], *Chequers*: Three beamed rooms, no frills but nicely old-fashioned, softly lit, clean and comfortable, with plenty of character, log fires, full Fullers range (rare around here) kept well, nice house wines, good coffee, good generous food inc some interesting exotic dishes, popular French-run evening restaurant, friendly efficient staff, lively atmosphere, no piped music; tables in courtyard *(D Irving, E McCall, R Huggins, T McLean, P and M Rudlin, Peter and Audrey Dowsett)*

Chipping Norton [High St], *Blue Boar*: Spacious and cheery well worn-in stone-built pub divided by arches and pillars, wide choice of food from separate servery, Courage Directors, Marstons Pedigree, John Smiths and a guest such as Wychwood, cheap coffee; juke box or piped music, fruit machines, TV, piano, separate beamed back restaurant, light and airy long flagstoned conservatory *(George Atkinson, Joan and Michel Hooper-Immins, G V Price)*; [High St], *Crown & Cushion*: Attractive homely and laid-back bar in handsome old-fashioned 16th-c hotel, some stripped stone and flagstones, well kept ales, bar food, flower-decked conservatory, tables in sheltered garden with suntrap terrace; children welcome, good bedrooms *(D Irving, E McCall, R Huggins, T McLean, Gordon, LYM)*; [High St], *Fox*: Dark low-lit lounge, clean, tidy and quiet, with lots of pictures, groups of seats, open fire, well kept Hook Norton ales, good coffee, reasonably priced bar food (lunchtime can use upstairs dining room for it); soft piped music, fruit machines, children welcome; well equipped good value bedrooms *(George Atkinson, David Carr, BB)*

☆ **Christmas Common** [signed from B480/B481; SU7193], *Fox & Hounds*: Unspoilt Chilterns cottage, cosy beamed bar with wall benches, bow-window seats, floor tiles and big inglenook log fire, locals' side bar, darts in third room (children allowed here), well kept Brakspears Bitter, Special and winter Old tapped from the cask in a back still room, friendly landlady, good home-made soup, wrapped sandwiches, tables outside *(PB, Derek Harvey-Piper, JP, PP, Joan Olivier, Gordon, LYM)*

☆ **Church Hanborough** [opp church; signed off A4095 at Long Hanborough, or off A40 at Eynsham roundabout; SP4212], *Hand & Shears*: Attractively done dining pub, long gleaming bar, steps down into spacious back eating area, another small dining room, wide choice of good brasserie-style food from simple bar dishes to fish and grills inc good thai curries, friendly attentive Australian staff, Adnams Broadside, Fullers London Pride and Morlands Original, decent wines, open fires, good atmosphere, soft piped music *(John Waller, Tim Barrow, Sue Demont, Mr and Mrs R Maggs, Mr and Mrs D Shier, Joan Olivier, John Waller, Kate Clear, BB)*

☆ **Clifton Hampden** [towards Long Wittenham, S of A415; SU5495], *Barley Mow*: Interesting thatched Chef & Brewer reopened end 1997 after three-month refurbishment, very low ancient beams, oak-panelled family room, Scottish Courage ales, piped music, restaurant, new kitchen; tables in well tended garden, short stroll from the Thames; bedrooms *(Joan Olivier, Gordon, JP, PP, LYM)*

Cothill [SU4699], *Merry Miller*: Large popular pub/restaurant contrived from 17th-c granary, stripped stone and flagstones, friendly efficient staff, wide choice of good value food inc sandwiches and children's dishes, no-smoking restaurant with wide-ranging menu inc vegetarian, well kept Hook Norton and a beer brewed for the pub, good choice of wines; disabled access *(Joan Olivier, Mrs B Kingley, Susan Trevaldwyn)*

Crays Pond [B471 nr junction with B4526, about 3 miles E of Goring; SU6380], *White Lion*: Clean and welcoming low-ceilinged pub with open fire, attractive conservatory, well kept Scottish Courage ales, good inventive if not cheap food (not Tues evening); big garden with play area, lovely setting *(Nicholas Holmes)*

☆ **Cropredy** [off A423 N of Banbury; SP4646], *Red Lion*: Old thatched stone pub charmingly placed opp churchyard, low beams, inglenook log fire, high-backed settles, brass, plates and pictures; popular home-made food from sandwiches up (two rooms set for eating, children allowed in restaurant part), well kept Scottish Courage ales, pub games; piped music, small back garden *(George Atkinson, Ted George, Peter and Anne Hollindale, Dr Paul Khan, Mr and Mrs R Maggs, Sheila and John French, LYM)*

☆ **Cumnor** [Abingdon Rd (B4017); SP4603], *Vine*: Busy and restauranty extended modernised pub with remarkably wide choice of enjoyable fresh food (starter would do as light lunch), carpeted back dining area, no-smoking area in conservatory, quick polite service, three well kept guest ales, good range of malt whiskies and wines, picnic-sets in attractive back garden *(W B Baker, Dick Brown, D and E Frewer)*

Curbridge [Bampton Rd (A4095); SP3308], *Lord Kitchener*: Good food cooked to order (so may be a wait), old local photographs, big log fire, end dining area, well kept Morrells Bitter and Varsity, friendly efficient service; piped music may be loud; garden with play area *(David and Marjorie Lamb)*

☆ **Deddington** [Horse Fair, off A4260/B4031; SP4631], *Deddington Arms*: 16th c, with pleasant atmosphere, black beams and timbers, mullioned windows, attractive settles and other comfortable country furnishings, fine log fire, nooks and crannies; some emphasis on good imaginative food, well kept real ales, good choice of wines by the glass, welcoming staff; children in eating area, spacious restaurant, small end games area; comfortable bedrooms, attractive village *(J Oakes, W M and J M Cottrell, Tim Brierly, Graham and Karen Oddey, Rev John Cooper, LYM)*

Deddington [Market Pl], *Unicorn*: 17th-c inn with inglenook bar, usual food inc inexpensive set lunch in oak-beamed restaurant, pleasant service, family room with separate games area; terrace, very nice walled back garden; bedrooms *(George Atkinson)*

☆ **Denchworth** [NW of Wantage; SU3791], *Fox*: Picturesque old thatched pub with two good log fires in low-ceilinged comfortable connecting areas, welcoming licensee, prompt service, good ample food from sandwiches up, Morlands ales, good house wines and coffee, reasonable prices, carvery in small beamed restaurant; nostalgic piped music, not too obtrusive; pleasant sheltered garden, isolated ancient village *(Marjorie and David Lamb)*

☆ **Dorchester** [High St; SU5794], *Fleur de Lys*: Busy 16th-c village pub opp abbey, two-level comfortably traditional interior, wide choice of good value home cooking, all fresh (not Mon; no sandwiches), Mansfield and Morlands Old Speckled Hen and Old Masters, friendly helpful service; unobtrusive piped music *(Simon Collett-Jones, W Osborn-King, TBB)*

☆ **Ducklington** [Standlake Rd; off A415, a mile S of Witney; SP3507], *Bell*: Thatched pub by village pond, recently attractively refurbished and doing well under very friendly newish licensees, with scrubbed tables, woodburner (and glass-covered well) in big flagstoned bar, further eating area, very well laid out restaurant (its beams festooned with hundreds of bells – these dominate the pub's decor); Morlands ales inc Old Speckled Hen, good house wines, wide choice of reasonably priced food, no piped music; garden behind with side play area; bedrooms *(Peter and Audrey Dowsett)*

☆ **East Hendred** [Orchard Lane, off A417 E of Wantage; SU4588], *Plough*: Good range of enjoyable food in beamed village pub's attractive and airy main bar, Morlands ales with a guest such as Charles Wells Bombardier, quick friendly service, farm tools; occasional folk nights, pleasant garden with good play area; attractive village *(A G Drake, Dick Brown, BB)*

☆ **Eaton** [off A420/B4017 W of Oxford; SP4403], *Eight Bells*: Friendly low-beamed small-roomed Tudor pub, good value food inc enjoyable baked potatoes, well kept Morlands, open fires, horse tack and brasses, helpful landlord, dining room (children allowed here) off cosy lounge; no dogs, tables in garden, tethering rail for horses, nice walks *(Joan Olivier, Maureen Hobbs)*

Ewelme [off B4009 about 5 miles SW of M40 junction 6; SU6491], *Shepherds Hut*: Simple extended local, cheery welcoming staff, good value pub food, quick service, well kept Morlands Bitter and Old Masters, decent coffee, pot plants, darts, small restaurant; piped pop music, fruit machine; children welcome, tables and swing in small pleasant side garden *(N S Holmes)*

Faringdon [Market Pl; SU2895], *Bell*: Relaxing well worn-in bar with red leather settles, inglenook fireplace with 17th-c carved oak chimneypiece, interesting faded mural in inner bar, well kept Wadworths ales, limited bar food, restaurant; piped music; children welcome, tables out among flowers in attractive cobbled back coachyard; bedrooms *(Gordon, D Irving, R Huggins, E McCall, T McLean, LYM)*; [Market Sq], *Crown*: Civilised old inn, flagstones, beams, panelling, leaded lights, woodburner, two bars and tiny comfortable hidden-away snugs, popular reasonably priced well presented food, efficient friendly staff, well kept ales; children welcome; good big quiet bedrooms overlooking lovely cobbled summer courtyard *(D Irving, R Huggins, E McCall, T McLean, Peter and Audrey Dowsett, Gordon, Sophie Prendergast, LYM)*

☆ **Fernham** [B4508, off A420 SW of Oxford; SU2992], *Woodman*: Heavily beamed 17th-c country pub, great log fire, candles, lots of atmosphere, well kept ales tapped from the cask, wide choice of food from lunchtime sandwiches and snacks to elaborate main dishes; children welcome *(Mr and Mrs B J Cox, LYM)*

☆ **Freeland** [Witney Rd; A4095 SW of Long Hanborough; SP4112], *Shepherds Hall*: Large comfortable bar with friendly prompt service, good choice of enjoyable sensibly priced food, open fire, gleaming copper, well kept Flowers IPA and Wadworths 6X, discreet piped pop music, back games room with two pool tables, garden with play area; comfortable bedrooms *(Peter and Audrey Dowsett, Joan Olivier)*

Garsington [Oxford Rd; SP5702], *Red Lion*: Good food, esp Sun lunch, very pleasant service *(Chris Bird)*; [The Green], *Three Horseshoes*: Largish village pub with delightful French licensees, wide choice of food inc delicious omelettes and proper chips, good salads, mainly Morrells beers, cheerful service; lovely views *(TBB)*

☆ **Godstow** [off A34 Oxford bypass northbound, via Wytham, or A40/A44 roundabout via Wolvercote; SP4809], *Trout*: Creeper-covered medieval pub, much extended and commercialised as big tourist draw, but nicely done, with fires in three huge hearths, beams and shiny ancient flagstones, furnishings to suit, attractive pictures, roomy extended dining area, back extension with Inspector Morse memorabilia and children's area; decent food inc good big pies, Bass and Worthington, winter mulled wine – at its best midweek out of season, but no denying the summer charm of its lovely terrace by a stream full of greedily plump perch, with peacocks in the grounds *(Mark Percy, Lesley Mayoh, TBB, M Rutherford, Steve Power, Mr and Mrs R Maggs, Gordon, Tim Brierly, LYM)*

☆ **Goring** [Manor Rd; SU6080], *John Barleycorn*: Endearing and well run low-beamed cottagey local in pretty Thames village, prints in cosy little lounge bar, good choice of well priced home-made food in adjoining eating area, well kept Brakspears, pool in end room, friendly helpful service; bedrooms clean and simple *(Paul Weedon, Ron Leigh, Mrs I Folkard-Evans, JP, PP, Gordon)*

Goring [Station Rd], *Catherine Wheel*: Good value food, well kept Brakspears, good informal atmosphere, very friendly staff, two cosy bars, good log fire; notable door to gents' *(Christine and Geoff Butler, TRS, Mrs I Folkard-Evans, Gordon)*

☆ **Great Tew** [off B4022 about 5 miles E of Chipping Norton; SP3929], *Falkland Arms*: Idyllic setting of untouched golden-stone thatched cottages; high-backed settles, stripped tables, flagstones and bare boards, shuttered stone-mullioned latticed windows, fine inglenook fireplace, panelling, nice old-fashioned touches, no-smoking dining room, well kept Wadworths ales with guests such as Adnams Broadside or Theakstons Old Peculier, farm cider, lots of malt whiskies and country wines, tables outside; children in eating areas, small bedrooms, open all day w/e and summer weekdays; now brewery-owned, shame it's lost the personal touch this sort of place really needs *(Paul Barnett, JP, PP, Kerry Law, Mr and Mrs R Maggs, Jenny and Michael Back, M and C Starling, John Bowdler, E A and D C Frewer, LYM)*

Hailey [Whiteoak Green, B4022 Witney—Charlbury; SP3414], *Bird in Hand*: Greatly extended old Cotswold pub, smart rather than pubby, popular for wide range of reasonably priced food in lounge or attractive restaurant, quick friendly service, well kept Boddingtons, Courage Directors and Marstons Pedigree, lots of wood, well chosen pictures and subdued lighting (inc candles on tables), nice views, unobtrusive piped music; comfortable cottage-style bedrooms, huge car park *(Dick Brown, Mimi and Alastair McNeil, Peter and Audrey Dowsett, Mrs S Evans, Gordon)*; [B4022], *Lamb & Flag*: Friendly little pub, good range of low-priced food prepared to order (so can be a wait if busy), attentive service, well kept Morlands Original and Old Speckled Hen *(David and Marjorie Lamb)*

Hailey [entirely different village from previous entry – leave Wallingford on A4130, turn left to Hailey 2 miles on; SU6485], *King William IV*: Attractive 16th-c Brakspears pub in charming peaceful countryside, beams and bare brickwork, big log fire, sturdy furnishings on tiled floor, wide choice of food (not cheap) *(LYM)*

Hampton Poyle [11 Oxford Rd; SP5015], *Gone Fish Inn*: Emphasis on simply cooked good fresh fish in spotless small beamed dining room with attractively set old oak tables, bar with two small snugs, settee and big log fire, Adnams, Arkells and another ale tapped from the cask, good choice of French wines by the glass, welcoming and obliging licensees, no piped music, bar billiards *(E A and D C T Frewer, Steve and Sarah de Mellow)*

Henley [Friday St; SU7882], *Anchor*: Cosy and relaxing informally run Brakspears local not far from Thames, homely country furniture and bric-a-brac in softly lit parlourish beamed front bar, huge helpings of reasonably priced food, well kept beers, friendly and obliging landlady; darts, bar billiards, piano and TV in room on right, back dining room; charming back terrace surrounded by lush vegetation and hanging vines *(Gordon, Gerald Barnett)*; [Greys Rd], *Bird in Hand*: Quiet, with good choice of well kept ales (free house – unusual here); big garden behind *(Tim Jenkins)*; [Bell St], *Little White Hart*: Long civilised but friendy and informal hotel bar overlooking Thames, lots of regatta pictures and bric-a-brac inc three suspended racing skiffs, gas lighting, good attractively priced food cooked in modern style (if bar full, can eat in candlelit river-view restaurant), prompt friendly service, welcoming landlady; bedrooms, most with own bathroom *(Susan and John Douglas)*; [West St], *Row Barge*: Friendly town local, cosy low-beamed bar dropping down the hill in steps, good value home cooking, well kept Brakspears, darts, big back garden *(Comus Elliott)*; [5 Market Pl], *Three Tuns*: Heavy beams and panelling, two rooms opened together around old-fashioned central servery with well kept Brakspears, straightforward generous home-cooked food all day, floodlit back terrace and separate games bar with pinball, juke box and fruit machine; no children *(David Carr, JP, PP, BB)*

☆ **Highmoor** [B481 N of Reading, off A4130 Henley—Oxford; SU6984], *Dog & Duck*: Cosy and cottagey low-beamed country pub with chintzy curtains, floral cushions, lots of pictures; relaxing bar on left, dining room on right, log fire in each, smaller dining room behind, fine choice of good generous food inc good vegetarian dishes, hard-working young licensees, well kept Brakspears PA, SB and Old; tables in garden *(D W Chesterman)*

☆ **Hook Norton** [SP3533], *Sun*: Convivial, well appointed and roomy conversion of two smaller pubs, keeping country atmosphere, well run, with good interesting blackboard food, all home-made from sandwiches up, pleasant no-smoking restaurant, well kept Hook Norton ales inc Mild from the nearby brewery, interesting reasonably priced wines, reasonable drinks prices, friendly efficient staff, darts; wheelchair access and disabled facilities, well equipped bedrooms *(R E Syrett, D and M Watkinson, Steve and Irene Law, Chris Raisin, Graham Doyle, Sue and Jim Sargeant)*

☆ **Kidmore End** [Chalkhouse Green Rd; signed from Sonning Common; SU6979], *New Inn*: Attractive and immaculate black and white pub by church, transformed by current licensees; very wide highly polished elm floorboards, beams, big fire, warm comfortable feel, lots of flowers in summer; pleasant restaurant with good sophisticated food, nicely presented, lighter meals in bar; well kept Brakspears PA, SB and Old, good range of wines, tables in attractive large sheltered garden with pond *(W Osborn-King, Richard Douglas, Canon and Mrs J Y Crowe)*

Kirtlington [Troy Lane; SP4919], *Oxford Arms*: Old-fashioned oak-beamed village pub with pews and woodburner in lounge, good interesting home-made food, real ales inc changing guest, good value French house wines, friendly landlord, wide mix of customers; separate dining area, games room with pool, small sunny back garden with barbecues *(E A and D C T Frewer, Sue and Jim Sargeant)*

Langford [SP2402], *Bell*: Village pub done up by new owners with pleasantly low-key decor, big log fire, books and magazines, fresh flowers, evening candles, sensibly short choice of enjoyable food with good veg, Wadworths 6X, proper coffee; no piped music *(Sandra Childress, Peter and Audrey Dowsett)*

☆ **Little Milton** [3 miles from M40, junction 7: A329 towards Wallingford; SP6100], *Lamb*: Pretty 17th-c thatched pub with beams, stripped stone, low windows, soft lighting, lots of tables for wide choice of food (all day Sun – very busy day) from sandwiches to good specials and steaks, well kept Bass, Benskins and Ind Coope Burton; no piped music, children in eating area (good choice for them), peaceful and attractive garden with swings, pleasant countryside *(Mr and Mrs R Maggs, TBB, LYM)*

Long Hanborough [A4095 Bladon—Witney; SP4214], *George & Dragon*: Late 15th-c partly thatched former farm building, low beams, good food in bar and restaurant; well behaved children allowed, watch for shallow step in bar *(Joan Olivier)*

☆ **Long Wittenham** [Fieldside, off A415 SE of Abingdon; SU5493], *Machine Man*: Unpretentious simple pub with friendly helpful landlord, good choice of genuine freshly made food esp fish, wide range of ales inc Hardy Royal Oak and Wadworths, decent wines, darts; bedrooms *(B Adams, Iain Robertson)*

☆ **Long Wittenham**, *Plough*: Enjoyable sensibly priced food in friendly low-beamed refurbished lounge with lots of brass, games in public bar, inglenook log fires, Ushers ales, good service, pool and children's room; Thames moorings at bottom of long spacious garden; bedrooms *(A Kilpatrick, Hazel and Michael Duncombe)*

☆ **Marston** [Mill Lane, Old Marston; SP5209], *Victoria Arms*: Attractive grounds by River Cherwell inc spacious terrace, good play area, punt moorings and hire; full Wadworths range and guest beers kept well, generous good food (not Sun evening in winter) from chunky sandwiches up inc children's dishes, attentive service, lots of tables in civilised main room and smaller ones off, real fires; soft piped music, children and dogs allowed; lavatory for disabled; beware sleeping policemen *(R T and J C Moggridge, BB)*

Middle Assendon [B480; SU7385], *Rainbow*: Pretty and cottagey Brakspears local, unspoilt friendly low-beamed bar split into two areas, well kept beers, short choice of unpretentious but tasty food, tables on front lawn *(Gordon, C J Bromage)*

☆ **Middleton Stoney** [B430/B4030; SP5323], *Jersey Arms*: Small 19th-c stonebuilt hotel, low and rambling, developing more of a role for its bar, cosy and traditional; beams, panelling, dark tables and chairs, good log fire in big fireplace, upmarket feel, good range of reasonably priced interesting home-made food from well filled baguettes up, Tetleys, Theakstons and Wadworths 6X, good coffee, friendly helpful staff; piped music, restaurant popular for business lunches; garden; bedrooms comfortable *(George Atkinson, E A and D C Frewer, Mrs J K Edwards)*

Milton Hill [A4130, junction A34 nr Didcot Power Stn; SU4790], *Packhorse*: Refurbished Morlands pub with piping hot food and friendly attentive waitresses in no-smoking restaurant, children welcome, disabled access (perhaps best from front); piped music turned down on request; big garden – no dogs – with floodlit terrace *(Joan Olivier)*

Milton under Wychwood [High St; SP2618], *Quart Pot*: Part-panelled in pine, with new back extension, usual pub food, well kept Morlands, friendly service, flame-effect gas fire; garden, attractive Cotswold village *(Simon Collett-Jones)*

☆ **Minster Lovell** [just N of B4047 Witney—Burford; SP3111], *Old Swan*: Old inn, interesting and atmospheric despite being rather geared to well heeled visitors and conference people, popular lunchtime for good if not cheap snacks and light meals (no sandwiches, asked to pay in advance, no puddings served in bar), Marstons ales, log fire, deep armchairs, rugs on flagstones, restaurant, tables in lovely garden; bedrooms *(Gordon Tong, Mike and Heather Thomas, A C Morrison, Paul S McPherson, Gordon, LYM)*

☆ **Moulsford** [Ferry Lane, off A329 N of Streatley; SU5983], *Beetle & Wedge*: More hotel/restaurant than pub (but still taking real trouble over walkers arriving soaked and muddy with children and dog), good filled baguettes and far from cheap leisurely meals, chatty Boathouse bar/restaurant by the Thames with well kept Adnams Best, Badger Tanglefoot and Wadworths 6X, good wines, pleasant waterside garden; well behaved children welcome, charming comfortable bedrooms *(Anthony Barnes, A J Bowen, LYM)*

Nettlebed [SU6986], *Rose & Crown*: Very welcoming licensees, good food, well kept beer *(Dr Gerald Barnett)*; [Watlington Rd], *Sun*: Friendly atmosphere, well kept Brakspears, lots of jugs hanging from old beams, good choice of food, dining room; sheltered attractive garden with climbing frame, swing and barbecue *(Paul McPherson)*

☆ **Newbridge** [A415 7 miles S of Witney; SP4001], *Maybush*: Low-beamed unpretentious local in lovely Thamesside setting, good range of food, welcoming efficient service, well kept Morlands Original and Old Speckled Hen, no piped music; children welcome, moorings, pretty and neatly kept waterside garden with terrace *(Lynda Payton, Sam Samuells, John Higgins, Mrs L M Jordan, LYM)*

☆ **Newbridge**, *Rose Revived*: Big pub well worth knowing for its lovely lawn by the upper Thames, across the road from our other entry here, prettily lit at night (good overnight mooring free); inside knocked through as busy dining pub – usual food all day inc Sun carvery, prompt polite service, helpful landlord, Morlands Original and Old Speckled Hen, Ruddles County; piped music, fruit machines; children welcome (summer bouncy castle), comfortable bedrooms with good breakfast *(James Nunns, Paul S McPherson, Miss M Oakeley, LYM)*

☆ **North Hinksey** [off A34 southbound just S of A420 interchange; SP4805], *Fishes*: Comfortable pub doing well under helpful new licensees who had previously made the Half Moon at Cuxham a popular main entry, good choice of reasonably priced enjoyable food (not Sun evening), well kept Morrells, decent house wines, Victorian-style open-plan lounge and pleasant no-smoking family conservatory; traditional games, soft piped music; big streamside garden with play area and two Aunt Sally pitches *(Joan Olivier)*

☆ **North Newington** [Banbury Rd; just W of Banbury; SP4139], *Roebuck*: Open fires, piped classical music and individual furnishings in attractive bistro-style dining bar, very wide range of good value interesting freshly made food, crisp fresh veg, themed dinners, well kept Morlands, good wines and country wines, welcoming attentive service; open fire in traditional public bar, children very welcome, good garden with play area; quiet village nr Broughton Castle *(D and E Frewer, John Bowdler, Mrs Tudor Hughes)*

Northmoor [B4449 SE of Stanton Harcourt; SP4202], *Red Lion*: Recently refurbished small 15th-c stonebuilt village pub, heavily beamed bar and small dining room off, welcoming log fire, good choice of very reasonably priced food inc good value Sun lunch, well kept Morlands Original, friendly staff, garden; no dogs *(Marjorie and David Lamb, Miss M Oakeley, James Nunns)*

☆ **Nuffield** [A4130/B481; SU6687], *Crown*: Food from sandwiches up inc daily fresh fish, country furniture and inglenook log fire in beamed lounge bar, well kept Brakspears Bitter, Special, Hop Demon and a seasonal ale; children in small family room, tables outside front and back, good walks *(David Dimock, J and B Cressey, Joan Olivier, LYM)*

☆ **Oxford** [Binsey Lane; narrow lane on right leaving city on A420, just before Bishops; SP4907], *Perch*: Lovely part-thatched pub doing well under current managers, pleasant setting with dozens of tables in big garden off riverside meadow; big, busy and spick and span, with low ceilings, flagstones, stripped stone, high-backed settles as well as more modern seats, good log fires, no-smoking eating area (children allowed), Tetleys and Marstons Pedigree, decent wine, friendly service; machines, piped music; open all day in summer, good play area (and giant chess), barbecues, landing stage, attractive waterside walks *(Gordon, Tim Brierly, John and Joan Wyatt, TBB, BB)*

☆ **Oxford** [North Parade Ave], *Rose & Crown*: Enthusiastic and concerned bearded landlord and particularly well kept Tetleys-related ales in friendly and unspoilt old local; limited but popular and well priced bar lunches inc Sun roasts, decent wine, prompt service; reference books for crossword buffs, no piped music or machines, jazz piano Tues; traditional small rooms, pleasant back yard with motorised awning and huge gas heater – children not allowed here or inside unless with friends of landlord *(P A Legon, John and Hazel Waller, Roger Crisp, Gordon, Terry Buckland, BB)*

☆ **Oxford** [Alfred St], *Bear*: Friendly little low-ceilinged and partly panelled rooms, not over-smart and often packed with students; massive collection of vintage ties, simple food most days inc sandwiches (kitchen may be closed Weds), good range of well kept Tetleys-related and other ales from centenarian handpumps on rare pewter bar counter, no games machines, tables outside; open all day summer *(J and P Maloney, TBB, Gordon, LYM)*

☆ **Oxford** [St Giles], *Eagle & Child*: Busy rather touristy pub (tiny mid-bars full of actors' and Tolkien/C S Lewis memorabilia), but students too; nice panelled front snugs, tasteful stripped-brick modern back extension with no-smoking conservatory, well kept Greene King Abbot, Marstons Pedigree, Morlands Old Speckled Hen and Tetleys, plentiful quickly served food, newspapers, events posters; piped classical music *(Christopher Glasson, SLC, Gordon, Nigel Woolliscroft, BB)*

☆ **Oxford** [Broad St], *White Horse*: Busy and cheerfully studenty, sandwiched between bits of Blackwells bookshop; single small narrow bar with snug one-table raised back alcove, mellow oak beams and timbers, ochre ceiling, beautiful view of the Clarendon building and Sheldonian, good lunchtime food (the few tables reserved for this), well kept Tetleys-related ales and Wadworths 6X, Addlestone's cider, friendly licensees *(Gordon, Walter Reid, TBB, BB)*

Oxford [St Clements St], *Angel & Greyhound*: Unpretentious bare-boards Youngs pub with well kept beer, scrubbed pine tables, bar billiards, good range of food, concrete tables in back garden; open all day *(Don Bryan, P A Legon)*; [17 Victor St, Jericho], *Bookbinders Arms*: Friendly and unpretentious little local, darts, cards and serious shove ha'penny, light snacks and some hot dishes, well kept Morrells *(PB)*; [Little Clarendon St, just off St Giles], *Duke of Cambridge*: Stylish cocktail bar/brasserie with high-tech minimal decoration, flamboyant efficient barmen, good range of drinks inc freshly squeezed juices *(Walter Reid)*; [Abingdon Rd], *Duke of Monmouth*: Thriving atmosphere, distinctive woodwork and windows, good food and beer, weekly meat raffles; garden with Aunt Sally *(B Adams)*; [Folly Bridge, between St Aldates and Christchurch Meadow], *Head of the River*: Civilised well renovated pub by river, boats for hire and nearby walks; split-level downstairs bar with stone and bare boards, Fullers Chiswick, ESB, London Pride and a seasonal ale, popular food inc children's, tables on terrace; bedrooms *(SLC)*; [Iffley Lock – towpath from Donnington Bridge Rd, between Abingdon Rd and Iffley Rd], *Isis*: Included for beautiful location (beer used to come by punt); early 19th-c former farmhouse with well kept Morrells, decent food, rowing mementoes, log fire, big garden with play equipment – lots of potential *(P A Legon)*; [Banbury Rd, Summertown], *Kings*: Bright clean almost transatlantic-feeling functional bar popular with young people, fast friendly service, well kept Adnams, good sandwiches and french sticks *(Tim Brierly, R T and J C Moggridge)*; [Woodstock Rd, opp Radcliffe Infirmary], *Royal Oak*: Maze of little rooms meandering around central bar, low beams, basic furnishings, Marstons Pedigree, Morlands Old Speckled Hen and Tetleys with guests like Arrols 80/-, Badger Tanglefoot, Greene King Abbot, Harwoods Porter and Theakstons XB, lunchtime food bar with good soup and doorsteps of bread, simple main dishes, daily papers, open fire, celebrity pictures in front bar, prints and bric-a-brac, games room with darts, pool etc; piped music may be loud, can get smoky; small back terrace; well used by doctors and nurses, open all day *(Gordon, SLC, R T and J C Moggridge)*; [Friars Entry, St Michael St], *Three Goats Heads*: Two friendly, individual and attractive bars, relaxed downstairs (with bare boards, TV, fruit machine and piped music – can be loud), more formal up; well kept cheap Sam Smiths, good choice of quick generous food, dark wood, booths and political prints *(David Carr, TBB, SLC)*; [272 Woodstock Rd], *Woodstock Arms*: Quiet, neat little local, friendly service, well kept Morrells Varsity, good house wine, good value simple food inc good Sun roast, separate bar with bar billiards, fruit machines and TV; seats outside front and back *(SLC, R T and J C Moggridge)*

☆ **Pishill** [B480 Nettlebed—Watlington; SU7389], *Crown*: Lovely wisteria-covered ancient building with black beams and timbers, log fires and candlelight, relaxed atmosphere, tasty home-cooked food (not Sun or Mon evenings) from sandwiches to steaks, separate restaurant, well kept Brakspears, Flowers Original and a guest beer, friendly service, picnic-sets on attractive side lawn, pretty country setting – lots of walks; bedroom in separate cottage; children allowed Sun lunchtime in restaurant *(Susan and John Douglas, Lesley Bass, M Borthwick, Mark Percy, Lesley Mayoh, JP, PP, LYM)*

Play Hatch [just off A4155; SU7476], *Crown*: Good choice of interesting attractively presented food in spacious rambling 16th-c pub, very popular with families; two bars and several rooms inc big no-smoking conservatory (which can get noisy), well kept Brakspears PA, SB and Old tapped from casks, decent wines, good service *(Betty Laker)*

Pyrton [SU6896], *Plough*: This attractive pub has been closed for conversion to a private house *(PJK)*

☆ **Rotherfield Peppard** [Gallowstree Rd, Peppard Common – off B481 N of Reading; SU7181], *Greyhound*: Low-beamed 17th-c pub in lovely setting nr green, big fireplace in spotless attractive bar with walking stick collection, dog prints, horsebrasses, friendly service, wide choice of good home-made food from baguettes and sandwiches to sizzlers, Bass and Morlands Old Speckled Hen, pine-furnished barn restaurant; tables out in front and at side, charming garden with terrace, arbour and boules *(Susan and John Douglas, Maysie Thompson, Mark Percy, Lesley Mayoh)*

☆ **Shilton** [off B4020 S of Burford; SP2608], *Rose & Crown*: Mellow and attractive 17th-c low-beamed stonebuilt village local with unusual choice of good value home-made food from sandwiches up, friendly attentive staff, well kept Morlands Old Masters and Old Speckled Hen, woodburner, soft piped music, darts in beamed and tiled public bar, restaurant; pretty village *(Joan Olivier, Marjorie and David Lamb, Peter and Audrey Dowsett, John Higgins, G W A Pearce)*

Shiplake Row [off A4155 W of Shiplake; SU7578], *White Hart*: Friendly Brakspears pub with good choice of good food, well kept beers, decent house wines, log fires; interestingly planted garden, nice location, fine views, good walks *(A J Bowen)*

☆ **Sibford Gower** [signed off B4035 Banbury—Shipston on Stour; SP3537], *Wykham Arms*: Pretty thatched cottage with comfortable open-plan low-beamed stripped-stone lounge, nice pictures, table made from glass-topped well, inglenook tap room, good service, well kept Banks's, Hook Norton and a guest ale, good coffee, decent wines, dominoes, wide food choice from sandwiches up, attractive partly no-smoking restaurant; children welcome;

country views from big well planted garden, lovely manor house opp; cl Mon lunchtime *(Mrs Tudor Hughes, Tim and Linda Collins, NWN, Ted George, Dave Braisted, LYM)*

☆ **Souldern** [Fox Lane (off B4100); SP5131], *Fox*: Charming beamed stone pub, cosy, spotless and comfortable; good interesting food from ploughman's to good value Sun lunch, well kept Hook Norton and other ales, decent wines, friendly helpful landlord, separate dining room; four comfortable bedrooms, good breakfast, delightful village *(Andy and Jill Kassube, Tom Williams, Margaret Dyke, Anne P Heaton, Tim Brierly)*

South Leigh [3 miles S of A40 Witney—Eynsham; SP3908], *Mason Arms*: Very restauranty and by no means cheap (£5 sandwiches, top-price beer); two big log fires, pictures on dusky red walls, candlelight and flagstones, sturdy antique furnishings, nice table linen in the main dining room; no children in bar, tables outside, cl Mon *(RJH, W B Baker, Alan and Susan Dominey, LYM)*

☆ **South Moreton** [High St, just W of Wallingford; SU5588], *Crown*: Cheerful open-plan rambling old village local with superbly kept Wadworths and guest ales, some tapped from the cask, good unpretentious food, faultless friendly service, spotless housekeeping; children allowed, discount scheme for OAPs, Mon quiz night, small garden *(John C Baker)*

Sparsholt [off B4507 W of Wantage; SU3487], *Star*: Good choice of good if not cheap freshly made food in comfortable and relaxed old local, Morlands Original, Worthington BB and a guest such as Brains SA, good atmosphere with horse-racing talk, log fire, attractive pictures, daily papers, subdued piped music, back garden; pretty village *(Marjorie and David Lamb)*

Stadhampton [Bear Lane, Brookhampton; signed off A329 in village; SU6098], *Bear & Ragged Staff*: Stylishly updated 16th-c pub, log fire, flagstones and polished bar, good food in bar and restaurant, good range of well kept beers, good wine and champagne by the glass, friendly staff; tables outside, barbecue; bedrooms *(J P O'Flaherty)*

Standlake [High St, off A415 SE of Witney; SP3902], *Bell*: Quiet pub with good original if not cheap food (no bar lunches Sun/Mon), well kept Morlands and a guest such as Charles Wells Bombardier, good value wine, unusual plush separate restaurant/bar area (evening, also Sun lunch) *(D WJ, Judith Madley)*

Stanton Harcourt [B4449 S of Eynsham; SP4105], *Harcourt Arms*: More restaurant than pub, nicely presented well cooked food in three welcoming, attractive, simply furnished and pleasantly informal dining areas with Spy cartoons and huge fireplaces, good choice of wines; piped music, service can slow; children welcome *(H W Clayton, LYM)*

☆ **Steventon** [The Causeway – central westward turn off main rd; village signed off A34; SU4691], *North Star*: Tiled passage leading to unchanging unspoilt main bar with built-in settles forming snug, steam-engine pictures, interesting local horsebrasses and other brassware; open fire in parlourish lounge, simple dining room; Morlands Mild, Bitter and Best tapped from casks in a side room, cheap weekday lunchtime bar food, cribbage; tables on grass by side *(Gordon, PB, JP, PP, Iain Robertson, R Huggins, D Irving, E McCall, T McLean, LYM)*

☆ **Steventon**, *Cherry Tree*: Good choice of good generous well priced food inc good vegetarian choice in spacious and relaxing interconnecting rooms, dark green walls, two or three old settles among more modern furnishings, interesting bric-a-brac; well kept Wadworths Farmers Glory and 6X and three guest beers, decent wines, friendly and courteous licensees and staff, log-effect gas fires; unobtrusive piped music in public bar, tables on newly extended terrace *(Dick Brown, Jeff Smith)*

☆ **Stoke Lyne** [off B4100; SP5628], *Peyton Arms*: Largely unspoilt stonebuilt pub with well kept Hook Norton beers (full range) tapped from casks behind small corner bar in sparsely decorated front snug, very friendly landlord and locals, limited lunchtime snacks, real fire, hops hanging from beam, bigger newly refurbished bar with traditional games, charity book store; dogs welcome, pleasant garden with Aunt Sally; cl Mon lunchtime *(Kevin Thorpe, CMW, JJW, Andy and Jill Kassube, JP, PP, PB)*

☆ **Stoke Row** [Newlands Lane, off B491 N of Reading – OS Sheet 175 map ref 684844; SU6884], *Crooked Billet*: Opened-up rustic beamed country pub/restaurant with wide choice of good interesting meals inc full vegetarian menu, relaxed homely atmosphere – like a French country restaurant; well kept Brakspears tapped from the cask, decent wines, good log fires, children welcome; big garden, by Chilterns beech woods *(C Baxter, James Nunns, Paul McPherson, JP, PP, Bob and Ena Withers, LYM)*

Stoke Talmage [signed from A40 at Tetsworth; SU6799], *Red Lion*: Basic old-fashioned country local, very friendly and cheerful, bare-boards public bar with well kept Hook Norton and lots of changing guest beers from small corner servery, open fire, prints, posters, darts, shove-ha'penny and other games, chatty landlord, carpeted modern lounge; pleasant garden, cl lunchtime Mon/Tues *(Kevin Thorpe, Iain Robertson, PB, JP, PP)*

Stratton Audley [off A421 NE of Bicester; SP6026], *Red Lion*: Welcoming thatched village local with four real ales, good choice of good food (not Sun evening), freshly made so may be a wait – but attentive service even when busy; log fire, stripped stone and beams, suitably old varnished wooden furniture, quiet piped music; small garden, pretty village *(CMW, JJW, Tim Brierly, David Regan)*

Sutton Courtenay [SU5093], *George & Dragon*: Good chatty atmosphere in friendly 16th-c pub, attractive mix of furnishings, good choice of fair-priced home-made food from thick sandwiches upwards inc popular Sun lunch, well kept Bass and Morlands Original and Old Speckled Hen, good range of decent wines, candles on tables, pewter mugs hanging from low beam; restaurant, big back terrace overlooking graveyard where Orwell is buried; no dogs *(R Huggins, D Irving, E McCall, T McLean, TBB)*

Swerford [A361 Banbury—Chipping Norton; SP3731], *Masons Arms*: Recently refurbished, with enjoyable food and wonderful country views *(H D Spottiswoode)*

☆ **Swinbrook** [back rd a mile N of A40, 2 miles E of Burford; SP2811], *Swan*: Dim-lit little beamed and flagstoned 16th-c country pub, gently smartened up, with antique settles, sporting prints and woodburner in friendly flagstoned tap room and back bar, carpeted dining room; enjoyable food (all day weekends), traditional games, Morlands Original and Wadworths 6X, farm ciders, no piped music; seats outside, nice surroundings *(Ted George, Walter Reid, Peter and Audrey Dowsett, Daren Haines, LYM)*

☆ **Sydenham** [off A40 NW of High Wycombe, and B4445 SE of Thame; SP7201], *Crown*: Relaxed rambling low-beamed village local, a little lamp in each small window, unusual choice of good interesting food, Morrells Best and Varsity with a guest such as Adnams, good choice of wines by the glass, friendly staff, children welcome, dominoes and darts; quiz nights, maybe piped radio; picturesque village, views of lovely church *(M and S Rollinson, C and T Stone, JP, PP, Jane and Andy Rankine, B R Sparkes)*

☆ **Tackley** [Medcroft Rd, off A4260 N of Kidlington; SP4720], *Gardeners Arms*: 17th-c village pub, comfortable spick and span lounge bar with beams, brasses and coal-effect gas fire in inglenook, well presented good value food from sandwiches up inc good vegetarian choice, charming Dickensian landlord, quick attentive service, well kept Morrells Bitter, Varsity and Graduate, good coffee, old photographs and cigarette cards; separate public bar with darts, TV and fruit machine, piped music, bookable skittle alley, picnic-sets on sunny terrace; handy for Rousham House *(George Atkinson, JJW, CMW, Ian Phillips)*

Thame [21 Cornmarket; SP7005], *Abingdon Arms*: Friendly family atmosphere, generous food inc home-made fresh pasta and speciality doorstep sandwiches, good service, well kept Bass, Brakspears, Fullers London Pride, good choice of bottled beers, small no-smoking front lounge and no-smoking bar, simple bright main bar with bare boards and oriental rugs, three real fires; piped music, busier and noisier evenings; open all day, tables in nice back garden with swings *(P Worth, James Chatfield)*; [9 Upper High St], *Swan*: Fine 15th-c coaching inn overlooking interesting market sq, comfortable sofas and other seats on bare boards, lots of antiques inc a boar's head, books and magazines to read, unusual piped music (maybe Stravinsky), well kept Brakspears and a guest such as Vale Haddas Spring Gold, good coffee, interesting friendly landlord; seats in courtyard *(George Atkinson, Andy and Jill Kassube)*

☆ **Thrupp** [off A4260 just N of Kidlington; SP4815], *Boat*: Unpretentious and relaxing 16th-c stone-built local in lovely canalside surroundings, good value genuine home cooking, quick friendly service, well kept Morrells Bitter, Varsity and Graduate, local paintings for sale, no piped music; restaurant, nice garden behind with plenty of tables, some in shade *(George Atkinson, Tim Barrow, Sue Demont)*

Upton [A417 Harwell—Blewbury; SU5186], *George & Dragon*: Welcoming little pub with well presented good food prepared to order, reasonable prices, Morlands Original, small end dining area *(Marjorie and David Lamb)*

Wallingford [St Leonards Ln; SU6089], *Little House Around the Corner by the Brook*: This engaging place has now closed *(GW)*

☆ **Warborough** [The Green South; just E of A329, 4 miles N of Wallingford; SU5993], *Six Bells*: Welcoming low-ceilinged thatched pub facing cricket green, with country furnishings in interconnecting seating areas off bar, wide choice of good value interesting well cooked food, well kept Brakspears and a guest beer, decent wines, big log fire, antique photographs and pictures; tables in back orchard *(Marjorie and David Lamb, E and D Frewer, LYM)*

☆ **West Hanney** [off A338 N of Wantage; SU4092], *Plough*: Unspoilt and pretty thatched local with attractive timbered upper storey, original timbers and uneven low ceilings, homely and welcoming panelled lounge with good log fire in stone fireplace, unusual plates, brasses and exotic butterflies, friendly staff, freshly made no-nonsense food inc good value Sun lunch, Tetleys-related ales, interesting whiskies, darts in public bar; back garden with aviaries; children welcome *(Margaret Dyke, Maureen Hobbs, Paul McPherson)*

West Hanney, *Lamb*: Friendly landlord, good choice of beers; very popular for attractive food choice *(Iain Robertson)*

☆ **Weston on the Green** [B430 nr M40 junction 9; SP5318], *Ben Jonson*: Thatched country pub with comfortable dark wood settles in welcoming beamed lounge bar, snug with roaring winter fire, wide choice of good value generous food inc vegetarian, well kept Bass and Flowers IPA, good house wine, daily papers, discreet pool room; usually open all day, children very welcome; big sheltered garden with occasional barbecues *(R T and J C Moggridge, E A and D C Frewer, Neil and Anita Christopher)*

Witney [Church Green; SP3510], *Angel*: Friendly well used extended 17th-c local, cheap Hook Norton Old Hookey and Red Bull, huge choice of attractively priced food, raging coal fire, nice pubby atmosphere, very quick service even when packed; pool room, coffee bar *(Peter and Audrey Dowsett, John and Hazel Waller, W W Burke)*; [Market Sq], *Eagle Vaults*: Popular and comfortable, with reasonably priced buffet-type meals, Bass-related ales, several adjoining lounges, family room, big back garden; open all day Thurs market day, fills with younger people evenings *(Peter and Audrey Dowsett)*

☆ **Woodstock** [Park St (just off A44); SP4416], *Bear*: Handsome old THF inn with relaxing heavy-beamed bar on right, cosy alcoves, tastefully casual mix of well worn wooden antique oak, mahogany and leather furniture, tartan curtains, chintz cushions, paintings, sporting trophies, blazing inglenook log fire, well kept Morrells, good fresh sandwiches, bar lunches, morning coffee, afternoon tea, helpful service; restaurant; good bedrooms *(George Atkinson, Liz Bell, Gordon, Dave Irving, Ewan McCall, Roger Huggins, Tom McLean, BB)*

Woodstock [59 Oxford St (A44)], *Queens Own*: Small attractive stone building, long friendly narrow bar done up with bare boards, stripped stone, beamery, antique settles, elderly tables, hops on beams, candles; well kept Hook Norton and several guest ales, country wines, wide range of homely food inc Italian (less in evening), reasonable prices, daily papers, discreet piped music; small back courtyard, lively Mon quiz night *(E A and D C T Frewer, Kevin Blake)*; [22 Market St], *Star*: Warm friendly atmosphere, decent food from sandwiches up; bedrooms clean and spacious, good breakfast *(M R Johnson, TBB)*

☆ **Woolstone** [off B4507 W of Wantage; SU2987], *White Horse*: Plushly refurbished partly thatched 16th-c pub, two big open fires in spacious beamed and part-panelled room with air of highly polished well cared-for antiquity, quickly served food inc several vegetarian dishes, well kept Wadworths 6X and a guest such as Hook Norton Best, decent wines, good coffee; children allowed in eating area, sheltered garden; four charming good value bedrooms, secluded interesting village, handy for White Horse and Ridgeway walkers *(J and P Maloney, M G Hart, Peter and Audrey Dowsett)*

☆ **Wootton** [Glympton Rd (B4027 N of Woodstock); SP4320], *Killingworth Castle*: Hard-working newish licensees, friendly and popular, in striking three-storey 17th-c inn, good local atmosphere, well kept Morlands Original and a guest beer, long narrow main bar with candles and log fire, bar billiards, darts and shove-ha'penny in smaller games end, generous food, pleasant garden; jazz Weds, folk Fri; bedrooms *(Pete Baker, Gordon, Michael Hyde)*

☆ **Wroxton** [Church St; off A422 at hotel – pub at back of village; SP4142], *North Arms*: Pretty thatched stone pub with bar food inc good value soup ad sandwiches, well kept Morrells, cheerful service, log fire, eclectic furnishings, lots of beer mugs; character restaurant (not Mon); piped music, darts, dominoes, fruit machine; attractive quiet garden, lovely village *(H D Spottiswoode, Dave Braisted, Keith Sheppard)*

The Post Office makes it virtually impossible for people to come to grips with British geography, by using a system of post towns which are often across the county boundary from the places they serve. So the postal address of a pub often puts it in the wrong county. We use the correct county – the one the pub is actually in. Lots of pubs which the Post Office alleges are in Oxfordshire are actually in Berkshire, Buckinghamshire, Gloucestershire or the Midlands.

Shropshire

After last year's good crop of new main entries here, we've found some more really enjoyable places this year: the pleasantly old-fashioned Castle in (or rather almost at the top of) Bishops Castle, the rambling old Kings Arms in Cleobury Mortimer, the attractive Crown at Wentnor tucked away in quiet countryside near the Long Mynd, and (making a return to the Guide after some useful new extensions) the Plough at Wistanstow – home of those excellent Woods beers. All these have good food, and other places we'd recommend particularly for an enjoyable meal out here are the restauranty Feathers at Brockton, the very friendly Burlton Inn at Burlton, the newish Cholmondeley Riverside at Cressage (doing very well indeed, in a great riverside position), the warmly welcoming Unicorn in Ludlow, the Old Three Pigeons at Nesscliffe (lots of fresh fish), the Hundred House at Norton (they make good use of herbs from its pretty cottage garden), the Armoury in Shrewsbury (excellent choice of wines by the glass and of malt whiskies), and the warm-hearted Wenlock Edge Inn on Wenlock Edge (good use of organic local produce). From this rich choice we name the Cholmondeley Riverside at Cressage the Shropshire Dining Pub of the Year. Some other pubs here have been standing out too in recent months, praised particularly by readers for other virtues: the Royal Oak at Cardington (a fine all-rounder, its former games area now an attractive new dining room), the Longville Arms at Longville (they have the knack of making people feel really at home – particularly for an overnight stay); and for good beer the Three Tuns in Bishops Castle and Crown at Munslow (both brewing their own), and the Horseshoe at Bridges (impressive range) and Willey Moor Lock near Whitchurch (interesting guest beers) – these last two gain a Beer Award this year. Drinks in Shropshire tend to be significantly cheaper than the national average; the cheapest places we found were the Castle in Bishops Castle and Kings Arms in Cleobury Mortimer, both stocking beers from small local brewers. The Lucky Dip section at the end of the chapter is well worth exploring. Prominent entries (all inspected and approved by us) are the Bear in Bridgnorth, Coalbrookdale at Coalbrookdale, Boat at Coalport, Black Lion in Ellesmere, Crown at Hopton Wafers, Crown at Newcastle and Stiperstones at Stiperstones. The Bear at Hodnet, not yet inspected by us, also sounds good, as does the Lion at Hampton Loade (its rather restrictive opening times this year foiled our third attempt to inspect it). There's a good choice in Ironbridge, and Shrewsbury has lots of possibilities – especially for real ale.

BISHOPS CASTLE SO3289 Map 6

Castle 🛏

The Square; just off B4385

In its commanding position at the top of the town, this substantial stone coaching inn dates from 1719, first used as a hotel in the 19th c. On the right is a clubby small beamed and panelled room glazed off from the entrance, with old local prints and sturdy leather chairs on its muted carpet; on the left a bigger room with maroon plush wall seats and stools, big Victorian engravings, a coal fire and nice table-lamps. Service too is old-fashioned, in the best sense – friendly and painstaking – Wellington the Basset Hound is very welcoming too. Besides good sandwiches (from £2), the landlady cooks tasty and generous food such as soup (£2.40), fish and chips (£5.95), lasagne (£6.25), steak and kidney pie or beef stew (£6.95) and game pie or sautéed loin of pork with a cider and apple sauce (£7.50); there is a dining room which is no smoking in the evening and Sunday lunchtime. Well kept Fullers London Pride, Hobsons, Worthington Best and Youngs Special on handpump, and over 40 malt whiskies; shove-ha'penny, cribbage and dominoes; a couple of picnic-sets out by flower tubs in front, with more in the sizeable back garden. The spacious rooms here are very attractively decorated with antique furniture. *(Recommended by Hazel and Michael Duncombe, Andrew Rogers, Amanda Milsom)*

Bass ~ Licensees David and Nicky Simpson ~ Real ale ~ Meals and snacks (12-1.45, 6.30-9) ~ Restaurant ~ (01588) 638403 ~ Children welcome ~ Open 12-2.30, 6(5 Fri, 5.30 Sat)-11; 12-3, 6.30-10.30 Sun ~ Bedrooms: £35B/£50(£60B)

Three Tuns

Salop Street

There's a lively bustling atmosphere, low-backed settles, heavy walnut tables, newspapers to read, and a good mix of customers in the simply furnished beamed rooms of this well converted building. Since 1642, beer has been brewed here. It's now produced in the many-storied Victorian brewhouse across the yard. Each stage of the brewing process descends from floor to floor within the unique tower layout (it's a Grade 1 listed building) and there are brewery tours by appointment. Well kept Three Tuns XXX, Offa and Sexton on old-fashioned handpump, with bottled Clerics Cure; they do home brew kits and carry-out kegs, sales by the barrel or cases of Clerics Cure – phone Steve Dunn the brewer on (01588) 638023. They hold an annual beer festival in July with Morris dancers in the yard; decent wine list. Good home-made bar food includes fish soup (£3), toasted goat's cheese salad (£5.50), seafood salad (£6.50), steak and kidney pie, fresh cod, fish pie (£7), rabbit casserole (£7.50) and fresh crevettes in garlic butter (£8); puddings like summer pudding and lemon tart (£2.75-£3.50). Dominoes, backgammon and cards. There's a small garden and terrace. We'd like to hear about the new holiday unit in the converted stable block which has its own garden and room for up to four people. *(Recommended by D Etheridge, Derek and Sylvia Stephenson, Nigel Woolliscroft, Andrew Rogers, Amanda Milsom, Pat and Tony Martin, Hazel and Michael Duncombe, Gary Roberts, P and M Rudlin)*

Own brew ~ Licensee Margaret Anthony ~ Real ale ~ Meals and snacks ~ Restaurant ~ (01588) 638797 ~ Children in eating area of bar ~ Occasional live music in upstairs room ~ Open 12-3; 5-11; 12-11 Fri in summer, and Sat; 12-10.30 Sun ~ Bedroom: £45/£90

BRIDGES SO3996 Map 6

Horseshoe £

Near Ratlinghope, below the W flank of the Long Mynd

There's a good choice of very well kept real ales at this attractive old local, which is charmingly set in good walking country, and now run by the second generation of the Muller family. They keep Adnams Broadside and Southwold, Hobson Town Crier, Shepherd Neame Spitfire and a guest or two on handpump, as well as several bottled beers. There's a genuinely unpretentious atmosphere in the comfortable bar which has interesting windows and a good log fire, with a small no-smoking dining room leading off. Lunchtime bar food now includes sandwiches and filled rolls (from £1.75), home-made soup (£1.85), a good traditional ploughman's (from £2.90), home-made vegetable lasagne (£3.25) and chilli (£3.50), good ham salad (£3.75), and home-made puddings. Darts, cribbage and dominoes. There are very pleasantly positioned tables outside by the little River Onny, and the pub's very handy for walks on the Long Mynd itself and on Stiperstones – despite its isolation, it can get very busy in summer. *(Recommended by Derek and Sylvia Stephenson, Gwen and Peter Andrews, Nigel Woolliscoft,*

Kerry Lawn, Simon Smith, G and M Stewart, Patrick Freeman)

Free house ~ Licensee Simon Muller ~ Real ale ~ Lunchtime meals and snacks ~ (01588) 650260 ~ Children in dining room ~ Open 12-2.30(3 Sat), 6-11; 12-3, 7-11 Sun; closed Mon lunchtime (and Tues-Thurs lunchtimes in winter)

BROCKTON SO5894 Map 4

Feathers

B4378

The charming beamed rooms at this stylish stone-built pub are very attractively decorated with stencilling on the terracotta or yellow colour-wash walls; comfortable seats, and there's a delightful conservatory. It's popular for its very good seasonally changing imaginative food, and for its relaxed restauranty atmosphere: soup (£2.75), garlic bread topped with chopped bacon, peppers and melted cheddar (£3.65), greek salad or chicken liver pâté (£3.95), pasta with spinach, tomato, and pumpkin seeds with mozzarella (£7.95), salmon in filo pastry (£8.95), chilli garlic chicken (£9.75), fresh fillet of fish with a lemon and chive crust and a lemon butter sauce or teryaki duck (£10.95), half shoulder of lamb with red wine and redcurrant sauce (£12.95), and puddings like bread and butter pudding and treacle, cherry and almond tart (£3.65); good Sunday lunch, and efficient and friendly waitress service. Two rooms are no smoking, and they have a policy not to sell cigarettes; piped music. Banks's Bitter and Morrells Varsity kept under light blanket pressure. *(Recommended by W Ruxton, Mike and Mary Carter, Alan and Paula McCully, Chris Gabbitas, Hugh McPhail; more reports please)*

Free house ~ Licensee Martin Hayward ~ Real ale ~ Meals and snacks (6.30-9.30) ~ (01746) 785202 ~ Children welcome ~ Open 6.30-11 (closed lunchtimes during the week); 12-2.30, 6.30-11 Sat/Sun; closed Mon

BURLTON SJ4626

Burlton Inn

A528 Shrewsbury—Ellesmere, near junction with B4397

Satisfied praise is the unanimous response from readers for the tremendous improvements the very friendly licensees have made at this most attractively restored old pub. Everything in the three fresh feeling cottagey connecting rooms seems meticulously arranged and cared for, from the flower displays in the brick fireplace or beside the neatly curtained windows, to the piles of *Country Living* and interior design magazines left seemingly casually in the corner. There are a few racing prints, spurs and brasses on the walls, and open fires in winter; dominoes, cribbage. Beautifully prepared bar food from a menu that changes about four times a year might include soup (£2.50), spinach and mushroom pancake or crab and gruyère tart (£3.95), lime peppered chicken kebab (£4.25), steak, kidney and beer pie or breaded plaice (£6.50), mixed bean chilli with a soft tortilla or fettucine with tomato, basil and coriander sauce (£6.75), chicken breast stuffed with stilton and wrapped in smoky bacon (£8.50), sirloin steak (£9.95), fried scallops with ginger, lime, chilli and cherry tomatoes and noodles (£8.95) and roast rack of lamb with redcurrant and mint sauce (£10.50). Well kept Banks's and four guests like Camerons Strongarm, Ridleys Rumpus and Morrells Graduate on handpump; obliging, helpful service. It's often rather peaceful at lunchtimes, though it gets much busier with cheery regulars in the evening; dogs welcome. There are tables on a small lawn behind, with more on a strip of grass beyond the car park; there's a climbing frame here too, and a new terrace has smart wooden furniture. The pub sign is a reminder of the days when this was known as the Cross Keys. *(Recommended by SLC, Sue and Bob Ward, Miss S P Watkin, P A Taylor, Sue and Bob Ward, Rita and Keith Pollard, Mr and Mrs F Carroll, Peter Astbury)*

Free house ~ Licensees Gerry and Ann Bean ~ Real ale ~ Meals and snacks (till 9.45 Mon-Sat; limited menu Mon lunch) ~ (01939) 270284 ~ Open 11-3, 6-11; 12-3, 7-10.30 Sun; cl bank hol Mon lunchtime

CARDINGTON SO5095 Map 4

Royal Oak £

Village signposted off B4371 Church Stretton—Much Wenlock, pub behind church; also reached via narrow lanes from A49

Doing very well under its friendly welcoming new licensees, this lovely old wisteria-covered white stone inn is now more spacious with a comfortable new dining area with exposed old beams and studwork – it was originally the games room. The friendly, rambling, low-beamed bar has a roaring winter log fire, cauldron, black kettle and pewter jugs in its vast inglenook fireplace, old standing timbers of a knocked-through wall, hops draped along the bar gantry, and gold plush, red leatherette and tapestry seats solidly capped in elm. Home-made bar food includes cauliflower cheese (£3), cottage pie or very tasty fidget pie (£4.75), meat or vegetable lasagne (£4.50) and fish and chips (£5.30), seafood lasagne (£5.50). Hobsons, Marstons Pedigree, Wadworths 6X and Woods Shropshire Lad kept under light blanket pressure; dominoes and cribbage in the main bar. There's a no-smoking area in the bar and in the restaurant. Tables in the rose-filled front courtyard have lovely views over hilly fields, and a mile or so away – from the track past Willstone (ask for directions at the pub) – you can walk up Caer Caradoc Hill which looks over scenic countryside. *(Recommended by John Cockell, Alan and Paula McCully, Dave Holcroft, DAV, TOH, Nigel Woolliscroft, David and Kathy Holcroft, Sue and Bob Ward, Patrick Hancock, Tim Barrow, Sue Demont, KC, SLC, Pat and Clive Sherriff, Edward Froggatt)*

Free house ~ Licensees David and Christine Baugh ~ Real ale ~ Meals and snacks (not Sun evening) ~ Children welcome in eating area of bar during meal times ~ (01694) 771266 ~ Open 12-2.30, 7-11; closed Mon except bank holidays ~ One bedroom: /£40B

CLEOBURY MORTIMER SO6775 Map 4

Kings Arms

Church Street (A4117 Bewdley—Ludlow)

Right on the village street, this inn is centuries older than its Georgian frontage suggests. It's open-plan inside but has kept lots of character, with an interesting mix of furnishings including various-sized pews on its broad floorboards, well spaced bar tables, a good log fire, an attractive longcase clock, pleasant lighting and lots of local pictures and Victorian music posters; big shuttered windows look across to the church. A step down through a snug little central heavily-beamed area takes you into the main back dining part, carpeted, and more low beams liberally hung with whisky water jugs and teapots. Besides sandwiches (from £1.70) and ploughman's (£3.80), food includes soup (£1.90), chilli con carne or tuna bake (£4.99), interesting vegetarian dishes such as mediterranean hotpot or blue cheese and sage fusilli (£4.99), chicken curry, seafood gratin or chicken and leek pie (£5.99), steak and kidney pie (£6.25) and salmon in a cream and white wine sauce (£7.50), with a few extra evening dishes like crispy duck breast with spicy plum sauce (£8.25); friendly attentive staff, well kept Hobsons Best and Town Crier and two or three guest beers such as Timothy Taylor Landlord and Wadworths 6X on handpump; maybe piped classical or operatic music. A simpler area on the right has a fruit machine. The bedrooms are well decorated, comfortable and good value, with a good breakfast (you may be asked to order the night before), but some walls could be thicker, and the floor of the front ones is the ceiling of the bar. *(Recommended by M Lavery, Derek and Sylvia Stephenson, G Coates, DAV, Michael Kirby)*

Free house ~ Licensee Michael Purnell ~ Real ale ~ Meals and snacks ~ Restaurant ~ (01299) 270252 ~ Children welcome at lunchtime ~ Open 11.30-11; 12-10.30 Sun ~ Bedrooms: £25B/£45B

All main entries have been inspected anonymously by the Editor or Deputy Editor. We accept no payment for inclusion, no advertising, and no sponsorship from the drinks industry – or from anyone else.

CRESSAGE SJ5904 Map 6

Cholmondeley Riverside

Off A458 SE of Shrewsbury, slightly before Cressage itself if coming from Shrewsbury

Shropshire Dining Pub of the Year

Run on very similar lines as its very succesful sister pub the Cholmondeley Arms near Bickley Moss, this neatly converted white hotel, now open for over a year, was the *Good Pub Guide's Newcomer of the Year* in 1998, and has more than proved itself worthy of that accolade. There's a decided emphasis on the good and rather unusual food. As well as home-made baguettes (£3.95) and soups such as carrot and orange (£2.95), you might find asparagus with smoked salmon and mousseline sauce (£5.25), king prawn tails grilled with garlic and parsley butter (£5.95), chicken, ham and mushroom pie with puff pastry crust (£7.50), chicken breast in a mushroom, dijon mustard and cream sauce (£8.95), calf liver fried with butter and sage (£9.25), grilled duck breast with port, spring onion and fresh ginger sauce (£9.95), and puddings like chocolate hazelnut charlotte or hot baked chocolate sponge with chocolate sauce (£3.95); booking is advised at weekends. The spaciously civilised bar has a variety of stripped pine and oak church pews, cushioned settles and tables dotted around the central servery, with a mix of country prints, plates and tapestries on the walls. Marstons Best and Pedigree on handpump, along with a couple of weekly changing guests; there's an excellent choice of interesting wines, as well as tea and coffee. French windows lead out to tables in a perfectly positioned garden overlooking a very pretty stretch of the Severn – in less amenable conditions you can have the same idyllic view down to the water from the big new conservatory. Coarse fishing on the river costs £4 a day, though it's free if you're staying. *(Recommended by Phil Revell, M Joyner, Basil J S Minson, Steve Whalley, W C M Jones, Liz and Andrew Camp)*

Free house ~ Licensees John Radford, John Patrick Wrigley ~ Real ale ~ Meals and snacks ~ (01952) 510900 ~ Children welcome ~ Open 11-11; 12-3, 7-11(10.30 Sun) in winter; closed 25 Dec ~ Bedrooms: £50B/£65B

LLANFAIR WATERDINE SO2476 Map 6

Red Lion

Village signposted from B4355 approaching eastwards; turn left after crossing bridge

Set near a good stretch of Offa's Dyke, this lovely old inn is very well positioned in an area of outstanding natural beauty with lots of good walks and cycle rides nearby. Inside, the landlord has carefully maintained a very traditional atmosphere, the rambling lounge bar has heavy beams, cosy alcoves, easy chairs, some long, low settles and little polished wooden seats on its turkey carpet, and a woodburning stove. Perhaps even nicer is the small black-beamed tap room, with plain wooden chairs on its flagstoned floor, and table skittles, dominoes, cribbage, shove-ha'penny, sensibly placed darts and piped music. Bar food includes soup (£2.10), lunchtime sandwiches (£2.30), salmon fishcakes (£4.95), ploughman's (£5.10), pasta dish of the day (£5.50), vegetable curry (£5.95), sirloin steak (£8.95) and daily specials like king prawns in filo pastry (£7.45), chicken breast dusted with sage leaves and layered with ham and melted cheese or grilled lamb cutlets with zucchini, tomato, garlic and rosemary topping (£8.20). The no-smoking back restaurant has views down to the River Teme, the border of England and Wales. Marstons Pedigree and Wye Valley Dorothy Goodbody on handpump, kept under light blanket pressure, and a good wine list; quoits. *(Recommended by TOH, Wendy Arnold; more reports please)*

Free house ~ Licensees Chris and Judy Stevenson ~ Real ale ~ Meals and snacks (not Sun evening) ~ Restaurant ~ (01547) 528214 ~ Children in eating area of bar ~ Open 12-2, 7-11(10.30 Sun); closed Tues lunchtime ~ Bedrooms: /£40(£45B)

Anyone claiming to arrange or prevent inclusion of a pub in the *Guide* is a fraud. Pubs are included only if recommended by genuine readers and if our own anonymous inspection confirms that they are suitable.

LLANYBLODWEL SJ2423 Map 6

Horseshoe

Village and pub signposted from B4936

Looking very much like most people's idea of a quaintly traditional English pub, this wonky old black and white timbered Tudor inn is in a lovely spot by the River Tanat. There are plenty of outside seats and you can buy a day ticket (£7.50) for a mile of fly-fishing. The simple low-beamed front bar has an old black range in the inglenook fireplace, traditional black built-in settles alongside more modern chairs around oak tables on a reclaimed maple floor, and lots of brass and china. In the rambling rooms leading off you'll find darts, pool, cribbage, dominoes, fruit machine. Tasty bar food includes good lunchtime baguettes (from £3), soup (£2.25), king prawns pan-fried in garlic butter (£4.95), mediterranean bean casserole (£5.50), steak and kidney pie (£5.95), grilled fresh fish of the day with lemon and dill butter (£6.50), game casserole (£6.95), and roast poussin with sherry and brandy sauce, grilled lemon sole, wild boar in plum and red wine sauce or chicken breast in a mushroom, cream and white wine sauce (£8.95), with puddings (which may be a bit small) like chocolate mousse (£3.25), and children's meals £2.75). The dining room is oak panelled. Marstons Best and Pedigree and Banks's Mild, and a range of malt whiskies. *(Recommended by Nigel Woolliscroft, Miss V Kavanagh Mr and Mrs Archibald, R J Bland, Pete Yearsley, David Edwards, Rob Whittle, K N Hay, Sue and Bob Ward, George Atkinson, D W Jones-Williams, Roger Byrne, David and Judy Walmsley)*

Marstons ~ Lease: Dennis Plant ~ Real ale ~ Meals and snacks (not Sun evening, not Mon except bank holidays) ~ Restaurant ~ (01691) 828969 ~ Children in eating area of bar at landlord's discretion ~ Open 11.30-3, 6.30-11; 12-3, 7-10.30 Sun; closed Mon lunch

LONGVILLE SO5494 Map 4

Longville Arms

B4371 Church Stretton—Much Wenlock

Once again this modest-looking inn – delightfully set in really beautiful countryside – is readers' favourite place to stay in this county. Bedrooms in a converted stable block are really comfortable, the conscientious licensees warmly welcoming hosts and the breakfasts marvellous. On the pub side of things, of the two spacious bars, the left one is simpler with sturdy elm or cast-iron-framed tables, newly covered banquettes, and a woodburning stove at each end. The right-hand lounge has dark plush wall banquettes and cushioned chairs, with some nice old tables. There's a wide range of good-value homely bar food, including sandwiches, soup (£1.50), deep-fried camembert with home-made chutney (£3.50), a vegetarian dish (£4.40), fresh grilled trout with almonds (£5.85), scampi (£5.95), cajun chicken (£6.30), sirloin steak (£7.90), and daily specials, and excellent puddings. Well kept Bass and Hobsons Best on hand or electric pump, with maybe a guest in summer, and several malt and Irish whiskies; cribbage, dominoes. There are picnic-sets under cocktail parasols in a neat terraced side garden, with a good play area and trampoline. The pub is well placed near to an excellent range of local attractions. They don't accept credit cards. *(Recommended by Mike Gorton, Mike and Mary Carter, Bruce Howells, Philip Champness, Mr and Mrs P Eastwood, Roger Byrne, Nigel Woolliscroft, TOH, Alan and Paula McCully, Charles Faragher, Miss Sarah Corlett, John Cumberland, Jeff Davies, Judy Wayman, Bob Arnett, the Harrowes, Edward Froggatt)*

Free house ~ Licensee Patrick Egan ~ Real ale ~ Meals and snacks ~ (01694) 771206 ~ Children welcome ~ Occasional live music Fri or Sun evening ~ Open 12-3, 7-11(10.30 Sun); closed Tues ~ Bedrooms: £20S/£40(£45S)

Most of the big breweries now work through regional operating companies, with different names. If a pub is tied to one of these regional companies, we put the parent company's name in brackets – in the details at the end of each main entry.

LUDLOW SO5175 Map 6

Unicorn

Lower Corve St, off Shrewsbury Rd

Beyond the car park of this very much enjoyed 17th-c inn, built in a row of black and white houses, there's a pretty little terrace with tables sheltering pleasantly among willow trees right next to the modest river Corve. Inside, the warmly atmospheric solidly beamed and partly panelled bar has a bustling atmosphere, a good mix of friendly locals and visitors, and a huge log fire in a big stone fireplace. There's also a timbered, candlelit no-smoking restaurant. Good, tasty, properly home-made bar food (you can also eat the restaurant food in the bar, too), might include lovely soup (£2.50), ploughman's (£4.95), lamb cutlets with onion sauce (£5.95), salmon and prawn bake or steak and kidney pie (£6.25), devilled kidneys (£7.50), wild boar with dry sherry and mushroom sauce (£8.75), venison with red fruit juice (£9.25) and half a roast duck with apple and ginger sauce (£11.25), and a splendid choice of home-made puddings like chocolate, toffee and rum gateau or sticky gingerbread; good breakfasts, and a good value Sunday lunch. Service is attentive, cheerful and willing. Well kept Bass and Worthington BB on handpump; dominoes. One or two readers have felt that the loos need refurbishing. *(Recommended by Ian Jones, Neil and Anita Christopher, Ann Williams, Tony Hughes, Janet Lee, Keith Sheppard, Gillian Jenkins, W W Burke, Wayne Brindle, Paul Robinshaw, Gwen and Peter Andrews, Alan and Barbara Mence, D Voller, Norman and Sarah Keeping, Andrew Shore, Theo, Anne and Jane Gaskin)*

Free house ~ Licensees Alan and Elisabeth Ditchburn ~ Real ale ~ Meals and snacks ~ Restaurant ~ (01584) 873555 ~ Children welcome in snug ~ Open 12-3, 6-11; 12-3.30, 7-10.30 Sun; closed 25 Dec ~ Bedrooms: £18(£25B)/£36(£50B)

MUCH WENLOCK SJ6200 Map 4

George & Dragon

High St

There are impressive collections of old brewery and cigarette advertisements, bottle labels and beer trays, George-and-the-Dragon pictures, and over one thousand water jugs hanging from the beams in the cosily atmospheric rooms at this unpretentious town local. It's furnished with a few antique settles as well as conventional furnishings, a couple of attractive Victorian fireplaces (with coal-effect gas fires), and an old till on the bar. At the back, the quieter snug old-fashioned rooms have black beams and timbering, little decorative plaster panels, tiled floors, a stained-glass smoke room sign, a big mural as well as lots of smaller pictures (painted by local artists), and a little stove in a fat fireplace. Very well liked bar food might include chicken liver pâté with redcurrant, orange and mint relish (£3.85), avocado, smoked salmon and prawn salad with coriander and lime vinaigrette (£3.95), home-baked ham with watercress, pear and shropshire blue sauce (£7.25) or honey glazed duck breast with orange and port sauce and onion and ginger marmalade (£9.50); no-smoking restaurant. Well kept Hook Norton Best and three often unusual guest beers from brewers like Everards, Hobsons, Lichfield or Timothy Taylor on handpump. *(Recommended by Nigel Woolliscroft, G Coates, John Andrew, Mr and Mrs P Eastwood, CMJ, JJW, M Joyner, Sam Samuells, Lynda Payton, DFL, Pat and Tony Martin, D Voller)*

Free house ~ Licensee Barry Blakeman ~ Real ale ~ Meals and snacks ~ Restaurant ~ (01952) 727312 ~ Well behaved children welcome ~ Open 11-2.30, 6-11; 12-3, 7-10.30 Sun

Talbot

High Street

The delightful little coach entry at this partly 14th-c civilised inn leads off the high street to white seats and tables in an attractive sheltered yard, and the entrance to the bar. Inside there are several neatly kept areas with comfortable green plush button-back wall banquettes around highly polished tables, low ceilings, and two big log fires (one in an inglenook); the walls are decorated with prints of fish and brewery paraphernalia; piped music. Lunchtime specials might include steak and kidney pie, fresh cod in mushroom and pepper sauce, pork and apricot pie or lasagne (£6.95), and evening specials like roast quail véronique, honey roast duckling or grilled halibut with tarragon and cream butter sauce (£12.95), and home-made puddings like pear, cherry and almond tart or sticky toffee pudding (£3.25); three course Sunday lunch (£10.95). The restaurant is no smoking. Well kept changing ales might include Courage Directors, John Smiths, and Theakstons on handpump or tapped from the cask, and several malt whiskies. *(Recommended by Janet and Peter Race, David and Kathy Holcroft, Geoff and Angela Jaques, Edward Froggatt, SLC, M Joyner)*

Free house ~ Licensees Sean and Cheryl Brennan ~ Real ale ~ Meals and snacks (not Sat evening) ~ Restaurant ~ (01952) 727077 ~ Children in eating area of bar ~ Open 10-3, 6-11; 12-3, 7-10.30 Sun ~ Bedrooms: £45B/£90B

MUNSLOW SO5287 Map 2

Crown

B4368 Much Wenlock—Craven Arms

Families are very welcome in the friendly rooms of this big old brewhouse which has a good children's menu, a donkey in the back yard, Sarge the cat and Tosh the friendly dog. Behind its imposing Georgian facade, there's a cosy Tudor interior with oak beams, nooks, and crannies. The warm and friendly split-level lounge bar has a pleasantly old-fashioned mix of furnishings on its broad flagstones, a collection of old bottles, country pictures, a bread oven by its good log fire, seats in a traditional snug with its own fire; the eating area has tables around a central oven chimney, stripped stone walls, more beams and flagstones. From their own microbrewery, they produce Munslow Boys Pale Ale, Munslow Hundred, and sometimes a third brew named after one of the locals; they also keep Marstons Pedigree on handpump. A wide choice of generously served home-made food includes filled french bread (from £1.75), soup (£2.25), vegetable gratin (£7.50), pork charcuterie or rump steak (£8.50), salmon normandy or asparagus chicken (£8.95) and thai tiger prawns (£10.95). Relaxed and friendly family service; games room with darts, table skittles, cribbage and dominoes; piped music. Tables outside. *(Recommended by A W and K J Randle, Mike and Mary Carter, Chris Gabbitas, Hugh McPhail, TOH, Dr B and Mrs P Baker, Edward Froggatt)*

Own brew ~ Licensees Vic, Mike and Zoe Pocock ~ Real ale ~ Meals and snacks ~ Restaurant ~ (01584) 841205 ~ Children welcome ~ Open 12-2.30, 7-11; 12-3, 7-10.30 Sun

NESSCLIFFE SJ3819 Map 6

Old Three Pigeons

A5 Shrewsbury—Oswestry

There are all sorts of things to see in the two acres of ground at this busy dining pub, from ducks and swans on the new lake, to a well stocked bird garden, a hen coop with rare laying hens (they use the eggs in the pub), to a Russian tank and other military hardware which they often lend to museums or shows; a few tables out here too. The long low building (parts of which are thought to be 14th c) looks quite big from the outside; the restaurant takes up much of the space, leaving two traditional bar areas separated by a brick pillar mostly covered by the food blackboard. These have brown cushioned sofas along the walls, a mix of plain wooden chairs and tables, log fires, and quite a few brasses on the walls or hanging from the ceiling. There's a food servery under the window, though it's generally used only for functions; the juke box by here isn't always switched on. Four real ales such as Boddingtons, Courage Directors, John Smiths and Morlands Old Speckled Hen kept under light blanket pressure, with about eight wines by the glass (including quite a few bin-ends); People come from quite some distance to eat here. The licensees hang and butcher their own meat, and fresh fish features heavily on the huge chalkboard menu, with cajun Scottish salmon, oak smoked haddock in a grain mustard sauce or swordfish in olive oil with garlic and herbs (£9.95), silver hake and roasted almonds (£10.95), whole oven baked bass (£13.95), alongside pork crumble, beef stroganoff and chicken breast wrapped in bacon and topped with a cream and cheese sauce (£9.95). There may be a wait at busy times; friendly service. It's handy for Kynaston Cave, and some good cliff walks. *(Recommended by Miss S P Watkin, P A Taylor, SLC, John Cumberland, Edward Froggatt, Sue and Bob Ward, J S M Sheldon)*

Free house ~ Licensee Dylan Brooks ~ Real ale ~ Meals and snacks ~ Restaurant ~ (01743) 741279 ~ Children welcome ~ Open 11.30-3, 6-11; all day Sat/Sun; closed all day Mon in winter

NORTON SJ7200 Map 4

Hundred House

A442 Telford—Bridgnorth

The cottagey gardens at this popular and very carefully run family business are delightfully pretty with unusual roses, trees, and herbaceous plants, and a very big working herb garden that supplies the kitchen. The neatly kept bar is divided into several separate areas, with old quarry tiles at either end and modern hexagonal ones in the main central part – which has high beams strung with hop-bunches and dried flowers. Steps lead up past a little balustrade to a partly panelled eating area where stripped brickwork looks older than that elsewhere. Handsome fireplaces have log fires or working Coalbrookdale ranges (one has a great Jacobean arch with fine old black cooking pots), and around sewing-machine tables are a variety of interesting chairs and settles with some long colourful patchwork leather cushions. From the brasserie menu, food includes sausage and mash (£5.95), lasagne (£6.50), steak and kidney pie (£6.95), coq au vin (£8.95) and 10oz sirloin (£12.95). Well kept Woods Shropshire Lad on handpump along with Ailrics Old, and Heritage Bitter (light and refreshing, not too bitter) brewed for them by a small brewery; also an extensive wine list with house wines by the carafe, half carafe, and big or small glass, and lots of malt whiskies; dominoes, piped music; the bedrooms here are particularly attractive. *(Recommended by Mike and Mary Carter, SLC, Dick Brown, Michael and Gillian Ford, David and Kathy Holcroft, Anthony Longden, Joyce McKimm, R Gorick, Andrew and Ruth Triggs, Yvonne and Peter Griffiths, Edward Froggatt, Ian Morley, Michael Begley)*

Free house ~ Licensee Henry Phillips ~ Real ale ~ Meals and snacks (till 10pm) ~ (01952) 730353 ~ Children welcome ~ Open 11-3.30, 6-11; 12-3.30, 7-10.30 Sun; cl 25 Dec evening ~ Bedrooms: £69B/£99B

PULVERBATCH SJ4202 Map 6

White Horse

From A49 at N end of Dorrington follow Pulverbatch/Church Pulverbatch signposts, and turn left at eventual T-junction (which is sometimes signposted Church Pulverbatch); OS Sheet 126 map reference 424023

The friendly rambling rooms in this bustling country pub have black beams and heavy timbering, as well as unusual fabric-covered high-backed settles and brocaded banquettes on its turkey carpet, sturdy elm or cast-iron-framed tables, and an open coalburning range with gleaming copper kettles. A collection of antique insurance plaques, big brass sets of scales, willow-pattern plates, and pewter mugs hangs over the serving counter, and there's even a good Thorburn print of a grouse among the other country pictures. Good bar food includes macaroni cheese (£3.95), plaice goujons (£4.50), lasagne (£4.75), chilli or chicken curry (£4.95), prawn and chicken curry (£6.25), sirloin steak (£7.50), and children's dishes (from £1.50). Well kept Boddingtons, Flowers Original and Wadworths 6X on handpump, several decent wines by the glass, and over 100 malt whiskies; friendly efficient service. The quarry-tiled front loggia with its sturdy old green leatherette seat is a nice touch. The entrance is around the back of the pub. *(Recommended by G Neighbour, Chris Gabbitas, Hugh McPhail, B Johnson, A Walsh)*

Whitbreads ~ Lease: James MacGregor ~ Real ale ~ Meals and snacks (till 10pm) ~ (01743) 718247 ~ Children welcome ~ Open 11.30-3, 7-11(10.30 Sun)

SHREWSBURY SJ4912 Map 6

Armoury 🍷

Victoria Quay, Victoria Avenue

Big arched windows overlooking the river light up the single airy room at this recently converted, enormous warehouse. The walls are packed with old prints, documents and other neatly framed ephemera, and glass cabinets show off collections of explosives and shells as well as corks and bottle openers. One entire wall is covered with copiously filled bookshelves, so that if you visit during a rare quiet moment it can look a little like a cross between a library and a museum. There's a mix of good heavy wooden tables, chairs and high-backed settles, interspersed by the occasional green-painted standing timber, and colonial fans whirring away on the ceiling. An eyecatchingly huge range of varied drinks served from behind the long bar counter includes well kept Boddingtons, Flowers Original, Wadworths 6X and Woods Shropshire Lad and a couple of guests like Batemans Valiant on handpump; a good wine list; includes around 25 by the glass; around 70 malt whiskies, a dozen different gins, lots rums and vodkas, a wide choice of brandies, and some unusual liqueurs. Tables at one end of the room are laid out for eating, while at the other is a grand stone fireplace; backgammon and draughts. Good bistro-style food includes chicken, asparagus and mushroom terrine with sweetcorn and coriander salsa (£4.95), breaded medallions of pork fillet on summer greens with tomato and chive sauce (£8.95) and guinea fowl breast with bacon, shallots and tarragon with dauphinoise potato and roast vegetables (£9.95). A convent stood on this site until the Dissolution, then in 1922 the current building was moved here brick by brick from its original position; it had its rather smart conversion to a pub in 1995. The place can get busy in the evenings, particularly at weekends. You can paddle boats along the Severn outside, escorted past rows of weeping willows by swans and gently quacking ducks. The pub doesn't have its own parking but they sell vouchers for parking on the road. *(Recommended by R J Bland, W W Burke, Dr H V Hughes, SLC)*

Free house ~ Managers Jill Mitchell and Eugene Millea ~ Real ale ~ Meals and snacks ~ (01743) 340525 ~ Open 11.30-3, 5-11 Mon-Fri; all day weekends

WENLOCK EDGE SO5796 Map 4

Wenlock Edge Inn ★ 🍴 🛏

Hilltop; B4371 Much Wenlock—Church Stretton, OS Sheet 137 map reference 570962

Although doing brilliantly well in all respects (it's a lovely place to stay), what makes this place so special is the genuinely warm welcome from the friendly landlord and his family, and the way visitors are immediately involved in the bar room chat. The cosy feel is perhaps at its best on the second Monday in the month (8pm) – story telling night, when the right hand bar is packed with locals telling tales, some true and others somewhat taller. In the right hand bar is a big woodburning stove in an inglenook, as well as a shelf of high plates, and it leads into a little dining room. The room on the left has pews that came from a Methodist chapel in Liverpool, a fine oak bar counter, and an open fire. Very popular bar food using local and organic produce, and delicious home-baked bread includes cream of asparagus soup (£2.75), garlic mushrooms (£3.85), steak and mushroom pie (£6.50), chicken, bacon and asparagus gratin (£6.90), salmon salad (£7.20), venison pie (£7.25), plaice fillet (£7.75), lamb casserole with redcurrant gravy (£7.85), sirloin steak (£9.90), and puddings like raspberry and apple crumble and rich chocolate roulade (£3.10-£3.40); good breakfasts. The dining room is no smoking. Well kept local Hobsons Best and Town Crier and a guest on handpump, interesting whiskies, decent wines by both glass and bottle, and lots of non alcoholic drinks like old-fashioned lemonade, ginger beer, raspberry and ginger brew, fruit cordials and cappuccino, and no music – unless you count the deep-throated chimes of Big Bertha the fusee clock. Water comes from their own 190 foot well. There are some tables on a front terrace and the side grass, and they are constructing a herb garden to fit in with the wildlife pond. The building is in a fine position just by the Ippikins Rock viewpoint and there are lots of walks through the National Trust land that runs along the Edge. *(Recommended by Joy and Peter*

Heatherley, M Joyner, SLC, Chris Brace, Mike and Mary Carter, Gwen and Peter Andrews, Dr Stephen Feast, Chris and Ann Garnett, Mike and Wena Stevenson, Mike Gorton, TOH, Gillian Jenkins, Alan and Paul McCully, Nigel Woolliscroft, Mr and Mrs G Lloyd, M Kershaw, Paul and Maggie Baker, Liz Bell, Ian Morley, Geoff and Angela Jaques, Fiona Jarman, Tim Barrow, Sue Demont, Mark Percy, Lesley Mayoh, Luke Worthington, Edward Froggatt, Pat and Clive Sherriff, Michael Begley, Mr and Mrs Lawson, Mr and Mrs Corelis; also in the Good Hotel Guide)

Free house ~ Licensee Stephen Waring ~ Real ale ~ Meals (not Mon except for residents) ~ Restaurant ~ (01746) 785678 ~ Children in restaurant, and in eating area of bar over 5 ~ Open 11.30-2.30, 6.30-11; 12-2.30, 6.30-10.30 Sun; closed Mon lunchtime; closed 24-26 Dec ~ Bedrooms: £45S/£70S

WENTNOR SO3893 Map 6

Crown

Village and pub signposted (not very clearly) off A489 a few miles NW of junction with A49

Very much a dining pub, this 16th-c place in a quiet out-of-the-way village has a fine view of the Long Mynd from picnic-sets and old-fashioned teak garden seats on its neat back lawn. Inside, one end has a snug area with two elderly sofas, pictures and a dresser filled with Portmeirion 'Botanic Garden' china, but the main bar area, with beams, standing timbers, a good log fire, some nice big prints and a collection of china and cut glass, is filled with a variety of tables set for food. Though not cheap, this is good value, running from sandwiches (from £1.50), soup (£2.30) and ploughman's (£4.75) through local sausages (£5.50), scampi (£6.50) and grilled salmon steaks with yoghurt and fresh dill mayonnaise (£8.50) to lamb Shrewsbury (£9.95) and a mixed grill (£10.25), with vegetarian dishes such as baked vegetables in a creamy cheese sauce (£6.95) and snacky things such as spinach timbale (£3.25) or oriental prawns (£3.50). There's also a cosy beamed no-smoking restaurant. Well kept Bass, Hobsons, Morlands Old Speckled Hen, Woods Shropshire Lad and Worthington on handpump, decent wines, very friendly helpful staff (the little spaniel's friendly, too). There may be piped music. Booking is suggested for Sunday lunch – and the bedrooms tend to get booked quite a way ahead. *(Recommended by SLC, Paul Robinshaw, TOH, R W Sheppard, S Phillips)*

Free house ~ Licensees David and Jane Carr ~ Real ale ~ Meals and snacks ~ Restaurant ~ (01588) 650613 ~ Well behaved children welcome in eating area of bar and restaurant ~ Open 12-3, 7-11(10.30 Sun) ~ Bedrooms: £25(£30B)/£45(£53B)

WHITCHURCH SJ5345 Map 7

Willey Moor Lock

Actually just over the Cheshire border, the pub is signposted off A49 just under two miles N of Whitchurch

The idyllic setting (across a little footbridge over the Llangollen Canal and its rushing sidestream), an interesting choice of well kept real ales, and the very welcoming landlady attract a good mix of customers of all types and ages to this lock keeper's cottage. Several neatly decorated low-beamed rooms have brick-based brocaded wall seats, stools and small chairs around dimpled copper and other tables, low ceilings, a large teapot collection and a decorative longcase clock, and two winter log fires. As well as well kept Theakstons Best there are four guest beers like Butterknowle Conciliation Ale, Hanby All Seasons, Salopian Shropshire Spires and Wychwood Fiddlers Elbow on handpump, and about 30 malt whiskies. Generous helpings of bar food such as battered cod (£4.95), steak pie or home-carved ham (£5) and mixed grill (£7). Fruit machine, piped music, and several dogs and cats. There are tables under cocktail parasols on a terrace, and a children's play area with swings and slides in the garden. *(Recommended by Nigel Woolliscroft, John Cockell, Graham and Lynn Mason, SLC, Chris Gabbitas, Hugh McPhail, David and Kathy Holcroft, Mike and Wena Stevenson, Wayne Brindle, Basil Minson)*

Free house ~ Licensee Mrs Elsie Gilkes ~ Real ale ~ Meals and snacks ~ (01948) 663274 ~ Children welcome away from bar area ~ Open 12-2.30(2 in winter), 6-11; 12-3, 7-10.30 Sun; closed 25 Dec

WISTANSTOW SO4385 Map 6

Plough 🍷

Village signposted off A49 and A489 N of Craven Arms

The delicious Wood beers Shropshire Lad, Special and a couple of seasonal brews are produced in a separate brew building behind this brick built tap house, where they are perfectly kept alongside a guest on handpump; also farm ciders, about 16 wines by the glass, and a fine display cabinet of bottled beers. The light and airy comfortable modern cafe-style interior has high rafters and bright lighting, and has recently been extended and freshly decorated. There's quite some emphasis on the popular home-made bar meals which might include big filled french sticks (£2.95), steak and kidney pie or baked mushrooms stuffed with stilton and leeks (£5.95); no credit cards. The games area has darts, pool, fruit machine and juke box. Outside there are some tables under cocktail parasols. *(Recommended by Jenny and Michael Back, Derek and Sylvia Stephenson, TOH, George Atkinson, Nigel Woolliscroft, Gwen and Peter Andrews, Chris Gabbitas, Hugh McPhail, Andrew Rogers, Amanda Milsom, Luke Worthington)*

Own brew ~ Managers Matthew Williams and Edward Wood ~ Real ale ~ Meals and snacks ~ (01588) 673251 ~ Children welcome ~ Open 12-3, 7-11(10.30 Sun)

Lucky Dip

Besides the fully inspected pubs, you might like to try these Lucky Dips recommended to us and described by readers (if you do, please send us reports):

☆ **All Stretton** [Shrewsbury Rd (B4370); SO4695], *Yew Tree*: Current owners doing good value changing food in comfortable beamed bars and dining room, well kept Bass and Worthington BB, quick helpful service, quiet piped music, dining room; children welcome, small village handy for Long Mynd *(TOH, J S Green, Robin Morton)*

Ash [Ash Magna; SJ5739], *White Lion*: Village pub with good choice of well kept ales inc guest beers such as Woods Woodcutter, Czech lager; antique golf club collection on lounge bar beams, brewery memorabilia, good atmosphere, friendly service, blazing log fires, sandwiches and snacks *(Sue and Bob Ward, SLC)*

Baschurch [Station Rd (B4397); SJ4222], *Boreatton Arms*: Modern pub with new no-smoking restaurant area (children welcome), wholesome tasty food, changing ales such as Everards Tiger and Hancocks HB, good wheelchair access *(G Coates)*

Bicton [Holyhead Rd; old A5 W of Shrewsbury; SJ4513], *Four Crosses*: Enterprising pub/restaurant with wide choice of generous reasonably priced food inc lunchtime and early evening bargains, good Sun lunches and fresh veg; big bar, raised eating area, restaurant, Bass and Worthington, reasonably priced wines, welcoming owners *(Dave and Kathy Holcroft)*

Billingsley [B4363 S of Bridgnorth; SO7185], *Cape of Good Hope*: Very popular, with bargain steaks in all sizes, help-yourself salads, Banks's ales *(Mr and Mrs D Lawson)*

☆ **Bridgnorth** [just past Northgate (B4373 N); SO7293], *Bear*: Particularly well run busy two-room pub with mix of wall banquettes, padded chairs and one or two settles, old notices and local pictures, french windows to small sheltered lawn with picnic-sets, good attractively priced food inc sandwiches, interesting specials, good fish and must-book Thurs gourmet nights, well kept changing ales such as Bathams, Blackbeard SJH, Hanby Love Bite, Holdens and Ruddles Best, good choice of wines; bedrooms *(Derek and Sylvia Stephenson, NWN, SLC, Tony Goff, Judy Van Der Sande, BB)*

☆ **Bridgnorth** [Stn; A458 towards Stourbridge], *Railwaymans Arms*: Good interesting real ales in converted waiting-room at Severn Valley steam railway terminus, bustling on summer days; simple summer snacks, coal fire, station nameplates, superb mirror over fireplace, seats out on platform; children welcome *(Nigel Woolliscroft, Barnie, Gwen and Peter Andrews, SLC, LYM)*

Bridgnorth, *Golden Lion*: Pleasantly decorated friendly traditional pub with well kept Banks's, decent coffee, hearty helpings of standard bar food; no music *(Gwen and Peter Andrews)*

Church Stretton [42 High St; SO4593], *Bucks Head*: Popular town pub with no-smoking open-plan eating area off bar, food inc generous bargain OAP lunch Weds *(TOH)*

☆ **Clun** [High St; SO3081], *Sun*: Friendly Tudor pub, timbers and beams, some sturdy antique furnishings, enormous open fire in flagstoned public bar, good food, well kept ales inc Banks's Bitter and Mild, Marstons Pedigree and Woods Special; children allowed in eating area, tables on sheltered back terrace; bedrooms, lovely village *(Steve Power, Edward Froggatt, Dagmar Junghanns, Colin Keane, LYM)*

Clun, *Buffalo*: Good range of beer, friendly welcome, good reasonably priced food from big filled baguettes up; tables in garden – dogs allowed *(Bob Medland)*

☆ **Coalbrookdale** [Wellington Rd, opp Museum of Iron; SJ6704], *Coalbrookdale*: Long flight of steps up to handsome dark brick 18th-c pub, simple, cheerful and bustling tiled-floor bar with local pictures, six or seven well kept changing ales such as Courage Directors, Enville, Flowers IPA and Original, Greene King Abbot and Theakstons XB from square counter also serving rather smaller carpeted room set more for the good value often imaginative food (not Sun); real fires, farm cider, country wines, good mix of people, piano, no piped music; dogs allowed, opens noon *(Sam Samuells, Lynda Payton, Barnie, CMW, JJW, BB)*

☆ **Coalport** [Salthouse Rd, Jackfield, nr Mawes Craft Centre; SJ6903], *Boat*: Cosy unspoilt waterside pub, quarry-tiled bar redecorated by hard-working newish licensees, coal fire in lovely range, good food inc local free-range pork, game and cheeses and good value Sun lunch, well kept Banks's Bitter and Mild, Camerons, Marstons and Morrells, Weston's farm cider, darts; summer barbecues on big tree-shaded lawn, in delightful part of Severn Gorge – though the footbridge to the china museum has been cl recently *(Basil Minson, B J Harding, Dr Steve Hugh, BB)*

☆ **Corfton** [B4368 Much Wenlock—Craven Arms; SO4985], *Sun*: Welcoming country local with good value food inc children's, lots of vegetarian, good fish and veg and bargain Sun lunch, well kept Whitbreads-related ales, pleasant lounge, lively and cheery bar, obliging service, dining room; tables on terrace and in good-sized garden with good play area; piped music; open all day, disabled access throughout *(Dr B and Mrs P B Baker, BB)*

Coton [Tilstock Rd; B5476 Wem—Whitchurch; SJ5234], *Bull & Dog*: Black and white open-plan Greenalls pub with screened-off dining area, good value food, Tetleys, pleasant service; piped music *(Sue and Bob Ward)*

Craven Arms [SO4383], *Stokesay Castle*: Friendly, with good fresh varied food from ploughman's to venison, good value; very accommodating over children's food; pleasant small dining room and bar, nice big garden *(Margaret Measures and family)*

Cressage [A458 Shrewsbury—Bridgnorth; SJ5904], *Eagles*: New landlord doing enjoyable food; well kept Banks's *(David Brammer)*

☆ **Ellesmere** [Scotland St (back car park on A495); SJ4035], *Black Lion*: Pleasantly relaxed and well run bar off tiled entrance corridor, interesting decor and some nice unusual features, quiet and comfortable roomy dining room, simple cheap substantial food all day inc bargains for children and OAPs, cheery service, well kept Marstons Bitter, Pedigree and Head Brewers Choice; piped music;; bedrooms, not far from canal wharf *(Dorothee and Dennis Glover, Miss S Watkin, P Taylor, S W Armstrong, BB)*

☆ **Hampton Loade** [off A442 S of Bridgnorth; SO7586], *Lion*: Warm and welcoming 17th-c stripped-stone inn tucked away down pot-holed lane, in very attractive spot overlooking River Severn; open fires, friendly efficient staff, good unusual food inc generous Sun lunch, good choice of well kept beer inc local Enville, Hook Norton Best and Simpkiss, country wines, good day-ticket fishing on River Severn, dining room; if anything the well worn in interior adds to the cosy feel; very busy in summer or when Severn Valley Rly has weekend steam spectaculars (quaint ferry crossing to stn), quiet otherwise; children welcome if eating lunchtime (or if booked to dine evening), picnic-sets outside; cl Mon, winter weekday lunchtimes, maybe some other times *(John Cumberland, Edward Froggatt, David and Kathy Holcroft, Sue and Bob Ward, Nigel Woolliscroft)*

Harmer Hill [SJ4822], *Bridgewater Arms*: Brewers Fayre pub with big dining area, decent food, Marstons Pedigree and a guest such as Wadworths 6X, refreshingly interested staff; play area *(Pat and Robert Watt, SLC)*

Heathton [SO8192], *Old Gate*: Wide choice of good food inc good choice of fresh fish in beautifully decorated pub with charming rooms on different levels, well kept Tetleys-related ales, good choice of wines, big attractive garden *(Nigel Roper)*

High Ercall [B5062; SJ5917], *Cleveland Arms*: Friendly, clean and tidy, with three real ales inc Mild, reasonable choice of good value straightforward fresh food, children welcome; picnic-sets in garden with quite a big play area *(CMW, JJW)*

☆ **Hodnet** [Drayton Rd (A53); SJ6128], *Bear*: Welcoming 16th-c pub with good range of reasonably priced well presented food from sandwiches up inc vegetarian, Scottish Courage ales, friendly helpful service; sofas and easy chairs in foyer, roomy refurbished bar with good solid furnishings and log fire, restaurant with small no-smoking area and corner alcove with glass-tile floor over unusual sunken garden in former bear pit; open all day, children welcome (high chairs and child-size cutlery), six good value comfortable bedrooms, opp Hodnet Hall gardens and handy for Hawkstone Park *(Keith and Janet Morris, Lawrence Bacon, Jean Scott, Ray Hebson, Edward Froggatt, Chris Gabbitas, Hugh McPhail, Neil and Anita Christopher, G Washington, SLC)*

☆ **Hopton Wafers** [A4117; SO6476], *Crown*: Friendly and attractive old creeper-covered inn with tables out on terraces and in garden running down to pond and stream with geese and ducks, warmly decorated beamed bar with big inglenook fire and woodburner, nice mix of individually chosen tables and chairs, interesting choice of well prepared good food, well kept Whitbreads-related ales with guests such as Fullers London Pride and Greene King Abbot, good house wines, courteous efficient staff, restaurant with no-smoking area; provision for children, comfortable and pretty timbered bedrooms *(George Atkinson, Alan and Barbara Mence, Paul and Maggie Baker, Mrs U Hofheinz, LYM)*

☆ **Ironbridge** [Blists Hill Open Air Museum – follow brown museum sign from M54 exit 4, or A442; SJ6704], *New Inn*: Rebuilt Victorian pub in this good heritage museum's re-created working Victorian community (shares its opening hours); informative licensees and friendly staff in period dress, well kept Banks's Bitter and Mild, pewter measure of mother's ruin for 2½d (money from nearby bank), good pasties, gas lighting, traditional games, good generous home cooking in upstairs tearoom; back yard with hens, pigeon coop, maybe children in costume playing hopscotch and skipping; children welcome *(Sam Samuells, Lynda Payton, CMW, JJW, LYM)*

Ironbridge [Wesley Rd, off Madeley Hill], *Golden Ball*: Friendly Elizabethan local with interesting range of reasonably priced food inc good vegetarian choice, at least five well kept ales, friendly licensees, real fire, pleasant terraced walk down to river; children welcome, comfortable bedrooms *(Christopher Glasson)*; [Wharfage], *Malthouse*: Clean, comfortable and relaxed, with unusual refreshing decor, welcoming attentive new young licensees and staff, well kept beer, some emphasis on creative choice of good country food (not Sun evening) using fresh produce in bar and restaurant, reasonable prices; bedrooms planned *(M Joyner, Peter and Janice Blackstaffe)*; [Buildwas Rd], *Meadow*: Popular and welcoming Severnside dining pub done up with old-fashioned beamery, cigarette cards, tasteful prints and brasses; wide choice of good value generous freshly prepared food in lounge and downstairs restaurant, quick service, well kept Scottish Courage ales and Marstons Pedigree, decent wines; pretty waterside garden *(SLC, M Joyner)*; [Waterloo St], *Olde Robin Hood*: Five comfortable and attractive connecting rooms with various alcoves inc barrel-vaulted dining room, lots of gleaming brass and old clocks, well kept changing ales such as Banks's Mild, Bass, Fullers London Pride, Golden Oval, Yorks Stonewall and Rauch, friendly service, good value standard food inc sandwiches; seats out in front, nice riverside setting by new road bridge, handy for museums complex; bedrooms, good breakfast *(Dave Braisted, SLC, M Joyner, B J Harding, Mike Gorton, Peter Smith)*; [The Square], *Tontine*: Friendly 18th-c hotel, not in best area but with good atmosphere, comfortable lounge bar and restaurant, lots of pictures, good choice of food inc sandwiches, baked potatoes, vegetarian and children's, Banks's Mild and Bitter, Bass; quiet piped pop music; reasonably priced bedrooms *(JJW, CMW)*

Ketley [Holyhead Rd (old A5); M54 junction 6, past Tesco; SJ6810], *Pudding*: One of the 'Little' pubs, cosy and informal, with bare boards, lots of bric-a-brac, jolly atmosphere, wholesome filling food inc big pies, good vegetarian and school puddings, well kept beers inc Lumphammer and interesting guests; Irish music, sometimes live; children welcome *(G Coates)*

Knockin [Main St; B4396 NW of Shrewsbury; SJ3422], *Bradford Arms*: Popular and busy modernised pub, good fresh standard food from huge ploughman's to Sun lunch, well kept Bass-related and guest ales, friendly service, reasonably priced restaurant; maybe piped radio *(Peter and June Gregory, R H Martyn)*

Leebotwood [A49 Church Stretton—Shrewsbury; SO4798], *Pound*: Attractive and comfortable beamed and thatched roadside pub, good choice of well presented food inc lots of specials and separately served veg in bar and big well laid-out no-smoking restaurant, well kept Woods Shropshire Lad, friendly staff, tables in garden *(TOH)*

☆ **Little Stretton** [Ludlow Rd; village well signed off A49; SO4392], *Green Dragon*: Well kept Tetleys, Wadworths 6X, Woods Shropshire Lad and quickly changing guest beers, reasonably priced straightforward food from good baguettes up, relaxed friendly staff, cheap house wine, malt whiskies, children in eating area and restaurant; tables outside, handy for Cardingmill Valley (NT) and Long Mynd *(Paul Robinshaw, R J Bland, Clive Petts, TOH, Nigel Woolliscroft, LYM)*

Little Stretton [Ludlow Rd], *Ragleth*: Neatly kept bay-windowed lounge, walkers and dogs welcome in brick-and-tile-floored bar with huge inglenook, very wide range of reasonably priced home-made food from sandwiches to steaks, quick service, well kept ales such as Morlands Old Speckled Hen and Charles Wells Bombardier (obliging staff will remove sparklers if asked), farm cider, tables on lawn by tulip tree; children welcome, restaurant *(Bob Medland, M Joyner, W Burke, LYM)*

Little Wenlock [SJ6507], *Huntsman*: Quiet village pub with bar, lounge and restaurant, horse paintings, ornamental central fireplace, good well presented food, Tetleys and interesting guest beers; well behaved children welcome, some tables outside; handy for Wrekin walks *(M Joyner)*

Longden [Longden Common; SJ4406], *Red Lion*: Three-room pub, good value food, Bass, Burtonwood and a guest beer, friendly staff, front games bar, tables outside; piped music *(SLC)*; *Tankerville Arms*: Good food inc Sunday carvery, restaurant and lounge/bar, well kept Ansells, Morlands Old Speckled Hen and Tetleys beers, darts and pool *(SLC)*

Loppington [B4397; SJ4729], *Dickin Arms*: Two-bar traditional country local in pretty village, open fire, well kept Bass, Wadworths and Youngers, enjoyable straightforward food inc Sun lunch, dining room; babies and dogs welcome, play area outside; pretty village *(Lorna and Howard Lambert, Mr and Mrs F Carroll)*

Ludlow [Bull Ring/Corve St; SO5175], *Feathers*: Superb timbered building, striking inside with Jacobean panelling and carving, fine period furnishings; sadly you'll probably be diverted to a fairly ordinary side bar for the good sandwiches and other decent bar food, or a casual drink – well kept Flowers Original and Wadworths 6X; pleasant service, restaurant, good parking; comfortable bedrooms, not cheap *(G Washington, Edward Froggatt, LYM)*; [Lower Broad St], *Wheatsheaf*: Nicely furnished traditional 17th-c beamed pub spectacularly built into medieval town gate, Bass, M&B Brew XI and Ruddles County, choice of farm ciders, restaurant; attractive bedrooms, warm and comfortable *(W W Burke)*

Madeley [Coalport Rd; SJ6904], *All Nations*: Spartan but friendly one-bar pub brewing its own distinctive well priced pale ale since the 1930s; good value lunchtime sandwiches, handy for Blists Hill *(Pete Baker)*

Marshbrook [over level crossing by B4370/A49; SO4489], *Station*: Roomy and unpretentious, attractively refurbished by new owners, good generous reasonably priced food inc really hot curries, quick friendly service, real ales; unobtrusive piped music *(TOH, Peter Salmon)*

Melverley [off B4393 W of Shrewsbury; SJ3316], *Tontine*: Pleasant atmosphere, good food running up to thai lemon chicken and steak, Bass, Hancocks HB and Worthington, bric-a-brac, pool in separate bar, conservatory, small garden *(SLC)*

☆ **Newcastle** [B4368 Clun—Newtown; SO2582], *Crown*: Good village atmosphere, welcoming licensees and good value usual food in quite spacious lounge bar with log fire and piped music, lively locals' bar with darts, pool and so forth in games room, well kept Tetleys, decent wines, efficient service, friendly great dane called Bruno; tables outside; charming well equipped bedrooms, good breakfast, attractive walks *(Philip and Katherine Carpenter, LYM)*

Northwood [SJ4634], *Horse & Jockey*: Quiet and friendly low-beamed country pub with simple decor, wide choice of good value food inc OAP bargains and good children's dishes, nice fire, lots of horse and jockey memorabilia; children and dogs welcome, play area *(Mr and Mrs F Carroll, Sue and Bob Ward)*

Norton in Hales [SJ7039], *Hinds Head*: Much-extended three-room country pub with emphasis on above-average food inc Sun lunch, but keeps its locals' bar; Bass, Hancocks HB and Worthington, open fire, prints and plates, pleasant staff; piped music *(Sue Holland, Dave Webster, SLC)*

☆ *nr* **Oswestry** [Candy, 5 miles W, just N of Trefonen; SJ2528], *Old Mill*: Expanding country dining pub with good inventive food – good value; well kept Bass, sells own sauces and pickles; on Offa's Dyke path *(Pete Yearsley, Brian Seller)*

Pentre [off A5 NW of Shrewsbury; SJ3617], *Grove*: Several rooms (atmosphere best when it's busy), with Bass, Worthingtons meals lunchtime and evening; piped music, play area outside, caravan park *(SLC)*

☆ **Picklescott** [off A49 N of Church Stretton; SO4399], *Bottle & Glass*: Warmly welcoming unspoilt early 17th-c country pub tucked away in delightful spot below N end of Long Mynd, pleasant quarry-tiled bar with log fire, well kept Bass and Worthington; new owners have now started to do good food esp home-made pies – must book Sun lunch; bedrooms *(TOH, Janet and Peter Race, David and Kathy Holcroft)*

☆ **Queens Head** [just off A5 SE of Oswestry, towards Nesscliffe; SJ3427], *Queens Head*: Emphasis on good value food (all day Fri and w/e) from speciality sandwiches to full meals, well kept Theakstons Best, XB and Old Peculier with a guest such as Woods Woodcutter, friendly very efficient staff, two dining areas with roaring coal fires, conservatory; garden by restored Montgomery Canal, country walks *(SLC, Jeff Davies, David and Kathy Holcroft, Basil Minson, Pete Yearsley)*

Rodington [SJ5914], *Bulls Head*: Generous food in village pub with well kept Burtonwood *(M Joyner)*

☆ **Ryton** [the one nr Dorrington, S of Shrewsbury; SJ4904], *Fox*: Smart country pub, very friendly and relaxed, with comfortable lounge bar and dining area, golfing prints, good range of tasty food esp fish, Bass and a guest such as Crown Buckley Rev James, friendly landlord; hill views *(TOH, SLC)*

Shifnal [SJ7508], *Beehive*: Welcoming local with cheap food *(David Brammer)*; [Victoria Rd; aka The Archway], *Jaspers*: Two snug bars with well kept beers such as Boddingtons, Everards, Fullers, Hobsons and Smiles Best, enjoyable eclectic food inc vegetarian, lots of puddings and particularly good Sun lunch in restaurant, separate lower-level bistro, very welcoming licensees, courteous staff, daily papers, terrace with barbecue *(David Holcroft, David Brammer)*; [High St], *White Hart*: Good value comfortable olde-worlde timbered local, good range of interesting changing well kept ales, promptly served standard food inc fresh veg, welcoming staff *(David Brammer)*

Shipley [Bridgnorth Rd; A454 W of Wolverhampton; SO8095], *Fox*: Banks's Milestone Tavern with old-world decor, pleasant location, varied good food all day, quick pleasant service, good choice of well kept ales and whiskies; children welcome *(W J Rixon)*

☆ **Shrewsbury** [Abbey Foregate; SJ4912], *M A D O'Rourkes Dun Cow Pie Shop*: Zany but homely decor, good range of good value food, friendly helpful staff, lots of jugs hanging from ceiling and enjoyably silly meat-pie and pig's-head memorabilia on walls, well kept Tetleys-related ales and Lumphammer, sharply trained attentive staff; attractive timber-framed building with enormous model cow on porch which looks pure O'Rourke but long predates his 'Little' chain *(M Joyner, SLC, John Honnor, BB)*

☆ **Shrewsbury** [New St/Quarry Park; leaving centre via Welsh Bridge/A488 turn into Port Hill Rd], *Boathouse*: Comfortably modernised pub in lovely position opp park by Severn, river views from long lounge bar, tables out on sheltered terrace and rose lawn; one of Whitbreads' Hogshead chain, with good changing choice of well kept real ales, friendly helpful staff, good range of standard food, darts in smaller bar; children welcome, summer barbecues, popular with young people evening; open all day *(G Coates, R J Bland, Mr and Mrs Jon Corelis, Andy and Jill Kassube, SLC, LYM)*

☆ **Shrewsbury** [4 Fish St], *Three Fishes*: Extensively refurbished heavy-beamed timbered pub, no smoking throughout – what a difference; well kept changing ales such as Bass,

Batemans XB, Fullers London Pride, Marstons Pedigree and Pridewood, Salopian Minsterley and Timothy Taylor Landlord, lunchtime food, lots of prints and bric-a-brac, friendly quick service; open all day, cl Sun *(Richard Lewis, David and Kathy Holcroft, SLC, John and Joan Wyatt, LYM)*

Shrewsbury [16 Castle Gates], *Castle Vaults*: Friendly old timbered local popular for wide choice of well kept changing esoteric ales such as Burntisland Dockyard Rivets, Hobsons Best, Inveralmond Independence and SP Sporting Grand Prix in proper lined glasses, good choice of wines and malt whiskies, farm cider, foreign bottled beers, central fire, good chatty landlord; generous helpings of good food in adjoining no-smoking Mexican restaurant, little roof garden with spiral staircase up towards castle; cl Sun lunchtime *(Richard Lewis, Andy and Jill Kassube, SLC)*; [Swan Hill/Cross Hill, nr old Square], *Coach & Horses*: Unspoilt Victorian pub with pine-panelled bar, two lounge areas, back restaurant with carvery, well kept Bass and two interesting guest beers, good home-made lunchtime food, attentive service; pretty flower boxes outside *(SLC, Richard Lewis, David and Kathy Holcroft, Mr and Mrs B Craig)*; [Dogpole], *Cromwells*: Pubby wine bar attached to hotel, Scottish Courage beers with several unusual guest beers, good value imaginative food from baguettes up, raised garden and terrace behind; piped music; open all day Sat; bedrooms *(R J Bland, SLC)*; [48 St Michaels St, A49 ½ mile N of stn], *Dolphin*: Recently refurbished early Victorian two-bar pub with five different well kept ales changing weekly such as Elgoods Golden Newt, Hoskins BOB, Mansfield Old Baily, Ridleys IPA and Ushers Autumn Frenzy, farm cider, foreign bottled beers, friendly staff; no food (apart from crisps etc), cl lunchtime Mon-Sat but opens 3 Fri/Sat *(Richard Lewis)*; [St Julians Friars], *Hop & Friar*: Former Acorn, refurbished by Banks's in olde-worlde style, their beers with guests such as Morrells, pleasant vibrant atmosphere, food, old red telephone box, some cinema seats, high stools; small conservatory *(SLC)*; [Church St], *Loggerheads*: Refurbished in old style by Banks's, one room with scrubbed-top tables and high-backed settles, others with lots of prints, real fire, food all day Mon-Sat till 6, friendly staff and locals, well kept Bitter, Mild, Fine Fettle and Camerons Strongarm, and a guest such as Bass *(Richard Lewis, SLC)*; [42 Wenlock Rd], *Peacock*: Split-level pub with prints in partly panelled lounge, full Marstons range and a guest Mild; piped music *(Chris Gabbitas, Hugh McPhail)*; [Smithfield Rd], *Proud Salopian*: Welcoming open-plan local with good choice of well kept mainstream changing ales, lunchtime food inc sandwiches, friendly landlord, darts, pool; wide screen TV, juke box, machines; open all day, cl Sun lunchtime *(Richard Lewis, SLC)*; [Battlefield Rd], *Red Lion*: Split-level Greenalls Millers Kitchen, with food till lateish, Greenalls Bitter and a guest such as Gales HSB, back bowling green; piped music, SkyTV *(SLC)*; [Frankwell], *Swan*: Recently refurbished, with pool in bare-boards back bar, Bass, Worthington and a guest such as Hanby Drawwell *(SLC)*

St Martins [Overton Rd (B5069); SJ3336], *Greyhound*: Good food, interesting memorabilia from nearby Ifton colliery; spacious garden with play area *(PG)*

☆ **Stiperstones** [village signed off A488 S of Minsterley – OS Sheet 126 map ref 364005; SO3600], *Stiperstones*: Very good value simple food served all day, inc vegetarian and their famous local whinberry pie, in welcoming little modernised lounge bar with comfortable leatherette wall banquettes, lots of brassware on ply-panelled walls, well kept Boddingtons, Flowers IPA and Woods Parish, good service, interesting landlord, darts in plainer public bar, maybe unobtrusive piped music; restaurant, tables outside; clean basic cheap bedrooms, good breakfast; good walking *(SLC, Edward Froggatt, Jeanne Cross, Paul Silvestri, Nigel Woolliscroft, BB)*

Telford [just off Horsehay roundabout; SJ6707], *All Labour In Vain*: Friendly old two-bar Greenalls pub with two real ales, bar food (not Mon/Tues), big screen TV; picnic-sets in big garden with play area and barbecue *(CMJ, JJW)*; [Long Lane (A442)], *Bucks Head*: Hotel bar with well kept Banks's and Tetleys, good quick food inc good value Sun lunch, family eating area and restaurant; piped music, fruit machine, pool; play area outside; bedrooms *(SLC, Chris Gabbitas, Hugh McPhail)*; [Market St, Oakengates; SJ7011], *Crown*: Seven or more ever-changing real ales, frequent beer festivals, knowledgeable staff, friendly locals, basic front bar, tables and barrels in side room, back room, sandwiches or rolls, friendly staff, pool table in public bar; tables outside *(Richard Lewis, G Coates)*; [Station Rd, Horsehay], *Station*: Comfortable banquettes, brass and bric-a-brac, no-smoking dining area, good choice of good value freshly prepared food (so may be a wait) inc children's, choice of Sun roasts, three real ales, quiet piped music; picnic-sets in fairly big garden; bedrooms *(CMW, JJW)*

☆ **Tilley** [just S of Wem; SJ5027], *Raven*: Well kept dining pub in pretty 18th-c black and white building, bright, clean and attractive, with good choice of good traditional home-made food inc lunchtime bargains, fine value Sun roasts, veg and cheeses from small local growers, Banks's and guest ales, welcoming landlord, log-effect gas fire, prints and bric-a-brac, separate restaurant (booking advised); nice terrace, beautiful village *(S Williamson, Mr and Mrs F Carroll, SLC, Pete Yearsley)*

☆ **Tong** [A41 just N of M54 junction 3, just beyond village; SJ7907], *Bell*: Good value food inc children's and Sun lunch in friendly and efficient Milestone Tavern dining pub, well kept reasonably priced Banks's and Marstons Pedigree, olde-worlde stripped brickwork, big family room, dining room, unobtrusive piped music, no dogs; pleasant back conservatory, big garden, attractive countryside nr Weston Park *(Edward Froggatt, M Joyner)*

Uckington [B5061; old A5 E of Atcham; SJ5810], *Horseshoes*: Food all day and good family atmosphere in big Brewers Fayre dining pub with Whitbreads-related ales, children's eating area and play area *(Chris Gabbitas, Hugh McPhail)*

Upper Farmcote [off A458 Bridgnorth—Stourbridge; SO7792], *Lion o' Morfe*: Country pub with log fire in plush lounge, coal fire in traditional public bar, carpeted pool room, conservatory, pleasant garden spreading into orchard; the Evanses who made this a popular main entry for very good value food and well kept beers have now retired and we wish them well *(LYM)*

Wall under Heywood [B4371 Church Stretton—Much Wenlock; SO5093], *Plough*: Popular for good value food served canteen-style in roomy and comfortable bar area, well kept Marstons Pedigree, efficient service, tables in garden *(TOH)*

☆ **Woore** [London Rd (A51); SJ7342], *Falcon*: Particularly hospitable licensees and polite young staff, outstanding choice of tasty nicely presented food inc lots of fish (best to book restaurant, esp weekends), well kept Ansells Mild and Marstons Bitter and Pedigree, comfortable cottagey bars, pristine copper-topped tables, interesting prints; bookmakers' in grounds, nr Bridgemere Garden World *(E G Parish, Sue Holland, Dave Webster, Richard Gibbs)*

Woore [London Rd (A51); SJ7342], *Swan*: Good food inc immaculate veg under current management, smart efficient service, neat public bar *(Sue Holland, Dave Webster)*

Stars after the name of a pub show exceptional character and appeal. They don't mean extra comfort. And they are nothing to do with food quality, for which there's a separate knife-and-fork rosette. Even quite a basic pub can win stars, if it's individual enough.

Somerset

Pubs which have been showing particularly well here in recent months are the bustling and attractive Globe at Appley, the well run Old Green Tree in Bath (lots of real ales), the cheerful Bell at Buckland Dinham (a new main entry, lots going on), the enjoyable old George in Castle Cary, the cottagey unspoilt Crown at Churchill (a favourite for many, with good beers), the unchanging Black Horse in Clapton in Gordano (full of character), the welcoming Wheatsheaf on the edge of its steep valley at Combe Hay (nice garden), the Strode Arms at Cranmore (good beer, thriving atmosphere), the Waggon & Horses near Doulting (interesting decor, great garden), the New Inn at Dowlish Wake (another favourite, particularly good staff), the civilised little Horse & Groom at East Woodlands, the extraordinary Old Station at Hallatrow (a new main entry – so much bric-a-brac you may get lost inside), the very relaxed Royal Oak at Luxborough (structural changes have gone down well), the friendly and very well run Notley Arms at Monksilver, the Bird in Hand at North Curry (new licensees – more relaxed furnishings and atmosphere, good food), the nicely laid out Carpenters Arms at Stanton Wick, the bustling Rose & Crown at Stoke St Gregory (very helpful licensees), the Cotley at Wambrook (this friendly dining pub is nice to stay in), the Crossways at West Huntspill (gains a Beer Award this year), the friendly well placed Royal Oak at Withypool, and another new main entry, the small-roomed Burcott Inn near Wookey. These pubs in their different ways have food that is at least enjoyable and at best superb. Among them, our choice as Somerset Dining Pub of the Year is the New Inn at Dowlish Wake. Of course, food is far from being everything. All the pubs we have mentioned so far have other charms, too. But Somerset also has such gems as the Rose & Crown at East Lyng (run by a landlord of decided character), the unspoilt little Tuckers Grave at Faulkland, the thatched Rose & Crown at Huish Episcopi (where the same family have been dispensing a great range of ciders for well over a century), the civilised Devonshire Arms at Long Sutton (a nice place to stay), the intriguing ancient Talbot at Mells, and the Halfway House at Pitney (excellent real ales). The Lucky Dip section at the end of the chapter also has a very strong choice: we'd particularly pick out the Square & Compass at Ashill (a firm main entry, losing its place this year only through a lack of reports), the Lamb in Axbridge, Inn at Freshford, Royal Oak at Over Stratton, Panborough Inn at Panborough, Greyhound at Staple Fitzpaine and Crown and Victoria at Tintinhull. There's a good choice in Bath and Bristol – and (led by the City Arms) in Wells. Drinks prices in Somerset are a little below the national average. The King William at Catcott (tied to Palmers) and New Inn at Blagdon (tied to Wadworths) had particularly cheap beer, and beers from the small Smiles brewery in Bristol are good value. Farm ciders are well worth searching out down here – and continue to thrive, despite the troubles of the bigger players such as Taunton Cider (whose closure was announced in the summer of 1998).

APPLEY ST0621 Map 1

Globe

Hamlet signposted from the network of back roads between A361 and A38, W of B3187 and W of Milverton and Wellington; OS sheet 181 map ref 072215

There are always plenty of locals in this busy, friendly pub – which is a good sign – as well as quite a few visitors, too. The simple beamed front room is relaxed and chatty, with benches and a built-in settle, bare wood tables on the brick floor, and pictures of magpies. As well as the restaurant, there's a further room with easy chairs and other more traditional ones; alley skittles. Good bar food includes sandwiches, home-made soup (£2.50), mushrooms in cream, garlic and horseradish (£3.50), a light cold egg pancake filled with prawns, celery and pineapple in marie rose sauce (£5), home-made steak and kidney pie in stout or savoury vegetable crumble (£6.25), steaks (from (£8.25), fresh salmon with chive, white wine and cream sauce (£8.50), chicken breast with pine nuts, bacon, raisins and apricots with a madeira sauce (£9.25), garlic king prawns (£11.75), children's dishes (from £3.25; some adult dishes can be served as half-helpings), and roast Sunday beef (£5.75). The restaurant is no smoking. A stone-flagged entry corridor leads to a serving hatch from where Cotleigh Tawny and guests like Butcombe Bitter and Wilmots, Cotleigh Barn Owl, and Teignworthy Reel Ale and Spring Tide are kept on handpump. Seats, climbing frame and swings outside in the garden; the path opposite leads eventually to the River Tone. *(Recommended by Adrian and Jane Tierney-Jones, the Didler, S G N Bennett, DJW, Douglas Miller, B J Cox, S G N Bennett, Patrick Renouf)*

Free house ~ Licensees A W and E J Burt, R and J Morris ~ Real ale ~ Meals and snacks (till 10pm) ~ Restaurant ~ (01823) 672327 ~ Children in eating area of bar and in restaurant ~ Open 11-3, 6.30-11; 12-3, 7-10.30 Sun; closed Mon lunchtime, except bank holidays

ASHCOTT ST4337 Map 1

Ashcott Inn

A39 about 6 miles W of Glastonbury

The attractive bar in this pleasant old pub has stripped stone walls and beams, some interesting old-fashioned seats among more conventional ones, a mix of oak and elm and other tables, and a log-effect gas fire in its sturdy chimney. Bar food includes sandwiches (from £2.10), home-made soup (£2.20), home-made chicken liver pâté (£3.45), ploughman's (£4.25), cider baked ham with two eggs (£5.25), beef in ale pie (£5.95), oriental stir fry (£6.25), steaks (from £6.95), grilled plaice (£7.25), daily specials such as mushrooms and bacon in garlic, cream and cheese (£3.95) and fillet steak stuffed with stilton, wrapped in bacon and served on a crouton with a port and cranberry sauce (£12.50), puddings (£2.95), and children's meals (£3.25); the restaurant is no smoking. Butcombe Bitter and guest beers like Flowers Original or Morlands Old Speckled Hen on handpump kept under light blanket pressure; cribbage, dominoes, shove-ha'penny, fruit machine, alley skittles, and piped music. Seats on the terrace, and a pretty walled garden with children's adventure play areas. *(Recommended by K H Frostick, Christopher and Mary Thomas, Veronica Brown, Dr and Mrs A K Clarke, Alan and Paula McCully, Jean and Richard Phillips, Donald Godden, Jack and Gemima Valiant)*

Heavitree (who no longer brew) ~ Managers Jon and Helen Endacott ~ Real ale ~ Meals and snacks ~ Restaurant ~ (01458) 210282 ~ Live entertainment monthly ~ Well behaved children welcome ~ Open 11-11; 12-10.30 Sun

BATH ST7565 Map 2

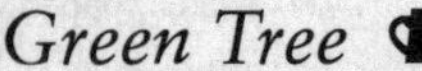

12 Green St

Very much enjoyed by readers, this is a genuinely unspoilt pub, well run by friendly licensees. The three bustling oak-panelled little rooms include a comfortable lounge on the left as you go in, its walls decorated with wartime aircraft pictures, and a no-smoking back bar. The big skylight lightens things up attractively. Good home-made lunchtime bar food includes soup (£3), filled baps (£3.30), good ploughman's (from £3.30), spaghetti with a rich tomato and parmesan sauce (£4.50), interesting salads, thai chicken curry or popular bangers and mash with tomato and onion or apple, cream, mustard and cider sauces (all £4.80), seafood platter (£6), and daily specials such as gazpacho (£3), spinach lasagne, fish pie, pesto pasta or beef rogan josh (all £4.80). There are usually five well kept beers on handpump such as Cottage Southern Bitter, Oakhill Black Magic, RCH Pitchfork, Uley Hogshead, and Wickwar Brand Oak Bitter, quite a few malt whiskies, a nice little wine list with helpful notes and 11 wines by the glass, bottled beers, a perry on draught, and a proper Pimms; chess, backgammon, shut the box, Jenga. The gents', though good, are down steep steps. *(Recommended by Matt Natton, Jack and Philip Paxton, Dave Irving, Ewan McCall, Tom McLean, Roger Huggins, J Sheldon, Rob Holt, Dr and Mrs A K Clarke, Simon and Amanda Southwell, David Wood, Mike Pugh, Giles Francis, John Hayter, David Peakall, Roger Wain-Heapy, Pat and John Millward, Richard Lewis, John and Lynn Busenbark)*

Free house ~ Licensees Sarah Le Feure and Nick Luke ~ Real ale ~ Lunchtime meals and snacks (not Sun) ~ (01225) 448259 ~ Children in eating area of bar at lunchtime if over 12 ~ Open 11-11; 7-10.30 Sun – closed Sun lunchtime, 25-26 Dec, 1 Jan, Easter Day

BECKINGTON ST8051 Map 2

Woolpack

Off A36 Bath—Warminster

New licensees again for this popular pub. The attractive no-smoking lounge has antique furnishings and pictures, a lively flagstoned public bar has stripped pine tables and a good log fire, and there's a cosy no-smoking dining room. Good if pricy bar food includes lunchtime home-made soup (£3.50), home-made chicken liver pâté (£4.25), sandwiches (from £4.10), omelettes (£6.50), good salads (from £6.75), deep-fried haddock (£7.25), chicken, leek and ham pie or pasta with roasted mediterranean vegetables and red pesto (£7.50), chilli marinated tuna steak with a lemon and ginger salsa (£8.95), daily specials, and puddings like home-made banoffee pie, crème brûlée or rich dark chocolate and rum truffle cake with a coffee bean sauce (£4.50). Well kept Courage Directors, Greene King IPA, and guest beers on handpump. This is part of the Old English Pub Co chain. *(Recommended by Dr and Mrs A K Clarke, Mrs S Evans, John and Lynn Busenbark, Sandria Parker, Andrew Shaw)*

Free house ~ Managers Ashley and Kim James ~ Real ale ~ Meals and snacks (till 10pm) ~ Restaurant ~ (01373) 831244 ~ Children welcome but must be over 13 in restaurant ~ Open 12-11; 12-10.30 Sun ~ Bedrooms: £55B/£65B

BLAGDON ST5059 Map 2

New Inn

Church Street, off A368

The setting here is lovely: you can see down over fields to wood-fringed Blagdon Lake and to the low hills beyond, from the picnic-sets at the back of this old-fashioned pub. Inside, the two characterful rooms have ancient beams decorated with gleaming horsebrasses and a few tankards, some comfortable antique settles – one with its armrests carved as dogs – as well as little plush armchairs, mate's chairs and so forth, and big logs burning in both stone inglenook fireplaces. Under the new manager, bar food includes lunchtime sandwiches, filled baked potatoes, and ploughman's (£5.50), as well as home-made soup (£2.25), deep-fried mushrooms with garlic mayonnaise (£2.95), home-cooked ham and eggs or home-made vegetable bake (£5.95), home-made steak and kidney pie (£6.25), trout and almonds (£7.50), chicken topped with cheese and ham (£7.75), steaks (from £9.50), daily specials, and puddings like home-made bread and butter pudding or apple crumble (from £2.50); six Sunday roasts. The restaurant is no smoking. Well kept Butcombe Bitter, Wadworths IPA and 6X, and a guest beer on handpump; darts, table skittles, cribbage, dominoes, fruit machine, trivia, and piped music. *(Recommended by Meg and Colin Hamilton, Comus Elliott, Philip and*

Jude Simmons, Mark and Heather Williamson, David Warrellow)

Wadworths ~ Manager Paul Chapman ~ Real ale ~ Meals and snacks ~ (01761) 462475 ~ Well behaved children in eating area of bar ~ Open 11.30-3, 7-11; 12-3, 7-10.30 Sun

BRADLEY GREEN ST2538 Map 1

Malt Shovel

Pub signposted from A39 W of Bridgwater, near Cannington; though Bradley Green is shown on road maps, if you're booking the postal address is Blackmoor Lane, Cannington, BRIDGWATER, Somerset TA5 2NE; note that there is another different Malt Shovel on this main road, three miles nearer Bridgwater

In a remote hamlet, this pleasant and friendly pub has a neatly kept straightforward main bar with window seats, some functional modern elm country chairs and sturdy modern winged high-backed settles around wooden tables, various boating photographs, and a black kettle standing on a giant fossil by the woodburning stove. There's also a tiny snug with white walls and black beams, a solid oak bar counter with a natural stone front, and red tiled floor. Decent bar food includes lunchtime sandwiches (£1.80, crusty rolls £2.25) and ploughman's (from £3.45), as well as good lamb provençale (£4.15), filled baked potatoes (from £4.30), pasta and spinach mornay (£3.95), home-made steak and kidney pie (£5), gammon and egg (£5.50), home-made fish pie (£6.25), steaks (from £8.95), daily specials like home-made cottage pie (£4), nut cutlet in provençale sauce in pastry or battered pork with sweet and sour sauce (£4.95), and scallops in wine and cream (£7.50), and children's menu (from £2.25). Well kept Butcombe Bitter, Morlands Old Speckled Hen, John Smiths, and a guest beer on handpump, and a fair choice of wines by the glass; sizeable skittle alley, dominoes, cribbage, and piped music. The family room opens on to the garden, where there are picnic-sets and a fishpond. No dogs inside. West of the pub, Blackmore Farm is a striking medieval building. *(Recommended by S H Godsell, Richard Gibbs, Maysie Thompson, G W Pearce, H Beck, JCW, Nick Lawless, K H Frostick, Eddie Edwards, Roger and Jenny Huggins, Jo and Gary Charlton)*

Free house ~ Licensees Robert and Frances Beverley, Philip and Sally Monger ~ Real ale ~ Meals (not Sun evening) and lunchtime snacks ~ Restaurant (not winter Sun evenings) ~ (01278) 653432 ~ Children in family room and in restaurant ~ Open 11-2.30(3 Sat), 6.30(7 winter)-11; 12-3, 7-10.30 Sun; closed Sun evening Nov-Feb ~ Bedrooms: £26.50B/£38B

BRISTOL ST5872 Map 2

Highbury Vaults £

St Michaels Hill, Cotham; main road out to Cotham from inner ring dual carriageway

In early Georgian days, this was used as the gaol where condemned men ate their last meal – the bars can still be seen on some windows. Today, it's a friendly place, and the bustling little front bar, with the corridor beside it, leads through to a long series of little rooms – wooden floors, green and cream paintwork, and old-fashioned furniture and prints, including lots of period Royal Family engravings and lithographs in the front room. It's one of the handful of pubs tied to the local Smiles brewery, so has all their beers on handpump at attractive prices, as well as changing guests such as Brains SA, Fullers London Pride, and Greene King IPA. Incredibly cheap bar food includes filled rolls, and hot dishes such as meaty or vegetable chilli, ratatouille, pork in mustard, lamb hotpot and beef in beer (all £3). Bar billiards, dominoes, and cribbage. The attractive back terrace has tables built into a partly covered flowery arbour that is heated on winter evenings; children must leave the garden by 9pm. *(Recommended by Simon and Amanda Southwell, Susan and Nigel Wilson, J Gowers, Tony and Wendy Hobden, Pat and John Millward, Mrs H Murphy)*

Smiles ~ Manager Bradd Francis ~ Real ale ~ Meals and snacks (12-2, 5.30-8.30; not Sat or Sun evenings) ~ (0117) 973 3203 ~ Open 12-11; 12-10.30 Sun; closed evening 25 Dec, 26 Dec, 1 Jan

BUCKLAND DINHAM ST7551 Map 2

Bell

High St

Particularly welcoming, hard-working licensees have made this attractive old pub an enjoyable place to be. There's a good bustling atmosphere throughout, and the narrow main bar has solid pine pink-cushioned country chairs, pine tables, a flowery cushioned window seat, and beams covered with beer mats, whisky bottle boxes, and hats; to the right is a huge stone fireplace with a woodburning stove, stripped modern pine high-backed settles creating booths, and wooden skis and golf clubs on the ceiling. Good bar food includes home-made soup (£2.50), sandwiches and filled french bread (from £2.75), filled baked potatoes (from £3.25), ploughman's (£3.95), vegetable lasagne (£4.35), home-cooked ham and egg (£4.50), omelettes (from £4.50), salad niçoise (£4.80), brunch (£4.95), steak, kidney and Guinness pie (£5.95), mixed warm seasonal seafood and shellfish (£12.95 for two people), children's meals (£3.50), and roast Sunday lunch (£4.95). Well kept Courage Best, Marstons Pedigree, Morlands Old Speckled Hen, John Smiths and Theakstons XB on handpump, a decent wine list, quite a few malt whiskies, a good choice of sherries and ports, freshly squeezed orange juice, and lots of different teas and coffees; cribbage, dominoes, and piped music, a news letter with listed forthcoming events, and a chalkboard with daily news. The comfortable partly no-smoking two-level dining room leads to the back garden: several small areas divided by low stone walls with a variety of seats (a couple of little stone ones for children), two side terraces with a few tables tucked into small secluded walled sections, and pretty flowers planted in a bicycle and a barrow; The two-acre field has a small wendy house and play area; boules. *(Recommended by Elizabeth John, Kenneth and Sarah McNaught, Susan and Nigel Wilson, W Marsh)*

Courage ~ Lease: Paul and Lynda Hartley-Nadhar ~ Real ale ~ Meals and snacks ~ Restaurant ~ (01373) 462956 ~ Children in eating area of bar ~ Live jazz Weds evenings ~ Open 11.45-3, 5.30-11; 12-3, 7-10.30 Sun

CASTLE CARY ST6332 Map 2

George 🛏

Market Place; just off A371 Shepton Mallet—Wincanton

This is a lovely thatched coaching inn set in the square of a historic village. The beamed front bar has a massive black elm mantlebeam over the log fire that is said to be over 1,000 years old. This is a cosy room, with a bow window seat, a cushioned high-backed settle by the fire, and just six or seven tables – they fill quickly at lunchtime, when there's a very civilised and relaxed atmosphere (despite the piped pop music). An inner no-smoking bar, separated by a glazed partition from the inn's central reception area, has a couple of big landscapes, some pictures made from butterfly wings, and a similarly decorous but busy feel. Good value food includes sandwiches (from £1.95; toasties 25p extra), soup (£2.50), 3-egg omelette (£4.25), honey-roast ham with egg or ploughman's (£4.75), smoked salmon pâté (£4.95), spicy vegetable tagine with couscous and lime chutney or steak and kidney in ale pie (£6.95), Mendip lamb cooked in red wine with local mushrooms (£7.50), confit of duck leg on garlicky butter beans cooked in wine and duck stock (£8.95), cold poached salmon with local asparagus (£10.95), chargrilled sirloin steak (£12.50), and home-made puddings (from £2.95). Well kept Butcombe and Wilmots on handpump, decent house wines with 10 by the glass, a fair range of malt whiskies and other spirits; pleasant staff. *(Recommended by Christopher Turner, Gordon, Richard Gibbs, Charles Gysin, Stephen Brown, John Knighton, Pamela Goodwyn, Janet Pickles)*

Free house ~ Licensees Sue and Greg Sparkes ~ Real ale ~ Meals and snacks ~ Restaurant ~ (01963) 350761 ~ Children in eating area of bar ~ Open 10.30-3, 6-11; 12-3, 7-10.30 Sun ~ Bedrooms: £45B/£75B

> If we know a pub has an outdoor play area for children, we mention it.

CATCOTT ST3939 Map 1

King William

Village signposted off A39 Street—Bridgwater

The spacious bar in this neatly kept cottagey pub has traditional furnishings such as kitchen and other assorted chairs, brown-painted built-in and other settles, window seats, Victorian fashion plates and other old prints, and one or two rugs on the stone floors; big stone fireplaces. Decent bar food includes sandwiches (from £1.80), home-made soup (£2.50), ploughman's (from £2.90), spinach and ricotta cheese cannelloni (£4.85), steak and kidney pie, curry or haddock in cider sauce (£4.95), Somerset pork (£6.95), steaks (from £8.65), duckling with orange and Grand Marnier sauce (£10.45), daily specials, and puddings. Well kept Palmers Bridport, IPA, and 200 on handpump, and a good range of malt whiskies; darts, cribbage, dominoes, and piped music. A large extension at the back includes a skittle-alley and a glass-topped well. *(Recommended by A C and J M Curry, Paul and Judith Booth, Stephen Brown, Dave Irving, Roger Huggins, Tom McLean, Ewan McCall)*

Palmers ~ Tenant Phillip Rowland ~ Real ale ~ Meals and snacks ~ Restaurant ~ (01278) 722374 ~ Children in eating area of bar and restaurant until 9pm ~ Open 11.30-2.30, 6-11; 12-3, 7-10.30 Sun

CHURCHILL ST4560 Map 1

Crown

Skinners Lane; in village, turn off A368 at Nelson Arms

'A lasting favourite' is how one reader describes this unspoilt cottagey pub – and all the other many supporters use similar descriptions. The small and local stone-floored and cross-beamed room on the right has a wooden window seat, an unusually sturdy settle, and built-in wall benches; the left-hand room has a slate floor, and some steps past the big log fire in a big stone fireplace lead to more sitting space. Well kept Bass, Cotleigh Batch Bitter (brewed by Cotleigh for them), Palmers IPA, Smiles Golden Brew, and guest beers such as Greene King Abbot or Palmers Tally Ho! all tapped from casks at the back, and country wines. Good value bar food (with prices unchanged since last year) includes tasty home-made soups like minestrone or stilton and celery (from £2.20), good rare beef sandwich (£2.50), a good ploughman's, chilli con carne or faggots (£3.95), and various casseroles (from £4.95); some of the meat comes from their own farm. They can be busy at weekends, especially in summer. There are garden tables on the front and a smallish but pretty back lawn with hill views; the Mendip Morris Men come in summer. Good walks nearby. *(Recommended by Stephen Brown, Tom Evans, Mike and Mary Carter, Michael Halsted, Alan and Paula McCully, Jenny and Roger Huggins, Mrs A Oakley, Barry and Anne, David Warrellow, Amanda and Simon Southwell)*

Free house ~ Licensee Tim Rogers ~ Real ale ~ Lunchtime meals and snacks ~ (01934) 852995 ~ Children in eating area of bar ~ Live entertainment on first Sun of month ~ Open 11.30-3, 5.30-11; 12-10.30 Sun

CLAPTON IN GORDANO ST4773 Map 2

Black Horse

4 miles from M5 junction 19; A369 towards Portishead, then B3124 towards Clevedon; in N Weston opp school turn left signposted Clapton, then in village take second right, maybe signed Clevedon, Clapton Wick

One reader has been coming to this characterful pub for 40 years – and is happy to tell us that little has changed. There's a good mix of locals and visitors in the partly flagstoned and partly red-tiled main room – as well as winged settles and built-in wall benches around narrow, dark wooden tables, pleasant window seats, a big log fire with stirrups and bits on the mantlebeam, and amusing cartoons and photographs of the pub. A window in an inner snug is still barred from the days when this room was the petty-sessions gaol; high-backed settles – one a marvellous carved and canopied creature, another with an art nouveau copper insert reading *East, West, Hame's Best*

– lots of mugs hanging from its black beams, and plenty of little prints and photographs. There's also a simply furnished room just off the bar (where children can go), with high-backed corner settles and a gas fire; darts, cribbage, and piped music. Bar food includes filled french bread (from £1.75), ploughman's (£3.60), and hot dishes like chilli con carne or lasagne (£4.50). Well kept Bass, Courage Best and Georges Bitter Ale, and Smiles Best on handpump or tapped from the cask, and Thatchers farm cider. The little flagstoned front garden is exceptionally pretty in summer with a mass of flowers in tubs, hanging baskets and flowerbeds; there are some old rustic tables and benches, with more to one side of the car park and in the secluded children's play area with its sturdy wooden climber, slide, rope ladder and rope swing. Paths from here lead up Naish Hill or along to Cadbury Camp. *(Recommended by Ian Phillips, Tom Evans, R Winn, Susan and John Douglas, Jack Morley, Adrian and Jane Tierney-Jones, Pamela Goodwyn, David Warrellow, Comus Elliott)*

Scottish Courage ~ Lease: Nicholas Evans and Alfonso Garcia ~ Real ale ~ Lunchtime meals and snacks (not Sun) ~ (01275) 842105 ~ Children in separate bar area ~ Live music Mon evenings ~ Open 11-3, 6-11; 11-11 Fri and Sat; 12-3, 7-10.30 Sun

COMBE HAY ST7354 Map 2

Wheatsheaf

Village signposted from A367 or B3110 S of Bath

A reliable place for a meal, this country pub is run by friendly, helpful licensees. It's in a pretty setting on the edge of a steep wooded valley (good nearby walks), and has three dovecotes built into the walls, and plenty of tables on the spacious terraced lawn looking down to the church and ancient manor stables. The pleasantly old-fashioned rooms have low ceilings, brown-painted settles, pews and rustic tables, a very high-backed winged settle facing one big log fire, old sporting and other prints, and earthenware jugs on the shelf of the little shuttered windows. Popular bar food includes home-made soup (£2.75), ploughman's (from £4.50), game terrine (£5.20), hot baked ham (£5.75), quiche (£5.95), seasonal pheasant (£8.75), fresh trout (£8.95), daily specials like chicken livers (£5.75), tagliatelle with wild mushrooms and peppers (£5.95), sautéed tiger prawns with garlic and whisky (£8.25), and home-made puddings like apple and fruit pie or tiramisu (£2.95). Well kept Courage Best and a guest like Butcombe Bitter or Morlands Old Speckled Hen tapped from the cask, several malt whiskies, and decent wines; shove-ha'penny and cribbage. *(Recommended by Lawrence Pearse, Howard and Barbara Clutterbuck, D S and J M Jackson, P and M Rudlin, Paul and Judith Booth, Mark and Heather Williamson, Andrew Chantrill, J P Anderson, Dr and Mrs A K Clarke, J C Simpson, Susan and Nigel Wilson)*

Free house ~ Licensee Mike Taylor ~ Real ale ~ Meals and snacks ~ Restaurant ~ (01225) 833504 ~ Children allowed away from bar ~ Open 11-2.30, 6(6.30 in winter)-10.30(11 Sat); 12-2.30, 7-10.30 Sun; closed 25-26 Dec ~ Bedrooms: £45B/£68B

COMPTON MARTIN ST5457 Map 2

Ring o' Bells

A368 Bath—Weston

Families will be pleased with the spacious no-smoking children's room here – it is decorated with Disney characters, they are giving crayons with drawing sheets or lucky bags to children who are very good, and there's a rocking horse; they have installed a Brio track, too. The snugly traditional front part of the bar has rugs on the flagstones, inglenook seats right by the log fire, and a warmly cosy atmosphere; up a step is a spacious carpeted back part with largely stripped stone walls and pine tables. Popular bar food includes sandwiches (from £1.35; toasties from £2.15), soup (£1.85), filled baked potatoes (from £2.95), stilton mushrooms (£3.25), omelettes (from £2.95), ploughman's (from £3.25), grilled ham and eggs (small £3.50, large £4.20), lasagne or mushroom, broccoli and almond tagliatelle (£4.75), beef in ale (£4.95), generous mixed grill (£9.35), daily specials like moussaka, good chicken curry, smoked seafood platter, and venison wellington, and children's meals (or helpings;

from £1). Well kept Butcombe Bitter, Wadworths 6X and guest beers such as Butcombe Wilmots Premium Ale on handpump or tapped from the cask. The public bar has darts and shove-ha'penny; table skittles and fruit machine. The large garden has swings, a slide, and a climbing frame. The pub is not far from Blagdon Lake and Chew Valley Lake, and is overlooked by the Mendip Hills. *(Recommended by Susan and Nigel Wilson, Tom Evans, Dr and Mrs A K Clarke, David Warrellow, JCW, C Sinclair, Gwen and Peter Andrews)*

Free house ~ Licensee Roger Owen ~ Real ale ~ Meals and snacks (till 10pm Fri/Sat) ~ Children in family room ~ (01761) 221284 ~ Open 11.30-3, 6-11; 12-3, 7-10.30 Sun

CRANMORE ST6643 Map 2

Strode Arms ★ 🍴 🍷

West Cranmore; signposted with pub off A361 Frome—Shepton Mallet

In a pretty setting by the village duckpond, this friendly early 15th-c former farmhouse is a reliable place for a meal – and a nice place if you just want a drink. The same menu is used in both the bar and restaurant: sandwiches (the ham in brown bread is very good), soup (£2.85), very good egg mayonnaise with prawns, capers, smoked trout, anchovy and asparagus tips (£4.15), fillet of pigeon breast with wild mushrooms in a piquant sauce (£5.50), ham and eggs (£6.25), tasty home-made steak and kidney pie (£7.25), smoked haddock and cod fishcakes (£7.75), wild mushroom tagliatelle (£7.95), breast of pheasant en croûte (£9.25), steaks (from £9.50), daily specials, Sunday roasts, and puddings like treacle tart or sticky toffee pudding (from £2.75); friendly service. There are charming country furnishings, a grandfather clock on the flagstones, fresh flowers (and pretty dried ones), pot plants, remarkable old locomotive engineering drawings and big black and white steam train murals in a central lobby, good bird prints, newspapers to read, and lovely log fires in handsome fireplaces. Well kept Flowers IPA, Fullers London Pride, Marstons Pedigree, and a guest such as Hook Norton Best on handpump, an interesting choice of decent wines by the glass and lots more by the bottle, and quite a few liqueurs and ports. The pub is an attractive sight in summer with its neat stonework, cartwheels on the walls, pretty tubs and hanging baskets, and seats under umbrellas on the front terrace; more seats in the back garden. On the first Tuesday of each month, there's a vintage car meeting, and the pub is handy for the East Somerset Light Railway. *(Recommended by Revd A Nunnerley, Peter and Margaret Frost, Susan and Nigel Wilson, M G Hart, Colin Thompson, Meg and Colin Hamilton, A C and J M Curry, A L and J D Turnbull, M G Hart, Evelyn and Derek Walter, P H Roberts, Luke Worthington, Mrs H Murphy, Mr and Mrs J McCurdy, Tom Evans, John and Lynn Busenbark)*

Free house ~ Licensees Rodney and Dora Phelps ~ Real ale ~ Meals and snacks (till 10pm Fri/Sat) ~ Cottagey restaurant ~ (01749) 880450 ~ Children in restaurant ~ Open 11.30-2.30, 6.30-11; 12-3, 7-10.30 Sun; closed Sun evening Oct-March

nr DOULTING ST6445 Map 2

Waggon & Horses 🍷

Doulting Beacon; eastwards turn off A37 on Mendip ridge N of Shepton Mallet, just S of A367 junction

This 18th-c inn promises well from outside, with its stone mullioned latticed windows, and pots of flowers lining an imposing external flight of stone steps. Inside lives up to expectations: a rambling bar with studded red leatherette seats and other chairs, a homely mix of tables including antiques, and paintings and drawings everywhere – not just for sale (as in so many pubs these days), but ones you actually want to buy. And those steps outside lead to a big raftered upper gallery where they have more formal art shows, besides two seasons of frequent classical recitals (Sept-Nov and Mar-Jun), also some jazz; this must be the only place where the pub piano is a carefully tuned Steinway grand. Two rooms are no smoking. Enjoyable, robustly flavoured food cooked by Mr Pajan (who comes from Austria) might include daily specials such as cauliflower soup (£2.90), duck liver pâté (£3.50), marinated herring with beetroot salad (£3.50), mediterranean hors d'oeuvres (£3.90), cassoulet of chicken (£7.90), escalope of veal in a madeira and cream sauce or grilled pork steaks marinated in soya and Chinese spices (£8.90), half a duck with peppers or grilled sea bass (£10.90), rump steak with wild mushrooms (£11.90), and puddings like squidgy chocolate pudding with chocolate sauce, lemon meringue pie or tiramisu (from £2.90); also, sandwiches (from £1.90), devilled mushrooms (£3.30, large £5.90), omelette (£5.90), ham and eggs (£6.20), steaks (from £9), and kiln-roasted Scottish salmon (£9.50). Quite often there will be Austrian, Spanish or Portuguese dishes, and they offer good fresh seafood on Thursday and Friday. Ushers Best and Founders and seasonal ales on handpump, a good choice of decent house wines, cocktails, cheerful service; chess and skittle alley. The big walled garden (with summer barbecues) is one of our favourites. Elderly tables and chairs stand on informal terracing, with picnic-sets out on the grass, and perennials and flowering shrubs intersperse themselves in a pretty and pleasantly informal way. There's a wildlife pond, and a climber for children. Off to one side is a rough paddock with a horse (horses are one passion of Mr Cardona, who comes from Colombia) and a goat called Dennis, and various fancy fowl, with pens further down holding many more in small breeding groups – there are some really quite remarkable birds among them, and the cluckings and crowings make a splendidly contented background to a sunny summer lunch. They often sell the eggs, too. *(Recommended by Brennig Jones, PR, UR, Mrs D M Graham, Alan and Lilian Meecham)*

Ushers ~ Lease: Francisco Cardona and Richard Pajan ~ Real ale ~ Meals and snacks ~ (01749) 880302 ~ Children in eating area of bar but must be well behaved ~ 4 or 5 classical music concerts in the spring and autumn, and some jazz also – phone for details ~ Open 11-3, 6-11; 12-3, 7-10.30 Sun; closed 25 Dec

DOWLISH WAKE ST3713 Map 1

New Inn

Village signposted from Kingstone – which is signposted from old A303 on E side of Ilminster, and from A3037 just S of Ilminster; keep on past church – pub at far end of village

Somerset Dining Pub of the Year

The licensees and their staff continue to offer a genuinely warm welcome to their customers – who often travel quite a way to come to this neatly kept village pub. The bar has dark beams liberally strung with hop bines, old-fashioned furnishings that include a mixture of chairs, high-backed settles, and attractive sturdy tables, and a woodburning stove in the stone inglenook fireplace. Good, enjoyable and reasonably priced bar food includes sandwiches (from £1.75), soup (£1.85), sausage and rosti (£3.35), pasta dishes (£3.45), warm duck salad, soft roes on toast or ploughman's (£3.50), omelettes (£3.75), all day breakfast (£4.50), liver with onion, bacon and mushrooms in wine sauce (£4.95), nut and lentil roast (£5.05), steaks (from £7.95), rack of lamb (£10.75), some Swiss specialities like raclette (£5.25) or charbonnade (£8.25), and small meals (from £1.75). Well kept Butcombe Bitter and two guests such as Theakstons Old Peculier and Wadworths 6X on handpump, a decent choice of whiskies, and Perry's cider. This comes from just down the road, and the thatched 16th-c stone cider mill is well worth a visit for its collection of wooden bygones and its liberal free tastings (you can buy the half-dozen different ciders in old-fashioned earthenware flagons as well as more modern containers; it's closed on Sunday afternoons). In a separate area they have darts, shove-ha'penny, dominoes, cribbage, bar billiards, table skittles as well as alley skittles and a fruit machine. The family room is no smoking. In front of the stone pub there's a rustic bench, tubs of flowers and a sprawl of clematis; the pleasant back garden has flower beds and a children's climbing frame. *(Recommended by Howard Clutterbuck, Joan and Michel Hooper-Immins, Douglas Allen, C P Scott-Malden, Jeanne and George Barnwell, Lynn Sharpless, Bob Eardley, Mr and Mrs H Quick, Stephen Brown, Galen Strawson, J M Lefeaux, Revd A Nunnerley, Ian and Villy White, Theo, Anne and Jane Gaskin, John Franklin, Ted George, Mr and Mrs Leslie Edie, Jo and Gary Charlton)*

Free house ~ Licensees Therese Boosey and David Smith ~ Real ale ~ Meals and snacks (not winter Sun evening) ~ (01460) 52413 ~ Children in family room ~ Open 11-3, 6-11; 12-3, 7-10.30 Sun

DUNSTER SS9943 Map 1

Luttrell Arms

A396

Based around a great hall built for the Abbot of Cleeve some 500 years ago, this is a civilised hotel. The comfortable back bar is the place to head for, with high beams hung with bottles, clogs and horseshoes, a stag's head and rifles on the walls above old settles and more modern furniture, and winter log fires. Ancient black timber uprights glazed with fine hand-floated glass, full of ripples and irregularities, separate the room from a small galleried and flagstoned courtyard. Under another new licensee, bar food includes home-made soup (£2.25), sandwiches (from £2.25; filled french bread from £3.65), ploughman's (£4.85), pasta with tomato and mushrooms a daily bake or ham and eggs (£4.95), chicken or vegetable curry (£5.75), chicken with barbecue sauce (£5.95), and sirloin steak (£10.75); both restaurants are no smoking. Well kept Bass and Exmoor Gold on handpump. In the gardens there are cannon emplacements dug out by Blake in the Civil War when – with Praise God Barebones and his pikemen – he was besieging the castle for six months. The town, on the edge of Exmoor National Park, is pretty and full of interest. *(Recommended by Richard Gibbs, R T and J C Moggridge, Tony Dickinson, Mrs Mary Woods, Steve Goodchild, Evelyn and Derek Walter)*

Free house ~ Licensee Kerry Smith ~ Real ale ~ Meals and snacks ~ Restaurant ~ (01643) 821555 ~ Children welcome ~ Open 11-11; 12-11 Sun ~ Bedrooms: £94B/£114B

EAST LYNG ST3328 Map 1

Rose & Crown

A361 about 4 miles W of Othery

Run by a landlord of character, this is a popular, enjoyable pub. The open-plan beamed lounge bar has a winter log fire (or a big embroidered fire screen) in a stone fireplace, a corner cabinet of glass, china and silver, a court cabinet, a bow window seat by an oak drop-leaf table, copies of *Country Life*, and impressive large dried flower arrangements. Good bar food includes sandwiches (from £1.75), soup (£2.10), ploughman's (from £3.50), home-cooked ham and egg (£4), omelettes (from £4.50), cashew and mixed nut paella or spicy chick pea and vegetable hotpot (£5.50), trout (£6.25), steaks (from £9.75), roast duckling with orange sauce (£11.50), and puddings like home-made treacle tart or sherry trifle (£2.75); pleasant waitress service. Well kept Butcombe Bitter, Hardy Royal Oak, and Wilmots Premium Ale on handpump; skittle alley and piped music. The back garden (largely hedged off from the car park) is prettily planted and there are picnic-sets. *(Recommended by Ann and Colin Hunt, Douglas Allen, Richard Dolphin, B J Harding)*

Free house ~ Licensee Derek Mason ~ Real ale ~ Meals and snacks ~ Restaurant ~ (01823) 698235 ~ Children in restaurant ~ Open 11-2.30, 6.30-11; 12-3, 7-10.30 Sun ~ Bedrooms: £27B/£44B

EAST WOODLANDS ST7944 Map 2

Horse & Groom

Signed off Frome bypass off A361/B3092 junction

This is a very quiet rural village and this small civilised pub offers a friendly welcome to all. The comfortable little lounge has a relaxed atmosphere (no games or piped music), an easy chair and settee around a coffee table, two small solid dining tables with chairs, and a big stone hearth with a small raised grate. The pleasant bar on the left with its stripped pine pews and settles on dark flagstones has Batemans XB, Greene King IPA, Hampshire King Alfred's, and Wadworths 6X tapped from the cask; good wines by the glass. Very well presented food includes filled home-made french bread (from £1.80), ploughman's (from £3.10), lovely liver, bacon and onion, asparagus and mushroom risotto or home-cooked ham with parsley sauce (all £5.25), prawn and spring onion pasta (£5.90), and smoked haddock topped with mozzarella or cod with mussels and prawns (£6.50); five or six interesting vegetables are served separately on a side plate, and super puddings like banana and date tart or chocolate pudding with chocolate and tia maria sauce (£3.25); helpful service. Shove-ha'penny, cribbage and dominoes. There are picnic-sets in the nice front garden by five severely pollarded limes and attractive troughs and mini wheelbarrows filled with flowers; more seats behind the big no-smoking dining conservatory. *(Recommended by A C and J M Curry, S G Bennett, M Joyner, J and E Gladston, Mrs C Jimenenz, John and Lynn Busenbark)*

Free house ~ Licensee Timothy Gould ~ Real ale ~ Meals and snacks (not Sun evening, not Mon) ~ Restaurant (not Sun evening, not Mon) ~ (01373) 462802 ~ Children in eating area of bar ~ Open 11.30-2.30(3 Sat), 6.30-11; 12-3, 7-10.30 Sun

FAULKLAND ST7354 Map 2

Tuckers Grave £

A366 E of village

For many years, this marvellously atmospheric and warmly friendly basic cider house has claimed the title of the smallest pub in the *Guide*, with a flagstoned entry that opens into a teeny unspoilt room with casks of well kept Bass and Butcombe Bitter on tap and Thatchers Cheddar Valley cider in an alcove on the left. Two old cream-painted high-backed settles face each other across a single table on the right, and a side room has dominoes and shove-ha'penny. There's a skittle alley and tables and chairs on the back lawn, as well as winter fires and maybe newspapers to read. Food is limited to sandwiches and ploughman's at lunchtime. *(Recommended by Pete Baker, John Poulter, Roger Huggins, Tom McLean, Dave Irving, Ewan McCall, Gordon)*

Free house ~ Licensees Ivan and Glenda Swift ~ Real ale ~ Lunchtime snacks (not Sun) ~ (01373) 834230 ~ Children welcome ~ Open 11-3, 6-11; 12-3, 7-10.30 Sun

HALLATROW ST6357 Map 2

Old Station

Wells Road (A39, close to junction with A37 S of Bristol)

A formidable collection of bric-a-brac has entirely taken over this pub: when you come in from the daylight, as your eyes gradually adjust to the dim light, you see more and more stuff simply everywhere. The forest of clutter hanging from the ceiling includes anything from sombreros and peaked caps to kites, from flags to fishnets, from ceramic charcoal stoves to sailing boats, from parasols to post boxes. Entertaining nonsenses abound, like the kilted dummy girl, the wall of car grills. The rather handsome island bar counter has well kept Ash Vine Challenger, Bass, Moles Best, Otter and Wickwar Brand Oak on handpump, and a mix of furnishings includes a sofa, high chairs around big cask tables, and small settles and dining or library chairs around more orthodox tables. Given the style of the place, it's quite a surprise to find such a wide range of enjoyable food: home-made soup (£1.95), avocado, mushroom and bacon bake (£3.95), deep-fried prawn and crab fritters with a sweet chilli dip (£4.65), thai-style chicken satay (£4.75), mushroom, courgette and beansprout stir fry (£4.95), steak and kidney pie or lasagne (£5.25), rack of lamb with a rosemary and redcurrant sauce (£7.50), chicken tandoori (£7.75), roast duck breast with a sweet and sour cherry sauce (£7.95), steaks (from £7.95), beef and asparagus in a black bean sauce (£9.25), daily specials and home-made puddings. Piped radio, fruit machine. Behind is a no-smoking railway carriage restaurant (photographs in the bar show the hair-raising difficulty of getting it here). The garden alongside has picnic-sets under cocktail parasols, and spreads back to a well equipped play area, with a recreation ground beyond. *(Recommended by Tom Evans, Alan and Paula McCully, Chris Plumb, DB, MK)*

Free house ~ Licensee Miles Redwood-Davies ~ Real ale ~ Meals and snacks (not 25 Dec) ~ Restaurant ~ (01761) 452228 ~ Children in eating area of bar and in restaurant ~ Open 11-3, 5(6 Sat)-11; 12-3, 7-11 Sun ~ Bedrooms: £30B/£42B

Waterside pubs are listed at the back of the book.

HINTON ST GEORGE ST4212 Map 1

Lord Poulett ♀

Village signposted off A30 W of Crewkerne; and off Merriott road (declassified – former A356, off B3165) N of Crewkerne; take care – there is another pub of the same name a mile or so away, at a roundabout on the former A303

Another new licensee has taken over this pleasant pub – and the emphasis is firmly placed on the good, imaginative food, with most tables now set for eating. The spacious main room has big black beams, stripped masonry, cushioned captain's chairs, lots of old settles, and nice old tables, and a log fire in the imposing stone fireplace; two cosy smaller rooms opening off – one with a big disused inglenook fireplace. Changing regularly, the food now includes sandwiches, home-made soup (£2.10), chicken liver pâté with gooseberry relish (£3.15), warm duck and mandarin salad (£3.75), potato and vegetable cakes with a garlic and herb cream sauce (£6.95), minted navarin of English lamb (£7.95), collops of beef in ale with caramelised onions (£8.20), baked loin of rabbit stuffed with apple and pistachio and served with a creamy mustard sauce (£8.45), honey roasted duck breast with a rich plum sauce (£8.95), and puddings (£2.50). Well kept Butcombe Bitter, Fullers London Pride, Otter Ale, and Wadworths 6X tapped from the cask, several malt whiskies, and farm cider; cribbage, dominoes, shove-ha'penny, and piped music, and a skittle alley with darts. The prettily planted back garden has some seats. This is largely a retirement village. *(Recommended by Mrs L McDonald, B Baxter, Stephen Brown, Galen Strawson, Dr and Mrs A J Newton, S Godsell, Theo, Anne and Jane Gaskin, Derek and Iris Martin; more reports please)*

Free house ~ Licensee Geoffrey Bussell ~ Real ale ~ Meals and snacks (not Sun evening) ~ Restaurant ~ (01460) 73149 ~ Children welcome ~ Open 12-3, 7-11; 12-2.30, 7-10.30 Sun

HUISH EPISCOPI ST4326 Map 1

Rose & Crown

A372 E of Langport

The locals all know this unspoilt thatched pub as 'Eli's' after the friendly landlady's father – Mrs Pittard's family has been here for well over 130 years. The atmosphere and character are determinedly unpretentious and welcoming, and there's no bar as such – to get a drink, you just walk into the central flagstoned still room and choose from the casks of well kept Bass and local guest beers such as Branscombe Vale Summa That, Butcombe Bitter, Moor Withy Cutter, and Teignworthy Reel Ale; farm cider (and local cider brandy) and country wines which stand on ranks of shelves all around (prices are very low); this servery is the only thoroughfare between the casual little front parlours with their unusual pointed-arch windows; genuinely friendly locals. Food is home-made, simple and cheap: generously filled sandwiches (from £1.70), a good choice of soups (£2.30), good filled baked potatoes (from £2.40), ploughman's (from £3.20), spinach lasagne (£4.95), and pork, apple and cider casserole or lamb hotpot (£5.25); good helpful service. Shove-ha'penny, dominoes and cribbage, and a much more orthodox big back extension family room has darts, fruit machine, trivia, and juke box; skittle alley and popular quiz nights. There are tables in a garden outside, and a second enclosed garden with a children's play area. George the dog will welcome a bitch but can't abide other dogs, though Bonny the welsh collie is not so fussy. A beer and music festival is held in the adjoining field every September, and on some summer weekends you might find the pub's cricket team (who always welcome a challenge) playing out here; good nearby walks, and the site of the Battle of Langport (1645) is close by. *(Recommended by Adrian and Jane Tierney-Jones, M Gardner, Pete Baker, Jack and Gemima Valiant, Hilarie Dobbie, Stephen Brown, Dave Irving, Roger Huggins, Tom McLean, Ewan McCall, Guy Thornington)*

Free house ~ Licensee Eileen Pittard ~ Real ale ~ Snacks (mainly 12-2.30, 5.30-8 but may be all day on summer weekends) ~ (01458) 250494 ~ Children welcome ~ Open 11.30-2.30, 5.30-11; 11.30-11 Fri/Sat; 12-10.30 Sun

KELSTON ST7067 Map 2

Old Crown

Bitton Road; A431 W of Bath

Butcombe have now taken over this traditional old place and installed a manager. The four small rooms are genuinely preserved and have beams strung with hops, interesting carved settles and cask tables on polished flagstones (attractively candlelit in the evenings), logs burning in an ancient open range (there's another smaller, open range and a Victorian open fireplace – both with coal-effect gas fires), and lovely tableau photographs. Well kept Bass, Butcombe Bitter and Wilmots, Smiles Best, and Wadworths 6X on handpump, and Thatchers cider; shove-ha'penny. Lunchtime bar food includes sandwiches, home-made soup, ploughman's, mushroom stroganoff or scampi (£4.95), 12 oz rump steak (£7.95), and puddings; helpful service. Picnic-sets under apple trees in the neat, sheltered back garden look out towards distant hills; you'd hardly believe you were just four miles from Bath's city centre. The car park is over quite a fast road. *(Recommended by Barry and Anne, Colin McKerrow, Simon and Amanda Southwell, Pat and John Millward; more reports on the new regime, please)*

Butcombe ~ Manager Chris Cole ~ Real ale ~ Lunchtime meals and snacks (not Sun or Mon evenings) ~ Restaurant (not Sun) ~ (01225) 423032 ~ Children in eating area of bar and in restaurant ~ Open 11.30-2.30, 5-11; 11.30-11 Sat; 12-10.30 Sun

KNAPP ST3025 Map 1

Rising Sun 🍷

Lower Knapp – OS Sheet 182 map reference 304257; off A38/A358/A378 E of Taunton

The wide choice of food continues to draw people to this lovely 15th-c longhouse. From the bar menu (not available on Friday or Saturday evenings), there might be home-made soup (£2.95), ploughman's (£4.50), open sandwiches (from £4.50), home-cooked ham and egg with sautéed potatoes (£5), and salmon and seafood tart (£5.75); there is also garlic mushrooms (£4), chicken liver pâté with cumberland sauce (£4.25), vegetable pancakes (£8.50), chicken breast stuffed with walnut and apricot with a honey and ginger sauce (£11), steaks (from £11), quite a few seasonal fish dishes like plaice fillets rolled with salmon mousse (£11.75), monkfish with a brandy, green peppercorn and cream sauce (£13), and whole dover sole (£16.25), puddings such as chocolate and hazelnut slice with raspberry coulis or treacle tart (from £3), and Sunday roast English beef (£6.50); part of the restaurant is no smoking. The big single room has two inglenook fireplaces (one with an old bread oven and range), well moulded beams, woodwork, and some stonework in its massive rather tilting walls, and a relaxed atmosphere. Well kept Bass, Boddingtons and Exmoor Ale on handpump, farm ciders, and a decent wine list. The staff (and dogs – Pepi the poodle and Pompey, who weighs in at nine stone) are very welcoming. The terrace is a suntrap in summer. *(Recommended by Sam Samuells, Lynda Payton, Ken Flawn, Theo, Anne and Jane Gaskin, Davie Warrellow, Mike Pugh, Simon Pyle, Mr and Mrs D Wilson, Keith Waters, Mr and Mrs C Roberts, D I Smith, Gethin Lewis, Tom Evans, E H and R F Warner)*

Free house ~ Licensee Tony Atkinson ~ Real ale ~ Meals and snacks ~ Restaurant ~ (01823) 490436 ~ Children in eating area of bar ~ Open 11.30(10.30 Sat)-2.30, 6.30-11; 12-3, 7-10.30 Sun ~ Bedrooms: £25/£36

LANGLEY MARSH ST0729 Map 1

Three Horseshoes ★

Village signposted off B3227 from Wiveliscombe

This is a nice little country pub with friendly licensees. The back bar has low modern settles and polished wooden tables, dark red wallpaper, planes hanging from the ceiling, banknotes papering the wall behind the bar counter, a piano, and a local stone fireplace. Well kept Fullers London Pride, Harveys Best, Otter Best, Palmers IPA, Wadworths 6X, and Youngs Bitter tapped from the cask, and Sheppeys farm cider; polite staff. Genuinely home-made food (they tell us prices have not changed for two years) includes filled rolls, soup (£1.50), pizzas (£3 or £3.95; can take away as well), butterbean bourguignon (£3.95), courgette and mushroom bake (£4.50), lamb in pernod or good steak and kidney pie (£4.95), pigeon breasts in cider and cream (£5.10), enjoyable fish pie (£5.25), popular steaks (from £7.95), daily fresh fish dishes like mussels in wine and cream, john dory or lemon sole (£7.95), and skate wings or smoked trout fillet (£8.95), and lovely puddings such as apple-filled pancake or lemon mousse (£2.10); no chips or fried food and some vegetables come from the garden. The no-smoking dining area has antique settles and tables and benches, and the lively front room has sensibly placed darts, shove-ha'penny, table skittles, dominoes, and cribbage; separate skittle alley, and piped music. The pub's elderly alsatian is called Guinness and the other is called Ruddles. You can sit on rustic seats on the verandah or in the sloping back garden, with a fully equipped children's play area and a view of farmland. In fine weather there are usually vintage cars outside. *(Recommended by David Lewis, Sarah Lart, the Didler, Patrick Freeman, Adrian and Jane Tierney-Jones, Wayne Wheeler; more reports please)*

Free house ~ Licensee John Hopkins ~ Real ale ~ Meals and snacks ~ (01984) 623763 ~ Well behaved children allowed away from bar ~ Occasional live entertainment ~ Open 12-2.30(3 Sun), 7-11(10.30 Sun)

LITTON ST5954 Map 2

Kings Arms

B3144; off A39 Bath—Wells

Children enjoy the excellent heavy wooden play equipment in the neat gardens here: a commando climbing net, slides, and baby swings; the River Chew runs through the bottom of the garden. Inside, there's a big entrance hall with polished flagstones, and bars lead off to the left with low heavy beams and more flagstones; a nice bit on the right beyond the huge fireplace has a big old-fashioned settle and a mix of other settles and wheelback chairs; a full suit of armour stands in one alcove and the rooms are divided up into areas by standing timbers. Good bar food includes sandwiches (from £2.95), garlic mushrooms (£3.50), lots of platters and salads (from £3.95; marinated pork ribs and potato skins with sour cream and barbecue sauces £7.50), daily vegetarian and pasta dishes, battered cod (£4.95), chilli (£6.95), lamb cutlets (£7.25), chicken and broccoli bake (£7.50), king prawns in garlic butter (£9.95), and steaks; children's colouring sheet menu with crayons. Well kept Bass, Courage Best, and Wadworths 6X on handpump. *(Recommended by Derek Patey, Philip and Jude Simmons; more reports please)*

Free house ~ Licensee Neil Sinclair ~ Real ale ~ Meals and snacks (12-2.30, 6.30-10; not 25 Dec) ~ (01761) 241301 ~ Children in two separate rooms ~ Open 11-2.30, 6-11; 12-3, 6-10.30 Sun; closed evenings 26 Dec and 1 Jan

LONG SUTTON ST4625 Map 1

Devonshire Arms 🛏

B3165 Somerton—Martock, just off A372 E of Langport

A nice place to stay, this tall gabled and solid stone inn has friendly licensees and is well known for its good food. The cosily old-fashioned front bar is separated from the rather smart restaurant area on the left by not much more than a sideboard – which makes for a very relaxed atmosphere. The built-in green plush corner seat is the prime spot, and there's a charming decor – deep green ceiling, lighter green walls, good sporting and country prints, fresh flowers and plants. There's also a flagstoned back bar, with horse tack, shelves of china, seats with lots of scatter cushions, and darts, dominoes, and juke box. Popular bar food changes daily, but might include sandwiches, prawns with a chilli and garlic sauce (£5.25), good salmon prawn mornay (£5.75), moules marinières, steak pie or smoked chicken salad (£5.95), tasty lamb casserole, and steaks. Well kept Flowers IPA and Wadworths 6X on handpump, decent wines, a good collection of malt whiskies, excellent coffee; friendly effective service. *(Recommended by Douglas Allen, John Evans, John Weeks, Stephen and Julie Brown, Roger Wain-Heapy, Mrs D Bromley-Martin, Mrs J Watts)*

Free house ~ Licensees David and Pam Naish ~ Real ale ~ Meals and snacks ~

Restaurant ~ (01458) 241271 ~ Children in eating area of bar ~ Open 12-2.30, 6-11(10.30 Sun) ~ Bedrooms: £45B/£55B

LUXBOROUGH SS9837 Map 1

Royal Oak ★

Kingsbridge; S of Dunster on minor rds into Brendon Hills – OS Sheet 181 map reference 983378

The refurbishments to this welcoming and well run inn have been most successful, and it's very much somewhere people enjoy staying the weekend – the breakfasts are first class, and the bedrooms (if not huge) are thoughtfully furnished and comfortable; each has its own teddy and ducks. Their Land Rover wildlife safaris are well liked, too. The two atmospheric bar rooms have beams and inglenooks, good log fires, flagstones in the front public bar, a real medley of furniture, and a friendly easy-going atmosphere; two characterful dining rooms. Well kept real ales such as Cotleigh Tawny, Exmoor Gold, Flowers IPA, and weekly guest beers on handpump, local farm cider, several malt whiskies, and a decent wine list. Good bar food includes home-made soup (£2.25), sandwiches (from £2.60), home-made port and stilton pâté (£3.95), filled baked potatoes (from £4), various ploughman's (from £4.50), chicken curry (£5.45), spinach and nut lasagne (£6.30), good venison burgers with home-made cumberland sauce, beef in ale pie (£5.75), and evening dishes such as fresh local trout pâté (£4.35), vegetarian filo parcels (£7.95), daily fresh fish dishes, pork fillet with apricots and a brandy cream sauce or venison casserole in a plum and cranberry sauce (£9.95), and steaks (from £10.95); puddings like banana and sticky toffee pudding or lemon cheesecake (£2.75), and children's meals. Pool, dominoes, cribbage, bagatelle, and shove-ha'penny – no machines or music; quiz Tuesday evenings. Tables outside and lots of surrounding walks. *(Recommended by John Voos, Sarah Bond, Adrian and Jane Tierney-Jones, Dave Braisted, Keith Moore, G Grant, Frank Davidson, Richard Gibbs, Murray and Jackie Hynd, Tamsin Turnbull, David Lewis, Sarah Lart, Lynn Sharpless, Bob Eardley, Paul Watt, Sue and Bob Ward, George and Jeanne Barnwell, Victoria Herriott, Simon Watkins, Steve Goodchild, M Fynes-Clinton, Jo and Gary Charlton, Anne Wine, Dagmar Junghanns, Colin Keane, J D Cloud, K Flack, Chris Tasker, Brian Barnes)*

Free house ~ Licensees Kevan and Rose Draper ~ Real ale ~ Meals and snacks (till 10pm) ~ Restaurant ~ (01984) 640319 ~ Children in restaurant and back bar ~ Folk music Fri evening ~ Open 11-2.30, 6-11; 12-2.30, 7-11(10.30 winter Sun) Sun ~ Bedrooms: £30(£50B)/£55(£65B)

MELLS ST7249 Map 2

Talbot

W of Frome; off A362 W of Buckland Dinham, or A361 via Nunney and Whatley

Run by a particularly convivial licensee, this popular 15th-c coaching inn is reached through an informally planted cobbled courtyard where there are cane chairs around tables. An attractive room leads off here, and has stripped pews, mate's and wheelback chairs, fresh flowers and candles in bottles on the mix of tables, and sporting and riding pictures on the walls, which are partly stripped above a broad panelled dado, and partly rough terracotta-colour. A small corridor leads to a nice little room with an open fire; piped music. Good bar food includes home-made soup (£2.25), chicken liver parfait with home-made chutney (£3.95), smoked salmon and scrambled egg or seafood crêpes (£4.50), home-made curry with poppadoms and so forth or hot vegetable pie (£7.50), steak and kidney in ale pie (£7.95), pot-roasted local rabbit with a grain mustard sauce (£8.25), poached salmon fillet with linguini pasta, vermouth and fresh herb sauce (£8.50), guinea fowl with potato rosti, oyster mushrooms, and rosemary cream sauce (£8.95), steaks (from £8.95), and roasted rack of local lamb coated in fresh herbs with garlic sauce (£9.95); Sunday roast, and nice breakfasts. Well kept Bass, Butcombe Bitter, and a changing weekly guest beer tapped from the cask, and good wines; well chosen staff. The two-roomed public bar has an appealing room nearest the road with big stripped shutters, a high dark green ceiling, a mix of chairs and a tall box settle, candles in bottles on the stubby pine tables, and a rough wooden floor; the locals' room has sports trophies, darts, cribbage, dominoes, and simple furnishings; skittle alley. They hold an Irish music weekend during the second week of September and a Daffodil Weekend with 350 members of the English Civil War over the Easter weekend. The village was purchased by the Horner family of the 'Little Jack Horner' nursery rhyme and the direct descendants still live in the manor house next door. The inn is surrounded by lovely countryside and good walks. *(Recommended by S G N Bennett, Paul S McPherson, Susan and Nigel Wilson, Walter Reid, Ellen McPherson, John and Lynn Busenbark)*

Free house ~ Lease: Roger Elliott ~ Real ale ~ Meals and snacks ~ Restaurant ~ (01373) 812254 ~ Children in eating area of bar and in restaurant ~ Open 12-2.30, 6-11; 12-3, 7-10.30 Sun ~ Bedrooms: £39B/£59.50B

MONKSILVER ST0737 Map 1

Notley Arms ★

B3188

At peak times, this bustling, friendly pub has people waiting for the doors to open – tables do fill up very quickly. The characterful beamed and L-shaped bar has small settles and kitchen chairs around the plain country wooden and candlelit tables, original paintings on the black-timbered white walls, fresh flowers, a couple of woodburning stoves, and maybe a pair of cats. Enjoyable bar food (with prices unchanged since last year) includes home-made soup (£2.25), sandwiches (from £2.50), very good ploughman's (from £3.25), home-made tagliatelle with ham, mushrooms, cream and parmesan cheese (£3.95), honey and mustard glazed chicken with roasted vegetables (£4.95), wild mushroom strudel with a sherry and cream sauce (£5.50), smoked haddock fishcakes with piquant crème fraîche sauce (£5.75), fresh salmon and asparagus bouchée (£5.95), lamb curry with spinach and tomato (£6.25), and puddings such as pear and almond tart or treacle tart (from £2.35); very good cheerful staff. Well kept Bass, Exmoor Ale, Ushers Best, and Wadworths 6X on handpump, and country wines; dominoes and trivia, and alley skittles. Families are well looked after, with colouring books and toys in the bright no-smoking little family room. There are more toys outside in the immaculate garden, running down to a swift clear stream. *(Recommended by Lesley Sones, J M and L M Lefeaux, Clive Steed, Dr Rod Holcombe, Russell Sunderland, W H and E Thomas, Paul Barnett, IHR, Mike and Mary Carter)*

Scottish Courage ~ Lease: Alistair and Sarah Cade ~ Real ale ~ Meals and snacks (see below) ~ (01984) 656217 ~ Children welcome ~ Open 11.30-2.30, 6.30-11; 12-2.30, 7-10.30 Sun; closed last week Jan, first week Feb

NORTH CURRY ST3225 Map 1

Bird in Hand

Queens Square; off A378 (or A358) E of Taunton

Enthusiastic new licensees have worked hard to revert this friendly place back to a proper village pub. And although the food is very good, they do not allow it to dominate – the tables that were set for eating have now been replaced by comfortable seating areas with deep sofas and so forth. They now have cricket and skittle teams, quiz nights, and fireside traditional story-telling on the first Thursday of each month. The bar has pews, settles, benches, and old yew tables (candlelit at night) on the flagstones, original beams and timbers, and log fires in inglenook fireplaces; the public bar has darts, cribbage, dominoes, and scrabble. Enjoyable bar snacks are served all week, with out of season à la carte main meals served only on Friday and Saturday evenings and Sunday lunchtime. Using fresh local produce and organic vegetables, the weekly changing dishes might include tomato, smoked bacon and lentil soup (£2.95), haddock kedgeree (£5.95), salad niçoise (£6.25), chicken club or BLT sandwiches (£5.25), risotto with asparagus, beans and peas (£7.25), braised fennel sausages with peppers (£7.95), cajun-style blackened salmon steak (£8.95), sirloin steak with brandy and peppercorns (£10.95), and puddings like lemon tart or summer pudding (£3.25); they have an Early Bird Club on Friday opening at 5.30 with free hors d'oeuvres until 7pm, and free hors d'oeuvres on Sunday lunchtimes. More formal dining is available in the separate restaurant area with conservatory. Well kept Badger Tanglefoot, Branscombe Vale Branoc, Butcombe Bitter, Cotleigh Tawny, Exmoor Ale, Otter Ale, and guests beers such as Adnams or Brakspears Ale on handpump or tapped from the cask, a thoughtful choice of wines with informal wine tastings, Rich's farm cider, and some interesting non-alcoholic drinks; skittle alley and piped music. Summer barbecues on the terrace. They hold a beer and music festival in October and May (Whit) bank holiday. *(Recommended by Mark Howard, the Haworth family, Adrian and Jane Tierney-Jones, Stephen Brown, John Barker, Lesley Pickles)*

Free house ~ Licensees Tom Cosgrove, Michael Gage ~ Real ale ~ Meals and snacks (not Sun evening or Mon lunchtime) ~ Restaurant ~ (01823) 490248 ~ Children in eating area of bar until 9pm ~ Trad jazz Sun lunchtime, blues/rock some Fri evenings ~ Open 12-3(4 Sat), 7-11(10.30 Sun); closed Monday lunchtime

PITNEY ST4428 Map 1

Halfway House

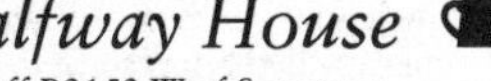

Just off B3153 W of Somerton

For real-ale lovers, this friendly old-fashioned pub is the place to head for. They keep six regulars tapped from the cask – Butcombe Bitter, Cotleigh Tawny, Hop Back Summer Lightning, Otter Bitter and Bright, and Teignworthy Reel Ale, with around another four as changing guests. They also have 20 or so bottled beers from Belgium and other countries, Wilkins farm cider, and quite a few malt whiskies. It's a friendly and cosy place, with plenty of space in the three rooms (all have good log fires), and the homely feel is underlined by a profusion of books, maps and newspapers; cards and chess. Good simple food includes sandwiches (from £2; the smoked salmon one is popular, as is the cream cheese and smoked salmon toasted bagels £2.50), filled baked potatoes (from £2.25), soup (£2.50), and a fine ploughman's with home-made pickle (from £3.95). In the evening they do about half a dozen home-made curries. There are tables outside. *(Recommended by P and M Rudlin, Adrian and Jane Tierney-Jones, Ian and Nita Cooper, R Brie, Stephen Brown, Chris Dower, Keith Darke)*

Free house ~ Licensees Julian and Judy Litchfield ~ Real ale ~ Meals and snacks (not Sun) ~ (01458) 252513 ~ Well behaved children welcome ~ Open 11.30-2.30, 5.30-11; 12-3, 7-10.30 Sun

RUDGE ST8251 Map 2

Full Moon

Off A36 Bath—Warminster

Opposite the now completed village green, this charming pub has fine views across the valley to Salisbury Plain and Westbury White Horse. The differently shaped rooms have a lot of character, and a gently upmarket but friendly atmosphere. The two rooms on the right have low white ceilings with a few black beams, a built-in settle by the bar, wheelbacks and slatback chairs around mainly cast-iron framed tables, a woodburning stove in a big stone fireplace with riding boots on the mantlebeam, and big shutters by the red velvet-cushioned window seats. Other rooms are similarly furnished except the smallish flagstoned dining room with stripped pine tables and high traditional settles; there's also a small plush restaurant and a big back carpeted extension alongside the skittle alley; shove-ha'penny and cribbage. Good bar food includes home-made soup (£2.25), caramelised red onion tart (£4.60), fried goat's cheese with cured ham (£5.25), stilton, spinach and mushroom vol au vent (£8.50), lemon and almond chicken (£9.50), Scotch steaks (from £9.50), fresh local trout with oatmeal (£10.50), roast tenderloin of pork with a crust of olive tomatoes and breadcrumbs (£10.95), rack of lamb with a white onion and mint cream sauce (£12.50), and puddings; Sunday roast lunch. Well kept Bass, Butcombe Bitter, and Fullers London Pride on handpump, local ciders, and several malt whiskies. *(Recommended by Bett and Brian Cox, Tom Evans, Peter and Audrey Dowsett, Susan and Nigel Wilson, Derek and Sylvia Stephenson, John and Lynn Busenbark, M G Hart, Pat and John Millward)*

Free house ~ Licensees Patrick and Christine Gifford ~ Real ale ~ Meals and snacks ~ Restaurant ~ (01373) 830936 ~ Children in eating area of bar and in restaurant ~ Open 12-11; 12-10.30 Sun; 12-3, 6-11 in winter ~ Bedrooms: £35B/£55B

SOUTH STOKE ST7461 Map 2

Pack Horse £

Village signposted opposite the Cross Keys off B3110, leaving Bath southwards – just before end of speed limit

The entrance alleyway that runs through the middle of this unpretentious 500-year-old gabled pub is still a public right of way to the church, and used to be the route along which the dead were carried to the cemetery. It stops along the way at a central space by the serving bar with its well kept Courage Best, and Ushers Best and Founders on handpump or tapped from the cask, and farm cider. The ancient main room has a good local atmosphere, a log fire in the handsome stone inglenook, antique oak settles (two well carved) and cushioned captain's chairs on the quarry-tiled floor, some Royalty pictures, a chiming wall-clock, a heavy black beam-and-plank ceiling, and rough black shutters for the stone-mullioned windows (put up in World War I); the cupboard in the fireplace used to be where they kept drunks until they sobered up. There's another room down to the left (with less atmosphere). Under the new licensees, good value bar food now includes home-made soup (£1.65), sandwiches (£2.10), filled baked potatoes (from £2.45), ploughman's (£3.30), ham and egg (£3.45), daily specials like nut roast (£4.25), cheesy garlic mushrooms with bacon and lyonnaise potatoes (£4.35), home-made steak and kidney or game pies, salmon steak with cucumber and cheese sauce, breast of chicken in stilton sauce or venison casserole (all £4.45), rump steak (£5.95), and puddings like home-made apple crumble (£2.20). Rather fine shove-ha'penny slates are set into two of the tables, and there's dominoes. The spacious back garden has new seats and pretty roses, and they keep chickens. *(Recommended by Jenny and Roger Huggins, Susan and Nigel Wilson, Luke Worthington, Tom McLean, Ewan McCall, Mrs H Murphy)*

Ushers ~ Tenants Michael and Kay Tibble ~ Real ale ~ Meals and snacks (served all day) ~ (01225) 832060 ~ Children welcome ~ Open 11-11; 12-10.30 Sun

SPARKFORD ST6026 Map 2

Sparkford Inn

High Street; just off A303 bypass W of Wincanton

The rambling series of softly lit rather low-beamed rooms here has a nice mix of old tables in varying sizes, good dining chairs, a colour scheme leaning towards plummy browns and dusky pinks, and plenty of worthwhile prints and other things to look at – including an intricate old-fashioned scrapbook screen; no-smoking areas. There's an indoor play room for children, open on Sunday lunchtimes. Decent food comes from a separate servery, and at lunchtime includes sandwiches (from £2.25; roast meat of the day £3.25), ploughman's (£4.50), a roast of the day (£6.15), and daily specials such as home-made cream of mushroom soup (£2.50), poached fresh salmon with white wine and pink peppercorn sauce (£7.95), baked duck breast with Drambuie sauce (£8), steaks (from £6.25), and home-made puddings; evening extras such as smoked salmon (£4.25), home-cooked ham and egg (£5.25), vegetable pie (£5.50), beef in Guinness (£5.80), and lemon chicken or cheese fondue for two (£6.50); the restaurant is no smoking. Well kept Bass and Worthington Best, and guest beers on handpump or tapped from the cask; country wines and local cider. Tables outside, with a good play area, and pretty tubs of flowers. *(Recommended by Mayur Shah, Stephen G Brown, Iain Robertson, Stephen, Julie and Hayley Brown, John Barker, Mrs Rushton)*

Free house ~ Licensees Nigel and Sue Tucker ~ Real ale ~ Meals and snacks (till 10pm) ~ Restaurant ~ (01963) 440218 ~ Children in eating area of bar and in restaurant ~ Open 11-3, 6.30-11; 12-3, 7-10.30 Sun; closed evening 25 Dec ~ Bedrooms: £29.50B/£39B

STANTON WICK ST6162 Map 2

Carpenters Arms

Village signposted off A368, just W of junction with A37 S of Bristol

This is an enjoyable place to stay – and the breakfasts are very good. It's well run and friendly, and the Coopers Parlour on the right has one or two beams, red-cushioned wall pews around heavy tables, fresh flowers, and swagged-back curtains and houseplants in the windows; on the angle between here and the bar area there's a fat woodburning stove in an opened-through corner fireplace. The bar has wood-backed built-in wall seats and some red fabric-cushioned stools, stripped stone walls, and a big log fire. Diners are encouraged to step down into a snug inner room (lightened by mirrors in arched 'windows'), or to go round to the sturdy tables angling off on the right; most of these tables get booked at weekends. Good bar food includes home-made soup (£2.50), pasta with three cheese sauce (£3.95), filled french bread (from £4.25; steak, onion and mushroom £5.95), terrine of pork, wild mushrooms and sun-dried tomatoes (£4.25), ploughman's (£4.50), smoked fillet of duck and chicken salad with crispy bacon (£4.75), home-made steak and kidney pie (£6.25), chargrilled ham and two eggs (£6.75), duck leg confit with mixed beans and toulouse sausage (£7.25), steaks (from £9.75), a stir fry of the day, and fresh fish from Cornwall. Well kept Bass, Butcombe Bitter, Wadworths 6X, and a guest beer on handpump, a decent wine list, and quite a few malt whiskies; cribbage, dominoes, fruit machine, piped music, and big satellite TV screen. There are picnic-sets on the front terrace, pretty flower-filled flower beds, and a new garden. *(Recommended by Howard Clutterbuck, John Knighton, Iain Robertson, JCW, Comus Elliott, Theo, Anne and Jane Gaskin, Robert Gomme)*

Free house ~ Licensee Nigel Pushman ~ Real ale ~ Meals and snacks (till 10pm) ~ Restaurant ~ (01761) 490202 ~ Children welcome (though no facilities for them) ~ Pianist twice a week ~ Open 11-11; 12-10.30 Sun ~ Bedrooms: £52.50B/£69.50B

STOGUMBER ST0937 Map 1

White Horse

From A358 Taunton—Williton, village signposted on left at Crowcombe

Set opposite the red stone church in a quiet village, this pleasant pub has a good friendly atmosphere and chatty locals. The neatly kept long bar room has old-fashioned built-in settles, other settles and cushioned captain's chairs around the heavy rustic tables on the patterned carpet, a warm winter coal fire, and piped classical music. Good, reasonably priced food includes sandwiches (from £1.20), home-made vegetable soup (£1.80), smoked mackerel pâté (£2.60), omelettes (£3.30), ploughman's or home-cooked gammon and egg (£3.50), vegetable pasty (£4.30), chicken with peaches or good steak and kidney pudding (£5.80), trout with almonds (£6.90), steaks (from £8.80), specials such as turkey curry (£4.50) or minted lamb chops (£4.80), and puddings like treacle tart, apple crumble or home-made pineapple ice cream (from £1.70); best to book for roast beef Sunday lunch (£5), and breakfasts are good; prompt service. Well kept Cotleigh Tawny, Otter Ale and a guest beer on handpump, and farm cider in summer. A side room has sensibly placed darts and a fruit machine; shove-ha'penny, dominoes, cribbage, and video game – as well as a separate skittle alley. The garden is quiet except for rooks and sheep in the surrounding low hills. *(Recommended by H Dickinson, F J Willy, Frank Davidson, K R Harris, K H Frostick, Mike and Mary Carter, Brian and Bett Cox, H O Dickinson, Mark Hydes, Eddie Edwards, Iain Robertson)*

Free house ~ Licensee Peter Williamson ~ Real ale ~ Meals and snacks (11-2, 6-10) ~ (01984) 656277 ~ Children in family room only ~ Open 11-2.30, 6-11; 12-3, 7-10.30 Sun ~ Bedrooms: /£40B

We accept no free drinks or payment for inclusion. We take no advertising, and are not sponsored by the brewing industry – or by anyone else. So all reports are independent.

TOKE ST GREGORY ST3527 Map 1

Rose & Crown

Woodhill; follow North Curry signpost off A378 by junction with A358 – keep on to Stoke, bearing right in centre – pub is behind a high hedge near the church

Even when busy – which this popular country cottage often is – the kind licensees offer a genuine welcome to both regulars and visitors. The neatly kept bar is decorated in a cosy and pleasantly romanticised stable theme: dark wooden loose-box partitions for some of the interestingly angled nooks and alcoves, lots of brasses and bits on the low beams and joists, stripped stonework, and appropriate pictures including a highland pony carrying a stag; many of the wildlife paintings on the walls are the work of the landlady, and there's an 18th-c glass-covered well in one corner. Mrs Browning's two sons are responsible for the good, honest cooking – using fresh local produce, fresh fish from Brixham, and their own eggs. At lunchtime, there might be sandwiches in home-made granary bread (from £1.75), soup (£1.95), local ham and egg (£4.25), omelettes (£4.50), grilled kidneys and bacon (£5.95), scrumpy chicken (£6), skate wings (£6.95), steaks (from £8.25), dover sole (£12.95), vegetarian dishes, and puddings (£2.50); in the evening, they offer a three-course meal for £12.99 with more elaborate dishes like stuffed burgundy snails, lobster soup, roast duckling with orange or roast rack of lamb. Plentiful breakfasts, and a good three-course Sunday lunch (£7.95). One small dining area is no smoking. Well kept Exmoor Ale, Hardy Country and Royal Oak, and Moor Withy Cutter on handpump, Thatchers farm cider, and decent wines; unobtrusive piped classical music, dominoes, and skittle alley. Under cocktail parasols by an apple tree on the sheltered front terrace are some picnic-sets; summer barbecues and a pets corner for children. In summer, residents have use of a heated swimming pool. The pub is in an interesting Somerset Levels village with willow beds still supplying the two basket works. *(Recommended by Roy Smylie, Paul McPherson, Mr and Mrs Broadhurst, Karen Eliot, Pat and John Millward, M G Hart, Mike and Wena Stevenson, Mr and Mrs R Banks, DMT, Bett and Brian Cox, P P and J Salmon, N C Hinton, Jo and Gary Charlton, Wayne Wheeler, Richard Dolphin, Theo, Anne and Jane Gaskin, J J M Davies Webb)*

Free house ~ Licensees Ron and Irene Browning ~ Real ale ~ Meals and snacks (till 10pm) ~ Restaurant ~ (01823) 490296 ~ Children welcome ~ Open 11-3, 6.30-11; 12-3, 7-10.30 Sun ~ Bedrooms: £25(£35B)/£38(£50B); s/c cottage

WAMBROOK ST2907 Map 1

Cotley

Village signposted off A30 W of Chard; don't follow the small signs to Cotley itself

Looking down on to the valley village, this stone-built pub is a popular place to stay, with lovely breakfasts, friendly licensees, and fine surrounding walks. There is a smart but unpretentious local atmosphere and the simple flagstoned entrance bar opens on one side into a small plush bar, with beyond that a two-room no-smoking dining area; several open fires. An extension is often used for painting sessions, and the results (complete with price-tags in case you see something you like) can be seen around the walls of the various rooms. Generous helpings of enjoyable food include sandwiches, home-made soup (£2.50), creamed mushrooms with tarragon or king prawns with garlic mayonnaise (£3.75), omelettes (from £4.95), vegetable and stilton crumble (£5.95), ham and egg (£6.20), kidneys in port and cream (£6.50), sweet and sour chicken (£6.95), chicken in a ginger and pumpkin sauce (£7.25), trout stuffed with prawns and cucumber (£8.95), three lamb chops with creamy mint sauce (£8.50), and a mixed grill (£10.25). The restaurant is no smoking. Flowers Original and Otter Ale on handpump kept under light blanket pressure, and a good choice of wines; pool, piped music, and skittle alley. Out in the garden below are some picnic-sets, with a play area and goldfish pool. *(Recommended by Ann and Colin Hunt, Mick Hitchman, Mr and Mrs J Bishop, J M Lefeaux, Richard and Margaret Peers, Mr and Mrs Broadhurst, Paul and Madeleine Morey, Chris Raisin)*

Free house ~ Licensee David Livingstone ~ Real ale ~ Meals and snacks (till 10) ~ Restaurant ~ (01460) 62348 ~ Children welcome ~ Open 11-3, 7-11; 12-3, 7-11 Sun ~ Bedrooms: £29B/£41B

WEST HUNTSPILL ST3044 Map 1

Crossways

2¾ miles from M5 junction 23 (A38 towards Highbridge); 4 miles from M5 junction 22 (A38 beyond Highbridge)

The atmosphere here is very relaxed and friendly, despite its popularity. The main part of the bar has dining-room chairs, a mixture of settles, and seats built into one converted brick fireplace, with good winter log fires in the others. At one end there's more of a dining room, attractively decorated with old farm machinery engravings, Albert and Chic cartoons (chiefly about restaurants), and 1920ish hunting prints – on Friday and Saturday evenings this area becomes a no-smoking bistro. The other end has an area with big winged settles making booths, and there's a family room with bamboo-back seats around neat tables. Good bar food includes generous sandwiches (from £1.80), lovely home-made soup (£2.50), garlic mushrooms (£3), ploughman's (£3.50), good faggots and marrowfat peas, nice macaroni cheese or broccoli, chicken and ham mornay (all £4.80), steak and kidney pie (£5), grilled fillet of salmon (£5.50), gammon and egg (£6.50), steaks (from £8.50), daily specials such as thai fishcakes, grilled fresh sardines, leek and stilton sausages, and rabbit in mustard and chives, children's meals (£2), and home-made puddings (£2.20); good breakfasts. Well kept Butcombe Wilmots Premium Ale, Flowers IPA, Hardy Royal Oak, Moor Merlins Magic, Smiles Best, and three guest beers on handpump, farm cider, and a decent wine list; darts, skittle alley, cribbage, dominoes, and fruit machine. There are picnic-sets among fruit trees in quite a big garden. If you're staying, the back rooms are quieter. *(Recommended by Roger and Jenny Huggins, Tom Evans, Nigel Flook, Betsy Brown, Pat Crabb, Mike and Karen England, Bronwen and Steve Wrigley, Adrian and Jane Tierney-Jones, Sue and Bob Ward, SHG, John and Elisabeth Cox, P H Roberts, C M Raybould, L W King, Comus Elliott, JCW, Chris and Shirley Machin, DJW, B J Harding, D Allsop, Nigel Clifton, Dave Irving, Roger Huggins, Tom McLean, E McCall, E J Mutter)*

Free house ~ Licensees Michael Ronca and Tony Eyles ~ Real ale ~ Meals and snacks (till 10pm Fri/Sat) ~ Restaurant (Fri/Sat evenings only) ~ (01278) 783756 ~ Children welcome away from main bar ~ Open 10.30-3, 5.30(6 Sat)-11; 12-3, 7-10.30 Sun; closed 25 Dec ~ Bedrooms: £24B/£34B

WINSFORD SS9034 Map 1

Royal Oak

In Exmoor National Park, village signposted from A396 about 10 miles S of Dunster

Looking at this immaculate and very pretty thatched inn in its quiet country setting, it's hard to believe that in the 17th c customers were regularly plundered by Exmoor highwayman Tom Faggus, whose exploits R D Blackmore, a frequent visitor, worked into *Lorna Doone*. The attractively furnished and cosy lounge bar has a cushioned big bay-window seat from which you can look across the road towards the village green and foot and packhorse bridges over the River Winn, tartan-cushioned bar stools by the panelled counter (above which hang horsebrasses and pewter tankards), the same cushions on the armed windsor chairs set around little wooden tables, and a splendid iron fireback in the big stone hearth (with a log fire in winter). Another similarly old-fashioned bar offers more eating space with built-in wood-panelled seats creating booths, fresh flowers, and country prints; there are several pretty and comfortable lounges. Bar food includes good home-made soup (£2.50), sandwiches (from £3.35; open ones from £3.95), home-made terrine (£3.95), ploughman's or mushroom, nut and pasta bake (£4), smooth chicken liver pâté with shallot confit (£3.95), ploughman's (£4.95), poached fillet of salmon with horseradish cream (£7.50), turkey, apricot and asparagus pie (£7.95), sirloin steak (£10.95), and home-made puddings (£2.95). Well kept Flowers IPA and Original on handpump with a guest beer such as Exmoor Ale or Shepherd Neame Spitfire tapped from the cask. They do a useful guide to Exmoor National Park identifying places to visit and there are good nearby walks – up Winsford Hill for magnificent views, or over to Exford. *(Recommended by Peter and Audrey Dowsett, Mrs J Murphy, Yavuz and Shirley Mutlu, Nigel Woolliscroft, Howard and Barbara Clutterbuck, Adrian and Jane Tierney-Jones, David and Jane*

Russell, Jim Winzer)

Free house ~ Licensee Charles Steven ~ Real ale ~ Meals and snacks ~ Restaurant ~ (01643) 851455 ~ Children in eating area of bar and in restaurant ~ Open 11-3, 6-11; 12-3, 7-10.30 Sun ~ Bedrooms: /£100B

WITHYPOOL SS8435 Map 1

Royal Oak

Village signposted off B3233

If you are staying in this bustling and friendly country village inn, there are plenty of marvellous surrounding walks, and the licensees can arrange riding, hunting, fishing, shooting, and Exmoor safaris; breakfasts are good, too. The smartly cosy beamed lounge bar has a fine log fire in a raised stone fireplace, comfortably cushioned wall seating and slat-backed chairs, and a stag's head, stuffed fish, several fox masks, paintings and other ornaments on its walls; another quite spacious bar is similarly decorated. Good bar food includes sandwiches, home-made soups such as chestnut and ginger or tomato and orange (£1.95), duck liver pâté or garlic mushrooms on a crouton (£3.50), fish gratinée (£4.75), venison casserole, fillets of pork in an artichoke and cream sauce, steak and kidney pie or beef curry (all £6.50), fresh fish such as skate, trout, plaice, crab or lobster (from £8), and home-made puddings like sticky toffee pudding, chocolate roulade or lemon meringue pie (£2.75). Well kept Exmoor Ale on handpump, several malt whiskies, a decent wine list, and a fair number of cognacs and armagnacs. It can get very busy (especially on Sunday lunchtimes), and is popular with the local hunting and shooting types; cribbage, dominoes, and piped music. There are wooden benches on the terrace, and just up the road, some grand views from Winsford Hill, with tracks leading up among the ponies into the heather past Withypool Hill. The River Barle runs through the village itself, with pretty bridleways following it through a wooded combe further upstream. This is another pub with a *Lorna Doone* connection; R D Blackmore stayed here while writing the book. *(Recommended by Lesley Sones, JKW, Sarah and Peter Godderham, Richard Gibbs, Dr Rod Holcombe, Harry and Doreen Payne, Ray Ryan, Brian and Bett Cox, Mark Hydes, Paul Barnett, Neil and Anita Christopher, David and Jane Russell)*

Free house ~ Licensees Richard and Jo-Anne Howard ~ Real ale ~ Meals and snacks ~ Restaurant ~ (01643) 831506 ~ Children in eating area of bar lunchtime only ~ Open 11-2.30, 6-11; 12-3, 7-10.30 Sun ~ Bedrooms: £33B/£74B; s/c cottage, too

WOOKEY ST5145 Map 2

Burcott Inn

Wookey Rd; B3139 W of Wells

Not far from Wells, this little roadside pub is neatly kept and friendly. The two simply furnished small front bar rooms are connected but different in character, with a square corner bar counter in the lounge, fresh flowers at either end of the mantlepiece above the tiny stone fireplace, Parker-Knollish brocaded chairs around a couple of tables, and high bar stools; the other bar has beams (some willow pattern plates on one), a solid settle by the window and a high backed old pine settle by one wall, cushioned mate's chairs and fresh flowers on the mix of nice old pine tables, dried flowers in a brass coal skuttle, old-fashioned oil-type wall lamps, and a hunting horn on the bressumer above the fireplace. A little room on the right has darts, shove-ha'penny, cribbage and dominoes, neat built-in wall seats, and small framed advertisements for Schweppes, Coke, Jennings and Oakhill, and there's a roomy back restaurant with black joists, stripped stone walls and sea-green check tablecloths. Nice bar food includes sandwiches (from £2.10; toasties from £1.95; open french sticks from £3.95), filled baked potatoes (from £3.25), ploughman's (from £4.25), home-made Spanish quiche or home-cooked ham and eggs (£4.95), home-made steak and kidney pie (£5.95), chicken in cream and mushrooms (£8.95), scampi in a brandy, tomato and cream sauce (£9.95), steaks (from £10.50), daily specials, and puddings. Well kept Cottage Southern Bitter, Exmoor Gold, and Morlands Old Speckled Hen on handpump. The sizeable garden is well spread and has picnic-sets and plenty of small trees and shrubs, and there's a paddock beyond. The window boxes and tubs at the front are pretty in summer. *(Recommended by P H Roberts, Bruce Bird, Andy and Jill Kassube)*

Free house ~ Licensees Ian and Anne Stead ~ Real ale ~ Meals and snacks ~ Restaurant ~ (01749) 673874 ~ Children in eating area of bar ~ Open 11-2.30(3 Sat), 6-11; 12-3, 7-10.30 Sun

Lucky Dip

Besides the fully inspected pubs, you might like to try these Lucky Dips recommended to us and described by readers (if you do, please send us reports):

Abbots Leigh [Pill Rd; A369, between M5 junction 19 and Bristol; ST5473], *George*: Friendly main-road dining pub with huge choice of attractively presented food from snacks up, real ales inc Marstons Pedigre; no children, good-sized enclosed garden *(J Osborn-Clarke, David Trump, LYM)*

Aller [A372 Bridgwater—Langport; ST4029], *Old Pound*: Well kept beer, good generous food in comfortable carpeted bar and restaurant, ex gunsmith owner – guns from muskets to machine guns; tables under cocktail parasols in side garden; bedrooms *(Rex Miller)*

☆ **Ashcott** [High St, signed off A39; ST4337], *Ring o' Bells*: Traditional three-room village local next to church with local Moors Withy Cutter or Merlins Magic and interesting West Country guest beers, Wilkins' farm cider, wide choice of good value well presented food inc some unusual dishes, vegetarian and build-you-up puddings, decent wines, chatty landlord and helpful service, welcoming regulars; skittle alley, fruit machines, small no-smoking restaurant with soft piped music *(Adrian and Jane Tierney-Jones, Veronica Brown, Robert and Sarah Sibson, Mr and Mrs K H Burton)*

☆ **Ashcott** [70 Bath Rd; A39/A361, SE of village], *Pipers*: Large cosy welcoming lounge, wide choice of good reasonably priced food from sandwiches to steaks inc vegetarian and children's in prettily set beamed dining area, well kept Bass, Courage Best and two local ales, prompt service, log fire, pleasant roadside garden *(Mrs Lynda Matthews, Alan Williams, F J and A Parmenter, Christopher and Mary Thomas)*

Ashcott [Ashcott Corner, nr Shapwick Hotel; ST4337], *Railway*: Unspoilt very basic Somerset levels peat-cutters' pub (no railway now – just bird-watchers and walkers), very obliging landlord, well kept Ruddles and a local guest ale, local farm cider; may open afternoon *(Veronica Brown, Keith Darke, Chris Dower)*

☆ **Ashill** [Windmill Hill; turn off A358 at Stewley Cross Garage; ST3116], *Square & Compass*: Friendly and unassuming tucked-away country pub with sweeping views, open fire, enjoyable and enterprising food from sandwiches through interesting snacks to carefully cooked main dishes, well kept Exmoor, Greene King Abbot, Marstons Pedigree, Morlands Old Speckled Hen and guest beers, traditional games, restaurant; children in eating areas, tables outside, good play area; only a shortage of recent reports keeps this good pub out of the main entries this year *(Derek and Iris Martin, Lynn Sharpless, Bob Eardley, LYM)*

☆ **Axbridge** [The Square; quite handy for M5; ST4255], *Lamb*: Welcoming old inn in attractive square, dark beams, rambling odd corners, good reasonably priced generous food (not Sun evening) inc good vegetarian choice and lots of puddings, well kept ales such as Bass, Butcombe and Wadworths 6X, Thatcher's farm cider, huge log fire, staff cheerful even when busy, pub games inc table skittles, pretty little garden, skittle alley; children in eating area; old-world spacious bedrooms, huge breakfast *(Alan and Paula McCully, Mrs D Graham, LYM)*

Backwell [Farleigh Rd; A370 W of Bristol; ST4968], *George*: Pleasantly modernised old coaching inn with soft lighting, well kept Ushers, well priced food inc good fresh fish in bar and separate restaurant, good choice of wines, good service; children welcome, pleasant terrace and garden with play area *(Alan and Paula McCully, Gwen and Peter Andrews)*; [West Town Rd], *New Inn*: Small pub/restaurant, clean and friendly, with impressive choice of good reasonably priced food inc great range of fish and good puddings; good service and atmosphere, no music *(Mr and Mrs J M Lefeaux)*

Banwell [Church St; ST3959], *Brewers Arms*: Very old, with good outside area inc ducks on little stream *(Dr and Mrs A K Clarke)*

☆ **Barrow Gurney** [Barrow St (B3130, linking A370/A38 SW of Bristol; ST5367], *Princes Motto*: Very welcoming cosy unpretentious local refurbished to make better use of long narrow room up behind snug traditional tap room, well kept Bass and other ales such as Boddingtons, Smiles Best and Wadworths 6X, cheap wholesome lunchtime snacks, pleasant garden; welcome improvements to parking area *(Alan and Paula McCully, Amanda and Simon Southwell, LYM)*

☆ **Batcombe** [off A359 Bruton—Frome, or A361 at Cranmore; ST6838], *Batcombe Inn*: Well furnished low-beamed 14th-c pub doing well under new management, wide choice of good home-made food inc vegetarian, well kept Butcombe, Flowers Original and Marstons Pedigree, big log fire and woodburning stoves, copper and brass, games room, comfortable minstrel's gallery; busy with families weekends (playroom, children's videos Sun), tables in fine walled garden with terrace and play area; behind church in pretty village *(Jill Bickerton, Gwen and Peter Andrews, K H Frostick)*

☆ **Bath** [Abbey Green], *Crystal Palace*: Cheerfully

busy modernised bar, sheltered courtyard with lovely hanging baskets, heated conservatory; good value freshly prepared straightforward food (not Sun evening) inc lunchtime snacks, speedy friendly service, well kept ales, log fire; fruit machines, video game, pinball, piped music *(GSB, Richard Lewis, DI, EMcC, RH, TMcL, Barry and Anne, Susan and Nigel Wilson, Neil Calver, Andrew Hodges, LYM)*

☆ **Bath** [23 The Vineyards; the Paragon, junction with Guinea Lane], *Star*: Genuinely friendly feel in four small interconnecting rooms separated by glass and panelling, a staunchly basic real unspoilt local unchanged by new landlord; particularly well kept Bass, Butcombe and Wadworths 6X in jugs from the cask, low prices, card-playing regulars in snug, dim lighting (famously bricked-in windows), no piped music *(D Irving, R Huggins, E McCall, T McLean, PB, Dr and Mrs A K Clarke, BB)*

☆ **Bath** [Midford Rd; ST7461], *Cross Keys*: Well refurbished dining lounge with end restaurant (best to book, high chairs for children), good cheap food cooked to order from home-made burgers and sausages through popular pies to duck with cherry sauce, good chips and veg, daunting choice of puddings, Courage Directors, Ushers Bitter and Founders, friendly service, locals' public bar; big garden with prettily populated aviary – great attraction for children *(Meg and Colin Hamilton, Neil Calver, Andy and Jill Kassube)*

☆ **Bath** [Mill Lane, Bathampton (off A36 towards Warminster or A4 towards Chippenham)], *George I*: Attractive creeper-covered canalside pub, well run and friendly, with wide choice of well presented usual food inc fish and vegetarian, good log fires, Bass, Courage Directors and Wadworths 6X; dining room by towpath, no-smoking family room, tables on quiet safe spacious back terrace with garden bar (interesting seats on front yard, but traffic noise there); can get crowded, esp weekends *(GSB, Dr and Mrs A K Clarke, Rob and Linda Davis, LM, H and D Payne)*

Bath [Walcot St], *Bell*: Musicians' pub, with well kept Butcombe, Wadworths 6X and guest beers, good cheap rolls, friendly efficient service; frequent free music *(Dr and Mrs A K Clarke, R Michael Richards)*; [17 Northumberland Pl, off High St by W H Smith], *Coeur de Lion*: Tiny single-room pub in charming flower-filled flagstoned pedestrian alley, cosy and friendly little bar, well kept mainly Whitbreads-related ales, lunchtime filled rolls in summer – perhaps Bath's prettiest pub, esp in summer *(Veronica Brown, Richard Lewis, Dr and Mrs A K Clarke, LYM)*; [11 Clevedon Pl W], *Curfew*: Warm welcome in busy low-ceilinged main bar, big table on landing down stairs, Bass and Wadworths IPA, no music *(R Huggins, D Irving, E McCall, T McLean)*; [1 Lansdown Rd], *Farm House*: Pleasant setting on hill overlooking Bath, good choice of food and well kept beer, jazz some evenings *(J Pettifer, Dr and Mrs A K Clarke)*; [6 Queen St], *Hacketts*: Daily-changing beers such as Batemans XXXB and Hook Norton at below-average prices, lunchtime food (not Sun); steps up to pub, and to lavatories; can get very busy Sat night *(G Coates)*; [47 St James's Parade], *Hobgoblin*: Bare boards, musical instruments and blues singer pictures, friendly staff, two well kept Wychwood beers, also Bath Gem and Marstons Pedigree; games machine, piped music may be quite loud, popular with students; pool table downstairs *(Dr and Mrs A K Clarke, Richard Lewis)*; [North Parade], *Huntsman*: Popular 18th-c pub claiming oldest stone shop front in Bath, long comfortable lounge, panelled side room, efficient friendly staff, wide choice of food inc well filled sandwiches, well kept Hardy beers; terrace *(Richard Lewis, Dr and Mrs A K Clarke)*; [1 Monmouth Pl], *Kings Arms*: Recently refurbished open-plan former coaching inn, bright pine, bric-a-brac, well kept Bass, Courage Best and Directors and a guest such as Smiles Exhibition, food inc Sun lunch, weekend live music, flagstoned entrance courtyard; bedrooms *(G Coates)*; [2 Saracen St], *Pig & Fiddle*: Small busy pub with good unusual choice of real ales from island bar, friendly service, two big open fires, clocks set to different time zones, very relaxed daytime, lively at night, good piped music, seats on big front terrace; home-cooked food here and in upper restaurant area, takeaways too *(Ben Hanna, Dr and Mrs A K Clarke, Susan and Nigel Wilson, DI, EMcC, RH, TMcL)*; [27 Daniel St], *Pulteney Arms*: Very small, with well kept Bass, Oakhill and Wadworths 6X, good chip baps and other food, jugs around walls; popular with Bath Rugby players, unobtrusive piped music or juke box; pavement tables *(Roger Wain-Heapy, Dr and Mrs A K Clarke)*; [Upper Borough Walls], *Sam Weller*: Well kept Bass and Wadworths 6X, good food cooked to order inc all-day breakfast, no-smoking area, friendly young staff, lively mixed clientele *(Dr and Mrs A K Clarke)*; [42 Broad St], *Saracens Head*: Beamed coaching inn with 19th-c prints inc mid-Victorian *Punch* title pages; well kept Scottish Courage ales, good well presented food at sensible prices inc generous Sat cold table, quick service; children in dining area *(Tony Dickinson, Dr and Mrs A K Clarke, Andrew Hodges)*

☆ **Bishops Lydeard** [A358 towards Taunton; ST1828], *Kingfisher*: Two neat communicating rooms, cottagey and relaxing, with quick cheerful service and concentration on food, from good beef sandwiches up; well kept local real ale, comfortably shaded tables outside *(Frank Davidson, Howard Clutterbuck, LYM)*

Blagdon Hill [4 miles S of Taunton; ST2217], *Lamb & Flag*: Cosy, clean and welcoming, tastefully and simply decorated in homely and relaxing country style keeping beams, settles etc; friendly newish licensees, good food, well kept Otter ales, log fire *(Mrs M N Brown, Rex Miller, David and Jean Hall)*

☆ **Brent Knoll** [2 miles from M5 junction 22; right on to A38, then first left; ST3350], *Red Cow*: Sensibly short choice of good well priced food inc proper veg and beautifully served Sun lunch in warmly welcoming spotless dining lounge where children allowed, with well spaced tables, quick pleasant staff, well kept Whitbreads-related ales, skittle alley, sheltered gardens *(Mark J Hydes, BB)*

Bridgwater [A38 N, just off M5 junction 23; ST3140], *Admirals Table*: Big new pub, good for motorway break *(Anon)*; [1 West Quay; ST3037], *Fountain*: Traditional tastefully extended 18th-c Wadworths town pub by River Parrett opp restored quay, their 6X and Farmers Glory kept well, also Badger Tanglefoot, Butcombe and guests such as Adnams, Cotleigh, Gales, twice-yearly beer festival; good value rolls, friendly licensees, bare boards, dark wood, old local prints *(Adrian and Jane Tierney-Jones)*

☆ **Bristol** [Upper Maudlin St/Colston St], *Brewery Tap*: Tap for Smiles brewery, small and busy – get there early for a seat; their beers kept well and sensibly priced, also interesting continental bottled ones, interesting unpretentious decor, good chatty atmosphere even when packed, log fire in no-smoking room, food inc filled rolls and vegetarian, no piped music; cl Sun *(Simon and Amanda Southwell, David Warrellow, Steve Willey)*

☆ **Bristol** [43 Corn St; ST5773], *Commercial Rooms*: Vast Wetherspoons establishment in impressive building, lofty ceiling, snug cubicles along one side, comfortable quieter no-smoking back room; reasonable prices, good real ales, food all day; very busy weekend evenings *(Simon and Amanda Southwell, Comus Elliott, Dr and Mrs A K Clarke)*

☆ **Bristol** [38 Jacobs Wells Rd, Clifton], *Hope & Anchor*: Character bare-boards 18th-c pub with plenty of atmosphere, hop bines, various sizes of old pine table, good choice of well kept ales such as Adnams Broadside, Badger Tanglefoot, Bath SPA, Fullers London Pride and Shepherd Neame Spitfire, fast efficient service by pleasant studenty staff, good generous food inc interesting dishes – very popular lunchtime; summer evening barbecues on good back terrace with interesting niches, occasional live music *(Dr and Mrs B D Smith, Dr and Mrs A K Clarke)*

Bristol [Hope Chapel Hill, Hotwells], *Adam & Eve*: Bass and Gibbs Mew ales, huge range of malt whiskies, good food, welcoming licensees and staff *(Patrick Godfrey)*; [18 Alma Vale Rd, Clifton], *Alma*: Cheerful town pub well refurbished without losing character, real ales such as Greene King Abbot, Theakstons XB and Wadworths 6X, good plain cheap food, friendly service, no music; popular upstairs theatre Tues-Sat – best to book *(Simon and Amanda Southwell)*; [Lower Clifton Hill], *Eldon House*: Lively, with good generous food cooked by landlady's husband, Ushers ales, Sun quiz night *(P B Godfrey)*; [32 Park St], *Le Chateau*: Big busy Smiles pub with their ales kept wall; Victorian feel, lots of pictures, open fires, roomy back conservatory, good home-made lunchtime food (many tables reserved Sat), more limited evening *(Simon and Amanda Southwell, Veronica Brown)*; [off King St/Welsh Back], *Llandoger Trow*: By docks, interesting as the last timber building built here, and making the most of its picturesque past in very cosy collection of small alcoves and rooms with original fireplaces and carvings; some concentration on food, draught sherries, eclectic array of liqueur coffees *(Val Stevenson, Rob Holmes)*; [59 Baldwin St], *Old Fish Market*: Ground floor of imposing red and cream brick building converted to Fullers pub, good mural showing it in 1790s along one wall, lots of wood inc rather ornate counter, parquet floor, lunchtime food inc sandwiches and home-baked pies, Fullers ales, good coffee, daily papers, quiet piped music *(Ian Phillips)*; [115 Whiteladies Rd, Clifton], *Penny Farthing*: Panelled pub with late Victorian bric-a-brac inc penny farthing, armchairs opp bar, lots of table seating, at least five real ales such as Butcombe and Wadworths 6X racked behind bar, home-made food lunchtime and evening, friendly helpful staff; can get very busy evenings *(Simon and Amanda Southwell)*; [15 Upper Maudlin St], *Sea Horse*: This Smiles pub has closed, for building of a children's hospital *(RIP)*; [35 Corn St], *Wig & Pen*: Converted commercial building with glass area at back and no-smoking area; friendly staff and well kept Smiles (and other) ale *(Dr and Mrs A K Clarke)*

☆ **Brompton Regis** [SS9531], *George*: Warmly welcoming pleasantly refurbished 17th-c ex-farmhouse in quiet village, reasonably priced home-made food inc good vegetarian choice, three real ales maybe inc bargain 12 Bore, organic wines, woodburners, skittle alley, quick friendly service; no juke box or machines, Exmoor views from garden by churchyard, dogs welcome, good walks *(Richard and Janet Fleming, Graham and Jill Wood, Chris Tasker)*

Cannington [12 High St (A39); ST2539], *Kings Head*: Vast blackboard choice of good food, friendly licensees, decent beers and wines; bedrooms *(Rex Miller, K H Frostick)*

Chard [Combe St; ST3208], *Bell & Crown*: Simple local with straightforward cheap food, three real ales, gas lighting, small back garden *(Ann and Colin Hunt)*; [High St], *Choughs*: Attractive 16th-c building (supposedly haunted by Judge Jeffreys) with friendly service, farm cider, cheap usual food *(R T and J C Moggridge)*; [Hornsbury Hill; A358 N; ST3310], *Hornsbury Mill*: Restaurant with rooms rather than pub, but also does snacks in comfortable bar (tidy dress); pond with ducks and turning mill wheel – good for children; bedrooms *(Howard Clutterbuck)*

☆ **Charlton Musgrove** [B3081, 5 miles SE of Bruton; ST7229], *Smithy*: Quiet open-plan 18th-c pub, roomy and sparkling clean, with stripped stone, heavy beams, log fires, plenty of pleasantly secluded corners, good range of cheap tasty home-cooked food inc Sun lunch and good vegetarian choice, well kept Bass and Butcombe, cheerful landlord, good service, walking sticks for sale; arch to small restaurant overlooking charming garden full of cottagey flower tubs and hanging baskets; skittle alley and pool table *(Brian Chambers, K R Harris,*

Alan and Paula McCully)
Chew Magna [back rd to Bishop Sutton; ST5763], *Pony & Trap*: Attractively refurbished Ushers pub in delightfully rural spot, warm cosy atmosphere, well kept ales inc seasonal, food inc good ploughman's *(Tom Evans)*
Chew Stoke [ST5661], *Stoke Inn*: Large welcoming family pub with good carefully cooked food from sandwiches to wonderful steaks, well kept Bass, local Butcombe, Courage, Smiles and Youngers, good fresh coffee, helpful smartly dressed staff, no-smoking restaurant; piped music, jazz Sun lunchtime in back room, side garden *(A C and J M Curry, J W G Nunns, Jenny and Michael Back)*
Chilton Polden [ST3739], *Toby Jug*: Welcoming atmosphere, good service, food from good sandwiches up, well kept Exmoor and Otter ale *(Colin Fisher)*
Clevedon [The Beach; ST4071], *Campbells Landing*: Good position opp restored Victorian pier, done up like old Campbells steamer with nautical items inc coastal charts and old local photographs, good choice of well kept beers inc Bass, Courage and guest ales, wide range of food; bedrooms *(Alan and Paula McCully)*; [Elton Rd], *Little Harp*: Promenade pub useful for low-priced food all day inc vegetarian, massive doorstep sandwiches and Sun lunch, views towards Exmoor and the Welsh hills from terrace and conservatory, pleasant no-smoking family area with mezzanine floor, well kept Marstons Pedigree, Mild, seasonal ales and guest beers, prompt service; one of our readers found it particularly cheering to be one of the youngest people in the room – at 72 *(Tom Evans, M Joyner, Alan and Paula McCully, JCW, Rev John Hibberd, Mike and Mary Carter)*; [15 The Beach], *Moon & Sixpence*: Substantial seafront Victorian family dining pub with good choice of generous usual food (puddings free to OAPs), quick friendly service, balconied mezzanine floor with good view of magnificently restored pier and over to Brecon Beacons, well kept Marstons Pedigree *(Veronica Brown)*
Clutton Hill [King Lane; off A39 Bristol—Wells; ST6360], *Hunters Rest*: Carefully extended stonebuilt pub with wide choice of bar food from interestingly filled rolls to steaks, several real ales, family room, no-smoking area, log fires, restaurant, big garden with play area, weekend miniature railway and view to Mendips; facilities for disabled *(Meg and Colin Hamilton, F J Willy)*
Combe St Nicholas [2½ miles N of Chard; ST3011], *Green Dragon*: Pleasantly refurbished, good value food (should book), welcoming service, well kept ales, decent wines, open fire; well behaved children allowed; open all day Sat, bedrooms *(Howard Clutterbuck)*
Congresbury [Brinsea Rd (B3133); ST4363], *Plough*: Unspoilt flagstoned local with three seating areas off main bar, two log fires, old prints, farm tools and sporting memorabilia; welcoming staff, lunchtime filled rolls, well kept Bass, Butcombe, Worthington BB and interesting guest beers, darts, table skittles, shove ha'penny and cards, jack russells called Pepper and Mustard, hair cuts 1st Sat of month; small garden with boules, aviary and occasional barbecues *(Alan and Paula McCully, Mike and Mary Cartern)*; [just off A370 from lights at W end of bypass], *Ship & Castle*: Big family area inc no-smoking room, oldish wooden furniture and couple of big settles, well kept Marstons ales at very sane prices, tasty food inc good-sized children's dishes, good pasta and vast mixed grill, attentive service; good play area *(the Sandy family, Tom Evans, Dr and Mrs A K Clarke)*; [Wrington Rd], *White Hart*: Welcoming modernised pub with cosy bar, conservatory extension, some concentration on generous tasty food inc vegetarian, full range of Badger beers, good service, terrace with Mendip views, big play area, aviary *(Mr and Mrs C Barker, Alan and Paula McCully, K R Harris)*
☆ **Corfe** [B3170; ST2319], *White Hart*: Welcoming licensees, son cooks good food inc vegetarian (worth the wait), priced in snack or full meal size, also sandwiches, ploughman's and unusual home-made ice creams; lounge with small stools, attractive small no-smoking dining room, friendly licensees, good choice of real ales (not cheap); children welcome *(Howard Clutterbuck, John Barker, Shirley Pielou, Sarah Armitage)*
Crewkerne [ST4409], *George*: Former coaching inn (the coach entry now opens into a shopping precinct); long bar, lounge and dining room, usual food inc very cheap, tasty and filling baguettes *(Janet Pickles)*; [Market Sq, opp Post Office], *White Hart*: 15th c, cosy, quiet and peaceful, newly redone with comfortable plain wooden furniture, fresh food and veg, wide choice of beers and spirits, efficient jolly staff *(Howard Clutterbuck)*
☆ **Croscombe** [A371 Wells—Shepton Mallet; ST5844], *Bull Terrier*: Cosy and clean, with beams, flagstones, parquet and carpet, flame-effect fires, three communicating rooms with a no-smoking family room, generous good value food from sandwiches to steaks (not winter Sun evening), well kept Butcombe Bitter, Smiles, a beer brewed for the pub and a guest such as Adnams, farm cider, decent wines, friendly service and border collie called Penny, traditional games; cl Mon in winter; comfortable bedrooms *(Mrs J Ravine, JE, Philip Orbell, Mr and Mrs R Fowler, Bruce Bird, Margaret and Douglas Tucker, LYM)*
Cross [ST4155], *White Hart*: Wide choice of evening food, very pleasant atmosphere, good service; landlord's wife is a professional wine taster *(Gethin Lewis)*
☆ **Crowcombe** [off A358 Combe Florey—Bicknoller; ST1336], *Blue Boar*: Taken over 1998 by the couple who made the Fitzhead Inn at Fitzhead (their last pub) our Somerset Dining Pub of the Year; friendly prompt service, good value food inc good veg, good beer range and coffee *(Dr P F A Watkins)*
Crowcombe, *Carew Arms*: Village inn dating

back several centuries, friendly, unspoilt and original, sensibly priced home-made food, Butcombe, Exmoor and Wilmots, Lane's farm cider; good refurbished bedrooms, nice spot at foot of Quantocks *(S P A Child, the Didler)*

Draycott [off A371, opp former stn; ST4750], *Strawberry Special*: Old high-backed settles, huge open fire, friendly welcome, reasonably priced plain food *(Alan and Paula McCully)*

☆ **Dulverton** [2 Bank Sq; SS9127], *Lion*: Generous food inc good value soup and specials in friendly and comfortably old-fashioned country-town pub with well kept Exmoor and Ushers, decent wine and coffee, helpful service, no music; children allowed in room off, pleasant setting *(W H and E Thomas, Dorothy and Leslie Pilson)*

☆ **East Coker** [ST5412], *Helyar Arms*: Well decorated spotless oak-beamed village pub in attractive setting, good atmosphere despite considerable extensions, good generous fairly cheap food, well kept beer, friendly staff *(D B Jenkin)*

East Harptree [B3134, SW; ST5655], *Castle of Comfort*: Mendip coaching inn, in same family for two generations, tree-trunk supporting beams in ancient unspoilt bar; very welcoming landlord, wide choice of good generous food, good range of real ales, pleasant atmosphere; attractively set out rooms in newish wing *(Veronica Brown)*

☆ **Easton in Gordano** [Martcombe Rd; A369 a mile from M5 junction 19; ST5276], *Rudgleigh*: Bustling roadside pub, attractive in summer with tables in big garden with willows, tamarisks and play area (but Tannoy food announcements); small nicely laid-out lounge with lots of commemorative mugs, other china, old guns, well kept Scottish Courage and Smiles ale, quick friendly service, wide range of prompt generous food; rather bleak little family room; open all day weekdays *(R W A Suddaby, B J Harding, Andrew Hodges, Douglas Miller, LYM)*

☆ **Edington Burtle** [Catcott Rd; ST4043], *Olde Burtle*: Good reasonably priced food inc fresh fish and steak sold by ounce, local veg and good Sun lunch in character bar, much refurbished lounge and comfortable restaurant, lovely log fire, well kept if not cheap Fullers London Pride, Wadworths 6X and an interesting guest beer; skittle alley *(Tom Evans, P H Roberts)*

Enmore [Enmore Rd; ST2434], *Enmore Inn*: Good food under new landlord *(Rex Miller)*

Evercreech [Evercreech Junction; A371 Shepton Mallet—Castle Cary; ST6438], *Natterjack*: Wide choice of generous enjoyable food, not expensive, friendly pleasant staff *(Mr and Mrs Ken Flawn)*

☆ **Exebridge** [B3222 S of Dulverton – pub over the river, in Devon; SS9224], *Anchor*: Well furnished, clean and comfortable rather hotelish pub in idyllic Exmoor-edge spot, big riverside garden with plenty of tables and play area; wide food choice from sandwiches up, well kept Courage Directors, Morlands Old Speckled Hen, Ushers Best and Wadworths 6X, local farm cider, above-average wines, some attractive furnishings and pictures; open all day summer w/e, children welcome, restaurant, smaller back games bar, skittle alley; comfortable bedrooms, good breakfast, fishing rights *(Ben and Sheila Walker, K Flack, John and Vivienne Rice, Mike Gorton, Tom Evans, Janet Pickles, LYM)*

☆ **Exford** [The Green (B3224); SS8538], *Crown*: Welcoming country hotel's cosy bar popular with farmers and smart local couples, generous food from good ploughman's to beautifully presented imaginative main dishes with lots of veg, well kept Brakspears, Exmoor and Wadworths 6X, decent wines, log fire, welcoming service, attractive streamside garden; comfortable bedrooms – in Good Hotel Guide 1999 *(Adrian and Jane Tierney-Jones, Mary Woods, Patrick Renouf, Nigel Harrison)*

☆ **Exford**, *White Horse*: Exmoor hotel with rustic-style open-plan Dalesman bar, hunting prints and trophies, pine tables and settles, very wide choice of food from filled baguettes to venison pie etc (procedure for getting it could perhaps be streamlined), generous Sun carvery, ales such as Bass, Cotleigh Tawny, Exmoor and Worthingtons, log fire, pleasant safe garden by River Exe; children in eating area, dogs allowed; open all day summer, lovely Exmoor village setting; bedrooms comfortable, stabling available *(Adrian and Jane Tierney-Jones, Richard Gibbs, LYM)*

Failand [B3128 Bristol—Clevedon; ST5171], *Failand Inn*: Well run cheerful and attractive beamed country pub, good choice of food (all day Fri-Sun), rooms for family dining off long bar, well kept ales such as Bass, Courage Best and Theakstons XB, decent house wines, friendly staff; no-smoking garden room, tables in pleasant garden; open all day, food all day Fri-Sun, children welcome if eating *(Gwen and Peter Andrews, Alan and Paula McCully, David Warrellow, JCW)*

Farleigh Hungerford [A366 Trowbridge—Norton St Philip; ST8057], *Hungerford Arms*: Well furnished pub with friendly licensees, decent food in main bar, more airy room off, and popular lower-level restaurant, well kept Courage Best and Morlands Old Speckled Hen; beautiful views from terrace *(Susan and Nigel Wilson, Ted George)*

Fitzhead [off B3227 W of Taunton; ST1128], *Fitzhead Inn*: New licensees in this tucked-away country pub are concentrating rather on the beer side, with Cotleigh Tawny, Fullers London Pride, Hook Norton, Tisbury Natterjack and two guests, also farm cider; besides bar food there are more elaborate evening dishes such as pheasant and monkfish; the previous people who scored such a hit with their food and wines are now at the Blue Boar at Crowcombe *(LYM)*

☆ **Freshford** [signed off B3108 – OS Sheet 172 map ref 790600; ST7960], *Inn at Freshford*: Welcoming comfortably modernised beamed pub, partly no smoking, friendly and obliging staff, well kept Ruddles County and Ushers, open fire, huge choice of good food from sandwiches up, restaurant (not Sun evening); children welcome, piped music; pretty gardens, nice spot by River Frome, walks to Kennet & Avon Canal *(Andrew Shore, Simon and Amanda Southwell, Meg & Colin Hamilton, LYM)*

☆ **Glastonbury** [Northload St; ST5039], *Who'd A Thought It*: Friendly town pub with interesting bric-a-brac and memorabilia, well kept ales such as Bass, Hardy Country and Porter and Palmers, decent wines, stripped brickwork, flagstones and polished pine, coal fires, pleasant staff, entertaining decorations in lavatories, popular varied food, no-smoking restaurant; bedrooms cosy and comfortable, good breakfast *(Jo and Gary Charlton, Adrian and Jane Tierney-Jones)*

Glastonbury [High St], *George & Pilgrims*: 15th-c inn with magnificent carved stone frontage, interesting front bar with heavy tables, handsome stone fireplace (flame-effect gas fire) and traceried stained-glass bay window; rest of pub more ordinary; well kept Bass and Wadworths 6X, decent food, helpful staff, children in buffet and pleasant upstairs restaurant, occasional live music; good clean bedrooms *(Tony Dickinson, LYM)*

Hambridge [B3168 S of Curry Rivel; ST3921], *Lamb & Lion*: Family-run, with good choice of real ale and good snacks *(Douglas Allen)*

☆ **Hardway** [rd to Alfreds Tower, off B3081 Bruton—Wincanton at Redlynch; pub named on OS Sheet 183 map ref 721342; ST7234], *Bull*: Pretty and welcoming beamed country dining pub, popular locally esp with older people weekday lunchtimes for wide choice of good generous food with fresh veg, warm comfortable bar, character dining rooms, log fire, well kept Butcombe and Wadworths 6X, farm cider; unobtrusive piped music, sell paintings and meringues; tables and barbecue in rose garden over road; bedrooms *(A Madden, D A Ellis, Mr and Mrs Gordon Turner)*

Haselbury Plucknett [ST4711], *Haselbury Inn*: New landlord in candlelit dining pub with heavy red-cushioned cask seats, chintz armchairs and sofas by the fire, good wines, wide choice of real ales, no-smoking restaurant; piped music may obtrude; children welcome, picnic-sets in garden; has been cl Mon *(Dr and Mrs A J Newton, Galen Strawson, Carole Smart, Andrew Jeeves)*

☆ *nr* **Haselbury Plucknett** [off A30 E of Crewkerne, towards Merriott; ST4611], *Old Mill*: Very modernised country dining pub in quiet spot, big picture windows looking over duck pond, good enjoyable food and well spaced tables in comfortable light and airy dining lounge, snug low-ceilinged bar on right, tables out on informal lawn by pretty stream; cl Sun *(Howard and Barbara Clutterbuck, BB)*

Hillfarance [ST1624], *Anchor*: Comfortable modernised pub with lots of flower tubs outside, good food inc children's and maybe free soup in eating areas off attractive two-part bar, good value evening carvery, well kept Butcombe, Exmoor and Rascals, family room with wendy house, speedy friendly service, garden with play area; bedrooms, caravan site, holiday apartments *(Mr and Mrs C Roberts, Bett and Brian Cox, Richard Dolphin)*

☆ **Hinton Blewett** [signed off A37 in Clutton; ST5957], *Ring o' Bells*: Charming low-beamed stone-built country local opp village green, very friendly landlord, good value home cooking (not Sun evening) inc some interesting dishes, well kept Wadworths 6X and three guest ales, log fire, pleasant view from tables in sheltered front yard; children welcome *(C Plumb, D, B and M Kolding, LYM)*

☆ **Hinton Charterhouse** [B3110 about 4 miles S of Bath; ST7758], *Rose & Crown*: Attractive panelled bar with well kept Bass, Butcombe and Smiles tapped from casks, wide choice of good value generous blackboard food inc plenty of fish and vegetarian in bar and restaurant, hard-working and amiable young owners, interesting new stone fireplace; open all day Sat *(Howard Clutterbuck, Mr and Mrs N Abraham, D Irving, E McCall, R Huggins, T McLean, Meg and Colin Hamilton)*

☆ **Holton** [off A303 W of Wincanton; ST6827], *Old Inn*: Charming rustic 16th-c pub, unassuming and friendly, with beams, ancient flagstones, log fire, hundreds of key fobs, attractive bric-a-brac, big open woodburner, plump cat; pleasant service, Butcombe, Wilmots and Wadworths 6X, food in bar and restaurant (must book Sun lunch); walking sticks for sale, tables ooutside, sheltered garden up steps *(James Nunn, BB)*

Ilminster [B3168 W; ST3614], *Lord Nelson*: Quiet, pleasant and friendly, good value bar food, good service, well kept beer, good garden; bedrooms *(Howard Clutterbuck)*

Kilve [A39 E of Williton; ST1442], *Hood Arms*: Woodburner in bar, cosy little plush lounge, no-smoking restaurant, wide choice of popular bar food (no sandwiches), friendly service, well kept Ushers Founders; skittle alley, tables on sheltered back terrace by garden; nice bedrooms – back are quietest *(M G Hart, K H Frostick, Dorothy and Leslie Pilson, David and Brenda Begg, LYM)*

☆ **Kingsdon** [off A303 at Podimore roundabout via A372 and B3151, then right opp village PO; ST5126], *Kingsdon Inn*: Attractive mix of country furnishings in three charmingly decorated communicating rooms, woodburner and open fires; new licensees doing usual bar food (not sandwiches), with more elaborate evening dishes (not cheap, not Sun evening), well kept Cotleigh Tawny and Harrier, Fullers London Pride, Oakhill Mendip Gold, local farm cider; children in eating area, traditional games, quiet piped music, picnic-sets outside *(Mike and Heather Watson, LYM)*

Knole [off A372; ST4825], *Limekiln*: Well furnished roomy flagstoned bar with eating areas inc family room, particularly well kept Bass and Ushers, reasonably priced quickly served bar food inc huge home-made burgers, good value restaurant; big garden, good setting *(Lesley Sones, Peter and Audrey Dowsett)*

Knowle [7 Axbridge Rd; ST6170], *Friendship*: Good estate pub, well kept Courage ales, tables

outside, play area *(Dr and Mrs A K Clarke)*
Mark [ST3747], *White Horse*: Spacious 17th-c pub, attractively old-world, with wide choice of home-made food (and of coffees), well kept Flowers and guest beers, good friendly service, some decent malt whiskies; good garden with play area *(H Beck, Mel Smith)*
Milborne Port [High St; ST6718], *Kings Head*: Very attractive and clean, with well kept ales inc Hardy, good food, friendly efficient staff; good bedrooms *(Stephen G Brown)*
Minehead [Esplanade; SS9746], *Hobby Horse*: Decent choice of food inc attractive dish of day, ales such as Bass and Flowers *(Don and Thelma Beeson)*; [Quay West], *Old Ship Aground*: Useful tourist pub with pleasant harbour views, ample menu esp fish, friendly staff, well kept Ruddles County, good coffee *(Peter and Audrey Dowsett)*
nr **Minehead** [Blue Anchor Bay; end of B3191, off A39 E; ST0343], *Blue Anchor*: Mellow building in spectacular clifftop setting, well run split-level hotel bars, friendly atmosphere, good range of food, beers inc Hardy, pleasant staff, big trim garden; children welcome, piped music; bedrooms clean, pretty and comfortable, site for touring caravans *(Gwyneth and Salvo Spadaro-Dutturi, Mary Woods)*
☆ **Misterton** [Middle St (A356); ST4508], *White Swan*: Spick and span small cottagey pub, hospitable and comfortable, with good choice of bar and restaurant food cooked by landlady, good range of well kept beers, no-smoking rooms, framed tapestries, collection of old wireless sets; attractive garden behind, skittle alley *(Mr and Mrs K W Johnson, Douglas Allen, Galen Strawson)*
☆ **Monkton Combe** [ST7762], *Wheelwrights Arms*: Small country inn with attractively laid-out bar, wheelwright and railway memorabilia, friendly service, wide choice of good reasonably priced home-made food, well kept ales such as Adnams, Butcombe and Wadworths 6X, big open fire, tiny darts room at end, fruit machine, quiet piped music; garden with valley view, well equipped small bedrooms in separate block *(Anthony Hoyle, LYM)*
☆ **Montacute** [The Borough, off A3088 W of Yeovil; ST4916], *Phelips Arms*: Roomy and airy, comfortably unpretentious, with varied good freshly cooked fair-priced food inc sandwiches and interesting specials, friendly efficient service, well kept Palmers; skittle alley, tables in appealing garden, delightful village, handy for Montacute House; bedrooms *(Dr S P Willavoys, Mr and Mrs J Russell, Galen Strawson, Stephen Brown)*
Montacute, *Kings Arms*: More hotel than pub, with blazing log fires, stripped 16th-c hamstone walls, mix of chintz, grey-gold plush and oak, food (not Sun evening) from filled baguettes up, no-smoking restaurants, decent wines; children welcome, bedrooms *(J H Jones, Theo, Anne and Jane Gaskin, Derek and Iris Martin, R C Morgan, D B Jenkin, Dr and Mrs B Smith, LYM)*
Moorland [1½ miles from M5 junction 24, via Huntworth; ST3332], *Thatchers Arms*: Remote and friendly, with small comfortable bar, second basic room with pool, woodburners, well kept Wadworths 6X and a guest beer, wide range of food inc basic cheap dishes, tables in garden; modern outside lavatories *(P and M Rudlin)*
☆ **Moorlinch** [Pit Hill Lane; signed off A39; ST3936], *Ring of Bells*: Fine old building, friendly and cosy, with log fire in attractive lounge, reasonably priced good hearty food, well kept changing ales such as Berrow, Bridgwater, Oakhill and Smiles, welcoming landlord; has been cl Mon-Thurs lunchtime in winter *(John Barker, Douglas Allen)*
Nailsea [Trendlewood Way; ST4670], *Old Farmhouse*: Attractive and spotless welcoming pub with restaurant in old barn, good for children; wide choice of home-made lunchtime food inc good carvery, Badger and other well kept ales, friendly service; beautiful garden with good play area, Sun quiz night *(Pat and John Smyth)*
Nether Stowey [Lime St; ST1939], *Ancient Mariner*: Large friendly pub opp Coleridge's cottage, varied good food inc own produce, well kept Butcombe, swift cheerful service; may be piped music at quiet times, children welcome *(Mr and Mrs B Tizard, Frank Davidson, G W A Pearce)*; [Keenthorne (A39 E of village)], *Cottage*: Warm and roomy local with good reasonably priced food, Butcombe and Flowers Original, friendly service, comfortable music-free dining lounge with woodburner, aquarium, interesting pictures; games room (children allowed here); skittle alley, tables on terrace *(Rex Miller, LYM)*
Newton St Loe [ST7064], *Globe*: Licensees with good GPG track record now doing food all day here, inc delicious puddings; good atmosphere, efficient service *(Meg and Colin Hamilton)*
North Perrott [ST4709], *Manor Arms*: Attractively modernised 16th-c pub on pretty village green, inglenook, beams and mellow stripped stone, good value imaginative freshly made food from sandwiches up in bar and cosy restaurant, well kept Boddingtons and Smiles, decent wines, good coffee, attentive service, cheerful atmosphere, pleasant garden with adventure play area *(Basil Minson)*
North Petherton [nr M5 junction 24; Taunton Rd (A38 towards Bridgwater); ST2932], *Compass*: Useful roadhouse with reasonably priced food inc generous sandwiches and vegetarian dishes, well kept Flowers Original; piped music may be loud *(Anon)*
Norton Fitzwarren [ST1925], *Cross Keys*: Well refurbished and extended, with wide choice of food showing much originality, well kept Theakstons *(Mr and Mrs W B Walker)*
Norton St Philip [A366 W of Trowbridge; ST7755], *Fleur de Lys*: 13th-c stone cottages joined centuries ago for many-roomed black-beamed flagstoned village local, huge fireplace, good value home-made food inc super veg, well kept Bass, Oakhill, Wadworths 6X and Worthington, friendly staff; children very welcome, skittle alley *(Brad W Morley, Nigel*

and Susan Wilson, Veronica Brown); *George*: As we write, this remarkable ancient building is a gutted shell, little more than just the walls and roof; the owners Wadworths hope to complete its internal rebuilding before the end of 1998 – and we hope the work turns out to have enhanced this former rather spectacular main entry, and not otherwise *(LYM)*

Norton sub Hamdon [ST4615], *Lord Nelson*: Cleverly refurbished, with good choice of real ales, and good food served without predominating; pretty village *(Douglas Allen)*

Oake [Hillcommon, N; off B3227 W of Taunton; ST1426], *Royal Oak*: Friendly atmosphere, efficient service, good food esp steak and ribs, great value, local beers; nice garden *(S J C Hill)*

☆ **Over Stratton** [S of A303 via South Petherton roundabout; ST4315], *Royal Oak*: Attractive and welcoming family dining pub, flagstones, prettily stencilled beams, scrubbed pine kitchen tables, pews, settles etc, log fires and rustic decor; impressive food choice, no-smoking restaurant, well kept Badger ales, helpful staff; open all day Aug, tables outside with barbecues and good play areas for toddlers and older children *(Guy Consterdine, Mike Gorton, Rob Chandler, LYM)*

☆ **Panborough** [B3139 Wedmore—Wells; ST4745], *Panborough Inn*: Genteel, quiet and spacious, almost a hotelish feel to the entrance, steps up to carpeted bar with plush wall banquette and other seats, beams, brasses, copper, some stripped stone, woodburner; neat dining area rambles round behind island servery (must book w/e), staff neat too; Butcombe and Courage Best, wide range of consistently good generous food inc vegetarian and splendid puddings; piped nostalgic pop music; some picnic-sets by car park and on front terrace *(J H Kane, A C and J M Curry, K R Harris, BB)*

☆ **Pitminster** [off B3170 S of Taunton (or reached direct); ST2119], *Queens Arms*: Peaceful village pub, cosy and unspoilt, with smiling service, log fire, seven well kept ales, interesting wines, good bar food from fine crab sandwiches up, wonderful fish restaurant in pleasant dining room; no music, dogs allowed, bedrooms with own bathrooms *(Howard Clutterbuck, D A C T Hancock, John Barker)*

Porlock [High St; SS8846], *Ship*: Picturesque thatched huge-chimneyed partly 13th-c pub, basic low-beamed locals' front bar with flagstones, inglenooks each end, hunting prints, back lounge, well kept Bass, Cotleigh, Courage Best and a local guest beer such as Bosuns Tackle, good country wines, easy-going service, bar food, pub games and pool table, garden; children welcome in eating area; bedrooms *(Adrian and Jane Tierney-Jones, Mr and Mrs R Maggs, LYM)*

☆ **Porlock Weir** [end of B3225, off A39 in Porlock; SS8547], *Ship*: Prettily restored old inn included for its wonderful setting by peaceful harbour, with tables in terraced rose garden and good walks (but no views to speak of from bars); usual bar food inc sandwiches, well kept ales such as Bass and Exmoor in straightforward Mariners Bar with family room; roaring fire, unusual space-age gents', attractive bedrooms *(John and Joan Calvert, Mr and Mrs T Crawford, Donald Mather, Sue and Bob Ward, M C and S Jeanes, LYM)*

☆ **Portishead** [High St; ST4777], *Poacher*: Popular with older lunchers for wide range of good reasonably priced freshly cooked food with real veg – get there early as many things sell out by 1ish, though they'll do the good trout much later; well kept Courage ales and guests such as Hook Norton Old Hookey, Shepherd Neame Spitfire, Smiles Best, very helpful staff – friendly and amusing; evening restaurant, cl Sun pm *(Tom Evans, K R Harris)*

☆ **Priddy** [from Wells on A39 pass hill with TV mast on left, then next left; ST5450], *Hunters Lodge*: Welcoming and unassuming walkers' and potholers' inn in same family for generations, well kept ales such as Butcombe and Exmoor tapped from casks behind the bar, simple good food inc bread and local cheese, low prices, log fire, flagstones; tables in garden; bedrooms, handy for Milton Lodge gardens *(Martin Grass, Veronica Brown, LYM)*

Priddy [off B3135; ST5250], *New Inn*: Bustling low-beamed pub, modernised but still traditional, with good log fire, spacious conservatory, good value food inc interesting dishes, well kept Fullers London Pride and Wadworths 6X, good local cider and house wines, skittle alley; motorcyclists made welcome; bedrooms comfortable and homely, tables outside facing quiet village green with famous hurdles *(David Warrellow, Alan and Paula McCully, Jean and Richard Phillips, LM)*

Rickford [off A368 (trickily from W); ST4859], *Plume of Feathers*: Unspoilt and cottagey, relaxed atmosphere, good basic food inc good choice of sandwiches under new managers, friendly service, well kept Ushers, log fire; seats in front garden, pretty hamlet setting *(David Warrellow, Alan and Paula McCully)*

Ridgehill [Crown Hill; off B3130 2 miles S of Winford; ST5462], *Crown*: Interesting old pub in deep country, authentically old-fashioned, with good food, attractive restaurant, skittle alley; lovely views from terrace, separate family area *(S E Paulley)*

Roadwater [off A39 at Washford; ST0338], *Valiant Soldier*: Large tucked-away family-run country inn with well kept Bass, good value generous interesting food, friendly service, pool table, darts, skittles; children welcome, streamside garden with play area; good value bedrooms, handy for sea and Exmoor *(Mr and Mrs D Beeson, Rex Miller)*

Rode [A361 Frome—Trowbridge; ST8153], *Bell*: Friendly landlord and service, smart decor, huge range of reasonably priced food inc lots of fish, well kept interesting changing ales, good coffee *(Bett and Brian Cox)*

Roundham [A30 Crewkerne—Chard; ST4209], *Travellers Rest*: Pleasant and quiet, well run by friendly ex-Navy landlord and wife, good choice of food all day cooked to order, ales such as Butcombe and Worthingtons BB, good wine choice; garden *(Howard Clutterbuck)*

☆ **Rowberrow** [about ½ mile from A38 at Churchill; ST4558], *Swan*: Good bar food from fine sandwiches up and quick courteous service in olde-worlde pub with good chatty atmosphere, comic hunting prints and ancient longcase clock, well kept Bass and Wadworths 6X; good walking country *(MRSM, GL, Alan and Paula McCully)*

Rumwell [A38 Taunton—Wellington, just past Stonegallows; ST1923], *Rumwell Inn*: Welcoming and comfortable, with old beams, lots of tables in several areas, very wide choice of well presented food inc good value specials and children's dishes, friendly efficient service, well kept ales such as Bass, Worthington and Branscombe Brandon, children's room, restaurant (should book Sat); tables outside, handy for Sheppy's Cider Museum; bedrooms *(P J Robbins, Shirley Pielou, F J Willy, Mel and Mick Smith)*

Shurton [ST2043], *Shurton Inn*: Small, delightfully unpretentious local in farming village, super food from really good sandwiches to bookable Sun lunch, pleasant licensees and service *(Jill Bickerton)*

Somerton [Mkt Pl; ST4828], *Globe*: Chatty two-bar local with log fire, wide choice of good bar food inc interesting ice creams, well kept ales inc Bass, good choice of wine, helpful friendly staff, dining conservatory, back pool room; no music, skittle alley, tables in garden *(Janet Pickles, John and Elspeth Howell)*; [Church Sq], *White Hart*: Attractive smallish 18th-c stonebuilt pub with welcoming service, friendly locals and cat, daily papers, good value food inc good steaks, Ushers ales, three bars, no-smoking dining room, back games room with pool *(Janet Pickles, John and Elspeth Howell)*

Standerwick [A36 Warminster—Bath; ST8150], *Bell*: Food inc super value Sun lunch – good choice, good veg *(Colin McKerrow)*

☆ **Staple Fitzpaine** [off A358 or B3170 S of Taunton; ST2618], *Greyhound*: Relaxing sophisticated atmosphere in interesting rambling country pub with antique layout, flagstones and inglenooks, welcoming log fires throughout, pleasant mix of settles and chairs; enthusiastic landlord, cheerful barmaid, well kept changing ales such as Badger Tanglefoot, Exmoor, Fullers London Pride and Otter, good food from soup and substantial fresh filled rolls up inc beautifully cooked fresh fish *(Mr and Mrs C Roberts, Paul and Judith Booth, Richard R Dolphin, LYM)*

Star [A38; ST4358], *Star*: Well kept Bass and lots of tables around big inglenook fireplace in real local, with Sun raffles – bar nibbles then inc pork scratchings and pigs' trotters *(Alan and Paula McCully)*

☆ **Stoke St Mary** [2¾ miles from M5 junction 25; A358 towards Ilminster, first right, right at T-junction then follow signs; ST2622], *Half Moon*: Roomy much-modernised village pub, five neat well decorated open-plan main areas, food from sandwiches to duck and steaks inc vegetarian, one no-smoking restaurant, friendly staff, well kept Bass, Butcombe, Flowers IPA, Fullers London Pride and Wadworths 6X, quite a few malt whiskies; bar billiards, maybe piped radio, children welcome, picnic-sets in well tended garden *(Richard Dolphin, F J Robinson, Comus Elliott, Derek and Iris Martin, Howard Clutterbuck, John Watt, Mr and Mrs C Roberts, LYM)*

Street [ST4836], *Bear*: Useful dining pub opp Clarks shoe museum and handy for shopping village, quick service, Hardy, Greenalls, Smiles and Tetleys; well equipped bedrooms, buffet breakfast *(N E Bushby, W Atkins, Marjorie and David Lamb)*; [Leigh Rd], *Two Brewers*: Pleasantly refurbished and welcoming, with wide choice of well cooked reasonably priced food, well kept Courage Best and Directors, Wadworths 6X and guests such as Archers Golden, Hook Norton Old Hookey and Timothy Taylor Landlord; garden with play area *(Julian Pearson)*

Tarr [Tarr Steps – OS Sheet 181 map ref 868322; SS8632], *Tarr Farm*: Nicely set for river walks, very cosy with huge tables made from slabs of wood, teas with good home-made scones, good choice of bar food, Flowers ale *(Dave Braisted)*

☆ **Taunton** [Magdalene St], *Masons Arms*: Fine friendly town pub, often very busy, with good changing range of well kept ales, good reasonably priced quick food (not Sun but served late other evenings) inc succulent sizzler steaks and interesting soups, no chips, comfortably basic furnishings, no music or pool tables; good bedrooms *(Howard Clutterbuck, Adrian and Jane Tierney-Jones, Andrew Brockbank, Barry Nowlan)*

Taunton [Deane Gate, Hankridge Way, nr Sainsbury; very handy for M5 junction 25], *Hankridge Arms*: Old-style new pub in modern shopping complex, well appointed, with good atmosphere and service, good choice of reasonably priced generous food in bar and restaurant, Badger ales *(Steve and Maggie Willey, Dr and Mrs A K Clarke, John Barker, Mr and Mrs W B Walker)*; [just off Fore St], *Millers*: Low-beamed Tudoresque building, two floors, friendly staff, good draught beers and wide choice of bottled beers and whiskies, sensibly priced wines, friendly staff, lovely roof garden – very busy on summer nights; good adjoining restaurant (not Sun evening) *(Ashley Comer)*; [Shuttern], *Pen & Quill*: Warm and cosy, with good sensibly priced food inc good choice of puddings, efficient friendly service, comfortably unhurried atmosphere *(John A Barker, Mr and Mrs D W Thomson)*; [Middleway, Wilton; across Vivary Park from centre], *Vivary Arms*: Pretty pub with good range of home-made fresh lunchtime bar food esp good soup and fish, in snug plush lounge and small dining room; prompt friendly service, no music; bedrooms with own bathrooms in Georgian house next door *(Shirley Pielou, Howard Clutterbuck)*

Tickenham [B3130 Clevedon—Nailsea; ST4571], *Star*: Dining pub with good range of food (can be a wait) inc early-eater bargains, good choice of beers such as Bass, Morlands Old Speckled Hen and Wadworths 6X, decent wines, friendly landlord, log fire, big family room, no-smoking conservatory; piped music, high chairs; garden with good play area *(Dave Braisted, Tom Evans, Alan and Paula McCully)*

☆ **Tintinhull** [Farm St; village signed off A303; ST4919], *Crown & Victoria*: Attractively opened up, with roomy, light and airy main bar, pleasant conservatory, wide choice of generous fairly priced food cooked to order inc big fish menu, afternoon teas too, good choice of local real ales, farm ciders, prompt service by courteous helpful staff; wheelchair access, well kept big garden with goldfish pool and good safe play area, handy for Tintinhull House (NT) *(Alan and Margaret Griffiths, Janet Pickles, LYM)*

Torre [ST0440], *White Horse*: Small family-run country pub, good food, quiet welcoming atmosphere, very friendly *(Mr and Mrs B S Matthews)*

Triscombe [signed off A358 NW of Taunton; ST1535], *Blue Ball*: Snug little unspoilt thatched pub tucked into Quantocks, tables out in colourful garden with peaceful hill views, neat beamed bar with sporting prints, no-smoking conservatory (children allowed), well kept Butcombe, Cotleigh Barn Owl, Exmoor and Otter, Sheppy's farm cider, quickly served food (no sandwiches, not Sun evening) inc unusual dishes, traditional games, skittle alley; piped music; bedroom suite in annexe; cl Sun evening in winter *(DMT, John Brightley, David Lewis, Sarah Lart, G W A Pearce, LYM)*

☆ **Trudoxhill** [off A361 Frome—Wells; ST7443], *White Hart*: Beams, stripped stone, friendly atmosphere, mainly table seating with a couple of easy chairs by one of the two log fires; main attraction the fine range of Ash Vine ales brewed here (you can usually visit the brewery), also Thatcher's farm cider and country wines; wide choice of bar food inc off-peak bargains, children in eating area, restaurant, picnic-sets in flower-filled sheltered side garden *(James Nunns, M Joyner, S G N Bennett, M G Hart, John and Lynn Busenbark, LYM)*

Tytherington [ST7645], *Fox & Hounds*: Roomy and tidy stripped stone bar with no-smoking annexe, interesting food inspired by German landlord inc vegetarian, welcoming service *(Charles and Pauline Stride)*

☆ **Upton** [B3190 E; ST0029], *Lowtrow Cross*: Isolated but very welcoming country inn with nice low-beamed bar, enormous inglenook, consistently good value home-made bar food, local real ale; neatly kept pool table, skittle alley, provision for children; small touring caravan site behind *(P M Brown, LYM)*

☆ **Upton Noble** [Church St; ST7139], *Lamb*: Small 17th-c stripped-stone village local with good range of real ales and good home-made food in comfortable bars; super landlady, good friendly staff, lovely views; big garden, cl Mon lunchtime *(K J Thurstans)*

Waterrow [A361 Wiveliscombe—Bampton; ST0425], *Rock*: Character pub with well kept ales inc Cotleigh Tawny and Exmoor Gold, wide choice of good home-made food, attractive prices, log fire in smallish bar exposing the rock it's built on, couple of steps up to lunchtime dining room doubling as evening restaurant, friendly helpful service; good well equipped bedrooms, charming setting in small valley village *(Cliff Blakemore)*

☆ **Wellow** [signed off A367 SW of Bath; ST7458], *Fox & Badger*: Friendly flagstoned bar with snug alcoves, small winged settles, flowers on the tables, three log fires, well kept Boddingtons, Butcombe, Wadworths 6X and a changing bargain beer, Thatcher's farm cider, well priced food, games and piped music in cosy public bar, restaurant, courtyard with barbecues; children in eating areas, open all day Thurs/Fri – can get very busy *(Susan and Nigel Wilson, Neil Calver, D Irving, E McCall, Jenny and Roger Huggins, T McLean, Wayne Wheeler, LYM)*

☆ **Wells** [High St, nr St Cuthberts; ST5545], *City Arms*: Good choice of good value food inc well prepared sandwiches and unusual dishes in big comfortable L-shaped rambling bar and upstairs restaurant of interestingly converted largely early 18th-c building – some parts even older (said to have been a Tudor jail); well kept Bass, Butcombe and guests from far afield, decent wines, welcoming prompt service, interesting bric-a-brac, attractive cobbled courtyard with well planted flower tubs etc; piped music *(N E Bushby, W Atkins, M G Hart, Peter and Audrey Dowsett, Veronica Brown, F C Johnston, Meg and Colin Hamilton, M Wellington, John and Lynn Busenbark, Bruce Bird)*

☆ **Wells** [St Thomas St], *Fountain*: Good value generous original food inc good value fresh fish and seafood and interesting ice creams in unpretentious downstairs bar with roaring log fire and popular upstairs restaurant (worth booking weekends, good Sun lunch); friendly quick staff, well kept Courage and Ushers, farm cider, good choice of wines with Spanish emphasis, good coffee; piped music; right by cathedral; children welcome *(D I Smith, Sylvia and Tony Birbeck, Veronica Brown)*

Wells [Market Pl], *Crown*: Big well spaced tables in connecting rooms around bar of fine old coaching inn just S of cathedral, imaginative use of architectural features inc magnificent fireplace behind bar, well kept Butcombe and Courage tapped from the cask, good choice of food from separate servery, high chair for children; William Penn connection, seats in back courtyard; bedrooms *(Walter Reid)*; [18 High St], *Star*: Attractively old-fashioned bar, part no smoking, off narrow cobbled yard (tables under the hanging baskets), with beams, dark panelling, cosy atmosphere of shoppers dropping in, well kept Bass and Butcombe, good food in bar and restaurant; piped music, fruit machine; bedrooms comfortable, with appropriate furnishings inc four-posters *(Walter Reid, BB)*

☆ **West Bagborough** [off A358 NW of Taunton; ST1633], *Rising Sun*: Welcoming local in tiny village below Quantocks, family service, short choice of fresh generous home-cooked food, well kept Exmoor and Oakhill, wide choice of wines, unobtrusive piped music, darts, table skittles, big log fires; bedrooms comfortable, with own bathrooms *(Veronica Brown, David Lewis, Sarah Lart)*

West Camel [ST5724], *Walnut*: Smartly upmarket inside, with friendly and comfortable country atmosphere, good choice of food inc fresh fish and good puddings, good service, several real ales; bedrooms *(John Barker, Beryl Morris)*

West Harptree [Harptree Hill; ST5657], *Wellsway*: Particularly carefully kept and served real ale *(Veronica Brown)*

West Monkton [ST2728], *Monkton Inn*: Spacious and comfortable low-beamed bar broken up into friendly snug areas, good choice of drinks inc Exmoor Gold and occasional beer festivals, good value food inc generous starters, welcoming quick service; unobtrusive piped music, pool and darts Tues and Thurs, Mon quiz night, some live bands; lots of tables in big lantern-lit garden with play area and summer pig roasts, peaceful spot *(Ashley Comer)*

West Pennard [A361 towards Pilton; ST5438], *Apple Tree*: Well renovated good value food pub, good choice inc pies fresh from a genuine oven and thoroughly cooked veg; flagstones, exposed brickwork, beams, good woodburner, comfortable seats, thatch above main bar, second bar and two eating areas; well kept Bass, Cotleigh and Worthington BB, good coffee, friendly service; can get crowded lunchtime; tables on terrace *(C and E M Watson, E H and R F Warner, Bett and Brian Cox)*

West Pennard [A361 E of Glastonbury], *Lion*: Good quickly served food using local ingredients in three neat dining areas opening off small flagstoned and black-beamed core with log fire in big stone inglenook, second log fire in stripped-stone family area, well kept Oakhill and Wadworths 6X; tables on big forecourt, bedrooms comfortable and well equipped, in neatly converted side barn *(J Holland, Walter Reid, Peter and Audrey Dowsett, BB)*

Westbury on Trym [17 Westbury Hill; ST5877], *Post Office Tavern*: Ten real ales and good menu in converted post office with lots of appropriate memorabilia; no-smoking area *(Dr and Mrs A K Clarke)*

Westbury sub Mendip [ST5048], *Westbury*: Doing well under present licensees, pleasant mellow interior with some character, dozens of old local photographs, pretty dining room, reasonably priced food, well kept Bass and guest beers *(Alan and Paula McCully, John Knighton)*

Weston super Mare [St Georges; just off M5, junction 21; ST3762], *Woolpack*: Olde-worlde 17th-c coaching inn with lively but relaxing local atmosphere, pleasant window seats and library-theme area, changing well kept ales such as Courage, Fullers and Oakhill, good well priced bar food inc home-made pies and some less usual dishes, keen efficient service, small but attractive restaurant; skittle alley *(Andy and Jill Kassube, Comus Elliott, Alan and Paula McCully, P and M Rudlin)*

Westonzoyland [Main Rd; ST3534], *Sedgemoor*: Small cosy pub, Royalist base before Battle of Sedgemoor; good atmosphere, interesting memorabilia inc Monmouth's declaration of his illegitimacy; bar food inc vegetarian, real ale, pleasant friendly service *(Paul S McPherson)*

☆ **Wheddon Cross** [A396/B3224, S of Minehead; SS9238], *Rest & Be Thankful*: Wide range of generous home-cooked food inc children's, friendly staff, comfortably modern two-room bar with buffet bar and no-smoking restaurant, well kept Morlands Old Speckled Hen, Ruddles, Theakstons XB and Ushers Best, two good log fires, huge jug collection, aquarium and piped music; communicating games area, skittle alley, public lavatory for the disabled; bedrooms *(Phil and Heidi Cook, Richard Gibbs, LYM)*

Wiveliscombe [10 North St; ST0827], *Bear*: Friendly, with home-cooked food, well kept local beers; has local beer festival with music and Morris dancers *(Adrian and Jane Tierney-Jones)*

Yeovil [A30, just W; ST5516], *Royal George*: Comfortable and welcoming, three real ales, friendly staff and locals *(Ann and Colin Hunt)*

If a service charge is mentioned prominently on a menu or accommodation terms, you must pay it if service was satisfactory. If service is really bad you are legally entitled to refuse to pay some or all of the service charge as compensation for not getting the service you might reasonably have expected.

Staffordshire

At last a worthwhile new entry here: the St George in Eccleshall, a charming small hotel well refurbished to keep and even enhance its 18th-c character – and as a bonus brewing its own good beers. Other worthies here are the two nicely placed Alstonefield pubs, both doing well, the Burton Bridge in Burton (bargain food, brewing its own good beers), the Yew Tree at Cauldon (a great favourite for Alan East's remarkable collections – very cheap well liked snacks and drinks, too), the Izaak Walton at Cresswell (a consistently good dining pub), the Swan With Two Necks at Longdon (first-class fish and chips), the charming old Holly Bush at Salt (good generous food from doorstep sandwiches up), the Greyhound at Warslow (bar carefully refurbished this year) and the Olde Royal Oak at Wetton (an enviable local – and home of toe-wrestling internationals). The usefully placed Moat House at Acton Trussell has opened a smart new bedroom wing (not cheap). Pubs currently finding particular favour with readers in the Lucky Dip section at the end of the chapter are the Crown in Abbots Bromley, Coopers Tavern in Burton, Black Lion at Butterton, Plough in Etruria, Worston Mill at Little Bridgeford (one of the best of Marstons Tavern Tables family dining pubs), Wolseley Arms near Rugeley, Stafford Arms in Stafford, Star in Stone, Crown at Wrinehill and Crown at Yoxall. We have inspected most but not all of these, and would be specially grateful for further readers' reports on them. This county is the heart of Britain's beer industry, with the waters of the River Trent making a powerful contribution to the products of the great breweries in Burton – Bass, Marstons and what till now has been Ind Coope (Carlsberg-Tetleys have now sold this brewery to Bass). Staffordshire drinks prices are well below the national average; besides the outstandingly cheap Yew Tree at Cauldon, we found good beer prices at the Burton Bridge at Burton on Trent and St George in Eccleshall (both brewing their own) and the Rising Sun at Shraleybrook (which normally brews its own, but has – we hope temporarily – interrupted this practice).

ACTON TRUSSELL SJ9318 Map 7

Moat House

Village signposted from A449 just S of Stafford; the right turn off A449 is only 2 miles (heading N) from M6 junction 13 – go through the village to find the pub on the W side, by the canal

Although this fine timbered building dates back to 1320 it has only been a pub for 11 years. It's attractively set in six acres of lovely landscaped grounds next to the duck-populated Staffordshire & Worcestershire canal, with mooring facilities for narrowboats, and picnic-sets in front by the water; some readers suggest that motorway noise can mar the atmosphere. It can get quite busy in the charmingly civilised oak-beamed bar which has a big open fireplace and comfortable armchairs. Well kept Banks's Bitter and Marstons Pedigree with two guests such as Morrells Varsity and Morlands Old Speckled Hen on handpump, a good wine list with about ten by the glass, and a decent range of spirits; friendly and efficient service. The family have a 400-acre farm which supplies some produce for the decent bar food which includes tomato and mozzarella salad with ratatouille and pesto sauce (£5.25), wild mushroom and potato wedge gratin (6.95), caramelised lemon chicken with pilau rice or deep-fried cod in beer batter (£7.25), skewered beef teriyaki with fried rice (£8.95) and steaks (from £9.50). No-smoking restaurant; fruit machine, piped music. They have now added bedrooms and we imagine that it would be a pleasant (if not cheap) place to stay – we await reports. *(Recommended by R T and J C Moggridge, David and Kathy Holcroft, Roy Butler, Paul and Diane Edwards, S J and C C Davidson, S Watkin, P Taylor, Karen Eliot, Basil Minson, Mike and Maggie Betton, David Hoult, DC, Thomas and Audrey Nott, Kate and Robert Hodkinson, George Atkinson, Peter and Jenny Quine, Suzanne and Steve Griffiths)*

Free house ~ Licensee G R J Lewis ~ Real ale ~ Meals and snacks (not Sat evening or Sun lunchtime) ~ Restaurant ~ (01785) 712217 ~ Children welcome in eating area of bar and restaurant ~ Open 11.30-3, 5.30-11; 11-11 Sat; 12-10.30 Sun; closed 26 Dec; Bedrooms: £90B/£99B

ALSTONEFIELD SK1355 Map 7

George

Village signposted from A515 Ashbourne—Buxton

Prettily positioned by the village green, from stone seats beneath the inn sign of this delightfully simple stone pub you can enjoy the tranquillity of this quiet farming hamlet. In the unchanging straightforward low beamed bar there's a collection of old photographs and pictures of the Peak District, and pewter tankards hanging by the copper-topped bar counter; locals, campers and hikers gather by the warm fire – although muddy boots and dogs may not be welcome. A spacious no-smoking family room has plenty of tables and wheelback chairs. Generous helpings of good straightforward bar food from a printed menu – you order at the kitchen door – include: sandwiches (£1.85), soup (£1.95), ploughman's (from £3.95), meat and potato pie (£5.10), smoked trout or Spanish quiche (£5.50), home-made lasagne or chicken (£5.75) and a couple of daily specials; home-made puddings. Well kept Burtonwood Bitter, Forshaws and a Burtonwood guest on handpump; dominoes and piped music. The big sheltered stableyard behind the pub has a pretty rockery with picnic-sets. You can arrange with the landlord to camp on the croft. *(Recommended by C J Fletcher, Hilary Dobbie, Barry and Anne, Nigel Woolliscroft, David Hoult, Graham and Karen Oddey, John and Christine Lowe, John and June Freeman, Hugh and Sarah McShane, John Waller, Victoria Herriott, Eric Locker, Paul Robinshaw)*

Burtonwood ~ Tenants Richard and Sue Grandjean ~ Real ale ~ Meals and snacks ~ (01335) 310205 ~ Children welcome in eating area ~ Open 11-3, 6.30(7 in winter)-11; 11-11 Sat; 12-10.30 Sun; closed 25 Dec

Watts Russell Arms

Hopedale

Popular with walkers and busy at weekends, this solid 18th-c stone pub is gloriously set down a quiet lane outside the village in a deep valley of the Peak District National Park; close to Dovedale and the Manifold. The cheerful beamed bar has brocaded wall banquettes and wheelback chairs and carvers, an open fire below a copper hood, a collection of blue and white china jugs hanging from the ceiling, bric-a-brac around the roughcast walls, and an interesting bar counter made from copper-bound oak barrels; no-smoking area. Generously served bar food includes filled baps (from £1.95, hot bacon and tomato £3.25), soup (£2) filled baked potatoes (from £3.25), English breakfast (£4.75), ploughman's or sausage and egg (£4.95), vegetable lasagne or home-made chilli (£5.25), scampi (£6.25), gammon and egg (£7.25), steak (£9.50) and daily specials such as lamb casserole with stilton dumplings or cod and parsley potato bake; children's meals (£2.95). Well kept Mansfield Best and Old Baily and a guest like Morlands Old Speckled Hen under light blanket pressure, and about a dozen malts; darts, table skittles, dominoes and piped music. Outside there are picnic-sets under red cocktail parasols on the sheltered tiered little terrace, and garden. *(Recommended by M Joyner, Jason Caulkin, Sue and Geoff Price, George Atkinson, Monica Shelley, Laura Darlington)*

Free house ~ Licensees Frank and Sara Lipp ~ Real ale ~ Meals and snacks (in winter not Sun evenings or Mon) ~ (01335) 310271 ~ Children welcome in eating area of bar ~ Open 12-2.30(3 Sat), 7-11(10.30 Sun); cl Mon lunchtime except during school holidays

BURTON ON TRENT SK2423 Map 7

Burton Bridge Inn £

24 Bridge St (A50)

The well kept Burton Bridge ales, brewed on the premises, are the main reason for seeking out this unpretentious and friendly brick local. The selection might include Bitter, XL, Porter, Festival, Old Expensive, Knot Brown Ale and Battle Brew. All are served on handpump in the simple little front bar, which has wooden pews, plain walls hung with notices and awards and brewery memorabilia; even when it's quiet people tend to spill out into the corridor; they also have about a dozen malt whiskies and country wines. Basic but good bar snacks include filled cobs (from £1, hot roast pork or beef £2), chips (£1), giant yorkshire puddings filled with pork or beef (£3.20), and other dishes (from £2 to £3); the panelled upstairs dining room is open at lunchtime only. There are seats outside and you can go round the brewery in the long old-fashioned yard at the back on Tuesdays if you book in advance. There's also a skittle alley (booked well in advance) and dominoes. (*Recommended by G Coates, Bronwen and Steve Wrigley, John Fahy, C J Fletcher, ALC, David Carr*)

Own brew ~ Tenant Kevin McDonald ~ Real ale ~ Lunchtime meals and snacks (not Sun) ~ (01283) 536596 ~ Children welcome lunchtimes and early evening ~ Open 11.30-2.15, 5.30-11; 12-2, 7-10.30 Sun; closed bank holiday Mondays till 7pm

CAULDON SK0749 Map 7

Yew Tree ★ ★ £

Village signposted from A523 and A52 about 8 miles W of Ashbourne; OS Sheet 119 map reference 075493

Tucked unpropitiously between enormous cement works and quarries and almost hidden by an enormous yew tree, this plain roadside local doesn't from the outside suggest any reason for stopping. Like Aladdin's cave the unassuming exterior gives no hint as to the treasures that are crowded within, mostly Victorian and all lovingly collected by the characterful landlord Alan East. The most impressive pieces are perhaps the working Polyphons and Symphonions – 19th-c developments of the musical box, often taller than a person, each with quite a repertoire of tunes and elaborate sound-effects; go with plenty of 2p pieces to work them. But there are also two pairs of Queen Victoria's stockings, ancient guns and pistols, several penny-farthings, an old sit-and-stride boneshaker, a rocking horse, swordfish blades, and even a fine marquetry cabinet crammed with notable early Staffordshire pottery. Soggily sprung sofas mingle with 18th-c settles and a four-person oak church choir seat with carved heads which came from St Mary's church in Stafford; above the bar is an odd iron dog-carrier (don't ask how it works!). As well as all this there's an expanding set of fine tuneful longcase clocks in the gallery just above the entrance, a collection of six pianolas (one of which is played most nights), with an excellent repertoire of piano rolls, a working vintage valve radio set, a crank-handle telephone, a sinuous medieval wind instrument made of leather, and a Jacobean four-poster which was once owned by Josiah Wedgwood and still has the original wig hook on the headboard. Remarkably cheap simple snacks, well liked by readers, include hot pork pies (65p), meat and potato pies, chicken and mushroom or steak pies (80p), hot big filled baps and sandwiches (from 85p), and quiche, smoked mackerel or ham salad (£3.10). Beers include very reasonably priced Bass, Burton Bridge and Mansfield Riding Mild on handpump or tapped from the cask, and there are some interesting malt whiskies such as overproof Glenfarclas; spirits prices are very low here, too. Darts, shove-ha'penny, table skittles (taken very seriously here), dominoes and cribbage. Dovedale and the Manifold Valley are not far away. (*Recommended by B Adams, Richard Gibbs, Nigel Woolliscroft, Ewan and Moira McCall, Sue Holland, Dave Webster,*

Kerry Law, Simon Smith, Justin Hulford, Simon Walker, John and Christine Lowe, Chris Raisin, Jerry and Alison Oakes, Graham and Karen Oddey, Victoria Herriott, Mike and Sue Walton)

Free house ~ Licensee Alan East ~ Real ale ~ Snacks (11-3, 6-9.30 but generally something to eat any time they're open) ~ (01538) 308348 ~ Children in Polyphon room ~ Occasional live folk music ~ Open 10-3, 6-11; 12-3, 7-10.30 Sun

CRESSWELL SJ9739 Map 7

Izaak Walton

Village signposted from Draycott in the Moors, on former A50 Stoke—Uttoxeter

There's a quiet and friendly atmosphere in the light and airy bar of this smart dining pub. Gently lit at night, it's prettily decorated with little country pictures, dried flowers on walls and beams, pastel flowery curtains, a little settee in one window and lots of uniform solid country-kitchen chairs and tables in polished pale wood. Well kept Marstons Pedigree and Best on handpump, and wines of the month on a blackboard. Consistently good bar food includes soup (£2.50), steak and kidney pie (£4.95), chicken and broccoli bake (£5.75), lasagne (£5.95), mushroom and stilton bake (£6.50), poached salmon (£7.50), mixed grill (£8.45), and daily specials like lamb and apricot curry (£5.95), duck and cranberry pie (£6.95), home-made salmon fishcakes (£7.50), grilled red snapper (£7.95) and game casserole or shoulder of lamb (£8.95); there is a £2 lunchtime and early evening discount on the menu prices (before 7 and not Sat or Dec). Piped music; the restaurant is no smoking. There's a surcharge of 2% on credit cards. *(Recommended by Paul and Maggie Baker, F C Johnston, John and Annette Derbyshire; more reports please)*

Free house ~ Licensees Anne and Graham Yates ~ Real ale ~ Meals and snacks (till 10; all day Sun) ~ Restaurant ~ (01782) 392265 ~ Well behaved children welcome ~ Open 12-3, 6(6.30 Sat)-11; 12-10.30 Sun; closed 25 Dec and evening 26 Dec

ECCLESHALL SJ8329 Map 7

St George

Castle Street; A519 S of Newcastle under Lyme, by junction with B5026

For many, the special feature of this 18th-c inn is the fact that it now brews its own good Slaters beers – Bitter, Mild, Original, Bees Knees, Top Totty, Premium, Supreme and Hi Duck (head brewer is the owners' son Andrew); good wines by the glass, and occasional beer festivals with a massive choice. The cosy beamed and carpeted bar has brocaded seats, an open fire in a big brick inglenook with a handsomely carved oak bressumer beam, and antique prints. A wide choice of enjoyable generous home-made food includes sandwiches (from £1.60), soup (£1.95), filled french bread (from £2.20), ploughman's (£4.95), pork and pepper suet pudding or vegetarian sausages (£6.25), chicken bolognese (£6.50), steaks (from £10.50) and specials such as mixed grill or creamed risotto of wild mushrooms with stilton (£10.95) and seafood stew (£12). There is a pleasant bistro restaurant; good service, friendly landlord; cribbage and piped music. *(Recommended by Richard Lewis, S J and C C Davidson, John Scarisbrick, Sue Holland, Dave Webster)*

Own brew ~ Licensees Gerard and Moyra Slater ~ Real ale ~ Meals and snacks (till 10; 12-10 Sat; 12-9 Sun) ~ Restaurant ~ (01785) 850300 ~ Children welcome till 8.30pm ~ Open 11-11; 12-10.30 Sun; closed 25 Dec ~ Bedrooms: £49B/£70B

LONGDON SK0714 Map 7

Swan With Two Necks

Brook Road; just off A51 Rugeley—Stafford

Readers enjoy the food and especially the superb fish and chips at this neatly kept atmospheric pub – cod (small £5, large £6). All well and freshly cooked by the French licensee, the bar menu also includes lunchtime sandwiches (from £1.80), soup (£1.60), lunchtime ploughman's (£4.10), seafood platter (£5), ham salad (£5.10), gammon and egg (£5.50), a good range of steaks (from £5.80), smoked salmon (£6.50), and daily specials such as vegetarian dishes (£4.50-£5.50), beef, ale and venison casserole or roast tenderloin of pork à l'orange (£5.50), wild trout or roast rack of lamb (£5.80) and escalope of veal (£7.20). The long quarry-tiled bar is divided into three room areas, with low beams (very low at one end), a restrained decor, five cosy warm coal fires and house plants in the windows; there's a two-room carpeted restaurant. Particularly well kept Ansells, Ind Coope Burton, a third beer from the brewer and three changing guests such as Fullers London Pride and Otter ale; decent wines, friendly helpful service; piped music. The garden, with a summer servery, has picnic-sets and swings, and the village is attractive. No children. *(Recommended by Martin Jones, S M Bradbury, Colin Fisher, Alan and Judith Gifford, Eric Locker; more reports please)*

Carlsberg Tetleys ~ Lease: Jacques Rogue ~ Real ale ~ Meals and snacks ~ Restaurant ~ (01543) 490251 ~ Open 12-2.30(3 Sat), 7-11; 12-3, 7-10.30 Sun

ONECOTE SK0555 Map 7

Jervis Arms

B5053, off A523 Leek—Ashbourne

In summer it's pleasant to sit outside in the gardens of this cheery bustling 17th-c pub. They run right down to the banks of the River Hamps, with picnic-sets under cocktail parasols on the ashtree-sheltered lawn, a little shrubby rockery and a footbridge leading to the car park. The new licensees are keen to attract families and have added a pets corner with pigmy goats; there are also slides and swings, two family rooms (one no smoking) with high chairs, and a mother and baby room. The irregularly shaped cosy main bar has white planks over shiny black beams, window-seats, wheelback chairs, two or three unusually low plush chairs, little hunting prints on the walls, and toby jugs and decorative plates on the high mantlepiece of its big stone fireplace. Bass, Everards Tiger, Marstons Pedigree, Stones and two weekly changing guests on handpump and maybe under light blanket pressure, and a fair range of malt whiskies. A changing selection of food might include soup, filled baked potatoes (from £3.95), ploughman's (£4.25), home-made pies (£4.50), leek and mushroom crumble (£4.95), steaks (from £4.95), pork in cider or chicken in stilton (£5.95), venison T-bone or minted lamb (£6.95); children's menu; one of the dining rooms is no smoking. Darts, dominoes, cribbage, fruit machine and piped music. A spacious barn behind the pub has been converted to self-catering accommodation. *(Recommended by Jenny and Michael Back, Nigel Woolliscroft; more reports on the new regime please)*

Free house ~ Licensees Pete and Rachel Hill ~ Real ale ~ Meals and snacks (till 10 Mon-Sat, til 9.30 Sun) ~ (01538) 304206 ~ Children welcome in family rooms ~ Open 12-3, 7(6 winter Sats)-11; 12-11 summer Sats; 12-10.30 Sun ~ Self-catering barn (with two bedrooms, sleeps five): £35 a night for the whole unit

SALT SJ9527 Map 7

Holly Bush

Village signposted off A51 S of Stone (and A518 NE of Stafford)

In summer pretty hanging baskets adorn the front of this thatched white-painted house. The oldest part dates back to the 14th c, and has a heavy beamed and planked ceiling (some of the beams attractively carved), a salt cupboard built in by the coal fire, and some nice old-fashioned touches – the antique pair of clothes brushes hanging by the door, attractive sporting prints and watercolours, the ancient pair of riding boots on the mantlepiece. Around the standing-room serving section several cosy areas spread off, including a modern back extension which blends in well, with beams, stripped brick work and a small coal fire; there are comfortable settees as well as more orthodox seats. The bar food is so popular that you may have to arrive early to be sure of a table. Prepared as far as possible from fresh local produce, the lunchtime menu includes very generous sandwiches (from £1.75, triple deckers £2.95), filled baked potatoes (from £2.25) and lunchtime specials such as leek and stilton sausages or lamb cobbler with herby pastry. The evening menu includes soup (£2.10), prawn cocktail (£3.25), gammon steak or greek lamb (£5.95), chicken piri-piri (£6.45), mixed grill (£6.75), and particularly good dishes of the day such as blackened cajun red snapper with a lime sauce (£7.50), venison steak with a redcurrant and cranberry jelly (£7.95), or whole rack of lamb with red wine and rosemary sauce (£8.45); home-made puddings (£2.50); Sunday roasts. Well kept Bass, Burtonwood Bitter and Forshaws on handpump, friendly and efficient service, maybe piped nostalgic pop music; darts, shove-ha'penny, cribbage, backgammon, Jenga, fruit machine. The big back lawn, where they may have traditional jazz and a hog roast in summer and a fireworks display on 5 November, has rustic picnic-sets, a rope swing and a busy dovecot; the village is attractive. *(Recommended by Janet Pickles, David Cooke, DAV, Dave Braisted, Peter and Jenny Quine, Graham and Lynne Mason, S J and C C Davidson, Dorothee and Dennis Glover, Gordon Tong)*

Free house ~ Licensee Geoffrey Holland ~ Real ale ~ Meals and snacks ~ (01889) 508234 ~ Children in eating area of bar till 8.30pm ~ Open 12-3, 6-11; 12-11 Sat; 12-10.30 Sun

SHRALEYBROOK SJ7850 Map 7

Rising Sun

3 miles from M6 junction 16; from A500 towards Stoke take first right turn signposted Alsager, Audley; in Audley turn right on the road still shown on many maps as A52, but now in fact a B, signposted Balterley, Nantwich; pub then signposted on left (at the T-junction look out for the Watneys Red Barrel)

As we went to press the licensees at this relaxed and friendly pub told us that ill health had temporarily forced them to stop brewing their own very popular beers. They still offer an impressive range of drinks – you can expect around six regularly changing ales on handpump such as Everards Tiger, Fullers London Pride, Greene King Abbot, Sherwood Forest Lionheart, Theakstons Old Peculier or Viking Summer Solstice; also over 120 malts, 12 cognacs and 100 liqueurs; and foreign beers from the Czech Republic, Belgium, Germany, Spain, Singapore and India. Simple but generous bar food includes omelettes (from £3.80), pizzas (from £3.50) and 17 vegetarian pot meals (£7). The well worn, casual bar has shiny black panelling and beams and timbers in the ochre walls, red leatherette seats tucked into the timberwork and cosy alcoves, brasses and some netting, dim lighting, curtains made from beer towels sewn together, and a warm open fire. Dominoes and piped music; camping in two paddocks. *(Recommended by Nigel Woolliscroft, Richard Lewis, Andy and Jill Kassube, Dr A C Williams, Dr F M Ellard, Richard Houghton, Sue Holland, Dave Webster)*

Free house ~ Licensee Mrs Gillian Holland ~ Real ale ~ Meals and snacks (till 10pm) ~ Restaurant ~ (01782) 720600 ~ Children welcome till 8.30 ~ Folk music second and fourth Thurs in month ~ Open 12-3.30, 6.30-11; 12-11(10.30 Sun) Fri, Sat and bank holidays; closed winter lunchtimes Mon-Thurs

WARSLOW SK0858 Map 7

Greyhound

B5053 S of Buxton

There's always a friendly welcome at this slated stone pub that takes its name from the Buxton—Uttoxeter coach which used to stop here. The long beamed bar has been refurbished, but the cushioned oak antique settles (some quite elegant), a log fire and houseplants in the windows remain. The pool room has darts, dominoes, cribbage, and fruit machine; piped music. Big helpings of good home-made bar food include sandwiches (from £1.80), filled baked potatoes (from £3.25), ploughman's (from £4.50), with blackboard specials like soup (£1.90), butterfly prawns with garlic dip (£3), vegetable lasagne (£5.25), steak, mushroom and ale pie or Caribbean vegetable hotpot (£5.50), chicken in leek and stilton sauce or pork and peaches in peppercorn sauce (£6); puddings include hot bakewell pudding or home-made fruit crumble (£2.25). Well kept Marstons Pedigree and a guest beer such as Charles Wells Bombardier or Timothy Taylor Landlord on handpump. There are picnic-sets under ash trees in the side garden, with rustic seats out in front where window boxes are a riot of colour in summer. The simple bedrooms are comfortable and clean, and breakfasts good. Handy for the Manifold Valley, Dovedale and Alton Towers. The licensees also run the Devonshire Arms in Hartington. *(Recommended by Cameron Watson, Mr and Mrs D Lawson, Derek and Sylvia Stephenson, Nigel Woolliscroft, Anthony Barnes, David Carr)*

Free house ~ Licensee David Mullarkey ~ Real ale ~ Meals and snacks (check opening times below) ~ (01298) 84249 ~ Children welcome in tap room ~ Live bands Sat night ~ Open 12-2.30(3 Sat), 7-11; 12-3, 7-10.30 Sun; closed Mon lunchtimes all year and Tues lunchtime Oct-May ~ Bedrooms: £16.50/£33

WETTON SK1055 Map 7

Olde Royal Oak

This white-painted and shuttered stone village pub is the international centre of the sport of toe wrestling – the official world championships are held here every year on the first Saturday in June. The rest of the year local enthusiasts are happy to explain the intricacies of the sport and you can taste Anklecracker, an ale brewed especially for them by Black Bull (in nearby Fenny Bentley) as a tribute to the importance of the event. There's also well kept Ruddles County and Rutland, Theakstons XB and a weekly guest beer on handpump, about 18 malt whiskies, Addlestone's cider and two wines of the month. There's a good mix of locals and visitors, and a timelessly relaxed atmosphere in the bar which has black beams – hung with golf clubs – supporting the white ceiling boards, small dining chairs sitting around rustic tables, a piano surrounded by old sheet music covers, an oak corner cupboard, and a log fire in the stone fireplace; this room extends into a more modern-feeling area with another fire which in turn leads to a carpeted sun lounge looking out on to the small garden. The good choice of straightforward bar food includes sandwiches (from £1.45), soup (£1.50), omelettes (£4.15), ploughman's (from £4.25), chicken (£4.65), lasagne (£5.25), cream cheese and broccoli bake or local trout (£5.45), gammon and egg or pineapple (£6.25) and steak garni (£9.50). Darts, dominoes, cribbage, shove-ha'penny and piped music. Wetton Mill and the Manifold Valley are nearby, and behind the pub is a croft suitable for caravans and tents. *(Recommended by Dorothee and Dennis Glover, Nigel Woolliscroft, Paul Barnett, David Carr, Paul Robinshaw)*

Free house ~ Licensee George Burgess ~ Real ale ~ Meals and snacks ~ (01335) 310287 ~ Children welcome in family room ~ Open 11.30-3, 6.30-11; 12-3, 6.30-10.30 Sun; 12-2, 7-11 in winter ~ Bedrooms: /£35S

Lucky Dip

Besides the fully inspected pubs, you might like to try these Lucky Dips recommended to us and described by readers (if you do, please send us reports):

☆ **Abbots Bromley** [Mkt Pl; SK0724], *Crown*: Welcoming 1970s-feel modernised lounge and bright public bar with games, food (not Sun evening) freshly cooked to order inc vegetarian, fish and interesting puddings, well kept Banks's Mild and unusual guest beers, entertaining landlords, good service; big mural of the pretty village's famous ancient Horn Dance (first Mon after first Sun in Sept); children welcome, good value clean bedrooms *(G Coates, Richard Lambert, DC, CMW, JJW, B R Dunn, LYM)*

Anslow [59 Hopley Rd; SK2125], *Burnt Gate*: Newish owners making great strides on the food side; pleasant lounge, Ind Coope Burton and Marstons Pedigree *(EJL)*

Appleby Parva [A444; half mile from M42 junction 11; SK3109], *Appleby Inn*: Large busy roadhouse (coach parties sometimes), plenty of tables in well divided areas around central bar, quick efficient friendly service, usual bar food all day well cooked and presented, inc sandwiches, vegetarian and children's, Bass beers; separate restaurant evening and Sun lunch; motel bedrooms, six suited to disabled; handy for Twycross Zoo, open all day *(M Borthwick)*

☆ **Ashley** [signed from A53 NE of Market Drayton; SJ7636], *Peel Arms*: Immaculate plush local with good atmosphere, olde-worlde touches such as warming old kitchen range, friendly licensees, well kept Marstons; no food Sun; lovely big garden with swings *(G Washington, Nigel Woolliscroft)*

Audley [Bignall End; SJ7951], *Plough*: Particularly well kept Banks's, Marstons Pedigree and interesting guest beers from customers' wish list, good range of food (not Sun evening) in dining area off lounge, lots of flowers outside; parking not always easy *(Sue Holland, Dave Webster)*; [Nantwich Rd], *Potters Lodge*: Extended Brewers Fayre family pub with indoor Lego play area, games machine for under-10s, wide choice of food, friendly service; outside play area too *(Sue*

Holland, Dave Webster)

Barton under Needwood [B5016 W; SK1818], *Top Bell*: Low-beamed pub with four Burtonwood ales, basic wholesome cheap food, good atmosphere, friendly landlord, popular jazz/blues nights (no food then) Weds and Fri-Sun; pool in small second bar *(G Coates)*

Branston [Tatenhill Lane; off A5121 just SW of Burton; SK2221], *Bridge*: Cosy canalside pub with good home-made food inc lots of veg, well kept Marstons Pedigree and Head Brewers Choice tapped from the cask; good moorings outside Bridge 34, basic supplies for boaters and caravanners *(C J Fletcher)*

Brocton [A34 Stafford—Cannock; SJ9619], *Seven Stars*: Big Steak pub with big indoor play area, well kept Ansells and Burtonwood, good service, reliable food up to 24oz steaks *(John and Christine Simpson)*

Burslem [Hamil Rd, off Leek Rd; SJ8749], *Vine*: Big comfortable open-plan local with well kept changing ales such as Courage Best, Jennings Sneck Lifter, Mansfield Grays, Ridleys Witchfinder Porter, Woods Wonderful; friendly staff *(Richard Lewis)*

☆ **Burton on Trent** [Cross St; SK2423], *Coopers Tavern*: Traditional counterless back tap room with notably well kept Bass, Hardys & Hansons Classic, Best and Mild and Marstons Pedigree straight from imposing row of casks (no serving counter), barrel tables, cheap nourishing lunchtime hot filled cobs, pie and chips etc (not Sun), comfortable front lounge with piano and coal fire, very friendly staff *(Richard Lewis, David Carr, LYM)*

Burton on Trent [51 Derby St], *Alfred*: Tied to local small Burton Bridge brewery, their full range kept well from central bar serving two spartan rooms, good beer-oriented food too; pool in back, friendly landlord, lots of country wines; cheap bedrooms *(C J Fletcher, Richard Lewis)*; [Station St], *Roebuck*: Comfortable pub with lots of well kept Tetleys-related ales and interesting changing guests, good value food, friendly staff, prints and artefacts; piped music, open all day weekdays; decent bedrooms *(Richard Lewis, David Carr, John Fahy)*

☆ **Butterton** [signed off B5053; SK0756], *Black Lion*: Charming homely and atmospheric low-beamed 18th-c stone inn in Peak District conservation village, welcoming Canadian landlady, fine old traditional furnishings, log fire, kitchen range in inner room, seven real ales, reasonably priced standard food, pleasant bistro; well lit pool room, darts, trivia etc, piped music (may be loud), TV; clean tidy bedrooms; has been cl Weds lunchtime *(B Adams, David Carr, Jason Caulkin, Mr and Mrs Paice, Vicky and David Sarti, Andrew and Carol Walker, Joan and Tony Walker, LYM)*

☆ **Cheddleton** [Basford Bridge Lane, off A520; SJ9651], *Boat*: Cheerful local with neat long bar, low plank ceilings, particularly well kept Marstons and other ales, good value simple food, interesting pictures, attractive fireplace in airy extension; handy for flint mill, railway museum and country park; children welcome, fairy-lit tables outside overlooking canal *(John Beeken, LYM)*

☆ **Copmere End** [W of Eccleshall; SJ8029], *Star*: Classic simple two-room country local in nice spot overlooking mere, Bass and guest ale, beautifully presented freshly made food from sandwiches up inc fine puddings and popular Sun lunch, very friendly service, picnic-sets in beautiful back garden full of trees and shrubs; children welcome *(Nigel Woolliscroft)*

Dilhorne [Draycott Cross Lane (A521 Cheadle—Longton, opp turn to village at Boundary); SJ9743], *Red Lion*: Nice atmosphere in traditional long bar, friendly staff, Marstons real ale, good value food from soup and baguettes up, separate dining room; piped music; on ridge overlooking the wooded Cheadle Hills with plenty of country walks, handy for Foxfield Steam Railway *(Tony and Wendy Hobden)*

☆ **Dovedale** [Thorpe—Ilam rd; Ilam signed off A52, Thorpe off A515, NW of Ashbourne; SK1452], *Izaak Walton*: Relaxing and informal low-beamed bar in sizeable hotel, some distinctive antique oak settles and chairs, good log fire in massive central stone chimney; Ind Coope Burton and two guest ales (hotel prices), efficient courteous service, ample nicely presented food in bar and restaurant, morning coffee and afternoon tea; very tranquil spot – seats on two spacious well kept lawns by sheep pastures, superb views; bedrooms comfortable *(George Atkinson, B and M Parkin, DC, LYM)*

Draycott in the Moors [56 Uttoxeter Rd; SJ9840], *New Plough*: Good food at very reasonable prices inc bargain lunches, exacting owners; back terrace has view of ostriches *(E G Parish)*

Eccleshall [SJ8329], *Royal Oak*: Ancient black and white local with friendly staff and good value meals; very popular and lively *(SH, DW)*

Edingale [off A513 N of Tamworth; SK2112], *Black Horse*: Two-bar village local, reasonable choice of food (not Sun) inc bargain specials, three real ales inc Mild, children welcome – popular with families w/e; quiet piped music, SkyTV, small fountain and fishpond by entrance, picnic-sets in small garden, separate play house with guinea pig *(CMW, JJW)*

☆ *nr* **Endon** [Denford, some way E, off A53 SW of Leek; SJ9553], *Holly Bush*: Friendly traditional pub on Caldon Canal, wide range of well kept beer, good value home-made food from sandwiches up, no piped music, real fires, superb position, dedicated landlady; dogs welcome, very busy in summer *(Denise and Quentin Thwaites, SH, DW)*

☆ **Etruria** [Hanley rd (off A53 opp Festival site); SJ8647], *Plough*: Small two-room pub, nice atmosphere and decor, coal fire, five well kept Robinsons beers inc the rare Old Stockport and bottled Old Tom, friendly licensees and staff, wide choice of food served till late esp steaks and hot sandwiches, will do anything on request; busy lunchtime and weekends *(Kerry Law, Smithy)*

☆ **Fradley** [Fradley Park signed off A38 Burton—Lichfield, OS Sheet 128 map ref 140140; SK1414], *Swan*: Cheery pub in picturesque canalside spot, very popular summer weekends; wide choice of quickly served food from sandwiches to Sun lunch inc vegetarian, friendly service, well kept Tetleys-related ales inc Mild, traditional public bar, quieter plusher lounge and lower vaulted back bar (where children allowed), lots of malt whiskies, real fire, cribbage, dominoes; waterside tables, good canal walks *(D A Goult, CMW, JJW, S P Watkin, P A Taylor, Chris Raisin, LYM)*

☆ **Grindon** [signed off B5033 N of A523; SK0854], *Cavalier*: 16th-c character pub with well kept Wards Best, decent straightforward food, pleasant service; smallish front bar with larger room behind and separate games room, good mix of locals and visitors; pleasant informal garden, attractive countryside; often closed – sure to be open Fri night, weekends and bank hol Mons *(NW, LYM)*

Hanley [65 Lichfield St; SJ8747], *Coachmakers Arms*: Unpretentious friendly town local, three small rooms and drinking corridor, well kept Bass and Worthington, popular darts, cards and dominoes, skittles *(SH, DW, Pete Baker)*; [Tontine St], *Tontine Alehouse*: Good generous lunchtime food, well kept Tetleys and Marstons Pedigree *(SH, DW, NW)*

Harlaston [off A513 N of Tamworth; SK2110], *White Lion*: Popular village pub with good choice of good value food inc lots of fish, OAP lunches, two real ales, L-shaped lounge with budgerigars, bar with pool; quiz night Fri, maybe quiet piped Irish music; children welcome *(CMW, JJW)*

Hartshill [296 Hartshill Rd (A52); SJ8545], *Jolly Potters*: Outstanding Bass in gently smartened-up four-room local with central bar, corridor to public bar (with TV) and three small homely lounges; very welcoming to strangers *(Sue Holland, Dave Webster, Pete Baker)*

☆ **Haughton** [Newport Rd (A518); SJ8620], *Shropshire*: Friendly and smart, with converted barn at one end of long narrow lounge, wide choice of well prepared food, well kept Ind Coope Burton, relaxed atmosphere, public bar; nice shady garden overlooking quiet pastures *(Paul and Maggie Baker)*

☆ **Hednesford** [Mount St; SJ9913], *West Cannock*: Wide choice of well kept reasonably priced beers inc guests and good varied food inc good value Sun lunch and Mon OAP bargain in cosy Victorian-style pub, good friendly service; tables outside *(John and Christine Simpson)*

☆ **High Offley** [towards High Lea; Bridge 42, Shrops Union Canal; SJ7826], *Anchor*: Unspoilt homely canal pub in same family for over a century, two simple homely rooms, well kept Marstons Pedigree and Owd Rodger and Wadworths 6X tapped in cellar, Weston's farm ciders, sandwiches; children welcome, seats outside, cl Mon-Weds winter; caravan/campsite *(Nigel Woolliscroft)*

Hill Chorlton [Stone Rd (A51); SJ7939], *Slaters*: Comfortable beamed bar, good standard bar food from sandwiches up inc vegetarian and Sun roasts, well kept Ansells Mild, Boddingtons and Marstons Pedigree, decent wines, upstairs restaurant, children's room; tables out in attractive garden, animals in barn; bedrooms *(Miss S Watkin, P Taylor, NW, LYM)*

Hoar Cross [off A515 Yoxall—Sudbury; SK1323], *Meynell Ingram Arms*: Welcoming traditional country pub, quiet and relaxing, log fire in each bar, good varied reasonably priced food inc popular Sun lunch, well kept Boddingtons and Marstons Pedigree, quick cheerful service *(C J Fletcher)*

Hopwas [SK1704], *Red Lion*: Pleasantly refurbished, with comfortable lounge, small dining room, good choice of reasonably priced decent food, pleasant landlord, prompt efficient service, well kept changing ales such as Ansells Mild; canalside garden with mooring *(Diane and Maurice Flint)*

☆ **Huddlesford** [off A38 2 miles E of Lichfield; SK1509], *Plough*: Extended and refurbished Greenalls canalside dining pub with wide choice of good value generous food from sandwiches through wild boar sausages to seafood and Sun roasts in four eating areas, well kept Bass, Greenalls Original and guest beers tapped from the cask, good range of wines, attentive young staff, games area; attractive hanging baskets, waterside tables *(Mark Sutcliffe, Dave Braisted, Colin Fisher)*

Hulme End [B5054 Warslow—Hartington; SK1059], *Manifold*: Comfortable 18th-c country pub nr river, spacious lounge bar with open fire, four well kept real ales, wide choice of generous popular food from superb stilton sandwiches to Sun lunch, separate dining room; children and cyclists welcome; new bedrooms in converted stone smithy in secluded back courtyard, disabled facilities *(Paul Robinshaw, C Fisher, BB)*

Ivetsey Bank [A5 Telford—Cannock, 5 miles from M6 junction 12; SJ8311], *Bradford Arms*: Well kept Banks's ales, good reasonably priced food esp local steaks, wide vegetarian choice, children's menu, old car prints, interesting specialist magazines, very friendly staff, disabled access; big garden with play area and animals (maybe potted plants for sale in car park); caravan/campsite *(Chris Gabbitas, Hugh McPhail)*

Keele [A525 W of Newcastle under Lyme; SJ8045], *Sneyd Arms*: Solid 19th-c stone building, formerly local court; Tetleys-related ales, wide choice of lunchtime food inc fish, friendly staff, good landlord; cribbage, pool, popular with students and conference delegates *(SH, DW)*

Kings Bromley [Manor Rd (A515); SK1216], *Royal Oak*: Three real ales and good choice of good value well presented generous food inc vegetarian and interesting specials, welcoming long-serving landlady, immaculate premises *(Brian Smart, D Toseland)*

☆ **Leek** [Blackshaw Moor (A53 NNE); SK0059], *Three Horseshoes*: Friendly family-run inn, lots of nooks and crannies, good homely atmosphere, open fire, no-smoking area, children's area, good service, good generous food inc self-service veg, good puddings, good range of real ales, sensible prices, candlelit beamed restaurant – Sat dinner-dance; bedrooms *(E G Parish, B Adams, B and M Parkin)*

☆ **Leek** [St Edward St], *Swan*: Comfortable old three-room pub with good reasonably priced lunchtime food, pleasant helpful staff, no-smoking lounge, well kept Bass and guest ales, occasional beer festivals, lots of malt whiskies, choice of coffees; now has downstairs wine bar; folk club, seats in courtyard *(John Scarisbrick, SH, DW)*

Leek [16 St Edward St], *Wilkes Head*: Basic two-room local, tap for well kept Whim ales, also Broughton and interesting guest ales; welcoming regulars and dogs, lunchtime rolls, good choice of whiskies, farm cider, pub games; children allowed in one room (but not really a family pub), tables outside *(Richard Lewis, SH, DW, Pete Baker)*

☆ **Lichfield** [Market St; SK1109], *Scales*: Cosy traditional oak-panelled bar with wooden flooring, screens, gas lights, sepia photographs of old Lichfield; welcoming service, reasonably priced food, well kept Bass, related ales and interesting guest beers, daily papers, darts; piped music, machines; suntrap back courtyard *(CMW, JJW, LYM)*

☆ **Little Bridgeford** [nr M6 junction 14; right off A5013 at Little Bridgeford; SJ8727], *Worston Mill*: Popular Marstons Tavern Table family dining pub, spacious and welcoming, in attractively converted 1814 watermill, wheel and gear still preserved; lots of oak and leather, well kept Marstons beers inc their fine Oyster Stout, good value wine, wide choice of reasonably priced good food from sandwiches up, welcoming efficient staff, conservatory; children well cared for inside and out – attractive garden with adventure playground and nature trail (lakes, islands etc); open all day, jazz some nights *(Richard Lewis, S J and C C Davidson, LYM)*

Longport [Station St; SJ8549], *Pack Horse*: Welcoming new licensees doing good fresh food up to huge mixed grill, bar with comfortable lounge one side and restaurant the other; nr Trent & Mersey Canal *(A J Martin)*

Milwich [Smallrice; B5027 towards Stone; SJ9532], *Red Lion*: Bar at end of farmhouse, Bass tapped from the cask, friendly welcome, log fire *(NW)*

Newcastle under Lyme [High St; SJ8445], *Albion*: Recently modernised and refurbished, well kept Marstons ales and unusual guest beers, freshly prepared lunchtime food *(Nigel Woolliscroft)*; [Hassell St], *Farrow & Firkin*: Usual Firkin style, with well kept ales, friendly staff, some live music; open all day *(Richard Lewis)*; [High St], *Golden Lion*: Good value simple home cooking weekdays in unpretentious comfortably refurbished pub with well kept Bass; handy for open market, haven for rugby players Fri/Sat *(Nigel Woolliscroft)*; [Liverpool Rd/High St], *Holy Inadequate*: Rock/heavy metal/motorcyclists' pub with unusual murals and decor – Triumph Bonneville on wall; well kept beer, pleasant bar staff, good music, quiz nights, good outside area; no food *(Janet Tideswell, NW)*; [Ironmarket], *Ironmarket*: Three-storey Hogshead alehouse with stairs up from entrance seating to long bar with bare boards and brick, up to 18 real ales inc some tapped by gravity from windowed still room, good range of wines and bottled Belgian beers, wide food choice, daily papers, friendly staff and locals; open all day *(Nigel Woolliscroft, Richard Lewis)*; [Bridge St], *Old Brown Jug*: Student pub with good range of well kept Marstons beers, cheap lunchtime food *(Nigel Woolliscroft)*

Oakamoor [Star Rd; B5417 towards A524; SK0645], *Old Blazing Star*: Well refurbished 16th-c pub with limited choice of bar food cooked to order and attractively presented, several real ales; within easy reach of Alton Towers and handy for Les Oakes's splendid museum (free) *(E G Parish)*

Onneley [Bar Hill Rd; A525 W of Newcastle; SK7543], *Wheatsheaf*: 18th-c country inn by enormous garden centre, traditional food and Spanish tapas dishes in lounge, Whitbreads-related ales, candlelit restaurant specialising in Spanish food; play area, open all day w/e and bank hols; bedrooms *(E G Parish)*

Pattingham [High St; SO8299], *Crown*: Homely and popular local transformed by current licensees, comfortable and cosy, with good atmosphere, well kept Banks's Bitter and Hansons Mild, pool room, tables out behind; occasional live music *(John and Steve Oates)*

☆ **Penkhull** [Manor Court St; SJ8644], *Greyhound*: Relaxed traditional two-room pub in hilltop 'village', particularly good value filling snacks, well kept Marstons Pedigree and Tetleys; children in eating area, picnic-sets on back terrace *(SH, DW, LYM)*

Penkhull, *Marquis of Granby*: Well kept Marstons in popular village local *(NW)*

Penkridge [Penkridge Lock, Cannock Rd; SJ9214], *Boat*: Particularly friendly landlady in bustling comfortably old-fashioned pub by Staffs & Worcs Canal (not very scenic here), real ales such as Ansells Mild and Bitter, Ind Coope Burton and Marstons Pedigree, usual food (not Sun), gentle piped music; tables out by car park *(Kate and Robert Hodkinson)*

☆ **Rudyard** [off A523 N of Leek; SJ9558], *Poachers*: Neatly kept, popular and comfortably furnished dining pub with wide choice of freshly made food, really helpful service, real ales; nr Rudyard Lake with its steamboat and narrow-gauge railway, lovely walks; good bedrooms *(E G Parish, LYM)*

☆ **Rugeley** [Wolseley Bridge; A51/A513 NW; SK0220], *Wolseley Arms*: Large and busy pleasantly modernised L-shaped bar with alcoves and raised dining area, wide choice of reasonably priced good straightforward food esp fish, good range of well kept ales, first-class attentive service, prints and farm tools, smart lavatories; no bar stools, you really have to sit at a table; garden runs down to Trent & Mersey Canal, handy for Shugborough (not to mention local arts, crafts, antiques and garden

centres) *(Derek and Margaret Underwood, Kate and Robert Hodkinson, Derek Stafford, S M Cutler)*
Shebden [signed off A519 N of Newport; nr Harpur Adams Ag Coll; SJ7626], *Wharf*: Welcoming and comfortable no-nonsense family pub, wide choice of good value simple food and of guest beers, bar billiards, games machines; children welcome, big garden and playground, below Shropshire Union Canal embankment (magnificent nearby aqueduct gives wonderful echo); cl winter lunchtimes *(Kate and Robert Hodkinson, John and Shirley Dyson, NW)*
☆ **Shenstone** [Birmingham Rd; A5127 Lichfield—Sutton Coldfield; SK1004], *Bulls Head*: Rambling 18th-c coaching inn recently roomily refurbished, low beams, flagstones, bare bricks, panelling, close-set old pine tables and mixed chairs in narrow rooms, good value well presented home-made food inc fish and chips and more unusual dishes, welcoming quick food service even when busy, well kept Bass, M&B Brew XI and a changing guest beer; children welcome, disabled facilities *(Paul and Maggie Baker, G Coates, Irene and Geoffrey Lindley)*
☆ **Stafford** [turn right at main entrance to station, 100 yards down; SJ9223], *Stafford Arms*: Busy but friendly and relaxing beamed real ale pub with full Titanic range well kept and two or three changing guest beers, farm cider, cheap simple food (all day weekdays; not Sun evening or Sat), chatty staff, daily papers, wide range of customers (no under-21s – exc babies); Titanic memorabilia, pool, bar billiards, juke box, skittle alley; barbecues and live bands during summer beer festivals; open all day, can be very busy *(Richard Lewis, Derek and Sylvia Stephenson, G Coates, SH, DW)*
Stafford [Mill St; Victoria Sq end], *Bird in Hand*: Very well kept Courage Best and Directors, John Smiths and Highgate Saddlers, annual beer festival, friendly staff, good menu, two bars, snug, back pool room, open fire, back terrace; open all day, can get very busy and smoky – nr university *(Richard Lewis, Dr and Mrs A K Clarke)*; [3 Eastgate St], *Forester & Firkin*: Typical bare floorboards, lots of barrels, print and brewery artefacts, framed beer mats on panelled walls, friendly staff, well kept beer, daily papers; open all day, machines, music evenings *(Richard Lewis)*; [Eastgate St], *Lord Nelson*: Big bustling local with well kept ales such as Bass, Boddingtons, Theakstons Best and XB and Youngers No 3, farm ciders, open fires, friendly staff, limited well priced food; open all day weekdays *(Richard Lewis, S J and C C Davidson)*; [Mill St], *Nags Head*: Friendly bare-boards local, well kept Bass, Highgate Old, Worthington Best and a guest, popular lunchtime for good choice of food inc vegetarian and cheap steaks; late evening loud juke box for young people *(Richard Lewis, Dr and Mrs A K Clarke)*; [Bridge St/Lichfield St], *Picture House*: Splendid Wetherspoons conversion of Grade II listed former cinema, well kept ales Courage Directors, Marstons Pedigree, Theakstons Best and XB, Wadworths 6X and guests such as Lichfield Steeplejack, farm cider, ornate ceiling, film posters, lots of comfortable seating, no-smoking areas, good choice of food all day, friendly efficient staff; good disabled facilities, spacious terrace *(Richard Lewis, G Coates, John and Christine Simpson)*
Stoke on Trent [Leek Rd; SJ8745], *Fawn & Firkin*: Usual Firkin bare boards and breweriana, their own Fawn, Golden Glory and Dogbolter kept well, usual food, friendly staff, games machine; doormen on busiest nights, open all day *(Richard Lewis)*; [Sideway Rd, Boothen; SJ8743], *Gardeners Retreat*: The allotments giving its name have yielded to industrialisation, but still has tables on lawn – and well kept Marstons Pedigree *(Sue Holland, Dave Webster)*; [Hill St], *Staff of Life*: Character Bass city local, welcoming even when packed, unchanging layout of three rooms and small drinking corridor; well kept ales *(SH, DW, PB)*; [Shelton; SJ8746], *Tap & Spile*: Constantly changing real ales, country wines, friendly new landlord, bare boards and bricks with lots of prints; pool, traditional games *(Richard Lewis, SH, DW, NW)*; [Corporation St], *Uncle Toms Cabin*: 1930s mock-Tudor, refurbished but still with interesting original features; Stoke City supporters' base, but welcoming to strangers; Marstons Pedigree *(Sue Holland, Dave Webster)*
☆ **Stone** [21 Stafford St (A520); SJ9034], *Star*: Welcoming 18th-c canalside pub, very popular with young families; good friendly staff, prompt service, home-made food (not Sun evening) from basic to more adventurous inc cheap children's and good value Sun bar lunch, well kept Banks's, Camerons and Marstons; canal photographs and exposed joists in intimate public bar, snug lounge and pleasant family room, open fire, nearby moorings; open all day Apr-Oct *(David and Ruth Shillitoe, Paul and Sandi Ellison, LYM)*
Stone [Old St], *Peasant*: Old-fashioned backstreet pub with Marstons ales, cosy nook *(Dave Braisted)*
Stowe [off A518 Stafford—Uttoxeter; SK0027], *Cock*: Village local with good servings of simple food given cricketing names in novelty upstairs Stumps restaurant, two small and friendly bars, cricketing pictures *(Bruce Braithwaite)*
Stramshall [SK0735], *Hare & Hounds*: Reliable and friendly stop-off, plain food well served, well kept beer *(DC)*
Talke Pits [Talke Rd; SJ8252], *Skylark*: Big estate pub with live bands and karaoke in busy bar, quieter comfortable lounge, great value daily specials and children's meals, well kept Bass, Joules Red Cross (from Bass Museum), M&B Mild and Worthington, friendly locals; open all day *(Richard Lewis)*
Trysull [Ebstree Rd; SO8594], *Hollybush*: Cosy and friendly traditional pub with good food (not Sun), open fires, lots to look at; organises a springtime charity Mud Run *(L Cherry)*
☆ **Tutbury** [High St; off A50 N of Burton; SK2028], *Olde Dog & Partridge*: Handsome Tudor timbered inn with comfortable bedrooms in separate block; the new licensees

are converting the old-fashioned bar into a second restaurant, keeping the extensive and highly organised popular carvery – so though they still have well kept Marstons Pedigree and a guest beer this no longer has any pub part; friendly service *(E J Locker, A Williams, Ian Phillips, Liz Picken, LYM)*

Uttoxeter [37 High St; SK0933], *Smithfield*: Clean and comfortable pub with good value lunchtime food inc Sun roast, Burtonwood Forshaws, Top Hat and Buccaneer, obliging staff; bedrooms *(G P Neighbour)*; [High St; opp cinema; SK0933], *Wellington*: The landlord who brought so much interest and individuality here has left, and under the new people this has become a more straightforward young person's pub, with pool and karaoke *(LYM)*

☆ **Weston** [The Green, off A518; SJ9726], *Woolpack*: Well modernised, open-plan but separate areas with low beams, cosy corners, well polished brassware and antique furniture inc high-backed settle; good varied fresh food inc very hot balti, well kept Marstons and guest ales, smart pleasant staff, extended dining room; secluded well tended garden *(Bill Sykes, S J and C C Davidson, Peter and Jenny Quine)*

Wetley Rocks [SJ9649], *Powys Arms*: Good value snacks, Tetleys ales, lurid tales of witches etc *(Dave Braisted)*

☆ **Whitmore** [3 miles from M6 junction 15 – A53 towards Mkt Drayton; SJ8141], *Mainwaring Arms*: Popular old place of great character, rambling interconnected oak-beamed rooms, stone walls, four open fires, antique settles among more modern seats; well kept Bass, Boddingtons, Marstons Pedigree, wide range of foreign bottled beers and ciders, friendly service, seats outside, children in eating area, no piped music; open all day Fri/Sat, picturesque village *(NW, LYM)*

Whittington [Main St (the one nr Lichfield); SK1608], *Bell*: Two smallish rooms, reasonable choice of food inc lunchtime snacks and sandwiches, more restauranty evening, four well kept real ales; picnic-sets on terrace, big well planted garden with play area, pleasant village; open all day w/e, cl Mon lunchtime *(CMW, JJW)*; *Dog*: Extensively refurbished, very popular at lunchtime for very wide choice of good value food from big filled rolls and baked potatoes up inc plenty of vegetarian dishes, service most efficient and friendly even when packed, well kept ales such as Tetleys *(Dorothee and Dennis Glover, Paul Robinshaw)*

Wombourne [sharp left after taking A449 village turn-off; SO8792], *Red Lion*: Locally very popular for good range of simple well done bar food; mainly Tetleys-related ales, stuffed animals in lounge, further eating area upstairs; TV in main public bar *(Paul and Sue Merrick)*

☆ **Wrinehill** [Den Lane; pub signed just off A531 Newcastle—Nantwich; SJ7547], *Crown*: Well kept beers such as Bass, Fullers London Pride, Marstons Best, India Export and Pedigree and Timothy Taylor Landlord, wide choice of good generous food inc vegetarian, in busy but cosy neatly refurbished beamed pub with friendly long-serving landlord and staff, plush seats but olde-worlde feel, interesting pictures, two big log fires, well reproduced pop music; children allowed lunchtime, early evening; cl weekday lunchtimes exc bank hols; tables in garden, lovely floral displays *(Richard Lewis, LYM)*

☆ **Yoxall** [Main St; SK1319], *Crown*: Warm, friendly and relaxed, with good landlord, good value fresh food inc bargain Sun lunch, well kept Marstons Pedigree, decent wines esp beaujolais choice, quick service, cosy refurbished lounge with log-effect gas fire, separate raised dining room; children welcome lunchtime *(Michael and Hazel Lyons, Mr and Mrs Maurice George)*

Please tell us if the decor, atmosphere, food or drink at a pub is different from our description. We rely on readers' reports to keep us up to date. No stamp needed: *The Good Pub Guide*, FREEPOST TN1569, Wadhurst, E Sussex TN5 7BR.

Suffolk

New entries here this year are two good country dining pubs, the Queens Head at Bramfield and the White Rose at Lindsey, also the thriving Bull in the charming village of Cavendish (enjoyable food here, too) and the Cornwallis Arms at Brome (rather unusual for us in being a hotel rather than a pub, but given properly pubby virtues since its tie to the go-ahead young St Peters Brewery). Other pubs currently on top form here include another St Peters pub, the beautifully restored De La Pole Arms at Wingfield, and also the quietly upmarket Six Bells tucked away on the edge of Bardwell, the atmospheric medieval Crown at Bildeston, the beautifully set Butt & Oyster near Chelmondiston, the Froize at Chillesford (this superb fish pub gains a Place to Stay award this year), the well run Trowel & Hammer at Cotton (so much more spacious than it looks from the road), the very welcoming old Queens Head at Dennington, the Ship at Dunwich (excellent fish and chips), the relaxing Queens Head at Erwarton, the restauranty Red Lion at Icklingham, the cheerfully civilised Angel in Lavenham, the gloriously old-fashioned Kings Head at Laxfield, the busy little Star at Lidgate with its Spanish food, the welcoming Brewers Arms at Rattlesden (gains a Food Award this year), the Crown at Snape (a good all-rounder), the Crown in Southwold (good food, excellent wines by the glass – as well as Adnams beers at their best), that fine dining pub the Angel at Stoke by Nayland, the Gardeners Arms at Tostock (the pub everyone would like as their local – enjoyable food, too), and the well run Angel at Wangford (a good retreat from the A12). Among all these very good pubs, many of them with excellent food, the Froize at Chillesford really excels for an enjoyable meal out, and for the second year running is Suffolk Dining Pub of the Year. This favoured county also has many fine entries in the Lucky Dip section at the end of the chapter. Ones that currently stand out are the Ship at Blaxhall, Plough at Blundeston, White Hart at Blythburgh, Eels Foot at Eastbridge, Old Chequers at Friston, Kings Arms at Haughley, Brewery Tap in Ipswich, Bull in Long Melford (good choice in this lovely village), Cock at Polstead and – a particular favourite – the Lord Nelson in Southwold (another place with a great choice). We have inspected and approved almost all of these. This is a good county for beer drinkers, with plenty of small breweries producing good ales, alongside the well known Adnams, Greene King and Tolly. However, beer prices are around or perhaps a little higher than the national average; the cheapest beer we found was in the Angel at Wangford (and the cheapest Adnams we found was in Southwold itself, the home of the brewery).

BARDWELL TL9473 Map 5

Six Bells 🍷

Village signposted off A143 NE of Bury; keep straight through village, then fork right into Daveys Lane off top green

This neatly kept 16th-c pub and its attractive surroundings were used in the filming of some episodes of *Dad's Army*. A photograph of the cast hangs in the cosy bar which has a comfortable mix of easy chairs and settees alongside other seats under its low heavy beams; its timbered walls have an attractive collection of decorative china, black and white etchings and old fashion plates, and the big fireplace has a coal-effect fire. The dining room to one side has been refurbished to serve as an additional bar with a coal effect gas fire, exposed stone walls and mixed armchairs, pine carvers and pine tables. The bigger restaurant on the other side has a no-smoking conservatory beyond. A very wide range of carefully cooked food includes lunchtime sandwiches, soup (£2.55), deep-fried brie with cranberry and orange relish (£4.95), suffolk pork sausages with onion gravy and mash (£4.95), ragoût of lamb kidneys and pork chipolatas in a rich mushroom sauce or roast stuffed shoulder of lamb (£5.50), chargrilled breast of chicken on black pudding mash with a spicy dressing (£7.50) and peppered steak stoganoff (£6.95); slightly more elaborate evening dishes might include medallions of venison with a tomato, rosemary and redcurrant sauce (£10.50), ragoût of monkfish with tiger prawns and mushrooms in a creamy tomato and basil sauce (£11.95) and pan-fried breast of barbary duck with a cranberry, orange and port sauce (£13.50); it is advisable to book for the popular three course Sunday lunch (£9.95). Well kept Adnams and Theakstons Best on handpump and a guest in the summer. As well as several malt whiskies they have five wines by the glass and about 40 by the bottle or half bottle; mulled wine in winter; maybe unobtrusive piped music; cribbage and board games. There are picnic-sets under cocktail parasols on a small front gravel terrace, and plastic tables on the back lawn, with a small wendy house and lots of young trees. The bedrooms are in the converted barn and stables. *(Recommended by George Atkinson, Bernard Stradling, Ronald Dodsworth, J F M West, David Gregory, Margaret and Nigel Dennis, Ian Phillips, Pamela Goodwyn, Charles and Pauline Stride)*

Free house ~ Licensees Carol and Richard Salmon ~ Real ale ~ Meals and snacks (12-1.30, 6.45-9; limited menu Mon lunchtime)~ Restaurant ~ (01359) 250820 ~ Children welcome away from the bar ~ Open 12-2, 6.30-10.30(11 Fri/Sat); 12-2.30, 6.30-11 Sun; closed 25-26 Dec ~ Bedrooms; £45S/£55S

BILDESTON TL9949 Map 5

Crown

104 High St (B1115 SW of Stowmarket)

It's quite a surprise to find a big and attractive garden behind this handsome timbered 15th-c inn on the village High Street; there are well spaced picnic-sets sheltering among shrubs and trees. The pub also boasts several ghosts and their histories are proudly displayed inside, but the real draw for most people is the wide choice of well prepared bar food. The menu includes sandwiches (from £2.25; three-tier ones from £3.95; toasties from £2.75), ploughman's (£4.25), omelettes or roast leg of cajun-spiced chicken (£4.95), steaks (from £10.95), and daily specials such as fish soup (£2.25), black olive pâté (£3.25), mushroom baked with stilton (£3.95), cod in beer batter (£4.95), vegetable stroganoff or lamb casserole (£5.95), steak and kidney pie (£6.25) and cumberland sausage (£6.95); part of the dining room is no smoking. The pleasantly comfortable bar has dark beams, dark wood tables with armchairs and wall banquettes upholstered to match the floral curtains, latticed windows, an inglenook fireplace (and a smaller more modern one with dried flowers). Well kept Adnams and Nethergate IPA and a weekly changing guest like Ridleys Rumpus or Tolly Cobbold Original Best tapped straight from the cask; several malt whiskies and fresh fruit juices. Darts, bar billiards, shove-ha'penny, cribbage, dominoes, fruit machine and piped music. Quiet and comfortable bedrooms. *(Recommended by Penny and Martin Fletcher, Quentin Williamson, Bill Pemberton, Paul and Sandra Embleton, Joan and Andrew Life, Charles and Pauline Stride, Patrick Trafford, Wayne Brindle, Mrs P Pearce)*

Free house ~ Licensees Dinah and Ted Henderson ~ Real ale ~ Meals and snacks ~ Restaurant ~ (01449) 740510 ~ Children welcome ~ Open 11-2.30, 6-11; 12-3, 7-10.30 Sun; closed evening 25 Dec ~ Bedrooms: £25(£39B)/£35(£59B)

Pubs with attractive or unusually big gardens are listed at the back of the book.

BRAMFIELD TM4073 Map 5

Queens Head

Church Farm Road (A144 S of Halesworth)

Before they took this over a year ago, the Corcorans had proved themselves at the Anchor at Sutton Gault in Cambridgeshire – he was chef, she was manageress. The responsibilities are not quite so firmly divided here, as it's Mrs Corcoran who produces the good puddings, such as lemon posset, apricot jam frangipane tart, fresh fruit and almond pavlova, or bread and butter pudding (£3.25-3.95), as well as running the bar. Mr Corcoran makes the other good food, including delicately flavoured starters such as thai style chicken, shii-take mushroom and coriander soup (£2.95) and grilled dates wrapped in bacon with a mild mustard sauce (£3.25) and main dishes such as seafood crumble or supreme of chicken with lemon and tarragon, very fresh-tasting fishcakes or wild boar sausages (£6.95), brioche filled with wild mushroom stroganoff (£7.95), roast duckling with spiced cherry glaze (£9.95) and roast rack of lamb or sirloin steak with lemon and parsley butter (£10.95). Hot dishes come piping hot, and pies have proper shortcrust pastry. They keep a good English cheeseboard, and good bread comes with fine unsalted butter. There's a pleasantly relaxed atmosphere in the high-raftered lounge bar, which has pine tables, a good log fire in its impressive fireplace, and a sprinkling of farm tools on the walls; a separate no-smoking side bar has light wood furnishings. Good friendly service (real linen napkins), well kept Adnams Bitter, Broadside and seasonal ales, good wines and coffee, local apple juices and organic cider and maybe home-made elderflower cordial; no piped music. The former back games bar is now a family room. *(Recommended by Tom Gondris, Pamela Goodwyn, Gwen and Peter Andrews)*

Adnams ~ Tenants Mark and Amanda Corcoran ~ Real ale ~ Meals and snacks (12-2, 6.30-10) ~ Children welcome ~ (01986) 784214 ~ Open 11.45-2.30, 6.30-11; 12-3, 7-10.30 Sun; closed 26 Dec

BRANDESTON TM2460 Map 5

Queens Head

Towards Earl Soham

Readers report good straightforward food and efficient and friendly service at this unpretentious country local. Bar food includes sandwiches (from £1.50), home-made soup (£2.50), ploughman's (£4.25), well liked local sausages (£4.50), mushroom and nut pancake (£4.95), chilli or home-baked gammon and egg (£5.25), breaded plaice (£5.50) and chicken kiev (£6.50); seasonal specials might include moroccan lamb, mexican chicken or pork cooked with apples and cider (£5.25); puddings (£2.75). The simply decorated open-plan bar is divided into separate bays by the stubs of former walls, and has some panelling, brown leather banquettes and old pews. Good range of Adnams ales kept under light blanket pressure; shove-ha'penny, cribbage, dominoes, backgammon and faint piped music. In the big rolling garden there are plenty of tables on the neatly kept grass among large flower beds; also, a play tree, climbing frame, and slide. There's a caravan and camping club site at the back and you can visit the nearby cider farm. *(Recommended by Pat and Tony Martin, I R Bell, J F Knutton, Pamela Goodwyn; more reports please)*

Adnams ~ Tenant Anthony Smith ~ Real ale ~ Meals and snacks (not Sun evenings) ~ (01728) 685307 ~ Children in family room ~ Jazz 3rd Mon in month ~ Open 11.30-2.30, 6-11; 12-2.30, 7-10.30; closed 25 Dec ~ Bedrooms: £18/£36

BROME TM1376 Map 5

Cornwallis Arms

Rectory Road; after turning off A140 S of Diss into B1077, take first left turn

The latest incarnation of this largely 19th-c country hotel is not unlike some of our Scottish entries, in the sense that although it is a hotel, its stylish and comfortable bar has all the virtues that you'd want in a civilised country pub. Formerly the privately owned Oaksmere Hotel, and then a Waveney Inn, the establishment has been taken over by the small newish local St Peters Brewery, and has their Best, Stong and Golden Ale tapped straight from the cask; also a large range of St Peters bottled ales. Service is welcoming, and good bar food includes sandwiches (from £4.75), wild mushroom and herb risotto with parmesan flakes and oil of truffle (£3.95), avocado and creamed flaked white crab (£4.50), home-made quiche or fresh penne with a medley of vegetables and pine nuts (£5.50), steak and kidney suet pudding, haddock in Golden Ale batter or chicken cooked in garlic, tomatoes and herbs and topped with mozzarella (£7.95) and steaks (from £11.95); home-made puddings include summer pudding and apple and sultana crumble (£3.25). The bar includes parts of the building's beamed and timbered 16th-c core; a step up from the tiled-floor serving area, through heavy timber uprights, takes you up to a relaxed carpeted area, attractively furnished with a good mix of old and antique tables, some oak settles alongside cushioned library chairs, a glazed-over well, and a handsome woodburning stove. A well planted Victorian-style side conservatory has coffee-lounge cane furniture, and there's an elegant restaurant. The grounds, originally laid out in the 17th c, are most attractive, with magnificent topiary. *(Recommended by D E Twitchett, R C Vincent)*

St Peters ~ Lease Ian Towler ~ Real ale ~ Meals and snacks (till 10 Fri and Sat) ~ Restaurant ~ (01379) 870326 ~ Children welcome ~ Open 11-3, 6-11; 11-11 Sat; 12-10.30 Sun ~ Bedrooms: £65B/£85B

BUTLEY TM3651 Map 5

Oyster

B1084 E of Woodbridge

This interesting old country pub stands alone on the road, rather outside the village itself. The low ceilinged bar is relaxed and airy; a pair of good coal fires in fine Victorian fireplaces, a medley of stripped pine tables, stripped pews, high-backed settles and more orthodox seats, and a spinning dial hanging below one of the very heavy beams, for deciding who'll buy the next round – the Adnams Bitter, Broadside Extra and their seasonal beers on handpump are well kept; darts and dominoes. A good selection of generously served food might include chicken liver pâté (£3.50), New Zealand mussels or hot and spicy nibbles (£4.50), ploughman's (from £3.20), cumberland sausage (£4.95), steak and kidney or game pie (£5.95), lamb kleftiko (£7.95), venison with pepper sauce (£8.95) and lobster or seafood platter (£12.95); children's helpings (£2.95), puddings (£2.50), and Sunday roast (£4.95). The back garden has picnic-sets and solid wooden tables and chairs, with budgerigars and rabbits in an aviary. *(Recommended by Mrs P Goodwyn, Ronald Dodsworth, Mike and Karen England)*

Adnams ~ Licensee Mr Hanlon ~ Real ale ~ Meals and snacks (not Sun evening) ~ (01394) 450790 ~ Children in restautant ~ Impromptu folk music Sunday evenings ~ Open 11.30-3, 6-11; 11.30-11 Sat; 12-3, 7-10.30 Sun

CAVENDISH TL8046 Map 5

Bull

High Street (A1092 Long Melford—Clare)

Charmingly set in a famously pretty village, this cheerful pub hides an attractive 16th-c beamed interior (and, they say, a ghost) behind its Victorian frontage. It's open-plan, but laid out well, with heavy standing timbers and attractive fireplaces; one room is no-smoking. There's a thriving bustling atmosphere – it can get quite crowded at lunchtime, but service stays smiling, attentive and efficient. Besides sandwiches (from £1.85) and ploughman's (from £3.50), three blackboards show a good range of good value food, such as chicken and pasta salad (£3.50), crispy duck with Chinese pancakes (£3.95), smoked salmon stuffed with prawns or tiger prawns in filo with a dip (£4.25), various curries or pasta and fennel bake (£5.95), baked lamb shank with Greek herbs and red wine served with a tasty greek salad (£8.95), breaded veal escalope topped with ham and mozzarella with a tomato and oregano sauce, a good mixed grill (£9.95) and steak (from £10.50); fish is delivered fresh daily, and might include squid with garlic and chillies (£4.95), grilled haddock, skate or cod (around £6.25), and lemon sole or scampi provençale (£8.95). Puddings are home-made, too. Well kept Adnams Bitter and Broadside, a good choice of wines by the glass; maybe piped music; tables can be booked. There are tables in the garden, with summer barbecues. *(Recommended by Gwen and Peter Andrews, Nick Holmes, Richard and Valerie Wright, Mrs M Dixon)*

Adnams ~ Tenants Gavin and Mo Crocker ~ Real ale ~ Meals and snacks (not Mon) ~ Restaurant ~ (01787) 280245 ~ Children welcome ~ Open 11-3, 6.30-11; 12-3 7-10.30 Sun

nr CHELMONDISTON TM2037 Map 5

Butt & Oyster

Pin Mill – signposted from B1456 SE of Ipswich

Marvellously placed by the River Orwell, this simple old bargeman's pub is attractive at any time and readers especially enjoy visits during the annual Thames Barge Race (end June/beginning July). From benches outside there are fine views of boats going up and down the water, and views to the wooded slopes beyond. The same can be had from the bay window inside, where there's quite a nautical theme to match the surroundings. The half-panelled timeless little smoke room is pleasantly worn and unfussy, with model sailing ships around the walls and high-backed and other old-fashioned settles on the tiled floor; the most unusual carving of a man with a woman over the mantlepiece is worth a glance. Good bar food includes lunchtime sandwiches (from £1.40), ploughman's (£3.25), ravioli (£3.75), tiger prawns in garlic butter (£5.65), honey-roast half duck (£6.95), daily specials like tuna and mushroom crumble, seafood provençale or Normandy pork (£4.50-£5), and popular hot and cold buffet on weekend lunchtimes. Tolly Cobbolds Bitter, IPA, Original, Shooter, and Mild, and occasional guest beers on handpump or tapped from the cask, and decent wines; shove-ha'penny, shut the box, cribbage and dominoes. *(Recommended by Penny and Martin Fletcher, Mrs P Goodwyn, Ian Phillips, Richard and Valerie Wright, Julian, Derek and Sylvia Stephenson, David Peakall, Thomas Nott)*

Pubmaster ~ Tenants Dick and Brenda Mainwaring ~ Real ale ~ Meals and snacks ~ (01473) 780764 ~ Children welcome except in main bar ~ Open 11-11; 12-10.30 Sun; 11-3, 7-11 Mon-Fri in winter

CHILLESFORD TM3852 Map 5

Froize

B1084 E of Woodbridge

Suffolk Dining Pub of the Year

Although the astonishingly wide choice of well prepared fresh fish from Lowestoft is the main attraction here, this well run place is not exclusively a dining pub. The very friendly and efficient licensees hope that now the new no-smoking dining room is complete there will be more room in the bar for those who wish to enjoy the wide and changing range of local ales that are well kept on handpump. Besides Adnams, Woodfordes, Mauldons and Greene King there may be brews from Brettvale, Buffys, Mighty Oak, Nethergates, Old Chimneys and St Peters; also a good range of wines by the glass. It also remains the place for a relaxed and civilised leisurely meal. Just a few examples from the very extensive menu and changing specials board are starters like home-made soup (£4.15), hot sea lettuce sautéed in olive oil with prawns, garlic and coriander (£6.15), sauté of squid with garlic, parsley, tomatoes and courgettes (£6.55) and pan-fried sardines in whole-ground flour with sun-dried tomatoes (£7.45); main courses might include home-made smoked fishcakes with a basil and leek sauce (£7.25), crab gratin (£7.95), home-made fish pie (£10.75), baked brill with crème fraîche, cherry tomatoes and parmesan cheese (£10.95), sea bream with a timbale of courgette and ginger with a citrus butter sauce and Cinzano and crispy orange strips (£13.60), medallions of monkfish wrapped in parma ham with a bed of roasted vegetables and a red pepper coulis (£13.95), whole grilled john dory with a wild mushroom, sweet sherry and brown butter sauce (£14.65), and lobster (from £17.95);

also a few non-fish dishes such as tomato and feta cheese tart (£7.65), stir-fried chicken with honey, ginger and garlic (£8.95), duck with a toffe apple galette and nectarine sauce (£9.45), rack of lamb with garlic and rosemary (£9.95) and steak (£13.60). Helpings are very generous, and there's a good choice of puddings including schoolboy treats. The licensee, Alistair Shaw, is in charge of the kitchen (popping out, apron and all, to see that everything's going well), while Joy Shaw runs the comfortable open-plan dining lounge (with gentle good humour, and help from the latest in a long succession of courteous young men from one particular village in the Loire valley). The bar has beams, a turkey carpet, a mix of mate's chairs and red-cushioned stripped pews around the dark tables, and a couple of housekeeper's chairs by the open stove in the big arched brick fireplace. This has a huge stuffed pike over it, and the big room is full of interesting things to look at; darts (league winter Weds), dominoes, shove-ha'penny and fruit machine. There are tables outside on a terrace and a play area; disabled loos, baby changing facilities. We have had such good reports about the bedrooms and the gargantuan breakfasts here that this year we have added a Stay Award to their list of accolades. *(Recommended by Mike and Karen England, John Fahy, MDN, C Fowler, R J and M M Cudmore, P F Whight, Roy Oughton, Ron Baden Hellard, John Wooll, Mr and Mrs J Heron, Tim and Linda Collins, Anthony Barnes, Paul S McPherson, John Richmond, Bill Pemberton, Helen Pickering, James Owen, Pat and Tony Martin, H T Conroy, Michael Hyde, Mr and Mrs A Albert, Charles and Pauline Stride, Richard Smith, Pamela Goodwyn, Derek and Sylvia Stephenson, Reg and Kate Wheaton)*

Free house ~ Licensees Alistair and Joy Shaw ~ Real ale ~ Meals and snacks (not Mon) ~ Restaurant ~ (01394) 450282 ~ Children in restaurant ~ Live entertainment occasional Sun evenings ~ Open 11-3, 6-11; 11-11 Sat; 12-10.30 Sun; closed Mon except bank holidays ~ Bedrooms: £30B/£50

COTTON TM0766 Map 5

Trowel & Hammer 🍷

Mill Rd; take B1113 N of Stowmarket, then turn right into Blacksmiths Lane just N of Bacton

A back extension makes this pub much larger than the little thatched cottage seen from the road. The large spreading lounge has wheelbacks and one or two older chairs and settles around a variety of tables, lots of dark beamery and timber baulks, fresh flowers, a big log fire, and at the back an ornate woodburning stove. There is an emphasis on the good and reasonably priced bar food: the daily-changing menu might include creamy asparagus soup (£2.25), greek salad in pitta bread (£3.25), goat's cheese, onion and walnut tart (£5.75), cumberland sausage with bubble and squeak and onion gravy or meat balls in a rich tomato sauce with tagliatelle (£5.95), steak, kidney and ale pie (£6.25), grilled kidneys and black pudding with dijon mustard sauce (£6.75), filo parcel of salmon with lemon, lime and coriander sauce or well liked klefitico (£6.95), lamb cutlets with mint and redcurrant sauce (£7.95) and medallions of monkfish with spinach and creamy star anise sauce (£9.25); friendly and efficient service, even when busy. Well kept Adnams, Greene King IPA and Abbot, and maybe Nethergate Bitter and a local guest on handpump or tapped from the cask, and an interesting wine list; pool, fruit machine and piped music. A pretty back garden has lots of roses and hollyhocks, neat climbers on trellises, picnic-sets and a fine swimming pool. *(Recommended by Peter Meister, Ronald Dodsworth, Pat and Tony Martin, Mrs P Goodwyn, Ian Phillips, Paul and Maggie Baker, Simon Morton, Ian and Nita Cooper)*

Free house ~ Licensees Julie Huff and Simon Piers-Hall ~ Real ale ~ Meals and snacks (11.30-2, 6.30-10) ~ Restaurant ~ (01449) 781234 ~ Children welcome but not in the restaurant ~ Live music some Fridays ~ Open 11.30-3, 6-11; 11.30-11 Sat; 12-10.30 Sun

If you see cars parked in the lane outside a country pub have left their lights on at night, leave yours on too: it's a sign that the police check up there.

DENNINGTON TM2867 Map 5

Queens Head

A1120

For centuries this lovely Tudor pub was owned by a church charity and inside the arched rafters in the steeeply roofed part of the bar are reminiscent of a chapel. The main L-shaped room, has carefully stripped wall timbers and beams – the great bressumer beam over the fireplace is handsomely carved – and new comfortable padded wall seats on the partly carpeted and partly tiled floor; well kept Adnams Bitter, Broadside and Summer Holiday and Wadworths 6X on handpump from the brick bar counters; friendly and welcoming landlord. Good bar food with prices unchanged from last year includes sandwiches (from £1.75) ploughman's (from £4.25), as well as soup (£2.25), tiger prawns in filo pastry and garlic dip (£3.55), vegetable curry (£4.25), fish pie (£4.65), chicken curry (£4.95), braised sausages in red wine (£5.50), steak and mushroom pie or layered sausage pie (£5.95), chicken and creamy asparagus sauce or salmon and prawn au gratin (£6.75), steaks (from £8.95), lots of puddings like apricot sponge pudding with butterscotch, pistachio and apricot sauce or treacle tart (£2.60); Sunday roast (£5.75); with some dishes, vegetables and chips are extra; they serve very good breakfasts too, from 9am; piped classical music. The pub is prettily set by the church and the side lawn, attractively planted with flowers, is sheltered by some noble lime trees and has picnic-sets; this backs on to Dennington Park where there are swings and so forth for children. *(Recommended by MDN, Gwen and Peter Andrews, Ian Phillips, Tony Gayfer, I R Bell, Pamela Goodwyn, Eric Locker, David and Laraine Webster)*

Free house ~ Licensee Ray Bumstead ~ Real ale ~ Meals and snacks ~ Restaurant ~ (01728) 638241 ~ Children in family area ~ Open 11.30-2.30, 5.30(6 Sat)-11; 12-3, 6.30-10.30 Sun; closed 25, 26 Dec

DUNWICH TM4770 Map 5

Ship ★

It's the fresh fish (straight from boats on the beach) with home-made chips that readers love at this delightful old brick pub (£5.10 lunchtime, from £6.75 in the evening); at lunchtime there are also simple dishes like home-made soup (£1.80), potato and onion bake (£4.25), pork and bean stew or chicken and cider pie (£4.75), ploughman's (£5.25); in the evening there's a wider choice of fish and several more elaborate dishes such as marinated sardines in a lime and dill dressing (£4.25), stilton and port cheesecake (£4.75), leg of lamb with redurrant gravy (£7.50), fish pie or steak and stout vol au vent (£8.25) and sirloin steak (£8.95); scrumptious home-made puddings (£3.25) and children's menu (fron £4.95). The cosy main bar is traditionally furnished with benches, pews, captain's chairs and wooden tables on its tiled floor, a woodburning stove (left open in cold weather) and lots of nautical memorabilia; darts, dominoes and cribbage. There's a good bustling atmosphere, especially at lunchtime, but the friendly, helpful staff and licensee manage to cheerfully cope with the crowds and make everyone feel welcome. Very well kept Adnams Bitter, Broadside, Extra and seasonal ales on handpump at the handsomely panelled bar counter. There's a conservatory and attractive, sunny back terrace, and a large garden with well spaced picnic-sets and an enormous fig tree. Comfortable rooms and generous breakfasts. Dunwich today is such a charming little place it's hard to imagine that centuries ago it was one of England's busiest ports. Since then fairly rapid coastal erosion has put most of the village under the sea, and there are those who claim that on still nights you can sometimes hear the old church bells tolling under the water. The pub is handy for the RSPB reserve at Minsmere. *(Recommended by John Wooll, S A Edwards, Ronald Dodsworth, Eric Locker, Mr and Mrs McKay, MDN, Tim and Linda Collins, Peter Plumridge, Nigel Woolliscroft, Pat and John Millward, CMW, JJW, Helen Crookston, Neil Calver, Derek Hayman, Gwen and Peter Andrews, Derek and Sylvia Stephenson, Fiona Duncan, Klaus and Elizabeth Leist, Peter Woolls, Colin and Joyce Laffan, P and M Pumfrey, Margaret and Nigel Dennis, June and Perry Dann, Joy and Peter Heatherley)*

Free house ~ Licensees Stephen and Ann Marshlain ~ Real ale ~ Meals and snacks (not

24/25 Dec) ~ Evening restaurant ~ (01728) 648219 ~ Children welcome away from bar ~ Open 11-3(3.30 Sat), 6(7 winter)-11; 12-3, 7-11 Sun; closed evening 25 Dec ~ Bedrooms: £36B/£51B

EARL SOHAM TM2363 Map 5

Victoria

A1120 Stowmarket—Yoxford

The new licensees at this friendly and unpretentious pub lease it from their predecessors who still operate the microbrewery that produces the Victoria Bitter, a mild called Gannet, and a stronger ale called Albert that are all well kept and served on handpump. The relaxed bar has kitchen chairs and pews, plank-topped trestle sewing-machine tables and other simple country tables with candles, tiled or board floors, stripped panelling, an interesting range of pictures of Queen Victoria and her reign, and open fires. Bar food under the new regime includes corned beef hash (£3.50), vegetarian pasta dishes (£4.25), curries (£4.95), fresh fish and shellfish (£5) and a Sunday roast in the winter. Shove-ha'penny, cribbage and dominoes; seats out in front and on a raised back lawn. The pub is close to a wild fritillary meadow at Framlingham and a working windmill at Saxtead. *(Recommended by Ian Phillips, CMW, JWW, Tony Gayfer, Pat and Tony Martin; more reports on the new regime please)*

Own brew ~ Lease: Paul Hooper and Clare Forster ~ Real ale ~ Meals and snacks (12-2, 5.30-10) ~ (01728) 685758 ~ Well behaved cildren welcome ~ Impromptu folk music Tues evenings ~ Open 11.30-3, 5.30-11; 12-3, 7-10.30 Sun

ERWARTON TM2134 Map 5

Queens Head

Village signposted off B1456 Ipswich—Shotley Gate; pub beyond the attractive church and the manor with its unusual gate (like an upturned salt-cellar)

There are fine views over the fields to the Stour estuary from this unassuming and relaxed 16th-c pub. The welcoming and comfortably furnished bar has bowed black oak beams in the shiny low yellowing ceiling, a cosy coal fire and several sea paintings and photographs. The same good food is served in the bar and more modern restaurant and includes sandwiches, home-made soup (£1.95), ploughman's (£3.75), home-made moussaka, chicken breast in peach and almond sauce or beef and ale casserole (£5.50), gammon and egg or breaded plaice stuffed with prawn, chardonnay and mushroom sauce (£6.95); daily specials might include game in season, and tuna steak with prawn and caper sauce or chicken, ham and mushroom pudding (£6.95); very friendly and efficient service; no-smoking area in restaurant. Very well kept Adnams Bitter and Broadside and Greene King IPA on handpump; a decent wine list with several half bottles, and a wide choice of malt whiskies. Darts, bar billiards, shove-ha'penny, cribbage, dominoes and piped music. The gents' has a fascinating collection of navigational maps. Picnic-sets under summer hanging baskets in front. Handy for Erwarton Hall with its peculiar gatehouse. *(Recommended by Mr and Mrs Albert, Mike and Mary Carter, Ian Phillips, Stephen Rudge, Pamela Goodwyn, A Albert, Peter Woolls, Colin Savill)*

Free house ~ Licensees Mr B K Buckle and Mrs Julia Crisp ~ Real ale ~ Meals and snacks ~ Restaurant ~ (01473) 787550 ~ Children welcome in restaurant ~ Open 11-3, 6.30(7 winter)-11; 12-3, 7-11 Sun; closed 25 Dec

FRAMSDEN TM1959 Map 5

Dobermann

The Street; pub signposted off B1077 just S of its junction with A1120 Stowmarket—Earl Soham

In summer there are lots of pretty hanging baskets and colourful window boxes outside this charmingly restored thatched pub. There's a friendly and relaxed atmosphere in the two spotlessly kept bar areas, which have very low, pale stripped beams, a big comfy sofa, a couple of chintz wing armchairs, and a mix of other chairs, and plush-seated stools and winged settles around polished rustic tables; there's a wonderful twin-facing fireplace, photographs of show rosettes won by the owner's dogs on the white walls, and maybe Tinker the friendly tabby. Well kept Adnams Bitter and Broadside and guests such as Bass, Mauldons or Morrels on handpump; efficient service. Shove-ha'penny, table skittles, cribbage, dominoes, and piped radio. Good bar food includes sandwiches (from £1.75), home-made soup or deep-fried squid (£3.25), home-made chicken liver pâté or brown shrimps (£3.45), huge ploughman's (from £4.95), spicy nut loaf with tomato sauce (£5.75), chilli or mixed grill (£6.95), scampi (£7.45), steak and mushroom pie (£7.75), venison pie (£9.95), steaks (from £10.95) and dover sole (£13.50). They play boules outside, where there are picnic-sets by trees and a fairy-lit trellis. No children. *(Recommended by JKW, Mike and Mary Carter, David Gregory, Ronald Dodsworth, Jenny and Brian Seller, David and Doreen Gregory, David and Laraine Webster)*

Free house ~ Licensee Susan Frankland ~ Real ale ~ Meals and snacks ~ (01473) 890461 ~ Open 12-3, 7-11(10.30 Sun) ~ Pianist some Sats ~ Bedroom: £25S/£35S

HARTEST TL8352 Map 5

Crown

B1066 S of Bury St Edmunds

Delightfully set by the village green and church (bell-ringing practice Thurs evening), there is a relaxed and chatty atmosphere at this comfortably modernised pink-washed dining pub. There's plenty of space for its many regular dark wood tables, and besides two no-smoking dining areas there's a family conservatory. Reliable, reasonably priced home cooking includes good sandwiches (from £2), soup (£2.25), ploughman's (£3.50), smoked salmon pâté with prawns (£4.25), omlettes (from £5), ricotta and spinach cannelloni, (£6), breast of chicken or plaice (£6.75), gammon and pineapple (£7.50), steaks (from £8.75), dover sole (£11) and daily specials; they do a Friday lunchtime fresh fish and pudding menu (£6.50). Well kept Greene King IPA, Abbot and maybe seasonal ales under light blanket pressure, decent house wines, quick and friendly black-tie staff; quiet piped music. The big back lawn has picnic-sets among shrubs and trees, and there are more under cocktail parasols in a sheltered side courtyard, by a plastic play treehouse. *(Recommended by JKW, George Atkinson, Gwen and Peter Andrews, Ronald Dodsworth, Ian Phillips, Nicholas Stuart Holmes, E A George, Pam Adsley, J F M West, B N F and M Parkin)*

Greene King ~ Tenant Paul Beer ~ Real ale ~ Meals and snacks ~ Restaurant ~ (01284) 830250 ~ Children welcome ~ Open 11-2.30, 6-11; 12-3, 7-10.30 Sun; closed 25/26 Dec

HORRINGER TL8261 Map 5

Beehive 🍷

A143

It's easy to miss this small cottage – the only sign is a beehive the size of a dog kennel in the front garden. There are some very low beams in some of the rambling little rooms that radiate from the central servery, as well as carefully chosen dining and country kitchen chairs on the coir or flagstones, one or two wall settles around solid tables, picture-lights over lots of 19th-century prints, stripped panelling or brickwork, and a woodburning stove. The gents' has a frieze depicting villagers fleeing from stinging bees. Bar food might include ham and puy lentil soup (£3.50), game terrine with a cumberland sauce (£4.50), ploughman's (£5.50), ham, cheese and onion hash (£7.50), wild mushroom risotto (£7.95), seared fresh tuna with salad niçoise (£8.95), bouillabaisse (£9.50), breast of duck with a grape and citrus sauce (£11.50) and rib steak in a madeira and wild mushroom sauce (12.95); puddings (£3.45). Well kept Greene King IPA and a monthly changing guest such as Greene King Abbot or Morlands Old Speckled Hen under light blanket pressure, and decent changing wines with half a dozen by the glass. An attractively planted back terrace has picnic-sets and more seats on a raised lawn. Their dog Muffin is very good at making friends, although other dogs are not really welcome. This has always been regarded as a particularly well run place with extremely helpful and friendly staff and quickly served, excellent food, but the licensees have now opened another pub just across the county border in Kirtling (see Cambs main entry) and this has meant some management reorganisation and a new chef here. In the early months of 1998 there were one or two signs that the new system had not yet settled in entirely satisfactorily, but the Kingshotts' track record gives us confidence that any rough edges will be quickly smoothed over. *(Recommended by Dr M Owton, Paul and Sandra Embleton, Ian Phillips, Mrs P Goodwyn, Gwen and Peter Andrews, Maysie Thompson, P and M Pumfrey, John Fahy)*

Greene King ~ Tenant Gary Kingshott ~ Real ale ~ Meals and snacks (not Sun evening) ~ (01284) 735260 ~ Children welcome ~ Open 11.30-2.30, 7-11; 12-2.30, 7-10.30 Sun

HOXNE TM1777 Map 5

Swan

Off B1118; village signposted off A140 S of Diss

As we went to press we heard that this carefully restored late 15th-c house was again under new management and now part of the Old English Pub Company chain. The relaxed bar has two solid oak counters, heavy oak floors, and a deep-set inglenook fireplace, with an armchair on either side and a long bench in front of it; you can still see the ancient timber and mortar of the walls. A fire in the back bar divides it from the no-smoking snug, and the dining room has an original wooden fireplace. Bar food under the new regime includes sandwiches (from £2.75), home-made soup (£2), chinese spring rolls (£3.45), cajun prawns with garlic dip (£3.75), ploughman's (£4.95), thai vegetable schnitzel (£6.75), salmon steak (£7.95), steaks (from £8.50), rack of lamb with port gravy, pork fillet with mushroom and port sauce or chicken in brandy and mushroom sauce (£9.95), and puddings (£3.25). Adnams Bitter, Courage Directors and IPA and Marstons Pedigree on handpump; pool, cribbage, dominoes and piped music. There is an extensive lawn behind used for croquet, and hand-made elm furniture sheltered by a willow and other trees and a shrub-covered wall. Nearby is the site of King Edmund the Martyr's execution; the tree to which he was tied for it is now reputed to form part of a screen in the neighbouring church. *(Recommended by Ronald Dodsworth, Gwen and Peter Andrews, Muriel and Peter Gleave, Pat and Tony Martin, Mr and Mrs N Chesher, R E and P Pearce, Pamela Goodwyn; reports on the new regime please)*

Free house ~ Manager: Jacqueline Malcolm ~ Real ale ~ Meals and snacks (all day) ~ Restaurant ~ (01379) 668275 ~ Children welcome ~ Live entertainment, usually 1st Sat in month ~ Open 11-11; 12-10.30 Sun

HUNDON TL7348 Map 5

Plough

Brockley Green – nearly 2 miles SW of village, towards Kedington

The courteous and friendly landlord represents the third generation of his family to run this extended and modernised pub. It's nicley positioned on top of one of the few hills in the area and commands fine views of the Stour valley. The neat carpeted bar has low side settles with Liberty-print cushions, pine kitchen chairs and sturdy low tables on the patterned carpet, lots of horsebrasses on the beams, and striking gladiatorial designs for Covent Garden by Leslie Hurry, who lived nearby; there's still a double row of worn old oak timbers to mark what must once have been the corridor between its two rooms. Decent bar food includes lunchtime sandwiches, pan-fried pork in wine sauce with ham and melted cheese (£9.95), prawn filled crèpes with mushroom and white wine sauce (£10.95), roast fillet of monkfish with lime and dill butter (£11.95) and breast of duckling with cherry and lime sauce (£11.95); seafood evenings on Tuesdays and Fridays. Well kept Adnams, Greene King IPA and maybe a guest beer under light blanket pressure, quite a few wines and malt whiskies, and freshly squeezed orange juice; piped music. Parts of the bar and restaurant are no smoking. Comfortable bedrooms and good English breakfasts. It's also a certified location for the Caravan Club, with a sheltered site to the rear for tourers. Behind there are five acres of landscaped gardens; as we went to press we heard that they had dug out a trout lake but were having problems filling it. There's also a terrace with a pergola and ornamental pool, croquet and putting; the pub's two friendly retrievers may be out here, too. *(Recommended by G Neighbour, Richard and Valerie Wright, Ron and Sheila Corbett, Gwen and Peter Andrews, F C Johnston, John and Karen Gibson, Heather Martin)*

Free house ~ Licensee David Rowlinson ~ Real ale ~ Meals and snacks ~ Restaurant ~ (01440) 786789 ~ Children welcome ~ Open 11(12 in winter)-2.30, 5.30-11; 12-3, 7-10.30 Sun ~ Bedrooms: £40B/£60B

ICKLINGHAM TL7772 Map 5

Red Lion

A1101, Mildenhall—Bury St Edmunds

There's a great emphasis on dining at this 16th-c thatched inn. Very popular bar food includes soup (£2.55), pâté (£3.25), Newmarket sausages (£5.25), lamb liver with bacon and onion gravy (£6.95), vegetarian dish of the day or steak and ale pie (£7.25), gammon steak with sweet and sour sauce (£7.55), pork chops with honey and mustard glaze (£8.70), local larkwood trout (£8.95), sirloin steak (£10.25), huntsman's grill (£10.65) and fresh lemon sole (£10.95). The beamed open-plan bar has a calm and civilised atmosphere, as well as turkey rugs on the polished wood floor, candlelit tables, a nice mixture of wooden chairs, two big fireplaces, daily newspapers, old fishing rods and various stuffed animals and piped classical music. Well kept Greene King IPA and Abbot and occasional guest beers on handpump, lots of country wines and elderflower and citrus pressé, and mulled wine in winter. In front (the pub is well set back from the road) old-fashioned white seats overlook the car park and a flower lawn; picnic-sets on a raised back terrace face the fields – including an acre of the pub's running down to the River Lark, with Cavenham Heath nature reserve beyond. Handy for West Stow Country Park and the Anglo-Saxon Village. *(Recommended by Paul and Sandra Embleton, Bill Pemberton, Ronald Dodsworth, R Wiles, DAV, Gwen and Peter Andrews, John Fahy, R Suddaby, J F M and M West, Scott Rumery, Ian Phillips)*

Greene King ~ Lease: Jonathan Gates and Ian Hubbert ~ Meals and snacks (till 10 Mon-Sat) ~ Restaurant ~ (01638) 717802 ~ Children welcome (but reports suggest not the warmest of welcomes for younger children) ~ Open 12-3, 6-11; 12-3, 7-10.30 Sun

LAVENHAM TL9149 Map 5

Angel ★

Market Pl

Readers are consistently delighted by the excellent friendly service and good bar food at this civilised and carefully renovated Tudor inn. The long bar area, facing on to the charming former market square, is light and airy, with plenty of polished dark tables and a buoyantly pubby atmosphere. There's a big inglenook log fire under a heavy mantlebeam, and some attractive 16th-c ceiling plasterwork (even more elaborate pargeting in the residents' sitting room upstairs). Round towards the back on the right of the central servery is a no-smoking family dining area with heavy stripped pine country furnishings. Changing twice a day, the well cooked food might include cream of mushroom soup (£2.75), chicken liver pâté (£3.95), ploughman's (£4.75), pork and leek sausages (£5.25), fresh crab salad (£6.95), steak and ale pie or asparagus and tomato tart (£6.75), grilled whole plaice (£7.25), skate wing with lemon and capers, lamb in paprika and cream or chicken breast with cider and apples (£8.25), and sirloin steak (£9.95); puddings such as vanilla terrine with raspberry sauce or chocolate fudge cake (£3.25); prices are slightly higher in the evenings. Well kept Adnams Bitter, Greene King IPA, Mauldons White Adder and Nethergate Bitter on handpump, quite a few malt whiskies, and several decent wines by the glass or part bottle (you get charged for what you drink). They have shelves of books, dominoes, cribbage and trivia; piped music. There are picnic-sets out in front over-looking the square, and white plastic tables under cocktail parasols in a sizeable sheltered back garden; it's worth asking if they've time to show you the interesting Tudor cellar. Comfortable bedrooms and enjoyable breakfasts. *(Recommended by Gwen and Peter Andrews, Dr M Owton, David and Kay Ross, Helen Pickering, James Owen, Mrs P Goodwin, David Heath, Ronald Dodsworth, Hugh O'Neill, Mrs P J Pearce, Chris Brace, R Wiles, Maysie Thompson, Bill Pemberton, Alan Barker, Claire Jenkins, Ian Phillips, Penny and Martin Fletcher, Bob and Maggie Atherton, Tony Hall, Melanie Jackson, J F Knutton, Alan Parsons, Fiona and John Richards, Dr I Crichton, Joy and Peter Heatherley, Lynn Sharpless, Bob Eardley, Simon Morton, Tina and David Woods-Taylor, Wayne Brindle, John Baker, John Saul, Simon Walker, Mike and Heather Watson, Margaret and Nigel Dennis)*

Free house ~ Licensees Roy and Anne Whitworth, John and Val Barry ~ Real ale ~ Meals and snacks ~ Restaurant ~ (01787) 247388 ~ Children welcome until 9 ~ Classical piano Fri evenings, jazz piano Sunday evenings (played by the landlord) ~ Open 11-11; 12-10.30 Sun; closed 25, 26 Dec ~ Bedrooms: £39.50B/£65B

Swan ★

This handsome timbered Elizabethan inn is one of the buildings which gives this once-prosperous wool town its great charm. It actually incorporates several lovely half-timbered buildings, including an Elizabethan house and the former Wool Hall. It's quite smart, but ideal for an atmospheric afternoon tea or for those who need that extra bit of luxury as it does have all the trimmings of a well equipped hotel (and not a cheap one). The peaceful little tiled-floor bar, buried in its heart, has leather chairs, a set of handbells that used to be employed by the local church bell ringers for practice, and memorabilia of the days when this was the local for the US 48th Bomber Group in the Second World War (many Americans still come to re-visit old haunts). From here armchairs and settees spread engagingly through a network of beamed and timbered alcoves and more open areas. Overlooking the well kept and sheltered courtyard garden is an airy Garden Bar. Well kept Adnams Best and Greene King IPA maybe under light blanket pressure; darts, cribbage, dominoes and piped music. Fairly limited and not particularly cheap bar food includes home-made soup (£2.95), sandwiches (from £3.50), British cheeses and biscuits (£4.95), honey-baked ham and roast turkey salad (£7.95), a vegetarian dish, and one or two daily hot dishes such as steamed salmon with citrus dressing, fillet of chicken with mushroom and tarragon sauce and fillet steak with peppercorn sacue (all £9.95), and home-made puddings (£3.50); also, morning coffee and good afternoon tea. There is also a lavishly timbered no-smoking restaurant with a minstrel's gallery. *(Recommended by Ronald Dodsworth, David Heath, Paul and Sandra Embleton, Maysie Thompson, K and J Brooks, J F M West, D E Twitchett, Pam Adsley)*

Free house ~ Licensee Elizabeth Combridge ~ Real ale ~ Meals and snacks ~ Restaurant ~ (01787) 247477 ~ Children welcome ~ Open 11-2, 6-11; 12-2, 7-10.30 Sun ~ Bedrooms: £85B/£140B

LAXFIELD TM2972 Map 5

Kings Head

Behind church, off road toward Banyards Green

Readers suggest that entering this thatched Tudor pub is like stepping back in time. The wonderfully old-fashioned front room is delightfully furnished with a high-backed built-in settle on the tiled floor and an open fire: a couple of other rooms have pews, old seats, scrubbed deal tables, and some interesting wall prints. Well kept Adnams Bitter, Broadside, Extra and winter Old and Tally Ho, and Greene King IPA tapped from the cask, and good James White cider; shove ha'penny and dominoes. Decent bar food with prices unchanged since last year includes parsnip and apple soup (£2.10), parfait of chicken livers with cranberry relish (£3.60), tagliatelle with roast pepper and pesto sauce or local pork and apple sausages with pickle (£4.95), salad of jellied bacon and parsley (£5.50), Norfolk dumpling filled with pork and thyme (£5.75), 8oz steak (£8.50), and puddings like sticky toffee pudding or rice pudding with toasted almonds (£2.95). Going out past the casks in the back serving room, you find benches and a trestle table in a small yard. From the yard, a honeysuckle arch leads into a sheltered little garden and the pub's own well kept and secluded bowling, badminton and croquet green. *(Recommended by Mike and Mary Carter, Tony Gayfer, Chris Mawson, A Ridgway, Gwen and Peter Andrews, CMW, JJW, Klaus and Elizabeth Leist, Ian and Nita Cooper, M R Hyde, Anthony Barnes, P and M Pumfrey, Richard Balls, David and Doreen Gregory, June and Perry Dann)*

Free house ~ Managers Adrian and Sylvia Read ~ Real ale ~ Meals and snacks ~ Restaurant ~ (01986) 798395 ~ Children welcome ~ Live music Tuesdays ~ Open 11-3, 6-11; 12-4, 7-10.30 Sun

LEVINGTON TM2339 Map 5

Ship

Gun Hill; village signposted from A45, then follow Stratton Hall sign

If you look carefully enough, there's a distant sea view from the picnic-sets in front of this charmingly traditional inn, and inside the rooms have quite a nautical theme. There are lots of ship prints and photos of sailing barges, beams and benches built into the walls, and in the middle room a marine compass set under the serving counter, which also has a fishing net slung over it. There are also a number of comfortably upholstered small settles, some of them grouped round tables as booths, and a big black round stove. The dining room has more nautical bric-a-brac, beams taken from an old barn, and flagstones; two no-smoking areas. Favourite bar meals can run out so it's worth arriving early for the tasty home-made bar food which might include broccoli, tomato and mushroom quiche (£5.50), salmon and crab fishcakes or kippers (£5.95), avocado bake, beef olives, caribbean chicken or pork with peaches (£6.25). Up to eight real ales on handpump or tapped from the cask include well kept Boddingtons, Greene King IPA, Ind Coope Burton and Tetleys with guests like Flowers IPA and Greene King Abbot; country wines. Service is friendly and unflustered. No dogs or children. *(Recommended by Ronald Dodsworth, Charles and Pauline Stride, Ian and Nita Cooper, Maggie and Derek Washington, MDN, Ian Phillips, Neil Calver, Paula Williams)*

Pubmaster ~ Tenants William and Shirley Waite ~ Real ale ~ Meals and snacks (not Sun/Mon/Tues evenings) ~ (01473) 659573 ~ Folk music first Tues of month ~ Open 11.30-3, 6-11; 12-3, 7-10.30 Sun

LIDGATE TL7257 Map 5

Star 🍴 🍷

B1063 SE of Newmarket

There's a surprisingly cosmopolitan feel to this little village pub – the chatty landlady is Spanish and in both food and decor there's a delightful mix of traditional English and Mediterranean influences. The small main room has lots of English pubby character, with handsomely moulded heavy beams, a good big log fire, candles in iron candelabra on good polished oak or stripped pine tables, bar billiards, dominoes, darts and ring the bull, and just some antique Catalan plates over the bar to give a hint of the Mediterranean. Besides a second similar room on the right, there's a cosy simple dining room on the left. The easy going atmosphere, and the changing bar menu with crisp and positive seasonings in some dishes, speak more openly of the South. There might be mediterranean fish soup or tomato and goat's cheese salad (£4.50), warm chicken liver salad (£5.90), roast lamb in garlic and wine, paella, home-made lasagne, monkfish marinière or lamb kidney in sherry (£9.50), wild boar (£10.50) and sirloin steak in stilton sauce (£12.50). Greene King IPA, Abbot, and a guest on handpump, enjoyable house wines; darts, bar billiards, dominoes, ring the bull and maybe unobtrusive background music. There are tables on the raised lawn in front and in a pretty little rustic back garden. *(Recommended by R Wiles, A J Bowen, A Albert, Sue Grossey, Richard and Valerie Wright, Richard and Robyn Wain, Gwen and Peter Andrews, John Fahy, Ronald Dodsworth, David Regan, N S Smith, Ian and Nita Cooper)*

Greene King ~ Tenants Maria Teresa and Anthony Axon ~ Real ale ~ Meals and snacks (till 10; not Sun evening) ~ Restaurant ~ (01638) 500275 ~ Children welcome

~ Open 11-3, 5-11; 11-3, 6-12 Sat; 12-3, 7-11 Sun; closed 1 Jan and evening 25 Dec

LINDSEY TL9744 Map 5

White Rose

Rose Green, which is SW of village centre; off A1141 NW of Hadleigh (and signposted from Kersey)

Pleasantly refurbished after a fire, this civilised thatched and timbered dining pub is tucked away in a quiet rural spot, well away from housing. The long beamed main bar has a good log fire in the inglenook, country chairs and pine tables. Attractively presented good food might include a home-made soup (£2.95), filled french bread (from £4), moules marinières (£4.20), power-packed liver and bacon or chargrilled orange talapia (£7.25) and a seafood platter (£22.50 for two people), with vegetarian dishes such as leek and stilton tartlet (£6.25); sauces are interesting, and they do small helpings for children; home-made puddings (£3.95). A cosy and comfortable second bar opens into a restaurant in a raftered former barn, with slightly higher prices and a wider choice. Well kept Adnams and Greene King IPA and Abbot on handpump or tapped from the cask, good wines, welcoming service; piped music. *(Recommended by Mrs P Goodwyn, Tom Gondris, Pat and Bill Pemberton)*

Free house ~ Licensee Richard May ~ Real ale ~ Meals and snacks (not Sun evening or Mon) ~ Restaurant ~ (01787) 210664 ~ Children welcome ~ Open 12-3, 6-11; cl Sun evening and Mon

ORFORD TM4250 Map 5

Jolly Sailor £

This aptly named and unspoilt smugglers' inn was built mainly from wrecked ships' timbers in the 17th c. The several snugly traditional rooms are served from counters and hatches in an old-fashioned central cubicle. There's an unusual spiral staircase in the corner of the flagstoned main bar – which also has 13 brass door knockers and other brassware, local photographs, and a good solid fuel stove; a small room is popular with the dominoes and shove-ha'penny players, and has draughts, chess and cribbage. Chatty and friendly staff serve well kept Adnams Bitter, Broadside and seasonal ales on handpump and good straightforward bar food such as local fish and chips, home-made steak pie or lasagne, home-cooked ham and egg, and daily roasts (all £4.75); the dining room is no smoking. One or two picnic-sets on grass by the car park. No children or credit cards. *(Recommended by Gwen and Peter Andrews, Jill Bickerton, Richard and Valerie Wright, Yavuz and Shirley Mutlu, Chris Mawson, Susan May, David and Doreen Gregory, Ian Phillips, Joy and Peter Heatherley, R E and P Pearce, Tom McLean)*

Adnams ~ Tenant Philip M Attwood ~ Real ale ~ Bar meals (not Mon-Thurs evenings Nov-Easter; not 25 Dec) ~ (01394) 450243 ~ Open 11.30-2.30, 7-11; 12-2.30, 7-10.30 Sun; closed 25 Dec evening ~ Bedrooms: /£35

RATTLESDEN TL9758 Map 5

Brewers Arms

Signposted on minor roads W of Stowmarket, off B1115 via Buxhall or off A45 via Woolpit

Although there is an emphasis on good, reasonably priced and interesting food at this 16th-c village local, the atmosphere remains friendly and very pubby. There is a small but lively public bar, and on the left, the pleasantly simple beamed lounge bar has horsebrasses, individually chosen pictures and bric-a-brac on the walls. It winds back through standing timbers to the main eating area, which is partly flint-walled, has a magnificent old bread oven and new more comfortable seating. The imaginative bar menu changes constantly but might include fresh tomato soup (£2.50), stuffed garlic mushrooms (£3.75), duck terrine in a port and brandy jelly (£3.95), mixed mushroom lasagne with ricotta and parmesan cheese (£7.50), thai fishcakes on a bed of aromatic noodles (£7.95), prawns in a spicy coconut and coriander sauce with orange and ginger rice (£8.25), pan-fried pork with caramelised onions and leeks and an asparagus, basil and sherry sauce (£8.50), calf liver with herb mashed potato and a port and red wine sauce (£10.95) and fillet steak with a stilton and walnut sauce (£10.95); no-smoking restaurant. Very welcoming and friendly service, and well kept Greene King Abbot and IPA and a monthly changing guest under light blanket pressure; decent wines. French windows open on to a garden edged with bourbon roses, with a boules pitch. *(Recommended by Gwen and Peter Andrews, Mrs P Goodwyn, Peter Dodd, J Pickett, P Green, Charles and Pauline Stride, David Gregory, Evelyn and Derek Walter, Pamela Goodwyn, Ian and Nita Cooper, Mrs B Gallagher, Mrs R Talbot)*

Greene King ~ Lease: Jeffrey Chamberlain ~ Real ale ~ Meals and snacks (not Tues or Sun evenings) ~ Restaurant ~ (01449) 736377 ~ Children welcome under parental supervision (but not babes in arms) ~ Open 12-2.30(3 Sat), 6.30-11; 12-3, 7-10.30 Sun; closed Mon

REDE TL8055 Map 5

Plough

Village signposted off A143 Bury St Edmunds—Haverhill

A lovely spot; sometimes the only sound at this welcoming partly thatched pub is birdsong from the aviary or surrounding trees, or perhaps the cooing from the dovecote; there maybe pheasants strutting across the lawn at the back. Readers enjoy the consistently good and interesting food here: there's quite an emphasis on game and always lots of fresh fish. The wide ranging and changing menu might include crab au gratin or guinea fowl in a red wine and tarragon sauce (£6.95), wild rabbit with coriander, spring onions and garlic, tuscany lamb with sun-dried tomatoes, wine and herbs, stuffed chicken pockets with stilton, celery and walnuts in a port sauce or highland beef in whiskey and horseradish sauce (£7.95), monkfish creole with prawns or pan-fried plaice topped with mushrooms and prawns (£8.95) and steaks (from £9.50); very friendly service and decent wines. The simple and traditional cosy bar has copper measures and pewter tankards hanging from low black beams, decorative plates on a delft shelf and surrounding the solid fuel stove in its brick fireplace, and red plush button-back built-in wall banquettes; maybe piped pop music. There are picnic-sets in front and a sheltered cottagey garden behind. *(Recommended by Ronald Dodsworth, MDN, Gwen and Peter Andrews, David Regan, R E and P Pearce, J F M West, Mr and Mrs N Chesher)*

Greene King ~ Tenant: Brian Desborough ~ Meals and snacks (not Sun evening) ~ (01284) 789208 ~ Children welcome ~ Open 11.30-3, 6.30-11; 12-3, 7-10.30 Sun

SNAPE TM3959 Map 5

Crown

B1069

There's a homely and warmly friendly atmosphere at this unspoilt smugglers' inn. Furnished with striking horseshoe-shaped high-backed settles around the big brick inglenook, spindleback and country kitchen chairs, nice old tables, it has old brick floors, an exposed panel which shows how the ancient walls were constructed, and lots of beams in the various small side rooms. Home-made and particularly good food might include goose breast salad with deep-fried parsnip crisps (£4.95), thai balls with soy chilli dip or crayfish tails in spicy sauce (£5.95), local cod on mash with garlic and parsley cream (£8.95), confit of duck thai red curry (£10.50) and monkfish on puy lentil risotto (£11.50); welcoming and attentive service. Well kept Adnams Bitter, Broadside and a seasonal ale on handpump, and a good thoughtful wine list with a dozen by the glass (including champagne). There are tables and cocktail parasols in the pretty roadside garden. No children. The clean and comfortable bedrooms are full of character with beamed ceilings, sloping floors and doorways that you may have to stoop through; good generous breakfasts. Handy for Snape Maltings. *(Recommended by John Akerman, David and Kay Ross, Mrs P Goodwyn, Brian and Jenny Seller, W K Wood, Penny and Martin Fletcher, MDN, Jill Hallpike, Carl Upsall, R Wiles, G Neighbour, Gwen and Paeter Andrews, Phil and Heidi Cook, Joy and Peter Heatherley, M H Pritchard)*

Adnams ~ Tenant Paul Maylott ~ Real ale ~ Meals and snacks ~ Restaurant ~ (01728)

688324 ~ Open 12-3, 6-11; 12-3, 7-10.30 Sun; closed 25 Dec and evening 26 Dec ~ Bedrooms: £35B/£50B

Golden Key ★

Priory Lane

Although the licensees here are Adnams' most longstanding tenants there are no signs that they are resting on their laurels – this year they have plans to add another bedroom and an extra dining room to this quietly elegant and rather civilised inn. There's quite an emphasis on the popular bar food which might include grilled sardines (£4.25), smoked haddock quiche (£6.25), steak, mushroom and Guinness pie (£6.95), fresh cod fillet with cream parsley sauce (£8.95), bass fillet with lemon and prawn butter (£10.95) and fresh vegetables and good home-made puddings (£3.25). The low-beamed stylish lounge has an old-fashioned settle curving around a couple of venerable stripped tables on the tiled floor, a winter open fire, and at the other end, some stripped modern settles around heavy Habitat-style wooden tables on a turkey carpet, and a solid fuel stove in the big fireplace. The cream walls are hung with pencil sketches of customers, a Henry Wilkinson spaniel and so forth; a brick-floored side room has sofas and more tables. Full range of well kept Adnams beers on handpump including the seasonal ones, as well as a good wine list, and about a dozen malt whiskies. There are plenty of white tables and chairs on a terrace at the front near the small sheltered and flower-filled garden. *(Recommended by David and Kay Ross, Phil and Heidi Cook, Jill Hallpike, Carl Upsall, Anthony Barnes, Peter Meister, Joy and Peter Heatherley, Lynn Sharpless, Bob Eardley, M R Hyde, Mike and Mary Carter, Gwen and Peter Andrews, D J Hayman, Peter Woolls, Nigel Wilkinson, Ian Phillips)*

Adnams ~ Tenants Max and Susie Kissick-Jones ~ Real ale ~ Meals and snacks ~ (01728) 688510 ~ Children allowed in dining room only ~ Open 11-3, 6-11; 12-3, 7-10.30 ~ Bedrooms: /£60B

Plough & Sail 🍴 🍷

Snape Maltings Riverside Centre

In 1965 the malting business finally ground to a halt here and the buildings known collectively as Snape Maltings, which now house the Plough and Sail, a famous concert hall, an art gallery and various shops, were bought by George Gooderham, a local farmer and relative of the present licensee. The pub itself is a buff-coloured long narrow building with the bar facing you as you walk through the door; beyond this on the right is a raised airy eating room with attractive pine furniture and – to one side – a settle in front of the open fire. To the left of the bar and down some steps is a quarry-tiled room with dark traditional furniture; also a busy little restaurant. There's a nice mix of customers and the atmosphere is relaxed and friendly; one room is no smoking. Well presented and imaginative food includes sandwiches (from £2.40), a choice of three home-made soups (£3.75), ploughman's (from £3.95), smoked local sprats (£4.25), aubergine, tomato and mozzarella bake (£6.25), Aldeburgh cod with a cheese crust and a white wine and mustard sauce (£6.95), chicken with asparagus and cream sauce (£7.95), pan-fried duck breast with apricot and almonds or fillet of pork with wholegrain mustard sauce (£8.75), ostrich steak with wild mushrooms (£9.25) and fillet steak with blue cheese wrapped in bacon (£11.95). Well kept Adnams ales on handpump, and a fine wine list with a few by the glass. The big enclosed back terrace has lots of picnic-sets and a giant chess set. *(Recommended by Mrs Romey Heaton, S A Edwards, John C Baker, Andy and Sarah Gillet, David and Kay Ross, Maggie and Derek Washington, Pamela Goodwyn, Ian Phillips, June and Perry Dann)*

Free house ~ Licensee G J C and G E Gooderham ~ Real ale ~ Meals and snacks ~ Restaurant ~ (01728) 688303 ~ Children in eating area of bar ~ Open 11-3, 5.30-11; 12-3, 7-10.30 Sun

Food details, prices, timing etc refer to bar food – not to a separate restaurant if there is one.

SOUTHWOLD TM5076 Map 5

Crown ★

High Street

Close to the brewery, this smart old inn is very much Adnams' flagship and earns praise from readers in almost every respect. As we went to press we heard that there was a new manager and head chef, but initial reports suggest that standards are being fully maintained. The elegant beamed main bar has a stripped curved high-backed settle and other dark varnished settles, kitchen chairs and some bar stools, pretty, fresh flowers on the mix of kitchen pine tables, newspapers to read, a carefully restored and rather fine carved wooden fireplace, and a relaxed atmosphere; the small no-smoking restaurant with its white cloths and pale cane chairs leads off. The smaller back oak-panelled locals' bar has more of a traditional pubby atmosphere, red leatherette wall benches and a red carpet; the little parlour on the left is also no-smoking; shove ha'penny, dominoes and cribbage. Perfectly kept Adnams Bitter, Broadside, Extra and Regatta on handpump; also a good choice of malt whiskies, tea, coffee and herbal infusions. There's a particularly carefully chosen wine list (they have the full Adnams range, well over 300), with a monthly changing choice of 20 interesting varieties by the glass or bottle kept perfectly on a cruover machine; you can get any of them from the cash and carry by the mixed dozen round the corner. The very popular and creative bar food changes daily but might include cream of carrot and coriander soup (£2.95), wild mushroom open ravioli in a tomato and red pepper sauce (£4.50), home-made saffron tagliatelle with basil pesto, roast tomato and spinach or venison sausages with mustard and herb mash (£8), braised knuckle of lamb with a red lentil and crisp bacon jus (£8.50) and bouillabaisse with spinach noodles and saffron rouille (£10.50); puddings include sticky toffee pudding with golden syrup sauce or poached pear in red wine syrup with clotted cream (£3.25). There are a few tables in a sunny sheltered corner outside. *(Recommended by Helen Pickering, James Owen, J and P Maloney, Mrs D P Dick, Pat and Tony Hinkins, A Ridgway, James and Pam Benton, Ronald Dodsworth, A C Curry, Jasper Sabey, Gwen and Peter Andrews, P A Legon, Pat and John Millward, Mr and Mrs McKay, Nigel Woolliscroft, Helen Crookston, Jill and Keith Wright, M Clifford, David and Anne Culley, J F M West, Evelyn and Derek Walter, P and M Pumfrey, Dr F M Halle, K and J Brooks, Mr and Mrs C H Phillips, Joy and Peter Heatherley, David and Doreen Gregory, J F Knutton, Robert Gomme, Wayne Brindle, Richard Balls, Dr B and Mrs P B Baker, Richard Siebert; more reports on the new regime please)*

Adnams ~ Manager Anna Bostedt ~ Real ale ~ Meals and snacks (12.15-2.30, 7-9.30) ~ Restaurant ~ (01502) 722275 ~ Children in eating area of bar ~ Open 10.30-3, 6-11; 12-3, 6-10.30 Sun; closed first week Jan ~ Bedrooms: £45B/£68B

STOKE BY NAYLAND TL9836 Map 5

Angel

B1068 Sudbury—East Bergolt; also signposted via Nayland off A134 Colchester—Sudbury

Few voices of dissent are ever heard amongst the heaps of praise for this elegant and stylish dining pub. The delicious and attractively presented food might include home-made soup (£2.75), griddled fresh sardines in oregano (£4.95), fresh dressed crab with home-made mayonnaise (£4.95), sauté of liver and bacon with madeira sauce (£6.50), home-made steamed steak and kidney pudding (£6.75), vegetable filo parcels with fresh tomato coulis (£6.95), chicken and king prawn brochette with yoghurt and mint dip (£9.50), steamed fillets of salmon and halibut with dill sauce (£9.75), brochette of scallops wrapped in bacon (£10.95) and honey glazed roast rack of lamb (£11.25); home-made puddings might include tuile basket of brown bread ice cream or steamed apple pudding with vanilla sauce (£3.45). You do need to arrive early or book if you don't want to risk having to wait for a table. The comfortable main bar area has handsome Elizabethan beams, some stripped brickwork and timbers, a mixture of furnishings including wing armchairs, mahogany dining chairs, and pale library chairs, local watercolours and older prints, attractive table lamps, and a huge log fire. Round the corner is a little tiled-floor stand-and-chat bar – with well kept Adnams, Greene King IPA and Abbot and a guest beer on handpump, and a thoughtful wine list. One no-smoking room has a low sofa and wing armchairs around its woodburning stove, and Victorian paintings on the dark green walls. There are cast-iron seats and tables on a sheltered terrace. Spacious well equipped rooms and good breakfasts. *(Recommended by Bob and Maggie Atherton, MDN, Mrs P Goodwyn, R Wiles, C L Kauffmann, David Gregory, J M Waller, Richard and Robyn Wain, Richard and Margaret Peers, Ronald Dodsworth, Jasper Sabey, Gwen and Peter Andrews, Peter Baggott, J F Knutton, Pat and John Millward, Ian Phillips, D E Twitchett)*

Free house ~ Licensee Peter Smith ~ Real ale ~ Meals and snacks ~ Restaurant ~ (01206) 263245 ~ Children in restaurant ~ Open 11-2.30, 6-11; 12-3, 7-10.30 Sun; closed 25 and 26 Dec ~ Bedrooms: £46B/£59.50B

THORNHAM MAGNA TM1070 Map 5

Four Horseshoes

Off A140 S of Diss; follow Finningham 3¼ signpost, by White Horse pub

There are new licensees at this handsome thatched pub and it is now part of the Old English Pub Company chain. Said to date back to the 12th c, the interior is full of charm and character, and because it rambles round so much is deceptively spacious. The extensive bar is well divided into alcoves and distinct areas, with very low and heavy black beams, some tall windsor chairs as well as the golden plush banquettes and stools on its spread of fitted turkey carpet, country pictures and farm tools on the black-timbered white walls, and logs burning in big fireplaces; the area with the inside well is no smoking, as is the restaurant. We have had very favourable reports on bar food under the new regime, which might include filled rolls (from £2.25), home-made soup (£2.75), hot filled baguettes (from £3.95), yorkshire puddings filled with sausages (£6.50), home-made beef and ale pie, cod in beer batter or mushroom and almond tagliatelle (£6.95), chicken, ham, apricot, walnut and mushroom pie or chicken kiev (£7.25), mixed grill (£8.25) and rump steak (£8.95); two course meal for OAPs (£4.95, not weekends); children's menu (£3.25). Well kept Adnams Southwold, Courage Directors, Morlands Old Speckled Hen, Nethergate Old Growler and Theakstons Old Peculier on handpump; piped music. In summer, you can sit at the picnic-sets beside the flower beds on a sheltered lawn. Nearby, Thornham Walks consists of nearly 12 miles of permissive footpaths on the beautiful and privately owned Thornham Estate and there is a half mile hard-surfaced path through the parkland, woodland and farmland which is suitable for wheelchairs and pushchairs as well as those with walking difficulties. The thatched church at Thornham Parva is famous for its ancient wall paintings. *(Recommended by Gwen and Peter Andrews, Trevor Moore, Mrs P Goodwyn, Peter Plumridge, Graham McNutty, M and M Carter; more reports on the new regime please)*

Free house ~ Managers: Mike and Maxine Hughes ~ Real ale ~ Meals and snacks ~ Restaurant ~ (01379) 678777 ~ Children in family room ~ Open 12-2.30, 7(6.30 summer Sat)-11; 12-3, 7-10.30 Sun ~ Bedrooms: £40B/£55B

TOSTOCK TL9563 Map 5

Gardeners Arms 

Village signposted from A14 (former A45) and A1088

The friendly licensees ensure that everyone feels welcome at this charmingly unspoilt pub. The smart lounge bar has a bustling villagey atmosphere, as well as low heavy black beams, and lots of carving chairs around the black tables, and in the lively tiled-floor public bar there's darts, pool, shove-ha'penny, dominoes, cribbage, juke box, and an unobtrusive fruit machine. Very well kept Greene King Abbot, IPA and seasonal beers on handpump. Consistently enjoyable and good value bar food from a fairly limited range includes lunchtime sandwiches (from £1.60), ploughman's (from £3.75), burgers (from £4.25), scampi (£5.75), gammon and egg (£6.25); daily specials such as hot chicken salad with sun-dried tomatoes, peppers and mushrooms (£5.75), beef and pickled walnut casserole or moroccan lamb (£6.25) and thai king prawn green curry on rice (£7.50). It's pleasant to sit outside on picnic-sets among the roses and other flowers on the sheltered lawn. *(Recommended by D R A Field, Ian Phillips, J F M*

West, T R Burden, Gwen and Peter Andrews, Bill and Sheila McLardy, Mrs P Goodwyn, Peter Meister, Charles Bardswell, Pat and Tony Martin, R E and P Pearce)

Greene King ~ Tenant Reg Ransome ~ Meals and snacks (not Mon or Tues evenings or Sun lunchtime) ~ Restaurant ~ (01359) 270460 ~ Children in eating area of bar ~ Open 11.30(11 Sat)-2.30, 7-11; 12-3, 7-10.30 Sun

WANGFORD TM4679 Map 5

Angel

High St; village signposted just off A12 at junction of B1126 to Southwold

There's a lovely friendly atmosphere at this neatly kept cream-painted 17th-c village inn. Good, well spaced, simple but substantial furniture includes some sturdy elm tables, cushioned winged wall benches, and a splendid old bar counter; old local photographs on the cream walls. Reasonably priced bar food might include sandwiches (from £2.25), hot filled french bread (£3.25), soup (£1.50), farmhouse pâté (£3), breaded plaice (£4.99), vegetable suet pudding (£5.50), chicken coated with a honey and mustard sauce or pork steak with apricot sauce (£6.50), minted leg of lamb (£6.75) and steaks (from £6.95); children's menu (£2.50). The restaurant is no smoking. Well kept Adnams, John Smiths, Morlands Old Speckled Hen, Theakstons Best and Youngs Special maybe under light blanket pressure, decent house wines from the Adnams list, good generous coffee; pleasant staff, maybe piped music; cribbage and a weekly quiz. The garden behind has picnic-sets under cocktail parasols. Comfortable and spotlessly clean bedrooms. *(Recommended by June and Perry Dann, Mr and Mrs P Bastable, Mrs P Goodwyn, D H Tarling, Gwen and Peter Andrews)*

Free house ~ Licensee Richard Pearson ~ Real ale ~ Meals and snacks (all day till 9.30) ~ Restaurant ~ (01502) 578636 ~ Children welcome ~ Open 12-11; 12-10.30 Sun ~ Bedrooms: £40B/£49B

WINGFIELD TM2277 Map 5

De La Pole Arms

Church Road; village signposted off B1118 N of Stradbroke

Readers report that this carefully restored village inn is well worth seeking out. Inside the decor is very traditional with interesting bric-a-brac, comfortable traditional seating, and no distraction by juke boxes, machines or flashing lights. Despite the deliberate simplicity there is a pleasantly civilised feel. Good bar food, with some emphasis on local fish and seafood, includes filled baguettes like smoked chicken and bacon or brie and sun-dried tomato (£4.95), fish platter (£6.95), fresh dressed cromer crab (£7.95), pan-fried rainbow trout stuffed with onions and chestnuts (£8.75), chicken and button mushroom sizzler (£8.95), and home-made puddings like hot chocolate brownie with clotted cream and traditional summer pudding (from £2.95). The well kept St Peters Best, Fruit Beer, Strong, and Wheat Beer on handpump and under light blanket pressure come from a newish small brewery at South Elmham, some 11 or 12 miles to the NE. Service is courteous and helpful; cribbage, dominoes and piped music. *(Recommended by Bob Arnett, Judy Wayman, D Twitchett, D S Marshall, Tom Gondris)*

St Peters ~ Manager Tom Harvey ~ Real ale ~ Meals and snacks ~ Restaurant ~ (01379) 384545 ~ Open 11-3, 6-11; 12-3, 7-10.30 Sun

Post Office address codings confusingly give the impression that some pubs are in Suffolk when they're really in Norfolk or Cambridgeshire (which is where we list them).

Lucky Dip

Besides the fully inspected pubs, you might like to try these Lucky Dips recommended to us and described by readers (if you do, please send us reports):

☆ **Aldeburgh** [Crabbe St; TM4656], *Cross Keys*: Busy low-ceilinged 16th-c pub with antique settles, Victorian prints, woodburners, food from soup and open sandwiches up, Adnams ales (the full range); can get smoky, fruit machine; open all day July/Aug, children in eating areas, tables in back yard which opens on to promenade and beach *(PGP, Thomas Nott, Maggie and Derek Washington, P and M Pumfrey, LYM)*

Aldeburgh [Market Cross Pl; opp Moot Hall], *Mill*: Friendly, with good value food cooked to order inc local fish; good service, well kept Adnams ales, decent coffee, locals' bar (can be rather smoky), cosy no-smoking beamed dining room with Gypsy Queen model, sea view; cream teas July/Aug; fruit machine, can get rather full in summer; bedrooms *(CMW, JJW)*

☆ **Aldringham** [B1122/B1353 S of Leiston; TM4461], *Parrot & Punchbowl*: Neatly kept beamed pub with food inc interesting vegetarian dishes from downstairs servery, dining-room meals Fri/weekend (must book then), lots of decent wines, well kept Adnams and Greene King IPA; children welcome, dogs allowed; pleasant sheltered garden with own servery and a couple of swings, nice craft centre opp *(Mrs Romey Heaton, Mrs P Goodwyn, BB)*

Barham [Old Norwich Rd; TM1451], *Sorrel Horse*: Cheerful and attractive pink-washed pantiled 17th-c country pub, nicely refurbished bar with magnificent log fire, lots of beams, lounge and two dining areas off, particularly well kept Tolly ales inc Cobbolds IPA, decent bar food inc interesting specials, prompt friendly service; good garden with big play area and barbecue, timber stables opp; well placed for walks *(John Baker)*

☆ **Barnby** [Swan Lane; TM4789], *Swan*: Plush beamed dining pub with very well presented food, emphasis on excellent choice of good fresh fish – not cheap but good value; well kept Courage Directors, good house wines, very efficient welcoming service, fishing decor *(Dorothee and Dennis Glover, Maggie and Derek Washington)*

Beccles [New Market; TM4290], *Kings Head*: Hospitable central hotel, handy for coffee or afternoon tea; Tudor behind 18th-c front, two welcoming busy bars, real ales such as Adnams Bitter and Old, Bass, Greene King IPA, reasonably priced food with fresh veg (two for one evening bargains), Sun carvery 12-5; bedrooms *(June and Perry Dann, Ian Phillips)*; [centre], *Swan House*: Several comfortable rooms and courtyard, good attentive service, chilled glass for unusual bottled beers from around the world, bar nibbles, short choice of imaginative well prepared food (worth booking) *(June and Malcolm Farmer)*; [Puddingmoor, off old mkt], *Waveney House*: Hotel with pleasant bar overlooking river, good choice of food inc Sun roasts and home-made puddings; bedrooms *(June and Perry Dann)*

Bentley [TM1138], *Case is Altered*: Well kept Greene King IPA and guest beers, good choice of bar food, sizeable dining area, bargain Sun lunch, interesting decor with oak beams, chalked bons mots and bottle collections; charming village *(Eddie Edwards)*

☆ **Blaxhall** [off B1069 S of Snape; can be reached from A12 via Little Glemham; TM3657], *Ship*: Welcoming and helpful landlord in spotless low-beamed traditional country local, log fire, generous home cooking with fresh veg in unassuming dining lounge, well kept Tolly and Marstons Pedigree, piped music, pool in public bar; children in eating area; self-catering cabins available, attractive setting; cl Mon lunchtime *(Derek and Maggie Washington, June and Perry Dann, LYM)*

☆ **Blundeston** [from B1074 follow Church Lane, right into Short Lane, then left; TM5197], *Plough*: Friendly staff and locals in smartly modernised old country pub which was the home of Barkis the carrier in *David Copperfield*; huge choice of good bar food inc plenty of fish, well kept Adnams; handy for Jacobean Somerleyton Hall *(Anthony Barnes, Mrs J Shillington)*

☆ **Blyford** [B1123 Blythburgh—Halesworth; TM4277], *Queens Head*: Thatch, very low beams, a well they still use, some antique settles alongside more modern conventional furnishings, huge fireplace, popular generous food inc bargain lunches (but no sandwiches), well kept Adnams Bitter, Mild, and Broadside; children allowed in no-smoking restaurant, tables outside with good play area, bedrooms *(Trevor Williams, J F Knutton, June and Perry Dann, David and Anne Culley, Mr and Mrs Charles Gysin, Gwen and Peter Andrews, Chris Mawson, P and M Pumfrey, John Wooll, Robert Turnham, LYM)*

☆ **Blythburgh** [A12; TM4575], *White Hart*: Welcoming open-plan family dining pub with fine ancient beams, woodwork and staircase, good fish, well kept Adnams Bitter, Old and Broadside, decent wines; children in eating area and restaurant, piped classical music, open all day Fri/Sat; spacious lawns looking down on tidal marshes, magnificent church over road *(Peter Plumridge, Derek and Maggie Washington, Colin and Joyce Laffan, Anthony Barnes, Klaus and Elizabeth Leist, Nigel Wilkinson)*

Brome [TM1376], *Brome Grange*: 16th-c core, with well kept Adnams, good bar food, helpful staff, restaurant; bedrooms spacious and comfortable, in courtyard *(Cliff Blakemore)*

Bungay [Broad St; TM3491], *Green Dragon*: Unpretentious local brewing its own fine well priced ales inc a Mild, food inc good filled baked potatoes, curry or Tex Mex nights, liberal attitude towards children; piped music may be loud, very popular with young people – side room quieter; Sun quiz night *(Rita and Keith Pollard, Ian Phillips)*

☆ **Bury St Edmunds** [Whiting St; TL8564], *Masons Arms*: Busy clapboarded pub with particularly good value home-made food from really good snacks up, three well kept Greene King ales from nearby brewery, prompt friendly service, busy but comfortable and relaxing dining lounge with lots of oak timbering, separate bar, no music, terrace tables; more of a local evenings *(PGP, Ian Phillips, Nigel Woolliscroft)*

Bury St Edmunds [Mount Rd; minor rd towards Thurston, parallel to A143; TL8967], *Flying Fortress*: Much enlarged former HQ of USAF support group, on edge of Rougham ex-airfield – the original for the film *Twelve O'Clock High*, with WWII bomber models and evocative black and white pictures; comfortable modern lounge area, well kept Adnams and other ales such as Flowers, Mauldons and Tetleys from long bar, decent food inc carvery (big echoic restaurant area), friendly staff, take-away wines, tables outside, old fire-engine for children to play on *(John Baker, Ian Phillips, Michael Hyde)*; [7 Out Northgate St, Station Hill], *Linden Tree*: Good bustling yet relaxed atmosphere and wide choice of generous cheap food in busy attractively renovated family dining pub with stripped pine bar, friendly quick service, well kept Greene King IPA and Rayments, wines in two glass sizes, freshly squeezed orange juice, popular conservatory restaurant (worth booking), good well kept garden *(J F M West)*; [Traverse, Abbeygate St], *Nutshell*: Quaint and attractive corner pub, perhaps the country's smallest inside, with particularly well kept Greene King IPA and Abbot, friendly landlord, lots of odd bric-a-brac – an interesting tourist attraction; cl Sun and Holy Days *(Robert Gomme, Richard and Valerie Wright, Comus Elliott)*; [39 Churchgate St], *Queens Head*: Opened-up Victorian pub keeping its Dutch tiles and bar panelling, particularly well kept Nethergate, Wolf and several other real ales mainly from small breweries, good snacks esp baguettes; popular with professional and elderly people lunchtime, more a young people's meeting place evenings; open all day all week, nr abbey ruins *(John Baker, David Lamb, Quentin Williamson)*

Carlton [Rosemary Lane; just N of Saxmundham; TM3864], *Poachers Pocket*: Neatly kept refurbished country pub with helpful service, well kept changing ales, well presented generous usual food, small dining area; garden with lovely country views; some live music *(Maggie and Derek Washington)*

Carlton Colville [The Street; A146 W of Lowestoft; TM5189], *Bell*: Deliberately simple decor in relaxed open-plan pub divided by log fire, well kept Greenjack ales (from nearby Oulton Broad) and a guest beer, Czech, German and Belgian beers on tap or bottled, wide choice of good varied food (can book), small conservatory, sizeable garden with play area *(David and Cathy Weaver)*; *Crown*: Comfortable friendly atmosphere, nice balance between ancient and modern, generous straightforward food inc vegetarian, real ales inc Adnams and John Smiths; very handy for East Anglian Transport Museum *(Quentin Williamson, Albert and Margaret Horton)*

Chelsworth [The Street; near Bury St Edmunds; TL9848], *Peacock*: Attractive and prettily set old dining pub, fairly intimate pubby decor, small bar by entrance kept for drinkers (well kept Adnams and Greene King IPA), lots of Tudor brickwork and exposed beams, big inglenook log fire, well spaced comfortable tables, nice small garden; open all day Sat; bedrooms – the two at the back are quieter; pretty village *(Pamela Goodwyn, Mike and Maggie Betton, LYM)*

☆ **Chevington** [off A143 SW of Bury; TL7860], *Greyhound*: Plain simply modernised village pub given character by masses of domestic bric-a-brac, particularly good real Indian cooking at reasonable prices, faultless service, Greene King IPA and Abbot, big woodburner, enthusiastic service, restaurant; garden with good play area *(John Baker)*

☆ **Clare** [High St (A1092 W of Sudbury); TL7645], *Swan*: Much modernised early 17th-c village local, lots of copper and brass and huge log fire, public bar with WWII memorabilia and another fire (dogs allowed here), friendly landlord, good value home-made food from huge bargain huffers, lovely flower tubs out behind; very special village, lovely church *(Nick Holmes, Patrick Hancock, Heather Martin, Richard and Valerie Wright, Mrs M Dixon, BB)*

☆ **Clare** [Market Hill], *Bell*: Large timbered inn with comfortably rambling lounge bar, splendidly carved black beams, old panelling and woodwork around the open fire, side rooms (one with lots of canal and other prints), well kept Nethergate ales inc Mild and maybe Umble coriander beer, also guests such as Courage Directors and Fullers London Pride, decent wines, food inc children's dishes in dining conservatory opening on to terrace; darts, pool, fruit machine; bedrooms off back courtyard, open all day, interesting village *(M A and C R Starling, Gwen and Peter Andrews, Pam Adsley, Richard and Valerie Wright, Pat and Tony Martin, LYM)*

Clare [Nethergate St], *Clare Hotel*: Smart but pleasantly pubby L-shaped bar with enjoyable food, well kept beer, decent service, conservatory/restaurant, attractive garden with shady areas; bedrooms *(Patrick Hancock, LYM)*

☆ **Cretingham** [TM2260], *Bell*: Comfortable pub mixing striking 15th-c beams, timbers and big fireplace with more modern renovations and furnishings, Adnams and changing guest beers, good generous food inc vegetarian and children's, attentive landlord; no-smoking lounge and restaurant with Sun lunch, traditional games in public bar, family room, may open all day in summer; seats out in rose garden and on front grass *(John Kirk, LYM)*

Dalham [TL7261], *Affleck Arms*: Good atmosphere in thatched village pub by stream (dry in recent summers), log fire in cosy low-beamed locals' bar, more comfortable and intimate rambling dining bar on right, wide choice of food inc vegetarian and children's, Greene King and other ales; service can slow when busy; picnic-sets out in front, fish pond and pets corner behind *(CMW, JJW, LYM)*

☆ **East Bergholt** [Burnt Oak, towards Flatford Mill; TM0734], *Kings Head*: Well kept attractive beamed lounge with comfortable sofas, interesting decorations, quick pleasant service, good value home-made bar food inc several vegetarian dishes, good starters and curry, well kept Tolly and guest beers, decent wines and coffee, piped classical music (juke box in plain public bar); lots of room in pretty garden, flower-decked haywain, baskets and tubs of flowers in front *(Mike and Mary Carter, Pamela Goodwyn, Mike and Heather Watson)*

☆ **Eastbridge** [off B1122 N of Leiston; TM4566], *Eels Foot*: Light modern furnishings in friendly country pub with wide choice of generous cheap food, well kept Adnams and other ales, darts in side area, neat back dining room; walkers, children and dogs welcome, more tables and swings outside, pretty village handy for Minsmere bird reserve and heathland walks; open all day in summer for coffee and cream teas *(Gwen and Peter Andrews, EJL, G Neighbour, Pamela Goodwyn, Maggie and Derek Washington, Tim and Linda Collins, Helen Pickering, James Owen, CMW, JJW, Amanda, Paul and Rebecca Longley, June and Perry Dann, LYM)*

Eriswell [TL7278], *Chequers*: Very wide food choice inc lots of Tex Mex and good value Sun lunch, warm welcome, very fast service *(N E and M A Jolley)*

Felixstowe [Church Rd; TM3034], *White Horse*: Recently rebuilt, with no-smoking dining room, wide choice of food inc vegetarian and very popular Sun lunch, pleasant staff, very helpful landlord, seats outside with play area *(Mrs J Deale)*

Felixstowe Ferry [TM3337], *Victoria*: Helpful licensees in child-friendly riverside pub, good food emphasising local seafood, competitively priced Adnams and guest beers, sailing charts in gents' *(Mrs P Goodwyn)*

Finningham [B1113; TM0669], *White Horse*: Friendly new licensees, well kept Flowers and Tolly, very big menu changing daily inc good vegetarian choice; handy for walkers *(Grahame McNulty)*

☆ **Framlingham** [Market Hill; TM2863], *Crown*: Traditional small inn now owned by Old English Pub Co, old-fashioned heavy-beamed public bar opening into hall and comfortable character lounge with armchairs by log fire, good bar and restaurant food (not cheap), real ales inc Adnams, decent wines, lively atmosphere on Sat market day; comfortable period bedrooms *(Ian Phillips, Mrs P Goodwyn, LYM)*

Framlingham [Castle Approach], *Castle*: Friendly old small pub with well kept Whitbreads and other ales, wide range of decent food from toasties and good omelettes to steaks; children welcome *(Helen Winter)*

☆ **Friston** [B1121; just off A1094 Aldeburgh—Snape; TM4160], *Old Chequers*: Welcoming dining pub with simple but stylish country pine furnishings, light and airy decor, good if not cheap interesting food (no wait, served from bain-marie) inc fish, game, vegetarian, light and tasty puddings, well kept Adnams, good wines and whiskies; good walk from Aldeburgh *(Simon Watkins, Mrs P Goodwyn, Joy and Peter Heatherley, Maggie and Derek Washington, Mrs Romey Heaton, P Whight, MDN, LYM)*

Gislingham [High St; TM0771], *Six Bells*: Real village pub, cheerful and spotless, friendly staff, good food combining tradition and invention, particularly well kept ales, reasonable prices *(John Baker)*

☆ **Great Glemham** [between A12 Wickham Mkt—Saxmundham, B1119 Saxmundham—Framlingham; TM3361], *Crown*: Friendly new licensees (no longer letting bedrooms), chatty open-plan beamed lounge with two enormous log fires, wooden pews and captain's chairs around stripped and waxed kitchen tables, local pictures, well kept Greene King IPA and Abbot and a guest beer from old brass handpumps, usual food from sandwiches up inc vegetarian in bar and no-smoking restaurant (children allowed), tables in garden *(Mrs P Goodwyn, Charles and Pauline Stride, LYM)*

Hadleigh [Mkt Pl; TM0242], *Ram*: Pleasantly unassuming, very friendly, with good food and service *(C L Kauffmann)*

Halesworth [Thoroughfare; TM3877], *White Hart*: Welcoming well restored open-plan local with well kept beer and good home-cooked food with local veg *(D S Marshall, June and Perry Dann)*

☆ **Haughley** [off A45/B1113 N of Stowmarket; TM0262], *Kings Arms*: Wide choice of good value home-made food inc interesting fish, good Greek dishes (landlady's mother comes from Cyprus) and puddings, airy beamed dining lounge with lots of shiny dark tables, restaurant area on left, busy public bar with games, log fire, well kept Greene King IPA, Abbot and Rayments, decent wines, friendly service; piped music; tables and play house in colourful back garden *(Norman Smith, John and Elizabeth Thomason, Simon Morton, Pamela Goodwyn, LYM)*

☆ **Hawkedon** [Rede Rd, between A143 and B1066; TL7952], *Queens Head*: Sympathetically refurbished 17th-c real village pub, cheerful and lively, with particularly well kept Mauldons, Woodfordes and interesting guest beers, energetic knowledgeable staff, log fire, good traditional sensibly priced food *(John Baker)*

Horringer [TL8261], *Six Bells*: Proper pub neatly done up by new licensees, well kept Greene King, good cheap food esp pies, pleasant staff, good conservatory and outside area – useful for children; darts, bar billiards *(Derek Field)*

Hulver Street [TM4687], *Hulvergate Lodge*: Large pub in pleasant countryside, good food in bar or restaurant, big terrace and garden with weekend barbecues *(June and Perry Dann)*

Huntingfield [TM3374], *Huntingfield Arms*: Neat pub overlooking green, light wood tables and chairs, pleasant combination of beams and stripped brickwork, good range of attractively presented bar food inc good fresh fish, well kept Adnams, friendly service, restaurant, games area with pool beyond woodburner *(Pamela Goodwyn, June and Perry Dann)*

☆ **Icklingham** [A1101 NW of Bury; TL7772], *Old Plough*: Attractively decorated brick and flint pub with well kept Adnams, Greene King IPA and a guest such as Wadworths 6X, good range of home-made food (cheaper early suppers), lots of cricketing memorabilia and books, bar billiards, subdued piped music; big garden with play area *(JJW, CMW, Scott Rumery)*

☆ **Ipswich** [Cliff Rd, by Tolly's Cliff Brewery; TM1744], *Brewery Tap*: Ground floor of early 19th-c building nestling under vast brewery, across rd from docks; a pleasant oasis in a difficult town, with decent food (not Sun/Mon evenings) from big Scotch eggs and filled baps up, well kept Tolly ales (and cases of bottled beers), helpful staff, very mixed customers, traditional games, children's room, brewery tours twice a day; piped music may obtrude (not in no-smoking room on right); open all day, wheelchair access *(Richard Houghton, E A Shortland Jones, Pete Yearsley, D H and M C Watkinson, John Fahy, Neil Calver, LYM)*

Ipswich [Spring Rd], *Fat Cat*: Reconstruction of basic genuine pub outstanding for well kept beer, with friendly first-rate service; adventurously filled rolls, lots of old advertisements *(John Baker)*; [Henley Rd/Anglesea Rd], *Greyhound*: Simple but comfortable Victorian decor, well kept Adnams and guest ales, good substantial home cooking inc plenty for vegetarians, quick service, helpful young staff; children welcome, quiet back terrace *(Joan and Andrew Life)*

Ixworth [just off A143 Bury—Diss; TL9370], *Pykkerel*: Several rooms off central servery, Elizabethan beams, attractive brickwork, big fireplaces, antique tables and chairs, persian rugs on gleaming boards, small back sun lounge, well kept Greene King IPA and Abbot and a guest beer under light carbon dioxide blanket, restaurant (no food Sun evening); children welcome *(Ronald Dodsworth, J F M West, LYM)*

Kentford [Bury Rd; TL7066], *Cock*: Comfortable and friendly, with inglenook log fire, welcoming young licensees, airy restaurant, consistently good modestly priced Swedish food, well kept Greene King beers; neat garden *(Mrs A Garnett, Mrs P Gorton)*

Kersey [TL9944], *Bell*: Quaint flower-decked Tudor building in picturesque village, low-beamed public side with tiled floor and log fire divided from lounge by brick and timber screen, good service, wide choice of bar food, well kept ales, decent house wines, restaurant, sheltered back terrace with fairy-lit side canopy; open all day (afternoon teas), children allowed, small caravan site *(Alan Parsons, D and J Tapper, C L Kauffmann, Mrs P Goodwyn, LYM)*

☆ **Kettleburgh** [Easton Rd, SW of Framlingham; TM2660], *Chequers*: Good food inc fresh fish and local quail, reasonable prices, Thurs evening bargains, well kept Whitbreads-related and other ales, decent wines; unrenovated lively bar with open fire, cosy panelled dining room, attentive courteous service *(John and Sara Wheatley, Mrs P Goodwyn)*

Knodishall [TM4261], *Butchers Arms*: Good reasonably priced home-cooked food in cheerful refurbished old local with well kept Adnams, pleasant airy dining room; darts, cribbage etc *(Norman Smith)*

☆ **Layham** [Upper St, Upper Layham, off B1070 S of Hadleigh; TM0240], *Marquis of Cornwallis*: Beamed 16th-c pub with plush lounge bar, nicely prepared food inc good ploughman's and fresh veg, popular lunchtime with businessmen and retired locals, friendly atmosphere, well kept beers such as Marstons Pedigree, good wines and coffee; good valley views, picnic-sets in extensive riverside garden, open all day Sat in summer; bedrooms handy for Harwich ferries *(C L Kauffmann)*

Little Glemham [The Street (A12); TM3458], *Lion*: Well kept Adnams, wide choice of attractively priced food, garden with animals and aviary *(June and Perry Dann)*

☆ **Long Melford** [B1064; TL8645], *Bull*: Medieval former manorial great hall, now a hotel, with beautifully carved beams in old-fashioned timbered front lounge, log fire in huge fireplace, antique furnishings, daily papers; more spacious back bar with sporting prints; good range of bar food from sandwiches to one-price hot dishes inc imaginative salads and fresh fish, no-smoking restaurant, well kept Adnams Best, Greene King IPA and Nethergate, good wines; children welcome, tables in courtyard, open all day Sat/Sun; comfortable if pricy bedrooms *(Maysie Thompson, J F Knutton, Ronald Dodsworth, Pam Adsley, Ian Phillips, J Warren, Helen Winter, Margaret and Nigel Dennis, D E Twitchett, LYM)*

Long Melford [Hall St], *Cock & Bell*: Attractive cream-washed pub, recently refurbished, with well kept Theakstons Best and Old Peculier, decent wine, tasty food such as cheese and vegetable wellington or rabbit with thyme sauce, even a home-made sauce in the prawn sandwiches, friendly service *(Gwen and Peter Andrews, Pam Adsley)*; *Crown*: Dark green ceiling and walls show off carefully chosen prints and nicely placed furniture, dusky pink banquettes on one side, big log fire, reasonably priced generous food cooked to order, well kept Bass, Greene King IPA and Morlands Old Speckled Hen, good open fire; quiet piped music; well equipped bedrooms, huge breakfast *(Ian Phillips, Pam Adsley, LYM)*; [High St, N end], *Hare*: Wide choice of reasonably priced food cooked to order by landlady, cheerful and attentive welcoming landlord, Greene King IPA and Abbot, decent wines, spacious main bar and dining area, log fire in small back bar, upstairs dining room; attractive garden with terrace *(Neil Colquhoun)*

Lowestoft [Pakefield St; TM5492], *Jolly Sailors*:

Generous well prepared food esp fish and friendly atmosphere in roomy bar and much-booked restaurant; popular Sun carvery, attentive service, sea view; looking well after redecoration outside *(Albert and Margaret Horton)*; [just off Somerleyton Rd], *Oak*: Two-bar estate pub reopened spring 1997 by former manager of Hobgoblin in Reading (Berks), with similar alehouse-style appeal though beer range not yet so adventurous *(R Houghton)*

☆ **Market Weston** [Bury Rd (B1111); TL9877], *Mill*: Well opened-up, combining restaurant and pub without clashes; interesting freshly made perfectly cooked food inc popular Sun lunch, very reasonable prices, well kept Adnams, Greene King IPA and an Old Chimneys beer from the village brewery, enthusiastic effective service; suitable for children *(John Baker, D R A Field, Mrs M Dallisson)*

☆ **Melton** [Wilford Bridge (A1153 E of Woodbridge); TM2950], *Wilford Bridge*: Light and roomy, with good value food inc local fish in bar and restaurant, steak nights Mon/Tues, takeaways, prompt friendly service even though busy, decent wines; nearby river walks *(Nicholas Wright)*

Mettingham [B1062 Bungay—Beccles; TM3589], *Tally Ho*: Popular and roomy food-oriented pub, comfortable if very refurbished, with exotic puddings, real ales such as Courage Directors and Morlands Old Speckled Hen, pleasant quick service *(N S Doolan)*

Middleton [The Street; TM4367], *Bell*: Delightful little welcoming take-us-as-you-find-us pub, part thatched and beamed, in pretty village; woodburner in comfortable lounge, Adnams ales tapped from the cask, good value simple food inc children's; darts and open fire in public bar (dogs allowed), small back dining room, picnic-sets in garden, camping; maybe piped radio, some folk nights, car boot sales some Suns; landlord keen on classic cars and motorcycles *(Richard Gibbs, CMW, JJW)*

Naughton [Whatfield Rd; TM0248], *Wheelers Arms*: Ancient low-beamed thatched pub in quiet hamlet, well kept Tolly ales, plenty of character (and locals), good bar food inc local game; pool room, garden, has been open all day Sat in summer *(John Prescott)*

Nayland [B1087, just off A134 Sudbury—Colchester; TL9734], *White Hart*: Smart carefully renovated 16th-c building behind 17th-c coaching frontage, more restaurant than pub – good upmarket country food inc good value Sun supper, scrubbed tables on partly glass floor looking down into cellar, also cosy back bar with big comfortable settee by blazing log fire; friendly service, Adnams and Greene King IPA, good value wines; bedrooms *(Gwen and Peter Andrews, Charles and Pauline Stride)*

Needham Market [TM0855], *Rampant Horse*: Well kept beer, good home-made food, friendly helpful service, terrace with barbecue behind *(Pete Yearsley)*

Newbourne [TM2643], *Fox*: Good atmosphere in 17th-c pub with straightforward home cooking using fresh local produce, well kept Tolly tapped from the cask, cosy unspoilt oak-beamed drinking area around log fire, separate family room, new dining room extension; pretty hanging baskets, lots of tables out in attractively redone garden with pond, musical evenings *(Pamela Goodwyn, Richard and Valerie Wright)*

Norton [Ixworth Rd (A1088); TL9565], *Tickled Trout*: Modern brick pub refurbished as single bar with restaurant – good food esp fish; cheerful and spotless, with faultless service, particularly well kept Hook Norton Best and guest ales *(John Baker, Derek Field)*

☆ **Orford** [Front St; TM4250], *Kings Head*: Bright cheerful feel in cleanly refurbished beamed lounge bar overlooking churchyard, well kept Adnams ales, good coffee, food inc lunchtime snacks, attractive dining room, decent wines, quietly welcoming new landlord, friendly staff and locals; live music Fri, character recently decorated bedrooms with own bathrooms *(P and J Banks, John Prescott, Tim and Linda Collins, CMW, JJW, David Child, Gwen and Peter Andrews, LYM)*

Orford, *Crown & Castle*: Comfortable and unassuming bars, reasonably priced food; bedrooms very pleasant, in garden chalet *(Tim and Linda Collins)*

☆ **Polstead** [The Green, off A1071 or B1068 E of Sudbury; TL9938], *Cock*: Friendly and unspoiled, with very civilised landlord, interesting reasonably priced food (not Sun evening) from good value imaginatively filled lunchtime big rolls and real soups through honest rewarding main courses to imaginative puddings, inc superb Sun lunch and their own smoked meats; low beams, woodburner and open fire, well kept ales such as Fullers London Pride, Greene King IPA, Mauldons and Woodefordes Wherry, good choice of wines, candlelit evening barn restaurant; piped music not too obtrusive, garden with side play area overlooking green; cl Mon; children welcome *(Mrs D Cox, Mrs S Wenlock, Michael Ellis, V J Parry, Keith and Janet Morris)*

☆ **Ramsholt** [Dock Rd, off B1083 – first turning after road to church; TM3041], *Ramsholt Arms*: Lovely isolated spot, but busy on summer weekends, with picture window nautical bars overlooking River Deben, good log fire, well kept Adnams and Flowers Original, several wines by the glass, bar food (not winter Sun evenings) inc fish and game, no-smoking restaurant, summer afternoon terrace bar (not Sun); longish steep walk down from car park; children welcome, comfortable and spacious recently done bedrooms, yacht moorings nearby *(David Peakall, Simon Cottrell, Pamela Goodwyn, Gwen and Peter Andrews, Ian Phillips, Mr and Mrs M Ashley Miller, LYM)*

Rattlesden [High St; TL9758], *Five Bells*: Cheerful modernised village pub with well kept Mansfield Classic, a Wadworths beer and an interesting guest, basic food, friendly helpful staff *(John C Baker)*

Rendham [B1119 Framlingham—Saxmundham; TM3464], *White Horse*: Open-plan bar filled with dining tables, well kept Flowers Original and Greene King IPA, plenty of whiskies (welcoming Scots landlord), good welcoming mix of customers, food from good home-made soup and sandwiches up *(Gwen and Peter Andrews)*

☆ **Risby** [slip rd off A14; TL7966], *White Horse*: Wide choice of food in bar and restaurant, welcoming landlords, obliging prompt service, good choice of real ales; log fire, beams, brickwork and panelling, mats on flagstones, attractive and interesting decor and furnishings *(W H and E Thomas, John Baker, LYM)*

☆ **Rumburgh** [NW of Halesworth; TM3481], *Buck*: New licensees in pretty and popular rambling country local, several rooms inc restaurant, good value food inc generous Sun roasts and fresh veg, lots of character, well kept ales such as Adnams Extra, friendly atmosphere, games in end room; quiet back lawn *(June and Perry Dann, Mrs P Goodwyn)*

☆ **Saxtead Green** [B1119; TM2665], *Old Mill House*: Roomy dining pub across green from working windmill, neat country look, brick servery, wooden tables and chairs, pretty curtains, good reasonably priced home-made food with crisp veg, well kept Adnams, Courage Best and Directors and Shepherd Neame Spitfire, decent wines; quiet piped music; sizeable garden, pretty back terrace, good play area *(Gwen and Peter Andrews, Pete Yearsley, Mrs P Goodwyn, LYM)*

Shottisham [TM3144], *Sorrel Horse*: Simple thatched two-bar pub in tucked-away village, well kept Tolly ales tapped from the cask, reasonably priced straightforward food lunchtime and early evening, friendly service, good fire; quiz nights some Sats, tables on green in front *(Pat and Tony Martin, Richard and Valerie Wright)*

Sibton [Halesworth Rd; TM3669], *White Horse*: Comfortable and attractively laid out 16th-c pub with interesting furnishings, well kept Adnams Bitter and Broadside, pleasant owners, attractive big garden with play area *(Richard Houghton, LYM)*

Snape [B1069 N of Maltings; TM3958], *Cross Keys*: Clean and well lit, with cosy main bar, smallish restaurant, good food, friendly cheerful atmosphere, Adnams; tables out under cocktail parasols *(Joan and Andrew Life)*

☆ **Southwold** [42 East St; TM5076], *Lord Nelson*: Bustling cheerful little local nr seafront, very well run, with low ceilings, panelling and tiled floor, spotless light wood furniture, lamps in nice nooks and crannies, super soda-syphon collection, particularly well kept Adnams Mild, Bitter, Extra, Broadside and Old, good generous basic lunchtime food freshly made from sandwiches up, attentive service, no music, sheltered back garden; open all day, children welcome *(Richard Balls, Gwen and Peter Andrews, Adrian and Jane Tierney-Jones, Tony Gayfer, Tom McLean, Nigel Woolliscroft, Eric Locker, J F M West, C R L Savill, John Wooll, J and P Maloney, Tim and Linda Collins, Ted George, A J Thomas, P J Keen, BB)*

☆ **Southwold** [7 East Green], *Sole Bay*: Homely and welcoming little Victorian local moments from sea, opp brewery (and the Sole Bay lighthouse), light wood furnishings, particularly good value simple lunchtime food (not Sun in winter) esp local smoked sprats, well kept full Adnams range, good house wines, chatty landlord, friendly locals and dogs, lots of polished seafaring memorabilia, unobtrusive piped music, caged birds; conservatory with cockatoos, tables on side terrace *(Tony Gayfer, Richard Balls, Dave Cave, Jean Southwell, Gwen and Peter Andrews, R T and J C Moggridge, June and Perry Dann, Pat and John Millward, John Wooll, BB)*

Southwold [Blackshore Quay; from A1095, right at Kings Head – pass golf course and water tower], *Harbour*: Popular basic harbour local, tiny low-beamed front bar, upper back bar with lots of nautical bric-a-brac – even ship-to-shore telephone and wind speed indicator; some imaginative food (not Sun evening, just fish and chips in newspaper Fri evening/Sat lunch), well kept Adnams Bitter and Broadside, coal fires, solid old furnishings, friendly service (though can slow at busy times), darts, table skittles, tables outside with play area, ducks and animals – can be a bit untidy out here *(Richard Balls, J and P Maloney, K and E Leist, LYM)*; [High St], *Kings Head*: Spacious dining pub with lots of maroon and pink plush, very wide choice of decent food esp fish and vegetarian, well kept Adnams, good house wines, friendly service, no-smoking area; comfortable family/games room with well lit pool table; jazz Sun night, decent bedrooms in house across road *(Mrs Romey Heaton, Ian Blackwell, John Wooll, Richard Balls, BB)*; [South Green], *Red Lion*: Tidy, comfortable and relatively quiet, with big windows looking over green to sea, ship pictures, brassware and copper, elm-slab barrel tables, pale panelling; well kept Adnams Bitter, Broadside and Mild, efficient service, good range of good value basic food inc vegetarian and good fish, family room and summer buffet room, tables outside; right by the Adnams retail shop; bedrooms small but comfortable *(Richard Balls, MDN, Dr B and Mrs P B Baker, BB)*; [Market Pl], *Swan*: Very much a hotel, with relaxed comfortable back bar, chintzy and airy front lounge, well kept Adnams and Broadside with the full range of their bottled beers, decent wines and malt whiskies, bar food; good bedrooms inc garden rooms where (by arrangement) dogs can stay too *(Gwen and Peter Andrews, Richard Balls, J F M West, Robert Turnham, LYM)*

☆ **Stradishall** [A143; TL7452], *Cherry Tree*: Two small traditional beamed bars, good home cooking inc vegetarian, pleasant atmosphere, open fires, Greene King beers under light pressure; friendly ducks and pond in huge rustic garden (dogs allowed here); outside gents' *(John and Karen Gibson, BB)*

Stratford St Mary [TM0434], *Swan*: Very cosy olde-worlde beamed pub with good choice of generous food cooked to order (so may be a

wait), well kept Tolly, log fire in big fireplace, friendly service; children welcome, some tables over road by River Stour *(C L Kauffmann)*
Stutton [Manningtree Rd (B1080); TM1534], *Kings Head*: Attractive pub with friendly and caring new licensees, several smallish individual beamed rooms, exposed timbers, woodburner; good choice of good value fresh well cooked no-frills food inc bargain lunches and children's helpings, real ales, good value house wines; children welcome; shady side garden with new play area, nr Alton Water reservoir and recreation area *(MDN)*
Theberton [B1122; TM4365], *Lion*: Cosy lounge with comfortable banquettes, lots of old photographs, pictures, copper, brass and plates, fresh flowers, good value freshly made food inc children's (may be a wait), friendly licensees, interesting changing guest beers as well as Adnams; piped radio, separate part with darts, pool and TV; garden with picnic-sets, small terrace and camp site *(CMW, JJW)*
Thorpe Morieux [TL9453], *Bull*: Pleasant inside and out, with Adnams, guest beer and Addlestone's cider, wide-ranging menu inc good steaks, friendly jovial landlord, small games room; conservatory, welcome for children *(Pamela Goodwyn)*
☆ **Walberswick** [B1387, off A12 S of Lowestoft; TM4974], *Bell*: Recently refurbished rambling pub with big open fire and woodburner; good bar food from interesting sandwiches to local fish and stir fries (service can slow when it's crowded), well kept Adnams Bitter, Broadside and Extra, no-smoking restaurant, family room, conservatory; children welcome, dogs allowed in flagstoned bar, darts, shove-ha'penny, and fruit machine; bedrooms with views, nr beach; open all day summer Sats, sizeable flower-filled garden, some folk nights *(Wayne Brindle, David and Anne Culley, Richard Gibbs, Pamela Goodwyn, Hugh O'Neill, John Wooll, LYM)*
Waldringfield [The Quay; nr Woodbridge; TM2844], *Maybush*: Riverside pub with sailing memorabilia inc Giles cartoons, wide range of generous well priced and well cooked food, quick friendly service, sizeable verandah with good views over River Deben and its bird-haunted sandbanks *(Joan and Andrew Life, Richard May)*
Wangford [A12 to Wrentham; TM4679], *Plough*: Welcoming stop with reasonably priced home-cooked food, well kept beers *(June and Perry Dann)*
☆ **Westleton** [B1125 Blythburgh—Leiston; TM4469], *Crown*: Upmarket extended beamed country inn with country chairs, attractive stripped tables, good local photographs and farm tools in smallish decorous bar area, six interesting real ales, lots of malt whiskies, good wines, farm cider, log fires, pleasant service, piped classical music; wide range of home-made food inc good vegetarian choice in big dining area opening off on left (children allowed) and in roomy no-smoking dining conservatory, pretty garden with aviary and floodlit terrace, beautiful setting, good walks nearby; 19 comfortable bedrooms, good breakfast *(Mrs Romey Heaton, June and Perry Dann, Margaret and Nigel Dennis, Gwen and Peter Andrews, J F Knutton, David and Anne Culley, Colin and Joyce Laffan, LYM)*
☆ **Westleton** [Darsham Rd, off B1125 Blythburgh—Leiston], *White Horse*: Less smart and cheaper than the Crown, friendly village pub with generous straightforward food (not winter Tues) in unassuming high-ceilinged bar and attractive no-smoking Victorian back dining room; agreeably busy decor, well kept Adnams Bitter and Broadside and seasonal ales, quiet piped music, friendly service; picnic-sets in cottagey back garden with climbing frame, and out by village duckpond); handy for Fisks clematis nursery, children in eating area, bedrooms *(June and Perry Dann, LYM)*
Wissett [The Street; TM3679], *Plough*: Popular open-plan 17th-c local, lounge area one end, well kept Adnams Bitter and Broadside, good food inc bargain Mon roast, good value Sun lunch; live music some Sats, buskers Thurs *(June and Perry Dann, N S Doolan)*
Woodbridge [opp quay; TM2749], *Anchor*: Good value food (not Mon-Weds evenings) inc sandwiches, vegetarian, good pies, well priced fresh local fish, well kept Greene King IPA and Abbot, friendly service *(Pat and Tony Martin)*; [Market Hill], *Kings Head*: Large character bar with lots of timbering, blazing inglenook log fire, big tables, good if not cheap choice of generous food from sandwiches up inc lots of fish, service efficient and cheery even during busiest lunchtime bustle, full Adnams range kept well, no loud music *(Peter Plumridge, Pat and Tony Martin, Richard and Valerie Wright)*; [New St, off Mkt Sq], *Olde Bell & Steelyard*: Unusual olde-worlde pub with steelyard still overhanging the street, well kept Greene King IPA and Old Harry, good service, very friendly atmosphere, home-made food inc monster bacon and brie baguette, welcoming licensees *(Jenny and Brian Seller)*; [Seckford St], *Seckford Arms*: Interesting pub with Mexican accent in decor and good food, well kept Adnams and often unusual guest beers, children welcome in garden lounge; open all day *(D and J Tapper)*

Bedroom prices normally include full English breakfast, VAT and any inclusive service charge that we know of. Prices before the '/' are for single rooms, after for two people in double or twin (B includes a private bath, S a private shower).

Surrey

Pubs currently generating a lot of enthusiasm here include the Plough at Blackbrook (good choice of house wines, enjoyable food, lovely garden), the ancient Cricketers on its pretty green just outside Cobham (back in these pages after a break – it gets almost incredibly busy in summer), the roadside Compasses at Gomshall (very popular for lunch), the bustling and prettily set White Horse at Hascombe, the King William IV on its steep hillside at Mickleham (a fine all-rounder, and for the second time running our choice as Surrey Dining Pub of the Year), the well run Royal Oak in Pirbright (more space in its small linked rooms this year, excellent beers), the Skimmington Castle on Reigate Heath (nicely cleaned up under its newish licensees, without losing its individuality), the friendly Fox & Hounds at South Godstone (another exemplary all-rounder), the charmingly set old Volunteer at Sutton (making it into the main entries for the first time), the rambling old White Lion in Warlingham, and the friendly Wotton Hatch at Wotton (another new main entry, establishing its appeal after a complete make-over a few years ago). The new landlord of the beautifully set Stephan Langton at Friday Street is now keeping it open all day; there are also new licensees at the Villagers tucked away in the woods at Chilworth, and the Fox & Hounds at Englefield Green has new owners – but the good manager is staying on. In this expensive county, particular praise to the attractive Dolphin at Betchworth for pricing both its food and its drinks so reasonably. And an unexpected find for the area is the Ram at Farncombe – a genuine country cider house, with a choice of two or three dozen. Pubs showing well in the Lucky Dip section at the end of the chapter are the Abinger Hatch at Abinger Common (promising new regime), William IV in Bletchingley, Queens Head at East Clandon, Prince of Wales in Esher, Parrot at Forest Green, Three Horseshoes at Laleham, Cricketers Arms at Ockley, Botley Hill Farmhouse in Warlingham and Brickmakers Arms in Windlesham; we have not yet inspected two or three of these, and would be particularly grateful for further readers' reports so as to narrow the choice down for this year's inspection shortlist. As we have said, this is an expensive county; typically, a pint of beer in a Surrey pub costs 20p more than the national average.

BETCHWORTH TQ2049 Map 3

Dolphin 🍷

The Street; 2½ miles W of Reigate on A25 turn left into Buckland, then take the second left

The homely front room of this friendly village local has kitchen chairs and plain tables on the 400-year-old scrubbed flagstones, and the carpeted back saloon bar is black-panelled with robust old-fashioned elm or oak tables. There are three warming fires, and a nice chiming longcase clock. Very good value bar food includes soup (£2), sausage and egg (£3.25), ploughman's (from £3.70), filled baked potatoes (from £3.95), meat or vegetable lasagne (£4.95), gammon steak (£6.25), and daily specials like spaghetti bolognese (£4.95) and chicken curry or steak and mushroom pie (£5.85), and puddings like spotted dick or apple pie (£2.05). Well kept Youngs Bitter,

Pale Ale, Special and seasonal brews on handpump; up to 18 wines by the glass; efficient service; darts, dominoes, cribbage, and fruit machine. There are some seats in the small laurel-shaded front courtyard and picnic-sets on a lawn by the car park, opposite the church and on the back garden terrace. No children inside. *(Recommended by G S Dudley, John Pettit, Andy and Jill Kassube, Rick Cottrell, Hilton Lord, G W Stevenson, Don Mather, DWAJ)*

Youngs ~ Managers George and Rose Campbell ~ Real ale ~ Meals and snacks (12-2.30, 7-10) ~ (01737) 842288 ~ Open 11-3.30, 5.30-11; 11-11 Sat; 12-10.30 Sun

BLACKBROOK TQ1846 Map 3

Plough 🍷

On byroad E of A24, parallel to it, between Dorking and Newdigate, just N of the turn E to Leigh

This neatly kept white pub, beautifully decorated with marvellous hanging baskets and window boxes in summer, is carefully run by attentive friendly licensees. There are fresh flowers on the tables and window sills of the large linen curtained windows in the partly no-smoking saloon bar, and down some steps, the public bar has brass-topped treadle tables, a formidable collection of ties as well as old saws on the ceiling, and bottles and flat irons; piped music. There are a good few tables, and children can play in the prettily painted Swiss playhouse furnished with tiny tables and chairs, in the secluded garden. Good bar food includes daily specials such as vegetable chowder (£2.65), mussel tartlet with lightly curried cream sauce (£4.25), hot spicy beef, lime and coconut curry or brioche of mixed mushrooms in port and red wine sauce (£6.95) and salmon fillet poached in raspberry vinegar (£9.95), and puddings such as lemon cream tart or spiced apple and sultana pancakes (£3.25); also, filled baked potatoes (from £3.75), ploughman's (£4.45), toasted bagels (from £4.45), breaded plaice (£5.45), ratatouille niçoise (£5.95), chicken curry with nan bread, mango chutney, and cucumber and yoghurt raita (£5.95), and sirloin steak (£10.45). Well kept King & Barnes Sussex, Broadwood, Festive, and seasonal beers on handpump, about 15 wines by the glass, freshly squeezed juice and several malt whiskies and port. The countryside around here is a particularly good area for colourful spring and summer walks through the oak woods. They usually have an atmospheric carol concert the Sunday before Christmas. No children inside. *(Recommended by Comus Elliott, John Pettit, Maggie and Derek Washington, Mrs G Sharman, G P Kernan, James Nunns, Don Mather, TOH, Colin Draper)*

King & Barnes ~ Tenants: Chris and Robin Squire ~ Real ale ~ Meals and snacks (not Mon evening) ~ (01306) 886603 ~ Open 11-2.30(3 Sat), 6-11; 12-3, 7-10.30 Sun; closed 25/26 Dec and 1 Jan

CHILWORTH TQ0346 Map 3

Villagers

Blackheath; off A248 SE of Guildford, by station, over level crossing – at Blackheath turn left

This half timbered old inn stands almost alone on a quiet lane through mixed woodland, and backing on to Blackheath. A small flagstoned room with a big fireplace by the entrance suits walkers, and beyond this the main beamed and carpeted bar rambles around among standing timbers, with a mix of furniture including cushioned pews and more orthodox chairs; a neat dining room is partly separated from this by a largely knocked-through wall. Bar food includes sandwiches (from £3.50), tomato and feta salad (£3.25), fresh battered calamari (£3.95), filled baked potatoes (from £4), steak, kidney and Guinness pie (£7.25), thai chicken curry (£7.95), fresh tuna steak with coriander and lemon butter or barnsley chop with fresh apricots (£9.95), and puddings such as almond, strawberry and poppy seed gateaux, white chocloate and strawberry truffle cake or orange terrine (£3.50); well kept Courage Best, Fullers London Pride, Hogs Back TEA, Morlands Old Speckled Hen on handpump, decent house wines, pleasant young staff, dominoes, trivia, unobtrusive laid-back piped music. There are tables on a sheltered back terrace bright with begonias, with steps up past roses to a good-sized lawn, and a short path through the trees to a cricket green. There are good walks all around – the table-mats show some. We have not yet heard from readers staying in the newly decorated bedrooms – but it's a nice quiet spot. *(Recommended by Mark Percy, Lesley Mayoh Gordon Stevenson, Herbie; more reports please)*

Free house ~ Licensee Mr N Booth ~ Real ale ~ Meals and snacks (all day Sat/Sun) ~ Restaurant ~ (01483) 893152 ~ Children in eating area of bar and restaurant ~ Jazz second Thurs in month ~ Open 12-3, 6-11; all day Sat/Sun ~ Bedrooms: £25

COBHAM TQ1060 Map 3

Cricketers

Downside Common; 3¾ miles from M25 junction 10; A3 towards Cobham, 1st right on to A245, right at Downside signpost into Downside Bridge Rd, follow road into its right fork – away from Cobham Park – at second turn after bridge, then take next left turn into the pub's own lane

If this bustling old pub is crowded in summer you can wander over to the attractive village green to enjoy your drink, or into the delightfully neat back garden with its standard roses, dahlias, bedding plants, urns and hanging baskets. The spacious open-plan interior has crooked standing timbers – creating comfortably atmospheric spaces – supporting heavy oak beams so low they have crash-pads on them. In places you can see the wide oak ceiling boards and ancient plastering lathes. Simple furnishings, horsebrasses and big brass platters on the walls, and a good atmospheric winter log fire; the stable bar is no smoking. At lunchtime most people are here to eat, with dishes listed on the blackboards: soup (£2.50), king prawns wrapped in filo pastry with teriyaki dip (£4.95), cold buffet with smoked fish, pies, quiches and cold meats (£5), sausages or vegetable lasagne (£5.75), fresh salmon and prawns tagliatelle (£5.95), steak, ale and mushroom pie (£6.50) and fresh grilled sole with prawn butter sauce (£8.95). It's worth arriving early to be sure of a table – especially on Sunday. Well kept Morlands Old Speckled Hen, Theakstons Best, Wadworths 6X and Websters Yorkshire on handpump, and several wines by the glass. Dogs welcome. *(Recommended by Ian Phillips, Colin Draper, Simon Collett-Jones, Mrs Jane Basso, John and Patricia White, Anthony Barnes, Lady M H Moir, Derek Harvey-Piper, Margaret and Nigel Dennis)*

Courage ~ Lease: Wendy Luxford ~ Real ale ~ Meals and snacks (till 10pm) ~ Restaurant (not Sun evening, or all day Mon) ~ (01932) 862105 ~ Children in Stable Bar ~ Open 11-2.30, 6-11; 12-3, 6(7 winter)-10.30 Sun

COLDHARBOUR TQ1543 Map 3

Plough

Village signposted in the network of small roads around Abinger and Leith Hill, off A24 and A29

Smartened up quite a lot since the last edition, the two bars at this well placed inn have stripped light beams and timbering in the warm-coloured dark ochre walls, with quite unusual little chairs around the tables in the snug red-carpeted games room on the left (with darts and pool), and little decorative plates on the walls and a big open fire in the one on the right – which leads through to the no-smoking restaurant. As well as a fine range of eight or nine real ales on handpump, such as Adnams Broadside, Hogs Back TEA, Ringwood Old Thumper, Shepherd Neame Master Brew, Bishops Finger and Spitfire, Wadworths 6X and a guest beer, the friendly licensees now brew two of their own beers – Crooked Furrow and Tollywhacker; they also keep country wines and Biddenden farm cider on handpump. Bar food includes cottage pie (£5), fried chicken breast with garlic and herbs, garlic and parsley mushrooms in filo pastry baskets, steak, onion and ale pie, lamb liver and smoked bacon in onion gravy, fisherman's pie or baby spinach leaf salad with bacon, avocado and chicken breast (£7) and griddled swordfish or griddled tuna steak in red wine and rosemary marinade (£9). Outside there are picnic-sets by the tubs of flowers in front and in the the terraced garden with fish pond and waterlilies. Good walks all around. *(Recommended by Mr and Mrs G Stonehouse, C Bromage, Tim Barrow, Sue Demont, Nick and*

Fiona Andrews-Faulkner, Derek Harvey-Piper, Mr and Mrs J Otten, Brian and Jenny Seller)

Free house ~ Licensees Richard and Anna Abrehart ~ Real ale ~ Meals and snacks ~ Restaurant ~ (01306) 711793 ~ Open 11.30-3, 6.30-11; 11.30-11 Sat, 12-10.30 Sun; cl 25/26 Dec and 1 Jan evening ~ Bedrooms: /£50S

COMPTON SU9546 Map 2

Withies

Withies Lane; pub signposted from B3000

Athough there's still a genuinely pubby atmosphere in the little bar at this smartly atmospheric 16th-c dining pub, it's mainly somewhere to come for a meal. The small low beamed bar has a massive inglenook fireplace with a roaring log fire, some attractive 17th-c carved panels between the windows, and a splendidly art nouveau settle among the old sewing machine tables. A short and straightforward choice of bar food includes soup (£2.50), sandwiches (from £3.25), a choice of pâté (£3.50), good ploughman's (from £3.75), cumberland sausages (£4.25), filled baked potatoes (from £4) and seafood platter (£6.50); the restaurant has a more elaborate and quite pricy menu, and is popular with business people during the week. Well kept Bass, Fullers London Pride, King & Barnes Sussex and Marstons Pedigree on handpump. The immaculate garden, overhung with weeping willows, has tables under an arbour of creeper-hung trellises, more on a crazy-paved terrace and yet more under old apple trees. The neat lawn in front of the steeply tiled white house is bordered by masses of flowers. (*Recommended by C J Machin, B Lake, Ian Phillips, James and Wendy Timms, Michael Sargent, John Evans, Derek Harvey-Piper, Martin and Karen Wake, Tom Mann, Miss A Drake)*

Free house ~ Licensees Brian and Hugh Thomas ~ Real ale ~ Meals and snacks (not Sun evening) ~ Restaurant ~ (01483) 421158 ~ Children welcome ~ Open 11-3, 6-11; 12-3 Sun; closed Sun evening

DUNSFOLD TQ0035 Map 3

Sun

Off B2130 S of Godalming

This elegantly built brick-fronted 18th-c pub, set by a quiet village green, has symmetrical arched double porches and neat twin bottle-glass bow windows – pleasant in summer to sit outside at one of the tables. Inside, there's a friendly old-fashioned atmosphere, scrubbed pine furniture, log fires, and Friary Meux Best, King & Barnes Sussex, and Marstons Pedigree on handpump – along with country wines and a decent wine list. Quickly served in generous helpings, the good popular home-made bar food includes sandwiches (from £1.90), home-made soup (£2.75), ploughman's (from £4.50), venison sausages in red wine (£5.95), rabbit casserole (£6.50), steak and kidney pie (£6.75), tandoori chicken (£6.95), steaks (from £10.50), fresh fish dishes, and puddings like hot pecan and white chocolate slice or blackberry and apple pie (£2.95); cottagey restaurant. Darts, table skittles, dominoes, and trivia. *(Recommended by Paul Williams, David Clifton, Mrs W D Morrison)*

Vanguard (Carlsberg-Tetleys) ~ Lease: Mrs Judith Dunne ~ Real ale ~ Meals and snacks (till 10pm) ~ Restaurant ~ (01483) 200242 ~ Children in eating area of bar and restaurant ~ Occasional live music Fri ~ Open 11-3, 6-11; 12-4, 7-10.30 Sun

EFFINGHAM TQ1253 Map 3

Sir Douglas Haig

The Street; off A246 W of Leatherhead

The ochre wood floors, beams, shelves and bar, and creamy floral wallpaper at this large open-plan pub give the interior a 1940's feel. At the lounge end of its single long room there are armchairs and a sofa by the coal fire, and books and a TV on wood shelves. The other end of the room also has a coal fire, as well as mixed new and old chairs and tables on a small turkey carpet. It's a reliable place for good value specials such as quiche (£5.25), fresh fish (from £5.50), steak and ale pie, lasagne or rabbit pie

(£5.75), pork escalope (£5.95) and home-smoked hickory ribs (£6.95), and puddings (£2.95). They serve a good choice of coffees including cappuccino. Well kept Boddingtons, Gales Best and HSB, King and Barnes Sussex and Wadworths 6X, and a changing guest. There's a back lawn and an attractive terraced area with seats and tables; fruit machine, piped music and a TV in the corner of the lounge. *(Recommended by DWAJ, John Pettit, Mrs G Sharman, D P and J A Sweeney, George Atkinson, Mrs D W Cook, T Pascall)*

Free house ~ Licensees Adam and Laurie Smart ~ Real ale ~ Meals and snacks (till 10 Fri/Sat; not Sun evening) ~ (01372) 456886 ~ Children in eating area of bar ~ Open 11-11; 12-10.30 Sun; cl 25 Dec evening ~ Bedrooms: £55B/£65B

ELSTEAD SU9143 Map 2

Woolpack

The Green; B3001 Milford—Farnham

Well kept Greene King Abbot and Fullers London Pride are tapped from the cask at this bustling, friendly pub. The nicely informal long airy main bar has fireplaces at each end, window seats and spindleback chairs around plain wooden tables, and a fair amount of wool industry memorabilia, such as the weaving shuttles and cones of wool that hang above the high-backed settles. Leading off here is a big room decorated with lots of country prints, a weaving loom, scales, and brass measuring jugs; the fireplace with its wooden pillars lace frill is unusual. A changing choice of bar food might include mushrooms stuffed with smoked cod, prawns and oyster sauce, prawns in lime, coriander and chilli butter or hallumi, tomato and onion with coriander, honey and chilli dressing (£4.95), swordfish in malaysian coconut and coriander sauce (£9.95) and ostrich steak in pesto, honey and mustard sauce (£11.95); Sunday lunch is popular; decent wine list. Dominoes and cribbage. A family room leads to the garden with picnic-sets and a children's play area. *(Recommended by Derek and Margaret Underwood, Roger and Valerie Hill, Nigel Wikeley, James and Wendy Timms, G C Hackemer, Miss J Broadhead, G and M Stewart, Helen Hazzard, Liz and Ian Phillips, Chris Elford, Mr and Mr T Bryan, Piotr Chodzko-Zajko, Andrew W Lee, Ian Jones, Mike Fitzgerald, P Gillbe, Mr and Mrs T A Bryan, Lady M H Moir, David Peakall, R Crail, Colin McKerrow, Margaret and Nigel Dennis)*

Ind Coope (Carlsberg-Tetleys) ~ Lease: J A Morris and S A Askew ~ Real ale ~ Meals and snacks ~ Restaurant ~ (01252) 703106 ~ Children in family room and restaurant ~ Open 11-2.30, 6-11; 12-3, 7-10.30 Sun; closed evening 25 Dec, all day 26 Dec

ENGLEFIELD GREEN SU9772 Map 2

Fox & Hounds

Bishopsgate Road; off A328 N of Egham

This smart 17th-c pub, on the edge of Windsor Park and a very short stroll from the main gate to the Savile Garden, was changing hands just as we went to press. As the present manager was staying on, and no major changes are planned (except for possibly all day opening in summer), we're hoping that it will continue doing as well as it has in the past. It's a simple but civilised place with good sturdy wooden tables and chairs, prints in sets of four, a good log fire in the big fireplace, and some stuffed animals and fading red gingham curtains. A simple and limited choice of bar food includes sandwiches (from £2.45), a good choice of baguettes (Saturday and Sunday only, from £2.75), soup (£3.95), and pâté (£5.95). An extensive list of more substantial – and expensive – dishes can be found in the attractive candlelit back dining room; friendly service. Well kept Courage Best and Directors and Fullers London Pride on handpump. There are picnic-sets on the neat and pretty front lawn, and more on a back terrace. *(More reports on the new regime please)*

Scottish Courage ~ Manager Mario Sala ~ Real ale ~ Meals and snacks ~ Restaurant ~ (01784) 433098 ~ Well behaved children welcome ~ Jazz Mon evening ~ Open 11-3, 6-11; 12-3, 7-10.30 Sun (possibly all day in summer); closed 25 Dec

FARNCOMBE SU9844 Map 3

Ram

Catteshall Lane; Off A3100 in Godalming; take Catteshall Road opp Leathern Bottle, leading into Catteshall Lane, then after Farncombe Boathouse take second left, then first right, followed by first left

Staff offer helpful tastings from the 30 different ciders, both cask and keg, that they keep at this lovely old 16th-c cider house. They do also keep Fullers London Pride and ESB and a guest such as Batemans XB on handpump, and quite a few country wines as well. Simple but wholesome bar food might include filled rolls and sandwiches, game pâté (£3.70), rabbit pie (£3.70), roast pheasant (£4.95), wild boar (£5.50), and puddings like treacle tart (£2.70); obliging service from friendly staff. The three simple small rooms have coal-effect fires in old brick hearths, heavy beams, and wooden tables and pews; there's a talking parrot in the public bar (which can be smoky), and maybe a huge german shepherd; dominoes and shove-ha'penny. The pub gets very popular with a younger set later in the evening. It's especially appealing in summer, when the big back garden proves very popular with families; a softly rippling stream runs through the middle, and there are a good few picnic-sets and tables and chairs beside the trees on the grass, and on a covered patio. Throughout the year, they hold various celebrations – St George's Day, May Day, Guy Fawkes, ceilidhs and so forth; there's a small play area, as well as a big carved wooden ram. *(Recommended by Pat and Tony Martin, Nigel Wikeley, Susan and John Douglas)*

Free house ~ Licensees Harry Ardeshir and Carolyn Eley ~ Real ale ~ Meals and snacks ~ (01483) 421093 ~ Children in eating area of bar ~ Folk music Mon and Weds evenings ~ Open 11-11; 12-10.30 Sun

FRIDAY STREET TQ1245 Map 3

Stephan Langton

Village signed off B2126, or from A25 Westcott—Guildford

In a beautifully peaceful spot, surrounded by good walks – Leith Hill is particularly rewarding – this busy country local has a comfortable bar and parlour-like lounge with fresh flowers. There are some handsome brass vases in front of the fireplace, amongst the mix of pub furnishings around it. There are plenty of tables in a front courtyard, with more on a back terrace. Bar food (under the new licensee) is listed on boards above the fireplace and might include soup (£2.65), filled baguettes (from £3), ploughman's (from £4), curry (£4.50), vegetable quiche (£4.75), sausage and egg (£4.95), steak (£9.50), and children's meals (from £2.85); Sunday lunch (£6.50); the restaurant has a no-smoking area. Well kept Bass, Stones Best and a couple of guests like Fullers London Pride and Greene King IPA on handpump, and half a dozen wines by the glass; darts, shove-ha'penny, cribbage and piped music. The village is so unspoilt they prefer you to leave your car in a free car park just outside, but if you don't fancy the lovely stroll there are a few spaces in front of the pub itself. *(Recommended by L Granville, Derek Harvey-Piper, Ian Phillips, Ian Jones, Steve Goodchild)*

Barr ~ Tenant Bernard Jenkyn ~ Real ale ~ Meals and snacks (all day) ~ Restaurant ~ (01306) 730775 ~ Children welcome ~ Open 11-11; 12-10.30 Sun

GOMSHALL TQ0847 Map 3

Compasses

Station Road (A25)

Though it's beside a main road, this has a pretty garden, with picnic-sets under cocktail parasols on a neat lawn sloping down to the mill stream that runs along beside the road, below three big weeping willows. Inside, the main focus is on the neat no-smoking dining area, which takes up most of the space, with primrose yellow tablecloths toning with the soft yellow patterned wallpaper and dark grey carpet. Good value generous well presented food includes sandwiches (from £2.45), filled french sticks (from £3.25), ploughman's (from £3.95), home-made crab cakes with sweet and sour dip (£6.45), grilled local trout fillets with honey and almond, steak and kidney pie or chicken and mushroom pie (£6.95) and sirloin steak (£9). The carpeted bar is relatively plain, with some farm tools on the high ceiling, simple pub furniture and some architectural drawings of historic sailing ships. Well kept Flowers IPA, Gibbs Mew Bishops Tipple, Marstons Pedigree and Theakstons XB on handpump from a modern servery, good value house wines; pleasant efficient service; dominoes, cribbage. Take care to park in the pub's spaces – other tempting places nearby risk clamping. *(Recommended by Andrew Worby, Tony Scott, R B Crail, Anna and Martyn Carey, D Mather)*

Enterprise Inns ~ Lease: Nicky Tullet ~ Real ale ~ Meals and snacks (all day) ~ Restaurant ~ (01483) 202506 ~ Children welcome ~ Live blues Fri ~ Open 11-11; 12-10.30 Sun ~ Bedrooms: /£45B

HASCOMBE TQ0039 Map 3

White Horse

B2130 S of Godalming

Tucked away in a pretty village among lovely rolling wooded country lanes on the Greensand way this attractive old rose-draped inn has simple but characterful rooms with a bustling, friendly atmosphere. The cosy inner beamed area has a woodburning stove and quiet small-windowed alcoves that look out onto the garden; there's also a conservatory with light bentwood chairs and peach coloured decor. Generous helpings of good, quickly served bar food include sandwiches (from £2.75), good proper ploughman's (from £4.25), steak burgers (£6) and fish pie (£7.95); best to get there early for a table at lunchtime, especially at weekends. Quick cheerful service. Well kept Badger Best, Marstons Pedigree and Youngs on handpump; quite a few wines. Darts, shove-ha'penny, dominoes, and fruit machine. There are quite a few tables on the spacious sloping back lawn, with more on a little terrace by the front porch. The village is pretty, and the National Trust's Winkworth Arboretum, with its walks among beautiful trees and shrubs, is nearby. *(Recommended by Mick Hitchman, LM, John Evans, Michael Sargent, Gordon Stevenson, Lady M H Moir, Chris and Kate Lyons, Mr and Mrs D Ross, Ian Phillips)*

Allied Domecq ~ Lease: Susan Barnett ~ Real ale ~ Meals and snacks (till 10(9.30 Sun)) ~ Restaurant ~ (01483) 208258 ~ Children in eating area of bar ~ Open 11-3, 5.30-11; 11-11 Sat; 12-10.30 Sun; cl 25 Dec, 26 Dec evening

LEIGH TQ2246 Map 3

Plough

3 miles S of A25 Dorking—Reigate, signposted from Betchworth (which itself is signposted off the main road); also signposted from South Park area of Reigate; on village green

Attractively set overlooking the village green, this pretty tiled and weatherboarded cottage is handy for Gatwick airport, and popular at lunchtime for its nicely presented bar food: sandwiches (from £2.15), soup (£2.50), fried breaded goat's cheese with cranberry sauce (£3.95), ploughman's (£4.25), prawn cocktail (£4.50), lasagne or vegetable lasagne (£5.75), 8oz sirloin (£10.25), daily specials like turkey curry (£5.50) and smoked haddock in cheese and egg sauce (£6.25), and puddings (£2.95). Well kept King & Barnes Bitter, Broadwood, Festive and seasonal ales on handpump, most kept under light blanket pressure, and a decent wine list (all bottles are available by the glass as well). On the right is a very low beamed cosy white walled and timbered dining lounge and on the left, the simple, more local pubby bar with a good bow-window seat and an extensive choice of games that takes in darts, shove-ha'penny, dominoes, table skittles, cribbage, trivia, a fruit machine and video game, Jenga, backgammon, chess and Scrabble; piped music. There are picnic-sets under cocktail parasols in a pretty side garden, fairy lights in the evening, and pretty hanging baskets. Parking nearby is limited. *(Recommended by David and Carole Chapman, Terry Buckland, DWAJ, D and J Tapper, Derek Harvey-Piper, Chris and Shirley Machin, David Peakall, Mike and Heather Watson, C P Scott-Dalden, G W Stephenson)*

King & Barnes ~ Tenant Sarah Bloomfield ~ Meals and snacks (till 10pm; all day Sun) ~ Restaurant ~ (01306) 611348 ~ Children in restaurant only ~ Open 11-11; 12-10.30 Sun

MICKLEHAM TQ1753 Map 3

King William IV

Byttom Hill; short but narrow steep track up hill just off A24 Leatherhead—Dorking by partly green-painted restaurant – public car park down here is best place to park; OS Sheet 187 map reference 173538

Surrey Dining Pub of the Year

Cut into a steep hillside, this friendly bustling pub has panoramic views down from the snug plank-panelled front bar. The more spacious back bar is quite brightly lit with kitchen-type chairs around its cast-iron-framed tables, log fires, fresh flowers on all the tables, and a serviceable grandfather clock. The lovely terraced back garden is neatly filled with sweet peas, climbing roses and honeysuckle and plenty of tables (some in an open-sided wooden shelter); a path leads straight up through woods where it's nice to walk after lunch – quite a few walkers do come here. Bar food might include ploughman's (from £4.25), filled baked potatoes (from £4.50), mushroom and aubergine bake or pasta and prawns in a tomato, mushroom and pepper sauce (£6.95), steak, kidney and mushroom pie or good seafood pie (£7.25), roast duckling with orange sauce (£8.25), roast rack of lamb with minted herb crust (£8.25), hot tandoori chicken (£8.95), and puddings like orange meringue pie, white and dark chocolate mousse or apple, sultana and pecan pie; the choice is more limited on Sundays and bank holidays. Well kept Adnams, Badger Best, Hogs Back TEA, Hop Garden Gold and a guest on handpump; quick and friendly service. Dominoes, and light piped music; no children after 1 April 1999. *(Recommended by B and M Parkin, Martin and Karen Wake, Anthony Hughes, LM, Barry and Marie Males, Kevin Flack, Brian and Jenny Seller, R T and J C Moggridge, Mr and Mrs G Turner, Lady M H Moir, Alan Griffiths, Gwen and Peter Andrews, Mrs D W Cook, James Nunns, Mr and Mrs B Hobden, Derek Harvey-Piper, Ian Jones, Simon Penny)*

Free house ~ Licensees C D and J E Grist ~ Real ale ~ Meals and snacks (not Mon evening) ~ (01372) 372590 ~ Open 11-3, 6-11; 12-3, 7-10.30 Sun; closed 25 Dec and 31 Jan

PIRBRIGHT SU9455 Map 2

Royal Oak

Aldershot Rd; A324 S of village

Now running their own cask-ale club, this lovely old cottage has up to nine changing real ales on handpump, serves over 100 beers a year and holds regular festivals. There might be well kept Boddingtons, Crown Buckley Merlins Oak, Flowers IPA and Original, Gales Hampshire Glory, Youngs Bitter and Special, Whitbread Fuggles and Wychwood Owzat on handpump; they also have around 15 wines by the glass and bottle. This year a bar extension has been added which overlooks the back garden and is joined on to the existing dining area. A rambling series of snug side alcoves has heavy beams and timbers, ancient stripped brickwork, and gleaming brasses set around the three real fires, and furnishings include wheelback chairs, tapestried wall seats, and little dark church-like pews around the trim tables; one area is no smoking. No noisy games machines or piped music. Bar food includes soup (£1.95), pâté (£2.75), ploughman's (£4.95), breaded plaice (£4.95), liver, ale and onions in a large yorkshire pudding (£5.35), steak and ale pie (£5.95), butterfly chicken breast coated in lemon and ginger sauce (£6.45), salmon with creamy butter and tarragon sauce (£6.95), sirloin steak (£8.95), and specials like chicken and filo parcels with plum sauce (£3.95) and thai pork curry (£5.95), and puddings like apple pie or chocolate fudge cake (£2.35). Children may be allowed to sit at limited tables in the dining area to eat with their parents. The front gardens are very colourful and look particularly attractive on fine evenings when the fairy lights are switched on. The big back garden leads down to a stream, and is less affected by noise from passing traffic; there may be barbecues and spit-roasts out here in summer. Good walks lead off in all directions, and the licensees are usually happy to let walkers leave their cars in the car park – if they ask first. *(Recommended by KC, P A Legon, George Atkinson, Guy Consterdine, Wayne Brindle)*

Whitbreads ~ Manager John Lay ~ Real ale ~ Meals and snacks (all day Sat and Sun) ~ (01483) 232466 ~ Children in no-smoking area, only if eating ~ Open 11-11; 12-10.30 Sun

REIGATE HEATH TQ2349 Map 3

Skimmington Castle

3 miles from M25 junction 8: through Reigate take A25 Dorking (West), then on edge of Reigate turn left past Black Horse into Flanchford Road; after ¼ mile turn left into Bonny's Road (unmade, very bumpy track); after crossing golf course fork right up hill

Minor renovations and a bit of tidying over the last year have not detracted from the individuality of this quaint old country local. The bright main front bar leads off a small central serving counter with dark simple panelling. There's a miscellany of chairs and tables, shiny brown vertical panelling, a brown plank ceiling, and well kept Flowers Original, Greene King IPA, Youngs Special and either Bass, Marstons Pedigree or Wadworths 6X on handpump, as well as lots of wines by the glass and cask conditioned cider. The cosy back rooms are partly panelled too, with old-fashioned settles and windsor chairs; one has a big brick fireplace with its bread-oven still beside it – the chimney is said to have been used as a highywayman's look-out. A small room down steps at the back has shove-ha'penny, cribbage, dominoes, board games and trivia; piped music. Popular bar food (you do need to arrive early for a table) includes brie and bacon sandwiches (£3.10), steak, ale and mushroom pie, fresh haddock, minted lamb cutlets, broccoli bake or thai chicken curry (£6.50). There are nice views from the crazy-paved front terrace and tables on the grass by lilac bushes, with more tables at the back overlooking the meadows and the hillocks. There's a hitching rail outside for horses, and the pub is handy for ramblers on the North Downs. *(Recommended by Ian Phillips, Paul and Pam Penrose, J L Torond, Rob Burnside, DWAJ, James Nunns; more reports on the new regime, please)*

Pubmaster ~ Licensee Tony Pugh ~ Real ale ~ Meals and snacks ~ (01737) 243100 ~ Children in cellar bar ~ Folk music second Sun of month ~ Open 11-3, 5.30(6 Sat)-11; 12-10.30 Sun; 12-4 7-10.30 winter Sun

SOUTH GODSTONE TQ3648 Map 3

Fox & Hounds

Tilburstow Hill Rd; just outside village, turn off A22 into Harts Lane, pub is at the end; handy for M25 junction 6

Very well run by a cheerful landlord and his chef wife, this pretty old-fashioned inn is in a pleasant spot on Tilburstow Ridge. It's bigger than its dark furniture, low beams and raised levels make it seem, with lots of little nooks and crannies to sit in. The cosy low-beamed bar has some fine antique high-backed settles amongst more modern ones, cushioned wall-benches and a window seat around the few low tables, racing prints on the walls, prettily arranged dried hops, and a big kettle on the woodburning stove; there are a couple more seats and tables around the tiny bar counter, up a step and beyond some standing timbers. Popular imaginative lunchtime bar food (although not cheap) might include sandwiches (from £4), soup (£4), spinach and tomato pasta (£4.50), ploughman's (£5.50), liver and bacon or pork, chorizo, black pudding and butterbeans (£5.75), fillet steak on garlic bread (£6), scampi (£7). You can reserve tables in the restaurant, which is the only part of the pub where food (more elaborate and not cheap) is served, some evenings only. Well kept Greene King IPA and Abbot on handpump, and a very extensive wine list; piped classical music. There are view from a good few picnic-sets out in the garden. *(Recommended by Maggie and Derek Washington, J Sheldon, Paul and Pam Penrose, Dick Brown, Jenny and Brian Seller, Mayur Shah, Margaret and Nigel Dennis)*

Greene King ~ Tenants David and Lorraine McKie ~ Real ale ~ Lunchtime bar meals and snacks ~ Restaurant ~ (01342) 893474 ~ Children welcome lunchtimes only ~ Open 11-3, 6-11; 12-3, 7-10.30 Sun

SUTTON TQ1046 Map 3

Volunteer

Water Lane, off Raikes Lane – just off and visible from B2126 1⅓ miles S of its junction with A25 at Abinger Hammer

Well modernised without losing its character, this has three low-ceilinged linked traditional rooms dating from the 17th c, with antique military prints, Wills cycling cigarette cards, big rugs on bare boards (red tiles by the servery and the entrance), shiny low ceilings, and a mix of furniture from typical pub tables and chairs to a pew and a biggish gateleg table. Good varied food might include french bread filled with brie and crispy bacon (£3.95), ploughman's or filled baked potatoes (from £4.25), chilli or cottage pie (£5.95), steak, ale and mushroom pie or fresh grilled cod (£7.25), cajun chicken (£7.95) and delicious puddings; no-smoking area. Badger IPA, Best, Tanglefoot and a seasonal beer kept under light blanket pressure, decent wines, courteous and obliging licensees and friendly staff, small coal fire, well chosen and reproduced piped music. It's a lovely quiet setting, good for walkers, with picnic-sets under cocktail parasols in front by the bright hanging baskets and window boxes of petunias, and more rustic tables and benches on suntrap grassy terraces spreading up behind among shrubs and hedges. Beyond is a paddock overrun with rabbits. The pub can get crowded at weekends. *(Recommended by R B Crail, Liz and Ian Phillips, Jenny and Brian Seller, B Lake, J S M Sheldon, Mr and Mrs C Fraser, Norman and Angela Harries)*

Hall & Woodhouse ~ Manager ~ Real ale ~ Meals and snacks (all day summer Sat/Sun) ~ Restaurant ~ (01306) 730798 ~ Children welcome away from bar ~ Open 11-3, 6-11; 11-11 summer Sat; 12-10.30 summer Sun ~ Bedrooms: £20/£35

THURSLEY SU9039 Map 2

Three Horseshoes

First registered as a beer house in 1841, this rather civilised tile-hung partly 16th-c, Georgian and Victorian cottage is run by hard-working and friendly licensees. The neatly kept dark, cosy beamed bar has log fires, fine old country furniture, including lovingly polished elm tables, and some Brockbank cartoons (he lived here). Well kept Gales Butser and HSB on handpump and served in lined glasses; maybe piped classical music. Good quickly served home-made bar food includes sandwiches (from £3.50; toasties £4; ploughman's or rare roast beef baguette (£5), salmon gratin or crab-filled mushrooms (£5.25), chicken and ham bake (£6.25) and beef madras or boeuf bourguignon (£7.95); part of the restaurant is no smoking. There are plenty of tables in the two acres of attractive garden, and pleasant views over the green. The village church is worth a visit. *(Recommended by R B Crail, J W G Nunns, Mr and Mrs C Simons, Martin and Karen Wake, David Peakall)*

Free house ~ Licensees Ann and Steve Denman ~ Real ale ~ Meals and snacks (not Sun or Mon evenings) ~ (01252) 703268 ~ Children over 5 in restaurant lunchtime only ~ Open 12-3, 6-11; 12-4, 7-10.30 Sun; closed Sun evening Sept-April

WALLISWOOD TQ1138 Map 3

Scarlett Arms

Village signposted from Ewhurst—Rowhook back road; or follow Oakwoodhill signpost from A29 S of Ockley, then follow Walliswood signpost into Walliswood Green Road

It's worth visiting this unspoilt little red-tiled country pub for the charmingly straightforwad way its carefully preserved original small-roomed layout takes you back in time. Its three neatly kept communicating rooms have low black oak beams, deeply polished flagstones, simple but perfectly comfortable benches, high bar stools with backrests, trestle tables, country prints, and two roaring winter log fires. Well kept King & Barnes Sussex, Broadwood, Festive and Mild on handpump. Darts, bar billiards, cribbage, shove-ha'penny, table skittles, dominoes and a fruit machine in a small room at the end. Usual bar food includes sandwiches (from £2.50), ploughman's (£3.95), mushroom stroganoff (£4.95), cod, trout or plaice (from £5.25), lasagne (£5.25), curries, steak and kidney pie or chicken and ham pie (£5.75), a daily roast

(£5.95), chicken and prawn salad (£6.25), steaks (from £7.95), half a shoulder of lamb (£10.50), and puddings (from £2.50). There are old-fashioned seats and tables with umbrellas in the pretty well tended garden. No children. *(Recommended by Maggie and Derek Washington, Colin Draper, Mike and Heather Watson, Alan and Brenda Williams, DWAJ, Derek Harvey-Piper, J S M Sheldon)*

King & Barnes ~ Tenant Jess Mannino ~ Real ale ~ Meals ~ (01306) 627243 ~ Open 11-2.30, 5.30-11; 12-3, 7-10.30 Sun; cl 25 Dec evening

WARLINGHAM TQ3658 Map 3

White Lion

B269

With a good pubby atmosphere, this unspoilt old pub is based on two 15th-c cottages, and has at its heart a fine Tudor fireplace enclosed by high-backed settles and a warren of friendly dark-panelled rooms with nooks and crannies, wood-block floors, very low beams, and deeply aged plasterwork. A side room decorated with amusing early 19th-c cartoons has darts, cribbage, trivia and fruit machine. Simple but good bar food is served in the bigger brighter no-smoking room at the end of the building, from a range including filled baked potatoes (from £3.25), curries (£4.50) and steak or roast (£4.95); quick service. Well kept (and well priced) Bass, Fullers London Pride, Hancocks HB, and guests like Gales Anniversary or Morlands Old Speckled Hen on handpump. Piped music in the eating area. The well kept back lawn, with its rockery, is surrounded by a herbaceous border; there may be outside service here in summer. *(Recommended by Christopher Wright, Kevin Flack, Anna and Martyn Carey, D and J Tapper, A Kilpatrick, Ian Phillips, Paul Hilditch)*

Bass ~ Manager Charlie Evans ~ Real ale ~ Meals and snacks (not Sun evening) ~ (01883) 624106 ~ Children in eating area of bar until 8pm ~ Open 11-11; 12-10.30 Sun

WOTTON TQ1247 Map 3

Wotton Hatch

A25 Dorking—Guildford; coming from Dorking, start slowing as soon as you see the Wotton village sign – the pub's round the first bend

There's a very friendly smiling welcome at this carefully run 17-c family dining pub. Its low-ceilinged rooms have cushioned wheelback chairs and rugs on timber, slate or carpeted floors, and to one side a handsome cocktail bar has medieval-style seats ranked around its panelled walls under a high frieze of plates; gentle piped classical or older style music. Bar food changes once a month and might typically include leek and potato or asparagus and mushroom soup (£2), pork and prune terrine (£2.95), sandwiches (from £3.65), ploughman's (£4) and beef pie (£5.95). The evening menu is more extensive and might include pork loin with stilton sauce (£6.75), chicken breast with cheese and bacon and cheese sauce or rump steak (£6.95) and baked fish and gooseberry salad (£7.50), as well as afternoon cream teas (£3). Well kept Bass and Fullers London Pride and a guest like Hancocks HB on handpump, and about ten wines by the glass; more than half the pub is no smoking. There are impressive views from the neatly kept garden; children's play area; no dogs. *(Recommended by Dick Brown, Neale and Sandra Dewar, Anna and Martyn Carey, Mrs W D Morrison)*

Bass ~ Manager Phil Conisbee ~ Real ale ~ Meals and snacks (12-10(9 Sun)) ~ Restaurant ~ (01306) 732931 ~ Children welcome away from bar ~ Occasional jazz in summer ~ Open 11-11; 12-10.30 Sun

Post Office address codings confusingly give the impression that some pubs are in Surrey when they're really in Hampshire or London (which is where we list them). And there's further confusion from the way the Post Office still talks about Middlesex – which disappeared in 1974 local government reorganisation.

Lucky Dip

Besides the fully inspected pubs, you might like to try these Lucky Dips recommended to us and described by readers (if you do, please send us reports):

☆ **Abinger Common** [Abinger signed off A25 W of Dorking – then right to Abinger Hammer; TQ1145], *Abinger Hatch*: Beautifully placed pub just taken over by the licensees who have previously done so well at the Stephan Langton over at Friday Street; several real ales, promising food, character bar with heavy beams, flagstones, basic furnishings, log fires; lovely setting nr pretty church and duck pond in clearing of rolling woods, with tables in nice garden *(Susan and John Douglas, LYM)*

☆ **Albury** [off A248 SE of Guildford; TQ0547], *Drummond Arms*: Comfortable and civilised panelled alcovey bar, conservatory (children allowed here) overlooking pretty streamside back garden with fountain and covered terrace; popular with older people lunchtime for food from sandwiches to steaks, well kept Courage Best and Directors, King & Barnes Broadwood, Festive and Sussex, and Youngs; piped music; bedrooms, attractive village, pleasant walks nearby *(P J Keen, John Pettit, Ian S Morley, Martin and Karen Wake, John and Lynn Busenbark, Wendy Arnold, LYM)*

☆ **Albury Heath** [Little London, off A25 Guildford—Dorking – OS Sheet 187 map ref 065468; TQ0646], *William IV*: Bustling take-us-as-you-find-us country pub in good walking area, old-fashioned character low-beamed flagstoned bar with big log fire, simple cafe-style dining area, close-packed tables in upstairs restaurant; home-made food from sandwiches up, monthly seafood nights and spitroasts, well kept ales such as Boddingtons, Fullers London Pride, Greene King Abbot, Wadworths 6X and local Hogs Back; shove-ha'penny and cards, children welcome, attractive front garden with long wall seat *(Jenny and Brian Seller, Don Mather, Ian S Morley, LYM)*

Bagshot [56 High St; SU9163], *Three Mariners*: Practical layout with pool and machines in side wing, Courage and Theakstons Best, useful food; piped pop music; small pleasant terrace *(Ian Phillips)*

Banstead [High St, off A217; TQ2559], *Woolpack*: Busy open-plan dining pub with very cheap food, well kept Scottish Courage ales with a guest such as Shepherd Neame Bishops Finger, good no-smoking area; open all day *(Don Mather)*

☆ **Bletchingley** [Little Common Lane; 3 miles from M25 junction 6, off A25 on Redhill side of village; TQ3250], *William IV*: Quaint old tucked-away country pub, prettily tile-hung and weatherboarded, with lots of bric-a-brac, comfortable little back dining room, wide choice of good food inc vegetarian, well kept ales inc Fullers London Pride, Harveys Best, Pilgrims Progress and Youngs Special, decent wines, good atmosphere, helpful staff; seats in nice garden with summer w/e barbecues *(Bruce Bird, James and Lynne House, Jane and Richard Doe, LYM)*

☆ **Bletchingley** [Outwood Lane], *Prince Albert*: Good sensibly priced food esp fish in attractive extended pub, several nooks and corners, well kept beer, smallish restaurant, welcoming attentive service; tables on terrace and in small pretty garden *(Sheila and John French, W A F Ruxton, Philip Cooper)*

☆ **Bramley** [High St (A281 S of Guildford); TQ0044], *Jolly Farmer*: Cheerful and lively, very popular for wide choice of good generous freshly prepared food, Theakstons Old Peculier and Pilgrim Talisman served by sparkler, welcoming service, two log fires, beer mat and banknote collections, big restaurant; bedrooms *(DWAJ, LYM)*

☆ **Brockham** [Brockham Green; TQ1949], *Royal Oak*: Attractively refurbished with comfortable lounge/dining area, bare boards and log fire on other side, good range of well kept beers such as Adnams, Gales HSB, Harveys, Morlands Old Speckled Hen and Wadworths 6X (Aug beer festival), reasonably priced interesting food inc good value sandwiches, local pictures for sale; good garden with play area, nice spot on green nr River Mole, below N Downs; children and dogs welcome, open all day *(Jenny and Brian Seller, James Nunns, David and Carole Chapman, Tony Scott)*

Brook [A286 N of Haslemere; SU9337], *Dog & Pheasant*: Busy low-beamed roadside pub in attractive spot opp cricket green nr Witley Common, quick friendly service, good range of well kept ales, good choice of reasonably priced food, shove-ha'penny, walking-stick collection; children welcome, small pretty garden *(Andrew W Lee, Derek and Margaret Underwood, Mike and Sue Todd)*

Burrowhill [B383 N of Chobham; SU9763], *Four Horseshoes*: Friendly and well run cottagey pub on village green, varied good value food all day in bar and expanded restaurant section, Scottish Courage ales, good service, snug bar for families; lots of picnic-sets (some under ancient yew), pleasant outlook *(Ian Phillips, Mr and Mrs B W Twiddy)*

Byfleet [155 High Rd; Old Byfleet; TQ0661], *Blue Anchor*: Refurbished pub worth knowing for wide choice of very reasonably priced straightforward food all day, lunchtime bargains *(W Marshall)*

☆ **Charleshill** [signed off B3001 Milford—Farnham nr Tilford; SU8944], *Donkey*: Old-fashioned beamed cottage pub in same family for three generations, simple reasonably priced home-made food (not Sun evening) from sandwiches up, well kept Morlands IPA and Old Speckled Hen with a guest such as Charles Wells Bombardier, country wines, traditional games, maybe quiet piped music; children allowed in no-smoking conservatory, attractive garden with play area, good walks *(Tony and Wendy Hobden, J Sheldon, Derek Harvey-Piper, David Shillitoe, LYM)*

Charlton [Charlton Rd; Ashford Common; off

B376 Laleham—Shepperton; TQ0869], *Harrow*: Comfortable newly rethatched 17th-c pub, lovely cultivated peaceful atmosphere despite fairly plain decor, short choice of generous interesting no-frills food (tables can be booked), good friendly service even when crowded, well kept Fullers London Pride and Morlands Old Speckled Hen *(Mayur Shah)*

Charlwood [Charlwood Rd; TQ2441], *Greyhound*: Greene King pub with good value food, crab net and bric-a-brac hanging from ceiling, sensible prices; open all day *(Tony Scott)*

Chertsey [Bridge Rd; TQ0566], *Boathouse*: Roomy and comfortable family chain pub, good Thames-side spot, efficient friendly staff, reasonably priced food, Theakstons, Wadworths 6X and changing beers such as Ringwood; bedrooms *(Ian Phillips, Sue and Mike Todd)*; [London St (B375)], *Crown*: Friendly and relaxed Youngs pub with button-back banquettes in attractively renovated high-ceilinged bar, well kept ales, separate food servery on right, good service; neatly placed darts, discreet fruit machines; garden bar with conservatory, tables in courtyard and garden with pond; children welcome; smart 30-bedroom annexe *(Ian Phillips)*; [Ruxbury Rd, St Anns Hill (nr Lyne); TQ0267], *Golden Grove*: Busy local with low beams, lots of stripped wood, cheap straightforward home-made food from sandwiches up (not Sat-Mon evenings) in pine-tabled eating area, well kept Adnams and Tetleys-related ales, cheerful service, coal-effect gas fire; piped music, fruit and games machines; big garden with friendly dogs and goat, play area, wooded pond *(Ian Phillips)*

☆ **Chiddingfold** [A283; SU9635], *Crown*: Picturesque old inn in attractive surroundings, worth a visit for its fine carving, massive beams, big inglenook log fire, tapestried panelled restaurant, simpler side bar, mulled wine, ales such as Badger Tanglefoot and Wadworths 6X, tables out on verandah; children allowed, has been open all day; good bedrooms *(A Hepburn, S Jenner, Martin and Karen Wake, M Kershaw, Simon Penny, LYM)*

Chiddingfold [Petworth Rd (A283 S)], *Rams Nest*: Comfortably traditional 18th-c inn, one fire by bar and eating area, another in cosy reading area with easy chairs, books and magazines; lots of antique furnishings, well rounded choice of well presented food, friendly service; children allowed in restaurant, tables on verandah, garden with adventure play area; bedrooms in separate block *(R K Nathan, W G Matters)*; [Petworth Rd], *Winterton Arms*: Four changing real ales, good food, big garden with tables and awnings; disabled access *(David and Brenda Tew)*

Chilworth [Dorking Rd; TQ0247], *Percy Arms*: Smart, clean and well run Greene King pub, roomy and well lit; their real ales, food inc good ploughman's, generous baguettes, pies and vegetarian, friendly young staff; piped music, smaller public bar; pretty views over vale of Chilworth to St Marthas Hill from big pleasant back conservatory and picnic-sets in tidy garden, pleasant walks *(Mark Percy, Lesley Mayoh, Gordon Prince, LM)*

☆ **Chipstead** [3 miles from M25, junction 8; A217 towards Banstead, right at second roundabout; TQ2757], *Well House*: Cottagey and comfortable partly 14th-c pub with lots of atmosphere, good straightforward lunchtime food (not Sun) from sandwiches up, welcoming staff, log fires in all three rooms, well kept Fullers ales; dogs allowed; attractive garden with well reputed to be mentioned in Doomsday Book (Tannoy calls you in when your food is ready), delightful setting *(Ian Phillips, W Ruxton, LYM)*

☆ **Chipstead** [Outwood Lane (B2032)], *Ramblers Rest*: Picturesque collection of partly 14th-c buildings, extensive range of different drinking areas with different atmospheres, panelling, flagstones and low beams, wide range of well kept mainly Whitbreads-related ales, good generous well presented freshly made food worth waiting for, family restaurant; big pleasant garden behind, decent walks nearby; piped music; open all day inc Sun, no dogs *(Marianne and Lionel Kreeger, Tony Scott)*

Chipstead [Hazelwood Lane], *White Hart*: Open-plan bar with cheap well presented food from sandwiches up, real ale such as Bass, Fullers London Pride and Greene King IPA, cheery staff; pleasant walled garden, maybe summer bouncy castle *(Ian Phillips)*

☆ **Cobham** [Plough Lane, towards Downside; TQ1059], *Plough*: Cheerful black-shuttered local with comfortably modernised low-beamed lounge bar, well kept Scottish Courage ales, helpful staff, pine-panelled snug with darts, lunchtime food from sandwiches up inc plenty of cold snacks and a few hot dishes (with French leanings); seats outside *(Gordon Prince, LYM)*

☆ **Compton** [B3000; SU9546], *Harrow*: This nice pub has priced itself out of our main entries now, but remains enjoyable for food (from sandwiches and filled baked potatoes up), drink and atmosphere, with well kept Greene King IPA and Abbot and Harveys Best; children welcome, open all day, cl Sun evening; bedrooms *(Derek Harvey-Piper, Lady M H Moir, Ian Phillips, J S M Sheldon, LYM)*

☆ **Cox Green** [Baynards Station Yard; Baynards Lane (W off B2128 just N of Rudgwick); TQ0734], *Thurlow Arms*: Tucked-away converted railway building with lots of railway and military memorabilia on walls and ceiling, well kept own-brew and Badger ales, good value food in extensive dining area, public bar with pool, darts and juke box, pleasant Danish barman, tables outside; former railway outside now Downs Link Path – busy summer weekends, when cyclists may turn up by the score; simple bedrooms available by prior arrangement *(A Hepburn, S Jenner, Peter Bourdon, Mike Fitzgerald)*

☆ **East Clandon** [just off A246 Guildford—Leatherhead; TQ0651], *Queens Head*: Small rambling connecting rooms, big inglenook log fire, fine old elm bar counter, bookcases, pictures, copperware; wide choice of good sensibly priced food inc lots of fish, friendly service, well kept ales, decent wines, no lunchtime piped music; children welcome, tables in quiet garden, handy for two NT properties *(John Evans, Hilarie Taylor, J Sheldon, Mrs T Bizat, KC, LYM)*

☆ **Effingham** [Orestan Lane (A246 Leatherhead—Guildford); TQ1253], *Plough*: Characteristic commuter-belt Youngs local with consistently well kept ales, honest home cooking (fresh veg and potatoes may be extra) inc enjoyable Sun lunch, two coal-effect gas fires, beamery, panelling, old plates and brassware in long lounge, no-smoking extension; popular with older people – no dogs, children or sleeveless T-shirts inside, no music or machines, attractive garden with play area; convenient for Polesdon Lacey (NT) *(John Pettit, J Sheldon, G W Stevenson, Alan and Brenda Williams, Annie and Will Dennis)*

Egham [38 High St; TQ0171], *Crown*: Busy simply furnished local with good reasonably priced promptly served basic food, half a dozen changing ales such as Adnams, Fullers and Gales, coal fires, restful walled back garden with noisy aviary and pretty pond *(Ian Phillips)*

Englefield Green [Northcroft Rd; SU9970], *Barley Mow*: Recently refurbished pub overlooking cricket green, reasonably priced food, back dining area with no-smoking section, Scottish Courage ales with a guest such as Marstons Pedigree, darts; pleasant garden *(A Hepburn, S Jenner)*; [Wick Lane, Bishopgate], *Sun*: Unpretentious welcoming local, well kept Courage Best, Greene King Abbot and Tetleys, decent wines, good choice of food inc lots of sandwiches and good Sun lunch, reasonable prices, daily papers, roaring log fire, biscuit and water for dogs; back conservatory, pleasant garden with aviary, handy for Savile Garden and Windsor Park *(Ian Phillips, Simon Collett-Jones, John Robertson)*

Epsom [Pikes Hill; TQ2160], *Barley Mow*: Friendly and attractive Fullers local, deceptively big, with well kept ales, decent food, conservatory and garden – very busy on warm summer evenings *(D P and J A Sweeney)*; [St Margaret Dr], *Haywain*: Recently opened Brewers Fayre, very family-friendly, with reasonably priced tasty food, nice outside play area *(R C Vincent)*; [opp race-course], *Tattenham Corner*: Big Beefeater worth knowing for food all day inc summer barbecues, garden with play fort; does get busy, esp on race days *(R C Vincent, J Sheldon)*

☆ **Esher** [West End La; off A244 towards Hersham, by Princess Alice Hospice; TQ1464], *Prince of Wales*: Victorian Chef & Brewer extended and smartly refurbished in attractive period style, cosy corners, open fires, turkish carpets, old furniture, prints and photographs, candlelight; massive choice of generous reasonably priced food, at least four well kept Scottish Courage ales, good wine choice, quick friendly staff, daily papers, family area; big garden, nr green and pond *(R B Crail, Susan and John Douglas)*

Esher [71 High St], *Bear*: Two landmark life-size bears behind roof parapet of much renovated Youngs pub with their full range kept well, bar food from cauliflower cheese to fillet steak *(Ian Phillips)*; [Alma Rd/Chestnut Ave; Weston Green; TQ1566], *Marneys*: Good varied food in friendly village atmosphere, family dining area, quick service, Scottish Courage ales, decent wines; very small – can get crowded; tables outside, charming spot overlooking duck pond by golf course *(Margaret Parker, John Crafts, Gordon Stevenson)*

Ewell [Kingston Rd; TQ2262], *Queen Adelaide*: Refurbished mainly as carvery restaurant, decent straightforward food in smallish bar, welcoming service; bedrooms in adjacent newly completed lodge *(DWAJ)*

Farnham [SU8544], *Duke of Cambridge*: Recently refurbished as free house, with good beer choice; bedrooms *(Iain Robertson)*; [Tilford Rd, Lower Bourne], *Spotted Cow*: Welcoming rural local with wide choice of consistently appetising home-made food inc lots of fish, well kept Adnams, Courage and Hogs Back TEA, decent wine, attentive friendly service, reasonable prices; play area in big garden *(Mrs J A Blanks, Ruth Gardner)*

☆ **Fickleshole** [Featherbed Lane; off A2022 Purley Rd just S of A212 roundabout; TQ3860], *White Bear*: Rambling interestingly furnished partly 15th-c family country pub with lots of small rooms, well kept Fullers London Pride and a guest beer, limited bar food such as burgers and good sandwiches, restaurant, fruit machine, video game, piped music; children welcome, jazz Weds, open all day Sat; play area in sizeable garden *(Jenny and Brian Seller, LYM)*

☆ **Forest Green** [nr B2126/B2127 junction; TQ1240], *Parrot*: Quaint rambling country pub, pleasant and comfortable, with pervasive parrot motif, well kept Courage Directors, Fullers London Pride, Hogs Back TEA, John Smiths and Wadworths 6X, good often interesting food (many tables reserved, giving it something of a restaurant feel in the evening), end locals' bar with open fire, pool and interesting bric-a-brac, good cheerful service even when crowded; children welcome, open all day; plenty of space outside by cricket pitch, good walks nearby *(James Nunns, Mike and Sue Todd, LYM)*

Frimley Green [SU8856], *Kings Head*: Bass Tavern with good value food, well kept beers, friendly service *(R B Crail)*; [205 Frimley Green Rd], *Old Wheatsheaf*: Good busy lunchtime pub with attractively priced generous food then, hard-working landlord, friendly staff, well kept Morlands ales and a guest such as Marstons Pedigree, good malt whiskies *(R B Crail)*

Godstone [handy for M25 junction 6; TQ3551], *White Hart*: Pleasant Beefeater with proper bar, abundant ancient beams, two enormous log fires, friendly service, well prepared food; pleasant views across green with pond *(Ian Phillips, Mrs G Sharman, LYM)*

Grayswood [A286 NE of Haslemere; SU9234], *Wheatsheaf*: Much modernised pub useful for consistently good food inc interesting dishes, amiable attentive landlord; restaurant; conference/bedroom extension *(Mrs J A Blanks)*

Great Bookham [Lower Rd; parallel to A246; TQ1354], *Anchor*: Quaint 19th-c pub, lots of character, good friendly atmosphere, Courage Best and Directors, Wadworths 6X and a guest beer from big central bar, good pub food, seats on small front terrace *(Ian Morley)*

Guildford [Shalford Rd, Millbrook; across car park from Yvonne Arnaud Theatre, beyond boat yard; SU9949], *Jolly Farmer*: Decent food all day from upstairs counter in big two-level pub by River Wey, extensive terrace and moorings, lots of picnic-sets, pleasant conservatory, Flowers and Marstons Pedigree, friendly young staff; some live music summer *(Tony Scott, David and Carole Chapman)*; [Old Portsmouth Rd], *Olde Ship*: Unusual layout around central bar, very old back part, log fires and candles, well kept Morlands, good range of fairly priced food inc good pizzas, decent wines, obliging service; no music *(Ian Phillips, P A Legon)*; [58 Epsom Rd], *Sanford Arms*: Unspoilt traditional pub with good simple food from sandwiches and ploughman's to cottage pie, ham and eggs and so forth (lunchtime, not Mon – fry-ups Sun); spotless, with very nice staff, no music *(Peter Lewis)*; [Millmead], *White House*: Refurbished riverside pub with well kept Fullers, pretty setting, pleasant helpful staff, hot and cold food, small upstairs no-smoking bar; for over-25s *(Tony Scott)*

Hambledon [Hambledon Rd, off A283 – OS Sheet 186 map ref 967391; SU9639], *Merry Harriers*: Homely country local with lovely inglenook log fire, dark wood and red decor, dark pine bar, pine tables, impressive collection of chamber-pots hanging from beams, well kept Tetleys-related ales with guests such as King & Barnes and Youngs Dirty Digger, reasonably priced freshly made food from sandwiches up, pool room; big back garden, picnic-sets in front and over road – caravan parking *(Martin and Karen Wake)*

Holmbury St Mary [TQ1144], *Kings Head*: 70s-feel pub awaiting redecoration in popular walking country, useful for well kept Ringwood Best and Fortyniner, local farm cider, bar food; pretty spot on village green, informal sloping back garden; pool, SkyTV, can be smoky *(B Lake)*

Horley [Brighton Rd, handy for M23 junction 9; TQ2842], *Air Balloon*: Big Steak pub with exceptionally speedy friendly service even when busy, good value food, good adjoining children's indoor play barn, small outdoor play area; handy for Gatwick *(R C Vincent, George Atkinson)*; [Church Rd], *Olde Six Bells*: Interesting building – part of heavy-beamed open-plan bar was probably a medieval chapel, and some masonry may date from 9th c; local atmosphere, reasonably priced food, Bass ales and a guest such as Fullers London Pride, upstairs raftered dining room, conservatory, tables out by bend in River Mole; open all day weekdays *(Tony Scott, Ian Phillips, LYM)*

Horsell [Horsell Birch; SU9859], *Cricketers*: Plenty of seats in clean bar and eating area, carpet and shiny boards, good choice of good food inc vegetarian, several real ales, children well catered for; big well kept garden, and seats out in front overlooking overgrown village green *(Gill and Keith Croxton)*

☆ **Irons Bottom** [Sidlow Bridge, off A217; TQ2546], *Three Horseshoes*: Friendly unassuming country local, food prepared with interest and care, menu reflecting landlord's time overseas; excellently kept Fullers London Pride and interesting guest ales, quiz or darts night Tues, summer barbecues *(Don Mather, Derek and Maggie Washington)*

Kingswood [Waterhouse Lane; TQ2455], *Kingswood Arms*: Big and busy, with wide variety of reasonably priced popular food, cheerful quick service (announcements when orders are ready), Scottish Courage ales, conservatory dining extension; spacious rolling garden with play area *(TOH, Mrs G Sharman)*

☆ **Laleham** [B376, off A308 W of M3 junction 1; TQ0568], *Three Horseshoes*: Popular and plushly modernised, but dating from 13th c, with flagstones, heavy beams, interesting history, lots of tables in enjoyable garden, and easy stroll to Thamesside lawns; generous usual bar food, well kept ales inc Fullers London Pride, decent wines, efficient service, piped music, restaurant; children in no-smoking conservatory, open all day *(Ian Phillips, D P and J A Sweeney, Derek Harvey-Piper, Ian Phillips, LYM)*

Laleham [The Broadway], *Feathers*: Friendly old cottage, roomy inside, with bar in single-storey front extension, traditional decor, lots of hanging pewter mugs, well kept ales such as Courage Best, Fullers London Pride, Highgate Foxs Nob and Morlands Old Speckled Hen, reasonably priced generous home-made food in beamed back dining area with evening roaring log fire; maybe piped music; small terrace and garden *(Ian Phillips, T I M Cusk)*

Leatherhead [5 North St; TQ1656], *Penny Black*: Busy Whitbreads Hogshead in converted post office, big partitioned beamed bar, framed stamp collections on brick walls, bare boards, lots of tables and chairs, solid fuel stove, wide choice of Whitbreads and guest ales, straightforward reasonably priced cheerfully served bar food; some seats outside, live entertainment some evenings *(J S M Sheldon, John Pettit)*; *Running Horse*: Small bar with about six real ales such as Ansells and Ind Coope Burton, usual food reasonably priced, no-smoking eating area *(Tony Hobden)*

☆ **Leigh** [S of A25 Dorking—Reigate; TQ2246], *Seven Stars*: Pretty country local, brightly refurbished with pine furniture in airy and spacious flagstoned bar, wide choice of good food from filled baguettes up (may be a longish wait), Youngs ales, woodburner in inglenook; flower-filled garden, maybe summer Sun barbecues *(John H L Davis, Mr and Mrs N B Dyson, John and Shirley Dyson, Eddie Edwards, LYM)*

Limpsfield Chart [TQ4251], *Carpenters Arms*: Tidy much modernised pub in delightful setting by village common, lovely walks, easy reach of Chartwell; good varied menu inc vegetarian, well kept Morlands Old Speckled Hen, very efficient friendly service *(R T and J C Moggridge, A Kilpatrick)*

Lower Kingswood [Brighton Rd; A217, 1½ miles from M25 junction 8; TQ2453], *Fox on the Hill*: Spacious refurbished bar, popular lunchtime for well presented straightforward good value food; friendly attentive staff; bedrooms *(D WAJ, Mrs G Sharman)*

Lyne [Lyne Lane; TQ0166], *Royal Marine*: Small, friendly and cosy free house, neat as a new pin, unpretentious well presented reasonably priced home-made food, real ales, most attractive small garden *(Ian Phillips)*

☆ **Mickleham** [Old London Rd, off A24 S of Leatherhead; TQ1753], *Running Horses*: Refurbished 16th-c beamed village pub well placed nr Box Hill, well kept Tetleys-related ales, cheerful service even when packed with impatient walkers, two lovely open fires, comfortable and attractive dining extension/conservatory; nice view from pretty courtyard garden *(Gordon Stevenson, R Worthing, G S and E M Dorey)*

☆ **Newdigate** [Parkgate Rd; village off A24 S of Dorking; TQ2042], *Surrey Oaks*: Interesting layout, rustic lantern-lit booth seating off flagstoned beamed core with big log fire, friendly atmosphere, good food inc interesting dishes and quality fresh ingredients, Youngs and several guest beers; piped music but no mobile phones; good big garden with thatched awning, rockery and water feature *(D and J Tapper, LYM)*

Newdigate, *Six Bells*: Good atmosphere in popular local with good range of well kept ales, enjoyable food, friendly service, a welcome for children; plenty of tables in pleasant garden, lovely outlook over church *(David and Helen Wilkins)*

Normandy [Guildford Rd E (A323); SU9351], *Duke of Normandy*: Well run Greene King pub with their ales inc seasonal brews, sensibly priced food quickly served by friendly staff, several malt whiskies *(R B Crail)*

☆ **Ockley** [Stane St (A29); TQ1439], *Cricketers Arms*: Pretty 15th-c stonebuilt village local with Horsham slab roof, flagstones, low beams, inglenook log fires, shiny pine furniture, good simple generous bar food inc good value Sun roast, well kept ales such as Fullers London Pride and Ringwood Best, country wines, friendly staff, quiet piped music, darts area, small attractive dining room with cricketing memorabilia; seats in delightful back garden with duck pond and play area *(Tony Scott, David and Carole Chapman, LYM)*

Ockley, *Old School House*: Fine school house attractively converted to popular and enjoyable dining pub, good value generous from sandwiches up inc vegetarian and fresh pasta and fish, polite service, well kept King & Barnes, good wines, wonderful log fire *(TOH, Tony and Wendy Hobden, Tony Scott, A Humphreys)*

Ottershaw [222 Brox Rd (off A320 N of Woking); TQ0263], *Castle*: Comfortable and friendly local, lots of farm tools etc, stripped brick and beamery, log fire; home-cooked food popular for business lunches (no-smoking dining area), well kept changing ales such as Adnams, Fullers London Pride, Greene King Abbot, Tetleys, Wadworths 6X and Youngs Special, Addlestone's cider; garden with tables in pleasant creeper-hung arbour *(Ian Phillips, JWGN)*

☆ **Outwood** [Prince of Wales Rd; turn off A23 at Station sign in Salfords S of Redhill – OS Sheet 187 map ref 312460; TQ3146], *Dog & Duck*: Rambling beamed country cottage with good relaxed atmosphere, settles, oak armchairs and more ordinary seats, stripped dark beams, rugs on quarry tiles, daily papers, Badger Best, IPA, Tanglefoot and Gribble Reg's Tipple under light CO^2 blanket, food all day from sandwiches up inc children's, pub games, unobtrusive piped music; open all day, children in eating area, picnic-sets outside with play area and country views *(M Owton, Andy and Jill Kassube, G Simpson, Paul and Pam Penrose, Tony Scott, Mayur Shah, LYM)*

☆ **Outwood** [Outwood Common, just E of village; TQ3245], *Bell*: Attractive extended 17th-c country dining pub, olde-worlde beamed bar and sparser restaurant area, good choice of well kept ales such as Youngs Dirty Duck, quick friendly service, log fires; children and dogs welcome, summer cream teas, has been open all day; pretty fairy-lit garden with country views, handy for windmill *(K and E Leist, Margaret and Nigel Dennis, Jenny and Brian Seller, Tony Scott, LYM)*

Oxshott [Leatherhead Rd (A244); TQ1460], *Bear*: Busy yet relaxed Youngs pub with well kept beer, big conservatory dining room, friendly courteous staff, usual pub food with fresh veg, good log fire, teddy bear collection, occasional barbecues in small garden *(James and Lynne House, J Sheldon)*

☆ **Oxted** [52 High St, Old Oxted; off A25 not far from M25 junction 6; TQ3852], *George*: Neat and tidy, with chatty atmosphere, attractive prints, pleasant restaurant area, generous food all day from sandwiches to steaks, well kept Badger Best and Tanglefoot and guest beers, decent wines and coffee, friendly helpful staff, welcoming fire; children welcome over 10 *(Michael and Hazel Duncombe, Dick Brown, D and J Tapper, Joan and Andrew Life, R T and J C Moggridge, LYM)*

Oxted [69 Tanhouse Rd, Broadham Green – off High St opp Old Bell], *Haycutter*: Huge garden, very friendly welcome, good straightforward food, well kept ales such as Marstons Pedigree *(James and Lynne House)*

Peaslake [off A25 S of Gomshall; TQ0845], *Hurtwood*: Small prewar country hotel in fine spot for walkers (no muddy boots inside, though), worth knowing for well kept ales inc local Hogs Back, also good malt whiskies; bar food, sizeable restaurant *(R B Crail, BB)*
Puttenham [Seale Lane; SU9347], *Good Intent*: Friendly and atmospheric country local, good range of attractively presented reasonably priced food, constantly changing range of ales, Inch's farm cider, roaring log fire; dogs allowed, no children *(G W Stevenson, Gordon Prince)*
Pyrford Lock [Lock Lane; 3 miles from M25 junction 10 – S on A3, then take Wisley slip rd and go on past RHS Garden; TQ0458], *Anchor*: Busy modern pub included for its position by bridge and locks on River Wey Navigation; big terrace, canteenish conservatory, picture-window bar, upstairs room with narrow-boat memorabilia; popular lunchtime with families and older people for usual food inc vegetarian and children's (may be queues and Tannoy announcements), Scottish Courage ales, juke box, sports TV, machines etc; open all day in summer *(D P and J A Sweeney, Derek Harvey-Piper, LYM)*
Redhill [44 Hatchlands Rd; A25 towards Reigate; TQ2650], *Hatch*: U-shaped Edwardian bar with blue decor, mirrors and lamps, pictures, fire, eight real ales, some rare, fine range of lagers and bottled beers, country wines, adjoining restaurant *(Tony Scott, David and Carole Chapman)*; [11 Church Rd, St Johns; TQ2749], *Plough*: Friendly old-world pub said to date from 13th c, neat and compact, with low beams, waggon wheels, brass and bric-a-brac, small lamps, flame-effect fires, little snug for two, well kept Tetleys-related and guest ales, good home-made blackboard food inc vegetarian, friendly efficient staff; back garden with terrace *(Tony Scott, David and Carole Chapman)*
Reigate [99 Reigate Hill Rd, ½ mile from M25; TQ2550], *Yew Tree*: Comfortable panelled pub, decent straightforward food, well kept Scottish Courage ales *(Tony Scott)*
Ripley [High St; TQ0556], *Ship*: Welcoming and comfortable 16th-c two-bar local with low beams, flagstones, cosy nooks, log fire in vast inglenook; well kept Courage Best and Wadworths 6X, sensible food from sandwiches up, small raised games area with bar billiards, window seats and stools rather than chairs; small high-walled terrace *(Dr and Mrs B D Smith, Martin and Karen Wake)*; [High St], *Talbot*: Pleasant service, well kept ales such as Adnams and Friary Meux, bar food from generous baguettes up, restaurant; piped music; bedrooms *(James Nunns, Tony and Wendy Hobden)*
Runfold [off A31 just NE of Farnham; SU8747], *Jolly Farmer*: Popular bar food, well kept sensibly priced Ushers ales, pleasant garden with good adventure playground – nice retreat from trunk rd; children in restaurant, no dogs *(Iain Robertson, LYM)*; *Princess Royal*: Good value straightforward food, very busy with families Sun lunchtime *(Iain Robertson)*
Sendmarsh [Marsh Rd – OS Sheet 186 map ref 045555; TQ0455], *Saddlers Arms*: Friendly low-beamed local very popular with older people lunchtime for good value straightforward food from sandwiches up inc vegetarian and Sun lunch; welcoming licensees and dog, well kept Tetleys-related ales with a guest such as Wadworths 6X, no-smoking area, toby jugs, brassware etc, quiet piped music, machines in separate bar; tables outside *(D W A J, S Mackenzie, Ian Phillips)*
☆ **Shepperton** [Shepperton Lock, Ferry Lane, off B375; TQ0867], *Thames Court*: Huge recently rebuilt pub well placed by Thames, galleried central atrium with separate attractive panelled areas up and down stairs, two good log fires, enjoyable generous food from snacks upwards all day, well kept Bass and Fullers London Pride, daily papers, friendly staff; children welcome, attractive riverside tree-shaded terrace with big gas radiant heaters *(Mayur Shah, Margaret and Nigel Dennis, Ian Phillips, R B Crail)*
☆ **Shepperton** [Russell Rd], *Red Lion*: Roomy, quiet and welcoming old wisteria-covered two-bar local across rd from Thames, plenty of tables on terrace among fine displays of shrubs and flowers, more on lawn over road (traffic noise) with lovely river views and well run moorings; wide choice of food in bars and restaurant, well kept Scottish Courage ales with guests such as Fullers London Pride, quick service, interesting prints, red-cushioned seating, restaurant *(D P and J A Sweeney, Mayur Shah)*
☆ **Shere** [signed off A25 3 miles E of Guildford; TQ0747], *White Horse*: Striking half-timbered medieval Chef & Brewer with uneven floors, massive beams, Tudor stonework, oak wall seats, two log fires, one in a huge inglenook; efficiently served food, King & Barnes and Theakstons; tables outside, children in eating area, open all day Sun – beautiful village *(Ian Phillips, Mrs G Sharman, Nigel Roper, Hazel and Michael Duncombe, LYM)*
☆ **Staines** [The Hythe; S bank, over Staines Bridge; TQ0471], *Swan*: The star is for the splendid Thamesside setting, with moorings, tables on riverside verandah, big back conservatory; good choice of food, cheerful service, well kept Fullers ales, two pleasantly refurbished bars and dining area, soft piped music; can be very busy Sun lunchtime and summer evenings; comfortable bedrooms *(Simon Collett-Jones, Ian Phillips)*
Staines [124 Church St], *Bells*: Now a Youngs pub, with well kept Bitter, Special and Winter Warmer, good prompt food from sandwiches up, friendly staff, cosy traditional furnishings and central fireplace, darts, cribbage, fruit machine, quiet juke box; plenty of seats in big garden *(Ian Phillips)*; [14 Church St], *Hobgoblin*: Former Clarence, now a Wychwood pub with their good attractively priced beers; bare boards, some atmosphere, food inc vast doorstep sandwiches, games end

with pool, loudish music *(Ian Phillips)*; [Leacroft], *Old Red Lion*: Vibrantly friendly and happy, crowded lunchtime with all ages; good value food, quick service, real ales inc Fullers London Pride, seats out on terrace opp small green *(Ian Phillips)*

☆ **Sunbury** [64 Thames St; TQ1068], *Magpie*: Lovely spot, with river views from upper bar and small terrace by boat club, good food from ploughman's up, well kept Bass, Boddingtons and Gibbs Mew Bitter and Bishops Tipple, decent wines, efficient antipodean service; bedrooms *(Martin and Karen Wake, Ian Phillips, James Nunns, D P and J A Sweeney)*

Tadworth [Dorking Rd (B2032); TQ2354], *Blue Anchor*: Busy, warm and homely, with cheerful helpful staff, varied good value generous food, well kept Bass, Fullers London Pride and Worthington, decent wine, log fires; piped music may obtrude *(Mrs G Sharman, TOH)*

Tadworth [Box Hill Rd; TQ2256], *Hand in Hand*: Roomy pub currently doing well, with good food inc Sun lunch in extended dining area, friendly service, well kept Courage; handy for Box Hill *(Mrs E I Barty)*

Tandridge [Tandridge Lane, off A25 W of Oxted; TQ3750], *Barley Mow*: Pretty whitewashed pub with window boxes and shutters, spacious refurbished bar, pleasant restaurant area, helpful welcoming staff, fairly priced home-made food, Badger ales tapped from the cask, log fires; no music or machines, big garden; interesting church nearby, good walks to Oxted or Godstone; well equipped small bedrooms, good breakfast *(Derek and Maggie Washington, Margaret and Nigel Dennis, Mike Pugh, Paul and Pam Penrose)*; [Tandridge Lane], *Brickmakers Arms*: Good friendly atmosphere in popular and pretty country dining pub, dating from 15th c but much extended and modernised, with good range of freshly made food inc their own smoked dishes and lots of fish, well kept Whitbreads-related ales, decent wines inc local ones, restaurant with good log fires, prompt friendly service *(R and S Bentley, C C S Reeves, WR)*

Tatsfield [Westmore Green; TQ4156], *Old Ship*: Big bar with lots of interesting pictures and bric-a-brac, well kept Bass, Greene King IPA and Worthington, prompt courteous service, kitchen refurbished for new chef/patron – enjoyable mix of pubby and restaurant food, small restaurant with log fire; pretty setting on green opp duck pond, with play area in big garden and good value holiday barbecue meals *(PP, Carol Bulled, Jenny and Brian Seller)*

Thames Ditton [Hampton Court Way; Weston Green; TQ1566], *Greyhound*: Food-oriented Wayside Inn, with good range of Whitbreads-related and guest ales, very popular Sun lunch, helpful staff, pleasant atmosphere, big pine tables in airy rooms; very busy after Twickenham internationals *(Christopher Wright)*; [Western Green], *Marneys Pond*: 18th c, overlooking village duck pond – lots of duck memorabilia inside, and beams, dried flowers, old fireplaces, wooden furniture; wide choice of blackboard food, good range of wines, well kept Wadworths 6X, side garden, some tables overlooking green *(Martin and Karen Wake)*

Thorpe [Sandhills Ln, Thorpe Green; TQ0268], *Rose & Crown*: Rebuilt and enlarged as Chef & Brewer with good changing home-made food, good atmosphere, real ales such as Courage Best and Directors, Morlands Old Speckled Hen and Theakstons XB, good choice of wines by the glass, piped classical music; can get crowded; good outdoor children's area *(Tom and Ruth Rees, Ian Phillips, RBC, Nigel and Sue Foster)*

☆ **Tilford** [The Green, off B3001 SE of Farnham; SU8743], *Barley Mow*: Good food esp vegetarian, well kept Scottish Courage ales, good log fire in big inglenook, comfortable traditional seats around scrubbed tables, interesting prints; small back eating area, weekend afternoon teas; darts, table skittles, no children; pretty setting between river and geese-cropped cricket green nr ancient oak, with waterside garden – village does get busy in summer though *(G and M Stewart, Martin and Karen Wake, Margaret and Nigel Parker)*

Tilford Common [former Duke of Cambridge; SU8742], *Hankley*: Former Duke of Cambridge extensively refurbished for American-theme family dining – spare ribs, cajun dishes, even catfish; pleasant terrace with country views *(Martin and Karen Wake, G and M Stewart)*

Virginia Water [Callow Hill; SU9969], *Rose & Olive Branch*: Small friendly Morlands pub with guest beer such as Charles Wells Bombardier, good if not always cheap home-made food inc unusual dishes (busy Fri night, best to book then), decent wines, welcoming helpful service, matchbox collection, quiet piped music; children allowed lunchtime, attractive garden *(John Athersuch, John Ince, Nina Randall, Ian Phillips, Nigel and Sue Foster)*

Walton on Thames [Station Approach; TQ1066], *Ashley Park*: Friary Meux, Ind Coope Burton and Tetleys, good range of reasonably priced food; popular with younger people; bedrooms *(R B Crail)*; [113 Manor Rd], *Old Manor House*: Friendly lively atmosphere in small old character local by medieval manor house nr Thames, good landlord *(Christine and Geoff Butler)*

☆ **Walton on the Hill** [Walton St], *Fox & Hounds*: Decent food esp puddings in chatty bar and pleasant adjoining restaurant (must book), well kept Bass, Fullers London Pride and two other ales, brisk service, nice surroundings; open all day Sun *(J S M Sheldon, Justin Hulford, LYM)*

☆ **Warlingham** [Limpsfield Rd; TQ3857], *Botley Hill Farmhouse*: Converted 16th-c farmhouse, more restaurant than pub, but attractively presented fresh bar food too; good food inc lots of fish and seafood, delicious puddings, modern presentation, well kept if not cheap ales such as Greene King IPA and Abbot,

Pilgrims and Shepherd Neame Spitfire, good house wines, open fire, friendly polite service; children welcome, with attractions for them, cream teas, wonderful North Downs views, good walking country; very busy weekends, with entertainments *(Mrs J Blanks, G Simpson, Carol Bulled)*

☆ **West Clandon** [The Street (A247 SE of Woking); TQ0452], *Onslow Arms*: Partly 17th-c rambling country pub, pricy but good and convivial; dark nooks and corners, heavy beams, flagstones, warm seats nr inglenook log fires, soft lighting, lots of brass and copper, efficient staff; eight well kept ales, decent wines, nicely presented sandwiches, carvery-style hot-lamp bar food servery (not Sun evening), partly no-smoking restaurant (popular Sun lunches), great well lit garden; children welcome, open all day *(Ronald Buckler, Susan and John Douglas, Mike and Heather Watson, Joy and Peter Heatherley, B Lake, B and M Parkin, LYM)*

☆ **West Clandon** [The Street], *Bulls Head*: Friendly and comfortably modernised 16th-c country local – retiring landlord's daughter and husband took over summer 1998, but no real changes; small lantern-lit front bar with open fire and some stripped brick, old local prints, raised rather canteenish back inglenook dining area very popular esp with older people lunchtime for good value enjoyable straightforward home-made food from sandwiches, ploughman's and baked potatoes to steak, efficient service, Courage Best and Marstons Pedigree, good coffee, no piped music, games room with darts and pool; lots of tables and good play area in garden, convenient for Clandon Park, good walking country *(DWAJ, Mr and Mrs D J Ross, R Lake, S Mackenzie)*

West Horsley [The Street, off A246 E of Guildford; TQ0753], *Barley Mow*: Modest village local with flagstones, beams, faded decor, extraordinary collection of pig ornaments, well kept ales such as Greene King, Ringwood and Youngs, decent wines and spirits, good value lunchtime food, comfortable little dining room, cheerful staff *(John Evans, R B Crail)*; [The Street], *King William IV*: Comfortable red plush banquettes in neatly secluded areas, very low beams, well kept Courage Best and Directors and Youngs Special, decent coffee, log fire, good disabled access, food inc children's; darts area, piped radio *(John Evans, Ian Phillips, J Sheldon, J E and L J Roth)*

Weybridge [Oatlands Chase; TQ0965], *Badgers Rest*: Former hotel well refurbished (with bare brick and very realistic beams) as warm and welcoming Bass Vintage Inn, already very popular with older people lunchtime for wide choice of good straightforward food from sandwiches up, Bass, Hancocks HB and Worthington, very helpful staff; pleasantly divided with tables for varying numbers, separate food counter, back area for smokers; tables on front lawn; immaculate bedrooms *(Ian Phillips, R B Crail, Minda Alexander)*; [Heath Rd/Waverley Rd], *British Volunteer*: Good pubby atmosphere, with good freshly cooked food (even the bangers and mash is interesting) inc good puddings in fresh tiled dining room, quick cheerful service, friendly landlady who knows her wines, well kept beer, good coffee; pool, small courtyard *(Minda Alexander)*; [Princes Rd], *Jolly Farmer*: Warm and cosy small local opp picturesque cricket ground, good interesting reasonably priced food esp sandwiches and snacks, well kept ales such as Courage Best, Fullers London Pride and three from Hop Back; lovely garden with terrace, marquee extension and barbecue *(Ian Phillips, Simon Penny)*; [Thames St], *Lincoln Arms*: Comfortable extended family pub with good inexpensive food from sandwiches up, real ales such as Greene King Abbot, Marstons Pedigree, Morlands Old Speckled Hen and Tetleys, friendly efficient staff; tables in pleasant front garden, water for dogs *(Ian Phillips, James Nunn)*; [83 Thames St], *Old Crown*: Friendly and well run old-fashioned three-bar pub, warm and comfortable, very popular lunchtime for reasonably priced generous straightforward food from sandwiches up esp fish (served evening too), freshly made so may be a wait; Scottish Courage ales and a guest such as Morlands Old Speckled Hen, no music or machines; children welcome, suntrap streamside garden *(DWAJ, R B Crail, J S M Sheldon)*

☆ **Windlesham** [Chertsey Rd (B386 E of Bagshot); SU9264], *Brickmakers Arms*: Popular well run dining pub with good interesting freshly made food esp ciabatta sandwiches and fish, not cheap but good value, cheerfully basic busy bar, well kept Scottish Courage and other ales, wide choice of wines inc interesting bin-ends, splendid service, daily papers; well behaved children allowed in restaurant, attractive garden with boules and barbecues, lovely hanging baskets *(Guy Consterdine, Malcolm Phillips, A Hepburn, S Jenner, Margaret and Nigel Dennis, Jerry Hughes)*

Windlesham [Church Rd], *Half Moon*: Big lively friendly local, good range of well kept ales inc Fullers London Pride, Wadworths 6X and many quickly changing guest beers, country wines, good value straightforward food inc good Sun family lunch, cheerful quick service, modern furnishings, log fires, piped music, silenced fruit machine, interesting WWII pictures; huge beautifully kept garden popular with families *(Dr M Owton, A Hepburn, S Jenner)*

Witley [Petworth Rd (A283); SU9439], *White Hart*: Tudor beams, good oak furniture, log fire in cosy panelled inglenook snug where George Eliot drank; well kept Shepherd Neame ales with a guest such as Marstons Pedigree, public bar with usual games, restaurant; piped music; seats outside, lots of pretty hanging baskets etc, play area *(James Nunns, LYM)*

Wood Street [White Hart Lane; SU9550], *White Hart*: Country local dating from 16th c, good food, helpful staff, good choice of well kept real ales inc five changing guests, big dining area *(Miss J Broadhead)*

Woodmansterne [Woodmansterne St; TQ2760], *Woodman*: Late 19th-c village pub, recently pleasantly enlarged, with good range of reasonably priced food in good dining area, Bass and Fullers London Pride, garden with play area *(Pam and Derek Higham)*

Worplesdon [Burdenshott Rd – heading N from Guildford on A320, turn left at Jacobs Well roundabout towards Worplesdon Stn; SU9854], *Jolly Farmer*: Beamed country pub dramatically refurbished and extended in 1997, with roomy and pleasant additional bare-brick dining area; enjoyable food esp fish, real ales; big sheltered garden *(Guy Consterdine, LYM)*

☆ **Wrecclesham** [Bat & Ball Lane; Boundstone – off Upper Bourne Lane, itself off Sandrock Hill Rd; SU8245], *Bat & Ball*: Cosy old pub with well kept Fullers, Youngs and local beers, good choice of food inc home-made baltis, pasta and generous sandwiches, Sun bar nibbles, polite welcoming service, good atmosphere; family extension, spacious terrace and gardens *(Iain Robertson, Andy and Jill Kassube)*

Wrecclesham [Sandrock Hill Rd], *Sandrock*: Up to eight well kept changing ales mostly from smaller breweries, often Midlands ones, in simply converted local with friendly knowledgeable staff; real fire, children welcome, games room and garden, no piped music, annual beer festival *(G C Hackemer, Andy and Jill Kassube, Iain Robertson)*

If you have to cancel a reservation for a bedroom or restaurant, please telephone or write to warn them. A small place – and its customers – will suffer if you don't. And recently people who failed to cancel have been taken to court for breach of contract.

Sussex

Sussex has more than its share of really nice unspoilt old pubs, carefully run by pains-taking licensees; there's plenty of good food, and a good choice of local beers led by Harveys and King & Barnes, with some interesting smaller breweries too. Pubs that currently stand out in our report files, with a particularly good postbag from readers, are the unchanging traditional Rose Cottage at Alciston (good food using organic vegetables, local fish and game), the foody but relaxed Bridge at Amberley and the friendly and chatty Sportsmans there (these are both new main entries this year – what is it about that small village that seems to sprout such good pubs?), the Fountain at Ashurst (taken over by two brothers who are making some useful changes), the charmingly unspoilt Murrell Arms at Barnham (filled with interesting knick-knacks during the licensee's long decades there – another new find for us), the timelessly old-fashioned Cricketers Arms at Berwick, the George & Dragon at Burpham (winning combination of good food and great location), the Black Horse at Byworth (another unspoilt pub, with a lovely garden), the friendly and bustling Six Bells at Chiddingly (very cheap food), the Old House at Home tucked away near Chichester Harbour at Chidham, the ancient George & Dragon near Coolham (good food, a lovely back garden – another new main entry), the cheerful good value White Harte in Cuckfield, the Elsted Inn at Elsted (super food, and bedrooms now), the very well run Griffin at Fletching (another place with excellent food – it's on something of a winning streak at the moment), the welcoming Queens Head at Icklesham (interesting decor, nice food and surroundings), the friendly and interesting old Two Sawyers at Pett (another new main entry – good beers from neighbouring microbrewery), the Peace & Plenty at Playden (a really nice dining pub), the Horse Guards at Tillington (very restauranty now, much enjoyed for its good imaginative food) and the Dorset Arms at Withyham (a proper pub, with proper home cooking). From among all these, and all the other Sussex pubs with strengths on the food side, we choose as Sussex Dining Pub of the Year the Griffin at Fletching. Two points of interest: the friendly Half Moon near the river at Kirdford has now taken its fish specialisation to the point of opening a fish shop nearby; and the eccentric – not to say hippy – Snowdrop in Lewes is becoming quite a favourite of readers with a taste for the unusual. Some pubs to pick out from the Lucky Dip section at the end of the chapter are the Old Vine at Cousley Wood, Crown & Anchor at Dell Quay, George at Frant, George & Dragon at Houghton, Cock at Ringmer, Best Beech near Wadhurst and Lamb at West Wittering; we have inspected and liked all these. The Cowdray Arms at Balcombe, not yet inspected, comes warmly recommended by trusted readers, and Brighton has a fine choice. Drinks prices here have at last begun to steady, but are still well above the national average. We found the Queens Head at Icklesham the cheapest for beer, followed by the Bull at Ticehurst (both of these stocking locally brewed beers) and the Golden Galleon at Seaford (brewing its own). In summer 1998 the small Sussex chain of Beards pubs was bought by Greene King of Suffolk. In general, Beards pubs have tended to be well above average, with a good deal of character and caring tenants. They include several main entries and quite a few of the Lucky Dip pubs at the end of the chapter. So we welcome Greene King's assurances that they will continue virtually unchanged.

ALCISTON TQ5005 Map 3

Rose Cottage

Village signposted off A27 Polegate—Lewes

Happily, little changes at this charming and very well liked country cottage. The house martins and swallows returned again to nest above the porch, seemingly unperturbed by the people going in and out beneath them, and what was a once-common Sussex tradition now lives on only at this pub, when every Good Friday lunchtime you can still see locals long-rope skipping to make the crops grow faster. The fresh fish still comes daily from a local fisherman at Eastbourne, eggs are from their own chickens, pheasants are shot by the landlord, and venison comes from the landlord's brother-in-law. Bar food remains quite a draw, the good daily specials might include cheesy topped mussels (£3.50; main course £6.25), very popular thai-style tiger prawns with a hot soy dip (£3.65; main course £6.25), rabbit and bacon or chicken and ham pies (£5.50), winter steak and kidney pudding (£5.95), chargrilled lamb cutlets with a honey and mint glaze, thai-style curries or barbecued spare ribs (£6.25), chicken in tomato and basil topped with mozzarella (£6.50), venison braised in port and Guinness (£7.95), and roast Sunday lunch (£6.95; the lamb marinated in red wine, rosemary and garlic is good); from the menu, there is home-made soup, lincolnshire sausages (£4.25), ploughman's (from £4.25), honey-roast ham with poached egg (£4.75), and steaks (from £9.50). Well kept Harveys Best and a monthly guest beer on handpump, decent wines including a 'country' of the month and six by the glass (or half litre), Merrydown and Biddenden ciders, and summer kir and pimms. Small and cosy, the relaxed and friendly bar soon fills up, so get there early for one of the half dozen tables with their cushioned pews – under quite a forest of harness, traps, a thatcher's blade and lots of other black ironware, with more bric-a-brac on the shelves above the stripped pine dado or in the etched glass windows. In the mornings you may also find Jasper, the talking parrot (it can get a little smoky for him in the evenings). There's a lunchtime overflow into the no-smoking restaurant area; log fires, dominoes, cribbage, and maybe piped classical music. There are some seats under cover outside, and a small paddock in the garden has ducks and chickens. *(Recommended by G Coates, Tim and Pam Moorey, Mrs M A Stevenson, Anthony Bowen, Glen and Nola Armstrong, Dave Carter, Timothy Galligan, Peter Meister, R J Walden, R and S Bentley, Colin Laffan, Mr and Mrs C Moncreiffe, Tony and Rachel Schendel, Mike and Heather Watson, P Rome, A Cowell, Wayne Brindle)*

Free house ~ Licensee Ian Lewis ~ Real ale ~ Meals and snacks (till 10pm) ~ Evening restaurant ~ (01323) 870377 ~ Children welcome – must be over 6 in evenings ~ Open 11.30-3, 6-11; 12-3, 7-10.30 Sun; closed 25/26 Dec ~ Self-catering flat

ALFRISTON TQ5103 Map 3

Star

The front of this smart old place is decorated with fine medieval carvings, and the striking red lion on the corner – known as Old Bill – was probably the figurehead from a wrecked Dutch ship. Inside, the front part is welcoming and full of atmosphere, and in the bustling heavy-beamed bar is a sanctuary post – holding it gave the full protection of the Church; in 1516 one man rode a stolen horse from Lydd in Kent to take advantage of the offer – and avoided the death penalty. Elegant furnishings include a heavy Stuart refectory table with a big bowl of flowers, antique windsor armchairs worn to a fine polish and a handsome longcase clock; the fireplace with its big log fire is Tudor. Some lounge areas are no smoking. Bar food includes soup (£2.50), sandwiches or filled baked potatoes (from £3), omelettes or yorkshire puddings with sausages and gravy (£5), grilled field mushrooms with bacon and red leicester (£6), and daily specials. Badger Tanglefoot and Bass on handpump. The comfortable bedrooms are in an up-to-date part at the back. *(Recommended by Janet and Colin Roe, Liz Bell, Paul and Sandra Embleton, Sue and Steve Griffiths, Ian Phillips)*

Free house ~ Managers James Leeming, Leo Morris ~ Real ale ~ Meals and snacks (snacks only Sun) ~ Restaurant ~ (01323) 870495 ~ Children in lounges ~ Open 11-11; 12-10.30 Sun; 11-2.30, 6-11 in winter ~ Bedrooms: £52B/£104B

AMBERLEY TQ0212 Map 3

Black Horse

Off B2139

This very pretty village pub has high-backed settles on the flagstones, beams over the serving counter festooned with sheep and cow bells, traps and shepherds' tools, and walls decorated with lots of old local prints and engravings; there are plenty of pictures too in the similar but more comfortable saloon bar; log fires at either end of the main bar and one in the lounge. Bar food (they tell us prices have not changed since last year) includes sandwiches (from £2.25), winter soup (£2.75), ploughman's, steak and kidney pie (£5.50), fresh fillet of plaice (£5.90), steaks (from £10), and daily specials; the restaurant is no smoking. Well kept Friary Meux and Ind Coope Burton with a guest beer on handpump; friendly, welcoming staff. Darts, cribbage, dominoes, fruit machine, trivia, and piped music; two big dogs and a sleepy cat. There are seats in the garden. The attractive village is close to the River Arun, with a castle, and the pub is handy for the South Downs Way and Amberley Industrial Museum.
(Recommended by Tim Barrow, Sue Demont, David and Carole Chapman, Neil Porter, John Beeken, Tony Scott, Mrs P M Jolins, N E Bushby, W Atkins)

Pubmaster ~ Tenant Chris Acterson ~ Real ale ~ Meals and snacks ~ Restaurant ~ (01798) 831700 ~ Children in eating area of bar and in restaurant ~ Open 11-3, 6-11; 12-3, 7-10.30 Sun

Bridge

B2139

Close to the old bridge and a pretty stretch of the meandering River Arun, this attractive old white-painted pub is popular for its good interesting food. The friendly and relaxed narrow bar has a couple of cushioned window seats and a mix of old wooden chairs by a few tables along one side, a group of brown velveteen bucket seats around a table at one end with a button-backed brown sofa beside them, candles in bottles creating a soft light, and a tiled bar gantry with fairy lights along it; a cosy small room with similar seats leads off the bar, and a delft shelf and beam with brass, copper, and lots of bottles leads to the attractively furnished two-roomed dining room; the walls throughout are covered with modern portrait art and impressionist-style paintings. Generous helpings of totally home-made changing bar food include starters like smoked salmon or salt beef open sandwiches, ploughman's, a huge bowl of good soup, prawn and papaya cocktail, and moules marinières (all £4), vegetarian dishes such as stuffed aubergine or tagliatelle (£6.25), chicken and stilton in filo pastry (£8.25), good steaks (from £9.50), around 8 fresh fish dishes such as sea bream, red snapper, fresh cod or salmon in various interesting sauces (£10.25), and puddings like marshmallow and meringue pie, steamed treacle pudding or summer fruit pudding (£2.50); a choice of 4 roast Sunday lunches (£7.50). Well kept Flowers Original, Gales Best, Harveys Best, King & Barnes Sussex, and Morlands Old Speckled Hen on handpump, and lots of cocktails; good, friendly service, and piped music. The summer hanging baskets are pretty and there are white plastic seats and tables in front of the pub, with more in a little side garden. Children are not allowed inside. *(Recommended by Mrs P Elkin, K and J Morris)*

Free house ~ Licensee Stephen Chandler ~ Real ale ~ Meals and snacks ~ (01798) 831619 ~ Open 11-3, 6-11; 12-3, 7-10.30 Sun

We say if we or readers have seen dogs or cats in a pub.

Sportsmans

Crossgates; Rackham Rd, off B2139

Panoramic views dropping away from tables on the decked terrace, little conservatory and bars at this unassuming village local lend a light and refreshing feel to the whole place. Its two friendly and chatty little lounge bars are simply decorated in a homely way with well used brocaded chairs on its light brown patterned carpet, and lots of little notices and pictures, and postcards from locals to the pub. As well as Miserable Old Bugger – brewed for the pub by Brewery on Sea, and named after a club that's based here – three well kept guests might be from Brewery on Sea, Fullers and Youngs. The brick floored public bar has a hexagonal pool table and darts, and the pretty little red-tiled conservatory is engagingly decorated with old local bric a brac. Home-made bar food includes sandwiches (from £2.25), local sausage in a french stick (£3.25), ploughman's (£3.60), scampi (£5.50), steak and kidney pie (£5.75), half roast chicken (£6.50), sirloin steak (£9.25), and daily specials like beef or vegetarian lasagne (£5.50), turkey and mushroom stroganoff or breaded devilled chicken breast (£5.75) and home-made puddings like bread and butter pudding, rich chocolate torte and toffee apple pancake (£2.50); possibly piped Irish folk music. (*Recommended by Mrs P Elkin, K and J Morris)*

Free house ~ Licensees Chris and Jenny Shanahan ~ Real ale ~ Meals and snacks ~ Children in conservatory and pool room ~ Open 11-2.30, 6-11; 12-3, 7.10.30 Sun; cl 25 Dec eve

ASHURST TQ1716 Map 3

Fountain

B2135 N of Steyning

Two brothers (who used to run the Gardeners Arms in Ardingly) have taken over this 16th-c country pub. They are moving the kitchens to the back and opening up that room (where they've discovered an inglenook fireplace) as a snug with flagstones, heavy beams, and simple furniture. The charmingly rustic tap room on the right has a couple of high-backed wooden cottage armchairs by the log fire in its brick inglenook, two antique polished trestle tables, fine old flagstones, and Courage Best, Harveys Best and John Smiths on handpump with changing guests like Flowers Original and Gales HSB tapped from the cask. A bigger carpeted room with its orginal beams and woodburning stove is where most of the good bar food is served. This now might include sandwiches (from £2.50), ploughman's (£4.75), smoked haddock and prawns in cheese sauce, home-made pies like steak, mushroom and ale or chicken and asparagus (£6.95), filo pastry parcel filled with broccoli, aubergine and roasted peppers (£7.50), fresh fish such as lemon sole, grilled marlin, baked salmon or tilapia (from £7.95), chicken breast in ginger and herbs (£8.50), winter game dishes such as rabbit casserole or pheasant braised in port and red wine (£8.50) or venison fillet with juniper berries and redcurrants (£8.95), steaks (from £10.50), and puddings like banana crêpes with toffee sauce, summer pudding or sticky toffee pudding (£2.95). Shove-ha'penny, cribbage, dominoes, and oak-beamed skittle alley. The garden is to have considerable work done on it, but includes seats by an attractive duckpond. No children. *(Recommended by Brian and Jenny Seller, Malcolm Taylor, Pat and Tony Martin; more reports on the new regime, please)*

Free house ~ Licensees Mark and Christopher White ~ Real ale ~ Meals and snacks (not Sun or Mon evenings) ~ (01403) 710219 ~ Open 11(11.30 Sat)-2.30, 6-11; 12-2.30, 7-10.30 Sun

BARCOMBE TQ4114 Map 3

Anchor

From village follow Newick, Piltdown sign, then turn right at Boast Lane leading to Anchor Lane, marked with a No Through Rd sign, then first left (by post box)

On a summer's day, this cheerful little pub is a very popular place to be. It's set by the River Ouse with neatly kept waterside lawns and a fairy-lit terrace with plenty of picnic-sets and white metal seats and tables, and you can hire boats on an unspoilt three-mile stretch of the river as it winds through the meadows (£3.20 an hour per adult, half price for children) – reckon on about two hours if you're going all the way to the fish ladder falls near Sutton Hall and back. A riverside kiosk serves cream teas and cold drinks, and there are barbecues most summer weekends. In winter the approach road can flood and cut the pub off – they leave out a boat or two then. Inside, there are two tiny bars decorated with a good few motor racing trophies won by the landlord's late father, along with some car models, and other racing and RAF memorabilia – meetings of the Jaguar Owners Club, Vintage Sports Car Club, and MG Club are held here. Bar food includes home-made soup (£2.60), sandwiches (from £2.25; filled french bread from £4.50), filled baked potatoes (from £3.95), ploughman's (from £4.75), creamy tomato and vegetable pasta (£4.95), home-baked ham and egg (£5.25), local pork sausages with onion gravy (£5.50), daily specials like smooth chicken liver pâté (£3.95), steak and kidney pudding (£6.50), poached halibut with citrus butter (£8.25), and sirloin steak with a wild mushroom and red wine sauce (£8.95), and puddings such as fresh fruit pavlova or spotted dick (£3.25). There's an intimate no-smoking candlelit restaurant. Well kept Badger Best and Tanglefoot, Harveys Best, and guest beers on handpump, and a decent wine list including some local English ones. Good friendly service; dominoes, shut the box, and Scrabble. The no-smoking family room has toys and children's videos. The pub has been run by the same family for over 35 years. *(Recommended by John Knighton, Bruce Bird, Anthony Byers, John Beeken, Jenny and Brian Seller, Comus Elliott)*

Free house ~ Licensees Graham and Jaci Bovet-White ~ Real ale ~ Meals and snacks (not 25 Dec; 12-3, 6-9.30) ~ Restaurant ~ (01273) 400414 ~ Children welcome away from bar ~ Open 10.30am -11pm; 12-10.30 Sun; 11-3, 6-11 in winter; closed 25 Dec, evening 1 Jan ~ Bedrooms: £32/£55

BARNHAM SU9604 Map 2

Murrell Arms

Yapton Rd; B2233

We were delighted to find this charming unspoilt pub, run by Mr and Mrs Cutten for 34 years. They believe in traditional pub values and have no piped music or noisy machines and serve no chips or 'rabbit food' salads. The two bar rooms are packed with mementoes collected by the licensees over the years: the saloon bar has some nice old farmhouse chairs, a very high-backed settle by the piano, and a mix of tables (including a fine circular Georgian one) on the partly turkey carpeted very old dark wood parquet floor, candles in bottles, hundreds of jugs, mugs, china plates and old bottles crammed along delft shelves, walls completely covered with little prints and pictures, agricultural artefacts hanging from the ceiling, an elderly grandfather clock, a collection of old soda syphons, and a huge polished half-barrel bar counter. To get to the cheerful public bar, you walk past the stillage room where the barrels of well kept Gales Bitter, Best, HSB, IPA and a changing guest are stored. A lively game of darts (they have keen men's and women's teams) was in progress at one end of the room on our evening visit, and a group of happy chatty youngsters were round a big table at the other; two open fires, lots of farming tools, old photographs and more pictures, an interesting Cox's change machine and Crystal Palace clock by the bar, and some old horsebrasses; a simple tiny snug over a half wall (the only place where really well behaved children are tolerated) has an enormous cartwheel on the ceiling; ring the bull. Straightforward bar food includes ploughman's (£1.50), local sausages, and a couple of changing daily specials such as suet bacon pudding or liver and bacon casserole (£2.95). From the car park you walk through a pretty flower-filled courtyard with a large cider press on one side, and fine ancient wooden benches and tables under a leafy grape vine on the other – note the huge bellows on the wall; there are picnic-sets on a cottagey little enclosed garden up some steps. *(Recommended by R T and J C Moggridge, John Donnelly, Tony Scott)*

Gales ~ Tenant Mervyn Cutten ~ Real ale ~ Meals and snacks ~ (01243) 553320 ~ Well behaved children in snug ~ Open 11-3, 6-11; 11-11 Sat; 12-10.30 Sun; closed evening 25 Dec

BERWICK TQ5105 Map 3

Cricketers Arms

Lower Rd, S of A27

With a peaceful and unhurried atmosphere, this delightful and unspoilt old flint cottage has unanimous appeal to readers. The three little similarly furnished rooms have simple benches against the half-panelled walls, a happy mix of old country tables and chairs, burgundy velvet curtains on poles, a few bar stools, and some country prints; quarry tiles on the floors (nice worn ones in the middle room), two log fires in little brick fireplaces, a huge black supporting beam in each of the low ochre ceilings, and (in the end room) some attractive cricketing pastels; helpful, friendly staff – even when really busy. Sound bar food includes home-made soup (£2.95), creamy garlic mushrooms (£3.95), ploughman's or filled baked potatoes (from £4.25), home-cooked honey ham and egg (£4.50), a vegetarian dish, fresh local cod in batter (£5.25), garlic and herb chicken quarter (£5.50), sirloin steak (£7.95), daily specials, and puddings like home-made fruit crumble (£2.75); they hold winter themed food evenings. Well kept Harveys Best, PA and seasonal ales tapped from the cask, and decent wine; darts, dominoes, cribbage, and an old Sussex game called toad in the hole. The old-fashioned garden is very pretty with mature flowering shrubs and plants, lots of picnic-sets in front of and behind the building, and little brick paths – idyllic on a sunny summer's day. The wall paintings in the nearby church done by the Bloomsbury group during WWII are worth a look. *(Recommended by Amanda Ariss, David and Carole Chapman, R D and S R Knight, Tony Scott, Anthony Bowen, Comus Elliott, Peter Meister, Lesley Sones, Rex Martyn, Stephen Harvey, A Cowell, John Beeken, Paul and Heather Bettesworth)*

Harveys ~ Tenant Peter Brown ~ Real ale ~ Meals and snacks ~ (01323) 870469 ~ Children in eating area of bar only ~ Open 11-3, 6-11; 11-11 summer Sat; 12-10.30 Sun

nr BILLINGSHURST TQ0830 Map 3

Blue Ship

The Haven; hamlet signposted off A29 just N of junction with A264, then follow signpost left towards Garlands and Okehurst

Tucked away down a country lane, this charmingly unpretentious pub has a cosy beamed and brick-floored front bar with a blazing fire in the inglenook fireplace and hatch service; a corridor leads to a couple of similar little rooms. Well kept King & Barnes Broadwood, Sussex and seasonal beers tapped from the cask. A games room has darts, bar billiards, shove-ha'penny, cribbage and dominoes. It can get crowded with a pleasant mix of customers, particularly at weekends; there may be a playful cat. Straightforward but enjoyable bar food includes sandwiches (from £2), winter soup (£2.75), ploughman's (from £3.80), macaroni cheese (£4.35), cottage pie (£4.55), and steak and kidney pie or scampi (£6.10). It's very nice in summer, when you can relax at the tree-shaded side tables or by the tangle of honeysuckle around the front door, and there's a play area for children. *(Recommended by David and Carole Chapman, Tony Scott, Dave Cupwell, Lady M H Moir, Guy Consterdine, Mr and Mrs C G Fraser)*

King & Barnes ~ Tenant J R Davie ~ Real ale ~ Meals and snacks (not Sun or Mon evenings) ~ (01403) 822709 ~ Children in two rooms without bar ~ Open 11-3, 6-11; closed evening 25 Dec

BLACKBOYS TQ5220 Map 3

Blackboys

B2192, S edge of village

As popular as ever, this bustling 14th-c weatherboarded house has antique prints and masses of bric-a-brac (including a collection of keys above the bar) in its string of old-fashioned and unpretentious little rooms, dark oak beams, bare boards or parquet, and a good inglenook log fire. Good waitress-served food includes home-made soup (£2.50), ploughman's (from £3.50), filled baked potatoes (from £3.75), home-smoked ham and egg (£4.95), vegetable curry (£5.50), nice seafood pancake, tagliatelle napolitana or steak and kidney pie (£5.95), entrecote steak (from £6.95), daily specials like mediterranean tartlets or home-cured salmon (£3.50) and lamb niçoise or fresh crab and prawn salad (£9.50), and puddings like treacle sponge or pot of chocolate and spiced rum mousse (£2.95); friendly, efficient staff even when busy. The restaurants are no smoking. Well kept Harveys Best, Pale Ale, Mild and seasonal brews on handpump; darts, dominoes, cribbage, fruit machine, video game, and juke box. Outside, there's masses of space, with rustic tables in the back orchard, some seats overlooking the pretty front pond, a play area with a challenging wooden castle and quite a few animals, and a barn with a big well equipped playroom; good Woodland Trust walks opposite the pub; handy for the Vanguard Way footpath. *(Recommended by Kevin Thorpe, Jenny and Brian Seller, John Beeken, Ros Barber, David Miles, Colin Laffan, Margaret and Nigel Dennis, Bruce Bird)*

Harveys ~ Tenant Nicola Russell ~ Real ale ~ Meals and snacks (till 10pm in summer; not Sun evening) ~ Restaurant ~ (01825) 890283 ~ Children in eating area of bar and in restaurant ~ Occasional Morris dancers and singers ~ Open 11-3, 6-11; 12-3, 7-11 Sun

BROWNBREAD STREET TQ6715 Map 3

Ash Tree

Village signposted off the old coach road between the Swan E of Dallington on B2096 Battle—Heathfield and the B2204 W of Battle, nr Ashburnham

This tranquil country local is hidden away down narrow country lanes in a charmingly isolated hamlet. The cosy beamed bars have nice old settles and chairs, stripped brickwork, two inglenook fireplaces, and evening candlelight. Good bar food includes sandwiches, home-made soup (£2.25), home-made smoked salmon mousse (£3.95), cottage pie (£4.25), liver and bacon (£5.95), chicken in tarragon and cream (£6.25), pheasant in wine and herbs (£7.95), steaks (from £9.90), fresh fish dishes, and Sunday roasts. They may do only full meals at some of their busiest times. Very well kept Harveys Best and a guest such as Fullers London Pride or Morlands Old Speckled Hen on handpump; cheerful, friendly service, and darts, pool, bar billiards, fruit machine, video game, juke box, and piped music in the simple games room on the left. There's a pretty garden with picnic-sets. *(Recommended by B and M Parkin, Ray Watson, Mike Fitzgerald, R J Walden, Mr and Mrs Jonathan Russell, D and J Tapper, Mr and Mrs R D Knight, Ken Frostick, D H and M C Watkinson)*

Free house ~ Licensees Malcolm and Jennifer Baker ~ Real ale ~ Meals and snacks (not Mon) ~ Restaurant ~ (01424) 892104 ~ Children in eating area of bar ~ Open 12-3, 7-11; 12-4, 7-10.30 Sun; closed Mon

BURPHAM TQ0308 Map 3

George & Dragon

Warningcamp turn off A27 a mile E of Arundel, then keep on up

This is a most attractive spot with plenty of surrounding walks – muddy boots to be left outside. The neatly kept and spacious open-plan bar has good strong wooden furnishings, lots of interesting prints, and a warm welcome from the friendly licensees. Bar food is very popular and good, and it's the daily specials that really stand out: excellent home-made soup, smoked haddock, egg and broccoli bake (£5.70), chicken in tarragon cream sauce (£5.80), turkey schnitzel (£5.95), lamb cutlets with a mint and redcurrant sauce (£6.95), whole trout with lemon and pine nut filling (£7.50), skate wing with capers (£8.95), and puddings like good chocolate orange terrine, sticky toffee pudding, white chocolate mousse or raspberry cheesecake (£3.50); tasty sandwiches. Many of the tables get booked up in advance, and service can slow down at peak times. Well kept Arundel ASB, Brewery on Sea Spinnaker Bitter, Cotleigh Tawny, Harveys Best, and Sharps Doom Bar on handpump; piped music. Plenty of pretty surrounding walks, and the nearby partly Norman church has some unusual decoration. *(Recommended by Alan Skull, Mrs P Goodwyn, Malcolm Taylor, Bruce Bird, Martin and Karen Wake, Comus Elliott, Tony Scott, Ian Phillips, Anna and Martyn Carey, Mrs Romey Heaton, Derek and Maggie Washington, Penny and Martin Fletcher, Tim and Pam*

Moorey, Mrs J A Powell, Tony and Wendy Hobden, R T and J C Moggridge, David Gould, David and Carole Chapman, Margaret and Nigel Dennis, Mark Matthewman, Jo and Gary Charlton, Bebba Smithers, Ian Jones, Pamela Goodwyn, Lawrence Pearse, B and M Kendall, J Reay)

Belchers Pubs ~ Tenants James Rose and Kate Holle ~ Real ale ~ Meals and snacks (not winter Sun evening) ~ Restaurant (not winter Sun) ~ (01903) 883131 ~ Well behaved children (preferably over 8) allowed in eating area of bar ~ Occasional jazz/cajun music ~ Open 11-2.30, 6-11; 12-3, 7-10.30 Sun; closed Sun evenings Oct-Easter; closed 25 Dec

BURWASH TQ6724 Map 3

Bell

A265 E of Heathfield

In summer, the hanging baskets and tubs in front of this friendly village pub are a marvellous sight; there are seats here that look across the busy road to the church. The relaxed L-shaped bar to the right of the main door has built-in pews and a mix of seats, all sorts of ironwork, bells and barometers on its ochre Anaglypta ceiling and dark terracotta walls, and a good winter log fire. Well kept Arundel ASB and Footslogger, Batemans XB, Cains Springbok Ale, Harveys Best, and Wadworths Easter Ale on handpump, a range of malt whiskies, and some new world wines. Darts, bar billiards, shove-ha'penny, ring the bull and toad in the hole, table skittles, cribbage, dominoes, trivia, and unobtrusive piped music. Generous helpings of decent bar food include sandwiches and 3-cheese ploughman's, tasty deep-fried camembert, good ham and two eggs (£4.50), broccoli, cheese and potato bake or chilli con carne (£4.95), crab and prawn platter or lamb madras (£5.95), nice salmon steak, and steaks. Car park at the back. This is a pretty village. *(Recommended by Mick and Hazel Duncombe, Comus Elliott, Joan and Andrew Life, T Pascall, A and A Dale, Graham and Lynn Mason)*

Beards (who no longer brew) ~ Lease: Colin and Gillian Barrett ~ Real ale ~ Meals and snacks (not Sun evening) ~ (01435) 882304 ~ Children welcome till 9.30 ~ Open 12-3.30, 6-11; 12-11 Sat; 12-10.30 Sun; closed evenings 25-26 Dec ~ Bedrooms: £25/£40

BYWORTH SU9820 Map 2

Black Horse

Signposted from A283

At weekends (especially in summer), this unspoilt old pub can get busy when people come to enjoy the lovely gardens. There are tables on a steep series of grassy terraces, sheltered by banks of flowering shrubs, that look across a drowsy valley to swelling woodland, and a small stream runs along under an old willow by the more spacious lawn at the bottom; dogs are welcome on a lead. Inside, there's a nice relaxed atmosphere in the simply furnished though smart bar with its pews and scrubbed wooden tables on the bare floorboards, and open fires; the no-smoking back dining room has lots of nooks and crannies and a tented curtain to keep out the draughts. Bar food includes sandwiches, good ploughman's (from £4.25), daily specials, puddings, and Sunday roasts. Well kept Brewery on Sea Spinnaker Mild, Fullers London Pride, Youngs Ordinary and maybe a guest or two on handpump kept under light blanket pressure. Darts, bar billiards, cribbage, dominoes, and piped music. *(Recommended by Ann and Colin Hunt, Bruce Bird, Juliet Winsor, MCG, David Gould, Keith Ward, Susan and John Douglas, Graham and Karen Oddey)*

Free house ~ Licensees Rob Wilson, Teri Figg ~ Real ale ~ Meals and snacks (not evening 24 Dec) ~ Restaurant ~ (01798) 342424 ~ Children in restaurant only ~ Open 11-2.30(3 Sat), 6-11; 12-3, 7-10.30 Sun

Please let us know of any pubs where the wine is particularly good.

CHIDDINGLY TQ5414 Map 3

Six Bells ★ £

Village signed off A22 Uckfield—Hailsham

Although this old-fashioned pub has a strong local following, visitors come from quite a way away to enjoy the bustling, informal atmosphere – and all are made very welcome by the friendly, chatty landlord. The characterful beamed rooms have solid old wood furnishings including some pews and antique seats, log fires, lots of fusty artefacts and interesting bric-a-brac, and plenty of local pictures and posters. A sensitive extension provides some much needed family space; dominoes and cribbage. The atmosphere is quite lively when they have live music evenings. A big draw is the remarkably low-priced bar food, straightforward but tasty, with dishes such as french onion soup (£1), a choice of grilled french breads (from £1.10), shepherd's pie (£1.85), ravioli with spicy sauce (£1.95), steak and kidney pie (£2.40), filled baked potatoes (from £2.70), ploughman's (from £3), tuna and pasta bake (£3.20), garlic prawns (£4), cajun chicken (£4.50), rack of ribs (£4.95), ham hock (£5.95), and puddings like treacle tart or banoffee pie (£2.40); vegetables are an extra 60p. Well kept Courage Best and Directors and Harveys Best on handpump or tapped from the cask. Outside at the back, there are some tables beyond a big raised goldfish pond, and a boules pitch; the church opposite has an interesting Jeffrey monument. Vintage and Kit car meetings outside the pub every week. This is a pleasant area for walks. *(Recommended by Ann and Colin Hunt, Dave Carter, David Lamb, Kevin Thorpe, Janet and Colin Roe, David Cullen, Emma Stent, Peter Meister, Jason Caulkin, Mr and Mrs R D Knight, Quentin Williamson, K M Thorpe, Wayne Brindle, LM)*

Free house ~ Licensee Paul Newman ~ Real ale ~ Meals and snacks (11-2.30, 6-10.30) ~ (01825) 872227 ~ Children in family room ~ Jazz Sun lunchtime, blues and other live music in the barn Tues, Fri, Sat and Sun evenings (from 9) ~ Open 11-3, 6-11; 12-3, 7-10.30 Sun

CHIDHAM SU7903 Map 2

Old House At Home

Cot Lane; turn off A27 at the Barleycorn pub

Not far from Chichester harbour, this charming pub (down a quiet country lane and part of a cluster of farm buildings) is liked by a good mix of customers. The homely bar has timbering and low beams, windsor chairs around the tables, long seats against the walls, and a welcoming log fire. At lunchtime, the good bar food includes filled french bread and ploughman's, soup (£3.25), fishcakes (£4.95), home-cooked ham and egg (£5.95), sausages with mash and onion gravy (£5.95), a pie of the day (£6.25), and fresh fillet of cod in beer batter (£6.50); also, warm salad of goat's cheese with a redcurrant vinaigrette (£4.25), smoked chicken breast on a light tarragon mayonnaise (£5.95), nut terrine (£6.95), grilled tuna loin steak (£9.95), half a roast duck with a sweet cherry sauce (£10.50), Scotch fillet steak (£12.95), and daily specials; best to book at weekends and on summer evenings. The eating area is no smoking. Well kept real ales such as Badger Best, Ballards Best, Ringwood Best and Old Thumper, Old House (Burts Nipper), and a weekly changing guest beer on handpump, as well as a good selection of country wines and several malt whiskies; there's a large friendly german shepherd. There are a couple of picnic-sets on the terrace, with many more in the garden behind. *(Recommended by June and Eric Heley, Mr and Mrs D E Powell, Tony Scott, Richard Dolphin, Derek Stafford, Peter Meister, J F Reay, Guy Lockton, Tim Abel, Ann and Colin Hunt, Mrs D Bromley-Martin, Janet and John Pamment, Gladys Howden, Jo and Gary Charlton, Victoria Herriott, R J Bland, N E Bushby, W E Atkins, Edward Froggatt, R J Walden)*

Free house ~ Licensees Cliff Parry and Terry Brewer ~ Real ale ~ Meals and snacks (not 25 Dec, not evening 26 Dec) ~ (01243) 572477 ~ Children in eating area of bar ~ Open 11.30(12 Sat)-3, 6-11.30; 12-4, 7-10.30 Sun

There are report forms at the back of the book.

nr COOLHAM TQ1423 Map 3

George & Dragon

Dragons Green; pub signposted off A272 between Coolham and A24

Stretching away behind this old tile-hung cottage, the big grassy garden is beautifully kept, with lots of rustic tables and chairs well spaced among fruit trees, shrubs and lovely flowers; the little front garden has a sad 19th-c memorial to the son of a previous innkeeper. The bustling bar has unusually massive beams (see if you can decide whether the date cut into one is 1577 or 1677), unpretentious furnishings, an enormous inglenook fireplace, as well as more modern features such as a fruit machine, darts, bar billiards, table skittles, shove-ha'penny, cribbage, and dominoes. Good totally home-made bar food includes sandwiches (from £2.50; not Sunday), soup (£2.95), ploughman's (£4.95), home-cooked cider ham, egg and super home-made chips, steak and kidney pie or a couple of vegetarian dishes (£5.50), sweet and sour chicken (£6.50), steaks (from £10), and puddings (£2.50). Well kept King & Barnes Broadwood, Festive and Sussex on handpump. *(Recommended by Tony and Wendy Hobden, David and Carole Chapman, Bruce Bird, Tony Scott)*

King & Barnes ~ Licensee Roger Nash ~ Real ale ~ Meals and snacks (not Sun evening) ~ (01403) 741320 ~ Children welcome ~ Open 11-3, 6(6.30 in winter)-11; 11-11 Sat; 12-10.30 Sun

COWBEECH TQ6114 Map 3

Merrie Harriers

Village signposted from A271

This white-clapboarded village pub was once a farmhouse. The friendly bar is beamed and panelled, and has a traditional high-backed settle by the brick inglenook, as well as other tables and chairs, and darts. There's quite an emphasis on the popular bar food which includes sandwiches, home-made soup (£2.80), home-made salmon mousse (£3.95), almond-coated brie with redcurrant jelly (£4.95), nut roast with tomato sauce (£5.75), salads (from £7.50), home-made steak and kidney in ale pie (£7.75), salmon steak with hollandaise sauce (£9.15), grilled breast of duck with a changing home-made sauce (£10.25), steaks (from £10.25), daily specials, and puddings like home-made fruit cheesecake (£2.95); Sunday roast. Well kept Flowers IPA and Harveys Best on handpump; charming, professional service. The brick-walled and oak-ceilinged back restaurant is no smoking. Rustic seats in the terraced garden. *(Recommended by Janet and Colin Roe, Colin Laffan; more reports please)*

Free house ~ Licensees J H and C P Conroy ~ Real ale ~ Meals and lunchtime snacks ~ Restaurant ~ (01323) 833108 ~ Children in restaurant ~ Open 11-2.30, 6-11; 12-3, 7-10.30 Sun

CUCKFIELD TQ3025 Map 3

White Harte £

South Street; off A272 W of Haywards Heath

At lunchtime, it's best to get here early if you want to eat, as many of the tables are already snapped up by 12.30. The comfortable beamed lounge has a good cheery atmosphere, a mix of polished floorboards, parquet and ancient brick flooring tiles, standing timbers, a few local photographs, padded seats on a slightly raised area, and some fairly modern light oak tables and copper-topped tables. Furnishings in the public bar are sturdy and comfortable with a roaring log fire in the inglenook, maybe the friendly cat, and sensibly placed darts. The straightforward meals (they tell us prices have not increased this year) include ploughman's (from £3.20), sausage and egg (£3.30), and salads, but most people tend to go for the five or so very good value home-cooked specials: pies like chicken and mushroom, fish, or steak and kidney, turkey breast in mushroom sauce, smoked haddock bake, or stilton and celery quiche (all £3.90). Well kept King & Barnes Bitter and Broadwood and a guest beer on handpump; fruit machine, shove-ha'penny. The village is attractive. *(Recommended by DWAJ, B and M Kendall, Terry Buckland, Elizabeth and Klaus Leist, Steve Willey, Mr and Mrs A Budden)*

King & Barnes ~ Tenant Ted Murphy ~ Real ale ~ Lunchtime meals and snacks (not Sun) ~ (01444) 413454 ~ Well behaved children in eating are of bar at lunchtime ~ Open 11-3, 6-11; 12-3, 7-10.30 Sun

DONNINGTON SU8502 Map 2

Blacksmiths Arms

Left off A27 on to A286 signed Selsey, almost immediate left on to B2201

On entering this homely little white roadside cottage, you will probably be greeted with a handshake by the friendly landlord and have your coats taken. The small down-to-earth rooms are crammed with bric-a-brac: low ceilings are densely hung with hundreds of jugs, pots and kettles (each scrupulously cleaned by the landlord every week), the walls crowded with Victorian prints and there's a grandfather clock and an interesting old cigarette vending machine on the sill of one of the pretty little windows. Solid and comfortable furnishings on the patterned carpet include several 1950s sofas; shove-ha'penny, dominoes, fruit machine. Well kept Bass, Badger Best, Fullers London Pride, Ringwood Best and occasional guest beers on handpump or tapped from the cask, sometimes kept under light blanket pressure. Enjoyable bar food (with prices almost unchanged since last year) includes sandwiches or crusty rolls (from £1.75), soup (£1.80), filled baked potatoes (from £3.75), pizzas (from £3.75), ploughman's (£3.95), a vegetarian dish of the day or home-made lasagne (£6.95), home-made steak and kidney pie (£7.25), Selsey crab salad (£8.95), puddings (from £2.80), and quite a choice of children's meals (from £1.75). The big garden has a well fenced play area with a plastic tree house, and swings. *(Recommended by D S and J M Jackson, Mrs Mary Woods, J Snell, Janet and Colin Roe, David Peakall, Ann and Colin Hunt, Edward Froggatt)*

Free house ~ Fergus and Gill Gibney ~ Real ale ~ Meals and snacks (till 10pm, not Sun evenings end Oct-beg May) ~ Restaurant (not winter Sun evenings) ~ (01243) 783999 ~ Children welcome ~ Open 11-2.30, 6-11; 12-3, 7-10.30 Sun

DUNCTON SU9617 Map 3

Cricketers

Set back from A285 N

The charming garden behind this pretty little white house has won several awards, and has a proper barbecue (summer Sunday lunchtime barbecues and jazz), picnic-sets, and an attractive little creeper-covered seating area. There's a separate skittle alley at the front to one side of the building, lovely flowering baskets and tubs, and a rope swing for children. Inside, the bar has a few standing timbers giving the room an open-plan feel, there's an inglenook fireplace at one end with a large summer dried flower arrangement and some brass pots and warming pans on either side of the grate, local photographs on the mantlepiece, half a dozen bar stools and a mix of country tables and chairs, and green-cushioned settles; wildlife pictures, a cartoon of the jovial and friendly licensee and his wife, and a relaxed, cheerful atmosphere. Down a couple of steps a similarly furnished room is set for eating and is decorated with farming implements, pictures, and cricketer cigarette cards. Good, popular bar food includes soup (£3.50), garlic mushrooms (£3.95), ploughman's, open granary sandwiches (from £4.25), oven-roasted vegetables and mozzarella cheese (£4.50), chicken liver pâté with onion confit (£4.75), fish terrine with prawn sauce (£4.95), vegetable pasta bake (£5.50), steak and kidney pudding (£7.25), chicken with oven-roasted tomatoes and rosemary (£7.95), oven-roasted salmon fillet with tomato and chives or sliced magret duck breast with orange and lemon sauce (£8.95), and puddings (£3). Well kept Archers Golden, Friary Meux Bitter, Gales HSB, Ind Coope Burton, Youngs, and guest beers on handpump, lots of malt whiskies, decent wines; cribbage. (*Recommended by John Fahy; more reports please)*

Free house ~ Licensee Philip Edgington ~ Real ale ~ Meals and snacks (not Sun or Mon winter evenings) ~ Restaurant ~ (01798) 342473 ~ Well behaved children in restaurant only ~ Open 11-2.30, 6-11; closed winter Sun evenings

EAST DEAN TV5597 Map 3

Tiger 🍷

Pub (with village centre) signposted – not vividly – from A259 Eastbourne—Seaford

The village green by this white tiled pub is particularly idyllic on a summer evening when you can sit on the grass and look back at the pretty window boxes, clematis and roses, big bright inn sign of a tiger on a branch, and rustic seats and tables on the brick front terrace. Inside, the smallish rooms have low beams hung with pewter and china, traditional furnishings including polished rustic tables and distinctive antique settles, and old prints and so forth. Well kept Adnams Best, Flowers Original, Harveys Best, and Timothy Taylor Landlord on handpump; also a fair choice of wines with several interesting vintage bin-ends and 6 good wines by the glass; cribbage and dominoes. A short but good choice of home-made bar meals, listed on a blackboard, might include local sausage ploughman's (£4.25), home-made smoked haddock, ginger and spring onion fishcakes (£5.95), steak in ale pie (£6.25), and whole local lobster (£10.95); their meat comes from the very good local butcher who wins awards for his sausages. The upstairs family room is no smoking. Morris dancers visit every bank holiday. The lane leads on down to a fine stretch of coast culminating in Beachy Head, and there are plenty of good walks. No children. *(Recommended by R J Bland, Tony Scott, Michael and Hazel Duncombe, David and Carole Chapman, John Voos, Charles Bardswell, Brian and Anna Marsden, John Beeken, Comus Elliott)*

Free house ~ Licensee Nicholas Denyer ~ Real ale ~ Meals and snacks ~ (01323) 423209 ~ Open 11-11; 12-10.30 Sun; 11-3, 6-11 in winter

ELSTED SU8119 Map 2

Elsted Inn ★ 🍴 🛏

Elsted Marsh; from Midhurst left off A272 Petersfield Rd at Elsted and Harting sign; from Petersfield left off B2146 Nursted Rd at South Harting, keep on past Elsted itself

Of course many people come here to enjoy the very good food, but it is still a simple and unpretentious village pub with good local beers, plenty of regulars, and a bustling chatty atmosphere (no noisy piped music or games machines). The two simple bars have country furniture on wooden floors, original shutters, old railway photographs (the pub was built to serve the railway when there was a station next door), and three open log fires; darts, shove-ha'penny, dominoes, cribbage, backgammon, and cards; the small restaurant (candlelit at night) has patchwork curtains, an old oak dresser, and restored old polished tables and chairs. They use the best ingredients for their good cooking: local game, Jersey cream from a local farm, hand-made bread from the National Trust bakery at Slindon, free range eggs, mainly free range chicken and duck, and local vegetables and fruit. The menu sometimes changes twice a day and might include sandwiches (from £2.50), macaroni cheese (£4.50), filled baked potatoes or ploughman's (£4.95), good mussels baked with garlic and cheese (£5.50), king prawns in garlic butter (£6), good local sausages, mushroom roulade or roast beef (£7.50), Sussex bacon pudding (£7.75), local rabbit in mustard sauce or salmon fishcakes (£8), braised venison (£8.25), quail in garlic (£9), and puddings like plum crumble, dark chocolate mousse and popular treacle tart (£4); winter Wednesday curry night (£10). As there isn't much space, they now reluctantly advise booking for meals. Well kept Ballards Trotton, Best, Wassail, summer Nyewood Gold, and winter Wild, Fullers London Pride, and guests such as Arundel Best, Cheriton Pots, and Hop Back Crop Circle on handpump; friendly, helpful staff; two big friendly dogs, Sam and Truffle, who welcome guests. The lovely enclosed garden has a big terrace, plenty of wooden garden furniture, a good view of the South Downs; summer barbecues. The new bedrooms are in the old brewery building. *(Recommended by David Cullen, Emma Stent, Jerry and Alison Oakes, William and Julie Ryan, R D Knight, Peter Meister, Derek Harvey-Piper, Ian Jones, N E Bushby, W E Atkins, Edward Froggatt, Paul Williams, Julie Peters, Colin Blinkhorn, Mark Matthewman, Tony Gayfer, Martin and Karen Wake, John Evans)*

Free house ~ Licensees Tweazle Jones and Barry Horton ~ Real ale ~ Meals and snacks ~ Restaurant ~ (01730) 813662 ~ Children in eating area of bar and in

restaurant ~ Folk music first Sun evening of the month ~ Open 11.30-3, 5.30(6 Sat)-11; 12-3, 7-11 Sun; closed evening 25 Dec ~ Bedrooms: £35B/£50B

Three Horseshoes ★

Village signposted from B2141 Chichester—Petersfield; also reached easily from A272 about 2 miles W of Midhurst, turning left heading W

The snug little rooms in this 16th-c pub are full of rustic charm, with ancient beams and flooring, enormous log fires, antique furnishings, attractive prints and photographs, and night-time candlelight. Good bar food includes home-made soup (£3.95), avocado with stilton and mushroom sauce topped with bacon (£5.50), generous ploughman's with a good choice of cheeses (£5), steak, kidney and ale pie or braised lamb with apples and apricots in a tomato chutney sauce (£8.95), fresh seasonal crab and lobster, and home-made treacle tart or grand marnier cheesecake (£3.95). Well kept changing ales racked on a stillage behind the bar counter might include Ballards Best, Cheriton Pots, Fullers London Pride, Hampshire King Alfreds, Hop Back Summer Lightning, and Ringwood Fortyniner, and summer cider; friendly service; dominoes. The garden is lovely with free-roaming bantams and marvellous views over the South Downs. *(Recommended by John H Davis, Ann and Colin Hunt, Mr and Mrs C Neve, N E Bushby, W E Atkins, John Evans, John and Joan Calvert, Lynn Sharpless, Bob Eardley, Jo and Gary Charlton)*

Free house ~ Licensees Andrew and Sue Beavis ~ Real ale ~ Meals and snacks (not winter Sun evenings) ~ Restaurant ~ (01730) 825746 ~ Well behaved children welcome ~ Open 11-2.30, 6-11; 12-3, 7-10.30 Sun; closed Sun evening Oct-May

FAIRWARP TQ4626 Map 3

Foresters Arms

Set back from B2026, N of northern Maresfield roundabout exit from A22

This pleasant local is in a pretty setting on a small green and close to the Vanguard Way and Weald Way at the south end of Ashdown Forest. Inside, it's homely and welcoming, with a comfortable lounge bar, a public bar with a big aquarium, a woodburning stove in a big stripped stone fireplace, and well kept King & Barnes Bitter, Festive, Mild, Old and Broadwood on handpump, Weston's cider, and a few malt whiskies. Decent bar food food includes sandwiches (from £2.50), ploughman's (£4.50), starters (from £4.50), bar snacks (from £4.95), roasts (£5.95), home-made curries or vegetarian dishes (from £5.95), home-made pies (from £6.50), fresh fish dishes (from £8.95), and children's meals (from £3.25); good popular Sunday lunch, and efficient service. Darts, pool, dominoes, fruit machine, video game, trivia, and piped music. There are some tables outside. *(Recommended by R D and S R Knight, R J Walden, Colin Laffan, Pat and Tony Martin, Sue and Steve Griffiths)*

King & Barnes ~ Tenants Mel and Lloyd West ~ Real ale ~ Meals and snacks ~ Restaurant ~ (01825) 712808 ~ Children welcome ~ Open 11-3, 6-11; 12-3, 7-10.30 Sun; closed evening 25 Dec ~ Bedrooms: £20/£30

FIRLE TQ4607 Map 3

Ram

Signposted off A27 Lewes—Polegate

Handy for exploring a particularly fine stretch of the South Downs, this 17th-c village pub has unspoilt bars with winter log fires, comfortable seating, soft lighting, and a relaxed atmosphere; the snug is no smoking. Well kept Batemans XXXB and Harveys Best on handpump; darts, shove-ha'penny, dominoes, cribbage and toad in the hole. The gents' has a chalk board for graffiti, and there are tables in a spacious walled garden behind. They have a fine ginger cat called Orange, and two comical geese. Bar food includes home-made soup, ploughman's, spinach, mushroom and tomato lasagne (£7), seafood pie (£9), and puddings; helpings are not huge. Nearby Firle Place is worth visiting for its collections and furnishings. *(Recommended by Dan Wilson, Kevin*

Thorpe, Simon Cottrell, Tony and Wendy Hobden, Wayne Brindle, Jo and Gary Charlton, Bruce Bird, Sue Demont, Tim Barrow)

Free house ~ Licensees Michael and Keith Wooller and Margaret Sharp ~ Real ale ~ Meals and lunchtime snacks ~ (01273) 858222 ~ Children in two rooms away from bar ~ Folk music 2nd Mon and 1st and 2nd Weds of month ~ Open 11.30-3, 7-11; 11.30-11 Sat; 12-10.30 Sun; closed evening 25 Dec ~ Bedrooms: /£60(£70S)

FLETCHING TQ4223 Map 3

Griffin ★ Ⓣ 🛏 🍷

Village signposted off A272 W of Uckfield

Sussex Dining Pub of the Year

The licensees and their staff really go out of their way to make customers feel welcome in this civilised old inn. There's a good bustling atmosphere and blazing log fires in the beamed and quaintly panelled bar rooms, as well as old photographs and hunting prints, straightforward furniture including some captain's chairs, china on a delft shelf, and a small bare-boarded serving area off to one side. A separate public bar has darts, pool, and fruit machine. Very good enjoyable bar food might include hot ciabatta sandwiches with fillings like roast mediterranean vegetables or salami, tomatoes and mozzarella (from £3.95), moules marinières or a light mousse of goat's cheese (£4.95), crab and prawn fritters with a coriander dip (£5.95), home-made hand raised pork pie (£6.50), pasta with wild mushrooms, roasted red onions, pesto and parmesan (£6.95), confit of duck on rocket leaves with a shallot and red onion sauce or pot-roasted local rabbit braised in cider with shallots and bacon (£7.50), local cod in beer with home-made chips (£7.95), and puddings like home-made elderflower and juniper sorbet, dark chocolate and coffee mousse or iced white chocolate parfait (£3.95); enjoyable breakfasts. Well kept Badger Tanglefoot, Ballards Best, Courage Directors, and Harveys Best on handpump, and a fine wine list with ten wines (including champagne) by the glass. There are tables in the beautifully arranged back garden with lovely rolling Sussex views, with more on a sheltered gravel terrace (used for dining). The barn has been developed to give four more bedrooms and to create an attractive room for private parties. The pub is in a pretty spot just on the edge of Sheffield Park.
(Recommended by Mr and Mrs R J Salter, Paul Williams, Richard Siebert, John and Joan Calvert, David Cullen, Emma Stent, Peter Meister, Evelyn and Derek Walter, Colin Draper, Colin and Joyce Laffan, Dr Paul Khan, R D and S R Knight, B K and R S Levy, A E Brace, Liz Bell, Margaret and Nigel Dennis, Peter Glenser, Charlie Ballantyne, Brian and Anna Marsden, Pat and Tony Martin, Kate and Robert Hodkinson, Sebastian Leach, Wayne Brindle, Betsy Brown, Nigel Flook)

Free house ~ Licensees Nigel Pullan and John Gatti ~ Real ale ~ Meals and snacks ~ Restaurant (not Sun evening) ~ (01825) 722890 ~ Children welcome ~ Piano/sax jazz Fri/Sat evenings and Sun lunchtime ~ Open 12-3, 6-11; 12-3, 7-10.30 Sun; closed 25 Dec ~ Bedrooms: £50S/£75B

HAMMERPOT TQ0605 Map 3

Woodmans Arms

Pub visible and well signposted on N (eastbound) side of A27 just under 4 miles E of A284 Arundel; heading westbound, go past pub until you can turn on to eastbound carriageway – after leaving the pub you can rejoin the westbound one almost immediately

Unless you're really well below 6ft, you really do have to stoop as you walk around the bar in this delightful 16th-c thatched flint pub – indeed, several are strung with fairy lights as a warning. The brick-floored entrance area has a chatty atmosphere, its seats including one cosy armchair by the inglenook's big log fire, with lots of brass, and genuine old photographs of regulars. On the right a carpeted dining area with candles on the tables has wheelback chairs around its tables, and cheerfully cottagey decorations; on the left is a small no-smoking room with a few more tables; the local flavour is at its best on occasional special evenings such as their annual home-made sloe gin competition. Good well presented home-made food in generous helpings includes sandwiches (from £2.45), ploughman's (£5.45), bacon and onion roly poly, celery and mushroom stroganoff or chicken casserole (all £5.90), curries (£6.95), light-crusted steak and kidney pie, weekend fresh fish such as whole plaice or dressed local crab (£7.50), poached salmon in dill sauce (£8.95), evening duck breast with port and cumberland sauce (£9.25), steaks (from £9.50), and puddings like apple pie or rhubarb crumble (£2.95); there is a partly no-smoking dining area. Well kept Gales Best, HSB and a changing beer on handpump or tapped from the cask; country wines, decent conventional wine, and good friendly service. Cribbage, dominoes and maybe some piped music. The yellow labrador is called Tikka. Despite road noise, the garden is a delight, with tables and picnic-sets on a terrace, under a fairy-lit arbour and on small lawns among lots of roses and tubs of bright annuals. They have a free map of a circular walk from the pub – best to phone ahead if you are a sizeable party of walkers. *(Recommended by Bruce Bird, Pat and Robert Watt, Colin Draper, Ann and Colin Hunt, Tony and Wendy Hobden, Mimi and Alastair McNeil, P R White)*

Gales ~ Tenants Malcolm and Anne Green ~ Real ale ~ Meals and snacks (not Sun evening) ~ Evening restaurant ~ (01903) 871240 ~ Well behaved children welcome ~ Folk club every 2nd Sun evening ~ Open 11-3(3.30 Sat), 6-11; 12-3.30, 7-10.30 Sun

HARTFIELD TQ4735 Map 3

Anchor

Church Street

On the edge of Ashdown Forest, this welcoming old pub dates from the late 15th c. The original bar has heavy beams, old advertisements and little country pictures on the walls above the brown-painted dado, houseplants in the brown-curtained small-paned windows, and a woodburner, and rambles informally around the central servery. Another bar (in what was the old kitchens) has more old beams, a flagstone floor, a dining area with good tables and chairs, and huge logs burning in an old inglenook fireplace. Well kept Bass, Flowers IPA and Original, Fullers London Pride, and Harveys Best on handpump. Good bar food includes sandwiches (from £1.75), home-made soup (£2.50), filled baked potatoes (from £3.25), ploughman's (from £3.75), moules marinières (£4), local sausages (£4.50), home-cooked ham and egg (£4.75), prawn and crab curry (£6), lamb kebab with yoghurt and mint (£8.75), sirloin steak (£10), good value daily specials, and puddings (from £2.50); children's meals (from £2); quick friendly service. Darts in a separate lower room; shove-ha'penny, cribbage, dominoes, and piped music. The front verandah soon gets busy on a warm summer evening. There's a play area in the popular garden. *(Recommended by LM, Colin and Joyce Laffan, Brian and Anna Marsden)*

Free house ~ Licensee Ken Thompson ~ Real ale ~ Meals and snacks (12-2, 6-10) ~ Restaurant ~ (01892) 770424 ~ Children welcome ~ Open 11-11; 12-10.30 Sun; closed evening 25 Dec ~ Bedrooms: £35S/£50S

nr HEATHFIELD TQ5920 Map 3

Star

Old Heathfield – head East out of Heathfield itself on A265, then fork right on to B2096; turn right at signpost to Heathfield Church then keep bearing right; pub on left immediately after church

The L-shaped beamed bar in this 14th-c inn is reached up some well worn brick steps, and is a cosy place on a winter day. It's got a lot of character, a log fire in the inglenook fireplace, panelling, built-in wall settles and window seats, just four or five tables, and a relaxed, chatty atmosphere; a doorway leads into a similarly furnished smaller room. A fair range of bar food is chalked up on a board (they tell us prices remain virtually unchanged) and includes ploughman's (£4.75), fresh mussels or cold meats with bubble and squeak (£6.25), good local cod with chips, fresh crab (£7.95), half a free range duckling (£11.95), fresh lobster (£15), and winter game dishes; efficient, friendly service. Well kept Harveys Best and Greene King IPA and guests such as Bass, Greene King Abbot, Hop Back Summer Lightning, and Youngs Special on handpump, some malt whiskies and farm cider; bar billiards, shove-ha'penny, cribbage, dominoes and piped music. The prettily planted sloping garden with its rustic furniture has year-round table service, and views of rolling oak-lined sheep pastures – Turner thought it fine enough to paint. The neighbouring church is rather interesting, with its handsome Early English tower. *(Recommended by Heather Simpson, Wayne Brindle, K M Thorpe, J S M Sheldon, Steve Goodchild, Margaret and Nigel Dennis)*

Free house ~ Lease: Mike and Sue Chappell ~ Real ale ~ Meals and snacks ~ Restaurant ~ (01435) 863570 ~ Children in eating area of bar ~ Jazz some Suns ~ Open 11.30-3, 5.30-11; 12-3, 7-10.30 Sun

HORSHAM TQ1730 Map 3

Black Jug

31 North St

Big windows light the airy open-plan turn-of-the-century-style room in this friendly town pub. There's a large central bar, a nice collection of heavy sizeable dark wood tables, comfortable chairs on a stripped wood floor, dark wood panelled dado above which are cream walls crammed with interesting old prints and photographs, and a warm terracotta ceiling. A spacious dark wood conservatory has similar furniture and lots of hanging baskets; dominoes and cribbage. Well kept Boddingtons, Courage Directors, Marstons Pedigree, John Smiths, and Wadworths 6X on handpump, two dozen malt whiskies, and nine chilled vodkas from Poland and Russia. The changing bar menu, densely written on a blackboard, includes sandwiches, soup (£2.95), spinach and ricotta tortellini with a creamy green olive and garlic sauce (£3.95), cumberland sausages with mustard mash and onion gravy (£5.25), thai salmon and crab fishcakes with chilli dressing (£5.95), steak and Guinness pie (£8.50), braised venison in a brown ale and juniper sauce (£9.25), sirloin steak with red wine and onion sauce (£10.50), fried breast of barbary duck with an orange and raspberry sauce (£10.95), grilled red mullet with a lemon and dill butter (£12.45), and raspberry crème brûlée, bread and butter pudding with apricot sauce or profiteroles with hot chocolate sauce (£3.25). There are quite a few tables sheltered under a pagoda outside on a back flower-filled terrace. *(Recommended by Ron Gentry, Tony Scott, David and Carole Chapman, G Simpson, R Cooper, Pat and Tony Martin)*

Courage ~ Manager Neil Stickland ~ Real ale ~ Meals and snacks (till 10pm) ~ Conservatory restaurant ~ (01403) 253526 ~ Children in conservatory weekends only until 6pm ~ Live entertainment Sun evening bank hol wknds ~ Open 11-11; 12-10.30 Sun; closed 26 Dec

ICKLESHAM TQ8816 Map 3

Queens Head

Small sign party obscured by plants off A259

Apart from having good, enjoyable food and an interesting decor, what readers really like about this comfortably relaxed old pub is the way the friendly licensees make both visitors and locals so welcome. The open-plan areas work round a very big serving counter, which stands under a vaulted beamed roof, the high beamed walls and ceiling of the easy-going bar are covered with lots of farming implements and animal traps, and there are well used pub tables and old pews on the brown patterned carpet. Other areas (one no smoking) are popular with diners – the bar food is very reasonably priced – and have big inglenook fireplaces. The generous helpings of food quickly served by friendly efficient staff include sandwiches (from £1.95; steak in french bread £4.50), home-made soup (£2.50), soft herring roes on toast (£3.95), ploughman's (£4.10), ham and egg (£4.75), cheesy ratatouille (£5.50), a curry of the day or steak and mushroom in ale pie (£6.50), steaks (from £9.50), and home-made daily specials such as sweet potato and vegetable bake (£5.95), pork in cider (£6.25), game and ale pie (£6.50), half a roast duck (£6.95), and fresh fish like skate, hake, halibut, cod, trout or salmon (£5-£8.50). From a constantly changing choice of at least four, the very well kept real ales might include Batemans XB, Courage Directors, Greene King Abbot, Old Forge Brothers Best, Harveys PA, Ringwood Old Thumper, Rother Valley Lighterman, Swale Kentish Pride, and Woodfordes Wherry; a good choice of wines by the glass, Biddenden cider, and sparking elderflower cordial; shove-ha'penny, dominoes, fruit machine, trivia, and piped music. There are broad views over the vast gently sloping plain of the Brede valley from wooden picnic-sets in the little garden, and a children's play area; boules. Good walks. *(Recommended by Kevin Thorpe, E G Parish, Brian and Jenny Seller, D Buckley, Janet and Colin Roe)*

Free House ~ Licensee Ian Mitchell ~ Real Ale ~ Meals and snacks (12-2.45, 6.30-9.45; not 25/26 Dec) ~ (01424) 814552 ~ Well supervised children welcome till 9pm ~ Open 11-11; 12-5, 7-10.30 Sun; closed evening 25 Dec, limited hours 26 Dec

KINGSTON NEAR LEWES TQ3908 Map 3

Juggs

The Street; Kingston signed off A27 by roundabout W of Lewes, and off Lewes—Newhaven road; look out for the pub's sign – may be hidden by hawthorn in summer

Covered with roses in summer, this bustling tile-hung cottage pub was named for the fish-carriers who passed through on their way between Newhaven and Lewes. The rambling beamed bar has an interesting mix of furnishings that ranges from an attractive little carved box settle, Jacobean-style dining chairs and brocaded seats and other settles to the more neatly orthodox tables and chairs of the small no-smoking dining area under the low-pitched eaves on the right. The cream or stripped brick walls are hung with flower pictures, battle prints, a patriotic assembly of postcards of the Lloyd George era, posters, and some harness and brass. Popular bar food includes home-made soup (£3.50), open sandwiches (from £3.50), ploughman's or sausages (£3.95), haddock and chips (£4.50), vegetable savoury (£5.75), pitta bread with chicken tikka (£5.95), home-made steak and kidney pudding (£8.75), steaks (from £8.50), daily specials, and home-made puddings (£2.95). On Sunday lunchtime food is limited to a cold buffet. One of the family rooms is no smoking. Service remains speedy and efficient (aided by a rather effective electronic bleeper system to let you know when meals are ready) even when the pub is very busy. Well kept Harveys Best, King & Barnes Festive, and a guest on handpump. Log fires, dominoes, shove-ha'penny. There are a good many close-set rustic teak tables on the sunny brick terrace; a neatly hedged inner yard has more tables under cocktail parasols, and there are two or three out on grass by a timber climber and commando net. *(Recommended by Mayur Shah, Derek Harvey-Piper, R and S Bentley, Jason Caulkin, R J Walden, Tony Hobden, Martin and Karen Wake, Bruce Bird)*

Free house ~ Licensees Andrew and Peta Browne ~ Real ale ~ Meals (not Sun lunchtime) and snacks ~ Restaurant ~ (01273) 472523 ~ Children welcome away from bar servery ~ Open 11-11; 12-10.30 Sun; 11-3, 6-11 in winter; closed evenings 25/31 Dec, 1 Jan and all day 26 Dec

KIRDFORD TQ0126 Map 3

Half Moon

Opposite church; off A272 Petworth—Billingshurst

The friendly licensees have now opened their own fish shop close to this sizeable tile-hung cottage – so you can order your fish, have lunch and go back to collect it to take home. The Morans have had links with Billingsgate for over 130 years, so it's not surprising that one of the main draws here is the interesting fresh fish dishes. There might be such rarities as tile fish, porgy, parrot fish, soft shell crabs, Morton Bay bugs, scabbard fish, razor shells, mahi mahi, and baramundi. But as fresh fish is seasonal, there may be times when the range isn't as big as you might hope: crab cakes with red pepper jam (£5.50), buffalo shrimp with cajun mayonnaise (£5.50), wing of skate with caper butter sauce (£8.50), salmon and tuna kebab with a yoghurt and mint dip (£10.95), and roasted scabbard fish and Spanish mackerel with mixed olives, garlic, rosemary and tomatoes (£14.50). Also, non-fishy things like filled french bread (from £3.60), roquefort, asparagus and chicken tart (£3.95), ploughman's (from £3.95), baked mushrooms stuffed with three cheeses and almonds (£4.95), spare ribs with barbecue sauce (£5.85), and steak and kidney pie (£6.50). Well kept Arundel Best, Greene King Abbot, King & Barnes Sussex, and Shepherd Neame Spitfire on handpump. The simple partly quarry-tiled bars are kept ship-shape and very clean, and there's a beamed eating area with an open fire; darts, pool, cribbage, dominoes, fruit machine, and jazz or classical radio. The restaurant is partly no smoking. There's a back garden with swings, barbecue area, tables, and big boules pitch, and more tables in front facing the pretty village's church. *(Recommended by Rod and Moyra Davidson, Guy Conseterdine, Mr and Mrs D Powell, Dr Paul Khan, Richard Tosswill, Mike Fitzgerald, Andrew W Lee, John Beeken, Kim Maidment, Philip Vernon)*

Whitbreads ~ Lease: Anne Moran ~ Real ale ~ Meals and snacks (not Sun evening) ~ Restaurant ~ (01403) 820223 ~ Children welcome until 9pm ~ Open 11-3, 7-11; 12-3, 7-10.30 Sun; closed evening 25 Dec ~ Bedrooms: £30B/£45(£55B)

LEWES TQ4110 Map 3

Snowdrop

South Street; off Cliffe High Street, opp S end of Malling Street just S of A26 roundabout

For a really different pub experience, you should come here. It's a unique place with a positively laid-back atmosphere, but is enjoyed by an extraordinarily mixed bunch of people of all ages. The interior is unusual to say the least with a glorious profusion of cast-iron tables, bric-a-brac and outlandish paraphernalia that no doubt owes much to the next-door antique shop. Unfolding the rather dreamlike maritime theme, downstairs there are three ships' figureheads dotted around, walls covered with rough sawn woodplank and upstairs a huge star chart painted on a dark blue ceiling, and a sunset sea mural with waves in relief. The pub is quiet at lunchtime but a young people's preserve, and lively to match, in the evenings, when the loudish juke box plays anything from Bob Dylan or Ella Fitzgerald to Indian chants. They serve no red meat, and the good value light-hearted menu includes sandwiches, burritos or large home-made pizzas (from £2.50, margherita pizza £4.75), paella (£6.50), fresh fish, and lots of well-priced vegan and vegetarian dishes like delicious hearty home-made tomato soup, hummus in pitta bread (£2.60), and cheesy tuna and pasta bake (£4.60); free range chicken is the Sunday roast, and they do children's helpings. Five well kept real ales such as Fullers ESB, Harveys Best, Hop Back Summer Lightning, and changing guests on handpump, good coffee, friendly licensees and staff; pool and juke box. There are a few tables in the garden. *(Recommended by Brad W Morley, Kevin Thorpe, K and J Morris, Anthony Bowen, Ann and Colin Hunt, R J Walden, Comus Elliott, Jan Wilson, Tony Scott, M and M Carter, Pat and Tony Martin, Sue Demont, Tim Barrow)*

Free house ~ Licensees Tim and Sue May ~ Real ale ~ Meals and snacks 12-3(2.30 Sun), 6(7 Sun)-9 ~ (01273) 471018 ~ Children in eating area of bar only ~ Live jazz Mon evening and other live music some weekends ~ Open 11-11; 12-10.30 Sun

LODSWORTH SU9223 Map 2

Halfway Bridge ★ 🍴 🍷 🍺

Just before village, on A272 Midhurst—Petworth

There's a lot going for this smartly civilised family-run pub – a friendly atmosphere, good real ales, and enjoyable food. The three or four comfortable rooms have good oak chairs and an individual mix of tables (many of them set for dining), and use attractive fabrics for the wood-railed curtains and pew cushions. Down some steps the charming no-smoking country dining room has a dresser and longcase clock. Log fires include one in a well polished kitchen range, and paintings by a local artist line the walls. Changing regularly, the interesting food includes lunchtime specials (not Sundays) like BLT open sandwich (£4.50), half rack of barbecue ribs with sweet pepper rice (£4.95), spinach and mushroom lasagne (£5.45), and roast beef salad (£5.95); there's also deep-fried camembert with gooseberry and red onion marmalade or chicken liver and cognac pâté (£3.50), green-lipped mussels stuffed with chilli, coconut and coriander (£4.95), pork and leek sausages with onion gravy (£5.95), mediterranean king prawns (£6.50), ricotta and herb tortellini with an artichoke sauce (£7.50), stir-fried beef in oyster sauce with noodles or steak, kidney, Guinness and mushroom pudding (£8.25), local rabbit braised with prunes (£8.50), warm salad of salmon and watercress with a lime and coriander dressing (£9.50), fillet steak (£14.20), daily specials such as carrot, courgette and coriander soup (£3.25), un-dyed smoked haddock with poached egg (£5.50), breast of chicken stuffed with spinach and wrapped in parma ham (£8.95), and puddings like tarte tatin, banana toffee pie or rhubarb fool (£3); popular Sunday roasts; polite service. A good range of well kept beers includes Cheriton Pots Ale, Fullers London Pride, Gales HSB, and guests from breweries such as Brewery on Sea, Hampshire Brewery, Harveys, Hogs Back or Pilgrim, farm ciders, and a thoughtful little wine list with a changing choice by the glass. Dominoes, shove-ha'penny, cribbage, backgammon, and other games like Jenga, bagatelle, and mah jong. Ralph the jack russell now wears a sign saying 'please don't feed me'. At the back there are attractive blue wood tables and chairs on a terrace with a pergola. They've bought another pub, the Cricketers Arms at Wisborough Green. *(Recommended by David Crafts, Ron Shelton, Martin and Karen Wake, Dennis Stevens, John Evans, C P Baxter, Paula Williams, Julie Peters, Colin Blinkhorn, Martin and Jane Wright, G C Hackemer, Edward Froggatt, Mr and Mrs G Turner, Simon Small, Lady M H Moir, Steve Goodchild)*

Free house ~ Licensees Sheila, Edric, Simon and James Hawkins ~ Real ale ~ Meals and snacks (till 10pm) ~ Restaurant ~ (01798) 861281 ~ Children over 10 in restaurant ~ Jazz every 2nd Sun evening in summer ~ Open 11-3, 6-11; 12-3, 7-10.30 Sun; closed winter Sun evenings

LOWER BEEDING TQ2225 Map 3

Crabtree

Brighton Rd; A281 S of village, towards Cowfold

You can drop into the cosy beamed bars in this busy pub for just a drink, but most people do come to eat. There's an air of civilised simplicity, and plenty of character in the back no-smoking restaurant (the only place where they do food in the evening). At its best, the food is very good indeed and might include sandwiches (from £1.95) leek and potato soup with croutons (£3.50), ploughman's (from £4), roasted quail stuffed with apricot, pine kernels and sage (£4.50), seared fillet of tuna fish with guacamole and tortilla layers (£4.75), fennel, pepper and watercress risotto with tomato dressing (£8), calf liver with crispy bacon on lentil purée with marsala sauce or roasted pork tenderloin with honey, soya and ginger on stir-fried vegetables (£9.50), and puddings like toffee pudding or bread and butter pudding (£3.50); they offer a one-course special such as tiger prawn and crunchy vegetable salad with roasted chilli and lime dressing or asparagus, spinach and quail's egg tart (£6.50) or a two-course special (£10.50). Well kept King and Barnes Sussex, Festive and seasonal brews on handpump, and good wines; cribbage and dominoes. A pleasant back garden has some seats. The pub is very handy for Leonardslee Gardens, which are closed in winter. *(Recommended by Colin McKerrow, John Fahy, Terry Buckland, Derek Harvey-Piper, R J Walden)*

King & Barnes ~ Tenants Jeremy Ashpool and Xanthe Woraker ~ Real ale ~ Lunchtime bar meals and snacks ~ Restaurant ~ (01403) 891257 ~ Well behaved children in restaurant ~ Open 10-3, 6-11; 12-3, 7-10.30 Sun

LURGASHALL SU9327 Map 2

Noahs Ark

Village signposted from A283 N of Petworth; OS Sheet 186 map reference 936272

Run by friendly licensees, this 16th-c local is charmingly set overlooking the village green – tables on the grass in front are ideal for watching summer cricket matches. The two neatly furnished bars have fresh flowers or warm log fires (one in a capacious inglenook), depending on the season, well kept Greene King Abbot, IPA and Rayments on handpump, and darts, pool, shove-ha'penny, table skittles, dominoes, and cribbage. Bar food includes sandwiches (from £3.75, toasties such as bacon and mushroom £3.95), ploughman's (from £4.50), tomato and vegetable tagliatelle (£5.75), steak and kidney pudding (£6.15), lamb cutlets (£7.50), calf liver and bacon (£7.95), smoked salmon salad (£8.75), and fillet steak (£12.50). The summer flowering baskets are splendid. *(Recommended by J Sheldon, Martin and Karen Wake, Mr and Mrs Carey, Mrs D W Cook, Derek Harvey-Piper, John Evans, James Nunns)*

Greene King ~ Lease: Kathleen G Kennedy ~ Real ale ~ Meals and snacks (not Sun evening) ~ Restaurant ~ (01428) 707346 ~ Children welcome ~ Open theatre annually, dances in garden in summer, in function room in winter ~ Open 11.30-3, 6-11; 12-3, 7-10.30 Sun; winter weekday opening is half an hour later

MAYFIELD TQ5827 Map 3

Middle House

High St; village signposted off A267 S of Tunbridge Wells

Set in the middle of a very pretty village, this handsome 16th-c timbered inn is Grade I listed. There's a largely original L-shaped beamed main bar dominated by a massive fireplace surrounded by menu boards at one end, with straightfoward pub furniture, fresh flowers, a chatty relaxed atmosphere, and well kept Fullers London Pride, Greene King Abbot, Harveys Best, and a guest like Badger Tanglefoot, Hook Norton Old Hookey or Hop Back Summer Lightning on handpump; local cider and decent wine list. The tranquil lounge has a cosy group of comfortable russet chesterfields set around a log fire in an ornately carved fireplace (disputedly by Grinling Gibbons). Generous helpings of good bar food include home-made sausages with mash, onions and gravy (£5.50), home-made steak and kidney pudding (£6.95), fresh pasta topped with salmon in a mornay sauce (£8.50), thai chicken and prawn curry (£8.95), pork fillet on caramelised apples and prunes or venison steak finished with sloe gin and sweet onions (£9.95), and roasted monkfish on chargrilled peppers with a garlic and lime butter (£11.95). Sunday 3-course roast lunch and Wednesday 3-course jazz evening menu (both £15.95); friendly service. One of the restaurants has some handsome panelling (and is no smoking), and another room was once a chapel; piped music. Afternoon tea is served in the fairly formal terraced back garden which has picnic-sets, white plastic sets with cocktail parasols, lovely views, and a slide and a log house for children. *(Recommended by Serena Hebeler, Robert Gibb, Mr and Mrs G J Cotton, Margaret and Nigel Dennis, Wayne Brindle, David Gittins; more reports please)*

Free house ~ Licensee Monica Blundell ~ Real ale ~ Meals and snacks ~ Two restaurants (not Sun evening) ~ (01435) 872146 ~ Children welcome ~ Live jazz Weds ~ Open 11-11; 12-10.30 Sun ~ Bedrooms: £35(£55B)/£45(£55B)

NUTHURST TQ1926 Map 3

Black Horse

Village signposted from A281 SE of Horsham

This year, the licensees have added new garden furniture to the front terrace here, and have renovated the much liked back woodland streamside garden; plenty of surrounding walks. Inside, it's old-fashioned and friendly, and the main bar has big Horsham flagstones in front of the inglenook fireplace, interesting pictures on the walls, and magazines to read. At one end it opens out into other carpeted areas including a dining room. Well kept Greene King IPA, Hardy Popes Traditional, Hop Back Summer Lightning, Wadworths 6X, Charles Wells Bombardier, and a weekly guest beer on handpump, and they hold beer festivals twice a year; Belgian fruit beers, country wines, and wines of the month. Bar food includes sandwiches, tomato and basil soup (£2.95), wild boar terrine with juniper berries and raspberry port coulis (£3.95), good bangers and mash, grilled goat's cheese with herbs on salad leaves or cannelloni romagna (£6.95), smoky fish crumble (£7.50), chicken tikka masala (£8.25). They hold themed food evenings; the restaurant is no smoking; cribbage, dominoes, Jenga, and piped music. *(Recommended by John Fahy, Eamonn and Natasha Skyrme, Simon Collett-Jones, R and S Bentley, Louise Lyons, Peter Elliot, Dr Jim Mackay, Susan and John Douglas)*

Free house ~ Licensees Karen Jones and Julian Clayton ~ Real ale ~ Meals and snacks ~ Restaurant (not Sun evening) ~ (01403) 891272 ~ Children welcome ~ Monthly live jazz trio ~ Open 11-3(3.30 Sat), 6-11; 12-3.30, 7-10.30 Sun

Pubs staying open all afternoon are listed at the back of the book.

OFFHAM TQ4012

Blacksmiths Arms

A275 N of Lewes; on left

This attractive red brick dining pub is kept spick and span, with most of the close-set tables in the open-plan bar set for enjoying the imaginative food. At one end of the gleaming central counter is a huge inglenook fireplace with logs stacked at one side, and at the other is the airy dining area. Nice old prints of London, some Spy prints and several old sporting prints decorate the walls above shiny black wainscoting. Bar snacks include ploughman's (from £4.25), filled baked potatoes (from £4.50), and ham and eggs (£5.25), plus soups such as cream of broccoli (£2.55), lamb and redcurrant pâté with crème fraîche and mint dressing (£4.50), curries (from £5.95), steak, kidney and mushroom pie (£6.95), chicken breast stuffed with prawn and lemon mousse with a tomato and dill cream sauce (£7.75), pork fillet with red onion, ginger and pineapple confit and sherry sauce (£8.25), cajun blackened fresh salmon fillet with smoked bacon and creamed leek sauce (£8.50), steaks (from £8.95), a vegetarian dish of the day, and puddings like home-made fresh fruit pie or chocolate bread and butter pudding with marmalade sauce (£3.50); careful efficient service. Well kept Harveys Best on handpump. French windows open on to a tiny little brick and paved terrace with a couple of flowering tubs and picnic-sets with umbrellas; beware of the dangerous bend when leaving the car park; spotless disabled lavatories. ***(Recommended by Mayur Shah, Dave Wilcock, Brian Carter, P Keen; more reports please)***

Free House ~ Licensee Jean Large ~ Real ale ~ Meals and snacks ~ (01273) 472971 ~ Children over five in restaurant ~ Open 11-3, 6.30-11; 12-3, 7-10.30 Sun; closed 25-26 Dec

OVING SU9005 Map 2

Gribble

Between A27 and A259 just E of Chichester, then should be signposted just off village road; OS Sheet 197 map reference 900050

It's their own-brew beers that most people come to enjoy at this charming rose-covered thatched cottage – Gribble Ale, Reg's Tipple, Black Adder II, Pigs Ear, Ewe Brew, and winter Wobbler on handpump; country wines, and farm cider. But there's also a good friendly atmosphere and enjoyable food, and the bar has lots of heavy beams and timbering, and old country-kitchen furnishings and pews. On the left, there's a no-smoking family/dining room with pews which provides one of the biggest no-smoking areas we've so far found in a Sussex pub. Home-made bar food includes ham and eggs (£4.95), chicken and broccoli lasagne (£4.95; bigger helping £5.95), chicken korma or stir-fried prawns with snow peas (£4.95; bigger helping £6.25), home-made burger with barbecue sauce (£5.75), fresh fish in lemon batter with chips (£5.95), lemon and pepper chicken or orange and basil pork steak (£7.25), steaks (from £10.25), and children's meals (£3.25). Darts, shove-ha'penny, cribbage, fruit machine and a separate skittle alley. There are seats in the pretty garden and a covered seating area. ***(Recommended by Tony and Wendy Hobden, Brad W Morley, David Gould, John Donnelly, Ann and Colin Hunt, Dr Alan Green, J Brisset, Lawrence Pearse, Mrs D Bromley-Martin, Bruce Jamieson)***

Own brew (Badger) ~ Managers Brian and Lyn Elderfield ~ Real ale ~ Meals and snacks ~ (01243) 786893 ~ Children in big family room ~ Open 11-3, 6-11; 11-11 summer Sat; 12-10.30 summer Sun

PETT

Two Sawyers

Pett Rd; off A259

It's always a joy for us to discover a genuine old country pub with a bit of real character. This is a place to spend a leisurely Sunday afternoon over a drink, possibly a pint of very well kept Old Forge Pett Progress or one of the other beers that the cheerful Old Forge brewmen brew to the sound of rock in a small building across the car park – you will probably be welcome to have a look round; two or three other changing real ales might include Flowers Original, Gales HSB, Old Forge Pett Arrow or Brothers Best; five wines by the glass. The meandering rooms of this unhurried low-beamed place are simply but genuinely put together, with black band saws on cream walls, handsome iron wall lamps and stripped tables on bare boards in its two simple bars, and dark wood pub tables and cushioned banquettes in a tiny low-ceilinged snug, with a very old painted flint wall on one side; a sloping old stone floor leads down to a low-beamed restaurant. Big helpings of bar food, cooked by the easy going young landlord, include filled baguettes (from £1.95, steak £3.75), soup (£2.50), pâté (£3), ploughman's (£3.70), quiche (£4.95), lasagne (£5.95), scampi or beef, cod and prawn pie or beer and mushroom pie (£6.25), rump steak (£9) and puddings (£2.50). Leisurely service is very friendly. An iron gate leads from a pretty suntrap front brick courtyard to an unaffected and restful back garden with shady trees, a few well spaced picnic-sets and children's play area; pétanque, darts, fruit machine shove-ha'penny. *(Recommended by K M Thorpe, E G Parish, Jenny and Brian Seller)*

Free House ~ Licensee Peter Neumark-Payne ~ Real ale ~ Meals and snacks ~ (01424) 812255 ~ Children welcome away from bar ~ Live folk, bluegrass or Latin funk Fri evening ~ Open 11-3, 6-11 (may be open all day in summer) Mon-Thurs; 11-11 Fri/Sat; 12-10.30 Sun; cl 25 Dec ~ Bedrooms: £18.50/£34

PETWORTH SU9719 Map 2

Badgers 🍷

Coultershaw Bridge; just off A285 1½ miles S

Of course most people come to this stylish dining pub to enjoy the very good food, but there is a small chatty drinking area by the entrance, with a couple of tables (and an attractive antique oak monk's chair) and some bar stools – and locals drop in regularly for a pint. All the rest of the space around the island bar servery is devoted to dining tables – well spaced, and an attractive mix of chairs and of tables, from old mahogany to waxed stripped pine. White walls, the deep maroon colour of the high ceiling, charming wrought-iron lamps, winter log fires, stripped shutters for the big Victorian windows, and a modicum of carefully chosen decorations including a few houseplants and dried flower arrangements induce a feeling of contented relaxation in the several linked areas; this is underlined by informal yet punctilious service. Besides the good if not cheap restaurant menu, the imaginative changing choice of attractively presented bar dishes might include good pasta with scallops, prawn tails and basil (£8.25), grilled salmon with sun-dried tomato sauce and roasted vegetables (£10.95), and an excellent fish and shellfish stew (£13.95). Please do record for us the price and details of any other dishes you particulary enjoy here. Well kept Badger Best, Hop Back Summer Lightning and Theakstons Best on handpump, with a good range of well chosen house wines and a fine list by the bottle; maybe faint piped music (the dominant sound is quiet conversation). A terrace by a waterlily pool has stylish metal garden furniture under parasols, and some solid old-fashioned wooden seats. No motorcyclists. *(Recommended by Martin and Karen Wake, James Nunns, Mrs D M Gray; more reports please)*

Free house ~ Real ale ~ Meals and snacks ~ Restaurant ~ (01798) 342651 ~ Children over 5 may be allowed away from bar

PLAYDEN TQ9121 Map 3

Peace & Plenty

A268/B2082

Charmingly decorated, this cottagey dining pub is much liked by readers. The deep pink walls and shelves are attractively crowded with lots of china, little pictures, brass implements, and cat paraphernalia, there are pot plants and dried flowers, small lamps creating a warm glow, a good mix of tables, and a woodburning stove in a big inglenook at one end with comfortable armchairs either side; gentle classical piped radio. There are two similarly cosy cottagey dining areas. Enjoyable bar food might include home-made soup or salmon fishcake with a light lemon sauce (£2.95; the creamy seafood soup is very good), roast ham and egg (£4.65), bangers and mash or moussaka (£5.95), lamb liver and bacon (£6.25), rump steak (£6.95), chicken tobago (in a hot citrus sauce, £7.05), very popular roast beef in a giant yorkshire pudding (£7.75), steak and kidney pudding (£7.95), and puddings like ginger and treacle pudding, lemon meringue pie or caramel apple granny (£2.95); attentive service. Well kept Greene King IPA, Abbot and Rayments on handpump from a small counter. The friendly little children's room has a comfy sofa, Sega games, toys, and books; cards, trivial pursuit, and mind trap on each table. There are seats in the pretty flowery garden though there is traffic noise. *(Recommended by D Buckley, Ray Watson, Mr and Mrs P Eastwood, G Washington, S Cutier, Paula Williams, Brenda and Stuart Naylor, B and M Parkin)*

Free house ~ Licensee Yvonne Thomas ~ Real ale ~ Meals and snacks (11-9.30) ~ Restaurant ~ (01797) 280342 ~ Children welcome ~ Open 11-11; 12-10.30; closed 25-26 Dec

nr PUNNETTS TOWN TQ6220 Map 3

Three Cups

B2096 towards Battle

This is just the place to end up after enjoying one of the many surrounding walks – and the pub dogs Monty and Lettie and the cat Hattie welcome other dogs (on a lead). It's an unspoilt traditional local, and the peaceful and friendly long low-beamed bar has attractive panelling, comfortable seats including some in big bay windows overlooking a small green, and a log fire in the big fireplace under a black mantlebeam dated 1696. A partly no-smoking back dining room leads out to a small covered terrace with seats in the garden beyond. Bar food is totally home-made and includes sandwiches (from £2), soup (£2.50), ploughman's (£4), ham and eggs (£3.95), meaty or vegetarian lasagne or steak in ale pie (£5.25), chicken in a mushroom and cream sauce (£6), grilled trout with almonds (£7), sirloin steak (£8.50), and puddings such as fruit crumble or banoffee pie (£2.50); Sunday roast (£5.25). Well kept Beards Best and Harveys Best and guests like Arundel Footslogger, Batemans XXXB or Fullers London Pride on handpump; darts, shove-ha'penny, cribbage, and dominoes. (*Recommended by Dave Braisted, K M Thorpe, Mr and Mrs R D Knight; more reports please)*

Beards ~ Tenants Barbara and Colin Wood ~ Real ale ~ Meals and snacks ~ (01435) 830252 ~ Children in eating area of bar only ~ Occasional solo singer or duo weekends ~ Open 11-2.30, 6.30-11; 11-11 Sat; 12-4, 7-10.30 Sun

RYE TQ9220 Map 3

Mermaid 🛏 🍷

Mermaid St

Even if you've never been to this lovely old inn, you're more than likely to have seen a postcard or photograph of its striking black and white timbered facade, with the distinctive sign hanging over the steeply cobbled street. The fine back bar remains unchanged with a mix of quite closely set furnishings including Victorian gothic carved oak chairs, older but plainer oak seats and more modern ones in character, and a massive deeply polished bressumer beam across one wall for the huge inglenook fireplace; three antique but not ancient wall paintings showing old English recipes and so forth, and a pleasant atmosphere with an easy-going mix of tourists and well-off locals. The cellars that hold the well kept Marstons Pedigree and Morlands Old Speckled Hen date back seven centuries; good wine list. Bar food includes soup (£6), filled french bread (£4.50), spinach and ricotta pasta (£6), local codling (£7.50), cold roast beef or ham salad (from £8), entrecote steak (£10.50), and puddings like pear and almond tart (£3). Piped music, chess and cards. There are seats on a small back terrace. *(Recommended by J Sheldon, Paul McPherson, Paula Williams, Mr and Mrs D Ross, T Pascall, Dorothee and Dennis Glover, David and Margaret Bloomfield, Betsy Brown, Nigel Flook, Kevin Thorpe, Paul Hilditch)*

Free house ~ Licensees Robert Pinwill and Mrs J Blincow ~ Real ale ~ Meals and snacks (11-6 in summer) ~ Restaurant ~ (01797) 223065 ~ Well behaved children welcome ~ Open 11-11; 12-10.30 Sun ~ Bedrooms: £45(£62B)/£90(£128B)

Ypres Castle 🍽 🍷

Gun Garden, off A259

What is interesting about this pub in its fine setting up near the 13th-c Ypres Tower, with a steep flight of stone steps down to the building, is that it has the atmosphere and feel of a good local but offers food that is considerably better than that. The style of the pub is fairly spartan, with basic furnishings, local events posters and so forth – what transforms it is the friendly atmosphere, which seems particularly warm and embracing on a blustery winter's night; and the three friendly labradors do their bit to help. The nicest place to eat is in a quieter room beyond the bar with simple but comfortable wall seats and local pictures. What's on the menu depends on what the landlord's found in the markets – not just the fresh local fish and seafood, but the products of his weekly trips to London. Besides good value filled baguettes (£1.75), it might include soup (£2.25), ploughman's (from £4.20), roast fillet of cod (£7.70), moules marinières (£7.95), excellent scallops in garlic butter (£8.95), and daily specials such as pasta with mushrooms and a cheesy garlic sauce or spicy tomato and pepper sauce (£5.65), roast duck in morello cherry and brandy sauce (£8.80), rack of local lamb with mint and redcurrant glaze (£9.60), and Scotch sirloin steak (£10.95); good fresh vegetables. Well kept Harveys Best and Mild, Old Forge Brothers Best, and changing guest beers on handpump, good value wine (especially by the bottle) with lots by the glass, and farm cider; maybe old yachting magazines to leaf through. Darts, shove-ha'penny, dominoes, cribbage, and piped jazz or classical music. In summer, there's the big bonus of a sizeable lawn; picnic-sets out here have a fine view out over the River Rother winding its way through the shore marshes. Ypres, pub and tower, is pronounced WWI-style, as Wipers. *(Recommended by S Groves, David Braisted, Betsy Brown, Nigel Flook, T Pascall, E P Gray)*

Free house ~ Licensee R J Pearce ~ Real ale ~ Meals and snacks ~ Restaurant ~ (01797) 223248 ~ Children in eating area of bar until 9pm ~ Blues Sun evening ~ Open 12-11; 12-10.30 Sun

SALEHURST TQ7424 Map 3

Salehurst Halt 🍷

Village signposted from Robertsbridge bypass on A21 Tunbridge Wells—Battle Rd

Close to the attractive 14th-c church, this little village local has a quiet, warmly friendly atmosphere. The L-shaped bar has good plain wooden tables and chairs on flagstones at one end, a cushioned window seat, beams, a little open brick fireplace, a time punch clock and olde worlde pictures; lots of hops on a big beam divide this from the beamed carpeted area with its mix of tables, wheelback and farmhouse chairs, and a half wall leads to a dining area with a grandfather clock. Nice home-made food includes, at lunchtime, filled baked potatoes (£3.90), burgers made with top minced rump with a choice of cheese, bacon or barbecue sauces (very popular, £5.50), home-baked ham with egg (£5.90), lasagne or chilli (£5.90), and steaks (£6.95), with evening dishes such as pâté or snails, spicy vegetable parcel or beef in ale pie (£7.95), beef stroganoff or seafood pie (£8.95), supper specials like beef curry, vegetable pie or a fish dish (£7.50), and puddings such as fruit crumbles, fudgecake or bread and butter pudding (£2.75). There are fresh flowers on the bar, well kept Harveys Best on handpump, good wines, and a relaxed and chatty atmosphere; piped music. The little garden with its terraces and picnic-sets is pleasant, and the window boxes and tubs are very pretty. *(Recommended by Peter Meister, Tony and Rachel Schendel, Sinclair Robieson, Paula Williams)*

Free house ~ Licensee Jane Steed ~ Real ale ~ Meals and snacks (not Mon or Tues) ~ (01580) 880620 ~ Well behaved children in eating area of bar ~ Open 12-3(3.30 Sat, 4 Sun), 7-11(10.30 Sun); closed Mon/Tues exc bank holidays

Children welcome means the pubs says it lets children inside without any special restriction; readers have found that some may impose an evening time limit – please tell us if you find this.

nr SCAYNES HILL TQ3623 Map 3

Sloop

Freshfield Lock; at top of Scaynes Hill by petrol station turn N off A272 into Church Rd, keep on for 1½ miles and then follow Freshfield signpost

Handy for the Bluebell Line steam railway and not far from Sheffield Park, this country pub has a long saloon bar with a simple mix of pine furniture and some comfortable old seats, and a warmly friendly atmosphere; there are benches in the old-fashioned brick porch. Bar food is home-made, good and popular, and might include filled french sticks (from £3.75), ploughman's (from £4.95), pancakes filled with spinach and cheese (£5.95), popular fish pie or Mexican chilli beef (£6.95), chicken in mustard and gruyère cheese sauce (£7.95), and daily specials such as chicken fricasee with vinegar and tarragon on wild rice (£8.95), salmon fillet with a lime and butter sauce (£9.95), thai beef salad with lemon grass, chilli and coriander (£10.50), fillet of lamb kebabs indonesian style with vegetable couscous (£11.50), and large whole crab salad with prawns (£12.50). Well kept Adnams Extra and Harveys Best and seasonal Knots of May on handpump, and a decent wine list; piped music. The basic but airy public bar has stripped woodwork and bare boards, and a small games room leading off with sensibly placed darts and bar billiards; piped music. This is a lovely spot beside what used to be the Ouse canal with a sheltered garden and lots of tables to enjoy the sunshine and birdsong. *(Recommended by John Knighton, P W Taylor, Lisa Day, Charles Parry, Simon and Sally Small, Mr and Mrs R D Knight)*

Beards ~ Tenant Ian Philpots ~ Real ale ~ Meals and snacks (not Sun evening) ~ (01444) 831219 ~ Well behaved children welcome ~ Open 11-3, 6-11; 12-3, 7-10.30 Sun; closed evenings 25-26 Dec, 1 Jan

nr SEAFORD TV4899 Map 3

Golden Galleon

Exceat Bridge; A259 Seaford—Eastbourne, near Cuckmere

They seem to be able to handle huge numbers of customers in this busy pub with remarkable efficiency – and particularly on a sunny day, it can get pretty packed. Two thirds of the premises is no smoking – there's a conservatory and river room, and a spreading main bar with high trussed and pitched rafters which create quite an airy feel. A fine choice of real ales includes their own from the little microbrewery on site. Brewed by the landlord's brother-in-law, they might include Cuckmere Haven Best, Guv'nor, Golden Peace, an old fashioned cask conditioned stout, Saxon King, and seasonal beers; they also brew their own keg conditioned lager, as well as keeping other ales like Harveys Armada, Gales HSB and Greene King Abbot and IPA, on handpump or tapped from the cask, and hold occasional beer festivals (the May Day one has 22 real ales and farm ciders); farm cider, good wines by the glass, a decent selection of malts, continental brandies, Italian liqueurs, and cappuccino or espresso coffee. Most people, however, come to enjoy the good food, with starters and small snacks such as home-made soups (£2.75), bruschetta romana (a chunk of garlic bread topped with warm plum tomatoes, garlic, onion, finely chopped celery, and fennel) or tuna fish and butter beans with capers, onion, garlic and parsley with olive oil (£3.25), Italian rarebit (toasted bread with melting cheddar, mozzarella and parma ham £3.95), insalata di frutti di mare (Italian seafood salad £4.50) or whole king prawns in garlic butter with aioli dip (£6.95), plus ploughman's (from £3.95), lunchtime baked potatoes (from £4.75), very good fresh local fish of the day (£6.25), chicken in tomato, fresh ginger and garlic sauce (£7.75), and Scottish steaks (from £9.75); they have their own smokery, and offer a children's menu. It's worth walking along the river to the sea or inland to Friston Forest and the downs, and there are tables in the sloping garden with views towards the Cuckmere estuary and Seven Sisters Country Park. *(Recommended by Lawrence Pearse, John Beeken, Janet and Colin Roe, Tim and Pam Moorey, Tony and Wendy Hobden, David and Carole Chapman, Simon Collett-Jones, N B Thompson, Tony Scott, P Rome)*

Own brew ~ Licensee Stefano Diella ~ Real ale ~ Meals and snacks (ploughman's/salads all day; no food winter Sun evenings) ~ (01323) 892247 ~ Children welcome ~ Open 11-11; 12-10.30 Sun; closed winter Sun evenings nr TICEHURST TQ6830 Map 3

Bull

Three Legged Cross; coming into Ticehurst from N on B2099, just before Ticehurst village sign, turn left beside corner house called Tollgate (Maynards Pick Your Own may be signposted here)

Close to Bewl Water and handy for visiting the lovely gardens of Pashley Manor, this 14th-c Wealden hall is a most pleasant place to spend a quiet lunchtime. A series of small flagstoned, brick-floored or oak parquet rooms run together, with heavy oak tables, seats of some character, and two big log fires; it's well liked by locals in the evening, when the friendly very low beamed rooms soon fill up. Well kept Harveys Best and Pale Ale, Morlands Old Speckled Hen, and locally brewed Rother Valley Level Best on handpump; friendly service. Bar food includes soup (£2.75), filled freshly baked french bread (from £2.75), and daily specials such as thai fishcakes (£4.75), beef sizzler (£5.50), lamb liver and bacon (£6.25), steak and kidney pie (£6.50), half shoulder of English lamb (£7.25), and puddings like sticky toffee pudding or crème brûlée (£3.25); Sunday roast beef, pork or lamb (£6.25). There's an unusual round pool table, as well as darts, bar billiards, pinball, dominoes, cribbage and piped music, and a couple of boules pitches. In summer the charming garden is a lovely place to sit at tables beside an ornamental fish pond looking back at the rose and clematis-covered building; outside bar and barbecue, and at weekends they usually have a bouncy castle for children. Maynards fruit farm is just up the road. *(Recommended by Comus Elliott, Bob and Maggie Atherton, Peter Meister, B and M Parkin, James and Lynne House, Paula Williams, C and M Starling)*

Free house ~ Licensee Mrs E M Wilson-Moir ~ Real ale ~ Meals and snacks (not Sun or Mon evenings) ~ Restaurant ~ (01580) 200586 ~ Children welcome ~ Live entertainment Sun evenings ~ Open 11-3, 6-11; 12-3, 7-10.30 Sun; closed winter Mon

TILLINGTON SU9621 Map 2

Horse Guards

Village signposted from A272 Midhurst—Petworth

Run by warmly friendly and experienced licensees, this neatly kept 300-year-old inn is very much somewhere to come for an enjoyable meal rather than a casual drink. It's in a pretty setting perched high over the lane and there's a lovely view beyond the village to the Rother Valley from the seat in the big black-panelled bow window of the cosy beamed front bar – which also has some good country furniture and a log fire. A wide choice of good, interesting food includes sandwiches (from £3.25), home-made soup (£3.95), ploughman's (£5.50), good caesar salad (from £5.25), chicken curry or mushroom stroganoff (£7.25), and seafood pie (£7.50) from the light bar menu, as well as lunchtime dishes like italian-style roasted vegetables with a balsamic and basil vinaigrette (£4.50), grilled black pudding with a whisky and wholegrain mustard dressing (£4.75), crab and spinach florentine with a thermidor sauce (£5.95), tagliatelle verdi with button mushrooms, spring onions and blue cheese sauce (£6.95), flavoured sausages with a white onion sauce and duchesse potatoes (£7.50), steak and kidney pie (£8.25), oven-baked haddock fillet with a chive, basil and sun-dried tomato crumble topping set on a vermouth sauce (£9.75), and extra evening specials like grilled langoustine with garlic butter (£6.95), marinated duck breast with orange and basil (£11.95), and grilled whole brill (£13.25); excellent Sunday roast beef with yorkshire pudding (£8.75). The good wine list usually has a dozen by the glass; well kept Badger Best and King & Barnes Best on handpump, and good espresso and cappuccino coffee. Darts, and cribbage. There's a terrace outside, and more tables and chairs in a sheltered garden behind. The church opposite is 800 years old. *(Recommended by R E Syrett, Brian Mills, W Ruxton, Evelyn and Derek Walter, L Granville, B and M Kendall, Wendy Arnold, Martin and Karen Wake, G D Sharpe, Mr and Mrs D E Powell, Sue Stevens, Clive Gilbert, Margaret and Nigel Dennis, Betsy Brown, Nigel Flook, K M Thorpe, Patrick Hall, Susan and John Douglas)*

Free house ~ Licensees Aidan and Lesley Nugent ~ Real ale ~ Meals and snacks (till 10pm) ~ (01798) 342332 ~ Children welcome but must be over 8 in evening ~ Open 11-3, 6-11; 12-3, 7-10.30 Sun ~ Bedrooms: /£65B

WEST ASHLING SU8107 Map 2

Richmond Arms 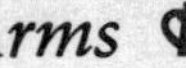

Mill Lane; from B2146 in village follow Hambrook signpost

Friendly new licensees have taken over this out-of-the-way village pub and have done some careful refurbishment without changing too much of the character – the locals seem pleased which is always a good sign. The main bar, dominated by the central servery, still has a 1930s feel with its long wall benches, library chairs, and black tables, there's now a dark wooden dado with a cream wall in one part and wallpaper in the other, wooden ducks on the picture rails and pictures on the walls, and an open fire in the now stripped brick fireplace. They still keep a good range of real ales on handpump – Arundel Gold and Beards Best, Harveys Best, King & Barnes Mild, Hop Back Summer Lightning, Timothy Taylor Landlord, and Woodfordes Wherry. Bar food includes filled french bread (£2.50), home-made steak and kidney pudding or home-cooked ham and eggs (£5.95), and sirloin steak (£7.95). Dominoes, cribbage, and skittle alley. There's a pergola, and some picnic-sets by the car park. *(Recommended by Ann and Colin Hunt, Bruce Bird, Phyl and Jack Street, D and J Tapper, Jo and Gary Charlton, Edward Froggatt; more reports on the new regime, please)*

Beards ~ Tenants Alan and Dianne Gurney ~ Real ale ~ Meals and snacks ~ (01243) 575730 ~ Children welcome ~ Open 11-2.30(3 Sat), 5.30-11; 12-3, 7-10.30 Sun

WEST HOATHLY TQ3632 Map 3

Cat

Village signposted from either A22 or B2028 S of East Grinstead

Mr and Mrs Shee run this pub with great care. Last year they bought the freehold from Beards and have created a relaxing environment with no pool, darts, fruit machines, loud music or fast food. There are polished tables with fresh flowers and candles, some beams and panelling, two roaring log fires, and quiet classical piped music. The food is aimed between good home-cooking and well presented restaurant food, and includes home-made soup (£3.25), home-made chicken liver pâté (£4.95), sausage and mash with onion gravy (£6.95), fresh grilled sardines in garlic butter (£7.95), mushroom stroganoff, steak and kidney pie or liver and bacon (£9.95), pork fillet in a creamy cider and apple sauce (£12.95), roast rack of lamb or halibut with fresh cheese sauce topped with salt water prawns and tomatoes (£14.95), and steaks (from £15.95). Well kept Harveys Best and Hardy Royal Oak on handpump, and a carefully chosen little wine list. Seats among the roses out in front are a good place to catch the sun, and there are fine views of the neighbouring old church nestling amongst its yew trees. No children. *(Recommended by Tony Scott, Derek Harvey-Piper, B J Harding, G Simpson; more reports please)*

Free house ~ Licensees Peter and Sue Shee ~ Real ale ~ Meals and snacks (not 25-26 Dec) ~ Restaurant ~ (01342) 810369 ~ Folk music Tues evening, piano most Fri/Sat evenings ~ Open 12-2.30, 6-11; 12-3, 7-10.30 Sun; closed evenings 25-26 Dec

WINEHAM TQ2320 Map 3

Royal Oak

Village signposted from A272 and B2116

It's always pleasing to come across delightfully old-fashioned places like this that remain unchanging and traditional and place the emphasis on drinking rather than eating. There are logs burning in an enormous inglenook fireplace, ancient corkscrews decorating the very low beams above the serving counter, racing plates, tools and a coach horn on the walls, and simple furnishings. Well kept beers tapped from the cask in a still room on the way to a little snug include Harveys Best and Marstons Pedigree; darts, shove-ha'penny, dominoes, cribbage. The limited range of bar snacks includes fresh-cut or toasted sandwiches (from £1.75, home-cooked roast beef £2 or lovely smoked salmon £2.50), home-made soup in winter, and ploughman's (from £3.50); courteous service – the pub has been in the same family for over 50 years. It can get very busy at weekends and on summer evenings. The charming frontage has a lawn with wooden tables by a well. On a clear day sharp-eyed male readers may be able to catch a glimpse of Chanctonbury Ring from the window in the gents'. No children inside. *(More reports please)*

Inn Business ~ Tenant Tim Peacock ~ Real ale ~ Snacks (available during opening hours) ~ (01444) 881252 ~ Open 11-2.30, 5.30(6 Sat)-11; 12-3, 7-10.30 Sun; closed evenings 25 Dec and 1 Jan

WITHYHAM TQ4935 Map 3

Dorset Arms

B2110

The bar in this bustling 16th-c inn has a traditional welcoming atmosphere, sturdy tables and simple country seats on the wide oak floorboards, and a good log fire in the stone Tudor fireplace. The good bar food is very popular, so it's best to get there early for a seat (or book in advance): quite a few sandwiches (from £2; toasties from £2.30), home-made soup (£2.35), ploughman's (from £3.75), filled baked potatoes (from £4.35), spinach and feta cheese goujons (£4.50), omelettes or crispy cod and chips (£4.95), home-roasted ham and egg (£5.35), fresh baked trout or rump steak (£6.95), and daily specials such as ratatouille (£4.95), smoked salmon flan, venison pie or lamb chop (£5.25), duck breast (£5.95), and half shoulder of lamb (£7.50), with puddings like sticky toffee pudding, caramel apple pie or lemon tart (£3); the restaurant is pretty. Well kept Harveys Best, Pale Ale, Mild and seasonal beers on handpump, and a reasonable wine list including some local ones. Darts, dominoes, shove-ha'penny, cribbage, fruit machine, and piped music. There are white tables on a brick terrace by the small green. The countryside around here is nice, and the nearby church has a memorial to Vita Sackville-West. (*Recommended by Martin Wright, Alan Kilpatrick, Tony Scott, Peter Meister, A Cowell, Ron Gentry, R D Knight)*

Harveys ~ Tenants John and Sue Pryor ~ Real ale ~ Meals and snacks (not Mon evening) ~ Restaurant (not Sun evening) ~ (01892) 770278 ~ Children in restaurant and lounge area ~ Open 11.30(11 Sat)-3, 5.30(6 Sat)-11; 12-3, 7-10.30 Sun

Lucky Dip

Besides the fully inspected pubs, you might like to try these Lucky Dips recommended to us and described by readers (if you do, please send us reports):

☆ **Alfriston** E Sus [High St; TQ5203], *George*: Welcoming 14th-c timbered inn, ancient low beams, huge inglenook, jovial landlord, hard-working staff, well kept Fullers London Pride, Harveys, Marstons, Morlands Old Speckled Hen and Theakstons; popular for home-made bar food inc lots of good fish and fresh veg in bar, intimate candlelit restaurant or garden dining room; comfortable attractive bedrooms, lovely village, fine riverside walks down to Cuckmere Haven *(Phyl and Jack Street, Mr and Mrs A Albert, G Hallett)*

Angmering W Sus [off main st opp Lamb, then 3rd left into cul de sac; TQ0704], *Spotted Cow*: Well kept ales inc one brewed for the pub, good bar food (very popular weekday lunchtimes with older people), friendly service, smuggling history; restaurant, roomy garden, good play area; lovely walk to Highdown hill fort *(Bruce Bird, R T and J C Moggridge, Tony and Wendy Hobden, Mrs P J Pearce)*

Ansty W Sus [A272/B2036, 2 miles from Ansty; TQ2923], *Ansty Cross*: Recently refurbished and extended under new owners, some concentration on enjoyable food, well kept Bass, Fullers London Pride and Harveys, inglenook log fire, very friendly courteous staff *(Terry Buckland)*

☆ **Ardingly** W Sus [B2028 2 miles N; TQ3429], *Gardeners Arms*: Immaculately refurbished olde-worlde dining pub very popular for consistently good if not cheap fresh home-made food, big inglenook log fire, service pleasant and cheerful even when crowded, well kept Boddingtons, Harveys and Theakstons, morning coffee and tea, attractive decorations, maybe soft piped music, no children; well spaced tables out among small trees, handy for Borde Hill and Wakehurst Place *(Tony and Wendy Hobden, Fred Chamberlain, Derek and Maggie Washington, Elizabeth and Klaus Leist, D Wilcox, Eamonn and Natasha Skyrme, Tony Scott, Lady M H Moir, John Pettit)*

☆ **Arlington** E Sus [off A22 nr Hailsham, or A27 W of Polegate; TQ5407], *Yew Tree*: Neatly modernised two-bar village local, colourful flowers out in front, reliable generous home cooking inc children's, well kept Courage Directors, Harveys Best and Morlands Old Speckled Hen, log fires, efficient cheery service, subdued piped music, darts; dining area with french windows to good big garden and play area, by paddock with farm animals *(John Beeken, R D and S R Knight, LM, Tony Scott, BB)*

☆ **Arlington** [Caneheath, E of village], *Old Oak*: 17th-c former almshouses, with relaxing and spacious open-plan L-shaped beamed bar, dining room, good reasonably priced home-made food inc puddings from cold counter, well kept Badger, Harveys and usually a guest beer tapped from the cask, friendly helpful landlord, log fires, no music, peaceful garden; children allowed, handy for Bluebell Walk *(Alan Skull, BB)*

Arundel W Sus [Mill Rd; keep on and don't give up!; TQ0107], *Black Rabbit*: Big touristy riverside pub, plenty of provision for families, best on a quiet day – lovely spot, with lots of tables out looking across to bird-reserve watermeadows and Castle; Badger Best and Tanglefoot and guest ales, log fires, restaurant, open all day in summer, doubling as tea shop then; summer boat trips here *(David and Carole Chapman, Tony and Wendy Hobden, David Gould, Tony Scott, Lady M H Moir, Pamela Goodwyn, A Pring, LYM)*; [36 Kings Arms Hill], *Kings Arms*: Straightforward local, popular with young people, with well kept ales inc Fullers, Youngs and a local guest, bar food, small back yard; open all day *(Tony Scott)*; [London Rd, by cathedral], *St Marys Gate*: Comfortable open-plan bar, alcoves, lots of horse-racing caricatures, generous good value home-made food from sandwiches up, well kept Badger Best and Tanglefoot and guest beer, friendly staff coping well with the coach parties, restaurant, no-smoking area, TV in small back room, unobtrusive piped music, picnic-sets on pleasant back terrace; bedrooms quiet and good value *(Norman and Sarah Keeping, Ian Phillips, Bruce Bird, K and J Morris)*; [High St], *Swan*: Well refurbished, with beatiful woodwork and attractive matching fittings, unusual beaten brass former inn-sign now in open-plan L-shaped bar, good choice of food inc vegetarian, full range of good Arundel beers (priced down weekday early evenings) with a guest such as Fullers London Pride, all well kept, friendly young staff; piped music can get loud – side room a bit quieter; restaurant, good bedrooms *(Mark Matthewman, Tony and Wendy Hobden, Bruce Bird, LYM)*

☆ **Balcombe** W Sus [London Rd (B2036/B2110); N of village; TQ3033], *Cowdray Arms*: Roomy country pub, popular for good choice of well prepared and presented food inc some interesting dishes, attentive welcoming service, well kept Beards, Harveys and guest such as Adnams, Buckleys or Thwaites Mild, occasional beer festivals, spacious no-smoking restaurant; children welcome, garden with good play area *(DWAJ, Dr and Mrs D J Walker, Bruce Bird, A Kilpatrick, Tony Scott)*

Bexhill E Sus [Turkey Rd; TQ7407], *Rose & Crown*: Good home-made food from baguettes and ploughman's to Sun lunch in friendly and clean suburban local with old-fashioned rather domestic atmosphere, no-smoking area, well kept Harveys Best; wheelchair access and disabled facilities, tables in garden with terrace and barbecue *(A L Budden, Alec and Marie Lewery)*

Billingshurst W Sus [High St; A29; TQ0925], *Olde Six Bells*: Picturesque partly 14th-c flagstoned and timbered pub with well kept King & Barnes, cheery service, inglenook fireplace, pretty roadside garden *(Tony and Wendy Hobden, TOH, LYM)*

☆ **Binsted** W Sus [Binsted Lane, off A27 about 2 miles W of Arundel; SU9806], *Black Horse*: Pretty 17th-c pub with ochre walls and open fire in big comfortable bar, seven or eight well kept ales, darts and pool one end, warmly welcoming licensees, bar food inc generous sandwiches and well presented freshly cooked specials, wider range in back conservatory restaurant, Gales HSB, Harveys Best, Marstons Pedigree and Hop Back Summer Lightning; idyllic garden, views over valley; bedrooms *(JDM, KM, Colin Draper, Mrs Romey Heaton, John Donnelly, BB)*

Blackham E Sus [A264 towards E Grinstead; TQ4838], *Sussex Oak*: Shepherd Neame pub doing very well under newish licensees and their son, she cooks good very generous plain food *(Colin Laffan)*

Boarshead E Sus [Eridge Rd; off A26 bypass; TQ5332], *Boars Head*: Unspoilt cosy old dim-lit stone-floored place next to pleasant farmyard, welcoming log fire, simple good value food, well kept ales, low 16th-c beams; very peaceful weekday lunchtimes (piped music turned down then if asked) *(R D and S R Knight)*

Bodle Street Green E Sus [off A271 at Windmill Hill; TQ6514], *White Horse*: Simply modernised country pub popular with older people midweek for good value generous lunches, friendly service, well kept Harveys and Shepherd Neame Spitfire, decent wines and malt whiskies, open fires, bar billiards, darts, cheery piped music; some tables outside *(Janet and Colin Roe, BB)*

Bognor Regis W Sus [56 London Rd; SZ9399], *Alex*: Friendly, warm, cosy and clean, good value generous food inc good daily specials, hot pork in home-baked bread (Sat) and Sun lunch, pleasant service, Scottish Courage and King & Barnes ales, huge mug and jug collection *(R Cooper, R T and J C Moggridge, Mrs V C Williams)*

Bolney W Sus [The Street; TQ2623], *Eight Bells*: Friendly, clean and comfortable, well kept Harveys and Flowers Original, good promptly served food, local paintings, open fires; occasional live music, garden *(Bruce Bird, Tony and Wendy Hobden)*

Bosham W Sus [High St; SU8003], *Anchor Bleu*: Lovely sea and boat views from low-beamed waterside pub, in attractive village; Scottish Courage beers, log-effect gas fire, seats outside; very popular with tourists – those parking on the hard standing below risk tidal inundation *(JDM, KM, Tony Scott, LYM)*

☆ **Brighton** E Sus [15 Black Lion St; TQ3105], *Cricketers*: Bustling down-to-earth town pub with ageing Victorian furnishings and lots of interesting bric-a-brac – even a stuffed bear; well kept Courage Directors, Morlands Old Speckled Hen and Wadworths 6X tapped from the cask, friendly staff, usual well priced lunchtime bar food inc vegetarian and fresh veg in upstairs bar, restaurant (where children allowed) and covered ex-stables courtyard bar; open all day, piped music may be loud *(Tony Scott, Ann and Colin Hunt, Klaus and Elizabeth Leist, Tony and Wendy Hobden, F Chamberlain, Tim Barrow, Sue Demont, Eddy Street, LYM)*

☆ **Brighton** [105 Southover St, Kemp Town], *Greys*: Buoyant atmosphere in very small basic single-room corner local with two or three rough and ready tables for eating – must book, strongly recommended for limited choice of good food lunchtime and Tues-Thurs evening, Belgian chef with some adventurous original recipes; very friendly landlord, well kept ale, well chosen and reproduced piped music, live music Sun lunchtime *(Graham Parker, R J Walden, BB)*

Brighton [Guildford Rd], *Battle of Trafalgar*: Friendly town local with well kept ales such as Wadworths 6X and Youngs, hearty typical food, piped jazz and blues, lovely big garden *(Dan Wilson)*; [10 New Rd, off North St], *Colonnade*: Small but beautifully kept, with velvet, shining brass, gleaming mirrors, theatrical posters and lots of signed photographs, good friendly service even when very busy, some snacks esp salt beef sandwiches (free seafood nibbles Sun lunchtime instead), Boddingtons, Flowers and Harveys (early-evening weekday happy hour), good choice of house wines, tiny front terrace; next to Theatre Royal, they take interval orders *(F Chamberlain, Tim Barrow, Sue Demont)*; [Clifton Hill], *Crescent*: Pleasant unpretentious local in conservation area, Courage ales, lunchtime food, interesting raised seating area, back terrace; no pool or loud music *(P A Legon)*; [Surrey St], *Evening Star*: Very popular for up to a dozen well kept interesting changing ales inc two brewed here; changing farm ciders, good lunchtime food (not Sun), old-fashioned atmosphere, bare boards, simple furnishings, good mix of customers, railway memorabilia; live music nights, friendly service; no food Sun *(Bruce Bird)*; [Union St, The Lanes], *Font & Firkin*: Sometimes wildly busy but worth the effort, clever circular church refurbishment (still has pulpit and bell pulls, alongside Sunday comedians and other live entertainment), sturdy old furnishings, some tables up on narrow balcony around cupola base, pleasant service, good choice of well kept ales inc some brewed here, decent food inc good value Sun roasts; good loud music *(Betsy Brown, Nigel Flook, Pat and Tony Martin, Anna and Martyn Carey, R Cooper, BB)*; [Trafalgar St], *George*: Recently refurbished, particularly well kept beers, inexpensive vegetarian dishes; children welcome *(Robert Heaven)*; [125 Gloucester Rd], *George Beard*: Quiet but opulently stylish town pub, welcoming and relaxing; good range of well kept ales inc Adnams, Harveys and guests; good value bar lunches Mon-Sat *(Dan Wilson)*; [Hangleton; TQ2607], *Hangleton Manor*: Medieval former manor house with impressive entrance, two bars, panelling, old photographs of its days as part of a farm, well kept guest beers such as Greene King Abbot, good bar menu from nicely served sandwiches up, pleasant service; big garden; bedrooms *(Mrs M Rice, R T and J C Moggridge)*; [First Ave, Hove], *Hove Place*: Mews pub with comfortably furnished panelled bars, heated Italian garden with loggia and statues, Bass, Flowers and Harveys, decent wines by the glass, good range of bar food *(Fred Chamberlain)*; [13 Marlborough Pl], *King & Queen*: Medieval-style lofty main hall with well kept Theakstons Best and XB from long bar, generous good value food, friendly service, pool table, flagstoned courtyard; good free jazz most evenings (when parking tends to be difficult) and Sun lunchtime; open all day Sun, good roasts *(Ann and Colin Hunt, LYM)*

Burwash Weald E Sus [A265 two miles W of Burwash; TQ6624], *Wheel*: Enjoyable food all day in friendly recently refurbished and extended open-plan pub with good inglenook log fire, comfortable banquettes, nicely framed old local photographs, well kept Harveys and other ales, games bar up a step or two behind, garden; lovely walks in valley opp *(Mr and Mrs R D Knight, BB)*

Bury W Sus [A29 Fontwell—Pulborough; TQ0113], *White Horse*: Recently refurbished, with well kept ale inc Fullers London Pride, good food inc superb tournedos in big sectioned dining area, friendly service, tables in pretty outside area *(Malcolm and Ann Grant, R T and J C Moggridge)*

Chailey E Sus [South St (A275); TQ3919], *Horns Lodge*: Unpretentious, with better than average food *(R D and S R Knight)*

Chalvington E Sus [signed off A27 and A22, then follow Golden Cross rd; TQ5209], *Yew Tree*: Isolated 17th-c proper country pub, two rooms, low beams, stripped bricks and flagstones, generous home cooking inc vegetarian (not Sun lunchtime), well kept Harveys and maybe others; children welcome if eating, can be packed weekends; attractive little walled terrace, extensive grounds inc own cricket pitch *(Guy Vowles, G Coates, BB)*

Charlton W Sus [village signed from A286 and A285, and from East Dean; SU8812], *Fox*: Cosy old low-beamed pub doing well again under friendly new young couple, good bar menu inc good vegetarian choice and generous Sun roasts, reasonable prices, three real ales, log fires, good atmosphere; no-smoking family extension, restaurant; open all day at least on Sun *(Ann and Colin Hunt, LYM)*

Chichester W Sus [St Pancras; SU8605], *Coach & Horses*: Comfortably refurbished open-plan pub, welcoming landlord, well kept King & Barnes inc Mild and seasonal ales, good lunchtime bar food, back garden *(Bruce Bird)*; [Whyke Rd], *Mainline*: Large pub with good food; evenings popular for discos and loud music *(DG)*; [3 St Pancras], *Nags Head*: Good local atmosphere, lots of panelling and old books, substantial good food in bar and eating area inc evening and Sun lunch carvery, friendly staff, well kept Boddingtons, Flowers Original, Fullers London Pride, Morlands Old Speckled Hen and Wadworths 6X, log fires; piped music can be a bit loud, live music some nights *(Mark Matthewman, David Gould)*; [Priory St, opp park], *Park*: Pleasant L-shaped bar with decent food from sandwiches up, Gales and a guest beer *(Tony and Wendy Hobden)*

Chilgrove W Sus [off B2141, Petersfield—Chichester; SU8214], *White Horse*: More smart restaurant than pub, lunches cheaper than evening, good food in bar too; remarkable list of outstanding wines, idyllic downland setting with small flower-filled terrace and big pretty garden *(Mrs D Bromley-Martin, Dennis Stevens, J Sheldon, Ann and Colin Hunt)*

☆ *nr* **Chilgrove** [Hooksway, signed off B2141 down steep track; SU8116], *Royal Oak*: Smartly simple country tavern in very peaceful spot, beams, brick floors, country-kitchen furnishings, huge log fires; home-made standard food inc vegetarian, well kept real ales, friendly service, games, attractive seats outside; provision for children, has been cl winter Mons, good walks *(Ann and Colin Hunt, David Cullen, Emma Stent, LYM)*

Climping W Sus [TQ0002], *Black Horse*: Good food from home-made soup and huge ploughman's up; skittle alley, walk to beach *(Mrs Romey Heaton)*

Cocking W Sus [A286 S of Midhurst; SU8717], *Blue Bell*: Friendly new licensees in unspoilt country local, wide choice of usual food inc children's helpings, roaring log fire, well kept Boddingtons and other ales; bedrooms, good walks – just off South Downs Way *(Ann and Colin Hunt)*

Coldwaltham W Sus [pub signed down lane S of Pulborough – OS Sheet 197 map ref 027167; TQ0216], *Labouring Man*: Clean, friendly and comfortable, with great atmosphere, good food, ales such as Fullers London Pride, Hardy Royal Oak, Wadworths 6X; children welcome *(Mrs L Phillips, Roger Stamp)*

Colemans Hatch E Sus [signed off B2026; or off B2110 opp church; TQ4533], *Hatch*: Nicely brightened-up traditional old Ashdown Forest pub doing well under current landlord, enjoyable food, Harveys ales, tables outside *(Colin Laffan, LYM)*

☆ **Compton** W Sus [B2146 S of Petersfield; SU7714], *Coach & Horses*: Spotless 15th-c former coaching inn, good atmosphere, well kept ales such as Cheriton Diggers Gold and King & Barnes Best, roomy walkers' bar, charming little plush beamed lounge bar with attractive restaurant, well presented appetising food, friendly Flemish landlady, attentive staff; tables out in front, small secluded back garden, attractive village; fine wooded hilly walking country *(Phyl and Jack Street, Ann and Colin Hunt)*

☆ **Cousley Wood** E Sus [B2100 Wadhurst—Lamberhurst; TQ6533], *Old Vine*: Attractive tastefully redecorated dining pub with lots of old timbers and beams, wide range of generously served modestly priced decent food, good house wines, four well kept ales, pleasant service; rustic pretty restaurant on right, pubbier bare-boards or brick-floored area with woodburner by bar, a few tables out behind *(Mr and Mrs J Ayres, Tina and David Woods-Taylor, R and S Bentley, BB)*

Cowfold W Sus [A281 S; TQ2122], *Hare & Hounds*: Welcoming refurbished pub, part flagstoned, with real ales such as Adnams, Harveys and Wadworths, amiable landlord, attractive food esp pies; children allowed if eating *(Terry Buckland)*

Crawley W Sus [6 Grand Parade, High St; TQ2636], *Jubilee Oak*: Wetherspoons pub with good range of beer and food all day, excellent prices, big no-smoking area *(R Cooper)*; [High St], *Old Punch Bowl*: Greene King pub in venerable much extended building, friendly staff, sensible food all day, no-smoking room; very popular lunchtimes and weekend evenings, cl Sun lunchtime *(Alec and Marie Lewery, Tony and Wendy Hobden, Tony Scott, David and Carole Chapman)*; [opp Three Bridges Stn], *Snooty Fox*: Newish purpose-built pub as upmarket replacement for former Fox, food-oriented with dining room partly no smoking; Tetleys *(Tony and Wendy Hobden)*; [High St], *White Hart*: Two-bar Harveys local with their full range, lunchtime food, friendly staff, comfortable saloon, pool and darts teams; open all day, busy market days (Thurs-Sat); jazz or Irish music w/e *(Tony Scott, Dave Cupwell)*

nr **Crawley** [B2036 2 miles N of Pound Hill; TQ2939], *Heathy Farm*: Smart new pub, part converted house, with good choice of well kept beers, extensive menu, efficient staff *(Terry Buckland)*

nr **Crowborough** E Sus [Lye Green, Friars Gate; Groombridge Rd; TQ5130], *Half Moon*: Pretty and cottagey refurbished country pub on edge of Ashdown Forest, tables out in front and in extensive back area with play area, full Shepherd Neame range, also Harveys, a fairly strong ale brewed for the pub, and a good guest beer; hard-working newish licensee, decent food inc good Sun lunch *(Colin and Joyce Laffan)*

Dallington E Sus [Woods Corner; B2096 E of Dallington; TQ6619], *Swan*: Country local with good log fires in both traditional front bars, inglenook fireplace, far views from plain but comfortable no-smoking back eating room, well kept Harveys, Flowers IPA and Wadworths 6X, decent food, pleasant staff; tables in back garden; bedrooms *(J Sheldon, Sussannah Anderson, BB)*

☆ **Danehill** E Sus [School Lane, Chelwood Common; off A275; TQ4128], *Coach & Horses*: Consistently good home-cooked food inc vegetarian in cottagey local with two small bars and roomy ex-stables dining extension, well kept Harveys, Greene King and guest beers, decent house wine, friendly service, good atmosphere, pews in bar, two big dogs; attractive big garden *(Ron Gentry, Geoffrey*

Lawrance, Susan and John Douglas, Mr and Mrs R D Knight)

☆ **Dell Quay** W Sus [SU8302], *Crown & Anchor*: Modernised 15th-c pub in good spot overlooking Chichester Harbour (on site of Roman quay), doing well under new landlord, with good food from sandwiches up esp plenty of fresh local fish; marina views from garden and comfortable bow-windowed lounge bar, panelled public bar with unspoilt fireplace, Courage Best, Marstons Pedigree and Wadworths 6X, restaurant *(JEB, Miss A Drake, Miss P M Stevenson, BB)*

Ditchling E Sus [2 High St; B2112; TQ3215], *Bull*: Beamed 14th-c inn with attractive antique furnishings in civilised main bar, old pictures, inglenook fireplace, well kept Whitbreads-related ales, good choice of malt whiskies, comfortable family room, no-smoking restaurant, fairly good wheelchair access; picnic-sets in good-sized pretty garden and on suntrap terrace, comfortable bedrooms, charming old village just below downs *(Peter Meister, LYM)*

☆ **Eartham** W Sus [signed off A285 Chichester—Petworth, from Fontwell off A27, from Slindon off A29; SU9409], *George*: Big popular pub newly refurbished in light wood, comfortable lounge opening on to new terrace, pubbier public bar with games, popular food from baguettes and baked potatoes to vegetarian, fish, steaks and interesting pies, well kept Gales Best, Butser, HSB, and maybe a guest beer, no-smoking restaurant; piped music; children welcome in eating areas, open all day summer w/e *(R J Walden, R T and J C Moggridge, B and M Parkin, Iain Robertson, Elizabeth and Klaus Leist, John and Barbara Howdle, Barry and Marie Males, Edward Froggatt, LYM)*

☆ **Easebourne** W Sus [off A272 just NE of Midhurst; SU8922], *Olde White Horse*: Cosy local with promptly served generous home-made food inc fresh veg, welcoming licensees, Greene King IPA and Abbot, small log fire, traditional games in tap room, tables on back grass and in courtyard *(G C Hackemer, LYM)*

East Chiltington E Sus [Chapel Lane; 2 miles N of B2116; TQ3715], *Jolly Sportsman*: Unpretentious unspoilt country pub, popular with walkers and cyclists, dining room off small bar, basic good value food from sandwiches and ploughman's up, real ales such as Courage Best, King & Barnes, Plumpton Rectors Revenge and John Smiths, very obliging landlord, pool room, big garden with extensive views and screened play area, nice spot next to small nursery run by landlord's father-in-law *(John Beeken, LM)*

East Hoathly E Sus [High St; TQ5216], *Kings Head*: Good reasonably priced food, well kept ales, good wines; former coach house, oak beams, log fires; beware the cat *(Mr and Mrs M J C Pilbeam, Peter Hardy)*

East Lavant W Sus [Pook Lane; signed off A286 N of Chichester; SU8608], *Royal Oak*: Simple furnishings, rugs on bare boards and flooring tiles, two open fires and a woodburner, attractively planted gardens, Gales real ales, country wines, short choice of food (not cheap, and may take a while), children welcome if eating; new licensees *(Martin and Karen Wake, JDM, KM, D B Jenkin, Bruce Bird, LYM)*

East Wittering W Sus [Church Rd; SZ7997], *Thatched Tavern*: Nicely refurbished, with good food, tables outside with play area, masses of flowers; gets very busy, Tues quiz night *(N E Bushby, W Atkins)*

☆ **Eastbourne** E Sus [The Goffs, Old Town; TV6199], *Lamb*: Two main heavily beamed traditional bars off pretty Tudor pub's central servery, spotless antique furnishings, good inglenook log fire, well kept Harveys ales, friendly polite service, well organised food bar, upstairs dining room (Sun lunch), no music or machines; dogs seem welcome, children allowed in very modernised side room; by ornate church away from seafront; popular with students evenings *(Tony Scott, Tony Hobden)*

Eastbourne [Grange Rd], *New Inn*: Roomy and friendly, with helpful staff, Bass, Courage Directors, Harveys, John Smiths and a guest beer; restaurant *(E Robinson, AB)*; [Holywell Rd, Meads – just off front below approach from Beachy Head], *Pilot*: Bustling, comfortable and friendly, prompt ample food, pleasant service, well kept real ales, good ship photographs; garden *(B and M Parkin)*

Etchingham E Sus [A265 Burwash—Hawkhurst; TQ7126], *De Etchingham Arms*: This pleasant pub has now closed, and is being sold for redevelopment *(RIP)*

Ewhurst Green E Sus [TQ7925], *White Dog*: Extensive and attractive partly 17th-c pub/restaurant in fine spot above Bodiam Castle with tables in big garden making the most of the view; cheerful unpretentious atmosphere, interesting choice of reasonably priced food (not Mon), well kept Fullers London Pride and Harveys, decent wines, helpful service, evening restaurant; walkers and children welcome, bedrooms *(P Howell, A Carey, Brian and Anna Marsden, LYM)*

Faygate W Sus [TQ2134], *Cherry Tree*: Attractive old pub with obliging landlord, King & Barnes real ales, nice atmosphere, reasonable food; just off dual carriageway *(Tony Scott, Ron Gentry)*

Felpham W Sus [102 Felpham Rd, just E of Bognor; SZ9599], *George*: Good food esp puddings, good friendly service, village pub atmosphere, attractive oak-beam decor, separate dining room; glorious garden with pond *(NM)*

Ferring W Sus [TQ0902], *Henty Arms*: Modest two-bar pub with wide choice of reasonably priced food, Youngs; no-smoking restaurant *(Tony and Wendy Hobden)*; [S Ferring], *Tudor Close*: Thatched former barn, rather upmarket, with Courage and Wadworths 6X, wide choice of food in bar or restaurant *(Tony and Wendy Hobden)*

☆ **Findon** W Sus [High St, off A24 N of Worthing; TQ1208], *Village House*: Good food inc fish and local game, not cheap but honest value, in welcoming converted 16th-c coach house, oak tables, panelling, pictures, racing silks from local stables, big open fire, well kept ales inc Courage and King & Barnes, good service, restaurant popular for Sun lunch, small attractive walled garden with terrace and fish pond; bedrooms, handy for Cissbury Ring and downland walks *(Tony and Wendy Hobden, John Beeken)*

Fishbourne W Sus [99 Fishbourne Rd; just off A27 Chichester—Emsworth; SU8404], *Bulls Head*: Interesting old building with fair-sized main bar, full Gales range kept well, unusual guest beers, friendly landlord and locals, good choice of food (not cheap but good value, not Sun evening), log fires, no-smoking area, children's area, skittle alley, boules pitch, restaurant *(K and J Morris, Bruce Bird)*

Fittleworth W Sus [Lower St (B2138); TQ0118], *Swan*: Prettily placed 15th-c inn with big inglenook log fire in friendly lounge, bar food in attractive panelled side room with landscapes by Constable's deservedly less-known brother George, well kept Boddingtons, attentive service; piped music, games inc pool in public bar; well spaced tables on big sheltered back lawn, good walks nearby; open all day Thurs-Sat, children in eating area *(Tony and Wendy Hobden, LYM)*

☆ **Fletching** E Sus [High St; TQ4223], *Rose & Crown*: Well run 16th-c pub locally popular for good home-made food with fresh veg in bar and small restaurant, friendly attentive service, real ales, beams, inglenooks and log fires, tables in pretty garden *(Derek and Maggie Washington, John Knighton)*

☆ **Frant** E Sus [High St, off A267 S of Tunbridge Wells; TQ5835], *George*: Tucked down charming quiet village st by ancient church and cottages, bar with several rooms rambling round servery, low ceiling, mix of seats inc pews, high-backed settles and a sofa, coal-effect gas fire in big inglenook, well kept Fullers London Pride, Greene King Abbot, Harveys and King & Barnes, decent wines and food inc bargain lunches, good coffee, darts in public bar; pleasant restaurant, picnic-sets in walled garden *(Paula Williams, Pat and Tony Martin, Colin Laffan, Gordon Tong, BB)*

☆ **Fulking** W Sus [off A281 Brighton—Henfield via Poynings; TQ2411], *Shepherd & Dog*: Charming partly panelled country pub with antique or stoutly rustic furnishings around log fire, attractive bow windows, bar food from sandwiches and lots of cheeses to steaks inc vegetarian choice (no chips or children's menu), well kept Harveys Best, Flowers Original and changing guest beers, good downs views from pretty streamside garden with upper play lawn; open all day Sat, can be packed out, no children in bar *(John Beeken, A Sutton, Gareth and Toni Edwards, Martin and Karen Wake, R J Walden, Colin Draper, Gordon Prince, Iain Robertson, LYM)*

Gatwick W Sus [Charlwood Rd; TQ2941], *Flight Tavern*: Former Aero Club, tastefully extended and modernised in rustic style complete with inglenook, some emphasis on good choice of good generous food, well kept Bass, helpful staff; children allowed in conservatory dining area, good for plane-spotting – 300 m S of runway *(Terry Buckland)*

Glynde E Sus [TQ4509], *Trevor Arms*: Doing well under hard-working new management, with well kept Harveys, good range of food, small dining room, great views, sizeable garden – very busy at weekends; nice spot, good walks *(Dan Wilson)*

☆ **Graffham** W Sus [off A272 or A285 SW of Petworth; SU9217], *Foresters Arms*: Very big helpings of good food (not cheap, but good value) in smallish very friendly traditional two-room pub with papers and magazines to read, well kept Gales HSB, big log fire, no music; walkers welcome, may be crowded weekends; pretty no-smoking restaurant (can be fully booked), tables in garden; bedrooms *(Susan Cutler, R D Knight)*

☆ **Gun Hill** E Sus [off A22 NW of Hailsham, or off A267; TQ5614], *Gun*: Big country dining pub under new management, close-set tables in several interesting rambling rooms, log fires (and an Aga on which they've done some of the cooking), good straightforward food, well kept Adnams Extra, Flowers Original, Harveys Best and Larkins, good wines, efficient pleasant service; children allowed in two no-smoking rooms, lovely garden with big play area, right on Wealden Way *(Janet and Colin Roe, Peter Meister, B and M Parkin, LYM)*

☆ **Halnaker** W Sus [A285 Chichester—Petworth; SU9008], *Anglesey Arms*: Welcoming service and quickly cooked genuine food with occasional interesting Spanish specialities in bar with traditional games (can be a bit smoky), well kept King & Barnes and Tetleys-related ales, good wines (again inc direct Spanish imports); simple but smart candlelit dining room with stripped pine and flagstones (children allowed), tables in garden *(Rex Martyn, John H Davis, Clive Gilbert, DC, LYM)*

Handcross W Sus [Plummers Plain; B2110 W; TQ2428], *Wheatsheaf*: Three King & Barnes real ales, good range of good food from sandwiches to steaks, inc children's, lots of horse tack, no-smoking dining area; big garden with play equipment *(Keith Widdowson)*

Hartfield E Sus [Gallipot St; B2110 towards Forest Row; TQ4634], *Gallipot*: Simple but comfortable L-shaped bar with new landlord-chef doing enjoyable food, a couple of well kept ales, log fire, obliging service, restaurant; away from the crowds on edge of attractively set village, good walks nearby *(Eamonn and Natasha Skyrme)*; [A264], *Haywaggon*: Spacious beamed pub with good value simple bar food all day (can be a wait), well kept ale *(G Simpson, Margaret and Nigel Dennis)*

☆ **Hastings** E Sus [14 High St, Old Town; TQ8109], *First In Last Out*: Congenial and chatty beer-drinkers' pub – even the cat is a character, holding his central armchair against all comers; open-plan bar attractively divided by settles, pews forming booths, posts and central raised log fire, good reasonably priced beers brewed here, guest ales, farm cider, friendly landlord, no games or juke box;

interesting simple lunchtime food, free Sun cockles; parking nearby difficult *(E G Parish, P R Morley)*

Hastings [All Saints St, Old Town], *Stag*: Early 17th-c former smugglers' pub on high pavement (up a few steps), low beams, bare boards, stout furniture, no frills; well kept Shepherd Neame beers, lots of malt whiskies, ex-fireman landlord, friendly long-serving staff, some fascinating stories; weekend bar food, folk nights Weds *(E G Parish, Jack and Philip Paxton)*

Haywards Heath W Sus [Butley Green Rd; TQ3324], *Dolphin*: Good standard food – a Bass Vintage Inn, with their beers *(Ian Phillips)*

Heathfield E Sus [A265 E; TQ5821], *Old Coach House*: More cross between animal home (outside) and restaurant than pub, but does have Harveys ales and good bar food, with charming service; bedrooms *(Colin and Joyce Laffan)*

Henfield W Sus [A281; TQ2116], *White Hart*: 16th-c village pub with comfortable L-shaped lounge and big no-smoking area, lots of panelling, tools hanging from low beams, horsebrasses, paintings, prints and photographs, log fire, large popular dining area with good choice of home-cooked food inc vegetarian and tempting puddings, staff friendly and efficient even on busy days, well kept Badger beers and Harveys Best; children welcome, garden with terrace and play area *(Bruce Bird)*

☆ **Hermitage** W Sus [36 Main Rd (A259); SU7505], *Sussex Brewery*: Pleasant stripped-brick bar with immense log fire, sawdust on boards and flagstoned alcove (this bit food-free Fri/Sat night), well kept ales such as Badger Tanglefoot, Shepherd Neame Spitfire, Timothy Taylor Dark Mild or Landlord, Youngs and one brewed for them, good local fish and vast choice of sausages inc vegetarian, no-smoking red plush dining room up a few steps; no machines or piped music, small walled garden; can get very busy, open all day Sat *(Ian Phillips, David Dimock, Tim Abel, Bruce Bird)*

Herstmonceux E Sus [Chapel Row, Church Rd; TQ6312], *Welcome Stranger*: Unspoilt country pub in same family for nearly a century, well kept Harveys Bitter and Old and a guest beer from small serving hatch *(Jack and Philip Paxton)*

Heyshott W Sus [off A286 S of Midhurst; SU8918], *Unicorn*: Very friendly small country local prettily placed by village green, well kept Ballards Best, generous bar food, good polite service, attractive restaurant, garden with barbecue; children allowed, reasonable disabled access; nearby walks *(J S Evans, P and S White, Ann and Colin Hunt)*

☆ **Holtye** E Sus [Holtye Common; A264 East Grinstead—Tunbridge Wells; TQ4539], *White Horse*: Unpretentiously refurbished ancient village pub with helpful polite staff, good value if not cheap food inc good vegetarian choices, well kept ales inc Brakspears, popular carvery restaurant with illuminated aquarium set into floor; good facilities for the disabled, marvellous view from back lawn; bedrooms *(Elizabeth and Klaus Leist, Barry Perfect)*

☆ **Hooe** E Sus [A259 E of Pevensey; TQ6809], *Lamb*: Prettily placed dining pub, extensively refurbished with lots of stripped brick and flintwork, one snug area around huge log fire and lots of other seats, very wide choice of generous popular food from well filled sandwiches up, children's dishes, well kept Bass and Harveys, quick friendly service *(Mrs S Wilkinson, B and M Parkin, Jenny and Brian Seller)*

Horsham W Sus [North Parade; Warnham Rd (A24); TQ1730], *Dog & Bacon*: Cosy and cottagey two-bar King & Barnes pub, pleasant local feel; no food Sat/Sun evening *(Tony Scott)*; [Carfax], *Olde Kings Head*: Rambling old hotel, well prepared usual food in bar with large open fire, coffee shop (not Sun), restaurant; bedrooms *(Margaret and Nigel Dennis, Tony Scott)*; [29 Carfax], *Stout House*: Small friendly unpretentious local with well kept King & Barnes Festive, Sussex and Broadwood, good lunchtime rolls, friendly licensees and regulars; cl Tues evening *(Tony Hobden, Tony Scott)*

Horsted Keynes E Sus [The Green; TQ3828], *Green Man*: Traditional village inn in attractive spot facing green, spotless but not too modernised, with well kept Adnams and Harveys, good usual food, reasonable prices; handy for Bluebell Line *(John C Baker, Tony Hobden)*

☆ **Houghton** W Sus [B2139; TQ0111], *George & Dragon*: New management in fine old timbered pub with civilised rambling heavy-beamed bar, nice comfortable mix of furnishings inc some antiques, pleasantly served reasonably priced meals from baked potatoes up, cheerful staff, well kept beers, log fire, good friendly staff, no-smoking room, charming garden with pretty views; children (and maybe dogs) welcome; handy for South Downs Way *(M J Dowdy, Mrs D Bromley-Martin, David and Carole Chapman, N B Thompson, LYM)*

Hunston W Sus [B2145 Chichester—Sidlesham; SU8501], *Spotted Cow*: Small but attractive, doing well under current landlord, flagstones and comfortable sofas, big fires, well kept Gales and guest ales, reasonably priced interesting food from lunchtime sandwiches to Chinese take-aways and more elaborate evening restaurant meals inc theme night; skittles, big garden; handy for towpath walkers *(N E Bushby, Miss W E Atkins, K Stevens)*

Ifield W Sus [Hyde Dr; TQ2437], *Mill House*: Conversion of beamed mill house, original watermill nearby, country-style bar and restaurant, Whibreads-related ales, nice garden; open all day *(Tony Scott)*; [Ifield St], *Plough*: Ancient King & Barnes local in pleasant spot nr 13th-c church recently comfortably refurbished, their full beer range kept well, good atmosphere, friendly staff, extended cosy saloon with lots of brass and wood, games in small public bar; tables out in front, handy for local Barn Theatre *(David and Carole Chapman, Tony Scott, Dave Cupwell)*

Isfield E Sus [Rose Hill (A26); TQ4516], *Halfway House*: Beams, fine fireplaces, well polished fittings, well kept Harveys Bitter and Old, good home cooking, good service, lovely cottage garden *(Tony Scott)*

Jevington E Sus [TQ5601], *Eight Bells*: Village pub opp South Downs footpath, well kept Adnams Broadside, Courage Best, Harveys Best, Shepherd Neame BB and a guest such as Rother Valley Level Best, central bar with pictures for sale by local artists, welcoming efficient staff, good cheap promptly served food inc home-grown veg, no music, walkers welcome (bags to cover boots), good garden with secluded paved and grassy alcoves *(Bruce Bird, John Beeken)*

Kingsfold W Sus [Dorking Rd; A24 Dorking—Horsham, nr A29 junction; TQ1636], *Dog & Duck*: Cosy and friendly old country pub, well kept King & Barnes and other ales, good value nicely presented food (not after 2 lunchtime) inc good sandwiches and popular lunches, very attentive service, open fires *(Jayne and Douglas McLuckie, R T and J C Moggridge)*

☆ **Lambs Green** W Sus [TQ2136], *Lamb*: Quaint old beamed pub well refurbished to give more space, friendly helpful staff, well kept beers such as Wadworths 6X and Youngs, good varied changing food, good value considering helping size, restaurant; nice log fire *(R Cooper, BB)*

☆ **Lavant** W Sus [Lavant Rd (A286); SU8508], *Earl of March*: Roomy village pub with well kept Ballards Best, Ringwood Old Thumper and guests such as Cottage Golden Arrow and Hampshire King Alfred, Weston's Old Rosie cider, good generous home-cooked food inc vegetarian (new no-smoking area by servery), staff cope very well even when busy, naval memorabilia, bric-a-brac and prints, games and puzzles, no piped music; dogs welcome, regular live music; good views from garden, good local walks *(Bruce Bird, David Gould)*

☆ **Lewes** E Sus [Castle Ditch Lane/Mount Pl; TQ4110], *Lewes Arms*: Charming unpretentious street-corner local below castle mound, cosy front lounge and two larger rooms (one with pool), particularly well kept Harveys, good orange juice, simple but unusual lunchtime food, friendly service, newspapers and tatty old books, no music – great place for conversation; comically small garden, so people migrate to pavement and street *(Janet and Colin Roe, Alan Skull, Sue Demont, Tim Barrow)*

Lewes [55 Western Rd], *Black Horse*: Nice two-bar local with well kept Harveys and other ales such as Brakspears, Fullers and Wadworths 6X, bar food, friendly service *(Tony Scott)*

Litlington E Sus [The Street; between A27 Lewes—Polegate and A259 E of Seaford; TQ5201], *Plough & Harrow*: Cosy beamed front bar in attractively extended flint local, six well kept Badger Tanglefoot, Harveys and Thwaites Chairman, decent wines by the glass, helpful staff; good home cooking, dining area done up as railway dining car (children allowed here); back lawn with children's bar, aviary and pretty views; live music Fri *(Gwen and Peter Andrews, LYM)*

☆ **Littlehampton** W Sus [Wharf Rd; westwards towards Chichester, opp rly stn; TQ0202], *Arun View*: Clean and comfortable 18th-c inn right on harbour with river directly below windows, Whitbreads-related ales, wide choice of reasonably priced decent bar food, restaurant strong on fish (wise to book), flower-filled terrace; summer barbecues evenings and weekends; bedrooms *(Clare and Roy Head, David and Carole Chapman, Christopher Gallop)*

☆ **Lodsworth** W Sus [off A272 Midhurst—Petworth; SU9223], *Hollist Arms*: Cosy and friendly bars, big cheerful dining room, good well priced home-made food, well kept Ballards and Arundel guest beer, two log fires, snug with darts, shove ha'penny etc; whole lamb barbecues *(E M Steinitz, Paula Williams, Mrs L Phillips)*

☆ **Loxwood** W Sus [B2133; TQ0431], *Onslow Arms*: Well refurbished, with lively young staff, well kept full King & Barnes range, good house wines, big helpings of good value simple food, picnic-sets in garden sloping to river and nearby canal under restoration *(Alan and Brenda Williams, Prof and Mrs S Barnett)*

☆ **Mayfield** E Sus [Fletching St – off A267 at NE end of village; TQ5827], *Rose & Crown*: Pretty weatherboarded old inn with cosy little low-beamed front rooms, big inglenook, wide choice of bar food from lunchtime toasties through well priced specials to duck and steak, well kept Greene King Abbot, Harveys Best and Morlands Old Speckled Hen, shove-ha'penny, restaurant; piped music; children welcome, attractive bedrooms, tables outside; open all day Sat *(Eddie Edwards, Wayne Brindle, Peter Meister, LYM)*

Merston W Sus [off A259 Bognor—Chichester; SU8902], *Kings Head*: Very pleasant friendly service, good lunch snacks, evening Greek specialities, good range of puddings, well kept Gales HSB, good house wine *(R T and J C Moggridge)*

Middleton on Sea W Sus [Elmer Sands; SU9800], *Elmer*: Well kept Gales Butser and HSB, nicely cooked well presented food inc plenty of good veg and enjoyable puddings, friendly efficient service *(C J Bromage)*

☆ **Midhurst** W Sus [South St; SU8821], *Spread Eagle*: This handsome and atmospheric old inn, mainy 17th c but partly much older and long a main entry, has completed its transformation into a restaurant-cum-hotel by removing the bar counter (and the real ale that went with it); bedrooms *(J S M Sheldon, Edward Froggatt, LYM)*

Midhurst [North St], *Angel*: Handsomely refurbished 16th-c coaching inn with sensibly priced well kept Gales and good food in pleasant bar, splendid brasserie and dining room, pleasant efficient service; comfortable bedrooms *(John A Barker)*

Milland W Sus [SU8328], *Rising Sun*: Gales pub with well kept ales, wide range of reasonably priced food (can get smaller helpings), two loudly welcoming parrots; garden with imaginative play area and animals *(Marjorie and David Lamb, David Cullen, Emma Stent)*

☆ **Milton Street** E Sus [off A27 Polegate—Lewes; ¼ mile E of Alfriston roundabout; TQ5304], *Sussex Ox*: Attractive family country pub beautifully placed below downs, big lawn and marvellous play area; good atmosphere inside, well kept Greene King Abbot and Harveys, reliably good food, pleasantly simple country furniture, hop-draped beams, brick floor, woodburner, friendly young staff, one lively and one quieter family room; can camp in nearby field, lots of good walks, busy weekends *(LM, LYM)*

New Bridge W Sus [off A272 W of Billingshurst; TQ0625], *Limeburners Arms*: Cosy, picturesque and very low-ceilinged, comfortable lounge side, enjoyable food from good doorstep sandwiches up, Gales ales, two friendly corgis, bar billiards on public side, nice little front garden; by well run modest-sized caravan and camping site, handy for Arun fishermen *(David and Carole Chapman)*

☆ **Newick** E Sus [The Green; A272 Uckfield—Haywards Heath; TQ4121], *Bull*: Welcoming, comfortable and peaceful for a midweek lunch, lots of beams and character, good value generous food inc interesting cooking and fresh Newhaven fish in sizeable eating area, inglenook log fires, cheerful welcoming staff, well kept mainly Scottish Courage ales; no music, booking advised w/e *(R and M Draper, G Simpson, Renee and Dennis Ball, Ann and Colin Hunt, BB)*

Newick [Church Rd], *Royal Oak*: Attractive village local with friendly licensees, well priced simple food from sandwiches up, King & Barnes Best; seats out in front *(Ann and Colin Hunt)*

Normans Bay E Sus [signed off A259 E of Pevensey, or off B2182 W out of Bexhill; TQ6806], *Star*: Massively extended modernised dining lounge, often very busy indeed (when service and even queue to order can slow), with huge choice of very generous cheap food inc local fish and fine changing range of ales such as Adnams, Batemans, Charles Wells Bombardier, Harveys Best, Hopback Summer Lightning, Marstons Owd Roger and Morlands Old Speckled Hen, also lots of continental bottled beers, good country wines, plenty of ciders etc; piped music, games in children's room, garden with good play area; open all day, jazz Tues, good walks inland away from the caravan sites *(Sue and Steve Griffiths, Jenny and Michael Back, Colin Laffan, A M Pring, LYM)*

☆ **Northchapel** W Sus [A285 Guildford—Petworth; SU9529], *Half Moon*: Beams, lots of farm tools, open fire, Friary Meux, Hampshire Uncle Sam, King & Barnes and Ringwood Old Thumper, home-made food inc choice of ploughman's; garden with tame goose, big red tractor, even old buses; live music last Mon of month *(J W G Nunns)*

Northiam E Sus [TQ8224], *Cafe du Moulin*: Dining place with good food and sizeable popular bar *(Paul McPherson)*

Nyetimber W Sus [Pagham Rd; SZ8998], *Lamb*: Bright pub beautifully kept by Portuguese couple, warm and attentive service, wide choice of consistently good food inc fresh seafood in bar and restaurant (must book Sat), good range of beers, decent wines *(R J Walden)*

Pagham W Sus [Nyetimber Lane; SZ8897], *Lion*: Cosy two-bar pub with friendly and efficient staff, good value food, wooden seating, uneven flooring, low beams, well kept beers, small restaurant, big suntrap terrace *(Lawrence Pearse, June and Malcolm Farmer)*

Patching W Sus [Arundel Rd; off A27 W of Lancing; TQ0806], *Fox*: Friendly enthusiastic landlord, well kept King & Barnes inc seasonal brews, good reasonably priced home-made food, lots of panelling, nice tree-shaded garden; occasional live music *(Bruce Bird)*

Pease Pottage W Sus [by M23 junction 11; TQ2533], *James King*: Welcoming and genuine, with good log fire, decent bar food, friendly willing service, well kept ale *(Tony Scott, David and Carole Chapman, BB)*

Peasmarsh E Sus [Main St; TQ8822], *Cock Horse*: Doing well under current well tried management, with pleasing bar, welcoming log fire, good well priced food inc delicious home-made puddings, good choice of well kept beers inc Harveys *(Derek Tennant)*

Pett E Sus [Pett Rd; TQ8713], *Royal Oak*: Doing well under new owners, with good value home cooking from filled baked potatoes to more elaborate dishes, lots of beams, good fireplace, well kept local beers at competitive prices; clean and well appointed *(Pat and Bruce Field)*

Petworth W Sus [North St; SU9721], *Stonemasons*: Above-average bar and restaurant food, traditional and contemporary, in comfortable roomy eating areas, reasonable prices, welcoming efficient staff; pleasant garden and terrace; opp Petworth House so best to book in summer; bedrooms *(Mr and Mrs G Dixon)*

Pevensey E Sus [High St; TQ6304], *Priory Court*: Hotel in shadow of Pevensey Castle with enjoyable plush-and-brasswork bar, welcoming log fire, well kept real ales, farm cider, decent wines, good bar food, extensive gardens with pond; bedrooms *(G Washington)*

Poynings W Sus [TQ2612], *Royal Oak*: Well kept Scottish Courage ales and King & Barnes, good generous food inc vegetarian and fish, service efficient even when very busy, cosy but plenty of room (inc no-smoking area), big attractive garden with barbecue and summer marquee *(Bruce Bird)*

Pulborough W Sus [99 Lower St; TQ0418], *Oddfellows Arms*: 17th-c, with stripped stonework, flagstones and low beams, good range of ales inc King & Barnes and Gales HSB, open fire dividing off public area with darts and bar billiards; open all day Tues-Sat, popular for food, garden with play area *(David and Carole Chapman)*

☆ **Ringmer** E Sus [Old Uckfield Rd; blocked-off

rd off A26 N of village turn-off; TQ4412], *Cock*: Very welcoming country pub, heavily beamed main bar with big inglenook log fire, pleasant modernised rooms off inc no-smoking lounge, restaurant, well kept Harveys Bitter and Mild, Morlands Old Speckled Hen and Ruddles Best, huge blackboard choice of enjoyable food, good service; children allowed in overflow eating area; piped music; tables on small terrace and in big sloping fairy-lit garden with shrubs, fruit trees and lots of spring flowers *(John Beeken, Colin Laffan, LYM)*

Ripe E Sus [off A27; TQ5010], *Barley Mow*: Good food inc curries and baltis, very reasonable prices, welcoming atmosphere, nice log fire *(Robert Heaven)*; [in village], *Lamb*: Interestingly furnished rooms around central servery, attractive antique prints and pictures, nostalgic song-sheet covers, Victorian pin-ups in gents'; generous food inc children's, well kept Scottish Courage ales and a guest such as Harveys, several open fires; pub games, pleasant sheltered back garden with play area and barbecues *(K M Thorpe, Anthony Bowen, LYM)*

☆ **Rogate** W Sus [A272; SU8023], *Wyndham Arms*: Small welcoming village local with well kept Ballards, King & Barnes, Ringwood and a guest ale tapped from the cask, good home-cooked food using fresh local ingredients, helpful staff; dogs and well behaved children welcome; bedrooms good value *(KC, David Cullen, Emma Stent)*

☆ **Rowhook** W Sus [off A29 NW of Horsham; TQ1234], *Chequers*: Unpretentious 16th-c beamed and flagstoned front bar with inglenook fire, step up to low-ceilinged lounge, good choice of bar food inc children's, quick friendly service, well kept Boddingtons, Flowers Original, Fullers London Pride and Whitbreads Fuggles, traditional games, restaurant; piped music, live Sun lunchtime; tables out on terraces and in pretty garden with good play area, attractive surroundings *(Mrs Romey Heaton, LYM)*

☆ **Rusper** W Sus [signed from A24 and A264 N and NE of Horsham; TQ2037], *Plough*: Padded very low beams, panelling and big inglenook, huge range of good value food, attractive dining area, well kept ales such as Courage Directors, local Dorking, Fullers London Pride and King & Barnes, lovely log fire, bar billiards and darts in raftered room upstairs; fountain in back garden, pretty front terrace, occasional live music; children welcome *(Tony Scott, LM, LYM)*

☆ **Selsfield** W Sus [Ardingly Rd; B2028 N of Haywards Heath, nr West Hoathly; TQ3434], *White Hart*: Heavy low 14th-c beams and timbers, big log fire, wide choice of food inc some original dishes, well kept Gales, King & Barnes and Tetleys, good service; tastefully converted barn restaurant, picnic-sets on side lawn above steep wooded combe, walks nearby; children welcome, handy for Wakehurst Place *(Terry Buckland, LYM)*

☆ **Shoreham by Sea** W Sus [Upper Shoreham Rd, Old Shoreham; TQ2105], *Red Lion*: Dim-lit low-beamed 16th-c pub with series of alcoves, enjoyable food, well kept Scottish Courage ales, King & Barnes, Wadworths 6X and interesting guest beers, occasional beer festivals, decent wines, farm cider, log fire in unusual fireplace, no-smoking dining room, pretty sheltered garden; piped music may obtrude; good walks and South Downs views *(Jackie and Alan Moody)*

Shoreham by Sea [signed off A27, A259], *Airport Bar*: Not a pub, but this small bar in 1930s art deco airport building has good beers brewed for it by local Brewery on Sea; relaxed atmosphere, well presented simple food, tables on terrace, uninterrupted views all round (plenty of light aircraft action); children welcome, small airport museum *(John Beeken)*

Shortbridge E Sus [Piltdown; TQ4521], *Peacock*: Comfortable and welcoming rebuilt beamed and timbered bar, big inglenook, very generous nicely presented bar food served piping hot, well kept Boddingtons and Morlands Old Speckled Hen, pleasant service; shame about the out-of-character piped music (they will turn it down); restaurant, children welcome, sizeable garden *(Mrs G M Deane, R D Knight, Alan Skull, Colin Laffan, BB)*

☆ **Sidlesham** W Sus [Mill Lane, off B2145 S of Chichester; SZ8598], *Crab & Lobster*: Old country local very much enjoyed by those in tune with its uncompromising individuality, log fire in chatty traditional bar, no-smoking plusher side dining lounge, charming back garden looking over to the bird-reserve of silted Pagham Harbour; limited choice of food (not Sun evening – can be good), well kept Archers Village and Gales Best and BBB, decent wines, country wines, traditional games; dogs welcome, no music or machines *(P R White, Brian Mills, Mr and Mrs K Sandiford, LYM)*

Singleton W Sus [SU8713], *Fox & Hounds*: Popular food, welcoming service, two small relaxed bars and eating area, real fires, friendly locals; handy for Weald & Downland Open Air Museum *(Ann and Colin Hunt)*; [A286], *Horse & Groom*: Friendly staff, well kept ales inc Cheriton Pots, generous promptly served reasonably priced home-made food, quiet piped classical music, no-smoking restaurant, garden; open all day Sun *(Bruce Bird, Ann and Colin Hunt)*

☆ **Slindon** W Sus [Slindon Common; A29 towards Bognor; SU9708], *Spur*: Popular and attractive 17th-c pub, good choice of good value food changing daily inc vegetarian, two big log fires, well kept Scottish Courage beers, friendly efficient staff, friendly dogs; children welcome, games room with darts and pool, sizeable restaurant, pretty garden *(Tony and Wendy Hobden, Jill Silversides, Barry Brown)*

Slindon *Newburgh Arms*: Congenial, comfortable and relaxed, with pleasantly homey furnishings, sizeable dining area with rows of tables for good value food from good ploughman's up, well kept Badger Best, lots of country wines; piped music; good area for downs walks *(Mark Matthewman, Richard Dolphin)*

☆ **South Harting** W Sus [B2146; SU7819], *White Hart*: Attractive unspoilt pub with good generous home cooking (may be a wait) inc vegetarian and sandwiches, lots of polished wood, hundreds of keys, big log fire in cosy snug, cheerful long-serving licensees, well kept Tetleys-related ales, good coffee, restaurant, separate public bar; well behaved dogs allowed, children welcome (toys in games room); good garden behind for them too, with spectacular downs views *(Ann and Colin Hunt, Tony and Wendy Hobden)*

South Harting [B2146], *Ship*: Very wide choice of good value food from good value toasties up in informal unspoilt 17th-c local with friendly efficient service, Hardy and Palmers Pope ales, good coffee, rather close-set tables, unobtrusive piped classical music, dominoes, maybe chestnuts to roast by public bar's log fire; nice setting in pretty village *(John Evans)*

Southbourne W Sus [A259; SU7806], *Travellers Joy*: Friendly roadside Gales pub, locals' public bar, lounge mainly dining – wide range of reasonably priced food inc Sun roasts and lots of puddings; garden *(Ann and Colin Hunt)*

Southwater W Sus [Two Mile Ash, a mile or so NW – OS Sheet 198 map ref 148273; TQ1427], *Bax Castle*: Old flagstoned pub pleasantly extended with ex-barn no-smoking restaurant, big fireplace in back room, well kept low-priced beer brewed for them by North Downs and others such as Brakspears, Fullers London Pride and John Smiths, good bar food inc children's helpings and good Sun lunch (best to book), no music, good big garden with play area; Downs Link Way walks on former rail track *(Bruce Bird, Tony Scott)*

St Leonards E Sus [Mercatoria; TQ8009], *Horse & Groom*: Pleasant and friendly traditional town pub in old Maze Hill area, uniform hats and caps, two bars, big back room, cheap and cheerful home-made food from sandwiches up, Courage Directors, Harveys Bitter and Best Marstons Pedigree; small garden *(Ian Phillips)*

Staplefield W Sus [Handcross Rd, just off A23; TQ2728], *Jolly Tanners*: Pleasant and comfortable bars, good reasonably priced varied home cooking, real ales such as Fullers London Pride, Harveys Best and Mild and King & Barnes, friendly efficient service even under pressure, attractive garden with lots of space for children; by green, quite handy for Nymans (NT) *(Mr and Mrs P A King, Ron Shelton, Tony Scott)*; [Warninglid Rd], *Victory*: Unpretentious whitewashed pub, dovecote in roof, picnic-sets and play area in garden overlooking cricket green; well kept Courage Best, Harveys and Wadworths 6X, decent wines, vast choice of good value food, welcoming staff, log fire, games area, decorative plates and horsebrasses; popular, get there early *(John Beeken, Brian and Anna Marsden, Tony Scott, LM)*

Steyning W Sus [41 High St; TQ1711], *Chequer*: Timber-framed Tudor pub with labyrinthine bars, friendly staff, good range of well kept Whitbreads-related beers, wide choice of generous food from good snacks up, friendly efficient service *(Guy Consterdine, Ron Gentry)*

☆ **Stopham** W Sus [off A283 E of village, W of Pulborough; TQ0218], *White Hart*: Friendly old beamed pub with hard-working and obliging new landlord, open fire in one of its three snug rooms, freshly made bar food, well kept Flowers Original and Whitbreads Strong Country, candlelit no-smoking restaurant; children welcome, play area over rd, with grass walks by pretty junction of Arun and Rother rivers *(David Cullen, Emma Stent, Graham Simpson, Comus Elliott, LYM)*

☆ **Stoughton** W Sus [signed off B2146 Petersfield—Emsworth; SU8011], *Hare & Hounds*: Much modernised pub below downs with reliably good home-made food (can take a while) in airy pine-clad bar, big open fires, half a dozen changing well kept ales such as Cottage Southern, Ringwood Best and Timothy Taylor Landlord, friendly staff, restaurant, back darts room; children in eating areas, tables on pretty front terrace and in back garden; nr Saxon church, good walks nearby *(Ann and Colin Hunt, Bruce Bird, LYM)*

☆ **Sutton** W Sus [SU9715], *White Horse*: Traditional country pub in attractive little hamlet nr Bignor Roman villa, island servery separating bare-boards bar from two-room dining area, simple decor and furnishings, good choice of plentiful food from good sandwiches to local game and fish, Arundel Best, Courage Best, Youngs and guest beers, log fire, friendly staff; tables in garden, good value bedrooms, comfortable and well equipped *(David Dimock, Phil Judge, Bruce Bird, LM, M S Catling, BB)*

☆ **Tangmere** W Sus [Arundel Rd (A27); SU9006], *Olde Cottage*: Homely and popular, with new licensees doing good helpings of outstanding food inc good value Sun lunch – can book tables but order from bar; reasonable prices, well kept Brakspears, pleasant dining room; tables under cocktail parasols on terrace and in tree-sheltered garden; has been cl Sun evening *(Eamonn and Natasha Skyrme, Clive Gilbert, Leonard White)*

Telscombe Cliffs E Sus [South Coast Rd (A259); TQ3901], *Badgers Watch*: Tastefully refurbished and extended former coastguard cottages on seaview clifftop, Bass and Fullers London Pride, good value hearty bar food inc vegetarian and Sun roast, helpful young staff, local pictures; piped music may obtrude; tables outside *(John Beeken, Lesley Sones)*

Turners Hill W Sus [Lion Lane; TQ3435], *Red Lion*: Simple pub with well kept Harveys, good value food (no cooking Sun), friendly staff, wonderful fireplace, pretty garden *(K and E Leist)*

☆ **Wadhurst** E Sus [Mayfield Lane (B2100 W); TQ6131], *Best Beech*: Well run dining pub, pleasant dim-lit bar on left with wall seats, quiet but individual decor and coal fire, cosy eating area with lots of pictures and china on right, well done fresh bar food (not Sun evening) from sandwiches to particularly good steaks, well kept Harveys and other ales, decent wines, quick friendly service; back restaurant, good value attractive bedrooms, good breakfast; cl Mon *(Jill Bickerton, Comus Elliott, Paul S McPherson, BB)*

Wadhurst [St James Sq (B2099)], *Greyhound*: Neatly kept village pub with wide choice of usual bar food and set Sun lunch in restaurant or pleasant beamed bar with big inglenook log fire, real ales such as Bass, Harveys and Youngs Special, no piped music; tables in well kept back garden; bedrooms *(James and Lynne House, Comus Elliott, LM, BB)*

Walderton W Sus [Stoughton rd, just off B2146 Chichester—Petersfield; SU7810], *Barley Mow*: Spacious flagstoned U-shaped bar with country bric-a-brac, good service, well kept ales such as Ringwood Old Thumper, Ruddles Best and Wadworths 6X, good choice of generous bar food inc vegetarian and good puddings, two log fires, cheerful staff, no music; children welcome, big pleasant garden with fish pond and aviary, good walks, handy for Stansted House *(Bruce Bird, Ann and Colin Hunt, N E Bushby, W Atkins)*

Warbleton E Sus [TQ6018], *Warbil in Tun*: Welcoming and pretty extended dining pub with beams and red plush, huge log fireplace, good value food inc very good puddings, well kept ales such as Flowers IPA and Harveys, good coffee, relaxed civilised atmosphere; tables on roadside green *(Michael Fullagar, David and Mary Mapp)*

Wartling E Sus [TQ6509], *Lamb*: Popular old inn, keeping a good deal of rustic charm; well kept Greene King ales, decent food inc cheaper helpings for children *(Jenny and Brian Seller)*

☆ **Washington** W Sus [just off A24 Horsham—Worthing; TQ1212], *Franklands Arms*: Well kept Whitbreads Wayside Inn, roomy and welcoming, with wide choice of food all day from warm baguettes to good puddings, well kept Flowers Original and Wadworths 6X, decent wine choice, log fires, prompt service; big bar, smaller dining area, games area with pool and darts, disabled facilities; tables in neat garden, quiet spot yet busy weekends *(R H Martyn, John Beeken, N B Thompson, M J Dowdy)*

☆ **West Chiltington** W Sus [Church St; TQ0918], *Elephant & Castle*: Impressive welcome and good changing freshly made food in tastefully extended and decorated old village pub behind ancient church in attractive village; well kept King & Barnes ales, helpful service, no music; children welcome, good garden with ducks and chickens *(D and J Tapper, Bruce Bird, Penny and Martin Fletcher, BB)*

West Dean W Sus [A286 Midhurst—Chichester; SU8512], *Selsey Arms*: Warm and friendly, log fire, lots of horse racing pictures and memorabilia, big dining lounge, well priced beers *(Ann and Colin Hunt)*

☆ **West Wittering** W Sus [Chichester Rd; B2179/A286 towards Birdham; SU7900], *Lamb*: Immaculate 18th-c country pub, several rooms neatly knocked through with tidy furnishings, rugs on tiles, good choice of well kept ales, decent wines, wide choice of reasonably priced food from separate servery, friendly staff; dogs on leads allowed, tables out in front and in small sheltered back garden – good for children, with outside salad bar on fine days; busy in summer *(Mrs S Fortescue, David Dimock, Ann and Colin Hunt, N E Bushby, W E Atkins, P R White, BB)*

West Wittering [Cakeham Rd], *Old House At Home*: Roomy, with log fires; dogs welcome *(David Gould)*

Westbourne W Sus [North St; SU7507], *Good Intent*: Friendly two-bar local with well kept Ballards, Dartmoor, Friary Meux Best and a guest beer, good value simple food, real fires, darts, juke box, monthly live music; barbecues *(Ann and Colin Hunt)*

Willingdon E Sus [Lower Willingdon; just off A22 Polegate—Eastbourne; TQ5803], *British Queen*: Two spacious attractively decorated and furnished bars, friendly welcome, well kept Courage ales, good value food, good service *(Dr and Mrs A K Clarke)*; [99 Wish Hill], *Red Lion*: Friendly local with Victorian feel, comfortable and attractive – settees, bar stools, well kept King & Barnes Festive and Broadwood, good reasonably priced food *(A J Thomas)*

☆ **Wilmington** E Sus [just off A27; TQ5404], *Giants Rest*: Unpretentious, with pine furniture and basic seating in small chatty rooms; good choice of imaginative sensibly priced home-made food, well kept ales such as Adnams, Harveys and Timothy Taylors, farm ciders, friendly service, no music; picnic-sets outside; very popular lunchtimes, cl Mon *(Thomas and Audrey Nott, Alan Skull)*

☆ **Winchelsea** E Sus [German St; TQ9017], *New Inn*: Variety of solid comfortable furnishings in well decorated bustling rambling beamed rooms, some emphasis on food inc good fresh fish (sandwiches too), well kept changing ales such as Everards Tiger, Harveys, Wadworths 6X and one brewed for them by Adnams, decent wines and malt whiskies, friendly service; separate public bar with darts, children in eating area, pretty bedrooms (some sharing bathrooms), delightful setting *(A Bradbury, R and M Bishop, Bob and Maggie Atherton, B J Harding, LYM)*

Winchelsea Beach E Sus [TQ9017], *Smugglers*: Attractive interior, with pleasant staff, three real ales inc an own brew, good lunches, sandpit outside for children; nr beach *(Quentin Williamson)*

Wisborough Green W Sus [Loxwood Rd; TQ0526], *Cricketers Arms*: Attractive old two-bar pub on green, low beams, bare boards, woodburner, five or six real ales; now taken over by the Hawkinses of the Halfway Bridge at Lodsworth (see main entries), with good prospects for the food side; old wooden benches outside *(David and Carole Chapman)*; [A272 W of Billingshurst], *Three Crowns*: Big clean and polished open-plan bar stretching into dining room, stripped bricks and beams, good reasonably priced food inc big ploughman's and popular Sun lunch, well kept ales such as Greene King Abbot, quick attentive service, sizeable back garden *(David and Carole*

Chapman)
Woodmancote W Sus [the one nr Emsworth; SU7707], *Woodmancote Arms*: Village local under friendly new licensee, three real ales, longish bar with pool one end, cosy little eating area with fire; play area *(Ann and Colin Hunt)*
Worthing [Broadwater Green (A24); TQ1303], *Cricketers*: Quiet, clean and friendly extended panelled pub with lower restaurant, well kept Bass, Fullers London Pride, Greene King IPA, Harveys and a guest beer, good food and staff; garden *(Bruce Bird)*; *Town Pride*: Modern pub with two bars downstairs and one up, local lifeboat pictures and memorabilia (pub named after one); popular with shoppers lunchtime, young people weekends; piped music *(Mrs M Rice)*; [High St, W Tarring], *Vine*: Cosy and comfortable unpretentious local with Badger and guest beers kept well, farm cider, good home-made lunchtime food; large attractive garden good for children *(Anna and Martyn Carey)*; [Warwick St], *Warwick Arms*: Former Hogshead, with seven well kept real ales, dark wood, big mirrors, good atmosphere, usual lunchtime food inc limited vegetarian, reasonable choice of wines *(Anna and Martyn Carey)*
Yapton W Sus [Maypole Lane; signed off B2132 Arundel rd – OS Sheet 197 map ref 977042; SU9704], *Maypole*: Friendly country pub with two log fires in lounge, good lunchtime bar food, well kept Ringwood Best and changing guests, many from small breweries, occasional brewery weekends and beer festivals, amusing dog called Sid; seats outside, skittle alley *(Bruce Bird)*

The letters and figures after the name of each town are its Ordnance Survey map reference. *How to use the Guide* at the beginning of the book explains how it helps you find a pub, in road atlases or large-scale maps as well as in our own maps.

Warwickshire (including Birmingham and West Midlands)

Four new entries here this year: the Fiddle & Bone in Birmingham (bone as in trombone – a new pub opened by two orchestral musicians, highly enjoyable), the Dun Cow at Dunchurch (a grand old coaching inn which has been handsomely refurbished), the extraordinary Castle on Edge Hill (a converted battlemented folly), and the Chequers at Ettington (its new owners have transformed it into a dining pub to be reckoned with). Other pubs here doing specially well these days are the Bell at Alderminster (this smart dining pub now has bedrooms), the friendly Fox at Great Wolford (gains a Food Award this year, but still very welcoming if all you want is just a drink), the Howard Arms at Ilmington (another very good dining pub, with lots of character), the Bell at Monks Kirby (especially if you like authentic Spanish food) and the unpretentious Plough at Warmington. The Fox & Hounds at Great Wolford is our choice as Warwickshire Dining Pub of the Year, in a close-run finish between it and the Howard Arms. After the death (at a venerable age) of its long-serving landlady, the Case is Altered at Five Ways continues to delight, carefully preserved by her granddaughter as an enjoyable anachronism. Traditionalists also have two other fine destinations here: the Vine in Brierley Hill and the Old Windmill in Coventry. A most unusual pub is the Crooked House in Himley – a very odd building worth seeing as a curiosity, besides being a good pub in its own right. The Little Dry Dock in Netherton is another engaging oddity, highly eccentric – and little changed though it's now tied to Ushers. Pubs currently finding particular favour in the Lucky Dip section at the end of the chapter are the Kings Head at Aston Cantlow, Haywaggon at Churchover, Red Lion at Claverdon, Black Swan in Stratford (which has a very good choice), Pie Factory in Tipton, Bell at Welford on Avon, Manor House in West Bromwich and Royal Oak at Whatcote; having inspected all these ourselves, we can give them the thumbs-up. Warwick has a good choice, the Golden Cross at Ardens Grafton is enjoyed for its collections of dolls and teddy bears, the Bulls Head at Wootton Wawen is still well worth knowing for good food (at a price), and the reliable White Hart at Newbold on Stour is kept out of the main entries only by a lack of readers' reports this year. Beer prices in this area are a bit lower than the national average – a lot lower in those pubs supplied by smaller local or regional breweries. Cheapest of all were the Crooked House in Himley (a Banks's pub) and the Vine in Brierley Hill (the tap for Bathams brewery).

ALDERMINSTER (War) SP2348 Map 4

Bell 🍴 🍷

A3400 Oxford—Stratford

You do need to book, or at least arrive early for a table at this friendly and fairly smart dining pub, and as it's only four miles from Stratford you could fit in a very pleasant supper here before the theatre. The imaginative menu changes monthly and dishes are produced as far as possible from fresh ingredients. There might be tomato, red lentil and basil soup (£3.25), home-made pâté (£5.25), cheese, lentil and tomato loaf (£7.95), sauté of lamb liver with mushrooms and cream and sherry sauce (£8.25), pork with lemon and coriander served with couscous (£8.50), braised lamb shank with mint and redcurrant gravy (£9.75) and duck breast with a blackcurrant and cassis sauce (£9.95), as well as several fresh fish dishes like mediterranean seafood pasta (£8.25), grilled lemon sole (£10.95), garlicky king prawns or fresh pan-fried scallops with mushrooms and brandy and cream (£11.95); good value weekday two course lunch (£6.50). The communicating areas of the neatly kept spacious bar have plenty of stripped slatback chairs around wooden tables on the flagstones and wooden floors, little vases of flowers, small landscape prints and swan's-neck brass-and-globe lamps on the cream walls, and a solid fuel stove in a stripped brick inglenook; apart from the small entrance bar the whole pub is no smoking. Well kept changing beers might include Courage Directors, Fullers London Pride, Greene King Abbot and IPA and Hook Norton Best on handpump, a good range of wines by the glass, freshly squeezed juice and a cocktail of the month. Civilised and friendly waitress service, and readers with children have felt particularly welcome here – they have high chairs but no children's menu. A conservatory and terrace overlook the garden and Stour Valley. There is an extensive programme of parties, food festivals, classical and light music evenings throughout the year. As we went to press they had just started doing B&B – we await reports. *(Recommended by Jack Houghton, Michael and Jeanne Shillington, P Lloyd, David and Ruth Shillitoe, Janet Arter, Roy Bromell, John Bowdler, P and D Carpenter, J H Kane, Dorothee and Dennis Glover, Brian Skelcher, Theo, Anne and Jane Gaskin, Hugh Spottiswoode, Maysie Thompson)*

Free house ~ Licensees Keith and Vanessa Brewer ~ Real ale ~ Meals and snacks ~ (01789) 450414 ~ Children welcome ~ Open 12-3, 7-11(10.30) Sun; closed evenings 24 Dec and 1 Jan ~ Bedrooms: £30B/£65B

BERKSWELL (W Midlands) SP2479

Bear

Spencers Lane; village signposted off A452 W of Coventry

A splendid example of how well the Chef & Brewer formula can work, this picturesque 16th-c timbered pub successfully combines a traditional relaxed atmosphere with a very wide choice of good value food. Inside there are comfortably snug low-beamed areas, alcoves, nooks and crannies, panelling, a longcase clock, bric-a-brac and prints, and roaring log fires in winter; in one place the heavy timbers show the slope of the cats'-slide eaves. All food is cooked to order, and besides well served doorstep sandwiches (from £2.60), filled ciabattas (from £3.85) and ploughman's (from £3.95), there maybe traditional fish and chips (£5.45), steak and kidney pudding (£6.05), wild mushroom penne (£6.25), lasagne (£6.50), haddock béarnaise hash (£7.20), turkey, ham and pork pie (£7.15), full rack of barbecue ribs (£10.70) and puddings such as apple pie (from £2.70). Well kept Theakstons Best and up to three guests; decent house wines and unusually for this chain quite a few by the glass; maybe piped music. There are tables behind on a tree-sheltered back lawn. The cannon in front is a veteran of the Crimean War and when it was last fired to mark Queen Victoria's Diamond Jubilee the blast shattered most of the windows in the locality. The village church is well worth a visit. *(Recommended by Brian Skelcher, Susan and John Douglas, Ted George, Stephen G Brown, Roy Bromell)*

Scottish Courage ~ Manager Ian Robinson ~ Real ale ~ Meals and snacks (all day) ~ (01676) 533202 ~ Well behaved children welcome if eating ~ Open 11-11; 12-10.30 Sun

BIRMINGHAM (W Midlands) SP0586 Map 4

Fiddle & Bone

4 Sheepcote Street; opposite National Indoor Arena South car park

Set up by two members of the City of Birmingham Symphony Orchestra, this remarkable converted schoolhouse is well worth a detour for the excellent live music they have every evening from 8, and some weekend afternoons as well – and has an enjoyably refreshing feel at other times of day, too. They'd only been open just over a year as we went to press, but already nearly 600 bands had livened up the stage at the end of the lofty main bar, mostly jazz, but also blues, soul, classical, and folk. They have activities you can join in, with a weekly choir practice, and salsa lessons for beginners and intermediates (there's a charge for these). On our last visit they blithely told us they were trying to be individual, and it's fair to say they've hit the right note. Various musical instruments hang from the ceiling or the walls, and along the bar counter trombones have been ingeniously converted into lights. Spotless varnished light pine tables with cushioned benches form little booths along each side of the bare-boards room, and a staircase in the middle leads down to the restaurant and a flagstoned bar area with a lighter cafe-bar feel. There are lots of picnic-sets outside here, but you get a better view of the activities and boats on the adjacent canal through the windows of another bar upstairs. Well kept Marstons Pedigree, Theakstons Best and Old Peculier, and Fiddlers Pluck, a beer named for them by Theakstons, on handpump, a short but good choice of wines by the glass, and unusual schnapps; efficient helpful staff. Good bar food, with most things available all day, includes soup (£2.50), filled baguettes (from £3.10), calamari rings with tartare sauce (£3.50), thick sliced toasted bread topped with mushroom and courgettes in scrambled egg (£3.85) or mussels with parsley and garlic (£4.30), spinach lasagne (£4.95), fish and chips (£5.75), wiener schnitzel or roast leg of lamb (£6.95), and hungarian goulash (£6.99); there may be a slight wait at busy times. Their website (www.fiddle-bone.co.uk) has a list of gigs coming up over the next month; there's usually good piped jazz when there isn't live music. Next door is a developing craft centre, and a waterbus stops just outside. Be prepared for high charges at the NCP car park opposite – best to think of them as a cover charge for the music; it's also handy for the National Sea Life Centre. *(Recommended by Jean and Richard Phillips, Jack Barnwell, Maggie and Peter Shapland)*

Free house ~ Licensee Werner Koder ~ Real ale ~ Meals and snacks (12-10) ~ Restaurant ~ (0121) 200 2223 ~ Children in restaurant ~ Live music every night at 8, some afternoons from 2 ~ Open 11-11; 12-10.30 Sun

BRIERLEY HILL (W Midlands) SO9187 Map 4

Vine £ ■

Delph Rd; B4172 between A461 and A4100, near A4100

Readers find this warmly welcoming pub archetypally English. Full of local characters, it serves really good value food and is also the tap for the next-door Batham brewery – so the Bitter and Mild, and Delph Strong in winter, are well kept and also very reasonably priced. It's a popular place so it can get crowded in the warmly welcoming front bar which has wall benches and simple leatherette-topped oak stools; the extended and refurbished snug on the left has solidly built red plush seats, and the back bar has brass chandeliers as well as darts, dominoes and fruit machine. Good fresh lunchtime snacks include samosas (60p), sandwiches (£1), pasta bake and salad (£1.80) and curry, faggots and peas, or steak and kidney pie (£2.50). The pub is known in the Black Country as the Bull & Bladder, from the good stained-glass bull's heads and very approximate bunches of grapes in the front bow windows. *(Recommended by Theo, Anne and Jane Gaskin, Andy and Jill Kassube, Chris Raisin, Graham Doyle, Pat and Tony Martin; more reports please)*

Bathams ~ Manager Melvyn Wood ~ Real ale ~ Lunchtime snacks (Mon-Fri only) ~ (01384) 78293 ~ Children welcome in children's room ~ Blues Sun evening ~ Open 12-11; 12-4, 7-10.30 Sun

COVENTRY (W Midlands) SP3379 Map 4

Old Windmill £

Spon Street

Unlike the rest of the buildings in the street – a collection of transplanted survivors from the blitz – this unpretentious timber-framed 15th-c pub is on its original site. Still known locally as Ma Brown's after a former landlady, it has a good local reputation as the friendliest pub in Coventry. The interior is full of character: one of the rambling series of tiny cosy old rooms is little more than the stub of a corridor, another has carved oak seats on flagstones and a woodburner in a fine ancient inglenook fireplace, and another has carpet and more conventionally comfortable seats. There are exposed beams in the uneven ceilings, and a back room preserves some of the equipment used when Ma Brown brewed here. Well kept Courage Directors, John Smiths, Marstons Pedigree, Morlands Old Speckled Hen, Websters and a couple of guests all kept under light blanket pressure; fruit machine, juke box. Good value food passed out straight from the kitchen door includes filled batches (from £1.20), soup (£1.75), faggots and mushy peas (£3.50), home-made cottage pie, chicken curry or cheesy cauliflower and broccoli bake (£3.60) and all day breakfast, gammon and egg, haddock, home-made steak pie or ploughman's (£3.75); no-smoking dining area. The pub is popular with students, extremely busy on Friday and Saturday evenings, and handy for the Belgrave Theatre. *(Recommended by G Washington, Thomas and Audrey Nott, John Brightley)*

Courage ~ Tenant: Lynne Ingram ~ Real ale ~ Lunchtime meals and snacks ~ (01203) 252183 ~ Children in dining area ~ Folk music 1st Tues in month ~ Open 11-11; 12-3, 7-10.30 Sun; closed 25 Dec and lunchtime 1 Jan

DUNCHURCH (War) SP4871 Map 4

Dun Cow

1⅓ miles from M45 junction 1: on junction of A45 and A426

This mainly Georgian coaching inn has undergone something of a face-lift since it last appeared as a main entry in the Guide. The decor is very traditional with welcoming open fires, rugs on the wooden floors, exposed oak beams and country pictures; it's all spotlessy kept and the staff are friendly and attentive. Bass and a guest such as Fullers London Pride on handpump; fruit machine and piped music. Well liked reasonably priced food includes sandwiches (£3.50), ploughman's (£3.75), soup (£1.95), fried shrimps with lemon mayonnaise (£2.95), salmon and crab fishcakes (£4.50) and main courses such as three shires sausages and mash (£4.50), hot chicken salad (£5.45), broccoli and brie pastry tart with sherry cream sauce (£5.95), mixed grill (£6.95), and steaks (from £6.95). Outside there are tables in the pretty coachyard and on a sheltered side lawn. *(Recommended by Patrick Tailyour, Michael Betton, George Atkinson, Anthea Robinson, Roy Bromell)*

Bass ~ Manager: Florie D'Arcy ~ Meals and snacks (all day) ~ (01788) 810305 ~ Children welcome ~ Open 11-11.30; 12-11.30 Sun

EDGE HILL (War) SP3747 Map 4

Castle

This was built in 1749 by an 18th-c Gothic Revival fanatic to mark the spot where Charles I raised his standard at the start of the Battle of Edge Hill, and it's said that after closing time at this crenellated octagon you can hear ghostly sounds of the battle, and there's even been the apparition of a cavalry officer galloping by in search of his severed hand. There are arched doorways and the walls of the warm and cosy lounge bar have the same eight sides as the rest of the main tower and are decorated with maps, pictures and civil war memorabilia. In the public bar there are old farming implements, as well as darts, pool, cribbage, dominoes, fruit machine, trivia, Aunt Sally and piped music. Full range of Hook Norton ales and a guest on handpump; country wines and around 30 malt whiskies. Bar food includes sandwiches (£2.10), ploughman's (£4.50), chicken curry or vegetarian pasta dishes (£5.25), home-made steak and kidney pudding (£5.95), mixed grill (£6.25), cajun chicken (£6.95) and steaks (£8.95); quick and friendly service. There is a large garden with splendid views across the battlefield. The bedrooms are in a separate tower. Upton House is nearby on the A422, and Compton Wynyates, one of the most beautiful houses in this part of England, is not far beyond. *(Recommended by Mike Gorton, Michael and Hazel Lyons, Susan and John Douglas, David Clifton, Allan and Philipa Wright)*

Hook Norton ~ Lease: Mr Blann ~ Meals and snacks ~ Children welcome ~ Open 11.15-2.30, 6-11; 12-3, 6-10.30 Sun ~ Bedrooms: £23B/£49.50B

ETTINGTON (War) SP2749 Map 4

Chequers

A422 Banbury—Stratford

Initial reports on the new regime at this village pub are very promising. The emphasis is very much on dining and well liked imaginative bar food includes filled french bread (from £3.75), spinach, bacon and crouton salad (£5.75), green-lipped mussels (£6.25), vegetable thai curry (£7.75), chargrilled peppers with couscous (£8), wild boar (£10.50), thai monkfish (£11.75) and steaks (from £13.50); puddings include home-made Baileys brûlée and summer pudding (£4). Hook Norton Best and a guest, usually from Whitbreads, on handpump; extensive wine list. The carpeted lounge bar is decorated with comic hunting scenes; friendly and welcoming service; piped music and no-smoking area. There's a spacious conservatory and in summer there are window boxes and flower tubs in front and tables under cocktail parasols in the neat back garden. *(Recommended by Hugh Spottiswoode, Gordon Hewitt, Miss A Aronica; more reports on the new regime please)*

Free house ~ Licensees Mr and Mrs Russell ~ Real ale ~ Meals and snacks (not Sun evening or Mon) ~ Restaurant ~ (01789) 740387 ~ Children welcome ~ Open 12-2, 6.30-10.30; closed Sun evenings and Mon

FARNBOROUGH (War) SP4349 Map 4

Butchers Arms

Off A423 N of Banbury

Prettily set well back from the road on the side of a hill, this creeper-covered village pub has a nice choice of carefully renovated rooms. The pleasant main lounge bar has lots of oak furniture and fittings, flagstone floors and some carpet, piped Classic FM. Bass, Hook Norton and a weekly guest like Wardens Best on handpump; decent wine list. There's a prettily countrified dining extension with big timbers, and a front public bar with darts; fruit machine. Bar food in generous helpings includes sandwiches (from £1.85), soup (£2.35), filled baguettes (£2.85), very well liked toasted bread filled with ham and cheese and topped with a fried egg, cod or home-made pâté (£3.85), ploughman's, omelettes, vegetable bake or lamb curry (£4.85), home-made steak and kidney pie or gammon and egg (£5.85) and home-made puddings (£2.85); friendly staff. Seats in garden as well as a veritable menagerie that includes rabbits, hamsters, parakeets and budgies. It's handy for Farnborough Hall. *(Recommended by Dave Braisted, David Toulson, Sheila Keene, Dr John Bassett, John Bowdler, Jill Bickerton)*

Free house ~ Licensee Kathryn Robinson ~ Real ale ~ Meals and snacks (till 10) ~ Restaurant ~ (01295) 690615 ~ Children welcome away from bar ~ Live music Fri evenings ~ Open 12-3, 7-11

FIVE WAYS (War) SP2270 Map 4

Case is Altered

Follow Rowington signposts at junction roundabout off A4177/A4141 N of Warwick

As we went to press we heard that Gwen Jones, who was the landlady here for many years, has sadly passed away. Her granddaughter was increasingly involved in the running of the pub over the last few years and plans to change very little. It is indeed the feeling that nothing ever changes here that is the real charm of this delightful white cottage that has been licensed to sell beer for over three centuries. There's no food, no children or dogs, and no noisy games machines or piped music – but you can be sure of a delightfully warm welcome from the cheery staff and regulars. The small, unspoilt simple main bar is decorated with a fine old poster showing the Lucas Blackwell & Arkwright brewery (now flats) and a clock with its hours spelling out Thornleys Ale, another defunct brewery; there are just a few sturdy old-fashioned tables, with a couple of stout leather-covered settles facing each other over the spotless tiles. From this room you reach the homely lounge (usually open only weekend evenings and Sunday lunchtime) through a door lit up on either side. A door at the back of the building leads into a modest little room, usually empty on weekday lunchtimes, with a rug on its tiled floor and an antique bar billiards table protected by an ancient leather cover (it takes pre-decimal sixpences). Well kept and very reasonably priced Ansells Bitter and Mild, Flowers Original, and guest ales at weekends served by rare beer engine pumps mounted on the casks that are stilled behind the counter. Behind a wrought-iron gate is a little brick-paved courtyard with a stone table under a chestnut tree. *(Recommended by Pete Baker, Ted George, Brian Skelcher, Stephen Brown, Andy and Jill Kassube; more reports please)*

Free house ~ Licensee Jackie M Willacy ~ Real ale ~ (01926) 484206 ~ Open 12(11.30 Sat)-2.30, 6-11; 12-2, 7-10.30 Sun

GREAT WOLFORD (War) SP2434 Map 4

Fox & Hounds ★

Village signposted on right on A3400 3 miles S of Shipston on Stour

Warwickshire Dining Pub of the Year

Readers are so enthusiastic about the food at this inviting 16th-c stone pub that this year we have given them a Food Award. Besides the usual pub fare such as sandwiches, soup and ploughman's, imaginative specials might include fresh sardines stuffed with onions and basil with provençal sauce (£3.50), smoked salmon terrine (£3.75), pork fillet wrapped in bacon and spinach with light green peppercorn sauce (£9.50), lamb kleftico (£9.95), grilled red snapper with provençal butter, capers and lemon (£11) and puddings like sticky toffee pudding (£2.95) and chocolate terrine or coconut parfait with an apricot coulis (£3.50). Despite the increasing emphasis on food locals and those who just want a drink feel very welcome in the cosy low-beamed old-fashioned bar which has a nice collection of chairs and candlelit old tables on spotless flagstones, old hunting prints on the walls, and a roaring log fire in the inglenook fireplace with its fine old bread oven. A small tap room serves a terrific choice of seven weekly changing beers like Black Sheep, Butcombe, Fullers London Pride, Hook Norton Best, Morlands Old Speckled Hen, Shepherd Neame Spitfire and Wychwood Dogs Bollocks on handpump, and over 200 malt whiskies. There's a well on the terrace outside. *(Recommended by K H Frosktick, Pam Adsley, Jerry and Alison Oakes, John Bowdler, J H Kane, Walter Reid, Martin Jones, R H Davies, Dave and Deborah Irving, Sheila Keene, Simon Walker)*

Free house ~ Licensees Graham and Anne Seddon ~ Meals and snacks ~ (01608) 674220 ~ Children in eating area ~ Open 12-3, 7-11; closed Sunday evening and Monday ~ Bedrooms: /£35S (breakfast not served)

HIMLEY (W Midlands) SO8889 Map 4

Crooked House ★

Pub signposted from B4176 Gornalwood—Himley, OS Sheet 139 map reference 896908; readers have got so used to thinking of the pub as being near Kingswinford in the Midlands (though Himley is actually in Staffs) that we still include it in this chapter – the pub itself is virtually smack on the county boundary

Here's one of the few pubs that really lives up to its name: you lose all sense of balance as you walk into this remotely set wonky old brick house. When subsidence caused by the mine workings underneath threw the pub 15 degrees out of true they propped it up, rehung the doors and straightened the floors. The result leaves your perceptions spinning in a way the landlord suggests is akin to being at sea. Inside on one table a bottle on its side actually rolls 'upwards' against the apparent direction of the slope, and for a 10p donation you can get a big ball-bearing from the bar to roll 'uphill' along a wainscot. There's a friendly atmosphere in the characterful old rooms, and at the back is a large, level and more modern extension with local antiques. Very reasonably priced Banks's Bitter and Dark Ale, Marstons Pedigree and maybe Banks's seasonal ales on hand or electric pump; dominoes, fruit machine and piped music. Good value bar food includes tasty and inexpensive rolls, smokies (£3.65) and steak and kidney pie (£4.25). The conservatory is no smoking at food times, and there's a spacious outside terrace; There may be Morris dancing outside in summer, when it can get very busy with coach trips. *(Recommended by M Borthwick, Ian Phillips, Mr and Mrs D Lawson, Jeanne Cross, Paul Silvestri)*

Banks's ~ Manager Gary Ensor ~ Real ale ~ Meals and snacks (12-2 every day; 6.30-8.30 Thurs; 5-8.30 Fri and Sat; not evenings Sun-Wed) ~ (01384) 238583 ~ Children welcome in conservatory during food times ~ Maybe Morris dancers during the summer ~ Open 11-11; 12-10.30 Sun; 11.30-2.30, 6.30-11 winter weekdays; 12-3, 7-10.30 winter Sun

ILMINGTON (War) SP2143 Map 4

Howard Arms

Village signposted with Wimpstone off A34 S of Stratford

Readers continue to enjoy the imaginative well prepared bar food at this smart golden-stone dining inn. It can get busy and the welcoming and efficient young staff cope well, although as food is prepared to order there may be delays. The menu changes constantly but there may be soup (£2.75), chicken liver pâté or butterfly prawns with garlic dip (£4.50), lamb liver with smoky bacon and onion gravy (£6.50), steak and kidney pie (£6.75), chicken balti (£7), baked aubergine with stir-fried vegetables topped with a goats cheese glaze (£8.25), chicken with tarragon cream sauce (£8.50), poached salmon with a vermouth and chive cream sauce (£8.95) and duck with an orange liqueur sauce (£10.95); puddings include summer pudding, steamed treacle sponge and home-made apple pie (£3.75); small helpings of some dishes for children. There's a cosy atmosphere in the friendly heavy-beamed bar (possibly full of shooting gents on Saturday) which has rugs on lovely polished flagstones, comfortable seats, highly polished brass, and open fires, a couple of tables in a big inglenook, screened from the door by an old-fashioned built-in settle). A snug area off here is no smoking. Well kept Everards Tiger, Marstons Pedigree and an interesting guest like Wychwood Fiddlers Elbow on handpump and under light blanket pressure, decent wines of the month, and excellent freshly pressed apple juice. Shove-ha'penny, cribbage, dominoes and Aunt Sally on Thursday evenings; piped music. The garden is lovely in summer with fruit trees sheltering the lawn, a colourful herbaceous border and well spaced picnic-sets, with more tables on a neat gravel terrace behind. It's nicely set beside the village green, and there are lovely walks on the nearby hills (as well as strolls around the village outskirts). *(Recommended by David Shillitoe, Maysie Thompson, Graham Tayar, Catherine Raeburn, Martin and Catherine Snelling, J H Kane, Martin Jones, Pam Adsley, Michael and Jeanne Shillington, Richard Sanders, G R Braithwaite, Roy Bromell, Dorothee and Dennis Glover, Nigel and Sue Foster, Martin and Karen Wake, J and P Maloney, Neil Porter, Simon Walker, Cyril Brown, Alan and Barbara Mence, John Bowdler, E V Walder, Pat and Roger Fereday)*

Free house ~ Licensee Alan Thompson ~ Real ale ~ Meals and snacks (not winter Sun evenings) ~ Restaurant (not winter Sun evenings) ~ (01608) 682226 ~ Well behaved children welcome ~ Open 11-2.30, 6-11; 12-3, 7-10.30 Sun; closed 25 Dec ~ Bedrooms: /£55B

LAPWORTH (War) SP1670 Map 4

Navigation

Old Warwick Rd (B4439 Warwick—Hockley Heath)

What really makes this bustling local special is its canalside setting, and in summer it comes into its own – canal-users and locals sit on a back terrace where they have barbecues, jazz, Morris dancers or even travelling theatre companies; outside hatch service, and it's all prettily lit at night. The friendly flagstoned bar is decorated with some brightly painted canal ware and cases of stuffed fish, and has high-backed winged settles, seats built around its window bay and a coal fire in its high-mantled inglenook. Another quieter room has tables on its board-and-carpet floor and a modern extension is nicely done with rugs on oak floors, cast-iron tables and bentwood chairs; delightful views over the sheltered flower-edged lawn, and on down to the busy canal behind. Bar food in very large helpings includes lunchtime sandwiches (from £2.50), chicken balti or large cod in beer batter (£5.95), beef, Guinness and mushroom pie (£6.50), steaks (from £7.95), grilled duck breast with plum sauce (£8.95), and traditional puddings made by the licensee's mother (£2.50). Service is cheery and efficient even when it's busy. Very well kept Bass, Highgate Dark Mild, M&B Brew XI, and up to two guests on handpump, and a guest farm cider; fruit machine, dominoes. *(Recommended by Tom McLean, Mike and Mary Carter, Mrs G Sharman, Dr Oscar Puls, Tony Hobden, Mr and Mrs C Moncreiffe, Brian and Anna Marsden, Lynn and Peter Brueton, Mike Gorton, Andy and Jill Kassube, John Franklin, Andrew Scarr, Joan and Tony Walker, M Joyner, Iona Thomson)*

M&B (Bass) ~ Lease: Andrew Kimber ~ Real ale ~ Meals and snacks ~ (01564) 783337 ~ Children welcome in eating area until 9 ~ Morris dancing and canal theatre in summer ~ Open 11-3, 5.30-11; 11-11 Sat; 12-10.30 Sun; cl 25, 26 Dec evenings

LITTLE COMPTON (War) SP2630 Map 4

Red Lion 🍷

Off A44 Moreton in Marsh—Chipping Norton

This attractive 16th-c stone inn is well liked for its reasonably priced tasty food, friendly welcome and good service. Bar food includes soup (£2.25), chicken liver pâté (£3.25), filled baguettes (from £2.95), ploughman's (£3.95), filled baked potatoes (from £3.50), plaice (£4.95), home-made lasagne (£5.75), or tagliatelle niçoise (£5.95) and daily specials like vegetable spring rolls with an oriental chilli dip (£3.25), avocado, prawn and crab salad (£4.95), chicken with bacon, mushrooms and tarragon and a white wine and cream sauce or salmon and broccoli filled crêpes (£6.95), chargrilled lamb steak in wholegrain mustard and honey marinade (£8.75) roast duck with orange and grand marnier sauce (£10.50) and steaks (from £8.95, 32oz £26.75). Booking is recommended on Saturday evenings especially; no-smoking dining area. The simple but civilised and comfortable low-beamed lounge has snug alcoves and a couple of little tables by the log fire. The plainer public bar has another log fire, and darts, pool, cribbage, fruit machine and juke box. Donnington BB and SBA under light blanket pressure and an extensive wine list; good service; maybe piped music. No dogs – even in the garden where there are tables and a children's play area. Conveniently positioned for exploring the Cotswolds. *(Recommended by Tim and Linda Collins, NWN, Tim Brierly, M G Swift, Gordon, Mr and Mrs H Quick, Dr A Drummond, Sheila and John French, BHP, Iona Thomson, John Franklin, Barry and Anne, H O Dickinson)*

Donnington ~ Tenant David Smith ~ Real ale ~ Meals and snacks ~ Restaurant ~ (01608) 674397 ~ Children welcome in eating area of bar ~ Open 12-2.30, 6-11; 12-3, 7-10.30 Sun ~ Bedrooms: £25/£38 (no under 8s)

LOWSONFORD (War) SP1868 Map 4

Fleur de Lys

Village signposted off B4439 Hockley Heath—Warwick; can be reached too from B4095 via Preston Bagot

As we went to press we heard that there were new licensees at this attractively set canalside pub. In summer it's pleasant to sit outside on the picnic-sets among tall weeping willows by the canal. In winter the big comfortable spreading bar is warmed by a log fire; also lots of low black beams in the butter-coloured ceiling, brocade-cushioned mate's, wheelback and dining chairs around the well spaced tables, and rugs on the flagstones and antique tiles. Bar food under the new regime includes soup (£2.25), sandwiches (£2.75) and ploughman's (from £4.95); on the changing specials boards there might be filo Japanese prawns (£3.25), filo brie (£3.45), tomato and basil quiche (£5.40), grilled trout (£7.25), cajun chicken sizzlers (£8.60), rack of lamb or skate wing (£8.95), and beef wellington or lemon sole (£10.95). Flowers Original, Fullers London Pride and Wadworths 6X under light blanket pressure. Children are welcome in the no-smoking family area and there's a good play area outside. *(Recommended by M G Swift, Paul and Judith Booth, D A Norman, Sue Rowland, Paul Mallett, Simon Hulme, Roy Bromell, Chris Walling, Brian Skelcher, D P Brown, John Franklin, C A Hall; reports on the new regime please)*

Whitbreads ~ Managers Ian and Maria Blackman ~ Real ale ~ Meals and snacks ~ (01564) 782431 ~ Open 11-11; 12-10.30 Sun

MONKS KIRBY (War) SP4683 Map 4

Bell

Just off B4027 (former A427) W of Pailton; Bell Lane

The very traditional appearance of this timbered and flagstoned old pub is rather deceptive, because with its chatty Spanish landlord the warmly comfortable and informal atmosphere is distinctly southern European. Besides the extensive tapas blackboard menu (£3.75-£4.25), the very wide ranging bar menu offers traditional pub food such as chicken kiev (£6.25), mushroom stroganoff (£6.50), scampi (£7.25), lamb cutlets (£8.25) and steaks (from £9.95), as well as a quite astonishing range of hugely tempting Spanish dishes such as chorizo cooked in garlic and white wine (£3.95), king prawns in garlic and chilli sauce (£4.95), paellas (from £8.25), speciality steak grills (from £10.75) and an amazing array of seafood dishes such as tuna cooked with tomatoes, white wine and prawns (£10.95), monkfish cooked in a clay dish with red peppers, herbs, garlic and white wine (£11.95) and sea bass in a white wine and shellfish sauce; no-smoking dining area; piped music. As well as well kept Boddingtons and Flowers Original on handpump there's a very good wine list, ports for sale by the bottle and a healthy range of brandies and malt whiskies. The plain little back terrace has rough-and-ready rustic woodwork, geese and chickens and a pretty little view across a stream to a buttercup meadow. *(Recommended by Brian and Anne Marsden, Dave and Deborah Irving, Brian Smart, Susan and John Douglas, Eric and June Heley, Roy Bromell, Stephen Brown, D P Brown, Heather Roberts, Michael Begley, Ted George, Luke Worthington)*

Free house ~ Licensees Paco and Belinda Garcia Maures ~ Real ale ~ Meals and snacks (during opening hours) ~ Restaurant ~ (01788) 832352 ~ Children welcome ~ 12-2.30, 7-10.30; closed Mon lunchtime; closed 26 Dec, 1 Jan

NETHERTON (W Midlands) SO9387 Map 4

Little Dry Dock

Windmill End, Bumble Hole; you really need an A-Z street map to find it – or OS Sheet 139 map reference 953881

Painted in red, white and blue, this lively and eccentric canalside pub began life as a boatyard. They didn't change much during the conversion – an entire narrow-boat is squeezed into the right-hand bar and used as the servery (its engine is in the room on the left), and there's also a huge model boat in one front transom-style window, winches and barge rudders flanking the door, marine windows, and lots of brightly coloured bargees' water pots, lanterns, jugs and lifebuoys; fruit machines and piped music. Ushers Best, Founders and Little Puck on handpump; friendly service. Simple good value bar food includes soup (£1.75), black pudding thermidor (£2.10), faggots and peas (£4.45), home-cooked ham with parsley sauce or chilli (£4.50), lasagne (£4.65), gammon and egg (£5.20), scampi or minted lamb pie (£5.25), steak and kidney in Guinness pie (£5.50), rump steak (£6.50) and mixed grill (£6.95), and traditional puddings (from £1.95). There are pleasant towpath walks nearby. *(Recommended by Ian Phillips, Chris Raisin, Graham Doyle, Andy and Jill Kassube, Daren Haines; more reports please)*

Ushers ~ Tenant Frank Pearson ~ Real ale ~ Meals and snacks (till 10pm) ~ (01384) 235369 ~ Children welcome ~ Irish folk music Mon evenings ~ Open 11-3, 6(5.30 Sat)-11; 12-3, 6-10.30 Sun

SAMBOURNE (War) SP0561 Map 4

Green Dragon

A435 N of Alcester, then left fork on to A448 just before Studley; village signposted on left soon after

Bedecked with colourful hanging baskets in summer, this welcoming village-green pub with its shuttered and timbered facade has long been a popular stop for good value lunchtime food. The bar menu includes sandwiches, omelettes (from £4.50), ploughman's, liver and bacon, sausages with bubble and squeak, home-made steak and Guinness pie, home-made lasagne or chilli (£5.50), stir-fried chicken (£6.50), gammon and egg (£6.95) and daily specials; there are far more elaborate dishes in the restaurant menu. The cheery modernised communicating rooms have low beamed ceilings, rugs on flagstoned floors, little armed seats and more upright ones, some small settles, and open fires; maybe piped music. Well kept Bass, Hobsons, and M & B Brew XI on handpump; friendly, attentive service. There are picnic-sets and teak seats among flowering cherries on a side courtyard, by the car park; bowls. The bedrooms are neatly decorated and well equipped. *(Recommended by Christopher Turner, J H Kane, Kay Neville-Rolfe, John Franklin, Ian Phillips, B Adams, Mike Gorton, Tom Gondris, Michael Begley, J H Kane)*

M & B (Bass) ~ Lease: Phil and Pat Burke ~ Real ale ~ Meals and snacks (till 10; not Sun) ~ Restaurant (not Sun) ~ (01527) 892465 ~ Children welcome ~ Open 11-3, 5.30(6 Sat)-11; 12-3, 7-11 Sun ~ Bedrooms: £48B/£60B

SHUSTOKE (War) SP2290 Map 4

Griffin

5 miles from M6, junction 4; A446 towards Tamworth, then right on to B4114 and go straight through Coleshill; pub is at Furnace End, a mile E of village

On the edge of a playing field, this charmingly unpretentious village local is popular with readers for the ten or so real ales served by the friendly licensee. One or two will always be from their own microbrewery which produces very tasty Church End, Choir Boy, Cuthberts, Old Pal, Vicar's Ruin or perhaps Pew's Porter. These are served alongside interesting guests such as Bathams, Exmoor Gold, Holdens, Otter Bright, Theakstons Mild and Old Peculier, Timothy Taylor Landlord, all from a servery under a very low, thick beam; country wine, mulled wine and hot punch also. There is always a good mixed crowd, even mid-week, in the low-beamed L-shaped bar; also an old-fashioned settle and cushioned cafe seats (some quite closely packed), sturdily elm-topped sewing trestles, lots of old jugs on the beams, beer mats on the ceiling, and log fires in both stone fireplaces (one's a big inglenook); the conservatory is popular with families. Good lunchtime bar food includes sandwiches (from £1.50), steak cob (£2.50), steak pie, curry of the day or chilli (£4.50), cod (£6), 8oz sirloin steak (£7) and a few blackboard specials; you may need to arrive early to get a table. There are old-fashioned seats and tables on the back grass, a children's play area, and a large terrace with plants in raised beds. *(Recommended by John Dwane, John Dinane, Kerry Law, Simon Smith, Peter and Gwyneth Eastwood, Mark Fennell, Lady M H Moir)*

Own brew ~ Licensee Michael Pugh ~ Real ale ~ Lunchtime meals and snacks (not Sun) ~ (01675) 481205 ~ Children welcome in conservatory ~ Open 12-2.30, 7-11; 12-2.15, 2-10.30 Sun; closed evenings 25/26 Dec

WARMINGTON (War) SP4147 Map 4

Plough £

Village just off B4100 N of Banbury

Very well placed in a delightful village a few yards up a quiet lane from a broad sloping green with duck pond and ducks, this unpretentious local looks especially pretty in the autumn, when the creeper over the front of the building turns a striking crimson colour. There's a nicely relaxed and cheery atmosphere in the warmly cosy bar which has old photographs of the village and locals, an old high-backed winged settle, cushioned wall seats and lots of comfortable Deco small armed chairs and library chairs, and good winter log fires. Well kept Hook Norton Best, Marstons Pedigree and a guest on handpump, and several malt whiskies; darts, dominoes, cribbage and piped pop music. Unambitious but good food includes locally made pork pie with chips and salad (£3.95), home-made cottage pie (£4.50), flavoursome home-baked ham, egg and chips (£5.50), and a popular Sunday lunch (although readers report that there may not be a choice of roasts). Very friendly licensee and staff. (*Recommended by M Joyner, Kerry Law, Simon Smith, CMW, JJW, J H Bell, John Bowdler, George Atkinson, Sheila and John French, Ted George*)

Free house ~ Licensee Denise Willson ~ Real ale ~ Meals and snacks (till 8.30pm; not Sun evening) ~ (01295) 690666 ~ Children in eating area lunchtimes and early evening ~ Open 12-3, 6-11; 12-3, 7-10.30 Sun; closed evening 25 Dec

Lucky Dip

Besides the fully inspected pubs, you might like to try these Lucky Dips recommended to us and described by readers (if you do, please send us reports):

Alcester [Kings Coughton; A435 towards Studley; SP0859], *Moat House*: Tudor beams and timbers, very nice atmosphere, lovely open fire, welcoming staff, well kept Courage Directors and Websters, plentiful food inc vegetarian; no-smoking room *(William Cunliffe)*

Aldridge W Mid [Chester Rd, Little Aston (A452 over Staffs border); SK0900], *Old Irish Harp*: Banks's Milestone Tavern, popular for their standard food inc vegetarian and children's; several rooms inc dining area, their Bitter and Marstons Pedigree, pleasant atmosphere, friendly efficient service, all ages; TV, quiz nights, open all day *(SLC)*

Allesley W Mid [73 Birmingham Rd; SP2981], *Rainbow*: Basic busy local in lopsided ancient building, a pub from the early 1950s, brewing its own ales, also Courage; good value food, friendly service, sunny garden; open all day, can be crowded with young people at night *(Edward Norris)*

Ansty [B4065 NE of Coventry, handy for M69/M6 junction 2; SP3983], *Rose & Castle*: Popular low-beamed pub with particularly good friendly service, wide choice of good value food, well kept Bass, Holt Plant & Deakins and other ales inc a rotating guest beer, some canal-theme decoration; not big, fills up quickly; children welcome, lovely canalside garden with play area *(Andy and Jill Kassube, Tony Hobden, Thomas and Audrey Nott, Brian Attmore)*

☆ **Ardens Grafton** [towards Wixford – OS Sheet 150 map ref 114538; SP1153], *Golden Cross*: Friendly L-shaped bar with Shakespearean murals, good choice of food here or in dining room with remarkable collection of world-wide and antique dolls, and no-smoking room with teddy bear collection; good choice of well kept ales such as Barrows 4Bs, Black Knight, Judges and Ouster, very welcoming efficient service, photographic magazines (local society meets here); unobtrusive piped music, fruit machine; seats outside, nice views *(June and Mike Coleman, Andy and Jill Kassube, Alan and Barbara Mence)*

☆ **Armscote** [off A3400 Stratford—Shipston; SP2444], *Armscote Inn*: Happy family-run pub, spotlessly clean, in picturesque Cotswold stone village, warm atmosphere, good well presented food using fresh produce in bar and restaurant inc vegetarian and choice of fish (refurbished kitchens), friendly service, well kept Greene King Abbot, Hook Norton Best and a guest, decent coffee *(J H Kane, Alan Jennings, Mike and Barbara Donaldson)*

☆ **Aston Cantlow** [Bearley Rd; SP1359], *Kings Head*: Attractively and comfortably refurbished beautifully timbered village pub not far from Mary Arden's house in Wilmcote, low beams, flagstones, inglenook log fire, enterprising choice of good generous freshly made food, fair prices, good value wines, well kept Whitbreads-related ales, cheerful staff *(Mary Walters, Mr and Mrs D Shier, Lord Sandhurst, LYM)*

Barston W Mid [Barston Ln; from M42 junction 5, A4141 towards Warwick, first left, then signed; SP2078], *Bulls Head*: Attractive partly Tudor village local, oak-beamed bar with log fires and Buddy Holly memorabilia, comfortable lounge with pictures and plates, dining room, friendly relaxed service, good value basic food, well kept Bass, M&B Brew XI and Tetleys, secluded garden, hay barn behind *(Joan and Tony Walker, Brian Skelcher, PB)*

Bearley [Bearley Cross; A3400 N of Stratford; SP1760], *Golden Cross*: Popular and friendly pub/restaurant, lovely old timbered bar with open fireplaces, soft lighting, good generous bar food, well kept Whitbreads-related ales, helpful staff; small restaurant *(Dave Braisted)*

Birmingham [308 Bradford St, Digbeth], *Anchor*: Perfectly preserved three-room Edwardian corner pub, carefully restored art nouveau glass, long high-ceilinged bar with basic seating, well kept Ansells Mild, Everards Tiger and Tetleys, interesting quickly changing guest beers, beer festivals; well priced simple food all day inc huge chip butties, friendly staff, back games room with pool, TV, juke box; tables outside, handy for coach stn *(Richard Lewis, Tony Hobden, SLC, John Dwane, G Coates)*; [Bennetts Hill], *Bennetts*: Converted bank, now like domed ballroom with Egyptian/French theme; comfortable dining area with sensibly priced specials, reasonable house wine, good coffee *(Roy Bromell)*; [16 Factory Rd, Hockley], *Black Eagle*: Four-room character late 19th-c pub, nicely furnished, with good varied low-priced home-cooked food, good friendly service, well kept Ansells, Marstons and guest beer *(John Dwane, E A Moore)*; [Bennetts Hill], *Factotum & Firkin*: Friendly and lively big hall with balcony, side bar, bare boards, lots of artefacts, red telephone box, friendly staff; good value food, well kept beers, good service, theme nights, stage for live music *(Richard Lewis, Ted George, Paul and Sue Merrick)*; [Cambrian Wharf, Kingston Row – central canal area], *Flapper & Firkin*: Popular bare-boards two-floor canalside pub behind Symphony Hall, typical Firkin features, lots of wood, own brew and guest ales, reasonably priced food, friendly staff; piped music may be loud, TV, some live entertainment, skittles Weds, tables outside *(SLC)*; [157 Barford St, Digbeth], *Lamp*: Two small well furnished rooms, cosy and intimate, lunchtime food, well kept ales such as Batemants Mild, Boddingtons, Stanway Stanney and Wadworths 6X; open 12-11 (cl Sun afternoon) *(SLC)*; [176 Edmund St], *Old Contemptibles*: Spacious and comfortable Edwardian pub with lofty ceiling and lots of woodwork, a bit spoilt by sales posters and loud piped music; well kept Bass, M&B Brew XI, Highgate Dark Mild and changing guest beers, friendly staff, food lunchtime and early evening (not Sat eve or Sun); open all day, cl Sun *(Richard Lewis, SLC, LYM)*; [Temple Row W], *Old Joint Stock*: Great new Fullers bank conversion with their ales from big Victorian-style central bar, food esp pies, upper balcony seating; popular with office workers, quiet debating atmosphere *(SLC, John Dwane)*; [Alcester Rd, Kings Heath], *Pavilions*: Tastefully converted big Victorian pub, well kept Banks's and other ales such as Marstons, straightforward food *(Jack Barnwell)*; [115 Corporation St], *Square Peg*: Roomy Wetherspoons pub, numerous areas inc no smoking, lots of old local prints, good choice of well kept ales inc guests from nearly 30-metre bar, farm cider, decent wines, good mix of people, no music, plenty of staff – efficient and friendly; open all day, their usual reliable food 11-10, sensible prices *(Richard Lewis, Mrs G Sharman, SLC, Daren Haines)*; [Brindley Wharf/Gas St], *Tap & Spile*: Nice canalside position, three levels, stripped brickwork and reclaimed timber, old pine pews and settles, lots of prints, friendly staff, good menu, good choice of well kept ales *(Richard Lewis)*; [276 Bradford St, Digbeth], *White Swan*: Unfussy but clean and comfortable friendly local with serving hatch to Victorian-tiled corridor, big bar, fire in small back lounge, charming staff, lovely fresh rolls, well kept Ansells Bitter and Mild and Tetleys *(Pete Baker, SLC, Ted George)*

Bishops Itchington [SP3857], *Butchers Arms*: Well kept beer, good food and atmosphere *(G Washington)*

Broom [off A46 N of Evesham, via B439 to Bidford; SP0853], *Broom Hall*: 16th-c, comfortable black-beamed lounge with double-sided fireplace, friendly staff, bargain lunches, real ales, good house wines and coffee; bedrooms *(Roy Bromell)*; [High St], *Broom Tavern*: Attractive 16th-c timber-framed pub, comfortable and relaxing, wide choice of good food cooked by Polish landlord in bar and two restaurant rooms (tables can be booked), Bass, Boddingtons, Flowers and Hook Norton, good value choice of wines, big log fire, hunting and country life cartoons, good service; children welcome *(June and Mike Coleman, S Needham)*

Bulkington [between Nuneaton and Coventry; SP3986], *Weavers Arms*: Friendly landlord, Bass-related ales and a guest beer, limited lunchtime food inc generous baguettes, big and small *(Tony and Wendy Hobden)*

☆ **Churchover** [handy for M6 junction 1, off A426; SP5180], *Haywaggon*: Carefully modernised old pub with good range of rather upmarket food with Italian leanings, esp seafood – Italian landlord; two snug eating areas, friendly atmosphere, must book Sun lunch; children's play area, on edge of quiet village, beautiful views over Swift valley *(Patrick Tailyour, John Brightley, BB)*

☆ **Claverdon** [B4095 towards Warwick; SP1964], *Red Lion*: Tasteful dining pub with rooms partly opened together, hop-hung beams, good home-cooked food (landlord ran restaurant in Spain), well kept Whitbreads-related ales and Marstons Pedigree, log fire, conscientious service, no-smoking back dining area with country views over sheltered back terrace and gardens; piped music *(George Atkinson, Mr and Mrs D Boynton, John Bowdler, BB)*

Coventry W Mid [Hill St/Berger St; SP3379], *Gatehouse*: Particularly well kept Bass and Brew XI, simple home-cooked food from giant doorstep sandwiches up (and maybe free coffee), friendly atmosphere; converted gatehouse for the Leigh Mills worsted factory, stained-glass decorations *(Chris Gabbitas, Hugh McPhail)*

Curdworth [A4097; SP1792], *Crown*: Smart dining pub with separate food counter, full menu from snacks up, Bass *(Tony and Wendy Hobden)*

☆ **Dorridge** W Mid [177 Four Ashes Rd; SP1775], *Drum & Monkey*: Comfortable newly refurbished and extended Greenalls Millers Kitchen family dining pub doing well under present hard-working landlady, wide choice of reliable good value food all day (£2 discounts for Lottery losers Mon-Thurs), well kept Tetleys-related ales, no-smoking area; big garden with play area *(Jack Barnwell)*

Earlswood W Mid [Lady Lane, past the Lakes; SP1274], *Red Lion*: Useful dining pub in imposing twin-gabled black and white Georgian pub, several small but high-ceilinged rooms each with its own character, sturdy tables and chairs, some wall settles, no-smoking back room with open fire, chandeliers and bigger tables, traditional food all day inc vegetarian and OAP menu, Bass and another beer such as Highgate Dark Mild, exemplary service, no loud music; disabled access, skittle alley, Stratford Canal moorings *(G Coates)*

☆ **Eathorpe** [car park off Fosse Way (B4455); SP3868], *Plough*: Big helpings of good food inc some bargain meals in long neat and clean split-level lounge/dining area with matching walls, carpets and table linen, huge piranha in tank by bar, good friendly chatty service; good coffee *(Roy Bromell)*

Ettington [Banbury Rd (A422 towards Stratford); SP2749], *Houndshill House*: Neat dining pub with welcoming landlord and modestly priced decent food in pleasant surroundings, very popular with families and OAPs; Scottish Courage ales, stripped stone and beams, good service, tables in big attractive garden, good views from front; children welcome, good well equipped bedrooms *(Maureen O'Neill)*

Fenny Compton [Wharf Rd; SP4152], *Wharf*: Recently refurbished two-bar pub by Bridge 136 of South Oxford Canal, Bass and guest beers, food (all day in summer) from filled hot baguettes up inc vegetarian, family room, restaurant, garden with terrace *(Anon)*

Gaydon [B4100, nr junction B4451 and M40 junction 12; SP3654], *Gaydon*: Quiet and pleasant, with real fire in lounge, two real ales, food inc OAP lunches and good Sun roasts, small no-smoking dining room; bar with darts, fruit machine and TV *(CMW, JJW)*

Grendon [A5 S of Tamworth; SK2900], *Black Swan*: Limited bar food inc tasty baguettes, Marstons *(Tony and Wendy Hobden)*

Halesowen W Mid [21 Stourbridge Rd; SO9683], *Waggon & Horses*: No-frills welcoming local with well kept Bathams, a house beer and up to a dozen or so interesting changing ales from small independent brewers; no food *(Paul Kelly, Dr and Mrs A K Clarke)*

Halford [A429; SP2545], *Halford Bridge*: Large and friendly old modernised stonebuilt hotel, woodburner in carpeted bar, stuffed fish, usual bar food, nice coffee, helpful staff, restaurant; bedrooms *(George Atkinson)*

Harborough Magna [Pailton Rd; 3 miles from M6 junction 1; SP4779], *Old Lion*: Tastefully modernised beamed Marstons dining pub, well run and spotless, with reasonable prices, well kept ales inc a seasonal one, particularly good quick cheerful service, small no-smoking area; restaurant popular for business lunches, piped music *(George Atkinson, Patrick Tailyour)*

Harbury [SP3759], *Dog*: Food inc good pork batch, most unusual sauces; Ansells, Bass and a guest such as Tisbury Archibald Beckett *(Dave Braisted)*

Harbury [Mill St, just off B4451/B4452 S of A425 Leamington Spa—Southam; SP3759], *Shakespeare*: Popular dining pub with good hospitable service and good choice of freshly cooked food (not Sun evening); linked beamed rooms, stripped stonework, well kept Whitbreads-related ales with guests such as Fullers London Pride and Timothy Taylor Landlord, inglenook log fire, horsebrasses, pleasant conservatory, separate pool room; children welcome; tables in back garden with aviaries *(Mrs B Sugarman, Roy Bromell)*

Hatton [Birmingham Rd (B4100); SP2467], *Falcon*: Isolated roadside low-beamed pub doing well under new regime, well refurbished for more concentration on very well cooked and presented reasonably priced food, but still cosy and warm, with big inglenook fireplace; well kept Bass, staff attentive, friendly and polite, big back garden and walled terrace *(Andy and Sarah Gillett)*

Hawkesbury W Mid [close to M6 junction 3, exit past Novotel northwards on Longford Rd (B4113), 1st right into Black Horse Rd, cross canal and into Sutton Stop; SP3684], *Greyhound*: Cosy unpretentious pub brimming with bric-a-brac, well kept Bass and Banks's Mild, coal-fired stove, unusual tiny snug; booking essential for the Pie Parlour – lots of canalia and quite private olde-worlde atmosphere; tables on attractive terrace with safe play area by junction of Coventry and N Oxford Canals – wonderful spot if you don't mind pylons, and can find it; children welcome *(P J Rowland)*

Henley in Arden [High St; SP1466], *Blue Bell*: Impressive timber-framed building with fine coach entrance; more modestly modern inside (despite the beams), with small bar, split dining area, limited food, real ales such as Boddingtons and Wadworths 6X; some tables in courtyard *(George Atkinson, SLC)*

☆ **Hockley Heath** W Mid [Stratford Rd (A34 Birmingham—Henley in Arden); SP1573], *Wharf*: Friendly modernised Chef & Brewer with lounge extension overlooking canal, quick good value generous food from hot meat rolls to carvery, Scottish Courage ales, plenty of seats, good canal photographs; darts, TV, games machines, piped pop music; children welcome; attractive garden with adventure playground by Stratford Canal, interesting towpath walks *(Alan and Barbara Mence, Dave Braisted)*

Iron Cross [A435 Evesham—Alcester; SP0552], *Queens Head*: Clean and comfortable, wide range of real ales inc Fat Gods brewed at the pub, good food range inc bargain specials and good Sun lunch, lots of antiques; open all day *(J Dwane)*

Kenilworth [Castle Hill; SP2871], *Clarendon Arms*: Busy dining pub with good cheap food inc vegetarian in several rooms off long partly flagstoned bar and in largish upstairs dining room; reductions for children and over-55s, efficient staff, good range of well served beers; opp castle *(S J Sloan)*; [High St], *Clarendon House*: Comfortable and civilised, with partly panelled bar, antique maps, prints, copper, china and armour, well kept Flowers IPA and Original and Hook Norton Best and Old Hookey, decent wines, friendly helpful bar staff, good value simple bar food, interesting restaurant specials *(Tony and Joan Walker)*; [Castle Green], *Queen & Castle*: Reliable Beefeater opp castle, quick well cooked food with good value OAP discounts, loyal local following, friendly staff, well kept Whitbreads-related ales, quaint corners, beams and pictures; piped pop music, games machines; extensive lawns, good play area *(G R Braithwaite)*; [High St], *Virgins & Castle*: Dark and basic, with several old-fashioned rooms off inner servery, simply furnished small snugs by entrance corridor, flagstones, heavy beams, some booth seating, coal fire, upstairs games bar, restaurant; cheap bar food (stops 1.45, not Sun/Mon evenings) from sandwiches up, well kept Bass, Greenalls Original and guest beers, good coffee; frequent live music, open all day, children in eating area, tables in sheltered garden *(Mark Fennell, Dr Oscar Puls, Michael and Gillian Ford, LYM)*

Kingswinford W Mid [Greensforge; out W of A449 by Staffs & Worcs Canal, over Staffs border; SO8688], *Navigation*: Comfortable lounge bar, separate public bar, reasonably priced generous food inc sandwiches, Banks's Mild, Bass and Tetleys; small garden, pleasant setting with boats working through the lock, nice towpath walks *(Dr A Drummond, DAV)*

Ladbroke [village signed off A423 S of Southam; SP4158], *Bell*: Cosy rambling Greenalls pub with good value lunchtime food, Bass and Tetleys, friendly staff, nice atmosphere; tables in garden, pleasant surroundings – very busy weekends *(Dave Braisted)*

Lapworth [Old Warwick Rd (B4439); SP1670], *Boot*: Busy canalside pub with two small attractive bars, good atmosphere, good if not cheap food inc imaginative dishes, also good filled baguettes, well kept beers, decent wines (big glasses); refurbished restaurant upstairs, nice garden, pleasant walks *(Barrie and Jayne Baker, Steve and Sarah Pleasance, Geoffrey and Penny Hughes)*

Leek Wootton [Warwick Rd; SP2868], *Anchor*: Busy and welcoming, with large helpings of good value food (all day Sat, not Sun) in bookable dining lounge and smaller bar, friendly efficient service, particularly well kept Bass and a guest ale, popular with older people, picnic-sets in pleasant garden behind *(Thomas and Audrey Nott, E V Walder)*

☆ **Lighthorne** [Bishops Hill; a mile SW of B4100 N of Banbury; SP3355], *Antelope*: Attractive 17th-c stonebuilt dining pub in very pretty uncrowded village setting, two comfortable and clean bars (one old, one newer) with Cromwellian theme, wide choice of good reasonably priced food inc old-fashioned puddings, separate dining area; well kept Flowers IPA and Wadworths 6X, pleasant service; piped music; little waterfall in banked garden *(Graham Tayar, Catherine Raeburn)*

☆ **Long Itchington** [Church Rd, off A423 S of Coventry; SP4165], *Harvester*: Unpretentious welcoming two-bar village local with 60s feel, quiet, neat and tidy (nothing to do with the chain of the same name), with efficiently served very cheap food from sandwiches to good steaks, three well kept Hook Norton and a guest ale, friendly landlord, fish tank in lounge bar, cosy relaxed restaurant *(Ted George, Pete Baker, Roger Mullis)*

☆ **Lower Brailes** [B4035 Shipston on Stour—Banbury; SP3039], *George*: Fine old inn in lovely village setting, attractively refurbished roomy flagstoned front bar with dark oak tables, nice curtains and inglenook log fire, darts, panelled oak-beamed back bar with soft lighting and green decor, smart country-style flagstoned restaurant; provision for children, renovated bedrooms, sizeable neatly kept sheltered garden; has had well kept Hook Norton and good freshly made food, but licensees who improved it so much left in summer 1998 – reports on new regime please *(John Bowdler, George Atkinson, LYM)*

☆ **Lower Quinton** [off A46 Stratford—Broadway; SP1847], *College Arms*: Wide range of good fresh food, well kept Whitbreads-related ales, welcoming efficient service, cosy well furnished eating area, spacious open-plan lounge with stripped stone and heavy beams, unusual highly polished tables inc one in former fireplace, leather seats, partly carpeted parquet floor, bric-a-brac; piped music, games in roomy public bar; on green of pretty village *(J Oakes, Ted George, George Atkinson)*

Loxley [signed off A422 Stratford—Banbury; SP2552], *Fox*: Welcoming pub in sleepy village, well kept ales such as Bass, Flowers and Hook Norton, wide range of good value homely cooking lunchtime and evening, settles, brocaded banquettes, tables outside; handy for Stratford *(Nigel and Sue Foster)*

Mancetter [B4111 N of Nuneaton; SP3196], *Plough*: Pleasant carpeted lounge with beams, small inglenook, settles, pictures, plants, brass and copper, good choice of good value food inc children's and bargains, four real ales inc very cheap house Bitter, picnic-sets in garden with play area *(CMW, JJW)*

Marston Jabbett [454 Nuneaton Rd; B4112 Nuneaton—Bulkington; SP3788], *Corner House*: Quickly served good usual food in big Marstons Tavern Table roadhouse (due for refurbishment), three real ales inc a seasonal brew *(JJW, CMW)*

Meer End W Mid [A4147 S of Balsall Common; SP2474], *Tipperary*: Recently refurbished low-ceilinged pub (what's happened to the enormous goldfish in the piano-aquarium?), bigger kitchen doing good fresh food, Greenalls ales with a guest beer, friendly service, children welcome; picnic-sets in garden *(Michael and Hazel Lyons, LYM)*

☆ **Newbold on Stour** [A3400 S of Stratford; SP2446], *White Hart*: Well run chain dining pub, wide range of tasty reasonably priced food (not Sun evening) in good-sized helpings, long and airy beamed and tiled bar divided by stub walls and big stone fireplace (good log fire), big bay windows, roomy back bar with pool and so forth, very well kept Bass and M&B Brew XI; picnic-sets and boules out in front, giant draughts at the back; children welcome, open all day Sat *(Colin Fisher, Ted George, John Bowdler, Dave Braisted, LYM)*

Nuneaton [SP3592], *Felix Holt*: New Wetherspoons, a real bonus for the town – good cheap beer, good cheap wine, nice surroundings, reasonable food; exemplary lavatories *(Ian Blackwell)*

☆ **Offchurch** [Welsh Rd; off A425 Radford Semele; SP3565], *Stags Head*: Low-beamed thatched village pub doing well under current landlord (Mervyn Hayes of *It Ain't 'alf 'ot Mum* – posters and photographs abound), good food inc good value Sun lunch, friendly service, well kept Bass and Morlands Old Speckled Hen, good coffee; tables in good-sized garden with play area *(Roy Bromell)*

Old Hill W Mid [132 Waterfall Lane; SO9685], *Waterfall*: Down-to-earth local, very friendly staff, well kept and well priced Bathams, Enville, Hook Norton, Marstons and three or four interesting guest beers, farm cider, country wines, cheap plain home-made food from good filled rolls to Sun lunch and special snacks Fri, tankards and jugs hanging from boarded ceiling; piped music, children welcome, back garden with play area; open all day w/e *(Julian Pearson, Wayne Wheeler, Dave Braisted)*

☆ **Oldbury** W Mid [Church St, nr Savacentre; SO9888], *Waggon & Horses*: Ornate Victorian tiles, copper ceiling and original windows in busy town pub with well kept changing ales such as Bass, Brains Bitter and SA, Everards Tiger and Nutcracker, Marstons Pedigree and Nailers OBJ, wide choice of generous food inc lots of puddings in bar and bookable upstairs bistro, decent wines, friendly efficient service even when busy, lively comfortable lounge with tie collection, side room with high-backed settles and big old tables, open fire, Black Country memorabilia; opens noon *(Richard Lewis)*

Pathlow [A3400 N of Stratford; SP1857], *Dun Cow*: Old country free house, flagstones, oak beams, inglenook log fires, lots of guest beers, properly cooked and presented locally produced food, fresh flowers, daily papers; dogs welcome *(Dennis D'Vigne)*

☆ **Priors Hardwick** [off A423 via Wormleighton or A361 via Boddington, N of Banbury; SP4756], *Butchers Arms*: Dark medieval oak beams, flagstones, panelling and antiques, huge choice of very well cooked and presented food (not cheap) in small welcoming bar with inglenook log fire, and in restaurant – arrive early for a table; keg beer, very welcoming licensee, good service, country garden *(H W Clayton)*

☆ **Priors Marston** [follow Shuckburgh sign, then first right by phone box], *Holly Bush*: Friendly character golden stone pub, small rambling rooms, beams and stripped stone, old-fashioned pub seats, up to three fires in winter, bar food from good range of baguettes to steaks inc children's and Sun roasts, well kept Bass, Hook Norton Best, Marstons Pedigree and guest beers, friendly elderly dogs, restaurant; darts, pool, games machines, juke box, piped music; children welcome, tables in sheltered garden, bedrooms *(George Atkinson, LYM)*

Rugby [Sheep St; SP5075], *Three Horseshoes*: Friendly Swiss-run hotel with good relaxed atmosphere in comfortable olde-worlde lounge, very well kept ales such as Boddingtons, Flowers Original and local Judges, decent coffee, usual food from sandwiches and good soup up, popular eating area; piped classical radio; bedrooms *(George Atkinson, Tony Hobden)*

Ryton on Dunsmore [High St; SP3874], *Blacksmiths Arms*: Friendly village local, good menu, Bass and M&B, no-smoking area *(Shirley Fletcher)*

☆ **Sedgley** W Mid [129 Bilston St (A463); SO9193], *Beacon*: Unspoilt 1930s-feel local with authentic 19th-c fittings, several unsmart Victorian rooms around unusual tiny hexagonal serving bar with stained-glass shutters, lots of character, no music or machines, family room and conservatory; brews its own good well priced Sarah Hughes Surprise Bitter and Dark Ruby Mild (packs a hefty punch for a Mild) in restored tower brewery, two or three other well kept ales; outside lavatories, seats on terrace *(Mr and Mrs I Rispin, Michael Begley, Colin Fisher)*

☆ **Shipston on Stour** [Station Rd (off A3400); SP2540], *Black Horse*: 16th-c thatched pub with interesting ornaments and coal fire in atmospheric low-ceilinged bar, decent range of interesting food inc small but tasty filled rolls and Mon-Thurs bargain meals, well kept Scottish Courage ales, friendly staff and locals, inglenook coal fire, small dining room, back garden with terrace and barbecue, newfoundland dog and a couple of cats *(Dr A Y Drummond)*

☆ **Shipston on Stour** [High St], *White Bear*: Massive settles and cheerful atmosphere in traditional front bar, recently refurbished back bistro-style restaurant, good value freshly home-made food inc good vegetarian choice and nicely filled baguettes, well kept Bass and Marstons Pedigree, log fires, friendly staff, tables in small back yard and benches on street; bedrooms simple but clean, with huge breakfast *(Mr and Mrs C Roberts, Tony Hughes, LYM)*

Shirley W Mid [Tanworth Lane; SP1078], *Cheswick Green*: Extensively refurbished spacious pub, family dining area, indoor children's play area (not intrusive), Bass and Hancocks HB, good range of wines by the glass, wide choice of food, big garden *(Jack Barnwell)*; [Haslucks Green Rd], *Drawbridge*: Roomy Greenalls pub by canal drawbridge worked by boatmen, waterside terrace, well kept Banks's, Greenalls Bitter and Original and a guest beer, good choice of food inc fish and OAP specials; open all day *(Jack Barnwell)*

Shustoke [B4114 Nuneaton—Coleshill; SP2290], *Plough*: Rambling local done up in olde-worlde style with brass galore, cheap lunchtime snacks, straightforward meals – often good value; Bass and M&B beers *(John and Liz Soden)*

Solihull W Mid [High St; SP1479], *Masons Arms*: Beams, Bass, M&B Brew XI, cheap spirits; cl 2.30 lunchtime *(Ian Phillips)*; [Station Rd], *Yates's Wine Lodge*: Spacious well designed conversion of former furniture store, friendly staff, good standard food till 6 (very

popular lunchtime), Boddingtons and Courage Directors *(Jack Barnwell)*
Stockton [High St; SP4363], *Crown*: Friendly village inn, two real fires, brasses and copper pans, assorted furniture inc armchairs and settee, at least six real ales (some unusual), good reasonably priced straightforward home-made food inc sandwiches and vegetarian; pool, darts and other games one end, piped music or juke box; restaurant in ancient barn, boules *(Tony Hobden)*
Stonnall W Mid [Main St; off A452; SK0703], *Old Swann*: Wide choice of good home-made lunchtime food inc fine sandwiches and bargain OAP meals, big newish dining extension (booking advised Sun), welcoming staff, cold Bass, M&B Brew XI and Worthington *(Cliff Blakemore, Jack Barnwell)*
Stourbridge W Mid [Brook Rd, Old Swinford; SO9283], *Labour in Vain*: Multi-roomed Banks's alehouse with lots of wood, nooks and crannies, colour-washed walls, guest ale such as Enville; friendly efficient staff, food all day from sandwiches to massive pies; sports TV, tables outside, climbing frame *(G Coates)*; [Brook Rd, nr stn], *Seven Stars*: Large Victorian pub with impressive high ceiling, lovely decor inc decorative tiles and ornate carving, good generous food inc all-day cold snacks in second bar's eating area or restaurant on left, well kept changing ales such as ABC, Courage Directors and Theakstons Best; comfortably bustling atmosphere, nice staff *(G Coates)*
☆ **Stratford upon Avon** [Southern Way; SP0255], *Black Swan*: Great atmosphere in very popular 16th-c pub nr Memorial Theatre – still attracts actors, lots of signed RSC photographs; wide choice of good plain wholesome food at moderate prices, Flowers and other Whitbreads-related ales, quick service, open fire, bustling public bar (little lounge seating for drinkers), children allowed in small dining area, no piped music; attractive little terrace looking over riverside public gardens – which tend to act as summer overflow; known as the Dirty Duck *(F J Robinson, Peter and Audrey Dowsett, SLC, Brian Skelcher, LYM)*
☆ **Stratford upon Avon** [High St, nr Town Hall], *Garrick*: Attractive ancient building with lots of beams and timbers, stripped stone, bare boards, lively evening theatrical character, cosy front bar, busier back one, central open fire, well kept Whitbreads-related ales with guests such as Fullers London Pride, good generous sensibly priced bar food in air-conditioned eating area, friendly efficient service, thoughtfully chosen piped music; children allowed away from bar *(Alan and Barbara Mence, Bett and Brian Cox, Bill Sykes, LYM)*
☆ **Stratford upon Avon** [Guild St/Union St], *Slug & Lettuce*: Open-plan bar with old pine kitchen tables and chairs on rugs and flagstones, period prints on stripped panelling, popular enterprising bar food, well kept Tetleys-related and guest beers, decent wines, daily papers, helpful staff, solid fuel fire; good lunchtime atmosphere, can get crowded with young people later, TV, piped music; floodlit two-level back terrace, children welcome, open all day Thurs-Sun *(Kathleen Newton, Julia Hiscock, James Morrell, J and P Maloney, Ted George, LYM)*
Stratford upon Avon [Waterside], *Arden*: Hotel not pub, but closest bar to Memorial Theatre, Courage Best and Directors, good baguettes and other bar food, smart evening bouncer; very popular, get there early; bedrooms good, not cheap *(SH, DW)*; [Church St], *Windmill*: Cosy old pub with town's oldest licence, beyond the attractive church; mix of quarry tiles, bare boards and carpet, wide choice of reasonably priced usual food inc vegetarian, well kept Whitbreads-related and interesting guest ales, efficient staff, good civilised mix of customers, dining area *(Sue Holland, Dave Webster, Ian and Jane Irving, SLC)*
☆ **Temple Grafton** [a mile E, towards Binton; off A422 W of Stratford; SP1255], *Blue Boar*: Country dining pub with beams and log fires, cheerful staff, well kept Courage Directors, Hook Norton Best, Morlands Old Speckled Hen and Theakstons XB, usual bar food from baked potatoes up, more elaborate restaurant dishes, good wine choice, traditional games in flagstoned stripped-stone side room, comfortable stripped-stone restaurant with no-smoking section; children welcome, open all day summer w/e, picnic-sets outside; bedrooms *(John Bowdler, R Davies, J H Kane, Roy Bromell, William R Cuncliffe, LYM)*
☆ **Tipton** W Mid [Hurst Lane, Dudley Rd; towards Wednesbury, A457/A4037; SO9592], *M A D O'Rourkes Pie Factory*: Exuberantly eccentric, a theme pub with a heart – probably lots of them actually, given all that esoteric ancient meat-processing equipment, strings of model hams, sausages, pigs' heads and so forth; good value hearty food inc children's, well kept Lumphammer (brewed for them by Tetleys) and Ansells Mild, Greene King Abbot, Marstons Pedigree and Tetleys, piped music, live Irish folk Sun lunchtime, jazz some evenings; children welcome, open all day, can get packed esp Fri/Sat night *(James Nunns, Stephen Brown, Daren Haines, Chris Raisin, Graham Doyle, LYM)*
Upper Gornal W Mid [Clarence St; SO9291], *Jolly Crispin*: Little old local, once a cobbler's shop, doing well under new landlord, with interesting particularly well kept changing ales such as Hobsons Best, PG Steam, Santa Fe *(Kerry, Carol and Philip Law)*
☆ **Warwick** [11 Market Pl; SP2865], *Tilted Wig*: Roomy and airy Georgian town pub divided into three areas, some stripped stone, neatly spaced light wood country-kitchen furniture on flagstones and bare boards with scattered rugs, good views over square; well kept Ansells, Tetleys and a guest ale, good range of wines, wide choice of good reasonably priced home-made food (not Sun evening), lively bustle, quick friendly service; tables in garden, live jazz and folk Sun evening, open all day Fri/Sat and summer *(Ted George, M Joyner)*
☆ **Warwick** [11 Church St], *Zetland Arms*: Pleasant and cosy town pub with short choice

of cheap but good bar food (not weekend evenings), well kept Bass and Davenports, decent wine in generous glasses, friendly quick service, neat but relaxing small panelled front bar with toby jug collection, comfortable larger eating area; small conservatory, interestingly planted sheltered garden; children may be allowed; bedrooms, sharing bathroom *(Graham Tayar, Catherine Raeburn, Ted George, LYM)*

☆ **Warwick** [90 West St], *Tudor House*: Attractive 15th-c beamed coaching inn opp castle car park (and priced to match its position), lots of black timber, tiles and parquet floor, suits of armour, big fireplace, superb minstrels' gallery, good generous well served food, Courage Directors, Ruddles Best and a guest such as Greene King Abbot, decent wine; piped music; tables in front and on back terrace; bedrooms with own bathrooms *(George Atkinson, Joan and Michel Hooper-Immins)*

Warwick [Lower Cape], *Cape of Good Hope*: Busy two-room pub on Grand Union Canal by Warwick Top Lock, attracting many boaters; smallish bar, larger dining room, wide choice of usual food, well kept Bass and Whitbreads-related real ales; seats out by water *(Tony and Wendy Hobden)*; [30 Market Pl], *Rose & Crown*: Recently refurbished and currently doing very well, with friendly staff and atmosphere, well kept M&B Brew XI, Highgate Mild and guest beers, farm cider, good range of good food; cosy and clean, with snug bar *(B and J Perrett, Patrick Tailyour)*

☆ **Welford on Avon** [High St (Binton Rd); SP1452], *Bell*: Dim-lit dark-timbered low-beamed lounge with open fire and polished copper, good value food inc generous imaginative sandwiches and good fish and vegetarian range, friendly keen staff, well kept Whitbreads-related ales, comfortable recently built restaurant and dining conservatory (children allowed here), flagstoned public bar with darts, pool and so forth; piped music; tables in pretty garden and back courtyard; attractive riverside village *(Chris Baldwin, Karen Arnett, Michael Gittins, Tim and Linda Collins, LYM)*

Welford on Avon [Binton Bridges; SP1455], *Four Alls*: Efficiently run busy friendly Wayside Inn by river, wide choice of generous food inc OAP specials and decent grills, no-smoking eating area, Whitbreads-related ales, nice garden *(Peter Lloyd, Philip and Trisha Ferris)*

☆ **West Bromwich** W Mid [Hall Green Rd, 2 miles from M6, junction 9; SP0091], *Manor House*: Remarkable genuinely medieval building in unexpected spot (ie modern housing estate), with moat and gatehouse; flagstoned no-smoking 13th-c great hall with massive oak trusses and beams, interesting snug upper rooms; a whole lot of mock-medieval paraphernalia, even knight on neighing horse, and apart from the building itself – which really is worth a visit – is best thought of as a jolly family dining pub, with very generous fair-priced meals (inc proper chips) and well kept Banks's Bitter and Mild; fruit machines, piped music may be loud; children welcome, open all day Sun *(R T and J C Moggridge, Chris Raisin, Graham Doyle, LYM)*

☆ **Whatcote** [off A422 Banbury—Stratford; SP2944], *Royal Oak*: Dating from 12th c, quaint low-ceilinged small room, huge inglenook, Civil War connections, lots to look at; wide choice of good food, welcoming service, well kept Hook Norton Best and Shepherd Neame Spitfire, picnic-sets outside; children welcome *(John Bowdler, Ann and Bob Westbrook, LYM)*

Whitacre Heath [Station Rd; off B4114 at Blyth End E of Coleshill; SP2192], *White Swan*: Refurbished pub with good value food, well kept Bass and M&B beers *(Dave Braisted)*

☆ **Whitnash** [Tachbrook Rd; SP3263], *Heathcote*: Comfortable Greenalls country pub fitted out with rustic memorabilia, lots of beams and woodwork, five well kept ales, another four interesting guest beers tapped from the cask, roaring fire, armchairs, good choice of good home-made food all day, pub games, SkyTV, friendly staff and locals *(Richard Lewis)*

☆ **Willey** [just off A5, N of A427 junction; SP4984], *Sarah Mansfield*: Hospitable and welcoming, with small bar area, lots of dining tables in two comfortable and spotlessly refurbished rooms mainly given over to eating, Laura Ashleyesque curtains, polished flagstones, stripped masonry, cosy corners, open fire; ambitious range of food from sandwiches up, pleasant young staff, well kept ales inc Adnams Broadside and a guest such as Exmoor Gold *(Ted George, Patrick Tailyour, George Atkinson)*

Wilmcote [The Green; formerly Swan House; SP1657], *Mary Arden*: Beams, pine boards, comfortable seats around good-sized tables, glass-topped well and woodburner, good food and service, well kept Theakstons Best and XB, tables on terrace overlooking Mary Arden's house, more in back garden, very attractive village; piped music; comfortable bedrooms *(George Atkinson, Alan and Barbara Mence, Joan and Michel Hooper-Immins)*

☆ **Withybrook** [B4112 NE of Coventry, not far from M6, junction 2; SP4384], *Pheasant*: Big busy dining pub with lots of dark tables, plush-cushioned chairs, wide choice of generous bar food inc good value specials, Scottish Courage ales under light carbon dioxide blanket, good coffee, blazing log fires; piped music; children welcome, tables under lanterns on brookside terrace *(Chris and Ann Garnett, Roy Bromell, H Paulinski, John Franklin, Michael Begley, LYM)*

☆ **Wixford** [off A46 S of Redditch, via A422/A435 Alcester roundabout, or B439 at Bidford; SP0954], *Three Horseshoes*: Roomy and nicely furnished, with consistently good generous food inc fresh fish, interesting choice (esp weekends, when it can get crowded), charming landlord and staff, good range of well kept mainly Whitbreads-related ales *(P Lloyd, W and E Thomas)*

Wolverhampton W Mid [38 Chapel Ash; SO9198], *Clarendon*: Banks's brewery tap with their Mild and Bitter and Camerons Strongarm, spacious comfortable split-level lounge, nice decor, smoke room, popular food (not Sat/Sun evening) inc good sandwich bar and breakfast from 8am; open all day, Sun afternoon closure *(Richard Lewis)*; [9 Princess St], *Feline & Firkin*: Bare boards, bench seating, barrel tables, own well kept ales (from sister pub in Stafford) inc a Mild, good menu, friendly staff, brewery prints etc, back games area inc pool; tables on terrace, open all day *(Richard Lewis)*; [Sun St, behind old low-level stn], *Great Western*: Three-bar pub with particularly well kept Bathams and Holdens, very promptly served good cheap food inc local specialities, lots of railway memorabilia, friendly staff; SkyTV; open all day, roomy back conservatory, tables in yard with good barbecues *(DAV, Richard Lewis)*; [Lower Green, Tettenhall Rd (A41)], *Mitre*: Small and comfortable, with Bass, Stones, Worthington and a guest such as Hook Norton Old Hookey; setting a pleasant oasis *(D Stokes)*; [53 Lichfield St], *Moon Under Water*: Busy but comfortable open-plan Wetherspoons (former Co-op) with long bar, panelling and lots of old Wolverhampton prints, their usual reliable all-day food inc 2 for 1 offers at certain times, good choice of ales at reasonable prices *(Richard Lewis)*; [A449, Penn; SO8996], *Penn Cottage*: Beefeater with a touch of individuality, food inc very crisp baguettes, Whitbreads-related ales *(Dave Braisted)*; [Lichfield St], *Posada*: Ornate tile and glass frontage, semi-circle central bar, lots of wood and glass, back room with games; well kept Greene King Abbot, Holt Plant & Deakins and Tetleys, friendly locals, helpful staff; open all day, busy with young people evening *(Richard Lewis)*; [Princess St], *Tap & Spile*: Recently refurbished bare-boards alehouse, basic seating, eight or so well kept interesting ales from central servery, Weston's Old Rosie cider, daily papers, pub games, friendly staff; open all day *(Richard Lewis)*

☆ **Wootton Wawen** [Alcester Rd; just off A3400 Birmingham—Stratford; SP1563], *Bulls Head*: Smart and attractive but expensive black and white Elizabethan dining pub now owned by Quintessential English Pub Co (licensee stays on as co-manager), good choice of good interesting food inc several fresh fish and unusual vegetarian dishes (beware, they charge extra for veg), low beams and timbers, rugs setting off good flagstones, well kept Banks's, Fullers London Pride, Marstons Pedigree and Wadworths 6X; pews in more austere tap room with dominoes, shove-ha'penny; children welcome, open all day Sun, tables on pleasant terrace – handy for Stratford Canal walks *(Brian and Bett Cox, Paul and Maggie Baker, Maysie Thompson, Mr and Mrs M J Bastin, M G Hart, Roy Bromell, Kim Maidment, Philip Vernon, James Nunn, Liz Bell, David and Ruth Shillitoe, Neville Kenyon, Karen Eliot, Rydon Bend, William R Cuncliffe, Sue Holland, Dave Webster, LYM)*

Real ale to us means beer which has matured naturally in its cask – not pressurised or filtered. We name all real ales stocked. We usually name ales preserved under a light blanket of carbon dioxide too, though purists – pointing out that this stops the natural yeasts developing – would disagree (most people, including us, can't tell the difference!).

Wiltshire

Full of good pubs, this county has plenty of fairly priced pub food – and great variety in terms of character and atmosphere. Current front-runners are the civilised Crown at Alvediston (imaginative food including lots of fresh fish – a new main entry), the Red Lion in Axford (another pub back among the main entries after a break – good fish here too), the beautifully placed Cross Guns near Bradford on Avon (often packed for its good value food), the Three Crowns at Brinkworth (imaginative often elaborate food), the Compasses at Chicksgrove (very welcoming new licensees, same good cook as before), the White Hart at Ford (first-class all round), the Angel at Heytesbury (lots of fresh fish and wines by the glass – but a good pubby atmosphere), the welcoming George in Lacock, the Woodbridge at North Newnton (quite extraordinary range of food, often a warning sign but not here – gaining its first Good Pub Guide main entry this year), the old-fashioned Vine Tree at Norton (good food, newish young licensees also gaining their first main entry), the Silver Plough at Pitton (good food – the people who took over a year or so ago have settled in very well), the friendly Raven at Poulshot, and the George and Dragon at Rowde (excellent food, especially fish). Finally, there's the Seven Stars near Woodborough; it has all the proper pubby virtues – including a warm welcome for walking parties – but also very good wines and fine food with strong French leanings; it is our Wiltshire Dining Pub of the Year. The Lucky Dip at the end of the chapter has a particularly fine choice of pubs this year. Among them we'd pick out the Waggon & Horses at Beckhampton, White Hart in Castle Combe and Salutation nearby (the only one of this group that we have not yet inspected ourselves – it comes with strong local recommendations), Horse & Groom at Charlton, Black Dog at Chilmark, Rising Sun near Lacock, Lamb at Semington, Golden Swan at Wilcot (kept out of the main entries only by a lack of reader reports this year) and Poplars at Wingfield. Drinks prices tend to be around the national average, perhaps even a shade higher. Generally (though not always) we found beer in pubs tied to Wadworths of Devizes quite a bit cheaper. The county has a fine range of other brewers, including Arkells and Ushers, and smaller but highly favoured ones such as Bunces, Hop Back, Moles and Tisbury. (The Gibbs Mew brewery in Salisbury has now closed, and Enterprise Inns who bought the firm are having the beers brewed elsewhere.)

ALVEDISTON ST9723 Map 2

Crown

Village signposted on left off A30 about 12 miles W of Salisbury

The three charming low beamed wood panelled rooms of this lovely old thatched inn are cosily painted deep terracotta, have two inglenook fireplaces, dark oak furniture and shelves crowded with bric a brac and antiques. Very good imaginative bar food – with plenty of fresh fish – might include fried brie wedges or salmon in honey, mustard and dill (£4.75), smoked duck with blackcurrant dressing (£4.95), prawns in filo (£5.25), seafood lasagne or chicken korma (£7.95), lemon sole (£9.95), monkfish

(£11.75), rack of lamb (£12.25) and Scotch fillet steak (£13.50). Well kept Bass, Courage Best, Wadworths 6X and a guest like Charles Wells Bombardier on handpump; darts and piped music. On different levels around a thatched white well, the attractive garden is nicely broken up with shrubs and rockeries among neatly kept lawns; it faces a farmyard with ponies and other animals, and there's a children's play area. *(Recommended by C N R Bateman, Dr and Mrs N Holmes, Clive Bonner, Jerry and Alison Oakes, Bryan and Jean Warland)*

Free house ~ Licensees Nickolas Shaw and Colin Jordan ~ Real ale ~ Meals and snacks ~ (01772) 780335 ~ Children welcome ~ Open 12-3, 7-11 ~ Bedrooms: £25/£45B; suite that sleeps 4 adults and 2 children £95

AXFORD SU2370 Map 2

Red Lion

Off A4 E of Marlborough; on back road Mildenhall—Ramsbury

The emphasis at this pretty flint-and-brick pub is very much on the good food and fresh fish, although drinkers are still made just as welcome as diners. A quite restauranty bar menu (they have the same menu in the bar and restaurant) includes soup (£2.50), baked brie with redcurrant jelly (£3.75), crevette platter or sirloin steak (£11.50), rack of lamb or grilled monkfish (£11.75), beef wellington with horseradish cream (£13.50), puddings from a trolley (£3.50), as well as daily specials like warm black pudding salad (£3.50), potted stilton and chestnut terrine (£3.95), guinea fowl breast baked in bacon with celery and bread sauce (£11.50) and several fresh fish dishes like skate (£11.50), and lobster (£22.50). There are comfortable cask seats and other solid chairs on the spotless parquet floor of the bustling beamed and pine-panelled bar, with picture windows for the fine valley view; the restaurant is no smoking. The well kept beers change all the time but might include Flowers Best, Hook Norton, Oakhill Bitter and 6X on handpump. The sheltered garden has picnic-sets under cocktail parasols, swings, and lovely views. *(Recommended by June and Tony Baldwin, Paul and Ursula Randall, David Gittins, M V and J Melling)*

Free house ~ Licensees Mel and Daphne Evans ~ Real ale ~ Meals and snacks ~ Restaurant ~ (01672) 520271 ~ Children in eating area of bar ~ Open 11.30-3, 6.30-11; 12-3, 7-10.30 Sun ~ Bedrooms: £35B/£50B

BARFORD ST MARTIN SU0531 Map 2

Barford

Junction A30/B3089

As well as special offers on their menu – such as a discount of £2 on a three-course meal – very reasonably priced bar food at this nicely old-fashioned pub includes soup (£2.25), filled ciabattas (from £2.50), fresh grilled fish fillet of the day with fresh creamy tomato sauce and herb crust, salmon fishcakes and fried wild boar steak with bubble and squeak and red wine gravy (£5.95), steak and kidney pie (£6.50), beef rogan josh (£6.95), fried pork tenderloin with apricot, mushroom and smoked bacon sauce or 8oz sirloin (£8.95), daily specials like chicken skewers with satay dip (£3.95), and roast chicken breast wrapped in puff pastry with mushroom and white wine cream sauce (£9.95), children's dishes (£3), and puddings like seasonal fruit crumble or home-made mango ice cream (from £3). Their Friday evening Israeli barbecues (all year round, from 7pm) are well liked. The various well cared for chatty interlinking rooms and bars all have dark wooden tables and red cushioned chairs. Generally busier in the evenings than at lunchtime, the front bar also has some interesting squared oak panelling, and a big log fire in winter; friendly attentive service. Badger Best and Tanglefoot kept under light blanket pressure, quite a few country wines, and lots of Israeli wines; darts; one reader found the piped pop music a bit loud. The restaurant is no smoking; disabled access and lavatories. There are tables on an outside terrace, and more in a back garden. *(Recommended by Mrs Thelma Ford, Mrs G Connell, Richard Etherington, R T and J C Moggridge, Graham and Lynn Mason, Lisette Collingridge, George and Jeanne Barnwell, Phyl and Jack Street, Steve Goodchild)*

Badger ~ Tenant Ido Davids ~ Real ale ~ Meals and snacks ~ Restaurant ~ (01722) 742242 ~ Children welcome ~ Open 11.30-11; 12-3, 7-11 Sun ~ Bedrooms: £35B/£45B

BERWICK ST JOHN ST9422 Map 2

Talbot

Village signposted from A30 E of Shaftesbury

There's a friendly welcome for locals and visitors alike at this unspoilt old village pub which is carefully run by attentive licensees. The single long, heavy beamed bar is simply furnished, with cushioned solid wall and window seats, spindleback chairs, a high-backed built-in settle at one end, and tables that are candlelit in the evenings. There's a huge inglenook fireplace with a good iron fireback and bread ovens and nicely shaped heavy black beams and cross-beams with bevelled corners. Freshly prepared bar food includes garlic mushrooms or sliced smoked trout (£4.75), ploughman's (£4.95), pasta dishes (from £5.95), steak and kidney pie, madras beef curry or chicken tikka masala (£8.50) and steaks (£14.95). Adnams Best and Broadside, Bass, and Wadworths 6X on handpump, farm cider, fresh juices and good wines; cribbage and dominoes. There are some tables on the back lawn; they do lock the car park when the pub is closed so check with the licensee if you wish to leave your car and walk in the Ebble Valley. *(Recommended by DP, Phyl and Jack Street; more reports please)*

Free house ~ Licensees Roy and Wendy Rigby ~ Real ale ~ Meals and snacks (not Sun) ~ Restaurant ~ (01747) 828222 ~ Children in eating area of bar at lunchtime ~ Open 12(11.30 Sat)-2.30, 7(6.30 Fri/Sat)-11; 12-2.30 Sun; cl Sun evening, and Mon except bank holidays

BOX ST8369 Map 2

Quarrymans Arms

Box Hill; coming from Bath on A4 turn right into Bargates 50 yds before railway bridge, then at T-junction turn left up Quarry Hill, turning left again near the top at grassy triangle; from Corsham, turn left after Rudloe Park Hotel into Beech Rd, then third left on to Barnetts Hill, and finally right at the top of the hill

Tucked away down a warren of lanes, this low stone building with its dramatic valley views is well worth finding. Although there's quite some emphasis on the beautifully prepared imaginative food, one pleasant modernised room with an open fire and interesting quarry photographs and memorabilia covering the walls is kept aside just for drinking the well kept Abbey Bellringer, Butcombe, Moles, Wadworths 6X on handpump, and a guest or two like Bath Barnstormer tapped straight from the cask, good wines, over fifty malt whiskies, and ten or so vintage cognacs. The very popular bar food might include cream of mushroom soup (£2.50), stilton and asparagus pancake (£3.50/£5.95), home-made crab cakes (£4.50), moules marinières (£5.25), warm salad of chicken and bacon (£6.50), broccoli, mushrooms and red peppers in white wine, cream and stilton sauce on tagliatelle (£6.95), fried pork medallions in cream and mustard sauce (£9.25), rack of lamb on port, redcurrant and thyme jus (£10.50), wild boar steak pan fried with garlic, on blueberry, maple syrup and whiskey sauce with bacon lardons (£12.50), and puddings like treacle tart or sticky toffee pudding (£3.50). Servce is helpful and friendly; darts, shove-ha'penny, cribbage, dominoes, fruit machine, video game, boules, cricket, and piped music. There are picnic-sets outside on an attractive terrace, and it's ideally situated for cavers, potholers and walkers, and runs interesting guided trips down the local Bath stone mine. *(Recommended by Jenny and Roger Huggins, Peter and Audrey Dowsett, Mrs Laura Gustine, Steven M Gent, Meg and Colin Hamilton, Brian and Anna Marsden, Lyn and Geoff Hallchurch, Susan and Nigel Wilson, Comus Elliott)*

Free house ~ Licensee John Arundel ~ Real ale ~ Meals and snacks (12-3, 6.30-10.30) ~ Restaurant ~ (01225) 743569 ~ Children welcome ~ Open 11-11; 12-10.30 Sun; 11-4, 6-11 Mon-Wed in winter ~ Bedrooms: £25/£50

nr BRADFORD ON AVON ST8060 Map 2

Cross Guns

Avoncliff; pub is across footbridge from Avoncliff Station (road signposted Turleigh turning left off A363 heading uphill N from river in Bradford centre, and keep bearing left), and can also be reached down very steep and eventually unmade road signposted Avoncliff – keep straight on rather than turning left into village centre – from Westwood (which is signposted from B3109 and from A366, W of Trowbridge); OS Sheet 173 map reference 805600

Fabulous views from the floodlit terraced gardens of this marvellously placed country pub take in the wide river Avon, with its maze of bridges, aqueducts (the Kennet & Avon Canal) and railway tracks that wind through this quite narrow gorge. With its great views, its atmospheric pubby feel, and its very good reasonably priced home cooking it's not surprising that it's so popular. There's a nice old-fashioned feel to the bar, with its core of low 17th-c, rush-seated chairs around plain sturdy oak tables (most of which are set for diners, and many of them reserved), stone walls, and a large ancient fireplace with a smoking chamber behind it. Well kept Courage Best, Millworkers (brewed for the pub), Ushers Best and a guest beer on handpump, about 100 malt whiskys and two dozen country wines; piped music. Generously served dishes might include filling sandwiches (from £1.80), good stilton or cheddar ploughman's (from £3.75), steak and ale pie or curry (£5.50), trout (£5.75), battered cod (£6), steaks (from £6.50) and poached salmon (£7.50). There may be a system of Tannoy announcements for meal orders from outside tables; good service. Walkers are very welcome, but not their muddy boots. The pub gets very busy, especially at weekends and summer lunchtimes, so if you want to eat it's probably best to book; readers have suggested that the ladies' lavatories could be smartened up.
(Recommended by Neil Spink, Daren Haines, P and S White, Jane Kingsbury, Alison and Mick Coates, Paul and Judith Booth, Meg and Colin Hamilton, Susan and Nigel Wilson, Peter and Rosie Flower, Charles and Pauline Stride)

Free house ~ Licensees Dave and Gwen Sawyer ~ Real ale ~ Meals and snacks (till 10.15) ~ (01225) 862335 ~ Children welcome ~ Open 10.30-3, 6.30-11; all day Sat/Sun in summer

BRINKWORTH SU0184 Map 2

Three Crowns

The Street; B4042 Wootton Bassett—Malmesbury

The highly imaginative changing menu at this village inn covers an entire wall. The very popular bar food isn't cheap but there are no complaints from readers who all agree that it's good value. Do get here early as they don't take bookings, and it does get very busy. There might be steak and kidney pie (£8.95), seafood or lamb and mint pie (£9.95), half a smoked chicken with rich sherry and cream sauce with dijon mustard (£12.95), roast sliced duck with mushroom, cream and madeira sauce or baked blue marlin with prawns and capers (£13.45), fried venison with spring onions, smoked bacon, juniper berries soaked in port and flamed in damson wine (£14.45), filo basket with strips of fried crocodile with stem ginger and flamed in ginger wine or fried ostrich with sun-dried tomato, oyster mushrooms and capers and flamed with apricot wine (£15.95). All dishes are served with half a dozen fresh vegetables; puddings might be crème brûlée, bread and butter pudding, strawberry shortbread or chocolate and orange truffle torte (from £3.75). Particularly nice is the way that this has remained very much a pub, despite its appeal to diners with well kept Archers Village, Boddingtons, Marstons Pedigree, Wadworths 6X and Whitbreads Castle Eden kept under light blanket pressure, just under 80 wines, with ten by the glass, and mulled wine in winter, most people choose to eat in the elegant no-smoking conservatory, so that the rambling bar is busy with drinkers too. There's a lovely traditional feel in all its little enclaves, as well as big landscape prints and other pictures on the walls, some horsebrasses on the dark beams, a dresser with a collection of old bottles, tables of stripped deal (and a couple made from gigantic forge bellows), big tapestry-upholstered pews and blond chairs, and log fires; sensibly placed darts, shove-ha'penny, dominoes, cribbage, chess, fruit machine, piped music. A terrace has a pond and fountain, and outdoor heating. The garden stretches around the side and back, with well spaced tables, and looks over a side lane to the village church, and out over rolling prosperous farmland. *(Recommended by Pat and Robert Watt, Janet Pickles, Evelyn and Derek Walter, Susan and Nigel Wilson, Tom Rees, Laura Bradley, B J Cox, D Godden, Tracy Lewis, T L Rees, Dr D G Twyman, Andrew Shore, Brian and Bett Cox)*

Whitbreads ~ Lease: Anthony Windle ~ Real ale ~ Meals and lunchtime snacks ~ (01666) 510366 ~ Children in eating area of bar until 9pm ~ Open 10-3, 6-11; 11-11 Sat; 12-10.30 Sun; cl 25 Dec

CHICKSGROVE ST9629 Map 2

Compasses

From A30 5½ miles W of B3089 junction, take lane on N side signposted Sutton Mandeville, Sutton Row, then first left fork (small signs point the way to the pub, in Lower Chicksgrove; look out for the car park); OS Sheet 184 map ref 974294

Doing really well under its very friendly welcoming new licensees this lovely timeless old thatched house, delightfully placed in a quiet rural hamlet, has received lots of good solid praise from readers over the last year. Very fairly priced bar food, home-made and better than ever might include sandwiches (£2.50), watercress and stilton soup (£2.95), ploughman's (£4.75), bouillabaisse, avocado and tiger prawns with peach mayonnaise or moules marinières (£4.95), steak and kidney pie or lasagne (£6.95), pork tenderloin with wholegrain mustard, wine and cream (£8.25), seafood tagliatelle (£8.95), sirloin steak, boned quail cooked with leeks, onions, grapes and port or beef stroganoff (£11.95), and good puddings like lemon flan (£2.75). The characterful bar has old bottles and jugs hanging from the beams above the roughly timbered bar counter, farm tools, traps and brasses on the partly stripped stone walls, and high-backed wooden settles forming snug booths around tables on the mainly flagstone floor. It's very pleasant sitting in the quiet garden or the flagstoned farm courtyard, and there's a nice walk to Sutton Mandeville church and back via Wadder Valley. Well kept Bass, Tisbury Peter Austin and Wadworths IPA and 6X on handpump. *(Recommended by C and A Moncreiffe, Brad W Morley, Jan R Watts, Jerry and Alison Oakes, Phyl and Jack Street, M Mackay, Dr and Mrs N Holmes, Jenny and Michael Back, Roger Byrne, Howard and Margaret Buchanan, Hugh Chevallier, John and Lynn Busenbark, Mark Percy, Lesley Mayoh)*

Free house ~ Licensees Dudley and Eileen Cobb ~ Real ale ~ Meals and snacks ~ (01722) 714318 ~ Children welcome ~ Open 11-3, 6.30-11; 12-3, 7-10.30 Sun; cl Mon except bank holidays ~ Bedrooms: £35B/£45B

CORSHAM ST8670 Map 2

Two Pigs

A4, Pickwick

For our readers who like their music blue and don't like to see children in pubs, this old-fashioned and characterful roadside drinking house is a rarity these days – a pub in the true old-fashioned sense of the word. Under 21s aren't allowed, the emphasis is firmly on drinking, the only piped music is the blues (with live blues Mon evenings), and they don't serve any food whatsoever. They keep an inspired range of beers, mostly from smaller independent breweries. Alongside Pigswill (from local Bunces Brewery) four changing guest beers might be Greene King Abbot, Hop Back Summer Lightning, RCH Pitchfork and Woods Shropshire Lad; also a range of country wines. The very narrow long dimly lit bar has stone floors, wood-clad walls and long dark wood tables and benches; a profuse and zany decor includes enamel advertising signs, pig-theme ornaments, and old radios, a bicycle and a canoe. The country atmosphere is lively and chatty the landlord (he's been here ten years now) entertaining, the staff friendly, and there's a good mix of customers, too. A covered yard outside is called the Sty. Beware of their opening times – the pub is closed every lunchtime, except on Sunday. *(Recommended by Dr and Mrs A K Clarke, Mrs Laura Gustine, Andrew and Eileen Abbess, Susan and Nigel Wilson)*

Free house ~ Licensees Dickie and Ann Doyle ~ Real ale ~ (01249) 712515 ~ Live blues Mon evenings ~ Open 7-11; 12-2.30, 7-10.30 Sun

DEVIZES SU0061 Map 2

Bear

Market Place

A chatty older set enjoy coffee in the calmly comfortable atmosphere of the big main bar with its roaring winter log fires, black winged wall settles and muted red button-back cloth-upholstered bucket armchairs around oak tripod tables, and good value meals at this rambling old coaching hotel. The traditionally-styled Lawrence room (named after Thomas Lawrence the portrait painter, whose father once ran the inn), separated from the main bar by some steps and an old-fashioned glazed screen, has dark oak-panelled walls, a parquet floor, shining copper pans on the mantlepiece above the big open fireplace, and plates around the walls; part of this room is no smoking. Straightforward bar food includes sandwiches (from £2.50), home-made soup (£2.50), filled baked potatoes (from £3.50), ploughman's (from £3.75), omelettes (from £4.50), ham, egg and chips (£3.95) and sausage and mash (£4.50), and home-made puddings (£2.25); there are buffet meals in the Lawrence room – you can eat these in the bar too. On Saturday nights they have a good value set menu. Well kept Wadworths IPA and 6X and a guest beer, wines by the glass and freshly squeezed juices are served on handpump from an old-fashioned bar counter with shiny black woodwork and small panes of glass, along with freshly squeezed juices, over a dozen wines by the glass, and a good choice of malt whiskies; especially friendly and helpful service. Wadworths brewery where you can buy beer in splendid old-fashioned half-gallon earthenware jars is within sight of the hotel. *(Recommended by Gwen and Peter Andrews, Francis Johnston, Martin and Barbara Rantzen, E J and M W Corrin, Ian Phillips, Alan and Paula McCully, Joan and Tony Walker)*

Wadworths ~ Tenant W K Dickenson ~ Real ale ~ Meals and snacks (not Sun lunch) ~ Restaurant ~ (01380) 722444 ~ Children in eating area of bar ~ Open 11-11; 10.30-3, 7-10.30 Sun; cl 25/26 Dec ~ Bedrooms: £54B/£80B

EBBESBOURNE WAKE ST9824 Map 2

Horseshoe

On A354 S of Salisbury, right at signpost at Coombe Bissett; village is around 8 miles further on

The pretty little garden at this delightfully set secluded old country pub has seats that look out over the steep sleepy valley of the River Ebble, and a paddock with three goats. The very friendly welcoming landlord also has a couple of entertaining dogs. There are fresh flowers from the garden on the tables in the beautifully kept bar, which also has lanterns, farm tools and other bric-a-brac crowded along its beams, and an open fire. Simple but well cooked home-made bar food is served by kind efficient staff and might include sandwiches (£2.95), a very good ploughman's (£4.50), trout pâté (£5.25), locally made faggots (£6.45), liver and bacon or steak and kidney pie (£6.95), fresh fish bake or venison pie (£7.25), duck and gooseberry sauce (£11.95), and excellent home-made puddings; good breakfasts and three course Sunday lunch. Well kept Adnams Broadside, Otter Best, Ringwood Best and Wadworths 6X tapped from the row of casks behind the bar, farm cider, country wines, and several malt whiskies; friendly service. Booking is advisable for the small no-smoking restaurant, especially at weekends when they can fill up quite quickly. The barn opposite is used as a pool room with darts and a fruit machine. *(Recommended by Eddie Edwards, Phyl and Jack Street, Tim Barrow, Sue Demont, Jerry and Alison Oakes, Richard Gibbs, Dr D Twyman, John Davis, Angus Lyon, John and Lynn Busenbark, Hugh Chevallier, R J Walden)*

Free house ~ Licensees Anthony and Patricia Bath ~ Real ale ~ Meals and snacks (not Mon evening or Sun) ~ Restaurant ~ (01722) 780474 ~ Children in eating area of bar and restaurant ~ Open 12-3, 6.30-11; 12-4, 7-10.30 Sun ~ Bedrooms: /£45B

FONTHILL GIFFORD ST9232

Beckford Arms

Off B3089 W of Wilton at Fonthill Bishop

There's a particularly good contrast between the rather sedately relaxed high-ceilinged Edwardian lounge bar, and the very simple public bar at this pleasant old inn. The lounge bar has a deeply comfortable leather chesterfield and armchair, some upright blond chairs on a maroon carpet by the bar, and a big log fire. It leads into a light and airy back garden room with similar furnishings but a high pitched plank ceiling, and picture windows on to a terrace. There are tables out here and more up in the garden which slopes away among shrubs and a weeping elm. Popular with locals, the straightforward public bar has darts, fruit machine, pool, TV and juke box. There's a pretty Laura Ashleyesque dining room. Well kept Courage Best and Directors, and a guest like Ringwood Fortyniner; piped music. The new licensee has introduced ten wines by the glass, and has extended the range of very reasonably priced food from the bar menu, specials board and à la carte menu. There might be sandwiches (from £2.25), ploughman's (£4.95), pork casserole, herbs, tomato and apple (£5.75) poached chicken breast with mushroom, white wine and coriander sauce (£5.95), chinese-style pork on a bed of noodles or whole plaice (£6.50), chicken roulade filled with spinach and ricotta with a tarragon sauce (£7.75), supreme of salmon with cream, dill and prawn sauce (£7.95), glazed pork tenderloin with sweet and sour jus (£8.25), and home-made puddings like apple pie or treacle sponge (£2.75). *(Recommended by Colin Fisher, Martin and Jane Wright, N Phillips, Alan and Paula McCully; more reports please)*

Free house ~ Licensee Paul Strasman ~ Real ale ~ Meals and snacks ~ Restaurant ~ (01747) 870385 ~ Children in Garden room ~ Open 11-3, 6-11; 12-3, 7-10.30 Sun ~ Bedrooms: £34.50S/£54.50S

FORD ST8374 Map 2

White Hart ★

A420 Chippenham—Bristol; follow Colerne sign at E side of village to find pub

Doing really well in all respects, this stone country inn – which is wonderful in summer with its a terrace by a stone bridge and trout stream – is a particular favourite for its splendid food (you will need to book), lively atmospheric bar, excellent range of well kept beers and really friendly accommodating welcome. There are heavy black beams supporting the white-painted boards of the ceiling, tub armchairs around polished wooden tables, small pictures and a few advertising mirrors on the walls, and an ancient fireplace (inscribed 1553). Despite the number of people eating it's still a place to come to just for a drink; they keep fine wines, farm ciders and a dozen malt whiskies, and up to ten well kept real ales might include well kept Badger Tanglefoot, Bass, Boddingtons, Flowers Best, Fullers London Pride, Hook Norton, Marstons Pedigree and Owd Roger, Shepherd Neame Spitfire and Smiles Heritage on handpump or tapped from the cask; pool and piped music. Served in particularly generous helpings, the weekly-changing menu might include lunchtime mushroom, lentil and tarragon soup (£1.95), ploughman's (£4.25), baked aubergine filled with ratatouille topped with mozzarella (£4.95), spicy lamb meatballs with couscous and a tomato, chilli and olive oil dressing, home-made pork spring rolls with ginger and chilli dipping sauce (£5.50) and chicken provençale with tomatoes, pepper and black olives (£6.25). They don't do bar snacks in the evening, but you can eat from the more elaborate restaurant menu at lunchtime and in the evening in the bar: carpaccio of beef fillet with asparagus, parmesan crisps and poached egg dressing (£5.75), fried loin of pork with mushrooms, shallots and peppercorn sauce (£9.95) and chicken breast with basil and parmesan potato cake, sweet garlic fritters and herbed juices or grilled lemon sole with lemon butter (£9.95). It's a particularly nice place to stay and there's a secluded swimming pool for residents. *(Recommended by Simon Penny, Dr and Mrs A K Clarke, Ann and Colin Hunt, D L Parkhurst, Dr D Twyman, JCW, J Sheldon, B J Harding, Tim Barrow, Sue Demont, Bernard Stradling, Nick and Meriel Cox, John and Christine Simpson, Mrs Laura Gustine, Comus Elliott, Mr and Mrs I Brown, KC, Pat and John Millward, Mr and Mrs*

Mark Hancock, Lyn and Geoff Hallchurch, Dr and Mrs I H Maine, D G Clarke, Mrs M Mills, Rob Holt, Yvonne and Peter Griffiths, Kerry Law, Kay McGeehan, Denise Harbord, Susan and Nigel Wilson, Paul and Nicky Clements, Barry and Anne, Steve Willey, Eddy Street, Luke Worthington, Dagmar Junghanns, Colin Keane, Derek Clarke, Suzanne and John Jones, Val and Rob Farrant, KC, Pat and Roger Fereday, Andrew Shore)

Free house ~ Licensees Chris and Jenny Phillips ~ Real ale ~ Meals and lunchtime snacks ~ Restaurant ~ (01249) 782213 ~ Children in restaurant at lunchtime ~ Open 11-3, 5-11; 12-3, 7-10.30 Sun ~ Bedrooms: £50B(£75 weekends)/£75B

HEYTESBURY ST9242 Map 2

Angel

High St; just off A36 E of Warminster

The best time to visit this enjoyably welcoming 16th-c inn is Tuesday or Friday when the fresh fish is delivered, although there's always a very good choice of up to ten very reasonably priced fresh fish dishes listed on the constantly changing blackboards. There might be whole salmon fishcakes with dill mayonnaise (£6.25), dressed crab (£7.25), roasted tuna on roasted vegetables, halibut fillet wrapped in parmesan, or whole sole (£8.95). Other very well prepared bar food, served with perfectly cooked vegetables, might include cream of watercress or very good carrot and coriander soup (£3.50), filled baguettes – made with authentic flour flown in from France – (£3.85), ploughman's (£4), a vegetarian tart such as asparagus tart (£5.75), wild boar and apple sausages (£6.25), rack of lamb (£9.75) and duck breast (£10.50); cappuccino. As well as about a dozen wines by the glass and freshly squeezed orange juice there's well kept Marstons Pedigree, Ringwood Best, Timothy Taylor Landlord and a guest on handpump. The cosy and homely lounge on the right, with well used overstuffed armchairs and sofas, flower and Japanese prints and a good fire, opens into a charming back dining room which is simple but smart with a blue carpet, blue-cushioned chairs and lots more flower prints on the white-painted brick walls. On the left is a long beamed bar with quite a vibrant atmosphere, a woodburner, some attractive prints and old photographs on the terracotta-coloured walls, and straightforward tables and chairs. The dining room opens on to an attractive secluded courtyard garden; hot nuts, cheerful young staff, maybe piped Phil Collins; cribbage. *(Recommended by Gwen and Peter Andrews, Barry and Anne, Pat and Robert Watt, B Kilcullen, Mrs C Jimenez, Simon and Alison Rudd-Clarke)*

Free house ~ Licensees Philip Roose-Francis, Sue and Tim Smith ~ Real ale ~ Meals and snacks ~ Restaurant ~ (01985) 840330 ~ Supervised children welcome ~ Open 11.30-3, 6.30-11; 12-3, 7-10.30 Sun; cl 25 Dec evening ~ Bedrooms: £37.50B/£49B

HINDON ST9132 Map 2

Lamb

B3089 Wilton—Mere

This solid old hotel, dating back in part to the 13th c, is prettily set near Fonthill Park and Lake, and very usefully open all day. It has a roomy long bar, split into several areas, with the two lower sections, now with a new slate floor, perhaps the nicest. There's a long polished table with wall benches and chairs, and a big inglenook fireplace, and at one end a window seat with a big waxed circular table, spindleback chairs with tapestried cushions, a high-backed settle and brass jugs on the mantlepiece above the small fireplace; up some steps, a third, bigger area has lots of tables and chairs. Bar food includes tomato, coriander and orange soup (£2.95), ploughman's (£3.95), stilton, broccoli and cauliflower bake or curried bean and lentil bake (£5.95), grilled cod with prawn mayonnaise, fried pork fillet with mustard sauce, glazed lamb chops with hawthorn jelly, venison and mushroom casserole, steak and kidney pie, grilled goat's cheese with bacon and smoked duck or chicken breast and garlic (£6.95), seared Cornish scallops with smoked bacon (£7.95) and grilled bass with roast red pepper and tomato (£10.95), and a well liked good value Sunday roast; the restaurant is no smoking. They usually do cream teas throughout the afternoon. Four real ales include Ash Vine and Wadworths 6X alongside two constantly changing guests like

Butcombe or Lionheart Ironside. They serve just under a dozen wines by the glass, and a range of whiskies includes all the malts from the Isle of Islay. Service can slow down when they get busy, but remains helpful and friendly. There are picnic-sets across the road (which is a good alternative to the main routes west). No dogs. *(Recommended by Phyl and Jack Street, John Evans, Tony Gayfer, Colin Laffan, Lynn Sharpless, Bob Eardley, C Scott-Malden, David and Ruth Shillitoe, Paul and Ursula Randall, K H Frostick, Gwen and Peter Andrews, Brad W Morley, Alan and Paula McCully, Susan and Nigel Wilson, Mrs Valerie Thomas, Mrs M Rolfe, Elven Money, Ann and Colin Hunt, James Nunns)*

Free house ~ Licensees John Croft and Cora Scott ~ Real ale ~ Meals and snacks (till 10pm) ~ Restaurant ~ (01747) 820573 ~ Children welcome ~ Open 11-11; 12-10.30 Sun ~ Bedrooms: £43B/£65B

KILMINGTON ST7736 Map 2

Red Lion

Pub on B3092 Mere—Frome, 2½ miles S of Maiden Bradley; 3 miles from A303 Mere turn-off

Don't be put off by the modest ivy covered exterior of this unpretentious but warmly welcoming 400-year-old local. The comfortably cosy low ceilinged bar is nicely individual, with a curved high-backed settle and red leatherette wall and window seats on the flagstones, photographs on the beams, and a couple of big fireplaces (one with a fine old iron fireback) with log fires in winter. A newer no-smoking eating area has a large window and is decorated with brasses, a large leather horse collar, and hanging plates. Simple lunchtime bar meals include home-made soup (£1.60), filled baked potatoes (from £2.50), toasted sandwiches (from £2.60), ploughman's (from £3.35), steak and kidney pie (£3.95), meat or vegetable lasagne (£4.85), and two daily specials such as very good home-cooked ham (£3.95). Butcombe and two guests like Cottage Our Ken and Oakhill Bitter under light blanket pressure; also farm cider, elderflower pressé, citrus pressé and monthly changing wines. Sensibly placed darts, dominoes, shove-ha'penny and cribbage. There are picnic-sets in the big attractive garden, and maybe Kim, the labrador. It's popular with walkers – you can buy the locally made walking sticks, and a gate leads on to the lane which leads to White Sheet Hill, where there is riding, hang gliding and radio-controlled gliders. It's also handy for Stourhead Gardens which are only a mile away. *(Recommended by Alan and Paula McCully, Mrs Stevens, Drs R A and B F Matthews, Mike Gorton, Mrs C Jimenez, Mr and Mrs D Ross)*

Free house ~ Licensee Chris Gibbs ~ Real ale ~ Lunchtime meals and snacks (till 1.50) ~ (01985) 844263 ~ Children in eating area of bar till 9pm ~ Open 11.30-2.30, 6.30-11; 12-3, 7-10.30 Sun ~ Bedrooms: £25/£30

LACOCK ST9168 Map 2

George

Not elaborate or fancy but jolly reliable with an unfailing friendly welcome, this lovely homely old place, which has been licensed continuously since the 17th c, and run by the present licensee for well over a decade, is really liked by readers. One of the talking points has long been the three-foot treadwheel set into the outer breast of the magnificent central fireplace. This used to turn a spit for roasting, and was worked by a specially bred dog called, with great imagination, a turnspit. Often very busy indeed, the comfortably welcoming bar has a low beamed ceiling, upright timbers in the place of knocked-through walls making cosy corners, candles on tables even at lunchtime, armchairs and windsor chairs, seats in the stone-mullioned windows and flagstones just by the bar. The well kept Wadworths IPA, 6X, and seasonal ale are very reasonably priced. There's a decent choice of wines by the bottle. Generous helpings of good value tasty bar food served with fresh vegetables and real chips might include sandwiches (£1.80), home-made soup (£2.10), filled french stick (from £2.95), prawn cocktail (£3.75), ploughman's (£3.95), 8oz sirloin (£8.25), and puddings like black cherry pie or raspberry hazelnut meringue roulade (£3.50); prompt and friendly service; no smoking barn restaurant; darts. There are picnic-sets with umbrellas in the back garden, as well as a play area with swings, and a bench in front that looks over the main street. It's a nice area for walking. The bedrooms (very highly praised by readers) are up at the landlord's farmhouse with free transport to and from the pub. *(Recommended by Alan and Paula McCully, Ann and Colin Hunt, Joan and Michel Hooper-Immins, Paul Cleaver, P and S White, Sheila Keene, Meg and Colin Hamilton, Paul and Sandra Embleton, Peter and Audrey Dowsett, J A Woolmore, Lawrence Pearse, Miss Veronica Brown, M G Hart, Mrs Laura Gustine, Janet Pickles, Pat and Roger Fereday, Susan and Nigel Wilson, Ian Phillips, Brian and Anna Marsden, JCW, Clare and Chris Tooley, John and Lynn Busenbark, Terry Griffiths, Derek Stafford, Brian and Bett Cox, Andrew Shore)*

Wadworths ~ Tenants John and Judy Glass ~ Real ale ~ Meals and snacks ~ Restaurant ~ (01249) 730263 ~ Children welcome ~ Open 10-3, 5-11 Mon-Thurs; 10-11(10.30 Sun) Fri-Sun ~ Bedrooms (see above): £25B/£40B

Red Lion

High Street; village signposted off A350 S of Chippenham

The other main entry in this lovely National Trust village is this imposing Georgian inn which is fairly plain from the outside but nicely spacious and welcoming inside. The comfortable long bar is divided into separate areas by cart shafts, yokes and other old farm implements, and old-fashioned furnishings including a mix of tables and comfortable chairs, turkey rugs on the partly flagstoned floor, and a fine old log fire at one end. Plates, paintings, and tools cover the walls, and there are stuffed birds, animals and branding irons hanging from the ceiling. Bar food includes soup (£2.25), sandwiches (from £2.85), pâté (£3.10), ploughman's (from £5.50), scampi (£6.75) salmon steak with white wine and cream sauce (£8.95) 8oz rump (£9.50), puddings (£2.50), and daily specials; one side of the dining area is no smoking. Well kept and priced Badger Tanglefoot, Wadworths IPA, 6X and seasonal beer on handpump, and several malt whiskies; darts, shove-ha'penny, table skittles, dominoes and fruit machine. It can get busy, and towards the latter half of the evening especially is popular with younger people. Close to Lacock Abbey and the Fox Talbot Museum. *(Recommended by Alan and Paula McCully, Ann and Colin Hunt, Peter and Audrey Dowsett, June and Tony Baldwin, Dr and Mrs B Smith, Tom Evans, Ian Phillips)*

Wadworths ~ Manager Peter Oldacre ~ Real ale ~ Meals and snacks ~ (01249) 730456 ~ Children welcome ~ Open 11.30-3; 6-11; 11-11 summer Sat; 12-10.30 summer Sun; 12-3, 6-10.30 winter Sun ~ Bedrooms: £45B/£65B

LIMPLEY STOKE ST7861 Map 2

Hop Pole

Coming S from Bath on A36 take B3108 at traffic lights signed Bradford on Avon, turn right of main road at sharp left hand bend before the railway bridge, pub is 100 yds on right (car park just before on left); OS Sheet 172 map reference 781610

Just a few minutes' walk to the Kennett & Avon canal, this picture book cream stone monks' wine lodge makes a good base for walks by the water. Welcoming and atmospheric, the homely dark-panelled room on the right has red velvet cushions for the settles in its alcoves, some slat-back and captain's chairs on its turkey carpet, lantern lighting, and a log fire. The spacious left-hand lounge (with an arch to a cream-walled inner room) also has dark wood panelling, and a log-effect gas fire. Well cooked and presented home-made bar food (you may need to book) includes filled baps (from £1.90), ploughman's or salads (from £3.75), a daily pie like steak and ale pie (from £5.50), local trout (£6.95), Scotch salmon (£7.95), bass (£8.55), duck breast in black cherry sauce (£8.95) and local game in season; children's meals (from £2.50), and Sunday roast (£5.25); friendly, courteous service. Part of the restaurant is no smoking. Bass, Butcombe, Courage Best and a changing guest on handpump, with a range of malt whiskies; darts, shove-ha'penny, cribbage, dominoes, trivia and piped music. There's an attractive enclosed garden behind with rustic benches, a terrace and pond; boules. *(Recommended by Dr and Mrs A K Clarke, JDM, KM, Brad W Morley, Susan and Nigel Wilson, Meg and Colin Hamilton, Janet Pickles, Howard Clutterbuck)*

Free house ~ Licensee Robert Williams ~ Real ale ~ Meals and snacks ~ Restaurant ~

(01225) 723134 ~ Children in restaurant at the landlord's discretion ~ Open 11-3, 6-11; 12-3, 7-10.30 Sun

LITTLE CHEVERELL ST9853 Map 2

Owl £

Low Rd; just off B3098 Westbury—Upavon, W of A360

Their very good value lunchtime special offer of two courses for £3.95 or three courses for £4.95 is a big draw at this delightfully cosy little local pub. Other good value food includes soup (£2.25), ploughman's (£3.75), spicy chicken wings (£3.95), breaded haddock (£4.75), poached salmon steak (£5.75), 8oz rump (£5.95), bass poached in white wine (£7.50), and puddings like lemon meringue pie or chocolate fudge cake (from £1.60). Very comfortable and relaxing, the peaceful and neatly traditional bar seems a lot bigger than it really is thanks to plenty of chairs, stools, high-backed settles and tables; a piano separates the main area from a snugger room at the back. There are fresh flowers on the tables, local papers and guides to read, a gently ticking clock, two or three stuffed owls behind the bar, a few agricultural tools on the walls, and noticeboards advertising local events and activities. As well as well kept Wadworths 6X there are three changing real ales from brewers like Ash Vine, Hambleton or Oakhill; a blackboard lists forthcoming brews, and there's usually a beer festival the last weekend in April and in early September. They also have country wines, maybe farm cider and jugs of Pimms in summer; friendly smiling service; the Stable is no smoking. It's set in a delightfully peaceful spot, with cooing woodpigeons in the lovely tall ash and willow tree lined garden behind, with its rustic picnic-sets on a long lawn that runs down over two levels to a brook; there are plastic tables and chairs on a terrace above here. A pergola with climbers and hanging baskets across the front of the pub makes another lovely area of tranquil seating. Dogs are welcome (they have their own, and a cat). *(Recommended by N Rushton, Susan and Nigel Wilson, David and Kay Ross, Colin and Joyce Laffan, Gwen and Peter Andrews, John Hayter, Lyn and Geoff Hallchurch)*

Free house ~ Licensee Mike Hardham ~ Real ale ~ Meals and snacks (till 10) ~ (01380) 812263 ~ Well behaved children welcome ~ Open 12-2.30, 7-11; 12-3, 7-10.30 Sun; cl Mon

LOWER CHUTE SU3153 Map 2

Hatchet

The Chutes well signposted via Appleshaw off A342, 2½ miles W of Andover

The enchanted appearance of this unchanging 16th-c thatched cottage ranks it alongside some of the country's most charming looking pubs. The especially low beams look down over a lovely mix of captain's chairs and cushioned wheelbacks set around oak tables. There's a splendid 17th-c fireback in the huge fireplace, with a big winter log fire in front. Good bar food includes sandwiches (from £2.25, steak £4.95), home-made soup (£2.50), thai crab cakes (£3.50), ploughman's (£3.95), chilli, spaghetti bolognese, giant filled yorkshire pudding or liver and bacon (£4.95), boeuf bourguignon or steak and stout pie (£5.45), moules marinières or scampi (£5.95), thai chicken (£6.25), and tasty puddings. Well kept real ales served by the friendly barmaid are Adnams, Marstons Pedigree and Timothy Taylor Landlord on handpump, and a range of country wines. Darts, shove-ha'penny, dominoes, cribbage, and piped music. There are seats out on a terrace by the front car park, or on the side grass, as well as a children's sandpit. *(Recommended by Jenny and Michael Back, Dr Alan Green, Phyl and Jack Street, John and Joan Calvert, Gordon, Stephen, Julie and Hayley Brown, G W A Pearce, Dr S P Willavoys, Peter Neate)*

Free house ~ Licensee Jeremy McKay ~ Real ale ~ Meals and snacks (till 9.45) ~ Restaurant ~ (01264) 730229 ~ Children in eating area of bar and restaurant ~ Open 11.30-3, 6-11; 12-3.30, 7-10.30 Sun ~ Self-contained flat: £45

Prices of main dishes usually include vegetables or a side salad.

LOWER WOODFORD SU1235 Map 2

Wheatsheaf

Leaving Salisbury northwards on A360, The Woodfords signposted first right after end of speed limit; then bear left

There's a welcoming and rather cosy feel to this 18th-c farm – part of the interior was originally the barn and stables – and though most of it is laid for dining there are a couple of tables by the front bar which are still used by drinkers. At the heart of the bar there's an unusual indoor pond with goldfish and to get from one part of the pub to the other you have to cross a miniature footbridge. The very wide choice of food includes home-made soups like spinach and broccoli (£2.20), filled baguettes with chips (£3.95), ploughman's or baked potatoes with nice fillings like stilton and bacon (£4.55), chicken, ham and mushroom pasta bake, prawn and smoked haddock fusilli or chicken or vegetable madras (£5.95), steak and mushroom pie or chicken, stilton and broccoli pie (£6.15), breaded plaice (£5.45), or grilled chicken breast with garlic and herb butter (£7.45), salmon steak with hollandaise and dill sauce (£8.95), sirloin steak (£10.95), and children's meals (from £2.50), daily specials like beef curry (£5.25), haddock goujons (£5.95), fresh trout (£6.50), game pie (£6.15), and traditional puddings like apple pie or raspberry meringue nest (from £3.25); most of the pub is no smoking; piped music. Well kept Badger Best, IPA and Tanglefoot on handpump are promptly served by helpful, friendly staff; darts, dominoes and cribbage. Good disabled access, and baby-changing facilities. The big walled garden has picnic-sets, a climber and swings, and is surrounded by tall trees. It's in a lovely setting only a few miles from Salisbury with lots of pretty walks in the Avon Valley, and it's handy for Old Sarum. *(Recommended by Phyl and Jack Street, A Lock, JCW, Susan and Nigel Wilson, Stephen, Julie and Hayley Brown, Mr and Mrs Peter Smith, Gordon, Colin and Alma Gent, Dr D G Twyman)*

Badger ~ Managers Ron and Ann May ~ Real ale ~ Meals and snacks (till 10pm) ~ (01722) 782203 ~ Children welcome ~ Open 11-3, 6.30(6 Fri, Sat)-11; 12-3, 7-10.30 Sun

MARLBOROUGH SU1869 Map 2

Sun

High Street

Run by a cheery extrovert landlord, this busy little 15th-c inn with its heavy sloping beams and wonky floors gives a charming sense of busy old time Marlborough. The attractively furnished and dimly lit characterful bar has brasses and harness hanging above the log fire, benches built into the black panelling, an antique high backed settle, and newspapers. Bar food might include chicken liver pâté or fish soup (£2.95), smoked salmon and prawn open sandwich (£3.95), very tasty fresh battered haddock (£6.10), sizzling chicken in black bean sauce (£7.25) and seafood platter (£7.50); no-smoking dining area. Well kept Bass and Courage Directors on handpump, and several reasonably priced wines; fruit machine and piped music. You can sit outside on a small sheltered back courtyard. Although bedrooms are fairly simple they are characterfully positioned, one in a garret with a lovely view of the High Street. The pub is nicely placed adjacent to the church of St Peter where Cardinal Wolsey was inducted as a priest. *(Recommended by Mrs Kay Neville-Rolfe, Michael and Jean Wilby, John Fahy, Tina and David Woods-Taylor, David Griffiths)*

Scottish Courage ~ Licensee Peter Brown ~ Real ale ~ Meals and snacks ~ Restaurant ~ (01672) 512081 ~ Children in eating area of bar and restaurant till 9pm ~ Open 11-11; 12-10.30 Sun ~ Bedrooms: £25(£35B)/£35(£45B)

Planning a day in the country? We list pubs in really attractive scenery at the back of the book.

NETHERHAMPTON SU1029 Map 2

Victoria & Albert

Just off A3094 W of Salisbury

The new licensees at this charmingly timeless thatched cottage are slowly working to restore the black beamed bar to resemble the painting over the fireplace which shows it as it was a decade ago, filled with gleaming brassware. There's already a good mix of individual tables, nicely cushioned old-fashioned wall settles and some attractive small armed chairs on the ancient polished floor tiles; darts, fruit machine and piped music. Alongside Courage Best and Directors and a beer from Wychwood they keep a guest like Morlands Old Speckled Hen on handpump. Bar food includes soup (£2.75), filled baguettes (£3.75), battered cod and chips (£4.95), ploughman's or steak and ale pie (£5.25), sausages, mash and onion gravy in a yorkshire pudding (£5.95), chinese-style pork (£6.50) and cajun chicken breast (£6.95), as well as puddings like plum crumble and spotted dick (£2.95). There's hatch service for the sizeable garden behind, with well spaced picnic-sets, a fountain and a big weeping willow. Handy for Wilton House (and Nadder Valley walks). *(Recommended by Stephen G Brown, Sally Sharp, Phyl and Jack Street, N Thompson)*

Free house ~ Licensees Harriet Allison and Pam Bourne ~ Real ale ~ Meals and snacks ~ (01722) 743174 ~ Children in snug ~ Open 11-3, 5.30(6 Sat)-11; 12-3, 7-10.30 Sun

NORTH NEWNTON SU1257 Map 2

Woodbridge 🍷

A345 Upavon—Pewsey

The warm decor here matches the enthusiasm of the cheerful licensees: blazing log fire, prints on terracotta walls, cosy touches such as the flowery cushions and curtains, daily papers and magazines to read, quite a collection of old wine bottles. It's on the food side that their enthusiasm really shows, with an enormous world-hopping choice of dishes, often spicy. In the early 1990s they were already ahead of the recent fad for Mexican food, and still rather specialise in it, especially with their fajitas – spicy beef, chicken, vegetables or prawns in a skillet, served with hot tortillas and soured cream (from £7.25). Other dishes, served generously, include soup (£2.50), sesame and ginger prawns, filled french sticks or ploughman's (£3.95), hot chicken liver and bacon salad (£4.25), steak and ale pie (£5.95), grilled pork fillet steaks topped with rich mushroom and brandy sauce, chicken breast topped with stilton sauce or white wine and grape sauce (£7.95), roast lamb on the bone with rosemary and redcurrant sauce (£9.50), and daily specials like cajun fish steak, liver, bacon and mash, mesquite salmon salad, seared shark with thyme butter sauce and monkfish and bacon brochettes with red pepper sauce. Their puddings, all home-made, are particularly good and might include ginger sponge with ginger sauce or pecan pie (from £3.25). The more elaborate dishes come at conventional mealtimes, but you can get straightforward bar food at any time of day (as well as afternoon teas and so forth). It's worth booking for Sunday lunch. Well kept Wadworths IPA, 6X, Farmers Glory and a seasonal guest beer, two dozen enjoyable wines by the glass, well served coffee, helpful friendly service; no dogs; piped music. The huge garden beside the River Avon has plenty of tables, boules pitches and a play area, and they have space for a few tents or caravans; a day's fly fishing pass is available at £25. Only one of the pleasantly furnished bedrooms has its own bathroom. *(Recommended by Gordon, Kevin Flack, June and Tony Baldwin, Michelle Hayles, C Baxter, Martin and Karen Wake, Helen Pickering, James Owen)*

Wadworths ~ Tenants Lou and Terri Vertessy ~ Real ale ~ Meals and snacks (11-2.30, 5.30-10.30) ~ (01980) 630266 ~ Seated children welcome ~ Open 11-3; 5.30-11; 12-3, 7-10.30 Sun; cl 25 Dec ~ Bedrooms: £35(£40B)/£40(£45B)

Tipping is not normal for bar meals, and not usually expected.

NORTON ST8884 Map 2

Vine Tree

4 miles from M4 junction 17; A429 towards Malmesbury, then left at Hullavington, Sherston signpost, then follow Norton signposts; in village turn right at Foxley signpost, which takes you into Honey lane

This pleasantly civilised dining pub is popular for its wide range of food which might include potato, cheese and onion soup (£2.65), sandwiches (from £2.95), houmous with pitta bread (£3.75), breaded brie with redcurrant jelly (£3.95), marinated smoked salmon strips with lemon cream (£4.25), fresh sardines with garlic, shallots and lemon (£4.25), moules (£4.50), fish pie or baked goat's cheese with honey and garlic croutons (£6.95), salmon and coriander fishcakes with apple and cider brandy chutney (£7.65), fish and chips (£7.25), pork tenderloin with stilton sauce (£8.95), red wine and juniper marinated lamb leg steaks with chilli dressing (£9.25), puddings like toffee apple and pecan pie (from £3.35) and children's meals (£2.95); Sunday roast (£6.50). Best to book, especially at weekends; one dining area is no smoking. Seeming much more remote than its proximity to the motorway would suggest, it's housed in an attractively converted 18th-c mill house. Three smallish rooms open together with plates, small sporting prints, carvings, hop bines, a mock-up mounted pig's mask (used for a game that involves knocking coins off its nose and ears), lots of stripped pine, candles in bottles on the tables (the lighting's very gentle), and some old settles. Well kept Archers Vine Tree, Bass and a guest like Moor Merlins Magic; service is efficient and chatty; piped music. There are picnic-sets under cocktail parasols in a vine-trellised garden with young trees and tubs of flowers, and a well fenced separate play area with a fine thatched fortress and so forth. *(Recommended by Stephen Alexander, Betsy and Peter Little, Dave Irving, Roger Huggins, Ewan McCall and Tom McLean, F C Johnston, Sheil and John French, Rona Murdoch)*

Free house ~ Manager Mark Gibbons ~ Real ale ~ Meals and snacks (till 10pm) ~ (01666) 837654 ~ Children in eating area of bar and in dining area ~ Open 11.30(11 Sat)-3, 6.30(6 Sat)-11; 12-10.30 Sun

PITTON SU2131 Map 2

Silver Plough 🍷

Village signposted from A30 E of Salisbury

Readers agree that the already very well prepared and imaginative food at this civilised dining pub has actually improved since the new licensees took over more than a year ago. It does get busy so booking is advised. From a wide choice, the warm chicken salad with ginger and sesame seed, and marinated herrings were particularly enjoyed. There might also be sandwiches (from £2.75), ploughman's (£4.25), pasta with smoked seafood, dill and horseradish (£5.25), yorkshire pudding filled with cumberland sausage (£5.45), roast aubergine filled with ratatouille with herby cheese crust and couscous (£5.25), moules marinières (£5.95), steak (£8.25), and daily specials like smoked sea trout on sliced avocado with grain mustard and poppy seed dressing (£3.75), fried duck breast coated with black cherry, orange and brandy sauce, grilled chicken breast on marsala and wild mushroom sauce or grilled whiting fillet on salad leaves with caper and lemon dressing (all £8.95); no-smoking area in the restaurant. Old jugs, glass rolling pins and other assorted curios hanging from the beamed ceilings in the main bar, paintings and prints on the walls, and comfortable oak settles. Well kept Badger Best, IPA and Tanglefoot and Wadworths 6X under light blanket pressure, a fine wine list including 10 by the glass and some well priced and carefully chosen bottles, a good range of country wines, and a worthy choice of spirits. There's a skittle alley next to the snug bar; alley skittles, cribbage, dominoes and piped music. Service is generally friendly and efficient, but can be a little disinterested at times. There are picnic-sets and other tables under cocktail parasols on a quiet lawn, with an old pear tree, and there are good downland and woodland walks.

(Recommended by Dr D Twyman, Charles Gray, Jerry and Alison Oakes, Phyl and Jack Street, Ian and Jacqui Ross, Mr and Mrs K Flawn, John Bowdler, Douglas and Jean Troup, Brian and Jill Bond, Richard and Rosemary Hoare, J Brisset, Roger and Valerie Tarren)

Badger ~ Manager Adrian Clifton ~ Real ale ~ Meals and snacks ~ Restaurant (not Sun evening) ~ (01722) 712266 ~ Children in eating area of bar till 9pm ~ Open 11-3, 6-11; 12-3, 7-10.30 Sun; cl 25 Dec evening

POULSHOT ST9559 Map 2

Raven

Village signposted off A361 Devizes—Seend

One reader found it a real treat sampling the particularly well kept Wadworths IPA, 6X and seasonal brews which are tapped straight from the cask at this splendidly tucked-away pub. It's prettily set across from the village green with a nice country welcome, thriving chatty atmosphere (no piped music here), smiling helpful service, and spick and span housekeeping. The two cosy and intimate rooms of the black-beamed bar are well furnished with sturdy tables and chairs and comfortable banquettes, and there's an attractive no-smoking dining room. The landlord keeps charge of the kitchen which produces the good value sandwiches (from £2.35), cream of vegetable soup (£2.40), ploughman's (from £3.10), creamy mushroom and broccoli risotto (£5.75), corned beef hotpot or scampi (£6.25), grilled chicken breast with smoked bacon and melted gruyère (£6.75), grilled lamb steaks with red wine and cranberry sauce (£7.40), poached fresh salmon with tarragon and dill sauce (£7.55), pork stroganoff (£8.35) and 10oz rump (£9.40), fried bass on a bed of leeks with cream herb sauce (£9.50); good fresh vegetables; and puddings like crème brûlée and sticky toffee pudding (£2.60). The gents' are outside. *(Recommended by G Washington, Ron Gentry, Gwen and Peter Andrews, Mr and Mrs Peter Smith, June and Tony Baldwin, Mrs Laura Gustine, MRSM, Colin and Joyce Laffan, John Hayter, Simon Collett-Jones)*

Wadworths ~ Tenants Susan and Philip Henshaw ~ Real ale ~ Meals and snacks ~ Restaurant ~ (01380) 828271 ~ Children in restaurant ~ Open 11-2.30(3 Sat), 6.30-11; 12-3, 7-10.30 Sun

RAMSBURY SU2771 Map 2

Bell

Village signposted off B4192 (still shown as A419 on many maps) NW of Hungerford, or from A4 W of Hungerford

Nicely positioned in a smartly attractive village, this comfortably civilised pub keeps a good range of drinks including well kept Hook Norton Best, Shepherd Neame Spitfire, Wadworths 6X and IPA and a guest on handpump, about fifty bin ends, and around 20 malt whiskies. Victorian stained-glass panels in one of the two sunny bay windows look out on to the quiet village street, and a big chimney breast with a woodburning stove divides up the smartly relaxed and chatty bar areas, nicely furnished with fresh flowers on the polished tables; evening piped music. Although the pub was about to change hands as we went to press the present chef was staying so bar meals should still include lunchtime sandwiches (from £1.75), soup (£2.75), king prawns in filo pastry with sweet and sour dip (£4.25), ploughman's (£4.75), toulouse sausage and mash, roasted vegetables with tomato and herb rice, fresh salmon fishcakes or thai green chicken curry (£6.95), tuscan chicken (£7.95), fillet of sea bream on a bed of aubergine (£8.50), and children's meals (from £1.95). Tables can be reserved in the restaurant, though the same meals can be had in the bar; one section is no smoking. There are picnic-sets on the raised lawn. Roads lead from this quiet village into the downland on all sides. *(Recommended by John Fahy, Tom Evans, M G Hart, P Neate, Yavuz and Shirley Mutlu, Tim Brierly, David Warrellow)*

Free house ~ Licensee ~ Real ale ~ Meals and snacks (not Sun evenings) ~ Restaurant ~ (01672) 520230 ~ Children in restaurant and room between bar and restaurant ~ Open 12-2.30(3 Sat) 6.30-11; 12-3, 7-10.30 Sun; cl winter Sun evenings

> You are now allowed 20 minutes after 'time, please' to finish your drink – half-an-hour if you bought it in conjunction with a meal.

ROWDE ST9762 Map 2

George & Dragon (🍴) 🍷

A342 Devizes—Chippenham

You will need to book to try the exceptionally good cooking at this warmly welcoming old dining pub because not surprisingly it's very popular. Ingredients are fresh, well chosen, and used to good effect, with fresh Cornish fish as a special highlight. The deftly inspired seasonally changing menu might include borlotti bean salad in olive oil and garlic (£4), provençale fish soup with rouille, gruyère and croutons or carpaccio of tuna, watercress, olive oil and balsamic vinegar (£5), beef kebab with couscous salad or pollock in beer batter with chilli soy sauce (£8), baked local ham with madeira sauce (£10), roast hake with grilled peppers and aioli (£11), fried swordfish with lemon and parsley (£12), fillet of john dory steamed with spinach and garlic (£15), Scottish langoustines grilled with garlic butter (£16), and puddings like chocolate and ginger roulade with lemon grass custard, brown sugar meringue with vanilla ice cream and chocolate sauce or sticky toffee pudding (£4); no-smoking dining room. The bar has some interesting furnishings, plenty of dark wood, and a log fire (with a fine collection of brass keys by it), while the bare-floored dining room has quite plain and traditional feeling tables and chairs. Four well kept local ales include Butcombe, Hop Back Crop Circle and Wadworths 6X on handpump, as well as a local farm cider and continental beers and lagers; friendly and efficient service; shove ha'penny, cribbage, dominoes and trivia. *(Recommended by Gwen and Peter Andrews, Dr D G Twyman, Tony Beaulah, Sheila Keene, Peter and Audrey Dowsett, Tina and David Woods-Taylor, Ron Gentry, W Burke, Mrs Laura Gustine, Lyn and Geoff Hallchurch, Dagmar Junghanns, Colin Keane, F and A Parmenter, John and Barbara Howdle, John Hayter, Pat and John Millward)*

Free house ~ Licensees Tim and Helen Withers ~ Real ale ~ Meals and snacks (till 10; not Sun or Mon) ~ Restaurant ~ (01380) 723053 ~ Children welcome ~ Open 12-3, 7-11(10.30 Sun); cl Mon lunchtime

SALISBURY SU1429 Map 2

Haunch of Venison ★

1 Minster Street, opposite Market Cross

A must if you're in the city – there's something about this marvellously atmospheric old building that lures visitors into a long and lingering visit. Built some 650 years ago as the church house for St Thomas's, just behind, it has massive beams in the ochre ceiling, stout red cushioned oak benches built into its timbered walls, genuinely old pictures, a black and white tiled floor, and an open fire; a tiny snug opens off the entrance lobby. A quiet and cosy upper panelled room has a small paned window looking down onto the main bar, antique leather-seat settles, a nice carved oak chair nearly three centuries old, and a splendid fireplace that dates back to the building's early years; behind glass in a small wall slit is the smoke-preserved mummified hand of an unfortunate 18th-c card player. Well kept Courage Best and Directors and a guest like Wadworths 6X on handpump from a unique pewter bar counter, with a rare set of antique taps for gravity-fed spirits and liqueurs; about 75 malt whiskies, decent wines (including a wine of the week), and a range of brandies; chess. Bar food, includes sandwiches (from £2.25), filled ciabatta (from £3.50), ploughman's (from £4.50), yorkshire pudding filled with venison sausage (£4.50), salmon and crab cakes (£3.95), venison cottage pie or goat's cheese crostini with mixed leaves and pine nuts (£4.95), and home-made puddings like treacle tart, bread and butter pudding or rhubarb crumble. The pub can get a little smoky. *(Recommended by Gordon, Howard England, David Peakall, Jerry and Alison Oakes, Stephen Brown, Mr and Mrs Carey, M Joyner, Tim Barrow, Sue Demont, Dr and Mrs J Hills, Frank Gadbois, Stephen and Julie Brown, Barry and Anne, Rupert Willcocks, Hanns P Golez, Lynn Sharpless, Bob Eardley, David Carr, Dr and Mrs A H Young)*

Courage ~ Lease: Antony and Victoria Leroy ~ Real ale ~ Lunchtime meals and snacks (not Sat) ~ Restaurant ~ (01722) 322024 ~ Well behaved children in restaurant and one side room ~ Nearby parking may be difficult ~ Open 11-11; 12-3.30, 7-10.30 Sun; cl evening 25 Dec

New Inn

New Street

The handsome interior of this ancient and creaky timbered town centre pub – it's completely no smoking throughout – has heavy old beams, horsebrasses, timbered walls, an inglenook fire in the largest room, and a panelled dining room, with quiet cosy alcoves, and a relaxing unpretentious atmosphere. A good range of well presented home-made food served throughout the pub includes soup (£2.45), sandwiches (from £3.25), smoked trout terrine (£3.95), ploughman's or asparagus quiche (£4.95), lamb liver with bacon and onions (£6.95), salmon steak with hollandaise and dill sauce (£7.95), chicken breast cooked with mushrooms in white wine and cream sauce (£8.95), pork tenderloin simmered in cider and apricots (£9.95), and duck breast cooked in honey with chestnut stuffing (£10.95); and good sturdy puddings (£2.95); friendly helpful licensees and staff, well kept Badger Dorset Best and Tanglefoot and Charles Wells Eagle on handpump, decent house wines; maybe piped Radio 2. Tables out in the sizeable pleasant walled garden look up to the nearby cathedral. The back bedrooms are quieter; no cooked breakfast. *(Recommended by Rona Murdoch, Tim Barrow, Sue Demont, N B Thompson, Mark Percy, Lesley Mayoh; more reports please)*

Badger ~ Tenants John and M G Spicer ~ Real ale ~ Meals and snacks (01722) 327679 ~ Children in eating area of bar and garden room ~ Open 11-3, 6-11; 11-11 Sat, 11-4, 7-10.30 Sun; cl 25 Dec ~ Bedrooms: £39.50B/£49.50B

SEEND ST9361 Map 2

Barge

Seend Cleeve; signposted off A361 Devizes—Trowbridge, between Seend village and signpost to Seend Head

The neatly kept waterside garden with its old streetlamps at this canalside pub is a perfect spot to watch the comings and goings of boats and barges on the Kennet and Avon Canal – there are moorings by the humpy bridge. Inside, the unusual barge theme decor in the friendly and relaxed bar is perhaps at its best in the intricately painted Victorian flowers which cover the ceilings and run in a waist-high band above the deep green lower walls. A distinctive mix of attractive seats includes milkchurns and the occasional small oak settle among the rugs on the parquet floor, while the walls have big sentimental engravings. The watery theme continues with a well stocked aquarium, and there's also a pretty Victorian fireplace, big bunches of dried flowers, and red velvet curtains for the big windows. A good range of bar food served in big good value helpings by cheery uniformed staff includes soup (£2.25), sandwiches (from £3.50), ploughman's (£4.50), pasta with leek, roquefort and wild mushroom sauce (£5.95), filo pastry filled with peppers, sun-dried tomatoes, mushrooms and slices of mozzarella cheese, steak and kidney pie or chicken, mushroom and ham pie (£6.95), venison steak with red currant and port sauce (£8.25) and 10oz sirloin (£8.95). In the evening dishes are served with fresh vegetables and a couple of additional dishes are a bit more restauranty; the restaurant extension is no smoking. They recommend booking for meals, especially at weekends. Well kept Bass, Badger Tanglefoot, Wadworths IPA and 6X, and a fortnightly changing guest beer; lots of malts and mulled wine in winter. Good service; trivia, fruit machine. Barbecues outside on summer Sundays. At the busiest times you may find queues to get in the car park, and service can slow down. *(Recommended by P and S White, Jerry and Alison Oakes, Mr and Mrs Peter Smith, R M Sparkes, R H Rowley, D G Clarke, Phyl and Jack Street, Luke Worthington, G W A Pearce, John and Vivienne Rice, Derek Clarke, Charles and Pauline Stride)*

Wadworths ~ Tenant Christopher Moorley Long ~ Real ale ~ Meals and snacks (till 10 Fri/Sat) ~ Restaurant ~ (01380) 828230 ~ Children welcome ~ Open 11-2.30(3 Sat), 6-11; 12-4, 7-10.30 Sun

Pubs in outstandingly attractive surroundings are listed at the back of the book.

SEMLEY ST8926 Map 2

Benett Arms 🍷

Turn off A350 N of Shaftesbury at Semley Ind Estate signpost, then turn right at Semley signpost

The genial Belfast born Joe Duthie and his delightful Irish wife have run this ruggedly charming village inn for the last 21 years now. Set right on the Dorset border, it's in a lovely setting just across the green from the church, with pretty countryside in all directions. Friendly and welcoming, the two cosy and hospitable rooms are separated by a flight of five carpeted steps, and have one or two settles and pews, a deep leather sofa and chairs, hunting prints, carriage lamps for lighting, a pendulum wall clock, and ornaments on the mantlepiece over the log fire. Down by the thatched-roof bar servery, the walls are stripped stone; upstairs, there's a dark panelling dado. Attractively presented bar food includes sandwiches (from £1.80), very good home-made soup (£2.95), ploughman's, smoked ham and salami with greek olives or grilled goat's cheese (£4.95), leek and cheese bake (£5.95), scampi (£6.95), salmon cooked in dry vermouth with dill, scallops and cream or mushroom stroganoff (£8.95), half a roast duckling with orange sauce or sirloin steak (£10.95), beef stroganoff (£13.95), and puddings like apple crumble and sherry trifle, several ice creams and caramelised maple syrup and walnut crunchies (£2.95). Four changing real ales might include Benskins, Gibbs Mew Bishops Tipple, Ruddles or Websters on handpump, kept under light blanket pressure, farm cider, four chilled vodkas, 18 malt whiskies, lots of liqueurs, and a thoughtfully chosen wine list, including a good few by the glass; helpful chatty landlord. Dominoes and cribbage, but no machines or music. There are seats outside. Well behaved dogs welcome. *(Recommended by Alan and Paula McCully, John A Barker, Mr and Mrs D E Powell, Phyl and Jack Street, Bruce Bird)*

Enterprise Inns ~ Tenant Joe Duthie ~ Real ale ~ Meals and snacks (till 10pm) ~ Restaurant ~ (01747) 830221 ~ Children in eating area of bar and restaurant ~ Open 11-3, 6-11; 12-3, 7-10.30 Sun; closed 25/26 Dec ~ Bedrooms: £31B/£48B

SHERSTON ST8585 Map 2

Rattlebone

Church St; B4040 Malmesbury—Chipping Sodbury

Despite quite an emphasis on the very well prepared imaginative food there's still a good pubby atmosphere at this cheery bustling old 16th-c inn: soup (£2.25), lunchtime ploughman's (£3.50), spicy crab and mushroom bake topped with grilled cheese (£3.95), slices of duck breast with toasted almonds and mango chutney, smoked salmon with a dill and mustard sauce or grilled goat's cheese on crispy crouton with honey and black pepper (£4.25), steak and kidney pie or creamy leek and smoked cheese crêpes (£6.50), scampi (£6.95), salmon fillet topped with roasted parmesan on a tomato coulis (£8.75), turkey escalope with garlic, white wine and mushroom sauce or roast chicken breast wrapped in bacon with a rich tarragon mustard sauce (£8.95), pork tenderloin with stilton and cream sauce with toasted cashew nuts (£9.50), and puddings like crème brûlée or home-made crumble (from £2.75); three course Sunday roast and coffee (£8.95); part of the dining area is no smoking. Several rambling rooms, nooks and crannies have pink walls, pews and settles, country kitchen chairs around a mix of tables, big dried flower arrangements, lots of jugs and bottles hanging from the low beams, and plenty of little cuttings and printed anecdotes. In the public bar there's a hexagonal pool table, darts, table football, Connect Four, shove-ha'penny, fruit machine, cribbage, dominoes and juke box; also table and alley skittles. Well kept Smiles Best and Golden and a guest like Fullers London Pride on handpump, over 50 malt whiskies, 20 rums, fruit wines, decent wines, and quick obliging service. The smallish garden is very pretty with flower beds, a gravel terrace, and picnic-sets under umbrellas. There are four boules pitches. *(Recommended by John Fahy, Derek and Sylvia Stephenson, Deborah and David Rees, Jacquie and Jim Jones, Peter Neate, Keith and Margaret Kettell, Charles and Pauline Stride, Janet Pickles, John and Elizabeth Cox, S H Godsell, Andrew Shore, Desmond and Pat Morris, MRSM, Margaret and Douglas Tucker, Nick and Meriel Cox, JCW, Tom McLean, Ewen McCall, Roger Huggins, Dave Irving, M G Hart, Pat and John Millward)*

Smiles ~ Manager David Baker ~ Real ale ~ Meals and snacks (till 10) ~ (01666) 840871 ~ Children in eating area ~ Open 10-11; 12-10.30 Sun

WOODBOROUGH SU1159 Map 2

Seven Stars

Off A345 S of Marlborough: from Pewsey follow Woodborough signposts, then in Woodborough bear left following Bottlesford signposts; OS Sheet 173, map reference 113591

Wiltshire Dining Pub of the Year

There's a really winning combination of leisurely but civilised pub atmosphere, traditional furnishings and really good Anglo-French country cooking at this lovely red brick thatched house. At first all seems straightforward: polished bricks by the bar counter, well kept Badger Dorset Best, Bunces Pigswill and Wadworths 6X on handpump, hunting prints, attractively moulded panelling, a hot coal fire in the old range at one end, a big log fire at the other, a pleasant mix of antique settles and country furniture, cast-iron-framed tables, cosy nooks here and there, a couple of pub dogs and a black cat. It's when you notice the strings of onions and shallots by one fireplace, and then the profusion of retired wine bottles on delft shelves – and perhaps the gingham tablecloths and decidedly non-standard art up steps in the attractive back dining area – that you realise all is not quite what it seems. So ask for the menu: changing daily, it might include soup (£2.75), sandwiches (from £2.95), ploughman's (£4.25), moules marinières or aubergine provençale (£4.75), steak and kidney pie (£5.75), mushroom stroganoff (£6.50), cassoulet (£7.25), jugged hare (£10.75), monkfish with cream and asparagus (£9.75), bouillabaisse (£10.75), and pudddings like tarte tartin (£3.50). At our inspection meal, mallard done with orange and local rabbit cooked in the Normandy style with cider and cream came with beautiful waxy French potatoes (they get regular supplies direct from France) and excellent leaf-wrapped cabbage patties. The wine list is exemplary, with about a dozen including plenty of French by the glass in the £1.80ish range, and interesting bin ends. There's an attractive restaurant with handsome Victorian pictures; maybe intelligent piped music. Seven acres of riverside gardens. *(Recommended by Dr Paul Khan, Martin and Karen Wake, TRS, G A Page, Fiona McLean)*

Free house ~ Licensees Philippe Cheminade and Kate Lister ~ Real ale ~ Meals and snacks ~ Restaurant ~ (01672) 851325 ~ Well behaved chidren in eating area of bar and restaurant ~ Open 12-2, 6-11; 12-3 Sun; cl Sun evening and Mon

Lucky Dip

Besides the fully inspected pubs, you might like to try these Lucky Dips recommended to us and described by readers (if you do, please send us reports):

☆ **Aldbourne** [The Green (off B4192)], *Blue Boar*: Ancient Tudor public bar, friendly and relaxed, with homely feel and boars head; extensive more modern lounge/dining area, busy at lunchtime, with good choice of inexpensive food from generous sandwiches up, fresh veg; nice furnishings, well kept Archers Village, Wadworths IPA and 6X, decent wine, quick friendly service, blazing log fire; quiet piped music; children welcome, neatly kept small back country garden, seats out facing pretty village green nr church *(Gordon, Peter and Audrey Dowsett)*

Avebury [SU0969], *Stones*: Good reasonably priced vegetarian restaurant in converted barn, not a pub but atmosphere not entirely unpubby – and has Bunces real ale *(June and Tony Baldwin)*

Badbury [off A345 S of Swindon; SU1980], *Bakers Arms*: Quiet, clean and comfortable village local doing well under current regime, with Arkells beers, nice food, fresh flowers, pleasant atmosphere; children welcome, garden *(Julia Cohen)*

☆ **Beckhampton** [A4 Marlborough—Calne; SU0868], *Waggon & Horses*: Friendly stone-and-thatch pub handy for Avebury and open all day, full range of Wadworths ales and a guest beer kept well, good coffee, old-fashioned unassuming bare-boards bar, understated Dickens connections, log fires, wide choice of popular good value bar food inc children's and imaginative dishes, teas, dining lounge, family room; side room with pool and machines, CD juke box, pleasant garden with good play area; parking over road, no dogs; bedrooms *(Lyn and Geoff Hallchurch, Chris Mawson, TRS, Paul and Diane Edwards, Neil Spink, LYM)*

☆ **Biddestone** [The Green, off A420 W of Chippenham; ST8773], *White Horse*: Busy simple village local, small cosy carpeted rooms, wide choice of cheap well cooked food and filled rolls, well kept Courage ales, quick friendly service; children welcome, shove-ha'penny, darts and table skittles; overlooks duckpond in picturesque village, tables in good garden with play area, aviary and chipmunks; bedrooms *(Mr and Mrs J Brown, Ann and Colin Hunt)*

☆ **Bishops Cannings** [off A361 NE of Devizes; SU0364], *Crown*: Carefully refurbished unassuming village local with friendly and enterprising licensees, good value well cooked food (new upstairs dining room), well kept Wadworths IPA and 6X, decent wines, enjoyable atmosphere; dogs welcome, next to handsome old church in pretty village, walk to Kennet & Avon Canal *(John and Chris Simpson, June and Tony Baldwin, Lyn and Geoff Hallchurch, Marjorie and David Lamb, Colin and Joyce Laffan)*

Bishopstone [the one nr Swindon, signed off A419/B4192 at Wanborough; SU2483], *Royal Oak*: Recently refurbished two-bar local in beautiful village, some beams and oak panelling, wood floors, settles, bookshelves, prints on striped wallpaper; warm and friendly, with Arkells Bitter, 2B and 3B, food inc organic meat and burgers, gourmet nights, cribbage, darts and chess, garden; quiz and murder mystery nights, handy for Ridgeway *(Sam Samuells, Lynda Payton)*; [High St], *True Heart*: Spacious old country pub with very wide choice of good food inc good vegetarian choice, friendly attentive service, Flowers and Wadworths tapped from the cask, decent coffee, light and airy bar with eating area up three steps, corridor to small dining room, fresh flowers; children welcome, own menu; picnic-sets in garden with terrace; darts, piped music; cl Mon lunchtime *(CMW, JJW)*

Bradford on Avon [17 Frome Rd (B3109 S); ST8261], *Barge*: Attractive child-friendly pub with good food, friendly staff and local atmosphere, good well priced food inc lunchtime baguettes, nicely set canalside garden with rabbit hutches, relaxing views; service can slow when busy; good value bedrooms *(Sian Hamilton, Susan and Nigel Wilson)*; [Masons Hill], *Dandy Lion*: Busy old-world pub with good lunchtime food, Bass, Wadworths IPA and 6X and a seasonal ale, espresso machine, friendly staff, popular upstairs evening restaurant specialising in steaks *(Nigel and Susan Wilson)*; [Silver St], *Kings Arms*: Back to a proper name (was briefly Sprat & Carrot); bare boards and rugs, ceiling loaded with fishing gear, smiling service, big open fire, popular dining area (some interesting dishes), well kept Greene King IPA, Abbot, Smiles Best and Theakstons Best, good choice of spirits *(Dr C C S Wilson, Susan and Nigel Wilson, Dr and Mrs A K Clarke)*

Bratton [B3098 E of Westbury; ST9052], *Duke*: Warmly welcoming and civilised, well refurbished, with comfortable lounge bar, public bar and nice small dining room, generous well cooked food inc outstanding Sun lunch, Moles ales (tied to them), experienced licensees and quick pleasant service, well behaved labrador called Wellington, exemplary lavatories; ancient whalebone arch to garden; bedrooms *(Colin Laffan, Lyn and Geoff Hallchurch)*

☆ **Broad Chalke** [North St; Ebble Valley SW of Salisbury; SU0325], *Queens Head*: Roomy and friendly, with heavy beams, inglenook with woodburner, padded settles and chairs, some stripped brickwork, wide range of home-made food from sandwiches up, welcoming service, well kept ales inc Fullers London Pride and Ringwood Best, decent wines and country wines, good coffee; maybe piped music; wheelchair access from back car park, tables in pretty courtyard; comfortable well equipped bedrooms in newish separate block *(Angus Lyon, Paul McPherson, John Davis)*

☆ **Broad Hinton** [High St; off A4361 about 5 miles S of Swindon; SU1076], *Crown*: Light and airy open-plan bar, plush and roomy eating area, good home-cooked food esp salads and puddings, friendly uniformed waitresses, well kept Arkells BB, BBB, Kingsdown and Mild, no-smoking area, interesting bric-a-brac, unobtrusive piped music; unusual gilded inn sign, attractive spacious garden with fishpond and play area; bedrooms *(June and Tony Baldwin, CMW, JJW, Martin Freeman, LYM)*

Brokerswood [ST8352], *Kicking Donkey*: Good sensibly priced food, fine range of beer such as Hook Norton Old Hookey, Oakhill, Smiles Golden, Tisbury and one brewed for them by Bunces, good service even on a busy Sun, several bars and various nooks, log fires; delightful lawn, lovely rural setting *(Colin Laffan, Derek and Sylvia Stephenson)*

Broughton Gifford [ST8763], *Bell on the Common*: Friendly and popular old stonebuilt pub in attractive spot, traditional furnishings, generous good value straightforward home-made food, well kept Wadworths and farm cider, copper bar counter with handpumps on back wall, big coal fire, public bar with darts, pool etc, pleasant restaurant; children welcome, garden, bowls club next door *(Trevor Owen)*

Burcombe [SU0730], *Ship*: Clean and comfortable, very popular for wide range of good generous reasonably priced food; welcoming staff, country wines, beautiful gardens *(Mary Blake)*

Burton [B4039 Chippenham—Chipping Sodbury; ST8179], *Old House At Home*: Spacious and attractive stonebuilt dining pub with wide choice of good but not cheap home-cooked food inc spicy vegetarian dishes, good-sized helpings, log fire, well kept Wadworths, good choice of wines by the glass; piped music, cl Tues lunchtime *(Andrew Shore)*

☆ **Castle Combe** [The Hill; signed off B4039 Chippenham—Chipping Sodbury; ST8477], *White Hart*: Pretty stonebuilt ancient pub, attractive inside, with beams, panelling, flagstones, seats in stone-mullioned window, big log fire, old photographs; Wadworths IPA, Farmers Glory and 6X and a guest such as Adnams, good service, interesting choice of decent food from well filled rolls up, good cream teas, smaller lounge, family room, games room; walkers welcome, tables in sheltered courtyard *(Andrew and Eileen Abbess, Barry and Anne, LYM)*

☆ *nr* **Castle Combe** [The Gibb; B4039 Acton Turville—Chippenham, nr Nettleton], *Salutation*: Good choice of attractively served good food inc vegetarian, popular fish and chips, Aberdeen Angus steaks in comfortable lounge bar and raftered thatched and timbered restaurant, jovial landlord, friendly staff, pubby locals' bar, Whitbreads-related ales, decent wines *(Desmond and Pat Morris, John Knighton, Ken Hull, Vanessa Mudge, MRSM)*

Chapmanslade [A3098 Westbury—Frome; ST8247], *Three Horse Shoes*: 16th-c beamed country inn with beautifully cooked food, well kept ales inc Wadworths 6X, sensibly priced good wines, big log fire, lots of brass and pewter, restaurant; pleasant garden with superb views, very helpful service *(Geoffrey Kemp)*

☆ **Charlton** [B4040 toward Cricklade; ST9588], *Horse & Groom*: Wide choice of good food in carefully refurbished dining pub, civilised and relaxing; friendly staff, good log fire, well kept Archers and Wadworths, farm cider, decent wines; restaurant (good value Sun lunch), tables outside; dogs welcome, has been cl Mon *(D G King, John and Pat Smyth, J and M de Nordwall, Mike and Heather Watson, LYM)*

Cherhill [A4 E of Calne; SU0370], *Black Horse*: Popular beamed dining pub, linked areas crowded with tables for wide range of very good value generous food (two evening sittings), prompt service, no-smoking area, huge fireplace, four Ushers ales, children welcome *(Tony Beaulah, Jerry and Alison Oakes, Colin and Joyce Laffan)*

☆ **Chilmark** [B3089 Salisbury—Hindon; ST9632], *Black Dog*: Well kept ales such as Bass, Tisbury and Wadworths 6X, Irish landlord, friendly staff, good food (different blackboards lunchtime and evening) and good local atmosphere in comfortably modernised 15th-c beamed pub with armchairs by lounge log fire, fossil ammonites in the stone of another room; restaurant *(Mr and Mrs T Bryan, R T and J C Moggridge, Ian Bradshaw, LYM)*

Chippenham [Malmesbury Rd; ST9173], *Cepen Arms*: Big modern Brewers Fayre family dining pub, good friendly service, well kept Whitbreads-related beer, fast food, play areas indoors and out *(Peter Neate, Dr and Mrs A K Clarke, Mr and Mrs G Snowball)*

Chitterne [ST9843], *Kings Head*: Nice local with enjoyable food, well kept Bass and Gibbs Mew; pretty village *(J W G Nunns)*

Cholderton [A338 Tidworth—Salisbury; SU2242], *Crown*: Cosy thatched low-beamed cottage with welcoming new licensees, simple choice of reasonably priced food, well kept Boddingtons, fast efficient service; L-shaped bar with nice open fire, bar billiards one end; seats outside *(David and Ruth Shillitoe, G Coates)*

Clyffe Pypard [SU0777], *Goddard Arms*: Interesting prints, paintings, sculptures, secondhand books and records for sale in 16th-c pub's small bar and lounge, changing art exhibition in back skittle alley (doubles as pool room, with busy music nights); friendly staff, well kept Flowers IPA, Greene King Abbot, Marstons Pedigree and Wadworths 6X, varied food inc good vegetarian choice, thai evening food, weekly vegetarian feast; sculpture garden, tiny pretty thatched village in lovely countryside *(Pete and Rosie Flower, Keith Wills, Mrs Laura Gustine)*

Collingbourne Ducis [A338 Marlborough—Salisbury; SU2453], *Last Straw*: Comfortable cottagey thatched pub with real ales, decent coffee, friendly service, good open fire; separate dining room *(Ann and Colin Hunt)*

☆ **Coombe Bissett** [Blandford Rd (A354); SU1026], *Fox & Goose*: Tasty reasonably priced food (interesting vegetarian, fine puddings) and Wadworths 6X and other ales in thriving spacious neatly kept open-plan pub by delightful village green; welcoming staff, rustic refectory-style tables, coal fires, old prints, hanging chamber-pots; can be very busy weekends, piped music (classical at lunchtime), children catered for, evening restaurant; picnic-sets on terrace and in garden with play area, good access for wheelchairs *(Jerry and Alison Oakes, Ian Phillips)*

Corsley [A362 Warminster—Frome; ST8246], *White Hart*: Pleasantly furnished, with good generous home-made food, well kept Oakhill ales, sensible prices, friendly landlord; handy for Longleat *(Mrs Stevens)*

Corsley Heath [A362 Frome—Warminster; ST8245], *Royal Oak*: Very popular lunchtime for good range of generous reasonably priced home-made food inc vegetarian and some unusual dishes, helpful friendly service, Bass and Wadworths 6X, roomy two-part bar, big pleasant back children's room, big garden, restaurant; handy for Longleat *(DWAJ, K R Harris)*

Cricklade [SU0993], *Vale*: Good atmosphere in pleasant, comfortable bar adjoining Georgian hotel; well kept ales such as Archers Village and Wadworths 6X, popular food; bedrooms *(D Irving, E McCall, R Huggins, T McLean)*

Crudwell [A429 N of Malmesbury; ST9592], *Plough*: Quiet lounge, bar with darts and juke box, pool room, dining area with comfortable well padded seats and more in elevated part; remarkably wide range of reasonably priced food, well kept ales such as Bass, Boddingtons, local Foxley, Morlands Old Specked Hen and Wadworths 6X, maybe open fires, pleasant side garden *(T McLean, E McCall, R Huggins, D Irving, P and D Carpenter, Geoffrey and Penny Hughes)*

Dauntsey [Dauntsey Lock; B4069 – handy for M4 junctions 16 and 17; ST9782], *Peterborough Arms*: Roomy pub in nice spot by old Wilts & Berks Canal, welcoming landlord, good value generous food, good changing range of real ales, pool, skittle alley; children welcome, sizeable garden with play area *(Patrick Godfrey)*

Derry Hill [nr Bowood House; ST9570], *Lansdowne Arms*: Very pleasant relaxed atmosphere in attractively refurbished Victorian pub, soft lighting, lots of candles, well kept Wadworths and a guest beer, good choice of good value wines by the glass, interesting reasonably priced food, open fire, restaurant; garden with good play area, handy for Bowood *(Mrs Laura Gustine)*

Devizes [Market Pl; SU0061], *Black Swan*: Comfortable town-centre pub with good friendly atmosphere, good value food, well kept Wadworths; good bedrooms *(John and Christine Simpson)*; [Long St], *Elm Tree*: Welcoming heavy-beamed local, Italian food esp pizzas, well kept Wadworths, decent house wines, no-smoking area; piped music; restaurant, clean and tidy bedrooms *(N Rushton)*

☆ **East Knoyle** [The Street, off A350; ST8830], *Seymour Arms*: Pretty 17th-c pub, quiet and comfortable, with immaculately polished tables, good food from huge granary baguettes to properly presented freshly made hot dishes, plenty of fresh veg and real chips, eating area on left, china display, quotations on beams, well kept Wadworths ales, friendly Welsh landlady, efficient service; tables in garden with play area; bedrooms good value *(John and Joan Nash, Colin Fisher, Mrs W Dillon)*

☆ **Farleigh Wick** [A363 Bath—Bradford; ST8064], *Fox & Hounds*: Good fresh food served quickly by friendly helpful staff in welcoming low-beamed rambling bar, highly polished old oak tables and chairs, gently rural decorations; attractive garden; can get packed weekends *(Susan and Nigel Wilson, MRSM, Meg and Colin Hamilton, Andrew and Eileen Abbess, Lyn and Geoff Hallchurch)*

Farley [The Street; SU2229], *Hook & Glove*: Small chatty bar, emphasis on larger lounge/restaurant with good value good food (Italian influence), careful housekeeping, efficient careful service; piped music may obtrude; fine wooded countryside, good walking *(Phyl and Jack Street, Howard and Margaret Buchanan)*

Fovant [A30 Salisbury—Shaftesbury; SU0128], *Cross Keys*: Attractive former coaching inn, relaxing old-fashioned bar with end restaurant, consistently good food, log fire, efficient friendly service, Adnams and Gales HSB, decent coffee; bedrooms *(Ann and Colin Hunt, C and E M Watson)*

Great Bedwyn [SU2764], *Cross Keys*: Spacious and relaxed village pub with comfortable chairs and settles, Wadworths ales, generous bar food inc delicious ice cream; bedrooms – good walking country nr Kennet & Avon Canal *(Richard Burton)*

☆ **Great Hinton** [3½ miles E of Trowbridge, signed off A361 opp Lamb at Semington; ST9059], *Linnet*: Village pub refurbished to maximise dining space, good value home-made food from sandwiches up inc vegetarian, children's and good Sun lunch, good tables and chairs, well kept Wadworths IPA and 6X, decent house wines, friendly efficient service, walking-sticks for sale, unobtrusive piped music; children welcome, picnic-sets on front terrace, pretty village *(Colin and Joyce Laffan)*

Great Somerford [ST9682], *Volunteer*: Friendly local with well kept beer and limited choice of sensibly priced food; quiet village *(Pete and Rosie Flower)*

☆ **Hannington** [off B4019 W of Highworth; SU1793], *Jolly Tar*: Wide choice of good value honest food, well kept Arkells BB, BBB and Kingsdown, decent wines, welcoming ex-sailor landlord, big log fire in relaxing lounge bar, ships' crests on beams, stripped stone and flock wallpaper; games bar, skittle alley, upstairs grill room; maybe piped music; good robust play area in big garden, tables out in front too; pretty village *(Peter and Audrey Dowsett, TRS, G W A Pearce, BB)*

Haydon Wick [SU1387], *Manor Farm*: New pub in pleasantly extended former farmhouse, in huge housing estate; Banks's and Camerons Strongarm, extensive well priced menu; unobtrusive piped music *(Peter and Audrey Dowsett)*

☆ **Heddington** [off A3102 S of Calne; ST9966], *Ivy*: Basic thatched village pub with good inglenook fireplace in low-beamed bar, timbered walls, well kept Wadworths real ales tapped from the cask, bar food, children's room; seats outside the picturesque house *(Jerry and Alison Oakes, Tony Beaulah, LYM)*

Highworth [Swanborough; B4019, a mile W; SU1891], *Freke Arms*: Clean, comfortable, airy and friendly, four rooms on different levels, well kept ales inc Arkells 3B, good house wine, food inc wonderful sandwiches and straightforward hot dishes (nothing expensive), quick service, no piped music; small garden with play area *(Peter and Audrey Dowsett)*

Hodson [not far from M4 junction 15, via Chiseldon; SU1780], *Calley Arms*: Doing well under friendly and efficient current management, relaxed and welcoming big bar with open fire and dining area, good well priced food (not Mon evening), good range of well kept Wadworths ales with a guest, good choice of whiskies, country wines; children welcome, pleasant walk from Coate Water country park *(Andy Larter, Jeff Davies, R Mattick)*

Honeystreet [SU1061], *Barge*: Unspoilt canalside pub with charming almost 18th-c atmosphere in bar, well kept ales, pleasant pictures, wide range of home-made food from sandwiches to fresh trout, good prices, log fires; garden, bedrooms – nice setting, good downland walks *(T G Brierly, K R Harris)*

Horton [off A361 Devizes—Beckhampton; SU0463], *Bridge*: Good interesting food changing daily, generous but not cheap, in spacious pub by Kennet & Avon canal, partitioned into four well furnished areas with carpets or flagstones, dark wood and warm colours, good atmosphere, Wadworths IPA and 6X tapped from the cask, decent wines, log fire, prompt service, good restaurant; disabled lavatories, tables in garden *(June and Tony Baldwin, Ian Phillips, J R Bieneman, Tony Beaulah)*

Kington St Michael [handy for M4 junction 17;

ST9077], *Jolly Huntsman*: Roomy, with scrubbed tables and old-fashioned settees, good range of well kept changing ales (friendly landlord interested in them), good value promptly served fresh-cooked food inc vegetarian, open fire; maybe sports on TV; two cheap bedrooms *(G V Price, Dave and Deborah Irving)*

Lacock [22 Church St; ST9168], *Carpenters Arms*: Rambling bar done up carefully to look cottagey and old-fashioned, quickly served good standard home-made bar food (no sandwiches), well kept ales, restaurant, children in eating area; shame there's no car park; bedrooms *(Ann and Colin Hunt, LYM)*

☆ *nr* **Lacock** [Bowden Hill, Bewley Common – back rd to Sandy Lane, OS Sheet 173 map ref 935679], *Rising Sun*: Lovely spot with pretty garden and great views, mix of old chairs and basic kitchen tables on stone floors, stuffed animals and birds, country pictures, open fires, friendly newish licensees and locals, good range of Moles ales, food from sandwiches up, provision for children *(Derek and Sylvia Stephenson, Herbert and Susan Verity, Dagmar Junghanns, Colin Keane, Roger and Valerie Hill, Brian and Anna Marsden, LYM)*

Liddington [Bell Lane, just off A419 a mile from M4 junction 15; SU2081], *Village Inn*: Comfortable, warm and friendly local, dark oak panelling, dark oak and brick partitions and bar surround, settles in stripped stone and beamed back extension, Arkells beers, wide choice of food inc wide vegetarian range and popular Sun roasts (booking may be advisable then), log fire, conservatory; no children; bedrooms simple but clean *(Sam Samuells, Lynda Payton, JJW, CMW)*

Limpley Stoke [A36; ST7760], *Rose & Crown*: Good choice of beers, friendly manager, pleasant valley-view restaurant, concentration on fish *(Graham Brooks)*

Little Bedwyn [off A4 W of Hungerford; SU2966], *Harrow*: This attractive little pub closed in 1998; we hope that – as after previous closures – it will reopen *(LYM)*

☆ **Lockeridge** [signed off A4 Marlborough—Calne just W of Fyfield; SU1467], *Who'd A Thought It*: Welcoming village pub revitalised by enthusiastic new licensees, good well presented food (popular with older people midweek lunchtime), well kept Wadworths, log fire, separate public bar, family room; pleasant back garden with play area, delightful scenery, lovely walks *(Tony and June Baldwin, Jenny and Brian Seller, G J Gibbs, Pat Crabb, Mrs Laura Gustine)*

Longbridge Deverill [A350/B3095; ST8740], *George*: Engaging chef/patron doing good reasonably priced food in simple village pub, spacious and quiet, with well kept Gales, small restaurant *(Richard Tabor)*

☆ **Malmesbury** [Tetbury Hill, just S off B4014; ST9388], *Suffolk Arms*: Cheerful efficient service in knocked-through bar and big no-smoking panelled dining room, well kept Wadworths IPA and 6X and a changing guest beer, log fire, usual food well prepared; children welcome *(Mark Percy, Lesley Mayoh, D Irving, E McCall, R Huggins, T McLean, Mike and Grete Turner, LYM)*

☆ **Malmesbury** [62 High St; ST9287], *Smoking Dog*: Cosy beamed and stripped stone local, rather upmarket weekends, with big stripped pine tables, a beer brewed for the pub and changing well kept ales from casks behind bar, farm ciders, decent wines, good coffee, log fires, daily papers, board games, reference books, soft piped music; back bistro, garden; open all day, bedrooms *(Mark Percy, Lesley Mayoh, Dave and Deborah Irving, TBB)*

Malmesbury [29 High St], *Kings Arms*: Popular 16th-c town pub with two bars, good choice of well presented home-made food inc seafood, good value specials and lots of puddings, Whitbreads-related ales, pleasant restaurant; good courtyard garden, jazz last Sat of month; comfortable bedrooms *(Eric and Margarette Sibbit, D Irving, R Huggins, T McLean, E McCall)*

☆ **Manton** [High St; SU1768], *Up The Garden Path*: Good interesting freshly made food in very friendly extended village pub with largish beamed bar and no-smoking restaurant; well kept ales, decent wines; gets its name from steep path *(Tony Beaulah)*

☆ **Marlborough** [1 High St], *Bear*: Rambling well worn in Victorian inn with impressive central log fire, main bar and lounges on separate levels, well kept Arkells ales, cheerful service, generous often interesting food inc huge baguettes and good fish in old-fashioned side bar, small front lunchtime tapas bar (evening restaurant), medieval-style banqueting hall for special occasions, skittle alley, tables in small back courtyard *(HNJ, PEJ, Lyn and Geoff Hallchurch, Graham Fogelman)*

☆ **Mere** [Castle St (B3095, off A303); ST8132], *Old Ship*: Interesting 16th-c coaching inn famous for 17th-c carved fireplace with Charles I portrait; cosy hotel bar, spacious separate more pubby bar across coach entry divided by standing timbers, mix of old tables and chairs, buttoned leather wingback chairs, well kept Badger ales and Wadworths 6X, bar food, pub games and piped music, good value timbered and raftered restaurant; children allowed in eating area; good value bedrooms, picturesque village *(Derek Harvey-Piper, Alan and Paula McCully, LYM)*

Mere, *Talbot*: 16th-c inn, very much modernised but friendly, comfortable and cosy with open fire, enjoyable bar food inc good Sun lunch, cream teas, well kept Badger, back bar with machines and pool; comfortable bedrooms *(Alan and Paula McCully, BB)*

Mildenhall [SU2069], *Horseshoe*: Pleasantly relaxed, three clean and attractive partly partitioned rooms and small dining room, tasty food from baguettes and usual bar dishes to Indonesian food done by Dutch chef, good puddings, picnic-sets out on grass *(Mrs A Storm)*

☆ **North Newnton** [A345 Upavon—Pewsey; SU1257], *Woodbridge*: Open all day for enormous world-hopping choice of generous good value food inc imaginative vegetarian dishes in bar and small restaurant (should book Sun lunch), also afternoon teas; well kept Wadworths ales, good wines and coffee, good friendly service, log fire, newspapers and magazines; big streamside garden with boules, fishing available; good value bedrooms, good breakfast, small camping/caravan site *(Gordon, Kevin Flack, June and Tony Baldwin, Michelle Hayles, C Baxter, Martin and Karen Wake, Helen Pickering, James Owen)*

☆ **Nunton** [off A338 S of Salisbury; SU1526], *Radnor Arms*: Good interesting food esp fish and local game in lovely ivy-clad village pub with friendly helpful staff, inexpensive beers; three pleasantly decorated linked rooms inc cheerfully busy yet relaxing bar and staider restaurant; log fires, very friendly labrador; can get rather smoky if crowded; attractive garden popular with children *(Dr David Tomlinson, Dr D Twyman, Mark Barker, Tony Shepherd)*

Ogbourne St Andrew [SU1974], *Wheatsheaf*: Refurbished by new owners, with wide choice of generous food from baguettes up, well kept Bass and Worthington, extensive wine list, relaxed welcoming atmosphere even when busy; children welcome; back terrace *(Malcolm Richardson)*

☆ **Potterne** [A360; ST9958], *George & Dragon*: Steep steps up to convivial and homely traditional beamed bar, pool and darts in games room, usual bar food, well kept Wadworths 6X, friendly landlady and cat; small collection of antique farm tools, unique indoor .22 shooting range (can be booked by groups), skittle alley, pleasant garden and suntrap yard; well behaved children in eating area, cl Mon lunchtime; bedrooms *(David Warrellow, John Hayter, W W Burke, Mrs Laura Gustine, Peter and Audrey Dowsett, LYM)*

Ramsbury [Crowood Lane/Whittonditch Rd; SU2771], *Crown & Anchor*: Friendly and relaxed beamed village pub, good food, well kept Bass, Tetleys and usually a guest beer, open fires, pool in public bar; no piped music, children welcome, garden with terrace *(Mr and Mrs Peter Smith)*

Redlynch [N of B3080; SU2021], *Kings Head*: Comfortable cottagey 16th-c pub with wide choice of good generous food inc several vegetarian dishes, Ushers Best and Founders, friendly and helpful staff; seats in garden *(Bill and June Howard, C A Hall)*

☆ **Salisbury** [Town Path, W Harnham; SU1328], *Old Mill*: Former mill in lovely setting, with floodlit garden by millpond, view of cathedral a stroll across the meadows; simple but comfortable beamed bars (can get rather crowded and smoky), over 500 china and other ducks, well kept Boddingtons, Flowers Original, Hop Back GFB and Summer Lightning and a guest beer, decent malt whiskies and wines, friendly helpful staff, bar food inc imaginative dishes and good seafood, restaurant; children welcome, comfortable bedrooms, good breakfast *(Neil and Angela Huxter, Mr and Mrs P Spencer, Paul McPherson, Ian and Jacqui Ross, Tim Barrow, Sue Demont, Dr D Twyman, LYM)*

Salisbury [Fisherton St], *Deacons*: Clean, basic free house (possibly converted from shop or house), small front bar and back games room, wooden floorboards and jovial atmosphere; well kept Gales HSB, Ringwood Old Thumper and Wadworths 6X; bedrooms *(Jerry and Alison Oakes)*; [St John St], *Kings Arms*: Creaky old Tudor inn, darkly panelled and heavily beamed, with friendly staff, comfortable furnishings, Whitbreads-related ales, good choice of wines, restaurant; comfortable bedrooms *(N Thompson, Gordon, LYM)*; *Old Ale House*: Marvellous choice of changing ales *(Jerry and Alison Oakes, Veronica Brown)*; [Milford St], *Red Lion*: Mix of old-fashioned seats and modern banquettes in two-roomed nicely local-feeling panelled bar opening into other spacious and interesting areas, medieval restaurant, well kept Bass, Ushers, Wadworths 6X and a strong guest beer, lunchtime bar food, loggia courtyard seats; children in eating areas; bedrooms comfortable *(Jerry and Alison Oakes, N B Thompson, LYM)*; [Harnham Rd (off A338)], *Rose & Crown*: Worth a visit for the view – almost identical to that in the most famous Constable painting of Salisbury Cathedral; elegantly restored inn with friendly beamed and timbered bar, real ales, good well presented food inc good value restaurant meals, charming Avon-side dining terrace, picture-window bedrooms in smart modern extension as well as the more traditional ones in the original building *(F Willy, LYM)*

Sandy Lane [A342 Devizes—Chippenham; ST9668], *George*: Neat stonebuilt pub with pleasant atmosphere, wide choice of food inc unusual dishes, well kept Wadworths, decent wines, pleasant efficient service, interesting decor, bons mots chalked on beams; car park on dodgy bend *(M Wellington, June and Tony Baldwin, Peter Neate, LYM)*

Seend [Bell Hill (A361); ST9461], *Bell*: Four-room refurbished pub with cosy lounge, friendly efficient service, well kept Wadworths IPA and 6X, food from sandwiches to steaks in bar and tasteful upstairs restaurant (with good views), no music *(Lyn and Geoff Hallchurch, Dr and Mrs A K Clarke, J S Green, Pat and Tony Martin)*

☆ **Semington** [The Strand; A361 1½ miles E of A360 roundabout, nr Keevil; ST9259], *Lamb*: Cheerfully pubby series of rooms with helpful service, popular good value bar food inc some interesting dishes, well kept Butcombe, Ringwood Best and Shepherd Neame Spitfire, decent wines, good coffee, woodburner and log fire, children in eating area, tables out in colourful walled garden; can be smoky, cl Sun evening *(Peter Neate, Mr and Mrs Broadhurst, Mike Brearley, Lyn and Geoff Hallchurch, LYM)*

South Marston [SU1987], *Carriers Arms*: Vast choice of well presented food (not Sun evening) in enjoyably compact bar or restaurant, good licensees, good choice of beers inc Arkells, decent wine; no piped music *(Mr and Mrs*

Garrett)

South Newton [A36; SU0834], *Bell*: Quiet 17th-c inn refurbished with extended dining area, attentive friendly licensees, good value generous bar food, two or three well kept ales, friendly dog expert at catching beer mats; bedrooms, pleasant countryside with nice walks *(Dr and Mrs N Holmes)*

South Wraxall [off B3109 N of Bradford on Avon; ST8364], *Longs Arms*: Cheerful cosily refurbished country local with welcoming landlord, wide-ranging good reasonably priced food, well kept Bass and Wadworths, log fire, pretty garden *(A G Chesterton, Lyn and Geoff Hallchurch)*

☆ **Stapleford** [Warminster Rd (A36); SU0637], *Pelican*: Long bar with big dining area, well kept ales inc Bunces, Wadworths and changing rarities such as Otter, bargain prices by the jug, wide choice of freshly prepared food inc good value monster mixed grill – book Sat night or get there early; big riverside garden with play area, pleasant despite nearby road *(Howard and Margaret Buchanan, Jerry and Alison Oakes)*

☆ **Stibb Green** [just off A338 S of Marlborough; SU2262], *Three Horseshoes*: Friendly and spotless old-world pub with good choice of good reasonably priced home-made food, warmly welcoming landlord and staff, inglenook log fire in comfortable beamed front bar, well kept Wadworths ales, country wines, farm cider, dining room with railway memorabilia and pictures *(G F Woodroffe, TRS, Tony Hobden)*

Stockton [just off A36 Salisbury—Warminster, nr A303; ST9738], *Carriers*: Pretty village pub in Wylye valley, well kept beer, decent wine, good service, very wide food choice inc good puddings; new owners *(PW, RW, Meredith and Don Binsacca)*

☆ **Stourton** [Church Lawn; follow Stourhead signpost off B3092, N of junction with A303 just W of Mere; ST7734], *Spread Eagle*: NT pub in lovely setting at head of Stourhead lake (though views from pub itself not special), front bar with open fire, settles and country decor, cool and spacious civilised back dining room popular mainly with older people; standard food, Ash Vine, Bass and Wadworths 6X, friendly waitress service, tables in back courtyard; bedrooms *(Alan and Paula McCully, Meg and Colin Hamilton, G W A Pearce, LYM)*

Swindon [Bridge St/Regent St; SU1485], *Father Teds*: Arkells pub, former Lamb & Flag newly done up in Irish theme, with matching food, Guinness (with shamrock) and music (can be loud); also Arkells BB and BBB, flagstones and mosaic tiles, panelling, screened seating areas, Victorian fireplaces, beamed back area *(Sam Samuells, Lynda Payton)*; [Emlyn Sq], *Glue Pot*: Bare-boards tap for Archers Brewery, with their Village, Best, Golden and Headbanger kept well, and a guest such as Moles Best; high-backed settles, friendly locals, pub games, seats outside – in Brunel's Railway Village; open all day (cl Sun afternoon) *(Richard Lewis, Andy and Jill Kassube)*; [Devizes Rd], *Hobgoblin*: Bare boards, dark wood, old brewery signs, well kept Wychwood Special and Fiddlers Elbow with guests such as Courage Best and Wadworths 6X, friendly staff, pinball; juke box, big screen TV, can get noisy, crowded and smoky; terrace, live music Thurs, open all day (cl Sun afternoon) *(Richard Lewis)*; [Wood St, Old Town], *Kings Arms*: Comfortable and spacious Victorian hotel with well kept Arkells Bitter, BB, BBB and Kingsdown, friendly staff, good reasonably priced lunchtime food, disabled access; bedrooms *(Richard Lewis)*; [6 Albert St], *Rising Sun*: Backstreet local with tiny flagstoned lounge, friendly welcome, well kept Courage Best and Ushers Best, Founders and a seasonal ale, darts, pool, juke box and TV in basic bar; open all day *(Richard Lewis)*; [Regent St], *Savoy*: Wetherspoons, with split-level seating areas in spacious converted cinema lined with books and film memorabilia, comfortable atmosphere, several real ales, decent wine, good menu and very moderate prices, quick friendly service; popular with all ages, no music, no-smoking areas *(Peter and Audrey Dowsett)*

Upavon [3 High St; A345/A342; SU1355], *Antelope*: Friendly pub with log fire and local RAF memorabilia in lounge bar, some emphasis on food in bar and restaurant, five well kept real ales, small bow-windowed games area; bedrooms *(Dr and Mrs A K Clarke, LYM)*

Upton Scudamore [ST8647], *Angel*: Old whitewashed village pub off the beaten track, with good food and beer; stained glass in main bar *(Pat and Robert Watt)*

Wanborough [Callas Hill, 2 miles from M4 junction 15; former B4507 towards Bishopstone; SU2083], *Black Horse*: Delightfully unspoilt country local with lovely downland views, beams and tiled floor, open fires in both bars, popular new licensees, lunchtime food, well kept competitively priced Arkells Bitter, BBB and seasonal ales; informal elevated garden with play area *(LP, SS, Andy Larter)*; [Burycroft, Lower Wanboro], *Cross Keys*: Doing well under friendly current management, well kept real ales, good choice of food *(Jeff Davies)*; [High St, Lower Wanboro], *Harrow*: Pretty thatched pub with friendly two-level refurbished beamed main bar, big stone fireplace and bay window alcoves, real ales such as Brakspears, Hook Norton Old Hookey, Morlands Old Speckled Hen, Youngs Special, bar food, simple stripped stone dining room; tables on small terrace *(Lynda Payton, Sam Samuells, E McCall, R Huggins, T McLean, Brian Clegg)*; [High St, Lower Wanboro], *Plough*: Long low thatched stone pub with good friendly atmosphere, three old-world rooms with huge centrepiece log fire in one, another more or less for evening dining; real ales inc Archers Village, Bass and Wadworths 6X, good interesting home-made food (not Sun), bar billiards; open all day Sat *(Andy and Jill Kassube, E McCall, R Huggins, T McLean)*; [Foxhill, 1½ miles towards Baydon; SU2381], *Shepherds Rest*: Remote, friendly and unassuming Ridgeway pub popular with local racing people, long lounge and dining extension, half a dozen well kept ales such as Badger and Flowers IPA, wide choice of reasonably priced food, log fire, lots of pictures, pool room, restaurant; piped music; picnic-sets and play area outside; children and walkers welcome, very busy in summer, camping *(Brian Clegg, HNJ, PEJ, JJW, CMW, Giles Francis)*

West Lavington [A360; SU0053], *Staging Post*: Ushers pub, former Wheatsheaf, with good choice of sensibly priced food, good evening menu, fairly young licensees *(Colin and Joyce Laffan, Dr and Mrs A Newton)*

Westwood [off B3109 S of Bradford on Avon; ST8059], *New Inn*: Cheerful beamed country pub with wide choice of good value home-made food running up to kangaroo and red mullet, several rooms attractively opened together, well kept Bass, Adnams and Wadworths 6X, lots of brasses, good fire; no-smoking cellar bar *(Susan and Nigel Wilson)*

☆ **Wilcot** [signed off A345 N of Pewsey, and in Pewsey itself; SU1360], *Golden Swan*: Very pretty old steeply thatched pub nr Kennet & Avon Canal, unpretentiously welcoming, lots of china hanging from beams of two small rooms, well kept Wadworths IPA and 6X and in winter Old Timer, friendly retriever and prize-winning cat, good value home-made bar food (not Sun evening or Mon), dining room, games room with bar billiards; rustic tables on pretty front lawn, field with camping, occasional folk and barbecue weekends, children welcome; good value simple bedrooms, big and airy *(Ann and Colin Hunt, Angus Lyon, LYM)*

Wilton [A30; SU0931], *Pembroke Arms*: Very courteous and efficient service in clean pub with good menu inc particularly good salads; leaving car park may be difficult *(C and E M Watson)*

Wilton [the much smaller village S of Gt Bedwyn; SU2661], *Swan*: Warm and friendly simple pub with wide variety of enjoyable food – good for family lunches; real ales such as Boddingtons, Hook Norton, Wadworths 6X, pool; children welcome, garden with small play area, picturesque village with windmill, handy for Crofton Beam Engines *(Paul Fleckney, Nick Holmes)*

☆ **Wingfield** [B3109 S of Bradford; ST8256], *Poplars*: Attractive and friendly country local with decent food inc fine steak sandwich, well kept Wadworths, quick pleasant service, enjoyable atmosphere, no juke box or machines, no children; own cricket pitch – new landlord a keen cricketer *(Steven Bertram, Susan and Nigel Wilson, BB)*

☆ **Winterbourne Bassett** [off A4361 S of Swindon; SU0975], *White Horse*: Attractively restored 1920s pub in lovely countryside, newish dining conservatory, well kept Wadworths and occasional guest beers, limited choice of decent fresh food (may be a wait if busy) inc several fish dishes, cheerful friendly service, huge goldfish in tank on bar; seats outside *(June and Tony Baldwin, CMW, JJW)*

Wootton Bassett [Swindon Rd; A420 just off M4 junction 16; SU1082], *Sally Pusseys*: Named for former landlady; good choice of generous unpretentious food at sensible prices from filled rolls to super puddings, helpful friendly staff, busy main bar, lower restaurant; mainly dining, but well kept Arkells, good coffee *(Mrs B Sugarman, Alan Vere, RL)*

☆ **Wootton Rivers** [signed off A345, A346 and B3087 S of Marlborough; SU1963], *Royal Oak*: Extended 16th-c thatched pub with wide choice of food in pleasantly furnished L-shaped dining lounge, games in area off timbered bar, well kept Wadworths 6X tapped from the cask and a guest ale on handpump, interesting whiskies, particularly good wines, restaurant, fresh flowers; children welcome, tables under cocktail parasols in back yard, bedrooms in adjoining house, attractive village *(C Baxter, Pat Crabb, Charles and Pauline Stride, Mrs Laura Gustine, Brian and Bett Cox, A C Curry, TRS, Dr Paul Khan, Julie Peters, Colin Blinkhorn, Mr and Mrs Tew, LYM; more reports please)*

☆ **Wylye** [High St; just off A303/A36 junction; SU0037], *Bell*: Nicely set in peaceful village, smartish feel, black beams, timbering, stripped masonry, three log fires, sturdy rustic furnishings, Badger beers, wide choice of food, no-smoking area, side eating area; may be piped music; children welcome, fine downland walks; bedrooms *(Carole Smart, Andrew Jeeves, Gordon, John and Vivienne Rice, Howard and Barbara Cluttbuck, Phyl and Jack Street, Pat and Robert Watt, Derek Stafford, LYM)*

Bedroom prices are for high summer. Even then you may get reductions for more than one night, or (outside tourist areas) weekends. Winter special rates are common, and many inns cut bedroom prices if you have a full evening meal.

Yorkshire

A fine crop of new entries here is headed by the relaxed and stylish Jefferson Arms at Thorganby (delightfully run by sisters who'd spent many years in Switzerland before returning here recently), and the Crown at Great Ouseburn (an engaging village pub run by an ex Leeds United man). Both have good food, as do the General Tarleton at Ferrensby and the interesting Boars Head at Ripley; while the Wellington at Lund is a reliable dining pub in a part of Yorkshire where such establishments are at quite a premium. The honours roll-call among longer-established main entries here is a long one: the friendly Ship at Aldborough (good all round), the Crab & Lobster at Asenby (exceptional food, but managing to keep a warmly pubby atmosphere), the interesting and well run Kings Arms at Askrigg (they have a good chef these days), the charmingly unspoilt Birch Hall at Beck Hole, the Black Bull in Boroughbridge (a really good all-rounder), the Malt Shovel at Brearton (another fine all-rounder, gaining a Beer Award this year, though its real forte is the very good food), the Red Lion in its prime spot at Burnsall (good food, nice place to stay), the rather restauranty Foresters Arms at Carlton, the Devonshire Arms at Cracoe (taken over by Jennings since it was last in these pages a few years ago, with a good manager), the stylish old Blue Lion at East Witton (super food), the friendly and enjoyable Horse Shoe tucked away at Egton Bridge, the Angel at Hetton (very popular for food), the beautifully set unchanging old George at Hubberholme, the George & Dragon in Kirkbymoorside (some careful refurbishments, good food, excellent wine list), the bustling Chequers at Ledsham (this old favourite now brews its own beer), Will's o' Nat's at Meltham (another really thriving place, well run and friendly), the nicely set Dawnay Arms at Newton on Ouse (its present management has settled in extremely well), the Three Tuns at Osmotherley (this little gem gains a Food Award this year), the White Hart at Pool (new manager doing well), the civilised and relaxing Yorke Arms at Ramsgill (gains both a Food Award and a Wine Award this year), the Kings Arms at Redmire (exemplary country local), the beautifully set Milburn Arms at Rosedale Abbey, the Fat Cat in Sheffield (splendid real ales yet not too beery – with really good value food, too), the Three Acres at Shelley (hardly a pub, but very enjoyable for food including exquisite sandwiches, and for beers and wine), the sparkling little Fox & Hounds at Starbotton (good food, a nice place to stay – and we can personally vouch for the hill walks over to the George at Hubberholme, though we admit to taking the short cut back, along the river), the St Vincent Arms at Sutton upon Derwent (lots of well kept beers, good friendly service, enjoyable food), the Wombwell Arms at Wass (emphasis on good imaginative food), and the friendly Duke of York overlooking the harbour, at the bottom of the Abbey Steps in Whitby. From among the pubs which stand out particularly for food in this distinguished group, we choose the Malt Shovel at Brearton as Yorkshire Dining Pub of the Year – a winning combination of friendly pub atmosphere with consistently rewarding cooking. The Lucky Dip section at the end of the chapter is rich in possibilities. Places which came out particularly well on inspection by us, or which readers have enthused strongly about (or more usually both), are the Plough at Allerthorpe, Falcon at Arncliffe, Cadeby Inn at Cadeby, Plough at Fadmoor, Kaye Arms at Grange Moor, Cow & Calf at Grenoside, Shears in Halifax, Star at Harome, Rat & Ratchet in Huddersfield, Fountain at Ingbirchworth, Shoulder of Mutton at Kirby Hill, Spite just above Otley, Cubley Hall at Penistone, Hare at Scawton, Railway at Spofforth, Rose & Crown at Sutton on the Forest, Tan Hill Inn at Tan Hill, Marton Arms at Thornton in Lonsdale and Rockingham Arms at Wentworth. The Cragg Lodge at Wormald Green deserves a special word for its unrivalled collection of malt whiskies, as do the Riverhead in Marsden and Crown in Malton for the beers they brew; the Black Sheep Brewery in Masham now has a fine visitor centre. Drinks prices here are well below the national average, but recently have been rising a little more quickly than elsewhere. We found pubs tied to the local Sam Smiths and Clarks were much cheaper than most, and also found cheap beer in the two Sheffield pubs, and in the St Vincent Arms in Sutton upon Derwent.

ALDBOROUGH (N Yorks) SE4166 Map 7

Ship

Village signposted from B6265 just S of Boroughbridge, close to A1

As well as being a focal point for the social life in the village this neatly kept and attractive old pub offers a friendly welcome to visitors, too. The heavily beamed bar has some old-fashioned seats around heavy cast-iron tables, sentimental engravings and lots of copper and brass on the walls, and a coal fire in the stone inglenook fireplace. Good bar food includes sandwiches (from £1.95; open ones from £4.25), home-made soup (£2), garlic mushrooms (£3.60), ploughman's (£4.75), giant yorkshire pudding with roast beef (£5.25), home-made steak and kidney pie or lasagne (£5.50), home-made chicken curry (£5.95), battered cod (£6.50), steaks (from £7.95), and good, often interesting daily specials; good breakfasts and friendly brisk service. Well kept John Smiths and Tetleys Bitter on handpump, and quite a few malt whiskies; shove-ha'penny, dominoes, and piped music. There are seats on the front terrace or on the spacious lawn behind. There's an ancient church opposite, and the pub is near the Roman town with its museum and Roman pavements. *(Recommended by Comus Elliott, Mrs P Forrest, John R Ringrose, Martin Hickes, A J L Gayfer, Michael Butler, T M Dobby, Mr and Dr J Harrop)*

Free house ~ Licensee Duncan Finch ~ Real ale ~ Meals and snacks (not Sun evening) ~ Restaurant (not Sun evening) ~ (01423) 322749 ~ Children in eating area of bar and in restaurant (not suitable for small children as no facilities) ~ Open 12-2.30, 5.30-11; 11-11 Sat; 12-3, 7-10.30 Sun ~ Bedrooms: £32S/£45S

APPLETREEWICK (N Yorks) SE0560 Map 7

Craven Arms

Village signposted off B6160 Burnsall—Bolton Abbey

This is a lovely spot and the creeper-covered pub is well liked by walkers. The view from the picnic-sets in front of the building is splendid, looking south over the green Wharfedale valley to a pine-topped ridge; there are more seats in the back garden. Inside, the small cosy rooms have roaring fires (one in an ancient iron range), attractive settles and carved chairs among more usual seats, beams covered with banknotes, harness, copper kettles and so forth, and a warm atmosphere; the landlord is quite a character. Bar food includes home-made soup (£2), sandwiches (from £2.10), potted shrimps (£3.20), ploughman's (£4), cumberland sausage and onion sauce (£5.20), home-made steak and kidney pie (£5.20), ham and eggs (£6.15), steaks (from £8.70); the little no-smoking dining room is charming. Well kept Black Sheep Bitter and Special, Tetleys Bitter, and Theakstons Best and Old Peculier on handpump, decent, keenly priced wines, and several malt whiskies; darts, cribbage, and dominoes – no music. They have a self-catering cottage. *(Recommended by K Hogarth, David Edwards, Richard and Valerie Wright, B and M Kendall, M Buchanan, P R White, Paul and Madeleine Morey, John Fazakerley, Judith Hirst, Gwen and Peter Andrews, Andrew and Ruth Triggs)*

Free house ~ Licensees Jim and Linda Nicholson ~ Real ale ~ Meals and snacks (not Tues evening) ~ Restaurant ~ (01756) 720270 ~ Children in eating area of bar ~ Open 11.30-3, 6.30-11; 12-3, 7-10.30 Sun

ASENBY (N Yorks) SE3975 Map 7

Crab & Lobster ★

Village signposted off A168 – handy for A1

The licensees continue to offer exceptional food in this very popular thatched dining pub while keeping a good pubby atmosphere – not an easy thing to achieve. There's a lot of character in the rambling, cosily cluttered L-shaped bar, and an interesting jumble of seats from antique high-backed and other settles through settees and wing armchairs heaped with cushions to tall and rather theatrical corner seats and even a very superannuated dentist's chair; the tables are almost as much of a mix, and the walls and available surfaces are quite a jungle of bric-a-brac, with standard and table lamps and candles keeping even the lighting pleasantly informal. Changing constantly, the much enjoyed food might include ravioli of spinach and ricotta with sage butter, terrine of charred vegetables or feta cheese and virgin olive oil (£5), seafood bruschetta, lunchtime fish club sandwich or chicken livers, queenie scallops and bacon salad (£5.50), thai fish salad (£6.50), baked goat's cheese and burnt onions in filo with honeycomb salad (£8.50), seafood paella or braised lamb with sausage moussaka (£10.50), fish wellington with shellfish cream (£11.50), crisp duck confit, black pudding and pineapple pickle (£12), calf liver, sage and onion rosti and crisp bacon (£12.50), and puddings like baked chocolate mousse with whisky cream, cherry bakewell tart with clotted cream or baked egg custard tart with nutmeg ice cream (£4.50); lovely chocolates with the coffee; good value set lunch, and usually nibbles on the bar counter. Bass, Black Sheep, Theakstons Best, and Timothy Taylor Landlord on handpump, and good wines by the glass, with interesting bottles; well reproduced piped music. There's a sizeable garden, and a mediterranean-style terrace in front of the pub for outside eating; wood-stove barbecues every Friday evening and Sunday lunchtime with entertainment during the spring and summer, weather permitting. A permanent marquee is attached to the no-smoking restaurant. The bedrooms are in the surrounding country house which has three acres of mature gardens, tennis court and 180 metre golf hole with full practice facilities. *(Recommended by Susan and John Douglas, ALC, Julie Sage, George Green, Allan Worsley, Walker and Debra Lapthorne, Nick and Alison Dowson, Tony Hall, Melanie Jackson, Pat Bruce, Stephen and Brenda Head, T Halstead)*

Free house ~ Licensees David and Jackie Barnard ~ Real ale ~ Meals and snacks ~ Restaurant ~ (01845) 577286 ~ Children welcome ~ Regular jazz/blues evenings ~ Open 11.30-3, 6.30-11; 12-11 summer Sun; 12-3, 6.30-11 winter Sun ~ Bedrooms: £58B/£68B

ASKRIGG (N Yorks) SD9591 Map 10

Kings Arms

Village signposted from A684 Leyburn—Sedbergh in Bainbridge

The fine countryside that surrounds this early 19th-c coaching inn (it was converted from its original use as a famous racing stables in 1810) probably inspired both Turner and Wordsworth who stayed here. There are three atmospheric, old-fashioned bars with lots of mementoes and photographs of the filming of James Herriot's *All Creatures Great and Small* – the inn itself, in the series, was the Drovers Arms. The very high-ceilinged central room has an attractive medley of furnishings that includes a fine sturdy old oak settle, 19th-c fashion plates, a stag's head, hunting prints, and a huge stone fireplace; a curving wall with a high window shows people bustling up and down the stairs and there's a kitchen hatch in the panelling. The small low-beamed and oak panelled front bar has period furnishings, some side snugs, and a lovely green marble fireplace. A simply furnished flagstoned back bar has yet another fire, and a juke box. Darts, pool, shove-ha'penny, dominoes, and cribbage. Enjoyable food can be eaten in the bars or the no-smoking, waitress-served Silks Grill Room, and under the new chef might include home-made soup (£2.50), pigeon en croûte (£3.25), stir-fried vegetables (£5), grated potato pancake with bacon and onions topped with cheese and poached eggs (£5.50), pasta with garlic and pimento baked under a salami and mozzarella crust (£6), cantonese chicken or steak in ale pie (£6.50), steaks (from £9.50), 16oz barnsley chop with a sherry and mushroom sauce (£9.95), daily specials, puddings like hot chocolate pudding with chocolate sauce or home-made cheesecake (£2.95), and children's dishes (from £1.95); good breakfasts. The Club Room is also no smoking. Well kept Dent Bitter, Morlands Old Speckled Hen, John Smiths, Theakstons XB, and Youngers No 3 on handpump, quite a few malt whiskies, and a very good wine list (including interesting champagnes); pleasant, helpful staff. The two-level courtyard has lots of tables and chairs. This is a lovely village. *(Recommended by B Kneale, K F Mould, Bob and Maggie Atherton, Suzy Miller, Bruce Bird, Walter and Susan Rinaldi-Butcher, RWD, R H Rowley, B Edgeley, Gwen and Peter Andrews, Andrew and Ruth Triggs; also in the Good Hotel Guide)*

Free house ~ Licensees Raymond and Elizabeth Hopwood ~ Real ale ~ Meals and snacks (served all day in summer) ~ Restaurants ~ (01969) 650258 ~ Children welcome but must be over 10 in main restaurant ~ Occasional live entertainment ~ Open 11-11; 11-3(5 Sat), 6.30-11 in winter; 12-3, 7-10.30 Sun ~ Bedrooms: £50B/£79B

AYSGARTH (N Yorks) SE0088 Map 10

George & Dragon

The lovely scenery of Upper Wensleydale surrounds this 17th-c coaching inn, and there are plenty of fine walks and woodland wildlife. The small, cosy and attractive bar has built-in cushioned wooden wall seats and plush stools around a few pubby tables, tankards, jugs, and copper pots hanging from the thick beams, portraits of locals by the landlord on the panelled walls, a warm open fire with a dark wooden mantlepiece, and high bar stools by the decorative wooden bar; well kept Black Sheep Bitter, John Smiths, Tetleys Bitter, and Theakstons Best on handpump. There's also a polished hotel lounge with antique china, and a grandfather clock; friendly obliging service. A lot of emphasis is placed on the food which can be eaten in the bar or two other attractive no-smoking dining areas. At lunchtime this might include home-made soup (£2.50), sandwiches (£2.95; hot baps from £3.75), home-made chicken liver or trout pâté (£3.95), filled baked potatoes (£4.25), three-egg omelettes (from £5.50), ploughman's (£5.95), cumberland sausage (£6.25), mushroom and tomato crumble (£6.50), fresh battered haddock (£6.95), gammon with two eggs (£7.95), and venison casserole (£8.75); a larger choice in the evening takes in king prawns in garlic and tomato butter (£3.95), sweet and sour chicken (£8.25), poached salmon with a cream and cucumber sauce (£8.95), duckling and orange sauce (£10.95), and steaks (from £10.95). Piped music, and a grey and white cat called Smokey. Outside on the gravelled beer garden are some picnic-sets and tubs of pretty flowers. *(Recommended by Mrs Y M Lippett, Ray and Liz Monk, Charles and Pauline Stride, David and Judy Walmsley, Clare Wilson, Hazel and Michael Duncombe, Pat and Clive Sherriff; more reports please)*

Free house ~ Licensees Nigel and Joanne Fawcett ~ Real ale ~ Meals and snacks (12-2, 6-9) ~ (01969) 663358 ~ Children welcome ~ Open 11-3, 6-11; 12-3, 6-10.30 Sun ~ Bedrooms: £32B/£57B

BARDSEY (W Yorks) SE3643 Map 7

Bingley Arms 🍷

Church Lane, off A58 Leeds—Wetherby

There are records of brewing here in 953 and this historic place was connected with Kirkstall Abbey and used by the monks. The large lounge area, with a huge fireplace (the chimney contains a priest hole), is divided into several more intimate areas including a no-smoking part, and there are all sorts of interesting features – most picturesque of all is the upstairs brasserie. There's a smaller public bar; darts, dominoes, fruit machine, TV, and piped music. Bought from the brewery only a couple of years or so ago, the inn seems to have come into its own now, with a really friendly atmosphere and speedy pleasant service. Totally home-made food using fresh produce changes daily and might include home-made soup (£2.50), filled ciabatta or french sticks (from £3.95), bangers and mash (£5.95), sweet and sour chicken (£5.95), popular jumbo haddock (£6.95), fresh fish dishes, steaks, and puddings; they offer a good value 2-course meal (between 5.30 and 6.45pm, £5.95). Well kept Black Sheep Bitter, John Smiths, and Tetleys Bitter on handpump, good wines. There are tables out in a charming quiet terraced garden, and barbecues out here run to inventive herby vegetarian dishes as well as the usual meats. *(Recommended by Roger Kiddier, Martin Hickes, Sue Blackburn, Drs A and A C Jackson, Andy and Jill Kassube; more reports please)*

Free house ~ Licensees Jim and Jan Wood ~ Real ale ~ Meals and snacks (12-2.30, 5.30-9.30) ~ Restaurant ~ (01937) 572462 ~ Well behaved children welcome ~ Live band Mon evenings ~ Open 12-3.30 5.30-11; 12-11 (10.30 Sun)Sat; closed Mon lunchtime

BECK HOLE (N Yorks) NZ8202 Map 10

Birch Hall

'Delightful' and an 'unspoilt haven' are just two descriptions used by readers here. It's a unique and unchanging pub cum village shop with two rooms – one is the shop selling postcards, sweeties and ice creams in between, and there is hatch service to both sides. Furnishings are simple – built-in cushioned wall seats and wooden tables and chairs on the floor (flagstones in one room, composition in the other), and well kept ales such as Black Sheep Bitter, Theakstons Black Bull, and local guest beers on handpump. Bar snacks such as butties (£1.80), locally-made pies (£1.20), and home-made scones and cakes including their lovely beer cake (from 60p); friendly, welcoming staff. Outside, an ancient mural hangs on the pub wall, there are benches out in front, and steep steps up to a charming little steeply terraced side garden with an aviary and a nice view. This is a lovely spot with marvellous surrounding walks – you can walk along the disused railway line from Goathland. *(Recommended by Bruce Bird, Andy and Jill Kassube, Nick and Alison Dowson, Peter Smith)*

Free house ~ Licensee Colin Jackson ~ Real ale ~ Snacks (available throughout opening hours) ~ (01947) 896245 ~ Children in small family room ~ Parking is difficult, so park in the nearest car park ~ Open 11-11; 11-3, 7.30-11 in winter; 12-10.30 summer Sun; closed winter Mon evenings

BEVERLEY (E Yorks) TA0340 Map 8

White Horse ('Nellies') £

Hengate, close to the imposing Church of St Mary's; runs off North Bar Within

This determinedly traditional old pub has a carefully preserved Victorian feel, though it dates from much earlier. The basic but very atmospheric little rooms are huddled together around the central bar, with brown leatherette seats (high-backed settles in one little snug) and basic wooden chairs and benches on bare floorboards, antique cartoons and sentimental engravings on the nicotine-stained walls, a gaslit pulley-controlled chandelier, a deeply reverberating chiming clock, and open fires – one with an attractively tiled old fireplace. Well kept and very cheap Sam Smiths OBB on handpump. Cheap, simple food includes sandwiches (from £1.30; toasties £2.30), home-made yorkshire pudding and gravy (£1.50), filled baked potatoes (£2.30), egg and bacon (£2.90), home-made steak pie or meaty or vegetarian lasagne (£3.95), a roast of the day, and puddings like fruit crumble or jam roly-poly (£1.75). A separate games room has pinball, fruit machine, juke box, and two pool tables – these and the no-smoking room behind the bar are the only modern touches. Those whose tastes are for comfortable modern pubs may find it a little spartan, anyone else will quickly feel at home. *(Recommended by David Carr, Pete Baker, Paul and Pam Penrose, Stephen, Julie and Hayley Brown, Rona Murdoch)*

Sam Smiths ~ Manager John Etherington ~ Real ale ~ Lunchtime meals and snacks (not Mon) ~ (01482) 861973 ~ Children welcome away from bar ~ Folk Mon, jazz Weds, poetry and music night 1st Thurs of month – all poets/musicians welcome ~ Open 11-11; 12-10.30 Sun; closed 25 Dec

BILBROUGH (N Yorks) SE5346 Map 7

Three Hares

Off A64 York—Tadcaster

By the time this book is published, new licensees will have taken over this busy dining pub. They were planning to keep on the same kitchen brigade and front of house staff, so we are keeping our fingers crossed that things won't change too much. The very good bar food has included home-made soup, chicken liver parfait with toasted onion bread and apple and mustard relish (£3.95), pan-seared king scallops, (£5.25), steak and mushroom casserole or Whitby fish pie (£6.95), stilton and onion tart with red pepper salsa (£7.95), sirloin steak or caramelised fillet of pork with couscous, roasted vegetables and sweet chilli sauce (£9.95), duck breast with wild mushroom risotto (£10.50), daily fish specials, and puddings like bread and butter pudding, summer fruit parfait with passion fruit coulis, and apple tart tatin with blueberry ice cream (£3.25). Well kept Black Sheep Bitter, and Timothy Taylor Landlord on handpump, and eleven wines by the glass. The old village smithy forms part of the no-smoking restaurant and the old forge and implement hooks are still visible; the prettily papered walls of the traditional bar are hung with pictures of the village (taken in 1904 and showing that little has changed since then), and there's plenty of polished copper and brass. The churchyard close to the pub is where Sir Thomas Fairfax, famous for his part in the Civil War, lies buried. *(Recommended by R Inman, Pat and Tony Martin, H Bramwell, R Grace, Joy and Peter Heatherley, William Cunliffe; more reports on the new regime, please)*

Free house ~ Lease: Peter and Sheila Whitehead ~ Real ale ~ Meals and snacks (not Mon) ~ Restaurant (not Sun evening or Mon) ~ (01937) 832128 ~ Well behaved children in eating area of bar and over 10 in restaurant, but must be gone by 8pm ~ Open 12-2.30, 7(6.30 Fri/Sat)-11; 12-3, 7-10 Sun; closed Mon (except bank holidays), 25 Dec and evenings 26 Dec and 1 Jan

BLAKEY RIDGE (N Yorks) SE6799 Map 10

Lion

From A171 Guisborough—Whitby follow Castleton, Hutton le Hole signposts; from A170 Kirkby Moorside—Pickering follow Keldholm, Hutton le Hole, Castleton signposts; OS Sheet 100 map reference 679996

At peak times, this isolated 16th-c inn does get very busy, but there's a good mix of customers, and the food remains reliably good. The views from here are stunning and the pub is said to be the fourth highest in England (1325 ft up). The cosy and characterful beamed and rambling bars have a bustling, friendly atmosphere, warm open fires, a few big high-backed rustic settles around cast-iron-framed tables, lots of small dining chairs on the turkey carpet, a nice leather settee, and stripped stone walls hung with some old engravings and photographs of the pub under snow (it can easily get cut off in winter). As well as lunchtime sandwiches (£2.45) and ploughman's (£4.45), the bar food includes soup or giant yorkshire pudding and gravy (£1.95), home-cooked ham and egg, pure beefburgers, home-made steak and mushroom pie, home-made vegetable lasagne, mushroom balti, and beef curry (all £5.95), deep-fried king prawns (£6.75), pork fillet with apple and white wine sauce (£6.95), sirloin steak (£8.95), puddings like sticky toffee pudding, treacle roly-poly or apple pie (£2.45), and children's menu (£3.25). One of the restaurants is no smoking. Well kept Morlands Old Speckled Hen, John Smiths, Tetleys Bitter, and Theakstons Best, Old Peculier, Black Bull and XB on handpump; dominoes, fruit machine and piped music. *(Recommended by M Borthwick, Piotr Chodzko-Zajko, Geoffrey and Irene Lindley, Paul Barnett, Brian Seller, Stephen, Julie and Hayley Brown)*

Free house ~ Licensee Barry Crossland ~ Real ale ~ Meals and snacks (8.30am-10.30pm) ~ Restaurant ~ (01751) 417320 ~ Children welcome ~ Open 10.30am-11pm; 10.30-10.30 Sun ~ Bedrooms: £16.50(£35B)/£47(£55B)

BOROUGHBRIDGE (N Yorks) SE3967 Map 7

Black Bull

St James Square (B6265, just off A1(M))

Apart from being a comfortable and enjoyable place to stay, this lovely 13th-c inn also has good, interesting food, well kept beers, and a friendly atmosphere. The main bar area, with a big stone fireplace and brown leather seats, is served through an old-fashioned hatch, and there's a cosy and attractive snug with traditional wall settles. The well presented food is totally home-made (bread rolls, pasta, sorbets, ice creams) and is served in the bar and extended dining room: soup (£2.25), lunchtime sandwiches (from £2.75; not Sunday; ciabatta rolls from £4.95), thai spiced noodle broth with peanuts and chilli (£3.50), omelettes (from £3.95), pasta with black olives and peppers and a tomato herb sauce (£4.95), yorkshire pudding filled with lamb casserole braised in real ale gravy (£5.75), home-made pie of the day (£5.95), stir-fried chicken and vegetables with a thai sweet and sour sauce (£6.75), chargrilled steaks (from £10.95), daily specials, puddings and warm chocolate pecan tart with whisky fudge sauce, caramelised apple tart tatin or tangy lemon cheesecake with a thick raspberry compote (£3.25); they hold themed food nights, too. Well kept Black Sheep Bitter, Hambleton Bitter, and John Smiths on handpump, enjoyable wines (with 10 by the glass), proper coffee – and they do afternoon teas (not on Sunday). Service is friendly and attentive; the fat ginger cat is called Sprocket. Cribbage, dominoes, shove-ha'penny, chess and Captain's Lady; classical piped music in the restaurant. The comfortable bedrooms are in a more modern wing; good breakfasts. *(Recommended by Richard and Robyn Wain, Alyson and Andrew Jackson, Phil Revell, Julie Peters, Michael and Hazel Duncombe, Roger Byrne, Miss J Hirst, James Nunns, Andy and Jill Kassube, Michael Butler)*

Free house ~ Licensees Margaret Chrystal, Terry McKenne ~ Real ale ~ Meals and snacks (not 25 Dec, 1 Jan) ~ Restaurant ~ (01423) 322413 ~ Children in eating area of bar ~ Open 11-11; 12-10.30 Sun ~ Bedrooms: £37B/£49B

nr BRADFIELD (S Yorks) SK2692 Map 7

Strines Inn

Strines signposted from A616 at head of Underbank Reservoir, W of Stocksbridge; or on A57 heading E of junction with A6013 (Ladybower Reservoir) take first left turn (signposted with Bradfield) then bear left

The children's playground here has been upgraded and safely fenced in, and they now have a permanent bouncy castle. From the picnic-sets there are fine views as the inn is on the edge of the High Peak National Park, and there are some rescued animals – pigs, goats, geese, hens, sheep, a rabbit called Budweiser, and a pair of free-roaming peacocks; well behaved dogs welcome. Inside, the main bar has a warmly welcoming and relaxed atmosphere, black beams liberally decked with copper kettles and so forth, quite a menagerie of stuffed animals, homely red-plush-cushioned traditional wooden wall benches and small chairs, and a coal fire in the rather grand stone fireplace; there's a good mixture of customers. A room off on the right has another coal fire, hunting photographs and prints, and lots of brass and china, and on the left, a similarly furnished room is no smoking. Tasty bar food includes home-made soup (£2.10), sandwiches (from £1.60; toasties from £1.80; hot pork £2.25), filled baked potatoes or omelettes (from £3), garlic mushrooms (£3.95), chilli in a giant yorkshire pudding (£4.50), ploughman's (£4.95), liver and onions (£5.95), spicy bean casserole or thai mushroom noodles (£5.35), steaks (from £8.25), daily specials such as steak in ale pie (£5.95), wine and cheese with olives, biscuits and fruit (2 people £12), and puddings such as hot pancakes with ice cream or apple crumble (from £2); Sunday roast lunch (£5.95; children £3). Well kept Flowers Original, Marstons Pedigree, Wadworths 6X, Wards Thorne, and Whitbreads Castle Eden on handpump, and several malt whiskies; good service, darts, and piped radio. The bedrooms have four-poster beds and two of the ensuite rooms have open log fires; breakfast can be served in your room. *(Recommended by RWD, M Borthwick, D Alexander, Anne and David Robinson, John and Joan Nash, Mr and Mrs D Hack)*

Free house ~ Licensee Jeremy Stanish ~ Real ale ~ Meals and snacks (12-9 in summer) ~ (0114) 2851247 ~ Well behaved children in eating area of bar until 9pm ~ Open 11-11; 12-10.30 Sun; 10.30-3, 7-11 winter weekdays ~ Bedrooms: £35B/£59.50B

BRANDESBURTON (E Yorks) TA1247 Map 8

Dacre Arms

Village signposted from A165 N of Beverley and Hornsea turn-offs

The rambling rough-plastered modernised bar here is vividly furnished, has a roomily comfortable feel, plenty of tables, and well kept Black Sheep, Courage Directors, Tetleys, and Theakstons Old Peculier tapped from the cask. A wide choice of bar food includes lunchtime sandwiches (not weekends), home-made soup (£1.65), filled baked potatoes (from £2.85), steak and kidney casserole (snack size £3.35, king size £4.85), chicken curry (snack size £3.60, king size £4.95), filled yorkshire puddings (from £4.45), omelette (£4.95), steaks (from £8.05), house specials like turkey and ham pie (£5.45), barbecued pork chops (£5.85), chicken wrapped in bacon with a spicy tomato and mushroom sauce (£6.65), and thai green king prawn curry (£7.85), and puddings (from £2.15). Darts and piped music. An inn has stood here since the 16th c and for some time it was one of the most important posting stations in the East Riding. *(Recommended by I Maw, Joan and Michel Hooper-Immins, C A Hall, Stephen, Julie and Hayley Brown)*

Free house ~ Licensees Jason and Liza Good ~ Real ale ~ Meals and snacks (12-2, 6-10; all day Sat/Sun) ~ Restaurant ~ (01964) 542392 ~ Children welcome ~ Open 11.30-2.30, 6-11; 11.30-11 Sat; 12-10.30 Sun; closed 25 Dec

BREARTON (N Yorks) SE3261 Map 7

Malt Shovel

Village signposted off A61 N of Harrogate

Yorkshire Dining Pub of the Year

'A good all-rounder' is one way of describing this 16th-c village pub. There's a warm welcome from the genuinely friendly, helpful licensees, a good choice of real ales, a nice little wine list, and most enjoyable food. Several heavily-beamed rooms radiate from the attractive linenfold oak bar counter with plush-cushioned seats and a mix of tables, an ancient oak partition wall, tankards and horsebrasses, both real and gas fires, and lively hunting prints. The very good food might include sandwiches (from £2.25), garlic mushroom bake (£4.75), nut roast with pesto sauce or rabbit and mushroom pie in port (£4.95), home-baked ham with grain mustard and honey sauce (£5.30), good haggis (£5.50), cajun fresh haddock (£5.80), a kilo of fresh mussels steamed in white wine, tomatoes and garlic (£5.95), venison sausage with red wine gravy (£6.25), lamb shanks braised in white wine with garlic and mint (£6.50), seared tuna steak with soy and balsamic dressing (£7.95), chargrilled rib-eye steak with green peppercorn sauce (£8.50), and puddings such as treacle tart, apple and blackberry crumble or fresh lime tart. Well kept Black Sheep Bitter, Daleside Nightjar, Theakstons Best, and two constantly changing guests on handpump, up to 30 malt whiskies, a small but interesting and reasonably priced wine list (they will serve any wine by the glass), and farm cider; they serve their house coffee (and a guest coffee) in cafetières. Darts, shove-ha'penny, cribbage, and dominoes. You can eat outside on the small terrace on all but the coldest of days as they have special heaters. There are more tables on the grass. *(Recommended by Janet Lewis, Andrew Low, R F and M Bishop, Vann and Terry Prime, David and Helen Wilins, Prof and Mrs S Barnett, Roger Byrne, Geoffrey and Brenda Wilson, Andrew and Ruth Triggs, Janet Edwards, Rita Horridge, Janet and Peter Race, Marian and Andrew Ruston, M Buchanan)*

Free house ~ Licensees Les and Charlotte Mitchell ~ Real ale ~ Meals and snacks (not Sun evening, not Mon) ~ (01423) 862929 ~ Children welcome ~ Open 12-3, 6.45(7 Sun)-11(10.30 Sun); closed Mon

BUCKDEN (N Yorks) SD9278 Map 7

Buck 🍷

B6160

Seats on the terrace of this attractive creeper-covered stone pub enjoy good surrounding moorland views, and there are lots of surrounding footpaths and lanes. The modernised and extended open-plan bar has upholstered built-in wall banquettes and square stools around shiny dark brown tables on its carpet – though there are still flagstones in the snug original area by the serving counter – local pictures, hunting prints, willow-pattern plates on a delft shelf, and the mounted head of a roebuck on bare stone above the log fire. Helpful uniformed staff quickly serve the popular bar food which includes sandwiches, home-made soup (£2.70), confit of duck breast terrine wrapped in pancetta with a soya and honey dressing (£4.75), braised local rabbit encased in leeks with foie-gras and a chive vinaigrette (£5.95), breast of corn-fed chicken with black pudding risotto and dijonnaise sauce (£8.25), roasted escalope of salmon (£8.40), sautéed pork medallions in a honey and mead sauce (£8.50), fried venison steak with a cranberry and port sauce (£11.70), and puddings such as spicy date pudding with hot toffee and ginger sauce, home-made chocolate truffle cheesecake or home-made ice creams and sorbets (from £3.25); the dining area and restaurant are no smoking. Well kept John Smiths Magnet, and Theakstons Best, Old Peculier, Black Bull and XB on handpump, a fair choice of malt whiskies, and decent wines; dominoes, piped music and fruit machine. The bedrooms have been upgraded this year. *(Recommended by David Edwards, Eddie Edwards, Greta and Christopher Wells, L Waler, R Inman, Andrew and Ruth Triggs, P Rome, Ann and Colin Hunt, Sue Blackburn, Vann Prime, Wm Van Laaten, Geoffrey and Brenda Wilson, Walter and Susan Rinaldi-Butcher)*

Free house ~ Licensee Nigel Hayton ~ Real ale ~ Meals and snacks (12-5, 6.30-8.30 Sun) ~ Evening restaurant ~ (01756) 760228 ~ Children welcome away from bar ~ Open 11-11; 12-10.30 Sun ~ Bedrooms: £36B/£72B

BURNSALL (N Yorks) SE0361 Map 7

Red Lion 🛏 🍷

B6160 S of Grassington, on Ilkley road; OS Sheet 98, map reference 033613

Well run and popular, this 16th-c former ferryman's inn stands in a lovely spot on the bank of the River Wharfe. The bustling main bar has sturdy seats built in to the attractively panelled walls (decorated with pictures of the local fell races), windsor armchairs, oak benches, rugs on the floor, and steps up past a solid-fuel stove to a no-smoking back area with sensibly placed darts; dominoes. The carpeted, no-smoking front lounge bar, served from the same copper-topped counter through an old-fashioned small-paned glass partition, has a log fire. A good choice of enjoyable bar food at lunchtime includes home-made soup (£2.75), sandwiches (from £3.50; open sandwiches £5.75), good Cumbrian air-dried ham cured in molasses and served with their own chutney or a light terrine of local game layered with pheasant, pigeon and duck (£4.25), ploughman's with home-made chutneys and relishes or ratatouille with blue wensleydale cheese (£6.95), steak and kidney in ale pie (£7.25), fillet of fresh cod with a lemon, parsley and sun-dried tomato crust (£7.95), braised shoulder of Herdwick lamb stuffed with garlic, rosemary, wild mushrooms and lemon (£9.50), and Aberdeen Angus sirloin steak (£10.75), with evening dishes such as hors d'oeuvres for two (£11.50), venison steak and sausage chargrilled and served with olive mash, fresh wild mushrooms and braised red cabbage (£9.50), and breast of duckling roasted with chinese five spice and served with their own mango chutney (£11.50), daily specials such as pot-roasted brisket of local Aberdeen Angus (£9.95), fresh halibut steamed and served on chive mash and topped with crispy leeks (£10.95), and 16oz dover sole with lemon and parsley butter (£13), and puddings like milk and plain chocolate amaretti truffle terrine served with a raspberry coulis, sticky toffee pudding with caramel sauce or crème brûlée (from £3.75). Well kept Morlands Old Speckled Hen, John Smiths, and Theakstons Best and John Bull on handpump, several malt whiskies, and a very good wine list with around 14 by the glass. The back terrace is lit by old gas lamps, and as well as fine views from here, you can also see the river from more seats on the front cobbles and from most of the bedrooms. Lots of fine surrounding walks, and fishing permits for 7 miles of river. *(Recommended by Gwen and Peter Andrews, Walter and Susan Rinaldi-Butcher, Richard and Valerie Wright, R Inman, D Goodger, Mr and Mrs V Ogilvie, Prof and Mrs S Barnett, Mr and Mrs D Stokes, B M and P Kendall, Mr and Mrs D J Ross, Gill and Keith Croxton, Bob and Maggie Atherton, David and Judy Walmsley, Simon Watkins, Prof and Mrs S Barnett, Pat and Clive Sherriff, P and M Morey)*

Free house ~ Licensee Elizabeth Grayshon ~ Real ale ~ Meals and snacks (12-2.30, 6-9.30) ~ Restaurant ~ (01756) 720204 ~ Children welcome ~ Open 11am-11.30pm; 12-10.30 Sun ~ Bedrooms: £42B/£84B

BYLAND ABBEY (N Yorks) SE5579 Map 7

Abbey Inn

The abbey has a brown tourist-attraction signpost off the A170 Thirsk—Helmsley

The setting for this well liked dining pub – opposite the abbey ruins – is lovely. The rambling, characterful rooms have big fireplaces, oak and stripped deal tables, settees, carved oak seats, and Jacobean-style dining chairs on the polished boards and flagstones, various stuffed birds, cooking implements, little etchings, willow-pattern plates and china cabinets, and some discreet stripping back of plaster to show the ex-abbey masonry; the big back room has lots of rustic bygones; piped music. Good lunchtime bar food includes tomato and orange soup (£2.50), sandwiches (£3.50), chicken liver and ginger parfait or stilton and pear mousse (£5), salmon and prawn quiche (£7), beef in ale pie or smoked haddock mornay (£7.50), and chicken breast with a white wine and mushroom sauce (£7.95), with evening dishes such as smoked duck breast with a spinach and raspberry mousse (£6), vegetable moussaka (£8.50), braised lamb with minted gravy (£10.50), and venison casserole in a port and blackcurrant sauce (£11.50); three-course roast Sunday lunch (£14). Well kept Black Sheep Bitter and Tetleys on handpump, and an interesting wine list. The grey tabby cat is called Milly and the black one, Woody. There's lots of room outside in the garden. *(Recommended by Tom Johnson, Mr and Mrs G Smallwood, SS, Geoffrey and Brenda Wilson, R Inman, Mr and Mrs K Hosen, Geoff and Angela Jaques, R F Grieve, Syd and Syn Donald, John Fahy, Mr and Dr J Harrop, Paul Barnett, Richard Fallon, Paul and Ursula Randall)*

Free house ~ Licensees Jane and Martin Nordli ~ Real ale ~ Meals and snacks (not Mon lunchtime) ~ (01347) 868204 ~ Children welcome ~ Open 11-3, 6.30-11; 11.30-3, 6.30-11 Sun; closed Mon lunchtime (except bank holidays) and 25 Dec

CARLTON (N Yorks) SE0684 Map 10

Foresters Arms

Off A684 W of Leyburn, just past Wensley; or take Coverdale hill road from Kettlewell, off B6160

Much of this comfortable ex-coaching inn is given over to eating, but locals are still welcome to drop in for a drink – which many do. There's a good, relaxed atmosphere, open log fires, and low beamed ceilings, and a wide choice of good enjoyable food from an extensive and imaginative menu. As well as lots of fish dishes such as moules marinières (£4.50), baked crab and asparagus gateau (£5.25), fillet of seabream with mussels provençale (£8.95), and roast monkfish tails with onion marmalade or mediterranean prawn salad with soy and lime vinaigrette (£9.95), there might be light lunch dishes like soup (£3.25), baked sweet onion and coverdale cheese tart (£5.25), sausage and mash with onion gravy (£6.50), and grilled ham and eggs or strips of chicken on a bed of mixed nut salad (£7.50), plus grilled goat's cheese with sun-dried tomato and seasonal salad (£5.95), chicken and wild mushroom lasagne (£9.95), duckling breast and confit leg with herb-butter sauce (£11.95), calf liver with leek mash and madeira sauce (£12.95), and puddings such as treacle tart with ginger ice cream, mousse of white chocolate with orange confit or sticky toffee pudding with butterscotch sauce (from £3.95); a choice of good cheeses with a glass of port (£8.50). Well kept Black Sheep Bitter, Ruddles County, John Smiths, and Theakstons Best on handpump, a good restauranty wine list, 40 malt whiskies, and freshly squeezed orange. The restaurant is partly no smoking. Darts, dominoes, and piped music. There are some picnic-sets among tubs of flowers. *(Recommended by Philip Cooper, Gwen and Peter Andrews, Bob and Maggie Atherton, Alan J Morton, K F Mould, David and Judy Walmsley, Mr and Mrs M Thompson, W James, A C Chapman, B and M and P Kendall, Jill Hallpike, Carl Upsall)*

Free house ~ Lease: Barrie Higginbotham ~ Real ale ~ Meals and snacks (not Sun evening, not Mon) ~ Restaurant (not Sun evening, not Mon) ~ (01969) 640272 ~ Children in eating area of bar and must be over 12 in restaurant ~ Open 12-3, 6.30-11; 12-3, 7-10.30 Sun; closed Mon lunchtime ~ Bedrooms: £35S/£60S

CARTHORPE (N Yorks) SE3184 Map 10

Fox & Hounds

Village signposted from A1 N of Ripon, via B6285

It's the enjoyable food that most people come to this neatly kept and friendly extended village pub for. As well as daily specials such as black pudding with caramelised apple and onion marmalade (£3.95), queen scallop and prawn mornay (£4.95), chicken curry or steak and kidney pie (£7.95), and honey-roast barbary duck breast with cloves and stem ginger (£10.95), the menu includes home-made stilton and onion soup (£2.55), home-made duck liver pâté in port jelly (£3.95), whole fresh dressed Whitby crab (£5.95), chicken breast filled with coverdale cheese in a creamy sauce (£8.95), rack of English lamb (£10.95), steaks (from £10.95), and puddings such as white chocolate and Irish cream cheesecake with home-made dark chocolate ice cream, passion fruit tart or steamed chocolate sponge with a rich chocolate sauce (£3.75; home-made ice creams £3.25). There is some theatrical memorabilia in the corridors, and the cosy L-shaped bar has quite a few mistily evocative Victorian photographs of Whitby, a couple of nice seats by the larger of its two log fires, plush button-back built-in wall banquettes and chairs, plates on stripped beams, and some limed panelling; piped light classical music. An attractive high-raftered no-smoking restaurant leads off with lots of neatly black-painted farm and smithy tools. Well kept John Smiths Bitter on handpump, and decent wines with quite a few by the glass. *(Recommended by K F Mould, F J Robinson, Geoffrey and Brenda Wilson; more reports please)*

Free house ~ Licensee Howard Fitzgerald ~ Meals and snacks (not Mon) ~ Restaurant (not Mon) ~ (01845) 567433 ~ Children welcome until 8pm ~ Open 12-2.30, 7-11(10.30 Sun); closed Mon and first week of the year

COXWOLD (N Yorks) SE5377 Map 7

Fauconberg Arms ★ 🍷

This is a pretty village with attractive tubs of flowers on the cobbled verges of the broad street. The old stone inn has a civilised atmosphere and the two cosy knocked-together rooms of the lounge bar have carefully chosen furniture – most of it is either Mouseman or the work of some other local craftsmen – or cushioned antique oak settles and windsor high-backed chairs and oak tables; there's a marvellous winter log fire in an unusual arched stone fireplace, and gleaming brass. For those wanting an informal drink and chat, there's also an old-fashioned back locals' bar. Good bar food includes home-made soup (£2.25), mousse of salmon and oak-roast sea trout (£4.25), steak and Guinness pie, asparagus and cashew nut filo pastry plait with a port, red onion and honey glaze or chicken barbados (£6.45), pork, apple and mushroom stroganoff (£6.75), deep-fried Whitby creel prawns with garlic and ginger (£7.50), sirloin steak (£9.75), and puddings like Grand Marnier white chocolate mousse, apricot crème brûlée or butterscotch pudding (£3.25). Well kept Theakstons Best and Black Bull on handpump or tapped from the cask, and an extensive wine list. Darts, dominoes, fruit machine, and piped music. The inn is named after Lord Fauconberg, who married Oliver Cromwell's daughter Mary. *(Recommended by David and Helen Wilkins, K F Mould, Nick and Alison Dowson, K and J Brooks, David Cooke, Syd and Wyn Donald, Peter and Ruth Burnstone, Howard England, P R White, Martin Harlow)*

Free house ~ Tenants Robin and Nicky Jaques ~ Meals and snacks ~ Restaurant ~ (01347) 868214 ~ Children welcome ~ Open 11-3, 6.30(6 Sat)-11; 12-3, 7-10.30 Sun; winter evening opening 7pm ~ Bedrooms: £30S/£55S

CRACOE (N Yorks) SD9760 Map 7

Devonshire Arms

B6265 Skipton—Grassington

Jennings have now taken over this comfortable long white pub, set in the middle of a small Dales village, and have installed a manager – readers seem most happy with the changes. The bar has low shiny black beams supporting creaky white planks, little stable-type partitions to divide the solidly comfortable furnishings into cosier areas, polished flooring tiles with rugs here and there, and gleaming copper pans round the stone fireplace. Above the dark panelled dado are old prints, engravings and photographs, with a big circular large-scale Ordnance Survey map showing the inn as its centre. Good bar food, generously served, includes home-made soup (£1.95), sandwiches (from £2.95; filled french sticks from £3.50), mushroom pot (£3.95), avocado and tuna bake (£4.25), ploughman's (£5.95), a pie of the day (£6.50), smoked haddock with saffron mash or leek, brie and walnut wellington (£6.95), roasted joint of lamb with minted gravy (£7.95), Aberdeen Angus steaks (from £9.25), and puddings. Well kept Jennings Bitter and Cumberland and a guest such as Black Sheep on handpump, and several malt whiskies; darts, dominoes, cribbage, and piped music. There are picnic-sets on a terrace flanked by well kept herbaceous borders, with more seating on the lawn; Monty the dog may watch you coming and going from his position on the roof. *(Recommended by Eddie Edwards, Ann and Rob Westbrook, Mr and Mrs Garrett, K and F Giles, P R White, Mike and Wendy Proctor; more reports please)*

Jennings ~ Manager Christopher Gregson ~ Real ale ~ Meals and snacks ~ Restaurant ~ (01756) 730237 ~ Children in restaurant ~ Open 11.30-11; 12-10.30 Sun ~ Bedrooms: £42.50B/£49.50B

CRAY (N Yorks) SD9379 Map 7

White Lion

B6160, Upper Wharfedale N of Kettlewell

1,100 ft up by Buckden Pike, this former drovers' hostelry is the highest pub in Wharfedale and is surrounded by some superb countryside; there are picnic-sets above the very quiet steep lane or on the great flat limestone slabs in the shallow stream which tumbles down opposite. Inside, the simply furnished bar has a traditional atmosphere, seats around tables on the flagstone floor, shelves of china, iron tools and so forth, a high dark beam-and-plank ceiling, and a warming open fire; there's also a no-smoking dining room. Bar food includes sandwiches (from £2.75), filled yorkshire puddings (from £2.95), madeira pork (£7.95), trout, chicken and prawns in white wine and garlic (£8.75), venison (£8.95), and steaks (£9.95); if you eat very early evening in summer, you get a 20% discount. Well kept Moorhouses Pendle Witches Brew and Black Cat, Tetleys Bitter, and a guest beer on handpump; dominoes and ring the bull. *(Recommended by B and M Kendall, Eddie Edwards, David and Judy Walmsley, Ann and Colin Hunt, David Varney, Vann Prime, Wm Van Laaten)*

Free house ~ Licensees Frank and Barbara Hardy ~ Real ale ~ Meals and snacks ~ (01756) 760262 ~ Children in dining room ~ Limited parking ~ Open 11-11; 12-10.30 Sun; 11-3, 6-11 in winter ~ Bedrooms: £27.50(£35S)/£40(£50S)

CROPTON (N Yorks) SE7588 Map 10

New Inn

Village signposted off A170 W of Pickering

The own-brewed beers are quite a draw to this neatly kept and comfortably modernised village inn, and the Cropton Brewery shop is very popular – you can take home packs of bottle conditioned beers and stout, and they encourage brewery trips, too. Their ales consist of Two Pints, King Billy, Monkmans Slaughter, Uncle Sams, Backwoods, Honey Gold, and Scoresby Stout (brewery trips are encouraged) on handpump; country wines. The airy lounge bar has Victorian church panels, terracotta and dark blue plush seats, lots of brass, and a small open fire, and a local artists has designed historical posters all around the no-smoking downstairs conservatory. Bar food includes lunchtime sandwiches (not Sunday), steak and mushroom in ale pie (£5.95), a chicken dish (£7.50), whole leg of lamb (from £7.95), and steaks (from £8); friendly staff. The elegant small no-smoking restaurant is furnished with genuine Victorian and early Edwardian furniture. Darts, dominoes, fruit machine, piped music, and pool room. There's a neat terrace and garden with pond. Comfortable, good value bedrooms. *(Recommended by Bruce Bird, Dr Paul Khan, Mr and Mrs P Spencer, Richard Lewis, Walter and Susan Rinaldi-Butcher, Andy and Jill Kassube, Christopher Turner, J and P Maloney, Andrew Hazeldine)*

Own brew ~ Licensee Sandra Lee ~ Real ale ~ Meals and snacks ~ Restaurant ~ (01751) 417330 ~ Children in conservatory and restaurant ~ Open 11-11; 12-3, 7-10.30 Sun; 11-3, 7-11 in winter ~ Bedrooms: £32B/£54B

DACRE BANKS (N Yorks) SE1962 Map 7

Royal Oak

Enjoyed by locals and visitors alike, this friendly and peaceful 18th-c stone pub is set in a village just above the River Nidd and with beautiful views; there are seats outside and a boules piste. Inside, it's open-plan and the two comfortable lounge areas have interesting old photographs and poems with a drinking theme on the walls, an open fire in the front part, and well kept Black Sheep Bitter, John Smiths, Theakstons, and a guest such as Daleside Old Legover on handpump. Generous helpings of good chip-free, home-made food include soup (£2.15), sandwiches (from £2.25), garlic mushrooms (£2.95), vegetarian moussaka (£5.25), steak, kidney and mushroom or rabbit, ham, and mushroom pies (£5.45), coq au vin or lamb kleftiko (£6.45), roasts such as honeyed lamb, pork or beef (from £5.25), daily specials, and puddings; the restaurant is no smoking. Darts, pool, cribbage, dominoes, and piped music. *(Recommended by Prof and Mrs S Barnett, Richard Lewis, Andrew and Ruth Triggs, E A George, P R White)*

Free house ~ Licensee Lee Chadwick ~ Real ale ~ Meals and snacks (not Sun evening) ~ Restaurant ~ (01423) 780200 ~ Children in eating area of bar and in restaurant; they do not cater for infants ~ Open 12-3, 7-11(10.30 Sun); closed 25 Dec

EAST MARTON (N Yorks) SD9051 Map 7

Cross Keys

A59

Friendly new licensees have taken over this attractive pub, just a few minutes' walk from the Leeds and Liverpool canal, which passes through quite a narrow valley here. Inside, high-backed old-fashioned settles divide the mainly open-plan bar into smaller areas, and there are pictures on the walls, horsebrasses on the heavy black beams, and a huge spit in front of the big winter open fire. Home-made bar food includes soup (£1.90), sandwiches (from £2.25), curries, mushroom stroganoff or three-cheese and broccoli bake (from £4.95), cajun chicken or haddock and prawn mornay (£5.25), gammon and egg (£5.95), steak pie (£5.90), steaks (from £7.50), and puddings like popular wavy gravy (plain, milk and white chocolate mousses with sponge fingers and a chocolate base, £1.95). Well kept Black Sheep, Theakstons Best, and John Smiths on handpump; darts, dominoes, and a fruit machine. There is a separate restaurant, a small lounge useful for families, and two private rooms (one, for small meetings, with a bar, the other a large functions room). Seats outside on the lawn. *(Recommended by WAH, Colin and Ann Hunt; more reports please)*

Free house ~ Licensees Pauline and Graham Wilkinson ~ Real ale ~ Meals and snacks ~ Restaurant ~ (01282) 843485 ~ Children in own room ~ Open 11-3, 6-11; 12-10.30 Sun

We mention bottled beers and spirits only if there is something unusual about them – imported Belgian real ales, say, or dozens of malt whiskies; so do please let us know about them in your reports.

EAST WITTON (N Yorks) SE1586 Map 10

Blue Lion

A6108 Leyburn—Ripon

Most people do come to this stylish place for a civilised meal but there is still some pubby atmosphere, and it does pay to get there early as you can't book a table in the busy bar (though you can, of course, in the restaurant), and there may be quite a wait. The big squarish bar has high-backed antique settles and old windsor chairs and round tables on the turkey rugs and flagstones, ham-hooks in the high ceiling decorated with dried wheat, teazles and so forth, a delft shelf filled with appropriate bric-a-brac, several prints, sporting caricatures and other pictures on the walls, a log fire, and daily papers; the friendly labradors are called Ben and Archie. Particularly good and very popular, the bar food might include sandwiches, home-made soup (£2.95), leek and bacon tart with aioli (£3.95), duck liver parfait with toasted brioche (£5), antipasti of cold meats, pickles and chutneys (£5.50), roast slices of king scallops in puff pastry case with leeks and fennel (£5.95), home-made tagliatelle carbonara (£6.75), roast fillet of cod with spring onion mash and a chive and tomato butter sauce (£10), cassoulet of pork rib, duck, toulouse sausage and pancetta with mashed potato or sirloin steak (£10.95), peppered duck breast with a port and blackberry sauce (£11.25), sautéed monkfish with spiced cabbage and oriental sauce (£11.50), chargrilled roe deer cutlet with a juniper and wine sauce (£13.75), and puddings such as rich chocolate tart with vanilla, raspberry and chocolate sauces, sticky toffee pudding with banana ice cream and butterscotch sauce or tart tatin of pears with honey ice cream (from £3.75); good breakfasts; no snacks on Sunday lunchtime. Well kept Black Sheep Bitter and Riggwelter, John Smiths, and Theakstons Best on handpump, and decent wines with quite a few by the glass. Picnic-sets on the gravel outside look beyond the stone houses on the far side of the village green to Witton Fell, and there's a big pretty back garden. *(Recommended by CRJH, John Read, RB, Vann and Terry Prime, John Oddey, Mike and Maggie Betton, Angela Copeland, John and Vivienne Rice, Walter and Susan Rinaldi-Butcher, David and Judy Walmsley, Susan and John Douglas, Richard Dolphin, Paul McPherson, Dr and Mrs I H Maine, Tim Halstead, Jill Hallpike, Carl Upsall)*

Free house ~ Lease: Paul Klein ~ Real ale ~ Meals and snacks ~ Restaurant (closed Sun evening) ~ (01969) 624273 ~ Children in restaurant ~ Open 11-11; 12-10.30 Sun ~ Bedrooms: £47.50B/£85B

EGTON BRIDGE (N Yorks) NZ8105 Map 10

Horse Shoe

Village signposted from A171 W of Whitby; via Grosmont from A169 S of Whitby

Much enjoyed by readers, this friendly inn has attractive gardens with pretty roses, mature redwoods and some comfortable seats on a quiet terrace and lawn beside a little stream with ducks, geese, and bantams; good surrounding walks and fishing available on a daily ticket from Egton Estates. Inside, the bar has high-backed built-in winged settles, wall seats and spindleback chairs around the modern oak tables, a big stuffed trout (caught near here in 1913), pictures on the walls, and a warm log fire. Generous helpings of bar food include lunchtime sandwiches, and dishes such as warm tartlet filled with trout and cheese (£3.80), warm salad of pigeon with walnut oil (£4.20), chicken and crab tart (£8.40), and duck breast with wild berry sauce (£10). Well kept Tetleys Bitter, Theakstons Best, and guests from local breweries like Cropton and Durham on handpump; darts, dominoes, and piped music. The bedrooms are being updated. Perhaps the best way to reach this beautifully placed pub is to park by the Roman Catholic church, walk through the village and cross the River Esk by stepping stones. Not to be confused with a similarly named pub up at Egton. *(Recommended by K F Mould, David Heath, Ian Phillips, Comus Elliott, Phil and Heidi Cook, RWD, Ian Piper, Tom Thomas, M Rutherford, Stephen, Julie and Hayley Brown)*

Free house ~ Licensees Tim and Suzanne Boulton ~ Real ale ~ Meals and snacks (not 25 Dec) ~ Restaurant ~ (01947) 895245 ~ Children in separate back bar ~ Open 11-11; 12-10.30 Sun; 11.30-3, 6.30-11 in winter ~ Bedrooms: £26(£30B)/£38(£45B)

ELSLACK (N Yorks) SD9249 Map 7

Tempest Arms

Just off A56 Earby—Skipton; visible from main road, and warning signs ¼ mile before

This 18th-c stone pub has a series of quietly decorated areas with small chintz armchairs, chintzy cushions on the comfortable built-in wall seats, brocaded stools, and lots of tables, quite a bit of stripped stonework, some decorated plates and brassware, and a log fire in the dividing fireplace. A fair choice of bar food includes home-made soup (£1.95), sandwiches (from £2.95), mushroom and stilton casserole (£3.35), chicken liver or cream cheese and herb pâté with home-made orange and onion chutney (£3.50), black pudding on an apple and parsnip purée mash with mild mustard sauce (£4.25), battered fresh haddock (£5.95), bangers and mash (£6.50), marinated shoulder of lamb with a mint and redcurrant gravy (£7.25), chicken dijon (£7.85), Aberdeen Angus sirloin steak (£9.25), and confit of duck with home-made stuffing (£9.95). Well kept Jennings Bitter, Cumberland, Snecklifter and guest beers on handpump, and quite a few malt whiskies and wines by the glass. Darts, dominoes, and quiz nights. Tables outside are largely screened from the road by a raised bank. *(Recommended by WAH, Richard and Valerie Wright, Ed Miller, Richard Butcliffe)*

Jennings ~ Managers Martin Clarkson and John Green ~ Real ale ~ Meals and snacks ~ Restaurant ~ (01282) 842450 ~ Children in eating area of bar and in restaurant ~ Open 11-11; 12-10.30 Sun ~ Bedrooms: £49.50B/£57.50B

FERENSBY (N Yorks) SE3761 Map 7

General Tarleton

A655 N of Knaresborough

Run by the same people as the Angel at Hetton, this smartly refurbished 18th-c coaching inn operates along very much the same lines, with the excellent food and wines a powerful draw. Making very good use of fresh local ingredients, the bar menu might features dishes such as soup (£2.95), particularly good starters such as chicken liver parfait (£3.95) or baked tomato tart (£4.25), risotto of basil, spinach and home-dried cherry tomatoes (£5.95), poached salmon (£7.95), tasty wild boar sausages with red cabbage and red wine jus (£8.35), thai-style pork with noodles (£9.95), chargrilled spring lamb on an Italian salad with rocket, roast vegetables and pesto (£10.95), and a huge blackboard menu with lots of fish and other daily specials. Another blackboard lists some of their extensive range of wines, around two dozen of which are available by the glass. Completely redecorated and refitted last year, the civilised beamed and carpeted bar has quite a bright feel in places, with brick pillars dividing up the several different areas to create the occasional cosy alcove, some exposed stonework, neatly framed pictures on the white walls, a mix of country-kitchen furniture and comfortable banquettes, and a big open fire; a door leads out to a pleasant tree-lined garden with smart green tables. Even early in the evening the tables inside can be almost full with people eating. Well kept Black Sheep, Tetleys and Timothy Taylor Landlord on handpump; efficient, almost formal service from well dressed staff. The courtyard eating area is no smoking (though you can hear kitchen activity from here). Like the Angel, they have regular events and gourmet evenings, and you can buy gift vouchers to use at both the pubs. The good bedrooms have their own separate entrance. *(Recommended by Alan and Janice Curry, Miss G Hume, M A Godfrey, Ann and Bob Westbrook, Alyson and Andrew Jackson)*

Free house ~ Licensee Denis Watkins ~ Real ale ~ Meals and snacks (12-2, 6-10) ~ Restaurant ~ (01423) 340284 ~ Children welcome ~ Open 12-3, 6-11; 12-10.30 Sun ~ Bedrooms: £49.50B per room

Please keep sending us reports. We rely on readers for news of new discoveries, and particularly for news of changes – however slight – at the fully described pubs. No stamp needed: *The Good Pub Guide*, FREEPOST TN1569, Wadhurst, E Sussex TN5 7BR.

FLAMBOROUGH (E Yorks) TA2270 Map 8

Seabirds 🍷

Junction of B1255 and B1229

Close to the open country above the cliffs of Flamborough Head, this straightforward village pub has a public bar with quite a shipping theme, and leading off here the comfortable lounge has a whole case of stuffed seabirds along one wall, as well as pictures and paintings of the local landscape, and a woodburning stove. Lunchtime bar food includes soup (£1.70), giant yorkshire pudding filled with onion gravy (£2.70), omelettes (from £4.85), leek and mushroom crumble (£5.95), and haddock mornay (£6.15), with evening extras like chicken and pork liver pâté (£3.05), gammon and eggs (£6.95) or steaks (from £11.35), and daily specials such as baked flat mushrooms filled with crabmeat and topped with mozzarella cheese (£3.95), halibut brochette with a prawn and dill sauce (£7.95), and fillet of plaice filled with lobster and asparagus mousse (£8.25). Well kept John Smiths and a weekly changing guest on handpump, and a wide range of malt whiskies. Friendly, hardworking staff; dominoes, fruit machine, and piped music. There are seats in the garden. *(Recommended by David Carr, William Cunliffe, Joan and Andrew Life, Stephen and Brenda Head)*

Free house ~ Licensee Jean Riding ~ Real ale ~ Meals and snacks (not Sun or Mon evenings in winter) ~ Restaurant ~ (01262) 850242 ~ Children in restaurant ~ Open 11.30-3, 7(6.30 Sat)-11; 12-3, 7-10.30 Sun; closed Mon evening in winter

GOOSE EYE (W Yorks) SE0340 Map 7

Turkey

High back road Haworth—Sutton in Craven, and signposted from back roads W of Keighley; OS Sheet 104 map ref 028406

The village is placed at the bottom of a steep valley with high-walled lanes, and this tucked away pub has various cosy and snug alcoves, brocaded upholstery, and walls covered with pictures of surrounding areas; the restaurant is no smoking. Generous helpings of decent bar food (they tell us prices have not changed since last year) include egg and tuna mayonnaise (£2.50), sandwiches such as hot beef (£2.75), cheese and onion quiche (£4.60), fillet of breaded haddock (£5.40), good steaks (from £7.20), daily specials like filled yorkshire puddings (£3.80), and puddings (from £2.10); Sunday roast beef (£5.80). Well kept Goose Eye Bitter, Greene King Abbot, Ind Coope Burton, Marstons Pedigree, and a guest beer on handpump, and 40 malt whiskies; piped music. A separate games area has pool, fruit machine, and video game. *(Recommended by WAH, M Buchanan, Piotre Chodzko-Zajko, Andy and Jill Kassube, Richard Fallon; more reports please)*

Free house ~ Licensees Harry and Monica Brisland ~ Real ale ~ Meals and snacks (not Mon) ~ Restaurant ~ (01535) 681339 ~ Children welcome until 9pm ~ Open 12-3(5 Sat), 5.30(7 Sat)-11; 12-3, 7-10.30 Sun; closed Mon lunchtime except bank holidays

GREAT OUSEBURN (N Yorks) SE4562 Map 7

Crown

Off B6265 SE of Boroughbridge

Well liked for its very good food, this cheery village pub was where Ambrose Tiller started his Tiller Girls dancing troupe when he was staying here with Barrett's Great American Circus. It's a notably friendly place – locals might start chatting to you as you stand at the bar, and the licensees and staff are very obliging. The warmly welcoming carpeted bar has lots of Edwardian prints and pictures around the walls, as well as a hefty old mangle, plenty of hops, flowers and greenery, cushions on the chairs and wall settles, some military badges, and assorted knick-knacks from a pair of china dogs to a model witch hanging beside the fireplace. Two no-smoking eating areas open off, one with plates and an old cooking range, the other with smart tablecloths and stripped stone walls. Beyond a third area laid out for eating is a sunny terrace with green plastic tables and chairs (and maybe summer barbecues), and behind that is a garden with a play area. Well kept John Smiths, Black Sheep, Timothy

Taylor Landlord and a changing guest on handpump; dominoes, piped music. The well presented meals include queen scallops with garlic butter and mozzarella (£4.95), smoked bacon, garlic and onion tartlet with melted brie and a tomato and chive coulis (£4.95), battered haddock (£6.50), vegetables and brie en croûte with provençale sauce (£6.95), seafood pie (£8.95), medallions of chargrilled pork with a creamy brandy, mushroom and tarragon sauce (£9.95), roast goose breast with wild mushroom and port sauce (£13.95), and specials such as venison and garlic sausage casserole or tuna steak in green peppercorn sauce; children's menu, filled baguettes weekend lunchtimes. They grow their own herbs and salads. The landlord used to play for Leeds United. Note they don't open weekday lunchtimes. *(Recommended by Annabelle Watling, C A Hall, Mr and Mrs Allen, Alan Morton)*

Free house ~ Licensees Steve Balcombe, Patricia Grant ~ Real ale ~ Meals and snacks ~ Restaurant ~ (01423) 330430 ~ Children welcome ~ Irish band St Patrick's Day and 1 Jan ~ Open 5-11 weekdays, 11-11 Sat, 12-10.30 Sun

HARDEN (W Yorks) SE0838 Map 7

Malt Shovel

Follow Wilsden signpost from B6429

The three spotlessly clean rooms in this handsome dark stone building have kettles, brass funnels and the like hanging from the black beams, horsebrasses on leather harness, blue plush seats built into the walls, and stone-mullioned windows; one room has oak-panelling, a beamed ceiling, and an open fire; one room is no smoking at lunchtime. Good value bar food includes sausage, mustard and onion sandwich (£2.75; the hot beef are £3), giant yorkshire pudding with sausages or beef and gravy (£3.50), omelettes (from £4.75), and home-made steak pie or chilli (£4.95). Well kept Tetleys on handpump, and efficient service; dominoes, Monday quiz nights, and piped music. This is a lovely spot by a bridge over Harden Beck, and the big garden is open to the public. *(Recommended by JDM, KM, Jane Aldworth, John Keeler, Mr and Mrs R Maggs; more reports please)*

Carlsberg Tetleys ~ Managers Keith and Lynne Bolton ~ Real ale ~ Lunchtime meals and snacks (not Sun) ~ (01535) 272357 ~ Children in eating area of bar ~ Open 12-3, 5-11; 12-11(10.30 Sun)Sat and summer Thurs/Fri

HEATH (W Yorks) SE3519 Map 7

Kings Arms

Village signposted from A655 Wakefield—Normanton – or, more directly, turn off to the left opposite Horse & Groom

Happily, little changes at this old-fashioned pub. The original bar has a fire burning in the old black range (with a long row of smoothing irons on the mantlepiece), plain elm stools and oak settles built into the walls, and dark panelling. A more comfortable extension has carefully preserved the original style, down to good wood-pegged oak panelling (two embossed with royal arms), and a high shelf of plates; there are also two other small flagstoned rooms, and the conservatory opens on to the garden. The restaurant is partly no smoking. Good value bar food (they tell us prices have not changed since last year) includes home-made soup (£1.75), sandwiches (from £1.65; hot sausage and onion £1.85), ploughman's or omelettes (£4.50), home-made lasagne or beef in ale pie, gammon and egg or battered haddock (all £4.75), puddings (£1.95), and children's meals (£2.50). As well as cheap Clarks Bitter and Festival, they also serve guests like Tetleys Bitter and Timothy Taylor Landlord on handpump. The pub is in a fine setting with seats along the front of the building facing the village green, picnic-sets on a side lawn, and a nice walled flower-filled garden. *(Recommended by Michael Butler, K Frostick, Dr A J and Mrs P G Newton, Tim Halstead)*

Clarks ~ Managers Terry and Barbara Ogden ~ Real ale ~ Meals and snacks ~ Restaurant ~ (01924) 377527 ~ Children welcome ~ Open 11.30-3(4 Sat), 5.30-11; 12-10.30 Sun; closed winter Sun afternoons

HECKMONDWIKE (W Yorks) SE2223 Map 7

Old Hall

New North Road; B6117 between A62 and A638; OS Sheet 104, map reference 214244

The former home of Nonconformist scientist Joseph Priestley, this interesting 15th-c building has lots of old beams and timbers, latticed mullioned windows with worn stone surrounds, brick or stripped old stone walls hung with pictures of Richard III, Henry VII, Catherine Parr, and Joseph Priestley, and comfortable furnishings. Snug low-ceilinged alcoves lead off the central part with its high ornate plaster ceiling, and an upper gallery room, under the pitched roof, looks down on the main area through timbering 'windows'. Bar food includes rolls (from £2.25), a pie of the day (£3.95), vegetable lasagne, chicken with cashew nuts, beef curry or chilli con carne (all £4.25), good beer-battered haddock (£4.95 medium, £5.95 jumbo), gammon and egg (£5.95), steaks (from £6.95), and puddings such as fruit crumbles or pies (£2.25). Well kept (and cheap) Sam Smiths OB on handpump; fruit machine, piped music, and sports or music quizes on Tuesday night and a general knowledge one on Thursday evening. *(Recommended by Derek and Sylvia Stephenson, Michael Butler, W W Burke, Tom Thomas, Andy and Jill Kassube, DC)*

Sam Smiths ~ Manager Robert Green ~ Real ale ~ Meals and snacks (all day Sun) ~ (01924) 404774 ~ Children welcome ~ Open 11-11; 12-10.30 Sun

HELMSLEY (N Yorks) SE6184 Map 10

Feathers

Market Square

A new licensee has taken over this handsomely solid three-storey stone inn with its comfortable lounge bar, Mouseman furniture and relaxed atmosphere. The friendly adjoining pub part is much lower and a good deal older: heavy medieval beams and dark panelling, unusual cast-iron-framed tables topped by weighty slabs of oak and walnut, a venerable wall carving of a dragonfaced bird in a grape vine, and a big log fire in the stone inglenook fireplace. Bar food includes sandwiches (from £3.50), soup (£2.25), home-made stilton and walnut pâté (£3.50), broccoli and stilton quiche (£5.95), deep-fried Whitby haddock (£6.50), home-made steak pie (£6.95), chicken stuffed with mozzarella, wrapped in bacon and and served with a vermouth sauce (£8.95), steaks (from £11.75), and puddings (£3.50). The restaurant is no smoking. Well kept John Smiths and Theakstons Old Peculier on handpump. There's an attractive back garden with seats and tables. Rievaulx Abbey (well worth an hour's visit) is close by. The pub can get very busy on Friday (market day). *(Recommended by Janet Pickles, Walker and Debra Lapthorne, Bruce Bird, Richard Fallon, Michael Switzer, Paul Barnett; more reports on the new regime, please)*

Free house ~ Licensee Graham Davies ~ Real ale ~ Meals and snacks ~ Restaurant ~ (01439) 770275 ~ Children in eating area of bar only ~ Open 11-11; 12-10.30 Sun ~ Bedrooms: £40B/£60B

HETTON (N Yorks) SD9558 Map 7

Angel ★ 🍴 🍷

Just off B6265 Skipton—Grassington

To be sure of a table, you must arrive at this friendly, very well run dining pub early – even during the week, as people drive from miles around for a special meal out. In summer, you may prefer to eat outside. Served by hard-working uniformed staff, there might be home-made soup (£2.95; lovely rustic fish soup with aioli £4.50), prawn and sesame toast with dipping sauce (£3.50), crispy tomato and cheshire cheese tart drizzled with pesto (£4.75), warm salad of crispy duck with spicy sausage and oriental plum sauce (£5.85), tagliatelle with mushrooms and cream (£6.50), salmon fishcake on a tomato salsa and lemon mayonnaise (£7.95), oriental pork hotpot (£8.95), seafood hors d'oeuvres (for two, £9.95), calf liver on creamed celeriac with crispy pancetta and roast shallots (£10.95), chargrilled ribeye of Scottish beef with caesar salad (£12.95), fresh fish and daily specials, and puddings such as chocolate tart with orange crème anglaise, cappuccino brûlée or sticky toffee pudding with butterscotch sauce (from £3.75). Well kept Black Sheep Bitter, Tetleys, and Timothy Taylor Landlord on handpump, 300 wines (with 24 by the glass, including two champagnes), and a good range of malt whiskies. The four timbered and panelled rambling rooms have lots of cosy alcoves, comfortable country-kitchen chairs or button-back green plush seats, Ronald Searle wine snob cartoons and older engravings and photographs, log fires, a solid fuel stove, and in the main bar, a Victorian farmhouse range in the big stone fireplace; the snug is no smoking (as is part of the restaurant). Sturdy wooden benches and tables are built on to the cobbles outside. *(Recommended by M Kershaw, WAH, GLD, Gwen and Peter Andrews, Michael Butler, Karen Eliot, Prof and Mrs S Barnett, Vann and Terry Prime, Prof P A Reynolds, Dr and Mrs I H Maine, Philip and Ann Falkner, Stephen and Brenda Head, Ann and Colin Hunt, Ron Gentry, David and Judy Walmsely, Tom Thomas, John Honnor, RJH, Allen Ferns, Jane Taylor, David Dutton, Julie and Steve Anderston, S P Watkin, P A Taylor, Fred and Christine Bell, Mrs D P Dick, M Holdsworth)*

Free house ~ Licensee Denis Watkins ~ Real ale ~ Meals and snacks (till 10pm) ~ Restaurant ~ (01756) 730263 ~ Well behaved children welcome ~ Open 12-2.30(3 Sun), 6-11(10.30 Sun); closed one week Jan

HUBBERHOLME (N Yorks) SD9178 Map 7

George

Village signposted from Buckden; about 1 mile NW

Moors rise all around this remote and unspoilt old inn, and there are seats and tables to enjoy the view – and to look on to a swirly stretch of the River Wharfe where they have fishing rights. The two neat and cosy rooms have genuine character: heavy beams supporting the dark ceiling-boards, walls stripped back to bare stone and hung with antique plates and photographs, seats (with covers to match the curtains) around shiny copper-topped tables on the flagstones, and an open stove in the big fireplace. Generous helpings of good bar food includes sandwiches, carrot and coriander soup (£2.30), home-made chicken liver pâté (£3.25), home-cured salmon with a warm potato salad and lemon and dill vinaigrette (£4.25), cumberland sausage (£5.25), steak and kidney pie (£6.50), gammon and two eggs (£6.90), chicken in a spicy peanut sauce (£6.95), stuffed red pepper (£7.20), dales lamb chops baked with rosemary and garlic (£9.95), venison steak with a port, redcurrant and lemon sauce (£10.75), and puddings like sticky toffee pudding with fudge sauce or raspberry crème brûlée (£3.25). Very well kept Black Sheep Special, Theakstons Black Bull and XB, and Youngers Scotch on handpump, over 20 malt whiskies, and decent wines; friendly service. Dominoes, and a game they call 'pot the pudding'. The pub is near the ancient church where J B Priestley's ashes are scattered (this was his favourite pub). *(Recommended by Greta and Christopher Wells, R Inman, Prof and Mrs S Barnett, K Frostick, T G Brierly, Chris and Sue Bax, Vann and Terry Prime, Gwen and Peter Andrews, Eddie Edwards, D Goodger, Tom Thomas, B M and P Kendall, David and Judy Walmsley, Paul and Madeleine Morey, Andy and Jill Kassube)*

Free house ~ Licensees Jerry Lanchbury and Fiona Shelton ~ Real ale ~ Meals and snacks ~ Restaurant ~ (01756) 760223 ~ Children in eating area of bar ~ Open 11.30-3, 6.30-11; 11.30-11 summer Sat; 12-10.30 summer Sun ~ Bedrooms: £26/£39(£49B)

HULL (E Yorks) TA0927 Map 8

Minerva

From A63 Castle Street/Garrison Road, turn into Queen Street towards piers at central traffic lights; some weekday metered parking here; pub is in pedestrianised Nelson Street, at far end

In fine weather you can sit at the picnic-sets outside this handsome pub and watch the harbour activity in the bustling marina. They also brew their own beers – Pilots Pride and occasional other brews such as Midnight Owl (available between December and February) and a Special Ale for their beer Festival in mid-August (they hold a mini one around Easter, too); also, guests such as Black Sheep, Everards or Charles Wells on handpump. You can visit the brewery (best to phone beforehand). The several rooms ramble all the way round a central servery, and are filled with comfortable seats, quite a few interesting photographs and pictures of old Hull (with two attractive wash drawings by Roger Davis) and a big chart of the Humber; the lounge is no smoking during mealtimes. A tiny snug has room for just three people, and a back room (which looks out to the marina basin) houses a profusion of varnished woodwork. Good sized helpings of straightforward bar food such as soup (£1.55), hot or cold filled french bread (from £2.45), filled baked potatoes (from £2.25), ploughman's (from £4.25), home-made steak in ale pie or home-made curry (£4.35), popular huge battered haddock (£4.75), and rump steak (£6.45), daily specials (several are vegetarian), children's specials, and puddings like home-made bread and butter pudding (from £1.85); Sunday roast (£4.45), and on summer Wednesdays they do a curry night. Darts, dominoes, cribbage, fruit machine, and piped music. *(Recommended by Andy and Jill Kassube, Mike and Mary Cater, Richard Fallon)*

Own brew (Carlsberg Tetleys) ~ Managers Eamon and Kathy Scott ~ Real ale ~ Meals and snacks (not Fri/Sat/Sun evenings) ~ (01482) 326909 ~ Children in eating area of bar at mealtimes only ~ Open 11-11; 12-10.30 summer Sun; closed 25 Dec

Olde White Harte ★ £

Off 25 Silver Street, a continuation of Whitefriargate (see previous entry); pub is up narrow passage beside the jewellers' Barnby and Rust, and should not be confused with the much more modern White Hart nearby

As we went to press, the new manager told us that this ancient tavern was to be closed in the early autumn for a careful revamp of its six bars – none of the fine old features will be changed though, but new fabrics and furnishings will smarten things up, and they were hoping to revert all the six gas-effect fires back to real ones. The downstairs bar has attractive stained-glass windows that look out above the bow window-seat, carved heavy beams support black ceiling boards, and there's a big brick inglenook with a frieze of delft tiles. The curved copper-topped counter serves well kept McEwans 80/- and Theakstons Old Peculier and XB on handpump. One menu will serve the whole building and will include sandwiches and snacks as well as proper pies, thai chicken, fresh fish, steaks, and daily specials. Seats in the courtyard outside. It was in the heavily panelled room up the oak staircase that in 1642 the town's governor Sir John Hotham made the fateful decision to lock the nearby gate against Charles I, depriving him of Hull's arsenal; it didn't do him much good, as in the Civil War that followed, Hotham, like the king, was executed by the parliamentarians. *(Recommended by Andy and Jill Kassube, William Cunliffe, Richard Fallon; more reports on the changes, please)*

Scottish Courage ~ Manager Neil Pigg ~ Real ale ~ Meals and snacks ~ (01482) 326363 ~ Children in restaurant ~ No nearby parking ~ Open 11-11; 12-10.30 Sun

KIRKBYMOORSIDE (N Yorks) SE6987 Map 10

George & Dragon

Market place

A few changes to this civilised 17th-c coaching inn this year include the refurbishment of the friendly pubby front bar which now has leather chesterfields as well as the brass-studded solid dark red leatherette armchairs set around polished wooden tables, dark green walls entertainingly covered with lots of photographs, prints, shields and memorabilia connected with cricket and rugby (the landlord's own interest), panelling stripped back to its original pitch pine, horsebrasses hung along the beams, and a blazing log fire; no games machines, pool or juke boxes, and the piped music is either classical or jazz, and not obtrusive. An attractive beamed bistro has been opened up, with more sporting prints on the terracotta walls, some wine paraphernalia, and candles in bottles, and the no-smoking restaurant has been redecorated. At lunchtime, the choice of food listed on blackboards might include filled rolls (they bake all their own bread; from £2.25), home-made soup (£2.50), spinach and cheese roulade with tomato coulis (£5.95), italian-style meatballs or steak and mushroom pie (£6.90), chicken breast with bacon and dijon sauce (£7.50), and salmon fillet with a creamy dill sauce or lamb liver, bacon and onions (£7.90). In the evening, dishes include creamy stilton pâté with crushed walnuts (£3.95), black pudding on a bed of apple purée and onions finished with chopped crispy bacon and apple slices (£4.95), sweet and sour vegetable stir fry on egg noodles (£7.50), home-made Scottish salmon and chive cakes with dill sauce (£7.90), seafood hotpot (£8.90), barbary duck breast on a raspberry jus (£10.50), pork slices layered with apple and walnut marmalade finished with a sherry sauce and served with a stuffed baked apple (£10.90), puddings like plum tatin, blackberry and apple crumble or chocolate mousse (£3.20), and daily specials like parsnip and carrot spicy croquettes on spinach with tomato coulis (£6.95) or rabbit braised in dijon mustard and green ginger sauce (£9.90); Sunday roasts (£6.90), and enjoyable breakfasts. Well kept Black Sheep Bitter, Marstons Pedigree, John Smiths, and Timothy Taylor Landlord on handpump, a fine wine list with 10 by the glass, and over 30 malt whiskies; dominoes, and shove-ha'penny. There are seats under umbrellas in the back courtyard and a surprisingly peaceful walled garden for residents to use. The bedrooms are in a converted cornmill and old vicarage at the back of the pub. Wednesday is market day. This is a nice place to stay. *(Recommended by Julie and Tony Warneck, Bruce Bird, IHR, Vann and Terry Prime, Walter and Susan Rinaldi-Butcher, John and Joan Wyatt, David Heath, T G Brierly, Mr and Dr J Harrop, Mrs P Hare, Bruce Jamieson, Michael Switzer, Richard Fallon, C Beadle, Joan and Andrew Life, R Gardiner, David and Ruth Hollands; also in the Good Hotel Guide)*

Free house ~ Licensees Stephen and Frances Colling ~ Real ale ~ Meals and snacks ~ Restaurant ~ (01751) 433334 ~ Well behaved children welcome ~ Open 11-3, 6-11; 12-3, 7-10.30 Sun ~ Bedrooms: £49B/£79B

KIRKHAM (N Yorks) SE7466 Map 7

Stone Trough

Kirkham Abbey

In good weather this attractively set inn is a fine place to sit after enjoying one of the many nearby walks – and there is a good outside seating area with lovely valley views. The inn is handy for Kirkham Abbey and Castle Howard. Inside, the several beamed and cosy rooms are neatly kept and attractive, with warm log fires, a friendly atmosphere, and well kept Jennings Cumberland, Tetleys, Theakstons Old Peculier, and Timothy Taylor Landlord on handpump; farm cider. Good bar food includes home-made soup (£2.95), interestingly filled fresh baked french bread (from £4.95), fresh tagliatelle with salmon, langoustine and prawns or lovely fresh Whitby haddock (£7.25), fried chicken breast with cracked flavoured oils (£7.50), medallions of beef fillet with a brandy, cream and peppercorn sauce (£9.95), daily specials, and home-made puddings (£3.25). The no-smoking farmhouse restaurant has a fire in an old-fashioned kitchen range. Darts, pool, shove-ha'penny, cribbage, and piped music. *(Recommended by Pat and Tony Martin, Chris Gabbitas, Hugh McPhail, Anthony Quinsee, Patrick Hancock, Christopher Turner)*

Free house ~ Licensee Holly Dane ~ Real ale ~ Meals and snacks (not Mon lunchtime) ~ Restaurant ~ (01653) 618713 ~ Well behaved children welcome ~ Open 12-2.30, 6-11(10.30 Sun); closed Mon lunchtime and 25 Dec

LEDSHAM (W Yorks) SE4529 Map 7

Chequers

Claypit Lane; a mile W of A1, some 4 miles N of junction M62

This is a really enjoyable village pub with a good bustling atmosphere and a cheerful welcome to all from the friendly licensee. The old-fashioned little central panelled-in servery has several small, individually decorated rooms leading off, with low beams, lots of cosy alcoves, a number of toby jugs, and log fires. Good, well liked straightforward bar food includes home-made soup (£2.45), sandwiches (from £3.10), ploughman's (£4.85), scrambled eggs and smoked salmon (£5.25), lasagne (£5.50), vegetable pasta bake (£5.95), generous grilled gammon and two eggs (£7.25), daily specials such as cumberland sausage (£4.95), chicken, pineapple and pasta salad (£5.25), wild mushroom and courgette risotto (£5.45), home-made steak and mushroom pie (£5.85), pork fillet in brandy, cream and peppercorn sauce (£5.95), and sirloin steak chasseur (£7.95), and puddings (from £2.75). They now brew their own Brown Cow Best Bitter, and also keep John Smiths, Theakstons Best, and Youngers Scotch on handpump. A sheltered two-level terrace behind the house has tables among roses (a sanctuary from a bad stretch of the A1), and the hanging baskets and flowers are very pretty. *(Recommended by Geoffrey and Brenda Wilson, Lawrence Pearse, Tony Gayfer, Joy and Peter Heatherley, Catherine and Martin Snelling, Pete Yearsley, John Fahy, T Loft, Carolyn Reynier, Miss S Watkin, P Taylor, Mike and Maggie Betton)*

Free house ~ Licensee Chris Wraith ~ Real ale ~ Meals and snacks (not Sun) ~ Restaurant (not Sun) ~ (01977) 683135 ~ Children allowed in eating area of bar only ~ Open 11-3, 5.30-11; 11-11 Sat; closed Sun

LEEDS (W Yorks) SE3033 Map 7

Whitelocks ★ £

Turks Head Yard; alley off Briggate, opposite Debenhams and Littlewoods; park in shoppers' car park and walk

Hardly changed since 1886, this is a marvellously preserved and atmospheric place. The long and narrow old-fashioned bar has polychrome tiles on the bar counter, stained-glass windows and grand advertising mirrors, and red button back plush banquettes and heavy copper-topped cast-iron tables squeezed down one side. And although it might be best to get here outside peak times as it does get packed, the friendly staff are quick and efficient. Good, reasonably priced lunchtime bar food includes yorkshire pudding and gravy (65p), filled baked potatoes (from £1.25), sandwiches (from £1.35), and home-made steak and potato pie or vegetable or meaty lasagne (£2.35). Well kept Courage Directors, Morlands Old Speckled Hen, Theakstons Best, XB and Old Peculier, Youngers IPA, Scotch and No 3 on handpump. At the end of the long narrow yard another bar is done up in Dickensian style. *(Recommended by Allan Worsley, Peter Plumridge, Reg Nelson, K F Mould, Steve Willey, Bob and Maggie Atherton, Andy and Jill Kassube, Martin Hickes, Graham and Karen Oddey)*

Scottish Courage ~ Manageress Donna Mayell ~ Real ale ~ Meals and snacks (all day; though only sandwiches after 8pm) ~ Restaurant ~ (0113) 245 3950 ~ Children allowed in restaurant only ~ Open 11-11; 12-10.30 Sun; closed 25-26 Dec, 1 Jan

LEVISHAM (N Yorks) SE8391 Map 10

Horseshoe

Pub and village signposted from A169 N of Pickering

This is a neatly kept, traditional pub with plenty of good surrounding walks. The bar has brocaded seats, a log fire in the stone fireplace, bar billiards, and well kept John Smiths, and Theakstons Best, XB and Old Peculier on handpump, and over 30 malt whiskies. Good bar food includes home-made soup (£2), sandwiches (from £2.95), black pudding and ham salad or home-made chicken liver pâté (£3.75), ploughman's (£4.95), venison sausages with red wine and onion gravy (£5.75), Whitby haddock or steak and kidney pie (£5.95), leek and mushroom crumble (£6.50), salmon with a rich tomato and basil sauce (£7.95), chicken with a wild mushroom and tarragon sauce (£8.75), steaks (from £10.95), children's menu (£3.25), and puddings; the dining room is no smoking. Bar billiards, cribbage, and piped music. On warm days, the picnic-sets on the attractive village green are a fine place to enjoy a drink. *(Recommended by Jerry and Alison Oakes, M Borthwick, Mark J Hydes, Comus Elliott, Don and Thelma Anderson, Colin Savill, Dr Morley, T M Dobby, Mrs P Hare, Piotre Chodzko-Zajko)*

Free house ~ Licensees Brian and Helen Robshaw ~ Real ale ~ Meals and snacks (not 25 Dec) ~ (01751) 460240 ~ Children welcome ~ Open 11(12 Sun)-3, 6.30-11(10.30 Sun); closed Mon ~ Bedrooms: £26B/£52B

All *Guide* inspections are anonymous. Anyone claiming to be a *Good Pub Guide* inspector is a fraud, and should be reported to us with name and description.

LEYBURN (N Yorks) SE1191 Map 10

Sandpiper

Market Place – bottom end

Dating back to 1640, this quiet little stone cottage is enjoyed, the licensees tell us, by the more mature customer – though very well behaved children are allowed. The bar has a couple of black beams in the low ceiling, a stuffed pheasant in a stripped-stone alcove, antlers, and just seven tables – even including the back room up three steps, where you'll find attractive dales photographs, toby jugs on a delft shelf, and a collection of curious teapots. Down by the nice linenfold panelled bar counter there are stuffed sandpipers, more photographs and a woodburning stove in the stone fireplace. There's also a spic-and-span dining area on the left. Traditional bar food at lunchtime (they tell us prices have not changed since last year) includes home-made soup (£1.95), sandwiches (from £1.95; toasties £2.25), filled baked potatoes (£2.95), ploughman's or cumberland sausage (£4.25), meaty or vegetarian lasagne (£5.25), daily specials, and evening dishes such as garlic mushrooms (£3.50), gammon with peaches and cheese (£9.50), and steaks (from £9.50). Well kept Black Sheep Riggwelter and Dent Bitter on handpump, around 100 malt whiskies, and a decent wine list. There are lovely hanging baskets, white cast-iron tables among the honeysuckle, climbing roses, and so forth on the front terrace, with more tables in the back garden. *(Recommended by Bruce Bird, John Fazakerley, Andrew and Ruth Triggs, Ann and Colin Hunt, Ian and Villy White)*

Free house ~ Licensees Peter and Beryl Swan ~ Real ale ~ Meals and snacks (not 25 Dec) ~ Evening restaurant ~ (01969) 622206 ~ Well behaved children may be allowed ~ Open 11-2.30, 6.30-11; closed 25 Dec ~ Bedrooms: £25B/£40B

LINTHWAITE (W Yorks) SE1014 Map 7

Sair

Hoyle Ing, off A62; 3½ miles after Huddersfield look out for two water storage tanks (painted with a shepherd scene) on your right – the street is on your left, burrowing very steeply up between works buildings; OS Sheet 110 map reference 101143

It's the fine range of own-brewed ales that most people come to this unspoilt and old-fashioned pub to enjoy, and if Mr Crabtree is not too busy, he is glad to show visitors the brewhouse: pleasant and well balanced Linfit Bitter, Mild, Special, Swift, Ginger Beer, Old Eli, Leadboiler, Autumn Gold, and the redoubtable Enochs Hammer; there's even stout (English Guineas), a porter (Janet St), and occasional Xmas Ale, Springbok Bier, and Smokehouse Ale. Westons farm cider and a few malt whiskies. The four rooms are furnished with pews or smaller chairs on the rough flagstones or carpet, bottle collections, beermats tacked to beams, and roaring log fires; one room is no smoking. The room on the right has shove-ha'penny, dominoes, Jenga, chess, and juke box; piano players welcome. There's a striking view down the Colne Valley – through which the Huddersfield Narrow Canal winds its way; in the 3½ miles from Linthwaite to the highest and longest tunnel in Britain are 25 working locks and some lovely countryside. No food. *(Recommended by Andrew and Ruth Triggs, Judith Hirst, John Plumridge, H K Dyson, Joan and Michel Hooper-Immins; more reports please)*

Own brew ~ Licensee Ron Crabtree ~ Real ale ~ (01484) 842370 ~ Children in three rooms away from the bar ~ Open 7-11 only on weekdays; 12-11 Sat; 12-10.30 Sun

LINTON (W Yorks) SE3947 Map 7

Windmill

Leaving Wetherby W on A661, fork left just before Hospital and bear left; also signposted from A659, leaving Collingham towards Harewood

The carefully restored small beamed rooms in this friendly pub are spotlessly kept and have walls stripped back to bare stone, polished antique oak settles around copper-topped cast-iron tables, pots hanging from the oak beams, a high shelf of plates, and log fires. Enjoyable generously served food includes home-made soup (£2.50), yorkshire pudding and onion gravy (£2.50), lunchtime sandwiches (from £2.80), fresh battered haddock (£5.95), beef and mushroom in ale pie (£6.50), wild boar sausages (£6.95), cajun chicken (£8.95), and steaks (from £8.95); they also offer a two-course menu between 5.30 and 7 during the week (£5.95). Well kept John Smiths, Theakstons Best and three or four weekly guest beers on handpump from breweries such as Daleside, Hambleton, Marston Moor, Rooster's, and Rudgate. The two black labradors are called Jet and Satchmo. The pear tree outside was planted with seeds brought back from the Napoleonic Wars and there is a secret passage between the pub and the church next door. *(Recommended by June and Malcolm Farmer, Rupert and Mary Jane Flint, Michael Butler, Mr and Mrs Curry, M Phillips; more reports please)*

Scottish Courage ~ Tenants Geoff Stoker and Daron Stoker ~ Real ale ~ Meals and snacks ~ (01937) 582209 ~ Children welcome until 8.30pm ~ Open 11.30-3, 5-11; 11-11 Sat; 12-10.30 Sun

LINTON IN CRAVEN (N Yorks) SD9962 Map 7

Fountaine

On B6265 Skipton—Grassington, forking right

This pub looks down over the village green to the narrow stream that runs through this delightful hamlet. The little rooms are furnished with stools, benches and other seats, and they have well kept Black Sheep Bitter, and Theakstons Best, Black Bull and Old Peculier on handpump; decent malt whiskies and farm cider. Bar food includes home-made soup (£2.95), home-made pâté (£3.95), open sandwich platters (from £4.50), vegetable risotto (£6.50), popular home-made lamb and apple pie (£6.75), bacon chops with fried egg (£6.95), supreme of chicken in lemon, prawn and chardonnay sauce (£7.25), and specials such as a medley of four fresh fish (£7.50), rack of lamb or half a duck with orange sauce (£8.95), and puddings like blueberry pie or summer pudding (£2.95); one small eating area is no smoking; friendly service. The pub is named after the local lad who made his pile in the Great Plague – contracting in London to bury the bodies. *(Recommended by Mrs Janet Annison, Roger and Christine Mash, Greta and Christopher Wells, Gwen and Peter Andrews, P R White, Ann and Bob Westbrook, David and Judy Walmsley, Andrew and Ruth Triggs, Julie and Steve Anderton, Vann and Terry Prime, P A Taylor, John Fazakerley, A N Ellis)*

Free house ~ Licensee Colin Nauman ~ Real ale ~ Meals and snacks ~ (01756) 752210 ~ Children in eating area of bar ~ Open 11-3, 6-11; 12-4, 7-10.30 Sun; may stay open longer if busy

LITTON (N Yorks) SD9074 Map 7

Queens Arms

From B6160 N of Grassington, after Kilnsey take second left fork; can also be reached off B6479 at Stainforth N of Settle, via Halton Gill

Picnic-sets in front of this attractive and friendly white-painted inn – and from the two-level garden – have stunning views over the fells, and there are fine surrounding walks, too – a track behind the inn leads over Ackerley Moor to Buckden and the quiet lane through the valley leads on to Pen-y-ghent. Inside, the main bar on the right has a good coal fire, stripped rough stone walls, a brown beam-and-plank ceiling, stools around cast-iron-framed tables on the stone and concrete floor, a seat built into the stone-mullioned window, and signed cricket bats. On the left, the red-carpeted room has another coal fire and more of a family atmosphere with varnished pine for its built-in wall seats, and for the ceiling and walls themselves. Decent bar food (they tell us prices have not increased since last year) includes sandwiches (from £2.45; hot or cold crusty rolls from £3), filled baked potatoes (from £2.80), ploughman's (£3.80), meaty or vegetable lasagne (£4.10), home-made pies (from £5.30), gammon and egg (£6.25), daily specials, a larger evening menu, and children's meals (from £2.20). Well kept Tetleys and, in summer, Black Sheep on handpump; darts, dominoes, shove-ha'penny, and cribbage. *(Recommended by D Goodger, Geoffrey and Brenda Wilson, Paul and Madeleine Morey, Neil and Anthony Huxter, Gwen and Peter Andrews, David and Judy Walmsley)*

Free house ~ Licensees Tanya and Neil Thompson ~ Real ale ~ Meals and snacks (not Mon except bank holidays) ~ (01756) 770208 ~ Children in family room ~ Open 12-3, 7(6.30 Sat)-11(10.30 Sun); closed Mon (except bank holidays); closed 1st wknd Jan-beg Feb ~ Bedrooms: £30B/£40(£50B)

LOW CATTON (E Yorks) SE7053 Map 7

Gold Cup

Village signposted with High Catton off A166 in Stamford Bridge or A1079 at Kexby Bridge

This is a friendly pub and the three neatly kept and comfortable communicating rooms of the lounge have open fires at each end, plush wall seats and stools around good solid tables, flowery curtains, some decorative plates and brasswork on the walls, and a very relaxed atmosphere. Generous helpings of good, reasonably priced food might includes soup, lunchtime sandwiches and ploughman's, nice Whitby haddock, and warm home-cooked ham with creamy mustard sauce, grilled salmon steak with lemon butter and a pie of the day such as lamb and apricot (£5.25); the no-smoking restaurant has pleasant views of the surrounding fields. Well kept John Smiths and Tetleys Bitter on handpump. The back games bar is comfortable, with a well lit pool table, dominoes, fruit machine, video game, and well reproduced music. There's a garden with a timber climing frame and grassed area for children, and the back paddock houses Annie and Billie the goats, Tina and Pony the shetlands, and Kandy the horse; they have fishing rights on the adjoining River Derwent. *(Recommended by Calum and Jane Maclean, B P White, Roger Bellingham)*

Free house ~ Licensees Ray and Pat Hales ~ Real ale ~ Meals and snacks (all day weekends; not Mon lunchtime) ~ Restaurant ~ (01759) 371354 ~ Children welcome ~ Open 12-2.30, 6-11; 12-11 Sat; 12-10.30 Sun; closed Mon lunch (except bank holidays); closed evening 25 Dec

LUND (E Yorks) SE9748 Map 8

Wellington 🍷

Off B1248 N of Beverley

Taking up one side of the green in a delightfully unspoilt little Wolds-edge village, this smartly refurbished pub is a popular lunchtime stop for quite a mix of customers. Though most people then have come to eat, in the evening the bar is food-free, and the several rooms take on a quite different feel. The most atmospheric part is the cosy Farmers Bar, a small heavily beamed room with an interesting fireplace and some old agricultural equipment; the neatly kept main bar is much brighter, with a brick fireplace and bar counter, well polished wooden banquettes and square tables, dried flowers, and local prints on the textured cream-painted walls. Off to one side is a plainer flagstoned room, while at the other end a York-stoned walkway leads to a room with a display case showing off the village's Britain in Bloom awards. The short range of well prepared lunchtime bar food might include several soups such as lettuce and smoked bacon or broccoli and blue cheese (£2.75), big sandwiches served with home-made chips (from £3.95), chargrilled pork loin with barbecue sauce (£6.95), smoked haddock fishcakes with a mild curried apple sauce (£7.50), chicken, mushroom and tarragon stroganoff (£8), and a popular Sunday roast (£6.25); good puddings such as banana and toffee crumble. Well kept Black Sheep, John Smiths and Timothy Taylor Landlord on handpump, and a good wine list, with a helpfully labelled choice by the glass. Briskly efficient service from uniformed staff; piped music, cribbage, pool, dominoes. A small courtyard beside the car park has a couple of benches. *(Recommended by N H White, H Bramwell, Gordon Thornton, Ian Morley)*

Free house ~ Licensees Russell Jeffery, Sarah Warburton ~ Real ale ~ Lunchtime meals (not Mon) ~ Evening restaurant (not Sun or Mon) ~ (01377) 217294 ~ Well behaved children in eating area until 8pm ~ Open 12-3, 7-11(closed Mon lunch); 12-3, 7-10.30 Sun

If you know a pub's ever open all day, please tell us.

MASHAM (N Yorks) SE2381 Map 10

Kings Head

Market Square

On Wednesday – market day – it's enjoyable to sit at the front windows of the two opened-up bar rooms of the neatly kept and spacious lounge bar here and watch the bustle. One room is carpeted and one has a wooden floor, and there are green plush seats around wooden tables, a big War Department issue clock over the imposing slate and marble fireplace, and a high shelf of Staffordshire and other figurines. New managers will have taken over here by the time this book is published, but the bar food has included home-made soup (£1.30), sandwiches (from £2.25; not Sunday), eggs with a spicy mango and curried mayonnaise (£2.25), three cheese and broccoli bake or a roast of the day (£5.95), lamb liver and bacon, chicken breast wrapped in bacon with a sherry cream sauce or Whitby cod (£6.95), rack of lamb (£7.95), steaks (from £8.95), daily specials, and puddings (£1.95); nice breakfasts. Well kept Theakstons Best, XB, and Old Peculier, and guest beers on handpump; fruit machine, dominoes, piped music. The handsome inn's hanging baskets and window boxes are most attractive, and there are picnic-sets under cocktail parasols in a partly fairy-lit coachyard. The bedrooms have been refurbished this year. *(Recommended by Malcolm and Helen Baxter, Rachel Sayer, Andrew and Ruth Triggs, James Nunns; more reports please)*

Scottish Courage ~ Real ale ~ Meals and snacks ~ Restaurant ~ (01765) 689295 ~ Well behaved children welcome until 9.30pm ~ Open 11-11; 12-10.30 Sun ~ Bedrooms: £50.50B/£71B

White Bear

Signposted off A6108 opposite turn into town centre

It's not surprising that the Theakstons Best, XB, Old Peculier and seasonal beers are well kept here, as the Theakstons old stone headquarters buildings are part of this pub and the brewery is just the other side of town; tours can be arranged at the Theakstons Brewery Visitor Centre (01765 689057, extension 4317, Weds-Sun); morning visits are best. The traditionally furnished public bar is packed with bric-a-brac such as copper brewing implements, harness, pottery, foreign banknotes, and stuffed animals – including a huge polar bear behind the bar. A much bigger, more comfortable lounge has a turkey carpet. Under another new licensee this year, the bar food might include home-made soup (£1.75), sandwiches (from £2.25), all-day breakfast (£4.45), fish pie or beef in ale with yorkshire pudding (£4.95), spinach and mushroom lasagne or chicken curry (£5.25), rump steak (£7.45), puddings like plum pudding with custard (£2.45), and children's menu (£2.45). Darts, dominoes, fruit machine and CD juke box. In summer there are seats out in the yard. *(Recommended by Vann Prime, Wm Van Laaten, Andrew and Ruth Triggs, Beryl and Bill Farmer; more reports please)*

Scottish Courage ~ Tenant M J Moon ~ Real ale ~ Meals and snacks (not Sat evening) ~ (01765) 689319 ~ Children welcome until 8pm ~ Live bands Sat evening ~ Open 12-11; 12-10.30 Sun; 12-3, 6-11 winter weekdays ~ Bedrooms: £30/£40

MELTHAM (W Yorks) SE0910 Map 7

Will's o' Nat's

Blackmoorfoot Road; off B6107; a couple of miles out of village to north west

Popular with walkers – the pub is situated on both the Colne Valley and Kirklees circular walks and close to Blackmoorfoot reservoir (birdwatching) – and with those arriving by car, this is a bustling place with friendly licensees. Most people come to enjoy the reliably good food which might include home-made soup (£1.35), lots of sandwiches (from £1.75; bacon and egg £2; steak with onions £4.50), yorkshire pudding with onion gravy (£2), ploughman's (from £3.95), deep-fried fresh haddock (£4.20), apple, cheese and onion bake or chicken curry (£4.30), steak and kidney pudding (£4.75), chicken in a leek and stilton sauce (£5.10), gammon and egg (£5.25), smoked salmon and prawn platter (£6.95), and steaks or grilled salmon (£12.95, Mondays and Tuesdays), puddings like chocolate and ginger cheesecake, raspberry torte or lemon meringue pie (from £2.25), a good choice of British cheeses with biscuits (£2.75), and children's meals (from £2.20). Well kept Old Mill Bitter and Tetleys Bitter and Mild plus guest beers on handpump, a good little wine list, and around 30 malt whiskies. By the bar there are comfortably cushioned heavy wooden wall seats around old cast-iron-framed tables, and the cream walls have lots of interesting old local photographs and a large attractive pen and wash drawing of many local landmarks, with the pub as its centrepiece. A slightly raised dining extension at one end, with plenty of well spaced tables, has the best of the views and is partly no smoking. Fruit machine and piped music (not obtrusive). The name of the pub means 'belonging to, or run by, William, son of Nathaniel'. *(Recommended by Bronwen and Steve Wrigley, Graham and Lynn Mason, Neil Townend, M Joyner, H K Dyson)*

Carlsberg Tetleys ~ Lease: Kim Schofield ~ Real ale ~ Meals and snacks (11.30-2.30, 6-9.30; not 25 Dec, not evenings 26 Dec or 1 Jan) ~ (01484) 850078 ~ Well behaved children welcome ~ Open 11.30-3, 6(6.30 Sat)-11; 12-3, 7-10.30 Sun; closed evenings 25/26 Dec, evening 1 Jan

MIDDLEHAM (N Yorks) SE1288 Map 10

Black Swan

Market Pl

The immaculately kept heavy-beamed bar in this 17th-c stone inn has a good cheerful local feel – as well as high-backed settles built in by the big stone fireplace, racing memorabilia on the stripped stone walls, horsebrasses and pewter mugs, and well kept John Smiths Bitter and Theakstons Best, Old Peculier, and XB on handpump; quite a few malt whiskies and decent little wine list. Bar food includes lunchtime sandwiches (from £1.95), filled baked potatoes (from £2.50), and ploughman's (from £3.50), as well as home-made soup (£1.80), egg mayonnaise (£1.95), battered haddock (£4.95), vegetable lasagne (£5.25), lasagne or chicken with a creamy spicy, coconut sauce (£5.50), and evening gammon with pineapple (£7.95), steaks (from £10.25), and children's dishes (£2.95). Darts, dominoes and piped music. There are tables on the cobbles outside and in the sheltered back garden. Good walking country. *(Recommended by J and H Coyle, William Cunliffe, Ann and Colin Hunt, Alan Morton)*

Free house ~ Licensees George and Susan Munday ~ Real ale ~ Meals and snacks (not 25 Dec) ~ Restaurant ~ (01969) 622221 ~ Children in eating area of bar until 9pm ~ Open 11-3.30, 6-11; 12-3, 6-10.30 Sun ~ Bedrooms: £26B/£46B

MOULTON (N Yorks) NZ2404 Map 10

Black Bull 🍴

Just E of A1, 1 mile S of Scotch Corner

For several readers, this decidedly civilised place is a firm favourite. It's very much somewhere to come for an enjoyable meal out, and has a lot of character, and the bar has a huge winter log fire, fresh flowers, an antique panelled oak settle and an old elm housekeeper's chair, built-in red-cushioned black settles and pews around the cast-iron tables (one has a heavily beaten copper top), silver-plate Turkish coffee pots and so forth over the red velvet curtained windows, and copper cooking utensils hanging from black beams. A nice side dark-panelled seafood bar has some high seats at the marble-topped counter. Excellent lunchtime bar snacks include lovely smoked salmon: sandwiches (£3.25), pâté (£4.95), and smoked salmon plate (£5.25); they also do a very good home-made soup served in lovely little tureens (£2.50), fresh plump salmon sandwiches (£3.25), black pudding and pork sausage with caramelised apple (£4.25), welsh rarebit and bacon (£4.75), pasta with queen scallops, chilli and garlic (£4.95), curried fish mornay (£5.25), tartlet of crab, leek, gruyère and walnut (£5.95), and puddings (£3). In the evening (when people do tend to dress up), you can also eat in the polished brick-tiled conservatory with bentwood cane chairs or in the Brighton Belle dining car – where they also do a three-course Sunday lunch. Good wine, and a fine choice of sherries. There are some seats under trees in the central court. *(Recommended by SS, J and G Dundas, Mr and Mrs A Bull, K F Mould, Chris Brace, John and Chris Simpson, Roger Bellingham, David Shillitoe, Cynthia Waller)*

Free house ~ Licensees Mrs A Pagendam and Miss S Pagendam ~ Lunchtime bar meals and snacks (not Sun) ~ Restaurant (not Sun evening) ~ (01325) 377289 ~ Children in eating area of bar if over 7 ~ Open 12-2.30, 6-10.30(11 Sat); closed Sun evening and 24-27 Dec

MUKER (N Yorks) SD9198 Map 10

Farmers Arms

B6270 W of Reeth

High in Swaledale, this unpretentious pub stands in grand scenery and has plenty of nearby rewarding walks – as well as interesting drives up over Buttertubs Pass or to the north, to Tan Hill and beyond. The cosy bar has a warm open fire and is simply furnished with stools and settles around copper-topped tables. Straightforward bar food includes lunchtime baps and toasties, soup (£1.80), home-made steak pie or chicken or vegetable curries (£4.95), gammon and pineapple (£5.95), steaks (from £8.20), puddings like caramel toffee cheesecake (£2.50), and children's meals (£2.80). Butterknowle Bitter, John Smiths Bitter, and Theakstons Best and Old Peculier on handpump; darts and dominoes. They have a self-catering studio flat to rent.

(Recommended by Vann and Terry Prime, Edward and Richard Norris, Mary Thompson, Ray and Liz Monk, Hazel and Michael Duncombe)

Free house ~ Licensees Chris and Marjorie Bellwood ~ Real ale ~ Meals and snacks ~ (01748) 886297 ~ Children welcome ~ Open 11-3, 6.30-11; 11-11 Sat; 12-10.30 Sun; winter evening opening 7

NEWTON ON OUSE (N Yorks) SE5160 Map 7

Dawnay Arms

Village signposted off A19 N of York

There's a good, friendly bustling atmosphere in this black-shuttered 18th-c inn, and usually, quite a crowd of customers enjoying the well liked bar food. On the right of the entrance is a comfortable, spacious room with a good deal of beamery and timbering and plush wall settles and chairs around wooden or dimpled copper tables. To the left is another airy room with plush button-back wall banquettes built into bays and a good log fire in the stone fireplace; lots of brass and copper. Good bar food includes sandwiches and ploughman's, soup (£2.25), home-made pâté (£2.95), deep-fried stilton mushrooms (£3.50), courgette provençal or home-made lasagne (£4.95), chicken mornay (£6.75), beef bourguignon or lamb liver (£7.50), grilled halibut steak (£8.95), venison steak (£9.95), steaks (from £10.95), and home-made puddings (£2.95); the restaurant is no smoking. Well kept Boddingtons, Flowers Original, Morlands Old Speckled Hen and Tetleys on handpump, and 40 malt whiskies; darts, pool, fruit machine, and unobtrusive piped music. The neat, sloping lawn runs down to the River Ouse where there are moorings for three or four cruisers; plenty of seats on the terrace. Benningbrough Hall (National Trust) is five minutes' walk away.

(Recommended by Paul and Ursula Randall, Janet and Peter Race, Mrs Frances Gray, Geoffrey and Brenda Wilson, Christopher Turner, J C Burley, M J Morgan, Piotr Chodzko-Zajko, Joan and Andrew Life, Andrew and Ruth Triggs)

Free house ~ Licensees Alan and Richard Longley ~ Real ale ~ Meals and snacks ~ (01347) 848345 ~ Children welcome ~ Open 12-3, 5.30(6 Sat)-11; 12-3, 7-10.30 Sun

NUNNINGTON (N Yorks) SE6779 Map 7

Royal Oak

Church Street; at back of village, which is signposted from A170 and B1257

The main draw to this spotlessly kept and attractive little dining pub remains the good enjoyable food. Served by friendly and efficient staff, there might be sandwiches (from £2.50), home-made soup (£2.70), spicy mushrooms or stilton pâté (£4), egg mayonnaise with prawns (£4.75), ploughman's or lasagne (£7), chicken in an orange and tarragon sauce or ham and mushroom tagliatelle (£8.25), fisherman's pot or steak and kidney casserole (£8.75), sirloin steak (£12), daily specials, and puddings like home-made apple pie or chocolate fudge cake (£2.75). Well kept Tetleys and Theakstons Best and Old Peculier on handpump. The bar has carefully chosen furniture such as kitchen and country dining chairs or a long pew around the sturdy tables on the turkey carpet, and a lectern in one corner; the high black beams are strung with earthenware flagons, copper jugs and lots of antique keys, one of the walls is stripped back to the bare stone to display a fine collection of antique farm tools, and there are open fires. Handy for a visit to Nunnington Hall (National Trust). *(Recommended by Mrs Frances Gray, Paul and Ursula Randall, R Inman, Trevor and Diane Waite, Walter and Susan Rinaldi-Butcher, Rita Horridge, R Gardiner)*

Free house ~ Licensee Anthony Simpson ~ Real ale ~ Meals and snacks (not Mon) ~ (01439) 748271 ~ Children in restaurant only, if over 8 ~ Open 12-2.30, 6.30-11; closed Mon

OSMOTHERLEY (N Yorks) SE4499 Map 10

Three Tuns

South End, off A19 N of Thirsk

Although much emphasis is placed on the very good food here served in the roomy, crisply stylish and comfortable back restaurant, the front part has a lot of pubby character and is just the place for a relaxed drink. It's hardly been knocked about at all, and is popular with walkers, and with visitors to this lovely village centred around Mount Grace Priory. It has a modest stone facade (with an old-fashioned wooden seat out by the door), and inside on the left is a simple small square bar and tap room, which fill quite quickly at weekends; attractive coal fire. Bar food includes good sandwiches and toasties (from £2.95), ploughman's with interesting cheeses from small producers and really good bread (£5.65), deep-fried camembert with fresh raspberry sauce (£5.25), grilled fresh sardines (£6.50), smoked salmon with scrambled eggs (£6.95), gammon and two eggs (£7.25), roast breast of barbary duck stuffed with pâté and herbs and a madeira sauce (£10.25), steaks (from £12.75), and daily specials such as cream of fresh lemon sole and lobster (£3.25), skewered tempura prawns (£4.95), mixed hors d'oeuvres (£6.75), roasted vegetable torte with tomato and basil sauce (£9.25), mini rack of pork with apricot and sage sauce (£9.50), grilled fresh halibut topped with cheese and prawns (£11.45), roasted half shoulder of local lamb with madeira sauce (£12.50), and puddings like bread and butter pudding, tia maria parfait or fresh strawberry and apple crumble with hazelnuts (£3.25). Well kept John Smiths, and Theakstons Best, XB and Old Peculier on handpump, and smart courteous and efficient service. Tables out in the pleasant back garden have lovely views. The bedrooms are well equipped and comfortable. *(Recommended by RB, Janet and Peter Race, Mr and Mrs W B Walker, Charles and Pauline Stride, Michael Butler)*

Free house ~ Licensee Hugh Dyson ~ Real ale ~ Meals and snacks (not Sun evening) ~ Restaurant ~ (01609) 883301 ~ Children welcome ~ Open 11.45-3.30, 6.45-11; 12-3.30, 7-10.30 Sun ~ Bedrooms: £49.50B/£65B

PICKHILL (N Yorks) SE3584 Map 10

Nags Head

Take the Masham turn-off from A1 both N and S, and village signposted off B6267 in Ainderby Quernhow

It's quite an achievement to successfully run a pub, restaurant and hotel without one part becoming over-dominant – but for over 28 years, the friendly Boynton brothers have done just that. The busy tap room on the left has beams hung with jugs, coach horns, ale-yards and so forth, and masses of ties hanging as a frieze from a rail around the red ceiling. The smarter lounge bar has deep green plush banquettes on the matching carpet, and pictures for sale on its neat cream walls, and another comfortable beamed room (mainly for restaurant users) has red plush button-back built-in wall banquettes around dark tables, and an open fire. Much enjoyed food includes soup (£2.50), chicken liver and walnut pâté or spicy lamb kebab with mediterranean salsa and minted yoghurt (£3.95), fried queen scallops with sun-dried tomatoes, wild mushrooms and beurre blanc (£4.50), mixed hors d'oeuvres (£5.50), large cod and mushy peas (£5.95), seafood lasagne (£6.95), gammon and egg (£7.25), smoked pork chop with sauerkraut (£8.50), super barnsley chops, fried pigeon breasts served on roasted peppers with pan juices (£9.95), szechuan king prawns or lovely grilled duck breast with a lime and gin sauce (£10.95), sirloin steak (£11.95), and puddings like rhubarb crumble with rum and raisin ice cream, pear and gingersnap glory and burnt oxford cream (£3.25); service can slow down under pressure; the refurbished restaurant is no smoking. Well kept Black Sheep Special, Hambleton Bitter, John Smiths, Theakstons Black Bull, and a guest beer on handpump, a good choice of malt whiskies, and good value wines (several by the glass). One table's inset with a chessboard, and they also have cribbage, darts, dominoes, shove-ha'penny, and faint piped music. *(Recommended by Neil Porter, Isobel Paterson, Barry and Marie Males, John and Christine Simpson, Julie and Tony Warneck, Susan and Nigel Wilson, R Macnaughton, Chris and Sue Bax, Walker and Debra Lapthorne, D W and J W Wilson, Paul and Ursula Randall, Sarah and Peter Gooderham, Andrew and Ruth Triggs, Andy and Jill Kassube, Sue and Geoff Price, Dave Braisted, Giles Francis, Helen and Andy, Stephen and Brenda Head)*

Free house ~ Licensees Raymond and Edward Boynton ~ Real ale ~ Meals and snacks (till 10pm) ~ Restaurant (closed Sun evening) ~ (01845) 567391 ~ Well behaved children welcome but small ones must be gone by 7pm ~ Open 11-11; 12-10.30 Sun ~ Bedrooms: £40B/£55B

POOL (W Yorks) SE2445 Map 7

White Hart

Just off A658 S of Harrogate, A659 E of Otley

Under the new manager, reports from readers have been most favourable. The four rooms have a restrained country decor, a pleasant medley of assorted old farmhouse furniture on the mix of stone flooring and carpet, and a quiet and comfortable atmosphere; there are two log fires, and a no-smoking area. Enjoyable bar food includes lunchtime sandwiches (from £3.50), sausages and cheddar mash with onion gravy (£4.75), and broccoli and brie pastry parcel (£5.50), as well as chicken soup (£1.95), savoury bacon and cheddar melt (£2.75), smokehouse platter (£4.65), beer in ale pie or lemon chicken (£5.25), stilton, chestnut and stout bake (£5.65), mustard pork loin steak (£6.50), rump steak (£6.95), and puddings such as good iced lemon caramel pudding; Sunday roast beef (£5.95). Well kept Bass, Stones, and Worthington Best on handpump, and a good choice of wines with quite a few by the glass; piped music. There are tables outside. This part of lower Wharfedale is a pleasant walking area. *(Recommended by Walter and Susan Rinaldi-Butcher, Michael Gittins, Julia Gorham, Anne and David Robinson, Rachael Ward, Mark Baynham, Lynne Gittins)*

Bass ~ Manager David Britland ~ Real ale ~ Meals and snacks (11-10) ~ (0113) 202 7901 ~ Open 11-11; 12-10.30 Sun

RAMSGILL (N Yorks) SE1271 Map 7

Yorke Arms

Take Nidderdale rd off B6265 in Pateley Bridge; or exhilarating but narrow moorland drive off A6108 at N edge of Masham, via Fearby and Lofthouse

To get the best out of this creeper-clad former shooting lodge, you must stay for a couple of days. The bedrooms are comfortable, the breakfasts marvellous, the food exceptionally good, and the owners courteous and friendly. The bars have fresh flowers and polish smells, two or three heavy carved Jacobean oak chairs, a big oak dresser laden with polished pewter and other antiques, and open log fires. Good imaginative food includes home-made soup (£3.50), thai spiced fishcakes (£4.95), sandwiches (from £4.95), a warm salad of black pudding, apple and poached egg or a choice of yorkshire cheeses with home-made relish (£5.20), freshly made pasta with chilli and chargrilled vegetables (£6.50), ham and eggs with sauté potatoes (£7.95), chicken breast stuffed with spinach on a root rostie and a saffron sauce (£8.50), fresh halibut with cheesy mash and prawns with a garlic sauce (£8.95), venison steak with celeriac, wild mushrooms and a port wine sauce (£8.95), sirloin steak (£12.25), and specials such as grilled vegetable tart tatin with pesto and parmesan (£4.95), pine nut, melon, smoked bacon and mozzarella salad (£5), bruschetta of beef, red onion, tomato and avocado and mustard mayonnaise (£7.20), sauté pork fillet with black pudding, pak choi, prune and armagnac (£8.20), and grilled breast of duck with butternut squash, balsamic and spinach (£8.50). Black Sheep on handpump, and a good wine list. They prefer smart dress in the no-smoking restaurant in the evening. You can walk up the magnificent if strenuous moorland road to Masham, or perhaps on the right-of-way track that leads along the hill behind the reservoir, also a bird sanctuary. *(Recommended by R Inman, Lesley, Peter and Alastair Barrett, B and M Kendall, Alan and Mandy Maynard, Janet and Peter Race, David and Judy Walmsley, John Plumridge)*

Free house ~ Licensees Gerald Atkins, Frances Atkins, John Tullett ~ Real ale ~ Meals and snacks (only for residents on Sun evening) ~ Restaurant ~ (01423) 755243 ~ Children in eating area of bar only ~ Open 11-11; 12-10.30 Sun ~ Bedrooms: £50B/£90B

REDMIRE (N Yorks) SE0591 Map 10

Kings Arms

Wensley—Askrigg back road: a good alternative to the A684 through Wensleydale

There's a good deal of character helped by friendly locals and licensees in this charming little pub, tucked away in an attractive small village. The simply furnished bar has cloth-covered wall settles and wall seats set around cast-iron tables, and there's a fine oak armchair (its back carved like a mop of hair) and a woodburning stove. Enjoyable bar food includes good soup (£2.25), sandwiches (from £2.45), breaded haddock (£4.95), vegetarian dishes (from £5.95), home-made lasagne (£6.45), good steak and kidney pie (£7.45), wild boar pie (£8.45), steaks (from £11.45), and Sunday roast (£5.45); the restaurant is no smoking and has local scenes on the wall painted by a local artist. Well kept Redmire Brew (brewed for the pub by Hambleton Ales), as well as Black Sheep Special, Richardson Brothers Four Seasons, John Smiths, and Theakstons Black Bull and Lightfoot on handpump, over 50 malt whiskies, and decent wines. The rather sweet staffordshire bull terrier is called Kim. Pool, dominoes, and cribbage; quoits. From the tables and chairs in the pretty garden here there's a superb view across Wensleydale; fishing nearby. Handy for Castle Bolton where Mary Queen of Scots was imprisoned. *(Recommended by Vann and Terry Prime, Bruce Bird, Mr and Mrs P Frost, K F Mould, Mary Thompson, Michele and Clive Platman, B Edgeley, Marion Tasker)*

Free house ~ Licensee Roger Stevens ~ Meals and snacks ~ Restaurant ~ (01969) 622316 ~ Children in eating area of bar until 9.30pm ~ Open 11-3, 6-11; 12-3, 7-10.30 Sun ~ Two bedrooms: £18B/£36B

RIPLEY (N Yorks) SE2861 Map 7

Boars Head

Just off A61 N of Harrogate

Ripley had three thriving inns until Sir William Ingilby, who owned the land, decreed that they should shut on Sundays to prevent churchgoers flocking in after the service. All three closed, and the delightful village was without a pub for 71 years. The story goes that when in 1990 the current landowner opened this luxurious hotel, such was the relief from locals that the vicar came in on the first night to bless the beer pumps. With a separate entrance at the side of the hotel (though you can walk through the public rooms to get there), the long flagstoned bar is very much like a smart bistro, with green checked tablecloths and olive oil on all the tables, most of which are arranged to form individual booths. The green walls have jolly little drawings of cricketers or huntsmen running along the bottom, as well as a boar's head (part of the family coat of arms), and a couple of cricket bats. The excellent bar food changes weekly, but typically includes lunchtime sandwiches, soup (£2.50), beef carpaccio with parmesan shavings and red onion salsa (£4.25), button mushroom stroganoff or poached plaice filled with spinach and wild mushrooms with a pesto dressing (£7.95), seared lamb liver with smoked bacon and a sage jus (£8.50), roast duck breast with chorizo and lentil cassoulet (£9.95), and puddings like sticky toffee pudding (£3.50);

they do a three-course set meal for £11.95. Though the emphasis seems to be on eating, drinkers are welcome too, and as well as an excellent wine list (with ten or so by the glass) and a good selection of malt whiskies, there's a very good choice of well kept real ales such as Theakstons Best and Old Peculier, Timothy Taylor Golden Best and Landlord, and their intriguing Crackshot – brewed to their own 17th-c recipe by Daleside. A pleasant little garden has plenty of tables. Part of the bar is no smoking. Some of the furnishings in the hotel came from the attic of next door Ripley Castle, where the Ingilbys have lived for over 650 years. Service was a little erratic on our own summer inspection visit, but readers' enthusiastic reports show that this is not the norm. *(Recommended by Walker and Debra Lapthorne, Miss L Hodson, P Stallard, Michael Butler, Geoffrey and Brenda Wilson, Peter and Jennifer Sketch)*

Free house ~ Licensee Sir Thomas Ingilby ~ Real ale ~ Meals and snacks ~ Restaurant ~ (01423) 771888 ~ Children welcome ~ Open 11-11; 12-10.30 Sun ~ Bedrooms: £90B/£105B

RIPPONDEN (W Yorks) SE0419 Map 7

Old Bridge 🍷

Priest Lane; from A58, best approach is Elland Road (opposite Golden Lion), park opposite the church in pub's car park and walk back over ancient hump-backed bridge

Mr Beaumont has carefully run this rather civilised 14th-c pub since 1963. It's set by the medieval pack horse bridge over the little River Ryburn, and the three communicating rooms are each on a slightly different level. There are oak settles built into the window recesses of the thick stone walls, antique oak tables, rush-seated chairs, a few well chosen pictures and prints, a big woodburning stove, and a relaxed atmosphere; fresh flowers in summer. Bar food includes a popular weekday lunchtime cold meat buffet which always has a joint of rare beef, as well as spiced ham, quiche, scotch eggs and so on (£8.50 with a bowl of soup and coffee); also, sandwiches, country-style terrine (£3.25), devilled crab (£3.95), stilton, mushroom and lentil canelloni (£4.50), pork stroganoff, fish pie or tagine of lamb with couscous (£4.75), and puddings like banana and toffee pancakes, cherry and almond frangipane tart and chocolate and brandy vacherin (£2.50). Well kept Black Sheep Special, Timothy Taylor Best and Golden Mild, and a weekly guest beer on handpump, 20 malt whiskies, a good choice of foreign bottled beers, and interesting wines with half a dozen by the glass. The popular restaurant is over the bridge. *(Recommended by ALC, Steve Goodchild, P H Roberts; more reports please)*

Free house ~ Licensee Ian Beaumont ~ Real ale ~ Meals and snacks (no bar meals Sat or Sun evening) ~ Restaurant ~ (01422) 822595 ~ Children in eating area of bar ~ Open 11.30-3, 5.30-11; 11.20-11 Sat; 12-10.30 Sun

ROBIN HOODS BAY (N Yorks) NZ9505 Map 10

Laurel 🍺

Village signposted off A171 S of Whitby

In a particularly pretty and unspoilt fishing village sits this charming little pub, set at the bottom of a row of fishermen's cottages. The friendly beamed main bar bustles with locals and visitors, and is decorated with old local photographs, Victorian prints and brasses, and lager bottles from all over the world; there's a roaring open fire. Bar food consists of lunchtime sandwiches (from £1.50) and winter soup. Well kept John Smiths and Theakstons Old Peculier and Black Bull on handpump; darts, shove-ha'penny, dominoes, cribbage, and piped music. In summer, the hanging baskets and window boxes are lovely. They have a self-contained apartment for two people. *(Recommended by David Carr, Comus Elliott, RWD, Richard Fallon, Stephen and Brenda Head, Rita Horridge, John Fahy, Paul Barnett, Stephen, Julie and Hayley Brown)*

Scottish Courage ~ Lease: Brian Catling ~ Real ale ~ Lunchtime snacks ~ (01947) 880400 ~ Children in snug ~ Open 12-11; 12-10.30 Sun

ROSEDALE ABBEY (N Yorks) SE7395 Map 10

Milburn Arms

The easiest road to the village is through Cropton from Wrelton, off the A170 W of Pickering

A very enjoyable place to spend a couple of days, this is a welcoming 18th-c inn run by a helpful, kind licensee. There's a good atmosphere and log fire in the neatly kept L-shaped and beamed main bar plus well kept Bass, Black Sheep Special and Riggwelter, and a monthly guest on handpump; 20 malt whiskies and eight good house wines by the glass. Generous helpings of good food served by smartly dressed waitresses include home-made soup (£2.50), good lunchtime sandwiches (from £2.75), chicken and duck liver pâté with a red onion and raisin relish (£4.25), pastry case of warm goat's cheese with sun-dried tomato and black olive salsa (£4.45), chargrilled wild boar sausage on leek and mustard mash with onion gravy (£4.50), confit of duck on braised cabbage and a green peppercorn sauce (£4.75), soft noodles with a sweet pepper and mushroom cream sauce with smoked goat's cheese (£6.25), chicken breast filled with salmon mousse on a champagne king prawn sauce or chargrilled fillet of salmon on crushed garlic potatoes in a lime butter sauce (£7.95), fried medallions of venison with roasted shallot jus (£9.25), and sirloin steak with a blue cheese sauce (£10.25); huge breakfasts. The restaurant is no smoking. Darts, shove-ha'penny, cribbage, dominoes, fruit machine, and piped music. The steep surrounding moorland is very fine and the terrace and garden have plenty of seats on which to relax. *(Recommended by David and Brenda Tew, Comus Elliott, Gethin Lewis, Pamela and Merlyn Horswell, Barbara Wensworth, Stephen, Julie and Hayley Brown, J and P Maloney, Chris and Sue Bax, Mrs G M Roberts, Geoffrey and Irene Lindley)*

Free house ~ Licensee Terry Bentley ~ Real ale ~ Meals and snacks ~ Restaurant ~ (01751) 417312 ~ Well behaved children in eating area of bar till 8.30pm ~ Open 11.30-3, 6.30-11; 11.30-11 Sat; 12-3, 6.30-10.30 Sun ~ Bedrooms: £41.50B/£76B

SAWLEY (N Yorks) SE2568 Map 7

Sawley Arms

Village signposted off B6265 W of Ripon

Fountains Abbey (the most extensive of the great monastic remains – floodlit on late summer Friday and Saturday evenings, with a live choir on the Saturday) is not far from this rather smart pub. The series of small turkey-carpeted rooms have been firmly run by Mrs Hawes for nearly 30 years now, and there are log fires and comfortable furniture ranging from small softly cushioned armed dining chairs and settees, to the wing armchairs down a couple of steps in a side snug; there may be daily papers and magazines to read, and two small rooms (and the restaurant) are no smoking. Good bar food includes lunchtime sandwiches, interesting soups such as leek and coconut or cauliflower and orange, salmon mousse or stilton, port and celery pâté, salmon pancake (£4.50), steak pie (£6.10), plaice mornay (£7.20), and puddings like lovely bread and butter pudding or meringue swans (£3.75). Good house wines and quiet piped music. The award-winning flowering tubs, baskets and gardens are quite spectacular. *(Recommended by Gwen and Peter Andrews, Janet and Peter Race, M A Buchanan, R L Gorick, Brian Wainwright, Peter and Ruth Burnstone, Mr and Mrs R Maggs, P R White, John Honnor)*

Free house ~ Licensee Mrs June Hawes ~ Meals and snacks (not winter Sun or Mon evenings) ~ Restaurant ~ (01765) 620642 ~ Well behaved children allowed if over 9 ~ Open 11.30-3, 6.30-10.30; 12-3, 7.30-10 Sun; closed Sun and Mon evenings in winter

Real ale may be served from handpumps, electric pumps (not just the on-off switches used for keg beer) or – common in Scotland – tall taps called founts (pronounced 'fonts') where a separate pump pushes the beer up under air pressure. The landlord can adjust the force of the flow – a tight spigot gives the good creamy head that Yorkshire lads like.

SETTLE (N Yorks) SD8264 Map 7

Golden Lion

A65

There's a surprisingly grand staircase that sweeps down into the spacious high-beamed hall bar of this handsome coaching inn. Also, an enormous fireplace, comfortable settles and plush seats, brass, prints and chinese plates on dark panelling, and a cheerful atmosphere. Enjoyable bar food includes soup (£2), sandwiches (from £2.60; hot roast sirloin of beef £3.85; prawns, banana and pineapple £4.25), filled baked potatoes (from £3.30), chicken liver terrine wrapped in bacon (£3.50), omelette of the day (£4.80), ploughman's with home-made chutney (£4.95), apple and brie parcels (£6.75), cajun chicken (£7.50), pork fillet on a bed of caramelised fruits with smoked Austrian cheese surrounded with apple and calvados sauce (£9.75), half a crispy duck with a brandy caramelised orange sauce (£10.50), baby leg of lamb (£10.95), and daily specials. Well kept Thwaites Bitter and Craftsman and a monthly guest beer on handpump kept under light blanket pressure, wines by the glass, bottle, litre or half-litre, and country wines; friendly helpful staff. The lively public bar has pool, fruit machine, and piped music; the labrador-cross is called Monty, and the black and white cat, Luke. *(Recommended by Arthur Williams, R T and J C Moggridge, Margaret and Arthur Dickinson, J H and S A Harrop, B M and P Kendall, Ann and Colin Hunt, Judith Hirst, Andrew and Ruth Triggs)*

Thwaites ~ Tenant Philip Longrigg ~ Real ale ~ Meals and snacks (untill 10pm) ~ Restaurant ~ (01729) 822203 ~ Children in eating area of bar until 9.30pm ~ Open 11-11; 12-10.30 Sun ~ Bedrooms: £22.50(£29.50B)/£45(£56B)

SHEFFIELD (S Yorks) SK3687 Map 7

Fat Cat £

23 Alma St

Of course the 10 real ales are the main draw here, but there's also a good, friendly and relaxed atmosphere that visitors can feel happy in. As well as their own-brewed, cheap Kelham Island Bitter, Pale Rider and another Kelham Island beer, and Timothy Taylor Landlord, there are seven interesting guest beers on handpump plus Belgian bottled beers (and a Belgian draught beer), British bottled beers, fruit gin, country wines, and farm cider. Good bar food (prices have not changed for two years now) includes sandwiches, soup (£1.30), vegetable cobbler, ploughman's, mexican mince, leek and butter bean casserole, and pork and pepper casserole (all £2.50), and puddings such as apple and rhubarb crumble or jam roly-poly (80p); well liked Sunday lunch. The two small downstairs rooms have coal fires, simple wooden tables and cushioned seats around the walls, and jugs, bottles, and some advertising mirrors on the walls; the one on the left is no smoking; cribbage and dominoes. Steep steps take you up to another similarly simple room (which may be booked for functions) with some attractive prints of old Sheffield; there are picnic-sets in a fairylit back courtyard. *(Recommended by David Carr, John McDonald, Ann Bond, Tony Hobden, Geoff and Sylvia Donald, the Didler, Ian Phillips, Christopher Turner, Richard Fallon, Andy and Jill Kassube, R N Hutton, Terry Barlow, Mike and Wendy Proctor, JJW, CMW, David and Fiona Pemberton)*

Own brew ~ Licensee Stephen Fearn ~ Real ale ~ Lunchtime meals and snacks (not 1 Jan) ~ (0114) 249 4801 ~ Children in upstairs room at lunchtime and early evening (if room is not booked) ~ Open 12-3, 5.30-11; 12-3, 7-10.30 Sun; closed 25-26 Dec

New Barrack

601 Penistone Road, Hillsborough (A61 N of centre)

As well as a fine choice of nine real ales well kept on handpump here – regulars such as Abbeydale Moonshine, Barnsley Bitter, John Smiths Magnet, and Stones, with five guest beers – there are five continental draught lagers, 20 continental bottled beers, over 20 malt whiskies, and farm cider. It's a big pub, and the comfortable front lounge has red leather banquettes, old pine floors, an open fire, and collections of decorative plates and of bottles, and there are two smaller rooms behind, one with TV and darts

– the family room is no smoking. Darts, cribbage, dominoes, and piped music. The good value simple food is all freshly made and might include sandwiches (from £1.20), home-made soup (£1.75), a huge satisfying ploughman's (£3.75), vegetarian dishes such as sweet potato and mozzarella loaf, a greek salad with stuffed vine leaves, feta cheese and so forth, and popular felafels (£3.75), meaty things such as sausage and tomato casserole, chilli, curries or steak sandwich (£3.95), steaks (£4.95), puddings such as peach crumble or cinnamon and carrot bake (£1.75), and a good value Sunday lunch. Service is friendly and competent; daily papers and magazines to read; maybe quiet piped radio. There are tables out behind. Local parking is not easy.

(Recommended by CMW, JJW, S E Paulley, Jack and Philip Paxton, Alan Paulley, Adam Dawson)

Free house ~ Licensee James Birkett ~ Real ale ~ Meals and snacks (12-2.30, 5.30-7.30; no food Sat/Sun evenings) ~ (0114) 234 9148 ~ Children welcome until 8pm ~ Folk music Mon evening, live blues/jazz Sat evening ~ Open 12-11 Mon-Thurs; 12-11(10.30 Sun)

SHELLEY (W Yorks) SE2112 Map 7

Three Acres

Roydhouse; B6116 and turn left just before Pennine Garden Centre; straight on for about 3 miles

Of course most people come to this civilised former coaching inn to enjoy the particularly good food, but the real ales are very well kept, it's a nice place to stay (super breakfasts), and the staff are friendly and efficient. The roomy lounge bar has a relaxed atmosphere, tankards hanging from the main beam, button-back leather sofas, old prints and so forth, and maybe a pianist playing light music. At lunchtime, the very enjoyable bar food includes interesting sandwiches (from £2.95; toasted ciabatta with roasted tomatoes, aubergines, basil, mozzarella and spinach salad £3.75; an open sandwich of smoked chicken breast, bacon, lettuce and tomato topped with a free-range poached egg £5.75), home-made prawn bisque topped with a prawn and rarebit crouton (£3.95), moules marinières (£5.25), salad of grilled lamb with lanark blue and warm mint dressing (£6.95), crispy japanese chicken with wok-fried greens, thread noodles and sweet chilli sauce (£7.95), steak, kidney and mushroom pie (£8.25), a roast of the day (£8.50), lots from the seafood bar such as Irish oysters (half a dozen £6.95), Loch Fyne queenie scallops with gruyère, grain mustard and garlic (from £6.95), fried king prawns in thai dressing (£12.95), and fresh Whitby lobster (from £15.95), and evening dishes such as duck, guinea fowl and rabbit liver terrine with spiced pear chutney (£4.95), ragout of corn fed chicken with a ravioli of wild mushrooms (£11.95), and seared fillet of beef with yorkshire pudding, caramelised onions, mustard and horseradish butter (£14.95); vegetarian dishes, and puddings. Well kept changing ales such as Adnams Extra, Mansfield Bitter and Riding, Morlands Old Speckled Hen, and Timothy Taylor Landlord on handpump, a good choice of malt whiskies, and exceptional (if not cheap) choice of wines. There are fine views across to Emley Moor, occasionally livened up by the local hunt passing.

(Recommended by Mr and Mrs G Turner, GLD, Neil Townend, Peter Marshall, Mike and Mary Carter, J and P Maloney, Derek and Sylvia Stephenson, Chris Platts, Andy and Jill Kassube, Michael Butler)

Free house ~ Licensees Neil Truelove, Brian Orme ~ Real ale ~ Meals and snacks ~ Restaurant ~ (01484) 602606 ~ Children in eating area of bar and in restaurant ~ Open 12-3, 7-11(10.30 Sun); closed Sat lunchtime and 25 Dec ~ Bedrooms: £50B/£65B

SNAITH (E Yorks) SE6422 Map 7

Brewers Arms

10 Pontefract Rd

It's the excellently kept Old Mill ales that draw readers here – all are brewed just around the corner (you can arrange a tour) using only natural ingredients for brewing and cleaning. The selection on handpump may include Old Mill Traditional, Mild,

Old Curiosity, Black Jack, Nellie Dean and Three Lions; unusually, they also do their own lager as well; quite a few malt whiskies. In the pleasant clean and bright open plan rooms of the bar there are old local photographs, exposed ceiling joists and a neat brick and timber bar counter. Straightforward bar food includes steak and kidney pie (£5), roasts (£5.50) and chicken à la crème (£5.95). There are also good value home-cooked restaurant meals in the fresh and airy conservatory-style no-smoking dining area with green plush chairs, a turkey carpet, a pine plank ceiling and lots of plants. Fruit machine and piped music; beware of joining the skeleton at the bottom of the old well. *(Recommended by Roger Bellingham, H K Dyson, Mr and Mrs B Hobden, Michael Butler; more reports please)*

Own Brew ~ Manager John McCue ~ Real ale ~ Meals and snacks ~ Restaurant ~ (01405) 862404 ~ Children welcome till 9pm ~ Singalong to organist Sun eve ~ Open 12-3, 6-11(7-10.30 Sun) ~ Bedrooms: £45B/£57B

STARBOTTON (N Yorks) SD9574 Map 7

Fox & Hounds

B6160 Upper Wharfedale rd N of Kettlewell; OS Sheet 98, map reference 953749

You can be sure of a friendly welcome from the landlord and other customers in this old-fashioned and notably well run inn. The bar has traditional solid furniture on the flagstones, a collection of plates on the walls, whisky jugs hanging from the high beams supporting ceiling boards, and a big stone fireplace (with an enormous fire in winter). Bar food is very good and popular so it's best to get here early to be sure of a seat: cream of onion soup (£2.25), stilton, sun-dried tomato and sweet roast pecan salad (£3.75), deep-fried king prawns with lemon mayonnaise (£4.95), turkey and coriander burger (£5.25), parsnip, chestnut and tomato crumble or mexican-style pork in a hot chilli sauce (£6.25), steak and mushroom pie (£6.50), good chicken, ham and mushroom crumble (£6.95), moroccan-style lamb (£7.50), and puddings like chocolate pudding with white chocolate sauce, sticky toffee pudding or apricot and almond tart with maple syrup ice cream (£2.25); at lunchtime there are also filled french sticks (from £2.95) and ploughman's and yorkshire pudding filled with mince or ratatouille (£4.75), and in the evening, extra dishes like baked salmon with a herb crust and creamy dill sauce (£8.25) or peppered venison steak with a port, lemon and redcurrant sauce (£9.95). The dining area is no smoking. Well kept Black Sheep Bitter, Theakstons Black Bull and Old Peculier, and Timothy Taylor Landlord on handpump, and around 60 malt whiskies. Dominoes, cribbage, and well reproduced, unobtrusitve piped music. Seats in a sheltered corner enjoy the view over the hills all around this little hamlet. *(Recommended by Chris and Sue Bax, Geoffrey and Brenda Wilson, Prof and Mrs S Barnett, Vann and Terry Prime, Gwen and Peter Andrews, WAH, Tim and Linda Collins, Chris Brace, Lesley, Peter and Alastair Barrett, Sheila and John French, Andrew and Ruth Triggs, David and Judy Walmsley, Ann and Colin Hunt)*

Free house ~ Licensees James and Hilary McFadyen ~ Real ale ~ Meals and snacks (see below) ~ (01756) 760269 ~ Children in eating area of bar ~ Open 11.30-3, 6.30-11; 12-3, 7-11 Sun; closed Mon evening all year, and all day Mon Oct-March ~ Bedrooms: £30S/£50S

STUTTON (N Yorks) SE4841 Map 7

Hare & Hounds

The lovely long sloping garden of this stone-built pub is quite a draw for families, and there are toys out here for children. Inside, there's a friendly welcome and cosy low-ceilinged rooms unusually done out in 1960s style. And as well as Sam Smiths OB on handpump, decent wine, and good, helpful service, there's a wide choice of very popular, good food set out on a huge blackboard in the lounge bar. With prices unchanged for two years, there might be home-made soup (£1.65), home-made pâté or deep-fried brie with raspberry sauce (£3.50), lunchtime haddock or home-made steak and mushroom pie (£4.95), roast lamb (£5.50), breast of chicken in a cheese and ham sauce (£5.95), and evening extras such as barnsley chops (£9.25), and fillet steak in a stilton and cream sauce (£13.50). Occasional piped music. It does tend to get crowded at weekends. *(Recommended by Janet Pickles, Tim Halstead, Andy and Jill Kassube, JJW,CMW; more reports please)*

Sam Smiths ~ Tenant Mike Chiswick ~ Real ale ~ Meals and snacks (not Sun or Mon evenings) ~ Restaurant ~ (01937) 833164 ~ Children welcome ~ Open 11.30-3.30, 6.30(6 Sat)-11; 12-3.30, 7-10.30 Sun; closed 26 Dec

SUTTON UPON DERWENT (E Yorks) SE7047 Map 7

St Vincent Arms

B1228 SE of York

Enjoyed by readers, this popular and cosy old pub keeps a fine range of around nine real ales on handpump: Banks's Bitter, Camerons Strongarm, Fullers London Pride, ESB, Chiswick, and a seasonal beer, John Smiths, Timothy Taylor Landlord, and Charles Wells Bombardier; also a range of malt whiskies, and very reasonably priced spirits. Good friendly service. Well liked bar food includes sandwiches (from £1.55), home-made soup (£1.90), filled baked potatoes (from £1.95), salmon fishcakes with a lemon and dill sauce (£3.50), ploughman's (from £3.50), good fillet of haddock in their own batter (£5.20), steak and kidney pie (£6.50), stir fry of the day (£8.50), steaks (from £9.50), and puddings like home-made treacle tart or apple pie (£2.20). One eating area is no smoking. The parlour-like, panelled front bar has traditional high-backed settles, a cushioned bow-window seat, windsor chairs and a coal fire; another lounge and separate dining room open off. No games or music. An attractive garden has tables and seats, and there are pleasant walks along the nearby River Derwent. The pub is named after the admiral who was granted the village and lands by the nation as thanks for his successful commands – and for coping with Nelson's infatuation with Lady Hamilton. *(Recommended by Paul and Pam Penrose, C A Hall, Peter Marshall, Margaret and Arthur Dickinson, Roger Bellingham, John Burley, Geoffrey and Brenda Wilson)*

Free house ~ Licensee Phil Hopwood ~ Real ale ~ Meals and snacks ~ Restaurant ~ (01904) 608349 ~ Children welcome (must be well behaved in restaurant) ~ Open 12-3, 6-11; 12-3, 7-10.30 Sun; closed evening 25 Dec

TERRINGTON (N Yorks) SE6571 Map 7

Bay Horse

W of Malton; off B1257 at Hovingham (towards York, eventually sigposted left) or Slingsby (towards Castle Howard, then right); can also be reached off A64 via Castle Howard, or via Welburn and Ganthorpe

Friendly and comfortable, this charming country pub has a good relaxed atmosphere, and enjoyable food and real ales. The cosy lounge bar has country prints, china on delft shelves, magazines to read, and a good log fire, and a traditional public bar has darts and dominoes. There's a dining area handsomely furnished in oak, and a back family conservatory has a collection of old farm tools on the walls. Well presented bar food includes lunchtime sandwiches, baps or crusty bread (from £2), filled baked potatoes (£2.45), and ploughman's (£5.40), as well as home-made soup (£1.90), Scarborough smokie browned with cream and parmesan (£3.55), terrine of duck with lime pickle (£3.75), leek, apple, stilton and walnut strudel in a wild mushroom sauce (£6), lamb hotpot or home-made steak and kidney pie (£6.30), grilled Ampleforth trout (£6.50), pork marinated in orange, wine and herbs and cooked with smoked sausage and button onions (£7.60), steaks (from £10.80), and puddings such as banana yoghurt cheesecake or home-made coffee, cream and brandy trifle (£2.65); children's dishes (from £1), and on Tuesday lunchtimes, they only serve soup and sandwiches. Well kept Courage Directors, John Smiths, and Theakstons Black Bull on handpump, and 62 blended and malt whiskies. There are tables out in a small but attractively planted garden. *(Recommended by Don and Thelma Anderson, Greta and Christopher Wells, Allan Worsley, Peter and Ruth Burnstone, Philip and Ann Falkner, Arthur and Margaret Dickinson)*

Free house ~ Licensees Robert and Jill Snowdon ~ Real ale ~ Meals and snacks (not Sun or Tues evenings) ~ (01653) 648416 ~ Restaurant ~ Children welcome if well behaved ~ Open 12-3, 6.30-11; 12-3, 7-10.30 Sun

THORGANBY (N Yorks) SE6942 Map 7

Jefferson Arms

Off A163 NE of Selby, via Skipwith

Giant daisies line the front of this handsome and surprisingly old village inn, which under its current licensees is going from strength to strength. The two sisters who run it are particularly friendly and helpful, taking everything in their stride, and working hard to make sure visitors have exactly what they want. They lived in Switzerland for 23 years before coming to Thorganby in 1997, and one has a Swiss husband responsible for the authentic rosti that plays such a prominent part in the menu. Very relaxed and stylish, the spacious main bar is distinctively decorated in a spotless mix of contemporary and traditional, with brick pillars and bar counter, dark wooden cushioned pews, several big mirrors on the green fleur-de-lys-patterned walls, and a couple of smart display chairs with huge sunflowers. A delightful little beamed lounge is more comfortable still, full of sofas and armchairs, as well as fresh flowers and potted plants, a fireplace with logs beside it, neat curtains, an antique telephone, and a pile of *Hello!* magazines. A long narrow conservatory is festooned with passion-flowers and grape vines. As well as a choice of rostis with various toppings (£4.90), the very good food might include sandwiches, soups such as curry with pineapple (£2.80), stuffed jalapeno peppers (£4.20), battered haddock with home-made chips (£5.80), Milanese potato gnocchi (£6.60), fried chicken breast with sage and parma ham (£7.90), grilled pork steak on a mushroom and bacon sauce with home-made German noodles (£8.90), poached salmon in a creamy orange sauce (£8.60), and quite a choice of ostrich dishes; you can eat from the same menu in the bar or restaurant. Well kept Black Sheep and John Smiths on handpump, and a thoughtful wine list, with a few half bottles; darts, chess, backgammon, soft piped music. The restaurant and conservatory are no smoking. There are tables in a porch area, and more in a side garden with roses and a brick barbecue. It's a nicely peaceful place to stay. *(Recommended by Peter Barnes, H Bramwell, Annabelle Watling)*

Free house ~ Licensee Margaret Rapp ~ Real ale ~ Meals and snacks ~ Restaurant ~ (01904) 448316 ~ Children in eating area of bar ~ Open 12-3, 6-11; 12-10.30 Sun; closed all day Mon ~ Bedrooms: £35B/£55B

THORNTON WATLASS (N Yorks) SE2486 Map 10

Buck

Village signposted off B6268 Bedale—Masham

There's always something going on at this warmly friendly village local – it might be a quoits match (the league has three divisions now), a game of cricket (they have their own team and not only does the pub border the village cricket green – one wall is actually the boundary), or live entertainment in the form of Saturday and Sunday evening country or 60s/70s music, and monthly Sunday lunchtime jazz. The sheltered garden has an equipped children's play area and there are summer barbecues – both quite a draw for families. If you wish to stay, they offer golfing, racing, and fishing breaks and there are plenty of good surrounding walks. The pleasantly traditional right-hand bar has upholstered old-fashioned wall settles on the carpet, a fine mahogany bar counter, a high shelf packed with ancient bottles, several mounted fox masks and brushes (the Bedale hunt meets in the village), a brick fireplace, and a relaxed atmosphere; piped music. Good, popular food at lunchtime might include light dishes such as mushroom rarebit with wensleydale cheese, Theakstons Ale, and a rasher of bacon (£3.75), ploughman's with good cheeses and home-made chutney, fresh crab and avocado salad or mussels in in a cream and pesto sauce (£4.50), steak and kidney pie or Whitby cod (£6.25), and lasagne (£6.50), evening dishes such as cheese and ale soup (£2.50), spicy Moroccan chicken (£7.95), and venison casserole (£8.25); chips are home-made, Sunday roasts are popular, and breakfasts are good. Well kept Black Sheep Bitter, John Smiths, Tetleys, Theakstons Best, and a local guest beer on handpump, and around 40 malt whiskies. The beamed and panelled no-smoking dining room is hung with large prints of old Thornton Watlass cricket teams. A bigger bar (refurbished this year) has darts and dominoes. *(Recommended by Andy and*

Jill Kassube, Bruce Bird, RB, Susan and Nigel Wilson, Miss L Hodson, Andrew and Ruth Triggs, Joan and Andrew Life, Derek and Sylvia Stephenson, David and Judy Walmsley, Elizabeth and Alex Rocke)

Free house ~ Licensees Michael and Margaret Fox ~ Real ale ~ Meals and snacks (not 25 Dec; served all day Sun) ~ Restaurant ~ (01677) 422461 ~ Well behaved children welcome ~ Live music Sat/Sun evenings, jazz monthly Sun lunchtime ~ Open 11-2.30, 6-11; 11-11 Sat; 12-10.30 Sun; closed evening 25 Dec ~ Bedrooms: £36S/£48(£54S)

WASS (N Yorks) SE5679 Map 7

Wombwell Arms

Back road W of Ampleforth; or follow brown tourist-attraction sign for Byland Abbey off A170 Thirsk—Helmsley

Reliably good for its imaginative food, this bustling pub is also well liked for its beers from local breweries and the warm welcome from the helpful licensees. The little central bar is spotlessly kept and cosy, and the three low-beamed dining areas are comfortable and inviting and take in an 18th-c former granary. At lunchtime, bar food might include sandwiches (from £2.25; hot or open ones £4.15), soups such as red pepper (£2.50), goat's cheese on a garlic crouton (£4.05), venison sausages with mustard mash and caramelised onions (£5.95), smoked haddock fishcakes with chive butter sauce (£6.15), and pasta with wild mushrooms (£6.75), with evening dishes like aubergine stuffed with garlic mushrooms and tomatoes and topped with parmesan breadcrumbs (£6.25), breast of chicken stuffed with blue cheese wrapped in pancetta (£8.35), cod baked with rosemary on leek mash or rack of lamb on chargrilled mediterranean vegetables (£8.50), chargrilled halibut steaks with citrus sauce (£8.95), and puddings such as banana and toffee crumble or pavlova with a wild berry coulis (£3.25); a plate of English cheeses (£3.75). One dining area is no smoking. Well kept Black Sheep Bitter, Timothy Taylor Landlord, and a guest such as Cropton Two Pints, Hambleton Stallion or York Stonewall on handpump, decent malt whiskies, and around 9 wines by the glass. *(Recommended by Walter and Susan Rinaldi-Butcher, Allan Worsley, Nick and Alison Dowson, Mr and Mrs D Price, Chris Brace, R Inman, R J Robinson, John Fahy, Simon Collett-Jones, John Honnor, Chris and Shirley Machin, Paul and Ursula Randall, Paul Barnett, Chris and Elaine Lyon)*

Free house ~ Licensees Alan and Lynda Evans ~ Real ale ~ Meals and snacks ~ (01347) 868280 ~ Children in eating area of bar (no under-5s evening) ~ Open 12-2.30, 7-11; 12-3, 7-10.30 Sun; closed winter Sun evening, all day Mon and 2 weeks Jan ~ Bedrooms: £29B/£49B

WATH IN NIDDERDALE (N Yorks) SE1467 Map 7

Sportsmans Arms

Nidderdale rd off B6265 in Pateley Bridge; village and pub signposted over hump bridge on right after a couple of miles

As well as opening up more bedrooms in an adjoining barn and stable block, most of this civilised restaurant-with-rooms was in the process of extensive refurbishment as we went to press. Mr Carter has been here for 20 years now, and many of his staff have been with him for over 10 years – it's that sort of reliably good place. Most people do come, of course, to enjoy the marvellous food or stay overnight – but there is a welcoming bar where locals do drop in just for a drink. Using the best local produce – game from the moors, fish delivered daily from Whitby, and Nidderdale lamb, pork and beef – the carefully presented and prepared food might include home-made soups (£3), lunchtime filled french bread (£4.75), and ploughman's (£5.50), calf liver on olive mash with bacon and red onion sauce, salmon with ginger and spring onions or chicken with gruyère and garlic (£8.75), lemon sole grenobloise (£8.95), fresh tuna in basil and tomato dressing (£9.50), turbot with asparagus and beurre blanc (£12.95), lobster (hot or thermidor £14.50), and puddings such as summer pudding or rich chocolate pots with chocolate ice cream (£3.75). The restaurant is no smoking. There's a very sensible and extensive wine list, a good choice of malt whiskies, several Russian vodkas, and attentive service; open fires, dominoes. Benches and tables outside. *(Recommended by Chris and Sue Bax, Ian Phillips, Brian Wainwright, Janet and Peter Race, Walker and Debra Lapthorne, Tony Hall, Melanie Jackson; also in the Good Hotel Guide)*

Free house ~ Licensee Ray Carter ~ Meals and snacks (not 25 Dec) ~ Evening restaurant ~ (01423) 711306 ~ Children in eating area of bar only ~ Open 12-2.30, 6.30-11(10.30 Sun); closed 25 Dec ~ Bedrooms: £30(£40S)/£50(£70S)

WHITBY (N Yorks) NZ9011 Map 10

Duke of York

Church Street, Harbour East Side

At the foot of the famous 199 Steps leading from the abbey, this bustling, popular pub overlooks the harbour entrance and the western cliff. There's a welcoming and comfortable beamed lounge bar and decorations that include quite a bit of fishing memorabilia, but it's the wide choice of good value fresh local fish on the menu itself which appeals most: there might be fresh crab sandwiches (£2.90), large fillet of fresh cod (£4.95), and fresh crab salad (£5.95), as well as sandwiches (£2.25), ploughman's or leek and stilton bake (£4.50), steak and mushroom pie, chicken tikka masala or lamb balti (£4.95), puddings (£2.25), and children's meals (from £2.50). Well kept Black Dog Abbey Ale and Special (brewed in Whitby), John Smiths and a guest beer on handpump, decent wines, 35 malt whiskies, and quick pleasant service even when busy; piped music, fruit machine. *(Recommended by Norma and Keith Bloomfield, Tony Scott, Janet Pickles, Mark Matthewman, Joan and Michel Hooper-Immins, Chris Gabbitas, Hugh McPhail, Martin Jones, David and Carole Chapman, David Carr, Beryl and Bill Farmer, M Rutherford, Denis and Margaret Kilner, David and Ruth Hollands)*

Free house ~ Lease: Lawrence Bradley ~ Real ale ~ Meals and snacks (12-9) ~ (01947) 600324 ~ Children welcome ~ Open 11-11; 12-10.30 Sun; closed 25 Dec ~ Bedrooms: /£25(£39B)

WIDDOP (W Yorks) SD9333 Map 7

Pack Horse

The Ridge; from A646 on W side of Hebden Bridge, turn off at Heptonstall signpost (as it's a sharp turn, coming out of Hebden Bridge road signs direct you around a turning circle), then follow Slack and Widdop signposts; can also be reached from Nelson and Colne, on high, pretty road; OS Sheet 103, map ref 952317

High up on the moorland, this isolated traditional pub has warm winter fires and a friendly welcome – and is a haven for walkers. The bar has window seats cut into the partly panelled stripped stone walls that take in the moorland view, sturdy furnishings, and well kept Black Sheep Bitter, Morlands Old Speckled Hen, Theakstons XB, Thwaites Bitter, and a guest beer on handpump, around 130 single malt whiskies, and some Irish ones as well, and decent wines; efficient service. Generous helpings of good bar food include sandwiches, soup, ploughman's, home-made steak and kidney pie, steaks, and specials such as vegetarian dishes, moussaka (£4.95), haddock mornay (£5.95), thai chicken curry (£6.95), rack of lamb (£8.95), and fresh fish. There are seats outside. *(Recommended by Ian and Nita Cooper, D Stokes, Rev John Hibberd; more reports please)*

Free house ~ Licensee Andrew Hollinrake ~ Real ale ~ Meals and snacks (see below) ~ (01422) 842803 ~ Children welcome until 8pm ~ Open 12-3, 7-11; 12-11 Sat/Sun; closed weekday lunchtimes and Mon Sept-Easter ~ Bedrooms: £28B/£40B

Please keep sending us reports. We rely on readers for news of new discoveries, and particularly for news of changes – however slight – at the fully described pubs. No stamp needed: *The Good Pub Guide*, FREEPOST TN1569, Wadhurst, E Sussex TN5 7BR.

YORK (N Yorks) SE5951 Map 7

Black Swan

Peaseholme Green; inner ring road, E side of centre; the inn has a good car park

This interesting building was quite plain and plastered until complete restoration before the last war revealed the splendid timbered and jettied façade and original lead-latticed windows in the twin gables. The busy black-beamed back bar (liked by locals) has wooden settles along the walls, some cushioned stools, and a throne-like cushioned seat in the vast brick inglenook, where there's a coal fire in a grate with a spit and some copper cooking utensils. The cosy panelled front bar, with its little serving hatch, is similarly furnished but smaller and more restful. The crooked-floored hall that runs along the side of both bars has a fine period staircase (leading up to a room fully panelled in oak, with an antique tiled fireplace); there is provision for non smokers. Decent good value bar food includes generously filled giant home-made yorkshire puddings (from £2.55), filled french sticks (from £3.45), and daily specials such as cumberland sausage, haddock or chicken with chips (from £4.25). Well kept Bass, Fullers London Pride, Shepherd Neame Spitfire, Worthington Best, and York Yorkshire Terrier on handpump, and several country wines; dominoes, fruit machine, trivia, and piped music. If the car park is full, it's worth knowing that there's a big public one next door. *(Recommended by Paul and Ursula Randall, Chris Gabbitas, Hugh McPhail, J and P Halfyard, Eric Larkham, Sue and Geoff Price)*

Bass ~ Manager Pat O'Connell ~ Meals and snacks (not Fri evening) ~ (01904) 686911 ~ Children in separate room ~ Folk Thurs evenings ~ Open 11-11; 12-10.30 Sun ~ Bedrooms: /£50B

Olde Starre

Stonegate; pedestrians-only street in centre, far from car parks

Very busy at peak times, this is the city's oldest licensed pub (1644), though parts of the building date back to 900. The main bar has original panelling, green plush wall seats, a large servery running the length of the room, and a large leaded window with red plush curtains at the far end. Several other little rooms lead off the porch-like square hall – one with its own food servery, one with panelling and some prints, and a third with cream wallpaper and dado; the tap room is no smoking. Well kept John Smiths Bitter and Magnet, and Theakstons Best, XB and Old Peculier on handpump, good coffee, and decent whiskies – most spirits are served in double measures for a single's price; friendly, helpful staff. Piped music, fruit machine, and video game. Good bar food includes filled rolls (from £2.55), battered haddock (£3.95), ploughman's (£4.30), cottage or steak and onion pie (£4.75), cumberland sausage or beef in ale (£4.80), mixed grill (£7.25), and puddings like blackberry and apple crumble or chocolate sponge (£1.95). *(Recommended by Rona Murdoch, M Borthwick, Colin Draper, Chris Gabbitas, Hugh McPhail, Andrew and Ruth Triggs, Howard England, Eric Larkham, SLC)*

Scottish Courage ~ Managers Bill and Susan Embleton ~ Real ale ~ Meals and snacks (11.30-8.30; not Fri/Sat evenings) ~ (01904) 623063 ~ Children welcome away from bar area ~ Open 11-11; 12-10.30 Sun

Spread Eagle £

98 Walmgate

As well as a large choice of good value food, this friendly pub is popular for its fine range of real ales on handpump: Mansfield Riding Bitter and Old Baily, Morlands Old Speckled Hen, Timothy Taylor Landlord, York Yorkshire Terrier and Stonewall, and six changing guests; several malt whiskies. The main bar is a dark vault with two smaller, cosier rooms leading off – lots of old enamel advertisements and prints on the walls, and a relaxed atmosphere. Well liked bar food under the new manageress includes filled rolls or hoagies (£1.99; hot beef sandwich with onion gravy £2.99), soup and a sandwich (£2.45), filled baked potatoes (from £2.50), burgers (from £3.25), steak and kidney pudding or mushroom stroganoff (£3.50), all-day breakfast (£4.25), fish and chips (£4.50), gammon and egg (£4.99), daily specials such as omelettes (£3.50), salmon en croûte, a pie of the day or home-made curries (£4.95), and vegetable lasagne (£5.65), and puddings like treacle sponge (£1.99). Fruit machine, trivia and juke box. *(Recommended by Ian Baillie, Chris Gabbitas, Hugh McPhail, Eric Larkham, Roger Bellingham, Thomas Nott)*

Mansfield Brewery ~ Manager Trudy Pilmoor ~ Real ale ~ Meals and snacks (12-2.30, 5.30-9.30; all day Sat; not Sun evening) ~ Restaurant ~ (01904) 635868 ~ Children welcome until 7pm ~ Live rock/blues Sun lunchtime ~ Open 11-11; 12-10.30 Sun

Tap & Spile £

Monkgate

As well as a refurbishment inside, this traditional pub now has an outside terrace with seats under parasols and outside heaters for cooler weather; there are more seats in the garden. But it remains the eight well kept real ales on handpump that most people come to enjoy – Black Sheep Bitter, Tap & Spile Premium, Old Mill Bitter and Theakstons Old Peculier, and five constantly changing guests on handpump from breweries such as Batemans, Daleside, Four Rivers, Roosters, and so forth; they also keep wheat beer, farm cider, and country wines. The big split-level bar has bare boards, brown or burgundy cushioned wall settles right around a big bay window, with a smaller upper area with frosted glass and panelling; darts, shove-ha'penny, dominoes, fruit machine, and piped music. Straightforward bar food includes sandwiches or toasties (from £1.50), home-made soup (£1.70), filled baked potatoes (from £1.80), omelettes (£3), chilli con carne (£3.25), vegetable lasagne (£3.75), gammon and egg (£4.25), and mixed grill (£5); daily specials, children's meals, and Sunday roast lunch. *(Recommended by Ian Baillie, Piotr Chodzko-Zajko, Andy Cunningham, Yvonne Hannaford)*

Century Inns ~ Manager Andy Mackay ~ Real ale ~ Meals and snacks (12-6.30 Mon-Sat; 12-2.30 Sun; not Sun evening) ~ (01904) 656158 ~ Well behaved children in eating area of bar until 7pm ~ Live music Sun evening ~ Open 11.30-11; 12-10.30 Sun

Lucky Dip

Besides the fully inspected pubs, you might like to try these Lucky Dips recommended to us and described by readers (if you do, please send us reports):

Aberford W Yor [Old North Rd; best to use A642 exit off A1; SE4337], *Swan*: Useful high-throughput dining pub, vast choice of good value generous food from sandwiches to carvery and display of puddings, lots of black timber, prints, pistols, cutlasses, stuffed animals and hunting trophies, well kept Boddingtons, Flowers, Tetleys and Timothy Taylor, generous glasses of wine, friendly uniformed staff, upstairs evening restaurant; children welcome, comfortable bedrooms *(Neil and Anita Christopher, Michael Butler, H Bramwell, Eddy and Emma Gibson)*

Addingham W Yor [SE0749], *Craven Heifer*: Consistently good food (not Mon lunchtime) in pleasant modernised lofty beamed lounge, friendly management and chef, two fireplaces, dark green plush, lots of country prints; good choice of usual food, Tetleys-related ales, piped music; steep steps from car park *(P T Parr)*; *Fleece*: Welcoming low-ceilinged 18th-c two-bar pub with eating area, big helpings of tasty food from baguettes to steak and cajun chicken, well kept ales inc Tetleys, open fires *(Michael Butler)*

Aislaby N Yor [SE7886], *Huntsman*: Carefully refurbished old pub with lots of pictures, cosy seating, wide choice of good value food inc superb sandwiches, fish, local produce, vegetarian and children's, very efficient friendly staff, well kept Camerons and Marstons, decent wines; piped music; busy weekends and holidays *(Richard Lewis)*

Aldbrough St John N Yor [off A1 signed to Piercebridge, then signed off to left; NZ2011], *Stanwick Arms*: Lovely country pub in good spot overlooking village green, happy staff, good food with Barbados influence in bistro and bar (bar food may stop if restaurant busy), Black Sheep and John Smiths Magnet, good log fire, all clean and tidy; seats outside; children welcome, bedrooms; cl Mon lunchtime *(B Kneale)*

☆ **Allerthorpe** E Yor [off A1079 nr Pocklington; SE7847], *Plough*: Clean and airy pub doing well under very friendly current managers, two-room lounge bar with snug alcoves, hunting prints, WWII RAF and RCAF photographs, open fires, wide choice of good sensibly priced food, well kept Theakstons Bitter, XB and Old Peculier, decent house wines, well served coffee, restaurant, games extension with pool, juke box etc; pleasant garden, handy for Burnby Hall *(Roger Bellingham, Stephen, Julie and*

Hayley Brown, Mrs M Hunt, LYM)
Ampleforth N Yor [Main St; SE5878], *White Swan*: Extensive modern lounge/dining bar in small attractive village, wide choice of generous food from good big filled buns to popular Sun lunch, front country bar with several real ales inc a guest beer, lots of malt whiskies, darts and a couple of fruit machines; restaurant, decent wines, good friendly service even on very busy Sat night; back terrace *(Denis and Margaret Kilner, Paul and Ursula Randall)*

☆ **Appletreewick** N Yor [off B6160/B6265 SE of Grassington; SE0560], *New Inn*: Welcoming stonebuilt pub with good value simple food inc good sandwiches, well kept John Smiths and Theakstons Best, imported beers, willing service, interesting photographs, pub games, family room, no music; in fine spot, lovely views, garden, good walking; bedrooms *(Judith Hirst, Gwen and Peter Andrews, LYM)*

☆ **Arncliffe** N Yor [off B6160; SD9473], *Falcon*: Classic old-fashioned haven for walkers, ideal setting on moorland village green, no frills, Youngers tapped from cask to stoneware jugs in central hatch-style servery, generous plain lunchtime and early evening bar snacks, open fire in small bar with elderly furnishings and humorous sporting prints, airy back sunroom (children allowed here lunchtime) looking on to garden; run by same family for generations – they take time to get to know; cl winter Thurs evenings; bedrooms (not all year), good breakfasts and evening meals – real value *(Neil and Angela Huxter, Vicky and David Sarti, LYM)*

Askham Bryan N Yor [SE5548], *Nags Head*: Well kept beer, good food and wine, good atmosphere *(G Washington)*

☆ **Askwith** W Yor [3 miles E of Ilkley; SD1648], *Black Horse*: Biggish open-plan family pub in lovely spot with superb Wharfedale views from terrace; wide choice of usual food cooked well (best to book Sun lunch), well kept Worthington, pleasant helpful staff, open fire *(Lynne Gittins, Michael Butler)*

Austwick N Yor [SD7668], *Game Cock*: Prettily placed below the Three Peaks, pleasant atmosphere in homely old-fashioned beamed back bar, sensibly priced simple bar food inc vegetarian, well kept Thwaites, good fire, welcoming landlady, smarter no-smoking restaurant, no music, seats outside with good play area; clean bedrooms *(T M Dobby, Margaret and Arthur Dickinson, Gwen and Peter Andrews, LYM)*

Bawtry S Yor [28 High St (A614); SK6593], *Turnpike*: Comfortable L-shaped flagstoned bar with alcoves and lots of wood, three real ales and a guest, good value food lunchtime and Tues-Thurs evening, open all day Sun; fruit machine, piped music *(CMW, JJW)*

Beal N Yor [off A645 E of Knottingley; SE5325], *Hungry Fox*: Pleasant mature atmosphere, cheerful efficient service, good generous food in bar and restaurant (pianist some nights), John Smiths and a guest beer; popular with older people *(V and J Davies)*

☆ **Beverley** E Yor [North Bar Within (A164); TA0340], *Beverley Arms*: Spacious traditional oak-panelled bar in comfortable and well run long-established hotel (ex THF, seems more approachable as a Regal), two bars, well kept ales, easy-going friendly atmosphere, choice of several decent places to eat inc interesting former coachyard (now enclosed) with formidable bank of the ranges that were used for cooking; good bedrooms, some with Minster view *(H Bramwell, Roger Bellingham, LYM)*

Beverley [North Bar Without], *Rose & Crown*: Prompt cheerful service even when busy, decent piping hot food inc outstanding speciality giant haddock, well kept Wards, good service; bedrooms *(Malcolm Baxter, I Maw)*; [1 Flemingate], *Tap & Spile*: Well done Tap & Spile with laid-back atmosphere, interesting range of ales often from small breweries, huge choice of country wines; by Minster *(Tim Barrow, Sue Demont)*

Birstall W Yor [Church Lane; from Bradford towards Dewsbury turn right at church – OS Sheet 104 map ref 218262; SE2126], *Black Bull*: Old building opp ancient Norman church, dark panelling and low beams, former upstairs courtroom, Whitbreads-related ales, good cheap home-made food inc bargain early meals, old local photographs; recent small extension *(Michael Butler)*

Blackshaw Head W Yor [Badger Lane; old Burnley rd, above Hebden Bridge; SD9527], *Top Shoulder*: Good imaginative food, very reasonable prices, pleasant village pub atmosphere *(Mrs J A Beale)*

Bolton Abbey W Yor [SE0754], *Devonshire Arms*: Comfortable and elegant hotel in marvellous position, limited choice of good bar food from sandwiches to Sun lunches (Dukes Bar very popular with walkers, can be a bit smoky), well kept beers, good wines, tables in garden; handy for the priory, walks in the estate and Strid River valley; smart restaurant, helicopter pad; good bedrooms *(Julia Gorham, Geoffrey and Brenda Wilson)*

Boroughbridge N Yor [Bridge St; SE3967], *Three Horseshoes*: Spotless traditional pub with character landlord, friendly locals, huge fire in lounge, darts, dominoes and cards in public bar, great atmosphere, good plain home cooking from sandwiches to steaks in bars and restaurant, well kept Black Sheep; bedrooms *(Pete Baker)*

Bradfield S Yor [Dale Rd, Low Bradfield; towards Strines – OS Sheet 110 map ref 253919; SK2592], *Haychatter*: Attractive and welcoming small stonebuilt country pub in lovely countryside, two real ales; views and walks *(CMW, JJW)*; [High Bradfield – OS Sheet 110 map ref 268927], *Old Horns*: Friendly old stonebuilt pub with comfortably refurbished divided L-shaped bar, lots of pictures, no-smoking area, good value food, busy but efficient service, ales such as Boddingtons, Courage Directors, John Smiths Magnet and Stones; quiet piped music, children welcome, picnic-sets and play area outside, hill village with stunning views, interesting church, good walks *(CMW, JJW)*

Bradford W Yor [Toller Lane (B6269), Heaton; SE1334], *Hare & Hounds*: Welcoming modern pub with well kept Stones, reasonably wide choice of good food inc early evening bargains, good friendly landlady *(Cliff Blakemore)*; [Easby Rd, nr Univ], *McCrorys*: Classic cellar bar reminiscent of late 1950s, a haven for bohemians, great acoustics for Weds/Sun blues bands, cajun or folk music; John Smiths real ales *(Reg Nelson)*

Brafferton N Yor [SE4370], *Farmers*: Friendly unspoilt local under newish licensees, pine country furniture, nice Yorkshire range with glowing fire, subtle lighting, good value food, small restaurant, Theakstons Best, XB and Old Peculier, comfortable games room with fruit machine and darts, tables in garden; bedrooms *(Nick and Alison Dowson, Janet Pickles)*

Brompton N Yor [just off A64 W of Scarborough; SE9582], *Cayley Arms*: Quiet and welcoming uncluttered pub in pretty village, swift friendly service, good freshly cooked generous food inc good choice of fish, reasonable prices, well kept ales inc Theakstons; garden *(A Burt, A M Pring, Peter Burton)*

Brompton N Yor [the one off A684 just N of Northallerton; SE3896], *Village Inn*: Wide range of hearty food, consistently good value, pleasantly served in long narrow room; bedrooms in motel wing behind, attractive countryside *(H Bramwell, Joseph Watson)*

Burniston N Yor [A171 N of Scarborough; TA0193], *Three Jolly Sailors*: Roomy lounge with eating area, public bar and conservatory, Bass, Worthington and a guest such as Morlands Old Speckled Hen, good varied generous food inc vegetarian, local fish and good value carvery *(Ann and Bob Westbrook)*

☆ **Burton Leonard** N Yor [off A61 Ripon—Harrogate; SE3364], *Hare & Hounds*: Attractive country pub with wide choice of generous food inc very popular steak and kidney pie, fresh veg and good chips; warm, comfortable and spotless beamed bar with paintings, copper and brass, big fairy-lit beech branch over ceiling, cosy coffee lounge, spacious restaurant, well kept Black Sheep, Tetleys and Theakstons, decent wines, very friendly attentive staff, no games or juke box *(Mrs D J Garvey, D V Clements)*

☆ **Cadeby** S Yor [off A1(M) via A630, then Sprotbrough turn; SE5100], *Cadeby Inn*: Biggish, with open fire, gleaming brasses and lots of house plants in back lounge, quieter front sitting room, no-smoking snug, separate games area; generous food from good hot beef sandwich to excellent value carvery, well kept ales inc Tetleys, Sam Smiths, John Smiths, and Courage Directors, over 200 malt whiskies, cheerful landlord, good service even when busy, seats out in front; children in eating area, open all day Sat *(Peter F Marshall, Nigel and Sue Foster, LYM)*

Caldwell N Yor [NZ1613], *Brownlow Arms*: Small friendly pub in isolated village, busy, with good home-cooked food, well kept John Smiths and a guest such as Bull Premium, reasonable prices; landlord was the vicar *(Mike and Sue Walton)*

☆ **Cawood** N Yor [King St (B1222 NW of Selby); SE5737], *Ferry*: Unspoilt but neatly kept 16th-c inn, smallish comfortable rooms, massive inglenook, stripped brickwork, bare boards, well kept Marstons, Timothy Taylor Landlord and local guest beers tapped from the cask, good reasonably priced food from refitted kitchen, tables out on flagstone terrace and grass by River Ouse swing bridge; cl weekday lunchtimes; good value bedrooms *(Simon Orme)*

☆ **Chapel le Dale** N Yor [B5655 Ingleton—Hawes, 3 miles N of Ingleton; SD7477], *Old Hill*: Basic stripped-stone flagstone-floor moorland bar with potholing pictures and Settle railway memorabilia, roaring log fire in cosy back parlour, well kept Dent and Theakstons Bitter, XB and Old Peculier, generous simple home-made food in separate room inc good beef sandwiches and pies, plenty of vegetarian; juke box; children welcome; bedrooms basic but good, with good breakfast – wonderful isolated spot, camping possible *(R H Rowley, Nigel Woolliscroft, LYM)*

☆ **Clifton** W Yor [Towngate/Coalpit Lane; off Brighouse rd from M62 junction 25; SE1622], *Black Horse*: Smart yet cosy dining pub, very popular for enormous choice of good generous traditional food in restaurant; comfortable oak-beamed bars, good service, at least four well kept Whitbreads-related beers, friendly service, open fire; bedrooms comfortable *(Andy and Jill Kassube, Michael Butler)*

Cloughton N Yor [N of village; TA0297], *Hayburn Wyke*: Included for position, nr NT Hayburn Wyke and Cleveland Way coastal path, lots of tables outside; very black and white L-shaped bar, restaurant and eating area beyond, well kept Scottish Courage beers, friendly informal service, well behaved children welcome; bedrooms *(Dave Braisted, M Borthwick)*

☆ **Cloughton Newlands** N Yor [A171; TA0196], *Bryherstones*: Several interconnecting rooms, well kept Theakstons, over 50 whiskies, good reasonably priced generous food in separate eating area, welcoming service, plenty of atmosphere; pool room, quieter room upstairs; children welcome, delightful surroundings *(S E Paulley)*

Collingham W Yor [SE3946], *Half Moon*: Good varied menu esp fish dishes such as monkfish in prawn sauce; children welcome, good choice for them *(Mrs E E Sanders)*

☆ **Colton** N Yor [off A64 York—Tadcaster; SE5444], *Old Sun*: Attractive and friendly 17th-c beamed local doing well under current landlord, popular for good reasonably priced food (not Mon); low doorways, old settles and banquettes, sparkling brasses, well kept Bass, Morlands Old Speckled Hen and John Smiths, decent wines, log fires, welcoming staff; picnic-sets out in front *(John Burley, CMW, JJW)*

Copt Hewick N Yor [off B6265 E of Ripon; SE3471], *Oak Tree*: Comfortable, with good choice of beers and of reasonably priced wines, wide choice of individually and perfectly cooked food, service carefully supervised by landlord *(Mr and Mrs A R Hawkins)*

☆ **Crayke** N Yor [off B1363 at Brandsby, towards Easingwold; SE5670], *Durham Ox*: Relaxed and well used old-fashioned flagstoned lounge bar with antique settles and other venerable furnishings, interestingly carved panelling, log fire in imposing inglenook, bustling public area with darts and fruit machine, decent food (not Sun evening) from sandwiches up, well kept Banks's, Camerons and Marstons Pedigree; restaurant, children welcome, bedrooms – attractive village *(Chris and Sue Bax, Nick and Alison Dowson, Philip and Ann Falkner, T Halstead, LYM)*

Cridling Stubbs N Yor [between junctions 33 and 34 of M62 – easy detour; SE5221], *Ancient Shepherd*: Cosy family-run pub with pleasant layout, friendly atmosphere and warm welcome; Boddingtons and John Smiths, huge sandwiches, good generous home-made evening bar meals, reasonable prices, comfortable banquettes, efficient service; quiz night Weds *(Catherine Smith, Catherine Cheetham, LYM)*

Darley Head N Yor [B6451; SE1959], *Wellington*: Tastefully extended and well decorated quaint old local, big room with open fire, two smaller rooms, old pews and tables, well kept Black Sheep, Tetleys and Theakstons, good bar food, great landlord, sweeping views from restaurant; bedrooms well furnished, lovely scenic drive here *(Janet and Peter Race, Rachael Ward, Mark Baynham)*

Deighton N Yor [A19 N of Escrick; SE6243], *White Swan*: Good food inc vegetarian from sandwiches and ploughman's to dressed crab, two very popular comfortable bars, separate restaurant, good choice of enjoyable wines by the glass; seats outside, but traffic noise *(Janet Pickles)*

☆ **Dewsbury** W Yor [Station, Wellington Rd; SE2523], *West Riding Licensed Refreshment Rooms*: Superb early Victorian station bar, celebrating 150th anniversary in 1998 – well worth missing a few trains for; three busy rooms with character despite bare floors and minimal decor, good range of real ales inc Batemans, good food inc interesting vegetarian dishes from nutritionist licensee, good value weekday lunches, popular pie and curry nights, steam-engine cigarette cards and framed antique time-tables; particularly well kept Batemans XB, XXXB and Mild and several guest beers from small breweries, occasional beer festivals, farm ciders, coal fires; open all day, no-smoking area till 6, jazz nights, disabled access *(the Didler, Andy and Jill Kassube, Richard Lewis, Michael Butler)*

Dewsbury [2 Walker Cottages, Chidswell Lane, Shaw Cross], *Huntsman*: Cosy converted cottages alongside urban-fringe farm, lots of brasses and appropriate bric-a-brac, low ceilings, friendly locals, wide choice of well kept beers inc Black Sheep and John Smiths; no food evening or Sun/Mon lunchtime, busy evenings *(Michael Butler)*

Doncaster S Yor [Leisure Park, Herten Way (off A638 S); SE5902], *Cheswold*: Brewers Fayre with masses for children inc big play room and outdoor play areas and children's shop – a mini leisure park, events all year; well kept Boddingtons, Marstons Pedigree, Morlands Old Speckled Hen and Wadworths 6X, comfortable open-plan seating, good food and friendly efficient staff; open all day *(Richard Lewis)*; [1 West St], *Leopard*: Lively pub with superb Warwicks & Richards tiled facade, well kept Courage Directors, Greene King IPA, John Smiths and Charles Wells Bombardier, local papers, friendly staff, pool in games room, good juke box, pub games, quiz nights, live music upstairs; lounge can get smoky *(Richard Lewis)*; [W Laith Gate], *Plough*: Quiet traditional two-room local with well kept Bass and Barnsley, old town maps, friendly staff and locals, pub games, tiny garden; open all day Tues, Fri and Sat *(Richard Lewis)*; [W Laith Gate], *Tut 'n' Shive*: Good choice of mainly Whitbreads-related ales and of popular food, good prices, friendly staff, bare boards and panelling, good juke box, games machine; open all day *(Richard Lewis)*; [Frenchgate – edge of central pedestrian precinct], *White Swan*: Front room so far below counter level that you need a high reach for your well kept local Wards ales, side passage leading to surprisingly big back bar/eating area – full range of cheap pub food *(Tony Hobden, BB)*

Dungworth S Yor [Loxley Rd (B6077) up nr Damflask Reservoir; SK2889], *Nags Head*: Good food in pleasantly busy rather isolated pub, Hardys & Hansons Bitter, plates and pictures, games room with pool and machines; can get a bit smoky *(CMW, JJW)*; [Main Rd (B6076 W of Sheffield)], *Royal*: Pleasant village local on edge of Peak District, food inc well priced Sun lunch, well kept Bass, John Smiths Magnet and local guest beers *(CMW, JJW, Andy and Jill Kassube)*

Easingwold N Yor [Market Pl; SE5270], *George*: Smart bar areas in market town hotel popular with older people, real ales such as Black Sheep, Marstons and local brews, good food in bar and restaurant inc Whitby fish and imaginative dishes, friendly enthusiastic service; bedrooms *(Dr B and Mrs P B Baker)*; [Knott Lane], *Station*: Victorian hotel surrounded by housing estate, brewing its own good appropriately named ales such as Steamcock and Express, tasteful decor with local steam railway memorabilia, friendly landlord, good lunchtime bar food, real fire; bedrooms comfortable, with own bathrooms *(Dr B and Mrs P B Baker, Nick and Alison Dowson)*

Egton Bridge N Yor [NZ8005], *Postgate*: Moorland village local tastefully refurbished by licensees new to the trade, relaxed atmosphere, simple good value food, real ales; traditional games in public bar, tables on sunny flagstoned terrace; has been open all day; bedrooms *(John Higgins, LYM)*

Emley W Yor [Chapel Lane; signed off A642 Hudderfield—Wakefield; SE2413], *White Horse*: Unpretentious village local with big tap room and smaller lounge, homely atmosphere and friendly staff; changing ales inc guests such as Bass, Tetleys, Theakstons and Stones, cheap plentiful food *(M Dickinson)*

☆ **Escrick** N Yor [E of A19 York—Selby; SE6442], *Black Bull*: Good atmosphere in unpretentious village pub with bar/dining area well opened up by newish owners, divided by arches and back-to-back fireplaces with flagstones on one side, mix of wooden tables with benches, stools and chairs, good value generous food here and in back dining room inc special deals, small helpings for children and OAPs, well kept John Smiths, Tetleys and Theakstons (weekday happy hour 5-7); bedrooms *(P R Morley, Roger Bellingham)*

Faceby N Yor [NZ4903], *Sutton Arms*: Dining pub with pleasant atmosphere, nice if not cheap food, well kept local beer, 30s and 50s bric-a-brac *(Chris and Sue Bax)*

☆ **Fadmoor** N Yor [off A170 in or just W of Kirkbymoorside; SE6789], *Plough*: Lovely spot overlooking quiet village green, for spick and span little pub doing well under its new licensees (formerly of the main entry Feathers in Helmsley); very tastefully refurbished, with extremely hospitable helpful landlady, ample helpings of beautifully presented bar food and restaurant meals, real ales, good open fire; children very welcome in restaurant; comfortable bedrooms *(Karen and Andy Hutton, LYM)*

☆ **Farndale East** N Yor [Church Houses, next to Farndale Nature Reserve; SE6697], *Feversham Arms*: Friendly pub in lovely daffodil valley (very busy then), two unspoilt but bright smallish rooms with flagstone floors and real fires, well kept Tetleys, good value home-cooked food, open fire, smart beamed and stripped-stone restaurant, friendly service; very popular weekends; walkers with wet boots and dogs not welcome; nice small garden, good bedrooms, big breakfast *(Maurice Thompson)*

Fewston N Yor [Norwood; B6451 5 or 6 miles N of Otley; SE2054], *Sun*: 18th-c inn with decent food, Theakstons XB, Best and Old Peculier, open fires, games room; children's play area; summer afternoon teas, Fri and Sat evening barbecue *(C A Hall)*

Firbeck S Yor [New Rd; SK5688], *Black Lion*: Tall old village pub, pleasantly modernised with two small rooms off bar, walls covered with hundreds of interesting photographs, half a dozen well kept Scottish Courage and other beers, some concentration on good generous reasonably priced food in bar and pleasant new back restaurant extension, real chips; two bedrooms, attractive village *(Nigel Brewitt, G P Kernan)*

Flamborough N Yor [Dog & Duck Sq; junction B1255/B1229; TA2270], *Royal Dog & Duck*: Welcoming local with two homely comfortable beamed rooms, well kept Bass, fair-priced usual food esp local fish, particularly well kept Bass; bedrooms *(Peter Plumridge, LYM)*

Flockton W Yor [Barnsley Rd; off A642 Wakefield—Huddersfield at Blacksmiths Arms; SE2314], *Sun*: Friendly beamed pub with lots of brasses and open fires in two comfortable little rooms, reasonably priced food inc delicious big yorkshire puddings, Stones and Worthington BB, tables outside; not far from M1 junction 38, via A637 *(John and Elspeth Howell)*

Follifoot N Yor [Main St; SE3452], *Lascelles Arms*: Welcoming and hospitable, with interesting reasonably priced food, very friendly atmosphere, good open fires, small cosy lounge area, well kept attractively priced Sam Smiths OB, decent wines *(James Marshall, BS)*

☆ **Gargrave** N Yor [Church St (off A65 NW of Skipton); SD9354], *Masons Arms*: Friendly and busy well run local, attractive and homely, well kept Whitbreads-related ales, generous quick bar food inc vegetarian and good sandwiches, copper-canopied log-effect gas fire dividing two open-plan areas; tables in garden, bowling green behind; children if well behaved; in charming village on Pennine Way, between river and church and not far from Leeds & Liverpool Canal *(Ann and Colin Hunt, Charles and Pauline Stride, Roger and Pauline Pearce)*

Gargrave [A65 W], *Anchor*: Useful spacious family place with wide range of real ales and simple reasonably priced food inc children's; pleasant service, lots of amusements, piped music; canalside tables and play area; restaurant; bedrooms in modern wing *(WAH, Ann and Colin Hunt, LYM)*

Goathland N Yor [opp church, off A169; NZ8301], *Mallyan Spout*: More hotel than pub, popular from its use by TV's *Heartbeat* cast, with three spacious lounges (one no smoking), traditional relaxed bar, good open fires, fine views, Malton PA and Double Chance, good malt whiskies and wines; children in eating area, usually open all day, handy for Mallyan Spout waterfall; comfortable bedrooms *(Stephen, Julie and Hayley Brown, Andrew Hazeldine, LYM)*

☆ **Grange Moor** W Yor [A642 Huddersfield—Wakefield; SE2215], *Kaye Arms*: Good civilised and busy family-run dining pub with imaginative proper food, courteous efficient staff, exceptional value house wines, hundreds of malt whiskies, no-smoking room; children allowed lunchtime, handy for Yorkshire Mining Museum; cl Mon lunchtime *(Michael Butler, Dave Braisted, Neil Townend, LYM)*

Grantley N Yor [off B6265 W of Ripon; SE2369], *Grantley Arms*: Attractive beamed stone pub in quiet Dales village, welcoming coal fires, good food running up to steaks, Tetleys and Theakstons, restaurant; children welcome if eating *(L Price)*

☆ **Grassington** N Yor [Garrs Lane; SE0064], *Black Horse*: Comfortable and cheerful open-plan modern bar, very busy in summer, with well kept Black Sheep Bitter and Special, Tetleys and Theakstons Best and Old Peculier, open fires, generous straightforward home-cooked bar food inc children's and vegetarian, darts in back room, sheltered terrace, small attractive restaurant; bedrooms comfortable, well equipped and good value *(Judith Hirst, Prof and Mrs S Barnett, Ron Gentry, BB)*

☆ **Grassington** [The Square], *Devonshire*: Well

kept welcoming hotel, comfortable lounge bar with good window seats overlooking sloping village square, interesting pictures and ornaments, open fires, good range of well presented food inc good Sun lunch in big well furnished dining room, good family room, attentive landlord, full range of Theakstons ales kept well, also Tetleys, tables outside; well appointed good value bedrooms, good breakfast *(Dick Brown, Judith Hirst, Gwen and Peter Andrews, Ann and Colin Hunt, LYM)*

Great Habton N Yor [NW of Malton; SE7676], *Grapes*: Cosy and friendly, with good food inc inventive recipes – esp beef; reasonable prices, well kept Theakstons, good service; best to book w/e *(Revd Denis Samways)*

☆ **Grenoside** S Yor [Skew Hill Lane, 3 miles from M1 junction 35 – OS Sheet 110 map ref 328935; SK3293], *Cow & Calf*: Neatly converted farmhouse, three friendly connected rooms, one no smoking, high-backed settles, stripped stone, brass and copper hanging from beams, plates and pictures, good value hearty home-made bar food (not Sun evening) inc sandwiches, children's and bargain suppers Fri, well kept Sam Smiths OB, tea and coffee; piped music, music quiz nights; family room in block across walled former farmyard with picnic-sets; splendid views over Sheffield, disabled access, open all day Sat *(CMW, JJW, David Carr, Michael Butler, Roy Butler, Don and Shirley Parrish, LYM)*

Grenoside [Main St], *Old Harrow*: Open-plan, with comfortable banquettes, plates, pictures and old photographs, adjoining flagstoned former tap room, good value lunchtime food, well kept Boddingtons, Stones and Whitbreads Castle Eden; fruit machine, TV, darts, maybe loud piped music; small garden with picnic-sets; children and dogs allowed *(G Washington, David Carr, Patrick Hancock)*; [210 Main St], *Old Red Lion*: Renovated open-plan stonebuilt pub with alcoves and separate areas, flagstones around bar, well kept ales inc Wadworths 6X, notice offering top-ups, good choice of inexpensive fresh food (all day Sat, not Sun evening) inc vegetarian and bargains Mon, Tues and Fri, good coffee; games machines, piped pop, TV, cash quiz Tues, live music Thurs; open all day, children and dogs seem welcome, picnic-sets out in front *(CMW, JJW, G Washington)*

☆ **Grinton** N Yor [B6270 W of Richmond; SE0598], *Bridge*: Welcoming and relaxed riverside inn in lovely spot opp Cathedral of the Dales, two bars, very friendly service, good range of good value simple well prepared food from decent sandwiches to good steaks, ales such as Black Sheep Special, John Smiths, Tetleys Imperial, Theakstons Best, XB and Old Peculier, decent wines; attractive tables outside, front and back; bedrooms with own bathrooms; dogs welcome, open all day, good walks *(Vann and Terry Prime, Anthony Barnes, Edward and Richard Norris, Philip and Caroline Pennant-Jones)*

☆ **Halifax** W Yor [Paris Gates, Boys Lane – OS Sheet 104 map ref 097241; SE0924], *Shears*: Hidden down steep cobbled lanes among tall mill buildings, dark unspoilt interior, well kept Timothy Taylor Landlord and Golden Best and a guest beer, welcoming knowledgeable landlord (not Tues), friendly staff; very popular lunchtime for good cheap food from hot-filled sandwiches to home-made pies, curries, casseroles etc; sporting prints, local sports photographs, collection of pump clips and foreign bottles; seats out above the Hebble Brook; good value food inc real chip and home-made pies *(Pat and Tony Martin)*

Halifax [Horsfall St, Savile Pk], *Big 6*: Old-fashioned Victorian mid-terrace pub with snugs, memorabilia, interesting bottle collection; quick friendly service, well kept Greene King Abbot, Marstons Pedigree and Old Speckled Hen, lunchtime sandwiches, pies etc; can get smoky *(Pat and Tony Martin)*; [Shibden Fold, off A58 at Stump Cross], *Shibden Mill*: Cottagey and welcoming riverside pub dating back to 17th c, smart inside with good bar lunches from sandwiches up, popular restaurant, Black Sheep and guest beers, good wine; hidden away in valley bottom, a picture when floodlit *(Greta and Christopher Wells)*; [Bradford Old Rd – off A647 at Ploughcroft, right at ski slope sign, up steep cobbles], *Sportsman*: Fine Calderdale views from prominent hilltop which this friendly and comfortable 17th-c pub shares with dry ski slope; good choice of bar food from sandwiches through cheap lunches to good value carvery, well kept Timothy Taylor Landlord, Tetleys and a beer brewed for the pub, children's room with plenty of games equipment *(Pat and Tony Martin)*; [Park Terr, Stump Cross], *Stump Cross*: Well run oldish stone building with pleasant modern furnishings, well kept beers, good range of modestly priced food *(W W Burke)*

Hampsthwaite N Yor [Main St; about 5 miles W of Harrogate; SE2659], *Joiners Arms*: Quietly welcoming spotless and nicely updated pub in pleasant village setting, stripped stone, back dining area, friendly staff, well kept John Smiths, decent wines, good food inc popular Sun lunch *(Ian and Nita Cooper)*

Harewood W Yor [Harrogate Rd (A61); SE3245], *Harewood Arms*: Busy hotel, former coaching inn, opp Harewood House; three attractive, comfortable and spaciously relaxing lounge bars with wide choice of good food from sandwiches up, friendly prompt service, well kept ales inc cheap Sam Smiths OB, decent house wines; coffee and afternoon tea *(Janet Pickles, Rachael Ward, Mark Baynham)*

☆ **Harome** N Yor [2 miles S of A170, nr Helmsley; SE6582], *Star*: Welcoming thatched beamed pub/restaurant with good if not cheap food inc interesting sandwiches and light lunches, fine steak and kidney pudding, game and fresh fish and seafood, attractive layout and furnishings inc aged Mouseman tables and bar stools, well kept Black Sheep and Theakstons, good wines by the glass, two wonderful log fires, daily papers and magazines *(Stephen Adams, Ann and Bob Westbrook, J and P Maloney)*

Harrogate N Yor [31 Tower St; SE3155], *Tap & Spile*: Basic but very friendly bare-boards stripped-stone pub, refreshing change from the town's Irish theme pubs and sports pubs; good local atmosphere, three clean and pleasant rooms, up to ten changing well kept and well described ales, helpful staff, cheap basic lunchtime bar food, daily papers; open all day Sat, packed on live band nights *(John Honnor, Vann and Terry Prime)*

Hartshead W Yor [15 Hartshead Lane; not very far from M62 junction 25; SE1822], *Grey Ox*: Doing well under new management, with wonderful Pennine views esp from garden with play area; generous well cooked food, well kept Tetleys-related ales, cosy fire *(Greta and Christopher Wells)*

Hawes N Yor [High St; SD8789], *White Hart*: Friendly, warm and cosy, busy around bar (esp weekends and Tues market day), quieter on left, wide choice of reasonably priced food in bar and restaurant, real fire, well kept John Smiths, welcoming service; bedrooms good value *(Mrs D P Dick, P A Legon)*

nr **Hawes** [nr High Shaw, off A684 N; SD8691], *Simonstone Hall*: Very accessible Game Tavern attached to country house hotel, walkers warmly welcomed, fantastic views, great food, tasteful furnishings; comfortable bedrooms *(Suzy Miller)*

Haworth W Yor [SE0337], *Three Sisters*: Roomy bars and smoking and no-smoking restaurant, varied interesting reasonably priced food from sandwiches to speciality big steaks, well kept ales such as Black Sheep and Theakstons, very helpful staff; open all day; bedrooms *(N Stansfield)*

Hebden Bridge W Yor [Keighley Rd (A6033); SD9927], *Nutclough House*: Friendly, cosy and comfortable bar, generous reasonably priced bar meals with good vegetarian choice, well kept Courage Directors, Timothy Taylor Landlord, Theakstons Best and a guest beer, fairly wide range of malt whiskies, side games room; handy for Hardcastle Crags; good value bedrooms *(Bruce Bird)*; [Bridge Gate], *White Lion*: Solid stonebuilt inn with hospitable landlord, comfortable bar and country-furnished bare-boards dining lounge, good choice of reasonably priced good generous food all day inc vegetarian, well kept Boddingtons and Timothy Taylor Landlord; bedrooms comfortable *(Andy and Jill Kassube, Kathy and Steve Barker)*

Hedon E Yor [9 Baxtergate; off A1033; TA1928], *Shakespeare*: Cosy village local with open fire in small L-shaped bar, well kept Morlands Old Speckled Hen, Tetlows Tummy Tickler and Vaux Samson, decent wine, good value food from sandwiches and toasties up inc decently cooked fresh veg, cheerful welcome, thousands of beermats on beams, old framed brewery advertisements, darts, games machines, small TV; gets very busy; bedrooms *(Paul and Ursula Randall)*

☆ **Helmsley** N Yor [Market Pl; SE6184], *Black Swan*: Smart and attractive hotel, not a pub, but pleasant beamed and panelled bar with carved oak settles and windsor armchairs, cosy and gracious lounges with a good deal of character, surprisingly reasonable bar lunch menu, courteous staff, charming sheltered garden; good place to stay – expensive, but comfortable and individual *(W H and E Thomas, BB)*

Helmsley [Market Sq], *Crown*: Simple but welcoming and pleasantly furnished beamed front bar opening into bigger unpretentious central dining bar, wide choice of food inc enjoyable teas, range of well kept beers, efficient staff, roaring fires, tables in sheltered garden behind with conservatory area; bedrooms pleasant *(Janet Pickles, Janet and Peter Race, W and E Thomas, BB)*; [Market Pl], *Royal Oak*: Comfortable and popular, with friendly staff, three well decorated rooms, antiques, good food inc superb roasts and filled yorkshire puddings (worth the wait if busy – no food orders after 8), well kept Camerons Bitter and Strongarm; piped music and TV (can be intrusive if both on); bedrooms good if not cheap *(K and E Leist, Bruce Bird)*

Helperby N Yor [Main St; SE4470], *Golden Lion*: Five interesting changing ales from smaller often distant brewers (but served through sparkler), wide choice of good if not cheap food, good fire, cosy atmosphere, friendly staff, no juke box or games; two beer festivals a year; busy Sat *(Nick and Alison Dowson)*

Holme on Spalding Moor E Yor [Old Rd; SE8038], *Olde Red Lion*: Well run village pub, clean and comfortable, good food with fish emphasis in old-world panelled L-shaped lounge bar and dining room, friendly attentive staff, eclectic range of wines, sunny terrace with koi carp; comfortable bedrooms in chalets behind *(Rona Murdoch, Michelle Hayles)*

Horbury W Yor [Queen St; SE3018], *Boons*: Former Woolpack transformed by Clarks, comfortably basic, with their beer and guests kept well, simple decor with some flagstones, bare walls, Rugby League memorabilia, very friendly young Australian licensees, back tap room with pool; very popular, can get crowded *(Michael Butler)*

Horsehouse N Yor [Coverdale rd Middleham—Kettlewell; SE0481], *Thwaite Arms*: Friendly little family pub popular for good simple food – only a few tables in pretty homely dining room, so worth booking; fine Sun roast, well kept Theakstons and John Smiths, farm cider, charming friendly landlord, chatty local farmers evening, good coal fire in cosy snug, bigger plainer locals' bar; early 19th-c former farm building in wonderful village setting nr beautiful little church, lots of paths to nearby villages and moors, great drive along dale; children welcome; two bedrooms *(Paul and Madeleine Morey, D W Stokes)*

☆ **Horton in Ribblesdale** N Yor [SD8172], *Crown*: Clean and pleasant low-ceilinged bar with dark woodwork, brasses and good fire, good value interesting food inc vegetarian (soups and specials particularly praised), very well kept ales such as Theakstons Old Peculier,

welcoming helpful staff, open fire; simple good value bedrooms *(Dagmar Junghanns, Colin Keane, A C and E Johnson, John Hobbs)*
Hotham E Yor [Main St; quite handy for M62 junction 38; SE8934], *Hotham Arms*: Friendly and busy, with comfortable banquettes, smallish back dining area partly no smoking, good value food (not Mon/Tues evenings), good-natured attentive service, real ales such as Black Sheep and Tetleys, TV and fruit machine, games room *(Mr and Mrs P Eastwood)*
☆ **Huddersfield** W Yor [40 Chapel Hill; SE1416], *Rat & Ratchet*: Bare-boards two-room local brewing its own beer (changing each month) alongside guest ales such as Adnams, Batemans Dark Mild, Caledonian 80/-, Greene King Abbot, Marstons Bitter, Pedigree and Winter Warmer, Morlands Old Speckled Hen, Timothy Taylor Best and Landlord; two more comfortable rooms up steps, basic well cooked cheap bar food inc outstanding sandwiches and popular Weds curry night; ambience more pleasant than you might guess from outside, open all day (from 3.30 Mon/Tues) *(Tony Hobden, Richard Lewis, Judith Hirst, Derek and Sylvia Stephenson, John Plumridge, Patrick Hancock)*
Huddersfield [Station Building], *Head of Steam*: Railway memorabilia, model trains and cars for sale, pies, sandwiches and Sun roasts, friendly staff, real ales such Boddingtons, Morlands Old Speckled Hen, Ridleys Rumpus and local Kitchen Town, Huddersfield Pride and Wilsons Wobble – open all day, an enterprising change from usual platform cafe *(Pat and Tony Martin, R J Bland, Richard Lewis)*; [Queen St], *Old Court Brew House*: High-ceilinged former court, bright and airy, original plasterwork and fittings such as gas lamps, long bar, plenty of open space, armchairs and sofas; a Whitbreads pub with half a dozen of their ales kept well, also three or four brewed here – the top of the brew copper, surrounded by glass, sticks up through the floor of the high-ceilinged public bar; games machines, food; open all day *(Richard Lewis, Joan and Michel Hooper-Immins)*; [Colne Bridge; B6118 just off A62 NE], *Royal & Ancient*: Marstons beers, good interesting food, log fires, golfing theme bar, school magazine photographs and football programmes in extended dining area, popular restaurant with Bette Davis memorabilia *(Michael Butler)*
Huggate E Yor [off A166 or B1246 W of Driffield; SE8855], *Wolds*: Attractively refurbished small 16th-c pub, mildly upmarket, wide range of decent if not cheap food, friendly staff, well kept real ale, benches out in front and pleasant garden behind with delightful views; has been cl Mon; bedrooms compact but clean and nicely appointed – lovely village, good easy walks *(Paul and Ursula Randall, JRR, H Bramwell)*
Hull E Yor [9 Humber Dock St; TA0928], *Green Bricks*: Early 19th-c inn overlooking marina, usually open all day, lunchtime and early evening meals, Bass and Stones, seating outside *(CMW, JJW)*; [Scale Lane], *Manchester Arms*: Small and comfortable, with lots of woodwork, good pub lunches inc sandwiches, unusual pitta bread sandwiches, vegetarian and other main dishes at attractive prices; unobtrusive piped music, quiz nights *(H Spencer)*; [11 Posterngate], *Mission*: Converted seamen's mission complete with minstrels' gallery, comfortable settees, very well priced food and Old Mill beers; handy for Princes Quay shopping centre; children welcome *(Andy and Jill Kassube); [77 Charles St],* New Clarence: Big U-shaped bar partitioned for some cosiness, dark panelling, stone floors, up to ten real ales from all over, such as Caledonian Deuchars, Greene King Abbot and Jennings; good well priced snacks; pool, games machines, juke box; open all day, handy for New Theatre *(Andy and Jill Kassube)*; [193 Cottingham Rd], *Old Grey Mare*: Former Newland Park, now a substantially extended partly no-smoking Tom Cobleigh family pub with friendly efficient service, good range of well prepared good value food inc vegetarian and two-for-one bargains 4-7, six real ales inc Theakstons XB; piped music, fruit machines, service can slow; bedrooms *(CMW, JJW)*; [5 Dock St], *Rugby*: Comfortable and fairly quiet, with well priced lunchtime food from hot beef sandwiches up, well kept Sam Smiths, pool, TV *(Andy and Jill Kassube, H Spencer)*; [roundabout Commercial Rd/Hessle Rd], *Whittington & Cat*: Well restored, many pictures of docks in their heyday, fine brasswork, leather banquettes, quality fittings; well kept cheap Mansfield Mild and Bitter, good value basic lunchtime food (not Sun/Mon); CD juke box, fruit machines, piped music; facilities for disabled *(CMW, JJW)*
Hutton le Hole N Yor [SE7090], *Crown*: Bustling friendly local with huge helpings of good food, good friendly service, well kept Camerons, lots of whisky-water jugs; children welcome; small pretty village with wandering sheep *(Jane Broadribb, Stuart Barlow)*
Ilkley W Yor [Leeds Rd (A65); SE1147], *Wharfedale Gate*: Brewers Fayre vastly improved by sensitive refurbishment – comfortable, with no-smoking area in lounge, Boddingtons and Wadworths 6X *(D W Stokes)*
☆ **Ingbirchworth** S Yor [Welthorne Lane; off A629 Shepley—Penistone; SE2205], *Fountain*: Neat and spacious red plush turkey-carpeted lounge, cosy front bar, comfortable family room, open fires; emphasis on generous good value varied bar food inc exotic salads and superb puddings; well kept Tetleys and Marstons Pedigree, well reproduced pop music, friendly service, tables in sizeable garden overlooking reservoir; bedrooms *(RWD, Richard Cole, BB)*
Kettlesing N Yor [A59, Kettlehead; SE2256], *Bulls Head*: Good value food all day in traditional country pub with well laid out long circular bar; interesting beers such as Vaux Waggle Dance, friendly staff *(Chris Johnson)*
☆ **Kettlewell** N Yor [SD9772], *Racehorses*: Comfortable and civilised, with very friendly attentive service, good well presented food, well

kept ales inc Theakstons XB, good choice of wines, log fires; well placed for Wharfedale walks; bedrooms good, with own bathrooms *(Dick Brown, LYM)*

Kettlewell, *Kings Head*: Lively and cheerful old character local away from centre, well kept ales such as Black Sheep, Tetleys, Timothy Taylor, good value food; pool room, bedrooms *(Tony Lewis, Ron Gentry, BB)*

Killinghall N Yor [Otley Rd (A59/B6161); SE2756], *Travellers Rest*: Good value food and well kept beer; handy for Harlow Carr gardens; piped music may be rather intrusive *(Joy and Peter Heatherley)*

☆ **Kilnsey** N Yor [Kilnsey Crag; SD9767], *Tennant Arms*: Good range of good food, well kept Tetleys and Theakstons Best and Old Peculier, open fires, friendly efficient staff, interesting decorations; piped music; beautiful Wharfedale setting, with views of spectacular overhanging crag from restaurant; comfortable immaculate bedrooms all with private bathrooms, good value; good walks *(John Higgins)*

☆ **Kirby Hill** N Yor [off A66 NW of Scotch Corner, via Ravensworth; NZ1406], *Shoulder of Mutton*: Friendly and unassuming village inn with green plush wall settles, stone arch to public bar, open fires, good bar food from lunchtime sandwiches to steaks, vegetarian dishes, good service, Black Sheep Bitter and Riggwelter, John Smiths and Websters Yorkshire, quite a few malt whiskies, restaurant; darts, dominoes, cribbage, piped music, Fri quiz night; children in eating area, fine views from picnic-sets in yard behind and from good value bedrooms (you do hear the – tuneful – church bell); cl Mon lunchtime *(Bruce Bird, Chris and Ann Garnett, B Kneale, LYM)*

☆ **Kirkby Overblow** N Yor [SE3249], *Star & Garter*: Cosy and quaint old country-feel pub very popular lunchtime with older people for generous good value bar food inc imaginative specials and good vegetarian choice, outstanding value 3-course Sun lunch, particularly well kept Camerons and Tetleys, two real fires, bluff no-nonsense Yorkshire landlord, first-rate service, dining room for evening meals; open all day *(Howard and Margaret Buchanan, Andy and Jill Kassube, Margaret and Arthur Dickinson)*

☆ **Knaresborough** N Yor [19 Market Pl; SE3557], *Blind Jacks*: Former 18th-c shop done out a few years ago as charming multi-floor traditional tavern, with simple but attractive furnishings, brewery posters etc, well kept Black Sheep, Hambleton White Boar and Nightmare Stout and Timothy Taylor Landlord with changing guest beers, farm cider and foreign bottled beers; well behaved children allowed away from bar, open all day, cl Mon till 5.30 *(G P Kernan, Peter Haines, Andy and Jill Kassube, Dr and Mrs B Baker, M Buchanan, Paul Hilditch, LYM)*

Knottingley W Yor [A1 Business Park, Pontefract Rd; SE5023], *Turnpike*: Smart new Brewers Fayre, good value food inc children's in pleasant surroundings, play areas indoors and out; bedrooms in adjoining Travel Inn *(R C Vincent)*

Langsett S Yor [A616 nr Penistone; SE2100], *Waggon & Horses*: Welcoming and comfortable main-road moors pub, helpful staff, blazing log fire, stripped stone and woodwork, good home cooking inc good value Sun lunch, well kept Bass and Stones, magazines to read, friendly small dog *(Peter and Mavis Brigginshaw)*

☆ **Langthwaite** N Yor [Arkengarthdale, N of village – aka the CB Inn; NY9902], *Charles Bathurst*: Long bar with clean and spartan bistro decor but immediately welcoming atmosphere, light pine, scrubbed tables, country chairs and benches, roaring fire, friendly helpful service, well kept John Smiths and Theakstons, good imaginative reasonably priced food using local ingredients, frequently changing menu, fairly short but interesting wine list; bedrooms, attractive spot with wonderful views *(Jennifer Oswald-Sealy, Revd J E Cooper, W James)*

☆ **Langthwaite** [just off Reeth—Brough rd], *Red Lion*: Cosy unspoilt 17th-c pub, individual and relaxing, in charming dales village with ancient bridge; local books and maps for sale, basic cheap nourishing lunchtime food, well kept Black Sheep Riggwelter and Theakstons XB, country wines, tea and coffee; well behaved children allowed lunchtime in very low-ceilinged (and sometimes smoky) side snug, quietly friendly service; good walks all around, inc organised circular ones from the pub *(Anthony Barnes, Judith Hirst, LYM)*

☆ **Lastingham** N Yor [off A170 W of Pickering; SE7391], *Blacksmiths Arms*: Attractively old-fashioned village pub opp ancient church, log fire in oak-beamed bar's open range, traditional furnishings, no-smoking dining area with food from sandwiches to steaks inc vegetarian (breakfasts for campers etc), well kept Black Sheep, Hambleton Stud and Websters Yorkshire, quite a few malt whiskies, separate games room with pool etc; well behaved children welcome, no-smoking bedrooms, lovely countryside *(Mrs P Hare, Tom Thomas, Richard Fallon, Chris and Sue Bax, LYM)*

Laughton en le Morthen S Yor [High St; off B6463 E of Sheffield; SK5288], *Hatfield Arms*: Good food lunchtime and evening (12-7 Sun – may need to book dining room then); lounge with comfortable banquettes, beamery and brasses, biggish tap room, four real ales, no piped music; quiz Weds, children welcome *(CMW, JJW)*

Laughton en le Morthen, *St Leger Arms*: Gently refurbished and extended, basic very cheap home-made food, real chips, memorable yorkshire puddings, popular all-day Sun carvery, good value meat sandwich; well kept cheap Barnsley Bitter and three other ales in lined over-sized glasses; games area, flower garden with picnic-sets, swings and lovely views; children welcome, occasional quiz nights; can get very busy, piped music may be rather loud *(CMW, JJW)*; [Brookhouse; towards Thurcroft; SK5188], *Travellers Rest*: Modern stonebuilt pub with good food inc Sun lunches, vegetarian and bargains (no food Sun evening), partly no-smoking dining room, Hardys & Hansons and Stones, children welcome, games room with pool, quiet piped music; streamside seats outside, play area; pleasant village *(CMW, JJW)*

☆ **Leeds** W Yor [Gt George St, just behind Town Hall; SE3033], *Victoria*: Well preserved ornate Victorian pub with grand etched mirrors, impressive globe lamps extending from the ornately solid bar, imposing carved beams, booths with working snob-screens, smaller rooms off; well kept Tetleys inc Mild and several well chosen guest beers, friendly smart bar staff, reasonably priced food in luncheon room with end serving hatch, no-smoking room; open all day *(Richard Lewis)*

Leeds [North St (A61)], *Eagle*: Well kept reasonably priced Sam Smiths, sensible food inc good sandwiches and speedy friendly service in 18th-c pub with choice of basic or plush bars; pleasant for lunch, good bands in back bar weekends, occasional beer festivals; bedrooms *(Peter Plumridge, LYM)*; [26 Gt George St], *Felon & Firkin*: Former court rooms, with decorated vaulted ceilings, fancy windows and cops and robbers decor along with the usual Firkin benches, barrels and breweriana; upper gallery shows microbrewery producing their Fuzz, Felon, Bobby, Dogbolter and a chocolate and orange Stout; bar food from big sandwiches up, table footer, games machines, big screen TV, live music and comedy nights, friendly staff, disabled access; open all day *(Richard Lewis, Andy and Jill Kassube)*; [9 Burley Rd, junction with Rutland St], *Fox & Newt*: Interesting choice of well kept mainly Whitbreads-related ales as well as several brewed in the cellar here, good value limited standard lunchtime food inc cheap Sun lunch, cheery neo-Victorian decor, well reproduced piped music; open all day, children welcome, pub dog called Buster – other dogs allowed evening; occasional quiz nights *(Richard Lewis, LYM)*; [Lower Briggate], *Hogshead*: Spacious open-plan Whitbreads pub with very wide choice of changing well kept guest ales, often quite recherché; bare wood, partitions, some upstairs seating, wide food choice, friendly staff, relaxing atmosphere; open all day *(Richard Lewis)*; [51 Headrow], *Horse & Trumpet*: Late Victorian, with fine period features inc superb snug, lunchtime food, Tetleys and half a dozen interesting changing guest ales, busy friendly staff; open all day *(Richard Lewis)*; [Lovell Pk Rd], *Londoner*: Open-plan Tetleys Festival Ale House done up tavern-style with alcove seating (part no smoking), dark wood, stained and sloganed walls; half a dozen interesting changing guest beers, friendly staff, lunchtime food, games area, tables outside; open all day (Sun afternoon closure) *(Richard Lewis)*; [Roundhay Rd, Oakwood; SE3236], *Roundhay*: Reopened after refurbishment as cheap and cheerful Foresters Feast dining pub, well kept Whitbreads-related beers, quick friendly service; handy for Roundhay Park and Tropical World *(Phil and Anne Smithson)*; [3 Bishopgate St], *Scarborough*: Impressive ornate art nouveau tiled frontage; bare boards, barrel tables, lots of wood, ten or so interesting changing real ales inc Milds in fine condition, farm cider, extensive cheap menu, friendly helpful staff, music-hall posters; open all day, Sun afternoon closure *(Richard Lewis)*; [Merrion Way], *Stick or Twist*: Roomy recent Wetherspoons conversion below casino, well kept ales inc four interesting guest beers, some unusual bottled beers, good choice of food all day inc two-for-one bargains, friendly staff, disabled facilities, no piped music, no-smoking area; open all day *(Richard Lewis)*; [top end of Merrion Centre, Merrion Way], *Tap & Spile*: Tiles and flagstones, stripped stone walls, prints of old Leeds, well kept changing ales such as Dent, Hambleton Stallion, Jennings, Old Mill Black Jack, Timothy Taylor Landlord and Whitbreads Castle Eden, lunchtime food; pool (this part can get smoky), TV, piped music; open all day, cl Sun *(Richard Lewis)*

Little Ouseburn N Yor [B6265 S of Boroughbridge; SE4461], *Green Tree*: Welcoming little pub with comfortable plush banquettes, friendly staff, well kept Timothy Taylor Landlord, Tetleys and guest beers, nicely cooked and presented standard food inc good value Sun lunch, reasonable prices, panelled dining room *(John Oddey)*

☆ **Long Preston** N Yor [A65 Settle—Skipton; SD8358], *Maypole*: Clean and friendly dining pub with spacious beamed dining room and comfortable lounge with copper-topped tables, stag's head, open fire; good choice of good value generous food inc home-made pies and Sun lunch, well kept Boddingtons, Timothy Taylor and Whitbreads Castle Eden, helpful service; bedrooms clean and comfortable, with own bathrooms *(Malcolm and Lynne Jessop, Gordon Neighbour)*

Low Bradfield S Yor [SK2692], *Plough*: Good value freshly made food inc children's, fish and chips take-aways and Sun lunch, comfortable banquettes, lots of brass and copper, old lamps and bric-a-brac, Whitbreads-related ales, two fires; pool in separate bar, restaurant, picnic-sets in garden; children welcome *(CMW, JJW)*

Low Row N Yor [B6270 Reeth—Muker; SD9897], *Punch Bowl*: Cheerful family bar, open all day in summer, with well kept Theakstons Best, XB and Old Peculier and guests, rows of malt whiskies, decent house wines, wide choice of good value generous food, log fire, games room; piped music; fine Swaledale views esp from terrace with quoits pitches below; popular tea room 10-5.30 with home-made cakes, small shop, bicycle and cave lamp hire, folk music Fri; good basic bedrooms, also bunkhouse, big breakfast *(Gwen and Peter Andrews, Judith Hirst)*

☆ **Malham** N Yor [off A65 NW of Skipton; SD8963], *Lister Arms*: Friendly easy-going open-plan lounge, busy weekends, relaxed attitude to children and dogs, fine choice of very enjoyable good value bar food inc vegetarian, well kept changing ales such as

Black Sheep, Ind Coope Burton and Wadworths 6X, even Liefmans fruit beers in summer, lots of malt whiskies, well worn-in furnishings and fittings, roaring fire, restaurant famous for steaks (good wine list), games area with pool and maybe loudish piped music; seats outside the substantial creeper-covered stone inn overlooking small green, more in back garden – nice spot by river, ideal for walkers; bedrooms *(Prof and Mrs S Barnett, Norman Portis, Neil Calver, Rita and Keith Pollard, Ian Phillips)*

Malham, *Buck*: Big village pub suiting walkers, wide range of quickly served good generous home-made food inc vegetarian, well kept Black Sheep, Theakstons Best and a guest beer, big log fire in comfortable lounge, roomy bar, separate candlelit dining room, picnic-sets in small garden; decent well equipped bedrooms, many good walks from the door *(Neil Calver, Ian Pendlebury, Ron Gentry, Dave Braisted, Cyril Brown, Ian Phillips)*

Malton N Yor [Wheelgate; SE7972], *Castle*: Friendly local, liked by racing enthusiasts, with excellently kept Malton ales, also John Smiths; simple food inc sandwiches *(Pat and Tony Martin)*; [12 Wheelgate], *Crown*: Unspoilt pub in same family for generations, good Malton Crown Double Chance, Owd Bob, Dark and Porter from brewhouse in back courtyard, good atmosphere, good food (not Sun, sandwiches only Tues, bookings only evenings); very popular with locals; good value bedrooms *(Alyson and Andrew Jackson)*

☆ **Market Weighton** E Yor [SE8742], *Londesborough Arms*: Old-fashioned market-town inn with two bars, John Smiths and Tetleys, interesting ambitious food in bars and bistro/restaurant, decent wine, good civilised atmosphere; comfortably refurbished bedrooms, good value *(John Prescott, LYM)*

☆ **Marsden** W Yor [2 Peel St; SE0412], *Riverhead*: Basic own-brew pub in converted grocer's, spiral stairs down to microbrewery producing good range of interesting beers named after local reservoirs (the higher the reservoir, the higher the strength) inc Mild, Stout and Porter, farm cider, friendly service and locals, unobtrusive piped music, no food (maybe sandwiches) or machines; wheelchair access, cl weekday lunchtimes, open all day w/e, nice stop after walk by canal or on the hills *(Stephen and Brenda Head, Richard Lewis, R J Bland, John Plumridge, Joan and Michel Hooper-Immins)*

Marsden, *Swan*: Well kept frequently changing beer and good bar food inc good value Sun lunches *(R J Bland)*

☆ **Masham** N Yor [SE2381], *Black Sheep Brewery*: Stylish modern bistro-style drinking area on top floor of maltings which now houses the brewery – not a pub, but likely to appeal to Good Pub Guide readers, together with a brewery visit; pleasant functional decor, upper gallery, good food all day, excellent service, some worthwhile beery tourist trinkets, and of course well kept Black Sheep Bitter, Special and Riggwelter; interesting brewery tour, good family facilities inc play area; cl 5 Mon, and late winter Sun evenings, can be very busy *(Susan and Nigel Wilson, Vann Prime, Wm Van Laaten, R C Vincent, Richard Lewis)*

Maunby N Yor [off A167 S of Northallerton; SE3586], *Buck*: Very attentive friendly staff, well kept ales such as Black Sheep, Courage Directors, Hambleton and John Smiths, good food; in out-of-way village by River Swale *(Alyson and Andrew Jackson)*

Meltham W Yor [A635; SE0910], *Ford*: Refurbished moors-edge pub doing well since reopening under new owners, with Ruddles and Theakstons, good generous freshly made food inc outstanding steak and kidney pie, long bar with old-fashioned fireplace at one end, comfortable settees and armchairs, picture windows with views towards Holme Moss, upstairs restaurant *(Neil Townend)*

Middlesmoor N Yor [up at the top of the Nidderdale rd from Pateley Bridge; SE0874], *Crown*: Remote inn with friendly landlord and family, simple but well presented food inc good sandwiches, particularly well kept Theakstons, coal fires in small cosy rooms, homely dining room, beautiful view over stonebuilt hamlet high in upper Nidderdale, tables outside; cheap bedrooms *(Mr and Mrs M Thompson, Trevor and Diane Waite)*

☆ *nr* **Midgley** W Yor [signed from Hebden Br, with evening/Sun bus to pub; coming from Halifax on A646 turn right just before Hebden Bridge town centre on to A6033 towards Keighley, take first right up steep Birchcliffe Rd and keep on to the top – OS Sheet 104 map ref 007272; SE0027], *Mount Skip*: Spectacular views of Pennines and mill-town valleys, welcoming staff, well kept Tetleys and Timothy Taylor Bitter, Landlord and Golden Best, good log fire, lots of prints and old photographs, china and brasses, generous cheap food inc vegetarian, Sun lunches and two sizes for children; games area, unobtrusive piped music, restaurant, benches outside – right by Calderdale Way footpath; children allowed (not late); open all day Sat, cl Mon lunchtime Oct-Easter, Tues lunchtime Jan-Easter *(Bruce Bird, Tony Hobden, LYM)*

☆ **Midhopestones** S Yor [off A616 W of Stocksbridge; SK2399], *Midhopestones Arms*: Cosy and friendly character 17th-c local, flagstones, stripped stone and pine, three small rooms, woodburner, pictures, assorted chairs, tables and settles; eight well kept ales inc Scottish Courage ones, Barnsley, Timothy Taylor Landlord and Wards, friendly staff, log fires, good value simple home cooking (not Sun evening, restricted Mon/Tues lunch) esp Sun lunch, breakfasts too; piped music; restaurant, seats outside; children welcome *(Peter Marshall, RWD)*

☆ **Mill Bank** W Yor [Cotton Stones; 1½ miles off A58 at Triangle pub – OS Sheet 110 map ref 025217; SE0221], *Alma*: Two cosy front rooms with pine furniture, old fishing tackle and plaques and plates with ceramic fishes, good home cooking inc outstanding chips, lots of home-made pizzas, Indian meals, good duck confit and fish, up to four real ales such as Kitchen, Timothy Taylor Landlord and Golden Best and Tetleys, good choice of bottled beers, small back pool room; cl lunchtime exc Weds, all day w/e *(Andy and Jill Kassube, Pat and Tony Martin)*

Mirfield W Yor [212 Huddersfield Rd (A644); SE2019], *Railway*: Lively and friendly open-plan local with well priced Bass, Stones, Worthington and guest beers, wide variety of good value food from double-decker sandwiches to tasty evening dishes, small front restaurant; piped music; a few tables out in front *(Michael Butler)*

Moorsholm N Yor [A171 nearly a mile E of Moorsholm village turnoff; NZ6914], *Jolly Sailor*: Long beams-and-stripped-stone bar with open fires, good value food, hard-working licensees, tables and play area looking out to the surrounding moors, restaurant; folk music w/e, may be cl winter weekday lunchtimes *(M Borthwick, LYM)*

Mytholmroyd W Yor [Cragg Vale; SE0126], *Hinchcliffe Arms*: Remote old stonebuilt pub with plenty of character, particularly good carvery (five or more joints), bar food too, well kept Scottish Courage beers; on road that leads only to a reservoir, very popular with walkers *(Dr Wallis Taylor)*; [38 New Rd (B6138)], *Shoulder of Mutton*: Comfortable and friendly stonebuilt local, popular for good value very generous home cooking (not Tues evening) inc fish, children's and good range of puddings, OAP and children's helpings, no-smoking and family dining areas; well kept Black Sheep, Boddingtons, Flowers IPA, Stones and guest beers, nice display of toby jugs and other china, small no-dining area for locals *(Ian and Nita Cooper, Andy and Jill Kassube, Tony Hobden)*

New Mill W Yor [Penistone Rd (A635); SE1808], *Crossroads*: Spacious and attractive roadside pub with Mansfield Riding and Old Baily, proper coffee, good reasonably priced food inc children's, friendly service, friendly staff, open fire and small aquarium in bar, kitchen range and darts in smaller tiled-floor room leading off, adjoining raftered partly no-smoking dining barn; nice garden with play area and country views; cl Mon *(B C Franklin, Michael Butler)*

North Grimston N Yor [SE8468], *Maltsters Arms*: Generous well presented food in pleasant dining area, good quick service, Tetleys *(Ian Hydes)*

North Newbald E Yor [SE9136], *Tiger*: Proper village pub on big green surrounded by rolling hills, handy for Wolds Way walking; roaring fire, good home-made food, well kept Black Sheep, Boddingtons and John Smiths; three bedrooms *(C A Hall, LYM)*

☆ **Nosterfield** N Yor [B6267 Masham—Thirsk; SE2881], *Freemasons Arms*: Friendly and civilised open-plan bar and dining area, two log fires, beams and flagstones, well kept Black Sheep, Timothy Taylor Landlord, Tetleys and Theakstons Best, decent wines, short choice of good food (not Mon evening), smiling service, Empire theme with interesting curios and WWI memorabilia; tables outside, very pleasant surroundings *(Alyson and Andrew Jackson, DC)*

☆ **Oakworth** W Yor [Harehills Lane, Oldfield; 2 miles towards Colne; SE0038], *Grouse*: Comfortable, interesting and spotless old pub packed with bric-a-brac, gleaming copper and china, lots of prints, cartoons and caricatures, dried flowers, attractively individual furnishings; very popular for limited choice of well presented good home-made lunchtime bar food (not Mon) from soup and sandwiches up, charming evening restaurant, well kept Timothy Taylor, good range of spirits, entertaining landlord, good service; fine surroundings and Pennine views *(Bruce Bird, WAH, Arthur and Margaret Dickinson)*

Osmotherley N Yor [The Green; SE4499], *Golden Lion*: Enjoyable food, well kept beers such as Fools Gold, John Smiths Magnet and Theakstons XB, good staff, fresh flowers, tables out overlooking village green; 44-mile Lyke Wake Walk starts here *(R F Grieve, Mike Smith, R J Bland)*

Ossett W Yor [47 Manor Rd, just off Horbury Rd; SE2820], *Victoria*: Very wide range of interesting evening food and popular Sun carvery, small dining room with washroom theme, well kept Tetleys and guest beers, decent wines, cosy bar (piped music may obtrude a bit); cl lunchtime Mon-Thurs, no lunchtime food Fri/Sat *(Michael Butler, M Borthwick)*

☆ **Otley** W Yor [Newall with Clifton; B6451 towards Blubberhouses, a mile N – just over N Yorks boundary; SE2047], *Spite*: Popular and welcoming low-beamed pub with wildfowl prints, walking stick collection, traditional furnishings, good log fire, good value honest food (not Sun or Mon evenings) from sandwiches to roasts in bar and restaurant, well kept Black Sheep and Websters with guest beers; children in eating area, open all day Sat, tables out in neat well lit rose garden, beautiful setting *(Rachael Ward, Mark Baynham, F J Robinson, John Saul, R Inman, LYM)*

☆ **Pateley Bridge** N Yor [Fellbeck; B6265, 3 miles E; SE2066], *Half Moon*: Friendly roadside pub in good setting handy for Brimham Rocks, open all day, with spaciously airy modernised decor, well kept Black Sheep Best, Theakstons and Timothy Taylor Landlord, decent wine, generous reasonably priced quick bar food inc children's, welcoming staff; piped music, fruit machines; children welcome, garden with play area; s/c holiday chalets *(Ian and Nita Cooper, G Washington, LYM)*

Pateley Bridge [Main St], *Crown*: Cosy lounge with railed-off dining area alongside, stripped stonework and horsebrasses, good generous food (separate lunchtime and evening menus) inc children's, friendly service, well kept John Smiths and Theakstons Best, public bar with back pool room, restaurant, good chatty service *(Richard Lewis)*

☆ **Penistone** S Yor [Mortimer Rd; outskirts, towards Stocksbridge; SE2402], *Cubley Hall*: Former grand Edwardian country house, panelling, elaborate plasterwork, mosaic tiling, plush furnishings, roomy conservatory, distant views beyond the neat formal gardens (with a good play house and adventure playground), wide choice of good generous neatly served food served all day from sandwiches up inc vegetarian and imaginative dishes, well kept Ind Coope Burton, Tetleys Bitter and Imperial and interesting guest beers, decent wines (wide choice by the glass), efficient good-humoured service, restaurant; piped music, children in restaurant and conservatory; very popular for w/e wedding receptions, comfortable bedrooms *(R T and J C Moggridge, L M and C J Clark, C Hinchcliffe, LYM)*

☆ **Pickering** N Yor [Market Pl; SE7983], *White Swan*: Attractive small hotel, former coaching inn, with two small panelled bars, good interesting well priced bar food inc lunchtime sandwiches and good vegetarian choice, well kept ales such as Black Sheep Bitter and Special and Hambleton, open fires, friendly helpful staff, busy but comfortable family room, good restaurant with interesting wines esp St Emilion clarets; bedrooms comfortable, good breakfast *(Eric Larkham, Norma and Keith Bloomfield, Stephen and Brenda Head, JWGN)*

Reeth N Yor [Market Pl (B6270); SE0499], *Kings Arms*: Popular beamed dining pub by green, pine pews around walls, huge log fire in 18th-c stone inglenook, quieter room behind; good reasonably priced food, friendly locals and efficient service, well kept full Theakstons range, John Smiths Bitter and Magnet; children very welcome, caged parrot, piped pop music may need turning down, maybe sports TV; bedrooms *(James Nunns, Brian Seller)*

Ribblehead N Yor [B6255 Ingleton—Hawes; SD7880], *Station*: Interesting and immaculate walkers' pub, very isolated, by Ribblehead Viaduct – ideal for railway enthusiasts, with appropriate decor in bar; friendly helpful licensees, good log fire in woodburner, well kept Theakstons, big helpings of bar food, dining room; open all day in season; comfortable bedrooms, good breakfast *(R Vincent, Dick Brown)*

Riccall N Yor [A19 10 miles S of York; Silver St; SE6238], *Hare & Hounds*: Good value cheap food (not Sun/Mon evening) from sandwiches up, old mining photographs, very friendly staff; Scottish Courage beers, decent wine *(Chris Gabbitas, Hugh McPhail)*

Richmond N Yor [Finkle St; NZ1801], *Black Lion*: Bustling local atmosphere in well used coaching inn with well kept ales inc Camerons Strongarm and Ruby, character beamed black-panelled back bar, nice no-smoking lounge, basic locals' bar, log fires, no-frills food in front dining room; bedrooms reasonably priced *(Hazel and Michael Duncombe, VP, TP, B Kneale)*; [Market Pl], *Castle Tavern*: Recently refurbished, with no-smoking dining area, good value food inc huge Sun lunch, Vaux Samson and Double Maxim; back bar with pool *(Mr and Mrs Edwards)*; [Victoria Rd], *Turf*: Friendly, with good generous reasonably priced food, attentive staff, nice atmosphere *(E P Hopkins)*

Ripon N Yor [Allhallow Gate; off Mkt Sq; SE3171], *Golden Lion*: Small, cosy and beautifully kept, with inviting exterior, enjoyable food from good value yorkshire pudding to interesting dishes such as marinated meats with rice and nan bread, staff very friendly without being overpowering, light and airy conservatory, well kept Theakstons *(Lesley, Peter and Alastair Barrett)*

☆ **Robin Hoods Bay** N Yor [King St, Bay Town; NZ9505], *Olde Dolphin*: Roomy 18th-c inn stepped up above sea front in attractive little town; unpretentious basic bar with friendly service, convivial atmosphere, good range of well kept Scottish Courage ales, good open fire, good value bar food inc vegetarian and local seafood, popular back games room; dogs welcome in bar if well behaved, piped music, can get smoky and crowded weekends, long walk back up to village car park; Fri folk club, bedrooms basic but cheap *(Hazel and Michael Duncombe, John and Liz Soden, John Higgins)*

Robin Hoods Bay [Bay Town], *Bay*: Included for the fine sea views from cosy picture-window bar; well kept John Smiths and Theakstons Black Bull, log fires, food in bar and separate dining area, welcoming staff; tables outside, cosy bedrooms (not many with own bath) *(David Heath)*

☆ **Rosedale Abbey** N Yor [300 yds up Rosedale Chimney; SE7395], *White Horse*: Cosy and comfortable farm-based country inn in lovely spot above the village, local feel in character bar with elderly maybe antique furnishings, lots of stuffed animals and birds, well kept John Smiths and Theakstons, quite a few wines and good choice of malt whiskies, friendly service, good generous home-made food esp range of pies, grand views from terrace (and from restaurant and bedrooms); children allowed if eating, open all day Sat; attractive bedrooms – a nice place to stay, good walks *(Mike and Grete Turner, Comus Elliott, LYM)*

☆ **Runswick Bay** N Yor [NZ8217], *Royal*: Super setting, lovely views over fishing village and sea from welcoming big-windowed plain front lounge with interesting marine fishtank, limited choice of good value food inc huge helpings of fresh local fish, well kept Black Sheep, good service, nautical back bar, cosy bustling atmosphere, terrace; bedrooms *(Malcolm and Helen Baxter, LYM)*

Saltburn by the Sea N Yor [A174 towards Whitby; NZ6722], *Ship*: Beautiful setting among beached fishing boats, sea views from tasteful nautical-style black-beamed bars and big plainer summer dining lounge; good range of bar food, quick friendly service, evening restaurant (not Sun), children's room and menu, seats outside; busy at holiday times, smuggling exhibition next door *(K and E Leist, Val Stevenson, Rob Holmes, BB)*

☆ **Saxton** N Yor [Headwell Lane; not far from A1 – B1217 towards Towton; SE4736], *Plough*: Smart but friendly dining pub, small bar with blazing coke fire and big dining room off, huge changing blackboard choice of good freshly made food (not Sun evening) from enterprising lunchtime snacks through carefully prepared interesting main dishes to beautifully presented puddings, friendly staff, well kept Theakstons, good choice of house wines, good coffee; seats outside, cl Mon; pleasant stone village with magnificent church *(Stephen Adams, P R and A M Caley)*

Saxton, *Crooked Billet*: Tidy and well run extended pub very popular for reasonably priced food inc good sandwiches and giant yorkshire puddings – get there early w/e for a seat, they're quite a cult; friendly comfortable atmosphere, well kept John Smiths, decent wine, pleasant efficient staff, conservatory dining extension *(Janet Pickles, D M and B K Moores, Michael Butler)*; [by church in village], *Greyhound*: Unchanging delectable local in attractive quiet village, Victorian fireplace in chatty tap room (children allowed here), traditional snug, corridor to games toom, well kept cheap Sam Smiths OB tapped from the cask, a couple of picnic-sets in side yard; open all day weekends *(LYM)*

Scaling Dam N Yor [Guisborough Rd (A171), opp reservoir; NZ7413], *Grapes*: Comfortable and friendly bar and new dining room off, traditional furniture, original range (with skull in side nook) *(M Borthwick)*

Scarborough N Yor [Vernon Rd; TA0489], *Hole in the Wall*: Unusual long pub, refreshing conversation and lively radical debate, well kept Malton Double Chance, Theakstons BB, XB and Old Peculier and good changing guest beers, country wines, no piped music or machines; cheap basic lunchtime food *(Reg Nelson)*; [Eastborough], *Jolly Roger*: Well done up as character pub, lots of beams and atmosphere, real ale; bedrooms *(Reg Nelson)*; [Westborough], *Lord Rosebery*: New Wetherspoons pub nr stn, in former local Liberal HQ; handsome decor inc galleried upper bar, well kept beers inc guests, reasonably priced good food; open all day, very busy evenings *(Simon Orme)*; [Burniston Rd], *Scalby Manor*: Spacious, friendly and efficient Brewers Fayre in converted 19th-c mansion, play areas indoors and out (inc summer bouncy castle), wide choice of food inc children's, Whitbreads-related ales kept very well; open all day, lots of tables outside *(Richard Lewis)*; [seafront, Scalby Mills], *Scalby Mills*: Fine views over North Bay towards the castle from small two-room seafront pub in 15th-c former watermill, good value food all day (at least in summer), interesting real ales from near and far; handy for Sea Life Centre *(Tony Scott)*; [1 North Terr], *Scarborough Arms*: Good atmosphere, good value filling meals, Banks's, Camerons, Marstons and a guest beer; open all day *(Tony Scott)*; [Queen St], *Talbot*: Well kept real ales, good atmosphere – esp on impromptu folk nights *(Reg Nelson)*; [Falsgrave Rd], *Tap & Spile*: Former White Horse very successfully given the old-world treatment, authentic lived-in feel, excellently kept real ales, useful no-smoking room, efficient good-humoured staff *(Reg Nelson)*

☆ **Scawton** N Yor [off A170 Helmsley—Thirsk; SE5584], *Hare*: Low and pretty, much modernised but not spoilt, with flagstones, a couple of cosy settees, simple wall settles, little wheelback armchairs, air force memorabilia; friendly service, well kept Black Sheep, Theakstons Best and XB, sensibly priced good generous food inc good vegetarian range, two friendly dogs, eating area, pool room; tables in big back garden with caged geese, nice inn-signs; children welcome, handy for Rievaulx *(Juliet Short, Geoffrey and Brenda Wilson, BB)*

Scotton N Yor [Main St; SE3359], *Guy Fawkes Arms*: Helpful and friendly landlord, well kept Hambleton, John Smiths and Tetleys, good basic lunchtime food (not Tues) *(Alyson and Andrew Jackson)*

Selby N Yor [Mkt Pl; SE6132], *Londesborough Arms*: Two bars, wide choice of reasonably priced food, morning coffee – handy for Selby Abbey; market day Mon *(Janet Pickles)*

Settle N Yor [Market Pl; SD8264], *Royal Oak*: Market-town inn with roomy partly divided open-plan panelled bar, comfortable seats around brass-topped tables, well kept Whitbreads-related ales with Timothy Taylor Landlord as a guest beer, generous bar food all day, restaurant; children welcome, bedrooms *(Anne and David Robinson, Mr and Mrs P Stainsby, Tom Thomas, LYM)*

Sheffield S Yor [Clarkehouse Rd; SK3386], *Aunt Sally*: Tom Cobleigh formula pub in attractively converted Victorian school, good food even Sun night inc children's and vegetarian, six real ales, garden with play area, disabled access; open all day Sun; fruit machine, piped pop music *(CMW, JJW)*; [Abbeydale Rd], *Broadfield*: Friendly Whitbreads pub with wide range of fresh good value food, at least eight changing guest beers; open all day, popular with students *(John Fahy)*; [537 Attercliffe Common (A6178); SK3788], *Carbrook Hall*: Dating from 1620, surviving part of even older building, popular with ghost-hunters; no-smoking dining room (children welcome here) with armour, helmets and Civil War artefacts, pool room with old bread ovens, Oak Room with panelling, beautiful carved fireplace and Italianate plaster ceiling (games machines, piped music etc); good value lunchtime bar food and Sun roasts, John Smiths Magnet and Stones, attractive small garden with dovecote and play area; open all day Fri *(CMW, JJW, Patrick Hancock, David Carr)*; [1 Henry St – Shalesmoor tram stop right outside], *Cask & Cutler*: Well refurbished small corner pub, coal fire in no-smoking bar on left, no juke box or machines, friendly licensees, half a dozen well kept beers from small breweries (plans to brew their own), regular beer festivals, farm cider, appropriate posters, good value home-made food till 6.30 inc popular cheap Sun lunch (booking advised), friendly dog called Topper; open all day Fri/Sat, wheelchair access, tables in nice back garden *(the Didler, Richard Lewis, Andy and Jill Kassube, Jack and Philip Paxton)*; [Cobden View Rd, Crookes], *Cobden View*: Friendly local popular with students, well kept Boddingtons and guest beers, pool room, juke box *(Patrick Hancock)*; [Worksop Rd, just off Attercliffe Common (A6178)], *Cocked Hat*: Largely open-plan, tasteful dark colours, brewery memorabilia, well kept Marstons Burton and Pedigree, good value lunchtime food *(Patrick Hancock)*; [400 Handsworth Rd (A57)], *Cross Keys*: Ancient friendly unspoilt local inside churchyard, well kept Stones, open fires; open all day *(Patrick Hancock, LYM)*; [Eccleshall Rd], *Devonshire*: Opp Wards Brewery, with well kept Vaux beers, partitions dividing bare-boarded front area from plusher back, interesting old Wards brewery memorabilia, dining conservatory; wide choice of decent good value food, open all day *(Patrick Hancock)*; [69 Broad Lane], *Fagans*: Warm and welcoming old pub with long bar, freshly made lunches inc massive fish platter, friendly staff, well kept Tetleys, wide range of malt whiskies, no juke box, live music Fri *(M Smith)*; [240 West St], *Foundry & Firkin*: Usual bare boards and breweriana, with good choice of ales brewed on the premises, reasonably priced food, friendly staff, games machines, ski machine, Jenga game; tables in garden, live music; on tram route, open all day *(Richard Lewis)*; [Division St/Westfield Terr], *Frog & Parrot*: Bare boards, lofty ceiling, huge windows, comfortable banquettes up a few steps, lively studenty cafe-bar atmosphere in evenings, friendly staff, interesting beers brewed on the premises (one fearsomely strong) and beers from parent Whitbreads, lots of malt whiskies and vodkas; open all day *(David Carr, Richard Lewis, LYM)*; [Trippet Lane], *Grapes*: Friendly three-room pub with Courage Directors and John Smiths, cheerful landlord, pool; live music nights upstairs *(Patrick Hancock)*; [26 Johnson St], *Harlequin*: Good corner local with Wards Best, pot-bellied stove, pool room, corridor drinking area, side room for live music *(the Didler)*; [25 Orchard St], *Hogshead*: Bare boards, breweriana, ten or more well kept ales inc unusual ones, plenty of Belgian bottled beers, country wines, malt whiskies, farm cider, wide choice of reasonably priced food, piped music, staff friendly and helpful even when very busy; also coffee, tea, pastries etc; open all day *(Richard Lewis)*; [Poole Rd, Darnall, not far from M1 junctions 33/34], *Kings Head*: Good-natured atmosphere, incredible choice of cheap but good basic bar food, much home-made; Stones and Tetleys *(CMW, JJW, Patrick Hancock)*; [1 Mowbray St], *Morrisseys Riverside*: Unspoilt three-room pub, one of small chain, with nice garden overlooking River Don, good choice of beers such as Adnams, Archers Golden, Timothy Taylor Landlord and Tom Woods Best from Highwood; folk nights upstairs *(the Didler)*; [94 Crookes], *Noahs Ark*: Six mainly Whitbreads-related ales and huge range of generous good value food (not Sun evening) all freshly prepared (so may be a wait) inc early evening bargains in friendly pub, open all day (not Sun) and popular with students; disabled lavatory; dominoes, pool, TV, quiet piped music *(JJW, CMW)*; [Crookes/Lydgate Lane], *Old Grindstone*: Busy refurbished Victorian pub, good value food inc choice of Sun roasts, Timothy Taylor Landlord, Vaux Waggle Dance and Wards, raised no-smoking area, teapot collection, obliging service, friendly black cat, games area with two pool tables and SkyTV etc, piped music; open all day all week, jazz Mon *(JJW, CMW)*; [145 Duke St], *Red Lion*: Welcoming and utterly traditional, central bar serving four separate rooms each with original ornate fireplace and coal fire, attractive panelling and etched glass; cosy and comfortable, well kept Burtonwood, no food *(PB)*; [Rock St, Pitsmoor], *Rock House*: Cosy traditional L-shaped lounge with tap room and smaller lower snug, friendly welcome, well kept John Smiths Bitter and Magnet and Stones, no juke box or games machines, Tues games night, Thurs quiz night, several dozen whiskies, two gardens – one with water feature; open 1-5, 8-11; opens noon Sat, all day Sun *(Richard Lewis)*; [Victoria Quays, Wharf Rd, off B6073 N of centre], *Sheaf Quay*: Fine old building in canal basin development nicely altered by Tom Cobleigh, relaxed atmosphere, good value cheerful bar food inc children's and vegetarian *(David Carr)*; [Waingate], *Tap & Spile*: Solidly traditional corner alehouse with around 10 real ales and ciders from all over, pool and darts in back room *(Patrick Hancock)*; [128 West St], *West Street Hotel*: Large comfortable open-plan pub, lots of wood and bare boards, well kept ales such as Black Sheep Special, Morlands Bills Spring Brew, Stones, good value good cheap food, friendly staff, juke box; open all day *(Richard Lewis)*; [57 Greenhill Main Rd], *White Swan*: Friendly four-room local with fair choice of food lunchtime and early evening (not Sun evening), five real ales; usually open all day *(JJW, CMW)*

Shepley W Yor [44 Marsh Lane; links A629 and A635, from village centre by Black Bull; SE2010], *Farmers Boy*: Homely beamed cottage conversion with well kept Bass-related beers, interesting food, simple country furnishings and woodwork, flower pictures, thriving atmosphere, back barn restaurant; very popular with youngish locals *(Michael Butler)*

Sheriff Hutton N Yor [The Square; SE6566], *Highwayman*: Cosy old coaching inn overlooking castle, food inc good value Sun lunch, log fires, snug bars, oak beams in lounge and dining room, decent range of beers, big garden; 12th-c church *(Philip and Ann Falkner, Pat and Tony Martin)*

Shiptonthorpe E Yor [A1079 Mkt Weighton—York; SE8543], *Crown*: Warm and comfortable, welcoming landlord, good straightforward food inc Sun lunch, well kept Stones Best, decent house wine *(Roger Bellingham)*

Sicklinghall N Yor [Main St – OS Sheet 104 map ref 363485; SE3648], *Scotts Arms*: Pleasantly refurbished Chef & Brewer, interesting layout, well kept Theakstons Best, XB, Old Peculier and Old Bull, reasonably attentive service, enthusiastic piped music; big garden with play area *(Janet and Peter Race, LYM)*

Silsden W Yor [Bell Sq; SE0446], *Punch Bowl*: Very friendly service and good value generous food *(M Borthwick)*

☆ **Sinnington** N Yor [off A170 W of Pickering; SE7586], *Fox & Hounds*: Two clean and welcoming bar areas, nice paintings and old artefacts, cosy fires, reasonably priced good food in bar and restaurant inc interesting veg, well kept Bass and Camerons, dining area, separate pool room; attractive village with pretty stream and lots of grass; warm comfortable good value bedrooms, good breakfast *(David and Ruth Hollands)*

Skelton N Yor [Shipton Rd; A19 just N of York ring rd; SE5756], *Riverside Farm*: Big Tom Cobleigh chain pub, well ordered and organised, with friendly staff, imaginative good value food inc children's and vegetarian, good coffee, well kept beers inc an interesting guest *(Roger Bellingham, Paul and Pam Penrose)*

Skerne E Yor [Wansford Rd (off B1249 SE of Driffield); TA0455], *Eagle*: Quaint unspoilt village local with two simple rooms either side of hall, coal fire, well kept Camerons from rare Victorian cash-register beer engine in kitchen-style servery, chatty locals, friendly landlord brings drinks to your table; no food, open 7-11 Mon-Fri, 12-2 weekends *(PB)*

☆ **Skipton** N Yor [Canal St; from Water St (A65) turn into Coach St, then left after canal bridge; SD9852], *Royal Shepherd*: Busy old-fashioned local in pretty spot by canal, well kept Whitbreads-related ales and guests such as Cains, decent wine, friendly service, unusual sensibly priced whiskies, open fires, low-priced standard quick food, ageing banquettes, photographs of Yorks CCC in its golden days, white cat called William; big bar, snug and dining room, tables outside, games and juke box; children welcome in side room *(L Dixon, Prof and Mrs S Barnett)*

Skipwith N Yor [signed off A163 NE of Selby; SE6638], *Drovers Arms*: Comfortably well worn two-room pub with good log fires, very friendly landlord, Boddingtons, John Smiths and Theakstons XB, fine range of house wines, good value food from sandwiches to choice of Sun roasts; separate dining room, children welcome (big toy box in lounge, tables out behind with play area); wheelchair access, cl Mon lunchtime *(Janet Pickles)*

Slaithwaite W Yor [Cop Hill; up Nabbs Lane then Holme Lane; SE0613], *Rose & Crown*: Marvellous Colne Valley and moor views, three refurbished rooms off bar, end restaurant, well kept Tetleys, Timothy Taylor Landlord and a seasonal beer, wide choice of malt whiskies, warm welcome, good bar food; good walks *(R J Bland)*

Sleights N Yor [180 Coach Rd; NZ8707], *Plough*: Pleasant two-bar stonebuilt pub with emphasis on food; good views, well kept John Smiths and Theakstons *(M Borthwick)*

Sneaton N Yor [Beacon Way; B1416 S of Whitby; NZ8908], *Sneaton Hall*: Comfortable old-fashioned hotel bar doing well under new owners, good changing choice of well cooked food in bar and elegant restaurant inc good Sun lunch, lovely views to Whitby abbey, dominoes and quoits, lots of malt whiskies, very friendly staff; tables on terrace; bedrooms *(M Borthwick)*; [Beacon Way], *Wilson Arms*: Sparkling clean and shiny, with warm welcome, good value generous food from sandwiches up inc local fish, Barnsley, Black Sheep and Theakstons, bright fires, neat staff, pleasant dining room; bedrooms with fine views *(M Borthwick, E C R and J Dicks)*

☆ **South Dalton** E Yor [off B1248 NW of Beverley; SE9645], *Pipe & Glass*: Friendly dining pub in charming secluded setting, with attractive conservatory restaurant overlooking Dalton Park, doing well under new management; interesting food (must book w/e), well kept Theakstons, some high-backed settles, old prints, log fires, beams and bow windows, children welcome, tables in garden with splendid yew tree and play area; bedrooms *(Paul and Pam Penrose, Peter Marshall)*

South Kilvington N Yor [SE4384], *Old Oak Tree*: Pleasant village pub with freshly made food inc good reasonably priced vegetarian range, landlord does the cooking and will adapt to dietary requirements; well kept beers, relaxed friendly and informal atmosphere, big back conservatory restaurant, secluded side restaurant *(Walter and Susan Rinaldi-Butcher)*

☆ **Sowerby** W Yor [Steep Lane; SE0423], *Travellers Rest*: Several cosy and comfortable little rooms, well kept Timothy Taylor, open fire, wide choice of good generous reasonably priced food, friendly service; fine country setting, good view over Halifax and Calderdale Valley from garden (lovely at night); gents' up steps *(David Tew)*

Sowerby Bridge W Yor [Bolton Brow; canal basin; SE0623], *Moorings*: Former canal warehouse, big windows overlooking boat basin, high beams, stripped stone, canal pictures, no-smoking family room; wide choice of food (not Sun evening) from filled cobs to steaks inc children's and vegetarian, welcoming staff, Moorhouses, Theakstons Best and XB, Youngers Scotch and guest beer, lots of bottled beers, pub games; new Belgian-style grill room, tables out on terrace, open all day Sat *(S E Paulley, M Buchanan, LYM)*; *Navigation*: Nr canal, house beers Navigator and No 2, friendly staff, books and magazines to read, good value freshly cooked food *(Tony Hobden)*

☆ **Spofforth** N Yor [High St; A661 Harrogate—Wetherby; SE3650], *Railway*: Small pub with exceptionally helpful friendly service, wide choice of good freshly made food at attractive prices, good helpings, well kept Sam Smiths, ordinary bar, simple unfussy lounge, real fires, no juke box; garden and play area *(Geoff Roberts, Graham and Helen Brown, Geoffrey and Brenda Wilson, Paul Gray, BB)*

☆ **Sprotbrough** S Yor [Lower Sprotbrough; 2¾ miles from M18 junction 2; SE5302], *Boat*: Interesting roomy stonebuilt ex-farmhouse with lovely courtyard in charming quiet spot by River Don, three individually furnished areas, big stone fireplaces, latticed windows, dark brown beams, good value generous meals (no sandwiches), well kept Scottish Courage beers, farm cider, helpful staff; piped music, fruit machine, no dogs; big sheltered prettily lit courtyard, river walks; restaurant (Tues-Sat evening, Sun lunch); open all day summer Sats *(Mike and Grete Turner, Barry and Marie Males, DC, LYM)*

☆ **Staithes** N Yor [off A174 Whitby—Loftus; NZ7818], *Cod & Lobster*: Basic pub in superb waterside setting in unspoilt fishing village under sandstone cliff, well kept beers inc Camerons Best and Red Dragon, good crab sandwiches, friendly service and locals, lovely views from seats outside; quite a steep walk up to top car park *(Andrew Hazeldine, Judith Hirst, LYM)*

☆ **Stanbury** W Yor [SE0037], *Old Silent*: Neatly rebuilt moorland village pub with several interconnecting rooms, stone floors, mullioned windows and open fires, conservatory, friendly restaurant, games room, juke box; good if not cheap food, friendly attentive staff, well kept Theakstons; bedrooms *(Bronwen and Steve Wrigley, LYM)*

Staveley N Yor [signed off A6055 Knaresborough—Boroughbridge; SE3663], *Royal Oak*: Prettily laid out beamed and tiled-floor pub, new landlord doing good home-made food inc unusual dishes in bar and restaurant, good choice of beers from local small breweries, broad bow window overlooking tables on front lawn *(Ann and Bob Westbrook, LYM)*

Stokesley N Yor [1 West End; NZ5209], *White Swan*: Cosy pub with outstanding range of cheeses, home-made pickle and several cheeses for its ploughman's, good pâtés too; five well kept ales inc two or three changing interesting guest beers, well worn-in but clean, comfortable and tidy split-level panelled bar, hat display, welcoming staff, friendly ridgeback called Bix and little black dog called Titch; midweek live blues and jazz *(Andy and Jill Kassube, Jim Cornish, Tim Abel)*

☆ **Sutton on the Forest** N Yor [B1363 N of York; SE5965], *Rose & Crown*: Picturesque and comfortable two-room dining pub with relaxed and informal bistro atmosphere, good fresh generous food, imaginative without being too clever, good steaks and lots of properly cooked veg, Theakstons ales, interesting wines, smart customers, welcoming licensees; charming wide-street village *(Mrs H Walker, Bill and Sheila McLardy, H Bramwell, Janet Lewis)*

Swainby N Yor [High St; NZ4802], *Black Horse*: Pleasant spot by stream, Tetleys and Theakstons, good home-made food inc good veg, service friendly and efficient even when busy; garden with children's play area *(Don and Shirley Parrish)*

Swinton S Yor [Warren Vale Rd (A633); SK4599], *Woodman*: Comfortable lounge with pictures and ornaments, good choice of good value food inc sandwiches and snacks, John Smiths in lined glasses, bar with pool and games, maybe piped pop radio; two seats out in front, walks nearby *(CMW, JJW)*

☆ **Tan Hill** N Yor [Arkengarthdale (Reeth—Brough) rd, at junction with Keld/W Stonesdale rd; NY8906], *Tan Hill Inn*: Wonderfully remote old stone inn on the Pennine Way – Britain's highest pub, nearly five miles from the nearest neighbour, basic, bustling and can get overcrowded, full of bric-a-brac and pictures inc good old photographs, simple sturdy furniture, flagstones, big log fires (with prized stone side seats); well kept Black Sheep Riggwelter and Theakstons Best, XB and Old Peculier (in winter the cellar does chill down – for warmth you might prefer coffee or whisky with hot water), big helpings of warm comforting food served by unstuffy and friendly staff, sandwiches too; children and dogs welcome, open all day at least in summer; bedrooms, inc some with own bathrooms in newish extension; often snowbound, with no mains electricity (juke box powered by generator); Swaledale sheep show last Thurs in May *(Bronwen and Steve Wrigley, Nigel Woolliscroft, Judith Hirst, LYM)*

Thirsk N Yor [Market Pl; SE4382], *Golden Fleece*: Comfortable two-room bar popular with locals, good food from sandwiches up, well kept Whitbreads-related ales, pleasant service, view across market pl from bay windows; restaurant, bedrooms *(W and E Thomas)*

Thixendale N Yor [off A166 3 miles N of Fridaythorpe; SE8461], *Cross Keys*: Small welcoming country pub in deep valley below the rolling Wolds, single L-shaped room with fitted wall seats, relaxed atmosphere, well kept Jennings and Tetleys, sensibly priced home-made food all from blackboard; popular with walkers, pleasant garden behind *(Mr and Mrs J R Ringrose)*

Thornhill W Yor [Combs Hill; off B6117 S of Dewsbury – OS Sheet 110 map ref 253191; SE2519], *Alma*: Relaxed local, comfortable and friendly, good choice of reasonably priced food, flagstones by counter, carpeting elsewhere, solidly attractive pine furniture and pink banquettes in partitioned bays, cigarette card collections, well kept Bass, Stones, Theakstons and Worthington BB; small popular restaurant *(Michael Butler)*

☆ **Thornton** W Yor [Hill Top Rd, off B6145 W of Bradford; SE0933], *Ring o' Bells*: Spotless 19th-c moortop dining pub noted for its success in pub catering competitions, wide choice of well presented good home cooking inc fresh fish, meat and poultry specialities, superb steaks, good puddings, bargain early suppers, pleasant bar, popular air-conditioned no-smoking restaurant; good range of Scottish Courage and other ales, friendly professional service, wide views towards Shipley and Bingley *(Geoffrey and Brenda Wilson, Donald and Margaret Wood, Andy and Jill Kassube)*

☆ **Thornton in Lonsdale** N Yor [just NW of Ingleton; SD6976], *Marton Arms*: Big welcoming beamed bar, stripped stone walls festooned with caving pictures, roaring log fire, good relaxed atmosphere, plain pine furniture, up to 15 well kept ales, farm cider, lots of malt whiskies, martinis to make your hair stand on end, good value generous food inc home-made pizzas, enormous gammon and daily specials, efficient friendly service even when busy; bar billiards room, children welcome, marvellous views from garden – attractive dales setting opp church where Conan Doyle was married; pleasant spacious bedrooms in annexe (one equipped for disabled), good breakfast, great fell walking country *(Alan Morton, Kevin and Amanda Earl, Andy and Jill Kassube, E G Parish, Stuart Steels, Bruce Bird, Vann Prime, Wm Van Laaten, Arthur and Margaret Dickinson)*

Thornton le Clay N Yor [SE6865], *White Swan*: Comfortable and welcoming old-fashioned family-run beamed dining pub with well presented fairly priced food inc vegetarian, well kept ales such as Black Sheep and Youngers Scotch, decent wines, good log fire, shining brasses, tables on terrace; good view from impeccable ladies', attractive countryside nr Castle Howard; cl Mon lunchtime *(Anon)*

☆ **Threshfield** N Yor [B6160/B6265 nr Grassington; OS Sheet 98 map ref 988637; SD9763], *Old Hall*: Three knocked-together rooms, high beam-and-plank ceiling with lots of chamberpots, cushioned wall pews, tall well blacked kitchen range, good bustling atmosphere, good food (not Mon or winter Sun evening) with unusual touches, well kept Timothy Taylor Bitter, Landlord, Golden Best and Dark Mild, dozens of malt whiskies, generally good service, darts, dominoes; piped music; neat garden with aviary, good base for dales walks – two s/c cottages; children in eating area, cl Mon lunchtime *(Vann and Terry Prime, Mr and Mrs Garrett, Ann and Colin Hunt, Martin Hickes, Lynne Gittins, Andrew and Ruth Triggs, Pat and Clive Sherriff, LYM)*

Thrintoft N Yor [SE3293], *New Inn*: Friendly 18th-c family-run village local with wide choice of good generous sensibly priced home-made food, well kept Black Sheep, restaurant *(Graham Hewitt)*

Thruscross N Yor [off A59 Harrogate—Skipton or B6255 Grassington—Pateley Bridge; SE1558], *Stone House*: Warm and cosy moorland pub with beams, flagstones, stripped stone, dark panelling and good log fire; good generous interesting food (separate dining room), well kept ales, traditional games, no music, sheltered tables outside; children welcome *(Prof and Mrs S Barnett, Cliff Blakemore)*

Thurgoland S Yor [Old Mill Lane; SE2901], *Bridge*: Old stonebuilt pub by River Don, wide choice of good value fresh home-made food inc children's and Mon/Tues bargain OAP lunch, Stones and a guest beer such as Marstons Pedigree, cosy and friendly atmosphere; quiet piped music, children and dogs in second room, big garden; handy for Forge Museum, good walks; no food Sun evening *(JJW, CMW)*

Tickhill S Yor [Sunderland St (A631 Bawtry rd); SK5993], *Scarbrough Arms*: Cheerful village local, small low-ceilinged central bar with coal fire, barrel tables and lots of brass, more conventional lounge, traditional public bar, good home-cooked lunchtime food (not Sun) inc imaginative vegetarian dishes (landlady and some staff have trained at Vegetarian Soc), well kept Scottish Courage beers with a changing independent guest, friendly efficient staff, tables out on lawn with swings; interesting village *(N J Worthington, S L Tracy)*

Timble N Yor [off Otley—Blubberhouses moors rd; SE1853], *Timble*: Unspoilt village pub in beautiful stone building, good cheap basic bar food, Scottish Courage ales, genuine Yorkshire atmosphere *(D Stokes)*

Tockwith N Yor [Marston Rd; SE4752], *Spotted Ox*: Welcoming traditional country local, particularly well kept Tetleys, interesting guest beers, home-made food *(Alan Ball)*

Tong W Yor [SE2230], *Greyhound*: Delightful low-ceilinged local by village cricket field, open-plan but with distinctive areas inc flagstones, good atmosphere, well kept Tetleys, popular food in bar and restaurant inc lots of specials *(Michael Butler)*

Ulley S Yor [Turnshaw Rd; 2 miles from M1 junction 31 – off B6067 in Aston; SK4687], *Royal Oak*: Friendly and cosy stonebuilt pub in lovely countryside by church, popularly priced bar food served till late, attractive and intimate inexpensive restaurant (must book); well kept cheap Sam Smiths OB, stable-theme beamed lounge with rooms off (can be smoky), quiet piped music, good children's room, big garden; can get packed on warm summer evenings, esp Sat *(Patrick Hancock, WAH)*

Wakefield W Yor [Newmillerdam (A61 S); SE3315], *Dam*: By reservoir dam, attractive walking country; neatly kept L-shaped stripped-stone bar with usual furnishings, busy Toby carvery/restaurant, well kept Bass-related beers, pleasant coffee lounge, good friendly service, generous usual food *(Michael Butler)*

Wales S Yor [Church St; SK4783], *Duke of Leeds*: Well kept Whitbreads-related ales, very generous inventive food, friendly licensee, no machines etc; not far from M1 junction 31, via A57 W, A618, B6059 *(G P Kernan)*

☆ **Walkington** E Yor [B1230; SE9937], *Ferguson Fawsitt Arms*: Mock-Tudor bars in 1950s style, with good choice of properly cooked good value food and good puddings from airy no-smoking flagstone-floored self-service food bar, very popular lunchtime with older people; friendly cheerful service, decent wine; tables out on terrace, games bar with pool table; delightful village *(K and J Brooks, H Bramwell, LYM)*

Walkington [B1230], *Dog & Duck*: Popular well run Mansfield dining pub with good choice of food from good value sandwiches up in long lounge bar or small restaurant, well kept Riding, warm welcome *(Peter Plumridge)*

Walsden W Yor [Rochdale Rd; SD9322], *Cross Keys*: Well kept Black Sheep Best, Tetleys and five changing ales mainly from small breweries (often inc a Mild), good generous home cooking (all day Sun) inc vegetarian, efficient, helpful and friendly service even when busy, friendly cat; conservatory overlooking restored Rochdale Canal, lots of good walks – nr Pennine Way *(Bruce Bird, Tony Hobden)*

Walton W Yor [off back rd Wetherby—Tadcaster; SE4447], *Fox & Hounds*: Clean and happy pub quite handy for A1, good choice of reasonably priced delicious plain home-made food, good service, John Smiths *(Edward Leetham)*

Weaverthorpe N Yor [Main St; SE9771], *Star*: Comfortable little inn in relaxing village setting, good straightforward bar food (more expensive restaurant), well kept Camerons and guest beers such as Banks's and Badger Tanglefoot, exceptionally welcoming staff; nice bedrooms, good breakfast; has been cl weekday lunchtimes *(Colin Savill, Rev J Hibberd)*

☆ **Wentworth** [3 miles from M1 junction 36; B6090, signed off A6135; SK3898], *Rockingham Arms*: Friendly new landlord in warmly welcoming country inn with comfortable traditional furnishings, hunting pictures, open fires, stripped stone, rooms off inc a dining room and family room, several well kept Scottish Courage ales, unpretentious home cooking; piped music; tables in attractive garden with own well kept bowling green; has been open all day; bedrooms *(Mark O'Hanlon, Andy and Jill Kassube, Roy Butler, LYM)*

☆ **West Witton** N Yor [A684 W of Leyburn; SE0688], *Wensleydale Heifer*: Comfortable genteel dining pub with low-ceilinged small interconnecting areas in front lounge, big attractive bistro, separate restaurant, good food inc interesting dishes and seafood (generous though not cheap), good log fire, attractive prints, pleasant decor, excellent service, no music; small bar with decent wines, well kept Black Sheep, John Smiths and Theakstons Best, and another fire; nice bedrooms (back ones quietest), good breakfast *(Malcolm Phillips, Ian Pendlebury, Gwen and Peter Andrews)*

Wetherby W Yor [34 North St, ⅓ mile from A1; SE4048], *Swan & Talbot*: Clean, comfortable and relaxing, very well decorated, with Bass, Black Sheep, John Smiths and Tetleys, pleasant chatty staff, good choice of usual food *(Ian Phillips)*

☆ **Whashton** N Yor [N of Richmond; NZ1506], *Hack & Spade*: Small immaculate pub/restaurant with marvellous choice of good food inc vegetarian in bar and dining area, friendly helpful staff, keg Theakstons, good coffee and house wine *(Rita and Keith Pollard, Duncan and Carole Small)*

Whiston S Yor [Turner Lane; nr M1 junction 33; SK4590], *Golden Ball*: Extended old food-oriented pub with good value food (not Sun evening) inc good beef baguettes and sensibly priced home-made puddings, well kept Greene King Abbot, Ind Coope Burton, Timothy Taylor Landlord and guests, one no-smoking eating area, relaxed atmosphere; TV, piped music *(Derek and Sylvia Stephenson)*

Whitby N Yor [Church St; NZ9011], *White Horse & Griffin*: Well priced food inc good choice of local fresh fish (you can't have just a drink), cosy candlelit ambience *(M Borthwick)*

☆ **Wigglesworth** N Yor [B6478, off A65 S of Settle; SD8157], *Plough*: Warm and friendly, with little rooms off bar, some spartan yet cosy, others smart and plush, inc no-smoking panelled dining room and snug; consistently good bar food inc huge sandwiches and children's dishes, conservatory restaurant (minimum price limit) with panoramic dales views, well kept Boddingtons and Tetleys, decent wines and coffee; attractive garden, pleasant bedrooms *(Mr J and Dr S Harrop, WAH)*

☆ **Wormald Green** N Yor [A61 Ripon—Harrogate; SE3065], *Cragg Lodge*: The exceptional draw here in this otherwise straightforward and rather reserved pub is the unique range of nearly 1,000 malt whiskies – probably the widest choice in the world – in 16 price bands, depending on rarity; also well kept Tetleys and Theakstons Best, XB and Old Peculier, distinguished brandies, mature vintage port; big open-plan bar popular with older people at lunch for bargain food, partly no-smoking restaurant; children in eating area, tables outside, bedrooms *(L Dixon, Piotr Chodzko-Zajko, LYM)*

Wortley S Yor [SE2900], *Bridge*: Unpretentious, clean and willing, with good food from sandwiches up inc Sun lunch (no other food then), very pleasant rural surroundings; handy for 18th-c Top Forge – preserved water-powered hammers, open Sun *(DC)*

Wragby W Yor [A638 nr Nostell Priory; SE4117], *Spread Eagle*: Very good food at most attractive prices, pleasant helpful staff, well kept Bass and Sam Smiths, four homely and friendly traditional low-beamed rooms inc atmospheric tap room with photographs of regulars as youngsters, evening restaurant; quiz night, popular weekends *(Walter and Susan Rinaldi-Butcher)*

☆ **York** N Yor [High Petergate], *Hole in the Wall*: Friendly rambling open-plan pub handy for Minster, beams, stripped brickwork, turkey carpeting, plush seats, well kept Mansfield beers, good coffee, cheap food noon onwards inc generous Sun lunch, prompt service; juke box, piped music not too loud; open all day *(Andy Cunningham, Yvonne Hannaford, Chris Gabbitas, Hugh McPhail, Tony Scott, LYM)*

☆ **York** [Tanners Moat/Wellington Row, below Lendal Bridge], *Maltings*: Rough-and-ready small pub with well kept Black Sheep and half a dozen or more quickly changing beers from small breweries, good choice of continental ones, farm ciders, country wines, decent well priced generous weekday lunchtime food, welcoming service, lots of woodwork inc odd salvaged fittings, old enamel advertisements, daily papers in gents', traditional games; piped radio, parking virtually impossible; open all day, handy for Rail Museum, jazz or folk Mon/Tues, piped radio, great beer festivals *(Richard Lewis, Howard England, Tony and Wendy Hobden, Eric Larkham, SLC, Richard Houghton)*

☆ **York** [26 High Petergate], *York Arms*: Snug little basic panelled bar (beware the sliding door), big modern no-smoking lounge, cosier partly panelled room full of old bric-a-brac, prints, brown-cushioned wall settles, dimpled copper tables and an open fire; quick friendly service, well kept Sam Smiths, good value simple food lunchtime to early evening, no music; by Minster, open all day *(Eric Larkham, BB)*

York [53 Fossgate], *Blue Bell*: Untouched traditional pub with corridor linking tiny front bar to back room not much bigger, well kept Vaux and a guest beer, good lively atmosphere; open all day, can get very busy *(Eric Larkham, SLC, PB)*; [Marygate], *Coach House*: Very clean, with good choice in pleasant bar, superb food, friendly atmosphere; bedrooms comfortable, handy for centre *(T and C Howard-Jones)*; [15 North St, opp Viking Hotel], *First Hussar*: One of the three independently franchised Tap & Spiles which, when Pubmaster sold the chain to Century Inns, stayed independent but had to change their names; very basic decor in three smallish rooms, wide range of well kept ales such as Old Mill and Theakstons, also guest beers and Weston's Old Rosie cider, lunchtime food inc nice sandwiches and cheap chips; machines, tables outside, open all day, Weds music night *(J A Halfyard, Thomas Nott, Eric Larkham)*; [9 Church St], *Golden Lion*: Big open-plan T J Bernards pub recently given stone-floored Edwardian refurbishment, dark with plenty of lamps; friendly efficient staff, Scottish Courage ales with good guest and lots of bottled beers, wide choice of generous lunchtime food; fruit machine, piped music *(SLC, Ann and Bob Westbrook)*; [4 King St], *Grapes*: Rather upmarket but very welcoming, Thwaites ales inc special brews; no nearby parking *(R Houghton)*; [24 Lendal], *Lendal Cellars*: Split-level Hogshead ale house down steps in broad-vaulted 17th-c cellars carefully spotlit to show up the stripped brickwork, hand-crafted furniture and cask seats on stone floor, interconnected rooms and alcoves, well kept Whitbreads and guest ales, farm cider, country wines, foreign bottled beers, friendly staff, interesting electrical lattice work in two rooms, open all day; children allowed while food being served, 11.30-7(5 Fri/Sat) *(Richard Lewis, Eric Larkham, LYM)*; [Goodramgate], *Old White Swan*: Victorian, Georgian and Tudor themed bars, delightful covered courtyard, enjoyable food, Bass-related ales, friendly staff; juke box, piped music, games machines – can get loudly busy towards w/e *(Ian Baillie, Eric Larkham)*; [7 Stonegate], *Punch Bowl*: Has been unspoilt friendly Bass local with small dim-lit rooms off corridor (almost Hogarthian, but for the piped music and flashing machines), but some refurbishment under way while this is being written; friendly helpful service, good generous lunchtime food inc vegetarian (no-smoking area by food servery), well kept ales inc guests such as York Stonewall and Yorkshire Terrier, farm cider, panelled lounge; open all day all week, some live music and quiz nights, good value bedrooms *(Rona Murdoch, G Washington, Ian Baillie)*; [Goodramgate], *Snickleway*: Snug little old-world pub, friendly landlord, well kept Morlands Old Speckled Hen and John Smiths, limited range of lunchtime food (not Sun) inc good value fresh sandwiches, lots of antiques, copper and brass, good coal fires, cosy nooks and crannies, unobtrusive piped music, prompt service, hilarious cartoons in gents' *(Paul and Ursula Randall)*; [12 Coppergate], *Three Tuns*: Smallish single room, subdued lighting, prints, well kept Mansfield and occasional guest beer, food inc vegetarian, juke box, machines; open all day, handy for Jorvik Centre *(Eric Larkham, SLC)*

Children welcome means the pub says it lets children inside without any special restriction. If it allows them in, but to restricted areas such as an eating area or family room, we specify this. Places with separate restaurants usually let children use them, hotels usually let them into public areas such as lounges. Some pubs impose an evening time limit – let us know if you find this.

London
Scotland
Wales
Channel Islands

London

Among London's vast number of pubs are a few dozen really good ones. Places showing particularly well these days include, in Central London, the Bishops Finger (EC1: a classily remodelled pub, with good food and atmosphere – a new main entry), the classic largely subterranean Cittie of Yorke (WC1), the charming little Grenadier tucked away in its Belgravia mews (SW1), the vibrant foody Eagle (EC1), the Jerusalem Tavern (EC1: another excellent recent remodelling in the old-fashioned mould; very good beers), the fine old Lamb in Lambs Conduit St (WC1), the civilised Leopard (EC1: another new entry, with good food from an open kitchen and a remarkable conservatory), the Moon Under Water spreading through Soho (WC2: a particularly good – and often crowded – Wetherspoons), that British Museum standby the Museum Tavern (WC1), the Old Bank of England (EC4: a great bank conversion by Fullers), the rambling Olde Cheshire Cheese (EC4) and the friendly little Olde Mitre (EC1: a favourite City pub). Particularly enjoyable pubs in North London include the busy foody Chapel (NW1), the nice little villagey Compton Arms (N1), and the very Hampstead Flask (NW3); in South London, the civilised Alma (SW18), the atmospheric old Anchor (SE1: it's planning to add bedrooms), that unexpected coaching inn the George (SE1), the beautifully set White Cross (Richmond) and particularly for families the Crown & Greyhound (SE21); in West London, the Anglesea Arms (SW7: this fine all-rounder is now open all day) and Dove (W6: but this charming old riverside pub is likely to be taken back into management by Fullers). Here in West London the food at the other Anglesea Arms (W6) is very good, and we always particularly like the Windsor Castle (W8). In East London, the Prospect of Whitby (E1) is fun, though touristy. London pubs have always had good sausages, but for years it was difficult to set your gastronomic sights much higher than that. Now, there's plenty of choice of decent pub food at reasonable prices, and quite a few pubs where the food is particularly appealing: to places we've already picked out for food we'd add the Fire Station and the Ship in our South London section. Overall, our choice as London Dining Pub of the Year is the Chapel in Chapel St, London NW1 – but be warned, like many of the younger generation of London's gastropubs it can be pretty noisy in the evenings. London drinks prices are terribly high – nearly 20p a pint higher than the national average. We found the cheapest beer in pubs tied either to the local Fullers or to Sam Smiths of Yorkshire; our Wetherspoons entries, though good value, are no longer the outstanding bargains they were last year. Wine used to be a bit of a black spot in London pubs. Now, many have a really good choice of wines by the glass, kept fresh, including the Bishops Finger, Eagle and Old Bank of England (Central), Compton Arms and Flask (North), and Alma, Bulls Head, Ship and White Cross (South). In the Lucky Dip section at the end of the chapter pubs we'd rate as well worth a visit are, in Central London, the Peasant, Pheasant & Firkin, Dirty Dicks and Hamilton Hall (EC1), Antelope, Buckingham Arms, Fox & Hounds and both Red Lions (SW1), Audley (W1) and Chandos and Salisbury (WC2); in North London, the Albion (N1), Euston Flyer (NW1),

Freemasons Arms (NW3) and Crockers (NW8); in South London, the Founders Arms (SE1), Mayflower (SE16) and Star (Maldon Rushett); in West London, the Chelsea Ram (SW10), the Strand on the Green pubs (W4) and Kings Arms (Hampton Court); and Hollands in East London (E1).

CENTRAL LONDON

Covering W1, W2, WC1, WC2, SW1, SW3, EC1, EC2, EC3 and EC4 postal districts

Parking throughout this area is metered throughout the day, and generally in short supply then; we mention difficulty only if evening parking is a problem too. Throughout the chapter we list the nearest Underground or BR stations to each pub; where two are listed it means the walk is the same from either

Albert (Westminster) Map 13

52 Victoria Street, SW1; ⊖ St James's Park

As busy as you might expect for a pub directly in between Westminster and Victoria, this splendid looking Victorian building is one of the great sights of this part of London, though it's rather dwarfed by the faceless cliffs of dark modern glass around it. Inside civil servants, tourists, and the odd (as in occasional) MP all add to the wonderfully diverse mix of customers in the huge open-plan bar, which has good solid comfortable furniture, and some gleaming mahogany. There's a surprisingly airy feel thanks to great expanses of heavily cut and etched windows along three sides, but though there's plenty of space, it can be packed on weekday lunchtimes and immediately after work. Service from the big island counter is generally swift and efficient (particularly obliging to overseas visitors), with Courage Best and Directors, Theakstons Best and a couple of well chosen guests on handpump. The separate food servery is good value, with sandwiches (from £1.40), soup (£1.75), salads (from £3.50) and five home-cooked hot dishes such as shepherd's pie, steak pie, fish and chips, chicken lasagne or a vegetarian dish (all £4.25). The upstairs restaurant does an eat-as-much-as-you-like carvery, better than average (all day inc Sunday, £14.95). The handsome staircase that leads up to it is lined with portraits of former Prime Ministers. They sound the Division Bell for those MPs who've popped in for a quick drink. Piped music, fruit machine. *(Recommended by George Atkinson, Tony Scott, Ian Phillips, Mark Baynham, Rachael Ward, Alan and Paula McCully, Gordon, M Walker, Robert Lester, John and Wendy Trentham, Wayne Brindle)*

Scottish & Newcastle ~ Managers Roger and Gill Wood ~ Real ale ~ Meals and snacks (11-10.30; 12-10 Sun) ~ Restaurant ~ (0171) 222 5577 ~ Children in eating area and restaurant ~ Open 11-11; 12-10.30 Sun; cl 25/26 Dec

Argyll Arms (Oxford Circus) Map 13

18 Argyll St W1; ⊖ Oxford Circus, opp tube side exit

Easy to spot by the profusion of plants and flowers festooning its frontage, this unexpectedly traditional Victorian pub is undoubtedly one of the best pubs in the area, much as it was when built in the 1860s. This is especially the case in the most atmospheric and unusual part, the three cubicle rooms at the front; all oddly angular, they're made by wooden partitions with distinctive frosted and engraved glass, with hops trailing above. A good range of changing beers typically includes Brakspears, Greene King IPA, Hook Norton Best, Tetleys and Timothy Taylor Landlord on handpump, and they may well have one or two more unusual guests; also Addlestone's cider, malt whiskies, and freshly squeezed orange and pineapple juice. A long mirrored corridor leads to the spacious back room, with the food counter in one corner; this area is no smoking at lunchtime. Chalked up on a blackboard (which may also have topical cartoons), the choice of meals includes unusual sandwiches like generously filled stilton and grape (£2.50), salt beef (£3.25), or roast chicken, bacon and melted cheese (£3.65), and main courses such as salads or a pie of the day. Prompt, efficient staff; two fruit machines, piped music. The quieter upstairs bar, which overlooks the busy pedestrianised street (and the Palladium theatre if you can see through the foliage outside the window), is divided into several snugs with comfortable plush easy chairs; swan's neck lamps, and lots of small theatrical prints along the top of the walls. The gents' has a copy of the day's *Times* or *Financial Times* on the wall. The pub gets very crowded, but there's space for drinking outside. *(Recommended by Stephen and Julie Brown, Jasper Sabey, John Fazakerley, TBB, Tony Scott, Mark Baynham, Rachael Ward, Ian Phillips, Wayne Brindle, Hanns P Golez, Christopher Gallop, Bob and Maggie Atherton, Thomas Thomas, John and Anne Peacock, David Carr, Richard Lewis)*

Nicholsons (Allied; run as free house) ~ Managers Mike Tayara, Regina Kennedy ~ Real ale ~ Meals (12-7.30) and snacks (till 9.30) ~ Restaurant ~ 0171-734 6117 ~ Children welcome ~ Open 11-11; 12-9 Sun; closed 25 Dec, 1 Jan

Bishops Finger 🍷 (City) Map 13

9-10 West Smithfield, EC1; ⊖ Farringdon

Rather grotty until only around a year ago, this has now been transformed into a swish little bar cum restaurant in a verdant square beside Smithfield Market. Laid back but classy, the well spaced out room has bright yellow walls (nicely matching the fresh flowers on the elegant tables and behind the bar), big windows, carefully polished bare boards, a few pillars, and comfortably cushioned chairs under a wall lined with framed prints. Distinctive food from an open kitchen beside the bar includes ciabatta filled with goat's cheese, pesto and beef tomato (£2.95), raw salmon sushi (from £3.25), bangers and mash (£4.25), tonkatsu (fried pork with rice and shredded cabbage in a fruity sauce, £4.95), baked pepper filled with rice and ratatouille (£5.50), oyakodunburi (chicken with eggs and peas in a soy and sweet rice wine sauce, £6.25), chargrilled lamb chump chop with mustard glaze and vegetable risotto (£7.95), and puddings like chocolate and pear brûlée (£2.95). Well kept Shepherd Neame Master Brew, Bishops Finger and Spitfire on handpump, with a wide choice of wines (eight by the glass), and several ports and champagnes; friendly service. Upstairs is another bar, which they hope to develop as an evening restaurant. There are a couple of tables outside. As we went to press they were hoping to introduce live jazz one evening a week.

Shepherd Neame ~ Manager Hannah Chalk ~ Real ale ~ Meals and snacks (12-3, 6-9) ~ 0171-248 2341 ~ Open 12-11 Mon-Fri; closed weekends

Black Friar (City) Map 13

174 Queen Victoria Street, EC4; ⊖ Blackfriars

Bigger inside than seems possible from the delightfully odd exterior, this unique pub has in its inner back room some of the best fine Edwardian bronze and marble art-nouveau decor to be found anywhere: big bas-relief friezes of jolly monks set into richly coloured Florentine marble walls, an opulent marble-pillared inglenook fireplace, a low vaulted mosaic ceiling, gleaming mirrors, seats built into rich golden marble recesses, and tongue-in-cheek verbal embellishments such as Silence is Golden and Finery is Foolish. See if you can spot the opium smoking-hints modelled into the fireplace of the front room. They've expanded the menu a bit since last year: as well as filled rolls (£2.50), and baked potatoes or ploughman's (£2.95), they do straightforward daily specials such as sausage and mash (£4.50), and a roast (£5.25); service is obliging and helpful. Well kept Adnams, Brakspears, Marstons Pedigree and Tetleys on handpump; fruit machine. The pub does get very busy, particularly after work, when lots of people spill out on to the wide forecourt in front, near the approach to Blackfriars Bridge. If you're coming by Tube, choose your exit carefully – it's all too easy to emerge from the network of passageways and find yourself on the other side of the street or marooned on a traffic island. They were experimenting with daytime weekend opening as we went to press, so if you're in the area then it's worth checking to see if they're open. *(Recommended by Chris Westmoreland, Eric and Jackie Robinson, Christopher Gallop, David Carr, Mark Baynham, Rachael Ward)*

Nicholsons (Allied) ~ Manager Mr Becker ~ Real ale ~ Lunchtime meals (11.30-2.30)

~ 0171-236 5650 ~ Open 11.30-11 weekdays; may have limited weekend opening, especially in summer

Cittie of Yorke (Holborn) Map 13

22 High Holborn, WC1; find it by looking out for its big black and gold clock ⊖ Chancery Lane

Very well liked by readers, this unique pub can take your breath away when you see the main back room for the first time. It looks rather like a vast baronial hall, with vast thousand-gallon wine vats resting above the gantry, big bulbous lights hanging from the soaring high raftered roof, and its extraordinarily extended bar counter stretching off into the distance. It does get packed in the early evening, particularly with lawyers and judges, but it's at busy times like these when the pub seems most magnificent. Most people tend to congregate in the middle, so you may still be able to bag one of the intimate, old-fashioned and ornately carved cubicles that run along both sides. The triangular Waterloo fireplace, with grates on all three sides and a figure of Peace among laurels, used to stand in the Grays Inn Common Room until barristers stopped dining there. Appealingly priced Sam Smiths OB on handpump (well below the cost of a typical London pint) and some unusually flavoured vodkas such as chocolate orange or pear and ginger; smartly dressed staff, fruit machine, video game and piped music. A smaller, comfortable wood-panelled room has lots of little prints of York and attractive brass lights, while the ceiling of the entrance hall has medieval-style painted panels and plaster York roses. There's a lunchtime food counter in the main hall with more in the downstairs cellar bar: as well as filled baps, ploughman's and salads, they have several daily specials such as steak and ale pie, lamb braised in red wine, chicken and spinach lasagne, sausage hotpot, and leek, stilton and mushroom bake (all £4.25). A pub has stood on this site since 1430, though the current building owes more to the 1695 coffee house erected here behind a garden; it was reconstructed in Victorian times using 17th-c materials and parts. *(Recommended by Tim Barrow, Sue Demont, J Fahy, David and Carole Chapman, Rachael Ward, Mark Baynham, Ted George, Ian Phillips, Greg Kilminster, Tony Scott, Nigel Wilson, Christopher Gallop, Mike Gorton, Alan and Paula McCully, R J Bland, Jill Bickerton, Val Stevenson, Rob Holmes, Eric and Jackie Robinson, Chris Westmoreland, Mick Hitchman, Jens Arne Grebstad, E A Thwaite, David Carr)*

Sam Smiths ~ Manager Stuart Browning ~ Real ale ~ Meals and snacks (12-9) ~ 0171-242 7670 ~ Children in eating area ~ Open 11.30-11; closed all day Sun

Dog & Duck (Soho) Map 13

18 Bateman St, on corner with Frith Street, W1; ⊖ Tottenham Court Rd/Leicester Square

A delightful little Soho landmark, this pint-sized corner house is a reassuring constant among the ever-changing restaurants and trendy bars lining this part of town. On the floor by the door is a mosaic of a dog, tongue out in hot pursuit of a duck, and the same theme is embossed on some of the shiny tiles that frame the heavy old advertising mirrors. The little bar counter is rather unusual, and serves very well kept Tetleys, Timothy Taylor Landlord, and a couple of guests on handpump; they do doorstep sandwiches (from £1.80). The chatty main bar really is tiny, though at times it manages to squeeze in a wonderfully varied mix of people; there are some high stools by the ledge along the back wall, and further seats in a slightly roomier area at one end. Upstairs is a snug bar overlooking the street, where they have a weekly Sunday evening club for deaf people; the barman has been on a sign language course. There's a fire in winter, and newspapers to read. In good weather especially there tend to be plenty of people spilling on to the bustling street outside. No machines or piped music – though if you fancy a few tunes Ronnie Scott's Jazz Club is near by. *(Recommended by Stephen and Julie Brown, Gerry Christie, Steve Harvey, David Carr, Maggie and Bob Atherton; more reports please)*

Nicholsons (Allied) ~ Manageress Mrs Gene Bell ~ Real ale ~ Snacks (not weekends) ~ 0171-437 4447 ~ Open 12-11; closed Sat and Sun lunchtimes, opening 6 Sat evening (7 Sun)

Eagle (City) Map 13

159 Farringdon Rd, EC1; opposite Bowling Green Lane car park; ⊖ Farringdon/Old Street

Once a pioneering novelty, now already something of an institution, the Eagle continues to serve some of the best pub food in London, its distinctive Mediterranean-style meals effortlessly superior to those in the welcome imitators that have sprung up all over the city. If anything, it's almost a little too successful, as we often hear from readers who've waited in vain during the week for a table to become available; anyone who's experienced that will be delighted to hear they now open on Sundays, when it should be a little easier to find a space. Made with the finest quality ingredients, typical dishes might include Tuscan white bean soup with Cavalo Nero and pesto (£4), pumpkin, sage and chilli risotto (£7), marinated rumpsteak sandwich (£8), a Spanish casserole of chicken, wine and garlic or scallops and chorizo on bruschetta, with rocket and piquilos peppers (£8.50), a good paella with mussels, squid, prawns, hake, clams, chicken, broad beans and peppers (£9.50), and grilled swordfish steak with an imaginative cauliflower, red onion, pine nut, raisin and mint salad (£11); they also do Spanish and goat's milk cheeses (£5), and Portuguese custard tarts (90p). Note they don't take credit cards. On weekday lunchtimes especially, dishes from the blackboard menu can run out or change fairly quickly, so it really is worth getting here as early as you possibly can if you're hoping to eat. Though the food is out of the ordinary, the atmosphere is still lively, chatty and pubby (especially in the evenings), so it's not the kind of place you'd go to for a smart night out or a quiet dinner. The open kitchen forms part of the bar, and furnishings in the single room are simple but stylish – school chairs, a rabndom assortment of tables, a couple of sofas on bare boards, and modern paintings on the walls (there's an art gallery upstairs, with direct access from the bar). There's quite a mix of customers, but at times there's quite a proliferation of media folk (*The Guardian* is based just up the road). Well kept Boddingtons, Flowers Original and Wadworths 6X on handpump, good wines including a dozen by the glass, good coffee, and properly made cocktails; piped music. *(Recommended by David Carr, Greg Kilminster, Yavuz and Shirley Mutlu, Mark Baynham, Rachael Ward, MB, Nick Rose, R J Bland, Sebastian Leach, James Macrae, Maggie and Bob Atherton, Dave Braisted)*

Free house ~ Licencees Michael Belben, Usha Ginda, Tom Norrington-Davies ~ Real ale ~ Meals 12.30-2.30(3.30 Sat), 6.30-10.30 ~ 0171-837 1353 ~ Children welcome ~ Open 12-11; 12-5 Sun; closed bank hols, Easter, and 10 days at Christmas

Grapes (Mayfair) Map 13

Shepherd Market, W1; ⊖ Green Park

Traditional and friendly, this chatty pub is bang in the middle of civilised Shepherd Market, and on sunny evenings you'll generally find the square outside packed with smart-suited drinkers. Much quieter at lunchtimes, the dimly lit bar is cheery and old-fashioned, with plenty of stuffed birds and fish in glass display cases, and a snug little alcove at the back. Bar food might include sandwiches (from £2.75), seafood platter or half roast chicken (£4.55), and ploughman's (£5.25); the eating area is no smoking at lunchtime. A good range of six or seven well kept (though fairly pricy) beers on handpump usually takes in Boddingtons, Flowers IPA and Original, Fullers London Pride, Greene King Abbot, Marstons Pedigree, and Wadworths 6X; fruit machine. Service can slow down a little at the busiest times. What was the restaurant is now a private members club, though membership is free and they say applications to join are welcome. *(Recommended by Rachael Ward, Mark Baynham, Ian Phillips, Peter Todd, Wayne Brindle, Thomas Nott, Tim Barrow, Sue Demont, Eric and Jackie Robinson)*

Free house ~ Licensees Gill and Eric Lewis ~ Real ale ~ Lunchtime meals and snacks (not Sun) ~ 0171-629 4989 ~ Children over 10 in eating area of bar lunchtime only ~ Open 11-11; 12-10.30 Sun; closed 25 Dec

Children – if the details at the end of an entry don't mention them, you should assume that the pub does not allow them inside.

Grenadier (Belgravia) Map 13

Wilton Row, SW1; the turning off Wilton Crescent looks prohibitive, but the barrier and watchman are there to keep out cars; walk straight past – the pub is just around the corner; ⊖ Knightsbridge

Famous for its Bloody Marys (from a long-kept-secret recipe) and well documented poltergeist (it's reckoned to be the capital's most haunted pub), this snugly characterful place is a real favourite with some readers, several of whom have been visiting regularly for over 30 years. Patriotically painted in red, white and blue, it was used for a while as the mess for the officers of the Duke of Wellington, whose portrait hangs above the fireplace, alongside neat prints of Guardsmen through the ages. The bar is tiny (some might say cramped), but you should be able to plonk yourself on one of the stools or wooden benches, as despite the charms of this engaging little pub it rarely gets too crowded. Well kept Courage Best, Marstons Pedigree, Theakstons Best and a regularly changing guest from handpumps at the rare pewter-topped bar counter, as well; service is friendly, but can be a little slow. Bar food runs from bowls of chips and nachos (very popular with after work drinkers), through good sausage and mash (£4.50) to hot steak sandwiches (£5.50); they may do a Sunday roast. The intimate back restaurant is quite pricy, but good for a romantic dinner. There's a single table outside in the peaceful mews, from where on a sunny summer evening it's lovely watching the slowly darkening sky, idly dreaming you might one day be able to afford one of the smart little houses opposite. *(Recommended by Christopher Wright, Guy Consterdine, Jasper Sabey, Susan and John Douglas, Ian Phillips, Stephen and Brenda Head, Tom McLean, Roger Huggins, Dave Irving, Ewan McCall, Gordon, Thomas, Suzanne and Therese Schulz)*

S & N ~ Managers Paul and Alexandra Gibb ~ Real ale ~ Meals and snacks (12-2.30, 6-10) ~ Restaurant ~ 0171-235 3074 ~ Children over 5 in restaurant ~ Open 12-11(10.30 Sun); closed 25 Dec

Jerusalem Tavern (City) Map 13

55 Britton St, EC1; ⊖ Farringdon

This carefully restored old coffee house is one of only a very few pubs belonging to the newish, small Suffolk-based St Peter's Brewery, and one of the highlights is the full range of their rather tasty beers: St Peter's Best, Extra, Fruit beer, Golden Ale, Grapefruit, Mild, Strong, Porter, Wheat beer, and Winter Spiced, all tapped from casks behind the little bar counter. If you develop a taste for them (and they are rather addictive) they also sell them to take away, in rather elegant distinctively shaped bottles. The pub itself is a vivid re-creation of an 18th-c tavern, and the architect has clearly done his homework; darkly atmospheric and characterful, it seems so genuinely old that you'd never guess the work was done only a couple of years ago. So convincing is the result that it was used to represent a turn of the century tavern in the recent film *The Wings of the Dove*. There's been a pub of this name around here for quite some time, but the current building was developed around 1720, originally as a merchant's house, then becoming a clock and watchmaker's. It still has the shop front added in 1810, immediately behind which is a light little room with a couple of wooden tables and benches, a stack of *Country Life* magazines, and some remarkable old tiles on the walls at either side. This leads to the tiny dimly lit bar, which has a couple of unpretentious tables on the bare boards, and another up some stairs on a discreetly precarious balcony; the atmosphere is relaxed and quietly chatty. A plainer back room has a few more tables, as well as a fireplace, and a stuffed fox in a case. Blackboards list the simple but well liked food: soup (£3), unusual sandwiches such as salami and red onion (£3.95), locally made sausages such as venison and red wine or lamb and mint (£4.25), spaghetti bolognese or vegetable kiev (£4.95), and carrot cake (£3); they open at 9am for breakfasts and coffee. A couple of tables outside overlook the quiet street. The brewery has another main entry at Wingfield in Suffolk. *(Recommended by Mark Baynham, Rachael Ward, David Carr, Sue Demont, Tim Barrow, Simon Allen, John Murphy)*

St Peter's ~ Manager Mike Robinson ~ Real ale ~ Meals and snacks (12-7) ~ 0171-490 4281 ~ Children welcome ~ Open 9am-11pm Mon-Fri; closed weekends

Lamb ★ (Bloomsbury) Map 13

94 Lamb's Conduit Street, WC1; ⊖ Holborn

Like the street, this old favourite is named for the Kentish clothmaker William Lamb who brought fresh water to Holborn in 1577. It's a unique and timeless survival, famous for its cut-glass swivelling 'snob-screens' all the way around the U-shaped bar counter. Sepia photographs of 1890s actresses on the ochre panelled walls and traditional cast-iron-framed tables with neat brass rails around the rim very much add to the overall effect, and when you come out you almost expect the streets to be dark and foggy and illuminated by gas lamps. Consistently well kept Youngs Bitter, Special and seasonal brews on handpump, and around 40 different malt whiskies; prompt friendly service, and a good mix of customers. Lunchtime bar food such as steak and ale or chicken and cider pie, sausage and mash, and ploughman's (all around £4.95); on Sunday lunchtimes the choice is limited to their popular Sunday roast (£4.95). There are slatted wooden seats in a little courtyard beyond the quiet room down a couple of steps at the back; dominoes, cribbage, backgammon. No machines or music. A snug room at the back on the right is no smoking. It can get very crowded, especially in the evenings. *(Recommended by J R Ringrose, Richard Lewis, Tony Scott, Rachael Ward, Mark Baynham, Nigel Williamson, Ian Phillips, Gordon)*

Youngs ~ Manager Richard Whyte ~ Real ale ~ Lunchtime meals and snacks (12-5) ~ 0171-405 0713 ~ Well behaved children up to early evening ~ Open 11-11; 12-10.30 Sun; closed evening 25 Dec

Lamb & Flag (Covent Garden) Map 13

33 Rose Street, WC2; off Garrick Street; ⊖ Leicester Square

The only pub in Covent Garden to celebrate St George's Day rather than St Patrick's, this old favourite is a well liked place for Londoners to meet after work, and even in winter you'll find plenty of people drinking and chatting in the little alleyways outside (often because they can hardly squeeze inside). Despite a few recent changes, it hasn't altered much since the days when Dickens described the Middle Temple lawyers who frequented it when he was working in nearby Catherine Street. The busy low-ceilinged back bar has high-backed black settles and an open fire, and in Regency times was known as the Bucket of Blood from the bare-knuckle prize-fights held here. It fills up quite quickly, though you might be able to find a seat in the upstairs Dryden Room. There may be darts in the plainer front bar. Well kept Courage Best and Directors, Greene King IPA, Marstons Pedigree, and Youngs on handpump; up till about 5 o'clock at least one of these will be a fair bit cheaper than later on in the day. Also, a good few malt whiskies. Lunchtime bar food includes a choice of several well kept cheeses and pâtés, served with hot bread or french bread, as well as doorstep sandwiches (£3.50), ploughman's (£3.50), and, upstairs, hot dishes like shepherd's pie or bangers and mash (£3.95). *(Recommended by Mick Hitchman, R J Bland, Ted George, Tim Barrow, Sue Demont, Alan and Paula McCully, RWD, Mark Baynham, Rachael Ward, Gordon, P A Legon, David Carr, Val Stevenson, Rob Holmes, Bob and Maggie Atherton)*

Courage ~ Lease: Terry Archer, Sandra and Adrian Zimmerman ~ Real ale ~ Lunchtime meals (till 2.30) and snacks (12-4.30); limited Sun ~ (0171) 497 9504 ~ Live jazz Sunday evening ~ Children in eating area of bar lunchtimes only ~ Open 11-11; 12-10.30 Sun; closed 25 Dec, 1 Jan

Leopard (City) Map 13

33 Seward St, EC1; ⊖ Farringdon

Don't be fooled by the inauspicious exterior; this smartly refurbished pub is rather civilised inside, especially in the unusual conservatory at the back. It's quite a surprise when the more traditional front part suddenly gives way to a soaring atrium – rather like an indoor garden – but it doesn't feel at all out of place. Plants cover the side walls and there are plenty of light wooden tables, with french windows leading to a small but not unappealing terrace. A green wrought-iron spiral staircase leads to another comfortable room, and a small outside drinking area. Back downstairs, the front of the pub has plenty of space and a comfortably relaxed feel, as well as a long dark wooden bar counter, a couple of big mirrors, fading rugs on the bare boards, and a neat tiled fireplace; soft piped music. The choice of beers is very good, with the four well kept real ales usually including a couple of guests that you'd be hard pushed to find anywhere else in the area; on our last visit as well as Greene King Abbot and Salisbury Best they had Vaux How's Your Father and Maclays Wallace IPA. The well chosen wine list takes in a dozen by the glass. An open kitchen serves good freshly prepared bar meals from a changing blackboard menu, which might include sandwiches, nachos (£4.50), various sausages with braised red cabbage and garlic mash (£5.50), seafood fishcake coated with sesame seeds with provençale sauce (£6.25), smoked salmon and roast vegetable risotto (£6.35), grilled lamb steak with garlic butter (£6.75), and sirloin steak with sweet pepper and anchovy butter (£7.45); friendly service. *(Recommended by Richard Lewis, Bridget Burgess)*

Free house ~ Manager Malcolm Jones ~ Real ale ~ Meals and snacks (12-9.30) ~ 0171-253 3587 ~ Children in eating area ~ Open 11-11 weekdays; closed weekends

Lord Moon of the Mall (Trafalgar Square) Map 13

16 Whitehall, SW1; ⊖ Charing Cross

Many of central London's highlights are within easy walking distance of this well converted former bank, making it an ideal pit stop for sightseers and visitors. It opened in 1872 as a wing of the rather exclusive Corks, Biddulph and Co, then was a branch of slightly less select Barclays before its transformation by Wetherspoons. The impressive main room has a very high ceiling and quite an elegant feel to it, with smart old prints, big arched windows looking out over Whitehall, and a huge painting that seems to show a well-to-do 18th-c gentleman; in fact it's Tim Martin, founder of the Wetherspoons chain. Once through an arch the style is recognisably Wetherspoons, but slightly classier than usual, with a couple of neatly tiled areas and nicely lit bookshelves opposite the long bar; black and white photographs of nearby sights are accompanied by brief historical notes. The three games machines don't quite fit in. The back doors are now only used in an emergency, but were apparently built as a secret entrance for account holders living in Buckingham Palace (Edward VII had an account here from the age of three); the area by the doors is no smoking. Courage Directors, Fullers London Pride, Theakstons Best and a couple of quickly changing guests such as Charles Wells Bombardier or Smiles on handpump. Bar food, from the standard Wetherspoons menu, is good value and reliable, ranging from soup (£2.35), filled baguettes (from £2.75), and baked potatoes (£3.15) to vegetarian pasta (£4.95), somerset pie ((£5.25), chicken balti (£5.45), and daily specials such as spicy bean casserole; Sunday roast. The terms of the license rule out fried food. As you come out of the pub Nelson's Column is immediately to the left, and Big Ben a walk of ten minutes or so to the right. Note they don't allow children. *(Recommended by Tim Barrow, Sue Demont, Rachael Ward, Mark Baynham, David Chamberlain, Meg and Colin Hamilton)*

Free house ~ Manager Diane Daglish ~ Real ale ~ Meals and snacks (11-10; 12-9.30 Sun) ~ 0171-839 7701 ~ Open 11-11; 12-10.30 Sun

Moon Under Water (Soho) Map 12

105 Charing Cross Rd, WC2; ⊖ Tottenham Court Rd/Leicester Square

Hardly a place to come for a quiet drink, this fiercely modern Wetherspoons pub has quickly established itself as one of the most popular pubs in this part of town. A breathtaking conversion of the old Marquee club, perhaps the most remarkable thing about it – apart from its size – is the intriguing mix of customers it attracts, from Soho trendies and students to tourists and the local after-work crowd; for people-watching it's hard to beat. The carefully designed main area is what used to be the auditorium, now transformed into a cavernous white-painted room stretching far off into the distance, with seats and tables lining the walls along the way. It effortlessly absorbs the hordes that pour in on Friday and Saturday evenings, and even when it's at its busiest you shouldn't have any trouble traversing the room, or have to wait very long to be served at the bar. Good value food and drinks are the same as at other Wetherspoons pubs (see previous entry), and they have regular real-ale festivals and promotions; friendly service. The former stage is the area with most seats, and from here a narrower room leads past another bar to a back door opening on to Greek St (quite a surprise, as the complete lack of windows means you don't realise how far you've walked). The small seating area upstairs is no smoking. Essentially this is a traditional pub that just happens to have a rather innovative design, so it's worth a look just to see the two combined; if you find it's not quite your style, at the very least it's a handy shortcut to Soho. *(Recommended by Chris Parsons, A Hodges, Stephen and Julie Brown)*

Free house~ Manager Lorenzo Verri ~ Real ale ~ Meals and snacks (11-10) ~ 0171-287 6039 ~ Open 11-11; 12-10.30 Sun

Museum Tavern (Bloomsbury) Map 13

Museum Street, WC1; ⊖ Holborn or Tottenham Court Rd

One of the main draws to this quietly civilised pub has always been its genuinely old-fashioned feel, and that's even more the case now that they've got rid of the fruit machine. It's directly opposite the British Museum, which explains why lunchtime tables are sometimes hard to come by, but it rarely gets too busy. In late afternoons especially there's a nicely peaceful atmosphere, with a good mix of locals and tourists, and unlike most other pubs in the area it generally stays pleasantly uncrowded in the evenings. Karl Marx is fondly supposed to have had the odd glass here, and it's tempting to think that the chap at the next table scribbling notes or with his nose in a book is working on a similarly seminal set of ideas. The single room is simply furnished and decorated, with high-backed benches around traditional cast-iron pub tables, and old advertising mirrors between the wooden pillars behind the bar. A decent choice of well kept beers on handpump usually takes in Courage Best and Directors, Theakstons Best and Old Peculier, and a more unusual guest, but even for this area they're not cheap – it's one of our more expensive central London entries. They also have several wines by the glass, a choice of malt whiskies, and tea, coffee, cappuccino and hot chocolate. Available all day from a servery at the end of the room, bar food might include cold pasties, pie or quiche with salads, sausages and chips (£4.99), ploughman's (£5.99), and hot dishes like tuna and mushroom bake or chicken and mushroom pie (£5.99); helpful service. It gets a little smoky when busy. There are a couple of tables outside under the gas lamps and 'Egyptian' inn sign. *(Recommended by Ted George, Gordon Prince, Mike Gorton, Sue Demont, Tim Barrow, Gordon, Jens Arne Grebstad, Steve Harvey, Mick Hitchman, Hanns P Golez, Hugh MacLean, David Carr)*

Scottish & Newcastle ~ Manager Lachlan Mackay ~ Real ale ~ Meals (11-10) ~ 0171-242 8987 ~ Children in eating area ~ Open 11-11; 12-10.30 Sun; closed 25/26 Dec, 1 Jan

Nags Head (Belgravia) Map 13

53 Kinnerton St, SW1; ⊖ Knightsbridge

Hidden away in an attractive and peaceful mews minutes from Harrods, this quaint little gem is one of the most unspoilt pubs you're likely to find in the whole of London, let alone so close to the centre. Indeed it really doesn't feel like London at all, and you could be forgiven for thinking you'd been transported to an old-fashioned local somewhere in a sleepy country village, right down to the friendly regulars chatting around the unusual sunken bar counter. Homely and warmly traditional, it's rarely busy, even at weekends, when even in summer there's a snugly relaxed and cosy feel. The small, panelled and low-ceilinged front area has a wood-effect gas fire in an old cooking range (seats by here are generally snapped up pretty quickly), and a narrow passage leads down steps to an even smaller back bar with stools and a mix of comfortable seats. There's a 1930s What-the-butler-saw machine and a one-armed bandit that takes old pennies, as well as rather individual piped music, generally jazz, folk or show tunes. The well kept Adnams and Tetleys are pulled on attractive 19th-c china, pewter and brass handpumps. Bar food includes sandwiches (from £3.50), ploughman's or plenty of salads (from £4.75), real ale sausage, mash and beans, chilli, or steak and mushroom pie (all £4.95) and specials like roasts (£4.95) or cod mornay (£4.25); there's a £1 service charge added to all dishes in the evenings. There are a few seats and a couple of tables outside. This has long been one of our favourite London pubs, but, in common with several readers, we have noticed in recent months that the service isn't quite what it was; they still greet you as you enter, and say goodbye when you leave, but the landlord gets unduly agitated whenever anyone dares try and put their coat or jacket over a chair rather than on a coathook. *(Recommended by Ian Phillips, Ted George, Pete Baker, M J Dowdy, Bob and Maggie Atherton, C Smith, James Nunns, B J Harding, Gordon, Peter Plumridge, Dave Irving, Roger Huggins, Ewan McCall, Tom McLean, Steve Harvey, Hanns P Golez, Virginia Jones, Hugh MacLean, Wayne Brindle, David Carr)*

Free house ~ Licensee Kevin Moran ~ Real ale ~ Meals and snacks (12-9.30) ~ 0171-235 1135 ~ Children in eating area ~ Open 11-11; 12-10.30 Sun

Old Bank of England 🍷 (City) Map 13

194 Fleet St, EC4; ⊖ Temple

Lots of pubs are converted from old banks these days, but few quite so spectacularly as this splendid place. A rather austere Italianate structure, it was until the mid-1970s a subsidiary branch of the Bank of England, built to service the nearby Law Courts; after that it was a building society before Fullers transfomed it into a pub in 1995. The opulent bar never fails to impress first and even second time visitors: three gleaming chandeliers hang from the exquisitely plastered ceiling high above the unusually tall island bar counter, and the green walls are liberally dotted with old prints, framed bank notes and the like. Though the room is quite spacious, screens between some of the varied seats and tables create a surprisingly intimate feel, and there are several cosier areas at the end, with more seats in a galleried section upstairs. The mural that covers most of the end wall looks like an 18th-c depiction of Justice, but in fact was commissioned specially for the pub and features members of the Fuller, Smith and Turner families. Fullers Chiswick, ESB and London Pride on handpump (the first of these very nicely priced for the area), along with a couple of changing guests, and around 20 wines by the glass; very good efficient service from neatly uniformed staff. Good generously served bar food includes soup (£2.50), deep-filled sandwiches (from £3.50), ploughman's, a pasta special or bean, celery and coriander chilli (£5.25), battered fish and chips (£5.95), and several pies like leek and potato, chicken, bacon and spinach, or a good game pie (from £5.25); they do cream teas in the afternoon. The dining room is no smoking at lunchtime. The pub is easy to spot in winter by the Olympic-style torches blazing outside; the entrance is up a flight of stone steps. Note they don't allow children. Pies have a long if rather dubious pedigree in this area; it was in the vaults and tunnels below the Old Bank and the surrounding buildings that Sweeney Todd butchered the clients destined to provide the fillings in his mistress Mrs Lovett's nearby pie shop. *(Recommended by Walter and Susan Rinaldi-Butcher, Tony Scott, J R Ringrose, Dr and Mrs A K Clarke, Chris Parsons, Robert Gomme, Simon Walker, David Carr)*

Fullers ~ Manager Peter Biddle ~ Real ale ~ Meals and snacks (12-8) ~ Restaurant ~ 0171-430 2255 ~ Open 11-11 Mon-Fr; closed all day weekends and bank holidays

Old Coffee House (Soho) Map 13

49 Beak Street, W1; ⊖ Oxford Circus

With a wider choice of meals than most other pubs in the area, this friendly pub is useful to know about for a decent well priced lunch. It was one of the first in London to pile itself high with bric-a-brac – not the boring bought-in bits that seem to come with the fixtures in so many places these days, but an intriguing jumble of nostalgic ephemera that all but fills the busy downstairs bar. The best time to see it properly is on a quiet lunchtime (it's generally so popular in the evenings you won't get an unbroken view), when you might find yourself sitting beside or under a stuffed pike or fox, a great brass bowl or bucket, or maybe one of the ancient musical instruments (brass and string sections both well represented). On the walls are a good collection of Great War recruiting posters, golden discs, death-of-Nelson prints, theatre and cinema handbills, and so forth – and there's even a nude in one corner (this is Soho, after all). Upstairs, the food room has as many prints and pictures as a Victorian study. Not especially unusual, but good value, bar food includes filled baked potatoes (from £2.50), burgers (£3.20), various salads (£4), quite a few hot dishes like chicken, ham and leek pie, chilli, lasagne, pasta and broccoli bake, or winter stews and casseroles (all £4.20), and puddings like treacle sponge (£1.85). Well kept Courage Best and Directors and Marstons Pedigree on handpump; fruit machine, piped music. *(Recommended by Ian Phillips, Jill Bickerton, Virginia Jones, David Carr, Wayne Brindle)*

Courage ~ Lease: Barry Hawkins ~ Real ale ~ Lunchtime meals and snacks (12-3; not Sun) ~ (0171) 437 2197 ~ Children in upstairs food room 12-3pm ~ Open 11-11; 12-3, 7-10.30 Sun

Olde Cheshire Cheese (City) Map 13

Wine Office Court; off 145 Fleet Street, EC4 ⊖ Blackfriars

Remarkably untouristy considering it's one of London's most famous old pubs, this 17th-c former chop house delights readers with its genuinely historic feel and dark, unpretentious little rooms. Over the years Congreve, Pope, Voltaire, Thackeray, Dickens, Conan Doyle, Yeats and perhaps Dr Johnson have called in, a couple of these probably coming across the famous parrot that for over 40 years entertained princes, ambassadors, and other distinguished guests. When she died in 1926 the news was broadcast on the BBC and obituary notices appeared in 200 newspapers all over the world; she's still around today, stuffed and silent. Up and down stairs, the profusion of small bars and rooms have bare wooden benches built in to the walls, sawdust on bare boards, and on the ground floor high beams, crackly old black varnish, Victorian paintings on the dark brown walls, and a big open fire in winter. It's been extended in a similar style towards Fleet St. Lunchtime bar food includes sandwiches, filled jacket potatoes, and ploughman's, and hot dishes such as shepherd's pie, home-made vegetarian quiche or chicken tikka (all £4.25). Well kept (and, as usual for this brewery, well priced) Sam Smiths OB on handpump, friendly service. Some of the Cellar bar is no smoking at lunchtimes. One reader visiting last year was persuaded by other customers to unpack his viola and play a few tunes, thus earning himself a steady flow of free drinks throughout the night. The pub is generally fairly quiet at weekends. *(Recommended by Jenny and Brian Seller, Giles Francis, Nigel Wilson, Tony Scott, Richard Fallon, Gordon, Graham and Karen Oddey)*

Sam Smiths ~ Licensee Gordon Garrity ~ Lunchtime meals and snacks (not weekends) ~ Two evening restaurants (not Sun) ~ 0171-353 6170 ~ Children in eating area of bar and restaurant ~ Open 11.30-11 Mon-Fri; 11.30-3, 5.30-11 Sat, 12-4 Sun; closed Sun evening and bank hols

Olde Mitre £ (City) Map 13

Ely Place, EC1; the easiest way to find it is from the narrow passageway beside 8 Hatton Garden; ⊖ Chancery Lane

As well as its distinctive character and history, what draws people back to this carefully rebuilt little tavern is the really exceptional service and welcome; the landlord clearly loves his job, and works hard to pass that enjoyment on to his customers. One of London's most special pubs, it's hidden away on the edge of the City, so you're always surprised to find so many other visitors enjoying its charms. The cosy dark panelled small rooms have antique settles and – particularly in the back room, where there are more seats – old local pictures and so forth. It gets good-naturedly packed between 12.30 and 2.15, filling up again in the early evening, but by around nine becomes a good deal more tranquil. Indeed one reader found the atmosphere so relaxing on a quiet late afternoon visit that she fell asleep. An upstairs room, mainly used for functions, may double as an overflow at peak periods. Well kept Friary Meux, Ind Coope Burton and Tetleys on handpump; notably chatty staff; darts. Popular bar snacks include really good value cheese sandwiches with ham, pickle or tomato (£1, including toasted), as well as pork pies or scotch eggs. There are some pot plants and jasmine in the narrow yard between the pub and St Ethelreda's church. The iron gates that guard Ely Place are a reminder of the days when the law in this district was administered by the Bishops of Ely; even today it's still technically part of Cambridgeshire. *(Recommended by Rachael Ward, Mark Baynham, Gordon, Tony Scott, Tim Heywood, Sophie Wilne, R J Bland, Mayur Shah, John Fazakerley, Chris Westmoreland)*

Allied ~ Manager Don O'Sullivan ~ Real ale ~ Snacks (11-9.45) ~ 0171-405 4751 ~ Open 11-11 Mon-Fri; closed weekends and bank hols

Orange Brewery (Pimlico) Map 13

37 Pimlico Road, SW1; ⊖ Sloane Square

Every week this lively and friendly pub produces over 500 gallons of their popular ales – SW1, a stronger SW2, and a seasonal Porter. They've been experimenting with different lager recipes in recent months, so their long-standing Victoria could be about to be superseded. You may also find a couple of guest beers, plus a good range of foreign bottled beers, including some Trappist brews. Above the simple wooden chairs, tables and panelling is some vintage brewing equipment and related bric-a-brac, and there's a nicely tiled fireplace; fruit machine, piped music. A viewing area looks down into the brewery, and you can book tours for a closer look. Some readers feel it's like a posh version of a Firkin pub, and its after-work appeal is such that there may be times when it's hard to find anywhere to sit; a few seats outside face a little concreted-over green beyond the quite busy street. The menu was about to change as we went to press (along with the manager) but typically features things like ploughman's (£2.75), three cheese pasta or a big cumberland sausage in gravy flavoured with their own beer (£3.75), chilli (£3.95), and steak and kidney pudding (£4.95). *(Recommended by Ian Phillips, Jasper Sabey, Rachael Ward, Mark Baynham, Martin Watts, Eddy and Emma Gibson, Dr S P Willavoys)*

Own brew (though tied to S & N) ~ Real ale ~ Meals and snacks (limited choice Sun) ~ 0171-730 5984 ~ Children welcome until 9pm ~ Open 11-11; 12-10.30 Sun

Princess Louise (Holborn) Map 13

208 High Holborn, WC1; ⊖ Holborn

Some big changes at this old-fashioned gin-palace over the last year: now a Sam Smiths pub, it no longer has the wide range of real ales it's had in recent years, but the two other main draws – the vibrant, bustling atmosphere, and the unique architectural appeal – haven't been affected at all. Readers often comment on the way the building has managed to keep its genuine period features intact; even the gents' has its own preservation order. The elaborate decor includes etched and gilt mirrors, brightly coloured and fruity-shaped tiles, and slender Portland stone columns soaring towards the lofty and deeply moulded crimson and gold plaster ceiling. Quieter corners have comfortable green plush seats and banquettes. Very nicely priced Sam Smiths OB on handpump from the long main bar, which might also have several wines by the glass; friendly service. Bar snacks such as onion rings (£1.70) or potato wedges (£1.80) with dips, as well as an upstairs lunchtime buffet, sandwiches, filled baked potatoes (£3.50), burgers (£3.95), chilli (£4), salads with home-made dressing (£4.25), gammon and egg (£4.95), and salmon steak or creamy vegetable kiev (£5.25). Fruit machine. Though it does get crowded during the week, it's usually quieter later on in the evening, or on a Saturday lunchtime. *(Recommended by Rachael Ward, Mark Baynham, Dr Oscar Puls, Tony Scott, Michael Sandy)*

Sam Smiths ~ Manager Timothy Buck ~ Real ale ~ Meals and snacks (12-9) ~ 0171-405 8816 ~ Open 11(12 Sat)-11; closed Sun, 25/26 Dec, and Good Fri

Red Lion (Mayfair) Map 13

Waverton Street, W1; ⊖ Green Park

In one of Mayfair's quietest and prettiest corners, this civilised place has something of the atmosphere of a smart country pub; only the presence of so many suited workers reminds you of its true location. The main L-shaped bar has small winged settles on the partly carpeted scrubbed floorboards, and London prints below the high shelf of china on its dark-panelled walls. Well kept Courage Best and Directors, Greene King IPA, and Theakstons Best on handpump, and they do rather good Bloody Marys (with a daunting Very Spicy option); also a dozen or so malt whiskies. Bar food, served from a corner at the front, includes sandwiches (from £2.50), cumberland sausage (£4.75), cod and chips or half rack of ribs with barbecue sauce (£6.95) and a couple of daily specials (£5). Unusually for this area, they serve food morning and evening seven days a week. It can get crowded at lunchtime, and immediately after work. The gents' has a copy of the day's *Financial Times* at eye level. *(Recommended by Rachael Ward, Mark Baynham, Gordon, Christopher Wright, Mike and Karen England, P R Morley)*

S & N ~ Manager Greg Peck ~ Real ale ~ Meals and snacks (12-2.30, 6-9.30) ~ Restaurant ~ 0171-499 1307 ~ Children in eating area of bar ~ Open 11.30-11 weekdays; 11-3, 6-11 Sat; 12-3, 7-11 Sun; closed 25/26 Dec, 1 Jan

Seven Stars £ (City) Map 13

53 Carey St, WC2; ⊖ Holborn (just as handy from Temple or Chancery Lane, but the walk through Lincoln's Inn Fields can be rather pleasant)

Hardly changed in the several hundred years it's stood here, this tranquil little pub faces the back of the Law Courts, but attracts a far wider range of customers than the barristers and legal folk you might expect. We're not using the word little lightly – it's not just mild temperatures that lead people to stand in the peaceful street outside. The door, underneath a profusion of hanging baskets, is helpfully marked General Counter, as though you couldn't see that the simple counter is pretty much all there is in the tiny old-fashioned bar beyond. Lots of caricatures of barristers and other legal-themed prints on the walls, and quite a collection of toby jugs, some in a display case, the rest mixed up with the drinks behind the bar. Friendly chatty licensees, Courage Best and Directors on handpump, several malt whiskies, and very good value bar snacks such as sandwiches (£1.50), pork pies and sausages, with maybe a couple of hot dishes like lamb curry, goulash, or cottage pie (£2.95); you may have to eat standing up, the solitary table and stools are on the left as you go in. A cosy room on the right appears bigger than it is because of its similar lack of furnishings; there are shelves round the walls for drinks or leaning against. Stairs up to the lavatories are very steep – a sign warns that you climb them at your own risk. *(Recommended by David Carr, Gordon, Tony Hobden, Chris Westmoreland)*

Courage ~ Lease: Geoffrey and Majella Turner ~ Real ale ~ Snacks and meals (all day) ~ 0171-242 8521 ~ Open 11-10 Mon-Fri; closed weekends

Star (Belgravia) Map 13

Belgrave Mews West – behind the German Embassy, off Belgrave Sq ⊖ Knightsbridge

Though it can get busy at lunchtime and on some evenings, this simple and traditional pub is another of those places that seems distinctly un-London, and there's a pleasantly quiet and restful local feel outside peak times. A highlight in summer is the astonishing array of hanging baskets and flowering tubs outside – though many pubs try hard with such displays, few end up with anything quite so impressive. The small entry room, which also has the food servery, has stools by the counter and tall windows; an arch leads to a side room with swagged curtains, well polished wooden tables and chairs, heavy upholstered settles, globe lighting and raj fans. The back room has button-back built-in wall seats, and there's a cosy room upstairs. Good value straightforward bar food might include sandwiches (from £2.35), sausage, chips and beans (£3.95), and a good ribeye steak(£6.95). Very well kept Fullers Chiswick, ESB and London Pride – the first at a particularly nice price for this part of town. *(Recommended by Bob and Maggie Atherton, Ian Phillips, LM, Jasper Sabey, Mr and Mrs Jon Corelis, Gordon, M J Dowdy, Mark Baynham)*

Fullers ~ Managers T and J Connel ~ Real ale ~ Meals and snacks ~ 0171-235 3019 ~ Children in eating area of bar ~ Open 11.30-11 weekdays; Sat 11.30-3, 6.30-11; Sun 12-3, 7-10.30; closed Dec 25/26

Westminster Arms (Westminster) Map 13

Storey's Gate, SW1; ⊖ Westminster

Unpretentious and friendly, this busy Westminster local is usually packed after work with government staff and researchers from the Houses of Parliament just across Parliament Square. The main draw is the choice of real ales, which generally includes Bass, Boddingtons, Brakspears PA, Gales IPA, Greene King Abbot, Theakstons Best, Wadworths 6X, Westminster Best brewed for them by Charringtons, and a monthly changing guest; they also do decent wines. Furnishings in the plain main bar are simple and old-fashioned, with proper tables on the wooden floors and a good deal of panelling; there's not a lot of room, so come early for a seat. Pleasant, courteous service. Most of the food is served in the downstairs wine bar (a good retreat from the ground floor bustle), with some of the tables in cosy booths; typical dishes include filled rolls (from £2.50), salads and ploughman's, lasagne or steak and kidney pie (£5.50), and fish and chips or scampi (£5.95). Piped music in this area, and in the more formal upstairs restaurant, but not generally in the main bar; fruit machine. There are a couple of tables and seats by the street outside. *(Recommended by Mark Baynham, Rachael Ward, Tim Barrow, Sue Demont, Ian Phillips, James Nunns, Gordon)*

Free house ~ Licensees Gerry and Marie Dolan ~ Real ale ~ Meals and snacks (all day weekdays, till 5 Sat/Sun) ~ Lunchtime weekday restaurant (not Weds) ~ 0171-222 8520 ~ Children in restaurant lunchtimes only ~ Open 11-11(8 Sat); 12-6 Sun; closed Dec 25-6

NORTH LONDON

Parking is not a special problem in this area, unless we say so

Chapel (Marylebone) Map 13

48 Chapel St, NW1; ⊖ Edgware Rd

London Dining Pub of the Year

Attractively refurbished and very cosmopolitan, this well liked food pub is particularly relaxed and civilised at lunchtimes, especially in summer, when tables on the terrace outside can be busy with chic, suited creative folk enjoying a break. Light and spacious, the cream-painted main room is dominated by the open kitchen, which produces unusual soups such as lemon and courgette, and generously served dishes like goat's cheese, tomato and oyster mushroom tart (£8), roast chicken stuffed with sun-dried tomatoes and peppers (£9.50), roasted john dory with artichoke and anchovy sauce (£12), roast guinea fowl breasts with sage (£12.50), and puddings such as an excellent tarte tatin. Prompt and efficient service from helpful staff, who may bring warm walnut bread to your table while you're waiting. Furnishings are smart but simple; there are plenty of wooden tables around the bar, with more in a side room with a big fireplace. At lunchtime most people come to eat (it fills up quite quickly, though you can book), but in the evening trade is more evenly split between diners and drinkers; the music can be rather loud then, especially at weekends. Adnams and Fullers London Pride on handpump (rather expensive, even for London), a good range of interesting wines (up to half by the glass), cappuccino and espresso, and a choice of teas such as peppermint or strawberry and vanilla. *(Recommended by Greg Kilminster, Tim Barrow, Sue Demont, Nick Rose, Charlie Ballantyne)*

Bass ~ Lease: Lakis Hondrogiannis ~ Real ale ~ Meals ~ 0171-402 9220 ~ Children welcome ~ Open 12-11; 12-3, 7-10.30 Sun

Compton Arms 🍷 (Canonbury) Map 12

4 Compton Avenue, off Canonbury Rd, N1; ⊖ Highbury & Islington

A tiny pub hidden away up a mews, this peaceful place has beautiful hanging baskets in front, and a delightfully relaxing little crazy paved terrace behind, with benches and cask tables among flowers under a big sycamore tree. They recently added a covered section to this part so you can still sit out if it's raining, and they plan to have heaters out here in winter. Well run by friendly staff, the unpretentious low-ceilinged rooms are simply furnished with wooden settles and assorted stools and chairs, with local pictures on the walls; free from games or music, it has a very personable, village local feel. Well kept Greene King Abbot, IPA, Rayments and Sorcerer on handpump, and around 22 wines by the glass. Good value bar food includes sandwiches, soup and the like, but majors on sausages, with half a dozen different types served with mashed potato and home-made gravy (£3.55). *(Recommended by Mark Baynham, Rachael Ward, Jenny and Roger Huggins, Caroline Wright)*

Greene King ~ Manager Paul Fairweather ~ Real ale ~ Meals and snacks (not Tues evening) ~ 0171-359 6883 ~ Children in back room ~ Open 12-11; 12-10.30 Sun

Flask 🍷 £ (Hampstead) Map 12

14 Flask Walk, NW3; ⊖ Hampstead

For many years a popular haunt of Hampstead artists, actors, and local characters, this civilised old local is just around the corner from the Tube, but miles away in spirit. The snuggest and most individual part is the cosy lounge at the front, with plush green seats and banquettes curving round the panelled walls, a unique Victorian screen dividing it from the public bar, an attractive fireplace, and a very laid back and rather villagey atmosphere. A comfortable orange-lit room with period prints and a few further tables leads into a much more recent but rather smart dining conservatory, which with its plants, prominent wine bottles and neat table linen feels a bit like a wine bar. A couple of white iron tables are squeezed into the tiny back yard. Unusual and good value daily changing bar food might include sandwiches, good soups such as pumpkin, pasta with artichoke hearts and creamy pesto sauce (£3.50), ham, egg, bubble and squeak (£3.70), and Jamaican curry or Moroccan lamb casserole (£3.90); everything is home-made, including the chips. Well kept Youngs Bitter, Special and seasonal brews on handpump, around 20 wines by the glass, and decent coffees – they have a machine that grinds the beans to order. A plainer public bar (which you can only get into from the street) has leatherette seating, cribbage, backgammon, lots of space for darts, fruit machine, trivia, and SkyTV; this is the favourite bit of the resident german shepherd dog, Lady. A noticeboard has the latest news of their darts and cricket teams. There are a few tables outside in the alley. The pub's name is a reminder of the days when it was a distributor of the mineral water from Hampstead's springs. *(Recommended by Jane and Robert Oswaks, Tony Scott, Gordon, Mr and Mrs Jon Vorelis, Pete Baker)*

Youngs ~ Manager John Orr ~ Real ale ~ Meals and snacks 12-3(4 Sat), 6-9; not evenings Sun or Mon ~ 0171-435 4580 ~ Children in eating area of bar till 9pm ~ Thurs comedy night ~ Open 11-11; 12-10.30 Sun

Holly Bush (Hampstead) Map 12

Holly Mount, NW3; ⊖ Hampstead

As we went to press we heard that the brewery was planning some big changes to this cheery old local; details were unclear, but it seems they're keen to make it more of a food pub, and there was talk of it closing for a couple of months for a big refurbishment. How this will affect things we don't know, but as we understand English Heritage have been advising on any alterations, we're keeping our fingers crossed that any changes will leave the timeless feel of the place intact. Real Edwardian gas lamps light the atmospheric front bar, there's a dark sagging ceiling, brown and cream panelled walls (decorated with old advertisements and a few hanging plates), open fires, and cosy bays formed by partly glazed partitions. Slightly more intimate, the back room, named after the painter George Romney, has an embossed red ceiling, panelled and etched glass alcoves, and ochre-painted brick walls covered with small prints and plates. Beers have typically included Benskins, Ind Coope Burton and Tetleys, with changing guests. The walk up to the pub from the tube station is delightful, along some of Hampstead's most villagey streets and past several of its more enviable properties. *(Recommended by Mick Hitchman, Gordon, Tom McLean, Mr and Mrs Jon Corelis; more reports please)*

Allied ~ Manager Carol Farren ~ Real ale ~ 0171-435 2892 ~ Nearby parking sometimes quite a squeeze ~ Open 12-3, 5.30-11; 12-11 Sat, 12-10.30 Sun

Olde White Bear (Hampstead) Map 12

Well Road, NW3; ⊖ Hampstead

With a new landlord since our last edition, this villagey and almost clubby neo-Victorian pub pulls off the rare trick of making all sorts of different types of people feel relaxed and at home. Next to the smart mother fussing over her student daughter you might find a builder with holes in his jumper and cement-encrusted boots, what could be the local bank manager, or maybe an elderly gentleman carefully rolling his cigarettes from a rusty old tin. Friendly and traditional, the dimly lit main room has lots of Victorian prints and cartoons on the walls, as well as wooden stools, cushioned captain's chairs, a couple of big tasselled armed chairs, a flowery sofa, handsome fireplace and an ornate Edwardian sideboard. A similarly-lit small central room has Lloyd Loom furniture, dried flower arrangements and signed photographs of actors and playwrights. In the brighter end room there are elaborate cushioned machine tapestried pews, and dark brown paisley curtains. Beers on handpump usually include Greene King IPA and Abbot, Tetleys, Wadworths 6X and a weekly changing guest; also 15 or so malt whiskies. Bar food is now served all day, with a seasonal menu including things like sandwiches (from £2.35), tomato and basil soup (£2.85), baked aubergine slices (£5.95), thai chicken curry (£6.50), beef bourguignon (£6.75), and chargrilled tuna steak with spiced lentil salsa (£6.95). Darts, cribbage, shove ha'penny, dominoes, fruit machine, piped music. Parking may be a problem – it's mostly residents' permits only nearby. *(Recommended by Tom McLean, Gordon, Ian Phillips, R Sheard)*

Allied ~ Lease: Gary Appleton ~ Real ale ~ Meals and snacks (12-9) ~ 0171-435 3758 ~ Open 11-11; 12-10.30 Sun

Spaniards Inn (Hampstead) Map 12

Spaniards Lane, NW3; ⊖ Hampstead, but some distance away; or from Golders Green station take 220 bus

Named after the Spanish ambassador to the court of James I, for whom it was built as a private residence, this comfortable and authentically old-fashioned former toll house juts out into the road like King Canute holding back the tide of traffic. The low-ceilinged oak-panelled rooms of the attractive main bar have open fires, genuinely antique winged settles, candle-shaped lamps in pink shades, and snug little alcoves. Behind is a very nice sheltered garden, with slatted wooden tables and chairs on a crazy-paved terrace opening on to a flagstoned walk around a small lawn, with roses, a side arbour of wisteria and clematis, and an aviary. Bar food might include sandwiches, various sauages with leek mash (£5.25), fish and chips or chargrilled salmon steaks (£5.65), and steak and Guinness pie (£5.95); on Sundays they just do a roast. The food bar is no smoking. A quieter upstairs bar may be open at busy times. Well kept Bass, Fullers London Pride, Hancocks BB and a guest like Timothy Taylor Landlord on handpump; piped classical music, newspapers, fruit machine, trivia. A couple of readers feel the pub is so popular with visitors that it's lost a little of its charm, and that prices are a little too high. The pub is very handy for Kenwood, and indeed during the 1780 Gordon Riots the then landlord helped save the house from possible disaster, cunningly giving so much free drink to the mob on its way to burn it down that by the time the Horse Guards arrived the rioters were lying drunk and incapable on the floor. Parking can be difficult – especially when people park here to walk their dogs on the heath. *(Recommended by Richard Fallon, Mr and Mrs Jon Corelis, Gordon, Michael and Hazel Lyons, Ian Phillips, JSMS)*

Bass ~ Manager T J McCormack ~ Real ale ~ Meals and snacks (12-9.30) ~ 0181-455 3276 ~ Children welcome ~ Open 11-11; 12-10.30 Sun

Waterside (King's Cross) Map 13

82 York Way, N1; ⊖ King's Cross

A useful place to know about if you're passing through what's not exactly an appealing area for visitors, this friendly little oasis has an unexpectedly calm outside terrace overlooking the Battlebridge Basin. The building really isn't very old but it's done out in firmly traditional style, with stripped brickwork, latticed windows, genuinely old stripped timbers in white plaster, lots of dimly lit alcoves (one is no smoking), spinning wheels, milkmaid's yokes, and horsebrasses and so on, with plenty of rustic tables and wooden benches. Some of the woodwork was salvaged from a disused mill. Boddingtons, Morlands Old Speckled Hen and Wadworths 6X on handpump; pool, pinball, fruit machine, TV for sports, and sometimes loudish juke box. The menu is these days a standard Berni one, with things like sandwiches, soup (£1.45), steak and mushroom pudding or lasagne (£4.25), vegetable curry (£4.85), and lots of steaks (from £4.95). There may be barbecues on the terrace on sunny days. No dogs inside. *(Recommended by Mark Baynham, Rachael Ward, Mr and Mrs A R Hawkins)*

Whitbreads ~ Manager John Keyes ~ Real ale ~ Meals and snacks (12-2.30, 6-9; not evenings Sat/Sun) ~ (0171) 837 7118 ~ Children in no-smoking part of eating area till 7pm ~ Open 11-11; 12-10.30 Sun; may be closed Dec 25/26

SOUTH LONDON

Parking is bad on weekday lunchtimes at the inner city pubs here (SE1), but is usually OK everywhere in the evenings – you may again have a bit of a walk if a good band is on at the Bulls Head in Barnes, or at the Windmill on Clapham Common if it's a fine evening

Alma 🍷 (Wandsworth) Map 12

499 York Road, SW18; ⇌ Wandsworth Town

Recently brightly redecorated, this stylish local is unexpectedly civilised, with an air of chattily relaxed bonhomie. There's a mix of chairs around cast-iron-framed tables, a couple of sofas, lots of ochre and terracotta paintwork, gilded mosaics of the Battle of the Alma, an ornate mahogany chimney-piece and fireplace, bevelled mirrors in a pillared mahogany room divider, and pinball and a fruit machine. The popular but less pubby dining room has a fine turn-of-the-century frieze of swirly nymphs; there's waitress service in here, and you can book a particular table. Even when it's very full with smart young people – which it often is in the evenings – service is careful and efficient. Youngs Bitter, Special and seasonal brews on handpump from the island bar counter, good house wines (with around 20 by the glass), freshly squeezed orange, mango and passion fruit juice, good coffee, tea or hot chocolate, newspapers out for customers. Unusual and tasty, the good value bar food might include sandwiches (from £2), croque monsieur (£3), mussels with tomato, basil, cumin and olive oil (£4.25), home-made sausages or asparagus, pecorino and rocket frittata (£6.50), sage smoked escalope of pork with pancetta and sugar snaps (£7.25), roast rib of beef on stir-fried mediterranean vegetables (£9.50), and daily specials such as grilled salmon or lamb steak with tomato and rocket salad (£7.95); the menu may be limited on Sunday lunchtimes. They've started opening at 10 at weekends to serve breakfasts, with everything from muesli and fruit to a full cooked meal (£4.75). If you're after a quiet drink don't come when there's a rugby match on the television, unless you want a running commentary from the well heeled and voiced young locals. Cribbage, pinball, dominoes, fruit machine. Charge up their 'smart-card' with cash and you can pay with a discount either here or at the management's other pubs, which include the Ship at Wandsworth (see below). Travelling by rail into Waterloo you can see the pub rising above the neighbouring rooftops as you rattle through Wandsworth Town. *(Recommended by David Carr, Ian Phillips, Jasper Sabey, Richard Gibbs, Richard Fallon)*

Youngs ~ Tenant Charles Gotto ~ Real ale ~ Meals and snacks (12-10.30; not Sun evening) ~ Restaurant ~ 0181-870 2537 ~ Children in restaurant ~ Open 11(10 Sat)-11; 10am-10.30pm Sun; closed 25/26 Dec

Anchor (South Bank) Map 13

34 Park St, Bankside, SE1; Southwark Bridge end; ⊖ London Bridge

Expect some interesting developments at the Anchor over the next few months: they tell us they'll be adding bedrooms and jazz nights. A warren of dimly lit little rooms and passageways, this atmospheric riverside spot has a hard to beat view of the Thames and the City from its busy front terrace; one couple we know was so captivated by the scene that they came back several times during a week over Christmas. The current building dates back to about 1750, when it was built to replace an earlier tavern, possibly the one that Pepys came to during the Great Fire of 1666. 'All over the Thames with one's face in the wind, you were almost burned with a shower of fire drops,' he wrote. 'When we could endure no more upon the water, we to a little ale-house on the Bankside and there staid till it was dark almost, and saw the fire grow.' Inside are creaky boards and beams, black panelling, old-fashioned high-backed settles, and sturdy leatherette chairs. Even when it's invaded by tourists it's usually possible to retreat to one of the smaller rooms. Bass, Flowers Original, Greenalls Original and rapidly changing guest beers such as Greene King Abbot on handpump or tapped from the cask; they also do jugs of Pimms and sangria, and mulled wine in winter. Cribbage, dominoes, three fruit machines, and fairly loud piped music. Bar food includes sandwiches (from £2.95) and salads, winter soup, and five changing hot dishes like steak and ale pie, braised liver and bacon, and chicken with a mustard and porter sauce (all around £4.50); they do a Sunday roast in the restaurant. The pub can get smoky, and service can slow down at busy periods. Tom Cruise enjoys a pint at the Anchor at the end of the film version of *Mission: Impossible.* Sword or Morris dancers may pass by on summer evenings, and there's an increasing number of satisfying places to visit nearby; the Clink round the corner is particularly good for history buffs. *(Recommended by Susan and John Douglas, Tony Scott, Mr and Mrs A R Hawkins, Mark Baynham, Rachael Ward, Ian Phillips)*

Greenalls ~ Real ale ~ Meals and snacks (12-9) ~ Restaurant ~ 0171-407 3003 ~ Children in eating areas and restaurant till 8.30 ~ Open 11-11; 12-10.30 Sun; cl 25 Dec

Bulls Head 🍷 £ (Barnes) Map 12

373 Lonsdale Road, SW13; ⇄ Barnes Bridge

Top class modern jazz groups performing every night are what draw the crowds to this imposing Thamesside pub, built in 1684. You can hear the music quite clearly from the lounge bar (and on peaceful Sunday afternoons from the villagey little street as you approach), but for the full effect and genuine jazz club atmosphere it is worth paying the admission to the well equipped music room. Back in the bustling bar alcoves open off the main area around the island servery, which has Youngs Bitter, Special and seasonal beers on handpump, over 80 malt whiskies, and a good range of decent wines, with 20 by the glass. Around the walls are large photos of the various jazz musicians and bands who have played here; dominoes, cribbage, Scrabble, chess, cards, and fruit machine in the public bar. All the food is home-made, including the bread, pasta, sausages and ice cream, and they do things like soup (£1.30), sandwiches, and pasta, pies, or a popular carvery of home-roasted joints (all £3.80); service is efficient and very friendly. Bands play 8.30-11 every night plus 2-4.30 Sundays, and depending on who's playing prices generally range from £3.50 to around £6. Given the quality of the music, it's amazing we don't receive more reports on this distinctive place. *(More reports please)*

Youngs ~ Tenant Dan Fleming ~ Real ale ~ Meals and snacks ~ Evening bistro (not Sun evening, though they do Sun lunch) ~ 0181-876 5241 ~ Children welcome ~ Jazz or blues every night, and Sun afternoon ~ Nearby parking may be difficult ~ Open 11-11; 12-10.30 Sun

Crown & Greyhound (Dulwich) Map 12

73 Dulwich Village, SE21 ⇌ North Dulwich

Imposing and astonishingly spacious, this grand place was built at the turn of the century to replace the two inns that had stood here previously, hence the unusual name. Readers like the way it caters so well for children, offering Lego and toys to play with as well as children's meals, and never making families feel like second-class citizens. They have baby changing facilities, and an ice cream stall in the very pleasant big two-level back terrace, which also has a new play area with sandpit, and a good many picnic-sets under a chestnut tree. It gets very busy inside in the evenings but there's enough room to absorb everyone without any difficulty. The most ornate room is on the right, with its elaborate ochre ceiling plasterwork, fancy former gas lamps, Hogarth prints, fine carved and panelled settles and so forth. It opens into the former billiards room, where kitchen tables on a stripped board floor are set for the good bar food. Changing every day, the lunchtime choice might include enormous doorstep sandwiches and toasties, ploughman's, and a range of specials like lamb and fennel casserole, chicken, broccoli and stilton bake, vegan nut loaf, and steak and kidney pie (all around £5.25). Best to arrive early for their popular Sunday carvery, they don't take bookings. A central snug leads on the other side to the saloon – brown ragged walls, upholstered and panelled settles, a coal-effect gas fire in the tiled period fireplace, and Victorian prints. Well kept Ind Coope Burton, Tetleys and Youngs on handpump, along with a monthly changing guest like Adnams or Morlands Old Speckled Hen; they have a wine of the month too. Dominoes, fruit machines, trivia, and piped music. Known locally as the Dog, the pub has long-established links with poetry groups (they still have well regarded readings today), and is handy for walks through the park. *(Recommended by Mike Gorton, Ian Phillips)*

Allied ~ Manager Barney Maguire ~ Real ale ~ Meals and snacks (12-2.30, 6-10; not Sun evening) ~ Evening restaurant (not Sun) ~ 0181-693 2466 ~ Children in restaurant and no-smoking family room ~ Open 11-11; 12-10.30 Sun; closed evening 25 Dec

Cutty Sark (Greenwich) Map 12

Ballast Quay, off Lassell St, SE10; ⇌ Maze Hill, from London Bridge, or from the river front walk past the Yacht in Crane St and Trinity Hospital

They've long been proud of the view of the Thames from this attractive late 16th-c white-painted house, and now that the Millennium Dome is almost complete (from the outside at least) there's plenty more to look at. Tables on a waterside terrace across the narrow cobbled lane from the pub are perhaps the nicest place to take it in, but you'll see more from inside through the big upper bow window, itself striking for the way it jetties out over the pavement. Despite a few recent changes the atmospheric bar still conjures up images of the kind of London we imagine Dickens once knew, with flagstones, rough brick walls, wooden settles, barrel tables, open fires, low lighting and narrow openings to tiny side snugs. Well kept Bass, Fullers London Pride and changing guests like Harveys Sussex and Youngs Special on handpump, a good choice of malt whiskies, and a decent wine list. An elaborate central staircase leads up to an upstairs area; fruit machine, trivia, juke box. Served in a roomy eating area, good bar food includes soup (£1.95), filled baguettes (from £2.99), very well liked boozy sausages (£5.50), roast vegetable lasagne (£5.50), battered cod (£6.25), jerk chicken (£7.95), a decent choice of children's meals, and daily specials; staff are helpful, but service can slow down at times. The pub can be very busy with young people on Friday and Saturday evenings, and fine summer evenings are also likely to draw the crowds. *(Recommended by Jill Bickerton, David and*

Carole Chapman, Robert Gomme, Brian and Anna Marsden, Mrs P J Pearce, John Fahy)

Free house ~ Managers Octavia Gleedwood and David Jackson ~ Real ale ~ Meals and snacks (12-9; 12-7 Sat) ~ 0181-858 3146 ~ Children upstairs till 9pm ~ Monthly live music ~ Open 11-11; 12-10.30 Sun

Fire Station (Waterloo) Map 13

150 Waterloo Rd, SE1; ⊖ Waterloo

Best known for the imaginative food served from the open kitchen in the back dining room, this bustling place is a remarkable conversion of the former LCC central fire station. It's hardly your typical local, but does a number of traditionally pubby things far better than anyone else nearby, and the two vibrantly chatty rooms at the front certainly seem to be the favoured choice for the area's after work drinkers. The decor is something like a cross between a warehouse and a schoolroom, with plenty of wooden pews, chairs and long tables (a few spilling on to the street outside), some mirrors and rather incongruous pieces of dressers, and brightly red-painted doors, shelves and modern hanging lightshades; the determinedly contemporary art round the walls is for sale, and there's a table with newspapers to read. Well kept Adnams Best, Brakspears, Youngs, a beer brewed for them by Hancocks, and a changing guest like Boddingtons on handpump, as well as a number of bottled beers, and a good choice of wines (several by the glass); helpful service. They serve a short range of bar meals between 12.30 and 6, which might include filled ciabattas (from £3.50), leek and fennel soup (£3.50), salads (£5.25), and half a dozen oysters (£6.50), but it's worth paying the extra to eat from the main menu. Changing every lunchtime and evening, this has things like chargrilled smoked cod with parsley mash and tomato and chilli salsa (£9.95), guinea fowl with risotto verde and courgette flowers (£10.50), and puddings such as peach and almond tart with custard sauce (£3.50); they don't take bookings, so there may be a slight wait at busy times. Piped modern jazz and other music fits into the good-natured hubbub. Those with quieter tastes might find weeknights here a little too hectic – it's less busy at lunchtimes and during the day. As we went to press they were considering opening Sunday evenings. *(Recommended by Mark Baynham, Rachael Ward, Tim Barrow, Sue Demont, Sebastian Leach, Paul Hilditch)*

Free house ~ Manager Peter Nottage ~ Real ale ~ Snacks (12-6.30) and meals (not Sun) ~ Restaurant ~ Children welcome away from the bar ~ Open 11-11; 12-5 Sun; closed one week at Christmas, Easter bank hols

George ★ (Southwark) Map 13

Off 77 Borough High Street, SE1; ⊖ Borough or London Bridge

We heard from one reader this year who was delighted to find this splendid-looking 17th-c coaching inn is just 100 yards from his office. Noted as one of London's 'fair inns for the receipt of travellers' as early as 1598, it's such a London landmark that it's easy to forget it's still a proper working pub. Rebuilt on its original plan after the great Southwark fire in 1676, it was owned for a while by Guys Hospital next door, and then by the Great Northern Railway Company, under whose stewardship it was 'mercilessly reduced' as E V Lucas put it, when the other wings of the building were demolished. Now preserved by the National Trust, the remaining wing is a unique survival, the tiers of open galleries looking down over a cobbled courtyard with plenty of picnic-sets, and maybe Morris men in summer. It's just as unspoilt inside, the row of simple ground-floor rooms and bars all containing square-latticed windows, black beams, bare floorboards, some panelling, plain oak or elm tables and old-fashioned built-in settles, along with a 1797 'Act of Parliament' clock, dimpled glass lantern-lamps and so forth. The snuggest refuge is the simple room nearest the street, where there's an ancient beer engine that looks like a cash register. They use this during their regular beer festivals (generally the third week of each month), when they might have around ten unusual real ales available; the ordinary range includes Boddingtons, Flowers Original, Fullers London Pride, Morlands Old Speckled Hen, and a beer brewed for them, Bishops Restoration. Also farm cider, country wines, and mulled wine in winter; darts, video game. Lunchtime bar food might include club sandwiches (£3), and ploughman's, roast vegetable lasagne, sausages and mash, and deep-fried cod (all £4.95). A splendid central staircase goes up to a series of dining rooms and to a gaslit balcony. One room is no smoking. Unless you know where you're going (or you're in one of the many tourist groups that flock here during the day in summer) you may well miss it, as apart from the great gates there's little to indicate that such a gem still exists behind the less auspicious looking buildings on the busy high street. *(Recommended by Philip Vernon, Richard Lewis, Tony Scott, Mark Baynham, Rachael Ward, Jasper Sabey, Paul Hilditch, Ian Phillips)*

Whitbreads ~ Manager John Hall ~ Real ale ~ Lunchtime bar meals and snacks ~ Restaurant (not Sun; often used for groups only – check first) ~ 0171-407 2056 ~ Children in restaurant ~ Nearby daytime parking difficult ~ Folk night first Mon of month (except bank hols); occasional Morris dancers in summer ~ Open 11-11; 12-10.30 Sun; closed 25/26 Dec, 1 Jan

Horniman (Southwark) Map 13

Hays Galleria, Battlebridge Lane, SE13; ⊖ London Bridge

The spacious gleaming bar of this elaborate pub is rather like a cross between a French cafe bar or bistro and a Victorian local. The area by the sweeping bar counter is a few steps down from the door, with squared black, red and white flooring tiles and lots of polished wood; from here steps lead up to various comfortable carpeted areas, with the tables well spread out so as to allow for a feeling of roomy relaxation at quiet times but giving space for people standing in groups when it's busy. There's a set of clocks made for tea merchant Frederick Horniman's office showing the time in various places around the world. Bar food includes a good few baguettes or sandwiches (from £2.70), baked potatoes (from £4), home-made quiches (£4.75), and daily changing hot dishes like steak and mushroom pie or a couple of vegetarian meals (£5). Well kept (though even for London quite pricy) Adnams Extra, Fullers London Pride, Morlands Old Speckled Hen, Timothy Taylor Landlord and maybe a couple of other guests on handpump. A tea bar serves tea, coffees, and other hot drinks, and Danish pastries and so forth; a hundred-foot frieze shows the travels of the tea. Fruit machine, trivia, pinball, table football, unobtrusive piped music. Wonderful views of the Thames, HMS *Belfast* and Tower Bridge from the picnic-sets outside. The pub is at the end of the visually exciting Hays Galleria development, several storeys high, with a soaring glass curved roof, and supported by elegant thin cast-iron columns; various shops and boutiques open off. It's busy round here in the daytime, but quickly goes quiet as the evening goes on. *(More reports please)*

Nicholsons (Allied) ~ Manager David Matthews ~ Real ale ~ Snacks and lunchtime meals ~ 0171-401 6811 ~ Children welcome till 6pm ~ Occasional live entertainment ~ Open 11-11 weekdays; 11-6 Sat; 12-6 Sun; closed 25 Dec, and some evenings Christmas week

Market Porter (Southwark) Map 13

9 Stoney Street, SE1; ⊖ London Bridge

Open between 6.30 and 8.30 am for market workers and porters (and anyone else who's passing) to enjoy a drink at the start of the day, this busily pubby place is particularly well liked for its range of well kept beers, one of the most varied in London. The seven ales on handpump usually include a combination of Bunces Pig Swill, Courage Best and Directors, Fullers London Pride, Gales HSB, Harveys Sussex, Thirsty Willey and Youngs Bitter. The main part of the atmospheric long U-shaped bar has rough wooden ceiling beams with beer barrels balanced on them, a heavy wooden bar counter with a beamed gantry, cushioned bar stools, an open fire with stuffed animals in glass cabinets on the mantlepiece, several mounted stags' heads, and 20s-style wall lamps. Sensibly priced simple bar food includes soup (£1.95), sandwiches (from £2.15), burgers (£3.95), lasagne or all day breakfast

(£4.25), fish and chips (£4.25), and daily specials; Sunday lunch. Obliging service; darts, fruit machine, video game, pinball, and piped music. A small partly panelled room has leaded glass windows and a couple of tables. Part of the restaurant is no smoking. The company that own the pub – which can get a little full and smoky – have similar establishments in Reigate and nearby Stamford St. *(Recommended by Richard Lewis, Mark Baynham, Rachael Ward, Mr and Mrs A R Hawkins, Greg Kilminster, Dr and Mrs A K Clarke)*

Free house ~ Manager Anthony Heddigan ~ Real ale ~ Meals and snacks (not Sat) ~ Restaurant (not Sun evening) ~ 0171-407 2495 ~ Children in restaurant ~ Open 11(12 Sat)-11; 12-10.30 Sun

Phoenix & Firkin ★ (Denmark Hill) Map 12

5 Windsor Walk, SE5; ⇌ Denmark Hill

One of the Firkin flagships, this vibrant place is an interesting conversion of a palatial Victorian railway hall, but it's the atmosphere, rather than the architecture, that draws so many varied people in. Lively, loud, and crowded with young people in the evenings, it has a model railway train running back and forth above the bar, along with paintings of steam trains, old-fashioned station name signs, a huge double-faced station clock (originally from Llandudno Junction in Wales), solid wooden furniture on the stripped wooden floor, plants, and old seaside posters and Bovril advertisements. At one end there's a similarly-furnished gallery, reached by a spiral staircase, and at the other arches lead into a food room; chess, dominoes, Twister, fruit machine, video game, pinball, and juke box. Two of the beers, Rail and the stronger Phoenix, are brewed on site, and they also have Dogbolter and Golden Glory from other Firkin pubs, and maybe one or two guest beers. Straightforward food includes big filled baps (usually available all day), a good cold buffet with pork pies, salads, quiche and so forth, and daily hot dishes like vegetable chilli (£3.95) or beef and Dogbolter pie (£4.50); they do a Sunday roast (£4.95). The pub can get smoky at times, and though the piped music can be noisy later in the day, it's much quieter at lunchtimes. There are a couple of long benches outside, and the steps which follow the slope of the road are a popular place to sit. *(More reports please)*

Own brew ~ Managers Mark and Lisa Fogg ~ Real ale ~ Meals and snacks (12-8) ~ 0171-701 8282 ~ Well behaved children welcome till 8.30 ~ Live music Saturdays, quiz night Thurs ~ Open 11-11; 12-10.30 Sun; closed 25 Dec

Ship 🍷 (Wandsworth) Map 12

41 Jews Row, SW18; ⇌ Wandsworth Town

Weather permitting, in summer there's a barbecue every day on the extensive two-level riverside terrace of this smartly bustling place, with vegetable kebabs and italian-style chicken as well as burgers and steaks (£5.50). It's then that the pub really comes into its own, with lots of picnic-sets, pretty hanging baskets and brightly coloured flower-beds, small trees, and an outside bar; there's a Thames barge moored alongside. Inside, only a small part of the original ceiling is left in the main bar – the rest is in a light and airy conservatory style; wooden tables, a medley of stools, and old church chairs on the wooden floorboards, and a relaxed, chatty atmosphere. One part has a Victorian fireplace, a huge clock surrounded by barge prints, and part of a milking machine on a table, and there's a rather battered harmonium, old-fashioned bagatelle, and jugs of flowers around the window sills. The basic public bar has plain wooden furniture, a black kitchen range in the fireplace and darts, pinball and a juke box. Youngs Bitter, Special and Winter Warmer on handpump, freshly squeezed orange and other fruit juices, a wide range of wines (a dozen or more by the glass) and good choice of teas and coffees. Relying heavily on free-range produce, the main bar menu might include sandwiches (not weekends), rabbit terrine with sweet pepper and ginger pickle (£4.25), home-made pork sausages with chive mash or lamb and spinach curry (£6.50), mussel and squid stew (£7), roast cod with clams (£8.40), pan-fried duck breast (£9.50), daily specials, and puddings like blueberry bread and butter pudding (£3.50). Service is friendly and helpful. The pub's annual firework display draws huge crowds of young people, and they also celebrate the last night of the Proms. Barbecues and spit roasts every weekend in summer, when the adjacent car park can get full pretty quickly. *(Recommended by Christopher Wright, David Carr, Richard Fallon)*

Youngs ~ Licensees Charles Gotto, Desmond Madden, R Green ~ Real ale ~ Meals and snacks (12-3, 7-10.30; all day Sun) ~ Restaurant ~ 0181-870 9667 ~ Children welcome ~ Open 11-11; 12-10.30 Sun

White Cross Ῡ (Richmond) Map 12

Water Lane; ⊖/⇌ Richmond

Under new management since our last edition, this busy old pub enjoys a perfect riverside position, delightful in summer, and with a certain wistful charm in winter as well. The best part is the paved garden in front, which on a sunny day feels a little like a cosmopolitan seaside resort; the plentiful tables are sheltered by a big fairy-lit tree (not so long ago identified by Kew Gardens as a rare Greek Whitebeam), and in summer there's an outside bar. Inside, the two chatty main rooms have something of the air of the hotel this once was, as well as comfortable long banquettes curving round the tables in the deep bay windows, local prints and photographs, an old-fashioned wooden island servery, and a good mix of variously aged customers. Two of three log fires have mirrors above them – unusually, the third is underneath a window. A bright and airy upstairs room has lots more tables and a number of plates on a shelf running round the walls; a couple of tables are squeezed on to a little balcony. Youngs Bitter, Special and seasonal beers on handpump, and a good range of 22 or so carefully chosen wines by the glass. From a servery at the foot of the stairs, home-made lunchtime bar food includes sandwiches and a variety of hot dishes from home-made sausages to venison. No music or machines – the only games are backgammon and chess. Boats leave from immediately outside to Kingston or Hampton Court. Make sure when leaving your car outside that you know the tide times – it's not unknown for the water to rise right up the steps into the bar, completely covering anything that gets in the way. *(Recommended by B J Harding, Comus Elliott, David and Nigel Pugsley, Tony Scott, David Peakall, Martin and Karen Wake, Jenny and Roger Huggins)*

Youngs ~ Manager Ian Heggie ~ Real ale ~ Lunchtime meals and snacks (12-4) ~ 0181-940 6844 ~ Children in upstairs room ~ Open 11-11; 12-10.30 Sun; closed evening 25 Dec

Windmill Ῡ (Clapham) Map 12

Clapham Common South Side, SW4; ⊖ Clapham Common/Clapham South

A few changes to this bustling Victorian inn since our last edition: the fish tank has gone and the conservatory is no longer no-smoking, but they've converted the courtyard barbecue into an outdoor bar so that in summer, when the pub seems to serve all the visitors to neighbouring Clapham Common, there's much less of a wait to be served. Spacious enough to mean that however busy it gets you should be able to find a quiet corner, the comfortable and smartly civilised main bar has plenty of prints and pictures on the walls, real fires, and a mix of tables and seating. Bar food such as sandwiches and baguettes (from £1.60), soup (£1.95), ploughman's (from £3.95), vegetable kiev (£4.75), chicken satay (£4.95), beef stroganoff (£5.95), daily specials, and chargrilled sirloin steak (£8.95); service is prompt and friendly. Youngs Bitter, Special and seasonal beers on handpump, a good choice of wines by the glass and plenty more by the bottle; fruit machine and video game. They still have their monthly opera nights in the conservatory, when the genre's rising stars perform various solos and arias; also good jazz and other music, nicely segregated from the main bar. A painting in the Tate by J P Herring has the Windmill in the background, shown behind local turn-of-the-century characters returning from the Derby Day festivities. It's a particularly nice place to stay, with very comfortable bedrooms. *(Recommended by Susan and John Douglas, Ian Phillips; more reports please)*

Youngs ~ Managers Peter and Jenny Hale ~ Real ale ~ Meals and snacks (12-2.30, 7-10 weekdays; 12-9 weekends) ~ Restaurant (not Sun evening) ~ 0181-673 4578 ~ Children in eating area of bar till 9~ Live opera first Mon evening of month, jazz second Thurs ~ Open 11-11; 12-10.30 Sun ~ Bedrooms: £86B/£96B, around £20 less at weekends

WEST LONDON

During weekday or Saturday daytime you may not be able to find a meter very close to either Anglesea Arms or to the Windsor Castle, and parking very near in the evening may sometimes be tricky with all of these, but there shouldn't otherwise be problems in this area

Anglesea Arms (Hammersmith) Map 12

35 Wingate St, W6; ⊖ Ravenscourt Park

Despite its out of the way location this busy place is one of the best-known of London's new breed of gastro-pubs. A number of smart locals come here just for a drink, but it's the food that encourages most people to seek it out. Changing every lunchtime and evening, the inventive menu might include several starters like catalan-style chorizo, garlic and eel gratin (£4.50), sautéed lamb sweetbreads, with pappardelle, pancetta, button onions and mushrooms (£4.50), deep-fried stuffed courgette flowers with wild goat's curd (£4.75), and pigeon and foie gras terrine (£4.95), and half a dozen or so main courses such as risotto primavera with shaved parmesan and salsa rossa (£6.75), stuffed saddle of rabbit with caramelised shallots (£8.25), chargrilled chump of lamb (£9.25), and toasted scallops with minted green split peas, bacon and tarragon (£9.25); good puddings, and some unusual farmhouse cheeses (£4.50). The eating area leads off the bar but feels quite separate, with skylights creating a brighter feel, closely packed tables, and a big modern mural along one wall; directly opposite you can see into the kitchen, with several chefs frantically working on the meals. You can't book, so best to get there early for a table. It feels a lot more restauranty than, say, the Eagle, and they clearly have their own way of doing things; though the food is excellent, the the service can be a little inflexible, and efficient rather than friendly. The bar is rather plainly decorated ('in a designer way' they insist) but cosy in winter when the roaring fire casts long flickering shadows on the dark panelling. Neatly stacked piles of wood guard either side of the fireplace (which has a stopped clock above it), and there are some well worn green leatherette chairs and stools. Courage Best and Directors, Marstons Pedigree and Theakstons XB on handpump, and a good range of carefully chosen wines listed above the bar. A couple of readers find the place a bit smoky. Several tables outside overlook the quiet street (not the easiest place to find a parking space). (*Recommended by SD, JD, Bob and Maggie Atherton, Sophie and Mike Harrowes)*

Courage ~ Lease: Dan and Fiona Evans ~ Real ale ~ Meals (12.30-2.45, 7.30-10.45) ~ 0181-749 1291 ~ Children welcome ~ Open 11-11; 12-10.30 Sun; closed a week over Christmas, and 1 Jan

Anglesea Arms (Chelsea) Map 13

15 Selwood Terrace, SW7; ⊖ South Kensington

Now open all day, it's nice to see this genuinely old-fashioned and delightfully chatty old favourite doing so well at the moment. Despite the surrounding affluence the pub has always been friendly and unpretentious, managing to feel both smart and cosy at the same time. The tidied-up bar has central elbow tables, a mix of cast-iron tables on the bare wood-strip floor, wood panelling, and big windows with attractive swagged curtains; at one end several booths with partly glazed screens have cushioned pews and spindleback chairs, and down some steps there's a small carpeted room with captain's chairs, high stools and a Victorian fireplace. The traditional mood is heightened by some heavy portraits, prints of London, a big station clock, bits of brass and pottery, and large brass chandeliers. On busy evenings customers spill out on to the terrace and pavement. A good choice of seven real ales might include Adnams Broadside, Brakspears SB, Fullers London Pride, Harveys Sussex, Wadworths 6X, and Youngs; they also keep a few bottled Belgian beers (the landlord is quite a fan), and several malt and Irish whiskeys. Bar meals might include soup (£2.75), filled baguettes (from £4), sausage and mash or deep-fried breaded camembert (£5.50), salmon fishcakes or avocado and garlic chicken (£6.50), and Sunday roasts £6; they were considering doing evening meals every night as we went to press. A singer they had in on St George's Day last year was reckoned by one reader to be as good as anyone at the Proms. The pub is very popular with well heeled young people, but is well liked by locals too; perhaps that's because many of the locals *are* well heeled young people. *(Recommended by Tony Scott, Tim Barrow, Sue Demont, Mick Hitchman, Mark Baynham, Rachael Ward, D E Twitchett, Lynda Payton, Sam Samuells)*

Free house ~ Licensee Andrew Ford ~ Real ale ~ Lunchtime meals and snacks (12-3), evenings too at weekends (6.30-9.30) ~ 0171-373 7960 ~ Children welcome till 7pm ~ Daytime parking metered ~ Open 11-11; 12-10.30 Sun; closed Dec 25/26

Bulls Head (Chiswick) Map 12

Strand-on-the-Green, W4; ⊖ Kew Bridge

The original building on the site of this well worn riverside pub served as Cromwell's HQ several times during the Civil War, and it was here that Moll Cutpurse overheard Cromwell talking to Fairfax about the troops' pay money coming by horse from Hounslow, and got her gang to capture the moneybags; they were later recovered at Turnham Green. The pleasant little rooms ramble through black-panelled alcoves and up and down steps, and the traditional furnishings include benches built into the simple panelling and so forth. Small windows look past attractively planted hanging flower baskets to the river just beyond the narrow towpath. Well kept Courage Directors, Greene King IPA, Theakstons XB and Old Peculier and Wadworths 6X on handpump; very cheery service. Bar food includes sandwiches, a vegetarian dish like spinach and ricotta cheese cannelloni (£5.50), a roast (£5.99), rack of ribs (£7.50), and 10 oz rump steak (£7.99); the food area is no smoking. A games room at the back has darts, fruit machine and trivia. The pub isn't too crowded even on fine evenings, though it can get busy at weekends, especially when they have a raft race on the river. Strand-on-the Green is a delight for those who frequent Thameside pubs, and it can be hard choosing between this and its even older neighbour the City Barge. *(Recommended by Gordon, Simon Collett-Jones, David and Carole Chapman, Jenny and Brian Seller, Eddy and Emma Gibson)*

Scottish & Newcastle ~ Manager Kate Dale ~ Real ale ~ Meals and snacks (12-10) ~ 0181-994 1204 ~ Children in eating area of bar ~ Open 11-11(10.30 Sun)

Churchill Arms (Kensington) Map 12

119 Kensington Church St, W8; ⊖ Notting Hill Gate/Kensington High St

They like to celebrate at this bustling place, whether it be Halloween, St Patrick's Day or even Churchill's birthday (November 30th), all are marked with some gusto; they're already hatching plans to commemorate the Millennium. At times rather like a busy village local, the pub's vibrant atmosphere owes a lot to the notably friendly (and chatty) Irish landlord, who works hard and enthusiastically to give visitors an individual welcome. One of his hobbies is collecting butterflies, so you'll see a variety of prints and books on the subject dotted around the bar. There are also countless lamps, miners' lights, horse tack, bedpans and brasses hanging from the ceiling, a couple of interesting carved figures and statuettes behind the central bar counter, prints of American presidents, and lots of Churchill memorabilia. The spacious and rather smart plant-filled dining conservatory may be used for hatching butterflies, but is better known for its big choice of really excellent Thai food: chicken and cashew nuts (£4.95) or Thai noodles, roast duck curry or beef curry (£5.25). Service in this part – run separately from the pub – isn't always particularly friendly. They also do things like lunchtime sandwiches, ploughman's, home-made steak and kidney pie, and Sunday lunch. Well kept Fullers ESB, London Pride, and very nicely priced Chiswick on handpump; cheerful service. The pub can get rather smoky. Shove-ha'penny, fruit machine, and unobtrusive piped music; they have their own cricket and football teams. *(Recommended by Susan and John Douglas, D J and P M Taylor, LM, David and Nina Pugsley, David Peakall, GM, Paul Hilditch)*

Fullers ~ Manager Gerry O'Brien ~ Real ale ~ Meals and snacks (12-2.30, 6-9.30; not Sun evening) ~ Restaurant (not Sun evening) ~ 0171-727 4242 ~ Children welcome ~ Open 11-11; 12-10.30 Sun; closed evening 25 Dec

Dove (Hammersmith) Map 12

19 Upper Mall, W6; ⊖ Ravenscourt Park

The nicest of the clutch of pubs punctuating this stretch of the river, this old-fashioned Thamesside tavern was about to become a managed house as we went to press, but we can't imagine the brewery will want to change much. Its best feature is the very pleasant tiny back terrace, where the main flagstoned area, down some steps, has a few highly prized teak tables and white metal and teak chairs looking over the low river wall to the Thames reach just above Hammersmith Bridge. If you're able to bag a spot out here in the evenings, you'll often see rowing crews practising their strokes. By the entrance from the quiet alley, the main bar has black wood panelling, red leatherette cushioned built-in wall settles and stools around dimpled copper tables, old framed advertisements, and photographs of the pub; well kept Fullers London Pride and ESB on handpump. No games machines or piped music. It's not quite so crowded at lunchtimes as it is in the evenings. *Rule Britannia* is said to have been composed here. A plaque marks the level of the highest-ever tide in 1928. *(Recommended by Tony Scott, Jasper Sabey, Mick Hitchman, David Carr, Greg Kilminster, D J and P M Taylor, Gordon)*

Fullers ~ Tenant Brian Lovrey ~ Real ale ~ Meals and snacks (12-2.30, 6-10) ~ 0181-748 5405 ~ Open 11-11; 12-10.30 Sun

Ferret & Firkin (Fulham) Map 12

Lots Road, SW10; ⊖ Fulham Broadway, but some distance away

Popular with a good mix of mostly young, easy-going customers, this unusually curved corner house has a very jolly and infectiously cheerful feel in the evenings; at lunchtimes it can have quite a different atmosphere, and on occasions is almost deserted then. The bar is determinedly basic, with traditional furnishings well made from good wood on the unsealed bare floorboards, slowly circulating colonial-style ceiling fans, a log-effect gas fire, tall airy windows, and plenty of standing room in front of the long curved bar counter. Several readers have described it as a sort of anglicised Wild-West saloon. Well kept beers brewed in the cellar downstairs include the notoriously strong Dogbolter, Balloonastic, and Ferret; with 24 hours' notice you may be able to collect a bulk supply. A food counter serves heftily filled giant meat-and-salad rolls (from £2.50, usually available all day), nachos (£3.95), and one or two hot dishes like tomato and pesto cannelloni or chilli con carne (£4.95); Sunday roast (£4.95). Good – and popular – juke box, as well as chess, backgammon, bar billiards, table football, fruit machine and video game. Several readers feel the Firkin puns (now immortalised on souvenirs for sale at the bar) are wearing a bit thin now. It's handy for Chelsea Harbour, which, to continue the Western analogies, at times feels rather like a ghost town. *(Recommended by Giles Francis, Gordon, Sue Demont, Tim Barrow)*

Own brew ~ Manager Graeme Macdonald ~ Real ale ~ Meals and snacks (12-8) ~ 0171-352 6645 ~ Daytime parking is metered and may be difficult ~ Live music Sat and Tues evenings ~ Children welcome till 9pm ~ Open 12-11(10.30 Sun)

It's very helpful if you let us know up-to-date food prices when you report on pubs.

Ladbroke Arms (Holland Park) Map 12

54 Ladbroke Rd, W11; ⊖ Holland Park

Close to Holland Park and Notting Hill, this popular food pub has a warm red hue to its neatly kept bar (especially up in the slightly raised area with fireplace), as well as simple wooden tables and chairs, comfortable red-cushioned wall-seats, several colonial-style fans on the ceiling, some striking moulding on the dado, colourful flowers on the bar, newspapers and *Country Life* back numbers, and a broad mix of customers and age-groups; soft piped jazz blends in with the smartly chatty atmosphere. The landlord deals in art so the interesting prints can change on each visit. The well kept beers are rotated from a range that takes in Courage Best and Directors, Everards Tiger, Greene King Abbot, and Morlands Old Speckled Hen; also a dozen malt whiskies. Chalked up on a couple of blackboards on the right hand side of the central servery, the imaginative range of home-made bar meals might typically include soup (£3.25), chicken liver and brandy pâté (£4.95), falafel or squid and baby clams sautéed with ginger and chilli on a bed of tagliatelli (£6.95), pork and garlic sausages (£7.25), and roasted vegetables with grilled brie (£7.50). Recent reports suggest a slight drop in standards in the last months; we hope it's just a blip, as for a while this was up amongst the best pubs for meals in London. Lots of picnic-sets in front, overlooking the quiet street. *(Recommended by Mick Hitchman, Ian Phillips, Sebastian Leach; more reports please)*

Courage ~ Tenant Ian McKenzie ~ Real ale ~ Meals and snacks (12-2.30, 7-10; all day weekends) ~ 0171-727 6648 ~ Children welcome ~ Open 11-3, 5.30-11; 11-11 Fri/Sat, 12-10.30 Sun; closed 25 Dec

White Horse 🍷 🍺 (Fulham) Map 12

1 Parsons Green, SW6; ⊖ Parsons Green

A recent innovation at this chatty and meticulously run pub has been the opening of an upstairs gallery, with changing exhibitions showing off work by established and new artists. The main attraction though continues to be the eclectic range of drinks: as well as particularly well kept Adnams Extra, Bass, Harveys Sussex, Highgate Mild and perhaps an unusual guest (with some helpful tasting notes), they have 15 Trappist beers and a good few other foreign bottled beers, a dozen malt whiskies, and good, interesting and not overpriced wines. It's usually busy (sometimes very much so), but there are enough smiling, helpful staff behind the solid panelled central servery to ensure you'll rarely have to wait to be served. Well liked weekday lunches might include sandwiches (from £3.50; some interesting cheeses), Tuscan white bean soup with fresh herbs (£3.25), ploughman's (£4), penne with tomato, stilton and spinach (£4.50), pork sausages and rosti (£5.50), broad bean and roasted tomato risotto (£6.50), egg noodle stir fry (£6.75), 8oz steak with peppercorn sauce (£10.75), and puddings like lemon tart (£3.25); in winter they do a very good Sunday lunch. The spacious and tastefully refurbished U-shaped bar has big leather chesterfields and huge windows with slatted wooden blinds; to one side is a plainer area with leatherette wall banquettes on the wood plank floor, and a marble fireplace. Several of the high-backed pews on the right hand side may be reserved for eating. Dominoes, cribbage, chess, cards, fruit machine. It's a favourite with smart young people, so earning the pub its well known soubriquet 'the Sloaney Pony'; many locals never refer to it at all by its proper name. On summer evenings the front terrace overlooking the green has something of a continental feel, with crowds of people drinking al fresco at the white cast-iron tables and chairs; there may be imaginative Sunday barbecues. They have quarterly beer festivals (often spotlighting regional breweries) – the best known is for strong old ale held on the last Saturday in November; lively celebrations too on American Independence Day or Thanksgiving. *(Recommended by D P and J A Sweeney, H Flaherty, A Hepburn, S Jenner, ALC, S Williamson, Derek Harvey-Piper)*

Bass ~ Managers Mark Dorber, Lucy Dunstan ~ Real ale ~ Meals and snacks (12-3.30, 6-10.30; all day weekends) ~ 0171-736 2115 ~ Children welcome ~ Jazz Sun evenings ~ Open 11-11; 12-10.30 Sun; closed 24-27 Dec

White Swan (Twickenham) Map 12

Riverside; ⇌ Twickenham

Picturesque and unspoilt, this 17th-c riverside house is built on a platform well above ground level, with steep steps leading up to the door and a sheltered terrace, full of tubs and baskets of flowers. Even the cellar is raised above ground, as insurance against the flood tides which wash right up to the house. Across the peaceful almost rural lane is a little riverside lawn, where tables look across a quiet stretch of the Thames to country meadows on its far bank past the top of Eel Pie Island. Reassuringly traditional, the friendly bar has bare boards, big rustic tables and a mixture of other simple wooden furnishings, and blazing winter fires. The photographs on the walls are of regulars and staff as children, while a back room reflects the landlord's devotion to rugby, with lots of ties, shorts, balls and pictures. Readers like the weekday lunchtime buffet, which in summer might include everything from cheese and ham to trout and smoked salmon; other bar food includes sandwiches (from £2), soup (£2), and winter lancashire hot pot or calf liver (£5). Well kept Charles Wells Bombardier, Courage Best, Marstons Pedigree, Morlands Old Speckled Hen and Websters on handpump, with around 10 wines by the glass; backgammon, cribbage, piped blues or jazz. They have an annual raft race on the river the last Saturday in July, and there's an equally enthusiastic Burns Night celebration. The pub can get busy at weekends and some evenings. It's a short stroll to the imposing Palladian Marble Hill House in its grand Thames-side park (built for a mistress of George II). *(Recommended by J Gibbs, Susan and John Douglas; more reports please)*

Courage ~ Real ale ~ Lease: Steve Roy and Kirsten Faul ~ Meals and snacks (not wknd evenings) ~ 0181-892 2166 ~ Folk duo fortnightly in winter ~ Open 11-11 (11-3, 5.30-11 Mon-Thurs in winter); 12-10.30 Sun

Windsor Castle (Holland Park/Kensington) Map 12

114 Campden Hill Road, W8 ⊖ Holland Park/Notting Hill Gate

Many London pubs promising a garden in truth have little more than a cramped and concreted yard, so the big tree-shaded area at the back of this unchanging old place is a real draw in summer (it's closed in winter). There are lots of sturdy teak seats and tables on flagstones – you'll have to move fast to bag one on a sunny day – as well as a brick garden bar, and quite a secluded feel thanks to the high ivy-covered sheltering walls. The series of unspoilt and small rooms inside all have to be entered through separate doors, so it can be quite a challenge finding the people you've arranged to meet – more often than not they'll be hidden behind the high backs of the sturdy built-in elm benches. Time-smoked ceilings and soft lighting characterise the bar, and a cosy pre-war-style dining room opens off. A few changes to the menu under the new management: they still do the range of often unusual sausages, and oysters and mussels, plus things like cream cheese and prosciutto ciabatta (£4.95), oyster mushroom stroganoff (£6.95), and lamb shank (£8.95). Bass and Fullers London Pride on handpump, along with decent house wines, various malt whiskies, and maybe mulled wine in winter; a round of drinks can turn out rather expensive. No fruit machines or piped music. Usually fairly quiet at lunchtime (when one room is no smoking), the pub can be packed some evenings, often with smart young people. Some of the mostly young staff can still leave you waiting alone at the bar for quite some time. *(Recommended by Susan and John Douglas, Jasper Sabey, Mick Hitchman, Jacqueline Orme, Gordon)*

Bass ~ Manager Carole Jabbour ~ Real ale ~ Meals and snacks (12-10.30) ~ (0171) 727 8491 ~ Children in eating area of bar daytime only ~ Daytime parking metered ~ Open 12-11; 12-10.30 Sun

> The knife-and-fork rosette distinguishes pubs where the food is of exceptional quality.

EAST LONDON

Grapes (Limehouse) Map 12

76 Narrow Street, E14; ⊖ Shadwell (some distance away) or Westferry on the Docklands Light Railway; the Limehouse link has made it hard to find by car – turn off Commercial Rd at signs for Rotherhithe tunnel, Tunnel Approach slip-road on left leads to Branch Rd then Narrow St

A peaceful spot well off the tourist route, this 16th-c tavern is one of London's most characterful riverside pubs. It was used by Charles Dickens as the basis of his 'Six Jolly Fellowship Porters' in *Our Mutual Friend*: 'It had not a straight floor and hardly a straight line, but it had outlasted and would yet outlast many a better-trimmed building, many a sprucer public house.' Not much has changed since, though as far as we know watermen no longer row out drunks from here, drown them, and sell the salvaged bodies to the anatomists as they did in Dickens' day. It was a favourite with Rex Whistler who came here to paint the river (the results are really quite special). The back part is the oldest, with the recently refurbished back balcony a fine place for a sheltered waterside drink; steps lead down to the foreshore. The partly-panelled bar has lots of prints, mainly of actors, some elaborately etched windows, and newspapers to read. Adnams, Tetleys, Ind Coope Burton and a changing guest on handpump, and a choice of malt whiskies. Bar food such as soup (£2.75), sandwiches (from £2.95), bangers and mash (£4.95), home-made fishcakes with caper sauce (£5.25), dressed crab (£6.95), and a Sunday roast (no other meals then); hard-working bar staff. Booking is recommended for the upstairs fish restaurant, which has fine views of the river. Shove-ha'penny, table skittles, cribbage, dominoes, backgammon, maybe piped classical or jazz; no under 14s. *(Recommended by A Hepburn, S Jenner, Bob and Maggie Atherton, David Carr, Tim Heywood, Sophie Wilne, John Fahy, R J Bland)*

Allied ~ Manager Barbara Haigh ~ Real ale ~ Meals and snacks (not Sun evening) ~ Restaurant (closed Sun) ~ 0171-987 4396 ~ Open 12-3, 5.30-11; 7-11 Sat; closed Sat lunchtimes, and bank hols

Prospect of Whitby (Wapping) Map 12

57 Wapping Wall, E1; ⊖ Wapping

Turner came to this entertaining old pub for weeks at a time to study its glorious Thames views, Pepys and Dickens were both frequent visitors, and in the 17th c the notorious Hanging Judge Jeffreys was able to combine two of his interests by enjoying a drink at the back while looking down over the grisly goings on in Execution Dock. With plenty more stories like these it's no wonder they do rather play upon the pub's pedigree, and it's an established favourite on evening coach tours (it's usually quieter at lunchtimes). The tourists who flock in lap up the colourful tales of Merrie Olde London, and only the most unromantic of visitors could fail to be carried along by the fun. Plenty of beams, bare boards, panelling and flagstones in the L-shaped bar (where the long pewter counter is over 400 years old), while tables in the waterside courtyard look out towards Docklands. Well kept Courage Directors, Marstons Pedigree and Theakstons XB on handpump, and quite a few malt whiskies; basic bar meals such as salads (£3.75) and roasts and the like (£4.75), with a fuller menu in the upstairs restaurant. One area of the bar is no smoking. Built in 1520, the pub was for a couple of centuries known as the Devil's Tavern thanks to its popularity with river thieves and smugglers. *(Recommended by A Hepburn, S Jenner, Tony Scott, James Nunns, David Carr, Sue Demont, Tim Barrow)*

Scottish & Newcastle ~ Manager Christopher Reeves ~ Real ale ~ Meals and snacks ~ Restaurant ~ 0171-481 1095 ~ Children in eating areas ~ Modern jazz first Weds evening of month ~ Open 11.30-3, 5.30-11 weekdays; 11.30-11 Sat, 12-10.30 Sun

There are report forms at the back of the book.

Town of Ramsgate (Wapping) Map 12

62 Wapping High St, E1; ⊖ Wapping

Despite its proximity to the City, this evocative old pub has kept a really unspoilt feel (how many other pubs can boast their own gallows?), and rarely gets crowded. It overlooks King Edward's Stairs (also known as Wapping Old Stairs), where the Ramsgate fishermen used to sell their catches. Inside, an enormous fine etched mirror shows Ramsgate harbour as it used to be. The softly lit panelled bar is a fine combination of comfort and good housekeeping on the one hand with plenty of interest on the other: it has masses of bric-a-brac from old pots, pans, pewter and decorative plates to the collection of walking canes criss-crossing the ceiling. There's a fine assortment of old Limehouse prints. Good value bar food (some of it cheaper than it was last year) includes sandwiches (from £1.95, steak £3.25), filled baked potatoes (£2.75), ploughman's (£2.95) and hot dishes like mixed grill, lasagne, fish and chips, and cumberland sausage and mash (£3.95); service is friendly, but not always fast. Well kept Bass, Fullers London Pride and Worthingtons Best, maybe under light blanket pressure; cribbage, trivia, unobtrusive piped music. There's a good sociable mix of customers. At the back, a floodlit flagstoned terrace and wooden platform (with pots of flowers and summer barbecues) peeps out past the stairs and the high wall of Olivers Warehouse to the Thames. *(Recommended by Geoff and Sylvia Donald, Marjorie and David Lamb, Sue Demont, Tim Barrow; more reports please)*

Charringtons (Bass) ~ Manager Julie Allix ~ Real ale ~ Meals and snacks (11.30-3, 6.30-9 weekdays; 12-9 Fri/Sat ~ (0171) 264 0001 ~ Children welcome ~ Open 11.30-11; 12-10.30 Sun

Lucky Dip

Besides the fully inspected pubs, you might like to try these Lucky Dips recommended to us and described by readers (if you do, please send us reports). We have split them into the main areas used for the full reports – Central, North, and so on. Within each area the Lucky Dips are listed by postal district, ending with Greater London suburbs on the edge of that area.

CENTRAL LONDON

EC1

[94 Ironmonger Row], *Britannia*: Very well kept Boddingtons, Fullers London Pride and ESB and Marstons Pedigree, comfortable, busy and friendly, lunchtime food, traditional games; open all day, live music w/e *(Richard Lewis)*

[Chiswell St], *Chiswell Vaults*: Very big cellar pub, lots of separate vaulted areas, nooks and crannies – pizza restaurant in one *(Dr and Mrs A K Clarke, BB)*

[14 Holborn], *Melton Mowbray*: Large pastiche of Edwardian pub done up with etched glass and booths, front opening in summer on to pavement cafe tables; well kept Fullers ales, friendly staff, sandwiches and simple hot dishes *(Ian Phillips, Greg Kilminster)*

[8 Tysoe St], *O'Hanlons*: Long and narrow, with bare boards and panelling, comfortable relaxing atmosphere, seats in back area, a real Irish welcome – friendly landlord and locals; interesting O'Hanlons beers such as Dry Stout, Port Stout, No 1, Myrica (brewed using bog myrtle and honey) and a seasonal ale from owner's Vauxhall microbrewery, good lunchtime food inc giant sausages and lots of fish, maybe even home-grown organic rhubarb pie and custard, no games or piped music; open all day *(Richard Lewis)*

[3 Baldwin St], *Old Fountain*: Welcoming old pub, popular for wholesome lunchtime food; interesting fish tank, well kept beer *(Dr and Mrs A K Clarke)*

☆ [240 St John St], *Peasant*: Elaborate, imaginative food in strikingly furnished upstairs restaurant or downstairs bar, rather trendily redone but still with some reminders of its days as a more traditional corner house, inc tiled picture of St George and Dragon; very helpful service, minimal furnishings and decor, polished bar with fresh flowers, mosaic floor, lights dim throughout evening; drinks limited (no real ale), and too expensive to merit a visit without eating; is a cheaper mezze menu too *(T Barrow, S Demont, BB)*

☆ [166 Goswell Rd], *Pheasant & Firkin*: Genuine local feel (a rare treat for EC1, as is the Sun evening opening), with down-to-earth concentration on good beer (own cheap light Pluckers, also good value Pheasant and powerful Dogbolter brewed here), and basic food at very reasonable prices; bare boards, plenty of bar stools, very friendly service, congenial company from all walks of life, daily papers, good cheap CD juke box *(Jane Keeton, Peter Plumridge, Sue Demont, Tim Barrow, LYM)*

EC2

[91 Moorgate], *Bishop of Norwich*: Pubby-feeling Davy's wine bar with their Best Bitter and Old Wallop, decent range of wines by the glass, food inc bangers and mash, steak and kidney pie and dish of day at City prices; very civilised and atmospheric, with sawdust on floor, pewter tankards, venerable doorman ensuring dignified, quiet and pleasant atmosphere; cl 9, also w/e and bank hols *(Ian Phillips)*

☆ [202 Bishopsgate], *Dirty Dicks*: Traditional City cellar with board floors and brick barrel-vaulted ceiling, interesting old prints inc one of Nathaniel Bentley, the original Dirty Dick; real ales, wine racks overhead, open sandwiches, baguettes and reasonably priced hot dishes, pleasant service, loads of character – fun for foreign visitors *(Ian Phillips, Tony Scott, Francis and Deirdre Gevers, BB)*

☆ [Bishopsgate/L'pool St Stn], *Hamilton Hall*: A Wetherspoons flagship, stunning Victorian baroque decor, plaster nudes and fruit mouldings, chandeliers, mirrors, upper mezzanine, good-sized upstairs no-smoking section (not always open, though – can get crowded and smoky downstairs), comfortable groups of seats, reliable food all day from well filled baguettes up brought to your table, well kept low-priced Scottish Courage and guest beers; fruit machine, video game but no piped music; open all day *(Tim Barrow, Sue Demont, D P Brown, J Fahy, Tony Scott, Dr and Mrs A K Clarke, LYM)*

[168 Old St], *Masque Haunt*: Impressive long Wetherspoons pub with lots of books in raised back area, no smoking areas, their usual food all day, efficient friendly staff, eight well kept ales most from small breweries; open all day *(Richard Lewis)*

EC3

[Crutched Friars, via arch under Fenchurch St Stn], *Cheshire Cheese*: Large pub with upstairs lounge, lots of tables and shelves for plates or glasses; busy lunchtime, with good choice of sandwiches and pies, other hot dishes, Bass, Fullers London Pride; big screen sports TV evening *(Ian Phillips)*

[133 Houndsditch], *Eastern Monk*: One of a chain of mainly City pubs, similar to Old Monk, EC3 – this one includes a Thai restaurant *(LP, SS)*

[47 Aldgate High St], *Hoop & Grapes*: Largely late 17th-c (dismantled and rebuilt 1983), with Jacobean staircase, carved oak doorposts and age-blackened oak serving counter; long narrow beamed and timbered bar, good food, well kept ales such as Adnams, Fullers and Jennings; cl Sun evening, open all day weekdays, very popular *(Tony Scott)*

[80 Leadenhall St], *Old Monk*: Below street level, with lots of glazed and panelled seating alcoves, good range of real ales inc Boddingtons, Beamish Red, Fullers London Pride and Theakstons Best, occasional interesting beer festivals, bar food inc filled baguettes and baked potatoes, burgers, omelettes, chilli and shepherd's pie all day weekdays; one of a small chain of similar City pubs, can get very busy lunchtime *(Sam Samuells, Lynda Payton)*

SW1

☆ [22 Eaton Terr], *Antelope*: Stylish panelled local, rather superior but friendly; bare boards, lots of interesting prints and old advertisements, well kept ales such as Adnams, Fullers London Pride, Marstons Pedigree and Tetleys, good house wines, sandwiches, baked potatoes, ploughman's and one-price hot dishes; quiet and relaxed upstairs weekday lunchtimes, can get crowded evenings; open all day, children in eating area *(Ian Phillips, LYM)*

☆ [62 Petty France], *Buckingham Arms*: Congenial Youngs local close to Passport Office and Buckingham Palace, lots of mirrors and woodwork, unusual long side corridor fitted out with elbow ledge for drinkers, well kept ales, decent simple food, reasonable prices, service friendly and efficient even when busy; SkyTV for motor sports (open Sat); handy for Westminster Abbey and St James's Park *(Mark Baynham, Rachael Ward, LYM)*

[4 Norris St], *Captains Cabin*: Large open-plan nautical-theme pub, Scottish Courage ales *(Robert Lester)*

☆ [29 Passmore St/Graham Terr], *Fox & Hounds*: Tiny unchanging unpretentious local, the last we know of in London with no spirits licence – just well kept ales such as Adnams, Bass, Greene King IPA and Harveys, also wines, sherries, vermouths etc; very friendly landlady and staff, narrow bar with wall benches, hunting prints, old sepia photographs of pubs and customers, some toby jugs and a piano – so near a wooden partition that it would be practically impossible to hit the bass notes; coal-effect gas fire; can be very busy Fri night, maybe quieter Sat *(Robert Lester, C F Fry, Gordon, Glynn Davis, BB)*

[Dean Bradley St], *Marquis of Granby*: Big open-plan pub, well kept Bass and guest beers, lunchtime food, very busy then and early evenings, with some interestingly indiscreet conversations to be overheard; open all day, cl weekends *(T Barrow, S Demont)*

☆ [58 Millbank], *Morpeth Arms*: Roomy Victorian Youngs pub handy for the Tate, old books and prints, photographs, earthenware jars and bottles; busy lunchtimes, quieter evenings – well kept ales, good choice of wines, food, helpful staff; seats outside (a lot of traffic) *(Tony Scott, Tim and Linda Collins, Eddy and Emma Gibson, BB)*

☆ [23 Crown Passage; behind St James's St, off Pall Mall], *Red Lion*: Small cosy early Victorian local tucked down narrow pedestrian alley nr Christies; friendly relaxed atmosphere, panelling and leaded lights, decent lunchtime food, unobtrusive piped music, real ales such as Adnams and Courage Directors *(James Nunns, John Fahy, B J Harding, BB)*

☆ [D of York St], *Red Lion*: Busy little pub notable for dazzling mirrors, crystal chandeliers and cut and etched windows, splendid mahogany, ornamental plaster ceiling – architecturally, central London's most perfect small Victorian pub; good value sandwiches, snacks and hot dishes, well kept Eldridge Pope Hardy Country and Tetleys *(J Fahy, Ian Phillips, LYM)*

☆ [Victoria Stn], *Wetherspoons*: Warm, comfortable and individual, a calm haven above the station's bustle, with very cheap ever-changing real ales, wide choice of reasonably priced decent food all day, prompt friendly service, good furnishings and housekeeping – and heaven for people-watchers, with glass walls and tables outside overlooking the main concourse *(Tony and Wendy Hobden, Mrs D Carpenter, Eddy and Emma Gibson, T Barrow, S Demont, Simon Penny)*

[14 Vauxhall Bridge Rd], *White Swan*: Lively pub handy for the Tate, well kept Theakstons XB, stuffed white swan by door, something of a rustic feel with sanded and scrubbed tables and real flowers in the tubs outside *(E McCall, R Huggins, D Irving, T McLean, BB)*

SW3

[29 Milner St], *Australian*: Good Nicholsons drinking pub, lots of woodwork, choice of well kept ales; can be a bit Sloaney *(Jasper Sabey)*

☆ [87 Flood St], *Coopers Arms*: Relaxed atmosphere, interesting style with country furnishings and lots of stuffed creatures, good food (not Sat/Sun evenings) inc some inventive hot dishes and attractive show of cheeses and cold pies on chunky deal table; well kept Youngs Bitter and Special, good choice of wines by the glass; under same management as Alma and Ship in South London (see main entries) *(Richard Gibbs, LYM)*

☆ [Old Church St], *Front Page*: Civilised local with good interesting bistro food, heavy wooden furnishings, huge windows and big ceiling fans for airy feel, good wines, well kept Boddingtons, Ruddles County and Websters Yorkshire; open all day *(Jasper Sabey, LYM)*

☆ [50 Cheyne Walk], *Kings Head & Eight Bells*: Attractive location by gardens across (busy) road from Thames, some tables outside; carefully refurbished to keep relaxing traditional local feel, clean, comfortable and friendly, with good value bar food, well kept ales such as Adnams, Boddingtons, Brakspears, Flowers, Greene King Abbot, Morlands Old Speckled Hen, Youngs and a seasonal brew, good staff; well behaved dogs allowed *(Tony and Wendy Hobden, Gordon, D J and P M Taylor, BB)*

☆ [Christchurch Terr], *Surprise in Chelsea*: Enjoyably unassuming, with well kept Bass and related ales, decent food, friendly service, and classic broad-spectrum mix of locals; often surprisingly quiet evenings, cosy and warm; not overly done up considering location, attractive stained-glass lanterns, mural around top of bar; well behaved dogs on leads *(David Dimock)*

W1

[37 Thayer St, bottom end of Marylebone High St], *Angel*: Clean and quite spacious, with art deco stained glass and repro oak panelling, broad stairs to big-windowed upstairs bar with food counter (usual range); Sam Smiths OB, goodish choice of house wines, decent service, log-effect gas fires *(Jill Bickerton, BB)*

☆ [41 Mount St], *Audley*: Roomy and solid, with High Victorian woodwork, clock hanging from ornate ceiling in lovely carved wood bracket, well kept Courage Best and Theakstons, good food and service, upstairs panelled dining room; open all day *(Tony Scott, LYM)*

[Wells St], *Champion*: Sam Smiths pub with upstairs dining area; very handy for shopping *(Mick Hitchman)*

[Kingly St], *Clachan*: Wide changing range of ales and above-average food in comfortable well kept pub with ornate plaster ceiling supported by two large fluted and decorated pillars, smaller drinking alcove up three or four steps; can get very busy and smoky *(DC, T Barrow, S Demont)*

[Bruton St], *Coach & Horses*: Fine old timbered pub stuck between modern buildings, small bar with upstairs dining room (not always open), Courage Directors, John Smiths, Theakstons and Youngers IPA, sandwiches *(James Nunns)*

[7 Duke St], *Devonshire Arms*: Very well designed and comfortable, plenty of regulars, very pleasant staff, obliging landlady, food inc enormous sandwiches and good pizzas, well kept Bass, quick table clearing; handy for Wallace Collection *(Sheila Keene)*

[Marylebone], *Devonshire Arms*: Comfortable new pub run by licensees of O'Conor Don, interesting tiled decor, good food esp fishcakes, friendly service *(Richard Gibbs)*

[45 Harrowby St], *Duke of York*: Cosy little two-bar pub with plenty of local colour, bustling at lunchtime; very friendly staff and landlord, well kept Hancocks HB, low spirits prices, bar food, big-screen sports TV *(Dan Wilson)*

[38 Gt Marlborough St], *Fanfare & Firkin*: Typical bare-boards Firkin, split-level back room, their own ales kept well, hot baps etc; music may be loud, lavatories down stairs *(SLC)*

☆ [42 Glasshouse St], *Glassblower*: Handy tourist refuge from Regents St, unfussy furnishings but neat and tidy, gaslight, busy bar and more relaxing upstairs lounge, good choice of simple food all day inc good filled baguettes, well kept Scottish Courage ales, a good few malt whiskies, prompt friendly service; fruit machine, video game, trivia, juke box; children in eating area, open all day *(Comus Elliott, Tim and Linda Collins, Mayur Shah, LYM)*

[30 Bruton Pl], *Guinea*: Well kept Youngs, bar food inc good pies and ciabatta-bread sandwiches, lunchtime suits spilling out into

mews *(Richard Gibbs, LYM)*
[Tottenham Ct Rd], *Jack Horner*: Fullers bank conversion with similar theme to Old Bank of England (see main entries), good atmosphere, their beers well kept, brisk service, interesting menu; very popular but spacious, no piped music *(Chris Parsons)*
[2 Shepherd Mkt], *Kings Arms*: Minimalist bare wood and rough concrete decor, dim upper gallery, friendly young staff, Theakstons and one or more guest beers such as Courage Directors, Greene King Abbot, Sam Smiths, standard bar food inc filled baguettes; piped music can be a little loud; summer pavement overflow *(Rachael Ward, Mark Baynham, LYM)*
☆ [Wardour St], *Moon & Sixpence*: Wetherspoons pub in former bank, original big arched windows giving very light feel in rather spacious main bar, big eating area, good choice of well priced real ales and of wines by the glass, decent food all day inc Sun, no smoking area, pile of board games, no music or machines; pleasantly quiet and relaxing Sat lunchtime *(Michael Sandy, Sue Demont, Tim Barrow, SLC, BB)*
☆ [88 Marylebone Lane], *O'Conor Don*: Genuinely Irish without being in your face about it, waitress drinks service (so you don't have to wait for your Guinness to settle), generous helpings of good straightforward food, no piped music; attractive formal upstairs dining room – Galway oysters flown in daily; good Irish folk music Sat *(Jim and Liz Meier, BB)*
[58-60 Goodge St], *One Tun*: Lively young person's pub with full Youngs range, lots of games and atmosphere; can be busy and smoky Fri night, with loud music *(Rachael Ward, Mark Baynham)*
[7 Greek St], *Pillars of Hercules*: Pleasantly old-fashioned, with ornate heavily painted plasterwork, good changing beer choice, specialised range of bottled beers, food esp pies; can get crowded *(C J Parsons)*
[Kingly St], *Red Lion*: Friendly, solidly modernised without being spoilt, with well kept Sam Smiths at a sensible price, reasonably priced food upstairs; video juke box *(Susan and Nigel Wilson, BB)*
[Wardour St], *Ship*: Corner pub, long bar with alley down one side, etched and cut glass, green and black Anaglypta ceiling, well kept Fullers, friendly service; some concentration on lunchtime food, busier pub atmosphere evenings; largely no smoking, but piped music can be loud *(Ian Phillips)*
[Langham Pl; take express lift in far corner of hotel lobby], *St Georges*: Not a pub, but the 15th-floor bar, now tastefully refurbished, is a most civilised place for a drink with a view – worth the extra cost; bedrooms *(TBB, BB)*
[8 Mill St], *Windmill*: Gilt plaster cherubs, pleasant clean and fresh downstairs dining area, Youngs ales, some emphasis on wines *(Ian Phillips)*

W2

[4 Bathurst St; opp Royal Lancaster Hotel], *Archery*: Homely, comfortable and very friendly genuine London pub with well kept Badger Best and Tanglefoot and a guest such as Black Adder II, food from ploughman's to lamb cutlets and so forth, board games, darts etc in back room, quiet and civilised piped music, picnic-sets outside – horses passing from stables behind *(Ian Phillips, Sue Holland, Dave Webster)*
[66 Bayswater Rd], *Swan*: Pleasant tree-shaded courtyard with big glass canopy looking across busy road to Kensington Gardens, old London prints, well kept Scottish Courage ales, busy food bar, quiet upper room at back *(Ian Phillips, BB)*
☆ [10a Strathearn Pl], *Victoria*: Interesting corner local, lots of Victorian royal and other memorabilia, *Vanity Fair* cartoons and unusual little military paintings, two cast-iron fireplaces, wonderful gilded mirrors and mahogany panelling, bare boards and banquettes, friendly managers, Fullers ales, well priced food counter; quiet piped music, pavement picnic-sets; upstairs (not always open) replica of Gaiety Theatre bar, all gilt and red plush *(Ian Phillips, LYM)*

WC1

☆ [38 Red Lion St], *Enterprise*: Lively no-frills pub with great decor of tiled walls, big mirrors, bare boards; good choice of Bass-related and guest ales, wide range of good value food, friendly staff, small back garden; gets busy evening *(Rachael Ward, Mark Baynham, Greg Kilminster)*
[High Holborn], *Penderals Oak*: Vast Wetherspoons pub with their usual food, but otherwise quite distinctive, with wonderful decor and woodwork; fine choice of real ales at sensible prices *(Rachael Ward, Mark Baynham)*
[Judd St], *Skinners Arms*: Nicely refurbished, with glorious woodwork in saloon bar, lots of London prints, comfortable back seating area, well kept Everards Tiger, Greene King IPA and Abbot and Wadworths 6X, friendly staff, bar food, pavement picnic-sets, interesting tiled frontage with hanging baskets; open all day, handy for British Library *(Richard Lewis)*

WC2

☆ [29 St Martins Lane], *Chandos*: Open all day from 9 (for breakfast), very busy downstairs bare-boards bar, quieter more comfortable upstairs with alcoves and opera photographs, low wooden tables, panelling, leather sofas, orange, red and yellow leaded windows; generally enjoyable food from sandwiches to Sunday roasts, well kept and priced Sam Smiths Mild, Stout and OB, air conditioning (but can get packed and smoky early evening), cheerful mainly antipodean service; children upstairs till 6, darts, pinball, fruit machines, video game, trivia and piped music; note the automaton on the roof (working 10-2 and 4-

9) *(Susan and Nigel Wilson, Gordon, John Fahy, Eddy and Emma Gibson, Mick Hitchman, Tony and Wendy Hobden, Peter and Pat Frogley, C Smith, LYM)*
[42 Wellington St], *Coach & Horses*: Small Irish pub with imported Dublin Guinness from old-fashioned copper-topped bar, food inc good lunchtime hot roast beef baps, barman with computer-like drinks order memory, well kept Courage Best; can get crowded *(Simon Walker, Dave Braisted)*
[Waldorf Hotel, Aldwych], *Footlights*: Good popular small bar (with own entrance), good sandwiches and hot pre-theatre dishes, well kept Bass and Stones, good choice of house wines; bedrooms *(J F M West)*
[Villiers St], *Griffin*: Recently refurbished, decent food, well kept beer *(M R D Foot, BB)*
[Betterton St/Drury Lane], *Hogshead*: Done up in olde-worlde tavern style, comfortable upstairs, with well kept Whitbreads-related ales and impressive choice of unusual guest beers, wide choice of wines, farm cider, basic cheap food, pleasant bustling atmosphere *(Mr and Mrs J Brown, T Barrow, S Demont, Simon Walker)*
[39 Bow St], *Marquess of Anglesey*: Large, expensively refurbished, quiet, light and airy, with good bar food at sensible prices, consistently well kept Youngs, seating upstairs, good service even when busy (they try to serve quickly if you're going to the theatre) *(John C Baker, Simon Walker)*
[Shaftesbury Ave/West St], *Marquis of Granby*: Plenty of panelling, windows look out on hustle and bustle, Theakstons Best, limited food; juke box *(SLC)*
☆ [90 St Martins Lane], *Salisbury*: Floridly Victorian, theatrical sweeps of red velvet, huge sparkling mirrors and cut glass, glossy brass and mahogany; decent food inc salad bar (even doing Sun lunches over Christmas/New Year), well kept Tetleys-related ales, decent house wines, no-smoking back room, friendly service; shame about the piped music and games machines *(Mark Baynham, Rachael Ward, John Fahy, BB)*
[Kingsway], *Shakespears Head*: Typical new Wetherspoons with their usual ales, wines and varied food; popular for its prices, and weekend opening *(Rachael Ward, Mark Baynham)*
[10 Northumberland St; Craven Pl], *Sherlock Holmes*: Well appointed pub decorated with Sherlock Holmes memorabilia, inc complete model of Mr Holmes' apartment; well kept ales, comfortable plush booths, friendly staff, upstairs restaurant; busy lunchtime *(M Hickman, BB)*

NORTH LONDON

N1

☆ [10 Thornhill Rd], *Albion*: Low ceilings, snug nooks and crannies inc cosy back hideaway, some old photographs of the pub, horsebrasses and tack recalling its coaching days, open fires, some gas lighting, no-smoking area, good range of real ales, enjoyable food, very friendly landlord, interesting Victorian gents'; flower-decked front courtyard, big back terrace with vine canopy *(A L Budden, BB)*
[Kings X Stn], *Coopers*: Nostalgia theme, real ales such as Courage Directors, John Smiths, Theakstons and Worthington, good value snacks; open all day from 7am (9 Sun) *(Dr Alan Green)*
[116 Cloudesley St], *Crown*: Gastropub given fashionably distressed look with ricketty tables; helpful friendly staff *(Tim Barrow, Sue Demont)*
[by Highbury & Islington tube], *Hedgehog & Hogshead*: Friendly bare-boards pub brewing its own lager and ales, wide choice of very varied food, simple decor; can get busy *(Mark Baynham, Rachael Ward)*
[87 Noel Rd], *Island Queen*: Good freshly made and often unusual food in amiable character pub with well kept Bass and Worthington BB, good value wines, upstairs restaurant, welcoming atmosphere, good juke box, big mirrors with appliqué jungle vegetation; handy for Camden Passage antiques area; children welcome; can get rather smoky, and a bit boisterous round the pool table *(Ian Phillips, Sue Demont, Tim Barrow)*
[26 Wenlock Rd], *Wenlock Arms*: Friendly and popular real ale pub with ten or so from small breweries, kept very well, quickly changed, always inc a Mild, also farm cider and perry, foreign bottled beers, snacks inc salt beef sandwiches, darts; open all day, jazz – modern Tues, trad Fri, piano Sun lunch *(Richard Lewis)*

N5

[26 Highbury Pk], *Highbury Barn*: Particularly well kept beers, good value food; recently refurbished, handy for Arsenal FC *(Nigel Woolliscroft)*

N6

☆ [77 Highgate West Hill], *Flask*: Comfortable Georgian pub, mostly modernised but still has intriguing up-and-down layout, sash-windowed bar hatch, panelling and high-backed carved settle tucked away in snug lower area (this original core which earns the star open only weekends and summer); usual food all day inc salad bar, good barman, Tetleys-related and Youngs ales, coal fire; very busy Sat lunchtime, well behaved children allowed, close-set picnic-sets out in attractive front courtyard with big gas heater-lamps *(Gordon, J S M Sheldon, Gordon Neighbour, LYM)*

NW1

[1 Randolph St], *Camden Brewing Co*: Unusual layout, with settees and coffee tables; not a brewery, but has well kept ales such as Greene King Abbot and Wadworths 6X; friendly, a bit yuppy *(Chris Glasson)*
☆ [Euston Rd; opp British Library], *Euston Flyer*: Spacious and comfortable, handy for

British Library across rd; well kept Fullers ales and guests such as Mauldons, Morrells Varsity, Tomintoul Stag and Ushers Best tapped from casks in side area, decent food inc vast baps with chips, friendly staff; open plan, but a reasonable degree of privacy if one wants it; unobtrusive piped jazz, early aircraft photographs, open all day *(M R D Foot, Richard Lewis)*
[120 Euston Rd], *Friar & Firkin*: Usual Firkin decor, bare boards, barrels, lots of wood and breweriana, their usual menu, well kept beers brewed on the spot, friendly staff; games machines; open all day, happy hour, quiz nights, live music *(Richard Lewis)*
[1 Eversholt St], *Head of Steam*: Large bar up stairs from bus terminus and overlooking it, fun for train/rail buffs with lots of memorabilia, also Corgi collection, interesting model trains and buses and magazines for sale; interesting well kept ales (also take-away), most from little-known small breweries (esp Northern and Scottish), Biddenham farm cider and lots of bottled beers; TV, bar billiards, downstairs restaurant; open all day *(Richard Lewis, SLC, Tony Scott, George Atkinson, T Barrow, S Demont, Richard Houghton, Simon Walker)*
[Gloucester Ave], *Pembroke Castle*: Split-level pub with trendy new blue decor, laid-back atmosphere, good mix of customers, well kept ales, daily papers; popular with young people w/e evenings *(Tim Barrow, Sue Demont)*

NW3

☆ [32 Downshire Hill], *Freemasons Arms*: Big recently refurbished pub with spacious but busy garden right by Hampstead Heath, good arrangements for serving food and drink outside; several comfortable rooms inside, well spaced variously sized tables, leather chesterfield in front of log fire; good staff, decent food served all day (prices almost make up for the local parking fees), lunchtime no-smoking eating area, well kept Bass and Fullers London Pride; children allowed in dining room, dogs in bar, open all day summer *(Comus Elliott, Mr and Mrs Jon Corelis, Jack Clarfelt, LYM)*
[154 Haverstock Hill], *Haverstock Arms*: Lively, with good mix of customers inc actors and musicians, good weekday food, endearing long-serving Irish tenant; sports TV for football *(GT)*
[North End Way], *Jack Straws Castle*: Three-storey pub/restaurant in London's highest spot, 18th-c coaching inn rebuilt after bomb damage in WW2, on site of pre-Roman earthworks, with panoramic views from upstairs restaurant; warm friendly bars, daily changing varied menu, Bass and other ales, big back terrace with summer barbecues; open all day; bedrooms *(Tony Scott)*
[Hampstead High St], *King William IV*: Long a gay pub, but by no means exclusively – hospitable and friendly, with well kept real ale *(GT)*
[28 Heath St], *Three Horseshoes*: Pleasant Wetherspoons pub in nice location, well kept sensibly priced beers, good staff, food all day, no-smoking area *(Anon)*
[30 Well Walk], *Wells Tavern*: Unpretentious Hampstead local handy for the Heath, roaring fires, Adnams, Boddingtons and Flowers, food inc great value sausage ploughman's; piped music, most local parking reserved for residents; comes into its own on a sunny day, picnic-sets in front and on both sides *(Mark Percy, Lesley Mayoh, BB)*

NW6

[Kilburn High Rd], *Goose & Granite*: Airy open-plan pub with big windows, plenty of tables, stool seating at shelving, simple good value food, Fullers London Pride and Just So, friendly staff; piped music *(SLC)*
[Kilburn High Rd], *Old Cock*: Greene King Irish-theme pub, lots of sign and distance posts, keg beer, Guinness, snacks, pool, TV *(SLC)*

NW7

[Hammer Lane, Mill Hill], *Three Hammers*: Roomy, with fireplaces, books, cosy no-smoking family area, friendly staff, good food inc good value Sun lunch with big pudding choice, nice garden, countrified setting *(Jane and Robert Oswaks)*

NW8

☆ **[24 Aberdeen Pl], *Crockers***: Magnificent original Victorian interior, full of showy marble, decorated plaster and opulent woodwork; relaxing and comfortable, with well kept Bass and wide range of other sensibly priced ales, friendly service, decent food inc vegetarian and good Sun roasts, tables outside *(Sue Demont, Tim Barrow, John Fahy, Tony Scott, LYM)*

ENFIELD

[Market Pl (A110)], *Kings Head*: Unpretentious and comfortable lunchtime or early evening pub with well kept ales inc Marstons Pedigree and Youngs, good tasty food in back dining area, fine choice of wines, darts and pool in games area; busy later *(Michael and Hilary Stiffin)*

PINNER

☆ [Waxwell Lane], *Oddfellows Arms*: Delightful small pub with friendly landlord, relaxed atmosphere, well prepared reasonably priced lunchtime food, good choice of well kept beers; lovely garden *(Chris Glasson, Derek Stafford)*
[High St], *Queens Head*: Traditional pub dating from 16th c, good value fresh food inc vegetarian, well kept changing ales such as Marstons Pedigree and Youngs Special, very friendly staff and landlord, no music or machines; welcome car park *(Chris Glasson)*

SOUTH LONDON

SE1

[8 Borough High St], *Barrow Boy & Banker*: Well organised new pub with good

competitively priced food, welcoming staff *(Charles Gysin)*
[48 Tooley St], *Cooperage*: Small character pub with original cobbles behind, Davys real ale; handy for London Dungeon *(M A Hickman)*
☆ [Bankside], *Founders Arms*: Sparkling view of Thames and St Pauls from spacious glass-walled plush-seat modern bar and big waterside terrace; well kept Youngs Bitter and Special, reasonable food, pleasant service, genuine feel *(David and Carole Chapman, T Barrow, S Demont, DJW, LYM)*
☆ [5 Mepham St], *Hole in the Wall*: No-frills drinkers' pub in railway arch virtually underneath Waterloo Stn – rumbles and shakes when trains go over; not a place for gastronomes or comfort-lovers but well worth knowing for its dozen well kept changing ales and nearly as many lagers, also good malts and Irish whiskeys; loudish juke box, pinball and games machines; basic food all day (cl w/e afternoons) *(LM, Richard Fallon, Mark Baynham, Rachael Ward, T Barrow, S Demont, LYM)*
[Jamaica Rd], *Liams Og*: Busy lunchtime pub nr Tower Bridge, reasonably priced food, Courage ales *(Anon)*
☆ [St Mary Overy Wharf; off Clink St], *Old Thameside*: Good pastiche of ancient tavern, two floors – hefty beams and timbers, pews, flagstones, candles; splendid river view upstairs and from charming waterside terrace by schooner docked in landlocked inlet; good choice of well kept ales such as Adnams Broadside and Marstons Tippeney, all-day salad bar, lunchtime hot buffet *(M A Hickman, LYM)*

SE10

[King William Walk, opp Cutty Sark], *Gypsy Moth*: Comfortable two-level circular dining lounge, brass lighting and fans, interesting artefacts on delft shelf, open all day for food – quite a good choice; well kept Adnams and Tetleys-related ales, polite efficient staff, not too crowded; picnic-sets in good garden *(Mayur Shah)*
[52 Royal Hill], *Richard I*: Quiet and friendly no-nonsense traditional two-bar local with particularly well kept Youngs, bare boards, panelling, good range of traditional bar food inc outstanding sausages, good staff, no piped music; tables in pleasant back garden with barbecues, busy summer weekends and evenings *(M Chaloner)*
[Crane St], *Yacht*: Friendly, clean and civilised, with good food and service, good river view from spacious upper room, light wood panelling, portholes, yacht pictures, cosy banquettes *(Mr and Mrs P L Spencer, David Carr)*

SE13

[Lewisham High St], *Yates's Wine Lodge*: Large clean wine bar/pub in former Co-op dept store, pleasant service, civilised feel; nearby parking not always easy *(A M Pring)*

SE16

☆ [Bermondsey Wall East], *Angel*: Superb Thames views to Tower Bridge and the City upstream, and the Pool of London downstream, esp from balcony supported above water by great timber piles; food from baguettes to impressive main meals, Gales HSB, kind friendly staff, upstairs restaurant where children allowed; nr remains of Edward III's palace, interesting walks round Surrey Quays *(Jenny and Brian Seller, LYM)*
☆ [117 Rotherhithe St], *Mayflower*: Friendly and cosy riverside local with black beams, high-backed settles and open fire, good views from upstairs and atmospheric wooden jetty, well kept Bass and Greene King IPA, Abbot and Rayments, decent bar food (not Sun night), friendly staff; children welcome, open all day; in unusual street with beautiful church *(Kevin Flack, LYM)*

SE22

☆ [Barry Rd, Peckham Rye], *Clock House*: Friendly and popular local with charming Victorian decor, two rooms with dark woodwork, carpets, plenty of ornaments inc lots of clocks and measuring instruments, no music; well kept Youngs, very welcoming – proper pub with diners in the minority, but has decent reasonably priced home-made bar food; some seating outside, lots of colourful flower baskets, tubs and window boxes *(Jenny and Brian Seller)*

SW2

[Brixton Rd], *Beehive*: Very friendly Wetherspoons pub, wide range of beers and lagers at affordable prices, piping hot food served with a warming smile *(Mr Clifford)*
[New Park Rd], *Sultan*: Unpretentious backstreet local with well kept Scottish Courage ales, friendly service, secluded and peaceful fairy-lit back garden *(T Barrow, S Demont)*

SW4

[Clapham Park Rd], *Bellevue*: Trendy dining bar, no real ales but good range of wines, comfortable sofas, armchairs, daily papers etc; innovative well priced food can be good, good atmosphere; piped music can be a little loud *(Sue Demont, Tim Barrow, BB)*
[Clapham Manor St], *Bread & Roses*: Food pub owned by Workers Beer Co, with its own Workers Ale brewed for it, good wine list, various leftish cultural events; piped music can be rather loud *(T Barrow, S Demont)*

SW8

[Thessaly Rd], *British Lion*: Traditional Victorian pub with preserved bar back, Courage ales, small library for locals *(Tony Hobden)*
☆ [169 South Lambeth Rd], *Rebatos*: Lots of Spanish customers, real Spanish feel, consistently good authentic food in front tapas bar and pink-lit mirrored back restaurant – great atmosphere, frequent

evening live music *(Susan and John Douglas, T Barrow, S Demont, BB)*

SW11

[Chatham Rd], *Eagle*: Attractive old side-street pub, Whitbreads-related and interesting guest ales, helpful landlord, paved back garden and seats in front; peaceful and relaxed unless big-screen sports TV on *(Tim Barrow, Sue Demont)*

[St Johns Hill], *Falcon*: Lots of glass and mirrors, comfortable back lounge, more spartan front bar, good welcoming staff, honest basic lunchtime food till 3, good range of well kept ales inc annual beer festival, cheap tea or coffee *(T Barrow, S Demont)*

☆ [opp Battersea Pk BR stn], *Masons Arms*: Trendy young people's local doubling as stylish food pub with short but interesting choice of well prepared food (esp Italian) from open-plan kitchen, good range of wines, light modern decor – battered wooden tables, spotlights, some armchairs and sofas behind; limited beer, may be loud piped music *(Sue Demont, Tim Barrow, BB)*

☆ [60 Battersea High St], *Woodman*: Busy, friendly and individual young people's local, with little panelled front bar, long main room, log-effect gas fires, lots of enamel advertising signs; Badger and guest beers, espresso machine, food inc Sun breakfast from 9.30, bar billiards, darts and games machines at one end, picnic-sets on partly covered back terrace with barbecue; good with children *(T Barrow, S Demont, BB)*

SW12

[97 Nightingale Lane], *Nightingale*: Welcoming, comfortable and civilised early Victorian local, good bar food, well kept Youngs, sensible prices, very friendly staff, attractive back family conservatory; children in useful small family area, small secluded back garden *(Ian Phillips, Sue Demont, Tim Barrow, BB)*

SW13

[7 Church Rd], *Sun*: Several areas around central servery, interesting pictures and decorations, Victorian-style wallpaper, pleasant atmosphere, six Tetleys-related and guest ales, usual home-cooked food, benches and tables over road overlooking duckpond; very popular in summer *(Susan and John Douglas, Sue Demont, Tim Barrow, MS)*

[The Terrace], *White Hart*: Youngs pub thoughtfully restored in clubby Edwardian mood, long-serving landlord, well kept beer, unusual range of good wines, popular home-made food, wonderful Thames terrace, no music *(Mr and Mrs J E Lockwood)*

SW17

[84 Upper Tooting Rd], *Kings Head*: Huge very well decorated Victorian pub, lots of small room areas, well kept real ales, food, friendly service *(Dr and Mrs A K Clarke)*

SW18

[East Hill], *Beehive*: Friendly traditional local, small and neat; well kept Fullers, efficient service, good mix of customers, unobtrusive piped music; very popular evenings esp weekend *(Sue Demont, Tim Barrow, LM, BB)*

[68 Wandsworth High St], *Brewery Tap*: Fine Victorian tap for Youngs Brewery, well refurbished so as not to ruin its atmosphere; their full range kept very well, lots of comfortable seating, relevant prints and artefacts, good choice of food inc lots of specials, good friendly staff; piped music; open all day *(Dr and Mrs A K Clarke)*

SW19

[Wimbledon Common], *Crooked Billet*: Popular olde-worlde pub by common, lovely spot for summer drinking, open all day; full Youngs range kept well, decent value bar food, pleasant helpful service, good relevant decor, restaurant in 16th-c barn behind *(Jenny and Brian Seller, Tony Scott, Colin McKerrow)*

[24 High St Wimbledon], *Dog & Fox*: Well kept Youngs, front terrace facing High St; Chinese restaurant *(Dr and Mrs A K Clarke)*

[Camp Rd], *Fox & Grapes*: By common, with good friendly service, softer lighting, warmer feel, lovely new mural behind food servery, new carpet; good choice of hearty food, Scottish Courage ales with a guest such as Wadworths 6X; piped music, big screen sports TV; open all day, children welcome till 7, pleasant on summer evenings when you can sit out on the grass *(Susan and John Douglas, Gregor Macdonald, LYM)*

[6 Crooked Billet], *Hand in Hand*: Very well kept Youngs (full range), straightforward food inc home-made pizzas and burgers, relaxed and cheerful U-shaped bar serving several small areas, some tiled, others carpeted, log fire; rather spartan no-smoking family annexe with bar billiards, darts etc; tables out in courtyard with vine and hanging baskets, benches out by common; can be very crowded with young people esp summer evenings *(Tony Scott, A M Stephenson, BB)*

[Merton Abbey Mills; Merantum Way; next to Savacentre], *William Morris*: Lively and popular two-floor modern pub on site of the old Wm Morris/Liberty mills by R Wandle, lots of corners, seats outside; interesting Wm Morris materials and old bicycle posters, good range of ales inc Theakstons XB and one brewed for the pub, good choice of reasonably priced food inc Thai dishes and traditional puddings (just filled rolls Sat), brisk service; open all day, can get crowded, handy for market and waterwheel – and steam train passes *(Jenny and Brian Seller)*

BEXLEY

[65 High St], *Kings Head*: Dating from 15th c, with lots of horse tack, post horns etc, good choice of cheapish bar food from sandwiches and baked potatoes up Mon-Sat, Sun lunch; municipal car park opp *(A Pring)*

[North Cray Rd], *White Cross*: Welcoming,

with good choice of bar food and proper meals, good service, well kept Scottish Courage ales *(Paul and Sharon Sneller)*

BROMLEY

[157 High St], *Royal Bell*: Former coaching inn, now Greenalls, with several big rooms, handy for food lunchtime or early evening; popular with younger people later, no nearby parking *(AP)*

CHEAM

[17 Park Rd], *Olde Red Lion*: Small low-ceilinged 16th-c pub, recently refurbished without being spoilt, popular lunchtime for good value nicely presented food (not Sun evening) from sandwiches up, ales such as Fullers London Pride, Hancocks HB, Morlands Old Speckled Hen and Worthingtons Best, island bar, tables out on terrace *(DWAJ)*

CHELSFIELD

[Church Rd], *Five Bells*: Little changed over the years, with ancient tables and chairs, old photographs of this Miss Read village, well prepared food inc good toasties, well kept Courage and a guest such as Tolly Original; newish restaurant *(Dave Braisted, Michael and Hazel Duncombe)*

[Well Hill], *Rock & Fountain*: Enlarged pub handy for Lullingstone Park, pleasant countryside nearby; food inc Sun roasts, dining room off main bar, tables under cocktail parasols on small terrace (rather a lot of steps); quiz nights *(A M Pring)*

CHISLEHURST

[Old Perry St], *Sydney Arms*: Good value bar food, Scottish Courage ales, efficient service, friendly atmosphere, big conservatory and pleasant garden – good for children; almost opp entrance to Scadbury Park – lovely country walks *(B J Harding)*

COULSDON

☆ [Old Coulsdon; Coulsdon Rd (B2030) on edge of Common], *Fox*: Busy partly 18th-c family dining pub with good value generous food all day, done to order, well kept real ale, decent wine, friendly efficient staff, good choice of beers and whiskies, log fires, no-smoking area, interesting uncluttered displays; good big enclosed play garden inc summer bouncy castle and ball pool, maybe a magician; handy for North Downs walks, but no dogs *(Mrs Janice Whitehead, D F T Gurner)*

CROYDON

[65 Leslie Park Rd; off Cherry Orchard Rd], *Builders Arms*: Friendly two-bar Fullers local, their beers kept well, decent food, pleasant garden with play area and attractive hanging baskets; open all day *(Tony Scott)*

CUDHAM

☆ [Cudham Lane], *Blacksmiths Arms*: Decent generous reasonably priced food inc interesting soups, good ploughman's, well kept Courage, Fullers London Pride and Morlands Old Speckled Hen, good coffee, quick friendly service; nearly always busy yet plenty of tables, with cheerful cottagey atmosphere, soft lighting, blazing log fires, low ceiling; big garden, pretty window boxes, handy for good walks *(B J Harding, R Boyd, Jenny and Brian Seller)*

FARNBOROUGH

[High St], *Change of Horses*: Useful main road pub, food lunchtime and evening; also hard-boiled eggs on the bar *(A M Pring)*

[A21 by hospital], *White Lion*: Old free house with good range of whiskies, lunchtime food inc 3-course lunch, nice pubby decor, tables on small terrace, garden *(A M Pring)*

KESTON

[Commonside], *Greyhound*: Roomy, with lots of china and bric-a-brac, wide choice of reasonably priced blackboard food, charity events, no-smoking area; big garden with Sat barbecues and play area, handy for walks on common and in woods *(AMP)*

KINGSTON

[2 Bishops Hall; off Thames St – down alley by Superdrug], *Bishop out of Residence*: Riverside Youngs pub with pleasant Thames views, big bar and eating area, lunchtime emphasis on wide range of good value quick food, well kept ales, decent house wines, customers of all ages; tables out on balcony *(John Wooll, GP)*

[88 London Rd], *Hog & Stump*: New name for large Edwardian own-brew pub (formerly Flamingo) much the same but smartened up, neater and tidier – even the beers seem fresher and crisper; polite friendly service *(Richard Houghton)*

[Eden St], *Kings Tun*: Useful Wetherspoons, with reasonable food, decent beer inc interesting guest beers, helpful and efficient young staff *(Sue and Mike Todd)*

LEAVES GREEN

Crown: Pleasant Shepherd Neame pub with wide choice of attractively priced food, side dining room (worth booking weekends); daily papers, games machines *(A M Pring)*

MALDEN RUSHETT

☆ [Chessington Rd; A243 just N of M25 junction 9], *Star*: Busy dining pub with well made reasonably priced generous food from sandwiches up inc vegetarian, sizeable no-smoking area, jovial long-serving ex-sea captain landlord, helpful quick friendly service, well kept King & Barnes and Scottish Courage ales, decent wines, maybe a splendid locally made elderflower champagne, big log fire; handy for Chessington World of Leisure, quickly fills at lunchtime *(DWAJ, J S M Sheldon)*

ORPINGTON
[High St], *Harvest Moon*: Useful Wetherspoons pub, with usual menu, guest beers etc; open all day *(A M Pring)*

PETTS WOOD
[Station Sq], *Daylight*: Spacious, well refurbished with lots of alcoves, reasonably priced lunchtime food inc good value Sun lunch, real ales such as Fullers London Pride, Hancocks HB and Morlands Old Speckled Hen, cheery management, provision for children, tables outside; evenings has loud music and young crowds *(B and M Kendall, Bridget Burgess, R Boyd)*
Sovereign of the Seas: Good Wetherspoons pub, wide choice of beers, very friendly atmosphere; gets crowded – lots of young people but no trouble *(A M Pring, R Boyd)*

RICHMOND
☆ [45 Kew Rd], *Orange Tree*: Interesting main bar with fine plasterwork, big coaching and Dickens prints, fine set of 1920s paintings; open all day, with theatre club upstairs, well kept Youngs, friendly service, good food all day (not Sun evening) in civilised and spacious cellar bar; pleasant tables outside *(Nigel Williamson, Tony Scott, LYM)*
☆ [Petersham Rd], *Rose of York*: Comfortable seats inc leather chesterfields, Turner prints on stripped pine panelling, old photographs, attractive layout inc no-smoking area, reasonably priced Sam Smiths ales, pleasant helpful service; high chairs, bar billiards, fruit machines, TV, piped pop music; bedrooms *(B J Harding, Tony Scott)*[17 Parkshot; just off shopping centre], *Sun*: Reliable Fullers local with pleasant atmosphere, good value food, well kept ales, masses of Rugby memorabilia; uncrowded at lunchtime *(C J Parsons)*
☆ [25 Old Palace Lane], *White Swan*: Pleasant setting for charming respite from busy Richmond, easy welcoming feel in dark-beamed open-plan bar, well kept Scottish Courage beers, good coal fires, good freshly cooked bar lunches; children allowed in conservatory; pretty paved garden, barbecues *(Comus Elliott, Mrs D W Cook, LYM)*

ST PAULS CRAY
[Main Rd; junction with A223 towards Bexley], *Bull*: Two-bar pub with pleasant service, sandwiches, ploughman's and some hot dishes, decent wines, garden; games machines, quiz night *(AMP)*

WEST LONDON
SW6
[235 New Kings Rd], *Duke of Cumberland*: Huge lavishly restored Edwardian Youngs pub opp Parsons Green, attractice decorative tiles and interesting panel fleshing out his life; well kept beer, cheerful at weekend lunchtimes, relaxed for weekday lunchtime food – not usually too busy *(Dr and Mrs A K Clarke, BB)*
[248 North End Rd], *Goose & Granite*: Much renamed and now taken over by Just So Pub Co; lots of little nooks, fairly big no-smoking area, young friendly helpful staff, well kept real ales *(Dr and Mrs A K Clarke)*

SW10
☆ [Burnaby St], *Chelsea Ram*: Very unusual for a Youngs pub, more like a wine bar with some emphasis on good if not cheap food changing daily, inc vegetarian, pasta, fish and Smithfield meat; well kept Youngs, interesting wines inc good choice by the glass, outstanding bloody mary, good Pimms; lively mix of customers, friendly service, lovely fire, pleasant golden walls, shutters, books, pine tables, no music, quiet back part; open all day Fri *(Mrs C Scrutton, Pippa Scott, Sue Demont, BB)*
[1 Billing Rd], *Fox & Pheasant*: Cosy, friendly and charmingly old-fashioned back-street local, feels like a country pub in middle of town; particularly well kept beer at sensible prices, decent food *(Dr and Mrs A K Clarke)*

W4
☆ [72 Strand on the Green], *Bell & Crown*: Big busy pub with several comfortable areas, very friendly feel, local paintings and photographs, simple good value food inc lunchtime hot dishes and lots of sandwiches, well kept Fullers, log fire, no piped music or machines; great Thames views esp from conservatory and picnic-sets out by towpath; open all day, good towpath walks *(David and Carole Chapman, Ian Phillips, Tony Scott, Eddy and Emma Gibson)*
☆ [27 Strand on the Green], *City Barge*: Small panelled riverside bars in picturesque partly 15th-c pub (this original part reserved for diners lunchtime), also airy newer back part done out with maritime signs and bird prints; good atmosphere, usual bar food (not Sun), well kept Courage Directors and Wadworths 6X, back conservatory, winter fires, some tables on towpath – lovely spot to watch sun set over Kew Bridge *(Chris Glasson, B J Harding, Eddy and Emma Gibson, LYM)*
[110 Chiswick Lane S, by Gt West Rd at Fullers Brewery], *Mawson Arms*: Open-plan Fullers brewery tap also known as Fox & Hounds, well kept ESB, London Pride and IPA, also full range of their bottled beers; lots of seating, bare boards, nice minimalist decor, settee at one end, daily papers, limited decent food, helpful friendly staff; open all day *(Ian Phillips)*
[2 Bath Rd, Bedford Pk], *Tabard*: No music, wide range of customers, helpful friendly staff, good choice of ales, wide choice of wines, William de Morgan tiles, William Morris wallpaper and carpets; good Thai restaurant, fringe theatre upstairs; disabled access, tables on terrace, well behaved children welcome *(John Mulcahy)*

W5
☆ [124 Pitshanger Lane], *Duffys*: Attractive and civilised, soft lighting, stripped floor, chess

tables, well kept Brakspears, Fullers London Pride and Wadworths 6X, good value bar food, good friendly staff, slightly separate small restaurant – appetising aromas *(Greg Kilminster)*
[Hanger Lane], *Fox & Goose*: Smart Fullers pub, good range of their beers, reasonable choice of bar food and wines; bedrooms comfortable and well priced *(Andy and Jill Kassube)*
[Elm Grove Rd, by Warwick Dene], *Grange*: Imposing mid-Victorian pub on Ealing Common, tall arched windows looking out over it, soft lighting, old local photographs on pastel wallpaper, comfortable seats and old wooden tables, food all day in big airy conservatory, Scottish Courage ales, picnic-sets in big courtyard with barbecues twice a week, friendly staff, daily papers; piped music *(Mark Percy)*
[43 The Broadway], *North Star*: Large busy suburban pub little changed since 1930s, particularly well kept Youngs and other ales, prompt enthusiastic service *(John C Baker)*
[St Marys Rd; just S of Ealing Broadway, opp BBC Ealing Film Studios], *Red Lion*: Good quiet Fullers local, welcoming to visitors, with particularly well kept London Pride and ESB, simple lunches, single small unspoilt bar with wooden floor and seating in low-backed booths, photographs of BBC studio stars *(Greg Kilminster)*
[Church Pl; off St Marys Rd], *Rose & Crown*: Good food and atmosphere in 1920s/30s pub with small public bar, fairly big lounge and conservatory, well kept Fullers ales, friendly efficient staff; games machines, unobtrusive piped country music, Sun quiz night; tables in back garden *(Dr M Owton)*
[Haven Lane], *Wheatsheaf*: Welcoming Fullers local, good choice of bar food inc Sun lunch – when there may be a small antiques auction *(Val Stevenson, Rob Holmes)*

W6

[Aldensley Rd], *Andover Arms*: Small intimate unspoilt local, particularly well kept Fullers London Pride, unobtrusive SkyTV *(Giles Francis)*
[Lower Mall], *Blue Anchor*: Friendly panelled pub right on Thames, oars and other rowing memorabilia, cheap generous bar lunches, Courage and guest beers, pleasant river-view upstairs restaurant; riverside tables, busy weekends *(Mick Hitchman, D J and P M Taylor, BB)*
[320 Goldhawk Rd], *Brook*: Former Queen of England refurbished as gastropub by owners of Chapel, NW1, kitchen team recruited from good restaurants doing good inventive food; well kept Fullers London Pride, good wine list *(Charlie Ballantyne)*
[40 Hammersmith Broadway], *Edwards*: Good helpful service, good modern pub food, well kept beer; stylish and comfortable, but character not its strongest point *(FG, DG, BB)*

W7

[Green Lane, Hanwell], *Fox*: Friendly open-plan 19th-c pub in quiet spot nr Grand Union Canal, well kept Courage Best and Directors and Marstons Pedigree, good reasonably priced home cooking inc Sun roasts, dining area, panelling, wildlife pictures, farm tools hung from ceiling; garden, occasional w/e barbecue *(Andrew and Eileen Abbess)*

W8

☆ [23a Edwardes Squ], *Scarsdale Arms*: Busy Georgian Chef & Brewer in lovely leafy square, keeping a good deal of character, with stripped wooden floors, two or three fireplaces with good coal-effect gas fires, lots of knick-knacks, ornate bar counter; Adnams, Shepherd Neame Bishops Finger and Theakstons, decent wines, back food servery with reasonably priced food; tree-shaded front courtyard with impressive show of flower tubs and baskets; open all day *(Tony Scott, LYM)*

W10

[13-15 North Pole Rd], *North Pole*: Very successfully converted in recent months, now a spacious, light and airy pub, surprisingly interesting given its location; wide range of imaginative food, polished bare boards, low-key chandeliers and other touches of laid-back elegance, table football; popular with BBC folk *(BB)*

W11

[46 Queensdale Rd], *Star*: Quiet backstreet pub with great panelling, lovely back garden, good food (short choice changing daily), well kept Fullers London Pride *(Charlie Ballantyne)*

W13

☆ [2 The Avenue; opp West Ealing stn], *Drayton Court*: Big Edwardian turreted stone building with two bars, friendly staff, lots of locals of all ages, full Fullers range kept well, good choice of fresh-tasting snacks and light lunches inc vegetarian and good Sun roasts, sensible prices; barbecues on terrace, balcony overlooking big garden with unobtrusive play area; downstairs theatre *(Dr Alan Green, Val Stevenson, Rob Holmes)*

W14

[24 Blythe Rd, Olympia], *Frigate & Firkin*: Typical Firkin – lots of wood, brewing memorabilia, bare boards, good choice of reasonably priced food, friendly staff, well kept ales in variety; open all day *(Richard Lewis)*

BRENTFORD

[Lion Way; behind Magistrates Court], *White Horse*: May date partly from 18th c, with Bass, Hancocks HB and Worthingtons, games area, new conservatory, garden overlooking first lock on Grand Union Canal *(Ian Phillips)*

CRANFORD
[123 High St; Cranford Lane off A312], *Queens Head*: Friendly local feel despite proximity to Heathrow, well kept Fullers inc seasonal ale *(Richard Houghton)*

EASTCOTE
[High Rd], *Case is Altered*: Attractive old pub in quiet setting, well kept ales, pleasant garden, wide choice of food *(Chris Glasson, Mark J Hydes)*

HAMPTON
[122 High St], *Dukes Head*: Friendly open-plan local with good home-made bar lunches from fresh sandwiches up (not Sun), and interesting full meals evenings (not Sun) and Sun lunchtime, inc popular Weds steak night; secluded restaurant, small pleasant terrace with good value barbecues; well kept Courage Best, Gales HSB, John Smiths and guest ales, dogs welcome subject to approval of Ben and Tessa resident golden retrievers *(Michael Gale, Chris Daly)*

HAMPTON COURT
☆ [Hampton Court Rd, next to Lion Gate], *Kings Arms*: Oak panels and beams, stripped-brick lounge with bric-a-brac and open fire one end, public bar the other end with stripped pine food servery beyond (eat where you like, food all day from 8.30); pleasant relaxed atmosphere, well kept Badger beers, upstairs restaurant; unobtrusive piped music, children welcome; open all day, picnic-sets on roadside cobbles *(Val and Alan Green, Susan and John Douglas, John Crafts, LYM)*

HAMPTON WICK
[High St; by Kingston Bridge], *White Hart*: Comfortable and friendly, with well kept Fullers, food from good baguettes to Thai dishes; children welcome, tables out in front *(Piotr Chodzko-Zajko, Ian Phillips)*

HATTON
[Green Man Lane; 30 yds from A30 crossroads at Bedfont], *Green Man*: Genuinely old pub in unpromising spot, with alcoves, low ceilings, secret room behind fireplace and tales of highwaymen; warm and welcoming, with Scottish Courage ales, half a dozen hot lunchtime specials – gets very busy then *(Ian Phillips, Mayur Shah)*

ISLEWORTH
[181 Twickenham Rd], *Chequers*: Clean, spacious and well appointed, with wide choice of beers and good low-priced traditional food – no smoking area at lunchtime; welcoming neat staff *(John and Elisabeth Cox)*
Town Wharf: Worth knowing for riverside position, splendid views from upstairs bar with lunchtime hot food and good range of beers; good waterside seating area; can be crowded, esp summer Fri lunchtimes *(SP)*

LONGFORD
[M4 junction 14; A3113, then left into A3044, then right at roundabout into Bath Rd], *White Horse*: Brasses on low black beams, fireplace between the two areas, comfortable seats, pot plants in windows, cosy atmosphere; good lunchtime bar food, efficient friendly service, well kept Scottish Courage ales; fruit machine, piped music; tables outside, open all day *(Mayur Shah)*

NORWOOD GREEN
☆ [Tentelow Lane (A4127)], *Plough*: Attractive old-fashioned low-beamed decor, cheerful villagey feel, well kept Fullers ales inc Chiswick, welcoming service, cosy family room, even a bowling green dating to 14th c; decent cheap lunchtime food, flame-effect gas fire; can get crowded weekends; occasional barbecues in lovely garden with play area, open all day, lavatories for the disabled *(Ian Phillips)*

OSTERLEY
[Windmill Lane; B454, off A4 – called Syon Lane at that point], *Hare & Hounds*: Well worn-in open-plan suburban Fullers pub in nice setting opp beautiful Osterley Park, lots of tables in good mature garden; reasonably priced straightforward bar lunches, prompt service; darts, piped music, chaps talking football *(Steve Power, D P and J A Sweeney)*

TEDDINGTON
[Adelaide Rd], *Adelaide*: Friendly corner local with three well kept real ales, good value food esp filled baguettes, back garden; popular lunchtime *(LM)*

TWICKENHAM
☆ [9 Church St], *Eel Pie*: Busy and unpretentious, open all day (not Mon afternoon), wide range of Badger and other ales, farm cider; usual bar food (lunchtime not Sun) and all-day sandwiches (not Sun), lots of Rugby player caricatures, bar billiards, pinball and other pub games, some seats outside; piped music may be loud; open all day (but cl at 8 on big Rugby days – when it can be very busy), children allowed till 6; nice street *(Comus Elliott, Steve Power, LYM)*
☆ [Cross Deep], *Popes Grotto*: Huge relaxing suburban local, helpful staff, good value lunchtime bar food from sandwiches to Sun roasts, well kept Youngs, good range of other drinks, no music, games in small public bar; tables in own garden, and attractive public garden over rd sloping down to Thames (cl at night); children in eating area *(Greg Kilminster, LYM)*
[Winchester Rd, St Margarets; behind roundabout on A316], *Turks Head*: Friendly local with full Fullers range kept well, home-cooked food changing daily; manic on Rugby days; stand-up comics Mon/Sat in hall behind *(Terry and Jayne Harmes, Ian Phillips, BB)*

EAST LONDON

E1

[Whitechapel Rd], *Blind Beggar*: 19th-c, refurbished in early 80s with lovely deep leather chairs, relaxed atmosphere, Scottish Courage ales, conservatory and small garden; open all day inc Sun *(S A Jenner)*

[St Katharines Way], *Dickens Inn*: Splendid position above smart docklands marina, well kept Scottish Courage ales, interesting baulks-and-timbers interior, several floors inc pricy restaurant; popular with overseas visitors *(A Hepburn, S Jenner, LYM)*

☆ [9 Exmouth St], *Hollands*: Well worth penetrating the surrounding estates for this unspoilt Victorian gem, friendly and entirely genuine, with lots of original fittings inc bar snob-screens and fine mirrors, interesting bric-a-brac, Youngs ales, simple bar food, darts; open all day *(David Carr, LYM)*

E3

[8 Coborn Rd], *Coborn Arms*: In Bow Heritage Area, with full Youngs range, straightforward lunchtime bar food, quiet friendly atmosphere; darts, piped music; some tables out in quiet front area; open all day inc Sun *(S A Jenner)*

E4

[Larkshall Rd], *Larkshall*: Attractive old-looking pub with various little rooms, big ornate eating area recently refurbished with lots of wood, Courage Best and Directors *(Robert Lester)*

[31 Mill Lane], *Rose & Crown*: Friendly and cosy, with extended upper bar, Boddingtons and Marstons Pedigree *(Robert Lester)*

E8

[Parkholme Rd], *Prince George*: Well kept Whitbreads-related and several other ales, the feel of a genuine pub, popular food inc choice of roasts for Sun lunch (good prawns free with it), friendly atmosphere, good mix of customers *(Chris Bird)*

E11

[31 High St Wanstead], *Cuckfield*: Highly refurbished, with lots of light-coloured wood, prominent lamps and lanterns – comfortable and smart; Bass and Worthington, real fire, good friendly atmosphere, conservatory; smart dress, no under-21s *(Ian Phillips, J Fahy, Robert Lester)*

[Wanstead High St], *George*: 18th-c coaching inn, vastly refurbished by Wetherspoons, always busy but never crowded, good range of changing ales, food typical Wetherspoons value; unsmoky and unpretentious, has become the area's premier pub *(Mark Baynham, Rachael Ward)*

[36 High St Wanstead], *Raffertys*: Former Clutterbucks made over as faux Irish, long narrow pine-panelled bar with comfortable chairs on boards or tiles, Tetleys, stouts, lagers etc, inexpensive limited food; one of Jack the Ripper's victims said to have been murdered in a next-door yard *(Ian Phillips)*

E17

[42 Orford Rd], *Queens Arms*: Open-plan 19th-c pub with Scottish Courage beers, darts, pool, garden *(Robert Lester)*

☆ [off Whipps Cross Rd], *Sir Alfred Hitchcock*: More atmosphere than usual round here, rather countrified, with well kept ales such as Boddingtons, Flowers, Fullers ESB, enthusiastic Irish landlord, big open fires, Chinese bar meals and restaurant, reasonable prices; TV in bar; dogs welcome, sunny terrace; bedrooms *(Rachael Ward, Mark Baynham)*

E18

[Woodford New R (A104, corner of Fullers Rd)], *Napier Arms*: Comfortable recently refurbished two-bar pub with Charrington IPA, Greene King IPA, snacks all times, terrace; quiz night Thurs *(Robert Lester)*

CHADWELL HEATH

[Billet Rd, Marks Gate; nr A112], *Crooked Billet*: Comfortable beamed and panelled saloon, Tetleys, darts, good friendly local atmosphere *(Robert Lester)*

HAINAULT

[720 New North Rd; A1112], *Oak*: Large modern pub opp Hainault Forest, a beer named for the pub, good friendly atmosphere, darts, pool, big screen sports TV *(Robert Lester)*

ILFORD

[308 Ley St; nr A123], *Bell*: Massive two-bar John Barras pub, very spacious and atmospheric; Scottish Courage ales, cheap food, big-screen TV; darts in public bar *(Robert Lester)*

ROMFORD

[260 London Rd (A110)], *Crown*: Friendly open-plan pub nr dog track done up in Victorian style; Tetleys *(Robert Lester)*

UPMINSTER

[Upminster Rd (A124)], *Bridge House*: Pleasant open-plan pub with fish theme, good food at very reasonable prices, good friendly service, Courage Best and Greene King IPA *(Robert Lester)*

WOODFORD

[735 Chigwell Rd (A113)], *Three Jolly Wheelers*: Large and friendly, completely refurbished in wooden mock-Tudor style, Bass and Hancocks HB, restaurant, newspapers framed in gents' *(Robert Lester)*

Scotland

This year we have far more new entries here than usual, including three pubs returning to these pages on fine form after a break: the grandly old-fashioned Abbotsford in Edinburgh (lots of beers, good food), the busy old George at Inveraray and the quirky and exceedingly Scottish Inverarnan Inn at Inverarnan. The complete newcomers are the Royal in Cromarty (a very likeable quietly traditional seaside hotel), the relaxed and pubby Drovers at East Linton (good beers, good food; we're glad to have found it open this time – the last time we tried to inspect it we found it closed for refurbishments!), the waterside Ship on the Shore in Leith, Edinburgh (some concentration on fresh fish), the bustling Auctioneers in Glasgow (interesting conversion of an auctioneers'), the vibrantly cosmopolitan Blackfriars there (unusual coffee specialities as well as good beers), the beautifully set Glenelg Inn at Glenelg (a favourite find this year), the foody and aptly named Waterside in Haddington (it looks very like the imaginary pubs we used to have on our covers before the 1998 edition), the Moulin in Pitlochry (good all round – and brewing its own good beers) and the Cabin in St Monance (excellent food, striking but cosy bar). Other pubs and inns currently doing particularly well here are the Applecross Inn at Applecross (great setting, good seafood), the friendly Galley of Lorne at Ardfern (upgraded bedrooms, nice breakfasts), the atmospheric Village Inn at Arrochar (a good all-rounder), the Byre at Brig o' Turk (enjoyable food), the Tigh an Truish at Clachan Seil (a nicely set welcoming local), the showy Guildford Arms, Kays Bar (food prices unchanged for the second year running) and the Starbank (good food and beers, great choice of wines by the glass), all three in Edinburgh, the bustling good value Lock in Fort Augustus, the very warm-hearted and civilised Babbity Bowster in Glasgow and (we think Wetherspoons' most impressive conversion) the Counting House there, the Tormaukin in Glendevon (a popular stop on a lovely route), the Traquair Arms in Innerleithen (good food, beer from Traquair House), the good value harbourside Steam Packet in Isle of Whithorn, the excellent if hard-to-get-to Kilberry Inn at Kilberry (you'd find us there almost every evening – if it weren't for the little matter of the 1,114-mile round trip from our office), the Portland Arms in Lybster (good food and service), the well run Burts Hotel in Melrose, the smart yet friendly Killiecrankie Hotel beautifully placed outside Pitlochry (good food), the idyllically sited Plockton Hotel at Plockton, the welcoming waterside Crown at Portpatrick (fine food and service), the Wheatsheaf at Swinton (outstanding food, service highly praised too), the Morefield Motel in Ullapool (still one of the best places we've found for seafood) and the newly decorated Ailean Chraggan at Weem. With food in so many Scottish pubs and inns now so very much better than it was even a few years ago, the competition for our award of Scotland's Dining Pub of the Year is becoming intense: this year the award goes to the Wheatsheaf at Swinton. There are plenty of good Scottish pubs and inns which are kept out of the main entries primarily by lack of page space, and the Lucky Dip section at the end of the chapter is particularly worth exploring (as the high proportion of starred entries shows). Ones we'd pick out are the Allanton Inn at Allanton, Craw at

Auchencrow, Horseshoe at Eddleston, Tibbie Shiels on St Marys Loch and Old Thistle at Westruther (Borders); Swan at Kingholm Quay, Anchor at Kippford, Black Bull in Moffat and George at Moniaive (Dumfries & Galloway); Crooked Inn at Crook of Alves and Towie Tavern at Turriff (Grampian); Dalrachney Lodge at Carrbridge, restored Old Inn at Gairloch and Royal in Kingussie (Highland); Hawes in Queensferry (Lothian); Oban Inn in Oban (Strathclyde); Nivingston House at Cleish and Kenmore Hotel at Kenmore (Tayside); and Sligachan Hotel and Stein Inn at Stein on Skye. Glasgow has a good choice of enjoyable pubs, and Edinburgh has a splendid one. Although malt whisky prices are often below what you'd expect to pay in an English pub, beer prices tend to be higher; the cheapest place we found was the Counting House in Glasgow. Incidentally, younger readers may need to know that /- is the sign for shilling – as in 80/- ale, which in days of even more stable prices than today cost 80 shillings (or £4) a cask.

ABERDEEN (Grampian) NJ9305 Map 11

Prince of Wales £

7 St Nicholas Lane

The cosy flagstoned area at the heart of this individual old tavern has the city's longest bar counter, and it's a good job too; some lunchtimes there's standing room only, with a real mix of locals and visitors creating a friendly bustling feel. It's furnished with pews and other wooden furniture in screened booths, while a smarter main lounge has some panelling and a fruit machine. A fine range of particularly well kept beers includes Bass, Caledonian 80/-, Orkney Dark Island, Theakstons Old Peculier, Youngers No 3, and guest ales on handpump or tall fount air pressure; good choice of malt whiskies. Popular and generously served home-made lunchtime food includes filled french bread (£2.70), filled baked potatoes (£3), macaroni cheese (£3.30), steak pie or lamb stew (£3.50), chicken curry (£3.95), and fresh breaded haddock (£4); cheery staff. Standing in the narrow cobbled lane outside it would be easy to forget that this is the very heart of the city's shopping centre, with Union Street almost literally overhead. *(Recommended by Ian and Nita Cooper, Andrew Rogers, Amanda Milsom)*

Free house ~ Licensee Peter Birnie ~ Real ale ~ Lunchtime meals and snacks (not Sun) ~ (01224) 640597 ~ Children lunchtime only ~ No nearby parking ~ Folk music Sunday eves ~ Open 11-midnight; 12.30-11 Sun

APPLECROSS (Highland) NG7144 Map 11

Applecross Inn

Off A896 S of Shieldaig

Wonderfully placed in a beautiful bay, this friendly compact inn is more popular than you might expect from the loneliness of the setting, and you'll usually find a number of cheerful locals in the simple but comfortable bar. Reached by a breathtaking drive over the 'pass of the cattle' (one of the highest in Britain), it's particularly well regarded for its meals, with the bar menu usually including sandwiches (from £1.50), home-made vegetable soup (£1.75), nice venison or cheese burgers (£2.15), garlic mushrooms (£2.50), fresh deep-fried cod or haddock (£4.95), squat lobster curry or half a dozen local oysters (£5.95), delicious queen scallops in a cream wine and mushroom sauce or dressed local crab salad (£7.50), sirloin steak (£9.95), and puddings like home-baked apple crumble (£2.50); you must book for the no-smoking restaurant. Darts, dominoes, pool (winter only) and juke box (unless there are musicians in the pub); a good choice of around 50 malt whiskies, and efficient service. There is a nice garden by the shore with tables. Bedrooms are small and simple but adequate, all with a sea view; marvellous breakfasts. They may warm food for babies, and highchairs are available. You can hire mountain bikes. *(Recommended by Paula*

Williams, Steve Radley, K M Crook, Mr and Mrs Archibald, Bronwen and Steve Wrigley, Andrew Hazeldine, E Locker, David and Judy Walmsley, D G Clarke)

Free house ~ Licensee Judith Fish ~ Meals and snacks (12-9 in summer; 12-2, 7-9 in winter) ~ Restaurant ~ (01520) 744262 ~ Children welcome until 8.30 ~ Open 11-11(midnight Fri, 11.30 Sat); 12-11 Sun (12-9 Nov-Mar); cl 2.30-5 Mon-Thur from Nov to Mar; closed 1 Jan ~ Bedrooms: £22.50/£45

ARDFERN (Strathclyde) NM8004 Map 11

Galley of Lorne

B8002; village and inn signposted off A816 Lochgilphead—Oban

A good mix of people enjoys this relaxing inn, ideally placed across from Loch Craignish; one reader spotted a retired colonel type supping with a dreadlocked gentleman with a nosering. Seats on a sheltered terrace have marvellous views over the sea and yacht anchorage, and on a cooler day you can appreciate the same outlook from the cosy main bar. There's a log fire, as well as old Highland dress prints and other pictures, big navigation lamps by the bar counter, and an unfussy assortment of furniture, including little winged settles and upholstered window seats on its lino tiles. Good bar food includes home-made soup (£1.95; soup and a sandwich £3.95), haggis with whisky and cream (£3.25), lunchtime open sandwiches (from £3.50), ploughman's or burgers (from £4.85), good moules marinières (£5.25; large £8.95), curried vegetables with rice (£5.75), home-made steak pie (£5.95), fresh battered sole fillets (£7.85), daily specials like haunch of local venison in port (£9.25) or Loch Craignish langoustines (£9.85), and puddings such as home-made banoffee pie (£3); children's menu (£2.75); spacious restaurant. Quite a few malt whiskies; darts, pool, dominoes, fruit machine, piped music. Count on a good breakfast if you're staying. *(Recommended by Richard Gibbs, Chris and Anne Garnett, John and Sheila French)*

Free house ~ Licensee Susana Garland ~ Meals and snacks ~ Restaurant ~ (01852) 500284 ~ Children welcome ~ Occasional folk music ~ Open 11-2.30, 5-11.30; 11-11.30 Sat; 12-11 Sun; closed 25 Dec ~ Bedrooms: £33.50B/£67B

ARDUAINE (Strathclyde) NM7910 Map 11

Loch Melfort Hotel

On A816 S of Oban and overlooking Asknish Bay

From the wooden seats on the front terrace of this comfortable cream-washed Edwardian hotel there's a magnificent view over the wilderness of the loch and its islands. The airy and modern bar has a pair of powerful marine glasses which you can use to search for birds and seals on the islets and on the coasts of the bigger islands beyond. The creamy walls are papered with nautical charts, there are wheelback chairs around wooden tables, a panelled bar counter, a wooden planked ceiling, a log-effect gas fire, and a relaxed atmosphere. An extensive bar food menu might include home-made soup or sandwiches (£2.95), large filled baguettes (£4.25), a good ploughman's (£5.25), Ormsary venison sausages with caramelised onions (£6.25), home-made burgers (£6.95), half a dozen Ardencaple oysters (£7), local langoustines with herb or garlic butter or their own cured gravadlax with dill and sweet mustard sauce (£9.50), Aberdeen Angus steaks (from £10.50), half a local lobster (from £12.25), and daily specials like chicken liver parfait with peppercorn dressing or freshly dressed local crab; home-made puddings (£3), and children's menu. The main restaurant is no smoking; good wine list and selection of malt whiskies. Passing yachtsmen are welcome to use the mooring and drying facilities, and hot showers. It's a short stroll from the hotel through grass and wild flowers to the rocky foreshore, where the licensees keep their own lobster pots and nets. From late April to early June the walks through the neighbouring Arduaine woodland gardens are lovely. The comfortable bedrooms have sea views. *(Recommended by Peter Marshall, Colin Thompson, John and Barbara Burns, Stephen Holman, Julie and Steve Anderton)*

Free house ~ Licensees Philip and Rosalind Lewis ~ Meals and snacks (12-2.30, 6-9) ~ Restaurant ~ (01852) 200233 ~ Children welcome ~ Open 10-11; cl from Hogmanay to mid Feb ~ Bedrooms: £72.50B/£105B

ARDVASAR (Isle of Skye) NG6203 Map 11

Ardvasar Hotel

A851 at S of island; just past Armadale pier where the summer car ferries from Mallaig dock

A good place for a meal, this friendly and comfortably modernised white stone inn sits on the edge of the Sound of Sleat, with fine views across the water to the dramatic mountains of Knoydart. The menu might include home-made dishes like country-style lamb and vegetable broth (£2.50), lentil and cheese bake with provençale sauce (£6.30), roast prime rib of Scottish beef with bordelaise sauce (£6.80), fresh dressed local crab (£8), roasted local pheasant breast with venison and apple and calvados sauce (£12.90), large baked scallops with grapes, cheese, mustard and wine sauce (£13.90), and puddings like warm apricot and marmalade almond flan or blueberry cheesecake (from £2.25). The simple public bar has stripped pews and kitchen chairs, while the smartly modern cocktail bar is furnished with plush wall seats and stools around dimpled copper coffee tables on the patterned carpet, and Highland dress prints on the cream hessian-and-wood walls. A room off the comfortable hotel lounge has armchairs around an attractive coal-effect gas fire; darts, dominoes, cribbage, pool, pinball, juke box, fruit machine, and background music. Well kept Reepham Velvet and maybe a weekly guest beer tapped from the cask, and lots of malt whiskies. The hotel is handy for the Clan Donald centre. *(Recommended by Colin Draper, Walter and Susan Rinaldi-Butcher, Stephen Holman; more reports please)*

Free house ~ Licensees Bill and Gretta Fowler ~ Real ale ~ Bar meals and snacks (12-2, 5-7 and 8-9) ~ Restaurant ~ (01471) 844223 ~ Children welcome until 8 ~ Live entertainment in winter ~ Open 12(12.30 Sun)-11; closed all day Mon; Jan/Feb open 5-11 only ~ Bedrooms: £45B/£70B

ARROCHAR (Strathclyde) NN2904 Map 11

Village Inn

A814, just off A83 W of Loch Lomond

The oldest part of this notably friendly place was built as a manse for the local church in the last century, but it's the more recent informal dining area that readers consider the real heart of the place. It's very comfortable and atmospheric, with a candle on each table, lots of bare wood, soft traditional piped music, and lovely views (over the shore road) of the head of Loch Long, and the hills around The Cobbler, the main peak opposite. Steps lead down to the bar, which has an open fire. Good home-made food includes large filled rolls, stilton and broccoli quiche (£4.70), haggis, neeps and tatties (£5.20), grilled trout with almonds (£6.40), venison, honey and mushroom pie (£7.55), excellent fresh fish such as herring in oatmeal and succulent steamed mussels, daily specials like roast duck breast on peach sauce with a citrus fruit dressing, and puddings such as sticky toffee pudding (£2.60); children's menu. Service is efficient but unobtrusive, and the sociable landlord makes a point of circulating – ready for a chat if customers want it. Well kept Maclays 70/-, 80/- and Wallace IPA, Heather Fraoch and three weekly changing guests on handpump, and 42 malt whiskies; piped music. Booking is recommended for the restaurant in the evenings. *(Recommended by Sarah and Brian Fox, Mrs Angela Power, Dr Jim Mackay, Simon and Karen Lemieux, James Paterson, Mr and Mrs Scott-Gall)*

Maclays ~ Manager Mrs Beverly Paterson ~ Real ale ~ Meals and snacks (12-10) ~ Restaurant ~ (01301) 702279 ~ Children welcome until 8pm ~ Occasional traditional music ~ Open 11am-midnight; 11am-1am Sat ~ Bedrooms: £35B/£50B

BRIG O' TURK (Central) NN5306 Map 11

Byre

A821 Callander—Trossachs

The name byre means cowshed, so this carefully converted place has come a long way since it was built in the 18th c; it's now a lovely secluded spot for a relaxed, tranquil meal. The setting is delightful, on the edge of a network of forest and lochside tracks in the Queen Elizabeth Forest Park – lots of walking, cycling, and fishing. The cosy, spotless beamed bar has prints and old photographs of the area, some decorative plates, stuffed wildlife, comfortable brass-studded black dining chairs, an open fire, and rugs on the stone and composition floor. Using fresh local produce, the good bar food includes home-made soup (£2.10), sandwiches (from £2.75), haggis, neeps and tatties (£2.95), filled baked potatoes (£3.25), mushroom stroganoff (£4.95), deep-fried haddock or wild game casserole (£5.95), chicken, bacon and haggis with a whisky and grain mustard sauce (£6.50), and puddings (£2.95); service is prompt and friendly. The more elaborate menu in the no-smoking restaurant is popular in the evenings – it's worth booking then. No bar food on Saturday evenings, though you can eat the restaurant menu in the bar. Well kept Maclays 70/-, Wallace IPA and guests on handpump, maybe under light blanket pressure, and 20 malt whiskies; traditional Scottish piped music. There are tables under parasols outside. *(Recommended by A Muir, Susan and John Douglas, Roger and Christine Mash, H L Dennis, Bill and Brenda Lemon)*

Free house ~ Licensees Liz and Eugene Maxwell ~ Real ale ~ Meals and snacks ~ Restaurant ~ (01877) 376292 ~ Children welcome ~ Open 12-3, 6-11 Mon-Sat (except cl all day Tues); 12.30-11 Sun; cl Mon-Thurs in winter

BROUGHTY FERRY (Tayside) NO4630 Map 11

Fishermans Tavern £

12 Fort St; turning off shore road

The well kept real ales can change daily at this unspoilt, bustling and friendly town pub. The impressive choice typically includes Belhaven 70/- and St Andrews, Boddingtons, Maclays 80/-, and three guests, all on handpump or tall fount air pressure; there's also a good choice of malt whiskies, some local country wines, and a draught wheat beer. The little brown-carpeted snug on the right with its nautical tables, light pink soft fabric seating, basket-weave wall panels and beige lamps is the more lively bar, and on the left is a secluded lounge area. The carpeted back bar (popular with diners) has a Victorian fireplace; dominoes and fruit machine, and an open coal fire. Lunchtime bar food includes filled rolls or home-made steak and gravy pie (£1.10), prawns in ginger and garlic breadcrumb coating (£2.25), filled jacket potatoes (£3.10), hot Mexican tortilla with spicy chicken, chilli and tomato filling (£3.25) and specials like haunch of venison in red wine sauce (£5.50); enjoyable breakfasts. Disabled lavatories, and baby changing facilities. The breakfast room is no smoking. The landlord also runs the well preserved Speedwell Bar in Dundee. The nearby seafront gives a good view of the two long, low Tay bridges. *(Recommended by R M Macnaughton, Susan and John Douglas, Tom McLean, Roger Huggins, L G Milligan, Eric Locker)*

Free house ~ Licensee Jonathan Stewart ~ Real ale ~ Lunchtime meals 12-2.30 and snacks all day (Jul/Aug no food exc high teas for guests; snacks only Sun) ~ Restaurant ~ (01382) 775941 ~ Children welcome ~ Open 11-midnight(1am Sat); 12.30-midnight Sun ~ Bedrooms: £19/£38

CANONBIE (Dumfries and Galloway) NY3976 Map 9

Riverside

Village signposted from A7

Good quality ingredients and suppliers are the rule at this civilised little inn, with most of the food free range and local; breads are organic, cheeses unpasteurised, and fresh fish delivered three times a week. Tables are usually laid for dining and the varied bar menu, on two blackboards, might include soups such as smoked ham and lentil, mushroom and mustard or tomato and orange (£2.20), with home-made breads like tomato and courgette or Guinness and treacle loaf; other dishes include potted guinea fowl with mushrooms or duck terrine (£4.25), stilton and leek crumble (£5.25), dressed crab salad (£5.75), half a corn-fed free-range chicken marinated in lemon, rosemary and balsamic vinegar, Loch Fyne oysters or fresh langoustines (£6.95), enormous Aga-roasted cod with cheese and onion (£7.95), thick barnsley chop (£8.95), rib-eye steak (£11.95), and fine puddings such as rhubarb and orange crumble or marmalade bread and butter pudding (£3.50). They do a three course

Sunday lunch. Well kept Yates Bitter on handpump – a fair bit cheaper than the average price for a pint in the area – along with maybe a guest beer or two, and a dozen or so malt whiskies. The range of properly kept and served wines has always been a highlight; they've recently changed their supplier, but continue to have a very wide choice, with quite a few by the glass or half bottle. The communicating rooms of the bar have a mix of chintzy furnishings and dining chairs, pictures on the walls for sale, and some stuffed wildlife; half of the bar and the dining room are no smoking. In summer – when it can get very busy – there are tables under the trees on the front grass. Over the quiet road, a public playground runs down to the Border Esk (the inn can arrange fishing permits), and there are lovely walks nearby. Though we receive more reports on this pub than just about any other in Scotland, over the last few months they haven't been as unswervingly enthusiastic as we've come to expect: readers don't always find the service and welcome as consistent as the food. *(Recommended by Dr Michael Allen, K F Mould, Vann and Terry Prime, K M Crook, R Macnaughton, Paul S McPherson, Peter Marshall, Joy and Peter Heatherley, Alan Lillie, Wm Van Laaten, Mr and Mrs G Dundas, John and Beryl Knight, John and Barbara Burns, Luke Worthington, Christine and Malcolm Ingram)*

Free house ~ Licensee Robert Phillips ~ Real ale ~ Meals and snacks ~ Children welcome ~ Restaurant (cl Sun) ~ (013873) 71512/71295 ~ Open 11-2.30, 6.30-11; closed 2 weeks in Feb and maybe Nov, Dec 25/26 and Jan 1/2 ~ Bedrooms: £55B/£78B

CARBOST (Isle of Skye) NG3732 Map 11

Old Inn

This is the Carbost on the B8009, in the W of the central part of the island

Useful for walkers and climbers, and in a nice spot beside Loch Harport, this straightforward old stone house is one of the most traditionally pubby places on the island. From the terrace, there are fine views of the loch and the harsh craggy peaks of the Cuillin Hills. The three simple areas of the main bare-board bar are knocked through into one, and furnished with red leatherette settles, benches and seats, amusing cartoons on the part-whitewashed and part-stripped stone walls, and a peat fire; darts, pool, cribbage, dominoes, and piped traditional music. A small selection of sustaining bar meals includes cock-a-leekie soup (£1.70), sandwiches, chestnut and stilton pâté with highland oatcakes (£2.25), haggis, neeps and tatties (£5.50), spinach and cashew nut strudel (£5.65), and fresh cod in beer batter (£6.45). Several malt whiskies – including Talisker, fresh from the distillery just 100 yards from the pub (there are guided tours, with samples, in summer). Children's play area. Non-residents can come for the breakfasts if they book the night before, and the bedrooms in a separate annexe have sea views. As we went to press they were building a new bunkhouse and shower block for the loch's increasing number of yachtsmen, and they plan to add a small restaurant and their own pontoon. *(Recommended by Nigel Woolliscroft, Steve Radley, Julie and Steve Anderton)*

Free house ~ Licensee Deirdre Cooper ~ Meals and snacks (12-2, 6.30-10) ~ (01478) 640205 ~ Children welcome till 8pm ~ Occasional live music ~ Open 11-midnight(11.30 Sat), 12.30-11 Sun; winter closed 2.30-5 ~ Bedrooms: £24.50B/£49B

CAWDOR (Highland) NH8450 Map 11

Cawdor Tavern

Just off B9090 in Cawdor village; follow signs for post office and village centre

Lots of improvements to this Highland village pub over the last few months, with changes to the bar, lounge and restaurant adding to the surprisingly stately feel of the place; it looks rather modern from the outside, so the elegant fittings inside are quite a surprise. Most impressive is the beautiful oak panelling in the substantial rather clubby lounge, gifted to the tavern by a former Lord Cawdor and salvaged from the nearby castle; more recent panelling is incorporated into an impressive new ceiling. The public bar on the right now has a brick fireplace housing an old cast-iron stove, as well as elaborate wrought-iron wall lamps, chandeliers laced with bric-a-brac, and an imposing pillared serving counter. Good bar food might include sandwiches, fresh mussels steamed with garlic, shallots, cream and white wine (£3.15), home-made salmon and crabcakes with a chive cream sauce (£3.25), smoked seafood platter (£4.25), seafood trio with white wine and dill sauce (£8.95), breast of pheasant wrapped in bacon with red wine and orange jus (£9.95), and puddings like sticky ginger pudding with home-made vanilla ice cream (£3.95); the restaurant is partly no smoking. They usually serve snacks all day in summer. Orkney Dark Island, Tetleys and Worthingtons on handpump, and over a hundred malt whiskies; darts, pool, cribbage, dominoes, board games, cards, fruit machine, video games, juke box, piped music. There are tables on the front terrace, with tubs of flowers, roses, and creepers climbing the supports of a big awning. *(Recommended by Neil Townend, Justin Hulford, Richard Dolphin, J G Kirby)*

Free house ~ Licensee Norman Sinclair ~ Real ale ~ Meals and snacks (12-2, 5.30-9) ~ Restaurant ~ (01667) 404777 ~ Children welcome away from public bar ~ Open 11-11 (12.30am Sat); 12.30-11 Sun; winter weekdays cl between 3 and 5; closed 25 Dec

CLACHAN SEIL (Highland) NM7718 Map 11

Tigh an Truish

This island is linked by a bridge via B844, off A816 S of Oban

Very much a traditional local, this 18th-c inn is near a lovely anchorage and set next to the attractive old bridge which joins Seil Island to the mainland. The unpretentious and informal L-shaped bar has pine-clad walls and ceiling, some fixed wall benches along with the wheelback and other chairs, tartan curtains for the bay windows overlooking the inlet, prints and oil paintings, and a woodburning stove in one room, with open fires in the others; pleasant service. Bar food includes home-made soup (£1.90), home-made nut burgers (£3.75), moules marinières (£4.95), steak and ale pie or sole mornay (£6.50), locally caught prawns with garlic mayonnaise (£6.95), and puddings such as treacle tart; the dining room is no smoking. Well kept McEwans 80/- and regular guest beers on handpump, and a good choice of malt whiskies; darts, dominoes and piped music. There are some seats in the small garden, and they have their own filling station just opposite. There's a rather jolly story about the origin of the pub's name. *(Recommended by Pamela and Merlyn Horswell, M A Buchanan, Paul and Ursula Randall, Julie and Steve Anderton, Jean and George Dundas)*

Free house ~ Licensee Miranda Brunner ~ Real ale ~ Meals and snacks 12-2.15, 6-8.30; no meals winter evenings ~ (01852) 300242 ~ Children in eating area ~ Occasional live music ~ Open 11am (12.30 Sun)-11.30pm; in winter open 11-2.30, 5-11.30; cl 25 Dec, 1 Jan ~ Self-catering twin/double flats: £40B

CREEBRIDGE (Dumfries and Galloway) NX4165 Map 9

Creebridge House

Minnigaff, just E of Newton Stewart

This sizeable country house hotel is set in three acres of gardens and woodland – a fine place to stay with lots to do nearby. Tables under cocktail parasols out on the front terrace look across a pleasantly planted lawn, where you can play croquet. The welcoming and neatly kept carpeted bar has Black Sheep, Orkney Dark Island and Timothy Taylor Landlord on handpump, as well as about 40 malt whiskies, and that great rarity for Scotland, a bar billiards table. Enjoyable brasserie-style food includes home-made soup (£2.10), lunchtime sandwiches (from £1.95; elaborate baguettes and filled rolls from £3.95), duck liver parfait with orange and apricot chutney (£3.95), mushroom risotto in a puff pastry case (£5.25), cod in beer batter or chicken curry (£5.95), beef stir fry (£6.95), filo parcels of lamb on onion marmalade with roast fennel and finished with a rich port jus (£9.50), and good steaks (from £10.95); daily specials, excellent fresh fish on Fridays, and Sunday lunchtime carvery in the comfortable restaurant. Meats are local and well hung, and presentation careful with good attention to detail. Fruit machine, comfortably pubby furniture, and maybe unobtrusive piped music. The garden restaurant is no smoking. They can arrange fishing, walking, pony-trekking, and complimentary golf at the local golf course.

(Recommended by Neil Townend, Julian Holland; more reports please)

Free house ~ Licensees Susan and Chris Walker ~ Real ale ~ Meals and snacks ~ Restaurant ~ (01671) 402121 ~ Children welcome ~ Open 12-2.30, 6-11.30; 12.30-2, 7-11 Sun; cl 26 Dec ~ Bedrooms: £55B/£90B

CRINAN (Strathclyde) NR7894 Map 11

Crinan Hotel

A816 NE from Lochgilphead, then left on to B841, which terminates at the village

Regular visitors say this beautifully positioned large hotel never rests on its laurels, and that instead there's always some sort of improvement going on. Picture windows in the two stylish upstairs bars make the most of the marvellous views of the busy entrance basin of the Crinan Canal, with its fishing boats and yachts wandering out towards the Hebrides. The simpler wooden-floored public bar (opening on to a side terrace) has a cosy stove and kilims on the seats, and the cocktail bar has a nautical theme with wooden floors, oak and walnut panelling, antique tables and chairs, and sailing pictures and classic yachts framed in walnut on a paper background of rust and green paisley, matching the tartan upholstery. The Gallery bar is done in pale terracotta and creams and has a central bar with stools, Lloyd Loom tables and chairs, and lots of plants. Very good bar food (lunchtimes only) might include home-made soup (£3.50), smoked haddock (£5.95), local mussels or cold ham salad (£8.95), locally smoked wild salmon (£10.75), seafood stew (£13.75), and a pudding such as lemon tart or chocolate roulade (£3.75); Scottish farmhouse cheddar (from a 75lb cheese) with oatcakes. You can get sandwiches and so forth from their coffee shop. Theakstons Best, a good wine list, a good few malt whiskies, and freshly squeezed orange juice. The restaurants are very formal. *(Recommended by Walter Reid, D P Brown; more reports please)*

Free house ~ Licensee Nicholas Ryan ~ Real ale ~ Bar meals lunchtime only (12-2.30) ~ Restaurants ~ (01546) 830261 ~ Children in eating area of bar ~ Open 11(12 Sun)-11; winter 11-2.30, 5-11 ~ Bedrooms: £60B/£120B

CROMARTY (Highland) NH7867 Map 11

Royal

Marine Terrace

A wonderfully relaxing place to stay, this friendly old-fashioned seaside hotel is pretty much the centre of things in this beautifully restored sleepy village at the tip of the Black Isle. Most of the rooms and a long covered porch area look out over the sea, and a couple of picnic-sets outside enjoy the same tranquil view. The comfortable lounge has quite a bright feel, as well as pink painted walls, cushioned wall seats and leatherette armchairs, small curtained alcoves with model ships, and old local photos; piped Scottish music. A room to the right with a fireplace is a bit like a cosy sitting room; it leads into an elegant lounge for residents. The basic public bar, popular with locals, has a separate entrance; pool, darts, cribbage, dominoes, TV, juke box. Good bar food includes deep-fried haggis balls (£3.95), local mussels with pâté and tomato sauce (£4.40), smoked salmon and prawn tagliatelle or vegetable risotto (£6.50), various crêpes such as chicken with spicy rice, curry sauce and coconut (£6.60), scampi, mussels and prawns sautéed with onions and bacon (£9.25), and daily specials such as venison in red wine or huge prawns (£9.95); children's menu. Around three dozen malt whiskies, and very friendly service – both the barmaid and the landlord spent a good while chatting to us on our recent visit. The porch (a nice bit to eat in) is no smoking. It's hard to believe Cromarty was once a thriving port; a nice little museum a short stroll away sparkily illustrates its heritage. You can get boat trips out to see the local bottlenose dolphins, and maybe whales too in summer. *(Recommended by Neil Townend, Paul and Ursula Randall)*

Free house ~ Licensees J and B Shearer ~ Meals and snacks (12-2, 5.30-9) ~ Restaurant ~ (01381) 600217 ~ Children welcome ~ Open 11-11; 12-11 Sun ~ Bedrooms: £35B/£58B

EAST LINTON (Lothian) NT5977 Map 11

Drovers

5 Bridge Street (B1407), just off A1 Haddington—Dunbar

Atmospheric and genuinely pubby, the main bar of this comfortable old inn feels a bit like a welcoming living room as you enter from the pretty village street. Comfortable armchairs and nostalgic piped jazz create a very relaxed air, with faded rugs on the wooden floor, a basket of logs in front of the woodburning stove, and fresh flowers and newspapers adding to the convivial appeal. There's a goat's head on a pillar in the middle of the room, plenty of hops around the bar counter, and a mix of prints and pictures (most of which are for sale) on the half panelled, half red-painted walls. A good range of six real ales, changing weekly, might include Adnams Broadside, Caledonian 80/-, Fullers ESB, Orkney Dark Island, Vaux Waggle Dance and Wadworths 6X; good service from the two sisters in charge and their smartly dressed staff. A similar room leads off, and a door opens on to a walled lawn with tables and maybe summer barbecues. Relying on fresh local ingredients delivered daily, the very good food might at lunchtime include soups such as carrot, parsnip and ginger (£2.25), skillet of black pudding in a bacon and tomato sauce (£3.95), blue cheese, celery and onion flan (£6.50), lamb, vegetable and potato casserole or dressed local crab (£6.95), and grilled salmon with herb and tomato butter (£7.25), with evening meals like caramelised salmon in a raspberry and balsamic jus (£10.95), bacon-wrapped scallops with risotto and a pepper sauce (£11.95), and their speciality chargrilled honey and ginger pig. Part of the upstairs restaurant is no smoking. The gents' has a copy of the day's *Scotsman* newspaper on the wall. The elaborate fountain on the village's tiny green is worth a look. *(Recommended by R M Corlett, Andy and Jill Kassube)*

Free house ~ Licensees Michelle and Nicola Findlay ~ Real ale ~ Meals and snacks (not Sat evening) ~ Restaurant ~ (01620) 860298 ~ Children welcome ~ Live music Weds evening at 9 ~ Open 11.30-2.30, 5-11; 12.30-midnight Sun; closed 25 Dec, 1 Jan

EDINBURGH (Lothian) NT2573 Map 11

The two main areas here for finding good pubs, both main entries and Lucky Dips, are around Rose Street (just behind Princes Street in the New Town) and along or just off the top part of the Royal Mile in the Old Town. In both areas parking can be difficult at lunchtime, but is not such a problem in the evening.

Abbotsford

Rose Street; E end, beside South St David St

Originally built for Jenners department store, this small and gently formal single bar pub is something of a long-standing institution for city folk. Friendly and cheerful, it has dark wooden half panelled walls, a highly polished Victorian island bar counter, long wooden tables and leatherette benches, and a welcoming log effect gas fire; there are prints on the walls and a notably handsome ornate plaster-moulded high ceiling. The range of well kept beers changes every week, but there are usually half a dozen guests like Aviemore Red Murdoch, Flowers Original, Greenmantle, and Inveralmond Ossians alongside the Caledonian 80/- and Deuchars IPA; they recently installed a set of air pressure tall founts to serve them in the true Scottsh fashion. Good, reasonably priced food includes soup (£1.30), haggis, neeps and tatties (£4.95; locals reckon it's amongst the best in town), curry (£4.95), a roast of the day (£4.95), breaded haddock (£5.25), medallions of pork with orange and ginger sauce (£6.10) and sirloin steak (£6.50). Over 50 malt whiskies, efficient service from dark-uniformed or white shirted staff. If you're English and they ask for a passport they're just kidding. *(Recommended by Colin Draper, Mr and Mrs Jon Corelis, A Jones, D Parkhurst, Amanda and Simon Southwell)*

Free house ~ Licensee Colin Grant ~ Real ale ~ Lunchtime meals and snacks ~ Restaurant ~ (0131) 2255276 ~ Children in eating area of bar and restaurant ~ Open 11-midnight; closed Sun

Bannermans £

212 Cowgate

A favourite with students, this busy city centre pub seems to be aiming very much at the younger end of the market under its new manageress. On some nights they describe themselves as a pre-club venue, and there might be a DJ with lasers and strobe light effects then. It's rather different in tone earlier in the day, when another innovation over the last few months has been the introduction of a lunchtime buffet (£3.50), with a range of hot and cold dishes like baked potatoes, chilli and curry, and make-your-own sandwiches. They do popular weekend breakfasts. Used to store oysters before it became a pub, it's set underneath some of the tallest buildings in the Old Town, and has a unique warren of simple crypt-like flagstoned rooms with barrel-vaulted ceilings, bare stone walls, wood panelling and pillars at the front, and quite a mixture of wrought iron and wooden tables and chairs. There may a big screen during sporting events. Well kept Caledonian 80/- and Deuchars IPA, and guests like Red McGregor, Theakstons Best, and Youngers No 3, and around 30 malt whiskies; dominoes, cribbage, trivia, cards and board games. *(Recommended by Mr and Mrs Jon Corelis, Terry Barlow, Jenny and Roger Huggins; more reports please)*

Free house ~ Licensee Kevin Doyle ~ Real ale ~ Lunchtime meals and snacks ~ (0131) 556 3254 ~ Children welcome until 7pm away from bar ~ Live music Weds/Sun evenings, maybe DJs Thurs/Fri/Sat ~ Open 11-1am; 11(licensed from 12.30)-midnight Sun

Bow Bar ★ £

80 West Bow

Handily placed just below the castle, this traditional drinking pub usually has between eight and a dozen very well kept real ales served from impressive tall founts made by Aitkens, Mackie & Carnegie, Gaskell & Chambers, and McGlashan, dating from the 1920s. A typical choice would take in Caledonian 80/- and Deuchars IPA, Dent Aviator, Fullers London Pride, Timothy Taylor Landlord, and various changing guests. The grand carved mahogany gantry has an impressive array of malts (over 140) including lots of Macallan variants and cask strength whiskies, as well as a good collection of vodkas (nine) and gins (eight), and, particularly, rums (24); they're an exclusive supplier of Scottish Still Spirit. Basic, but busy and friendly, the spartan rectangular bar has a fine collection of appropriate enamel advertising signs and handsome antique trade mirrors, sturdy leatherette wall seats and heavy narrow tables on its lino floor, cafe-style bar seats, an umbrella stand by the period gas fire, a (silent) prewar radio, a big pendulum clock, and a working barograph. Look out for the antiqued photograph of the bar staff in old-fashioned clothes (and moustaches). Simple, cheap bar snacks – steak pies (£1.20). Cheery and knowledgeable service, and no games or music – just relaxed chat, and the clink of glasses. *(Recommended by Peter Marshall, Andy and Jill Kassube, D Parkhurst, Vann and Terry Prime, A Jones, the Didler)*

Free house ~ Licensee Lee Thorbers ~ Real ale ~ Lunchtime snacks 12-4 (not Sun) ~ (0131) 226 7667 ~ Open 11-11.30; 12.30-11 Sun; closed 25/26 Dec, 1/2 Jan

Guildford Arms

West Register St

Though its choice of beers is quite a draw, this most enjoyable Victorian city pub stands out for its friendly, bustling atmosphere – and its exquisite decor. The main bar has lots of mahogany, glorious colourfully painted plasterwork and ceilings, big original advertising mirrors, and heavy swagged velvet curtains at the arched windows. Refurbished after some recent flooding, the snug little upstairs gallery restaurant gives a dress-circle view of the main bar (notice the lovely old mirror decorated with two tigers on the way up), and under this gallery a little cavern of arched alcoves leads off the bar. They keep a very fine choice of up to eleven real ales on handpump, most of which are usually Scottish, with Belhaven 60/-, Caledonian Deuchars IPA and 80/-, Harviestoun 70/- and Ptarmigan, Orkney Dark Island, and changing guests (three of which are always English). During the Edinburgh festival they usually hold a beer and folk festival. Good choice of malt whiskies; fruit machine, lunchtime piped jazz and classical music. Bar food includes chargrilled steak burger (£4.75), home-made steak pie (£4.85), breaded haddock (£4.95), and daily specials (all under £5); on Sundays they only do filled rolls. It is very popular, but even at its busiest you shouldn't have to wait to be served. No children. *(Recommended by A Jones, Susan and John Douglas, Mr and Mrs Jon Corelis, Neil Townend, the Didler, P Rome, Andy and Jill Kassube, Eric Larkham, Roger Huggins)*

Free house ~ Licensee David Stewart ~ Real ale ~ Lunchtime meals and snacks ~ (0131) 556 4312 ~ Open 11-11(midnight Thurs/Fri/Sat); 12.30-11 Sun

Kays Bar £

39 Jamaica St West; off India St

A favourite with some readers, this cosy and atmospheric little back street pub is bigger than you might think from the outside. John Kay was the original owner selling whisky and wine; wine barrels were hoisted up to the first floor and dispensed through pipes attached to nipples which can still be seen around the light rose. As well as various casks and vats there are old wine and spirits merchant notices, gas-type lamps, well worn red plush wall banquettes and stools around cast-iron tables, and red pillars supporting a red ceiling. A quiet panelled back room leads off, with a narrow plank-panelled pitched ceiling; very warm open coal fire in winter. A good range of constantly changing and interesting real ales might include well kept Belhaven 80/-, Boddingtons, Exe Valley Devon Glory, Exmoor Ale, McEwans 80/-, Theakstons Best and XB, Tomintoul Wild Cat, and Youngers No 3 on handpump; up to 70 malts, between eight and 40 years old and 10 blended whiskies. Simple, good value lunchtime bar food (the price of which never seems to alter) includes soup (95p), haggis, neeps and tatties, chilli or steak pie (£2.60), filled baked potatoes (£2.75) and chicken balti, lasagne or mince and tatties (£3); dominoes and cribbage. *(Recommended by Ian Phillips, A Jones, the Didler, John Cockell, Roger Huggins, David Carr)*

Scottish Courage ~ Tenant David Mackenzie ~ Real ale ~ Lunchtime meals and snacks (12-2.30) ~ (0131) 225 1858 ~ Children in back room until 5pm (must be quiet) ~ Open 11-12(1am Fri/Sat); 11-11 Sun

Ship on the Shore

26 The Shore, Leith (A199)

Easy to spot by the delightfully intricate ship model that serves as a sign, this lovely old pub is right in the heart of what in recent years has become a really rather appealing part of town. In the heyday of Leith's docks (well represented in a reproduction engraving in the dining room) the Ship was a hotel that enjoyed a somewhat bawdy reputation; these days it's well regarded for its very good meals, with quite an emphasis on locally caught fish and seafood. At lunchtime they do a bargain three-course meal for £6.50, as well as soup (£1.95), sandwiches (from £4) and fish and chips (£4.95), while the evening menu might include things like rainbow trout with almond butter (£10.50), stir-fried medallions of monkfish with walnut oil and tomato and courgette brunoise, and grilled black bream on a bed of chinese leaves (£13.95); popular Sunday breakfasts (£5.25). The bar has a number of old painted signs for companies like the East India Bay Co, or Podgie Mullen, fishmonger and greengrocer, as well as wooden chairs, floors and wall benches, ship's lanterns, and compasses and other nautical equipment; piped music. Well kept Caledonian Deuchars IPA and 80/- and Courage Directors on handpump, and a few malt whiskies. Oars and fishing nets hang from the ceiling of the nicely panelled dining room. Tables outside are well placed for the late evening sun. *(Recommended by A Muir, David Unsworth)*

Free house ~ Licensees Kenny Gordon, Roy West ~ Real ale ~ Meals and snacks ~ Restaurant ~ (0131) 555 0409 ~ Children over 8 ~ Open 12-midnight

Starbank ♀ £ ☕

67 Laverockbank Road, off Starbank Road; on main road Granton—Leith

Marvellous views over the Firth of Forth from the picture windows in the neat and airy bar of this comfortably elegant pub, well regarded by readers for its friendly atmosphere and excellent choice of properly kept beers. The range changes all the time, but might include Belhaven 80/-, St Andrews and Sandy Hunters, Broughton Special, Harvieston, Marstons Pedigree, Thwaites, and Timothy Taylor Landlord. A good choice of wines too (all 30 are served by the glass), and 25 malt whiskies. Well presented and tasty home-made bar food (with prices unchanged for the second year running) includes soup (£1.20), madeira herring salad (£2.50), a daily vegetarian dish (£4.25), lasagne or sausage casserole (£4.50), ploughman's (£4.75), baked haddock mornay (£5.25), mixed seafood salad or roast lamb (£5.50), and poached salmon with lemon and herb butter (£6.50). Service is helpful, the conservatory restaurant is no smoking, and there are no noisy games machines or piped music; sheltered back terrace. *(Recommended by Roger Huggins, M A Buchanan, Neil Townend, Ian Phillips, Andy and Jill Kassube)*

Free house ~ Licensee Valerie West ~ Real ale ~ Meals and snacks (12-2.30, 6-9.30; 12-9.30 Sat/Sun) ~ Restaurant ~ (0131) 552 4141 ~ Children welcome till 8pm ~ Monthly jazz ~ Open 11-11(12 Thurs/Fri/Sat); 12.30-11 Sun

ELIE (Fife) NO4900 Map 11

Ship

Harbour

The setting of this welcoming harbourside pub is hard to beat if you like the seaside, as tables on the terrace behind look directly over Elie's broad sands and along the bay. In summer there's a barbecue out here, and it's a fine spot for watching the Sunday matches of the pub's successful cricket team, who use the beach as their pitch. Tables in the restaurant enjoy the same view. The villagey, unspoilt beamed bar has a lively nautical feel, as well as friendly locals and staff, coal fires, and partly panelled walls studded with old prints and maps; there's a simple carpeted back room. Good bar food – decent value for the area – includes dishes such as soup (£1.50), king prawns in garlic butter (£4.50), vegetable crumble (£6), fresh local haddock and chips (£6.20), steak pie (£6.95), poached salmon with lime mayonnaise (£7.50), Scottish steaks (from £12), and puddings (£3.50); children's menu, and Sunday lunch (£7.95; children £3.95). Well kept Belhaven Best and 80/-, and Theakstons Best; darts, dominoes, captain's mistress, cribbage and shut-the-box. Bedrooms are next door, in a guesthouse run by the same family; if you stay there are concessions on the pub's food and wine. *(Recommended by Eric Locker; more reports please)*

Free house ~ Licensees Richard and Jill Philip ~ Real ale ~ Meals ~ Restaurant ~ (01333) 330246 ~ Children welcome (not in front bar) ~ Open 11-midnight(1am Fri and Sat); 12.30-11 Sun; closed 25 Dec ~ Bedrooms: £30B/£50B

FORT AUGUSTUS (Highland) NH3709 Map 11

Lock

Once the village post office, this is a proper pub, full of locals and characters and with a welcoming and amusing landlord. Well placed at the foot of Loch Ness, it's right by the first lock of the flight of five that start the Caledonian Canal's climb to Loch Oich. The atmosphere is lively and cheerful, especially in summer when it can be packed in the evenings with a good mix of regulars and boating people (it can get a bit smoky then). Good value substantial food, with generous helpings of chips, includes a pint of mussels (£4.50), seafood chowder or fresh Mallaig haddock (£4.95), seafood stew (£5.95), game casserole (£6.50), grilled sea trout (£7.95), salmon steak in filo pastry (£10.50), venison (£11.25), and daily specials; quite a bit of the space is set aside for people eating – one part is no smoking. The fish dishes – particularly good in the upstairs restaurant – are very fresh indeed, and no wonder: Mr MacLennen has his own fishmonger's shop next door. The bar is homely and comfortable, with a gently faded decor and some stripped stone, a big open fire, and unobtrusive piped music; Tetleys and a beer named for the pub under light blanket pressure, and a fine choice of about 100 malt whiskies (in generous measures). The restaurant is no smoking. *(Recommended by Justin Hulford, Simon and Amanda Southwell, Neil Townend, Mrs Kay Neville-Rolfe, Colin Draper, P R and S A White, Sue and Bob Ward)*

Free house ~ James MacLennen ~ Real ale ~ Meals (12-3, 6-10) and snacks ~ Evening restaurant ~ (01320) 366302 ~ Children in eating area of bar and in restaurant ~ Folk music Mon, Tues and Weds evenings ~ Open 11-midnight(11.30 Sat); 12.30-11 Sun; cl 25 Dec and 1 Jan

GIFFORD (Lothian) NT5368 Map 11

Tweeddale Arms

High St

Probably the oldest building in this quiet Borders village, this efficiently run hotel is well liked by readers for its good food and relaxed atmosphere. The comfortably modernised lounge bar has cushioned wall seats, chairs and bar chairs, dried flowers in baskets, Impressionist prints on the apricot coloured walls, and a big curtain that divides off the eating area. Lunchtime bar food typically includes very good soups (£1.50), deep-fried haggis on creamed onion sauce or smoked trout mousse (£3.75), battered haddock (£5.50), creamed leeks and mushrooms in puff pastry (£5.75), sautéed chicken strips and vegetables in garlic butter (£5.95), leg of lamb in wholegrain mustard sauce (£6), Aberdeen Angus steak (£9.50), and puddings (£2.40); sandwiches are available all day (except Sundays). In the evening you may be able to order dishes in the bar from the restaurant. The well kept Belhaven Best and guest beers such as Borders SOB, Broughton Black Douglas, and Morlands Old Speckled Hen are usually rather cheaper in the public bar than in the lounge; cheerful service. Quite a few malt whiskies, and charming, efficient and friendly service; dominoes, fruit machine, cribbage, and piped music. If you're staying, the tranquil hotel lounge is especially comfortable, with antique tables and paintings, chinoiserie chairs and chintzy easy chairs, an oriental rug on one wall, a splendid corner sofa and magazines on a table. The inn looks across the peaceful green to the 300-year-old avenue of lime trees leading to the former home of the Marquesses of Tweeddale. *(Recommended by Nick and Meriel Cox, R M Macnaughton, Neil Townend, Comus Elliott, Paul and Ursula Randall, John and Joan Wyatt)*

Free house ~ Licensee Mrs W Crook ~ Real ale ~ Meals and snacks ~ Restaurant ~ (01620) 810240 ~ Children welcome ~ Open 11-11(midnight Sat/Sun) ~ Bedrooms: £42.75B/£65B

GLASGOW (Strathclyde) NS5865 Map 11

Auctioneers £

6 North Court, St Vincent Place

Sir Winston Churchill and William Burrell are just two of the figures who passed through these auction rooms when they were still serving their original purpose, the latter returning a painting because he couldn't afford it. The building has been very well converted into a pub, with the valuation booths around the edges of the main high-ceilinged flagstoned room transformed into intimate little booths, and plenty of junk and antiques dotted about as if they were for sale, with lot numbers clearly displayed. You'd probably be most tempted to bid for the goods in the smarter red-painted side room, which rather than the old lamps, radios, furnishings and golf clubs elsewhere has framed paintings, statues, and even an old rocking horse, as well as comfortable leather sofas, unusual lamp fittings, a big fireplace, and an elegant old dresser with incongruous china figures. There's quite a bustling feel in the bar (especially in the evenings), which has lots of old sporting photos, programmes and shirts along one of the panelled walls. Well kept Caledonian 80/- and Deuchars IPA, Orkney Dark Island and a changing guest on handpump, and over 40 malt whiskies; friendly service. Bar food includes soup (£1.45), hot filled baguettes or baked potatoes (from £2.95), haggis, neeps and tatties or vegetable curry (£3.95), fish and chips or steak pie (£4.45), and ribeye steaks or Louisiana chicken (£4.95). Walking past you might not instantly spot this is a pub: the windows still look like a shop front, replete with more junk and a shop dummy. Another impressive conversion, the Counting House (see below), is just around the corner. *(Recommended by Richard Lewis, A Muir)*

Bass ~ Manager Ian Donnelly ~ Real ale ~ Meals and snacks (11-9.45) ~ (0141) 229 5851 ~ Children in side room if eating, until 8pm ~ Open 11am-midnight; 12.30-12 Sun

Babbity Bowster £

16-18 Blackfriars St

One of our favourite Glasgow pubs, this lively but stylish 18th-c town house feels rather like a continental cafe bar. Welcoming yet cosmpolitan, the simply decorated light interior has fine tall windows, well lit photographs and big pen-and-wash drawings in modern frames of Glasgow and its people and musicians, dark grey stools and wall seats around dark grey tables on the stripped wooden boards, and an open peat fire. The bar opens on to a small terrace which has tables under cocktail parasols, and boules. All day food includes several home-made soups in three sizes (from £1.50 to £3.95), croque monsieur (£3.25), haggis, tatties and neeps (£3.75; they also do a vegetarian version), vegetable chilli hot pot (£4.50), stovies (from £4.75), pork, garlic and bean casserole or ratatouille (£4.75), west coast mussels (£5.50), and daily specials. They serve good value breakfasts from 8am to 10.30 (till 12.30 Sunday), and there are more elaborate meals in the airy upstairs restaurant. Watch out for special offers on food and drinks at various times of the day. Well kept Maclays 70/- and 80/-, and changing guest beers on air pressure tall fount, a remarkably sound collection of wines, malt whiskies, freshly squeezed orange juice and good tea and coffee. Enthusiastic service is consistently efficient and friendly, taking its example from the energetic landlord. They have live Celtic music at weekends (piped at other times); dominoes. Car park. *(Recommended by Vann and Terry Prime, Walter Reid, A Muir, Eric Larkham, Monica Shelley, Nigel Woolliscroft, Ian Phillips, Andy and Jill Kassube, Stephen Holman, Richard Lewis)*

Free house ~ Licensee Fraser Laurie ~ Real ale ~ Meals and snacks (12-10) ~ Restaurant ~ 0141 552 5055 ~ Children welcome ~ Acoustic music at weekends ~ Open 11-midnight; 12-midnight Sun; closed 25 Dec and 1 Jan ~ Bedrooms: £45B/£65B

Blackfriars £

36 Bell Street

The imaginative range of drinks at this relaxed and cosmopolitan corner house has something for everyone: as well as half a dozen real ales, some from smaller independent breweries, they have 10 wines by the glass, 30 or so malt whiskies, and, more unusually, a blackboard menu listing a dozen different coffees, from Brazilian Santos to Colombian Supremo, all with helpful tasting notes. With its newspaper rack, candles on tables, and big shop-front windows looking over the street, the vibrant bare-boards bar manages to combine the atmosphere of a traditional pub with a younger cafe-like buzz, and though it's definitely somewhere students feel at home (there's the usual city-centre array of posters for plays and arts events), you'll usually find a real range of types and ages scattered about the spacious room. Opposite the long bar itself is a big interestingly framed mirror above a cushioned wallseat, while elsewhere are a couple of tables fashioned from barrels, and up by the coffee menu a section with green cloths on all the tables; piped music, loudish some evenings. Changing regularly, the well kept beers might include Arrols 80/-, Belhaven 60/-, Caledonian Deuchars IPA, Houston Killellan, Isle of Skye Wee Ferry and Tetleys; they have a good range of European bottled beers too, and farm cider. Lunchtime bar food such as sandwiches, a vegetarian pasta dish (from £3.50), sausages in red wine gravy with mustard mash (£3.95), and steak and ale pie (£4.95); in the evening they have pizzas (from £3.50), and a snackier 'tapas' menu with nachos, dips and the like; popular Sunday brunch menu. Friendly service. In the basement is a long established

Sunday night comedy club, with jazz on a Thursday (cover charge for these); on weekend evenings they might have free jazz in the bar as well. *(Recommended by Richard Lewis, SLC, Andy and Jill Kassube, David Unsworth)*

Free house ~ Licensee Alan Cunningham ~ Real ale ~ Meals and snacks ~ (0141) 552 5924 ~ Children in daytime if eating ~ Live jazz some weekend evenings in bar, every Thurs in basement; Sun comedy night ~ Open 11-midnight

Counting House £

24 George Square

Breathtakingly grand, and astonishingly roomy, this imposing place is a remarkable conversion by Wetherspoons of what was formerly a premier branch of the Royal Bank of Scotland. It's a perfect antidote for those who get a slight feeling of claustrophobia in some other Glasgow pubs. A lofty richly decorated coffered ceiling culminates in a great central dome, with well lit nubile caryatids doing a fine supporting job in the corners. There's the sort of decorative glasswork that nowadays seems more appropriate to a landmark pub than to a bank, as well as wall-safes, plenty of prints and local history, and big windows overlooking George Square. As soon as it opens there's a steady stream of people coming for coffee or early lunches, but there's endless space to absorb them; away from the bar are several carpeted areas (some no smoking) with solidly comfortable seating, while a series of smaller rooms, once the managers' offices, lead around the perimeter of the building. Some of these are surprisingly cosy, one is like a well stocked library, and a few are themed with pictures and prints of historical characters like Walter Scott or Mary, Queen of Scots. It's all kept spotless, and you can practically set your watch by the rounds of the polisher, who wipes each table several times an hour. The central island servery has a particularly good range of well kept ales on handpump, such as Caledonian 80/- and Deuchars IPA, Courage Directors, Theakstons Best, and a couple of guests such as Hop Back Summer Lightning or Stillmans 80/-, with a good choice of bottled beers and malt whiskies, and 12 wines by the glass. Sound efficiently served food includes burgers (from £2.95), chicken, ham and leek pie or chicken balti (£4.75), evening steaks (£6.95), daily specials such as chicken goujons (£3.75) or vegetable lasagne (£4.25), and puddings like chocolate cake or cheesecake (£1.95). Fruit machine, video game. *(Recommended by Ian Baillie, Richard Lewis)*

Free house ~ Licensees Philip and Andrea Annett ~ Real ale ~ Meals and snacks (11-10; 12.30-9.30 Sun) ~ (0141) 248 9568 ~ Open 11am-midnight; 12.30-12 Sun

GLENDEVON (Tayside) NN9904 Map 11

Tormaukin

A823

A popular stop on one of the most attractive north-south routes through this part of Scotland, this remote but well run hotel still fulfills much the same role as it did when first built as a drovers' inn. It's a comfortable and neatly kept place, and the softly lit bar has plush seats against stripped stone and partly panelled walls, ceiling joists, and maybe gentle piped music; log fires. Good imaginative bar food includes soup (£2.10), chicken liver and herb pâté (£3.85), lunchtime ploughman's (£4.75), fresh haddock (£6.50), local venison sausages (£6.75), mediterranean vegetable paella or creamed leek and tarragon crêpes (£7.25), good salads (from £7.45), chicken in cajun sauce with peppers (£7.50), crispy duck legs with orange glaze or brochette of king prawns and monkfish (£8.95), steaks (from £9.50), and puddings (£3.40); children's menu (from £2.65), good breakfasts. Three well kept real ales on handpump such as Harviestoun 80/-, Ptarmigan 85/-, Montrose or Schiehallion, and Ind Coope Burton, a decent wine list, and quite a few malt whiskies; efficient service, even when they're busy. Some of the bedrooms are in a converted stable block. Loch and river fishing can be arranged, and there are plenty of good walks over the nearby Ochils or along the River Devon – plus over 100 golf courses (including St Andrews) within an hour's drive. *(Recommended by Basil J S Minson, Andrew Low, Jean and George Dundas, IHR, Colin Draper, Julian Holland)*

Free house ~ Licensee Marianne Worthy ~ Real ale ~ Meals and snacks (12-2, 5.30-9.30; all day Sun) ~ (01259) 781252 ~ Restaurant ~ Children welcome ~ Live music some winter Fri evenings ~ Open 11-11; 12-11 Sun; closed two weeks mid Jan ~ Bedrooms: £53B/£75B

GLENELG (Highland) NG8119 Map 11

Glenelg Inn

Unmarked road from Shiel Bridge (A87) towards Skye

As the landlord says, the atmosphere in Glenelg is unique, and especially in the pub. Even getting there is an adventure, the single-track road climbing dramatically past heather-strewn fields and mountains with spectacular views to the lochs below. Just when we thought we'd made it, we were held up by a big flock of sheep who commandeered the lane as they sauntered lazily back to their field. Glenelg is the closest place on the mainland to Skye (there's a little car ferry across in summer) and on a sunny day tables in the inn's beautifully kept garden have lovely views across the water. Instantly welcoming, the unspoilt red-carpeted bar has an overwhelming impression of dark wood, with lots of logs dotted about, and a big fireplace – it feels a bit like a mountain cabin; there are only a very few tables and cushioned wall benches, but crates and fish boxes serve as extra seating. Black and white photos line the walls at the far end around the bar billiards table, and there are various jokey articles and local information elsewhere. A blackboard lists the very short range of good bar meals such as hoagies (£2.50), chicken supreme with a creamy haggis and whisky sauce (£6) or baked salmon on a grapefruit jus (£7.50); in the evening they do an excellent three course meal in the no-smoking dining room (£22), making very good use of fresh local ingredients. A good choice of malt and cask strength whiskies; enthusiastic service. They may occasionally have fiddlers playing in the bar; if not, the piped music is in keeping with that theme. They can organise local activities, and there are plenty of excellent walks nearby. The bedrooms are excellent, and certainly much improved since Dr Johnson wrote 'We did not much express much satisfaction' after staying here in 1773. *(Recommended by Dr A Kelly, Colin Thompson)*

Free house ~ Licensee Christopher Main ~ Meals and snacks (April-Oct; Sat evening only Nov-March) ~ Restaurant ~ (01599) 522273 ~ Children welcome till 8 ~ Open 11-midnight; cl lunchtime Nov-March ~ Bedrooms: £84B/£128B including three course dinner

HADDINGTON (Lothian) NT5174 Map 11

Waterside

Waterside; just off A6093 at E end of town

On a sunny summer's day this really is a beautiful spot, with plenty of tables outside the long two-storey white house enjoying a perfect view across the water to the church and narrow little bridge, and on Sundays maybe a jazz band playing on the side terrace. The scene is captured rather well on an unusual glass engraving in the comfortably plush carpeted bar, which also has curtains swagged back around little windows, shaded lamps on the window sills beside square wooden tables, a woodburning stove, and quite a mix of decorations on the walls (among the prints and pictures is a CD presented to them by the singer Fish). Across the hall a similar room has bigger tables and long cushioned benches, and there's a more formal stripped-stone conservatory. Most people come here to eat (several tables have reserved signs), with the good bistro menu taking in soup (£1.95), smoked haddock and leek fishcakes or deep-fried haggis in whisky sauce (£3.50), mussels done in a variety of ways (£3.95), chicken in pepper sauce (£6.25), usually five vegetarian dishes, steak and Guinness pie, chicken and asparagus tagliatelle, or salmon with puff pastry and a white wine sauce (all £6.95), and pork cutlet with apple and cider sauce (£7.95). Admans Broadside, Belhaven 80/-, Caledonian Deuchars IPA and Wadworths 6X on handpump, and a good range of wines. There's a family connection with another new entry, the Drovers at East Linton. If you're driving, the gap under the adjacent bridge is very small; it's much nicer to park a short distance away and walk. There are almost more tables outside than in the bar, but if they're all full you can sit on the wall beside the river, or, as we did on our midsummer visit, over the wall on the grass right by the water, opposite an old dovecote. *(Recommended by R M Corlett, Anna Bissett)*

Free house ~ Licensee Jim Findlay ~ Real ale ~ Meals and snacks (all day Sun) ~ Restaurant ~ (01620) 825674 ~ Children welcome ~ Open 11.30-3, 5-midnight Mon-Fri; all day weekends

INNERLEITHEN (Borders) NT3336 Map 9

Traquair Arms

Traquair Rd (B709, just off A72 Peebles—Galashiels; follow signs for Traquair House)

Popular with locals and visitors alike, this pleasantly modernised inn is a hospitable and welcoming place, highly praised in recent months for its food. Making good use of fresh local ingredients, the enjoyable meals might include home-made soup (£1.60), filled baked potatoes (from £3), omelettes (from £4), vegetarian dishes (from £5.30), ploughman's (£5.75), chicken stuffed with haggis in a creamy apple, onion and celery sauce (£5.95), venison casserole (£6.25), salmon with avocado (£6.30), mussels with potato and spiced sausage (£6.50), steaks (from £11.75), and traditional puddings. The simple little bar has a warm open fire, a relaxed atmosphere, and well kept Greenmantle and (from Traquair House) Traquair Bear on handpump; several malt whiskies and draught cider, friendly staff. A pleasant and spacious no-smoking dining room has an open fire and high chairs for children if needed. No music or machines. *(Recommended by Colin Draper, Ian and Nita Cooper, Andy and Jill Kassube, Colin Thompson)*

Free house ~ Licensee Hugh Anderson ~ Real ale ~ Meals and snacks (12-9) ~ Restaurant ~ (01896) 830229 ~ Children welcome ~ Open 11-midnight ~ Bedrooms: £48B/£70B

INVERARAY (Strathclyde) NN0908 Map 11

George £

Main Street East

Run by the same family for over 130 years, this atmospheric and comfortably modernised hotel is a central part of the little Georgian town that's stretched along the shores of Loch Fyne in front of Inveraray Castle. Often busy, the friendly stone-flagged bar has a nicely traditional feel, particularly on a dark winter's evening, with exposed joists, old tiles and bared stone walls, modern winged settles as well as cushioned stone slabs along the walls, nicely grained wooden-topped cast-iron tables, lots of curling club and ships' badges, and a cosy log fire. Lunchtime bar food includes soup (£1.80), ploughman's (from £3.25), sweet pickled herring (£3.95), fried haddock (£4.50), home-made steak pie (£4.95), and daily specials like Irish stew (£4.50) or cod in filo pastry and mornay sauce (£6.50), with evening dishes such as grilled Loch Fyne salmon (£7.50), and steaks (from £10.75); good local cheeses, and a choice of coffees. Two rotating real ales such as Caledonian Deuchars IPA or Orkney Raven on handpump, and over 80 malt whiskies; cheerful service, darts, pool, dominoes, and juke box. The inn is well placed for the great Argyll woodland gardens – the rhododendrons are at their best in May and early June – and there are good walks nearby. *(Recommended by Dave Braisted, Neil Townend, R Macnaughton, David Hoult, Walter Reid)*

Free house ~ Licensee Donald Clark ~ Real ale ~ Meals and snacks (12-9) ~ Restaurant ~ (01499) 302111 ~ Children welcome ~ Open 11-12.30; noon-12.30 am Sun; cl 25 Dec, 1 Jan ~ Bedrooms: £30B/£55B

INVERARNAN (Central) NN3118 Map 11

Inverarnan Inn £

A82 N of Loch Lomond

Unusual is the word readers most often use to describe this warmly friendly and atmospheric old drovers' inn, though they frequently follow that up with amazing, or idiosyncratic. The staff wear kilts to serve, accompanied by piped traditional Scottish music, and the long bar feels a little like a small baronial hall, unchanged for at least the last hundred years (some of the fusty furnishings and fittings look as if they could have been around even longer). Log fires burn in big fireplaces at each end, and there are green tartan cushions and deerskins on the black winged settles, Highland paintings and bagpipes on the walls, and a stuffed golden eagle on the bar counter. Lots of sporting trophies (such as a harpooned gaping shark), horns and so forth hang on the high walls of the central hall, where there's a stuffed badger curled on a table, and a full suit of armour. A wide range of good malts – 60 in the gantry and 60 more in stock, and farm cider. Bar food includes good broth (£1.20), pâté (£1.50), burgers (£3), steak sandwich (£3.25), scampi (£4.50) and fresh salmon (£6.95). Tables outside on a back terrace, with more in a field alongside – where you might come across a couple of ponies and geese. A stream runs behind. *(Recommended by Walter Reid, Nigel Woolliscroft, Richard Gibbs, T M Dobby, Bronwen and Steve Wrigley, Don and Shirley Parrish, Paul and Ursula Randall, Mr and Mrs I Keenleyside)*

Free house ~ Licensee Duncan McGregor ~ Meals and snacks (12-2, 6-8.30) ~ (01301) 704234 ~ Well behaved children allowed until 9 ~ Occasional live music ~ Open 11-11(midnight Sat); closed 25 Dec, 1 Jan ~ Bedrooms: £17/£34

ISLE ORNSAY (Isle of Skye) NG6912 Map 11

Tigh Osda Eilean Iarmain

Signposted off A851 Broadford—Armadale

Gaelic is truly the first language of the charming staff at this civilised little inn, many of whom have worked here for some years; even the menus are bilingual. Friendly and relaxed, it's a particularly nice place to stay, attractively positioned overlooking the sea in a picturesque part of Skye. The cheerfully busy bar has a swooping stable-stall-like wooden divider that gives a two-room feel: good tongue-and-groove panelling on the walls and ceiling, leatherette wall seats, brass lamps, a brass-mounted ceiling fan, and a huge mirror over the open fire. There are about 34 local brands of blended and vatted malt whisky (including their own blend, Te Bheag, and a splendid vatted malt, Poit Dhubh Green Label, bottled for them but available elsewhere), and an excellent wine list; darts, dominoes, cribbage, and piped music. Bar food might include home-made soup (£1.75), lunchtime sandwiches, local mussels in whisky (£3.50), herring in oatmeal (£5.50), pork, fennel and mushroom casserole (£5.75), local crab with mozzarella (£6), fillet of lamb with redcurrants, juniper and rosemary (£7.50), grilled sea bass with lime and fennel (£8.50), puddings like baked lemon tart (£2.50), and children's menu (£3.50). They have their own oyster beds and every day send a diver to collect fresh scallops. The pretty, no-smoking dining room has a lovely sea view past the little island of Ornsay itself and the lighthouse on Sionnach (you can walk over the sands at low tide). Some of the bedrooms are in a cottage opposite. The most popular room has a canopied bed from Armadale Castle. *(Recommended by Don and Shirley Parrish, Colin Draper)*

Free house ~ Licensee Sir Iain Noble ~ Meals and snacks (12-2.30, 6.30-9.30) ~ Restaurant ~ (01471) 833332 ~ Children welcome (but only till 8.30 in the bar) ~ Live music Thurs evenings ~ Open 12-12 Mon-Fri, 12-2.30, 5-12 Sat; 12-2.30, 6.30-12 Sun ~ Bedrooms: £70B/£950B

ISLE OF WHITHORN (Dumfries and Galloway) NX4736 Map 9

Steam Packet £

Good views of the picturesque natural working harbour from the big picture windows of this welcoming modernised inn – there's usually quite a bustle of yachts and inshore fishing boats. Inside, the homely low-ceilinged bar is split into two: on the right, plush button-back banquettes and boat pictures, and on the left, green leatherette stools around cast-iron-framed tables on big stone tiles, and a wood-burning stove in the bare stone wall. Bar food can be served in the lower-beamed dining room, which has a big model steam packet boat on the white walls, excellent colour wildlife photographs, rugs on its wooden floor, and a solid fuel stove, and there's also a small eating area off the lounge bar. The good value bar meals might include soup (£1.45), filled rolls (from £1.30), vegetable dimsum (£2.85), haggis (£3.95), chicken curry (£4.25), vegetable lasagne or breaded haddock stuffed with prawns, cheese and mushrooms (£4.95), a good mixed seafood platter (£8.75), steaks (from £10.75), and well liked seafood and game specials; local cheeses, children's menu. Unusually, you can take food away. Well kept Theakstons XB on handpump, with a guest such as Caledonian Deuchars IPA or Batemans XB; two dozen malt whiskies; pool, dominoes and piped music. Dogs welcome. White tables and chairs in the garden. The back bar and conservatory are no smoking. Every 1½ to 4 hours there are boat trips from the harbour; the remains of St Ninian's Kirk are on a headland behind the village. *(Recommended by Mr and Mrs D Price, Anthony Longden, Joyce McKimm, Neil Townend, Francis and Deirdre Gevers)*

Free house ~ Licensee John Scoular ~ Real ale ~ Meals and snacks (not 25 Dec) ~ Restaurant ~ (01988) 500334 ~ Children welcome away from public bar ~ Occasional folk music ~ Open 11-11; 11-2.30, 6-11 in winter; 12-11 Sun ~ Bedrooms: £25B/£50B

KELSO (Borders) NT7334 Map 10

Queens Head £

Bridge Street (A699)

This 18th-c Georgian coaching inn has a very pleasant atmosphere in the roomy and attractive back lounge, with its comfortable mix of modern and traditional. Tables fill quickly at lunchtime for the wide choice of good generous food, which might include sandwiches (from £1.95), ploughman's (£3.25), haddock in breadcrumbs (£4.55), steak pie (£4.65), daily specials such as duck stir fry or a pasta dish (from £4), evening dishes like chargrilled cajun salmon (£6.95), medallions of pork loin (£7.75) and sizzling mixed grill (£12.25), and puddings (£2.50); service is by courteous waitresses, with very helpful and efficient licensees. There's also a small simpler traditional streetside front bar, with a lively local atmosphere; pool. Well kept Courage Directors, Morlands Old Speckled Hen, Marstons Pedigree, and Whitbreads Castle Eden on handpump; dominoes, fruit machine, video game, and piped music; they can arrange golf, fishing and horse riding. *(Recommended by Nigel Woolliscroft, Michael Wadsworth, R T and J C Moggridge, James Nunns)*

Free house ~ Licensee Ian Flannigan ~ Real ale ~ Meals and snacks (12-2, 6-9) ~ Restaurant ~ (01573) 224636 ~ Children welcome ~ Open 11-2.30, 4.45-11; 11-12 Sat; 11-11 Sun ~ Bedrooms: £35B/£50B

KILBERRY (Strathclyde) NR7164 Map 11

Kilberry Inn

B8024

The inventive home-made food at this whitewashed former post office is easily among the best of any pub in Scotland, a feat all the more remarkable given the place's remote location. Local produce arrives by taxi, and we can only assume that from then on the landlady spends all her time cooking: as well as the meals, she makes all their own breads, muesli, pickles and chutney. You can buy some of these to take away, and indeed one reader seems to treat each visit like a trip to the supermarket, stocking up on jams and cakes each time he leaves. A typical menu might include home-made malted granary garlic bread (£1.95), cream of broccoli soup with home-made bread (£2.75), port and stilton pâté (£4.50), country sausage pie (£7.50), freshly baked stilton and walnut pie (£7.95), medallions of pork in a calvados and cream sauce (£12.95), baked rump steak cooked in red wine and topped with stilton (£13.95); puddings such as freshly baked apple and raspberry pie, or ice cream made with genuine Blackpool rock. They appreciate booking if you want an evening meal. The small relaxed dining bar is tastefully and simply furnished but warmly friendly, with a good log fire. No real ale, but a good range of bottled beers and plenty of malt whiskies; the family room is no smoking. It's a lovely place to stay with neat, cosy bedrooms, and particularly attentive and welcoming service. Breakfasts are hearty, with a different home-made marmalade each day. The pub is on a delightful slow winding and hilly circular drive over Knapdale, from the A83 S of Lochgilphead, with breathtaking views over the rich coastal pastures to the sea and the island of Gigha beyond. Note it isn't open in winter. *(Recommended by Andrew Guthrie, Dr M Allen, John and Barbara Burns, Dr D G Twyman, Derek and Maggie Washington)*

Free house ~ Licensee John Leadbeater ~ Meals and snacks ~ (01880) 770223 ~ Well behaved children in family room ~ Open 11-2, 5-10; closed Sun, and closed all mid-Oct-Easter ~ Bedrooms: £36.50S/£63B

KILMAHOG (Central) NN6108 Map 11

Lade Inn 🍷

A84 just NW of Callander, by A821 junction

Feeling like a proper pub – rather than the hotel bars more prevalent around here – this well run place is set in the beautiful richly wooded surroundings of the Pass of Leny, with high hills all around and the Trossachs not far off. The wide range of interesting bar food is all freshly made, with no frozen things at all, not even peas. The choice takes in lunchtime sandwiches (from £3.75) and baked potatoes (from £4.75), as well as vegetable pancake (£5.99), steak pie (£6.35), haggis, neeps and tatties (£6.40), game casserole or chicken curry (£7.35), salmon with dill butter (£8.95), rack of lamb (£13.95), daily specials, and puddings like crannachan (a rich mousse with whisky) or bread and butter pudding (£2.99); children's menu (£3.99). Well kept Broughton Greenmantle, Heather Fraoch Ale, and Orkney Red MacGregor on handpump, and a wine list strong on New World ones); cheerful informal service, dogs allowed. The main carpeted dining bar has blond wood chairs around pine tables, with beams, some panelling, stripped stone and Highland prints; a no-smoking room opens on to the terrace and attractive garden, where they have three ponds stocked with fish, and hold summer evening barbecues; piped Scottish music. *(Recommended by Dr John Bassett, H L Dennis; more reports please)*

Free house ~ Licensee Paul Roebuck ~ Real ale ~ Meals and snacks (12-2.30, 5.30-9) ~ Restaurant ~ (01877) 330152 ~ Children in eating area till 9pm ~ Ceilidh Sat evenings ~ Open 12-11(midnight Sat); 12-3, 5.30-11 in winter; 12.30-11 Sun

KIPPEN (Central) NS6594 Map 11

Cross Keys Hotel 🛏

Main Street; village signposted off A811 W of Stirling

The friendly licensees at this relaxed and comfortable 18th-c inn really make an effort to make you feel at home. Popular with locals, the straightforward but welcoming lounge has a good log fire, and there's a coal fire in the attractive family dining room. Generously served food, using fresh local produce, includes home-made soup (£1.80), home-made bramble and port liver pâté (£3.15), omelettes (from £3.30), lamb stovies (£4.50), venison burgers (£5.95), steak pie (£6.85), poached salmon with a lemon and dill sauce (£6.95), Aberdeen Angus sirloin steak (£11.75), and puddings like bread and butter pudding (£2.95) and clootie dumpling (£3.10); smaller helpings for children. Well kept Broughton Greenmantle on handpump, and quite a few malt whiskies; dominoes, shove-ha'penny, fruit machine, and juke box, with darts and pool in the separate public bar. The garden has tables and a children's play area. Booking is essential for the restaurant. *(Recommended by Graham and Lynn Mason, Neil Townend, Ian Jones)*

Free house ~ Licensees Angus and Sandra Watt ~ Real ale ~ Meals (12-2, 5.30-9.30) ~ Restaurant ~ (01786) 870293 ~ Children in restaurant ~ Open 12-2.30, 5.30-11(midnight Sat); 12.30-11 Sun; closed evening 25 Dec, 1 Jan ~ Bedrooms: £19.50/£39

All main entries have been inspected anonymously by the Editor or Deputy Editor. We accept no payment for inclusion, no advertising, and no sponsorship from the drinks industry – or from anyone else.

KIRKTON OF GLENISLA (Tayside) NO2160 Map 11

Glenisla Hotel

B951 N of Kirriemuir and Alyth

In one of the prettiest of the Angus Glens, this friendly 17th-c former posting inn has new owners this year. They're keen to promote local produce, with the beers, wines, and cheeses all coming from nearby suppliers. The real ales Independence, Lia Fail and Ossians – from the small Inveralmond brewery in Perth – are proving especially popular. The simple but cosy carpeted pubby bar has beams and ceiling joists, a roaring log fire, wooden tables and chairs, decent prints, and a rather jolly thriving atmosphere. The lounge is comfortable and sunny, and the elegant high-ceilinged dining room has rugs on the wooden floor, pretty curtains, candles and fresh flowers, and crisp cream tablecloths. Carefully prepared bar food at lunchtime might include soup (£2.50), Orkney herrings in dill (£3.15), home-baked ham with freee range eggs (£5.25), chilli (£5.50), ploughman's (£5.95), and lamb cutlets with mint sauce (£6.25), with evening dishes such as leek and mushroom risotto (£6.95), duck breast on a bed of red onion marmalade (£8.95), and fillet of halibut with a hazelnut crust and cheese and chive sauce (£9.95). The landlord has a keen interest in whiskies (he used to work for a distiller) so can advise on their 50 or so malts; also local fruit wines. A refurbished stable block has darts, dominoes, cribbage, and a TV and video for children. The bedrooms are attractively individual, and they can arrange fishing in local lochs. No smoking in dining room. *(Recommended by Carole Smart, Andrew Jeeves, Susan and John Douglas, Mrs R Scholes; more reports please)*

Free house ~ Licensees Shona Carrie, Steve Higson ~ Real ale ~ Meals ~ Restaurant ~ (01575) 582223 ~ Children in eating area and games room ~ Traditional Ceilidhs, folk or country muasic Sun 4-8pm ~ Open 11-11; 12-11 Sun; open 11-2.30, 6-11 wkdys Oct-June; closed 24-26 Dec ~ Bedrooms: £46.50B/£77B

LINLITHGOW (Lothian) NS9976 Map 11

Four Marys £

65 High St; 2 miles from M9 junction 3 (and little further from junction 4) – town signposted

Named after the four ladies-in-waiting of Mary Queen of Scots, who was born at nearby Linlithgow Palace, this atmospheric and friendly pub has masses of mementoes of the ill-fated queen, such as pictures and written records, a piece of bed curtain said to be hers, part of a 16th-c cloth and swansdown vest of the type she'd be likely to have worn, and a facsimile of her death-mask. The L-shaped bar also has mahogany dining chairs around stripped period and antique tables, a couple of attractive antique corner cupboards, and an elaborate Victorian dresser serving as a bar gantry. The walls are mainly stripped stone, including some remarkable masonry in the inner area. A good choice of around eight constantly changing well kept real ales on handpump might take in Belhaven 70/- and 80/-, Boddingtons, Caledonian Deuchars IPA, Fullers London Pride, Harviestoun Ptarmigan and Schiehallion, and Orkney Dark Island; friendly and helpful staff. Bar food includes soup (£1.45), toasties or sandwiches (from £1.50), filled baked potatoes (£2.95), haggis, neeps and tatties (£3.95), and fresh fried or smoked haddock (£4.95). When the building was an apothecary's shop, David Waldie experimented in it with chloroform – its first use as an anaesthetic. Parking can be difficult. *(Recommended by Ian Phillips; more reports please)*

Belhaven ~ Manageress Mrs E Forrest ~ Real ale ~ Meals and snacks (12-2.30, 5.30-8.30; not Sun evening) ~ (01506) 842171 ~ Children in eating area of bar till 8.30 ~ Open 11-11(11.45 Sat); 12.30-11 Sun

LYBSTER (Highland) ND2436 Map 11

Portland Arms

A9 S of Wick

A good base for the area, renowned for its spectacular cliffs and stacks, this staunch old granite hotel is our most northerly main entry. The knocked-through open plan bar is comfortable and attractively furnished, and there's also a small but cosy panelled cocktail bar. Consistently reliable bar food (often the same as in the restaurant but cheaper) includes soup (£1.85), chicken liver pâté (£3.95), liver and bacon, smoked haddock tagliatelle, baked fillet of sole or generous fresh salmon salad (all £5.95), steaks (from £11.95), and popular puddings (£2.95); good Sunday lunch. Friendly and obliging owners and staff. They keep 40 or more malt whiskies (beers are keg). They can arrange fishing and so forth. *(Recommended by Mr and Mrs Dewhurst, Chris and Anne Garnett, Sarah Markham, Neil Townend, Richard Dolphin, Dr G Craig)*

Free house ~ Licensee Gerald Henderson ~ Meals and snacks ~ Restaurant ~ (01593) 721208 ~ Children welcome ~ Open 11-11 ~ Bedrooms: £45B/£68B

MELROSE (Borders) NT5434 Map 9

Burts Hotel

A6091

Very popular with readers at the moment, this comfortable and rather smart old hotel is a civilised place to stop for a good meal, but it's best to get there early – it can get very busy indeed. Served by professional, hard-working staff there might be lunchtime sandwiches, soup (£1.80), parfait of hare with a tropical fruit chutney (£3.95), deep fried haddock (£6.25), parma ham, wild mushroom and leek risotto or a vegetarian dish like butternut, leek and courgette casserole (£6.95), pan-fried liver with garlic mash and root vegetable and redcurrant sauce, or salmon and prawn spring roll with orange fillets and a herb crème fraîche (£7.95), and puddings like baked ice cream croissant with ragoût of seasonal fruits, or warm courgette and nutmeg loaf with apricot ice cream (£3.95); extremely good breakfasts. Recently renovated, the comfortable and friendly L-shaped lounge bar has lots of cushioned wall seats and windsor armchairs on its turkey carpet, and Scottish prints on the walls; the Tweed Room and the restaurant are no smoking. Well kept Bass and Belhaven 80/- and Sandy Hunters on handpump, 70 malt whiskies, and a good wine list; dominoes. There's a well tended garden (with tables in summer). Melrose with its striking ruined abbey is probably the most villagey of the Border towns; an alternative if distant way to view the abbey ruins is from the top of the tower at Smailholm. *(Recommended by Ian and Nita Cooper, R Macnaughton, K F Mould, Pamela and Merlyn Horswell, Comus Elliott, Alan J Morton, Ray and Chris Watson, R T and J C Moggridge)*

Free house ~ Licensee Graham Henderson ~ Real ale ~ Meals and snacks ~ Restaurant ~ (01896) 822285 ~ Children welcome till 8pm ~ Open 11-2.30, 5-11; 12-2.30, 6-11 Sun; closed 26 Dec ~ Bedrooms: £48B/£82B

MOUNTBENGER (Border) NT3125 Map 9

Gordon Arms

Junction A708/B709

Sir Walter Scott and James Hogg used to meet in this remotely set and warmly welcoming inn, and letters from both are displayed on the walls of the comfortable public bar, along with an interesting set of period photographs of the neighbourhood (one dated 1865), and some well illustrated poems. Well kept Greenmantle, Broughton Oatmeal Stout, and maybe summer guest beers on handpump, 56 malt whiskies, and a fair wine list. Bar food includes sandwiches (lunchtime only), vegetarian dishes, and home-made steak pie (£5.50), roast beef and yorkshire pudding (£5.95), braised steak (£6.50) and lamb chops (£7.50); children's dishes and summer high teas in the dining room. Winter fire; pool, dominoes, and trivia. The resident family of friendly bearded collies are called Misty, Morar and Coll. A cheery sight amidst splendid empty moorlands, the inn has its own petrol station, and in addition to the hotel bedrooms has a bunkhouse providing cheap accommodation for hill walkers, cyclists and fishermen, all of whom should find this area particularly appealing. *(Recommended by Neil Townend, Dr A C Williams, Dr F M Ellard; more reports please)*

Free house ~ Licensee Harry Mitchell ~ Real ale ~ Meals and snacks ~ Restaurant ~ (01750) 82232 ~ Children in eating areas till 8pm ~ Accordion and fiddle club third Weds every month ~ Open 11-11(midnight Sat); 12.30-11 Sun; closed Tues end Oct-Easter ~ Bedrooms: £26/£42

PITLOCHRY (Tayside) NN9458 Map 11

Moulin

11 Kirkmichael Rd, Moulin; A924 NE of Pitlochry centre

Now a quiet village overshadowed by bustling Pitlochry, Moulin used to be by far the busier place, a boozy market town where every house was said to be an ale house. Now there's only this impressive white-painted 17th-c inn, especially worth a visit for the delicious real ales made in their little stables brewery across the street: Braveheart, Ale of Atholl and the stronger Old Remedial. The pub has been much extended over the years, but the bar (in the oldest part of the building) still seems an entity in itself rather than just a part of the hotel. Above the fireplace in the smaller room is an interesting painting of the village before the road was built, while the bigger carpeted area has a good few tables and cushioned banquettes in little booths divided by stained-glass country scenes, another big fireplace, some exposed stonework, fresh flowers, and local prints and golf clubs around the walls; bar billiards, shove ha'penny, dominoes, fruit machine. A wide choice of popular bar food includes soup (£1.95), lunchtime sandwiches and baked potatoes (from £3.50), steak and ale pie (£5.75), root vegetable and lentil bake or leek and sweet pepper pasta (£5.95), venison casserole (£6.50), minute steak stuffed with haggis (£6.95), and daily specials such as grilled rainbow trout with garlic and parsley butter (£6.95) or Isle of Skye langoustines (£9.95); prompt friendly service. They keep around 40 malt whiskies. Picnic-sets outside are surrounded by tubs of flowers, and look across to the village kirk. Groups can tour the brewery by arrangement, and they have good value three night breaks out of season. Rewarding walks nearby. *(Recommended by Pauline and Jim Welch, Ruth Holloway, Andrew Hazeldine, Kate and Robert Hodkinson)*

Own Brew ~ Licensee Heather Reeves ~ Real ale ~ Meals and snacks (12-9.30) ~ Restaurant ~ (01796) 472196 ~ Children in eating area till 9 ~ Celtic music winter Fri eves and Sun afternoons ~ Open Sun-Thurs 11.30-10.45; Fri/Sat 11.30-11.30 ~ Bedrooms: £45B/£68B

nr PITLOCHRY (Tayside) NN9162 Map 11

Killiecrankie Hotel

Killiecrankie signposted from A9 N of Pitlochry

Dramatic views of the mountain pass from the lovely peaceful grounds of this smart but relaxed country hotel, well run by warmly welcoming licensees. The attractively furnished bar has some panelling, upholstered seating and mahogany tables and chairs, as well as stuffed animals and some rather fine wildlife paintings; in the airy conservatory extension (which overlooks the pretty garden) there are light beech tables and upholstered chairs, with discreetly placed plants and flowers. Unfailingly good bar food is served by friendly staff and might at lunchtime include soup (£2.40), sweet cured herrings (£4.30), ploughman's and salads (from £5.95), deep-fried fresh haddock in beer batter or popular cumberland sausage with hot onion chutney (£7.25), and oak-smoked chicken breast with minted mango and papaya compote (£8.95); evening extras such as tagliatelle with salmon, mussels and prawns (£8.25). The restaurant is no smoking. Decent wines and lots of malt whiskies, coffee and a choice of teas. The grounds have a putting course, a croquet lawn – and sometimes roe deer and red squirrels. *(Recommended by J F M West, Dr D Twyman, Roger and Christine Mash, Ray Watson, Sue and Bob Ward, Bill and Brenda Lemon, Joan and Tony Walker, Susan and John Douglas, James Nunns)*

Free house ~ Licensees Colin and Carole Anderson ~ Meals and snacks (12.30-2, 6.30-9.15) ~ Evening restaurant ~ (01796) 473220 ~ Children in eating area of bar ~ Open 11-2.30, 5.30-11; 12-2.30, 6.30-11 Sun; closed one week mid Dec, all Jan/Feb ~ Bedrooms: £52B/£104B

The details at the end of each main entry start by saying whether the pub is a free house, or if it's tied to a brewery (which we name).

PLOCKTON (Highland) NG8033 Map 11

Plockton Hotel

Village signposted from A87 near Kyle of Lochalsh

A few changes are planned at this friendly little hotel over the next year or so; they recently bought the next building along its elegant row of pretty stone-built houses, which they hope to convert into extra bedrooms and a courtyard dining area. The setting is lovely, in a delightful National Trust village, looking out past the palm trees and colourfully flowering shrub-lined shore, and across the sheltered anchorage to the rugged mountainous surrounds of Loch Carron. The comfortably furnished, bustling lounge bar has window seats looking out to the boats on the water, as well as antiqued dark red leather seating around neat Regency-style tables on a tartan carpet, three model ships set into the woodwork, and partly panelled stone walls. The separate public bar has pool, darts, shove-ha'penny, dominoes, and piped music. Popular promptly served bar food includes home-made soup (£1.80, with their own bread), sandwiches, filled baked potatoes, chicken liver and whisky pâté (£3.25), venison casserole or poached smoked fillet of haddock (£6.75), leg of lamb marinated in wine and rosemary (£7.25), a vegetarian dish of the day, prawns fresh from the bay (starter £6.25, main course £12.50), monkfish and prawns in a creamy vermouth, chive and ginger sauce (£10.25), local scallops (£10.50), and steaks (from £11.50); children's menu (from £2.25). It's worth booking, as they do get busy. Good breakfasts; small no-smoking dining room. Tennents 80/- on tall fount air pressure, a good collection of malt whiskies, and a short wine list. *(Recommended by T M Dobby, K M Crook, Mr and Mrs J E Murphy, Chris and Ann Garnett, Paula Williams, Mr and Mrs Archibald, Dr D G Twyman, Stephen Holman, Eric Locker, David and Judy Walmsley, Joan and Tony Walker, Lynn and Peter Brueton)*

Free house ~ Licensees Tom and Dorothy Pearson ~ Real ale ~ Meals and snacks (not 25 Dec) ~ Restaurant ~ (01599) 544274 ~ Children in eating area of bar ~ Occasional ceilidh band ~ Open 11-midnight(11.30 Sat); 12.30-11 Sun; closed 1 Jan ~ Bedrooms: £27.50B/£55B

PORTPATRICK (Dumfries and Galloway) NX0154 Map 9

Crown ★

Very well liked by readers at the moment, this bustling and atmospheric harbourside inn remains welcoming and efficient even at its busiest. The rambling old-fashioned bar has lots of little nooks, crannies and alcoves, and interesting furnishings such as a carved settle with barking dogs as its arms, an antique wicker-backed armchair, a stag's head over the coal fire, and shelves of old bottles above the bar counter. The partly panelled butter-coloured walls are decorated with old mirrors with landscapes painted in their side panels. Under the new head chef there isn't quite so much emphasis on seafood as before, but you'll still find extremely fresh local prawns, lobster, and monkfish tails and scallops (£11.40), as well as sandwiches (from £1.70; toasties from £1.90), soup (£2), and other dishes; good breakfasts. Carefully chosen wine list, and over 250 malt whiskies; maybe piped music. An airy and very attractively decorated early 20th-c, half no-smoking dining room opens through a quiet no-smoking conservatory area into a sheltered back garden, and you can sit outside on seats served by a hatch in the front lobby and make the most of the evening sun. *(Recommended by Neil Townend, Christine and Malcolm Ingram, Stan and Hazel Allen, Ian Potter, Nigel Woolliscroft, Pamela and Merlyn Horswell, Paul and Nicky Clements, Richard Holloway, Patrick Osborne)*

Free house ~ Licensee Bernard Wilson ~ Meals and snacks (till 10) ~ Restaurant ~ (01776) 810261 ~ Children welcome ~ Open 11-11.30; 12-11 Sun ~ Bedrooms: £48B/£72B

If you report on a pub that's not a main entry, please tell us any lunchtimes or evenings when it doesn't serve bar food.

SHERIFFMUIR (Central) NN8202 Map 11

Sheriffmuir Inn

Signposted off A9 just S of Blackford; and off A9 at Dunblane roundabout, just N of end of M9; also signposted from Bridge of Allan; OS Sheet 57 map reference 827022

Remotely set in the middle of lonely moorland, this isolated drovers' inn enjoys wonderful views, not too dramatically changed since it was built in 1715, the same year as the Battle of Sheriffmuir commemorated in a couple of the prints on the walls inside. The welcoming L-shaped bar is basic but comfortable, with pink plush stools and button-back built-in wall banquettes on a pink patterned carpet, polished tables, olde-worlde coaching prints on its white walls, and a woodburning stove in a stone fireplace; there's a separate no-smoking room. Well kept Arrols 80/-, Marstons Pedigree and always two guests on handpump, kept under light blanket pressure, and a good choice of whiskies; piped music. Promptly-served by particularly friendly and efficient staff, lunchtime bar food includes home-made soup, steak pie (£6.50), and battered haddock or chicken korma (£6.95); they can get busy at lunchtimes so it's worth getting there early. There are tables and a children's play area outside. *(Recommended by Paula Williams, K M Crook, Mark and Heather Williamson; more reports please)*

Free house ~ Licensee Roger Lee ~ Real ale ~ Meals ~ Restaurant ~ (01786) 823285 ~ Children welcome ~ Open 11.30-2.30, 5.30-11; 11.30-11 Sat; 12-11 Sun; closed Mon Oct-Mar

SHIELDAIG (Highland) NG8154 Map 11

Tigh an Eilean 🛏

Village signposted just off A896 Lochcarron—Gairloch

Though this is very much a hotel with a tiny locals' bar attached, it stands out for its delightful waterside setting, looking out over the Shieldaig Island – a sanctuary for a stand of ancient Caledonian pines – to Loch Torridon, and then out to the sea beyond. It's a comfortable place to stay, with easy chairs, books and a well stocked help-yourself bar in the neat and prettily decorated two-room lounge, and an attractively modern dining room specialising in tasty and good value local shellfish, fish and game. Quickly served, simple bar food includes home-made soup, sandwiches, smoked salmon parcels or spring lobster marie rose (£3.75), fresh halibut in batter or pork en croûte with apricot (£6.75), and puddings like apple charlotte (£2); Tennents 80/- on air pressure. The bar is very simple, with red brocaded button-back banquettes in little bays, and picture windows looking out to sea; winter darts, juke box. A sheltered front courtyard has three pinic-sets. The National Trust Torridon estate and the Beinn Eighe nature reserve aren't too far away. *(Recommended by Ian Jones, Anthony Barnes, D G Clarke, Dr D G Twyman)*

Free house ~ Licensee Mrs Elizabeth Stewart ~ Meals and snacks (12-2.15, 6-8.30) ~ Restaurant ~ (01520) 755251 ~ Children in eating area of bar until 8pm ~ Open 11-11; 11-2.30, 5-11 in winter; 12.30-2.30 Sun – closed Sun evening; closed all day winter Sun ~ Bedrooms: £45B(no view)/£100B

SKEABOST (Isle of Skye) NG4148 Map 11

Skeabost House Hotel ★ 🛏

A850 NW of Portree, 1½ miles past junction with A856

Set in twelve acres of secluded woodland and gardens, this civilised and rather grand-looking hotel has glorious views over Loch Snizort, said to have some of the best salmon fishing on the island. One of the draws is the excellent lunchtime buffet (£7.95) served in the the spacious and airy conservatory, with a very wide choice of cold meats and fresh salmon; they also do home-made soup (£2), good filled baked potatoes (from £2.95), baguettes (from £2.99), haggis with oatcakes (£3.90), and a few main courses like strips of chicken in tomato and basil sauce with tagliatelle, olives and peppers (£5.80), lamb casserole (£5.95), and Scottish sirloin steak (£13.95); children's meals (from £2.40). All the eating areas are no smoking; best to dress fairly smartly in the main dining room. The bustling high-ceilinged bar has a pine counter and red brocade seats on its thick red carpet, and a fine panelled billiards room leads off the stately hall; there's a wholly separate public bar with darts, pool, fruit machine, trivia, juke box, piped music (and even its own car park). A fine choice of over 100 single malt whiskies, including their own and some very rare ones. *(Recommended by E Locker, Walter and Susan Rinaldi-Butcher, David and Judy Walmsley, Joan and Tony Walker, Jane Taylor, David Dutton; more reports please)*

Free house ~ Licensee Iain McNab ~ Meals and snacks (12-1.30, 6.30-9.30) ~ Restaurant ~ (01470) 532202 ~ Children in eating area of bar ~ Accordion/fiddle in public bar Sat evening ~ Open 12-2, 6-12(11 Sat); 12.30-3, 6-11 Sun; cl Nov-Mar ~ Bedrooms: £48B/£104B

ST MONANCE (Fife) SO5202 Map 11

Cabin

16 West End; just off A917

Though it's not cheap, the excellent seafood in the back restaurant here is among the finest in the area – quite a surprise unless you're in the know, as from the outside you'd think the place quite ordinary. The snug front bar is immaculate yet warmly cosy, the well polished light wooden panelling and fittings and lack of windows creating something of a below-decks feel. On the mantlepiece above a smart tiled fireplace is a gleaming ship's bell, and there are a few seafaring models and mementoes on illuminated shelves, as well as turn-of-the-century photos of local life around the walls. Well kept Belhaven 80/- and St Andrews and a changing guest like Wadworths 6X on handpump; also a wide range of wines, several malt whiskies (including a malt of the month), and freshly squeezed fruit juices. Very friendly service. A plainer public bar is popular with local salts – several came in wearing waterproofs and wellies on our summer visit. Lunchtime bar food such as soup (from £2.50), half a dozen oysters (£6.50), fettucine with fresh or smoked seafood (£6.95) and grilled langoustines (£11.95); they do a two course lunch for £13. In the evenings they do food only in the airy restaurant (except in summer when you may be able to eat outside on the terrace), with its big windows overlooking the harbour and the Firth of Forth; meals then might include cullen skink (£2.85), corn-fed chicken filled with mango and grilled with blue cheese (£11.95), roast salmon on a bed of saffron and herb mash with white truffle scented vinaigrette (£12.95), rolled fillets of sole and scampi tails in a leek and ginger sauce (£13.50), and lobster and avocado salad with Tuscan salt bread, and a basil and olive oil dressing (£18.25). The restaurant is no smoking. *(Recommended by Eric Locker, Paul and Ursula Randall, David Unsworth)*

Free house ~ Licensee Tim Butler ~ Real ale ~ Meals and snacks ~ Restaurant ~ (01333) 730327 ~ Children in restaurant till 8pm ~ Open 11-11; 12.30-11 Sun; closed Mon, and three weeks in Jan

nr STONEHAVEN (Grampian) NO8493 Map 11

Lairhillock 🍷

Netherley; 6 miles N of Stonehaven, 6 miles S of Aberdeen, take the Durris turn-off from the A90 (old A92)

The unusual freshly prepared food is what brings most visitors to this smart but relaxed and friendly extended country pub. In the bar, this might include soup (£2.25), cullen skink (£3.75), a changing terrine or pâté (£4.15), filled baguettes (£4.65), lunchtime ploughman's (£5.45), curry of the day or potato and ham pie (£6.95), vegetarian dishes, venison and wild boar lasagne (£7.95), monkfish and king prawn stir-fry or pheasant breast stuffed with wild mushroom and chive mousse (£8.95), chicken stuffed with haggis in a whisky sauce (£9.50), fresh fish, steaks (from £12.25) and puddings (£2.95); Sunday buffet lunch. The cheerful beamed bar has panelled wall benches, a mixture of old seats, dark woodwork, harness and brass lamps on the walls, a good open fire, and countryside views from the bay window. The spacious separate lounge has an unusual central fire; the traditional atmosphere is always welcoming, even at the pub's busiest. Well kept Boddingtons, Courage Directors,

Flowers IPA, McEwans 80/-, and changing guest beers on handpump, over 50 malt whiskies, and an extensive wine list; friendly efficient staff; darts, cribbage, dominoes, shove-ha'penny, trivia, and piped music. The cosy restaurant – reckoned by some readers to be one of t he finest in the Aberdeen area – is in a converted raftered barn behind. Panoramic southerly views from the conservatory. ***(Recommended by Steven Bertram, John Poulter, Isabel McIntyre; more reports please)***

Free house ~ Licensee Frank Budd ~ Real ale ~ Meals and snacks (12-2, 6-10) ~ Restaurant ~ (01569) 730001 ~ Children in restaurant/conservatory ~ Pianist in restaurant/singing and accordion Fri ~ Open 11-2.30, 5-11 weekdays and winter weekends, 11-midnight summer Sats, 11-11 summer Suns; closed 25/26 Dec, 1/2 Jan ~ Single bedroom: £60

SWINTON (Borders) NT8448 Map 10

Wheatsheaf

A6112 N of Coldstream

Scotland's Dining Pub of the Year

Once again readers are united in high praise for the excellent food at this extremely well run and rather civilised place, in a pretty village surrounded by rolling countryside. At lunchtime the daily changing menu might include sandwiches, chicken and spring vegetable soup (£2.25), moules marinières (£4.35), baked avocado with seafood in cheese sauce (£4.85), filo pastry basket with monkfish, leeks and coriander (£5.80), lamb and vegetable casserole (£6.25), confit of duck with puy lentils (£6.85), asparagus and artichoke ravioli in a mull cheddar sauce (£6.90), roast tenderloin of pork with apricots (£7.25), local seafood, and delicious puddings, with evening dishes like chicken supreme on stir-fried oriental vegetables and noodles (£11.25) and fillet of venison on roasted vegetables with a bramble, juniper and port jelly sauce (£14.25). Booking is advisable, particularly from Thursday to Saturday evening. Well kept Caledonian 80/- and Deuchars IPA, alternating with Greenmantle, a decent range of malt whiskies and brandies, good choice of wines, and cocktails. Service is friendly, unhurried and genuinely welcoming. The carefully thought out main bar area has an attractive long oak settle and some green-cushioned window seats, as well as wheelback chairs around tables, a stuffed pheasant and partridge over the log fire, and sporting prints and plates on the bottle-green wall covering; a small lower-ceilinged part by the counter has pubbier furnishings, and small agricultural prints on the walls – especially sheep. The front conservatory has a vaulted pine ceiling and walls of local stone, while at the side is a separate locals' bar; dominoes. The garden has a play area for children. The dining areas are no smoking. Bedrooms are simple but comfortable, and, not surprisingly, they do very good breakfasts. ***(Recommended by Nick and Meriel Cox, Andrew Low, Christopher Beadle, Ian S Morley, Mrs M Wood, John and Kathleen Potter, Alan Morton, Mike Doupe, Comus Elliott, Bill Wood, Christine and Malcolm Ingram)***

Free house ~ Licensees Alan and Julie Reid ~ Real ale ~ Meals and snacks (12-2, 6-9.30; not Mon, exc for residents) ~ Restaurant ~ (01890) 860257 ~ Children welcome ~ Open 11-2.30, 6-11 weekdays, 11-11 Sat, 12.30-3, 6.30-10.30 Sun; in winter closed Sun eves, all day Mon (exc for residents), 25 Dec and 1 Jan ~ Bedrooms: £34(£45S)/£58(£72S)

TAYVALLICH (Strathclyde) NR7386 Map 11

Tayvallich Inn

B8025, off A816 1 mile S of Kilmartin; or take B841 turn-off from A816 two miles N of Lochgilphead

Fresh seafood is the highlight of the menu at this simply furnished cafe/bar, brought in by local fishermen from the bay of Loch Sween just across the lane. The choice typically includes home-made soup (£1.95), moules marinières (£3.50), fillet of haddock or stir-fried vegetables (£4.50), baked goat's cheese and roasted peppers (£4.90), beef curry or cajun chicken (£5.50), half a dozen Loch Sween oysters or locally smoked salmon (£7), sirloin steak (£12), fried scallops (£12.50), the very popular seafood platter (£15.50), and home-made puddings (£3); half helpings for children. Decent wines and Islay malt whiskies. Service is friendly, and people with children are very much at home here. The small bar has cigarette cards and local nautical charts on the cream walls, exposed ceiling joists, and pale pine upright chairs, benches and tables on its quarry-tiled floor. It leads into a no-smoking (during meal times) dining conservatory, from where sliding glass doors open on to a terrace with pinic-sets and lovely views over the yacht anchorage and water. There's a garden, too. *(Recommended by Mr and Mrs D Lee, Neil Townend, Colin Thompson, John and Barbara Burns)*

Free house ~ Licensee John Grafton ~ Meals and snacks ~ Restaurant ~ (01546) 870282 ~ Children welcome until 10pm ~ Open 11-11(midnight Sun, 1am Fri/Sat); 11-2.30, 6-11 in winter; closed Mon Nov-Mar

THORNHILL (Central) NS6699 Map 11

Lion & Unicorn

A873

A reliable place for consistently good food (they describe the style as contemporary Scottish), this pleasant inn still has some parts dating back to 1635; in the restaurant you can see the original massive fireplace, six feet high and five feet wide. The constantly changing menu might at lunchtime include soup such as carrot and coriander (£1.95), baguettes and baked potatoes (from £3.50), deep-fried brie with cranberry sauce (£3.75), ostrich burger (£4.50), herring fried in oatmeal (£5.75), steak, mushroom and Guinness pie (£5.95), Aberdeen Angus steaks on big sizzling platters (from £11), puddings like strawberry parfait or bread and butter pudding (from £2.95), and children's helpings (from £3). They do a set two course lunch for £6, or two course dinner for £10. Well kept Inveralmond Independence and Ossians, and maybe a guest like Broughtons IPA on handpump, with a fine range of malt whiskies, and a good choice of wines (mostly New World). The open-plan front room has a warm fire, beams and stone walls, and comfortable seats on the wooden floors, while the beamed public bar has stone walls and floors, and darts, cribbage, and dominoes. The restaurant is no smoking. Very nice in summer, the garden has a children's play area, tables, and summer Sunday barbecued spit-roasted whole pig, lamb or venison (weather permitting). A couple of readers have found the pub closed at unexpected times in winter – it may be best to check first then. *(Recommended by Neil Townend, Justin Hulford, Mrs J Kemp, Dr A C Williams, Dr F M Ellard, Susan and John Douglas)*

Free house ~ Licensees Walter and Ariane MacAulay ~ Real ale ~ Meals and snacks (12-10pm) ~ Restaurant ~ (01786) 850204 ~ Children welcome ~ Open 12-12(1am Fri/Sat); 12.30-midnight Sun ~ Bedrooms: £40/£60

TUSHIELAW (Borders) NT3018 Map 9

Tushielaw Inn 🛏

Ettrick Valley, B709/B7009 Lockerbie—Selkirk

In a pleasantly remote setting by Ettrick Water, this friendly and traditional country inn is a good base for walkers or for touring, with its own fishing on Clearburn Loch up the B711. Readers particularly like the welcome, and the well prepared home-cooked food such as pan-fried liver and bacon with onion gravy (£7.95), baked chicken breast with brie and bacon (£8.50), roast rack of local lamb with honey, rosemary and garlic sauce (£10.95), and Aberdeen Angus fillet steak with haggis and red wine sauce (£11.95); Sunday roasts. The unpretentious but comfortable little bar has decent house wines, a good few malts, an open fire, local prints and photos, and an antique brass till; it opens on to an outside terrace with tables. Darts, shove-ha'penny, cribbage, dominoes, and piped music. The dining room is no smoking. Note they don't open weekday lunchtimes. *(Recommended by A N Ellis, Sue and Bob Ward, Peter and Anne Cornall, Rita and Lionel Twiss, Chris Rounthwaite, M J Morgan, Wayne Brindle; more reports please)*

Free house ~ Licensees Steve and Jessica Osbourne ~ Meals and snacks ~ Restaurant ~ (01750) 62205 ~ Children welcome ~ Open 7-11, plus 12.30-2 weekends (closed weekday lunchtimes); closed all day Mon-Thurs in winter ~ Bedrooms: £25B/£42B

ULLAPOOL (Highland) NH1294 Map 11

Ceilidh Place

West Argyle St

Plenty of varied things going on at this pretty, rose-draped white house, in a quiet side street above the small town. Rather like a stylish arty cafe-bar – but with a distinctly Celtic character – there's an art gallery, bookshop and coffee shop, and regular jazz, folk, ceilidh and classical music. The eclectic furnishings and decor include bentwood chairs and one or two cushioned wall benches among the rugs on the varnished concrete floor, spotlighting from the dark planked ceiling, attractive modern prints and a big sampler on the textured white walls, magazines to read, venetian blinds, and houseplants; there's a woodburning stove, and plenty of mainly young upmarket customers. The side food bar – you queue for service at lunchtime – does good food from fresh ingredients, such as varied and original salads, home-made soups and breads (from £2), baked potato (£3.25), and venison mince (£3.95); there's always a good choice for vegetarians. Decent wines by the glass, an interesting range of high-proof malt whiskies, and a choice of cognac and armagnac that's unmatched around here; dominoes, piped music. There's an attractive no-smoking conservatory dining room, where the appealing menu has quite a few fish dishes. Tables on a terrace in front look over other houses to the distant hills beyond the natural harbour. The bedrooms are comfortable and pleasantly decorated. *(Recommended by Paula Williams, Mrs Jean Dundas, J G Kirby, Andrew Hazeldine, Stephen Holman)*

Free house ~ Mrs Jean Urquhart ~ Meals and snacks 11-9(6 winter) ~ Evening restaurant ~ (01854) 612103 ~ Children in eating area of bar ~ Regular traditional and folk music (not Sun) ~ Open 11-11; 12.30-11 Sun ~ Bedrooms: £45(£50B)/£90(£110B)

Morefield Motel (Ⓨ)

North Rd

For several hours a day everyone who visits here is coming to enjoy the excellent fresh fish and seafood, and there can be quite a scramble for a table. The owners (themselves ex-fishermen and divers) have a ship-to-shore radio in the office which they use to corner the best of the day's catch before the boats have even come off the sea. Depending on availability, the generously served meals might include soup (£2.50), oak-roasted smoked salmon (£5.75), a basket of prawns (£6.25), crisp battered haddock (£6.95), moules marinières (£8.95), seafood thermidor (£8.75), scallops with bacon (£9.50), a marvellous seafood platter (£16.75), and daily specials such as monkfish, turbot, fresh dressed brown crab, bass with fresh ginger, and giant langoustines with garlic or herb butter. Non-fishy dishes also feature, such as chicken done in various ways (from £7.25), fillet steak with haggis and Drambuie sauce (£14.50), and various vegetarian meals. The smarter Mariners restaurant has a slightly more elaborate menu. In winter the diners tend to yield to local people playing darts or pool, though there's bargain food then, including a very cheap three-course meal. Well kept Courage Directores, Morlands Old Speckled Hen and Orkney Raven on handpump, and nearly 100 malt whiskies, some nearly 30 years old; decent wines and friendly tartan-skirted waitresses. The L-shaped lounge is mostly no smoking and the restaurant is totally no smoking, and there are tables on the terrace; they recently added an air-conditioned conservatory. All the bedrooms have been extensively refurbished and remain popular with hill-walking parties; enjoyable breakfasts. *(Recommended by Ian Baillie, Neil Townend, H Dickinson, Alastair C Fraser, Neil and Angela Huxter)*

Free house ~ Licensee David Smyrl ~ Real ale ~ Meals and snacks (12-2, 5.30-9.30) ~ Restaurant ~ (01854) 612161 ~ Children welcome (but not in restaurant under 12) ~ Occasional live music winter Fri ~ Open 11-11; winter open 11-2.30, 5-11; closed 25/26 Dec, 1/2 Jan ~ Bedrooms: £40B/£50B

It's against the law for bar staff to smoke while handling food or drink.

WEEM (Tayside) NN8449 Map 11

Ailean Chraggan

B846

This family-run hotel is an enjoyable place to stay – small and friendly and set in two acres with a lovely view to the mountains beyond the Tay, sweeping up to Ben Lawers (the highest in this part of Scotland). The good food is a big draw, with the changing menu typically including sandwiches (from £2.45), soup (£2.45), excellent cullen skink (£3.75), moules marinières (£4.25), mediterranean vegetable parcels (£7.50), venison casserole, grilled lamb chops, or baked cod with spicy yoghurt and coriander dressing (£8.25), chicken breast with leek and stilton sauce (£8.50), a lovely platter of whole prawns from Loch Etive (£12.50; the barman apparently drives over every week and buys up the entire catch), and puddings such as hazelnut and passionfruit roulade or pineapple truffle torte (£3.50). Very good wine list, over 100 malt whiskies, and separate children's menu. The modern lounge has recently been redecorated and refitted, with new carpets and striped wallpaper; a dining room shares the same menu, and there are two outside terraces (one with an awning) to enjoy the view. Winter darts and dominoes. *(Recommended by Susan and John Douglas, Ron and Sheila Corbett, Andrew Low, Mr and Mrs P Spencer, Roger and Christine Mash, Chris and Ann Garnett, Dr D G Twyman, Sue and Jim Sargeant, Ann Bolton, Paul and Ursula Randall)*

Free house ~ Licensee Alastair Gillespie ~ Meals and snacks ~ (01887) 820346 ~ Children welcome ~ Open 11-11; closed 25/26 Dec, 1/2 Jan ~ Bedrooms: £35B/£70B

Lucky Dip

Besides the fully inspected pubs, you might like to try these Lucky Dips recommended to us and described by readers (if you do, please send us reports):

BORDERS

☆ **Allanton** [B6347 S of Chirnside; NT8755], *Allanton*: Comfortable and traditional stone terraced inn with creaky swinging sign, changing choice of real ales such as Belhaven 80/-, Charles Wells Bombardier and Greene King IPA, good food from daily changing menu in side dining room, children's menu; attentive service from friendly smartly dressed staff, brick fireplace in homely front bar, local honey for sale, public bar with darts and pool, tables in garden behind; occasional beer and folk festivals; bedrooms, open all day weekends *(Peter and Anne Cornall, BB)*

☆ **Auchencrow** [not far from A1 via B6438 from Reston; NT8661], *Craw*: Cottagey roadside pub in small village, wide choice of interesting good food with some emphasis on fresh fish and seafood; cosy bar with leather-cushioned wall seats, fresh flowers, tables set for eating, woodburner, beams covered in horse show rosettes won by licensee's daughter; helpful flexible service, well kept Border Special, decent wines, more formal lounge; children welcome; bedrooms *(Simon Heafield, A N Ellis, Mr and Mrs G McNeill, BB)*

☆ **Bonchester Bridge** [A6088; NT5812], *Horse & Hound*: Wide range of good home cooking, well kept changing ales such as Courage Directors and Orkney Dark Island, interesting building, splendid open fire in each bar, very pleasant service, evening restaurant, children's area; bedrooms; cl Tues in winter *(R T and J C Moggridge)*

☆ **Eddleston** [A703 Peebles—Penicuik; NT2447], *Horseshoe*: Civilised old beamed pub, good bar and restaurant meals, friendly helpful staff, soft lighting, gentle music, comfortable seats, well kept ale, good choice of wines and whiskies; well equipped bedrooms in annexe *(Mrs C Scrutton, LYM)*

Eyemouth [NT9564], *Ship*: Straightforward pub in interesting position in pretty fishing village, harbour view from upstairs dining room, good home-made soups and local fish, well kept Caledonian 70/- and local Border, friendly service; bedrooms *(Andy and Jill Kassube)*

☆ **Kelso** [7 Beaumont St; NT7334], *Cobbles*: Small two-room dining pub with wall banquettes, some panelling, warm log and coal fires, good value food inc good home-made soups and puddings; very courteous quick service, real ales such as Boddingtons, Caledonian 70/- and McEwans 80/-, decent wines and malt whiskies; piped music; disabled lavatory *(Pamela and Merlyn Horswell)*

Melrose [High St; NT5434], *Kings Arms*: Late 18th-c, with old chairs, interesting ornaments and cosy log fire in beamed bar, well kept Tetleys-related and other ales, good choice of malt whiskies, wide choice of good food inc some local dishes and good fish soup, good children's menu (they're welcome); attentive friendly service even when busy; bedrooms *(Hazel and Michael Duncombe, Kit Ballantyne)*

☆ **St Boswells** [A68 just S of Newtown St Boswells; NT5931], *Buccleuch Arms*: Well established sandstone inn emphasising wide choice of imaginative well prepared bar food (not Sun), sandwiches all day; Georgian-style no-smoking pink plush bar with light oak panelling, well kept Greenmantle, restaurant, tables in garden behind; children welcome, bedrooms *(CD, LYM)*

☆ **St Marys Loch** [A708 SW of Selkirk; NT2422], *Tibbie Shiels*: Down-to-earth inn with interesting history in wonderful peaceful setting by a beautiful loch, handy for Southern Upland Way and Grey Mares Tail waterfall – quite a few caravans and tents in summer; stone back bar, no-smoking lounge bar, straightforward waitress-served lunchtime bar food, well kept Belhaven 80/- and Greenmantle, several dozen malt whiskies, traditional games; children welcome, restaurant, open all day (cl Mon/Tues Nov-Mar); bedrooms *(Jane Keeton, Peter and Anne Cornall, Ian S Morley, Richard Gibbs, Andy and Jill Kassube, Sheila and John French, LYM)*

☆ **Westruther** [B6456, off A697 just SE of the A6089 Kelso fork; NT6450], *Old Thistle*: A firm recommendation for its superb local Aberdeen Angus steaks, besides other food from sandwiches up; a thoroughly nice pub, with intriguing little 18th-c traditional bar, games room, thriving local atmosphere, comfortable two-room lounge and restaurant; cl weekday lunchtime but food all day w/e, children welcome, refurbished bedrooms *(LYM)*

CENTRAL

☆ **Drymen** [The Square; NS4788], *Clachan*: Lively cottagey pub, licensed since 1734, friendly and welcoming; original fireplace with side salt larder, tables made from former bar tops, former Wee Free pews along one wall; decent food in tartan-carpeted lounge, well kept Belhaven Best, 80/- and Stout, hard-working friendly licensee, lots of old local photographs; piped music; on green of attractive village, handy for Loch Lomond and Trossachs *(Paul and Ursula Randall, Michael Butler, Walter Reid)*

Drymen [The Square], *Winnock*: A hotel but has a popular pubby L-shaped bar dating from 17th c, reasonably priced food, good choice of malt whiskies, big garden with picnic-sets; decent bedrooms, ceilidh Sun *(Michael Butler)*

Stirling [Baker St; NS7993], *Hogs Head*: Done out in basic alehouse style with stripped wood and mock gaslamps, eight real ales on handpump, more tapped from the cask, usual lunchtime food, friendly staff; open all day *(Julian Holland, Chris and Ann Garnett)*; [St Marys Wynd], *Whistlebinkies*: Much modernised town pub originally built as stables for castle in late 16th c, but now only exterior shows much sign of its age; three comfortable levels linked by wooden staircase, some bargain dishes on mostly standard menu, quite a few mirrors, lots of posters and leaflets for local and student events; Morlands Old Speckled Hen, newspapers, piped pop music, weekly quiz night; tables on slightly scruffy sloping garden behind, handy for castle and old town *(H L Dennis, BB)*

DUMFRIES AND GALLOWAY

Annan [High St; NY1966], *Blue Bell*: Good genuine local with Scots pictures, maps and ornaments on panelled walls, games area on different level, well kept Belhaven, St Andrews, Theakstons and beer brewed for the pub, attractively priced whiskies *(Pamela and Merlyn Horswell, PB)*

Auchencairn [NX7951], *Old Smugglers*: Friendly and popular 18th-c inn, comfortable and attractive with clean white woodwork, good pub food at sensible prices inc outstanding puddings and cakes, quick competent staff, good juke box, pretty garden and terrace; children welcome *(GF)*

Creetown [off A75; NX4758], *Lairds*: Useful stop associated with caravan site; good bar with guest beers, reasonably priced food, friendly staff *(Stan and Hazel Allen)*

Haugh of Urr [B794 N of Dalbeattie; NX8066], *Laurie Arms*: Warmly welcoming local with lounge and public bars, real ales such as Bass and Tetleys, decent wine, good plain food esp steaks; tables outside, new bedrooms *(Vicky and David Sarti)*

☆ **Kingholm Quay** [signed off B725 Dumfries—Glencaple; NX9773], *Swan*: Small dining pub in quiet spot on River Nith overlooking old fishing jetty, well kept dining lounge (children welcome), comfortable newly decorated public bar, very friendly staff, Theakstons and Youngers, wide choice of good value food esp fish, good puddings, also high teas; restaurant, quiet piped music, children welcome, tables in small garden; bedrooms – handy for Caerlaverock nature reserve *(M A Buchanan, Mrs M McGurk, Christine and Malcolm Ingram)*

☆ **Kippford** [signed off A710 S of Dalbeattie; NX8355], *Anchor*: Good reasonably priced generous bar food inc children's (served all day in summer) in waterside inn facing yacht anchorage, traditional back bar with lots of varnished woodwork, plush front dining bar with lots of prints on stripped stone walls, friendly licensee, good service even when busy, log fire, Scottish Courage real ales; games room, seats out facing water; open all day summer *(P R MacCrimmon, Stan and Hazel Allen, LYM)*

☆ **Kirkcudbright** [Old High St; NX6851], *Selkirk Arms*: Quiet modern decor in cosy and comfortable partly panelled lounge with good local flavour; good reasonably priced food, recently extended dining area, friendly efficient service, real ale inc local Solway Criffel, tables in good spacious garden; fishing; children in restaurant and lounge; good value bedrooms *(Stan and Hazel Allen, LYM)*

☆ **Moffat** [1 Churchgate; NT0905], *Black Bull*: Attractive and well kept, with quick friendly service, generous hearty food from sandwiches up, well kept McEwans 80/-, friendly public bar with railway memorabilia and good open fire (may be only bar open out of season), plush softly lit cocktail bar, simply furnished tiled-floor dining room, side games bar with juke box; children welcome, tables in yard, open all day; bedrooms comfortable and good value *(Alan Wilcock, Christine Davidson, Colin Draper, Stephen Holman, E Locker, LYM)*

☆ **Moffat** [High St], *Moffat House*: Well run extended Adam-style hotel with good value reliable food in spacious old-fashioned plush lounge, relaxed and quiet; prompt helpful service, real ale all year; comfortable bedrooms with good breakfast *(Nick and Meriel Cox, Neil Townend)*

☆ *nr* **Moffat** [signed off A74 towards Beattock; NT0905], *Auchen Castle*: Beautifully appointed country-house hotel (so dress appropriately) in lovely quiet spot with spectacular hill views, well cooked and presented food in peaceful and comfortable bar, decent wines, choice of malt whiskies, cheerful helpful staff – kind to children; trout loch in good-sized grounds; bedrooms superbly decorated, wonderful views *(Nick and Meriel Cox)*

☆ **Moniaive** [High St (A702); NX7790], *George*: 17th-c inn with interesting no-frills old-fashioned flagstoned bar of considerable character; well kept beer, reasonably priced lunchtime snacks, friendly staff and locals, simple bedrooms *(Stan and Hazel Allen, Ian and Villy White, LYM)*

FIFE

Aberdour [NT1985], *Foresters Arms*: Welcoming bar with very friendly staff, old cigarette cards, sporting memorabilia, pool, lunchtime toasties; Rab's Bell over the bar sounds last orders, bought by regulars in memory of Robert Littlejohn who died aged 29 in the Piper Alpha disaster *(Jenny and Roger Huggins)*

☆ **Anstruther** [Bankwell Rd; NO5704], *Craws Nest*: Well run popular hotel with good value bar meals inc outstanding fresh haddock in attractive light long lounge, photographs, paintings for sale, maybe a real ale such as Maclays Wallace, good service; bedrooms *(Paul and Ursula Randall)*

Anstruther [Cellardyke], *Haven*: Welcoming good value pub/restaurant with charming garden, plenty of atmosphere, interesting old local photographs *(Eric Locker)*

Auchtermuchty [NO2311], *Forest Hills*: Tiny parlour-like bar of small 18th-c hotel used for recent filming of *Dr Finlay's Case Book*, in centre of quiet village; copper-topped tables and cushioned seating, locals watching TV, straightforward food in bar and dining room; bedrooms *(Gordon Neighbour, BB)*

Carrick [A919 NW of St Andrews; NO4423], *St Michaels*: Attractive red-walled pine-furnished bar, more rustic public bar (good for families), two dining areas, good value well presented food all day, helpful friendly staff; gentle piped music, can get very busy lunchtime; attractive back terrace and big garden with picnic-sets; open all day, bedrooms *(Susan and John Douglas)*

Ceres [Main St (B939 W of St Andrews); NO4011], *Meldrums*: Small hotel with pleasant respectable atmosphere in cottagey parlour bar, clean and attractive beamed dining lounge with good choice of well prepared and presented reasonably priced bar lunches, prompt friendly service even when busy; bedrooms *(Susan and John Douglas)*

☆ **Falkland** [Mill Wynd; NO2507], *Stag*: Cosy long low white-painted 17th-c house in delightful setting opp charming green, round corner from medieval village square; dimly lit and pubby, with dark wooden pews and stools, exposed stone, copper-topped tables, stone fireplace, antlers and line drawings on wall, and some stained glass above bar; Ind Coope Burton, coffee cocktails, decent food (not Tues or Sun eve), toasted sandwiches and take-away pizzas available most of day, helpful service, dining room with masses of posters; bar billiards, fruit machine, TV, unobtrusive piped music, children welcome *(Susan and John Douglas, BB)*

Falkland, *Hunters Lodge*: Chatty low-ceilinged inn opp Falkland Palace (NTS); neatly kept brightly lit roomy bar, friendly local feel, Maclays Liberty, back eating area with good value straightforward food from sandwiches and baguettes to steaks; fruit machine, piped pop music *(Deborah and Ian Carrington, BB)*

Kettlebridge [NO3007], *Kettlebridge*: Separate dining room with good menu, four real ales *(Dallas Seawright)*

☆ **Kingsbarns** [A917 St Andrews—Crail; NO5912], *Cambo Arms*: Friendly small inn with real fires in armchair lounge and simple front bar, real ales such as Belhaven 80/-, Brains Dark and St Andrews, homely books and pictures, good food all home-cooked to order using much local produce in bar and (not every evening) tiny restaurant – steaks from own beef herd; well equipped bedrooms in former back stables/outbuildings *(Paul and Ursula Randall)*

Lower Largo [The Harbour; NO4102], *Crusoe*: Useful harbourside inn with good food from sandwiches up, beams and stripped stonework, settees in bays, open fire, well kept Scottish Courage beers, quick service; separate lounge bar with Crusoe/Alexander Selkirk mementoes, restaurant; bedrooms spacious and comfortable, with good sea views *(Paul and Ursula Randall)*

North Queensferry [A90; NT1380], *Queensferry Lodge*: Useful motorway break with good views of Forth bridges and the Firth from modern hotel lounge, McEwans real ale, good value bar food inc good buffet 12-2.30, 5-10; bedrooms good *(Neil Townend)*

St Andrews [South St; NO5116], *Ogstons*: Cafe-bar/bistro, marble tables in vestibule and gallery over main bar, real ales such as Bass and Caledonian, good espresso coffee etc, daily papers, friendly willing service, more or less continental snacks most of the day, pleasant airy conservatory dining area, evening Italian restaurant *(Paul and Ursula Randall)*

☆ *nr* **St Andrews** [Grange Rd (off A917) a mile S; NO5114], *Grange*: More restaurant than pub, new French chef doing good choice of enjoyable food in spotless small beamed and flagstoned bar too, affable service, good range of malt whiskies, decent wines (but keg beers), good coffee, furniture in keeping with the age of the building, attractive setting; cl Mon/Tues Nov-Mar *(John Honnor, George Dundas)*

Tayport [Dalglish St; NO4528], *Bell Rock*: Simple old-fashioned fisherman's pub in cottage overlooking harbour, old local photographs and nautical bric-a-brac – really friendly and cheerful, with well kept Scottish Courage ales, home-made food, masses of photographs – local railways, RAF, submarines, tankers *(Paul and Ursula Randall, Susan and John Douglas)*

☆ **Wormit** [Newton Hill – B946/A92 S of Dundee; NO4026], *Sandford*: Golfing hotel's cosy and attractive bar with Highland paintings and bay window seat overlooking the handsome former mansion's grounds, very good inventive bar lunches and suppers (inc children's helpings) served till late, very obliging newish owner; bedrooms good *(Susan and John Douglas)*

GRAMPIAN

Banchory [North Deeside Rd (A93 E); NO6995], *Scott Skinners*: Locally very popular, with friendly efficient staff, comfortable lounge bar, snug, sandwiches and limited but well priced hot dishes, well kept Bass and three guest beers, restaurant; children very welcome, play area and games room; piped music *(Ian and Nita Cooper)*

Braemar [A93; NO1491], *Fife Arms*: Big Victorian hotel on the coach routes, comfortable sofas and tartan cushions, reasonably priced reliable pub food (self-service), huge log fire; children and dogs welcome, piped music, massive ski run game; bedrooms warm and comfortable with mountain views, pleasant strolls in village *(Susan and John Douglas)*

☆ **Crook of Alves** [Burghead Rd, just off A96 Elgin—Forres; NJ1362], *Crooked Inn*: Generous enjoyable food (all day Sun) inc vegetarian, good steaks and Sun roasts in bustling beamed village inn with built-in high-backed brocaded settles, lots of prints and bric-a-brac, open fires, some stripped stone, well kept Theakstons Best, decent wines, friendly service, chess; children in eating area; cl lunchtime Mon-Thurs, cl Mon in Oct, Nov and Jan *(G C Hackemer, LYM)*

Cullen [NJ5167], *Cullen Bay*: Good locally produced food inc good value Sun lunch, good beer range inc Belhaven, up to 30 malt whiskies, beautiful bay view; comfortable bedrooms *(Ian and Sandra Thornton)*

Dyce [Overton Circle; part of Marriott Hotel; NJ8812], *Bon Accord*: Good atmosphere, friendly staff, keg beers but good choice of good wines by the glass, good food in both restaurants inc local fish and beef, efficient service; comfortable bedrooms, handy for airport *(Mike and Karen England)*

☆ **Findhorn** [NJ0464], *Crown & Anchor*: Useful family pub with food all day inc imaginative and children's dishes (model train takes orders to kitchen), up to six changing real ales, big fireplace in lively public bar, separate lounge, friendly individual staff; bedrooms comfortable, good boating in Findhorn Bay (boats for residents) *(Andrew Rogers, Amanda Milsom, LYM)*

Monymusk [signed from B993 SW of Kemnay; NJ6815], *Grant Arms*: Comfortable well kept inn with good Don fishing, log fire dividing dark-panelled lounge bar, lots of malt whiskies, S&N real ales, games in simpler public bar, very good bar food (wide choice), restaurant; children welcome, open all day weekends; bedrooms *(Neil Townend, LYM)*

Stonehaven [Shorehead; NO8786], *Ship*: Overlooking harbour, with simply furnished bar, smarter back dining area, games in side room; good reasonably priced food, well kept Orkney Dark Island and guest beers *(Neil Townend)*

☆ **Turriff** [Auchterless; A947, 5 miles S; NJ7250], *Towie*: Comfortable and warmly welcoming dining pub, good interesting home-made food (all day Sun), reasonable prices, elegant no-smoking dining room, helpful service, well kept Theakstons Best and a weekly changing guest beer, decent wines, lots of malt whiskies; children welcome, darts, pool, shove-ha'penny, cribbage, dominoes, trivia, and piped music; handy for Fyvie Castle (NTS) and Delgatie Castle, open all day w/e *(Neil Townend, LYM)*

HIGHLAND

☆ **Achiltibuie** [NC0208], *Summer Isles*: Popular bar with fresh carefully made food – menu limited because of remoteness, but might include baguettes, venison in red wine, huge seafood platter and good puddings; Lairg or Orkney Raven real ale, very friendly service, mix of locals, incomers and visitors; hotel side warm, friendly and well furnished, with pretty watercolours and flowers; bedrooms comfortable and good value, though the cheapest are not lavish *(Anthony Barnes)*

Aultbea [NG8689], *Drumchork Lodge*: Competitively priced good food and well kept real ale in hotel lounge or very roomy public bar (underpopulated since winding-down of nearby NATO base) with massive log fire, pool and darts; well kept real ale; also open all year; bedrooms *(Chris and Ann Garnett)*

Aviemore [Coylumbridge Rd; NH8912], *Olde Bridge*: Well kept and attractive inn, recently extended, with good value bar food inc four-course meals (whisky for the haggis), cheerful mainly antipodean waitresses, changing real ales such as Caledonian and Lairds, Tues ceilidh; pleasant surroundings *(James Nunns, EJL)*

☆ **Carrbridge** [nr junction A9/A95 S of Inverness; NH9022], *Dalrachney Lodge*: Consistently good reasonably priced food and friendly staff in pleasantly relaxed traditional shooting-lodge-type hotel with simple bar, comfortable lounge with books and log fire in ornate inglenook, plenty of malt whiskies, well kept McEwans 70/-, old-fashioned dining room; very busy with locals weekends; children welcome, bedrooms, most with mountain and river views; open all year *(David Dolman, R F and M K Bishop, Neil Townend)*

Dornoch [Church Rd; NH8089], *Mallin House*: Good well priced food inc tasty local fish and superb langoustine in welcoming lounge or restaurant, well kept Theakstons Best and other Scottish Courage beers, good range of malt whiskies, friendly service, interesting collections of whisky-water jugs and golf balls; comfortable bedrooms *(Mick Hitchman)*; [Argyle St], *Sutherland House*: Bar/restaurant rather than pub, but well worth knowing for very welcoming service, pleasant surroundings and good food from sandwiches, filled baked potatoes and other bar food at sensible prices to steaks, venison, wild salmon and so forth *(Jean Perree, Thelma Dover)*

Fort William [Glen Nevis; NN1272], *Glen Nevis*: Good value food in comfortable modern lounge bar, handy for campsite and Ben Nevis walkers; good restaurant *(Mike Jones)*; [66 High St], *Grog & Gruel*: Done out in traditional alehouse style, half a dozen interesting changing well kept ales, upstairs restaurant with wide range of enjoyable food inc vegetarian and non-standard dishes, starters available as bar snacks downstairs, helpful waiters; children welcome; in pedestrian part *(Hazel and Michael Duncombe, Mike Jones)*

☆ **Gairloch** [just off A832 near bridge; NG8077], *Old Inn*: Attractive inn in nice spot, comfortable two-room lounge and public bar well renovated following 1996 fire damage – cosy and softly lit; friendly landlord and staff, a good few malts, up to eight real ales in summer, popular good value bar food, games in public bar; open all day, picnic-sets and rope swing in streamside garden, lovely woodland walks; comfortable bedrooms *(Mr and Mrs P L Spencer, Neil and Angela Huxter, Bronwen and Steve Wrigley)*

Garve [A835 some miles N; NH3969], *Inchbae Lodge*: Snug friendly bar with lots of dark woodwork, good generous food inc imaginative main dishes; hotel side has attractive dining room, good wines, sitting room with plush chairs and sofas; comfortable bedrooms, beautiful setting *(Anthony Barnes)*

☆ **Glen Shiel** [A87 Invergarry—Kyle of Lochalsh; NH0711], *Cluanie*: Hotel in lovely wild setting by Loch Cluanie (good walks), big helpings of good simple freshly prepared bar food in three knocked-together rooms with dining chairs around polished tables, overspill into restaurant; friendly efficient staff, good fire, well kept interesting ales, no pool or juke box; children welcome; big comfortable modern bedrooms nicely furnished in pine, stunning views and good bathrooms – great breakfasts for non-residents too *(Nigel Woolliscroft)*

Glencoe [old Glencoe rd, behind NTS Visitor Centre; NN1256], *Clachaig*: Spectacular setting, surrounded by soaring mountains, inn doubling as mountain rescue post and cheerfully crowded with outdoors people in season, with walkers' bar (two woodburners and pool), pine-panelled snug, big modern-feeling lounge bar; snacks all day, wider evening choice, lots of malt whiskies, well kept ales such as Arrols 80/-, Maclays 80/-, Marstons Pedigree, Theakstons Old Peculier, Tetleys and Youngers No 3; children in no-smoking restaurant; frequent live music; simple bedrooms, good breakfast *(David Trump, John and Beryl Knight, LYM)*; [off A82 E of Pass], *Kings House*: Alone in a stupendous mountain landscape, with simple bar food inc children's dishes, well kept McEwans 80/-; choose your bar carefully – the dark climbers' one at the back (sometimes rather draughty) has very basic furnishings, loud pop music, pool and darts, the central cocktail bar has cloth banquettes and other seats around wood-effect tables; open all day; bedrooms in inn itself, and in cheaper dormitory-style bunkhouse *(CG, AG, BB)*

Invergordon [NH7168], *Marine*: Useful stop, with food inc decent filled rolls, reasonably priced drinks, cheerful service *(Chris and Ann Garnett)*

☆ **Invermoriston** [A887/A82 NE of Fort Augustus; NH4117], *Glenmoriston Arms*: Cosily comfortable lounge, cheery stables bar, well kept McEwans 80/-, lots of malt whiskies, decent straightforward bar food, friendly quick staff; good restaurant with imaginative fresh food (book ahead); fishing and stalking by arrangement, handy for Loch Ness; bedrooms good, open all year *(Mr and Mrs J E Murphy, LYM)*

☆ **Kentallen** [A828 SW of Ballachulish; NN0057], *Holly Tree*: Comfortable hotel converted from Edwardian railway station, and much extended since, in lovely quiet setting by Loch Linnhe, with pleasant grounds stretching a mile taking in their own grassy pier and slipway; neat little carpeted bar, some railway prints and photographs; good fish and game in modern dining room, looking out over water; bedrooms all have loch views *(Mrs L Foster, BB)*

☆ **Kingussie** [High St (A86); NH7501], *Royal*: Big former coaching inn, the highlight these days the half dozen or so interesting real ales and lager brewed in their own Iris Rose Brewery in the stables; also 200 malt whiskies, spacious open-plan bar with banquettes and stage for evening entertainment, standard well priced food inc good baguettes, friendly helpful staff, no-smoking area; juke box; children welcome, open all day; bedrooms *(M Thompson, G Neighbour, E Locker, BB)*

☆ **Kylesku** [A894, S side of former ferry crossing; NC2234], *Kylesku Hotel*: Useful for this remote NW coast (but in winter open only weekends, just for drinks), rather spartan but pleasant and busy local bar (unusual in facing the glorious view, with seals often in sight), friendly helpful service, short choice of reasonably priced food from sandwiches to wonderfully fresh local seafood, delicious substantial garnishes; open all day in summer, comfortable seaview restaurant, outside tables with sea view too, well refurbished peaceful bedrooms, good breakfast; boatman does good loch trips *(J and S French, R C Morgan, Colin Thompson)*

Melvich [A836; NC8765], *Melvich*: Food from simple sandwiches to fresh wild salmon in civilised lounge bar or restaurant, relaxed atmosphere and service, peat or log fire; lovely spot, beautiful sea and coast views; bedrooms *(Dr D G Twyman, Neil Townend, CG, AG)*

☆ **Plockton** [Innes St, off A87 or A890 NE of Kyle of Lochalsh; NG8033], *Creag Nan Darach*: Fresh substantial well cooked food inc superb fish, real chips and veg done just right, well kept McEwans 80/- and Theakstons, good range of malt whiskies, pleasant efficient service, congenial bustling atmosphere even in winter; some live traditional music, modestly comfortable bedrooms *(D Stokes, H Dickinson)*

☆ *nr* **Spean Bridge** [A82 7 miles N; NN2491], *Letterfinlay Lodge*: Well established hotel, lovely view over Loch Lochy from big comfortably modern main bar with popular lunchtime buffet and usual games, small smart cocktail bar, no-smoking restaurant; good malt whiskies, friendly service, children and dogs welcome, pleasant lochside grounds, own boats for fishing; clean and comfortable bedrooms, good breakfast; gents' have good showers and hairdryers – handy for Caledonian Canal sailors *(Sue and Bob Ward, Mike Jones, Colin Draper, K M Crook, LYM)*

Strontian [NM8161], *Ben View*: Good bar food and beer in simple pine-panelled bar with open fire; bedrooms, peaceful setting *(Mrs L Foster)*

Talladale [A832 Kinlochewe—Gairloch; NG8970], *Loch Maree*: Good lochside setting, comfortable bar running the length of the hotel, friendly family management, good food, decent wines, coal fire; bedrooms, open till early Nov *(Alistair Taylor)*

Tongue [A836; NC5957], *Ben Loyal*: Lovely views up to Ben Loyal and out over Kyle of Tongue, good value bar food, Tennents 80/-, friendly owners, small but imaginative choice of restaurant food using local (even home-grown) produce; traditional live music in lounge bar in summer; comfortable good value bedrooms *(Mr and Mrs A Dewhurst, Dr D G Twyman)*

☆ **Ullapool** [Shore St; NH1294], *Ferry Boat*: Simple, friendly and busy pubby bar, harbour and sea views, well kept changing ales such as Greenmantle, Isle of Skye Red Cuillin and Black Cuillin, Orkney; coal fire in quieter inner room, honest lunchtime bar food from sandwiches up, no-smoking evening restaurant; open all day, children in eating areas, Thurs folk night, well equipped bedrooms *(Ian Baillie, Andrew Hazeldine, LYM)*

LOTHIAN

Aberlady [Main St; NT4679], *Old Aberlady*: Spotless comfortable traditional pub, friendly efficient service, good varied food, well kept beer, restaurant *(S L Randle)*

Balerno [22 Main St (off A70); NT1666], *Grey Horse*: Late 18th-c small stonebuilt pub with unspoilt panelled bar, friendly lounge, Belhaven, Boddington and Caledonian Deuchars, dominoes, cards; open all day *(the Didler)*; [64 Johnsburn Rd], *Johnsburn House*: Lovely old-fashioned beamed bar in 18th-c former mansion with ornate ceiling by Robert Lorimer, Caledonian Deuchars, Orkney Dark Raven and guest beers, coal fire, panelled dining lounge with good food inc shellfish, game and vegetarian, more formal evening dining rooms; children welcome, open all day w/e, cl Mon *(the Didler)*

Champany [NT0279], *Champany Inn*: Group of converted farm buildings, more restaurant than pub, but does have Belhaven real ales as well as good food (inc delectable puddings); good service even when packed; bedrooms *(A Muir)*

☆ **Cramond** [Cramond Glebe Rd (off A90 W of Edinburgh); NT1876], *Cramond Inn*: Softly lit little rooms with comfortable brown-and-brass decor, traditional English-style pub furnishing but Scottish bric-a-brac, good coal and log fires, prompt friendly service, Sam Smiths OB, emphasis on good generous well priced salads, grills etc; very popular with retired couples at lunchtime; in picturesque waterside village *(Ian and Villy White, Neil Townend, LYM)*

☆ **Dirleton** [B1345 W of N Berwick; NT5184], *Open Arms*: Apt name – very welcoming hotel, small and comfortable; not a place for just a drink, but good for bar food inc generous snacks and well presented hot dishes with good fresh veg; lovely little sitting room with good open fire, helpful service, fine position facing castle; good bedrooms *(P Rome, Ian Phillips)*

☆ **Dunbar** [Old Harbour; NT6878], *Starfish*: Brightly redecorated bistro, perhaps now more restaurant than pub, with good waitress-served food esp good chowder, paella and (expensive) fresh fish and lobster specials, good chowder; changing wines, malt whiskies, bottled beer only; nice wood fittings, orange-painted walls and ceiling, friendly staff, relaxed atmosphere *(Peter*

O'Malley, David Unsworth, BB)

Dunbar [Old Harbour], *Volunteer*: Busy red-painted house with outside tables looking down to harbour; good value bar food, seafood restaurant; takes its name from volunteer lifeboatmen, RNLI flag outside *(BB)*

☆ **Edinburgh** [8 Leven St], *Bennets*: Elaborate Victorian bar with wonderfully ornate original glass, mirrors, arcades, panelling and tiles, well kept Caledonian Deuchars and other ales from tall founts (even the rare low-strength Caledonian 60/-), lots of uncommon malt whiskies, bar snacks and simple lunchtime hot dishes, children allowed in eating area lunchtime; open all day, cl Sun lunchtime *(the Didler, Andy and Jill Kassube, LYM)*

☆ **Edinburgh** [St Georges Sq/George St], *Dome*: Opulent Italianate former bank, huge main bar has magnificent soaring dome, elaborate plasterwork and stained glass; central servery, pillars, lots of greenery, mix of wood and cushioned wicker chairs, Caledonian Deuchars IPA and 80/-, smart dining area with interesting food; smaller and quieter art deco Frasers bar (may be cl some afternoons and evenings early in week) has atmospheric period feel, striking woodwork, unusual lights, red curtains, lots of good period advertisements, piped jazz, daily papers, same beers – also wines (rather pricy) and cocktails; bedrooms in hotel complex – no reports on these yet *(Vann and Terry Prime, W D Christian, BB)*

☆ **Edinburgh** [55 Rose St], *Rose Street Brewery*: Malt-extract beer brewed on the premises, mild-flavoured though quite potent Auld Reekie 80/- and stronger sticky 90/-, also Brewhouse Reserve and AGM 80/- – tiny brewery can be seen from upstairs lounge (cl at quiet times); back-to-basics downstairs bar open all day, with well reproduced (maybe loud) pop music from its CD juke box, machines; usual food, good friendly service, tea and coffee, live music some evenings *(Susan and Nigel Wilson, Eric Larkham, the Didler, Andy and Jill Kassube, Roger Huggins)*

☆ **Edinburgh** [Rose St, corner of Hanover St behind Jenners], *Milnes*: Well reworked 1992 as traditional city pub, rambling layout taking in several areas downstairs and even in yard; busy old-fashioned bare-boards feel, dark wood furnishings and panelling, cask tables, lots of old photographs and mementoes of poets who used to meet here, wide choice of mostly Scottish Courage beers with well kept Caledonian 80/- and some unusual bottled ones, good value lunches inc various pies charged by size; cheerful staff, lively atmosphere, esp evening *(Nick and Meriel Cox, Eric Larkham, the Didler, Mr and Mrs Jon Corelis, Roger Huggins, BB)*

☆ **Edinburgh** [George St], *Standing Order*: Busy former bank, well converted by Wetherspoons in the style of the Counting House in Glasgow, enormous main room with splendidly colourful and elaborate ceiling, lots of tables, smaller side booths; no-smoking room with well stocked bookshelves, comfortable green sofa, Adam fireplace, and portraits; good value food, coffee and pastries, decent choice of beers; extremely popular Sat night *(Andy and Jill Kassube, W D Christian, BB)*

☆ **Edinburgh** [W Register St], *Cafe Royal*: Can be noisy and crowded – go at a quiet time to take in the superb Doulton tilework portraits of 19th-c innovators, showy island bar counter and other Victorian details; well kept McEwans 80/-, Morlands Old Speckled Hen, Theakstons Best and a weekly guest beer, lunchtime carvery (not Sun) with hot sandwiches carved to order, daily papers; children allowed in restaurant, open all day *(Eric Larkham, Roger Huggins, LYM)*

Edinburgh [232 Canongate], *Canons Gait*: Smart Royal Mile bar with pleasant atmosphere, good choice of real ales inc Isle of Skye and Orkney, well priced food inc local produce *(Andy and Jill Kassube)*; [Broughton St], *Cask & Barrel*: No-frills traditional drinkers' pub, good choice of beers, helpful service, good value bar food esp stovies Mon-Fri, Thai lunch Fri *(William Angold, BB)*; [26 Broughton St], *Cloisters*: Parsonage turned alehouse, mixing church pews and gantry recycled from redundant church with bare boards and lots of brewery mirrors; Caledonian Deuchars and 80/-, guests such as Courage Directors, Flying Firkin Aviator, Inveralmond Lia Fail and Village White Boar, friendly atmosphere, good food choice; open all day *(the Didler)*; [1 Cumberland St], *Cumberland*: Classic unpretentious old-fashioned bar, seven real ales such as Bass, Caledonian 80/-, Fullers London Pride, and Hopback Summer Lightning, lots of malt whiskies, busy chatty feel, good service, daily papers, lunchtime food; leather seating, brewery memorabilia and period advertisements, cosy side room, bright lighting, plain modern back extension; space in front for outside drinking *(Vann and Terry Prime, Andy and Jill Kassube, BB)*; [9 Grassmarket], *Fiddlers Arms*: Unspoilt traditional pub with McEwans ale, free Scottish live music with primarily local audience (has been Mon) *(Mr and Mrs Jon Corelis)*; [102 Constitution St, off Leith Walk], *Homes*: No-frills one-room pub with five real ales, friendly staff, antique tin boxes, lunchtime toasties; open all day (till late on Fri/Sat folk nights) *(the Didler)*; [James Court, by 495 Lawnmarket], *Jolly Judge*: Interesting and comfortable basement of 16th-c tenement with traditional fruit-and-flower-painted wooden ceiling, friendly service, Caledonian 80/- and a guest beer, changing malt whiskies, hot drinks, lovely fire, quickly served lunchtime bar meals and afternoon snacks; piped music, games machine; children allowed at lunchtime in eating area; cl Sun lunchtime; space outside in summer *(Roger Huggins, LYM)*; [The Shore, Leith], *Leith Oyster Bar*:

Comfortable pub overlooking water in restored Docks, one of the cheapest places for food in area, with short choice of reliable, simple and good value meals, inc breakfasts; pleasant candlelit bar with wooden floors, real ales, decent wines *(Walter Reid, BB)*; [Lindsay Rd, Newhaven], *Peacock*: Good straightforward food esp fresh seafood in neat plushly comfortable pub with conservatory-style back room leading to garden, McEwans 80/- and a guest such as Orkney Dark; very popular, best to book evenings and Sun lunchtime; children welcome, open all day *(Ian and Villy White, M A Buchanan, LYM)*; [13 Ettrick Rd], *Royal Ettrick*: A nice place to stay, with view over brook in green quiet area; but also good food in glazed dining area overlooking bowling greens, fine collection of real ales such as Bass, Buckleys Rev James, Caledonian Deuchars, 80/- and Tempus Fugit, Harviestoun Ptarmigan, Maclays Kanes Amber and Tomintoul Culloden; bedrooms *(Vann and Terry Prime)*; [118 Biggar Rd (A702), Hill End], *Steading*: Popular modern pub, several cottages knocked together at foot of dry ski slope, a dozen well kept Scottish and English real ales inc Timothy Taylor Landlord, consistently good varied generous food 10am-10pm, relatively cheap, in bar, restaurant and conservatory – dining pub atmosphere evening; friendly staff *(Mr and Mrs T Bryan, M A Buchanan)*; [1 St Andrews Sq], *Tiles*: Exquisitely tiled cafe/bar, waiter service to outside seats and tables creating rather continental feel; several real ales such as Broughton Merlin, Caledonian Deuchars IPA, Courage Directors and Harviestoun, good wine list with a dozen by the glass; black and white checked chairs and floor, interesting plasterwork, fresh flowers on bar, bistro-style menu, daily papers, efficient service, busy, with wide mix of customers *(Eric Larkham, BB)*

Gullane [East Links Rd; NT4882], *Old Clubhouse*: Two bars, old pictures, memorabilia, stuffed birds, open fire, three Maclays real ales, wide range of bar food, fast friendly service, views over golf links to Lammermuirs; open all day *(R M Corlett)*

Haddington [Sidegate; NT5174], *Maitlandfield House*: Interesting varied good food, well kept Belhaven, pleasant conservatory; bedrooms good *(D L Parkhurst)*

Musselburgh [78 N High St; aka Staggs; NT3472], *Volunteer Arms*: Same family since 1858, unspoilt busy bar, dark panelling, old brewery mirrors, great gantry with ancient casks, Caledonian Deuchars, 60/- and 80/- and guest beers; open all day (not Tues/Weds, cl Sun) *(the Didler)*

☆ **Queensferry** [South Queensferry (B924, just off A90); NT1278], *Hawes*: Featured famously in *Kidnapped*, now comfortably modernised, with fine views of the Forth bridges (one rail bridge support in car park), friendly staff, well kept Arrols 80/-, Ind Coope Burton and guest beers such as Caledonian 80/- from tall founts, decent usual food from efficient servery, games in small public bar, no-smoking family room, restaurant, children welcome; tables on back lawn with play area; good bedrooms, esp Duke of Argyll suite *(D Parkhurst, LYM)*

☆ **Ratho** [Baird Rd; signed off A8, A71, B7030 W of Edinburgh; NT1370], *Bridge*: Very welcoming extended 18th-c pub enjoyed by all ages, food all day inc vegetarian, good children's dishes and tactful range of food for those with smaller appetites, choice between quick Pop Inn menu and more expensive things, well kept Belhaven 80/- and Summer Ale, pleasant helpful and chatty staff; garden by partly restored Union Canal, good well stocked play area, own canal boats (doing trips for the disabled, among others); open all day from noon, very busy in summer *(Dr A C Williams, Dr F M Ellard, Neil Townend, Ian and Villy White)*

STRATHCLYDE

Balloch [Fisherwood Rd; NS3981], *Tullichewan*: Attractive big hotel opp boat trip pier, drawing-room feel in lounge bar with wide choice of food from soup and sandwiches to steak inc reasonable vegetarian choice, small dining room, separate big restaurant, Scottish Courage beers; bedrooms *(Michael Butler)*

☆ **Bothwell** [27 Hamilton Rd (B7071); a mile from M74 junction 5, via A725; NS7058], *Cricklewood*: Smartly refurbished dining pub with good bar food, Scottish Courage real ale, restful atmosphere, neat decorations inc old carved wooden trade signs on stairway, complete sets of cigarette cards in gents'; open all day; bedrooms *(A Muir)*

Carnwath [A721 E of Carstairs; NS9846], *Wee Bush*: Extensively renovated and rethatched, with welcoming atmosphere, stone floors, good food such as herring in mustard sauce or venison and chicken, Tennents 70/-; Burns wrote Better a Wee Buss Than Nae Bield outside *(Pamela and Merlyn Horswell)*

Colintraive [opp the Maids of Bute; NS0374], *Colintraive*: Clean, bright and friendly small family-run hotel in lovely spot overlooking the Maids of Bute, by ferry to Rhubodach on Bute; straightforward food inc nice puddings; bedrooms immaculate and attractive, with huge baths and good breakfast *(NW)*

☆ **Connel** [North Connel; NM9134], *Lochnell Arms*: Attractive hotel with cosy public bar, small lounge, conservatory extension; good value food inc good seafood, friendly service, bric-a-brac, plants, beautiful views over Loch Etive; waterside garden; bedrooms *(Andrew Low)*

☆ **Glasgow** [17/19 Drury St], *Horseshoe*: Classic high-ceilinged pub with enormous island bar, gleaming mahogany and mirrors, snob screens and all sorts of other Victorian features – well worth a good look round; friendly service, well kept Bass, Greenmantle and Caledonian 80/-, lots of malt whiskies; games machines, piped music; amazingly cheap food in plainer upstairs bar, no-smoking restaurant (where children allowed); open all day *(Richard Lewis, A Muir, LYM)*

☆ **Glasgow** [12 Ashton Lane], *Ubiquitous Chip*: Well placed mirrors giving feeling of space, striking raftered roof, bustling chatty atmosphere, minimal decoration except for some stained glass and carefully carved wooden chests and pews, Caledonian 80/- and Deuchars, a dozen or more wines by the glass, chilled vodkas, farm cider, 120 malt whiskies, helpful service; good bistro menu in adjacent rooms or on pleasant balcony overlooking well known downstairs restaurant; very popular, can be packed with university people *(Monica Shelley, Stephen Holman, Walter Reid, David Unsworth, BB)*

☆ **Glasgow** [83 Hutcheson St], *Rab Ha's*: Well converted Georgian townhouse in same family as Babbity Bowster (see main entries), quite trendy, with loud music and mostly young customers in evening; candlelit tables, interesting paintings and art, plain wooden tables and chairs, panelled walls one end, stone the other, can get busy; good imaginative bar food with lots of salads and distinctive toasted sandwiches and pasta, and reasonably priced meals in upstairs bistro (cheap set menus Mon-Weds); Caledonian beers, coffee machine, decent wines, daily papers; fruit machine; bedrooms elegant and immaculate *(Ian Phillips, BB)*

☆ **Glasgow** [153 North St], *Bon Accord*: Attractively done up in Victorian kitchen style, busy and friendly, with Marstons Pedigree, McEwans 80/-, Theakstons Best and Old Peculier, Youngers No 3 and several guest beers, good choice of malt whiskies and wines, good value simple bar food all day, traditional games; restaurant, Weds quiz night, open all day *(Chris and Sue Bax, Ian Jolly, LYM)*

☆ **Glasgow** [154 Hope St], *Cask & Still*: Comfortable and welcoming, with bare boards and panelling, big carpets, raised leather seating area, reasonably priced food all day (menu limited evenings) with well kept ales such as Caledonian Golden Promise, Theakstons Best, Tomintoul Caillie and Youngers No 3, lots of unusual bottled beers, shelves and shelves of malt whiskies, Bulmer's cider, decent wines, friendly helpful staff, interesting prints, good piped music; open all day (cl lunchtime Sun) *(Richard Lewis, BB)*

Glasgow [1153 Cathcart Rd], *Clockwork Beer Co*: Comfortable brightly decorated two-level cafe-bar with microbrewery on view brewing interesting Lager, Red and Amber, also five good guest beers on tall fount air pressure, good range of continental beers, speciality fruit schnapps, country wines from Moniack Castle, Cairn o' Mohr and Lindisfarne, good conventional wines and masses of malt whiskies; good food all day, half helpings for children, friendly service; open all day *(Richard Lewis)*; [12 Brunswick St], *Mitre*: Unspoilt small Victorian pub with horseshoe bar and coffin gantry, three or four real ales such as Belhaven, Orkney Dark Island, St Andrews and one brewed for the pub, also unusual Belgian and other bottled beers; friendly sports-loving staff, wholesome cheap food, upstairs restaurant; open all day, cl Sun *(SLC, Richard Lewis)*; *Printworks*: Whtibreads Hogshead pub with usual wide choice of well kept beers inc microbrews, also Belgian bottled beers, country wines; interesting multi-level building keeping features of former trade, good menu, friendly staff; open all day *(Richard Lewis)*; [11 Exchange Pl], *Rogano*: Elegant art deco restaurant with smart downstairs front bar area popular for a discreet drink – good cocktails and wines; piped jazz, sophisticated atmosphere, bar menu less expensive than the good restaurant (mostly seafood), but still not cheap; cushioned seats in booths, big ceiling fan, decor echoes the Clyde-built liner *Queen Mary (Walter Reid, BB)*; [Airport], *Tap & Spile*: Well done in the style of a traditional pub, with plenty of seats and good service even when packed; well kept beers such as Batemans XXXB, Calders Dark, Caledonian 70/-, Everards Tiger, Federation Original and Youngs, decent malt whiskies, good snacks inc fresh sandwiches, no-smoking area *(Monica Shelley, Ian Phillips)*; [Byres Rd], *Tennents*: Big lively high-ceilinged pub with well kept Caledonian 70/- or 80/-, Greenmantle, Theakstons Best and lots of interesting changing guest ales, also plenty of good malt whiskies, decent house wine, quick good-humoured service, usual food *(Monica Shelley)*; [141 Dumbarton Rd, Kelvinhall], *Three Judges*: Maclays and several quickly changing well kept guest ales, Addlestone's cider, basic food, friendly licensees, staff and locals (with their dogs), plenty of seating in long civilised back bar, massive pump clip collection; open all day *(Richard Lewis, Eric Larkham, Walter Reid)*

☆ **Houston** [Main St (B790 E of Bridge of Weir); NS4166], *Fox & Hounds*: Village pub with quick friendly service, good atmosphere (busy evening, quieter daytime), several interesting changing well kept ales such as Heather Fraoch, Isle of Skye Red Cuillin, Moorhouses Premier and Tomintoul Wildcat, occasional beer festivals, clean plush hunting-theme lounge, comfortable seats by fire, sandwiches in bar, wide range of food upstairs, no-smoking areas, piped music; separate livelier bar with video game and pool; open all day, children welcome *(Walter Reid, K M Crook, LYM)*

Inverkip [NS2072], *Inverkip*: Well organised dining pub, enjoyable food, smooth efficient bar service, comfortable surroundings *(Pamela and Merlyn Horswell)*

Kilfinan [B8000, Cowal Peninsula; NR9379], *Kilfinan*: Friendly sporting hotel halfway down Cowal Peninsula, nr Loch Fyne shore; small public bar (used by locals) with communicating lounge, good choice of bar food, restaurant; comfortable bedrooms *(John*

Knighton)
Lochwinnoch [Main St; NS3558], *Black Bull*: Traditional village inn restored with restraint, hard-working new owners, blackboard aphorisms on drink, stripped stonework, fine range of whiskies and ever-changing ales *(Walter Reid)*
Luss [A82 about 3 miles N; NS3593], *Inverbeg*: Across road from Loch Lomond with tables overlooking it, lounge often crowded for straightforward waitress-served food inc several haggis dishes (also restaurant), well kept real ales, friendly staff, games in simple public bar; bedrooms *(Bronwen and Steve Wrigley, LYM)*
Milngavie [Main St; NS5574], *Talbot Arms*: Pleasantly refurbished, wide choice of reasonably priced lunchtime food from substantial sandwiches up, five real ales such as Alloa Talbot 80/-; handy for start or finish of West Highland Way; TVs in bar *(Ian Baillie, Bronwen and Steve Wrigley)*
☆ **Oban** [Stafford St, nr North Pier; NM8630], *Oban Inn*: Friendly bustling traditional pub, beams and slate floor downstairs, quieter upstairs with banquettes, panelling and stained glass, no-smoking family area; hard-working staff, well kept McEwans 70/- and 80/-, lots of whiskies, sandwiches downstairs, cheap food upstairs 11-9 inc vegetarian and good fish and chips, traditional and modern games, juke box or piped music; open all day, folk Sun, singer most w/e *(David Warrellow, Chris and Ann Garnett, Paul Hilditch, Dr A C Williams, Dr F M Ellard, P R and S A White, Julie and Steve Anderton, Hazel and Michael Duncombe, LYM)*
Otter Ferry [B8000; NR9384], *Oystercatcher*: Newish pub and restaurant in old building, outstanding spot overlooking Loch Fyne with lots of tables out on spit; spacious, light wood furnishings, good bar food and seafood restaurant, good wines, local oysters *(Walter Reid)*
Prestwick [Main St; NS3525], *Finbarr Flanagans*: Genuine Irish manager, great bar staff, McEwans 70/- and continental lagers as well as the beers you'd expect, weekday happy hour 5-8, good range of wines and whiskies, bargain three-course meals *(Alistair Taylor)*
Sorn [NS5526], *Sorn Inn*: Trim, well kept inn in conservation village, friendly family service, well kept McEwans 60/- and other beers; wide choice of good food in restaurant; comfortable bedrooms *(Walter Reid)*
☆ **Strachur** [A815 N of village; NN0901], *Creggans*: Welcoming little hotel in lovely countryside by Loch Fyne, tweedy cocktail bar (partly no smoking) with cappuccino machine and home-baked produce for sale, no-smoking conservatory, lively public bar with games room, SkyTV, juke box; good choice of malt whiskies and wines, popular good value bar food inc local seafood, no-smoking restaurant; children welcome, monthly live entertainment summer, open all day; comfortable bedrooms *(John and Beryl Knight, Walter Reid, Chris and Ann Garnett, Pamela and Merlyn Horswell, LYM)*
☆ **Symington** [Main St; just off A77 Ayr—Kilmarnock; NS3831], *Wheatsheaf*: Charming and cosy 18th-c pub in quiet pretty village, popular lunchtime for consistently good original food esp fish and local produce, Belhaven beers, friendly quick service; tables in garden *(Christine and Malcolm Ingram)*
Taynuilt [a mile past village, which is signed off A85; NN0030], *Polfearn*: Hotel with pleasant lounge bar, picture windows making most of setting by loch with Ben Cruachan towering over, well kept beers, relaxed atmosphere, welcoming landlord, good food esp local mussels and fish soup; tables in garden, bedrooms *(Mr and Mrs J Batstone)*
Uplawmoor [Neilston Rd; A736 SW of Neilston; NS4355], *Uplawmoor*: Comfortable atmosphere, friendly staff and owners, good well priced food, particularly well kept ales such as Bass and Caledonian 80/-, separate cocktail bar and attractive restaurant; tables out on terrace *(Mrs C Scrutton, Andy and Jill Kassube)*

TAYSIDE

Abernethy [NO1816], *Crees*: Comfortably refurbished, with four well kept ales, good whiskies, good home-made lunches inc scrumptious puddings, real fire; monthly folk music, handy for Pictish tower nearby; bedrooms planned in adjoining barn *(Dallas Seawright, Catherine Lloyd)*
Blairgowrie [Lower Mill St; NO1745], *Cargills*: Coffee shop/gift shop not pub (no bar, drinks brought to table), but given its position well worth knowing for wide choice of food from modern pasta concoctions to Angus beef, salmon, venison and super puddings; very pleasant service, good coffee, pretty spot by river *(Jean and George Dundas)*
☆ **Broughty Ferry** [Shore Terr/Fishers St; NO4630], *Ship*: Small busy local by lifeboat station, handsomely refurbished in burgundy and dark wood, stately model sailing ship and other mainly local nautical items; open all day for enjoyable food inc massive good value seafood platter, good service, pleasant upstairs dining room with lovely waterfront view, friendly staff; keg beer *(Susan and John Douglas, L G Milligan)*
Broughty Ferry [48 Gray St], *Old Anchor*: Friendly and comfortable carpeted town pub with nautical-theme partitioned bar, ceiling fans, very child-friendly no-smoking eating area, good range of daily specials, generous helpings, Scottish Courage ales with a guest such as Broughton Merlin; open all day *(Ian and Nita Cooper)*
☆ **Cleish** [2 miles from M90 junction 5, off B9097 W; NT0998], *Nivingston House*: Hospitable and relaxing country hotel, well presented reasonably priced bar lunches, rich wallpaper and furnishings, log fire, separate no-smoking lounge, welcoming efficient service, good evening meals, Alloa Calders

tapped from the cask, dozens of malt whiskies, decent wines, snooker; children in eating area, good bedrooms, handsome gardens *(Neil Townend, IHR, Bill and Sylvia Trotter, Ray and Chris Watson, LYM)*

Dundee [100 Commercial St; NO4030], *Mercantile*: Converted bank, much use of repro Charles Rennie Mackintosh style glass in pretty pinks and greens, several levels inc three balconies, lots of old local photographs, wide choice of Scottish real ales, inexpensive food till 8 inc soup and sandwiches, restaurant upstairs; jazz Sun 1-5 *(Susan and John Douglas)*; [Brook St], *Royal Oak*: Pubby bar with stripped stone, old furniture, well kept Ind Coope Burton and several other changing ales, open fire; more like Indian restaurant behind, with sombre dark green decor, tasty curries, also wide choice of more general food; can be very busy weekends, and weekday food may stop around 8ish *(Susan and John Douglas, Neil Townend)*

Dunkeld [NO0243], *Atholl Arms*: Small Victorian hotel overlooking river and bridge, elegant relaxing lounge bar via main entrance with smartly modern servery, antique furnishings, rather grand fireplace, dining area with massive oval table; bedrooms *(Susan and John Douglas)*

☆ **Eassie** [A94 Coupar Angus—Forfar; NO3547], *Castleton House*: Country-house hotel under new ownership, elegant high-ceilinged armchair bar with big log fire, consistently good food, very pleasant service, spacious candlelit L-shaped conservatory restaurant and separate no-smoking dining room; beautiful grounds, bedrooms; fairly handy for Glamis Castle *(Jean and George Dundas, Susan and John Douglas)*

☆ **Errol** [The Cross (B958 E of Perth); NO2523], *Old Smiddy*: Emphasis on good food inc fresh local ingredients and interesting recipes, well kept Belhaven 80/-, lots of country wines, attractive heavy-beamed bar with assorted old country furniture, farm and smithy tools inc massive bellows, good service; pleasant village setting, open all day Sun, cl Mon/Tues lunchtime *(Susan and John Douglas)*

Forfar [45a Queen St; NO4550], *Queen St Bar*: Small, neat, warm and well furnished, with small but attractive menu of well cooked promptly served food; very popular lunchtime, but no rush *(George Dundas)*

Glamis [NO3846], *Strathmore Arms*: Smart hotel with warm and bustling traditional pub bar, stripped stone, fairy-lit twig arrangements, enjoyable food inc interesting dishes (people eat early here), prompt service; bedrooms *(Susan and John Douglas, Jean and George Dundas)*

☆ **Kenmore** [A827 W of Aberfeldy; NN7745], *Kenmore Hotel*: Civilised and quietly old-fashioned small hotel beautifully set in pretty 18th-c village by Loch Tay; layout recently improved – main bar now the front room with long poem hand-written by Burns on the wall, also old fishing photographs, china, panelling, tartan furnishings; good helpful service, enjoyable food from good sandwiches up, cosy upmarket feel; children welcome, back garden with great Tay views; bedrooms, elegant residents' rooms and back dining room, own fishing *(Susan and John Douglas, Nick and Meriel Cox, David Atkinson, Neil Townend, LYM)*

☆ **Kinnesswood** [A911 Glenrothes—Milnathort; NO1703], *Lomond*: Well appointed and friendly small inn with lovely sunset views over Loch Leven, good value bar and restaurant food strong on fresh local produce, delicious puddings, well kept Belhaven, Jennings and guest beers such as Greene King Abbot, quick thoughtful service, log fire; bedrooms comfortable *(Andy and Jill Kassube, R M Macnaughton)*

Lawers [A827; NN6739], *Ben Lawers*: Small well kept inn, friendly new owners doing good reasonably priced food in pleasant dining room; bedrooms *(Mrs Maureen Robertson)*

☆ **Memus** [N of Forfar, off B955 or B957; NO4259], *Drovers*: Pretty rose-covered cottage with lovely orchard garden, bar with ancient flagstones, cosy fire in old range, stripped pine dado, Victorian bric-a-brac, Maclays 70/- and McEwans 80/-, choice of wines and whiskies, good choice of food inc vegetarian, pleasant service in small candlelit dining area (can be busy) *(Susan and John Douglas)*

Perth [off A85 W; NO0724], *Huntingtower*: Plush decoration – even the conservatory overlooking streamside hotel gardens; good reasonably priced bar food, small range of beers; bedrooms *(Ray Watson, IHR)*

Pitlochry [Mill Lane; NN9459], *Old Mill*: Roomy town pub with bar food, good choice of beers, tables out in semi-pedestrianised area *(Nick and Meriel Cox)*

St Fillans [12 miles W of Crieff; NN6924], *Achray House*: Stunning lochside position, good friendly service, good varied reasonably priced food esp puddings, extensive wine list; bedrooms *(Ian and Sandra Thornton, IHR)*

Wester Balgedie [A911/B919 nr Milnathort; NO1604], *Balgedie Toll*: Beamed bar with good food, friendly helpful service, well kept Ind Coope Burton and Tetleys, coal fire; motorcyclists welcome *(Dallas Seawright, David Logan)*

Woodside [A94 Burrelton—Coupar Angus; NO2037], *Woodside*: Anglicised inside, with neatly laid tables on smart green carpet, wide choice of food from good soup with home-baked rolls to king prawns and smoked venison, welcoming waitress service *(George Dundas)*

THE ISLANDS

Arran

Whiting Bay [NS0426], *Kinscadale*: Sun lounge with fine view of bay and mainland; good food; bedrooms *(Dave Braisted)*

Bute

Rothesay [Albert Pl; NS0864], *Black Bull*: Comfortable three-room seafront pub, good value bar food inc sizzle steaks and vegetarian choice, Greenmantle ale, fine choice of malt whiskies, friendly efficient service, attractive pictures of Clyde pleasure steamers *(Dave Braisted)*

Islay

Port Charlotte [NR2457], *Port Charlotte*: Fine refurbishment (large injection of American money), warm peat fire, friendly staff, good range of malt whiskies, good restaurant with local steaks, fish and seafood, sailing ship prints, lovely lochside views; piped music; bedrooms *(Peter and Jacquie Bradbury)*

Skye

Ardvasar [Armadale; A851 towards Broadford; NG6203], *Clan Donald Centre*: More attractive cafeteria/restaurant than pub (part of museum with lovely woodland gardens and walks), but does have a bar, as well as very good value good food and efficient friendly service; good family day out *(Walter and Susan Rinaldi-Butcher)*

Portree [harbourside; NG4843], *Pier*: Down-to-earth fishermen's bar, language to match sometimes, keg beers, good generous fish suppers, welcoming landlord, occasional live music, pipers during Skye games week; bedrooms good value *(Nigel Woolliscroft)*

☆ **Sligachan** [A850 Broadford—Portree, junction with A863; NG4830], *Sligachan Hotel*: Remote inn with almost a monopoly on the Cuillins, capacious and comfortable, with well laid-out huge modern pine-clad bar (children's play area, games room, red telephone ox) separating the original basic climbers' and walkers' bar from the plusher more sedate hotel side; well kept McEwans 80/- and two ales brewed on Skye, dozens of malt whiskies on optic, quickly served bar food inc particularly fresh seafood, fine log fire, good meals in hotel restaurant, good home-made cakes and coffee; very lively some nights, with summer live entertainment and big campsite opp; bedrooms good value, cl winter *(Nigel Woolliscroft, BB)*

☆ **Stein** [end of B886 N of Dunvegan; NG2556], *Stein Inn*: Down-to-earth small inn delightfully set above quiet sea inlet, tables out looking over sea to Hebrides (great sunsets), peat fire in flagstoned and stripped-stone public bar, really welcoming licensees and locals, well kept Isle of Skye Cuillin Red, good malt whiskies, bar food (in winter only for people staying); bedrooms thoroughly renovated *(Jens and Birgitte Hoiberg, D Prodham, LYM)*

Uig [NG3963], *Ferry*: Tiny, friendly and unpretentious lounge bar, reasonably priced limited food from soup and toasties to good fresh fish; clean and comfortable bedrooms overlooking pier and water *(Chris and Ann Garnett, BB)*; [A87], *Uig*: Lovely spot overlooking harbour and sea, good basic food with some interesting dishes, friendly staff, tartan chairs and fire in recently refurbished lounge; modern bedrooms in new annexe with good views *(Jean Panepinto, Bill Cote, Mr and Mrs D Parrish, BB)*

South Uist

☆ **Pollachar** [S end of B888; NF7414], *Pollachar Hotel*: Comfortably modernised and extended 17th-c inn in glorious shoreside setting with fantastic views to Eriskay and Barra, dolphins, porpoises and seals; big public bar, separate dining room, good bar meals; very helpful friendly staff and locals (all Gaelic speaking); 12 well renovated bedrooms with own bathrooms, good breakfast *(NW)*

If a service charge is mentioned prominently on a menu or accommodation terms, you must pay it if service was satisfactory. If service is really bad you are legally entitled to refuse to pay some or all of the service charge as compensation for not getting the service you might reasonably have expected.

Wales

The new entry we have most enjoyed finding here this year has been the friendly and pleasantly idiosyncratic little Rose & Crown tucked away at Graianrhyd, setting a splendid example by staying open all day even when it expects little afternoon trade. Other enjoyable newcomers, or pubs finding their way back into the Guide after a break, are the Bryn Tyrch at Capel Curig in the heart of Snowdonia (a favourite with vegetarians), the homely White Hart just outside Crickhowell (good home cooking), the warm-hearted old Royal Oak at Gladestry (handy for the Offa's Dyke Path), Kilverts in Hay on Wye (civilised and rather sophisticated, without being pretentious about it), the extremely ancient Plough & Harrow at Monknash (remarkable choice of real ales), the George III beautifully placed at Penmaenpool on the Mawddach estuary, the lively Ship in Porthmadog (many dozen malt whiskies, and good beer), and the Tynycornel at Talyllyn – a hotel, but in an irresistibly nice spot. In the last few months readers' praise has been particularly warm for several of the existing main entries, too: the Bear in Crickhowell (great character, good all round), the Nantyffin Cider Mill just outside (first-class food), the Pen-y-Gwryd up above Llanberis (this mountain inn is another great all-rounder), the sophisticated Pant-yr-Ochain in Gresford, the Walnut Tree at Llandewi Skirrid (great food of rare quality, variety and imagination – yet they couldn't be kinder to grubby walkers and stranded taxi-less boaters), the welcoming Druid at Llanferres (imaginative food, a nice place to stay), the Clytha Arms just outside Raglan (another very well run all-rounder), the attractive thatched Bush at St Hilary (reliably good value food), and with its mountain and river views the carefully run Groes at T'yn y Groes (good food and drink, a nice place to stay). Besides the pubs already mentioned for good food, we'd also pick out the waterside Penhelig Arms in Aberdovey (fresh fish delivered daily), the Queens Head near Llandudno Junction (good fresh fish here too), and the Ferry Inn at Pembroke Ferry (the new licensee is keeping up its tradition of a wide choice of simply cooked fresh fish). Among all these, the pub that this time carries off the honours as Wales Dining Pub of the Year is the Nantyffin Cider Mill near Crickhowell. It's worth mentioning, incidentally, that around the main walking areas pub food here tends to be very generous. The Lucky Dip section at the end of the chapter has some prime prospects this year (most of them already inspected and approved by us): the Gazelle and Liverpool Arms at Menai Bridge (Anglesey); White Horse at Cilcain, White Lion at Llanelian yn Rhos and Sun at Rhewl (Clwyd); Harbourmaster at Aberaeron, Druidstone near Broad Haven, Sloop at Porthgain and Wolfe at Wolfs Castle (Dyfed); Prince of Wales at Kenfig (Mid Glamorgan) and Bear in Cowbridge (S Glamorgan); Abbey Hotel at Llanthony, Hostry at Llantilio Crosseny and Nags Head in Usk (Gwent); Royal Oak in Betws y Coed, Kings Head in Llandudno, Ty Coch at Porth Dinllaen and Golden Fleece at Tremadog (Gwynedd); and Blue Boar in Hay on Wye and Red Lion at Llanfihangel nant Melan (Powys). Beer prices in the Principality are a bit lower than the national average, with tied pubs – unusually – tending to be cheaper than free houses. Most unusually of all, it was a pub tied to a national brewer (the Rose & Crown at Graianrhyd, tied to Whitbreads) that we found the cheapest for beer. Pubs tied to Burtonwood and Lees were also relatively cheap, as was the Old House at Llangynwyd (tied to Whitbreads but stocking a local beer more cheaply). The three main independent Welsh brewers are Brains and Buckley (now joining forces), and Felinfoel; Hancocks HB is a Bass beer. Increasingly, there are also beers from smaller-scale Welsh brewers to be found here now, such as the enjoyable Tomas Watkin beers from the Castle in Llandeilo (see Dyfed Lucky Dip entries).

ABERDOVEY (Gwynedd) SN6296 Map 6

Penhelig Arms

Opp Penhelig railway station

Fresh fish is delivered to this mainly 18th-c hotel from the local fishmonger daily. Very well prepared and served, there might be marinated herring fillets with beetroot in a cream mayonnaise (£3.95), fresh dressed local crab (£5.50), delicious fish pie (£6.50), fresh salmon and asparagus salad with a coral sauce or cod fillet grilled with peppers, anchovies and cheese with tomato sauce (£6.95), plaice fillet steamed with prawns with a velouté sauce (£7.50), as well as sandwiches (from £1.95), cream of tomato and pepper soup (£1.95), filled baguettes or stilton cheesecake with melon (£3.95), lamb braised in a barbecue sauce (£6.50), steak and mushroom pie (£6.75), and puddings like banana mousse with chocolate sauce or treacle tart (£2.75); children's helpings; no-smoking restaurant. The excellent wine list has over 40 half bottles, and about 14 wines by the glass, two dozen malt whiskies, fruit or peppermint teas, and coffee. The small original beamed bar has a cosy feel with winter fires, changing real ales such as Bass, Morlands Old Speckled Hen and Tetleys on handpump, and about two dozen malt whiskies; dominoes. In summer you can eat out on a terrace by the harbour wall while you take in the lovely views across the Dyfi estuary – same views from the comfortable bedrooms. *(Recommended by Sue and Bob Ward, J H Jones, J Sheldon, Basil Minson, Amanda and Simon Southwell, Peter Lewis, Yvonne and Peter Griffiths, Mike and Wena Stevenson, Dr M Owton, Jacquie and Jim Jones)*

Free house ~ Licensees Robert and Sally Hughes ~ Real ale ~ Meals and snacks ~ Restaurant ~ (01654) 767215 ~ Children in eating area of bar and restaurant till 9.30 ~ Open 11-4, 5.30-11; 12-4, 7-10.30 Sun; cl 25/26 Dec ~ Bedrooms: £39B/£69B

ABERGORLECH (Dyfed) SN5833 Map 6

Black Lion

B4310 (a pretty road roughly NE of Carmarthen)

There's a simple Welsh charm at this friendly old-fashioned white house, its windows and sides outlined in black paint, with many of the locals speaking Welsh in the plain but comfortably atmospheric stripped-stone bar. It's traditionally furnished with plain oak tables and chairs, high-backed black settles facing each other across the flagstones by the log-effect gas fire, horsebrasses on the black beams, and some sporting prints; a restaurant extension has light oak woodwork. It's delightfully placed in the beautiful Cothi Valley with the Brechfa Forest around; picnic-sets, wooden seats and benches across the quiet road luxuriate in the views. The garden slopes down towards the River Cothi where there's a Roman triple-arched bridge; the licensee has fishing rights and the river is good for trout, salmon and sea trout. Straightforward bar food includes crispy coated camembert (£2.95), ginger and garlic prawns (£3.50), mussels (£3.75), wild mushroom lasagne (£5.50), fresh fish (£6.50), roast duck with orange sauce (£9.50) and fillet steak (£11.75), and children's meals; in summer there may be afternoon teas with a selection of home-made cakes, and Saturday barbecues. Well kept Worthingtons Best on handpump, and Addlestone's cider; good friendly service; sensibly placed darts, cribbage and unobtrusive piped music. Remy the jack russell loves to chew up beer mats. Lots of good walks nearby. *(Recommended by Jenny and Brian Seller, Miss J Reay, Jack and Gemima Valiant, Richard Siebert)*

Free house ~ Licensee Mrs Brenda Entwistle ~ Real ale ~ Meals and snacks ~ Restaurant ~ (01558) 685271 ~ Children welcome ~ Open 11.30-3.30, 7-11; 12-3.30, 7-10.30 Sun; cl Mon except bank hols

nr ABERYSTWYTH (Dyfed) SN6777 Map 6

Halfway Inn

Pisgah (not the Pisgah near Cardigan); A4120 towards Devil's Bridge, 5¾ miles E of junction with A487

The genuinely old-fashioned and peaceful charm of this enchanting old place has been comfortably retained by the friendly new Scottish licensees. The atmospheric beamed and flagstoned bar has stripped deal tables and settles and bare stone walls, as well as darts, pool, dominoes, trivia and piped music (classical at lunchtimes, popular folk and country in the evenings), and a well kept beer from Badger alongside Felinfoel Double Dragon, Hancocks HB and weekly guests on handpump. There may be up to four draught ciders, and a few malt whiskies. Tables can be reserved in the dining room/restaurant area. Generously served with fresh vegetables, bar food includes soup (£1.50), filled baked potatoes (from £1.75), sandwiches (from £2.50), ploughman's (£4), breaded scampi (£5.75), chicken, mushroom and ham pie (£5.50), steak and ale pie (£5.95) 8oz sirloin (from £9.75), daily specials like brie and broccoli pie (£5.50), home-made puddings, and children's meals (£2.75). With its panoramic views down over the wooded hills and pastures of the Rheidol Valley from picnic-sets under cocktail parasols it's not surprising that it does get busy in summer. There's a very simple play area, free overnight camping for customers, a new nursery, and a baling rail for pony-trekkers. *(Recommended by Joan and Michel Hooper-Immins, Dr Oscar Puls, Christopher Gallop, Jack and Gemima Valiant, Patrick Freeman, David Peakall)*

Free house ~ Licensee David Roberts ~ Real ale ~ Meals and snacks ~ Restaurant ~ (01970) 880631 ~ Children in eating area of bar and restaurant ~ Occasional live music Fri ~ Open 12-3, 7(6.30 Sat)-11(10.30 Sun) ~ Bedroom: £19S/£38S

BEAUMARIS (Anglesey) SH6076 Map 6

Olde Bulls Head ★ 🍷

Castle Street

The quaintly old-fashioned rambling bar at this smartly cosy old inn is full of reminders of its long and interesting past: a rare 17th-c brass water clock, a bloodthirsty crew of cutlasses, even the town's oak ducking stool. There's also lots of copper and china jugs, snug alcoves, low beams, low-seated settles, leather-cushioned window seats and a good open fire. The entrance to the pretty courtyard is closed by the biggest simple hinged door in Britain. Very good daily changing lunchtime bar food might include sandwiches (from £1.80), home-made cream of parsnip and cumin soup (£2.25), good ploughman's with Welsh cheeses (£4.50), cold poached salmon with mayonnaise (£4.95), warm leek and bacon quiche, steak, Guinness and mushroom pie, grilled gammon with apricots and sage, casserole of duck legs in rich orange sauce or grilled fillet of cod with pesto and herb crust (£5.50), and puddings such as rhubarb tart with cinnamon crumble topping and brandied bread and butter pudding with honey ice cream (£2.25). There is also a smart no-smoking restaurant. Very well kept Bass, Worthington Best and a guest on handpump, a good comprehensive list of over 220 wines (with plenty of half bottles), and freshly squeezed orange juice; cheerful, friendly service; chess and cards. The simple but charming bedrooms (with lots of nice little extras) are named after characters in Dickens's novels. *(Recommended by Anthony Bowen, J H Jones, G C Hackemer, Pamela and Merlyn Horswell, David Peakall, Chris and Shirley Machin, Dr D G Twyman)*

Free house ~ Licensee David Robertson ~ Real ale ~ Meals and snacks (not evenings or Sun lunch) ~ Restaurant ~ (01248) 810329 ~ Children in eating area of bar till 8pm ~ Jazz last Fri in month ~ Open 11-11; 12-10.30 Sun; cl evening 25/26 Dec, 1 Jan ~ Bedrooms: £49B/£79B

Sailors Return

Church Street

Very popular with all ages, this bright and cheerful place, more or less open-plan, is nowadays often packed with happy diners, especially in the evenings (lunchtimes tend to be quieter); all the tables in the dining area on the left can be booked. The food, done well, with fresh vegetables includes filled butties (from £2), soup (£2.25), garlic mushrooms or prawn cocktail (£3.95), ploughman's (£5.50), broccoli and cream cheese bake or chicken curry (£5.65), roast chicken breast with sage and onion stuffing or grilled plaice (£5.95), sirloin steak (£9.45), daily specials like leek and ham pie or chicken in leek and bacon pie, and puddings like lemon lush pie or banoffee meringue roulade (£2.35). Furnishings include comfortable richly coloured banquettes. There's a quaint collection of china teapots, and maps of Cheshire among the old prints and naval memorabilia betray the landlord's origins; the Green room to the left of the bar is no smoking; well kept Boddingtons, Marstons Pedigree, Morlands Old Speckled Hen and Tetleys on handpump. Helpful friendly service (you get the feeling the landlord really enjoys his calling); maybe unobtrusive piped music. ***(Recommended by Jill Bickerton, Peter and Anne Hollindale, Diana Smart, J D and J A Taylor, Joy and Peter Heatherley, Mark Percy, Lesley Mayoh, E Evans)***

Free house ~ Licensee Peter Ogan ~ Real ale ~ Meals and snacks ~ (01248) 811314 ~ Children welcome during food serving times ~ Open 11.30-3, 6-11; 12-3, 7-10.30 Sun

BETWS-Y-COED (Gwynedd) SH7956 Map 6

Ty Gwyn

A5 just S of bridge to village

This cottagey coaching inn is worth visiting for its generously served tasty meals including lots of fresh fish, as the terms of the licence do mean that you must eat or stay overnight (it's well placed for the area's multitude of attractions) if you want a drink. Fresh fish might include herring fillets marinated in madeira (£3.25), potted shrimps with toast (£3.50), fresh calamari with sweet chilli dip (£3.75), battered cod (£6.50), trout with whiskey and prawn sauce (£7.95), king scallops thermidor (£11.95) and whole lobster thermidor (£15.95), served alongside good soup (£2.50), port and hazelnut pâté (£3.50), curry, lasagne, mushroom and nut fettucine or chicken breast with lemon and garlic (£5.95), roast leg of pork bordelaise (£6.95), fresh lamb kidneys stroganoff (£7.95) and sirloin steak (£11.95). There's a nice personally welcoming atmosphere in the beamed lounge bar which has an ancient cooking range worked in well at one end, and rugs and comfortable chintz easy chairs on its oak parquet floor. The interesting clutter of unusual old prints and bric-a-brac reflects the fact that the owners run an antique shop next door; highchair and toys available. Theakstons Old Peculier on handpump, maybe two friendly cats; piped music. ***(Recommended by J H Jones, KC, Keith and Margaret Kettell, C McKerrow, R J Bland, Gordon Theaker, Dr Jim Mackay, Joy and Peter Heatherley, B M and P Kendall, Eric Locker)***

Free house ~ Licensees Jim and Shelagh Ratcliffe ~ Real ale ~ Meals and snacks ~ Restaurant ~ (01690) 710383 ~ Children welcome ~ Open 12-2, 7-9.30(8.30 winter); cl Mon-Wed Jan ~ Bedrooms: £20(£30B)/£35(£52B)

BODFARI (Clwyd) SJ0970 Map 6

Dinorben Arms 🍷

From A541 in village, follow Tremeirchion 3 signpost

Clinging to the side of the mountain this friendly black and white inn is well known for its incredible range of about 300 malt whiskies (including the full Macallan range and a good few from the Islay distilleries). They also have plenty of good wines (with several classed growth clarets), vintage ports and cognacs, and quite a few unusual coffee liqueurs. As well as a glassed-over well, the three warmly welcoming neat flagstoned rooms which open off the heart of this carefully extended building have plenty of character, with beams hung with tankards and flagons, high shelves of china, old-fashioned settles and other seats, and three open fires; there's also a light and airy garden room. Well kept Aylesbury Best, Tetleys and a couple of guests kept under light blanket pressure. There are lots of tables outside on the prettily landscaped and planted brick-floored terraces, with attractive sheltered corners and charming views, and there's a grassy play area which – like the car park – is neatly sculpted into the slope of the hills. It can get very busy (it's advisable to book) with people here for the lunchtime smorgasbord which includes a changing range of hot soups, main courses and puddings (£8.50). Other snacks include home-made steak and kidney pie or chicken, ham and mushroom pie (£4.85), scampi (£5.20), lasagne (£5.75), grilled salmon (£6.50), seafood mornay (£6.95), sirloin steak or Welsh lamb chops (£7.95). One child can eat free if both parents are dining (except on Saturday nights). A no-smoking area in the upstairs Badger Suite has a carvery on Friday and Saturday (£12.95) and a good help-yourself farmhouse buffet on Wednesday and Thursday (£8.95). *(Recommended by KC, W C M Jones, Mr and Mrs Irving, John Fazakerley, Liz Bell)*

Free house ~ Licensee David Rowlands ~ Real ale ~ Meals and snacks (12-2, 6-10; Sun lunchtime smorgasbord only) ~ Restaurant ~ (01745) 710309 ~ Children welcome ~ Open 12-3(4 Sat), 6-11; 12-11 Sun

BOSHERTON (Dyfed) SR9694 Map 6

St Govans

Village signed from B4319 S of Pembroke

Not surprisingly this beautifully placed comfortably modernised inn is very popular with walkers and climbers comparing climbs and there are lots of very good climbing phototgraphs. It's a lovely area, quite close by there's a many-fingered inlet from the sea, now quite land-locked and full of water-lilies in summer, while some way down the road terrific cliffs plunge to the sea. The south wall of the bar of this comfortably modernised inn is decorated with murals of local beauty spots painted by a local artist, W S Heaton. Stone pillars support the black and white timbered ceiling of the spacious bar which has a woodburning stove in a large stone fireplace, plenty of button-back red leatherette wall banquettes and armed chairs around dimpled copper tables, and stags's antlers; darts, pool, cribbage, dominoes, fruit machine, trivia, juke box and board games. A small but useful choice of mostly home-made bar food might include gammon, crab or trout (£6.50), bass (£7) and sirloin steak (£10.75). About a quarter of the pub is no smoking. Well kept real ales include Bass, Crown Buckley Reverend James, Fullers London Pride, Shepherd Neame Bishops Finger, Wadworths 6X, Worthington Best on handpump and about a dozen malt whiskies. There are a few picnic-sets on the small front terrace. *Recommended by Jean and Richard Phillips, Mr and Mrs S Thomas; more reports please*

Free house ~ Licensee Sheila Webster ~ Real ale ~ Meals and snacks ~ (01646) 661311 ~ Children welcome till 9pm ~ Open 11-11; 12-3, 6.30-10.30 Sun; 12-2, 7-11 in winter ~ Bedrooms: £17.50S/£35S

CAPEL CURIG (Gwynedd) SH7258 Map 6

Bryn Tyrch

A4086 W of village

On our inspection visit to this comfortable Snowdonian country inn we found the polite barman offering advice on local climbs – and explaining how he fitted climbing in around his work schedule. It is very much a place for walkers and climbers. We had a seat at one of the big picture windows which run the length of one wall, with views across the road to picnic-sets on a floodlit patch of grass by a stream running down to a couple of lakes; in the distance is the Snowdon

Horseshoe. There are several easy chairs round low tables, some by a coal fire with magazines and outdoor equipment catalogues piled to one side, and a pool table in the plainer hikers' bar. Wholesome food, with an emphasis on vegetarian and vegan dishes, is generously served to meet the healthy appetite of anyone enjoying the local outdoor attractions – or you could try one of the many coffee blends (listed on a blackboard) or Twinings teas with a piece of vegan fruit cake. The seasonally changing menu might include ciabatta sandwiches, apple and stilton soup (£2.95), garlic mushrooms with stilton sauce (£3.85), breakfast (£4.50), vegetable and lentil cottage pie or vegetable and kidney bean chilli (£6.25), spinach and feta cheese pie (£6.65), shortcrust free-range chicken and mushroom pie (£7.15), fried venison sausage (£7.85) and duck breast with orange, garlic and pepper sauce (£9.50); well kept Flowers IPA, Wadworths 6X and Whitbreads Castle Eden; more tables on a steep little garden at the side; no-smoking dining room. *(Recommended by Howard James, KC, S P Watkin, P A Taylor)*

Free house ~ Licensee Rita Davis ~ Real ale ~ Meals and snacks (12-9.30) ~ (01690) 720223 ~ Children welcome ~ Open 12-11 ~ Bedrooms: £24.50(£27.50B)/£41(£49B)

CAREW (Dyfed) SN0403 Map 6

Carew Inn

A4075 just off A477

In a good setting just opposite the imposing ruins of Carew Castle, this simple old inn is a positively friendly place with a good deal of character. It's now so popular that in summer they put a marquee in the garden to help accommodate the summer crowds, they also have live music in here on Thursday and Sunday nights. There's a notably cheery welcome in the very characterful little panelled public bar and comfortable lounge, as well as old-fashioned settles and scrubbed pine furniture, and interesting prints and china hanging from the beams. The no-smoking upstairs dining room has an elegant china cabinet, a mirror over the tiled fireplace and sturdy chairs around the well spaced tables. Generously served, reasonably priced bar food includes mussels in white wine with garlic and herbs (£4.50), chicken, leek and mushroom pie (£5.95), local dressed crab (£6.95) and gammon steak (£7.50). Local mackerel and sea bass can be caught and served within two hours. Well kept Crown Buckley Reverend James, Worthington Best and a couple of guests, sensibly placed darts, dominoes, cribbage, piped music. Dogs in the public bar only. The back garden has a wheelchair ramp and is safely enclosed, with a sandpit, climbing frame, slide and other toys, as well as a remarkable 9th-c Celtic cross. Seats in a pretty little flowery front garden at this popular and unchanging inn look down to the river where a tidal watermill is open for afternoon summer visits, it's also opposite the imposing ruins of Carew Castle. *(Recommended by IHR, Dr M Owton, Ben and Sheila Walker, Graham Baker, Chris Brace, Jack and Philip Paxton, Ian Phillips, Charles and Pauline Stride, Mike and Mary Cartern, Michael Sargent, T L Rees, Joan and Michel Hooper-Immins, Jack and Gemima Valiant, Brian and Anna Marsden, Tony Pounder)*

Free house ~ Licensee Mandy Hinchliffe ~ Real ale ~ Meals and snacks ~ Restaurant ~ (01646) 651267 ~ Children in eating area of bar at lunchtime and restaurant ~ Live music Sun, and Thurs evening in summer ~ Open 11-11; 12-10.30 Sun; 12-3, 4.30-11(10.30 Sun) in winter

CILGERRAN (Dyfed) SN1943 Map 6

Pendre

Village signposted from A478

Thought to be one of the oldest in West Wales, this unspoilt traditional pub has massive stripped 14th-c medieval stone walls above a panelled dado, with armchairs and settles on a beautifully polished slate floor; piped music. Bar food under the new licensee includes filled rolls (£1.20), home-made soup (£1.95), quiche (£2.50), cottage, fisherman's or steak and ale pie (£4.75), scampi (£4.95) and sirloin steak (£6.95). Well kept Carmarthen Tomas Watkins Whoosh and Old Style Bitter on handpump and lots of malt whiskies; personal service from the licensee and staff.

The public bar has darts. There are seats outside, with an enclosed play area. The other end of the town leads down to the River Teifi, with a romantic ruined castle on a crag nearby, where coracle races are held on the Saturday before the August bank holiday. There's a good local wildlife park nearby, and this is a good area for fishing. *(Recommended by David and Natasha Toulson, Ben and Sheila Walker, Peter Lewis; more reports please)*

Free house ~ Licensee Sandra Tucker ~ Real ale ~ Meals and snacks (12-9) ~ Restaurant ~ (01239) 614223 ~ Children in eating area of bar and restaurant ~ Open 11-2.30, 6-11; 11-11 Sat, 12-2.30, 7-10.30 Sun

COLWYN BAY (Clwyd) SH8578 Map 6

Mountain View

Mochdre; take service-road into village off link road to A470, S from roundabout at start of new A55 dual carriageway to Conwy; OS Sheet 116 map reference 825785

Well regarded in the area for its big helpings of good value bar food, this neatly kept plush pub still attracts locals for a chat and its well kept real ales including Burtonwood Bitter, Buccaneer, James Forshaws and Top Hat on handpump; also over two dozen malt whiskies. The spreading carpeted interior is divided into areas by arched walls, with a big picture of the Aberglaslyn Pass hanging near the entrance, and several others of Conwy Castle hung throughout. There are quite a few houseplants (and bright window boxes in the large windows); darts, pool, dominoes, fruit machine, table football and juke box. The raised seating area is no smoking. From a fairly extensive menu and specials board there might be broccoli soup (£2.25), mushroom and pepper tagliatelle (£5.25), plaice in pernod, home-made gammon, peppered pork steak on a bed of mushrooms and onions or whole plaice (£6.95), strips of beef and scampi in lobster sauce (£7.25) and roast duck or devilled rack of Welsh lamb (£7.95). *(Recommended by KC, S P Watkin, P A Taylor, Roger Byrne; more reports please)*

Burtonwood ~ Tenant Malcolm Gray ~ Real ale ~ Meals and snacks ~ (01492) 544724 ~ Children in eating area of bar ~ Open 11.30-3, 6-11; 12-5, 7-10.30 Sun

CRESSWELL QUAY (Dyfed) SN0406 Map 6

Cresselly Arms

Village signposted from A4075

Year in, year out nothing changes at this marvellously traditional old Welsh-speaking creeper-covered local. There are seats outside facing the tidal creek of the Cresswell River, and if the tides are right you can get here by boat. There's a relaxed and jaunty feel in the two simple comfortably unchanging communicating rooms, which have red and black flooring tiles, built-in wall benches, kitchen chairs and plain tables, an open fire in one room, a working Aga in the other, and a high beam-and-plank ceiling hung with lots of pictorial china. A third red-carpeted room is more conventionally furnished, with red-cushioned mate's chairs around neat tables. Well kept Worthington BB is tapped straight from the cask into glass jugs by the landlord, whose presence is a key ingredient of the atmosphere; fruit machine and winter darts. *(Recommended by Pete Baker, Jack and Philip Paxton, Ian Phillips)*

Free house ~ Licensees Maurice and Janet Cole ~ Real ale ~ (01646) 651210 ~ Children welcome in back room ~ Open 12-3, 5-11; 11-11 Sat; 12-3, 7-10.30 Sun

CRICKHOWELL (Powys) SO2118 Map 6

Bear ★

Brecon Road; A40

This faultlessly run old coaching inn is the sort of enticing place readers go back to again and again. There's a calmly civilised atmosphere in the comfortably decorated, heavily beamed lounge, which has lots of little plush-seated bentwood armchairs and handsome cushioned antique settles, and a window seat looking down on the market

square. Up by the great roaring log fire, a big sofa and leather easy chairs are spread among the rugs on the oak parquet floor; antiques include a fine oak dresser filled with pewter and brass, a longcase clock and interesting prints. It can get terribly busy, but service remains more than welcoming and friendly; piped music. Beautifully presented freshly cooked bar meals from a changing menu, and made as much as possible from local ingredients, might include soup (£2.75), smoked mackerel pâté or filled baguettes (£3.95), welsh rarebit on olive bread with bacon (£4.20), sausage and mash (£4.50), chicken, ham and leek pie (£5.95), fresh gnocchi in tomato and basil sauce with melted parmesan (£6.25), fresh salmon fishcakes with lemon and tarragon (£6.75), moroccan spiced lamb or steak and kidney pie (£6.95), goat's cheese and fried onion pie with mediterranean vegetables and garlic bread (£7.25), oak smoked salmon cutlet on green leaves (£7.95),braised hock of braised Welsh lamb (£8.75) and sirloin steak (£10.95); very good puddings like steamed treacle sponge pudding with butterscotch sauce or home-made ice cream with stem ginger liqueur in a brandy snap barrel (all £3.25) or Welsh cheeses. The family bar is partly no smoking. Well kept Bass, John Smiths, Ruddles Best and County on handpump; malt whiskies, vintage and late-bottled ports, and unusual wines (with about a dozen by the glass) and liqueurs, with some hops tucked in among the bottles. The back bedrooms – particularly in the quieter new block – are the most highly recommended, though there are three more bedrooms in the pretty cottage at the end of the garden. Lovely window boxes, and you can eat in the garden in summer; disabled lavatories.
(Recommended by Dr and Mrs A J Newton, Pamela and Merlyn Horswell, Jackie Orme, RKP, Dr and Mrs Cottrell, D and N Pugsley, D and L Berry, J H Jones, Peter Meister, Derek and Margaret Underwood, Roy Smylie, Gordon Tong, Gordon Theaker, Chris Philip, Wayne Brindle, Adrian Levine, Mrs M Mills, B M and P Kendall, Adrian and Jane Tierney-Jones, Liz Bell)

Free house ~ Licensee Mrs Judy Hindmarsh ~ Real ale ~ Meals and snacks (till 10pm) ~ Restaurant ~ (01873) 810408 ~ Children welcome ~ Open 10-3, 6-11; 12-3, 7-10.30 Sun ~ Bedrooms: £45B/£59B

nr CRICKHOWELL (Powys) SO2118 Map 6

Nantyffin Cider Mill

1½ miles NW, by junction A40/A479

Wales Dining Pub of the Year

The beautifully presented food (relying wherever possible on local and organic meat and vegetables – with quite a lot coming from a relative's nearby farm) at this handsome pink-washed inn is easily of restaurant standard. The menu changes constantly but might include starters such as home-made soup (£2.95), spicy moroccan lamb cakes with couscous and apricot salsa (£4.75), fresh open ravioli with leeks and goat's cheese with light cream leek sauce (£4.95), risotto with fresh crab and summer greens (£5.25), roasted rib eye of beef baguette filled with sauté mushrooms and onions topped with roast garlic dressing with chips (£5.95), open prawn sandwich on chargrilled bread (£6.50), crab, ginger and spring onion omelette with stir-fried vegetables (£6.95), roasted boneless chicken leg stuffed with green onion and herbs served with caramelised onions and roast tomato pistou (£7.50), fresh salmon and spinach fishcakes (£7.95), barbecued pork loin (£8.25), fillets of red mullet with warm salad of sugarsnap peas, broad beans and asparagus with pesto dressing (£12.50), roast rack of welsh lamb with sautéed wild mushrooms, herb crust and rosemary garlic sauce (£14.50), chargrilled Cornish lobster (£15.95), and puddings like tart au citron, sticky toffee pudding and coconut parfait with apricot coulis and rum ice cream (from £3.25); children's meals or smaller helpings. The look of the place is smartly traditional – almost brasserie style, with a woodburner in a fine broad fireplace, warm grey stonework, cheerful bunches of fresh and dried flowers, and good solid comfortable tables and chairs. The bar at one end of the main open-plan area has three well kept changing real ales such as Brains SA, Marstons Pedigree and Tomas Watkins Old Style Bitter on handpump, and three draught ciders like Dunkertons, Mendip Magic and Thatchers Dry, American wines (several by the glass or half bottle), and popular home-made lemonade and Pimm's in summer, and hot punch and mulled wine in winter. A raftered barn with a big cider press has been converted into quite a striking restaurant. The building faces an attractive stretch of the River Usk (the other side of a fairly busy road), and has charming views from the tables out on the lawn above its neat car park. A ramp makes disabled access easy. *(Recommended by J H Jones, Pat and John Millward, Gethin Lewis, David and Nina Pugsley, N H E Lewis, Deirdre Goodman, Dr Oscar Puls, Mr and Mrs Pyper, J Goodrich, Chris Philip, B M and P Kendall, David Gregory, Mike Pugh, Nic and Meriel Cox, Gordon Theaker, Margaret and Nigel Dennis, D and L Berry, George and Brenda Jones, Liz Bell)*

Free house ~ Licensees Glyn Bridgeman, Sean Gerrard ~ Real ale ~ Meals and snacks (till 10pm) ~ Restaurant ~ (01873) 810775 ~ Children welcome ~ Open 12-2.30(3 Sat/Sun), 6(7 Sun)-11; cl Mon

White Hart

Brecon Rd (A40 W)

A quieter, more homely and very reasonably priced alternative to the often busy Bear, this friendly little family-run pub used to be a toll house – as the interesting tariff sign outside shows. The cosy little spic-and-span bar, with stripped stone, beams and flagstones, is flanked by an eating area on one side (with TV) and sizeable no-smoking restaurant on the other. A friendly neatly dressed barman serves very well kept Bass, Brains, Hancocks HB and Theakstons XB on handpump from the bar that runs the length of the room opposite the entrance. Enjoyable home-made bar food includes sandwiches (from £1.50), home-made leek and potato soup (£2.50), fresh mushrooms in stilton sauce, welsh rarebit or glamorgan sausage with leeks, caerphilly cheese, egg and breadcrumbs (£3.50), chicken curry (£4.95), home-made lasagne or steak and stout pie (£5.20), roast leg of Welsh lamb in local honey (£5.95) and roast goose breast in madeira (£10.25); cribbage, dominoes, trivia, fruit machine, quiz Mon eve; piped classical music. There are tables with parasols on a suntrap terrace above a few parking bays by the road: beware of the blind exit from the small side car park on the other side of the pub. *(Recommended by Mr and Mrs J Williams, Christopher and Mary Thomas)*

Free house ~ Licensees Mike and Vanessa Griffin ~ Real ale ~ Meals and snacks (till 9.45) ~ (01873) 810473 ~ Children welcome in eating area of bar (till 9pm) and restaurant ~ Open 12-3, 6-11; 12-11 Sat; 12-4, 7-10.30 Sun

EAST ABERTHAW (South Glamorgan) ST0367 Map 6

Blue Anchor ★

B4265

Famous throughout Wales for its tremendous age and character, this thatched and creeper-covered stone pub has a warren of snug, low-beamed rooms dating back to 1380. Nooks and crannies wander through massive stone walls and tiny doorways, and there are open fires everywhere, including one in an inglenook with antique oak seats built into its stripped stonework. Other seats and tables are worked into a series of chatty little alcoves, and the more open front bar still has an ancient lime-ash floor; darts, dominoes, fruit machine and trivia machine. Bar food includes sandwiches (from £1.95), cream of white onion and stilton soup (£2.50), filled baked potatoes (from £3), celery, grapes and flaked salmon in lemon mayonnaise (£3.25), beef curry (£5.25), cajun spiced pork chop or fresh linguine pasta (£5.50), baked salmon fillet with aubergine crust on a crab and prawn bisque (£5.95), peppered 8oz rump steak (£7.50); they do a three-course roast lunch (£9.45) on Sundays, for which it's best to book. Carefully kept Boddingtons, Buckleys Best, Flowers IPA, Marstons Pedigree, Theakstons Old Peculier and a guest on handpump. Rustic seats shelter peacefully among tubs and troughs of flowers outside, with more stone tables on a newer terrace. From here a path leads to the shingly flats of the estuary. The pub can get packed in the evenings and on summer weekends, and it's a shame the front seats are right beside the car park; readers have suggested that the lavatories could do with some attention. *(Recommended by David Lewis, Sarah Lart, Mr and Mrs S Thomas, David and Nina Pugsley, I J and N K Buckmaster, R Michael Richards, Daren Haines, D and L Berry)*

Free house ~ Licensee Jeremy Coleman ~ Real ale ~ Meals and snacks (12-2, 6-8 Mon to Fri, no food Sat, Sun evening) ~ Evening restaurant ~ (01446) 750329 ~ Children welcome till 8pm in eating area of bar (later if eating) ~ Open 11-11; 12-10.30 Sun

GLADESTRY (Powys) SO2355 Map 6

Royal Oak

B4594 W of Kington

Just below the Hergest Ridge, this nicely old-fashioned village pub is a welcome sight to walkers on the Offa's Dyke Path. On the evening we inspected, enthusiastic locals were meticulously laying out a green felt cloth for a game of cribbage in the simple roomy bar, with its beams, stripped stone and flagstones (there's also a cosy turkey-carpeted lounge). More locals wandered in and gathered in a friendly chatty group around the bar, where a beaming barman drew well kept Bass and Hancocks HB from handpump. In spite of the dreary weather we warmed up nicely at our small table next to the log fire. Bar food includes sandwiches (from £1.20), ploughman's (£3.25), cottage pie (£4.25), broccoli and cheese bake or lasagne (£4.50), mixed grill (£6) and sirloin steak (£8.50). No-smoking restaurant; darts, pool, cribbage, dominoes, video game, juke box, quoits, piped music; camping available on the helpful licensees' hill farm. *(Recommended by David Gittins, Brian Seller, Ian Jones, Edward Leetham, DC)*

Free house ~ Licensees Mel and Chris Hughes ~ Real ale ~ Meals and snacks ~ Restaurant ~ (01544) 370669 ~ Children welcome ~ Open 12-2(3 Sat and Sun), 7-11(10.30 Sun) ~ Bedrooms: £20B/£40B

GRAIANRHYD (Clwyd) SJ2156 Map 6

Rose & Crown

B5430 E of Ruthin; village signposted off A494 and A5104

The sort of place you'd almost certainly go straight past if you weren't in on the secret, this simple building in a remote part of the Clwydian Hills hides within it a really enjoyable pub. The bar sparkles with carefully chosen eclectic bric-a-brac. One small room has hundreds of decorative teapots hanging from its beams, the other has steins and other decorative mugs; there are 1950s romantic prints, Marilyn Monroe memorabilia, antlers, china dogs (and a real one called Doris), highly ornamental clocks, a fiddling cherub, cottagey curtains and two warm coal fires. For once we found the piped music (well reproduced light rock) a decided plus, though perhaps not everyone would agree; it goes well with the very relaxed chatty atmosphere, locals and informal young landlord making sure strangers don't feel left out. A wide choice of bar food includes sandwiches and toasties (from £1.50), soup (£1.95), filled baked potatoes (from £2.05), whitebait (£2.95), lasagne (£4.25), vegetarian dishes such as nutburger or moussaka (£4.95), steak and kidney pie, lamb rogan josh or lasagne (£4.95) and 10oz sirloin (£8.95). Well kept Boddingtons, Flowers IPA and Marstons Pedigree on handpump, tea and coffee; darts, dominoes, trivia, fruit machine. Picnic-sets out on a rough terrace by the car park have pretty hill views. *(Recommended by Ray and Liz Monk)*

Whitbread ~ Licensee Tim Ashton ~ Real ale ~ Meals and snacks (12-2.30, 6-10) ~ (01978) 780727 ~ Children welcome ~ Open 12-11; 12-10.30 Sun

GRESFORD (Clwyd) SJ3555 Map 6

Pant-yr-Ochain 🍷

Off A483 on N edge of Wrexham: at roundabout take A5156 (A534) towards Nantwich, then first left towards the Flash

Feeling more like a manor house than a pub, this spacious old country house stands in its own beautiful grounds with a small lake and some lovely trees. Its light and airy rooms are stylishly decorated, with a wide range of interesting prints and bric-a-brac on its walls and on shelves, and a good mix of individually chosen country furnishings including comfortable seats for chatting as well as more upright ones for eating. There are good open fires, and the big dining area is set out as a library, with books floor to ceiling. Consistently good, interesting food from a menu that constantly develops might include home-made soup (£2.95), chicken, pork and brandy pâté or ploughman's (£4.95), fishcakes (£5.25), steak, red wine and smoked bacon pie (£7.95), roasted aubergines stuffed with tomato and vegetable ratatouille or grilled plaice (£8.75), chicken with cashew nut and ginger sauce or malaysian fruit curry (£8.95), roast fillet of salmon on a bed of stir-fried vegetables (£9.25), and braised half shoulder of lamb with redcurrant, port and rosemary sauce (£10.75). They have a good range of decent wines, strong on up-front New World ones, as well as Boddingtons, Flowers Original, Fullers London Pride, Plassey Bitter and Shepherd Neame Spitfire and a good collection of malt whiskies. Service is polite and efficient. This is in the same small family of pubs as the Grosvenor Arms at Aldford (see Cheshire main entries), and not dissimilar in style and gently up-market atmosphere; one room is no smoking. *(Recommended by Mark Howarth, Quentin Williamson, Andrew and Anna Schuman, Mark Jones)*

Free house ~ Licensee Duncan Lochead ~ Real ale ~ Meals and snacks (12-9.30) ~ (01978) 853525 ~ Children in eating area of bar at lunchtime only ~ Open 12-11; 12-10.30 Sun

HALKYN (Clwyd) SJ2172 Map 6

Britannia

Pentre Rd, off A55 for Rhosesmor

Fabulous views from the partly no-smoking dining conservatory and terrace at this warmly welcoming old farmhouse stretch to Liverpool and the Wirral, and on a clear day you may even be able to pick out Blackpool tower and Beeston Castle; it's best to book if you want a window table. The cosy unspoilt lounge bar has some very heavy beams, with horsebrasses, harness, jugs, plates and other bric-a-brac; there's also a games room with darts, pool, dominoes, fruit machine, juke box and board games. Very good value reliable bar food in generous helpings includes home-made soup (£1.20), sandwiches served on Rhes-y-Cae bread (from £2.50), black pudding and mustard sauce (£2.95), cumberland sausage (£4.50), scampi, lamb and rosemary and redcurrant casserole or beef and ale pie (£5.25), pork escalopes in pepper sauce (£5.95), and daily specials. Lees Bitter, GB Mild and Moonraker on handpump or tapped from the cask, a dozen or so malt whiskies, and a choice of coffees. Attractions for the children include Jacob, a 26-year-old donkey, tame goats, Fleur the oxford sandy and black, and various breeds of ducks and chickens – you can usually buy fresh eggs. *(Recommended by Alan and Paul McCully, Andy and Jill Kassube, Dave Braisted, KC, David Hoult; more reports please)*

J W Lees ~ Tenant Keith Pollitt ~ Real ale ~ Meals and snacks ~ Restaurant ~ (01352) 780272 ~ Children welcome ~ Open 11-11; 12-10.30 Sun

HAY ON WYE (Powys) SO2342 Map 6

Kilverts

Bullring

The informal relaxed atmosphere in the airy high-beamed bar of this friendly town pub made for an enjoyably restful pause during our busy Welsh inspection trip. The easy-going but efficient pony-tailed barman made us good cappuccinos, and chatted with a couple of locals at the bar. In line with the understated civilised feel of the place – some stripped stone walls, *Vanity Fair* caricatures, a couple of standing timbers, candles on well spaced mixed old and new tables, and a pleasant variety of seating – the menu is thoughtful. Lunchtime bar food includes french sticks or sandwiches (from £2.50), crab pâté with dill sour cream sauce (£4.25), ploughman's (from £4.95), spinach and mushroom roulade filled with cream cheese and chives on a bed of sweet peppers (£7.95) and gammon steak (£7.95). In the evening there are several weightier dishes like roast brace of quail with wild mushroom sauce (£9.50) and braised lamb hock in root vegetable and redcurrant sauce (£10.50). The specials board might include moules marinières (£4.10), chargrilled squid with wild mushroom and tarragon cream sauce (£4.25), charcuterie (£4.25), steak, mushroom and Guinness pie (£4.95) and skate wing with capers and black butter (£9.50). Well kept Bass, Hancocks HB and Highgate Saddlers on handpump, Bulmer's farm cider, local Welsh wines, and freshly squeezed orange juice in summer; maybe piped pop radio. There are tables out in a small front flagstoned courtyard. *(Recommended by Jack and Gemima Valiant, J and B Coles, Malcolm Baxter, John Cockell)*

Free house ~ Licensee Colin Thomson ~ Real ale ~ Meals and snacks ~ (01497) 821042 ~ Restaurant ~ Children welcome till 9pm ~ Open 11-11; 12-10.30 Sun ~ Bedrooms: £30B/£60B

Old Black Lion

26 Lion St

The smartly civilised and attractive bar at this atmospheric old pub is particularly lovely at night when candles on old pine tables cast a cosy inviting glow over the red carpet, black panelling, oak and mahogany bar counter, and two old timber and glass screens. Readers really enjoy the thoughtfully prepared bar meals which might include sandwiches (from £2.95), home-made soup (£3.25), ploughman's or filled baked potatoes (from £5.25), vegetarian dishes such as hungarian vegetable goulash (£6.95) or nut roast (£7.55), tempura battered plaice (£7.85), braised lamb with Indian spices (£8.50), spicy peppered venison (£8.95), 8oz sirloin (£11.95), a good selection of specials like Loch Fyne herring fillets or loin of wild boar with black pepper and brandy cream; Sunday 3-course lunch, and special breakfasts for fishermen (with Loch Fyne kippers), and puddings like chocolate brandy cake or warm apple pie. The cottagey restaurant, also candlelit, is no smoking. Well kept Wadworths 6X, Wye Valley Supreme and their own Black Lion (made for them by the Wye Valley brewery) on handpump – as well as an extensive, good value wine list, several malt whiskies, and decent coffee. Service is good but this is a firmly run place and they do like food orders to be in promptly, and to shut the bar at closing time in the evening. A sheltered back terrace has some tables. The inn has trout and salmon fishing rights on the Wye, and can arrange pony trekking and golf. *(Recommended by Derek and Margaret Underwood, Brian Seller, Nicholas Stuart Holmes, Malcolm Baxter, Robert Gomme, Gwen and Peter Andrews, Martin Jones, Mrs P Goodwyn, Tim Barrow, Sue Demont, Nicholas Holmes, Barry and Anne, J A Riemer, Dorothee and Dennis Glover, Jack and Gemima Valiant)*

Free house ~ Licensees John and Joan Collins ~ Real ale ~ Meals and snacks ~ Restaurant ~ (01497) 820841 ~ Children over 5 in eating area of bar ~ Open 11-11; 12-3, 7-10.30 Sun ~ Bedrooms: £23B/£49.90B

LITTLE HAVEN SM8512 Map 6

Swan

Set in one of the prettiest coastal villages in west Wales, and right on the coast path, this delightful little inn has lovely views across the broad and sandy hill-sheltered cove from seats in its bay window, or from the sea wall outside (just the right height for sitting on). The two communicating rooms have quite a cosily intimate feel, as well as comfortable high-backed settles and windsor chairs, a winter open fire, and old prints on walls that are partly stripped back to the original stonework. Cooked by the genial landlord (who's now been here over a decade), the compact choice of well-liked lunchtime bar food includes sandwiches (from £1.50), home-made soup (£2.50), traditional Welsh lamb and vegetable soup (£3.50 – with cheese on the side £3.75), ploughman's (from £4.25), crab bake (£4.75), sardines grilled with spinach, egg and mozzarella (£4.95), chicken curry (£5.50), locally smoked salmon or fresh local crab (£6.95), and home-made puddings (£2.95). Well kept Bass, Wadworths 6X and Worthington BB on handpump from the heavily panelled bar counter, and a good range of wines and whiskies; pleasant, efficient service; no children, dogs or dirty boots. *(Recommended by Martin Jones, Jeremy Brittain-Long, H and D Payne, John and Enid Morris, Carole Smart, Andrew Jeeves, Malcolm and Helen Baxter, Hilarie Dobbie, Mr and Mrs M J Bastin, IHR, Jack and Gemima Valiant)*

James Williams (Narberth) ~ Tenants Glyn and Beryl Davies ~ Real ale ~ Lunchtime meals and snacks ~ Restaurant ~ (01437) 781256 ~ Open 11-3(2.30 winter), 6(7 winter)-11; 12-3, 7-10.30 Sun

LLANBEDR-Y-CENNIN (Gwynedd) SH7669 Map 6

Olde Bull

Village signposted from B5106

Perched on the side of a steep hill, this delightful little 16th-c drovers' inn has splendid views over the Vale of Conwy to the mountains beyond, from seats in the particularly lovely herb garden with its big wild area with waterfall and orchard, and hanging baskets round the terrace. Inside, the knocked-through rooms are full of massive low beams (some salvaged from a wrecked Spanish Armada ship), elaborately carved antique settles, a close crowd of cheerfully striped stools, brassware, photographs, Prussian spiked helmets, and good open fires (one in an inglenook). Well kept Lees Bitter and Mild on handpump from wooden barrels, and several malt whiskies; friendly service. Generous helpings of bar food include soup (£1.95), big filled french sticks (from £2.50), prawn cocktail (£3.50), vegetarian bean bourguignon or curries (£5.50), steak and kidney or chicken and mushroom fresh crusty bread pot (£5.95), evening steaks (from £10.95) and nice old-fashioned home-made puddings like fruit crumble or bread and butter pudding (£2.50); children's menu (£2.50); the dining area is no smoking. The pub is popular with walkers. Darts and dominoes. Lavatories are outside. *(Recommended by Roger Byrne, Liz Bell, S P Watkin, P A Taylor; more reports please)*

Lees ~ Tenants John and Debbie Turnbull ~ Real ale ~ Meals and snacks ~ Restaurant ~ (01492) 660508 ~ Well behaved children welcome ~ Open 12-5, 7-11(10.30 Sun in winter)

nr LLANBERIS (Gwynedd) SH6655 Map 6

Pen-y-Gwryd

Nant Gwynant; at junction of A498 and A4086, ie across mountains from Llanberis – OS Sheet 115 map reference 660558

There's a hospitably welcoming atmosphere in the homely slate-floored log cabin bar of this magnificently set old climber's pub, which doubles as a mountain rescue post. A snug little room with built-in wall benches and sturdy country chairs lets you contemplate the majestic surrounding mountain countryside – like precipitous Moel-siabod beyond the lake opposite. A smaller room has a collection of illustrious boots from famous climbs, and a cosy panelled smoke room more climbing mementoes and equipment. Like many other mountaineers, the team that first climbed Everest in 1953 used the inn as a training base, leaving their fading signatures scrawled on the ceiling. There's a hatch where you order lunchtime bar meals: good value robust helpings of home-made food such as soup (£1.80), ploughman's using home-baked french bread, quiche lorraine or pâté (£3.50), with casseroles in winter. You will need to book early if you want to stay here. Residents have their own charmingly furnished, panelled sitting room and a sauna out among the trees, and in the evening sit down together for the hearty and promptly served dinner (check on the time when you book); the dining room is no smoking. As well as Bass and mulled wine in winter, they serve sherry from their own solera in Puerto Santa Maria; friendly, obliging service; table tennis, darts, pool, bar billiards and shove-ha'penny. *(Recommended by Robert Pettigrew, J H Jones, Martin Pritchard, Quentin Williamson, Roger Byrne, G C Hackemer, Brian and Anna Marsden, Mark Percy, Lesley Mayoh, Jacquie and Jim Jones, DC)*

Free house ~ Licensee Jane Pullee ~ Real ale ~ Lunchtime meals and snacks ~ Evening restaurant ~ (01286) 870211 ~ Children welcome ~ Open 11-11; cl Nov/Dec, open weekends only Jan/Feb ~ Bedrooms: £21(£26B)/£42(£52B)

We say if we know a pub has piped music.

LLANDEWI SKIRRID (Gwent) SO3416 Map 6

Walnut Tree ★ 🍴 🍷

B4521

We continue to include this very well known restaurant for its very relaxed atmosphere, and the caring hands-on approach of the licensees who're quite happy if people just pop in for a glass of very good value tasty wine. The excellent imaginative food – not cheap – combines strong southern European leanings with an almost fanatical pursuit of top-class fresh and often recherché ingredients. It includes carefully prepared soups such as asparagus and tarragon (£4.85), crispy crab pancakes (£5.45), rissotto with spring vegetables (£5.85), marinated smoked herring, celeriac, remoulade and new potatoes (£5.95), and main courses like baked aubergine stuffed with pasta (£9.50), duck with celeriac gratin and sweet and sour pumpkin or red mullet with braised fennel and pesto (£14.95), cold crab with lemon dressing (£15.85), fricassee of lobster and monkfish (£17.85), lobster thermidor (£19.85) and seafood platter (£28.90); vegetables are £2.75 extra. Puddings are delicious – especially the Toulouse chestnut pudding (£5.55); no credit cards, and £1 cover charge. The attractive choice of wines is particularly strong in Italian ones (they import their own), and the house wines by the glass are good value. The small white-walled bar has some polished settles and country chairs around the tables on its flagstones, and a log-effect gas fire. It opens into an airy and relaxed dining lounge with rush-seat Italianate chairs around gilt cast-iron-framed tables. There are a few white cast-iron tables outside in front. *(Recommended by A C Morrison, Helen Pickering, James Owen, Gwen and Peter Andrews, Jackie Orme, RKP, A J Bowen, I J and N K Buckmaster, Dr and Mrs Cottrell, J H Jones, R C Morgan, Michael Coshall, Pamela and Merlyn Horswell, Liz Bell, Gordon Theaker, Stan and Hazel Allen, David Peakall, A E Brace, Nick and Meriel Cox, Candida Leaver)*

Free house ~ Licensees Ann and Franco Taruschio ~ Meals and snacks (12-3, 7-10) ~ Restaurant ~ (01873) 852797 ~ Children welcome ~ Open 12-4, 7-12; cl Sun and Mon; cl one week at Christmas and two weeks in Feb

LLANDRINDOD WELLS (Powys) SO0561 Map 6

Llanerch £ 🛏

Waterloo Road; from centre, head for station

Set in a quiet leafy spot on the edge of a spa town, this low-ceilinged 16th-c inn has peaceful mountain views looking over the Ithon Valley. There's a really cheerful local atmosphere in the busy squarish beamed main bar which has old-fashioned settles snugly divided by partly glazed partitions, and a big stone fireplace that's richly decorated with copper and glass; there are more orthodox button-back banquettes in communicating lounges (one of which is no smoking). Popular lunchtime dishes include soup (£1.95), sandwiches (from £1.95), filled baked potatoes (from £2.50), ploughman's (£3.50), fisherman's pie, lasagne, or vegetable lasagne (£3.50), chicken curry or steak, kidney and mushroom pie (£4.95), mixed grill (£7.95), and children's meals (from £1.75), and evening extras like chicken breast cooked in white wine and cream sauce with grapes (£5.95) or Welsh lamb slowly baked in garlic and redcurrant sauce (£7.25). Well kept Hancocks HB and two regularly changing guests on handpump; there may be up to 20 real ales during their late August Victorian Festival. Service is prompt and generally friendly; piped music. A separate pool room has a fruit machine, darts and dominoes. A front play area and orchard give it the feel of a country pub, and there are delightful views from the terrace, which leads to a garden (with boules). *(Recommended by Joan and Michel Hooper-Immins; more reports please)*

Free house ~ Licensee John Leach ~ Real ale ~ Meals and snacks ~ Restaurant ~ (01597) 822086 ~ Children welcome ~ Live music two Sats and one Thurs each month ~ Open 11.30-2.30; 6-11; 11.30-11 Sat; 12-10.30 Sun ~ Bedrooms: £27.50B/£45B

nr LLANDUDNO JUNCTION SH8180 Map 6

Queens Head

Glanwydden; heading towards Llandudno on B5115 from Colwyn Bay, turn left into Llanrhos Road at roundabout as you enter the Penrhyn Bay speed limit; Glanwydden is signposted as the first left turn off this

At first it may seem that this friendly modest-looking village pub is geared solely for serving food, but locals do pop in here for a drink – although you will need to book or get here early for a table if you're eating. Carefully prepared and generously served imaginative home-made food from a weekly changing menu, with fresh local produce firmly in evidence, might include soup such as fresh pea and mint (£2.15), open rolls (from £3.50), home-made pâté (£3.95), green lipped mussels sautéed in garlic butter (£4.25), open prawn sandwich (£4.35), lasagne (£5.95), salmon and pasta bake (£6.50), pancake with fresh herbs filled with mushroom and asparagus, topped with napoli sauce (£6.95), steak and kidney pie (£7.25), chicken breast filled with brie with a wild mushroom and tarragon sauce (£8.50) or braised Welsh beef in tomato and ginger sauce (£8.95), and several extra fish specials like fish soup (£2.95), crab salad (£8.50) and monkfish on a cucumber bed with lime and basil salsa (£8.95). Delicious puddings include chocolate nut fudge pie or poached pear with port and rosemary (£2.75). Well kept Benskins, Ind Coope Burton and Tetleys on handpump, decent wines including several by the glass, several malts, and good coffee (maybe served with a bowl of whipped cream and home-made fudge or chocolates). The spacious and comfortably modern lounge bar has brown plush wall banquettes and windsor chairs around neat black tables and is partly divided by a white wall of broad arches and wrought-iron screens; there's also a little public bar; the dining area is no smoking; piped music. There are some tables out by the car park. No dogs. *(Recommended by Bronwen and Steve Wrigley, Pamela and Merlyn Horswell, Mike and Wena Stevenson, Mike Jones, M Meadley, Liz Bell, KC, Abigail Dombey, Kate Naish, Brian and Lis Whitford, Paul Hilditch, Neville Kenyon, Basil Minson, Joy and Peter Heatherley, S P Watkin, P A Taylor)*

Carlsberg Tetley (Ansells) ~ Lease: Robert and Sally Cureton ~ Real ale ~ Meals and snacks ~ (01492) 546570 ~ Children over 7 in garden ~ Open 11-3, 6-11; cl 25 Dec

LLANFERRES (Clwyd) Map 7 SJ1961

Druid

A494 Mold—Ruthin

Nothing is too much trouble for the friendly staff and licensees at this delightfully set extended 17th-c inn. It's particularly popular for its interesting range of very good changing bar food – almost Food Award standard – which might include tomato soup (£2.25), delicious granary baps filled with mozzarella and mushrooms, chicken fillet and lemon mayonnaise or pepperoni and mozzarella (£3.45), clam chowder (£3.50), stilton-stuffed mushrooms, mussels and mozzarella cheese in a creamy pesto sauce or steak and mushroom pie with good pastry (£5.95), smoked haddock and poached eggs or lamb balti (£6.95), poached salmon wrapped in smoked bacon with hollandaise sauce (£8.50), braised shoulder of lamb with red wine and vegetables (£8.95) or swordfish steak with pimento sauce (£8.95), fillet steak (£11.50), and good vegetarian dishes such as baked mushrooms and sweet peppers with mozzarella (from £5.95); vegetables are fresh and generous. Tables sheltered in a corner by a low wall with rock-plant pockets outside make the most of the view looking down over the road to the Alyn valley and the Craig Harris mountains beyond, as does the broad bay window in the civilised and sympathetically refurbished smallish plush lounge. You can also see the hills from the bigger welcoming beamed back bar, also carpeted (with quarry tiles by the log fire), with its two handsome antique oak settles as well as a pleasant mix of more modern furnishings. The attractive dining area is relatively smoke-free. Well kept Burtonwood Best, Bucaneer and Top Hat on handpump, decent malt whiskies and wine list; games area with darts and pool, also dominoes, shove-ha'penny, bagatelle, Jenga and other board games; maybe unobtrusive piped music. *(Recommended by Mr and Mrs Archibald, KC, Sue and Bob Ward, P Thomas, Susan Mullins)*

Burtonwood ~ Tenant James Dolan ~ Real ale ~ Meals and snacks (12-3, 6-10; all day Sat, Sun and bank hols) ~ Restaurant ~ (01352) 810225 ~ Children welcome ~ Traditional piano sing-along first Sat of month ~ Open 12-3, 5.30-11; 11.30-11 Sat and bank hols; 12-10.30 Sun ~ Bedrooms: £22.50/£36.50

LLANFRYNACH (Powys) SO0725 Map 6

White Swan

Village signposted from B4558, just off A40 E of Brecon bypass

Stylishly done up, the rambling bar at this tranquil village pub is cool and calm in summer with its flagstoned floor and partly stripped walls. There are plenty of well spaced tables – each with a blue aluminium lamp above – in its series of softly lit alcoves, as well as a roaring log fire in winter and maybe piped classical music. An idyllically secluded terrace behind is green and shady with plenty of stone and wood tables, is attractively divided into sections by low privet hedges, roses and climbing shrubs, and overlooks peaceful paddocks. A short list of well prepared bar food includes french onion soup (£2.60), ploughman's (from £4.75), lasagne, ratatouille, or macaroni and broccoli cheese (£4.75), fisherman's pie, cottage pie or hot chicken curry (£7), lamb chops marinated in garlic and herbs (£10.50), Welsh-style grilled trout with bacon (£11.25), well hung steaks (from £11.50), puddings such as sherry trifle (from £2), children's dishes (£3.90), and maybe weekend specials; nicely cooked vegetables. Service is courteous and efficient; well kept Brains Bitter and Flowers Original on handpump, and good value South African house white wine. The churchyard is across the very quiet village lane. *(Recommended by Mr and Mrs B Craig, Jackie Orme, RKP, A J Bowen, David and Nina Pugsley, KC, Margaret and Nigel Dennis; more reports please)*

Free house ~ Licensees David and Susan Bell ~ Real ale ~ Meals and snacks ~ (01874) 665276 ~ Children welcome ~ Open 12-3(2.30 Sun), 7-11(10.30 Sun); cl Mon (except bank hols), and last three weeks of Jan

LLANGATTOCK (Powys) SO2117 Map 6

Vine Tree

A4077; village signposted from Crickhowell

Tables under cocktail parasols at this friendly well run dining pub give an enchanting view of the splendid medieval stone bridge over the River Usk, and a short stroll takes you to our Crickhowell main entry, the Bear. The front part of the bar has soft seats, some stripped stone masonry, and brass ornaments around its open fireplace. The back is set aside as a dining area with windsor chairs, scrubbed deal tables, and decorative plates and Highland cattle engravings on the walls; most of the tables are set out for eating. Fresh fish comes twice a week from Cornwall, and they use local meat and vegetables in the wide range of carefully prepared dishes, served in huge helpings, such as stockpot soup (£2.15), pâté (£3.95), prawn cocktail or smoked venison with cranberry sauce (£4.75), roast chicken (£5.45), half a dozen vegetarian dishes like lasagne or curry (all £5.75), home-made steak and kidney pie (£6.95), gammon in parsley sauce or scampi (£8.95), lamb chops in garlic, rosemary and marsala cream sauce, pheasant in cream, grape and white wine sauce or venison and red wine casserole (£9.95), pork stuffed with apricots in a tangy orange sauce (£8.35) and salmon in a creamy leek sauce, wrapped in filo pastry (£10.95). Well kept Boddingtons, and Wadworths 6X on handpump and air pressure. *(Recommended by Jackie Orme, Pat Brown, Connie Fisher, D and N Pugsley, D and L Berry, Daren Haines, Margaret and Nigel Dennis, B M and P Kendall, George and Brenda Jones, Paul Robinshaw, Pamela and Merlyn Horswell)*

Free house ~ Licensee I S Lennox ~ Real ale ~ Meals and snacks (till 10pm) ~ Restaurant ~ (01873) 810514 ~ Children welcome ~ Open 12-3, 6-11(7-10.30 Sun)

Pubs with attractive or unusually big gardens are listed at the back of the book.

LLANGEDWYN (Clwyd) SJ1924 Map 6

Green

B4396 SW of Oswestry

In a lovely spot in the Tanat Valley, just inside Wales, this ancient place is very well run as a dining pub. Kept spotless inside, it has a nice layout, with various snug alcoves, nooks and crannies, a good mix of furnishings including oak settles and attractively patterned fabrics, and a blazing log fire in winter; there's a pleasant evening restaurant upstairs. In summer this road is well used as a scenic run from the Midlands to the coast, so the pub sees a lot of business then – but that's when its attractive garden over the road comes into its own, with lots of picnic-sets down towards the river. An impressive range of good home-made food includes sandwiches (from £1.40), ploughman's (£3.85), chicken curry, steak and kidney, chicken and mushroom or cottage pie (£4.90), scampi (£5.25), fresh local trout (£5.45) and several home-made daily specials like shepherd's pie (£5.45), game pie (£6.45), fresh salmon steak with tarragon sauce (£6.95) sirloin steak (£7.95) and daily specials, as well as tasty puddings like syrup pudding, trifle and meringue (from £2.50). Well kept Boddingtons and about five guests like Courage Directors, Fuggles IPA, Morlands Old Speckled Hen, Theakstons Old Peculier and Woods Special on handpump, a good choice of malt whiskies and farm cider, friendly quick service; darts, dominoes, cribbage and piped music; the restaurant is no smoking. The pub has some fishing available to customers, a permit for the day is £5. *(Recommended by Paddy Moindrot, Pearl Williams; more reports please)*

Free house ~ Licensee Mrs R G Greenham ~ Real ale ~ Meals and snacks (till 10pm) ~ Restaurant ~ (01691) 828234 ~ Children welcome ~ Open 11-3(4.30 Sat/Sun), 6-11

LLANGYNIDR (Powys) SO1519 Map 6

Coach & Horses

B4558

This popular old inn, with plenty of tables over the road on a well fenced lawn running down to a lock and moorings, is an ideal base for walking the Monmouth to Brecon Canal, and is a good value well liked place to stay – the breakfasts are good and hearty. The spacious turkey-carpeted lounge has small armchairs and comfortable banquettes against the stripped stone walls, and in winter a big open fire. A useful choice of very good bar food includes sandwiches (from £2.50), filled baguettes (from £2.75), ploughman's (£3.50), several chicken curries (from £7.50), as well as lots of fresh fish on the specials board like salmon and asparagus bake (£4.95), cod and prawn mornay (£8.95), poached Wye salmon (£10.95) and grilled halibut (£11.95); puddings (£3.75); no-smoking area in restaurant. Well kept Bass, Hancocks and a guest like Morlands Old Speckled Hen on handpump; pool, fruit machine, video game and piped music. *(Recommended by Neil Graham, Iorwerth Davies, Roger and Fiona Todd, Gordon Theaker)*

Free house ~ Licensee Derek Latham ~ Real ale ~ Meals and snacks (till 10pm) ~ (01874) 730245 ~ Well behaved children welcome ~ Open 12-11(10.30 Sun); cl 25 Dec evening ~ Bedrooms: £25B/£50B

LLANGYNWYD (Mid Glamorgan) SS8588 Map 6

Old House

From A4063 S of Maesteg follow signpost Llan ¾ at Maesteg end of village; pub behind church

They now stock an incredible 400 whiskies, as well as well kept Brains, Flowers Original, Whitbreads and Worthington Best on handpump, and a choice of wines by the glass at this lovely thatched pub which dates back to 1147. They've built up quite a reputation for well cooked fresh fish – the landlord goes to the local fish market regularly – and for their reasonably priced bar food such as generously served soup (£1.90), steak sandwich (£2.25), pâté (£2.70), prawn cocktail (£3), scampi (£3.75), ploughman's (£3.80), steak and kidney pie (£4.60), beef or chicken curry (£4.70), trout and almonds (£6.90), poached salmon (£8.50), prawn provençale (£10.50), 16oz sirloin (£11.15), and puddings from a trolley (£2), daily specials, and children's meals (from £1.25). Although much modernised, the two cosy rooms of its busy bar still have some comfortably traditional features, high-backed black built-in settles, lots of china and brass around the huge fireplace, shelves of bric-a-brac, and decorative jugs hanging from the beams; piped music. An attractive conservatory extension (half no smoking) leads on to the garden with good views, play area, and a soft ice-cream machine for children. The Welsh inn sign with a painting of the Mari Lwyd refers to the ancient Mari Lwyd tradition which takes place here at Christmas. *(Recommended by John and Joan Nash, Michael and Alison Sandy, Ian Phillips, George and Brenda Jones, David and Nina Pugsley; more reports please)*

Whitbreads ~ Lease Richard and Paula David ~ Real ale ~ Meals and snacks (till 10pm) ~ Restaurant ~ (01656) 733310 ~ Children welcome ~ Open 11-11; 12-10.30 Sun

LLANNEFYDD (Clwyd) SH9871 Map 6

Hawk & Buckle

Village well signposted from surrounding main roads; one of the least taxing routes is from Henllan at junction of B5382 and B5429 NW of Denbigh

This welcoming little hotel is perched over 200m up in the hills, and in very clear weather you can see as far as the Lancashire coast, possibly even Blackpool Tower 40 miles away, from most of the modern comfortable and well equipped bedrooms. The long knocked-through black-beamed lounge bar has comfortable modern upholstered settles around its walls and facing each other across the open fire, and a neat red carpet in the centre of its tiled floor. The lively locals' side bar has darts and piped music. Bar food is well above average, with a choice of home-made dishes like toasted sandwiches (from £2.25), soup (£2.25), ploughman's (£3.95), steak and kidney pie or various vegetarian dishes like mushroom and nut fettucine (£5.95), chicken madras, lasagne or turkey and ham pie (£5.95), lemon sole (£7.95) and sirloin steak (£9.45); good Spanish house wines; the dining room is no smoking. Friendly licensees, two cats and a friendly labrador. There's an attractive mosaic mural on the way through into the back bedroom extension. *(Recommended by Ben Hill, Paul Hilditch, S P Watkin, P A Taylor; more reports please)*

Free house ~ Licensees Bob and Barbara Pearson ~ Meals and snacks ~ Restaurant ~ (01745) 540249 ~ Children in eating area of bar till 8.30pm ~ Open 12-2, 7-11(10.30 Sun); cl Mon lunchtimes; cl lunchtime Mon-Fri Oct-May ~ Bedrooms: £40B/£50B; no children under 8

LLANYNYS (Clwyd) SJ1063 Map 7

Cerrigllwydion Arms

Village signposted from A525 by Drovers Arms just out of Ruthin, and by garage in Pentre further towards Denbigh

The rambling interior of this lovely old place is a maze of atmospheric little rooms, filled with dark oak beams, a good mix of seats, old stonework, interesting brasses, and a collection of teapots. As well as Bass and Tetleys on handpump they keep a good choice of malt whiskies, liqueurs and wines; darts, dominoes and unobtrusive piped music. Besides sandwiches and standard bar snacks, food includes home-made soup (£1.75), and changing dishes of the day such as asparagus spears rolled in home-made ham in cheese sauce (£5.65), dressed crab salad (£6.40), baked pork chops in apple and cider sauce (£6.60), duck in port and brandy sauce (£8.80), roasted lamb in mint and redcurrant sauce (£8.90), and a big mixed grill (£10.50); the restaurant is no smoking. Across the quiet lane is a neat garden with teak tables among fruit trees looking across the fields to wooded hills. The adjacent 6th-c church has a medieval wall painting of St Christopher which was discovered under layers of whitewash in the 60s. *(Recommended by Roger and Christine Mash, Paul Hilditch, KC, D W Jones-Williams)*

Free house ~ Licensee Brian Pearson ~ Real ale ~ Meals and snacks (not Mon evening) ~ Restaurant ~ (01745) 890247 ~ Children in restaurant ~ Open 12-3, 7-11(10.30 Sun); cl Mon lunchtime

LLWYNDAFYDD (Ceredigion) SN3755 Map 6

Crown

Coming S from New Quay on A486, both the first two right turns eventually lead to the village; the side roads N from A487 between junctions with B4321 and A486 also come within signpost distance; OS Sheet 145 map reference 371555

The friendly, partly stripped-stone bar at this attractive white-painted 18th-c pub has red plush button-back banquettes around its copper-topped tables, and a big woodburning stove; piped music. Reliably good home-made bar food includes decent lunchtime sandwiches (from £1.70), as well as soup (£2.30), garlic mushrooms (£2.95), pizzas (from £5.45), vegetarian lasagne or steak and kidney pie (£5.65), salads (from £5.95), local trout (£5.95), steaks (from £7.55), and daily specials prepared from local produce, such as lamb pie or chicken, stilton and broccoli pie (£5.95), and fresh salmon with roast pepper butter or fresh plaice with watercress, orange and aioli (£6.25); children's meals (from £2); the choice may be limited at Sunday lunchtime, when they do a roast. Very well kept Boddingtons, Flowers IPA and Original and Wadworths 6X on handpump, a range of wines, and good choice of malt whiskies. The pretty tree-sheltered garden has won several awards with its delightfully located picnic-sets on a terrace above a small pond among shrubs and flowers, as well as a good play area for children. The side lane leads down to a cove with caves by National Trust cliffs. *(Recommended by David and Natasha Toulson, J H Jones, Mr and Mrs K Fawcett, David and Michelle James, Mr and Mrs G Turner)*

Free house ~ Licensee Keith Soar ~ Real ale ~ Meals and snacks ~ Restaurant ~ (01545) 560396 ~ Children welcome ~ Open 12-3, 6-11(10.30 Sun)

LLYSWEN (Powys) SO1337 Map 6

Griffin ★ 🛏 🍷

A470, village centre

One reader describes how the bright enthusastic personality of the welcoming licensee and his huge mastiff Amber light up this peaceful well run ivy-covered inn. A soundly imaginative range of very good hearty country cooking relies firmly on local produce, some from their own gardens. Most days after Easter they serve brown trout and salmon, caught by the family or by customers in the River Wye just over the road, and they're well known for very good seasonal game such as pheasant or jugged hare. In the evenings you may find a range of tapas, and they do regular wine tasting nights. Excellent lunchtime meals from a sensible choice might include delicious home-made soups such as carrot and sweetcorn (£2.95), duck liver pâté (£3.95), cottage pie (£5.25), ploughman's (£5.50), curry and rice (£6.50), bangers and mash (£6.75), chicken in white wine and mushrooms (£6.95) and crispy leg of duck on apple (£7.25). Evening meals are more elaborate and might include hot smoked salmon on mixed leaves (£4.50), stuffed loin of Welsh lamb on a greengage, garlic and rosemary jus (£10.50) and sirloin steak with chargrilled vegetables or in a madeira sauce (£11.50), good puddings like strawberry pavlova or sticky toffee pudding (£3.25). Crown Buckley Reverend James, Flowers IPA, Tomas Watkin (a local beer) and a guest on handpump, and a good varied wine list with several half bottles. The Fishermen's Bar is popular with chatty locals; it's decorated with old fishing tackle and has a big stone fireplace with a good log fire, and large windsor armchairs and padded stools around tables; at lunchtime there's extra seating in the no-smoking dining room for bar meals; other dogs are allowed. You can shoot or fish here – they have a full-time ghillie and keeper. Service is friendly and helpful. Pretty comfortable bedrooms and great breakfasts. *(Recommended by J H Jones, David Cullen, Emma Stent, Chris Brace, Dr Oscar Puls, Wayne Brindle, Jason Caulkin)*

Free house ~ Licensees Richard and Di Stockton ~ Real ale ~ Meals and snacks (not Sun) ~ Restaurant ~ (01874) 754241 ~ Children welcome ~ Open 12-3, 7-11(10.30 Sun) ~ Bedrooms: £40B/£70B

MAENTWROG (Gwynedd) SH6741 Map 6

Grapes

A496; village signposted from A470

There's something to suit almost everyone at this rambling old inn. It's well geared for families and people out for a reliable meal, but at the same time is quite a favourite with Welsh speaking locals here for the lively pubby bar. From the good-sized sheltered verandah you can see trains on the Ffestiniog Railway puffing through the wood, beyond the pleasant back terrace and walled garden (there's a fountain on the lawn). Hearty bar food includes lunchtime sandwiches (not Sun, from £1.75), soup (£2.10), lentil, mushroom and hazelnut pâté (£3.50), steak burgers (£5.25), spicy vegetable stew (£6), mushroom stroganoff, lasagne or pork ribs (£6.25), lamb chops with a creamy leek and stilton sauce (£8), beef and bacon in a red wine and mushroom sauce (£8.25), and good specials tending to concentrate on fresh fish. Four changing beers on handpump might include well kept Bass, Fullers London Pride, Greene King and Plassey Dragons Breath on handpump, good house wines, over 30 malt whiskies, and good coffee. All three bars are attractively filled with lots of stripped pitch-pine pews, settles, pillars and carvings, mostly salvaged from chapels. Good log fires – there's one in the great hearth of the restaurant where there may be spit-roasts. An interesting juke box in the public bar, where there's also an intriguing collection of brass blowlamps. The dining room is no smoking; disabled lavatories. *(Recommended by Pamela and Merlyn Horswell, J H Jones, A J Bowen, D Goodger, Anthony Bowen, George Atkinson, Keith and Margaret Kettell, Roger Byrne, Mike Pugh, Paul Barnett, Mark Percy, Lesley Mayoh, Tim Barrow, Sue Demont, Jack and Gemima Valiant, John Baker, John Scarisbrick, Howard James)*

Free house ~ Licensees Brian and Gill Tarbox ~ Real ale ~ Meals and snacks (12-9.30 Sat/Sun) ~ (01766) 590365 ~ Children in eating area of bar and verandah ~ Open 11-11; 12-10.30 Sun ~ Bedrooms: £25B/£50B

MONKNASH (S Glamorgan) SS9270 Map 6

Plough & Harrow

Signposted Marcross, Broughton off B4265 St Brides Major—Llantwit Major – turn left at end of Water Street; OS Sheet 170 map reference 920706

This unspoilt country pub is in a peaceful spot not far from the coast near Nash Point (we have enjoyed the walk from the pub down to the sea, where you can pick up a fine stretch of the coastal path). It's a basic place (as is the gents'), and the main bar seems hardly changed over the last 60 or 70 years: a delightful find for those who enjoy really old-fashioned traditional pubs. It was originally part of a monastic grange and dates from the early 12th c: the stone walls are massively thick. The main bar (which used to be the scriptures room and mortuary) has a log fire in its huge fireplace with a side bread oven big enough to feed a village, as well as a woodburning stove with polished copper hot water pipes. The heavily black-beamed ceiling has ancient ham hooks, there's an intriguing arched dorrway to the back, and on the broad flagstones is a comfortably informal mix of furnishings that includes three fine stripped pine settles. A simple choice of good value food includes filled rolls (£1.20), faggots, chips, peas and gravy (£4.50), ploughman's, steak and ale pie and a salad or pasta bowl (all £4.95). Up to fourteen well kept ales might include Bass, Brains, Buckleys, Felinfoel, Greene King Abbot, Shepherd Neame Spitfire, and Worthington on handpump or tapped from the cask; daily papers, sensibly placed darts. The room on the left has pool, juke box and a fruit machine; piped music. Very quiet on weekday lunchtimes, the pub can get crowded and lively at weekends; it's popular with families. There are picnic-sets in the small front garden. *(Recommended by RMR, Mr and Mrs S Thomas, David Lewis, Sarah Lart, David and Nina Pugsley – no relation)*

Free house ~ Licensee: Pugsley (nickname) ~ Real ale ~ Lunchtime meals and snacks ~ (01656) 890209 ~ Children in eating area of bar till 8.30pm ~ Acoustic music at the weekend ~ Open 12-11; 12-10.30 Sun

PEMBROKE FERRY (Dyfed) SM9603 Map 6

Ferry Inn

Nestled below A477 toll bridge, N of Pembroke

We're hoping that the new licensee at this unaffected old sailor's haunt will keep cooking the same extensive range of very fresh fish in the same simple way that's proved so appealing in the past – the list of specials he gave us as examples suggests he will. There might be cod and chips (£5.25), plaice (£6.50), shell on prawns, green lip mussels and crispy fried clams on a platter (£6.95), scallops, prawns and mushrooms in a creamy sauce (£7.25) and dover sole or sea bass (£9.95), served alongside the menu which includes a pint of prawns (£3.25), moules marinières (£4), cumberland sausage (£4.95), lamb kebabs marinated in honey and mint or vegetarian lasagne (£5.25) and sirloin steak (£8.95), and puddings (£2.50). The bar has a buoyantly pubby atmosphere, nautical decor to suit its past, and good views over the water. Well kept Bass, Hancocks HB and Worthingtons on handpump, and a decent choice of malt whiskies. There are tables outside on a terrace by the water. Efficient service, fruit machine, unobtrusive piped music. *(Recommended by Charles and Pauline Stride, Graham Lynch-Watson, Michael Sargent)*

Free house ~ Licensee Colin Williams ~ Real ale ~ Meals and snacks (12-2, 7-10 Mon-Sat; 12-1.30, 7-9 Sun) ~ (01646) 684927 ~ Children in dining area ~ Open 11.30-2.45, 6.30(7 Mon)-11; 12-2.45, 7-10.30 Sun; cl Dec 25/26

PENMAENPOOL (Gwynedd) SH6918 Map 6

George III 🛏

Just off A493, near Dolgellau

The tidal Mawdacch estuary stretches away below the beautifully situated stone terrace of this popular hotel, and on a summer evening you can watch the sun go down over the water, catching the heather on the opposite hillside as it slowly disappears from view. Inside, the beamed and partly panelled welcoming upstairs bar opens into a cosy lounge where armchairs face a big log fire in a stone inglenook and there's an interesting collection of George III portraits. The downstairs bar (recently extended to cope with the demand for bar food) has long green leatherette seats around plain varnished tables on the flagstones, heavy beams, and stripped stone walls. Well kept Courage Directors, John Smiths, Marstons Pedigree and Ruddles Best on hand or electric pump. Darts, dominoes, fruit machine and maybe piped classical music. Home-made bar food includes soup (£2), home-made chicken liver pâté (£4.30), ploughman's (£5.25), chicken pancake or ratatouille (£5.60), hake fillet in mild mushroom sauce or steak and kidney pie (£5.95), six king prawns in garlic butter or grilled tuna steak (£6.65), smoked fish platter (£6.85), pork schnitzel with garlic butter and lemon (£7.25), half a roast crispy duckling with bramley apple sauce (£12.25), and puddings like apricot and apple crumble or bread and butter pudding (£2.95); the restaurant and cellar bar are no smoking. Some bedrooms are in a very comfortable award-winning conversion of what used to be an adjacent station, and most have stunning views over the water. There are fine walks in the forested hills around, such as up the long ridge across the nearby toll bridge. The hotel has fishing rights and can reserve sea-fishing trips from Barmouth, and there's an RSPB reserve next door. *(Recommended by Sarah and Peter Gooderham, Dave Braisted, Dr and Mrs Rob Holcombe, Mike and Wena Stevenson, Rob Whittle, J H Jones, Philip Campness, Rosie Davies, Patrick Freeman)*

Free house ~ Licensees John and Julia Cartwright ~ Real ale ~ Meals and snacks (12-2.30, 6.30-10) ~ Restaurant ~ (01341) 422525 ~ Well behaved children in cellar bar and restaurant ~ Open 11-11; 12-10.30 Sun ~ Bedrooms: £50B/£94B

PONTYPOOL (Gwent) ST2998 Map 6

Open Hearth

The Wern, Griffithstown; Griffithstown signposted off A4051 S – opposite British Steel main entrance turn up hill, then first right

This well run welcoming local is worth visiting for its splendid range of up to nine changing real ales – much better than you'll find anywhere else in the area, which include Archers Golden, Boddingtons, Brains Reverend James, Greene King Abbot, Hancocks HB and three guest ales on handpump, as well as a good choice of wines and malt whiskies. The comfortably modernised smallish lounge bar has a turkey carpet and big stone fireplace, and a back bar has leatherette seating. Reliable good value bar food includes soup (£2.15), filled baked potatoes (from £2.85), various curries (from £4.50), vegetable stir fry (£4.75), scampi or cod (£5.50), steak and ale pie (£5.45), pork glazed in a fresh ginger and orange sweet caramel (£6.95), lamb chops served on tarragon and Pernod scented potato (£8.95), sirloin steak cooked in a Mexican sauce (£9). Service is very friendly and efficient – they do their best to try and suit you if you want something not on the menu, and the downstairs no-smoking restaurant is something of a local landmark; cribbage, dominoes, and piped music. You can watch the comings and goings on a stretch of the Monmouthshire & Brecon Canal from seats outside, and the garden has swings, shrubs and picnic-sets, and boules in summer. *(Recommended by David Lewis, Sarah Lart, Mike Pugh, Pamela and Merlyn Horswell)*

Free house ~ Licensee Gwyn Philips ~ Real ale ~ Meals and snacks (till 10) ~ Restaurant ~ (01495) 763752 ~ Children in eating area of bar and restaurant ~ Open 11.30-3.30, 6-11; 11.30-11 Sat; 12-4.30, 7-10.30 Sun

PORTHMADOG (Gwynedd) SH5639 Map 6

Ship

Lombard Street; left turn off harbour rd, off High Street (A487) in centre

This roomy well run local – easy-going and relaxed, and known around here as Y Llong – has lots of attractive ship prints, photographs and drawings in its two dimly lit bars, quite a bit of brass nautical hardware, and candles in bottles. It's sturdily furnished, with pews, mate's chairs and so forth, and has well kept Burton Ale, Greene King Abbot, Marstons Pedigree, Morlands Old Speckled Hen, Tetleys Bitter and Mild and a guest on handpump (they have a beer festival in early October), and over 70 malt whiskies. A wide choice of generous nicely cooked bar food includes sandwiches (from £1.50), soup (£1.95), port and stilton pâté (£3.25), ploughman's (£4.30), lasagne (£5.85), chilli or wild mushroom lasagne (£5.95), scampi (£6.25), seafood crumble (£6.50), beef casserole or pork cooked in creamy mustard sauce (£6.85) and 8oz sirloin (£8.35); there's also an attractive no-smoking bistro-style back restaurant. TV, silenced fruit machine, dominoes. It's not a long walk from the Ffestiniog Railway terminus. *(Recommended by Tony Hobden, George Atkinson, Peter and Anne Hollindale, Joan and Michel Hooper-Immins)*

Free house ~ Licensees Robert and Nia Jones ~ Real ale ~ Meals and snacks ~ Restaurant ~ (01766) 512990 ~ Children in eating area of bar till 8pm(9 if eating) ~ Open 11-11; Sun 12-10.30

PRESTEIGNE (Powys) SO3265 Map 6

Radnorshire Arms

High Street; B4355 N of centre

Although part of a small chain of hotels this rambling, timbered place never seems to change its old-fashioned charm and individuality. Renovations have revealed secret passages and priest's holes, with one priest's diary showing he was walled up here for two years. Discreet modern furnishings blend with venerable dark oak panelling, latticed windows and elegantly moulded black oak beams, decorated with horsebrasses. Reasonably priced bar food might include good sandwiches (from £1.95), home-made soup (£2.25), filled baguettes (from £3.65), vegetarian dish of the day (£5.75), pie of the day or lamb liver and bacon (£5.95), whole breaded plaice (£6.25), breast of chicken with mushrooms and tarragon (£6.50), poached salmon with dill and white wine sauce (£6.95), grilled rump steak (£8.25), and puddings (£2.25); children's helpings (from £2.25). Well kept real ales include Bass, Cains and Yates on handpump, several malt whiskies, and welcoming attentive service; separate no-smoking restaurant, morning coffee, afternoon tea. There are some well spaced tables on the sheltered flower-bordered lawn, which used to be a bowling green. *(Recommended by Pamela and Merlyn Horswell, Graham and Karen Oddey; more reports please)*

Free house ~ Manager Philip Smart ~ Real ale ~ Meals and snacks ~ Restaurant ~ (01544) 267406 ~ Children welcome ~ Open 11-11; 12-10.30 Sun; 12-3, 7.10.30 winter Sun ~ Bedrooms: £45B/£90B

nr RAGLAN (Gwent) SO3608 Map 6

Clytha Arms

Clytha, off Abergavenny road – former A40, now declassified

Standing in its own well cared for extensive grounds (they're a mass of colour in spring) this fine old country inn impresses readers with its easy gracious comfort, excellent food and fine range of beers. The changing choice of very appealing fresh food is well prepared and presented, and might include soup (£3.80), seafood soup (£4), faggots and peas with beer and onion gravy (£4.25), black pudding with apple and mustard sauce, moules marinières or leek and laverbread rissoles (£4.95), wild boar sausage with potato pancakes (£5.25), ploughman's or salmon burger with tarragon and mayonnaise (£5.95), wild mushroom ragoût with pasta (£5.75), duck cassoulet (£6.90) or mixed shellfish grill (£7.95), and delicious home-made puddings (£3.50); good value three-course Sunday lunch in the no-smoking restaurant. A well stocked bar serves well kept Bass, Banks's, Hook Norton, Felinfoel Double Dragon and Uley Old Spot all on handpump as well as Weston's farm ciders and home-made perry. You will find locals in the tastefully refurbished bar which has a good lively atmosphere, with solidly comfortable furnishings and a couple of log fires. This is a real favourite with readers as a place to stay with its interested licensees, and charmingly helpful staff; darts, shove ha'penny, boules, table skittles, cribbage, draughts and chess. *(Recommended by Mr and Mrs I Rispin, Mike and Wena Stevenson, David and Nina Pugsley, Brian and Lis, Wayne Brindle, Dennis Heatley, Michael Coshall, Barry and Anne, Malcolm Taylor, Gwyneth and Salvo Spadaro-Dutturi, Peter and Audrey Dowsett)*

Free house ~ Licensees Andrew and Beverley Canning ~ Real ale ~ Meals and snacks (not Sat or Sun evening) ~ Restaurant ~ (01873) 840206 ~ Children welcome ~ Open 12-3, 6-11; 12-11 Sat; 12-4, 6(7 in winter)-10.30 Sun ~ Bedrooms: £45B/£50B

RED WHARF BAY (Anglesey) SH5281 Map 6

Ship

Village signposted off B5025 N of Pentraeth

Tables on the front terrace of this very popular family-run 16th-c house look down over ten square miles of treacherous tidal cockle-sands and sea, with low wooded hills sloping down to the broad bay. Inside is old-fashioned and interesting, with lots of nautical bric-a-brac in big friendly rooms on each side of the busy stone-built bar counter, both with long cushioned varnished pews built around the walls, glossily varnished cast-iron-framed tables and welcoming fires. Enterprising and well presented daily changing bar food might typically include cream of celery and stilton soup (£2.40), hot spicy avocado (£4.20), ploughman's (£4.75), cottage pie (£5.25), baked stuffed onions (£5.75), chicken breast with wholegrain mustard and tomato sauce (£6.85), ham shank with creamy dijon mustard sauce (£7.20), dressed crab (£7.65), salmon steak with horseradish crust (£8.15), and puddings like rhubarb and ginger crumble or sticky toffee pudding (£2.75). There may be delays at busy times (it can be quite crowded on Sundays, when food service stops promptly at 2, and you do need to arrive early for a table), but service is always friendly and smiling; the cheery licensee has been here now for over 20 years. The family room, dining room and cellar room are no smoking. Very well kept Burtons, Friary Meux, Marstons Pedigree, Tetleys Bitter and a guest beer on handpump with a sparkler; a wider choice of wines than usual for the area, and about 30 malt whiskies. Darts and dominoes in the back room; piped music. There are rustic tables and picnic-sets by an ash tree on grass by the side. *(Recommended by George Atkinson, M Meadley, J H Jones, GLD, Alan and Paula McCully, G S and E M Dorey, S P Watkin, P A Taylor, Mark Percy, Lesley Mayoh, Chris and Shirley Machin, Joy and Peter Heatherley)*

Free house ~ Licensee Andrew Kenneally ~ Real ale ~ Meals and snacks ~ (01248) 853568 ~ Restaurant ~ Children welcome in eating area of bar ~ Open 11-11; 12-10.30 Sun; 11-3.30, 7-11 winter Mon-Fri

ROSEBUSH (Dyfed) SN0630 Map 6

New Inn

B4329 Haverfordwest—Cardigan, NW of village

There's a quietly relaxed atmosphere at this attractively restored 17th-c drovers' inn. Three cosy cottagey rooms have interesting stripped stonework, simple antique oak country furniture on handsome slate flagstones or red and black diamond Victorian tiles, and a couple of coal fires – one in a quite cavernous fireplace. There is a small garden room. A short choice of good bar food using carefully chosen local ingredients might include soup (£2.75), a half pint of prawns (£3), cawl with cheese (£3.50), garlic mushrooms (£4.50), crostini of cockle and bacon with laver sauce or polenta with herbed local goat's cheese and parsley salsa (£5), seafood lasagne (£6), outstanding thai red curry pork or mushroom stroganoff (£6.75), as well as puddings such as bread and butter pudding (£3.75), and good local cheeses. As the food is freshly prepared there may be a wait; no-smoking restaurant. Very well kept real ales include Crown Buckley Reverend James, Dorothy Goodbody Blonde Bombshell and Greene King Abbot on handpump; well chosen wines by the bottle or glass, Weston's farm cider and friendly staff; darts, piped music. There are tables outside, and plenty of good walks nearby. *(Recommended by John and Enid Morris, R Mattick, Richard Siebert, Nick and Meriel Cox, Mr and Mrs M J Bastin, Jack and Gemima Valiant)*

Free house ~ Licensee Diana Richards ~ Real ale ~ Meals and snacks ~ Restaurant ~ (01437) 532542 ~ Children welcome ~ Live music Mon ~ Open 12-3, 6-11(10.30) Sun; cl Sun eve Nov-Easter, and second week in Jan

SHIRENEWTON (Gwent) ST4894 Map 6

Carpenters Arms

B4235 Chepstow—Usk

Handy for Chepstow, this building was originally a smithy. Once inside past the eye-catching array of hanging baskets, it's well worth wandering around this hive of small interconnecting rooms before you settle: there's plenty to see, from chamber-pots and a blacksmith's bellows hanging from the planked ceiling of one lower room, which has an attractive Victorian tiled fireplace, through an interesting case of sugar-tongs, to a collection of chromolithographs of antique Royal occasions under another room's pitched ceiling (more chamber-pots here, too). Furnishings run the gamut too, from one very high-backed ancient settle to pews, kitchen chairs, a nice elm table, several sewing-machine trestle tables and so forth. Food includes faggots and onion gravy (£4.25), stilton and vegetable crumble (£4.95), steak and mushroom pie or beef stroganoff (£5.95) and chicken supreme in leek and stilton sauce (£6.75); Sunday lunch is good value. Well kept Boddingtons, Flowers IPA, Fullers London Pride, Marstons Pedigree and Owd Rodger, and Wadworths 6X on handpump; a good selection of over 50 malt whiskies; cheerful service, darts, shove-ha'penny, cribbage, dominoes and maybe loudish piped pop music. *(Recommended by I J and N K Buckmaster; more reports please)*

Free house ~ Licensee James Bennett ~ Real ale ~ Meals and snacks (not winter Sun eves) ~ (01291) 641231 ~ Children in family area ~ Open 11-2.30(3 Sat), 6-11; 12-3, 7-10.30 Sun

ST HILARY (S Glamorgan) ST0173 Map 6

Bush £

Village signposted from A48 E of Cowbridge

Set in an attractive village, this genuinely old-fashioned 16th-c thatched pub is a friendly atmospheric place. The comfortable and snugly cosy low-beamed lounge bar has stripped old stone walls, and windsor chairs around copper-topped tables on the carpet, while the public bar has old settles and pews on aged flagstones; darts and subdued piped music, and a warming wood fire. Very reasonably priced good bar food includes sandwiches (from £1.75), home-made soup (£2.20), laverbread and bacon (£2.95), welsh rarebit (£3.35), spinach and cheese crêpe (£3.55), ploughman's (£3.95), trout fillet grilled with bacon or liver with onion gravy (£4.50), chicken curry and rice or steak and ale pie (£4.95), mixed grill (£7.50), and good daily specials; the restaurant menu is available in the bar in the evenings, with meals like trout fried in sherry (£8.95) or breast of duck in orange (£11.95); they will do smaller helpings for children. Well kept Bass, Hancocks Best and Morlands Old Speckled Hen on hand or electric pump, with a range of malt whiskies and a farm cider; efficient service. There are tables and chairs in front, and more in the back garden. *(Recommended by N H Lewis, Rob Holt, M Joyner, C D Jones, Jeremy Brittain-Long, David and Nina Pugsley, I and N Buckmaster, D and L Berry, R B Mowbray)*

Bass ~ Tenant Sylvia Murphy ~ Real ale ~ Meals and snacks (till 3 Sun; not winter Sun evenings) ~ Restaurant ~ (01446) 772745 ~ Children welcome ~ Open 11.30-11; 12-10.30 Sun ~ Bedrooms: £20/£30

STACKPOLE (Dyfed) SR9896 Map 6

Armstrong Arms

Village signposted off B4319 S of Pembroke

Recently taken over by a mother and daugher team, this delightful rather Swiss-looking inn is tucked away on the Stackpole estate. One spacious area has new pine tables and chairs, with winter darts and pool, but the major part of the pub, L-shaped on four different levels, is given over to diners, with neat light oak furnishings, and glossy beams and low ceilings to match; piped music. Lunchtime bar food, served by cheerful black-and-white-uniformed waitresses, includes soup (£2.95), ciabatta filled with smoked salmon and cream cheese (£3.95), lasagne, crêpes filled with spinach and stilton or salmon and leek mornay or lamb liver lyonnaise with parsley mashed potatoes (£4.95), spinach and lentil roulade on a tomato coulis (£4.95). A more elaborate evening menu includes mushroom and cranberry en croûute (£5.25), moules marinières (£5.50), beef, Guinness and mushroom pie (£6.95), grilled chicken supreme with garlic and herb butter or cheese sauce (£7.25), rack of Welsh lamb with port, cranberry and orange sauce or leek cream (£8.95) and rib eye steak with chasseur sauce (£9.75). Puddings include crème brûlée or chocolate and raspberry roulade (£3.25). Well kept Charles Wells Bombardier and Crown Buckley Best and Reverend James on handpump, and several malt whiskies. There are tables out in the attractive gardens, with colourful flower beds and mature trees around the car park; no credit cards or dogs. *(Recommended by H and D Payne, Patrick Wintour, Carole Smart, Andrew Jeeves, Jeremy Brittain-Long, Deirdre Goodman, Graham Lynch-Watson, Mr and Mrs M J Bastin, T L Rees, Michael Sargent, Nick and Meriel Cox, Brian and Anna Marsden)*

Free house ~ Licensees Margaret and Valerie Westmore ~ Real ale ~ Meals and snacks (not Sun lunchtime) ~ Restaurant ~ (01646) 672324 ~ Children in restaurant and inglenook room till 8.30 ~ Open 11-11; 11.30-3, 6-11 winter Mon-Sat; 12-3, 7-10.30 winter Sun

Please tell us if any Lucky Dips deserve to be upgraded to a main entry and why. No stamp needed: *The Good Pub Guide*, FREEPOST TN1569, Wadhurst, E Sussex TN5 7BR.

TALYBONT-ON-USK (Powys) SO1122 Map 6

Star £

B4558

They keep an incredible twelve changing real ales at this old-fashioned little canalside pub. There might be Boddingtons, Felinfoel Double Dragon, Freeminer, Hartleys, Marstons Pedigree and Old Peculier, Theakstons Best and Wye Valley Dorothy Goodbody, as well as farm cider on handpump too. Several plainly furnished pubby rooms – unashamedly stronger on character than on creature comforts – radiate from the central servery, including a brightly lit games area with pool, fruit machine and juke box; roaring winter fires, one in a splendid stone fireplace. Cheerily served hearty bar food includes soup (£2), ploughman's (£3.50), ham with parsley sauce (£4), lasagne, faggots, peas and chips (£4.50), daily roast, chilli, chicken curry, pork goulash or lamb liver casserole (£4.95), carbonnade of beef (£6.50), sirloin with savoury sauce (£7.95), and vegetarian dishes such as vegiburger (£3.50) and spinach and leek pasta bake (£4.95); children's meals (£2). You can sit outside at picnic-sets in the sizeable tree-ringed garden or walk along the tow path, and the village, with both the Usk and the Monmouth & Brecon Canal running through, is surrounded by the Brecon Beacons national park. *(Recommended by David Lewis, Sarah Lart, Charles and Pauline Stride, Jack and Philip Paxton)*

Free house ~ Licensee Joan Coakham ~ Real ale ~ Meals and snacks (till 9.30) ~ (01874) 676635 ~ Children welcome till 9pm ~ Live blues/rock Weds evenings ~ Open 11-3, 6-11; 11-11 Sat; 12-10.30 Sun ~ Bedrooms: £25B/£45B

TALYCOED (Gwent) SO4115 Map 6

Halfway House

B4233 Monmouth—Abergavenny; though its postal address is Llantilio Crossenny, the inn is actually in Talycoed, a mile or two E

A huge wisteria surrounds the handsome ancient door of this pretty 17th-c country inn. Inside, a step up on the left takes you into a cosy little no-smoking dining room with burgundy furnishings and carpet, sporting and other prints, and black kettles around its hearth. The main bar is also snug and cosy: soft lighting, bare boards, polished brasses around a nice old stone fireplace, wall settles, a few red plush bar stools, and a back area with a couple of antique high-backed settles and enormous foresters' saws. Lovers of picturesque old inns will recognise many old friends in their collection of Wills cigarette cards. Carefully presented bar food includes mussels in white wine and garlic (£3.25), avocado and corn bake (£5.80), steak and stout pie (£5.95), chicken breast in port and mushroom sauce (£6.30), venison with red wine and redcurrant sauce (£7.85) and duck in orange and cointreau sauce (£8.40); welcoming service; no-smoking area in dining room. Well kept Bass and Felinfoel Bitter and Double Dragon on handpump; darts, maybe quiet piped radio. All is neat and clean, including the outside gents'. There are picnic-sets out on a front terrace with a big barbecue, and in a neatly kept garden; there's a cricket field in front (home to a succesful team), and two or three caravans behind. *(Recommended by Gethin Lewis; more reports please)*

Free house ~ Licensees Mr and Mrs L G Stagg ~ Real ale ~ Meals and snacks (not Sun eve) ~ (01600) 780269 ~ Well behaved children welcome ~ Open 12-3, 6-11(7-10.30 Sun); cl winter lunchtimes ~ Bedrooms: £25/£37

TALYLLYN (Gwynedd) SH7209 Map 6

Tynycornel

B4405, off A487 S of Dolgellau

As soon as you step out of your car here you're enveloped in peace: the hotel looks out over a charming lake nestling below high mountains – Cadair Idris opposite (splendid walks), Graig Goch behind you. In the evening all you hear is birdsong, sheep, wavelets lapping under the moored boats (for guests to hire). It's very civilised inside, not at all pubby, but relaxed and friendly, with deep armchairs and sofas to sink into around the low tables, a central log fire, and big picture windows looking out over the water (the serving bar, with keg beer, is tucked away behind); there's floral wallpaper, good big bird prints, local watercolours. Good well served food includes soup (£1.85), sandwiches (£2), chicken liver and brandy pâté (£2.95), ploughman's (£4.75), scampi or breaded king prawns (£5.75) and gammon (£6.95), and daily specials like battered cod or haddock and prawn in cheese sauce (£5.50), beef curry or a pasta dish (£5.75), and puddings (£2.50); afternoon tea (£3); helpful uniformed staff; no-smoking restaurant and conservatory. An attractively planted side courtyard has good teak seats and tables. Guests also have the use of a sauna and outdoor swimming pool, and fishing facilities. *(Recommended by D W Jones-Williams, Sarah and Peter Gooderham, J H Jones, M Joyner, J Sheldon)*

Free house ~ Manager Mr Rolands ~ Meals and snacks (12-2, 7-8.30 maybe till 9; not Sun) ~ Restaurant ~ (01654) 782282 ~ Children in bar area ~ Open 11-11; 12-10.30 Sun ~ Bedrooms: £47B/£94

TY'N Y GROES (Gwynedd) SH7672 Map 6

Groes

B5106 N of village

Bedrooms (some with terraces or balconies) at this very well run inn have magnificent views over the mountains or scenic reaches of the Conwy River. You get the same views from the no-smoking airy verdant conservatory, and from seats on the flower decked roadside. The homely series of rambling, low-beamed and thick-walled rooms are beautifully decorated with antique settles and an old sofa, old clocks, portraits, hats and tins hanging from the walls and fresh flowers. A fine antique fireback is built into one wall, perhaps originally from the formidable fireplace which houses a collection of stone cats as well as winter log fires. A very good range of traditional country cooking, with lots of local produce, might include french onion soup (£2.75), sandwiches (from £3), Welsh cheese board (£4.95), soup and a sandwich (£5.95), lasagne, chicken curry or steak (£6.75), steak and kidney pot with thyme dumplings (£6.95), fillet of poached salmon and grilled plaice with hollandaise sauce (£8.75), daily specials like ham, pork and turkey rolled in bacon or braised marrow provençale (£6.50), crab or local salt marsh lamb (£8.50) and fresh Conwy lobster (£18.50), and lots of tasty puddings like fresh fruit pavlova, treacle tart, bread and butter pudding (£3.30), and tempting home-made ice creams like lemon curd or caramelised pears with maple syrup (£2.95). Well kept Banks's and Marstons Pedigree on hand and electric pump and kept under light blanket pressure, a good few malt whiskies, kir, and a fruity Pimms in summer; cribbage, dominoes and light classical piped music at lunchtimes (nostalgic light music at other times). It can get busy, but this shouldn't cause any problems with the efficient friendly service. There are seats in the pretty back garden with its flower-filled hayricks. *(Recommended by Dave Braisted, Mrs P Goodwyn, Roger and Christine Mash, Roger Byrne, Tim Harper, Paul Hilditch, Liz Bell, Dr Phil Putwain, Gordon Theaker, R H Sawyer, D L Evans, Pearl Williams, Joy and Peter Heatherley, Eric Locker)*

Free house ~ Licensees Dawn, Tony and Justin Humphreys ~ Real ale ~ Meals and snacks ~ Restaurant ~ (01492) 650545 ~ Children in eating area of bar till 8pm ~ Open 12-3, 6.30-11(10.30 Sun) ~ Bedrooms: £63.25B/£80.50B

USK (Gwent) SO3801 Map 6

Royal

New Market Street (off A472 by Usk bridge)

Described by one reader as a haven in a barren land, this characterful and unspoilt Georgian country-town pub was once owned by John Trelawney and frequented by Mary Shelley. The two simple open-plan rooms of the homely old-fashioned bar are still furnished with some original pieces. The left-hand room is the nicer, with a cream-tiled kitchen range flush with the pale ochre back wall, a comfortable mix of tables and chairs, a rug on neat slate flagstones, plates and old pictures on the walls, china cabinets, a tall longcase clock, and open fires; piped music. Particularly well kept Bass, Felinfoel Double Dragon, Hancocks HB and a guest such as Adnams Broadside on handpump, and an extensive wine list. Tasty bar meals, served in big helpings, are popular and might include deep-fried breaded plaice or half a roast chicken (£6.50), cold home-baked ham or mushroom, cashew nut and tagliatelle pie (£6.75), lasagne verdi or beef and beer pie (£6.95), grilled lamb chops or breast of chicken in a cream, tarragon and white wine sauce (£7.95) and lovely tender steaks (from £10.50); they do a popular Sunday lunch (£6.95) (when the ordinary menu isn't available). Service can slow down at busy times. *(Recommended by J W Hackett, H L Dennis, George and Brenda Jones, Pamela and Merlyn Horswell, Gwyneth and Salvo Spadaro-Dutturi, Jenny and Brian Seller)*

Free house ~ Licensee Anthony Lyons ~ Real ale ~ Meals and snacks (not Sun evening and Mon lunchtime) ~ (01291) 672931 ~ Well behaved children welcome ~ Open 12-3, 7-11; cl Mon lunchtime

Lucky Dip

Besides the fully inspected pubs, you might like to try these Lucky Dips recommended to us and described by readers (if you do, please send us reports):

ANGLESEY

Dulas [A5025 N of Moelfre; SH4687], *Pilot Boat*: Good food and service, enthusiastic and pleasant young licensees, limited choice of reasonably priced wines, sensible prices, warm, friendly and clean; restaurant *(Mr and Mrs T Pitwell, Dr J H Jones)*

☆ **Menai Bridge** [Glyngarth; A545, half way towards Beaumaris; SH5572], *Gazelle*: Outstanding waterside situation looking across to Snowdonia, steep and aromatic sub-tropical garden behind, lively main bar and smaller rooms off popular with yachtsmen, short choice of bar food and restaurants, well kept Robinsons Best and Mild, helpful staff; children allowed away from serving bar; bedrooms *(J S M Sheldon, LYM)*

☆ **Menai Bridge** [St Georges Pier, by Straits], *Liverpool Arms*: Unpretentious old-fashioned four-roomed local with cheerful relaxed atmosphere, low beams, interesting mostly maritime photographs and prints, panelled dining room, conservatory catching evening sun, one or two tables on terrace; good value bar food, well kept Greenalls Special and Best, welcoming landlord, good service; no music *(T G Thomas, D Goodger, Dr J H Jones)*

CLWYD

Bersham [SJ3049], *Elephant & Castle*: Cosy bar with good value food, well kept Gales HSB *(Tom Evans)*

Broughton [The Old Warren; old main rd towards Buckley; SJ3263], *Spinning Wheel*: Very wide choice of good freshly made well served food, pleasant surroundings now the road's closed to through traffic, efficient staff, good choice of beers and malt whiskies; piped music may be obtrusive *(KC)*

☆ **Bylchau** [A543 3 miles S; SH9863], *Sportsmans Arms*: Wide views from highest pub in Wales, straightforward food with fresh veg and vegetarian dishes, well kept Lees Traditional and Best Dark Mild; Welsh-speaking locals, cheerful and welcoming prompt service, good log fire, old-fashioned high-backed settles among more modern seats, darts and pool, no piped music, harmonium and Welsh singing Sat evening; children allowed in eating area, cl Mon/Tues lunchtimes in winter (and maybe other lunchtimes then) *(NAK, LYM)*

Carrog [B5436, signed off A5 Llangollen—Corwen; SJ1144], *Grouse*: Small unpretentious local, local pictures, very friendly staff, Lees Bitter, attractively priced food from good sandwiches and hearty soup up, splendid River Dee view from bay window and tables on terrace with pretty walled garden; pool in games room, piped music; bedrooms *(Jenny and Michael Back, George Atkinson, Ray and Liz Monk)*

☆ **Cilcain** [signed from A494 W of Mold; SJ1765], *White Horse*: Very attractive homely country local with several rooms, low joists, mahogany and oak settles, roaring inglenook fire, quarry-tiled back bar allowing dogs, reasonably priced home-made food inc interesting dishes, vegetarian and lots of puddings, well kept changing ales such as Marstons Pedigree, Morlands Old Speckled Hen or Timothy Taylor Landlord, pub games; no children inside, picnic-sets outside; delightful little village *(Mathew Bailey, Sue and Bob Ward, Anthony Hoyle, LYM)*

Cwm [S of Dyserth; SJ0677], *Blue Lion*: Family-owned 16th-c pub in lovely hill setting with views over Vale of Clwyd towards Snowdonia, son cooks good food with local produce, very friendly efficient service, well kept Marstons, plenty of wines and spirits, inglenook log fires, beams crowded with chamber pots, lots of brasses and china; restaurant; garden, just off Offa's Dyke Path *(Mr and Mrs Archibald, Brian Seller)*

Erbistock [signed off A539 W of Overton, then pub signposted; SJ3542], *Boat*: This enchantingly placed 16th-c riverside pub has closed, with the intention of reopening as an Italian restaurant *(LYM)*

Gwernymynydd [SJ2263], *Swan*: Friendly staff, good choice of food inc plenty of vegetarian *(KC)*

Holywell [Brynford Hill; SJ1875], *Llyn y Mawn*: Charming comfortable country pub based on 15th-c coaching inn with sympathetic recent extension (inc evening restaurant), warmly welcoming licensees, good home cooking with fresh veg, well kept ales inc Buckleys, summer farm cider; quiz and music nights *(Andy and Jill Kassube)*
Lixwm [B5121 S of Holywell; SJ1671], *Crown*: Well kept early 17th-c village inn, good choice of real ale inc changing guest beers, reasonably priced bar food cooked to order every evening and weekend lunchtimes, pleasant licensees, nice atmosphere; children allowed in dining room, open all day Sun, cl weekday lunchtimes; colourful front flower tubs and baskets; bedrooms *(Basil Minson, Mr and Mrs D Jackson)*
Llanbedr dyffryn Clwyd [SJ1359], *Griffin*: Charming pub with good freshly made food from sandwiches to steaks (they'll even do breakfast by prior arrangement), well kept real ales, log fires, colouring things for children, pool and TV in family room, big garden; cl Tues lunchtime; bedrooms and overnight camping, attractive surroundings *(D and G Williams)*
Llandegla [Ruthin Rd (A525); SJ1952], *Crown*: Quickly served good value food inc vegetarian in comfortable bright bar with good set of Hogarth prints, well kept Lees, good helpful service, popular restaurant; on Offa's Dyke Path *(Brian Seller)*
Llanelian yn Rhos [S of Colwyn Bay; signed off A5830 (shown as B5383 on some maps) and B5381; SH8676], *White Lion*: Family-run 16th-c inn, traditional flagstoned snug bar with antique settles and big fire, dining area on left with jugs hanging from beams, teapots above window, further more spacious dining area up broad steps, wide choice of good reasonably priced bar food from sandwiches and big tureen of home-made soup up, well kept Marstons Bitter, Pedigree and a seasonal beer, good range of wines, lots of malt whiskies; dominoes, cribbage, piped music; rustic tables outside, good walking nearby; children in eating areas; bedrooms *(Jenny and Michael Back, LYM)*
Llanelidan [B5429 just E of village; signed off A494 S of Ruthin – OS Sheet 116 map reference 110505; SJ1150], *Leyland Arms*: This beautifully set interesting old pub has been giving readers a lot of pleasure, for its enjoyable food in charming surroundings, but as we went to press was under temporary management, with no news on its future operation *(LYM; news please)*
Llangollen [Horseshoe Pass (A542 N); SJ2045], *Britannia*: Included for position, with lovely Dee Valley views from picturesque though much extended pub, two quiet bars and brightly cheerful dining areas (one no smoking), Whitbreads-related ales; well kept garden; good value attractive bedrooms *(Alan and Barbara Mence, E G Parish)*; [Mill St; A539 E of bridge (N end)], *Sarah Ponsonby*: Large pub next to canal museum on quieter side of the Dee, pleasant staff, good choice of good value generous food, well kept Theakstons, no-smoking area; pleasant garden overlooking park *(S W Armstrong, KC)*; [Trevor Uchaf, off A539 E; SJ2442], *Sun Trevor*: Spectacular views over River Dee and canal, enjoyable proper food in bar and restaurant, friendly staff, well kept Scottish Courage ales, no piped music *(KC)*
Llansilin [B4580 W of Oswestry; SJ2128], *Wynnstay*: Pleasant unpretentious village pub, small lounge with range and sparkling brasses, larger locals' bar, welcoming licensees and friendly staff, well kept Marstons Pedigree, good cheap simple food; bedrooms comfortable *(Dr B and Mrs P B Baker, Pete Yearsley)*
Marchwiel [A525/A528 SE of Wrexham; SJ3648], *Red Lion*: Comfortable feel, nice decor, bar, small lounge and attractive back dining lounge (children allowed here) with country view, Marstons Bitter and seasonal ale, enjoyable food, helpful staff, facilities for disabled *(Jenny and Michael Back)*
Mold [A541 Denbigh rd nr Bailey Hill; SJ2464], *Bryn Awel*: Popular good value dining pub, good choice of satisfying food inc vegetarian, huge helpings, good service, cheerful bustling atmosphere, attractive decor, good no-smoking area; no piped music *(KC)*; [Loggerheads; A494, 3 miles towards Ruthin; SJ1962], *We Three Loggerheads*: Comfortable two-level bar, games area, pleasant young staff, decent usual food, unobtrusive piped music; open all day in summer; picnic-sets out on side terrace overlooking river *(S P Watkin, P A Taylor, KC, LYM)*
Northop [SJ2468], *Soughton Hall*: Recently opened country pub in attractive and extensively renovated stable block of comfortable country house hotel, real ales, wide choice of wines, freshly made bistro-style food; bedrooms *(Anon)*
Overton Bridge [A539; SJ3643], *Cross Foxes*: Warm and friendly 17th-c coaching inn in attractive setting on Dee, small entrance room, lounge on left, small back bar and games room, Marstons Bitter and Pedigree, good value generous straightforward home cooking with some interesting specials *(Jenny and Michael Back)*
Penley [SJ4240], *Dymock Arms*: Very old and full of character, well kept unusual beers and farm cider, food inc bargain Sun lunch *(Mr and Mrs F Carroll)*
☆ **Rhewl** [the one off A5 W of Llangollen; SJ1744], *Sun*: Unpretentious little cottage in lovely peaceful spot, good walking country just off Horseshoe Pass, relaxing views from terrace and small pretty garden; simple good value food from sandwiches to good Sun lunch, well kept Felinfoel Double Dragon, Worthington BB and a guest beer, old-fashioned hatch service to back room, dark little lounge, portakabin games room – children allowed here and in eating area *(Ray and Liz Monk, Joan and Michel Hooper-Immins, KC, LYM)*

St George [off A55 nr Abergele; SH9576], *Kinmel Arms*: Interesting building, clean and comfortable, with short but good choice of freshly made food often using unusual local ingredients (plenty of time needed, as everything cooked for you); good range of real ales with weekly guest; bedrooms, attractive village *(KC)*

☆ **Trofarth** [B5113 S of Colwyn Bay; SH8470], *Holland Arms*: Good value generous food inc lunchtime bargains in old-fashioned 17th-c former coaching inn, warm cosy atmosphere, prompt friendly service, Ansells Mild and Tetleys, farm tools in one room, stuffed owls in the other, raised dining area open when busy; some tables outside with valley and mountain views; handy for Bodnant *(Roger Byrne)*

DYFED

☆ **Aberaeron** [Quay Parade, just off A487; SN4462], *Harbourmaster*: Reopened under pleasant new licensees and doing well, good interesting reasonably priced lunchtime bar food inc very fresh crab sandwiches in home-baked brown bread, Brains and Buckleys real ale, cosy bar with lots of ship memorabilia, simple refurbished restaurant; bedrooms comfortably refurbished too, lovely harbourside setting *(Jill Young, Gwyneth and Salvo Spadaro-Dutturi, IHR)*

Aberaeron [10 Market St], *Cadwgan Arms*: Late 18th c, with well kept beer and friendly licensees; open all day *(Gwyneth and Salvo Spadaro-Dutturi)*; [Market St], *Monachty Arms*: In same family for over a century but recently refurbished, lovely warm welcome, abundant reasonably priced food, well kept Tetleys, separate pool room and dining room, garden; bedrooms simple *(Gwyneth and Salvo Spadaro-Dutturi)*; [Queen St], *Prince of Wales*: Cosy backstreet pub, welcoming and unfussy, with open fires, friendly ex-butcher landlord, good steaks, well kept Felinfoel Double Dragon *(Gwyneth and Salvo Spadaro-Dutturi)*

Amroth [SN1607], *Amroth Arms*: Smart locally popular dining pub, good value meals inc Sun lunch, seats out on pavement overlooking sea *(Pam Adsley, M and M Carter)*

☆ *nr* **Broad Haven** [N of village on coast rd, bear L for about 1½ miles then follow sign L to Druidstone Haven – inn a sharp left turn after another ½ mile; OS Sheet 157 map ref 862168, marked as Druidston Villa], *Druidstone*: Very unusual and a favourite place to stay for many; its club licence means you can't go for just a drink and have to book to eat there (the food is inventively individual home cooking, with fresh ingredients and a leaning towards the organic; restaurant cl Sun evening); a lived-in informal country house alone in a grand spot above the sea, with terrific views, spacious homely bedrooms, erratic plumbing, cellar bar with a strong 1960s folk-club feel, well kept Worthington BB tapped from the cask, good wines, country wines and other drinks, ceilidhs and folk jamborees, chummy dogs (dogs welcomed), all sorts of sporting activities from boules to sand-yachting; cl Nov and Jan; bedrooms *(Gerald Barnett, LYM)*

Cardigan [leaving centre southwards on right after bridge; SN1846], *Eagle*: Very popular lively local, bright and cheerful, rugs on tiled floor, hop-festooned beams, thousands of beer mats on ceiling, lots of bric-a-brac, entertaining verses in poet's corner, well kept Buckley, good straightforward food from outstanding ham rolls to real blowouts *(Mr and Mrs K Fawcett)*

Carmarthen [Lammas St; SN4120], *Drovers Arms*: Small family-run hotel with homely bar where women feel happy, very reasonably priced usual bar food, well kept Felinfoel Double Dragon, welcoming service; bedrooms comfortable, good breakfast inc cockles and laverbread *(Mike and Wena Stevenson)*

Cenarth [A484 Cardigan—Newcastle Emlyn; SN2641], *Three Horseshoes*: Welcoming family-run village pub with friendly attentive staff, good choice of generous reasonably priced home-made food – most people here to eat; medieval alehouse at the back *(Mr and Mrs K Fawcett, C H and B J Owen)*

☆ **Cwm Gwaun** [Pontfaen; Cwm Gwaun and Pontfaen signed off B4313 E of Fishguard; SN0035], *Dyffryn Arms*: Classic unspoilt country tavern, very basic and idiosyncratic, run by same family since 1840 – charming landlady Bessie has been here 40 years herself; plain deal furniture, well kept Bass and Ind Coope Burton served by jug through a hatch, good sandwiches if you're lucky, Great War prints, draughts-boards inlaid into tables, coal fire, very relaxed atmosphere; pretty countryside *(Jack and Philip Paxton, Kevin Thorpe, LYM)*

Dale [SM8105], *Griffin*: Friendly no-frills waterside pub by Milford Sound, popular with yachtsmen and sailboarders; limited choice of well cooked simple food inc seafood, three real ales, friendly service, good view of boats in estuary, can sit out on sea wall; children allowed when eating *(Mr and Mrs T A Bryan, Jeremy Brittain-Long)*

Fforest [Heol Fforest; A48/A4138; SN5704], *Black Horse*: Good smiling service, well kept Brains SA, Bitter and Dark, generous piping hot food inc midweek bargains in neat dining room *(Joan and Michel Hooper-Immins)*

Fishguard [The Square, Upper Town – OS Sheet 157 map ref 958370; SM9537], *Royal Oak*: Busy but well organised, with low-beamed narrow front bar, woodburner and pictures commemorating defeat here of second-last attempted French invasion, steps down to big picture-window dining extension with well spaced tables, decent food inc some unusual dishes and good potatoes and veg, well kept Buckleys and other ales *(Anne Morris, Peter Lewis, Dr Oscar Puls)*

☆ **Haverfordwest** [24 Market St; SM9515], *Georges*: Unusually wide choice of generous home-made food using good meat and fresh veg in attractive bar with character stable-like furnishings, informal relaxed atmosphere and good choice of well kept ales such as Bass, Ind Coope Burton and Marstons Pedigree; more sophisticated evening restaurant, good friendly service; no dogs *(IHR)*

Lampeter [A482 towards Pumpsaint; SN5748], *Tafarn Jem*: Very welcoming new landlord in isolated country pub with lovely views over steep valley, particularly good food inc outstanding local steaks; children welcome *(David and Natasha Toulson, BB)*

Little Haven [off B4341 W of Haverfordwest; SM8512], *Castle*: Well placed by green looking over sandy bay, limited enjoyable food inc local fish, well kept Worthington BB, quick friendly service, beams and stripped stone, big oak tables, castle prints, restaurant, outside seating; children welcome *(David and Nina Pugsley, Martin Jones, Tony Pounder, LYM)*

Llanarthne [B4300 E of Carmarthen; SN5320], *Paxton*: Cosy and friendly dimly lit bar with two cats and loads of bric-a-brac, more sober restaurant, helpful service, wide choice of generous bar food, well kept Buckley, farm cider, decent malt whiskies; folk, jazz and blues nights; opp wood leading to Paxtons Tower (NT); open all day w/e *(Pete Baker, Lynda Payton, Sam Samuells, Jack and Gemima Valiant)*

Llanddarog [aka Yr Hedd Gwyn, B4310 just off A48 E of Carmarthen; SN5016], *White Hart*: Friendly ancient stone-built thatched dining pub with heavy beams, lovely carved settles, Welsh tapestries and so forth; above-average generous food running up to sizzling venison, kangaroo and crocodile, well kept real ale, restaurant area; piped nostalgic music (even in the garden) *(Miss J Reay, A J Bowen, R B Mowbray, J Taylor)*

Llandeilo [Pentrefelin (A40 towards Carmarthen); SN6023], *Nags Head*: Pleasantly refurbished dining pub, roomy open-plan bar with log fire and lots of horsey prints and brasses, good interesting food inc local fish and game, well kept ales such as Boddingtons, Flowers IPA and Worthington BB, decent house wines, good friendly service, well appointed back dining room; piped music *(Anne Morris)*

Llandeilo, *Castle*: Brews its own very good value T Watkin beers, with other guest beers kept well; big bar, several tidily renovated rooms, reasonably priced good basic food, tables in spacious yard *(Jack and Gemima Valiant, David Brammer)*

Llandybie [6 Llandeilo Rd (A483 N of Ammanford); SN6115], *Red Lion*: Wide choice of good generous fresh food inc fish and Sun lunch in attractive and welcoming inn's tastefully modernised, spacious and comfortable bar and restaurant; several well kept Whitbreads-related ales, local pictures for sale; bedrooms *(DAV, R B Mowbray, Jack and Gemima Valiant)*

Llangain [Old School Rd; B4312 S of Carmarthen; SN3816], *Pantydderwen*: Good varied food, freshly cooked (so may be a wait); weekends very busy – worth booking *(Mr and Mrs G J Garrett)*

Llanwnnen [B4337 signed Temple Bar from village, on A475 W of Lampeter; SN5346], *Fish & Anchor*: Snug bar with lots of stripped pine, enthusiastic landlord, friendly service, well kept ales, good collection of whiskies, good value bar food inc lots of local specialities and fresh veg; pretty little country dining room, views from garden with good play area; children allowed *(Mr and Mrs K Fawcett, LYM)*

Mathry [Brynamlwg; off A487 Fishguard—St Davids; SM8732], *Farmers Arms*: Good food esp fresh local fish and seafood, fair prices, Bass, Buckley and Worthington; tables in small walled garden, safe for children, and has been open all day in summer: in winter much more of a village local, when it may be cl Sun *(Mike Pugh, John and Enid Morris)*

Milton [just off A477; SN0303], *Milton Brewery*: Cosy ex-brewery with attractively unfussy olde-worlde decor, panelling and stripped stonework, popular food, well kept Bass and Worthington BB, friendly staff, open fire each end; seats outside *(C H and B J Owen)*

Nantgaredig [A40 Llandeilo—Carmarthen; SN4921], *Last Chance*: Large open-plan food pub with wide choice of bar food, separate restaurant, well kept Worthington and Tomas Watkin PSB; play area *(Jack and Gemma Valiant)*

Nevern [B4582; SN0840], *Trewern Arms*: Extended inn in lovely setting nr notable church and medieval bridge over River Nyfer, dark stripped-stone slate-floored bar, rafters hung with rural bric-a-brac, high-backed settles, plush banquettes, usually several Whitbreads-related ales, food ordered from bright modern kitchen, tables in pretty garden; loudish games room, lunchtime service can stop too promptly; restaurant, comfortable bedrooms, big breakfast *(Bill Hyett, Jack and Gemima Valiant, R Mattick, LYM)*

Newport [East St; SN0539], *Llwyngwair Arms*: Friendly straightforward local with good food inc smoked local trout from its own smokery and genuine Indian dishes (takeaways too), well kept Worthington and a cheap house beer, coal-effect fire, lots of rugby and rowing mementoes; copes well with the busy holiday season *(Michael Richards)*

Newquay [Glanmor Terr; SN3859], *Black Lion*: Partly 17th c, with low ceilings, stripped stone, well kept ales inc Courage Directors, lots of malt whiskies and Irish whiskeys, bar food, restaurant with Celtic dishes; big garden overlooking Cardigan Bay, with play area and boules; weekend folk music, bar can be a bit smoky when busy; bedrooms *(Thomas Hunter)*

☆ **Pont ar Gothi** [A40 6 miles E of Carmarthen; SN5021], *Cresselly Arms*: Cosy low-beamed restaurant overlooking river, step up to tiled bar area with fishing memorabilia and copper-topped tables around the edges, another step to relaxing lounge area with woodburner and TV; good value bar food, well kept Whitbreads-related ales, welcoming service, riverside walks *(Jack and Gemima Valiant, Dr and Mrs G H Lewis, R B Mowbray)*

Pontarsais [A485 Carmarthen—Lampeter; SN4428], *Stag & Pheasant*: Welcoming and unpretentious, with good range of reasonably priced food from cawl to more substantial meals, decent choice of real ales, pleasant decor *(Mr and Mrs K Fawcett)*

Ponterwyd [A44 nearly 2 miles E; SN7781], *Dyffryn Castell*: New management doing good food in comfortably unpretentious inn dwarfed by the mountain slopes sweeping up from it; bedrooms clean, comfortable and good value *(CHO, BJO, LYM)*; [A44 about quarter-mile W of A4120 junction; SN7480], *George Borrow*: Lounges at front and back of bar with old copper objects, good food esp chicken korma, homely welcoming atmosphere, restaurant; children welcome, nice views – in fine spot by Eagle Falls and gorge, so gets lots of summer visitors; comfortable bedrooms *(Margaret and Andrew Leach)*

☆ **Porthgain** [off A487 at Croes-goch; SM8132], *Sloop*: Recently extended pub in interesting village, close to old harbour; friendly relaxing local atmosphere, dark bare stone, alcoves, nautical and wreck memorabilia, family/eating area; well kept Felinfoel Double Dragon and Worthington, good value food (all day in summer) inc nice full crab sandwiches, lots of polite young staff, afternoon teas, tables outside *(Steve Thomas, C H and B J Owen, Simon Watkins, Jeff Davies, Joan and Michel Hooper-Immins)*

Rhandirmwyn [SN7843], *Royal Oak*: Good lively family bar, usual food running up to decent steaks; good area for walks; big bedrooms with superb views – good value *(David Lewis, Sarah Lart)*

Robeston Wathen [B4314 S; SN0815], *Bridge*: Cottagey and comfortable, with well kept beer, wide choice of good food esp Sun lunch, friendly attentive staff, separate dining room; weekend live entertaiment *(C H and B J Owen)*

Rosebush [SN0729], *Tafarn Sinc*: Unpromising (a big zinc shed) but really interesting inside – reconditioned railway halt, full of local history, with well kept beer too; life-size dummy passengers in big garden *(Jack and Gemima Valiant, John and Enid Morris)*

☆ **Saundersfoot** [Wogan Terr; SN1304], *Royal Oak*: Friendly unspoilt local, well kept Bass, Boddingtons and Flowers Original, many dozen malt whiskies, no music or machines, two rooms used for very good generous food esp fresh fish (booking advised in season); tables outside (with overhead heaters) to watch the seaside bustle *(D Prodham)*

☆ **Solva** [Lower Solva; SM8024], *Cambrian Arms*: Attractive and interesting dining pub with pleasant atmosphere, bar food inc authentic pasta and popular Sun lunch, decent Italian wines, Tetleys-related ales, efficient service, log fires; no dogs or children *(Simon Watkins, Martin Jones, IHR, Gerald Barnett, Dr D G Twyman, John and Enid Morris)*

St Clears [Lower St; SN2716], *Butchers Arms*: Young and enthusiastic new licensees doing good beautifully presented food in small cosy freshly painted pub; Felinfoel beer, log fires with oven for roasting potatoes and chestnuts *(Mr and Mrs Cyril Davison, P Manning)*

St Davids [Goat St; SM7525], *Farmers Arms*: Cheerful and busy genuine pub, good straightforward food, well kept Flowers and Worthington BB, cathedral view from tables in tidy back garden *(N H E Lewis, Simon Watkins)*; [centre], *Old Cross*: Reliable food inc good ploughman's with local cheese, sensible prices, polite service, genteel atmosphere, good position – get there before the tourist coaches arrive; pleasant garden, bedrooms *(IHR)*

St Dogmaels [SN1645], *Ferry*: Old stone building with modern additions overlooking Teifi estuary, character bar, pine tables, nice clutter of bric-a-brac inc many old advertising signs; well kept Marstons Pedigree and Wadworths 6X, generous bar food inc crab sandwiches and enjoyable baked Welsh goat's cheese (pay with your order), restaurant; children welcome, tables out on terrace *(N P Smith, Rita and Keith Pollard, LYM)*

St Florence [SM0801], *Old Parsonage Farm*: Friendly family dining pub with big attractive eating area, good choice of quick well presented home-made food inc good value Sun lunch, colourful garden; bedrooms *(Pam Adsley)*; *Sun*: Small friendly village pub with well kept Buckley, very reasonable drinks prices, decent usual food (not Sun lunchtime); children welcome *(Pam Adsley)*

Talsarn [SN5456], *Red Lion*: Old-fashioned Welsh local under new owners, good fresh food lunchtime and evening (all day Sat), inc Sun lunch *(Jill Young)*

☆ **Tenby** [Quay Hill; SN1300], *Plantagenet House*: Unusual nicely renovated medieval building with marvellous old chimney, three floors with stripped stonework, tile and board floors, interesting food inc fine soups, good baguettes, fresh local crab and fish, Welsh cheeses; friendly service, Flowers Original and Wadworths 6X (licence allows alcohol service only with food), upstairs restaurant; fine Victorian lavatories; open all day in season, but cl lunchtime out of season *(Lynda Payton, Sam Samuells, Martin Jones, Gordon Theaker)*

☆ **Tresaith** [off A487 E of Cardigan; SN2751], *Ship*: Tastefully decorated bistro-style pub on Cardigan Bay with magnificent views of sea, beach and famous waterfall; interesting generous home-made food inc good ploughman's with local cheeses, local specialities and children's menu, good range of beers inc Buckleys and unusual English

guest beers, good photographs *(Rita and Keith Pollard, Jeff Davies, R Mattick)*
White Mill [A40 Carmarthen—Llandeilo; SN4621], *White Mill*: Attractive whitewashed building with shutters and flowers, clean inside with comfortable plush wall seats, beams and tiles, warmly welcoming licensees, good food inc wild salmon, interestingly cooked lamb, Hancocks HB and Worthington; children welcome *(Mr and Mrs G J Garrett)*
Wolfs Castle [A40 Haverfordwest—Fishguard; SM9526], *Wolfe*: Wide choice of good fresh home-made food (not Sun or Mon evenings in winter) in comfortable dining lounge, garden room and conservatory, well kept Worthington, decent wines, obliging service, attractively laid out garden; simpler public bar with darts, restaurant; children welcome; bedrooms *(Malcolm and Helen Baxter, LYM)*

GLAMORGAN – MID

Caerphilly [Cardiff Rd; ST1587], *Courthouse*: 14th-c pub with splendid castle views from light and airy modern back cafe/bar and tables on grassy terrace; character original core has rugs on ancient flagstones, stripped stone walls, raftered gallery, food all day (not Sun evening, not after 5.30 Mon, Fri or Sat) inc several vegetarian and children's dishes, good choice of well kept ales such as Greene King Abbot and Youngs Ramrod, good coffee, partly no-smoking restaurant; children welcome in eating areas, pub games, piped pop music (can be a bit loud), open all day *(S P Bobeldijk, M G Hart, Ian Phillips, David and Nina Pugsley, Jacquie and Jim Jones, LYM)*
Creigiau [ST0781], *Caesars Arms*: Fine display of good value fish cooked in open kitchen, with tasty starters and tempting puddings; good wine and coffee, very busy *(J H Jones)*
Kenfig [2¼ miles from M4 junction 37; A4229 towards Porthcawl, then right at roundabout leaving Cornelly; SS8383], *Prince of Wales*: Interesting ancient pub among sand dunes, heavy settles and open fire in stripped stone bar, well kept Bass, Worthington and maybe a guest ale tapped from the cask, good choice of malt whiskies, simple home-made food (can be a wait) from large filled rolls or sandwiches up inc fresh fish and their own eggs and summer veg, traditional games, small dining room; handy for nature reserve and walks, children welcome *(Mr and Mrs T A Bryan, John and Joan Nash, Brian and Anna Marsden, Gordon Theaker, Mr and Mrs G Turner, David and Nina Pugsley, Steve Thomas, Ian Phillips, LYM)*
Pontneddfechan [High St; SN9007], *Old White Horse*: Small pub with pleasant staff, good generous bar food, interesting beer range inc Buckleys, restaurant; handy for nearby waterfall walk *(J Morrell)*
Rudry [ST1986], *Maenllwyd*: Comfortably furnished traditional lounge in low-beamed Tudor pub with log fires, good reasonably priced food, well kept ales, good choice of wines, friendly staff, spacious restaurant; provision for children, pleasant countryside nearby *(Lisa Huish, LYM)*
Taffs Well [ST1283], *Fagins*: Wide changing range of real ales from handpump or tapped from the cask, friendly olde-worlde atmosphere, benches on flagstones, good bar meals, reasonably priced restaurant *(David Lewis, Sarah Lart)*
☆ **Thornhill** [A469 towards Caerphilly; ST1484], *Travellers Rest*: Carefully enlarged attractive old thatched pub with great views, wide choice of good value popular substantial food all day inc vegetarian, good veg, Bass-related and a guest ale, sensibly priced wine, good service even when busy, daily papers and magazines; huge fireplace and nooks and crannies in atmospheric low-beamed bar on right, other bars more modernised; piped music; tables out on grass, good walks *(I and N Buckmaster, R Michael Richards, G Coates, Hugh and Shirley Mortimer)*

GLAMORGAN – SOUTH

Cardiff [10 Quay St], *City Arms*: Warm welcome, well kept Brains Bitter, Dark and SA kept to perfection, limited range of rolls – good sandwich shop virtually opp; perfect for Arms Park, great atmosphere – esp Sat night when half Cardiff seems to be here, with disco in one room and bouncers on door *(Ian Phillips, Andy and Jill Kassube)*; [St Marys St, nr Howells], *Cottage*: Well kept Brains SA, Bitter and Dark Mild and good value home-cooked lunches, long bar with narrow frontage and back eating area, lots of polished wood and glass, good cheerful service, relaxed friendly atmosphere (even Fri/Sat when it's crowded; quiet other evenings), decent choice of wines; open all day *(P A Legon, Andy and Jill Kassube, Jack and Gemima Valiant)*; [Thornhill rd, Llanishen; ST1781], *Nine Giants*: Pleasant surroundings, friendly staff, good value home cooking; big garden popular in summer – the giants are the surrounding trees *(I Buckmaster)*; [St Johns Sq/Castle St], *Owain Glyndowr*: Typical Hogshead woody style, good choice of well kept ales inc Youngs Sweet Chariot (brewed for this chain), Old Hazy cider, good choice of reasonably priced food 12-6, friendly staff, live music some nights – open till midnight Fri/Sat; children welcome daytime, disabled access; open all day *(Richard Lewis)*; [10 Adam St], *Vulcan*: Largely untouched Victorian local with good value lunches (not Sun) in sedate lounge with some original features inc ornate fireplace, well kept Brains Bitter and Dark Mild; maritime pictures in lively sawdust-floor public bar with darts, dominoes, cards and juke box – can be a little loud *(Pete Baker)*; [Atlantic Wharf], *Wharf*: Big Victorian-look pub in pleasant largely residential setting by old dock, paddle-steamer prints and authentic nautical memorabilia downstairs, small lounge bar, maybe restaurant upstairs, family room tricked out like station platform, Brains and changing guest ales, lunchtime bar food; piped music can be noisy, local bands weekends, sometimes Thurs *(Jack and Gemima Valiant, I and N Buckmaster, Peter Neate)*

☆ **Cowbridge** [High St, signed off A48; SS9974], *Bear*: Neatly kept old coaching inn with Brains Bitter and SA, Hancocks HB, Worthington BB and a guest beer, decent house wines, friendly young bar staff, flagstones, panelling and big log fire in beamed bar on left, pool and pin table in back games area, quieter lounge with old leather club chairs and sofas by the log-effect gas fire, busy lunchtime for usual bar food from sandwiches up; children welcome; barrel-vaulted cellar restaurant, bedrooms quiet and comfortable, good breakfast *(Pamela and Merlyn Horswell, I and N Buckmaster, David and Nina Pugsley, LYM)*

☆ **Craig Penllyn** [off A48 W of Cowbridge; SS9777], *Barley Mow*: Welcoming, with good value food and well kept varied real ales; bedrooms comfortable *(David and Nina Pugsley, I and N Buckmaster)*

Dinas Powis [Station Rd; ST1571], *Star*: Attractively refurbished village pub with stripped stone walls or panelling, heavy Elizabethan beams, modernised restaurant; well kept Brains, usual food *(ST, Jack and Gemima Valiant, LYM)*

Lisvane [ST1883], *Griffin*: Pretty and busy, with well kept Brains SA and guest beers such as Blackawton Devon Gold and Fullers London Pride, reasonably priced traditional food inc vegetarian, chairs and settles in long beamed bar with raised eating area, upstairs children's room; facilities for disabled, a couple of benches out in front *(G Coates)*; [Cherry Tree Cl; towards Thornhill], *Old Cottage*: Charmingly converted well decorated old barn on edge of new housing estate, Tetleys-related ales, good value food in bar and restaurant, no-smoking area; open all day, handy for Cefn Onn Park, lovely walks any time of year but best in May *(I and N Buckmaster)*

Llancadle [village signed off B4265 Barry—Llantwit just E of St Athan; ST0368], *Green Dragon*: Attractively rebuilt after fire, traditional bar on left with hunting and other country prints, copper, china and harness, well kept Bass, Hancocks HB and an interesting guest beer, friendly uniformed staff, maybe piped pop music; good value generous food, comfortably relaxed dining lounge on right with nice pictures; picnic-sets on covered back terrace *(R B Mowbray, BB)*

☆ **Llancarfan** [signed off A4226; can also be reached from A48 from Bonvilston or B4265 via Llancadle; ST0570], *Fox & Hounds*: Prettily set dining pub by interesting church, streamside tables out behind; neat comfortably modernised open-plan bar rambling through arches, traditional settles and plush banquettes, coal fire, well kept Hancocks HB and guest ale, bar food inc interesting dishes, candlelit bistro; children welcome, darts, fruit machine, unobtrusive piped music; open all day w/e, but may not always open some lunchtimes out of season *(David and Nina Pugsley, I and N Buckmaster, Mr and Mrs S Thomas, LYM)*

Penarth [Esplanade; ST1871], *Chandlers*: Busy pub/bistro, good value fish and meat barbecues, salad bar, service unfailingly attentive *(Pamela and Merlyn Horswell)*

Pendoylan [2½ miles from M4 junction 34; ST0576], *Red Lion*: Friendly village pub recently refurbished under new management, good standard home-made food, well presented, in bar and restaurant; cheerful staff, well kept Flowers IPA and Original; good garden with enterprising play area, next to church in pretty vale *(F J Willy)*

☆ **Penmark** [off A4226 W of Barry; ST0568], *Six Bells*: Relaxing and friendly 18th-c village pub with good imaginative well presented food inc crisp veg in bar and rather upmarket recently renovated restaurant; interesting relics of Hancocks Brewery in small public bar with darts and open fire, well kept Hancocks HB, good wines *(Nigel Clifton, Heather March)*

☆ **Sigingstone** [off B4270 S of Cowbridge; SS9771], *Victoria*: Friendly and spotless neo-Victorian country pub/restaurant with quickly served good value food inc nice veg, good upstairs restaurant, well kept Bass (though not the sort of place to go to for just a drink), pleasant surroundings, good service *(James Young, C D Jones, David and Nina Pugsley)*

GLAMORGAN – WEST

☆ **Kittle** [18 Pennard Rd – B4436 W of Swansea; SS5789], *Beaufort Arms*: Good food inc wide choice of fish (also sandwiches) in attractive old pub below ancient chestnut tree, plenty of character in carefully renovated saloon with low beams and dark walls, comfortably cushioned settles, quick friendly service, well kept Brains SA, Buckley Best and a summer guest beer, small family area, TV in public bar, restaurant *(Michael Sandy, D Crowle)*

Scurlage [Gower; SS4587], *Countryman*: Modern pub with good menu, well kept beers, swift service, chatty staff, good provision for families, popular Tues quiz night, occasional entertainment – very busy summer evenings *(Dr Einar Williams)*

Upper Cwmtwrch [Heol Gwys; SN7511], *George IV*: Good atmosphere, friendly service, well kept Boddingtons and Flowers IPA, good home-made usual food, good house wines *(Dr H R Long)*

West Cross [A4067 Mumbles—Swansea; SS6089], *West Cross*: Comfortably refurbished with steps up to glassed back dining extension with great view over Mumbles Bay, garden below by pedestrian/cycle way around bay; good home-made food inc fine fish and chips, well kept Wadworths 6X, friendly staff *(John and Vivienne Rice, R B Mowbray)*

GWENT

Abergavenny [Flannel St; SO3014], *Hen & Chickens*: Small well worn traditional local, Bass and Brains, basic wholesome cheap lunchtime food (not Sun; shame about all the young smokers), friendly staff, popular darts, cards and dominoes *(Pete Baker)*; [B4598, 3 miles E], *Lamb & Flag*: Generous good value food inc some unusual dishes, children's meals and fresh veg in roomy and comfortable modern lounge bar or two dining rooms, well kept Brains Bitter and SA, good service; children welcome, high chairs; open all day in summer, country views – tables outside with play area; comfortable if not cheap bedrooms *(Joan and Michel Hooper-Immins, Sidney and Erna Wells, Steve Thomas)*; [Pantygelli – old rd NE, W of A465], *Olde Crown*: Good food, real ales, good landlord *(Alison and Mick Coates)*

Bassaleg [2 Caerphilly Rd; handy for M4 junction 28; A468 towards Caerphilly; ST2787], *Tredegar Arms*: Vast range of well kept real ales, enthusiastic landlord, good eating area, family and outdoor areas *(Dr and Mrs A K Clarke, David Lewis, Sarah Lart)*

Bryngwyn [off old A40 W of Raglan; SO3909], *Cripple Creek*: Refurbished and reopened, with friendly family service, good reasonably priced food inc splendid chips, nice dining room, real ales such as Brains and Tetleys; play area, open all day *(Alan Baird)*

Grosmont [SO4024], *Angel*: 17th-c village pub on attractive steep single street within sight of castle, seats out by ancient market hall, not far from 13th-c church; welcoming atmosphere, well kept Batemans XXXB and Buckleys, Bulmer's cider, nice well priced specials, very friendly service and local atmosphere *(R T and J C Moggridge, Neil and Anita Christopher, BB)*

Llandenny [SO4104], *Raglan Arms*: Spacious open-plan refurbished bar with comfortable settees and armchairs, real fire, Italian chef doing good food inc unusual dishes, pasta and steaks, three well kept real ales, well chosen wines, conservatory restaurant; tables in garden *(Colin Mansell, Mrs D Olney)*

Llanfihangel Crucorney [village signed off A465; SO3321], *Skirrid*: Among the oldest pubs in Britain, with parts dating from 1110; ancient studded door lets you into high-ceilinged main bar, all stone and flagstones, dark feel accentuated by furniture inc pews (some padded), big open fire; panelled dining room, good generous bar food from sandwiches up (may be a wait), well kept Ushers Best, Founders and seasonal brews; darts, pool and piped music; open all day summer, children welcome, tables on terrace and small sloping back lawn, well equipped bedrooms *(Dr A Drummond, JKW, LYM)*

Llanthony [off A465, back rd Llanfihangel Crucorney—Hay; SO2928], *Abbey Hotel*: Enchanting peaceful setting in border hills, lawns among Norman abbey's graceful ruins; basic dim-lit vaulted flagstoned crypt bar, well kept Bass, Flowers Original, Ruddles County and Wadworths 6X, farm cider in summer, simple lunchtime bar food, no children; occasional live music, open all day Sat (and Sun in summer); in winter cl Sun evening and weekdays exc Fri evening; evening restaurant, bedrooms *(A C Morrison, Wayne Brindle, Jack and Gemima Valiant, LYM)*

Llanthony, *Half Moon*: Basic country inn suiting this unspoilt valley with its great walks and pony-trekking centres, decent plain food, real ales such as Bull Mastiff Son-of-a-Bitch and Flowers Original; bedrooms not luxurious but clean and comfortable *(Jack and Gemima Valiant, David Lewis, Sarah Lart)*

☆ **Llantilio Crosseny** [signed off B4233 Monmouth—Abergavenny; SO3915], *Hostry*: 15th-c pub nr Offa's Dyke Path, flagstones and grey carpet, bowed Tudor beams, traditional pubby bar furnishings, some stripped stonework, guns above one fireplace, Rolls-Royce cigar cards; interesting landlord, good home cooking inc good ploughman's, wide vegetarian choice and good value Sun lunch, neat dining room, well kept ales such as Wye Valley, table skittles; children welcome; bedrooms comfortable – very quiet village; may cl lunchtime if no walkers expected *(Brian Seller, Warren Marsh, BB)*

Llanwenarth [A40 Abergavenny—Crickhowell; SO2714], *Llanwenarth Arms*: Beautifully placed 16th-c riverside inn with views of hills, old-fashioned dark wood in bar, several real ales, good food in light and airy modern restaurant with good hill views, conservatory, terrace; first-class service, children welcome; 18 comfortable bedrooms overlooking Wye *(Steve Thomas, Pamela and Merlyn Horswell)*

Michaelston y Fedw [a mile off A48 at Castleton; ST2484], *Cefn Mably Arms*: Tastefully refurbished local with changing real ales, friendly efficient service, enjoyable freshly made food inc fish and vegetarian in bar and restaurant, tables in garden – country setting *(I and N Buckmaster, Michael Richards)*

☆ **Monmouth** [Lydart; B4293 towards Trelleck; SO5009], *Gockett*: Extended country pub just along rd from ostrich farm, with hops in rafters of light and airy room on left, houseplants, sliding doors to pleasant garden, no-smoking dining room with low beams, some stripped stone, coaching prints and log fire, enjoyable generous efficiently served food inc interesting dishes, well kept Bass and a guest such as Hardys & Hansons or Hook Norton; children welcome; bedrooms with own bathrooms, good breakfast *(LM, R T and J C Moggridge, BB)*

☆ **Monmouth** [Agincourt Sq], *Punch House*: 17th-c market-town pub with relaxed and chatty open-plan beamed bar, red leatherette settles, old bound *Punch* volumes (even the dog is called Punch), big fireplace, no-smoking area; generous straightforward food inc four roasts, prompt friendly service, well kept Bass, Hancocks HB, Wadworths 6X and Worthington Best, decent wines; restaurant, tables out on cobbles overlooking square; children in eating area, occasional live entertainment, open all day (exc Sun afternoon) *(Pamela and Merlyn Horswell, Daren Haines, LYM)*

Mynyddbach [B4235 Chepstow—Usk; ST4994], *Carpenters Arms*: Many rooms, good food, at least five real ales inc Marstons Owd Rodger *(P B Godfrey)*

Newport [22 Stow Hill; ST3188], *Pen & Wig*: Recently refurbished, with plenty of seats in no-smoking area, wide choice of food Mon-Sat, Sun lunch, well kept Whitbreads-related and other ales, wide choice of foreign beers inc special offers, friendly staff, tables outside; jazz Fri, live music Sun, disco Fri/Sat till 2am, fortnightly folk nights, big screen TV; no children *(Richard Lewis)*; [Cambrian Centre], *Rat & Parrot*: Big, airy and comfortable new two-floor pub, well kept Scottish Courage ales, smart dress required – bouncers; open all day *(Richard Lewis)*; [10 Cambrian Centre], *Wetherspoons*: Large open-plan pub with solid decor, lots of tables inc no-smoking areas; friendly and relaxing, with half a dozen well kept ales inc guests, usual Wetherspoons food; open all day *(Richard Lewis)*

Penallt [SO5211], *Bush*: 17th-c stone pub with interesting home-made dishes as well as good value usual food, Bass and Hancocks HB, well furnished big lounge, conservatory, pool room; extensive garden with play area; bedrooms with own bathrooms *(Dr B and Mrs P B Baker)*

The Narth [off B4293 Trelleck—Monmouth; SO5206], *Trekkers*: Log cabin high in valley, unusual and welcoming, esp for children; lots of wood with central fire, helpful licensee, good generous food inc vegetarian and fun ice creams, good range of well kept Felinfoel Double Dragon, Freeminers and a guest such as Adnams or Shepherd Neame, skittle alley family room, facilities for the disabled; dogs, long back garden *(LM, Dr B and Mrs P B Baker, Margaret and Nigel Dennis)*

Tintern [Devauden Rd; off A446 about ¾ mile W of main village; SO5301], *Cherry Tree*: Quaint unspoilt country pub in quiet spot by tiny stream, steps up to simple front room, well kept Hancocks HB and farm cider, cards and dominoes, bar billiards in second room, charming garden; children welcome *(Pete Baker, Paul and Heather Bettesworth)*

☆ **Trelleck** [SO5005], *Village Green*: Comfortable and welcoming beamed restaurant/bistro in sensitively preserved old building, cosy little front bar, well kept Bass and Worthington, good wines, prints, lots of dried flowers, reliable food using local produce; bedrooms in well converted former stables *(Pamela and Merlyn Horswell)*

☆ **Trelleck Grange** [minor rd St Arvans—Trelleck; SO4902], *Fountain*: Tucked away on a back road through quiet countryside, unassuming inn with well kept Boddingtons and Wadworths 6X in cheerful dark-beamed bar, roomy and comfortable dining room, popular food from good fresh sandwiches up (service can slow); maybe nostalgic piped pop music, darts, decent malt whiskies and wines; children allowed away from bar, small sheltered garden with summer kids' bar; bedrooms *(LM, Pat and John Millward, LYM)*

☆ **Usk** [The Square; SO3801], *Nags Head*: Relaxed beamed front bar, comfortable and well kept, with lots of brassware, old saws and other rustic artefacts, tables set for food (drinkers tend to head for the back bar), welcoming family service, well kept Brains and Buckley Rev James, good choice of whiskies, wide choice of generous tasty food inc home-made pies, Usk salmon and game in season *(LM, Christopher and Mary Thomas, Mike Pugh, David and Nina Pugsley, Malcolm Taylor, A E Brace, June and Peter Gregory)*

Usk [The Square], *Castle*: Useful for food all day, with generous helpings and Whitbreads-related ales *(Mike Pugh, David and Nina Pugsley)*

GWYNEDD

Abergynolwyn [Tywyn—Talyllyn pass; SH6807], *Railway*: Lovely setting esp outside on a warm day or evening, good value main dishes, well kept beer *(Dr Rod Holcombe)*

Bangor [by old Menai Bridge; SH5973], *Antelope*: Pleasantly refurbished Greenalls pub with superb views over Menai Bridge to Anglesey, good atmosphere and service, wide range of good value generous home-made food; open all day *(Alan and Paula McCully)*

Barmouth [Church St; SH6116], *Last*: 15th-c harbourside local behind modern front with new harbour mural, low beams, flagstones, nautical bric-a-brac, little waterfall down back bar's natural rock wall, wide choice of good cheap bar lunches inc vegetarian, well kept Marstons Pedigree, friendly if not always speedy service; roadside tables overlooking harbour and bay *(E G Parish, Joan and Michel Hooper-Immins)*

☆ **Beddgelert** [A498 N of Porthmadog; SH5948], *Tanronen*: Comfortably and attractively refurbished hotel bar, good choice of good value bar food, attentive staff, well kept Robinsons, restaurant; walkers welcome, good bedrooms overlooking river across road, or fields and mountains behind *(Paul and Sharon Sneller, Gordon Theaker, BB)*

Beddgelert, *Prince Llewelyn*: Plush hotel bar with log fire and raised dining area, simpler summer bar, good atmosphere, wide choice of good value generous bar food, well kept Robinsons, rustic seats on verandah overlooking village stream and hills – great walking country; piped music, busy at peak holiday times, children allowed at quiet times; bedrooms pleasant, with good breakfast *(George Atkinson, Howard James, BB)*; *Royal Goat*: Old-fashioned place, very friendly, with generous bar food, competent service; good accessible bedrooms, good breakfast *(Pamela and Merlyn Horswell)*; *Saracens Head*: Cheerful hotel popular with coach parties and outdoor pursuits courses, usual bar food, back locals' bar with pool, front saloon with live entertainment most Sats, Robinsons beers; comfortable bedrooms *(Roger Byrne)*

Bethel [B4366 NE of Caernarfon; SH5365], *Y Bedol*: Consistently well cooked food, Scottish Courage beers, modern plush lounge bar with local paintings, public bar with games, Snowdon views from garden; children allowed; busy on music nights *(Mike Jones)*

Betws y Coed [A5; SH7956], *Royal Oak*: Huge well organised tiled-floor Stables Bar with good facilities for family eating (partly no smoking, good disabled access), attractive decor and some interesting pictures, popular food inc good original specials and local fish, very long bar counter with Boddingtons, Flowers IPA and Morlands Old Speckled Hen, espresso machine, friendly helpful service; one end with pool, darts, TV and fruit machine, tables on verandah and big terrace; open all day, jazz Thurs, male voice choir alternate Fri; bedrooms – and the substantial hotel has its own comfortable bar *(Jack and Gemima Valiant, Roger Byrne, G S and E M Dorey, BB)*

Betws y Coed [A5 next to BP garage and Little Chef], *Waterloo*: Wide choice of well served generous food, even mountain mutton sometimes, good obliging service even when busy, freshly squeezed orange juice, no piped music; bedrooms *(KC)*

Capel Curig [A5 NW of Betws y Coed; SH7258], *Cobdens*: Good varied satisfying food inc home-made bread and interesting vegetarian dishes, sensible prices, well kept local Cambrian and Scottish Courage beers, pleasant service, bare rock in back bar; lovely river scene across road, good walks all around; bedrooms *(Jack and Gemima Valiant, Mike Pugh)*

Dinas Mawddwy [aka Red Lion; just off A470 E of Dolgellau; SH8615], *Llew Coch*: Genuine country local with charming timbered front bar sparkling with countless brasses, well kept Bass, quick friendly service, cheap cheerful food inc trout or salmon from River Dovey just behind; plainer inner family room lively with video games, pool and Sat evening live music, lounge extension (open at busy times), good wheelchair access, tables out on quiet lane; surrounded by steep fir forests, good walks *(Howard James, Richard Lewis, LYM)*

Dolgarrog [Conwy Rd; SH7767], *Lord Newborough*: Very welcoming, with log fire, good food, welcoming staff *(Mrs D W Jones-Williams)*

Ganllwyd [SH7224], *Tyn-y-Groes*: Friendly old inn owned by NT in lovely Snowdonia setting, fine forest views, old-fashioned furnishings in partly panelled beamed lounge, well kept Boddingtons and Flowers, quite a few malt whiskies, good choice of generous straightforward food, woodburner, small pleasant family dining room, separate no-smoking restaurant; may not open till 7 evenings; comfortable well equipped bedrooms, salmon and seatrout fishing, good walks *(M Mason, D Thompson, Amanda and Simon Southwell)*

Glandwyfach [A487; SH4843], *Goat*: Doing well under new tenants, with good food and friendly service *(Mrs D W Jones-Williams)*

Harlech [SH5831], *Castle*: Handy for the impressive castle, with decent beer, wine and food; bedrooms *(Peter and Audrey Dowsett)*

☆ **Llandudno** [Old St, behind tram stn; SH7883], *Kings Head*: Friendly rambling pub, much extended around 16th-c core, spaciously open-plan, bright and clean, with comfortable traditional furnishings, red wallpaper, dark pine, wide range of generous food, well kept Tetleys-related ales, good choice of wines, quick friendly service, huge log fire, smart back dining room up a few steps; children welcome, open all day in summer, seats in front overlooking quaint Victorian tramway's station *(GLD, Keith and Margaret Kettell, LYM)*

Llandudno [Madoc St; SH7883], *Cross Keys*: Good choice of reasonably priced food, good choice of Whitbreads beers, friendly service; clean and tidy *(S J Biggins)*

☆ **Llandwrog** [aka Ty'n Llan; ½ mile W of A499 S of Caernarfon; SH4456], *Harp*: Welcoming lounge bar with irregular shape giving cosy corners, well kept Whitbreads-related ales, good value food inc Sun roast, cheerful separate dining room, picnic-sets among young fruit trees; opp imposing church in quiet village; good bedrooms *(Douglas and Jean Troup, Mr and Mrs R Head, BB)*

☆ **Porth Dinllaen** [beach car park signed from Morfa Nefyn, then a good 15-min walk – which is part of the attraction; at high tide better to park at golf course; SH2741], *Ty Coch*: Stunning spot on curving beach, far from the roads, with great view along coast to mountains; pub itself full of attractive salvage and RNLI memorabilia; keg beer, decent coffee, usual food; may be closed much of winter, but open all day summer and very popular then – on a hot still day this is an idyllic spot *(Peter and Audrey Dowsett, LYM)*

☆ **Tremadog** [off A487 just N of Porthmadog; SH5640], *Golden Fleece*: Neat and clean stonebuilt inn on attractive square, friendly attentive staff, well kept Bass, Mild and Marstons Pedigree, decent wines, cosy partly partitioned rambling beamed lounge with open fire, nice little snug (reserved seats for regulars Fri/Sat night), enjoyable separate back bistro (children allowed here and in small family room), good value generous bar food inc fish and vegetarian, games room, intriguing cellar bar, tables in sheltered inner courtyard; has been cl Sun *(George Atkinson, S and J Gay, Tony Hobden, LYM)*

Tremadog [The Square], *Madoc*: Pleasant pub/hotel, friendly landlord *(Peter and Audrey Dowsett)*; [The Square], *Union*: Cosy, clean and tidy traditional stone-built pub, attractive furnishings in panelled and carpeted lounge bar, big fireplace, good atmosphere, popular OAP lunches Weds and Fri, Marstons Pedigree, good coffee, pleasant back restaurant *(George Atkinson)*

☆ **Tudweiliog** [Nefyn Rd; B4417, Lleyn Peninsula; SH2437], *Lion*: Cheerful village inn with wide choice of decent food inc well prepared vegetarian dishes and good puddings in bar and no-smoking family dining conservatory (small helpings for children), fast helpful service, well kept Boddingtons, Marstons Pedigree, Ruddles Best and Theakstons Best and Mild, lots of whiskies, games and juke box in lively public bar; pleasant garden, good value bedrooms *(Jack and Gemima Valiant, J Sheldon, LYM)*

POWYS

Abermule [off A483 NE of Newtown; SO1594], *Abermule Inn*: Basic cheerful roadside local with cheap home-made food, Bass and Worthington on sparkler, plain lounge, lino-floored public bar with TV, radio, juke box and fruit machine, rookery behind garden with swings and climbing frames; open all day, camp site *(Paddy Moindrot, BB)*

Berriew [SJ1801], *Lion*: Neatly kept timber-framed country inn with very friendly staff, good home-cooked food in bar and restaurant, Bass and Worthington with guest beers such as Greene King and Shepherd Neame, decent house wines, fairly smart atmosphere, friendly attentive service, separate public bar; well equipped cottagey bedrooms, quiet attractive village *(Paul and Maggie Baker)*

☆ **Bleddfa** [A488 Knighton—Penybont; SO2168], *Hundred House*: Log fire in small, quiet and relaxed lounge's huge stone fireplace, new wall seats in L-shaped public bar with attractively flagstoned lower games area, lacy tablecloths and enjoyable food in little dining room with another vast fireplace, well kept Woods Shropshire Lad and Worthington; tables in garden with barbecue – very quiet spot, dropping steeply behind to small stream – lovely countryside; bedrooms simple but comfortable, good breakfast *(Dorsan Baker, Graham and Karen Oddey, BB)*

Brecon [George St; SO0428], *George*: Well kept Greene King Abbot and Morlands Old Speckled Hen, food inc ploughman's with three local cheeses and generous salads, pleasing ambiance, attentive service, attractive dining room *(Chris Parsons)*

Buttington [A458; SJ2509], *White Horse*: Popular trunk road stop, and on Offa's Dyke Path, with Bass Special, decent food at reasonable prices, helpful chatty staff; back garden with various animals inc vietnamese pot-bellied pig *(Brian Seller)*

Bwlch [A40 W of Crickhowell; SO1522], *Kestrel*: Wonderful views, Hancock HB, tempting food *(Pat and Robert Watt)*

☆ **Carno** [A470 Newtown—Machynlleth; SN9697], *Aleppo Merchant*: Plushly modernised stripped stone bar, small lounge with open fire, unusual tapestries by landlady, no-smoking area, games in public bar, decent food from sandwiches to steaks, well kept Boddingtons, occasional guest beer, restaurant (well behaved children allowed here), tables in garden; piped music; good value comfortable bedrooms *(Gerald Fleit, Peter and Audrey Dowsett, K Andrews, LYM)*

Church Stoke [Brompton (A489); SO2794], *Blue Bell*: A pleasant anachronism, where to hear the local news (if not find real ale), maybe beef or cheese evening sandwiches, proper old-fashioned landlady *(Brian Seller)*

Craig y Nos [A4067 Swansea—Brecon; SN8315], *Gwyn Arms*: Idyllic riverside setting, comfortable and spacious; good range of food inc kangaroo, venison and lots of curries, Whitbreads and some local ales; handy for Dan-yr-Ogof caves *(K R Harris)*

☆ **Crickhowell** [New Rd; SO2118], *Bridge End*: Chatty and darkly attractive roomy local in good spot by many-arched bridge over weir of river Usk, straightforward food, well kept Bass and Worthington BB; open all day *(David and Nina Pugsley)*

☆ **Cwmdu** [A479 NW of Crickhowell; SO1823], *Farmers Arms*: Friendly country local, popular with walkers, with welcoming homely service, unpretentious partly flagstoned bar with attractive prints and stove in big stone fireplace, well kept changing ales such as Dorothy Goodbodys, SP Sporting Ales Doves Delight and Wye Valley Brew 69, good value hearty home cooking, plush restaurant, tables in garden; bedrooms with good breakfast – handy for pony-trekkers and Black Mountains *(Brian Seller, BB)*

☆ **Derwenlas** [A487 Machynlleth—Aberystwyth; SN7299], *Black Lion*: Cosy and welcoming 16th-c country pub, heavy black beams, thick walls and black timbering, attractive pictures and lion models, tartan carpet over big slate flagstones, log fire, popular straightforward food inc vegetarian, well kept Tetleys, decent wines; piped music; garden up behind with play area and steps up into woods; bedrooms *(BB)*

☆ **Glasbury** [B4350 towards Hay, just N of A438; SO1739], *Harp*: Snug welcoming log-fire lounge and airy games bar with picture windows over garden sloping to River Wye, usual bar food inc children's (children very welcome), well kept ales inc local Breconshire Valhalla; good value simple bedrooms, good breakfast *(Salvo and Gwyneth Spadaro-Dutturi, BB)*

☆ **Hay on Wye** [Castle St/Oxford Rd; SO2342], *Blue Boar*: Mix of pews and country chairs in attractively individual if sometimes smoky panelled bar, log fire, pleasant relaxed atmosphere with nice mix of customers inc children, separate light and airy long dining room with lots of pictures for sale, bright tablecloths and cheery decor, big sash windows, good choice of generous straightforward home cooking, well kept Whitbreads-related ales, decent wines, good coffees and teas *(S Watkin, P Taylor, Tim Barrow, Sue Demont, Gwyneth and Salvo Spadaro-Dutturi, Nigel Woolliscroft, BB)*

Hay on Wye [Broad St], *Three Tuns*: Charming old-fashioned pub with fireside settle and a few old tables and chairs in tiny dark quarry-tiled bar in one of Hay's oldest buildings, landlady knowledgeable about local history, well kept Worthington tapped from the cask, Edwardian bar fittings, lots of bric-a-brac; no food *(Kevin Thorpe, Jack and Philip Paxton)*

Knighton [Broad St; SO2972], *George & Dragon*: Dark-panelled back parlour bar with two fine old carved settles, stone fireplace, dozens of hanging jugs and mugs, stags' heads, old pictures, brassware, swords; similar if simpler front public bar, well kept Woods Shropshire Lad, good choice of food inc interesting dishes, friendly staff, small restaurant; good stop-off for Offa's Dyke Path *(Brian Seller)*

Knighton [SO2972], *Red Dragon*: Well kept beer, good bar food, restaurant, hard-working licensees; handy for Offa's Dyke Path *(Chris Parsons)*

Knucklas [off B4355 Knighton—Newtown; SO2574], *Castle*: Old-fashioned main bar, dining room off, good home-made food, good value (the friendly family share the cooking), well kept ales inc Hancocks HB; bedrooms – handy for Offa's Dyke Path *(S E Paulley and family)*

Libanus [A470 SW of Brecon; SN9925], *Bull*: Popular local with well kept Hancocks HB, good value plain food, very friendly staff; bedrooms well appointed and comfortable, great breakfast – good base for walking weekends *(Bruce Howells, G W A Pearce)*

Llanbedr [nr Crickhowell; SO2420], *Red Lion*: Quaint old pub in pretty little village set in dell, log fires and well kept ales such as Felinfoel Double Dragon, but rather too many instruction notices; good walking country *(Gwyneth and Salvo Spadaro-Dutturi)*

Llandrindod Wells [Temple St (A470); SO0561], *Metropole*: Big Edwardian hotel's comfortable front bar with glassed-in terrace, useful for all-day snack service; well kept Brains SA, Marstons Pedigree and Flowers Original; bedrooms *(Joan and Michel Hooper-Immins)*

Llanfihangel nant Melan [A44 10 miles W of Kington; SO1858], *Red Lion*: Warm and friendly stripped-stone 16th-c roadside pub with good individual cooking, unpretentious but well presented, in roomy main dining area beyond standing timbers on right, smaller room with small pews around tables, back bar with pool, well kept changing ales such as Hook Norton, decent wines, some tables in front sun porch, sensible prices; main entry quality, but restricted hours (cl Tues-Thurs lunchtime, Tues evening) are a drawback; comfortable simple chalet bedrooms, handy for Radnor Forest walks *(Paul Catcheside, Sarah and Peter Gooderham, B M Baker, BB)*

Llanfyllin [High St (A490); SJ1419], *Cain Valley*: Old coaching inn with very relaxed friendly atmosphere, welcoming helpful staff, decent food inc fresh veg and well kept Bass and Brains in hotelish beamed and dark-panelled lounge bar, good restaurant; handsome Jacobean staircase to comfortable bedrooms, good breakfast *(George Atkinson, Martin Jones)*

☆ **Llanwrtyd Wells** [The Square; SN8746], *Neuadd Arms*: Comfortably relaxed turkey-carpeted bar with plush seats, big log fire and local pictures, separate tiled public bar with craft tools and splendid row of old bells, well kept reasonably priced Hancocks HB, Felinfoel Double Dragon and a guest such as Batemans Jollys Jaunt, lots of interesting bottled beers, popular food inc vegetarian and theme nights; beer festival Nov, various other events; bedrooms pleasant and well equipped; tables out on front terrace, engaging very small town – good walking area, mountain bike hire *(Joan and Michel Hooper-Immins, G Coates, BB)*

Llanwrtyd Wells [The Square], *Belle Vue*: Stripped stone L-shaped bar with glass partitions and decor reminiscent of 1970s house, corner pool table and large-screen sports TV, Brains beers, varied food inc vegetarian from separate servery with dining area; tables outside, reasonable disabled access; bedrooms with own bathrooms, also provision for tents *(G Coates)*; [Dolecoed Rd], *Stonecroft*: Friendly Victorian pub with wholesome simple reasonably priced food, Brains SA and Youngers Scotch (and twice-yearly beer festival), big riverside terrace with barbecues and evening events; bedrooms – dormitory type, popular with walkers *(G Coates)*

Llanyre [SO0462], *Bell*: Old but modernised inn, comfortable and well kept, with wide choice of usual food, well kept ales inc Hancocks HB, friendly obliging landlord, pool, restaurant; bedrooms *(Eddie Edwards)*

☆ **Machynlleth** [Heol Pentrerhedyn; A489, nr junction with A487; SH7501], *White Lion*: Big country-town bar with pink and maroon decor, plush seats, shiny copper-topped tables, big bay window seats overlooking main street, inglenook log fire, end eating area with usual food inc vegetarian (and high chairs – children welcome), well kept Banks's Bitter and Mild, Marstons Pedigree and a guest such as Morlands Old Speckled Hen, service brisk and cheerful even on busy Weds market day; piped pop music, silenced fruit machine; pretty views from picnic-sets in attractive back garden, some tables out by road too; neatly modernised stripped pine bedrooms *(Howard James, M Joyner, BB)*

Machynlleth, *Wynnstay*: Busy well staffed bar, interesting beer choice, reasonably priced food; bedrooms *(Pamela and Merlyn Horswell)*

☆ **Montgomery** [The Square; SO2296], *Dragon*: 17th-c timbered hotel with attractive prints and china in beamed bar, attentive service, well kept Woods Special and guest beer, good coffee, sensibly priced food from sandwiches to steaks inc vegetarian and children's, board games, unobtrusive piped music, restaurant; jazz most Weds, open all day; comfortable bedrooms, very quiet town below ruined Norman castle *(Alan and Barbara Mence, Walter and Susan Rinaldi-Butcher, LYM)*

Newtown [Broad St; SO1191], *Elephant & Castle*: Popular 16th-c timbered inn with comfortable dining room, adjoining riverside sun lounge; bedrooms *(E G Parish)*

☆ **Old Radnor** [signed off A44 W of Kington; SO2559], *Harp*: Superb peaceful hilltop position, with lovely views and good walks nearby, fine inglenook and elderly seats in slate-floored lounge, stripped-stone public bar with a smaller log fire and old-fashioned settles, sandwiches and ploughman's, normally good value hot dishes too (not Mon), well kept Woods and maybe other ales, decent wines, character dining room with antique curved settle and other high-backed seats, friendly service; seats outside with play area, pleasant bedrooms, good breakfast *(David Edwards, Graham and Karen Oddey, David Gittins, LYM)*

Pencelli [B4558 SE of Brecon; SO0925], *Royal Oak*: Two small polished flagstone bars, welcoming service, well kept Boddingtons and Flowers and farm cider, good food Thurs-Sat pm and w/e lunchtimes inc half-price children's helpings, log fires, simple dining room; charming terrace backing on to canal and fields, lovely canal walks *(Donna and Ian Dyer, Martin and Alison Stainsby)*

☆ **Penderyn** [off A4059 at Lamb to T-junction then up narrow hill; SN9408], *Red Lion*: Old stonebuilt Welsh local high in good walking country, open fires, dark beams, flagstone floors, antique settles, blazing log fires, well kept ales such as Bass, Brains, Everards and Marstons Pedigree, welcoming landlord; children allowed if they sit quietly, dogs too (on leads); great views from big garden *(Gwyneth and Salvo Spadaro-Dutturi, LYM)*

Rhayader [North St (A470); SN9768], *Crown*: Pleasant 17th-c inn with beamed bar partitioned for eating areas, good helpings of reasonably priced food from snacks to steaks, Hancocks HB and Tomas Watkin OSB, very helpful and obliging licensees; soft piped music *(Jenny and Michael Back, Gethin Lewis)*

☆ **Talybont on Usk** [SO1122], *Travellers Rest*: Beautiful setting with valley views, well kept beer inc four guests, above-average generous food running to wood pigeon and maybe lobster, big dining area, good sloping garden by Monmouthshire & Brecon Canal towpath; bedrooms *(Rob Holt, Jackie Orme, RKP)*

Three Cocks [A438 Talgarth—Hay-on-Wye; SO1737], *Old Barn*: Long spacious converted barn with central bar, good choice of food from sandwiches up, two pool tables, SkyTV, Flowers IPA, Original and three other ales, very friendly staff; seats outside with good play area and barbecue, open all day at least in summer; parent inn across rd has reasonably priced clean and tidy bedrooms with good breakfast *(Simon and Amanda Southwell, LYM)*

Welshpool [Raven Sq; SJ2208], *Raven*: Decent home-made food inc vegetarian in lounge bar/restaurant, Bass-related beers; handy for steam railway *(Mr and Mrs McKay)*

Ystradfellte [SN9213], *New Inn*: Homely pub with attractive bar, plenty of seating, polished brass, woodburner and friendly twinkly landlord; well kept Flowers Original, wide choice of promptly served food inc good value Sun lunch, woodburner, Flowers Original; handy for Brecon Beacons *(Ian Phillips)*

Post Office address codings confusingly give the impression that some pubs are in Gwent or Powys, Wales when they're really in Gloucestershire or Shropshire (which is where we list them).

Channel Islands

The islands' pubs are at their best out of season. On weekend evenings in summer the main centres are thronged with lively packs of teenagers – with many pubs blasting out high-decibel music for them. However, even then the pubs we include as main entries have a more civilised appeal. A particular draw is the low price of drinks, with beer prices typically 35p a pint cheaper than on the mainland; the local breweries are Ann Street, Guernsey Brewery (which produces a remarkable variety of different brews) and Randalls. On Guernsey, the Fleur du Jardin at Kings Mills is currently doing particularly well, after a refurbishment; and the Hougue du Pommier tucked away in Castel is a well tried favourite. We'd also mention the Ship & Crown in St Peter Port and Atlantique in St Saviour (from the Lucky Dip section at the end of the chapter). On Jersey, the quaintly attractive Old Smugglers in St Brelade and the Admiral in St Helier (good value food) are on fine form, and the Old Portelet in St Brelade and Les Fontaines at St John, both very well run, have good facilities for children. The charmingly set Old Court House at St Aubin has been carefully redecorated this last year, and its main dining room has been extended. Lucky Dip entries here we'd pick out particularly are the Dolphin in Gorey, Chambers in St Helier (losing its place in the main entries merely because of a lack of recent reports from readers) and La Pulente, beautifully placed on St Ouens Bay (we had actually decided to promote it to the main entries this year, but had to put the promotion on hold when it changed hands and was radically refurbished). Other Lucky Dip entries to single out are the Harbour Lights on Alderney and Ship on Herm. Most Guernsey pubs close on Sunday; those pub/restaurants that do open will serve alcohol only to customers spending at least £3 on food. On Jersey, Sunday is a day when many of the island's residents like to eat out for a family lunch – so it's wise to book lunch then.

CASTEL (Guernsey) Map 1

Hougue du Pommier

Route de Hougue du Pommier, off Route de Carteret; just inland from Cobo Bay and Grandes Rocques

The name of this calmly civilised and well equipped hotel (Apple Tree Hill) commemorates the fact that a cider mill stood here in the 18th c. The oak-beamed bar is quite roomy, with leatherette armed chairs around wood tables, old game and sporting prints, guns, sporting trophies and so forth; the bar counter itself is attractively carved. The nicest seats are perhaps those in the snug area by the big stone fireplace with its attendant bellows and copper fire-irons; piped music; part of the bar is no smoking. Good bar food includes sandwiches (from £2.40), soup (£2.20), filled warm french bread (from £4.20), ploughman's (£4.80), mushroom stroganoff on saffron rice (£4.80), steak and kidney pie (£4.95), chicken and ale casserole (£5.25), pork and apple cobbler with strong cider (£5.50), spicy thai crab cakes (£5.80), steaks (from £8.20) and daily specials; seven wines by the glass or bottle. A conservatory with cane furniture overlooks fruit trees shading tables on the neatly trimmed lawn. There are more by the swimming pool in the sheltered walled garden, and in a shady flower-filled courtyard. Leisure facilities include a pitch-and-putt golf course and a putting green (for visitors as well as residents), and for residents there's free temporary membership to the Guernsey Indoor Green Bowling Association (the stadium is next door and rated as one of the best in Europe); daily courtesy bus into town. No dogs. *(Recommended by Andy and Jill Kassube, R Davies; more reports please)*

Free house ~ Licensee Stephen Bone ~ Meals and snacks (not Sun evening) ~ Restaurant ~ (01481) 56531 ~ Children welcome ~ Singer/guitarist Fri evening ~ Open 11.30-2.30, 6-11.45; 12-2.45 only Sun ~ Bedrooms: £44B/£88B

GREVE DE LECQ (Jersey) OS 583552 Map 1

Moulin de Lecq

This black-shuttered old mill was commandeered by the Germans during the Occupation of Jersey and used to generate power for their searchlight batteries in this part of the island. Today it is a well liked pub with plenty of local custom and a warm and pleasant atmosphere. There's a good log fire, toasting you as you come down the four steps into the cosy bar, as well as plush-cushioned black wooden seats against the white-painted walls; piped music. Well kept Guernsey Sunbeam Bitter, Jersey Old Jersey Ale and Tipsy Toad Ale and Jimmy's Bitter on handpump. Good generously served bar food might include soup (£1.75), pâté (£2.50), ploughman's (£3.95), chilli, home-made lasagne or vegetarian moussaka (£4.95), cod in home-made batter or gammon steak with pineapple (£5.25), half a chicken with barbecue sauce (£5.75) and steaks (£7.95); children's menu (£2.50). Most people eat in the former granary upstairs. The massive restored waterwheel still turns outside, with its formidable gears meshing in their stone housing behind the bar. The terrace has picnic-sets under cocktail parasols, and there's a good children's adventure playground. The road past here leads down to pleasant walks on one of the only north-coast beaches. *(Recommended by George Atkinson, Sue Rowland, John Evans; more reports please)*

Jersey Brewery ~ Manager Shaun Lynch ~ Real ale ~ Meals and snacks (12-2.15, 6-8.30; 12.30-3 only Sun) ~ (01534) 482818 ~ Children welcome ~ Open 11-11 (inc Sun)

KINGS MILLS (Guernsey) Map 1

Fleur du Jardin

Kings Mills Rd

The cosy and sensitively refurbished rooms at this old-fashioned inn have low-beamed ceilings and thick granite walls, a good log fire in the newly refurbished public bar which is still popular with locals, and individual country furnishings in the lounge bar on the hotel side. As well as sandwiches (from £1.95, hot chargrilled steak £4.95), soup (£1.95), mushroom stroganoff or steak, kidney and ale pie (£4.95), pan-fried chicken breast with mushroom and cream sauce (£6.45) and seared lamb cutlets with a thyme jus (£7.45) from the menu there are various imaginative daily specials such as fricassee of baby artichoke and cherry tomatoes in a provençale butter or skate wing with a walnut and herb butter (£5.95) and duck breast in a raspberry vinegar jus (£8.25). Well kept Guernsey Sunbeam and their winter or summer ale on handpump, and maybe other guest beers, decent wines by the glass or bottle; friendly efficient service; unobtrusive piped music. Part of the restaurant is no smoking. In the two acres of beautiful gardens picnic-sets are surrounded by flowering cherries, shrubs, colourful borders, bright hanging baskets, and flower barrels. There is a swimming pool for residents. *(Recommended by Mark Percy, Lesley Mayoh, Gordon Neighbour, David and Jane Russell, R Davies)*

Free house ~ Licensee Keith Read ~ Real ale ~ Meals and snacks ~ Restaurant ~ (01481) 57996 ~ Children welcome ~ Open 11am-11.45pm; 12-2, 6.30-10.30 Sun ~ Bedrooms: £39.75B/£79.50B

ROZEL (Jersey) Map 1

Rozel Bay

Just out of sight of the sea, this pub is set on the edge of a sleepy little fishing village. The new licensee has redecorated throughout and extended the no-smoking upstairs dining area. In the snug and cosy small dark-beamed back bar they have stripped back the tables and the bar counter to their original light wood finish; also an open fire, old prints and local pictures on the cream walls, dark plush wall seats and stools. Leading off is a carpeted area with flowers on big solid square tables; darts, pool, cribbage and dominoes in the games room; piped music. Bar food under the new regime includes home-made soup (£1.95), an impressive range of sandwiches (from £2), ploughman's (£3.95), spinach and mushroom lasagne (£4.95), thai green chicken curry (£5.25), home-made sausages or beefburgers (£5.60) and beef in oyster sauce (£6.20); the specials board always includes a catch of the day; puddings such as home-made cheesecake or honey, apple and almond pudding (£2.50). Bass, Boddingtons and Courage Directors under light blanket pressure. There are tables under cocktail parasols by the quiet lane and in the attractive steeply terraced hillside gardens behind, where there may be barbecues on summer Sundays. *(Recommended by George Atkinson, J R Hawkes, Mr and Mrs S Davies, Ewan and Moira McCall, Mr and Mrs D G Parry, Steve and Carolyn Harvey, Mrs D Benham; more reports on the new regime please)*

Randalls ~ Lease: Gus McInnes ~ Real ale ~ Meals and snacks ~ Restaurant ~ (01534) 863438 ~ Children welcome ~ Open 10am-11pm

ST AUBIN (Jersey) OS 607486 Map 1

Old Court House Inn

This charming 15th-c inn is steeped in history – the front part of the building used to be the home of a wealthy merchant, whose cellars stored privateers' plunder alongside more legitimate cargo, while the upstairs restaurant still shows signs of its time as a courtroom. The conservatory which overlooks the tranquil harbour, with views stretching past St Aubin's fort right across the bay to St Helier, now houses the Westward Bar which is elegantly constructed from the actual gig of a schooner. The atmospheric main basement bar has cushioned wooden seats built against its stripped granite walls, low black beams and joists in a white ceiling, a turkey carpet and an open fire; it can get crowded and smoky at times. A dimly lantern-lit inner room has an illuminated rather brackish-looking deep well, beyond that is a spacious cellar room open in summer. Good value bar food includes open sandwiches (from £3.25), soup (£2.20), lasagne (£4.75), roast chicken (£4.95) and scampi (£5.50); lunchtime set menu (2 courses £8.50, 3 courses £9.95); in the evening you can eat off the more elaborate à la carte menu throughout the pub – dishes include salmon and cod fishcakes (£5.25), grilled goat's cheese on a sun-dried tomato crouton (£5.95), vegetable strudel (£7.95), chicken breast filled with goat's cheese and chives, wrapped in ham with a saffron sauce (£10.95) and medallions of venison with poached pear and ginger (£12.50). Well kept Marstons Pedigree and maybe a guest on handpump; cribbage, dominoes, scrabble, chess, shut the box, piped music, and darts in winter. The bedrooms, individually decorated and furnished, are small but comfortable, and you might get one on the harbour front. *(Recommended by Richard and Robyn Wain, George Atkinson, K G and J Archer)*

Free house ~ Licensee Jonty Sharp ~ Meals and snacks (not Sun evening) ~ Restaurant ~ (01534) 46433 ~ Children welcome till 9pm ~ Open 11-11.30 ~ Bedrooms: £45B/£90B

If you enjoy your visit to a pub, please tell the publican. They work extraordinarily long hours, and when people show their appreciation it makes it all seem worth while.

ST BRELADE (Jersey) OS 603472 Map 1

Old Portelet Inn

Portelet Bay

This 17th-c clifftop farmhouse is unashamedly aimed at families and beach visitors and is ideally positioned to do so. There's a sheltered cove right below which is reached by a long flight of steps with glorious views across Portelet (Jersey's most southerly bay) on the way down. The atmospheric low ceilinged, beamed downstairs bar has a stone bar counter on bare oak boards and quarry tiles, a huge open fire, gas lamps, old pictures, etched glass panels from France and a nice mixture of old wooden chairs. It opens into the big timber ceilinged family dining area, with standing timbers and plenty of highchairs. Reliable bar food includes sandwiches (from £1.40), ploughman's (£3.95), tuna filled baked potatoes (from £3.60), soup (£1.60), mushrooms poached in beer with mild mustard and cheese sauce (£3.50), lasagne (£4.50), chilli (£4.80), spicy chicken and tomato penne or steak and mushroom pie (£4.95), half roast duckling with orange sauce (£6.95), and steaks (from £7.60); children's meals (including baby food), and a large range of liqueur coffees and hot chocolates. Efficient service from friendly and neatly dressed staff. Well kept Adnams, Boddingtons, Courage Directors and Marstons Pedigree under light blanket pressure, and reasonably priced house wine; plenty of board games in the wooden-floored loft bar. No-smoking areas, disabled and baby changing facilities, and a superior supervised indoor children's play area (entrance 50p); pool. Outside there is another play area and picnic-sets on the partly covered flower-bower terrace by a wishing well as well as in a sizeable landscaped garden with lots of scented stocks and other flowers. *(Recommended by Steve and Carolyn Harvey, George Atkinson, John Evans, Sue Rowland)*

Randalls ~ Manageress Tina Lister ~ Real ale ~ Meals and snacks (12-2.10; 6-9) ~ (01534) 41899 ~ Children in family dining room ~ Live music most nights in summer, Fri night in winter ~ Open 10(11 Sun)-11

Old Smugglers

Ouaisne Bay; OS map reference 595476

Once old fishermen's cottages, this friendly, extended place then became a small residential hotel until after World War II when it emerged as a popular pub. It's in a pretty position on the road down to the beach and even on the days when it is really busy, the staff remain calmly helpful and food is quickly served. There's a genuinely relaxed, pubby atmosphere, as well as thick walls and black beams, open fires, and cosy black built-in settles. Two well kept real ales might include Bass and Ringwood Best on handpump; sensibly placed darts as well as cribbage and dominoes. Well liked bar food includes home-made soup (£1.95; local seafood chowder £2.50), ploughman's (£3.50), filled baked potatoes (from £3.95), burgers (from £3.95), vegetarian lasagne (£4.50), steak and Guinness pie (£4.75), grilled lamb chops with rosemary sauce (£4.95), poached haddock in a cream, wine and prawn sauce (£5.50), home-made chicken kiev (£5.75), chicken satay with spicy peanut sauce (£6.25) and king prawns in various sauces like black bean (£7.50), and fresh fish specials. A room in the restaurant is no smoking. Close by are some attractive public gardens. *(Recommended by Mr and Mrs S Davies, George Atkinson, Sue Rowland, John Evans)*

Free house ~ Licensee Nigel Godfrey ~ Real ale ~ Meals and snacks (not winter Sun evenings) ~ Restaurant ~ (01534) 41510 ~ Children welcome till 9pm ~ Open 11am-11.30pm

ST HELIER (Jersey) Map 1

Admiral £

St James St

This impressive candlelit pub is packed with interesting memorabilia and curios. As well as dark wood panelling, attractive solid country furniture, and heavy beams – some of which are inscribed with famous quotations – there are old telephones, a clocking-in machine, copper milk churn, enamel advertising signs (many more in the small back courtyard which also has lots of old pub signs) and an old penny 'What the Butler Saw' machine; daily papers to read. Quickly served and very good value bar food includes soup (£1.90), filled baked potatoes (from £2.75), half a spit-roast chicken or scampi (£4.25), steak and kidney pie (£4.30) and half a dozen daily specials; four course Sunday lunch (£7.95). Well kept Boddingtons and maybe a guest on handpump; dominoes, cribbage and piped music. There are plastic tables outside on a flagged terrace – quite a suntrap in summer. The pub is busier in the evenings, when it is well liked by a younger set. *(Recommended by George Atkinson, Mr and Mrs S Davies, Sue Rowland)*

Randalls ~ Manager Joanna Dyke ~ Real ale ~ Meals and snacks (12-2, 6-8; not Fri or Sun evening or all day Sat) ~ Restaurant ~ (01534) 30095 ~ Children welcome till 9pm ~ Open 11-11; closed 25 Dec evening

Tipsy Toad Town House

New Street

Although now owned by the Jersey Brewery, this attractive 1930s pub still stocks Tipsy Toad, Horny and Jimmy's – beers brewed at its sister pub, the Star & Tipsy Toad in St Peter. They used to brew here as well until the on-site microbrewery that filled the glass-windowed central room was removed to make way for additional restaurant seating. The pub is on two floors; downstairs the traditional bar has old photographs, solid furnishings, some attractive panelling and stained glass, and heavy brass doors between its two main parts to allow in more light; there's wheelchair access and loos; piped music. Upstairs has at least as much space again and is very well planned with a lot of attention to detail; baby changing facilities and high chairs. The new manager told us that the bar menu is likely to change soon, but as we went to press bar food included lunchtime filled baguetttes (from £1.85), sausages and mash or warm salads such as chicken liver or bacon lardons (£4.95), haggis, neeps and tatties (£5.95), stir-fried king prawns (£7.50), very popular fajitas with salsa, guacamole and cream dips (from £7.75), chargrilled steaks (from £8.95), lots of fresh fish and daily specials on the blackboard and children's meals (from £2); no-smoking area in restaurant. The house wines are sound, and the whole place is immaculate, running like clockwork; it can get busy in the evenings. *(Recommended by Tim and Chris Ford, Stephen Holman, Stephen and Jean Curtis)*

Jersey ~ Manager Dennis Murphy ~ Real ale ~ Meals and snacks (12.30-2.30, 6.30-10.30; not Mon evening or Sun) ~ Evening restaurant ~ (01534) 615000 ~ Children welcome ~ Disco Sun evening ~ Open 9am-11pm; cl 25 Dec

ST JOHN (Jersey) OS 620564 Map 1

Les Fontaines

Le Grand Mourier, Route du Nord

To be sure not to miss the best part of this pub – the distinctive public bar, and particularly the unusual inglenook by the large 14th-c stone fireplace – look for the worn and unmarked door at the side of the building, or as you go down the main entry lobby towards the bigger main bar slip through the tiny narrow door on your right. There are very heavy beams in the low dark ochre ceiling, stripped irregular red granite walls, old-fashioned red leatherette cushioned settles and solid black tables on the quarry-tiled floor, and for decoration antique prints and Staffordshire china figurines and dogs; look out for the old smoking chains and oven by the granite columns of the fireplace. The main bar is clean and carpeted, with plenty of wheelback chairs around neat dark tables, and a spiral staircase leading up to a wooden gallery under the high pine-raftered plank ceiling. For families a particularly popular feature is the supervised play area for children, Pirate Pete's (entry £1), though children are also made welcome in the other rooms of the bar. A wide range of bar food includes soup (£1.60), sandwiches (from £1.70), pâté (£2.25), ploughman's or cumberland sausage (£4.50), chicken kiev (£4.60), steak and mushroom pie or chicken and ham pie (£4.95), battered cod (£5.25), steaks (from

£7.45) and up to 10 daily specials; children's meals (£2). One large area is no-smoking; dominoes, cribbage and piped music. Adnams Best and Courage Directors under light blanket pressure. This pub is attractively set on the northernmost tip of the island, where the 300-feet-high granite cliffs face the distant French coast. Seats on a terrace outside, although noisy lorries from the nearby quarry can mar the atmosphere. There are good coastal walks nearby. *(Recommended by Tim and Chris Ford, George Atkinson; more reports please)*

Randalls ~ Manager Sandra Marie King ~ Real ale ~ Meals and snacks ~ (01534) 862707 ~ Children welcome ~ Open 10am-11pm

ST PETER PORT (Jersey) OS 595519 Map 1

Star & Tipsy Toad

In village centre

It's the very well kept own-brew beers that draw readers to this popular and unpretentious pub. Besides occasional seasonal brews you should find Horny Toad, Jimmys, and Tipsy Toad on handpump, and a guest such as Bass. There are tours of the on-site microbrewery every day and at other times you can see the workings through a window in the pub. The sensitively refurbished cottagey bar which has plenty of panelling, exposed stone walls, tiled and wood-panelled floors. A small games room has darts, pool, cribbage, dominoes, pinball, video game, fruit machine and piped music, and there's a good family conservatory, and children's playground and terraces. Tasty bar food includes home-made soup (£1.70), lunchtime doorstep sandwiches (from £1.75), sausage, egg and chips (£3.15), mozzarella sticks in beer batter with a red Russian dip (£3.55), lunchtime ploughman's (£3.95), gammon and pineapple (£5), lamb and mint suet pudding or steak and Horny ale pie (£5.50), cajun chicken (£5.60), sea bass (£5.95), steaks (from £6.25) and children's meals (£2). Friendly staff; wheelchair access and disabled lavatories. They often have a well regarded World Music Festival. See also the Tipsy Toad Town House in St Helier. *(Recommended by Richard and Robyn Wain, S J Barber, Stephen and Jean Curtis; more reports please)*

Own brew (Jersey) ~ Manager John Dryhurst ~ Real ale ~ Meals and snacks (12-2.15, 6-8.15; not Sun; not winter Mon evenings) ~ (01534) 485556 ~ Children welcome ~ Live bands Fri, Sat evenings in summer, Sat only in winter ~ Open 9am(11 Sun)-11pm

Lucky Dip

Besides the fully inspected pubs, you might like to try these Lucky Dips recommended to us and described by readers (if you do, please send us reports):

ALDERNEY

☆ **Newtown**, *Harbour Lights*: Welcoming, clean and well run hotel/pub in a quieter part of this quiet island, doing very well under current management, recently refurbished bar with varied good bar food esp fresh local fish and seafood, attractive prices, well kept Guernsey Bitter; caters particularly for families; terrace in pleasant garden, bedrooms *(Michael Inskip, D Godden, Mr and Mrs B Craig)*

GUERNSEY

Castel [Rue du Friquet], *Le Friquet*: Country hotel, bar open all day opening into attractive gardens, popular restaurant with renowned seafood platter, good value carvery with help-yourself veg, well kept Randalls; bedrooms good value *(Andy and Jill Kassube)*

St Andrew [nr Little Chapel], *Last Post*: Largeish, with comfortable lounge, genuine public bar, friendly staff, Randalls beer, locally popular reasonably priced food (not Sun/Mon evenings); open all day, handy for German Underground Hospital *(Gordon Neighbour)*

☆ **St Martin** [La Fosse], *Bella Luce*: Former 12th-c manor with lovely gardens, more hotel than pub, but has a super small and cosy bar with old-world pubby traditional atmosphere, good service, decent wines and reasonably priced food in bar and restaurant; keg beer; comfortable bedrooms *(Rudy Jacobs)*

☆ **St Peter Port** [North Esplanade], *Ship & Crown*: Lively town pub with bay windows overlooking harbour, very popular with yachting people and smarter locals, sharing building with Royal Guernsey Yacht Club; interesting photographs (esp concerning WWII German occupation, also boats and ships), good value food from sandwiches through fast foods to steak, well kept

Guernsey Bitter, welcoming prompt service even when busy *(John Knighton, Judith Hirst, Alan Green, LYM)*
St Peter Port [Le Charroterie], *Drunken Duck*: Particularly good choice of real ales such as Gales, Ringwood, Theakstons and Wadworths 6X, popular bar food until early evening, pleasant young Irish landlord, bar billiards; local bands, quiz nights, little nearby parking *(Howard England, Andy and Jill Kassube, Stephen Holman)*; [Lower Pollet], *Thomas De La Rue*: Smartly refurbished, with nautical bric-a-brac, good choice of reasonably priced generous food from baguettes to burgers and pizzas etc, wide choice of beers inc local Guernsey ale; music gets louder after 8 *(Andy and Jill Kassube, Stephen Holman)*
St Saviour [rue de la Perelle, Perelle Bay], *Atlantique*: Wide choice of good value food inc good seafood in stylish bar and restaurant, well kept Guernsey Bitter, no smoking area; comfortable bedrooms *(Gordon Neighbour)*

HERM
[Harbour], *Ship*: Charming pub in enchanting spot, plenty of seating outside in pretty courtyard, nautical bar (with friendly South African staff), upstairs restaurant with carvery, buffet and excellent local seafood; a house beer, good wines, distant sea view if you choose your viewpoint carefully; bedrooms *(Mark Percy, Lesley Mayoh, Judith Hirst)*

JERSEY
Gorey [The Harbour], *Dolphin*: Basic fishing theme (nets etc) in two long beamed bar areas looking across harbour, friendly pubby atmosphere, good fish and seafood inc scallops, big prawns, grilled sardines, seafood platter, children's dishes; restaurant; very busy indeed Sun lunchtime; piped music may be loud, difficult to park nearby; comfortable bedrooms *(George Atkinson, Ian and Villy White, Mr and Mrs S Davies, LYM)*
St Helier [Mulcaster St], *Chambers*: Impressive heavy-beamed pub with well done courts theme, separate areas (one with panelling, club chairs and daily papers), imposing paintings, prints and mirrors, candlelit tables, massively long bar counter with well kept Courage Directors, Marstons Pedigree and Theakstons XB and Old Peculier, decent wines, good value food, neat staff, separate gallery dining room; children welcome till 8, live music – open till 1 am *(LYM)*
St Helier [Halkett St], *Dog & Sausage*: Comfortable and neatly refurbished local in pedestrianised shopping area, welcoming staff, snug small rooms, dark green decor, fans, old photographs, and lots of Victorian and Jersey Railway memorabilia; piped music not too intrusive, tables outside *(Sue Rowland, Tim and Chris Ford, BB)*; [Bath St], *Original Wine Bar*: Informal environment, with casual decor and comfortable sofas; real ales inc Jersey Brewery's new Naomh Padraigs Porter, good choice of food, wines, coffees and teas, friendly efficient service, relaxing cheerful atmosphere *(Steve and Carolyn Harvey)*
☆ **St Lawrence** [Main Rd], *British Union*: Cottagey beamed and panelled lounge bar, no-smoking snug with woodburner and toys cupboard, second bar with darts, separate games room; good bar food from filled baked potatoes to steaks and fresh seafood, well kept Ann Street ale, efficient thoughtful service; piped music, children welcome; open all day, live music Sun evening *(LYM)*
☆ **St Martin** [Grande Rte de Faldouet (B30)], *Royal*: Roomy family local by church in untouristy village, toys and video games in small children's room off extended lounge, games in public bar, attractive upstairs restaurant, old prints and bric-a-brac; wide choice of generous popular well priced food inc children's, well kept Boddingtons, Marstons Pedigree and Theakstons; piped music may obtrude; tables out on big terrace with play area, open all day *(LYM)*
☆ **St Ouens Bay** [Five Mile Road; OS map ref 562488], *La Pulente*: Just over the road from the island's vastest beach; under new management and entirely refurbished, with pastel decor, wooden tables and chairs, Caribbean theme, bar food and upstairs seafood restaurant, Bass and Randalls, conservatory and tables on terrace; children welcome, open all day *(BB; reports on new regime please)*
Trinity, *Trinity Arms*: Large cheap basic meals, friendly staff and well kept Guernsey and Old Jersey ale in cheery country local, spacious and comfortable turkey-carpeted lounge and rambling quarry-tiled public bar with pool, video game and juke box or piped music; tables outside, handy for Jersey Zoo *(Ewan and Moira McCall, BB)*

SARK
☆ *La Moinerie*: Attractive stone house with woodburner in small low-ceilinged lounge bar, mix of eating-height tables with appropriate chairs and lower tables with settees and easy chairs, good reasonably priced bar food, swift efficient service, Guernsey Captains Bitter, restaurant with open fire; tables out on good-sized sloping lawn; pleasant bedrooms, peaceful spot *(Steve and Carolyn Harvey)*

Please let us know what you think of a pub's bedrooms. No stamp needed: *The Good Pub Guide*, FREEPOST TN1569, Wadhurst, E Sussex TN5 7BR.

Overseas Lucky Dip

We're always interested to hear of good bars and pubs overseas – preferably really good examples of bars that visitors would find memorable, rather than transplanted 'British pubs'. We start with ones in the British Isles (but over the water), then work alphabetically through other countries. A star marks places we can be confident would deserve a main entry. Note that the strong £ currently makes the best bars in foreign capitals (often very pricy) a good deal more accessible than previously.

IRELAND

☆ **Belfast** [Gt Victoria St; opp Europa Hotel], *Crown*: Bustling 19th-c gin palace with pillared entrance, opulent tiles outside and in, elaborately coloured windows, almost church-like ceiling, handsome mirrors, individual snug booths with little doors and bells for waiter service, gas lighting, mosaic floor – wonderful atmosphere, very wide range of customers (maybe inc performers in full fig from Opera House opp); good lunchtime meals inc oysters, Hilden real ale, open all day; National Trust *(More reports please)*

☆ **Dublin** [Merrion Row; off St Stephens Green], *O'Donoghues*: Small old-fashioned Victorian bar with dark panelling, mirrors, posters and snob screens, musical instruments and other bric-a-brac on ceiling, bank-note collection behind long side counter; superb atmosphere, good friendly service even when busy – popular with musicians – maybe an impromptu riot of Celtic tunes played on anything from spoons to banjo or pipes; fine Guinness, gets packed but long-armed owner ensures quick friendly service; plainer back bar has live music too; open all day *(Mayur Shah, Chris Raisin, Martin Ellis, Christine)*

Dublin [Harry St; off Grafton St], *Bruxelles*: Cosy and friendly upstairs Victorian bar with dark panelling, mirrors and outstanding Guinness; downstairs much more modern, Celtic symbols, grey/black/red decor, seats in alcoves and around central pillars, dim lighting; rock music can be very loud *(Mayur Shah, Chris Raisin)*; [East Essex St, Temple Bar], *Fitzsimons*: Very comfortable and welcoming if not genuine 'old Dublin', highly geared to tourists esp downstairs – free all-day traditional music, periodic dancers; good Guinness, friendly staff, lots of varnished wood, polished floor and bar counter, good bar food *(Chris Raisin, Mayur Shah)*; [Dame St], *Mercantile*: One of the best, dim-lit, with wall stools and huge barrels on bare boards, ceiling fans, primarily young couples (maybe loud rock music), lovely stairs to gallery over bar; coupled with O'Briens Bar – long side counter, raised end area, big fish tank *(Mayur Shah, Chris Raisin)*; [17 Anglesea St, Temple Bar], *Old Dubliner*: Very popular and friendly, well kept and served Guinness, traditional interior, snob screens, wall settles, round cast-iron-framed tables, wall paintings cleverly enhance the feeling of age; TV may obtrude *(Chris Raisin, SK)*; [Anglesea St, Temple Bar], *Oliver St John Gogarty*: Large popular bare-boards bars, bric-a-brac inc bicycle above counter, good Guinness, good if not cheap food in fairly small cosy upper-floor restaurant, very friendly efficient service; live music upstairs *(Mayur Shah, Chris Raisin)*

Glasson, *Murrays*: Unchanged over its long history; good Guinness *(S G Brown)*; *Village Inn*: Brilliant atmosphere, great for a traditional Sunday night out *(S G Brown)*

Loughrea [N6 about 15 miles E of Galway], *Meadow Court*: More restaurant than pub, but useful journey break with good well presented food, very fair prices, well stocked bar *(H C Holman)*

Portmagee, *Moorings*: Strong emphasis on fish and seafood inc fresh oysters and lobster, good range of wines, view of harbour and Valentia Island, live music in bar next door; bedrooms in old cottage adjoining, recently done up to high standard – just off Kerry Ring *(Susan Mullins)*

Shankill [Shangana Rd], *Byrnes*: Recently remodelled, very quaint, good local atmosphere, excellent staff; occasional weekend entertainment *(Kemberlee)*

ISLE OF MAN

Castletown [Victoria Rd; SC2767], *Sidings*: By steam railway station, bar food usually inc choice of good fresh fish, wide range of beers – usually about ten *(Derek and Sylvia Stephenson)*

Douglas [N Quay; SC3876], *Blazers*: Wine bar overlooking harbour, splendid choice of good food, reasonable prices, good service; parking difficult *(D H and M C Watkinson)*

Kirk Michael [SC3291], *Mitre*: Former

coaching inn, oldest surviving pub on island; home-made food inc fresh sandwiches, good service, cheerful landlord, well kept local Okells *(Diana Brumfit, Betty Taverner)*

☆ **Laxey** [Tram Station – OS Sheet 95 map ref 433846; SC4484], *Mines Tavern*: Beamed pub in lovely woodland clearing where Manx electric railway and Snaefell mountain railway connect, just below the Lady Isabella wheel (largest working water wheel in the world); splendid old tram photographs, advertisements and other memorabilia in one bar with counter salvaged from former tram, other bar dedicated to mining; fresh sandwiches and reasonably priced home cooking, well kept local Bushys and Okells, maybe Tetleys from the mainland; piped music, darts, fruit machines (public bar not lounge); lovely sitting outside to watch Victorian trams *(More reports please)*

☆ **Peel** [Station Pl/North Quay; NX2484], *Creek*: Recently refurbished dining pub in lovely setting on the ancient quayside opp new Manannan heritage centre, very helpful courteous landlord and staff, wide choice of good food inc fish fresh from the boats and several unusual dishes, local Okells beers; wheelchair access *(D H and M C Watkinson, Derek and Sylvia Stephenson)*

Peel [Shore Rd], *Marine*: Wide choice of food in bar and restaurant (both very busy) from good shepherd's pie to tender lamb cutlets (five at a time), fish and lobster, quick very cheerful service, well kept Okells *(Diana Brumfit, Betty Taverner)*

Ramsey [West Quay; SC4594], *Trafalgar*: Food inc excellent local queenies (small scallops); well kept Cains (from Liverpool) as well as local Bushys *(Derek and Sylvia Stephenson)*

LUNDY

☆ *Marisco*: One of England's most isolated pubs (yet full every night), great setting, atmospheric galleried interior with lifebelts and other paraphernalia from local shipwrecks; brews its own tasty beer, also others and Lundy spring water on tap, good value house wines, welcoming staff, good if not cheap range of home-cooked food using island produce, with lots of seafood and vegetarian; children welcome, tables outside, self catering and camping available; souvenir shop, and doubles as general store for the island's few residents *(Richard Gibbs, Dave Braisted)*

AUSTRALIA

☆ **Sydney** [81 Lower Fort St, The Rocks], *Hero of Waterloo*: Delightful old stonebuilt pub dating from 1845, with considerable character – touristy, but good atmosphere, genuine and uncontrived (even in the haunted basement function room, scene of several murders in the old days); stools along long bar, adjacent sitting area, imports such as Bass, Newcastle Brown and Guinness on tap as well as Fosters, Resch, Tookeys Old, New and Blue and Victoria Bitter, well presented generous food in bar and restaurant; English singalong Sun evening; as close to a typical British pub as you'll find abroad *(Derek Stafford)*

☆ **Sydney** [Argyle Pl, The Rocks], *Lord Nelson*: Solid stone, with beams and bare floorboards – the city's oldest pub; brews its own Nelsons Revenge, Three Sheets, Trafalgar and Victory, and has tastings first Weds of month (not Jan); good choice of other Australian beers, great easy-going service, interesting reasonably priced home-made food, nautical theme, upmarket atmosphere, pine furniture; open all day, gets touristy; attractive bedrooms *(Andrew and Eileen Abbess)*

Sydney [176 George St, opp Regent Hotel], *Jacksons on George*: Essentially a restaurant with four floors of entertainment, but ground floor has marvellous pubby bar with imposing rank of keg taps on long counter (they claim to sell 101 beers from 27 countries), cubicle seating, Tiffany-style lamps *(Derek Stafford)*

AUSTRIA

Vienna [Baekerstrasse 9], *Alt Wien*: Comfortably bohemian, largely undiscovered by tourists – student/folkie 60s time warp *(Mr and Mrs Jon Cornelis)*; [Kaertner Str 10], *American Bar*: Tiny cocktail lounge in art deco architectural gem by Adolf Loos – soft lighting, piped retro jazz, slightly dowdy stylishness of the decor all work towards ideal atmosphere; good if expensive drinks, dress decorously to match *(Mr and Mrs Jon Cornelis)*; [Hernalser Hauptstr 212], *Schweigers Bierbeisl*: Genuine locals' bar with lots of panelling, good beers inc Austrian rarities on tap, also foreign bottled beers (esp from former Hapsburg Empire) – landlord happy to talk beers, at least in German *(John C Baker)*; [Siebensterngase 19], *Siebenstern Brau*: Massive vaulted cellar with rambling side rooms, good beers inc Hanfbier (hemp instead of hops), good local dishes and Nurnberg bratwurst, lots of chatting locals – something of a bierkeller atmosphere, with enthusiastic if rushed service *(John C Baker)*

BELGIUM

Beersel [Herman Teirlinckplein 3; just off E19 junction 14], *Dree Fonteinen*: One of the few microbreweries producing lambic beer, the sharpish Gueuze, sweetend Faro and cherry Kriek made in the cellar going well with excellent choice of classic Belgian country dishes; big restaurant and bar with extra back room, cl Tues, Weds *(Joan and Michel Hooper-Immins)*

☆ **Bruges** [Kemelstraat 5; SW of centre], *Brugs Beertje*: Excellent little tavern known as the Beer Academy, serving over 300 of the country's beers, in each beer's distinctive glass; table menus, helpful English-speaking staff, good basic bar food *(Amanda Hill, David Halliwell)*

☆ **Bruges** [off Breidelstraat], *Garre*: Attractive and welcoming 16th-c timbered building, stripped brickwork, upper gallery, very relaxed atmosphere, well over 100 local beers inc five Trappists and its own draught beer – each well served in its own glass with cheese nibbles; knowledgeable helpful staff, unobtrusive piped classical music, light snacks; children welcome *(Amanda Hill, David Halliwell)*

Bruges [Kemelstraat 8; SW of centre], *Hobbit*: Cluttered bar, lively and bustling, with good choice of local beers and of whiskies, attentive staff, good generous food inc pasta, grills and seafood; candlelit tables, subdued lighting *(Amanda Hill, David Halliwell)*

☆ **Brussels** [R Montagne aux Herbes Potageres], *Mort Subite*: A local institution, under same family since turn of the century, long Belle Epoque room divided by two rows of pillars into nave with two rows of small tables and side aisles with single row, huge mirrors on all sides, leather seats, swift uniformed waiters and waitresses scurrying from busy serving counter on right; their own Gueuze, Faro, Kriek, Peche and Framboise brewed nearby, good food inc omelettes and croques monsieur, no piped music *(Joan and Michel Hooper-Immins)*

CANADA

Aurora [Yonge St; Ontario], *Filly & Firkin*: Style and atmosphere like an English pub, good service, food inc some English favourites, televised quizzes, tables on terrace *(Dr Gerald Barnett)*

Banff [206 Wolf St; Alberta], *St James Gate*: Recently opened olde Irish pub with good value food inc fish (excellent) and chips, Traditional and Rose Brown real ales – good, but served too cold for British tastes *(Derek and Sylvia Stephenson)*

Carp [2193 Richardson Side Rd], *Cheshire Cat*: Formerly small rural school, now a good try at reproducing the ambience of a small English village pub, comfortable and relaxing *(John Roué)*

Lions Head [Ontario], *Lions Head*: Small friendly family-run pub with good wide-ranging food inc several vegetarian dishes, nice terrace overlooking lake; handy for Bruce Trail *(Patrick Renouf)*

Merrickville, *Gads Hill*: Comfortable and pleasant, nice place for reflective pint in a somewhat Dickensian/Victorian atmosphere; small restaurant attached *(John Roué)*; [118 Main St E], *Sam Jakes*: Tall and handsome old stone inn with some concentration on dining room; beers from local microbreweries, good choice of wines and malt whiskies; bedrooms handsomely furnished in period style *(John Roué)*

Whistler [4270 Mountain Sq; British Columbia], *Blacks*: Upstairs bar nr ski resort's main gondolas, spectacular view from full-length windows, Bass, John Smiths and Guinness on draught, over 20 malt whiskies, interesting good value food inc good soups with hefty sandwiches, usual good Canadian hospitality *(John and Joan Nash)*

CANARY ISLANDS

Lanzarote [Costa Teguise], *Cutty Sark*: Good service, good food inc breakfast – superb helpings; keg Stones and Guinness *(D Jeynes)*; *Dolphin*: Good pub atmosphere, staff and food; reasonable prices *(D Jeynes)*

CZECH REPUBLIC

Prague, *Nebozizek*: Pub/restaurant at top of funicular rly – wonderful view over city; good beers and food, popular so best to book; walk down through woods and fields via Strahov monastery *(Jane Kingsbury)*; [Kremencova 11], *U Fleku*: Brewing its own strong flavoursome black ale since 1843 (some say 1499) – usually served with a short; huge, with benches and big refectory tables in courtyard after courtyard, dark beams, very popular and atmospheric; good basic food – sausages, pork, goulash with dumplings; open early morning to late night, with early evening piano and drums, later brass band; very popular with tourists at weekends *(M A and C R Starling, Ian Phillips)*

DOMINICAN REPUBLIC

Sosua, *Britannia*: Travesty of an English pub, but quite respectable for the area; English customers welcome, reasonably priced food all day, good range of the reasonable local beer, plenty of rum; nr beautiful beaches *(Jenny and Brian Seller)*

EGYPT

Aswan, *Old Cataract*: Grand hotel with minimum charge in bars but well worth it: superb Nile and desert view from Elephantine Bar (with quiet piped music) especially atmospheric at night, live local music in Terrace Bar, lagers and all types of food; New Cataract (same site) has bar with no minimum charge, also duty-free shop – useful for stocking up on Nile cruise *(Ian Phillips)*

Luxor [part of Hotel Mercure], *Le Sarab*: Bar of international hotel, spilling on to waterside terrace by Nile moorings, European and local bottled beers and good wine, moderate prices *(Ian Phillips)*

FRANCE

Alpe d Huez [Ave des Jeux], *Avalanche*: Pleasant comfortable corner bar opp highly heated open-air winter swimming pool, good piped jazz (live late night), Belgian draught beer *(I M Phillips)*

Oz en Oisans [Station], *Causerie*: Small comfortable piano bar between two ski cable stations, off-duty Alpine troops and ski instructors, Hoegarden, Fischer and Jupiter on draught; piped music – live evenings *(I M Phillips)*

Vaujany [La Villete], *Airelles*: Mountain bar/restaurant, ancient beams of family's former cattle byre snugged against vast rock, good beer and food, outside tables, friendly pleasant staff, photogenic husky *(I M Phillips)*

GERMANY

Bamberg [Dominikaner Str], *Schlenkerla*: Tap for delicious smoky Rauchbier from tiny 17th-c Heller brewery, inc wondrous strong Bock version; two marvellous rooms, one stone-vaulted, the other heavy-beamed, reasonably priced typical German pub food *(Stephen Pine, Alfred Lawrence)*

Passau [Heiliggeistgasse 4], *Heilig Geist Stift Schenke*: Very interesting old Bavarian pub with own vineyards, wide choice of beers, beer mug collection, stained-glass windows; good local cooking *(Jane Kingsbury)*

GREECE

Chania [8 Katechaki Sq; Crete], *Kapnario*: Good restaurant in old harbour area, Greeks as well as tourists giving authentic atmosphere – very busy, get there early to avoid queue *(Mr and Mrs B Thomas)*

Frangocastello [Crete], *Oasis*: At end of sandy beach, breath-taking south coast views, food good; bedrooms clean, friendly staff speak some English *(Mr and Mrs B Thomas)*

HONG KONG

Hong Kong [Hutchison House], *Bull & Bear*: Good British-style pub, wide choice of food inc good steak and kidney pie at reasonable prices, good decor, good choice of beers with early happy hour *(Alison Hunt)*

Kowloon [Pratt St], *Delaneys*: Good beer, very friendly Western staff, good food from traditional breakfast to huge beef and ale pies, big screen sports TV – can get excitable *(Piotr Chodzko-Zajko)*

ITALY

Torbole, *La Guillotine*: Enjoyable young people's Lake Garda bar, beams, tiled floor, prints and mirrors, Bass and Guinness as well as cocktails etc, medium prices, music, caged bird *(Terry Barlow)*

JAPAN

Kyoto [2nd floor, Shobi bdg; opp Keihan-Sanjo Stn, Sanjo-Dori], *Pig & Whistle*: Tired of sushi, sake and sitting on tatami mats? This Britpub is v popular with ex-pats of all ages, and young Japanese, with Bass and Guinness on tap, huge choice of whiskies, darts, fish and chips; those taller than (Japanese) average should watch out for the suspended rowing boat *(Martin and Karen Wake)*; [Kiyamichi Dori], *Tudor Inn*: Another place for the homesick – very well done transplant, with nice cat theme, good bottled beer *(Dr and Mrs A K Clarke)*

MADEIRA

Funchal [Rua do Favila; off main rd W, just before Reids – on left, coming from town], *Red Lion*: Don't be put off by the name – in fact a pleasant restaurant and bar, doing good reasonably priced food esp espada (scabbard fish) and espatada (skewered beef); friendly attentive English-speaking service, local Coral beer, open-air tables; handy for Quinta do Magnolia gardens *(George Atkinson)*

Ribeiro Frio, *Old Trout*: Single-storey wooden building in cool and attractive mountain setting, idyllic garden terrace overlooking woodside river; very pubby log-cabin atmosphere, snug little candlelit Victorian-style bar with open fire, rugs, cosy sofas, lots of flowers; rustic softly lit restaurant area with pine furnishings on quarry tiles, big windows overlooking stream, very trout-based food; open 9-5 *(Susan and John Douglas)*

MAJORCA

☆ **Cala d Or** [carrer d'en Rito 12; formerly listed as Fowlers, which is still the name of the bar], *Hostal Cala Llonga*: Exquisitely furnished (remaining stock of owner's former antique shop), lots of marble busts, wonderful paintings, oriental rugs, objets, extravagant flower arrangements, candles everywhere, glossy magazines, colourful lanterns; good choice of drinks inc remarkable range of Spanish brandies, coffee in antique silver and Wedgwood bone china (with Bendicks mint), well reproduced opera or jazz (if landlady not playing operetta on the corner grand piano); terrace with pretty balcony overlooking marina, and now have bedrooms and a small s/c flat *(Susan and John Douglas)*

MAURITIUS

Flic en Flac, *Mer de Chine*: Chinese restaurant, but OK to have just a drink; on beautiful beach, two sides open – ideal for sunset sipping *(Bill and Sylvia Trotter)*

NETHERLANDS

Amsterdam [Funenkade], *'t Ij Brouwerij*: Cafe brewing its own fine beers in vast copper vats, from real Pils to dauntingly strong Columbus, also exceptional autumn Bok and midwinter Nieuwjaarsbier *(Giles Francis)*; [Egelantiersgracht 12; Jordaan], *Smalle*: Typical Dutch pub in old distillery in lovely canalside spot nr Westertoren; small and often crowded, streetside summer tables, friendly owners and staff, lots of regulars, good snacks and light dishes all hours – wide enough choice to put together an informal full meal; good choice of wines by the glass, interesting Belgian beers *(Mr and Mrs Jon Cornelis)*

NEW ZEALAND

Auckland [Mount Eden Rd], *Galbraiths*: The closest thing to a British pub in NZ, British beers brewed on site as well as imported such as Boddingtons, lively atmosphere, consistently friendly service, simple wholesome food from traditional British pub dishes to Pacific rim; in former public library – as portico shows; open all day, very busy early Fri evening or Eden Park match days *(Graeme Perry)*; *Loaded Hog*: Essentially a drinking bar, friendly and lively, part of a chain of this name, stocking Loaded Hog, Red Dog and other cold beers in chilled glasses; good quick food in good-sized helpings, big room with central bar open to street, balcony, good cheerful service *(Derek Stafford, DAV)*; [Customs St E], *Rose & Crown*: Pleasant pub with friendly barman, good value food (not Sat lunchtime) such as quiche or steak and kidney pie; beware big surcharge for half-pints instead of pints *(DAV, Derek Stafford)*

Christchurch [opp Victoria Park], *Oxford on the Avon*: Busy bar and cafeteria, huge range of very popular plain food inc outstanding value and quality lamb from carvery, good range of nicely served local beers, decent wine by the glass, quite a pub-like atmosphere; food all day from good value breakfasts on (bar opens later), tables out by the river with evening gas heaters *(A Albert, DAV)*

Rotorua [Tutanekai/Haupapa St; North Island], *Pig & Whistle*: Former 40s police station with appropriate murals and memorabilia, high ceilings, tall windows, three beers brewed upstairs, food such as chowder, pumpkin soup, BELT club sandwich with fries – the sort of place where you drop in for happy hour, end staying all night *(DAV, Andrew and Eileen Abbess)*

Russell [Bay of Islands], *Duke of Marlborough*: Good traditional pubby bar, good service and range of beers, delightful big verandah overlooking beach and Pacific; 19th-c colonial-style hotel *(Derek Stafford)*

OMAN

Muscat [Intercontinental Hotel], *Al Ghazal*: Terrific atmosphere, two pool tables, lots of little booths, Guinness and various keg beers, drinkable wines, long early-evening happy hour, good friendly service; this very heavily Indian-influenced country is not strictly Moslem, so there's the unusual sight of very happy men in full Arab dress downing pints of lager; happy hour 6-8 *(Mike and Karen England)*

SINGAPORE

☆ **Singapore** [Beach Rd], *Raffles*: Magnificent national monument, lavishly restored: Long Bar well worth a visit for its atmosphere, Singapore slings and underfoot peanut shells, sedate Billiards Bar, Tiffin Room with elaborate changing buffets, more expensive meals in the Writer's Room, and five other food outlets each with its own style of cooking; cultural and Raffles displays; even with the strong pound prices can be daunting if you stay *(Dr and Mrs A K Clarke)*

Singapore [Holland Village], *Bobs Tavern*: Bar/restaurant with lots of British food for homesick ex pats, efficient service, keg Tiger; rather fierce air conditioning, but nice tables out on verandah – more peaceful out here than in bustling centre *(Mike and Karen England)*; [off Orchard Rd], *Five Emerald Hill*: Old colonial-style bar among lovely old buildings of historic Peranakan area, long bar, bare boards, wooden ceiling fans, good mix of locals, ex pats and tourists – can get busy evenings; free peanuts – shells go on the floor; speciality Rocket Fuel is chillies soaked in vodka; piped jazz or (more appropriately for the current mood here) blues *(Mike and Karen England)*; [Millenia Walk], *Paulaner Brauhaus*: Authentic-feeling Munich bierkeller with beer brewed in house by a genuine Bavarian – great beer, amazing prices *(Dr and Mrs A K Clarke)*; [B2-09/10 Tanglin Shopping Centre, Tanglin Rd], *Treffpunkt Cafe*: Two basement Singaporean-run bars with chatty cheerful staff, good friendly atmosphere, character barman Mr Foo, relatively cheap keg Tiger, full menu till 3 then snacks – some quite sizeable; open all day, very lively Fri evening (mainly locals, some tourists); cl Sun *(Mike and Karen England)*

SOUTH AFRICA

Cape Town [St Georges Mall], *Loco*: Central cafe with bar in old Blue Train carriage; reasonable snacks and meals *(Bill and Sylvia Trotter)*

Dullstroom [Mpumalanga], *Dullstroom Inn*: Lovely old-world atmosphere, seats out on stoep, cheap food, friendly staff, welcome stop on Jo'burg route to Pilgrims Rest or Graskop – signed from main rd *(Bill and Sylvia Trotter)*

Wilderness [Holiday Inn Garden Ct], *Murphys*: Irish pub that works, real pubby atmosphere, good snacks and meals, walk through hotel garden to idyllic beach *(Bill and Sylvia Trotter)*

TENERIFE

Puerto de la Cruz [Camino El Durazio 3; La Orotava], *Casa Fifo*: Delightful bar and small restaurant above botanic gardens, typical decor, delicious food, usual lagers, super dry white wines, lots of locals and tourists *(J F M West)*

UNITED STATES

Bar Harbor [36 Rodick St; Maine], *Lompoc*: Very jolly pub with its own fruity yet well hopped Atlantic Brewing Co Special, also Coal Porter, Ginger Wheat Beer, Blueberry Ale and seasonal brews, as well as other microbrews and Guinness; explanatory brewery tours, eclectic choice of good food from exotic sandwiches to main dishes inc Middle Eastern, live music some evenings *(Hazel Morgan)*

Bethlehem [Union Blvd; Pennsylvania], *Old Brewery*: Lots of microbrewery beers; home of a musikfest *(James Flamish)*

Boston [33 Stuart St; Massachussetts], *Jacob Wirth*: More restaurant than bar, but good choice of German beers and handy for tour of Boston on foot; nice atmosphere *(Paul Noble)*

Gig Harbor [Harborview Pa; about 30 miles S of Seattle; Washington], *Tides*: Old waterfront building, deck area on harbour, good choice of draught microbrews, good pub food; the town is worth the trip *(Tim Jacobson)*

Hoosick Falls [Main St; New York], *Man of Kent*: Surprising bit of England, very pubby, with Fullers ESB and Morlands Old Speckled Hen as well as Guinness, German and US beers, keenly priced food, geese, ducks and a vietnamese pot-bellied pig called Lucy in pleasant back garden overlooking creek; cl Tues, Weds *(Paul Noble)*
Laguna Beach [Beach Blvd; California], *Laguna Beach Brewing Co*: Lively fashionable upstairs bar/restaurant with tables on balcony, copper brewing equipment viewed from back bar, own Beach Blonde (a German-style Kolsch), Victoria ESB (brave attempt at a British Bitter, served cold), and imported Belgian beers; good food *(Paul and Cait O'Reilly)*
New York [93 South St, Seaport], *North Star*: Good imitation two-room English pub, busy and lively, with dark green lincrusta ceiling, wall mirrors, oak furniture, handpumps for the Bass, Boddingtons and Fullers ESB, good choice of English bottled beers and Scotch malt whiskies, fish and chips, steak and kidney pie, good bangers and mash; obliging and friendly staff; attractive location in group of restored warehouses and quays with a couple of full-rigged ships as background *(Graham Reeve)*
New York [156 E 34th St], *Brews*: Olde-worlde, with antique light fittings, wide choice of keg beers inc several English ones, good choice of food from snacks to huge steaks, sensible prices, two no-smoking areas, upstairs room, superb service; handy for Empire State Building *(Graham Reeve)*; [15 East 7th St], *McSorleys*: Lots of dark wood, old-fashioned concrete floor, close-set chairs around nicely worn pub tables, walls packed with old photographs and interesting framed news clippings; one reader has been coming here for 50 years *(John Roué)*; [977 2nd Ave], *Murphys*: Relaxed atmosphere, bentwood chairs, high-backed bar stools, old-country pictures, globe lamps, Guinness, cheerful Irish barman, restaurant *(John Roué)*; [Hudson/11th St], *White Horse*: Built 1880, one of city's last wooden buildings; where Dylan Thomas had his last drink *(John Roué)*
Norcross [Jones Mill Rd; Gwinnett County], *Poor Richards*: Very good beer choice, nice people, good darts, tasty menu; cool bands *(James Walls)*
Rapid City [610 Main St; S Dakota], *Firehouse Brewing Co*: Microbrewery in former 1915 firehouse, brewery view from downstairs and upstairs bars, good varied food inc bangers and mash, interesting seasonal brews inc Oktoberfest beer festival with live music; some seats outside *(Lynda Payton, Sam Samuells)*
San Francisco [California], *Thirsty Bear*: Microbrewery, with a new cask-conditioned ale each Tues at 5.30; good tapas *(Joel Dobris)*; [Columbus, nr Broadway], *Vesuvio*: In bohemian/Italian North Beach neighbourhood, and little changed since its days of 50s beatnik fame; largely unspoiled despite tourist popularity, combining art gallery with Victorian atmosphere and good choice of draught beers *(Mr and Mrs Jon Cornelis)*
Sioux Falls [North Philip Ave; S Dakota], *Sioux Falls Brewing Co*: Stripped brickwork, bare boards, seasonal and other ales from microbrewery behind glass inc sample trays, inspired food inc great seafood cauldron; basement live music, huge upstairs function room *(Lynda Payton, Sam Samuells)*
Spearfish [506 5th St; S Dakota], *Bozys*: Western-style log cabin pub with bare boards, beam and plank ceiling, tractor-seat bar stools, chairs around big tables, bearskins and log fires, good collection of American microbrews and imports; hotel has atmospheric 'great room' pine log furniture, skins and rugs; log cabin bedrooms around central courtyard with hot tub *(Lynda Payton, Sam Samuells)*
Syracuse [New York], *Colemans*: Large house converted into Irish pub/restaurant, pleasantly faded 1930s decor, very efficient pleasant service, substantial satisfying food *(John Roué)*

We accept no free drinks or payment for inclusion. We take no advertising, and are not sponsored by the brewing industry – or by anyone else. So all reports are independent.

Special Interest Lists

PUBS WITH GOOD GARDENS

The pubs listed here have bigger or more beautiful gardens, grounds or terraces than are usual for their areas. Note that in a town or city this might be very much more modest than the sort of garden that would deserve a listing in the countryside.

Bedfordshire
Bolnhurst, Olde Plough
Milton Bryan, Red Lion
Riseley, Fox & Hounds

Berkshire
Aldworth, Bell
Hamstead Marshall, White Hart
Holyport, Belgian Arms
Hurley, Dew Drop
Waltham St Lawrence, Bell
West Ilsley, Harrow

Buckinghamshire
Amersham, Queens Head
Bledlow, Lions of Bledlow
Bolter End, Peacock
Fawley, Walnut Tree
Ford, Dinton Hermit
Hambleden, Stag & Huntsman
Little Horwood, Shoulder of Mutton
Northend, White Hart
Skirmett, Frog
Waddesdon, Five Arrows
West Wycombe, George & Dragon

Cambridgeshire
Fowlmere, Chequers
Great Chishill, Pheasant
Heydon, King William IV
Horningsea, Plough & Fleece
Madingley, Three Horseshoes
Swavesey, Trinity Foot
Wansford, Haycock

Cheshire
Aldford, Grosvenor Arms
Bunbury, Dysart Arms
Lower Peover, Bells of Peover
Macclesfield, Sutton Hall
Weston, White Lion

Cornwall
Helford, Shipwrights Arms
Philleigh, Roseland
St Agnes, Turks Head
St Kew, St Kew
St Mawgan, Falcon
Tresco, New Inn

Cumbria
Barbon, Barbon
Bassenthwaite, Pheasant
Bouth, White Hart
Eskdale Green, Bower House

Derbyshire
Birch Vale, Waltzing Weasel
Buxton, Bull i'th' Thorn
Melbourne, John Thompson
Woolley Moor, White Horse

Devon
Avonwick, Avon
Berrynarbor, Olde Globe
Broadhembury, Drewe Arms
Clyst Hydon, Five Bells
Dartington, Cott
Exeter, Imperial
Exminster, Turf
Haytor Vale, Rock
Kingskerswell, Bickley Mill
Lower Ashton, Manor
Lydford, Castle
Sidford, Blue Ball
South Zeal, Oxenham Arms
Weston, Otter

Dorset
Christchurch, Fishermans Haunt
Corfe Castle, Fox
Farnham, Museum
Kingston, Scott Arms
Marshwood, Bottle
Nettlecombe, Marquis of Lorne
Osmington Mills, Smugglers
Plush, Brace of Pheasants
Shave Cross, Shave Cross
Tarrant Monkton, Langton Arms
West Bexington, Manor

Essex
Castle Hedingham, Bell
Chappel, Swan
Coggeshall, Compasses
Great Yeldham, White Hart
Hastingwood, Rainbow & Dove
High Ongar, Wheatsheaf
Mill Green, Viper
Stock, Hoop
Toot Hill, Green Man
Wendens Ambo, Bell
Woodham Walter, Cats

Gloucestershire
Amberley, Black Horse

Ampney Crucis, Crown of Crucis
Blaisdon, Red Hart
Ewen, Wild Duck
Great Rissington, Lamb
Greet, Harvest Home
Gretton, Royal Oak
Kilkenny, Kilkeney
Kineton, Halfway House
Minchinhampton, Old Lodge
Nailsworth, Egypt Mill
North Nibley, New Inn
Oddington, Horse & Groom
Old Sodbury, Dog
Redbrook, Boat
Sapperton, Daneway
Tewkesbury, Old Black Bear
Withington, Mill

Hampshire
Alresford, Globe
Battramsley, Hobler
Bramdean, Fox
Longparish, Plough
North Gorley, Royal Oak
Ovington, Bush
Owslebury, Ship
Petersfield, White Horse
Steep, Harrow
Tichborne, Tichborne Arms
Whitsbury, Cartwheel

Hereford & Worcester
Aymestrey, Riverside
Bretforton, Fleece
Much Marcle, Slip Tavern
Sellack, Lough Pool
Ullingswick, Three Crowns
Woolhope, Butchers Arms

Hertfordshire
Ayot St Lawrence, Brocket Arms
Walkern, White Lion

Isle of Wight
Chale, Clarendon (Wight Mouse)
Shorwell, Crown

Kent
Biddenden, Three Chimneys
Bough Beech, Wheatsheaf
Boyden Gate, Gate
Chiddingstone, Castle
Dargate, Dove
Fordcombe, Chafford Arms
Groombridge, Crown
Ickham, Duke William
Linton, Bull
Newnham, George
Penshurst, Bottle House
Ringlestone, Ringlestone
Selling, Rose & Crown
Smarden, Bell
Toys Hill, Fox & Hounds
Ulcombe, Pepper Box

Lancashire (inc Greater Manchester, Merseyside)
Darwen, Old Rosins
Newton, Parkers Arms
Whitewell, Inn at Whitewell

Leicestershire
Braunston, Old Plough
Exton, Fox & Hounds
Medbourne, Nevill Arms
Old Dalby, Crown

Lincolnshire
Newton, Red Lion
Stamford, George of Stamford

Norfolk
Great Bircham, Kings Head
Reedham, Ferry
Sculthorpe, Sculthorpe Mill
Stow Bardolph, Hare Arms
Titchwell, Manor
Woodbastwick, Fur & Feather

Northamptonshire
Ashby St Ledgers, Olde Coach House
East Haddon, Red Lion
Eastcote, Eastcote Arms
Wadenhoe, Kings Head

Northumberland, Durham, Tyneside & Teeside
Belford, Blue Bell
Blanchland, Lord Crewe Arms
Diptonmill, Dipton Mill
Thropton, Three Wheat Heads

Nottinghamshire
Caunton, Caunton Beck
Colston Bassett, Martins Arms
Kimberley, Nelson & Railway
Upton, French Horn

Oxfordshire
Binfield Heath, Bottle & Glass
Broadwell, Five Bells
Burford, Lamb
Chalgrove, Red Lion
Chinnor, Sir Charles Napier
Clifton, Duke of Cumberlands Head
Finstock, Plough
Fyfield, White Hart
Hook Norton, Gate Hangs High
Hook Norton, Pear Tree
Kelmscot, Plough
Maidensgrove, Five Horseshoes
Shipton-under-Wychwood, Shaven Crown
South Stoke, Perch & Pike
Stanton St John, Star
Tadpole Bridge, Trout
Watlington, Chequers
Westcott Barton, Fox
Woodstock, Feathers

Shropshire
Bishops Castle, Three Tuns
Cressage, Cholmondeley Riverside
Norton, Hundred House

Somerset
Ashcott, Ashcott
Bristol, Highbury Vaults
Combe Hay, Wheatsheaf

Compton Martin, Ring o' Bells
Dunster, Luttrell Arms
Litton, Kings Arms
Monksilver, Notley Arms
South Stoke, Pack Horse
West Huntspill, Crossways

Staffordshire
Acton Trussell, Moat House
Onecote, Jervis Arms
Salt, Holly Bush

Suffolk
Bildeston, Crown
Brandeston, Queens Head
Dennington, Queens Head
Hoxne, Swan
Lavenham, Angel
Lavenham, Swan
Laxfield, Kings Head
Rede, Plough

Surrey
Chilworth, Villagers
Coldharbour, Plough
Compton, Withies
Farncombe, Ram
Gomshall, Compasses
Hascombe, White Horse
Mickleham, King William IV
Pirbright, Royal Oak
Sutton, Volunteer
Warlingham, White Lion
Wotton, Wotton Hatch

Sussex
Amberley, Black Horse
Ashurst, Fountain
Barcombe, Anchor
Berwick, Cricketers Arms
Blackboys, Blackboys
Byworth, Black Horse
Coolham, George & Dragon
Elsted, Three Horseshoes
Firle, Ram
Fletching, Griffin
Hammerpot, Woodmans Arms
Heathfield, Star
Kirdford, Half Moon
Mayfield, Middle House
Oving, Gribble
Scaynes Hill, Sloop
Seaford, Golden Galleon
Wineham, Royal Oak

Warwickshire
Edge Hill, Castle
Ettington, Chequers
Farnborough, Butchers Arms
Ilmington, Howard Arms
Lowsonford, Fleur de Lys

Wiltshire
Alvediston, Crown
Bradford-on-Avon, Cross Guns
Brinkworth, Three Crowns
Chicksgrove, Compasses
Ebbesbourne Wake, Horseshoe
Lacock, George
Little Cheverell, Owl
Lower Woodford, Wheatsheaf
Netherhampton, Victoria & Albert
North Newnton, Woodbridge
Norton, Vine Tree
Salisbury, New Inn
Seend, Barge
Woodborough, Seven Stars

Yorkshire
East Witton, Blue Lion
Egton Bridge, Horse Shoe
Heath, Kings Arms
Osmotherley, Three Tuns
Stutton, Hare & Hounds
Sutton upon Derwent, St Vincent Arms

London, Central
London W 1, Red Lion

London, North
London N 1, Waterside
London NW 3, Spaniards

London, South
London SE21, Crown & Greyhound
London SW18, Ship

London, West
London W 6, Dove
London W 8, Windsor Castle
Twickenham, White Swan

London, East
London E 1, Prospect of Whitby

Scotland
Ardfern, Galley of Lorne
Arduaine, Loch Melfort
Creebridge, Creebridge House
Edinburgh, Starbank
Gifford, Tweeddale Arms
Glenelg, Glenelg
Haddington, Waterside
Kilmahog, Lade
Pitlochry, Killiecrankie
Skeabost, Skeabost House
Thornhill, Lion & Unicorn

Wales
Aberystwyth, Halfway
Bodfari, Dinorben Arms
Crickhowell, Bear
Crickhowell, Nantyffin Cider Mill
Llandrindod Wells, Llanerch
Llanfrynach, White Swan
Llangedwyn, Green
Llangynidr, Coach & Horses
Llwyndafydd, Crown
Presteigne, Radnorshire Arms
St Hilary, Bush
Stackpole, Armstrong Arms
Tyn y Groes, Groes

Channel Islands
Castel, Hougue du Pommier
Kings Mills, Fleur du

Jardin
Rozel, Rozel Bay

WATERSIDE PUBS
The pubs listed here are right beside the sea, a sizeable river, canal, lake or loch that contributes significantly to their attraction.

Bedfordshire
Linslade, Globe
Odell, Bell

Berkshire
Great Shefford, Swan

Cambridgeshire
Cambridge, Anchor
Holywell, Old Ferry Boat
Sutton Gault, Anchor
Wansford, Haycock

Cheshire
Chester, Old Harkers Arms
Wrenbury, Dusty Miller

Cornwall
Bodinnick, Old Ferry
Cremyll, Edgcumbe Arms
Falmouth, Quayside & Old Ale House
Helford, Shipwrights Arms
Mousehole, Ship
Mylor Bridge, Pandora
Polkerris, Rashleigh
Polruan, Lugger
Port Isaac, Port Gaverne
Porthallow, Five Pilchards
Porthleven, Ship
St Agnes, Turks Head
Trebarwith, Port William
Tresco, New Inn

Cumbria
Ulverston, Bay Horse

Derbyshire
Shardlow, Old Crown

Devon
Avonwick, Avon
Dartmouth, Royal Castle
Exeter, Double Locks
Exminster, Turf
Instow, Boathouse
Plymouth, China House
Topsham, Passage House
Torcross, Start Bay
Tuckenhay, Maltsters Arms
Weston, Otter

Dorset
Chideock, Anchor
Lyme Regis, Pilot Boat

Essex
Burnham-on-Crouch, White Harte
Chappel, Swan
Heybridge Basin, Jolly Sailor

Gloucestershire
Ashleworth Quay, Boat
Great Barrington, Fox
Redbrook, Boat
Tewkesbury, Old Black Bear
Withington, Mill

Hampshire
Alresford, Globe
Bursledon, Jolly Sailor
Langstone, Royal Oak
Ovington, Bush
Portsmouth, Still & West
Wherwell, Mayfly

Hereford & Worcester
Aymestrey, Riverside
Knightwick, Talbot
Wyre Piddle, Anchor

Hertfordshire
Berkhamsted, Boat

Isle of Wight
Bembridge, Crab & Lobster
Cowes, Folly
Seaview, Seaview
Shanklin, Fishermans Cottage
Ventnor, Spyglass

Kent
Deal, Kings Head
Faversham, Albion
Oare, Shipwrights Arms
Whitstable, Pearsons Crab & Oyster House

Lancashire (inc Greater Manchester, Merseyside)
Garstang, Th'Owd Tithebarn
Manchester, Dukes 92
Manchester, Mark Addy
Whitewell, Inn at Whitewell

Lincolnshire
Brandy Wharf, Cider Centre

Norfolk
Reedham, Ferry
Sculthorpe, Sculthorpe Mill

Northamptonshire
Oundle, Mill
Wadenhoe, Kings Head

Oxfordshire
Tadpole Bridge, Trout

Shropshire
Cressage, Cholmondeley Riverside
Llanyblodwel, Horseshoe
Ludlow, Unicorn
Shrewsbury, Armoury
Whitchurch, Willey Moor Lock

Staffordshire
Acton Trussell, Moat House
Onecote, Jervis Arms

Suffolk
Chelmondiston, Butt & Oyster

Sussex
Barcombe, Anchor

Warwickshire
Lapworth, Navigation
Lowsonford, Fleur de Lys
Netherton, Little Dry Dock

Wiltshire
Bradford-on-Avon, Cross Guns
North Newnton, Woodbridge
Seend, Barge

Yorkshire
Hull, Minerva
Newton on Ouse, Dawnay Arms
Whitby, Duke of York

London, North
London N 1, Waterside

London, South
London SE 1, Anchor
London SE 1, Horniman
London SE10, Cutty Sark
London SW13, Bulls Head
London SW18, Ship

London, West
London W 4, Bulls Head
London W 6, Dove
Twickenham, White Swan

London, East
London E 1, Prospect of Whitby
London E 1, Town of Ramsgate
London E14, Grapes

Scotland
Ardfern, Galley of Lorne
Arduaine, Loch Melfort
Carbost, Old Inn
Clachan Seil, Tigh an Truish
Crinan, Crinan
Edinburgh, Starbank
Elie, Ship
Fort Augustus, Lock
Glenelg, Glenelg
Haddington, Waterside
Isle Ornsay, Tigh Osda Eilean Iarmain
Isle of Whithorn, Steam Packet
Plockton, Plockton
Portpatrick, Crown
Shieldaig, Tigh an Eilean
Skeabost, Skeabost House
St Monans, Cabin
Tayvallich, Tayvallich

Wales
Aberdovey, Penhelig Arms
Abergorlech, Black Lion
Cresswell Quay, Cresselly Arms
Little Haven, Swan
Llangedwyn, Green
Llangynidr, Coach & Horses
Pembroke Ferry, Ferry
Penmaenpool, George III
Pontypool, Open Hearth
Red Wharf Bay, Ship
Talyllyn, Tynycornel

Channel Islands
St Aubin, Old Court House
St Ouens Bay, La Pulente

PUBS IN ATTRACTIVE SURROUNDINGS

These pubs are in unusually attractive or interesting places – lovely countryside, charming villages, occasionally notable town surroundings. Waterside pubes are listed again here only if their other surroundings are special, too.

Bedfordshire
Linslade, Globe

Berkshire
Aldworth, Bell
Frilsham, Pot Kiln
Hurley, Dew Drop
Waltham St Lawrence, Bell

Buckinghamshire
Bledlow, Lions of Bledlow
Brill, Pheasant
Frieth, Prince Albert
Hambleden, Stag & Huntsman
Ibstone, Fox
Little Hampden, Rising Sun
Northend, White Hart
Skirmett, Frog
Turville, Bull & Butcher

Cheshire
Barthomley, White Lion
Bunbury, Dysart Arms
Langley, Leathers Smithy
Lower Peover, Bells of Peover
Marbury, Swan

Cornwall
Boscastle, Cobweb
Chapel Amble, Maltsters Arms
Helston, Halzephron
Lamorna, Lamorna Wink
Morwenstow, Bush
Porthallow, Five Pilchards
Ruan Lanihorne, Kings Head
St Agnes, Turks Head
St Breward, Old Inn
St Kew, St Kew
St Mawgan, Falcon
Tresco, New Inn

Cumbria
Askham, Punch Bowl
Bassenthwaite, Pheasant
Boot, Burnmoor
Bouth, White Hart
Braithwaite, Coledale
Broughton in Furness, Blacksmiths Arms
Caldbeck, Oddfellows
Cartmel, Cavendish Arms
Chapel Stile, Wainwrights
Coniston, Black Bull
Crosthwaite, Punch Bowl
Dent, Sun

Elterwater, Britannia
Garrigill, George & Dragon
Grasmere, Travellers Rest
Hawkshead, Drunken Duck
Ings, Watermill
Lanercost, Abbey Bridge
Langdale, Old Dungeon Ghyll
Little Langdale, Three Shires
Loweswater, Kirkstile
Melmerby, Shepherds
Mungrisdale, Mill
Scales, White Horse
Seathwaite, Newfield
Troutbeck, Mortal Man
Troutbeck, Queens Head
Ulverston, Bay Horse

Derbyshire
Brassington, Olde Gate
Froggatt Edge, Chequers
Hardwick Hall, Hardwick
Kirk Ireton, Barley Mow
Ladybower Reservoir, Yorkshire Bridge
Little Hucklow, Old Bulls Head
Over Haddon, Lathkil
Woolley Moor, White Horse

Devon
Beer, Anchor
Blackawton, Normandy Arms
Branscombe, Fountain Head
Broadclyst, Red Lion
Chagford, Ring o' Bells
Dunsford, Royal Oak
Exminster, Turf
Haytor Vale, Rock
Holbeton, Mildmay Colours
Horndon, Elephants Nest
Horsebridge, Royal
Iddesleigh, Duke of York
Kingston, Dolphin
Knowstone, Masons Arms
Lower Ashton, Manor
Lustleigh, Cleave
Lydford, Castle
Meavy, Royal Oak
Peter Tavy, Peter Tavy
Postbridge, Warren House
Rattery, Church House
Stokenham, Tradesmans Arms
Widecombe, Rugglestone
Wonson, Northmore Arms

Dorset
Abbotsbury, Ilchester Arms
Askerswell, Spyway
Burton Bradstock, Three Horseshoes
Corfe Castle, Fox
Corscombe, Fox
East Chaldon, Sailors Return
Farnham, Museum
Kingston, Scott Arms
Loders, Loders Arms
Marshwood, Bottle
Milton Abbas, Hambro Arms
Osmington Mills, Smugglers
Plush, Brace of Pheasants
Worth Matravers, Square & Compass

Essex
Fuller Street, Square & Compasses
Little Dunmow, Flitch of Bacon
Mill Green, Viper
North Fambridge, Ferry Boat

Gloucestershire
Amberley, Black Horse
Ashleworth Quay, Boat
Bisley, Bear
Bledington, Kings Head
Chedworth, Seven Tuns
Chipping Campden, Eight Bells
Cold Aston, Plough
Coln St Aldwyns, New Inn
Great Rissington, Lamb
Guiting Power, Hollow Bottom
Minchinhampton, Old Lodge
Miserden, Carpenters Arms
Nailsworth, Weighbridge
North Nibley, New Inn
Sapperton, Daneway
St Briavels, George
Stanton, Mount

Hampshire
Alresford, Globe
East Tytherley, Star
Hawkley, Hawkley
Micheldever, Dever Arms
North Gorley, Royal Oak
Ovington, Bush
Petersfield, White Horse
Tichborne, Tichborne Arms

Hereford & Worcester
Aymestrey, Riverside
Kidderminster, King & Castle
Knightwick, Talbot
Much Marcle, Slip Tavern
Pensax, Bell
Ruckhall, Ancient Camp
Sellack, Lough Pool
Walterstone, Carpenters Arms
Weobley, Olde Salutation
Woolhope, Butchers Arms

Hertfordshire
Aldbury, Greyhound
Ashwell, Bushel & Strike
Westmill, Sword in Hand

Isle of Wight
Chale, Clarendon (Wight Mouse)

Kent
Boughton Aluph, Flying Horse
Brookland, Woolpack

Chiddingstone, Castle
Groombridge, Crown
Newnham, George
Selling, Rose & Crown
Toys Hill, Fox & Hounds

Lancashire (inc Greater Manchester, Merseyside)
Blackstone Edge, White House
Conder Green, Stork
Downham, Assheton Arms
Fence, Forest
Newton, Parkers Arms
Whitewell, Inn at Whitewell

Leicestershire
Exton, Fox & Hounds
Glooston, Old Barn
Hallaton, Bewicke Arms
Upper Hambleton, Finches Arms

Lincolnshire
Aswarby, Tally Ho

Norfolk
Blakeney, White Horse
Blickling, Buckinghamshire Arms
Burnham Market, Hoste Arms
Great Bircham, Kings Head
Heydon, Earle Arms
Horsey, Nelson Head
Thornham, Lifeboat
Woodbastwick, Fur & Feather

Northamptonshire
Chapel Brampton, Brampton Halt
Harringworth, White Swan

Northumberland, Durham, Tyneside & Teeside
Allenheads, Allenheads
Bamburgh, Lord Crewe Arms
Blanchland, Lord Crewe Arms
Craster, Jolly Fisherman
Diptonmill, Dipton Mill
Etal, Black Bull
Great Whittington, Queens Head
Haltwhistle, Milecastle
Haltwhistle, Wallace Arms
Romaldkirk, Rose & Crown
Stannersburn, Pheasant

Nottinghamshire
Laxton, Dovecote

Oxfordshire
Ardington, Boars Head
Burford, Mermaid
Chalgrove, Red Lion
Checkendon, Black Horse
Chinnor, Sir Charles Napier
Kelmscot, Plough
Maidensgrove, Five Horseshoes
Oxford, Kings Arms
Oxford, Turf Tavern
Shenington, Bell
Shipton-under-Wychwood, Shaven Crown

Shropshire
Bridges, Horseshoe
Cardington, Royal Oak
Llanfair Waterdine, Red Lion
Wenlock Edge, Wenlock Edge

Somerset
Appley, Globe
Blagdon, New Inn
Combe Hay, Wheatsheaf
Cranmore, Strode Arms
Luxborough, Royal Oak
Stogumber, White Horse
Wambrook, Cotley
Winsford, Royal Oak

Staffordshire
Alstonefield, George

Suffolk
Dennington, Queens Head
Dunwich, Ship
Lavenham, Angel
Levington, Ship
Snape, Plough & Sail

Surrey
Blackbrook, Plough
Chilworth, Villagers
Cobham, Cricketers
Dunsfold, Sun
Englefield Green, Fox & Hounds
Friday Street, Stephan Langton
Mickleham, King William IV
Reigate Heath, Skimmington Castle
Sutton, Volunteer

Sussex
Amberley, Black Horse
Barcombe, Anchor
Billingshurst, Blue Ship
Brownbread Street, Ash Tree
Burpham, George & Dragon
Burwash, Bell
East Dean, Tiger
Fletching, Griffin
Heathfield, Star
Kirdford, Half Moon
Lurgashall, Noahs Ark
Mayfield, Middle House
Seaford, Golden Galleon
West Hoathly, Cat
Wineham, Royal Oak

Warwickshire
Edge Hill, Castle
Himley, Crooked House
Warmington, Plough

Wiltshire
Alvediston, Crown
Axford, Red Lion
Bradford-on-Avon, Cross Guns
Ebbesbourne Wake, Horseshoe

Yorkshire
Appletreewick, Craven Arms
Askrigg, Kings Arms
Beck Hole, Birch Hall
Blakey Ridge, Lion
Bradfield, Strines
Buckden, Buck

Burnsall, Red Lion
Byland Abbey, Abbey
Cray, White Lion
East Witton, Blue Lion
Heath, Kings Arms
Hubberholme, George
Levisham, Horseshoe
Linton in Craven, Fountaine
Litton, Queens Arms
Lund, Wellington
Masham, Kings Head
Meltham, Will's o' Nat's
Middleham, Black Swan
Muker, Farmers Arms
Ramsgill, Yorke Arms
Ripley, Boars Head
Robin Hoods Bay, Laurel
Rosedale Abbey, Milburn Arms
Shelley, Three Acres
Starbotton, Fox & Hounds
Terrington, Bay Horse
Thornton Watlass, Buck
Wath-in-Nidderdale, Sportsmans Arms
Widdop, Pack Horse

London, Central
London EC 1, Olde Mitre

London, North
London NW 3, Spaniards

London, South
London SE 1, Horniman
London SE21, Crown & Greyhound
London SW 4, Windmill

Scotland
Applecross, Applecross
Arduaine, Loch Melfort
Brig o Turk, Byre
Clachan Seil, Tigh an Truish
Crinan, Crinan
Haddington, Waterside
Kilberry, Kilberry
Kilmahog, Lade
Mountbenger, Gordon Arms
Pitlochry, Killiecrankie
Sheriffmuir, Sheriffmuir
Tushielaw, Tushielaw

Wales
Abergorlech, Black Lion
Aberystwyth, Halfway
Bosherston, St Govans
Capel Curig, Bryn Tyrch
Carew, Carew
Crickhowell, Nantyffin Cider Mill
Llanbedr-y-Cennin, Olde Bull
Llanberis, Pen-y-Gwryd
Llangedwyn, Green
Maentwrog, Grapes
Penmaenpool, George III
Red Wharf Bay, Ship
Talyllyn, Tynycornel

Channel Islands
St Brelade, Old Portelet
St Brelade, Old Smugglers
St John, Les Fontaines

PUBS WITH GOOD VIEWS

These pubs are listed for their particularly good views, either from inside or from a garden or terrace. Waterside pubs are listed again here only if their view is exceptional in its own right – not just a straightforward sea view, for example.

Berkshire
Chieveley, Blue Boar

Buckinghamshire
Brill, Pheasant

Cheshire
Higher Burwardsley, Pheasant
Langley, Hanging Gate
Langley, Leathers Smithy
Overton, Ring o' Bells

Cornwall
Cremyll, Edgcumbe Arms
Polruan, Lugger
Ruan Lanihorne, Kings Head
St Agnes, Turks Head

Cumbria
Braithwaite, Coledale
Cartmel Fell, Masons Arms
Hawkshead, Drunken Duck
Langdale, Old Dungeon Ghyll
Loweswater, Kirkstile
Mungrisdale, Mill
Troutbeck, Queens Head
Ulverston, Bay Horse

Derbyshire
Over Haddon, Lathkil

Devon
Instow, Boathouse
Postbridge, Warren House

Dorset
Kingston, Scott Arms
West Bexington, Manor
Worth Matravers, Square & Compass

Gloucestershire
Amberley, Black Horse
Cranham, Black Horse
Gretton, Royal Oak
Kilkenny, Kilkeney
Sheepscombe, Butchers Arms
Stanton, Mount

Hampshire
Beauworth, Milbury's
Owslebury, Ship

Hereford & Worcester
Pensax, Bell
Ruckhall, Ancient Camp
Wyre Piddle, Anchor

Isle of Wight
Bembridge, Crab & Lobster
Ventnor, Spyglass

Kent
Linton, Bull
Penshurst, Spotted Dog
Tunbridge Wells, Beacon

Ulcombe, Pepper Box

Lancashire (inc Greater Manchester, Merseyside)
Blackstone Edge, White House
Darwen, Old Rosins

Northumberland, Durham, Tyneside & Teeside
Haltwhistle, Wallace Arms
Seahouses, Olde Ship
Thropton, Three Wheat Heads

Shropshire
Cressage, Cholmondeley Riverside

Somerset
Blagdon, New Inn

Suffolk
Erwarton, Queens Head
Hundon, Plough
Levington, Ship

Sussex
Amberley, Sportsmans
Byworth, Black Horse
Elsted, Three Horseshoes
Fletching, Griffin
Icklesham, Queens Head
Rye, Ypres Castle

Wiltshire
Axford, Red Lion
Box, Quarrymans Arms

Yorkshire
Appletreewick, Craven Arms
Blakey Ridge, Lion
Bradfield, Strines
Kirkham, Stone Trough
Litton, Queens Arms
Meltham, Will's o' Nat's
Shelley, Three Acres
Whitby, Duke of York

London, South
London SE 1, Anchor

Scotland
Applecross, Applecross
Ardvasar, Ardvasar
Arrochar, Village
Crinan, Crinan
Cromarty, Royal
Edinburgh, Starbank
Glenelg, Glenelg
Isle Ornsay, Tigh Osda Eilean Iarmain
Kilberry, Kilberry
Pitlochry, Killiecrankie
Sheriffmuir, Sheriffmuir
Shieldaig, Tigh an Eilean
Tushielaw, Tushielaw
Weem, Ailean Chraggan

Wales
Aberdovey, Penhelig Arms
Aberystwyth, Halfway
Bodfari, Dinorben Arms
Capel Curig, Bryn Tyrch
Halkyn, Britannia
Llanbedr-y-Cennin, Olde Bull
Llanberis, Pen-y-Gwryd
Llanferres, Druid
Llangynwyd, Old House
Llannefydd, Hawk & Buckle
Penmaenpool, George III
Talyllyn, Tynycornel
Tyn y Groes, Groes

Channel Islands
St Aubin, Old Court House

PUBS IN INTERESTING BUILDINGS
Pubs and inns are listed here for the particular interest of their building – something really out of the ordinary to look at, or occasionally a building that has an outstandingly interesting historical background.

Buckinghamshire
Forty Green, Royal Standard of England

Cornwall
Morwenstow, Bush

Derbyshire
Buxton, Bull i'th' Thorn

Devon
Dartmouth, Cherub
Harberton, Church House
Rattery, Church House
Sourton, Highwayman
South Zeal, Oxenham Arms

Hampshire
Beauworth, Milbury's

Hereford & Worcester
Bretforton, Fleece

Lancashire (inc Greater Manchester, Merseyside)
Garstang, Th'Owd Tithebarn
Liverpool, Philharmonic Dining Rooms

Lincolnshire
Stamford, George of Stamford

Northumberland, Durham, Tyneside & Teeside
Blanchland, Lord Crewe Arms

Nottinghamshire
Nottingham, Olde Trip to Jerusalem

Oxfordshire
Banbury, Reindeer
Fyfield, White Hart

Suffolk
Lavenham, Swan

Sussex
Alfriston, Star
Rye, Mermaid

Warwickshire
Himley, Crooked House

Wiltshire
Salisbury, Haunch of Venison

Yorkshire
Hull, Olde White Harte

London, Central
London EC 4, Black Friar
London WC 1, Cittie of Yorke

London, South
London SE 1, George
London SE 5, Phoenix & Firkin

Scotland
Edinburgh, Guildford Arms

PUBS THAT BREW THEIR OWN BEER

The pubs listed here brew their own brew on the premises; many others not listed have beers brewed for them specially, sometimes to an individual recipe (but by a separate brewer). We mention these in the text.

Berkshire
Frilsham, Pot Kiln

Cornwall
Helston, Blue Anchor

Cumbria
Cartmel Fell, Masons Arms
Cockermouth, Bitter End
Coniston, Black Bull
Dent, Sun
Hawkshead, Drunken Duck

Derbyshire
Derby, Brunswick
Melbourne, John Thompson

Devon
Branscombe, Fountain Head
Hatherleigh, Tally Ho
Holbeton, Mildmay Colours
Horsebridge, Royal
Newton St Cyres, Beer Engine

Gloucestershire
Apperley, Farmers Arms
Sapperton, Daneway

Hampshire
Cheriton, Flower Pots
Southsea, Wine Vaults

Hereford & Worcester
Aymestrey, Riverside
Knightwick, Talbot

Lancashire (inc Greater Manchester, Merseyside)
Manchester, Lass o' Gowrie
Manchester, Marble Arch

Leicestershire
Somerby, Old Brewery

Norfolk
Woodbastwick, Fur & Feather

Nottinghamshire
Nottingham, Fellows Morton & Clayton

Shropshire
Bishops Castle, Three Tuns
Munslow, Crown
Wistanstow, Plough

Staffordshire
Burton on Trent, Burton Bridge
Eccleshall, St George
Shraleybrook, Rising Sun

Suffolk
Earl Soham, Victoria

Surrey
Coldharbour, Plough

Sussex
Oving, Gribble
Seaford, Golden Galleon

Warwickshire
Birmingham, Fiddle & Bone
Brierley Hill, Vine
Shustoke, Griffin

Yorkshire
Cropton, New Inn
Hull, Minerva
Linthwaite, Sair
Sheffield, Fat Cat
Snaith, Brewers Arms

London, Central
London SW 1, Orange Brewery

London, South
London SE 5, Phoenix & Firkin

London, West
London SW10, Ferret & Firkin

Scotland
Pitlochry, Moulin

Channel Islands
St Helier, Tipsy Toad Town House
St Peter, Star & Tipsy Toad

OPEN ALL DAY (AT LEAST IN SUMMER)

We list here all the pubs that have told us they plan to stay open all day, even if it's only on a Saturday. We've included the few pubs which close just for half an hour to an hour, and the many more, chiefly in holiday areas, which open all day only in summer. The individual entries for the pubs themselves show the actual details. A few pubs in England and Wales, allowed to stay open only in the last two or three years, are still changing their opening hours – let us know if you find anything different.

Berkshire
East Ilsley, Crown & Horns
Hare Hatch, Queen Victoria
Lambourn, Hare & Hounds
Sonning, Bull
West Ilsley, Harrow

Buckinghamshire
Bledlow, Lions of Bledlow
Brill, Pheasant
Cheddington, Old Swan
Easington, Mole & Chicken
Great Missenden, George
Skirmett, Frog
Wheeler End, Chequers
Wooburn Common, Chequers

Cambridgeshire
Cambridge, Anchor
Cambridge, Eagle
Etton, Golden Pheasant
Godmanchester, Black Bull
Holywell, Old Ferry Boat
Huntingdon, Old Bridge
Peterborough, Charters
Wansford, Haycock

Cheshire
Aldford, Grosvenor Arms
Barthomley, White Lion
Broxton, Egerton Arms
Bunbury, Dysart Arms
Chester, Old Harkers Arms
Cotebrook, Fox & Barrel
Higher Burwardsley, Pheasant
Langley, Hanging Gate
Langley, Leathers Smithy
Macclesfield, Sutton Hall
Marbury, Swan
Nantwich, Crown
Plumley, Smoker
Tarporley, Rising Sun
Wettenhall, Boot & Slipper
Whitegate, Plough
Wrenbury, Dusty Miller

Cornwall
Bodinnick, Old Ferry
Boscastle, Cobweb
Chapel Amble, Maltsters Arms
Cremyll, Edgcumbe Arms
Edmonton, Quarryman
Falmouth, Quayside Inn & Old Ale House
Helston, Blue Anchor
Lamorna, Lamorna Wink
Lostwithiel, Royal Oak
Mithian, Miners Arms
Mousehole, Ship
Mylor Bridge, Pandora
Pelynt, Jubilee
Polperro, Old Mill House
Polruan, Lugger
Port Isaac, Golden Lion
Port Isaac, Port Gaverne
Porthleven, Ship
St Agnes, Turks Head
St Just in Penwith, Star
St Keverne, White Hart
St Mawes, Victory
Trebarwith, Port William
Tresco, New Inn
Truro, Old Ale House

Cumbria
Ambleside, Golden Rule
Askham, Punch Bowl
Bowland Bridge, Hare & Hounds
Bowness on Windermere, Hole in t' Wall
Braithwaite, Coledale
Brampton, New Inn
Broughton in Furness, Blacksmiths Arms
Buttermere, Bridge
Caldbeck, Oddfellows
Cartmel, Cavendish Arms
Cartmel Fell, Masons Arms
Chapel Stile, Wainwrights
Coniston, Black Bull
Crosthwaite, Punch Bowl
Dent, Sun
Elterwater, Britannia
Eskdale Green, Bower House
Grasmere, Travellers Rest
Heversham, Blue Bell
Keswick, Dog & Gun
Kirkby Lonsdale, Snooty Fox
Kirkby Lonsdale, Sun
Langdale, Old Dungeon Ghyll
Little Langdale, Three Shires
Loweswater, Kirkstile
Mungrisdale, Mill
Penrith, Agricultural
Seathwaite, Newfield
Sedbergh, Dalesman
Threlkeld, Salutation
Tirril, Queens Head
Troutbeck, Mortal Man
Troutbeck, Queens Head
Ulverston, Bay Horse

Derbyshire
Ashbourne, Smiths Tavern
Beeley, Devonshire Arms
Buxton, Old Sun
Buxworth, Navigation
Castleton, Castle
Derby, Alexandra
Derby, Brunswick
Derby, Olde Dolphin
Fenny Bentley, Coach & Horses
Froggatt Edge, Chequers
Hardwick Hall, Hardwick
Hope, Cheshire Cheese
Ladybower Reservoir, Yorkshire Bridge
Over Haddon, Lathkil
Wardlow, Three Stags Heads
Whittington Moor, Derby Tup

Devon
Abbotskerswell, Court Farm

Beer, Anchor
Branscombe, Masons Arms
Cockwood, Anchor
Dartmouth, Cherub
Dartmouth, Royal Castle
Exeter, Double Locks
Exeter, Imperial
Exeter, White Hart
Exminster, Turf
Haytor Vale, Rock
Iddesleigh, Duke of York
Lustleigh, Cleave
Newton St Cyres, Beer Engine
Plymouth, China House
Postbridge, Warren House
Rackenford, Stag
Ringmore, Journeys End
Stoke Gabriel, Church House
Topsham, Passage House
Torcross, Start Bay
Torrington, Black Horse
Tuckenhay, Maltsters Arms
Ugborough, Anchor
Wonson, Northmore Arms
Woodland, Rising Sun

Dorset
Abbotsbury, Ilchester Arms
Bridport, George
Chideock, Anchor
Christchurch, Fishermans Haunt
Corfe Castle, Greyhound
Dorchester, Kings Arms
East Chaldon, Sailors Return
Kingston, Scott Arms
Loders, Loders Arms
Lyme Regis, Pilot Boat
Norden Heath, Halfway
Osmington Mills, Smugglers
Tarrant Monkton, Langton Arms
West Bexington, Manor
Worth Matravers, Square & Compass

Essex
Burnham-on-Crouch, White Harte
Dedham, Marlborough Head
Heybridge Basin, Jolly Sailor
High Ongar, Wheatsheaf
North Fambridge, Ferry Boat
Saffron Walden, Eight Bells
Stock, Hoop
Stow Maries, Prince of Wales

Gloucestershire
Amberley, Black Horse
Ampney Crucis, Crown of Crucis
Awre, Red Hart
Bisley, Bear
Blockley, Crown
Chedworth, Seven Tuns
Chipping Campden, Eight Bells
Chipping Campden, Noel Arms
Clearwell, Wyndham Arms
Coln St Aldwyns, New Inn
Ewen, Wild Duck
Ford, Plough
Great Barrington, Fox
Guiting Power, Hollow Bottom
Nailsworth, Egypt Mill
North Woodchester, Royal Oak
Old Sodbury, Dog
Oldbury-on-Severn, Anchor
Redbrook, Boat
Sheepscombe, Butchers Arms
South Cerney, Eliot Arms
Stanton, Mount
Tetbury, Gumstool
Withington, Mill

Hampshire
Bentworth, Sun
Boldre, Red Lion
Bursledon, Jolly Sailor
Droxford, White Horse
Froyle, Hen & Chicken
Langstone, Royal Oak
Locks Heath, Jolly Farmer
North Gorley, Royal Oak
Owslebury, Ship
Portsmouth, Still & West
Rotherwick, Coach & Horses
Sopley, Woolpack
Southsea, Wine Vaults
Titchfield, Fishermans Rest
Well, Chequers
Wherwell, Mayfly
Winchester, Wykeham Arms

Hereford & Worcester
Bredon, Fox & Hounds
Bretforton, Fleece
Kidderminster, King & Castle
Knightwick, Talbot
Ledbury, Feathers
Lugwardine, Crown & Anchor
Pensax, Bell
Walterstone, Carpenters Arms
Weobley, Olde Salutation

Hertfordshire
Aldbury, Greyhound
Ashwell, Bushel & Strike
Ashwell, Three Tuns
Ayot St Lawrence, Brocket Arms
Berkhamsted, Boat
Knebworth, Lytton Arms
Walkern, White Lion
Watton at Stone, George & Dragon

Isle of Wight
Arreton, White Lion
Chale, Clarendon (Wight Mouse)
Cowes, Folly
Rookley, Chequers
Shorwell, Crown
Ventnor, Spyglass
Yarmouth, Wheatsheaf

Kent
Barfrestone, Yew Tree
Bough Beech, Wheatsheaf
Boughton Aluph, Flying Horse
Chiddingstone, Castle
Deal, Kings Head
Groombridge, Crown
Iden Green, Woodcock
Ightham Common, Harrow
Langton Green, Hare
Luddesdown, Cock
Oare, Shipwrights Arms
Ringlestone, Ringlestone
Tunbridge Wells, Beacon
Tunbridge Wells, Sankeys
Whitstable, Pearsons Crab & Oyster House

Lancashire (inc Greater Manchester, Merseyside)
Bispham Green, Eagle & Child
Chipping, Dog & Partridge
Conder Green, Stork
Croston, Black Horse
Darwen, Old Rosins
Fence, Forest
Garstang, Th'Owd Tithebarn
Liverpool, Philharmonic Dining Rooms
Lytham, Taps
Manchester, Dukes 92
Manchester, Lass o' Gowrie
Manchester, Marble Arch
Manchester, Mark Addy
Manchester, Royal Oak
Newton, Parkers Arms
Raby, Wheatsheaf
Ribchester, White Bull
Stalybridge, Station Buffet
Yealand Conyers, New Inn

Leicestershire
Empingham, White Horse
Glaston, Monckton Arms
Loughborough, Swan in the Rushes
Redmile, Peacock
Somerby, Old Brewery
Upper Hambleton, Finches Arms
Wing, Kings Arms

Lincolnshire
Coleby, Bell
Grantham, Beehive
Lincoln, Victoria
Lincoln, Wig & Mitre
Stamford, George of Stamford

Norfolk
Bawburgh, Kings Head
Blakeney, Kings Arms
Burnham Market, Hoste Arms
Fakenham, Wensum Lodge
Hunworth, Blue Bell
Kings Lynn, Tudor Rose
Larling, Angel
Mundford, Crown
Norwich, Adam & Eve
Norwich, Fat Cat
Reedham, Ferry
Sculthorpe, Sculthorpe Mill
Snettisham, Rose & Crown
Swanton Morley, Darbys
Thornham, Lifeboat
Tivetshall St Mary, Old Ram
Winterton-on-Sea, Fishermans Return

Northamptonshire
Ashby St Ledgers, Olde Coach House
Badby, Windmill
Chacombe, George & Dragon
Great Brington, Fox & Hounds
Oundle, Ship

Northumberland, Durham, Tyneside & Teeside
Allendale, Kings Head
Craster, Jolly Fisherman
Etal, Black Bull
Haltwhistle, Wallace Arms
New York, Shiremoor House Farm
Newcastle upon Tyne, Crown Posada
Seaton Sluice, Waterford Arms
Thropton, Three Wheat Heads

Nottinghamshire
Beeston, Victoria
Caunton, Caunton Beck
Kimberley, Nelson & Railway
Normanton on Trent, Square & Compass
Nottingham, Fellows Morton & Clayton
Nottingham, Lincolnshire Poacher
Nottingham, Olde Trip to Jerusalem

Oxfordshire
Bampton, Romany
Banbury, Reindeer
Bloxham, Elephant & Castle
Burford, Mermaid
Clifton Hampden, Plough
Cuddesdon, Bat & Ball
Cuxham, Half Moon
Dorchester, George
Duns Tew, White Horse
East Hendred, Wheatsheaf
Exlade Street, Highwayman
Finstock, Plough
Kelmscot, Plough
Oxford, Kings Arms
Oxford, Turf Tavern
Shipton-under-Wychwood, Shaven Crown
Stanton St John, Talk House
Wytham, White Hart

Shropshire
Bishops Castle, Three Tuns
Cleobury Mortimer, Kings Arms
Cressage, Cholmondeley Riverside

Nesscliffe, Old Three Pigeons
Shrewsbury, Armoury

Somerset
Ashcott, Ashcott
Bath, Old Green Tree
Beckington, Woolpack
Bristol, Highbury Vaults
Churchill, Crown
Clapton in Gordano, Black Horse
Dunster, Luttrell Arms
Huish Episcopi, Rose & Crown
Kelston, Old Crown
Rudge, Full Moon
South Stoke, Pack Horse
Stanton Wick, Carpenters Arms

Staffordshire
Acton Trussell, Moat House
Alstonefield, George
Cresswell, Izaak Walton
Eccleshall, St George
Onecote, Jervis Arms
Salt, Holly Bush
Shraleybrook, Rising Sun

Suffolk
Butley, Oyster
Chelmondiston, Butt & Oyster
Chillesford, Froize
Cotton, Trowel & Hammer
Lavenham, Angel
Wangford, Angel

Surrey
Betchworth, Dolphin
Chilworth, Villagers
Coldharbour, Plough
Effingham, Sir Douglas Haig
Farncombe, Ram
Friday Street, Stephan Langton
Gomshall, Compasses
Hascombe, White Horse
Leigh, Plough
Pirbright, Royal Oak
Reigate Heath, Skimmington Castle
Sutton, Volunteer
Warlingham, White Lion
Wotton, Wotton Hatch

Sussex
Alfriston, Star
Barcombe, Anchor
Berwick, Cricketers Arms
Burwash, Bell
Coolham, George & Dragon
East Dean, Tiger
Firle, Ram
Hartfield, Anchor
Horsham, Black Jug
Icklesham, Queens Head
Kingston near Lewes, Juggs
Lewes, Snowdrop
Mayfield, Middle House
Oving, Gribble
Pett, Two Sawyers
Playden, Peace & Plenty
Punnetts Town, Three Cups
Rye, Mermaid
Rye, Ypres Castle
Seaford, Golden Galleon

Warwickshire
Berkswell, Bear
Brierley Hill, Vine
Coventry, Old Windmill
Himley, Crooked House
Lapworth, Navigation
Lowsonford, Fleur de Lys

Wiltshire
Barford St Martin, Barford
Box, Quarrymans Arms
Bradford-on-Avon, Cross Guns
Brinkworth, Three Crowns
Devizes, Bear
Hindon, Lamb
Lacock, Red Lion
Marlborough, Sun
Norton, Vine Tree
Salisbury, Haunch of Venison
Salisbury, New Inn
Sherston, Rattlebone

Yorkshire
Allerthorpe, Plough
Asenby, Crab & Lobster
Bardsey, Bingley Arms
Beck Hole, Birch Hall
Beverley, White Horse
Blakey Ridge, Lion
Boroughbridge, Black Bull
Bradfield, Strines
Brandesburton, Dacre Arms
Buckden, Buck
Burnsall, Red Lion
Cracoe, Devonshire Arms
Cray, White Lion
Cropton, New Inn
East Marton, Cross Keys
East Witton, Blue Lion
Egton Bridge, Horse Shoe
Elslack, Tempest Arms
Ferrensby, General Tarleton
Great Ouseburn, Crown
Harden, Malt Shovel
Heath, Kings Arms
Heckmondwike, Old Hall
Helmsley, Feathers
Hubberholme, George
Hull, Minerva
Hull, Olde White Harte
Ledsham, Chequers
Leeds, Whitelocks
Linthwaite, Sair
Linton, Windmill
Linton in Craven, Fountaine
Low Catton, Gold Cup
Masham, Kings Head
Masham, White Bear
Muker, Farmers Arms
Pickhill, Nags Head
Pool, White Hart
Ramsgill, Yorke Arms
Ripley, Boars Head
Ripponden, Old Bridge
Robin Hoods Bay, Laurel
Settle, Golden Lion
Sheffield, New Barrack
Thorgansby, Jefferson Arms
Thornton Watlass, Buck
Whitby, Duke of York
Widdop, Pack Horse
York, Black Swan
York, Olde Starre

York, Spread Eagle
York, Tap & Spile

London, Central
London, Bishops Finger
London EC 1, Eagle
London EC 1, Olde Mitre
London EC 4, Black Friar
London EC 4, Old Bank of England
London EC 4, Olde Cheshire Cheese
London EC1, Jerusalem Tavern
London SW 1, Albert
London SW 1, Grenadier
London SW 1, Lord Moon of the Mall
London SW 1, Nags Head
London SW 1, Orange Brewery
London SW 1, Star
London SW 1, Westminster Arms
London W 1, Argyll Arms
London W 1, Dog & Duck
London W 1, Grapes
London W 1, Old Coffee House
London W 1, Red Lion
London WC 1, Cittie of Yorke
London WC 1, Lamb
London WC 1, Moon Under Water
London WC 1, Museum Tavern
London WC 1, Princess Louise
London WC 2, Lamb & Flag
London WC 2, Seven Stars

London, North
London N 1, Compton Arms
London N 1, Waterside
London NW 1, Chapel
London NW 3, Flask
London NW 3, Olde White Bear
London NW 3, Spaniards

London, South
London SE 1, Anchor
London SE 1, Fire Station
London SE 1, George
London SE 1, Horniman
London SE 1, Market Porter
London SE 5, Phoenix & Firkin
London SE10, Cutty Sark
London SE21, Crown & Greyhound
London SW 4, Windmill
London SW13, Bulls Head
London SW18, Alma
London SW18, Ship
Richmond, White Cross

London, West
London SW 6, White Horse
London SW10, Ferret & Firkin
London W 4, Bulls Head
London W 6, Anglesea Arms
London W 6, Dove
London W 8, Windsor Castle
London W11, Ladbroke Arms
Twickenham, White Swan

London, East
London E 1, Prospect of Whitby
London E 1, Town of Ramsgate

Scotland
Aberdeen, Prince of Wales
Applecross, Applecross
Ardfern, Galley of Lorne
Arduaine, Loch Melfort
Ardvasar, Ardvasar
Arrochar, Village
Brig o Turk, Byre
Broughty Ferry, Fishermans Tavern
Carbost, Old Inn
Cawdor, Cawdor Tavern
Clachan Seil, Tigh an Truish
Crinan, Crinan
Edinburgh, Abbotsford
Edinburgh, Bannermans Bar
Edinburgh, Bow Bar
Edinburgh, Guildford Arms
Edinburgh, Kays Bar
Edinburgh, Ship on the Shore
Edinburgh, Starbank
Elie, Ship
Fort Augustus, Lock
Gifford, Tweeddale Arms
Glasgow, Auctioneers
Glasgow, Babbity Bowster
Glasgow, Blackfriars
Glasgow, Counting House
Glendevon, Tormaukin
Haddington, Waterside
Innerleithen, Traquair Arms
Inveraray, George
Inverarnan, Inverarnan
Isle Ornsay, Tigh Osda Eilean Iarmain
Isle of Whithorn, Steam Packet
Kelso, Queens Head
Kilmahog, Lade
Kippen, Cross Keys
Kirkton of Glenisla, Glenisla
Linlithgow, Four Marys
Lybster, Portland Arms
Mountbenger, Gordon Arms
Plockton, Plockton
Portpatrick, Crown
Sheriffmuir, Sheriffmuir
Shieldaig, Tigh an Eilean
St Monans, Cabin
Swinton, Wheatsheaf
Tayvallich, Tayvallich
Thornhill, Lion & Unicorn
Ullapool, Ceilidh Place
Ullapool, Morefield Motel
Weem, Ailean Chraggan

Wales
Beaumaris, Olde Bulls Head
Bodfari, Dinorben Arms
Bosherston, St Govans
Capel Curig, Bryn Tyrch
Carew, Carew
Cilgerran, Pendre
Colwyn Bay, Mountain View
Crickhowell, White Hart
East Aberthaw, Blue Anchor
Graianrhyd, Rose & Crown
Gresford, Pant-yr-Ochain
Halkyn, Britannia
Hay on Wye, Kilverts
Hay on Wye, Old Black Lion
Llanberis, Pen-y-Gwryd
Llandrindod Wells, Llanerch
Llanferres, Druid
Llangynidr, Coach & Horses
Llangynwyd, Old House
Maentwrog, Grapes
Monknash, Plough & Harrow
Penmaenpool, George III
Pontypool, Open Hearth
Porthmadog, Ship
Presteigne, Radnorshire Arms
Raglan, Clytha Arms
Red Wharf Bay, Ship
St Hilary, Bush
Stackpole, Armstrong Arms
Talybont-on-Usk, Star

Channel Islands
Greve de Lecq, Moulin de Lecq
Kings Mills, Fleur du Jardin
Rozel, Rozel Bay
St Aubin, Old Court House
St Brelade, Old Portelet
St Brelade, Old Smugglers
St Helier, Admiral
St Helier, Tipsy Toad Town House
St John, Les Fontaines
St Peter, Star & Tipsy Toad

NO SMOKING AREAS
So many more pubs are now making some provision for the majority of their customers – that's to say non-smokers – that we have now found it is worth listing all the pubs which have told us they do set aside at least some part of the pub as a no-smoking area. Look at the individual entries for the pubs themselves to see just what they do: provision is much more generous in some pubs than in others.

Bedfordshire
Houghton Conquest, Knife & Cleaver
Keysoe, Chequers

Berkshire
Binfield, Stag & Hounds
Boxford, Bell
Bray, Fish
East Ilsley, Crown & Horns
Frilsham, Pot Kiln
Hamstead Marshall, White Hart
Hare Hatch, Queen Victoria
Lambourn, Hare & Hounds
Sonning, Bull
Waltham St Lawrence, Bell
West Ilsley, Harrow
Yattendon, Royal Oak

Buckinghamshire
Amersham, Queens Head
Bledlow, Lions of Bledlow
Bolter End, Peacock
Cheddington, Old Swan
Easington, Mole & Chicken
Fawley, Walnut Tree
Forty Green, Royal Standard of England
Great Missenden, George
Hambleden, Stag & Huntsman
Ibstone, Fox
Little Hampden, Rising Sun
Long Crendon, Angel
Prestwood, Polecat
Skirmett, Frog
Waddesdon, Five Arrows
West Wycombe, George & Dragon

Cambridgeshire
Barnack, Millstone
Bythorn, White Hart
Cambridge, Anchor
Cambridge, Eagle
Cambridge, Free Press
Cambridge, Live & Let Live
Elsworth, George & Dragon
Etton, Golden Pheasant
Fowlmere, Chequers
Godmanchester, Black Bull
Gorefield, Woodmans Cottage
Heydon, King William IV
Hinxton, Red Lion
Holywell, Old Ferry Boat
Horningsea, Plough & Fleece
Huntingdon, Old Bridge
Keyston, Pheasant
Stilton, Bell
Sutton Gault, Anchor
Swavesey, Trinity Foot
Wansford, Haycock
Woodditton, Three Blackbirds

Cheshire
Bunbury, Dysart Arms
Cotebrook, Fox & Barrel
Higher Burwardsley, Pheasant
Langley, Hanging Gate
Langley, Leathers Smithy
Marbury, Swan

Peover Heath, Dog
Plumley, Smoker
Pott Shrigley, Cheshire Hunt
Weston, White Lion
Wrenbury, Dusty Miller

Cornwall
Bodinnick, Old Ferry
Boscastle, Cobweb
Chapel Amble, Maltsters Arms
Constantine, Trengilly Wartha
Cremyll, Edgcumbe Arms
Edmonton, Quarryman
Egloshayle, Earl of St Vincent
Helston, Halzephron
Lanlivery, Crown
Mithian, Miners Arms
Mylor Bridge, Pandora
Polruan, Lugger
Port Isaac, Port Gaverne
Ruan Lanihorne, Kings Head
St Agnes, Turks Head
St Breward, Old Inn
St Just in Penwith, Star
St Mawes, Victory
St Mawgan, Falcon
Trebarwith, Port William
Treburley, Springer Spaniel
Tresco, New Inn

Cumbria
Ambleside, Golden Rule
Appleby, Royal Oak
Armathwaite, Dukes Head
Barbon, Barbon
Bassenthwaite, Pheasant
Beetham, Wheatsheaf
Boot, Burnmoor
Braithwaite, Coledale
Broughton in Furness, Blacksmiths Arms
Buttermere, Bridge
Caldbeck, Oddfellows
Cartmel, Cavendish Arms
Casterton, Pheasant
Chapel Stile, Wainwrights
Coniston, Black Bull
Crosthwaite, Punch Bowl
Dent, Sun
Elterwater, Britannia
Eskdale Green, Bower House
Garrigill, George & Dragon
Grasmere, Travellers Rest
Hawkshead, Drunken Duck
Heversham, Blue Bell
Ings, Watermill
Kirkby Lonsdale, Snooty Fox
Kirkby Lonsdale, Sun
Lanercost, Abbey Bridge
Little Langdale, Three Shires
Melmerby, Shepherds
Mungrisdale, Mill
Scales, White Horse
Seathwaite, Newfield
Sedbergh, Dalesman
Tirril, Queens Head
Troutbeck, Mortal Man
Troutbeck, Queens Head
Ulverston, Bay Horse
Yanwath, Gate

Derbyshire
Barlow, Trout
Beeley, Devonshire Arms
Birchover, Druid
Brassington, Olde Gate
Castleton, Castle
Derby, Brunswick
Derby, Olde Dolphin
Fenny Bentley, Coach & Horses
Froggatt Edge, Chequers
Hardwick Hall, Hardwick
Hope, Cheshire Cheese
Kirk Ireton, Barley Mow
Ladybower Reservoir, Yorkshire Bridge
Melbourne, John Thompson
Over Haddon, Lathkil
Wardlow, Three Stags Heads
Whittington Moor, Derby Tup
Woolley Moor, White Horse

Devon
Ashprington, Durant Arms
Axmouth, Harbour
Beer, Anchor
Berrynarbor, Olde Globe
Blackawton, Normandy Arms
Branscombe, Fountain Head
Branscombe, Masons Arms
Chardstock, George
Chittlehamholt, Exeter
Clyst Hydon, Five Bells
Cockwood, Anchor
Coleford, New Inn
Dartington, Cott
Dartmouth, Cherub
Dartmouth, Royal Castle
Doddiscombsleigh, Nobody
Dolton, Union
Drewsteignton, Drewe Arms
Dunsford, Royal Oak
Exeter, Imperial
Exeter, White Hart
Exminster, Turf
Harberton, Church House
Hatherleigh, Tally Ho
Haytor Vale, Rock
Holbeton, Mildmay Colours
Horsebridge, Royal
Kingskerswell, Bickley Mill
Kingston, Dolphin
Knowstone, Masons Arms
Lustleigh, Cleave
Lydford, Castle
Marldon, Church House
Peter Tavy, Peter Tavy
Ringmore, Journeys End
Sidford, Blue Ball
Sourton, Highwayman
South Zeal, Oxenham Arms
Staverton, Sea Trout
Topsham, Passage House
Torcross, Start Bay
Ugborough, Anchor
Widecombe, Rugglestone

Woodland, Rising Sun

Dorset
Abbotsbury, Ilchester Arms
Askerswell, Spyway
Bridport, George
Burton Bradstock, Three Horseshoes
Chideock, Anchor
Christchurch, Fishermans Haunt
Church Knowle, New Inn
Colehill, Barley Mow
Corscombe, Fox
Cranborne, Fleur-de-Lys
Dorchester, Kings Arms
East Chaldon, Sailors Return
East Knighton, Countryman
East Morden, Cock & Bottle
Evershot, Acorn
Kingston, Scott Arms
Loders, Loders Arms
Lyme Regis, Pilot Boat
Marnhull, Blackmore Vale
Norden Heath, Halfway
Osmington Mills, Smugglers
Plush, Brace of Pheasants
Puncknowle, Crown
Shave Cross, Shave Cross
Tarrant Monkton, Langton Arms
West Bexington, Manor

Essex
Castle Hedingham, Bell
Chappel, Swan
Clavering, Cricketers
Dedham, Marlborough Head
Fyfield, Black Bull
Great Yeldham, White Hart
Hastingwood, Rainbow & Dove
Horndon-on-the-Hill, Bell
Rickling Green, Cricketers Arms
Toot Hill, Green Man
Wendens Ambo, Bell
Youngs End, Green Dragon

Gloucestershire
Almondsbury, Bowl
Amberley, Black Horse
Ampney Crucis, Crown of Crucis
Awre, Red Hart
Barnsley, Village Pub
Bisley, Bear
Blaisdon, Red Hart
Bledington, Kings Head
Brimpsfield, Golden Heart
Chipping Campden, Eight Bells
Chipping Campden, Noel Arms
Clearwell, Wyndham Arms
Cold Aston, Plough
Coln St Aldwyns, New Inn
Duntisbourne Abbots, Five Mile House
Great Rissington, Lamb
Greet, Harvest Home
Gretton, Royal Oak
Hyde, Ragged Cot
Kilkenny, Kilkeney
Kineton, Halfway House
Little Washbourne, Hobnails
Littleton upon Severn, White Hart
Meysey Hampton, Masons Arms
Minchinhampton, Old Lodge
Miserden, Carpenters Arms
Nailsworth, Egypt Mill
Naunton, Black Horse
North Woodchester, Royal Oak
Oakridge Lynch, Butchers Arms
Oddington, Horse & Groom
Old Sodbury, Dog
Oldbury-on-Severn, Anchor
Sapperton, Daneway
Sheepscombe, Butchers Arms
South Cerney, Eliot Arms
St Briavels, George
Stanton, Mount
Withington, Mill

Hampshire
Alresford, Globe
Boldre, Red Lion
Bramdean, Fox
Bursledon, Jolly Sailor
Chalton, Red Lion
Droxford, White Horse
East Tytherley, Star
Ibsley, Old Beams
Langstone, Royal Oak
Locks Heath, Jolly Farmer
Micheldever, Dever Arms
North Gorley, Royal Oak
Pilley, Fleur de Lys
Portsmouth, Still & West
Sopley, Woolpack
Sparsholt, Plough
Titchfield, Fishermans Rest
Wherwell, Mayfly
Wherwell, White Lion
Winchester, Wykeham Arms

Hereford & Worcester
Bredon, Fox & Hounds
Bretforton, Fleece
Brimfield, Roebuck
Dorstone, Pandy
Kempsey, Walter de Cantelupe
Lugwardine, Crown & Anchor
Ombersley, Crown & Sandys Arms
Ruckhall, Ancient Camp
Sellack, Lough Pool
St Owens Cross, New Inn
Stockton Cross, Stockton Cross
Ullingswick, Three Crowns
Upton Bishop, Moody Cow
Weobley, Olde Salutation
Winforton, Sun
Woolhope, Butchers Arms

Woolhope, Crown

Hertfordshire
Aldbury, Greyhound
Ashwell, Bushel & Strike
Ayot St Lawrence, Brocket Arms
Burnham Green, White Horse
Flaunden, Bricklayers Arms
Knebworth, Lytton Arms
St Albans, Rose & Crown
Walkern, White Lion
Watton at Stone, George & Dragon
Westmill, Sword in Hand

Isle of Wight
Arreton, White Lion
Bonchurch, Bonchurch
Chale, Clarendon (Wight Mouse)
Cowes, Folly
Rookley, Chequers
Seaview, Seaview
Shorwell, Crown
Ventnor, Spyglass
Yarmouth, Wheatsheaf

Kent
Boughton Aluph, Flying Horse
Boyden Gate, Gate
Groombridge, Crown
Oare, Shipwrights Arms
Smarden, Bell
Tunbridge Wells, Sankeys
Ulcombe, Pepper Box

Lancashire (inc Greater Manchester, Merseyside)
Bispham Green, Eagle & Child
Chipping, Dog & Partridge
Croston, Black Horse
Darwen, Old Rosins
Downham, Assheton Arms
Fence, Forest
Goosnargh, Bushells Arms
Manchester, Lass o' Gowrie
Mellor, Oddfellows Arms
Newton, Parkers Arms
Raby, Wheatsheaf
Ribchester, White Bull
Yealand Conyers, New Inn

Leicestershire
Braunston, Old Plough
East Langton, Bell
Empingham, White Horse
Glaston, Monckton Arms
Glooston, Old Barn
Hose, Rose & Crown
Loughborough, Swan in the Rushes
Lyddington, Old White Hart
Old Dalby, Crown
Redmile, Peacock
Sibson, Cock
Somerby, Old Brewery
Thorpe Langton, Bakers Arms
Upper Hambleton, Finches Arms
Wing, Kings Arms

Lincolnshire
Allington, Welby Arms
Coleby, Bell
Dyke, Wishing Well
Gedney Dyke, Chequers

Norfolk
Bawburgh, Kings Head
Blakeney, Kings Arms
Blakeney, White Horse
Burnham Market, Hoste Arms
Burnham Thorpe, Lord Nelson
Colkirk, Crown
Fakenham, Wensum Lodge
Great Bircham, Kings Head
Hempstead, Hare & Hounds
Heydon, Earle Arms
Hunworth, Blue Bell
Kings Lynn, Tudor Rose
Larling, Angel
Norwich, Adam & Eve
Reedham, Ferry
Ringstead, Gin Trap
Stiffkey, Red Lion
Stow Bardolph, Hare Arms
Swanton Morley, Darbys
Titchwell, Manor
Tivetshall St Mary, Old Ram
Upper Sheringham, Red Lion
Warham, Three Horseshoes
West Beckham, Wheatsheaf
Winterton-on-Sea, Fishermans Return
Woodbastwick, Fur & Feather

Northamptonshire
Ashby St Ledgers, Olde Coach House
Chacombe, George & Dragon
Clipston, Bulls Head
Eastcote, Eastcote Arms
Farthingstone, Kings Arms
Fotheringhay, Falcon
Harringworth, White Swan
Oundle, Mill
Oundle, Ship
Sulgrave, Star
Wadenhoe, Kings Head

Northumberland, Durham, Tyneside & Teeside
Allenheads, Allenheads
Alnmouth, Saddle
Bamburgh, Lord Crewe Arms
Carterway Heads, Manor House
Cotherstone, Fox & Hounds
Great Whittington, Queens Head
Haltwhistle, Wallace Arms
New York, Shiremoor House Farm
Newton on the Moor, Cook & Barker Arms

Rennington , Masons Arms
Romaldkirk, Rose & Crown
Seahouses, Olde Ship
Seaton Sluice, Waterford Arms
Stannersburn, Pheasant

Nottinghamshire
Beeston, Victoria
Kimberley, Nelson & Railway
Laxton, Dovecote
Nottingham, Lincolnshire Poacher

Oxfordshire
Ardington, Boars Head
Bampton, Romany
Banbury, Reindeer
Barnard Gate, Boot
Blewbury, Red Lion
Broadwell, Five Bells
Burcot, Chequers
Burford, Lamb
Burford, Mermaid
Chinnor, Sir Charles Napier
Clanfield, Clanfield Tavern
Clifton, Duke of Cumberlands Head
Clifton Hampden, Plough
Cumnor, Bear & Ragged Staff
Duns Tew, White Horse
Exlade Street, Highwayman
Fyfield, White Hart
Lewknor, Olde Leathern Bottel
Maidensgrove, Five Horseshoes
Murcott, Nut Tree
Oxford, Kings Arms
Oxford, Turf Tavern
Ramsden, Royal Oak
Shipton-under-Wychwood, Lamb
Shipton-under-Wychwood, Shaven Crown
South Stoke, Perch & Pike
Stanton St John, Star
Steeple Aston, Red Lion
Woodstock, Feathers
Wootton, Kings Head
Wytham, White Hart

Shropshire
Bishops Castle, Three Tuns
Bridges, Horseshoe
Brockton, Feathers
Cardington, Royal Oak
Llanfair Waterdine, Red Lion
Ludlow, Unicorn
Much Wenlock, George & Dragon
Much Wenlock, Talbot
Wenlock Edge, Wenlock Edge
Wentnor, Crown

Somerset
Ashcott, Ashcott
Bath, Old Green Tree
Blagdon, New Inn
Buckland Dinham, Bell
Castle Cary, George
Compton Martin, Ring o' Bells
Doulting, Waggon & Horses
Dowlish Wake, New Inn
Dunster, Luttrell Arms
East Woodlands, Horse & Groom
Hallatrow, Old Station
Knapp, Rising Sun
Langley Marsh, Three Horseshoes
Monksilver, Notley Arms
Sparkford, Sparkford
Stoke St Gregory, Rose & Crown
Wambrook, Cotley
West Huntspill, Crossways

Staffordshire
Acton Trussell, Moat House
Alstonefield, George
Alstonefield, Watts Russell Arms
Cresswell, Izaak Walton
Onecote, Jervis Arms

Suffolk
Bardwell, Six Bells
Bildeston, Crown
Bramfield, Queens Head
Chillesford, Froize
Dunwich, Ship
Erwarton, Queens Head
Hartest, Crown
Hundon, Plough
Lavenham, Angel
Lavenham, Swan
Levington, Ship
Orford, Jolly Sailor
Rattlesden, Brewers Arms
Snape, Crown
Snape, Plough & Sail
Southwold, Crown
Stoke by Nayland, Angel
Thornham Magna, Four Horseshoes
Wangford, Angel

Surrey
Blackbrook, Plough
Cobham, Cricketers
Coldharbour, Plough
Friday Street, Stephan Langton
Gomshall, Compasses
Reigate Heath, Skimmington Castle
Sutton, Volunteer
Thursley, Three Horseshoes
Warlingham, White Lion

Sussex
Alciston, Rose Cottage
Alfriston, Star
Amberley, Black Horse
Amberley, Sportsmans
Barcombe, Anchor
Blackboys, Blackboys
Burwash, Bell
Byworth, Black Horse
Chidham, Old House At Home
Cowbeech, Merrie Harriers
Firle, Ram
Hammerpot, Woodmans Arms
Icklesham, Queens Head
Kingston near Lewes, Juggs
Kirdford, Half Moon
Lodsworth, Halfway Bridge
Lower Beeding, Crabtree

Lurgashall, Noahs Ark
Mayfield, Middle House
Nuthurst, Black Horse
Oving, Gribble
Punnetts Town, Three Cups
Rye, Ypres Castle
Seaford, Golden Galleon

Warwickshire
Alderminster, Bell
Coventry, Old Windmill
Himley, Crooked House
Ilmington, Howard Arms
Little Compton, Red Lion
Lowsonford, Fleur de Lys
Monks Kirby, Bell

Wiltshire
Axford, Red Lion
Barford St Martin, Barford
Brinkworth, Three Crowns
Devizes, Bear
Ebbesbourne Wake, Horseshoe
Hindon, Lamb
Kilmington, Red Lion
Lacock, Red Lion
Limpley Stoke, Hop Pole
Little Cheverell, Owl
Lower Woodford, Wheatsheaf
Marlborough, Sun
Norton, Vine Tree
Pitton, Silver Plough
Poulshot, Raven
Ramsbury, Bell
Rowde, George & Dragon
Salisbury, New Inn
Seend, Barge
Sherston, Rattlebone

Yorkshire
Appletreewick, Craven Arms
Asenby, Crab & Lobster
Askrigg, Kings Arms
Aysgarth, George & Dragon
Beverley, White Horse
Bilbrough, Three Hares
Blakey Ridge, Lion
Bradfield, Strines
Buckden, Buck
Burnsall, Red Lion
Carlton, Foresters Arms
Carthorpe, Fox & Hounds
Cray, White Lion
Cropton, New Inn
Dacre Banks, Royal Oak
Egton Bridge, Horse Shoe
Goose Eye, Turkey
Harden, Malt Shovel
Helmsley, Feathers
Hetton, Angel
Hull, Minerva
Kirkbymoorside, George & Dragon
Kirkham, Stone Trough
Levisham, Horseshoe
Linthwaite, Sair
Linton in Craven, Fountaine
Low Catton, Gold Cup
Meltham, Will's o' Nat's
Newton on Ouse, Dawnay Arms
Pickhill, Nags Head
Pool, White Hart
Ramsgill, Yorke Arms
Redmire, Kings Arms
Rosedale Abbey, Milburn Arms
Sawley, Sawley Arms
Sheffield, Fat Cat
Sheffield, New Barrack
Snaith, Brewers Arms
Starbotton, Fox & Hounds
Sutton upon Derwent, St Vincent Arms
Thornton Watlass, Buck
Wass, Wombwell Arms
Wath-in-Nidderdale, Sportsmans Arms
York, Black Swan
York, Olde Starre

London, Central
London EC 4, Olde Cheshire Cheese
London SW 1, Lord Moon of the Mall
London W 1, Argyll Arms
London W 1, Grapes
London WC 1, Lamb
London WC 1, Moon Under Water

London, North
London NW 3, Spaniards

London, South
London SE 1, George
London SE21, Crown & Greyhound

London, West
London SW10, Ferret & Firkin
London W 4, Bulls Head

London, East
London E 1, Prospect of Whitby

Scotland
Applecross, Applecross
Arduaine, Loch Melfort
Brig o Turk, Byre
Canonbie, Riverside
Cawdor, Cawdor Tavern
Clachan Seil, Tigh an Truish
Crinan, Crinan
Edinburgh, Starbank
Fort Augustus, Lock
Glasgow, Counting House
Innerleithen, Traquair Arms
Isle Ornsay, Tigh Osda Eilean Iarmain
Isle of Whithorn, Steam Packet
Kilberry, Kilberry
Kilmahog, Lade
Kirkton of Glenisla, Glenisla
Linlithgow, Four Marys
Melrose, Burts
Pitlochry, Killiecrankie
Plockton, Plockton
Portpatrick, Crown
Sheriffmuir, Sheriffmuir
Skeabost, Skeabost House
Swinton, Wheatsheaf
Tayvallich, Tayvallich
Thornhill, Lion & Unicorn
Tushielaw, Tushielaw
Ullapool, Ceilidh Place

Ullapool, Morefield Motel

Wales

Aberdovey, Penhelig Arms
Beaumaris, Olde Bulls Head
Bodfari, Dinorben Arms
Bosherston, St Govans
Capel Curig, Bryn Tyrch
Carew, Carew
Colwyn Bay, Mountain View
Crickhowell, Bear
Crickhowell, White Hart
Gladestry, Royal Oak
Gresford, Pant-yr-Ochain
Hay on Wye, Old Black Lion
Llanbedr-y-Cennin, Olde Bull
Llanberis, Pen-y-Gwryd
Llandrindod Wells, Llanerch
Llandudno Junction, Queens Head
Llangedwyn, Green
Llangynidr, Coach & Horses
Llangynwyd, Old House
Llanynys, Cerrigllwydion Arms
Llyswen, Griffin
Maentwrog, Grapes
Penmaenpool, George III
Pontypool, Open Hearth
Porthmadog, Ship
Presteigne, Radnorshire Arms
Raglan, Clytha Arms
Rosebush, New Inn
Talycoed, Halfway House
Tyn y Groes, Groes

Channel Islands

Castel, Hougue du Pommier
Kings Mills, Fleur du Jardin
Rozel, Rozel Bay
St Brelade, Old Smugglers
St Helier, Tipsy Toad Town House
St John, Les Fontaines

PUBS CLOSE TO MOTORWAY JUNCTIONS

The number at the start of each line is the number of the junction. Detailed directions are given in the main entry for each pub. In this section, to help you find the pubs quickly before you're past the junction, we give in abbreviated form the name of the chapter where you'll find them in the text.

M1

14: Moulsoe (Bucks) 1¼ miles
18: Crick (Northants) 1 mile; Ashby St Ledgers (Northants) 4 miles
24: Kegworth (Leics) under a mile; Shardlow (Derbys) 2½ miles
26: Kimberley (Notts) 3 miles
29: Hardwick Hall (Derbys) 4 miles

M3

5: Mattingley (Hants) 3 miles; Rotherwick (Hants) 4 miles
7: Dummer (Hants) ½ mile

M4

8: Bray (Berks) 1¾ miles
9: Holyport (Berks) 1½ miles
12: Stanford Dingley (Berks) 4 miles
13: Chieveley (Berks) 3½ miles
14: Great Shefford (Berks) 2 miles; Lambourn (Berks) 5 miles
18: Old Sodbury (Gloucs) 2 miles
21: Aust (Gloucs) ½ mile; Littleton upon Severn (Gloucs) 3½ miles

M5

7: Kempsey (Herefs & Worcs) 3¾ miles
9: Bredon (Herefs & Worcs) 4½ miles
16: Almondsbury (Gloucs) 1¼ miles
19: Clapton in Gordano (Somerset) 4 miles
23: West Huntspill (Somerset) 2¾ miles
28: Broadhembury (Devon) 5 miles
30: Topsham (Devon) 2 miles; Woodbury Salterton (Devon) 3½ miles; Exeter (Devon) 4 miles

M6

13: Acton Trussell (Staffs) 2 miles
16: Barthomley (Cheshire) 1 mile; Shraleybrook (Staffs) 3 miles; Weston (Cheshire) 3½ miles
19: Plumley (Cheshire) 2½ miles
29: Brindle (Lancs etc) 3 miles
32: Goosnargh (Lancs etc) 4 miles
33: Conder Green (Lancs etc) 3 miles
35: Yealand Conyers (Lancs etc) 3 miles
40: Yanwath (Cumbria) 2¼ miles; Stainton (Cumbria) 3 miles; Tirril (Cumbria) 3½ miles; Penrith (Cumbria) ¾ mile; Askham (Cumbria) 4½ miles

M9

3: Linlithgow (Scotland) 2 miles

M11

7: Hastingwood (Essex) ¼ mile
10: Hinxton (Cambs) 2 miles

M25

8: Reigate Heath

(Surrey) 3 miles; Betchworth (Surrey) 4 miles
10: Cobham (Surrey) 3¾ miles
18: Flaunden (Herts) 4 miles

M27
1: Cadnam (Hants) ½ mile
8: Bursledon (Hants) 2 miles
9: Locks Heath (Hants) 2½ miles

M40
2: Beaconsfield (Bucks) 2 miles; Wooburn Common (Bucks) 2 miles; Forty Green (Bucks) 3½ miles
5: Ibstone (Bucks) 1 mile; Bolter End (Bucks) 4 miles
6: Lewknor (Oxon) ½ mile; Watlington (Oxon) 3 miles; Cuxham (Oxon) 4 miles
11: Chacombe (Northants) 2½ miles

M45
1: Dunchurch (Warwicks) 1⅓ miles

M50
3: Upton Bishop (Herefs & Worcs) 2 miles

M56
12: Overton (Cheshire) 2 miles

Key to map areas

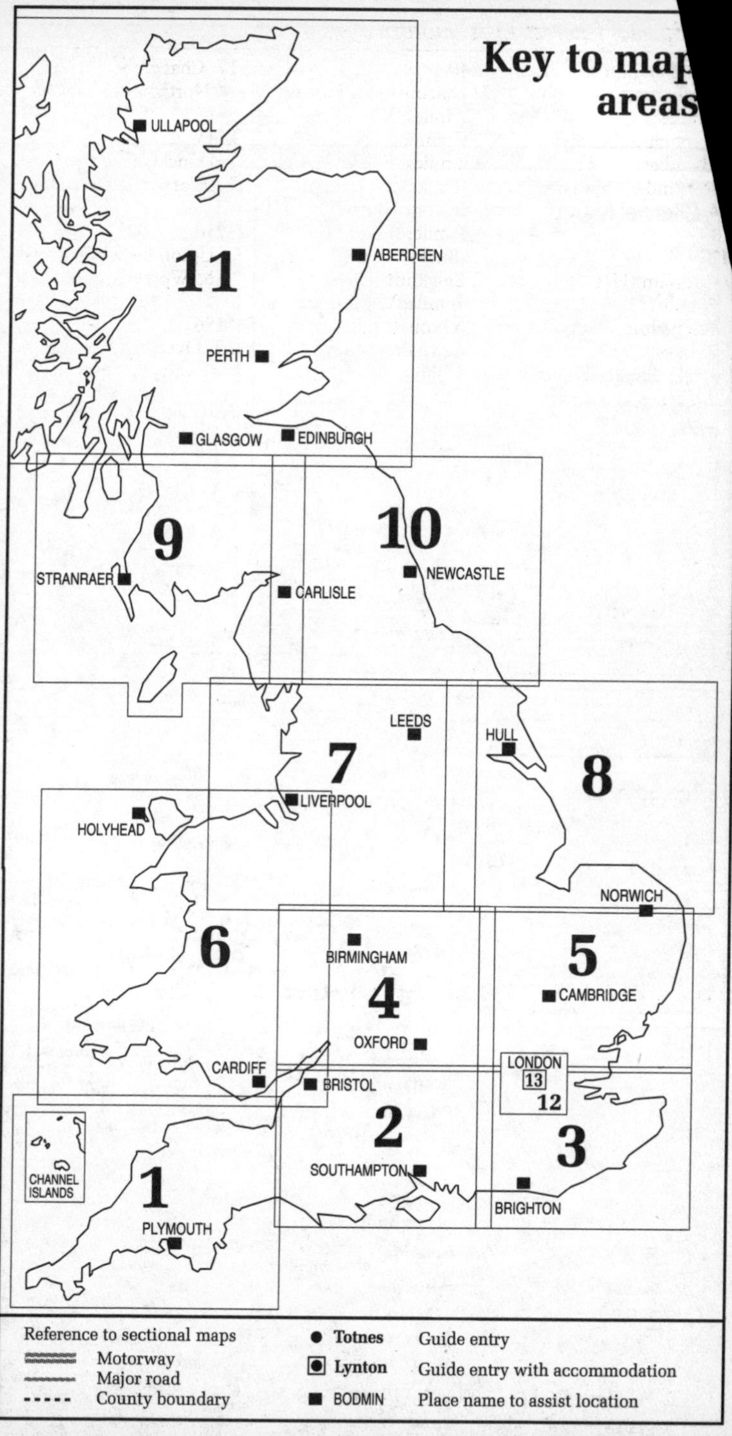

Reference to sectional maps

Motorway
Major road
County boundary

● **Totnes** Guide entry
⊙ **Lynton** Guide entry with accommodation
■ BODMIN Place name to assist location

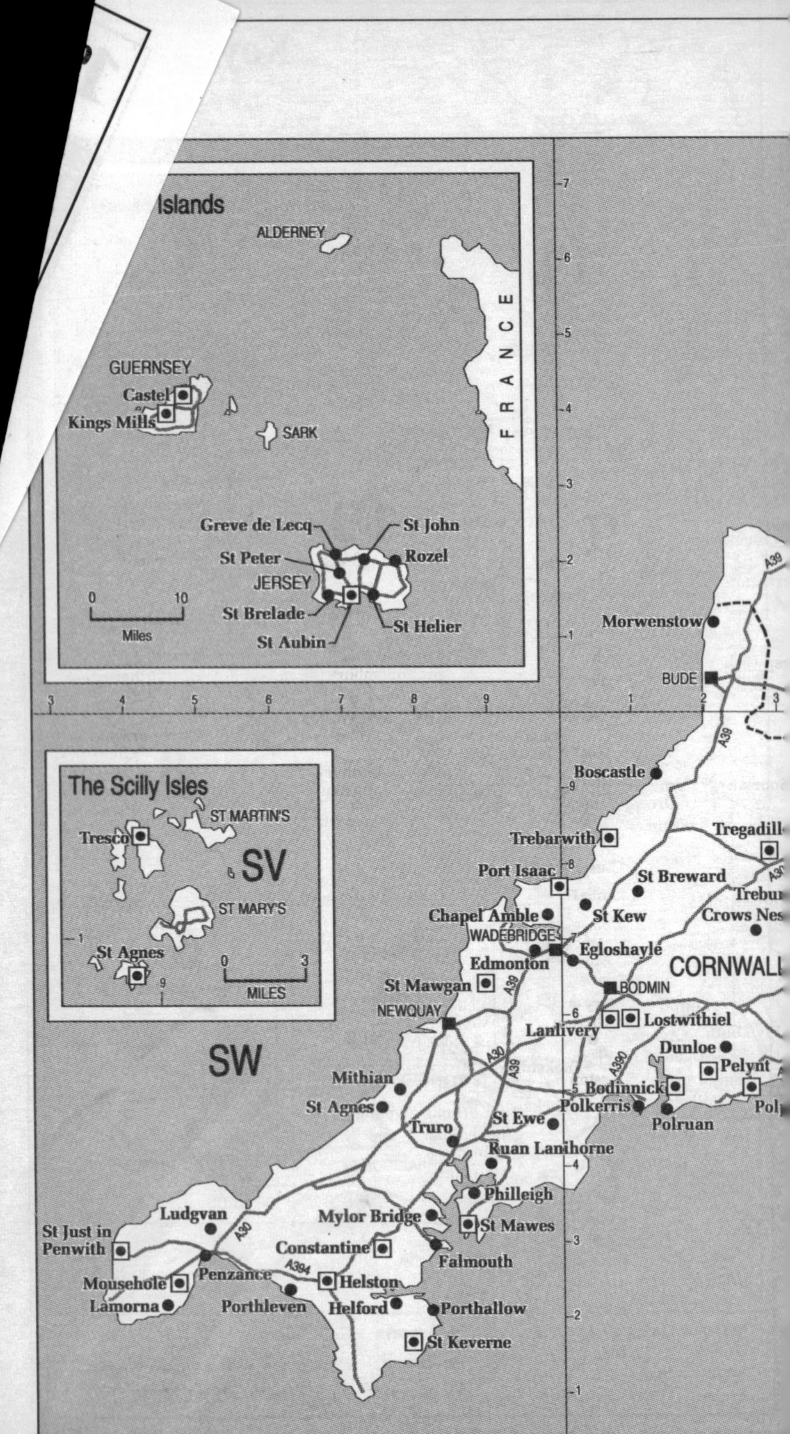

Islands
ALDERNEY
GUERNSEY
Castel
Kings Mills
SARK
FRANCE
Greve de Lecq
St John
St Peter
Rozel
JERSEY
St Brelade
St Helier
St Aubin
0
10
Miles
Morwenstow
BUDE
The Scilly Isles
ST MARTIN'S
Tresco
SV
ST MARY'S
St Agnes
0
3
MILES
SW
Boscastle
Trebarwith
Tregadill
Port Isaac
St Breward
Trebu
Chapel Amble
St Kew
Crows Nes
WADEBRIDGE
Egloshayle
Edmonton
CORNWALL
St Mawgan
BODMIN
NEWQUAY
Lanlivery
Lostwithiel
Dunloe
Pelynt
Mithian
Bodinnick
St Agnes
Polkerris
Polruan
St Ewe
Truro
Ruan Lanihorne
Philleigh
Ludgvan
Mylor Bridge
St Mawes
St Just in
Penwith
Constantine
Falmouth
Mousehole
Penzance
Helston
Lamorna
Porthleven
Helford
Porthallow
St Keverne
A39
A30
A390
A394

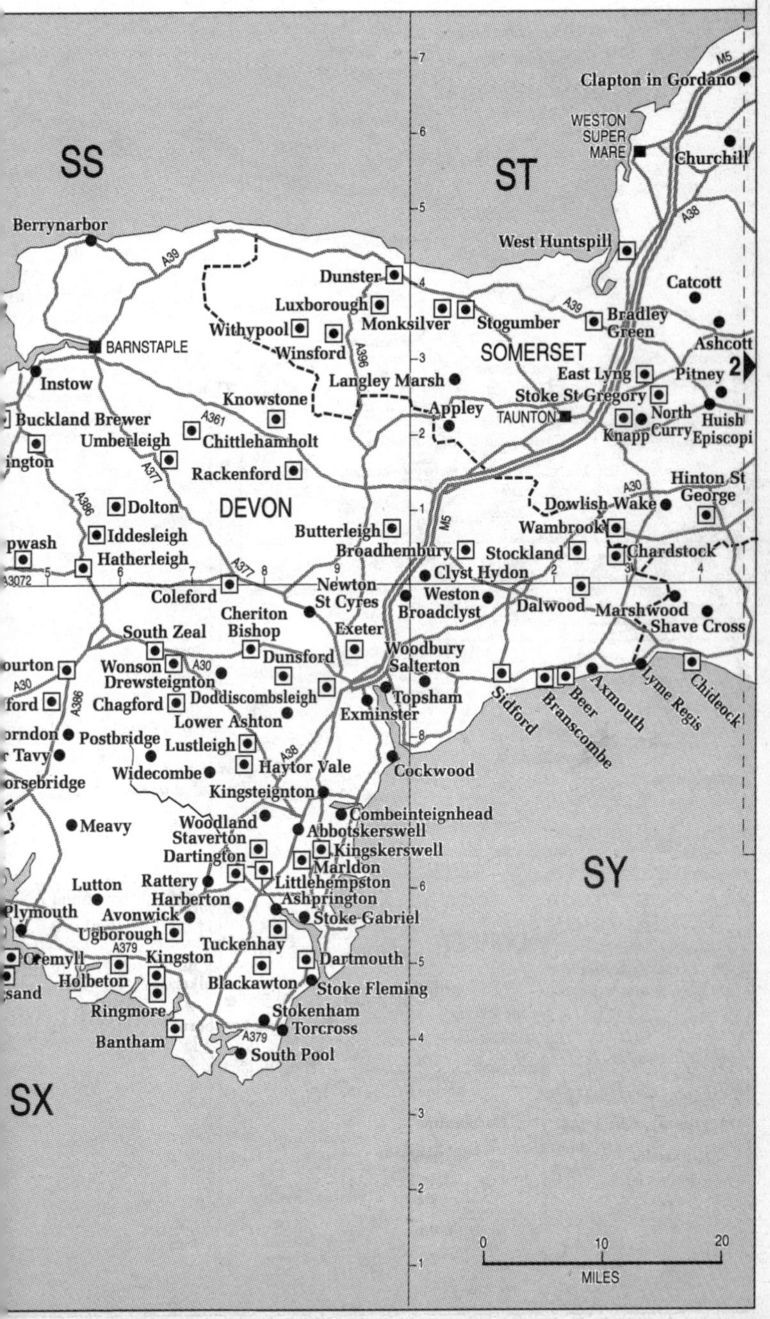

SS
ST
SX
SY
SOMERSET
DEVON
BARNSTAPLE
WESTON SUPER MARE
TAUNTON
Clapton in Gordano
Churchill
West Huntspill
Catcott
Ashcott
Bradley Green
Pitney
East Lyng
Stoke St Gregory
North Curry
Knapp
Huish Episcopi
Hinton St George
Dowlish Wake
Wambrook
Chardstock
Stockland
Dalwood
Marshwood
Shave Cross
Chideock
Lyme Regis
Axmouth
Beer
Branscombe
Sidford
Berrynarbor
Dunster
Luxborough
Monksilver
Stogumber
Withypool
Winsford
Langley Marsh
Appley
Instow
Knowstone
Buckland Brewer
Umberleigh
Chittlehamholt
Rackenford
Dolton
Iddesleigh
Hatherleigh
Butterleigh
Broadhembury
Clyst Hydon
Newton St Cyres
Weston
Broadclyst
Coleford
Cheriton Bishop
South Zeal
Exeter
Woodbury Salterton
Wonson
Drewsteignton
Dunsford
Chagford
Doddiscombsleigh
Topsham
Exminster
Lower Ashton
Postbridge
Lustleigh
Haytor Vale
Widecombe
Cockwood
Kingsteignton
Combeinteignhead
Meavy
Woodland
Staverton
Abbotskerswell
Kingskerswell
Dartington
Marldon
Rattery
Littlehempston
Lutton
Harberton
Ashprington
Avonwick
Stoke Gabriel
Plymouth
Ugborough
Tuckenhay
Cremyll
Kingston
Dartmouth
Holbeton
Blackawton
Stoke Fleming
Ringmore
Stokenham
Torcross
Bantham
South Pool
M5
A38
A39
A396
A361
A377
A386
A30
A3072
A379
2
MILES
0
10
20

2

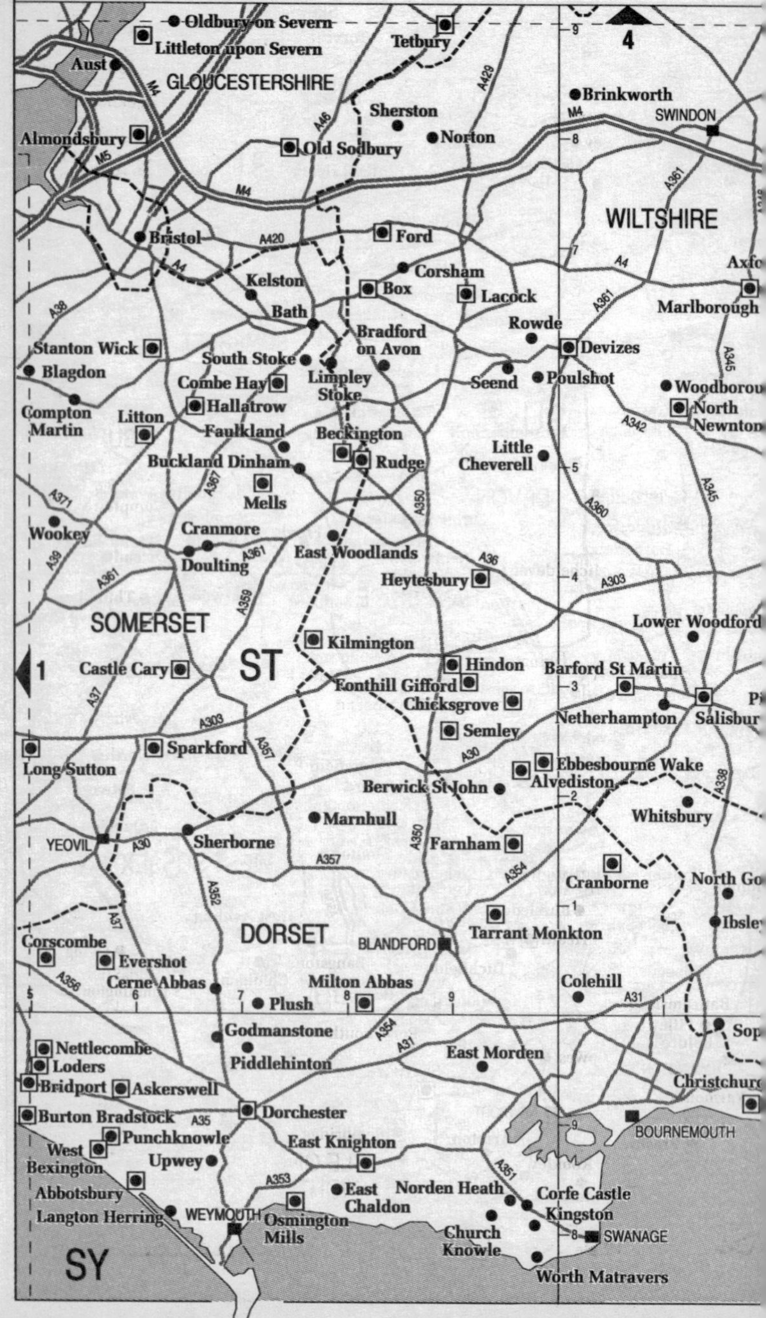

Oldbury-on Severn
Littleton upon Severn
Tetbury
Aust
GLOUCESTERSHIRE
Brinkworth
Sherston
SWINDON
Almondsbury
Norton
Old Sodbury
WILTSHIRE
Bristol
Ford
Axfo
Corsham
Kelston
Box
Lacock
Marlborough
Bath
Rowde
Bradford on Avon
Devizes
Stanton Wick
South Stoke
Blagdon
Limpley Stoke
Seend
Poulshot
Woodborou
Combe Hay
North Newnton
Compton Martin
Hallatrow
Litton
Faulkland
Beckington
Little Cheverell
Buckland Dinham
Rudge
Mells
Wookey
Cranmore
East Woodlands
Doulting
Heytesbury
SOMERSET
Lower Woodford
Kilmington
Castle Cary
ST
Hindon
Barford St Martin
Fonthill Gifford
Chicksgrove
Netherhampton
Salisbur
Semley
Long Sutton
Sparkford
Ebbesbourne Wake
Alvediston
Berwick St John
Whitsbury
Marnhull
YEOVIL
Sherborne
Farnham
Cranborne
North Go
Ibsley
Tarrant Monkton
DORSET
BLANDFORD
Corscombe
Evershot
Cerne Abbas
Milton Abbas
Colehill
Plush
Sop
Godmanstone
Nettlecombe
Loders
Piddlehinton
East Morden
Bridport
Askerswell
Christchurc
Burton Bradstock
Dorchester
BOURNEMOUTH
Punchknowle
West Bexington
East Knighton
Upwey
Abbotsbury
East Chaldon
Norden Heath
Corfe Castle
Langton Herring
WEYMOUTH
Osmington Mills
Kingston
Church Knowle
SWANAGE
SY
Worth Matravers
M4
M5
A46
A429
A420
A4
A38
A361
A345
A342
A371
A367
A350
A360
A39
A36
A303
A359
A37
A357
A30
A338
A354
A352
A356
A31
A35
A351
A353
4
1

2

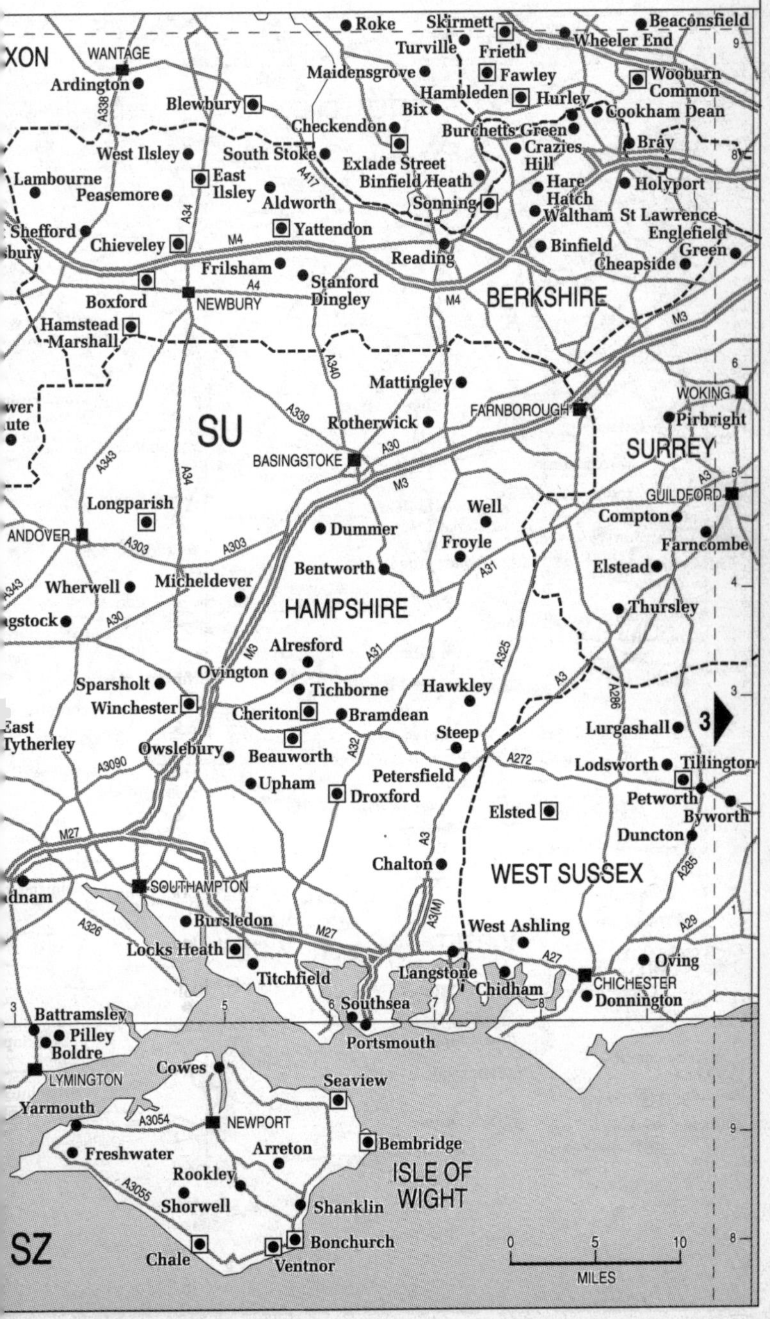

Roke
Skirmett
Beaconsfield
Turville
Frieth
Wheeler End
XON
WANTAGE
Maidensgrove
Fawley
Wooburn Common
Ardington
Hambleden
Hurley
Blewbury
Bix
Cookham Dean
A338
Checkendon
Burchetts Green
Bray
West Ilsley
South Stoke
Exlade Street
Crazies Hill
Lambourne
East Ilsley
A417
Binfield Heath
Hare Hatch
Holyport
Peasemore
Aldworth
Sonning
Waltham St Lawrence
Shefford
A34
Yattendon
Englefield Green
Chieveley
M4
Binfield
Reading
Cheapside
Frilsham
Stanford Dingley
A4
Boxford
NEWBURY
M4
BERKSHIRE
Hamstead Marshall
M3
A340
Mattingley
WOKING
A339
FARNBOROUGH
Pirbright
SU
Rotherwick
A343
BASINGSTOKE
A30
SURREY
M3
A3
A34
GUILDFORD
Longparish
Well
Compton
ANDOVER
Dummer
Farncombe
A303
A303
Froyle
Bentworth
Elstead
A343
Wherwell
Micheldever
A31
HAMPSHIRE
Thursley
A30
M3
Alresford
A31
A325
Ovington
Sparsholt
Tichborne
Hawkley
A3
A286
Winchester
Cheriton
Bramdean
3
East Tytherley
Steep
Lurgashall
Owslebury
Beauworth
A32
A272
A3090
Petersfield
Lodsworth
Tillington
Upham
Droxford
Petworth
Elsted
Byworth
M27
Duncton
A3
Chalton
WEST SUSSEX
SOUTHAMPTON
A285
A3(M)
A326
Bursledon
M27
West Ashling
A29
Locks Heath
A27
Oving
Titchfield
Langstone
Chidham
CHICHESTER
Southsea
Donnington
Battramsley
Pilley
Portsmouth
Boldre
Cowes
LYMINGTON
Seaview
Yarmouth
A3054
NEWPORT
Bembridge
Freshwater
Arreton
ISLE OF WIGHT
Rookley
A3055
Shorwell
Shanklin
Bonchurch
SZ
Chale
Ventnor
0
5
10
MILES

3

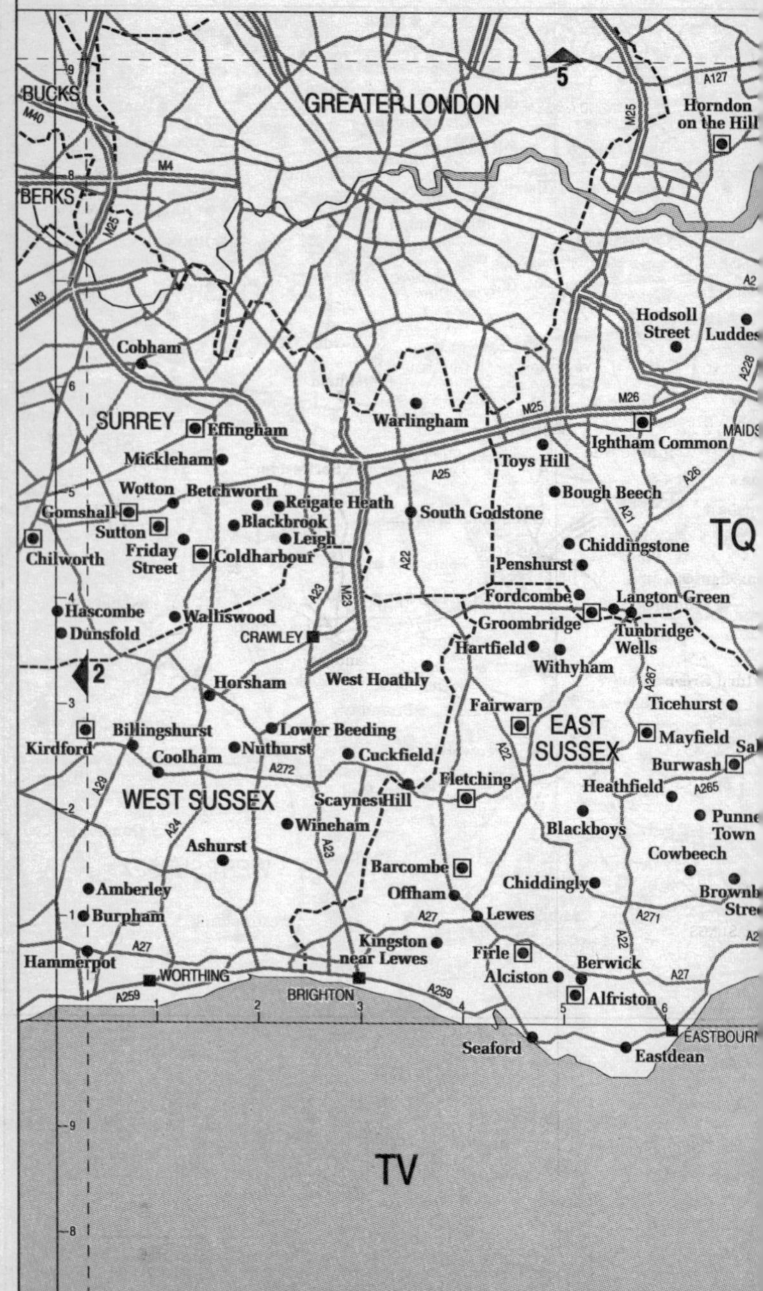

5
BUCKS
M40
BERKS
M4
M25
M3
GREATER LONDON
M25
A127
Horndon on the Hill
A2
Hodsoll Street
Luddes
A228
M26
Cobham
SURREY
Effingham
Warlingham
M25
Ightham Common
MAIDS
Mickleham
Toys Hill
A25
A26
Wotton
Betchworth
Bough Beech
Gomshall
Reigate Heath
South Godstone
A21
Sutton
Blackbrook
Chilworth
Friday Street
Leigh
Coldharbour
Chiddingstone
TQ
A22
Penshurst
A23
M23
Fordcombe
Langton Green
Hascombe
Walliswood
Groombridge
Tunbridge Wells
Dunsfold
CRAWLEY
Hartfield
Withyham
2
Horsham
West Hoathly
A267
Fairwarp
Ticehurst
Kirdford
Billingshurst
Lower Beeding
EAST SUSSEX
Mayfield
Nuthurst
Coolham
Cuckfield
Burwash
A272
A22
A29
Fletching
Heathfield
A265
WEST SUSSEX
Scaynes Hill
A24
Wineham
Blackboys
Punne Town
Ashurst
A23
Cowbeech
Barcombe
Amberley
Offham
Chiddingly
Burpham
A27
Lewes
A271
A22
Kingston near Lewes
Firle
Hammerpot
A27
Berwick
WORTHING
Alciston
A27
A259
BRIGHTON
A259
Alfriston
Seaford
EASTBOURN
Eastdean
TV

3

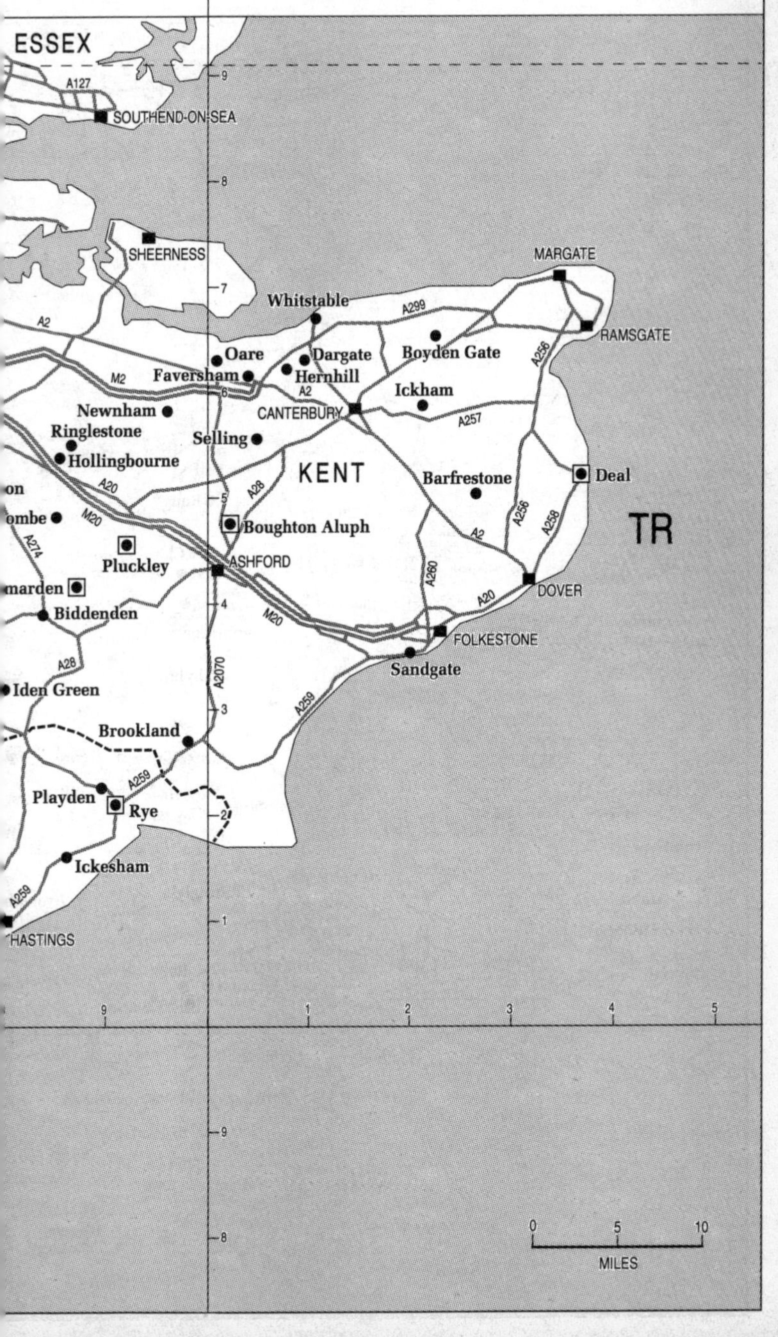
ESSEX
A127
SOUTHEND-ON-SEA
SHEERNESS
MARGATE
RAMSGATE
Whitstable
A299
A2
M2
Oare
Dargate
Boyden Gate
Faversham
Hernhill
A256
A2
Ickham
Newnham
CANTERBURY
A257
Ringlestone
Selling
Hollingbourne
KENT
Deal
Barfrestone
on
A20
A28
ombe
M20
A256
A258
TR
Boughton Aluph
A274
A2
Pluckley
ASHFORD
A260
DOVER
marden
A20
Biddenden
M20
FOLKESTONE
A28
Sandgate
A2070
Iden Green
A259
Brookland
A259
Playden
Rye
Ickesham
A259
HASTINGS
0
5
10
MILES

4

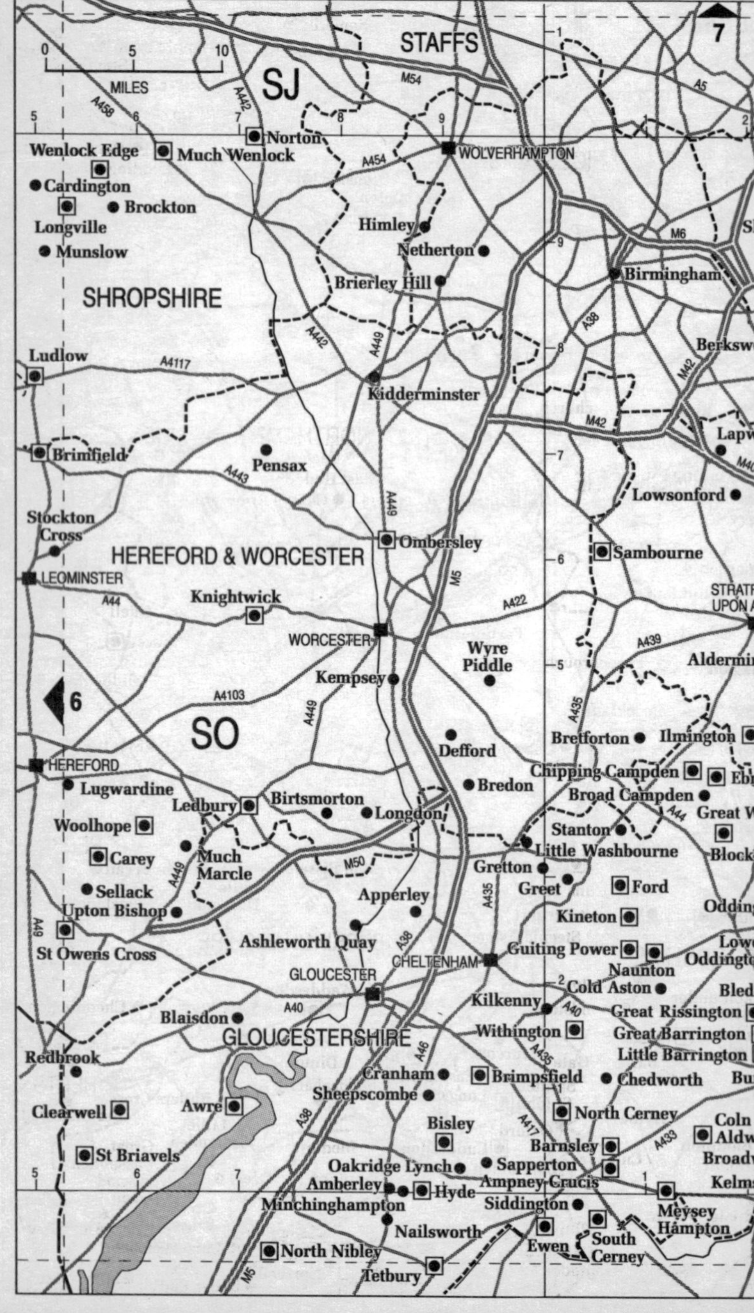

STAFFS
SJ
SO
7
6
0 5 10
MILES
SHROPSHIRE
HEREFORD & WORCESTER
GLOUCESTERSHIRE
Norton
Much Wenlock
Wenlock Edge
Cardington
Brockton
Longville
Munslow
WOLVERHAMPTON
Himley
Netherton
Brierley Hill
Birmingham
Berkswe
Ludlow
Kidderminster
Brimfield
Pensax
Lapw
Lowsonford
Stockton Cross
Ombersley
Sambourne
LEOMINSTER
Knightwick
WORCESTER
STRATF UPON AV
Wyre Piddle
Aldermin
Kempsey
Defford
Bretforton
Ilmington
HEREFORD
Lugwardine
Bredon
Chipping Campden
Ebri
Broad Campden
Great W
Ledbury
Birtsmorton
Longdon
Woolhope
Stanton
Carey
Much Marcle
Little Washbourne
Blockl
Gretton
Greet
Ford
Sellack
Apperley
Upton Bishop
Kineton
Odding
Ashleworth Quay
Guiting Power
Lowe Oddingto
St Owens Cross
CHELTENHAM
Naunton
GLOUCESTER
Cold Aston
Bledi
Kilkenny
Blaisdon
Great Rissington
Withington
Great Barrington
Redbrook
Little Barrington
Cranham
Brimpsfield
Chedworth
Bur
Sheepscombe
Clearwell
Awre
North Cerney
Bisley
Coln S
Aldwy
Barnsley
St Briavels
Broadw
Oakridge Lynch
Sapperton
Kelms
Amberley
Hyde
Ampney Crucis
Minchinghampton
Siddington
Meysey Hampton
Nailsworth
Ewen
South Cerney
North Nibley
Tetbury
M54
A5
A458
A442
A454
M6
A38
M42
A4117
A449
M42
M40
A443
M5
A44
A422
A439
A4103
A435
A44
M50
A49
A40
A46
A417
A433

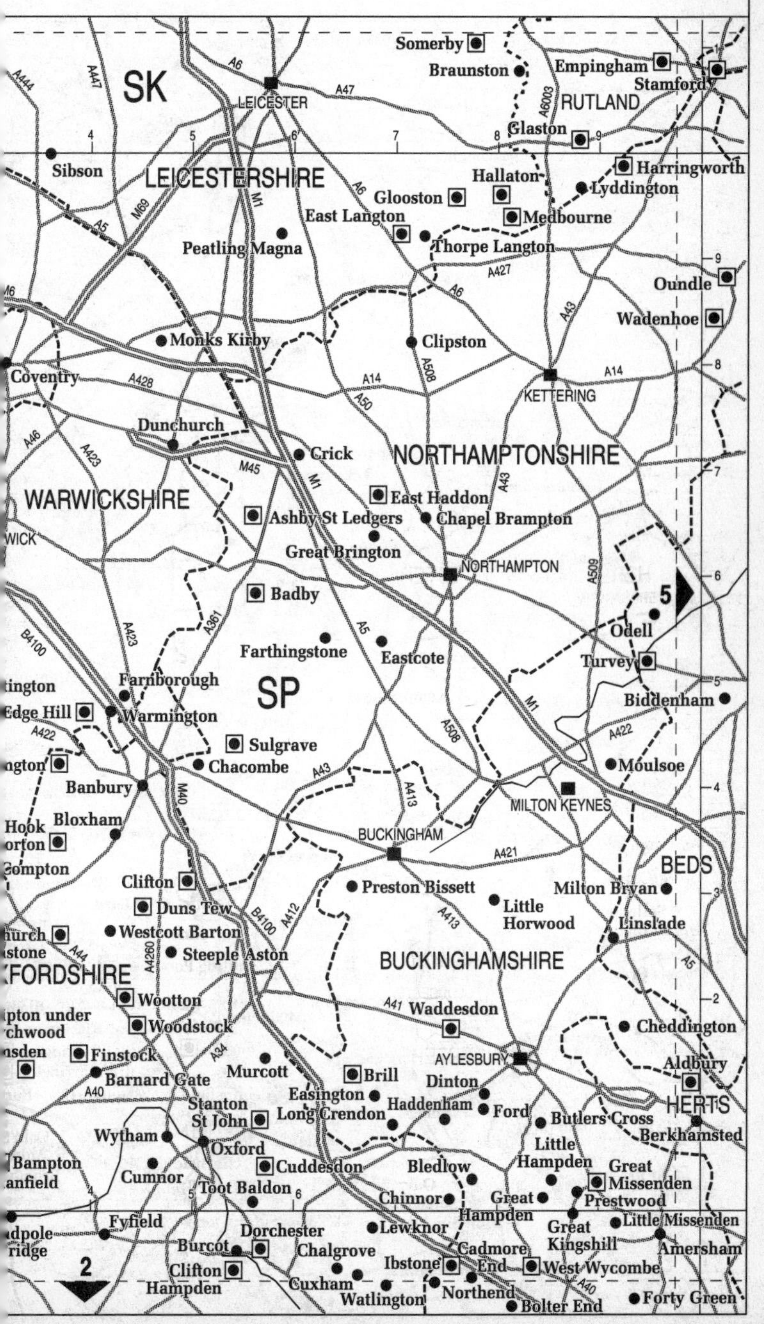

SK
Somerby
Braunston
Empingham
Stamford
A444
A447
A6
LEICESTER
A47
A6003
RUTLAND
Glaston
Sibson
LEICESTERSHIRE
M69
M1
A6
Hallaton
Harringworth
Lyddington
Glooston
East Langton
Medbourne
A5
Peatling Magna
Thorpe Langton
A427
Oundle
M6
A6
A43
Wadenhoe
Monks Kirby
Clipston
Coventry
A428
A14
A508
A50
A14
KETTERING
Dunchurch
A46
A423
Crick
NORTHAMPTONSHIRE
M45
M1
A43
WARWICKSHIRE
East Haddon
Ashby St Ledgers
Chapel Brampton
WICK
Great Brington
NORTHAMPTON
A509
5
Badby
B4100
A423
A361
A5
Odell
Farthingstone
Eastcote
Turvey
tington
Farnborough
SP
Biddenham
Edge Hill
Warmington
M1
A422
A508
A422
Sulgrave
ngton
Chacombe
Moulsoe
Banbury
M40
A43
A413
MILTON KEYNES
Hook
Bloxham
orton
BUCKINGHAM
Compton
A421
BEDS
Clifton
Preston Bissett
Milton Bryan
Duns Tew
Little Horwood
B4100
A412
A413
Linslade
hurch
Westcott Barton
stone
A44
Steeple Aston
A4260
BUCKINGHAMSHIRE
FORDSHIRE
A5
Wootton
pton under
chwood
A41
Waddesdon
Woodstock
Cheddington
A34
nsden
Finstock
AYLESBURY
Aldbury
Murcott
Brill
Barnard Gate
Dinton
A40
Easington
HERTS
Stanton
St John
Long Crendon
Haddenham
Ford
Butlers Cross
Berkhamsted
Wytham
Oxford
Little
Hampden
Bampton
Cuddesdon
Bledlow
Great
Missenden
Cumnor
anfield
Toot Baldon
Chinnor
Great
Hampden
Prestwood
Fyfield
Great
Kingshill
Little Missenden
dpole
ridge
Dorchester
Lewknor
Burcot
Chalgrove
Cadmore
End
Amersham
2
Clifton
Hampden
Ibstone
West Wycombe
Cuxham
A40
Watlington
Northend
Forty Green
Bolter End

5

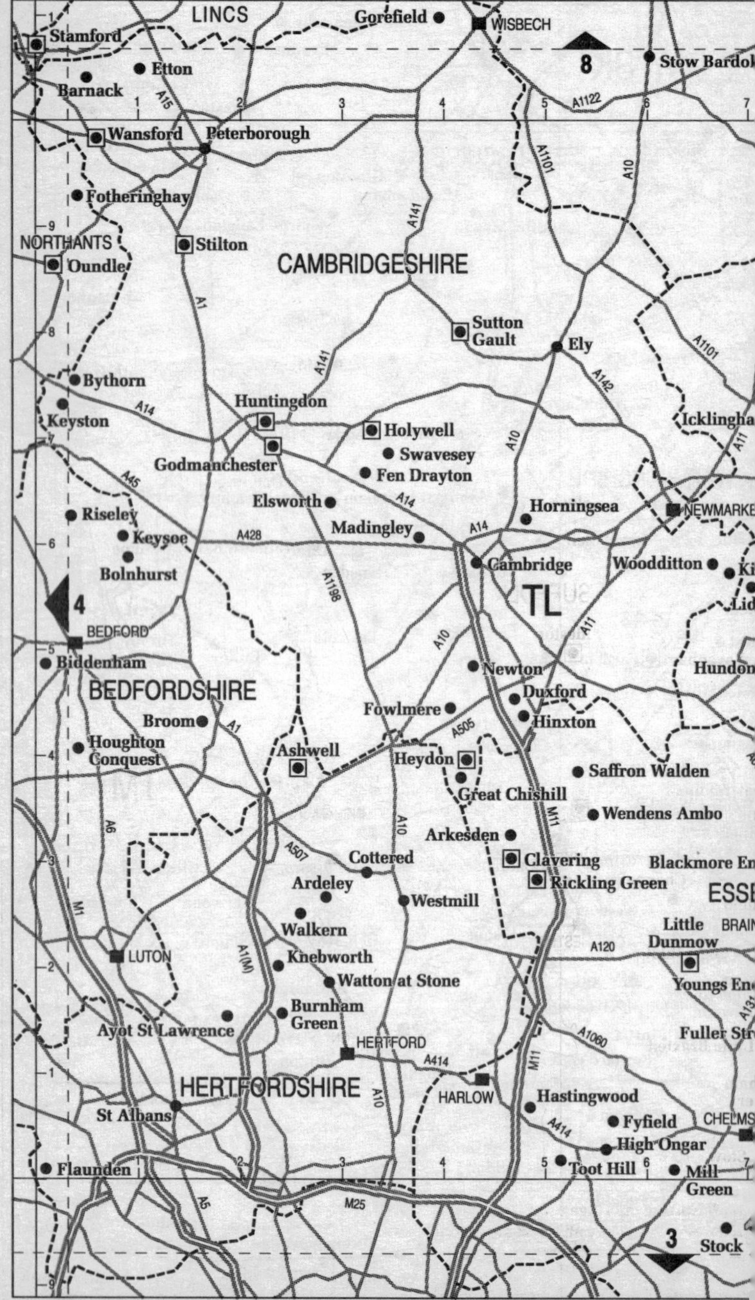
LINCS
Gorefield
WISBECH
Stamford
Etton
Barnack
Stow Bardol
8
Wansford
Peterborough
Fotheringhay
NORTHANTS
Stilton
Oundle
CAMBRIDGESHIRE
Sutton Gault
Ely
Bythorn
Keyston
Huntingdon
Holywell
Swavesey
Fen Drayton
Godmanchester
Icklingha
Elsworth
Horningsea
NEWMARKE
Riseley
Keysoe
Madingley
Cambridge
Woodditton
Bolnhurst
TL
4
BEDFORD
Biddenham
Newton
BEDFORDSHIRE
Duxford
Hundon
Fowlmere
Hinxton
Broom
Houghton Conquest
Ashwell
Heydon
Saffron Walden
Great Chishill
Wendens Ambo
Arkesden
Clavering
Blackmore En
Cottered
Rickling Green
Ardeley
Westmill
ESSE
Walkern
Little Dunmow
BRAIN
LUTON
Knebworth
Watton at Stone
Youngs En
Burnham Green
Ayot St Lawrence
Fuller Str
HERTFORD
HARLOW
HERTFORDSHIRE
Hastingwood
St Albans
Fyfield
CHELMS
High Ongar
Flaunden
Toot Hill
Mill Green
3
Stock
A15
A1122
A1101
A10
A141
A1
A1101
A142
A14
A11
A45
A428
A1198
A10
A11
A1
A505
M11
A6
A507
A10
M1
A1(M)
A120
A1060
A414
M11
A10
A414
A5
M25

5

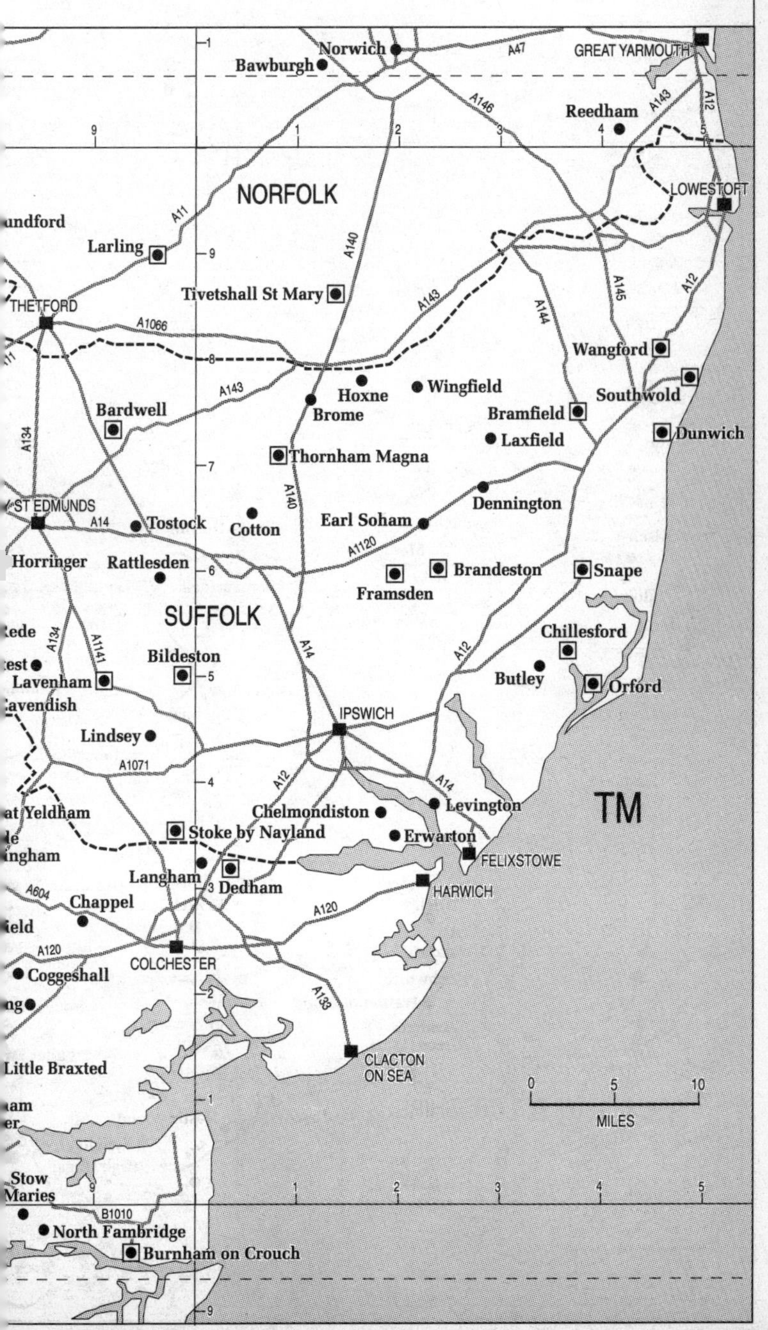

Norwich
Bawburgh
A47
GREAT YARMOUTH
A146
A143
A12
Reedham
NORFOLK
LOWESTOFT
A11
Larling
A140
Tivetshall St Mary
A143
A144
A145
A12
THETFORD
A1066
Wangford
A143
Hoxne
Wingfield
Southwold
Bardwell
Brome
Bramfield
Dunwich
A134
Laxfield
Thornham Magna
Dennington
ST EDMUNDS
A14
Tostock
Cotton
A140
Earl Soham
A1120
Horringer
Rattlesden
Brandeston
Snape
Framsden
SUFFOLK
Chillesford
A134
A1141
Bildeston
A14
A12
Butley
Lavenham
Orford
IPSWICH
Lindsey
A1071
A12
A14
Levington
TM
Chelmondiston
Stoke by Nayland
Erwarton
FELIXSTOWE
Langham
Dedham
HARWICH
A604
Chappel
A120
A120
COLCHESTER
Coggeshall
A133
CLACTON
ON SEA
Little Braxted
0
5
10
MILES
B1010
North Fambridge
Burnham on Crouch

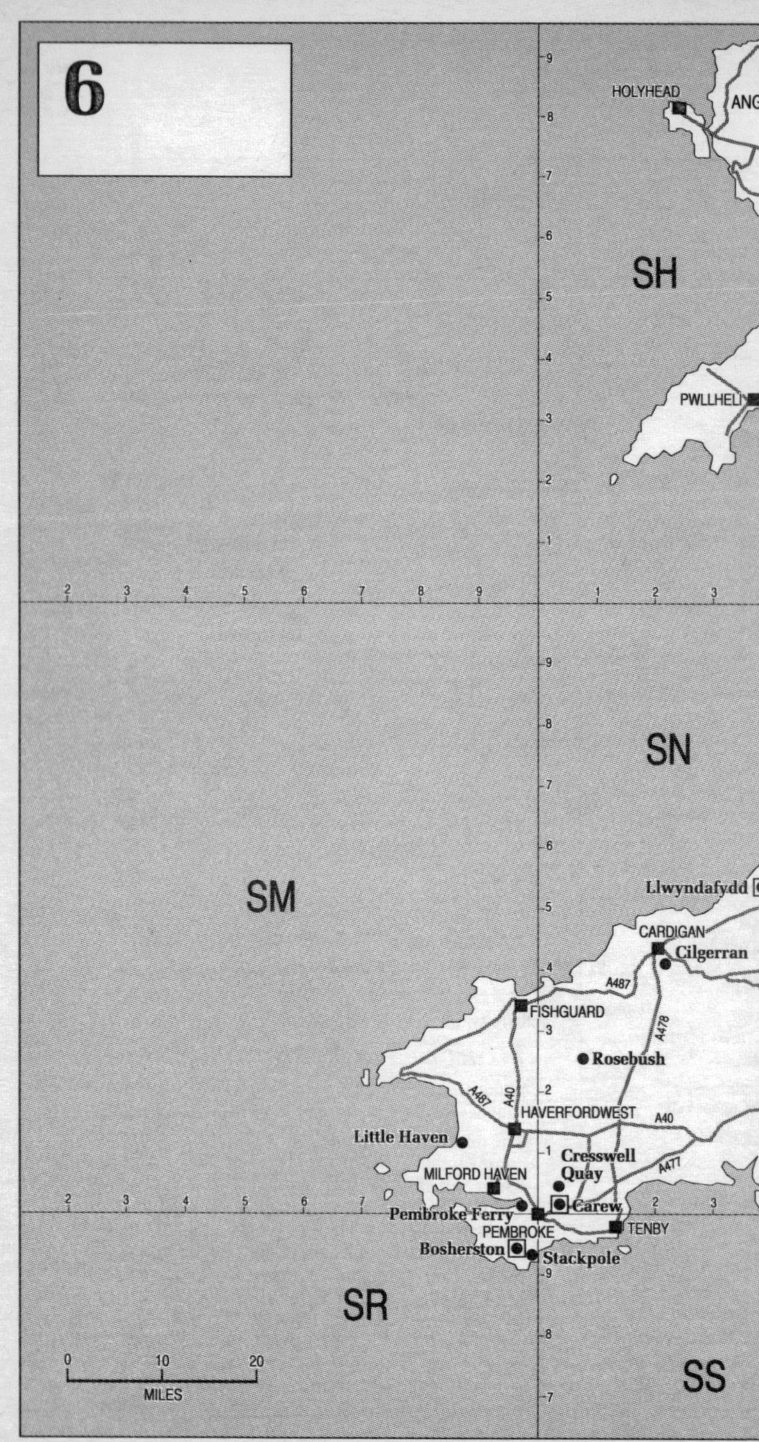
6
HOLYHEAD
ANGL
SH
PWLLHELI
SN
SM
Llwyndafydd
CARDIGAN
Cilgerran
A487
FISHGUARD
A478
Rosebush
A487
A40
HAVERFORDWEST
A40
Little Haven
Cresswell
Quay
A477
MILFORD HAVEN
Carew
Pembroke Ferry
PEMBROKE
TENBY
Bosherston
Stackpole
SR
SS
0
10
20
MILES

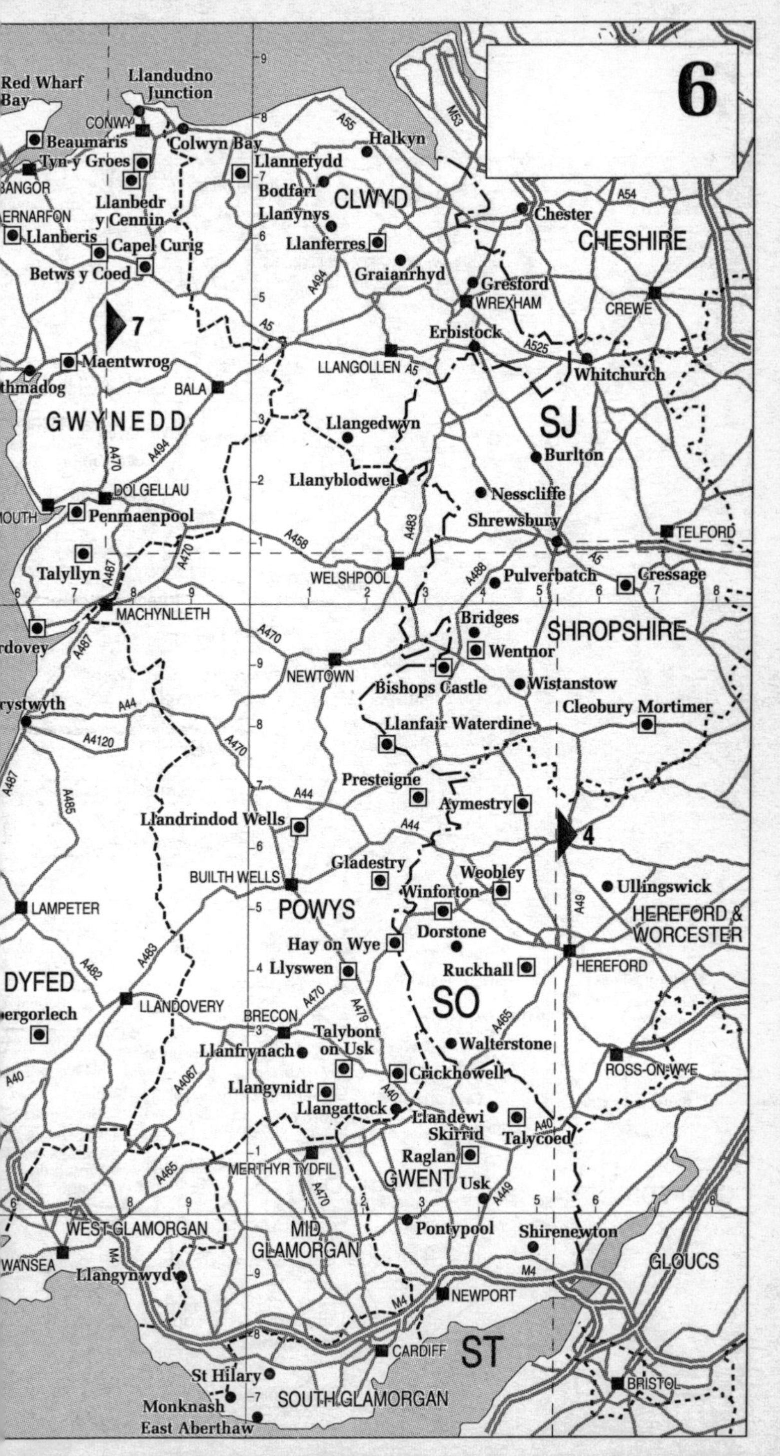

6
Red Wharf Bay
Llandudno Junction
CONWY
Colwyn Bay
Beaumaris
Tyn y Groes
BANGOR
Llanbedr y Cennin
Llanberis
Capel Curig
Betws y Coed
Halkyn
Llannefydd
Bodfari
CLWYD
Llanynys
Llanferres
Graianrhyd
Chester
CHESHIRE
Gresford
WREXHAM
CREWE
Erbistock
Whitchurch
LLANGOLLEN
Maentwrog
BALA
GWYNEDD
Llangedwyn
SJ
Burlton
Llanyblodwel
Nesscliffe
DOLGELLAU
Penmaenpool
Shrewsbury
TELFORD
Talyllyn
WELSHPOOL
Pulverbatch
Cressage
MACHYNLLETH
Bridges
Wentnor
SHROPSHIRE
NEWTOWN
Bishops Castle
Wistanstow
Cleobury Mortimer
Llanfair Waterdine
Presteigne
Aymestry
Llandrindod Wells
4
7
Gladestry
Weobley
BUILTH WELLS
Winforton
Ullingswick
LAMPETER
POWYS
HEREFORD & WORCESTER
Dorstone
Hay on Wye
Llyswen
Ruckhall
HEREFORD
DYFED
SO
LLANDOVERY
BRECON
Talybont on Usk
Llanfrynach
Walterstone
ROSS-ON-WYE
Crickhowell
Llangynidr
Llangattock
Llandewi Skirrid
Talycoed
Raglan
MERTHYR TYDFIL
GWENT
Usk
WEST GLAMORGAN
MID GLAMORGAN
Pontypool
Shirenewton
GLOUCS
Llangynwyd
NEWPORT
CARDIFF
ST
St Hilary
BRISTOL
Monknash
SOUTH GLAMORGAN
East Aberthaw

7

9
Ulverston
Cartmel
Beetham
Casterton
Kirkby Lonsda
Yealand Conyers
BARROW-IN-FURNESS
M6
A65
Settle
SD
0
10
20
MILES
Conder Green
LANCASHIRE
A6
Garstang
Whitewell
Newto
Downham
Chipping
Wharles
BLACKPOOL
Goosnargh
Ribchester
M55
PRESTON
Lytham
Brindle
Croston
Darw
SOUTHPORT
A59
M61
Belmor
Bispham Green
M6
GREATE
MANCHES
A6
A580
MERSEYSIDE
M6
Liverpool
M62
Llandudno
Junction
Colwyn Bay
CONWY
Raby
M53
CHESHIRE
A55
Overton
Plumley
Tyn y Groes
Bodfari
Halkyn
Whitegate
Llanbedr y
Cennin
Llannefydd
Delamere
Peover
CLWYD
Chester
Cotebrook
A470
A525
Llanferres
Tarporley
Llanynys
A494
Aldford
Handley
Wettenhall
A5
Betws y Coed
Graianrhyd
Higher Burwardsley
A49
Bunbury
Barthomley
Gresford
Llanelidan
Broxton
Nantwich
A5
WREXHAM
Bickley Moss
Shraleybrook
Wrenbury
GWYNEDD
SJ
Marbury
Aston
LLANGOLLEN
A5
Erbistock
Whitchurch
BALA
A41
A53
A483
A528
6
A49
A41
Llanyblodwel
A494
Burlton
A5
A495
Nesscliffe
SHROPSHIRE
Shrewsbury

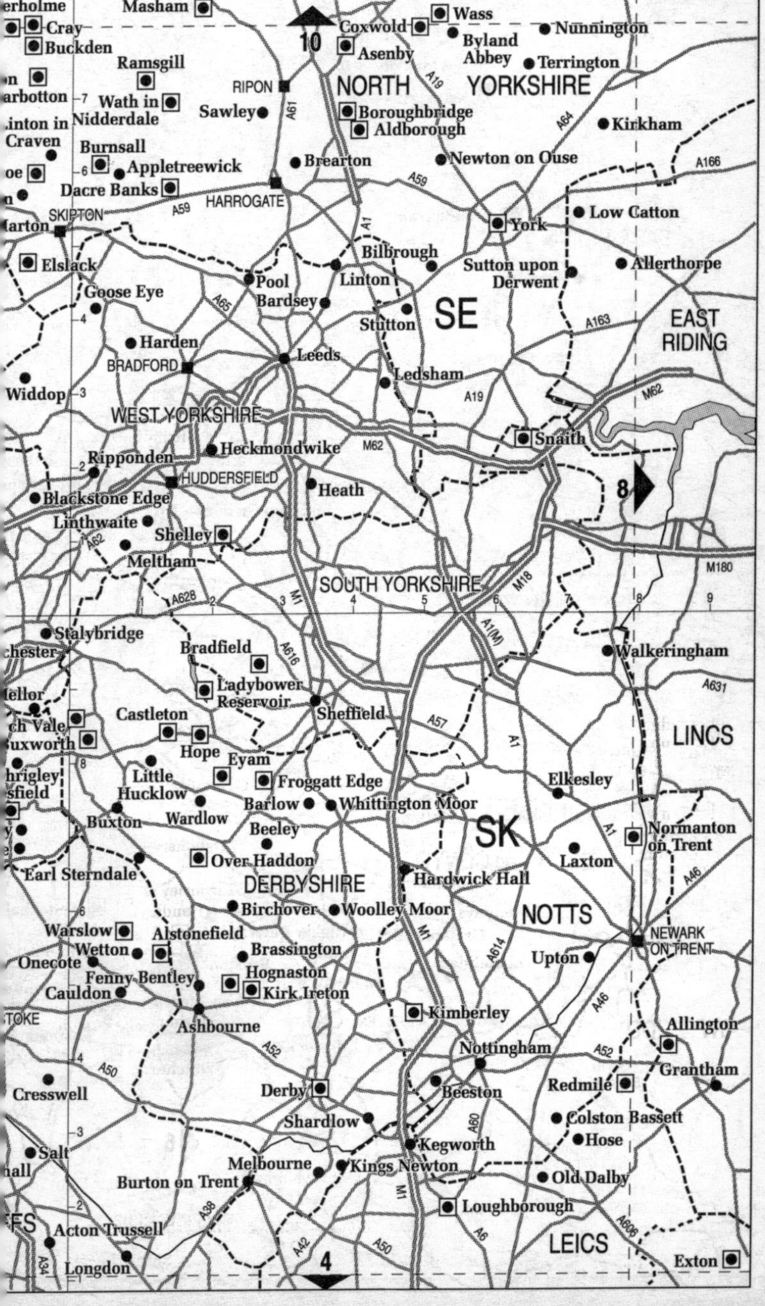
Masham
Wass
Coxwold
Nunnington
Cray
Buckden
10
Asenby
Byland Abbey
Terrington
Ramsgill
RIPON
NORTH YORKSHIRE
A19
Wath in Nidderdale
Sawley
A61
Boroughbridge
Aldborough
A64
Kirkham
Burnsall
Appletreewick
Dacre Banks
Brearton
Newton on Ouse
A166
HARROGATE
A59
SKIPTON
Low Catton
York
A1
Elslack
Bilbrough
Sutton upon Derwent
Allerthorpe
Goose Eye
Pool
Linton
A65
Bardsey
SE
Stutton
A163
EAST RIDING
Harden
Leeds
BRADFORD
Ledsham
Widdop
A19
M62
WEST YORKSHIRE
Snaith
Heckmondwike
M62
Ripponden
HUDDERSFIELD
Heath
8
Blackstone Edge
Linthwaite
Shelley
A62
Meltham
M180
SOUTH YORKSHIRE
M18
A628
M1
Stalybridge
A1(M)
Bradfield
Walkeringham
A616
Ladybower Reservoir
A631
Sheffield
Castleton
A57
LINCS
Hope
A1
Eyam
Little Hucklow
Froggatt Edge
Elkesley
Barlow
Whittington Moor
Wardlow
Buxton
A1
Normanton on Trent
Beeley
SK
Laxton
Over Haddon
Earl Sterndale
A46
Hardwick Hall
DERBYSHIRE
Birchover
Woolley Moor
NOTTS
M1
Warslow
Alstonefield
NEWARK ON TRENT
Wetton
Brassington
A614
Upton
Onecote
Hognaston
Fenny Bentley
Cauldon
Kirk Ireton
A46
Kimberley
Ashbourne
Allington
A52
Nottingham
A52
A50
Grantham
Redmile
Cresswell
Derby
Beeston
Shardlow
A60
Colston Bassett
Hose
Kegworth
Salt
Melbourne
Kings Newton
Old Dalby
Burton on Trent
M1
Loughborough
A38
A606
Acton Trussell
A42
A6
LEICS
A50
A34
4
Exton
Longdon

8

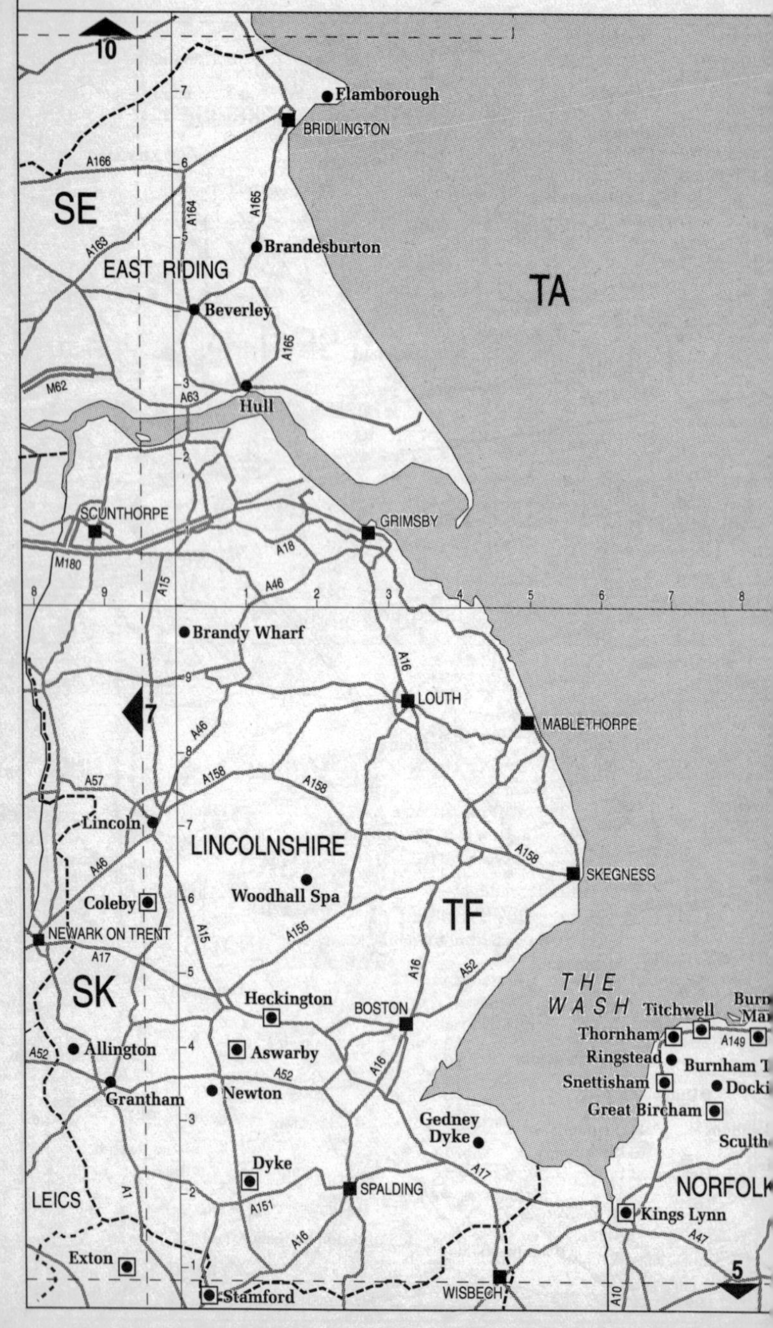

10
Flamborough
BRIDLINGTON
A166
SE
A164
A165
A163
Brandesburton
EAST RIDING
TA
Beverley
A165
M62
A63
Hull
SCUNTHORPE
GRIMSBY
A18
M180
A15
A46
Brandy Wharf
A16
LOUTH
MABLETHORPE
A46
A57
A158
A158
Lincoln
LINCOLNSHIRE
A158
SKEGNESS
A46
Woodhall Spa
Coleby
TF
A155
NEWARK ON TRENT
A15
A17
A16
A52
THE WASH
SK
Heckington
BOSTON
Titchwell
Thornham
A149
Allington
Aswarby
Ringstead
A52
A52
A16
Snettisham
Grantham
Newton
Great Bircham
Gedney Dyke
Dyke
A17
NORFOLK
LEICS
A1
SPALDING
A151
Kings Lynn
A16
A47
Exton
5
Stamford
WISBECH
A10

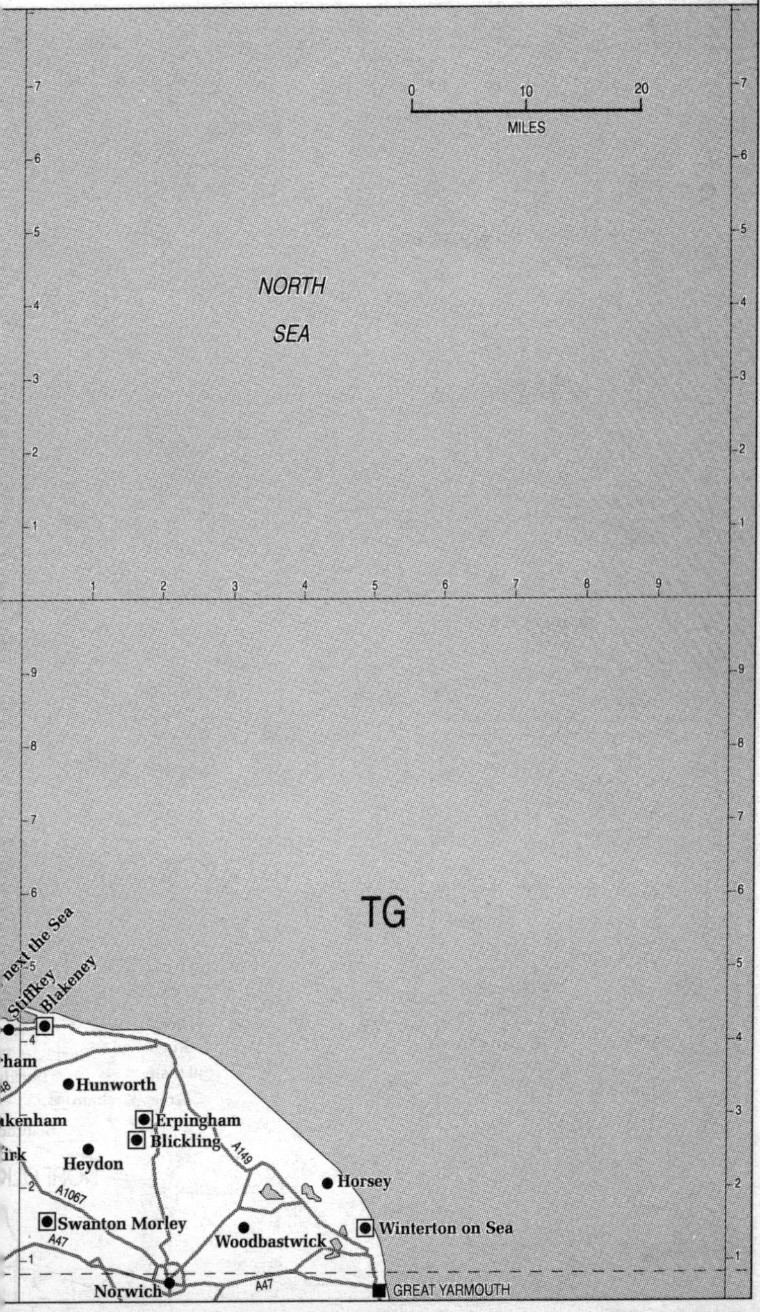

0
10
20
MILES
NORTH
SEA
TG
next the Sea
Stiffkey
Blakeney
ham
Hunworth
kenham
Erpingham
Blickling
A149
irk
Heydon
A1067
Horsey
Swanton Morley
Woodbastwick
Winterton on Sea
A47
Norwich
A47
GREAT YARMOUTH

9

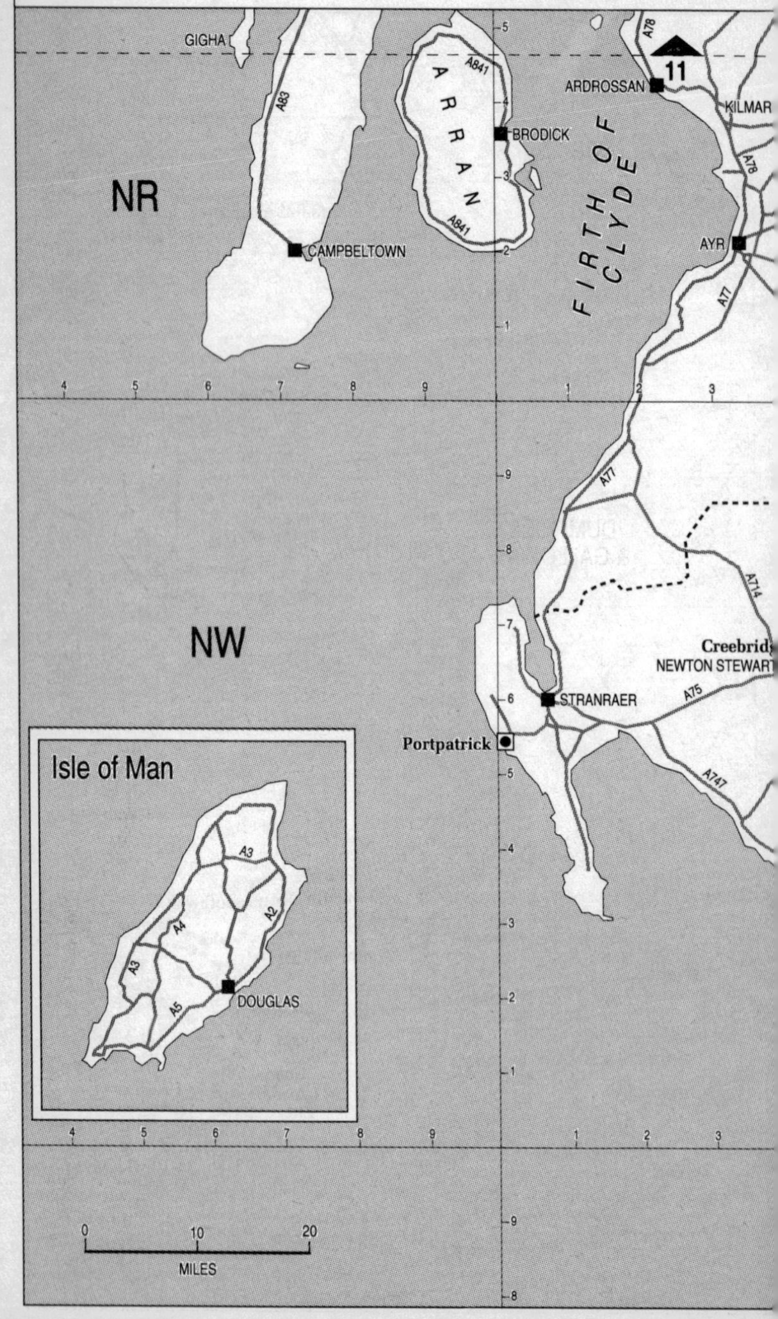

GIGHA
A83
CAMPBELTOWN
ARRAN
A841
BRODICK
FIRTH OF CLYDE
ARDROSSAN
11
A78
KILMAR
AYR
A77
NR
NW
Creebrid
NEWTON STEWART
A714
A75
STRANRAER
Portpatrick
A747
Isle of Man
A3
A2
A4
A5
DOUGLAS
0
10
20
MILES

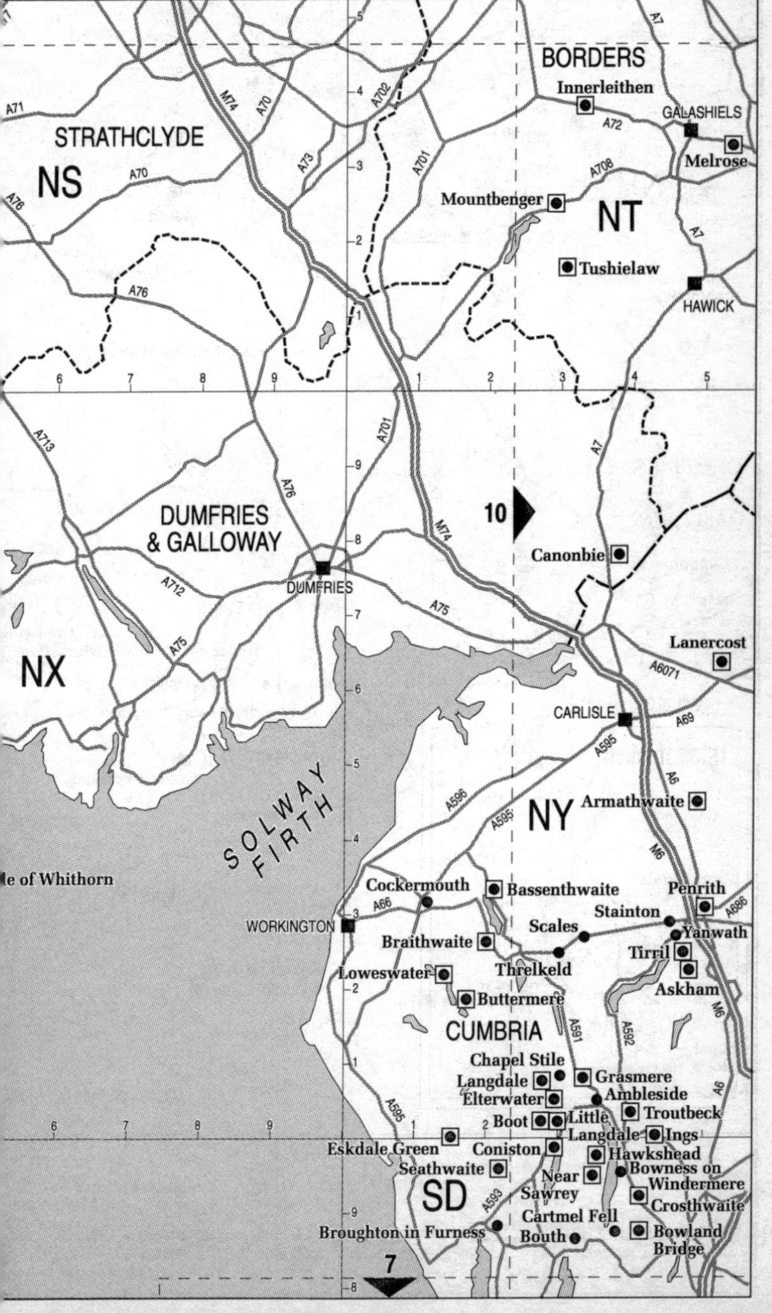

BORDERS
Innerleithen
GALASHIELS
Melrose
A72
A708
Mountbenger
NT
Tushielaw
HAWICK
A7
STRATHCLYDE
NS
A71
A70
A76
M74
A73
A702
A701
DUMFRIES
& GALLOWAY
DUMFRIES
A713
A712
A75
NX
10
Canonbie
Lanercost
A6071
CARLISLE
A69
A595
A596
A6
M6
NY
Armathwaite
SOLWAY
FIRTH
e of Whithorn
Cockermouth
Bassenthwaite
Penrith
A686
Stainton
Yanwath
Scales
WORKINGTON
A66
Braithwaite
Tirril
Askham
Threlkeld
Loweswater
Buttermere
CUMBRIA
A591
A592
Chapel Stile
Langdale
Grasmere
Elterwater
Ambleside
Boot
Little
Langdale
Troutbeck
Ings
Eskdale Green
Coniston
Hawkshead
Seathwaite
Near
Sawrey
Bowness on
Windermere
Crosthwaite
SD
A593
Cartmel Fell
Broughton in Furness
Bouth
Bowland
Bridge
7

10

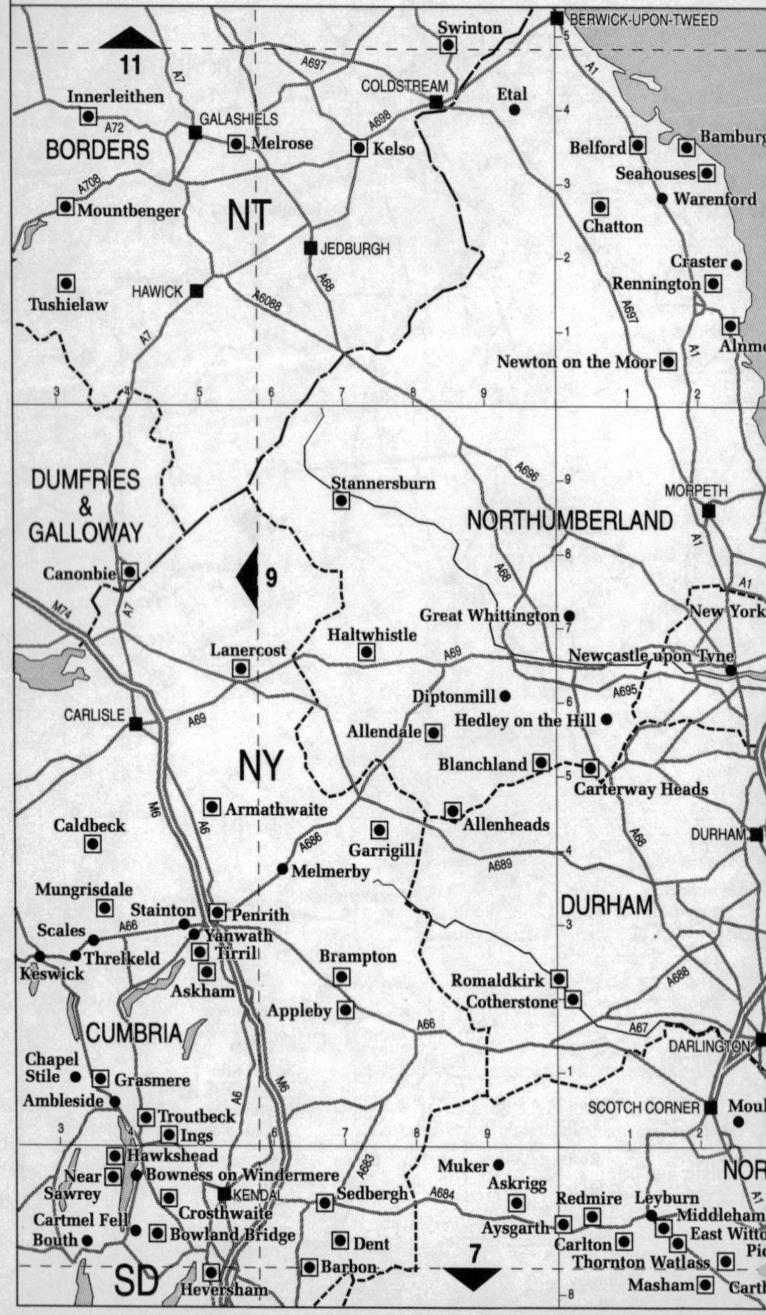

BERWICK-UPON-TWEED
Swinton
11
Innerleithen
GALASHIELS
COLDSTREAM
Etal
Melrose
Kelso
BORDERS
Belford
Bamburg
Seahouses
Warenford
Mountbenger
NT
Chatton
JEDBURGH
Craster
Rennington
HAWICK
Tushielaw
Alnmo
Newton on the Moor
DUMFRIES & GALLOWAY
Stannersburn
MORPETH
NORTHUMBERLAND
Canonbie
9
Great Whittington
New York
Haltwhistle
Lanercost
Newcastle upon Tyne
Diptonmill
CARLISLE
Hedley on the Hill
Allendale
Blanchland
NY
Carterway Heads
Armathwaite
Allenheads
Caldbeck
Garrigill
DURHAM
Melmerby
Mungrisdale
DURHAM
Stainton
Penrith
Scales
Yanwath
Threlkeld
Tirril
Keswick
Brampton
Askham
Romaldkirk
Cotherstone
Appleby
CUMBRIA
Chapel Stile
Grasmere
DARLINGTON
Ambleside
Troutbeck
SCOTCH CORNER
Moul
Ings
Hawkshead
Muker
NOR
Near Sawrey
Bowness on Windermere
Askrigg
KENDAL
Sedbergh
Redmire
Leyburn
Crosthwaite
Middleham
Cartmel Fell
Aysgarth
East Witto
Bouth
Bowland Bridge
Dent
Carlton
Pic
Thornton Watlass
Barbon
7
SD
Heversham
Masham
Carth
A7
A72
A697
A698
A708
A6088
A68
A1
A696
M74
A69
A695
M6
A6
A686
A689
A66
A688
A67
A683
A684

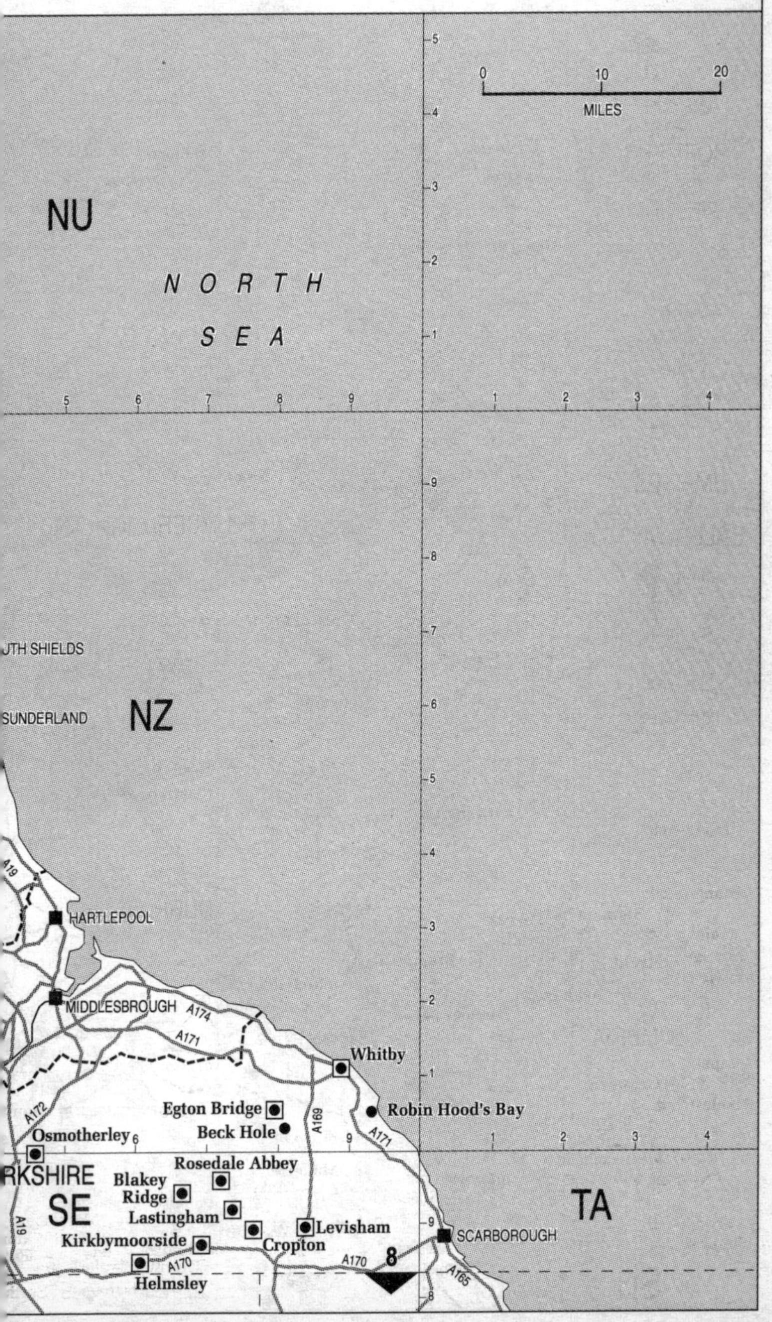

0
10
20
MILES
NU
NORTH
SEA
NZ
UTH SHIELDS
SUNDERLAND
HARTLEPOOL
MIDDLESBROUGH
A174
A171
A19
A172
A169
Whitby
Robin Hood's Bay
Egton Bridge
Beck Hole
Osmotherley
Rosedale Abbey
Blakey Ridge
Lastingham
Levisham
Cropton
Kirkbymoorside
Helmsley
A170
RKSHIRE
SE
TA
SCARBOROUGH
A165
8

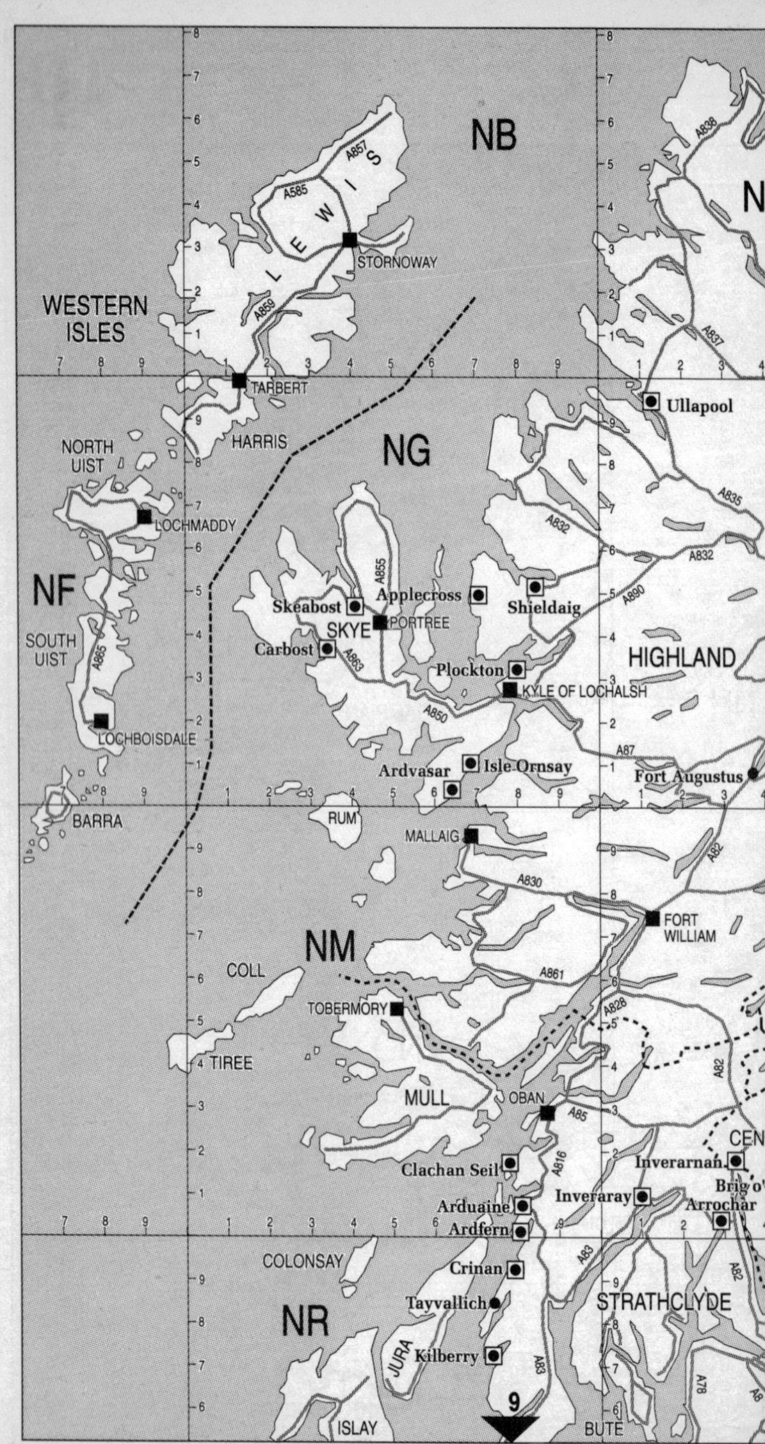

NB
LEWIS
A857
A585
STORNOWAY
A859
WESTERN ISLES
TARBERT
HARRIS
NORTH UIST
LOCHMADDY
NG
NF
SOUTH UIST
A865
LOCHBOISDALE
BARRA
Skeabost
SKYE
PORTREE
A855
Carbost
A863
A850
Applecross
Shieldaig
Plockton
KYLE OF LOCHALSH
Ardvasar
Isle Ornsay
RUM
MALLAIG
A830
A832
A835
A838
A837
A890
A87
Ullapool
HIGHLAND
Fort Augustus
A82
FORT WILLIAM
NM
COLL
TOBERMORY
A861
A828
TIREE
MULL
OBAN
A85
A816
Clachan Seil
Arduaine
Ardfern
Inverarnan
Inveraray
Arrochar
Brig o'
CENT
COLONSAY
Crinan
Tayvallich
STRATHCLYDE
NR
JURA
Kilberry
A83
A78
ISLAY
BUTE
9

11
THURSO
WICK
Lybster
ND
MILES
DORNOCH
BANFF
FRASERBURGH
Cawdor
INVERNESS
NJ
NK
NH
GRANTOWN-ON-SPEY
GRAMPIAN
Aberdeen
Stonehaven
Kirkton of Glenisla
MONTROSE
Pitlochry
Weem
TAYSIDE
NO
DUNDEE
Broughty Ferry
PERTH
ST ANDREWS
FIFE
Elie
Sheriffmuir
Glendevon
STIRLING
NT
Edinburgh
Linlithgow
Gifford
LOTHIAN
BORDERS
BERWICK UPON TWEED
10

12

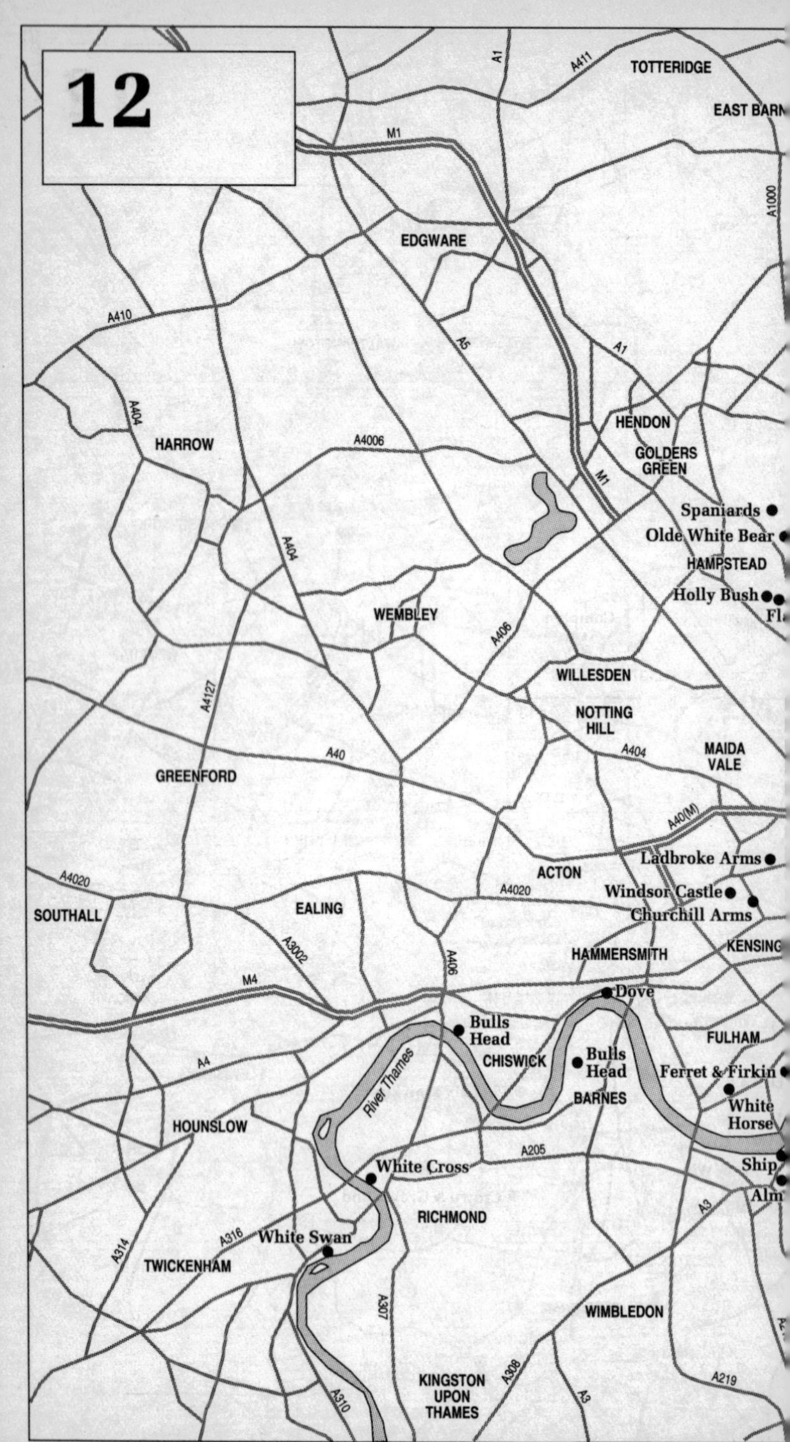

TOTTERIDGE
EAST BARN
A1
A411
M1
A1000
EDGWARE
A410
A5
A1
A404
HENDON
HARROW
A4006
GOLDERS GREEN
M1
Spaniards
Olde White Bear
HAMPSTEAD
A404
Holly Bush
Fl
WEMBLEY
A406
WILLESDEN
A4127
NOTTING HILL
A404
MAIDA VALE
A40
GREENFORD
A40(M)
Ladbroke Arms
A4020
ACTON
Windsor Castle
A4020
SOUTHALL
EALING
Churchill Arms
KENSING
A3002
HAMMERSMITH
A406
M4
Dove
Bulls Head
FULHAM
A4
River Thames
CHISWICK
Bulls Head
Ferret & Firkin
BARNES
White Horse
HOUNSLOW
A205
Ship
White Cross
Alm
A3
RICHMOND
A316
White Swan
A314
TWICKENHAM
A307
WIMBLEDON
KINGSTON UPON THAMES
A308
A310
A3
A219

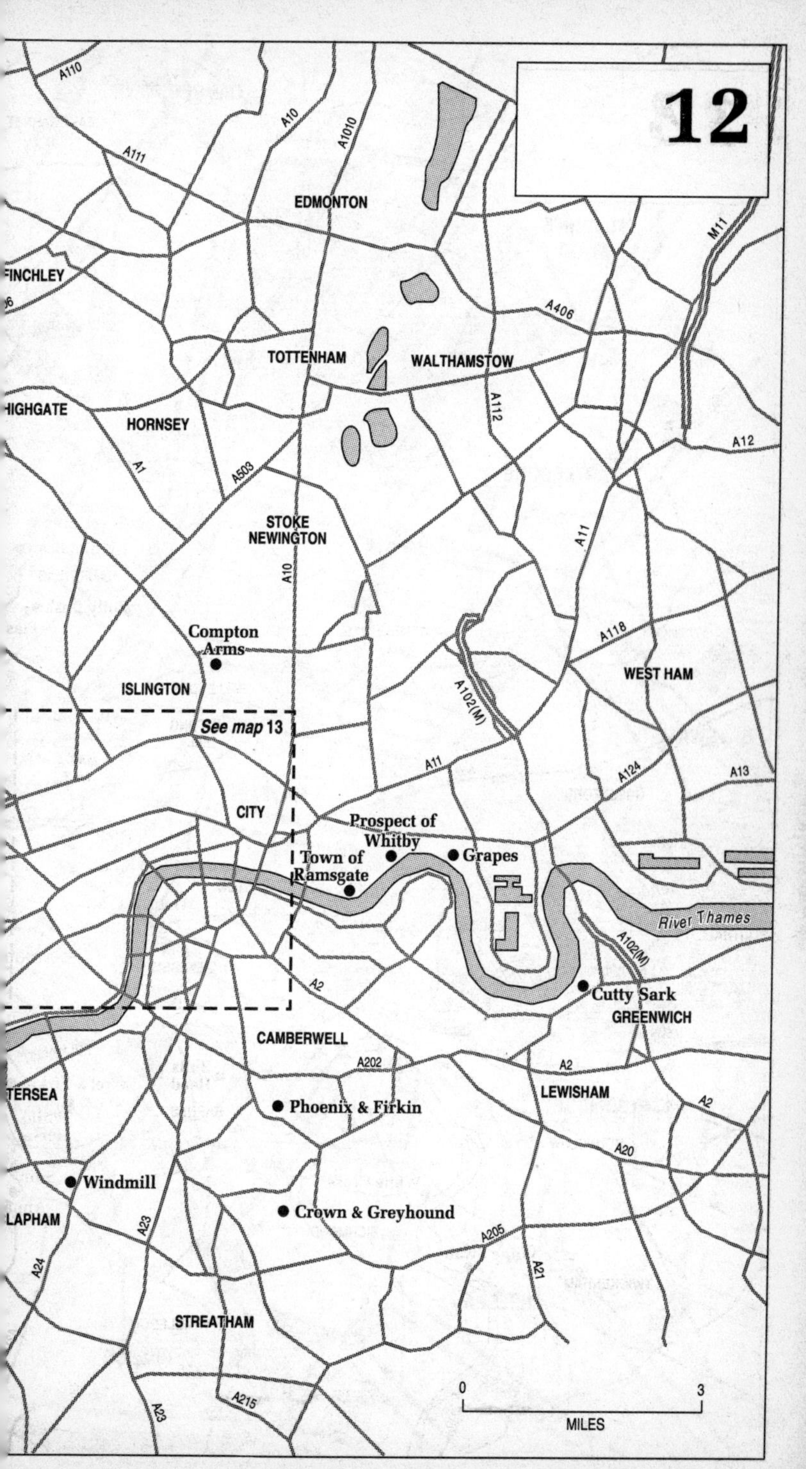
12
A110
A10
A1010
A111
EDMONTON
FINCHLEY
M11
A406
TOTTENHAM
WALTHAMSTOW
HIGHGATE
HORNSEY
A112
A12
A1
A503
STOKE
NEWINGTON
A11
A10
Compton
Arms
A118
WEST HAM
ISLINGTON
A102(M)
See map 13
A11
A124
A13
CITY
Prospect of
Whitby
Town of
Ramsgate
Grapes
River Thames
A102(M)
A2
Cutty Sark
GREENWICH
CAMBERWELL
A202
A2
TERSEA
LEWISHAM
A2
Phoenix & Firkin
A20
Windmill
Crown & Greyhound
LAPHAM
A23
A205
A24
A21
STREATHAM
A215
A23
0
3
MILES

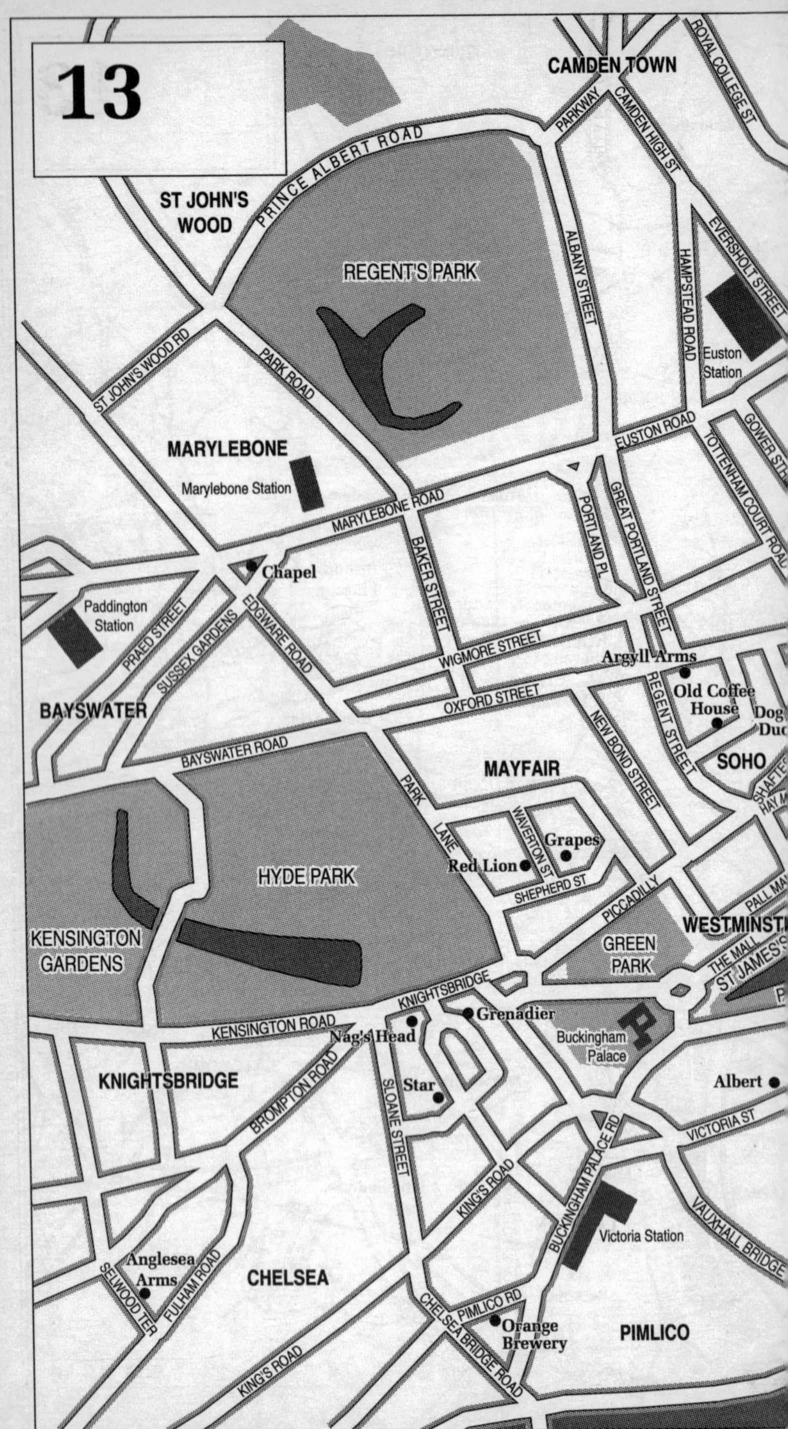

13
CAMDEN TOWN
ROYAL COLLEGE ST
PARKWAY
CAMDEN HIGH ST
PRINCE ALBERT ROAD
ST JOHN'S WOOD
REGENT'S PARK
ALBANY STREET
HAMPSTEAD ROAD
EVERSHOLT STREET
Euston Station
ST JOHN'S WOOD RD
PARK ROAD
EUSTON ROAD
GOWER ST
TOTTENHAM COURT ROAD
MARYLEBONE
Marylebone Station
MARYLEBONE ROAD
PORTLAND PL
GREAT PORTLAND STREET
BAKER STREET
Chapel
Paddington Station
PRAED STREET
SUSSEX GARDENS
EDGWARE ROAD
WIGMORE STREET
Argyll Arms
Old Coffee House
REGENT STREET
OXFORD STREET
BAYSWATER
NEW BOND STREET
SOHO
BAYSWATER ROAD
MAYFAIR
PARK LANE
WAVERTON ST
Grapes
Red Lion
HYDE PARK
SHEPHERD ST
PICCADILLY
KENSINGTON GARDENS
GREEN PARK
WESTMINST
THE MALL
KNIGHTSBRIDGE
Grenadier
KENSINGTON ROAD
Nag's Head
Buckingham Palace
KNIGHTSBRIDGE
SLOANE STREET
Star
Albert
BROMPTON ROAD
BUCKINGHAM PALACE RD
VICTORIA ST
KING'S ROAD
Victoria Station
VAUXHALL BRIDGE
Anglesea Arms
SELWOOD TER
FULHAM ROAD
CHELSEA
PIMLICO RD
Orange Brewery
PIMLICO
CHELSEA BRIDGE ROAD
KING'S ROAD

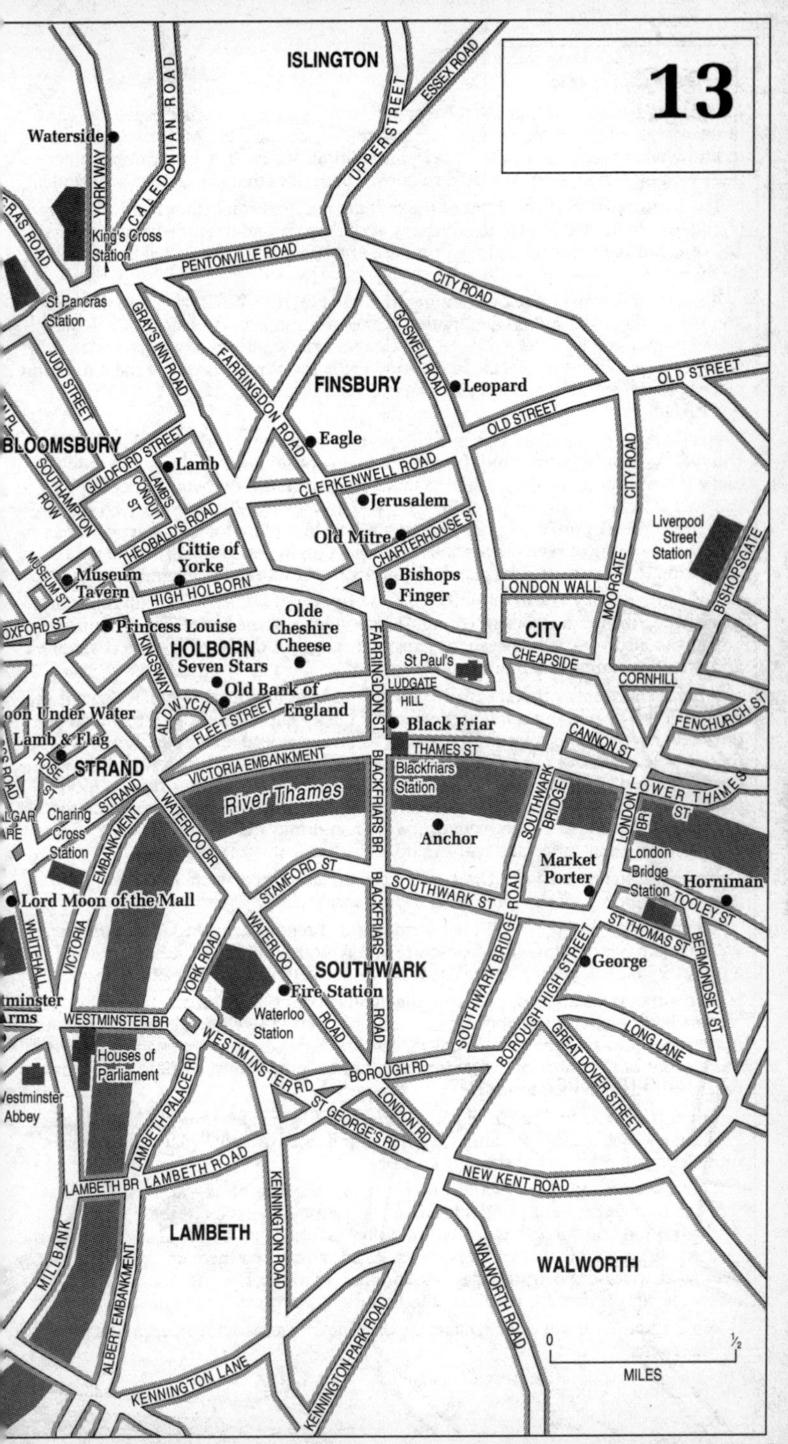
13
ISLINGTON
Waterside
King's Cross Station
St Pancras Station
FINSBURY
Leopard
Eagle
BLOOMSBURY
Lamb
Jerusalem
Old Mitre
Cittie of Yorke
Museum Tavern
Bishops Finger
Princess Louise
HOLBORN
Olde Cheshire Cheese
Seven Stars
Old Bank of England
St Paul's
CITY
Liverpool Street Station
Black Friar
STRAND
Lamb & Flag
Blackfriars Station
River Thames
Charing Cross Station
Anchor
Market Porter
London Bridge Station
Horniman
Lord Moon of the Mall
George
SOUTHWARK
Fire Station
Waterloo Station
Houses of Parliament
LAMBETH
WALWORTH
0
½
MILES
PENTONVILLE ROAD
CITY ROAD
GOSWELL ROAD
OLD STREET
FARRINGDON ROAD
CLERKENWELL ROAD
CHARTERHOUSE ST
HIGH HOLBORN
LONDON WALL
CHEAPSIDE
CORNHILL
FENCHURCH ST
CANNON ST
LUDGATE HILL
THAMES ST
FLEET STREET
ALDWYCH
KINGSWAY
VICTORIA EMBANKMENT
LOWER THAMES ST
SOUTHWARK BRIDGE
LONDON BR
WATERLOO BR
STAMFORD ST
SOUTHWARK ST
TOOLEY ST
ST THOMAS ST
BERMONDSEY ST
LONG LANE
BOROUGH HIGH STREET
GREAT DOVER STREET
SOUTHWARK BRIDGE ROAD
BLACKFRIARS ROAD
WATERLOO ROAD
YORK ROAD
WESTMINSTER BR
WESTMINSTER RD
BOROUGH RD
LONDON RD
ST GEORGE'S RD
NEW KENT ROAD
LAMBETH PALACE RD
LAMBETH ROAD
LAMBETH BR
KENNINGTON ROAD
KENNINGTON PARK ROAD
KENNINGTON LANE
WALWORTH ROAD
ALBERT EMBANKMENT
MILLBANK
WHITEHALL
VICTORIA EMBANKMENT
STRAND
ROSE ST
OXFORD ST
MUSEUM ST
SOUTHAMPTON ROW
THEOBALD'S ROAD
GUILFORD STREET
LAMB'S CONDUIT ST
JUDD STREET
GRAY'S INN ROAD
YORK WAY
CALEDONIAN ROAD
UPPER STREET
ESSEX ROAD
CITY ROAD
MOORGATE
BISHOPSGATE
OLD STREET
FARRINGDON ST
BLACKFRIARS BR

Report forms

Please report to us: you can use the tear-out forms on the following pages, the card in the middle of the book, or just plain paper – whichever's easiest for you. We need to know what you think of the pubs in this edition. We need to know about other pubs worthy of inclusion. We need to know about ones that should not be included.

The atmosphere and character of the pub are the most important features – why it would, or would not, appeal to strangers, so please try and describe what is special about it. But the bar food and the drink are important too – please tell us about them.

If the food is really quite outstanding, tick the FOOD AWARD box on the form, and tell us about the special quality that makes it stand out – the more detail, the better. And if you have stayed there, tell us about the standard of accommodation – whether it was comfortable, pleasant, good value for money. Again, if the pub or inn place is worth special attention as a place to stay, tick the PLACE-TO-STAY AWARD box.

Please try to gauge whether a pub should be a main entry, or is best as a Lucky Dip (and tick the relevant box). In general, main entries need qualities that would make it worth other readers' while to travel some distance to them; Lucky Dips are the pubs that are worth knowing about if you are nearby. But if a pub is an entirely new recommendation, the Lucky Dip may be the best place for it to start its career in the *Guide* – to encourage other readers to report on it, and gradually build up a dossier on it; it's very rare for a pub to jump straight into the main entries.

The more detail you can put into your description of a Lucky Dip pub that's only scantily decribed in the current edition (or not in at all), the better. This'll help not just us but also your fellow-readers gauge its appeal. A description of its character and even furnishings is a tremendous boon.

It helps enormously if you can give the full address for any new pub – one not yet a main entry, or without a full address in the Lucky Dip sections. In a town, we need the street name; in the country, if it's hard to find, we need directions. Without this, there's little chance of our being able to include the pub. **Even better for us is the postcode**. And with any pub, it always helps to let us know about **prices** of food (and bedrooms, if there are any), and about any lunchtimes or evenings when food is **not** served. We'd also like to have your views on drinks quality – beer, wine, cider and so forth, even coffee and tea; and do let us know if it has bedrooms.

If you know that a Lucky Dip pub is open all day (or even late into the afternoon), please tell us – preferably saying which days.

When you go to a pub, don't tell them you're a reporter for the *Good Pub Guide*; we do make clear that all inspections are anonymous, and if you declare yourself as a reporter you risk getting special treatment – for better or for worse!

Sometimes pubs are dropped from the main entries simply because very few readers have written to us about them – and of course there's a risk that people may not write if they find the pub exactly as described in the entry. You can use the form at the front of the batch of report forms just to list pubs you've been to, found as described, and can recommend.

When you write to *The Good Pub Guide*, FREEPOST TN1569, WADHURST, East Sussex TN5 7BR, you don't need a stamp in the UK. We'll gladly send you more forms (free) if you wish.

Though we try to answer letters, there are just the four of us – and with other work to do, besides producing this *Guide*. So please understand if there's a delay. And from June till August, when we are fully extended getting the next edition to the printers, we put all letters and reports aside, not answering them until the rush is over (and after our post-press-day late summer holiday). The end of May is pretty much the cut-off date for reasoned consideration of reports for the next edition.

We'll assume we can print your name or initials as a recommender unless you tell us otherwise.

I have been to the following pubs in *The Good Pub Guide 1999* in the last few months, found them as described, and confirm that they deserve continued inclusion:

Continued overleaf

PLEASE GIVE YOUR NAME AND ADDRESS ON THE BACK OF THIS FORM

Pubs visited continued...

Your own name and address *(block capitals please)*

Please return to
The Good Pub Guide,
FREEPOST TN1569,
WADHURST,
East Sussex
TN5 7BR

REPORT ON *(pub's name)*

Pub's address

☐ YES MAIN ENTRY ☐ YES *Lucky Dip* ☐ NO don't include

Please tick one of these boxes to show your verdict, and give reasons and descriptive comments, prices etc

☐ Deserves FOOD award ☐ Deserves PLACE-TO-STAY award 99:1

PLEASE GIVE YOUR NAME AND ADDRESS ON THE BACK OF THIS FORM

REPORT ON *(pub's name)*

Pub's address

☐ YES MAIN ENTRY ☐ YES *Lucky Dip* ☐ NO don't include

Please tick one of these boxes to show your verdict, and give reasons and descriptive comments, prices etc

☐ Deserves FOOD award ☐ Deserves PLACE-TO-STAY award 99:2

PLEASE GIVE YOUR NAME AND ADDRESS ON THE BACK OF THIS FORM

Your own name and address *(block capitals please)*

DO NOT USE THIS SIDE OF THE PAGE FOR WRITING ABOUT PUBS

Your own name and address *(block capitals please)*

DO NOT USE THIS SIDE OF THE PAGE FOR WRITING ABOUT PUBS

REPORT ON *(pub's name)*

Pub's address

☐ **YES** MAIN ENTRY ☐ **YES** ***Lucky Dip*** ☐ **NO don't include**

Please tick one of these boxes to show your verdict, and give reasons and descriptive comments, prices etc

☐ Deserves FOOD award ☐ Deserves PLACE-TO-STAY award 99:3

PLEASE GIVE YOUR NAME AND ADDRESS ON THE BACK OF THIS FORM

REPORT ON *(pub's name)*

Pub's address

☐ **YES** MAIN ENTRY ☐ **YES** ***Lucky Dip*** ☐ **NO don't include**

Please tick one of these boxes to show your verdict, and give reasons and descriptive comments, prices etc

☐ Deserves FOOD award ☐ Deserves PLACE-TO-STAY award 99:4

PLEASE GIVE YOUR NAME AND ADDRESS ON THE BACK OF THIS FORM

Your own name and address *(block capitals please)*

DO NOT USE THIS SIDE OF THE PAGE FOR WRITING ABOUT PUBS

Your own name and address *(block capitals please)*

DO NOT USE THIS SIDE OF THE PAGE FOR WRITING ABOUT PUBS

REPORT ON *(pub's name)*

Pub's address

☐ **YES** **MAIN ENTRY** ☐ **YES** ***Lucky Dip*** ☐ **NO don't include**

Please tick one of these boxes to show your verdict, and give reasons and descriptive comments, prices etc

☐ Deserves FOOD award ☐ Deserves PLACE-TO-STAY award 99:5

PLEASE GIVE YOUR NAME AND ADDRESS ON THE BACK OF THIS FORM

REPORT ON *(pub's name)*

Pub's address

☐ **YES** **MAIN ENTRY** ☐ **YES** ***Lucky Dip*** ☐ **NO don't include**

Please tick one of these boxes to show your verdict, and give reasons and descriptive comments, prices etc

☐ Deserves FOOD award ☐ Deserves PLACE-TO-STAY award 99:6

PLEASE GIVE YOUR NAME AND ADDRESS ON THE BACK OF THIS FORM

Your own name and address *(block capitals please)*

DO NOT USE THIS SIDE OF THE PAGE FOR WRITING ABOUT PUBS

✂ ....

Your own name and address *(block capitals please)*

DO NOT USE THIS SIDE OF THE PAGE FOR WRITING ABOUT PUBS

REPORT ON *(pub's name)*

Pub's address

☐ **YES MAIN ENTRY** ☐ **YES *Lucky Dip*** ☐ **NO don't include**

Please tick one of these boxes to show your verdict, and give reasons and descriptive comments, prices etc

☐ Deserves FOOD award ☐ Deserves PLACE-TO-STAY award 99:7

PLEASE GIVE YOUR NAME AND ADDRESS ON THE BACK OF THIS FORM

REPORT ON *(pub's name)*

Pub's address

☐ **YES MAIN ENTRY** ☐ **YES *Lucky Dip*** ☐ **NO don't include**

Please tick one of these boxes to show your verdict, and give reasons and descriptive comments, prices etc

☐ Deserves FOOD award ☐ Deserves PLACE-TO-STAY award 99:8

PLEASE GIVE YOUR NAME AND ADDRESS ON THE BACK OF THIS FORM

Your own name and address *(block capitals please)*

DO NOT USE THIS SIDE OF THE PAGE FOR WRITING ABOUT PUBS

Your own name and address *(block capitals please)*

DO NOT USE THIS SIDE OF THE PAGE FOR WRITING ABOUT PUBS

REPORT ON (*pub's name*)

Pub's address

☐ YES MAIN ENTRY ☐ YES *Lucky Dip* ☐ NO don't include

Please tick one of these boxes to show your verdict, and give reasons and descriptive comments, prices etc

☐ Deserves FOOD award ☐ Deserves PLACE-TO-STAY award 99:9

PLEASE GIVE YOUR NAME AND ADDRESS ON THE BACK OF THIS FORM

REPORT ON (*pub's name*)

Pub's address

☐ YES MAIN ENTRY ☐ YES *Lucky Dip* ☐ NO don't include

Please tick one of these boxes to show your verdict, and give reasons and descriptive comments, prices etc

☐ Deserves FOOD award ☐ Deserves PLACE-TO-STAY award 99:10

PLEASE GIVE YOUR NAME AND ADDRESS ON THE BACK OF THIS FORM

Your own name and address *(block capitals please)*

DO NOT USE THIS SIDE OF THE PAGE FOR WRITING ABOUT PUBS

✂ ....

Your own name and address *(block capitals please)*

DO NOT USE THIS SIDE OF THE PAGE FOR WRITING ABOUT PUBS

REPORT ON (*pub's name*)

Pub's address

☐ YES MAIN ENTRY ☐ YES *Lucky Dip* ☐ NO don't include

Please tick one of these boxes to show your verdict, and give reasons and descriptive comments, prices etc

☐ Deserves FOOD award ☐ Deserves PLACE-TO-STAY award 99:11

PLEASE GIVE YOUR NAME AND ADDRESS ON THE BACK OF THIS FORM

REPORT ON (*pub's name*)

Pub's address

☐ YES MAIN ENTRY ☐ YES *Lucky Dip* ☐ NO don't include

Please tick one of these boxes to show your verdict, and give reasons and descriptive comments, prices etc

☐ Deserves FOOD award ☐ Deserves PLACE-TO-STAY award 99:12

PLEASE GIVE YOUR NAME AND ADDRESS ON THE BACK OF THIS FORM

Your own name and address *(block capitals please)*

DO NOT USE THIS SIDE OF THE PAGE FOR WRITING ABOUT PUBS

Your own name and address *(block capitals please)*

DO NOT USE THIS SIDE OF THE PAGE FOR WRITING ABOUT PUBS

REPORT ON *(pub's name)*

Pub's address

☐ YES MAIN ENTRY ☐ YES *Lucky Dip* ☐ NO don't include

Please tick one of these boxes to show your verdict, and give reasons and descriptive comments, prices etc

☐ Deserves FOOD award ☐ Deserves PLACE-TO-STAY award 99:13

PLEASE GIVE YOUR NAME AND ADDRESS ON THE BACK OF THIS FORM

REPORT ON *(pub's name)*

Pub's address

☐ YES MAIN ENTRY ☐ YES *Lucky Dip* ☐ NO don't include

Please tick one of these boxes to show your verdict, and give reasons and descriptive comments, prices etc

☐ Deserves FOOD award ☐ Deserves PLACE-TO-STAY award 99:14

PLEASE GIVE YOUR NAME AND ADDRESS ON THE BACK OF THIS FORM

Your own name and address *(block capitals please)*

DO NOT USE THIS SIDE OF THE PAGE FOR WRITING ABOUT PUBS

Your own name and address *(block capitals please)*

DO NOT USE THIS SIDE OF THE PAGE FOR WRITING ABOUT PUBS

REPORT ON (pub's name)

ub's address

☐ YES MAIN ENTRY ☐ YES *Lucky Dip* ☐ NO don't include

lease tick one of these boxes to show your verdict, and give reasons and escriptive comments, prices etc

☐ Deserves FOOD award ☐ Deserves PLACE-TO-STAY award 99:15

LEASE GIVE YOUR NAME AND ADDRESS ON THE BACK OF THIS FORM

EPORT ON (pub's name)

ub's address

☐ YES MAIN ENTRY ☐ YES *Lucky Dip* ☐ NO don't include

ease tick one of these boxes to show your verdict, and give reasons and scriptive comments, prices etc

Deserves FOOD award ☐ Deserves PLACE-TO-STAY award 99:16

EASE GIVE YOUR NAME AND ADDRESS ON THE BACK OF THIS FORM

Your own name and address *(block capitals please)*

DO NOT USE THIS SIDE OF THE PAGE FOR WRITING ABOUT PUBS

Your own name and address *(block capitals please)*

DO NOT USE THIS SIDE OF THE PAGE FOR WRITING ABOUT PUBS

REPORT ON (pub's name)

Pub's address

☐ YES MAIN ENTRY ☐ YES *Lucky Dip* ☐ NO don't include

Please tick one of these boxes to show your verdict, and give reasons and descriptive comments, prices etc

☐ Deserves FOOD award ☐ Deserves PLACE-TO-STAY award 99:17

PLEASE GIVE YOUR NAME AND ADDRESS ON THE BACK OF THIS FORM

REPORT ON (pub's name)

Pub's address

☐ YES MAIN ENTRY ☐ YES *Lucky Dip* ☐ NO don't include

Please tick one of these boxes to show your verdict, and give reasons and descriptive comments, prices etc

☐ Deserves FOOD award ☐ Deserves PLACE-TO-STAY award 99:18

PLEASE GIVE YOUR NAME AND ADDRESS ON THE BACK OF THIS FORM

Your own name and address *(block capitals please)*

DO NOT USE THIS SIDE OF THE PAGE FOR WRITING ABOUT PUBS

Your own name and address *(block capitals please)*

DO NOT USE THIS SIDE OF THE PAGE FOR WRITING ABOUT PUBS

REPORT ON (*pub's name*)

Pub's address

☐ YES MAIN ENTRY ☐ YES *Lucky Dip* ☐ NO don't include

Please tick one of these boxes to show your verdict, and give reasons and descriptive comments, prices etc

☐ Deserves FOOD award ☐ Deserves PLACE-TO-STAY award 99:19

LEASE GIVE YOUR NAME AND ADDRESS ON THE BACK OF THIS FORM

EPORT ON (*pub's name*)

ub's address

☐ YES MAIN ENTRY ☐ YES *Lucky Dip* ☐ NO don't include

ease tick one of these boxes to show your verdict, and give reasons and scriptive comments, prices etc

Deserves FOOD award ☐ Deserves PLACE-TO-STAY award 99:20

EASE GIVE YOUR NAME AND ADDRESS ON THE BACK OF THIS FORM

Your own name and address *(block capitals please)*

DO NOT USE THIS SIDE OF THE PAGE FOR WRITING ABOUT PUBS

Your own name and address *(block capitals please)*

DO NOT USE THIS SIDE OF THE PAGE FOR WRITING ABOUT PUBS

REPORT ON (*pub's name*)

Pub's address

☐ YES MAIN ENTRY ☐ YES *Lucky Dip* ☐ NO don't include

Please tick one of these boxes to show your verdict, and give reasons and descriptive comments, prices etc

☐ Deserves FOOD award ☐ Deserves PLACE-TO-STAY award 99:21

PLEASE GIVE YOUR NAME AND ADDRESS ON THE BACK OF THIS FORM

EPORT ON (*pub's name*)

ub's address

☐ YES MAIN ENTRY ☐ YES *Lucky Dip* ☐ NO don't include

ease tick one of these boxes to show your verdict, and give reasons and scriptive comments, prices etc

Deserves FOOD award ☐ Deserves PLACE-TO-STAY award 99:22

EASE GIVE YOUR NAME AND ADDRESS ON THE BACK OF THIS FORM

Your own name and address *(block capitals please)*

DO NOT USE THIS SIDE OF THE PAGE FOR WRITING ABOUT PUBS

Your own name and address *(block capitals please)*

DO NOT USE THIS SIDE OF THE PAGE FOR WRITING ABOUT PUBS

.PORT ON (*pub's name*)

b's address

YES MAIN ENTRY ☐ YES *Lucky Dip* ☐ NO don't include

ase tick one of these boxes to show your verdict, and give reasons and criptive comments, prices etc

Deserves FOOD award ☐ Deserves PLACE-TO-STAY award 99:23

EASE GIVE YOUR NAME AND ADDRESS ON THE BACK OF THIS FORM

PORT ON (*pub's name*)

›'s address

YES MAIN ENTRY ☐ YES *Lucky Dip* ☐ NO don't include

ase tick one of these boxes to show your verdict, and give reasons and criptive comments, prices etc

Deserves FOOD award ☐ Deserves PLACE-TO-STAY award 99:24

:ASE GIVE YOUR NAME AND ADDRESS ON THE BACK OF THIS FORM

Your own name and address *(block capitals please)*

DO NOT USE THIS SIDE OF THE PAGE FOR WRITING ABOUT PUBS

Your own name and address *(block capitals please)*

DO NOT USE THIS SIDE OF THE PAGE FOR WRITING ABOUT PUBS

REPORT ON (pub's name)

Pub's address

☐ YES MAIN ENTRY ☐ YES *Lucky Dip* ☐ NO don't include

Please tick one of these boxes to show your verdict, and give reasons and descriptive comments, prices etc

☐ Deserves FOOD award ☐ Deserves PLACE-TO-STAY award 99:25

PLEASE GIVE YOUR NAME AND ADDRESS ON THE BACK OF THIS FORM

REPORT ON (pub's name)

Pub's address

☐ YES MAIN ENTRY ☐ YES *Lucky Dip* ☐ NO don't include

Please tick one of these boxes to show your verdict, and give reasons and descriptive comments, prices etc

☐ Deserves FOOD award ☐ Deserves PLACE-TO-STAY award 99:26

PLEASE GIVE YOUR NAME AND ADDRESS ON THE BACK OF THIS FORM

Your own name and address *(block capitals please)*

DO NOT USE THIS SIDE OF THE PAGE FOR WRITING ABOUT PUBS

Your own name and address *(block capitals please)*

DO NOT USE THIS SIDE OF THE PAGE FOR WRITING ABOUT PUBS

REPORT ON *(pub's name)*

Pub's address

☐ YES MAIN ENTRY ☐ YES *Lucky Dip* ☐ NO don't include

Please tick one of these boxes to show your verdict, and give reasons and descriptive comments, prices etc

☐ Deserves FOOD award ☐ Deserves PLACE-TO-STAY award 99:27

PLEASE GIVE YOUR NAME AND ADDRESS ON THE BACK OF THIS FORM

EPORT ON *(pub's name)*

ub's address

☐ YES MAIN ENTRY ☐ YES *Lucky Dip* ☐ NO don't include

ease tick one of these boxes to show your verdict, and give reasons and scriptive comments, prices etc

Deserves FOOD award ☐ Deserves PLACE-TO-STAY award 99:28

EASE GIVE YOUR NAME AND ADDRESS ON THE BACK OF THIS FORM

Your own name and address *(block capitals please)*

DO NOT USE THIS SIDE OF THE PAGE FOR WRITING ABOUT PUBS

Your own name and address *(block capitals please)*

DO NOT USE THIS SIDE OF THE PAGE FOR WRITING ABOUT PUBS

.PORT ON (*pub's name)*

b's address

YES Main Entry ☐ YES *Lucky Dip* ☐ NO don't include

ase tick one of these boxes to show your verdict, and give reasons and criptive comments, prices etc

Deserves Food award ☐ Deserves Place-to-stay award 99:29

EASE GIVE YOUR NAME AND ADDRESS ON THE BACK OF THIS FORM

PORT ON (*pub's name)*

's address

YES Main Entry ☐ YES *Lucky Dip* ☐ NO don't include

ase tick one of these boxes to show your verdict, and give reasons and criptive comments, prices etc

Deserves Food award ☐ Deserves Place-to-stay award 99:30

ASE GIVE YOUR NAME AND ADDRESS ON THE BACK OF THIS FORM

Your own name and address *(block capitals please)*

DO NOT USE THIS SIDE OF THE PAGE FOR WRITING ABOUT PUBS

Your own name and address *(block capitals please)*

DO NOT USE THIS SIDE OF THE PAGE FOR WRITING ABOUT PUBS